THE JUCO CLASSIC

Publishing Consultant Susan C. McDonald
Printed by Taylor Publishing Company
                Dallas, Texas

Library of Congress Catalog Card Number: 88-62470
ISBN 0-943335-02-7 (Standard Edition)
ISBN 0-943335-03-5 (Collectors Edition)

TABLE OF CONTENTS

George E. Killian

WELCOME

The NJCAA was founded on May 14, 1938, by a handful of California junior college representatives in Fresno, California.

While founded by California men, there was no intention that the NJCAA be just a "West Coast Organization." This became apparent when Trinidad College of Trinidad Colorado, hosted the 1941 Track Championship in Denver, Colorado.

In 1945, the NJCAA, weakened by the war and not yet ready to renew activities, gave its blessing to an invitational basketball tournament at Compton, California. The tournament mushroomed into a national activity by 1947 with teams participating from as far away as Washington and Louisiana. Other schools from the Great Lakes area, the Middle West, and the East Coast clamored for invitations that could not be provided. Clearly, a nationwide basketball program, sponsored by the NJCAA, was a necessity.

Compton invited the NJCAA to call a special meeting in connection with its 1947 tournament, to consider a national basketball program, from which grew the present regional and national tourney plan.

Hutchinson, Kansas, became the eventual site for the NJCAA Championship Basketball Tournament. Co-sponsors, the Lysle Rishel Post of the American Legion and Hutchinson Junior College hosted this event for the first time in 1949. In subsequent years the Lysle Rishel Post became the sole host and, in 1988, celebrated 40 years of conducting the Juco Basketball Championship.

The membership growth in the NJCAA corresponded with the planned growth of the junior college movement throughout the nation. In 1968 the membership stood at 419. Twenty years later the membership stands at 535.

In 1988 the NJCAA is recognized as the leader in administrating junior college athletic programs across the nation. It has become involved not only in national programs but has also made its mark on the international scene.

The NJCAA Basketball Tournament has grown in concert with the overall growth of the junior/community college movement. It has had a "sold out" sign hanging in its window for the past 10 years. Every basketball buff in the country knows where Hutchinson, Kansas, is because it has become synonymous with the Juco Basketball Tournament.

This publication, long overdue, will highlight one of America's premier sporting events. It will give you a firsthand, factual account of each year's tournament; each one more exciting than the other. Furthermore, it will give you an insight into the lives of so many who have made their mark in the junior college basketball world.

The NJCAA is deeply indebted to Michael L. Johnson for bringing the chronicle of this sports spectacle to the American public.

Thank you Michael.

George E. Killian
Executive Director
National Junior College Athletic Association

(Top, left) ABC Sportscaster Gary Bender

(Top, right) Herbert L. "Herb" Bender, Gary's father, who coached Dodge City Junior College in five consecutive tourney appearances from 1948-1952.

PREFACE

I admire people with vision. I admire people even more who follow their vision to completion. Therefore, I am indebted to Mike Johnson for allowing me to relive such an important time in my life, the National Junior College Basketball Tournament.

I was privileged to be a son of a coach (Herb Bender) who took his Dodge City, Kansas, team to the Juco Tournament five straight years. I remember Convention Hall, the tourney's first site in Hutchinson. To me it had to be the biggest place on earth. Seeing teams with strange sounding names, enjoying the thrilling moments of the Stockton, California, team throwing oranges to the crowd, or the exciting beat of the tom-toms representing the Apaches of Tyler, Texas. What impact it had on a seven-year-old.

You can imagine what further impact it had on me, when some 15 years later, in my first job, I was given the opportunity to broadcast this very same NJCAA Tournament. As a broadcaster I vividly remember the tourney's first big giant, Artis Gilmore, and the defensive genius of Cotton Fitzsimmons' Moberly, Missouri, teams.

There has been a lot said and written about the love of sport. That love is nowhere more evident than in the people of Hutchinson, the hosts, who each year open their arms to the nation's best juco teams.

If you have never been to the Juco Tournament, your total sports experience just hasn't been completed. But, let me warn you, it can be one of the toughest tickets around.

Ralph Waldo Emerson once said, "Man tends to become what he thinks most about." In my case it is true! Sitting on my dad's team bench, I began to realize my challenge was to in some way report all the excitement about me.

This book is the way it was. I hope you enjoy it as much as I have.

Gary Bender
ABC Sports

Gary Bender (left) with younger brother Kelly in Dodge City gym in 1950.

ACKNOWLEDGEMENTS

When I started this project, I took care to note everyone who helped me in any way. After five years, that list grew to 12 pages. It is impossible to thank everyone individually in this limited space, but I am grateful nonetheless, particularly since many have become newfound friends.

However, there are those without whose help this book would never have been completed. My deepest gratitude to the following:

Dr. Michael W. Mould, for his doctorial dissertation, *A History of the National Junior College Athletic Association: 1937 through March 1969,* which delineated the NJCAA's early development and problems;

Bill Goldsmith, for his master's thesis, *The History of the National Junior College Athletic Association National Basketball Tournament,* which provided a detailed account of the Western States Basketball Tournament, the forerunner of the national event;

The Hutchinson News and its sports staffs throughout the years — in particular, Fred Mendell, Barbara Caywood, Larry Feese, Robert Lyster, and Dana McBratney — for providing excellent coverage of the Juco Tournament the past 40 years;

The following newspapers, for supplemental tournament coverage — *Aberdeen (Wash.) Daily World, Arkansas City (Kan.) Daily Republican-Traveler, Burlington (Iowa) Hawk-Eye, Casper (Wyo.) Tribune, Compton (Calif.) Journal, Coffeyville (Kan.) Journal, The Daily Freeman* (Kingston, N.Y.), *The Daily Journal* (Kankakee, Ill.), *The Daily Spectrum* (St. George, Utah), *Dallas Morning News, Dodge City (Kan.) Daily Globe, El Dorado (Kan.) Times, Ephraim (Utah) Enterprise, The Evening Sun* (Baltimore, Md.), *The Evening Times* (Trenton, N.J.), *Garden City (Kan.) Telegram, Hannibal (Mo.) Courier-Post, Hibbing (Minn.) Daily Tribune, Independence (Kan.) Reporter, Jackson (Miss.) Daily News, Kilgore (Tex.) News Herald, Lawton (Okla.) Constitution, Los Angeles Times, Midland (Tex.) Reporter-Telegram, Moberly (Mo.) Monitor-Index, New York Times, Ogden (Utah) Standard-Examiner, Orlando (Fla.) Sentinel, Paducah (Ky.) Sun-Democrat, Parsons (Kan.) Sun, Pasadena (Tex.) News Citizen, Poplar Bluff (Mo.) Daily American Republic, Pratt (Kan.) Tribune, Pueblo (Colo.) Star-Journal, Quincy (Ill.) Herald-Whig, St. Louis Globe-Democrat, San Angelo (Tex.) Standard-Times, San Francisco Chronicle, Seattle Post-Intelligencer, Seattle Times, Southwest Times Record* (Fort Smith, Ark.), *Springfield (Mo.) Daily News, Springfield (Mo.) Leader-Press, Sunday Times Advertiser* (Trenton, N.J.), *The Times Herald* (Middletown, N.Y.), *Topeka (Kan.) Capital Journal, Trentonian (Trenton, N.J.), Twin Falls (Ida.) Times-News, Vincennes (Ind.) Sun-Commercial, Washington Post,* and *Wichita Eagle-Beacon;*

The Hutchinson Public Library and Highline Community College (Midway, Wash.) Library, for securing microfilm of newspapers from around the nation through interlibrary loan;

George Killian and his staff at the NJCAA office, for opening their door to me and providing whatever information I needed at a moment's notice;

The American Legion members of Lysle Rishel Post 68 who made me feel at home at the tournament during the final years of my research and who were the first to show their faith in my work by helping to financially guarantee *The Juco Classic's* publication;

All the individuals, institutions, and newspapers who donated pictures;

The more than 200 coaches, players, referees, tourney officials, and other former participants whose input made this work more than just a collection of dry facts and numbers;

Lorian Choate and Ed Eaton, for the laborious task of editing a monster manuscript;

Jerry Kershaw and Tony Jimenez, for their support, and for making people aware of *The Juco Classic's* existence;

Andrew Biggs, for providing legal advice at a bargain rate;

Susan McDonald, without whose effort and guidance this work would still be in manuscript form on my desk;

Bob Gilliland, for spearheading the drive to guarantee *The Juco Classic's* publication, something he believed in from Day 1;

Steve Drach, for being an ever-reliable right-hand man, doing whatever I couldn't do from 1,500 miles away;

Gary Bender and Cotton Fitzsimmons whose friendship and encouragement throughout helped me over some tough times;

And, finally, my family — Pat and Dave and Mom, for being there whenever I needed them; Matthew, for being patient during the many hours when Daddy's door was closed; and Linda, for being a loving wife who recognized I had a dream I needed to fulfill.

Michael L. Johnson

A very special thanks goes to those whose financial assurances made the JUCO CLASSIC possible.

Lysle Rishel Post No. 68, American Legion

Greater Hutchinson Chamber of Commerce

Eugene E. Bogash

Leon Schartz

Dillon Companies, Inc.

Jerry R. Blocher

Central Bank & Trust Company

Hutchinson National Bank & Trust Company

KWBW Radio

Gene E. Schmidt

John E. Neal

Virginia H. Rayl

Dr. Jack L. Perkins

Steve A. Drach

Brad Dillon

The First National Bank of Hutchinson

William D. Davis, M.D.

Charles L. Gilliland

Bob Gilliland

Richard L. Cooper

Charles Studt

Dr. Don Miller

Cotton Fitzsimmons

INTRODUCTION

I've spent 15 years coaching in the NBA. I've enjoyed every moment of it and hope to continue doing so for many years to come.

But, I've said this many times, and I say it with all honesty: If I quit coaching in pro basketball tomorrow and want to continue to coach, you won't find me going to a major university. You'll find me at some community college.

I wouldn't go to the best, though. I would want to go to a school that needs to build a program, that wants to reach the pinnacle of junior college basketball — that wants to go to Hutch!

The National Junior College Athletic Association Basketball Tournament has been in existence for 41 years and for 40 of those years its home has been in Hutchinson. The event has put the town on the map.

Everyone connected with the basketball profession has heard of Hutchinson and the Juco Tournament. Ask the big names in college basketball — the Bobby Knights, the John Thompsons, the Larry Browns, the Lou Carneseccas — if they've been there. Then ask them, if they weren't recruiting players, would they go again just for the fun of it?

The answers would be unanimously positive.

What's the attraction? How can a city of only 45,000 sitting in the middle of the Kansas plains be such an appealing sports mecca when there's the NAIA and the NCAA tournaments happening elsewhere?

It wasn't always that way. That's what this book is all about.

I still remember my introduction to the mystique of Hutchinson and the Juco Tournament in 1952 when I was a freshman at Hannibal-LaGrange College which was competing in the national event for the first time.

We drove out to Kansas from Missouri, a trip that really felt like an excursion into the Land of Oz.

The first thing I noticed was the vastness of the land and how it took a long time to get anywhere because the wind kept pushing you back.

Next there were the large, green fields of wheat.

Then, as we approached Hutchinson, there were the big, white grain elevators in the horizon. They're not hard to spot since there are 15 skirting the city, one of them being nearly half-a-mile in length, one of the largest in the world. They became a beacon for us on later trips; any time you saw those elevators, you knew you were getting close to Hutch.

The lasting first impression I have of Hutchinson was that the streets were so wide. In today's terms they don't seem so wide what with six- and eight-lane highways everywhere. But, at the time, having grown up in Bowling Green, Missouri, which had 2,600 people, and going to school in Hannibal, which was 19,000, the streets in Hutch seemed huge.

My top memory of that first tournament was where we played. For its first three years in Hutch, the tournament had been housed in old Convention Hall, a small, inadequate facility. We were the first to play in the Hutchinson Sports Arena, a modern-day field house which had just been completed the week before. Junior colleges didn't play basketball in field houses in those days. They played in gyms. Having the opportunity of playing before thousands of fans was a rare and special experience.

And who could forget the weather? On Thursday, everyone was enjoying the first day of spring in shirt-sleeves. Then, that night, we were hit by a fierce ice storm and the next day the temperature barely warmed to freezing.

The drastic change was typical of the weather I encountered in seven later tourney trips to Hutchinson. On Tuesday, the weather might be beautiful, but, on Wednesday, we would get hit by a dust storm. And Thursday we would have a shower to cool things down. Then, on Friday, it would snow. Of course, Saturday was the championship game and by then nobody cared about the damn weather.

Which leads to the one negative memory I have about that 1952 tournament. Not winning. In fact, two consecutive years our Hannibal-LaGrange Trojans made it to the semifinals only to lose, eventually finishing third both times. Having played so hard, come so far, gotten so close, and not won it all always made me wonder, "What if . . ." It also provided me with the incentive to want to come back and win it all as a coach.

Whatever bad feelings I retained about that year's tournament, however, they were completely overshadowed by the good. I've been to a lot of tournaments as a player and as a coach and under no circumstances did anybody treat you more first-class than the people of Hutchinson.

The NJCAA made a great move when they picked Hutch as the site of the Juco Tournament. The people of Hutchinson have nurtured the Tournament as though it were a rose. When they needed a better playing facility, they built the Sports Arena. When they didn't have sufficient hotel space, they built the Baker Hotel and later the Holidome. When the Arena began to show its age, they refurbished it. No matter the cost, Hutchinson has taken care of its pride and joy.

I was fortunate to have met the men who sparked the Tournament's early success: Charley Sesher, who had the foresight to see that Hutchinson was the place for the Tournament and the wherewithal to make it happen; and Bud Obee, Guy Holt, and all the guys at the American Legion, who at the time were young, energetic veterans of World War II, the kind of driving leadership which made the Tournament work. Since 1949, the Legion has sponsored the Tournament, giving each participant and fan a feeling that is unique to sports today — a feeling of being home.

Step into the Sports Arena during Tournament week and you can sense tradition oozing from the walls. It's something communities like Tyler, Texas; Burlington, Iowa; Casper, Wyoming; Vincennes, Indiana; Twin Falls, Idaho; Independence, Kansas, and Moberly, Missouri, live and die for.

When I coached at Moberly Junior College in the 60s, it wasn't uncommon for people there to pull down the shades on the store and put a sign up saying, "Gone to the National Tournament. Be back next week." What's unreal is that they still do it today.

Every basketball fan should experience the uniqueness of the Juco Tournament just once. The atmosphere that Hutchinson and its people create is the best argument I can think of for why the NCAA Final Four should be played on a university campus and not in the Superdome.

My junior college experience was a big part of my life which I've never forgotten and never intend to. I'm still a juco man.

I have always felt that junior college was the best place for a lot of players, not only academically, but also psychologically. A lot of players need nurturing and tender loving care. For me, junior college was a chance to get my feet on the ground as a student for two years before being thrown to the wolves. If more basketball players took the juco route, there would be more degrees earned today.

Nobody can take away those junior college days. When you talk to ex-juco guys — I don't care if it's Freddie Brown, Bob McAdoo, Foots Walker, Rickey Green, Spud Webb, or whoever — mention their junior college experience and their eyes light up. It was a youthful, carefree time in their life. Junior college basketball was important to them. And at the center was one terrific week in Hutchinson.

A couple years ago when I was honored to be inducted into the NJCAA Basketball Hall of Fame, I told the players about to participate in that year's Tournament:

"I want you to know that you will have the greatest week of your entire life. And I mean that sincerely. I have played on the junior college level. I have coached on the junior college level. I have played in the NAIA tournament. I have coached teams in the NCAA tournament. I have coached teams in the NBA play-offs. And I'm telling you now, you will have the greatest week of your entire life. You will love this tournament so much because of the people that are involved with the tournament. This is something you will remember the rest of your life. You will never forget this week."

There are no losers at the Juco Tournament. Only winners.

Cotton Fitzsimmons
Head Coach
Phoenix Suns

here is anything?"

This or similar comments have been uttered many times before. This time the speaker is Jack Alofs, head coach of Herkimer County Community College, Herkimer, New York, a first-time participant in the National Junior College Athletic Association basketball Tournament.

For the past 39 years, the tournament has been held in the south-central Kansas town of Hutchinson, population 45,000. Though Hutchinson has an airport, no major airlines service it. Like other participants too far from Kansas to drive, Alofs' squad has had to fly to Wichita, rent vans or station wagons, then drive the 50 miles to Hutchinson (or "Hutch" as they've heard the locals refer to it).

The ride from Wichita is bleak, particularly on an overcast mid-March Sunday afternoon. How can a place be so flat and colorless? The land around Herkimer is also farmland, but nothing like this.

There is no confirmation that Kansas is the "Land of Ahs," as the state tourist commission proclaims, until the Herkimer team's hour-long drive nears its end and then it is only because of the oddity of seeing the occasional horse and buggy in the Mennonite community of Yoder just south of Hutch.

Finally, the New York squad reaches its destination, the Hutchinson Holidome. It is a new Holiday Inn, complete with indoor swimming pool, hot tub, and arboretum. At least the players will have a nice place to stay.

Is this the mecca that Alofs' has heard so much about? Says Alofs, "I heard [Hutchinson] was the place to go to play junior college basketball: where you see some good competition, play some good teams, kids get some good exposure, and it's big-time junior college basketball." But after the ride through nowhere, there is doubt in his voice.

MONDAY — PRACTICE

Herkimer County is one of 16 teams to travel to Hutchinson from as far east as Waterbury, Connecticut, as far west as Twin Falls, Idaho, as far north as Bismarck, North Dakota, and as far south as Pasadena, Texas, (just outside Houston) to vie for the junior college basketball crown.

For the most part, the schools represented have had little, if any, national publicity during the year. Often they are unknowns locally. The average seating capacity for the home floors of the teams in the 1987 Juco Tournament is approximately 2,000, but their average attendance is much less.

There are a few Cadillac facilities like the one in Midland, Texas, a beautiful 6,000-seat facility adorned in Midland College's colors of green and gold or the underground field house in Twin Falls, Idaho, which holds 3,800-4,200, depending on how many get by the fire marshall's notice.

There are also some clunkers. Bismarck Junior College plays in an old armory affectionately called "The Pit." For Brewton-Parker College of Mount Vernon, Georgia, home is "The Barn," an old brick building which holds 500 max.

Then there is the home court of Kankakee Community College of Kankakee, Illinois. The Cavaliers play in an 85-year-old National Guard armory "that is falling down around us," says Coach Denny Lehnus. "There are a lot of pillars and very few unobstructed-view seats. It has an antiquated heating system

Among San Jacinto's talent-laden 1987 squad is John Hudson (No. 44) who will be second-team all-Metro Conference the following year at South Carolina. (Photo courtesy of the **Hutchinson News***)*

that has no thermostat. You either have heat or you have none. The temperature at game time for Vincennes [in the game played for the right to come to Hutchinson] was 84 degrees."

Hutchinson's Sports Arena is a Taj Mahal in comparison. Though 35 years old, the Arena is bright and colorful. For the Juco Tournament, seating is on the plus side of 7,000. With standing-room-only, attendance can approach the 8,000 mark. There are no obstructed views.

Traditionally, Monday of tournament week has been set aside as a practice day, giving everyone an equal opportunity to experience the openness of the Arena. Each participant is allowed a half-hour practice in the Arena's full-sized practice gym, then another half-hour on the main floor.

As the newcomers first step inside the Arena, they begin to realize the Juco Tournament may be the special experience they've heard about.

John Salerno, athletic director for Mattatuck Community College (which has no home court, but plays home games at three different local high schools in Waterbury, Connecticut) says, "This facility is gorgeous. You don't expect something like this."

"We're all kind of in awe," says Bismarck Coach Tom Kirchoffner. "Most of our players are kind of on a bubble, floating around."

Throughout the day the stands are dotted with local fans and several four-year college coaches. The largest grouping appears around 10:30 in the morning. Scheduled to practice: No. 1-ranked San Jacinto College from Pasadena, Texas.

The Ravens are an anomaly in the world of junior college basketball. With a front-page article to appear the following day in, of all places, *The Wall Street Journal,* San Jacinto (or "San Jac" to tourney veterans) is one junior college that *does* receive national media attention. The school is tied for most national titles and has produced so many later collegiate and professional stars that every street kid in New York City has filed away the name for future references should things not work out in their attempt to play at a major college. The current Raven squad owns a juco record 70-game win streak and is laden with potential Division I talent; so much so that Lenzie Howell, a former high school All-American, spends most of his time on the bench.

After San Jac's workout, the audience remains at its peak for another two hours as a few Hutchonians take lunch at the Arena. The crowd's constituency is always in flux, people coming and going. Few remain throughout.

One of those that does is no stranger to the Sports Arena. Just last year he brought Gloucester County College of Sewell, New Jersey, here to compete. Now Ronald "Fang" Mitchell is head coach at Coppin State College, a newly designated Division I school in Baltimore. Like others trying to build a new program, Mitchell is looking for immediate help from the juco ranks and has come to Hutchinson to recruit. But, two days early?

"I love the atmosphere here," Mitchell says. "The people of Hutchinson have always treated me especially nice. As soon as I arrived, I just got the feeling of being back home. If I have to come to Hutchinson, Kansas, once a year just to find happiness, then I'm willing to come."

The small Arena crowd is even smaller now, but Mitchell smiles broadly and with a dreamy look gestures around the building. "Even when it's empty, you can feel the emotion in here because you know what it's going to be like."

That evening at the Converse-sponsored player banquet, the young men who will be competing for a national title get further clues about the significance of the week ahead.

On the agenda is the honoring of the newly inducted members to the NJCAA Basketball Hall of Fame. One of those who took the time out of a busy schedule to accept the honor in person is Darrell Floyd, a two-time NCAA All-American at Furman, who has not been back to Hutchinson since playing in the Juco Tournament in 1952. In fact, Wingate College, the North Carolina school he played for, is no longer a junior college. Yet Floyd has returned because, "this was quite an opportunity to play out here. It was really a stepping stone to greater things. Without this opportunity, I probably wouldn't have gone on to a senior college."

Finally, there is the guest speaker. Just yesterday he was in Atlanta where his Southwest Missouri State Bears upset Clemson then nearly upset Kansas in the NCAA Southeast Regional. Now a media celebrity, Charlie Spoonhour still makes time to recognize his roots.

Spoonhour's comments are brief and funny. His main point is just because you play or coach on the junior college level, does not mean you can't compete at the major college level. Hard work often pays off with unexpected dividends.

He also indicates everyone should pay particular attention to the men in Legion hats, members of the local American Legion, Lysle Rishel Post 68, sponsors of the tournament for 39 years. "They're honestly trying to make this tournament better for you. You go to these other tournaments and you're sort of herded like cattle." Then with earnest emphasis he says, "Fellows, this is the greatest tournament in the world."

TUESDAY — THE WAITING ENDS

At 10 a.m., an hour-and-a-half before ticket windows open, fans begin to congregate outside the Arena doors. Within 30 minutes there are as many as 50 people at each end of the building. Some, like first-in-line Marion Lehnus, cousin of Kankakee Coach Denny Lehnus, are new to the tournament, and having heard that tickets are scarce, want to be sure of getting in. Most, however, are veterans who know that the afternoon session is

all general admission and rarely sold out. They have come early simply because they are eager for the proceedings to begin.

By tip-off time, the crowd numbers 1,000. Though the players and referees are on the court ready to go, tourney officials hold the opening jump ball for the hands of the clock to point straight up noon, the scheduled start time, prompting one impatient fan to yell, "If you're waiting on me, you can get started."

Noon.

The 40th NJCAA Basketball Tournament begins.

The opener is between Wabash Valley College (29-7) and Kankakee Community College (32-4). Both are unranked though Kankakee has been in the NJCAA poll most of the year, at one time rated as high as No. 2. It is Kankakee's second trip to the nationals and, for the second time, the Cavaliers open the tournament against another team from their own state.

Since the curtain-raiser of any event creates its own pressure, the two Illinois schools intensify it by pressing each other throughout. The game is uptempo but not picturesque with 40 turnovers. In the end it is 24 turnovers and only eight free throws out of 20 attempts that dooms Kankakee. Wabash Valley wins, 82-75, a mild upset.

The crowd grows during the matinee feature between No. 7 Herkimer County (30-2) and No. 12 Gloucester County (22-3). Says Gloucester Coach Howard Horenstein of the turn-out, "It's wonderful. We're lucky to get 25, 50 people out to our games."

What is not so wonderful for the New Jersey squad is the result of the game. Three Herkimer players score 20 or more, led by All-American Jim Smith, who compiles the best individual stats of the day with 37 points and 8 rebounds. The Generals clobber Gloucester, 99-80.

The afternoon audience peaks for the finale. Four thousand fans grace the stands, leading one newly arrived visitor to say, "Doesn't anyone have a job in this town?"

The reason for the sizable crowd is the debut of odds on favorite, No. 1 San Jacinto (33-0). The Ravens' first-round opponent is No. 18 Westchester Community College (26-8) of Valhalla, New York. It is an unfortunate pairing since San Jac Coach Ronnie Arrow and Westchester Coach Ralph Arietta are good friends, having twice worked together at ABA-USA tournaments in Colorado Springs. But, all's fair when the national crown is on the line. Says Arrow, "We're friends, but I don't deduct them off income tax."

It seems particularly unfair to Westchester since the Westcos have been in four tournaments with San Jacinto and this is their fourth meeting. However, as Arietta rationalizes, "If you're going to play a team like San Jacinto, you better play them the

*After a disappointing 1986 tournament, San Jacinto's Greg "Boo" Harvey (No. 10) captures the Obee Small Player Award in 1987 before moving on to St. John's University with backcourt mate Michael Porter. (Photo courtesy of the **Hutchinson News**)*

first game because they'll get tougher as the tournament goes on.''

Arietta, a veteran of six previous tournaments, also sees another advantage to the pairing. ''You know what it's like out here. People come out and always root for the underdog. And we're definitely the most logical [choice].''

Sure enough, the Arena lends full vocal support to Westchester. With the backing, the Westcos proceed to take control of the tempo, playing stingy zone defense and showing patience on offense, so much so they receive a shot-clock violation for holding until the last second before attempting to score. When reserve Tony Smith hits a three-pointer from the top of the key at the buzzer, giving Westchester a surprise 36-34 halftime lead, fans are primed for a major upset.

A two-time All-Tourney selection, Michael Porter (No. 12) will join his San Jacinto teammate in the backcourt at St. John's University the following year. (Photo courtesy of Hutchinson News)

However, the closeness of the game gains the attention of the powerful Ravens. With 19 each from the guard tandem of Greg ''Boo'' Harvey and Michael Porter (who will be the starting guards for St. Johns University next year), the top-ranked Ravens take over in the second half, claiming victory, 82-69.

The evening session tips off promptly at 6 p.m. with the day's best 20 minutes of action. As fans straggle into the Arena, No. 9 Midland College (30-3) and No. 13 Three Rivers Community College (32-4) of Poplar Bluff, Missouri, exchange the lead 16 times. Tough man-to-man defenses force missed shots. The biggest lead of the half comes at the end with Midland on top, 30-26.

But, like the games that preceded it, Game 4 does not hold together. In the early minutes of the second half, three Three Rivers starters pick up their fourth fouls. When Jeff Ford, the Raiders' leading scorer, fouls out with 10:21 to go, Midland is comfortably in front, 58-47. Superior quickness and depth eventually give the Chaparrals a convincing 81-66 win.

By the time David Norman sings the National Anthem before the evening feature, the Arena is virtually full. To the uninitiated, it is a surprising turnout, considering the teams playing.

On one side of the court is Westark Community College (28-9), nine-time tourney participant and former champ from Ft. Smith, Arkansas, which defeated the local Hutchinson Community College squad to get to the ''Sweet 16.''

On the other side is newcomer Mattatuck Community College (26-1) of Waterbury, Connecticut. Though ranked No. 10, the Chiefs are from the New England region which has won less than a quarter of its games in the tournament.

Even the Mattatuck administration has little faith. In order to save money, ''Super Saver'' airline tickets were purchased back in December with a return date of Friday, a day before the tournament's completion. It assumed the region's representative would lose two and go home.

The large crowd is also a factor. According to Mattatuck Athletic Director John Salerno, the turnout is ''only 7,900 more fans than we're used to.'' Confirms Coach Bob Ruderman, ''This is more people than we've played before in two years total.''

The Arena audience proves to be a boon for the Chiefs, however. Always hungry to root the underdog, the crowd gets

behind Mattatuck, especially after the Chiefs dominate the middle, outrebounding Westark, 29-10, to take a 42-33 half-time margin.

Then after leading by as much as 12 during the final period, Mattatuck almost lets the game slip away. The combination of Lewis Jones' three-point shots (5 of 8 for the game) and only one Mattatuck point from three one-and-one situations, brings Westark within two, 74-72, with 2:10 remaining.

The Chiefs hang on, though. Behind freshman center Brent Dabbs' 24 points and 9 rebounds, Mattatuck scores an 83-72 upset victory.

Since the match-up is less than inspiring and there is a long week yet ahead, the large crowd does not stay long for the final game. The decision proves wise. Mesa Community College (27-5) blows out Bismarck (22-10), 87-58, led by John Jerome's 32 points and 13 rebounds.

For the most part, those in attendance have headed for bed and rest. For a few select visitors, however, there is still the annual Converse-sponsored Shrimp Feed. All day long, fans have scanned the stands to glimpse celebrity faces. They are all here now in the Holidome's ballroom — head coaches and assistants from all over the United States. It is a mini-NCAA Final Four convention which grows in size each year. Last year Converse listed 75 in attendance; this year 250.

Among the name figures is Larry Brown from nearby Kansas University. Why is he here when his Jayhawks are preparing to meet Georgetown in the NCAA Southeast Region semifinals later in the week? ''I have a lot of respect for the junior college system and the coaching and I think it's important for the kids that are playing in the tournament to see Division I coaches here.''

For others it is strictly a working proposition. Pat Foster has frequently recruited juco players in the past at Lamar and now at Houston. To him the Juco Tournament ''gives us a chance to see all the players in one setting, in a pressure situation, in a short period of time.''

Still others look at coming to Hutchinson as something more than a job. Arkansas' Nolan Richardson once guided a team to a national title on the Arena floor and has returned every year since, not only to recruit as a four-year coach, but to relive the past.

''The fans are tremendous,'' says Richardson. ''This is the biggest week probably in their entire year. Christmas doesn't even match this!''

WEDNESDAY — A TEXAS SHOOT-OUT

The final two opening-round contests are played Wednesday afternoon.

The first proves how quickly the three-point field goal, making its first tourney appearance this year, can change a game. After trailing No. 14 Brewton-Parker College (30-2) most of the way, No. 5 Allegany Community College (25-2) from Cumberland, Maryland, attempts a comeback led by Rudy Archer, one

After two outstanding tournaments as a top assist man, Allegany's Rudy Archer (No. 11) will become a starting guard at the University of Maryland. (Photo courtesy of the Hutchinson News)

of the most heavily recruited juco players in the country. In the final six minutes, Archer hits three three-pointers, all from NBA distance, to pull the Trojans within one, 77-76, with 1:30 left.

Allegany needs one more three-pointer to tie the game in the final minute, but Archer can no longer connect. His first attempt rims away. Then with 11 seconds showing, his shot from too far out grazes the underside of the net. Brewton-Parker pulls off the biggest upset yet, knocking off one of the lower-bracket favorites, 81-78.

In the final opening-round game, heavily favored No. 2 College of Southern Idaho (33-1) manages only 32 percent from the field while much smaller Northeast Mississippi Junior College (27-4) holds its own on the boards. Led by 6-2 Wayne Sears' 10 points and 7 rebounds the Tigers build a 10-point first-half margin over CSI.

Southern Idaho rectifies the problem with Dale Karst's steal and three-pointer with six seconds left in the first period and the first five points of the second. Though the Golden Eagles continue to look lackluster, falling behind by as much as seven in the final period, they notch a 73-65 win. It is CSI's second-lowest winning total of the year.

Southern Idaho's performance is typical of the first-round. No team has played to its potential for a complete game. There are more bad moments than good. Is this the caliber of play at the Juco Tournament?

Allegany Coach Bob Kirk has an explanation: "I think every team knows that you have to win that first one to get into the finals. [So] they try so hard it just gets away from them."

The opening quarterfinal later that night, appears to confirm Kirk's assessment. Herkimer County plays near perfect basketball, hitting 77 percent from the field to take a 50-34 halftime advantage over Wabash Valley.

Then fouls hurt the Generals who have little bench strength. Wabash Valley comes from 17 down to take a three-point lead.

Herkimer responds with clutch three-point shooting (5 of 8 in the second half) and a final 67 percent from the field. Led by Jim Smith's 31 and Mitchell Williams' 27, the Generals squeak by Wabash Valley, 87-84.

It is the most thrilling game yet. But, it is boring in comparison to what is to come.

Everyone concedes that San Jacinto has the best talent in the 16-team field. Many figure the Ravens to breeze all the way to the finals. However, because there are enough who think San Jac's toughest competition is in the quarterfinals, the Arena is full for the evening finale.

The reason is San Jacinto's opponent — cross-state rival Midland. Twice in the past five years, the Ravens have prevented Midland from coming to Hutch in inter-regional play. Last year's loss was particularly hard since at the time the Chaparrals were undefeated and ranked No. 2. Four Midland starters have not forgotten, nor has Coach Jerry Stone who later admits to breaking a cardinal rule of coaching. "We talked about San Jac before we ever came up here and we prepared a little bit for them."

The contest is uptempo, but tightly fought from the outset; there are seven ties and seven lead changes in the first 11 minutes. Then Midland goes cold. During a four-minute stretch San Jac reels off 13 unanswered points. It looks like another win for the Ravens.

Reserve forward Alex Stanwood changes matters quickly, scoring 11 straight during a Chaparral rally. Midland only trails, 43-42, with 2:57 left in the half. San Jacinto halts the Chaparral's momentum, taking a 50-45 lead at intermission, but not before one fact is established — the Ravens' have their hands full.

The underdog-loving fans take to Midland. They are fully behind the Chaparrals when they finally complete their comeback on a three-pointer by Todd Duncan, tying the game at 60-all with 16:07 remaining.

The intensity has now reached a fever pitch. The lead is exchanged nine more times with both sides having to erase threatening deficits (Midland one of five, San Jac one of four). During one minute toward the end, the teams trade baskets at such a rapid clip that it is like two heavyweights standing toe to toe, neither one wanting to go down.

Then a bad pass and a pair of fouls give the advantage to Midland. After Daron "Mookie" Blaylock's two free throws at the 1:34 mark, the Chaparrals are on the verge of a great victory, leading 92-89.

With 1:21 to go, Moses Scurry scores inside for San Jacinto

and is fouled by Bruce Nix, his fifth. Scurry misses the potential tying free throw, however, and Midland regains a three-point advantage with two more Blaylock free throws at the 1:09 mark.

Again Scurry scores inside. Midland calls time. There are 32 seconds on the clock. Can the Chaparrals hold on?

With 20 seconds left, Michael Porter picks up his fourth foul in the past 2½ minutes, sending Blaylock to the line again.

For the game Midland has missed only one free throw. Blaylock is 6-for-6 for the half. But, just when the Chaparrals can assure nothing less than a tie, Blaylock misses.

San Jacinto rebounds, moves the ball quickly across the mid-court line, and calls time. With 13 seconds to go, the Ravens have a chance to preserve their phenomenal win streak.

In the Midland huddle, Coach Stone tells the Chaparrals to switch from man-to-man to a "13" defense, the team's match-up zone. At the last second he changes his mind. But, before he can instruct his players, freshman forward Billy Ray Smith says, "No, coach, 13."

San Jacinto plays the ball in from the right side then tries to move it out front to Boo Harvey, noted for making things happen. Just as the pass comes from the right wing, Lincoln Minor darts out from the lane, spears the ball, and takes off for the other end. The stunned Ravens remain in place. The Arena audience stands as one. Minor passes up a dunk for a sure lay-up.

The steal by Midland's Lincoln Minor (No. 11) in the final moments of the quarterfinal with San Jacinto, ends the Ravens' record 71-game win streak. Minor will be a member of the NCAA champion Kansas Jayhawks in 1988. (Photo courtesy of the **Hutchinson News**)

In the following pandemonium, San Jac tries to call time while the clock runs down to two seconds before the scorers' table acknowledges the request. After a discussion at the table, the clock is reset to :05.

However, the Midland bench is already celebrating. It's an apparent premature display to most fans, considering that a three-pointer could tie it.

Then everything becomes clear — San Jacinto has no more time outs. Todd Duncan hits two technical free throws to complete the Chaparral upset, 98-93.

There is no mass rush for the exits. Fans linger, milling around, rehashing the game. The discussions will continue for hours . . . for days. Later, the *Hutchinson News* will describe the contest as "one of the greatest games ever played in the NJCAA Tournament."

Even knowledgeable basketball men are impressed. University of Maryland Coach Bob Wade, making his first trip to Hutch, says the game "should have been on national television."

"Forget about [whether] it's junior college basketball, high school, college, or pro," says Minnesota's Clem Haskins, "That's one of the finest games I've ever witnessed."

Says Midland's Stone, "I think I'm in a dream."
This is what the Juco Tournament is all about.

THURSDAY — GOOD BASKETBALL, NICE PEOPLE

The NJCAA Basketball Tournament is unique in format. Where the NCAA, the NIT, and the NAIA use a win-or-else single-elimination structure, the Juco Tournament uses a "false" double-elimination bracket. As in standard double-elimination tournaments, it requires two losses to be eliminated from competition. However, once a team loses, it cannot win its way back through the bracket as in a "true" double-elimination tournament like the College World Series.

Besides being practical for junior college administrations with limited budgets, having a team play more than once lets college recruiters have an additional look at players and gives fans more basketball to enjoy.

Getting a team up after losing a chance to win a national crown is not easy for coaches, however. The day's afternoon consolation fare reflect the fact with three uninspiring contests.

Yet, there is an audience to watch. Though not as big as the previous two afternoons, the crowd is still larger than most junior colleges are used to. Why?

"People here just really love juco basketball," says Jerry Mullen, who has been going to the tournament for 20 years as a high school coach, a junior college coach, and now as the head of his own scouting service. "People take vacations . . . I mean it's a happening in the Midwest."

The spectators are not all from Hutchinson either. Buddy Riemann, who has his own jewelry business in Paducah, Kentucky, closes his store twice a year; once to go to the Poconos and once for the Juco Tournament in Hutchinson. He has been doing it every year since 1969 simply "to see good basketball" and because "You have the finest people here. I love your people. I love your town."

Leonard Isaacs from Brownfield, Texas, an annual tourney watcher since 1974, agrees. "All these wonderful people that I've met. Believe you me, there are a lot of wonderful friends and I really appreciate it."

The atmosphere is addictive according to Tony Jimenez who, as a member of the working press, has covered the tournament since 1971 and is doing so this year for *USA Today, Basketball Weekly, Off the Glass,* and both wire services. "This [tournament] is like a nice warm cozy house to me. It has a friendly aura. [The Final Four] is like you meet somebody who's real wealthy, real well-to-do and you go to their house and you're afraid to sit on their chairs. But with this tournament, it's almost like you can take your shoes off, kick back, relax, and really enjoy yourself."

The enjoyment continues with the evening's first quarterfinal which features 22 lead changes and six ties. Cinderella Mattatuck again proves it is a better team than anyone thought. They lead in virtually every statistical category including a 39-28 rebound advantage. However, 29 Chief turnovers allow Mesa to stay in the game.

With 1:27 remaining and only seven seconds on the shot clock, Doug Lewis hits a three-pointer to put Mesa on top, 62-60, and immediately follows with a steal. With :27 showing and one second on the shot clock, Van Mayes scores from inside, giving the Thunderbirds a comfortable four-point margin.

Mattatuck doesn't give up, getting two from Rufus Freeman with 10 seconds left. Immediately, Emmett Lewis intentionally fouls Mesa's Kirk Hatch. Hatch misses two free throws. The Chiefs hustle the ball up court, Calvin Glenn pulling up in traffic. The shot bounds away no good at the buzzer. Mesa survives, 64-62.

The remaining quarterfinal is less exciting. Brewton-Parker scores the first basket of the game, but never leads again. Favored Southern Idaho has good leadership in sophomore forward Erick Newman (26 points, 11 rebounds) and exceptional athletic ability as shown by super dunker Joey Johnson (brother of Boston Celtic Dennis Johnson) who gets so high receiving an alley-oop pass, all he has to do is drop it for two.

Yet, the Golden Eagles continue to be inconsistent. Mauro Gomes, one of the best shooters in the nation, hits 1 of 14 from the field, including 1 of 8 from three-point range. Brewton-Parker outrebounds the Eagles, 48-41. It isn't pretty, but Southern Idaho advances to the semifinals, 89-78.

FRIDAY — THE KILLER

In early January, Mesa Community College annually hosts the Rotary Shootout, an eight-team tournament many consider the best juco tournament next to the nationals. Schools are invited from as many states as possible and are typically among the best in the country. To prove the point, three of the 1987 semifinalists played in this year's Shootout.

Having already dispatched the nation's No. 1 team and having downed both Herkimer County and Mesa to win its second consecutive Shootout, Midland is the clear favorite. The Chaparrals have three guards (Mookie Blaylock, Lincoln Minor, and Todd Duncan) who can hit from three-point range with regularity and the deepest bench that Jerry Stone (who already has one national crown to his credit) has ever had.

As for Herkimer, "everybody's got a better bench," says Coach Jack Alofs. In fact, without superstars Jim Smith and Mitchell Williams, the Generals are just an average team. Alofs' hope is that the lucky Indian tie clasp a Herkimer fan gave him at the Shootout will extend the Generals' 21-game win streak.

The other semifinal match-up is equally unequal. Mesa has a solid starting five in floor general Doug Lewis, hard-working Kirk Hatch, spot-player Van Mayes, quick-jumping all-conference Caleb Davis, and heavily recruited, versatile John Jerome. But, compared to the depth and athletic prowess of Southern Idaho, the Thunderbirds appear to fall short.

CSI has Region 18 Player of the Year Erick Newman, a potential Olympic high jumper in Joe Johnson, two Brazilian whizzes in 6-8 Edwardo Drewnick and 6-7 Mauro Gomes, three quick guards (Keith Jackson, Keith Reynolds, and Gerald Collins) who can be used interchangeably, and a steady, reliable reserve. Five Golden Eagles saw action in last year's semifinals, giving CSI a big edge in pressure experience. Besides, Southern Idaho has beaten Dixie College twice which in turn beat Mesa twice.

If there is any speculation that Midland will still be high from the San Jacinto victory and overlook the opening semifinal, it is quickly dispelled. Herkimer plays with the Chaparrals for eight minutes then gradually falls to the wayside. Midland hits 11 of 16 three-pointers including 6 of 7 by Todd Duncan and 4 of 6 by Mookie Blaylock and rolls to an easy 107-75 win.

The other semifinal is less straightforward. Southern Idaho continues erratic, leads most of the way by comfortable margins, but is unable to deliver the killing blow.

After taking a 41-28 advantage with 15:58 left, the Golden Eagles have trouble with Mesa's match-up zone and slowly lose the lead. When Caleb Davis hits a half hook with 1:58 remaining, the crowd explodes as the underdog Thunderbirds edge ahead, 53-51.

Mauro Gomes hits his fifth three-pointer of the night, this time from NBA distance on the left side, to regain the lead for CSI with 1:11 to go.

Two free throws by Van Mayes with 47 seconds left returns the advantage to Mesa.

Then comes the killer. With 14 seconds on the shot clock, 15 in the game, CSI's Keith Jackson launches from the top of the key, losing control at the last instant. The ball bangs off the backboard, hammers the front rim, and drops for three points.

John Jerome tries to duplicate the shot at the Mesa end, but it bounds away to teammate Doug Lewis whose last second heave is not even close. Southern Idaho squeezes by, 57-55.

SATURDAY — THE EIGHT BEST

Having survived the week, the teams playing on trophy day are assured recognition as the eight best junior college teams in the nation. It bears out what Allegany's Bob Kirk told his players after losing in the opening round, "Now for 24 hours, you're in the losers' bracket. But, tomorrow we're going to be in the winners' bracket again."

In the battle for seventh-place, Allegany defeats Kankakee, 72-61, led by John Turner's 19 points and 17 rebounds and Rudy Archers' 14 points and 8 assists. It is the third straight year the Trojans have been winners on the final day of the tournament. Kankakee has reason for pride, too, having set a new school record for wins (34) during the week.

After the heart-breaking loss to Midland, San Jacinto Coach Ronnie Arrow tells the press, "You just hope your guys are mature enough to understand that it's not the end of the world.

There are still a hell of a lot of people that would like to be in our situation.''

The Ravens respond accordingly, racking up consecutive 100-plus point totals, including a 113-93 fifth-place victory over Brewton-Parker. For the losing Barons, there is also reason for congratulation since their sixth-place finish is the highest in the school's history.

Win or lose, the opponents in the third-place contest are definitely winners. Neither were expected to come so far. Says Herkimer County's Jack Alofs, ''We didn't have the horses that some or most of the teams participating in the tournament had, but as Charlie Spoonhour said at the opening banquet, if you play hard, there is no telling how far you can go.''

Mesa, one of the top-10 defensive squads in the country, succumbs to Herkimer's upbeat tempo, allows Jim Smith and Mitchell Williams 39 and 30 respectively, but still manages to outmaneuver the Generals, 104-92, for third.

One more game remains.

Then, Midland reaches down and comes up with a brilliant comeback. Southern Idaho scores only twice more. Meanwhile, Lincoln Minor hits two three-pointers and Todd Duncan registers a rare four-pointer when Gomes fouls him on a basket from beyond the three-point line. With 26 seconds left, the CSI advantage is one — 69-68.

Erick Newman tries to extend the lead but misses. Midland rebounds, outlets quickly, and races upcourt with a clear fast break advantage.

Suddenly, Gomes fouls the lead man at midcourt. It is heads-up play since Midland is not yet in a one-and-one situation and must inbound the ball from the right side with seven seconds showing and no time outs.

The ball immediately comes in to Minor. He was the hero against San Jacinto and leads all scorers in the title game with 20. Everyone knows who will take the last shot.

Minor drives left, then right and — with two seconds left — pulls up from 19 feet out without faking. CSI's Joey Johnson is

Herkimer County's Mitchell Williams (No. 44) is second to teammate Jim Smith in the race for most points in the 1987 tournament with 105. (Photo courtesy of the **Hutchinson News**)

Midland plays the championship game without the services of playmaker Daron ''Mookie'' Blaylock (No. 10) who will be ''Newcomer of the Year'' in the Big Eight next year at Oklahoma. (Photo courtesy of the **Hutchinson News**)

The first MVP in 17 years not from the championship squad, Herkimer County's Jim Smith (No. 22) leads the 1987 tournament in scoring (125) and is second in rebounds (39). (Photo courtesy of the **Hutchinson News**)

The tournament has been well attended despite the fact the contests overall have not been inspiring (the average point spread for each game has been 12.4, the fourth-widest margin in tourney history). Therefore, it is not surprising that the final contest attracts the biggest audience of the week — a standing-room-only crowd.

The pairing is a good one. After knocking off San Jacinto, Midland has become everyone's favorite to win the crown, particularly since Southern Idaho, the bottom-bracket favorite has not played well in three victories.

However, a late development has thrown the outcome up in the air. In the latter stages of the semifinal contest against Herkimer, Mookie Blaylock, Midland's floor leader, suffered a stress fracture in his right foot. He is dressed but hobbles along the sidelines, quiet, unsmiling. In fact, there are no smiles at the Chaparral end of the floor.

The mood is 180 degrees different at the CSI end. The Golden Eagles have yet to play to their potential and feel they have something to prove.

The emotional difference is apparent once the game starts. Southern Idaho is confident, aggressive in its pursuit of victory. Midland is tentative, trying not to lose. The first half is close throughout, but midway in the period, Midland can no longer secure the lead. When Mauro Gomes banks a wild three-point shot off the glass with two seconds left and a man hanging on him, the Golden Eagle contingent — the largest of the 16 participants, completely filling the east end bleacher — is charged to the max with CSI on top, 40-34.

The surge continues in the final frame with the Eagles building a margin of 13 twice, the last at 65-52 with 7:45 remaining.

right there, however, jumping so high that his blocking arm is extended outward rather than upward when it rejects the ball.

The bleachers on the east end erupt. Southern Idaho has claimed the junior college basketball crown.

THE AFTERMATH — HANDING OUT ACCOLADES

The Juco Tournament is rich in tradition because of its stable environment. Hutchinson has hosted the event for 39 years. Throughout that time the American Legion has sponsored the event with a legion of willing volunteers headed by Guy Holt, its chairman for the past 36 years.

One of the more visible symbols of the continuity of personnel which has made this tournament a success is the awards ceremony emcee. For the 35th time, a silver-haired Hod Humiston conducts the proceedings with dignity and occasional humor.

Unlike after the Final Four when the audience leaves en masse once a national champ is crowned, a large majority of Juco Tourney fans remain for the entire awards ceremony, applauding those honored.

As the top four teams receive their trophies, each team's coach says his thank-yous, making sure to recognize their team host, who has all but lived with them throughout the week, and also the fans. Says Midland's Jerry Stone, ''We really appreciate people who understand basketball.''

Then everywhere programs are opened and lists checked to see if personal All-Tournament Team picks match those officially selected. After all 12 have been introduced alphabetically and their pictures taken, Humiston says the same thing he's said for 35 years, ''How'd you like to have a team like that?''

The drama is similar to that of Oscar night, particularly when it comes to the final four individual awards. It is enhanced when Jerry Stone is chosen Coach of the Tournament, only the fourth time the winner has not been the one who guided his team to a championship. Says a stunned Stone, "How 'bout that, Mama?"

The Sesher Sportsmanship and Obee Most Outstanding Small Player Awards go to Mattatuck's Paxton Cobb and San Jacinto's Boo Harvey, respectively. The two recipients are unsure how to react since the awards are unique in the collegiate sports world. It is only after they are showered with applause and have a chance to see the names of previous recipients such as Sam Williams, Ollie Taylor, Ray Williams, and Spud Webb that they realize how significant the honors are.

Finally, there is the announcement of the French MVP award. For the first time in 17 years the honor goes to someone not on the championship squad. But, since he led all scorers with 125 points and was the second-leading rebounder averaging 9.8 a game, it is hard to deny Herkimer County's Jim Smith the honor.

It is over for another year. As people leave, choruses of "See you next year" can be heard throughout the Arena. For its devoted followers, it is reassuring to know that, like Christmas, the tournament will always come again next year.

Is the experience that important?

Just ask the people in Twin Falls, Idaho, who gathered in festive Super Bowl party-type groups to watch the event on television, only to be denied seeing all but a few minutes of the beginning and end because of a satellite problem. (Fortunately, they will get to see the championship game in its entirety as the second half of a doubleheader broadcast following the NCAA championship game a week later.)

Or ask Eddie Trenkle, Coach Fred Trenkle's next youngest son, who could not control the tears of joy that streamed down his face as he sat amidst the victorious Golden Eagle players, posing for their championship photograph.

Or ask the Southern Idaho players themselves. All year long, after every practice, after every game, they have met at midcourt, joined hands, and yelled the same phrase. Now with the first-place trophy theirs they go to midcourt to do it once more, screaming "NATIONAL CHAMPIONSHIP!" as proudly as they can.

***

Has the NJCAA Basketball Tournament always been successful? Who have been its stars? What has made it unique?

For those who have experienced the Juco Tournament's past, this book will rekindle fond remembrances. For everyone else, it is an introduction to a rich tradition.

Tournament Results

Day		Game	
Tuesday:	Game		
		1	Wabash Valley — 82 Kankakee — 75
		2	Herkimer County — 99 Gloucester County — 80
		3	San Jacinto — 82 Westchester — 69
		4	Midland — 81 Three Rivers — 66
		5	Mattatuck — 83 Westark — 72
		6	Mesa — 87 Bismarck — 58
Wednesday:	Game		
		7	Brewton-Parker — 81 Allegany — 78
		8	Southern Idaho — 73 NE Mississippi — 65
		9	Kankakee — 100 Gloucester County — 78
		10	Herkimer County — 87 Wabash Valley — 84
		11	Midland — 98 San Jacinto — 93
Thursday:	Game		
		12	Westchester — 75 Three Rivers — 65
		13	Westark — 105 Bismarck — 80
		14	Allegany — 93 NE Mississippi — 74
		15	Mesa — 64 Mattatuck — 62
		16	Southern Idaho — 89 Brewton-Parker — 78
		17	San Jacinto — 121 Wabash Valley — 102
Friday:	Game		
		18	Kankakee — 82 Westchester — 64
		19	Allegany — 79 Westark — 75 OT
		20	Brewton-Parker — 83 Mattatuck — 81
		21	Midland — 107 Herkimer County — 75
		22	Southern Idaho — 57 Mesa — 55
Saturday:	Game		
		23	Allegany — 72 Kankakee — 61
		24	San Jacinto — 113 Brewton-Parker — 93
		25	Mesa — 104 Herkimer County — 92
		26	Southern Idaho — 69 Midland — 68

How They Finished in 1987

1. College of Southern Idaho — Twin Falls, Idaho
2. Midland College — Midland, Texas
3. Mesa Community College — Mesa, Arizona
4. Herkimer County Community College — Herkimer, New York
5. San Jacinto College, Central Campus — Pasadena, Texas
6. Brewton-Parker College — Mt. Vernon, Georgia
7. Allegany Community College — Cumberland, Maryland
8. Kankakee Community College — Kankakee, Illinois

All-Tournament Team

Daron "Mookie" Blaylock — Midland College
Lee Campbell — Brewton-Parker College
Mauro Gomes — College of Southern Idaho
Greg "Boo" Harvey — San Jacinto College, Central Campus
John Jerome — Mesa Community College
Joey Johnson — College of Southern Idaho
Doug Lewis — Mesa Community College
Lincoln "Ice" Minor — Midland College
Michael Porter — San Jacinto College, Central Campus
Jim Smith — Herkimer County Community College
John Turner — Allegany Community College
Mitchell Williams — Herkimer County Community College

Coach of the Tournament

Jerry Stone — Midland College

French Most Valuable Player

Jim Smith — Herkimer County Community College

Sesher Sportsmanship Award

Paxton Cobb — Mattatuck Community College

Bud Obee Outstanding Small Player Award

Greg "Boo" Harvey — San Jacinto College, Central Campus

1987 TOURNAMENT BRACKET

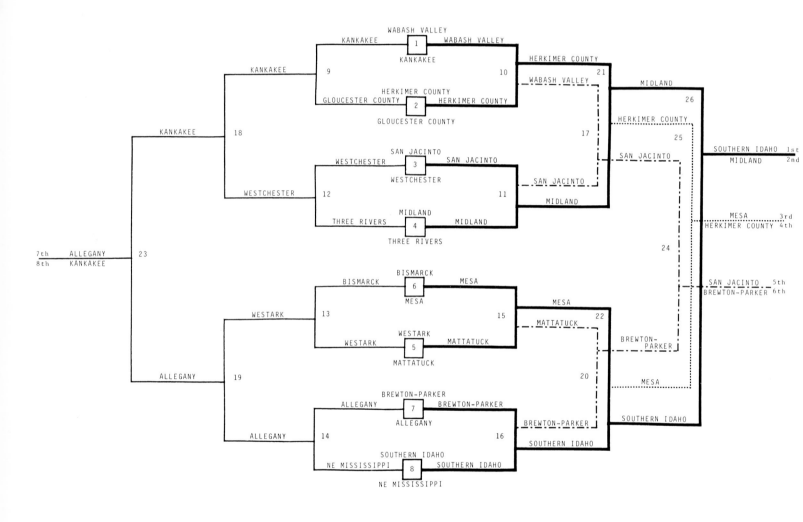

arle J. "Goldie" Holmes was a short man with a grand vision. As athletic director of Compton College, he developed a national reputation for his feisty drive toward excellence in junior college athletics. Not satisfied with putting on the small local Compton Invitational, he dreamed of an intersectional basketball tournament of national proportions. But, in 1945, with a war on, there was little interest in such an ambitious venture.

Instead, with the blessings of the National Junior College Athletic Association, whose activity had ceased because of the war, Holmes organized and directed the Western States College Basketball Tournament held in Decker Gymnasium on the Compton campus. Because of travel restrictions imposed by the war effort, the event was hardly on the grand scale he envisioned. Only nine junior colleges participated with seven of the nine schools from in and around the Los Angeles area. Only the inclusion of Modesto Junior College from Northern California and Phoenix Junior College from Arizona gave any intersectional semblance to the competition.

Still, the tournament was a huge success with a packed house every night. By the time Pasadena Junior College copped the title, more than 10,000 spectators had viewed the event during its four-day run and efforts were already underway for its return the following year.

Then the war ended and travel regulations were relaxed. Suddenly, a season-ending intersectional tournament was now appealing. Many colleges wanted invitations to the Western States Tournament, making the selection process difficult. In the end 16 teams representing junior colleges in Utah, Arizona, and California were invited to Compton for the second annual event.

The 1946 tourney — which saw the defending champs beaten by Sacramento City College in the final — was even more popular than its predecessor. More than 20,000 took in some portion of the five-day event with some sessions drawing turnaway crowds.

The third Western States Tournament came very close to fulfilling Goldie Holmes' dream. The number of teams wanting entrance to the 1947 edition made the selection process an unpopular chore. Regardless of the criteria employed, deserving teams felt slighted. In the end, 16 teams from nine states met the first week of March in Compton. The fact that only schools west of the Mississippi were represented kept it from being a truly national event.

Not only had the tournament grown in relation to its cross-sectional representation, it had also grown as a promotion. Ticket prices were raised and a $5.00 reserved-seat season ticket was introduced. The number of awards was increased to include the presentation of wristwatches and silver basketballs to each member of the championship team. Besides the team trophies for placing in the tournament, trophies were also awarded to the team displaying the best sportsmanship, to the outstanding player, and to the members of the All-Tourney Team. The event had become a topflight production.

The increased interest in the Compton tournament and the rapid growth of junior colleges after the war confirmed the need for a nationwide basketball program. At the invitation of Compton College, NJCAA President Paul Wilhelmsen called a special business meeting during the 1947 Western States Tournament to discuss a regional and national tournament plan. As a result

Goldie Holmes, Athletic Director of Compton College and "Father" of the NJCAA Basketball Tournament, never played a major role in the NJCAA or the tournament after its inception though he remained loyal to his brainchild until his death. Holmes officiated early tournaments and took a minor role in the organization as Director of the NJCAA Service Bureau from 1953-1960, long after the rest of California had turned its back on the NJCAA. (Photo courtesy of Ken Fagans)

of this meeting, the United States was divided into eight regions with vice presidents appointed and assigned responsibility for organizing regional tournaments the following year. Regional winners and runners-up would then participate in the Association's first national basketball tournament.

In order to reduce travel time for as many teams as possible, it was agreed to locate the national tournament in the central United States. Captain E.P. "Chink" Coleman, director of athletics at Wentworth Military Academy in Lexington, Missouri, was elected president of the association and was delegated to select a site and organize the tournament.

The first National Junior College Athletic Association Basketball Tournament was eventually scheduled for March 23-27, 1948, at the Southwest Missouri State Teachers College Field House in Springfield.

Goldie Holmes' dream became reality.

THE PARTICIPANTS

Region	Team
Pacific Northwest	Marin Junior College — Kentfield, California
	*Moberly Junior College — Moberly, Missouri
Western	Compton College — Compton, California
	Glendale College — Glendale, California
Southwest	Murray State School of Agriculture — Tishomingo, Oklahoma
	Tyler Junior College — Tyler, Texas
Southeast	State Agricultural and Mechanical College, Third District — Magnolia, Arkansas
	Brewton-Parker Junior College — Mount Vernon, Georgia
Midwest	Fort Scott Junior College — Fort Scott, Kansas
	McCook Junior College — McCook, Nebraska
North Central	Morton Junior College — Cicero, Illinois
	Duluth Junior College — Duluth, Minnesota
Eastern	Bluefield College — Bluefield, Virginia
	*Dodge City Junior College — Dodge City, Kansas
Northeast	Central City Business Institute — Syracuse, New York
	*Jackson Junior College — Jackson, Michigan
*Invited to fill bracket	

Though the NJCAA had been in existence a decade, it was still little more than a loose confederation of schools with minimal structure. Putting on a basketball tournament with national scope required a complex coordination of elements. It was quickly apparent the fledgling association had a lot to learn.

To begin with, it had been assumed profits from regional tournaments would finance the trips for the national entries. The Association soon found out interest in junior college sports was not as well developed nationally as it was in Southern California. Many regional tourneys had trouble just finding teams to compete, let alone draw crowds. Consequently, several were miserable financial failures.

A notable example of the dilemma facing many tourney entries was the case of Marin Junior College, winner of the Pacific Northwest region. The school was located in Kentfield below Mount Tamalpais in the heart of Marin County, California. The cost of transporting the team halfway across the continent plus providing food and lodging for a little more than a week was estimated at $2,400. The regional held in Sacramento was a flop, netting only $675 for the winner's trip. The nearly $1,800 deficit was more than the school could afford.

With a week to go before the nationals, a contribution drive was organized to make up the difference. The student body, the school administration, the San Rafael *Independent,* the San

Francisco newspapers, and Ira Blue, radio newscaster for station KGO in San Francisco, all got behind the effort to send the Mariners to Springfield.

Armed with milk bottles to hold donations, the student assembled a car caravan to canvas the county. They staged a giant rally on the steps of the county courthouse. They engaged the faculty in a benefit basketball game. Everyone from the school's president down to the team water boy participated in the effort to solicit financial support for the team.

While the people of Springfield were reading about the virtues of the two local favorites — teams who had only a relatively short distance to travel to reach the upcoming national tournament — the Mariners were desperately trying to make ends meet. On Thursday morning the fund was still short $700. A deadline was set for 7 p.m. the next day, the team's scheduled departure time.

The deadline was not needed however. By noon the goal was reached and, by the time the team's train left for Springfield more than $4,300 had been collected.

Other schools in the same situation did not fair as well. The advanced publicity provided by the Springfield press the week before the tournament reflected the tenuous situation as the slate of participants changed from one day to the next. Depending on which day you picked up the paper, one of the North Central regional representatives figured to be either Austin Junior College, Duluth Junior College, or a "team yet to be named."

The first qualifiers to definitely say they were not able to come were South Jersey College of Camden, New Jersey, and Stockton Junior College of Stockton, California (runner-up to Marin in the Pacific Northwest regional failure). Two teams were "invited" to replace them — Jackson Junior College from Michigan and Moberly Junior College from Missouri. The promoters took quick advantage of the fact Moberly was the only home state product in the tournament and designated it "host team."

The scramble to find enough teams willing and able to fill out the tournament bracket continued all week, culminating with the last minute withdrawal of Beckley College of Beckley, West Virginia, just three days before the event's scheduled start. Grabbing for the best — and closest — team available, President Chink Coleman selected Dodge City Junior College, conference champions of neighboring Kansas.

Since the participants remained in question up to the last moment, there was little pre-tourney publicity about the teams coming to Springfield. What press was allocated to tournament coverage was mostly given to the teams considered "local favorites" — an obvious ploy to generate interest in the local populace.

The primary recipient of newsprint was "host" invitee, Moberly. The Greyhounds had failed to earn their way to the tournament when they lost by two points to McCook Junior College, another tourney participant, in the semifinals of the Midwest regional. It was their only loss of the season to a junior college foe, making their 27-3 record overall an impressive one.

More important to tournament organizers was the fact several Moberly players had already participated before Springfield audiences at the state high school tournament. One of them, Don Gosen, the number two scorer for Moberly, had led his Hermann High team to a fourth-place finish just the year before.

The Greyhounds also possessed the most sought-after basketball player in the state in Huntsville native, Bill Gardiner, a 6-7 center who averaged just under 19 points a game. According to the Moberly public relations department, no fewer than 10 colleges and universities had already made bids for his services for the following year. The local papers jumped on the bandwagon, using Gardiner as a prime example of the talent to be found in the tournament by the numerous college scouts expected to attend. Consequently, Gardiner received more advance press than most of the teams entered in the tournament.

By virtue of the fact it was just across the Kansas border and, therefore, the closest participant to Springfield, Fort Scott Junior College also garnered prime pre-tourney publicity. Also nicknamed Greyhounds, Fort Scott was a tall team for that era with seven members over six-feet and owned an excellent 22-4 record, including the Midwest regional championship.

The only other team to receive much attention prior to the tournament was Compton College. The Tartars were immediately tagged as the pre-tourney favorites. Eight members, including four starters, were returnees from the previous year's team, winner of the Western States Tournament. Compton qualified for the trip to Springfield by winning the Western regional, placing three men on the region's all-tournament team — center Carl Kraushaar, and forwards Bob Crowe and Dan Ducich. The trio was the core of a blistering fast-break offense which had streaked past opponents 33 times in 41 games. The "Terrible Tartars" were definitely the team to beat.

The Southern California schools participating in the 1948 Juco Tournament were accorded early favorite status because of tradition and talent. Compton and Glendale players comprised half of the 1948 Western States All-Tourney Team: top row — far left, Carl Kraushaar (Compton); second from left, Dan Ducich (Compton); bottom row — far left, Ward Coburn (Glendale); second from left, Gene Haas (Glendale); middle, Bob Crowe (Compton). (Photo courtesy of the NJCAA)

TUESDAY — HISTORY BEGINS

Compton College and Arkansas A&M of Magnolia had the distinction of playing in the first game in the history of National Junior College Basketball Tournament competition. Since Southwest Missouri State Teachers College hospitably opened the doors of its field house for the momentous occasion, it was only fair the tournament also provide a first for the hosts.

In 1947, Jackie Robinson broke the color line in Major League baseball. Earlier in the month, the NAIB[1] tournament in Kansas City rescinded a long-standing rule which banned the participation of "Negroes" when two colleges withdrew from the competition to protest the practice. The end of segregation in sports was rapidly at hand and the NJCAA Tournament helped it along by bringing integration with it. Compton's Bob Crowe was the first black ever to play on Southwest Missouri State's court.

Crowe was a superb athlete. The 23-year-old southpaw from Franklin, Indiana, had been clocked in 9.9 for the 100-yard dash and 48.6 for the quarter-mile. His explosive speed was the crux of the Compton fast-break attack.

Though he had a tough shooting game against the quintet from Magnolia, Crowe's crowd-pleasing floor play sparked Compton's offense to an easy 61-51 win. The only threat came from the 20-point stellar performance of Duddy Waller, leading scorer for the Mule Riders from Arkansas. Still, Tartar Coach William Schleibaum substituted freely in the second half. The win solidified Compton's role as tournament favorite.

The team from Duluth, Minnesota — on the shores of Lake Superior — brought a five-gallon container of drinking water with them which appeared to have magical powers. The Bluejays came from behind in the last seven minutes to defeat Blue-field, Virginia, 57-50, in the second game of the day after three Bluefield starters went to the bench with five personals. The turning point came when the Ramblin' Reds' 6-8 center, Warren Butterworth, who dominated the boards throughout the game, fouled out with 2½ minutes remaining and the score knotted at 48-all. From then on Bluefield managed only two points. Duluth forward Carl Gustafson upped the individual tourney scoring mark, leading the Bluejays with 23 points.

The final afternoon contest was close even though the outcome was never really in question. The McCook Indians put up a game fight, trailing by only two at the half and never by more than six. They tied the score twice in the second half but were unable to capture the lead as the Murray State Aggies went on to win their 20th game in 21 starts, 53-49.

A small, hustling crew from Jackson, Michigan, opened the evening session with the tournament's first upset. The Maroons jumped out to a 35-21 halftime lead and never slackened their aggressive pace. The Bookkeepers from Central City Business Institute wore down, suffering their second defeat of the year, 70-55. Jackson center Phil Martin topped the day's newly established individual scoring record by netting 25. Guard Bill Gulgulian, who did double duty filling in for CCBI's ailing coach, Robert Ralston, scored 21 for the losers before fouling out.

In the evening feature, Glendale College — runner-up to Compton in the Western regional — gave notice it was also a title threat. Maintaining the advantage throughout the game, the Glendale Vaqueros had little trouble beating Brewton-Parker, 58-42. The ease with which Glendale won confirmed Southern California basketball was as good as advertised.

The day's finale was a frustrating disappointment for the 200 Fort Scott rooters who followed their team to Springfield. Fortune turned against the Greyhounds from the beginning when they played without the services of leading scorer, Gerald Beaman, who remained in Kansas because his wife was having a baby.

Despite the drawback, Fort Scott had plenty of opportunities, especially after Tyler lost four players to fouls. The Greyhounds failed to capitalize, however, missing 13 free throws. The Kansas crew was never closer than four points, falling to the victorious Apaches, 66-60.

Fort Scott's loss was particularly discouraging for tournament promoters. The day's activity had opened to a sparse afternoon crowd. The evening audience was only slightly better. The total attendance for both sessions was less than 1,200. With one of the local draws no longer in the winner's bracket, the signs for financial success were not good.

Compton's Bob Crowe, who later played at San Jose State, was the first black athlete to play on Southwest Missouri State's floor. (Photo courtesy of San Jose State University.)

---

[1] The National Association of Intercollegiate Basketball (NAIB) was the forerunner of the National Association of Intercollegiate Athletics (NAIA).

WEDNESDAY — WHERE IS THE CROWD?

The opener on the tournanment's second day gave the organizers reason to smile. As a last minute replacement, Dodge City Junior College was not expected to do much more than fill out the bracket. However, the way the southwestern Kansas squad bombed Illinois state champ, Morton Junior College, convinced many the dark horse team should not be overlooked. After leading 26-18 at the half, the Dodge City Conquistadors ripped the nets for 50 points, a total only slightly less than the average most tourney entries boasted for an entire *game*. Led by center Don Heiland's 19 and forward Eddie Gibbon's 18, the Kansans established a new team high for tourney scoring, winning 76-45.

Just as tournament backers were beginning to smile, the last first-round game put back the frowns. Trailing for most of the contest, Moberly still had a chance to win when the Greyhounds pulled into a 47-all tie with 2½ minutes to play. Then a free throw by the Mariners from Kentfield followed by three successive field goals crushed Moberly hopes. Bill Gardiner, Moberly's sensational center, was held to just five field goals by Marin center Ray Snyder. Snyder also equaled Gardiner's 15-point total, thus negating the big man's effect on the game. The player and team who most sparked local fan curiosity lost, 59-50, and were relegated to consolation play.

***

Springfield had been selected as the site of the NJCAA Tournament for several reasons: It was centrally located in the United States. In the Southwest Missouri State Field House, it had an excellent facility with available playing dates. And, since it had successfully hosted the Missouri State basketball tournament, it appeared to have a good community interest in basketball.

Southwest Missouri State Field House, site of the first Juco Tournament. (Photo courtesy of Mark Stilwell, SID Southwest Missouri State University.)

The only drawback to Springfield's hosting the tournament was its lack of exposure to the sport at the junior college level. No junior colleges were located in Springfield.

The NJCAA hoped the caliber of talent and play plus the national scope of the event would be sufficient to tantalize public interest and attract a sizable audience. The regional tournament failures were evidence the NJCAA underestimated the drawing power of junior college basketball. The national tournament's modest first day crowd appeared to confirm the fact for Springfield as well.

The last hope for selling the tournament to the local audience was to appeal to regional bias. With Moberly's loss, even this promotional tactic was rendered useless. Now the only Midwestern team left in the winner's bracket was the Cinderella squad from Dodge City, Kansas — a town more than 300 miles from Springfield.

In an editorial in the Wednesday evening *Springfield Leader and Press,* sports editor Perry E. Smith chided the local citizenry by saying, "The support Springfield is giving the national junior college basketball tournament does not befit our town's status as 'hotbed' of the sport in these hyar [sic] parts." Though he

built up the superior quality of the basketball being exhibited and the interest shown by the press from all over, it was evident from the tone of the article that the tournament was in danger of being a flop.

If the column chastened anyone who read it, it didn't show in the Wednesday night box office receipts. Not many shared the interest of college coaches such as Kansas University Head Coach Phog Allen who was there scouting talent. According to news accounts, "barely 400 fans" watched the evening session which featured two contrasting quarterfinal match-ups.

Pre-tourney favorite Compton was extended in its game with Duluth, falling behind twice in the second half before recovering to win, 44-37. The loss of Duluth's hot-shooting guard, Rudie Brandstorm, to fouls midway in the final period provided the impetus for Compton's revival. The score was the lowest in the tournament to that point, in sharp contrast to the 50-point one-half total chalked up by Dodge City earlier in the day.

It also contrasted sharply with the record-setting single-game total established by the Murray State Aggies in the nightcap. The Oklahomans overwhelmed a much smaller Jackson team, streaking to a lopsided 79-39 victory. The win represented the Aggies 21st consecutive victory — a streak which had begun after a season-opening loss to the Oklahoma A&M "B" squad — and set up an excellent semifinal match between the champions of the West and Southwest.

THURSDAY — A PREVIEW OF THINGS TO COME

Since Tyler had finished second in the Southwestern regional and Glendale was runner-up in the West, the Thursday afternoon quarterfinal served as a preview of the upcoming Murray State-Compton contest. Tyler trailed 28-25 at halftime, but quickly took the lead in the first five minutes after intermission. A game-ending stall ordered by Tyler Coach Floyd Wagstaff — who wore a hat all through the tournament to cover his balding head — almost backfired. Clever maneuvering by Glendale forced several steals, enabling the Californians to close to within two. But, Tyler's output from the free throw line proved the difference. Outshot from the field, Tyler chalked up a 20-12 advantage in charities and held on to win, 50-46. Considering the strength of the California contingent, the Apache victory was viewed with mild surprise.

The Thursday night feature proved to be the best quarterfinal and the best contest of the day. Using a balanced attack, Marin took a 10-point margin into the dressing room at the half, then quickly built it to 15 once the Californians returned to the floor.

Then, just as they had in the last half of their opening-round game, the Dodge City Conquistadors cut loose behind Eddie Gibbons, who hit 17 of his 19-point total in the second frame.

Moberly's Bill Gardiner, who later played at St. Louis University, was the first player to break the 30-point barrier. His 33 against Morton Junior College was the tourney record for two years. (Photo courtesy of St. Louis University.)

Gibbons made the game interesting when he hit three consecutive long set shots to bring Dodge City within a field goal of the Mariners with three minutes left. After Marin's Ray Snyder stifled the rally momentarily with a clutch fielder, Gibbons came right back with another bull's-eye. At the 1:40 mark, Dodge City trailed, 50-48.

Snyder, who had been a hero the day before in the Mariner win over Moberly, put on the mantle again with another clutch field goal, ending the Conquistador rally for good.

As exciting as Thursday night's feature was, few people witnessed it. As in the two previous days, the Southwest Missouri State Field House had more empty seats than occupied. Even the presence of "host" Moberly in the nightcap was not enough to lure an audience. Consequently, the single best individual performance of the tournament went virtually unnoticed.

Living up to his pre-tourney publicity, Bill Gardiner led the Greyhounds to a 77-65 consolation win over Morton with an outstanding offensive show and 33 points. The total was exceptional for that era of the sport and would serve as a tournament standard of excellence for two years.

FRIDAY — WEST VERSUS SOUTHWEST

Events were rapidly coming to a head for the first National Junior College Basketball Tournament with two very promising semifinals scheduled for Friday. Both featured match-ups between teams from the West and the Southwest. The afternoon semifinal pitted fast-breaking, tourney favorite Compton College against an explosive group of Murray State Aggies who were riding a long winning streak. The evening semifinal matched two teams with similar well-balanced scoring attacks — Tyler and Marin. The cream was rising to the top.

Though action on the court was building toward an exciting Saturday climax, there was no corresponding buildup of an audience to view it. The situation was so desperate, Chink Coleman announced that the weekday special 50-cent student admission price would be extended to include the championships on Saturday night. It was an obvious maneuver to attract as many Southwest Missouri State students as possible to fill the empty fieldhouse.

However, the same small crowd chose to attend Friday's games. It was too bad, since the two semifinal contests lived up to the championship caliber expected at the final stages of tournament play.

The first half of the Compton-Murray State game demonstrated how evenly matched the two teams were with six ties and five lead changes. At the half, it was Murray State in front of favored Compton, 26-21.

The second half opened with a flurry resembling championship volleys at Wimbledon. In a four-minute span, the two teams exchanged buckets at a five-points-a-minute pace. When the flurry ended, Murray State was still on top by three.

The game continued close until less than five minutes remained. Then, with Murray State ahead, 47-45, the Aggies began a parade to the foul line. When Dan Ducich, Compton's leading scorer, fouled out at the 2:47 mark, the end was no longer in doubt. Murray State advanced to the championship game, 56-49.

The first half of the Tyler-Marin game closely paralleled the earlier semifinal with eight lead changes before Tyler broke away at the end of the period to lead by seven.

Having traveled further than anyone else to get to the tournament, the Mariners from Kentfield did not give up without a fight. Encouraged by their cheering entourage — 10 fellow students who made the nearly 2,000-mile trip by car — the California quintet launched into a fast-break attack, outscoring their Texas opponents, 10-2, in the first six minutes of the second half. Tyler regained the lead momentarily with a field goal, but then a pair of two-pointers by guard Walt Moreno put the Mariners out in front for good.

It was no wonder Coach Floyd Wagstaff was losing his hair. For Tyler, the second half was a nightmare best forgotten.[2] Five minutes into the last period, the Apaches lost their rebounding strength when center Dave Rodriguez fouled out. Then they lost three more starters — two more to fouls and one, swift guard Jose Palafox, to an ankle injury.

On the Mariner behalf, it was truly a team victory. In the first half, Herb Jotter, Marin's play-making guard, dazzled the crowd with his floor work. He, along with forward Bob McCune, who took game honors with 18, carried the scoring load during the opening period. Then in the final stretch, it was eight timely baskets by Walt Moreno and the dominating board work of Ray Snyder which provided the winning margin, 62-53.

The Mariner followers had put together many dollars for the team to travel many miles. The players repaid the show of faith by putting Marin in the finals.

SATURDAY — AN END TO A BEGINNING

Saturday's march for tournament trophies began with a replay of the Midwestern regional championship. In their earlier match, Fort Scott outlasted McCook, 45-44. The battle for fifth place in the nation was much the same. Led by Charley Watt's 13-point outburst down the stretch, the Greyhounds rallied from a seven-point halftime deficit and again nipped McCook, this time by two, 60-58. Watt wound up with 21 for game-high honors while McCook's Ray "Cub" Jussel led the Indians with 20, giving him a four-game total of 72 for the tourney scoring title.

Another Kansas team and another rally were also featured in the final afternoon match-up. This time, however, the Kansans were not the ones who rallied. Dodge City seemed to be comfortably in front, 52-38, with 2:05 to go when Duluth — which had been as cold as a Minnesota winter — finally warmed up. The Bluejay's Rudie Brandstorm caught fire, hitting 10 points in 60 seconds and another six before the end of the game. Despite his remarkable effort, Dodge City held on for a 58-54 victory and fourth-place.

Another rally highlighted the third-place game. Trailing Tyler 31-18 at half and by as many as 10 points in the second period, Compton pulled even with 2:45 remaining on a long field goal by Bob Crowe. The Tartars made their comeback complete, winning the closest finish of the tournament, 67-66.

With a 22-game win streak on the line and an impressive win over the pre-tourney favorite in the semifinals, Murray State was the team to beat in the championship contest. The Aggies' size and stingy defense had made beating the best look easy.

In contrast, the road to the finals had been a long arduous struggle for Marin, both on and off the court. Not only had the Mariners scrambled by seven post-season opponents to get to where they were, they had also overcome the financial burden others had been unable to do.

The final tilt began as most pressure championship affairs do; both teams were extremely tight and played accordingly. A listless first half ended in a 19-15 Marin advantage.

The second half was a different story. Cranking up their fast break, the Mariners outscored the Oklahomans, 13-2. After the game-breaking spurt, first-year coach Irwin "Red" Diamond had his charges play it safe. The Californians were never again challenged, chalking up a conservative 48-34 final tally.

The National Junior College Athletic Association Basketball Tournament crowned Marin Junior College its first national champion.

THE AFTERMATH — COUNTING THE RECEIPTS

On Tuesday evening following the tournament, passengers on the S.P. Daylight out of Los Angeles had trouble getting through the mass of people packing the outer portions of San Francisco's Third and Townsend railway terminal. Two-thirds of Marin's student body and hundreds of fans were on hand to greet their heroes and to proudly parade them down Market Street. It was a demonstration befitting any national championship.

---

[2] Years later, Wagstaff was able to recount complete histories of each of his players, could recall having played the other two California teams, but was completely surprised to find out Tyler had played Marin in the semifinals.

The Marin Mariners from Kentfield, California, first champs of the NJCAA Basketball Tournament, traveled farther than any other participant in tourney history. (Photo courtesy of Irwin "Red" Diamond.)

For the first time, junior colleges from all over the country had come together to compete for the right to be called the nation's best. It was a major accomplishment.

Back in Springfield, however, there were doubts. Would it ever happen again?

The NJCAA incurred a debt of between $3,000 and $3,500 putting on the tournament. Among the bills was a $1,000 outlay for prizes, including trophies patterned after the ones awarded by the NCAA.

As the story unfolded in the newspapers, President Chink Coleman first reported that by "cutting expenses" he expected to cover the NJCAA's financial obligations. This was an optimistic statement, since prior to Saturday's sessions, it was obvious the box office take would not cover the outstanding debt.

A week-and-a-half later, Coleman's story had changed. The NJCAA was now estimating a loss of "several hundred dollars." With a total paid attendance of fewer than 3,800, the five-day national tournament had been a financial disaster.

Then began a series of recriminations. Who was responsible for the failure?

Shortly after the tournament, Coleman made a statement to the press saying, "With the exception of the Chamber of Commerce, every agency that was asked for help in putting across our tournament cooperated wonderfully. The hotels, press, radio, and especially those folks at SMS, gave us fine treatment."

In a board meeting of the Springfield Chamber of Commerce, Manager Louis Reps replied by openly criticizing the way Coleman handled the tournament.

Coleman rebutted Reps in a letter, charging the Chamber with making promises it never kept.

The details behind the tournament's financial failure have become muddled by time and lack of documentation. A true accounting of what happened is impossible. Needless to say, the problems of the first National Juco Basketball Tournament plagued the NJCAA for sometime. Lawsuits were contemplated and it was not until three years later that matters were finally brought to rest.[3] Even then, the financial embarrassment of the first tournament remained a black eye for the association in its bid for respectability.

Wentworth's New Director of Athletics

IN 1941, COACHES, WRITERS AND PLAYERS OF NEW MEXICO VOTED HIM THE STATE'S OUTSTANDING COACH

CAPT. E. P. "Chink" COLEMAN

KNOWN FOR HIS TRIPLE SPINNER - THE SPIN HAS BEEN INSTRUMENTAL IN BRINGING MANY FOOTBALL VICTORIES TO COLEMAN'S TEAMS

"FILL THAT GAP, CHINKER!"

"CHINK" IS NOT A CHINAMAN - IN HIGH SCHOOL, THE COACH CALLED COLEMAN A CHINKER, BECAUSE HE PLUGGED IMPORTANT HOLES IN THE LINE - "CHINKER" TOOK ON AND FOLLOWED HIM TO COLLEGE, LATER ABBREVIATED TO "CHINK"

Studied at St. Edwards U., Texas Christian U., and New Mexico State. During 12-year period, his teams won 88, tied 1, and lost 31 games.

LEXINGTON, Mo.—Capt. E. P. (Chink) Coleman, college football and basketball coach at Wentworth Military Academy here since 1942, has been upped to director of athletics at the school.

Welcome to the

NATIONAL JUNIOR BASKET-BALL CHAMPIONSHIP TOURNAMENT

Sponsored by the National Junior College Athletic Association

The program of the NJCAA is planned and guided by athletic administrators from junior colleges having membership in the association. It is completely democratic in that a regional vice-president of each region and state chairmen from every state select representatives to represent their areas in the national tournament.

A national program is rapidly developing in all sports. The NJCAA will sponsor national meets in Basketball, Swimming, Track and Field, Tennis, and Golf. Through the years I can visualize the addition of Boxing, Baseball, and our own Coaching School.

I wish to thank the Southwest Missouri State College of Springfield, Missouri, for the wonderful facilities; the coaches and administrators for their assistance in putting on the tournament.

CAPT. E. P. COLEMAN,
President NJCAA.

Executive Committee

PRESIDENT—

Capt. E. P. "Chink" Coleman
Wentworth Military Academy
Lexington, Missouri.

SECRETARY-TREASURER—

George "Dutch" Hoy,
Phoenix Junior College.
Phoenix, Arizona.

NJCAA Districts with Regional Vice Presidents

WESTERN—	NORTHEAST—	NORTH CENTRAL—	SOUTHWEST—
Earl J. Holmes, Compton College, Compton, Calif.	Phillip H. Clarke, Hillyer Junior College, Hartford, Connecticut.	Charles D. Smidl, Woodrow Wilson College, Chicago, Illinois.	Bob Carter, Amarillo College, Amarillo, Texas.
MIDWEST—	PACIFIC NORTHWEST—	SOUTHEAST—	EASTERN—

The 1948 program was a hastily constructed item with team photographs often found several pages from team rosters. However, there was plenty of space for a prominent (page 1) write up of E.P. "Chink" Coleman, the NJCAA's flamboyant new president and tourney organizer. (Photo courtesy of the NJCAA)

[3] The lack of information regarding the NJCAA's early financial problems is directly related to its loose, almost informal organization at the time. Documentation of officer responsibilities was sketchy. Communication between member institutions was minimal. It was a year before a majority of the membership became fully aware of the Springfield disaster. (Referring to his 1949 election as president of the NJCAA, Reed Swenson said, "Had I known the mess the NJCAA was in I might not have accepted the position.")

At the annual meeting held simultaneous to the 1949 tournament, Chink Coleman resigned. In the following year, two lawsuits were contemplated — one by Southwest Missouri State against the NJCAA for outstanding debts and one by the Association against Coleman for misappropriation of funds. None of the suits were ever brought to court, however, for the simple reason no written contracts ever existed.

When asked by the NJCAA to give a financial accounting of his tenure as president, Coleman took almost a year to comply. Since he had not been required to keep detailed records of his actions, he had to piece together the account from scratch.

It was not until the annual meeting in March of 1951 that the affair was finally brought to rest when the NJCAA formally accepted Coleman's accounting. Subsequently, all parties involved agreed to drop the matter.

A positive note to the tournament's failure was that the NJCAA learned from the experience. Undaunted by the initial lack of success, the Association made immediate plans for a second national championship. This time the NJCAA was taking no risks. At the conclusion of the Springfield tournament, President Coleman announced the NJCAA would require a $5,500 guarantee from the host of the 1949 version of the event. Eight cities were bidding for the tournament, but only one remained serious once the requirement of a guarantee was established.

Attending the tournament at Springfield was Charley Sesher, basketball and football coach for Hutchinson Junior College, who had been delegated by the school to try to obtain a regional tournament for Hutchinson, Kansas. Before one of the daily NJCAA meetings, Sesher was approached by his good friend Herb Bender, coach of Dodge City: "Why don't you go after the nationals?"

Sesher was an astute observer with a quiet, unassuming personality — a sharp contrast to the NJCAA's flamboyant promoter, Chink Coleman. Though he saw the cool reception the tournament received at Springfield, he quickly recognized its possibilities. When asked if Hutchinson would be interested in hosting the affair, he said yes. This was a bold move for such an unpretentious individual. Sesher had no assurance of support at home.

With the Springfield papers already saying Hutchinson had offered to underwrite the next year's tournament, Sesher returned to Hutchinson to sell the idea. After getting the approval of the Hutchinson Junior College administration, he approached various civic organizations in search of a sponsor for the venture. The Chamber of Commerce was interested in the idea, but did not have the funds. The Elks Club had the money, but had already committed it to the local baseball team. Lyse Rishel Post 68 of the American Legion was the only remaining organization in the city financially solid enough to take on the project.

When approached by Sesher, the post's executive committee was enthusiastic about hosting the tournament. However, the organization's by-laws required expenditures over $1,000 be approved by the general membership. It took several weeks to convince the Legion to commit the $5,500 needed to sponsor the event.[4] Working without fanfare, Sesher helped Legion officials sell the proposal, then ironed out promotional and financial details with the NJCAA.

On May 7th at the conclusion of the NJCAA Track and Field competition in Phoenix, it was announced Hutchinson would be the site of the 1949 basketball championship. On January 10, 1949, a contract was signed between the NJCAA, the American Legion, and Hutchinson Junior College.

The National Junior College Basketball Tournament was given a second chance.

Tournament Results

Tuesday:	Game	
	1	Compton — 61 Arkansas A&M — 51
	2	Duluth — 57 Bluefield — 50
	3	Murray St. — 53 McCook — 49
	4	Jackson — 70 CCBI-Syracuse — 55
	5	Glendale — 58 Brewton-Parker — 42
	6	Tyler — 66 Fort Scott — 60
Wednesday:	Game	
	7	Dodge City — 76 Morton — 45
	8	Marin — 59 Moberly — 50
	9	Arkansas A&M — 61 Bluefield — 42
	10	Compton — 44 Duluth — 37
	11	Murray St. — 79 Jackson — 39
Thursday:	Game	
	12	McCook — 58 CCBI-Syracuse — 51
	13	Tyler — 50 Glendale — 46
	14	Duluth — 66 Jackson — 56
	15	Fort Scott — 47 Brewton-Parker — 41
	16	Marin — 56 Dodge City — 51
	17	Moberly — 77 Morton — 65
Friday:	Game	
	18	McCook — 60 Arkansas A&M — 49
	19	Fort Scott — 54 Moberly — 40
	20	Murray St. — 56 Compton — 49
	21	Dodge City — 49 Glendale — 32
	22	Marin — 62 Tyler — 53
Saturday:	Game	
	23	Fort Scott — 60 McCook — 58
	24	Dodge City — 58 Duluth — 54
	25	Compton — 67 Tyler — 66
	26	Marin — 48 Murray St. 34

How They Finished in 1948

1. Marin Junior College
2. Murray State School of Agriculture
3. Compton College
4. Dodge City Junior College
5. Fort Scott Junior College
6. Tyler Junior College
7. Duluth Junior College
8. McCook Junior College

All-Star Squad

Curtis Beaman — Fort Scott Junior College
Bob Crowe — Compton College
Dan Ducich — Compton College
Eddie Gibbons — Dodge City Junior College
Roy D. Irons — Murray State School of Agriculture
Herb Jotter — Marin Junior College
Negial King — Murray State School of Agriculture
Carl Kraushaar — Compton College
Walt Moreno — Marin Junior College
Herb Richardson — Tyler Junior College

To friends and acquaintances, Charley Sesher was the "perfect gentleman." Without his foresight and diplomacy, the Juco Tournament might not have survived its inaugural event. (Photo courtesy of the NJCAA)

---

[4] If the Legion had been approached just one year earlier, it is questionable whether the proposal would have gained favor with its membership. In 1948 the organization was in a period of transition with Veterans of World War II swelling its ranks. When Sesher appealed to the Legion for support, a majority of the post's executive committee were newly installed World War II vets. John Kline was the organization's first World War II commander. The new guard was more dynamic than the older, conservative World War I membership. Many of the executive committeemen had played major college basketball or had seen the sport at a high competitive level. They could envision how a well-run national tournament would excite people and were willing to accept the risks involved in sponsoring the event.

Olympic's Ted Tappe, the 1949 Tournament's top scorer with 81 points, was an all-round athlete. After finishing his collegiate basketball career at Washington State University, he played professional baseball with the Chicago Cubs and Cincinnati Reds. (Photo courtesy of Linc Perry.)

n the March 20, 1949, *Hutchinson News-Herald,* two days before the start of the first NJCAA Basketball Tournament in Hutchinson, Kansas, the tournament was described as "the biggest sports event Hutchinson has ever entertained." In retrospect, given the growth of the NJCAA and the success of the national tournament, this statement would appear more than accurate. However, at the time, coming on the heels of the previous year's financial disaster, there was considerable concern as to how big an event the tournament really would be. Promoters selling $6.25 season tickets at the Class B state high school tournament in Hutchinson the week before met repeated rejection accompanied with comments such as "What's so special about junior college basketball?" In a day when newspapers cost a nickel and a five-room house could be purchased for as little as $6,000, the unknown fate of the $5,500 guarantee put up by the American Legion co-sponsors was enough to cause a degree of apprehension.

There was one potential bright spot. If Hutchinson Junior College were in the tournament, ticket sales would automatically go up, making financial success more likely. Hutchinson had not qualified for regional play, having taken fourth in the Western Division of the Kansas Juco Conference. However, in an arrangement with the NJCAA, if any of the regional qualifiers could not make the trip, Hutchinson would be the first "invited" to fill out the bracket.

During the week preceding the tournament, the *News-Herald* described the Hutchinson fans as "getting a rough ride on the rough front edge of the anxious seat." One by one regional winners were certified as coming until only one position was left unclaimed; the one belonging to Region 16 champion, Ricker Junior College of Houlton, Maine. Located near the U.S.-Canadian border some 1,600 miles from Hutchinson, the school was situated about as far away as you could get and stay within the boundary of the United States. The school had until the Wednesday prior to the tournament to accept.

Tournament sponsors heaved a collective sigh when distance proved to be too much of an obstacle. Ricker relinquished its spot in the bracket, allowing Hutchinson to enter the tournament.

THE PARTICIPANTS

Outside of the local team, the only other ballclub familiar to Hutchonians was Dodge City Junior College which competed against Hutchinson during the regular season. There was no real interest in junior college basketball outside of that played in Hutchinson's own back yard. Interest had to be generated to make the tournament successful.

In order to inform the Hutchinson fans and, in the process, sell the tournament, the *News-Herald* devoted extensive coverage to the upcoming event. The paper printed every scrap of information — which often was not much — that trickled in about the participating teams. When the hard news dried up, details were provided on how the teams were traveling, when they would arrive, and where they would stay once they got there.

Region	Team
1	Compton College — Compton, California
2	Grant Technical College — Del Paso Heights, California
3	Olympic Junior College — Bremerton, Washington
4	Weber College — Ogden, Utah
5	Sayre Junior College — Sayre, Oklahoma
6	Dodge City Junior College — Dodge City, Kansas
7	Tyler Junior College — Tyler, Texas
8	Abraham Baldwin Agriculture College — Tifton, Georgia
9	Campbellsville College — Campbellsville, Kentucky
10	Campbell College — Buies Creek, North Carolina
11	Webster City Junior College — Webster City, Iowa
12	Joliet Junior College — Joliet, Illinois
13	Brainerd Junior College — Brainerd, Minnesota
14	Junior College of Benton Harbor — Benton Harbor, Michigan
15	Bayonne Junior College — Bayonne, New Jersey
16	*Hutchinson Junior College — Hutchinson, Kansas
	*Invited to fill bracket

If press was the measuring stick by which a team was to be judged, the Compton College Tartars would have won going away. The institution flooded the newspaper with reams of publicity material. There were plenty of facts, though, to back up the claim that Compton was the team to beat.

Compton College was an established name in the world of junior college athletics. The Tartars had twice won the Little Rose Bowl championship in football and were a power in track and field. They had won the 1947 Western States Basketball Tournament, forerunner of the national contest, and had placed third the previous year in Springfield. The team represented a region where junior college sports were significantly more advanced and better organized than the rest of the country. Compton's 35-3 record was even more impressive considering the Californians played some of the toughest competition in the land and had earned their right to participate in the national tournament by winning a grueling 16-team regional tourney.

Compton was not the only team figured to have a better-than-fair shot at the championship. Given its first-class mode of transportation to the tournament, it was not difficult to perceive that Tyler Junior College was also a first-class ballclub. Consisting of several Texas high school stars, Tyler was a carefully assembled scoring machine with affluent backers. One of them, H.W. Snowden, a Dallas oil man, donated his private DC-3 to ferry the players to the tournament. Despite a forced landing at Winfield, Kansas, because of bad weather, the team traveled in luxury. Tyler was the only entry to fly to Hutchinson.

A sixth-place finisher in the tournament the year before, Tyler sported a record of 32-1 and had earlier won the highly regarded Texas A&M Juco Invitational. The team's only loss on the year was to the SMU freshmen. The Apaches rebounded from the lone defeat to win 30 straight. Tyler was definitely a top contender.

Where Compton (established in 1927) and Tyler (established in 1926) represented the old guard of junior colleges, Olympic Junior College, the other pre-tourney favorite, represented the new. Olympic was typical of many schools created shortly after World War II to accommodate the mass release of servicemen with G.I. Bill benefits at their disposal. Located in Bremerton, Washington, sight of the Puget Sound Naval Shipyard, the school had been in existence only three years.

Unlike Compton or Tyler, Olympic did not have a reputation nor a recruiting budget with which to construct a championship team. Instead the school relied on local standouts. Two team members, in fact, had played on the Bremerton High School team which placed second in the Class A state tournament the year before. Nevertheless, the Bremerton school brought an excellent 29-1 record to the tournament. The only loss for the Rangers was to an undefeated University of Washington frosh team which they later avenged by giving the Washington team *its* first loss.

Good ballclubs did not end there. From the East came Abraham Baldwin which had won the Georgia state title three years running, averaged over 70 points a game,[1] and owned a respectable 27-3 record.

The East also offered a team of "giants" from Campbellsville, Kentucky. Eight players were over six-feet tall. Six-foot, eight-inch center Jack Nash was the tallest player in the tournament.

From the West, Grant Tech (32-5) of Del Paso Heights, a northern suburb of Sacramento, gained respect after defeating regional favorite City College of San Francisco, 56-50; just after the San Franciscans had hammered College of Marin, defending national champs, 73-47.

Weber College of Ogden, Utah, was also a threat, having survived a wild scoring Region 4 tournament in which scores over 80 points were common.

To the north, Webster City Junior College had recently gained nationwide notoriety in its regional tournament game against Bloomfield (Iowa) Junior College. When Bloomfield would not come out of a tight zone defense, Webster City forward Marvin Jacobson held the ball near the half court for 9½ minutes. The result was a scoreless quarter and unhappy fans. However, the Iowans' 21-2 record — both losses by only one point — proved they could play basketball.

Though they had not played as many games as most tourney entries, the other northern club, the Red Raiders from Brainerd, Minnesota, possessed a decent 16-3 record and featured a legitimate scoring star in forward Chuck Warnberg who averaged 18.6 points per game.

Closer to home, the Sayre, Oklahoma, Yellowjackets represented the area of the country which had produced the previous year's No. 2 team, the Murray State Aggies. Sayre's 26-10 record did not look overly impressive until one considered the fact the Oklahomans were 23-1 against junior college competitors.

The local pick was Kansas champion, Dodge City, a veteran club which appeared to have improved over the previous year's tournament team. Having placed fourth in 1948, it was expected the Conquistadors would do even better this year.

The other four entries in the tournament were enigmas. What advance publicity Campbell College received came from having traveled the furthest by automobile. The appropriately nicknamed Camels motored to Hutchinson in a caravan of cars from Buies Creek, North Carolina, an exhausting distance of more than 1,100 miles. Outside the fact the Bayonne team clamored for good Kansas steak dinners when they first arrived, the only insight into the team's ability came from Coach Bernie Ockene's admonition that his players were "conceding nothing to any rival." As for Joliet and Benton Harbor, the most said about either was that Benton Harbor represented a region noted for being a "hot-bed" of basketball.[2]

Although next to nothing was known about these teams, they were at least accorded a chance of winning. This was not the case for the Hutchinson Blue Dragons. Everyone was grateful that Hutchinson had been granted a place in the tournament bracket. It was a just reward for the players, who had had a tough season, and for the city, which had taken the risk of hosting a tournament with a financial albatross dangling around its neck. Still, no one had any illusions about Hutchinson's chances. The Dragons had a mediocre record of 10-8, 8-7 against junior college opponents. They had no stars. Their leading scorer, Glenn Smyth, owned a modest 11.2 average. It was taken for granted they would play two games and quietly watch the rest of the proceedings from the sidelines. Drawing a good crowd for the first night of the tournament was all that was expected of the local squad. Tournament officials hoped, given a taste of the action, the fans would be hooked for the rest of the week; enough so at least to break even.

---

[1] A 70-point score in 1949 was roughly equivalent to a 100-point score today. To illustrate the point, the scoreboard for Convention Hall, the site of the tournament its first years in Hutchinson, had an upward limit of 70.

Lower scores were partly due to less developed skills in players as compared with today. A more important factor, however, were the rules governing play. For example, game time was kept on a continuously running clock. (For championship bracket contests in the tournament, this rule was waived to allow the clock to be stopped for dead-ball situations in the last two minutes of regulation and overtime periods.) Another rule which helped lower scoring allowed the team fouled the option of shooting a free throw or retaining possession of the ball.

[2] Joliet Junior College, in fact, was not a regional winner. The Wolves, losers to Wright Junior College of Chicago 60-58 in the Region 12 final, received the opportunity to play in Hutchinson when Wright declined to come.

TUESDAY — ONLY ONE SURPRISE

With the exception of one game, the first day's set of six went as expected. Compton became the first team to break the 80-point barrier in the tournament's short history, smashing Benton Harbor 81-49 in the opener. Led by center Allan Lamont, who scored 19 of his 21 points in the first half, Compton took a 43-19 halftime lead then coasted, using second stringers for most of the final period.

Olympic's 6-5 Ted Tappe was a high school all-stater the prior or two years and a state and regional all-star during the current campaign. He was a good-looking, well-developed kid who had celebrated his 18th birthday just the week before the tournament. His superior ability made up for the fact he was the youngest player on the court. Using an extremely accurate left-hand hook shot, Tappe topped all scorers with 27, spearheading a 72-48 Ranger rout of Webster City.

Two other favorites also had little trouble: Dodge City bested Campbellsville, 65-50, and Tyler overwhelmed Bayonne, 64-42. Both verified their top-notch credentials, employing balanced scoring attacks and steady play to subdue their opponents.

The only close contest occurred in the last afternoon game. The lead changed hands five times in the closing 10 minutes before Brainerd edged Campbell, 70-68.

The one surprise came in the day's finale.

Convention Hall was ill-suited for basketball. The court was extremely small. There were bleachers on the sidelines, close enough players had to avoid spectators' legs when inbounding the basketball. A stage three feet from the west end and risers with seats behind the east basket further hemmed in the court. The playing area was so small it was joked that, on fast breaks, players had to go down court three rows deep.[3]

The claustrophobic conditions obviously affected Sayre in the nightcap. The lean and lanky Yellowjackets appeared stage struck, disconcerted by their surroundings. The Hutchinson Blue Dragons put their home court advantage to good use, stunning the Oklahomans, 68-50.

The first day's results excited local fans and encouraged American Legion sponsors. Including advance and general admission sales, the $5,500 guarantee to the NJCAA was already in the till. With Hutchinson's upset win, the Legion was no longer worried about covering expenses.

WEDNESDAY — THE TOURNAMENT'S FIRST OVERTIME

The Wednesday afternoon first-round contests were notable for two excellent scoring performances.

In the first game, Abraham Baldwin's Buck Brannen hit from all over the court, tallying 27. But, it was not enough as Weber won, 70-64.

Hampered by a bandaged bad knee which cut down his mobility, Grant Tech's Jim Loscutoff lacked the finesse of Brannen and other top scorers in the tournament. Most of his points came from under the basket on rebounds or driving lay-ups as his solid, 215-pound frame dominated the middle. In the final opening-round game, Loscutoff horsed in 32, one shy of the tourney record, leading the Saracens to an easy 67-47 win over Joliet.

The high point of the day and one of the best games of the tournament came in the first quarterfinal that evening. From a point in the second half when Sid Ryen rallied the Rangers to a 34-all tie, until Olympic forward Jim Day hit a free throw to knot the score in the closing seconds, Compton and Olympic exchanged the lead five times and shared it seven in a tight defensive struggle. A 55-all tie at the end of regulation necessitated the tournament's first overtime.

With three minutes to play in a cautiously played extra period, the Rangers led Compton, 59-55. Forward Ed Tucker rescued the Tartars, scoring the next two buckets, the last with 37 seconds left. A Tucker free throw then vaulted Compton into the lead.

Unruffled, Olympic moved the ball up court. With 15 seconds showing, Day canned one from the corner, only his second field goal of the game, and was fouled. After a time out, Olympic elected to inbounds the ball rather than shoot a free throw.

With scant seconds left, the jubilant Rangers tossed the ball in play from the midcourt line into backcourt, made a couple passes, dribbled once — then threw one awry. Compton's Allan Lamont leaped in the air to intercept, landed, spun around, and fired from just beyond the free throw circle. The ball swished the net, just beating the final gun.

Instantly team emotions flip-flopped. The once joyous Rangers were in tears. The Tartars were ecstatic.

"It was really something," said Compton Coach Ken Fagans. "I had to go back and send a telegram to the Compton newspaper and I could hardly write the telegram down. About half-an-hour after the game I was still shaking."

Grant Tech's "Jungle Jim" Loscutoff was the first tourney alumnus to reach the pro ranks. He graduated from the University of Oregon where he led the northern division of the Pacific Coast Conference in scoring and was named first-team all-conference as a senior. Loscutoff then enjoyed a successful pro career with Boston (above, middle — signing contract with Celtic owner Walter Brown) from 1956 to 1964, a period in which the Celtics won seven NBA Championships. (Photo courtesy of Jim Loscutoff)

[3]The court dimensions were 88'x48'. A regulation court today is 94'X50'.

The game was bound to be a heartbreaker with such evenly matched teams: Each was led in scoring by a true All-American — Ted Tappe netting a game-high 23 and Allan Lamont matching his opening-game total of 21. Each possessed a scrappy, play-making guard — Ernie Bond for Compton and Olympic's Darwin Gilchrist, who was unimpeded despite having only one eye. And each had players who excelled in the clutch — Ryen and Day for the Rangers and Lamont and Tucker for the Tartars. Most observers felt that, if the teams had been in opposite

Allan Lamont, who scored the winning basket for Compton in the tournament's first overtime game, later played for the USC Trojans. (Photo courtesy of Ken Fagans)

brackets, this game would have been for the championship, such was the high caliber of play exhibited.

The historic Compton-Olympic contest overshadowed the quarterfinal which followed. Fast-breaking Tyler raced past a less talented Brainerd club, 78-63. Guard Jose Palafox, the swiftest racehorse in the Tyler stable, led all scorers with 26.

THURSDAY — RIVALS MEET AGAIN

There were six games scheduled for Thursday. Only one held any interest for Hutchinson fans.

After the Blue Dragons' upset win over Sayre, tournament officials scrambled to take advantage of the propitious turn of events. They quickly announced a change in the Thursday program, moving the Hutchinson-Dodge City game from its originally scheduled 2:30 matinee slot to the last game of the day. Ticket sales increased accordingly.

There was only one distraction for the anxious hometown fans. The afternoon opener, a consolation match between Campbell and Bayonne, became the first and only scheduled game in tournament history not played. The reason: one of the teams was not there to play.

Bayonne Coach Bernie Ockene was a colorful fire-eater. In an age when coaches were vocally shackled, restricted from even talking to their players except during time-outs,[4] Ockene's short, stocky frame often violated the playing floor as he vigorously disputed officials' calls during Bayonne's first-round encounter with Tyler. In one instance, he stormed the court to protest a goal which he declared had not been properly credited to his team. Though he argued with intensity commensurate to game-winning import, this was hardly the case. The game was never in question. As the 64-42 final indicated, the Tyler Apaches far outclassed their eastern opponents, holding them to the lowest team total of the tournament. However, Bayonne's mentor, disgusted with the outcome, packed up his team, and put it on a train back to New Jersey. Campbell advanced without having to suit up.

In the first quarterfinal game of the evening, Grant Tech advanced to the semifinals with an impressive 68-58 win over Weber. Saracens Ed Rueda, Bob Stein, Carl Youngstrom, and

Bayonne Junior College's firebrand, Bernie Ockene, later coached at St. Peter's College, Jersey City, New Jersey. (Photo courtesy of St. Peter's College)

Jim Loscutoff, each hit double figures with Loscutoff again high man with 20.

Though the Grant Tech-Weber game was closely contested, the less-than-capacity Convention Hall crowd fidgeted, awaiting the next contest. Everyone felt Dodge City was better than Hutchinson. Still, the local fans had reason for guarded optimism. In the two previous conference match-ups between the teams, Hutchinson had lost by the slim margins of one and five points. Even Conquistador backers were aware the third encounter would not be easy.

Even though the Blue Dragons owned a home court advantage, the Hutchinson upset of Sayre demonstrated the team had improved since last meeting Dodge City. Much of this improvement had to be credited to Coach Charley Sesher's decision to enter his team in an A.A.U. tournament in Wichita at the end of the regular season while junior college regional champs were being decided elsewhere. Against amateur squads featuring many ex-college stars, Hutchinson had won its way to the quarterfinals before succumbing.

The payoff for the additional experience became quickly evident. From the opening tip, the Blue Dragons were the aggressors, deploying a tenacious ball-hawking defense. The intensity of play was reflected in the bevy of fouls called. Five Blue Dragons and four Conquistadors narrowly missed expulsion with four fouls apiece.

Don Heiland's six second-period goals kept Dodge City in the hunt as they trailed by only two with five minutes remaining. Hutchinson padded its advantage with the expert free throw shooting of Rich Mercer and LeRoy Esau. Then, in the final three minutes of play, the Conquistadors sealed their fate, failing to score. The result: Hutchinson — 55, Dodge City — 48.

Hutchinson, a last minute replacement which was expected to lose its first two games, had instead won two. The local team was now only two games away from a national title.

Paralleling the home team's success, the tournament's financial picture looked rosier with each passing day. The first night's attendance, having only "approached" Convention Hall's 2,500 seating capacity,[5] grew steadily each successive evening. With Hutchinson in the semifinals, a Friday night full house was guaranteed.

Despite the poor playing conditions of Convention Hall and the small seating capacity, everyone was pleased with the management of the tournament and the support of the fans. Even visitors from towns competing for the position of tournament host were impressed. According to Jim Dean, sports editor of the Tyler *Courier Times,* "This is the place for it. I have to admit our facilities for handling a tournament like this aren't as good as yours."

NJCAA officials were also happy. Insiders seemed to think that, if Hutchinson were to pass the bond issue for a new field house which was on the spring ballot, not only would it host the tournament next year, but for many years to come.

---

[4]The rule had been newly instituted for the 1948-1949 school year. Prior to then, coaches could only talk to their players at halftime.
[5]Attendance figures reported by the press used 2,500 as the seating capacity of Convention Hall. The actual number of seats available for sale was 2,060.

FRIDAY — BATTLE FOR THE MAYOR'S SHIRT

Unlike the previous evening when the partisan crowd quietly waited through preliminary games, the Hutchinson fans were totally involved in the opening Friday night semifinal contest between Compton and Tyler. The packed house cheered vigorously, going through feature bout warm-ups, its sentiments heavily favoring the Texans. Tyler was the beneficiary of the support, not only because they were the underdog, but also because earlier in the school year Tyler fans had shown the same favoritism for the Hutchinson football squad which faced rival Kilgore College in the Texas Bowl at Tyler.

Compton dominated the early going, establishing a 19-8 lead after 10 minutes. Then, to the delight of the crowd, Tyler mounted a swift passing attack which closed the gap to 23-19 at halftime. Led by the spectacular one-hand, overhead shooting of center Bryan Miller, who was complemented by speedster Jose Palafox and floor general Jerry Champion, the Apaches gained the lead shortly after intermission, then gradually increased their margin to eight. Though the Tartars rallied several times during the half, they never caught up. The Apaches avenged the previous year's third-place loss to Compton with a 62-52 triumph.

The Tyler upset fired up the house. The crowd wanted more of the same, not only to prolong Hutchinson's euphoric climb to the summit of the junior college basketball world, but also to save the mayor's shirt.

Before the tournament started, North Sacramento Mayor Kenneth R. Hammaker wagered his shirt with Will S. Thompson, mayor of Hutchinson, pronouncing Grant Tech would win the title. City pride and mayoral wardrobe were at stake in the Friday night feature.

Tension mounted rapidly for hometown rooters as Grant Tech controlled the lead from the beginning. Behind the leadership of hook-shot artist Carl Youngstrom, the Saracens led by five at half, expanded their advantage to 48-40 with five minutes left, and still held a five-point margin with two minutes to go.

"Sesher's Sensations," already having done more than was expected of them and having nothing to lose, played the last two minutes with reckless abandon. A pair of free throws and a field goal by Blue Dragon forwards, Bob Lees and Glenn Smyth, pulled Hutchinson to within one with 45 seconds on the clock.

After a free throw by guard Cliff Davis with 30 seconds remaining, Grant Tech tried to nail the coffin shut by holding the ball for the duration of the contest. In the next 15 seconds the Saracens were fouled three times. Passing up a free throw opportunity each time, they kept possession of the ball in order to run out the clock.

The strategy failed, however, when Hutchinson regained control of the basketball. Guard LeRoy Esau, noted for his uncanny ability to attract fouls, drove to the basket and was immediately violated. He calmly sank two charities, tying the score.

Hutchinson had a chance to win the contest at the line when the other Blue Dragon guard, Rich Mercer, was given two free throw attempts. He missed both tosses but immediately made up for it by hitting a long one from outside the free throw circle, putting Hutchinson on top by two.

With pandemonium erupting around them, Grant Tech desperately passed the ball under its basket, shot and missed, tipped the ball back, shot again, and missed as the gun sounded. The court instantly flooded with joyous partisans, exuberant over having witnessed their favorite sons perform their third straight miracle.

The celebration was premature, however. On the final play of the game, Grant Tech's Jim Loscutoff was fouled trying to tie the count. It took three minutes to clear the floor of disbelieving spectators so the big center could shoot the two free throws awarded him.

When the first free throw missed, nothing could hold back the throng. Delirious Hutchonians swarmed around Loscutoff as he dejectedly threw the meaningless second shot at the basket.

The unreal had become real.

Three days earlier, no one would have given the Hutchinson Blue Dragons a chance of winning one game let alone of making their way to the championship. Not many would have even wagered the tournament would be a money-maker. Yet on the eve of the final day of the tourney, Hutchinson fans went home dreaming of a Cinderella story to beat all Cinderella stories while tournament sponsors gloated over their rapidly filling coffers.

Given the jubilation that preceded it, the last game of the day was anti-climactic. The consolation pitting Campbellsville and Campbell for fifth place was truly a game of the "forgotten." All week, fans had trouble keeping straight which team was which. Now with a possible championship just a game away for the hometown, the ecstatic crowd, uncaring as to which "Campbell" won, quickly piled out of Convention Hall, leaving Campbellsville to defeat Campbell, 62-54, in front of nearly empty seats. As though the lack of attention was not enough, both squads were exhausted from having played earlier in the day, a requirement forced by scheduling experimentation common in the tourney's first years.

SATURDAY — CINDERELLA TO THE END

Hutchinson's Friday night win affected ticket sales the way a spring thunderstorm swells a mountain stream. Boren's Sporting Goods, center for tournament ticket sales, was deluged with calls Saturday morning. The calls came with such frequency store personnel dispensed with normal phone courtesy, answering simply, "Sorry, no more tickets."

A ticket for Saturday night's final quickly became a cherished commodity. In order to satisfy as many fans as possible, the American Legion decided to sell 1,300 standing-room tickets, a total more than half the seating capacity of Convention Hall.

A half hour before the evening's first game, the lucky ones who had obtained a ticket crushed through the doors of Convention Hall and raced up the ramps in a gold rush dash to stake out those standing areas with the best advantage. The fact the game everyone came to see was not to be played for another 3½ hours was testimony to how rabidly Hutchinson fans jumped on the local team's bandwagon.

Considering the crush of humanity — violating several fire codes — and its overwhelming partisan sentiments, the decorum of the crowd during the final three contests was exemplary. This may have been due in part to Fred Mendell's Saturday morning *News-Herald* article which severely castigated the hometown fans for their "unruly" behavior the night before.

During the heated play of the Hutchinson-Grant Tech semifinal, an indiscreet few had thrown popcorn boxes and programs to register disapproval with officials' calls and heckled Grant Tech players as they shot free throws, characteristics which, Mendell noted, were not desirable of fans looking to host the tournament in the future.

Whether sufficiently chastened by the article or simply preoccupied with jockeying for a better view of the championship to come, the crowd was particularly quiet during the first two games. There were only two outbursts of enthusiasm before the finale.

The first came just prior to the opener when members of the Olympic team passed out apples to the crowd. The fruit, though grown in Washington, had made its way to the Bremerton squad through the donation of a Hutchinson grocery store. Regardless of its origins, the fans were appreciative, giving their support to the Rangers who made up an early deficit to eventually defeat Dodge City, 61-53, for fourth place.

The crowd stirred again when the dean of Grant Tech presented Mayor Hammaker's shirt to Hutchinson's mayor. Mayor Thompson acknowledged the gift with a shirt of his own, bought especially for the occasion. The expression of good will plus a tinge of guilt feeling may have swayed sentiment toward Grant Tech in the penultimate game of the evening. Even so, local fans made little noise as they politely watched Compton again live up to its pre-tourney publicity, winning convincingly, 61-47.

The stage was set for the final act. Would the tournament end the way of a Hollywood script — "Underdog Comes From Nowhere To Win It All!" — or would logic finally prevail?

There was no question which side of the coin the crowd was rooting for. Convention Hall was a mad house of screaming fans as the home team took the floor. Enthusiasm remained fever pitched even as the Tyler club immediately took control of the game. The fact that the Apaches could only manage a five-point

4-29 halftime lead was reason enough for the locals to stoke the fires of hope.

Then, when a red hot Blue Dragon team came out of the dressing room to knot the score at 34 after the intermission, the most die-hard of skeptics had a difficult time not believing the ultimate sports miracle was just around the corner.

Tyler met the challenge, however, and again moved ahead.

Not to be discouraged, the Blue Dragons tied it at 45-all.

Repeatedly the Apaches tried to shake Hutchinson. Three times Bryan Miller's beautiful arching hook shots broke the deadlock. Once Jose Palafox pushed his team ahead. Another time it was Ramon Orona. Each time Tyler tried to pull away, the scrappy, determined Blue Dragons persisted, clawing their way back into contention.

One by one, key players on both sides fouled out, victims of intense play. By game's end, Miller, Palafox, and Champion, the core of the Apache team, and Smyth, Lees, and Esau, the prime movers of the Blue Dragons, were whistled to the bench.

With three minutes left, Tyler gained a 63-57 advantage. The end in sight, Coach Floyd Wagstaff ordered his Apaches to play it safe.

Led by LeRoy Esau's 19, 8 in the championship game, Hutchinson set a team record for tourney free throws (74) which lasted until 1953. Esau later starred for the University of Wyoming, leading the Cowboys to a West Region runner-up spot in the 1952 NCAA tournament. (Photo courtesy of the University of Wyoming)

LeRoy Esau hit a free throw for Hutchinson.

Buddy Matthews matched it for Tyler.

Esau hit another, his eighth in nine trips to the line. Then Glenn Smyth fired a long one. The Blue Dragons were within three, 64-61, a minute-and-a-half to play.

Tyler worked the ball, looking for scoring opportunities. None appeared. They extended their lead with a free throw by Miller.

Bob Lees countered for Hutchinson.

Matthews made his second free throw in as many minutes, his total output for the game. Tyler 66. Hutchinson 62. Time was running out.

Hal Davis, subbing for Lees, had a prayer answered, narrowing the margin to a single bucket with 10 seconds left on the clock.

Miraculously, Hutchinson got the ball back with time enough to get two more shots off. The Tyler defense stiffened for the final onslaught. Both shots went wide of their mark.

The clock struck midnight for Cinderella.

The fans, limp from the prolonged tension, were not entirely dismayed by the outcome. Many had stood for five hours just to see the top offensive team in the tournament (Tyler) meet the top defensive team (Hutchinson); to see a group of courageous Blue Dragons with no outstanding star battle to almost even terms a star-laden Apache crew; to see deserving winners extended to the limit to prove their championship mettle; to see equally deserving losers prove they had been erroneously maligned and were capable of playing with the best; to see good basketball. They got more than they paid for — a truly excellent championship contest.

THE AFTERMATH — FINDING A HOME

The first national tournament held in Hutchinson grossed $10,900. The sum was $1,200 less than the Class B state tournament drew the week before, but was a windfall compared to the receipts from the first tournament in Springfield. The American Legion netted nearly $1,000 after all expenses were paid.

The tournament had been financially successful despite a poor playing area and limited seating. City officials, American Legion sponsors, and officials of the NJCAA all realized better conditions had to be established if the tournament was to have a future in Hutchinson.

The city fathers' answer to the problem was to build a new field house. To that end, a $994,000 bond issue had been placed on the April 5th ballot.

Just prior to the awards ceremony, with the crowd flush from the excitement of the championship contest, outgoing NJCAA President Chink Coleman and City Councilman Loren Baird made a pitch for the proposal. Throwing questions to the throng, they stirred the fans into a revival meeting fervor — "How would you like to have the tournament come to Hutchinson every year?" — "Do you think we should build a new field house?" — "Would you like to have the bond issue pass?" The queries were met with booming choruses of "Yes!"

On April 5th, the bond issue for the new sports arena passed by a vote of more than two-to-one. On the same ballot, a bond issue for curb-side garbage collection narrowly won approval by a 400-vote margin. Hutchinson citizens had their priorities.

At the NJCAA Track and Field Championship held in Phoenix in May, Hutchinson was awarded the 1950 tournament.

In 1948 a dying tournament stumbled into new life when enterprising men from Hutchinson, Kansas, offered to take the risk of playing host to it. With the good fortune of an unbelievable Cinderella performance, the tournament survived. Hutchinson fans witnessing the event would never forget its excitement. They were hooked.

The NJCAA Basketball Tournament had a home.

Tournament Results

Tuesday: Game

    1   Compton — 81 Benton Harbor — 49
    2   Olympic — 72 Webster City — 48
    3   Brainerd — 70 Campbell — 68
    4   Tyler — 64 Bayonne — 42
    5   Dodge City — 65 Campbellsville — 50
    6   Hutchinson — 68 Sayre — 50

Wednesday: Game

    7   Weber — 70 Abraham Baldwin — 64
    8   Grant Tech — 67 Joliet — 47
    9   Webster City — 55 Benton Harbor — 51
    10   Compton — 62 Olympic — 61 OT
    11   Tyler — 78 Brainerd — 63

Thursday: Game

    12   Campbell advanced by forfeit
    13   Joliet — 64 Abraham Baldwin — 57
    14   Olympic — 71 Brainerd — 65
    15   Campbellsville — 68 Sayre — 57
    16   Grant Tech — 68 Weber — 58
    17   Hutchinson — 55 Dodge City — 48

Friday: Game

    18   Campbell — 59 Webster City — 52
    19   Campbellsville — 76 Joliet — 62
    20   Dodge City — 68 Weber — 54
    21   Tyler — 62 Compton — 52
    22   Hutchinson — 55 Grant Tech — 53
    23   Campbellsville — 62 Campbell — 54

Saturday: Game

    24   Olympic — 61 Dodge City — 53
    25   Compton — 61 Grant Tech — 47
    26   Tyler — 66 Hutchinson — 64

How They Finished in 1949

1. Tyler Junior College
2. Hutchinson Junior College
3. Compton College
4. Olympic Junior College
5. Campbellsville College
6. Grant Technical College
7. Dodge City Junior College
8. Campbell College

All-Tournament Team

Jerry Champion — Tyler Junior College
LeRoy Esau — Hutchinson Junior College
Darwin Gilchrist — Olympic Junior College
Allie F. "Buddy" Gilvin — Campbellsville College
Allan Lamont — Compton College
Bryan Miller — Tyler Junior College
Jose Palafox — Tyler Junior College
Ted Tappe — Olympic Junior College
Ed Tucker — Compton College
Carl Youngstrom — Grant Technical College

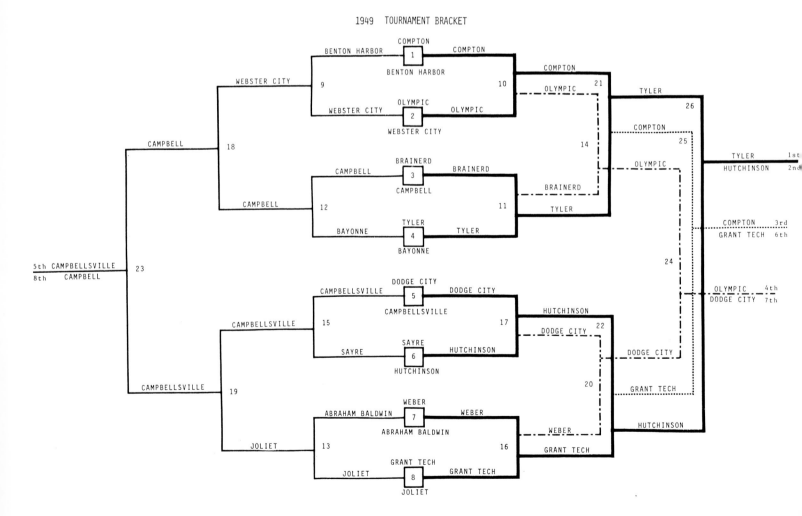

1949 TOURNAMENT BRACKET

f there were any lingering doubts whether Hutchinson was capable of supporting the National Junior College Basketball Tournament, the rush for tickets to the 1950 event quickly dispelled them. Season-ticket purchasers bought two-thirds of Convention Hall's seating capacity prior to the opening of single-session sales tournament week. To further underscore the point, the enthusiastic display by hometown fans came in spite of Hutchinson Junior College's failure to qualify for tournament play.

Enthusiasm for the tournament was not strictly a local phenomenon. In the tournament's first year, NJCAA officials had had to ask schools to compete. Now in its third year of competition, the circumstances were reversed — teams were begging for the chance to participate. The tournament committee even received a request to compete from as far away as the Panama Canal Zone. The increased interest in the tournament helped swell NJCAA membership ranks to 196 institutions. On the eve of its 1950 edition, the fledgling Juco Tournament appeared healthy and ready to take wing.

The 1950 tournament was not without controversy, however. Distance continued to be too much of a financial burden for many qualified teams, particularly in the East. The NJCAA coped with the problem during the tournament's first two years by inviting teams to fill out the bracket. No set policy existed for offering invitations. Teams were generally selected based on their drawing power at the box office. With the tournament's success and rising popularity, this arbitrary method of completing the tournament bracket came under question.

After Hutchinson Junior College's spectacular showing in the 1949 tournament as an invited entry, the NJCAA adopted a rule which specified that the hosting school had to earn its way into the tournament, the same as any other school. Though the NJCAA's ruling was an attempt to rectify the inequities of the tournament selection process, it didn't go far enough. The rule did not specify what method was to be used to determine who was to receive the invitation should a vacancy occur. Instead, the vice president of the hosting region was responsible for certifying the substitute team.

To avoid potential controversy at the end of the season, Region 6 Vice President Herb Bender, coach of Dodge City Junior College, announced in January that, should the situation arise, the invitation would go to the runner-up in the regional tourney. As coincidence would have it, Dodge City placed second in the Region 6 Tournament, then received an invitation to the national when Region 16 failed to field a representative for the second straight year.

The irony of the situation was that Dodge City had not "earned" its way into the regional tourney, having placed third in the Western Kansas Juco Conference. Unlike its rule regarding the host of the national tournament, the NJCAA encouraged the participation of the regional host to help increase the gate at the regional tournament. To add to the controversy, Hutchinson had beaten Dodge City in the Western Kansas race, placing second.

The inadequacies of the Association's rules were further illustrated when Region 14 representative, Keystone Junior College of LaPlume, Pennsylvania, advised the tournament committee it was unable to make necessary arrangements to attend the

N.E. Mississippi's Gene Garrett was the tourney's first offensive star, the first to score 100 points in four games. Garrett later played at Murray State University in Kentucky. (Photo courtesy of Gene Garrett)

tournament. There were no provisions for *two* vacancies in the tournament bracket.

The NJCAA executive committee solved the immediate problem by inviting the defending national champs from Tyler, Texas. It was hard to fault the selection. After an opening loss, Tyler had won 35 straight before losing its last two. The Texans were unquestionably one of the best teams in the country. Still, they were not even runner-up in their region, having lost to Hinds Junior College of Raymond, Mississippi, in the semifinals. Consequently, formal complaints were lodged to the executive committee by Hinds and Region 7 host McNeese Junior College of Lake Charles, Louisiana.

Growth had its pains.

THE PARTICIPANTS

Region	Team
1	Los Angeles City College — Los Angeles, California
2	City College of San Francisco — San Francisco, California
3	Olympic Junior College — Bremerton, Washington
4	Weber College — Ogden, Utah
5	Amarillo College — Amarillo, Texas
6	Garden City Junior College — Garden City, Kansas
7	Northeast Mississippi Junior College — Booneville, Mississippi
8	Jacksonville Junior College — Jacksonville, Florida
9	Campbellsville College — Campbellsville, Kentucky
10	Wingate Junior College — Wingate, North Carolina
11	Grand View College — Des Moines, Iowa
12	Flint Junior College — Flint, Michigan
13	Virginia Junior College — Virginia, Minnesota
14	*Tyler Junior College — Tyler, Texas
15	Bayonne Junior College — Bayonne, New Jersey
16	*Dodge City Junior College — Dodge City, Kansas

* Invited to fill bracket

For the first time, the National Juco Tournament was not a novelty to the spectators viewing it. Most of those purchasing tickets to the event had been to the tournament the year before. They were already familiar with six of the 1950 entries, repeaters from the previous year. In addition, nearly half the teams had played each other sometime during the season so comparisons could be made between regions. With the tourney's financial success assured, speculation about what was going to happen on the court took precedence over off-court proceedings.

If pre-tourney coffee shop prognostications were correct, the 1950 slate of competitors looked to be the best to date. There were many favorites to choose from. When comparisons were made, however, all were eventually measured against the defending national champs.

For the third year in a row, Tyler Coach Floyd Wagstaff had assembled an exceptional basketball team. Only two starters remained from the previous year's championship squad — sparkplug Jerry Champion and reliable forward Ramon Orona. Because Wagstaff was a tireless recruiter, Orona no longer started. Instead, Wagstaff's replacements included three all-staters — top-scoring center O'Neal Weaver, 6-5 forward Royce Ray, and diminutive sharpshooter Tommy Hancock.

In December the Tyler squad took its act on the road in a five-city, six-day barnstorming tour. Hutchinson fans were the first to realize Tyler's power as the Texans easily handled the Blue Dragons, 77-65. On the tour, two eventual tourney entrants — Dodge City and Olympic — were similarly introduced to Tyler's prowess.[1] In the highly competitive Texas A&M Invitational, Tyler also dispatched another national contender, Amarillo. Tyler followers insisted the current band of Apaches were the best yet. Few were willing to dispute the fact.

As strong as the Tyler squad appeared on paper, it was hard to believe the Texans had not qualified for the national tournament. Wagstaff, not one to make excuses, claimed the team had simply been beaten by a better team. Though the competition may have been tough, the truth was Tyler had not played at full strength. Ankle injuries to Hancock and Orona and a team bout with the flu had handicapped the Apaches. Reports were the team was back to health, however. If so, Tyler was indeed the measuring stick by which other tournament teams would be gauged.

The team most often compared to Tyler was Northeast Mississippi Junior College. The Tigers from Booneville matched up well on two counts. First, they succeeded where Tyler failed defeating Hinds Junior College to win the Region 7 tourney. Secondly, while Tyler's 38-game schedule was ruggedly impressive, it paled in comparison with the Booneville squad's. The Tigers competed in 54 contests during the year; two and three times as many as most other tournament teams. The extraordinary number of games led many observers to comment, "When do they have time to go to school?" Even more remarkable was that Northeast Mississippi played a wide open fire-department-drill style of basketball, guaranteed to tire any team over the course of a season. Booneville's 46 victories — mostly high-scoring affairs — were testimony to the team's endurance.

Since changes in rules and playing styles had opened up the game, higher scoring averages were a common denominator among several tourney entries. Hundred-point contests were no longer unheard of. A prime example of this kind of play was Bayonne Junior College (22-3). The Clippers massacred Trenton Junior College twice, 111-49 and 116-38. Some considered Bayonne a serious contender for the national title on the strength of several wins against four-year schools. Although the team made an early departure the previous year, the veteran squad was expected to stay longer this time.[2]

High scores were not the sole dominion of the East. The West also produced high-powered offenses. Weber College (24-7) won the northern division of the Intermountain Collegiate Athletic Conference, setting a conference scoring record with 88 points against Ricks College. Like Tyler, Weber was well-traveled. Coaching in his 16th season, Reed Swenson (president of the NJCAA) prepared his team by arranging a trip to Mexico. The team won four out of six games against some of the leading Mexican basketball teams, including the University of Mexico. The Wildcats ended the season by winning a particularly tough Region 4 tourney, including a victory over highly regarded Trinidad Junior College, a two-time winner over national entrant Garden City.

As usual, the California schools were accorded favorite status sight unseen. But, in both cases there were sufficient credentials to support the claim.

Under Coach Ralph Hillman's guidance, City College of San Francisco (24-6) had won five different championships over the past four years. The preceding year they had been the team to beat in Region 2, before being upset in the regional final by Grant Tech. This year was different. The squad was loaded with conference all-stars and was a legitimate contender.

And, any team who survived the brutal 16-team Region 1 tournament had to be considered a top competitor. While pre-tourney favorites Fullerton Junior College and Compton College — an improved version of the excellent team which placed third in the nation the year before — were being upset, the Cubs from Los Angeles City College mauled Palo Verde, 90-36[3], and knocked off Phoenix, 65-52. In the final, Los Angeles took a commanding 11-point lead over Ventura Junior College with 12 minutes to go, then sweated out the finish. Ventura slowly eroded the margin with driving lay-ups which the Cubs were powerless to stop, since all three front-liners were burdened with four fouls. Los Angeles barely survived, 58-56.

Though Los Angeles' 20-10 record was not particularly impressive, word was LACC's fortunes had drastically improved after the addition of three new players at the semester break —

---

[1] It was easy to see why Tyler Junior College was always able to land such superb talent. A cross-country plane trip was a rarity in 1950, especially for a junior college. The extravagance raised a lot of envious eyebrows. Whenever it was suggested Wagstaff might be hiring his players, he rejoined, "If I was gonna hire 'em, I'd a gotten bigger ones."

Tyler had substantial fan support because Wagstaff worked at it. The plane the team used on the trip west was owned by a heater manufacturing company out of Huntington, West Virginia, with a local office in Tyler. Arrangements for the plane were made by Brady Gentry, a U.S. Congressman from Tyler. Tyler's expenses were for the pilot and the gas. The team made stops for games in Hutchinson, Dodge City, Denver, Boise, and a best two-out-of-three series in Bremerton, Washington. The return trip was to have included stops in Los Angeles, San Diego, and Phoenix, but the plane was called back to Tyler before the rest of the tour could be completed.

[2] After Bayonne's voluntary quick exit the year before, the NJCAA passed a resolution, reprimanding Coach Bernie Ockene. The admonition was effective. Ockene was significantly less vocal during the 1950 tournament.

[3] The mauling was literal as well as figurative. The Cubs poured it on throughout the game, trying to atone for a 51-50 tourney upset to the Palo Verde Pirates the year before. With nine minutes to play, Los Angeles led, 80-33. The Cubs were certain to break the regional record of 90, set earlier in the day by Ventura.

Completely outclassed, the Pirates proceeded to stall to prevent Los Angeles from setting the record. They passed up easy lay-ups and took the ball out of bounds rather than shoot free throws on fouls.

Finally, Richard Williams, a Los Angeles sub, grabbed the ball and took off down the court. He collided with a Palo Verde player and hit the floor violently. Humiliation and year-old resentment exploded. The benches poured on to the court and a massive fist fight ensued.

guard Rollen Hans and forwards Jimmy Powell and Hal Uplinger, all starters. Those who witnessed the team's arrival at tournament headquarters in the American Legion's Bisonte Hotel could see why. Los Angeles had the tallest starting line-up in the tournament. Talk among coaches in the Bisonte lobby indicated the Cubs were the team to beat.

Local supporters were naturally disgruntled when circumstances prevented Hutchinson Junior College from making an encore appearance at the national tournament. The fans, however, held no animosity toward the two teams which represented Kansas. Both became "Cinderella" favorites with the hometown crowd. In the case of Garden City Junior College (20-5), the epithet was appropriate. The school had never won a major sports championship before copping that year's Western Kansas Juco Conference crown. While other tourney contenders boasted offensive capabilities, the Broncbusters emphasized defense. In the Western Kansas race, they held opponents to a stingy 35.7 points per game. During the year, they had defeated tourney entries Amarillo (three times) and Dodge City (twice). All but two of their losses came when one or more of their starters were unable to play. Despite its "Cinderella" label, Garden City had a very real chance.

None of the other tournament entries appeared strong enough to take the title. Three repeaters from the 1949 tournament — Dodge City Junior College (15-7), Campbellsville College (18-6), and Olympic Junior College (19-8) — looked to be weaker than they had been the year before when they took home trophies for their performances. Two others — Wingate Junior College (25-6) and Amarillo College (23-8) — had plenty of game experience and a star performer, but little else. The other four teams — Jacksonville Junior College (21-2), Virginia Junior College (18-2), Flint Junior College (14-2), and Grand View College (15-4) — were definite long-shots. All had good records but did not measure up to a team like Tyler.

TUESDAY — OUT OF THE BLOCKS

On Tuesday morning a crowd gathered in a snow-encrusted field just east of Hutchinson Junior College to watch NJCAA President Swenson, Hutchinson Mayor Loren Baird, and Harry Faris, head of the local school board, break ground for the new Sports Arena. Among those witnessing the auspicious occasion was a very cold George "Dutch" Hoy, NJCAA secretary. It never occurred to Hoy to bring a topcoat to Hutchinson, having left the 85-degree warmth of Phoenix.

Hoy wasn't the only visitor surprised by the vagaries of Kansas weather. The chilly scene outside seemed to creep into the small confines of Convention Hall as San Francisco and Flint opened the third annual NJCAA Basketball Tournament. Both teams were cold, missing easy shots. Then, midway through the first half, San Francisco thawed. Kevin Duggan started arching shots from the 25-foot range, hitting six before the end of the period. By halftime the Rams were comfortably in front, 31-17, and never looked back.

In the second contest, Garden City posted a convincing 76-52 win over the Dolphins from Jacksonville. Spearheaded by the precise passing and accurate overhead shooting of pivot man John Keller, Garden City's tally demonstrated the Broncbusters had more than just an exceptional defense.

In the final afternoon contest, Tyler confirmed its champion nettle by overwhelming the Virginia Greyhounds in every phase of play. Early in the contest, Jerry Champion and Tommy Hancock, Tyler's pair of 5-7 guards, shredded the Greyhound defense with sensational passing and spectacular long shots. As the game progressed, Jimmy Browning, O'Neal Weaver, and Royce Ray, the Tyler front line, began to hit from short range. Five Tyler players hit double figures in racking up the team's 82 points. The figure not only surpassed the day's two previous winning totals, but also improved on the tournament record. The only negative was the recurrence of Hancock's bad ankle, forcing the speedster to the Tyler bench for most of the second half. Spectators were convinced the loss of such a valuable starter was of no consequence, though, when the Tyler reserves played the last 10 minutes with little depreciation in team effectiveness. As if to emphasize the point, reserve guard Bobby Madrid zipped the cords from far beyond the centerline just as time ran out to give Tyler a 28-point victory.

If anyone felt Tyler was a shoo-in, they had second thoughts after the first game of the evening session. The game turned into a tennis match for spectators as both teams traded long passes, setting up fast-break attacks. In a close game from beginning to end, Northeast Mississippi downed Campbellsville, 88-85. Not only was Tyler's newly established scoring record toppled by the winner, but by the loser as well. The 173-point total smashed by 31 the old record for two teams set in 1948. Nine players scored double figures with Northeast Mississippi's Gene Garrett grabbing game-high honors with 29. Garrett might have set a new individual record had he not spent the last seven minutes on the bench because of fouls.

From the day's opening tip off, each winning team had outshone the previous winner's performance. The pace of play quickened until attaining heart-racing speed in the Northeast Mississippi-Campbellsville contest. As though sensing the fans were in need of a rest, the two teams in the feature switched gears. Unfortunately the gear they shifted to was neutral. Both teams suffered through more than one cold spell. For long stretches, it looked as if neither Amarillo nor Dodge City possessed an offense. At times it appeared keep-away was the game being played; the ball was passed around the perimeter with no hint of a goal attempt. Finally, with seven minutes remaining, Amarillo came to life, beating Dodge City for the third time that year, 54-45.

The pace picked up again in the day's finale. In a mild surprise, Weber raced pass Bayonne, 76-49. The New Jersey ballclub was not the team described by advance press. Though the Clippers showed occasional flashes of good basketball, their play was generally disorganized. Passes and shots often went wildly astray. Even lay-ups were hard to come by. In contrast, the Utah crew proved consistent throughout with the game-high scoring of center Jerry Downs (17), forward Lawrence Stone (16), and guard Darrell Tucker (16) demonstrating Weber's balance.

WEDNESDAY — THE PACE QUICKENS

After taking fourth place in the 1949 tournament with a veteran squad, Olympic Coach Phil Pesco had the unenviable task of completely rebuilding his team. Gone were all-star performers Ted Tappe and Darwin Gilchrist, the foundation of the previous year's team. Instead, the current platoon of Rangers displayed better balance. They had little trouble disposing of Grand View in Wednesday's opening game, 62-47. Scoring honors were grabbed by Olympic forward Bob Dotson who shattered Grand View's tight, drawn-in defense with 23 points, mostly from far out.

The final first-round contest was still in question five minutes into the second period. Then, with Los Angeles leading Wingate, 33-32, Al Roges started hitting from the post. Shortly, all the blue-shirted Californians were making scoring contributions. The result was an 83-47 rout. Though Los Angeles had failed to impress anyone with its play early on, no one doubted the team's championship caliber after the Cubs reeled off 50 points in the last 15 minutes.

The first round was notable for its preponderance of lopsided games. Only one contest had been close throughout. The games were not uninteresting, though. Fans were treated to excellent exhibitions with significantly higher scores. Clearly the best teams had advanced to the championship bracket.

With the prospect of superb quarterfinal match-ups in the offing, spectators poured into Convention Hall, jamming it for the Wednesday night session. Many came to back the Kansas dark horse from Garden City against the favored San Francisco squad. Just as many wanted to witness the impending footrace between the Region 7 opponents from Booneville and Tyler. Fan expectations for a thrilling evening did not go unfulfilled.

In the opener, Garden City put its checking man-to-man defense to work, keeping San Francisco from hitting for five minutes. Then with Garden City leading, 13-3, San Francisco's Skip Carnegie began firing mortar shells over the defense. The bombs hit home, pulling the Rams within four, 19-15.

Garden City managed to maintain a slight distance on the Californians until midway through the second half. Kevin Duggan, Carnegie, and little Frank Sampson then connected in rapid succession for the Rams, cutting the Kansans' lead to 38-35 with eight minutes remaining. Up to that point, Broncbuster Coach

Ed Hall had done little substituting. Though the score was low, the pace had been fast. Garden City appeared to be tiring.

Before the Broncbusters had a chance to fade into extinction, however, forward Don McGillivray hit from the side. Then, Frank Kinney hit from the other side. Gaining new life, Garden City endured, upsetting San Francisco, 58-45.

The Wednesday finale could be described in one word — fast! Everything happened fast: passing, scoring, fouling. The court was constant motion.

Northeast Mississippi took the early advantage when Gene Garrett swished three long shots in the first minute to put the Tigers on top, 6-0. Tyler matched Booneville's speed with some of its own and charged back to knot the score at 12-all three minutes later. The two teams sprinted the rest of the half, exchanging the lead six times and sharing it five. Momentum of play might have reached hurricane velocity had the referees not whistled 28 infractions. At halftime with Northeast Mississippi leading Tyler, 42-38, two Tigers and one Apache were within one of fouling out.

A minute into the second period, Royce Ray, Tyler's tallest player at 6-5, was sidelined, having met the limit for personals. The breakneck tempo continued with no hint of slackening. Northeast Mississippi kept up the pressure, zipping passes the length of the court, converting them to buckets. Garrett and center Ken Robbins led the attack up the middle, using either hand to bank in shots on the gallop. When Tyler tightened up the middle, guard Walter Johnson and forward Ken Lindsey spread the defenders with long-range shots.

The defending champs gamely struggled to keep pace. The effort produced fouls. Three more Apaches followed Ray to the bench. The Northeast Mississippi lead fluctuated between four and 14 through the half, and, at the two-minute mark, it was apparent Tyler's reign over junior college basketball was at an end.

Convention Hall fans were limp from one of the best exhibitions of basketball they had ever witnessed. A new champion was to be crowned Saturday night. Most agreed the boys from Booneville had the inside track for the coronation.

THURSDAY — A BREATHER

Thursday's games provided a respite for tournament followers already drained by the ever-accelerating action of the first two days. Only two games were close and neither impacted crowd emotions as had the previous day's contests.

The dramatic high point of the day came in the consolation match opening the evening session. Hometown favorite Dodge City and eastern powerhouse Bayonne fought to the closest decision of the 1950 tournament.

With one minute remaining, the score was tied at 55. As the clock wound down to the 30-second mark, Don Taylor canned one from 25-feet, giving Dodge City the lead. In the ensuing scramble, the Conquistadors regained control of the basketball. With time running out, Bayonne's James Smith batted the ball from the hands of a Dodge City player, picked it up on the dribble, raced the length of the court, then missed an easy, uncontested lay-up as time expired. The 57-55 loss eliminated Bayonne.[4]

The quarterfinal contest between Amarillo and Weber was a seesaw affair from the start. Weber jumped out to a 14-7 advantage early on, but Amarillo climbed back in the game, gaining the halftime lead, 34-32. Amarillo was still in front, 60-56, with seven minutes remaining when Wildcat forwards Keith Sewell and Lawrence Stone hit a pair to help knot the score at 61-all. Star guard Buddy Travis put the Badgers back on top, but then Sewell calmly sank two free throws, followed by a sizzling fielder. Weber never trailed again, winning 72-67.

In the last quarterfinal, Los Angeles duplicated its first-round performance with a lackluster first half. After leading Olympic, 31-29, at intermission, the trio of Hal Uplinger, Rollen Hans, and Al Roges kicked into gear. The Cubs possessed a comfortable 11-point margin with eight minutes remaining and coasted to a 74-57 win. Uplinger topped all scorers with 22, while Roges and Hans added 19 and 17, respectively.

FRIDAY — THE RACE RETURNS FOR FIVE MORE YEARS

Big news greeted local fans as they filed into Convention Hall for Friday's opening session. The NJCAA, the Lysle Rishel American Legion post, and Hutchinson Junior College had signed a contract awarding Hutchinson the national tournament for the next five years. The success of the current tournament prompted unanimous agreement. As if to mark the momentous occasion, fans were treated to a historic performance.

Buddy Travis, Amarillo's 6-2 guard, was a versatile scorer. He could hit from both long and short range with equal efficiency. He was also strong. He scored his record-setting 40th point while being knocked to the court. The superhuman effort wasn't enough, however. With two minutes to play and trailing Olympic, 65-61, Travis fouled out. Olympic went on to eliminate Amarillo, 69-65.

The crowd packed into Convention Hall Friday night to see the opening semifinal contest between Garden City and Northeast Mississippi. It was a dream match. Garden City had distinguished itself as the premier defensive team, holding a quick, explosive San Francisco attack to a mere 45 points in the quarterfinals. In contrast, the Booneville squad's offense drew rave reviews from local fans. According to tournament committeeman John Kline, a former Kansas University player, "I've never seen a team anywhere play as fast and yet maintain such uncanny accuracy." Tempo would be the key to the issue.

During the first half, it was Garden City who dictated the rhythm of play. The Broncbusters played ball-control offense, kept action at their end of the court, and led throughout, at one point attaining a 27-16 advantage.

Holding down the Booneville scoring machine was like sitting on a lighted powder keg. By halftime, the Tigers had sliced the margin to four. In the first two minutes after the break, Ken Robbins tipped in a bucket and Gene Garrett swished one from the corner, tying the score. Garrett then gave the Tigers the lead with two field goals and a free throw.

Before the Mississippi squad could grab momentum completely, John Keller sparked the Broncbusters with a three-point play, tying the score at 32-all.

There were 10 more ties, the last coming at the two-minute mark, 53-all.

John Keller continued his collegiate playing career at Kansas University where he was a member of the Clyde Lovelette-led Jayhawks who won the 1952 NCAA Tournament. The Jayhawks later took second behind the national A.A.U. Champion Peoria Catepillars in the U.S. Olympic Trials, eventually placing seven players on the Olympic team. Keller became the first former NJCAA Tournament player to earn a gold medal in the Olympics. (Photo courtesy of Kansas University)

---

[4]The game's inept ending foreshadowed the New Jersey school's demise. A year later on June 20, 1951, Bayonne Junior College closed its doors because of insufficient funds.

Then, the powder keg blew. In rapid succession, Tiger reserve forward, Edd Burks hit a jumper, Garrett flipped in an underhand miracle, followed by a driving lay-up. In the space of 30 seconds, the outcome was decided.

Garden City's defense had been begrudging throughout, holding Northeast Mississippi to its lowest total in three games. Yet it had not stopped the dynamo output of Garrett. The speedy forward accounted for 35 of the Tigers' 61 points, including 11 for 16 from the line. Another factor in Garden City's loss was the disqualification of two of the tallest Broncbusters — 6-2 center Keller and 6-4 forward Don McGillivray — down the home stretch. The board work of Keller, McGillivray, and Dale Horton had been a major reason the Tiger offense never fully got out of the starting blocks.

Kansas fans faced further disappointment in the game for fifth place. As in the previous year, consolation bracket winners were forced to play twice in the same day. In Dodge City's case was too much to endure. The Conquistadors had fought a hard, close battle with Wingate in the afternoon, using only five players the entire game. Against Jacksonville, their stamina quickly flagged. The Dolphins grabbed the lead in the first three minutes, then outlasted the Kansans for a 58-43 victory.

Winning the day's finale meant a chance at the national championship. But, it was the same old script as far as Los Angeles was concerned. The first half was another dogged performance by the Cubs. Then during intermission, the Californians donned their shooting clothes and, on cue, took center stage. Using a three-pronged attack Los Angeles scored at will, crushing Weber's hopes of a title, 80-57. Forward Jimmy Powell led the Cub charge with 25, fired mostly from mid-range. Hal Uplinger, his stablemate on the other side of the lane, potted long one-handers to the tune of 19. And in the middle, Al Roges continued his steady play with 22. For the third time, double figures separated the Californians from their opponents.

SATURDAY — CROSSING THE FINISH LINE

Championship night opened with the third meeting of the year between Tyler and Olympic. In December, Olympic had hosted the Apaches at the end of their cross-country barnstorming tour, the Rangers twice falling victim to the Texans, both times by the score of 65-54. In the battle for fourth place, Olympic came closer to beating its old nemesis than ever before, but was still unable to do the job. With the 65-58 victory, Tyler took home its third trophy in as many years, recouping its pre-tourney respect.

Garden City also gained renewed esteem with another magnificent defensive performance. Employing a checking man-to-man defense, the Broncbusters throttled Weber's offense, holding the Wildcats to a meager 37 points. The total was the fewest given up by a team since the low-scoring 1948 affair. Considering the increased scoring in the tournament, Garden City's four-game defensive average of 48.8 was an awesome achievement. The third-place finish was a credit to the ball club. Still, many fans could not help shake their heads and wonder, "If only . . ."

A Kansas win in the low-scoring preliminary had the local crowd charged up, ready for a change-of-pace in the finale. Los Angeles and Northeast Mississippi epitomized offense. Both teams had scored almost as many points in three games as others had in four. Although the Booneville squad owned the tourney record for a single game, Los Angeles held a four-point edge in total points. However, the Californians had not had to face the defensive-minded crew from Garden City. It was tough to predict the winner.

As similar as their records appeared, there *were* contrasts. The most obvious difference was the source of each team's offense. Balanced scoring characterized the Cub attack. Three different individuals had led Los Angeles' point production in its previous outings. Though Ken Robbins and Ken Lindsey were capable of hitting the hoop if required there was no question who ignited the Northeast Mississippi offense. In three games Gene Garrett had scored 94 points — 13 more than Ted Tappe's tournament record for *four* games.

Another difference between the two teams may have swayed the Convention Hall crowd slightly toward the Mississippi side of the ledger. The Tigers were the pride of a Booneville student body which totaled just over 500. The Los Angeles team, on the other hand, represented a school with the largest junior college enrollment in the nation — 14,000. Regardless of who favored whom, everyone expected to smell burning rubber for the next 40 minutes. What transpired disappointed many.

To begin with, Booneville was forced to alter its game plan. Los Angeles' quick guards, Rollen Hans and Ed Bartolomea, repeatedly intercepted the long looping, floor-length passes, which fueled the Tiger fast break, converting them into easy buckets for the Cubs.

Secondly, the Mississippi squad lost its firepower. Garrett picked up three quick fouls, forcing him to sit out most of the first half. To make matters worse, he hurt his knee in a tumble and was never up to par from then on.

With three minutes remaining in the opening half and Los Angeles leading, 31-22, the outlook for Northeast Mississippi appeared bleak. However, the Booneville cause gained new hope when the Tigers scored the next seven points. Northeast Mississippi went into the locker room at halftime, trailing by only two.

After winning the championship for Los Angeles City College, Rollen Hans (front row center), Al Roges, and Hal Uplinger (second and third from left, back row) attended Long Island University, then spent two years together playing service ball at Los Alamitos Naval Air Station. They reunited again as members of the NBA's Baltimore Bullets, under their former LIU coach, Clair Bee. Uplinger gained later notoriety as the television producer for Bob Geldolf's "Live Aid Concert." (Photo courtesy of the NJCAA)

Momentum continued to favor the Tigers after intermission. Behind four quick goals by center Ken Robbins, Northeast Mississippi grabbed the lead, 38-36.

The Cubs retaliated led by center Al Roges — who seemed to make a practice of having a hot second period. With 12 minutes remaining, the Californians were back in control, 48-40.

Northeast Mississippi challenged, pulled within two, but lost Robbins to fouls in the process. Without their big man, the Tigers were at the mercy of Roges and Hal Uplinger who owned the boards. The Booneville squad was never close again.

Uplinger led the Cubs with 25, mostly sensational jump shots from the corners and the edges of the key. Roges supported with 23 from tip-ins and fade-away one-handers in the middle. With Garrett managing only six tallies, Northeast Mississippi was no match for the new champs from Los Angeles.

THE AFTERMATH — CORRECTING PROBLEMS

According to most observers, the Los Angeles City College Cubs of 1950 were the best team to play in the tournament in its first half-dozen years. Four of their five starters were legitimate stars whose individual glows were diminished because they shared the limelight. Three of them would eventually play professional basketball.

Yet, with so much going for them, with the junior college basketball world at their feet, the new champs had reason to envy those they had vanquished. As one Los Angeles player told the *Hutchinson News-Herald*, "I have to admit the 'school spirit' back home doesn't compare with that hereabouts. A championship squad of 10 boys gets plenty of attention in small schools — but not much when the squad is just 10 of 14,000." To emphasize the point, he related that only about 25 people were at the train station to see the team off for the national event.

The team must have been thoroughly dumbfounded when it arrived at Los Angeles' Union Station the following Monday. Three hundred enthusiastic well-wishers greeted their heroes, then escorted them by motorcade to City Hall. Before a cheering throng on the steps outside, Mayor Fletcher Bowron congratulated the Cubs, saying "Los Angeles is very proud of the men who brought back the bacon. We appreciate what Los Angeles City College has done for Los Angeles."

***

The 1950 NJCAA Basketball Tournament was a resounding success: new attendance and gross receipts records were established; the signing of a new contract insured a home for the next five years; and the construction of a new playing facility promised even better results in the future. Everything looked rosy. Even the tournament's weak points appeared resolved.

No more trouble was anticipated regarding future tournament invitations. During the week's business sessions, the NJCAA restructured its regions, allowing better tournament representation, and established a specific selection process for filling vacancies in the bracket.

When it was discovered that one team's roster included a high school student,[5] the Association immediately went to work and adopted a set of long overdue eligibility rules.

All in all, tournament week had been profitable and productive. NJCAA officials had good reason to believe their actions alleviated the organization's growing pains. One year later, they would realize their work was just beginning.

Tournament Results				
Tuesday:	Game			
		1	San Francisco — 64 Flint — 52	
		2	Garden City — 76 Jacksonville — 52	
		3	Tyler — 82 Virginia — 54	
		4	NE Mississippi — 88 Campbellsville — 85	
		5	Amarillo — 54 Dodge City — 45	
		6	Weber — 76 Bayonne — 49	
Wednesday:	Game			
		7	Olympic — 62 Grand View — 47	
		8	Los Angeles — 83 Wingate — 47	
		9	Jacksonville — 64 Flint — 60	
		10	Garden City — 58 San Francisco — 45	
		11	NE Mississippi — 84 Tyler — 79	
Thursday:	Game			
		12	Virginia — 79 Campbellsville — 75	
		13	Wingate — 66 Grand View — 51	
		14	Tyler — 66 San Francisco — 61	
		15	Dodge City — 57 Bayonne — 55	
		16	Los Angeles — 74 Olympic — 57	
		17	Weber — 72 Amarillo — 67	
Friday:	Game			
		18	Jacksonville — 82 Virginia — 75	
		19	Dodge City — 54 Wingate — 51	
		20	Olympic — 69 Amarillo — 65	
		21	NE Mississippi — 61 Garden City — 55	
		22	Jacksonville — 58 Dodge City — 43	
		23	Los Angeles — 80 Weber — 57	
Saturday:	Game			
		24	Tyler — 65 Olympic — 58	
		25	Garden City — 55 Weber — 37	
		26	Los Angeles — 67 NE Mississippi — 63	

How They Finished in 1950

1. Los Angeles City College
2. Northeast Mississippi Junior College
3. Garden City Junior College
4. Tyler Junior College
5. Jacksonville Junior College
6. Weber College
7. Olympic Junior College
8. Dodge City Junior College

All-Tournament Team

Kevin Duggan — City College of San Francisco
Gene Garrett — Northeast Mississippi Junior College
John Keller — Garden City Junior College
Chuck Koon — Olympic Junior College
Kenneth Lindsey — Northeast Mississippi Junior College
Jim Powell — Los Angeles City College
Buddy Travis — Amarillo College
Darrell Tucker — Weber College
Hal Uplinger — Los Angeles City College
O'Neal Weaver — Tyler Junior College

---

[5]Robert "Cob" Jarvis, the player in question, was the star of the Booneville High School team which had won Mississippi's class AA title the week prior to the Juco Tournament. Like many schools at the time Booneville's high school and junior college were housed in the same building. Nothing underhanded was intended by his play in the national tournament, since, under Mississippi Junior College Association rules, Jarvis was eligible. The incident simply illustrated how lax the NJCAA had been regarding eligibility rules.

1951:

SKELETON IN THE CLOSET

O n February 19, 1951, front pages across the country carried a news story which rocked the sports world. Three City College of New York basketball players were arrested on charges of bribery. All admitted accepting payoffs from a gambler for throwing three contests at Madison Square Garden.

The incident was just the latest in a series of scandals involving college basketball. It stunned the public for two reasons. First, the gambler in question was known to have underworld connections. Second, CCNY represented the pinnacle of college basketball, having swept both the NIT and NCAA tournaments the year before. If organized crime was so pervasive as to have permeated a citadel of American sports, how safe was the moral fiber of the nation's youth?

The question was asked often. For the next few months, newspaper coverage of the unfolding CCNY scandal, including the subsequent investigation by Estes Kefauver's Senate Crime Commission, spawned similar stories of misconduct. Served up almost on a daily basis, the stories painted a disquieting picture of disintegrating integrity in sports. With the Cold War now heated to full-fledged military conflict in Korea, these revelations did little to relieve the insecurity of Americans.

In the midst of the unsure emotional climate surrounding it, the 1951 National Juco Tournament seemed a sanctuary of dependability. For the second year in a row, financial success was assured before play began. Hutchinson fans, entranced with the tournament, quickly made tickets scarce commodities. If there was a question yet unanswered, it was whether or not another attendance record would be set.

Even the bone of contention which fueled controversy in the past was now resolved. The NJCAA's restructuring at the end of the previous tournament proved successful. For the first time in the tournament's short history, every region was represented by its certified champion.

The NJCAA Tournament appeared to be the perfect distraction from the oppressive mood hovering over the country. Everyone welcomed the diversion of good, competitive basketball played in a dissension-free atmosphere.

THE PARTICIPANTS

Region	Team
1	Ventura Junior College — Ventura, California
2	Stockton Junior College — Stockton, California
3	Olympic Junior College — Bremerton, Washington
4	Weber College — Ogden, Utah
5	Amarillo College — Amarillo, Texas
6	Dodge City Junior College — Dodge City, Kansas
7	Northeast Mississippi Junior College — Booneville, Mississippi
8	South Georgia College — Douglas, Georgia
9	Tiffin University — Tiffin, Ohio
10	Wingate Junior College — Wingate, North Carolina
11	Norfolk Junior College — Norfolk, Nebraska
12	Junior College of Benton Harbor — Benton Harbor, Michigan
13	York Junior College — York, Pennsylvania
14	Tyler Junior College — Tyler, Texas
15	New York State Institute of Applied Arts and Sciences — Binghamton, New York
16	Moberly Junior College — Moberly, Missouri

Though his national tournament play was disappointing overall, Nield Gordon enjoyed a distinguished career in basketball. He finished his collegiate education at Furman where he starred with the legendary Frank Selvy. In Gordon's senior year, Furman became the first NCAA school to average 90 points per game during a season.

Gordon was drafted by the New York Knicks, but missed an opportunity to play in the NBA because he was drafted by the Army.

At 25 Gordon, entered the coaching profession as the head coach of Belmont Abbey College (preceding later NBC sportscaster Al McGuire), then preceded later Florida State coach Joe Williams as assistant coach at Furman. He achieved his greatest success at Newberry College where he coached three teams to the NAIA tournament in 14 years. Gordon retired in 1986 after starting the program at Winthrop College, after compiling 489 wins in 24 years of coaching. (Photo courtesy of Furman University)

Basketball was changing. Rules, playing strategies, and shooting styles were rapidly modifying the sport. As evidenced by the 1950 tournament, scores were climbing higher. The game was loosening up.

As team scores elevated, so did individual totals. Many ball clubs now focused their offense around the point production of one individual. In the previous tournament, Buddy Travis of Amarillo and Gene Garrett of Northeast Mississippi exemplified the type of marksmen employed in this stratagem. The game plan proved sound. The three teams favored to win the 1951 NJCAA Basketball Tournament brought with them the three top scorers in junior college ranks.

Always tough Region 1 again produced a championship caliber team. Ventura Junior College (33-4) made a habit of winning honors. At mid-season the Pirates won the California State Juco meet at Modesto. Later they won the Utah Juco Invitational. During the year they also dethroned perennial favorite Compton College as champs of the Western States Conference, trouncing them twice by more than 20 points. After they disposed of Compton a third time to add the regional prize to their string of laurels, only the national title remained. It appeared theirs for the taking. The fact Ventura twice downed the defending national champs from Los Angeles City College — the last time convincingly, 71-41 — gave credence to the claim that the California team was the best in the country.

Ventura's offense was built around its brilliant post man, Ernie Hall. At 6-2, Hall was short for his position. Whatever he lacked in height, he made up for in speed, agility, and tremendous leaping ability. His mastery of the jump shot set him apart from other players and made him a prime offensive weapon in the middle.[1] Not only was Hall Ventura's scoring leader, but its emotional leader as well. His facial expressions were very animated, reflecting the intensity with which he approached the game. His enthusiasm often rubbed off on his teammates, sparking the team's winning ways.

Ventura's advance press, credited Hall with national junior college scoring honors for the past two seasons. The claim was only partly accurate. Hall's 673-point accumulation was the top junior college mark for 1950. However, his 732 total for 1951 placed him third behind two other tournament participants.

According to the December 1950 *Juco Review* — which did not include Ventura's statistics — the leading junior college scorer in 1950 was Neild Gordon of Wingate Junior College. Though an honorable mention selection for the All-Tournament Team that year, the 6-6 center had not lived up to his credentials. Likewise his team's performance was not exceptional. This year was expected to be a different story. Wingate owned the best record among national contenders — 38-2.

The team's final two contests demonstrated it had improved and Gordon was a key element in its success. After winning Region 10, the Bulldogs arranged an exhibition game with the Wake Forest varsity in order to raise funds for their trip to Hutchinson. In a true barn-burner, Wingate embarrassed the four-year school, winning, 98-97, in double overtime. Gordon dominated with 36 points. Wanting revenge, Wake Forest asked for a second engagement. In the return match, Wake Forest attempted to stop Gordon, putting a heavy guard on him. The tactic failed. Gordon topped his previous total with 37 and the Bulldogs won again, 84-79.

Gordon was a regional all-star, having led tournament scoring with a 29.0 average. He amassed 738 points during the 1951 campaign, putting him ahead of Ventura's Hall. Still, he was almost 50 points away from the nation's leader.

O'Neal Weaver had very large hands. They were a major asset for the husky 6-4½ post man from tiny Martins Mill, Texas. Besides being a top point producer, he was an exceptional ball handler, an expert passer.[2] He triggered the Tyler Junior College offense. When the guards fed Weaver at the post, he either passed off for an assist or turned to his right to loft a pin-point left-handed hook shot. In 1950, Weaver — who ranked just behind Wingate's Gordon in scoring — had been selected to the All-Tournament Team, having led his team to a fourth-place finish. In the current season, no one came close to his 826-point total.

If Weaver was the best in the country, there was every reason to believe the Tyler Apaches were also the best. They possessed the top scorer in the land, a crafty veteran coach in Floyd Wagstaff, an impressive 32-3 record, and a history of four straight tourney appearances, including a national title. No one questioned their chances for the current campaign.

No other team had a player like Hall, Gordon, or Weaver. All other competitors were, therefore, automatically accorded only an outside chance of grabbing the junior college crown.

Besides Tyler and Wingate, seven schools had previously participated in the nationals. Five were returnees from the 1950 event: Northeast Mississippi Junior College (47-9); Weber College (32-9); Olympic Junior College (24-2); Dodge City Junior College (18-6); and Amarillo College (19-9). Two others were earlier contestants: Moberly Junior College (22-3) in the Springfield tournament and Junior College of Benton Harbor (19-3) in the inaugural meet in Hutchinson. Of these, the team rated best was the squad from Booneville, Mississippi.

For the second year in a row, Northeast Mississippi played and won more games than any other junior college in the nation. Its 56-game schedule was two better than its 1950 total. Still, with an impressive record and a runner-up trophy from the previous year, the Tigers were not in the same class as the three tourney favorites. Why? Super scorer Gene Garrett was no longer around to spark the explosive Booneville attack, having moved on to play at Murray State College. Without Garrett, Northeast Mississippi lost to Tyler four times during the year.[3]

In addition to Ventura, the tourney newcomers included Binghamton State Tech (28-2), Stockton Junior College (26-5), South Georgia College (23-6), Norfolk Junior College (14-6), York Junior College (14-7), and Tiffin University (8-12). By virtue of the fact the team hailed from California, only Stockton showed potential for surprising the favorites.

TUESDAY — END OF AN ERA

The weekend before the tournament, Convention Hall's old fan-shaped, metal backboards were replaced with regulation glass boards intended for Hutchinson's new Sports Arena. The change heralded an end of an era. With the Arena due for completion in December, the 1951 NJCAA Basketball Tournament was the last major sports event held in the close confines of barn-like Convention Hall.

The tournament began with a lively tip-off between Hutchinson Mayor Loren Baird, representing the team from Tiffin, Ohio, and Mayor M.W. Smith of Booneville, Mississippi. The odds favored the Tiffin Dragons on the ceremonial jump ball, since Baird stood an even six feet and Smith measured only 5-7½. Unfortunately, that advantage did not carry over to the opening contest.

Though the green-clad Dragons remained close through the first 10 minutes of play, Northeast Mississippi gradually pulled away, easily winning, 78-61. The boys from Booneville looked like the same team which had burned up the court the year before, with one exception. Instead of Gene Garrett leading the fast break, it was 5-10 Gerald Caviness, an elusive sharpshooter who led all scorers with 25.

It was more of the same in the second game. Benton Harbor managed to stay with Wingate for 15 minutes, before Wingate guard Darrell Floyd — who played as well inside as out — began flipping in baskets from every range up to 30 feet away. He hit seven field goals in the first half and five in the second, totaling 26 points for game-high honors. It was a good thing, since Neild Gordon, Wingate's star center, had trouble getting untracked. Though his rebounding was an important factor in Wingate's first-half surge, he tallied only 11 points for the game while collecting four fouls. He watched much of the Bulldogs' 79-62 winning performance from the bench.

In the final afternoon contest, Amarillo owned a considerable size advantage over Norfolk with two starters measuring 6-6. Norfolk's tallest player was 6-3. Although Al Hutchinson and Jim Burris dominated the backboards at both ends of the court, the Amarillo Badgers had to withstand an early second-period rally before eventually subduing the Nebraskans, 63-52.

---

[1] In 1951, the one-handed jump shot was still a rarity. From outside, the two-handed set shot was in vogue while the hook shot was favored in the middle. The jump shot was not coached. In the early years of the tournament, anyone using the shot was labeled a "hotdog". The success of players like Hall led coaches to reconsider the jumper, since it was difficult to guard against.

[2] According to Cotton Fitzsimmons, a later teammate of Weaver's at Midwestern University in Wichita Falls, "He was the greatest passer I've ever seen . . . I have never been associated with a person who could pass the ball more accurately — get it to you in a tight area — than O'Neal Weaver."

At times Weaver would perform Globetrotter antics, passing through his legs, over his shoulder, or one-handed with the flick of the wrist. In an NAIA tournament game, Fitzsimmons scored 16 straight points for Midwestern — all off passes from Weaver.

As good as Weaver was, he had no ambition to play the sport other than for fun. He was drafted by the Boston Celtics but chose not to accept their offer. Instead, he played A.A.U. ball for a lumber company in Lake Charles, Louisiana.

[3] The season schedule for Tyler, Northeast Mississippi, and McNeese Junior College of Lake Charles, Louisiana, included four games against each other. The winner of the unintentional round robin was Tyler — but barely. Tyler beat Northeast Mississippi four times, Northeast Mississippi took three of four from McNeese, and McNeese bested Tyler three of four, handing the Texas team its only three losses for the year.

Another tournament favorite took to the court in the first game of the evening session and quickly demonstrated its advanced billing was not distorted. Ventura's whirlwind offense netted 50 points in the first 15 minutes against Weber, before taking a monumental 58-32 margin into the dressing room at half. The Pirates might have become the first team to crack the century barrier in tourney play had Coach Elmer McCall not put his bench into action most of the second period. Instead, Ventura settled for a new game high of 98. The short, quick Pirate front line proved the difference in Ventura's win with forwards Ed Millan (5-11) and Jim Crockom (6-4) and center Ernie Hall (6-2) all scoring 20 points or better.

The feature contest was a much colder affair. Tyler did not hit a field goal in the first four minutes, yet managed a 6-4 advantage over South Georgia. Then, while everyone else on the court remained frost-bitten, the Apaches' O'Neal Weaver took charge. His 14 first-half points helped give the Texans an eight-point margin at intermission.

The Georgians began to warm up in the second half behind the leadership of their captain, Billie Tillman. The Tiger rally might have succeeded had it not been for the continued hot shooting of Weaver. With two minutes remaining and Tyler leading, 55-50, the game cooled off again. Thanks to a semi-stall by the Apaches, Tyler froze out the Georgians for a 57-52 victory.

The win belonged to Weaver. The big man controlled every phase of the game, leading all scorers with 26 — nearly half his team's total — and assisting many of his teammates' baskets with fabulous one-handed passes. He even directed Tyler's spread offense at the end of the game.

The decibel level generated by partisan Hutchinson fans, a train-load of 300 Dodge City rooters, plus the 92-piece Conquistador band, threatened to blow the roof off Convention Hall during the day's finale. Although Stockton was a newcomer to the tournament, the Mustangs were favored over tourney-wise Dodge City, a surprise regional winner.[4] Dodge City's underdog status was an additional inducement for local fans to cheer on the Kansas team.

The Conquistadors continued to surprise people by shutting down the Stockton attack while building a 19-13 lead midway through the first period. The vocal crowd quieted as Stockton's Gene Sosnick — at 5-7, the shortest player in the tournament — began firing away from long range over the zone. By halftime, the Mustangs evened the score 26-all.

Dodge City's fast break kicked into gear after intermission. The Conquistadors regained the lead by eight, only to see it evaporate to one with five minutes remaining. After driving layups by Leon Vann and Paul Sexton gave Dodge City some breathing room, the Kansans froze the ball. A free throw by Vann was the only score in the last three minutes.

Stockton not only had the smallest player in the tournament, but also the tallest — 6-8 Ted Romanoff. Romanoff's height had been no advantage, though, against Vann, Dodge City's 6-4 center. Like Ventura's Ernie Hall, Vann had developed an excellent one-handed jump shot. From 10 feet out he was deadly. His game-high 23 points led Dodge City to a 58-53 victory. For the third year in a row, a Kansas team had upset a Northern California team in tournament play.

WEDNESDAY — AN UNHERALDED DISCOVERY

The second day's action began with the closest tournament game in two years. The one-point thriller did not start out as an exciting contest. The Binghamton Hornets took command early, established a 12-point margin at the half, and extended it to 15 with 12 minutes remaining. At that point, Ken Deardorff, York's leading scorer — who had been held to just three free throws in the first half — started potting shots from outside. Deardorff's marksmanship opened up Binghamton's defense,

inspiring the Flying Dutchmen from Pennsylvania to a crowd-pleasing rally.

With six minutes to go, Binghamton tried to protect its dwindling three-point lead by stalling. York pressured, forcing a free throw. Goals by Gerald Strine and Deardorff for York tied the game, 53-all. Moments later the Pennsylvanians took the lead for the first time on a bucket by Harold Berger. The score was deadlocked at 55 and 57 as Binghamton's Bob Ross and York's Berger matched baskets. At the 15-second mark, Deardorff stepped to the free throw line and sank the last point. It was his 18th tally for the half. His 21-point total led all scorers.

The York win was followed by an equally surprising final first-round contest. The unheralded Moberly Greyhounds jumped out to a quick lead and expanded it to 16 at the half over the veteran squad from Bremerton, Washington. Olympic attempted several second-half rallies but without the services of its leading scorer, 6-5 Ed Halberg — who fouled out early in the period — the Rangers could get no closer than nine.

The 72-56 Moberly victory impressed many observers. The Greyhounds were a well-balanced ball club with height and board strength led by two 6-7 giants — Don Anielak and Richard Gott — who alternated at the post. Their offense was keyed around the best guard tandem in the tournament; Jerry Andress engineered the offense with ambidextrous ball handling while Glenn Cafer set the scoring tempo with spectacular set shots from far out. The duo scored over half Moberly's total against Olympic. The ease with which Moberly handled the tourney-wise Washington team generated a consensus that the Greyhounds should not be overlooked as a contender in the lower bracket.

A standing-room-only crowd packed Convention Hall Wednesday evening, expecting to see two high-scoring offenses outrace one another. Instead, they witnessed one of the lowest scores of the tournament.

Neither Northeast Mississippi nor Wingate performed as they had in the first round, because tight officiating slowed action to a crawl. By the end of the game, three Booneville starters — Jack Martin, Edd Burks, and Gerald Caviness — plus Neild Gordon, Wingate's star, were whistled to the bench. Though Northeast Mississippi recorded 11 more fouls than Wingate, the Tigers were less affected by the frigid tempo. They took a 26-21 lead into the locker room at half and never trailed thereafter. Gordon epitomized Wingate's cold shooting. The Bulldog's leading scorer continued his disappointing play in tournament action, missing 10 of 12 free throws. In all, Wingate hit only 6 of 22 charities, one of the worst performances from the line in tournament history.

In the day's final game Ventura overwhelmed a taller Amarillo squad, 78-46. Again the key to the win was Ventura's small front line. Ernie Hall (20), Jim Crockom (16), and Ed Millan (15) dominated play, totaling more than the entire Amarillo team. The Pirates were clearly the class of the tournament.

THURSDAY — OLD HANDS THRILL THE CROWD

Midweek of the tournament was a time for fans to catch their breath as consolation games filled most of the day's schedule. The afternoon contests were all routine affairs. Weber, Olympic, and Wingate encountered little difficulty eliminating Norfolk, Binghamton, and Amarillo, respectively. Only a late rally provided any excitement in the consolation match opening the evening session, as Stockton held off South Georgia, 56-49.

But, if anyone stayed home because they felt Thursday's quarterfinals would follow the same pattern, they regretted it when they picked up the paper the next day.

Though the evening's first quarterfinal paired two dark-horse winners, it was not expected to be an even match. The Moberly Greyhounds had impressed everyone in their defeat of the tough, experienced crew from Olympic. On the other hand,

---

[4]Dodge City led a charmed existence when it came to getting into the national tournament. Twice before the Conquistadors failed to win their way into the event only to be reprieved at the last second by an invitation. In 1951 the strongest team in Region 6 was Garden City Junior College, winner of the Western Kansas Juco Conference and third-place finisher in the national tournament the year before. The Broncbusters were prevented from encoring, however, when Coffeyville College surprised them, 67-64, in overtime in first-round regional action. The upset paved the way for Dodge City's fourth straight tournament appearance.

the Flying Dutchmen from York not only had good fortune shine on them in their come-from-behind victory over Binghamton, but they were also the only team in the tournament who represented their region without winning a regional tourney.[5]

Any doubts about the Pennsylvania squad's legitimacy were quickly erased once play began, however. The first half of the Moberly-York contest showcased the best brand of basketball yet seen in that year's tournament. It was a hectic tussle between two teams who excelled in every facet of the game. After 20 minutes of brilliant play, York trailed Moberly by a slim two points.

Unfortunately, the Flying Dutchmen were unable to maintain Moberly's perfect pace in the second period. The Greyhounds systematically dismantled the York defense. Curly redheaded Jerry Andress quarterbacked Moberly's precision attack, contributing seven second-half field goals. As Moberly continued to sparkle, York slowly faded. At the conclusion of the game, most observers were ready to concede Moberly would be facing Ventura in Saturday's finale.

The excellent basketball displayed in the Moberly-York quarterfinal set the stage for the most thrilling game of the tournament. For only the second time in tourney play, two teams fought to even terms, forcing an overtime period. It was fitting that the two teams represented the only two schools to have participated in the tournament all four years of its existence — Dodge City and Tyler.

Since the Hutchinson Blue Dragons had beaten Dodge City twice during the year, the contest was of particular interest to local fans. Convention Hall was solidly behind the Conquistadors from the outset. The support pushed the underdog Kansas team into the role of aggressor. By halftime Dodge City led one of the best teams in the country, 33-25.

After intermission Dodge City's domination dissolved. Tyler constantly chipped away at the lead, tying the score at 38-all with 15 minutes remaining. From then on, the game was a toss-up, the two teams virtually trading baskets for the next 14 minutes.

With 45 seconds left, Dodge City enjoyed a 59-58 lead. Tyler worked desperately for an open shot, spending 25 valuable seconds trying to crack Dodge City's tough zone defense. Finally, Tyler guard Jimmy Browning cut loose from 30-feet out.

The basket was good.

The tension in Convention Hall reached a peak as Dodge City scrambled to match the Texas goal. It eased with sighs of relief from the crowd when the referee's whistle blew Tyler for a foul just seconds before the final gun. With salvation riding on the shot, reserve Paul Owings stepped to the line and hit his only free throw of the night to send the game into overtime.

Relief for the Kansas partisans was short-lived. As soon as play resumed, Tyler guard Jack Mosher snuck behind Dodge City's zone for an easy lay-in. Freddie Whillock followed, driving the middle for another basket.

The Kansans battled back, Leon Vann tipping in a basket, then adding his 21st point of the night, hitting one of two free throws. With two minutes to go, Dodge City was down, 64-63.

At the Tyler end of the court, O'Neal Weaver calmly put the Apaches back on top by three with a basket from close in.

With time running down, guard Paul Sexton hit a long set shot. The Conquistadors were within one again. Forty-five seconds remained.

Tyler worked the ball carefully, protecting it from the scrapping Kansans. With 15 seconds on the clock, forward Eliseo Flores broke open for another sleeper. The game was over.

For the second time in as many games, O'Weaver topped the scoring charts, this time with 25. His leadership and poise under pressure exemplified the winning difference between Tyler and Dodge City.

FRIDAY — A DAY FOR TEARS

With two days to go, tournament officials faced the pleasant prospect of another attendance record. Because of Convention Hall's limited seating capacity, this was not an easy achievement. The tournament had played before a full house every night in 1950 to set the current mark. The only way to improve on it was to increase the turnout at the afternoon sessions.

Hutchinson fans obliged. They were beginning to realize consolation contests were just as entertaining as championship bracket affairs. Friday's afternoon session illustrated this perfectly, keeping the spectators guessing during all three games.

In the first, a veteran Weber squad attacked a comfortable Benton Harbor lead, chewing the margin from 14 down to three in the space of 7½ minutes. Thoroughly rattled and in danger of complete collapse, the all-freshman team from Michigan desperately held on to the ball for the last 30 seconds, thwarting Weber's rally, 71-68.

The Olympic-Stockton game which followed was a defensive struggle, featuring the lowest score of the tournament. Olympic held the advantage until the two-minute mark when Stockton tied the score. Two field goals by Stockton's Ray Mosher — the first putting the Californians ahead for the first time, 40-39, and the second clinching the victory with 20 seconds to go — provided the winning difference. A last second long shot by Olympic's Wayne Backlund was too little, too late. For the first time in three years, the disappointed Rangers were going home before the final day of play.[6]

The final afternoon game was marked by another aborted rally. True to their previous style of play, the Flying Dutchmen from York battled from behind throughout and were in the midst of another rally when time expired. The Pennsylvanians never succeeded in catching Dodge City because of Leon Vann's unstoppable jump shot. His game-high 33 points lifted the Conquistadors to trophy row for the fourth straight year.

The impending results of the semifinals were a foregone conclusion for many. Northeast Mississippi won an easy first-round game but struggled against Wingate. Tyler had tough going in both its matches, since O'Neal Weaver seemed to be the only Apache who could find the range consistently. In contrast, flawless basketball characterized the victories of Ventura and Moberly.

The evening's opener began as expected. Ventura continued its championship form forging a 37-31 halftime score.

Things were not as easy for the Pirates in the second period, however. The boys from Booneville came out of the locker room red-hot, with passing and shooting reminiscent of their last year's performances. Northeast Mississippi stalked the lead, caught the tourney favorites, then passed them. With five minutes to go, the Tigers were poised at their opponent's jugular with a 61-52 advantage.

Throughout the year Ernie Hall had been the life force behind Ventura. His determination was contagious. Just as hope was fading for the Pirates, Hall hit three baskets, rallying the Californians. With 2½ minutes to go, Ventura regained the lead, 64-63.

The next two minutes became a mad dog scramble. The score was tied three times, the lead changing hands five. With 35 seconds on the clock, Northeast Mississippi's J.R. Stroud tallied, putting the Tigers on top, 69-68.

Ventura quickly came down the court and set up its offense for a game-winning shot. It came with 10 seconds remaining — and missed. Northeast Mississippi gained possession.

The Californians chased after the ball as the Tigers tried to ice

[5]Plans for Region 13's tournament fell through. York — which had been prepared to travel to Hutchinson the previous year before losing to Keystone Junior College in a play-off — was anxious to attend the national. Since York was one of the best teams in the area, Region 13 Vice-President Frank Rubini of Bethesda, Maryland, compared scores of the top teams in the region. He verified York's claim to the regional title and certified the Flying Dutchmen as region 13's representative to the national tournament.

[6]Olympic's disappointment was magnified by the problems the team experienced getting to Hutchinson. The economic travails of travel from the coast still plagued the NJCAA. Olympic was forced to organize a fund raising drive much like Marin Junior College had in 1948. The local Chamber of Commerce, radio station KVRO, and various auxiliary organizations supported the campaign with promotions, including a dollar-a-plate smorgasbord which attracted a thousand people. Support came from as far away as Tyler, Texas, where U.S. Congressman Brady Gentry contributed $100 to help defray the team's expenses.

Gentry's gesture was homage to Olympic's popularity. The Rangers were a crowd favorite. The team's practice of tossing apples to the stands had won the support of fans and started a tournament tradition (California schools brought oranges, Tyler passed out roses, Northeast Mississippi tossed tiny bales of cotton, etc.). With Olympic's elimination, the tradition ended. It was the last tournament appearance for the Bremerton school.

the game. At the last second, Booneville's Edd Burks fired from center court. The ball was at the top of its arch as the gun sounded. The final bucket swished the net, completing the coup de grace.

Ernie Hall personified Ventura's heart-crushing despair. He sat down at the end of the court, his back against the stage, his arms covering his face, and wept.

Though Hall led all scorers with 27, it was a new-found star for Northeast Mississippi who was the difference in the game. According to school sources, J.R. Stroud had missed the Tigers' first two games because he had remained home to await the birth of his first child. Fortunately, they had been able to fly him to Hutchinson just in time. Stroud's 24 points — which had come from all points of the compass — and his overall skill solidified an already talented Tiger team. Without him in the line-up, Northeast Mississippi might not have triumphed. With him, the Tigers looked even better than last year's second-place finishers.

The other semifinal remained a toss-up for three quarters of play. Then, Coach Maury John's lucky gray garbardine suit began to work its charm?[7] His Moberly Greyhounds started a streak which carried them to a 61-53 lead that threatened to grow.

Then, with less than five minutes remaining, the Tyler guards halted the Moberly onslaught. Glen Pearson — substituting for starter Jimmy Browning who fouled out — and Jack Mosher took turns gunning at the basket. A 10-footer by Mosher tied the game at 61-all with 2½ minutes to go. Thirty seconds later, Pearson tight-rope-walked the baseline and cashed in another two-pointer to put the Apaches ahead.

Tyler tried to run out the clock, but Moberly was able to get the ball back twice. Unfortunately, on both occasions the Greyhounds came up empty on long shots, the only ones available to them.

With 20 seconds remaining, Mosher drove the middle for the clincher. Tyler would have the opportunity to become the first two-time champion in Juco Tournament history.

SATURDAY — GRUDGE MATCH

On Saturday morning, the *Hutchinson News-Herald* printed a short innocuous sounding article titled "Jr. Colleges Redistricted". Those who took the time to read it were puzzled. The opening line read, "The NJCAA executive board Friday took care of its California problem child." What was the problem with California?

As the article outlined the new regional structure, it explained the reason for the action. California's junior college administrators were threatening to ban Golden State schools from participating in NJCAA sponsored events. The redistricting was simply a precaution to make sure each region would have representation at the next year's tournament, in case the California threat was carried out. Though there was nothing alarming in the tone of the article, it was the first inkling the general public received that all was not right within the organization.

By coincidence, Saturday's opener featured one of the two California teams still in the tournament. Stockton had played well since its opening-round loss in spite of a handicap. In the Mustangs' second game, Gene Sosnick — the team's pint-sized floor general — twisted his ankle. He saw limited action against Olympic and was still slowed to half-speed. The weakened guard position cost Stockton a fifth-place trophy.

In a 90-second spree, Benton Harbor's John Stevens stole the ball three times, hit two field goals and a free throw, and pulled the Indians into a 50-all tie with a minute remaining. The Indians' Norman Reidel gave them the victory with another free throw 30 seconds later. Stockton had two tries at the win, but both shots failed.

In the contest for fourth place, Wingate's Neild Gordon displayed his awesome scoring ability for the first time in Juco

Tournament play. He banged in 25 to lead the Bulldogs to a 78-58 rout of Dodge City. Gordon's offensive barrage was set up by teammate Jack Musten who connected on six first-period two-handed push shots from near midcourt. The long bombs forced Dodge City to spread its tight drawn-in zone, opening the middle for Gordon to work at will.

The only bright spot for Dodge City was another brilliant performance by center Leon Vann. His 27 led all scorers and gave him a new record for most points in a tournament with 104, breaking the mark set by Gene Garrett the year before.

The teams most people expected to see in the finale played for third instead. The game was a championship caliber contest nonetheless. After Ventura jumped out to a commanding 38-25 halftime lead, the Moberly Greyhounds raced back into contention. Don Anielak's looping hook shot with 1:45 to go brought Moberly within one, 63-62. The Greyhounds tried desperately to get the ball away from Ventura's stall, but twice allowed Ernie Hall backdoor buckets. The baskets iced the game for the Pirates. If the story in the morning paper was correct, Ventura's third-place trophy would be the last honor won by a California team.

Though the championship game involved two surprise participants, it was of sufficient interest that an estimated 3,800 people jammed into tiny Convention Hall. Everybody wanted to witness the grudge match par excellence.

Both Tyler and Northeast Mississippi had additional incentive for winning besides the distinction of being crowned the best in the country. Tyler wanted revenge for being upset by the Booneville squad in the quarterfinals the previous year. In Northeast Mississippi's case, it was a matter of redemption after losing to the Apaches four times during the current season. The teams had changed since those defeats, however. The differences seemed to favor the Mississippi school.

First, most of Northeast Mississippi's nine season losses occurred early in the year during a period when team captain Ken Lindsey was out of action with a finger injury. Though Lindsey was not an overpowering scoring threat, he was an exceptional leader. The Tigers' cohesiveness deteriorated without his presence.[8]

The other difference was quickly noticeable once play began. J.R. Stroud — Northeast Mississippi's newly uncovered star — put on a shooting clinic that amazed everyone. His assortment of scoring weapons included a two-handed set-shot from long range, a one-handed push from close in, and hook shots put up with either hand under the basket. The 24-year-old freshman's superior shooting ability netted him a tournament record 44 points in the championship game.

Stroud's success was due in part to the defensive strategy of Floyd Wagstaff. When the wily Tyler coach realized he had no one who could guard the phenomenal Mississippi shooter without picking up fouls, he ordered his team to concentrate its defense on the other Booneville players. Consequently, Stroud was allowed to put on one of the best shooting exhibitions in tournament history.

Wagstaff's strategy proved sound, however. Only one other Northeast Mississippi player scored in double figures — Edd Burks with 11. On the other hand, four Apaches accomplished the feat — O'Neal Weaver (24), Freddie Whillock (22), Jack Mosher (18), and Jimmy Browning (13). Despite Stroud's outstanding performance, Tyler smashed the Tigers, 93-75.

Tyler Junior College took home its second national title in four years.

THE AFTERMATH — THE SKELETON FALLS OUT

The fourth annual National Junior College Basketball Tournament was another rousing success. Gross receipts were up $1,000 and attendance had increased by 2,000. There was no way to improve until the tournament moved into the new Sports Arena.

---

[7]John had worn the suit since Moberly clinched its fourth straight Missouri state championship. It was just one of his many superstitions. He always wore a red tie (Moberly's school colors were red and gray). His car remained unwashed since the beginning of regional play. He also set his watch ahead one hour before each game, because the team won when he mistakenly did it on another occasion. It was hard to fault his beliefs, though. Moberly's record over the past four years was 101-16.
[8]Lindsey's leadership was recognized by those with basketball acumen. He was a two-time selection to the All-Tournament Team, despite not appearing at the top of any statistical category. Lindsey later became president of cross-state Northwest Mississippi Junior College at Senatobia.

Action during the week had been exciting and entertaining, the perfect distraction from unsettling front-page headlines. The tournament was not totally isolated from current events, however. In the Northeast Mississippi cheering section Friday night was Sgt. Randall Howell, an injured veteran of Korea who was recuperating in a hospital at Hot Springs, Arkansas. He had been granted leave to attend the tournament to see his former schoolmates battle in the semifinals. His presence was a vivid reminder that the tournament was only a temporary diversion.

Though the games were hard-fought, the closest yet in the tournament's history, play was sportsmanlike. It had been a week free from controversy. The NJCAA's showcase event for basketball had come of age.

This illusion was shattered the following week.

Hutchinson fans opened their March 30th newspapers to find Northeast Mississippi had used a "ringer" during the tournament. J.R. "Johnny" Stroud, the star of the Tigers' final two games, had played professionally for two years in the Southern Basketball Association. To local fans, the deception was obvious. Besides appearing late to avoid early detection, Stroud was listed on the team roster in the program while another player wore his jersey in the team picture.

Surprisingly, Northeast Mississippi denied any wrongdoing. The school's president, J.O. Stringer, contended no regulations had been broken. Though he was technically correct, those who witnessed Ernie Hall's heart-breaking emotions after Ventura's loss to the Booneville team questioned the Mississippi school's ethics.

Even people from the institution's own state criticized its priorities. Carl Walters, sports editor for the *Jackson Daily News*, described Northeast Mississippi's 60-game schedule "overemphasis — with a vengeance." He called for regulatory action by the Mississippi Junior College Conference, limiting the number of games a team could play in a season. He also challenged the NJCAA: "If the National JC event is the kind where pro cagers can compete, then Mississippi junior college teams have no business entering it. If it is not . . ., then Northeast deserves a rebuke."

After lengthy investigation, the NJCAA tended to the dilemma. During Executive Committee sessions held concurrent with the association's annual track and field meet in May, the committee ruled the regulation restricting the play of professionals had never been officially rescinded. It was still operative even though missing from copies of the eligibility rules sent to member schools. The committee stripped Northeast Mississippi of its runner-up trophy, elevated Ventura to second place in the standings, and suspended the Booneville school from participation in the association's 1952 event.[9]

The Stroud incident was disillusioning to fans who felt "it can't happen here." It was embarrassing to the NJCAA. Still, the consequences of the affair did not threaten the organization's existence. That was *not* the case with the association's "California problem".

On the recommendation of the Athletic Committee of the California State Junior College Association, California junior colleges were barred from further competition in NJCAA sponsored events after September 1, 1951. Though the NJCAA insisted it would continue to function with or without California's participation, the move hurt. Not only was NJCAA membership immediately reduced by one-fourth but the organization's viability as a "national" entity suffered. It would be several years before the association fully recovered from the setback.[10]

		Tournament Results	
Tuesday:	Game		
		1	NE Mississippi — 78 Tiffin — 61
		2	Wingate — 79 Benton Harbor — 62
		3	Amarillo — 63 Norfolk — 52
		4	Ventura — 98 Weber — 69
		5	Tyler — 57 South Georgia — 52
		6	Dodge City — 58 Stockton — 53
Wednesday:	Game		
		7	York — 58 Binghamton St. — 57
		8	Moberly — 72 Olympic — 56
		9	Benton Harbor — 74 Tiffin — 57
		10	NE Mississippi — 54 Wingate — 44
		11	Ventura — 78 Amarillo — 46
Thursday:	Game		
		12	Weber — 87 Norfolk — 74
		13	Olympic — 73 Binghamton St. — 59
		14	Wingate — 65 Amarillo — 55
		15	Stockton — 56 South Georgia — 49
		16	Moberly — 65 York — 57
		17	Tyler — 68 Dodge City — 65 OT
Friday:	Game		
		18	Benton Harbor — 71 Weber — 68
		19	Stockton — 42 Olympic — 41
		20	Dodge City — 59 York — 53
		21	NE Mississippi — 71 Ventura — 68
		22	Tyler — 65 Moberly — 62
Saturday:	Game		
		23	Benton Harbor — 51 Stockton — 50
		24	Wingate — 78 Dodge City — 58
		25	Ventura — 67 Moberly — 62
		26	Tyler — 93 NE Mississippi — 75

[9]Public sentiment at the time heavily disfavored Northeast Mississippi's actions. Many of the local fans had adopted the Tigers and felt betrayed. These negative feelings persisted for several years and even washed over onto other tourney teams from Mississippi. They might have been tempered had certain facts about the Stroud episode been available to the general public.

First, according to Ken Lindsey, the reason given for Stroud's early absence from the team was legitimate. Coach Bonner Arnold fully intended using Stroud in the regional and national tournaments but was prevented from doing so because Stroud chose to stay home and await the birth of his daughter.

Second, after Northeast Mississippi used a high school player in the 1950 tournament, the NJCAA revised its eligibility rules. When the new code was disseminated to member institutions, the clause restricting the use of professionals was inadvertently omitted. Northeast Mississippi officials followed previous NJCAA guidelines which allowed conference eligibility standards to prevail at the national level. The Booneville school belonged to two conferences: the Mississippi Junior College Association (which banned professionals) and the Mississippi Valley Conference (which had no professional limitations in basketball). The use of Stroud was predicated on the latter.

The Stroud incident was a learning experience for everybody. Stated Lindsey, "He [Bonner Arnold] really liked to win. [But,] I'm sure that if he had that [using Stroud] to do over, he'd a never done it." As for the NJCAA, standardized eligibility requirements in junior college sports finally became a top priority.

[10]Though the general public was not aware of it, the NJCAA's "California problem" was an old one, dating back to the end of World War II. The principal adversaries in the disagreement were the coaches and administrators from California where the NJCAA originated.

The NJCAA had been the brainchild of the coaches. Men like Compton's Goldie Holmes had wanted the destiny of junior college sports controlled through a national athletic organization run by the coaching fraternity. The California junior college administrators were in opposition to the idea, feeling they had dominion over all athletic functions since they controlled the purse strings. Personalities were also involved.

The feud built until the California Junior College Association took its 1951 action (the actual recommendation came in October of 1950). Its reasons for pulling out were: (1) participation in the NJCAA's "so-called" national events was too expensive; (2) California junior colleges supplied the greatest number of competitors in the events; (3) the events were, therefore, unnecessary replays between California schools; and (4) the NJCAA was undemocratic in its organization.

Only the first claim had validity. The growth of the NJCAA and the continued success of events like its national basketball tournament in Hutchinson were rapidly making the California Association's second and third objections invalid. The final point had been invalidated in 1950 when the NJCAA called for regional meetings to select regional vice-presidents rather than having them appointed by the Executive Committee. But by 1951, the feuding between the two factions had produced too many festering sore spots.

In a December 5, 1950, letter to Region 7 Vice-President Wayne Cusic, Goldie Holmes remarked, "California's action in boycotting the NJCAA . . . is regrettable, but as I see it, it will only be the Golden State colleges that are hurt by this action and that it will really strengthen the National Association as it will give other regions where the junior college athletic program is just getting started a better opportunity to place in our championship activities . . . I am sure that in a few years the California colleges will be requesting re-admittance into our Association."

Holmes' final prediction never occurred. Both the NJCAA and the California Association have grown and flourished independently.

1951 TOURNAMENT BRACKET

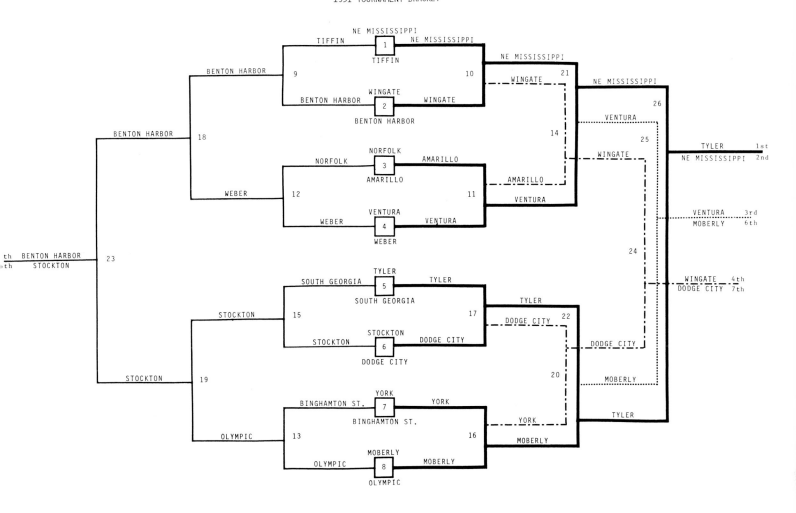

How They Finished in 1951	**All-Tournament Team**
1. Tyler Junior College	Jerry Andress — Moberly Junior College
2. Ventura Junior College	Cliff Appleget — Junior College of Benton Harbor
3. (Vacated)	Ken Deardorff — York Junior College
4. Wingate Junior College	Darrell Floyd — Wingate Junior College
5. Junior College of Benton Harbor	Ernie Hall — Ventura Junior College
6. Moberly Junior College	Kenneth Lindsey — Northeast Mississippi Junior College
7. Dodge City Junior College	Jack Mosher — Tyler Junior College
8. Stockton Junior College	Gene Sosnick — Stockton Junior College
	Leon Vann — Dodge City Junior College
	O'Neal Weaver — Tyler Junior College

1952:

UNDER A NEW ROOF

Inside the new Hutchinson Sports Arena, as pictured in the 1953 NJCAA basketball tournament official program. (Photo courtesy of NJCAA)

Outside Hutchinson Sports Area. (Photo courtesy of the **Hutchinson News**)

ollowing four years of steady growth, the NJCAA was forced to retrace some steps. The withdrawal of California cut deeply into the Association's membership list. The number of member institutions dropped from 185 in 1951 to 137 in 1952. The organization's image as a national clearing house for junior college sports was also tarnished. For President Reed Swenson and the other Executive Committee members, 1952 was a year for regrouping. Fortunately, circumstances provided the perfect rallying point for selling the organization. The National Junior College Basketball Tournament had an impressive new home.

After two years of construction, the Hutchinson Sports Arena was ready for use. Built by Foy Construction Company on 25 acres of land on the city's northeast edge, it was an architectural marvel for its time. Described as "modern functional" by Mann and Company, local designers of the facility, the Arena employed huge beam arches instead of the usual steel trusses. The effect was an open view for all spectators, an inside "arena" measuring 260' by 210'. There were 3,964 permanent seats affixed to concrete platforms around the floor. An additional 924 seats were on movable platforms just off the playing surface. The total seating capacity of 4,888 was more than double that of old Convention Hall. In a pinch, temporary bleachers could be moved in to expand seating to 7,000. Next to the Kansas State field house, it was the second largest building of its type in the state.

Cost overruns pushed the price of the structure over the million dollar mark. The people of Hutchinson got their money's worth, however. Besides the spacious seating area, the Arena contained 70 rooms. There were six offices, 12 storage areas, 21 dressing rooms and toilets, six press and radio booths hanging from the ceiling against the south wall, and a practice gym, containing a regulation basketball court. Compared to Convention Hall, the Sports Arena was a Taj Mahal.[1]

The facility reaped praises after its christening, the successful hosting of the Kansas state class B and BB tournaments the week before the nationals. The comments of *Salina Journal* Sports Editor, Bill Burke, were typical. "Salina has probably seen the last of state tournaments. . . We've known it for a long time but the final realization hit hard when we stepped into the beautiful million dollar Arena at Hutchinson . . . Because Hutchinson erected this giant building, it is now one of the leading basketball cities in the midwest."

Wichita — with a population five times that of Hutchinson — was probably the most envious. When the new Sports Arena was selected as the playing site of a potential Big Seven play-off between Kansas and Kansas State, *Wichita Beacon* Sports Editor Bob Donaldson reprehended the city's lack of foresight. "Such a playoff would have been a natural for Wichita. A natural for the city, yes. For the Forum? No. Our neighbor northwest of us

---

[1] Two of the Arena's features were particularly appreciated —
  (1) the dressing facilities: Convention Hall's facilities were non-existent. Teams generally dressed at their hotel rooms before coming to play.
  (2) the press facilities: According to Fred Mendell who covered the event at Convention Hall for the *Hutchinson News-Herald,* "I'd sit up in the seats, actually, and try to type up there with cheerleaders all behind me and a whole cheering section behind me. i tell you, it was awful."

is going to grab off many basketball attractions that might have been Wichita's and all because as a city it knew more about building buildings than our own does."

Community curiosity about the new structure was reflected in tournament ticket sales. As early as February 22 — almost a month before the event — gross receipts were reported to have topped the previous year's record. The people of Hutchinson were busting their buttons. Even though the 1952 National Juco Tournament was to be the closest affair to date, the Hutchinson Sports Arena stole the show.

THE PARTICIPANTS

Region	Team
1	*Dodge City Junior College — Dodge City, Kansas
2	Graceland College — Lamoni, Iowa
3	Grays Harbor College — Aberdeen, Washington
4	Branch Agricultural College — Cedar City, Utah
5	Connors State Agricultural College — Warner, Oklahoma
6	Garden City Junior College — Garden City, Kansas
7	Junior Agricultural College of Central Arkansas — Beebe, Arkansas
8	Abraham Baldwin Agricultural College — Tifton, Georgia
9	Campbellsville College — Campbellsville, Kentucky
10	Wingate Junior College — Wingate, North Carolina
11	Hibbing Junior College — Hibbing, Minnesota
12	Joliet Junior College — Joliet, Illinois
13	*Moberly Junior College — Moberly, Missouri
14	Wharton County Junior College — Wharton, Texas
15	*Campbell College — Buies Creek, North Carolina
16	Hannibal-LaGrange College — Hannibal, Missouri

* Invited to fill bracket

To go along with the tournament's new surroundings was a new cast. Though eight of the schools represented had previously participated, only three were returning contestants from the 1951 event. Since Tyler Junior College was not one of them, a new junior college kingpin was also assured.

The only clear-cut favorite was the fourth-place finisher from the previous year. Wingate Junior College went undefeated in North Carolina conference play, owned one of the two top scoring averages in the country (87.3), and again sported an exceptional record — 34-2. The school also claimed the only returning tournament all-star — 6-2 forward Darrell Floyd.

In the 1951 tournament, Floyd finished fourth among all scorers. His marksmanship and overall floor play had far outshone his more publicized teammate, Neild Gordon. In 1952, Floyd continued his all-star ways, leading Wingate in scoring with a 26.6 average. Coming into the tournament, he had amassed 931 points, outdistancing the top total of Tyler's O'Neal Weaver from the past year. If he lived up to his advance billing, sometime during the tournament he would become the first junior college player to breach the 1,000-point milestone for a season.

After Wingate, the field was wide-open, strewn with legitimate title contenders. Among them were the other two returnees from 1951, two teams who beat them, four upstarts, and a host of excellent records.

For the fifth year in a row, Dodge City Junior College graced the tournament roll. The Conquistadors were third-place finishers in the Western Kansas Juco Conference, owned an unimposing 14-7 record, and were only an invited entry, having been a runner-up in the Region 6 tournament.[2] Still, no one discounted the team's chances. Dodge City had brought similar credentials to the tournament before and had walked away with four trophies in as many years.

Like Dodge City, Moberly Junior College (22-5) was also an invited entry. The Greyhounds, however, owned an impeccable recommendation for inclusion in the tournament. Earlier in the year, Moberly won the Western States Invitational Tournament, beating Stockton Junior College and host Compton College — two of California's top teams. Moberly's presence gave

Though Darrell Floyd's two-year tourney average of 21.1 points per game was excellent, it did not compare to what he achieved as a collegian. As an All-American at Furman, Floyd led the nation for the 1954-55 and 1955-56 basketball seasons with 35.9 and 33.8 per-game averages, respectively. (Photo courtesy of Furman University)

the tournament a certain legitimacy as a "national" event.

The two teams who beat Dodge City and Moberly in regional play were obvious candidates for favorite status. Garden City Junior College (21-9) was again the best in Region 6, the Kansas state champion for the third straight year. Hannibal-LaGrange College (22-5) defeated Moberly three times in a 10-day period, usurping Moberly's Missouri state crown by winning a best two-out-of-three series, then quickly topping the Greyhounds again for the regional title.

Four tourney newcomers were considered title threats on the basis they survived regions noted for perennially producing top competitors. Wharton County Junior College (30-4) ended Tyler Junior College's domination of Region 14, dumping the defending champions in the first round of regional play.[3] Grays Harbor College (22-4) won impressively over Olympic College in the Region 3 finals at Bremerton to end a three-year string of tourney appearances for the Rangers. Likewise, Branch Agricultural College (27-7) replaced three-time participant Weber College. From the region which produced suspended Northeast Mississippi Junior College came a surprise winner from Beebe, Arkansas. Junior Agricultural College of Central Arkansas (22-13) knocked off top-rated East Mississippi Junior College of Scooba and Holmes Junior College of Goodman, Mississippi, to take over Northeast Mississippi's regional crown.

Four more teams presented superb records for their credentials — first-timers Hibbing Junior College (27-1) and Connors State Agricultural College (24-4) and veterans Joliet Junior College (26-1) and Campbellsville College (21-3).

Only Campbell College (23-10) — a runner-up to Wingate and another invited team — Abraham Baldwin Agricultural College (22-8), and Graceland College (13-6) appeared to be long shots.

With seven tournament teams having cracked the 100-point barrier during the year, the 1952 National Juco Tournament

---

[2]Though the NJCAA tried to head off the possibility of tournament bracket vacancies, the Association's 1951 restructuring went for naught. Phoenix College, the representative from Region 1 — which had previously produced top caliber Southern California squads — was unable to make the trip to Hutchinson. Likewise, the two Eastern Seaboard regions failed to send teams. The NJCAA was forced to extend three invitations, the most since the tournament's first year.
[3]Describing the early years of regional play, Tyler Coach Floyd Wagstaff said, "Back then we had to beg people to come [to the regional tournament] . . . They laughed at me about it and called it 'the Wagstaff Follies'. I made a mistake a few years later when I carried a whole bunch of these coaches to the national tournament at Hutchinson, Kansas. Then they all come back and give me trouble the rest of the time, trying to win." Wharton County was only the first of Wagstaff's problems. It would be four years before he would lead Tyler back to the national tournament.

promised to be a closely contested, high-scoring event.

TUESDAY — HOLD THAT TRAIN

In 1952, junior college teams did not play basketball in spacious field houses. They played in gyms, before generally small audiences. To perform in a magnificent structure like the Sports Arena in front of large, enthusiastic crowds was an awesome experience for most players. Walking into the Arena's cavernous interior for an opening-round game, the first step toward a possible national crown, could easily petrify a team.

When the Hibbing Cardinals took the floor for the tournament's inaugural game in the Arena, spectators immediately concluded the team would fold from the pressure. Hibbing looked like a YMCA team not a national junior college contender. The team's uniforms were little more than undershirts and shorts. Besides, the Minnesotans had brought only eight players.

Shortly after the opening tip, everyone admitted they had made a mistake. Hibbing did not need flashy uniforms nor more than eight players. The Cardinals had Dick Garmaker.

The 6-4 forward excelled at everything: His shooting was accurate from any distance, with either hand; his dexterity made him an excellent passer; and his solid frame, muscular torso, and powerful legs, combined with natural quickness and agility, made him an extraordinary rebounder. Garmaker was by far the best all-around talent showcased by the tournament in its first five years.

The opener was close for one quarter.[4] Then in the second

Dick Garmaker was one of two players (the other Wingate's Darrell Floyd) who first brought attention to the junior college ranks as a source of talent for university recruiters. After graduating from Hibbing, Garmaker became an All-American at the University of Minnesota, then starred in the NBA for six years. (Photo courtesy of Bob Peterson, University of Minnesota)

period, Garmaker scored 16 of his eventual 37 points. Campbell College crumbled. Hibbing romped, 95-66.

Garmaker's fabulous one-man show gave way to a total team effort in the second game. Connors State Coach Bob Rogers was a student of the Hank Iba style of basketball, having played for the legendary coach at Oklahoma A&M. The Aggies from Warner, Oklahoma, were a disciplined crew which maximized its scoring opportunities while minimizing those of its opponent.

With speed and quickness, the Aggie defense shut down Wingate's patented fast break. The slow tempo bothered the North Carolina team. What few open shots the Bulldogs

received refused to fall. They scored no more than four field goals in any one quarter. In the final period, Connors State employed Iba's Oklahoma A&M stall. The result was a crushing 57-40 Aggie upset.

Besides sharing the same nickname, the Branch Aggies also mirrored the Oklahomans in style, using the same cautious ball handling and careful shot selection. Unlike Connors State, however, Branch did not resort to a stall to ice the game. Instead, the Utah team took advantage of Graceland's pressing defense to run up 27 points in the last quarter of the afternoon finale to rack up another lopsided win, 81-60.

The tournament's drawing power in its new surroundings received its first test that evening when a concert at Convention Hall, featuring Guy Lombardo, competed with the event. Lombardo's music won as 5,622 packed the tournament's former home. Basketball in the Sports Arena held its own, however. In its first day of use, the Arena accommodated 6,000 fans — the most people to see a day's action in the tournament's history. Those who opted for athletics over aesthetics were properly rewarded. The evening session was loaded with record-breaking performances.

The opener began as if the only record in danger of being broken was the one for lowest score. Grays Harbor and Abraham Baldwin managed only one bucket apiece in the first 2½ minutes of play. Then, the two teams shook off opening-game jitters and broke from the gate.

Both Grays Harbor and Abraham Baldwin eschewed defense. The race to put points on the scoreboard was so frenzied that players often waited impatiently for the ball to go through the net so they could hustle it down to the other end of the court to hike up the score there. The scoring pace peaked in the last 10 minutes when the two teams combined for 64 points.

The final tally completely rewrote the record book. Grays Harbor became the first team in tournament history to crack the 100-point barrier, posting a total of 112. Abraham Baldwin was not far from the century mark with 90. Together they set a new record for total score — 202. The top performance by an individual also fell. Despite the game-long failure of his favorite hook shot, Grays Harbor center, Tony Vlastelica — a towheaded 6-6 ex-Marine who had played most of his basketball tha

Utilizing his trademark hook shot, Tony Vlastelica upped the single-game scoring mark to 42 in a first-round game against Abraham Baldwin, the tourney's first 100-point contest. Vlastelica later starred for the Oregon State Beavers. (Photo courtesy of Tony Vlastelica)

---

[4] For three years starting with 1952, junior college games were played in four 10-minute quarters rather than two 20-minute halves.
[5] Johnny Stroud's 44-point total in the 1951 championship game was disallowed when the NJCAA sanctioned Northeast Mississippi.

year at Camp Pendleton — passed Buddy Travis' old mark, hitting 42.[5]

The curtain-raiser was exhilarating for the fans. It put them in the perfect mood for the final two contests, featuring both Kansas entries. The highly partisan crowd, including 200-plus loyal Dodge City followers who had chartered their annual special train to Hutchinson, had plenty to cheer.

Though the feature game was close through three quarters of play, Dodge City was in the driver's seat from the second quarter on. Led by 5-11 forward Carlos Taylor — who scored all of his game-high 26 points on field goals — the Conquistadors again worked their familiar tournament magic, upsetting the favored squad from Beebe, Arkansas, 69-57.

Santa Fe Railroad officials had guaranteed the group of Dodge City rooters their train would not leave before the end of the final game between Garden City and Hannibal-LaGrange. They probably regretted the promise, however, when the day's finale proved to be one of the longest games in tournament history.

The contest did not begin as a classic. Hannibal-LaGrange jumped out to a quick 23-10 first-quarter lead, quieting the partisan fans. The cheering grew, though, as Garden City struggled back. By halftime the Broncbusters trimmed the margin to six. At the three-quarter mark, they were behind by one.

The Arena was charged with edge-of-your-seat electricity in the fourth period. The score was tied at 49, 51, 53, and 55. Hannibal took the lead 57-55 near the two-minute mark on a field goal by Lowell "Cotton" Fitzsimmons. The 5-6 blond whiz from Bowling Green, Missouri, then attempted to dribble out the clock. Instead, Garden City trapped Fitzsimmons against the midcourt line. Mort Highlander stole the ball and fed it to Harold Patterson whose easy lay-in tied the score for the fifth time in the period.

With 1:29 to go the Kansans regained the basketball and held it for a final shot. Unable to see the clock on the huge four-sided scoreboard overhead, the Broncbusters relied on teammates on the bench to keep them informed of the remaining time. Garden City's push for the final basket came with only four seconds left; only enough time for Patterson to get off a long overhead hook which missed everything.

Three quick Hannibal field goals put Garden City behind the eight ball in the overtime. Again the Kansans fought back. Field goals by reserves Tom Williams and Darrell Almond plus three points by Patterson in the last 40 seconds rescued the Broncbusters. Garden City again had a chance to win the game with a final shot, but on a fast break with 19 seconds remaining, Almond — who could not see the clock — uncorked an unnecessary desperation heave on the dead run. At the end of the overtime, the score was still knotted, 64-all.

Players and fans alike were wilting from the strain. Describing his own fatigue, Fitzsimmons later said, "I wondered if it [the game] was ever going to get over . . . I said, 'Heh! If they're all going to be like this, it truly *is* a national championship.'"

The tension did not let up. With less than two minutes remaining and one point separating the two teams, Garden City's Marvin Deckert was fouled. He hit two free throws, giving the Broncbusters their first lead of the game, 72-71.

With time running out, fate intervened. Hannibal forward Ray Schumann, closely guarded by Garden City's Ted Blue, launched a jumper from the side of the free throw circle. Despite the fact Blue deflected it, the ball hit its target. A foul was called on the play and the Trojans elected to retain possession of the basketball. Another Schumann field goal clinched the game for Hannibal-LaGrange.

The last two scores typified Schumann's leadership. He tallied 12 of his 31 points in the two overtimes without a miss. Schumann shared top honors with Garden City's Patterson, a 6-1 jumping jack who seemed to score best when the Broncbusters were in the hole. The heroics of both men exemplified the epic proportions of the contest. Many spectators wished the game had been played for the championship.

WEDNESDAY — AFTER TIME RAN OUT

Those able to tear themselves away from the spring-like weather outside were given a clue to why Tyler was not in the tournament. The Wharton County Pioneers did not have

One of the Juco Tournament's most successful alumni, Harold Patterson later starred in both basketball and football at Kansas University. Afterwards, he continued his athletic career in the Canadian Football League where he enjoyed 14 seasons as one of the league's top receivers. His many honors include the Schenley Most Outstanding Player Award for 1956. He holds several CFL receiving records and is the league's No. 3 all-time receiver. On November 25, 1971, Patterson achieved his greatest honor, induction into the Canadian Football Hall of Fame. (Photo courtesy of Ray Patterson, taken by Tom Bochsler Photography, Hamilton, Canada)

exceptional height — the front line all measured 6-3 — nor imposing physiques. One observer described the team as "a bunch of skinny Texans with sideburns." Still, the Pioneers played sound, steady basketball.

Except for the contest's initial stages, Wharton County led Moberly by comfortable margins throughout the Wednesday afternoon opener. The key to the 71-64 Pioneer win was Moberly's inability to stop hot-shooting Jim Payne. The Wharton County forward began firing successfully from long range, then shortened his attack when the defense came out to meet him. Payne took scoring honors with 30, all from the field.

The final first-round game was a complete mismatch. The Joliet Wolves were the tallest team in the tournament, with four starters standing 6-2 or better. They towered over the Campbellsville Tigers, whose personnel included the tourney's smallest player — 5-5, 115-pound Jackie Houk. The Kentucky squad tried to make up the size difference with speed, but the strategy was doomed from the start. With 6-6 forward Don Laketa and 6-4 center Bob Jenkins sweeping the backboards at both ends of the floor, Joliet wore out the quicker Tigers, 78-63. Laketa — a bench-warmer for Kansas State before transferring to his hometown junior college — led the scoring roll with 22.

The evening session started with a replay of the Region 10 final. Wingate shook off its opening-round loss and returned to its championship form, beating Campbell for the sixth time that season.

Anticipating the opening elimination contest would be the blase affair it was, many people took a little extra time eating supper, wanting to be primed for two very interesting quarterfinal match-ups later.

Forty-five-hundred fans piled into the Arena Wednesday night to see the first round's two highest powered offenses paired in quarterfinal matches with two teams who displayed a decided preference for control basketball. The evening feature also contrasted differing scoring philosophies. Hibbing relied on one big gun while Connors State pelted their opponents with peashooters.

In the first quarter, Oklahoma teamwork prevailed. The Aggie offense ignited while its defense — which held opponents to only 40.1 points per game during the year, the best in the tournament — froze out Hibbing. Connors State took the advantage, 23-15.

Then, the Aggies became uncharacteristically careless. Hibbing took advantage of the lapse and jumped back into contention. Leo Hartmann — a 6-5 tree in the middle — proved Hibbing had more than just Dick Garmaker, poking home eight quick points in the second period, leading the Minnesota team to a 36-33 halftime edge.

The third quarter was disastrous for Connors State. Not only did Garmaker take control of the game for Hibbing, but the Aggies handcuffed themselves with foul trouble. The Oklahoman's best rebounder, 6-6 center Jim Miller, went to the bench for good with a full seven minutes remaining in the period. Wayne Mulkey, another Connors starter, also picked up his fifth foul in the quarter. With 10 minutes left to play, Hibbing was in command, 51-45.

Three minutes later, Hibbing had extended the lead to nine. The Cardinals appeared on the road to victory. Then, Clarence Lynch caught fire for the Aggies, lifting them to within two.

Garmaker quickly held the Oklahomans at bay with six points. At the 3:30 mark, Hibbing held a 64-58 lead.

The Aggies refused to give up hope. Lynch and H.O. Hoover closed the gap to two. With tension building, the teams traded baskets. Finally, with 1:20 remaining, a beautiful hook shot by reserve Raymond Gann pulled Connors State even at 66-all.

With 50 seconds to go, Hibbing called time. Taking a page out of the Connors State playbook, the Minnesotans decided to hold for one last shot.

The Cardinals passed the ball around the perimeter, their passes cautious and sure. Seconds ticked slowly off the clock. Everyone in the Arena knew who was going to get the ball last.

The final shot came with one second showing. Garmaker caught a deflected pass and drove the middle. The ball was in the air as the buzzer sounded.

The shot was good.

Hibbing players swarmed Garmaker. However, their jubilation quickly gave way to confusion. Something was wrong. As the officials conferred at the scorer's table, players on both sides congregated along the sidelines, trading expressions of joy and despair.

The basket was disallowed. A foul had been blown against Connors before the buzzer. No one had heard it because, in the game-ending excitement, the whistle had popped out of the referee's mouth.

The floor was cleared for the free throw attempt. A hopeful group of Aggies watched helplessly as Hibbing's premier point producer toed the line.

Dick Garmaker confidently popped the net. The game was over.

Connors State held the Hibbing scoring wizard to 22 points. He was even topped by the Aggies' own Clarence Lynch who totaled 28. It was no consolation. The Oklahomans left the court, heads bowed in utter disappointment. Feeling worst of all was Raymond Gann. The 6-4 substitute had replaced center Jim Miller admirably, scoring the final Connors basket, the one which tied the game and gave the Aggies new hope. All that was forgotten, though. Gann made his way to the dressing room, a towel draped over his head to hide his tears. It was Gann who had fouled Garmaker.

Even though the day's finale featured an exciting rally, the game was a let down for the crowd after the previous thriller. Grays Harbor — cold for most of the contest — managed to make the game interesting during the third period, scoring 22 points in seven minutes. The Chokers[6] were behind by two at the end of three periods, then edged in front of Branch, 67-66. It was their first lead since the opening moments of the game.

The turning point came moments later. Tony Vlastelica drove around his man for an easy lay-up. The ball banged off the glass, whirled around the lip, dangling motionless for what seemed like several seconds, then fell away. Instead of leading by three points, Grays Harbor was again protecting a precarious one-point lead.

The Choker advantage toppled quickly. Instead of opting to take the ball out of bounds on fouls, the Washington team

insisted on challenging the charity stripe — and kept missing. Baskets by Neil Christiansen and Roger Olpin plus a pair of free throws by Boyd Adams gave Branch a 74-67 margin with three minutes remaining. The rest was routine. Grays Harbor scored only two more points. The Branch Aggies advanced to the semifinals with a 76-69 victory.

THURSDAY — THE FIRST DAY OF SPRING

Five coatless high school girls smiled from the front page of the *Hutchinson News-Herald*. It was warm and beautiful, perfect for the first day of spring. Whether it was the sunny day or the traditional need for a breather on the tournament's "hump day", only a thousand people attended the afternoon session — the lowest total of the tournament.

The afternoon consolation games warmed to the temperature outside. After Graceland won a nip-and-tuck match with Abraham Baldwin, 67-61, Moberly eliminated Campbellsville 67-65, on a last-second tip-in by Gerald Anderson. Then, the action turned downright hot!

The final afternoon match-up between Connors State and Grays Harbor was not a game but a war. One of the battle's most serious casualties was Bill Shahan of Connors State. While going up for a loose ball, Shahan was undercut. He fell, landing on his tail bone, cracking his head on the floor, the jarring tumble momentarily paralyzing him. After feeling returned, he spent the rest of the game in pain on the bench.

Fouls escalated. Grays Harbor center Tony Vlastelica fouled out on the opening jump ball of the fourth quarter. From then on a steady stream of Grays Harbor players made their way to the bench. Of the 52 fouls called, 36 were whistled against the tired team from Washington. With 1:03 remaining, Coach Dan Melinkovich was left with only four eligible men.

In an act of sportsmanship, opposing coach Bob Rogers pulled the Oklahoman's top scorer, Clarence Lynch, to even the sides. The move did not matter. Grays Harbor managed just four points in the final period. Connors State eliminated the Chokers, 64-51.

Attendance was also down for the evening session. It was possible fans were not ready for more tension, after the cliff hangers of the previous two evenings. They had nothing to fear however. Though the quarterfinal games were tightly contested, the night's program was dull viewing.

Those who showed up saw Garden City completely outclass Central Arkansas in a consolation game, 88-60. They quietly watched Wharton County use smooth ball handling and quick teamwork under the bucket to subdue a taller Joliet squad, 74-63. They became restless from boredom as Hannibal-LaGrange dominated the first half of the day's finale. Then, they were aroused by the only excitement of the night.

Continuing their magical ways, the underdog Dodge City Conquistadors fired out of the locker room, charged from behind, and took a comfortable 56-48 margin into the fourth quarter.

Then, the magic began to wear. A bad pass here. A steal there. Within minutes Hannibal had tied the game. When Ray Schumann hit a field goal — two of his 37 points for the night — the Missouri team was back in front, 58-56.

Dodge City fought desperately to hold on, tying the score twice more. But, there were no more rabbits in the hat.

As the game gradually slipped from the Conquistadors' grasp, fans filed out of the Arena, chilled by the near upset. They had a colder surprise waiting for them outside.

FRIDAY — WINTER RETURNS

Gale force northerly winds and freezing drizzle hit Hutchinson Thursday night. By morning, trees, telephone poles, and car windshields were layered with ice. At 11 a.m. Friday, the thermometer had only warmed to 30. For visitors, the second day of spring was a cruel joke. For the locals, it was typical Kansas weather.

At a crucial point in the afternoon contest between Garden City and Moberly, the storm knocked out radio station KWHK's

---

[6]Aberdeen, Washington, home of Grays Harbor College, is a lumbering community. The school's nickname derives from the industry. A "choker setter" is a person who puts a large cable (a "choker") around a log when it is ready to be pulled out. The job is difficult and dangerous.

feed of the game. Outside of that one incident, the activities inside the Arena were not affected by the frigid weather. In fact, those who braved the elements were treated to a series of radiant exploits.

In the day's opener, Darrell Floyd became the first junior college player to score 1,000 points in a season, doing it in grand fashion. After Graceland took a seven-point advantage at the end of three periods, Floyd led a Wingate fourth-quarter comeback, sending the game into an extra period. He then scored all seven of his team's tallies in overtime to secure an 82-77 win for the Bulldogs. Of Wingate's last 30 points, Floyd was responsible for 20 — half his game-high total of 40.

The high point parade continued with two more superb afternoon performances. Garden City's Harold Patterson contributed 35 in leading the Broncbusters past Moberly, 75-64, and Joliet's Don Laketa tallied 32 in the Wolves' 84-72 win over Dodge City.

In spite of freezing rain and the threat of snow, 5,000 fans persevered to take in the evening semifinals. They were rewarded with another outstanding individual scoring feat.

Though Hibbing was in control most of the way, the evening's opener was anything but smooth sailing for the Cardinals. The contest was tied 10 times and the lead switched hands six before Hibbing took the advantage for good. Even then the Minnesota team had to stave off a late Branch rally to pull out a 70-68 victory.

There was no question why Hibbing won. *Half* the Cardinal points were scored by Dick Garmaker. It was the third spectacular game for the splendid sophomore.

There were no 30-point performances in the remaining semifinal. After topping that mark in both prior games, Hannibal's Ray Schumann turned cold, scoring just six points in the opening half. His icy touch characterized a complete chill by the Trojans. Hannibal hit only 18 percent of its shots in the first two periods.

Schumann returned to form in the second half, managing 23 points for the game. Cotton Fitzsimmons helped make up Schumann's reduced point production, cranking in 21. But a 15-point Wharton County halftime advantage was too much to overcome. What hurt the Missouri state champs most was the lack of help from anybody else. Only one other Trojan — center Charles Hutchens who totaled seven — scored more than two points.

In contrast, four Wharton County players hit double digits — Jim Payne (24), Roy Green (19), Dan Gilder (12), and Charles Brown (11). Besides the better balanced scoring, the quicker Texas front line dominated the middle, controlling the backboards throughout the game. Despite their lack of size, the "skinny" Pioneers were in the finals.

SATURDAY — FROM SEVENTY FEET AWAY

It was snowing as the crowd left the Arena after Friday night's games. By morning the ground was blanketed with a two-inch accumulation. Snow on top of the previous night's ice was more than most telephone lines could bear. Three-quarters of the toll lines out of Hutchinson were out of commission. Travel was treacherous. The forbidding conditions were not conducive for a big turnout at the tournament.

But in spite of the weather, Saturday evening's championship session was sold out. Response for tickets was so overwhelming, temporary bleachers were erected on the main floor and 500 general admission tickets were made available on a first-come-first-served basis. Hutchinson fans proved they loved good basketball.

The trophy battle kicked off Saturday afternoon with an inspiring win for Kansas partisans. After Garden City trailed Wingate through the first half, sharp shooting by Harold Patterson and Marvin Deckert lifted the Broncbusters, making it anybody's game. Garden City gradually pulled away in the final period and posted a comfortable 66-56 win for fifth place.

Indicative of Garden City's tough defense — the second best in the tournament behind the slow-down basketball of Connors State — Wingate's national junior college scoring leader, Darrell Floyd, was held to 16. Game honors went to the Broncbusters' Harold Patterson with 23. His four-game total of 115 surpassed the previous tourney high set by Leon Vann the year before.

The contest for fourth place was exciting despite being the lowest scoring game in the tournament. Joliet led at all the quarter breaks before a Connors State rally in the final period knotted the sore at 45 with 1:08 to go.

For the Connors Aggies, the last minute must have seemed like déjà vu. As in the Aggies' game with Hibbing, Joliet played

For many of the seventh-place Connors State Aggies, success came later. Four of the Aggie starters — Clarence Lynch, Wayne Mulkey, Jim Miller (left to right, front row), and H.O. Hoover (far right, front row) — followed Coach Bob Rogers to East Texas State. There they, along with Shelby Metcalf who later succeeded Rogers as head coach at Texas A&M, combined to produce a national championship, winning the 1955 NAIA Tournament in Kansas City.

Another Aggie, reserve Louis Henson (second from right, front row) achieved later success as head coach at New Mexico State and the University of Illinois. (Photo courtesy of Clarence Lynch, Connors State College)

for one last shot. With time wearing down, the pressing Aggies were again called for a foul. This time the clock did not run out on them. Thirteen seconds still remained when Joliet guard Ron Fagan stepped to the line.

The Aggie fortunes brightened as the basketball bounded away, no good. Then, center Bob Jenkins slipped behind the Connors State front line for a tip-in. Joliet was on top by two.

Connors State scrambled to inbounds the ball and get it down the court for a shot before time ran out. In their haste, Joliet's Jess Gutirrez stole the ball, dribbled to the basket unmolested, and laid in the clincher.

One of the top thrills of the day came just before halftime of the third-place game Saturday night. After a free shot by the Branch Aggies, Hannibal-LaGrange took the ball out under the Branch basket with next to no time on the clock. Hannibal guard Cotton Fitzsimmons signaled his teammate, cut for the middle, took the inbounds pass at the Branch charity stripe, dribbled once, then let loose with a two-handed shot. The ball sailed over two-thirds the length of the court, rattled between the back and front of the rim, and fell through. It was the longest shot ever made in tournament history. Though sinking a 70-foot shot was an incredible feat in itself, most observers found it

One of the most popular participants in tourney history, Lowell "Cotten" Fitzsimmons holds the record for the longest shot made — 70 feet. In the second game of the 1952 Missouri state championship play-off against Moberly, Fitzsimmons also delivered from long distance, hitting from 52 feet away. (Photo courtesy of Donnie Crim, **Quincy Herald-Whig***)*

even harder to believe it had been accomplished by the smallest man on the court — Hannibal's "cotton top".

The contest's thrills did not stop there. After trailing Hannibal-LaGrange the entire ballgame, Branch rallied to tie the Missouri team 60-all, on a field goal by Boyd Adams with 30 seconds to play. Hannibal had two opportunities to win in the closing seconds but failed.

With two key players — center Charles Hutchens and quarterback Fitzsimmons — on the bench with five fouls for Hannibal, the extra period was a long stall for the last shot. Going into the final seconds of play, only two free throws — one by each team — had been put on the scoreboard. Then, Hannibal's Ray Schumann dribbled to the edge of the free throw circle, arched a long left-handed push shot, and cashed in the winning basket. His 26th point of the night not only gave Hannibal-LaGrange the third-place trophy, but nudged Schumann ahead of Harold Patterson in the race for top tourney honors with 117.

The opponents for the 1952 NJCAA basketball crown would not have been considered champions based on their appearance. Neither Wharton County's slight builds nor Hibbing's rag-tag uniforms inspired awe. If either team had participated in any of the previous national tournaments, they would have been regarded as definite underdogs. Still, both were winners. They had survived where others had not, overcoming handicaps to do so.

In every one of its tournament outings, Wharton County's

front line — center Charles Brown plus forwards Jim Payne and Roy Green — played against taller counterparts. The Pioneers had negated the height disadvantage with teamwork, quickness, and consistency. Only once did all three front-liners fail to score double figures.

Hibbing's handicap was less evident. The Cardinals' regular coach, Joe Milinovich, did not make the trip to Hutchinson. He remained in Minnesota, hospitalized with a case of pneumonia so severe he was not allowed to listen to broadcasts of his team's games. In his place, the Cardinals were guided by the Hibbing High School mentor, Mario Retica, who had been recruited to fill the position at the last moment.

Picking a favorite was difficult. The only significant difference between the two teams was their approach to putting points on the scoreboard. Hibbing's attack depended solely on the production of its star forward, Dick Garmaker. Wharton County's scoring was evenly distributed among all five starters. When Wharton County supporters suggested their team had a better chance of winning since all Hibbing had was Garmaker, Hibbing backers responded, "But that's enough." Anyone who saw Garmaker play was hard pressed to argue the point.

As one observer described it, the title tilt was "a real cat fight. They clawed and scratched at one another. There were a lot of fouls. First one team would be ahead then the other. It really hung the fans on the edge of their seats."

The argument regarding the disparity of scoring balance between the two teams proved moot. Both squads placed four men in double figures. In the final analysis, it was simply a matter of one championship team outlasting another. Only one basket separated the two at the game's conclusion.

Dick Garmaker did not disappoint his admirers. His final performance was truly champion. He hit 15 field goals and four free throws to take game honors while establishing a new four-game scoring record of 128 points. When Hibbing was down seven points with three minutes to go, it was Garmaker who led the Minnesotan's charge to the finish. Unfortunately, the stretch drive fell short.

Wharton County's patience, quick ball handling, and teamwork proved the deciding factor. For the third time in five years a team from the Lone Star State laid claim to the NJCAA basketball title.

THE AFTERMATH — DOUBLE THE MONEY

The Sports Arena's effect on gate receipts was astounding. Gross proceeds for the 1952 National Juco Tournament neared $25,000 — double the previous year's record. Following a similar success at the Class B and BB state tournaments, the local citizenry wondered whether they had built the Arena large enough.

The new construction was not without its problems. The uncooperative weather had highlighted the most serious of these — parking. The Arena's parking area was nothing more than a dirt field. Inclement conditions turned it into a quagmire. Long term plans called for paving the surface around the Arena. In the meantime, if the weather was wet, fans parked several blocks from the facility, then walked or caught special buses to the tournament. A long walk in freezing rain hammered home the inconvenience.

Minor annoyances aside, the NJCAA was very happy with the Sports Arena. The Association's revitalization would not be hurt by eye-popping descriptions passed word-of-mouth to the hinterlands by tourney participants.

However, during tournament week, the NJCAA took a more active step toward guaranteeing the organization's resurgence by adopting most of the recommendations of the American Association of Junior Colleges, a national administrative organization which sought to establish equitable rules of conduct in athletics. By following the AAJC's lead, the NJCAA hoped to gain eventual recognition as the national voice for junior college athletics. At the same time, the Association wanted to pave the way for reentry of the California schools. With cooperation between the NJCAA and the AAJC firmly established, it was felt that California administrators would have no further reason to boycott NJCAA activities. There was strong optimism that Golden State schools would be playing in the 1953 tournament.

1952 champs — the "skinny Texans" from Wharton County from left to right: Elton Cox, Dan Gilder, Franklin Knebel, Floyd Sheen, Roy Green, Charles Brown, Jim Payne, Charles Christiansen, George Hatch, John Smyrl, Coach Johnnie Frankie. (Photo courtesy of Gene Bahnsen, Wharton County Junior College)

Tournament Results

Tuesday: Game

1	Hibbing — 95 Campbell — 66
2	Connors St. — 57 Wingate — 40
3	Branch — 81 Graceland — 60
4	Grays Harbor — 112 Abraham Baldwin — 90
5	Dodge City — 69 Central Arkansas — 57
6	Hannibal-LaGrange — 75 Garden City — 72 2OT

Wednesday: Game

7	Wharton County — 71 Moberly — 64
8	Joliet — 78 Campbellsville — 63
9	Wingate — 79 Campbell — 61
10	Hibbing — 67 Connors St. — 66
11	Branch — 76 Grays Harbor — 69

Thursday: Game

12	Graceland — 67 Abraham Baldwin — 61
13	Moberly — 67 Campbellsville — 65
14	Connors St. — 64 Grays Harbor — 51
15	Garden City — 88 Central Arkansas — 60
16	Wharton County — 74 Joliet — 62
17	Hannibal-LaGrange — 65 Dodge City — 63

Friday: Game

18	Wingate — 82 Graceland — 77 OT
19	Garden City — 75 Moberly — 64
20	Joliet — 84 Dodge City — 72
21	Hibbing — 70 Branch — 68
22	Wharton County — 70 Hannibal-LaGrange — 62

Saturday: Game

23	Garden City — 66 Wingate — 56
24	Joliet — 49 Connors St. — 45
25	Hannibal-LaGrange — 63 Branch — 61 OT
26	Wharton County — 78 Hibbing — 76

How They Finished in 1952

1. Wharton County Junior College
2. Hibbing Junior College
3. Hannibal-LaGrange College
4. Joliet Junior College
5. Garden City Junior College
6. Branch Agricultural College
7. Connors State Agricultural College
8. Wingate Junior College

All-Tournament Team

Charles Brown — Wharton County Junior College
Ron Fagan — Joliet Junior College
Darrell Floyd — Wingate Junior College
Dick Garmaker — Hibbing Junior College
Roy Green — Wharton County Junior College
Leo Hartmann — Hibbing Junior College
Clarence Lynch — Connors State Agricultural College
Don Marshall — Branch Agricultural College
Harold Patterson — Garden City Junior College
Ray Schumann — Hannibal-LaGrange College

SUNFLOWER SHOWDOWN

*The tournament's all-time leading scorer, Ray Schumann scored 276 points in two tournaments (34.5 average), including a record 159 points (39.8 average) in four games of the 1953 tournament, all against the tough competition of the championship bracket. (Photo courtesy of Donnie Crum, **Quincy Herald-Whig**)*

In the 1948 National Juco Basketball Tournament, the average game score totaled 108. In 1952, the average had climbed to 137 points per game. The steady increase reflected a national trend at all levels of the sport. Rules had been introduced to speed up the game, allowing more opportunities for putting points on the scoreboard. Coaches altered their philosophies to take advantage of the changes, stressing offense over defense. Most importantly, playing ability improved drastically. Players were now taller, quicker, and stronger. No longer were two hands needed to guide the ball toward the basket. To be successful, a player's arsenal required a one-hand push, a jumper, and a hook shot.

Player improvement was particularly noticeable in the junior college ranks. Though earlier tournament participants later enjoyed successful college careers and, in a few instances, entered the pro ranks, none made the transition from the two-year to the four-year level more dramatically than two 1952 Juco Tournament stars — Dick Garmaker and Darrell Floyd. Both became first-team collegiate All-Americans. Their impact on the sport at the national level helped change the attitude of college mentors toward junior college transfers.

College recruiters descended on the 1953 National Juco Basketball Tournament in record numbers. There was good reason. Participating teams were loaded with bigger and better talent than ever before. Those who witnessed the event were treated to the finest basketball to date. Scores were the highest yet; competition, the toughest. The level of play was so exceptional, standards were set which still stand.

The 1953 Juco Tournament offered top excitement — and more than a few surprises.

THE PARTICIPANTS

Optimism regarding the return of California to the NJCAA fold was so high during the Association's 1952 annual restructuring, the Golden State was accorded a region all its own. It came as a disappointing surprise, therefore, when California administrators continued to boycott the national tournament. The resulting Region 1 vacancy in the 1953 tournament bracket was only the beginning.

After a one-year hiatus as the top team in the Northwest, the Olympic College Rangers regained their previous form, winning the Region 3 tournament. However, while Coach Phil Pesco returned to Hutchinson to represent the region at the NJCAA's annual meeting, his team did not. Newly instituted rules by Washington Junior College Conference administrators forbade league schools from competing after March 15th.

The snub by the two regions accentuated the battle which had been heating up between college administrators and athletic departments across the country. Many educators felt sports should be de-emphasized. To this end, organizations like the American Council of Education and the American Association of Junior Colleges sought to curtail post-season competition. Besides keeping the student out of the classroom, collegiate athletics was becoming too expensive.

The validity of the latter argument was hard to deny. Even schools with national repute often found it difficult to field a team in the tournament. The case of Wingate Junior College was a good example. A tournament participant for the past three years, the school failed to raise the necessary travel

Region	Team
1	*El Dorado Junior College — El Dorado, Kansas
2	Hannibal-LaGrange College — Hannibal, Missouri
3	*Jacksonville Junior College — Jacksonville, Florida
4	Eastern Arizona Junior College — Thatcher, Arizona
5	Howard County Junior College — Big Spring, Texas
6	Arkansas City Junior College — Arkansas City, Kansas
7	East Central Junior College — Decatur, Mississippi
8	Brewton-Parker Junior College — Mount Vernon, Georgia
9	LaJunta Junior College — LaJunta, Colorado
10	*Eastern Oklahoma Agricultural and Mechanical College — Wilburton, Oklahoma
11	Fairbury Junior College — Fairbury, Nebraska
12	Concordia College — Fort Wayne, Indiana
13	North Dakota State School of Science — Wahpeton, North Dakota
14	Lon Morris College — Jacksonville, Texas
15	New York State Institute of Applied Arts and Sciences — Brooklyn, New York
16	Moberly Junior College — Moberly, Missouri

* Invited to fill bracket

expenses for another try at the title.

For the second year in a row, three invitations were required to complete the tournament bracket. Though the vacancies represented important problems still facing the organization, the NJCAA had no trouble interesting schools to participate in the season-ending event. In fact, the opposite was true. The desire of teams to come to Hutchinson was so great it made the Association's orderly system for filling bracket slots resemble a carnival wheel-of-fortune game.

The first open position was filled without difficulty. The California no-show was replaced by Region 6 runner-up, El Dorado Junior College.

Filling the other two slots was not as straightforward. The Washington-Oregon slot was supposed to go to the runner-up of the Region 8 tournament. Because of a confusing set of circumstances regarding player eligibility, this vacancy was first offered to the third-place team. After region officials ironed out the controversy, runner-up Jacksonville Junior College was allowed to make the trip to Hutchinson it had rightfully earned.[1]

The final bracket opening was offered to Broome County Technical Institute of Binghamton, New York — a previous tournament participant in 1951 as Binghamton State Tech. Broome County was actually the *winner* of the Region 15 tournament, having defeated Brooklyn State Tech in the final. Brooklyn protested the game, however, because an ineligible player had been used.[2] Region officials bumped Broome County from the tournament's summit.

When Wingate announced it was not able to come to the tournament, the next choice for filling the bracket fell to the Region 15 runner-up — the demoted region champ, Broome County. Unfortunately, the offer came too late for the school to raise the necessary funds for the trip. The remaining slot was finally awarded to Eastern Oklahoma A&M College of Wilburton.

With all the hoopla surrounding the invitation process, none of the three invitees figured to be contenders. El Dorado (20-7), Jacksonville (15-5), and Eastern Oklahoma (18-13) were runners-up to more impressive teams. Still, the 1953 tournament field appeared wide open — the best yet. Coaches polled at the Monday night Chamber of Commerce steak dinner — thrown annually to welcome participating teams to Hutchinson — all agreed: No one team could be tagged a favorite. Six ballclubs

were considered formidable, however, and would be the pace-setters for the competition.

The first team mentioned as a yardstick for comparison was East Central Junior College of Decatur, Mississippi. The Warriors won the Mississippi Juco Conference with a 19-3 record. They possessed a high-powered, run-and-gun offense which averaged 81.4 points per game. In three Region 7 contests, Decatur zapped its opponents by an average margin of 36, including an 87-65 shellacking of tourney favorite, Northeast Mississippi Junior College in the final.[3]

East Central's potent offense was not tops among tourney contenders. That honor belonged to Hannibal-LaGrange College. The Trojans racked up some very large scores on their way to compiling a 25-7 record, reaching the 100-point plateau five times, including a high of 122. In a best-of-three regional play-off, they pummeled Centralia (Illinois) Junior College, 94-55 and 115-82. Since Hannibal's starting line-up was the tallest in the tournament, it was easy to understand why the team owned an 87.6 scoring average.

Hannibal's offensive strength did not come from its height, however. Sixty percent of Trojan scoring originated from the team's shortest starters — 6-1 Ray Schumann (28.5 points per game) and 5-6 Cotton Fitzsimmons (25.3). The two were the core of a veteran squad which placed third in the nation the year before. Hannibal's prior tournament experience gave the Trojans the edge over other contenders as far as local fans were concerned.

Rivaling Hannibal in height was Lon Morris College of Jacksonville, Texas (33-6). The Bearcats featured one of the best centers in junior college ranks — 6-7 freshman, Bob Burrow. With Burrow dominating the middle, the Bearcats won everything in sight: the Texas Junior College Athletic Conference tournament; the TJCAC league; and the Ranger Invitational tournament. They iced a spot in the nationals with a 17-point victory over Tyler Junior College at Tyler in the Region 14 final. Emerging from a region which had produced three national champions in five years gave Lon Morris tremendous credibility as a top power.

While Lon Morris was king of eastern Texas, Howard County Junior College was the best in the west. Winner of the West Texas Junior College Conference, Howard County owned the tournament's premier record — 31-4. Three of the Jayhawks' victories came in a tough Region 5 tournament, which they barely survived, winning the title in a one-point thriller against invited national tourney entry, Eastern Oklahoma.

Kansas pride appeared well represented by Region 6 champs, Arkansas City Junior College. The Tigers compiled an excellent 25-4 record while vying for honors against rugged Western Kansas Juco Conference competition, considered by many to be the best in a decade. To prove the point, league play ended in a three-way tie for the title. Arkansas City shared the crown with tourney participant El Dorado and always tough Dodge City College.

The sixth pre-tourney favorite, as labeled by the *Hutchinson News-Herald*, was Brooklyn State Tech. The only visible evidence supporting the claim was the team's respectable 21-6 record and the fact the Techsans represented the largest school (2,400 students) in the tournament. Otherwise, the choice of Brooklyn as a favorite appeared only a reflection of the enigmatic aura surrounding Eastern basketball.[4]

If the favorites faltered, other teams were waiting in the wings. Though they had unimpressive records, Brewton-Parker

---

[1] After the opening round of play in the Region 8 tournament, a complaint was lodged against Jacksonville for using two ineligible transfer students. Jacksonville dropped the two players, replayed and won its first-round contest, then proceeded to place second in the tournament.

The invitation to the national did not go to Jacksonville, though. Pensacola Junior College, host of the regional and third-place finisher, claimed the runner-up ranking on the basis of Jacksonville's earlier misconduct. Region officials agreed. Jacksonville was required to forfeit its second-place trophy, even though it had subsequently taken the runner-up spot without the ineligible players. The opportunity to compete for the national crown was extended to Pensacola.

To further confuse the matter, it was determined that the Jacksonville players in question *were* eligible. Jacksonville petitioned the region for return of its second-place prize and the right to play in Hutchinson. Though already certified, Pensacola yielded.

[2] With Brooklyn State leading 51-48 with nine minutes to go, Binghamton substituted Ford Baker who promptly tallied nine crucial points, boosting Broome County to victory. Brooklyn protested the game because Baker had signed a professional baseball contract two years earlier, a violation of NJCAA eligibility rules.

[3] After a year of suspension, Coach Bonner Arnold's Tigers from Booneville were back on the scene with another championship caliber team. Though Northeast Mississippi's dream of returning to Hutchinson was sabotaged by East Central, the obdurate Arnold did not give up without a fight. He challenged Decatur's championship, citing East Central for using an ineligible player — the same reason the boys from Booneville had spent a year in the NJCAA's dog house. The focus of Arnold's objection was Decatur's star center, 22-year-old Denver Brackeen who enrolled late after returning from a tour of duty in Korea. Under normal circumstances, the objection would have been valid. But since the country was in the midst of war, newly instituted NJCAA eligibility rules gave special consideration to servicemen. Arnold's protest was disallowed.

Junior College (12-10) and Eastern Arizona Junior College of Thatcher (15-13) were respected because of the regions they represented. Moberly Junior College (22-7) was a potential threat solely on the basis the school was making its third straight tournament appearance. The three invitees were also in the second wave of contenders.

Only the teams from Fairbury (15-4), Wahpeton (15-4), LaJunta (13-4), and Ft. Wayne (7-13) were clearly dark horses. With its losing record, Concordia College — one of the oldest institutions in the country[5] — immediately acquired the role of "Cinderella". Even here records were deceiving. None of Concordia's players measured less than six-feet. Since there were few junior colleges near Ft. Wayne, the school was forced to compete with many four-year colleges, hence its poor record.

Picking a winner was a pot shot at best. Anything could happen.

TUESDAY — BIG BANG BEGINNING

The 1953 Juco Tournament did not waste time living up to expectations. A crowd of 800 — supplemented by a large contingent of area high school basketball teams — were treated to an exhilarating tip-off contest.

The highly favored Lon Morris Bearcats jumped out to a quick 15-6 lead over El Dorado and maintained steady control during the first half.

Then, momentum shifted. After trailing by 10 at intermission, the underdog Grizzlies pressured Lon Morris all over the court. By the end of the third quarter, El Dorado had reduced the deficit to four points.

The Grizzlies continued their assault on the Texans' lead, tying the count at 48, then at 50. With a little more than half the final period remaining, Dick Smith sank a free throw, giving El Dorado its first lead of the game. Len Wilson followed with a tip-in. Dick Rippee added a free throw. After the Kansans again gained control of the basketball, the partisan crowd tensed with the possibility of a major upset.

El Dorado's margin was a slim 54-50. Two Grizzly starters were on the bench with five fouls. The clock showed 3:26 to go. Coach Dave Weatherby had only one option open to him — hold the ball for the rest of the game.

The ploy was successful for the next minute or so. Then, Boyd Sylestine broke the stall and drove for the hoop. Lon Morris was within one basket.

El Dorado continued to freeze the ball. Again it melted. This time, however, Lon Morris missed the resulting opportunity to tie the game. It was the Bearcats' last chance. El Dorado kept the ball and the advantage.

The tournament was off to a stirring start.

Playing a brand of basketball reminiscent of that utilized by their rivals at Booneville, the Warriors from Decatur, Mississippi, brought tourney action back to its predicted pattern in the afternoon feature. Behind Denver Brackeen's 36 points and Howard Sessums' 20, East Central raced passed the overmatched crew from Wahpeton, 99-78.

The night before, three LaJunta players were thrown into the street when the sideboard of the pickup they were riding broke rounding a corner. Fortunately, the only injury was a slight cut over one of the boys' eyes. LaJunta could have used some of that good fortune in the afternoon finale. After trailing throughout the game, the Rattlers staged a gallant fourth-period rally only to see Brewton-Parker hold on for a 65-63 win.

Another pre-tourney favorite lived up to its advanced notices in the evening opener. Hannibal-LaGrange dispatched Cinderella Concordia with relative ease thanks to the remarkable scoring skill of its two stars. All but 18 of the Trojans 87 points came from Cotton Fitzsimmons (35) and Ray Schumann (34).

The invitation to play in the nationals came as a pleasant surprise for the Mountaineers from Eastern Oklahoma A&M; particularly since the Wilburton team had lost a heart-breaking Region 5 final by a single point. As fate would have it, though, the region they replaced was paired with the team which had orchestrated that disappointing defeat — pre-tourney favorite, Howard County. The 3,000 fans who turned out for the feature contest anticipated the rematch would be another hard-fought affair. They were not disappointed. For the second year in a row, they were treated to an opening-night marathon thriller.

Eastern Oklahoma's vengeful zeal was apparent from the outset. The Mountaineers grabbed the lead and held it tenaciously. Though the game was close throughout, everything Howard County tried failed to dislodge the Oklahomans from the advantage. Leading 68-64 with 30 seconds left, it appeared Eastern Oklahoma had avenged the Texans.

Bang-bang action changed the picture in a hurry. First, long-shooting guard Chuck Warren gave Howard a chance with a high archer. On the in-bounds pass, the Jayhawks stole the ball. Casey Jones scored immediately. Eastern Oklahoma held the ball for one final shot, but missed. The score was deadlocked 68-all.

In the overtime, Howard County again found itself a step short of the aggressive Mountaineers from Wilburton. But, the Jayhawks continued to battle back. By the end of the first extra period, the contest was still a draw.

For 45 minutes, the Oklahomans had been in the driver's seat; Howard County had barely hung on. Shortly after the start of the second overtime, the teams switched roles. Jones hit a pair of free throws, putting the Jayhawks into the lead for the first time.

The advantage was short-lived. Guard Ken Ferguson flashed down the sideline and popped one from the corner for Eastern Oklahoma, putting the two teams back in a basket-trading mode.

With a minute to go, the game was still undecided, neither team giving up.

Since both ball clubs were haggard from the long ordeal, Howard County sought to end it with one last shot. The Oklahomans foiled the plan, stole the ball and imposed a stall of their own. Eastern Oklahoma's tie-breaking attempt came with 12 seconds on the clock. It missed.

Howard County grabbed the rebound, hurried the ball down the court, and lofted a long one. The shot caromed off the glass right into the waiting hands of a perfectly positioned Casey Jones. In heroic fashion befitting his name, Jones saved the day, tipping the ball back up and in just as the final buzzer sounded. Howard County broke the hearts of the Oklahomans for a second time, 80-78.

Besides draining the emotions of the crowd, the tremendous Howard County-Eastern Oklahoma battle put the tournament 45 minutes behind schedule. Most patrons had to go to work early the next morning. Few wanted to stay up past midnight to watch a contest destined to be dull after the one just completed. Consequently, only a sparse handful watched Eastern Arizona squeak by a determined Fairbury quintet, 63-57, in the nip-and-tuck finale.

---

[4]The awe Midwesterners held for the Eastern teams in the early years of the tournament was a carry-over from the superiority of Eastern basketball at the collegiate level. In reality, junior college basketball in the East was weak in comparison to the rest of the country. Prior tournaments bore this out. Despite bringing excellent records to the national meet, Eastern schools collectively owned an unimposing 1-9 mark. In fact, their only win was against another Eastern team.

The reason for this competitive gap was that junior colleges were just emerging as a part of the educational scene in the East. The glut of older four-year institutions along the Eastern Seaboard had made junior colleges unnecessary items. This changed after World War II and Korea. Veterans flooded the educational market, G.I. Bill benefits in hand.

Brooklyn State Tech offered the perfect example of what playing junior college basketball in the East meant. The junior college was basically a trade school. The team consisted primarily of ex-servicemen who played the game simply for "the fun of it." Sports were not only considered secondary but incidental. The school had no gym, home games being played at a "cross town" YMCA. Since the distance involved made daily practice impractical, the team "practiced" in regular competition. Home games were free to students, but, if 100 people showed up for a game, it was deemed "a crowd." The Brooklyn State student body backed the team's effort to get to the national tournament by raffling off a television. The $1,000 raised provided the team with transportation to Hutchinson — a three-day, two-night bus ride.

[5]Concordia College, a Lutheran school, was established in 1839. Three other institutions represented in the 1953 tournament shared Concordia's antiquity and religious affiliation: Hannibal-LaGrange (established in 1858) and Brewton-Parker (1904) were Baptist; Lon Morris (1873) was Methodist.

WEDNESDAY — THE FIREWORKS CONTINUE

Brooklyn State's Benny Bessen was not a member of the Techsan squad until February. Coach Gerry Anderson had never seen him in action but had heard he was an excellent high school player. His first glimpse of the young man came the day Bessen joined the team — during warm-ups prior to a game. Anderson told him, "Get in there and win." Bessen did just that.

In the Wednesday first-round opener, Bessen was again the team's spark plug. Twice the 5-11 barrel-shaped guard rallied Brooklyn against the Dolphins from Jacksonville. The first rally came in the third quarter when Bessen canned eight points to erase all but one of Jacksonville's seven-point halftime margin.

Jacksonville returned the favor with nine unanswered points at the beginning of the final period. Bessen went back to work. On three successive trips down the floor, he drove the lane twice for lay-ups, then launched a successful bomb. The spurt ignited the Techsans. Bessen went on to score 14 of his game-high 26 in the fourth frame, leading Brooklyn from behind to a 67-63 win.

The first 20 minutes of the final first-round contest transpired as expected. The fleet Tigers from Arkansas City zipped around the Moberly Greyhounds, forging a comfortable 39-26 halftime lead.

However, Moberly was not intimidated by Arkansas City's quickness nor the lack of support from the highly partisan Kansas crowd. After intermission, the Greyhounds' Dave Slaughter coolly cracked the cords with four long, beautiful left-handed push shots. The 5-9 guard's offensive display perked up the Missouri crew, giving the third quarter to Moberly. The Greyhounds outscored Arkansas City, 28-14, to go ahead by a point.

Arkansas City was kept from sinking into oblivion by the "never-say-die" spirit of reserve guard Seymour Seitchick who scored five of his total nine points at crucial moments in the fourth period. With a minute-and-a-half to go, Arkansas City was still in the game, tied 64-all.

Slaughter donned the hero's wreath again for Moberly, swishing a long arching shot. The Missourians immediately regained the ball on an Arkansas City miscue and chose to sit on it. Nervous Kansas fans watched the clock tick down. When Slaughter was fouled with 15 seconds remaining, the dismal end was in sight.

Slaughter stepped to the line and promptly went from hero to goat, missing both free throws. On the final miss, Arkansas City grabbed the rebound and whipped the ball the length of the court. A sprinting Lafayette Norwood caught the ball and dropped in an easy lay-up, sending the game into overtime.

Points were grudgingly exchanged during the extra period and, at the 1:41 mark, the game was still even 70-all. It appeared the first round would have a second double overtime game.

Such was not the case, however. The game breaker came shortly after the Kansans gained possession following another pair of missed Moberly free throws. The Tigers worked the ball into center Ray Potter, who fired the winning bucket with 23 seconds to play. Moberly had an opportunity to tie but missed, allowing Arkansas City to dribble out the clock for a 74-72 victory.

Despite two close scrapes, the first round ended as predicted — with one exception. El Dorado's shocking upset over Lon Morris gave the hometown crowd plenty to look forward to. Not since 1949 had two Kansas teams won in the opening round. Back then, the two had been required to face each other in the next outing. If El Dorado and Arkansas City met this year, it would be for the championship. It was a promoter's dream.

But dreams are not reality. El Dorado had been fortunate to survive against Lon Morris. The Texans had handcuffed themselves with poor foul shooting, hitting only 10 of 22 from the line. El Dorado could not expect the same generosity from its next opponent. Against the power-laden squad from Decatur, the Grizzlies were earmarked for extinction.

The 3,500 fans who filed into the Sports Arena for Wednesday evening's quarterfinal match-ups anticipated a Mississippi style up-and-down-the-court contest in the feature. To their surprise, East Central's speed-oriented machinery never clicked into gear. The patient, aggressive Grizzlies slowed the tempo and took command. For three quarters El Dorado held the Warriors at bay, maintaining a slim margin. Leading 53-49 with one period to go, the Kansans still had a chance to win.

Denver Brackeen and Howard Sessums brought the high hopes of the crowd back down to earth, rallying the Warriors to a 55-all tie. Three East Central free throws followed. When the Decatur crew adopted a keep-away game to run out the clock, fans accepted the inevitable.

The Grizzlies were not through, though. El Dorado broke the stall with Dick Smith cashing in a charity and Len Wilson adding a field goal to knot the game at 58-all.

No one scored in the next three minutes. Each team wasted a minute-and-a-half, playing for a sure shot only to come up empty. It was nail-biting time for the crowd.

The final 60 seconds passed quickly. First, Johnny Gragg hit a bucket for El Dorado. Seconds later, his teammate Smith deposited two free shots. East Central tried to regroup behind a two-pointer by Bill Livengood, but the game was over. With four seconds on the clock, Gragg sealed the win for the Kansans with two charities.

The Grizzlies' second upset over a highly regarded opponent amazed everyone. No one on El Dorado could match the talent of either Brackeen or Sessums for East Central. Yet, the Kansas squad had put together a solid team effort and effectively dismantled the Warriors' well-oiled offensive machine.

Center Mike Girrens led the Grizzlies in scoring, netting 22. Both Gragg and Smith rescued El Dorado in the final minutes of play with clutch free throwing. The real hero for the Grizzlies, however, was Wilson, a 6-2 silky-smooth athlete with quick reflexes. His defensive skills were so acute, Coach Weatherby always assigned him the task of guarding the top scorer on the opposing team. Therefore, it had been Wilson's job to stop East Central's Brackeen, a 30-point-per-game dynamo. Brackeen scored 17.

In the day's finale, Hannibal-LaGrange exploded for 37 points in the fourth period to break open a close contest with Brewton-Parker. Key to the Trojan victory was Ray Schumann's record setting 47-point performance. The 6-1 forward netted nearly half his team's 101, but it was not a new experience for him. Earlier that year he had amassed an unbelievable 62 points against Springfield (Illinois) Junior College. El Dorado's Wilson was going to have his hands full on his next assignment.

THURSDAY — ANYONE HAVE A LIGHT?

Thursday was a day of extremes. The first two games were white-knucklers: Concordia outlasted LaJunta, 71-66, in overtime; then Moberly pulled out a tight, 63-56 win over Jacksonville in the last six minutes. The next two contests were nowhere near as close.

In the final afternoon game, East Central drubbed Brewton-Parker 114-79, setting a new tournament high for team scoring in a game. Decatur's Denver Brackeen played unselfishly, feeding others when he could have scored himself, but still managed 53 points to top the tournament's individual mark.

In the evening opener, Mountaineer Jerrel Logan also tallied big, sinking 37 — over half his team's 72 — as Eastern Oklahoma doubled the score on an outclassed Fairbury squad. The back-to-back blowouts were two of the widest margins of victory in tournament history, allowing tourney goers an extra long supper break.

When local fans returned to the Arena, they had a difficult choice to make. The partisan Kansans naturally wanted to see their region do well against topflight competition. On the other hand, they were smitten by the colorful New York crew whose players described the object of the game as putting "pents" on the scoreboard. Besides, Arkansas City — a mere 100-mile jaunt down the road — had brought a large gallery of fans. The men from Brooklyn — 1,500 miles from Hutchinson — had only themselves as supporters.

The most the crowd could ask for was what it received — a close, well-played game. The largest lead enjoyed by either team through the first three quarters was five points. When Arkansas City built an eight-point advantage early in the fourth period, Brooklyn matched it with a spurt of its own. With two minutes remaining and the score knotted 65-all, the stage was set for an exciting race to the wire. Two factors prevented it from happening.

First, Arkansas City possessed the quickest guard tandem in the tournament. Five-six Lafayette Norwood and 5-10 Linwood

Burns were water bugs on the court. Consequently, the Tigers were a running team.

Second, Brooklyn's conditioning was suspect. Earlier in the week at the Chamber of Commerce dinner, Hutchonians had been shocked to see the Brooklyn players light up "smokes".[6] It was reported that the Techsans even smoked during halftime intermission in the dressing room.

When Brooklyn employed a full court press against the swift Arkansas City team in the final two minutes, it spelled immediate doom. As Brooklyn Coach Jerry Anderson stated later, "They ran us to death."

Norwood and Burns set up camp at the foul line as three winded Techsans fouled out trying to catch the two speedsters. Both men went to the line 11 times during the course of the game. Norwood hit nine of his opportunities, Burns all 11. Their exceptional free throw accuracy proved the winning difference.

With two Kansas teams already in the semifinals, there was little to hold the crowd's interest in the last quarterfinal. When the game turned ragged in the first half, the fans quickly faded from the Arena. By halftime, with Howard County in command 43-29 over Eastern Arizona, only 250 diehards remained. Those who stayed were rewarded with a determined Eastern Arizona rally in the fourth quarter. The drive was insufficient, though, to overcome the Howard County bulge. The Texans took the tournament's best record into the semifinals with an 80-74 victory.

FRIDAY — UP AGAINST THE ODDS

Considering the numbers alone, odds were 50-50 Kansas would be represented in the championship tilt. When comparing team strengths and tournament performances, however, the odds were much lower. If El Dorado pulled off a third upset against a top tourney contender, it would be a feat rivaling Hutchinson Junior College's 1949 miracle. And unless Arkansas City developed playing consistency, its chances were slim against the proven Howard County Jayhawks.

In Friday night's first semifinal match, Arena patrons were kept guessing: Would El Dorado accomplish the improbable?

Hannibal-LaGrange established control early, gaining the first quarter advantage, 21-17. El Dorado bounced back with an excellent second period to take a 36-35 margin to the locker room. In the third frame it was Hannibal again charging to the front. With 10 minutes remaining and a 59-53 lead, the Trojans were ready to smash El Dorado's impossible dream.

But, Hannibal had problems. First, the Trojans lost their top rebounder when 6-6 center Charles Hutchens fouled out with nearly four minutes left in the third period. Second, Cotton Fitzsimmons — the ignition switch for the Missouri crew's offense — was not penetrating the defense as frequently, his mobility significantly reduced by a blood blister on his foot. There was a chink in Hannibal's armor; El Dorado wedged a knife in the opening.

Clutch one-and-one free throw tosses by Len Wilson, Dick Rippee, and Dick Smith plus the unexpected outside shooting of reserve Bill McAdoo slowly dissolved Hannibal's margin then vaulted the Grizzlies to the lead. Despite the last moment heroics by Hannibal's Ray Schumann — who continued his phenomenal scoring pace with a game-high 37 — El Dorado prevailed, 75-69.

The reason for El Dorado's victory rested at the foul line. The Kansans displayed tremendous composure shooting charities under pressure, hitting 75 percent from the line. Leading the Grizzlies in that department were starters Smith (7 for 9), Mike Girrens (10 for 13), and Johnny Gragg (6 for 9). For the third time, underdog El Dorado proved a well-balanced unit could compete against superior talent.

Not since Hutchinson's appearance in 1949 had crowd sentiment been so intimately involved with action on the court. The vocal support Arkansas City received in the remaining semifinal was overwhelming. It seemed to visibly set fire to the Tigers' offense. After fighting to a near standoff in the first period,

Arkansas City charged past Howard County and never looked back. The Tigers scored 53 points in the first half and 50 in the second. Coach Dan Kahler substituted an entire new crew midway through the final period and still the onslaught continued. When the dust finally settled, all 10 Arkansas City players had scored. The Kansans embarrassed the Texans, 103-76.

Regardless of Saturday's play, the championship of junior college basketball belonged to the Sunflower State.

SATURDAY — SALVOS BEFORE THE SHOOT-OUT

The dream game on tap for later that night completely overshadowed the rest of Saturday's action. Still, the three consolation trophy games preceding it had plenty to offer basketball fans.

For example, the day's opener could be considered a preview of the championship. Lon Morris and Moberly had lost their first-round match-ups to the national finalists. The fact both had succumbed by a mere basket attested to the tight competition in the tournament. If the battle for fifth place was a true indication of things to come, fans were in for an unpredictable finale.

The teams traded leads, Moberly winning the first quarter, 18-16, Lon Morris taking a 39-31 advantage at intermission, and Moberly rebounding in the third frame. With one period remaining, nothing was resolved, the score knotted 50-all.

The lead switched hands five teams in the last quarter before Lon Morris leapfrogged ahead for good with 1½ minutes to go. The one-point victory margin was testimony to the equality of the two teams.

Headliner for the contest was Bearcat center, Robert Burrow. The freshman topped all scorers with 29, bringing his four-game total to 103. His performance moved him temporarily into first place in the tourney scoring derby and set the tone for the day's consolation play.

East Central center Denver Brackeen was three inches shorter than Burrow but no less effective in the middle. He possessed speed and quickness (traits commonly associated with Mississippi players) plus extraordinary jumping ability. His favorite weapon was the jump shot. He had been an all-stater in high school at Hickory, Mississippi, and a two-time all-star in the Mississippi Junior College Conference. His 1953 Juco Tournament achievements earned him further honors.

The Juco Tournament's first MVP award-winner was East Central's Denver Brackeen, the 1953 tourney's second-leading scorer (134 points), including a then record 53 points in a consolation game against Brewton-Parker. Brackeen was later an All-American at the University of Mississippi. (Photo courtesy of Denver Brackeen)

---

[6]The most prominent Techsan in this regard was Benny Bessen. The wise-cracking guard favored cigars. It was only one of the colorful traits which endeared him to local fans. Just before the New York team's train left for home, a group of Hutchonians gave Bessen a cowboy hat, dubbing him "the cowboy from Brooklyn." The presentation was made in appropriate surroundings for the "hell-for-leather" group of New Yorkers — at a bar near the railroad station.

In the contest for fourth place, East Central stormed past Eastern Arizona, 79-58, Brackeen leading the way. His game-high 48 boosted his tournament total to 134. The sum not only exceeded Burrow's point accumulation but also surpassed Dick Garmaker's individual mark set the year before. His superb play and unselfish attitude garnered him a spot on the All-Tournament Team and the tourney's first MVP award.[7]

When Cotton Fitzsimmons joined his teammates on the bench before Hannibal's third-place match with Howard County, he was stunned by the ovation he received. The crowd numbered nearly 7,000 — a fifth of Hutchinson's population. The tribute not only conveyed fan appreciation for the small blond guard's prior tourney exploits but was also an expression of sympathy. Fitzsimmons was in street clothes and on crutches.

During Hannibal's first-round game against Concordia, a blister had developed on Fitzsimmons' right little toe. After a small hole was cut in the side of his shoe to relieve the pressure, Fitzsimmons went on to lead all scorers with 35 points.

In Hannibal's second game, the blister grew. A larger hole was cut in the shoe. Fitzsimmons scored 25.

Against El Dorado, not only was the hold cut even larger, but Fitzsimmons received a shot of novocaine. The foot was stepped on in the first quarter and the resulting pain indicated the novocaine had not worked. In the time-out between quarters, Fitzsimmons went to the dressing room for another shot. His point production dropped to 19.

After the game, the team doctor noticed red streaks running up the young guard's leg. He was hustled to the hospital and treated for blood poisoning.

The preliminary to the championship was expected to be no contest; Hannibal-LaGrange was not the same team without Fitzsimmons engineering the offense. The prognostication held true. Twenty-one points separated the winner from the loser. But who won surprised everybody — the Trojans, 90-69.

All nine Hannibal players scored at least three points. Reserves who had seen little action in the past performed like starters. The Trojan effort was truly inspiring.

Hannibal would not have won, however, had it not been for the guiding hand of Ray Schumann. Despite persistent double-teaming by the Texans, Schumann managed 41 points — one less than Howard's top two scorers combined. It was the sophomore forward's fourth-straight superhuman performance. His remarkable tournament total of 159 shattered Denver Brackeen's newly established record and set a high-water mark which still stands.[8]

The tension associated with championship play was notably missing prior to the Saturday finale. For a majority of the Arena crowd, the Arkansas City-El Dorado match was a no-lose situation; local fans already felt a sense of victory just by having two Kansas teams in the finals.

Another factor contributing to the lack of pre-game anxiety was the fact few doubted the game's outcome. Everyone considered El Dorado's chances poor at best. The Arkansas City Tigers had beaten the Grizzlies three-out-of-four during the year, owned a 19-game win streak, and had proved their readiness for the crown with a devastating win over a tough Howard County club in the semifinals. The Grizzlies, on the other hand, could only point to three consecutive close surprises. The argument failed to sway crowd opinion. Most observers were willing to concede El Dorado was better than anticipated, but few would bet on the chances of another miracle.

Fan support appeared to bear out the forecast; the 2,000-some Arkansas Citians rooting for the Tigers outnumbered the El Dorado contingent, 4-1. Arkansas City fans were so convinced of the contest's inevitable outcome they announced plans for a victory celebration later that evening. The announcement was made at halftime over the Arena's PA system and came on the heels of a rugged first half in which Arkansas City struggled from behind to gain a one-point advantage.

The battle remained a toss-up through much of the third period. Then, frustrated by the limitations imposed by El Dorado's tough man-to-man defense, the Tigers' don't-let-the-grass-grow-under-your-feet offense stumbled. Bad passes resulted. By the end of the third quarter, El Dorado possessed a six-point margin.

The Grizzlies continued the pressure, losing two All-Tournament selections — Len Wilson and Dick Smith — to fouls in the process. Still, Arkansas City miscues mounted. While El Dorado poured in points, the Tigers could hit nothing. When the final tally was posted, Arkansas City was on the short end by 18 — the widest margin to date in championship play.

Four games. Four upsets. The 1953 Juco crown belonged to Cinderella — El Dorado Junior College, the only invited team ever to win the tournament.

THE AFTERMATH — WHAT HAPPENED?

The city of El Dorado exploded twice Saturday night: once at approximately 10:30 when news of the Grizzly victory was official; and again four hours later when the caravan of cars carrying team and fans was met at the city limits. Coach Dave Weatherby was transferred to an ambulance and the whole horn-honking procession was led by screeching siren to a downtown theater for a victory celebration. On Monday schools and businesses closed to honor the heroic Grizzlies with a parade. Unexpected or not, El Dorado was proud of its championship.

Back in Hutchinson, people were feeling as though they had been fleeced; unheralded El Dorado had copped the crown jewels right out from under everyone's nose. They were at a loss to explain how it happened.

According to Coach Weatherby, there was no mystery. "Let's face it. We were at home." In all four contests, El Dorado was the benefactor of crowd support because it was a Kansas school and/or because it was the perpetual underdog. More importantly, Weatherby sheltered his players from normal tournament to-do; the team drove home 75 miles to El Dorado every night. The reversion to regular routine reduced team tension.

Finally, Weatherby provided additional inducement by telling his players, "This is it." Not only was it the last year of junior college for most of the team, Weatherby had told school officials earlier in the year this season would be his last (he later reneged, staying in coaching one more year). The Grizzlies rallied around the thought and played beyond their potential. Mike Girrens best exemplified the team's response. The 6-3 center received little publicity prior to the tournament, yet led El Dorado scoring in its last three games, including a brilliant 28-point effort in the final. When key men like defensive demon Len Wilson or rugged rebounder Dick Smith fouled out, players came off the bench to play their best ever. The resulting championship was a tribute to team basketball.

***

---

[7]Though several sources list MVPs for every year of the tournament, the first such honor was not officially bestowed until the 1953 event. The "Player of the Year" trophy was awarded by the Hutchinson Junior Chamber of Commerce. The award was given to the best individual example of "sportsmanship, personal ability, and team support" in the tournament. The trophy was presented to Brackeen by Chamber president, John Alden, at the awards ceremony following the title game.

[8]Compared to other top players in the Juco Tournament, Ray Schumann was an unlikely candidate for setting a record which would remain untouched for more than 30 years. Though an outstanding high school athlete at Kampsville, Illinois, Schumann gained most of his basketball knowledge from play in independent amateur leagues. He received little formal training. Consequently, his playing style was unorthodox. He released his favorite left-hand jump shot from the side of his head, just off his ear. His ability to handle the ball was limited. He rarely dribbled more than twice and then only when moving to his left.

These deficiencies were offset by superior physical assets. Schumann was mature (he was 26) and always in peak condition (he could "run forever" and was noted for wearing out hitter after hitter, shagging fly balls). His brute strength made him an above-average rebounder despite a lack of height. He compensated for his poor ball-handling skills with exemplary speed. Asked whether Schumann's prior military experience had been served in Korea, former teammate Cotton Fitzsimmons responded, "No. But it wouldn't have mattered. They couldn't have shot him because he was too quick." Added to these physical attributes was Schumann's unbelievable shooting eye. Fitzsimmons swore that, when Schumann fired from his favorite spot in the corner, "he shot a curve ball" around the backboard.

The poker-faced forward's greatest asset, however, was his ability to rise to the occasion. He had a nose for the ball and could be counted on for a bucket whenever his team needed it most. It is to Schumann's credit that he established the tournament's premier scoring record against topflight competition in the championship bracket.

The 1953 El Dorado Grizzlies were the only invited team ever to win the NJCAA Basketball Tournament. Back row (left to right): Len Wilson, Bill McAdoo, and Jack Wickers. Second row: Coach Dave Weatherby, Dave Ellis, Mike Girrens, and Richard Smith (captain). Third row: Danny O'Brien, Bill Elliott, and Ray Reep. Front row: Pat Kinney, Johnny Gragg, and Dick Rippee. (Photo courtesy of Dave Weatherby)

The 1953 Juco Tournament was the best yet. With the aid of an all-Kansas finale, another attendance record was set. Play was marked by unrivaled individual and team performances which rewrote the record book. It appeared the only way to improve the event was to make it easier for teams to attend. To this end, the NJCAA Executive Committee decided to schedule the 1954 tournament two weeks earlier. The Association hoped the move would appease school administrators, particularly those on both coasts, and prevent further erosion of the organization's support.

The strategy proved fruitful immediately: the NJCAA gained recognition from the American Association of Junior Colleges. The two organizations showed a unified spirit by jointly issuing a "Statement of Principles Conducting Junior College Athletics."

Though the schedule change was positive politically, it proved negative in other ways. One year later, the NJCAA would have second thoughts.

How They Finished in 1953

1. El Dorado Junior College
2. Arkansas City Junior College
3. Hannibal-LaGrange College
4. East Central Junior College
5. Lon Morris College
6. Howard County Junior College
7. Eastern Arizona College
8. Moberly Junior College

All-Tournament Team

Denver Brackeen — East Central Junior College
Linwood Burns — Arkansas City Junior College
Robert Burrow — Lon Morris College
Lowell "Cotton" Fitzsimmons — Hannibal-LaGrange College
Lafayette Norwood — Arkansas City Junior College
Ray Schumann — Hannibal-LaGrange College
Howard Sessums — East Central Junior College
Dave Slaughter — Moberly Junior College
Richard Smith — El Dorado Junior College
Len Wilson — El Dorado Junior College

Player of the Year

Denver Brackeen — East Central Junior College

Tournament Results

	Game	
Tuesday:	1	El Dorado — 54 Lon Morris — 52
	2	East Central — 99 NDSSS-Wahpeton — 78
	3	Brewton-Parker — 65 LaJunta — 63
	4	Hannibal-LaGrange — 87 Concordia — 74
	5	Howard County — 80 Eastern Oklahoma A&M — 78 2OT
	6	Eastern Arizona — 63 Fairbury — 57
Wednesday:	7	Brooklyn St. — 67 Jacksonville — 63
	8	Arkansas City — 74 Moberly — 72 OT
	9	Lon Morris — 84 NDSSS-Wahpeton — 73
	10	El Dorado — 64 East Central — 60
	11	Hannibal-LaGrange — 101 Brewton-Parker — 75
Thursday:	12	Concordia — 71 LaJunta 66 OT
	13	Moberly — 63 Jacksonville — 56
	14	East Central — 114 Brewton-Parker — 79
	15	Eastern Oklahoma A&M — 72 Fairbury — 36
	16	Arkansas City — 76 Brooklyn St. — 68
	17	Howard County — 80 Eastern Arizona — 74
Friday:	18	Lon Morris — 93 Concordia — 73
	19	Moberly — 59 Eastern Oklahoma A&M — 48
	20	Eastern Arizona — 94 Brooklyn St. — 82
	21	El Dorado — 75 Hannibal-LaGrange — 69
	22	Arkansas City — 103 Howard County — 76
Saturday:	23	Lon Morris — 66 Moberly — 65
	24	East Central — 79 Eastern Arizona — 58
	25	Hannibal-LaGrange — 90 Howard County — 69
	26	El Dorado — 82 Arkansas City — 64

For the past five years Hutchinson had opened its arms to the Juco Tournament, giving visiting players, coaches, and fans the warmest of welcomes. The 1954 tournament was no different. Merchants went out of their way to make visitors feel at home. The Fox Theatre invited team members to a special morning movie. Anticipating the influx of students on "limited budgets," several eating establishments engaged in a "hamburger war," offering as many as a dozen of the grilled favorites for a dollar.

The traditional illustration of the city's hospitality was the Hutchinson Chamber of Commerce dinner held Monday evening prior to tourney action. Chamber members treated participating players and coaches like visiting royalty, feting them with a lavish steak dinner. The fourth annual affair received kudos not only for the sumptuous spread but also for the resplendent surroundings. In prior years, the kick-off dinner had been served in the less than luxurious 4-H Building at the Kansas State Fairgrounds. In 1954 it was held in the city's newest addition — the Baker Hotel.

Plans for a major hotel in Hutchinson were developed at about the same time as those for the Sports Arena. However, problems in financing delayed their implementation. Construction did not begin until late summer of 1952 after the Arena's debut. The Baker officially opened on February 13, 1954, just in time for the tournament.

At 156 feet (12 stories), the structure was the largest building in Hutchinson. It contained 175 rooms capable of sleeping 450. There were six private dining rooms, a ballroom, a banquet room, two kitchens, three elevators, and a coffee shop. No other lodging in the city could match the size or luxury of the Baker. Hutchinson finally had first-class accommodations to match its first-class playing facility.

The reaction to Hutchinson's hospitality was summed up best by NJCAA Secretary Hobart Bolerjack at the Chamber of Commerce dinner: "No city can surpass the fine accommodations, the courtesy and friendliness of Hutchinson to the NJCAA tournament and I hope we can continue the tournament here for many years." The comment received a rousing ovation.

John Woods, the No. 2 scorer in the 1954 tournament (111 points, including a tourney-high 38 versus Lon Morris), finished his basketball career at Hillsdale College in Michigan. (Photo courtesy of John Woods)

In 1954, the Baker Hotel replaced the old Bisonte Hotel as the principal lodging for tourney participants. Later it would also house the first offices of the NJCAA. (Photo courtesy of the NJCAA)

THE PARTICIPANTS

Region	Team
1	Eastern-Arizona Junior College — Thatcher, Arizona
2	Hannibal-LaGrange College — Hannibal, Missouri
3	*Centralia Junior College — Centralia, Illinois
4	Snow College — Ephraim, Utah
5	Connors State Agricultural College — Warner, Oklahoma
6	Arkansas City Junior College — Arkansas City, Kansas
7	Northeast Mississippi Junior College — Booneville, Mississippi
8	Brewton-Parker Junior College — Mount Vernon, Georgia
9	Fort Lewis Agricultural & Mechanical College — Hesperus, Colorado
10	Campbell College — Buies Creek, North Carolina
11	Fairbury Junior College — Fairbury, Nebraska
12	Junior College of Benton Harbor — Benton Harbor, Michigan
13	Bismarck Junior College — Bismarck, North Dakota
14	Lon Morris College — Jacksonville, Texas
15	Trenton Junior College — Trenton, New Jersey
16	Moberly Junior College — Moberly, Missouri

*Invited to fill bracket

Even though the Juco Tournament was just seven years old, coming to Hutchinson was already a tradition for many. The 1954 lineup included several familiar faces. Seven teams returned from the previous year. Only five schools were making their tourney debut — the lowest total to date.

Tradition played a major role in the *Hutchinson News-Herald's* selection of pre-tourney favorites. Since Region 14 had produced a national champion in three of the first six tournaments, it was safe to assume the current representative would be a top contender. Lon Morris College did more than survive in the battle for supremacy in Texas, however. In the regional tournament, the Bearcats demolished San Antonio College, 107-82, upended tourney favorite Wharton County Junior College, 89-61, then slipped by a strong Tyler Junior College team, 77-71. The Bearcats followed with three more victories to take home the Texas crown in the state plays-offs. In a two-week period, Lon Morris downed six of the Lone Star State's best by an average margin of 20 points. The Bearcats' 36-5 overall record against such tough competition was an achievement demanding respect.

The primary factor in the Texas school's success was the play of its star center, Bob Burrow. An All-Tournament selection from the previous year, Burrow continued to rack up honors during the 1953-54 campaign. The 19-year-old sophomore was voted the most valuable player in an early season tournament at Big Springs, Texas, and in the state play-offs. He was all-zone, all-conference, and all-region. His 1,072 total points and 30.6 per-game average topped all scorers in Texas.

Lon Morris encountered few serious challenges with Burrow's 6-7 frame dominating the middle. If the opposition was foolhardy enough to put up a fight, all Coach O.P. Adams had to do was bring in Ken Roach, another 6-7 giant. Facing twin towers was a nightmare that brought quick capitulation.

The other *News-Herald* pre-tourney pick was one of the teams which had experienced that bad dream. Only two blemishes spotted Northeast Mississippi Junior College's record: an 87-84 squeaker to East Mississippi Junior College of Scooba; and the 90-71 nightmare to Lon Morris. The two defeats were easily forgiven, however. Bonner Arnold's Tigers were a top-flight crew. Their 40 victories — more than any other tourney team — included four triumphs over Tyler, one of Lon Morris' nemeses.

Like Lon Morris, the Booneville squad was led by a star point-producer — Charles Floyd. The Mississippi center was a hook-shot artist supreme who boasted an average just under 30 points per game and had been the author of a 56-point masterpiece against Athens (Alabama) College. During the season, Floyd contributed 1,274 points to the Tigers, 3,587-point accu-

mulation; both were new junior college records.

Northeast Mississippi's 85-point average was imposing, b▮ not tops. That honor belonged to Hannibal-LaGrange Colleg▮ the leading contender in the second-wave of the local paper▮ pre-tourney favorites. Hannibal accomplished its high-scorin▮ exploits despite the loss of Ray Schumann and Cotton Fitzsim mons.[1] The new Trojans were a free-wheeling troop that did n▮ know how to slow down. The Missouri squad broke the 10▮ point barrier nine times during the year, helping account for i▮ 94.4-point average.

Hannibal's regional play epitomized the Trojans' ability t▮ score. Hannibal kicked into high gear immediately, flattenin▮ Junior College of Flat River, 120-80, in the semifinals. By hal▮ time in the finale, the Trojans had already sped to 75 point▮ They cracked 100 in the third period. When the dust settle▮ four Trojans had scored 25 points or better. The final read: Har nibal-LaGrange — 145, Campbellsville College 102. Both th▮ combined score and the amazing Hannibal total were new jun▮ or college highs.

The Trojans had one of the best records in the tournament – 27-4. It was one of those losses, however, which placed th▮ excellent Hannibal squad a step down from the two tourne▮ favorites. Earlier in the year, Northeast Mississippi easily beste▮ the Trojans, 84-69.

The *News-Herald's* other four second-line favorites did n▮ appear to be in the same class as Hannibal. Though Mober▮ Junior College was making its fourth consecutive tourne▮ appearance, the Greyhounds were not as strong as in the pas▮ Moberly's 18-8 record was indicative of the team's inconsister▮ play throughout the year. Junior College of Benton Harbc▮ (20-4), Trenton Junior College (18-3), and Bismarck Junior Co▮ lege (16-3) possessed better records than Moberly's but onl▮ Trenton carried additional credentials to support the paper▮ claim. The newcomers from New Jersey averaged more than 8▮ points per game and featured one of the country's top score▮ — James Fennelli (25.5). The Vikings demonstrated their sco▮ ing prowess earlier in the year by routing Bergen Junior Colleg▮ 129-76, Fennelli leading all scorers with 46.

Whether because of regional modesty or because of a psy▮ chological ploy, the paper chose to exclude an obvious favorit▮ from its pre-tourney picks. The Arkansas City Junior Colleg▮ roster included six players from its 1953 second-place tean▮ Among the Tiger returners were the dynamic duo of Linwoo▮ Burns and Lafayette Norwood, both All-Tournament selection▮ the year before. Since the Kansas crew compiled a superb 23-▮ record against stiff Region 6 competition, it was difficult t▮ understand why Arkansas City was not considered a top con▮ tender. Still, the Tigers were relegated to the role of underdo▮

Joining Arkansas City as anticipated also-rans were 195▮ repeaters, Brewton-Parker Junior College (26-5), Eastern Arizo na Junior College of Thatcher (13-13), and Fairbury Junior Col lege (10-10); previous tourney participants, Campbell Colleg▮ (24-7) and Connors State Agricultural College (13-4); and new comers, Snow College (17-8), Fort Lewis A&M College (12-12▮ and Centralia Junior College (11-11).

TUESDAY — A NEW SCHEDULE

In the early years of the tournament, an hour and a half wa▮ considered sufficient time to complete a contest. Since ther▮ the rules had changed, particularly regarding free throw shoot ing. The clock stopped more frequently, extending playin▮ time. When games went into extra periods, starting times fell b▮ the wayside. After two years of continuously falling behin▮ schedule, American Legion sponsors opted to allot an hour an▮ forty-five minutes per game. To accommodate the change▮ afternoon and evening sessions started a half hour earlier.

It was high noon when Benton Harbor and Eastern Arizon▮ tipped off the 1954 event. In keeping with the new time stric▮ tures, the Indians from Michigan fell into cadence and estab▮ lished a steady scoring pace. By quarters, Benton Harbor parte▮

---

[1]Schumann and Fitzsimmons completed their college education at Midwestern State University in Wichita Falls, Texas, where they joined forces with several players recently released from active duty in the Army. Their teammates included: O'Neal Weaver, Tommy Hancock, and Freddie Whillock (former Tyler Junior College performers); Rogers Morgan (a former player at Cameron State Agricultural College); and Fitzsimmons' older brother (who had also played junior college basketball). The combined playing experience of the group was awesome. (When Fitzsimmons was a senior, he was the youngest starter — at 24 years of age.) Asked why he would not schedule the team, E.O. "Doc" Hayes, S.M.U.'s venerable mentor replied, "Well, let me tell you something. They got a couple of guys over at Midwestern playing for them who were playing for Doctor Naismith when he laced up the first one."

the net for 23, 22, 21, and 21, respectively. Though the Gila Monsters from Thatcher canned 27 of 32 free throws, they were no match for the Indians. Behind the accurate hook shots of center John Woods — who led all scorers with 25 — Benton Harbor outshot Eastern Arizona, 32-21, from the field, winning 87-71.

Three-time participant Hannibal-LaGrange was not expected to have any trouble with newcomer Bismarck in the afternoon feature. However, when the Trojans found themselves clinging to a slim three-point lead with five minutes to go, they decided to take drastic measures. The high-scoring, run-and-gun ballclub chose to ice the game. For the next two minutes, 5-7 guard Ron Fisher entertained the crowd with a brilliant dribbling exhibition, thwarting the North Dakota school's attempts to grab the ball. None of the Trojans looked at the basket unless they were wide open. Hannibal was content to run out the clock.

Then, Bismarck broke the freeze twice. With Hannibal leading, 82-80, and 1:45 left on the clock, Bismarck's John Campagna sliced the margin to a sliver with a free throw. Moments later Hannibal's Bill Rittman regained the point with one of two charities.

The Mystics from Bismarck called time with 45 seconds to go, hoping to find magic on the bench. Coach Cliff Nygard instructed them to play for a tie. The North Dakotans carefully worked through a set offense, their patience eventually paying a dividend when a Bismarck player strolled to the basket off a perfectly executed play. But, the ball bounced off the glass, rolled around the hoop, and rimmed out. Hannibal held the ball for the win.

The two teams in the final afternoon contest shared a common trait — good defense. Both Connors State and Snow put barbed wire around the middle, preventing encroachment. The result was the lowest score in the 1954 tournament. Snow led from beginning to end, holding the Connors Aggies to six field goals in the first 20 minutes of play. The Utah team's 53-46 victory was considered a mild upset.

The highlight of the six o'clock game was the 35-point performance of Northeast Mississippi's Charles Floyd. The Booneville pivotman was not only adept at potting hook shots from close range, but frequently roamed to either side of the lane to hook them over his head as he faded away from the bucket. After Floyd netted several of the unguardable shots from 15 feet, the Aggies from Fort Lewis gave in. Northeast Mississippi was never pressed, winning 84-61.

Fairbury Coach C. L. "Red" Grovert received news of his father's death shortly before the Chamber of Commerce dinner Monday evening. Grovert promptly planned a return home, leaving the ballclub in the hands of Pete Biederman, the Fairbury High School mentor. The sad tidings affected the Bombers in the Tuesday night feature. Lon Morris steamed ahead of Fairbury, taking an overpowering 50-29 halftime advantage. Coach O. P. Adams substituted freely in the second period to keep the Bearcat rout from appearing too obvious. Both Bob Burrow and guard Jim Emerson — who combined for 54 of Lon Morris' 82 points — spent the final period resting on the bench. Even so, the Texans coasted to an 82-58 victory.

Though the opening moments were nip and tuck, the day's finale was just as predictable as the other evening games. Brewton-Parker possessed a strong inside game, generally counting on 6-4 forward Bill Groover and 6-4 center Curtis Gleaton to control the boards. The big men received quite a surprise, however, when they were challenged by a man a half foot shorter — Arkansas City's jumping jack, Linwood Burns. With Burns and running mate, Lafayette Norwood, providing the impetus, the Tigers' patented whirlwind offense took off. There was little the Barons from Georgia could do but watch. Brewton-Parker's Gleaton won the individual scoring battle with 26, but Arkansas City won the game, 70-54.

WEDNESDAY — UNVEILING CINDERELLA

The Centralia Blue Devils did not find out they were a tourney entry until the Monday before the tournament.[2] A hastily planned trip to Hutchinson and a sudden introduction to the spacious Sports Arena caused a bad case of opening-game jitters, the Illinois team playing well only in spurts. A decided height advantage for Moberly kept Centralia from rebounding missed shots. As the game progressed, Moberly gradually increased its lead, finishing with a 67-51 victory.

The difference might have been greater had the Greyhounds not displayed a few jitters of their own. Moberly guard Jim Carey later described playing in the expansive Arena for the first time as awe-inspiring: "I remember, I took a shot — I was a fair shooter — and the thing only got halfway to the bucket."

The sluggish performance by the Missouri squad was due in part to Carey's foul trouble. The six-foot catalyst of the Greyhound offense picked up three fouls in the first eight minutes. The team's momentum ground to a crawl until he returned to the lineup in the second half.

Coach Maury John summed up Moberly's lackluster showing stating, "Our play today will certainly scare no one."

The best first-round game was the last. In the first half, The Vikings from Trenton outclassed the Campbell Camels as anticipated, taking a 10-point lead into the locker room at intermission. But, a 1,600-mile 29-hour train ride from New Jersey began to tell in the third frame. The tired Vikings worked the ball to perfection only to see their shots bound away, no good.

The door was wide open for an exciting Campbell comeback. Forward Len Maness guided the Camel surge, sinking 18 of his game-high 26 points in the second half. An effective stall in the final two minutes, assured Campbell's 66-63 upset.

An estimated 3,500 fans turned out for the Wednesday evening quarterfinals. The head count was well below comparable figures from the past two tournaments but considerably more than a disappointing opening-night attendance. The increased interest was due largely to the feature contest — a match race between two thoroughbreds.

Since the fast-break was the prime ingredient in the game plan of both Hannibal-LaGrange and Arkansas City, everyone envisioned streaking colors on the court and large numbers on the scoreboard. Fouls undermined the crowd's expectations. Arkansas City's Linwood Burns and Tony Rendulich picked up their third personal fouls early in the second period. From that point Arkansas City players were hesitant about getting in the way of the hard-driving Hannibal team. The Trojan lead gradually increased from one after the first period, to three at intermission, to 10 with a quarter to play.

The Tigers regained some of their fire in the final period, narrowing the margin to four with three minutes to go. Hannibal foiled the rally, however, with a cautious passing game. The Trojans played for good shots and got the best available — free throws. Three Arkansas City players fouled out trying to break Hannibal's stall. When the final results were tabulated, Arkansas City and Hannibal tallied 25 field goals apiece. The six-point Hannibal victory margin came from the line, a result of 31 Arkansas City personal fouls.

The Kansas team's loss sent many of the local crowd on their way home. The chagrined fans who remained had reason to smile shortly thereafter. Lightly regarded Snow College was on the verge of being blown away by Northeast Mississippi when spring thaw set in. Trailing 12-5 in the first quarter, the Badgers came out of hibernation to tie the score at the end of the period. To the delight of the small gallery remaining, Snow continued challenging the heavy favorites. At the half, the Utah crew held the edge, 40-39.

Northeast Mississippi pulled back out in front after intermission but could not shake the tenacious Badgers. With the Tigers in the lead by three and one period to go, Snow still had a chance.

That chance waned when the boys from Mississippi upped the margin to six. Fans filed out of the Sports Arena, figuring the fun was over. Those who happened to turn on their car radio before leaving the Arena parking lot were fortunate. They had the opportunity to dash back into the building to catch the tail end of an amazing finish. Snow stunned Northeast Mississippi, 72-69.

---

[2] For the second year in a row, the Washington-Oregon region failed to send a representative to the tournament. The resulting vacancy belonged to the Region 2 runner-up — Campbellsville College. An appeal was lodged after regional play, however, upon the disclosure that Campbellsville had used two ineligible players, forcing a last-minute invitation to third-place finisher, Centralia.

The key to the magnificent upset was the Badgers' solid defense. Though Charles Floyd continued his brilliant tourney play with 34 points, the Utah team kept everyone else on the Booneville squad from scoring. Northeast Mississippi's final figure was 16 points below the Tigers' season average.

On the offensive side of the ledger, Snow received strong performances by forward Hal Jensen (22) and center Joe Kirby (19). Not only did the pair do their share in the point column, but also in the rebound department. Both powered the boards, giving Snow a decided advantage in the middle.

Fans left the Sports Arena in a felicitous mood. The 1954 Juco Tournament had just unveiled its Cinderella.

THURSDAY — DUSTING OFF THE TOURNAMENT

The most thrilling contest to date in the 1954 tournament came in Thursday's matinee feature, a consolation tilt between Trenton and Centralia. The lead swung back and forth in an ever widening arch until Trenton took a commanding eight-point advantage in to the final quarter. At that point, Centralia's Fred Johnson took charge. Held to just three points in three quarters, the six-foot guard rallied the Blue devils, scoring 17 in the fourth period. His heroics set up a nail-biting conclusion.

With 30 seconds remaining, Johnson broke a 70-all tie with a perfect shot from the top of the key.

Trenton hustled down the court and, at the 10-second mark, Fred Gmitter was fouled. The Viking guard calmly toed the line and sank two pressure free throws.

Centralia's in-bounds pass went to Johnson. Avoiding a Viking picket fence, he dribbled past midcourt and let fly from 30-feet out. The ball cut cleanly through the cords, just as the buzzer sounded.

Though Johnson was the man of the hour, he would not have had the chance if it had not been for Centralia's brilliant small forward — Robert Welch. The versatile 5-11 leaper — who never played the game until coming to Centralia — carried the Blue Devils through most of the contest, topping all scorers with 29.

A battle of Tigers followed. Both Northeast Mississippi and Arkansas City played like their nicknames. The game was fierce, close until the finish. In the end, balance prevailed. Charles Floyd continued his amazing hook shot exhibition, flinging them in from a distant post[3], totaling 28 to lead all scorers. But only one other Booneville player cracked double figures — long-shooting guard Jerry Ritchey (24). In comparison, five Arkansas City players managed the feat — Jim Reed (18), Linwood Burns (17), Lafayette Norwood (16), J. C. Louderback (12), and Reece Bohannon (10). For the first time in three tournament appearances, the Mississippi school was eliminated before trophy play.

Fans who attended the afternoon session stepped into a different world when they left the Sports Arena for the supper break. At 5 p.m. the temperature read a mild 78 degrees. Shortly thereafter the mercury began to slide downward as winds peaked to 78 miles per hour. The result resembled dust bowl conditions of the 1930s.

Blowing dust and a dipping thermometer reduced attendance at Thursday evening's session. Those who stayed home did not miss much in the quarterfinal feature between Moberly and Campbell. After a jittery opening-round game, Moberly was ready to play. The Greyhounds dogged Campbell all over the court, smothering the Camels defensively. On offense, hard-charging Jim Carey penetrated at will. The crowd favorite accounted for at least a dozen assists to go along with a game-high 21 points. Moberly was never threatened, winning easily, 68-50.

According to Benton Harbor Coach Gene Morgan, Lon Morris was guilty of psychological warfare prior to their quarterfinal match-up. That morning a chartered bus load of Lon Morris coeds checked into the Baker Hotel and were assigned rooms on the same floor as the Benton Harbor team. ''While I was trying to prepare them for a real tough ballgame, they were ogling the pretty Texas gals,'' complained Morgan.

If the ploy was knowingly conceived by Lon Morris, it did n[o] work. The Benton Harbor Indians were well prepared. The[y] sniped at the top-rated Bearcats, staying close. Near the end [of] the third period, they took the lead, 56-55.

With 4:30 remaining, Benton Harbor was still in the driver['s] seat, 65-64. The crowd tensed for a possible upset.

A tip-in by Bob Burrow. A free throw by James Emerson. [A] lay-up by Ken Roach. At the three-minute mark, thoughts of a[n] upset were forgotten. Lon Morris had regained control. Th[e] Texans padded their lead with free throws and easy lay-up[s,] winning 77-67.

For the most part, the game had been a war between center[s.] Like battleships firing salvos at one another, Benton Harbor['s] John Woods and the Bearcats' Burrow bombarded the baske[t.] Burrow matched his season average with 30. Woods, anoth[er] tourney hook shot artist, outdid the All-American with 38, th[e] highest individual total in the 1954 tournament.

FRIDAY — AN ANSWERED PRAYER

Overnight the mercury continued its plunge. The blowin[g] dust acquired a white partner — snow. In the morning Hutchin[son] residents awoke to a bizarre black and white tableau.

Despite the foul weather, 4,000 fans attended the Frida[y] night semifinals. Considering the apparent mismatche[s] involved, it was a surprisingly high figure. Though the Sno[w] Badgers had upended a tourney favorite, they were obvious[ly] not in the same league as the explosive Hannibal-LaGrang[e] Trojans. And no one could be certain which side of the Mober[ly] team's Jekyll-and-Hyde personality would be playing in th[e] contest against heavily favored Lon Morris. Instead of lopside[d] blow-outs, however, the two games were just compensatio[n] for the courageous souls who braved the elements.

The crowd was fully behind the underdogs from Utah an[d] was pleasantly surprised when Snow quickly took command [of] the evening feature. Playing control basketball and stingi[ng] defense, the Badgers led, 14-9, after one quarter. By halftim[e] Snow had extended its margin to seven.

Facing a tough uphill fight, Hannibal stepped up its scorin[g] pace. Snow countered with Eddie Lewis. The Pocatello, Idah[o] reserve took shots from far outside Hannibal's perimete[r.] Though his shots were uncharacteristically adventuresome fo[r] the cautious Badgers, Lewis was confidently accurate. Fou[r] long field goals in the third period demoralized the Troja[n] defense.

Only one quarter remained. Even though the Cinderel[la] Utahans were still dominant by seven, everyone expected Han[nibal] to mount a rally at any moment. The Trojans pressed t[o] make up ground. They only succeeded in making matte[rs] worse. Fouls sent Snow to the line with frustrating regularit[y.] When the final buzzer sounded, Hannibal had failed to reac[h] the finals for the third year in a row.

The Trojans had been off track from the beginning. Every[-] thing was out of sync: tempo, timing, shooting. The Sno[w] defense confused and denied the Missouri team at every tur[n.] Bill Bradley — till then Hannibal's leading scorer in the tourna[-] ment — managed only five points before fouling out. The Tr[o-] jans' final total of 59 was 35 points below their average.

Two Snow players had shone on offense.

Eddie Lewis' sensational shooting netted him a game-high 2[2] points. The exceptional performance was a surprise to the Are[-] na fans, but not to his Snow teammates. The freshman sub w[as] noted for his ability to come in cold off the bench and heat u[p] the game. He was the Badgers' fourth leading scorer and ha[d] been named to the all-star team of the Region 4 tournament.

The other outstanding Snow player was Joe Kirby. The 6[-] post — who looked too gangly to play as well as he did [—] enjoyed his best game thus far, matching Lewis' total of 22 whi[le] powering the boards at both ends of the court.

Though the play of these two Badgers stood out from the res[t,] it had been a complete team victory. Snow's tightfisted defen[se] was indicative of a close team unity, the kind displayed by pre[-] vious tournament champions.

---

[3] Floyd's unbelievable ability to hook from long distance even fascinated opposing players. Boyd Grant, a Snow College reserve, likened viewing Floyd's unique talent to the first time he ever saw someone dribble behind his back: ''We'd all run to the game because we couldn't believe that someone could dribble behind his back. And this guy (Floyd) was the same way . . . We all ran to every game he played . . . The first game we watched him play we just . . . why, he was kind of like a space guy. It was a Dr. J. We'd never seen anything like it!''

The Lon Morris-Moberly semifinal was a rematch of the teams who battled for fifth place the year before. That game had been tight from beginning to end with Lon Morris eking out a single-point victory. Friday's finale was equally close, equally exciting. The score was tied 15 times, the lead passing hands the same number. Not until the closing seconds was the winner determined.

The unpredictable Greyhounds put on their Dr. Jekyll masks to start the game, the first quarter ending with Moberly trailing Lon Morris by a mere digit. The close scuffle threatened to be a walk-away in the second period as the Missouri crew switched to its Mr. Hyde role. Lon Morris bounded to a nine-point margin. Just as quickly, Moberly regained form. Discarding their nefarious side for good, the Greyhounds charged to the front, taking a 41-40 edge into the locker room at intermission.

The Moberly advantage grew. Early in the final quarter, the Greyhounds were comfortably in front, 66-58.

Now it was the Texans' turn to stage a comeback. Bob Burrow started the surge with a pair of free throws. Field goals by Jim Emerson and Ken Roach pulled Lon Morris within a basket. The Texans acquired another charity. The margin was one.

Moments later the rally was complete. Aggressive Jim Carey hacked Burrow as he banked in a two-handed shot. The bucket was good. So was the subsequent free throw. The Bearcats were on top, 68-66.

Moberly bounced back. Reserve Ed Flynn hit his only goal of the game — a sensational button-hook lay-up. The tying basket was shortly followed by more Greyhound good news; Burrow — who represented most of the Texans' offense, having contributed 27 points — was whistled for his fifth foul. With 6:30 left, Lon Morris was up against the wall.

After Dick Warren swished one of two free throws awarded him on Burrow's foul, guard Billy Tubbs gave Lon Morris the upper hand again with a pair of charities of his own.

Without Burrow guarding him, 6-8 Warren found shooting much easier in the middle for the Greyhounds. He hit a bullseye, putting Moberly back on top, 71-70.

The Bearcats worked hectically for shots, but could not connect. They *were* fouled, however, Tubbs and forwards Dean Evans and John Clark were all successful from the line. With three minutes to go, it was Lon Morris — 73, Moberly — 71.

Moberly calmly worked the ball, finally finding Dana Sharp all alone in the corner. The sophomore forward tiptoed down the baseline and tied the score.

Despite the prolonged tension and the loss of a valuable player for the Texans, both teams looked confident. Overtime was likely.

Then came a killing blow for the Bearcats. In an effort to crash through Moberly's solid defense, Lon Morris' Clark was called for carrying the ball. As the game entered its final minute, all-important ball possession went to the Missouri squad.

Carey set up the Moberly attack, dribbling in backcourt. A long pass hit Sharp in the corner. Sharp passed up a shot and lobbed the ball to Warren crossing the lane. Warren whipped it across the middle to the opposite side. Forward Gordon Sulltrop caught the ball and jumped. The shot was true and clean. Moberly was on top with 42 seconds left.

The Texans sped to their end of the court and rushed through their offensive set. Both Evans and Tubbs hurried shots, but missed. Moberly grabbed the final rebound and held the ball until the buzzer.

Jubilant fans — strangers as well as Moberly diehards — stormed the court, mobbing the surprise victors. The Greyhound dressing room was equal bedlam. Players hooted and hollered, "We did it! We did it! We did it!"

When asked about the game by reporters, Coach Maury John — tears in his eyes — could barely choke out, "We beat a great ball club." After a few more tearful moments, he added, "You know, I was praying that last 30 seconds."

John's prayers had been answered. For the first time in five tries, he was taking a team to the final.

SATURDAY — SOMETHING SPECIAL

Saturday's trophy parade began with an exciting fifth-place contest between Brewton-Parker and Eastern Arizona. The teams switched leads at the quarters, the largest margin coming shortly into the final period when the Gila Monsters from Thatcher increased their 10-point third-quarter advantage to 13.

Then, Brewton-Parker's Jim Fetterman awakened the Georgia Barons. The 6-5 Fetterman — who saw limited action throughout the tournament — was not given an opportunity to play against the Arizona squad until the fourth quarter. He promptly tallied nine points, rallying his team to within two with 10 seconds to go.

Center Carl Wheeler held off the Baron comeback with a lay-up to salvage a 74-70 win for Eastern Arizona.

The fourth-place contest was a major disappointment for local fans. The Arkansas City Tigers did not look like a championship ball club which had won second the year before. The ubiquitous tandem of Linwood Burns and Lafayette Norwood — tourney all-stars a year ago — labored throughout the game. Burns added only a single bucket and that in the first quarter. He collected three fouls early in the first half and spent most of the second half on the bench. The one-hand push shots of Norwood also failed to connect. Norwood managed just nine points. Consequently, the final total of 46 was one of the lowest scores for the Tigers all year.

On the other hand, the victorious Benton Harbor Indians received another splendid outing from their star center, John Woods. His game-high 26 — almost half Benton Harbor's total — gave him 111 points for the tournament, moved him into the record books as one of the top-10 tourney scorers to date, and insured his presence on the All-Tournament Team.

The anticipated showdown between Lon Morris and Hannibal-LaGrange was as exciting as a championship contest though the prize was only third place. Hannibal maintained the advantage over the course of the game, but not by much. Whenever the Trojans threatened to extend the lead, Lon Morris retaliated with its twin towers of Bob Burrow and Ken Roach, who took game honors with 34 and 25, respectively. With 60 seconds left, down 73-71, and in the midst of another Lon Morris surge, Burrow fouled out. Hannibal extinguished the threat with a game-ending stall and claimed its third third-place trophy in as many years.[4]

The first dominate big man in tourney history, MVP Bob Burrow was later an All-American at Kentucky where he led the Wildcats to a runner-up finish in the 1956 NCAA Mideast Regional, scoring 64 points in two games. After college he played briefly in the NBA with Rochester and Minneapolis. (Photo courtesy of the University of Kentucky)

---

[4]Though the highly regarded Texans placed sixth, many veteran observers still consider the 1954 Lon Morris team as one of their all-time favorites. The Bearcats earned fan respect because of their class, their unwillingness to give up.

No other Lon Morris player exemplified this more than Bob Burrow. The broad-shouldered blond combined strength and finesse. He was adept at turn-around jumpers and hook shots, going either direction. According to former teammate Billy Tubbs (later head coach at Oklahoma University), "He was the closest thing to Wayman Tisdale I've been around . . . When you got the ball inside he would score . . . I liked to play with him . . . I'd shoot it and holler 'Off to the right' and he'd go fetch it and put it back in."

Burrow's soft touch garnered a tourney-high 116 points. But, besides tremendous ability, he exhibited a winning personality. The two assets made him a unanimous choice for MVP.

The two Friday night upsets set up a second straight dream finale as far as Hutchinson fans were concerned. Having backed both unheralded outsiders, the hometown crowd felt satisfied regardless of the outcome. The fact that Snow was making its first tournament appearance while Moberly was an old hand was the only reason for one team's receiving more attention than the other. Otherwise, the squads were so comparable it was difficult to tell them apart. The two schools owned near-identical records. Both possessed similar playing styles: cautious offense and stubborn defense. In fact, both teams had given up an identical 174 points in three games — an average of 58 points per game, the best in the tournament. Both were guided by mentors with similar coaching philosophies and displayed conspicuous team unity.[5] It was hard not to like either team and impossible to decide which was better.

The differences in the two teams revolved around their offensive strengths. For Snow, it was the big men who carried the scoring load. Guards Lewis Monson and Halbert Christensen were unselfish playmakers whose principal task was to feed the heart and soul of the Badger offense — line-drive shooting forward Hal Jensen and hard-working pivotman, Joe Kirby. Though 6-8 center Dick Warren was a capable player on the inside, Moberly depended on the leadership of guard Jim Carey to spearhead the Greyhound offense. If Carey clicked, Moberly clicked.

The Badgers attacked Moberly's strong point from the outset. Reserve Boyd Grant was inserted into the lineup with specific instructions: "Don't let him [Carey] get the ball." Wherever Carey went, so did Grant. Often the Moberly guard was double-teamed. Snow was so successful in denying him the ball that at one point in the contest, Carey called in frustration to Coach John, "What'll I do, Coach? What do you want me to do?"

Snow did not make effective use of the disruptive attention given Carey, however, After one quarter, the Badgers were on top by only one. In fact, at half, *Moberly* held the lead, 27-25. Only in the third period did the tactic begin to pay off. Late in the quarter, Snow gained a six-point margin, the largest by either team.

As close as the game had been to that point, there was very little to excite the crowd. Two thrilling upsets the night before made the championship tilt seem anticlimactic. Play by both teams was not as sharp. Both looked tired, particularly Moberly. Then, just before the end of the third quarter, the Greyhounds caught a second wind and pulled to within one. The crowd came to life, sensing something special was about to happen.

Moberly's momentum carried into the final period. Behind the fancy hook shots of Warren — who took over Carey's scoring leadership, hitting a game-high 18 — the Greyhounds forged to a six-point advantage with two minutes remaining.

It was Snow's turn to catch second wind. First, reserve Kent Anderson hit two pressure free throws. Then, Jensen maneu-vered for a lay-up. Finally, with 28 seconds on the clock, Anderson scored from long distance to tie the game, 46-all.

Moberly, obviously tired and on the verge of collapse, brought the ball downcourt and wasted a chance to win the game. Snow grabbed the rebound and immediately called time.

Coach Williams instructed the Badgers to work it to the big men for the game winner. But, the plan went awry. As time evaporated, Eddie Lewis — Snow's hero from the night before — found himself with the ball. The freshman dribbled to the right side of the court in front of the team bench, turned from 25 feet out, and cut loose a half-jump, half-set shot. The rotation was perfect. The trajectory true.

"I was standing right under the basket," Boyd Grant said later, "and I would have bet every dollar I had — which was only about one then — that it was going through."

The buzzer sounded just as ball met rim and silenced as the winning bucket lipped out, no good.

The Sports Arena was momentarily devoid of sound. Everyone was stunned by the sudden ending. Then an adrenal rush slowly surged through the crowd as realization of what was taking place finally sank in. For the first time, a championship game was going into overtime.

Raw tension filled the Arena as the players lined up for the tip-off. Weary from four pressure games in five days, the teams opened the extra period flustered, not really comprehending what was happening. Both teams missed easy shots.

Then, Moberly's Dan Sonnenberg broke the ice with a free throw. The basket triggered a Greyhound awakening. The previously near-silent Carey — who was playing on nothing but nervous energy — swished two buckets to lead Moberly's roll. Snow never recovered. The Badgers were down five points with just under a minute to play before they scored their first basket. By then it was too late.

After five tries, Moberly Junior College wore the National Juco crown at last.

THE AFTERMATH — DEALING WITH LOWER ATTENDANCE

When the buzzer sounded concluding the 1954 championship game, the Arena floor flooded with happy Moberly rooters. Among the first to reach the Greyhound players with back-slapping congratulations were the Hannibal-LaGrange Trojans — Moberly's long-time Missouri rivals. Past hatred was swept away by mutual enjoyment of the Show-Me State's victory. The excitement was so intense, a tearful Maury John began to bleed from the nose. It was a minor annoyance, however, compared to the thrill of the moment.

The magnitude of the team's accomplishment did not hit home fully until the Greyhounds returned to Moberly. The caravan of cars carrying the squad first encountered jubilant townspeople as far west as Keytesville, 27 miles away. Other

The 1954 Moberly Greyhounds — winners of the tournament's first overtime championship game. (Photo courtesy of Dan Callahan)

[5]Jim Carey and Boyd Grant, both described their former coaches Maury John and Jim Williams, similarly: they were tough disciplinarians. According to Grant, "You did what he told you to do. There were no exceptions." Still, both shared undying respect for their junior college mentors. Carey about John: "He was an outstanding coach . . . He watched out for his kids, made sure they went to college." Grant about Williams: "He was a tremendous coach. I think that he stood for all of the things I felt were important . . . Didn't make any difference who you were on the team, you got treated just the same." The two men were honest, fair-minded, and well-liked as their later success demonstrated: Maury John coached at Drake for 13 years and Iowa State for three before succumbing to cancer; Jim Williams led Colorado State for 26 years before retiring.

cars parked at various vantage points along the route home joined the caravan. By the time the lead vehicle reached the city limits, the procession had grown to seven miles in length. The spontaneous demonstration illustrated how important winning was to the people of Moberly.

***

Despite a suspenseful drama which built to an overtime climax, the 1954 Juco Tournament was not as successful as those before it. For the first time since moving the event to Hutchinson, receipts were down from the previous year. Attendance was 5,000 to 6,000 lower, reducing revenue $6,350. Two factors were thought to have caused the drop: bad weather and competition with state regional basketball tournaments during the same week throughout Kansas. The scheduling conflict had been anticipated; the unpredictable Kansas weather had not.

Though the heavy drop in income was discouraging to NJCAA and American Legion officials, no one was overly alarmed. The tournament had never been viewed as a moneymaking venture. Financial success was achieved as long as costs were recovered and visiting team expenses were defrayed as much as possible. Besides, junior college administrators across the nation who had pushed for the schedule change were pleased with the new arrangement. Teams were no longer obliged to extend practice for three weeks after league play as they had had to do in the past. Since regional tournaments were still meeting with failure,[6] additional cost cuts insured team participation.

Everyone was optimistic about the future. A proposal to televise the 1955 championship game was suggested. There was even talk that California administrators were seriously considering allowing teams into the tournament again.

Still, the NJCAA was not taking chances. Caution governed when the organization decided to change its regional structure. California along with recently truant Washington and Oregon were lumped into Region 4 which previously comprised most of Idaho, Utah, and Montana. The leftover Region 3 was then assigned to eastern Kansas. The move gave the Sunflower State two representatives in the national tournament and improved the odds for financial success.

Tournament Results

	Game	
Tuesday:	1	Benton Harbor — 87 Eastern Arizona — 71
	2	Hannibal-LaGrange — 83 Bismarck — 81
	3	Snow — 53 Connors St. — 46
	4	NE Mississippi — 84 Fort Lewis A&M — 61
	5	Lon Morris — 82 Fairbury — 58
	6	Arkansas City — 70 Brewton-Parker — 54
Wednesday:	7	Moberly — 67 Centralia — 51
	8	Campbell — 66 Trenton — 63
	9	Brewton-Parker — 80 Bismarck — 76
	10	Hannibal-LaGrange — 78 Arkansas City — 72
	11	Snow — 72 NE Mississippi — 69
Thursday:	12	Connors St. — 78 Fort Lewis A&M — 62
	13	Centralia — 74 Trenton — 72
	14	Arkansas City — 86 NE Mississippi — 74
	15	Eastern Arizona — 79 Fairbury — 53
	16	Moberly — 68 Campbell — 50
	17	Lon Morris — 77 Benton Harbor — 67
Friday:	18	Brewton-Parker — 75 Connors St. — 70
	19	Eastern Arizona — 79 Centralia — 72
	20	Benton Harbor — 78 Campbell — 61
	21	Snow — 69 Hannibal-LaGrange — 59
	22	Moberly — 75 Lon Morris — 73
Saturday:	23	Eastern Arizona — 74 Brewton-Parker — 70
	24	Benton Harbor — 57 Arkansas City — 46
	25	Hannibal-LaGrange — 77 Lon Morris — 71
	26	Moberly — 55 Snow — 49 OT

How They Finished in 1954

1. Moberly Junior College
2. Snow College
3. Hannibal-LaGrange College
4. Junior College of Benton Harbor
5. Eastern Arizona Junior College
6. Lon Morris College
7. Arkansas City Junior College
8. Brewton-Parker Junior College

All-Tournament Team

Bill Bradley — Hannibal-LaGrange College
Robert Burrow — Lon Morris College
Jim Carey — Moberly Junior College
James Emerson — Lon Morris College
Charles Floyd — Northeast Mississippi Junior College
Bill Groover — Brewton-Parker Junior College
Hal Jensen — Snow College
Gordon "Joe" Kirby — Snow College
Dick Warren — Moberly Junior College
John Woods — Junior College of Benton Harbor

Player of the Year

Robert Burrow — Lon Morris College

---

[6]Regional tournaments across the country faced widely varying financial success. They ranged from the remunerative Region 14 tourney at Tyler, Texas, which netted $2,066.64 to the profitless Region 15 meet at Trenton, New Jersey, which showed a $10 loss. For most, success meant *not* failing. The Region 16 tournament at Jefferson City, Missouri, turned a profit. However, the minimal amount of $86.25 was all that was given to the winner — the eventual national champion from Moberly — to pay for its trip to Hutchinson.

1955:

A "DULL" YEAR

Moberly's Jim Carey, a 1985 NJCAA Basketball Hall of Fame inductee, is the only tourney participant to have played and coached on a national champion. (Photo courtesy of Moberly Monitor-Index)

On March 7, the day before the 1955 National Jun College Basketball Tournament, an atomic device was deton ed at the Yucca Flats testing sight in Nevada. The predawn fla unleashed a furious 20-second fireball seen virtually from b der to border throughout the western United States. The exp sion was the largest in a succession of atomic tests that year

In world news, Chaing Kai-shek's Nationalist Chinese l Nanki, a bleak, barren, six-square-mile island at the north e of a chain near the China coast in the East China Sea. The Co munist victory was the third in six weeks. The continu Nationalist Chinese retreat had stimulated a U.S. promise defend Taiwan against Red aggression earlier in the month.

Closer to home, Vice-President Richard Nixon and fam were in the midst of a 28-day, 10-country goodwill tour throu Mexico, Central America, and the Caribbean. Pictures of a sm ing, hand-shaking Nixon with government leaders such as C ta Rica's Colonel Jose "Pepe" Figueres and Nicaragua's Gene Anastasio "Tacho" Somoza — hated enemies since the Nica gua-based invasion of Costa Rica in January — created t impression that the Western Hemisphere stood united in t Cold War.

These were exciting, albeit, scary times and people we becoming increasingly aware of it. This was due to an upsur in television sales. There were 10 times as many TV sets American homes as at the start of the decade. As the ads sa "True Magnavox quality can be yours for as little as $149.50 only $1.54 per week)."

While a few regaled tourney guests at the annual Chamber Commerce dinner Monday night, a majority of Hutchonia were comfortably ensconced in their favorite easy chairs home. Some were tuned to the most popular program on t airwaves — "I Love Lucy." Like one out of every two Ame cans, however, most were watching the first Broadway musi ever aired live on television. All across the nation people m velled at Mary Martin flying through the air as "Peter Pan." T spectacular was talked about for weeks.

The phenomenon was not new. On playgrounds all over t country, a familiar refrain was being sung in unison by coonsk clad children: "Davy . . . Davy Crockett — king of the wild fro tier." An audience of nearly 40 million (mostly between t ages of five and 15) had recently viewed weekly episodes of t frontier hero's story on Walt Disney's "Disneyland." A fad major proportions followed. Two versions of the series' the song (one by Bill Hayes and the other by the "real" Davy Cro ett — Fess Parker) competed for playing time on the radio. P ents were having a hard time hearing *their* favorite — "Since ly" by the Maguire Sisters.

Television's impact was felt everywhere. Though no statist exist to draw exact correlations, the rapid emergence of t novel diversion was probably an important factor in keepi spectators at home. As a consequence, the 1955 National Ju Tournament drew the smallest attendance ever to the Spo Arena.

THE PARTICIPANTS

The day before the opening of the 1955 Juco Tourname American Legion officials announced ticket sales were dov from the previous year. According to Guy Holt, tourname general chairman, "Apparently the reason is that more perso

e planning to buy individual game tickets rather than a season
ook.''

The disinterest in the tournament was even reflected in the
utchinson News-Herald's pre-tourney coverage. Though the
aper devoted as much space as it had in the past, what was
inted failed to excite the reader. The newspaper candidly
cked one team as the team to beat; all others were given short
rift. It required a discerning eye to pick out the top contend-
s.

Region	Team
1	Phoenix College — Phoenix, Arizona
2	Hannibal-LaGrange College — Hannibal, Missouri
3	Coffeyville College of Arts, Science, and Vocations — Coffeyville, Kansas
4	Boise Junior College — Boise, Idaho
5	Howard County Junior College — Big Spring, Texas
6	Arkansas City Junior College — Arkansas City, Kansas
7	East Central Junior College — Decatur, Mississippi
8	Jacksonville Junior College — Jacksonville, Florida
9	Pueblo Junior College — Pueblo, Colorado
10	*McCook Junior College — McCook, Nebraska
11	Graceland College — Lamoni, Iowa
12	Joliet Junior College — Joliet, Illinois
13	Eveleth Junior College — Eveleth, Minnesota
14	Tyler Junior College — Tyler, Texas
15	New York City Community College — Brooklyn, New York
16	Moberly Junior College — Moberly, Missouri

* Invited to fill bracket

The News-Herald's choice for winning the tournament was
ler Junior College (26-6). The paper's reason for selecting the
paches was not because of their tournament legacy (two
tional titles in four previous appearances) nor the fact they
presented Region 14 (the most successful region in national
mpetition). Tyler was selected solely on the basis of one static; the team averaged 96.1 points per game, tops among the
tion's junior colleges.

Tyler's offensive average was an impressive figure consider-
g the stiff rivalries the school faced regularly. Still, it was not
gnificant enough to justify excluding other teams with equally
pressive credentials —

East Central Junior College of Decatur, Mississippi, boasted
e best winning percentage in the tournament. The Warriors
wned a 30-3 record compiled in another region noted for pro-
ucing nationally competitive teams.

The Hannibal-LaGrange College Trojans possessed a better
cord than Tyler (29-6), were close behind the Apaches in
oring with a 91.3 average (third-best in the country), plus
ere making their fourth-straight trip to Hutchinson.

Howard County Junior College also sported a better record
an Tyler, racking up 28 wins against only three losses, includ-
g championships in four out of five Texas tournaments.

The team most would have figured to be an obvious threat,
owever, was virtually ignored by the press: Moberly Junior
ollege owned an excellent 25-4 record, was making its fifth
onsecutive tourney appearance (tying a tournament record),
s sixth overall (also a record), and featured three members
om the 1954 team — including All-Tournament selection Jim
arey — all of which were starters on the current squad. Above
l, the Greyhounds were the defending national champs.

Missing the opportunity to exploit the Missouri team's title
efense, the News-Herald instead focused on the team's
eight. The Greyhounds were the tallest team in the tournaent. Nine members stood six-feet or better, among them 6-10
oger King and 6-9 Carol Fleming. While the paper emphasized
e size of King and Fleming, it neglected to mention that the
vo were reserves. King, in fact, remained in Moberly thanks to
1 untimely case of mumps. Moberly did have superior size in
s lineup, but the Greyhounds were nowhere near the giants
ictured in print.

Height was the paper's rallying point for introducing the 1955
ourney participants to the public. Howard County had 6-8

Wiley Brown. Region 6 champ Arkansas City (23-7) had 6-8
Skippy Cleaver. McCook (19-4) carried 6-7 Max Winters and
Hannibal 6-7 Kelly Owens. Several teams featured 6-6 players
on their roster; Jack Lesan of Pueblo (23-5); Hal Hellerman of
New York City (22-5); Ron Ehler of Boise (18-8); and Sherald
Gordon of Joliet (16-4). Both East Central and Eveleth (27-2)
started 6-5 centers James Griffin and Tony Krall, respectively.

Two teams not only had size but bulk. Jacksonville (20-6)
started 6-6 Chuck Brendler and 6-5½ Larry Strom, both of
whom weighed in at 220 pounds. Six-five Bill Tipton of Coffeyville (18-4) was a tad bigger, tipping the scales at 225.

Considering the paper's emphasis of height, it was interesting
to note that the favored Tyler Apaches were among the shortest
squads in the tournament. Six-four-and-a-half Russell Boone
was the tallest of the Texans. Only the teams with the poorest
records ranked shorter. The tallest players for Phoenix (15-10)
and Graceland (12-9) were 6-4 Jon Gustason and 6-3 Walt Denny, respectively.

All in all, tourney patrons were given little to peak their curiosity and no advanced warning that an explosive drama was
about to unfold.

TUESDAY — THE BEST FIRST

At the Monday night Chamber of Commerce banquet, toast-
master Bud Detter flatly predicted, "The first round of play will
surely be the best ever." It was a fairly safe prognosis. Four of
the top five teams faced each other in the first round.[1]

The other prime contender also had its hands full. The lanky
crew from Decatur, Mississippi, faced a tremendous disadvantage under the backboards. The front line for Jacksonville averaged 6-5 and 210 pounds. Unless the Warriors were extremely
accurate, the tourney opener might resemble a scrimmage
between a dainty ballerina and an obstinate pachyderm.

The size disparity actually proved an advantage for the Warriors. Unlike previous Mississippi teams who stressed run-and-
gun offense, East Central played ball control. Since Jacksonville
was not particularly speedy, the Dolphins were content to follow the Warrior's lead, the contest becoming a tight, basket-
matching affair. At halftime, the score was 21-all.

The turning point came midway in the second half.[2] Unable
to penetrate Jacksonville's stone wall middle, Warrior guard
Darrell Thomas took the overhead route. He launched four successive bombs from far beyond the extremities of the Jacksonville defense. All four were on target, demoralizing the Dolphins. With seven minutes to go and a nine-point lead, East
Central employed a delay game to secure a 52-46 victory.

The Bees from New York City Community College (formerly
Brooklyn Tech) were again a colorful bunch. Though the team
received generous fan support, the New Yorkers were their
own best rooting section. Whenever the team scored, players
on the court would yell and leap in the air while teammates on
the sidelines emitted a chorus of whoops.

The Bees had plenty to cheer about early in the matinee feature. Using a fast-break attack, New York raced to a quick 13-
point lead over Pueblo. Then, a rash of charging fouls slowed
the New Yorkers, allowing Pueblo to rebound to a 42-40 halftime advantage.

A three-minute spurt in the first 10-minutes of the second half
proved the game breaker. Four different players contributed to
a Bee rally which shot the New Yorkers in front of Pueblo by
seven. New York never trailed again.

Center Hal Hellerman paced New York, hammering the
boards at both ends of the court while tallying 23 points for
game honors. Guard Al Weiss complemented Hellerman's
inside play, charming the crowd with six spectacular two-hand,
overhead, long distance push shots, adding 21 to the Bee total.
New York's 79-73 win was a mild surprise.

The forecast for a close-fought opening round was amply fulfilled in the final afternoon contest. Neither Eveleth nor Graceland could find the winning measure. The teams were tied after
20 minutes, 28-all. After another 20 minutes, the game was
again deadlocked, 51-all. Given an additional five minutes to

---

[1]Since the beginning, teams participating in the National Junior College Basketball Tournament have never been seeded. Positions in the tournament bracket
are drawn by lot, usually as much as a year in advance. Consequently, top ballclubs occasionally pair off in opening rounds.
[2]In 1955, junior college games were again played in two 20-minute halves.

decide matters, the two continued at a stalemate, 57-all.

Hoping to settle matters quickly, Eveleth's Jim Lakso launched a beautiful long archer to put the Tigers on top in the second overtime.

Graceland's Charles Hughes tossed in two free throws.

Eveleth switched tactics, letting the clock wind down, stalling for one shot. Another overtime appeared likely.

But, with three seconds remaining, Graceland's Chuck Foster slipped and fell, landing across the legs of Don Suomi.

Suomi — who had already distinguished himself by scoring all six of Eveleth's points in the first overtime — calmly cashed in two charities.[3]

Graceland called time. A strategy was formulated for one last desperation shot. Fortunately, the Iowans were able to get the shot off. Unfortunately, the long heave from near midcourt bounded off the rim just as the final buzzer sounded. Eveleth survived, 61-59.

Earlier in the year, the Phoenix Bears were led by five sophomores. Then, according to 23-year-veteran Coach Dutch Hoy, 'I dumped them when we apparently were going nowhere.' Though the move paid off in a trip to the nationals, it appeared to backfire in the first half of the evening opener, the Phoenix squad's inexperience allowing Joliet to grab a comfortable 10-point margin.

However, Hoy's faith in his all-freshman charges — ''This bunch of youngsters has the best boys that I've had in the last 15 years'' — was duly placed. Early in the second frame, the Bears roared from hibernation, caught and passed Joliet, then coasted to a 60-51 victory.

The most anticipated game in the first round was the opening-night feature. Coffee shop table talk during the day had focused on the regrettable pairing of Tyler and Hannibal-LaGrange so early in the tournament. The grumblings did not last long, though. Who could complain about seeing two of the nation's top offenses go at one another?

With the combined talents of ''Mr. Inside'' and ''Mr. Outside,'' it was easy to see why Tyler had the highest scoring average in the country. Well-built, number ''99'', center Russell Boone patrolled the middle, hitting unguardable fall-away jumpers with steady ease. Bespectacled guard Milton Williams — described by Coach Floyd Wagstaff as ''one of the finest shooters I ever coached'' — matched Boone's consistency with shots from long range, keeping the defense honest.

Hannibal countered with equally impressive performers. The leader of the Trojans was muscular, good-looking Danny Dotson. Besides being an excellent shooter, the 6-3 forward was a quick, effective ball handler. If covered, he found a way of getting it into Hannibal's 6-5 post, Bob Ebker.

In one respect, the Tyler-Hannibal contest was everything the fans expected; plenty of points were put on the scoreboard. For the Apaches, Boone scored 31 and Williams 27, their output comprising nearly 70 percent of Tyler's total. In the duel for game honors, Dotson barely lost out to Boone, netting 30 while Ebker contributed a creditable 20 to the Trojan cause. As the *News-Herald* stated later, ''All appeared to have the range at whatever spot they found themselves with the ball and a free arm.''

What the crowd did not expect was that most of those points would come from Hannibal. The Trojans stunned Tyler, 100-86. The key to the difference was Hannibal's superior size. While the Apaches had superb shooters, they lacked rebound power. Coach Wagstaff described the result succinctly: ''They tore us up.''

Though the day's finale featured a Kansas team, few fans stayed past the first half. Arkansas City was not the exciting crew it had been when led by speedsters Lafayette Norwood and Linwood Burns. There were no stars on the Tigers; all five starters carried modest scoring averages of seven to 14. Nothing in the Tiger arsenal was spectacular. Even so, Arkansas City had fashioned one game-winning formula after another during the year.

In the opening-round match-up against McCook, the Tigers again failed to impress. A tough McCook defense kept Arkansas City's offense in check, holding the margin of difference close throughout. With 2:16 remaining, the score was 52-all.

Then, with a short jumper, Tiger forward Bill Embry broke the tie. A minute later, Del Smith, Embry's counterpart on the other side of the lane, stole the ball and dribbled the length of the court for an easy lay-up. A little control basketball, a last-second clincher by Smith, and just like that, Arkansas City was in the win column again, 58-54. The victory put the Tigers in the championship bracket for the third year in a row.

WEDNESDAY — SETTING SIGHTS

The other first-round pairing looked forward to by most kicked off Wednesday's action. Like the Hannibal-Tyler game, it was an unfortunate early showdown between two top contenders. The contest featured a solid squad from Big Spring, Texas — all five Howard County starters averaged in double figures — and the defending national champions from Moberly, Missouri. Few of the 1,500 matinee spectators who played hooky from work were quibbling, however.

The first 12 minutes was a picture-perfect skirmish between champions. The score was tied three times and on 11 occasions the teams traded advantages. The crowd edged forward in their seats, preparing for a wire-to-wire tussle. What followed jolted everyone, inducing head shakes of disbelief.

Late in the first half, Moberly corrected earlier defensive lapses and unveiled a smoothly coordinated attack which produced amazingly effective patterns. The precision-like Greyhounds galloped past Howard County, grinding the Jayhawks into the earth. The final: Moberly — 111, Howard County — 66.

Mouths were agape all over the Arena. Not only had Moberly defeated one of the best teams in the country, but had done so convincingly — by *45 points*.

Skepticism regarding Moberly's qualifications for title consideration vanished. The current Greyhound unit was much improved. To illustrate how much stronger Moberly was compared to the championship squad of the year before, Jim Carey, previously the vanguard of the Greyhound offense, was no longer required to score. When the popular All-American fouled out of the Howard County contest with nine minutes remaining, only eight points were beside his name in the score book.

The offensive load had shifted to Moberly's front line where center Dan Sonnenberg and forwards Bill Wynn and Red Murrell shared scoring chores. Against Howard County, Wynn cap-

''Mr. Outside'' of Tyler's inside-outside scoring duo, Milt ''Chief'' Williams (No. 21) was later an AP Little All-America selection at Centenary. (Photo courtesy of Centenary)

[3]Suomi's on-court heroics seemed inconsequential compared to the battle he had previously won off the court. Two years before, he was crippled by polio. Though advised to give up sports, Suomi was determined to keep up his physical activity. He drove himself and eventually regained the use of his legs. His only lingering handicap was a slight limp that developed whenever he tired.

tured game honors with 36 while Sonnenberg and Murrell hit for 22 and 20, respectively. The balance was formidable.

Though still the catalyst for the Greyhounds, the gritty Carey no longer needed to worry about carrying his team in this department either. His performance in the opener had been admittedly substandard, but the effect on the outcome was insignificant. The reason: Dan Callahan, Carey's running mate at guard, was the mirror image of Carey. Both were terrific play-makers.

Even the Moberly bench was impressive. When Coach Mau-

The starting five for the defending champion Moberly Greyhounds — left to right: Dan Callahan, Philip "Red" Murrell, Dan Sonnenberg, "Bullet" Bill Wynn, and Jim Carey. (Photo courtesy of Stan Isle, photo taken by V.T. Goode, the **Moberly Monitor-Index**, Moberly, Missouri)

ry John rested his regulars with five minutes left in the game, the reserves handled the Texans with equal aplomb, outscoring the disheartened Jayhawks, 15-7.

There appeared to be no chinks in Moberly's armor. The chances for a second consecutive Greyhound crown looked very good.

Coming on the heels of Moberly's awesome accomplishment, the final first-round game received only passing attention. Coffeyville and Boise were making their tournament debut and both suffered from the tension. The contest remained close until Boise opened a six-point spread shortly into the second half.

Despite being from Kansas, the Coffeyville Red Ravens were not automatic favorites with the local crowd. Coffeyville represented the eastern half of the state — the first team to do so since Fort Scott Junior College in the inaugural event at Springfield — and Eastern Kansas basketball was an unknown quantity to the Sports Arena. Coffeyville had to earn fan endorsement.

The Red Ravens promptly did so, quickly erasing the Boise margin, soaring to a 10-point lead. During a three-minute scoring spree — engineered by Coffeyville's Rich Pruitt and John Catone — Boise failed to register a single point. The Red Ravens held on for a 78-70 victory.

The first round was everything it had been billed to be. All but two of the games had been closely fought throughout. Still, the games which had roused the most fan interest were the two lopsided wins by the Missouri schools. Though it was again possible for two Kansas schools to meet in the finals, the thought was barely discussed. Everyone had their sights set on an old-fashioned "hillbilly shootout" between Hannibal and Moberly for the championship.

If there were observers who needed additional convincing, they received it in the opening quarterfinal game Wednesday night. The contest was a schizoid struggle between two radical personalities. The tempo of the first half was slow, methodical, the Decatur crew's preferred style of play. East Central grabbed a quick four-point margin, then maintained the pace and the lead for the first 17 minutes.

However, Hannibal-LaGrange had proved its defensive abilities earlier in the year in a game with Bethany Lutheran of Mankato, Minnesota, in which the Trojans held the Mankato squad

to *one* field goal in the first half while building a 54-18 advantage. Against East Central, that same tough defense kept the score close.

Then, just before halftime, Hannibal gambled with a few medium- and long-range attempts, hoping to open the action. The shots connected. The Trojans went into the locker room with a 33-31 lead and the pace was never the same.

From the opening tip-off in the second half, Hannibal's fast-break offense was at full throttle. No longer on the leading edge of the score, East Central was forced to drop its strategy of patience. The Warriors were ill-equipped for the game's new rhythm. Led by Danny Dotson and Bob Ebker — who led all scorers with 21 and 20, respectively — Hannibal-LaGrange ran away from the pre-tourney favorite, winning 82-65.

The other Wednesday quarterfinal was equally uneven, going from basket-trading to blow-out. Phoenix kept the game close for most of the first half. Then, the Arkansas City Tigers leaped to a nine-point halftime lead. By game's end, Phoenix was in ashes by 22. Despite the satisfying win for the Kansans, the crowd remained relatively subdued. Arkansas City had looked much better than in its first outing, but everyone knew the Tigers needed a lot more improvement if they were going to beat their next opponent — Hannibal-LaGrange.

THURSDAY — DESTINY LOOMS

The sports headline for the Thursday evening *News-Herald* read: "Two Missouri Teams Loom As Tournament Favorites." The distinct possibility affected the tournament's hump-day turn-out at the Sports Arena. Only 2,800 fans showed to see the remaining quarterfinals. Those who stayed away were fortunate. They were saved the frustration of watching a maddeningly dull feature between Moberly and Coffeyville.

The underdog Red Ravens immediately employed a tight zone defense to slow down Moberly's attack. Unperturbed by the stratagem, the Greyhounds ignored the fenced up middle, firing with abandon from outside. Moberly quickly mounted a 10-point advantage.

Late in the first half, tired of fighting the zone, the Greyhounds decided to hold the ball at midcourt. Coffeyville failed to respond, pulling its defense in even tighter. Though down by a large margin, the Red Ravens appeared content to lose, just as long as it was not by 45 points.

Boos hailed the court. Galling periods of inaction occupied most of the game's remainder. By the time Moberly finally secured an easy 79-56 victory, the crowd was thoroughly irritated.

Those with an eye to the future, however, noted that the Missouri squad again demonstrated superb balance. Four players hit double figures — Red Murrell (19), Dan Sonnenberg (17), Bill Wynn (17), and Dan Callahan (12). Though handicapped with another cold shooting night, Jim Carey executed splendid floor play, orchestrating the Greyhounds keep-away tactics. It appeared only a miracle would stop Moberly from having another try at the title.

Two teams desperately wanted a shot at that unlikely occurrence. Consequently, the quarterfinal match between New York and Eveleth — the largest (2,500 students) and the smallest (80) schools, respectively, in the tournament — was the best. Like its predecessor, the contest featured more evasion than aggression. However, the heated ending made up for all the evening's cold inactivity.

Except for the early stages of the game, the advantage remained on the side of Eveleth. The Minnesotans built a 10-point lead at halftime and maintained the margin in the second period.

Then, with seven minutes remaining, New York's Fred Henderson and Gil Friedman started finding the range. By the 3:25 mark, the Bees had rallied to the fore, 45-44. Hal Hellerman, New York's big post, took over scoring duties with a field goal and three free throws, putting the Bees comfortably in front, 50-46, with time running out.

Eveleth's Jim Intihar cut the margin in half with a do-or-die 20-footer with 33 seconds to go.

At the 21-second mark, Intihar was fouled. He sank the first free throw, missed the second. However, the rebound deflected away right into Intihar's waiting hands at the free throw line.

He jumped and scored, putting Eveleth back on top with 19 seconds remaining.

New York scrambled to the other end of the court. A last ditch shot was tried.

It missed.

The rebound was tipped back up.

It missed

Two more tips.

Two more misses.

The buzzer sounded.

It had taken Intihar over 15 minutes to score his first eight points. His last five required less than 15 seconds, earning the Eveleth Tigers the right to face Moberly in the semifinals.

FRIDAY — COLLISION COURSE

The dominance of Hannibal-LaGrange and Moberly and their destined confrontation for the championship clearly influenced Friday attendance. Only the semifinals interested fans. Afternoon consolation contests were wholeheartedly ignored by the public, disappointing tourney officials. In contrast, a respectable crowd of 4,000 showed up for the evening session.

The two Missouri schools were on a collision course. Based on recent history, however, regular patrons had come to expect the unexpected. Derailments were definite possibilities when glory was the goal just around the bend. No team knew this better than Hannibal-LaGrange. For the past three years, the Trojans had been on the inside track for a shot at the crown only to be upset at the last moment.

Hannibal's semifinal jinx was paramount in the minds of the fans as the evening opener tipped off. Determined to disprove the hex, the Trojans immediately took the lead and built it to 10. The unspectacular Arkansas City Tigers called time to regroup, then scraped and clawed their way back. By halftime, Hannibal held only a four-point advantage, 42-38. Uncertainty hung in the air.

Doubt increased in the second half. Arkansas City continued to rally, tying the score at 56-all, taking the lead on a Tony Rendulich free throw, then trading baskets with Hannibal for five minutes. With 7:44 on the clock, Arkansas City held the edge, 63-62.

At that point, the Trojans took the reins of destiny firmly in hand. Bob Ebker hit an open lay-up followed by three free throws, Danny Doston added a field goal and two charities, and Lee Godsey connected on a jumper. Arkansas City was unable to counter. Hannibal-LaGrange was comfortably in front, 73-63, with 2½ minutes remaining. The jinx was broken.

The standout again for the Trojans was Dotson, son of a Leadwood, Missouri, mine safety inspector. Besides taking game honors with 32, Dotson spearheaded the Hannibal defense with brilliant thefts and helped insure the Trojan victory with a fancy dribbling exhibition to close out the contest. He and his Hannibal teammates were obviously primed for a title showdown with Moberly.

Of course, another group of Tigers had a say in whether that eventuality would take place. The only two Eveleth loses during the year had come at the hands of the University of Manitoba, a four-year school in Winnipeg, Canada. No junior college had cracked the Tigers' stout defense.

Moberly quickly made light of the issue, splurging to a substantial 13-point lead.

The Minnesotans were not intimidated. Though outnumbered by the aggressive Moberly front line, Tiger pivotman Tony Krall domineered the backboards at both ends of the court. When the Greyhounds became erratic in their shooting, Eveleth crept back into contention. By halftime, the margin was cut to six. With 13:25 to go, Jim Intihar canned a field goal to eliminate the difference completely, tying the score, 41-all.

Moments later, reserve Tom Flom tossed in a free throw, giving Eveleth the lead.

Moberly's Bill Wynn countered twice from the opposite charity stripe.

Then disaster struck. Though Krall had been successful pounding the boards, the Tiger post had also hammered the Greyhounds. Krall picked up his fifth foul with a full 12 minutes remaining. The loss left a large void in Eveleth's lineup.

Bill Wynn took advantage of the hole, scoring the next nine Moberly points. After Dan Sonnenberg added a free throw, Wynn then reeled off four more tallies. Moberly surged ahead, 57-50.

Their composure regained, the Greyhounds settled into a semi-stall for the last five minutes and increased their lead. At the 1:52 mark, Moberly was safely in front, 60-50. Don Suomi and Intihar hit desperate 24-footers to inspire a last minute Eveleth charge, but time ran out before real damage could be inflicted.

The ideal tug-of-war between two stubborn Missouri mules was to be.

SATURDAY — THE HAVES VS. THE HAVE-NOTS

The impending battle between Moberly and Hannibal-LaGrange was the foremost topic of discussion on the streets of Hutchinson and had been all week. Anyone not already stimulated by the prospect became so after watching three rousing games prior to the finale.

In the opener, Boise dictated the tempo from the outset, using a methodical passing attack, patiently working around Tyler's defensive perimeter, setting up sure shots. For 30 of the game's 40 minutes, the Broncos maintained full control of the basketball. Consequently, Tyler's offense never had the chance to shift into gear. The Apaches' Russell Boone and Milton Williams — two of the top scorers in the tournament — managed only 16 and 12 points, respectively. Boise took fifth place, holding high-powered Tyler to a mere 54 points.

The stall had been an often used — and much maligned — tactic in the 1955 tournament. But, in no game did it generate excitement like it did in the fourth-place contest between Coffeyville and East Central.

With two minutes to go and the score tied, 71-all, the Warriors decided to hold for one final shot, pulling the ball to midcourt. As in its game with Moberly, Coffeyville refused to abandon its drawn in defense. Play was frozen.

After a time out with 10 seconds left, East Central maneuvered for the game-winner. The Warriors got off a shot at the free throw line just as time expired, but the attempt missed.

The two teams traded a pair of points in overtime before events repeated themselves. East Central snatched a rebound and slowly brought the ball upcourt, halting just beyond the midcourt line. Action stopped as the Warriors held the ball, no one moving until the closing seconds. Again East Central fired a jumper from the free throw line just as time ran out. And again the attempt missed.

The crowd was restless as the tip for the second overtime launched skyward. The Mississippi team controlled the loose ball, pulled up short, and, to no one's surprise, held fast. Coffeyville was equally persistent. The Red Ravens refused to pressure the Warriors. For four minutes and 46 seconds the only action in the Sports Arena was in the stands where fans stood and booed.

As the clock wound down to its final ticks, East Central set up a third last chance goal. With two seconds remaining, reserve Leo Russell lofted a shot from the side. The ball parted the net at the buzzer, ending the crowd's frustration.

The third-place contest was more to fan liking. Playing its best basketball of the tournament, Arkansas City set a furious pace out of the blocks. Eveleth matched points for 15 minutes. Then, the slower, more deliberate Minnesotans petered out. The Kansans took an 11-point lead into the locker room at half and built on it once play resumed. By game's end Arkansas City had run away with victory, 94-69.

The time had finally come.

Few people questioned who the two best teams were after first-round play. Attendance was down partly due to that conviction. But, basketball aficionados were out in force for the championship. The assemblage of skilled players on the court was enough to make any sports fiend salivate. Five thousand eager fans filed into the Sports Arena for one reason, though: to watch a dog fight.

Hannibal-LaGrange and Moberly were bitter rivals, top dogs competing for territorial rights on the same block; only 66 miles separated Hannibal from Moberly. Though their closeness was sufficient reason for a long-standing feud, developments in cent years had fueled the conflict to epic proportions.

In 1952, Hannibal-LaGrange emerged as a prime force in Missouri basketball, winning both state and regional titles, usurping Moberly's previous mantle of superiority.

Being second-best did not set well with Moberly tradition. At the NJCAA meetings during tournament week that year, Coach Maury John insured against the incident's recurrence. Using his considerable influence in junior college politics, he asked that the Missouri region be restructured, sliced in two. The greater portion of the pie went to Region 16 which again became Moberly's private domain. Hannibal was relegated to Region 2 where it would compete with teams from Illinois and distant Kentucky. The implied slight deepened animosity between schools.

Despite the fact the two teams were evenly matched — Moberly and Hannibal-LaGrange had split during the year, Moberly winning at Moberly, 60-57, and Hannibal at Hannibal, 9-85 — the 1955 title tilt took on the aura of the teams' historical backdrop. The nouveau riche was trying to supplant the old guard; the haves were holding off the have-nots. This classic struggle resulted in one of the greatest championship games in tournament history.

True to the script, Moberly immediately took charge, keeping the upstart Trojans at arm's length. The Greyhounds maintained four- or five-point margin over the first 20 minutes, taking a 9-24 lead into the locker room.

Hannibal succeeded in closing the gap in the first five minutes of the second frame, tying the game at 36-all. But, three consecutive free throws by Bill Wynn again gave the Greyhounds breathing room.

The contest resembled a chess match played with live pieces. Fouls became a problem. Key players on both sides — Jim Carey, Red Murrell, and Wynn for Moberly and Danny Dotson, Bob Ebker, and Lee Godsey for Hannibal — were in danger of elimination. Moberly's Coach John and Hannibal's Howard Dewell entered tactics, shifting personnel. For 35 minutes, John's Greyhounds held the upper hand. The best Hannibal could manage was to stay within striking distance.

Then, the Trojans struck in earnest. Two buckets by Al Dunbar and a hook by Ebker put Hannibal on top for the first time with 3:59 to go.

The final minutes of battle took place at the free throw line. First, Ebker fouled Dan Sonnenberg. The Moberly pivotman had been coolly consistent all through the tournament and remained so with the championship on the line, swishing two free throws, giving Moberly a 53-52 advantage.

Sonnenberg was equally charitable at the other end of the floor, bumping Hannibal's Godsey as the Trojan forward drove for the basket. Godsey missed his first attempt, then tied the score with his second.

With 1:19 left, Moberly froze the ball for one shot. As the clock moved inside the 30-second mark, the Greyhounds maneuvered for the game breaker. The try was errant. Moberly's Murrell grabbed the rebound, spotted Carey streaking for the basket, and made a perfect pass. The bucket was off, but Carey was hacked.

Eighteen seconds remained when Jim Carey stepped to the line. The sparkplug guard had experienced a miserable tournament. Two free throws meant retribution and very likely another Moberly title. Nerves knotted his stomach.

He missed both chances.

Hannibal raced down the court, but failed to score. For the second year in a row, extra time was required to decide the championship.

The new start rejuvenated Hannibal. The Trojans quickly took the lead and held it. With 1:17 to go in the overtime, Hannibal was on top, 60-56. The Arena crowd, which had supported the "have-not" Trojans throughout, sensed victory was at hand. Even a field goal by Moberly's Wynn, cutting the lead in half, failed to diminish the rising elation along the sidelines. There was good reason. The Trojans were going to dribble off the last seconds. Handling the chore was Dotson — a superb ball handler and the tournament's eventual MVP.

Tourney MVP and leading scorer (103 points), Hannibal's Dan Dotson later played at the University of Houston. (Photo courtesy of Howard Dewell)

Thirty-four seconds remained as Dotson confidently moved the ball upcourt. As he crossed the center line, reserve Joe Barksdale met him head on. Dotson turned to protect the ball and was immediately pinched from the opposite side by Wynn. Wynn batted the ball away on the bounce, roared to the opposite end just in front of his pursuit, and banked the ball off the glass and in, tumbling into the goal support in the process.

There were still nearly 30 seconds left, plenty of time for Hannibal. Wynn slowly regained his feet. The prime candidate for the Trojans' final shot was Dotson, Wynn's man.[4]

As time ticked off Dotson, indeed, took possession of the ball. He drove deep in the corner and forced a shot over Wynn. The ball rimmed out. Moberly grabbed the rebound and an additional five minutes of play.

Wynn's stirring announcement that Moberly was not yet ready to abdicate the crown left the Arena limp. Hannibal, too, was sapped. When Sonnenberg drove in for a close bank shot after the opening tip, it signaled a cloudburst of Moberly points. In the next two minutes, Wynn, Murrell, and Callahan hit jumpers. During the same period, Hannibal netted neither points nor rebounds. The Trojans simply folded. The final stanza was an 11-4 rout.

Moberly Junior College accomplished the unprecedented, winning back-to-back national titles.

THE AFTERMATH — THE WHEELBARROW RIDE

The intensity of the Missouri shoot-out was felt far beyond the confines of the Sports Arena. Pfc. Donald Ray Schaffer, a paratrooper stationed at Fort Campbell, Kentucky, was so anxious to know how his hometown school had done he called his parents in Moberly. Seven minutes remained in regulation when his parents answered. They placed the receiver by the radio and the young serviceman stayed on the line for 35 minutes until the game's climax.

St. Louis was beyond the range of the Moberly radio broadcast. Hence, a nervous Mrs. Ray Bayens, Sr. — mother of one of the Greyhound reserves — decided to telephone the *Hutchinson News-Herald*. Because of the game's added length, it required three phone calls before her anxiety was relieved. On hearing the final result, Mrs. Bayens told the reporter on the other end of the line, "If I were there, I'd kiss you."

Her reaction was typical. At the conclusion of the game, 200 adoring Moberly fans rushed onto the Arena floor, pouring hugs

---

[4]Wynn later confessed that, when he realized he would not be able to get back on defense to prevent a Hannibal fast break, he resorted to playacting: "I just stayed there. The referee thought I was hurt and whistled an official time-out. And that gave me time to get my breath and we had a chance to set up a full defense."

and kisses of adulation on the victors. Tears were plentiful. Team Manager Rick Thornburg sobbed into a towel which he had used only moments before to dry the sweaty faces of the Moberly players.

Among the well-wishers, none was happier than Mrs. W.M. Wynn who had traveled all night Friday on a 12-hour bus ride from Salem, Missouri, just to see her son in the championship game. The tears of joy streaming down her face were the best reward a hero could receive.

The approbation the citizens of Moberly showed the team exceeded that given the champions the year before. Like the previous year, fans drove to meet the returning Greyhounds. But, this time the motorcade formed at Brunswick, 35 miles west of Moberly. At Clifton Hill, 12 miles west, the players were transferred to convertibles. An impromptu parade eight-miles long was already in progress by the time the procession entered the city.

The highlight of the celebration came just before the parade's end. Saturday afternoon, Mayor John R. Schroder of Hannibal had wired Moberly Mayor Earl B. Noel with the following challenge: "If by chance the Greyhounds win tonight's game, I will come to Moberly, at the date designated by you, and push you in a wheelbarrow on level ground, one yard for each point your team scores, provided you will come to Hannibal and do likewise when notified of the Hannibal-LaGrange Trojan victory." Dressed in hat and topcoat, legs dangling, a broad smile on his face, Mayor Noel traveled the last 71 yards to the victory observance at the Municipal Auditorium in a wheelbarrow pushed by Mayor Schroder.

As the *Moberly Monitor-Index and Democrat* later concluded, given such magnificent local support "the Greyhounds might 'make a habit' of winning the national championship."

* * *

Two years of declining attendance was enough for tournament sponsors. The NJCAA took action to curtail the trend.

First, no longer placing credence in west coast assurance that their schools would soon be returning to national competition, the NJCAA restructured its western region even further. Where the year before it had lumped the three west coast states into Region 4, it now added more. In 1956, Region 4 would also include Nevada and half of Wyoming — a total area encompassing virtually all of the western United States.

Second, rescheduling the tournament two weeks earlier — a move initiated two years before primarily at the insistence of west coast teams — had placed the event in direct competition with Kansas high school regional tournaments and the NAIA tournament in Kansas City. The NJCAA eliminated the conflict moving the 1956 tournament to its previous dates, just after Kansas state high school championship play.

Finally, the NJCAA changed its policy for filling vacancies in the tournament bracket.[5] As Hibbing Junior College Coach Joe Milinovich, Region 13 representative at the NJCAA meetings put it, "I . . . can't see why it should be necessary to import an 'alternate' team from many miles away when a good alternate is right in the host city." Hutchinson Junior College was, therefore, awarded the first invitation if needed in the 1956 tournament. The action recognized the city's devoted support for the past seven years. Milinovich summed up the feelings of all by stating, "I marvel at the attendance here when Hutchinson hasn't had a tournament entry since 1949. These fans are real basketball fans."

Tournament Results

Day		Game		
Tuesday:	Game	1	East Central — 52 Jacksonville — 46
		2	New York City — 79 Pueblo — 73
		3	Eveleth — 61 Graceland — 59 20T
		4	Phoenix — 60 Joliet — 51
		5	Hannibal-LaGrange — 100 Tyler — 86
		6	Arkansas City — 58 McCook — 54
Wednesday:	Game	7	Moberly — 111 Howard County — 66
		8	Coffeyville — 78 Boise — 70
		9	Tyler — 87 Jacksonville — 76
		10	Hannibal-LaGrange — 82 East Central — 65
		11	Arkansas City — 76 Phoenix — 54
Thursday:	Game	12	McCook — 73 Joliet — 61
		13	Boise — 70 Howard County — 63
		14	East Central — 61 Phoenix — 51
		15	Pueblo — 67 Graceland — 57
		16	Moberly — 76 Coffeyville — 59
		17	Eveleth — 51 New York City — 50
Friday:	Game	18	Tyler — 99 McCook — 90
		19	Boise — 74 Pueblo — 61
		20	Coffeyville — 90 New York City — 69
		21	Hannibal-LaGrange — 77 Arkansas City — 69
		22	Moberly — 61 Eveleth — 57
Saturday:	Game	23	Boise — 60 Tyler — 54
		24	East Central — 75 Coffeyville — 73 20T
		25	Arkansas City — 94 Eveleth — 69
		26	Moberly — 71 Hannibal-LaGrange — 64 20T

How They Finished in 1955

1. Moberly Junior College
2. Hannibal-LaGrange College
3. Arkansas City Junior College
4. East Central Junior College
5. Boise Junior College
6. Eveleth Junior College
7. Coffeyville College of Arts, Science, and Vocations
8. Tyler Junior College

All-Tournament Team

Russell Boone — Tyler Junior College
Dan Dotson — Hannibal-LaGrange College
Bob Ebker — Hannibal-LaGrange College
Jim Intihar — Eveleth Junior College
Don Moore — Boise Junior College
Phillip "Red" Murrell — Moberly Junior College
Tony Rendulich — Arkansas City Junior College
Bill Tipton — Coffeyville College of Arts, Science, and Vocations
Milton Williams — Tyler Junior College
Bill Wynn — Moberly Junior College

Player of the Year

Dan Dotson — Hannibal-LaGrange College

---

[5] Only one invitation was required in 1955. McCook Junior College received the nod when neither of the two top teams in Region 10 (West Virginia, Virginia, North Carolina, and South Carolina) could afford the trip to Hutchinson.

1956:

AN "ENTERTAINING" EVENT

The 1956 season was one of steadily increasing excitement for Blue Dragon fans. The current Hutchinson Junior College team was the best the school had yet fielded. The squad averaged over 80 points a game, twice cracking the 100-point barrier, and was a top contender in the West Juco Conference. At one point in the year, Hutchinson was even ranked 16th nationally. It was possible the local squad might finally win its way into the national tournament. Should the Blue Dragons falter along the way, though, they had the added assurance of an invitation should a bracket vacancy occur. Since all 16 regions had been represented only once in the tournament's eight-year history, a berth in the NJCAA Basketball Tournament appeared inevitable.

Fan optimism diminished the day before Region 6 play began. The *Hutchinson News-Herald* announced that Blue Dragon starting guard Billy Arnold had broken his foot in practice. Despite the loss, Hutchinson won its first-round game, easily downing Pratt Junior College, 79-67. Hopes surged as the Blue Dragons were victorious in their semifinal match against Dodge City College, 91-81. Then, fan ardor hit the ceiling. In the companion semifinal, Garden City Junior College — an up-and-down team with a losing record in conference play — overcame an early 30-15 deficit to upset Arkansas City Junior College, the No. 1 team in the country, 71-64.

With a sure berth in the nationals for sale at a bargain price, the Blue Dragons took the court for the regional final, full of confidence — and promptly misjudged the cost. After racing to a commanding 51-35 halftime lead, Garden City gallantly held on to eke out a 78-74 win.

Though a golden opportunity had been squandered, Hutchinson still had the NJCAA's invitation insurance policy. That, too, proved nonbankable. For the first time since 1950, all regions sent a representative to the national tournament.

The Juco Tournament's downward attendance trend would have to be reversed without the draw of the hometown school.

THE PARTICIPANTS

Region	Team
1	Eastern Arizona Junior College — Thatcher, Arizona
2	Hannibal-LaGrange College — Hannibal, Missouri
3	Coffeyville College of Arts, Science, and Vocations — Coffeyville, Kansas
4	Boise Junior College — Boise, Idaho
5	Cameron State Agricultural College — Lawton, Oklahoma
6	Garden City Junior College — Garden City, Kansas
7	Arkansas State College, Beebe Branch — Beebe, Arkansas
8	Jacksonville Junior College — Jacksonville, Florida
9	Pueblo Junior College — Pueblo, Colorado
10	North Greenville Junior College — Tigerville, South Carolina
11	Graceland College — Lamoni, Iowa
12	Chicago City Junior College, Wright Branch — Chicago, Illinois
13	Itasca Junior College — Coleraine, Minnesota
14	Kilgore College — Kilgore, Texas
15	New York City Community College — Brooklyn, New York
16	Moberly Junior College — Moberly, Missouri

*Prior to attending Hannibal-LaGrange, Art Day had been a **Picture Week** magazine first-team All-American his senior year at Chicago's John Marshall High School. He played for Hannibal one year then transferred to the University of San Francisco, following Bill Russell as the Dons starting center. (Photo courtesy of Howard Dewell, photo taken by Don W. Sigler Studio, Hannibal, MO)*

In 1956, the NJCAA Service Bureau — a large, network-sized sounding organization consisting of one person, Compton College's Goldie Holmes — distributed weekly ratings of junior college teams to newspapers and wire services around the country. The inaugural "coaches' poll" gave fans exposure to the progress of top teams in the nation throughout the season. Since intersectional play was still uncommon, valid comparisons between regions were limited, making the rankings arbitrary at best. When it came to selecting the favored team in the ninth annual National Juco Tournament, however, a scientific poll was not required.

Hannibal-LaGrange College was ranked in the top three all year, finishing in the No. 2 slot. The Trojans compiled a record of 31 wins — the most for any tourney participant — against only four losses. It was the fifth consecutive appearance for the Missouri school. A showcase full of trophies — three third-place and one second — was testimony to Hannibal's consistent strive for excellence.

The current Trojan team was the best to date. According to the *News-Herald*, Hannibal was "big, talented, fast, and sharp." Four squad members were over 6-5, the tallest, 6-9 freshman center Art Day. Combining superior quickness and agility with towering height, Day was an imposing court presence, epitomizing the team's power.

In the final Region 2 play-off game, Hannibal-LaGrange demolished Centralia (Illinois) Junior College, 133-87. The Trojans were primed for a national championship.

"It was really bitter to lose to them," said Coach Howard Dewell about Hannibal's taking second-place to Moberly the year before. "Losing to anybody in the United States wouldn't have been nearly as bad as losing to a team 50 miles away. We went into it [the 1956 tournament] with the idea, 'By golly! We were slapped down last year. There's no question we're the best now. We're going to walk through this thing like we own it.'"

The second choice for "team to beat" proved the NJCAA coaches' poll was not taken seriously. Seven tournament teams outranked Kilgore College (23-5). During the season, the Rangers suffered a humiliating 88-71 loss to archrival Tyler Junior College — generally considered the best in the region — before avenging the defeat, 85-81, at home, and gaining a share of the Longhorn Junior College Conference title. The conference co-champs were expected to meet in an old-fashioned Texas shoot-out for the Region 14 crown at Tyler, but the Apaches were ambushed by Lon Morris, 96-93, in a run-and-gun semifinal contest. In the finale, Kilgore played its finest game of the year, using an air-tight defense to shut down the running Bearcats convincingly, 81-63. Though the No. 14 Rangers were making their first trip to Hutchinson, tourney veterans were playing the odds. Any team able to survive the cutthroat competition of East Texas, the "region of champions," had to be good.

Hannibal-LaGrange and Kilgore — the two tallest teams in the meet — literally stood head and shoulders above the competition. As far as media pre-tourney prognostications were concerned, all other contenders were categorized as only "possible challengers" or simply discounted.

Leading the list of teams to watch was the defending two-time national champ, Moberly Junior College. Unlike the previous year when the champion Greyhounds were overlooked by the press as possible repeaters, this year's assessment appeared correct. Moberly's 18-8 record was mediocre compared to the school's previous standards. A mid-season bout with illness was given as a reason for the team's unimposing credentials, but a more likely explanation was the ballclub's lack of height. With only one starter — guard Dan Callahan — returning from the 1955 champion squad, Moberly was simply not as potent. Still, the Greyhounds could not be slighted; with Maury John — one of the best coaches in junior college basketball — masterminding the way, 12th-ranked Moberly was making an unparalleled sixth consecutive trip to the nationals. Since the Greyhounds already owned a win over tourney favorite Hannibal-LaGrange, a third title was not impossible.

Three other returnees from 1955 also warranted watching.

On paper, No. 7 Jacksonville Junior College (21-2) looked best, since its big front line remained intact from the previous year. The Dolphins were second in scoring in the nation with a 98.9 points-per-game average and possessed the highest individual scorer in the tournament, center Chuck Brendler (27.4).

Next in line was Pueblo Junior College (19-5) which had steadily improved during the year, finishing No. 13 in the NJCAA poll. Three starters returned from Pueblo's 1955 tourney team.

The last of the group was 10th-rated Boise Junior College which had finished fifth the year before, the highest placing of a returning team outside of Moberly and Hannibal-LaGrange. However, with only two starters from the 1955 squad and an unimpressive 18-8 record, Boise did not appear as strong.

According to the press, the only other tourney participant with potential was newcomer, No. 6 Itasca Junior College (18-3). Itasca's contender status was bolstered by the fact that the school came from the headwaters of the Mississippi River in northern Minnesota, the same area which produced 1952 runner-up Hibbing Junior College.

Among those disregarded for title contention were three clubs with excellent records and high ratings: No. 4 Wright of Chicago — which owned a 23-1 record, the best in the 16-team field — was omitted from consideration because it was a tourney newcomer, representing a region with an inconsistent track record; No. 8 New York City Community College (22-3) had flashed similar credentials before and was 2-4 against national competition to show for it; and, despite No. 17 Eastern Arizona Junior College's impressive 23-3 record, a team from a region with only one other school could not be taken seriously.[1]

The NJCAA coaches' poll was particularly suspect when it tried to rate more than 20 teams. Two teams sporting exceptional records received poor ratings: newcomer North Greenville Junior College (25-4) and veteran Graceland College (24-5) were rated 24th and 28th, respectively. Since Cameron State (19-6) of Lawton, Oklahoma, had not even won its region,[2] it appeared to have been ranked 31st as an afterthought. The poll lost total credibility, however, when it rated Coffeyville College — a team with a losing record (11-12) — as the 39th best in the country.

The poll *did* appear correct in one respect: the teams it failed to rank. Garden City Junior College (14-9) and Arkansas State College of Beebe (10-13) were definite underdogs.

With two solid front runners and both Kansas schools clearly outclassed by the competition, circumstances were not auspicious for attracting a good gate to the 1956 Juco Tournament.

TUESDAY — THE QUEEN AND HER COURT

The chances for another repeat championship for Moberly were seriously hurt just before the regional tournament when the Greyhounds lost 6-7 Richard Harvey, the tallest player on the team, due to scholastic ineligibility. Then, prior to the kick off of the 1956 Juco Tournament, those chances diminished further when two more Greyhounds were left home with academic problems. Fortunately, starter Al Morton and reserve C.L. Henke were able to rectify their scholastic standing — a matter of making up missed school work — and rejoined the team in time for the opener.

After trailing Eastern Arizona, 39-37, at halftime, Moberly crashed the boards with bullish 6-3 center Dave Rashcke and the nearly ineligible Morton, an agile 6-1 leaper, dominating the middle. Morton's game-high 32, including 11 straight free throws, led the Greyhounds to an 80-67 victory, their ninth consecutive in tourney play.

Though nine of their losses were against four-year schools, the Minutemen from Beebe, Arkansas, were not a national caliber team. Two second-half Minuteman rallies were all that entertained the crowd in the lopsided afternoon feature as Arkansas State-Beebe fell to Boise, 70-57. Top point producer for Boise was 6-6 center, Nick Panico, who tallied 17 of his game-high 25 in the first half. The star of the game, however,

[1] The NJCAA's California problem forced continuous experimentation in regional structuring in the sparsely populated West. Consequently, from 1954 to 1956, Phoenix College and Eastern Arizona were fortunate to have a region all their own.

[2] The top team in Region 5 was Amarillo College which beat Cameron State, 72-68, in the final. Amarillo forfeited the regional championship when one of its star players, Charles Brown, was discovered to be ineligible. According to former Amarillo Coach Bob Carter, prior to coming to Amarillo Brown attended the University of San Francisco for one semester, enrolled a second semester, but then withdrew before attending classes. One professor, however, kept him on his roll. Brown received three hours of "B" without attending a class. The additional hours made Brown ineligible under the NJCAA's transfer rule and kept the 11th-ranked Badgers from coming to Hutchinson.

Ironically, had Amarillo not been honest and volunteered the information to the NJCAA, the incident would probably have gone unnoticed. Because it had no permanent staff, the NJCAA was lax in policing its eligibility rules. To illustrate the point, Moberly's Dan Callahan and Jacksonville's Chuck Brendler both had attended four-year schools prior to junior college. Callahan briefly attended the University of Detroit while Brendler went to the University of Wisconsin for a year on a basketball scholarship. Though not aware of it, neither was technically eligible to participate in the 1956 tournament. The additional enrollments later cost Callahan a semester and Brendler a year of eligibility at Drake University and the University of Florida, respectively.

was the Broncos' Don Moore, a 5-10 bespectacled guard who scored several critical baskets and sparkled with steals and assists, before fouling out with 22 points.

In the final afternoon contest, Coffeyville's seven-game win streak was in serious jeopardy, since four of Graceland's starters were taller than the Red Ravens' tallest man — 6-2 Jack Haskins. But, as the *Coffeyville Journal* quoted first-year coach Jack Hartman: "We aren't too much worried about Graceland's height and we aren't much worried about being overconfident. With one or two exceptions, we have been the shortest team on the court all season. And no team has to worry about being overconfident after losing its first six games like we did this year."[3]

Coffeyville stayed close to Graceland and even held the lead through most of the second half. But with 1:40 remaining and down by one, Coffeyville's lack of height finally hurt. Two quick buckets by 6-4 Gary Hannaman and a tip-in by 6-3 Dick Gilberts wrapped up a Graceland closing rally which downed the Red Ravens, 64-59.

The day before, it had taken only 73 minutes to arrest the man who stole $3,000 from the Citizens State Bank of Cheney, Kansas. The quick success was due to an elaborate system of roadblocks set up by the Kansas State Highway Patrol to locate the robber's blue and white Chevy station wagon. Mrs. Joe Turner, wife of Kilgore's coach, and a traveling companion were stopped twice by the roadblocks, the first time by shotgun brandishing police. The reason: the two were driving a blue and white Chevy station wagon.

The Kilgore Rangers felt their chance for a national title was also roadblocked when Jacksonville scored the first six points of the evening opener. In the first eight minutes, the Dolphins hit 70 percent of their shots while Kilgore bounced the ball off the backboard.

Then, the Rangers clicked into their offensive groove. By halftime, Kilgore led, 41-38. In the second half, the margin expanded to 12. At the 10-minute mark, Coach Joe Turner ordered the Rangers to slow the game down.

Kilgore relaxed. Jacksonville heated up. With 3:44 to go, the Dolphins were within one, 64-63.

Baby-faced sophomore guard Ted Whillock took over for Kilgore, scoring the next four points on a field goal and two free throws.

Jacksonville closed, outscoring the Rangers 4-1 in free shots through the last minute-and-a-half. With five seconds remaining, the Dolphins' big burly center, Chuck Brendler, launched a last-ditch uncontested 20-foot hook which connected, giving Brendler top honors with 24 points. Victory, however, went to Kilgore, 70-69.

The other pre-tourney favorite had an easier time of it. After Garden City missed its first seven shots, Hannibal-LaGrange coasted, winning 95-71. Although the Trojans' Al Dunbar — a wiry, driving guard — topped all scorers with 22, it was Art Day who received the crowd's accolades. Playing little more than half the game, the big center effortlessly tallied 17 while dominating the boards. He was everything the media had publicized.

During the year, each NJCAA member school nominated a student judged to be "the prettiest junior college girl in America." Pictures of the nominees were then given to Naval Aviation cadets at the Hutchinson Naval Air Station south of the city for final selection. The winner was Elaine Cortez, a native Puerto Rican whose father owned a delicatessen and grocery in Manhattan. The 19-year old freshman at New York City Community College was crowned "Queen of the NJCAA Basketball Tournament" by an honor guard of Naval cadets just prior to the opening-day finale. Queen Cortez then watched her court jesters entertain.

The 1956 edition of the New York City Bees was every bit as colorful as previous teams. Using a style of play similar to the Harlem Globetrotters, the New Yorkers dazzled the crowd. Guard Furney Pressley and center Bernie Tiebout put on a shooting clinic, hitting 16 and 15, respectively, for the first half. New York built a 43-32 lead over Itasca by halftime, then pushed the lead to 16 early in the second period.

Elaine Cortez told the **Hutchinson News-Herald,** "The coming week promises to be one that I shall never forget," but also added, "I have never liked contests of any sort." Evidently no one else did either. Cortez was the only "Queen of the NJCAA Basketball Tournament." (Photo courtesy of the NJCAA)

Then the cold, blizzard conditions, which crippled their home state and had earlier delayed the queen's arrival in Hutchinson, hit the New Yorkers. The Itasca Vikings stormed the Bees, 20-6, closing to within two with 6:35 to go.

The Brooklyn team pulled out of the slump, only to have the Minnesotans rally again. With 1:42 remaining, the New York lead slipped to a single, icy digit, 69-68.

The Bees froze the ball until Richard Cananza broke behind the defense for an easy two. Then, Bob Keller tipped in a bucket. Finally, Pressley iced the game with four free throws. New York survived the cold, 77-71.

WEDNESDAY — LOOKING FOR TALENT

The best conclusion to a first-round game came in Wednesday afternoon's curtain raiser. After Eugene Poston, Pueblo's leading scorer (26.9), fouled out with seven minutes to play, North Greenville staged an inspired rally. Behind the outside shooting of Willard Fowler and the driving lay-ups of Harvard Riddle, the Mountaineers erased a 10-point Pueblo lead, pulling even at 84-all with 22 seconds to go.

Then, with one second on the clock, Pueblo freshman forward Dale Allen was fouled and calmly sank two free throws.

The Carolinians were able to get the ball inbounds to Riddle for a desperation half-court heave, but, though the 5-11 guard had already connected for 30 points, the tournament's second-highest total, he was unable to add a miracle. The ball bounded away as the gun sounded.

The final first-round game unveiled another contender for the title. As the *News-Herald* put it, previously unpublicized Cameron State displayed "a tight defense, a sharp group of shooters, and a methodical attack that manufactured points in a steady stream." The Aggies overpowered Wright of Chicago, 91-71. With the poor showing by the Kansas contingents, local fans found something to cheer about in the Aggies as Cameron forward Fran Siebuhr, an all-state performer from Topeka, topped all scorers with 24.

Earlier in the month, former tourney star Darrell Floyd, now at Furman, was named first-team All-American. His success, plus that of several other former Juco Tournament stars, prompted an influx of coaches to the tournament. One in par-

---

[3]Coffeyville's early season schedule was a nightmarish greeting for a rookie coach. Hartman's indoctrination included losses to the Pittsburg State "B" team (twice), Arkansas City (ranked No. 1 in the country), Hutchinson (in the unfriendly confines of the Sports Arena), and the Tulsa freshmen. The Red Ravens finally broke out of the slump with a win over Joplin, a team which had previously dispatched Coffeyville, 97-65. Even then, winning did not come easy. The final: Coffeyville — 90, Joplin — 89 — in overtime.

ticular caught the crowd's eye — Halstead, Kansas, native Adolf Rupp, the most prominent figure in collegiate coaching. His reason for attending the tournament was easily explained: "After our luck with [Bob] Burrow [former star with Lon Morris] I've got to say that my interest in junior college boys has improved tremendously."

Coaches from Maryland, Idaho, UCLA, Houston, Georgia Tech, Miami, Tulane, Bradley, and others, were treated to a thriller in the first quarterfinal contest. Moberly's nine-game tournament win streak was put to the test as Boise overcame a six-point halftime deficit to take a 43-36 lead with 10 minutes to go.

Moberly bounced back behind the shooting of veteran Dan Callahan, tying the game, 46-all, just before Callahan fouled out with two minutes remaining. The Greyhounds regained the lead at the 40-second mark on the second of two free shots by Dave Raschke.

Unperturbed, forward Ron Fitzgerald coolly cashed in two free throws at the Boise end of the court. With 20 seconds on the clock, the Broncos were on top, 51-50.

Moberly called time. The Greyhounds worked the ball inside to Al Morton. After a sensational first-round game, Morton had been ineffectual against the tight Bronco defense, scoring only 11. Again he was closed off from the basket.

The ball came back out front to Joe Gummersbach. As time ticked away, the reserve guard fired from long range. The shot cracked the cords, giving Moberly a chance at a third crown and Gummersbach a new nickname; from then on, his teammates referred to the redheaded hero as "The Man with the Golden Arm" after Frank Sinatra's current hit film.

Kilgore solidified its role as co-favorite in the day's finale with an impressive 85-63 drubbing of Graceland. In its previous outing, Graceland had been the tallest team on the court. Against Kilgore, the role changed. Averaging two inches per man taller on the front line, The Texans were in total control throughout, finishing the game with reserves.

The Rangers scored the victory using an effective 1-2 punch. After a miserable, stage-struck first game in which he tallied only one field goal, his lowest total of the year, 6-9 center Ed Erickson dominated the middle, hawking caroms and tossing in soft hooks to the tune of 20 rebounds and 28 points. Floor leader Ned Duncan provided the outside artillery with amazingly accurate shooting from long distance. The sophomore guard had fans oohing and ahing as he hit seven of nine in the first half. He eventually totaled 23 for the game.

The Moberly Greyhounds were going to have a tough time making it 11 in a row.

THURSDAY — HIGH ROLLERS

Hump day was a day for top scoring. Jacksonville's strong, bulky Chuck Brendler started things rolling with a powerful 43-point effort in the Dolphins' 81-73 elimination of Coffeyville. In the day's second consolation match, North Greenville's will-o'-the-wisp guard Willard Fowler outdrew Wright's Walter Olsen, 32 to 30, as the Mountaineer's shot down the Chicagoans, 88-77.

The preeminent performance of the day came in the evening's first quarterfinal contest as Pueblo's Eugene Poston took the ballgame in hand, engineering an 86-77 upset of Cameron State. Though small for a center, the 6-4 sophomore possessed superior leaping ability, quickness, and timing and was a master of positioning under the basket where he completely commanded play. His game-high 39 points was not the top tally for the day, but it would have been higher, had he not missed nine free throws and been less unselfish.

In the day's finale, Hannibal's Art Day and New York's Robert Keller posted more impressive individual totals, dueling to a near standoff. Day carried the first half with 28 points and Keller the second with 23 as the two tallied 38 and 37, respectively, for the game. The competition between the teams was not as close, however. Hannibal-LaGrange sprinted to a 64-44 halftime margin and was never challenged. The 109-89 final was the second-highest point total for two teams to date in tournament history.

The lopsided battle was marred by an unfortunate incident in the last 20 seconds of play when Hannibal's speedy Al Dunbar was low-bridged on a driving lay-up and sent crashing into the goal standard. The valuable sophomore was stunned, required

stitches to sew up a cut to his arm, but, otherwise, was ready for Hannibal's drive for the national championship.

FRIDAY — INCREASING INTEREST

As the two pre-tourney favorites moved closer to a final showdown, fan interest climbed. Between 4,500 and 5,000 spectators had watched Thursday night's quarterfinal match-ups. For the semifinals, the total was 5,500, the largest turnout of the year in the Sports Arena.

Both Friday evening pairings had appeal. In the first, two-time champion Moberly faced a tough hurdle on its road to a third straight title in the favored Kilgore Rangers, a talented squad with a considerable height advantage. And, in the finale, top-rated Hannibal-LaGrange would not only have its hands full with Eugene Poston-led Pueblo, but would also have to contend with the crowd, the Coloradans having picked up considerable Cinderella support from the local fans in its upset of Cameron State. Since pre-tourney favorites had a history of failure, it was obvious the larger audience expected a surprise or two.

There were no surprises in the first half of the Moberly-Kilgore contest, however. Stout defense by the taller Rangers smothered Moberly's point production. The Greyhounds hit one field goal in the first 10 minutes and only five in the first period. Kilgore was in total control, 39-23.

Matters worsened in the second half. With 12:48 left, Kilgore led by 23. Moberly's shot at another championship was running away.

Then, things began to happen.

First, Kilgore was in foul trouble. Starters Hunter Barton and Ted Whillock picked up infractions early — Whillock was called for four fouls in a little more than 7½ minutes — and watched most of the first half from the bench. In the second period two other starters — Bob Laskowitz and Ed Erickson — also neared expulsion. For a team which rarely substituted, the potential loss of so many key individuals represented impending disaster.

Secondly, Kilgore altered its offensive strategy. As he had done in the opener against Jacksonville, Coach Joe Turner called for a slowdown to preserve victory. All year long the Rangers had been plagued with at least one prolonged dry spell in every game. The change in tempo hastened the drought against Moberly.

The Greyhounds sniped back into contention. Behind a remarkable effort by Dan Callahan — who eventually led all scorers with 28 — Moberly closed the gap. With 1:44 to go, the Missourians trailed by four, 63-59.

A third try at a Greyhound crown was not to be, though. In the final rush, Kilgore's stall held. Two Ned Duncan buckets and an Erickson free throw, versus one field goal for Moberly, secured a Ranger victory.

In the day's finale, the solidly pro-Pueblo crowd suffered through three silent minutes when the Indians could not buy a shot, falling behind, 10-0. In the next six minutes, Pueblo outscored Hannibal, 20-10. From then on, the game was a mad scramble. Goals were matched through six more ties before a free throw put the score at odds. Continued goal-matching jockeyed the lead back and forth. At halftime, with underdog Pueblo in the lead, 43-38, the local fans were zestfully optimistic.

Pueblo continued its mastery over the bigger Trojans, extending its advantage to eight.

Then, halfway through the final period, Pueblo went cold again. Hannibal scored the next 12 points on six consecutive field goals, taking the lead, 67-63, with just under eight minutes to play.

But, four points was the largest margin the Missourians could muster. Pueblo battled back, tying the score, 71-all.

The teams matched points through five more ties.

With 45 seconds remaining and the game at an 81-all draw, Hannibal-LaGrange held for a final shot. Al Dunbar took the game-winning try at the six-second mark.

The shot missed.

However, Dunbar was fouled on the play and promptly hit the first charity. Though the second failed, it did not matter. The ball was loose on the court when time ran out.

The Trojans had played well. Art Day and Dunbar, Hannibal's premier players, bettered their season averages, hitting 28 and 7, respectively. Still, the highly favored Missouri team was barely able to survive. Why?

Eugene Poston.

Though giving away five inches, the Pueblo leader outscored and outrebounded Day, his taller counterpart. Poston was a wizard under the basket, amazing everyone with his fluid ability. After capturing game honors with 32, the *News-Herald* tagged Poston "the likely choice for the most valuable player award."

SATURDAY — ENTERTAINING TO THE END

One of the steps the American Legion co-sponsors initiated to help improve attendance was the inclusion of halftime entertainment during the evening sessions. Two full pages of the tournament program were devoted to the entertainment schedule. Besides the crowning of a beautiful queen, tourney goers could see everything from Boy Scout Indian dancing on Tuesday to a grand finale by the California headliners Saturday.

Though Compton College was unable to participate in the NJCAA Basketball Tournament, the school was well represented. The "Comettes," Compton's flashy drill team, were nationally renowned, having appeared in the Little Rose Bowl and on television during the National Football League's Pro-Bowl game. The squad consisted of 51 girls selected "on a point basis covering appearance, posture, dexterity, personality, ability to learn, rhythmic qualifications" and academic standing. The attractive co-eds garnered considerable publicity in the local press.

The halftime diversions were a pleasant plus. However, for most, basketball was sufficient entertainment.

The fifth-place game was interesting solely because it featured the tournament's top scorer — Chuck Brendler. Jacksonville's talented hook-shot artist again led all scorers with 31, giving him a four-game total of 121 and placing him fourth among tournament scorers to date, just behind Dick Garmaker then playing for Minneapolis in the NBA. With Brendler forging the way, the taller Dolphins ran away from North Greenville, 95-74.

All week long the Bees from New York had captivated fans with their own brand of entertainment — good basketball mixed with a touch of comedy. The game for fourth featured their *piece de resistance*. To the crowd's delight, the New Yorkers took to the court armed with squirt guns, dousing players and officials alike. Even after the water weapons were finally confiscated, it took time for the Bees to get serious. When they did it was to the wholehearted cheers of the fans. New York rallied in the last seven minutes to defeat Graceland, 77-70.

Championship night proved good basketball attracted a good audience. A standing-room-only crowd estimated at 4,200 packed the Arena.

The huge assemblage, though disappointed by the outcome, enjoyed superb play in the evening's opener. As in its semifinal against Hannibal-LaGrange, Pueblo started cold, the first six points going to Moberly. Since the two teams played even from then on, the Greyhounds' opening spurt proved the winning difference. Moberly took third place, 72-66.

Star for the Missouri squad was again team leader Dan Callahan who tallied 30 points in his final appearance in a Greyhound uniform. Unfortunately, he had to share the limelight with another 30-point performer — Pueblo's Eugene Poston. Though Poston's four-game point production of 119 left him shy of Chuck Brendler's top total, it made him unanimous choice for the tournament's Most Valuable Player award.[4]

The two teams predicted to be the best had survived to face each other. Consequently, the final decision process attracted a large Saturday night turnout. Those interviewed on local radio were divided: some picked Hannibal-LaGrange; others favored Kilgore. Comparison of the two teams verified the uncertainty of the question.

After leading all scorers with 121 points in the 1956 tournament, Jacksonville's Chuck Brendler (No. 24) played at the University of Florida. (Photo courtesy of Chuck Brendler)

Though Kilgore was the taller squad, Hannibal had the taller starting lineup. Giant 6-9 Art Day was flanked by a pair of 6-6 bookends — Lee Godsey and Bud Harbin. Kilgore matched part of Hannibal's front-line height with 6-9 Ed Erickson and 6-6 Hunter Barton, but fell off at the other front-line position. Ranger Bob Laskowitz was out of place not only because, as a semester transfer from the state of New York, he was a lone Yankee among four native Texans, but also because, he was a 6-1 guard masquerading as a forward.

The 1956 tourney's second-leading scorer (119 points) and MVP, Gene Poston (No. 32) later played at Western State College in Gunnison, Colorado. (Photo courtesy of J.W. Campbell, Western State College)

---

[4] The plaudits for Poston's talents are universal: Harry Simmons, Poston's former coach: "[He was] one of the better players I've ever had or seen;" Hod Humiston, former Hutchinson broadcaster: "The first time he walked on the court you could tell he was one of the better players in the tournament . . . Underneath the basket, he was wicked;" Hunter Barton, Kilgore forward who witnessed Poston's play only as a spectator: "He was about the smoothest ballplayer I ever saw in junior college . . . [He was] like a well-oiled ball bearing . . . If the ball hung on the rim, he got it."

Poston was recruited by more than 100 major colleges, including the University of Kentucky, but he selected Tulane. According to Coach Simmons, Poston remained at the Louisiana school for only a few weeks, then left, dissatisfied with the climatic and cultural changes from his native Colorado. Too late to follow up with any other offer, Poston followed two of his Pueblo teammates to Gunnison, Colorado, where he finished his collegiate career at Western State.

Still, it was anybody's guess who would win the battle for the boards. Barton was one of the top rebounders in junior college ranks and the 215-pound Erickson possessed outstanding strength. Earlier in the year during practice, a barrel-chested reserve weighing about the same as Erickson and running at full tilt, crashed into the big center. Though standing normally, unbraced, Erickson did not move while the reserve crumpled. Considering Day's limber quickness, it was a matter of Hannibal's finesse versus Kilgore's power.

The guard position was also a toss-up. Sid Bradley and, in particular, Al Dunbar gave the Missouri team superior quickness. The Rangers, however, possessed better outside shooting. Ned Duncan and Ted Whillock were both marksmen from any distance.

Though Coach Joe Turner's preferred style was run-and-gun, the Rangers lacked the greyhounds to do so. Consequently, Kilgore played a slow, deliberate game with set patterns. Hannibal-LaGrange was a speed team. Tempo would be a key factor.

The Texans had one clear advantage, though. The 40 fans who made their way from Kilgore to cheer the Rangers were not alone. A majority of the Arena crowd backed the Lone Star team. Rooting for newcomers over tourney veterans was becoming a local custom.

The many Kilgore supporters had little to cheer about once the game began. In the past, the Rangers' habitual cold streak came when the team was riding a big lead. But, against Hannibal, frigid conditions caught the Texans head on. Kilgore opened hitting only 27 percent of its shots. The Rangers also lost the battle in the middle as Day used his great quickness to control the backboards. At the half, Kilgore faced a 35-25 deficit.

Then, it was the Trojans turn to feel the chill. In a nine-minute stretch, Hannibal managed only a Bradley field goal and four Day free throws.

In contrast, Kilgore put its act together. Having failed to run their set patterns in the first half, often playing sluggishly, the Rangers were now executing as a unit, outscoring Hannibal, 24-10, in the first 10 minutes of the second half. Though the margin fluctuated, the Trojans were unable to come closer than three thereafter.

After the 68-65 final was posted, Stetson-hatted fans converged on the victors. East Texas had again proved its superiority in the junior college basketball world.

THE AFTERMATH — END OF A TREND

Joe Turner rarely displayed emotion. After being hoisted to the shoulders of several Ranger football players in a victory celebration immediately following the final buzzer, Turner's feelings were apparent only in his misty eyes. Happiness was there, nonetheless. As he told the *Kilgore News Herald,* "I'm just glad I'm alive."

Turner had reason to be proud of his players. Bob Laskowitz, more noted for his defensive talents than his scoring, sparked the Texans' comeback, hitting all but one of his 15 points in the final period. The Ranger defense was spectacular, particularly across the front line. Ed Erickson and Hunter Barton — a "defensive genius" who was always assigned the opposition's toughest scorer — pinched Art Day, allowing Hannibal's leading scorer only four points in the second half.[5] Erickson and Barton also did yeoman's work on the boards, sweeping away errant shots at both ends of the court.

Kilgore's leading scorer and team leader, Ned Duncan later played for the SMU Mustangs. (Photo courtesy of SMU)

But, if there was a single reason the Rangers won, it was Ned Duncan. Though he was the team's leading scorer and again topped the scoring roles with 23, his greatest asset was his ability to lead. He was crafty, smart, a perfectionist who gave 1— percent and made sure his teammates did likewise. Duncan was the glue holding Kilgore's unity together. As one observer remarked, "Gene Poston might have been the most 'outstanding' player in the tournament, but Ned Duncan was the most 'valuable.'"

* * *

According to the *Hutchinson News-Herald,* the 1956 National Juco Tournament "was 'aired' and 'papered' as never before." Ten radio stations carried live or recreated versions of tourney games. Besides national coverage by the Associated Press and the United Press, newspapermen from all over filed stories. Even Wichita and Dallas, cities without special interest in a particular team, sent representatives to cover the event. The developing interest in the tournament was also reflected at the box office. After two years of declining attendance, gate receipts were up. The NJCAA's showcase attraction was again healthy.

---

[5] The reason for Art Day's ineffective second half is a mystery. Though Kilgore's defense deserved considerable credit, even Kilgore's Hunter Barton suggested more was involved than met the eye. By Barton's own admission, Day was "out-quicking me" in the first half when the Hannibal center dominated play in the middle. Then, shortly into the final period, Day grabbed a defensive rebound. Barton knocked the ball out of Day's hands and into the goal. According to Barton, "[After that] Day just quit."

A possible explanation was given by the former Kilgore forward. After the Rangers beat Moberly in the semifinals, "the Moberly players told us to beat hell out of 'em [Hannibal-LaGrange]." They "detested" Hannibal and suggested that if Kilgore roughed up Day, he would fold. One Kilgore player followed the advice. Throughout the game, he nudged Day with verbal taunts and elbows.

Hannibal Coach Howard Dewell corroborates the story. Dewell described Day as "moody," "not an aggressive individual," the type of person who would become "passive when confronted with racial slurs." Dewell complained to officials on several occasions about the name-calling.

Though bothered by Day's lackluster performance, Dewell was reluctant to place responsibility for the loss on the big center's shoulders, however. "I credit myself with just a poor last-half coaching job . . . We should have won . . . They slowed us down, controlled the tempo."

What happened to Art Day in those final 20 minutes remains a question mark.

What happened to Hannibal-LaGrange is not. Hannibal de-emphasized sports when Coach Dewell left to become a high school teacher and coach in Quincy, Illinois. After five consecutive appearances, five excellent showings, a remarkable tourney record of 15-5, Hannibal-LaGrange never returned to the nationals.

The 1956 champion Kilgore Rangers: back row (left to right) Harry Bullard, Ned Duncan, Bob Laskowitz, Ed Erickson, Hunter Barton, Ted Whillock, Joe Turner; bottom row — Sonny Hatton, George Everett, Rondell Van Cleve, Bobby Barton, Dennis Creech, David McCool, Bob Pace. (Photo courtesy of Gerald Pinson, Kilgore College)

Tournament Results

Tuesday: Game

1	Moberly — 80	Eastern Arizona — 67
2	Boise — 70	Arkansas St-Beebe — 57
3	Graceland — 64	Coffeyville — 59
4	Kilgore — 70	Jacksonville — 69
5	Hannibal-LaGrange — 95	Garden City — 71
6	New York City — 77	Itasca — 71

Wednesday: Game

7	Pueblo — 86	North Greenville — 84
8	Cameron St. — 91	Chicago-Wright — 71
9	Eastern Arizona — 76	Arkansas St-Beebe — 55
10	Moberly — 52	Boise — 51
11	Kilgore — 85	Graceland — 63

Thursday: Game

12	Jacksonville — 81	Coffeyville — 73
13	North Greenville — 88	Chicago-Wright — 77
14	Graceland — 63	Boise — 58
15	Garden City — 77	Itasca — 69
16	Pueblo — 86	Cameron St. — 77
17	Hannibal-LaGrange — 109	New York City — 89

Friday: Game

18	Jacksonville — 88	Eastern Arizona — 75
19	North Greenville — 96	Garden City — 87
20	New York City — 79	Cameron St. — 78
21	Kilgore — 68	Moberly — 61
22	Hannibal-LaGrange — 82	Pueblo — 81

Saturday: Game

23	Jacksonville — 95	North Greenville — 74
24	New York City — 77	Graceland — 70
25	Moberly — 72	Pueblo — 66
26	Kilgore — 68	Hannibal-LaGrange — 65

How They Finished in 1956

1. Kilgore College
2. Hannibal-LaGrange College
3. Moberly Junior College
4. New York City Community College
5. Jacksonville Junior College
6. Pueblo Junior College
7. Graceland College
8. North Greenville Junior College

All-Tournament Team

Chuck Brendler — Jacksonville Junior College
Dan Callahan — Moberly Junior College
Arthur Day — Hannibal-LaGrange College
Al Dunbar — Hannibal-LaGrange College
Ned Duncan — Kilgore College
Edward Erickson — Kilgore College
Willard Fowler — North Greenville Junior College
Robert Keller — New York City Community College
Eugene Poston — Pueblo Junior College
Fran Siebuhr — Cameron State Agricultural College

Player of the Year

Eugene Poston — Pueblo Junior College

1957:

BLONDS HAVE MORE FUN

The top four-game total (106 points) was amassed by Gene Wells who, after the 1957 tournament, followed his Brewton-Parker coach, Glenn Wilkes, to Stetson University. (Photo courtesy of Stetson University)

F or the past seven years, Hutchinson fans had supported the National Junior College Basketball Tournament while their team watched the proceedings from the sidelines. In 1956, a berth in the tournament just eluded the Blue Dragons. In 1957, the carrot was dangled tantalizingly closer.

Hutchinson Junior College continued to improve its basketball fortunes. Ranking as high as fourth in the NJCAA coaches' poll during the current campaign, the Blue Dragons battled Arkansas City Junior College for the top spot in the Western Juco Conference throughout the year, only conceding the race after a humbling 74-55 road defeat to Dodge City College in its next to last conference game.

After giving the Wichita University freshmen their second loss of the season and first to a junior college, the Blue Dragons entered the Region 6 tournament full of fire. They crushed their first two opponents by a combined margin of 43. Against Arkansas City, Hutchinson went all out, taking aim at the basket 16 more times than the Tigers and dominating the boards, 50-39. Unfortunately, the Blue Dragons failed to convert their opportunities. They hit a paltry 32 percent from the field and a miserable 53 percent from the line. Arkansas City won the title, 69-65.

When every region reported it would be sending a representative to the tournament, Hutchinson Junior College was again shut out. The team was dismissed, many to participate in track. Since he was retiring from coaching to become the Blue Dragons' athletic director, Coach Charley Sesher collected team uniforms and packed them away for the last time.

Then, word came from Region 15 that one of the players on champion New York City Community College was scholastically ineligible. Runner-up Broome Technical Community College of Binghamton, New York, had made no plans for financing a trip to the nationals. The NJCAA was forced to extend an invitation to complete the bracket.

Hutchinson grabbed the carrot.

THE PARTICIPANTS

Region	Team
1	Boise Junior College — Boise, Idaho
2	Murray State Agricultural College — Tishomingo, Oklahoma
3	Northeastern Oklahoma Agricultural & Mechanical College — Miami, Oklahoma
4	Eastern Arizona Junior College — Thatcher, Arizona
5	San Angelo College — San Angelo, Texas
6	Arkansas City Junior College — Arkansas City, Kansas
7	Arkansas State College, Beebe Branch — Beebe, Arkansas
8	Brewton-Parker Junior College — Mount Vernon, Georgia
9	Pueblo Junior College — Pueblo, Colorado
10	North Greenville Junior College — Tigerville, South Carolina
11	Grand View College — Des Moines, Iowa
12	Joliet Junior College — Joliet, Illinois
13	Hibbing Junior College — Hibbing, Minnesota
14	Tyler Junior College — Tyler, Texas
15	*Hutchinson Junior College — Hutchinson, Kansas
16	Moberly Junior College — Moberly, Missouri

*Invited to fill bracket

The NJCAA Basketball Tournament had grown considerably since its unpromising beginning in Springfield. In 1957, only one regional tournament failed financially (the Region 7 tournament in Marion, Alabama, lost $170). In fact, the invitation given to Hutchinson Junior College proved to be the last required to fill a bracket. In nine years, 80 schools from 29 different states had participated in the affair. Once tasted, the excitement of national competition was habit-forming. The roster for the 10th anniversary of the Juco Tournament demonstrated that coming to Hutchinson was now a customary way of life for many.

Topping the list was the school which best exemplified the tournament's growing tradition. Moberly Junior College was a fixture in the tournament program. Under Maury John's guidance, the two-time national champion Greyhounds were making their seventh consecutive trip to Hutchinson. They had failed to reach the event only twice.

Just behind the Missouri school in number of appearances was the only other two-time titlist — Tyler Junior College. It was the Apaches' sixth tournament.

Four teams were making their fourth appearance — Arkansas City Junior College, Brewton-Parker Junior College, Joliet Junior College, and Eastern Arizona Junior College of Thatcher (second consecutive).

Three teams were in their third tournament — Arkansas State College of Beebe (second consecutive), Boise Junior College (third consecutive), and Pueblo Junior College (third consecutive).

Five schools were trying for a crown a second time — Grand View College, Hibbing Junior College, Hutchinson Junior College, Murray State Agricultural College, and North Greenville Junior College (second consecutive).

Only two schools were making their tourney debut — San Angelo College and Northeastern Oklahoma A&M College of Miami.

The 1957 Juco Tournament was not only filled with familiar faces but also blessed with its finest field to date. Seven of the top eight teams ranked in the final NJCAA coaches' poll were in attendance: No. 1 Moberly (27-3); No. 2 Brewton-Parker (27-3); No. 3 Boise (22-5); San Angelo (27-2) and Tyler (24-12) tied No. 4; and Pueblo (29-5) and Eastern Arizona (27-5) tied No. 6.

Four teams — North Greenville (26-4), Arkansas City (26-5), Northeastern Oklahoma (20-4), and Joliet (21-8) — possessed impressive won-lost credentials and were considered formidable foes despite their lack of ranking.

In addition, though their records were not awe-inspiring, Murray State (19-7), Hutchinson (18-6), and Hibbing (10-8) could not be discounted. All had been runners-up in their only other tourney appearance.

The only teams with no apparent chance at a title were Grand View (16-6) and Arkansas State of Beebe (7-3 versus junior colleges). Neither had won a game in previous tourney tries.

With the inclusion of Hutchinson in the line-up of participants, with wide open competition anticipated, and with large delegations of rooters expected from Moberly, Tyler, Arkansas City, Pueblo, and Miami, Oklahoma, tournament officials prepared for record attendance.

TUESDAY — PREDICTABLE PATTERN

In two previous appearances, the school from Beebe, Arkansas, waged battle in the Sports Arena under the nickname Minutemen and suffered four successive defeats. In the 1957 opener, the Minutemen were now Indians looking to ambush a win from the favored Mountaineers of North Greenville. The new identity was no more successful. The Indians gave a good account of themselves through the first half, then faltered. Midway through the final period, a 22-point lead in hand, North Greenville's Dick Campbell cleared his bench. The 82-69 Mountaineer triumph set the pattern for the tournament's first day.

Like Arkansas State-Beebe, Hibbing also stayed within striking distance for one period. Then, San Angelo's superior talent took control. With 13 minutes remaining, the Rams were in charge, 59-41. Hibbing made one last push, but the Texans slowed play, padding their lead with free throws. Hibbing succumbed, 73-63. Another pre-tourney favorite had won with relative ease.

Since Coach Gerald Stockton was a graduate of Oklahoma A&M, the Murray State Aggies played Hank Iba control basketball, a style not conducive to building excessive margins. Consequently, the close score of the afternoon finale left the impression that the decision was less than clear-cut. In fact, Pueblo dominated throughout. The Indians held off the tough Oklahomans, built an insurmountable 14-point advantage with three minutes to go, then coasted to a 69-63 victory.

Joliet's strategy for upending a tourney favorite was 180 degrees from that of Murray State. According to Coach "Pop" Wills, the best defense in basketball was to put the ball through the hoop. Frequently, he exhorted his players to "Shoot! Shoot!" Since, the plea sometimes started as soon as the basketball crossed the half-court line, the hustling Wolves usually took no more than two passes before firing at the bucket.

Unfortunately, the Moberly Greyhounds were also built to run. Though the race was close, Moberly was always in front. Forced to press at the end, the tired Wolves fouled. The Greyhounds widened the difference with free shots, winning 97-85. One more underdog failed.

All year long, Arkansas City had had problems with tight, drawn in defenses. Against Boise, the Tigers faced one of the best in the nation. With broad, hefty 6-7 Dave Shelby, 6-5 Nick Panico, and 6-3 Oliver McCord clogging the middle, preventing penetration, Arkansas City's running game slowed to a standstill. Even so, the Tigers gave the partisan Arena crowd reason to cheer in the evening feature.

After trailing by eight and nine points through most of the first half, Arkansas City rallied to knot the score at intermission. The Tigers continued stepping up the pace, keeping the game tight. Then a six-point burst with just over four minutes remaining put Boise in command. The staunch defense of the Broncos jammed the center court and held. Though the 68-63 final was the closest yet, the favorite again prevailed.

The evening finale developed into a scoring duel between Tyler's 6-4 center, Kelly Chapman, who was accurate from any distance up to 20 feet, and Grand View's 5-10 John Cisna, who was within range as soon as he stepped over the midcourt stripe. First, Chapman got hot, guiding Tyler to a 10-point lead. Then, it was Cisna's turn to sizzle from outside, leading the stubborn Vikings from behind. Twice Grand View caught the Apaches, grabbing the advantage at halftime, 37-35, and tying the score with 4:50 to go. Then, four quick jump shots by Chapman settled matters. While Chapman and Cisna topped all scorers for the day, Chapman won the personal battle 44 to 35. Tyler also won the war, 88-78.

WEDNESDAY — MIRACLES ARE RARE

Considering the developing pattern of play, the future did not loom bright for the Golden Norsemen from Miami, Oklahoma. Just prior to regional tournament play, Coach Red Robertson suffered a heart attack. Though assistant coach Jack Rucker guided Northeastern Oklahoma to an upset of Coffeyville College to reach the nationals, his trials were just beginning. Starting guard Don Wofford was struck down with food poisoning and was unavailable for play. Another team member was sidelined with a leg injury. To top it off, NEO faced the No. 2 team in the country in the opener. The Norsemen were in desperate need of good fortune.

What they did not need was Gene Wells. The 6-2 sophomore guard from Ludowici, Georgia, was the best shooter in Brewton-Parker history, owning both the school's one- and two-year scoring records. Against Northeastern Oklahoma, Wells was unstoppable. Even after picking him up at midcourt in the second half, the Norsemen could not prevent Wells from gunning. Wells topped all scorers with 35, leading Brewton-Parker to a 92-71 rout of the hard-luck Oklahomans.

The trend of first-round contests was firmly established: there were no thrilling close calls. The underdog might put up a struggle, but, in the end, the favorite was assuredly on top.

The pattern should have dampened the enthusiasm of local fans. The Gila Monsters from Thatcher, Arizona, Hutchinson's first-round opponent, possessed one of the top defenses in the nation, one which limited opponents to less than 55 points per game. Under Coach Bruce Larson's leadership, Eastern Arizona was a seasoned tourney veteran, unlikely to fold under the pressure of national competition. The leaves in the teacup did not read favorably for the home crowd.

But, nothing could erode the optimism of Hutchinson fans. It had been eight long years since the city had had something personal to cheer about in the tournament. Besides, after the Cinderella effort in 1949, everyone believed in miracles.

Living in the shadow of a legend is not easy. Face terrific half-court pressure and the best of hopes can go quickly awry. The Blue Dragons were jittery, playing far below their regular season form. Fifteen times they lost the ball on their side of the court without taking a shot. Still, with two minutes remaining and Eastern Arizona's top two players on the bench with five fouls, Hutchinson was down by a mere four points.

Miracles are rare, however. The team from Thatcher stalled, compelling the Blue Dragons to pressure — and foul. Eastern Arizona walked away to victory, 61-52.

Though the predictable first-round failed to generate much excitement, it did set up interesting possibilities. The first quarterfinal fulfilled those expectations.

Using superior height and quickness, North Greenville executed a tight zone defense, holding favored San Angelo in check, keeping the score close throughout. The turning point came with a little more than six minutes to go and the game tied. San Angelo's Frank Trevino hit the first of two free throws, then missed the second. Ram guard Jay Hawley snuck around the North Greenville rebounders, picked off the carom, and put it back in. The three-point cushion forced the all-freshmen Mountaineers to press. San Angelo added free throws, employed a weaving stall, and waited out the clock.

When the final figures were posted, North Greenville had outscored San Angelo from the field, 25-24. The Mountaineer zone held Hawley, the Rams' leading scorer, to only three field goals. However, the blanket-like defense had spawned fouls. While Hawley's 19 was considerably down from the 31 he tallied in the Texans' opener, the 6-3 sophomore still managed to lead Ram scoring, hitting 13 of 16 charities. Phil Addison — a speedy, soft-spoken point guard noted for playing best in the clutch — was just behind Hawley, contributing 18, connecting with five critical free throws near the end to seal San Angelo's 70-66 victory.

The other Wednesday quarterfinal was equally absorbing — for 25 minutes. Three times No. 3 Boise built leads of as much as eight points and three times No. 6 Pueblo rallied. After the final Indian charge, Boise went cold, going scoreless for three minutes, and never recovered. Pueblo won the battle for the West, massacring Boise, 72-54.

THURSDAY — DUEL OF THE PATRIARCHS

About the time the Thursday afternoon feature was to start, San Francisco's Golden Gate Bridge was sent swaying and shaking by the worst earthquake to hit the city since the devastator of 1906. The rocker tipped 5.5 on the Richter scale and injured 12.

The shock waves appeared to extend all the way to Kansas, since the consolation match on tap also did its share of rumbling. The grueling defensive struggle between Hutchinson and Northeastern Oklahoma produced poor shooting and 50 fouls. Despite having trailed most of the contest, Hutchinson found itself in a winning position with time running out.

Then, the Golden Norseman received an unusual stroke of good luck when forward Don Ward, left unattended under the basket, added an easy lay-up, sending the game into overtime.

However, NEO's good fortune was short-lived. The Oklahomans missed four crucial free throws in the extra period. To the delight of an exceptionally large (2,000) afternoon crowd, Hutchinson eliminated hapless Northeastern Oklahoma, 60-57.

Those who came early to the evening session were treated to a stimulating outside shooting exhibition, featuring Grand View's John Cisna, who again hooked up in a scoring duel. This time the small guard challenged someone closer to his size – Joliet's 5-8 Tom Broderick. The results were the same, howeve Cisna lost the individual shooting contest 34 to 27 while Gran View was again outclassed, 95-74.[1]

In the evening feature, the Gila Monsters from Thatche proved their opening win over the hometown team had bee no fluke. Employing the same aggressive defense, Eastern Ar zona shackled the No. 2 Blue Barons from Brewton-Parker, on of the best running teams in the tournament, holding the Geor gians 24 points below their per-game average of 86. None of th Blue Barons could solve the Gila Monsters' pressure from out side. Gene Wells, the All-American guard who had such an out standing opener with 32, was handcuffed, hitting only eigh Brewton-Parker's Ralph Miller topped all scorers with 22, bu only because his point total was augmented by a remarkabl 14-for-19 night at the free throw line.

On the Eastern Arizona side of the ledger, flashy Joe Ge maine set the scoring pace with 20, all in the first half. Joh Nicoll, the Gila Monsters' rugged center, picked up the scorin load in the second period with 14, tying Germaine for team honors. Though the game was close throughout, Eastern Arizo na's defense dictated the 69-62 outcome.

The only sour note for the Thatcher squad was the early sec ond half ankle injury to Germaine. While not the team's leadin scorer, the sophomore forward was the heart and soul of Eas ern Arizona's aggressive spirit. The sprain was severe, Ge maine's chances of further play, doubtful; without him, so wer the Gila Monsters' chances of winning.

In the last quarterfinal, it was the old patriarch versus the new Although they counted 14 appearances between them, Mobe ly and Tyler had met only once before in tournament compet tion, in 1951, when the Apaches downed Moberly in the semif nals, just before capturing their second national crown. At th time, Tyler was without question the kingpin of the junior co lege basketball world, Moberly, an unknown. Since ther Moberly had made five more trips to Hutchinson and grabbe two titles, while Tyler, struggling for domination on the toug battlefields of East Texas, had returned only once. The Grey hounds were now top dog.

The historical import of Thursday's final contest was not lo on the Arena crowd. More than 5,000 fans turned out for th evening's competition, mostly to see the battle between th only two-time champs in the tournament's short history. Th result was a letdown.

Both teams played with the style and grace of champion However, the Greyhounds hit and the Apaches did not. At hal time, Moberly led, 45-29. With 10 minutes remaining, the ma gin was still 15. Though Jimmy Cheshier — who grabbed gam honors with 27, 19 of which came in the second half — led Tyler rally which pulled the Apaches to within six with thre minutes to go, Moberly substantiated its No. 1 ranking. Playin superb team basketball, the poised Greyhounds finessed th ball, securing a 78-71 victory.

FRIDAY — CRESCENDO OF EXCITEMENT

The first three days of competition in the 1957 Juco Tourn ment did not live up to fan expectations. Despite the high cal ber of talent on the court, play was routine; the unfolding dra ma, uneventful. On Friday, the tenor of the meet change crescendoing in intensity and excitement.

Using superior front-line height and backcourt quicknes Arkansas City demolished Hibbing, 80-57, in the curtain raise The runaway roused the partisan crowd.

Another Kansas victory followed when the Hutchinson Blu Dragons beat the Joliet Wolves at their own game, outrunnin them, 78-64, after trailing by nine at halftime. The locals wer ecstatic.

The accelerating pace continued in the final afternoon con test. Tyler's Kelly Chapman and Brewton-Parker's Gene Wel engaged in a shooting match which produced the highest ind

---

[1] John Cisna was the first player ever selected to the All-Tournament Team after playing in only two games. But, it was ironic that Cisna was honored for his spectacular shooting performances. When Coach Dave Sisam recruited him from high school in Des Moines, the gutsy guard was an unaccomplished shooter who preferred to drive the lane. During the summer, Sisam told Cisna to shoot 200 jump shots a day, five days a week. He was also required to shoot 50 shots before and after practice. Natural ability combined with the additional work, turning Cisna into a bonafide scorer.
Sisam also achieved unique distinction in the 1957 tournament. He was the first individual to play in the tournament (with Grand View in 1950) then return as a coach.

dual and team totals in the tournament. Though Chapman's 5 — the third-highest total to date in tourney history — pped Wells' 35, Brewton-Parker's 100 beat Tyler's 92.

The fans were now primed for the two best games of the tournament.

Tyler's Kelly Chapman not only topped all 1957 scorers nationally with more than 1,000 points, but also took Juco Tournament scoring honors with 112 points in only three games, the second largest three-game total in tourney history. Chapman later played briefly for Kentucky, then finished his collegiate career at Texas A&M. (Photo courtesy of Floyd Wagstaff)

According to pre-tourney prognostications, the favorite in the upper bracket was the team from the sheep production center of San Angelo, Texas. The Rams — the nickname was taken from "rambouillet," the most important breed of sheep in the San Angelo economy — were undefeated against junior college opposition and owned the best winning percentage in the country. Many tourney observers, however, felt San Angelo was living on borrowed time. The Rams had no big man, no appreciable height, and no depth. Besides, it was the first trip to the nationals for the West Texas school.[2]

In contrast, it was the third consecutive trip to Hutchinson for Larry Simmons' Indians from Pueblo. Though only one man (Dale Allen) returned from the previous year's team, Pueblo was considered a veteran squad, with intelligent, capable personnel. Four team members were slated to attend the Air Force Academy after graduation. Pueblo's biggest advantage over San Angelo was in the middle. The Indians possessed one of the most sought-after players in the country — 6-5, 220-pound Ken Anderson, an 18-year-old freshman honor student who had been an all-state, All-American prep performer in high school at Moline, Illinois. Despite nursing an ankle injury during much of the season, Anderson led Pueblo in rebounds and scoring (22.6). In his first two tourney outings, he had tallied 52 points, 1 of which came against the tough, defensive-minded crew from Boise.

San Angelo's first two victories had hinged on the Rams' ability to gain the advantage and control the tempo of play, particularly at the end of the game. The same strategy was in effect against Pueblo. The Texans jumped out to a quick 10-5 lead. The next 3½ minutes destroyed their game plan, however. Employing a tight man-to-man defense, Pueblo put the clamps on the Rams, outscoring them, 15-2.

Though Pueblo's aggressive play shut down San Angelo's scoring from the field (the Rams hit under 30 percent of their shots in the first half), it also produced fouls. Twelve of 14 free throws, including 10 consecutive by Jay Hawley, pulled San Angelo within one at intermission.

The two teams played to a virtual draw through the first 13 minutes of the second period, tying 11 times.

The turning point came at the 6:40 mark when Al Miranda, the Rams' sixth man, canned two free throws followed by successive field goals by Hawley and Phil Addison. With a working margin, San Angelo engaged its patented end-game stall. Pueblo scored only four points in the last five minutes. The resulting 78-65 final did not indicate the closeness of the emotionally charged contest.

The hero for the Texans was Hawley, team leader and backbone of the Ram offense. Pueblo frequently double-teamed the 6-3 sophomore, forcing him to improvise shots. Three field goals came from superhuman underhand tosses. Despite the heavy defense, Hawley managed 27 points to lead all scorers. His 13-for-16 effort from the line epitomized San Angelo's winning difference.[3] For the second straight time the Rams were beaten from the field (23-22), but won because they converted free throws (34 of 42).

Like San Angelo, the lower bracket favorite had also not lost to a junior college opponent. The Moberly Greyhounds were not newcomers to tourney competition, however. Many observers felt the current crew was the best Maury John had yet assembled. Without Joe Germaine's inspirational leadership, Eastern Arizona's chances against the nation's top-ranked team were rated nil. Only a pocket full of surprises could keep the game interesting.

The first surprise came early. Germaine *did* start for the Gila Monsters. He played only a few minutes, contributed a lone field goal, then sat down for the remainder of the game, his ankle injury proving too painful. However, his presence gave Eastern Arizona a needed emotional lift.

The second surprise was Dustan Evermon. The little used reserve, whose previous role had been to spell the Gila Monster front-liners, filled Germaine's shoes admirably, scoring 15 points, his highest total for the year.

Another surprise centered around play inside. Evermon's timely performance coupled with the bull-like board work and game-high 22 points of John Nicoll gave Eastern Arizona an unexpected edge in the middle against the Greyhounds, the tallest team in the tournament.

The biggest surprise of all was not that the men from Thatcher beat heavily favored Moberly, but that they did so *decisively*. The Gila Monster defense was artistically magnificent. None of the Greyhounds could consistently find the range. Jim Mudd, who had scored 57 points in two games including 33 in the opener, was limited to five field goals, all in the first half. Another Moberly gun, Al Morton, was held to two field goals and nine total points. Even Joe Gummersbach, the Greyhound's floor general, was stymied. Though he led his team with 18, he was continually frustrated by Eastern Arizona's pressure and hit a poor percentage of his shots.

---

[2] The only advance knowledge the San Angelo team received regarding what to expect at the tournament came from word-of-mouth. During a practice session the Monday before the tournament, the Rams were introduced to the Sports Arena and were duly impressed. One player remarked, "Man, this is sure a big ol' place." Coach Phil George responded with one of the more lasting quotes in tourney history: "Yeah, but you just wait till they fill it full of eyes."

[3] According to Coach Phil George, the fact that Hawley was even able to play was "totally amazing." In San Angelo's final home conference game, the hard-driving guard crashed into the wall, fracturing his fibula. The injury went untreated for several days because Hawley told the coaches it was simply a bruise. When the pain finally became unbearable, Hawley was sent to the doctor, the proper condition diagnosed, and a walking cast put on the leg. Hawley was considered through for the year.

But, as George related, because Hawley "was so doggone competitive" and "had a very tremendous pain threshold," he took the cast off a week later of his own volition. Afraid Hawley might permanently injure himself, George required him to get doctor's permission to play. "He was so persuasive . . . [though] . . . I think he worked on that doctor's mind to clear him." Since the fracture was hairline and not separated, a new light-weight abbreviated cast was put on. Hawley played sparingly in the last two regular season games, but was still the leading scorer in the Rams' finale. The cast was removed prior to the Region 5 tournament. Though his mobility was hindered and his exceptional jumping ability significantly hampered, Hawley led his team to the nationals, copping all-regional tournament honors in the process. At Hutchinson, the injury continued to restrict Hawley's physical accomplishments, but did nothing to diminish his determination.

Even though the crowd solidly backed the Gila Monsters, everyone in the Arena was stunned by the outcome. Eastern Arizona's 67-55 defensive masterpiece was a memorable upset.

SATURDAY — GOLDEN UNITY

Playing for fifth place is not as glamorous as playing for a championship. However, for the 2,500 Hutchinson fans who attended Saturday afternoon's consolation trophy battles, winning meant more than national ranking — it meant retribution.

Arkansas City had been a longtime nemesis of the Hutchinson Blue Dragons. The Tigers had won the Western Juco Conference title five consecutive years, claiming the Region 6 crown four of those five years. Early in the season, Hutchinson was humiliated by the Tigers, 87-57, at Arkansas City. The Blue Dragons later redeemed their pride with a spine-tingling 54-48 thriller at Hutchinson. Then, came the Region 6 title game in which the Blue Dragons outplayed the Tigers, but still lost. The fifth-place contest represented an opportunity to even the score.

Hutchinson's chances did not appear good. Besides the fact Arkansas City owned a considerable size advantage over the Blue Dragons, Hutchinson was without the services of starting guard Bill Lovitt, sidelined because an insect bite on the calf of his leg became infected.

The local fans need not have worried. Lovitt's duties were capably handled by Glenn Hamilton, whose key free throws and 12 points helped Hutchinson take a 55-50 advantage with 52 seconds to go.

Arkansas City's Dave Dunbar pulled the Tigers within a basket with three of four free throws. Then, on the last play, Dunbar lofted the tying shot from midcourt and watched the basketball swish the air just short of the goal.

Joyous sighs filled the Arena. With a winning season behind them, the local crowd was free to enjoy the day's trophy parade.

First, they marvelled as Boise overhauled Brewton-Parker's running game with an exacting defense, installed a sharp, clever passing attack, which reaped 64 percent shooting from the floor in the first half, and dominated from beginning to end. The Broncos claimed fourth place, 81-74.

Then came an exceptionally rough third-place contest in which 48 fouls were called and five players finished the game on the bench. The frustration of just missing a chance at a national title plus heavy body contact caused by Moberly's tight screening offense led to hard feelings. The officials were forced to stop play and deliver severe warnings when players finally "squared off." The grudge match was eventually won by Pueblo, 93-83, primarily because of the 37-point performance of sophomore forward Dale Allen. The win avenged the Indians' loss to Moberly in the previous year's third-place game.

Compared to the semifinals and the other trophy matches, the 1957 Juco Tournament finale was a big disappointment. Neither Eastern Arizona nor San Angelo had shown any flair for adventure in their earlier outings. When paired with each other, a languorous tempo was inevitable. Both teams played with extreme caution, keeping the score low. The leading scorer in the game — Eastern Arizona's John Nicoll — only tallied 18. The effort was sufficient to earn Nicoll the tournament's MVP award, but was not enough to excite the 6,000 fans who viewed the championship tilt.

Still, the winners deserved respect, if not for their play, at least for their attitude. All year long the team had played with a unified spirit. The unity developed after the team leaders talked their fellow players into peroxiding their crew cuts. When the coach saw the results, he blew up. The instigators argued it was simply an act meant to generate team pride. To prove it, they agreed to return their hair to its natural color after their next loss. That loss did not occur until the final regular season game. By then, the coach had been won over and waived the agreement.

When the all-blond "Anglos" from San Angelo took to the court they were a smooth-running, well-balanced unit which rarely relinquished the lead once gained. Against Eastern Arizona, the Rams held the advantage all but twice, both times early in the contest. With seven minutes remaining, they were in complete command, 50-35. San Angelo's 63-51 victory gave Texas its fifth national title in 10 years.

According to former Eastern Arizona coach Bruce Larson, 1957 tourney MVP John Nicoll, "couldn't shoot a lick. He couldn't do anything but score. He was about as wide as the backboard, had good hands, a great pair of shoulders, and could muscle his way to the basket." Nicoll was one of the first players Larson ever recalled using a power lay-up, a very useful move in picking up three-point plays. Nicoll was later an All-Skyline Conference center at Brigham Young University. (Photo courtesy of John Nicoll)

THE AFTERMATH — THE LONG TRIP HOME

Despite Hutchinson's early elimination from title contention the 1957 NJCAA Basketball Tournament was a resounding success. New attendance standards were established for afternoon consolation contests, primarily because the Blue Dragons headlined the "sunshine league." Though no overall attendance record was set, gate receipts continued to increase from their 1955 low. For many, tournament week had been a pleasant, memorable experience. For some, the trip home was even more unforgettable.

Late Saturday night, the western half of Kansas was hit by the worst snow storm in 25 years. Thirty to 50 mile-per-hour wind kicked at a foot of snow, creating blizzard conditions from Oklahoma to Nebraska. Hutchinson was on the leading edge of the storm.

Teams heading east departed without incident. Others were forced to stay put in their warm, comfortable hotel rooms or brave the harrowing elements.

Two teams were stranded. On Monday, the team from Thatcher, Arizona, finally decided to avoid the snow-packed roads west and take a circuitous route through Oklahoma and Texas — a route whose weather, though snow-free, was only marginally better. The party from Pueblo did not head home until shortly after noon on Tuesday. Even then the Kansas Highway Patrol was advising that roads were only open to emergency one-way traffic. For many in the group, emergency conditions did exist; they had run out of funds.

The weather was indiscriminate in its choice of victims; it affected winners as well as losers. Hoping to beat the brunt of the storm by flying out of Wichita, the national champions from San Angelo left Hutchinson by bus in the early hours of Sunday morning. Halfway there, the bus broke down. In the midst of gale-force winds and freezing temperature, a resourceful Jay Hawley fixed the problem.

Coach Phil George later recalled, "I can still remember standing out in that cold, snow, ice, and everything . . . holding that thing [the rear grill hood where the engine was housed] up while that rascal was climbing in there in the night, freezing to death, trying to figure out how to make that thing run." He jokingly added, "That's the reason we had him on the team; we had to have a mechanic."

Jay Hawley (No. 10) not only led the San Angelo Rams to a 1957 national title with 94 points, but was also a ringleader in the team's bleached-blond look, setting a precedent for the next seven or eight years. Said Coach Phil George, "Peroxided hair became our identity." (Photo courtesy of Phil George)

The plane ride was not any smoother. On the final leg of the trek from Dallas to San Angelo, the plane encountered a huge dust storm. As Jim Cope — the *San Angelo Standard-Times* sportswriter who accompanied the team — described later in the paper: "The plane pitched, rocked and plowed onward. Its tail whipped and the young mother in the back hugged her baby and buckled tighter in her seat. Clouds rolled thickly and underneath dust boiled angrily. The ground was just something everyone hoped was farther below; it couldn't be seen."

Though having traveled for almost 12 hours, the team's spirits were still at fever pitch. "Everybody was so fired up, so excited that I don't remember anybody getting air sick," said George.

The pilot felt the high winds were too much for the DC-3 and wanted to reroute to Abilene. However, the expected welcoming party below and the high emotion of his passengers convinced him to try it.

"He bounced it pretty good . . . hung it kind of crooked in the air and all," remembered George. Once the plane was safely on the ground, the cheers of 700 wind-blown San Angeloans made it all worthwhile.

How They Finished in 1957

1. San Angelo College
2. Eastern Arizona Junior College
3. Pueblo Junior College
4. Boise Junior College
5. Hutchinson Junior College
6. Moberly Junior College
7. Brewton-Parker Junior College
8. Arkansas City Junior College

All-Tournament Team

Ken Anderson — Pueblo Junior College
Pete Carlisle — North Greenville Junior College
Kelly Chapman — Tyler Junior College
John Cisna — Grand View College
Joe Gummersbach — Moberly Junior College
Jay Hawley — San Angelo College
John Nicoll — Eastern Arizona Junior College
Nick Panico — Boise Junior College
Charley Reynolds — Hutchinson Junior College
Gene Wells — Brewton-Parker Junior College

Player of the Year

John Nicoll — Eastern Arizona Junior College

Tournament Results

Tuesday:	Game		
	1	North Greenville — 82 Arkansas St-Beebe — 69
	2	San Angelo — 73 Hibbing — 63
	3	Pueblo — 69 Murray St. — 63
	4	Moberly — 97 Joliet — 85
	5	Boise — 68 Arkansas City — 63
	6	Tyler — 88 Grand View — 78
Wednesday:	Game		
	7	Hibbing — 70 Arkansas St-Beebe — 62
	8	Brewton-Parker — 92 NE Oklahoma A&M — 71
	9	Eastern Arizona — 61 Hutchinson — 52
	10	San Angelo — 70 North Greenville — 66
	11	Pueblo — 72 Boise — 54
Thursday:	Game		
	12	Arkansas City — 66 Murray St. — 52
	13	Hutchinson — 60 NE Oklahoma A&M — 57 OT
	14	Boise — 94 North Greenville — 78
	15	Joliet — 95 Grand View — 74
	16	Eastern Arizona — 69 Brewton-Parker — 62
	17	Moberly — 78 Tyler — 71
Friday:	Game		
	18	Arkansas City — 80 Hibbing — 57
	19	Hutchinson — 78 Joliet — 64
	20	Brewton-Parker — 100 Tyler — 92
	21	San Angelo — 78 Pueblo — 65
	22	Eastern Arizona — 67 Moberly — 55
Saturday:	Game		
	23	Hutchinson — 55 Arkansas City — 53
	24	Boise — 81 Brewton-Parker — 74
	25	Pueblo — 93 Moberly — 83
	26	San Angelo — 63 Eastern Arizona — 51

1958:

CUTTING IT CLOSE AGAINST CLASS

When Hutchonians opened their Sunday paper March 9, 1958, some glanced at the front page headlines: "State Supreme Court Outlaws Fair Trade Act by 6-1 Vote"; "Snow Hits South Central Kansas Area; Heads East." Others skimmed further to learn of Cuban rebel leader Fidel Castro's threat to call a general revolutionary strike; to find out the specifics of President Eisenhower's program for ending the current economic slump; to discover that Wichita was one of the fastest growing job areas in the country. Most, however, turned immediately to page 15 — the sports section.

The fact that All-American Wilt Chamberlain had led the Kansas Jayhawks to a 61-44 upset of No. 1 Kansas State was temporarily ignored. Only one headline mattered: "Dragons Nip Conqs; Qualify for National." The article described how Hutchinson center Merle Harris scored with 30 seconds to go, lifting the Blue Dragons to an 82-81 victory over Dodge City College and giving them the Region 6 title. Hutchinson Junior College students planned a "Greet the Champs" welcome for the victorious Blue Dragons. The city responded accordingly.

There would be no need for an invitation this year. Hutchinson had finally "earned" its way into the NJCAA Basketball Tournament.

THE PARTICIPANTS

Region	Team
1	Weber College — Ogden, Utah
2	Cameron State Agricultural College — Lawton, Oklahoma
3	Coffeyville College of Arts, Sciences and Vocation — Coffeyville, Kansas
4	Joliet Junior College — Joliet, Illinois
5	Frank Phillips College — Borger, Texas
6	Hutchinson Junior College — Hutchinson, Kansas
7	Snead Junior College — Boaz, Alabama
8	Brewton-Parker Junior College — Mount Vernon, Georgia
9	Mesa County Junior College — Grand Junction, Colorado
10	North Greenville Junior College — Tigerville, South Carolina
11	Fairbury Junior College — Fairbury, Nebraska
12	Flint Junior College — Flint, Michigan
13	Ely Junior College — Ely, Minnesota
14	Kilgore College — Kilgore, Texas
15	Broome Technical Community College — Binghamton, New York
16	Moberly Junior College — Moberly, Missouri

In the past, the *Hutchinson News*[1] had habitually predicted that the current tournament would provide "the toughest competition yet" as a come-on to fans. The statement was made even when the tourney roll included a losing record or two. But, there was no need for false claims in building up the 1958 event, since the 16 entrants brought the best set of records yet compiled by a tourney field.

Topping the list was the first undefeated team to reach the national tournament — No. 1 Cameron State of Lawton, Oklahoma (25-0). The Aggies possessed the four ingredients necessary to maintain perfection: height, speed, a sharp-shooting offense, and a rugged defense. There were no weak spots in the Aggie starting lineup. The makeup of the Pioneer Conference all-star squad proved it. The Aggies placed three men (Bud Sahmaunt, Homer Watkins, and Gene Miller) on the first team and two (Jackie Martin and Gerald Hertzler) on the second. Cameron was the consensus choice to win the tournament.

The prime opposition for the Aggies came from two previous titleholders. For the eighth year in a row, Moberly Junior College (25-3) was among the nation's elite. Many considered the current squad the best yet. The Greyhounds returned three starters from their sixth-place team of a year ago: two of them — 6-8 Dave Terre and 6-7 Jim Mudd — gave Moberly the tallest front line in the tournament; the other — 5-7 Corky Alderson — personified the team's quickness. Kilgore College (23-2) was equally impressive with wins over the freshman squads of Baylor, SMU, TCU, and North Texas State. The Rangers also split with the Houston frosh. The only defeat Kilgore suffered to a junior college was on the road against Longhorn Conference rival Lon Morris College.

Which of the two former champions would challenge Cameron State for the title would be decided early; Moberly and Kilgore faced each other in the opening round. The additional balanced pairings of Hutchinson (19-6) vs. Mesa County Junior College (17-6), Snead Junior College (20-4) vs. Flint Junior College (20-4), and Brewton-Parker Junior College (23-6) vs. Broome Technical Community College (23-2), promised interesting first-round action in the lower bracket. None of the lower bracket opposition matched the potency of Moberly or Kilgore, however. The Moberly-Kilgore winner was expected to breeze to the championship game.

Cameron State's road to the title tilt was more difficult. The most prominent obstacle was North Greenville Junior College which owned the second-best record in the tournament (28-2), started the tallest lineup, and carried the most experience, returning its entire tourney squad from the year before. Other potential roadblocks included Coffeyville College (25-3), Kansas state champs for the second straight year; Joliet Junior College (23-4), the best team ever fielded by the five-time tourney participant; Weber College (25-6), a strong defensive club from the West; and Frank Phillips College (18-6), the representative from the region which produced the previous year's national champion. Only Ely Junior College and Fairbury Junior College — the tournament's "weak sisters" with identical 13-7 records — were no threat to Cameron's unblemished record.

TUESDAY — DARK HORSE AGAIN

Coffeyville Coach Jack Hartman spent most of Monday watching tourney entries go through 30-minute workouts on the Arena floor. He told the *Coffeyville Journal*, "The longer they come out, the taller they get."

Height was a concern for Hartman. The Red Ravens were one of the smallest teams in the tournament. Hartman's tallest starters were forward Gib Scranton and center Vencent Knight, both 6-2.

---

[1]On April 8, 1957, Hutchinson's only newspaper moved into a modern new facility on West 2nd Street. To mark the occasion, the publication changed its name from the *News-Herald* to its original masthead.

Fairbury, Coffeyville's first-round draw, was not much taller. To overcome their lack of height, both employed tight zone defenses. Consequently, the tip-off for the 1958 Juco Tournament was a cautious contest with more passing than shooting. The resulting 57-47 Red Raven victory did little to excite the 500 fans who turned out for the curtain raiser.

The afternoon feature was even less exciting. The only interesting aspect of the game was that it gave the local crowd its first glimpse of the No. 1 team in the country. All five Cameron State starters hit double figures — Bud Sahmaunt (17), Jackie Martin (17), Homer Watkins (15), Gene Miller (13), and Gerald Hertler (13). The Aggie defense was equally impressive, holding the Joliet Wolves 35 points below their season average. Cameron's crushing 82-52 triumph confirmed why the Aggies were undefeated.

After two dull games, fans trickled out of the Sports Arena to have an early supper before the evening session. Those who left missed nothing. Like Cameron State, North Greenville exhibited a balanced attack with four Mountaineers scoring 18 points or better. The Carolinians jumped to a 15-point lead in the first eight minutes, maintained a 10-point advantage from there on, and easily downed Frank Phillips, 86-75.

The evening opener was expected to be another lopsided match. Only 130 students were enrolled at Ely Junior College while Weber's faculty alone totaled 196. Everyone was surprised, however, when the Ironmen from Ely kept abreast of Weber, trailing the Wildcats by only three with 8:35 to go.

Then, in the next five minutes, the roof caved in. Weber exploded for 18 points while the Ironmen tallied two free throws by center John Sayovitz. The favored Utahans coasted to a 68-51 victory.

With the predictable first-round upper bracket games out of the way, fans prepared for the evenly matched pairings of the lower bracket. Kicking off the close competition was the contest Hutchinson fans had anxiously waited for all day. The mood of the 6,000 loyal supporters who showed for the opening-night feature reflected a confidence not shown in previous appearances. In the past, Hutchinson's tourney participation had been a gift. This time the Blue Dragons had earned their spot.

Hutchinson's record was not notable when compared with records such as Cameron State's. However, it failed to take into account, the Blue Dragons' improved play towards the end of the season when they closed with 12 consecutive victories before losing to Dodge City in the state play-offs — an anticlimactic endeavor since Hutchinson had just secured a berth in the nationals with the Region 6 crown.

The team's height was not formidable; its speed *was*. Against Mesa County, Hutchinson blistered the court. In the first 20 minutes, the Blue Dragons raced by the Coloradans, 51-21. With reserves stocking the lineup, Hutchinson's second half was less artistic but no less effective. The hometown rejoiced to walloping 91-62 romp. Because the local squad was sharp and poised, the press again confidently labeled Hutchinson the tournament's dark horse.

The day's finale matched unknown quantities with identical records. Snead of Boaz, Alabama, had never been to the tournament. The last trip for Flint was a brief two-game stint in 1950. The curious few who remained after Hutchinson's pleasing victory were rewarded with the best game of the day. The largest lead by either team was Flint's eight-point bulge with three minutes remaining in the first half. After Snead rebounded, the two battled even to the wire. When the final buzzer sounded the score read: Snead — 78, Flint — 76.

The game was not over, though. Flint's Bob Morin was fouled on the last play and was awarded two free throws. The floor was cleared and the Michigan guard, who had made two pressure shots in the latter stages of the contest, stood alone at the line. His teammates had already missed three crucial charities in the losing minute-and-a-half.

His first shot was clean and through.

The second hit the back edge of the rim hard, bounced against the front edge, then lipped up and out. Morin crumpled to the floor in tears.

WEDNESDAY — RIDING THE ROLLER COASTER

The day's opener was full of ups and downs. Brewton-Parker initiated the pattern, jumping to a 15-5 advantage.

Then, while the Georgians cooled off, Broome Tech fired up. The Hornets caught and passed Brewton-Parker, taking a comfortable 45-30 lead into the locker room.

The Georgia Barons pulled out of the nose dive behind the heroics of Pete McDuffie, a 5-9 forward who scored only three points in the opening frame. McDuffie's 20-point final period, plus the loss of four Broome Tech players to fouls, secured a 79-72 victory for Brewton-Parker.

When Coach Joe Turner found out who Kilgore was playing in the first round, he remarked, "Isn't that just our luck to draw a team like that." Those sentiments could easily have been ascribed to his opponents, the Moberly Greyhounds. Besides being the only teams in the tournament with previous championships, Moberly and Kilgore represented the two regions which combined had won two-thirds of the national titles in the past nine years.

The match-up drew so much pre-tourney attention, the game was shifted from its originally scheduled afternoon time slot to the Wednesday evening opener. Fans eagerly responded to the move. Fifty-five hundred — a large total for a midweek night in which no local favorite appeared on the agenda — ate supper early or skipped it all together in order to catch the 6 p.m. battle. Their sacrifice was rewarded.

Like the earlier Broome Tech-Brewton-Parker contest, the Moberly-Kilgore game was a roller coaster ride of emotions. Kilgore was the first to ride to the top, building a 24-14 lead with 8:40 to go in the first half, the largest held by either team during the contest.

Then, Moberly hopped in the upward climbing car, pulled even at 26-all, then forged a one-point advantage as the half neared completion.

In quick succession, Pat Stanley hit a free throw and Sid Cohen and Wilmer Cox each canned field goals. Kilgore spurted to a 38-34 halftime edge.

The hot hand switched after intermission with the Greyhounds tallying the first 10 points, taking their biggest lead of the game, 44-38.

Again the momentum turned, the next nine tallies going to Kilgore. Riding the crest, the Rangers gained their largest margin in the second half, 58-49, with 11:25 remaining.

The Greyhounds' next surge was not enough to overcome the Kilgore advantage. Moberly pulled to within two just before Don Stanley contributed a field goal and two free throws to give the Rangers breathing room at 64-58.

The pivotal point came with 7:44 to go when Sid Cohen, Kilgore's operations director and principal ball handler, was whistled for his fifth foul.

The door was open for the Greyhounds. However, in the next 4½ minutes, all Moberly could shave from the Kilgore lead was two points.

With three minutes remaining, Coach Turner ordered the Rangers to stall. The Greyhounds were forced to foul. While Corky Alderson field goals kept hopes alive at the Moberly end, Kilgore sank free throws. At the six-second mark, Lonnie Willoughby tossed in two clinching charities, his only points of the game. Kilgore won the battle of champions, 78-74.

A key element shared by a majority of the first-round winners was balanced point production and Kilgore was no different. All five starters hit double digits — Cox (17), Don Stanley (17), Cohen (15), Red Walling (14), and Pat Stanley (13). The total team effort was also reflected in the rebounding figures. Walling and the two Stanley's — identical twins whose only distinguishing feature was the number on their jersey — outhustled the taller Moberly front line and won the board war, 42-41.

Despite Kilgore's team play, one Ranger stood out. When Cohen sat down with his fifth foul, the responsibility for running Kilgore's floor plan fell to Cox, a 6-3 Houston native who put on a dribbling exhibition to prolong the Ranger stall in the nerve-racking waning minutes. As Coach Turner put it for the *Kilgore*

News Herald: "Wilmer played the best clutch ball I've ever had played for me. He did a helluva job."[2]

Moberly, too, had a hero. At 5-7, Corky Anderson had been the smallest man on the floor. He was also the quickest. His speed and maneuverability combined with an undefendable jump shot made him illusive prey on the court. The Moberly native single-handedly kept the Greyhounds alive at the end, hitting 12 of Moberly's final 16 points. His game-high 30 was the highest individual total in the first round. However, the Moberly guard received the best praise from his Kilgore defender — Cox: "I hope there aren't any tougher players than that Alderson."

After the tension of the Moberly-Kilgore contest, the Arena audience was allowed to catch its breath. The opening quarterfinal featured two defensive teams that stressed ball control and the pace slowed considerably.

Coffeyville surprised everyone by holding the advantage over Cameron State during most of the opening period, though the margin of difference was small.

The Aggies did not catch fire until the 1:20 mark of the half. A long field goal by Gene Miller, two free throws by Bud Sahmaunt, and another fielder by Miller tied the score, 28-all. Then, with eight seconds remaining, Homer Watkins — a 6-7 physical specimen with huge shoulders and arms — intercepted a Red Raven pass, dribbled from midcourt, and crammed the basketball two-handed. Though it gave Cameron a mere two-point advantage, the Watkins stuff crushed Coffeyville. The Aggies toyed with the Kansans throughout the second period, forcing numerous Red Raven errors with full-court pressure. The result was an unspectacular but easy 63-53 Cameron win.

The Wednesday finale began as a blowout. Weber waltzed to a 38-25 halftime advantage over North Greenville, then quickly built it to a margin of 18 at the beginning of the second period. Most of the Arena crowd gave up and headed home.

But, with few witnesses, the South Carolinians stole back into contention, making up 10 points of the deficit in five minutes and finally tying the score at 64-all with 3:48 remaining. When North Greenville regained control of the basketball, Coach Dick Campbell decided to play for one final shot.

While time crept slowly off the clock, both teams engaged in a staring contest. Then, as the final seconds neared, Weber tightened its defense while the Mountaineers moved in for the kill.

The game-ending shot by Melvin Quick split the cords, but was ruled to have been launched too late.

The overtime was a mini-version of regulation play. Weber jumped ahead, 75-69, before North Greenville mounted a closing rally. Then, with 11 seconds to go, the Mountaineers down, 75-74, two free throws by Jim Brittain sealed the victory for Weber.

THURSDAY — BEWARE THE DRAGON!

Since the Blue Dragons were slated to play last, Thursday was an anxious day of waiting for Hutchinson fans. Fortunately, the other hump day contests provided excellent distraction.

The shocker of the tournament occurred in the afternoon feature when Broome Tech downed No. 2 Moberly, 69-64. Using a spread offense, the New Yorkers slashed through Moberly's half-court pressure, pulled the much taller Greyhounds away from the basket, and upstaged the Missouri team in evey department. The most important factor in the upset, however, was the emotional state of the Moberly players who suffered a tremendous psychological letdown after the loss to Kilgore. Only Corky Alderson — whose second 30-point performance led all scorers and secured him a position on the All-Tournament Team — appeared motivated to play winning basketball. Consequently, for the first time in its illustrious tourney history, Moberly was eliminated from competition after two games.

The afternoon finale gave Kansas partisans a chance to warm up for the Blue Dragon game. Forsaking their usual defensive ways, the Coffeyville Red Ravens went to the offensive and led North Greenville wire-to-wire, chalking up a 92-82 win. Coffeyville forward Gib Scranton took game honors with 29, including 12 in the second half.

The evening started with a bang when 5-11 guard Norman Schulz came off the bench, quarterbacked the Mesa County

attack, led the Coloradans' assault on the boards, and topped the team's scoring with 20, enabling the Mavericks to edge Flint, 79-76, in an overtime thriller.

If the Mesa County-Flint cliff-hanger prolonged the agony of waiting for local fans, the evening feature intensified it. With the crowd supporting them, the Brewton-Parker Barons battled heavily favored Kilgore to near even terms through three quarters of the game.

Then, Don Stanley went on a scoring spree. Kilgore gradually pulled away to win, 95-88.

Two factors figured in the Texans' victory. First, Kilgore only fouled 13 times, outpointing Brewton-Parker, 23-12, from the free throw line. Secondly, Stanley — who had set a Texas state tournament record with 51 points in one game the previous year for his hometown Buna, Texas, high school — put together the best game any Ranger had played all year. Employing a soft, deadly jump shot, the freshman rolled up 37 points to lead all scorers. Twenty-three of his tallies came in the second half and 12 were fired in the critical final 10 minutes. When Stanley fouled out with 2:19 to go, the Arena crowd showed appreciation for his effort with a loud ovation.

The demonstration was polite compared to the raucous cheering which accompanied the Blue Dragons as they took the court for the remaining quarterfinal. The crowd's enthusiasm infected Hutchinson during a tight first period. By halftime the local squad had built a nine-point lead over Snead.

The coup de grace came five minutes into the second half. With Hutchinson leading by 20, 6-5 Don Owens, Snead's tallest man, fouled out. From then on, the Blue Dragons were merciless. By game's conclusion, Hutchinson's advantage had ballooned to 38. The final: Hutchinson — 96, Snead — 58.

Though Hutchinson center Merle Harris equaled the earlier 37-point performance of Kilgore's Stanley, praise for the victor was lauded on the entire squad. The hometown crew had again displayed tremendous speed and depth. A staunch Blue Dragon half-court defense held the Alabama Parsons far below their offensive average. When somebody asked Brewton-Parker Coach Jim Harley — who had watched from the stands — what he thought of Hutchinson's half-court pressure, he responded in a syrupy southern drawl, "Half-cowt, Hell! They get on ya when ya get off the bus and they don't get off until ya get back on."

Talk from all quarters revolved around the same thought: Watch out for the Blue Dragons!

FRIDAY — A STACKED DECK

When Hutchinson entered the semifinals in 1949, local fans were elated with the unexpected achievement, but prayerful when regarding the unpromising possibilities for further advancement. In 1958, the hometown was brimming with confidence. The Blue Dragons were on a tear. In the opening rounds, Hutchinson had outdistanced the opposition by an average 33.5 points per game while pre-tourney favorite Kilgore barely squeaked by, edging Moberly and Brewton-Parker by nine points total. Even Kilgore followers were apprehensive. According to Ted Allen, sports editor for the *Kilgore News Herald,* "Hutchinson . . . is the most underrated team in the tournament . . . [The Blue Dragons] will be difficult to handle anywhere, but particularly so on their home floor . . . The deck is stacked against [the Rangers] . . ."

The bright prospect brought out the hometown crowd. The fire department's limit of 6,500 Arena spectators was reached midway through the opening semifinal. For the first time since moving out of small Convention Hall, scores of eager ticket buyers were turned away from the tourney gate.

With everyone's attention focused on the upcoming Kilgore-Hutchinson contest, the other semifinal went unnoticed. Once the lucky ticket-holders finally settled in their seats and glanced up at the scoreboard, their interest was peaked; the undefeated Cameron State Aggies trailed underdog Weber.

Even with a 10-point deficit with 10 minutes to go, everyone expected Cameron to rally. However, Weber denied close shots and only the Aggies' Bud Sahmaunt showed consistent success from the perimeter. When the final 74-61 verdict was rendered, Cameron State — owner of the only remaining perfect record in collegiate basketball — bowed to its first conqueror.

[2]Cox was fortunate to be playing. Just prior to the Region 14 tournament, he was stricken with a serious case of food poisoning. He lost 10 pounds during the illness and required intravenous feeding. The Rangers missed his services in only one game, however, his quick recovery credited to superior physical condi-

The difference in the game was Weber's tenacious defense. At one point the usually poised Aggies gave up the ball four times in a row on bad passes forced by the purposeful Utahans. By game's end, Cameron's errors numbered 17 to Weber's eight.

Weber's upset charged the crowd. The winner of the Kilgore-Hutchinson semifinal would not have to face the No. 1 team in the nation.

To the two dozen or so Ranger fans in attendance, playing the Aggies would have been preferable to facing the Blue Dragons. The small group was lost in the overpowering support for Hutchinson. The Kilgore players could have easily been overwhelmed by the circumstances. Instead, the Rangers ignored the hoopla and knuckled down to business.

The task was not easy. Though the Rangers led through most of the first half, they could not shake the fired-up Blue Dragons. It took a free throw by Sid Cohen and a last second tip-in by reserve Charles Eads to salvage a 39-37 halftime edge.

Hutchinson persisted in the first four minutes of the second half, taking three brief leads. Then, Cohen and Don Stanley bottomed the net with increasing regularity. With nine minutes remaining, Kilgore had defused the explosive crowd with a commanding 67-58 advantage.

The Rangers were not allowed to ease back in the saddle, though. Hutchinson's Glenn Hamilton stole the ball and scored, quickly added another field goal, then was supported by Dick Gisel who canned a bucket from the side. With the Kilgore margin down to three, the crowd regained its enthusiasm.

During the next five minutes the two teams traded points. A bomb from the edge of the court by Billy James and a jumper by Maurice Schrag completed the Blue Dragon rally. At the 2:47 mark, the score was tied, 72-all.

When Kilgore missed its next attempt, Hutchinson grabbed the rebound and decided to play for the game-winner. A minute-and-ten seconds later, the Blue Dragons lost the ball on a bad pass.

It was Kilgore's turn to hold for one. The seats were filled with squirming fans as time ticked off. With three seconds remaining, Mickie Heinz threw a wrench in the Ranger machinery, knocking the ball out of bounds. Kilgore was unable to fire a shot before the final buzzer.

The electric mood of the crowd built during the time-out. It intensified in the cautiously played opening moments of overtime. Then, Red Walling — who had just two other field goals to his credit in the game — dampened Blue Dragon hopes, twice popping the cords from the corner. With Kilgore in control, Hutchinson was forced to scramble. Fouls followed. In the final minutes, the Rangers hit seven of 10 free throws to clinch their second title shot, 83-78.

SATURDAY — A FLURRY OF FOULS

The Joliet Wolves battled health problems all through the tournament. In their first outing, forward Jerry Keigher was weakened from a bout with the flu. The other forward, Matt Vigliocco, aggravated a previous knee injury in the opening minutes, sidelining him for the rest of the week. Then, on the last day of the meet, guard Larry Waddell was hospitalized with severe stomach cramps.

When Joliet faced Broome Tech for fifth place Saturday afternoon, only eight Wolves were available for play. The lack of personnel did not prevent the Illinois crew from a peak performance, though. In 51 trips to the line, Joliet free throwers hit a remarkable 42. The landmark achievement also pushed Joliet's tournament total to 111, another record setter. With 30 more points from the charity stripe than their opponents, the Wolves easily downed Broome Tech, 88-74.

After cheering the Coffeyville Red Ravens to a 70-60 fourth-place triumph over Brewton-Parker, local fans were in full voice for the evening session. The third-place showdown between Hutchinson and Cameron State was as eagerly awaited as the championship tilt later. Consequently, for the second night in a row, empty-handed ticket purchasers were turned away at the door.

The full-house throng was entertained by a record-setting, overtime thriller in the opener. Referees Tom Glennon and Steve Gergeni played a major role in the drama. With 11:31 left in the game, they whistled Hutchinson starting guard Keith Gaeddert to the bench with five fouls. Seventeen seconds later forward Dick Gisel joined him — the only time the sophomore ever fouled out of a junior college contest.

The calls were not one-sided. The Aggies' Homer Watkins and Ronnie Howard picked up their limit of fouls trying to hog-tie Hutchinson's Merle Harris. The Blue Dragon center — a late bloomer whose recent development paralleled Hutchinson's season-ending success — marched repeatedly to the free throw line, sinking 13 of 15 in the first half and 17 (one off the record) for the game. When Harris, too, fouled out with 5:43 to go, his game-high 31 points gave him a four-game total of 101, the tournament high.

A fourth Blue Dragon, Mickie Heinz, totaled five personals before time expired in regulation. Three more Aggies — Gene Miller, Gerald Hertzler, and Bill Flurry — reached the limit in overtime. In all, 65 fouls were called — a new tourney record.

Though the excessive number of infractions were evenly split (Cameron — 33, Hutchinson — 32), their effect was unequal. Throughout the tournament, Coach Ted Owens had stayed with his starting five as much as possible. Hutchinson, on the other hand, had shown good bench strength. In the overtime, Blue Dragon reserves scored all Hutchinson's points, including 10 for 10 from the line. Hutchinson outlasted Cameron State, 97-88.[3] Besides a beautiful third-place trophy, the Blue Dragons also won the distinction of having scored more points than any other team to date, their four-game sum of 362 surpassing East Central Mississippi's 1953 total by 10.

After Weber's semifinal upset of Cameron State, Kilgore's close calls against three opponents, and an exciting third-place

Kilgore's Sid Cohen was the first tourney MVP selected from the winning team. Though the Brooklyn native was not the Rangers leading scorer, few questioned his floor leadership. Cohen later starred at the University of Kentucky and was drafted by the Boston Celtics. (Photo courtesy of the University of Kentucky)

---

[3]Cameron State's sixth-place finish was a tremendous disappointment after having remained undefeated for so long. The Aggies later made up for it, though. On returning to Lawton, Coach Ted Owens asked his players, many of whom also played baseball, if they wanted to start a team. They agreed. The team borrowed uniforms from the 5th Field Artillery Battalion at Ft. Sill, qualified for the national tournament held at Northeast Oklahoma A&M in Miami, and became the NJCAA's first national champions in baseball.

contest preceding it, the championship game proved anticlimactic. Kilgore, in particular, found it difficult getting started, falling behind Weber, 17-10, halfway through the first period.

Then, sparked out of lethargy by Sid Cohen, who tallied 14 of his game-high 22 in the first half, the Rangers narrowed the difference to one by intermission.

While Weber showed less of the sharpness which vaulted the Wildcats past the No. 1 team in the country, Kilgore continued to play loose. Five minutes into the final period, the Rangers opened a 41-36 margin. In another five minutes, the advantage was 10. Weber never threatened thereafter.

With the 68-57 victory, Kilgore College copped its second National Junior College Basketball crown.

THE AFTERMATH — A NEW ATTENDANCE HIGH

After the finale, the easiest of the Rangers' four contests, Kilgore players looked gaunt and tired. The week-long pressure of national competition had taken its toll. Coach Joe Turner was described as "a man suffering a living death" from the strain. Red Walling sprained an ankle in the Brewton-Parker contest. Sid Cohen — the first individual from a winning team to be honored as the tournament's Most Valuable Player — suffered a charley horse in his right thigh and had a front tooth knocked out in the rugged overtime tilt with Hutchinson. All were emotionally and physically drained.

Kilgore's fatigue was testimony to the tournament's team balance. The fact that the Rangers' total four-game victory margin was the lowest to date for a champion further confirmed it.

The 1958 version of the Juco Tournament had been one of the best yet and the turnstiles agreed. Though tourney gross receipts were under 1953's top figure, more than 22,000 had entered the Sports Arena during the five-day competition — a new record.[4]

Tournament Results

Day		Game		Result
Tuesday:	Game			
		1	Coffeyville — 57	Fairbury — 47
		2	Cameron St. — 82	Joliet — 52
		3	North Greenville — 86	Frank Phillips — 75
		4	Weber — 68	Ely — 51
		5	Hutchinson — 91	Mesa County — 62
		6	Snead — 78	Flint — 77
Wednesday:	Game			
		7	Brewton-Parker — 79	Broome Tech — 72
		8	Joliet 108	Fairbury — 83
		9	Kilgore — 78	Moberly — 74
		10	Cameron St. — 63	Coffeyville — 53
		11	Weber — 77	North Greenville — 74 OT
Thursday:	Game			
		12	Frank Phillips — 77	Ely — 66
		13	Broome Tech — 69	Moberly — 64
		14	Coffeyville — 92	North Greenville — 82
		15	Mesa County — 79	Flint — 76 OT
		16	Kilgore — 93	Brewton-Parker — 88
		17	Hutchinson — 96	Snead — 58
Friday:	Game			
		18	Joliet — 101	Frank Phillips — 71
		19	Broome Tech — 55	Mesa County — 49
		20	Brewton-Parker — 90	Snead — 80
		21	Weber — 74	Cameron St. — 61
		22	Kilgore — 83	Hutchinson — 78 OT
Saturday:	Game			
		23	Joliet — 88	Broome Tech — 74
		24	Coffeyville — 70	Brewton-Parker — 60
		25	Hutchinson — 97	Cameron St. — 88 OT
		26	Kilgore — 68	Weber — 57

How They Finished in 1958

1. Kilgore College
2. Weber College
3. Hutchinson Junior College
4. Coffeyville College of Arts, Science, and Vocations
5. Joliet Junior College
6. Cameron State Agricultural College
7. Brewton-Parker Junior College
8. Broome Technical Community College

All-Tournament Team

Corky Alderson — Moberly Junior College
Frank Berrett — Weber College
Sid Cohen — Kilgore College
Dick Gisel — Hutchinson Junior College
Merle Harris — Hutchinson Junior College
Allen Holmes — Weber College
Ted James — Joliet Junior College
Vencent Knight — Coffeyville College of Arts, Science, and Vocations
Joseph "Bud" Sahmaunt — Cameron State Agricultural College
Don Stanley — Kilgore College

Player of the Year

Sid Cohen — Kilgore College

---

[4]General admission prices were higher and more reserved seat tickets were sold in 1953 than in 1958, thus accounting for the higher receipts.

oberly Junior College's early success in the National Junior College Basketball Tournament correlated directly to Maury John's coaching abilities. The Sweet Springs, Missouri, native started his tenure with the 1946-47 season in which he coached both Moberly's senior high and junior college. He inherited poor material on the junior college squad and ended with a paltry 6-13 record for his first year's effort. After that, Moberly never experienced a losing season under his head. In John's 12 seasons as the mentor of the Greyhounds, Moberly won 280 and lost 75 — a winning percentage of .789. John guided nine teams to the national tournament in 11 years and returned home with six trophies, including back-to-back championships.

The Greyhounds' ignoble 1958 finish signaled the end of an era. At the close of the school year, John accepted the head coaching position at Drake University. Without him, the 1958-1959 Greyhounds struggled. Coming into the Region 16 tournament, Moberly had barely won half its games. It required a victory in the meaningless third-place contest to salvage a winning season for the once mighty Greyhounds. Moberly's string of eight consecutive national tourney appearances — an all-time record — came to an end.

THE PARTICIPANTS

Moberly Junior College was not the only familiar name absent from the tournament's 1959 roster. After 11 years of steady growth and building tradition, the event received an infusion of new blood; 11 schools made their first trip to Hutchinson.

The plethora of fresh faces should have made predicting a winner a nightmarish task. The opposite was true, however. The *Hutchinson News* had no trouble zeroing in on "the big three."

Heading the list of top contenders was everyone's No. 1 team — Weber College (30-3). The choice was logical. Besides having been top-rated most of the year, Weber, with five previous appearances, was the most veteran of any tourney participant and the runner-up from the 1958 event.

The Wildcats also possessed the preeminent player in junior college ranks — Allen Holmes. An All-Tournament selection the year before, the 6-3 forward was a first-team Juco All-American, top scorer in the Intermountain Collegiate Athletic Conference, and owner of the third-highest average (25.9) coming into the tournament. Though he was Weber's only returning starter, he made all the difference.

Two of the Utahans' losses came early in the year at the end of a long road trip. Since then, Weber had been virtually unstoppable, felling 15 consecutive victims. In the best-of-three play-off series with Phoenix College for the Region 1 title, Weber squeaked by on a tip-in with 12 seconds remaining in the first contest, learned from the experience, then bombed the Arizonans, 72-47. The Wildcats knew what it took to win a national title.

The only tourney newcomer in "the big three" was Paris Junior College (25-4). Though unproven in national competition, no one doubted Paris's ability to compete with the best. In the Region 14 tournament, the Dragons downed No. 2 Lon Morris College in the semifinals, then edged No. 3 Kilgore College, the defending national champions, 62-61, in the final.

Before leaving for the big time at Drake University and later Iowa State, Maury John compiled a phenomenal .789 winning percentage at Moberly Junior College, guiding the Greyhounds to nine Juco Tournament appearances in 11 years, including the tourney's first back-to-back titles. He remained a fixture at later tournaments, recruiting heavily from the Juco ranks. In 1984, John was an inaugural inductee into the NJCAA Basketball Hall of Fame. (Photo courtesy of Iowa State University)

Rounding out "the big three" was Cameron State of Lawton, Oklahoma. The choice of the Aggies as a pre-tourney favorite was based as much on the lasting impression of the team's excellent record from the previous year as it was on its current accomplishments. Though the team was loaded with talent, the Aggies returned no starters from their 1958 sixth-place squad and had compiled an unimpressive 19-7 record. Even so, Cameron was well-coached, well-disciplined, and well-respected.

According to *Hutchinson News* sports editor Fred Mendell, the team joining "the big three" in the semifinals would be Independence Community College (19-4). Though it was the first trip to the nationals for the Pirates, there was supporting evidence that the Kansans would do well. Independence possessed height, speed, and marksmanship and, in rebounding power alone, was rated better than the Kansas representatives from the year before.

In addition, the Pirates played best under pressure. In one week's time, Independence chalked up five crucial victories, sewing up the Region 3 crown and winning its first state title in

Region	Team
1	Weber College — Ogden, Utah
2	Cameron State Agricultural College — Lawton, Oklahoma
3	Independence Community College — Independence, Kansas
4	LaSalle-Peru-Oglesby Junior College — LaSalle, Illinois
5	San Angelo College — San Angelo, Texas
6	Pratt Junior College — Pratt, Kansas
7	The Marion Institute — Marion, Alabama
8	Chipola Junior College — Marianna, Florida
9	Mesa County Junior College — Grand Junction, Colorado
10	North Greenville Junior College — Tigerville, South Carolina
11	Eagle Grove Junior College — Eagle Grove, Iowa
12	Henry Ford Community College — Dearborn, Michigan
13	Bethany Lutheran College — Mankato, Minnesota
14	Paris Junior College — Paris, Texas
15	State University of New York Agricultural & Technical Institute at Alfred — Alfred, New York
16	Lindsey Wilson College — Columbia, Kentucky

18 years. Among the season's booty were three Pirate victories over highly regarded Coffeyville College. However, Independence's most cherished treasure and best credential was its overtime triumph of top-rated Weber.

Only two other teams possessed credentials for possible title consideration. One was veteran San Angelo College (20-5), the only past champion in the tournament. The other was new to the national event, but not to Hutchinson. Earlier in the year on the Sports Arena floor, the local Blue Dragons downed Bethany Lutheran of Mankato, Minnesota, 66-54, one of only two losses all year for the Vikings. With 25 victories to their credit, the top-10 rated Minnesotans owned the best record in the tournament.

It was anybody's guess how the remaining 10 squads would do. Two were tourney veterans with litte to inspire prognosticators: North Greenville Junior College (23-5) was making its fouth consecutive trip to Hutchinson, but had graduated its entire starting lineup from a year ago; Mesa County Junior College (17-6) returned four starters from its 1958 tournament team, but had been easy pickings for Weber twice during the season, 75-58 and 76-53. The rest were novices to the proceedings: Henry Ford Community College (19-3), Eagle Grove Junior College (19-4), and The Marion Institute (13-7) were the latest entries from regions with poor previous showings; the old haunt of Joliet Junior College was now represented by LaSalle-Peru-Oglesby Junior College (15-4); Broome Technical Community College and New York City Community College lost their grip on the East to Alfred Tech (18-5); Chipola Junior College (16-6) ended Brewton-Parker Junior College's string of tourney appearances; Lindsey Wilson College (24-9) looked to be the heir apparent to Moberly's domain; and Pratt Junior College (18-7) became the last Western Kansas Junior College Conference school to earn a trip to the national tournament.

TUESDAY — DO-OR-DIE

Paris coach Boyd Converse was well aware teams often entered first-round games of the national tournament tight. He told the *Hutchinson News*, "I've been dreading this first one since the regionals." His opponent was North Greenville, a top-rated team, possessing tournament experience and featuring one of the top scorers in the country — Joe Parker (26.6).

Converse's fears proved well-founded. The Dragons failed to loosen up even though supported by the only cheerleading squad attending the afternoon session — three Southern Belles clad in buckskin skirts. The 1959 curtain raiser remained close through the first period and the opening minutes of the second half. Then, with 16:25 to go and North Greenville leading, 35-34, Paris exploded for 10 consecutive points. Despite Joe Parker's game-high 36, the South Carolinians, were unable to overcome the Dragon splurge. Paris entered championship bracket play as expected, 73-68.

A well-balanced Henry Ford crew made it look easy against Eagle Grove in the matinee feature, jumping out to a 14-point margin in the first half and expanding it to 19 with nine minutes left in the game.

In desperation, Eagle Grove employed a full-court press. Behind the leadership of center Mike Rawson, who tallied 17 of his game-high 25 points in the second frame, the Pirates hacked away at the lead, whittling the Henry Ford advantage to five with 1:30 to go.

However, the penalty for pressure piracy was exhaustion. Tired Eagle Grove players fouled or gave up unguarded goals, allowing Henry Ford to ease away to a 79-70 victory.

Advance press compared the team from Mankato with the only other Minnesota team to do well in the tournament — the 1952 Dick Garmaker-led, Hibbing Cardinals. Though Bethany Lutheran did not have a Garmaker on its roster, the Vikings were considered the best junior college basketball team the state had yet produced.

The publicity failed to impress the Statesmen from Alfred Tech. The New Yorkers battled the Mankato five to even terms through most of the first half of the afternoon finale and, with time running out, led by four.

Then, Bethany Lutheran guard Denny Kale blasted a 40-footer as time expired. The shot ignited the Minnesotans. After a lethargic six-point first half, 6-3 guard Chad Coffman showed his leaping prowess by cracking his head on the backboard and his scoring ability with 21 second-period points. His game-high performance led the Vikings to a 53-point half as Bethany Lutheran bombed Alfred, 85-65.

The best first-round game opened Tuesday evening's session with neither Chipola nor Independence able to muster a lead greater than seven. Chipola's seven-point advantage came in the first half when the Indians surprised Independence with their speed and accurate passing. Independence repaired its defense, awakened its offense to gain the halftime lead, 32-31, then climbed to its seven-point edge with 8:30 remaining.

Because of the closeness of the contest, Independence Coach Bob Sneller decided to install the Pirates' give-and-go control game. The move destroyed the Kansan's momentum. In the next five minutes, Independence missed six field goals and a free throw while Chipola swished four of five from the field. Two free throws by Max Kirkland with 2:07 to go gave Chipola the lead, 60-58.

Independence halved the margin on a Larry Knackstedt free throw at the 1:53 mark.

Seeking breathing room, Chipola shot and misfired, Pirate forward Gary Sebbert pulling down the rebound.

At the Independence end of the court, Sebbert drove for the basket and was whistled for charging — a close call. A minute and 10 seconds remained.

Again Chipola attempted to widen the difference.

Again Sebbert grabbed the carom.

With :38 on the clock, the Pirates called time and decided to hold for a do-or-die shot. At the six-second mark, another time-out was called to set up the end-game strategem which called for Independence floor general, Larry Knackstedt, a deadly outside shooter, to take the game-winner.

The Pirate players executed the play perfectly. Knackstedt passed to center Tom Russell who immediately dumped it back to Knackstedt. The 5-9 guard drove for a short jumper. The Indian defense converged. The shot was off balance, hitting the rim wide to the right. To the dismay of the heavily partisan Kansas crowd, Chipola survived, 60-59.

Another squeaker followed, the heavily favored San Angelo Rams finding the team from Marion, Alabama, much tougher than expected. With Colonel Leo Curtin, in military dress, commanding the Cadets from the sidelines and 6-9 Terry Litchfield, the tallest man in the tournament, calling the shots under the boards, Marion dominated play early. San Angelo struggled to grab a 47-46 halftime edge.

The Rams continued on top in the second half, but could not shake loose from the belligerent Cadets. With 10 minutes remaining, San Angelo held a bare two-point margin.

Frustrated by the Alabama team's superior size and continued determination, Coach Phil George called for slowdown tactics, a surprising move for the run-and-gun Rams. The midcourt freeze insured a photo finish.

With 1:15 to go, San Angelo took a 75-71 lead, the largest advantage of the half.

Marion's Neal Adkinson slashed the margin in two with a field goal at the 45-second mark. Twenty-two seconds later, John Stanhagen tied it up with a beautiful 20-footer.

San Angelo regained the advantage with 12 seconds left on a two-pointer by forward Jerry Ray — his only field goal of the game.

Marion diligently worked for the tying bucket. With four seconds to go, Stanhagen found an opening and was fouled. The 6-2 guard stepped to the line with a chance to knot the score.

His first free throw hit.

His second missed.

Time ran out on the Cadets as players scrambled for the rebound. San Angelo advanced to the championship bracket, 77-76.

For 35 minutes, the opening-day finale progressed as predicted, sending spectators home in droves. The Cameron Aggies opened up a 10-point margin on the team from LaSalle, Illinois, at halftime and maintained the difference until five minutes remained.

With no where to turn, the LaSalle Apaches launched an all-out attack. For a while the maneuver worked, Cameron's lead dwindling to three. Then, the over aggressive Apache pressure backfired; unguarded Aggies snuck in for easy buckets, widening the gap. Cameron eased to victory, 76-70.

WEDNESDAY — TO THE SALT MINES

Wednesday morning, Hutchinson Junior College staged an assembly to entertain the visiting teams. As a part of the ceremonies, each squad was introduced by its coach. When it was Cameron State's turn, a Cameron student announced that Coach Ted Owens had taken his crew on a tour of Hutchinson's salt mines. A LaSalle-Peru-Oglesby player, still remembering his team's loss to Cameron the previous night, took the rostrum next. With a smile he asked, "Where do they send them when they lose if they go to the salt mines when they win?"

Win or lose, the Weber Wildcats knew their destiny. Earlier that day Utah Governor George D. Clyde signed a bill which would make Weber a four-year state school beginning with the fall of 1962. Ogdenites had been trying to elevate Weber's status for more than 10 years. The good news could only be topped by the Wildcats winning the national crown.

In Wednesday's opener, Bruce Larson's charges climbed to the first plateau of that dream. After eight shaky minutes, Weber started to roll. By halftime the Wildcats led Lindsey Wilson, 35-29. With three minutes to go, Weber had the game safely in hand, 70-47. Coach Larson cleared his bench. Lindsey Wilson outscored the Wildcats, 16-2, in the final few minutes, but Weber won, 72-63.

Although All-American Allen Holmes was outstanding with 8 points and 14 rebounds, he was not the star for Weber. That honor fell to Gordon Millerberg, a husky 6-4 center who scored 12 of his game-high 21 points in the first half when his teammates were still trying to find the range of the Arena goals. Playing his best game of the year, Millerberg sparkled in all departments, contributing 9 of 10 from the line and joining Holmes in Weber's domination of the middle with 10 caroms.

However, the key to Weber's success was defense. Wildcat defenders stopped Lindsey Wilson cold at the start of the second half and the Blue Raiders never recovered. As Larson told the Hutchinson News, "Everything went pretty well . . . but then it usually seems to when you win."

Pratt Junior College was a surprise entry in the tourney field, the favored Region 6 team having been the hometown Hutchinson Blue Dragons. But, in regional play, three Hutchinson starters were crippled by ankle injuries. The Beavers — who had only achieved a 4-6 record in the Western Kansas Juco Conference — pounded the local squad, 69-50, then slipped by El Dorado Junior College, 72-71, for the region crown.

There were no hard feelings from Hutchonians, though. In fact, since Pratt was a neighbor just 50 miles to the southwest, the Hutchinson Chamber of Commerce formally adopted the Beavers as "home team."

Both Pratt and Mesa County felt the pressure of national competition in the final first-round contest. The opening 10 minutes were marred by bad passes, traveling calls, and poor shooting. After the two teams overcame their nervousness, Pratt forged to a 30-25 halftime advantage. Making good use of the local support and their superior board strength, the Beavers opened the gap to 12 with five minutes to go.

Mesa County chipped at the lead. With a little more than a minute remaining, the Mavericks narrowed the margin to four.

Then, forward David Stonebraker drove all the way through the Mesa County half-court pressure for an easy basket. Pratt triumphed, 65-60.

Warmed by the Pratt victory, the crowd of 5,000 was ready for the evening's main events. Neither quarterfinal match looked close, however. Paris was heavily favored over Henry Ford and Bethany Lutheran had impressed enough spectators in its opener to gain the nod over Chipola.

As though sensing the desperate situation, Henry Ford students sent a telegram Wednesday afternoon to fire up the team. The wire read: "Remember the Alamo!"

The Hawks flew out of the dressing room to attack the Texans. Paris led through most of the first half, but at intermission found the persistent Hawks just two points behind.

Henry Ford became the advantage-taker in the second period, though the game remained close. With three minutes to go, the score was tied, 61-all.

Then, Wayne Annett, Paris's playmaker, fouled out. The Dragon offense ground to a halt.

With fortune on their side, the Hawks stalled. The over-zealous Paris defense produced fouls, allowing Henry Ford to pad its margin with free throws. To the delight of the Arena crowd, the Hawks pulled off the first major upset of the 1958 tournament, winning 73-66.

The day's finale was a wild free-for-all with Chipola and Bethany Lutheran both utilizing the fast break to generate points. Their hard charging styles lead to major collisions. Players tumbled after midcourt crashes and tempers flared in the war under the boards. Bethany Lutheran coach Dwain Mintz received a technical foul when he exploded, trying to get time called after one of his players was poked in the eye. In all, 58 personal infractions were whistled and an unbelievable 97 free throws attempted. When truce was declared by the final buzzer, it was the team with the better percentage at the charity stripe which was pronounced winner. Bethany Lutheran's 32 for 47 outpointed Chipola's 29 for 50, giving the Mankato school a slim 82-79 victory.

THURSDAY — BIG GIFTS COME IN SMALL PACKAGES

Among those in attendance for Thursday's evening session, were Mr. and Mrs. Louis Mini from Dalzell, Illinois, a town of 300, five miles from LaSalle. The prime object of their attention was their son, 19-year-old James Mini, whose performance in the opening consolation contest between LaSalle-Peru-Oglesby and Marion gave them a memory they would never forget.

The year before, Mini had been the leading scorer in the nation, averaging 31 points per game. His 1958-1959 average had dropped to 24 per game, but he was still the top scorer for the LaSalle Apaches. Against Marion, he immediately proved his importance to the team, hitting 15 of LaSalle's first 16 points. The solo effort was not enough to give the Apaches the advantage; Marion led, 20-16.

Then, Mini's teammates came to life, tying the score. The contest was tied six more times before the Apaches broke away. At halftime, LaSalle was comfortably in front, 59-44. Leading the Apache charge was Mini with a staggering 20-minute output: 13 long-range field goals and 6 of 7 from the line for a whopping total of 32. His amazing shooting exhibition kept the apparent runaway interesting for fans.

Mini continued thrilling the crowd, hitting three quick field goals to open the second period, LaSalle's margin growing to 17.

The clean-cut Cadets from Marion were not ready for elimination, though. Behind the powerful inside play of their big post, Terry Litchfield, the Cadets rallied, reducing the Marion deficit to one, 80-79, with five minutes remaining.

LaSalle went to the stall. Marion pressured and fouled. Given the opportunity to ice the game from the line, the Apaches coolly connected. In the final minutes, Mini hit seven free throws and teammate Bob Walsh added five. LaSalle triumphed, 91-83.

Individual totals for the game were imposing. All but two of Terry Litchfield's 38 came from the field as the big Cadet dominated the middle. LaSalle's Bob Walsh contributed a respectable 25 in a supporting role for the Apaches. The star of the show, however, was Mini. The Apache leader tallied 16 field goals and 16 free throws. His game-high 48 was the highest total reached by an individual since Denver Brackeen's record 53 in 1953. Many considered Mini's performance more impressive. Brackeen was a center who achieved his total from close range. As his name implied, Mini was a mighty mite — he measured only 5-7. His long-distance missile shots required radar guidance, making his effort one of the most outstanding in tournament history.

In the feature quarterfinal, the Pratt Beavers quickly found out why Weber was the top team in the country. In the first eight minutes, the Wildcats demonstrated poise and skill, outclassing the Kansan, 20-8. Hitting at a 50 percent clip, Weber continued to dominate, taking a 10-point margin into the locker room at the half. The partisan Arena crowd found little more to cheer in the second period. The Beavers' fate was sealed with three minutes left when Pratt center Don Steinhart, the second leading scorer (26.4) coming into the tournament, picked up his fifth infraction on a double foul with Weber's Allen Holmes. The Wildcats rolled to easy victory, 81-66.

Besides displaying the characteristics required of a champion team, Weber's play showcased the tourney's best individual talent in Holmes who again lived up to his All-American credentials. The sophomore forward was the best in all categories: rebounding, steals, assists, and scoring. In the first half alone, Holmes hit 72 percent of his shots, mostly from the 20 to 30-foot range. His game-high 40 points was nearly half his team's total output. With Holmes at the helm, Weber was a sure bet for the title.

Cameron State and San Angelo belonged to the Pioneer Conference and had faced each other twice during league play; San Angelo won at home, 77-71, while the Aggies returned the favor at Lawton, dumping the Rams hard, 84-63. The last quarterfinal represented the rubber match between the two schools.

The game was nip and tuck. As long as the excellent shooting Rams hit for a high percentage, San Angelo held the advantage; in the first half, the Texans outshot Cameron 50 percent to 37 percent and led, 44-42. However, when Ram accuracy fell off, San Angelo was in trouble. Besides being taller than their Ram counterparts, Cameron State forwards John Bryant (6-4) and Tom King (6-3) and center Oscar McGuire (6-5) were all superb leapers. The trio controlled the backboards, giving San Angelo only one shot at the basket.

With 1:39 to go, nothing was decided, the score deadlocked, 77-all. Then, Cameron's inside superiority took over. Bryant, a transfer from Kansas State, capped the evening's series of brilliant individual performances, breaking the tie with his 37th point. Moments later teammate Tom King, another Kansas State transfer, tipped in a missed Aggie shot. The back-to-back goals were the final margin of difference as Cameron edged San Angelo, 83-79.

FRIDAY — DROOPY DRAWERS

The Independence Pirates started the day's action rolling with their second straight blowout, overwhelming North Greenville, 99-67. In their second tourney game, the Pirates had bombed Alfred Tech, 112-79, tying the second highest score to date in tournament history. Local fans were shaking their heads, wondering what might have happened had Independence not played one of its poorer games of the year against Chipola in the opener.

The Lindsey Wilson Blue Raiders found a surprise waiting for them when they dressed for their consolation contest with La-Salle-Peru-Oglesby. After pulling them on, their uniform pants sank to an embarrassingly low level. The uniforms had returned from the cleaners with the elastic waistbands dissolved.

With substitute attire hurriedly rounded up by team host Stew Oswalt, Lindsey Wilson took to the court and convincingly dispatched LaSalle, 96-82.

The win for the Kentuckians was achieved despite another brilliant performance by LaSalle's James Mini. The pint-sized Illinois guard was magnificent from the free throw line, canning 16 consecutive charities before missing his last attempt.

Though he only played in three games, Mini set a record for fr throws, hitting 39 for the tournament. His game-high 32 ga him a total of 103 points, placing him second in scoring for 1959 event, and assuring his selection on the All-Tournam Team.

The San Angelo Rams were a team fully capable of qui surges when behind. In one rugged road trip, San Angelo play three league games in four nights, won two games by one po and one by two, and came from behind in each to do so. La in the Region 5 final, the Rams overcame a six-point deficit w 30 seconds remaining to defeat tourney favorite Howard Cou ty Junior College.

In their consolation match with Pratt, the Rams again mou ed a furious rally. After chopping the Beavers' 15-point adva tage to two, San Angelo had the opportunity to complete t comeback with 10 seconds to go. The Rams threw it away wi a bad pass.

The errant play was typical of the sloppy execution throug out the game. The disappointment of having been eliminat from championship play the previous night was evident both sides. The consolation contest was also marred by fouls. Because they scored more points from the free throw li than from the field (33-28), the Pratt Beavers survived, 61-5

In recent years, the semifinals had provided the best ente tainment of the tournament. From the size of the crowd 6,000 eager fans — it was apparent everyone felt the 19 event would be no different.

The first paired surprise elements in the developing dram As newcomers, Henry Ford and Bethany Lutheran had bo gained a measure of local support because of their underdo status. It was only fair the two return the adoration with one the best games of the week.

The evenness of the match was established in the first h when there were 10 lead changes and 17 ties. The largest ma gin held by either team came just before halftime when Bethar Lutheran forged ahead, 47-43. Two free throws by Henry Ford Dick Halleen and a last-ditch field goal by Tim McIntyre, aft a bad pass by the Minnesotans, quickly erased the differenc deadlocking the teams at intermission.

There were fewer lead changes and fewer ties in the secor period, but the action was no less exciting. The men from Ma kato took control of the game, edging ahead, 59-50, in the fir four minutes of the half. Henry Ford countered with McInty who rallied the Hawks to a 69-all draw with half the period play.

Bethany Lutheran again inched ahead. The Hawks playe catch-up. With four minutes to go, the game was still up fc grabs, 80-all.

When the Vikings hit six straight free throws to open a si point margin with 25 seconds remaining, it appeared Henr Ford had finally reached the end of the line. Then, Joe Skaisg potted two from the charity stripe. A Hawk steal and foul unde the basket gave Henry Ford's Tony Aquino two more free toss es. After Aquino hit the first and missed the second, the Haw secured the loose ball. As time ran out, Jerry Callaway wa fouled going to the bucket. Though he calmly made both fre throws, it did not matter. Bethany Lutheran edged Henry Forc 90-89.

The other semifinal matched two veterans and the only pre tourney favorites still in contention. In fact, it was a rematch c one of the previous year's semifinals. In that game, Weber ha upset an undefeated Cameron State. This year the roles wer reversed; Weber was the heavy favorite. Still, everybody fe Cameron was the best challenge to the Wildcats title chance

The respect the teams felt toward each other was reflected i the tempo of the game. Carefully executed patterns and stou defense characterized the chess match played by Weber Bruce Larson and the Aggies' Ted Owens. Larson's Wildcat earned the early advantage, taking a 35-28 lead into the locke room.

When Gordon Millerberg picked up his fourth foul early i the second frame, Weber's fortunes turned. With their husk center on the bench, the Wildcats were at the mercy of Camer on's tall front line. Tom King, John Bryant, and Oscar McGuir all contributed to an Aggie rally which put the Oklahomans o top, 42-39, with 11:31 to go.

The pressure was on the Utahans. It was the cue for Allen Holmes. Shooting jump shots from 10-15 feet away, the splendid sophomore nailed four field goals and three free throws to account for all of Weber's scoring in the next seven minutes. Behind Holmes solo effort, Weber regained the advantage, 50-45, with 3:30 remaining.

Cameron battled desperately to close the gap. With 41 seconds, Tom King hit a close-in shot, apparently shearing the deficit to one. Unfortunately, the officials ruled offensive goaltending; John Bryant had put his hand above the cylinder as the ball went through the net, nullifying the basket. A free throw and a field goal by Weber's Richard Connolly quickly followed. For the second year in a row, Cameron's drive for the crown was stopped by the Wildcats, this time by a narrow 55-51 margin.

There was no question what was the key to Weber's victory. In amassing his game-high 26 points, Allen Holmes had been spectacular from the field (50 percent) and perfect from the line (6 for 6). It was a consensus feeling that the Wildcats not only had a lock on the crown, but the MVP award as well.

SATURDAY — STIFLED YAWNS

The 1959 "Trophy Day" was one of the least exciting in tournament history.

The Blue Raiders from Columbia, Kentucky, opened the series of runaways by jumping on the Independence Pirates for an early 10-point advantage. Hitting a remarkable 67 percent of their shots, the scorching hot Lindsey Wilson five built the margin to 18 by halftime. Independence mounted a second half rally, but could pull no closer than seven. The Blue Raiders' 53 percent shooting percentage from the field and 79 percent from the line earned the Kentuckians a breezy 98-86 fifth-place victory.

In the battle for fourth, the Pratt Beavers ran out of gas, recording nine turnovers which led to a nine-point deficit by halftime, then scoring a lone field goal in the first 10 minutes of the second half. Paris won easily, 78-49. Epitomizing Pratt's frustration was the substandard performance of their leading scorer. Hampered by ankle and hip injuries, center Don Steinhart managed only 16 points, his lowest total in four games.

Despite the day's earlier blowouts and the strong odds for two more that evening, 6,500 fans turned out for the tournament's finale. Their faithful support was rewarded with the only close action of the day.

The first half of the third-place contest was a tight affair made more interesting by the fact that upstart Henry Ford took a one-point edge over favored Cameron State into intermission.

The second period, however, fell into the day's appointed pattern. The Hawks opened the final frame with a shooting exhibition from the field and closed with another exhibition from the line. The Michigan crew was led by All-Tournament selection Tim McIntyre who topped all scorers with 35, including 17 for 19 from the foul stripe. He was ably assisted by the twin brother combination of Terry and Jerry Callaway who added 23 and 15, respectively, including Terry's perfect 13 for 13 from the line. Henry Ford outshot the Aggies by 10 percent from the field and zeroed in for 85 percent from the line. The Hawks' easy 91-69 victory surprised everyone.

The only similarities between the 1959 finalists were the character-building road trips each had taken early in the season and their excellent records, the best in the tournament.[1] In all other respects, Bethany Lutheran and Weber were worlds apart.

The Mankato squad was offensive minded, the third-leading point producer in the nation, averaging more than 90 points per game. Weber, on the other hand, stressed defense. The highest total given up by the Wildcats was 68 to Coffeyville College on their tiring swing through Kansas. Through 36 contests, Weber opposition had averaged a meager 52.1 points per game, second-best in the country.

The emotions displayed after the semifinals also contrasted the two titlists. The Viking locker room was a bedlam of elation, the Minnesotans happy to have a second-place trophy assured in their first trip to the nationals. Weber players were more subdued, matter-of-fact. After tasting the bitter wine of second-best the previous year, the Wildcats would only be satisfied by wearing the crown.

There was one other difference, one which stood out more than the rest: Bethany Lutheran did not have an Allen Holmes.

The task of handling Holmes fell to Chad Coffman, a 6-3 guard better known for his defense, though he had been a scoring dynamo for the Vikings throughout the tournament. Through two-thirds of the opening period, the defensive alignment proved effective. Coffman held Holmes in check and Bethany Lutheran edged ahead, 14-12, with 6:37 remaining in the period.

But, two factors crushed Vikings hopes of an upset. First, mid-

The 1959 national champion Weber Wildcats. In six tourney appearances with Eastern Arizona and Weber, Bruce Larson squads never finished lower than seventh. As the only individual in tourney history to guide teams to the championship game in three successive years, Larson was a deserving recipient of the tournament's first Coach of the Year Award in 1959. He later coached 11 years at the University of Arizona. (Photo courtesy of Bruce Larson)

[1] There was nothing glamorous about traveling at the junior college level. Since extensive travel was far beyond the financial means of most junior colleges, the team from Mankato was one of the first Minnesota schools to take its basketball team on the road, trekking all the way to Texas two years in a row. When asked whether the lengthy excursions were made because Bethany Lutheran was a private institution, former coach Dwain Mintz (later head coach at Wisconsin-Stout) replied, "It was because we were crazy, not because we were private. We didn't have a dime to make those trips. We talked them into taking care of us for 50 cents a player a night in motels. We talked restaurants into giving us practically free meals."

way in the opening period, Denny Kale, Coffman's running mate at guard and Bethany Lutheran's second-leading scorer in the tournament, twisted and broke his ankle after landing awkwardly on another player's foot. Secondly, Holmes slipped by Coffman's excellent defense for an easy lay-up.

With a dispirited Coffman on the court and a useless Kale on the bench, the Viking backcourt became easy pickings for Weber's quick Joe Carter. The 5-10 guard masterminded three straight thefts which set up Wildcat fast breaks. Weber vaulted to a 24-15 lead.

Bethany Lutheran tried to counter Weber's slow, deliberate game with pressure in the second half. Matters only worsened. After 10 minutes, Weber's margin grew to 46-30. Three Holmes field goals led a Wildcat rally which expanded the difference to 20 with five minutes remaining. Reserves finished the game for both sides.

With a 57-47 triumph, Weber College wore the laurel crown of junior college basketball.

THE AFTERMATH — THIRD TIME THE CHARM

Developing a winning formula had not been easy for Coach Bruce Larson. He had guided Eastern Arizona Junior College to the final in 1957 and Weber the year before only to fall short of the crown. Now, on his third successive try, Larson had finally copped the title. His patience was doubly rewarded. After the final buzzer, Larson's victorious Wildcats showed their adoration for their coach by carrying him from the floor on their shoulders. Later during the awards ceremony, fans and rivals alike paid their respects with a warm round of applause as Larson was honored with the tournament's first Coach of the Year award.

Coach Larson later said, "Because of previous tournament experience, I felt strongly [that] to win that tournament, to win four games, and to maintain consistency, defense was going to have to carry you in a game or two." Weber's defense proved itself in *all four* games, allowing only 56.8 points per game, the lowest figure since the tournament's early days when lower scoring prevailed.

Even with Larson's excellent coaching and the Wildcats' superb defense, most observers felt Weber wore the crown for only one reason — Allen Holmes. As San Angelo coach Phil George put it, "He was the talk of the tournament." No player since Hibbing's Dick Garmaker was so instrumental to a team's success. The lean, lanky forward — his teammates nicknamed him "Stretch" — led the Wildcats in every statistical category, including a tourney-high 115 points. His offensive prowess alone guaranteed his consideration for the tournament's top individual honor. Holmes was the unanimous recipient of the MVP award, however, for another reason: He excelled in the clutch. Bethany Lutheran coach Dwain Mintz paid the Weber star the highest compliment: "So much was demanded of him. [Yet,] as the pressure mounted, he just got better." To prove the point, in the championship game, Holmes tallied 31 points — more than half his team's total.[2]

Weber's Allen Holmes was one of the most dominating players in Juco Tourney history and one of the easiest MVP selections. He led all scorers with 115 points and topped every Weber statistical category, including more than half the team's offensive output in the title contest. He finished his collegiate career at the University of Utah, but a tragic auto accident prevented a future in the pros. (Photo courtesy of Bruce Woodbury, University of Utah)

---

[2] No narration of the National Junior College Basketball Tournament's history would be complete without including the full story of Allen Holmes. His ability to overcome adversity exemplifies the spirit of junior college sports.

Holmes' parents died when he was young. From the age of 13, he lived in four foster homes. He worked part-time jobs to put himself through high school. Though one of Arizona's top players at Phoenix Union High School, he was unable to qualify for a spot on a major university squad because of poor grades.

Bruce Larson brought Holmes with him when he moved from Eastern Arizona to Weber. In Ogden, Holmes found a home and blossomed on the court, bringing himself and Weber national recognition. As Harlem Globetrotter Bobby Milton told the *Ogden Standard-Examiner* during the 1959 tournament, "Before he finishes his college career he will write his name alongside of Wilt The Stilt Chamberlain and Oscar Robertson."

Four-year college doors all over the country stood wide open for Holmes when he graduated from Weber. Instead, he opted to stay in Utah and play for the Utes at Salt Lake City.

The 1959-60 Utah squad compiled an excellent 26-3 record, making it to the semifinals of the NCAA western regional. With Holmes and sophomore sensation Billy "The Hill" McGill returning, Utah was a strong candidate for the national title the following year.

Then, during the summer, tragedy ended Holmes's dreams. He was seriously injured in a car wreck, nearly losing his right leg. Doctors told him he would never play basketball again.

Holmes proved them wrong. After a year of rehabilitation, he rejoined his Utah teammates. As former Utah coach Jack Gardner told Ensign Ritchie for a December 26, 1982, *Standard-Examiner* article: "He made the greatest comeback I have ever seen in my life. I played him in the post his senior year because he couldn't move well. He was better on one leg than many were on two."

Basketball had been Holmes's life. With no chance to pursue his goal of playing professionally, Holmes faced another crisis. As he told Ritchie, he spent the next 15 years "kicking round at various jobs while drinking excessively. At one point I became paranoid."

Allen "Stretch" Holmes overcame that adversity, too, and later helped others lick similar problems as ethnic minority specialist and vice president of Project Re-Entry at the Utah State Prison.

1959 TOURNAMENT BRACKET

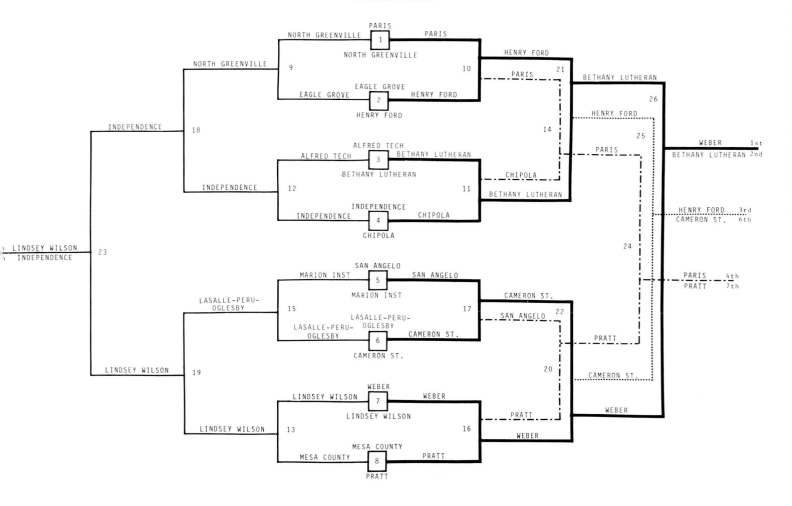

Tournament Results

Tuesday: Game

1. Paris — 73 North Greenville — 68
2. Henry Ford — 79 Eagle Grove — 70
3. Bethany Lutheran — 85 Alfred Tech — 65
4. Chipola — 60 Independence — 59
5. San Angelo — 77 Marion Inst. — 76
6. Cameron St. — 76 LaSalle-Peru-Oglesby — 70

Wednesday: Game

7. Weber — 72 Lindsey Wilson — 63
8. North Greenville — 101 Eagle Grove — 79
9. Pratt — 65 Mesa County — 60
10. Henry Ford — 73 Paris —66
11. Bethany Lutheran — 82 Chipola — 79

Thursday: Game

12. Independence — 112 Alfred Tech — 79
13. Lindsey Wilson — 83 Mesa County — 76
14. Paris — 88 Chipola — 66
15. LaSalle-Peru-Oglesby — 91 Marion Inst. — 83
16. Weber — 81 Pratt — 66
17. Cameron St. — 83 San Angelo — 79

Friday: Game

18. Independence — 99 North Greenville — 67
19. Lindsey Wilson — 96 LaSalle-Peru-Oglesby — 82
20. Pratt — 61 San Angelo — 59
21. Bethany Lutheran — 90 Henry Ford — 89
22. Weber — 55 Cameron St. — 51

Saturday: Game

23. Lindsey Wilson — 98 Independence — 86
24. Paris — 78 Pratt — 49
25. Henry Ford — 91 Cameron St. — 69
26. Weber — 57 Bethany Lutheran — 47

How They Finished in 1959

1. Weber College
2. Bethany Lutheran College
3. Henry Ford Community College
4. Paris Junior College
5. Lindsey Wilson College
6. Cameron State Agricultural College
7. Pratt Junior College
8. Independence Community College

All-Tournament Team

Wayne Annett — Paris Junior College
John Bryant — Cameron State Agricultural College
Joe Carter — Weber College
Chad Coffman — Bethany Lutheran College
Allen Holmes — Weber College
Benny Howell — Lindsey Wilson College
Larry Knackstedt — Independence Community College
Jim McIntyre — Henry Ford Community College
James Mini — LaSalle-Peru-Oglesby Junior College
Don Steinhart —Pratt Junior College

Coach of the Year

Bruce Larson — Weber College

Player of the Year

Allen Holmes — Weber College

1960:

NOTHING BUT COTTON

One of the most popular players in Hutchinson Junior College history, Bill French finished his career at the University of Wyoming. On November 30, 1968, French and his wife were killed in an automobile accident. The following spring, the Juco Tournament honored French by naming its MVP trophy after him. (Photo courtesy of Chuck Bell, University of Wyoming)

fter tasting tournament action with a 1959 eight place finish, the Independence Community College Pirate were eager to return to national competition. They set a bliste ing pace and by the time the last NJCAA coaches' poll w announced for 1960, the Pirates were ranked No. 1. The on loss for the southeastern Kansas school was to a Dave Sta worth-led Wichita University freshman team.

One more conference game remained on the Independenc schedule. If the Pirates beat Parsons Junior College — a tea they had defeated twice previously — on the Cardinals hor court, they would become the undisputed kings of the Easte Jayhawk Juco Conference.

Parsons bombed Independence, 82-62.

The Pirates' loss necessitated a play-off for the conferenc title in neutral Altamont, Kansas, a small country town 25 mil east of Independence and 10 miles south of Parsons. Usir slowdown tactics to counter Parsons's excellent running gam Independence kept the score low and close. The winning sh was in the air as time expired. The Pirates lost, 41-39.

In their final regular season game, a noticeably tired crew Pirates again experienced defeat, this time convincingly, 84-6 at the hands of Western Jayhawk Juco Conference powe house, Hutchinson Junior College. Going into the regional pla Independence rode a three-game losing streak.

All was not bleak for the Pirates, however. Independence w still the top seed in the Region 3 tournament. Since the eve was to be held on the Pirates' home floor, where they had n lost in two years, a second consecutive trip to Hutchinso loomed in the offing.

Independence creamed Chanute Junior College, 97-63, the first round, setting up the Pirates' fifth meeting of the ye with Parsons. But, for the third straight time, Independence w upended by the Cardinals, this time 70-66.

In 10 days' time, Independence's magnificent 20-1 record fe to 21-5, proving a No. 1 ranking did not guarantee a reserve seat at the National Juco Basketball Tournament.

THE PARTICIPANTS

Being the defending national champion was also not a sa bet for making the NJCAA Tournament's 16-team fiel Although Allen Holmes-less, Weber College was again a pow erful ballclub. However, the No. 2 Wildcats squandered a 1(point second-half advantage in the Region 1 final and wei nipped by Phoenix College, 77-76.

With the surprise demise of the two top clubs in the countr the *Hutchinson News* was reluctant to go out on a limb in its pri tourney predictions. The paper selected the teams most likel to make it to the semifinals, but sidestepped the issue of whic was best.

Since No. 1 and No. 2 had bitten the dust, it was natural t include the nation's No. 3 team as one of the favorites, particu larly since Broome Technical Community College possesse the best record in the tourney field. Unlike the inflated recor of previous eastern teams who faced weak competition Broome Tech's excellent 25-1 record had been compile against tough opposition. Early in the year the Hornets stun

Region	Team
1	Phoenix College — Phoenix, Arizona
2	Cameron State Agricultural College — Lawton, Oklahoma
3	Parsons Junior College — Parsons, Kansas
4	Chicago City Junior College, Wilson Branch — Chicago, Illinois
5	Howard County Junior College — Big Spring, Texas
6	Hutchinson Junior College — Hutchinson, Kansas
7	Arkansas State College, Beebe Branch — Beebe, Arkansas
8	Chipola Junior College — Marianna, Florida
9	Pueblo Junior College — Pueblo, Colorado
10	Louisburg College — Louisburg, North Carolina
11	Grand View College — Des Moines, Iowa
12	Henry Ford Community College — Dearborn, Michigan
13	Virginia Junior College — Virginia, Minnesota
14	Tyler Junior College — Tyler, Texas
15	Broome Technical Community College — Binghamton, New York
16	Lindsey Wilson College — Columbia, Kentucky

Region 4 power Joliet Junior College and always tough Tyler Junior College, the latter by a whopping 25 points. The New Yorkers were the best team yet from the East.

Also among the chosen four was No. 4 Cameron State (19-6). The Aggies were not as strong as in past years, but because of two consecutive sixth-place finishes, they were included in the pre-tourney elite. Besides, there were hundreds of followers traveling from Lawton, Oklahoma, 300 miles away, not to mention many local supports, who believed the Aggies would finally be successful in their fourth quest for a national crown.

Because they had dethroned the defending national champs, Phoenix (24-4), too, was considered a top contender. The strength of the Bears was illustrated by their having beaten several top California teams, losing only once to a junior college during the season.

Rounding out the "big four" was the school with the longest tradition in the meet. In seven trips to the nationals, the Tyler Apaches had posted a 15-7 record and grabbed five trophies, among them two crowns. Though their 28-9 season record included the humbling loss to Broome Tech, no one doubted the Texans' chances.[1] Tyler possessed one of the tallest squads in the 16-team field, had more games under its belt than any other club, and represented the most successful region in tournament history.

In other years, Tyler would easily have gained the pre-tourney favor of the local paper. Part of the reason the News took no definitive stand in 1960 was the tough opposition the Apaches were sure to face. Both Phoenix and Tyler were in the "killer" bracket. Among their competition: Pueblo Junior College (26-3), ranked No. 6; Henry Ford Community College (19-3), third-place finisher in 1959; Lindsey Wilson College (27-7), fifth-place team from the previous year with four of its starting five returning; and the local Blue Dragons (21-3) who owned an imposing 23-game win streak in the Sports Arena. Only Chipola Junior College (17-10), a repeater from the year before, and Wilson of Chicago (19-5), one of only three tourney newcomers, were considered long shots in the upper bracket.

Broome Tech and Cameron State had an easier row to hoe. Howard County Junior College (31-3), another tall Texas team with the second-best record in the tournament, and upstart Parsons (21-6), the Pirate-killers from southeastern Kansas, were the only prime opposition in the lower bracket. Veterans Arkansas State-Beebe (17-7), Virginia Junior College (17-7), and

Grand View College (14-10) plus newcomer Louisburg College (17-10) were discounted as title threats.

Still, as the examples of Independence and Weber demonstrated, nothing was certain.

TUESDAY — WHITE WELCOME

Mother Nature sent a special greeting to the National Juco Basketball Tournament Monday — 2½ inches of snow. To further show her giving spirit, she added another four inches Tuesday. The fluffy white moisture provided a marvelous experience for some of the Chipola cheerleaders from Marianna, Florida, who had never seen that type of precipitation before. For the people of Hutchinson, however, the common cry was "Enough is enough already!" Under the recent accumulation was another eight to 10 inches from Mother Nature's earlier unselfish moments. In fact, Hutchonians had been recipients of 41 inches of generosity since Christmas.

Surprisingly, city officials hoped for continued freezing temperatures throughout tournament week. As the *Hutchinson News* put it, "Freezing weather means the difference between parking or sinking in the Arena parking lot." The new levels of white came at a particularly unpropitious time for city commissioners. After early plans to pave the area around the Sports Arena, nothing was implemented. Just the Friday before, they had tabled a $221,500 proposition to pave the 1,600-car lot. The decision was a major topic of discussion all week as fans slogged through the mire to watch basketball.

The courageous few who braved the elements to catch the tourney opener were given an early glimpse of the kind of basketball they would see. Favored Phoenix controlled the game from the start, but was unable to shake the Lindsey Wilson Blue Raiders. With two minutes remaining and Phoenix ahead, 70-67, Lindsey Wilson's Doug Pendygraft pushed his game-high total to 27 with a 20-footer. Moments later a Blue Raider steal and a David Cowan jumper put the Kentuckians on top.

At the eight-second mark, Lindsey Wilson's Keith Brown had a chance to salt away the win from the free throw line, but missed the back end of a one-and-one.

Trailing 72-70, Phoenix hustled down the court and worked the ball to 6-8, 240-pound center Darnel Haney who launched a desperation heave from 25 feet. The shot banged off the rim at the buzzer.

Lindsey Wilson's come-from-behind upset of Phoenix set the tone for the tournament.

The day's second contest provided as much entertainment off the court as on. One side featured five Indian maidens and one four-year-old blonde miniature, all clad in feathered headdress. The personable Chipola cheerleaders passed out small packets of salted peanuts to advertise the principal product of their Florida Panhandle home and banged bongo drums to incite the Indians in their opener. Equally entertaining on the other side of the court were 10 energetic Chicagoans who engaged in what the paper described as "the wiggliest cheerleader antics seen for some time." In an age when "cheerleading" was just that, the crowd was thoroughly entranced by the Wilson pep group which performed remarkable acrobatic routines as a part of their yells.[2]

The game itself was less spectacular. When Chipola or Wilson *did* exhibit flashes of brilliance, one or the other would dart ahead. Most of the time, however, the action was rough and ragged, marred by excessive fouling. Controversy also plagued

---

[1] Early in the year Tyler made a week-and-a-half long swing through the eastern section of the United States, making stops in Alabama, Tennessee, New York, the Carolinas, and Mississippi. The game against Broome Tech came in the middle of the long road trip, following a contest in Buffalo. After sightseeing at Niagara Falls, the Apaches started out late for Binghamton the morning of the game, then encountered a snow storm which slowed their progress. Tyler arrived in Binghamton late that afternoon. According to former coach Floyd Wagstaff, the obviously tired Texans "played lousy." Never one to make excuses, however, Wagstaff quickly added, "We didn't get gypped out of the game, [though]. We just got beat."

[2] The Wilson players and cheerleaders received particular attention from the crowd, but for a reason other than their performance on the Arena floor; Both squads were all-black.

Black players had been a part of the NJCAA Basketball Tournament from its opening tip-off in Springfield, Missouri. Some of the best and most popular players had been black. However, the number on each team was limited, the effect of the prevailing racial prejudice in the country.

The people of Hutchinson were neither better nor worse than the rest of the nation when it came to racial prejudice. In the Convention Hall days of the tournament, blacks had suffered the indignity of not being allowed to stay in certain Hutchinson hotels or eat in certain restaurants, as was the case in many areas of the country. As the rest of the United States became more tolerant, so did the south central Kansas city.

When the all-black Wilson squad took to the Arena floor in 1960, it was a novelty. It had been only the year before that Cameron State brought to the national event the first team to start more blacks than whites. During tournament week 1960, the *Hutchinson News* ran articles covering an Atlanta restaurant sit-in and a *Sports Illustrated* story which described major league baseball as only being integrated *on* the field. All were evidence of the burgeoning civil rights movement. The crowd's reaction to the Wilson players and cheerleaders reflected that awakening racial consciousness. It was a mixture of natural curiosity and the unease of adjusting to changing conditions.

play. As time expired in the first half, Wilson's Sam Jones was whistled for offensive goaltending at the end of an exciting fast break. The Red Raiders argued loudly with the officials as the teams headed for the dressing rooms, but their complaints went unheard. Chipola owned a 43-41 halftime advantage.

The score remained close through the first five minutes of the second period. Then, sophomore John Sodec led an Indian charge which pulled Chipola to a comfortable 13-point margin. The Indians coasted to an 80-70 victory with game-ending free throws, the result of 30 Wilson fouls.

In the final afternoon game, Henry Ford played a flawless first half, dominating the boards against a much taller Tyler team. A cool, erratic performance by the Texans helped the Hawks from Michigan soar to a 42-30 halftime lead. An upset was in the making.

Then, the Tyler Apaches sprang to life. Guards Bud Forman and Bobby Weddle, who had been held scoreless in the opening period, began hitting from outside. The tall Texas front line of Folly Malone, Pete Petrou, and Ardie Dixon roamed the middle, piling up rebounds and points. Every bounce seemed to go Tyler's way. Halfway through the period the Apaches drew even. When the final buzzer sounded, Tyler had grounded the Hawks, 83-72.

The evening curtain raiser followed much the same pattern. Utilizing its superior height to best advantage, Howard County powered to a 32-22 edge at intermission. Then, the Indians from Beebe, Arkansas, staged an ambush similar to that of their Apache cousins from Tyler. Nine minutes into the second period, Arkansas State-Beebe pulled even. Howard County lost its height advantage a minute later when 6-9 Thomas Garrison picked up his fifth foul. The remainder of the contest was close combat.

In the final minute-and-a-half, Howard Lamb — the engineer of the Beebe squad's rally with 18 second-half points — completed the Indian raid, breaking a 52-all tie with two field goals. The 6-4 forward totaled a game-high 28, leading Arkansas State-Beebe to a 56-54 major upset.

When Hutchinson jumped out to a quick 36-20 lead over Pueblo with six minutes to go in the first half of the evening fea-

ture, the 4,000 hardy souls who braved the snow were warmed by elation.

Cold soon leaked through the Arena doors, however. Pueblo's Curtis Jimerson, a swift 6-2 forward, steadily swished shots from 10 to 20 feet or whipped sharp passes to opposite-side forward Waymond Dean for easy lay-ups. By halftime, Hutchinson's lead had been carved to five.

Blue Dragon fans shivered. There were two reasons for concern: First, when Hutchinson easily defeated Pueblo, 60-47 earlier in the season, Jimerson was injured and did not play. Pueblo was a much better ballclub with the El Paso native on the court. Second, in three of the four previous first-round contests, second-period rallies overcame halftime leads. To make matters worse, two of those comebacks were executed by Pueblo's blood brothers — teams with nicknames relating to a native American heritage. Pueblo's Indians were also on the warpath.

The Blue Dragons regained their composure in the locker room and continued to maintain their lead, again warming the crowd. The only chilling moment came at the 7:30 mark when Bill French, Hutchinson's top scorer, was ushered to the bench with five fouls. When Dean Brown, Hutchinson's second-leading scorer, and Tom McKain, a hard-driving reserve guard, took over Blue Dragon scoring chores, fearful uncertainty finally vanished. With five minutes remaining, the home team was in command, 78-62. Hutchinson basked in the glow of an 85-78 victory.

Heated competition kept Arena patrons warm in the final Tuesday contest, as well, as the unheralded Virginia Greyhounds kept pace with heavily favored Cameron State, trailing by a mere 41-40 margin at halftime. The Minnesotans maintained pressure in the second half, pulling even at 48-all with 15 minutes to go and finally darted ahead, 57-56, a few minutes later on a driving lay-up by center Bob Stevens.

With a little more than four minutes left, the Cameron Aggies were behind, 72-68, and in danger of losing their first opening-round contest ever.

Enter Bobby Joe Parrish.

Though the talented freshman from Bowling Green, Kentucky, had played before crowds numbering 14,000 in two years of Blue Grass State high school tournament competition, he had appeared unnerved when first introduced to the spacious surroundings of the Sports Arena and its vocal audience. The 5-10 guard missed four consecutive first-half shots, a couple by wide margins, and was exiled to the bench.

With the game on the line, the Cameron reserve reentered the lineup and promptly popped a long field goal. Moments later he added a short jumper. After teammate Richard Hall tallied a free throw with three minutes remaining, the Aggies were back on top.

Virginia's magnificent battle had been waged by the same starting five. As time ran down, the Greyhounds tired, allowing Cameron's Hall and Carl Cabbiness to hit a wide-open Parrish twice for easy baskets out of the Aggie control offense. The gutsy, clutch performance by Parrish elevated Cameron State to a 77-73 victory and into the championship bracket for the third year in a row.

WEDNESDAY — THE "COME-FROM-BEHIND" SYNDROME

Close, tense first-round play continued in the Wednesday opener. After Parsons took the early lead, Broome Tech's Wendy Terry went on a tear, scoring four goals in the space of 2½ minutes. The favored Hornets opened a 29-25 halftime margin.

Parsons erased the deficit in the first three minutes of second-half action. Then, behind the outside marksmanship of Leonard Kelley, the Cardinals took the advantage. Midway in the second period, Parsons extended its lead to eight, the widest gap of the game.

Again the tide turned. Parsons center Bill Johnson, the Cardinals' top rebounder and second-leading scorer, fouled out with 6:34 to go. Moments later, Broome Tech's Terry stole the ball, engineered a Hornet fast break, scored, and was fouled. He converted the free throw, putting the New Yorkers back on top, 53-52.

Kelley's sharp shooting pulled Parsons even at 55 and 57. Then, with 3:40 to go, Kelley slipped a double team in back-

Pueblo's Curtis Jimerson was later an All-Skyline Conference selection at the University of Wyoming. (Photo courtesy of the University of Wyoming)

court and drove all the way to the basket. Fouled on the shot, the 5-11 guard completed the three-point play, giving Parsons the controlling edge. Two Broome Tech miscues and free throws resulting from Hornet pressure helped Parsons clinch a 63-59 upset win.

Coming into the tournament, Grand View of Des Moines was touted as the best team ever to come out of the Iowa-Nebraska region. Yet, the Vikings owned a mediocre 14-10 record. The reason for the unimpressive mark was the forfeiture of several early games because of the use of an ineligible player. That player was the key to Grand View's claim to superiority.

As Grand View Coach Dave Sisam later described him, 6-6 Marvin Torrence was "tremendous, ahead of his time. [He was] a fantastic jumper with a great scoring instinct. He scored a lot from the outside and could run the floor well. He played in the 60s like players in the 80s do. He was just an all-round player with unlimited talent."

Though his size dictated that Sisam play him at center, Torrence possessed an extensive array of abilities; he could easily play any position on the court. From the oohs and aahs emitted by the afternoon crowd watching the final opening-round contest, it was evident the sophomore transfer from Michigan State was something special. Torrence effortlessly hooked, tapped, and dunked the basketball for a game-high 32 points. Grand View encountered no trouble downing Louisburg, 92-65.

Other than the Grand View-Louisburg blowout, first-round action was characterized by dramatic momentum shifts and thrilling late rallies. The pattern left fans guessing what surprises lay ahead. Those who caught the consolation contest preceding Wednesday night quarterfinals soon found out.

Trailing Phoenix, 79-72, with 1:30 remaining, Pueblo Coach Harry Simmons ordered his charges to apply full-court pressure. His instructions were a matter of form, not from a deep conviction that they would succeed. In fact, Simmons was really thinking about how his team would make its quick exit home after being the first eliminated in tourney play. His lack of confidence revolved around his limited manpower. Curtis Jimerson, Pueblo's top player, was benched with five fouls. Reserve center Phil Coulter — a top college prospect before he lost part of the thumb on his shooting hand in a summer accident — was an excellent screener and rebounder but not suited to fast action. Finally, Les Pollock, his principal outside playmaker and defensive specialist, was rendered ineffectual because of a dislocated shoulder suffered in regional play; the 5-10 guard played with one arm strapped to his side, his hand free but not really usable.

But, to Simmons' amazement, the Indians forced Phoenix into passing errors, stealing the ball three times in 15 seconds. Baskets by Pollock, Coulter, and Waymond Dean, pulled Pueblo within one. After recovering a missed Phoenix shot, Pueblo completed its sparkling rally with an easy Coulter bucket.

At the 14-second mark, Pollock stepped to the free throw line to ice the win. Forced to shoot one-handed because of his injury, he missed. In the rebound scramble, Dean was fouled and delivered two pressure charities. Phoenix forward Frank Mass dribbled the length of the court for an uncontested lay-up as time expired, but for naught. Pueblo had overtaken the Bears, 82-81.

Through the first 30 minutes of the opening quarterfinal, hometown hopes rose as Hutchinson gained and maintained the advantage over a tough Lindsey Wilson squad. Full-fledged faith was held in check, though. Considering the come-from-behind epidemic which had infected tourney action, the Arena crowd was unsure of the slim 63-59 Blue Dragon margin, especially since the Kentuckians had already engineered a late winning rally against pre-tourney favorite Phoenix.

Then, a field goal and a pair of free throws by Bill French and a two-pointer by John Channell buoyed fan optimism. With a 10-point cushion, the Blue Dragons let guards Tom McKain and Ken Sears control the ball. Fan insecurity evaporated as Hutchinson pulled away to an impressive 91-75 triumph.

Tyler supporters went through the same agonizing uncertainty in the evening's other quarterfinal. The highly favored Apaches barely managed a 42-all draw with Chipola through the first half. Then, as they had in their opener against Henry Ford, the tall and balanced Texans went on a second-period binge, swamping Chipola, 103-80.

THURSDAY — NO LEAD SAFE

The opening Thursday night quarterfinal was expected to be a close fought battle, since both combatants were well-stocked from the same arsenal; Grand View's Marvin Torrence and Parsons' front line of Carl Hancock, Bill Johnson, and Leon Harris all hailed from Chicago. Their similar size and power led to a near stalemate.

Neither team was able to measure the other through the first period until Parsons sprinted to a 36-28 advantage just before intermission. Grand View returned the favor to open the second half, taking a 41-40 edge after six minutes. Then, the contest settled into a taut, basket-trading affair.

The intensity of play was recorded in the foul column. With five minutes to go, all starters on both teams had three or four fouls apiece. Consequently, when Parsons pulled ahead, 58-52, on a spree by Hancock and Leonard Kelley, the Cardinals chose to play it safe.

Responsibility for guiding the Parsons stall fell to Kelley. The freshman guard took charge, forcing Grand View to gamble for steals. The result: Kelley scored nine of the Cardinals' last 11 points, all but two from the free throw line. Parsons held on for a 69-60 victory.

One of the keys to the Kansans' win was their grudging defense. Though Torrence approached his 30-points-per-game average with 26, he did not shine as he had in the Vikings' first game. Twelve of his shots missed the mark against Parsons' tough front line.

The most important factor in the victory, however, was Kelley. Playing his second brilliant game in a row, the clutch playmaker tallied 34 points to lead all scorers.

Arkansas State-Beebe had pulled two major upsets to reach the national quarterfinals. The first was in the Region 7 final against Snead Junior College — reported to be Alabama's greatest junior college club ever. The second was the first-round, come-from-behind masterpiece over the tall Texans from Howard County. The Indians were intent on making it three in a row against pre-tourney favorite Cameron State.

Beebe's Howard Lamb immediately made the goal feasible, hitting his first five shots from the field, propelling the Indians to a quick 12-0 lead. Flawless execution and shot selection marked the Arkansas squad's offensive attack while a solid Indian defense forced 13 Cameron turnovers. By halftime, Arkansas State-Beebe led, 35-22, and was in perfect position for another upset.

Behind the eight ball, the Aggies broke from the locker room and applied full-court zone pressure, catching the Beebe five off guard. The previously poised and confident Indians made careless errors and were prone to successful Aggie thievery. Proving again that no lead was safe in national competition, Cameron reeled off 15 consecutive points during the first 9½ minutes of the second half to take the lead. Arkansas State-Beebe never regained form. Shooting a spectacular 68 percent from the field in the final period, Cameron escaped an Indian uprising with a 69-62 victory.

FRIDAY — STRESS TEST

Afternoon consolation play featured three outstanding performances: Curtis Jimerson's 28 sparked Pueblo past Henry Ford, 62-59, in an otherwise lackluster affair. Harold Henson improved on Jimerson's total, netting 30, leading Howard County to an easy 85-69 victory over Broome Tech. Then, Marvin Torrence achieved the 1960 tournament's best individual tally so far, notching 41 as Grand View powered by Arkansas State-Beebe, 86-74. Had he been less generous with passes to his teammates and more accurate than 7 for 18 from the free throw line, the "Big M" might have challenged the tourney record.

Few witnessed the talented display, however. With two Kansas teams still in the running for a national crown, one of them representing the hometown, all eyes focused on the semifinals.

The Blue Dragons were first on the card. The atmosphere in the standing-room-only full house was an incongruous mixture of confidence and trepidation. On one hand, the current Hutchinson squad was the best yet assembled. The Blue Dragons' 25-game win streak in the Arena was an imposing obstacle for any opponent. In the back of everyone's mind, however, was the historical pattern of Hutchinson's tournament play. The Blue Dragons were 3-1 in each of their previous appearances — one misstep away from a title. The fact that Tyler was the team which had stopped the local crew from its nearest brush with the championship was not lost on the partisan crowd. A more pertinent reason for concern was the size of the Texans — Hutchinson gave away more than two inches per man on the front line.

The significance of the height difference was evident from the start. In Hutchinson's previous two outings, every Blue Dragon shooter had been hot. Against Tyler, no one could find the range consistently. When Hutchinson missed, the tall Apaches were there for the rebound, 6-5 Folly Malone, 6-9 Pete Petrou, and 6-4 Ardie Dixon controlling the middle and the game. Four consecutive Dean Brown free throws allowed the Blue Dragons a brief 17-15 advantage, but it proved to be the high-water mark of the dismal first half for the local squad. By intermission, the Apaches were in command, 35-25.

The partisan crowd's agony did not abate in the second half as Tyler immediately hiked the margin to 14.

Hope was not totally abandoned, however. If there was an underlying theme to the 1960 tournament, it was that no lead was secure until the final buzzer. With 17 minutes to go, Tyler leading, 45-33, momentum shifted. Hutchinson scored 10 unanswered points. The Sports Arena went from near quiet to a full-volume roar.

The Apaches were not overwhelmed by the crowd's thunder, squelching the rally before Hutchinson could threaten the lead. Hometown supporters squirmed in their seats as the Texans continued to hold the Blue Dragons at arm's length.

Then, another rally pulled Hutchinson abreast of the Apaches with two minutes to go.

The offensive game plan for the Texans was to get the ball to their big man, Pete Petrou. The gangly center had overpowered his five-inch smaller counterpart, Bill French, all night long. With the Arena bursting with noise, Petrou again proved unstoppable. Another two-point Tyler edge turned down the crowd's volume.

The waning moments were pure anxiety for local fans. Hutchinson matched a pair of Art Fiste free throws with a pressure duo by French. But, as time slipped away, the Blue Dragons were still a bucket short.

Matters were desperate. Only two ticks showed on the clock when freshman John Channell finally saved the day with a clutch jumper, sending the game into overtime.

The Blue Dragon's last loss in the Arena had been an extra-period thriller against Kilgore College in the 1958 semifinals. The first win in their current homecourt streak had also been a nerve-racking overtime gem the following evening against Cameron State. Local fans were experienced in added minutes of tension.

Their stress stamina was put to the test, though, in the additional five minutes against Tyler. The lead changed eight times. First, Petrou would can one over the outstretched arms of Hutchinson defenders. Then, French would counter with his beautiful, left-handed hook. The two centers hit three field goals apiece in the extra period. The only other tallies from the field were an outside poke by Hutchinson's Ken Sears and a late sleeper by Tyler's Bud Forman.

When the final totals were posted, Hutchinson and Tyler were nearly dead even. The Blue Dragons had 27 field goals and 28 fouls; so did Tyler. The sole difference in their statistics decided the contest. Hutchinson was 26 for 42 from the line, Tyler, 28 for 44. In the overtime, the Apaches converted three of five charities while Hutchinson made only one of five. With the 82-80 victory, Tyler advanced to the title game for the third time.

Bitter disappointment silenced the Arena. The crowd recovered slightly as Parsons and Cameron State engaged in a close fight, knotting the score five times in the early going of the other semifinal. However, when Cameron reeled off 10 straight points after a 20-all tie and Bill Johnson — Parson's tallest player and leading rebounder — picked up his fourth foul with 8:58 left in the first half, quiet gloom settled over the stands.

The turning point came in the final 1:23 of the opening period. After Parsons forward Leon Harris shaved a 37-32 Cameron edge to one with two free throws and a field goal, Leonard Kelley — held scoreless from the field by the determined defense of the Aggies' Bobby Joe Parrish — added a free throw to tie the game with 21 seconds to go. Carl Hancock contributed another fielder. Finally, Ed Lesniewski drove for a bucket as time expired. The Cardinals suddenly held a 41-37 halftime advantage.

Having lost in the semifinals the previous two years, the Aggies came out of the locker room determined to dispel talk of a jinx. They employed the same full-court zone pressure which had been so successful in their come-from-behind win over the

(Bottom, left) According to Grand View Coach Dave Sisam, Marvin Torrence was "ahead of his time. He played in the 60s like players in the 80s do." Overshadowed by Doug Pendygraft's record-setting performance in the battle for fourth, few remember that Torrence's 49 in the same game, tied for third-highest individual performance all-time and that his 148 points for the week were only six away from Pendygraft's top total. Torrence concluded his collegiate career at Drake University. (Photo courtesy of Drake University)

(Bottom, right) After capturing tourney scoring honors with 154 points, including an all-time single game record 63 against Grand View, Doug Pendygraft was a cinch MVP selection. He later played at the University of Kentucky, becoming the third tourney MVP to play for the legendary Adolph Rupp. (Photo courtesy of the University of Kentucky)

eebe Indians. Guard Bobby Pollan played his heart out, tallying a game-high 35 points, the largest single-game total of any Cameron player all year.

But, the Cameron press failed to ruffle Cardinal guards Fred Strathe and Kelley. And Pollan was the only Aggie able to hit with regularity. When Cameron missed, the Aggies were no match for Parsons' leaping front line. Hancock, Harris, and particularly Johnson, who played the entire final period without drawing a fifth foul, dominated the second-half board game. Parsons opened a 13-point gap and eased to an 85-80 victory, lifting the pall hanging over the hometown crowd.

SATURDAY — SEEKING REVENGE

The two afternoon trophy bouts were full of fireworks despite lopsided results.

In the first, a tough Howard County zone manned by tall Texans prevented Pueblo from hitting the basket with consistency. On offense, the Texans' firepower was provided by Harold Henson. After contributing a scant seven points in Howard's opening-round upset loss to Arkansas State-Beebe, the 6-4 forward steadily improved his performance, producing 91 points in his final three outings. His game-high 32 against Pueblo marked his highest tally of the tournament, led Howard County to an easy 75-60 fifth-place win, and secured him a place on the All-Tournament team.

The crowd forgot Henson's outstanding total, however, after the next contest. Going into the game, Grand View's Marvin Torrence and Lindsey Wilson's Doug Pendygraft led all tourney scorers with 33.0 and 30.3 averages respectively. The fact that each was the offensive fulcrum of his team was substantiated in the first period: Torrence hit half of the Vikings' 38 while Pendygraft bettered his per-game average, scoring 32 of Wilson's 56.

Torrence upgraded his effort in the final frame, canning 30 of Grand View's 56. His overall figure of 49 was just four shy of Denver Brackeen's tournament record.

At the same time, Pendygraft's second-half effort fell off — by one point. The 6-2 sophomore was responsible for 31 of the Blue Raiders' final 54. His grand total of 63 shattered the existing mark.[3]

The fact that Lindsey Wilson topped Grand View, 110-94, for fourth place was inconsequential. Their combined total of 204, a new game high for two teams, also went unnoticed. Those viewing the contest were agog for only one reason: Two men had accounted for 112 points.

The opponents in the third-place game were teams with similar styles. Cameron State and Hutchinson both preferred to score off the fast break set up by their man-to-man pressure defense. When the two confronted one another, their aggressive play produced spectacular results. In the third-place game two years before, the two racked up 185 points and a record 65 personal fouls. Their 1960 rematch followed much the same pattern.

By halftime, 112 points were on the scoreboard. The principal reason Cameron owned a 57-55 advantage was because the Aggies hit 31 of 36 free throws, the product of 20 Hutchinson fouls.[4]

The totals after the second 20 minutes, though not as high as in the 1958 battle, were no less formidable. A final 56 fouls and 82 points were entered in the scorebook. The victor tallied the same 97 points as had 1958's winner. The identity of the winner had changed, however.

Disappointment over their loss to Tyler the previous night weighed heavily on the Blue Dragons who looked tired in the second half. Cameron took advantage, opening a 10-point gap.

Hutchinson was able to halve the margin with a mid-period rally, but could muster no more. After two successive failures, the Aggies took home a third-place trophy, downing Hutchinson, 97-85.

The curtain raised on the championship drama. As the audience settled, the cast was introduced.

First was the odds on favorite for becoming the first school to win three national titles — Tyler Junior College. The Apaches were brimming with confidence, their size and balance, intimidating.

The second principal was tournament newcomer Parsons. No one had expected the Cardinals to win one game let alone three. Even the Parsons players were surprised at their success. They felt fortunate to be competing for the title and were in as much awe of Tyler as the public. The prevailing attitude on the team was, "How are we going to beat these guys?"

Finally, though not listed on the marquee, a third character played an important role in the drama — the Sports Arena itself.

Hutchinson fans were noted for their vocal displays. The power of their support was understood by any team who faced the Blue Dragons at home. Twenty-five consecutive opponents could give witness to the fact, showing their recent lack of success in the Arena as evidence. Tourney teams able to attract even a portion of the Arena following when Hutchinson was not playing gained a definite inspirational edge.

In the 1960 championship game, Parsons was given that support wholeheartedly. The level of endorsement reached a passionate extreme previously reserved for the local squad only. There were several obvious reasons: The Cardinals were from Kansas; Parsons was the affirmed underdog; Tyler had won two titles, Parsons none. These were superficial rationalizations; the real motive behind the crowd's fervor was *revenge*.

Despite having a decided homecourt advantage, Hutchinson had not produced a winner in the 12 years of its hosting the Juco Tournament. The fact was particularly irksome to local fans since the Blue Dragons had come close in every tourney appearance. The current team had been the city's best chance yet at a title. The latest crop of Blue Dragons was talented and popular — one of the most popular teams in the school's history. At the core of that popularity was Bill French, an All-American player with an All-American personality and All-

Tyler's 6-8 ¾" Pete Petrou ushered in a new era as one of the first "giants" of junior college basketball. He later played at the University of Houston. (Photo courtesy of Floyd Wagstaff)

---

[3] Doug Pendygraft's accomplishment reaped immediate reward: He was named the tournament's MVP.

However, over the years his untouchable feat has drawn much criticism. His detractors point out that the record-breaking performance came in a consolation contest which was never close; had it been a tight championship-bracket game, Pendygraft would not have scored as easily nor as frequently. They also argue that, though he was a gifted all-round player, capable of brilliant outside shooting (he joined Adolph Rupp's Kentucky Wildcats after graduating from Lindsey Wilson), Pendygraft was the recipient of several "gift" buckets against Grand View; as he neared the record, his teammates made it a point to get the ball to him whenever possible.

One person is unwilling to cheapen Pendygraft's achievement, though. Former Grand View coach Dave Sisam described Pendygraft's effort as "one of the best individual performances I've ever seen. We put different people on him. I even think we put Marvin [Torrence] on him for a while." The different strategies obviously failed. As Sisam put it, "[It was] my most embarrassing moment as a coach. I've gotten a lot of ribbing over the years over that one."

[4] Former Cameron coach Ted Owens related that during intermission, he intercepted Hutchinson Coach Sam Butterfield and complained, "I really think we're getting hometowned." As Owens returned to the floor the public address announcer declared that Cameron State had just shot the most free throws in a half in tournament history. According to Owens, "I was embarrassed that I'd said anything . . . [The incident] showed how you lose objectivity [when coaching a close contest.]"

American good looks. He inspired his teammates by playing the sport in spite of doctors' warnings that, as an extreme diabetic, he reduced his life expectancy with each game. Behind French's leadership, the team won the hearts of local fans.

Hutchinson's loss to Tyler in the semifinals was a crushing blow to the community. Most felt the Blue Dragons had been robbed of their rightful chance at a Juco crown. A major reason for their bitter feelings was an incident during the closing stages of regulation time. As Hutchinson's Tom McKain came upcourt, he suddenly stopped just past the midstripe. Tyler's giant Pete Petrou — nearly a foot taller than McKain — plowed over the small guard's back. No whistle sounded. The crowd was incensed by the oversight. Normally upstanding, reserved citizens required physical restraint. The missed foul would have been Petrou's fifth and, since the big center went on to lead all scorers with 32, including seven of 11 Tyler points in overtime, many considered the no-call the difference in the game.[5]

When the title match began to follow the script of the Hutchinson-Tyler semifinal, supreme frustration fueled the crowd's furor. The Apaches were again the advantage-takers. Though Parsons tied the score seven times during the opening 20 minutes, Tyler's superior size prevailed. Just as they had against Hutchinson, the Texans opened a 10-point gap. Only a brief Parsons rally at the end of the first period prevented the game from becoming a runaway.

Inspired by the crowd's enthusiasm, the Cardinals continued to whittle at the lead after intermission, tying the score at 52 and 55. No amount of cheering from the stands could push the Kansans over the hump, though. Tyler remained king of the hill.

Then, a new page was slipped into the script. At the 10:57 mark, Petrou picked up his fifth foul. Parsons' Leon Harris swished the ensuing free throw to tie the game at 56-all. With 11 minutes to go, justice had finally been rendered.

The Apaches were not a one man team, however. Tyler continued to press the advantage and, with 2:44 remaining, was still on top, 70-67. A sense of foreboding ate at the crowd's ardor.

It was time for Leonard Kelley to bring the Arena to life. Held to six points to that point, the Parsons playmaker scored his first points of the half on a jumper with 2:32 to go. After Art Fiste added a free throw to the Tyler cause, Kelley answered with two charities, tying the game at 71-all.

Action on the court slowed. Tension mounted. A bad pass or a missed shot at this juncture might prove fatal.

Tyler's leading scorer was Folly Malone, a deadly accurate shooter from the corners. With 1:08 on the clock, Malone found himself open in his favorite position.

Remarkably, he missed.

Bill Johnson pulled down the rebound for Parsons and Coach Gene Schickel immediately called time. The five Cardinals huddled alone in the middle of the floor, choosing to play for one shot.[6]

In the expert hands of Kelley and Fred Strathe, the Parsons control game was smooth and effective. Tyler applied a measure of pressure to prevent an easy bucket, but not enough to risk fouling. The Apaches were content with a tie.

Inside the 10-second mark, Parsons tried to work the ball into the middle. Tyler closed off easy access to the basket. The best shot the Cardinals could find was a high arching, Johnson 25-footer over the outstretched arms of Malone on the wing.

The ball bounded off the rim, in a line toward Malone and Johnson. Racing from his position deep in back court, Kelley intercepted the rebound. Almost in a single motion, he braked, half-turned, jumped off his right foot, and returned the ball to flight, falling backwards. The shot arched through the air from an improbable angle, narrowly missing the edge of the back-

board. It touched nothing but cotton at the buzzer.

The Sports Arena exploded.

Parsons Junior College had unbelievably upset Tyler for the national junior college crown.

Considered by many to be the "true" MVP of the 1960 tournament, Leonard Kelley led Parsons with 92 points including the winning basket at the buzzer in the finale, the only such occurrence in the tourney's title game. Kelley later joined Ralph Miller's Shockers at Wichita. (Photo courtesy of Leonard Kelley)

THE AFTERMATH — THE STATE TITLE

The eruption in the Sports Arena after Leonard Kelley's dramatic shot could not have been greater had Hutchinson won the title instead of Parsons. Pandemonium ruled. Fans flooded the floor lifting the Kansas hero to their shoulders. As Kelley later remarked, "I didn't really think it was that big of a deal. [Then] everybody went wild."

Anyone watching the following awards ceremony might have construed that Hutchinson *had* played for the title. As Fred Mendell stated in his *Hutchinson News* column, "In concluding ceremonies, speakers wavered more between praise and condolence for Hutchinson, finishing sixth in the tournament, than in acknowledging the greatness of those teams which finished above Hutchinson." The topper came during Region 3 Director Wendell McMurry's trophy presentation to the Cardinals when he implied that "luck" had been an important factor in Parsons' championship.[7]

Letters rolled into the *News*. For a week, Fred Mendell's column allowed the public to rehash the tournament. Nothing was mentioned about Parsons' poise and maturity nor Leonard Kelley's coolly perfect shot under extreme duress. Instead, the principal items of debate were fan decorum and "poor officiating" during the Tyler-Hutchinson semifinal. Behind the com-

---

[5] In the author's many hours of interviews, the Petrou-McKain incident ranks as the second most mentioned controversial play in tournament history. It is an excellent example of selective memory. Few fans remembered the missed opportunities Hutchinson had at the free throw line in the overtime. Even fewer remembered that a few minutes before the questionable play Bill French had been saved from expulsion when a close call under the basket was ruled blocking by a Tyler player instead of charging on French. The fact that Tyler's cornerstone, Folly Malone — who had not fouled out in 38 previous games that year — was later the first whistled to the bench (four of his five fouls were charges) also adds to the irony.

Speaking of the 1960 tournament, former Tyler coach Floyd Wagstaff said, "That was the only time I felt we weren't treated very well." It was a lone unfortunate occurrence in an otherwise long friendly rivalry. But, as Wagstaff was quick to add, "If anybody in the country has a right to be down on us [Tyler], it would be the basketball fans of Hutchinson. We always beat them."

[6] When asked why he allowed his players to select their own strategy in such a critical stage of a championship game, former Parsons coach Gene Schickel responded, "They could operate pretty well without me. They were smart enough to do that [set up an end-game strategy]. It was their ballgame. I never did believe in killing their spirit."

[7] McMurry later apologized in an open letter to Parsons Coach Gene Schickel, stating, "At the presentation ceremonies at the National Tournament, you and your team were done a grave injustice, and the presentation by me was inappropriate and inadequate."

The 1960 national champion and Kansas state champion Parsons Cardinals: back row (left to right) — Terrell Jackson, Carl Hancock, Bill Johnson, Mike Healy, Leon Harris, and Coach Gene Schickel; front row — Fred Strathe, Ed Lesnieski, Bill Stover, Leonard Kelley, and Harrison Stover. (Photo courtesy of Gene Schickel)

ments was an underlying opinion that had Hutchinson met Parsons in the title game, the Blue Dragons would have won.

By an ironic twist of fate, Hutchinson fans had an opportunity to see their point proved. Normally, the state play-off between the winners of the Eastern and Western Jayhawk Juco Conferences was scheduled for the week following regional action, just before the nationals. When, the two 1960 conference champs could not come to terms on dates and sites, the play-off was postponed until after the Juco Tournament. In an ultimate example of anticlimax, Parsons and Hutchinson faced each other in a two-out-of-three series to determine the best junior college team in Kansas.

The first game was held at Parsons. Without the services of star Bill French, who Coach Sam Butterfield said was "worn out" after four games of national competition, Hutchinson forced the Cardinals into overtime before succumbing, 80-77.

French was more than available for the second game in the Sports Arena. His game-high 26 plus 10 crucial second-half points by reserve zone-breaker, Paul Vega, produced a more favorable result for Hutchinson fans. The Blue Dragons evened the series with an 85-72 victory.

According to conference rules, Hutchinson was entitled to host the deciding game. A previously booked "Home Show" prevented use of the Arena, however. The "neutral site" of Buhler, 16 miles from Hutchinson, was picked for the final confrontation.

Though Buhler's high school gym was brand new, it required considerable packing to get 1,800 fans into the facility. Many were turned away. The fortunate few in attendance saw a brilliant rebounding exhibition by the Parsons front line. They saw spectacular shooting by Leonard Kelley and Bill Johnson, who netted 33 and 30, respectively. They saw the question of who was best in the country finally laid to rest. Parsons downed Hutchinson, 88-81.

Tournament Results

		Game	
Tuesday:		1	Lindsey Wilson — 72 Phoenix — 70
		2	Chipola — 80 Chicago-Wilson — 70
		3	Tyler — 83 Henry Ford — 72
		4	Arkansas St-Beebe — 56 Howard County — 54
		5	Hutchinson — 85 Pueblo — 78
		6	Cameron St. — 77 Virginia — 73
Wednesday:		Game	
		7	Parsons — 63 Broome Tech — 59
		8	Grand View — 92 Louisburg — 65
		9	Pueblo — 82 Phoenix — 81
		10	Hutchinson — 91 Lindsey Wilson — 75
		11	Tyler — 103 Chipola — 80
Thursday:		Game	
		12	Henry Ford — 92 Chicago-Wilson — 87
		13	Broome Tech — 77 Louisburg — 69
		14	Lindsey Wilson — 104 Chipola — 75
		15	Howard County — 80 Virginia — 71
		16	Parsons — 69 Grand View — 60
		17	Cameron St. — 69 Arkansas St-Beebe — 62
Friday:		Game	
		18	Pueblo — 62 Henry Ford — 59
		19	Howard County — 85 Broome Tech — 69
		20	Grand View — 86 Arkansas St-Beebe — 74
		21	Tyler — 82 Hutchinson — 80 OT
		22	Parsons — 85 Cameron St. — 80
Saturday:		Game	
		23	Howard County — 75 Pueblo — 60
		24	Lindsey Wilson — 110 Grand View — 94
		25	Cameron St. — 97 Hutchinson — 85
		26	Parsons — 73 Tyler — 71

All-Tournament Team

Bill French — Hutchinson Junior College
Harold Henson — Howard County Junior College
Curtis Jimerson — Pueblo Junior College
Bill Johnson — Parsons Junior College
Leonard Kelley — Parsons Junior College
George "Folly" Malone — Tyler Junior College
Sam Parker — Arkansas State College, Beebe Branch
Doug Pendygraft — Lindsey Wilson College
Bobby Pollan — Cameron State Agricultural College
Marvin Torrence — Grand View College

Coach of the Year

Floyd Wagstaff — Tyler Junior College

Player of the Year

Doug Pendygraft — Lindsey Wilson College

How They Finished in 1960

1. Parsons Junior College
2. Tyler Junior College
3. Cameron State Agricultural College
4. Lindsey Wilson College
5. Howard County Junior College
6. Hutchinson Junior College
7. Grand View College
8. Pueblo Junior College

1961:

A CHIROPRACTOR, A CLOWN,

AND A CROWN

The 1961 tournament's top scorer (135 points), Willie Murrell was later All-Big Eight at Kansas State and played three years in the ABA. (Photo courtesy of Anna Vee Hill, Eastern Oklahoma State)

he bracket for the 1961 NJCAA Basketball Tournament was drawn during the annual meeting held simultaneous to the 1960 event. Attending the drawing were coaches Sam Butterfield and Floyd Wagstaff. As the opponents for Game 5 were picked from the hat, the two grimaced. The feature game on opening night would match the representatives of Region 6 and Region 14. Should they win their respective regional tournaments — a likely possibility considering the talent returning on both ballclubs — Hutchinson Junior College and Tyler Junior College would renew their rivalry in the first round.

THE PARTICIPANTS

The field for the 1961 Juco Tournament was the most illustrious to date. The roll call of participants read like a Who's Who of junior college basketball. Included were five former national champions, eight of the top 10 teams in the latest NJCAA poll, and the six schools with the most tourney appearances. Only three institutions made their debut.

Heading the list of former titleholders was the reigning champ — Parsons Junior College. The Cardinals were still flying high with two All-Tournament selections from 1960 (Leonard Kelley and Bill Johnson), a better record (20-4), and a No. 4 national ranking.

Right in line behind them were 1959 titlist, Weber College, and 1957 winner, San Angelo College. Both were surprise entrants, however. Weber (20-10) started the year poorly, going winless on a December trip through Colorado and Kansas, while San Angelo (25-5) was an upset winner in Region 5, scoring 20 points in overtime to down No. 8 Howard County Junior College, 91-79.

Rounding out the list of former champions were the tournament's only double winners and its most veteran performers. After a two-year hiatus, Moberly Junior College (24-3) was back in the limelight, making its 10th tournament appearance. For Tyler Junior College (29-7), it was trip number eight. Moberly was ranked No. 2 and had not lost to a junior college foe. Tyler featured Folly Malone and Pete Petrou, the backbone of 1960's runner-up team. Both teams had excellent shots at an unprecedented third title.

The top 10 squads included No. 1 Broome Technical Community College (29-0), the only undefeated team in the meet; No. 3 Eastern Oklahoma A&M (21-4), victor over Oklahoma powerhouse Cameron State; No. 5 Pueblo Junior College (27-2), eighth-place finisher in 1960; No. 6 Joliet Junior College (23-3), the leading offensive team in the country; No. 7 Young Harris College (30-1), a tourney newcomer whose only loss was to the University of Georgia frosh; and No. 10 Snead Junior College (25-1), the tallest team in the tournament, averaging just over 6-7 across the front line.

The less notable also brought impressive credentials: Bethany Lutheran of Mankato, Minnesota, owned a 23-2 record, sec-

Region	Team
1	Weber College — Ogden, Utah
2	Eastern Oklahoma Agricultural and Mechanical College — Wilburton, Oklahoma
3	Parsons Junior College — Parsons, Kansas
4	Joliet Junior College — Joliet, Illinois
5	San Angelo College — San Angelo, Texas
6	Hutchinson Junior College — Hutchinson, Kansas
7	Snead Junior College — Boaz, Alabama
8	Young Harris College — Young Harris, Georgia
9	Pueblo Junior College — Pueblo, Colorado
10	Brevard College — Brevard, North Carolina
11	Burlington College — Burlington, Iowa
12	Flint Community Junior College — Flint, Michigan
13	Bethany Lutheran College — Mankato, Minnesota
14	Tyler Junior College — Tyler, Texas
15	Broome Technical Community College — Binghamton, New York
16	Moberly Junior College — Moberly, Missouri

ond-best in the school's history, just behind its 1959 national runner-up squad; Flint Community Junior College (21-2) boasted two 20-point-plus performers in Dale Lucas and James Atkinson; Brevard College (21-4), another tourney debutant, featured Thomas Barbee, a hot-shooting forward who canned 43 points in Brevard's regional triumph over North Greenville Junior College; and newcomer Burlington College (18-8), though dubbed the tournament's "Cinderella," possessed one of the top point producers in the country — Ira Harge (38.8).

Even the hometown representative looked good. In their fifth try at a national crown, the Hutchinson Junior College Blue Dragons brought a splendid 24-2 record, their best yet.

Since each team had won, on average, 86 percent of its games, the *Hutchinson News* flatly refused to choose any favorites. Reporters covering the event made a stab at likely victors in the first round, but admitted "they could be wrong." The only sure winners were tourney ticket holders. With the best congregation of talent yet assembled and an advance ticket sale $4,000 ahead of any previous year, prospects for an exciting and successful tournament were never better.

TUESDAY — REMEMBER THE ROSES

The San Angelo Rams opened the 1961 Juco Tournament by scoring the first point of the five-day event on a free throw. The 1-0 start was their only lead of the game. Broome Tech opened a 10-point gap late in the first half, extended it to 15 in the second, and coasted to a 73-62 win, the 30th straight for the Hornets.

The afternoon feature started as if it would be a matter-of-fact affair as well. After 4½ minutes, Pueblo owned a 13-1 lead over the much taller Snead Parsons. Then, 6-8 Harold Morris sparked a Snead rally that tied the score at 16-all. Suddenly, the contest was interesting.

It remained so until a little more than six minutes were left. A three-minute Pueblo spurt inflated a three-point margin to 10. The rest was a celebration for the Indians. With 30 seconds remaining, happy-go-lucky Robert Warlick capped a 27-point, game-high scoring performance with a slam dunk. Led by a broadly grinning Warlick, a happy band of Indians exited the court, an 80-62 opening-round victory under their belt.

The first two contests did little to enthuse the 2,500 fans viewing the afternoon session. Many, in fact, were more entertained by a talented heckler along the sidelines. The heckler was in full glory during the Pueblo-Snead game when a well-dressed man with a tournament badge on his lapel sat down next to him. The heckler sheepishly asked, "Are you a tourney official?" The well-dressed man answered, "Yes. In a way. I'm going to referee the next game and I just wanted to get on your side before I started."

The heckler's antics were again in demand in the third game. Weber set a runaway pace, building an 11-point lead over Eastern Oklahoma in the early minutes of play. Then, 6-6 Willie Murrell took over the show. The talented freshman leaper contributed six field goals to an Eastern rally which narrowed the Weber lead to one at halftime.

The Wildcats maintained a slim advantage through nine more minutes of the second period, then lost the edge on a Murrell field goal. The final minutes belonged to the Oklahomans. East-

ern Oklahoma opened a 10-point gap and eased to a 72-66 win, Murrell leading all scorers with 29.

With two Kansas teams on the agenda, fans hoped the evening's action would improve on the afternoon's lack of excitement. It appeared their wish was granted in the opener. After Brevard broke on top of the defending national champions, 7-2, Parsons quickly evened the score and sprinted away from the North Carolina newcomers, opening a 36-21 margin with six minutes remaining in the half.

Before crowd boredom had a chance to set in, Brevard's Thomas Barbee stirred up a storm. The whirlwind forward tallied 18 first-half points as the Tornados razed the Parsons lead to four at intermission. Brevard completed the rally after the break, knotting the score at 40-all with two minutes gone in the period.

After having applied a half-hearted two-man full-court press throughout the contest, Parsons' Leonard Kelley and Carl Hancock suddenly started to work in earnest. In a five minute period, Brevard lost the ball six times on bad passes. Parsons won easily, 83-71. A year had not diminished Parsons' poise under pressure. Cardinal scoring was paced by Kelley (31), Bill Johnson (23), and Hancock (12) — the team's three returning starters.

The evening feature had been anxiously awaited since the bracket drawing the year before. Not everyone was happy to see the match-up. Stated Tyler Coach Floyd Wagstaff, "I'd much rather play anybody else than Hutchinson." It was a sentiment shared by most tourney coaches. According to Wagstaff, since Hutchinson was "one of the finest basketball towns in the country," its fan support could overwhelm an opponent, especially when accompanied by jitters. After the crowd's reaction to Hutchinson's semifinal loss to Tyler the previous year, Wagstaff was doubly worried.

Crowd decorum also concerned *Hutchinson News* sports editor, Fred Mendell. In his column the week before the tournament, he cautioned local supporters that they were not only "fans" but "hosts" during the upcoming week. "The most lasting impression visitors will carry away will be of the big arena, filled with fans, and the attitude and antics of those fans." He finished with a gentle reminder that, "the rose bushes in front of the Arena were gifts from Tyler, Tex."

The mood of the Sports Arena Tuesday night was unexpected. Hutchinson fans were in full voice when rooting for the Blue Dragons, but their cheers lacked the intensity of the previous year. There was no vindictiveness as there had been in the 1960 championship game. Instead, there was an underlying current of fatalism.

A deadeye from the corner, Tyler's George "Folly" Malone was a two-time All-Tournament selection, scoring 147 points. He continued his collegiate career at the University of Houston. (Photo courtesy of Floyd Wagstaff)

Size had been a key factor in the Blue Dragons' loss to Tyler the year before. Hutchinson Coach Sam Butterfield had rectified that problem with taller personnel, including the front line of 6-5 John Channell, 6-4 Warren Vogel, and 6-6 Jerry Williams. Hutchinson gained additional height advantage with 6-4 sophomore Herb Stange, now a starter. It was the tallest Blue Dragon starting lineup to date.

Unfortunately, Tyler had also grown. Six-four forward Ardie Dixon had moved on to play at North Texas State, but his replacement, John Keats, was three inches taller. Keats' height added to the already prodigious front-line frames of Folly Malone and Pete Petrou who, according to the program, had grown a half inch each in the past year and now stood at 6-5½ and 6-9½, respectively. It was an imposing wall.

From the game's outset, height was again the telling difference. Hutchinson's Vogel picked up four first-half fouls trying to contain the half-foot taller Petrou on the inside. Though the Blue Dragons fought valiantly, trailing by only two at halftime, Hutchinson fans feared the gap would widen.

With the Apaches dominating the boards at both ends of the court, Tyler opened a 10-point margin with 13:31 to go. A late Hutchinson rally was foiled by Apache accuracy from the line. Tyler hit 10 of 11 free throws in the last two minutes and marched into the championship bracket with an 81-75 victory. Petrou and Malone were again the Blue Dragons' nemeses, leading all scorers with 28 and 20, respectively.

Downcast Hutchinson fans quickly filed out of the Arena after the evening feature. Few stayed to watch the day's finale. It made no difference that Young Harris picked up its 31st win of the season, downing Joliet convincingly, 96-78.

The hometown was not to have a crown again this year.

WEDNESDAY — THE ACTION PICKS UP

After a two-year absence from tournament competition, Moberly looked to have a healthy basketball program again. The Greyhounds were now under the guidance of mentor Cotton Fitzsimmons, formerly a tourney all-star with Moberly rival Hannibal-LaGrange College.[1] The tall and swift Missourians ran away from Bethany Lutheran in the day's opener, taking an insurmountable 50-24 halftime lead, making the second period a formality. Moberly demoralized the Minnesotans, 93-67.

The final afternoon contest featured the premier individual performance of the first round. From the opening tip, Burlington's 6-8 Ira Harge played above the heads of everyone else. He scored the first two points of the game, then dazzled the fans to the tune of 42. Unfortunately, the Blackhawks possessed little beyond the big center. Harge's first bucket gave Burlington its only lead. The better balanced Flint Bears controlled the game thereafter. Five Flint players hit double figures as the Bears easily dispatched Burlington, 86-66.

None of the first-round games were close enough to generate an adrenalin rush. Even when the scores *were* in question, there had been no doubt which was the better team. Considering its build-up, the 1961 tournament was becoming a major disappointment to fans.

Those feelings evaporated as second-round play began.

Snead dogged San Angelo throughout the consolation game opening evening action, never allowing the Rams to pull away. With 1:21 to go, the score tied at 64-all, the winner was still up for grabs. San Angelo stalled for the final shot. Six-one guard Bubba Bailey drew the honor, letting fly from 20-feet with three ticks on the clock. The ball cracked the cords.

The exciting conclusion ignited the crowd, priming the 4,000 Arena patrons for the evening quarterfinals.

Pueblo was also primed, despite the fact the Coloradans faced the unenviable task of upending the undefeated, No. 1

team in the nation with the best Indian player in subpar condition. In one of Pueblo's final practices before the tournament, Sam Smith, the Indians' leading scorer and rebounder, injured his back. Because of the ailment, he missed 10 minutes of action in Pueblo's opener.

Against Broome Tech, the injury continued to plague the big center. Smith, in obvious pain, struggled, managing only seven points, 12 under his average. His creditable rebound total of 10 was due solely to his size; at 6-8, he was the tallest player on the floor.

Plagued by back trouble during the 1961 tournament, Sam Smith (No. 54) later starred for Wichita State. (Photo courtesy of Wichita State University)

His teammates picked up the slack. On numerous occasions, agile 6-4 Robert Warlick moved from his forward spot to spell the ailing center. Though his point production suffered, he turned in a capable effort in an unfamiliar position.

The majority of the scoring load shifted to guards Gregg Smith and Norm Colglazier. During the season, the two compiled a 14-point average *combined*. However, against Broome Tech, the duo was deadly from outside. Colglazier hit eight of nine attempts from the field for a 17-point total while Smith netted seven of eight to lead the Indians with 19.[2]

Pueblo built a quick 14-point edge and maintained a 10-point or better spread into the second period. A Broome Tech spurt cut the Pueblo lead to five with 12:50 to go, but Colglazier led an Indian retaliation with sterling defense and four baskets, pushing the Pueblo advantage to 13. A final Broome Tech rally was too little, too late. The Indians handed the New Yorkers their first loss of the year, 69-64.

In the opening moments of the day's finale, Parsons held the lead twice, the last at 15-14. Then, Guy Curry put Eastern Oklahoma in front with a long field goal, Willie Murrell added two from the top of the free throw circle, and Wilkie Berry hit two free throws and three consecutive jumpers. In the final minutes

[1] The choice of Cotton Fitzsimmons as the Greyhounds' head coach met resentment from Moberly fans. As Fitzsimmons related, "First of all, I'm replacing a legend in Maury John. Secondly, they're replacing that legend with a guy they really despise. Nobody who played against one of the teams I played on could ever really say they liked me because I would do about anything I could to win the game." The fact that only one player, a non-starter, was a holdover from Maury John's 1958 tournament team, did not help Fitzsimmons' cause. "It took a little while at Moberly. When we didn't go to the nationals two straight years, I thought maybe the lynching party was going to come out." But, according to former *Moberly Monitor-Index* sportswriter Stan Isle (later a senior editor with the *Sporting News*), fan resentment soon disappeared. "When Cotton left [Moberly], he was more popular than Maury."

[2] The production of the two backcourt men did not surprise former Pueblo coach Harry Simmons. "Those two would screen like hell." Norm Colglazier's shooting ability, in particular, was vastly underrated. "Colglazier could have scored 25 points a game if he had wanted." Instead, the 6-2 floor general chose the role of unsung hero, assisting, rebounding, or scoring as needed. Simmons related that one of the greatest disappointments in his tournament experience was that Colglazier never made the All-Tournament team.

of the first half, the Mountaineers from Wilburton outscored Parsons, 21-5, to take a commanding 37-20 halftime lead.

The onslaught continued after intermission. Executing flawless ball control while working for percentage shots, Eastern Oklahoma built a gigantic 53-29 margin over the defending national champions with 12:22 to go. The predominately Kansas crowd squirmed. There was no way Parsons was that bad.

Suddenly, two long Leonard Kelley bombs ignited the Cardinals. In addition, Parsons' full-court press clicked. The defending titlists finally showed their championship mettle. Netting seven and five field goals apiece, Cardinal stalwarts Kelley and Bill Johnson led a brilliant stretch drive which shaved the Eastern Oklahoma advantage to a single bucket with 55 seconds to play.

Then, the comeback fizzled. Three Curry free throws to only one by Parsons gave the 69-65 squeaker to the Oklahomans. Ironically, Parsons outpointed the Wilburton squad from the field. The champs lost their chance to repeat at the charity stripe. The normally excellent free throw shooting Cardinals hit a miserable 11 for 24.

THURSDAY — LAST MINUTE DECISIONS

The tournament's hump day matinee session drew a particularly small crowd. After watching Weber's sharp defense and excellent offense outclass Brevard, 83-61, in the opener, the 1,000 fans in attendance wondered whether they, too, should be elsewhere. The two barn burners that followed provided the answer.

In the first period of the afternoon feature, Bethany Lutheran built a commanding 40-26 lead. Burlington slowly rallied, a long outside shot by Blackhawk Dave Mattson finally tying the score at 71-all late in the game.

The Vikings from Mankato played for the last shot. But, with 24 seconds remaining, Keith Johnson, Mattson's running mate at guard, batted a pass away and drove the length of the court, giving Burlington the lead. Bill Schlicher's free throw with nine seconds to go iced the game for the Iowans. A last second jumper by Bethany Lutheran's Larry Berke was meaningless.

The Burlington comeback was virtually a one-man show. Johnson's crucial tally was his only field goal of the game. Mattson fired four long bombs principally to draw the defense away from the middle. The rest of the second-half field total came from Ira Harge. The Blackhawk big man netted 47 of Burlington's 74, bettering his initial outing by five.

Ira Harge's 117 points in 1961 ranks as the highest three-game total in tourney history. Harge completed his collegiate career at Bowling Green and the University of New Mexico and spent six years in the ABA. (Photo courtesy of Loren Walker)

There were 14 lead changes and five ties in the first half of the final afternoon contest before Parsons broke away to a 44-38 halftime advantage over Broome Tech. The Cardinals maintained a four-to-six-point edge for the next eight minutes. Then, Broome Tech rallied, tying the game at 56-all with half the period remaining. Again Parson sprinted ahead, taking the biggest

lead of the game, 71-64, at the 4:22 mark. A jumper by Don Heller and three free throws by George Zurenda cut the margin to two.

Having gradually inched forward during the course of the tight battle, the few fans in the Arena now perched precariously on the edge of their seats. Charities by Leonard Kelley and Carl Hancock gave Parsons breathing room with 43 seconds to play. When the Cardinals regained possession of the basketball, everyone eased off their chairs and toward the exits.

A quick succession of events halted their progress. The Hornets' Zurenda stole the ball and scored. He immediately stole the ball on the inbounds pass and scored again. With nine seconds remaining, the game was tied, 73-all.

Without calling time-out, Parsons whipped the ball downcourt on two passes to Bill Johnson who unleashed a jumper from deep on the side. The shot rang true with three seconds showing, giving the Cardinals the game.

The building momentum of tourney action slowed in the consolation game opening the evening session. For the second year in a row, a loss to Tyler had ended Hutchinson's dreams of winning a crown. The whole town's depression was reflected in the Blue Dragon's ragged first-half. The running Wolves from Joliet took advantage of the situation, sprinting to a 19-point margin with 6:32 to go in the half. Though a late Blue Dragon surge cut Joliet's margin to 10 at intermission, the Hutchinson squad still showed little sign of life.

At halftime, Coach Sam Butterfield talked to his players about the good things that had happened during the year. "We can either hang our heads and write ourselves off or we can come back with character and win this ballgame."

The talk — plus a well-executed Blue Dragon half-court trap — had its effect. In the final 20 minutes, Hutchinson outscored Joliet, 62-31, to win, 88-67.

Later that evening, Pueblo's Harry Simmons asked Joliet's "Pop" Wills, "Pop, what in the world happened to your defense in that second half?"

The colorful Wills who was noted for eschewing defense in favor of a blistering running game, replied, "Not a damn thing that a bourbon and seven won't cure."

Hutchinson's victory enlivened the crowd. Everyone was in excellent humor for the remaining quarterfinals.

Height was a factor in both contests. In the first, Moberly held a big advantage over Flint, the smallest team in the tournament, averaging only six feet per man. In the second, Young Harris gave away more than three inches per man on the front line to the towering Tyler Apaches. Crowd sentiment favored the smaller teams.

Flint's size disadvantage was offset by tremendous team speed and quickness. The swift Bears jumped on top of Moberly by seven with 7:38 left in the opening period of the evening feature before the taller Moberly front line of Roscoe White, McCoy McLemore, and Lawrence Rucker took over, rallying the Greyhounds to a 32-30 halftime lead.

The second half featured tight action and several ties before Moberly began to pull away. With 5:49 to go, the Greyhounds led, 60-54.

In the next 4½ minutes Flint outpointed Moberly, 8-4, setting the stage for the most critical call of the game.

As Moberly's Ken Triplett brought the ball across midcourt, an aggressive Bear bumped him back across the center line. Referee Bill Osburn blew his whistle. What most expected to be a foul was ruled a backcourt violation. Moberly lost possession with 45 seconds remaining.

Eight seconds later, Dale Lucas, Flint's leading scorer, erased the difference on a 15-footer.

Moberly slowed for one.

Lucas, playing with the burden of four fouls, slapped the ball away. Teammate Lawrence Collins retrieved it and quickly returned it to a streaking Lucas. The Flint native laid in the go-ahead basket with 19 ticks on the clock. A Moberly traveling call and a last second free throw by Lucas added the finishing touch to the tournament's biggest upset yet.

There was no hint of an upset during the first 30 minutes of the nightcap. After leading by as much as 13, Tyler took a 48-42 halftime edge over Young Harris, then built it to 10 with eight minutes to go.

Suddenly, the Apaches shot blanks. Free throws by Young Harris' Larry Howell and Don Wade, a lay-up by Larry Cart, a

30-footer by Wade, and another lay-up by Wade pulled the Georgians into a 72-all tie with six minutes remaining.

John Keats rekindled the Apache attack with three consecutive field goals. With 2:42 to go and an 83-75 advantage, Tyler held the ball.

Again the Mountain Lions clawed back. In the next minute, double doses from the free throw line by Cart and Phil Meadows plus an easy bucket by Howell narrowed the deficit to two.

Guard George Wanamaker opened breathing space for Tyler with a field goal.

Meadows countered with a 20-footer for Young Harris.

Keats bagged a corner jumper for the Texans.

Howell grabbed a missed Young Harris shot and banged it back in.

With 24 seconds left, Folly Malone was fouled. Tyler's steadiest player was given two free throws to ice the Apache victory. He missed both.

Young Harris hurried down the floor to tie the game, but the Georgians hurried too fast. Whistles stopped play as the officials signaled Young Harris for traveling.

The Mountain Lions desperately scratched for the ball and, with six seconds to go, fouled Tyler's Wanamaker. After motioning to the bench that there was nothing to fear, the confident Texan toed the line and canned both free tosses.

The Apaches vacated the floor, allowing Young Harris two quick passes to Cart who drove for the final points. Tyler survived, 89-87.

FRIDAY — NINETEEN FROM THE LINE

Friday's curtain raiser matched Thursday's nail-biting tempo. After 39 minutes and 34 seconds of tight play and constant maneuvering from the sidelines, Weber called time, leading 90-88. Coach Dick Motta wanted to make sure the Wildcats had their plans straight for salting away the win.

However, his end-game strategy was never executed. As soon as the ball was put in play, San Angelo stole it.

"I've always said the Juco Tournament is the most outstanding basketball tournament in America." Dick Motta coached Weber in the 1961 and 1962 tournaments, then remained on to coach the Wildcats through their transition to the four-year level. However, he enjoyed his experience in Hutchinson so much he returned every year the next six years. "I went to that tournament every day. I got there two days early and stayed a day late." Motta later became one of the deans of the NBA, coaching for more than 19 years, including winning the NBA crown with the Washington Bullets in 1978. (Photo courtesy of Weber State College)

With five seconds remaining, the Rams asked for a time-out of their own in which Motta's counterpart, Phil George, diagramed a play designed to use San Angelo's top player, Bubba Bailey — who had scored a last chance bucket against Snead — as a decoy.

Weber foiled the plan, smothering Bailey and the Ram's designated shooter, Mack McCoulskey. Guard Bobby Shuffield had nobody to pass to. Instead, the little 5-9 reserve drove for the tying basket at the buzzer.

The game-long chess match between the two coaches continued in overtime. As Motta later stated, "It got to the point where it was bordering on the ridiculous. It was our third game. We were tired. There was a call and he [San Angelo's George] ran up by the 10-second line and I ran up by the 10-second line. I said, 'If you cross that 10-second line, I'm putting a full-court press on you.' He said, 'I'm too tired.' Then he jumped across and jumped back."

The teams traded buckets in the first two minutes of the extra period. After Weber failed twice to break the tie, Coach George signaled San Angelo to its control game. The Rams waited for the clock to wind down, but waited too long.

The second overtime started with more basket trading, as the two teams raced for the century mark. Weber won the race with a 109-102 final, a new record for combined score. Individual honors went to the winner's Bob Belka with 40. San Angelo was led by their shooting sensation, Bailey, who hit 19 of his 35 from the free throw line, another new record.[3]

Burlington's Ira Harge seemed bent on breaking all sorts of records in the first half of the afternoon feature, tallying 22. He also netted four fouls. His output dropped radically in the second period, allowing Hutchinson to make easy work of the Blackhawks, 67-56. Harge's game-high 28 gave him a three game total of 117 — 60 percent of Burlington's point production.

The afternoon's exhilarating entertainment was topped off by another thriller in which Moberly outlasted Young Harris in overtime, 66-63.

But, just as the tournament neared its climax, emotional momentum unexpectedly retarded. Only one of the two evening semifinals managed to keep the sellout crowd guessing.

The opener appeared doomed from the beginning. Everybody had been impressed with the crew from Wilburton, Oklahoma, especially Mountaineer forward Willie Murrell. Pueblo had also played well, but was handicapped with the Indian's top player, Sam Smith, still ailing.

As anticipated, Murrell scored at will, hitting his favorite jump shot from the top of the key. Smith, on the other hand, was ineffective. He sat down with 4:42 left in the first half, then was summoned to the bench for good with 14:15 remaining in the game when it was obvious he was in great pain. His total point production for the evening was two free throws. The fact that the game was no contest surprised no one.

The surprise was that the Pueblo Indians went on a second half rampage, opened a 10-point gap with 14 minutes to go, then widened it to an 81-58 canyon eight minutes later.

The only remaining question was how many points Murrell would score. Pueblo Coach Harry Simmons established a strategy of allowing the 6-5 freshman whatever he wanted while the Indians closed off the rest of the Eastern Oklahoma squad. Consequently, Murrell led all scorers with 45. The only other Mountaineer to hit double figures was Wilkie Berry — who actually had a bad game despite tallying 22.

In contrast, five Indians broke double digits — Robert Warwick (20), Norm Colglazier (17), Gregg Smith (16), Ron DeLeon (15), and Waymond Dean (14). In spite of Sam Smith's bad back, Pueblo won easily, 91-79.

The other semifinal's surprise came early. Though Tyler owned more than a four-inch height advantage per man, Flint proved quicker out of the blocks, sprinting to a 23-3 lead in the first nine minutes.

Then, Tyler's sleeping front-line giants awakened. In eight minutes the Apaches reduced the deficit to five. Another disastrous four minutes for Flint saw Tyler score 11 unanswered

---

[3] According to former San Angelo coach Phil George, the 1960-61 Rams were an excellent free throw shooting team. There was no question who was the best, however. "He [Bubba Bailey] would win all the guys desserts by staying after practice and beating them in free throw contests."

points to take the lead. By halftime, the Apaches were in command, 50-40.

Led by James Atkinson — who the *Hutchinson News* described as possessing "just about every shot in the book and some which haven't yet been explained in detail" — Flint battled back. As the game wore down, the Bears tied the score at 68, 72, and 74. With one minute remaining, they were still in contention, trailing the Texans, 82-79.

However, a lead, a substantial height superiority, and the option to play for only good shots, gave Tyler advantages too sizeable to overcome. The Apaches held on, winning 88-83.

Free flowing Atkinson led Flint with 32, but was overshadowed by Tyler's ever-present twosome, Pete Petrou and Folly Malone, who nailed 35 and 25, respectively, putting the Apaches into the championship game for the second year in a row.

SATURDAY — A BAD BACK VS. A DEADEYE

With both Kansas teams in action, the Saturday afternoon trophy matches drew a good crowd. Most came to see the opening contest between the local Blue Dragons and the Wildcats from Weber.

Spirits ran high when Center Warren Vogel scored five straight points, igniting a scorching Blue Dragon attack. With 11:30 to go, Hutchinson led by 17 and the rejoicing began. Though a fifth-place finish was lower than desired, most were satisfied. Hutchinson's 90-73 victory over Weber was the Blue Dragons' 27th win of the year, representing the best season yet for the local squad.

The predominately Kansas crowd had little to cheer in the first half of the fourth-place tilt in which Moberly's front-line trio of Roscoe White, Lawrence Rucker, and McCoy McLemore dominated every phase of the game. At intermission, the Greyhounds held a commanding 37-25 lead over Parsons, then opened the gap to 18 with less than 16 minutes to go. Fans began to leave the Arena.

Then, as in their quarterfinal loss to Eastern Oklahoma, the Cardinal full-court press started to click. Leonard Kelley and Carl Hancock haunted Moberly passing lanes, repeatedly stealing the ball. With 9:32 remaining, Parsons closed to within nine. Fan attention returned.

A pattern was established. Cardinal guards, Kelley (three times) and Ed Lesniewski (once), stole the ball at one end of the court and fed Bill Johnson for two at the other. With 3:12 on the clock, Kelley sank a beautiful 20-footer to tie the score at 57-all. He immediately swiped another Moberly pass, drew a foul, and hit the front end of a one-and-one, giving Parsons the lead for the first time since the early moments of the game.

With Moberly continuing to have trouble with its passing and Parsons having problems at the charity stripe, the result remained in doubt until the end.

When Moberly again lost control of the basketball, the ball bouncing high in the air along the sidelines, Parsons' Kelley jumped and batted the ball into a Greyhound player standing out of bounds. On the inbounds play, Kelley was fouled, sank a free throw — his 22nd point of the game — and secured a brilliant 61-57 come-from-behind victory for the Cardinals.

Fans had come to expect the third-place game to be little more than two teams going through the motions in an unsuccessful attempt to overcome the disappointment of missing a shot at the title. Consequently, championship night crowds often took their time filing into the Sports Arena.

The 1961 third-place match was no different. For much of the game, Eastern Oklahoma and Flint fumbled passes and missed shots. Then, as though sensing the growing audience, the two picked up the action.

With 45 seconds to go, Flint's Dale Lucas fired a 20-footer, tying it at 66-all, sending the contest into overtime.

Wilkie Berry put Eastern on top first in the extra five minutes with a pair of free throws. Then, Flint's James Atkinson hit a 30-foot bomb. Throughout the tournament, the 6-1 forward had drawn roars from the crowd with phenomenal behind-the-pack passes and 15-and-20-foot hook shots, both basic elements of his game. He was liquid motion.

During the overtime, Atkinson was again everywhere, dazzling the fans with his offense and defense, but to no avail. Though he registered his second straight 30-plus game with 31, Atkinson was again surpassed, this time by Eastern Oklahoma's

Willie Murrell who tallied 37, including six in the extra period, leading the Mountaineers to a 79-75 triumph.

Hutchinson fans had become increasingly conciliatory toward Tyler as the tournament progressed. There were a few stubborn anti-Tyler holdouts, but most were willing to let bygones be bygones. Many, in fact, favored an Apache title out of respect for the two Tyler veterans, Pete Petrou and Folly Malone, who had barely missed out on a well-deserved crown the year before. Everyone wanted a close, hard-fought championship game. However, there was considerable doubt whether it would occur.

Pueblo's Harry Simmons was one who shared that doubt. Because of Sam Smith's bad back, Simmons' biggest and best player had been ineffective all week. Even with Smith in the lineup, the Indians were up against a tremendous Tyler height advantage. Without him, they would be small fry at an Apache barbecue.

Uneasiness about the Pueblo big man's health quickly evaporated once the title tilt got under way. Week-long chiropractic care had eased the strain on Smith's back, returning him to his usual powerful self. Though carrying 240 pounds, he possessed the grace and leaping ability of a gazelle. His long arms — he required a size 48 extra long team blazer — and giant hands further extended his range of control. He tallied 18 first-half points, scoured the boards clean of missed shots, and totally stifled Petrou, his counterpart at center. Only a heroic 15-point effort by deadeye Malone kept Tyler in the game.

Though Pueblo held a comfortable 41-33 halftime lead, no one relaxed in the Indian dressing room. While dominating the middle during the opening period, "Big Sam" garnered four fouls — and reinjured his back. An ailing Smith accounted for only four points in the second half.

At the other end of the floor, Tyler's Malone continued his deadly shooting, swishing jumpers that narrowed the gap after intermission and eventually snared him game-high honors with 29.

Just as the tables were about to turn, however, a clown took the center ring.

Pueblo's Simmons described Robert Warlick as being often unpredictable, always the showman. A prime example occurred late in a game at LaJunta, Colorado. With Pueblo enjoying a sizeable lead, Warlick grabbed the basketball, tucked it under his arm, zigzagged up the court like a halfback in open field, dunked the ball, then held onto the rim, scratching himself like a monkey. Though thoroughly embarrassed by Warlick's antics, Simmons admitted, "You couldn't get mad at him. The crowd loved him."

However, with a national title on the line, the effervescent Warlick was all business. In a seven-minute stretch, the Pueblo forward hit seven field goals, including four straight to change a three-point cliff-hanger into a 15-point runaway. A game-ending semi-stall preserved the Indians' championship, 79-66.

Pueblo's "clown prince" Robert Warlick parlayed his 1961 Tourney MVP performance into an All-WCAC selection at Pepperdine University and four years in the NBA. (Photo courtesy of the NJCAA)

THE AFTERMATH — GROWTH AND CHANGE

During the impromptu post-game courtside celebration, the Indians hoisted to their shoulders in turn Sam Smith, Coach Harry Simmons, and reserve Jack Milam, the latter in order to cut down the net. The souvenir cords eventually made their way around the neck of the tournament's MVP. Robert Warlick accepted the award draped in cotton, his face plastered with his trademark — a broad smile.

Everyone was smiling. Since the school had a long tournament heritage and was long overdue, the Indians' championship was a popular one. Pueblo had been one of the first non-California participants in the Western States Tournament at Compton, the forerunner of the present national event. The Indians were a Midwest regional favorite in 1948, the national tournament's first year, before a snowstorm stranded them in Greensburg, Kansas, forcing them to forfeit a first-round game. Four subsequent trips to Hutchinson produced three consolation trophies and a strong desire to attain the summit. It was fitting that the school earn the top prize in its last tourney appearance. Two years later, Pueblo Junior College became a four-year institution as the University of Southern Colorado.

Tournament sponsors were also smiling. Gate receipts for the 1961 NJCAA Basketball Tournament totalled $29,250, breaking the previous 1953 high by more than $3,000. The event had definitely grown from its lowly origins. As outgoing NJCAA President Reed Swenson told the *Hutchinson News*, "This tournament is different from 13 years ago. Now every team wants to come."

Growth necessitated change.

For many years, Region 15 (the northeastern United States) had been a questionable entry with few schools, little interest, and no money. Invitations had often been extended to fill the region's vacancy.

Now, the junior college movement was blossoming, particularly in the East. Region 15 now represented 48 institutions. In contrast, Regions 3 and 6 — which had given Kansas two tourney representatives six out of the last seven years — consisted of eight schools apiece. Consequently, regional directors decided to combine the two Kansas regions and give the remaining region to the upper half of Region 15. The move made tournament participation more equitable nationwide — and initiated instant rivalries between eastern and western Kansas schools.

When Weber College expanded to a four-year curriculum, Reed Swenson retired as the NJCAA's President. From 1949-1962, Swenson was chiefly responsible for keeping the organization from crumbling and giving it legitimacy. (Photo courtesy of Bob Gilliland)

Tournament Results

Tuesday:	Game		
	1	Broome Tech — 73 San Angelo — 62	
	2	Pueblo — 80 Snead — 62	
	3	Eastern Oklahoma A&M — 72 Weber — 66	
	4	Parsons — 83 Brevard — 71	
	5	Tyler — 81 Hutchinson — 75	
	6	Young Harris — 96 Joliet — 78	
Wednesday:	Game		
	7	Moberly — 93 Bethany Lutheran — 67	
	8	Flint — 86 Burlington — 66	
	9	San Angelo — 66 Snead — 64	
	10	Pueblo — 69 Broome Tech — 64	
	11	Eastern Oklahoma A&M — 69 Parsons — 65	
Thursday:	Game		
	12	Weber — 83 Brevard — 61	
	13	Burlington — 74 Bethany Lutheran — 73	
	14	Parsons — 75 Broome Tech — 73	
	15	Hutchinson — 88 Joliet — 67	
	16	Flint — 67 Moberly — 64	
	17	Tyler — 89 Young Harris — 87	
Friday:	Game		
	18	Weber — 109 San Angelo — 102 2OT	
	19	Hutchinson — 67 Burlington — 56	
	20	Moberly — 66 Young Harris — 63 OT	
	21	Pueblo — 91 Eastern Oklahoma A&M — 79	
	22	Tyler — 88 Flint — 83	
Saturday:	Game		
	23	Hutchinson — 90 Weber — 73	
	24	Parsons — 61 Moberly — 57	
	25	Eastern Oklahoma A&M — 79 Flint — 75 OT	
	26	Pueblo — 79 Tyler — 66	

How They Finished in 1961

1. Pueblo Junior College
2. Tyler Junior College
3. Eastern Oklahoma Agricultural & Mechanical College
4. Parsons Junior College
5. Hutchinson Junior College
6. Flint Junior College
7. Moberly Junior College
8. Weber College

All-Tournament Team

James Atkinson — Flint Junior College
Garland "Bubba" Bailey — San Angelo College
John Channell — Hutchinson Junior College
Ira Harge — Burlington College
Don Heller — Broome Technical Community College
Bill Johnson — Parsons Junior College
George "Folly" Malone — Tyler Junior College
Willie Murrell — Eastern Oklahoma Agricultural & Mechanical College
Don Wade — Young Harris College
Robert Warlick — Pueblo Junior College

Coach of the Year

Harry Simmons — Pueblo Junior College

Most Valuable Player Award

Robert Warlick — Pueblo Junior College

1962:

PERFECTION

L umping Region 3 into Region 6 made it doubly difficult for Kansas schools to secure a berth in the 1962 NJCAA Basketball Tournament. Two tournament levels were required to name a representative.

Winning the western sub-regional — which had been the Region 6 tournament before — was hard enough with three Western Jayhawk Juco Conference foes tied for the crown. Since all three titleholders had downed each other twice, the tournament was a free-for-all. The law of averages prevailed. Arkansas City Junior College defeated Hutchinson Junior College for the first time, 86-83 in the semifinals, and in the final, Dodge City College solved Arkansas City for the first time, 71-63.

The eastern sub-regional was more straightforward. After capturing the Eastern Jayhawk Juco Conference crown without loss, Coffeyville College continued its domination of eastern Kansas opponents, easily defeating Parsons Junior College, 69-48, and Independence Junior College, 77-61.

Coffeyville was again the heavy favorite in the Region 6 tournament in Hutchinson's Sports Arena. The Red Ravens had twice beaten their opening opponent, Arkansas City, walloping the Tigers, 81-50, at Coffeyville and squeaking by, 66-64, at Arkansas City. Now the court was neutral, the stakes greater. A cold, tight Coffeyville crew escaped the law of averages, barely nipping the Tigers, 53-51.

The road was even rougher in the final. Ignoring Coffeyville's No. 2 national ranking, the Dodge City Conquistadors marched to a 34-25 halftime advantage and extended it to 12 with 16:45 left in the game, forcing the Red Ravens to struggle from behind. Coffeyville did not take its first lead of the second half until 2:20 remained.

Dodge City did not roll over. Guard Jerry Couch, the Conquistadors' top scorer, canned one with :57 left to put the underdogs back in front, 58-57.

Coffeyville shot and missed, Dodge City grabbing the rebound. A major upset was in the offing.

With 40 seconds remaining, Couch was called for charging. The reprieve gave Coffeyville the ball with sufficient time to work for a good shot. The one the Red Ravens took was not the best. At the 18-second mark, forward Paul Fortin lofted an arching 15-foot hook. It banged off the glass — and in.

Dodge City called time. When play resumed, the Conquistadors worked the ball inside. With two seconds showing, Elmer Walker fired from under the basket. The ball rolled off the side of the rim, no good.

The Red Ravens heaved a collective sigh. They were in the national tournament. Their record: 28-0.

THE PARTICIPANTS

Normally, a perfect record coming into the tournament would have garnered rave notices from the press and a favorite's role far in front of the field. In 1962, Coffeyville shared the spotlight. The Red Ravens were not the only undefeated team in the nation.

Young Harris College brought even more impressive credentials than it had the year before with three starters returning

Later an All-Missouri player at Drake University and an eight-year veteran in the NBA, McCoy McLemore led Moberly Junior College, scoring 86 points in four games. (Photo courtesy of Drake University)

Region	Team
1	Weber College — Ogden, Utah
2	Cameron State Agricultural College — Lawton, Oklahoma
3	Broome Technical Community College — Binghamton, New York
4	Lincoln College — Lincoln, Illinois
5	San Angelo College — San Angelo, Texas
6	Coffeyville College of Arts, Science, and Vocations — Coffeyville, Kansas
7	Fort Smith Junior College — Fort Smith, Arkansas
8	Young Harris College — Young Harris, Georgia
9	Trinidad State Junior College — Trinidad, Colorado
10	Wilmington College — Wilmington, North Carolina
11	Creston Community College — Creston, Iowa
12	Flint Community Junior College — Flint, Michigan
13	Bethany Lutheran College — Mankato, Minnesota
14	Lon Morris College — Jacksonville, Texas
15	New York City Community College — Brooklyn, New York
16	Moberly Junior College — Moberly, Missouri

from the 1961 Mountain Lions, including second-team All-American Larry Cart. The Georgians owned the third-highest offense in the nation (95.5) and had downed opponents by an average 30.5 points per game, tops among junior colleges. Their 30-0 record earned them the No. 1 spot in the NJCAA basketball poll — one step above Coffeyville.

Though their record was not spotless, the No. 8 Cameron State Aggies (24-3) were also considered in the pre-tourney elite. The reason: Jim Barnes. The 6-8, 246-pound sophomore was one of the most heavily touted players ever to participate in the event. Not only was he the tallest man in the tournament, but one of the fastest, having reputedly run the 100 in 10 flat. His 30.6 average was one of the best in the country. He had twice scored 50 in a game and was capable of much more. During breakfast one morning, Barnes showed off to reporters present, downing *24 eggs*. He was an animal. The press loved it. When fans saw Barnes' massive bulk displayed at the top of the sports page, no one questioned Cameron's chances at a crown.

Rounding out the "top four" was Moberly Junior College. Since they sported a less impressive record (25-5) than the other favorites, were only rated 15th in the nation (eight other tourney teams ranked higher), and returned only one starter (center McCoy McLemore) from the previous year's seventh-place team, the Greyhounds were added to the competitive cream based on their past track record; the two-time national champs were making their 11th tournament appearance in 15 years.

The competition did not slack off after the top four. Seven other nationally ranked teams graced the tournament roster: No. 7 Lon Morris College (28-8), the representative from Region 14, the region which had placed a team in the championship contest four out of the last six years; No. 10 Trinidad State Junior College (23-4), the highest-ranked tourney newcomer and the deposer of Pueblo Junior College, the defending national champion; No. 12 Broome Technical Community College (24-4), a familiar tourney veteran, making its third consecutive appearance; No. 14 Bethany Lutheran College (21-4), a repeater from 1961 with three returning starters, including honorable mention All-American Larry Berke; and No. 18 Creston Community College (22-5), a tourney debutant with one of the top offenses (88.4) and scorers (Dick Rishel, 28.5) in the country.

Though not ranked, Flint Junior College (17-6) and Weber College (21-10) also deserved consideration. They were among the top eight finishers in 1961, Flint having placed sixth, the highest finish of any tournament repeater, and Weber having notched eighth.

The rest of the roster was a question mark. Four-time tourney participant and former champion San Angelo College (22-7) was a surprise winner in Region 5, having knocked off No. 9 Howard County Junior College for the second year in a row. New York City Community College, also making its fourth trip to Hutchinson, was even more of a surprise. The Bees possessed a .500 record (11-11), making them an obvious long shot. The remainder of the field, all newcomers, represented the long and short of the competition; Wilmington College (20-4) had the tallest starting five, averaging just over 6-3 per man, while Lincoln College (29-5) and Fort Smith Junior College (24-11) started the smallest crews, averaging an even six-foot across the board.

TUESDAY — TOURNAMENT FEVER

Tournament fever struck Hutchinson early. One week before the start of the five-day event, advance season ticket sales were 30 percent greater than ever before. Only 30 reserved seats remained for championship night. After viewing exciting competition for the past 13 years, local fans did not want to miss any of the action.

Three thousand — one of the largest opening afternoon crowds yet — showed up early for the tip-off. They were eager to see two favorites collide right out of the starting gate.

The anticipated gold mine of thrills did not pan out. Young Harris jumped to a brief early lead before the Moberly Greyhounds shifted gears, caught, then passed the Georgians. By intermission, Moberly's advantage was 14. Shortly into the second period, the margin grew to 17. The undefeated Georgia squad made a valiant run at the Missourians, cutting the difference to six. Tight Greyhound defense and the loss of two Young

Harris starters to fouls ended the rally. Moberly won easily, 7 58.

The star for the Greyhounds was 6-6 sophomore McC McLemore who led all scorers with 26 and, along with forwa Andy Hubbard, dominated board play. Also key to the victo was the Greyhounds' stingy defense which held the No. 1 tea in the land 37 points below its offensive average. Moberl selection as a pre-tourney favorite was no mistake.

The afternoon feature was more to fan liking. After trailing small margins throughout the first half, Flint grabbed the ha time advantage from Creston on a pair of long-distance bom by Pat Manley and Clarence Shuett. The Bears then sprint ahead twice in the second period, attaining an eight-point ed with three minutes gone and a nine-point margin with 10 mi utes to go.

The Creston crew gave the crowd its money's worth, boun ing back from both deficits. Additional excitement was provi ed during the Iowan's second rally when the scoreboard tim failed with 9:04 to go. The final minutes were measured by st watch, the time periodically announced over the pub address system. As the 3:30 marked was called, Creston pull to within one, 64-63, on a 20-footer by reserve Rick Crawfo

The Golden Bears from Iowa regained control of the baske ball 30 seconds later, and, after a time-out, worked for the g ahead basket. The shot hit the rim and bounded high over t backboard and out of bounds. The lid remained on Cresto bucket for the rest of the game. Flint tallied the final sev points for a 71-63 victory.

The most exhilarating contest of the day followed. F Smith's Jim Bob Weir canned the first shot of the game, givi the Lions the opening lead. The advantage lasted precisely o minute and 15 seconds. The Lincoln Lynx raced by the Arkans five, building a 32-14 bulge.

At intermission the Fort Smith deficit was still 12. Then, in t first 10 minutes of the second half, the Lions outscored Linco 20-8, tying the score at 47-all.

Lincoln broke away again, going on top by six.

Fort Smith rallied to within one.

The tournament's two smallest teams then engaged in bask trading.

With 26 seconds to go, Fort Smith's Pat Martin finally tied t game with a free throw.

Fourteen seconds later, Lincoln's Al Hoffert hit one of tv free tosses to put the Lynx back in front, 67-66.

Fort Smith worked quickly for the go-ahead bucket. T long-distance attempt missed.

The rebound was immediately tied up. Only three secon remained as the jump ball was tossed in the air. The basketb was batted twice. At the last possible moment, Fort Smit Martin grabbed the loose sphere and shot. The ball roll around the rim — and stopped.

The buzzer sounded.

For nearly two full seconds the basketball remained ine Then it fell.

The basket was good. It was Martin's only field goal of t game and gave Fort Smith only its second lead, the one tf counted most.

The fortunes of the New York City Bees rested firmly on t shoulders of Herb Bacon. After the 6-3 forward broke his fc in NYCCC's third game of the year, the Bees entered a tailsp They did not pull out until Bacon returned to the lineup shor before regional action, just in time to earn an unexpected trip the nationals.

When Bacon reinjured his foot in the early minutes of t evening opener, Bee chances looked bleak. Everyone figur they would slowly fade against Lon Morris, one of the top-rat teams in the country.

By halftime, however, the New Yorkers trailed by only s Employing hit-and-run tactics the Bees rallied further. A Puma fielder with 10:37 to go tied the contest at 47-all.

In the next two minutes, hope for a major upset glimmer then vanished. Lon Morris built an eight-point marg stretched it to 15 five minutes later, then repelled a last di Bee attack, cruising to a 64-53 win.

The pressure of an unblemished record was terrific. O undefeated team had already fallen under its weight. Coffey le's unimpressive Region 6 outings proved the Red Ravens the stress, too, playing tight and tentative.

After the tournament, Coach Jack Hartman tried to relieve [th]e pressure by giving the team two days off to relax and get [a]way from basketball.

The strategy apparently worked. Coffeyville exploded from [th]e blocks, sprinting to a 16-5 lead before the men from Manka[to], Minnesota, realized the evening feature had started. A Beth[an]y Lutheran rally pulled the Vikings to within four with 1:17 left [in] the half, but a free throw by Paul Henry and a field goal by Jer[ry] Burton opened a seven-point halftime margin for the Kan[sa]ns.

The second half was all Coffeyville. In the first five minutes, [Be]thany Lutheran managed to squeeze only three field goals in [be]tween a Red Raven barrage. Coffeyville hit 21 of 41 second [ha]lf shots and steadily built an insurmountable lead, winning [co]nvincingly, 84-61.

Coffeyville's team balance impressed everyone. All five Cof[fe]yville starters hit double figures; Paul Henry (23), Lou Wil[lia]ms (19), Jerry Burton (14), Paul Fortin (12), and Ken Hendrix ([1]0). All contributed to Red Raven domination of the boards: [W]illiams (16 rebounds), Henry (12), Burton (10), Fortin (7), and [H]endrix (6). The Kansans gave notice that it would take a [su]perb effort to knock them from the ranks of the unbeaten.

The final game of the day sent the crowd home early. San [A]ngelo's 6-5 Kirby Pugh and 6-6 Bruce Tibbets manhandled [sm]aller Broome Tech, leading the Rams to a 12-point halftime [a]dvantage. Broome Tech never countered. San Angelo [a]dvanced with an easy 84-64 victory.

WEDNESDAY — BAD NEWS

Friends of the national tournament received the sad news [W]ednesday that Compton College's Goldie Holmes, the [ev]ent's founding father, was hospitalized in California. Holmes, [a] stout supporter of the tournament despite his school's exclu[si]on from NJCAA sponsored activities, had returned every year [un]til his advancing arthritic condition made it impossible for [hi]m to travel. Now, his hospital stay was reported to be "indefi[ni]te." He would later die on August 8th at the age of 54.

The Weber Wildcats also received bad news Wednesday — [in] the person of Cameron State's Jim Barnes. In the first half of [th]e day's opener, the giant center scored 32 and was principally [re]sponsible for the Aggies' other 16, dishing off repeatedly to [Ji]mmy Jones and John Reier. Cameron opened a comfortable [2]2-point gap at halftime.

Barnes cooled off in the second period because of foul trou[bl]e, but Mike Bryant picked up the slack, hitting 12 of 12 from [th]e line. When Barnes fouled out with 3:30 to go, a game-high [4]0 beside his name in the scorebook, Cameron State was in no [da]nger. A game which had been anticipated as one of the best [of] the first round ended up a 92-74 Aggie rout.

The final opening-round contest also looked like a romp as [Tr]inidad State lagged behind the Wilmington Seahawks [th]roughout. The Coloradans were down by as much as seven in [th]e first half, trailed 32-28 at intermission, then fell to their low[es]t depth, a 13-point deficit, with 13 minutes to go.

At the three-minute mark, Trinidad still needed 10 points to [pu]ll even. There seemed to be no way the Trojans could upset [W]ilmington's smoothly executed control pattern. A Charles [Li]ndsey free throw barely put a dent in the margin. But, a tip-in [by] Joe Price, followed by a beautiful reverse lay-up by Lindsey, [t]ightened the situation considerably. Trinidad trailed, 68-63, [wi]th 1:30 left.

Then came the break the Trojans needed. After Wilmington [w]as whistled for a foul, the player charged argued the call, [dr]awing a technical. Price notched both ends of a one-and-one [an]d Lindsey, who had hit eight straight from the line, made it [on]e with the technical. Trinidad played the ball inbounds. [Pr]ice was again fouled. Though he missed the second half of the [on]e-and-one, Trinidad was back in the game, trailing by one [wi]th a minute to go.

Wilmington's Albert Thiry widened the gap with a short [ju]mper.

Bob Johnson countered with a driving lay-up, but was called [fo]r a foul after he crashed into the Seahawks' Eugene Bogash [af]ter the goal. Bogash returned the margin to three with a pair [of] free throws.

Johnson connected again — this time without fouling.

Wilmington scrambled to inbounds the ball against pressure, [bu]t Trinidad's Lindsey intercepted a pass at midcourt and drove

for an easy lay-up. With 11 seconds remaining, the Coloradans owned their first lead of the half, 73-72.

The Seahawks' final shot hit the rim and fell away, becoming a much sought-after loose ball. A jump ball was called with two seconds on the clock. Trinidad's Price grabbed the tip, wrapped his arms protectively around the ball, and preserved the come-from-behind win for the Trojans.

The first round had been a series of runaways with a couple of last-second barn burners thrown in for spice. Interest was keen as fans sized up the field. Near sellouts for Friday and Saturday nights demonstrated that everyone expected the best games to come later.

Few figured Wednesday's quarterfinal action would be among them. Flint and Fort Smith were heavy underdogs to Moberly and Lon Morris, respectively. Consequently, the crowd was the smallest evening audience of the 1962 tournament.

Flint had also been a heavy underdog the year before when the Bears pulled the upset of the tournament, downing Moberly in the quarterfinals. Cotton Fitzsimmons' Greyhounds were determined that it would not happen again. Their confidence was shaken, however, when Flint held a 35-34 halftime lead.

Upset was on everybody's mind as the Bears continued to claw and scratch. The first 10 minutes of the second half saw six ties and five lead changes.

Then, Moberly's Joe Mimlitz broke the duel, hitting three consecutive field goals from 10 to 15 feet. Flint was only able to counter with a solitary free throw.

The Greyhounds continued to rain points. In an eight-minute period, Moberly outscored Flint, 20-4. With 1:38 remaining, the Greyhounds were in command, 73-57. Flint rallied in the latter moments, but the disadvantage was too great, the seconds left, too few. Moberly avenged the previous year's upset, 75-66.

The big gun for the Greyhounds was again McCoy McLemore. Besides leading all scorers with 27, the Moberly center displayed exceptional versatility, playing outside in the second half, feeding Mimlitz — who was second-high with 26 — for many of his crucial buckets.

The critical baskets of the finale were fired by Lon Morris' Jerry Wade and Ken Norman. Wade netted 17 of his total 23 in the first half and Norman followed with 19 second-period points to account for 24. The Bearcats completely outclassed Fort Smith, opening up a 15-point halftime margin before spreading it to 25 midway through the final frame. The small Arena crowd left en masse. Only about 400 diehards stayed to the bitter end as Lon Morris slaughtered the Lions, 96-65.

THURSDAY — UPSET

The day's first two games featured top individual scoring and little else. Lincoln's husky 6-4 center, Tom Flynn, nailed 28 of his game-high 35 in the first half, leading the Lynx to a runaway 83-62 victory over New York City. Then, Eugene Bogash (33) and Albert Thiry (23) combined for 70 percent of Wilmington's point production as the Seahawks flew by Weber, 78-64.

The latter loss marked Weber's last game in the Sports Arena. After seven appearances and a national title, the Wildcats' long tournament heritage would come to an end in the fall when the school added a junior year to its academic program in its expansion to a four-year curriculum.

Points were dear in the afternoon finale, especially for the team from Flint, Michigan. The Fort Smith Lions shredded holes in the Bear zone defense, tearing open a 22-5 gap after the first 10 minutes. Flint switched to a man-to-man and narrowed the deficit to six in less than four minutes, but could not break Fort Smith's grip on the lead.

Flint still trailed, 60-58, late in the game when Fort Smith's Pat Martin crashed into Bear reserve Ronald Morlan who banged his head into the floor and was knocked unconscious. Morlan, revived but groggy, sank two free throws, tying the score. After each side added another pair of charities, the score stood 62-all with 1:45 to go.

In the next 60 seconds Flint stole the ball twice. But, with victory within reach, the Bears could not find the range, missing both attempts at the tie-breaker.

At the 40-second mark, Fort Smith's Bill Meek put the Lions on top with a free throw.

Flint again had a chance to take the advantage. And again missed.

Fort Smith grabbed the rebound, held the ball for the last 25 seconds, and won its second nail biter in a row.

The evening opener was equally tense, though the game-ending action was static as Bethany Lutheran and Broome Tech engaged in a free-throw-shooting contest. The men from Mankato closed out an excellent 22-for-26 night at the line with eight of nine in the final 2:46, outlasting Broome Tech, 70-68.

Though the two quarterfinals on tap were not expected to be as close, the Arena was nearly jammed. Everyone was eager to see the tournament's top talent in the feature and the nation's only remaining undefeated team in the finale.

Jim Barnes' powerful performance in Cameron State's initial outing had stirred tongues all over town. No individual on Trinidad State, let alone in the whole field of participants, could match his awesome court presence. The sympathies of the Arena crowd were fully extended to the underdog Trojans.

The unexpected fan support sparked Trinidad State while a sagging defense prevented Barnes from getting the ball, keeping the Trojans in the game. By halftime, Cameron's advantage was only one. In the first 12 minutes of the second period, the score was tied four times and the lead changed hands 10. The crowd's enthusiasm geared up.

Then, three consecutive baskets by Bruce Gray, John Reier, and Jimmy Jones opened a seven-point gap for Cameron. Three-and-a-half minutes of hard work did not close the deficit for Trinidad. With 3:30 left, leading, 69-63, Cameron slowed the action, playing for sure shots.

Only Aggie momentum was slowed, however. Trinidad's Joe Price stole the ball, drove the length of the court, and scored an uncontested lay-up. He stole the ball again, passed off to Dennis Lee, and watched the Trojans gain another easy basket. When Larry Antonsen tipped in a missed shot moments later, Trinidad evened the score at 69-all.

On the next two trips down court, Cameron lost the ball on charging calls. Trinidad's Price made good on the first possession with a driving lay-up. The Trojans cashed in at the free throw line on the other. Scoring the last 11 points, Trinidad State upended Cameron State, 74-69.

It was a stunning upset. Most unbelievable of all was that Jim Barnes had hardly been a factor. The big man netted only 11 and did not take a shot in the final 10 minutes.

In contrast, three Trojans tallied 20 or better: Price (21), Bob Johnson (20), and Dennis Nickle (20).

The Trinidad State balance was insignificant when compared to that of Coffeyville in the day's finale against San Angelo. For the second game in a row, all Red Raven starters hit double-digits: Paul Henry (22), Paul Fortin (14), Ken Hendrix (14), Jerry Burton (13), and Lou Williams (10). For the second straight time, Coffeyville dominated board play: Williams (16), Burton (10), and Fortin (10). For the 30th consecutive time, the Red Ravens were victorious. As the *Hutchinson News* described it, Coffeyville's "deadeye shooting [52.8 percent from the floor] and skin-tight defense" was too much for the Rams. San Angelo quietly succumbed, 82-69.

FRIDAY — THE PERFECT HALF

In the day's opener, Lincoln's Mike Lumpp upped the 1962 tournament's best individual total, netting 43, including 13 perfect tries from the line. On the other side of the floor, Young Harris's Larry Cart celebrated his 22nd birthday with two halves of brilliant basketball. In the first period, the All-American set up easy baskets for his teammates with a variety of showy, picture perfect passes. Then in the final frame, he unveiled his sharp, long-range shooting eye, hitting 21 of a total 27, including 16 in a six-minute stretch. The two outstanding efforts sparked a battle royal. Only two points separated the combatants with 54 seconds to go. A pair of baskets by Roger Arrington clinched a 90-86 triumph for Young Harris.

Individual excellence continued in the afternoon feature. Despite sitting out the final minutes because of a scratched retina from an errant finger, Bethany Lutheran's Larry Berke fired 27 of his game-high 38 to lead the Vikings past Wilmington, 85-67.

The tournament's premier individual performance capped the afternoon's entertainment. As San Angelo coach Phil George remembered, "[Jim] Barnes was a man among boys. He

was awesome to look at. He had such size and talent, quickness and mobility that he could pretty much do what he wanted to when he got ready to do it. If they gave him the ball when he got his rhythm going, he was just about impossible to stop. You had to hit him with an ax handle to hold him down. We couldn't have stopped him with a train."

The big man roamed at will, scoring 49. The disdain for defense led to an all-out run-and-gun show. The Aggies galloped to a 57-46 halftime lead on their way to the century mark with 5:22 to go. When Barnes fouled out, the Cameron total was 112, a basket shy of the tournament record. Mike Ash replaced Barnes, cashed in a free throw, then potted a field goal at the buzzer, giving the Aggies a record-breaking 115-93 victory.

Friday night tickets disappeared long before the semifinalists were known. The standing-room only audience was not disappointed in its speculation. For most, mainly Kansas partisans, the investment became worthwhile as soon as Coffeyville earned a final four berth. The companion feature's coupling of the representatives from the tourney's two most successful regions was a bonus.

In the opener, Region 14's Lon Morris and Region 16's Moberly gave the crowd championship caliber excitement — but, it took time to develop. Behind Jerry Wade's 16 first-half points, the Bearcats beat the Greyhounds out of the gate, opening a 31-18 bulge with four minutes to go in the period.

Then, Moberly gained ground. By intermission, the margin was narrowed to eight. The Greyhounds continued their run after the break, reducing the deficit to one with 12:45 remaining. Three minutes later, Moberly was on top, 51-45.

Lon Morris was in serious trouble. Bill Gasway and his backup, James Hahn — the two top Bearcat rebounders — had collected four fouls apiece, trying to contain Moberly's McCoy McLemore. The agile Greyhound was simply too quick for the Lon Morris centers, especially when he roamed outside the lane for his shots. When both fouled out in the next two minutes, Moberly comfortably settled into the driver's seat, leading 52-47 with 6:29 to go.

After Gasway and Hahn were whistled to the bench, the task of guarding McLemore fell to the Bearcat's do-it-all guard Wade. Despite giving away four inches to the Moberly center, the 6-2 Wade possessed long arms and strong determination. McLemore did not score the rest of the game.

Meanwhile, the Bearcats stalked the lead. Reserve John Thompson hit a long fielder. Forward Ken Norman connected from the side. Thompson potted another 15-footer. Wade added a bomb. The rally continued until Lon Morris held a 58-57 advantage with 1:36 to go.

Then the Bearcats let the air out of the ball. Jim Bob Smith took control of the Lon Morris delay, forcing Moberly to pressure and foul. Free throws preserved a 65-60 Texan victory.

No one expected the other semifinal to be much of a contest, particularly since Trinidad State had lost one of its stars to injury. Just before intermission in Trinidad's quarterfinal match with Cameron State, Charles Lindsey crashed to the floor after a driving lay-up, landing on his hip. A doctor suggested he might be able to "walk it out" and return to the game. However, the injury was so painful, Lindsey did not want to try. He suffered on the bench while his teammates upset Cameron. The next day x-rays revealed a hip fracture.

Though the odds of Trinidad pulling off a second major upset in consecutive nights were excessive, the unforeseen occurrence was no stranger to semifinal action. What followed astonished everybody.

Throughout the season, Jack Hartman's Coffeyville squad had worked diligently on its defense. In the final NJCAA rankings, the Red Ravens rated third-best in stinginess, allowing opponents an average 53.9 points per game. Against Trinidad State, those defensive skills were honed to razor sharpness.

The five Coffeyville starters were like well-oiled parts, moving precisely in an intricate machine. Wherever the Trinidad players went, they were shadowed by a Red Raven. Eyeball to belly, hand in the face, the Coffeyville defensemen forced the Trojans away from the bucket. Open shots rarely presented themselves. High percentage attempts never materialized. At one point, after several Trinidad passes failed to find a chink in the Coffeyville armor, a Trojan launched a desperation 25-foot heave when he was left open for the barest instant. The Arena audience applauded the effort even though it missed.

The first Trinidad field goal did not come until 7:44 remained in the half. By then, the equally precise Coffeyville offense had opened a 32-5 chasm. Frustration was carved in every Trojan face. The Coloradans appeared relieved just to get the ball away whether it scored or not. When the first 20 minutes finally lapsed and the totals added up, Trinidad's shooting chart showed only four of 36 shots (11 percent) successful from the field. The Trojan deficit: *41 points.* Coffeyville led, 56-15.

The second half was unnecessary. The crowd, lulled to complacency by Coffeyville's machine-like exactness, sifted out of the Arena. The Red Raven starters, after 20 minutes of masterful consistency, lost their sharp edge and relinquished their spots on the floor to one substitute after another. Even the Trinidad players relaxed. With the pressure of winning no longer a factor, the Trojans played more in line with their previous form. They regained a measure of self-respect, outscoring Coffeyville by 19 in the second period. It was not enough to overcome the Red Ravens' first-half masterpiece.

The 89-67 victory sent Coffeyville into the title contest with an unblemished 31-0 record.

SATURDAY — TODAY'S OUR DAY

With all eyes focused on Coffeyville's attempt at an unprecedented undefeated national crown, the remaining trophy day match-ups received only passing attention. The only contest which aroused fan interest was the first.

When Young Harris scored 59 points in the opening period, then hit the century mark 10 seconds earlier than Cameron State had in its record-breaking effort the day before, tournament officials readied their erasers over the record book. The Georgians' 120-101 fifth-place victory over Bethany Lutheran set three scoring marks: most points by one team in a game (breaking Cameron's previous 115-point effort); most points by two teams in a game (topping the 211 posted by Weber and San Angelo the year before); and most points for a team in a tournament (moving the Mountain Lions three points ahead of Hutchinson's 1958 total of 362).

Ten players (five on each team) notched double figures. The Vikings were led by their All-American candidate, Larry Berke, who fired 27 points despite having one eye heavily bandaged. On the other side of the fence, four Young Harris players tallied 20 points or better. Three of them would not have scored as high had it not been for the spectacular assists of the game's leading scorer — Larry Cart (28).

Bethany Lutheran Coach Dwain Mintz's chief concern going into the game against Young Harris was not Cart's scoring potential, but his passing. "He would get inside real tight and give it to the big men. If you didn't take him, he'd put it up on you." Mintz described Cart's hands as being so quick when shuffling the ball off, "he would have made a great double play man."

The Mountain Lion sophomore tossed balls in every conceivable fashion with expert control, often leaving his teammates with nothing but empty space separating them from an easy two points. Cart was one of the greatest assistmen ever to play in the tournament.

The other two trophy battles were significantly less interesting.

The fourth-place contest was a mismatch between the Jim Barnes-led Cameron Aggies and the much smaller Fort Smith Lions. Even though Barnes hit below his average, Cameron encountered little difficulty, downing the Arkansas team, 78-66. Barnes' 23 gave him the tournament scoring title with 122.

In the game for third, Moberly's Joe Mimlitz led all scorers with 28, including 12 of 14 from the line, as the Greyhounds made short work of a demoralized Trinidad State, 83-66.

Only the title game remained.

The Coffeyville Red Ravens had impressed everyone during the week. Their efficient manner in overhauling class opponents often tranquilized the audience. On more than one occasion, Coffeyville's artful defense sent fans toward the exits long before the game's completion. The team's balance was eerie. Only once did all five starters not score double figures (Lou Williams missed double digits by one field goal in the Trinidad match). There were few in the sold-out Sports Arena who were not convinced Coffeyville was on the verge of making tournament history.

Among those non-believers were the members of the Lon Morris squad. The Bearcats were brimming with confidence. They had come too far not to believe in themselves. Just a few weeks earlier, their season was a disaster. After having been ranked as high as No. 1, the Bearcats ended their regular schedule with six consecutive defeats. They entered sub-regional play at the nadir of self-confidence.

An opening victory in front of hometown fans lifted the Bearcats' spirits and helped them regroup. Then, in consecutive nights, Lon Morris edged regional favorites Tyler Junior College and Kilgore College —both in overtime. The Bearcats were on a roll. They swept San Antonio College in a best-two-of-three play-off for the region crown, won their first two national tournament games with ease, then rallied to beat a solid Moberly ballclub in the semifinals.

The team felt invincible. Since the odds of going through an entire season without a defeat was so great, the pressure was on Coffeyville. Besides, Region 14 representative's had more championship game appearances and national crowns than any other region. The clincher was that earlier in the day the Cincinnati Bearcats had crushed Ohio State for the NCAA title. The Lon Morris Bearcats felt "today's our day, too."

One of the reasons the team developed such a positive attitude was because Coach Leon Black had sequestered the squad away from the tournament's hoopla. The Bearcats lived a regimented existence, doing everything together on a specified timetable. Their only exposure to tournament proceedings other than the games they played was through radio broadcasts and newspaper stories. They had no physical perception of Coffeyville's talent.

Their introductions to the Red Raven defense came as a rude awakening. The opening moments of the championship tilt played like the Coffeyville-Trinidad semifinal. The Red Ravens completely shut down Lon Morris. The Bearcats went nearly six minutes before hitting their first field goal.

After the initial shock dissipated, Lon Morris regained composure and battled back. The Bearcats pulled within two with 9:25 left in the half.

Then it happened again. Coffeyville's pressing man-to-man shackled the Texans. A Bill Gasway free throw was the sole Lon Morris score in the next five minutes. The Red Ravens sprinted to a 23-12 advantage. Lon Morris never pulled closer than nine points from then on.

With a 76-49 victory, Coffeyville College became the first undefeated champion in Juco Tournament history.

The 1962 champion Coffeyville Red Ravens were the first undefeated champions in the Juco Tournament. (Photo courtesy of Jack Hartman)

THE AFTERMATH — ASSEMBLING THE PERFECT TEAM

Though it is difficult to compare teams from different eras, many longtime tourney observers agree that the Coffeyville starting five was the best unit they ever saw. They were not physically overpowering. Instead, their strengths were superb finesse, flawless execution, and solidarity.

Stated San Angelo's Phil George, who experienced Red Raven perfection first-hand, "That bunch was so well-coached, played so well together, you couldn't find a weak seam. You know, the grouping of talent is always secondary to how the talent within a group plays. If they complement each other to where you don't actually realize what they're doing, then you've run against a great ballclub. In that light, I think you have to consider Coffeyville one of the greatest."

The achievements of the 1962 Red Ravens were awe inspiring: 32 wins without a loss; the largest average winning margin in four tournament games (20.8, an all-time record); and the largest winning margin in a championship game (25, also an all-time record). In fact, Coffeyville trailed only *once* in the whole tournament. (Ironically, Trinidad State grabbed an initial 1-0 advantage before being crushed by the Kansans.) The fact those accomplishments were attained by basically a five-man unit showed the team's remarkable cohesiveness.

Coach Jack Hartman was responsible for putting together the perfect team. His easiest recruiting chore was Coffeyville native Ken Hendrix, the Ravens' reliable No. 2 guard. Acquiring East High star Jerry Burton — an excellent swing man, who was comfortable playing inside as well as out — required several trips to Wichita. George Washington Coach Bill Reinhardt put Hartman in touch with his farthest acquisition, ambidextrous Paul Fortin (the 6-5 sophomore shot his crowd-pleasing, looping hooks left-handed but shot free throws right-handed), a forward from Lewiston, Maine. Former Moberly coach Maury John (then coaching at Drake) directed Hartman to the team's best jumper — Indianapolis' Shortridge High standout, Lou Williams. It was Williams who delivered the final cog to Hartman's basketball machine. After agreeing to attend Coffeyville, Williams wrote Hartman asking if he could bring along a friend. That "friend" turned out to be the team's star player — Paul Henry.

It was not incongruous to call Henry the "star" of a squad which stressed unity over individuality. Paul Henry epitomized team play. His unselfish attitude, intensity, alertness, and determination were the same characteristics his teammates possessed. In Henry, they were just more highly attuned. Hard work made him a better-than-average rebounder for his size (6-1½) and intelligence made him team leader on defense.

When Hartman later reflected on how he acquired Henry, he said, "I couldn't believe how fortunate I was." Yet, after coaching Henry for four years (Henry accompanied Hartman when he took the head coaching job at Southern Illinois the following year), Hartman stated, "I could see how he could be overlooked. He was such an unselfish player, you might not notice him in a ballgame. He probably could have scored a lot more had he been so inclined. He just took what came his way. When we needed a bucket, [however,] Paul would go get it for us."

Henry's importance to Coffeyville's success was best illustrated in the championship game. Everyone noticed his offensive prowess — a game-high 30 points, all from the field. It was his defensive leadership, however, which decided matters. Henry was assigned the task of guarding Jerry Wade, Lon Morris' top scorer, holder of a 25-point average in three tournament games. With Henry dogging him at every turn, Wade's total output was *one* field goal. Henry's feat destroyed the Texans' confidence, paved the way for Coffeyville's victory, and secured his unanimous endorsement as the tournament's Most Valuable Player.

* * *

While Coffeyville was making tournament history, the NJCAA tended to business. The previous year the organization sought equal representation for its membership. At the 1962 annual meeting, Association officials tackled equality in player participation.

Eligibility rules were clarified and teeth put in the regulations. Mid-year high school graduates were no longer eligible. All transfers — from four-year as well as from two-year institutions — were required to sit out two semesters (or three quarters). Students who falsified academic records were "ineligible for further competition at any time." Finally, any member college "which knowingly uses an ineligible player or players or violates the sport season game rules shall automatically forfeit their right to participate in Regional and National sponsored events of the NJCAA in all sports for at least one calendar year."

This renewed emphasis of standard eligibility came on the eve of the most disruptive moment in tournament history.

After winning the 1962 Juco title with Coffeyville, Coach of the Tournament Jack Hartman (center) took Red Raven stars Paul Henry (left) and Lou Williams (right) with him to Southern Illinois. He coached there eight years, then moved to Kansas State for 16 years before retiring in 1986. (Photo courtesy of Southern Illinois)

Though he was third-high scorer in the 1962 tournament with 101 points, Paul Henry was one of the first MVP recipients to be recognized as much for his defense as his offense. In the championship game, Henry held Jerry Wade, Lou Morris' leading scorer to one field goal. (Photo courtesy of Southern Illinois)

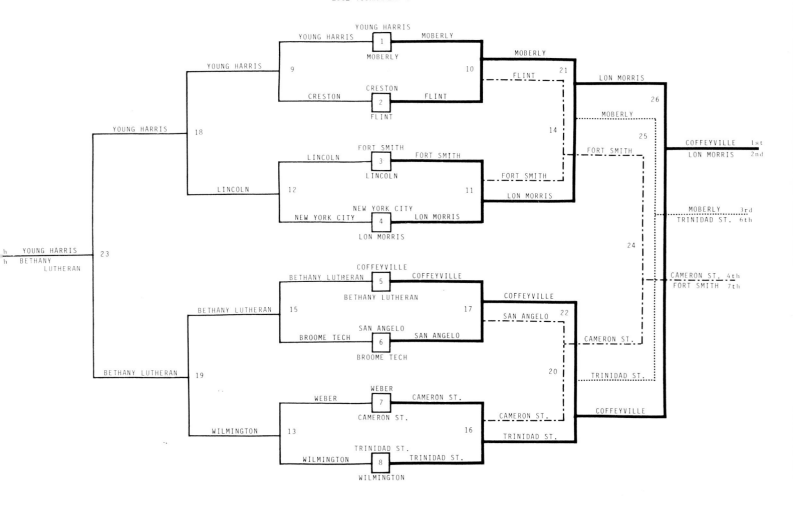

Tournament Results

Tuesday: Game

1. Moberly — 74 Young Harris — 58
2. Flint — 71 Creston — 63
3. Fort Smith — 68 Lincoln — 67
4. Lon Morris — 64 New York City — 53
5. Coffeyville — 84 Bethany Lutheran — 61
6. San Angelo — 84 Broome Tech — 64

Wednesday: Game

7. Cameron St. — 92 Weber — 74
8. Trinidad St. — 73 Wilmington — 72
9. Young Harris — 97 Creston — 76
10. Moberly — 75 Flint — 66
11. Lon Morris — 98 Fort Smith — 65

Thursday: Game

12. Lincoln — 83 New York City — 62
13. Wilmington — 78 Weber 64
14. Fort Smith — 63 Flint — 62
15. Bethany Lutheran — 70 Broome Tech — 68
16. Trinidad St. — 74 Cameron St. — 69
17. Coffeyville — 82 San Angelo — 69

Friday: Game

18. Young Harris — 90 Lincoln — 86
19. Bethany Lutheran — 85 Wilmington — 67
20. Cameron St. — 115 San Angelo — 93
21. Lon Morris — 65 Moberly — 60
22. Coffeyville — 89 Trinidad St. — 67

Saturday: Game

23. Young Harris — 120 Bethany Lutheran — 101
24. Cameron St. — 78 Fort Smith — 66
25. Moberly — 83 Trinidad St. — 66
26. Coffeyville — 74 Lon Morris — 49

How They Finished in 1962

1. Coffeyville College of Arts, Science, and Vocations
2. Lon Morris College
3. Moberly Junior College
4. Cameron State Agricultural College
5. Young Harris College
6. Trinidad State Junior College
7. Fort Smith Junior College
8. Bethany Lutheran College

All-Tournament Team

Jim Barnes — Cameron State Agricultural College
Larry Berke — Bethany Lutheran College
Eugene Bogash — Wilmington College
Larry Cart — Young Harris College
Tom Flynn — Lincoln College
Paul Henry — Coffeyville College of Arts, Science, and Vocations
Jim Jay — Fort Smith Junior College
Bob Johnson — Trinidad State Junior College
McCoy McLemore — Moberly Junior College
Jerry Wade — Lon Morris College

Coach of the Year

Jack Hartman — Coffeyville College of Arts, Science, and Vocations

Player of the Year

Paul Henry — Coffeyville College of Arts, Science, and Vocations

1963:

ENDURANCE MEET,

ENDURING MEMORIES

Though his 115 points in five games was not enough to lead Burlington to a title, Bobby Joe Hill eventually experienced the thrill of winning a national crown. In 1966, Hill made two lightning quick thefts and two driving lay-ups in 10 seconds to break open a close NCAA championship game. Topping all scorers with 20, Hill led the Texas Western Miners to a 72-65 upset victory over Kentucky. (Photo courtesy of Loren Walker)

Region	Team
1	Phoenix College — Phoenix, Arizona
2	Murray State Agricultural College — Tishomingo, Oklahoma
3	Broome Technical Community College — Binghamton, New York
4	Chicago City Junior College, Wilson Branch — Chicago, Illinois
5	Amarillo College — Amarillo, Texas
6	Independence Community College — Independence, Kansas
7	Southern Union College — Wadley, Alabama
8	Chipola Junior College — Marianna, Florida
9	Casper College — Casper, Wyoming
10	Wilmington College — Wilmington, North Carolina
11	Burlington Community College — Burlington, Iowa
12	Muskegon Community College — Muskegon, Michigan
13	Hibbing Junior College — Hibbing, Minnesota
14	South Texas College — Houston, Texas
15	New York City Community College — Brooklyn, New York
16	Moberly Junior College — Moberly, Missouri

*W*ebster's New Collegiate Dictionary defines drama a "a state, situation, or series of events involving interesting c intense conflict of forces." Since combatants oppose on another in an episodic framework leading to a climactic resolu tion, a tournament is a natural setting for drama.

Each NJCAA Basketball Tournament has offered its ow brand of drama, stirring emotions to varying degrees. None however, have been more dramatic than the 1963 event. Clos competition (the third-closest average winning margin pe game in tourney history) and intense play (an all-time recor number of overtimes) were the basic fuels of conflict. High dra ma was not reached, though, until a volatile ingredient was add ed to the fire.

Controversy.

THE PARTICIPANTS

Since none of the top-ranked teams survived regional pla the *Hutchinson News* forsook the NJCAA poll in picking th 1963 tournament's likely front-runners. Team records were als ignored. Instead, the paper selected pre-tourney favorite based on region strength, past tournament form, and commo sense.

At the beginning of the season, Independence Communit College figured to place no higher than third in the East Jayhaw Juco Conference. However, the Pirates proved their mettle tying for the league crown, then systematically downing th four top teams in Region 6. In sub-regional play they defeate former national titleholder Parsons Junior College, 70-66, an defending national champion Coffeyville College, 52-46. I regional play they topped West Jayhawk Juco co-champ Arkansas City Junior College, 63-59, and Hutchinson Junio College, 49-47. Considering their arduous road to the nationals the Pirates' 22-3 record had to be respected and their lowly No 15 ranking questioned.

Moberly Junior College (23-5) ranked even lower. The inclu sion of the 19th-rated Greyhounds among the tourney elite wa no surprise, however. Moberly was the most successful schoc in tournament history. The Greyhounds were making their 12t appearance in 16 years and had taken home more souveni hardware than any other participant. Though the current tean was one of the smallest in the school's history, local fans accept ed the Greyhounds as contenders out of habit.

The newspaper's final candidate for possible crowning glor *was* a surprise. On paper, Phoenix College did not have rega credentials. The Bears were unranked and owned an unprepos sessing 21-11 record. They did possess size and speed, howev er. It took one glimpse of the Arizonans in a pre-tourney work out to convince the *News* sports staff that Phoenix wa definitely championship caliber.

The favorites' prime opposition would likely come from th other ranked teams: No. 5 Hibbing Junior College and No. •

New York City Community College, holders of the tournament's best records (21-2 and 23-2, respectively); No. 9 Murray State Agricultural College (23-3), the fifth-best defensive team in the country (55.0); No. 10 Broome Technical Community College (24-5), owner of the nation's third-best defense (52.3); No. 11 Burlington Community College (22-3), a top offensive squad with two expert goal producers — Bobby Joe Hill (26.0) and Jim Boyce (24.9); and No. 17 Wilson of Chicago (27-7), ranked fifth offensively (90.7) in the final NJCAA poll.

More worrisome for the favorites, however, was the rest of the tourney field. The remaining seven teams were ticking time bombs:

Amarillo College (20-9) had dumped No. 1 ranked San Angelo College, 67-61, to earn a trip to Hutchinson;

Newcomer Casper College (24-4) had upset No. 8 Pueblo Junior College in overtime on Pueblo's home court on the way to a Region 9 crown;

Tourney debutant South Texas College (21-4), a school without playing facilities, had slipped by two-time national champion, 18th-rated Kilgore College in a close, best-two-out-of-three series;

Chipola Junior College (24-7) had edged Norman College of Norman Park, Georgia, 82-80, in overtime for the Region 8 title after only placing fourth in the Florida state tournament;

Unheralded Muskegon Community College (17-5) had earned its first berth in the nationals, breezing through Region 12 competition, downing Spring Arbor College, 110-83, and Jackson Junior College, 82-59;

Wilmington College (14-8), a repeater from 1962, had surprised North Greenville Junior College in a regional play-off, All-American Eugene Bogash leading the way with 73 points in two games;

And, most unpredictable of all, Southern Union College of Wadley, Alabama, had won four straight Region 7 contests after entering post-season play with a woeful 4-14 record.

The prospects for topflight competition were born out by public response to pre-tourney ticket sales. All reserved seats were sold two weeks before the event. A new attendance record was virtually assured.

TUESDAY — A MARATHON BEGINNING

There was only a hint of explosive action in the curtain raiser. Though never in front other than after the opening bucket, the Cinderella Bisons from Wadley, Alabama, showed the scrap that put them into the nationals despite a losing record. Southern Union stayed close to taller, quicker Phoenix, forcing the Bears to keep a constant eye to their flanks. A second-half Southern Union spurt pulled the Bisons within four. Then, Phoenix star Richard Ervin, a sleek, well-proportioned guard, engineered a three-point play, stopping the Bison charge for good. Ervin's 23 spearheaded a well-balanced Phoenix attack which produced an 83-70 victory.

The afternoon feature was a barn-burner even though the damp hay inside was relit several times before igniting, neither team finding the range during a dull first half. Broome Tech's shuffle offense created numerous opportunities but infrequent success while Wilmington's point production was only slightly better. At halftime, the score read 23-16 in favor of the Seahawks.

Wilmington opened up 10-point gaps twice in the second half before the smell of smoke signaled the impending conflagration. Held scoreless in the first half, Broome Tech's Charles Georgia found his shooting touch, hitting 18 second-period points to rally the Hornets. With 3:42 to go, Broome Tech took its first lead since the opening moments.

The New Yorkers could not hold it, however, the game ending in a 54-all deadlock. After Broome Tech twice failed to convert last chance opportunities in two overtimes, the score was still knotted, 71-all.

The Hornets did not get a last chance to win in the third extra period. Wilmington opened with a field goal by Tom Cole, two free throws by Eugene Bogash, another pair of charities by Wil-

liam Harris, and a two-pointer by Harry Buzzell. The outburst jumped the Seahawks ahead, 79-73, a deficit Broome Tech could not overcome. Wilmington won the longest game to date in tournament history, 83-79.

The heat from the Wilmington-Broome Tech bonfire did not abate in the afternoon finale. Speedy, aggressive Wilson of Chicago maintained the lead over Burlington through much of the first half, taking a 39-35 advantage to the locker room. The margin quickly evaporated once play resumed when Burlington's top guns, Bobby Joe Hill and Jim Boyce, hit for two and three, respectively, to tie the game at 40-all. The score was tied four more times and the lead changed hands six before Burlington rallied from four down with four minutes remaining to win by four, 75-71.

The hero for the Blackhawks was their lightning-quick point guard, Bobby Joe Hill. Hitting from far outside when his man failed to challenge or, when the defense closed in, driving, launching skyward, legs tucked beneath his floating body, and delivering easy lay-ups, the 5-10 freshman scored 20 of his game-high 30 points in Burlington's come-from-behind second half.

Guard play was also the key to victory in the evening opener. Going into the contest, however, Moberly's Cotton Fitzsimmons was more concerned about his opponents' advantage inside. With 6-9 Warren Young and 6-7 Jim Jones up front, South Texas averaged nearly three inches taller per man on the front line. The tallest Greyhound was 6-4 Gary Goss.

The Region 14 champion Seahawks immediately put their height to good use, muscling to a 29-21 lead. Then, Moberly guards Joe Mimlitz and Harold Cebrun connected from outside. The South Texas edge disappeared in three minutes. By halftime, the Greyhounds were up by seven.

The Texans failed to stop Moberly's two-pronged long distance attack in the second half as well. The Seahawks also lost their rebounding leverage. Shifting to a 2-1-2 zone, the smaller, hustling Greyhounds controlled the boards, opened a 21-point margin, and coasted to a 75-61 win. Coach Fitzsimmons' earlier anxiety had been for naught. Sharpshooters Mimlitz and Cebrun, two of the shortest men on the floor, hit 24 and 21 points, respectively, accounting for 60 percent of Moberly's total.

The evening feature paired teams with similar styles. In February, Independence Coach Bob Sneller had authored a *Juco Review* article titled "The Psychology of Ball Control". Murray State Coach Gene Robbins followed the precepts of Oklahoma State's Henry Iba, the godfather of deliberate play. Both directed teams equally capable of holding the basketball for long stretches. Since both were excellent from the charity stripe,[1] the balance of power rested in who possessed the ball and the lead near the end.

Independence grabbed the advantage first and held it for 14 minutes. Then, Murray State hit seven of its last nine shots from the field and sprinted to a 33-28 halftime lead.

A five-point margin for the deliberate Aggies was like a 15-point advantage for any other club. Independence was forced to apply pressure.

The Pirates played with poise. Two fade-away jumpers by Elroy Moore and a free throw by Bob Fedorko tied the game at 33-all.

Murray State countered with six unanswered points. At the 12-minute mark, Independence had it all to do again.

The Pirates did it quickly. Guard Bill Gaertner hit a free throw. Reserve George Knittle took a chunk out of the difference with a three-point play. Gaertner added a two-pointer. Then, another Gaertner free throw inched Independence ahead, 40-39, with 10:24 to go.

The Aggies became cautious. Too cautious. Fedorko stole the ball and fed Gaertner for an easy two. The end-game advantage was squarely on the Kansans' side of the court.

The expected Independence stall came with 6:43 on the clock. Murray State was unable to thaw the freeze. Easy buckets and free throws followed as the Pirate delay secured a 60-52 victory.

---

[1] Independence's exceptional free throwing ability was demonstrated in the sub-regional semifinals against Parsons when the Pirates sank 44 of 48 free throw attempts. The following night against Coffeyville they hit 18 of 22. For the year, Independence was 71.5 percent from the line, with five players bettering the team average.

The day's finale started and ended slowly. Chipola lingered in the blocks as Muskegon raced to a 25-17 lead after 10 minutes. Then, as the *Hutchinson News* described it, the Indians from Marianna, Florida, "got the sand out of their shoes and the moss off their feet." Chipola took a 35-34 lead into the locker room.

Gary Bryan took over once play resumed. The 6-3 Chipola sophomore tallied 10 while Muskegon mustered only a pair of free throws. The Indians opened an 11-point gap. Muskegon succumbed, unable to solve the Chipola offense. Indian guards repeatedly broke down the middle to score or dish off, forcing Gene Visscher, Muskegon's big man, to pick up five fouls trying to divide his attention. Scoring totals reflected Visscher's dilemma. Bryan (guard) and Austin Robbins (center) shared team-honors with 23 apiece, leading Chipola past Muskegon, 76-67.

WEDNESDAY — NO SURPRISES

The day's opener was filled with roughhouse action not always involving opposing players; in one instance, Casper teammates Mickey Hartsburg and Gary Eckhardt crashed together, nearly knocking each other unconscious. The numerous impacts led to 53 fouls and many free throws. Although New York City hit 89 percent (24 of 27) from the line — including a perfect 15 for 15 by game-high scorer Ray Amalbert (29) — Casper received more opportunities. The Thunderbirds triumphed, 80-74.

The other afternoon contest featured high and low points for both combatants. Hibbing's low came at the start when it took five minutes for the Cardinals to hit a field goal. Trailing Amarillo, 10-1, Hibbing then shifted to high gear and charged from behind, grabbing the lead 19-18.

Amarillo countered with six-foot guard Bob Dibler who capped a brilliant shooting exhibition (eventually netting him a game-high 30) by sinking a 40-footer just before halftime, giving the Badgers a 35-33 lead.

The second period followed the first half's pattern, only with the roles reversed. Amarillo started slowly, allowing Hibbing to build a 49-41 advantage before the Badgers rallied, knotting the score at 53-all.

From then on the teams played cautiously, trading baskets. After regulation time, the two were even at 57-all.

Another five minutes found them again tied, 60-all.

Finally, two pressure free throws by Don Stahl with six seconds left iced a 66-63 win for Hibbing.

A double overtime. A triple overtime. The closest opening competition in 10 years. Those who reserved their seats early were getting their money's worth. The only crowd-pleasing element missing was the upset. But, because no first-round win came easy, everyone anticipated that championship bracket play would test the best.

Phoenix was tested first. The chief concern for the Bears was how to combat Wilmington's Eugene Bogash. Despite Broome Tech's frequent double- and even triple-teaming, the All-American had tallied 34 in the Seahawk opener, the top individual point production of the first round. Stopping Bogash meant stopping Wilmington.

The Bears found the task easier said than done. Lofting two-hand push shots and unguardable overhead hooks, Bogash took up where he left off against Broome Tech. The only recourse for Phoenix was to match the effort. Six-one guard Luther Harper accepted the challenge, drawing "oohs" and "aahs" from the crowd by nailing a succession of long shots on the way to 18 first-half points. With better scoring support from his teammates than Bogash received from fellow Seahawks, Harper led Phoenix to a 42-34 halftime advantage. When the Bears expanded the margin to 15 midway through the final period, a Phoenix victory looked secure.

There was no denying Wilmington's cornerstone, however. Bogash, ably assisted by reserve Harry Buzzell, the only other Seahawk sophomore, chipped away at the Phoenix lead. With 1:35 to go, Wilmington trailed by a single basket.

But, three Seahawk attempts to tie failed. Despite Bogash's game-high 45 points, Wilmington fell to Phoenix, 78-76.

Moberly's assignment was similar to that of Phoenix — only doubly so. To stop Burlington, the Greyhounds had to shackle two of the best junior college players in the nation. As Cotton Fitzsimmons told his Moberly charges, "Keep Jim Boyce away

from the boards as much as possible and don't let Bobby Joe Hill go crazy penetrating us."

In the first period, the Greyhounds were only half successful. Harold Cebrun put the clamps on Hill outside, but Boyce roamed free inside, scoring 18 points. Moberly was forced to unleash its not-so-secret weapon — Joe Mimlitz. The left-hander fired pin-point accurate mortar shells for 22 points, leading the Greyhounds to a 10-point halftime edge.

The Missourians were more successful against the "gruesome twosome" in the second half. Cebrun continued to put a damper on Hill's electric moves, holding him to 13 for the game. The hardworking Greyhound's also closed off Boyce, allowing him a third of his first-half output. The only time the Blackhawk stars posed a threat was during a mid-period rally when Burlington pulled to within four. Missed free throws and mechanical errors, forced by Moberly's aggressive defense, stymied further gains.

The continued marksmanship of Mimlitz — who led all scorers with 36 — and the unexpected firepower of Gary Goss — who played his greatest game as a Greyhound, scoring 12 of a game-total 17 in the final 16 minutes, hitting seven for seven from the line, and grabbing nine rebounds — provided the offensive impetus to a convincing 86-71 Moberly triumph.

THURSDAY — WAITING FOR THE AXE TO FALL

After an absorbing beginning, the tournament settled into a casual pace, marking time until the championship was on the line. Afternoon action was close, but not inspiring.

Wilson's small but quick Raiders employed a man-to-man press, scampered to a 15-point halftime advantage, then held on with free throws, edging foul-prone South Texas, 85-81.

The most memorable occurrence in Amarillo's 78-73 victory over New York City was that the final 12 seconds seemingly lasted forever, officials delaying action 15 minutes so the Amarillo bench could patch a cut over center Tobie Hall's eye.

The afternoon finale was even slower. The game aggravated fans who had expected to see three of the best scorers in the tournament fire at will. What they saw was cautious inconsistency. Burlington's Jim Boyce led all scorers with the low figure of 19. The Blackhawks' Bobby Joe Hill and Wilmington's Eugene Bogash managed disappointing totals of 12 and 10 after averaging 22 and 40, respectively, in their first two outings. The contest was a tedious, leap-frogging affair in which Wilmington leaped last, eliminating Burlington, 59-55.

The day's best consolation action opened evening play. With less than a minute remaining and both leading scorers — Muskegon's Gene Visscher (31) and Murray State's Don Henry (23) — on the bench with five fouls, Murray State trailed by one, 56-55. At the 40-second mark, Muskegon's Tom Grams missed a free shot. Murray State's Gene Wilmoth grabbed the ball, charged the length of the court, and scored.

As tense seconds slipped away, Muskegon worked for a game-winning effort. With nine ticks left, reserve Bob Sydnor connected for the second time in as many minutes — his entire point production — giving the Jayhawks the edge.

In a race against the clock, Aggie guard Arthur Guess tore up the floor, caught a long pass at the free throw line, and, off balance, tried a lay-up off the glass. The ball rolled around the rim and out at the buzzer. Muskegon survived, 58-57.

The evening's first quarterfinal was an avian battle with swooping scoring sprees. The Hibbing Cardinals took wing first, flying to a 7-0 advantage. Casper spent nine minutes taxiing. Once airborne, the Thunderbirds streaked by Hibbing, soaring to a 15-point elevation. The Minnesotans pursued, pulling to within three by intermission.

Then, the Cardinals lost altitude. In the first six minutes of the second half, Hibbing hit one field goal and a pair of free throws. Meanwhile, the Thunderbirds swished the cords. Casper opened a 12-point gap and was never threatened again. Hibbing crashed in flames, 77-64.

It had been a quiet evening despite the largest crowd thus far. Those in attendance were politely attentive, but not moved to emotional outbursts by the action on the court. With a Kansas representative in the nightcap, the predominately Hutchinson audience was more inclined to cheer.

Local fans remained contrary, however, electing to back out-of-state Chipola over Region 6 champion Independence.

When the Pirates' Rick Park blasted the nets for 32 first-period points, leading Independence to a 51-34 runaway halftime advantage, the sounds echoing through the Sports Arena came solely from the Independence delegation.

Several patrons left for home. More followed when the margin grew to 20 points with 15 minutes to go. Since several Chipola starters were a whisker away from elimination due to excess fouls, the inevitable was in sight.

Then, Chipola applied full-court pressure. The crowd stirred. Backed by the roar of local supporters, the Indians made a run at the Kansans. In one of the greatest comebacks in tournament history, Chipola caught Independence, knotting the score at 79-all with 4:09 remaining.

The noticeably shaken Pirates did not collapse, however. Just as Chipola was ready to swamp Independence title hopes, Elroy Moore scored from underneath the basket, was fouled, and converted the free shot. The three-point play stemmed the Indian charge.

To the disapproving boos of the crowd, Independence engaged its delay game. One by one the Chipola starters fouled out. With perseverance, free throws, and Rick Park's game-high 45 points, Independence advanced to the semifinals, defeating Chipola, 93-83.

Independence Coach Bob Sneller later described his feelings during the Chipola game: "I thought we were finally going to have one of those games where everyone could relax a bit. Here's this 20-point lead. I'm already thinking about what we're going to do in the semifinals. Then all of a sudden, we're tied. I'm in a state of shock. I'm well aware that it's one thing to get beat and another thing to blow a 20-point lead in a national tournament. I'm thinking I'm going to have to live with this the rest of my life. I was scared to death. Then, here these guys, 18, 19 years old, the crowd screaming for Chipola, and they win by 10 points. I've said this many times, of all the things we did that year, turning the tide against Chipola was our greatest accomplishment."

THE AXE FALLS

All day Thursday the Arena buzzed with rumors. In the second half of the tight final afternoon game between Burlington and Wilmington, someone approached the Wilmington bench and said, "Don't worry too much about this one. There's going to be a disqualification." According to the circulating gossip, one of the teams in the championship bracket had used an ineligible player. Coach Bill Brooks was not sure what to believe.

Shortly before 9:00, during the Chipola-Independence quarterfinal warm-up, the rumors were confirmed. With heads huddled around transistor radios in an otherwise still Arena, fans listened to Public Relations Chairman Hod Humiston tell the local radio audience that Phoenix was disbarred from the tournament. Moments later public address announcer Joe Hardy repeated the news for the 5,000 Arena patrons who were already humming with whos, whys, and hows.

The *Hutchinson News* supplied details the next day. The player in question was Richard Ervin, the Bears' leading scorer. NJCAA Secretary Hobart Bolerjack disclosed that, after graduating from Louisville Central High School in 1959, the all-city and all-state basketball star had played for Wenatchee Valley Junior College in Washington in the winter of 1960. According to Bolerjack, Ervin admitted falsifying his entrance application and eligibility sheet when he enrolled as a freshman at Phoenix, hoping to avoid a year of ineligibility under the NJCAA's transfer rule.

The revelation stunned everyone, fueling street corner discussions. "Did Phoenix officials know about Ervin's ineligibility before hand?" "Who blew the whistle?" "Why was the fact not uncovered until the tournament was over half completed?"[2]

While fans gnawed on the controversy, NJCAA and American Legion officials quickly and professionally made order out of havoc. Thanks to a little good luck, the steps taken to rectify the hole in the tournament bracket were straightforward. Four teams were involved. Only one game, possibly two, needed to be replayed.

The first team affected was Southern Union from Wadley, Alabama, opening-round victim of Phoenix. The second was Wilmington, the Bears' second-round opponent. The Seahawks had played three games in three days and were ready to relax before their shot at a fourth-place finish on Saturday. Wilmington was not to have a day off, however. Tournament officials ordered a replay of the upper bracket quarterfinal, slating it for Friday morning. The winner of the Wilmington-Southern Union contest would face Moberly in the semifinals later that evening.

The third team involved was Broone Tech. The Hornets were the first team eliminated from tourney competition, having lost to Southern Union in consolation play Wednesday. Normally, a team eliminated that early was already on its way home. Tourney officials were fortunate that, because of prior travel commitments, Broome Tech was still in town. When notified of their reinstatement team members were happy for the reprieve. Despite the misgivings of Coach Dick Baldwin, who disliked the tournament's consolation format — "If the team hadn't wanted to play, we wouldn't have played" — the Hornets replaced Southern Union in the losers' bracket.

The reinstatement of Burlington, the fourth team involved, was dependent on the outcome of the Wilmington-Southern Union quarterfinal replay. The Blackhawks, packed and ready to return to Iowa when informed of the Phoenix ouster, waited nervously in the wings. If Southern Union won, the Blackhawks did not have to unpack, having been eliminated from tourney competition earlier Thursday by Wilmington. If Wilmington won, Burlington would square off against the team from Wadley in a late, late show following Friday night semifinal action.

To most fans, the disruption so close to the end of tournament week was a bit bewildering. The week's worth of drama that was crammed into the next two days made up for it.

FRIDAY — THE LONGEST DAY

Basketball aficionados had no time to loll in bed Friday morning. The day's first game started at 9:30.

The replay of the upper bracket quarterfinal was a unique occurrence in the annals of sports. After having been eliminated from championship competition, Wilmington and Southern Union were being granted a rare second chance at a national title. Both squads possessed long suits. Wilmington was taller; the Wadley troops, fresher. Both were grateful for the resurrection and showed it.

Southern Union threw a press at Wilmington, hoping to catch the battle weary Seahawks off guard. Wilmington responded with a tight zone. In the first half, neither team held a lead larger than five. The first four tallies after intermission gave Wilmington the largest advantage of the game, 39-31.

Southern Union fought back tying the score 47-all with a little more than 14 minutes to go. The scoreboard registered five more ties before Wilmington surged ahead, 70-65, with 3:06 remaining and two Wadley players on the bench with five fouls.

But, the Bisons surged back, a Bryan Atkins bucket tying the score with a minute left. After regaining possession, the Wadley five waited out the clock, but waited too long. The tournament's extra game required extra time.

---

[2]According to Phoenix College, there was no complicity on the school's behalf. Aware that three years had passed since Ervin's graduation from high school, Phoenix officials took extra care in checking Ervin's credentials, even contacting Ervin's Louisville high school. Of the four colleges to which the high school had sent transcripts, none were Wenatchee Valley. On three occasions during the year Ervin signed statements indicating no prior college experience. People in Phoenix were as shocked as anybody else by the abrupt revelation in Hutchinson. Embarrassed school officials wired apologies to tournament directors and to the two schools Phoenix had beaten in regional play. They also dismissed Ervin.

As for who blew the whistle, initial newspaper accounts fingered Bennie Franz, coach at Pratt Junior College. Franz had at one time been interested in recruiting Ervin, but dropped the idea after talking with Ervin's high school coach who told him of Ervin's enrollment at Wenatchee Valley. The *News* later reneged, saying Franz's input had only been supplementary evidence in the NJCAA's investigation. Franz later confirmed that he made no official statement to the NJCAA. He indicated that several other Kansas coaches shared the same knowledge and hypothesized that courtside note comparison led to the rumor. NJCAA Executive Director George Killian (then editor of the *Juco Review* and a member of the NJCAA Executive Committee), verified that no single individual was responsible for the organization's investigation. The NJCAA Executive Committee took action solely on the basis of the widespread rumor. A telegram correspondence with Wenatchee Valley Thursday obtained the clinching proof.

Why it took so long for the rumor to surface remains a mystery.

Though Southern Union was without two starters, the overtime favored the Bisons. Wilmington's primary point producer — Eugene Bogash, the game's leading scorer (26) — had picked up his fifth foul late in regulation.

However, the Seahawks demonstrated mental toughness in Bogash's absence. Led by Tom Cole's two field goals and Marshall Hamilton's clinching free throws with 1:06 to go, Wilmington topped Southern Union, 80-74, earning the dubious privilege of playing again eight hours later.

In the interim —

Broome Tech became the only team in history to suffer three defeats in a single tournament, falling short of Wilson, 79-71;

Muskegon stopped Amarillo, 76-71, in a clean contest, featuring a record-tying low number of fouls (8 for Muskegon, 11 for Amarillo);

And, Chipola led wire-to-wire, routing Hibbing, 87-67, sending spectators home to an early supper.

Revitalizing sustenance was mandatory since the evening guaranteed to be long.

* * *

Because of the Phoenix disqualification, an endearing Cinderella story was unfolding. Lost and forgotten in the drudgery of consolation play, the Wilmington Seahawks had been tapped by a fairy godmother's magic wand, whisked to the Prince's ball, and given a second chance at the glass slipper. Wilmington had already played four games, the normal maximum for a tournament. Two of those games required overtime, adding another half's-worth of playing time. The semifinal match-up with Moberly was the Seahawks' fifth contest in four days, their third in a little more than 36 hours. It was no wonder squad members complained of blisters on their feet. Despite a friendly godmother standing by, Wilmington's chances against pre-tourney favorite Moberly were slim at best.

Local fans fell in love with the North Carolinians. The focal point of their adoration was the Seahawks' star — Eugene Bogash.

The 6-5 sophomore did not look like a modern basketball player. His moves were ragged, unorthodox, his favorite hook shot, more a jump-hook. Many scouting coaches discounted his abilities on a single viewing. More than once he was described in terms similar to that of Moberly's Cotton Fitzsimmons: "He looked like an ol' country boy pulling a plow." The description was apropos. Bogash grew up on a mint farm in North Jetson, Indiana. His basketball skills were self-taught, honed through many hours of basket-shooting in a hayloft. Dedication produced accomplishment. Going into the Friday night opener, Bogash was the tournament's leading scorer, averaging just under 30 points a game.

When the Wilmington ace began pouring in points from all angles against Moberly, building excitement infused the crowd. A 20-point first-period by Bogash led Wilmington to a surprise 35-31 halftime edge.

Backed by cheers from a strong local following, the Seahawks struggled to maintain the advantage. Moberly pulled within one, 47-46.

Then, Bogash scored five consecutive field goals and a pair of free throws. Moberly countered with a solitary bucket.

Infatuated Wilmington supporters edged forward in their seats. The supposedly tired Seahawks looked fresh.[3] Their superior height controlled the boards. Moberly was beset by foul trouble. Everything was going Wilmington's way — the storybook fantasy was coming true.

In contrast, the Greyhounds lived in the shadow of a different story — Moberly tradition. They were fed it daily from the moment they first put on "the Red and Gray." Just before leaving for Hutchinson, the Moberly paper ran an article, listing every player to represent the city in 11 previous appearances in national competition. The current squad had a 13-game winning streak — the longest in Moberly history. The Greyhounds believed in themselves and refused to admit defeat.

Steadily, Moberly crept back into contention. Joe Mimlitz led the rebellion, scoring 17 second-half points. Wilmington, too,

aided the comeback, missing the front end of four one-and-ones in the final three minutes. The Greyhounds' biggest break, however, came with a minute to go, Moberly trailing, 72-69.

In an attempt to steal the ball, Mimlitz crashed into Wilmington's Tom Cole, sending him reeling backward. Mimlitz also fell, accidentally kicking Cole in the stomach. Thinking the blow was intentional, Cole jumped up, fists swinging. The altercation was brief, but, when the two players were separated, the officials ruled double foul. Instead of shooting free throws, Wilmington lost the ball on a jump at center court.

Dwight Yaeger — the replacement for Mimlitz who fouled out on the controversial double foul — hit a free shot, narrowing the margin to a single basket with 28 seconds left. At the eight-second mark, the skinny sophomore plugged the gap with a clutch jump shot. For the third time in the tournament, the second time that day, Wilmington was forced to overtime.

Three of Moberly's most talented players (Mimlitz, Robert Johnson, and Ken McCowan) sat on the bench with five fouls. Wilmington still had Bogash. Forty-one points were already marked by his name in the scorebook. Despite the amount of time they had spent on the court, the Seahawks appeared in a good position to win.

Butch Mantle's free throw gave Moberly first crack at the lead, the first Greyhound advantage since early in the game.

Wilmington's Harry Buzzell answered with a successful hook.

Mantle hit a lay-up.

Seahawk guard Bill Harris hit a jumper from the corner.

Moberly reserve Walker Belcher nailed a jumper in return.

Then, the jockeying for the lead ended. Harris missed for Wilmington, Moberly grabbing the rebound. Holding a 77-76 edge, the Greyhounds froze the ball.

Forced to foul, Wilmington sent Moberly's Gary Goss to the line with 56 seconds left. The Greyhound center hit the first free toss, missed the second. However, Moberly outmaneuvered the Seahawks for the rebound and again played with the clock.

With 17 seconds left, Wilmington sent Belcher to the charity stripe. Two missed attempts gave the Seahawks the ball with plenty of time to tie.

As Wilmington worked the ball around the perimeter, the crowd pleaded, "Give it to Bogash!" The All-American had been held scoreless for nearly eight minutes.

His chance to save the day never came. A traveling call on the Seahawks ended all hope for Cinderella. Moberly squeaked by, 78-76.

Though the ouster of Phoenix focused attention on the developing upper bracket drama, the lower bracket was not without its own controversy. The flap had its origins before the national event began.

The 1963 Blue Dragons were one of the most talented teams yet fielded by Hutchinson Junior College. It was a tall squad with 6-7 Larry Cooper — later a star at Indiana — centering a powerful front line. The Blue Dragons counted among their victims current national finalist Moberly and defending titleholder Coffeyville; the former, a rare easy win (73-62) on the Greyhounds' home court; the later, a 78-52 drubbing in the Region 6 semifinals. With one game to go, chances for a national berth and a possible crown were better than ever.

In the first half of the regional final at Parsons, Independence grabbed a narrow lead. In order to draw the taller Dragons out of a packed zone, Coach Bob Sneller ordered his Pirates to hold the ball. For nearly eight minutes nothing happened. Independence took a 16-9 advantage into the locker room at intermission.

A Hutchinson full-court press opened up the game in the second half. Then, with 7:30 to go, Independence started its delay again. The Pirates rode excellent free throw shooting to a 49-47 upset victory.

The next day's *Hutchinson News* reflected the gall of Blue Dragons fans. The paper's game account described the Independence stall as "set[ting] the game of basketball back a quarter of a century" and was accompanied by a three-inch, two column "artist's conception of game action" — a blank space.

---

[3] According to former Wilmington coach Bill Brooks, the Seahawks were used to physical stress. There were only nine squad members, so everyone saw his fair share of action. They were also all-round athletes. Six were members of Wilmington's strong baseball team. All were in excellent shape. Besides, as Brooks put it, "They were not the alibiing type. They would get out there and battle you even if they had to play four times a day."

When tournament time rolled around, Hutchinson fans reg-
ered their lingering bitterness, rooting for Pirate opposition
d roundly booing any Independence attempt to control the
ll. As the week passed, the obvious lack of local support for
e Kansas school became a source of rancor. On Friday, the
dependence Daily Reporter ran a front page commentary,
mplaining that the Pirates "are booed and jeered every time
ey take the Hutchinson court," and describing the "atrocious
splay" as "unsportsmanlike conduct" fomented by a bad
se of "sour grapes." The article did nothing to stanch the
ror.

Animosity flowed free in the remaining semifinal. Not only
d Independence have to battle the crowd, but also a tough
pponent. In two outings, Casper — the first team to represent
yoming in national competition — had downed the two top-
ed teams in the tournament.

Casper broke on top first, Independence scoring only two
ints in four minutes. After digging an initial 8-2 hole, the
rates slowly climbed out, Rick Park's 20-footer, putting Inde-
endence on top for the first time with 11 minutes left in the
lf. The teams traded points and the lead (eight times) the
mainder of the period before a Sam Williams field goal with
seconds to go gave Casper a 33-31 halftime advantage.

Williams extended the Thunderbird lead with a two-pointer
ter intermission. Then, the Pirates' Rick Park fired a barrage —
ree consecutive 20-foot jump shots. While Park reloaded,
lvin Taylor nailed a sleeper. Park loosed another broadside,
field goal and a free throw, a short jumper, then a long one.
on, the entire Pirate ballclub joined in the bombardment. A
tented Independence stall was never needed; the objecting
os of Hutchinson fans, never a factor.[4] The Pirates scored 51
cond-half points to demolish Casper, 82-54.

It was close to 11:30 before the tip off of the day's final game.
eryone was tired. Having already worked two games apiece,
feree teams Jerry Pooler and Red Weir, and Johnny Overby
d Ron Keefer agreed to share officiating chores, each working
minutes of each half. Of the 700 gluttons for punishment still
atching Arena action, two were fast asleep, draped across the
ck row seats of the first balcony. After losing a heartbreaker
rlier that day, no one expected the Wadley Bisons to have
uch left either.

But, Southern Union amazed all, playing with courageous
unk, tying Burlington, 34-all, at the half. Then, as the clock on
e Arena's north wall tolled the wee hours of Saturday morn-
g, the Bisons faded. Bobby Joe Hill (36) and Jim Boyce (20)
ere too much to handle. Burlington outscored the tired Ala-
amians 19 points in the second frame, topping Southern
nion, 88-69. The final buzzer merifully ended the longest day
tournament history.

SATURDAY — NO RESPITE FOR THE WEARY

It had been a long, grueling week for fans, players, and coach-
s. A slow, anticlimactic finish might have been expected and
elcomed. There was no surcease, however; if anything, the
tensity level increased.

The first 20 minutes of the day's opener epitomized the tour-
ey's relentless tightness. Muskegon and Wilson freewheeled
an even clip, tying the score nine times.

After Muskegon took a 50-46 margin to the dressing room at
termission, the pattern of close battles appeared to break
own. The Jayhawks remained hot; Wilson did not. Muskegon
uilt a 19-point advantage, allowing Coach Rudy Bartels to
ear his bench.

However, almost before the Muskegon starters had a chance
catch their breath, they were back on the court. Wilson's
uick Raiders sliced the lead to nine. The tournament's high
nsion level returned.

With the Jayhawk mainstays back in the game, Wilson's last
tch charge stalled. A Willie Lucas field goal in the last second
play pulled the Raiders as close as they got. Muskegon took
ome the fifth-place trophy, 90-85.

The fourth-place game also exhibited tension free moments.
hipola made numerous mechanical errors and joined the
rowing list of teams unable to solve the board work of Jim Boy-

ce and the outside shooting of Bobby Joe Hill. Burlington
grabbed a 38-30 halftime advantage and expanded it to 14 with
12:47 to go.

Then, the contest slowly tightened. Chipola chipped at the
lead, reducing it to five with 9:53 remaining. At the two-minute
mark, the deficit was three. With 29 seconds left, the margin
was a lone basket.

After a time out, Chipola immediately fouled guard Larry
Mills who promptly missed the front end of a one-and-one.
Chipola grabbed the rebound. Before the Indians could capital-
ize, however, Gary Bryan was called for charging.

Chipola's Charles Clark quickly fouled Mills again.

Again Mills missed an opportunity to ice the game.

The Indians pulled down the rebound with 11 seconds to tie,
but missed three attempts.

The Burlington crew drew breath with a whisper-thin 70-68
victory. It was a fitting ending for a team which had gained
reprieve from an early trip home. The chances that the Blackhawks would return to Hutchinson seemed certain, however:
Burlington was an all-freshman squad. Having combined for
223 points in five games, the deadly duo of Jim Boyce and Bobby Joe Hill was expected to be heard from again.

The Sports Arena filled early Saturday evening. Many were as
interested in the third-place contest as the championship tilt.
The reason: the Wilmington Seahawks were playing.

Few anticipated victory. Even the greatest of constitutions
had to feel the effects of six games and five overtime periods in
five days. Besides, the Seahawks had used only eight players.
Fans were there to demonstrate their affection and to show
respect for the team's remarkable stamina and determination.

All were happily astounded with what followed. Wilmington
took to the court as though it were Day One of the tournament.
Casper was caught flat-footed. The Seahawks opened a 12-
point gap and played with the lead. With 6:41 left in the game,
Wilmington possessed an unbelieveable 70-55 cushion.

Since Eugene Bogash had four fouls and had played more
minutes than any other Wilmington player, Coach Bill Brooks
decided to give his ace a well-deserved rest. The move opened
the door for Casper.

As the Thunderbirds pecked at the lead, the previously loyal
Wilmington crowd switched allegiance. Once the gap was narrowed to a single point and Bogash reinserted into the Seahawk
lineup, fan sentiments again flip-flopped. Hutchinson fans
loved close games as much as underdogs.

The strong support did not help. Myriad minutes of playing
time finally caught up with the Seahawks. Wilmington struggled
to maintain the advantage. Every time the North Carolinians
opened breathing space, Casper closed it. After Ed Samelton
crashed in for two with 30 seconds remaining, the Thunderbird
deficit was again a single digit.

Wilmington moved the ball up court, hoping to either hold it
or spread the difference with an easy basket. Instead, the
Seahawks were tied up. Casper controlled the tip.

Though a step slower than at the game's beginning, Wilmington players geared up for the final onslaught. Casper was unable
to get the ball inside. With time running down, reserve Craig
Kelley could wait no longer. He launched a 20-footer that
scored.

Wilmington called time.

There were a bare three ticks left on the clock. The situation
called for desperation strategy. While the Thunderbirds celebrated at the other end of the floor, Coach Brooks outlined the
following: Wray Ware, noted for his fine pitching arm — later
that spring at Grand Junction, Colorado, Ware was the winning
pitcher in the final game of the NJCAA Baseball Tournament as
Wilmington won its second title in three years — would heave
the basketball the length of the floor and against the glass backboard; Bogash would post up high, fake, and hook around his
man; if the timing was right, the ball would meet Bogash with a
clear path to the winning goal.

Play resumed. Ware lined up behind the end line. He faked
short then wound up, firing a strike the length of the court.
Simultaneously, Bogash outmaneuvered his man. Just as Coach
Brooks designed it, there was nobody between Bogash and the

---

[4] Coach Bob Sneller related that the negative reaction of Hutchinson fans was actually a plus for the Pirates: "I tried to take whatever happened and turn it
to our advantage. The kids understood that when anybody you're trying to beat is happy with what you're doing, they're probably beating you. The more they
holler or complain or cry out or boo is a direct measure of how successful you are. [Consequently,] boos were like applause to us . . . like music to our ears."

basket. Unfortunately, Ware's toss was a bullet. The basketball shot off the backboard and between the up-raised hands of the All-American. Casper won, 82-81.

The end of a long week was at hand. In spite of close shaves and controversy, two pre-tourney favorites had advanced to within a step of the winner's circle. Their similarities were uncanny and not necessarily characteristic of potential national champs.

Their strongest attribute was a top-notch scorer. Independence's Rick Park and Moberly's Joe Mimlitz were both pure shooters, expert marksmen from the field or the line, ranking near the top in tournament point production with 89 and 81 points, respectively.

There were other team high points: for Moberly, Harold Cebrun's defense; for Independence, Elroy Moore's leaping ability; for both, excellent bench support.

Their low points, however, were more numerable. Neither squad demonstrated natural quickness. Both teams were relatively small. Independence's 6-7 Calvin Taylor, the tallest player on either team, was only third in Pirate rebounding. Moberly center Gary Goss was a poor jumper, a "banger." Greyhound forward Robert Johnson, who appeared to have excellent physical assets, was only in his second year of organized basketball and played inconsistently, not yet having realized his full potential. Pirate guard Bill Gaertner, who looked to have no assets at all, played because of a symbiotic relationship with Independence's leading scorer — Gaertner would not have started without Rick Park in the lineup and Park would not have scored as well without Gaertner's feeds.

Even in their strengths there was weakness: Mimlitz was slow of foot; Park, suspect on defense.

With so many faults, why were they playing for a national championship? The answer: discipline, teamwork, and an intense desire to win, the latter exemplified most by unsung heroes.

Independence's catalyst was Bob Fedorko. The 6-3 sophomore from Shamokin, Pennsylvania, had not even been a member of the traveling squad as a freshman. Through determination he developed, overcoming a gimpy knee in the process. He was the Pirates third-leading scorer (12.0) and second-leading rebounder (7.6). Though his presence on the court often did not stand out in a box score, it *was* felt. Fedorko's teammates called him "Fab," the Independence newspaper, "Mr. Clutch." His importance to the team was reflected in the one statistical category he did top, one that rarely made headlines: He was the Pirates' assist leader.

Moberly's heart and soul was also a top assist man. As Coach Cotton Fitzsimmons put it, Larry "Butch" Mantle was "the bailing wire, the glue to our ballclub." His principal claim to fame was that he was the younger brother of New York Yankee star Mickey Mantle. He possessed none of Mickey's physical char-

The "bailing wire" for the 1963 Moberly Greyhounds, Larry "Butch" Mantle, younger brother of Mickey Mantle, later played at Central State University in Edmond, Oklahoma. (Photo courtesy of Central State University)

acteristics, however. He was rawboned, knees-and-elbows skinny. Fitzsimmons joked that "when he stood sideways during the introduction, they thought we only had four players out there." What the 6-3 sophomore *did* share with his famous brother was a tremendous competitive drive. Once, after a rare loss at Moberly, Fitzsimmons returned to the locker room to

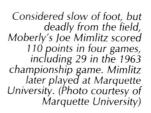

Considered slow of foot, but deadly from the field, Moberly's Joe Mimlitz scored 110 points in four games, including 29 in the 1963 championship game. Mimlitz later played at Marquette University. (Photo courtesy of Marquette University)

find Mantle on the floor atop two other teammates. He had ta[k]en exception to their casual acceptance of defeat. His grittine[ss] was further demonstrated on the court. Though lacking size a[nd] bulk, he was Moberly's leading rebounder.

With the will to win equitably distributed to both teams, Ar[e]na fans were in store for a classic confrontation. Ironically, t[he] standing-room-only crowd was apathetic. The predominate Hutchinson audience did not feel warmly toward the Kans[as] representative. And, through years of rooting for the underdo[g] they were conditioned to cheer against the perennial entra[nt] from Moberly. Consequently, they sat on their hands.

It was a difficult feat. Action exploded from the outset. Pa[rk] grabbed the opening tip, dribbled around a screen at the top [of] the circle, and drove for an easy lay-up, catching Moberly fla[t] footed. Moberly answered with three points, but it was the on[ly] Greyhound lead of the period. Behind Park's steady salvo[s,] Independence held the Hounds at bay, building a seven-poi[nt] advantage with 6:45 left in the half.

Mimlitz responded to the challenge, almost single-handed[ly] rallying Moberly to within four at intermission. The crow[d] showed more enthusiasm, mostly for the Greyhounds.

The Pirates continued a step ahead in the opening minutes [of] the second half.

Then, Mimlitz hit a corner shot and Johnson added a fr[ee] throw. With 14:15 remaining, the score was tied, 39-all.

After Park broke the deadlock with a 20-footer, Mober[ly] knotted it again at 41, 47, and 49. When a Johnson 10-foot[er] gave the Greyhound's their second lead of the game a[nd] reserve Walker Belcher extended it to three with a free thro[w,] crowd sentiment swung toward Independence.

The Pirates regained the lead on pairs of free throws [by] reserves Bob Faulkner and George Knittle.

Moberly countered with back-to-back field goals by sixt[h] man Ken McCowan and steadfast Mimlitz.

Park drove the left baseline for two.

McCowan answered.

Then, Independence's Moore broke free, drove for an ea[sy] two, and was fouled from behind. He sank the free shot, tyi[ng] the game at 59-all with three minutes to go.

Suddenly, who won was not important. The Arena was aliv[e,] caught up in the terrific tug-of-war on the floor.

Action slowed as tension built.

Mimlitz sank two charities for Moberly.

Park launched another successful field goal. Tied again at 6[1.]

With 1:52 left, Mimlitz missed from the top of the key. Ind[e]pendence grabbed the rebound and called time. Coach Snell[y] pulled Park — who had to be rested frequently throughout t[he] tournament because of swollen tonsils which obstructed h[is] breathing — instructing the Pirates to hold the ball. For the fir[st] time in the game, the patented Independence delay became [a] factor.

Silent anxiety hemmed the court as the Kansans engaged the Missourians in a staring contest.

With five ticks left, Independence called time again for one purpose — to get a rested Park back in the game.

Knowing full well that Park would take the last shot, the Greyhounds tried to keep him from getting the ball. They failed. However, they did prevent the Pirate ace from firing at close range. Park's final attempt was launched from 40 feet. The trajectory was on line, but the distance short, the ball bouncing off the front rim.

The longest tournament yet would run longer still.

Where Independence led the dance through most of regulation, Moberly took the first step in overtime, Mimlitz nailing a 15-footer. Park kept alive the personal duel between the scoring duo with a driving lay-up.

Then came the game's most critical call. Driving from the left wing, Moberly's McCowan weaved through the Independence defense, pulled up in front of the basket, shot, then landed on the Pirate's Knittle who fell to the floor. Knittle was awarded two free throws and canned both.

The potential four-point swing changed the complexion of the game. With Independence again holding the upper hand, threatening to stall at any moment, Moberly was forced to gamble.

Mimlitz evened the game at 65-all with another clutch 20-footer.

Fedorko shot a short one-hander which bounced off everything before falling for the Pirates.

Then, with 1:35 to go Mimlitz missed from the left corner and Independence grabbed the rebound. Enter the Pirate stall.

The game had been a continual chess match between Sneller and Fitzsimmons. The two coaches frequently shuffled pieces, fully utilizing their benches. With Independence in a strong end-game position its delay team on the floor, Fitzsimmons inserted four guards into his lineup. Their strategy: Get the ball without fouling.

It was an impossible assignment. Sneller's charges revelled in their specialty roles, particularly when it came to free throw shooting. The delay team (Park, Fedorko, Gaertner, Knittle, and Faulkner) had a combined percentage from the line of 78.8. Every time the Greyhounds fouled, it backfired. With the pressure of a national championship on the line, the Pirates were perfect. Faulkner (6-for-6 for the game) hit a pair. Knittle — his teammates called him "Ice Water" because his team-leading 86 percent free-throw-shooting average was compiled under pressure situations — added four more, giving him 8-for-8 for the game, 6-for-6 in overtime.

By downing Moberly, 73-68, Independence became the third Kansas school in four years to win a national crown.

THE AFTERMATH — HANDING OUT THE ACCOLADES

The 1963 NJCAA Basketball Tournament filled the record book with new marks and many asterisks. Financially, it was the greatest event yet with new highs in attendance and gate receipts. The many fans who had immersed themselves in a long week of human drama expressed their feelings during the awards ceremony.

The first response was one of the loudest. As they wearily shambled to the floor to receive their sixth-place trophy, the Wilmington Seahawks were showered with an ovation fit for a champion. It was appropriate. Six games in five days. Three losses by a total margin of five points. The "Cardiac Kids" had definitely shown the hearts of champions.

The third-place Casper Thunderbirds were greeted with polite, appreciative acknowledgement. They were the new kids on the block whose star was just beginning to rise.

The crowd response to Moberly's runner-up award was warm, filled with heartfelt sympathy. The Greyhounds had played far beyond their talents. Falling a step short of glory hurt nonetheless.

In any other year, Rick Park's 128 points, including a tourney record 39 for a title contest, would have easily secured an MVP award. But, because of the odd occurrences of the 1963 tournament, Park had to settle for a national title and an All-Tourney selection. He was later All-Missouri Valley at the University of Tulsa. (Photo courtesy of Independence Community College)

The 1963 champion Independence Pirates. Back row (left to right): Coach Bob Sneller, Bob Fedorko, Jim Rash, Calvin Taylor, Bill Dougherty, Elroy Moore, Jim Beck, and Manager John Chacoma. Front row: George Knittle, Bill Todd, Bill Gaertner, Bob Faulkner, Jim Murray, and Rick Park. (Photo courtesy of Bob Sneller)

The applause for the champion Pirates was cathartic for Hutchinson fans. It rose from silent deep-seated bitterness and envy to full-bodied, respectful acclaim. The victors were entitled their due.

One by one, the All-Tournament Team was announced and paid homage. Names like "Bogash", "Boyce", "Mimlitz", and "Park" were no surprise. The name "Fedorko" was. It did not appear among the top 10 in any scoring category. Bob Fedorko's reward was earned because of timely team leadership.

Bob Sneller was grateful for the additional weight that the Coach of the Year award supplied. He had lost 12 pounds in the pressure-packed past few weeks. The crowd's appreciation also offset the criticism he had received for his "whatever-it-takes-to-win" methods.

The final award was for Player of the Year. Based on statistics, Independence's Rick Park appeared a shoo-in. The Sayre, Pennsylvania, native had averaged 32 points per game, including a game-high 39 in the championship. He had achieved as much as, if not more than, any previous MVP.

But, 1963 was not a typical year. A unique occurrence created a unique situation. One man had carried his team through six games and three overtimes, scoring a tournament record 182 points, receiving very little rest. He was so important to the team's effort that a refrain was coined by adoring fans, to be screamed when circumstances seemed most desperate. Bud Janner repeated it in announcing the MVP award: "Give it to Bogash!"

All over the Arena, eyes glistened as the crowd gave Eugene Bogash the rarest of accolades — a standing ovation.

Cotton Fitzsimmons described him as looking like "An ol' country boy pulling a plow." Indeed, 1963 MVP Eugene Bogash performed like a workhorse, scoring a remarkable 182 points in six games in five days, a tourney record. Bogash completed his collegiate career at Drake University. (Photo courtesy of Drake University)

Tournament Results

Tuesday:	Game		
		1	Phoenix — 83 Southern Union — 70
		2	Wilmington — 83 Broome Tech — 79 3OT
		3	Burlington — 75 Chicago-Wilson — 71
		4	Moberly — 75 South Texas — 61
		5	Independence — 60 Murray St. — 52
		6	Chipola — 76 Muskegon — 67
Wednesday:	Game		
		7	Casper — 80 New York City — 74
		8	Hibbing — 66 Amarillo — 63 2OT
		9	Southern Union — 58 Broome Tech — 49
		10	Phoenix — 78 Wilmington — 76
		11	Moberly — 86 Burlington — 71
Thursday:	Game		
		12	Chicago-Wilson — 85 South Texas — 81
		13	Amarillo — 78 New York City — 73
		14	Wilmington — 59 Burlington — 55
		15	Muskegon — 58 Murray St. — 57
		16	Casper — 77 Hibbing — 64
		17	Independence — 93 Chipola — 83
Friday:	Game		
		10R	Wilmington — 80 Southern Union — 74 OT
		18	Chicago-Wilson — 79 Broome Tech — 71
		19	Muskegon — 76 Amarillo — 71
		20	Chipola — 87 Hibbing — 67
		21	Moberly — 78 Wilmington — 76 OT
		22	Independence —- 82 Casper — 54
		14R	Burlington — 88 Southern Union — 69
Saturday:	Game		
		23	Muskegon — 90 Chicago-Wilson — 85
		24	Burlington — 70 Chipola — 68
		25	Casper — 82 Wilmington — 81
		26	Independence — 73 Moberly — 68 OT
	R — Replay		

How They Finished in 1963

1. Independence Community College
2. Moberly Junior College
3. Casper College
4. Burlington Community College
5. Muskegon Community College
6. Wilmington College
7. Chipola Junior College
8. Chicago City Junior College, Wilson Branch

All-Tournament Team

Ray Amalbert — New York City Community College
Eugene Bogash — Wilmington College
Jim Boyce — Burlington Community College
Gary Bryan — Chipola Junior College
Bob Dibler — Amarillo College
Bob Fedorko — Independence Community College
Joe Mimlitz — Moberly Junior College
Rick Park — Independence Community College
Ed Samelton — Casper College
Gene Visscher — Muskegon Community College

Coach of the Year

Bob Sneller — Independence Community College

Player of the Year

Eugene Bogash — Wilmington College

Since 1960, tournament gross receipts had inched steadily higher, setting a new record each year. The increases were due to greater afternoon attendance and standing-room-only purchases, the only areas ticket sales had flexibility to improve. Fourteen hundred unreserved seats were regularly gobbled up shortly after going on sale before each evening session, a condition resulting from the fact that the 4,000 reserved-seat season tickets sold out prior to the tournament, disappearing at a faster rate each year. In 1964, the demand was so great that all season tickets were claimed 10 days after hitting the market. As the *Hutchinson News* put it, "The seat situation is catch-as-catch-can."

Interest in the tournament as a recruiting mecca also increased. Forty-nine four-year college coaches were already registered with the tournament committee before the 1964 event tipped off, many arriving early to see Monday's practice sessions.

Newsmen converged from opposite ends of the country. Most — like Howard Sudduth of the Jasper, Alabama, *Daily Mountain Eagle* — were there to cover a local participant. Others — like Don Miles of *The Journal Advocate,* of Sterling, Colorado, a city which had never sent a representative, but hoped to do so in the near future — were there to experience something unique and generate interest in their readership.

The *News* also reported that all but three teams would have radio broadcasts of their games sent back home. And, according to tournament publicity director Hod Humiston, "The other three might show up before it starts."

There were also numerous junior college coaches in attendance. Even though their teams failed to earn their way to Hutchinson, Gene Robbins of Murray State, Al Rochelle of Southern Union, Dick Baldwin of Broome Tech, and Jerry Anderson of New York City Community College — all mentors of 1963 entries — found it hard to stay away.

In its 17th year, the NJCAA Basketball Tournament had become a hard habit to shake.

After scoring 95 points in three games of the 1964 tournament, Eastern Arizona's Freddie Lewis scored 963 points, pulled down 344 rebounds, and shot 79.4 from the free throw line as an Arizona State Sun Devil. He then became an 11-year pro, a two-time all-star, and one of only three players to play in the ABA from its inception until it merged with the NBA. (Photo courtesy of Arizona State University)

THE PARTICIPANTS

The Burlington Community College Blackhawks had impressed everyone with their 1963 all-freshman unit, so few were surprised to see them as pre-tourney favorites in 1964. The No. 3 Iowans possessed the tallest starting five (averaging just over 6-4 per man), the tallest player (6-9 Mel Daniels), All-American Jim Boyce (one of five members back from their 1963 fourth-place squad),[1] and the best record in the meet (28-1). Though *Hutchinson News* sportswriter Barbara Caywood tagged three other teams as co-favorites, Burlington was the talk of the town.

The Blackhawks' chief contender was the Kansas representative, Dodge City College (25-2). The Conquistadors ranked one step below Burlington in the NJCAA poll and was further distinguished by having knocked off No. 1 Coffeyville College. Dodge City won the best two-of-three Region 6 play-off with the former champs, winning the final match, 65-62, on Coffeyville's noisy home court. Unfortunately, if both survived upper bracket competition, Burlington and Dodge City would face each other in the semifinals.

According to Caywood, the lower bracket picks were No. 7 Lon Morris College (29-4) and unrated Chipola Junior College (23-4). Of the two, Lon Morris was the more likely candidate. The Bearcats represented always strong Region 14 and had placed in all three previous tourney appearances, including a

---

[1] As good as the Blackhawks were, they might have been better. Burlington was missing an essential cog from its 1963 machine — Bobby Joe Hill. According to Jim Boyce (later head coach at Eastern Michigan), "Bobby Joe was pretty bright [130 I.Q.]. He prided himself on going to classes without opening the books. He did it for one year. The second year it kind of collapsed on him."

Fortunately, Don Haskins, coach at Texas Western (now University of Texas-El Paso), had seen Hill play. He suggested Hill transfer to Texas Western and work on his grades. His faith in Hill paid off. As Haskins related, "It was unbelievable how he could make things go. I've had two great point guards — Nate Archibald and Bobby Joe Hill. And Bobby Joe was as good as Nate. He was the kind of guy all the other guys believed in. He was an intense leader."

That leadership was evident early in the 1966 NCAA final. Lightning quick Bobby Joe Hill made two thefts and two driving lay-ups in 10 seconds to break open a tight game. Hill topped all scorers with 20, leading the Miners to a 72-65 upset victory over Kentucky.

runner-up finish in 1962. The highest finish for the Chipola Indians in three trips was seventh-place in 1963. Since only one starter (6-8 Austin Robbins) returned from that team, Chipola's inclusion in the pre-tourney elite appeared questionable.

There were five ranked teams with better possibilities: No. 5 Eastern Arizona Junior College (26-2); No. 11 Trenton Junior College (29-6); No. 13 Bacone College (26-3); No. 16 Brevard College (22-5); and No. 17 Casper College (21-5). All but Bacone had experienced national tournament competition. The most recent participant appeared the strongest. The Casper Thunderbirds returned three starters from their 1963 third-place team, including All-American and All-Tournament selection Ed Samelton.

Lurking in the shadows of the top-rated teams were four squads with excellent records: Centralia Junior College (26-1), a potent offensive squad with two of the top-10 scorers in the country — Russ Coleman (35.1) and Don Duncan (27.9); Jackson Junior College (21-2), a possessor of another top-10 gunner — honorable mention All-American Bobby Thompkins (27.8); San Angelo College (26-3), the only former champion in the meet; and, Leicester Junior College (20-3), a tournament newcomer.

Only three teams sat at the bottom of the barrel: first-time participant Southwest Baptist College (20-9) of Bolivar, Missouri, a surprise last-second winner over No. 9 Moberly Junior College; North Dakota State School of Science from Wahpeton (20-11), a veteran participant with no tourney victories; and Walker College of Jasper, Alabama, a debutant with the poorest record in the meet — 15-12.

TUESDAY — FIGHT FOR LIFE

The Trenton Vikings were an averaged-sized ballclub, but against their opening-round opponent, appeared to be giants. The Jackson Maroons were one of the smallest teams in tournament history. Their starting lineup averaged under six foot, their tallest player measuring 6-1.

What Jackson lacked in size it made up for in speed. After Trenton opened a nine-point gap early, the Maroons applied full-court pressure and turned the contest into a nip and tuck affair. With four minutes remaining and a three-point edge, Trenton held the ball, spreading the Jackson defense and the margin. The Vikings opened the 1964 tournament with a 79-69 victory.

Trenton Coach Howie Landa later described how his game strategy against Jackson developed: "They were really an excellent team and we tried to get a scouting report on them. I picked up one of those basketball scholastic magazines and here it had 'Zone Offense' by Jackson, Michigan's basketball coach [Chet Eicher]. I swear he did exactly what it said in the magazine. That's why we beat them. They had a great shooter [Bobby Thompkins]. They would send him through against our zone and we would follow him. He was never open all night."

The next contest was the most heavily touted in the first-round, featuring the tournament's two best offenses; Centralia was the nation's top scoring squad with an astounding 115.9 average while Burlington ranked third, producing 95.8 points per game. Each had lost only one game during the year. It was expected to be a high-flying shoot-out. It proved to a lopsided mismatch.

Centralia's tallest player was 6-4 — the average height of Burlington's starting lineup. The Blue Devils stayed close for 2 minutes, then buckled. With 6-9 Mel Daniels and 6-5 Jim Boyce patrolling the middle, Burlington romped, 99-76. Boyce le everybody with 32 points and 17 rebounds. Though hampere with three first-period fouls, Daniels contributed a creditable 2 points, 16 rebounds, and five blocked shots. The awesome di play sent warning shock waves through the other tourne encampments.

During practice sessions on the Arena floor Monday, men bers of the Eastern Arizona team complained to official "Those baskets are too high." A tape measure was produce One basket was four inches off, the other a full *two feet* too hig

In Tuesday afternoon's finale, the Thatcher squad must hav thought that officials failed to adjust the baskets, since none of the Gila Monsters could hit. San Angelo ran away to a 12-poir lead with five minutes left in the first half before Eastern Arizon struggled to reduce the margin to eight by intermission.

Then, Freddie Lewis, the Gila Monsters' top scorer, found th range. A three-point play by the small, quick forward gave th Thatcher crew a 40-39 lead with 15 minutes to go.

San Angelo immediately bounced back, opening a five-poir gap which took Eastern Arizona nearly 10 minutes to clos With a 62-60 advantage, the Gila Monsters stalled. Easy bucke and free throws gained Eastern its biggest margin, 66-61, wit 2:40 remaining.

It was San Angelo's turn to rally. An Eddie Pruitt tip-in, a Gar Jellison jumper, and two Charles Spieker free throws gave th Rams a 67-66 edge with just under two minutes remaining.

A Lewis 15-footer regained the lead for Eastern Arizona When San Angelo failed to score, the Gila Monsters returned t their delay and, with 15 seconds on the clock, San Angel fouled. Joe Pennington stepped to the line and calmly sank tw free throws, clinching a 70-67 win for Eastern. Freddie Lewis le all scorers with 27, 21 in the second half.

Chipola opened the evening session in fine form again: Bacone, taking a 48-45 halftime margin and extending it to eigl three minutes into the second period.

Then, four straight Tom Davis jumpers from outside 15 fee and a basket by Roosevelt Milton put Bacone in the lead, 60-58 with 15:03 to go. It was all Bacone and Harold Aldridge from then on. Aldridge camped at the free throw line, hitting 17 of 2 charities, leading all scorers with 31. His teammates wer equally hot, all five Bacone starters hitting double figures. Wit 1:40 remaining, the Warriors broke the century barrier on the way to a 107-84 rout. The only bright spot for Chipola was Aus tin Robbins' 30-point effort.

Suddenly, the decibel level increased. In the tournament Convention Hall era, Dodge City gained a reputation for bring ing one of the largest and loudest followings. A 12-year absenc had not diminished the enthusiasm of Conquistador suppor ers. The Sports Arena rang with noise from the moment th team took the court. Booming cries of "We're No. 1!" demor strated fan confidence. Their faith was not misplaced. Dodg City took command early, building a 12-point margin.

Then the situation changed. In the final 2½ minutes, under dog Southwest Baptist charged from behind, pulling to withi four at intermission. The partisan crowd became restive.

The engineer of the Southwest Baptist rally had been Harol Burton, a 6-3 forward who hit six of seven from the 25-foc range, scoring 15 of the Missourians' last 19 points. When pla resumed, Burton picked up where he left off. The Bolivar Bea cats clawed at the Dodge City lead until a Burton jumper tie the game at 46-all.

Conquistador fans drew breath as the Kansans spread the di ference to five.

Southwest Baptist persisted, knotting the game at 57-all mi way through the period.

Three more ties and four lead changes followed as Dodg City followers squirmed. The Conquistadors were in an une> pected fight for life.

With 3:37 remaining, Reggie Greene, Dodge City's floc leader, sank a 15-footer to put the Conquistadors ahead, 68-6: Bolivar missed, giving the ball back to the Kansans who stalle

The final minutes were excruciating for Conquistador fan Greene missed an easy lay-up. A free throw lipped off the rin In all, Dodge City gave Southwest Baptist five chances to tie d ain the lead. The Missourians were equally generous, missing very opportunity. When the 73-68 final was posted, Dodge ity backers felt fortunate to have won.

As Coach Chuck Brehm told the *Dodge City Daily Globe,* We just couldn't do anything right out there." Among the onquistador low points were 16 turnovers and 32.6 percent om the field, 15 percentage points below the team average.

Fortunately, there were also high points: 17 for 21 from the ee throw line and center Carl Head's domination of the mid-le. The only way Southwest Baptist had been able to stop the -4 jumping jack was with official help when Head was whistled r two goaltending calls. Otherwise, he roamed free, topping ll scorers with 30, edging Bolivar's Burton by two for the honor.

For local fans, the evening finale was anticlimactic. Few ayed until the end, even though favored Brevard fell behind e Wahpeton Wildcats at the start of both halves. The final 10 inutes bore out their expectations. The Brevard Tornadoes utscored NDSSS-Wahpeton, 26-12, blowing the North Dako-ns, away 76-62.

WEDNESDAY — WHAT RANKING MEANS

The 1964 Juco Tournament featured an oddity in its bracket-g. All first-round parings matched ranked teams against nranked teams. In Tuesday action, every rated squad won, but e two remaining favorites were hard put to continue the string Vednesday afternoon.

In the opener, Leicester outplayed Casper through 20 min-tes, taking a 34-29 lead, then extending it to 11 early in the sec-nd period.

Forced to play catch-up, Casper applied full-court pressure. 2½ minutes, the Thunderbirds erased a nine-point deficit, oving ahead, 46-45, with 10:41 to go.

The teams traded baskets for five minutes. Then a string of six onsecutive free throws — four by Ed Samelton and two by Mickey Hartsburg — plus a field goal gave Casper a five-point ushion.

Leicester rallied to within one with a little more than a minute emaining before Casper introduced a stall. With the Minute-en forced to foul, Casper hit six of eight free throws in the final 5 seconds to survive.

The stat sheet showed the Thunderbirds' good fortune. eicester outscored Casper by 14 points from the field, but anaged 17 more fouls. Superb shooting from the line (30 for 7) and 21 more charity opportunities were the difference. The hunderbirds breathed easier with the 72-65 victory.

The remaining ranked team had just as much difficulty. The rst half of the final opening-round contest featured 11 ties and ight lead changes with the Lon Morris Bearcats barely clutch-g a three-point lead at the end.

The Walker Rebels from Jasper, Alabama, continued their prising, tying the game three more times once play resumed. hen the rebellion fizzled. In the final 12 minutes, Lon Morris utscored Walker, 29-9. With a 76-58 victory, the Bearcats ecame the eighth ranked team to advance to the quarterfinals.

Excitement had surfaced in all first-round games, but emained afloat until the end in only a couple. With ranked eams exclusively in the championship bracket, fans expected he pace to accelerate. Few, however, figured the opening uarterfinal to be a heart-stopper.

The Burlington-Trenton pairing was considered a mismatch, ince traditionally, Eastern teams were weaker than their record r ranking indicated. Trenton was a good example why. The chool offered no athletic scholarships and possessed no play-g facilities. The team practiced from 10 to midnight at a local 'MCA. "Home" games were played at various neighboring unior high and high school gymnasiums. Asking the ragtag ikings to upend the tourney's acknowledged "team to beat" vas asking for a miracle.

Hoping to catch the taller more talented Blackhawks off uard, Trenton immediately applied full-court pressure. The naneuver achieved mixed results, but did keep the Vikings lose. At intermission, Burlington's advantage was only 40-36.

Then, as everybody in the Arena anticipated would happen ooner or later, the roof caved in on Trenton. After the Vikings bandoned their press, William Dunson fired from outside, Mel Daniels looped hooks in the middle, and Jim Boyce slammed

two powerful two-hand dunks. Burlington opened a 62-49 gap with 12 minutes to go.

The only edge Trenton had demonstrated over Burlington was hustle. Accordingly, Coach Howie Landa reinstated full-court pressure. To the encouraging cheers of fans eager for an upset, the Vikings took control. Burlington continued playing its normal game with no hint of slowing the tempo while the scrap-py Trenton squad hijacked passes, picked pockets, and team-tackled rebounds. Slowly the gap closed. A 15-footer by Carl Anderson with 2:03 remaining pulled the Vikings even for the first time since the opening tip. Two Anderson free throws 19 seconds later gave Trenton its first lead of the game. When the Vikings regained control of the ball, they played keep away.

The shoe was on the other foot. Burlington pressed — and fouled, Jim Cornwall hitting two free throws.

Daniels answered with one, cutting the Blackhawk deficit to a basket.

Anderson was fouled, hit the front end of one-and-one and missed the second. But, with two seconds showing, Bill Smith snuck around Burlington's big men and tipped the ball back up and in, performing the coup de grace. The final score: Trenton — 85, Burlington — 79. It was the first major upset in two years and one of the biggest ever.

Eastern Arizona demonstrated similar thoughts of upset in the nightcap. Erratic play by Dodge City and the outstanding abili-ties of Freddie Lewis lifted the Gila Monsters to an early six-point lead.

The Kansans settled down, however, after 6-6 Gerald Jacobs, Eastern's tallest player, picked up his fourth foul with seven minutes left. The Dodge City front line went to work, taking turns potting buckets. A rare 25-footer by Carl Head at the buzzer gave the Conquistadors a comfortable 46-37 halftime cushion. When Dodge City opened the gap to 14 in the next six minutes, fans headed for the exits.

Then, like Trenton before them, the Gila Monsters pressured and picked at the lead. A 20-footer by Harvey Polk with 1:07 to go pulled the Thatcher crew to within a single basket.

Dodge City tightened the screws further by failing to inbounds the basketball in the required five seconds. Eastern Arizona played for the tie.

However, the staunch Conquistador defense held. With 40 seconds remaining, Galen Frick gave Dodge City control with a steal, forcing Eastern to foul.

One of the Conquistador's strong points in their first outing had been free throw shooting. Against Eastern Arizona, that bright spot dimmed and nearly flickered out, sending chills through the Dodge City congregation. With 26 seconds left, Head hit only the second of two charities. With 10 seconds to go, Bob Selby missed the front end of one-and-one. Fortunate-ly, the Conquistadors secured the rebound. Two free throws by Larry Soice — his only points of the game — sewed up victory. Dodge City survived another scare, 89-84.

For the game, the Conquistadors hit only 47 percent of its free shots (15 for 32). This was offset by the superior front-line work of Head, Frick, and Robert Pipkin who dominated the boards and piled up points, all three scoring 20 or more. Still, the Con-quistadors needed to show more consistency in their total game plan if they wanted a national title.

THURSDAY — A DREARY DAY

The pace slowed as the tournament climbed its midweek hump. Only top individual performances highlighted the day's consolation play.

In the last afternoon contest, Eastern Arizona did not have enough inside strength to combat Burlington's Mel Daniels. And on the other side of the ledger, nobody on Burlington could handle Eastern's swift Freddie Lewis. At one point the Black-hawks' even tried smothering six-foot Lewis with 6-9 Daniels (who was later a teammate of Lewis in the ABA on the Indiana Pacers from 1968 to 1974 and on the Memphis Sounds in 1975). It failed. Lewis won the individual battle, 43 to 36, but Burling-ton won the war, 91-88.

Chipola's Austin Robbins and NDSSS-Wahpeton's Henry Holte also engaged in a scoring duel in the evening opener, Robbins winning, 33-32. However, the contest was not as close. Chipola opened 24-point gaps in both periods, then relaxed, easing to an 89-80 win.

Burlington's Mel Daniels completed his collegiate career at the University of New Mexico, before becoming the ABA's Rookie of the Year in 1968. The following year he was the league MVP. Daniels was one of the top-five rebounders in the ABA from 1968 to 1974 and holds league records for career rebounds (9,494) and career two-point field goals attempted (9,886) and made (4,692). (Photo courtesy of Loren Walker)

The best game of the day figured to be the evening feature between Lon Morris and Casper. The contest played true to form for 28 minutes, both teams jockeying for the lead. Then, all hell broke loose. In a seven-minute period, Casper outscored Lon Morris, 18-2.

Two factors contributed to the spurt. One was the leadership of 5-11 guard Mickey Hartsburg who, after a terrible tournament the year before, seemed more at home in front of the big Arena crowd, scoring 20 of his game-high 24 points in the final period. Casper's other winning ingredient was its board strength. Led by Sam Williams, who recovered 11 caroms, the Thunderbirds dominated the middle, allowing Lon Morris only one shot at the basket each trip up the court. The Bearcats were perfect from the line (13 for 13, including 10 for 10 by Gary Cornelison) but dismal from the field. Casper crushed the Texans, 76-59.

After scoring 177 points in two tournaments, Chipola's Austin "Red" Robbins (shown with Coach Milt Johnson) finished his college days at Tennessee before enjoying considerable success in the newly formed ABA playing eight years. The pencil-thin center was a top rebounder and a three-time ABA all-star. (Photo courtesy of Milt Johnson)

An all-day rain had held the evening's attendance to the lowest figure of the tournament. With the threat of further bad weather and the lack of stimulating action, the crowd of 5,50 quickly dispersed. Those few that did stay changed their mind as the remaining quarterfinal progressed.

Brevard scored the first six points. Then, Bacone rallied, tie the score twice, and sprinted ahead, securing a comfortable 48 38 halftime edge. In the second period, the Warriors' lead fluc tuated, rising to 13 three times, but never falling below six. Bre vard fell easily, 82-69.

FRIDAY — AT THE BUZZER

Friday's opener contained more action than all Thursday contests combined. Playing a pro-transition type game — stat ed San Angelo Coach Phil George, "We passed each othe going opposite directions." — Centralia and San Angelo race neck and neck at a hare-footed pace. At halftime both team had poured 54 points apiece through the nets.

The helter-skelter scramble continued to the wire. After tyin the game at 102-all with a free throw, Don Duncan stole the ba and drove for two, giving Centralia the edge with 24 seconds t go.

San Angelo's Charles Spieker answered with an heroic 20 footer with 12 seconds left.

Then, just as the final buzzer sounded, Duncan swished on from 30-feet.

It was a fitting climax to a nearly dead-even ballgame. Bot teams had identical free throw shooting statistics — 26 for 32 San Angelo had super efforts from Charles Morton (35) an Gary Jellison (24); Centralia, from Russ Coleman (24) and Dun can. Appropriately, the game-winner came from the game leading scorer, Duncan, whose 44 was the highest total of th 1964 tournament.

The following contest ended with the same frenetic tempo After overcoming Leicester leads of 10 and 8, Chipola rallied t gain an 83-79 edge with 1:08 remaining.

Leicester's Paul Anger cut the margin in two with a jumper a the 50-second mark. After the basket, Chipola lost the ball ou of bounds. With 33 seconds left, Tom Quinn knotted the score A David Atkins free throw with 19 seconds gave the Minutemen the advantage.

Donnie Carter hit a two-pointer with seven seconds on th clock, leapfrogging Chipola to the lead.

Finally, just as had happened in the preceding game, a las second swisher, an 18-footer by Quinn, decided the game Despite Austin Robbins' game-high 39 (all but one from th field), Leicester edged Chipola, 86-85.

Hopes were high for continued breakneck action in the eve ning's semifinals. Though they supported Dodge City in its pre vious two outings (Hutchinson Junior College cheerleader joined Dodge City cheerleaders in their yells), local fans wer enamored with the team from Trenton, New Jersey, and it miraculous upset of Burlington. Public sentiment was reflecte in the newspaper's tag for the Vikings — "Battling Orphans."

Another miracle looked possible at the start of the evenin feature when Dodge City took two minutes to score its first fiel goal, Trenton jumping in front, 4-1.

Then, dreams of upset evaporated. Dodge City's quickness rebounding strength, and aggressive man-to-man defens throttled the Vikings. With 10 minutes left in the opening peri od, the Conquistadors opened a 22-8 chasm.

The hustling Vikings were forced to press and fouled as result. Facing a 30-point deficit with five minutes to go, a frus trated Coach Howie Landa let loose, picking up two technica fouls in a nose-to-nose shouting match with Referee J.C. Bain The emotional outburst was not without cause. For the game Trenton matched Dodge City from the field, each hitting 39 field goals. The final difference was due to 26 more Conquista dor trips to the line.

There were two other factors more important to Dodge City victory, however. Only two Vikings — Bill Smith (35) and Jim Cornwall (29) — hit double figures while four Conquistadors — Carl Head (28), Robert Pipkin (23), Reggie Greene (19), and Galen Frick (17) — managed the feat. The most telling statistic though, was rebounding. Trenton grabbed only five offensive rebounds in the game's first 35 minutes. Dodge City won easily 110-86.

One opening for a title shot remained. While attention was focused on upper bracket play, Casper and Bacone had quietly scored impressive victories. It was anybody's guess which team would win.

The two squads kept the question in doubt for five minutes. Then, Casper opened up its offense, building an 18-point advantage. At intermission, the Thunderbirds were still comfortably in front, 49-37. When Casper continued to coast, spreading the gap to 15, fans quickly evacuated the premises.

Suddenly, the floor collapsed under the Thunderbirds. In a five-minute period, Casper threw the ball out of bounds three times, gave away four interceptions, and was burgled twice. Bacone scored 18 unanswered points to take a 59-56 lead.

The Thunderbirds pulled out of the nose dive, slowing action. Spurred by a Mickey Hartsburg three-point play, the Casper squad regained composure and edged ahead, 66-65, with six minutes remaining. The Thunderbirds surrendered the lead once more to Bacone, but reclaimed it for good with 1:50 to go. Casper's delay game and Roger Hessler's four free throws in the final 35 seconds preserved a 76-72 win.

SATURDAY — THE CLOSEST DAY

The 1964 tournament ended with a bang as all four trophy games were nail-biters, featuring exciting come-from-behind rallies. A total 10 points separated the winners from the losers. It was the closest day in tournament history.

Leicester took the early advantage in the battle for fifth, opening 10-point gaps several times. Centralia mounted rallies to close to within one or two but did not pull even until three minutes into the second period. The contest was tight from then on with five ties and frequent lead changes.

The final tie came inside the minute mark when Tom Quinn, the hero of Leicester's previous victory, hit a field goal, knotting the score at 97-all. A subsequent free throw by the 6-2 guard put the Minutemen ahead. With 23 seconds remaining, Quinn was fouled again and hit two more clutch free throws. Russ Coleman scored with 13 seconds to go, but Centralia could cash in no further. Leicester edged the Blue Devils, 100-99.

Though Leicester won the game, Centralia claimed most of the honors. Coleman took game-honors with 33, nudging out Leicester's Quinn (32) and Knute Haglund (31). Don Duncan, the other half of the Blue Devil's sensational guard tandem, tallied 28, giving him tournament honors with 114. Centralia also set two tournament records: most points (383) and most field goals (152) in four games.

In the other afternoon contest, Burlington fell 17 points behind Lon Morris with five minutes left in the half before the Blackhawks reduced the deficit to 10 by intermission. Nine minutes later the score was even, 65-all. The Blackhawks then gained the upper hand, building a seven-point margin with two minutes remaining.

It was Lon Morris' turn to rally, taking advantage of several Burlington miscues. Unfortunately, time ran out before the Bearcats could shave the difference completely. Burlington held on for fourth, 89-87.

Both sides received heroic efforts. Wayne Ballard led Lon Morris' early charge with 20 first-half points, ending the game with 31. Mel Daniels, Burlington's star in previous games, picked up four fouls early and did not see much action, notching only 16 points. The Blackhawk banner was instead raised by 28-year-old sophomore Jim Boyce, who netted 15 in the first half and 18 in the second, sparking Burlington's come-from-behind effort. Boyce's 100-point 1964 total added to his 108 from the year before, moved him into fifth-place on the tourney's list of top two-year scorers.

Though a modern four-sided scoreboard dangled from its ceiling, the Sports Arena was like most basketball courts in the country. Player foul accumulation was signaled to the benches manually. Thanks to Warren H. Laughlin, an assistant cashier at the Geneseo (Kansas) Citizens State Bank, that situation changed. Laughlin donated his recent invention, an electronic foul light, for use at the 1964 tournament. When a player fouled, all an official at the scorer's table had to do was flip a console switch and one of five numbers on the box-like vertical post, located at the end of the table, would light, indicating the player's foul status.

The innovation was much in evidence in the evening opener; 57 fouls were called. Coaches Ken Hayes of Bacone and Howie Landa of Trenton wore ruts in the sideline boards, during the hectic contest.

Landa's ruts were deeper. As in their upset win over Burlington, the Vikings spotted their opponent a large second-half lead, trailing, 71-55, with 11 minutes remaining, before the New Jersey crew decided to change matters. It was not until the final two minutes, though, that the Vikings put the oars into full-stroke.

Jim Cornwall hit from the wing then went one for two from the line. John Massielo scooped in a two-hand shot. Cornwall hit a 15-footer from the side, stole the ball, and added two free throws after a subsequent foul. Bacone missed two charities. Cornwall contributed another jumper. With 14 seconds to go, Trenton had narrowed the gap to two, 94-92.

As Bacone brought the ball upcourt, a Warrior smashed into Trenton's ever-present Cornwall. The officials whistled charging.

The Vikings took possession with six ticks on the clock. Bacone closed off the middle. Unable to find an open man, Massielo launched from 25 feet. The ball hit the front edge of the rim and fell to the floor, attracting a massive pile-up. Time expired. Bacone survived Trenton's late rush for third-place.

The 1964 NJCAA basketball crown was up for grabs. Casper and Dodge City had each staged impressive, lopsided victories and weathered close calls. Size was no factor since both starting lineups were almost identical in height. On paper, each possessed the talent to be national champions.

Dodge City's strength was its front line. Robert Pipkin, Carl Head, and Galen Frick had dominated board play in all three Conquistador games. They also combined for 195 points, an average of over 20 points per man per game. Head — an exceptional leaper for his size (6-4) — led the triumvirate, averaging 11 rebounds a game. Containing Head would be a prime requirement for a Casper win.

If the Conquistadors had a weakness, it was inconsistency. This played into Casper's strong point — experience. The Thunderbirds were anchored by three members from the previous year's third-place team — Mickey Hartsburg, Sam Williams, and Ed Samelton. Williams and Samelton (both from South Bend, Indiana) were top rebounders. Hartsburg (from Indianapolis, Indiana) was the team's spark plug at guard. The trio knew what to expect in pressure packed national competition. It was their leadership which had guided the Thunderbirds to the title game.

One factor was against Casper, however; the predominately Kansas crowd gave Dodge City a virtual home court advantage.

The Thunderbirds neutralized it from the start, taking control of the tempo and the game. Casper's defensive strategy against Dodge City's powerful front line was a box-and-one zone. Four Thunderbirds monitored the corners of the zone while 6-6 Al-Dee Konopnicki shadowed Head. The Utah State transfer, whose previous play had been unspectacular, successfully dogged the Dodge City star, holding Head to five first-half points.

At the other end of the court, Hartsburg continually eluded his man behind a high screen at the top of the key. He scored 15 for the period.

The Casper game plan was working perfectly — except for one thing; nobody could stop Galen Frick.

The 6-4 forward from Durham, Kansas, kept Dodge City out of serious trouble, tallying all 10 Conquistador points in the final 4½ minutes. His basket with 15 seconds left pulled Dodge City even, 32-all, at intermission. Then, Frick gave the Kansans their first lead of the game with the first point of the second half, a free throw.

Buckets by Hartsburg and Samelton quickly put Dodge City back in the hole.

Frick to the rescue again. A field goal and a three-point play vaulted the Kansans to a 38-36 advantage.

Sixteen successive points by one man in a little over 6½ minutes. It was time for the rest of the Conquistadors to join the effort. After Casper's Konopnicki picked up his fourth foul, the door opened for Head and company. The Dodge City lead steadily grew, reaching 13 points with 6:45 remaining.

Switching to a three-quarter-court man-to-man press, Casper fought back, Hartsburg and guard counterpart Roger Hessler leading a Casper rally which closed the gap to 66-63 with three minutes left.

In two other close calls, Dodge City's youthful corps had overcome inconsistent play just in time to thwart losses. Coach Chuck Brehm ordered his charges to hold the ball and crossed his fingers.

In the face of championship pressure, the Conquistador stall pattern was expertly effective. It found Head open three times and Frick once for easy baskets.

Dodge City College secured the title, 73-68.

THE AFTERMATH — MORE TO COME

Despite momentary lapses, the 1964 NJCAA basketball champion was a poised and disciplined ballclub. Its biggest asset, however, was balance. As *News* sportswriter Barbara Caywood put it: "You just can't pick out one member of that Dodge City club and say he's head and shoulders above the rest (except maybe Carl Head when he's jumping). If one or two of the starters faltered somewhat, there was always two or three other fellas there to carry the load . . . All five starters on the Dodge City team could easily have been put on the All-Star Tournament team."

The Conquistador balance posed a problem for tournament MVP selectors. Consequently, the award defaulted to the steady, resourceful captain of runner-up Casper — Mickey Hartsburg.

Though surprised at the selection, no one was up in arms about it. Local fans, in particular, were more than content with tourney results. First, the event was again a whopping financial success, setting a gross receipt record for the fourth straight year. Second, the Sports Arena was now two-thirds paid for; at the present rate, the bonds for the structure would be completely retired in six years. Finally, with Dodge City's triumph, Kansas schools had won four out of the last five national titles.

More was expected. There was a reason for the Conquistadors' occasional inconsistency and it foretold a bright future. All five Dodge City starters were *freshmen.*

How They Finished in 1964

1. Dodge City College
2. Casper College
3. Bacone College
4. Burlington Community College
5. Leicester Junior College
6. Trenton Junior College
7. Lon Morris College
8. Centralia Junior College

Tournament Results

	Game	
Tuesday:	1	Trenton — 79 Jackson — 69
	2	Burlington — 99 Centralia — 76
	3	Eastern Arizona — 70 San Angelo — 67
	4	Bacone — 107 Chipola — 84
	5	Dodge City — 73 SW Baptist — 68
	6	Brevard — 76 NDSSS-Wahpeton — 62
Wednesday:	7	Casper — 72 Leicester — 65
	8	Lon Morris — 76 Walker — 58
	9	Centralia — 102 Jackson — 78
	10	Trenton — 85 Burlington — 79
	11	Dodge City — 89 Eastern Arizona — 84
Thursday:	12	San Angelo — 98 SW Baptist — 85
	13	Leicester — 66 Walker — 63
	14	Burlington — 91 Eastern Arizona — 88
	15	Chipola — 89 NDSSS-Wahpeton — 80
	16	Casper — 76 Lon Morris — 59
	17	Bacone — 82 Brevard — 69
Friday:	18	Centralia — 106 San Angelo — 104
	19	Leicester — 86 Chipola — 85
	20	Lon Morris — 92 Brevard — 75
	21	Dodge City — 110 Trenton — 86
	22	Casper — 76 Bacone — 72
Saturday:	23	Leicester — 100 Centralia — 99
	24	Burlington — 89 Lon Morris — 87
	25	Bacone — 94 Trenton — 92
	26	Dodge City — 73 Casper — 68

All-Tournament Team

Harold Aldridge — Bacone College
Wayne Ballard — Lon Morris College
James Boyce — Burlington Community College
Jim Cornwall — Trenton Junior College
Donald Duncan — Centralia Junior College
Mickey Hartsburg — Casper College
Carl Head — Dodge City College
Freddie Lewis — Eastern Arizona Junior College
Thomas Quinn — Leicester Junior College
Austin Robbins — Chipola Junior College

Coach of the Year

Charles "Chuck" Brehm — Dodge City College

Player of the Year

Mickey Hartsburg — Casper College

The all-freshman national champion Dodge City Conquistadors; Back row (left to right) — Rex Trauer, Larry Kerbs, Robert Pipkin, Carl Head, Jesse Hensel, Galen Frick, Roger Allen, Bob Selby, Coach Chuck Brehm; front row — Dwight Negley, Don Gepner, Artie Hall, Reggie Greene, Larry Soice, Ron Coleman. (Photo courtesy of Chuck Brehm)

ACROSS THE MISSISSIPPI

With the increasing interest in advance reserved-seat tickets, the American Legion sponsors of the Juco Tournament decided to make ticket buying easier. Reserved-seat purchases for the 1965 event were to be handled entirely through mail orders. Fans were to submit their requests no earlier than February 14.

The response stunned Legion officials. The ticket committee was swamped by an avalanche of mail. After requests with morning postmarks for the 14th were worked, the supply of reserved seats was exhausted. One-hundred-and-five orders with afternoon postmarks plus nearly 1,500 dated February 15 remained.

To accommodate those requests imprinted with the 14th, Legion officials made an unprecedented move, opening the arena's upper balcony for reserved seating, leaving only 1,000 general admission seats for sale each night. The committee then faced the unpopular task of returning nearly $10,000 worth of unfilled requests.

In 17 years, the National Junior College Basketball Tournament had gone from poverty to prosperity, acquiring a loyal following along the way. The ticket request deluge came *three weeks before a single participant was known.*

THE PARTICIPANTS

Region	Team
1	College of Eastern Utah — Price, Utah
2	Murray State Agricultural College — Tishomingo, Oklahoma
3	State University of New York Agricultural and Technical Institute at Canton — Canton, New York
4	Joliet Junior College — Joliet, Illinois
5	Howard County Junior College — Big Spring, Texas
6	Dodge City College — Dodge City, Kansas
7	Arkansas State College, Beebe Branch — Beebe, Arkansas
8	Manatee Junior College — Bradenton, Florida
9	Northeastern Junior College — Sterling, Colorado
10	Ferrum Junior College — Ferrum, Virginia
11	Burlington Community College — Burlington, Iowa
12	Vincennes University — Vincennes, Indiana
13	Willmar Community College — Willmar, Minnesota
14	Kilgore College — Kilgore, Texas
15	Robert Morris Junior College — Pittsburgh, Pennsylvania
16	Moberly Junior College — Moberly, Missouri

Though they did not know for sure who would be in the tournament, season-ticket buyers did have solid expectations. From pre-season until its final week, the NJCAA poll rated defending champion Dodge City College No. 1. A national title and an additional year of play had matured the Conquistadors. They were no longer plagued by occasional spells of freshmanitis. All five starters were mentioned on one all-star listing or another. The only blemish on Dodge City's 26-1 record was to strong Kansas State frosh squad. Local fans bought their tickets, fully anticipating the recent string of Kansas titles would continue.

Dodge City's road to a second straight championship would not be easy, though. Two other former champs were excellent candidates for the crown — and, like the Conquistadors, both were in the tourney's lower bracket.

One of the potential roadblocks was No. 2 Kilgore College. The Rangers were undefeated in 29 games and possessed a potent weapon — Donald Kruse. In two sub-regional games,

the 6-8 center powered home 100 points. With Kruse at its fulcrum, the current Ranger crew was considered better than either of Kilgore's previous two national titlists. It was reported to be the best team yet to come out of Region 14 — a region which had produced more national finalists than any other.

The other obstacle was perennial favorite, No. 9 Moberly Junior College (25-3). It was the 13th appearance for the two-time champions and, as was usually the case, the Greyhounds were gifted with talent. This time they were also tall; five squad members measured 6-6 or better.

The final member of the *Hutchinson News* "big four" was out of place when compared with the tradition and reputation of the other three; Robert Morris was unranked and making its first trip to Hutchinson. The inclusion of the Pittsburgh school in the pre-tourney elite appeared to be a token gesture in recognition of its superlative 27-0 record. However, since the Colonials were in the upper bracket, they faced an easier trip to the finals than their more illustrious co-favorites.

The 1965 tournament featured an interesting blend of old and new. Half the field had never participated in the nationals before. The other half had made two or more appearances.

The veterans were more predictable. No. 5 Joliet Junior College (25-3), No. 14 Murray State Agricultural College (21-4), and No. 17 Burlington Community College (23-4) figured to give stiff competition to the top contenders. Howard County Junior College (24-10) and Arkansas State College of Beebe (14-16) were the tournament's long shots. Howard had upset No. 3 Cisco Junior College, 97-94, in two overtimes in the Region 5 final. The Beebe squad had slipped through Region 7 competition after all the seeded teams lost in early rounds.

The newcomers, including co-favorite Robert Morris, were harder to gauge. Three were ranked: No. 13 Canton Tech (24-1); No. 16 Northeastern of Sterling, Colorado (25-6); and No. 18 Willmar Community College (25-3). The records of the others ranged from excellent to passable: Ferrum Junior College, 20-2; Vincennes University, 24-6; Manatee Junior College, 21-8; and College of Eastern Utah at Price, 19-8. From their numbers alone, the first-timers were assured at least one success. Which of them would achieve glory and whether it would be as national champs was anybody's guess.

TUESDAY — GOALTENDING

Though the kick-off game was between Eastern unknowns, fans congregated outside the Sports Arena doors long before they opened. They were not concerned about getting good seats; they were just eager to savor another tournament week.

Near the head of the line were Mr. and Mrs. George Meece. The elderly Hutchinson couple (77 and 73, respectively) had not missed a tournament since its move to the "Salt Capital." They kept their string intact, entering the Arena promptly at 11:25 when it opened.

Seated in their usual front row seats behind the scorer's table, the Meece's watched Robert Morris' 6-5 Rod Jones outjump Canton Tech's 6-3 John Jenkins for the opening tip. It was the only advantage the Colonials held in the first half. With three minutes remaining, Canton opened a 33-21 margin.

Robert Morris rallied, cutting the halftime deficit to one. The Colonials continued to surge, grabbing a 43-38 lead with 16:29 to go.

Canton countered with Charles Murdaugh. The Brooklyn native hit two baskets in 15 seconds, lifting the Northmen to a 49-48 edge.

Ben Urso pumped one in for Robert Morris.

Then, a lid fell over the Colonial basket. Canton jumped ahead, spreading the margin to five. A three-point play by Mark O'Malley brought Robert Morris within a bucket, but it was as close as the Colonials could get. Canton steadily increased its lead, reaching a maximum difference of 14. Led by Murdaugh's 30 and Willie Shields' 23, the Northmen coasted to an 80-71 victory, handing Robert Morris its first defeat.

One game, one upset. The tournament was off and running.

In the next contest, Manatee stalked the Vincennes Trailblazers for 30 minutes, never leading, but never far behind. Then, like the Colonials before them, the Lancers went cold, hitting only four points in seven minutes. Meanwhile, Vincennes' Bob Pritchett and Larry Cobb combined for 17. The guard tandem eventually totaled 28 and 24, respectively, leading the Indians to an 82-64 runaway.

Run-and-gun was the name of the game in the afternoon finale. Joliet's "Pop" Wills lived and died by the fast break. His teams were never tall, but always speedy. The 1965 version of the Wolves was one of the swiftest. Joliet ranked fourth among the nation's top offenses with a 102.5 points-per-game average.

The 1965 edition of the Joliet Wolves was the last team A.A. "Pop" Wills brought to Hutchinson, though he attended several later tournaments as a fan. In his 33 years at Joliet Junior College, Wills compiled a record of 659 wins and 203 losses. He was the third winningest coach in NJCAA history. Wills passed away in November, 1983, four months before becoming a charter inductee in the NJCAA Basketball Hall of Fame. (Photo courtesy of the **Hutchinson News***)*

The Wolves broke from the gate. Howard County stayed close for five minutes, then fell off the rapid pace. Joliet fired 99 shots at the basket, hitting 39, with six Wolves snaring double figures. Joliet opened a 19-point gap with eight minutes to go and eased to an 87-76 victory.

Earlier in the week, a Roanoke, Virginia, sportswriter had called tourney publicity director Hod Humiston with a plea for help. "I've located Hutchinson, but I can't find Ferrum, Va., on the map anywhere." Ironically, Ferrum was less than 40 miles from Roanoke. As Ferrum Coach Jim Hartbarger later told the *Hutchinson News,* "We're out in the middle of nowhere. In fact, the boys say we're nine miles from civilization [Rocky Mount, Virginia]." Ferrum Junior College's 856 enrollment actually surpassed by 56 the population of the small furniture manufacturing town.

The basketball team reflected Ferrum's size. The tallest squad member was 6-4. The starting lineup was one of the smallest in the tourney field, averaging a shade over six-foot per man. Despite their lowly stature, the Panthers had achieved distinction. Ferrum was not only the first team from Virginia to appear in the NJCAA Basketball Tournament, but also the first Virginia team to appear in *any* post-season basketball tournament since 1939.

In the evening opener, Ferrum gave away nearly four inches per man to the Warriors of Willmar. The Panthers also spotted the Minnesotans an early 11-4 advantage. Using superior speed, expert ball handling, and bull's-eye target shooting, the Virginians closed the gap, tying the game at 13, 15 and 16. Ferrum fell behind once more, 17-16. Then, in the next 10 minutes the Panthers outdistanced Willmar, 23-3. The closest the Warriors could get from then on was nine points. Ferrum won easily, 79-59, becoming an instant Cinderella favorite.

The most anticipated game of the day followed. Dodge City and Burlington were the only two teams encoring from the previous year's tournament. A Dodge City-Burlington meeting had been eagerly expected the year before when the two teams had been co-favorites. An upset of Burlington squashed the showdown. This year's match-up did not figure to be as even. Burlington was without stars Jim Boyce and Mel Daniels who had matriculated to Detroit and New Mexico, respectively. The Blackhawks were further weakened by the loss of Phil Harris, a 6-9 post man who left school one week before the tournament. The all-freshman squad did not appear to pose a serious threat to the veteran national champs.

The opening period surprised the full-house turnout. Burlington outplayed the Kansans in every phase of the game. Center Roger Blalock and forward Sam Williams controlled the boards. Guards Milan Vorkapich and Virgil "Tennessee" Watkins along with Williams, provided steady Blackhawk firepower. Twice the Conquistadors were caught sleeping, allowing easy back door buckets. Midway through the period the Blackhawks' Blalock rejected a Carl Head jumper — the first time in the 6-4 leaper's 59-game career that anyone had blocked his shot. Burlington secured an early lead and held it. Only a 19-point effort by Head kept Dodge City from being further behind than 43-40 at intermission.

Conquistador fans were not concerned, however. On more than one occasion during the season, Dodge City had trailed at halftime only to roll over the opposition in the final frame. When Head and Reggie Greene nailed back-to-back baskets to open the second half, giving the Conquistadors their first lead since the opening moments, Dodge City supporters smiled knowingly.

Burlington scored the next five points.

The partisan Arena audience fidgeted until Dodge City tied it at 48-all. Another Conquistador spurt, lifted the Kansans to a five-point margin. Suddenly, Burlington caught a bad case of freshman fumblitis. The veteran Conquistadors took advantage with three consecutive lay-ups by Greene in less than a minute, raising a 10-point bulge. Dodge City followers relaxed. All was well.

Then, Williams and Watkins got hot for Burlington. In the next six minutes, the Blackhawks outscored Dodge City, 18-2. With less than 2½ minutes to go, the defending national champs were in a fight for life, trailing 80-73.

Dodge City pressed and whittled at the lead. The emotional intensity in the Arena increased correspondingly. A 15-footer by Robert Pipkin with 14 seconds to go tied the score, 83-all.

Burlington brought the ball upcourt quickly. The Blackhawks passed around the perimeter, looking for an opening. With six seconds left, Williams fired. The ball bounded away, no good, slipping through frantic fingers. Just before going out of bounds Blalock rescued it. The Blackhawk center put the ball back in flight in a do-or-die leap from behind the backboard. Out of nowhere sprang Head, smacking the ball away at the buzzer. The Conquistadors had five more minutes to rectify the situation.

Or did they?

Referee Buford Goddard raced toward the scorer's table, signaling emphatically. His ruling: Head's apparent block was goaltending.

Dodge City's Carl Head scored 189 points in two tournaments (10th-best all-time), but will be most remembered for being called for goal-tending at the buzzer in the Conquistador's 1965 first-round upset loss to Burlington. Head later starred at West Virginia University. (Photo courtesy of Chuck Brehm, taken by Kenneth Seals, Dodge City, KS)

Burlington players launched towels skyward, jumping for joy. The rest of the Arena was a tomb of silence. The only rush of movement beyond the Burlington bench was Head's angry charge at Goddard. Teammate Galen Frick restrained the distraught big man, guiding him toward the dressing room. Most reactions were like Reggie Greene's. The Dodge City playmaker — who had kept the Conquistadors in the game with 20 second-period points — slumped to the floor in a daze. He did not move until a concerned fan helped him from the court.

In the Dodge City locker room, Coach Chuck Brehm kicked dejectedly at used tape as he told the *Dodge City Daily Globe*, "He [Goddard] called it as he saw it. What beat us was our lack of reaction both on offense and defense. We didn't control the boards as we should have and we took some shots in the late going that should have been passed up. We were beat by a fine team that didn't make many mistakes and didn't quit."

Goddard's game-ending call fueled debates for days, weeks, months, and years to come. It was without question the most controversial play in tournament history.[1] Regardless of whether fans agreed or disagreed, however, all shared the sentiments best expressed by a Moberly newsman covering the event: "What a hell of a way for a champion to lose."

Burlington's upset of Dodge City was full of ironies:

It was the Conquistadors' second loss of the season, coming after 13 consecutive wins. Dodge City's only other defeat also came after 13 successive victories.

Burlington's victory put the Blackhawks in a position to do what Dodge City had done the year before — win a crown with an all-freshman starting lineup.

Most ironic of all, Head had blocked a similar shot in the critical final minutes of the 1964 championship contest against Casper College — with impunity. Casper Coach Swede Erickson described the Goddard call as "poetic justice"; "My assistant coach still has pieces of his watch out on the floor where he jumped and hopped so much [after the no-call] he broke it."

A subdued crowd watched the day's finale. Moberly briefly fell behind Northeastern of Sterling, Colorado, then sprinted to a nine-point lead midway through the period. The Greyhounds maintained margins of eight to 11, continuing to outdistance the Coloradans into the final frame. Three consecutive goals by Shannon Reading lifted Moberly to its largest lead, 53-39.

Then, behind the marksmanship of guard Mike Good, center J.R. Craig, and reserve Joe Hollowell, the Plainsmen shot holes in the Moberly advantage. The Sterling squad tied the game, 68-all, with 28 seconds to go. Moberly played for one, but was unable to get the shot off in time. Like the Conquistadors before them, the Greyhounds were in an unexpected fight for their lives.

Moberly took control early in overtime on a short jumper by Jim Chapman. The tough Greyhound defense closed off easy Northeastern attempts. Two minutes passed before Hollowell fired from 20-feet to pull the Plainsmen even.

A battle of free throws ensued. Moberly's Matthew Aitch — the game's leading scorer with 22, all from the field — collected his fifth foul.

With 1:29 remaining, Craig hit a turn-around hook, nudging the Sterling quintet ahead by one. Good followed shortly thereafter with a 15-footer. At the 15-second mark, Craig stuffed the ball.

The coupe de grace was nullified, however, by an official whistle; Craig was guilty of holding on to the rim. Rodney Jones sank the technical free shot, narrowing the Moberly deficit to three.

Forced to foul, the Greyhounds sent Keith Gentry to the line. The freshman hit two charities, icing the game. Northeastern prevailed, 78-75.

Shell-shocked fans vacated the Sports Arena for the security of home. One day of play and already three favorites were obliterated from the title race.

WEDNESDAY — THE CHILL SETS IN

It was apparent Eastern Utah of Price did not want to fall victim to the developing upset pattern, particularly against a team with a losing record. The Eagles took early control of the day's curtain raiser, opening a 47-27 gulf between them and Arkansas State-Beebe. The Indians helped out by hitting only 10 of 46 shots in the first half.

Harold Scifres, Beebe's leading scorer, reversed the trend after the break, nailing his first four attempts. Then the Indians went on a rampage, reducing the gap to 12 in less than two minutes.

With 10:08 remaining, Albert Brown stole the ball and drove for an easy lay-up, cutting the Price margin to 64-62. The Eagles suddenly found themselves in a battle for self-preservation.

After the men from Beebe took their first lead since the opening moments on a Bill Shaw bucket at the 3:09 mark, the advantage began to teeter-totter. With 1:27 to go, a Don Denson score seesawed Eastern Utah on top. A 30-footer by Ralph Mabry put Arkansas State on top 17 seconds later.

Finally, the basket exchange stopped. Eastern Utah missed and the Beebe Indians engaged their stall.

With 19 seconds remaining, Denson fouled Scifres. The Beebe center was the leading scorer in the game with 27, his 18 second-half points having sparked the Indians' rally. He had swished nine straight free throws.

Scifres' free toss missed, the ball bounding back in his hands. He shot again and missed, the ball trickling out of bounds, Eastern Utah's possession.

---

[1] In the author's many hours of interviews, no other play was more vividly retold than Buford Goddard's goaltending call against Carl Head. Everyone who saw it, remembers it distinctly. Interestingly enough, after 20 years, opinions remain divided, even crossing the bounds of partisanship. Despite the person's viewpoint, all generally agree on two facts: the basket would probably have been no good had Head not touched the ball; and, making such a critical call under the circumstances took "a lot of guts" on the part of Goddard.

The Springfield, Missouri, native later related, "It took an awful lot of people to get us [Goddard and fellow referee Joe L. Shosid] out of the Arena. I was called names I've never been called since. They had to play a complete game before I could get out of my dressing room."

As for whether he still felt the call (technically basket interference) was correct, Goddard replied that he had no doubts, particularly after viewing the game film the following day. "It had to be made."

His courage under adverse conditions proved rewarding. "There were a lot of college coaches there [at the tournament]. I immediately had offers from a couple major colleges when I got home." Goddard admitted that that one call served as his springboard to the Big Eight where he officiated for 12 years.

The Eagles cautiously worked the ball for an opening. With four seconds left, Denson fired from the right at an angle, 15 feet away.

The basket was good.

Eastern Utah dodged Arkansas State-Beebe's bullet, 88-87.

The preceding near upset appeared to have a chilling effect on the final first-round game. Neither Kilgore nor Murray State could find the basket with regularity, both teams managing only 50 percent from the line. Because Kilgore's cold 31 percent from the field topped Murray's ice-bound 22 percent, the Rangers took the halftime lead, 27-22.

When play resumed, Murray State thawed while Kilgore remained cold. The Aggies tied the game at 34-all with 12 minutes to go. The score was knotted again at 36, 38, 40, and 42. Then, back-to-back goals by Ardel England and Junious Simon gave Murray a four-point edge.

Enger the Aggie weave. Scoring lanes opened and fouls accumulated. Both Kilgore's twin towers — first 6-7 George Roderick then 6-8 Donald Kruse — fouled out. In the final seven minutes, Murray State hit both halves of six two-shot or one-and-one situations. The Aggies went 19 for 23 from the line in the second half, handing Kilgore its first defeat in tournament competition, 67-55.

Four favorites lay by the wayside, casualties of one of the most devastating first rounds in tournament history. Fans were in a quandary. Only three veterans remained in the championship bracket and two were surprises. The most eagerly awaited games would happen in the consolation bracket — if they happened at all.

In keeping with the tone of the first round, the Kansas weather pulled a switch. Tuesday was a cloudy, damp, but comfortable 58-degree day. The high Wednesday, 45 degrees, occurred at 2 a.m. Then, the mercury plummeted. Frigid temperatures and winds gusting to 25 m.p.h. held evening attendance to its lowest level of the tournament. Less than 5,000 watched sparkling guard play in the first two quarterfinals.

In the feature, 5-10 Charles Murdaugh topped scoring, hitting 32 and sparking a mid-game rally which gained the Canton Tech Northmen a 44-43 edge over Vincennes 2½ minutes into the second period.

Murdaugh was outnumbered, however. Vincennes guards Larry Cobb and Bob Pritchett tallied 27 and 17, respectively, leading the Trailblazers to a convincing 84-77 victory.

The finale featured a shooting exhibition par excellence. Ferrum blistered Joliet's zone, cashing in on 64 percent of its shots. Leading target practice was freshman John Quinn, a 5-9 guard who repeatedly ignored the drawn-in Joliet perimeter, firing from long range. Each time the basketball swished the net. With each swish, the crowd's reaction grew. By the time Quinn hit his 11th consecutive basket, the volume was deafening. The native New Yorker sank 12 of 15 from the field, leading the Cinderella Panthers to a 49-36 halftime advantage.

At intermission, Joliet's venerable Pop Wills made a change. The Wolves returned to the floor, defending man-to-man. Ferrum hit only 29 percent from the field in the second half. Though he ended up the leading scorer with 37, Quinn cooled to only 5 of 12 from outside. The balanced — all five Joliet starters scored double figures — running Wolves doubled Ferrum's second-half output, winning going away, 94-78.

Fans left the Arena feeling double distress. First, in a year of upsets, the underdog they had most wanted to win, had lost. Second, it was 17 degrees outside, the low for the day.

THURSDAY — QUARTERFINAL CLIFF-HANGERS

With the first-round defeat of so many pre-tourney favorites, 1965 consolation action drew above-average attention. Two of the one-time elite bounced back from adversity — one, with a vengeance.

In the matinee feature, Arkansas State-Beebe fell into an initial 5-0 hole which deepened at an alarming rate. The Indians only scored four points in the first 13 minutes. Meanwhile, Kilgore piled it on. At halftime the score read 46-22 in favor of the Rangers. Kilgore went into overdrive in the final period, hitting the century mark with 4:42 remaining. The Rangers opened the widest gap of the game at the final buzzer, exterminating the Beebe Indians, *112-59*. The 53-point difference was an all-time record for widest margin of victory.

The eagerly awaited Dodge City-Moberly match-up reflected its devalued status as an elimination contest. Both squads struggled early. Reggie Greene's 20-point output was the only luster in Dodge City's lackluster 36-35 first-half lead.

A switch to zone appeared to invigorate the Conquistadors. Dodge City kept the taller Greyhounds off the boards, mounting 11-0 and 14-2 spurts in the final frame. Led by Greene's glittering 34 points, Dodge City eliminated Moberly, 79-64.

Greyhound Coach Cotton Fitzsimmons later remarked, "Dodge City taught me a good lesson, one of the best lessons I ever learned as a young coach: Don't have slow people. That was the biggest team I took [to Hutchinson]. We were big — big and slow. After that I went for quickness and was more successful."

Sandwiched in between the comeback performance of the No. 1 and No. 2 teams was the tightest game of the tournament thus far. The contest between Canton Tech and Ferrum featured 11 ties, the final coming at the end of regulation at 59-all. A free toss by Canton's Willie Shields at the beginning of the overtime threw the game into a leapfrogging race to the wire. John Jenkins hopped last, hitting an easy shot under the basket with 20 seconds to go. Ferrum fired twice and missed. Canton Tech edged the Virginians, 64-63.

With the demotion of the tournament's top teams, local fans had developed an ambivalent "wait and see" attitude toward a "tainted" championship-bracket field. Their indifference vanished after the evening quarterfinals.

Murray State, a team with good height and tremendous leapers, did a lot to loosen the crowd's disposition. In a set pregame warm-up routine starting at midcourt, the Aggies one by one slammed the ball through the basket. The powerful dunking demonstration — which always packed the Aggies' home gym 45 minutes before game time — elicited oohs and aahs from the Arena audience and inspired initial interest in the evening feature. A close contest and an exciting, albeit bizarre, ending held it throughout.

With eight seconds remaining and Eastern Utah leading, 56-52, Murray State's Hal Grant — at 6-9, the tallest player in the tournament — tapped in a missed shot. On the succeeding inbounds pass, the ball hit a player's leg. Grant picked up the loose ball and laid it in, sending the game into overtime.

The extra period was cautiously played. Then, when Murray State grabbed a 58-57 edge on a Grant bucket — the reserve's third consecutive tally and his total output of the game — Aggie Coach Gene Robbins' became actively involved in the proceedings.

"I guess I was acrobatic on the sides," Robbins later related. "My actions on the sidelines were not intentional. I would go into a ballgame and say to myself, 'I'm going to sit here calmly tonight and cross my legs just like other coaches do.' I could do that — until they tossed the ball up."

When Murray State retrieved an Eastern Utah miss, Robbins high-jumped out of his chair, signaling for time out. Distracted, the Aggie with the ball stopped and looked toward the bench. The Eagle's Vince Colbert stripped the ball, dribbled once, and scored. A subsequent free shot by Dan Jordan saved the embarrassed Aggies, necessitating another five minutes of play.

Eastern Utah's Don Denson and Aggie Alvie Nelson traded baskets in the first 30 seconds of the second overtime. Then Nelson and Eagle Norman Hayden matched 20-footers. With 1:37 to go, Coach Robbins called for time — this time without incident. He ordered the Aggie weave.

The clock wound down. With 11 seconds showing, Nelson fired and missed. In the traffic jam under the basket, Ardel England was fouled. The 6-7 Aggie center missed two free throws. The men from Price took possession with nine seconds remaining.

The Eagles raced upcourt. Firing from eight feet away on the baseline, Denson connected with the winner, his second in as many games. Eastern Utah squeaked by, 65-63.

Rapidly beating hearts received no rest in the finale. As they had in their opening-round upset of Moberly, the Plainsmen from Sterling, Colorado, mounted a second-period rally, sparked by J.R. Craig and Bob Smith, tying Burlington, 59-all, with six minutes to go.

Seven lead changes followed.

With 59 seconds remaining, Smith hit a 10-footer, giving the Sterling five a 71-70 edge.

On Burlington's possession, the Blackhawks worked the ball to Sam Williams, the game's leading scorer with 26, 22 from the field. Williams shot and missed, grabbed the rebound, shot, and missed again. Northeastern took control of the ball with 38 seconds on the clock and called time.

In the huddle in front of the Northeastern bench, Coach Roy Edwards reminded his charges that all they had to do was hold the ball to win. It was agreed that no one was to take a shot, no matter how certain its success.

The Plainsmen returned to the floor and purposefully played keep-away. Then, with 27 seconds showing, Keith Gentry found himself with the ball and an open line to the goal. The freshman — who had coolly iced the victory against Moberly with two clutch free throws — forgot the situation. He shot instead of passed.

Burlington hauled down the rebound.

Again the Blackhawks went to their top gun, Williams. With 15 seconds remaining, the freshman forward was fouled in the act of shooting. Burlington Coach Lloyd Haberichter nervously shredded adhesive tape — a longtime game habit — as his ace stepped to the line.

Williams hit the first, tying the score.

The second bounded away, into the hands of Blackhawk center Roger Blalock. The 6-6 Chicago native, a second-stringer all season, threw in his second straight game-winner — this time without official aid. A desperation heave by Northeastern's Mike Good with four seconds remaining fell short. Burlington survived the bell again, 73-71.

FRIDAY — BREAKING WITH TRADITION

Thursday night's quarterfinal cliff-hangers revived fan enthusiasm toward the championship bracket. General interest in lower bracket play was limited to the afternoon match-up between Dodge City and Kilgore, the No. 1 and No. 2 teams in the country.

The game was not a champion struggle as might have occurred in the upper bracket. Both squads exhibited the disappointment of their lowered stature. Play was ragged with 53 fouls called. Despite the large number of personals, only one man fouled out. Donald Kruse sat down with nearly four minutes to play, having topped Kilgore in scoring with 24 points, including 14 of 15 from the line, and having spearheaded Ranger control of the boards.

It was not enough to win, however. Kilgore could not contain Dodge City's backcourt wizard Reggie Greene who nailed 23. And, though he helped win the rebound war, Kruse lost the battle at the post. Carl Head took game honors with 29 and wowed the crowd, blocking seven of Kruse's shots, while giving away four inches to the Ranger center. Dodge City advanced to the consolation championship, 88-76.

Attention was now fully directed toward the title contenders. Fans had adjusted to the early surprises and eagerly anticipated the evening's action, packing the Sports Arena. But, in keeping with the 1965 tournament's unpredictable nature, the tempo shifted. In the past, the semifinals had been sure bets for excitement, often the best games of the meet. Friday night's semifinals broke with tradition.

Though the opener offered a fast pace, no one chewed their nails while awaiting the final outcome. Joliet fired 101 shots, hitting 36 percent of them. Vincennes, meanwhile, launched 25 fewer attempts, but made them count at a 60 percent clip. The Trailblazers raced to a 52-44 halftime advantage, survived an early second-half Joliet rush, then coasted. A violent stuff by Nat Shields near the end punctuated Vincennes' easy 101-87 triumph.

There were two heroes for the Indianans. Freshman guard Bob Pritchett was the more visible star, firing a game-high 34 points, mostly from crowd-pleasing distances outside.

His less visible running mate was equally important to the win, however. Though his 17 points (all but one from the field) were alone a respectable contribution, Larry Cobb's primary input to the Vincennes victory was the silencing of Willie Boyce, Joliet's top scorer, who was held to 13, half his game average.

Blessed with the best backcourt tandem in the tournament, Vincennes appeared to have the inside track to the crown.

The other semifinal featured a pair of survivors; Burlington and Eastern Utah each owned two last-second victories. Accordingly, the nightcap was expected to be another nail biter.

However, two doses of nerve-racking tension was evidently too much to bear. Though the contest was closer than its predecessor, it lacked the intensity of the duo's earlier heart-stoppers. A six-point spurt — two outside goals by Virgil Watkins and a steal and score by Sam Williams — in the final minute of the first half proved the eventual difference. Burlington joined Vincennes in the title match, winning 93-87.

SATURDAY — A FIRST

Trophy day opened with a listless contest. After drawing 36-all at halftime, Dodge City and Howard County scored only 10 points apiece in 10 minutes. Dodge City came alive long enough for a two-minute, nine-point spurt, giving the Conquistadors a 69-60 victory.

There was little joy in the locker room after the win, however. A plot to throw team manager Dwight Negley into the showers was never executed. As one Conquistador told the *Dodge City Daily Globe*, "Why do it after finishing fifth."

Disappointment mingled with melancholy. A majority of the squad had been together for two years, had worked hard compiling brilliant back-to-back 29-2 seasons, had shared the heady experience of winning a national title. Everyone regretted having to part. Even Coach Chuck Brehm was leaving. After five years at Dodge City, a peerless record of 111-29, Brehm was slated for the head coaching position at Fort Hays State. He reflected the downcast feelings of his team, stating, "I'm sad to be leaving this fine bunch of men."

A silent chill pervaded the fourth-place game. At one point in the first half, the clock froze on time out. It went unnoticed for half a minute before action was halted to reset it. The squads from Sterling, Colorado, and Canton, New York, too, experienced cold spells. Canton's was more extensive, however. Northeastern built a 20-point second-period lead and coasted to a 77-67 victory. Canton Tech's only bright spot was the game-high, 23-point performance of Charles Murdaugh which netted him tournament scoring honors with 105.

Considering that Pop Wills' running Joliet Wolves were involved, it was inevitable the pace would pick up in the evening opener. Eastern Utah was equal to the task. Though both teams enjoyed comfortable leads in the wide-open sprint match, Eastern's kick lasted longer. The Eagles broke the tape, 106-100, grabbing third.

The 47 points by Eastern Utah's Ron Cunningham (No. 40) in the third-place game was one of the top-10 scoring performances in tourney history. Cunningham later played at the University of Utah. (Photo courtesy the **Hutchinson News**)

The star of the game was Eastern center Ron Cunningham. Noted more for his rebounding — he set a school record with 27 rebounds in a regional contest — than for his marksmanship, the 6-6 freshman from Washington, D.C., was on target all night, scoring 26 in the first half and 21 in the second. It was the top single-game performance of the tournament. Ironically, the total was only one less than Cunningham's combined output in three previous outings.

The finalists were not only surprises to local tourney followers, but to their own fans as well.

In its first session of 1806, the Indiana Territorial Legislature passed an act incorporating the first collegiate-level institution in the Indiana Territory, "to be called and known by the name and style of 'The Vincennes University'."

Though it had a long and proud tradition, Vincennes had yet to make an impact nationally in basketball. Coach Allen Bradfield had come close with his 1955-56 and 1956-57 squads which posted identical 26-3 records and were considered two of the best teams ever fielded by the Trailblazers. But, in 1956, Vincennes lost to No. 4-ranked and eventual Region 12 representative Wright of Chicago, 81-76, in the semifinals and, the following year, was upset by Pop Wills' Joliet Wolves, 92-88, in the final.

Since the Vincennes *Sun-Commercial* had never covered the event, the Trailblazers entered the nationals not knowing what to expect. Radio station WAOV sent Bill Kepler and Gus Stevens to broadcast the games — the first time the station had aired away contests in a decade.

When Trailblazer Larry Cobb saw the two announcers outside Convention Hall prior to Monday night's welcome dinner for the teams, he ran up to them and said, "Boy! Are you guys going to be here for the whole tourney?"

Stevens replied, "No, Larry. Soon as you lose two we have to go back."

Though the Blackhawks were tourney veterans, Burlington fans held equally bleak expectations. From prior experience, they knew there was nothing auspicious about facing the defending national champs in the opening round with an all-freshman squad and without their 6-9 starting center. Consequently, only the most devoted made the approximately 450-mile trip from the banks of the Mississippi River just to see a massacre.

Circumstances changed, however. With each victory, Vincennes fans were treated to increased newspaper coverage. Sportswriter John Bedford painted glowing pictures of the enthusiasm of the record crowds, the red-carpet treatment by Hutchonians, and the beautiful playing facilities in the Sports Arena. Though only seven carloads of Trailblazer supporters made the trip to Hutchinson, radio broadcasts and newspaper stories generated building excitement back home.

Victory had a more profound effect on Burlington fans. After the upset of Dodge City, Blackhawk supporters descended on Hutchinson in droves — only to find there was no room at the inn. Hotels and motels were packed with tourney visitors and participants in the Southwest Bowling Tournament which was in its fifth and final weekend of play. Caught in the overflow, Burlington students and townspeople camped out in the lobby and meeting rooms of the Baker Hotel. The Leon Hotel provided dormitory accommodations for 40 in sample rooms. Sleeping arrangements were so stretched that five avid, but unprepared, fans asked the Hutchinson Police Station if they could spend the night in jail. The duty officer turned them away, but not before contacting Burlington team host Don Miller. After a few early-morning phone calls, Miller, a local podiatrist, secured room for them in the old cabin cottages of the Elwood Motel, the property of one of his regular patients.

Blackhawk loyalty was in full voice during the championship contest and a good portion of the local crowd joined in, sentimentally favoring the Iowans. One reason for the support was that it was to be Coach Lloyd "Hobbie" Haberichter's final game. The LaPorte City, Iowa, native was retiring after 35 years of coaching, 20 at Burlington. Another reason was the team's unexpected success. In a tournament filled with surprises, the Blackhawks were the biggest surprise of all. Besides, there was something endearing about a team whose center, thrust to the forefront after riding the bench most of the year, scored the

winning basket in two games while wearing distinctive black high-topped shoes he had worn for two years.

Burlington enthusiasm was slapped down immediately, however. After gaining the tip, Vincennes quickly moved the ball upcourt to Nat Shields who promptly canned a 20-footer from the wing. The Blackhawks rebounded to a 3-2 advantage, then stumbled. Vincennes opened a 18-9 gap, threatening to run away with the crown.

After a time out, the Burlington five settled down. Nine consecutive points by Sam Williams pulled the Blackhawks within two, 22-20.

Dan Sparks ignited a Vincennes counter rally. Using his gangly long arms to good advantage, the 6-7 center scooped up rebounds and potted occasional looping right-hand hooks off the glass. Playing his best basketball of the tournament, the freshman netted 15, leading the Trailblazers to a 37-31 halftime edge.

Vincennes center Dan Sparks (No. 50) was plagued with nagging injuries throughout the 1965 tournament. After returning to his hometown in Bloomington, Indiana, "I went to my doctor," recalled Sparks, "and had my foot x-rayed. I had broken my arch." Sparks ended his collegiate days at Weber State, spent time in the professional ranks as a player and assistant coach, then returned to Vincennes, first as an assistant then as head coach. (Photo courtesy of the **Hutchinson News***)*

In the next five minutes, Burlington cut the margin to two. Enter Nat Shields. Though the sophomore forward had averaged just under 20 points in his first three outings, his output had been overshadowed by the spectacular play of the Vincennes guards. He possessed a hair-trigger release and needed only an inch of daylight to fire. In the second half Shields received all the time he needed, repeatedly finding himself open around the key. His on-target goals off the heal of the rim boosted the Trailblazers to five-point margins three times, 54-49, 56-51, and 60-55.

With 8:51 to go John Olsen, a defensive standout for Vincennes, fouled out. Burlington drew even 62-all on a 15-footer by Milan Vorkapich. Another Vorkapich field goal ended the torment of Blackhawk fans.

The relief was brief. Sparks and Shields combined for the next eight points. Then, Larry Cobb drove the middle. His shot was batted out of bounds by center Roger Blalock — goaltending. Vincennes was comfortably in front, 72-64.

Burlington made one more charge. A three-point play by Williams — giving him game honors with 30 — pulled the Blackhawks within a lone digit, 75-74, with 2:05 to go. It was their last hurrah.

Cobb ended a dazzling keep-away dribbling exhibition with an easy lay-up. Forced to foul, Burlington sent the Trailblazers to the line three times for two-shot intentionals. Though the Indianans hit only half of them, it was enough to ice victory.

With an 80-76 win, Vincennes University became the first school east of the Mississippi to sit atop the NJCAA basketball throne.

Of the three Vincennes players most felt deserved to be named MVP, the award went to the flashiest, Bob Pritchett, who led the Trailblazers with 89 points. Pritchett finished his collegiate career at Old Dominion. (Photo courtesy of Gus Stevens, Vincennes University)

The 1965 Vincennes Trailblazers, the first NJCAA champs from east of the Mississippi: back row left to right) — Fred Kuestler, John Olsen, Dan Sparks, Jim Housel, Steve Snider, and Bill Simmons; front row — Manager Fritz Levenhagen, Randy Weber, Larry Cobb, Nat Shields, Bob Pritchett, and Coach Allen Bradfield. (Photo courtesy of Gus Stevens, Vincennes University)

THE AFTERMATH — SPAWNING TRADITION

As soon as the awards ceremonies ended at about 11:15, the Burlington Blackhawks were whisked to the Santa Fe station to catch the 12:05 Grand Canyon Limited. While waiting to board, the sting of bitter cold (temperature in the teens) hammered home the sting of defeat. Blackhawks hero Roger Blalock stood in the shadows, fighting uncontrollable tears.

In contrast, the victors reaped the spoils. Bob Pritchett was voted the tournament's MVP over Larry Cobb, his less flashy running-mate at guard, and Nat Shields, the Trailblazers' reliable gunner. All three were equally deserving of the honor, having ranked among the tourney's top 12 scorers.

Coach Allen Bradfield — a graduate of Vincennes who never played basketball, yet compiled a respectable 245-98 (.714) record in 13 years as a head mentor — received the accolades of his players, riding their shoulders after the final buzzer, and the nod of the tournament selection committee, picking up the Coach of the Year award.

The 700-mile car trip back home — starting at 6 a.m. the next morning — went swiftly. The jubilant Trailblazers sang all the way. At Olney, Illinois, 32 miles west of Vincennes the team was joined by a caravan of cars. In the city, the players were transferred to a fire engine for an impromptu parade through downtown, several thousand welcoming them along the route. The celebration ended at Belees Gym on the university campus.

When called upon to summarize his feelings, Coach Bradfeld told the gathering, "We are tired; we have had a long trip. Before you leave I want each and every one of you to walk slowly around the trophy [points to huge trophy] and read what it says, but don't get too close [laughter]. It says 'National Junior College champions of the United States, Vincennes University'." With that he tossed one of the souvenir nets from the Sports Arena into the air. The crowd went wild.

It was a scene that had played many times before in different locales — the kind of scene which sewed the seeds of destiny.

How They Finished in 1965

1. Vincennes University
2. Burlington Community College
3. College of Eastern Utah
4. Northeastern Junior College
5. Dodge City College
6. Joliet Junior College
7. SUNY Agricultural and Technical Institute at Canton
8. Howard County Junior College

Tournament Results

		Game	
Tuesday:	Game	1	Canton Tech — 82 Robert Morris — 71
		2	Vincennes — 82 Manatee — 64
		3	Joliet — 87 Howard County — 76
		4	Ferrum — 79 Willmar — 59
		5	Burlington — 85 Dodge City — 83
		6	Northeastern — 78 Moberly — 75 OT
Wednesday:	Game	7	Eastern Utah — 88 Arkansas St-Beebe — 87
		8	Murray St. — 67 Kilgore — 55
		9	Robert Morris — 86 Manatee — 71
		10	Vincennes — 84 Canton Tech — 77
		11	Joliet — 94 Ferrum — 78
Thursday:	Game	12	Howard County — 73 Willmar — 64
		13	Kilgore — 112 Arkansas St-Beebe — 59
		14	Canton Tech — 64 Ferrum — 63 OT
		15	Dodge City — 79 Moberly — 64
		16	Eastern Utah — 65 Murray State — 63 2OT
		17	Burlington — 73 Northeastern — 71
Friday:	Game	18	Howard County — 94 Robert Morris — 80
		19	Dodge City — 88 Kilgore — 76
		20	Northeastern — 62 Murray St. — 58
		21	Vincennes — 101 Joliet — 87
		22	Burlington — 93 Eastern Utah — 87
Saturday:	Game	23	Dodge City — 69 Howard County — 60
		24	Northeastern — 77 Canton Tech — 67
		25	Eastern Utah — 106 Joliet — 100
		26	Vincennes — 80 Burlington — 76

All Tournament Team

Ron Cunningham — College of Eastern Utah
Carl Head — Dodge City College
Donald Kruse — Kilgore College
Thomas Moran — Joliet Junior College
Charles Murdaugh — SUNY Agricultural and Technical Institute at Canton
Bob Pritchett — Vincennes University
John Quinn — Ferrum Junior College
Bob Smith — Northeastern Junior College
Ben Urso — Robert Morris Junior College
Samuel Williams — Burlington Community College

Coach of the Year

Allen L. Bradfield — Vincennes University

Player of the Year

Bob Pritchett — Vincennes University

1966:

NUMBER THREE

Later an All-Big 10 performer and Player of the Year at the University of Iowa and a two-year pro with the Milwaukee Bucks, Burlington's Sam Williams (No. 40) led all scorers in the 1966 tournament with 149 points, fourth-highest in tourney history. His two-year total of 245 ranked him third all-time. Williams was also the first recipient of the Sesher Sportsmanship Award. (Photo courtesy of Dick Shadley)

Region	Team
1	Dixie Junior College — St. George, Utah
2	Cameron State Agricultural College — Lawton, Oklahoma
3	Leicester Junior College — Leicester, Massachusetts
4	Chicago City Junior College, Wilson Branch — Chicago, Illinois
5	Dallas Baptist College — Dallas, Texas
6	Hutchinson Community Junior College — Hutchinson, Kansas
7	Cumberland College of Tennessee — Lebanon, Tennessee
8	Chipola Junior College — Marianna, Florida
9	Casper College — Casper, Wyoming
10	Ferrum Junior College — Ferrum, Virginia
11	Burlington Community College — Burlington, Iowa
12	Alpena Community College — Alpena, Michigan
13	North Dakota State School of Science — Wahpeton, North Dakota
14	Tyler Junior College — Tyler, Texas
15	Wesley College — Dover, Delaware
16	Moberly Junior College — Moberly, Missouri

n April of 1965, Burlington Community Colle replaced retiring coach Lloyd Harberichter with Edward L. Sp. ling.

Sparling was a colorful, sometimes audacious figure who h started his coaching career in an orphanage. His most rece position had been at St. Leo College in St. Leo, Florida. In fo years the institution progressed from a prep school, to a juni college, to its current four-year level. Sparling handled the tra sition with aplomb, developing a basketball team good enou; to be ranked No. 3 in the final NJCAA poll of 1963. He broug the same abundant energy to the Burlington Blackhawks.

At the time, Iowa junior colleges were not allowed to off basketball scholarships. To acquire funds for the team, Sparli organized his players into window-washing crews who offere their services all over Burlington at a dollar a window. In add tion, he and local supporter Dick Shadley buttonholed dow town businessmen. In three Saturday forays, Sparling and Sha ley raised more than enough to cover the year's expenses. Tl effort cemented an already excellent relationship between tl school and the community and founded one of the stronge junior college booster clubs in the country.

In order to ensure "that at least once or twice a week they h. a good meal," Sparling invited two squad members a day to l house for supper. The relationship between the team and i new coach grew close.

By tournament time, players and fans alike had forgotten pa disappointment. Ed Sparling's Burlington Blackhawks we 21-2 — the top-rated team in the country.

THE PARTICIPANTS

Burlington's climb to the top of the NJCAA poll was not une pected. Though Ed Sparling was a talented motivator, he w. also blessed with an inheritance of four returning starter Heading the corps of veterans was Sam Williams — an A Tournament selection and honorable mention All-Americ: from the previous year and owner of the seventh-best scorir average in the country (29.3). With the addition of freshm: Steve Shumaker, a horse in the middle, Burlington was an intim idating force. The Blackhawk starting lineup measured 6-4, 6- 6-4, 6-7, 6-7. Pre-tourney hype tagged the Iowan squad as th consensus favorite.

Burlington's opposition was equally impressive, howeve Most threatening were three other top-five teams, all vetera: of previous tourney wars: No. 3 Cameron State Agricultural Co lege (24-3), winner of a power-laden Oklahoma region; No. Wilson of Chicago (24-0), possessor of the second most pote: offense in the country (107 points per game) and the only und feated team in the meet; and No. 5 Moberly Junior Colleg (25-5), the most veteran member of the 16-team field with 1 previous appearances and seven players from its 1965 tourne squad.

Two ranked newcomers also appeared strong contender No. 10 Dallas Baptist College (23-3) and No. 15 Wesley Colleg (23-1). Dallas Baptist's solid record was compiled against st: competition and included wins over Cameron State and No. Murray State Agricultural College. Wesley, the first Delawa: representative to the tournament, boasted the top offense the nation (109.2 per-game average) and no losses to a junic college foe.

Even the unrated posed concern. Veterans Ferrum Junior College (27-4), Leicester Junior College (21-5), Casper College (23-7), Tyler Junior College (26-9), and Chipola Junior College (21-8) and newcomers Alpena Community College (22-3) and Dixie Junior College (21-4) were all due serious consideration. Ferrum, Casper, and Alpena deserved particular watching: Ferrum returned four starters from its 1965 tourney team; Casper upset No. 2 Lamar Junior College in regional play; and Alpena dethroned Vincennes University, the defending national champs.

Only three teams were regarded as long shots: Cumberland College of Tennessee (17-9), a tourney newcomer from a usually unimpressive region; North Dakota State School of Science at Wahpeton (8-17), a third-time participant with no previous wins in national competition; and hometown Hutchinson Community Junior College (19-6), a starless wonder reminiscent of Hutchinson's 1949 Cinderella team.

Having learned from the previous year's experience, Burlington fans planned ahead, many arriving in Hutchinson early. Though confident in their team's ability, the Iowa contingent was wary. To cover all bases, they brought with them Father James Quinlan, pastor of St. Paul's Catholic Church in Burlington. The longtime Blackhawk booster provided each team member a shamrock shipped directly from Ireland by his brother and sister. The good luck tokens were considered necessary equipment, hedges against an initial bit of Blackhawk misfortune. By luck of the draw, Burlington's first opponent was the second-highest rated team in the competition — No. 3 Cameron State.

TUESDAY — SEA OF RED

The 19th edition of the NJCAA Basketball Tournament opened to great weather. Fans arrived at the Sports Arena in springtime conditions, the temperature in the 60s. The bountiful sunshine prompted Burlington's Ed Sparling to throw a curve at tourney officials — he requested convertibles for his team.

It was not the first brash act for the Blackhawk mentor. On Monday, a traditional practice day designed to allow the teams to familiarize themselves with the Arena floor and the fans to familiarize themselves with the teams, Sparling shooed spectators from the sidelines. It was the first closed practice session in the tournament's history.

Later, Arnold Lewis and his undefeated Wilson Raiders followed suit. When the No. 4-rated Chicago squad took to the court to kick off the event, they were a mystery team to fans.

Not so to their opponents. In the first five minutes, Dallas Baptist opened a surprising 17-2 lead.

Wilson switched to a zone press. Sparked by five baskets by Nat Mason, the Raiders rallied, tying the game, 46-all, at halftime.

The Chicagoans took an early three-point advantage in the second period.

Dallas Baptist solved the press, reeling off 11 unanswered points.

Wilson's Sylvester Coleman scored three buckets in a spurt which pulled the Raiders to within one with 8:30 to go.

Then David Nash's domination of the middle and the defense of Wendel Hart and John McCormick proved too much for the Chicagoans. Dallas Baptist spread the difference to 10 points. With all five starters in double figures, including Hart's game-high 31, Dallas Baptist eased to a 91-83 upset victory.

The tournament was again off to a rousing start.

The large Wahpeton, North Dakota, delegation — which included a 30-piece band — hoped their team could duplicate Dallas Baptist's feat. They knew that the losing record of the underdog Wildcats was deceiving; during the season, North Dakota State School of Science competed in the North Dakota College Athletic Conference which was composed entirely of four-year rivals.

Early action encouraged Wildcat supporters. The Wahpeton crew played even with Leicester through the first half, then opened a 50-45 gap with 17 minutes to go.

Then the Wildcats lost their grip on the game. The cold North Dakotans (35 percent from the field) could not keep pace with the Minutemen from Massachusetts. Led by Tony Koski, who fired in a game-high 30, including 13 of 19 from the field, Leicester came from behind, opened a 13-point advantage, and eventually won, 81-73.

The early going also looked promising for the underdog in the afternoon finale. Veteran Moberly played like a stage-frightened newcomer, missing its first eight shots from the field, while first-time participant Alpena executed with confidence. The Lumberjacks from Michigan tied the game six times and led by three before Moberly gained composure. The Greyhounds took a 23-21 lead with 6:47 left, extending it to six by intermission.

Led by Tom Richardson, who scored a game-high 24 and nabbed 16 rebounds, Alpena remained close. Then an 11-point Moberly spurt with five minutes remaining decided matters. The Greyhounds slowed things down and coasted to a 78-69 win.

The most exciting game of the day opened the evening session. The Casper Thunderbirds flew to a quick 10-1 advantage, putting Tyler — the second most successful school in tourney history — in the unfamiliar position of playing catch-up. The Apaches caught Casper twice at 10- and 21-all, but did not gain the lead until the 2:33 mark on Harry Bostic's corner jumper. Casper immediately responded, gaining a 39-36 margin at halftime.

The second period was more of the same. Casper repeatedly took go-ahead steps, forcing the Apaches to catch up. With 2:15 to go, Tyler's Vernon Lewis — the son of University of Houston head coach Guy Lewis — stole the ball and scored, tying the game. Another steal by Lewis and a free throw by Terry Stillabower gave the Apaches their first lead of the half, 72-71. Forty-eight seconds remained.

Casper worked the ball to its leading scorer, Ralph Brisker who fired twice and missed. In the scramble for the loose ball, Brisker fouled the ubiquitous Lewis. With nine seconds showing, the Tyler guard potted the first free shot, missed the second. The Apaches grabbed the rebound, however, and the 73-71 win.

Anticipating a "king size" rush for 1,350 unreserved seats, tournament officials earlier announced that tickets for the evening session would go on sale as soon as the afternoon crowd cleared the Arena. The rush never materialized. Fearing a long fruitless wait in line, hundreds of potential ticket buyers stayed home. Midway through the Casper-Tyler contest, play-by-play broadcasters announced that 300 seats were still unsold. The remaining tickets were gobbled up within the hour. By start of the feature, all 8,042 seats were occupied by red-coated, red-sweatered, red-shirted, red-dressed fans. The largest opening night audience yet had turned out to cheer on the local Blue Dragons.[1]

The current Hutchinson squad was not one of its best. There were no super stars. Mike Jones, the Blue Dragons' leading scorer (15.3), ranked only 15th in the Western Kansas Juco Conference. The team's popularity derived from the fact most of the players were products of the area. Two members were graduates of Hutchinson High. Starting forward Gene Gipson — oddly enough, a native of Tyler, Texas — was the only player hailing from out of state.

Another reason for fan fervor was the rumored departure of Coach Sam Butterfield, who was expected to become Hutchinson's athletic director, replacing retiring Charley Sesher. The previous year, the Blue Dragons had managed a mediocre 13-12 record, the worst in Butterfield's nine-year tenure. The hometown wished a better farewell for the fiery mentor.

---

[1] The "Blue" Dragon fan custom of dressing in red was not as anomalous as it sounded. Hutchinson's colors were blue *and red*. The tradition started soon after Sam Butterfield became head coach when the Blue Dragons made a Christmas swing through Texas. According to former assistant coach Bill Goldsmith, "We had lost a game or two down there and were down in the mouth. We were playing Amarillo on a Saturday night and we [Butterfield and Goldsmith] were downtown Saturday morning just kind of loafing around with Tom Hedrick, who was broadcasting the games and was also the president of the Quarterback Club. We walked by this men's store which had these real red blazers hanging in the window. Sam said, 'Maybe we ought to go buy some of those and wear 'em. They might change our luck.' Hedrick said, 'If you guys will wear them, the Quarterback Club will just buy them for you.' We walked in and, sure enough, they had sizes to fit us both. We got them, wore them that night and won, came back home, and wore them at every ballgame. And then *everybody* started wearing red."

Against the high-powered Wesley Wolverines, Hutchinson prospects were not auspicious. The Blue Dragon offensive average was nearly 30 points below that of the Dover squad.

Hutchinson turned the tables on the Wolverines, however, sprinting to a 49-34 halftime edge.

Wesley initiated a full-court press and quickly trimmed the Blue Dragon lead by eight.

Then, center Larry Berry and reserve guard John Markle — who hit five straight from the 10-15 foot range — sparked a Hutchinson spurt which opened a 25-point gap. The Blue Dragons shot 51.2 percent from the field and dominated the boards, smashing the top offense in the nation, 102-78. It was the first 100-point game of the year for Hutchinson.

Though the winner of the evening's finale would be the next Blue Dragon opponent, few remained to watch. Joyous local supporters exited the Arena, leaving the previous year's sentimental favorite to struggle alone. In spite of John Quinn's game-high 29, Ferrum was surprised by a poised Cumberland crew, 83-69.

WEDNESDAY — TRIALS AND TRIBULATIONS OF THE FAN

Burlington fan hunger for a crown was second only to Hutchinson's. Like the Blue Dragons, the Blackhawks had come close enough to taste the title without the privilege of savoring it. Burlington boosters, feeling 1966 was their year, made reservations at the Baker Hotel as early as September. One hundred and seventy five students signed up for a three-car train special to arrive in time for the semifinals, further augmenting an already large delegation from the banks of the Mississippi. Supporters even paid for a full-page ad in the *Hutchinson News* to run Saturday before the championship.

All their plans and dreams were immediately placed in jeopardy. Cameron State opened a quick five-point margin and lost the lead only three times during the first period of the day's curtain raiser. Burlington's biggest lead was 32-28 with approximately eight minutes remaining in the half.

Matters worsened after intermission when Cameron outscored the Iowans, 14-6, to take a commanding 58-44 lead. Then the Aggies slowed the pace.

Behind Roger Blalock and Sam Williams, the heart of the Iowa squad, Burlington rallied, pulling to within four with nine minutes to go.

Cameron scored the next seven points.

Williams tried to ignite another Blackhawk surge with a field goal.

The Aggies responded with seven more unanswered points.

At the two-minute mark, the hopes of Burlington fans were shattered. Cameron State led, 84-68. With a convincing 85-76 victory, the Aggies usurped the role of tourney favorite.

Like Burlington, the Chipola Indians also had faithful support — Mr. and Mrs. Charlie Bales. The year before, Bales, holder of the controlling interest in the Foundation Life Insurance Company of Atlanta, built the team a $75,000 dormitory, complete with swimming pool. When Chipola won the regional, he chartered a 47-seat commercial plane to fly the squad and its cheerleaders to Hutchinson.

With the Bales and five Indian maiden cheerleaders providing the sole support for the Florida squad, Chipola rallied from six down to tie the final first-round game 70-all with 4:13 remaining. Bob Trammell had an opportunity to put the Indians on top, but missed two free throws. He quickly redeemed himself, stealing the ball and scoring with 56 seconds to go.

Dixie's Wayne Nelson retaliated with a jumper at the 23-second mark.

The two Indian angels in the stands held their breath. With three ticks left, 6-3 guard Harry Dunn launched a 20-footer.

It was good. Chipola advanced to the championship bracket, 74-72.

Since the hometown Blue Dragons had the night off, the evening's quarterfinals played to a significantly reduced audience.

There was little to enthuse in the opener. Dallas Baptist opened a 13-point gap over Leicester with four minutes left in a dull first half. A brief Minuteman spurt lowered the difference to nine at intermission.

Then the pace picked up. Behind the shooting of Ken Burns and reserve John Bancroft, who hit five of six from the field, Leicester pulled to within one, 70-69, with 7:57 to go.

Dallas extended the lead to six.

Burns and Bancroft fired away again. A pair of free throws by Burns with 1:17 remaining brought the Minutemen again within one.

Inside the minute mark, the teams scrambled for control of the ball. Burns grabbed possession and scored, sending Leicester to the lead, 85-84, with 44 seconds on the clock.

With the seconds dwindling to single digits, Dallas Baptist's Wendel Hart drove for a lay-up. Burns prevented a sure two with his fifth foul. The Minuteman star departed with a game-high 27 points, leaving Dallas with its leading scorer at the line.

Hart missed both charities.

The battle for the final miss was tied up. Dallas called time. Coach Dennis Walling and his Indian band discussed a seemingly impossible situation; to have a chance, 6-0 Hart had to outjump Leicester's 6-8 Tony Koski.

Unbelievably, the Dallas guard got the tip. The ball bounced for the corner. Indian reserve Gale Rhine snatched it and frantically launched a 30-footer. The shot cleared the net just ahead of the buzzer.

The small contingent of Dallas Baptist supporters stormed the court. Suddenly, 19-year-old Linda Barnum, an Indian cheerleader, collapsed. A fire department resuscitator revived her two minutes later. A severe asthmatic, Barnum had suffered an attack induced by the heat of the Arena and the excitement of the last-second thriller.

There was no health threatening tension in the evening finale. The battle between the only two former champs in the 16-team field and the two most frequent and successful tourney participants was a major disappointment. Moberly's Tom Johnson skied for the opening tip and nine seconds later Tom Thoenen scored. Tyler was never closer. The eight-man Apache crew — Coach Floyd Wagstaff had kicked two key starters off the team after the regionals for breaking training — was no match for the Greyhounds' checking man-to-man defense and superior board strength. Led by Johnson's 23 points and 21 rebounds, Moberly opened a 43-27 halftime gap and breezed to a 79-64 victory.

THURSDAY — A RED ST. PATRICK'S DAY

Blustery 10-25 mile-per-hour winds tarnished the tournament's otherwise beautiful 70-degree weather, but had no effect on the Burlington Blackhawks. Showing none of the disappointment normal to first-round losers, the Iowans regained their top-rated form, blowing by Dixie, 97-79.[2]

The following contest was one of the best of the tournament. In the first period Leicester held the advantage seven times, Tyler six. After the Apaches took a 52-47 halftime edge, the largest lead by either team in the game, the two teams returned to "horse trading." With 1:40 remaining, the score was tied 78-all. Each team took three shots from the field and Tyler an extra try from the line, but neither could crack the tie.

Both played tentatively in overtime. The result: an 84-all deadlock.

Again, the two carefully measured each other. After the second overtime, the score was still even, 90-all.

Finally, frustrated with the nerve-racking close calls, Coach Floyd Wagstaff abandoned his cautious strategy, telling his charges, "Dang! Let's get out there and play. If you get a shot, put it up. Relax and let's get them." In the third five-minute extra period, Tyler exploded for 25 points, downing Leicester, 115-100. It was the second most points scored by two teams in a tourney game.

---

[2] According to Ed Sparling, whenever his 1965-66 team lost, "it was always a shock to them. They were such good kids and so close. Most of the time they would feel *me* let them down." After the heartbreaking defeat in the tourney opener, Sparling's first job "was to make them understand that the sun's going to come up in the morning and life's going to go on." He found that he had inadvertently contributed to their depression. During the year, Sparling intercepted scholarship offers from four-year schools so that his players could concentrate on the season. "I had two wastepaper baskets full of offers for them." After the loss to Cameron State, one squad member dejectedly told Sparling, "Gee, coach now we'll never get any scholarships." The team had assumed no one was interested and played with the additional pressure without telling Sparling.

The parade of high scores continued in the evening opener s Wesley's free-wheeling offense got back on track, breaking pen a close game midway through the final frame. The Wolerines eliminated Ferrum, 99-84.

The opening few minutes of the evening feature were tense, ne lead seesawing as Cameron State's Bill Bullock and hipola's Harry Dunn traded baskets. Chipola's biggest lead as 21-18 with 10:43 to go. Cameron's largest was seven short-y before intermission. Two baskets by Joe Sova pulled the Indis within three at the break.

Chipola continued within reach for the next 13 minutes. hen, Frank Judge got hot. The Aggie southpaw fired in 11 to ne wire for a game-high total of 29. Cameron used just five layers to defeat Chipola, 83-69, further solidifying its role as he team to beat.

A huge St. Patrick's Day crowd settled in for the remaining uarterfinal, but there was little green in evidence. An ocean of d-clad, eager Blue Dragon fans obliterated all verdancy. ccording to American Legion treasurer George Pankratz, it as the largest turnout in the Sports Arena's 14-year history.

Local rooters raised the roof as Hutchinson quickly jumped ut to a 12-point advantage. Then, Cumberland's taller front ne quieted Blue Dragon gunners as the Bulldogs chewed their vay back to within two at halftime.

As Barbara Caywood described it for the *Hutchinson News*, ne next 13 minutes "were about as lively as a mortuary." Both eams potted eight points apiece, then froze. Hutchinson was he coldest. After a Mike Jones jumper at the 14:42 mark, the lue Dragons did not score from the field for 7½ minutes. Cumerland was only slightly better, taking its first lead of the game, 3-41, with 7:35 remaining.

Larry Berry immediately initiated a Hutchinson thaw, driving or a lay-up to tie. While Berry, Charlie Griffie, and Gene Gipon continued to pace the offense, tenacious Blue Dragon efense forced Cumberland into errors. Hutchinson outscored he Tennessee crew 17-5 the rest of the way, winning convincgly.

The 60-46 final reflected the poor shooting by both sides: Cumberland hit 30.3 percent (17 of 56) from the field; Hutchinon 29.5 percent (21 of 71). Hutchinson's John Markle — who it 6 of 7 from outside in the Blue Dragon opener, but failed in hree attempts against Cumberland — told *News* reporter Chuck Woodling, "I don't think I even drew iron. Those baskets nust have been 11 feet high."

FRIDAY — JUDGMENT

The pretenders to the crown had been narrowed to four. Two vere pre-tourney favorites; two were surprises. A tremendous sychological homecourt advantage was a strong factor in Hutchinson's unexpected ascension to the final four. Dallas aptist's rise was based purely on talent. A virtual unknown at he start of the event, many fans now considered the Indian tarting five the best in the tournament.

There were two hubs to the Dallas squad.

The outside was commanded by Wendel Hart, a Dallas ative, who was the team leader on offense and defense. As one pposing coach stated, "As goes Hart, so goes Dallas Baptist."

The inside was patrolled by David Nash, a 245-pound bruiser rom St.Louis, who was a former high school classmate of Moberly's Tom Johnson, though he had not played with Johnon. The 17-year-old was a product of the playgrounds where Coach Dennis Walling had recruited him. His lack of experince was offset by superior height and quickness. The *Moberly Monitor-Index* described his moves and jumping ability as reminiscent of the Boston Celtics' Bill Russell." Listed at 6-9, he paper noted that Nash "appears to have grown since that neasurement." He was the tallest and most intimidating player n the tournament.

Moberly was the nominal favorite against Dallas Baptist in the rst semifinal. However, most observers felt that the Greyounds would have to prove it.

Behind the shooting of Larry Peirick and Harrison Stepter, the Missourians proceeded to do just that. Moberly took the early ead, opening a nine-point gap at the 8:35 mark.

Nash responded, hitting three field goals and a pair of free

throws. John McCormack's swishing free throw with six seconds left gave Dallas Baptist a 31-30 halftime edge.

The advantage changed hands repeatedly in the next seven minutes. With 10:40 to go, Dallas took its largest lead of the game, 49-45.

Two free throws by Peirick and one by Jim Chapman pulled the Greyhounds to within one. A clutch three-point play by Stepter regained the lead for Moberly.

After a Dallas Baptist free throw, Moberly called time. Coach Cotton Fitzsimmons told his Greyhounds to slow the pace. Moberly held the ball for more than a minute before Johnson found himself open, shot, and missed.

After scoring 112 points in four games, 1966 tourney MVP Frank Judge later played at the Universities of New Mexico and Houston. (Photo courtesy of the NJCAA)

Nash grabbed the rebound for the Indians. Dallas Baptist missed a chance to tie at the free throw line and Moberly regained possession.

Then, came the turning point of the game. On three successive trips up the floor, Johnson, Stepter, and Chapman canned jumpers. Moberly's advantage expanded to seven with 3:37 to play. A Greyhound stall forced a desperate Dallas squad to foul. Free throws secured a 64-60 Moberly victory and a fourth trip to the title game, tying Tyler for the most by one school.

When ticket windows closed five minutes before the Dallas Baptist-Moberly game, nearly 1,000 more general admission tickets were sold than seats were available. The take topped the previous night's record.

Though the hometown fans were enthusiastic about the Blue Dragon's chase of a dream, they were also realistic. Man for man, Hutchinson did not compare with Cameron State. Of special concern was the Aggies' star — Frank Judge.

The New York freshman was gifted beyond his 19 years. He had total command of every phase of the game. Chipola Coach Milt Johnson observed that Judge was "the kind of player who could beat you a lot of different ways." At 6-2, he had the leaping ability to compete with much taller players on the boards. His shooting range was unlimited. And his ball-handling capabilities alone were worth the price of admission. Frequently he would excite the crowd with agile maneuvers such as effortlessly dribbling the ball between his legs. With 57 points to his credit in two games, there appeared no way Judge could be contained.

Sam Butterfield's strategy against the scoring dynamo was simple: "Give him 30 points and hope maybe by concentrating on everybody else we might squeak it out."

The plan was a shaky gamble from the outset. In the first half, Judge hit 7 of 13 from the field, leading Cameron to a comfortable 45-37 lead.

Hutchinson fought back, pulling to within four in the next five minutes.

Appearing to toy with the Blue Dragons, Cameron then dangled the carrot 10 points away with 12:40 to go.

The local squad continued to chip at the lead. In a three-minute period, Mike Jones hit two free throws, Gene Gipson two field goals, Larry Berry two free throws, Gipson a field goal, and Charlie Griffie two free throws. With three minutes remaining, the Blue Dragons were down one, 76-75.

Showing total disdain for the tense situation, reserve Tony Miles ended the Cameron drought with a jumper. Judge immediately followed with a three-point play, extending the lead to six and nailing the lid on the Blue Dragon coffin.

The principal factors in Cameron State's 91-86 victory: superior Aggie board strength (51-36) — and Judge's game-high 35 points.

SATURDAY — THE BIG SHOW

Both Burlington and Wilson enjoyed comfortable cushions in the first trophy day contest. Wilson led by nine twice while Burlington's biggest advantage was 67-61 midway in the final period.

The Blackhawks were still in the driver's seat at the end when reserve guard Clarence Smith — "Dollar Bill" to his teammates — hit two clutch free throws with 56 seconds left, giving Burlington an 87-84 edge.

Wilson hustled down the court and took five shots at the basket before Geoff Porter finally nailed one with 26 seconds to go.

Coach Ed Sparling ordered the Blackhawks to hold the ball. They held it for 16 seconds before misfortune struck. Smith — who had little playing time during the year, but during the tournament seemed to be involved in every crucial Burlington situation — dribbled the ball off his foot and out of bounds.

Raider Coach Arnold Lewis called time. Lewis' strategy: get it to the hot hand — Porter. With three seconds on the clock, the 6-1 forward split the cords from 15 feet away in right forecourt, giving him a game-high 37 and Wilson the lead.

The Blackhawks immediately yelled time. Their plan was the same as the Chicagoans'. The hot hand for Burlington was Sam Williams with 36. However, there was not time for a good shot. The Blackhawk forward's 40-foot heave banged off the glass, no good.[3] Wilson took fifth-place, 88-87.

In two previous trips to Hutchinson, Chipola Coach Milt Johnson had admired the trophies displayed in a storefront window downtown. "If you got one of those [big trophies] for four on up, you were kind of pushing in on the elite. I always selfishly wanted to bring back one of those trophies."

Johnson's desires were stymied through the first 15 minutes of the fourth-place game. Led by Harry Bostic, who topped all scores with 30, Tyler opened margins of two to six.

Then a three-point play by Chipola's Bob Flowers turned the game around. With four minutes left, the Indians took a 35-34 lead. From that point until intermission, Chipola outscored Tyler, 11-2. The Floridians upped the advantage to 16 early in the second period then coasted. The Indians gave Coach Johnson his trophy, winning 80-73.

The evening opener was a typical slow-developing third-place game which neither team seemed to want to win. Hutchinson dominated early and held a 42-33 margin over Dallas Baptist with 16:48 to go.

Then the pace accelerated.

Jim Allen and David Nash sparked a Dallas rally which tied the game at 44-all. Seven more ties followed as the lead seesawed. The last tie came on a Wendel Hart basket for Dallas with 2:05 remaining.

Hutchinson decided to play for one, but, with 47 second left, lost the ball.

Dallas tried the same. With five seconds showing, Ha attempted the game-winner and missed.

As the Indians pulled down the rebound, Hutchinson' appropriately named Mike Fast stole the ball and raced th clock for the opposite end, just missing at the buzzer.

With 1:12 remaining in the overtime, Hutchinson again hel for one. Larry Berry drew the call and missed with 15 seconds t go.

Dallas rebounded. The Indians' Gale Rhine, already credite with one last-second game-winner, fired with two ticks left. missed.

At the 1:38 mark of the second overtime, Terry Delp, wh had just come off the bench following Berry's fifth foul, scram bled and scored, giving Hutchinson a 74-71 edge, the wide margin either team had held for 10 minutes.

Tom Traylor countered for Dallas with two free throws at th 47-second mark.

Then, with 32 seconds showing, the Blue Dragons' Delp wer from hero to goat, fouling Rhine.

Rhine donned horns, too, missing the front-end of one-and one.

Dallas Baptist grabbed the rebound and Hutchinson's Gen Gipson fouled Gary Beymer in the act of shooting. Beyme joined the growing list of could-have-been heroes, missin both charities.

Reliable Mike Jones pulled down the rebound for the Blu Dragons, but could not make the outlet pass. The officials calle jump ball with 10 seconds remaining.

Dallas grabbed the tip and called time. When play resume the Indians worked the ball to their top scorer — Hart. He sh from 20 feet.

No good.

Traylor, in perfect rebound position, tipped it back up.

No good.

The buzzer sounded.

As the many missed opportunities attested, the protracte third-place game reflected a long, tiring week for players an fans. The grind was particularly hard on the nerves of coache Blue Dragon assistant Gene Keady, drenched in sweat, brace himself after the final buzzer, thinking the contest was goin into a third overtime. He then looked at the scoreboard to di cover Hutchinson had won, 74-73.

Another coach also double-checked the scoreboard after th final buzzer. Twice Cotton Fitzsimmons had brought h Moberly Greyhounds to the floor alongside the director's tab located at the southwest corner of the playing area, just befor the supposed end of the game, only to turn around and ush them back to the dressing room for another five-minute wait

On the final trip from the dressing room, Fitzsimmons jokin ly asked then Assistant Tournament Director Al Wagler, "Is th thing ever going to end or what. Let's get on with the big show.

Wagler — whose 6-8 son, Bill, played for the Blue Dragons – smiled and said, "This is the big show."

The Greyhounds and more than 500 of their fans were eag for the finale. All week long, Moberly had taken backseat in th press and in street corner and coffee house klatches. No on denied that the Greyhounds were good. Moberly was alwa good. The Greyhounds simply did not have the crowd-pleasir sparkle that the Frank Judge-led Aggies possessed. After opening-round defeat of Burlington, Cameron State w already wearing the crown for many. In fact, between 200 an 300 Aggie fans had arranged for a steak and champagne dinn in the Baker Hotel's Grand Ballroom, following the champio

---

[3] Sam Williams' missed final shot in his final game for Burlington was virtually his only personal failure in the tournament. The 6-4 leaper put together a spectacular set of performances. Coach Ed Sparling related the reason why. According to tourney tradition, "you're playing through Saturday" was the Blackhawk theme. After the devastating opening-round loss to Cameron State, Williams approached Sparling and said, "Don't worry, Coach. I won't let you get embarrassed." In the Blackhawks' next outing, Williams improved his game-high 29 against Cameron with a game-high 35 against Dixie. In Burlington's 119-95 race with Wesley, the All-American registered a tourney-high 49. In four games, Williams totaled 149, fourth-highest in tournament history. His two-year total of 245 ranked him third all-time. According to Sparling, "He was so good, they had to figure out a new award for him."

   In 1966, the tournament committee inaugurated the Sesher Sportsmanship Award to honor Charley Sesher, retiring athletic director at Hutchinson Community Junior College and the man most responsible for moving the tournament to Hutchinson.

   It was propitious timing that Williams, one of its most deserving recipients, was its first. According to John Johnson, a Juco Tourney participant the following year and later a 13-year pro who followed Williams at the University of Iowa, "Before the game's over with, he was going to say hello to everybody in the arena. Come into a restaurant, Sam would be the last one to have a seat. He was going to talk to everybody. Everybody loved him."

   As Sparling put it, "Samuel loved the game. He played it for the sheer enjoyment of it. I always considered him the greatest player I ever had and I had 29 high school, junior college, and college All-Americans."

hip.

The game started as expected. After Cameron grabbed the opening tip, Judge immediately engineered a three-point play. The quick aggressive Oklahomans in their green tops and white pants pushed the tempo, opening a 17-12 gap midway through the period.

Though appearing a step faster, the Aggies could not outdistance Moberly. A field goal and two free throws by Tom Johnson lifted the Greyhounds to their first lead, 22-21 with 6:27 remaining. The score was tied at 24, 26, 28, and 30. Surprisingly, Moberly held a 36-32 halftime edge.

Cameron State was playing its best basketball. How could the Aggies be behind?

There were two reasons.

First, Moberly's Fitzsimmons left himself wide open for second-guessing, benching starter Tom Thoenen in favor of Jim Chapman. Thoenen was slower, hampered by a bad knee injured in high school. Additionally, Chapman was 6-6. By putting the four-inch taller Chapman on Judge, Fitzsimmons forced the Aggie scoring leader to loft his shots from farther out and at a higher angle. Judge continued to score but at a much reduced pace from previous games. Chapman and Johnson also kept Judge, a usually aggressive rebounder, off the boards, blocking out with consistent precision.

Second, Cameron misjudged the outside shooting capabilities of Moberly's taller troops. The Aggie 2-3 zone applied pressure to Harrison Stepter and Bill Mozee out front, closed off the deep middle and sides, but allowed a crease in the 15- and 18-foot range around the key. Chapman, Thoenen off the bench, and, in particular, Larry Peirick — a slow-footed, almost lumbering 6-7 center, who played his greatest game as a Greyhound, hitting 11 of 17 from the field and leading all scorers with 25 — were repeatedly left unguarded in the area. In one instance, Chapman double-clutched before shooting, not believing how open he was. Each promptly bottomed the net.

In the Greyhound locker room, Fitzsimmons told his charges, "We have taken everything they've thrown at us and they haven't put us away. They cannot play any better than they played. Now, let's go out there and break it open."

The Moberly squad's demeanor was immediately apparent. Brimming with confidence, the Greyhounds appeared to gain the step they were behind in the first half. They engaged a "prison-like" defense, forcing six Cameron missed shots to open the period. Meanwhile on offense, the Greyhounds executed crisp passes and perfect patterns. In five minutes, Moberly extended its lead to 15, forcing Cameron out of its zone. At the 11:55 mark, the score read 62-43. Aggie hopes petered out.

With a 90-66 triumph — the second-widest margin all-time in a championship game — Moberly Junior College became the first school to win three national titles.

THE AFTERMATH — TEN MORE YEARS

For his masterful maneuverings, Cotton Fitzsimmons was named Coach of the Year, becoming the first individual to be honored by the tournament as a player and a coach.

Despite being held to 20 points in the championship game, his low in four games, Frank Judge was named the tournament's MVP, a surprise to no one.

The biggest reward, however, came to the Hutchinson fans. Partly because of the unexpected success of the local Blue Dragons, the 1966 meet drew the largest attendance to date. Interest in the tournament continued to grow and and NJCAA officials had no desire to stop it. Consequently, shortly after noon Friday, the organization signed a new contract with tourney sponsors Lysle Rishel Post No. 68 of the American Legion and Hutchinson Community Junior College.

The National Junior College Basketball Tournament would be Hutchinson's for the next decade.

Tournament Results

Tuesday:	Game			
		1	Dallas Baptist — 91 Chicago-Wilson — 83	
		2	Leicester — 81 NDSSS-Wahpeton — 73	
		3	Moberly — 78 Alpena — 69	
		4	Tyler — 73 Casper — 71	
		5	Hutchinson — 102 Wesley — 78	
		6	Cumberland — 83 Ferrum — 68	
Wednesday:	Game			
		7	Cameron St. — 85 Burlington — 76	
		8	Chipola — 74 Dixie — 72	
		9	Chicago-Wilson — 94 NDSSS-Wahpeton — 69	
		10	Dallas Baptist — 86 Leicester — 85	
		11	Moberly — 79 Tyler — 64	
Thursday:	Game			
		12	Casper — 78 Alpena — 72	
		13	Burlington — 97 Dixie — 79	
		14	Tyler — 115 Leicester — 100 3OT	
		15	Wesley — 99 Ferrum — 84	
		16	Cameron St. — 83 Chipola — 69	
		17	Hutchinson — 60 Cumberland — 46	
Friday:	Game			
		18	Chicago-Wilson — 88 Casper — 65	
		19	Burlington — 119 Wesley — 95	
		20	Chipola — 77 Cumberland — 72	
		21	Moberly — 64 Dallas Baptist — 60	
		22	Cameron St. — 91 Hutchinson — 86	
Saturday:	Game			
		23	Chicago-Wilson — 88 Burlington — 87	
		24	Chipola — 80 Tyler — 73	
		25	Hutchinson — 74 Dallas Baptist — 73 2OT	
		26	Moberly — 90 Cameron St. — 66	

How They Finished in 1966

1. Moberly Junior College
2. Cameron State Agricultural College
3. Hutchinson Community Junior College
4. Chipola Junior College
5. Chicago City Junior College, Wilson Branch
6. Dallas Baptist College
7. Tyler Junior College
8. Burlington Community College

All-Tournament Team

Harry Bostic — Tyler Junior College
Wendel Hart — Dallas Baptist College
Mike Jones — Hutchinson Community Junior College
Frank Judge — Cameron State Agricultural College
Tony Koski — Leicester Junior College
Geoffrey Porter — Chicago City Junior College, Wilson Branch
Tom Richardson — Alpena Community College
Joe Sova — Chipola Junior College
Harrison Stepter — Moberly Junior College
Samuel Williams — Burlington Community College

Coach of the Year

Lowell "Cotton" Fitzsimmons — Moberly Junior College

Player of the Year

Frank Judge — Cameron State Agricultural College

Sesher Sportsmanship Award

Samuel Williams — Burlington Community College

1967:

TWENTY YEARS AND A KING

Dodge City's Roland "Fatty" Taylor later starred for LaSalle College before spending eight years in the pros. (Photo courtesy of LaSalle College)

Region	Team
1	Boise Junior College — Boise, Idaho
2	Cameron State Agricultural College — Lawton, Oklahoma
3	Broome Technical Community College — Binghamton, New York
4	Wright Junior College — Chicago, Illinois
5	Ranger Junior College — Ranger, Texas
6	Dodge City Community Junior College — Dodge City, Kansas
7	Hiwassee College — Madisonville, Tennessee
8	St. Johns River Junior College — Palatka, Florida
9	Northwest Community College — Powell, Wyoming
10	Ferrum Junior College — Ferrum, Virginia
11	Burlington Community College — Burlington, Iowa
12	Vincennes University — Vincennes, Indiana
13	Rochester State Junior College — Rochester, Minnesota
14	San Jacinto College — Pasadena, Texas
15	Trenton Junior College — Trenton, New Jersey
16	Moberly Junior College — Moberly, Missouri

At the NJCAA Basketball Tournament's inaugural in Springfield, sponsors had scrambled to find someone willing to purchase a ticket. On the eve of the event's 20th anniversary, it was the ticket buyers doing the scrambling.

The first hopefuls arrived at Hutchinson's 1st Avenue Post Office at 9 p.m. Sunday, February 19. By 11 p.m. the number had risen to 300. At midnight, one minute before the opening postmark deadline for ticket applications, approximately 1,000 pushing and shoving fans overflowed the Post Office's small lobby.

Seven postal workers handled 927 envelopes in the first 15 minutes after the deadline. According to ticket chairman Bill Lehr, at an average five requests per envelope, all reserved seats were sold in the first half hour.

THE PARTICIPANTS

On the NJCAA Basketball Tournament's 20th anniversary, it was apropos that the event's most successful participant be among the favored. It was the 15th trip to the nationals for Moberly Junior College. Coach Cotton Fitzsimmons' latest crew was considered the best. The defending national champs took up residence at the top of the season's first NJCAA poll and remained there, compiling a 27-2 record — tops in the school's history — against topflight competition, including four tourney representatives. A second back-to-back title appeared a strong possibility.

The Greyhounds' chief opposition was No. 2 San Jacinto College. Though only in its fifth year of operation, the Pasadena, Texas, school had already made major strides in developing an excellent sports program. The basketball squad's rapid improvement was due in part to Coach Tom Sewell's back-breaking scheduling. In order to gain quick experience, the Ravens had played 10 more games than any other team in the meet. Despite being a first-time participant, the Ravens' impressive 39-4 record — compiled against the tough competition of Region 14, the most successful region in tourney history — established San Jacinto as a solid challenger to the Moberly throne.

According to the *Hutchinson News,* four teams would contend with the co-favorites.

No. 3 Cameron State Agricultural College (24-3) and No. 8 Northwest Community College (28-2) were not surprise selections. With 6-7 Simmie Hill, a much sought-after transfer from Wichita State, having replaced 1966 tourney MVP Frank Judge (who had moved on to the University of New Mexico), the Cameron Aggies continued their tourney tradition as a tall, experienced ball club. The Northwest Trappers from Powell, Wyoming, although newcomers to Hutchinson, also possessed potential, sporting one of the top-10 offenses in the nation, averaging 101.4 points per game.

The other two choices were questionable. Burlington Community College (23-8) and Vincennes University (21-8) were both unranked, unexpected regional winners. Burlington, a two-time loser to Moberly during the year, needed a third-effort tip-in by freshman Larry Woods to outlast Webster City Junior College, 90-88, in overtime in the Regional 11 final. Vincennes possessed better credentials with a season victory over Moberly and a regional semifinal upset over No. 4 ranked, previously undefeated Port Huron Junior College. Still, the Trailblazers went into the regional final as underdogs, barely squeaking by Flint Community Junior College, 78-76, in overtime. The inclusion of both as pre-tourney favorites appeared a tribute to each's recent success in the nationals and overlooked the fact that freshmen predominated both squads.

There were also notable exclusions: No. 13 Rochester State Junior College (29-0), the leading point-producer in the meet (101.6 per game) and the only remaining undefeated team in junior college ranks; No. 10 Broome Technical Community College (28-3), the eighth-rated defensive team in the nation (63.0 points per game) and a seven-time tourney participant; and most surprising of all, No. 4 Ranger Junior College (27-2), an exciting, high-powered squad which owned a win over Cameron State. The three were unceremoniously demoted to "the rest of the field", joining Ferrum Junior College (25-3), St. Johns River Junior College (29-4), Wright Junior College (22-5), Boise Junior College (25-8), Trenton Junior College (24-8), Hiwassee College (21-10), and Dodge City Community Junior College (19-13).

No one totally discounted the chances of any of the 16 teams, however. The front-runners were particularly leery. As Cotton Fitzsimmons told the *Moberly Monitor-Index* just prior to the tournament: "I don't mind the role of favorite . . . but it's sometimes 'the kiss of death' to good ballclubs."

TUESDAY — THE UPSET BUG

The potential for the fatal kiss of upset was evident from the beginning. Freshman guard Bob Sands possessed a hot hand, firing four quick field goals, leading Trenton to an unexpected 13-5 advantage over heavily favored San Jacinto in the opener. The No. 2 Ravens did not appear ready.

Hoping to shake his troops out of lethargy, Coach Tom Sewell switched the Ravens to zone. Trenton did not score for the next 5½ minutes. Meanwhile, Steve Cutillo, Percy Anderson, and Ollie Taylor paced a San Jacinto spree, lifting the Texans to a seven-point edge.

Trenton recovered, pulling to within one. Then the Ravens put on another point barrage, blowing the game wide open. At half, the San Jacinto margin was 23. Led by Anderson's game-high 29, the Ravens destroyed any upset possibilities, coasting to a 91-75 victory.

The hint of upset remained razed during most of the matinee feature. With 5:50 remaining, Rochester's 29-game win streak was safely in hand, the Yellowjackets comfortably on top of Wright, 89-73.

Then, Grady Butts, a top Rochester front-line rebounder, was tagged for foul number five. At the 4:43 mark, 6-3 Robert Gorham, the tallest Yellowjacket and the team's leading scorer with 25 was whistled to the bench.

Wright whittled at the Rochester lead.

Finally, just inside the three-minute mark, Mike Savoy, the Yellowjackets' only remaining front-line starter, fouled out.

Wright struck in earnest. At the minute mark, the Rams were within four. With 48 second left, Buddy Haines hit his seventh field goal of the game, reducing the deficit to two.

James Williford broke the Rochester drought with a free throw.

Wright's Harvey Murphy responded with a short hook. The difference was one.

Holding on for dear life, Rochester attempted to freeze the ball for 35 seconds. One of the Yellowjackets foiled the effort, accidentally stepping on the out-of-bounds line.

With 11 seconds showing, Haines drilled a short jumper, giving Wright the lead.

Rochester hurried the inbounds pass. A Ram deflected it — into the hands of Haines. While everyone else was running in the opposite direction, Haines calmly laid in the final basket. Wright triumphed, 97-94, giving the 1967 tournament its first brush with "death."

Vincennes deterred thoughts of upset in the first half of the afternoon finale with perfect six-for-six free throw shooting while Ranger fired nine blanks out of 10. The Trailblazers built a nine-point advantage and maintained it until 14:08 remained.

Then, the Rangers puckered for the fatal kiss, steadily reducing the difference. With 7:54 to go, Larry Robertson engineered a three-point play, tying the game at 55-all. Vincennes held the lead twice more, but only briefly. Ranger moved ahead, 59-58, at the 5:48 mark and stayed there. Despite a horrid ordeal at the line (10 for 29 compared to 11 for 12 for the Trailblazers), the Rangers downed pre-tourney pick Vincennes, 72-61.

The evening opener was expected to be a refreshing breeze for the Burlington Blackhawks. The Hiwassee Tigers appeared tame game compared to Burlington's hard-luck first-round draws of Dodge City and Cameron in the prior two tournaments. But, as fortune would have it, Burlington had to contend with the upset bug which seemed to be infecting the tourney field.

Behind the spectacular shooting of Johnny Swann — he hit his first eight attempts, all from 20-feet and beyond, and eventually netted a game-high 25 — the Tennessee Tigers remained in the hunt. There were five ties and 13 lead changes. The widest margin held by either team was five.

After Larry Woods broke a 57-all deadlock with 2½ minutes to go, Coach Ed Sparling ordered his Blackhawks to slow it down. More used to running than ball control, Burlington repeatedly surrendered the sphere.

So did Hiwassee. The Tigers missed three shots and turned the ball over twice in an effort to tie. A final try came with five seconds left, Hiwassee controlling the ball out-of-bounds. On the inbounds pass Burlington's Bernie Williams broadjumped, intercepted, and held the ball. The Blackhawks survived, 59-57.

It was difficult for the "kiss-of-death" syndrome to have much effect on the evening feature since, on paper, neither team was favored. The 6,500 fans in attendance *did* have a preference. The Dodge City Conquistadors had earned the respect of local fans by being the only West Juco Conference team to defeat Hutchinson's Blue Dragons.

The Arena audience soon felt symptoms of the epidemic, however, as Boise blistered the cords. Keith Burke hit 7 of 10 from the field on a variety of shots before sitting down with three fouls midway through the first half. Then, Wendell Hart took over scoring chores for the Broncos. The Boise advantage gradually grew.

With 9:45 remaining in the game, Dodge City faced a 71-51 uphill battle. A brief Conquistador rally led by Roland Taylor halved the difference.

Then Boise's Renee Ruth delivered the coup de grace. In the final five minutes, the 6-1 sophomore scored all 14 Bronco points, giving him game honors with 24. Boise's 59 percent shooting from the field resulted in an impressive 91-77 victory.

With upset fever still alive, fans anxiously awaited the evening finale between Moberly and Broome Tech. During the season, the Greyhounds had barely escaped with a 60-55 win over the New Yorkers. Another tourney surprise was a distinct possibility.

Moberly's Cotton Fitzsimmons was genuinely concerned — but, not for the obvious reason. The close call at Binghamton had come in the notoriously rabid confines of Broome Tech's "Hornets' Nest" at the end of a four-game New York swing in which the Greyhounds had traveled 200 miles each day by car. Fitzsimmons' concern was, instead, based on the condition of two of his top players. Just after the Greyhounds' Region 16 victory, All-American Harrison Stepter's shoulder popped out in practice, a recurrence of a mid-season injury. Then, sophomore center Bernie Copeland injured *his* shoulder in another practice fall. Both starters were tender and sore.

The upset strain continued virulent. Broome Tech scored the first three points of the nightcap.

Then, Moberly introduced a vaccine — defense. The Greyhounds limited Broome Tech to five field goals and three free throws the rest of the half. On offense, Copeland convinced Fitzsimmons his shoulder was no problems, hitting all eight of his shots from the field. Moberly built a 38-16 halftime edge, improved it to 60-29 midway through the final period, and eased to a 73-52 victory.

The "kiss-of-death" epidemic died.

WEDNESDAY — RUNNING RANGERS

Cameron State's brush with upset came just before the tournament with rumors that the Aggies' top player, Simmie Hill, was ineligible. A hurried investigation followed. Region 2 Director Leo Canaday secured documents from Wichita State showing that Hill's grade average met the NJCAA's minimum transfer requirement. Cameron State officials also sent a telegram verifying that Hill had started classes 11 days after the school opened, inside the 14-day limit imposed by the national organization. The day before the tourney's tip-off, Hobart Bolerjack, the NJCAA's commissioner of eligibility pronounced, "Simmie Hill is perfectly eligible," to the relief of Aggie fans.

Cameron's controversial Simmie Hill took tourney scoring honors in 1967 with 98 points, but was unaccountably left off the All-Tournament Team (only the second such occurrence in tourney history), even though one week later he was named a 1st-Team Juco All-American. Hill finished his collegiate career at West Texas State University, then spent four years in the ABA. (Photo courtesy of West Texas State University)

In Wednesday's opener, Hill showed his gratitude by canning 7 of 11 from the field in the first half and all eight attempts in the second. His game-high 35 propelled Cameron State past Ferrum, 75-62.

The final first-round game was close for 28 minutes. Then, favored Northwest of Powell gradually pulled away from St. Johns River, opening a 10-point gap with just under six minutes to go. The Powell Trappers held back a final surge by the Floridians, winning 91-86.

Talk of upset was completely buried once the quarterfinals began. The better teams had gained confidence with advancement and showed it. Ollie Taylor and Steve Cutillo — who eventually hit 27 and 23, respectively — paced hot San Jacinto shooting as the Ravens opened a 10-point halftime spread over Wright, then extended it to 15. Buddy Haines — the game's leading scorer with 33 — tallied 12 straight points, sparking a second-period Wright rally, but the closest the Rams could get was seven. San Jacinto confirmed its favorite status, advancing 89-78.

The outcome of the day's other quarterfinal was a shocker for those who saw the score, but not the game. Those viewing the contest quickly became aware that the newspaper had erred in its pre-tourney team evaluation.

It was not so much that Burlington was overrated, but that Ranger had been overlooked. The Texans were run-and-gunners with a decided Harlem Globetrotter persuasion. First night nerves had obviously blunted their attack against Vincennes. Against another fast-break club like Burlington, the running Rangers were at their best. There were occasional miscues (17 in all). More often there was simply high-speed entertainment. Ranger poured in points, opened an unbelievable 59-30 gap at halftime, and was never pressed thereafter. Six Rangers hit double figures, including Ric Cobb's game-high 26, leading Ranger to a 98-68 Burlington humiliation.

Coach Ed Sparling summed up the Blackhawks' frustration: "On the first fast break of the game [for Ranger], the guy in the middle passed it, hit [his teammate] in the head, and it bounced in — went in just like a lay-up. That's when you know you're in big-time trouble. I used all my time-outs in the first half."

The Texans immediately became everyone's "team to watch."

THURSDAY — BIDING TIME

The semifinal participants were a forgone conclusion for many. Consequently, the tourney's hump day was a slow-paced formality, the top excitement coming in consolation play.

One of the best individual scoring duels of the tournament occurred during the afternoon finale when Burlington's Larry Woods hit 12 for 12 from the line, edging Wright's Buddy Haines, 36 to 34, for scoring honors. The team battle was not as close as Burlington rode the driver's seat throughout, eliminating the Chicagoans, 91-77.

The closest action of the day came in the evening opener. On the strength of 38 free throws, Dodge City outlasted Broome Tech, 86-82, in overtime.

With John Johnson hitting 15 of his team-leading 20 in the second half, Northwest of Powell gave Cameron State a run for its money in the evening feature, the Trappers trailing by only four with five minutes to go. However, pressure free throw shooting by Cameron gave the Aggies an 89-79 victory.

Unlike in its opening victory, the key for Cameron was not Simie Hill. The big forward picked up three fouls in the first nine minutes and was constantly double-teamed. He ended the evening with only 14 points, 12 below his average.

The Aggies' top gun was instead Bill Bullock, a stocky, bull-like sophomore guard who possessed surprising quickness and could fake and fire his favorite turn-around jumper in either direction. The Columbus, Ohio, native copped game honors with 35, matching Hill's opening-game output and demonstrating that the Aggies had more than a one-man attack.

The remaining quarterfinal was close only in the early going. The score was tied 17-all midway in the opening period before Moberly went on a 17-3 tear. The nearest Boise got from then on was seven shortly after intermission.

The difference in the contest was defense. While the Broncos had been feverishly hot against Dodge City in their opener, they were bone-chilling cold against Moberly. The Greyhounds' patented defense held the Broncos to 36 percent from the field. Moberly won easily, 70-50.

FRIDAY — BLOOD GAME

The four best teams in the nation had funneled through the championship bracket. It was a predictable occurrence which rarely happened, a promoter's dream. The semifinal pairings pitted No. 2 versus No. 4 and No. 1 versus No. 3. One was a battle for bragging rights in Texas; the other, a grudge match between the previous year's finalists. An exciting evening seemed assured.

Some, however, felt the opener would not be close at all.

After the demolition of Burlington, many local fans adopted Ranger as their favorite. The Rangers' brand of basketball was not only devastating, but entertaining.

Ranger Coach Ron Butler described the origins of his popular ballclub: "At that time, there were not a lot of black players in junior college in the state of Texas. I was fortunate to know a ouple of guys who lived in the New Jersey-New York area who new talent. There were not a lot of colleges recruiting [that] rea. These guys convinced me I could bring in three or four ids who hadn't been recruited. We put a team together that ad come off the playgrounds of New York City.

"The fans in the Southwest had never seen this type basket-all played. It was a novelty to them. We had standing-room-nly crowds in our gym. We were 325 miles from Houston and e had people in attendance who were from Houston. We ere a population of 3,000 people and we'd sell out every ame."

According to Butler, the Rangers gained such popularity that prominent Texas sports magazine rated the squad as the third est in the state behind the University of Houston (with Elvin ayes) and Stephen F. Austin (with George Johnson).

It was commonly felt that Ranger would bomb San Jacinto. aid San Jacinto Coach Tom Sewell to the *Hutchinson News*: People've been saying it, we've been hearing it and I know a ot of people have been thinking it that haven't said it."

When Ranger opened an early five-point gap, it appeared the ans were correct.

Then, consecutive baskets by Richard Vasquez, Percy Ander-on, and Steve Cutillo ignited the Ravens. The rest of the period ras all San Jacinto. Led by Anderson's 19 points, 18 from the eld, the Ravens burned the nets at a 67 percent clip. Against ne tenacious Raven zone, Ranger managed a meager 35 per-ent. San Jacinto went into the locker room at halftime with a omfortable 46-36 margin.

The Ranger cause continued worrisome. Behind by 11 with :25 to go, the situation deteriorated to hopeless.

Ranger center Ric Cobb — whose second-half performance ncluded eight straight field goals and 23 points — snared back-o-back buckets to improve matters.

San Jacinto countered with a stall, forcing Ranger to foul.

A pattern emerged. Ranger repeatedly sent San Jacinto to the ree throw line for one-and-one. Invariably, the Ravens hit the irst, missed the second. Ranger then grabbed the rebound and uickly scored. With 31 seconds remaining, the Ranger deficit ras reduced to one.

Then the pattern broke. Richard Vasquez converted two free hrows for San Jacinto.

Cobb answered at the Ranger end with a field goal.

With eight seconds showing, Larry Robertson picked up his ifth foul, sending the Ravens' Ollie Taylor to the line. Momen-arily, the old pattern returned. Taylor made the first charity, nissed the second.

The Rangers failed to grab the carom, however. The ball ounded back into Taylor's hands. An inconsequential foul at he buzzer and two free throws by Larry Pitre ended play. San acinto advanced to the championship game, 89-85.

If blood pressures had not risen during the first semifinal, they vere sure to in the second. There was no love lost between Cameron State and Moberly. The Aggies still smarted from their inexpected 24-point humiliation in the final the year before. Revenge was a key factor to the intense play that followed.

Simmie Hill scored the first three of his game-high 29 to open he contest. Cameron held the advantage until the 16:22 mark vhen Moberly's Harrison Stepter converted a three-point play. The Greyhounds then sprang ahead, scoring the next six points. A reverse hook by Hill temporarily broke the Cameron drought. Moberly then fired eight more unanswered points. Behind the nside pokes of Tom Thoenen (5 of 8) and the outside bombs of Frank Price (5 of 10), the Greyhounds opened a 32-21 bulge vith 2:01 left in the half. Cameron regained a measure of espect, reducing the deficit to seven by intermission.

The start of the second half resembled the beginning of the inal period in the 1966 championship contest — with the roles eversed. A purposeful Aggie crew outscored Moberly 9-1 to ake the lead, 36-35.

The battle lines were now firmly drawn.

In the next six minutes, Cameron and Moberly exchanged he lead seven times. The largest gap was three.

Emotions were strained. At the 10:10 mark, Greyhound David Lawrence was slapped with a technical for protesting his ourth foul. The resulting free throws boosted Cameron's lead o four.

Moberly did not threaten until back-to-back buckets by Step-er and Lawrence tied the game at 50-all.

Hill responded with a powerful two-hand dunk off an Aggie break.

Thoenen answered with two for Moberly.

Bill Bullock — who missed his first four shots then stopped shooting — regained confidence with a field goal. Center Maurice Savage added another. With 5:58 to go, Cameron State led, 56-52.

Again, Moberly refused to fold, tying it at 56.

Aggie reserve Terry Carlson broke the deadlock with a 12-footer with 3:22 remaining.

Thoenen halved the difference with a free throw.

Then, momentum shifted.

Center Bernie Copeland — Moberly's leading scorer in its first two outings, but a silent presence against Cameron's collapsing zone — banked in a short jumper off the glass, giving Moberly the lead. Clutch free throw shooting and Copeland's workman-like rebounding maintained it.

With 14 seconds left, Cameron State trailing, 67-64, Bullock stepped to the line for the Aggies. The reliable sophomore coolly sank the first, then purposely missed the second, banging it off the backboard. Ten players converged on the carom.

An official's whistle halted play. Aggie Joe Hayes was singled out for fouling Moberly's Lawrence.

Since Lawrence had ended on top of Hayes at the play's completion, the call drew unfavorable notices from the crowd. Previously impartial Hutchinson fans showered the court with boos. Someone behind the Cameron State bench tossed a pillow in the air. Thinking that Aggie Coach Red Miller was the perpetrator, officials assessed a technical.

Amidst a general uproar, Lawrence sank two free throws.Thoenen converted the technical. On the inbounds pass, Lawrence was left unguarded under the basket. He received the ball and an easy two. The five gifts gave Moberly a 72-65 victory.

Though the conclusion of the 1967 Cameron State-Moberly semifinal remained one of Coach Miller's most exasperating memories, he did not demean Moberly's right to the victory: "I don't want to sound like a guy with sour grapes. I don't think any one particular incident turned things around."

Miller specifically noted Cameron's poor play in falling behind in the first half. If there was a single key factor, however, it was Moberly's clutch free throw shooting. The Greyhounds hit 20 for 23, including their last 11 in a row.

For some, however, the outcome remained unresolved. At the final buzzer Moberly and Cameron partisans rushed onto the court. Three separate skirmishes ensued. Though the damage inflicted was minor, police were required to clear the floor. It was one of the few instances of overt fan rowdiness in the tournament's history.

SATURDAY — NO. 1 VERSUS NO. 2

The fifth-place contest started as a tight, basket-trading affair with 11 ties in the first 15 minutes. Then, a six-point spurt by Vincennes opened up the game. The Trailblazers took a 38-33 margin into the locker room and outscored Dodge City, 10-3, on their return to the floor. Despite a pair of brief rallies, the Conquistadors could not surmount the difference, pulling no closer than five. Vincennes won, 73-64.

The other afternoon game was a free-wheeling scoring derby led by sophomore Steve Shumaker who hit 11 of 14 from the field, tallying 26, as Burlington took a 50-46 halftime edge over Northwest of Powell.

The Trappers made an adjustment at intermission, assigning John Johnson and Jessie Jefferson double-team duties on Shumaker. The big center's output dropped to 10 in the second period.

Meanwhile, the Powell squad gained control of the boards and opened up its offense. Led by Johnson, who scored 33 for the game, including 13 of 16 from the line, Northwest outscored Burlington, 56-35, in the final period. The Trappers took fourth-place, 102-85.

The second Blackhawk bombing of the tournament was too much. Since Powell players had been given twice as many charity attempts (42 to 21) than had the Blackhawks, frustrated Burlington fans focused their anger on two striped-shirted men. Consequently, for the second time in as many days, police were required to escort the officials from the floor.

After attending Northwest Community College of Powell, Wyoming, John Johnson became an All-American at the University of Iowa and a 13-year veteran of the NBA. (Photo courtesy of the University of Iowa)

The evening opener was a disappointment to many. For the second time in a row, Ranger's exciting offense was shackled — this time by a Cameron full-court press. The Aggies overcame an early 7-3 Ranger margin, opened an eight-point gap at halftime, and were never threatened thereafter. Cameron State captured third, 91-77.

Never in its history had the tournament's filtering process worked so perfectly. For the first time, the No. 1 and No. 2 ranked teams had survived to the end.

Comparison of Moberly and San Jacinto revealed interesting similarities. Each possessed excellent starting units, but weak benches.[1] Each was capable of putting points on the board via the fast break. Most importantly, each had strong defenses.

Here the similarities became contrasts. San Jacinto favored a 2-3 zone. Moberly preferred man-to-man.

The greatest contrast between the two, though, was in their traditions. If there was any dominate school in the tournament's first 20 years, it was Moberly Junior College. The Greyhounds had appeared in three-fourths of the events and had earned more hardware than any other participant, including the most titles. San Jacinto, on the other hand, was receiving its baptism of fire. Few expected the Ravens to weather the initiation rights.

The closeness of the championship game surprised no one. The erratic play did. Tough defense on both sides accounted for many air balls and high, bounding rim shots. Stress, however, was an equally important factor. San Jacinto obviously suffered from a case of debutante nerves. Since three Moberly starters were members of its 1966 champion squad, the only explanation for the Greyhounds tightness was the old maxim: "It's harder to win the second than it is the first."

Pressure mounted through a tight, leap-frogging first half. San Jacinto held the advantage six times, Moberly four. The widest spread came with just under seven minutes to go. Harrison Stepter and Frank Price executed a beautiful 2-on-1 fast break, never letting the ball touch the floor. A successful lay-up gave Moberly a 24-19 lead. The Ravens responded, however, providing the period's only tie, 28-all at halftime.

A basket exchange renewed the tightening pressure after intermission. Then three successive long jump shots by Tom Thoenen threatened to crack the game open. With 15:58 remaining, Moberly took a 36-31 lead.

Two crucial breaks gave San Jacinto new life. At the 13:17 mark, Stepter, the Greyhound floor leader, was whistled for his fourth foul. A little more than two minutes later, Moberly center Bernie Copeland notched *his* fourth. Faced with a hard decision, Coach Cotton Fitzsimmons benched his top rebounder, but opted to leave his experienced floor general in the game.

After Raven guard Steve Cutillo tied the score 40-all with nine minutes to go, the contest was a Mexican standoff. Ties followed at 41, 43, 44, 46, 50, and 55, the last coming with 21 seconds remaining.

During that stretch, fans squirmed with increasing tension.

They saw brilliantly executed plays: Cutillo driving the left lane from the top of the circle off a beautiful screen by Wayne Wedemeyer; Price zipping a pass from the right backcourt to Stepter standing all alone just left of the basket.

They saw incredible saves: lean, lanky goateed Percy Anderson snatching a Price corner shot from mid-air, tight-roping the end line, and outletting it to Cutillo for a fast break; David Lawrence, about to fall out of bounds after grabbing a wild alley-oop toss from Price, passing across the lane under the basket to a wide open Thoenen for an easy two.

More often, they saw missed shots and defensive rebounds, the consequences of taut defense and strained nerves.

San Jacinto held the lead only once, 49-48, when Anderson spun around his man at the free throw line and drove the lane for an easy left-hand lay-up. Otherwise, it was the Greyhounds who took the step ahead.

As the contest entered its closing seconds, Moberly again controlled the basketball.

San Jacinto pressed. Just as Stepter crossed the midcourt stripe, Cutillo fouled him from behind.

Fourteen seconds remained. With his shaved head a symbol of his cool demeanor, Stepter calmly sank the first free shot, giving Moberly a 56-55 edge.

The second went in — then out.

Anderson skied for the rebound and hit the outlet for a quick trip up the court. But, before the fast break had a chance to develop, play stopped, the San Jacinto bench ordering a time-out.

When play resumed, the Raven guards met stiff pressure from Stepter and Price. Precious seconds evaporated. Once the ball crossed midcourt, Moberly surprisingly fell back into a 2-3 zone, a Greyhound rarity.

San Jacinto playmaker Richard Vasquez dribbled to the left wing, eyeing a Copeland-draped Anderson. Unaccountably he stopped. Finally, he lofted a pass to the Raven center. Out of nowhere, Thoenen crossed from the opposite side of the lane and intercepted.

Time expired.

Moberly was again king of the junior college world.[2]

THE AFTERMATH — CLASS ACT

The victors were royally rewarded for their achievement.

In appreciation for his splendid floor leadership, Harrison Stepter was selected to the All-Tournament Team for a second

---

[1] San Jacinto starting forward Wayne Wedemeyer had, in fact, spent much of the season on the bench himself. According to former coach Tom Sewell, the Ravens did not bring their best player with them — first-team All-American Tom Mitchell. At mid-season, Mitchell "dislocated his knee cap, tore the ligament. His knee cap moved about a foot up his leg. He had a very serious knee problem and it took him a long time to recover from it. We don't know what would have happened had he been with us."

[2] When San Jacinto called time after Stepter's missed free throw, the ball was in the hands of Raven guard Richard Vasquez. Though not as quick laterally as Moberly's Price or Stepter, there was no one on the court as fast from end line to end line. As Tom Sewell later said, "If we hadn't taken a time-out and let Vasquez take it the length of the floor, Vasquez would have gotten us an offensive opportunity some how."

Cotton Fitzsimmons agreed: "I thought they had us backpedaling. They might have come down and gotten an easy shot."

Fitzsimmons added that it taught him a good lesson as a young coach: "I never do that [call time in the final seconds of a close game when a potential break situation is developing] anymore. I've even carried it through in my pro career. If I've got time, we get it up and go with it. It [a time out] gives the other team time to set their defense."

The lesson was a hard one for San Jacinto. Stated Sewell, "I've always told Ron [assistant coach Ron Rucker], 'if you and I hadn't coached that last nine seconds, we probably would have won that national championship.' "

ne, the only individual to receive the honor as a back-to-back champion.[3]

Tom Thoenen's inclusion in the select 10 was also a welcome gesture. No one had wanted the Mexico, Missouri, native when he graduated from high school because he was considered too ow, his mobility hindered by a bad knee. Undeterred, the quiet, unassuming young man went about his business, becoming he Greyhounds' leading scorer. Recognizing his consistent ay in the clutch, the selection committee designated Moberly's "Silent Eagle" the tournament's Most Valuable Player.

The third Greyhound to receive honor was probably the most opular. From his playing days as a Hannibal-LaGrange Trojan o his return as mentor of the most envied school in junior college ranks, Cotton Fitzsimmons was always a fan favorite. He as not only a gifted coach, but a refreshing off-court presence. is being named Coach of the Year for the second straight year, tourney first, came as no surprise. It was a fitting farewell. The ollowing spring, Fitzsimmons accepted an assistant coaching osition at Kansas State University, the second stop in a successful career that culminated with over 15 years in the NBA.

Fitzsimmons later described his 1967 champion squad as the most talented team I had [at Moberly]. I loved all my eams, but that was the best. Because we'd won the national he previous year], that team had more pressure on it than any eam I coached. As you start into the season, you're rated No. — and you've got to try to maintain that rating. We played the oughest schedule of any junior college in America at that age.[4] [Entering the tournament] you have the same apprehensions you always have. But, you also have the same confidence. We *were* Moberly. We *did* believe in ourselves. In order or somebody [else] to win, they were going to have to beat us."

Nobody did. In the Juco Tournament's first 20 years, Moberly Junior College was the class of the field.

The only individual in tourney history to be selected twice to the All-Tournament Team as a member of a champion, Moberly's Harrison Steptor completed his collegiate career at Michigan State, played briefly for the Harlem Globetrotters, then later died of sickle-cell anemia. (Photo courtesy of Michigan State University)

Moberly's "Silent Eagle," tourney MVP Tom Thoenon went on to play at the University of Missouri. (Photo courtesy of the **Moberly Monitor-Index**)

[3]Cotton Fitzsimmons described Harrison Stepter as "the best collegiate point guard I ever had. Basically, I just turned the ballclub over to him." Ironically, the St. Louis native was not a guard when Fitzsimmons recruited him. According to Fitzsimmons, Stepter played forward and center on the same high school team as Jo Jo White, later an All-American at Kansas University. "Jo Jo played guard and did all the shooting. Nobody even thought much about Stepter. I really liked him. I saw him as a guard even then."

When White graduated at mid-term, Fitzsimmons began to worry. "They only had about four games left. Stepter, instead of being the center and staying under the basket, took it upon himself to bring the ball up. Not only did he bring the ball up, he started scoring. He had some games like 30 points. I was afraid all the other [coaches] would come out of the woodwork, see what I'd seen earlier, and I'd lose him."

[4]Despite the tough schedule, Moberly nearly compiled a perfect record. The Greyhounds two defeats came when Harrison Stepter was hurt. Since "only Jack Hartman had been able to take an undefeated team [to the title]," Cotton Fitzsimmons looked on the Stepter injury as "a blessing in disguise."

As Fitzsimmons told it: "We were playing Jefferson County Community College. Stepter drives to the basket and a guy cuts him off, just reaches around and grabs him. He falls and dislocates his shoulder.

"The next night we play Mineral Area [College, Flat River, Missouri]. Stepter [his shoulder in a sling] plays basically with his left hand. He plays a fine game, but he's playing left-handed. He can't hardly do anything. They beat us. That's our first loss. I'll never forget, they carried [Coach Bob] Sechrest all around the gym. It was the first time that Mineral Area had ever beaten Moberly. You would have thought they had won the national championship.

"Now we go to Vincennes. Vincennes is tough. They used to have these twin brothers that worked all the games. On every jump ball, before it ever got to the player's nose, Vincennes would tip it. They never called it. You couldn't get a jump ball in the building. I think we lost that game, 72-58.

"Because Stepter's hurt, I know why we lost to Vincennes. But, I wasn't happy with the Vincennes game in general. I had already ordered a meal [after the game]. So my team doesn't use Stepter as an excuse, I pay the people for the meal, but we don't eat it.

"The next morning we're up early and we have no breakfast. The only stop we make is in St. Louis 150 miles or so away. I guess maybe they have a Coke and candy bar while I'm not looking. I drive back the next 150 to Moberly, pull in in late afternoon, pull in behind the gym, get out, and say, 'Get 'em on.' This is on a Sunday. We practice and we practice and I'm on them bad.

"I remember when we were done — I forget how much I gave them, but I think it was close to $10 — I told them, 'Now you can go eat. But, I don't want to have that kind of play again ever.'

"Well, Monday we go play Burlington, who is by far better than any of those teams [we lost to]. We kick Burlington's ass. We never lose another game and we win the national championship."

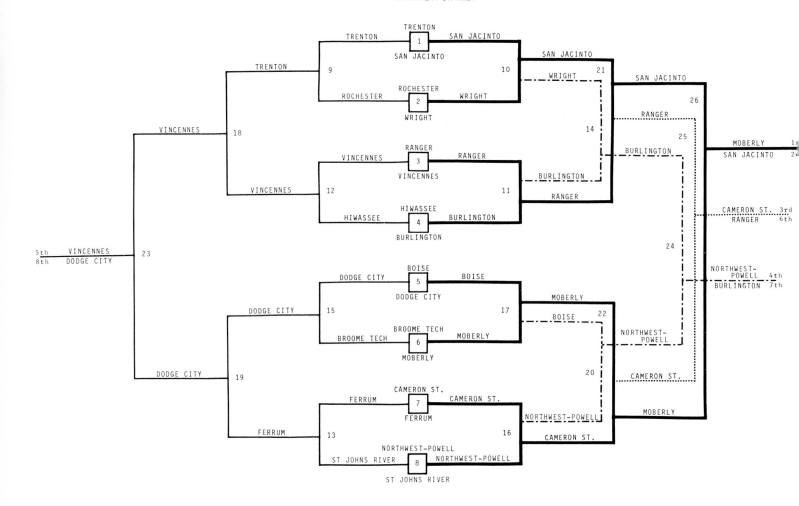

1967 TOURNAMENT BRACKET

Tournament Results

Tuesday: Game

1. San Jacinto — 91 Trenton — 75
2. Wright — 97 Rochester St. — 94
3. Ranger — 72 Vincennes — 61
4. Burlington — 59 Hiwassee — 57
5. Boise — 91 Dodge City — 77
6. Moberly — 73 Broome Tech — 52

Wednesday: Game

7. Cameron St. — 75 Ferrum — 62
8. Northwest-Powell — 91 St. Johns River — 86
9. Trenton — 94 Rochester St. — 80
10. San Jacinto — 89 Wright — 78
11. Ranger — 98 Burlington — 68

Thursday: Game

12. Vincennes — 63 Hiwassee — 51
13. Ferrum — 83 St. Johns River — 64
14. Burlington — 91 Wright — 77
15. Dodge City — 86 Broome Tech — 82 OT
16. Cameron St. — 89 Northwest-Powell — 79
17. Moberly — 70 Boise — 50

Friday: Game

18. Vincennes — 70 Trenton — 59
19. Dodge City — 73 Ferrum — 67
20. Northwest-Powell — 84 Boise — 71
21. San Jacinto — 89 Range — 85
22. Moberly — 72 Cameron St. — 65

Saturday: Game

23. Vincennes — 73 Dodge City — 64
24. Northwest-Powell — 102 Burlington — 85
25. Cameron St. — 91 Ranger — 77
26. Moberly — 56 San Jacinto — 55

How They Finished in 1967

1. Moberly Junior College
2. San Jacinto College
3. Cameron State Agricultural College
4. Northwest Community College
5. Vincennes University
6. Ranger Junior College
7. Burlington Community College
8. Dodge City Community Junior College

All-Tournament Team

Percy Anderson — San Jacinto College
Bill Bullock — Cameron State Agricultural College
Wayne Canaday — Vincennes University
Walter "Buddy" Haines — Wright Junior College
John Johnson — Northwest Community College
Steve Shumaker — Burlington Community College
Harrison Stepter — Moberly Junior College
Oliver Taylor — San Jacinto College
Tom Thoenen — Moberly Junior College
Jerry Venable — Ferrum Junior Colleg

Coach of the Year

Lowell "Cotton" Fitzsimmons — Moberly Junior College

Player of the Year

Tom Thoenen — Moberly Junior College

Sesher Sportsmanship Award

Oliver Taylor — San Jacinto College

he American Legion faced a challenge: Its three-year-old season ticket mail order system was not working.

The Hutchinson Post Office complained about the yearly crush of humanity outside its doors before each ticket-purchasing deadline. Fans were equally unhappy. Wrote one disgruntled line waiter to the *Hutchinson News*, "When you stand in line at the Post Office for two hours and you are about number 20 you feel pretty certain you are going to get tickets. Then 10 days later here comes your 'Dear John' letter with your unopened envelope."

The Legion's answer?

Three weeks before the 21st annual event, on Sunday, February 25, season tickets would go on sale at the Sports Arena. First come, first served.

The lineup started at 2:30 a.m. Saturday. Armed with sleeping bag, protective plastic covering, canvas tarpaulin, and a fuel heater, Fred Parrish, a Hutchinson cabinet maker, settled in for the nearly 35-hour wait.

Four hours later, Floyd Drolte joined him.

The numbers steadily increased. By nightfall, 500 tourney faithful were camped in line outside the Arena.

Inside, guests to the Fireman's Ball warmed to the music of Toby Stout and his band. Outside, avid basketball fans watched Kansas play Kansas State on television or heard Hutchinson Community Junior College play Pratt on the radio, their ardor tested by steady drizzle, an occasional heavy shower, and a 38-degree temperature.

When the doors opened at 1 p.m. the following afternoon, those who had braved the wait eagerly filed into the warm confines of the Arena. Their prime thoughts were not on physical comfort, however. Everyone wondered what kind of seating would be available when their turn came.

In a little more than three hours, Legion officials processed 960 requests for 3,830 season tickets. Despite the long wait, the new system was deemed the best yet. As Mrs. Ray Robertson told the *News*, "If you want them bad enough to wait for them, you deserve them."

THE PARTICIPANTS

The courage of the hardy season-ticket purchasers did not go unrewarded. The field for the 1968 NJCAA Tournament was the best yet. Combined, the 16 regional representatives had won just under 88 percent of their games. Eleven were rated in the top 20.

Heading the list was 1967 runner-up San Jacinto College. It was a different Raven club from the year before, though. Only one starter returned — Ollie Taylor. Head coaching chores had also changed with Tom Sewell now in the school's administration. In order to build quick experience, new coach Ron Rucker, Sewell's former assistant, pulled a chapter out of his boss' playbook. With Taylor's 33-point average leading the way, San Jacinto plowed through a punishing 42-game schedule, culminating in a grueling three game Region 14 play-off with No. 3 Tyler Junior College. Since the Ravens incurred only two losses, few questioned their top ranking.

In contrast, No. 2 Vincennes University returned eight members from its previous year's fifth-place team, including four starters. Led by All-American Wayne Canady and hot-shooting

Northeastern's Cliff Meely (No. 40) was later an All-Big 8 selection at the University of Colorado and a five-year veteran of the NBA. (Photo courtesy of Northeastern Junior College)

freshman Willie Humes, the Trailblazers had blazed to a 23-1 record, the best in the school's history. The only former champs in the meet had their sights on a second national title.

As the two top-rated teams in the country, San Jacinto and Vincennes were automatically accorded the roles of co-favorites. The chance of a second consecutive meeting of No. 1 and No. 2 in the championship was unlikely, however. Nine other ranked teams posed formidable obstacles for the favorites:

No. 4 Boise College (25-3), the fifth-best defensive club in the country (61.7) with five returning members from its 1967 tourney team;

No. 6 Mercer County Community College (27-2), another 1967 tourney veteran (as Trenton Junior College) with no losses to a two-year school in the current campaign;

Region	Team
1	Boise College — Boise, Idaho
2	Murray State College — Tishomingo, Oklahoma
3	Broome Technical Community College — Binghamton, New York
4	Robert Morris College — Carthage, Illinois
5	Christian College of the Southwest — Mesquite, Texas
6	Hutchinson Community Junior College — Hutchinson, Kansas
7	Paducah Junior College — Paducah, Kentucky
8	Miami-Dade Junior College, North Campus — Miami, Florida
9	Northeastern Junior College — Sterling, Colorado
10	Gardner-Webb College — Boiling Springs, North Carolina
11	Iowa Central Community College — Fort Dodge, Iowa
12	Vincennes University — Vincennes, Indiana
13	Bismarck Junior College — Bismarck, North Dakota
14	San Jacinto College — Pasadena, Texas
15	Mercer County Community College — Trenton, New Jersey
16	Missouri Baptist College of St. Louis — St. Louis, Missouri

No. 7 Hutchinson Community Junior College (24-1), possessor of the nation's longest winning streak (23 games) and a decided home court advantage;

No. 8 Gardner-Webb College (30-1), a tourney newcomer with two *Scholastic Magazine* High School All-Americans (Artis Gilmore and Ernie Fleming) and the country's best record;

No. 13 Robert Morris College (33-3), another debutant and owner of the nation's fourth-best defense (60.5);

No. 14 Northeastern Junior College (22-4), survivor of the most competitive regional with wins over No. 9 Trinidad State Junior College and No. 11 Lamar Junior College;

No. 15 Paducah Junior College (28-2), a first-timer with only one loss to a junior college foe;

No. 16 Murray State College (27-4), winner of always tough Region 2 with a victory over No. 12 St. Gregory's College; and

No. 20 Broome Technical Community College (25-5), another top defensive squad (64.9, 10th-best in the nation) and the "old man" of the field with seven previous appearances.

Four unranked newcomers also deserved serious regard: Christian College of the Southwest (30-6) had upended 1967 Region 5 representative Ranger Junior College; Iowa Central Community College (25-5) had downed Southeastern Iowa Area Community College (formerly Burlington Community College) — architect of the single losses for Vincennes and Hutchinson — and No. 5 Ellsworth Junior College; Miami-Dade Junior College (24-5) had defeated DeKalb Junior College, one of the top teams in the Southeast, 89-87 in two overtimes; and Missouri Baptist College of St. Louis (23-6) had crushed No. 18 Crowder College, 83-68.

Most years Bismarck Junior College's 20-8 record would have earned respect. But, representing a notoriously weak region in a year of super teams, the North Dakotans were simply discounted. The fact that Bismarck's first-round opponent was the hometown Blue Dragon quintet insured an early exit for the Mystics.

TUESDAY — A SEVEN-FOOTER AND A TRAFFIC JAM

With expectations of close, exciting competition running high, the opener was a surprise. For 5½ minutes Mercer County completely shut down Robert Morris scoring, building an early 22-7 cushion. Despite the brilliant outside shooting and game-high 31 points of Leonard Brasfield, Robert Morris never recovered. Mercer County's easy 79-63 victory gave the crowd time to renew old friendships — and to talk about the upcoming contest.

The opening session had attracted a larger than usual crov because of Gardner-Webb's star center, Artis Gilmore — tl first legitimate seven-footer to play in the tournament. Cou side fans were awed by his towering 7-2 presence.

Not so his opponents. The Northeastern Plainsmen forc the freshman giant into four fouls in the first 11 minutes. G more watched most of the remaining action from the bench

Ironically, when Gilmore picked up his final infraction wi seven minutes left in the game, his teammates came to li Having trailed most of the way, the Boiling Springs Bulldo suddenly showed snarl, forcing the Plainsmen to overtime.

The reprieve was short-lived. Behind the one-two punch Don Edwards (23) and Cliff Meely (21), Northeastern held Gardner-Webb, 83-80, in a mild upset.

A *major* upset brewed in the afternoon finale. Underdo Paducah waged a bitter battle with longtime rival Vincenne taking a 32-28 halftime lead and holding it for 12 minutes. The nine unanswered Trailblazer points in the next four minut doomed Paducah. Pre-tourney favorite Vincennes survive 62-59.

In previous years, the Region 6 representative had bee scheduled to play in the opening night feature to draw a goo crowd. After the 1967 tournament, NJCAA officials chose drop the tradition, letting the luck of the draw set the schedul The decision eventuated a rarity in Hutchinson — a traffic jar

Local fans not wanting to miss any of the Blue Dragons' 6 p.r opener converged on the Sports Arena at the same time mar non-fans were on their way home from work. Lines of cars fou blocks deep surrounded the Arena in every direction, causir an occasional frayed nerve and several late arrivals.

When the latecomers were finally seated, they found the heavily favored Dragons in an unexpected close fight. Bismar pestered the local squad, tying the game five times befo Hutchinson could create breathing room. Then the Blue Dra ons opened a 46-33 halftime edge and took wing. All 12 Hutc inson squad members played and all but one scored. Th hometown rejoiced with the team's 24th consecutive victor a 103-72 rout.

Tension returned in the evening feature. In a contest destine to go into overtime, Murray State and Missouri Baptist me sured each other to the tune of 19 ties. The final deadlock cam on an 18-foot fall-away jumper by the St. Louis squad's Joh Simmons with eight seconds left in regulation.

Missouri Baptist's good fortune ended there. The Troja failed to score in the first three minutes of overtime, allowin favored Murray State to eke out a 66-62 win.

The nightcap began as a tight defensive struggle befor upstart Miami-Dade went on a 23-3 rampage. With five mir utes left in the half, No. 4 Boise was in a 30-9 hole. Fans exite the Arena in droves. The Idaho squad made a valiant attempt climb back into the game, but could only reduce the deficit t a final 62-55 margin.

Boise Coach Murray Satterfield later stated that, with th experience of the 1967 tournament behind him and five return ing players, "I really had a lot of confidence. I really felt they [hi players] knew what it took [to win].

"I didn't have an assistant at the time so Eddie Sutton, th coach at College of Southern Idaho [later head coach at th Universities of Arkansas and Kentucky] said, 'Hey! I know you players as well as you do. How about letting me set on th bench with you.' I welcomed him.'

Then came Miami-Dade's 23-3 spurt. "Golly, we played bac I couldn't believe it! That's when Sutton left. He left with th rest of the crowd."

The Boise loss was the only shocker of the day.

WEDNESDAY — JUST WATCHING

Hutchinson's first day of spring was blustery and cold, the mercury hovering in the mid- to upper-30s. The chill appearec to have little effect on the heat of battle inside the Arena Broome Tech All-American Frank Streety was particularly hot

---

[1]Paducah and Vincennes first competed with one another in 1952. They were once members of the old Kentuckiana Conference and met regularly. Then in 1965 in a controversial game at Vincennes, Paducah walked off the court with more than six minutes left to play. The two schools fulfilled contractual obligations to meet the following year, then discontinued scheduling each other when Vincennes pulled out of the conference. The 1968 opening-round game was their first meeting since and generated considerable emotion on both sides.

hitting 55 percent of his shots from the field, accumulating a game-high 32 points. With three minutes remaining, the Hornets were comfortably in front of the Christian Trojans, 72-66.

Then cold nipped the New Yorkers. Christian scored 12 unanswered points to cop the win. Eight came from the line and explained the surprise victory. Slapped with a 21-8 disparity in fouls, Broome Tech was unable to overcome a 30-6 Christian advantage from the charity stripe.

Having challenged throughout and trailing by only four with 10 minutes to go, the Iowa Central Panthers held high hopes of duplicating Christian's feat. Top-rated San Jacinto responded by amassing 31 points to the gun, bursting the Iowans' balloon, 89-73.

The key to the Raven victory was Iowa Central's inability to top Jeff Halliburton and Ollie Taylor. The inside duo scored 28 of the first 29 San Jacinto points on the way to game-high totals of 33 and 29, respectively.

With only one major surprise in the first round, fans anticipated tremendous competition in the championship bracket. The opening quarterfinal did not disappoint them. The Mercer County-Northeastern match-up was intense from beginning to end with five technicals whistled. Both sides lost key personnel in the struggle to dominate: 6-8 center Wayne Sokolowski, Mercer's tallest man, departed at the 7:30 mark, the Vikings leading, 58-57; Don Edwards, the leading scorer in Northeastern's opener, followed a minute later, the Sterling crew ahead, 60-59. The latter loss hurt more. Without the services of their best playmaker, the Plainsmen failed to score for four minutes. Led by Bobby Sands' 32, Mercer County advanced, 82-71.

The time was at hand. The Arena was packed solid, overflowing into the aisles. The fire department complained about the flagrant disregard for existing fire codes, all for naught. There could be only one reason for such a staggering turn-out for a mid-week tourney session.

Hutchinson was playing.

Through the years of frustration, Blue Dragon fans had remained loyal, perpetually optimistic. Since the current Hutchinson squad possessed the school's best credentials to date, many believed that their day was finally just around the corner — provided they could get by Vincennes.

The Trailblazers were equally serious about the confrontation. Leading scorer Willie Humes was suited and ready for war though weakened by a bout with strep throat which had relegated him to civilian status in the Vincennes opener.

The conflict was a battle royale, the advantage switching sides in grand sweeps. Hutchinson jumped out to a 15-9 lead before Vincennes responded, taking a 45-39 halftime edge. The

The 1968 Sesher Sportsmanship Award-winner, Wayne Canady later played at the University of Miami. (Photo courtesy of Gus Stevens, Vincennes University)

combatants continued trading blows, first one, then the other spurting from behind to grab the lead. Finally, with 3:30 remaining, score tied 77-all, the stage was set for the clincher. Back-to-back pairs of free throws by Humes and Ron Burnett followed by a turn-around jumper by Wayne Canaday foretold the outcome. Employing a stall to force Hutchinson into fouls, Vincennes outscored the Blue Dragons 15-5 down the home stretch, claiming an 89-82 victory.

One man was unimpressed with the epic quarterfinal — Ed Sparling, whose Burlington Blackhawks had failed to make it to the tournament despite handing Hutchinson and Vincennes their only regular season defeats.

According to former Vincennes radio broadcaster Gus Stevens: "I saw him [Sparling] after the game. He had called it. He thought Vincennes would win. I said, 'Well, Ed. How did you like the Vincennes-Hutchinson game?' Of course, I was all smiles. He looked at me as only he can and said, 'Baby, when you're a loser, you don't *like* it, you just go to watch.'"

THURSDAY — UNWINDING

After the previous evening's tense finale and disappointing conclusion, Hutchinson fans found it hard to rouse enthusiasm for the tourney's Thursday bill of fare. The day's lackluster play reflected their mood.

The first two contests were boring blow-outs. Paducah never trailed, eliminating Bismarck, 93-56, and Iowa Central coasted in its 91-78 victory over Broome Tech.

Fans generated a modicum of fervor when Hutchinson and Northeastern exchanged leads 16 times and tied six in the first half of the afternoon finale. They were unable to sustain it, however. The Sterling squad outscored the downhearted Blue Dragons, 20-7, during a four-minute stretch and earned a 97-88 win, avenging an earlier season loss to Hutchinson.

The day's most exciting action was equally uninspiring. Boise nearly blew an 18-point lead in the final 11 minutes, squeaking by Missouri Baptist, 66-64.

Quarterfinal play followed suit.

All-American Joe Hamilton lived up to claims that he was "the greatest outside player in basketball today" with field goals from all distances and a 1968 tourney-high 39 points. Though his shooting feats entertained the crowd, they did not promote a Christian win. San Jacinto opened a 19-point halftime gap and eased to a 106-94 triumph. All five Raven starers hit double figures, topped by Jeff Halliburton's 35 and Ollie Taylor's 27.

After Murray State broke open a close contest with Miami-Dade just before intermission, fans poured out of the Arena. By the time the Aggies posted a 78-59 win, fewer than 400 remained. Those who persevered, however, left with the knowledge that the following evening's action would be more interesting. With the inside work of Mike Johnson (29) and Danny Hester (21) and the outside marksmanship of Dale Blaut (21), Murray State demonstrated it possessed the tools to challenge the nation's No. 1 team.

FRIDAY — DROOPY SOCKS

For the second year in a row, the country's top two teams were on a collision course. The possibility attracted a sizable semifinal crowd. Most speculators felt San Jacinto's road to the championship was bumpier and were there to see the Ravens' nightcap match-up with Murray State. Few gave Mercer County a chance against Vincennes. There were two reasons why the evening opener figured to be cut and dry.

First, though Eastern teams often ranked high in the NJCAA poll, courtside touts still considered them weak in comparison to the rest of the country. Mercer County offered no scholarships. The school's success was directly attributed to Viking Coach Howie Landa, an effervescent go-getter with the uncanny ability to mold a "silk purse" squad out of "sow's ear" local talent. One look at his current crop was enough to discourage any wagerer. The Vikings were a collection of elbows and kneecaps with the finesse of a charging bull. Their deficiencies were accentuated by their socks — droopy relics whose dwindling elasticity barely kept them above the ankle.

More importantly, with almost the same personnel on each squad, Vincennes had overcome a 22-6 deficit to down Mercer

County 70-59 in consolation play the previous year.

Their 1968 rematch followed a similar pattern. After four ties early, Mercer County reeled off 10 straight points to take a 24-14 advantage. Threatening to duplicate its feat of a year ago, Vincennes responded with eight unanswered points.

The Trailblazer charge went no further. With the Hutchinson crowd sentimentally backing the underdog, the Vikings held off Vincennes' attack, opened a 43-38 halftime edge, and main-

Allen Bradfield's exhortations from the sidelines did not prevent Mercer County's upset of Vincennes in the 1968 semifinals. (Photo courtesy of Gus Stevens, Vincennes University)

After capturing tourney scoring honors in 1968 with 114 points, San Jacinto's Jeff Halliburton completed his collegiate career at Drake University, then spent two years in the NBA. (Photo courtesy of Drake University)

tained a two- to eight-point spread the rest of the way. Displaying heart, determination, and an abundance of hustle, Mercer County defeated No. 2 Vincennes, 80-72.

The upset primed the crowd for another. Early action indicated the possibility existed.

After San Jacinto jumped on top with the first four points, Murray State slowly retaliated, finally grabbing a 19-18 edge. In the next two minutes, the lead changed hands eight times, with no misses at either end of the court. The Aggies came through the toe-to-toe exchange full of confidence, opening three-point leads twice.

However, just before intermission, San Jacinto got hot, sprinting ahead, taking an eight-point margin to the locker room.

Returning to the floor with renewed purpose, Murray State whittled the difference to two. Ollie Taylor single-handedly rebuilt it with three successive baskets. When the San Jacinto lead grew to 12 with half the period remaining, fan hopes for another upset waned.

Then came a critical moment of the game. In a scramble for a rebound under the basket, Raven center Jeff Halliburton caught an elbow in the mouth. Blood flowed freely. There was no question he needed medical aid. San Jacinto's leading scorer in its first two outings and its tallest player, exited the court for the dressing room.

The loss of Halliburton was such a serious blow to the Raven cause that Coach Ron Rucker accompanied his star, leaving floor strategy to his assistant. Tournament physician, Dr. Jack Perkins, who made a habit of carrying a suture kit with him, was summoned and quickly stitched the cut — so quickly that when Halliburton returned many fans wondered if the red they had seen previously had been an illusion.

The damage was already done, however. While Halliburton was being tended to, San Jacinto went flat, the momentum shifting to Murray State. Slowly, inexorably the Aggies reduced the deficit. With 46 seconds to go, Ron Robertson sank a corner shot to bring Murray State within a basket.

San Jacinto held the ball. The Aggies fouled, sending Larry Pitre to the line. The sophomore guard calmly sank the first, missed the second.

The Aggies grabbed the rebound and sped up the court. Danny Hester fired and missed. On the carom, the ball hit a San Jacinto player and went out of bounds.

Murray State Coach Gene Robbins called time and tried to dream up a miracle. When play resumed, San Jacinto allowed

Hester to drive to the bucket uncontested. A full-court pass a[t] up the remaining two seconds. With the 71-70 final, San Jacin[to] posted its 43rd win of the year — one away from a title.

SATURDAY — PESKY GNATS

An NJCAA experiment proved inconsequential in the troph[y] day opener. The use of three officials neither hindered n[or] helped Robert Morris. The Eagles simply were unable to ove[r]come an early cold streak, conceding fifth-place to Iowa Cen[n]tral, 75-62.

Miami-Dade also succumbed to chills in the fourth-plac[e] contest, hitting only 9 of 37 field goals and 6 of 14 free throw[s] in the first half. Northeastern of Sterling jumped out to an 18-[0] lead and poured it on, massacring the Floridians, 99-60.

The turning-point in the third-place game came when Murra[y] State's Mike Johnson nailed four successive second-half fiel[d] goals, pulling the Aggies out of "we-could-have-won-it-all["]doldrums and back into the game. The Oklahomans grabbe[d] the lead, slowed the tempo, and thrived off a Vincennes pres[s,] winning 67-58.

Most observers considered the Mercer County-San Jacint[o] championship tilt a mismatch comparable to a PT boat attac[k]ing a battleship. The difference was illustrated in the stars [of] both squads.

San Jacinto's Ollie Taylor was a war-horse, a superb physic[al] specimen. His leaping ability was the greatest tourney followe[r] had ever seen. When Taylor launched skyward for a reboun[d] he generally retrieved it, coming down with legs splayed an[d] elbows out, clearing a wide swath. Though only 6-2, he playe[d] as if he were 6-9. The Bronx sophomore was a consistent Roc[k] of Gibraltar, epitomizing the Ravens' style.

In contrast, Mercer County was a swarm of pesky gnats. Hus[n]tle was the name of the Vikings' game and Bobby Sands wa[s] their head hustler. Wherever the ball went, the good-lookin[g] Trenton sophomore always seemed near it. On offense, he wa[s] the team's leading scorer, the first down on a fast break. O[n] defense, his quick hands repeatedly stripped balls loose, eithe[r] setting up Mercer sprints down the court or destroying th[e] opponent's rhythm. At 6-3, Sands possessed none of Taylor['s] physical attributes. Instead, he relied on acutely develope[d] court savvy to guide his unglamorous, often awkward team[s]mates.

The rational choice was San Jacinto; the emotional one, Me[rcer]

...er County. With its beloved Blue Dragons on the sidelines, the predominately Hutchinson audience loaned its heart to the latter.

The overwhelming crowd response immediately took effect. Mercer County's normal aggressive, reaching, slapping defense accelerated. Previously poised San Jacinto fell victim to the scrambling style. Appearing in a hurry to finish matters early, the Ravens neglected their patterned offense, made numerous errant passes, and committed a rash of charging fouls. With Coach Howie Landa's animated exhortations from courtside delighting fans, the Vikings took control, building a 34-27 margin just before intermission.

In the locker room at halftime, Coach Ron Rucker confronted his Ravens. "You're 20 minutes away from winning it all. But, you're not going to do it playing the way you did the first half. This is the worst you've played in the entire tournament. You've got to suck it up and get it together for 20 minutes. You can be national champions."

The chastisement worked. San Jacinto restored its offensive game plan. Raven board domination, which had gone unnoticed in the first half because of Mercer County's many easy fast-break chances, became a prevalent factor; when the Vikings did not score on their first shot, they did not receive a second. Within five minutes of returning to the floor, San Jacinto evened matters and threatened to break the game open.

Under the heat of pressure, Coach Landa shed his coat and increased his sideline antics, flailing at the air with bare arms under his short-sleeved white shirt. His Viking charges responded, pulling from the same reserve of determination they had displayed against Vincennes.

The contest developed into a nip-and-tuck battle, neither team giving way.

The climax came in the final minute. After Ollie Taylor's three-point play gave San Jacinto a 64-62 lead with 2:03 to go, the Ravens gained control of the ball and held it. With 41 seconds remaining, Mercer County was forced to foul. Freshman guard Terry Mullin calmly sank two free throws, upping the advantage to four.

A 20-foot prayer by James Fitzgerald gave the Vikings renewed life. San Jacinto broke Mercer County's press, setting up Jeff Halliburton for a short jumper which missed. The Vikings regained possession.

With time evaporating, Fitzgerald tried another prayer from beyond the key. It hit the heel of the rim, bouncing high to the right wing. Fitzgerald raced to the rebound, took a step, and returned the ball to flight with a wild hook. The ball hit the top of the backboard and bounded away as time expired.

San Jacinto College ascended the junior college basketball throne, 66-64.

THE AFTERMATH — NO RESPECT

There were few long faces at the tournament's conclusion. The NJCAA and American Legion were elated by a new gross receipt record of nearly $50,000, a 10 percent increase over 1967's take. Hutchonians were smiling with the news that the Sports Arena, a foresighted gamble in 1949 and now the envy of many communities, was less than $100,000 from being paid for. Happiest of all were the fans. Standing in line for hours to buy season tickets to see excellent talent (eight of the 10 All-Tournament Team selections were eventually drafted by the pros), topflight competition, and an exciting ending was more than worthwhile.

Even the losers had reason to feel good. Reflecting the sentiments of Hutchinson fans who were enamored with the gutsy Cinderella club from New Jersey, the awards committee named Howie Landa Coach of the Year and Bobby Sands the Most Valuable Player. The unexpected honors drew loud approval from the Arena audience and appreciative grins from the recipients. As Landa told the *Hutchinson News*, if his team could not win, "the next best thing is being awarded two of the top three trophies."

The only shades of disappoint came from the unlikeliest corner — the champions. San Jacinto players and fans were baffled by the choices of the awards committee. Considering the team's accomplishments in only his first year at the helm, they

Howie Landa's selection as Coach of the Year and Bobby Sand's selection as MVP were major surprises, reflections of fan sentiments toward the droopy-socked Mercer County Vikings. Sands finished his collegiate career at Pepperdine University. (Photo courtesy of Howie Landa)

felt Ron Rucker deserved the Coach of the Year honor, particularly since only once before had the award gone to someone other than the coach of the winning squad. And, anybody who had watched Ollie Taylor's tourney performance and leadership was hard pressed to argue against his being the best talent in the event. Even Mercer County's Landa admitted, "Ollie Taylor killed us." Though enthroned at the pinnacle of junior college basketball, the Ravens were hurt by the lack of recognition those awards implied.

To the average tourney observer, San Jacinto had entered the event as the top-rated team and simply won as predicted. Few understood that the 44 Raven victories, the most ever by a national collegiate champion at any level, were produced with the almost exclusive use of *five* players — Jeff Halliburton, Ollie Taylor, Jeff Lake, Larry Pitre, and Terry Mullin — the tallest of which (Halliburton) was only 6-4.

As Rucker later stated, "I had a tremendous amount of respect for this ballclub. They performed miracles. We went

In the words of Mercer's Howie Landa, "Ollie Taylor killed us." Considered the "legitimate" 1968 MVP, Taylor had exceptional leaping ability for 6-2, good enough, in fact, to allow him to play alongside Elvin Hayes on the front line of the Houston Cougars. Taylor later spent four years in the ABA. (Photo courtesy of Kenny Bernard)

through a grueling season. All these kids were extremely tired and banged up. Even though they were hurt and sick, they would not quit. People did not realize the punishment they went through in the three play-off games with Tyler. Tyler was very physical. When you played Tyler, you put down 6-8, 6-7, 6-6, 6-5, and 6-3 [for them] and matched that with 6-4, 6-2, and three six-footers [for us]. That doesn't match up."

San Jacinto's problems began when three 6-6 recruits recanted one week before school started. The Ravens were left with nine squad members. Practice scrimmages were possible only when the student manager suited up.

The resulting void placed tremendous pressure on San Jacinto's only remaining height — Halliburton and Taylor. As their tourney performances witnessed, the pair responded with superhuman efforts inside. They ranked first and third in scoring with 114 and 97 points, respectively, their combined total representing over 60 percent of the Ravens' output. Always outmanned in the middle, the two used their abundant physical skills and courage to win rebounding wars. With Mercer County measuring 6-8, 6-6, and 6-5 across the front line, and with Halliburton weakened due to a liquid diet imposed by stitches in his mouth and bothered by a bandaged bruised thigh, the Raven duo dominated the boards, leading San Jacinto to a 44-33 rebounding edge in the title tilt.

Lack of depth also tethered the Raven starters with the burden of not fouling. According to Rucker, "the game we lost to Tyler at mid-season, Ollie fouled out. The game we were beat at Tyler the first game of the play-offs, Ollie fouled out. These five kids knew if they ever got in foul trouble, we had had it. There wasn't any margin for error." During the tournament, San Jacinto committed only 50 fouls, including a low 10 in the championship contest. No Raven fouled out in four games.

Only San Jacinto fans fully appreciated the team's achievement. They demonstrated it the following day. When the victorious Ravens arrived at Hobby (Houston International) Airport, a cheering throng of 2,500 was there to greet them.

Tournament Results

Tuesday:	Game		
		1	Mercer County — 79 Robert Morris — 63
		2	Northeastern — 83 Gardner-Webb — 80 OT
		3	Vincennes — 62 Paducah — 59
		4	Hutchinson — 103 Bismarck — 72
		5	Murray St. — 66 Missouri Baptist — 62 OT
		6	Miami-Dade North — 62 Boise — 55
Wednesday:	Game		
		7	Christian — 78 Broome Tech — 72
		8	San Jacinto — 89 Iowa Central — 73
		9	Robert Morris — 82 Gardner-Webb — 80
		10	Mercer County — 82 Northeastern — 71
		11	Vincennes — 89 Hutchinson — 82
Thursday:	Game		
		12	Paducah — 93 Bismarck — 56
		13	Iowa Central — 95 Broome Tech — 78
		14	Northeastern — 97 Hutchinson — 88
		15	Boise — 66 Missouri Baptist — 64
		16	San Jacinto — 106 Christian — 94
		17	Murray St. — 78 Miami-Dade North — 59
Friday:	Game		
		18	Robert Morris — 68 Paducah — 61
		19	Iowa Central — 85 Boise — 68
		20	Miami-Dade North — 86 Christian — 75
		21	Mercer County — 80 Vincennes — 72
		22	San Jacinto — 71 Murray St. — 70
Saturday:	Game		
		23	Iowa Central — 75 Robert Morris — 62
		24	Northeastern — 99 Miami-Dade North — 60
		25	Murray St. — 67 Vincennes — 58
		26	San Jacinto — 66 Mercer County — 64

How They Finished in 1968

1. San Jacinto College
2. Mercer County Community College
3. Murray State College
4. Northeastern Junior College
5. Iowa Central Community College
6. Vincennes University
7. Miami-Dade Junior College, North Campus
8. Robert Morris College

All-Tournament Team

Wayne Canaday — Vincennes University
Russell "Bo" Clarke — Hutchinson Community Junior College
Jeff Halliburton — San Jacinto College
Joe Hamilton — Christian College of the Southwest
Danny Hester — Murray State College
Cliff Meely — Northeastern Junior College
Robert Sands — Mercer County Community College
Wayne Sokolowski — Mercer County Community College
Frank Streety — Broome Tech Community College
Oliver Taylor — San Jacinto College

Coach of the Year

Howie Landa — Mercer County Community College

Most Valuable Player

Robert Sands — Mercer County Community College

Sesher Sportsmanship Award

Wayne Canaday — Vincennes University

Deciding to get an even bigger jump on 1969's Juco Tournament season-ticket buyers, Fred Parrish, 1968's first in line, arrived at the Sports Arena on Friday, February 21 at 8 p.m., 5½ hours before the start of his previous year's 35-hour vigil. He was surprised to find his prime station already taken.

At 8:30 that morning, almost 12 hours earlier, Mark Brown, a ninth grader at Central Junior High School, staked out the head position, unloading the obligatory line-waiting equipment — tent, sleeping bag, and camp heater — in preparation for a 52½-hour endurance test.

Madness had again struck basketball fanatic Hutchonians.

By Saturday evening a seven- to eight-block line serpentined around the Arena's south lot. The conditions were anything but ideal. Temperatures were in the low 30s; cold enough to require huddling to keep warm, but warm enough to melt the remnants of the previous week's eight-inch snowfall. Besides the mire of mud and slush, line-waiters were also inconvenienced by a lack of rest room facilities. Noting the occasional makeshift cardboard shelter mixed among the various sized tents, one thoughtful tenant erected a sign, labeling the encampment "Resurrection City II."

As a later *Hutchinson News* editorial described the event, "They were a sorry looking lot . . . It had all the appearance of a community disgrace . . . Obviously, if they were red-blooded, upstanding, patriotic American citizens, they would find something more constructive to do with their time.

"But appearances are deceiving, and what is obvious is not always true. They simply were patient sports enthusiasts, making do as best they could while waiting to get tickets to Hutchinson's biggest sports show."

THE PARTICIPANTS

Region	Team
1	Phoenix College — Phoenix, Arizona
2	Murray State College — Tishomingo, Oklahoma
3	Johnson & Wales Junior College of Business — Providence, Rhode Island
4	Robert Morris College — Carthage, Illinois
5	Howard County Junior College — Big Spring, Texas
6	Hutchinson Community Junior College — Hutchinson, Kansas
7	Paducah Community College — Paducah, Kentucky
8	Brevard Junior College — Cocoa, Florida
9	Northwest Community College — Powell, Wyoming
10	Gardner-Webb College — Boiling Springs, North Carolina
11	Southeastern Iowa Area Community College — Burlington, Iowa
12	Vincennes University — Vincennes, Indiana
13	Miles Community College — Miles City, Montana
14	San Jacinto College — Pasadena, Texas
16	Moberly Junior College — Moberly, Missouri
19	Robert Morris Junior College — Pittsburgh, Pennsylvania

When the first NJCAA poll of the 1968-69 season was released, basketball fans noted a conspicuous omission. The previous year's national champion was normally included in the top 20 as a matter of formality, even if graduation had decimated its ranks. San Jacinto College returned three starters, including All-Tournament selection Jeff Halliburton, and possessed

The Juco Tournament's first seven-footer, Artis Gilmore (No. 54) had a disappointing tourney experience two straight years. Afterwards, Gilmore attended Jacksonville University where he had better success, leading the Dolphins to a runner-up finish in the 1970 NCAA Final Four. He later played more than 17 years in the pros. (Photo courtesy of Jim Wiles, Gardner-Webb College)

one of the best records at any level of the sport over the past two seasons. Why were the Ravens not considered one of the country's best?

Pollsters soon reconsidered. San Jacinto won its first 13 games, lost to Tyler Junior College, then reeled off 29 more wins, sweeping the Region 14 play-off series with Tyler in two games. The Ravens entered the Juco Tournament with a remarkable three-year mark of 128-8. With the highest offensive average in the school's history (95.0) and the lowest defensive average in the nation (59.3), San Jacinto was definitely the No. 1 team in junior college circles. Odds appeared good that, for the third year in a row, the top-rated entrant would grab the title.

Though the Ravens were unanimously established tourney favorites by the press, there were 15 other contenders ready to dispute San Jacinto's top ranking. Heading the list were No. 2 Phoenix College and No. 4 Robert Morris Junior College of Pittsburgh. With perfect 32-0 and 27-0 records, respectively, the two held legitimate claim to a shot at the crown.

No. 6 Murray State College (26-4), No. 7 Southeastern Iowa Area Community College of Burlington (27-6), No. 8 Paducah Community College (25-2), No. 15 Vincennes University (19-5), No.16 Robert Morris College of Carthage, Illinois (28-5), and No. 18 Howard County Junior College (29-3) also felt strongly about their chances. Of these, the *Hutchinson News* favored Robert Morris of Carthage as the tourney "sleeper" based on the fact that the Eagles returned six members from their 1968 eighth-place squad and had already downed four tourney participants during the regular season. Many insiders, however, were more fearful of Ed Sparling's Burlington Black-hawks,[1] a physical ballclub led by All-American guard Fred Brown and high-scoring forward Dick Gibbs.

The unranked with potential included: Gardner-Webb College (30-3), the third-best offensive team in the nation (103.8), led by 7-2 All-American Artis Gilmore; newcomer Brevard Junior College (26-3), owner of an impressive win over the nation's top-scoring squad, No. 3 Indian River Junior College of Fort Pierce, Florida; and, Northwest Community College of Powell (26-7), engineer of an upset regional victory over No. 5 Northeastern Junior College of Sterling, Colorado.

The two unranked teams which frightened the competition most, however, were Moberly Junior College (23-8) and Hutchinson Community Junior College (21-9). Though neither possessed outstanding marks, both had shown steady improvement throughout the season. More importantly, Moberly's 16 tourney appearances and four national titles commanded respect. And, no one envied the squad which faced the Hutchinson Blue Dragons and their fervid fans in the Sports Arena.

Only two ballclubs were labeled long shots: Johnson & Wales Junior College of Business (24-2) and Miles Community College (14-9). Being the tournament's first representatives from Rhode Island and Montana, respectively, the two were expected to be stagestruck by the proceedings and no factor to the outcome.

TUESDAY — REAL SCARED

Interest in the National Junior College Basketball tournament was at an all-time high. If the long lineup for season tickets was not a sure indication, then the first reported incidence of ticket scalping was. Radio and newspaper coverage peaked. No fewer than nine of the participating teams brought broadcast crews to cover games, forcing improvised partitioning of press box facilities. The caliber of talent expected to perform on the Arena floor was also corroborated by a huge influx of four-year coaches and scouts. All signs pointed to an exhilarating week ahead.

The anticipated excitement immediately translated into the largest afternoon crowd to date in tournament history. Red-clad Hutchinson fans played hooky from school and work, packing the Arena. They patiently watched Paducah lead almost from beginning to end, downing Moberly, 80-76.

Then, they went deliriously crazy.

One Miles City student who traveled more than 800 miles from southeastern Montana to experience the first-time effort of the Pioneers, later told the *Hutchinson News*, "We didn't have any idea what we'd be up against. We talked to the boys just before the game and they were real scared."

The fears were well-founded. With the Arena audience roaring its approval at every turn, Hutchinson exploded to an 11-2 advantage. At halftime, the Blue Dragons led, 57-39. With 5:51 to go, they cracked the century mark. A missed free throw and four unsuccessful tip tries at the end prevented a new team scoring high. As it was, the 120-103 final tied the record for most points by a team in a game and set a new mark for two teams. The tournament was off to a spirited start.

The crowd petered out after the Hutchinson feature, leaving few to see Murray State win a streak scoring contest with Howard County, 71-68. It slowly regrouped during Burlington's 86-70 demolition of Northwest of Powell. By the time the teams took to the court for the evening feature, it had returned to full strength. The large turnout was primarily due to curiosity. Few expected any surprises. They were there just to see how good the top two teams in the country were.

No. 1 San Jacinto confirmed its ranking early, dashing to a 39-26 halftime edge over lowly Johnson & Wales. It was smooth sailing for the Ravens.

Then lightning struck. The Wildcats from Providence scored the first seven points of the second half and steadily slashed the lead. A basket by John Crenshaw with 12:07 to go, tied the score, 49-all.

In a fight for survival, San Jacinto could muster a lead no greater than four and even trailed briefly. Then with eight seconds remaining, Providence's Mike Polite politely popped the cords deadlocking the two teams at 70-all. It appeared the defending champs would be extended to overtime.

The Wildcats pressed with everyone up court. Suddenly, San Jacinto's Jeff Halliburton broke free. Raven guard Jimmy Green lofted a long pass over the defense into Halliburton's waiting hands. An easy lay-up thwarted San Jacinto's near embarrassment.

No. 2 Phoenix did not fare as well. Unimpressed with the undefeated credentials of the Bears, Robert Morris of Carthage jumped out to a 15-4 lead, maintained the difference through halftime, then increased it to 16. A Phoenix rally led by Denny Layton and Leroy Cobb reduced the deficit to six, but no more. Five Robert Morris players scored double figures, handing Phoenix its first loss, 84-75, and notching the tourney's first upset.

WEDNESDAY — I THOUGHT IT COUNTED

The tournament's other undefeated team also had its untainted record threatened in Wednesday's opener. After building a 15-point margin with 12 minutes to go, Robert Morris of Pittsburgh hit a scoring drought while the tenacious bulldogs of Gardner-Webb steadily closed the gap. A Steve Kebeck 20-footer with 3:45 to go tied the game, 79-all.[2]

Then reserve Chris Jones ended the Robert Morris tailspin nailing a short jumper. Momentum switched back to the Colonials who preserved their unblemished record with an 88-8? victory. Five Robert Morris players snagged double figures including Perry Johnson's game-high 32. The Pittsburgh crew also displayed excellent board power, outrebounding Gardner-Webb, 37-28, in spite of the lofty presence of Artis Gilmore.

The final first-round contest showcased the tourney's other seven-footer, Brevard's Pembrook Burrows. However, it was the guard play of Vincennes that stole the show. The Trailblazers dominated the boards, running circles around the Brevard defense. The dazzling backcourt pair of Oscar Evans and Willie Humes shared game honors with 24 points apiece, guiding the Trailblazers to an easy 97-83 win.

With only one surprise in the opening round, championship flight play figured to be top-notch. Though No. 1 San Jacinto and No. 4 Robert Morris of Pittsburgh appeared on a collision course in the lower bracket, the close shaves both squads had survived proved "anything could happen." The statement was particularly apropos in the upper bracket. Any one of the four teams had a shot at the finals. Since Hutchinson was one of them, a Wednesday evening sellout was assured.

As the Pioneers of Miles City discovered in their opener, facing a screaming mass of red was more than a little disconcerting. A key for any Hutchinson rival was to take the crowd out of the game. Thanks to the Blue Dragon's opening strategy, Paducah was able to do just that.

In Paducah's first outing, Moberly had successfully reduced a 12-point Indian lead to two in less than two minutes using a full-court press. Thinking that the Kentucky club had trouble handling pressure, Coach Gene Keady ordered his Blue Dragons to do the same. The quicker Indians slashed through the defense with ease, mounting a 14-point margin, putting a lid on the crowd.

Hutchinson fans were only temporarily silenced, however. Behind the one-two punch of sophomores Ray Willis and B? Clarke, the Blue Dragons rallied to within two at intermission. Willis evened matters with the first basket of the second half. From then on neither team dominated.

The final two minutes exemplified the second period'

---

[1] Though the institution officially became Southeastern Iowa Community College (later Southeastern Community College) and even moved to a brand new campus in West Burlington in 1973, locals plus the rest of the junior college world still referred to the school as "Burlington" and its basketball team as the "Burlington Blackhawks."

[2] During the tense moments of the Gardner-Webb comeback, latecomers to the afternoon session ran into an unexpected sight in the Arena parking lot — Robert Morris Coach Gus Krop. Somebody asked, "What the hell are you doing out here? Your team's playing!" Krop later explained, "My problem was that I'd get so damned excited. I felt like I was going to vomit. They later found out it was [caused by] diabetes."

tense defensive struggle. Paducah forced two five-second counts, gaining possession on the ensuing jump balls. Hutchinson coerced three Indian turnovers, the final coming with nine seconds on the clock, the Blue Dragons trailing, 86-85.

No remaining Hutchinson time-outs impelled guard Kenny Wiens to take matters into his own hands. He drove from center court, was tripped at the free throw line, and was bumped again as he went up for a lay-up. The basket was good. The Arena erupted.

In the midst of the reigning pandemonium, a whistle sounded. Wiens was ushered to the line. Unable to hear the desperate cries from the Blue Dragon bench, the 6-2 sophomore passively prepared to put the icing on the Blue Dragon win. It was only after the ball slid off the rim no good and time expired that Wiens found out what all the uproar was about: The infraction had been called *before* the shot. Wiens' apparent winning basket had been erased. His missed free throw put an end to another year's hopes for a Hutchinson championship.

Wiens later described the closing moments of the game as a "chaos situation": "[After the final buzzer,] I came back to the bench, happy, kind of jumping up and down. I thought we'd won. About that time I saw Coach Keady. I had no idea what had happened. Then I saw his eyes."

"That was really a bizarre deal," confirmed Keady later after he became the head coach at Purdue University. "He (Wiens) still apologizes to me every time he sees me. But, there wasn't anything he could do about it because there was so damn much noise."

The next week, Wiens' teammates would vote him the Blue Dragons' "Most Inspirational Player." He would later play at Cornell University, becoming the first tournament alumnus to graduate from the Ivy League.

But for the moment, the hometown crowd was crushed. Those who stayed for the day's finale watched in stunned silence while an outstanding talent show ensued. Mike Johnson repeatedly lifted Murray State off the canvas, leading all scorers with 31 while Burlington's Dick Gibbs joined the Blackhawk's elite 1,000-point scoring club with 22, pushing his career total to 1,014. The man who stirred the fans from dolor, though, was Burlington guard Fred Brown. Launching 20-25 foot bombs, the 6-3 sophomore burned the nets for 25, 22 from the field. Mur-

Often overshadowed by teammate Fred Brown, Southeastern Iowa's Dick Gibbs scored over 1,000 for the Blackhawks before completing his collegiate career at the University of Texas-El Paso. Gibbs spent five years in the NBA. (Photo courtesy of Loren Walker)

ray State contested throughout, but Burlington advanced, 67-62.

THURSDAY — A SLEEPER AWAKES

With three seconds left in regulation, Hutchinson's Dean Barr hit his only basket of the game — a long field goal similar to the one he fired in like circumstances to win a Region 6 semifinal — throwing the afternoon finale with Murray State into

overtime. The Blue Dragons jumped in front in the extra period, but were unable to stay there, missing the front end of two crucial one-and-ones. Behind Mike Johnson's tourney-high 41, Murray State eliminated Hutchinson, 88-86.

The other consolation contests were lopsided bores. Outside of outstanding individual totals — Gardner-Webb's Artis Gilmore (36), Brevard's Harold Fox (36), Phoenix's Dennis Layton (34), and Johnson & Wales' Nate Adger (34) — the only occurrence of note came in the afternoon matinee when the seven-foot centers of Gardner-Webb and Brevard squared off at center court for the opening tip.[3]

The evening quarterfinals were another matter.

Undefeated Robert Morris of Pittsburgh dug a deep hole, falling behind Vincennes, 27-11, in the feature. Then, behind star Perry Johnson's brilliant outside shooting — he eventually led all scorers with 36, becoming the sixth player of the day to break the 30-point barrier — the Colonials rallied, outscoring Vincennes, 16-1. From then on, it was a nip-and-tuck battle, ending in a 68-all tie.

The overtime decision came quickly, Robert Morris scoring the first five points. The Trailblazers fought back, but were doomed when they hit only two of six free throws in the final two minutes. Robert Morris walked away with a 77-76 squeaker, its 29-game win streak intact.

A 30-game win skein was on the line in the nightcap. Like the Colonials before them, the San Jacinto Ravens had their hands full with eight ties and 10 lead changes in the first half before Robert Morris of Carthage took a 36-35 halftime edge.

The situation did not brighten for the Texans in the second period. Robert Morris maintained control with accurate shooting, extending the lead to seven twice, the last coming with eight minutes to play. San Jacinto found itself in a rare position — trailing in the final minutes.

Abandoning its packed in 3-2 zone, the Ravens applied full-court pressure. The Robert Morris advantage slowly dissolved until San Jacinto finally managed a tie at 65-all. The score deadlocked four more times, the last coming when Jeff Halliburton flipped the ball in from under the basket with 50 seconds to go. Then the Eagles threw the ball away, trying to break the San Jacinto press. The defending champs were now in control of their destiny.

Coach Ron Rucker called time. With his Ravens huddled around him, he laid out the end-game plan; stall, run out the clock, and put up one last shot. The worst that could happen was an overtime. His final admonition: "Whatever you do don't turn it over."

When play resumed, San Jacinto stalled. Time wound off the clock. Then, with 15 seconds showing, forward Jeff Lake inexplicably broke from the Raven holding pattern and drove the the lane. A whistle sounded. Traveling.

San Jacinto's only recourse was to apply heavy pressure to keep Robert Morris from getting a final shot. The press was so effective, the Eagles barely beat the 10-second count getting the ball across the center line.

Since there was no time to set up an offensive play, Robert Morris called time. Coach Joe Ramsey outlined an inbounds play designed to get one last shot. Quick passes found Rhea Taylor at the top of the key. With two seconds showing, the 6-6 freshman turned and fired, lofting his trademark, a high archer. The ball hung at its apex, then descended. It hit the heel of the rim, ricocheted between back and front, then fell threw — at the buzzer. In its first two outings, Robert Morris of Carthage, the *Hutchinson News'* "sleeper", had downed the top two teams in the country.

FRIDAY — WHICH ROBERT MORRIS?

The afternoon consolation session marked time — with one exception. Sandwiched between routine wins by Moberly and San Jacinto over Howard County and Vincennes, respectively, was an offensive slugfest. Seven players — Leroy Cobb (35), George Watson (21), and Dennis Layton (20) for Phoenix and Ernie Fleming (27), Artis Gilmore (25), George Adams (24), and

---

3   Ironically, Artis Gilmore and Pembrook Burrows became teammates the following year at Jacksonville University (formerly Jacksonville Junior College, a four-time tourney participant). They were the nucleus of a Dolphin squad that went all the way to the NCAA championship game before losing to UCLA.

Steve Kebeck (21) for Gardner-Webb — scored 20 points or better as Phoenix outlasted Gardner-Webb, 108-106, in three overtimes. It was a perfect example of the caliber of talent in this year's tournament, a tasty hors d'ouvre before the day's exciting main fare.

When the Paducah Indians took the floor for the evening opener, they were bewildered by their reception. Two nights previous, a packed Arena had rooted almost *in toto* against the Kentuckians as they edged out the local favorites. Now that same full house was backing the Indians. Why the sudden turnabout?

One reason was that, against the power-ladened Burlington Blackhawks, Paducah was the underdog. Another was that, the higher the Indians placed, the better the hometown ballclub looked. The most significant reason, however, was undissipated anger. Only twice before had Hutchinson fans let a previous Blue Dragon loss color their emotions, upsetting their general impartiality during the tournament. In neither case were local sentiments so vivid as they were against Burlington.

The stimulus for the lingering animosity happened on January 4. Two weeks earlier, Hutchinson had upended the then No. 9 Blackhawks, 90-84, at Hutchinson in a rough, football-like contest in which 53 fouls were called. The return contest at Burlington was a grudge match in which another 50 infractions were whistled.

The most violent occurrence came early. On a Hutchinson fast break, Bo Clarke dished off to fellow guard Kenny Wiens, then plowed into Burlington's Gerard Fisher. Wiens, traveling at full speed, launched upward for a lay-up. He was suddenly hit from behind by Blackhawk forward Dick Gibbs, undercut by the downed Fisher, and flipped, his feet nearly scraping the backboard. He crashed head-first into the court. The officials ruled Clarke had charged. They admitted not seeing the latter collision.

The Blue Dragon bench and the few Hutchinson fans in attendance were incensed, viewing the action as a deliberate push by Gibbs, an act of retaliation for being ejected after a shoving incident with Wiens during the prior contest at Hutchinson. Coach Gene Keady pressed for Gibbs' banishment, threatening to pull his players from the court. The officials refused to take action and, after Hutchinson players voted to continue, play resumed. While Wiens was being administered to at a local hospital, Burlington dropped Hutchinson, 92-83.

The following day the *Burlington Hawk-Eye* cited the Blackhawk version of the incident. Said Coach Ed Sparling, "The referee made the right call. It was definitely a charging foul. The guy hit Gibbs. Dick went flying into the kid that was hurt. I'm sorry it happened. I never like to see accidents happen, but

One of the most colorful coaches in tourney history, the Burlington Blackhawks' Ed Sparling contrived a "cold, arrogant" exterior to help draw hatred from opposing fans and attention to his team. "The team would come out first and get a smattering of applause and a few boos, but nothing unkind," described Sparling of Blackhawk appearances in Hutchinson. "Then I would come out. That's when everybody got happy." (Photo courtesy of Loren Walker)

that's what it was — my guys will never deliberately hit someone from behind."

Hutchonians who had only heard about the incident on the radio or read it in the newspaper, were not convinced. One look at their fallen warrior was enough to instill bitter hatred. Wiens suffered from two broken teeth, a broken nose, and a sprained back.

The opening period of the Burlington-Paducah semifinal released the pent up fury of Hutchinson fans. Riding the overwhelming vocal support plus the hot shooting of Bobby Jones, Haywood Hill, and Rex Bailey, Paducah stunned the Blackhawks, building a 50-36 halftime lead.

Burlington revived in the locker room. Behind guard Fred Brown's hot hand, the Blackhawks reeled off 12 unanswered points.

The Iowans could not control the smaller, quicker Indians, however. Unrattled by Burlington's spurt, staying with its original game plan, Paducah gradually relengthened the advantage, taking a seven-point edge into the final minute.

Brown incited a last ditch Blackhawk surge, cashing in twice in 30 seconds. Then, he picked up his fifth foul, sitting down with a game-high 35. The resulting two free throws by Indian reserve Jim Johnson proved the clinchers. Though the Iowans received two easy buckets in the final 12 seconds, it was not enough. To the clamorous approval of the Hutchinson crowd, Paducah downed Burlington, 79-78.

With emotions running high, the Arena audience settled in for the media event of the tournament: Robert Morris versus Robert Morris.

The two Robert Morrises possessed like names because of similar origins. In 1921, John R. McCartan bought the Pittsburgh School of Accountancy and changed its name to Robert Morris after the colonial financier who signed the Declaration of Independence and later became the governor of Pennsylvania. In 1964, McCartan's company also purchased Carthage College, a four-year Lutheran institution in Illinois. It, too, was dubbed Robert Morris. The 1969 semifinal match-up marked the first meeting of the two schools.

The game was a nightmare for radio broadcasters, but a fantasy come true for the press. Everyone had fun with the pairing, predicting "Robert Morris should win." The statement was not only a joke, but a hedge.

The two teams had more than just names in common. Both were well-balanced. Each possessed a topflight scoring star, Perry Johnson for the Pennsylvania Robert Morris; L.C. Brasfield for the Illinois Robert Morris. Though the Pittsburgh squad had better height, the Carthage squad had greater experience. With consecutive wins over the top two teams in the country, the Carthage Eagles had demonstrated they were in the same league as the No. 4 Colonials of Pittsburgh. Few cared to delineate further which Robert Morris would prove superior.

The contest lived up to its pre-game hype. Robert Morris was equal to Robert Morris. The two battled to 16 ties and two overtimes. Each side placed four players in double figures. Three Eagles topped the 20-point mark: Rhea Taylor (27), John Lindsey (22), and Brasfield (21). The Colonials were led by Johnson's game-high 36 points and the outstanding overall performance of Dave Werthman with 24 points and 20 rebounds, the latter, half the team's total. The largest lead of the game, seven points, came seven seconds from the final score. Robert Morris of Pittsburgh finally outlasted Robert Morris of Carthage, 96-91.

SATURDAY — RUNNING OUT OF GAS

After sitting on the bench for three minutes because of a second-half leg injury, Dennis Layton returned to action, hit four baskets in a four-minute Phoenix drive, and broke open a close contest with Moberly. Layton's game-high 38 propelled the Bears to a record shattering 102-83 fifth-place victory. Phoenix became the first tourney team to average more than 100 points in four games, setting new marks for field goals (171) and total points (402).

The fourth-place tilt was close, but not very exciting. Murray State and San Jacinto played methodically, shot poorly, and threw the ball away frequently. Mike Johnson's seven of eight free throw chances in the final 1:39 salted away a 65-58 Murray State win. Johnson's game-high 24 moved him into sixth place on the two-year scoring rolls with 209. San Jacinto's Jeff Halliburton had 12 — his lowest total in eight tourney performances — but also joined Johnson in the tourney's elite 10 scorers of all time with a two-year total of 189.

Fred Brown again displayed *his* impressive scoring ability, hitting a game-high 28 (all but four from the field), setting a new Burlington school record with a career total of 1,672 points, breaking the old mark of 1,662 held by former Juco All-

Dennis "Mo" Layton's 115 points spearheaded the Phoenix Bear offense, the first tourney team to average 100 points in four tourney games. Layton later attended the University of Southern California, then spent five years in the pros. (Photo courtesy of the University of Southern California)

neither could put the other away. With 4:32 remaining, Robert Morris led, 67-66.

Then, the pressure of attaining an undefeated season plus the strain of playing four games and three overtime periods in four days caught up with the Colonials. When Robert Morris' Perry Johnson missed from outside, Paducah forward Gary Sundmacker grabbed the rebound, dribbled the length of the floor, passing everyone, and laid the ball in off the backboard. On the ensuing Robert Morris possession, Indian Bobby Jones swiped the ball, put a spinning one-on-one move on Colonial Joe Butler, and swished a jumper from the wing. Robert Morris countered with a field goal, but another pair of back-to-back goals by Sundmacker and Jones decided matters.

In an anticlimactic ending to an otherwise extremely competitive week, Paducah eased to a 79-76 victory, becoming the second tourney champ from east of the Mississippi.

THE AFTERMATH — OUR WEEK

The 1969 Juco Tournament was a gold mine for recruiters. Later that spring, leading scorer Perry Johnson — younger brother of Baltimore Bullet Gus Johnson — became one of the first players drafted by the pros right out of junior college. Sixteen more of his fellow performers would also be drafted. Nine would eventually enjoy successful professional careers: George Adams and Artis Gilmore (Gardner-Webb); Fred Brown and Dick Gibbs (Burlington); Charles Dudley (Moberly); Harold Fox (Brevard); Jeff Halliburton and Bob Nash (San Jacinto); and Dennis "Mo" Layton (Phoenix).

The superior talent gave Arena patrons their fair share of excitement. While the tournament's average game margin of 8.8 was the second lowest to date, the best had been saved until last. The margin of victory in the seven championship flight contests averaged just over 2.5 points per game. The fact that Paducah won by an all-time low total of nine points over four contests bore out the closeness of the competition. As Sonny Haws told local supporters on his return to Paducah, "If we played the same tournament over next week, there'd probably be another winner. If we played the next week, there'd be another. I think

American Sam Williams. Brown's heroics were not enough to win, however. Leading by two with four minutes to play, Robert Morris of Carthage stalled, forcing the Blackhawks to gamble. Easy baskets and free throws lifted the Eagles to a 62-53 victory — their third on the year against Burlington — and a third-place trophy.

The championship tilt fell into the close-fought pattern of the quarter- and semifinals. Both Robert Morris of Pittsburgh and Paducah enjoyed wild scoring sprees and 10-point bulges, but

(Left) Despite his potent 111-point offensive show in the 1969 tournament, the NJCAA Basketball Hall of Famer who later became known as "Downtown" Freddie Brown did not shot willingly. According to his former mentor Ed Sparling, "Freddie could do whatever he wanted to. He could rebound, could score, play defense, pass . . . [But] the thing that always stuck out in my mind about Freddie — the guys had to beg him to shoot."

Former tourney star John Johnson — Brown's teammate the following year at the University of Iowa and also later during Brown's 13-year tenure with the Seattle Supersonics — reiterated Sparling's observation. During Brown's first year at Iowa, Johnson noted that Brown was a playmaker: "He was one of the most acrobatic players I ever saw. Fred played basketball like a ballet dancer. He was always so light on his feet. It was like 'Now you see me; now you don't.' You couldn't pressure him because he was so clever with the basketball. People didn't realize how great a shooter Freddie was until he got to the pros." (Photo courtesy of the University of Iowa)

(Right) The 1969 tournament's leading scorer (133 points), Robert Morris' Perry Johnson was the first Juco player to be drafted by the pros. Johnson passed up the honor, finishing his collegiate career at Duquesne University. (Photo courtesy of Gus Krop, Robert Morris College)

The 1969 French MVP winner, Bobby Jones later starred for Drake University which was runner-up in the NCAA Midwest Regionals in 1970 and 1971. (Photo courtesy of Drake University)

there were certainly 11 teams who could have won it if they had had the breaks. It happened to be our week.''

Because the Indians were weeklong underdogs, the Paducah championship was a popular one. The Kentuckians were a balanced, team-oriented squad that was fun to watch. Fans appreciated that Bobby Jones (88 points) was recognized for his all-round skills and leadership, being named French Most Valuable Player[4] over top scorers Perry Johnson (133), Mike Johnson (120), Dennis Layton (115), and Fred Brown (111). They also applauded the inclusion of Rick Ragland on the All-Tournament Team. Since Ragland scored only 46 points in four games in a year when the lowest top-10 individual offensive performance was 34, it was acknowledgement that defensive skills were also a part of the game. Their only disappointment was that there was not enough room on the All-Tourney Ten for super sub Haywood Hill. The 6-2 sophomore had repeatedly inspired teammates and fans alike with heroic efforts off the bench, including a team-leading 21 points in the championship fray.

The Hutchinson fan support was not unappreciated. In his acceptance speech for Coach of the Year honors, Paducah's Sonny Haws recognized the championship caliber Hutchinson crowd, saying, ''I know what it's like to have you against me — and I know what its like to have you for me.''

Tournament Results

Tuesday:	Game	
	1	Paducah — 80 Moberly — 76
	2	Hutchinson — 120 Miles City — 103
	3	Murray St. — 71 Howard County — 68
	4	SE Iowa-Burlington — 86 Northwest-Powell — 70
	5	San Jacinto — 72 Johnson & Wales — 70
	6	Robert Morris (IL) — 84 Phoenix — 75
Wednesday:	Game	
	7	Robert Morris (PA) — 88 Gardner-Webb — 83
	8	Vincennes — 97 Brevard — 83
	9	Moberly — 85 Miles City — 66
	10	Paducah — 86 Hutchinson — 85
	11	SE Iowa-Burlington — 67 Murray St. — 62
Thursday:	Game	
	12	Howard County — 83 Northwest-Powell — 71
	13	Gardner-Webb — 107 Brevard — 93
	14	Murray St. — 88 Hutchinson — 86 OT
	15	Phoenix — 117 Johnson & Wales — 86
	16	Robert Morris (PA) — 77 Vincennes — 76 OT
	17	Robert Morris (IL) — 75 San Jacinto — 73
Friday:	Game	
	18	Moberly — 87 Howard County — 77
	19	Phoenix — 108 Gardner-Webb — 106 3OT
	20	San Jacinto — 85 Vincennes — 68
	21	Paducah — 79 SE Iowa-Burlington — 78
	22	Robert Morris (PA) — 96 Robert Morris (IL) — 91 2OT
Saturday:	Game	
	23	Phoenix — 102 Moberly — 83
	24	Murray St. — 65 San Jacinto — 58
	25	Robert Morris (IL) — 62 SE Iowa-Burlington — 53
	26	Paducah — 79 Robert Morris (PA) — 76

How They Finished in 1969

1. Paducah Junior College
2. Robert Morris Junior College (Pennsylvania)
3. Robert Morris College (Illinois)
4. Murray State College
5. Phoenix College
6. Southeastern Iowa Area Community College
7. San Jacinto College
8. Moberly Junior College

All-Tournament Team

Fred Brown — Southeastern Iowa Area Community College
Mike Johnson — Murray State College
Perry Jonson — Robert Morris Junior College (Pennsylvania)
Bobby Jones — Paducah Junior College
Dennis Layton — Phoenix College
Bob Nash — San Jacinto College
Rick Ragland — Paducah Junior College
Rhea Taylor — Robert Morris College (Illinois)
Dave Werthman — Robert Morris Junior College (Pennsylvania)
Ray Willis — Hutchinson Community Junior College

Coach of the Year

Claud ''Sonny'' Haws — Paducah Junior College

French Most Valuable Player Award

Bobby Jones — Paducah Junior College

Sesher Sportsmanship Award

Perry Johnson — Robert Morris Junior College (Pennsylvania)

---

[4] On November 30, 1968, former Juco All-American Bill French and his wife were killed in a tragic automobile accident. In honor of one of the most popular players in Hutchinson history, the local Junior Chamber of Commerce named their annual MVP trophy the ''William B. French Most Valuable Player Award.''

fter 31 years of nomadic existence, the National
Junior College Athletic Association established a permanent
home. Since the Juco Tournament played such an important
part in the organization's growth, it was fitting that the site of the
new headquarters was Hutchinson. On August 1, 1969, newly
appointed Executive Director George E. Killian, former athletic
director at Erie County Technical Institute of Buffalo, New York,
and the NJCAA's most recent president, opened the doors to
the new office located in the Hilton Inn (formerly the Baker
Hotel). The operation was not large — Killian's staff consisted
of one secretary — but, it was to be the nerve center of all
NJCAA functions, finally giving the organization a sense of legitimacy.

At the time of the 1968 annual meeting when the creation of
central office was approved, the organization had grown to
19 members — more than double the membership when the
Juco Tournament first moved to Hutchinson in 1949. Besides
the obvious need for a permanent controlling headquarters, the
necessity for region realignment was also evident.

During the 1968 spring meeting, NJCAA officials added three
new regions: Region 17 (Alabama and Georgia) was separated
from Region 8 (Florida); Region 18 (Idaho, Oregon, and Washington) was carved from Region 1 (the rest of the West); and,
Region 19 (Delaware, Maryland, New Jersey, and Pennsylvania)
was split from Region 15 (Connecticut and lower New York).

The new regional structure presented a problem, however.
How do you squeeze 16 participants out of 19 regions? The
dilemma was sidestepped for the 1969 tournament; the newly
loned regions simply played their parent region for the right to
go to Hutchinson. But, with the 1970 tournament, a new system
was devised. Drawn by lot, three pairs of adjacent regions met
in play-offs to determine who earned the trip to the nationals.
The results: Broome Technical Community College (Region 3)
bested Suffolk County Community College (Region 15);
Moberly Junior College (Region 16) downed defending national
champ Paducah Community College (Region 7); and, most
importantly, Casper College (Region 9) defeated Independence Community College (Region 6). For the first time in its
23-year history, the tournament did not have a Kansas representative.

THE PARTICIPANTS

Though Vincennes University entered the 1970 Juco Tournament with the highest ranked quintet, the former national
champ was not automatically accorded "the team to beat" status. Headlines for the *Hutchinson News* pre-tourney analysis
flatly stated, "Clear-Cut Favorite Absent." One reason was that,
after topping the NJCAA poll for most of the year, the Trailblazers had lost three of their final four regular season games, falling
to No. 2 in the rankings. A greater factor was that Vincennes
faced "murderer's row" competition.

Luck of the draw had placed six of eight ranked tourney
teams in the lower bracket. If it was to put a second title on the
mantle, Vincennes would have to survive against the likes of
No. 3 Christian College of the Southwest (29-5), No. 5 Casper
(27-2), No. 9 College of Southern Idaho (30-3), No. 13 Kennedy-King College (27-3), and No. 18 Ferrum Junior College
(24-0). There was also unranked Lake City Junior College (26-6)
to contend with. The debutant Timberwolves had the distinc-

*Though his teams only won five times in the nine Juco Tour-
nament appearances, Dick Baldwin is college basketball's all-time
winningest coach with 879 victories. Baldwin was an initial inductee into the NJCAA Basketball Hall of Fame in 1984. (Photo
courtesy of Dick Baldwin)*

tion of upending No.1 Brevard Junior College in Region 8
action, handing the Floridians their only loss of the year. Even
Vincennes' opening opponent, newcomer Brandywine College (23-5) — the first tourney participant from Delaware —
looked respectable. "They're not an exceptionally big team,
nor do they score a lot of points," Trailblazer Coach Allen Bradfield told the *Vincennes Sun-Commercial*, "but they play solid
ball and have good overall team quickness."

While a dog fight brewed in the lower bracket, the upper
bracket figured to be decided early. The winner of the first-
round battle between No. 12, two-time titleholder Tyler Junior
College (33-5) and unranked, four-time champion Moberly
(28-7) was considered a shoo-in for the title game. The only other ranked team potentially standing in the way was No. 19
Broome Tech (31-6). However, since the Hornets had compiled a meager 4-17 record in eight previous tourney appearances, few deemed the New Yorkers a real threat. Likewise the
rest of the field: Grand View College (25-5), North Dakota State
School of Science (21-6), Northeastern Oklahoma A&M College (24-7), Gadsden State Junior College (25-13), and Snow
College (15-14).

With lop-sided bracketing and no Kansas representative,
local tourney fans wondered if any excitement was in the offing.

Region	Team
1	Snow College — Ephraim, Utah
2	Northeastern Oklahoma Agricultural and Mechanical College — Miami, Oklahoma
3	Broome Technical Community College — Binghamton, New York
4	Kennedy-King College — Chicago, Illinois
5	Christian College of the Southwest — Mesquite, Texas
8	Lake City Junior College and Forest Ranger School — Lake City, Florida
9	Casper College — Casper, Wyoming
10	Ferrum Junior College — Ferrum, Virginia
11	Grand View College — Des Moines, Iowa
12	Vincennes University — Vincennes, Indiana
13	North Dakota State School of Science — Wahpeton, North Dakota
14	Tyler Junior College — Tyler, Texas
16	Moberly Junior College — Moberly, Missouri
17	Gadsden State Junior College — Gadsden, Alabama
18	College of Southern Idaho — Twin Falls, Idaho
19	Brandywine College — Wilmington, Delaware

TUESDAY — BATTLING SNOW

Northeastern Oklahoma Coach Cletus Green worried in his Hilton Inn room. He had preceded his squad to Hutchinson to attend meetings of the NJCAA Coaches Association, arriving over the weekend along with most of the other tourney teams. Since the Miami, Oklahoma, school was the closest participant (200 miles), Green's players, under the guidance of assistant coach Gene Prevett, waited until the day before the tournament to follow. But, as the Monday night player banquet neared, Green's team was nowhere in sight.

The reason?

During the day a surprise storm dumped more than a foot of snow across the southern tier of Kansas. It was reported that Baxter Springs, 25 miles from Miami, was buried under 30 inches. Green's concern was that his team would not only miss the banquet, but the tournament as well.

Just as the Convention Hall proceedings were about to start, the Golden Norsemen arrived. Tired and unkempt after a harrowing 10-hour ride, they received a thankful greeting from their coach, a warm meal, and an inspiring talk by guest speaker Jesse Owens.

The unpredictable Kansas weather, a tournament staple, had little effect on the other participants. Showing disdain for the unseasonable cold and paying little attention to defense, the Wahpeton Wildcats tipped off the event, winning their first tourney contest in seven tries, out-blazing newcomer Gadsden State, 103-99.

The second game was equally hot, though Grand View took longer to warm up, needing the last-ditch heroics of guard Don Watts to tie Broome Tech in regulation. Then forward Bob Hanson drove for a lay-up off the overtime tip, giving the Vikings their first lead of the game. Broome Tech stayed with the Iowans until Hanson — the game's top scorer with 32 — hit two field goals and two free throws in the final minute-and-a-half, leading Grand View past the New Yorkers, 99-93.

In the afternoon finale, Northeastern Oklahoma faced another battle with snow — Snow College. As they had the day before, the Oklahomans struggled. With under eight minutes remaining, NEO was blanketed by a 10-point Snow-fall. Using guard Larry Brown — the game's leading scorer with 25 — as their shovel, the Golden Norsemen plowed from behind, removing the Snow threat, 89-86.

The highlight of the day, the "championship of the first round," almost failed to live up to its advance billing. Moberly hit 15 of its first 19 shots from the field and sprinted to a commanding 42-31 first-half advantage over Tyler. The unusually large audience, most of whom had skipped supper to attend the 6 p.m. tilt, showed its disappointment by shifting attention to neglected stomachs.

Then Tyler rallied.

The final six minutes dissolved any interest in food, the two teams switching leads or tying on nearly every possession in a race to the wire. The Greyhounds broke the tape first on Charles Dudley's game-winner at the 16-second mark. Tyler had one final chance, but missed. With the 95-94 squeaker, Moberly became the team to beat in the upper bracket.

The rest of the evening was a bust, sending many fans hom early for late snacks. The only eventful happenings in the fe ture were a technical foul on Lake City's Terry Wallace for n reporting to the scorer's table, a technical foul on Kenned King for having six men on the floor, an accidental punt off th knee of Kennedy-King's burly center Sam Allen which lande in the Arena's second balcony, and the always snazzy, crow pleasing routines of the Kennedy-King (formerly Wilson Juni College) cheerleaders. Otherwise, the action was straightfo ward. Lake City never trailed, winning its tourney debut, 72-6

The only excitement in the nightcap came at the end of th first half when Casper's Abe Steward stepped over the midcou line and launched a desperation heave for two. The spectacul bucket ignited the Thunderbirds. After having trailed most the game, Casper outscored Christian, 25-8, in the final eigl minutes and rolled to an easy 83-69 win.

WEDNESDAY — NOTHING EARTH-SHAKING

The people of Twin Falls, Idaho, showed enthusiasm for the first tourney appearance by sending the 30-piece Southern Id ho band to Hutchinson with donations raised at the la moment. The noisy contingent spurred on the Golden Eagles the day's opener — but, for naught. In a game which neithe team was capable of gaining a clear upper hand, Ferrum pre served its undefeated record, edging the Idaho squad, 80-79.

Brandywine from faraway Wilmington, Delaware, did n bring a band, but attracted a large following nonetheless. Th afternoon crowd was fully behind the debutante Patrio against veteran Vincennes. They applauded the efforts of 6-center Terry Provonsha, whose awkward, but effective of balance shot produced a game-high 33 and stymied the mor talented Trailblazer front line, keeping Brandywine in the hun It required the late-game heroics of sophomore Jerry Dunn who hit 10 of his team-leading 27 in the final seven minutes, t silence the locals. Vincennes advanced, 89-79.

The first round yielded no earth-shaking revelations. Th games which had been expected to be toss-ups, were. Likewis the mismatches. Even though half the games had not bee decided until near the end, tourney drama had unfolded rou tinely. There was little encouragement that the opening qua terfinals would be any different. Grand View and Moberly wer heavy favorites.

The beginning of the Wednesday night feature confirme suspicions. Both squads shot poorly from the field (36 percen in a lackluster first period. The difference in scores came fron the fact that Grand View threw up 13 more shots than the Wild cats from Wahpeton. The Iowans opened a 16-point margi and coasted to a comfortable 46-35 halftime cushion.

Then the game's complexion changed. The North Dakot squad returned to the floor with hot hands, outscoring Gran View, 18-7, in the first five minutes. The Arena crowd stirre from lethargy.

The NDSSS comeback was only a tease, however. The Wild cats pulled abreast, but could not pass Grand View. The insid work of Jim Abernathy and the outside shooting of Bob Hanso kept the Vikings one step ahead. The Wahpeton squad had tw chances to tie near the end, but a missed free throw and a Do Watts steal and lay-up on a Wildcat inbounds pass in the fina minute — his second in like circumstances in two games — pre vented an upset. Grand View won, 88-84.

The nightcap followed a similar pattern. Moberly jumped ou to a 15-point lead just before intermission. Then behind flash penetrating guard Larry Brown, Northeastern Oklahoma scram bled back, tying the Greyhounds with four minutes to play i the game. Unlike the Wahpeton Wildcat comeback, NEO' charge did not peter out, forcing Moberly to an extra period.

Brown continued his heroics in overtime with two fre throws and a field goal, giving the Golden Norsemen the earl advantage. Fan delight at the turnabout was short-lived, how ever. A three-point play by Andy Knowles and a theft and lay-u by Larry "Gator" Rivers returned the lead to Moberly.

As the lead seesawed, tension reached its highest peak in tw days. Suddenly, it was all over. A basket by Charles Dudley an a 20-footer by Knowles put the Greyhounds on top to sta Despite Brown's game-high 38, Moberly downed Northeaster Oklahoma, 107-103.

Donald "Slick" Watts was already a slick operator for Grand View in the 1970 tournament, making critical steals for lay-ups in the Vikings' first two games. Watts completed his collegiate career at Xavier University of Louisiana, then spent six years in the NBA. (Photo courtesy of the Hutchinson News)

THURSDAY — STOMACH CRAMPS

The day's consolation play was a series of lopsided clashes: Tyler scored 14 unanswered second-half points, lifting the Apaches from three down to 11 up on the road to an 81-73 victor over Snow; Southern Idaho led by as much as 21, coasting to an 87-68 win over Brandywine; and Northeastern Oklahoma built a 20-point margin in the first 10 minutes, crushing the NDSSS Wildcats, 108-82.

The capper came in the evening opener. Behind the 29-point first-period effort of 6-8 center Steve Davidson, the Christian Trojans opened an insurmountable 60-39 gap over Kennedy-King. When the run-and-gun show ended, Davidson had tallied tourney-high 40 and Christian had eliminated the Chicagoans, 116-107. The combined score tied a tournament record.

By the time the quarterfinal feature between Ferrum and Vincennes tipped off, fans were ready for some close hard-fought action. Both opponents hoped the same. However, there was serious concern in the Vincennes camp.

Part of the reason the highly favored Trailblazers had had such a difficult time with first-time participant Brandywine in their opener was that Bob McAdoo, the team's leading scorer (19.3), netted only five points. The freshman center was ineffective throughout because of extreme pain. When he doubled up afterwards in the dressing room, the Vincennes squad could feel its chances at a second national title slipping away.

McAdoo was taken to tournament physician Dr. Jack Perkins. After an examination, Perkins diagnosed McAdoo's ailment as kidney infection and prescribed medication.

When Vincennes took the floor against Ferrum, McAdoo still suffered from nausea and stomach cramps, but, appeared better. His actions proved it. To the relief of Trailblazer fans, the lean 6-10 pivotman, hammered the boards with his usual aplomb and scored with regularity, grabbing game honors with 27.

Every point was needed. Ferrum tenaciously battled to preserve its unblemished record. The Panthers erased a six-point Vincennes margin in the final three minutes, pulling to within one. When Trailblazer forward Roy Simpson missed two free throws with 34 seconds to go, the door was opened for another Ferrum win.

The rapidly elapsing seconds immersed the crowd in the edge-of-your-seat excitement it had longed for. Then, with four ticks remaining, McAdoo picked up his fifth foul. Worse yet, he sent Sam Oglesby, Ferrum's leading scorer, to the charity stripe for a one-and-one. The Trailblazers had their backs to the wall.

Oglesby calmly toed the line, bounced the basketball, and fired. The ball hit the front of the rim and fell away. Vincennes reserve Jose DeCausey soared high for the rebound, dribbled to the corner, and held on until the buzzer. The Trailblazers escaped with a 78-77 victory.

The pattern through 16 games had been one of high-powered scoring. There were already six 100-point totals, one less than the tourney record. The day's finale was an interesting change of pace.

Casper was the top defensive club in the nation, allowing opponents just under 60 points per game. Lake City, an offensive-minded squad with a 93-point average, was forced to adjust. The Tiberwolves adapted well to the slow pace, however. So well, that they held Casper to 19 points through 20 minutes. With a commanding 17-point margin at the midpoint, Lake City upped the tempo. Guards Don Jackson and Jesse Hillman riddled the Thunderbird defense with quick passes, setting up numerous wide-open baskets. The Floridians won with surprising ease, 74-56, holding Casper to the lowest total of the week. Lake City's victory over No. 1 Brevard had been no fluke.

FRIDAY — WATER ON THE COURT

Over the years, the semifinals had proven to be exciting and competitive, often overshadowing championship night. The evening's full-house turnout demonstrated that longtime tourney fans expected to see the best basketball games of the week.

Their eagerness was intensified when the opening tip-off was delayed. Earlier, *Hutchinson News* photographer Bill Wempe climbed up into the scoreboard to take a fish-eye lens shot of the court. A light was removed and set aside to allow room for the camera. While Wempe took pictures, the hot bulb started a fire. Though it was quickly extinguished, it took 20 minutes to clear the overflow which puddled at center court.

When the opener between Grand View and Moberly finally commenced, water continued to drip. Towels were left on the court to sop up the excess, forcing players to tread cautiously around the midcourt area. Since Grand View relied heavily on team speed and the quickness of guard Don Watts and Harold Lee, the problem had a particular dampening effect on the Viking offense. Only center Jim Abernathy — who eventually led all scorers with 37 — found the range consistently, notching 21 points by halftime. Moberly guards Andy Knowles and Charles Dudley proved better mudders, combining for 29, leading the Greyhounds to a 45-37 edge.

Water on the court was less of a problem in the second period. It did not improve the Grand View cause, however. The Vikings pulled to within three twice only to see Moberly go on an 11-0 spurt. With 3:05 to go, the Greyhounds were in complete command, 92-76. Though the Vikings' Watts made the score more respectable with nine points in the final 2:30, Moberly entered the title tilt with a 99-90 triumph.

Despite the abundance of wetness in the opener, fan thirst for excitement had not been quenched. It remained unslaked following the nightcap. Since the water problem had dried up by the end of the Moberly-Grand View semifinal, the only reason for Lake City's early turnovers was Vincennes' aggressive 1-3-1 match-up zone. The miscues left the Timberwolves in arrears by 11 at intermission. Vincennes finished the job early in the second period, outscoring the Floridians, 23-7. The disappointed crowd departed shortly thereafter. Led by front-liners Roy Simpson (30), Bob McAdoo (16), and Jerry Dunn (14), the Trailblazers demolished Lake City, 95-64.

SATURDAY — RUBBER MATCH

Southern Idaho committed 14 first-half turnovers and handed control of the fifth-place contest to Tyler. The Apaches won easily, 104-91. It was Tyler's 21st 100-point game of the year and the ninth century-plus score of the week.

Casper staged an inspired rally against Northeastern Oklahoma, erasing a 17-point deficit with 16 minutes remaining to capture fourth place, 79-77.

The star of the game, however, was NEO's Larry Brown. The six-foot guard's game-high 37 garnered him tourney honors with 126. His hard charging style, which sent him into the trees in the middle where he was frequently knocked on his backside, won him popularity with fans. His ability to pick himself up with a smile earned him the Sesher Sportsmanship Award.

However, when Brown arrived at Northeastern Oklahoma, no one would have guessed he would later win a sportsmanship award. According to his coach, Cletus Green, "He was the hardest one to corral . . . Down deep he was a sweet kid, but he had a chip on his shoulder in so many things. He thought most of the time when an official called a foul . . . well he just knew the official was wrong, particularly if it was on him."

After several run-ins with officials, Green told Brown that, in order to continue playing, he would have to change his attitude. Since Brown had such "a nice smile," Green told him to pick up the ball and hand it to the official with a smile every time he was called for a foul. Brown complied and soon found referees returning his smile and the number of infractions against him markedly reduced. Brown's demeanor completely changed. By the time of the 1970 tournament, his smile had become a permanent fixture and a fan favorite.

The 1970 tournament's leading-scorer (126 points) and Sesher Sportsmanship Award winner, Larry Brown completed his collegiate career at the University of Houston. (Photos courtesy of Cletus Green)

The third-place contest was a back-and-forth tussle from beginning to end, the critical play coming with 35 seconds remaining when Grand View lofted a imprudent floor-length pass which was intercepted by Lake City's Larry Quarles. The 6-3 forward was immediately fouled and sank two free throws, icing victory. With the 78-74 win, Lake City became the highest Florida finisher to date.

As inveterate underdog rooters, local tourney fans had little emotional interest in the championship tilt. Moberly and Vincennes were top names in junior college circles with excellent winning traditions. Both had appeared in five of the last six national tournaments. Each had won titles.

However, as basketball aficionados, the local crowd turned out in force. Most felt the best two teams were playing for the crown. The fact that the title match represented the season rubber match between the two schools further whetted curiosity. The large winning margins in the previous two meetings — Moberly won, 100-83, at Moberly and Vincennes, 108-91, at Vincennes — sparked heated debate as to which was better.

Moberly's strength was Andy Knowles and Charles Dudley, the most potent guard tandem in the tournament. The 5-10 Knowles elicited frequent oohs and aahs from the crowd with his high-arching, space shots from well beyond the circle. Dudley was also a gifted outside shooter, but, because of his 6-3 height and muscle, was equally fond of driving for two. The pair had collected 79 and 58 points, respectively, nearly half Moberly's total.

Vincennes' advantage was in the middle. In three outings, 6-10 Bob McAdoo, 6-9 Roy Simpson, and 6-5 Jerry Dunn, plus 6-5 Jose DeCausey off the bench, combined for 70 percent of the Trailblazer's offense while manhandling their opponents, 128-83, on the boards.

Based on overall talent and balance, Vincennes appeared the better team. But, longtime courtside touts gave Moberly the edge. The Greyhounds were on an 18-game roll. Few were willing to bet against Moberly's proven tourney track record.

Little was decided in the first half. After eight lead changes, Vincennes benefited from a controversial late tip-in and took a 42-37 halftime margin to the locker room. The Trailblazers continued to build the lead, opening a 58-43 gap with 11:52 to play.

Then Moberly made its run at the title. Replacing a foul-plagued Dudley, speedster Larry Rivers sparked the emotionally down Greyhounds, upping the tempo. Moberly outscored Vincennes, 14-3, in four minutes.

Just as the Greyhounds pulled back into contention, their game fell apart. Vincennes fired 16 unanswered points, opening an insurmountable 20-point bulge with two minutes to go. With their 1-3-1 match-up zone holding Moberly to 39 percent from the field and with their superb front line controlling the boards, 52-39, the Trailblazers claimed the crown, 85-67.

THE AFTERMATH — THE WOMAN BEHIND THE MAN

The high powered 1970 tournament set two all-time records: the most 100-point games (9) and the highest average combined score per game (172.2). With the nets swishing so frequently it was not surprising that the team with the best defensive average (71.8) won.

It was also not surprising when one considered the talent on Vincennes. As Vincennes Coach Allen Bradfield later confided, "By 1970 I had been around just long enough . . . I had a pretty good idea what was required. I had the best assistant coach anybody ever had [Jerry Reynolds, later head coach of the Sacramento Kings]. We had every reason to suspect, if we did our job, we'd be around and contend for the national championship."

Paramount in the Vincennes collection of talent was Bob McAdoo. Acquiring the slender forward was a major coup for Bradfield. He spent eight months recruiting the much-sought-after big man, finally sending Reynolds south to McAdoo's home in Greensboro, North Carolina. His parting words: "Take your sleeping bag with you. You can call me anytime. But, don't come back across the Mason-Dixon line without McAdoo."

Though only a freshman, McAdoo already displayed the abilities that would make him an NCAA tourney all-star two years later at North Carolina and the NBA's leading scorer for three consecutive seasons (from 1973 to 1976). He was at his best in the title tilt, scoring a game-high 27[1]. Despite the outstanding effort, he was not picked on the All-Tournament Team. Considering that McAdoo would later become an initial inductee in the NJCAA Basketball Hall of Fame, it remains one of the more ironic non-selections in tourney history.

The one Trailblazer who did make the elite 10, deserved the honor. According to Bradfield, "Jerry Dunn was one great ballplayer." He was the team catalyst on defense, playing the back position on Vincennes' tenacious 1-3-1 zone. Because of his aggressive style of play, he led the Trailblazer rebounding corps despite being the smallest member of the front line. Whenever games became tight, he could also be counted on to do "whatever had to be done on the court." Given the caliber of Dunn's teammates — eventual pro McAdoo and pro draftees Oscar Evans and Roy Simpson — Bradfield paid Dunn the supreme tribute when he told a victory gathering of Trailblazer supporters on their return to Vincennes, "As of 1970, I'm calling Jerry Dunn the best ever to play for the Blue & Gold."

Since nine out of the past 11 Coach of the Year honors had gone to the winning coach, the selection of Bradfield as the top mentor was not unexpected. Bradfield did not treat it lightly, however, telling the Arena audience, "I think it is extremely significant that my colleagues selected me as the coach of the year.

---

[1] The Moberly player who guarded McAdoo in the championship game was Tom O'Connor. After the contest, Coach Rich Daly [later an assistant coach at Missouri] spoke to the 6-9 freshman about his defense. "Tom, you did a pretty good job, but that's something you're going to have to work on in the off season." A few years later after McAdoo achieved immediate success in the NBA, O'Connor wrote Daly, "Coach, maybe he was just better than I was."

(Left) After attending the University of Washington, Moberly's Charles Dudley later wore a championship ring as a member of the 1975 NBA champion Golden State Warriors. (Photo courtesy of the University of Washington)

(Right) Though the first player inducted into the NJCAA Basketball Hall of Fame, Bob McAdoo (No. 51) ironically did not make the 1970 All-Tournament Team. McAdoo was later an All-American at North Carolina and a 14-year star with the NBA. (Photo courtesy of the **Hutchinson News**)

I hope I'm worthy of this award." He thanked his assistants, the Vincennes fans and cheerleaders, and the school's administration, then ended, saying, "I also want to thank my wife Polly for her courage during this tourney."

The significance of an understanding, supportive wife for those in the coaching profession was never better illustrated than by the example of Polly Bradfield. She attended every practice, sat on the bench next to her husband at every game, and kept the team stats, the ones he relied on at halftime in the dressing room.

Her importance to the squad extended far beyond just being a statistician. "We always had a standing rule that, if I were ill, nobody would touch that team. Mrs. Bradfield would coach it." Bradfield cited one particular case. "One wild night in Centralia, Illinois, a couple worthies wearing striped shirts found good sufficient reason to remove my carcass from the premises — in my younger and more volatile days. They didn't seem to want to negotiate about it after a certain point. That same night the president got evicted. She ran the basketball team that night for sure." Though Bradfield was noted for being a strict disciplinarian, there was no lessening of respect by team members when Mrs. Bradfield took over practices while her husband was on scouting trips. "You could hear a pin drop in that gym when she had them."

During the tournament, Polly Bradfield was instrumental in encouraging team leader Jerry Dunn, staying up into the early morning hours, consoling him after his uninspiring effort against Ferrum. Then she received news that her father had died. She flew to Vincennes for the funeral in Noble, Illinois, missing the Trailblazer semifinal against Lake City. In spite of her grief, she immediately returned and was beside her husband for the championship game.

All-Tournament Team

Jim Abernathy — Grand View College
Larry Brown — Northeastern Oklahoma Agricultural and Mechanical College
Steve Davidson — Christian College of the Southwest
Jerry Dunn — Vincennes University
Steve Hegens — College of Southern Idaho
Jim Jenkins — North Dakota State School of Science
Andrew Knowles — Moberly Junior College
Bob Lackey — Casper College
Larry Quarles — Lake City Junior College and Forest Ranger School
Bobby Thompson — Tyler Junior College

Coach of the Year

Allen Bradfield — Vincennes University

Tournament Results

Tuesday:	Game	1	NDSSS-Wahpeton — 103 Gadsden St. — 99
		2	Grand View — 99 Broome Tech — 93 OT
		3	NE Oklahoma A&M — 89 Snow — 86
		4	Moberly — 95 Tyler — 94
		5	Lake City — 72 Kennedy-King — 63
		6	Casper — 83 Christian — 69
Wednesday:	Game	7	Ferrum — 80 Southern Idaho — 79
		8	Vincennes — 89 Brandywine — 79
		9	Broome Tech — 84 Gadsden St. — 80
		10	Grand View — 88 NDSSS-Wahpeton — 84
		11	Moberly — 107 NE Oklahoma A&M — 103 OT
Thursday:	Game	12	Tyler — 81 Snow — 73
		13	Southern Idaho — 87 Brandywine — 68
		14	NE Oklahoma A&M — 108 NDSSS-Wahpeton — 82
		15	Christian — 116 Kennedy-King —107
		16	Vincennes — 78 Ferrum — 77
		17	Lake City — 74 Casper — 56
Friday:	Game	18	Tyler — 102 Broome Tech — 89
		19	Southern Idaho — 101 Christian — 95 OT
		20	Casper — 87 Ferrum — 75
		21	Moberly — 99 Grand View — 90
		22	Vincennes — 95 Lake City — 64
Saturday:	Game	23	Tyler — 104 Southern Idaho — 91
		24	Casper — 79 NE Oklahoma A&M — 77
		25	Lake City — 78 Grand View — 74
		26	Vincennes — 85 Moberly — 67

How They Finished in 1970

1. Vincennes University
2. Moberly Junior College
3. Lake City Junior College and Forest Ranger School
4. Casper College
5. Tyler Junior College
6. Grand View College
7. Northeastern Oklahoma Agricultural and Mechanical College
8. College of Southern Idaho

French Most Valuable Player Award

Andrew Knowles — Moberly Junior College

Sesher Sportsmanship Award

Larry Brown — Northeastern Oklahoma Agricultural and Mechanical College

1971:

GLIDING TO A CROWN

Despite the worst snow storm in a decade, Juco Tournament fans still made their annual pilgrimage to the Sports Arena to buy season tickets for the 1971 event. (Photo courtesy of Kenny Bernard)

Region	Team
2	Bacone College — Muskogee, Oklahoma
3	Niagara County Community College — Niagara Falls, New York
4	Robert Morris College — Carthage, Illinois
5	Hill Junior College — Hillsboro, Texas
6	Hutchinson Community Junior College — Hutchinson, Kansas
7	Columbia State Community College — Columbia, Tennessee
8	Gulf Coast Community College — Panama City, Florida
9	Casper College — Casper, Wyoming
10	Ferrum Junior College — Ferrum, Virginia
11	Ellsworth Community College — Iowa Falls, Iowa
13	Bismarck Junior College — Bismarck, North Dakota
14	Tyler Junior College — Tyler, Texas
15	Manhattan Community College — New York, New York
16	Three Rivers Junior College — Poplar Bluff, Missouri
18	College of Southern Idaho — Twin Falls, Idaho
19	Robert Morris College — Caraopolis, Pennsylvania

t started snowing in Hutchinson at 4 a.m., Sunday February 21. Around 6 a.m. wind was added. At noon, a full fledged blizzard was in progress.

By day's end, the entire state of Kansas was in a holding pattern, virtually every road closed. In larger cities such as Wichita the National Guard was mobilized to aid in emergency relief efforts.

In Hutchinson, the blowing snow burned out a coil at KWBW's radio transmitter, knocking the station off the air for more than 24 hours. Employees on the morning shift at both hospitals worked double and sometimes triple shifts until their relief could straggle in. *Hutchinson News* photographer Jim Morris, a National Guard sergeant, commandeered a Guard truck to pick up *News* employees, but gave up by early evening. Local media were inundated by so many Monday closures that they quit compiling lists, assuming that everything in town was shut down. Stated veteran newsman Alvin Dumler, "This is the most completely I've seen the town paralyzed since April of 1938."

One endeavor was not at a standstill, however.

In spite of the worst winter storm in Kansas in a decade, National Juco Tournament fans somehow made their annual pilgrimage to the Arena, creating the traditional waiting line for season tickets. Though only 1,800 purchases were made — forcing a supplementary sale three weeks later — it was another example of Hutchinson's devotion to junior college basketball.

THE PARTICIPANTS

Every year it could be counted on that at least half and frequently more than half of the top-rated teams in the NJCAA poll would fail to survive regional play. The 1971 campaign was different only in the fact that one of those casualties had been considered a shoo-in for a repeat appearance in Hutchinson. Not only did No. 4 Vincennes University return a solid nucleus from its 1970 championship team, including All-American candidates Bob McAdoo and Roy Simpson, but Coach Allen Bradfield had also recruited a talented crop of freshmen who were sure to make the Trailblazers a contender again in 1972. When Vincennes fell 83-75 to unheralded Southwestern Michigan College of Dowagiac in the Region 12 semifinals, it was a shocking surprise to tourney followers.

Still, had they advanced, the Trailblazers would not have been the team to beat. that distinction belonged to No. 1 College of Southern Idaho.

After an eighth-place finish in their tourney debut the year before, Coach Jerry Hale's Golden Eagles were primed for a national crown. Their front line included 6-8 Ron Behagen and 6-7 Tim Bassett, returning starters, plus 6-7 Ralph Palomar, a 1970 reserve who was now the team's leading scorer. The backcourt also offered experience in the presence of 6-2 Steve Hegens, a 1970 All-Tourney selection and 1st-Team All-American. The lone newcomer was Victor Kelly, a flashy 5-6 penetrator who was so good, he had usurped Hegens' role as floor leader.

The Eagles were 33-2 on the year and had not been defeated by a junior college foe. The fact that No. 5 Casper College (25-3), the second-highest ranked team in the tournament, was

(Top, left) Southern Idaho's Tim Bassett (No. 13) was later a star at the University of Georgia and spent seven years in the pros. (Photo courtesy of the **Hutchinson News**)

(Top, right) All-Tournament selection, Ron Behagen (No. 33) ended his collegiate career at the University of Minnesota then spent seven years in the NBA. (Photo courtesy of the **Hutchinson News**)

ne of its victims, further widened the gap between the Idahoans and the rest of the field.

Southern Idaho's only dilemma was the same which Vincennes faced the year before: the pre-tourney favorite was in a top-heavy bracket. Among Southern Idaho's potential opponents were:

No. 6 Columbia State Community College, a first-timer, but owner of the best record in the field (26-1);

No. 8 Robert Morris of Illinois (29-4), possessor of one of the nation's top scorers — 6-7 Clyde Turner (27.6);

No. 11 Gulf Coast Community College, another newcomer, but considered the best team yet from Florida, owning wins over Vincennes (the then No. 1-rated Trailblazers' first loss of the season), No. 10 Miami-Dade Community College-North, and No. 17 Jefferson State Junior College, the latter two earning the Commodores a trip to Hutchinson;

No. 12 Robert Morris of Pennsylvania (25-3), victor over 1970 tourney participant and 17th-rated Brandywine College in region play;

Tyler Junior College (23-7), unranked, but a fifth-place finisher the year before, the most veteran participant, and the only former champ in the field;

And Ferrum Junior College (26-4), unranked, but also a repeater from 1970 in which the Panthers barely lost to eventual champ Vincennes in the quarterfinals.

The only apparent weak team in the upper bracket was Southern Idaho's first-round draw, newcomer Manhattan Community College (23-9).

Casper's road to the title game — and a possible rematch with Southern Idaho — was less treacherous. Of the four first-time participants in the lower bracket, three were unranked: Ellsworth Community College (22-7), Hill Junior College (25-8), and Three Rivers Junior College (23-9). The other, No. 13 Niagara County Community College (30-2), was discounted because the Frontiersmen represented notoriously weak region 3.

The lone unranked veteran possessed none of the respect-inducing mystique that a two-time titleholder like Tyler did in the upper bracket. Bismarck Junior College not only had the worst record in the field (21-10), but had not won a game in two previous tourney appearances.

Only two teams figured to pose problems for the Thunderbirds. One was Bacone College (31-3), tied for 13th with Niagara County and the nation's leading offense in the final poll (109.1). The other was local favorite Hutchinson Community Junior College. The Blue Dragons were always a threat on their home floor, but particularly so when ranked 19th in the nation with a 26-4 record. Fortunately for Casper, only one of the two had chance of survival past the opening round: Bacone and Hutchinson were paired in their first outing.

TUESDAY — CONFUSING THE ISSUE

The topflight battle between No. 6 Columbia State and No. 12 Robert Morris actually started the day before the 1971 tourney tip-off. Though Columbia State ranked higher than the Pennsylvanians, local touts favored Robert Morris. Colonial Coach Gus Krop was a veteran who knew the ins and outs of the hoopla in Hutchinson. In addition, he could play four players who were either 6-5 or 6-6. Columbia State's Gene McBee could match only one of them with 6-5 center Benny Newsom. The next tallest starter for the Chargers was 6-2.

Hoping to find a way to counter the size disparity, McBee scouted the Colonials during their half-hour Monday workout on the Arena floor. Aware that McBee was in the stands, Krop split his team into two squads, mixing starters with non-starters and further confusing matters by having one crew consist of *six* men. As Krop later related, "He was sitting there, trying to figure out how the hell one guy was getting open all the time."

McBee solved the mystery, however. Columbia State compensated for its lack of height with superior quickness, a game-long harassing full-court zone press, and excellent free throw shooting. Though outgunned from the field, 35-29, the Chargers canned 30 of 36 charities, downing Robert Morris, 88-83. Six of the seven Columbia State players who saw action hit double figures. Only starting guard Terry Martin, who left the game after taking ill, failed to score.

Size was also a factor in the afternoon feature. Outmanned Manhattan was unable to duplicate Columbia State's success in the opener, however. Southern Idaho laid back in a zone, forcing the Panthers to shoot from outside, then dominated the boards when they missed. Though the Golden Eagles were not impressive, at times seeming to play only well enough to win, they were definitely the superior team, winning easily, 75-57. Ron Behagen and Tim Bassett topped all scorers with 17 each and led Southern Idaho's board brigade which outrebounded Manhattan, 48-34.

Since the first two winners had used zone defenses, Ferrum's prospects did not appear encouraging when Tyler immediately came out in a zone in the afternoon finale. The Panthers countered with a one-man delay. Five-ten guard Bobby Stevens dribbled out front for nearly three minutes until backcourt mate Charlie Thomas broke loose for an easy two. After scoring the first four points, Ferrum was ready to dictate the tempo.

Then turnovers led to seven straight Tyler points. Though they shot well over Tyler's zone, the Panthers never recovered. Tyler advanced, 88-79, using only five men, four of whom hit 19 or better.

The most exciting first-round contest opened the evening session. After falling behind, 44-37, at intermission, No. 8 Robert Morris of Illinois continued to trail No. 11 Gulf Coast by as much as nine. Then, late in the game, the Eagles made a run. All-American center Clyde Turner — who copped game honors with 26 — scored Robert Morris' final six points, including a pair of clutch free throws with 11 seconds left, giving the Illinois school a final 77-76 margin and its only lead of the period.

There had been no real surprises in the upper bracket's first-round play. The higher rated teams advanced and in the one contest between unranked opponents, Tyler, with a prior tourney record of 26-12, downed Ferrum which was 3-8 against the nation's best.

Things were different in the bottom bracket.

In the second half of the evening feature, Bismarck guards Mike Montgomery and Brent Wallender slowed the tempo, playing catch or dribbling until a teammate found an opening, and deliberately picked apart Hill's defense. In the final minutes, several three-quarter-court-length Mystic passes found open targets. Behind Montgomery's game-high 23, including 11 of 12 from the line, Bismarck recorded the tournament's first upset, upending Hill, 88-76. It was only the second win by a North Dakota school in 14 tries.

Audience eyebrows remained raised as unheralded Ellsworth blasted No. 5 Casper, 17-2, in the first six minutes of the evening finale.

Overcoming the initial shock, the Thunderbirds gradually climbed back in the game and eventually took the lead, 34-33, after scoring the first seven points of the final period.

Ellsworth regained the lead, however, and never relinquished it. After a pair of successful steals in the final 1:30, Casper squandered opportunities to take the lead, immediately returning the ball to the Panthers on turnovers. Ellsworth held on, stunning the Thunderbirds, 63-60.

WEDNESDAY — A TRAUMATIC EXPERIENCE

In the two tourney appearances since Gene Keady took over the head coaching job at Hutchinson, his Blue Dragons had outscored lesser first-round opponents, 223-175. If statistics were any indication, Hutchinson would have to maintain that 110-plus scoring average to beat top-scoring Bacone.

Hutchinson fans were ready to lend full-volume vocal support to the effort, especially after Casper's upset the night before. If Hutchinson could get by Bacone, it appeared clear sailing for the Dragons to the title game.

Consequently, the Arena was jammed for the Wednesday opener. Though the newspaper later quoted an attendance figure of 7,250, there was no way to accurately measure the crowd's number since there were no reserved seats for afternoon sessions and since season ticket holders were allowed free admittance. Many longtime tourney followers agree, however, that it was not only the largest afternoon crowd, but also one of the largest overall in tourney history. Red-clad Hutchinson fans were everywhere. Every inch of the press facilities was occupied, forcing a Tulsa sportswriter who arrived late to stand. The mass of yelling humanity was overwhelming, leading a Niagara County cheerleader, whose Frontiersmen played next, to state, "It scared the life out of us."

The effect on the opposition was predictable. "It was a traumatic experience," Bacone Coach George Hauser said. "I think we had eight people there and the rest were for Hutchinson."

Inspired by the massive support, the Blue Dragons played near perfect basketball. By intermission, Hutchinson held a 17-rebound advantage and led, 57-39.

Then, the Dragon game plan fell apart. In the next 10 minutes, Hutchinson committed 11 turnovers after recording only five in the first period. In addition, Rich Morsden and Stan Blackmon, the core of the Dragon rebounding power, sat down with four fouls apiece. In an eight-minute stretch, Bacone reduced a 22-point deficit to four.

To the crowd's relief, Hutchinson pulled out of the tailspin, outrebounding Bacone, 65-43, and outscoring the Oklahomans, 106-94. Hutchinson's offensive output was 18 better than its average; Bacone's was 15 points less.

With one game remaining, the opening round was one upset away from a clean sweep in the lower bracket. There was no suspense in the final surprise, however. By the time Niagara County scored its first field goal, the 13th-rated Frontiersmen were down, 18-3. Unranked Three Rivers won easily, 100-75.

* * *

Columbia State's fortunes had done a complete flip-fl[o] under frosh coach Gene McBee. The prior year the Charg[e] finished eighth in a 10-team league with an 8-12 mark. Und[er] McBee, the current Columbia State club had lost once in [ ] games. In each, the Chargers were decided underdogs [in] height, making up the difference with quickness and aggressi[ve] defense. Columbia State's continued success rested on that fo[r]mula working once more. In the opening quarterfinal match-[up] with top-rated Southern Idaho, the Chargers faced their stiffe[st] challenge to date against one of the best front lines in the cou[n]try.

The task appeared almost impossible from the outset [ ] Southern Idaho quickly opened a 20-5 gap. Then the Charg[er] formula took effect. Columbia State's press gradually whittl[ed] the difference to two at halftime. With 10:44 left to play, t[he] Chargers were in control, 61-58.

One thing the Chargers had not counted on, however, w[as] that Southern Idaho might match their quickness. In fact, t[he] quickest and smallest player on the floor was not a Charger; [it] was Southern Idaho's Victor Kelly.

CSI Coach Jerry Hale, later head coach at Oral Rober[ts] described Kelly as, "probably the most exciting player, day [in] and day out, I've ever seen. If you weren't careful, he wou[ld] take the ball away from you three times before you ever got [ ] to halfcourt."

Besides his defensive prowess, Kelly was also a fearless driv[er] up the middle, an act that always stirred the crowd because [of] his 5-6 size. With Columbia State positioned to pull off the bi[g]gest upset yet in the tournament, Kelly repeatedly penetrate[d] the lane, dishing off to his taller teammates for baskets. Eig[ht] unanswered points doomed the Chargers. With the Golde[n] Eagle front line combining for 62 points, Southern Idah[o] downed Columbia State, 77-72.

The evening's other quarterfinal exhibited even mo[re] impressive scoring performances. With center Clyde Turner f[ir]ing in a tourney-high 36 on the inside and guard Lee Gilbe[rt] drilling from outside for 32, Robert Morris of Illinois easi[ly] solved Tyler's zone. The Eagles opened a 14-point halftim[e] lead, extended it to 20, before winning 101-86, the fourth cen[ ]tury-mark breaker of the day.

THURSDAY — THE BIG BLOWOUT

Weather stole the show on hump day. A massive, intense lo[w] centered in northern Kansas created a huge cyclone across th[e] state, causing "snirt" storms (snow and blowing dirt) in th[e] northwest and dust bowl conditions elsewhere. Western sta[ ]tions reported straight winds of 50-60 miles per hour with gus[ts] to 90. Hutchinson reporter Alvin Dumler described it as th[e] state's "worst sustained, hours-long buffeting in a century."

Hutchinson's peak occurred at 1 p.m. with winds measure[d] at 41 miles per hour, gusting to 55. The generated force, com[ ]bined with the extreme low barometric pressure, popped [ ] windshields out of parked cars in the lot outside the Sports Are[ ]na.

Those inside were not exempted from the storm's fury. A[t] 1:10, with 13:04 remaining in the consolation game betwee[n] Gulf Coast and Ferrum, the Arena was suddenly plunged i[n] darkness. Fortunately, no one was shooting. Players who wer[e] bringing the ball upcourt at the time, simply stopped and waite[d] until light returned 20 minutes later.

When play resumed Gulf Coast outlasted Ferrum, 85-82. Th[e] streak-scoring contest provided the day's only excitement o[n] the court.

The quarterfinals were particularly uninspiring. In keepin[g] with the weather conditions outside, both were blowouts.

Hutchinson's fast break kicked into high gear in the secon[d] period of the evening opener, extending a six-point halftim[e] lead over Three Rivers to 20 with three minutes to go. Blu[e] Dragon Martin Terry led all scorers with 27, 19 in the final fram[e] after picking up his fourth foul, as Hutchinson won easily, 99[-] 82.

In the nightcap, Bismarck tied Ellsworth twice in the first 1[0] minutes. Then the Iowans bombed the North Dakotans, 33-8[,] building an insurmountable 47-22 halftime edge. Fans depart[ ]ed, leaving the Mystics at the mercy of the Ellsworth barrag[e.]

The Panthers opened the gap to 45 with five minutes remaining before blowing Bismarck away, 101-67.

FRIDAY — WALKING WOUNDED

To the casual observer, Southern Idaho's predicted title shot was on course. Though the Golden Eagles exhibited some lackluster moments in their first two outings, their talent was evident. No other tourney team could match CSI's starting five.

There was no certainty in the Southern Idaho camp, however. Coach Jerry Hale knew his team was good — provided it remained healthy. And the Eagles were far from that.

Hale's worries began in the Region 1/18 best-of-three playoff against Arizona Western College. Ralph Palomar, the Eagles' leading scorer, severely twisted an ankle in the first game and missed the rest of the series. Despite contributing 23 points in CSI's quarterfinal with Columbia State, the El Paso native was still hobbled by the injury and well below his season standard of play.

Then in the opener against Manhattan, Steve Hegens also sprained an ankle. The All-American sat out the final 18 minutes and was used sparingly in the quarterfinal.

To make matters worse, Hegens' replacement, 5-8 Gary Quesnell — who stole the ball four times and added seven points against Manhattan, duplicating a similar heroic effort in regional play — fell on his elbow late in the game against Columbia State. The joint promptly swelled, making it difficult to bend.

The other Eagle starters were also nursing afflictions: Tim Bassett, a problem knee; Victor Kelly, back spasms; and Ron Behagen, a recently developed cold.

The fact that Southern Idaho *had* won two games despite lack of health was testament to its superior talent. But, against Robert Morris of Illinois, the Golden Eagles would need more.

Joe Ramsey's Carthage Eagles were an up-and-coming powerhouse. Robert Morris regularly scheduled games with tournament mainstays such as Moberly, Burlington, and Vincennes and held its own. It was the school's third trip to Hutchinson in four years and Ramsey's best squad to date. The core of the team was outside-inside combo, guard Lee Gilbert and All-American center Clyde Turner. In Robert Morris' first two games, the duo combined for 65 percent of the Eagles' offense, running the opposition ragged between covering the perimeter and the middle. Southern Idaho's physical condition would be tested from the start.

If the Golden Eagles were hurt, it never showed. Jerry Hale played his starting five throughout, all scoring double figures. Kelly continued where he left off, continually penetrating the middle for feeds to Behagen, Palomar, and Bassett. On defense, CSI held Gilbert and Turner to their lowest totals of the tournament (20 and 17, respectively), Turner's being 10 points below his average. Robert Morris led twice early, rallied briefly in the second half, but was never really in the game. Southern Idaho completely dominated, winning 87-70, looking ever more like national champs.

Two teams still had a shot at preventing that inevitability, however, and were eager for the opportunity. Consequently, the remaining semifinal was the most exciting — and loudest — game in the tournament.

The 150 Ellsworth fans in attendance were almost inaudible in comparison to the volume of the standing-room-only Hutchinson backing. The support was so intense that it repeatedly appeared to lift the Blue Dragons out of desperate situations.

In spite of its disproportionate cheering advantage, Hutchinson was unable to shake Ellsworth. The largest lead by either team was six. With 2:13 remaining, the Dragons were barely in front, 66-64.

Fifteen seconds later it was all over. Ellsworth's Benny Clyde, the Blue Dragons' game-long nemesis to the tune of 30 points, completed a three-point play, giving the Panthers a 67-66 edge. Though the pace was fast and furious the rest of the way, neither team scored again. Ellsworth missed four opportunities to ice the victory with free throws. Hutchinson's Martin Terry missed a potential game-winner with 25 seconds left and teammate Stan Blackmon failed with seven seconds showing.

As the loss became apparent, the previously deafening crowd silenced. Upstart Ellsworth had prolonged local fan frustrations for at least another year.

SATURDAY — SNATCHING THE CROWN

Casper tipped off the trophy day parade with a demonstration of its nation-leading defense. The Thunderbirds allowed Robert Morris of Pennsylvania only one 15-second lead in the first half before downing the Colonials, 63-58, for fifth place.

Three Rivers came from 16 down with 15 minutes remaining to tie Columbia State on an 18-footer by Paul Hale with 20 seconds left, sending the fourth-place contest into the 1971 tourney's only overtime. Reserve John Johnson scored the Raiders' next six points, putting Three Rivers in control in the extra period. The Missourians held their biggest lead of the game, 96-90, with two minutes left and won, 102-99. Columbia State's Harry Gilmore topped all scorers with 35.

Hutchinson fans were out in full force for championship night activities, but their hearts were not in it. After missing another in a long line of opportunities for a national title, the hometown was emotionally flat as were the Blue Dragons. Hutchinson led, 6-2, but quickly fell behind and never threatened again. Behind Lee Gilbert's 25 and Clyde Turner's 22, Robert Morris of Illinois rolled over the Dragons, 93-74, for third.

Most felt the title match was cut and dry, particularly after Southern Idaho's masterful handling of Robert Morris in the semifinals. The No. 1 Golden Eagles appeared destined to wear the crown.

Ellsworth immediately reopened the question. There were five lead changes and six ties in the first half, the last deadlock coming at 31-all, three minutes before the break. Then, the Panthers leveled the psychological blow of the game, reeling off eight unanswered points. Ellsworth took confidence and a 39-31 advantage into the locker room at intermission.

Stated Ellsworth Coach Jim Carey, "In the first half, when I saw all five of them [Southern Idaho] bringing the ball down the floor, they weren't running like they usually did. All five of them were jogging down the floor. I said, 'Hey! We're going to win.'"

After Ellsworth's outburst, Southern Idaho never looked the same. The injury plagued Eagles seemed sluggish in comparison to the fired-up Iowa squad.

On offense, Ellsworth was deliberate, working the ball repeatedly to Benny Clyde in the middle, the assist generally coming from guard Wendall Taylor who had broken Oscar Robertson's high school assist mark at Crispus Attucks in Indianapolis. When Clyde was closed off, Taylor fired from outside. Described Carey, "We put everybody to sleep, but we ran our offense." Clyde scored 28 and Taylor 21.

More important was the Panther defense. According to Carey's game plan, "If they beat us, they were going to have to beat us from outside." With 6-7 jumping jack Clyde anchoring the middle, the Ellsworth 2-1-2 zone was extremely effective, particularly out front. Taylor and Jerry Tetzlaff outplayed their more illustrious counterparts, Steve Hegens and Victor Kelly, limiting Kelly's penetration and holding the duo to 8 and 11, respectively.

Southern Idaho's lone outstanding performance came from Ron Behagen with 24. When the personable young man sat down with his fifth foul late in the game, he broke down in tears. It was an emotional display which summed up the Eagles' disappointment, one with which local Hutchinson fans could readily identify.

Unranked Ellsworth snatched the crown away from top-rated Southern Idaho, 80-71.

THE AFTERMATH — THE GLIDE

While Ellsworth's championship trophy was a surprise to many, the other awards were not.

Late in the tourney tip-off between Columbia State and Robert Morris of Pennsylvania, Colonial forward Jim Dashield was decked by Columbia State's Harry Gilmore and carried unconscious from the floor. While Gilmore was ejected, Dashield became the front-runner for the Sesher Sportsmanship award.

The choice was appropriate. Dashield possessed a pleasant, non-aggressive demeanor. In fact, Robert Morris Coach Gus Krop complained, "I didn't think he was belligerent enough."

Krop did not know what provoked Gilmore's punch, but suspected that it involved freshman center Jonathan Marshall, the complete opposite of Dashield in temperament. But, at 175 pounds, Dashield was a safer target than Marshall's 220. "The guy was too smart to hit Marshall. He might hit back."

Ironically, Columbia State, which had downed Robert Morris, relinquished its seventh-place trophy to the Colonials six weeks later. The same Harry Gilmore who had socked Dashield was ruled ineligible for having neglected to tell the school that he

Coach of the Tournament Jim Carey (left) was able to get more out of his star Benny Clyde (with trophy) than Clyde's later mentors at Florida State and the Boston Celtics. (Photo courtesy of Mary Lee, the Lees Studio)

"I didn't think he was belligerent enough," said Robert Morris Coach Gus Krop. Therefore, Jim Dashield had the perfect temperament for the Sesher Sportsmanship Award. Dashield completed his collegiate career at Penn State. (Photo courtesy of Mary Lee, taken by Alex Lee)

had played basketball for Mesa College in Grand Junction, Colorado, from 1961 to 1963.

The French Most Valuable Player Award was also a foregone conclusion. Benny Clyde, the tournament's leading scorer with 103 points, had been unstoppable, especially when it counted.

"We didn't have anybody who could match up with him," related Hutchinson Coach Gene Keady. "We couldn't shut him down." Consequently Clyde's 30-point performance was the principle factor in Hutchinson's semifinal demise.

With players like Tim Bassett and Ron Behagen — who later played at Georgia and Minnesota, respectively, before matriculating into the professional ranks — Southern Idaho *did* have the talent to match Clyde, but the results were no different. "We said, 'We can't give him the 15-18 foot shot.' And we didn't," stated CSI Coach Jerry Hale. "He just hit the 22-30 [footer]." Added Hale, "If he'd gone on and played as well as he did in that tournament, he'd still be playing."

Though only a freshman, Clyde had a repertoire that caused opposing coaches to cringe. At 6-7 he was an in-between size. Yet he was agile and quick enough to play guard in Ellsworth's delay game while at the same time capable of consistently outjumping his taller counterparts at center. Clyde's coach Jim Carey, who was later a Division I coach at Nevada-Reno, described him as "probably the best talent I've ever seen." It was his picture of Clyde as a rebounder that most tourney fans remember. "He would go up, get it, curl it, and kick it out, all in the same motion." It was the type of fluid movement that earned him the nickname "The Glide."

No one questioned Carey's Coach of the Tournament honor either. Taking an unranked tourney newcomer all the way to the championship was sufficient. Carey was not new to the winning experience, however. As a star of Moberly's 1954 and 1955 national champs, he had learned what it took to be on top, pointing out that it was Moberly mentor Maury John who said, "If you're not playing in a national tournament in the last game of the season, it hasn't been a success." By guiding Ellsworth to the title, Carey became the only individual to play on and coach a national junior college champion, a fact for which he was later cited when inducted into the NJCAA Basketball Hall of Fame.

Tournament Results

	Game		
Tuesday:			
		1	Columbia St. — 88 Robert Morris (PA) — 83
		2	Southern Idaho — 75 Manhattan — 57
		3	Tyler — 88 Ferrum — 79
		4	Robert Morris (IL) — 77 Gulf Coast — 76
		5	Bismarck — 88 Hill — 76
		6	Ellsworth — 63 Casper — 60
Wednesday:			
		7	Hutchinson — 106 Bacone — 94
		8	Three Rivers — 100 Niagara County — 75
		9	Robert Morris (PA) — 103 Manhattan — 83
		10	Southern Idaho — 77 Columbia St. — 72
		11	Robert Morris (IL) — 101 Tyler — 86
Thursday:			
		12	Gulf Coast — 85 Ferrum — 82
		13	Niagara County — 98 Bacone — 81
		14	Columbia St. — 88 Tyler — 79
		15	Casper — 83 Hill — 75
		16	Hutchinson — 99 Three Rivers — 82
		17	Ellsworth — 101 Bismarck — 67
Friday:			
		18	Robert Morris (PA) — 88 Gulf Coast — 72
		19	Casper — 65 Niagara County — 55
		20	Three Rivers — 106 Bismarck — 81
		21	Southern Idaho — 87 Robert Morris (IL) — 70
		22	Ellsworth — 67 Hutchinson — 66
Saturday:			
		23	Casper — 63 Robert Morris (PA) — 58
		24	Three Rivers — 102 Columbia St. — 99 OT
		25	Robert Morris (IL) — 93 Hutchinson — 74
		26	Ellsworth — 80 Southern Idaho — 71

How They Finished in 1971

1. Ellsworth Community College
2. College of Southern Idaho
3. Robert Morris College (IL)
4. Three Rivers Junior College
5. Casper College
6. Hutchinson Community Junior College
7. Robert Morris College (PA)
8. (Vacated)

All-Tournament Team

Tim Bassett — College of Southern Idaho
Ron Behagen — College of Southern Idaho
Dennis Bell — Gulf Coast Community College
Stan Blackmon — Hutchinson Community Junior College
Benny Clyde — Ellsworth Community College
Roy Fields — Three Rivers Junior College
Lee Gilbert — Robert Morris College (IL)
Rick Hockenos — Niagara County Community College
Abe Steward — Casper College
Clyde Turner — Robert Morris College (IL)

Coach of the Tournament
Jim Carey — Ellsworth Community College

French Most Valuable Player Award
Benny Clyde — Ellsworth Community College

Sesher Sportsmanship Award
Jim Dashield — Robert Morris College (PA)

1972:

THE BUTLER DID IT

O n March 2, the ABA held a "secret" draft in order to get a head start in its annual college recruiting war with the NBA. Unfortunately, only three teams kept their selections secret. For the first time, teams were allowed to choose one non-senior and the Virginia Squires immediately took advantage of the new rule, announcing a North Carolina junior forward as the draft's first pick — former juco All-American Bob McAdoo.

The graduation of a 6-9 future NJCAA Hall of Famer, NCAA All-American, and NBA great would have created an unfillable hole for most schools. Vincennes University was not most schools, however. Under Coach Allen Bradfield, the Trailblazers had carved out a Midwestern dynasty, earning five national tourney trips in seven years and two championships. Solid recruiting was behind Bradfield's consistent program and the loss of McAdoo meant only that Vincennes opponents would have to adjust to a new set of talented faces.

Bradfield's 1971-72 squad appeared the best edition yet. Though lacking the height of earlier versions, the current Vincennes team compiled an unparalleled record. In their next to last regular season game, the Trailblazers downed Southeastern Community College of Burlington, 79-77, to set a school record for consecutive wins with 24. The streak remained intact when they arrived in Bay City, Michigan, for the Region 12 tournament. They quickly extended it, rolling over Oakland Community College-Orchard Ridge, 99-65, Lansing Community College, 110-80, and Lorain County Community College, 94-77. Then, they avenged the previous year's regional upset, downing Southwestern Michigan College, 85-77, earning a trip to Hutchinson.

Vincennes entered the 1972 Juco Tournament ranked No. 1 with a 29-0 record.

THE PARTICIPANTS

Since the tourney's top-rated team had won the championship four of the past six years, odds heavily favored Vincennes. But, for the third straight year, luck of the draw placed the pre-tourney favorite in a very precarious position. Six of the 10 top-10 teams in the field were in the upper bracket, including the top three.

Like Vincennes, No. 2 Dalton Junior College and No. 3 Arizona Western College had compiled remarkable win streaks during the year. Arizona Western (31-2) duplicated the Trailblazer's string, winning 29 between losses in its first and last regular season games. Dalton even bettered the Vincennes feat, entering the tournament with an unblemished 34-0 mark. The two contenders had one drawback, however. Unlike the seasoned two-time former champion Trailblazers, Dalton and Arizona Western were facing tourney competition for the first time.

The other ranked team in the upper bracket did not share that handicap. No. 10 Paducah Community College (24-5) was a former titleholder and a longtime Vincennes rival. No. 11 Casper College (27-4) was making its sixth appearance and its third in a row, having placed fifth the year before. No. 19 Gulf Coast Community College (29-4) was also a veteran of the 1971 tournament and had handed the 1970-71 Trailblazer squad its first loss.

The only weak spots in the upper bracket were tourney new-

Richard Morsden, the second-leading scorer in Hutchinson Community College history, was later All-Missouri Valley at Wichita State. (Photo courtesy of Wichita State University)

Region	Team
1	Arizona Western College — Yuma, Arizona
2	Seminole Junior College — Seminole, Oklahoma
3	Erie Community College — Buffalo, New York
4	Robert Morris College — Carthage, Illinois
6	Hutchinson Community Junior College — Hutchinson, Kansas
7	Paducah Community College — Paducah, Kentucky
8	Gulf Coast Community College — Panama City, Florida
9	Casper College — Casper, Wyoming
10	Ferrum Junior College — Ferrum, Virginia
11	Southeastern Community College — Burlington, Iowa
12	Vincennes University — Vincennes, Indiana
14	Tyler Junior College — Tyler, Texas
15	Ulster County Community College — Stone Ridge, New York
16	State Fair Community College — Sedalia, Missouri
17	Dalton Junior College — Dalton, Georgia
18	College of Southern Idaho — Twin Falls, Idaho

comers Erie Community College (23-13), Vincennes' first opponent, and State Fair Community College (22-13).

The bottom bracket appeared more wide open. No. 6 Seminole Junior College (29-3) and No. 7 College of Southern Idaho (26-3) were the highest rated contenders, but both possessed weaknesses. While Seminole was one of the leading offensive teams in the country (102.6), the Trojans were newcomers in only their second year of competition. On the other hand, Southern Idaho was making its third consecutive trip to Hutchinson. Unfortunately, the Golden Eagles returned only super sprite Victor Kelly from its 1971 runner-up squad.

The strength of the lower bracket appeared to belong to No. 9 Ferrum Junior College (31-3) and No. 15 Hutchinson Community Junior College (22-4). Each was blessed with key experience from disappointing 1971 tourney performances. Ferrum returned the quick, savvy backcourt tandem of 6-3 Charlie Thomas and 5-10 Bobby Stevens while Hutchinson brought back its entire starting front line — 6-7 Tyrone Pryor, 6-4 All-American candidate Richard Morsden, and 6-7 1971 All-Tournament selection Stan Blackmon.

The rest of the bracket was unranked and suspect. Tyler Junior College (28-6), SECC of Burlington (26-5), and Robert Morris of Illinois (21-14) were tourney veterans, but did not appear to possess the same high caliber squads of past years, having engineered upsets in order to reach Hutch: Tyler surprised No. 8 San Jacinto College in Region 14 play, then upended 1st-Team All-American Larry Kenon-led Amarillo College in a play-off with Region 5; SECC-Burlington downed No. 17 Worthington State Junior College in a play-off with Region 13; and Robert Morris ousted No. 14 Triton College in Region 4 play. The other lower bracket team, tourney newcomer Ulster County Community College (27-2), was discounted simply because it represented traditionally weak Region 15.

The bottom bracket favorite would be decided early — Ferrum faced Hutchinson in the opening round. If Hutchinson won, championship fever would hit an all-time high for local Blue Dragon fans. It might prove the most difficult obstacle in Vincennes' quest for an undefeated title.

TUESDAY — OPENING THE DOOR

Those who showed up at the Sports Arena doors for the 1972 tip-off did so more out of tradition than actual interest in the opener. They were entertained by a scoring duel between Casper's Ken Morgan Clark and State Fair's Jim Lassiter, who shared game honors with 31 each, but found the rest predictable. Except for a 16-all tie, Casper led throughout, winning easily, 79-65.

It was the other two afternoon games which stimulated fan curiosity. No. 2 Dalton faced No. 19 Gulf Coast and No. 3 Arizona Western went against No. 10 Paducah in two of the better first-round match-ups.

Eyes were immediately opened when the Dalton players came out for warm-ups, an effect which had been planned. "We were just starting out [with a basketball program]," explained Dalton Coach Mel Ottinger. "I was doing everything I could to get things stirred up. So we started wearing one white shoe and one blue shoe [the school colors were white and navy blue]. It seemed to have a psychological effect on the other team because when we came out and warmed up, they all stopped and quit concentrating on the game." Ottinger carried the tactic further by having his players switch shoes at halftime. Another Ottinger break with convention was that each Dalton starter shook hands with the opposing coach after being introduced at the start of each game.

The apparent net effect of the psych job was an immediate Dalton seven-point advantage. Then Gulf Coast did some psyching of its own, holding the Roadrunners to a single free throw in an eight-minute stretch. Powered by center Butch "Super Blue" Taylor, who led everyone with 26 points and 13 rebounds, the Commodores opened a 20-point gap. Dalton attempted a comeback against Gulf Coast reserves late in the game, but eventually fell, 78-69.

The other top afternoon tilt was more hotly contested. Only three points separated Arizona Western and Paducah at intermission, the edge to the latter. Then the two really fired up. In the final period, Paducah shot 65 percent from the field and the

Matadors 59 percent. The difference in the game was a five minute Arizona Western cold snap, in which Paducah outscored the Matadors, 11-2. Paducah won, 86-78.

With the No. 2 and No. 3 teams early upset victims, the pa[th] to an undefeated title was already less cluttered for Vincenne[s] Trailblazer hopefuls were eager to get the opener again[st] Region 3 pushover Erie out of the way.

The Kats had a different view of the matter. Seven sopho[o]mores still felt the humiliating sting of a 119-77 regular-seas[on] thrashing at the hands of Vincennes the year before. With th[e] memory fresh in mind, Erie took control early, led most of th[e] first half, before relinquishing the edge just prior to intermi[s]sion.

The Trailblazers were not out of the woods yet. Behind 6-[?] 252-pound center Calvin Murphy, who led all scorers with 2[?] Erie continued to give Vincennes fits, regaining the lead, 62-6[?] with 14:10 remaining.

The Trailblazers forged ahead by seven.

The Kats clawed back within four.

Then Vincennes superior quickness took its toll. Led b[y] guards Dennis Shidler, who had a team-high 24, and Clarenc[e] "Foots" Walker, who surprised everyone with his leaping abili[i]ty, taking rebound honors with 14, the Trailblazers scored 1[?] unanswered points. Vincennes won comfortably, 107-83, [?] five starters hitting 16 or better.

Another decided underdog took sights at a major upset in th[e] evening feature. Unheralded Ulster County shot 57 percent [in] the first half and built a shocking 47-31 advantage over No. [?] Southern Idaho.

Then, as Ulster County Coach Mike Perry later described i[t] "Victor Kelly became miraculous." After being held to only sev[v]en first-half points, including a cold 2 of 7 from the field, Sout[h]ern Idaho's half-pint dynamo warmed up, almost single[e] handedly bringing the Golden Eagles back. He hit 10 of 13 fro[m] the field in the final frame, scoring a tourney-high 38 point[s] including 14 of 15 from the line. Confessed Perry, "I had Jack[y] Knowles punch him and slap him and kick him. The ball woul[d] still go in the basket. It was an incredible performance . . . a[n] incredible performance." Behind Kelly's heroics, Southern Id[a]ho downed Ulster, 85-75.

The nightcap was the game of the day as far as local fans we[re]

*The 1972 tournament's leading scorer with 118 points, 5-6 Victor Kelly (No. 44) later starred for the University of Southern California. (Photo courtesy of the **Hutchinson News**)*

concerned. Hutchonians were more encouraged than ever [of] Blue Dragon prospects. Height, tradition, and a huge followi[ng] were on their side. Coach Gene Keady confirmed the promisi[ng] outlook when he called for a scouting report from Robert Mor[ris] of Pennsylvania Coach Gus Krop, whose Colonials had lost [to] Ferrum in a region play-off. "Gus said we wouldn't have a[ny] problems beating them since we were playing at home."

The prediction held true in the opening period as Hutchinso[n] burned the cords at a 62-percent clip, taking a 46-41 lead.

The Panthers were unperturbed, however. While the Dra[?]

s started hot, Ferrum was more consistent, committing fewer turnovers and firing at a steady 44 percent throughout. More important, the disciplined Panther defense cooled down the Hutchinson offense in the second half. In one six-minute stretch, Ferrum tallied 15 points while Hutchinson went scoreless. Blue Dragon big men Richard Morsden and Stan Blackmon, whose combined average was more than 47 points, were shackled to less than half that amount before both fouled out. Despite the career high 34 points of guard Bobby Joe Jackson, Hutchinson fell to Ferrum, 82-72.

The Blue Dragon loss not only prolonged Hutchinson's frustrating pursuit of the junior college crown, but also opened the door wider for a Vincennes undefeated season.

WEDNESDAY — PLAYING SCARED

John Moody, SECC of Burlington's fourth all-time leading scorer, kept the Blackhawks in the game during the first half of the day's opener, notching 20 points. However, in the final period, Seminole's 1-3-1 zone sagged in, holding the 6-6 sophomore to only seven. Seminole won, 59-56, despite hitting only 37.7 percent from the field, one of the coldest shooting performances in tourney history. The Trojans were saved by a whopping 55-39 rebound advantage.

The final first-round contest was an excellent pairing of tournament veterans. Through the first 20 minutes, Tyler held a slim 41-39 edge over Robert Morris. Then, a minute-and-a-half into the second period, Tyler went on a 17-3 tear. With Clyde Turner now an All-Big Ten performer at Minnesota, only one half of Robert Morris' dynamic scoring duo of the previous year remained — All-Tourney selection Lee Gilbert. The six-foot sophomore was unable to carry the load alone, hitting only 7 of 19 from the field for 15 points, six under his average. Led by Jerry Ahart (33), Charles McKinney (26), and Jack James (20), Tyler won easily, 95-79.

Since seven of the eight quarterfinalists were ranked, the second round appeared a sure bet for close competition. Fans had to wait awhile before excitement materialized in the opening quarterfinal, however.

Gulf Coast controlled action from the outset, building a 12-point advantage with just under 13 minutes remaining. Then Jasper rallied, tying the score at 72-all. A missed hook shot from the free throw line by Thunderbird Ken Morgan Clark at the buzzer sent the game into overtime. A lay-up by Gulf Coast's Butch Taylor with 12 seconds left extended the contest another five minutes. The even battle was finally decided with 23 seconds remaining in the second overtime when Gulf Coast's Joe Johnson tipped in teammate Moe Rivers' missed free throw, giving the Commodores a five-point lead and clinching a hard-earned 89-86 victory.

Even though Paducah was ranked No. 10, few felt Vincennes would have any difficulty earning its 31st consecutive win in the nightcap. In fact, with the demise of No. 2 Dalton, No. 3 Arizona Western, and hometown favorite Hutchinson in the first round, many picked the Trailblazers to stroll to the crown.

Vincennes Coach Allen Bradfield felt differently. "Did I think we could win [the tournament]? Yes. Was I scared we wouldn't? You bet. I never went into a game I wasn't scared. I tried to train my players to be that way. If we were going to play four old ladies, all of whom are eight months pregnant, we were going out there and be scared to death." And in longtime rival Paducah, the Trailblazers had reason to be serious. Stated Bradfield, "I have the utmost respect when I see that Paducah uniform. That's scary even yet to think about playing Paducah."

The Indians dogged Vincennes throughout. It was not until the Trailblazers opened a nine-point spread with four minutes remaining and employed their stall that the contest was secure from doubt.

For the second straight game, all five Vincennes starters scored double figures, illustrating the balance which had been season-long team characteristic. It was surprising, therefore, that one player stood out from the rest. Center Bill Butler had been perfect in the second half, hitting 9 of 9 from the field and 5 for 5 from the line. His season-high 34 led all scorers and propelled Vincennes to a 96-85 triumph.

THURSDAY — HUMP DAY LULL

Hump day's best contest occurred in the afternoon consolation feature. SECC-Burlington and Robert Morris tied each other 14 times and exchanged the lead 21. With seven seconds left, the game tied 74-all, Walt Herrod hit two free throws for SECC. Robert Morris then called a time out it did not have. The subsequent technical sealed a 77-74 Blackhawk win, the third in four outings against Robert Morris that year.

The day's only other fireworks took place in the quarterfinals, though the excitement generated was due more to the contests' importance in terms of the tournament's final outcome rather than the play of the teams competing.

Tyler shot miserably in the first half of the evening feature, falling behind Seminole, 50-34. The Oklahomans returned the favor in the second period. Trailing by 10 with 12:12 remaining, Tyler scored 15 unanswered points. The Apaches went on to win, 87-81, in a mild upset.

The nightcap was closer throughout, but even less well-played. Neither Ferrum nor Southern Idaho scored in the last minute-and-a-half of a tense one-point game, largely because of costly turnovers. Epitomizing the poor play was Southern Idaho's Victor Kelly, who had just come off a sparkling 38-point opening performance. Though he again led all scorers with 20, Kelly hit only 7 of 24 from the field and missed the potential game-winner twice in the final 10 seconds. Ferrum won, 61-60.

FRIDAY — HE WAS BEAT AND DIDN'T KNOW IT

Most people would have thought that maintaining a perfect record and a No. 1 ranking would be sufficient motivation for any team, but, not so the Vincennes Trailblazers. According to Coach Allen Bradfield, "I'm sure Gulf Coast was more on our minds than an undefeated season. We just hoped they didn't get beat and we'd get a crack at them."

Hard feelings between the two schools dated back to the previous year. On its annual swing through Florida, Vincennes lost its first game of the year, falling to Gulf Coast, 101-84, at Panama City. The outcome was marred by rough play, injuries to Vincennes players, and what the *Orlando Sentinel* agreed were " 'homer' calls." After the loss, Bradfield vowed to the press, "I won't play in Panama City as long as Jack Jackson is the coach."

True to his word, Bradfield did not schedule Gulf Coast, one of the best teams in the country, during Vincennes' Florida trip the next year. This led to accusations by the Florida press that Vincennes had earned its No. 1 ranking and undefeated record against a "snap" schedule.

Thus the stage was set for the key match-up of the 1972 tournament, a battle between teams who disliked each other intensely.

From a height standpoint, Gulf Cost appeared better equipped to win the war. The Commodores held nearly a three-inch per-man advantage over Vincennes whose tallest starter was 6-3. Stated Coach Jackson to the *Vincennes Sun-Commercial*, "There's no way they [the Trailblazers] could handle our size . . . Vincennes is living on its past reputation and they certainly are overrated."

Gulf Coast quickly took the lead.

But, as Bradfield later stated, "He [Jackson] was beat before he left the dressing room and didn't know it. There are some things that are going to happen. He could have had half the Russian Army and we'd still have beat them."

The Trailblazers played with extreme poise, executing their full-court pressure defense with precision. Vincennes forced Gulf Coast into 16 turnovers, gained the lead with a 9-0 spurt, and opened a 45-35 gap by intermission. Spearheading the attack was six-foot guard Foots Walker who was all over the court, stealing the ball numerous times, scoring 15 points, and forcing the Commodores into uncharacteristic conservatism.

Jackson later told the press, "Vincennes has truly an amazing team . . . They have tremendous overall quickness and team scoring balance . . . it's almost impossible to spot a team like Vincennes that much of a lead." In the second half, Gulf Coast never got closer than five, eventually losing, 89-81.

It was another team victory for the Trailblazers. Guard Dennis Shidler had been the floor general. Walker and 6-3 Harold Miles — who was credited with holding 6-9, 220-pound Butch Taylor to 16, nine under his average — were the defensive stars. Bill Butler (23) and Tony Byers (22) were the offensive standouts, though for the third straight game all five Vincennes starters scored double figures. The most telling statistic, however, was that the smallest team in the tournament won the battle of the boards, 34-28. Summarized Gulf Coast's Jackson, "I have no doubt that they will win it all."

With the impressive victory keeping Vincennes on track for an undefeated crown, the other semifinal was anticlimactic. After a close 13 minutes, Ferrum outscored Tyler, 14-0, took a 38-27 lead, built it to 14 by halftime, and won going away, 84-60.

SATURDAY — TWELVE QUICK POINTS

With everyone expecting the Vincennes Trailblazers to breeze in the championship game, the three consolation trophy games provided a fan bonus.

In the fifth-place match, Hutchinson overcame a nine-point halftime deficit to tie Arizona Western at the end of regulation. The Blue Dragons then forged ahead in overtime only to see Arizona Western reel off seven straight points. The Matadors won, 99-94.

Hometown disappointment was offset by the splendid performance by forward Richard Morsden. The Kansas City native took game honors with 33, including a perfect 17 for 17 from the free throw line, moving him into the top spot in career scoring at Hutchinson with 1,377 points. Teammate Stan Blackmon was not far behind with 1,041 points, third-best in Blue Dragon history.

In the other afternoon contest, Southern Idaho established an all-time tourney record, committing only 46 fouls in four games. Fittingly, the fourth-place trophy was decided at the line.

With Southern Idaho leading, 71-70, and 10 seconds remaining, Casper fouled Victor Kelly. After Kelly hit the first free throw, Casper Coach Swede Erickson called time out.

When everyone settled at the free throw lane a second time, Erickson again called time. CSI Coach Jerry Hale looked down at Erickson who smiled and said, "Hale, I still got one left."

Sure enough, just as the referee was about to hand Kelly the ball, Erickson called his third straight time out.

The psychological ploy was ineffective, however. Kelly hit the free throw, icing the win. Kelly also iced game honors with 30, taking the scoring championship with 118. Casper's Ken Morgan Clark, the tourney's Sesher Sportsmanship Award-winner, ended action with an uncontested bucket.

With Tyler leading by 10 early in the second half of the third-place game, Butch Taylor scored back-to-back three-point plays, igniting a 13-2 Gulf Coast surge. The Commodores quickly captured the lead and an 85-81 victory.

Fans turned out in full-house numbers for championship night. Throughout the week everyone's attention had been drawn to Vincennes' overall team quickness, its frequently debilitating defensive pressure, and its surprising leaping ability despite lack of height. It had been 10 years since the tournament crowned its only undefeated champion and most expected to see it happen again.

Vincennes' final obstacle had slipped unnoticed into the title tilt. All three Ferrum opponents viewed poor play on their own part as the reason for losing: Hutchinson had committed untimely fouls; Southern Idaho too many costly turnovers; and Tyler simply could not find the target. Since Ferrum was offensively uninspiring, few gave the Virginians much chance.

Those who did cited one cause for all Panther opponent maladies — good defense. In its three outings, Ferrum held opposition scoring to a tourney low 64 points per game, forcing each to shoot a cool 40 percent from the field.

One of those believers was Kenny Gray, a Vincennes assistant the following year. With the Vincennes contingent elated from the win over Gulf Coast, Gray worked on players and coaches alike to take Ferrum seriously. After an evening, a morning, and an afternoon, Gray's effort struck home, bringing the Trailblazers down to earth. Stated Coach Allen Bradfield,

"We finally went in that [championship] night playing scared."

There was sufficient reason for fear. Ferrum started hot opening a quick 17-9 lead, forcing Vincennes to play catch-up.

Behind the offensive efforts of Foots Walker and Tony Byers the Trailblazers battled back, tying the game 19-all. There were four more ties. Then a 20-footer by Byers and a tip-in by Bill Butler gave Vincennes a 31-27 cushion at intermission.

Things tightened again as soon as play resumed. Baskets by Bobby Stevens and Lew Hill brought Ferrum within one, 32-31.

Then came the game's breaking point.

According to Bradfield, "I had a match-up, full-court defense we could use the whole game that I had never been able to use before or since. There were times we literally scored 20 points without the other team getting out of backcourt." Similar spurts had opened up the games in Vincennes' first three outings. It was the same against Ferrum. Twelve quick points sealed the outcome.

The Trailblazers played poised control ball to the finish, winning their 33rd consecutive game of the year, 73-61.

THE AFTERMATH — PERFECTION II

Comparisons between the 1972 Vincennes and the 1962 Coffeyville undefeated champions were unavoidable. Basically, the two were very similar. Both lacked height. Both were lightning quick. And, above all, both were disciplined machines, each part complementing the other.

Asked to evaluate his third national champ, Allen Bradfield stated, "I've had a lot of great ball teams. I've always wondered which one was the best. I think that if I were going to coach against the teams I had, that one [the 1971-72 squad] would scare me more than any other."

Since all five starters averaged double figures for the four tourney games and had contributed at least one heroic effort, choosing Trailblazer representatives on the All-Tournament team was a difficult task.

Forward Harold Miles, the blue collar worker on the team, had been a defensive stalwart, especially in the key win over Gulf Coast.

The other wing man, Tony Byers, the team's leading scorer throughout the season, had continued his consistent offensive output, despite the handicap of broken thumb on his non-shooting hand. A quick outside shooter, the 6-3 sophomore was particularly effective in the title game, scoring a game-high 23. Related former Ferrum player Bobby Stevens (later an assistant coach at Virginia Tech), "Our scouting report said he couldn't shoot the ball from 18-feet. [Instead] he just shot the lights out. I had problems with him. Charlie [Thomas] had prob-

Backcourt mates Charlie Thomas and Bobby Stevens (left and right respectively holding Ferrum's second-place trophy) achieved notoriety the following year as starters for Virginia Tech when the Gobblers stunned the college basketball world by winning the NIT in dramatic fashion. First, Thomas canned the winner with 33 seconds left in Virginia Tech's 65-63 upset of New Mexico. Next, Thomas and Stevens both made heroic last-minute efforts in the Gobblers' 74-73 come-from-behind upset of Alabama. Finally, Stevens swished a last-second jumper to defeat Notre Dame, 92-91, in overtime for the title. (Photo courtesy of Mary Lee, Alex Lee photographer)

lems with him. The more we tried to do with him, the better shooter he became. I seemed to always be at the bottom end of his jump shot."

For many, the team's unsung hero had been Foots Walker. On defense, the cat-quick sophomore was forever harassing

he opposition, batting the ball away for a steal or simply dis-
rupting the offensive flow. At the other end of the court, people
held their breath in anticipation knowing something exciting
would happen if he touched the ball. Not only was he a definite
All-Tourney prospect, but also an MVP candidate. Unfortu-

Vincennes' driving force on the court, Clarence "Foots" Walker later earned another championship crown with West Georgia in the NAIA Tournament before spending 10 years in the NBA. (Photo courtesy of Gus Stevens, Vincennes University)

French MVP Bill Butler (No. 35) Vincennes' 6-2 center, had remarkable spring in his legs and epitomized the 1972 Trailblazers' ability to make things happen despite lacking size. (Photo courtesy of the Hutchinson News)

nately, he earned neither recognition.

The All-Tournament selection committee opted for Walker's
backcourt mate Dennis Shidler, the emotional cornerstone for
Vincennes. The six-foot transfer from the University of Texas
had directed action on the court, picking up the slack offensively or defensively when needed. It was his 18 second-half points,
all from the field, which dispatched stubborn Erie in the Trailblazer opener.

Vincennes' other All-Tourney selection and the French Most
Valuable Player was a popular choice. At 6-2, Bill Butler was
probably the smallest legitimate center playing collegiate basketball at the time. His jumping ability amazed and delighted
everyone. Often he would be obscured in the pack under the
basket only to pop up above everyone to snatch a rebound or
to pull down a pass. He frequently jumped two or three times
to everyone else's one. According to Coach Bradfield, "His second jump was as good or better than his first."

The effect Butler had on the opposition was dramatic.
Described Vincennes Sports Information Director Gus Stevens,
"Butler had a phantom ability to play with the 6-8 to 7-0 players
and play with them on their level. That was demoralizing to
them. They had gone all through their high school careers and
their junior college careers just dominating little guys that were
6-2. They just could not accept [Butler's ability] and usually that
threw them off their game immediately."

A perfect example occurred in the semifinals when Butler
blocked the first couple shots of 6-9 Gulf Coast center Butch
Taylor (who set a tourney record with 60 rebounds in four
games). Said Coach Bradfield, "He just put Butch's head
between his legs."

"He played that same way at Louisville [the next two years],"
said Ferrum's Bobby Stevens. "They started him at guard on the
defensive end, but offensively, he went down in on the
blocks."

Unsurprisingly, the Coach of the Tournament went to Bradfield, the first to receive the honor three times. But, according
to the Vincennes mentor, "They [Ferrum] may have had the
very best coach in the tournament."

Ferrum Coach Bob Watson had been the co-captain of VMI's
1964 NCAA Tournament team and had just completed two
tours of Vietnam. "There was no question in my mind that he
was one of the bright upcoming young coaches in the country,"
said Watson's former player Stevens. "He had a tremendous
mind as far as strategy for the game. But, his biggest [attribute]
was in communication with the players. He had the ability to

just crawl all over you for making a mistake and, in two seconds,
turn around and put his arm around you. You felt nothing
towards him as far as hatred or anger. He had a way of getting
a player to play at his maximum . . . He was destined for great
things."

In 1977, Watson got his chance as an NCAA head coach,
landing the job at Evansville which had just graduated to the
Division I level. His great opportunity did not last long. On
December 13, 1977, the chartered DC-3 carrying Watson and
the Evansville basketball team crashed in a dense fog after take
off from Dress Regional Airport, killing all 31 on board.

Ferrum's Bob Watson was an up-and-coming young coach when he accepted the job at the University of Evansville in 1977. Later that year Watson perished with his team in an airplane crash. (Photo courtesy of the University of Evansville)

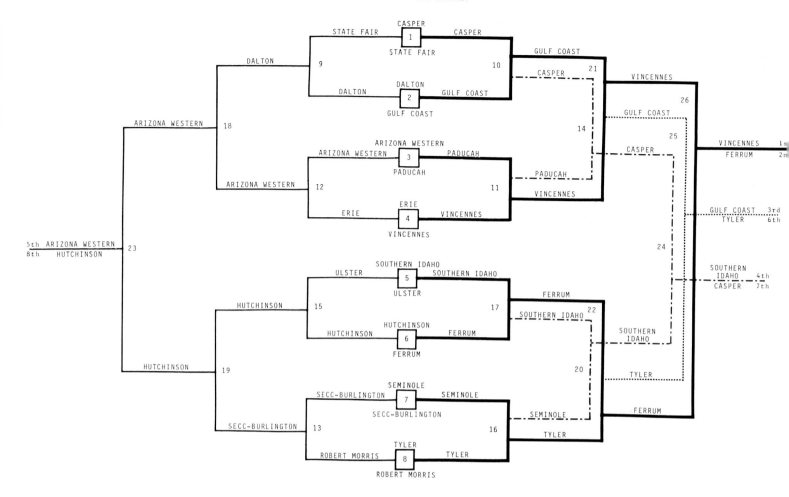

1972 TOURNAMENT BRACKET

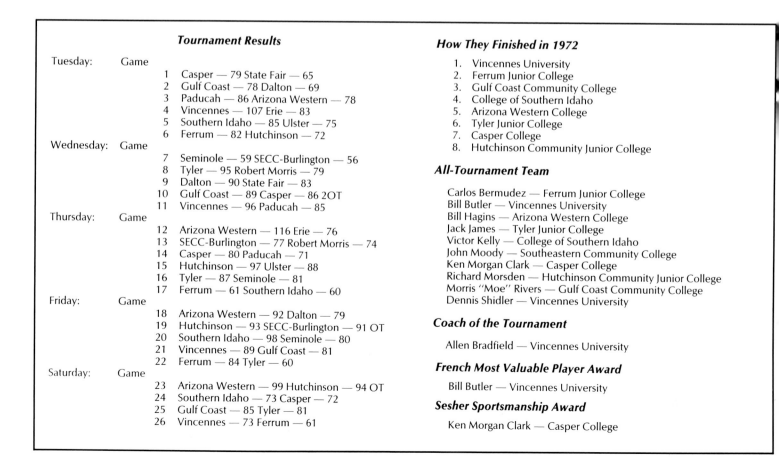

Tournament Results

Tuesday: Game

1. Casper — 79 State Fair — 65
2. Gulf Coast — 78 Dalton — 69
3. Paducah — 86 Arizona Western — 78
4. Vincennes — 107 Erie — 83
5. Southern Idaho — 85 Ulster — 75
6. Ferrum — 82 Hutchinson — 72

Wednesday: Game

7. Seminole — 59 SECC-Burlington — 56
8. Tyler — 95 Robert Morris — 79
9. Dalton — 90 State Fair — 83
10. Gulf Coast — 89 Casper — 86 2OT
11. Vincennes — 96 Paducah — 85

Thursday: Game

12. Arizona Western — 116 Erie — 76
13. SECC-Burlington — 77 Robert Morris — 74
14. Casper — 80 Paducah — 71
15. Hutchinson — 97 Ulster — 88
16. Tyler — 87 Seminole — 81
17. Ferrum — 61 Southern Idaho — 60

Friday: Game

18. Arizona Western — 92 Dalton — 79
19. Hutchinson — 93 SECC-Burlington — 91 OT
20. Southern Idaho — 98 Seminole — 80
21. Vincennes — 89 Gulf Coast — 81
22. Ferrum — 84 Tyler — 60

Saturday: Game

23. Arizona Western — 99 Hutchinson — 94 OT
24. Southern Idaho — 73 Casper — 72
25. Gulf Coast — 85 Tyler — 81
26. Vincennes — 73 Ferrum — 61

How They Finished in 1972

1. Vincennes University
2. Ferrum Junior College
3. Gulf Coast Community College
4. College of Southern Idaho
5. Arizona Western College
6. Tyler Junior College
7. Casper College
8. Hutchinson Community Junior College

All-Tournament Team

Carlos Bermudez — Ferrum Junior College
Bill Butler — Vincennes University
Bill Hagins — Arizona Western College
Jack James — Tyler Junior College
Victor Kelly — College of Southern Idaho
John Moody — Southeastern Community College
Ken Morgan Clark — Casper College
Richard Morsden — Hutchinson Community Junior College
Morris "Moe" Rivers — Gulf Coast Community College
Dennis Shidler — Vincennes University

Coach of the Tournament

Allen Bradfield — Vincennes University

French Most Valuable Player Award

Bill Butler — Vincennes University

Sesher Sportsmanship Award

Ken Morgan Clark — Casper College

1973:

THE YEAR OF THE DRAGON

During the 1972 NJCAA Basketball Tournament, *The New York Times* ran a feature article on the event, in particular, noting the vast amount of talent that lured four-year college coaches to Hutchinson year after year. Also, for the first time, *Sports Illustrated* mentioned the tournament in its season-ending summary of college basketball.

While national interest in the event was reaching new highs, local interest appeared to wane. For the second straight year there was no sellout on season tickets. Crowds still packed the Sports Arena, but more and more were buying tickets for single evenings rather than for the whole week.

The American Legion and the NJCAA attributed the decline to increasing dissatisfaction with the way season tickets were sold. Fans tired of having to wait in line for hours or having to pay someone else to do the waiting for them. Those who lived outside the Salt Capital — many took vacations in Hutchinson tourney week — were equally disgruntled. The change from a mail-in ticket order system had prevented these loyal followers from gaining season tickets unless they knew someone in Hutchinson.

Tourney sponsors first attempted to rectify the problem prior to the 1972 tournament by setting aside 1,200 tickets for mail order customers. Then for the 1973 event, they simply made all seats reserved, upping the ticket limit per customer from four to eight.

It was hard to tell whether the new arrangements were effective, since tickets for the 1973 tournament would have sold out no matter what method was used. The reason: Hutchinson Community Junior College was 26-3, ranked No. 1 in the nation, the highest year-end ranking for a Blue Dragon team yet.

It was believed in most quarters that 1973 would finally be the year of the Dragon.

THE PARTICIPANTS

Hutchinson's starting five had the look of a champion:

At one guard was 6-0 Greg Hill, a hard-nosed defensive player. At the other was 6-4 Charles Terry, whose quick hands delivered steals on defense and whose soft touch broke zones on offense.

Charles' older brother, 6-5 John Terry, a blue-collar rebounder and garbage man under the basket, played one forward. The other was 6-5 Teko Wynder, the best shooter on the team, despite the fact he shot cockeyed, from the side of his head rather than from in front.

The prime ingredient in Blue Dragon title chances was a good big man. Rudy Jackson had "future pro" written all over him. The 6-9 center was the team's leading scorer with a 23.4 average and its leading rebounder with 14.7 per game. He was versatile enough to shoot accurately from outside and fluid enough to bring the ball up court on a fast break, though Coach Gene Keady preferred he did not.

Optimism of Hutchonians was at an all-time high, not only because they backed a solid quintet, but because, for once, luck of the draw favored the Blue Dragons. In 10 previous appearances, misfortune had placed the locals against the best; Hutchinson had lost to the eventual champions on four occasions and to the eventual runner-up on five. Now the Dragons finally had

The top scorer in the 1973 tournament (111 points) and one of Hutchinson Community College's all-time leading scorers, Teko Wynder later attended Mercer University in Georgia before completing his collegiate career at Tulsa. (Photo courtesy of the University of Tulsa taken by Lassiter Shoemaker Photography, Tulsa, Oklahoma)

a break. The only other ranked team in Hutchinson's bracket was No. 14 Brevard Community College (22-2).

The rest belonged to the unranked: Dixie College (23-3), Bacone College (32-5), Olney Central College (28-6), North Greenville College (25-6), Paducah Community College (24-7), and Southeastern Community College of West Burlington (20-11). Former champion Paducah and the always competitive Burlington Blackhawks possessed the only long-standing tourney traditions among the veterans with Olney the lone newcomer. No team in the bottom bracket appeared the caliber of Hutchinson.

The upper bracket was another matter.

Region	Team
1	Dixie College — St. George, Utah
2	Bacone College — Muskogee, Oklahoma
4	Olney Central College — Olney, Illinois
5	McLennan Community College — Waco, Texas
6	Hutchinson Community Junior College — Hutchinson, Kansas
7	Paducah Community College — Paducah, Kentucky
8	Brevard Community College — Cocoa, Florida
9	Platte Junior College — Columbus, Nebraska
10	North Greenville College — Tigerville, South Carolina
11	Southeastern Community College — West Burlington, Iowa
12	Vincennes University — Vincennes, Indiana
15	Ulster County Community College — Stone Ridge, New York
16	Three Rivers Community College — Poplar Bluff, Missouri
17	Dalton Junior College — Dalton, Georgia
18	College of Southern Idaho — Twin Falls, Idaho
19	Mercer County Community College — Trenton, New Jersey

First of all, there was No. 18 Ulster County Community College (31-4), a 1972 tourney veteran with four returning starters and an 18-game win streak.

Second, there was No. 11 Mercer County Community College (30-3), a four-time veteran with an 11-game win streak.

Third, there was No. 6 College of Southern Idaho (29-3), making its fourth consecutive trip to Hutchinson.

And finally, there was No. 2 Vincennes University (26-3), the defending national champ and most successful tourney participant in the past 10 years.

Add to these unranked Dalton Junior College (26-6), which had made an impressive debut the previous year, and a dog fight could be expected. Only tourney veteran Three Rivers Community College (26-9) and newcomers McLennan Community College (26-5) and Platte Junior College (27-6) were discounted.

Hutchinson fans hoped that, while the Dragons were sweeping through the lower bracket, the other top contenders would be chewing each other to pieces in the upper. By championship night, the crown would just be sitting there, theirs for the wearing.

TUESDAY — THROWING IN THE TOWEL

The year before, Ulster County lost its first-round game after blowing a 16-point lead. The 1973 opener was déjà vu for the Senators. Ulster County quickly built a 20-4 advantage only to see Platte battle back, tying the score at 22-all. The game remained close until midway in the second half. Then Ulster prevented a repeat of history, outscoring the Raiders, 16-2. Behind Coleman Link's game-high 28 points and 11 rebounds, the favored Senators advanced, 89-77.

The second contest was not only the best first-round match-up, but one of the key games of the tournament. True to its billing, the first half saw the lead exchanged 21 times with neither No. 6 Southern Idaho nor No. 11 Mercer County managing an advantage greater than three.

In the second period, Mercer took control, building the margin to nine twice. Then with 5:22 remaining, the Vikings in front, 57-52, the scoreboard failed.

A short intermission followed as Al Wagler, in his first year as tournament director, hurriedly organized repairs. When it was apparent the clock would not be fixed in a reasonable time, officials decided to conclude the contest using a stop watch. Public address announcer Terry Messing would periodically appraise everyone of the time remaining and the score.

Had it been a less critical game or had the margin of difference been maintained, the problem with the scoreboard would not have been germane. But, almost as soon as play resumed, Southern Idaho mounted a rally, led by sophomore guard Ricky Sobers, who scored eight of the Eagles' last 10.

Points soon became crucial and seconds dear. CSI's Jerry Hale and Mercer's Howie Landa called frequent time-outs. Each pause produced huddles around the scorer's table where confusion reigned. At the beginning of one time-out, it was announced that 28 seconds remained. When the players returned to the floor, they were told 52 seconds were left.

With seven seconds to go, Southern Idaho's Willie Willia[ms] tied the game 64-all with two free throws. Mercer hurried t[he] ball downcourt and called time with three seconds left. A fir[st] Viking shot missed just as a towel was flung onto the court to si[g]nal the end of regulation.

Before the extra five minutes began, partial repairs were com[pleted on the scoreboard. Only the East side of the four-side[d] structure worked, however. Both benches were still in the da[rk] regarding the time and score, making play in the overtime aga[in] tentative.

Southern Idaho gained its first leads since the opening peri[od] on a pair of free throws and a 15-foot jumper by Williams.

Mercer countered each time with easy buckets, the first [by] Melvin Weldon after his steal, and the second by Connie Whi[te] after patient passing by the Vikings.

The Eagles decided to work the unseeable clock. With [2] seconds to go, CSI passed inside to 6-10 center Vincent Volmu[t] Mercer's 6-5 White outjumped him, intercepting the ball.

It was the Vikings' turn to milk the clock. Landa called tim[e] twice in the final seconds, partly to set up a final play, partly [to] insure his players knew the time remaining.

It was Landa's intention that the Vikings hit White low for [a] lay-up. But, as White later told Trenton's The Evening Time[s,] "Their guy forced me to the outside and when I got the ball[,] just started counting down the seconds in my mind. When it g[ot] to three I just shot it." The shot was from 20-feet away, outsi[de] White's normal range. It swished, nonetheless, giving Merc[er] County a 70-68 win.

The clock was in working order for the afternoon finale, b[ut] its importance went unnoticed in the first half. The period w[as] marred by sloppy play and 27 fouls, including a perfect footb[all] clip to Dalton's Tony Ingle who was immediately taken to th[e] hospital. Led by Ron Johnson's 20 points, including 16 for 1[7] from the line, Three Rivers mounted a 42-37 advantage.

The clock became a factor only after Dalton took its first lea[d] of the game with 14 minutes remaining. From then on, the lea[d] seesawed.

As time dwindled, Dalton's Harold Albany, Ingle's replace[ment], fired from the baseline, missing. Roadrunner captai[n] Roger Rome grabbed the rebound and tried to put up the game[-]winner, but was fouled at the buzzer. With time expired, Rom[e] stepped to the line, missed the first charity, then hit the secon[d] giving Dalton an 83-82 victory.

After an exciting afternoon session, things calmed dow[n] McLennan's only lead of the evening opener came at 2-1. Afte[r] 10 minutes, Vincennes had powered ahead, 29-13, havin[g] effectively used alley-oop passes to set up 6-8 center Ph[il] Spence. McLennan rallied to within four in the final period, the[n] faded. The defending champion Trailblazers won easily, 87-7[0.]

The evening feature's biggest thrill came when America[n] Legion officials tried to collar a dog which wandered onto th[e] court during the game. Otherwise, it was a lot of munched pop[-]corn and stifled yawns. Olney Central's patient, methodic[al] offense set up high-percentage shots, but not much action. Th[e] Blue Knights hit 59 percent from the field and never traile[d,] defeating Dixie, 85-71.

The most entertaining contest that night was the finale. Bot[h] teams exhibited Globetrotter showmanship, especial[ly] Bacone's 5-10 freshman guard, John Henry. The Warriors over[-]came a 12-point first-half deficit and a 15-point disadvantage i[n] the second half to down Paducah, 85-80.

WEDNESDAY — CAUGHT IN THE DRAGON'S FLAME

Anxious Hutchonians crowded into the Sports Arena as soo[n] as the doors opened. The packed house fidgeted while th[e] highly favored Blue Dragons mustered only a 49-45 halftim[e] edge over SECC of Burlington. Then the mass of red held it[s] breath as star Rudy Jackson picked up his fourth foul.

The anxiety was for naught. While Jackson missed nearly nin[e] minutes of the final period, Hutchinson burned the nets at a 60[-] percent clip. The lone bright spot for the opposing Blackhawk[s] was Joe Cosey who canned 21 of his game-high 32. Behin[d] Teko Wynder's 26 and Jackson's 24, the Dragons torche[d] SECC, 107-88.

The first-round's final game produced its only upset. Margi[n] fluctuated in an otherwise close contest with No. 14 Brevard holding the upper hand through the early going. Then, with 3:44 remaining, Gregg Ashorn hit a pair of free throws to put North Greenville in the lead for good. The Mounties played control ball for the final five minutes, using two more Ashorn charities to ice the game with 33 seconds left. North Greenville upended Brevard, 79-74.

Early in the season, Mercer County defeated Ulster County, 84-77, in the final of the Mercer Christmas Tournament. The uco Tournament's opening quarterfinal was a rematch of the two rivals, featuring a one-on-one pairing of two of the East's best guards — Mercer's Melvin Weldon (from Jersey City) and Ulster's Jackie Knowles (from the Bronx). Both respected each other with Weldon even telling the press he felt the New York talent was his better.

Weldon refuted his own argument early, scoring the game's first four points as Mercer built an 8-0 advantage. From then on, the Vikings played cat-and-mouse, pulling ahead whenever Ulster threatened. Weldon led Mercer with 17, holding his counterpart Knowles to only a pair of free throws. The Senators' Ike Chestnut made things interesting with a game-high 25 points, mostly from long bombs in the first half, but Mercer County won going away, 75-62.

Once word spread that Dalton's Tony Ingle was definitely out of action for the rest of the tournament — the sparkplug guard was scheduled for knee surgery the following day with reports that he would never play again — the night's other quarterfinal did not figure to be close.

However, inspired by the loss, the Roadrunners gave top-rated Vincennes trouble, overcoming a nine-point deficit to grab a 48-47 halftime edge. In the second half, Dalton extended the advantage to eight. Though Vincennes remained composed, firing off a 12-2 spurt, Dalton did not succumb, taking a 74-71 lead with 4:11 left.

Then a Dave Edmonds turnaround jumper and three consecutive Phil Spence baskets underneath doomed the Roadrunners. Harold Miles hit the clincher with 10 seconds left. Despite George Jackson's game-high 33, Dalton fell to Vincennes, 81-76.

THURSDAY — THE JUGGERNAUT CONTINUES

Though the Hutchinson juggernaut seemed ineffective at times during the day's opening quarterfinal, the resulting destruction was the same. North Greenville led only once early. Teko Wynder's game-high 30 (all but two coming from the field) and Rudy Jackson's 29 powered the Blue Dragons to a convincing 99-90 victory. Jackson also set a new record with 24 rebounds, leading Hutchinson's overwhelming 58-34 assault on the boards.

In the other quarterfinal, Olney Central added a workmanlike defense to its already demonstrated efficient offense. After trading baskets with Bacone to a 14-all tie, the Blue Knights clamped down. Seven minutes later Olney led, 31-18. The well-disciplined Illinois squad proved its Region 4 upset of No. 1 Wilbur Wright College of Chicago was no fluke, shooting 58 percent from the field, while holding the Warriors to 39 percent. Olney smothered Bacone, 88-64, winning the dubious distinction of being the next opponent in the path of the rampaging Blue Dragons.

FRIDAY — CHEERING AWAY ANXIETY

The semifinals were a sure draw. One was an intriguing rematch of the 1968 semifinal between Vincennes and Mercer County. The other would have attracted a full house even if Hutchinson's opponent had been the most inept team in history. As it was, the Blue Dragons faced a very popular Olney Central squad, the tournament's Cinderella.

In 1968, Mercer County had been Cinderella. The scraggy Vikings and their droopy socks were the darlings of the crowd, especially after they upended then No. 2 Vincennes, leading almost all the way.

Again in 1973, Vincennes was No. 2 and Mercer the underdog. This time, though, the Vikings had better personnel: two top front-liners in Connie White and Jerome Young and a superb backcourt leader in Melvin Weldon. Most felt the opening semifinal would be a close contest.

They were surprised when Mercer County faltered out of the gate. After Weldon sank the second of two free throws to put the Vikings on the board, Mercer missed 15 consecutive shots from the field, failing to score for 9½ minutes. Vincennes tallied 12 unanswered points and took command.

Then the Trailblazers became careless. With the help of Vincennes turnovers and the support of the Arena crowd, Mercer reduced an 11-point deficit with five minutes left in the half to a single bucket with 27 seconds showing.

With five seconds left, Weldon fired from 20 and missed. Vincennes' Mike Darrett rebounded. Instantly, Weldon rushed from his backcourt position, stripped the ball from Darrett's hands, and laid it in. At intermission, it was a new ballgame, tied 25-all.

The second period was almost an exact replay of the first, Vincennes firing out to a nine-point advantage.

Forced to its full-court press, the Vikings again battled back. On a long floor-length pass, setting up a three-point play by Weldon, Mercer grabbed its first lead of the game, 43-41.

The two teams exchanged the lead until a pair of free throws by guard Rich Freda, another pair by Weldon, a Freda lay-up off an inbounds pass, and a Weldon steal and crip shot opened a seemingly comfortable 60-53 Mercer margin with 1:22 to go.

Vincennes made it interesting to the wire, however. Ertha Faust hit a long bomb and Darrett added a three-point play to reduce the difference to two with 34 seconds remaining.

Mercer went to its control game, forcing the Trailblazers to foul. Facing a similar situation to two he had faced and failed at in the opener, Freda canned two free shots, icing a 62-58 Viking victory.

The predominantly pro-Hutchinson crowd showed exuberant confidence in between semifinals. It was almost as though fans were trying to chase away lingering insecurity. In 10 previous appearances, the Blue Dragons made it to the title game only once, 24 years prior. Recent one-point losses to eventual champs Paducah in the 1969 quarterfinals and Ellsworth in the 1971 semifinals were still fresh in mind.

It was with great relief then when Hutchinson started out playing its best basketball of the year against Olney. The Blue Dragons hit 7 of their first 10 shots, continuing the 70-percent pace throughout the first half, Teko Wynder leading the barrage with 10 of 12 from the field. Hutchinson opened an 18-7 gap in the first eight minutes and expanded it to 42-18 with 3:26 remaining in the half. Gaining the championship game appeared a certainty.

Hutchinson fans were so buoyed by confidence that they became magnanimous, applauding the efforts of the Blue Knights. It was a sincere display.

Olney Central became one of the most popular teams in tourney history almost the moment the squad first walked into the Arena Tuesday. In an era when self-indulgence reigned, dress was casual, and hair was either puffed up in an Afro or straggling to the shoulder, the Blue Knights were unique, a cultural throwback.

It was Coach Gene Duke's policy that Olney players would never go anywhere in groups less than six. This meant the team went everywhere together.

Wherever they went, they wore the same slacks, the same shirts, the same ties, and the same light blue blazers. Above all, they wore the same hairdo. According to team member Roger Morningstar (later a star at Kansas), "An inch-and-a-half was the limit on our hair . . . He [Coach Duke] would think it would be getting a little long every three weeks. In practice, he'd pull out his ruler, just have a little check, and we'd all head back down to the barber shop."

The Blue Knights' strict regimentation even included having to fold and stack their warm-ups neatly at the end of the bench. It had its dividends, however. Olney was a self-disciplined machine that executed faultlessly, making up for a lack of talent in many of its parts.

It was partly due to this discipline that Olney reduced the deficit to 17 by halftime. In the second frame, the Blue Knight comeback continued. Hutchinson center Rudy Jackson again experienced foul difficulty and spent most of the period on the bench. In his absence, Olney forward Robert Taylor burned the cords, netting 25 of his tourney-high 38. Hutchinson fan magnanimity mutated to acute anxiety as the Blue Knights reduced the margin to three with 5:10 to go.

Fortunately, the Blue Dragons regrouped. In the next 4½ minutes, Hutchinson outscored Olney, 11-4. With an 83-75 triumph, Hutchinson was one step away from its coveted national crown.

SATURDAY — DRAGON HUNTING

Three Rivers hit 25 of 35 free throws, including a pair by Mark Baker with two seconds left to tie Brevard 83-all in regulation of the trophy day opener. Another pair by Baker with four seconds left in overtime gave the Raiders a 91-89 victory and fifth place. Three Rivers shot 41 percent from the field, just slightly better than its 39.8 percent for four games, an all-time tourney low.

The fourth-place contest was not as exciting, Ulster County leading from start to finish, downing North Greenville, 79-75. North Greenville's effort was not without honor, however.

On October 15, 1972, V.C. "Bud" Obee died from a heart attack. He had been tournament director since the event's move to Hutchinson in 1949. To recognize Obee's role in the tournament's success, tourney officials inaugurated an award in his name. Each year's recipient would be the player showing "good character, leadership, and loyalty to his fellow players and coaches." Defensive ability was also a criteria. To be eligible, the candidate could not be taller than 6-1.

Five months earlier, V.C. "Bud" Obee (left), the Juco Tournament's director since 1949, died unexpectedly of a heart attack. The memory of his efforts in making the tournament a success was commemorated in 1973 with the presentation of the first Obee Small Player Award. (Photo courtesy of Bob Gilliland)

The Bud Obee Outstanding Small Player Award reflected Juco Tourney fan appreciation for the finer aspects of the game of basketball: a player's worth was not always measured by his height or scoring punch. North Greenville's 5-10 Phil Garrett was the first to receive this unique honor.

* * *

The city of Hutchinson was bursting at the seams. Blue Dragon fans resembled children on Christmas Eve: There was a giant, gaily wrapped gift with their name on it just sitting there under the tree, within sight, within reach, but inaccessible. They had to wait until Christmas morning to know the delights inside. And the waiting seemed interminable.

Few doubted that the championship was Hutchinson's for the taking. The facts were overwhelming: Mercer County was from the East and no Eastern school had ever won the title; Hutchinson owned at least an inch advantage at every position; Hutchinson had manhandled the opposition, averaging 96 points through three outings, the highest in the tournament; and, most importantly Hutchinson was playing at home.

Wichita television stations, whose sports reports in the pas had given only token acknowledgement of the event just 50 miles away, took special notice of the situation and flatly pre dicted in their Saturday evening broadcasts that Hutchinson would finally win the championship after many years of trying.

Still, there had to be one more win before the present coulc be opened — and a third-place game to watch before that. For tunately, it was a welcome diversion.

Next to the Blue Dragons, Olney Central was the team o favor with local fans. In their battle against traditional power house Vincennes, the underdog Blue Knights could expect ful volume support from the crowd. With it, Olney launched a determined attack, opening a 35-27 gap at halftime. Fans sa back, smiled, and enjoyed. Everything was going their way.

Then Vincennes mounted a steady comeback, finally taking the upper hand with 11:26 remaining. Olney kept pace, bu could not pass the Trailblazers. With a one-point edge and 35 seconds left, Vincennes went to an all-out stall. The Arena audi ence, which had become more and more involved in the game as it progressed, tensed for the final seconds.

Olney fouled Dave Edmonds. Edmonds missed the free throw, but Vincennes grabbed the rebound.

With five seconds left, Trailblazer Mike Darrett was fouled.

As Darrett stepped to the charity stripe for one-and-one, Blue Knight Roger Morningstar, the eventual Sesher Sportsmanship Award-winner, lined up in the first position on the left-hand side of the lane and wiped the bottoms of his shoes with his hands, a peculiar habit he performed during every game break

Darrett missed.

Morningstar described the subsequent action: "The ball came off to my side. It was not a big deal. I just jumped up, rebounded the ball. I think I took two dribbles out to the right-hand side and saw Rick [Bussard] way over to the left on our side of the half-court line. I threw the ball. He took one dribble and lunged at the basket. It hit the glass and went right through . . . The place just came unglued."

The explosion which followed Bussard's 50-foot game-winner at the buzzer could not have been louder had it been made on Hutchinson behalf in the title game. It was one of the most electrifying moments in tourney history. Fans stood and cheered as the six-foot hero was carried around the floor on the shoulders of his teammates. Hutchinson fans smiled knowingly to each other. The Olney win was just another omen, signaling success for the Blue Dragons.

The noise continued even after Hutchinson and Mercer County came out for pre-game warm-ups, adding to the tension already felt on both sides. Viking Coach Howie Landa was well aware of how influential the crowd could be in the Sports Are-na. The only support Mercer County appeared to have was from Burlington fans who unfurled a make-shift, bedsheet banner at midcourt, proclaiming their allegiance with "All the Way Vikings." Landa cautioned his players before the game, "Just imagine the noise is for you."

Then the cheering stopped.

It was replaced by an ever increasing murmur. All through the Mercer introductions, it grew. It reached its peak when Hutchinson reserve Paul Shoemaker was introduced as a starter. Suddenly hearts were in throats and "Where's Rudy?" on everyone's lips.

The answer was back in the dressing room. During the warm-ups, center Rudy Jackson had acquired an untimely nose bleed from an incidental bump. It had happened before during the year, but had never been a problem. This time the bleeding would not stop. By the time Jackson emerged to the thunderous relief of Blue Dragon fans, the damage was already done.

Though he missed only two minutes and 25 seconds, Jackson's absence had a decided impact on the game. First, Coach Gene Keady was unable to initiate his game plan of working the ball inside to his big man, a strategy which had been instrumental in opening early margins in Hutchinson's three previous victories. More important, it took the crowd out of the game.

Hutchinson fans had started the evening like a balloon ready to explode. Rick Bussard's dramatic shot released some of its emotional air. The momentary loss of Jackson released even more. Now the crowd's cheering had a desperate ring to it, lacking its earlier confidence.

The Blue Dragons played accordingly on the court, exhibiting none of the forcefulness which had dominated three other opponents. Their actions were tentative, defensive. The game was tight.

Then, with 4:23 left in the half, the score tied 28-all, Mercer's Rich Freda stole the ball at midcourt off a man-to-man full-court press, scoring a lay-up. Immediately afterwards, Melvin Weldon intercepted in the Hutchinson lane and lofted a long pass to Freda for another easy two. The Vikings went on a roll, taking a 39-28 halftime advantage.

A Woody Allen look-alike, Rich Freda (No. 14) was an unexpected thorn for Hutchinson throughout the 1973 title game, leading Mercer with 23 points. Freda completed his collegiate career at Hartwick College in New York. (Photo courtesy of Howie Landa)

After intermission, Teko Wynder and Charles Terry missed badly for Hutchinson. Weldon initiated a rare Viking fast break, making a spectacular feed to Connie White for an easy lay-up. Freda then tallied a three-point play. Twenty-two seconds into the final period, Hutchinson was down, 44-28.

From then on, every time the Blue Dragons tried to up the tempo, Weldon patiently slowed it down again. Hutchinson put up poor selections from outside while Mercer County employed well-executed plays, producing 12 lay-ups out of 14 second-half goals.

When the final score was posted, the Vikings had slain the Dragons, 80-61.

THE AFTERMATH — BEATING A DEAD DRAGON

"I always felt good about coming to the tournament because we were playing at home and we had pretty talented teams," stated Hutchinson Coach Gene Keady years later. "It was frustrating because we could never get over the hump." The 1973 championship was the worst. Keady — later head coach at Western Kentucky and the 1984 U.S. Basketball Writers' Association "Coach of the Year" at Purdue — described it as "probably the most frustrating game in my life."

The statement summed up the heartache felt by the Hutchinson crowd. The awards ceremony was one of the most subdued in tourney history. The disappointment was so evident Mercer County Coach Howie Landa almost apologized for winning, accepting the first-place trophy with, "I'm sorry it had to be Hutch, but these kids of mine deserve to be number one."

The Vikings did, indeed, deserve the title. They had defeated four ranked opponents, including the three top-rated squads, holding them to a tourney-low 62 points per game. In the title match, Mercer County lost 6-5 Connie White and 6-8 Jerome Young, the team's top rebounders, with more than eight minutes left in the game, yet maintained its cool and a decided advantage to the end. The reason was Melvin Weldon.

The six-foot sophomore completely dominated the game. As Landa told *The Trentonian,* "He ran our whole offense, handled the ball practically all of the time and played super defense." Whenever the Blue Dragons had the ball, they ran with it. When Mercer gained control, the ball immediately went to Weldon who waited until everybody was downcourt before *walking* the ball across the 10-second line. If he was pressured, he would elude the defender, then dribble out front until things were again calm. He had the patience of Job. If a Viking play did not work, he stopped action, dribbled the ball with one hand while reorganizing his troops with the other. He had nine assists in the game, most to Woody Allen look-alike Rich Freda who led Mercer with 23, a majority on uncontested lay-ups. There was little doubt that Weldon was the French Most Valuable Player.

* * *

Eligibility was a major concern for the NJCAA during the 1972-73 season.

In the fall, 6-9 Warren Wynn, a transfer student at Forest Park Community College in St. Louis, was declared ineligible for one year, in accordance with NJCAA regulations, after transferring from Southeastern Community College in West Burlington. Wynn charged the organization's ruling was unfair since he had not been academically eligible while at SECC. Wynn won an injunction which was later overturned on appeal. It was the first time the NJCAA was taken to court over one of its edicts.

At the tournament, the talk was about the recent change in NCAA eligibility standards. Previously, an athlete had to predict to a 1.6 average, i.e. through a combination of high school grades and national test scores, show he was able to maintain a 1.6 average in college. Now scholarships could be awarded to anyone maintaining a 2.0 or C average in high school. Many felt the looser eligibility rule would mean a decline in the caliber of talent seen at the tournament which had recently produced current pro stars Fred Brown, John Johnson, Artis Gilmore, and Bob McAdoo.

After leading Mercer County to an NJCAA championship with 22 points and 9 assists in the title game versus Hutchinson, Melvin Weldon (No. 10) played on the U.S. representative team to the 1974 World Games and was later captain of the Boston College Eagles. (Photo courtesy of Howie Landa)

Finally, the NJCAA had a problem with falsified transcripts. There were two major incidents:

In late October 1973, the organization declared Ulster County Community College sophomore Bob Miller ineligible for not having completed high school, after discovering that the high school transcript filed with Ulster was forged. Since he had been a member of the Senators' 1973 tourney team, Ulster County was required to forfeit its fourth-place trophy.

The other incident was uncovered at approximately the same time. An October 30 memo, signed by President A.H. Elland and Athletic Director Sam Butterfield and disseminated to all 1972-73 Hutchinson opponents, described how Wichita State coaches encouraged Hutchinson to admit Rudy Jackson to its program. Hutchinson officials were agreeable, provided Jackson had proper credentials. "He [Jackson] was registered on a provisional basis pending the receipt of an official high school transcript from John Bowne High School of Flushing, New York." The transcript later arrived showing Jackson having graduated 403rd in a class of 809 with a 2.33 grade-point average.

When Jackson transferred to Wichita State for the 1973-74 season, a routine check by the university discovered that John Bowne did not list Jackson as a graduate. Subsequent investigation determined that the transcript sent to Hutchinson was forged. A recruiter, who had brought Jackson to Wichita's attention, submitted an official statement accepting responsibility for the forgery.

The memo concluded: "Therefore, in keeping with the rules of the Kansas Jayhawk Junior College Conference and the National Junior College Athletic Association, we are forfeiting all basketball games played during the 1972-73 season and returning all trophies won."

With a few strokes of a pen, Hutchinson's best season to date was reduced to its worst ever.

Tournament Results

Tuesday:	Game		
		1	Ulster County — 89 Platte — 77
		2	Mercer County — 70 Southern Idaho — 68 O
		3	Dalton — 83 Three Rivers — 82
		4	Vincennes — 87 McLennan — 70
		5	Olney Central — 85 Dixie — 71
		6	Bacone — 85 Paducah — 80
Wednesday:	Game		
		7	Hutchinson — 107 SECC-Burlington — 88
		8	North Greenville — 79 Brevard — 74
		9	Southern Idaho — 70 Platte — 67
		10	Mercer County — 75 Ulster County — 62
		11	Vincennes — 81 Dalton — 76
Thursday:	Game		
		12	Three Rivers — 100 McLennan — 74
		13	Brevard — 93 SECC-Burlington — 85
		14	Ulster County — 82 Dalton — 80
		15	Paducah — 84 Dixie — 75
		16	Hutchinson — 99 North Greenville — 90
		17	Olney Central — 88 Bacone — 64
Friday:	Game		
		18	Three Rivers — 89 Southern Idaho — 87
		19	Brevard — 85 Paducah — 74
		20	North Greenville — 101 Bacone — 97
		21	Mercer County — 62 Vincennes — 58
		22	Hutchinson — 83 Olney Central — 75
Saturday:	Game		
		23	Three Rivers — 91 Brevard — 89 OT
		24	Ulster County — 79 North Greenville — 75
		25	Olney Central — 72 Vincennes — 71
		26	Mercer County — 80 Hutchinson — 61

How They Finished in 1973

1. Mercer County Community College
2. (Vacated)
3. Olney Central College
4. (Vacated)
5. Three Rivers Community College
6. Vincennes University
7. North Greenville College
8. Brevard Community College

All-Tournament Team

Gregg Ashorn — North Greenville College
Ike Chestnut — Ulster County Community College
George Jackson — Dalton Junior College
Rudy Jackson — Hutchinson Community Junior College
Ron Johnson — Three Rivers Community College
Roger Morningstar — Olney Central College
Phil Spence — Vincennes University
Larry Warren — Brevard Community College
Melvin Weldon — Mercer County Community College
Teko Wynder — Hutchinson Community Junior College

Coach of the Tournament

Howie Landa — Mercer County Community College

French Most Valuable Player Award

Melvin Weldon — Mercer County Community College

Sesher Sportsmanship Award

Roger Morningstar — Olney Central College

Bud Obee Outstanding Small Player Award

Phil Garrett — North Greenville College

1974:

DEFENSE

ith a national trophy on the mantle, Mercer County Community College went from a lovable orphan to an envied rich kid. Everyone was out to get the champs. First, Essex County College ended a 30-game Mercer win streak over two seasons. Later, Robert Morris College of Pennsylvania stopped the Vikings' home win skein at 55.

They were the only blemishes on Mercer County's record, however. The Vikings were ranked No. 1 in the first NJCAA poll and retained a high rating all season, finishing No. 5. They breezed through Region 19 play, trouncing Keystone Junior College, 91-57, and Wesley College, 95-59, before avenging their first loss, defeating Essex County, 82-71, in the final.

Normally, the Vikings would have started packing their bags for Hutchinson. The defending champs received no such privilege in 1974.

With the NJCAA's continued membership growth, more and more regional play-offs were required to narrow the tourney field to 16. Since the newest region, Region 20 (Maryland and the western half of Pennsylvania), had been carved from Region 19, the NJCAA decided that the parent and its child should meet in a play-off, until the overall regional play-off scheme was updated at the next annual meeting.

Consequently, Mercer County met No. 15 Community College of Allegheny County, Pittsburgh, in Cantonsville, Maryland, for one game. The Vikings barely escaped with an 85-83 victory, after Spencer Hood's lay-up at the buzzer bounced twice before falling.

Mercer still had not won a trip to the nationals, however. Under the old regional play-off structure, Region 19 was scheduled to face Region 10. Three days later, the Vikings were back on the court, this time at the Baltimore campus of the University of Maryland. Their opponent: No. 6 Anderson College, one of the biggest and most powerful teams in the country.

The outcome was stunning. Mercer outrebounded the taller Trojans, 40-33, and won convincingly, 57-42. After the game Viking Coach Howie Landa told reporters, "This may have been our greatest victory ever. I think we proved how great we really are. We ran our plays perfectly and did virtually everything right."

Though a regional crown, two tough play-off victories, and a 28-2 record were impressive credentials, they only meant that the defending champs had earned the opportunity to prove it all over again.

THE PARTICIPANTS

After creating seemingly unfair roadblocks to the nationals, Dame Fortune changed her tune once Mercer County reached Hutchinson. The only other ranked team in the upper bracket besides the Vikings was No. 9 Northeastern Oklahoma A&M College (29-2).

Three of Mercer's potential opponents were upset winners in regional play: newcomer Copiah-Lincoln Junior College (26-2) knocked off No. 4 Cumberland College, 72-71; former champion Dodge City Community College (20-12), making its first appearance in seven years, upended No. 12 Johnson County Community College, 67-65; and veteran Hill Junior College (26-10) surprised No. 14 Howard County Junior College, 107-100.

In a 1974 consolation game with Hill Junior College, Dodge City's Larry Dassie (No. 52) not only led all scorers with 35 points, but set an all-time record with 28 rebounds. Dassie later starred for former tourney coach Jack Hartman at Kansas State University. (Photo courtesy of Dick Brown)

Veterans Northeastern Junior College of Sterling (21-10) and Niagara County Community College (23-8) possessed unimpressive records. In fact, Mercer had slaughtered Niagara, 90-59, in the Vikings' first game of the season in the Erie Community College Invitational.

Five-time participant Grand View College appeared the only other upper-bracket threat outside of Northeastern Oklahoma. Though unranked in the final poll, Grand View had cracked the top-20 on several occasions during the year. Mercer's high-powered Viking kin owned a 96.7 scoring average, topping the century mark 13 times. Each win in the Des Moines Viking's 25-3 record was by almost a 23-point margin. If both Viking crews won, they would clash in the quarterfinals.

Provided it was able to survive its early battles, Mercer County's biggest obstacle to defending the title would come at the end. The bottom bracket was loaded with six top-20 teams, including three former champions whose long winning traditions totaled more tourney wins than the rest of the field combined: 1968 champ and No. 1-rated San Jacinto College (32-4 on the year and 9-3 in tourney competition), the early co-favorite with Mercer, averaging nearly 100 points a game; three-time champion Vincennes University (28-4 and 20-7), back for the eighth time in 10 years, bringing a respectable No. 7 ranking; and No. 19 Moberly Junior College (29-7 and 40-22), the most successful school in the tournament's history with four national crowns.

Region	Team
1	Arizona Western College — Yuma, Arizona
2	Northeastern Oklahoma Agricultural & Mechanical College — Miami, Oklahoma
3	Niagara County Community College — Sanborn, New York
5	Hill Junior College — Hillsboro, Texas
6	Dodge City Community College — Dodge City, Kansas
7	Copiah-Lincoln Junior College — Wesson, Mississippi
8	Chipola Junior College — Marianna, Florida
9	Northeastern Junior College — Sterling, Colorado
11	Grand View College — Des Moines, Iowa
12	Vincennes University — Vincennes, Indiana
13	Normandale Community College — Bloomington, Minnesota
14	San Jacinto College — Pasadena, Texas
15	New York City Community College — New York, New York
16	Moberly Junior College — Moberly, Missouri
17	Alexander City State Junior College — Alexander City, Alabama
19	Mercer County Community College — Trenton, New Jersey

The other ranked teams in the lower bracket were Arizona Western College (33-4) tied with Vincennes at 7th, New York City Community College (24-3) at 15th, and Chipola Junior College (25-4) tied with Moberly at 19th. Each was a legitimate threat.

The only apparent hopeless cases were Normandale Community College (23-3) and Alexander City State Junior College (19-8). In the august company of six schools with a combined 38 years of previous tourney experience, the two newcomers were expected to make an entry, then leave quietly after two games.

TUESDAY — WATCHING THE ELEPHANTS

In 1970, the last time Northeastern Oklahoma appeared in the nationals, Coach Cletus Green had worried in his hotel room, wondering where his snow-stranded team was. In 1974, Green was again pondering the whereabouts of his team. This time the problem was not weather.

After NEO lost a heartbreaking 85-84 regional final to No. 19 Seminole Junior College, Green had dismissed his team for spring break. He then received word that Seminole had used an ineligible player, requiring the school to forfeit all its games, including the regional title.

Just as Green was about to round up his team the NJCAA Office of Eligibility reinstated Seminole, overturning Region 2 Director Jack Rucker's ruling. The Seminole player in question, Leonard Whitted, had failed to note he had previously played for Pershing College in Beatrice, Nebraska, during the 1970-71 season. However, since he had played only six games before Pershing closed its doors because of bankruptcy, the Office of Eligibility felt there had been no "intent to defraud" and declared Whitted's omission not a falsification of records.

The matter was appealed once more, this time to the NJCAA's Executive Committee. In a conference call on March 15, the Committee reversed the decision a final time. Coach Green had three days to find his players and get them to Hutchinson.

When finally assembled, the NEO Golden Norsemen were an imposing force. Four players measured 6-8 and three 6-6. Northeastern Oklahoma used this superior size to advantage in the tourney opener, outrebounding Dodge City, 45-33. The only rebounding power for Dodge City was forward Larry Dassie, who topped everyone with 13. Dassie picked up three fouls in the first 11 minutes, however, and was used sparingly thereafter before finally fouling out. Northeastern Oklahoma advanced, 78-70.

The second contest featured a top offense versus a top defense. Hill averaged 98.8 points per game while Northeastern of Sterling limited opponents to 67.5, including a stingy 48.5 in its last 10 games.

It was defense that won. Northeastern held Hill to 26 points in the first half, then rode an 8-for-8 binge by Mike Shine to a 51-39 advantage with nine minutes remaining. The Rebels rallied to within two, but Northeastern repelled further encroach-

ment, winning 73-66.

On Monday, fans had opened their copies of the *Hutchins News* to find the beginning of a tradition with the paper — insert on the tournament. The 24-page "Tournament Speci. was filled with facts of past tournaments and bits and pieces information about the 16 teams competing for the 1974 crow including comments from the coaches.

One of the most popular quotes came from M.K. Turk, coa of newcomer Copiah-Lincoln: "I think this first time we'll ju come to the circus and watch the elephants."

Copiah-Lincoln had an "elephant" of its own in 6-8, 21 pound All-American Marion Hillard. When Hillard picked his third foul with 9:27 left in the opening period of the afte noon finale, the Wolves were in trouble. Six-six sophomore L Dixon tried to pick up the slack, hitting 27 of an eventual tou ney-high 37, but the best Copiah-Lincoln could do was mat. Grand View at 45-all. Led by 5-7 mouse Earl Hinton and star fo ward Curt Forrester (22 points each), the Vikings edged ahe. at intermission, then raced to a 100-87 victory.

The real "elephants" appeared later that night. The eveni. session included four dominant names in junior college baske ball: Mercer County, San Jacinto, Moberly, and Vincenne With San Jacinto and Moberly squaring off in the feature, . excellent turnout was expected.

The crowd was slow in arriving. Most felt the only way Niag ra County could beat Mercer County was if the defendi. champs suffered a mental let down.

There was little danger of that, according to Mercer soph more Marty Prendergast. "That's what this game is all about he told *The Trentonian*. "Confidence and cockiness. We're perfect shape mentally . . . At least three of us know the rope We've played before 8,000 people before. We know the cou and the town. That is, what there is of the town . . . There's r place to stay up and miss curfew."

With nothing more to do than concentrate on the task hand, the Vikings were eager to play — so eager that startin. guard Terry Mason left his sneakers at the hotel.

Mercer County took control immediately. As Niagara Coac. Dan Bazzani put it, "School was out the first few minutes of th second half . . . We just went through a meatgrinder." Th Vikings built a 33-point margin twice on the way to an 80-! rout.

Stated Bazzani afterwards, "I didn't think Mercer cou improve [since beating Niagara by 31 in the first game of th season] but they have. I'll be shocked if they don't win this thir again. I can't see anybody beating them. They do too mar things right."

It was four-time champ Moberly which did everything right the first half of the evening feature, pleasing Greyhound fa who, according to Coach Charlie Spoonhour, had had "the bags packed for four years" and "were starting to get a little res less." Six-four Ray Sills, 6-7 John Gordon, and 6-8 Vernon Di. on banged the boards, leading Moberly to a 27-18 reboun advantage, while the Greyhound man-to-man defense hel high-scoring San Jacinto in check.

Moberly's 10-point halftime margin grew to 12 before th top-rated Ravens finally got their act together. Led by guar. Ray Williams and Kenny Stewart, San Jacinto rallied, pullin within one twice, the last at 73-72 with 1:56 remaining.

Moberly stalled, working the ball inside to Gordon for two San Jacinto added a free throw.

Then turnovers took over with both sides coughing up th basketball. San Jacinto received one last opportunity to tie afte a Greyhound miscue with 17 seconds left. Stewart immediate! slipped while dribbling, losing the ball back to Moberly. Th Greyhounds held on for the opening round's first upset, 75-7.

The nightcap was short and sweet. Vincennes gained the lea moments after the opening tip and never trailed, manhandlin Normandale. Julius Norman and Tom Harris combined for 4 points and 21 rebounds, dominating play at both ends. Wit eight minutes remaining Coach Allen Bradfield removed h starters, leading 71-37. The Trailblazers won easily, 79-63.

WEDNESDAY — THE BEST I'VE SEEN

In the day's opener, favored Chipola lost the lead only onc to Alexander City State, just before intermission. The Indian uickly regained the advantage on a tip-in by John Billips, then uilt an 11-point margin in the second half. Chipola kept Alexander City at a comfortable distance until the final two minutes hen the Indians went to a delay game. The move proved near-disastrous, Chipola barely holding on for a 65-63 win. The key victory was a 55-37 Indian rebound advantage, led by Lester wis' game-high 17.

Rebounding was also a factor in the final first-round game. espite giving up an average four inches per man on the front e, No. 15 New York City outrebounded No. 7 Arizona West-n, taking a surprising 41-34 halftime edge. Then, when Otis nn, the Bees' leading scorer, sat down with foul trouble, placement Leroy Brown hit eight crucial points to protect the ad. Led by 6-4 center Jose Nava's game-high 26 points and 13 bounds, New York City upset Arizona Western, 75-66.

But, the top rebounding performance of the day and the tour-ment, came in the consolation game kicking off evening ction. Dodge City's 6-5 Larry Dassie recorded 35 points and 28 bounds, the latter an all-time tourney mark, rallying the Con-uistadors into a tie with Hill at the end of regulation. Unfortu-ately, his heroics did not extend to overtime. With Dassie held coreless, Hill edged Dodge City, 84-83.

The yo-yoing fortunes of Northeastern Oklahoma made a ownswing after the Golden Norsemen's win in Game 1. Lead-g scorer Steve Washington had severely injured an ankle in e contest and was diagnosed as unable to play in the opening uarterfinal.

The yo-yo bobbed back up when sophomore guard Leon lvoid took over team leadership, tallying a game-high 24, lead-g NEO to a 51-37 advantage over Northeastern of Sterling ith 11 minutes to play.

Down again went the yo-yo when the Colorado Plainsmen llied to within a basket with 2:15 remaining.

Finally, a tip-in by Bob Johnson, a steal and pass by Steve reen (Coach Cletus Green's son) to Johnson for another two, nd two Green free throws, stopped the yo-yo on an upswing, utting NEO out of reach, 67-61. Two long goals by Plainsman oger Plank were not enough. Northeastern Oklahoma dvanced to the semifinals, 67-65.

The most anticipated game of the day followed.

Once the darling of tourney crowds, Mercer County was now e villain. One mark against the Vikings was their style of play. hough Coach Howie Landa's well-designed deliberate ffense and match-up zone defense were super efficient, they id not excite audiences.

The major reason for the shift in loyalties, however, was that ourney fans were inveterate underdog rooters. Many felt rand View was the perfect answer in foiling Mercer's attempt t back-to-back titles. The Des Moines squad was not tall, but ossessed great overall quickness, led by speedster guard Earl linton. If Grand View gained the lead, the Iowa Vikings would asily outrun the Vikings from New Jersey. As Grand View oach Dave Sisam remembered it, "There were a lot of people aying, 'Hey! Grand View is going to upset Mercer.' They even aid it on television."

What happened was a shocker. Stated Sisam, "As a coach, ou never think it's going to happen . . . [but] it happens. We ad a disastrous ballgame. It was a nightmare. What really hurt s early in the ballgame was that 8 or 9 times down the floor in row we got great shots and we were 0 for 8 or 9. And they urned around, went down the floor, and everything went in. All f a sudden — Boom! We lost our patience."

From the 15:10 mark to 1:38 left in the first half, Grand View nanaged only two free throws. While Mercer's defense dis-nantled the Iowans' floor game, its equally precise offense gar-ered basket after easy basket from well-patterned plays. Mer-er County outscored Grand View, 29-2, taking an nsurmountable 41-15 halftime lead.

The crowd quickly shrank from 7,000 to 300. Substitutes layed out the remainder of the contest. When the final score vas posted, the Mercer County Vikings had vanquished the rand View Vikings, 83-48, holding the Iowa squad to under alf its scoring average. Grand View shot an arctic cold 23.5 per-cent from the field (16 for 68), setting an all-time tourney low. he masterful exhibition of defense led Sisam to tell the press, 'Mercer is the best junior college team I've ever seen."

THURSDAY — DANCING BEES

Mid-week consolation play was strictly routine:

Marion Hillard lived up to his All-American credentials, firing in 34 points and grabbing 14 rebounds to lead Copiah-Lincoln past Niagara County, 106-92.

Arizona Western led from beginning to end, downing Alex-ander City State, 84-75.

And, paced by Ray Williams outside and Art Johnson inside, each with 29 points, San Jacinto outraced Normandale, 109-81.

Only the afternoon finale held fan interest. There were 17 lead changes and no margin greater than five through the first 35 minutes. Then, it too faded to insignificance. Grand View pulled away, eliminating Northeastern of Sterling, 70-59.

After the first round each year, local fans adopted one team as a Cinderella favorite. The 1974 choice was New York City. There were two reasons the Bees got the nod: they were a scrappy bunch from the playgrounds of New York whose tallest starter was only 6-4 — and they had the most entertaining cheerleading squad the tournament had yet seen.

Every break when the nine young women from Brooklyn stepped on the court, all eyes in the Arena turned their way. Their routines were novel, incorporating acrobatics as well as hand-clapping, foot-stomping choreography — all understand-able since Asenath Sapp, their coach, had a background in dance.

On the sidelines, their chanting often gained more attention than the game. They were so popular that young boys, who usu-ally roamed the stands seeking player autographs, instead pes-tered the girls to sign programs from the time the squad warmed up in the hall 30 minutes before a game until it left with the team afterwards.

John Smith, head basketball coach at Panhandle State Col-lege in Goodwell, Oklahoma, was so taken by the Bee cheer-leaders that he offered scholarships to the entire group, telling Mrs. Sapp, "If we had your cheerleaders, we wouldn't have any trouble getting basketball players."

Their importance to the team's success was not lost on New York City Coach John Carty. When the school administration said the squad would not accompany the team to the nationals, Carty and his players flatly refused to make the trip to Hutchin-son. The school relented.

The extraordinary support did not help the Bees in their quar-terfinal, however. New York City hit only 30 percent from the field in the first half, falling behind Chipola, 37-26. The Bees sealed their fate by scoring only six points in the next 10 min-utes. With Albert Gardner tallying 28 and John Billips 21, Chipola outshot the New Yorkers 46 percent to 35 percent, downing the Bees, 73-55.

The remaining quarterfinal was a classic confrontation between the two most successful schools in tourney history. After Ray Sills opened the second half with a 20-footer, giving Moberly its largest lead of the game, 37-25, Vincennes fought back. Three free throws by Trailblazer Rickey Green finally closed the gap to a pair. Then, Moberly held the ball for the last 1:09, padding its lead with free throws, holding on for a 63-59 win. The victory gave the Greyhounds a 2-1 edge in season meetings with Vincennes and vaulted Moberly into the semifi-nals for the 11th time in 18 tourney appearances.

FRIDAY — CONSOLATION GRIT

From the beginning, the tournament's double-elimination format had drawn its fair share of supporters and detractors. Those in favor enjoyed seeing outstanding teams and players more than once, responding, in particular, to those who showed character after suffering a loss. Those opposed cited the fact that consolation games generally lacked the sparkle and heroics of championship bracket competition. Friday's after-noon feature was a denial of the latter.

With just under 15 minutes to play, San Jacinto star guard Ray Williams received an elbow to the right eye, opening a deep gash. The Mt. Vernon, New York, native was removed to the dressing room, the Ravens leading Arizona Western, 49-36.

Despite an intense aversion to needles, Williams allowed tourney physician Dr. Jack Perkins to sew up the cut on the spot. He returned to the floor with 6:02 remaining to find the San

Jacinto edge reduced to 59-58.

In a wild scramble to the finish, Williams scored the last nine Raven points, including the game-winner with nine seconds left. San Jacinto downed Arizona Western, 70-69. The championship determination of the 6-1 freshman, in a game in which the victor earned the right to place no higher than fifth, assured Williams' selection as the Obee Small Player of the Tournament.

According to most prognosticators, the title game would be played between former champs. Mercer County seemed indomitable. With Northeastern Oklahoma's leading scorer still on the bench with an ankle injury, few were betting against the Vikings in the opening semifinal. In the other, they were sticking with tradition. Moberly was the tournament's only four-time champ. Chipola represented a region which had never made it past the semifinals, the Indians themselves having never made it past the quarterfinals in five previous tries.

The predictions proved accurate as the evening began. Mercer's Connie White hit a 15-footer, canned a baseline jumper 17 seconds later, then teammate Terry Mason followed with back-to-back lay-ups. The Vikings were off to an 8-0 blitz of NEO.

The loss of Steve Washington was immediately felt by the Norsemen from Miami, Oklahoma. The 6-6 sophomore forward was NEO's release valve against full-court pressure and a key outside shooter against zones. Without him, the Oklahomans committed 13 turnovers and were unable to penetrate Mercer's masterful defense.

With 5:04 left in the opening period, the Vikings led, 20-8. They expanded the margin to 15 by intermission. With the first five points of the second half, they doubled the score on their Norsemen brothers, 40-20.

The only flaw in Mercer County's game plan came when Coach Howie Landa — decked out in a natty turtleneck and eye-catching checkered suit — ordered a delay. NEO rallied to within nine with 3:35 remaining. Mercer rode 9 for 12 shooting from the line in the final minutes, however, to preserve a 64-51 win.

The second half of the evening bill was not as straightforward. In fact, it was a cliff-hanger throughout with underdog Chipola holding a 56-52 advantage inside the two-minute mark.

Sherman Curtis hit a long bomb, pulling Moberly within a bucket. The Greyhounds then forced Chipola into a 10-second violation. While working for the tie, guard Kern McKelvey traveled with 44 seconds remaining.

Chipola held the ball, forcing Moberly to foul Lester Lewis. With 13 seconds showing, the Mobile, Alabama, forward hit the first charity, missed the second.

Curtis then fired another long swisher, reducing the Mober deficit to one.

But, time was almost gone. Chipola's Albert Gardner held th ball out-of-bounds while the final seconds ticked off. In frustra tion, Greyhound David Miller slapped the ball from his hand drawing an automatic foul. Gardner's free throw gave Chipo a 58-56 victory.

SATURDAY — MAKING A GAME OF IT

Four days into spring, Mother Nature gave tourney fans small reminder of the season past — two to three inches snow. The winter-like weather was brief, however. By afte noon, the snow was already melting outside the Sports Aren while the crowd inside warmed to blazing competition.

The opener was one of the fiercest battles in consolation pla The reason for the intense action was not so much the fifth place trophy that was up for grabs, but bragging rights in th Lone Star State. Hill blew a 14-point second-half lead, the needed six consecutive free throws in the final two minutes down San Jacinto, 94-89.

The fourth-place contest was even tighter. Neither Vir cennes nor Grand View led by more than six, spending most the final period trading advantages. With six seconds left Gran View's Larry Pittman hit a free throw, sending the game int overtime. With 12 seconds left in the extra period, Viking Ji Carlson sank a 25-footer, deadlocking the result again.

Then, Vincennes blew the game open, outscoring Gran View 12-1 in the first 2:13 of the final overtime, coasting to a 97 86 win. The victory was a signal to the rest of the junior colleg community for the following year. Leading all scorers wer Trailblazers Rickey Green (30), Tom Harris (28), and Julius Nor man (24) — all three first-year performers in an all-freshma starting line-up.

The fortunes of Northeastern Oklahoma continued to bob i the third-place game. NEO broke fast, opening a 20-8 margi

The rest of the contest, however, belonged to Moberly. Th Greyhounds edged in front 30-28 at halftime, built a 13-poir cushion in the next seven minutes, then won going away, 81 62. The key to victory was a huge 55-31 Moberly reboun advantage led by John Gordon — the Sesher Sportsmanshi Award-winner — who topped everyone with 20, giving him tourney-high 55.

The title tilt's standing-room-only crowd was not as large the previous year's, but considerably larger than had bee expected given the circumstances: Mercer County appeare destined to repeat as national champs.

(Bottom, left) The 1974 French MVP, Connie White (No. 20) completed his collegiate career at the University of California. (Photo courtesy of Howie Landa)

(Bottom, right) An imposing force defensively for Mercer County, Jerome Young (No. 30) later played for the California Golden Bears. (Photo courtesy of Howie Landa)

The core of Coach Howie Landa's Viking squad consisted of three sophomores.

Connie White, the most visible, was a quiet, 6-4 1st-Team All-American, who led the team in scoring with a 20.7 average and was at his best in the clutch.

Jerome Young was a 6-9 unsung hero whose scoring skills were still developing. He was only in his second year of organized basketball, having competed in track in high school. His native instincts were tremendous, however. It was his talent as a shot rejector that kept the opposition outside the Viking zone.

The third was firebrand Marty Prendergast, the team's emotional leader, who Landa affectionately referred to as a "hoodlum," "a tough, hard-nosed kid out of Jersey City."

The trio had already experienced the thrill of wearing a national crown. But, winning a second seemed more important. It was as though they had to prove that the first — against the hometown favorites — was no fluke. Consequently, all week fans marveled at how well-prepared the Vikings were.

Facing this determined bunch was underdog Chipola. The Indians had reached a higher plateau than any previous Florida tourney participant. They were not flashy, had not sparked fan imagination in three previous outings, despite an impressive victory over Moberly in the semifinals. Chipola was simply a nice, well-rounded team.

Out front were two quick guards, 6-2 Albert Gardner, the team's leading scorer (19.3), and 5-7 Albert Culver, Coach Milt Johnson's press-breaker and playmaker. The wing was 6-4 John Billips, a muscle man on the boards with a soft touch from outside. At low post was 6-6 Lester Lewis who was effective inside despite only weighing 190 pounds. The glue to the unit was high post Quinton Bell. According to Coach Johnson, the 6-8 2nd-Team All-American "had to control the boards, particularly the defensive boards. He was the catalyst in our running game."

The large turnout hoped Chipola would at least make a game of it, lending its full support to the Indians in the effort.

It did not help. Chipola led twice briefly before Mercer County rolled to a 34-26 halftime edge.

One of the keys to Chipola's previous successes had been its ability to adapt to game situations. At the start of the second half, Coach Johnson ordered his Indians to drop out of their zone into a man-to-man. Said Johnson, "You know I'm really not sure if that [switching to man-to-man] was a factor or not. I just know that we were eight points down and I certainly didn't want to stay in a zone and find myself 12 points down with 15 minutes to play. If we were going to make a move, we had to start making it immediately . . . because, against a team like Mercer, I didn't feel we could catch up in five minutes."

Chipola fell 10 down with 13 minutes remaining. Then, the Indians' quickness took over. Behind the outside shooting of the two Alberts (Gardner and Culver), Chipola outscored Mercer, 10-2, giving fans what they wanted — a close contest.

A tip-in by Chipola's Billips finally tied the score at 50-all with 5:12 to go. Three more ties followed, the last at the 1:56 mark on a tip-in by the Indians' Lewis.

With 1:20 remaining, Mercer's White hit reserve Spencer Hood, who had snuck behind the defense, for an easy two. Chipola called time.

When play resumed, the Indians worked the ball cautiously only to have a pass inside tipped away by White. Mercer's Prendergast retrieved the loose ball and was fouled, sinking two free throws. With time running out, the defending champs were in charge, 60-56. Chipola called time again.

During the break, Viking Coach Landa told Prendergast, who had taken over responsibility for bringing the ball up court after the Chipola comeback, "If they put it in, just throw the length of the court, we'll get the two points back and it'll be all over."

With 14 seconds left, Billips tipped in a Gardner miss, slicing the Chipola deficit to two. As instructed, Prendergast stepped out of bounds, wound up, and fired to Harry Ley who was streaking all alone behind the Indian press.

Unfortunately, the ball curved out of bounds, untouched. It was one of the few mistakes the Vikings had made during the week, but it had the potential for being the most costly: Chipola took possession under its own basket with eight seconds left to tie the game.

Coach Landa paced the sidelines. Coach Johnson shouted encouragement. The Arena crowd held its breath.

The Indians worked the ball into Gardner, the game's leading scorer with 20. At the four-second mark, he fired. The ball bounced away, no good. Leaping high, his legs spread-eagled, went Mercer's Young. His authoritative retrieval produced a sigh from Landa and a second straight crown for Mercer County.

THE AFTERMATH — RISING STAR TO FALLING METEOR

One of the highlights of the awards ceremony came during the All-Tournament Team introductions. Northeastern Oklahoma's Leon Alvoid, the first selection announced, drew oohs from the crowd as he stepped on the court dressed in a checked suit, large bow tie, and knee-length top coat with lush, furry collar and cuffs.

The crowd reaction doubled when the next selection stepped forward. Local favorite Larry Dassie of Dodge City wore a dazzling pink suit which he made himself.

The fashion parade prompted NEO Coach Cletus Green to tell Dodge City Coach Dick Brown, "We won the ballgame [the tourney opener], but you won the best-dressed contest."

The French MVP Award was no surprise. According to Mercer County Coach Howie Landa, Connie White, a normally reserved individual, boldly predicted after the Vikings' 1973 title, "Coach, I'm going to be the Most Valuable Player in the country." Landa responded, "I hope you are, son. Because that means we'll be in the finals."

In two tournaments, White had been a steady, reliable force in the Mercer machine, often coming up with the key play of the game. Reflected Landa, "I remember to this day when they put that net around his neck and they called his name."

The Coach of the Tournament, too, was no surprise. Landa joined Vincennes' Allen Bradfield as the only individual to receive the award three times.

The occasion was tinged with sadness, however. Earlier in the week, Landa had told his many friends in Hutchinson, "This is it for me." He was leaving Mercer, taking a year's sabbatical.

An animated actor on the sidelines with a mode of dress matching his loud mannerisms, Landa had become very popular with tourney crowds. He was recognized for his coaching genius, particularly regarding defense. His 1974 championship

All-Tournament selection Larry Dassie caused quite a sensation at the 1974 awards ceremony accepting his honor in a dazzling pink suit of his own creation. (Photo courtesy of Dick Brown)

squad held four opponents to an average *34.2 percent* from the field, not only an all-time tournament record, but a remarkable accomplishment at any level of basketball.

His peers also recognized his abilities. The following week Landa was scheduled to give a clinic at the NCAA Tourney Final Four in Greensboro, North Carolina, the only junior college coach asked to do so.

But, it was his players who admired him most. He had molded successful teams using individuals few others wanted, hindered by not being able to offer scholarships like national powers such as Moberly, Vincennes, or San Jacinto. He did it with integrity. As Marty Prendergast told *The Trentonian,* "He fills your needs personally, as well as athletically. If you have a problem, Howie won't just slip out like a lot of coaches. He'll listen to both sides of an issue." Said Connie White to Trenton's *The Evening Times,* "Howie's one of the greatest persons I've known. He's done so much for me and I hope in a way I've given him something in return."

Many of the Vikings came to Trenton just to have Landa as coach. Stated freshman Harry Ley, "I may go to another school after he leaves." It was the feeling of many tourney observers that Mercer County's rapidly rising star would soon become a falling meteor.

The inimitable Howie Landa was always popular with tourney fans because of his animated acting along the sidelines. A three-time Coach of the Tournament, Landa was inducted into the NJCAA Basketball Hall of Fame in 1986. (Photo courtesy of Howie Landa)

Tournament Results

Tuesday:	Game	
	1	NE Oklahoma A&M — 78 Dodge City — 70
	2	Northeastern — 73 Hill — 66
	3	Grand View — 100 Copiah-Lincoln — 87
	4	Mercer County — 80 Niagara County — 58
	5	Moberly — 75 San Jacinto — 73
	6	Vincennes — 79 Normandale — 63
Wednesday:	Game	
	7	Chipola — 65 Alexander City St. — 63
	8	New York City — 75 Arizona Western — 66
	9	Hill — 84 Dodge City — 83 OT
	10	NE Oklahoma A&M — 67 Northeastern — 65
	11	Mercer County — 83 Grand View — 48
Thursday:	Game	
	12	Copiah-Lincoln — 106 Niagara County — 92
	13	Arizona Western — 84 Alexander City St. — 7
	14	Grand View — 70 Northeastern — 59
	15	San Jacinto — 109 Normandale — 81
	16	Chipola — 73 New York City — 55
	17	Moberly — 63 Vincennes — 59
Friday:	Game	
	18	Hill — 99 Copiah-Lincoln — 84
	19	San Jacinto — 70 Arizona Western — 69
	20	Vincennes — 109 New York City — 95
	21	Mercer County — 64 NE Oklahoma A&M — 5
	22	Chipola — 58 Moberly — 56
Saturday:	Game	
	23	Hill — 94 San Jacinto — 89
	24	Vincennes — 95 Grand View — 86 2OT
	25	Moberly — 81 NE Oklahoma A&M — 62
	26	Mercer County — 60 Chipola — 58

How They Finished in 1974

1. Mercer County Community College
2. Chipola Junior College
3. Moberly Junior College
4. Vincennes University
5. Hill Junior College
6. Northeastern Oklahoma Agricultural & Mechanical College
7. Grand View College
8. San Jacinto College

All-Tournament Team

Leon Alvoid — Northeastern Oklahoma Agricultural & Mechanical College
Larry Dassie — Dodge City Community College
Barry Davis — Hill Junior College
Albert Gardner — Chipola Junior College
John Gordon — Moberly Junior College
Rickey Green — Vincennes University
Marion Hillard — Copiah-Lincoln Junior College
Lester Lewis — Chipola Junior College
Marty Prendergast — Mercer County Community College
Connie White — Mercer County Community College

Coach of the Tournament

Howie Landa — Mercer County Community College

French Most Valuable Player Award

Connie White — Mercer County Community College

Sesher Sportsmanship Award

John Gordon — Moberly Junior College

Bud Obee Outstanding Small Player Award

Ray Williams — San Jacinto College

BROKEN FINGER, TWISTED ANKLE

he 1973-74 season was a long one for Hutchinson fans. It started on the heels of the announcement that the school had forfeited all its games for the previous year, returning its 1973 tourney second-place trophy, and culminated when the then 18th-ranked Blue Dragons were upset by Independence Community Junior College in the Region 6 semifinals.

Prospects for the 1974-75 season were not encouraging either. Eight-year coach Gene Keady resigned after accepting an assistant coaching position with Eddie Sutton at Arkansas. Dick Gisel, one-time Hutchinson tourney star and Keady's assistant, took over the Blue Dragon reins, inheriting four sophomores and no true stars.

Gisel responded to the imposing situation by introducing what he called "a one-count offense": "If you aren't moving after one count, you're doing something wrong." The pace was so taxing that, according to assistant coach Gene Torczon, "A player can only go at full tilt for about eight minutes and then he needs that four minute break. That has given a lot of other kids a chance to get a lot of game action." Gisel frequently used his full complement of players. Many times, all 12 scored, with as many as seven hitting double figures. The fact that all five starters averaged in low double digits and that the highest individual tally during the season was 23 illustrated the team's balance.

The up-tempo system quickly caught on with Hutchinson fans. Recent misfortunes were forgotten. The Blue Dragons were again fun to watch.

Of course, it did not hurt fan morale that the new system produced wins. And more wins. Hutchinson's first loss came in its next-to-last regular-season game against Dodge City Community College, 81-80, on the road. By then, the Blue Dragons had amassed 24 consecutive wins, a school record.

In Region 6 play, Hutchinson left St. John's College of Winfield and Kansas City Kansas Community College players gasping for air, racing away to 107-61 and 121-87 victories, respectively. The Blue Dragons then avenged the previous year's regional upset, downing Independence, 91-90, for the title.

The next test was the toughest of the year: a best-two-of-three play-off with Region 2 champ Seminole Junior College. The season had long since surpassed fan expectations. A Blue Dragon win over the richly talented Oklahomans would simply be a bonus.

Hutchinson downed Seminole in two straight, 106-95 and 90-88. The Blue Dragons entered the Juco Tournament with a 26-1 record, the most wins in the school's history, and a No. 1 ranking in the NJCAA poll.

THE PARTICIPANTS

Though Hutchinson had fielded strong teams in the past, the Blue Dragons had never entered the Juco Tournament with a top ranking. Nor had they been the most senior of 16 participants (11 previous appearances).

Of course, only one previous tourney experience placed a team in exclusive company for the 1975 event. There were 10 schools making their first trip to the nationals, the largest group of newcomers since 1959. Included were No. 3 Anderson College (29-1), No. 4 Westchester Community College (33-1), No. 6 Western Texas College (32-1), No. 11 Lake Land College (32-3), and No. 14 DeKalb Community College-South (32-6). The unranked debutantes were Utica Junior College (29-3),

One of the quickest men to bring the ball up the court in tourney history, Vincennes' Rickey Green was later an All-American at the University of Michigan, runner-up to Indiana in the 1976 NCAA Final Four. Green later played more than 10 years in the NBA. (Photo courtesy of Gus Stevens, Vincennes University)

Essex County Community College (28-3), Waukesha County Technical Institute (28-5), Housatonic Community College (29-7), and Sheridan College (22-8).

There was even newness among the veterans, though the faces were familiar. Besides Hutchinson's Dick Gisel, rookie coaches guided No. 2 San Jacinto (35-3), No. 8 College of Southern Idaho (24-2), and No. 15 Arizona Western College (28-2): Wayne Ballard, who played for Lon Morris College in the 1964 tournament, had most recently assisted Dean Evans at San Jacinto; Boyd Grant, who played for Snow College in the 1954 championship game, came to CSI from the University of Kentucky where he had been an assistant in charge of recruiting for Adolph Rupp; and Arizona Western's Bob Banfield had recently been Jerry Hale's assistant at Southern Idaho.

Only two schools were veteran all the way. No. 10 Vincennes University (28-3) and unranked Grand View College (26-4) were the only repeaters from the 1974 tournament. Vincennes, a fourth-place finisher, returned five sophomores, including four starters. Grand View, a seventh-place finisher, returned seven sophomores, including three starters. They were also led by the most experienced mentors in the field: Allen Bradfield in his 23rd year at Vincennes and Dave Sisam in his 20th at Grand View.

Region	Team
1	Arizona Western College — Yuma, Arizona
4	Lake Land College — Mattoon, Illinois
5	Western Texas College — Snyder, Texas
6	Hutchinson Community Junior College — Hutchinson, Kansas
7	Utica Junior College — Utica, Mississippi
9	Sheridan College — Sheridan, Wyoming
10	Anderson College — Anderson, South Carolina
11	Grand View College — Des Moines, Iowa
12	Vincennes University — Vincennes, Indiana
13	Waukesha County Technical Institute — Pewaukee, Wisconsin
14	San Jacinto College, Central Campus — Pasadena, Texas
15	Westchester Community College — Valhalla, New York
17	DeKalb Community College, South Campus — Decatur, Georgia
18	College of Southern Idaho — Twin Falls, Idaho
19	Essex County College — Newark, New Jersey
21	Housatonic Community College — Bridgeport, Connecticut

But, ranking and experience were moot factors in picking a favorite. The field included 10 of the top 20, seven of the top 10, and the top four. Ranked teams were equitably distributed in the brackets with five in the upper and five in the lower. No one appeared to have a distinct advantage. Everyone would have at least one tough match and probably several. To prove the point, the combined won-loss percentage for the entire 16 participants was just under 90 percent, the highest in tournament history.

With the tourney field a class act headed by the hometown favorite, tickets for the 1975 event were cherished commodities. So much so, they were one of the few items that Harold Ghormley saved when his house burned to the ground in nearby Partridge.

TUESDAY — WHAT AM I DOING HERE?

The city of Hutchinson was again struck with basketball madness. The line-up for 400 general admission tickets for the tip-off session began forming at 7 a.m. — 4½ hours before the doors opened. Even those who already possessed afternoon passes arrived as early as 9:15 to insure they had the best seats, since none were reserved. Businesses all over town saw employees go to lunch and not return. There was only one thing on everyone's mind:

The top-rated Blue Dragons faced three-time champ Vincennes in the afternoon finale.

Southern Idaho Coach Boyd Grant was still able to find a seat in the bleachers after Kenny Davis' 22 points and 18 rebounds led the Golden Eagles past Sheridan, 78-62, in the opener.

Westchester's Ralph Arietta was not so lucky. After the Vikings downed Lake Land, 85-66, Arietta could only find standing room in the "nose-bleed" section.

Both, however, were impressed with what they saw. Said Coach Grant, "Both teams did things so well that I went home wondering whether we could play either one . . . I thought to myself, 'What am I doing here?' It was a tough game for either team to lose."

Two schools with long traditions and high rankings fueled the intensity level on and off the court, before and during the game, raising it to the equivalent of a championship contest.

Hutchonians had dreaded the meeting, cursing their misfortune. They were tight, as were the Blue Dragons. Hutchinson hit only 5 of its first 20 shots.

Meanwhile Vincennes hit 12 of 18, led by roommate guards Rickey Green and Dale Slaughter, and took a commanding 25-10 lead after 11½ minutes.

The Blue Dragons pulled themselves together, rallied to within five, then fell to a 54-45 deficit at intermission.

In the first 1:10 of the second half, Hutchinson cut the margin to three. Vincennes responded by increasing it to 11.

The Blue Dragons' principal strength all year long had been Coach Dick Gisel's ability to substitute fresh troops almost endlessly without degradation in play. Hutchinson had won many of its games by simply wearing out its opponent.

Vincennes Coach Allen Bradfield preferred to stick with h starters. When three of them encountered foul difficulty in th final period, Hutchinson's depth became a factor. The Blu Dragons gradually closed the gap, pulling within two, 76-7 with 4:31 remaining.

It was their last hurrah. Vincennes outscored Hutchinson 11-4, the rest of the way, winning 87-78.

The Blue Dragons received a magnificent performance from sophomore forward Randy Boyts. Despite being only 6-4 an weighing a slight 165, the Hesston, Kansas, native shared gam honors with 24 points and topped everyone in rebounds wit 17.

Guard Alvin Green, who hit 18, was the only other Hutchin son player in double figures, however. In comparison, Vin cennes placed five in that category, led by Tom Harris (24) an Green (20).

The key to victory was quickness out front. Said Gisel abou a future Michigan All-American and NBA star, "I thought w had some pretty fast guards. But, that Green went by us like w were standing still."

The evening session resembled the afternoon: two yawner followed by a blockbuster finale.

Alonzo Bradley's game-high 31 points and 14 rebounds le the Utica Bulldogs past Essex County, 73-63, in the opener.

In the feature, Western Texas ran off strings of 12 and 1 unanswered points to build an overwhelming 48-21 halftime advantage over Housatonic. Led by Bob Miller's 25 and Eugene Harris' 20, the Westerners won easily, 91-57.

Then came the nightcap, No. 2 San Jacinto versus No. Anderson, the game everyone came to see. Before Karlton Hil ton's three-point play gave Anderson a 43-41 halftime edge there were nine ties, keeping fans in their seats.

When San Jacinto scored the first eight points of the final peri od, the crowd began to trickle out. Anderson never led again.

Though lacking Anderson's size, the Ravens won the rebound war, 45-31, sparked by center Mike Schultz's game high 13.

Their strongest attribute, however, was out front. Ray and Sam Williams, brothers of All-American Gus Williams at the University of Southern California, were considered one of the best guard combos in the nation. Ray, the 1974 tourney's Obee Small Player Award-winner, averaged 21.5 points per game, shooting 60 percent from the field. Younger brother Sam was San Jacinto's leading scorer with a 21.8 average and the hottest hand most recently, having tallied 91 points in the three-game play-off with Henderson County Junior College for the Region 14 title.

It was Ray who was the star against Anderson, though. The 6-2 sophomore hit 16 of 22 shots from the field, nabbing game honors with 34. San Jacinto downed the Trojans, 84-79, joining Vincennes as tourney favorite.

WEDNESDAY — BULLDOG DEFENSE

Early in the day's opener, Arizona Western switched from man-to-man to zone, breaking the game wide open, forging a 52-35 gap at intermission. Led by Al Green's game-high 3 points, including 16 of 22 shooting from the field, and Jerome Shanks' game-high 15 rebounds, the Matadors coasted to a 97-75 victory over Waukesha County Tech.

The most exciting first-round contest was saved until last.

Behind forward David Purdue's 21 first-half points, Grand View took a 42-39 edge over DeKalb-South and maintained i through the second half. With 2:30 remaining, the Vikings were comfortably in front, 88-81.

Then the DeKalb Eagles mounted a rally. The turning point came with 1:08 to go when Grand View's 5-8 speedster playmaker Earl Hinton was whistled for a foul in a drive to the basket. Six-seven center Calvin Bowser sank a free throw, reducing the DeKalb deficit to a lone basket.

Eagle reserve Rus Willingham then stole the ball from the usually elusive Hinton and drove for the tying bucket with 40 seconds left.

Grand View held for one.

With five seconds showing DeKalb's Bowser intercepted in the middle and immediately called time.

Before the tournament started, Eagle Coach Roger Couch had told the press that his star Mike Dickerson was "the best wingman in the country — bar none." The 6-5 sophomore helped validate Couch's argument by leading all scorers in the game with 33 points. Everyone knew who would take the last shot.

Grand View's Dave Sisam countered by assigning Dillet Montgomery, his most aggressive defender, to cover Dickerson. When play resumed, the ball went to Dickerson as anticipated. But, as Sisam described, Montgomery was right there, "in his face," forcing the Decatur, Georgia, native to the deepest part of the corner. Dickerson shot over Montgomery, anyhow, drilling it at the buzzer. DeKalb-South downed Grand View, 90-88.

The quarterfinals began with an excellent exhibition of defense. After a 9-all tie, Southern Idaho held Westchester scoreless for 11½ minutes, opening a 26-9 lead. Though Westchester put up 25 more shots than the Golden Eagles, the New Yorkers never recovered, hitting only 30 percent for the game. Southern Idaho advanced, 69-51.

The defense in the nightcap was even more impressive. Before the contest, Utica Coach Robert Moreland acknowledged his team's underdog role, stating that "Vincennes probably has the best talent in the tournament." It came as a total surprise then when a solid Bulldog zone forced Vincennes to miss its first 10 shots. The Trailblazers hit only 4 of 19 in the first 10 minutes and 9 for 39 for the half. Utica took a shocking 33-19 advantage to the locker room.

Vincennes rallied in the second half, pulling as close as six. However, guard Marcello Singleton (21 points and 4 assists) and forward Alonzo Bradley (24 points and 14 rebounds) recaptured momentum for the Bulldogs. Utica stunned the favored Trailblazers, 74-59, holding them to 33 percent from the field.

Vincennes Coach Allen Bradfield later cited one reason for the upset was that the intensity of the opening-round game with Hutchinson had taken its emotional toll on the Trailblazers. He also admitted the possibility that he overlooked Utica because it was not a traditional powerhouse.

Said Coach Moreland with satisfaction, "It [success in the tournament] let me know that we were on a par with all the other junior colleges throughout the country."

THURSDAY — HEART-STOPPER II

Any time Texas schools squared off in the tournament, game intensity increased a few degrees above normal. The evening feature was no exception.

After Western Texas broke on top, 10-2, brothers Ray and Sam Williams rallied San Jacinto to the front, 17-16. The teams traded baskets.

Then a star was born.

In the next two minutes, Western Texas scored eight unanswered points, six by guard Bob Miller. The 6-5 sophomore's shots were not cheap, but from a distance. "I mean *long* range," described Western Coach Mike Mitchell, "three-point ABA land."

The crowd grew more and more excited with each long bomb. In the first five minutes of the second half, three long swishers by Miller brought fans out of their seats. The Seaford, New York, native then showed he could handle the ball on the move, sinking a double-clutch short jumper followed by a driving reverse lay-up.

The outburst lifted Western Texas to a 53-42 margin, breaking the game open. San Jacinto pulled no closer than four thereafter. Led by Miller's 16 for 25 mostly long-distance shooting and game-high 35 points, the Westerners advanced, 79-70.

The finale also featured top-notch scoring from Arizona Western's Al Green (31) and DeKalb-South's Mike Dickerson (28), both of whom battled to the finish.

After Green tied the score at 76-all with a pair of free throws with 46 seconds left, DeKalb turned the ball over. The Matadors took possession and played for the game-winner.

With eight seconds remaining, Green was fouled. The 6-2 Bronx native hit the first free throw, but missed the second, giving Arizona Western only a sliver of a lead.

For DeKalb it was the Grand View game all over again. In similar circumstances in that first-round contest, the Eagles had gone to their ace, Dickerson. One shot away from triumph or defeat in the quarterfinals, they gave the ball to him again.

But, just as Dickerson was about to fire, he spotted center Jarvis Reynolds open under the basket. Dickerson threaded a pass through three defenders to Reynolds for an easy lay-up. The 6-7 frosh missed — then immediately tipped it back in with one second left, giving the Eagles a 77-76 victory, their second heart-stopper in a row.

FRIDAY — SMASHING RESULTS

The defeat of Vincennes and San Jacinto, the only former champs in the field, guaranteed the national junior college crown would eventually rest on a new head. Three of the Final Four were tourney newcomers. Only Southern Idaho had experienced competition in Hutchinson, having reached the championship tilt four years earlier. The Golden Eagles, however, were not the favorite, at least among tourney fans.

After its dismantling of veteran Vincennes in the quarterfinals, Utica was adopted by the Arena audience as the Cinderella choice for 1975. Many were convinced the Bulldogs would win it all. They possessed a steady pilot on the floor in 6-1 guard Marcello Singleton, a converted high school center. They possessed a powerful scoring and rebound threat in 6-6 forward Alonzo Bradley, one of the most talented players in the tournament. Most of all, they possessed one of the most poised, disciplined defenses in the event's history.

It was not surprising that the halftime score of the opening semifinal was a low 32-27. Fans were bewildered, however, that Utica was behind and had trailed most of the period, one time by as much as eight.

When the Bulldogs scored the first two baskets of the final frame, pulling within one, everything appeared back in order.

Then, behind Kenny Davis' blue-collar work inside and Gary Yoder's soft touch outside, Southern Idaho outdistanced Utica, 16-4. With a nine-point cushion, the Golden Eagles spread to a four-corners offense, designed to work the clock or create easy back-door baskets. Off Yoder assists (11 for the game), CSI padded its lead to 67-49, coasting to a 69-55 victory.

Though Davis (22) and Yoder (19) were the offensive heroes, the key to the win came on defense. Coming into the contest, Eagle Coach Boyd Grant had faced the problem of how to stop Bradley, Utica's leading scorer. Normally, Grant would have assigned 6-4 forward Bob Durham, his best defender on the front line, to guard Bradley. Unfortunately, according to Grant, "We had lost him with a sprained ankle [in late February]. He did not play hardly at all in the national tournament." Instead, the task of defending Bradley went to 6-5 sophomore Dwight Boyles. Said Grant, "[It was] probably the best game that Dwight Boyles ever played for CSI." Bradley finished the game with seven points, only two coming in the second half.

The crowd braced for further disappointment in the nightcap. Throughout the evening word passed via the airwaves that Western Texas' Bob Miller, the Westerners' long-range bomber, leading scorer, and a particular fan favorite, had been injured in a freak accident and was doubtful for the semifinals.

The incident happened that afternoon when the Westerners were "killing some time watching some early games," described Coach Mike Mitchell. "I was going to stay and told the players to go back to the hotel to get some rest. They went out to get in the van." The next thing Mitchell knew, "He [Miller] came back in, his elbow bent, blood all over the place." In trying to jockey the van door closed, Miller's little finger on his shooting hand had been caught. "It had a slight break in it. But, the biggest problem was that it smashed his nail and it was just so sore to touch."

Though Miller did start for the Westerners, his shooting and ball-handling were definitely hampered by the splint on his little finger. His contribution was further handicapped by early foul trouble.

Despite the misfortune, Western Texas looked strong. The Westerners jumped on DeKalb-South, leading 36-25 by intermission, expanding it to 46-29 with just under 16 minutes remaining.

The game was not out of reach for DeKalb, however. After two whisker-thin wins at the buzzer, fans had dubbed the Eagles "the cardiac wonders." And for good reason. In the next

11½ minutes, DeKalb scrambled back, a feat made more amazing by the fact the Eagles attempted the run without the services of floor leader Scott Langford, side-lined earlier by an elbow to the eye requiring stitches. With 4:16 remaining, DeKalb took the lead 54-53 on a tip-in by Tony Williams.

Basket-trading followed: Eugene Harris hit a baseline jumper for Western Texas. Jarvis Reynolds countered for DeKalb. Miller swished one from 25-feet for the Westerners. Reynolds regained the lead again for the Eagles.

After Harris' 20-footer put Western on top with 1:40 left, the seesawing stopped, DeKalb's Rus Willingham missing from the baseline. During the rebound scramble, Western center Norman Barnes was fouled. He hit both ends of one-and-one, giving the Texans a three-point edge they maintained to the end. The final: Western Texas — 63, DeKalb-South — 60.

SATURDAY — A TWIST OF FATE

After its disappointing opening-round loss to Vincennes, Hutchinson returned to its normal leave-'em-in-the-dust form, downing Essex County, 99-75.

Then the machine began to run out of gas. Against determined Lake Land — whose two coaches, 6-7½ head coach Howard Garrett and 6-9 assistant Clyde Lovellette (a former Kansas All-American and ex-pro), were taller than any of their players — the Blue Dragons needed 29-for-35 free throw shooting to escape with an 89-86 victory.

By week's end, Hutchinson's tank looked empty. Behind the outside shooting of Dillet Montgomery (a game-high 24 points) and the offensive board work of Curt Forrester (a game-high 14 rebounds), Grand View made things look easy, mounting a 79-64 advantage with 8:14 to go.

Showing heart and courage, the tired Blue Dragons fought back, reducing the deficit to a lone point inside the minute mark. The effort fell short, however. Grand View held on, grabbing fifth-place, 91-89.

In the fourth-place contest, San Jacinto struggled just to trail Westchester, 29-27, at halftime. Then, Ray Williams scored 15 second-period points to lead the Ravens to a 61-56 win. Williams topped everyone with 23 points and 15 rebounds, just another in a long line of heroic tourney performances fans had come to expect from the brilliant sophomore. It was not his last. Williams left San Jacinto to become an All-American at Minnesota before spending 11 years in the NBA.

The third-place game also featured future notables. Utica's tight zone and super efficient offense (only five turnovers) broke open a close battle in the second half. The Bulldogs gradually widened the difference in the last 10 minutes, downing DeKalb-South, 80-66. Utica was again led by Marcello Singleton, the eventual Sesher Sportsmanship Award-winner — who shared game honors with DeKalb's Mike Dickerson with 20 — and Alonzo Bradley, whose 14 points and game-high nine rebounds, added to his previous outstanding totals, reserved a place for him on the All-Tournament Team.

But, real glory for the duo came later. The next year Singleton and Bradley followed Coach Robert Moreland to Texas Southern where, as seniors, they led the Tigers to an NAIA national title. Bradley, a two-time, 1st-Team NAIA All-American, was named the tourney MVP.

* * *

The championship tilt was eagerly awaited. Southern Idaho and Western Texas were evenly matched, two of the best defensive units in the tournament. The size difference between the two was negligible. Each had a top rebounder: Kenny Davis for the Golden Eagles and Eugene Harris for the Westerners. Each also possessed a good big guard: 6-4 Gary Yoder for CSI and 6-5 Bob Miller for Western.

The only negative threatening the equal pairing was Miller's broken finger. If Miller played up to the 30-point-per-game average of his first two outings, many felt Western Texas held a slight edge. If not, the scales tipped toward Southern Idaho.

When Miller came out, playing tentatively, passing up shots he normally took, momentum immediately swung to the Eagles.

When 6-7 Davis sat down with three fouls at the 10:53 mark of the first half, momentum shifted. Western Texas quickly

Since he was the consummate team leader, Gary Yoder's sprained ankle in the 1975 championship game may have cost Southern Idaho the crown. Yoder later starred at the University of Cincinnati. (Photo courtesy of the University of Cincinnati)

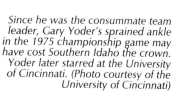

went from three down to five up.

Then came the crushing blow of the game. Yoder, the E floor leader, severely twisted his ankle.

His loss was critical to Southern Idaho's chances. Said E Coach Boyd Grant, later head coach at Fresno State and Col do State, "Of all the players I've coached, even at the m [college] level, he [Yoder] was probably the smartest play ever had, with the most ability for his smartness . . . He wa excellent penetrator and a great passer. He could see ev body . . . He was a coach on the floor."

Even more important was his attitude. Grant described Yc as a "very unselfish player. He was not a guy who worried at scoring. He worried about winning." In fact, Grant had o told the sophomore from Topeka, Indiana, that he thought should be scoring more. Replied Yoder, "Coach, when game is on the line, [then] I'll look for my shot."

Summed up Grant, "He didn't take the whole doughnut shared it. That was probably the secret of our [success] beca he brought that togetherness to the team."

Even tough Yoder returned to the floor in the second half ankle heavily taped, Southern Idaho was never the same three-point play by Andre Wakefield with just over two min gone, pulled the Eagles within a bucket, but it was a to threat. Western Texas reeled off a 12-1 spurt, eight coming f forward Brian Minor's work inside against foul-plagued D who was whistled for his fourth. Southern Idaho fought galla from a 42-29 deficit with 12:29 remaining, but came no clo than six.

Western Texas claimed the title, 65-57.

THE AFTERMATH — LUCK

After the game, Region 5 Director Buddy Travis, a forr tourney participant as player and coach, came up to M Mitchell, the young, well-dressed, good-looking mentor Western Texas, shook his hand and said, "This doesn't me near as much to you now as it will a lot of years from now.'

In only his second year as a head coach, Mitchell had alre achieved a national championship. It was an honor coveted coaches with 10 times his experience. Yet, it had come so e ly.

Looking back on it, Mitchell felt there were two reasons his team's success: "First of all, you have to be good to win. E you also, I think, have to have a little luck. You have to hav break or two here or there."

The week was replete with examples of Dame Fortur intervention, the timely injury to Gary Yoder and the con nient foul trouble of Southern Idaho's best rebounder, Ker Davis, in the title match, heading the list. However, Mitchell ed three other instances that were less obvious, all coming the semifinal against DeKalb-South.

The first was the play of DeKalb's star forward, Mike Dick son. "Thank goodness, he had an awful game against us," s Mitchell. "He just didn't make a shot [10 for 32]." Wa because of Western's excellent defense? "You'd like to that. We started manning them, but then we got in foul trout We played zone the whole second half and he just could make a shot. In all honesty, a lot of the shots he missed h been making."

Then there were the critical late free throws which gave the Westerners their eventual margin of victory. "Norman Barnes was about a 40-percent foul shooter for the year," explained Mitchell. "Barnes gets fouled. A one-and-one. I tried to substitute for him because there's no way he can make a free throw. [But] the officials wouldn't let me . . . And he makes them both. I mean, he strings them both. Both are dead center! He couldn't do that again at two o'clock in the afternoon with nobody in the gym and no pressure."

Finally, there was the clutch play of Eugene Harris, who Mitchell felt "could have been an NBA player" had he been a better shooter. With time running out, DeKalb forced Harris to the corner. "Eugene gets in a trap down along the baseline and it looks like we're going to get a held ball," described Mitchell. "He just jumps up, turns around, and shoots about a 22-footer and makes it between two guys. Sometimes you'd rather be lucky than good."

But, according to CSI Coach Boyd Grant, good fortune was not the only factor in the Western Texas title. "Mike Mitchell had a very good team. Physically, they were a much better team than we were. I had a lot of respect for Mike and the job that he did. He earned his way there. I really do believe they deserved to be the champions."

No one questioned the key to the Westerner squad, though. "Bob Miller was a great player, one of the very best to come through that tournament," stated Mitchell. "Anyone would be hard pressed to go back through the years of that tournament and list an all-time 1st-Team, 2nd-Team, 3rd-Team, etc. There were lots of great players and the thing that's hard to evaluate is how great is a player in terms of the roll he fills for his team . . . We had great rebounders. We had very intelligent players. [But] beyond Bob Miller, we didn't really have a good shooter on that team."

The fact that Miller was still able to play within himself and contribute despite a painful injury assured his selection as French MVP.

Other honorees that evening *were* surprises.

There was an abundance of candidates for the Obee Small Player Award that year, with Utica's 6-1 Marcello Singleton and San Jacinto's 5-11 Sam Williams among the more prominent. The selection committee, however, abided by the award's title, choosing one of the smallest players, a young man who had zipped around in front of tourney audiences for two years — Grand View's 5-8 Earl Hinton.

The other surprise was made more so by the way it was announced. Longtime awards ceremony emcee, Hod Humiston, broke with his traditional alphabetic introduction of the All-Tournament Team, by saving the first on the list till last, creating one of the all-time highlight moments for Hutchinson fans.

Because of his slight build, the final All-Tourney recipient was not in the same league physically as the other nine selected. He was not among the tops in any statistical category for the week. Yet, his dedication and gutsy play had caught the attention of opposing coaches. Said Grand View Coach Dave Sisam, "He was a really hard-working kid. His fundamentals were solid. He shot the same way every time, never got out of alignment."

He was a top student, a team leader. His own coach, Hutchinson's Dick Gisel, could find no other words to express his warm feelings toward him other than to summarize him as "a class individual." An example of his character came after Hutchinson's heart-breaking loss to Vincennes. Tired from a 24-point, 17-rebound, Herculean performance, disappointed after his team's fall from the pinnacle of a No. 1 ranking, the 6-4 sophomore congratulated each member of the victorious Vincennes squad, then, long after everyone else had left the floor, stayed to sign programs of young autograph-seekers, his perspiration-soaked hair dripping all the while.

When Humiston read the name "Randy Boyts," the Arena audience stood as one, giving the future TCU star a heartfelt standing ovation.

(Bottom, left) The French MVP, Bob Miller did not live up to his 1975 tourney credentials the following year at Louisiana State University (due in part to a bout with mononucleosis), but returned to form as a senior All-Southeast Conference selection. (Photo courtesy of Mike Mitchell, taken by Jim Tully, Snyder, TX)

"A class individual" according to Hutchinson Coach Dick Gisel, 1975 All-Tournament selection Randy Boyts later starred at Texas Christian University. (Photo courtesy of Texas Christian University)

Tournament Results

Tuesday: Game

1 Southern Idaho — 78 Sheridan — 62
2 Westchester — 85 Lake Land — 66
3 Vincennes — 87 Hutchinson — 78
4 Utica — 73 Essex County — 63
5 Western Texas — 91 Housatonic — 57
6 San Jacinto — 84 Anderson — 79

Wednesday: Game

7 Arizona Western — 97 Waukesha County — 75
8 DeKalb-South — 90 Grand View — 88
9 Lake Land — 89 Sheridan — 71
10 Southern Idaho — 69 Westchester — 51
11 Utica — 74 Vincennes — 59

Thursday: Game

12 Hutchinson — 99 Essex County — 75
13 Anderson — 78 Housatonic — 69
14 Grand View — 92 Waukesha County — 78
15 Westchester — 70 Vincennes — 54
16 Western Texas — 79 San Jacinto — 70
17 DeKalb-South — 77 Arizona Western — 76

Friday: Game

18 Hutchinson — 89 Lake Land — 86
19 Grand View — 83 Anderson — 65
20 San Jacinto — 83 Arizona Western — 75
21 Southern Idaho — 69 Utica — 55
22 Western Texas — 63 DeKalb-South — 60

Saturday: Game

23 Grand View — 91 Hutchinson — 89
24 San Jacinto — 61 Westchester — 56
25 Utica — 80 DeKalb-South — 66
26 Western Texas — 65 Southern Idaho — 57

How They Finished in 1975

1. Western Texas College
2. College of Southern Idaho
3. Utica Junior College
4. San Jacinto College, Central Campus
5. Grand View College
6. DeKalb Community College, South Campus
7. Westchester Community College
8. Hutchinson Community Junior College

All-Tournament Team

Randy Boyts — Hutchinson Community Junior College
Alonzo Bradley — Utica Junior College
Kenny Davis — College of Southern Idaho
Mike Dickerson — DeKalb Community College, South Campus
Al Green — Arizona Western College
Eugene Harris — Western Texas College
Bob Miller — Western Texas College
Allen Thompson — Westchester Community College
Ray Williams — San Jacinto College, Central Campus
Gary Yoder — College of Southern Idaho

Coach of the Tournament

Mike Mitchell — Western Texas College

French Most Valuable Player Award

Bob Miller — Western Texas College

Sesher Sportsmanship Award

Marcello Singleton — Utica Junior College

Bud Obee Outstanding Small Player Award

Earl Hinton — Grand View College

1975 TOURNAMENT BRACKET

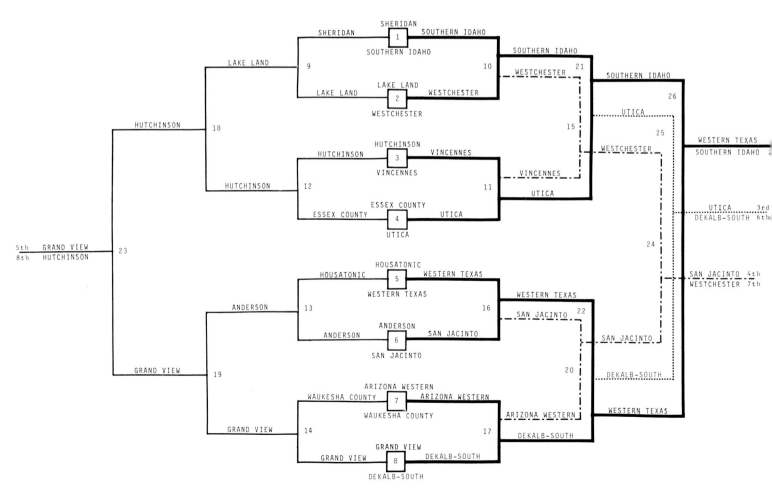

THE MARATHON BEGINS

After the California pull-out in 1951, the National Junior College Athletic Association continually grew, its biggest membership increases coming in the late 60s. In order to insure that everyone had a fair opportunity to compete in the national tournament, the organization realigned, creating three new regions in 1969 and another two in 1974.

More regions meant the development of a system of play-offs to pare the tourney field to 16. The play-offs drew ire from the coaching fraternity, however. Their thinking — if you won your region, you deserved the right to play in Hutchinson.

So, at the 1975 annual meeting, the NJCAA elected to try a bold experiment. With the agreement of the co-sponsoring Lyle Rishel American Legion Post, the tournament was expanded from a 16-team, five-day, 26-game event to a 21-team, six-day, 35-game endurance test.

The change required several immediate adjustments for longtime tourney followers.

The first involved dipping deeper into the pocketbook; season ticket prices increased to $18, a still remarkable bargain (51 cents per game) in comparison to costs nationwide, but a 20-percent elevation over the good thing fans had come to expect.

Secondly, the addition of another day to the event eliminated the traditionally popular Monday practice sessions which informally introduced fans to the participants.

Finally, there was the new bracket. The construction was bizarre and confusing. Ten teams played in the opening-round while 11 received first-round byes. Yet, a pseudo-double-elimination format was retained. The result, described a local editorial, "looks more like a drawing explaining integrated circuits rather than a tournament bracket."

There were other, more serious effects, however. The recent closing of the Kansas Inn (formerly the Baker Hotel) because of bankruptcy proceedings, significantly reduced the available housing for incoming teams and fans who arrived in greater numbers than ever before. Several participants were required to stay in outlying communities, thus negating some of the financial benefits the city of Hutchinson normally received from the annual event.

But, most ominous, as far as tourney sponsors were concerned, was the 15-percent decline in initial season ticket sales.

THE PARTICIPANTS

The new format did provide one distinct plus for fans: 21 open slots maximized the chances of seeing the best teams in junior college basketball. The 1976 tourney field included 11 of the top-20, tying the largest representation of ranked squads in history.

The participants were also experienced. There were only four newcomers with a third of the 21 having played in Hutchinson the year before. Fans were not only going to see a lot of basketball, but also a lot of good, competitive basketball.

The best conflicts appeared scheduled for the upper bracket where seven of the 11 ranked teams were assigned, including:

No. 1 College of Southern Idaho (29-1), the 1975 runner-up;

No. 4 DeKalb Community College-South (28-4), the previous year's sixth-place finisher;

No. 6 Westchester Community College (30-3), the second-best defensive squad in the nation (58.1) and another repeater from 1975;

Region	Team
1	Arizona Western College — Yuma, Arizona
2	Connors State College of Agriculture and Applied Science — Warner, Oklahoma
3	Jamestown Community College — Jamestown, New York
4	Lake Land College — Mattoon, Illinois
5	McLennan Community College — Waco, Texas
6	Johnson County Community College — Overland Park, Kansas
7	Columbia State Community College — Columbia, Tennessee
8	Chipola Junior College — Marianna, Florida
9	Casper College — Casper, Wyoming
10	Anderson College — Anderson, South Carolina
11	Southeastern Community College — West Burlington, Iowa
12	Henry Ford Community College — Dearborn, Michigan
13	Bismarck Junior College — Bismarck, North Dakota
14	San Jacinto College, Central Campus — Pasadena, Texas
15	Westchester Community College — Valhalla, New York
16	State Fair Community College — Sedalia, Missouri
17	DeKalb Community College, South Campus — Decatur, Georgia
18	College of Southern Idaho — Twin Falls, Idaho
19	Mercer County Community College — Trenton, New Jersey
20	Community College of Allegheny County, Boyce Campus — Monroeville, Pennsylvania
21	Rhode Island Junior College — Warwick, Rhode Island

No. 8 McLennan Community College (30-3), the winner of the region which produced the 1975 champ;

No. 11 Chipola Junior College (25-5), the 1974 runner-up;

No. 14 Southeastern Community College of West Burlington (26-4), the most veteran participant with 10 tourney appearances; and

No. 15 San Jacinto College-Central (30-5), a former champion and the fourth-place finisher in 1975.

Also included were Arizona Western College (25-7) and Lake Land College (24-12), both repeat performers from 1975. Only newcomers Jamestown Community College (28-4) and Johnson County Community College (28-8), a surprise representative from Kansas, were discounted as upper bracket contenders.

In comparison, the lower bracket appeared the private reserve of Mercer County Community College. After a year's absence, during which Howie Landa had taken a sabbatical to coach a professional team in Italy, the two-time champion Vikings were back in top form with a 29-2 record and a No. 3 ranking. Their stiffest competition would come at the outset against No. 9 Anderson College (27-2). After that it was relatively clear sailing. Columbia State Community College (24-4), rated tied for 15th with San Jacinto, and State Fair Community College (31-4), rated 19th, were the only other certified obstacles in Mercer's path to the title game.

The rest of the challengers were unranked: veterans Casper College (26-7), Henry Ford Community College (23-8), Connors State College (21-8), and Bismarck Junior College (15-11), and newcomers Rhode Island Junior College (25-2) and Community College of Allegheny County-Boyce (24-4).

One look at the week's schedule clearly illustrated that bringing all 21 teams to Hutchinson gave recognition to the regional victors, but did not necessarily make the championship process any more fair. A square peg still did not fit into a round hole. And with the NJCAA's continued insistence on filling bracket slots by lot, the hole was irregular.

Southern Idaho, which would have been the unquestionable favorite most other years, was considered just one of the pack in 1976. In order to capture the crown, the Golden Eagles would have to win a grueling five games in six days.

On the other hand, if Mercer County survived Anderson in Monday night's finale, the Vikings would need only three more wins and would not have to play again until Thursday night.

MONDAY — INKLINGS OF A LONG HAUL

There was no better way to tip-off an exciting week of basketball than to begin it with a good, old-fashioned Texas shoot-out. McLennan and San Jacinto had already faced each other twice during the year, splitting the decisions. The pairing was also interesting because the coaches of the two teams — Jim Haller of McLennan and Wayne Ballard of San Jacinto — had been teammates on Lon Morris' 1964 seventh-place squad.

Pre-game analysis slightly favored McLennan because of the Highlanders' six-foot freshman guard Vinnie Johnson, the leading scorer (27.6) coming into the tournament. Said San Jacinto's Ballard, "Last time we played them we 'held' him to just 35 points."

When the Ravens held Johnson to eight first-half tallies, a close contest was assured. There were 18 ties in the game. The

McLennan's prolific Vinnie Johnson (No. 14) finished his collegiate career at Baylor University and played more than eight years in the NBA. (Photo courtesy of Kenny Bernard)

largest margin came with 3:05 remaining, San Jacinto on top, 85-79. The Ravens needed four clutch free throws by 6-2 freshman forward Ollie Mack down the stretch, however, to secure a 91-90 victory.

Just as Southern Idaho was about to be introduced for the matinee feature, a short circuit plunged the Arena into semidarkness. It was another symbolic thumb-of-the-nose at the No. 1 Golden Eagles. Lake Land showed the same disrespect by playing the highly favored Idaho squad tough, forcing four ties and 13 lead changes.

Then midway in the second half, Southern Idaho's 1-3-1 trap defense produced three consecutive steals, contributing to eight unanswered points. Lake Land pulled no closer than three from then on, falling 71-66.

The afternoon finale began with 10-0 spurts by both teams before settling into a close match. Arizona Western took the upper hand in the second period opening a 53-46 gap over Westchester with 7:50 to go.

Then the Matadors went cold, scoring only once more in the game with 5:20 remaining. At the 1:50 mark, Westchester's Larry Rhodes hit a 25-footer, pulling the Vikings within one, 55-54.

Trying to hang on for dear life, Arizona Western carelessly turned the ball over 10 seconds later.

Westchester slowed for one and was tied up. The Vikings won the tip but lost the ball on a turnover with 44 seconds left.

Again Arizona Western tried to protect the ball. With eight seconds showing, Westchester's Ray Knox fouled Richie Winslow. The Matadors were not in the bonus situation, however, and retained possession out of bounds.

Then, on the inbounds pass, Westchester's Knox intercepted and drove for the winning basket.

After three tight afternoon battles, fans needed a breather. CCAC-Boyce obliged, building a 34-19 halftime lead in the evening opener. The Saints coasted the rest of the way, downing Henry Ford, 69-59, in the easiest win of the day.

The possibilities of a major upset restimulated the crowd in the evening feature. No. 4 DeKalb-South exhibited first-half jitters against the underdog Kansans of Johnson County and the supportive predominately-Kansas audience, trailing by as much as 10.

The Eagles regrouped, however. Led by All-American candidate Jarvis Reynolds' 37 points and 14 rebounds, DeKalb-South won, 74-67.

The evening session ended with the most eagerly awaited match-up of the day: No. 3 Mercer County versus No. 9 Anderson.

First, Mercer County overcame a seven-point deficit to take a 32-30 halftime advantage.

Then, Anderson made a similar comeback in the final period when 6-6 sophomore forward Karlton Hilton scored six straight points to pull the Trojans within one, 67-66, with 1:42 remaining.

The outcome was resolved at the line. Clutch one-and-one free throw shooting by Tony Rubino with 31 seconds left and Joe McKeown with 11 seconds left preserved a 71-68 Mercer victory.

The day had started and ended with a nail-biter. In between there had been only one dull contest. It had been one of the closest days in tourney history. With the prospects of five more action-packed days ahead, fans left the Arena wondering how their stamina would hold.

TUESDAY — AN EVENING OF WILD FINISHES

After Reno Gray's game-high 32 points led Lake Land past McLennan, 99-91, in the opening consolation match, the afternoon session recorded the tourney's first major surprises.

Connors State used an effective full-court press to stun State Fair, the team with the most wins coming into the tournament, 90-63.

Then, Bismarck dueled Casper to a 54-all draw before upsetting the Thunderbirds, 63-58, in overtime.

The day's excitement was only beginning.

The evening opener started innocently enough. SECC Burlington led from the tip, building a 62-48 margin with 13 minutes left in the game.

San Jacinto had proven during the year that it was capable of coming back, however, having overcome 21-point deficits for wins on two different occasions. In the next three minutes, the Ravens outscored the Burlington squad, 12-2.

The Blackhawks reopened the gap to 72-60.

San Jacinto rallied again, pulling within a bucket, 78-76, with 3½ minutes to go. A three-point play by Ollie Mack on the next sequence gave the Ravens their first lead of the game.

SECC tied the game 82-all with 1:24 remaining, sending the game into point-trading mode. Twice, San Jacinto's Chris Gonser hit a pair of free throws, followed by a field goal by Jerry Luckett, the Blackhawks' leading scorer.

With the game deadlocked at 86, the Iowans gained control and worked for the final shot. The ball went to Luckett for an easy short jumper. The shot slid off the rim at the buzzer. Said Blackhawk Coach Charlie Spoonhour, "It was unbelievable. Jerry hadn't missed anything, I think, since December."

More basket trading followed in overtime. With the game again tied and time running out, SECC stole the ball and immediately dribbled out of bounds, losing it. On the ensuing play "they [San Jacinto] baseballed it across the court," described Spoonhour. "I thought, 'What in the world are they doing that for?' I found out pretty soon — it was Ollie Mack who shot it in."

Mack's 20-footer at the buzzer capped a brilliant 40-point performance, the high for the 1976 tournament. He and Gonser combined for 11 of San Jacinto's 13 in overtime, leading the Ravens to a 99-97 win.

The evening feature picked up where the opener left off. Neither Southern Idaho nor Chipola led by more than five throughout the contest. There were 12 lead changes in the first half and nine in the second, including four in the final 54 seconds.

With 11 seconds remaining, Miller Butler — a replacement for the Indians' leading scorer, 6-8 Dorian Dent, who saw limited action because of a knee injury — gave Chipola a 66-65 edge on an inside move to the bucket.

"When the ball went in," stated Southern Idaho Coach Boyd Grant, "I thought, 'Oh my gosh! I ought to get time out.' " But, before Grant could attract the Eagles' attention, guard Andre Wakefield was already on a kamikaze course upcourt.

"They [Chipola] did not make good transition other than a couple of kids [who] kind of had their backs to him," continued Grant. "He went right down the floor and I could see him charging. I knew he was going to take the ball to the basket. In the last second, they tried to play the ball and he jumped in the air and floated. He had his legs up . . . and just laid the ball right up over the rim."

Chipola wing man Paul Hamilton tried to duplicate Wakefield's floor-length drive on the next play, but CSI's Ed Nickols planted himself squarely in his path. Two Nickols' free throws gave Southern Idaho a 69-66 victory.

The nightcap produced yet another wild finish. Jamestown made-up an 11-point deficit in 11 minutes to take a 73-71 lead just before Westchester's Jewell Pendleton tied the game with 1:53 remaining.

George Cheatum, the game's leading scorer with 34, put the Jamestown Jayhawks back on top with 34 seconds left.

Westchester's Mike Lawrence knotted the score again with 8 ticks showing.

On the next play, the Vikings stole the ball just as they had in their opener against Arizona Western. Jamestown changed the script, however, blocking the potential game-winner out of bounds.

With three seconds to go, Westchester had just enough time for one precisely executed play. The Vikings used one they had practiced many times, hitting Larry Rhodes in the corner. His perfect shot gave Westchester a 77-75 win, its second at-the-buzzer triumph in a row.

WEDNESDAY — ST. PATRICK'S DAY SPECIAL

The newly expanded tournament had already provided fans two overtimes, more than a handful of last minute decisions, and only two victory margins 10 points or greater. And the week was not yet half over.

Close action continued in Wednesday's consolation opener. Casper squandered leads of eight and 10, needing four clutch free throws by Gerald Campbell in the final two minutes, before eliminating State Fair, 65-59.

SECC-Burlington, too, blew a large second-half lead, its second in as many days, and was forced into overtime. Led by Everne Carr's 34 and Jerry Luckett's 32, the Blackhawks barely edged Johnson County, 107-106.

Then, guard Kevin Odoms scored Jamestown's final five points and put on a dribbling exhibition to run out the clock as the Jayhawks squeaked by Chipola, 79-77.

Suspense finally tapered off in the evening session. The opener was extremely sloppy, setting all-time tourney record for turnovers with 78, 41 by Connors State. Despite the errors, the Cowboys recorded their second straight easy win, downing Rhode Island, 91-76.

The most interesting aspect of the evening feature was its unique celebration of St. Patrick's Day: it was the 17th game of the tournament — and both teams wore green.

Otherwise, the contest was a mismatch. Columbia State totally dominated Bismarck on the boards, 46-21. Using a 10-0 spurt to gain a 53-39 advantage with 8:55 remaining, the Chargers coasted to a 73-63 victory.

In previous years, fans had measured the tournament's progress by the day of the week: the opening round was Tuesday and Wednesday; the quarterfinals Wednesday and Thursday; the semifinals Friday; and the championship Saturday.

The new expanded version altered that pattern. After nearly three days of continuous competition, fans were still confused,

The 1976 tournament's leading scorer with 110 points in four games, Ollie Mack (in air) later starred for the Pirates of East Carolina before spending three years in the NBA. (Photo courtesy of Rob Ludwig)

having to consult their programs to tell whether they were watching a first-round, second-round, or consolation contest.

With the evening finale, the official midpoint of the 1976 tournament, the fog cleared. The game between San Jacinto and DeKalb-South marked the tourney's first quarterfinal.

There was nothing landmark about the action, however. Despite problems at the guard position — Mike Maddox had a fever and Greg Stephens, foul trouble — DeKalb pressure forced San Jacinto into 37 turnovers. The Eagles overcame a nine-point deficit in the first-half to win, 75-65. Outstanding performances by San Jacinto's Ollie Mack and DeKalb's Jarvis Reynolds, each sharing game-honors with 28, provided the only major diversions.

THURSDAY — SLOW DOWN

With the opening rounds finally out of the way, the tournament was at a point when fan interest usually picked up. But, like Wednesday's nightcap, the other quarterfinals failed to match the intensity level of the first two days' play. The crowd even resorted to booing in the evening opener.

After Southern Idaho built a 26-12 advantage midway in the first period, Westchester gradually whittled the deficit to 30-28 with 14:43 left in the game before CSI extended the margin to 38-32.

As the score indicated, both sides were not in a hurry to put points on the board. With 10:30 to go, the contest went from first gear to neutral. Boyd Grant ordered his Golden Eagles to hold the ball. Westchester's Ralph Arietta countered by stubbornly keeping his Vikings packed in their 2-1-2 zone. For five minutes the only animation in the Arena came from the sidelines where fans vented their displeasure. Finally a referee's whistle interceded. Westchester was charged a technical for failing to force action.

Once action renewed, Southern Idaho quickly upped its advantage to 13 and coasted to a 57-47 victory.

In the evening feature, Mercer County fell behind Connors State by six early, before rallying to take an 11-point advantage. Deliberate as ever, Howie Landa's Vikings controlled the tempo, allowing Connors only one run in the second half. However, after the Cowboys pulled within four, 56-52, a floor-length pass to Lonnie Legette for an easy lay-up quashed the threat. Mercer County won, 64-54, holding Connors State 28 points below its average. The sole highlight for the Cowboys was James Bradley's game-high 25 points and 10 rebounds.

The most interesting game of the evening came last. Columbia State and Allegheny-Boyce remained abreast for most of the contest. Then, with 5:50 remaining, Willie Goldstone, Boyce's leading scorer, picked up his fifth foul. After Columbia State's Larry Cartwright made the first free throw, the officials noticed that the Saints had not substituted for Goldstone. A technical was called. Cartwright hit his second free throw plus the technical. Willie Wright followed with a field goal. The Chargers suddenly had a 66-61 lead and control of the game, eventually winning 79-72.

FRIDAY — THE BEST SURVIVE

Despite the increase in participants, and therefore, higher odds for upsets, the tournament's convoluted sorting process proved efficient. The four highest-ranked teams in each flight advanced to the semifinals.

Though two-time winner Mercer County remained in the race for the title, many considered the opener between No. 1 Southern Idaho and No. 4 DeKalb-South the true championship game. Both squads were familiar with the situation, having reached the same plateau the previous year. Each had experienced sophomore leaders: Kenny Davis and Andre Wakefield for the Golden Eagles and Jarvis Reynolds and Mike Maddox for DeKalb.[1] Stated DeKalb Coach Roger Couch of CSI, "They were well-coached and well-prepared. I didn't want to play him [Southern Idaho Coach Boyd Grant], and I don't think he wanted to play us."

One of the keys of the game was whether CSI could stop DeKalb's Jarvis Reynolds, one of the most highly-touted big men in junior college ranks. In two outings, the 6-8 center had already tallied 65 points and 25 rebounds.

Coach Boyd Grant's solution was that two hands were better than one. Working in shifts so they were always fresh, centers Ed Nickols and Gene Bowen held DeKalb's All-American candidate to one field goal and four points in the first half. Only 60-plus percent shooting, including long bombs by Ike and Andrew Osby, Tim Britt, and Tommy Bigby, kept the Georgians in the hunt, trailing 35-31 at intermission.

Bigby continued hot in the second period, lifting DeKalb into four ties with CSI.

Then, with 14:51 remaining, 6-6 Kim Goetz raced down the court, stopped on a dime at his wing position, and swished a 25-footer. It was only one of several for the excellent outside shooter — who had been relatively quiet in his three previous games — eventually netting him a game-high 25. More importantly, it gave Southern Idaho a lead it never again relinquished.

Boyd Grant's strategy worked. Nickols and Bowen held DeKalb's Reynolds to 12 points and 4 rebounds, effectively blocking off the middle, allowing Golden Eagle teammate Kenny Davis to grab rebounding honors with 11. With the 70-63 victory, Southern Idaho entered the title match for the second year in a row.

The other semifinal was not anticipated to be close. Mercer County had played for a championship two out of the past three years and three times since 1967. Columbia State's only previous tourney experience landed a seventh-place trophy in 1971, which was later forfeited.

The Chargers had demonstrated balanced scoring and excellent board strength in their first two games, however. When 6-10 Michael Davis, Mercer's only appreciable height, picked up three quick fouls, Columbia State took control. The Tennessee squad built a surprising 38-26 halftime advantage, then upped the margin to 15 early in the final period.

If tourney fans had been asked to state one characteristic which defined a Howie Landa team, their overwhelming reply would have been "scrappy." Even when winning back-to-back championships, Mercer County always seemed to be on the short end regarding natural talent. Yet, the Vikings were able to negate this disadvantage with poise and discipline, especially on defense.

With Davis playing with four fouls, Mercer County buckled down. Led by Phillip Mayo, who topped all scorers with 23, including 11 for 15 from the field, the Vikings went on a 21-

point tear in nine minutes. Columbia State scored only two.

Mercer County earned a 75-66 win and a chance at an unprecedented third title in four years.

SATURDAY — BECOMING A BRIDE

Among the trophy day afternoon crowd was one very interested spectator — Mrs. Auda L. Bell, grandmother of Lake Land Coach Chuck Bell. She pounded her cane in encouragement as the Lakers opened a 28-18 halftime lead and coasted to a 68-60 victory over Casper for sixth place. Said Coach Bell afterwards, "I am very proud of her and I'm sure she has seen more excitement here than in all her 83 years."

Bell expanded further on the tournament: "This has probably been nine of the best days of my life . . . The hospitality that the Hutchinson people have shown has been just great. I wouldn't mind living in Hutchinson someday."

The respect was mutual. Despite losing in the opening round, the Lakers became a crowd favorite. Lake Land possessed noticeable talent, in particular, 6-7 sophomore Doug Jemison, who won the tourney rebound crown with 42 in four games. But, it was team character which endeared the Lakers to fans.

One example was center Jim "Bull" Bramlett. According to Bell, the 6-5 freshman was "a rejected young man [who] lived at times in empty, abandoned cars in the ghettos of Decatur, Illinois. I found him to be a wonderful kid. Extremely strong. He did what he could do and stayed away from the things he couldn't." Because of his rough background, however, major colleges shied away. When Lake Land accepted him, "it just turned his life around," said Bell. "I had a real love for that kid, a real purpose for my stop in Lake Land."

The other shining example was 6-2 forward Chuck White. Bell described the Effingham, Illinois, frosh as a "very handsome blond-headed kid [who] had enough strength and wherewithal he could have pinched somebody's head off." Instead, in Lake Land's second game, with his man continually spitting in his face, White went about his business. "He maintained his composure which allowed us to win," said Bell. "They fell in love with him over that incident." Enough so that White was the hands-down recipient of the Sesher Sportsmanship Award.

With fans showing the effects of sitting through 30-plus games, the rest of the consolation trophy battles were contended without fanfare:

SECC of Burlington broke open a close game with a 14-4 spurt five minutes into the second half before downing Anderson, 84-74, for fifth;

Two tight zone defenses produced the lowest score of the week, as Allegheny-Boyce defeated Westchester, 54-45, for fourth;

And, after trailing for most of the first 27 minutes, DeKalb-

The 1976 tournament's leading assist man with 33 in four games, Obee Small Player Award winner Joe McKeown completed his collegiate career at Kent State University. (Photo courtesy of Kent State University)

---

[1] Mike Maddox, a Decatur, Georgia, native, did not play for DeKalb his freshman year, but had actually been a starting guard for the Hutchinson Blue Dragons. Wanting to return to his hometown, Maddox decided to transfer to DeKalb. Normally under NJCAA rules, he would not have been eligible his sophomore year. However, Hutchinson signed a release, allowing Maddox to play for the Eagles. There was one stipulation, though. By "gentleman's agreement," Maddox would not play should Hutchinson and DeKalb ever meet.
That meeting did occur in November in the Blue Dragon Classic. With Maddox on the bench, DeKalb won, 87-75.

outh scored 10 unanswered points to take command, beating Columbia State, 76-70, gaining third.

* * *

On paper, the 1976 championship belonged to Southern Idaho. The Golden Eagles were a solid, well-rounded squad with depth. They had quickness out front in Andre Wakefield and Dwight Williams, both superb defenders who often broke games open with steals. They had terrific scoring punch at the wings in Kim Goetz and Kenny Davis. And they had the oxen pair of Gene Bowen and Ed Nickols to share banging duty in the middle. In addition, there was Eric Hovey, who possessed Gary Koder-like intelligence and could be counted on to break up zones coming off the bench.

On the other hand, it was the same old story for Mercer County. Howie Landa had plenty of bodies with above average quickness to run in and out of the lineup, but only three key people to build on. Out front was 5-11 regional MVP Joe McKown, the Viking floor leader, who was noted for his crowd-pleasing assists. Scoring was primarily handled by 6-4 forward Phillip Mayo, a 1975 honorable mention All-American. And in the middle, muscular 6-10 Michael Davis took care of the boards at the rate of 12.7 rebounds a game.

But, even in the Vikings' strengths there was weakness. McKown was quick of hand, but slow of foot in comparison to CSI's guards. Mayo was an excellent talent, but had broken a leg earlier in the year and was still not up to his 1975 form. And Davis, a transfer from Shaw College in Detroit, was still developing, only in his second year of the sport.

Yet, with all the indicators pointing toward Southern Idaho, the title match was rated even. CSI had made five appearances in the past six years, had been highly ranked on each occasion, but had not won a crown, failing twice in the championship game. In comparison, Mercer County's Landa had gained a reputation as a master illusionist, who had already pulled two rabbits out of the hat and probably had a third hidden away somewhere.

There was one characteristic shared by both squads. Through the late 60s and early 70s, the Juco Tournament was noted as a run-and-gun show. The mid-70s still showcased several potent offenses, but a new pattern had developed. For the past two years, the teams with the best defensive averages played for the crown. In 1976 the pattern continued. Southern Idaho had held four opponents to a 60.5 average. Mercer's average against three was 62.7.

A conservative, deliberate pace was established immediately. Open shots were extremely limited (for the game, CSI shot 47 times, Mercer 49). It was the type of tempo where a 10-point lead was the equivalent to a 20-point margin in normal circumstances.

Though Southern Idaho held the edge all but twice in the first half, neither team was in definite command. After Mercer County took the lead 32-31 with 16:30 left in the game, CSI scored six straight, opening the biggest gap to that point. However, with 11:58 remaining, the Vikings were back within a pair.

Then came the key point in the contest. For 6½ minutes, Southern Idaho held Mercer scoreless. Led by Wakefield, the Golden Eagles surged to a 52-39 advantage, the largest of the game. From then on CSI simply protected the ball and shot free throws.

With a 62-50 victory, Southern Idaho, the perpetual bridesmaid, finally became a bride.

THE AFTERMATH — A SIGNIFICANT MEMORY

Though it was physically taxing and more expensive, the 1976 Juco Tournament gave fans their money's worth. Despite playing nine more games than usual, it was the closest event in tourney history with an average game margin of 7.2.

It also culminated in what many consider the best defensive title game ever. No Mercer County player hit double figures. Still, it required nearly flawless execution (only 8 CSI turnovers) to win.

Reflecting on the tournament, Boyd Grant stated, "I came in here [to Hutchinson] feeling we really had a good chance. I liked my team defensively. I liked my team's smartness. And, I liked our ability to shoot the ball. I really did feel positive for me, because I'm the most negative person in the world. I always think I'm going to have a losing season."

French MVP Kenny Davis' 91 points and 32 rebounds finally led Southern Idaho to a national championship after two previous Golden Eagle failures. Davis later played for the Arizona Wildcats. (Photo courtesy of the University of Arizona)

Two individuals in particular contributed to Grant's optimism.

One was sophomore guard Andre Wakefield, who, despite leading all scorers in the title contest (17), was most noted for his defense. Described Grant, "I've never coached anybody, even now, who could play defense any better than Andre could."

The 6-2 Chicago native was also the team leader. However, his disciplined approach to the game was newly acquired. Grant related that, as a freshman, Wakefield had terrible personal habits, including watching television until three or four in the morning. But, "by the time he was a sophomore," said Grant, "he'd beat me to breakfast and I would usually be to breakfast by 6:00 or 6:30. He would already have run four or five miles and already have drunk two or three bottles of orange juice. That was the type of conditioning that guy had. In fact, when they were recruiting him, all the coaches were shocked that he had such good habits."

The other key to Southern Idaho's success was Kenny Davis. The 6-8 sophomore led the Golden Eagles in scoring and rebounding, but his performances often went unnoticed. Even during the year, Twin Falls fans frequently commented that "Well, Kenny really didn't have a good game tonight" even though he might have scored 25 points and grabbed 15 rebounds. The reason for the oversight, Grant explained, was that Davis "played the whole game. In other words, it wasn't five or six minutes where he got six baskets and six rebounds." Grant likened him to a worker who never took a rest. "He labored the whole day, but did it at his own pace, instead of the guy who maybe worked hard for an hour, then took it easy for 15 minutes. It just seemed that no matter whether there was pressure or stress, he played with the same confidence."

Davis' contribution was not overlooked in the tournament, however. The selection committee chose him the French MVP.

One other person played an important role in the title, though he was reluctant to admit it. "Out in my hallway, the trophy sits where I was the National Junior College Coach of the Year in 1976," stated Grant. "I always take that trophy as [my] personal trophy for those kids winning the tournament rather than my coaching the win."

Still it was a significant accomplishment for Grant. "Probably I've had two great moments in coaching. One was winning the NIT [with Fresno State in 1983] . . . When they interviewed me after the NIT, they said, 'Is this the greatest honor you've ever received?' I said, 'Yes. One of them. The other one was when the team I coached won the National Junior College championship.'"

1976 TOURNAMENT BRACKET

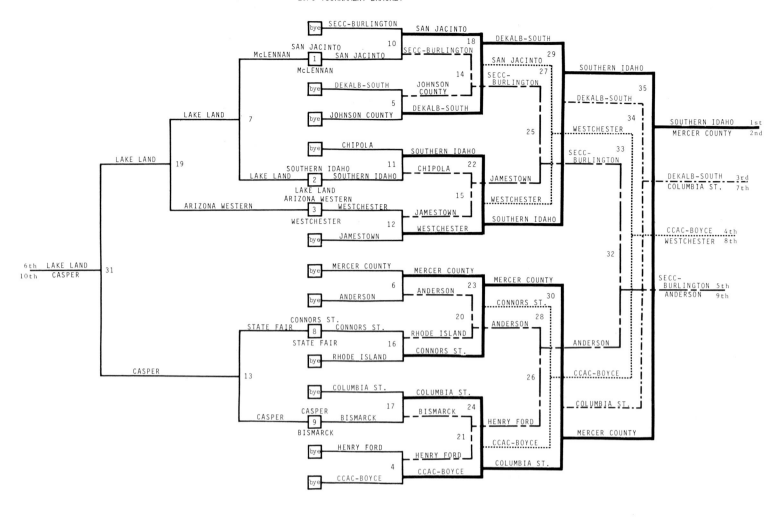

Tournament Results

Monday: Game
- 1   San Jacinto — 91 McLennan — 90
- 2   Southern Idaho — 71 Lake Land — 66
- 3   Westchester — 56 Arizona Western — 55
- 4   CCAC-Boyce — 69 Henry Ford — 59
- 5   DeKalb-South — 74 Johnson County — 67
- 6   Mercer County — 71 Anderson — 68

Tuesday: Game
- 7   Lake Land — 99 McLennan — 91
- 8   Connors St. — 90 State Fair — 63
- 9   Bismarck — 63 Casper — 58 OT
- 10   San Jacinto — 99 SECC-Burlington — 97 OT
- 11   Southern Idaho — 69 Chipola — 66
- 12   Westchester — 77 Jamestown — 75

Wednesday: Game
- 13   Casper — 65 State Fair — 59
- 14   SECC-Burlington — 107 Johnson County — 106 OT
- 15   Jamestown — 79 Chipola — 77
- 16   Connors St. — 91 Rhode Island — 76
- 17   Columbia St. — 73 Bismarck — 63
- 18   DeKalb-South — 75 San Jacinto — 65

Thursday: Game
- 19   Lake Land — 78 Arizona Western — 70
- 20   Anderson — 93 Rhode Island — 87
- 21   Henry Ford — 61 Bismarck — 47
- 22   Southern Idaho — 57 Westchester — 47
- 23   Mercer County — 64 Connors St. — 54
- 24   Columbia St. — 79 CCAC-Boyce — 72

Friday: Game
- 25   SECC-Burlington — 78 Jamestown — 74
- 26   Anderson — 68 Henry Ford — 59
- 27   Westchester — 81 San Jacinto — 78
- 28   CCAC-Boyce — 79 Connors St. — 77
- 29   Southern Idaho — 70 DeKalb-South — 63
- 30   Mercer County — 75 Columbia St. — 66

Saturday: Game
- 31   Lake Land — 68 Casper — 60
- 32   SECC-Burlington — 84 Anderson — 74
- 33   CCAC-Boyce — 54 Westchester — 45
- 34   DeKalb-South — 76 Columbia St. — 70
- 35   Southern Idaho — 62 Mercer County — 50

How They Finished in 1976

1. College of Southern Idaho
2. Mercer County Community College
3. DeKalb Community College, South Campus
4. Community College of Allegheny County, Boyce Campus
5. Southeastern Community College
6. Lake Land College
7. Columbia State Community College
8. Westchester Community College

All-Tournament Team

James Bradley — Connors State College
Kenny Davis — College of Southern Idaho
Michael Davis — Mercer County Community College
Larry Fitzgerald — Columbia State Community College
Doug Jemison — Lake Land College
Jerry Luckett — Southeastern Community College
Ollie Mack — San Jacinto College, Central Campus
Phillip Mayo — Mercer County Community College
Jarvis Reynolds — DeKalb Community College, South Campus
Andre Wakefield — College of Southern Idaho

Coach of the Tournament

Boyd Grant — College of Southern Idaho

French Most Valuable Player Award

Kenny Davis — College of Southern Idaho

Sesher Sportsmanship Award

Chuck White — Lake Land College

Bud Obee Outstanding Small Player Award

Joe McKeown — Mercer County Community College

Southern Idaho's All-Tourney selection Kim Goetz completed his collegiate career at San Diego State University. (Photo courtesy of San Diego State University, taken by Ernie Anderson)

Start with a three-day Class 3A Kansas State High School Tournament. End with a six-day National Juco Tournament. Sprinkle in a few NCAA tourney games and NBA games on the tube for good measure. Nearly 60 viewable basketball games in 10 days. For a basketball junkie, it was a heavenly recipe.

But, for the average fan living in Hutchinson it was too much. Despite being a memorable event, the 1977 expanded format of the NJCAA Basketball Tournament followed the previous year's lead. More and more fans decided against purchasing a season ticket, preferring to take their chances securing admission on selective evenings.

Besides the attendance decline, there was also disgruntlement in the ranks of the volunteers who put on the event. An extra day and nine additional games tipped the scales from an enjoyable communal experience to a taxing week of drudgery.

Neither the American Legion nor NJCAA co-sponsors liked the results. With the 1977 annual meeting, the tournament's experiment in expansion ended.

THE PARTICIPANTS

The final year of the expanded format again produced a top-flight tourney field highlighted by champions from the past seven years and eight of the last nine.

Heading the list of dignitaries was the consensus favorite — defending national champion College of Southern Idaho. Though the Golden Eagles returned only one starter (forward Kim Goetz), Coach Boyd Grant had done an excellent job of rebuilding; four CSI players were Region 18 all-stars. The Eagles started the year No. 1 and stayed there. They entered the national tournament 31-0, having established a 48-game win streak, a new junior college record, breaking the old mark of 42.

Southern Idaho's chief competition would come from the other former titleholders: No. 4 Western Texas College (31-3), featuring All-American candidate Lawrence Butler who scored 102 points in three Region 5 contests; No. 5 Independence Community Junior College (29-2), considered the best Kansas

Region	Team
1	Arizona Western College — Yuma, Arizona
2	Westark Community College — Fort Smith, Arkansas
3	Fulton-Montgomery Community College — Johnstown, New York
4	Lincoln Trail College — Robinson, Illinois
5	Western Texas College — Snyder, Texas
6	Independence Community Junior College — Independence, Kansas
7	Shelby State Community College — Memphis, Tennessee
8	Pensacola Junior College — Pensacola, Florida
9	Sheridan College — Sheridan, Wyoming
10	North Greenville College — Tigerville, South Carolina
11	Ellsworth Community College — Iowa Falls, Iowa
12	Vincennes University — Vincennes, Indiana
13	Normandale Community College — Bloomington, Minnesota
14	San Jacinto College, Central Campus — Pasadena, Texas
15	State University of New York Agricultural and Technical College at Farmingdale — Farmingdale, New York
16	Mineral Area College — Flat River, Missouri
18	College of Southern Idaho — Twin Falls, Idaho
19	Mercer County Community College — Trenton, New Jersey
20	Potomac State College of West Virginia University — Keyser, West Virginia
21	Rhode Island Junior College — Warwick, Rhode Island
22	Lawson State Community College — Birmingham, Alabama

representative in the past several years; No. 18 Vincennes University (25-4), guided by three-time Coach of the Year Allen Bradfield in his 25th year at the Trailblazer helm; San Jacinto College, Central Campus (30-6), featuring the 1976 tournament's leading scorer, Ollie Mack; Mercer County Community College (25-6), another defensive gem fashioned by Howie Landa; and Ellsworth Community College (23-8), going for a double after ranking first in the final football poll.

The other former participants — Arizona Western College (29-4), Normandale Community College (23-4), Westark Community College (25-6), North Greenville College (22-7), and Sheridan College (23-9) — were not in the same class. Their combined tourney record was 14-23. Only Westark, which appeared as Fort Smith Junior College in 1962, was above sub-.500 play in the nationals with a 2-2 mark. The highest any had finished was fifth by Arizona Western in 1972.

If a dark horse was to win the crown, it was more likely to come from the nine newcomers: Rhode Island Junior College (26-0), Lawson State Community College (30-2), Fulton-Montgomery Community College (30-3), SUNY-Farmingdale (26-3), Pensacola Junior College (28-4), Potomac State College (18-3), Shelby State Community College (26-5), Lincoln Trail

College (28-7), and Mineral Area College (22-10). No. 8 Rhode Island, No. 10 Lawson State, and No. 15 Pensacola, three of the top offensive squads in the country, appeared the best bets of keeping the former champions from adding to their trophy cases.

MONDAY — AWESOME LAWSON

The 30th annual NJCAA Basketball Tournament began with a bang. Powered by sophomore forward Larry Knight's game-high 29 points and 15 rebounds, unranked Ellsworth built a 17-point cushion in the first half, then held on to upset No. 18 Vincennes, 68-65.

The second game also featured fireworks, though of the lady-finger variety. Committing 10 turnovers in the first 10 minutes, Shelby State fell behind Potomac State by 11. Then, 5-9 Cleveland "Pee Wee" Jackson took charge, scoring a game-high 26, rallying the Saluqis to a 65-59 victory.

Outbursts were confined to one side in the afternoon finale. Establishing a new record for field goal percentage (68.4 percent), Mercer County disposed of Fulton-Montgomery with little trouble, 88-69. The only excitement came when the Vikings' ever-exuberant Howie Landa was whistled for two technical fouls, adding to his already prodigious total in tourney play.

The biggest explosion of the day occurred next.

Mention the name "Lawson State" to a longtime tourney fan today and it immediately conjures up a vision of blurred speed and popping nets. But, even when the Cougars entered the 1977 tournament, there were hints of their run-and-gun style; they had led the nation in scoring for two years and were currently second with a 101.2 average.

North Greenville matched baskets with the Alabamans — all 12 Lawson State players lived within a two-mile radius of the school — for 30 seconds of the evening opener. Then, the Cougars tore away on a 15-2 sprint and never slowed. By intermission, Lawson State was out in front, 69-46.

By game's end, the Lawson State totals were monumental: 120 shots, 63 field goals, 75 rebounds, and 137 points. Only the rebounding total was not an all-time tourney record. Seven Cougars hit double figures led by Edsel Brooks (27), Johnny High (23), and Keith McIntosh (20). It was their 22nd 100-point game of the year and one shy of their highest point production.

When asked what it felt like to score 90 points, more than any other team except Lawson State in the tournament's first two days, yet lose by 47, the second-widest margin in tourney history, North Greenville Coach Larry Wall could only respond, "It was very humbling."

Before the day began, the evening feature had been the game fans most wanted to see. When it became apparent that Independence's superior height, scoring balance (11 of 12 Pirates who played scored four or more points), and excellent pressure defense outclassed Rhode Island, fan attention wavered. The topic on everyone's tongue was the unbelievable performance by "Awesome Lawson." Consequently, Independence received little fanfare, handing Rhode Island its first loss of the year, 87-59, holding the Knights nearly 40 points below their average.

Sheridan's 82-76 defeat of Arizona Western in the nightcap went completely unnoticed.

TUESDAY — NAIL-BITING DIVERSIONS

Over morning coffee and rolls, the preferred topic of conversation was still the exploits of Lawson State. Fans were eager to see the running Cougars again, but had to wait until Wednesday to do so. In the meantime, four consecutive cliff-hangers provided excellent diversion.

The nail-biting action started with the matinee feature when Mark Gulmire made a last-second 20-footer to lift North Greenville over Rhode Island, 80-79, in consolation play.

Unranked Ellsworth made the afternoon finale interesting by overcoming a nine-point deficit to take a 30-26 halftime lead over No. 4 Western Texas.

Then, with 17:06 remaining, Ellsworth on top 35-34, Panther Coach Bud Fischer was slapped with two technicals for protesting a call which erased a Larry Knight basket after the ba[ll] bounced off the top of the backboard and through. Alle[n] Corder hit three of four penalty shots and Western Texas adde[d] six more unanswered points, putting Ellsworth back in the hol[e] 43-35.

With 10:56 to go, trailing by 10, the Panthers made anoth[er] run. At the 3:50 mark, Knight hit a turnaround jumper to tie th[e] score, 55-all. A minute later he hit again from the baseline, pu[t]ting Ellsworth back on top. The Panthers then held on, downin[g] Western Texas, 65-62.

Though 6-7, 225-pound Knight played an important role [in] the key moments of the contest, Western Texas stifled Ell[s]worth's inside game, outrebounding the Panthers, 43-34, 6-[?] Westerner forward Larry Orton leading the effort with 17.

The upset was triggered instead by terrific guard play. Sa[id] Ellsworth's Fischer, "We lived and died with the jump shot th[e] first part of the season before we got Knight [who transferre[d] from Indiana State] and it came through for us today." Th[e] backcourt tandem of Dennis Van Mathis and John Jones led a[ll] scorers with 24 and 23, respectively.

Action in the third consecutive tension-builder began eve[n] before the opening tip. After a San Jacinto player dunked durin[g] warm-ups (a no-no at the time), Shelby State took a pre-gam[e] one-point advantage with Pee Wee Jackson's successful pena[l]ty shot.

When the contest officially started, it quickly developed int[o] a basket-trading affair and remained so until San Jacinto gaine[d] control down the stretch.

With 3:54 to go, Shelby's Jackson was fouled, pulling a le[g] muscle in the process. Despite the injury, he sank two fre[e] throws, drawing the Saluqis within a basket.

San Jacinto held the ball.

At the 1:58 mark, Shelby's LeRoy Stokes stole the ball an[d] drove for the tie at 77-all.

Again, San Jacinto held the ball.

Shelby State fouled three straight times. The first two had n[o] effect since the Saluqis were under the foul limit. The fin[al] infraction came with four seconds showing. Ollie Mack calm[ly] hit both free attempts, giving him a game-high 29 points and lif[t]ing San Jacinto to a 79-77 win.

The fourth successive nerve-racker was the best.

The evening feature pitted two-time national champion Me[r]cer County against first-time participant SUNY-Farmingdal[e.] Beforehand, no one figured it to be close. But, the Aggies fro[m] Farmingdale played tough throughout. With 2:08 remainin[g,] the New Yorkers were even with Mercer, 61-all, and held po[s]session. For underdog-loving Hutchinson fans, it was the ide[al] Cinderella scenario.

The Aggies were in serious trouble, however. At the begin[n]ing of the year, Coach Tom Galeazzi had started with 12 pla[y]ers, then lost three to academic ineligibility. Another quit tw[o] weeks before the end of the season to work for the U.S. Post[al] Service. What remained was an excellent starting five — all ha[d] registered a 30-point game during the year — but little els[e.] Described Galeazzi, "The biggest guy on the bench was me an[d] I'm only about 5-10 or -11."

With the most important victory in Farmingdale's histor[y] within reach, Galeazzi had already dipped into his meag[er] reserves. His two tallest players and best rebounders, 6-5 Ma[rk] Graebe and 6-4 Reggie Parker, were beside him with five foul[s.] Another player was close to joining them with four.

Under the circumstances, Galeazzi had only one logic[al] option — hold for the last shot. "I honestly felt, if we gave th[e] ball back to Mercer, even [if] we were ahead, we could get i[nto] a situation where they put the ball inside and we'd get caug[ht] with a three-point play."

Then, with 1:03 remaining, Galeazzi's plan was foiled. Fo[r]ward Richard Hall drove the lane and scored, giving Farming[s]dale the lead.

In the next few seconds, Galeazzi and the heavily partisa[n] audience sweated as Mercer took aim twice and missed. Fina[l]ly, with 21 seconds left, Mercer fouled Charles Aydelott. Th[e] freshman guard hit the front end of one-and-one, sealing th[e] upset. The final: Farmingdale — 66, Mercer County — 61.

The day's finale was less exacting on fans. There was an exci[t]ing dunking show between Lincoln Trail's 6-11 Richard Johnso[n] and Southern Idaho's 6-8 Antonio Martin. But, otherwise, it wa[s] another straightforward win for the nation's No. 1 team. Led by Kim Goetz's 23 points, CSI extended its winning streak to 49, downing Lincoln Trail, 76-66.

WEDNESDAY — JUST STANDING AROUND

Normally, a Kansas entrant attracted a good crowd whenever it played. But, with the tournament nearing its midpoint and the high-powered Lawson State Cougars on tap later that evening, few were interested in rousing early to catch an 11 a.m. game which most expected to be one-sided.

After taking a 17-point first-half lead, Independence also displayed problems with motivation. The Pirates did little to stop what Mineral Area Coach Bob Sechrest called his "GMA" offense — "General Milling Around" — and did even less to put points on the board themselves. In the final five minutes, Independence scored only once from the field (that on a goal-tending call) and hit only three of seven free throws, including missing the front end of two one-and-ones. The No. 5 Pirates were fortunate to survive with a 67-61 victory.

In contrast, fans had no motivational problems getting to the tip-off of the evening session at 5:30 p.m. Offices were left early and suppers skipped in favor of witnessing the talk of the tournament — Awesome Lawson.

What the early-arrivers saw was not what they expected. With 8:40 left in the opening period, Lawson State trailed Normandale, 29-28.

Lawson Coach Eldridge O. Turner was equally unhappy. "That first bunch was standing around and you can't play basketball standing around."

Following wholesale substitutions, the results were more to fan liking. In the final 8:40 of the half, Lawson State scored 33 points, taking a commanding 61-39 advantage.

To the delight of the crowd, the Cougar's high-speed express continued in the second half, producing more unbelievable totals: 102 shots, 69 rebounds, and 113 points. Normandale fared better than North Greenville, Lawson's first victim, but still fell short by 22.

Run-and-gun was also the name of the game in the evening feature. Westark entered the tournament as the nation's top defense, allowing 59 points per game. By intermission, Pensacola had already netted 43. The second half was even worse, the Pirates romping past Westark, 95-61.

In the day's finale, the opening quarterfinal, Ellsworth built a comfortable 57-45 lead with 12:45 to go only to see Sheridan slice it to three. Ellsworth rebuilt the advantage to 11, but the Generals again rallied, drawing within three, 75-72, with 4:22 remaining.

Bothered by Sheridan's zone press, the Panthers went to a control game. The delay first produced an easy Jeff Miller layup. Then a powerful dunk by Larry Knight, his third such authoritative score of the night, decided matters. Ellsworth won, 83-76, led by Knight's game-high 23 points and 12 rebounds.

THURSDAY — SUPER SUBS, SUPER DEFENSE, SUPER WIN

Each of the remaining quarterfinals offered something of interest for everyone. The opener featured Cinderella favorite SUNY-Farmingdale. Next came the showdown between local favorite Independence versus No. 1 Southern Idaho. Finally, there was highly popular Lawson State in a running rematch with Pensacola, one of only two teams to outrace the Cougars during the year.

The first contest was a game of spurts, neither team able to sustain an advantage. The deciding spurt came with 14 minutes to play. San Jacinto led Farmingdale, 56-52, when forward Ollie Mack hit six of eight unanswered Raven points.

With 6-11 center Alton Lister on the bench with four fouls, San Jacinto decided to slow the tempo to protect the comfortable lead through the final 10 minutes. Fouls and free throws widened the Raven advantage. Behind Mack's game-high 24 points and Lister's game-high 14 rebounds (part of a 47-29 Raven board blitz), San Jacinto downed Farmingdale, 85-68.

The feature was a raucous battle even before the opening tip, the Independence and Southern Idaho bands trying to top each other in volume. The decibel level on the local side reached new highs as Independence started fast, taking an early 22-16 advantage.

The Southern Idaho Golden Eagles put a damper on the proceedings, calmly collecting themselves and gaining control of the game. With 3:15 remaining in the half, CSI was on top, 34-27.

Then came the key point in the contest. In rapid succession, Kevin Eberhart hit an 18-footer, Leslie McLeod scored a three-point play on a spectacular give-and-go fast break, and Thomas Louden netted three free throws, putting Independence back on top, 35-34, with 1:22 left.

After Rennie Kelly stole the ball, the Pirates held for the final shot. As time wound down, the ball ended in the hands of McLeod, an excellent, hard-nosed defensive player, but the least likely Pirate to be shooting under such circumstances — and especially from deep in the corner. The 6-4 New York frosh cooly drilled it at the buzzer.

The building exploded as if the game had ended. The Pirates raced to the dressing room on an emotional high which did not dissipate once play resumed. By the 6:08 mark, Independence had rolled to a commanding 69-52 margin, signaling the end of Southern Idaho's nearly two-year reign atop the junior college basketball world and the end of the Eagles' magnificent 49-game win streak.

Two factors keyed the Pirates' impressive 74-66 victory.

First was superb depth. Independence reserves outscored starters, 39-35, with super sub Louden leading all Pirates with 16.

Second was ever present defensive pressure. CSI Coach Boyd Grant attributed the latter to opposing mentor, Dan Wall. "He didn't just press you one way. He hit you with about three different presses and, about the time you thought you had something solved, he'd press you a different way . . . I just thought he did a masterful job of coaching."

The emphasis switched from defense to offense in the nightcap as Lawson State again exercised its brilliant running attack, sprinting to a 69-51 halftime lead.

Then sophomore guard Russell Saunders, who hit 19 of his team-leading 31 in the final period, rallied Pensacola. With 2:10 remaining, Scott Thomas hit a jumper to pull the Pirates within four, 104-100.

Ironically, the greatest offensive team in the tournament's history decided to slow it down. Pensacola was forced to foul. Lawson State scored its final nine points from the line, preserving a 113-104 victory.

FRIDAY — TURNING THE TABLES

With all eyes focused on the semifinals, Friday's consolation action normally attracted little attention. In 1977, there were two notable exceptions.

In the afternoon finale, the Farmingdale Aggies saw a nine-point lead evaporate in the final 3½ minutes, then breathed a sigh of relief when a bad pass prevented Sheridan from attempting the potential game-winner. Farmingdale escaped with an 84-83 win.

Though the Aggies' Mark Graebe and Reggie Parker shared game honors with 23 apiece, it was Graebe who was the star. The Holbrook, New York, sophomore hit 13 of 16 from the line and pulled down a game-high 12 rebounds.

Coach Tom Galeazzi described Graebe as a "super competitor" who epitomized his scrappy team. "We had a race that we ran at the end of practice. We called it 'The Suicide.' We had a couple of quick black kids on the team. [But] he [Graebe] never once lost a race the entire year — and he was our biggest guy."

Graebe was an accomplished punter, an All-Long Island split end in high school, and had been offered a football scholarship at North Carolina. From a basketball standpoint, no one was interested. Said Galeazzi, "There wasn't one Division I school recruiting him till we went to Hutchinson." Efforts like that against Sheridan not only won Graebe a starting position at Pepperdine, but also caught the attention of the tournament awards committee which later honored him with the Sesher Sportsmanship Award.

The other consolation game of note opened the evening session. Pensacola overcame Southern Idaho's early domination to overtake the Golden Eagles, eliminating the defending champs, 76-65. It was the only time in Boyd Grant's tenure at CSI (he accepted the head coaching job at Fresno State later that spring) that the Eagles lost two in a row.

With early-round upsets of ranked teams and with Lawson State and Independence hogging the headlines in the lower bracket, the upper bracket gained the reputation during the week as having weaker teams. Interestingly enough, however, the upper bracket furnished the closer, more exciting games. The opening semifinal was no exception.

Trailing Ellsworth by three with just under eight minutes remaining, San Jacinto decided to press, a strategy which Coach Wayne Ballard had wanted to save until later. The move produced immediate results, though.

First, the Ravens forced Ellsworth into a five-second count on an inbounds play, Ken Logan following with a field goal.

Then, David Williams stole the subsequent inbounds pass, Arthur Ross converting for another two.

Finally, San Jacinto pressure kept Ellsworth from crossing midcourt in 10 seconds. With the ensuing Ollie Mack jumper, momentum swung entirely to the Raven side. San Jacinto slowed the tempo and held on, winning the tight duel, 72-71.

The predominantly Kansas crowd only hoped the other semifinal would be as close. The facts, however, appeared insurmountable. In three games, Lawson State had already scored 363 points and grabbed 198 rebounds — just 39 and 12 off the all-time records for each category, respectively. At their current pace, the Cougars would shatter both marks long before halftime.

In terms of speed and quickness, Lawson State was peerless. In terms of depth, the Alabamans were at least on a par with Independence, the deepest squad in the tournament. Coach Eldridge O. Turner proved in the Normandale game that, no matter who he substituted, the ball still went through the net at an incredible rate. Only in terms of defense, did the Cougars appear to have a weakness.

Could Awesome Lawson be stopped?

The answer came quickly. After Rennie Kelly scored the first basket 20 seconds into the game, Independence never looked back.

The Pirates totally shut down Lawson's lauded running attack. "They would start to come up the floor on their break," explained Independence Coach Dan Wall, "and we had a ¾- or a half-court trap with [6-10] Chester [Giles] at the point. It really slowed them down just a little bit more than they wanted. They ended up firing a shot that they didn't want to shoot."

Giles' work in the middle was particularly impressive. Besides contributing 20 points and 20 rebounds, he blocked several shots and altered many more. Said Lawson assistant Russell Jackson, "Our kids were shooting their shots high to get them over Giles and that hurt our percentage [44 percent]."

The constant Pirate pressure had its effect. Related Wall, "Johnny High [a future NBA player who was Lawson's top scorer and rebounder] later told me in an all-star game in San Antonio that it was the most frustrated he'd ever been."

At the offensive end, Independence introduced a fast break attack of its own, scoring at will, turning the tables on the Cougars, 101-87.

SATURDAY — WASN'T MEANT TO BE

Vincennes and North Greenville tipped off trophy day by combining for only 10 fouls, an all-time tourney low. North Greenville's record four fouls allowed just two free throw opportunities (both of which were missed), helping the Mounties surprise Vincennes, 85-72, for seventh-place.

In the battle for sixth, Lincoln Trail's Tom Gable set a four-game tourney record for assists (39) and teammate Michael "Fly" Gray outdueled Western Texas's Lawrence Butler, 33 to 24, to take the four-game scoring title with 109 points (to Butler's 103).[1] However, it was the Westerners who took the prize, coming from eight down in the second half to win, 92-87.

After one of the more lackluster games of the week, fifth-place went to Pensacola, 76-70, over SUNY-Farmingdale.

Before the third-place game, Ellsworth Coach Bud Fischer told his team to "run back on defense and walk up on offense." It was the Panthers only chance against Lawson State.

Partly because the strategy was well-executed and partly

Six-four John Jones had one of the few bright moments for Ellsworth in semifinal match with San Jacinto, dunking over 6-11 Alton Lister. Jones wo[uld] later matriculate to Stephen F. Austin University while Lister went on to sta[te] Arizona State University and spend over 6 years in the NBA. (Photo courtes[y] Bud Fischer)

because Lawson showed the effects of playing five games in [5] days, Ellsworth prevented any long runs by the Cougars. Wi[th] 2:17 remaining, the Panthers led, 69-67. Key free throws [by] guards Dennis Van Mathis and John Jones preserved an 82-[??] Ellsworth win.

The Panther's star was again Larry Knight. The Detroit nati[ve] led everyone with 30 points and 16 rebounds. His 113-poi[nt] total for the week was one shy of the tourney leader. Howeve[r,] his 65 rebounds stood all alone, an indication of the NCAA to[p-] 10 average he would carry the next two years at Loyola of C[hi-] cago.

Though held to 19, his lowest total of the week, Lawso[n] State's Johnny High edged Knight for the tourney scorin[g] crown. The 6-3 sophomore drew attention to himself not on[ly] with smooth, all-round excellent play, scoring 114 points an[d] grabbing 46 rebounds, but also because he wore gold tassles [on] his shoes. It was a trademark he took with him to Nevada-Re[no] (coached by former juco tourney champion Jim Carey) whe[re] High and Lincoln Trail's Michael "Fly" Gray became the fas[t-] paced, tassled twosome known popularly as "The Fly and Hi[gh] Show."

* * *

It had been 14 years since Independence's last tourne[y] appearance. Pirate fans were eager and confident that the 19[??] event would end the same way — with a title.

Consequently, the small southeastern Kansas communi[ty] experienced a mass exodus. Followers dropped everything a[nd] travelled the nearly 200 miles to Hutchinson with no guarant[ee] of entrance into the Sports Arena on arrival. Though appro[xi-] mately 1,000 were squeezed in — one of the largest no[n-] Hutchinson contingents in tourney history — several made t[he] trip only to listen to the championship game on their car rad[io] in the Arena parking lot.

After stopping the longest winning streak in junior colle[ge] history, then downing the greatest offensive squad in tourn[ey] annals in back-to-back nights, Independence was the conse[n-] sus favorite of the 8,000-strong crowd. Many predicted a blo[w]out.

Independence Coach Dan Wall also feared a lopsided mat[ch] — the other way. "I feared a blow out [by San Jacinto] becau[se] we had blown our wad. I didn't know if our kids had enou[gh] left." The Pirates had played four games in five days to reach t[he] title tilt; San Jacinto, only three.

The Ravens also possessed excellent talent in All-Americ[ans] Ollie Mack and center Alton Lister, both of whom would lat[er]

---

[1] Lawrence Butler got his just reward two years later when he led the nation in scoring at Idaho State, averaging 30.1 points per game — over two points better than Indiana State's Player of the Year, Larry Bird.

Ellsworth's Larry Knight (No. 32) fell one point short of winning the 1977 scoring title, netting 113 points in five games, but did win the rebound title with 65 boards. The next two years, Knight was a top-10 rebounder in the NCAA at Loyola-Chicago. (Photo courtesy of Bud Fischer)

play in the NBA.

The most overlooked factor, however, was San Jacinto's competitive spirit. Two of the Ravens' tourney wins were by character-building, whisker-thin margins. An even better example was the final play-off game of the Region 14 championship. Trailing by eight with 3:20 left in regulation, San Jacinto rallied, forcing four overtimes before downing Henderson County Junior College, 80-78. The Ravens played with such determination that afterwards the victor's locker room was as silent as the loser's, everyone having collapsed in exhaustion.

It was that same dogged determination which sparked San Jacinto from an eight-point deficit, the largest of the game. At intermission the Independence advantage was down to 40-36. After Chris Gonser's swishing 20-footer and Mack's breakaway jam dunk in the first 1:03 of the final period, the Ravens served notice that the crown could only be won at a price.

Because both teams pressed, action took place from end line to end line. Aggressive defense resulted in numerous steals and offensive charges. Neither side was able to maintain an advantage for long. It all came down to the final minute.

With 1:03 remaining, Lister beat Chester Giles down low for stuff, pulling San Jacinto within a basket, 71-69.

On the subsequent play, Independence's Leslie McLeod drove from the left wing. As Lister blocked the shot cleanly, a whistle blew. When the accusing finger pointed in his direction, Lister charged the official. He did not realize that the call was for a foul away from the play and that the culprit was actually teammate Arthur Ross who was standing in a direct line between Lister and the official. Nonetheless, Lister's reaction drew a technical.

It was a controversial call in such a critical situation. Stated Raven Coach Wayne Ballard, "He [Lister] didn't cuss him or do anything but say, 'Who? Me?' [The official NJCAA game film confirms this.] Something like that, a show of emotion in a national championship game, you let the players decide it, not with a technical."

Rennie Kelly, who was already six for six from the line, calmly hit three more, extending Independence's lead to 74-69 with :53 seconds to go.

The game was not over, however. After Pirate Thomas Louden missed the front end of one-and-one, Mack broke free

underneath for two, reducing the gap to three with 21 seconds left.

On the ensuing inbounds play, Raven David Williams tied up Louden. Independence won the tip, but Kelly's fast break outlet was picked off by Mack. To stop a break the other way, Kelly fouled Williams.

After Williams hit the first free throw, Coach Ballard called the final San Jacinto time-out. He instructed the Mt. Vernon, New York, freshman — younger brother of former Ravens Ray and Sam — to purposely miss to Lister's side of the lane.

The plan could not have worked better. Williams banged the second free throw hard off the heel of the rim. The ball bounded wildly toward Lister and, in the rebound scramble, was knocked out of bounds off an Independence player. San Jacinto had 10 seconds to score the tying basket.

The Ravens again executed to Ballard's specifications, working the ball inside to Lister. The freshman faked right, turned left, and went up for a 10-footer.

The shot did not count, however. Lister was whistled for travelling. Said Ballard, "He was just doing what he was taught and they called walking on him . . . One of those, I guess, that wasn't meant to be."

With four seconds left, San Jacinto could only foul. Louden stepped to the line, made the first, missed the second, but immediately raised his arm and waved it around, heralding Independence's 75-72 victory.

THE AFTERMATH — WE'LL BE BACK

Though teammate Chester Giles won the French Most Valuable Player Award, Rennie Kelly was the heart of the Independence Pirates. The 6-4 Chicago native hurt his back during the Southern Idaho game and aggravated it further against Lawson State. In the title game, he was heavily taped and hurting. But, according to Coach Dan Wall, "He was such a gutty, great competitor that he played through that pain." He was the leading scorer for the Pirates with 21.

More important, he was a calm, rational leader. Toward the end of the title game, between Lister's walking violation and Louden's being fouled, no time ran off the clock, causing Coach Wall to race to the scorer's table in angry protest.

"The next thing I knew," said Wall, "I had two big hands around me, carrying me back to the bench. I look around and it was Rennie. He grabbed me, took me over to the chair, sat me down, put his finger in my chest, and said, 'You sit there and be quiet. We don't need a technical. We're going to win this.' "

With the loss of Kelly, Giles, and four other sophomores after graduation, it was understandable that Coach Wall would accept the first-place trophy with the remark, "We're very thankful we could win." With a bench of freshmen which had contributed 42 percent of Independence's tourney scoring, it was also no surprise that he ended with, "We'll be back next year."

The heart and soul of the 1977 champs, Rennie Kelly led Independence scoring with 71 points, including nine crucial free throws in the title tilt. Kelly continued his collegiate career at UCLA. (Photo courtesy of Independence Community College)

Tournament Results

Monday: Game

1	Ellsworth — 68 Vincennes — 65
2	Shelby St. — 65 Potomac St. — 59
3	Mercer County — 88 Fulton-Montgomery — 69
4	Lawson St. — 137 North Greenville — 90
5	Independence — 87 Rhode Island — 59
6	Sheridan — 82 Arizona Western — 76

Tuesday: Game

7	Vincennes — 80 Potomac St. — 61
8	North Greenville — 80 Rhode Island — 79
9	Ellsworth — 65 Western Texas — 62
10	San Jacinto — 79 Shelby St. — 77
11	SUNY-Farmingdale — 66 Mercer County — 61
12	Southern Idaho — 76 Lincoln Trail — 66

Wednesday: Game

13	Independence — 67 Mineral Area — 61
14	Western Texas — 93 Arizona Western — 59
15	Vincennes — 92 Fulton-Montgomery — 72
16	Lawson St. — 113 Normandale — 91
17	Pensacola — 95 Westark — 61
18	Ellsworth — 83 Sheridan — 76

Thursday: Game

19	Lincoln Trail — 75 Mineral Area — 70
20	Westark — 76 Normandale — 69
21	Mercer County — 73 Shelby St. — 61
22	San Jacinto — 85 SUNY-Farmingdale — 68
23	Independence — 74 Southern Idaho — 66
24	Lawson St. — 113 Pensacola — 104

Friday: Game

25	Western Texas — 58 Mercer County — 52
26	Lincoln Trail — 73 Westark — 70
27	SUNY-Farmingdale — 84 Sheridan — 83
28	Pensacola — 76 Southern Idaho — 65
29	San Jacinto — 72 Ellsworth — 71
30	Independence — 101 Lawson St. — 87

Saturday: Game

31	North Greenville — 85 Vincennes — 72
32	Western Texas — 92 Lincoln Trail — 87
33	Pensacola — 76 SUNY-Farmingdale — 70
34	Ellsworth — 82 Lawson St. — 76
35	Independence — 75 San Jacinto — 72

How They Finished in 1977

1. Independence Community Junior College
2. San Jacinto College, Central Campus
3. Ellsworth Community College
4. Lawson State Community College
5. Pensacola Junior College
6. Western Texas College
7. North Greenville College
8. State University of New York Agricultural and Technical College at Farmingdale

All-Tournament Team

Lawrence Butler — Western Texas College
Chester Giles — Independence Community Junior College
Mark Graebe — State University of New York Agricultural and Technical College at Farmingdale
Michael "Fly" Gray — Lincoln Trail College
Kim Goetz — College of Southern Idaho
Johnny High — Lawson State Community College
Rennie Kelly — Independence Community Junior College
Larry Knight — Ellsworth Community College
Ollie Mack — San Jacinto College, Central Campus
Russell Saunders — Pensacola Junior College

Coach of the Tournament

Dan Wall — Independence Community Junior College

French Most Valuable Player Award

Chester Giles — Independence Community Junior College

Sesher Sportsmanship Award

Mark Graebe — State University of New York Agricultural and Technical College at Farmingdale

Bud Obee Outstanding Small Player Award

Russell Saunders — Pensacola Junior College

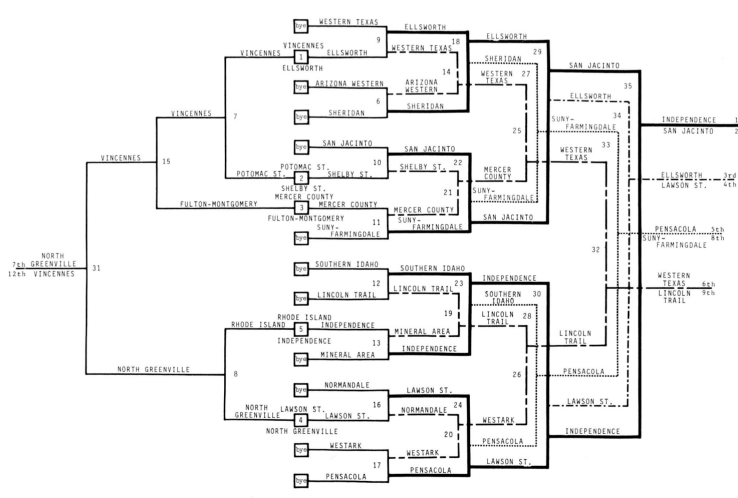

1977 TOURNAMENT BRACKET

an Wall was unable to back up the prediction he made on accepting Independence's 1977 first-place trophy. Later that spring, he moved to San Marcos, Texas, as head coach at Southwest Texas State.

When Missouri Western assistant Lynn Cundiff arrived on the scene as Wall's replacement, however, he immediately echoed Wall's confidence, stating, "The Pirates will win back-to-back national titles."

Later, Cundiff admitted that he made the remark "without really knowing." Since the city of Independence was still on a championship high, it appeared the wise thing to say. When asked by the press back at Missouri Western if taking over the head job of a defending champion was a dangerous career step, Cundiff replied, "Dangerous? It is suicide. All the people expect to win again."

The pressure was its worst when Independence started 7-4.

Then, three players became eligible at semester. Cundiff's Pirates steadily improved, entering the Region 6 tournament with a 22-7 mark and a six-game win streak. They knocked off No. 18 Cowley County Community College, 75-74, in overtime on Cowley's home floor, then traveling to Dodge City, topped the Conquistadors, 83-74, for the title and a chance to become the first Kansas team to repeat as national champion.

THE PARTICIPANTS

Region	Team
1	Mesa Community College — Mesa, Arizona
2	Westark Community College — Fort Smith, Arkansas
3	Niagara County Community College — Sanborn, New York
5	Western Texas College — Snyder, Texas
6	Independence Community Junior College — Independence, Kansas
7	Columbia State Community College — Columbia, Tennessee
8	Palm Beach Junior College — Lake Worth, Florida
9	Casper College — Casper, Wyoming
10	Anderson College — Anderson, South Carolina
12	Vincennes University — Vincennes, Indiana
16	Three Rivers Community College — Poplar Bluff, Missouri
17	Middle Georgia College — Cochran, Georgia
18	North Idaho College — Coeur d'Alene, Idaho
19	Essex County College — Newark, New Jersey
20	Community College of Baltimore — Baltimore, Maryland
22	James H. Faulkner State Junior College — Bay Minette, Alabama
Lost in First-Round Play-Offs:[1]	
4	Wabash Valley College — Mt. Carmel, Illinois
11	Grand View College — Des Moines, Iowa
13	Inver Hills Community College — Inver Grove Heights, Minnesota
14	Navarro College — Corsicana, Texas
15	New York City Community College — New York, New York
21	Post College — Waterbury, Connecticut

The No. 3 scorer in the 1978 tournament (84 points), Independence's Bobby Potts later starred at North Carolina-Charlotte, leading the Forty-Niners in scoring with 20.9 average for the 1981-82 season. (Photo courtesy of UNC-Charlotte)

Only six of the top 20 junior college teams made it to Hutchinson in 1978: No. 2 Casper College (32-3), No. 6 Community College of Baltimore (30-2), No. 7 Essex County Community College (28-3), No. 8 Niagara County Community College (22-0), No. 15 Anderson College (25-5), and No. 17 Vincennes University (26-5).

Of these, only Casper, with a runner-up trophy in seven appearances, and three-time champ Vincennes, making its 11th appearance in 14 years, possessed proven tourney credentials.

The others were question marks. Baltimore was making its first trip to the nationals. Essex County had yet to win a game in national competition. And Niagara County and Anderson had yet to win in the first round.

---

[1] With the end of the tourney's expanded format, the NJCAA went back to a system of play-offs to reduce 22 (later 24) regional winners to a 16-team field. Unlike before, these one-game play-offs, held at varying sites around the country, were designated "the first round" of the national tournament. This change in nomenclature led to confusion regarding participation records. Though all NJCAA regional winners have "officially" qualified for the national tournament since 1978, for the purposes of this book, all records are based on only those schools which participated at Hutchinson.

Given these circumstances — plus the fact that the 16-team field had a combined winning percentage of 78.2 percent, the lowest in 25 years — it was understandable that unranked defending champion Independence was immediately considered a top contender.

Of the other unranked former participants, only 1975 champ Western Texas College (27-7, with new head coach Nolan Richardson at the helm) had made its mark in tourney annals. Columbia State Community College (26-5), Westark Community College (25-8), and Three Rivers Community College (26-10) were all past trophy winners, but had yet to make a big splash.

Besides Baltimore, the only newcomer of note was North Idaho College (24-6) which downed 1976 titleholder College of Southern Idaho (now headed by former Western Texas coach Mike Mitchell), 60-54, in overtime in the Region 18 final. The rest were anomalies: Mesa Community College (21-9), Middle Georgia College (19-11), Faulkner State Junior College (20-15), and Palm Beach Junior College (15-15). The success of the latter two was especially unaccountable.

In the Region 22 tournament, George C. Wallace State Community College of Selma started a game wearing all even-numbered uniforms though the scorebook listed odd numbers. Since six Wallace State players saw action, six technicals were called. Faulkner State made four of them and won, 56-55. Then, in the final, the Red Eagles upset No. 9 John C. Calhoun State Community College in overtime.

Even more inexplicable was Palm Beach which lost six players, one a 6-10 center, to grades after the first semester. With only eight men on the roster, the Pacers upended the top three seeds in the Region 8 tournament, including No. 13 Florida College of Temple Terrace, 78-74, in the final.

There were no sure bets.

TUESDAY — A BOULDER OUT OF CONTROL

The cheering sections Eastern schools normally brought to Hutchinson were small at best. In the case of Community College of Baltimore, besides five cheerleaders, the following consisted of one fan. That lone rooter made a difference, however.

Dressed in a red sweat suit and red T-shirt with "Jerry Phipps CCB Red Devils" emblazoned in red across the front, a bearded Ron Berry came alive during time-outs, wending his way from his position on the Baltimore bench to the opposite end of the court. There he would employ a menacing leer and an assortment of finger waggles to put a whammy on the opposing team. It was an act that was not only appreciated by the audience, but also by the Red Devil squad. After winning the state tournament, the Baltimore team presented Berry with a trophy and a piece of the victory net.

The efforts of the "Super Hexer" appeared effective at the beginning of the tourney opener. Behind Leroy Loggins' 12 points, Baltimore jumped on top, 14-6.

Then Red Devil errors allowed Westark to tie it at 14-all.

From then on, it was a slow grind, with two of the top defenses in the country efficiently at work. The score at halftime was 26-all. Eight minutes later each team had added only four points apiece.

In order to bring Westark out of its zone, Coach Phipps told his Red Devils to play a semi-delay. With five minutes remaining, Baltimore squeezed ahead, 36-32.

Westark switched to a half-court trap, causing more Baltimore miscues. In less than 30 seconds, the Lions were within two.

Then Baltimore's Loggins, the game's leading scorer with 18, sat down with five fouls. Westark quickly captured the lead, then added to it, upsetting the No. 6 Red Devils, 47-40.

Baltimore's 40 points were the fewest in a tourney game in 25 years. The combined score was the lowest since 1951. The total was so low that a short in the scoreboard wiring, which would not allow the 10s digit to go higher than "4," was not discovered until the second half of the following game. By then fans were deeply involved in another excellent tug of war.

The matinee feature began with a Vincennes spurt, led by Tony Fuller's two dunks, lifting the Trailblazers to a 24-14 advantage with 9:32 remaining in the half.

Then, as Three Rivers Coach Gene Bess remembered,

"[Danny] Foster threw one up from about 34 and it glassed went in off the glass . . . It was the kind of shot you cringe when you see somebody throw it up."

From then on, the 6-5 sophomore forward was unstoppable. He hit nine baskets without a miss. One was a baseline jumper from behind the backboard. Another was a driving lay-up. However, most were long range bombs, exciting the crowd. Behind Foster's 20-point spree, Three Rivers led at intermission, 44-41.

The Raiders kept favored Vincennes on the run in the second half. Though appearing to play tentatively, the Trailblazers were able to forge a two-point edge with 28 seconds left. Three Rivers' Gene Deckard erased the difference with two free throws. A bouncing miss off the rim by Vincennes' Eric Duhart with five seconds to go sent the game into overtime.

Two more Deckard free throws gave Three Rivers the early advantage. However, with 3:13 remaining, Vincennes looked assured of regaining the tie. On a Three Rivers miss, the Trailblazers quickly outlet the ball to center Warrel Simmons on a breakaway.

Unfortunately, Deckard had planted himself at midcourt. Simmons steamrollered the sophomore guard, knocking him unconscious.

James Smith, Deckard's replacement, hit the front end of one-and-one. Shortly thereafter, Foster added another mortar shot. Duhart reduced the difference to two with a three-point play, but a turnaround jumper by Otto Porter and two more free throws by a resurrected Deckard sealed the Raider victory. Three Rivers upset Vincennes, 87-82.

After tipping off the week's action with a pair of impressive surprises, the afternoon finale gave tourney fans a chance to get an early supper. Mesa shot only 28.4 percent (21 of 74) from the field as Columbia State won easily, 72-60.

By intermission of the evening opener, fans were back in their seats ready for more excitement. A glance at the scoreboard told them they would have to wait. The halftime score was a miserly 28-16. Establishing a slow, patient tempo, No. 2 Casper had outshot much taller Western Texas 48 percent to 26 percent to take control.

The Thunderbirds' conservative pace backfired in the second half. Western Texas grabbed the momentum and gradually reduced the deficit to one, 44-43, with eight minutes remaining, giving the crowd what it wanted.

The Westerners' rally was exacted at a price, though. Three starters picked up their fifth fouls. Eight free throws down the stretch and three Kevin Sprewer stuffs in the final minute-and-a-half clinched a 61-57 Casper victory.

When the NJCAA decided to return the tournament to its original 16-team format, it also decided to reinstitute the old custom of reserving the opening night feature for the Region 6 champion. Consequently, fans were out in force, eager to see Independence begin its title defense.

After a week-and-a-half lay-off since the regional championship, the Pirates looked disappointingly rusty. Unheralded Faulkner State traded leads with the defending champs 15 times in the early going. With 3:52 left in the first period, Independence could only muster a two-point edge.

Then, like a boulder rolling down hill, the Pirates gained steam after a cumbersome start. By the time Robert Smith made a last-second tip-in before intermission, the Independence advantage had shot to 10, 42-32. With 14:18 remaining in the game, it had grown to 19. Then the Pirate boulder achieved bone-crushing momentum. In the final 4:10, Independence outscored Faulkner State, 26-1. Ten Pirates played and all scored four or more, led by Bobby Potts' 25. Independence demolished the Red Eagles, 101-64.

Another tourney favorite had its troubles in the nightcap. After one period, four Niagara County players had three fouls and one, floor leader Duane "Duke" Richardson, had four. Thanks to an excellent effort from his bench, however, Coach Dan Bazzani's Frontiersmen only trailed Palm Beach, 43-39.

The second half was a nail-biting struggle. Then, with seven minutes to go, the Frontiersmen outscored Palm Beach, 10-2, to take command. Led by Michael "Chick" Lyles' game-high 24 points and 16 rebounds, Niagara County preserved its unbeaten record, 79-72.

WEDNESDAY — EXCELLENT DEFENSE, SUSPECT OFFENSE

A great comeback tipped off the second day of action when North Idaho lost its poise, allowing Middle Georgia to rally from 5 down with eight minutes to play. On a pair of free throws by Larry Turner with four seconds to go, the Warriors made the comeback complete, edging North Idaho, 70-68.

The only pairing of ranked teams in the first round came last. For No. 15 Anderson it was another case of bad luck of the draw. In 1975, the Trojans had faced No. 2 San Jacinto in their opener. In 1976, it was No. 3 Mercer County. Now it was No. 7 Essex County. But, according to Coach Jim Wiles, "That was the first time I felt we had a better than even chance of winning the first game."

Indeed, Essex County proved no match for Anderson's powerful front line. After forward Ron White scored nine straight points to break open a close first half, the Trojans never looked back. Six-three White, 6-6 212-pound Tommy Wimbush, and 6-8 210-pound Reggie Small combined for 57 points and 27 rebounds, leading Anderson to a convincing 80-69 win.

The lone consolation game of the day was a lackluster affair. The only exciting moments were three technicals, including one on Vincennes Coach Allen Bradfield for waving a handkerchief in protest of a double-foul call. Behind Leroy Loggins' game-high 27, Baltimore eliminated Vincennes, 61-52.

The intensity level did not increase much with the opening quarterfinal. Though the game was close throughout, Three Rivers did not appear as emotionally involved as it had been in its upset of Vincennes. Seeming content to let Westark stay a step ahead, the Raiders did not contest the lead until Gene Deccard's jumper with 14:26 remaining, giving Three Rivers a 49-48 edge. From then on, the two teams traded advantages. Finally, in the last three minutes, the Raiders came alive, outscoring Westark, 8-2. Led by Otto Porter's 24 and Danny Foster's 23, Three Rivers advanced, 79-74.

Stimulation was saved for the nightcap.

Independence Coach Lynn Cundiff described his team as "excellent defensively, suspect offensively," partly because the Pirates lacked a big man like 6-10 Chester Giles and a pure shooter like Rennie Kelly from the previous year's championship squad, and partly because they spent most of their practice time defensing the upcoming game. Against No. 2 Casper and its tough zone, the Independence offense would face its sternest test in defense of its title.

The seriousness of the contest was reflected in tight, nervous play and several quick fouls. There were eight ties in the opening period. Despite hitting only one of seven free throws, Independence held a 31-29 edge at intermission.

The Pirates enjoyed the first spurt of the game to start the final frame, jumping to a 39-31 lead.

The Casper zone went to work, holding Independence at bay while steadily reducing the deficit. The Thunderbirds finally went ahead, 50-49, on a three-point play by Gerald Mattinson. The game was tied at 54 and 56.

Then Independence exploded for 12 unanswered points. After the outburst, the Pirates reversed their poor free throw shooting tendency — in the Region 6 semifinal against No. 18 Cowley County, Independence missed 30 free throws, including 11 in a row in the final 5½ minutes — hitting eight for eight (four by Thomas Louden and four by Bobby Potts) in the final two minutes. The Pirates downed Casper, 78-64.

The star of the game was Louden. The New York native led all scorers with 25, including 14 in the second half in critical situations. He hit two of the first baskets in the Independence run and added 10 of 12 from the line down the stretch. He also contributed nine rebounds and six assists. Already confident of the final results, the *Independence Reporter* touted Louden as "among the top candidates for the MVP award."

THURSDAY — ALPO AT THE TRAINING TABLE

"I think we stunk the gym up that five-minute span today. I thought I was going to have to go out and buy a can of Alpo to feed the team because we have been playing like dogs."

The quote was from Western Texas Coach Nolan Richardson. It referenced the Westerners second-half lapse when Faulkner State reduced a 20-point margin to two.

To Richardson's satisfaction, however, Western Texas rectified the situation, shooting a record-tying 68.4 percent from the

field, outscoring Faulkner, 23-10, in the final nine minutes, and eliminating the Red Eagles, 84-67.

In the other hump day consolation matches:

Palm Beach capitalized on 30 of 40 from the line to down Mesa, 68-58.

North Idaho outscored Essex County, 26-8, in the last seven minutes and coasted to a 79-59 victory.

And Casper overcame a 42-29 halftime deficit to overtake Westark, 76-75, on a 30-foot jump shot by Duane Trares with two seconds left.

The Casper comeback proved the high point of the day in terms of excitement. Neither quarterfinal was inspiring, though the first had its opportunities.

Niagara County scored the first 10 points, sizzled with 69 percent from the field, and opened a 47-26 halftime advantage over Columbia State.

Then the Chargers reversed their 23.5 percent first-half shooting and rallied. Midway in the final period, Columbia State cut Niagara's lead to 53-48.

At that point, according to Niagara Coach Dan Bazzani, "We just circled the wagons." Employing an unintriguing delay game, the Frontiersmen held on, preserving their 25th consecutive win without defeat, 74-70.

Anderson entered the nightcap with a purpose. Four of the five Trojan losses had come against teams from Georgia. Given the circumstances, Middle Georgia did not stand a chance. Paced by balanced scoring (five Trojans hit double figures) and superior front-line strength (Ron White, Tommy Wimbush, and Reggie Small outscored their counterparts by 15), Anderson downed Middle Georgia, 77-69.

FRIDAY — THEY WERE INCREDIBLE

Human interest stories made the afternoon consolation fare an appealing menu.

In the opener, Baltimore's Ron Berry was nearly upstaged when the Western Texas cheering squad surrounded the Super Hexer at midcourt and attempted to ward off his evil spells with white crosses. One of the hexes made it through their defenses, however. Baltimore overcame a 66-57 deficit in the final five minutes to win, 69-68, on Leroy Loggins' last-second 15-footer.

Next followed the tourney Cinderella — Palm Beach. Though often the brunt of jokes, the Pacers' small roster was an immediate fan favorite. One of Palm Beach's three assistant coaches (a practice necessity) referred to the squad as "the Eight Dwarfs." Dr. Edward M. Eissey, school president, demonstrated his loyalty, anyway, cheering from the stands, wearing a sign proclaiming "Eight Is Enough."

In the matinee feature Palm Beach's numbers were even less. With one reserve reportedly sidelined with an illness, the Pacers could not afford to foul. Instead, they limited themselves to nine infractions, allowing North Idaho only two free throws. Outscoring the Cardinals, 18-1, from the line, Palm Beach advanced to the consolation championship, 78-69.

The attraction in the afternoon finale was not one of the players, but one of the coaches. Columbia State's Gene McBee, a country-western singer back home in Tennessee where he headed the Gene McBee Family Singers, gained a following after performing at several Hutchinson night spots during the week. He was in specially good voice after Roger Hayes' 30 and Ken Offutt's 22 led the Chargers past Middle Georgia, 88-82.

Fans only hoped the evening session would hold as much interest. In the opening semifinal, defending champion Independence was the overwhelming pick over Three Rivers, the tourney sleeper. And though No. 8 Niagara County outranked No. 15 Anderson, Anderson's front line had impressed everyone, making the Trojans the heavy favorite in the nightcap.

Independence had the bigger problem. Three Rivers posed a double threat in "Mr. Inside" and "Mr. Outside" — Otto Porter and Danny Foster. The Raider forwards had scored 45 and 53, respectively, in their first two outings. "We were concerned about their rebounding, the Porter kid shooting in the middle, and, of course, Foster from outside," analyzed Indy Coach Lynn Cundiff. "We had to take something away and we didn't think Foster was very quick."

Cundiff's solution was to assign sophomore defensive specialist Leslie McLeod to Foster. "We played basically man[-to-man] defense," described Cundiff, "[and] did some stunting out of it. We ran stunts for McLeod. I believe that the first three times Foster touched the ball, McLeod stole it for a lay-up." McLeod limited Foster to 10 shots and 13 points, 10 below his average.

Overall team quickness was also a factor. Always appearing a step or two behind, Three Rivers resorted to reaching and grabbing to slow the Pirates. As a result, Independence cashed in 26 of 39 free throw attempts. Led by Bobby Potts' game-high 25 and Thomas Louden's 17 points and five assists (making him the top assist man in Independence history), the Pirates built a 19-point advantage midway in the final period, then coasted to a 84-68 victory.

The argument that Anderson should be highly favored in the other semifinal was not contested by opposing coach Dan Bazzani. "I thought they were the greatest club I had ever seen on the junior college level," said the Niagara County mentor. "They were incredible." The Trojans were so physically impressive that Bazzani did not want his players to see them when they shared the Arena's small practice gym prior to the evening's final contest, saying to himself, "If they see this club, they're going to die."

Niagara County's only chance was to gain an early lead and force Anderson out of its zone. Otherwise, it would be a long evening for the Frontiersmen.

Niagara executed the formula perfectly, scoring the first eight points. After George Turmon's 18-footer broke the ice for Anderson, the Frontiersmen went on another brief spree, opening a 13-2 advantage.

"[Then], we spread them out, made them play us man-to-man," recalled Bazzani. The Frontiersmen were so much quicker that they frequently eluded the defense. Said Bazzani, "I'll never forget [6-4 Michael] Lyles going up the lane twice and slam dunking on this 6-8 Reggie Small. Chick just blew up the middle twice in a row and slammed two of them. I remember the place going nuts."

Though the gap was closed several times, Anderson could never pull close enough. Shooting 65 percent from the field and 75 percent from the line, Niagara County extended its dream unbeaten season with a surprising 70-62 triumph. Summarized Bazzani, "We played probably the best ballgame of any club I've ever coached."

SATURDAY — THE DREAM DISSOLVES

Playing again with only seven players, Palm Beach was extended to the limit before defeating Baltimore, 77-76, in overtime for seventh-place.[2]

Baltimore's Leroy Loggins and the Pacers' Mike Bennett shared game honors with 21 each, but it was Bennett who stood out. The 5-11 sophomore hit the tying basket in regulation (a 20-footer with 41 seconds left) and scored six of his team's eight points in the extra period (one a twisting lay-up to open the period, one a 25-footer from the right side to regain the lead, and the last a double-clutch 10-footer to cap Palm Beach scoring with 42 seconds remaining.)

Though Gene McBee was forced to bench two starters for missing bed check, Columbia State played hard before succumbing to Casper, 86-84, in the fifth-place game.

In the third-place contest, the "Mr. Inside and Mr. Outside Show" proved too much for Anderson. Behind Otto Porter's 25 and Danny Foster's 23, Three Rivers downed the Trojans, 88-74.

For many tourney fans, most of them Kansans, the title match was no contest. Though unranked, Independence possessed the experience of a defending titleholder from a region that had produced six national champions. No. 8 Niagara County came from Region 3 whose representatives had compiled an undistinguished 9-28 record since 1962 with no finish higher than fifth. The success of the Frontiersmen was considered a fluke.

There were other reasons why the New Yorkers should not have been playing for a national crown. Niagara County gave no scholarships. Coach Dan Bazzani's annual recruiting budget was $100 or "whatever I could pay out of my pocket." The limitations were best illustrated when Bazzani tried to recruit 6-9

Cleveland native Tony Felder, a Casper reserve. "Of cou Casper flies him out for a visit, shows him the school. We d out to Cleveland and show him a picture of Niagara Commu College over a pint of ice cream."

No Niagara player made the Region 3 all-star team. Yet, Frontiersmen were one win away from an undefeated sea: Why?

Speed and quickness had a lot to do with it. But, mostly it comradeship. Coach Bazzani arranged for the team to together in an old house furnished with donated furniture. house was eight miles from the school. There was only one Either the car made multiple trips or the players hitchhiked

Fan support was minimal. The Sanborn campus was loca in the country seven miles equidistant between Niagara F and Lockport where most of the students lived. Described E zani, "It's an open area. Wind blows through there and si drifts are incredible. The students don't want to go to sch until three o'clock, then drive back seven miles or so, t come back [later] for a ballgame."

Through adversity, the team grew close. They were their c cheerleaders, their own fans.

In their previous two outings, the Frontiersmen used t quickness to gain the advantage and control the game. Aga Independence, they tried to do the same. Niagara Cou scored the first four points, then opened a quick 12-6 lead.

Independence Coach Lynn Cundiff had warned his play about Niagara's quick outlet passes to speedy guard Du Richardson for easy fast-break buckets. After a couple of | fect examples, the Pirates took the warning seriously and cu the passing lanes. Independence tied the game as 12-all, t moved ahead, opening a seven-point gap. With the first points of the second half, the Pirates were in command, 41-

Niagara County's Duane "Duke" Richardson later set school records at Canisius for steals in a game (7), steals in a season (66), and assists in a season (215). (Photo courtesy of Canisius College)

Then the heart of the Frontiersmen began to shine.

Richardson sandwiched two buckets around one by Mich Lyles, bringing Niagara back in the game. The Frontiersn continued to whittle the lead, finally tying it at 51-all. With 8 remaining, James White swished one from the corner, giv Niagara its first lead of the period.

Independence quickly regained the advantage on baskets Robert Smith and Thomas Louden.

When Niagara center Barry Wright received a cut above eye, Lyles returned to the line-up, having spent several minu on the bench with four fouls. For the next three minutes he | sonally dueled Independence, hitting four consecutive kets, each in a must situation. With 2:54 to go, Independer was only on top by one, 62-61.

---

[2] With the return of the 16-team double-elimination tourney format, officials changed the scheme for award placement. The consolation champion (first-round losers' bracket) received seventh instead of fifth. The second-round losers' champion won fifth instead of fourth. And the loser of the third-place game received fourth instead of sixth.

The spirit of the Frontiersmen did not go unnoticed. Fans who started the game rooting for Independence were now torn. With every point a potential game-winner, nerves were frayed.

At the 1:33 mark, Independence's Leslie McLeod missed the front end of one-and-one.

With 40 seconds left, Jerry Williams missed a turnaround jumper along the right lane for Niagara.

Lyles immediately fouled, sending guard Clifton Lewis to the line. The Pirates missed another front end of one-and-one.

With nine seconds remaining, Niagara's Williams missed again from 10 feet.

For the third straight time, the Frontiersmen fouled, this time sending center Calvin "Bubba" Coleman to the line for another Pirate one-and-one. Just as the referee was about to hand Coleman the ball, Niagara used its last time out.

In the huddle, Coach Bazzani spoke with optimistic fervor. "Chaney [reserve Bernard], he's going to miss. The ball's coming off to the right. I want you to grab that rebound and look to your right. Richardson, I want you at the free throw line extended, at the outlet position. We're going to grab this thing, we're coming down with the break, and we're going to win this one at the buzzer."

Like a dream, the scene unfolded just as Bazzani predicted. Coleman missed. Chaney rebounded, kicking it off to Richardson. The Frontiersmen broke for the other end.

Then the dream began to dissolve. Independence hurried back on defense, creating a three-on-three situation. With no one to feed to, Richardson pulled up at the free throw line and fired, crashing into Pirate Bobby Potts and falling to the floor. The ball caromed away. A wild rebound attempt by Williams was blocked by Coleman at the buzzer.

Independence had defended its title.

THE AFTERMATH — TEARS AND CHEERS

Still on the floor as the game ended, Duane Richardson rolled over on his stomach, put his head in the crook of his arm, and cried. Around him, Independence players leaped in the air and Pirate fans flooded the court.

While Dan Bazzani tried to console his heartbroken players as they slumped on the bench, the Independence squad congregated at center court, knelt, and prayed.

The stage was set for one the most moving awards ceremonies in tourney history.

As Niagara County and Independence received their trophies, the Sports Arena rocked with thunderous ovations.

The crowd's emotional vent continued with the Obee Small Player Award. Mike Bennett, by no means an extrovert [described Palm Beach Coach Joe Ceravolo: "The most I could ever get out of him was 'Yes, sir,' 'No, sir' for a long time."], was overwhelmed by the response, shyly ducking his head when the official photograph of the ceremony was taken.

The Sesher Sportsmanship Award-winner was also poplar. In fact, the whole Niagara County team had displayed perfect decorum throughout the week. But, ironically, a year earlier no Frontiersman would have been considered a candidate for such an honor.

During a loss in the 1977 Region 3 tournament, the Frontiersmen received more than their fair share of questionable calls. Related Coach Bazzani, "They [the Niagara players] started jawing with the officials. They started jawing with the fans. It was a disgrace and I was embarrassed."

At the beginning of the 1977-78 campaign, Bazzani vowed such an incident would never happen again. "We're going to kill them with kindness," Bazzani told his players. "If you say one word to an official, anything at all, you'll come sit next to me. If you get a technical, don't even turn and look, just run over to the bench and sit down because you're coming out. You're not playing again."

As the season progressed, the team's back-biting attitude changed 180 degrees. Said Bazzani, "Those kids learned a lesson that year."

Typifying that new attitude was the Sesher Award-winner. Throughout tourney week he was a goodwill ambassador on the court. When called for a foul, he handed the ball to the official, smiled, and patted him on the back. After a particularly rough foul in the championship game, he picked up the oppos-

ing player, hugged him, then patted him on the butt. "That was no show," said Bazzani. "He was the kind of kid who loved to play and had a good time playing."

His supreme gesture of sportsmanship came in the waning moments of the title game. When notified of his fifth foul, he raised up from his position along the free throw line, shook the hands of all the Independence players on the floor, walked over to the Independence bench, shook everyone's hand there, then headed for the Niagara bench. His teammates stood and applauded him. The Arena audience spontaneously joined them.

When Michael Lyles stepped on the floor to receive the Sesher Sportsmanship Award, they stood again.

Michael "Chick" Lyles led Cinderella Niagara County to a second-place finish in the 1978 tournament with 76 points and 37 rebounds, but will be most remembered for his stirring act of sportsmanship in the closing minutes of the championship game. Lyles later completed his collegiate career at Niagara University. (Photo courtesy of Niagara University)

The French Most Valuable Player Award was also richly deserved. The winner was the epitome of team leadership. Described Independence Coach Lynn Cundiff, "He just refused to lose and he wouldn't let anybody around him lose. You can see by his average, he was not a great scorer. But, when it got time to play in the clutch, he was the guy who wanted to play."

The best example of his will-to-win attitude came in the final moments of the Region 6 semifinal. With Independence holding a one-point edge in overtime, he grabbed a rebound, receiving an unintentional elbow to the jaw in the process. Though dazed, he dribbled the ball for the final four seconds. When time ran out, he collapsed. Said Cundiff, "He would not collapse while the game was going on. He was that kind of tough. That's the way he played and that's the way he lived."

When tough-guy Thomas Louden accepted his MVP plaque and was showered with cheers, there were tears in his eyes.

A super-sub with the 1977 champs, Thomas Louden came into his own in the 1978 tournament and was selected the French MVP. Louden completed his collegiate career at the University of Hawaii. (Photo courtesy of Independence Community College)

1978 TOURNAMENT BRACKET

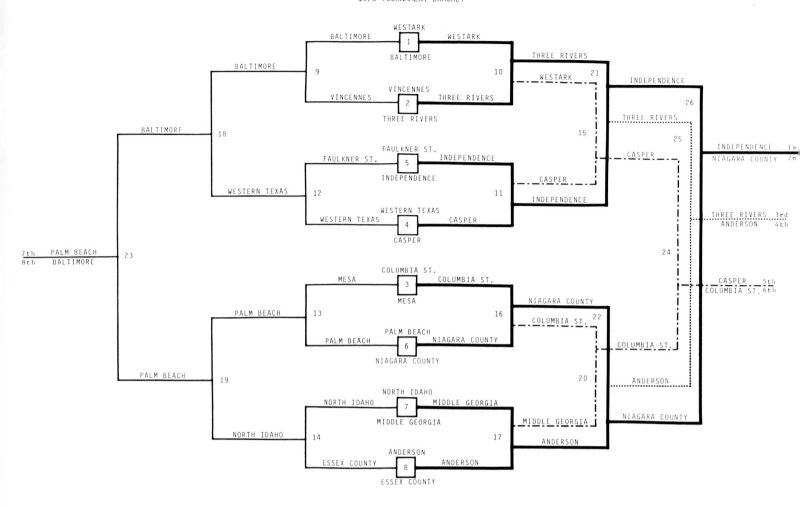

Tournament Results

Tuesday: Game

1. Westark — 47 Baltimore — 40
2. Three Rivers — 87 Vincennes — 82 OT
3. Columbia St. — 72 Mesa — 60
4. Casper — 61 Western Texas — 57
5. Independence — 101 Faulkner St. — 64
6. Niagara County — 79 Palm Beach — 72

Wednesday: Game

7. Middle Georgia — 70 North Idaho — 68
8. Anderson — 80 Essex County — 69
9. Baltimore — 61 Vincennes — 52
10. Three Rivers — 79 Westark — 74
11. Independence — 78 Casper — 64

Thursday: Game

12. Western Texas — 84 Faulkner St. — 67
13. Palm Beach — 68 Mesa — 58
14. North Idaho — 79 Essex County — 59
15. Casper — 76 Westark — 75
16. Niagara County — 74 Columbia St. — 70
17. Anderson — 77 Middle Georgia — 69

Friday: Game

18. Baltimore — 69 Western Texas — 68
19. Palm Beach — 78 North Idaho — 69
20. Columbia St. — 88 Middle Georgia — 82
21. Independence — 84 Three Rivers — 68
22. Niagara County — 70 Anderson — 62

Saturday: Game

23. Palm Beach — 77 Baltimore — 76 OT
24. Casper — 86 Columbia St. — 84
25. Three Rivers — 88 Anderson — 74
26. Independence — 62 Niagara County — 61

How They Finished in 1978

1. Independence Community Junior College
2. Niagara County Community College
3. Three Rivers Community College
4. Anderson College
5. Casper College
6. Columbia State Community College
7. Palm Beach Junior College
8. Community College of Baltimore

All-Tournament Team

Mike Bennett — Palm Beach Junior College
Sammie Ellis — Middle Georgia College
Leroy Loggins — Community College of Baltimore
Thomas Louden — Independence Community Junior College
Michael "Chick" Lyles — Niagara County Community College
Gerald Mattinson — Casper College
Ken Offutt — Columbia State Community College
Otto Porter — Three Rivers Community College
Bobby Potts — Independence Community Junior College
Ron White — Anderson College

Coach of the Tournament

Lynn Cundiff — Independence Community Junior College

French Most Valuable Player Award

Thomas Louden — Independence Community Junior College

Sesher Sportsmanship Award

Michael "Chick" Lyles — Niagara County Community College

Bud Obee Outstanding Small Player Award

Mike Bennett — Palm Beach Junior College

1979:
A COMMUNITY VICTORY

t was a common sight for the second weekend in February in Hutchinson: people dressed in every form of cold-weather clothing, forming a line more than 24 hours before the annual season-ticket sale for the National Juco Tournament.

But, there was more incentive to be first this year.

"We're trying to make this as easy and as fair as we can for the fans," said NJCAA Executive Director George Killian, as he and Tournament Chairman Guy Holt announced the newest ticket plan. The new setup resembled the procedure used by most professional football teams: season ticket holders would have until the end of May each year to renew their option for reserving the same seats for next year's tournament. Said Killian, "It amounts to having a lifetime seat of your choice because you can renew the tickets on a year-to-year basis."

Since city ordinances now forbade camping at the Arena, those in line made do with lawn chairs, blankets, and thermoses of hot liquid, braving the elements for the last time.

THE PARTICIPANTS

Region	Team
1	Dixie College — St. George, Utah
3	Niagara County Community College — Sanborn, New York
4	Belleville Area College — Belleville, Illinois
5	Western Texas College — Snyder, Texas
6	Coffeyville Community Junior College — Coffeyville, Kansas
7	Lindsey Wilson College — Columbia, Kentucky
8	Brevard Community College — Cocoa, Florida
9	Nebraska Western College — Scottsbluff, Nebraska
10	Brevard College — Brevard, North Carolina
11	Southeastern Community College — West Burlington, Iowa
12	Vincennes University — Vincennes, Indiana
13	Willmar Community College — Willmar, Minnesota
15	Westchester Community College — Valhalla, New York
16	Three Rivers Community College — Poplar Bluff, Missouri
19	Mercer County Community College — Trenton, New Jersey
21	Tunxis Community College — Farmington, Connecticut
	Lost in First-Round Play-Offs:
2	Claremore Junior College — Claremore, Oklahoma
14	Panola Junior College — Carthage, Texas
17	Truett-McConnell College — Cleveland, Georgia
18	College of Southern Idaho — Twin Falls, Idaho
20	Allegany Community College — Cumberland, Maryland
22	Chattahoochee Valley State Community College — Phenix City, Alabama

"We were ranked about 3 or 4 all season long," recalled Westchester Community College Coach Ralph Arietta. "Then the last week of the season, every team above us got beat. All of a sudden, bing, we're No. 1." The Westcos (formerly the Vikings) entered the national tournament 32-2. But, because they possessed only one starter over 6-3 and had enjoyed only moderate success (a seventh and an eighth) in two previous tourney appearances, they were not clear-cut favorites.

Among the notable challengers were the second- and third-place finishers from the previous year — No. 16 Niagara County Community College (24-3) and No. 4 Three Rivers Community College (33-3). There was also two-time champs No. 15 Mercer County Community College (24-4) and unranked Vincennes University (24-6) and single-time winners No. 20 Western Texas College (31-3) and unranked Coffeyville Community Junior College (23-6). Rounding out the serious contenders was No.

The 1979 tournament's No. 2 scorer with 90 points in only three games, Craig Tucker finished his collegiate career at the University of Illinois. (Photo courtesy of the University of Illinois)

10 Southeastern Community College of West Burlington, Iowa, (29-3) and No. 12 Brevard Community College of Cocoa, Florida (25-3).

The rest of the field was uncertain.

Three of the four remaining tourney veterans had earned the trip to Hutchinson through upset: Dixie College (25-3) had upended No. 17 College of Southern Idaho, 72-70, in overtime on CSI's home floor in a first-round play-off; Lindsey Wilson College knocked off No. 5 Chattahoochee Valley State Community College, 76-74, also in play-off action; and Willmar Community College (17-10) surprised No. 14 Suomi College of Hancock, Michigan, 75-74, in overtime in the Region 13 final. The other tourney vet, Brevard College of Brevard, North Carolina, (24-8) seemed to be thrown in just to confuse fans with the other Brevard.

Of the three newcomers — Tunxis Community College (27-2), Nebraska Western College (30-5), and Belleville Area College (28-7) — only Belleville had cause to feel optimistic. As a co-member of the Midwest Juco Athletic Conference, the Dutchmen could point at a league victory over highly-regarded Three Rivers.

The muddled waters of competition would settle early, however. Two-time champs Mercer County and Vincennes, No. 10

SECC of West Burlington and No. 20 Western Texas, and No. 1 Westchester and No. 4 Three Rivers all faced each other in the opening round.

TUESDAY — HAIL STORM

For most fans, the main opening-day attractions were in the evening. Along with the opener for the Kansas representative, Coffeyville, there were the top-flight Mercer County-Vincennes and Burlington-Western Texas match-ups.

The afternoon session held its own in terms of excitement, however.

During 40 minutes of action in the tip-off game, Niagara County and Brevard, North Carolina, tied 13 times with neither team gaining a lead greater than four. Each time Niagara took control down the stretch, Brian "Chico" Horton — the game's leading scorer with 24 — pulled the Tornadoes even, hitting four consecutive baskets. At the end of regulation, the score was tied, 61-all.

Niagara jumped ahead again in overtime. Brevard fought back, pushing the game into another five-minute period on Kevin Herron's 30-foot swisher at the buzzer.

Again, Niagara took the lead only to see Brevard respond — this time for good. The Tornadoes upset Niagara County, 77-75.

In the matinee feature, Dixie put on a shooting exhibition, topping its excellent 56-percent season average from the field by four percentage points. Willmar forward Bob Larson led all scorers with 33, but only one other Warrior hit double figures. Led by Johnny Gilbert's 19, Dixie placed five in double digits. All 10 Rebels who played, scored. Dixie won easily, 96-72.

The afternoon finale was another overtime thriller. Down 63-54 with 6:11 to go, Nebraska Western rallied, tying Lindsey Wilson, 67-all, in regulation. Then, after Terry Triplett and Derryl Williams made back-to-back three-point plays, the Cougars took their largest lead of the game, 79-74, with 48 seconds remaining. Four consecutive Kevin McNamara free throws in the final 15 seconds preserved an 84-80 Nebraska Western victory.

After the 1977-78 season, Mercer County Coach Howie Landa resigned. Picked to fill his shoes was his assistant of one year, Arch Freeman, whose only other coaching experience was at the high school level.

It was a tough task following in the footsteps of a legend, especially when the three-time Coach of the Tournament was still teaching at Mercer. But, Freeman was smart enough not to make drastic changes.

"Obviously his [Landa's] system was tried and tested," said Freeman. "My top two players had played a full season under his system. I thought that would be a good starting point. I decided to build around them and keep his essential offenses and defenses. I cut down the number of things that we did, because I had a tough time absorbing them. Howie knew them from years and years of coaching. Basically we were using the whole Mercer system. It was all Howie's stuff."

Consequently, though Landa was nothing more than an interested spectator, it was the same old Landa-style team on the court. The patient, stingy Vikings controlled the tempo in the evening opener, taking a quick 11-3 lead over Vincennes, building it to 36-26 at intermission.

Though a Mercer cold streak and several turnovers allowed Vincennes to close early in the final period, the Trailblazers never challenged the lead until the end. With 34 seconds remaining, Eric Duhart stole the ball for an easy lay-up, putting Vincennes on top for the first time, 59-58.

Both teams blew opportunities at the line, missing the front end of one-and-ones. Then Mercer guard Jeff Rocke drove the lane and missed an easy five-footer. In perfect position, using both hands, freshman forward Jeff Carrion tipped it back in with four seconds showing.

Warrel Simmons' desperation 45-foot heave at the buzzer rimmed out. It was the third straight opening-round loss for Allen Bradfield's Trailblazers and the third consecutive time they had fallen to Mercer County in tourney competition.

Nerves played an important role in the first half of the evening feature. It had been 17 years since Coffeyville had made a tourney appearance. For the Tunxis Tomahawks, it was their first exposure to an event which drew nearly 7,000 enthusiastic Kansas partisans.

The score remained close until the final minutes of the period. Then the Red Ravens took off, hitting 10 unanswered points, mounting a 42-32 halftime advantage. The closest Tunxis came thereafter was eight. Coffeyville ended the Tomahawks' 27-game win streak, 89-65.

Through the first half, the nightcap failed to live up to its advanced billing. SECC-Burlington dominated, building a 42-31 margin.

Then, with 17 minutes remaining, Western Texas switched to a full-court zone trap with 6-5 freshman forward Paul Pressey at the point.

"You can't simulate playing against a team pressure like what Western Texas put on you," described Blackhawk Coach Charlie Spoonhour. "Unless you've ever been in a hail storm, you can't really know how hard it is to dodge all those little bullets coming down."

At first, the Burlington squad handled the press. Then Pressey's long arms began deflecting passes. Western Texas tied the game, 61-all, with 9:18 to go.

The Blackhawks regrouped, hitting eight unanswered points.

Western Texas pressure was unrelenting. The Westerners tied it at 75, 77, and 79, the last with 1:30 remaining.

Spoonhour decided to hold for one. SECC never got that chance, however. With 20 seconds left, Western Texas stole the ball again, creating the Blackhawks' 17th turnover of the period. A 10-footer by Bill Patterson with three seconds showing gave the Westerners an 81-79 victory. It was their only lead of the game.

WEDNESDAY — SLAM, SLAM

The most awaited contest of the opening-round, led off the day's action. It was an excellent paring. No. 1 Westchester possessed the top offense in the tournament (91.0), No. 4 Three Rivers, the top defense (57.5). Three Rivers held a distinct height advantage. The Westcos were quicker. The one factor that tipped the scales slightly was each team's knowledge of the other. Three Rivers Coach Gene Bess had flown to New York to see the Westcos in the Region 15 final. All Westchester Coach Ralph Arietta had to go on was the Raiders' brief 30-minute workout during Monday's Arena practice sessions.

Once on the court, superior rebounding and a slow tempo favored Three Rivers. The Raiders gained control and held it, building a nine-point margin in the second half.

Behind Felix Tertulien, who hit 18 of his game-high 22 in the final frame, Westchester rallied, edging ahead 51-50 with 7:22 remaining.

Three Rivers regained the advantage, taking a 64-60 lead with just over a minute to go.

Then Allen Collins, the Westcos leading score, came to life. With only two field goals and two free throws to his credit to that point, the 6-3 sophomore sank back-to-back jumpers to even the score with 27 seconds left.

Quickness and pressure had brought Westchester back. With time running out and the game tied, the Westcos stayed with their press. Three Rivers broke it, creating a two-on-one situation. As the lone Westchester defender went for the ball, Pat Niemczyk dished it off. Robert Kirby took it all the way for a one-hand slam.

The Westcos still had time for a basket and a tie. But, just as Michael Kelly crossed midcourt, Niemczyk stole the ball. This time Mark Guethle got the slam.

With two dramatic dunks, Three Rivers rocked top-rated Westchester, 68-64.

In the final first-round match, Keith Lewis hit 20 of his game-high 26 in the first half to keep Belleville in contention. The Brevard Titans were too quick, however, finally prevailing, 81-75.

* * *

Losing in the opener after nearly winning a national crown the year before, was a crushing blow for the Niagara County Frontiersmen. Afterwards, Coach Dan Bazzani just had to get away on his own.

First, he went for a long walk. Then, he grabbed the car keys and took a long ride. Finally, he decided to go to a movie to take his mind off the loss. He entered the theater not knowing that the movie he had chosen was a mad-slasher thriller — "Halloween." Said Bazzani, "That kind of jolted me back to reality."

In the first consolation game, Niagara slashed Bob Larson's 30-plus average over the last eight games to a game-high 21, while eliminating Willmar, 76-70.

The rest of the evening agenda produced different endings after similar beginnings.

Dixie scored the first seven points of the opening quarterfinal before Brevard, North Carolina, rallied to within one. Then Johnny Gilbert, the game's leading scorer with 26, hit 10 points in the next four minutes, leading Dixie to a 21-12 margin. Brevard came no closer than six the rest of the way. Continuing their torrid shooting (38 for 68 — 56 percent), the Rebels advanced, 84-74.

The nightcap also started close with a tie at 11-all. Then, like Dixie, Mercer County went on a tear. Combining a stiff zone with hot shooting, the Vikings outscored Nebraska Western 18-4 over a 5½-minute stretch to take control.

Like Dixie, Mercer continued its dominance in the final stanza, maintaining a 10-point gap — but, only for 12 minutes. Fatigue and a Nebraska Western press took its toll. With just under two minutes remaining, the Cougar deficit was down to 61-58. Mercer needed four consecutive free throws (a pair each by Jeff Carrion and Daryl Devero) and a slam dunk by Andre Allen to preserve a 67-60 win.

THURSDAY — MOST CONVINCING

After Vincennes opened the day with a 77-76 overtime win over Lindsey Wilson, the tournament slipped into its traditional mid-week lull.

SECC-Burlington forced Belleville into 15 second-half turnovers on the way to an 83-60 rout.

A partial player revolt saw four Tunxis players, including two starters, benched because they wanted to wear shoes given them by a salesman. Undermanned, the Tomahawks were outclassed, 83-68, by Westchester.

The front line of Benton "Gorilla" Wade, Larry Jewell, and Chico Horton combined for 50 points and 38 rebounds as Brevard, North Carolina, overpowered Nebraska Western, 75-63.

The importance of quarterfinal competition did little to elevate the level of play. There were 69 turnovers in the evening feature. Still, things were close until Western Texas scored 12 unanswered points to take a 12-point lead with 13:40 remaining.

The Brevard Titans responded with a 14-2 spurt of their own, tying the score 48-all with 10:18 to go.

Then the Westerners' 6-8 freshman center, Greg Stewart, slammed one home, was fouled, and converted the three-point play. Momentum swung back to the Texans. With two minutes left, the Westerners were in total command, 80-63. Besides committing 37 miscues, Brevard hurt its chances by converting only 18 of 34 free throws. Western Texas advanced, 84-72.

The most convincing win of the tournament followed.

Back in 1973, Coach Gene Duke's Olney Central Knights became a tournament hit with their crew cuts, blue blazers, and team discipline. Six year later, Duke had mellowed. The hairstyles of his Coffeyville Red Ravens were longer, their playing style much freer.

In Region 6 action, the Ravens downed two-time defending champ Independence, 100-93, in overtime, ambushed No. 20 Cowley County, 118-114, in overtime, then ended No. 3 Dodge City's 28-game win streak, winning 90-84 in the final. In a first-round play-off, they defeated Claremore Junior College for the first time in three tries, 112-102. Averaging just under 102 points in its last five outings against some of the stiffest competition in the nation, Coffeyville represented an imposing obstacle for No. 4 Three Rivers. Particularly since, as Raider Coach Gene Bess stated, "We were fine defensive players. [But], we struggled to score."

To Bess' surprise, the Raiders scored the first eight points and took off running. With 7:52 left in the first period, Three Rivers had outraced the Red Ravens, 34-10. The closest Coffeyville came thereafter was 11.

For the game, Three Rivers outshot the Kansans 58 percent to 48 percent and outrebounded them, 44 to 33. The only bright spot for the Ravens was guard Craig Tucker. The six-foot freshman was unstoppable. At one point, Bess turned to assistant Roger Pattillo and asked, "Why don't we get somebody on him and stop him." Pattillo replied, "Coach, we're up 30. What do you want?"

Despite Tucker's game-high 40 points, Three Rivers swamped Coffeyville, 110-81.

FRIDAY — GAME OF THE TOURNAMENT

Late Thursday afternoon, the temperature dropped 10 degrees in 15 minutes and the barometer fell to 28.85 inches. The wind shifted to the north, gusting to 50 miles per hour, downing power lines. Mother Nature was not yet ready for spring.

During the night, Hutchinson was dusted by blowing snow mixed with rain. The accumulation was only an inch, but for most of the Brevard Titans from Cocoa Beach, Florida, it was the first white precipitation they had ever seen.

Whether inspired by the new experience or simply too cold to stand still, the Titans warmed the Arena in afternoon consolation action. Brevard's Steve Swank (37) outgunned Coffeyville's Craig Tucker (29) as the Titans outraced the speedy Kansans, 95-91.

The No. 3 scorer in the 1979 tournament with 87 points, Obee Small Player Steve Swank finished his collegiate career at Upsala College in New Jersey. (Photo courtesy of Steve Swank)

In other consolation play, SECC-Burlington held off Westchester, 81-69, and Niagara County eliminated Vincennes, 75-70. The latter marked the final tourney appearance of Coach Allen Bradfield. Later that spring he retired, having compiled a 608-176 record, including three national champions, in 27 years at Vincennes.

The opening semifinal was a clash of styles. On one side was the free-wheeling, excellent-shooting Dixie Rebels; on the other, defense-minded Mercer County.

In the first period, the tempo was compromised, Dixie taking a 32-29 edge into the locker room.

Mercer Coach Arch Freeman was unhappy with what he saw. The Vikings looked tired. They were playing too much one-on-one basketball, definitely not the Mercer way.

Restrained from aggressive sideline coaching because of a cast protecting an Achilles tendon injury, Freeman unloaded during his halftime talk. First, he told his team they had all summer to rest. Then, he told them they better start playing together if they wanted to get into the title game. Summarized Freeman, "Ten years from now, nobody is going to remember who scored the most points."

It was a different Viking squad in the second half. During a five-minute stretch, Mercer put Dixie in a deep freeze, allowing only two Johnny Gilbert free throws. With 12:21 remaining, Mercer County was on top, 41-36, and in command of the game. The Vikings held previously hot-shooting Dixie to 43 percent from the field while sizzling for 66 percent themselves. Winning 69-57, Mercer County advanced to the championship game for the fifth time in 12 years.

The other semifinal was the game of the tournament.

Both teams had acquired a fair share of backers during the week. Three Rivers had produced the more impressive victories. Western Texas had exhibited the more impressive talent.

Nolan Richardson's Westerners were tall and quick. They were also young. On 22 occasions during the year, they entered the dressing room behind at intermission only to come away with victory at game's conclusion. After 20 minutes of play against Three Rivers, the Westerners were again in arrears, 47-42. With 4:36 remaining, they were still down, 80-72.

Then Western Texas made its patented come-from-behind move. With 19 seconds left, the Texans trailed by only a basket. After the teams traded turnovers, Western's Dwight Williams stole the ball at midcourt and passed to Paul Pressey. Pressey shot from long distance and missed. The ball bounced back to Pressey who passed to Williams. Williams took two dribbles, then canned a 15-footer with two seconds showing, tying the game, 84-all.

Momentum shifted to the Westerners in overtime. When Greg Stewart opened scoring with a tip-in, the Texans took their first lead of the game.

Three Rivers traded baskets with Western throughout the period, however. With six seconds left, Marvin "Moon" McCrary swished a 20-footer, tying the score again, 93-all.

Marvin "Moon" McCrary swished a 20-footer with six seconds left in overtime of the Three Rivers-Western Texas semifinal, sending the game into an extra period. McCrary later starred for the University of Missouri. (Photo courtesy of Gene Bess)

Though the psychological edge was back on the side of the Raiders in the second extra period, Western remained in contention. With 13 seconds left, Three Rivers leading by a basket, the Westerners were again in position to extend playing time, Michael Smith at the line for a one-and-one.

Smith missed. Three Rivers rebounded, outletting the ball to Thurlon "Sam" Weaver deep down the sidelines. Weaver took it all the way for two and was fouled intentionally on the play. Two more free throws made the final: Three Rivers — 109, Western Texas — 103.

SATURDAY — WRONG NUMBER

In the opening trophy battle, SECC-Burlington scored the first eight points and led by as much as 13 before Niagara County came to life. From the 8:14 mark until 2:01 remained in the game, the Frontiersmen netted 11 unanswered points to take a 60-55 edge. Niagara County grabbed seventh, 65-59.

"Everyone had visions of the year before," said Niagara Coach Dan Bazzani, "but, I was proud of them because they did come back and win three straight."

The fifth-place game was the most confusing match for announcers since the Robert Morris-Robert Morris pairing 10

years earlier. Brevard (Florida) forced Brevard (North Carolin into three consecutive turnovers to open the final peric cashed in on each possession, and took a 42-37 advantage never relinquished. The Cocoa, Florida, Titans won, 83-79.

Dixie regained its collective shooting eye in the third-pla tilt, burning the nets at a 60-percent clip. Freshman guard Br Heaps hit eight clutch points down the stretch, including tw free throws with seven seconds left, to lead the Rebels pa Western Texas, 100-99. Westerner Greg Stewart took gam honors with 22 rebounds and 37 points, giving him the tourn scoring crown with 120.

With two top-rated defenses facing each other, the champ onship contest was guaranteed to be low scoring. The favori was hard to determine, however.

On the strength of three impressive wins, the edge shou have gone to Three Rivers. However, the semifinal agair Western Texas had been very exacting. "I've never seen a tea so tired," described Coach Gene Bess. "We went out to sho about 12 o'clock noon [Saturday]. Those kids would come u and say, 'We can't even shoot a jump shot.'" The fatigue fact seemingly tipped the scales toward Mercer County.

But, the Vikings had their own problem. "I thought the shouldn't stay in a motel all day," recalled Mercer Coach Ar Freeman. "They'd get too nervous." So Freeman took his pla ers to the Arena's practice gym to loosen up." "Jeff [Carrio was shooting around on the side and decided to jump off th side mat," said Freeman. "The mat fell and he twisted his ankl By that night, it puffed up about triple size." The loss of the 6-200-pound forward put a big dent in the Mercer front lin reducing the Vikings' offensive punch.

Fatigue proved the harsher burden as the contest unfolde Three Rivers was flat. Mercer County's defense controlled th tempo and held the Raiders to 28 percent from the field. Lea ing by as much as 14, Mercer went into the locker room with 26-16 halftime advantage.

With a large Poplar Bluff contingent chanting "Raiders dor quit," Three Rivers played more aggressively in the secor period, moving the ball better against the Mercer zone. Still, took over 13 minutes for the Raiders to cut the deficit in hal Finally, with 2:28 remaining, Marvin McCrary evoked a choru of "Mooooon, Moooooon" with a jumper from the free thro line, tying the game at 45-all.

Mercer County maintained poise. Andre Allen hit from abov the free throw line and, after a successful Three Rivers one-and one, Jeff Rocke converted both ends of a bonus situation. Wit 24 seconds left, the Vikings led, 49-47.

Three Rivers worked it to McCrary on the right wing, but th Raiders' leading scorer was heavily guarded. The ball cam back out to Thurlon Weaver at the top of the key. With Rock pressuring him on his right all the way, Weaver drove to the le wing, stopped, jumped from 20-feet out, and knocked it i dead center, tying the game with 10 seconds showing.

Back on defense, Three Rivers applied ¾-court pressure. E Fireall, a 5-9 Viking reserve, weaved his way upcourt an rimmed a short running one-hander at the buzzer.

The pace picked up in overtime. After two more ties, the di ference went to an odd number and the two teams traded one point leads. A pair of free throws by sub forward Greg Rucke gave Mercer a 58-57 edge with 34 seconds left, setting the stag for one of the most bizarre endings in tourney history.

At the 13-second mark, Daryl Devero reached around Robe Kirby and tried to bat away a Three Rivers pass into the middle The freshman forward was whistled for a foul, his fifth. Mercer leading scorer sat down joining two other Vikings in like circum stances.

With Carrion unable to play, Coach Freeman was left with choice between 6-6 sophomore John Rauchut and 6-4 fresh man Kenneth Widgeon. Neither had seen action in the tourna ment. Freeman opted for the sophomore. "My thinking wa that Rauchut was very big and wide and strong. For a defensiv rebound [on the free throw attempt], I felt he would be bette to block out than Widgeon."

Rauchut checked in at the scorer's table. But, before he coul enter the game the buzzer sounded. While the crowd humme in confused conversation, the officials and coaches huddle around the score book.

The problem was Rauchut's jersey number, "54." The scor book listed him as "52." "During the early games in Decem er," explained Freeman, "his uniform was stolen. We gave im a new uniform. We never thought about it and never put it on this [official NJCAA registration] form. Three months later vhen we got ready to go to the nationals, we sent in the form vhich I signed. Nobody thought about that his uniform number aad been changed."

Unfortunately, in the final seconds of Mercer's most important game of the year, the oversight cost a crucial technical foul. Vith a chance at three potential charities and possession of the all, Three Rivers appeared to have been given the national crown.

However, Kirby hit only the front end of one-and-one and Weaver missed the technical. The game was tied 58-all.

Then came another Mercer error. In the midst of the uproar over the uniform controversy, Freeman lost track of the score. Thinking his Vikings' were now behind, he instructed them to oul as soon as the ball went in play. Milton Woodley hit two ree throws, giving Three Rivers the lead with 10 seconds left.

Mercer had one last chance. Rocke, a strong, physical 5-11 guard, drove down the left side of the lane. His shot missed. Three Rivers' Mark Guethle was called for blocking, though. Rocke stepped to the line for one-and-one with one second eft.

The first shot swished.

Everyone in the Arena tensed. "Honestly, I was calling on the good Lord to help us any way he could while Rocke was shooting that last free throw," related Three Rivers' Bess. "I'm not proud; I wanted all the help I could get. The kid had hit so many free throws [8 in 11 tries], I was almost ready to believe we were going into double overtime again."

Rocke's second shot hit the front of the rim. A desperate tip by Widgeon fell short and to the left.

Three Rivers won the title, 60-59.

THE AFTERMATH — SORROW AND JOY

The loss was devastating for Mercer County, especially for he Vikings' freshman coach. Throughout the awards ceremony, Arch Freeman sat on the bench with his face buried in his hands, his players in turn consoling him.

"I was crestfallen," reflected Freeman. "It really left me in hock. But, it wasn't anyone's fault. The rules are the rules."

Still, it was a bitter pill to swallow. "It was crushing," said Freeman. "I would rather have gotten to the last game and been beaten cleanly and just feel, 'Well, they were better.' But, when you have your kid who's playing the best out for the whole game and you have this other freakish thing happen, it just kind of haunts you. I have to admit I had nightmares about the game for months afterwards. I'd wake up in the middle of the night with a few minutes left and I'd play it over and over. It's very hard to shake it off because you only get to a place like that once in your lifetime."

In athletic competition, one man's sorrow is another man's joy.

For the small southeastern Missouri town of Popular Bluff, the national crown meant escape from anonymity. "We're a community of 20,000 people with another 80,000 around here that kind of identify with us," described Three Rivers Coach Gene Bess. "I really think that we had a majority of those people listening or interested. This is their college team. We're the only college within 85 miles of here. I can't think of another town that supports a junior college like Poplar Bluff and vicinity supports us."

Bess was partly responsible for the Raiders' close ties with their fans. It was standard policy after each Three Rivers home game for the team to remain on the court for 15 minutes or so — win or lose.

Consequently, after suffering through three anxious close calls, including three overtime periods in the final two games, Raider fans were ready to rejoice. When their heroes returned, they packed the Popular Bluff high school gym to show their appreciation.

One of those receiving the loudest ovation was tourney MVP, Thurlon Weaver. He, more than any other player, symbolized the Three Rivers team. "He was injured, had a leg problem, for a pretty good portion of that year and didn't make the all-conference team," explained Bess.

Yet, when it counted most, he was there. Twice in the final two games, he fired what could have been the Raiders' final shot, only to connect, sending the contest into another period. Said Bess, "Sam was not a real quick kid. He had long arms and was not a particularly good shooter. But, he was a money player." His nickname "Iceman" was for a reason.

Like Weaver, the entire squad had achieved success despite adverse conditions. "We [the Three Rivers campus] were just in a downtown storefront facility," said Bess. "We used the high

The 1979 champion Three Rivers Raiders: back row (left to right) — Assistant Coach Roger Pattillo, Manager Rick Alsup, Thurlon "Sam" Weaver, Don Brown, Mark Guethle, Robert Kirby, Sylvester James, Marvin "Moon" McCrary, Dale Purnell, and Coach Gene Bess; front row — Milton Woodley, Pat Niemcyzk, Chuck Johnson, and Dwayne Walker. (Photo courtesy of Gene Bess)

school gym for games. We ended up practicing every which place around. We practiced at different high schools. There's a little correctional institution [the Sears Youth Center] up here north of town about nine miles and they let us have their gym. They put up glass backboards and everything just to help us.

"We also lived in an old dorm downtown that was really condemnable at the time. It was really a poor place to house kids." A national trophy was their just reward for endurance. Summarized Bess, "I think maybe adversity brings out the best in people."

Thurlon "Sam" Weaver not only won a net for a championship prize, but also the 1979 French MVP Award. Weaver completed his collegiate career at Henderson State University in Arkansas. (Photo courtesy of Gene Bess)

Tournament Results

Tuesday:	Game		
	1	Brevard (NC) — 77 Niagara County — 75 2OT
	2	Dixie — 96 Willmar — 72
	3	Nebraska Western — 84 Lindsey Wilson — 80 OT
	4	Mercer County — 60 Vincennes — 59
	5	Coffeyville — 89 Tunxis — 65
	6	Western Texas — 81 SECC-Burlington — 79
Wednesday:	Game		
	7	Three Rivers — 68 Westchester — 64
	8	Brevard (FL) — 81 Belleville — 75
	9	Niagara County — 76 Willmar — 70
	10	Dixie — 84 Brevard (NC) — 74
	11	Mercer County — 67 Nebraska Western — 60
Thursday:	Game		
	12	Vincennes — 77 Lindsey Wilson — 76 OT
	13	SECC-Burlington — 83 Belleville — 60
	14	Westchester — 83 Tunxis — 68
	15	Brevard (NC) — 75 Nebraska Western — 63
	16	Western Texas — 84 Brevard (FL) — 72
	17	Three Rivers — 110 Coffeyville — 81
Friday:	Game		
	18	Niagara County — 75 Vincennes — 70
	19	SECC-Burlington — 81 Westchester — 69
	20	Brevard (FL) — 95 Coffeyville — 91
	21	Mercer County — 69 Dixie — 57
	22	Three Rivers — 109 Western Texas — 103 2O
Saturday:	Game		
	23	Niagara County — 65 SECC-Burlington — 59
	24	Brevard (FL) — 83 Brevard (NC) — 79
	25	Dixie — 100 Western Texas — 99
	26	Three Rivers — 60 Mercer County — 59 OT

How They Finished in 1979

1. Three Rivers Community College
2. Mercer County Community College
3. Dixie College
4. Western Texas College
5. Brevard Community College (Florida)
6. Brevard College (North Carolina)
7. Niagara County Community College
8. Southeastern Community College

All-Tournament Team

Andre Allen — Mercer County Community College
Percy Brown — Southeastern Community College
Daryl Devero — Mercer County Community College
Ron Ence — Dixie College
Marvin "Moon" McCrary — Three Rivers Community College
Greg Stewart — Western Texas College
Steve Swank — Brevard Community College
Craig Tucker — Coffeyville Community Junior College
Thurlon "Sam" Weaver — Three Rivers Community College
Barry Wright — Niagara County Community College

Coach of the Tournament

Gene Bess — Three Rivers Community College

French Most Valuable Player Award

Thurlon "Sam" Weaver — Three Rivers Community College

Sesher Sportsmanship Award

Brian "Chico" Horton — Brevard College

Bud Obee Outstanding Small Player Award

Steve Swank — Brevard Community College

THE COME-FROM-BEHIND KIDS

t was no surprise that Western Texas College was ranked No. 2 in the first NJCAA basketball poll of the 1979-80 season. Nolan Richardson's Westerners featured 10 sophomores, seven of whom returned from the previous year's fourth-place team. Included were 6-8 Greg Stewart, the tourney's scoring champ, and 6-5 Paul Pressey, whom many considered one of the best defensive players ever to play in the Sports Arena.

"Usually you say [to your players], 'Hey, we'll take one game at a time,' " stated Richardson. "But their goals were set on winning the national championship. That's all they talked about. 'We're going back to Hutch and we're gong to win it.' "

When tournament time rolled around, the Westerners were in perfect position to make good on their goal. Western Texas came to Hutchinson with a 33-0 record, ranked No. 1.

Coach Jerry Stone, whose No. 8 Midland College team lost four times to Western, including a 21-point shellacking in the Region 5 final, felt the Westerners were not invincible, however. "All you have to do is stop their top eight players."

THE PARTICIPANTS

There were two principal threats to an undefeated Western Texas crown — No. 3 Westark Community College (32-3) and No. 6 Three Rivers Community College (32-4).

Westark was an up-an-coming name in junior college circles, making its third trip to Hutchinson in four years. Under Coach Gayle Kaundart, the Lions were consistently one of the top defensive teams in the country and currently No. 1, holding opponents to just more than 50 points per contest. If the tourney went as expected, Westark's defensive average would face the Westerners' top offensive average (100.0) in the lower bracket semifinals.

The upper bracket appeared the private domain of the defending national champs from Poplar Bluff. Led by 1979 All-Tourney selection Marvin "Moon" McCrary, Three Rivers was the latest in Gene Bess' excellent squads, which had yet to lose

Though he experienced a disappointing two games in the 1980 tournament, Westark's Darrell Walker (No. 20) spent a successful three years at the University of Arkansas and later in the NBA. (Photo courtesy of Westark Community College)

more than one game in a tournament. Few doubted that the Raiders would be Western Texas' opponent in the championship game.

The competition dropped off considerably after Westark and Three Rivers.

The chances of the other ranked teams were in reverse order of their rankings. No. 18 Anderson College (22-5), making its fourth appearance in six years, had its best bracket draw to date, facing unranked newcomers in its first two rounds, while No. 17 Community College of Baltimore (29-5) and No. 13 Middle Georgia College (29-4) clashed with Westark and Three Rivers, respectively, in their openers.

The top unranked veteran was Tyler Junior College (29-6), making its 13th appearance in the tournament, though for the first time since Floyd Wagstaff's retirement. Now under the guidance of second-year coach Ned Fowler, the Apaches were a definite lower-bracket threat, having started the year ranked No. 1.

Veterans Northeastern Junior College of Sterling, Colorado, (26-8) and Westchester Community College of Valhalla, New York, (30-4) exhibited potential, having downed No. 5 Casper College and No. 11 Nassau Community College, respectively, in regional competition.

However, North Idaho College (28-5) and Lincoln College (26-7), both making their second tourney appearance, were discounted. Each was in the direct path of Western Texas in the first two rounds.

Region	Team
1	Yavapai College — Prescott, Arizona
2	Westark Community College — Fort Smith, Arkansas
3	Monroe Community College — Rochester, New York
4	Lincoln College — Lincoln, Illinois
5	Western Texas College — Snyder, Texas
6	Cloud County Community College — Concordia, Kansas
7	Northwest Mississippi Junior College — Senatobia, Mississippi
9	Northeastern Junior College — Sterling, Colorado
10	Anderson College — Anderson, South Carolina
14	Tyler Junior College — Tyler, Texas
15	Westchester Community College — Valhalla, New York
16	Three Rivers Community College — Poplar Bluff, Missouri
17	Middle Georgia College — Cochran, Georgia
18	North Idaho College — Coeur d'Alene, Idaho
20	Community College of Baltimore — Baltimore, Maryland
22	Jefferson State Junior College — Birmingham, Alabama

Lost in First-Round Play-Offs:

8	Brevard Community College — Cocoa, Florida
11	Kirkwood Community College — Cedar Rapids, Iowa
12	Vincennes University — Vincennes, Indiana
13	Anoka-Ramsey Community College — Coon Rapids, Minnesota
19	Gloucester County College — Sewell, New Jersey
21	Housatonic Community College — Bridgeport, Connecticut

Cloud County Community College (25-7) and Monroe Community College (27-5) were the only newcomers to gain pre-tourney attention. Cloud County was the Kansas representative and possessed Ronnie Joyner, whose 30.1 average was fourth-best in the nation, tops coming into the tournament. Monroe had upset No. 2 Broome Community College in Region 3 action.

Northwest Mississippi Junior College (28-4), Jefferson State Junior College (21-9), and Yavapai College (21-12) were long shots.

All in all, Western Texas faced an undistinguished field. Its quest for a national title seemed easily attainable. The Westerners would not be truly tested until the later rounds.

TUESDAY — SLUGGISH START

There was nothing inspiring about the first day of play. All but one of the six games ended with a margin greater than 10 and the only surprises were minor ones.

In the opener, Yavapai controlled the tempo, dominated the boards (48-30), and led from start to finish, downing Northeastern of Sterling, 60-49. Mike Hitchcock led Yavapai scoring with only 11 points, but four other Roughriders tallied 10.

The matinee feature was one of the top pairings of the opening round and, for the most part, lived up to its billing. Three Rivers and Middle Georgia traded leads through nearly 15 minutes of the first half before two individual spurts determined the outcome.

While the Georgians were missing the front end of three bonus situations, Three Rivers' Marvin McCrary scored 10 straight points, giving the Raiders a 38-34 advantage at intermission.

Then, just as Middle Georgia's David Smart reduced the difference to two with the first basket of the final period, Three Rivers 6-3 freshman Tony Wallace went on a tear, hitting four field goals in a row. From then on, the Raider lead was never less than four. Three Rivers advanced as expected, 80-67.

The closest game of the day followed. The largest margin was eight, held by Monroe twice early in the second half. Late free throws and a Monroe cold spell, however, gave the victory to Jefferson State, 75-70.

The opening-night session was a sellout, the first such occurrence with Hutchinson not in the tournament. The reasons for the turnout were the debut outings of Kansas-favorite Cloud County and tourney-favorite Western Texas.

It was *not* because of the opener. After a modest 36-28 halftime edge, Anderson exploded for 57 points, routing Northwest Mississippi, 93-62.

The first period of the evening feature showcased the talents of 6-6 sophomore forward, Ronnie Joyner. The Memphis native was well on his way to his 30-point average with 18, all from the field. To the delight of the partisan crowd, Cloud County led, 44-42, at intermission.

Then Lincoln Coach Allen Pickering made a defensive change, moving 6-3 freshman Mike Goeken to cover the scoring phenom. Joyner's output was cut in half. Meanwhile Julius Poinsette and Fred Watkins sparked the Lynx offense, hitting 16 and 14, respectively. Lincoln won going away, 89-77.

The nightcap epitomized the unexciting first day of play. After a 13-day lay-off, top-rated Western Texas looked sluggish. Scoring in streaks, the Westerners built a 51-35 halftime advantage only to see North Idaho trim it to 74-72 with nine minutes remaining. Then Western's lauded press took over, giving the Texans a comfortable 108-94 winning margin.

WEDNESDAY — THERE'S A CAR IN MY BED

It had also been awhile since Jerry Phipps' CCB Red Devils had faced competition — 16 days. However, unlike Western Texas, Baltimore was ready for action. Said Phipps, "It gets a little old playing yourself."

In a contest pitting two top-10 defenses, the Red Devils held Westark to 15 percent shooting from the field and opened a 25-15 halftime lead.

The Lions improved their marksmanship to 32 percent after the second period, led by Darrell Walker's game-high 25 points, but Baltimore continued in control. The Red Devils spread the margin to 20 before spearing victory, 66-54.

The opening round culminated in another breeze. Tyler bui[lt] a commanding 46-27 advantage at intermission, then coaste[d] to a 102-83 win over Westchester.

If a chance at a national crown could not entice excitemen[t] then a shot at a lesser prize was not likely to produce any. Con[se]quently, the first consolation match extended the pattern o[f] unspectacular play.

The Middle Georgia Warriors were anything but warlike i[n] taking a 39-33 halftime advantage over Northeastern of Ster[ling]. As the press described them, the Georgians looked "ver[y] dead," later allowing Northeastern to tie the game in regulatio[n]. Though Middle Georgia led from start to finish in overtime, it[s] 89-85 triumph was nothing to brag about.

With highly-favored Three Rivers and Anderson facin[g] unranked newcomers in the opening quarterfinals, fans won[dered if there would ever be any reason to stir from their seat[s] other than for popcorn and hot dogs.

It was especially the feeling after Three Rivers broke open [a] close feature game with the first eight points of the second hal[f]. With 12:35 remaining, the Raiders were comfortably in fron[t], 44-33.

Then Yavapai switched from zone to pressure man-to-ma[n]. Led by guards Casper Ware and Raphael Dirden and reserv[e] center John Van Uden, a native of Auckland, New Zealand, th[e] Roughriders made a spirited comeback. The three combine[d] for all but four of Yavapai's second-half points, pulling the Ar[i]zona squad back in the game. Von Uden, who possessed inte[r]national experience as a member of the New Zealand nationa[l] team, capped the drive with a 12-foot baseline jumper and tw[o] pressure free throws. Despite the 25-point effort of Raider Mar[vin McCrary, including 13 of 13 from the line, Yavapai upende[d] the defending champs, 62-59.

"We just weren't mentally prepared for the game," Thre[e] Rivers Coach Gene Bess told the press. "I can't explain why."

Said Yavapai Coach Dave Brown, "I'm still in a state o[f] shock."

Until the Three Rivers upset, the only thing shocking in th[e] tournament had happened off the court. At 2:30 a.m. Wednes[day morning Steve Hedden, sixth-man for Jefferson State, an[d] roommate yell leader Perry Wynn were awakened by the soun[d] of breaking glass. Their next realization was that they wer[e] pinned beneath spinning wheels. A car driven by tourney refe[r]ee Lynn Shortnacy had crashed through their first-floor room a[t] the Royal Inn Motel.

Luckily, both young men only received cuts. Hedden's wa[s] the more serious. He was taken to the hospital where h[e] received 110 stitches to close a four-inch-long gash, ending h[is] availability for the tournament.

The loss of Hedden was not only unsettling to his parent[s] who had traveled from Plainsborough, New Jersey, to see hi[m] in action, and to Jefferson State Coach Bill Lankford, whos[e] bench strength was suddenly lessened, but also to the whol[e] team. "We didn't get any sleep hardly at all that night," state[d] Lankford.

Under the circumstances, few gave the already underdo[g] Pioneers much chance against Anderson in the nightcap. Bu[t] surprisingly, Jefferson State took control late in the openin[g] period, gained a 36-30 halftime edge, then, capitalizing on 2[6] of 36 free throw attempts, smashed Anderson, 83-67.

THURSDAY — THE PARTY'S OVER

Though the two upsets in Wednesday's quarterfinals brough[t] life to the proceedings, the tournament figured to return to i[ts] matter of fact course with Thursday night's feature. By every[one's standards, shorter and less-talented Lincoln was a mi[s]match for No. 1 Western Texas.

Consequently, when Lincoln jumped out to a 10-point lea[d] — by outrunning the quick Texans no less — mouths droppe[d] open.

"I remember at that point," recalled Lincoln Coach Alle[n] Pickering, "I looked at my assistant coach and I said, 'I don['t] really believe this is happening.' He looked at me and said, 'Ju[st] keep coaching.'"

Sure enough, the Westerners awakened with their patente[d] press. A few Lynx turnovers helped cose the gap. By halftim[e] the score was deadlocked, 45-all.

Still, a tie with the tourney favorite after 20 minutes was

moral victory for Lincoln. Said Pickering, "We were not awed by Western Texas. Those people at Hutch knew what they had, but to be honest, I never heard of Western Texas. [Beating] Vincennes [in the regionals] was a 10 times bigger deal to me."

Then came the second half.

During intermission, Nolan Richardson told his Westerners to switch to a 2-3 zone in order to protect several players in foul trouble. "We figured if they hit the outside shots," said Richardson, "they hit them. But, if they didn't, then we could rebound and fast break."

"I recall," said Pickering, "they got the tip and a slam. We threw the ball in and they took it away. They got another basket before I could even call time-out. Then the party was over."

Western Texas outscored Lincoln, 13-2, in the first four minutes. After the Lynx cut the margin to five, Western then tallied 18 points in four minutes, blowing the game wide open. The Westerners scored 55 second-period points, downing Lincoln, 100-79.

A similar eruption decided the remaining quarterfinal. After building a modest 33-27 halftime edge over Baltimore, Tyler outscored the Red Devils, 12-2, in the first four minutes of the final period. Baltimore never recovered. Tyler won easily, 73-59, setting up a good, old-fashioned Texas showdown in the semifinals.

FRIDAY — YOU WANT TO LOSE IT?

After three days of generally lackluster play, the tournament finally heated up. Friday's session was one of the closest days in tourney history, starting with three one-point decisions in consolation action.

In the opener, Tony Webster led all scorers with 27, including a game-winning jumper with 25 seconds to go, lifting Monroe over Middle Georgia, 85-84.

The matinee feature started out uninteresting. Then, after North Idaho built a 50-33 margin with just under 13 minutes remaining, Westchester mounted a do-or-die rally. When North Idaho missed the front end of one-and-one with 10 seconds left, the Westcos trailed by only one.

With three seconds showing, Westchester center Aldo Rowe missed the potential game-winner. In the rebound scramble, Rowe was fouled. A successful bonus conversion would give the Westcos one of the best come-from-behind victories tourney fans had ever seen.

But, according to Westchester Coach Ralph Arietta, "They couldn't have picked a better guy to foul because Aldo was the worst free throw shooter I ever had."

Rowe missed the first free throw, falling backwards on his rump. North Idaho survived, 70-69.

Desite having little experience outside of street ball, 6-5 forward Fred Watkins, a freshman walk-on from Chicago, was Lincoln's leading scorer and rebounder with 48 points and 26 rebounds in two previous outings. In the afternoon finale, Watkins again amassed game-high totals with 27 points, including 15 of 20 from the line, and 12 rebounds.

It was not enough, however. Baltimore allowed Lincoln only 43 shots from the field, clipping the Lynx, 58-57.

Fans did not know what to expect in the opening semifinal since Yavapai and Jefferson State were major surprises. Both had entered the competition with no prior tourney experience, with the most losses (12 and 9, respectively) in the 16-team field, and yet had defeated defending national champ Three Rivers and 18th-ranked Anderson. It was a toss-up who would advance to the title game.

Jefferson State took the early lead with a 10-point spurt, allowing the Pioneers to build a 39-29 halftime margin.

Then the Alabamans went cold, hitting only two of their next 12 shots. Yavapai pulled even at 53 and 55.

After guard Fred Freeman hit an 18-footer from the corner, the Pioneers went on another roll. Because of superior quickness, a varied and well-executed defense, and accurate (17 for 19) free throw shooting, Jefferson State downed Yavapai, 71-63.

The nightcap was the most eagerly awaited game of the week. Most considered the match between the former titleholders from Texas the championship game.

The contest was particularly important to Tyler. After losing their No. 1 ranking early in the year to Western Texas, the Apaches had fallen into the obscurity of the unranked. They wanted very much to prove they were just as good as their cross-state rivals.

Consequently, the Apaches completely dominated the first half. Tyler outshot the Westerners 55 percent to 37 percent, outrebounded them, 31-15, and outplayed them to a commanding 41-29 halftime advantage. It was a convincing performance.

The second half was even more convincing.

"It seemed to me, this team never was ahead at halftime," reflected Nolan Richardson of his Westerners. "The fans in Snyder would hardly pay attention to the first half of a game. They'd get up, walk around, go get some popcorn. We might be down. No worry."

A colorful man both in dress and personality, Western Texas Coach Nolan Richardson was a particular favorite of tourney fans who continued to follow his later success at the Universities of Tulsa and Arkansas. (Photo courtesy of the University of Tulsa)

Though only playing in three games, Fred Watkins was the fifth-leading scorer (75) and second-leading rebounder (38) in the 1980 tournament. The Lynx walk-on played one more year for Lincoln before finishing his collegiate career at the University of Detroit. (Photo courtesy of the University of Detroit)

Their confidence was based on the team's reaction to a threat. "Ohhhhhh!" said Richardson. "If you put the fear of losing in them, if they came out and thought they were going to lose, they'd beat you [by] 25."

During intermission, all Richardson needed to say was "You want to lose it, right?" When the Westerners returned to the floor, their eyes were wide. They hit 12 of their first 13 shots, pulling even with Tyler at 48-all in less than four minutes.

From then on it was no contest. Holding the Apaches to just 11 second-half points, Western won, 67-52, extending its undefeated string to 36 games — one away from a title.

SATURDAY — DAVID AND GOLIATH REWRITTEN

Monroe team captain Tony Webster saved his best performance until last, scoring a tourney-high 31 points, giving him the scoring title with 94, as the Tribunes claimed seventh, 95-76, over North Idaho.

Four clutch free throws in the final seconds by Marvin McCrary helped Three Rivers maintain its string of five tourney appearances with no more than one loss as the Raiders edged Baltimore, 57-56, for fifth.

The third-place contest had its typical slow start with Tyler dominating the first half. Then 5-10 Casper Ware, the tourney's Obee Small Player Award-winner, sparked Yavapai, lobbing a high pass to 6-6 Warren Webb for a spectacular slam dunk to open the final period. There were 15 ties or lead changes in the second half before a driving lay-up by Raymond Bell with 1:01 to go and a pair of free throws by Elton Webster with 23 seconds left gave the win to Tyler, 69-65.

Few were foolhardy enough to bet on the championship game.

Jefferson State had a nice, symmetrical team (5-11, 5-11, 6-6, 6-4, 6-4). Guards Mike Anderson and Fred Freeman were super scorers. Bill Lankford's Pioneers were quick and disciplined and crowd favorites. But, this David was no match for Goliath Western Texas.

The taller Westerners, averaging two-inches better at each position, were just as quick.

One example was Phil Spradling, a 6-4 transfer from New Mexico. The El Paso native was nicknamed "the Road Runner" because as Coach Nolan Richardson described, "The guy never ever stopped running. He couldn't have played unless he played on a team that ran because he couldn't slow down." How could a 5-11 counterpart contain him?

"The Road Runner" from El Paso, Sesher Sportsmanship Award winner Phil Spradling was another of the Western Texas squad to follow Coach Nolan Richardson to the University of Tulsa. (Photo courtesy of the University of Tulsa)

Then there was Paul Pressey, a forward who thought he wa a guard. Said Richardson, "Once the ball was in his hand something was going to happen. He was either going to dribble going to score a lay-up, or he was going to penetrate and kick off to somebody... [Center Greg Stewart] became our leadin scorer, but he became that because of a guy named Pau Pressey."

Even more fearsome was Pressey's defensive ability. Place at the point on the press, Pressey's long arms seemed to gro every time Western needed a steal. How could the Pioneers ge around him if nobody else could?

The biggest disparity between the two clubs, however, was i depth. After the loss of 6-5 Steve Hedden, Jefferson was le with 6-4 Tony Gaston — who had led the Pioneers in scorin (18) and rebounds (10) in the semifinal against Yavapai — as th only quality off the bench. In contrast, Western Texas was s loaded with talent that 6-6 David Brown and 6-4 Bill Patterso traded starting assignments. Combined, the two had alread scored 91 points, just three shy of the tourney leader. Nola Richardson had flexibility when fouls became a problem; Bi Lankford did not.

Despite the overwhelming odds, Jefferson State outplaye the Westerners in the first half. Western Texas hit only 35 per cent from the field and 43 percent from the line and trailed th Pioneers by as much as eight. Behind Freeman's 18, Jefferso led, 38-31, at intermission.

However, foul trouble by Anderson, Jefferson's floor genera combined with Western's Pressey-led press, produced a famil iar cat-and-mouse Western Texas game pattern. The Pioneer retained the advantage for another 11 minutes before Brow stole and dunked, tying it at 57-all. The score was knotted onc more at 59. Then Stewart put Western in front for good.

Nolan Richardson's Westerners made it a perfect 37-0, win ning 85-72.

THE AFTERMATH — SUCCESS CONTINUES

In sweeping to a title, Western Texas also cleaned up at the awards ceremony. Paul Pressey and Greg Stewart were selectec to the All-Tournament team, Stewart for the second time. Phi Spradling was honored with the Sesher Sportsmanship Award Nolan Richardson was Coach of the Tournament. And Pressey was tabbed French Most Valuable Player.

All were popular choices and not unexpected, especially Pressey's MVP selection. Though only among top-10 tourney leaders in the categories of free throws and assists, there was nc question the future NBA star was the reason the Westerners clicked. It was the 11th time in 12 tournaments over a two-year span that the Richmond, Virginia, native was named MVP. Stat ed Richardson, "He was maybe one of the best junior college players ever to play the game."

As happened when the 1962 Coffeyville Red Ravens and the 1972 Vincennes Trailblazers rolled to a crown with an undefeat ed slate, everyone asked, "Is Western Texas the best ever?" Normally, the question was merely cannon fodder for a lively discussion. But events of the following season, provided suffi cient argument that, indeed, the 1979-80 Westerners were the best junior college team ever assembled.

Prior to the 1980 tournament, Richardson had accepted the head coaching position at the University of Tulsa. Afterwards he recruited four of his Western Texas players (Pressey, Stewart, Spradling, and David Brown) plus Mike Anderson, Jefferson State's quick playmaker, to join him. The five junior college transfers immediately turned the Golden Hurricane program around. Tulsa had a 20-win season for the first time in 26 years. The school's attendance at home games more than doubled. Sports Illustrated featured Richardson and his charges in a story. Richardson was named Missouri Valley Coach of the Year and Pressey the Newcomer of the Year. Their remarkable success was capped when Tulsa won the NIT.

However, one of the biggest successes of the year came early in the season when the Hurricanes met Louisville. In a dream match for juco fans, starters from the 1980 NJCAA champs minus one (point guard Ronald Portee) defeated the starters of the defending NCAA champs minus one (Darrell Griffith), 68-60.

Western Texas' Paul Pressey was one of the few chosen tourney MVP not because of his scoring prowess, but because of his ability to make things happen at both ends of the court. After following Westerner Coach Nolan Richardson to the University of Tulsa where he was an All-Missouri Valley selection, Pressey became a top assist and steal man in the NBA with the Milwaukee Bucks. (Photo courtesy of the University of Tulsa)

* * *

"I played junior college basketball at Eastern Arizona," recalled Nolan Richardson, "and I always dreamed of going to Hutch. I was very disappointed I didn't get to go as a player, but that made it all the more special going as a coach. It was like Christmas when I was a little boy. I could hardly wait for the tournament to come."

Winning the Juco Tournament was even more significant. But, since he was expected at Tulsa immediately, Richardson did not have much chance to enjoy it. Mother Nature did her part to extend the time he did have, however.

Sunday on the trip home to Snyder, a blizzard stranded the Westerners in Minneola, a small town (population 654) in southwestern Kansas. For 15 or so hours — spent partly in a truck stop, partly sleeping in a local church — Richardson and his players shared their success in togetherness.

As they left, Richardson said, "This has been nice. Everyone here has been great to us. We'll never forget the people in Mineola."

Tournament Results

Day		Game	Result
Tuesday:	Game		
		1	Yavapai — 60 Northeastern — 49
		2	Three Rivers — 80 Middle Georgia — 67
		3	Jefferson St. — 75 Monroe — 70
		4	Anderson — 93 NW Mississippi — 62
		5	Lincoln — 89 Cloud County — 77
		6	Western Texas — 108 North Idaho — 94
Wednesday:	Game		
		7	Baltimore — 66 Westark — 54
		8	Tyler — 102 Westchester — 83
		9	Middle Georgia — 89 Northeastern — 85 OT
		10	Yavapai — 62 Three Rivers — 59
		11	Jefferson St. — 83 Anderson — 67
Thursday:	Game		
		12	Monroe — 89 NW Mississippi — 62
		13	North Idaho — 97 Cloud County — 91
		14	Westchester — 54 Westark — 50
		15	Three Rivers — 96 Anderson — 75
		16	Western Texas — 100 Lincoln — 79
		17	Tyler — 73 Baltimore — 59
Friday:	Game		
		18	Monroe — 85 Middle Georgia — 84
		19	North Idaho — 70 Westchester — 69
		20	Baltimore — 58 Lincoln — 57
		21	Jefferson St. — 71 Yavapai — 63
		22	Western Texas — 67 Tyler — 52
Saturday:	Game		
		23	Monroe — 95 North Idaho — 76
		24	Three Rivers — 57 Baltimore — 56
		25	Tyler — 69 Yavapai — 65
		26	Western Texas — 85 Jefferson St. — 72

How They Finished in 1980

1. Western Texas College
2. Jefferson State Junior College
3. Tyler Junior College
4. Yavapai College
5. Three Rivers Community College
6. Community College of Baltimore
7. Monroe Community College
8. North Idaho College

All-Tournament Team

Claude Butler — North Idaho College
Raphael Dirden — Yavapai College
Fred Freeman — Jefferson State Junior College
Marvin "Moon" McCrary — Three Rivers Community College
Calvin Oldham — Middle Georgia College
Paul Pressey — Western Texas College
Greg Stewart — Western Texas College
Fred Watkins — Lincoln College
Elton Webster — Tyler Junior College
Tony Webster — Monroe Community College

Coach of the Tournament

Nolan Richardson — Western Texas College

French Most Valuable Player Award

Paul Pressey — Western Texas College

Sesher Sportsmanship Award

Phil Spradling — Western Texas College

Bud Obee Outstanding Small Player Award

Casper Ware — Yavapai College

1981:

REMOVING THE SMELL

Tied for the 1981 tourney scoring title with 90 points, Three Rivers' Tony Wallace later played at Tulane University. (Photo courtesy of Tulane University)

Region	Team
1	Mesa Community College — Mesa, Arizona
2	Westark Community College — Fort Smith, Arkansas
3	Jamestown Community College — Jamestown, New York
4	Lincoln College — Lincoln, Illinois
5	Cooke County College — Gainesville, Texas
7	Hiwassee College — Madisonville, Tennessee
8	Chipola Junior College — Marianna, Florida
9	Nebraska Western College — Scottsbluff, Nebraska
10	Anderson College — Anderson, South Carolina
11	Southeastern Community College — West Burlington, Iowa
12	C.S. Mott Community College — Flint, Michigan
13	Golden Valley Lutheran College — Minneapolis, Minnesota
15	Fashion Institute of Technology — New York, New York
16	Three Rivers Community College — Poplar Bluff, Missouri
17	Gainesville Junior College — Gainesville, Georgia
19	Gloucester County College — Sewell, New Jersey
Lost in First-Round Play-Offs:	
6	Hutchinson Community College — Hutchinson, Kansas
14	Tyler Junior College — Tyler, Texas
18	College of Southern Idaho — Twin Falls, Idaho
20	Community College of Baltimore — Baltimore, Maryland
21	Roxbury Community College — Roxbury, Massachusetts
22	Walker College — Jasper, Alabama

The top memory of those who participated in the 1952 National Juco Tournament was the brand new Hutchinson Sports Arena. One of them, Cotton Fitzsimmons, recalled "There weren't many field houses in those days that junior colleges played in. They played in gyms. [Playing in the Sports Arena], that was big!"

However, 29 Juco Tournaments had come and gone. The Arena was showing its age. In fact, despite Hutchinson's continued excellent support at the box office, there were even rumors that the event might be moved.

So, in the midst of a nationwide recession, Hutchonians went to the November polls in 1980 and helped Ronald Reagan soundly defeat Jimmy Carter for President. They barely passed a $7.9 million school bond. But, they left no doubt about their community pride in and love for the Juco Tournament. A $1.4 million bond issue for extensive renovations of the Sports Arena passed by a 2-1 margin.

THE PARTICIPANTS

No longer was Missouri the private reserve of the Moberly Greyhounds. During the season, Three Rivers Community College won 35 straight games before losing to Crowder College, 69-66, in the second of a best-of-three series for the Region 16 crown. Gene Bess' Raiders returned to Hutchinson for the fourth consecutive year, bringing a tourney record of 16-4 with five trophies.

When the Raiders won in 1979, they were nobodies. Now the school was located in a new facility and the name "Three Rivers" recognized nationally in junior college ranks as a basketball powerhouse. The Raiders were consensus favorites for the 34th annual Juco Tournament ranked No. 1 with a 36-1 record.

After Three Rivers, familiar names were sparse in the 16-team field. The only other ranked team with more than two previous appearances was No. 19 Anderson College (27-4), making its fifth trip to the nationals in seven years.

The most veteran schools were among the unranked. Southeastern Community College of West Burlington (25-6) and Chipola Junior College (25-4) were making their 12th and 8th appearances, respectively, both having finished as high as second.

The only other schools with more than two appearances were Lincoln College (30-4), Westark Community College (28-5), and C.S. Mott Community College (26-6). But, even here, the names were not necessarily recognizable. Mott's four previous trips to Hutchinson had been as Flint Community Junior College.

Three Rivers was the only former champ in the field and, with the exception of the Burlington Blackhawks, the only team with a winning record in tourney competition. The Raiders' challenge would most likely come from unfamiliar quarters.

There were two undefeated squads: No. 4 Hiwassee College (29-0) and No. 17 Golden Valley Lutheran College (27-0). The other ranked teams included No. 6 Fashion Institute of Technology (31-2), No. 10 Mesa Community College (30-2), and No. 13 Gloucester County College (31-3). Of these, Hiwassee and Mesa had one previous tourney experience.

Unranked Jamestown Community College (27-6) and Nebraska Western College (28-7) had also been seen by tourney fans only one other time. However, like unranked newcomers Cooke County College (31-4) and Gainesville Junior College (22-6), they were not considered threats.

Despite the lack of big names, the week promised excitement. The field's combined won-lose percentage (88.3 percent) was the second-highest to date. Since all ranked teams faced unranked opponents in the opening round, the best games could be expected in the later rounds.

TUESDAY — OVERTURNING THE APPLE CART

The Golden Valley Royals nearly made it to Hutchinson in 1980. The key to their success was 6-8 center/forward Nelson Johnson, the second-leading rebounder in the nation (16.5) and an honorable mention All-American. In the Region 13 final against Anoka-Ramsey Community College, Johnson scored 57 points, grabbed 31 rebounds, and blocked 15 shots. Said Royal Coach Phil "Flip" Saunders, "He did everything but win the game." Golden Valley lost, 111-110, on a last second shot.

This year there was no denying the Royals. The Minnesotans were undefeated, principally because of Johnson's 22.5 points, 15.5 rebounds, 5 blocked shots, and 3 dunks per game, the kind of credentials that would later place him on the NJCAA's All-American 1st-Team.

A 1981 1st-Team All-American, Golden Valley's Nelson Johnson completed his collegiate career at Drake University. (Photo courtesy of Drake University)

In the tourney opener, Johnson again carried the load, hitting his first four shots. With five veterans from its 1980 tourney team, including four starters, Lincoln looked more like the newcomer, playing sloppily, allowing Golden Valley to take control. Then, as he had the previous year against Cloud County scoring phenom Ronnie Joyner, Lynx forward Mike Goeken put the clamps on Johnson. With 13:27 left in the period, Johnson picked up foul number four. Lincoln tied the score, 28-all, with 3:47 to go, then added the final six points of the half.

Golden Valley never came closer. Playing only four minutes of the second period before fouling out, Johnson totaled 12 points and no rebounds. Said Coach Saunders, "We're not going to beat very many people with our All-American on the bench." Lincoln handed the No. 17 Royals their first loss, 76-63.

Jamestown's Roland Rucker was a one-man army in the afternoon feature, firing 23 first-half points, leading the Jayhawks to a 50-39 advantage. The 6-3 freshman added another 22 in the second period. However, a tourney-high 45 points, all but three from the field, was not enough.

Southeastern of West Burlington rallied, scoring 11 unanswered points midway in the final frame. Then a 15-foot baseline jumper by Victor Jordan with three seconds remaining gave the Blackhawks a 97-95 victory.

When someone mentioned the long-standing traditions of junior college basketball in Texas, names like "Tyler," "Kilgore," and "Lon Morris" were generally the ones most referred

to. But, in fact, the oldest junior college in the Lone Star State was Cooke County College in Gainesville. Until Coach Jim Voight came along, however, the best season record the Lions had managed was 15-15.

Now in his fourth year at Cooke County, Voight had molded the best Lion team yet. Despite losing two starters who averaged 30 points and 20 rebounds between them at the Christmas break, Cooke County won the North Texas Junior College Conference. In the Region 5 final, the Lions beat No. 8 Midland College, 97-86. Then, in a first-round play-off with Region 14 winner Tyler Junior College, Cooke upset the No. 3 team in the nation, earning its first trip to the nationals.

Things did not get any easier at Hutchinson; in the afternoon finale, Voight's Lions faced top-rated Three Rivers.

Unexpectedly, it was a tight, close match-up between similar quick, defensive-minded squads. There were seven ties in the opening period. A jumper by James Helmich with seven seconds left, gave Cooke County a 32-30 halftime edge.

The Lions remained on top until midway in the final stanza when Three Rivers went on a nine-point binge, taking a 51-43 advantage.

Then Cooke rallied, finally tying the Raiders, 65-all, with 47 seconds left on a 25-foot bomb by Bruce Tipton.

Three Rivers regained the lead on one of two free throws by Alan Barnett with 18 seconds remaining.

Cooke County called time.

In the huddle, Voight designed a play to give Tipton the final shot. The plan worked perfectly. But, as the 6-4 guard went up, he changed his mind, afraid his shot might be blocked. At the last moment, he dished off to reserve guard Russell Taylor. Taylor's 15-footer barely beat the buzzer.

Cooke County upset Three Rivers, 67-66.

"It just seemed like we had the weight of the world on our shoulders out there," reflected Raider Coach Gene Bess. "The No. 1 ranking and the great fans we have make it kind of hard to keep things in perspective sometimes."

With the pre-tourney pick out of the way, the roll of favorite now fell to No. 4 Hiwassee. The undefeated Tigers readily accepted the new status. Behind O'dell Mosteller's game-high 26 points, Hiwassee ran away from Nebraska Western, opening a 39-22 halftime gap before breezing to a 93-68 win.

As an academic institution Fashion Institute of Technology was much respected in the fashion industry of New York City. The school offered an excellent curriculum, including courses in textiles, modeling, marketing, and other fashion-related businesses.

As a basketball powerhouse, however, FIT was a nonentity. Tourney fans viewed the Tigers as oddities, something for trivia buffs in later years. Despite their No. 6 ranking, few expected the New Yorkers to survive the pressures of a first appearance in the Sports Arena, especially under the prime-time scrutiny of a nearly full house.

Sure enough, as Coach Marvin Rippy remembered, "The experience was a little overwhelming." With 8:27 remaining in the first half, trailing by only four, FIT fell apart. While Westark's staunch defense took the Tigers out of their transition game, its offense scored 16 unanswered points. Westark held a 45-26 bulge at intermission and coasted to an 87-55 victory. Five Lions hit double figures led by DeWayne Shepard's game-high 22. The aggressive Westark zone held Fashion Institute to 34.7 percent from the field while committing just nine fouls.

The evening finale was a game of spurts. Chipola overcame a 10-point deficit in the first half, Mesa an 11-point disadvantage in the second. The turning point came with 8½ minutes remaining, Mesa on top, 53-52. In the next seven minutes, Chipola outscored the Thunderbirds, 14-3. Paced by Willie Jackson's 20 points, 7 rebounds, and 4 blocked shots, Chipola upended No. 10 Mesa, 70-62.

WEDNESDAY — WHAT'LL I DO?

With four upsets of ranked teams in the first day of play, the two remaining top-20 squads had reason for concern. Consequently, No. 13 Gloucester County wanted to leave no doubts in Wednesday's opener. The Roadrunners raced to a 17-point lead over C.S. Mott midway in the first half.

The Mott Bears rallied, however, taking a 40-39 halftime edge.

Again Gloucester tried to outdistance the Bears, building a 14-point margin in the final period.

Again Mott rallied, pulling within a basket, 75-73, with 4:25 remaining.

Then, while Gloucester Coach Ronald "Fang" Mitchell paced the sidelines — he stood throughout the game — three Mott players fouled out. Since there were only eight members on the Bear squad, it was the telling blow. Gloucester avoided upset with an 89-85 win.

There were no questions about the outcome of the final opening-round contest. Anderson's half-court trap took effect in the last two minutes of the first half, allowing the No. 19 Trojans to pull away from Gainesville, 49-38, at intermission. Anderson continued the onslaught in the second period, racking up a convincing 102-78 victory. Six Trojans tallied double figures, led by the massive front line of John Toms (6-5, 200 pounds), Windfred King (6-10, 240), and David Henderson (6-6, 209), each with 19.

In the consolation interlude before the opening quarterfinals, Nelson Johnson returned to form, hitting 11 of Golden Valley's first 13. Then the Cleveland, Ohio, native went cold, scoring only once more the rest of the period. The Royals fell behind Jamestown, 38-22, at halftime.

Golden Valley rallied in the final frame, gaining a 42-all tie with 11:03 to go on back-to-back three-point plays by Johnson. The Royals and Johnson continued hot, opening a 13-point gap. Jamestown answered with 12 straight points, but was unable to go ahead. Led by Johnson's 33 points, 12 rebounds, and 2 blocked shots, Golden Valley held on, 68-64.

According to Lincoln Coach Allen Pickering, "My first six or eight years [at Lincoln], we averaged 85 to 95 points a game and gave up 80. Defense to me was just kind of something you put up with until you had a chance to shoot again."

Then, in 1978, Pickering hired assistant coach Billy Hoagland, a former hard-nosed defensive player at Lincoln. Hoagland became the architect of the Lynx defense. "He was in charge of defense and I was in charge of offense," said Pickering. That division of power left Lincoln in a precarious position in the opening quarterfinal.

The Lynx interspersed several leads with eight ties before gaining a 47-45 edge at intermission. For the next 12 minutes, Southeastern of Iowa continued to keep pace, led by the hot shooting of point guard Handy Johnson (12 for 17 from the field and 29 points).

Earlier in the contest, defensive specialist Mike Goeken had received a severely cut lip, forcing Hoagland to accompany him to the hospital. With Lincoln unable to shake the Blackhawks, "I look up and down and, heck, I've got to coach the game myself," realized Pickering. "I haven't coached a whole game in four or five years."

Luckily he received timely advice from point guard Chris Jones who was resting on the bench. "Coach, I think we can trap for the next minute." Pickering called time, inserted Jones into the lineup, and instructed his team to trap just before the midcourt line. "We got a couple quick steals and turned the game around," recalled Pickering.

When Hoagland returned with five or six minutes remaining, Pickering gave a sigh of relief saying, "I'm glad you're back to take over." Hoagland replied, "You're ahead! I'm not going to do anything."

Lincoln's superior quickness and the dynamic scoring duo of Fred Watkins and Julius Poinsette proved too much for SECC-Burlington. Paced by Watkins' 32 and Poinsette's 26, the Lynx advanced to the semifinals, 88-82.

In the day's finale, Cooke County went after its second tourney favorite in two days. Though they rarely led, the Lions pestered Hiwassee from start to finish. Even after Jack Bedford's free throw gave Hiwassee a comfortable 94-89 lead with 29 seconds left, Cooke applied pressure. Bruce Tipton hit a 15-footer at the 20-second mark and Tommy Brown tipped in a Tipton miss at the buzzer. However, because of game-high 32-point totals by O'dell Mosteller and Al Cole, Hiwassee had sufficient cushion to edge the Lions, 94-93.

THURSDAY — CLIFF-HANGER CITY

The day's opening consolation contests were dull and sloppy bores, Three Rivers eliminating Nebraska Western, 91-73, and Fashion Institute doing the same to Mesa, 70-57.

Then the action intensified.

In the afternoon finale, Gainesville rallied from a six-point deficit with less than two minutes left only to miss two shots in the final 10 seconds. C.S. Mott squeaked by the Georgians, 90-88.

Action was hot in the first half of the evening curtain raiser, but not as hot as it would get after the break. When the two teams returned to the floor, SECC-Burlington hit 10 straight field goals while Cooke county canned 8 of 9.

With 12:56 remaining, the Burlington Blackhawks opened a 59-48 gap. Cooke closed it, taking a 79-78 margin on a long bomb by 5-7 Jeff Ray. The Blackhawks regained the lead on a driving goal by Handy Johnson with 47 seconds left. Finally, with five seconds showing, James Helmich won the game with an 18-footer. The final: Cooke County — 81, SECC — 80.

Despite the losses of forward Tommy Daniels — who hit his first shot, then left the game because of chest pains later diagnosed as pleurisy — and of center Willie Jackson — who was whistled for three fouls in the first 10 minutes — Chipola played Westark tough in the opening period of the evening's first quarterfinal. There were eight ties and neither team led by more than four. A last-second jumper by Glen Mays gave Westark a 30-26 advantage at intermission.

With Daniels in the hospital and Jackson back in the lineup but ineffectual, held scoreless for the half, Chipola began to lose ground in the final frame. Westark built a 50-43 margin with 6:54 remaining.

Then forward Mel Roseboro and guard Phil Green connected from outside. A 20-footer by Roseboro with 1:33 to go gave Chipola the lead, 53-52.

With 1:05 to go, a baseline jumper by Brian Kelleybrew returned the advantage to Westark.

Chipola failed to respond on its possession when Roseboro was called for charging.

At the 15-second mark, Chipola fouled Ronnie Wennberg. Coach Milt Johnson called two successive time-outs, hoping to freeze Westark's leading scorer.

Wennberg missed and the resultant scramble led to a jump ball between Westark's 6-5 Kelleybrew and 6-6½ Indian reserve Bill Nealy. Chipola won the tip with plenty of time to negotiate a game-winner.

However, the normally patient Indians hurried the ball upcourt. Ten feet past the 10-second stripe, Lion point guard Scott Bigott, rarely a headline-grabber, stripped the ball from Roseboro and the game from Chipola. Westark advanced, 54-53.

There were no indications that the nightcap would be similarly close. Continuing to impress, Anderson took a 41-31 halftime lead, sending many fans home.

But, because of foul trouble, the Trojans were forced to abandon their highly successful half-court trap. Led by Jeff Tucker, who hit 15 of his game-high 25 in the final frame, Gloucester County gradually reduced the deficit, finally taking its first lead since the opening bucket, 64-63, with 6:20 remaining.

The lead then seesawed. At the 1:10 mark, Winfred King gave the edge to Anderson, 75-74, with two free throws, setting up the fourth slam-bang finale in a row.

With 10 seconds left, Gloucester's Darnell Martin fired and missed. Roadrunner forward Earl "Helicopter" Harrison rebounded and immediately put it back up. The shot was blocked.

Harrison tried again. Again it was blocked. This time Anderson secured the rebound — and the win, the tourney's third consecutive one-point nail-biter.

FRIDAY — IF YOU ONLY KNEW

The day's action was delayed 15 minutes when both Three Rivers and Golden Valley came out wearing gold uniforms. After Golden Valley switched to its purple road attire, Three Rivers proceeded to hold All-American Nelson Johnson to 13 points and the Royals to the lowest total of the week, eliminating Golden Valley, 60-40.

The second game was a run-and-gun race, featuring an outstanding 30-point performance by C.S. Mott's Kevin Strozier, as the Bears downed Fashion Institute, 105-84.

The afternoon finale was an excellent, well-played contest until the end. In the final 80 seconds of a one-point thriller, both ides committed costly turnovers, failed to convert the front end of crucial one-and-one free throws, and missed potential game-winners from the field.

With one second showing, Gloucester County's Earl Harrison was fouled trying to score off an offensive rebound. Using a strategy which had worked against Westark the night before, Chipola Coach Milt Johnson called three consecutive time-outs, hoping to upset Harrison at the line.

Consistent with the last few moments of action, Harrison's first attempt fell short. His second hit long off the heel of the rim. Chipola survived, 77-76.

After the opening-day upsets, most observers tabbed No. 4 Hiwassee and No. 19 Anderson as the eventual championship game opponents. Anderson possessed a super half-court trap defense and the tallest, bulkiest front line in the field. Hiwassee was smaller, but quicker with excellent leapers and one of the top scorers in the nation — O'dell Mosteller (27.0 average at the start of the week). They were also the two best rebounding teams in the tournament. Neither Lincoln nor Westark were given much chance in the semifinals.

While many local fans were glued to TV sets in the Arena halls, watching an NCAA regional match between Wichita State and Kansas, Hiwassee faced its first man-to-man defense of the week — and could not crack it. Lincoln held the Tigers to 31 percent from the field and opened an unexpected 35-24 half-time advantage. Indicative of Hiwassee's frustration was that Mosteller picked up three fouls, adding only two free throws to the Tiger cause.

Dennis Murphy and David Wright led a Hiwassee rally which netted 12 straight points and a 44-43 lead with 11:44 remaining.

But, after the Tiger edge grew to four, two free throws by Tom Townslay and a three-point play by Fred Watkins returned the lead to Lincoln, 57-56, with 3:39 to go. From then on the contest became a game of "catch-me-if-you-can" with Hiwassee "it."

There was only one moment of concern for the Lynx. "We're holding the ball in a crucial part [of the game]," recalled Lincoln Coach Allen Pickering, "and Chris Jones goes for a lay-up. Chris was the world's worst shooter unless you put money on the line and then he was one of the greatest. He goes back door for a wide open lay-up to pretty much seal it — like make it a five-point game instead of a three-point game in the last minute or so — and he misses the lay-up. They kicked the ball out of bounds and I called time-out. I wanted just to punch him in the nose. Instead I put my arm around him and said, 'Hey, that's okay. No big deal.'

"Some lady heard that," continued Pickering, "wrote me a letter and said that was one of the greatest sportsmanship talks she had ever heard. I always wanted to write her back and say, 'If you only knew what was really in my heart.'"

Sesher Sportsmanship Award winner Chris Jones (No. 22) finished his collegiate career at Quincy College in Illinois. (Photo courtesy of Quincy College)

Lincoln prevailed, upsetting the Tigers, 70-63. Besides winning, the Lynx also surprised everyone by dominating the boards, 48-37, led by Fred Watkins 20 caroms (to go with 22 points). Hiwassee top gun O'dell Mosteller was held to only six points. Said Pickering, "This one was for my sister. She lives in Tennessee and I couldn't have stood the harassment I would have gotten from her if we had lost to a team from Tennessee."

The nightcap was even more shocking.

Led by Brian Kelleybrew, Westark jumped out to a quick 12-6 advantage, then held off a late Anderson rally. At intermission, Westark was in front, 39-35.

Anderson remained four to eight points in arrears for another six minutes. Then the Lions went on a 13-3 tear. With 7:15 remaining, Westark was in total command, 64-50. Behind a trio of outstanding performances — Kelleybrew (24), DeWayne Shepard (20), and Ronnie Wennberg (20) — Westark coasted to a stunning 78-66 victory.

"They made us look bad," summed up Anderson Coach John Edwards. "They just played a super game."

SATURDAY — TWO EXTREMES

During the week, the quick, running eight-man squad of C.S. Mott became a crowd favorite. However, the lack of personnel combined with foul trouble to hurt the Bears in the battle for seventh. Paced by Tony Wallace's game-high 36, Three Rivers easily controlled the contest, winning 104-86.

In the fifth-place game, 29 points by Willie Jackson and four free throws in the final 12 seconds by Mel Roseboro lifted Chipola over Cooke County, 85-79.

Anderson blew a 21-point first-half lead, then had to rally from five down with 2:30 remaining before defeating Hiwassee, 92-87, for third. Trojan David Henderson led all scorer's with 30 while Hiwassee's O'dell Mosteller hit 26, giving him 90 for the week, tying him with Three Rivers' Wallace for the tourney scoring title.

After a week of upsets, the championship match was a fitting pairing of two teams which had started the week among the unheralded also-rans. In the interim, Lincoln handed the only two undefeated entrants their first loss while Westark held three opponents to an average 58 points per game. There was no clear-cut favorite for the crown and, since the week had provided eight one- or two-point finishes, a new tourney record, everyone expected a close, exciting finale.

Unfortunately, what followed was anticlimatic.

The contest was close for seven minutes. Then behind the outside shooting of Ronnie Wennberg and the inside play of Brian Kelleybrew and DeWayne Shepard, Westark reeled off 10 unanswered points, opening a 25-11 gap. With 2:13 remaining, the difference was 20.

Though Julius Poinsette gained a hot hand, scoring the Lynx's first 10 points of the second half, Lincoln could only reduce the deficit to 12. "I think when I really knew it was all over was somewhere around nine minutes to go in the ballgame," recalled Lincoln Coach Allen Pickering. "We made a little rush at them . . . Poinsette steals the ball on a press, goes in for a lay-up, and it hangs on the front of the rim. 'Should I' or 'Shouldn't I?' And it said, 'No.' I thought, 'This is it. We're never going to catch them.'"

For the contest, Westark shot 67.5 percent from the field and Lincoln 33.3 percent, both extremes tourney records for a championship tilt.

Westark captured the crown, 67-50.

THE AFTERMATH — LASTING MEMORIES

Despite the disappointing loss, the week was a rewarding experience for the Lincoln Lynx, particularly for Chris Jones, winner of the Sesher Sportsmanship Award.

"He looked like a nice kid," described Coach Allen Pickering. "He was clean cut. He did nice things, picked opponents up. He was a classy player. I think that people there [at Hutchinson] especially pick up on that. That's just the way he played. I felt very fortunate that somebody else recognized that."

For Pickering, the week was equally memorable, his feelings toward the tournament and the city that supported it reflecting similar experiences of past participants. "It's a big deal and they treat it as a big deal. We went to talk to some classes and the thing that amazed me was how innovative their teachers were. There was a little girl assigned to Lincoln, Illinois. Where were we? What did we do? What state did we come from? What was the bird? What was the flower? They tied the whole thing in. It was a community project. We play a game in Lincoln, Illinois, and the fifth grade kids don't even know we're playing. But, at Hutchinson, it's different."

Pickering cited one example which summarized how special the week had been. Clyde Townslay, father of reserve Tom Townslay, constantly kidded Pickering during the season about the fact that, since Lincoln gave no scholarships, it cost him "$50,000" (an exaggeration) to have his son play for the Lynx. But, as he later told Pickering, "When I stood in that hallway [of the Arena] and I saw five kids climbing on my son wanting his autograph, it was the most dramatic single event in my entire life."

Nothing could top the sensation of winning it all, however.

Scott Bigott, the team sparkplug. Glen Mays, a converted high school center, learning the ropes at guard. Ronnie Wennberg, the zone-breaker. And the leaping inside tandem of Brian Kelleybrew and DeWayne Shepard, either of which deserved the MVP trophy though it went to the latter. Singularly, the Westark Lions were not exceptional. But, as a unit, they played nearly flawlessly, holding opponents to a tourney-low 40 percent from the field, allowing only 56 points per game, while hitting 57.8 percent from the field themselves, a new record.

Coach Gayle Kaundart had crafted excellent defensive teams in the past, but in three previous tournaments had only won two out of six games. Why the sudden jump to the top?

One reason was the tough Lion schedule of past years. "We were playing in a double conference then," explained Kaundart. "We had 30 conference games during the year and every one of them was a grind. Everybody liked to play their conference games after Christmas. We played nine weeks straight of three conference games a week and then went into play-offs. We had a state tournament. We had a regional two-best-out-of-three. Then we generally had to play a Kansas team [in an inter-region first-round play-off]. So we were absolutely worn out."

At the beginning of the 1980-81 season, Westark dropped out of one conference and returned to a normal two-games-a-week schedule. Despite still having to play 11 play-off games to get to the nationals, including a tough first-round pairing against Hutchinson Community College, the Lions were fresher for the wars of the tournament.

The other reason for Westark's success was a strong determination to bury past embarrassments. With a No. 3 ranking, the best defense in the nation, and led by a future pro in Darrell Walker, the Lions came to Hutchinson the previous year only to lose two straight.

When Kaundart accepted his Coach of the Tournament Award, he said, "I told the players the Arena was going to be renovated after the tournament was over, but I told them what they smelled when they walked into the Arena wasn't from the old building. It was the smell we left last year. I think we got rid of that."

Westark's Scott Bigott (No. 20 versus Lincoln's Chris Jones in the championship game) later played in the NCAA tournament with Houston Baptist. (Photo courtesy of Frank Deming)

How They Finished in 1981

1. Westark Community College
2. Lincoln College
3. Anderson College
4. Hiwassee College
5. Chipola Junior College
6. Cooke County Junior College
7. Three Rivers Community College
8. C.S. Mott Community College

French Most Valuable Player Award

DeWayne Shepard — Westark Community College

Sesher Sportsmanship Award

Chris Jones — Lincoln College

Bud Obee Outstanding Small Player Award

Kevin Strozier — C.S. Mott Community College

Tournament Results

Day		Game	
Tuesday:	Game		
		1	Lincoln — 76 Golden Valley — 63
		2	SECC-Burlington — 97 Jamestown — 95
		3	Cooke County — 67 Three Rivers — 66
		4	Hiwassee — 93 Nebraska Western — 68
		5	Westark — 87 Fashion Institute — 55
		6	Chipola — 70 Mesa — 62
Wednesday:	Game		
		7	Gloucester County — 89 C.S. Mott — 85
		8	Anderson — 102 Gainesville — 78
		9	Golden Valley — 68 Jamestown — 64
		10	Lincoln — 88 SECC-Burlington — 82
		11	Hiwassee — 94 Cooke County — 93
Thursday:	Game		
		12	Three Rivers — 91 Nebraska Western — 73
		13	Fashion Institute — 70 Mesa — 57
		14	C.S. Mott — 90 Gainesville — 88
		15	Cooke County — 81 SECC-Burlington — 80
		16	Westark — 54 Chipola — 53
		17	Anderson — 75 Gloucester County — 74
Friday:	Game		
		18	Three Rivers — 60 Golden Valley — 40
		19	C.S. Mott — 105 Fashion Institute — 84
		20	Chipola — 77 Gloucester County — 76
		21	Lincoln — 70 Hiwassee — 63
		22	Westark — 78 Anderson — 66
Saturday:	Game		
		23	Three Rivers — 104 C.S. Mott — 86
		24	Chipola — 85 Cooke County — 79
		25	Anderson — 92 Hiwassee — 87
		26	Westark — 67 Lincoln — 50

All-Tournament Team

David Henderson — Anderson College
Brian Kelleybrew — Westark Community College
O'dell Mosteller — Hiwassee College
Julius Poinsette — Lincoln College
Mel Roseboro — Chipola Junior College
Roland Rucker — Jamestown Community College
DeWayne Shepard — Westark Community College
Kevin Strozier — C.S. Mott Community College
Jeff Tucker — Gloucester County College
Tony Wallace — Three Rivers Community College

Coach of the Tournament

Gayle Kaundart — Westark Community College

A BAD CASE OF SPUDITIS

hough the 35th edition of the National Junior College Basketball Tournament was one of the most dramatic weeks in the event's history, longtime fans often found keeping their eyes on the action difficult. The reason?

The tournament had flashy new surroundings.

During the year, the Hutchinson Sports Arena had undergone a major face-lift. With the exception of the men's and women's dressing rooms which were the responsibility of Hutchinson Community College, every inch of the building's interior was changed. Nearly 4,000 gallons of paint had removed the accumulated drabness of 30 years. A scheme using gold, blue, red, and white, the colors of the local high school and community college, gave the building a cheerful freshness. The halls were covered with rubberized red tile and the walls adorned with modern graphics, a map of Kansas with the past state high school champions noted, a map of the United States pinpointing all the NJCAA champions, and most appropriately, a full-length color portrait of Charley Sesher — the man most responsible for bringing the tournament to Hutchinson — who had recently passed away.

There were two new features: an extensive sports medicine complex in the basement and the Humiston Administration Center, containing offices for the community college athletic department. The latter, named after Hod Humiston, a longstanding community leader and the tourney's awards ceremony emcee for the past 28 years, also held the Sports Arena's original jump circle, preserved as a centerpiece for the Center's hospitality area.

With a $12,500 sound system and an $85,000 computerized scoreboard, the "new" Sports Arena was ready for another 30 years of championship play.

THE PARTICIPANTS

Region	Team
1	Dixie College — St. George, Utah
2	Westark Community College — Fort Smith, Arkansas
3	Jamestown Community College — Jamestown, New York
5	Midland College — Midland, Texas
7	Volunteer State Community College — Gallatin, Tennessee
8	Miami-Dade Community College, North Campus — Miami, Florida
9	Nebraska Western College — Scottsbluff, Nebraska
10	Ferrum College — Ferrum, Virginia
12	Vincennes University — Vincennes, Indiana
14	Henderson County Junior College — Athens, Texas
16	Moberly Junior College — Moberly, Missouri
18	College of Southern Idaho — Twin Falls, Idaho
19	Mercer County Community College — Trenton, New Jersey
20	Allegany Community College — Cumberland, Maryland
21	Tunxis Community College — Farmington, Connecticut
22	John C. Calhoun State Community College — Decatur, Alabama

Lost in First Round Play Offs:

Region	Team
4	Illinois Central College — East Peoria, Illinois
6	Dodge City Community College — Dodge City, Kansas
11	Southeastern Community College — West Burlington, Iowa
13	Lake Region Community College — Devils Lake, North Dakota
15	State University of New York Agricultural and Technical College at Farmingdale — Farmingdale, New York
17	Abraham Baldwin Agricultural College — Tifton, Georgia

The first native Haitian to play collegiate basketball in the U.S., Miami-Dade's Yvon Joseph parlayed a 1982 All-Tournament selection into a starring role at Georgia Tech and a brief tenure with the New Jersey Nets in the NBA. (Photo courtesy of Georgia Tech, photo taken by Jack Reimer)

Making its third straight appearance, defending champ Westark Community College (31-3) looked like a sure bet for a repeat title. The Lions were deeper and quicker with better leapers than the year before and again possessed the best defense in the nation (51.8). They returned three starters, including tourney MVP DeWayne Shepard, whom Coach Gayle Kaundart described as "stronger, more consistent, and more aggressive." Yet, Westark was only ranked 12th and considered just one of many pre-tourney favorites.

Heading the list of top contenders were two undefeated squads. No. 1 Miami-Dade Community College-North (30-0) and No. 9 Tunxis Community College (26-0).

Other ranked veteran schools with strong possibilities included: No. 6 Jamestown Community College (30-2), possessing a top-10 defense (57.5) and the widest average winning margin in the field (26.1); No. 15 Vincennes University (31-4), making its 13th trip to Hutchinson, the first under head coach Dan Sparks; and No. 17 College of Southern Idaho, featuring the tallest front line in the competition, including 7-1 Rick Tunstall, one of two seven footers in the tournament, the first since Artis Gilmore and Pembrook Burrows in 1969.

There were also three ranked newcomers with potential: No. 3 Henderson County Junior College (31-2), which won tough Region 14 with two wins over No. 13 San Jacinto College; No.

8 Allegany Community College (31-3), which beat No. 7 Community College of Allegheny County, Pittsburgh, in Region 20 action; and No. 19 Calhoun State Community College (26-3), which won the North Division of the Alabama Junior College Conference with a perfect record and owned a 20-game win streak.

Two unranked veterans drew respect on their names alone: two-time former champ Mercer County Community College (27-3), making its 10th appearance, this time guided by Howie Landa who was returning to coaching after a three-year "retirement"; and four-time champ Moberly Junior College (30-5), returning for the 19th time after an eight-year absence, the longest in the school's history.

Veterans Dixie College (28-4), Ferrum College (20-8), and Nebraska Western College (28-7) were questionable, but not discounted: Dixie averaged 58.2 percent from the field; Ferrum was on a roll, winning the Region 10 tournament despite being seeded 8th; and Nebraska Western, with seven-footer Dave Cecil, upset No. 15 Southeast Community College of Fairbury, Nebraska, in Region 9 play.

Newcomers Volunteer State Community College (28-4) and Midland College (30-4) were the only apparent long shots. Volunteer State was given virtually no advance publicity and what notoriety Midland received was due to the team's 89.5 offensive average, tops in the field, and its 5-6 point guard who reputedly averaged 1.5 dunks a game.

TUESDAY — A WORLD RECORD

Tunxis' quickness caused several Ferrum turnovers, allowing the Tomahawks to forge a 20-2 advantage to start the first tourney game in the "new" Arena. Led by James Williams' game-high 32, Ferrum reduced the deficit to 12 twice, once in each half, but no further. After holding a 49-28 halftime margin, Tunxis used free throws from Ferrum's desperation fouls to post a 90-75 victory, extending its undefeated string to 27.

At the end of the regular season schedule, Coach Dan Sparks, who had been in the winner's circle as a player (1965) and as an assistant coach (1972), tried to instill the tradition of Vincennes basketball by showing his players films from past Trailblazer championships. The strategy apparently worked. Vincennes rolled through five Region 12 games, then smashed Illinois Central, 88-65, in a first-round play-off.

The Trailblazers were not as inspired in their opener in Hutchinson, however. Both Vincennes and Nebraska Western shot poorly, denying either the opportunity for any extended run. There were nine lead changes in the first half and no margin greater than four with Nebraska Western holding a 29-27 edge at intermission.

Then the fire of past Vincennes successes began to glow. The Trailblazer defense forced seven Nebraska Western turnovers in the next seven minutes. Cougar Coach Ron Brillhart repeatedly called time-outs to curb Vincennes' momentum, but was unsuccessful. The Trailblazers surged past Nebraska Western, 50-28, in the second half, giving Sparks his first tourney victory as head coach, 77-55.

Jamestown went on a 10-2 spree, overtaking Moberly 38-37 midway through the afternoon finale. The Jayhawks remained on top for another 5½ minutes. Then 6-6 guard Gerald Wilkins and 6-5 center Jerome Clayton attacked the middle of the Jamestown defense. Moberly outscored the New Yorkers, 14-2, taking control of the game.

Down nine with under two minutes remaining, Jamestown mounted a rally similar to that at the end of the first half. A driving lay-up by Carl Jeter and a three-point play by Sam Winley trimmed the difference to four with 1:11 to go.

Malcolm Thomas' powerful slam dunk with :58 showing appeared to seal a Moberly win, but three missed Greyhound one-and-ones left the outcome in doubt until the end. Though failing at the line down the stretch, Moberly hit 17 of 24 charities for the game compared to Jamestown's 9 of 16, giving the Greyhounds sufficient cushion for a 77-73 victory. Moberly's Wilkins, brother of Georgia All-American Dominique, led all scorers with 24.

The evening curtain raiser was one of the most bizarre contests in tourney history.

In the first half, Mercer County committed 14 fouls, including five by reserve forward Charles Thomas, and fell behind Dixie 45-26.

The Vikings were even more aggressive in the final period, piling up 22 more violations, not to mention three technicals. Four more Mercer players joined Thomas on the bench. Since Coach Howie Landa had lost two starters and a sixth man to grades at the semester and Michael Dobson, the team's regular center, to a severe ankle sprain in Monday's practice, the Vikings finished the contest with only three players on the floor.

Dixie responded magnificently to Mercer's charity. While Mercer was outscoring the Rebels, 33-23, from the field, Dixie hit 44 of 51 foul shots. Sophomore forward Chris McMullin paved the way with an unbelievable *29 for 29* — not only an all-time tourney record, but one which would later be listed in *The Guinness Book of World Records*.[1] Behind McMullin's tourney-high 39, Dixie downed Mercer County, 90-82.

Chris McMullin set a world record in Dixie's opener against Mercer County with 29 free throws without a miss. McMullin finished his collegiate career at Utah State University. (Photo courtesy of Utah State University)

If the events of the previous game did not make the crowd sit up and take notice, the evening feature surely did. Led by 6-4 forward Puntus Wilson and 6-6 center Chester Smith, each with 10, unheralded Midland mounted a patient attack, hit 65 percent from the field, and built a 13-point margin, before carrying a 32-22 advantage over defending champion Westark to the dressing room at intermission. Then, with diminutive point guard Anthony "Spud" Webb spearheading their running game, the Chaparrals extended the margin, racing to a 55-34 lead midway in the final period.

Midland's domination of the former champs was so complete, fans relaxed in their seats, showing no further interest, assuming an upset was inevitable. Their apathy did not last.

"When we went up there [to Hutchinson], it had been put in their paper that we had a little bitty guy who could dunk the ball," recalled Midland Coach Jerry Stone. "People would come up to me during practice and say, 'Which one is this Webb?' I'd point to him and they'd say, 'He can dunk the ball?' I'd say, 'Yeah.' And they'd say, 'Ohhhhh.' They flat didn't believe me. They thought it was a big publicity hype."

Then, against Westark, at a time when things were most boring, the 5-6 freshman stole the ball. "I thought, 'Well, he's going to dunk it,' " described Stone. "But, he stopped and went off both feet. He went up and I thought, 'He's going to try to dunk like that? My gosh, he's going to embarrass himself!' "

---

[1]With under five minutes remaining in the game and Dixie in obvious command, Coach Neil Roberts decided to rest McMullin. As he escorted McMullin's substitute to the scorer's table, one of the scorekeepers said, "No, coach. Don't take him out. He's got 29 straight free throws. It's a new NJCAA record."
Roberts called McMullin to the sidelines and said, "Chris, you've got 29 in a row and I know you're going to get some more. Do you want to stay in and keep this thing going?"
McMullin replied, "Nah. I'll probably miss the next one anyway."
In Dixie's next outing, McMullin received only one free throw attempt — and missed it.

Instead, Webb tomahawked the ball through the basket. "I mean just slammed it down," said Stone. "One of the best dunks I've ever seen him do. And I tell you, the roof went off that place . . . That's when they fell in love with him."

Just as the crowd adopted its new mini-hero, two factors changed the complexion of the game. First, Glen Mays and reserve Drexal Walls began hitting over the Midland zone. Second, the Chaparrals began missing free throws. In the final period, Midland hit only 13 of 27 free throws, many the front halves of bonus situations.

Though Webb dazzled fans with spectacular ball-handling, flashy assists to Wilson for dunks, and a pair of incredible dunks himself, Westark steadily reduced the margin. With 1:16 remaining, the Lions were only down two, 70-68.

The final seconds were the equal of any Hitchcock thriller. On four occasions, Midland players stepped to the line for one-and-one and missed. Only Webb, a victim of one of the missed opportunities himself, was able to connect, hitting one of two with :55 to go. With 24 seconds left, Tony Kelleybrew's 15-footer sliced the Westark deficit to one.

In the final 15 seconds, Midland's Wilson twice missed potential clinching one-and-one attempts. On the last, Westark grabbed the rebound.

Trying to redeem himself, Wilson attacked the Lions in backcourt. Westark outlet the ball anyway, eventually getting it in the hands of Kelleybrew who was left all alone under the basket. The Lions were an easy lay-up away from a win.

Suddenly out of nowhere, covering nearly three-quarters of the court in the blink of an eye, Wilson flew through the air, slapping the ball against the backboard at the buzzer. Though Westark players and fans pleaded for goaltending, no whistle blew.

Led by Webb's 21 and Wilson's 20, Cinderella Midland upset the defending champs, 71-70.

The only way the nightcap could top the other evening performances was if the No. 1 team in the country was also upended. Sure enough, the pressure of an undefeated record appeared a heavy burden. Miami-Dade North quickly fell behind Southern Idaho, 11-2, before hitting 10 straight. Southern Idaho regained the edge, however, and led the rest of the half. A last-second 20-foot heave by sophomore center Yvon Joseph, pulled Miami-Dade within three, 33-30.

The pace slowed in the second period as Southern Idaho tried to pull the Falcons out of their zone. There were several lead changes before the contest culminated in a second straight nail-biter.

With Miami-Dade on top by one in the closing seconds, CSI's Mike Elliott fired a jumper from the lane which hit the front of the rim. Two subsequent tips by the Golden Eagles also failed. Led by Joseph's game-high 18 points and 9 rebounds, Miami-Dade survived, 60-59.

WEDNESDAY — THE WEARING OF THE GREEN

David Smith stole the ball with five seconds left and drove for a lay-up, giving Volunteer State a 39-35 halftime lead and a definite emotional edge in the St. Patrick's Day opener. After intermission, the Pioneers rolled to a 59-45 advantage with 14 minutes remaining, then coasted to a 97-74 upset of Allegany. It was the worst loss in Coach Bob Kirk's 11-year career at Allegany.

Adversity was a way of life for Coach Leon Spencer, however. In his 18 years at Henderson County, he compiled a 384-169 record, but until 1982, never made it to Hutchinson, always failing to negotiate tough Region 14 competition. He came close in 1975 and 1976, then lost in the regional finals to eventual national runner-up San Jacinto in a spectacular four-overtime affair in 1977.

The current edition of Spencer's Cardinals was a well-balanced, quick squad led by a pair of speedy guards, 5-10 Niles Dockery and 6-3 Stan Cloudy, and a powerful forward, 6-5 Pat Marshall, a streak shooter who hit 18 of 21 field goals in Henderson's final match with San Jacinto.

Led by Marshall's 26 points and 11 rebounds, the Cardinals engineered the most impressive win of the opening round, never trailing, winning easily over Calhoun State, 86-57.

Along with introducing a new playing environment in the rejuvenated Sports Arena, tourney officials also initiated a new schedule. Ever since the tournament moved to Hutchinson

consolation play always began with the Wednesday evening opener. With the 1982 tournament, that contest was moved to the end of the afternoon session.

In it James Williams bettered his opening-game performance, scoring a game-high 38, leading Ferrum to a 99-87 win over Nebraska Western.

With only the two quarterfinals now on tap for the evening session, the starting time was pushed back from 6:00 to 6:30. It was still too early for Tunxis.

In a complete turnabout from a 20-2 start in their first outing, the Tomahawks fell behind Vincennes, 17-4. Though Tunxis played aggressively in the second period, it was never able to overcome that initial handicap.

Part of the Tomahawk dilemma was that Vincennes forward Robert Lewis held Tunxis' leading scorer, Alex Hooper, to only six first-half points. With Courtney Witte leading the offense with 28 and with the front line of Witte, Lewis, and Rodney Nealy snaring 37 rebounds compared to Tunxis' total team effort of 40, Vincennes handed the Tomahawks their first defeat, 94-78.

In the other quarterfinal, Midland led throughout but squandered several six- to 10-point advantages. Dixie erased a seven-point deficit in the final frame, tying the game, 50-all.

Then Midland's Chester Smith turned into a one-man wrecking crew, firing in two free throws, a lay-up, and three consecutive corner shots to open a 63-53 Chaparral lead.

Dixie fought back again, tying the score at 67-all on a long bomb by Brent Wade.

A Smith tip-in ignited another 10-5 Midland spurt highlighted by Spud Webb's breakaway dunk, further endearing the small guard to the fans.

With a little Irish luck plus two clutch free throws in the final six seconds by Puntus Wilson — offsetting the bad memory of his misses in like circumstances the previous night — the green-clad Chaparrals held off a final Dixie surge, winning 85-82.

Wilson (25 points and 17 rebounds) and Webb (16 points and 7 assists) were again instrumental in the Midland victory. But, it was Smith who was the star. The Dallas native tallied a personal high 28 points, grabbed eight rebounds, and held Dixie's leading scorer, Chris McMullin to 10 points.

THURSDAY — CLINGING TO PERFECTION

The day's consolation fare was typical. Mercer County eliminated the listless defending champs from Westark, 66-57, holding the Lions to 33 percent from the field. Calhoun State won a sloppy contest with Allegany, 67-64. And Dixie blew a 16-point advantage, trailed by three with 1:17, then turned things around, winning 86-82 in overtime, after four Tunxis players fouled out.

The lone exception was the matinee feature. For the second straight time, a last-second shot — this one a 30-footer by Ron Beach — failed to connect for Southern Idaho. Overcoming a huge height disparity with superior quickness and a record 71.8 percent from the field, Jamestown edged the Golden Eagles, 68-66.

Another close contest opened the evening's quarterfinal action.

To reach Hutchinson, Miami-Dade North nudged Florida Junior College of Jacksonville, 66-63, in the Region 8 final and barely slipped past Abraham Baldwin Agricultural College of Tifton, Georgia, by a bucket in a first-round play-off. Then, in their Tuesday opener, the Falcons fell behind early before edging Southern Idaho by one.

Against Moberly, Miami-Dade had a better start, taking a 10-4 advantage. Then Malcolm Williams, the Falcon mainstay during the early going, picked up his third foul. It took a last-second shot by Yvon Joseph for the Floridians to manage a 26-24 halftime edge.

Miami-Dade upped the margin immediately to eight when play resumed. Moberly cut into the difference on several occasions, but with 3:53 remaining still trailed by eight.

Then Malcolm Thomas, Jerome Clayton, Johnny Holman, and Gerald Wilkins all contributed to a spree which pulled Moberly within one with :28 to go.

Miami-Dade was again forced to hold on for dear life.

Thanks to four free throws by Tracy Stringer in the final 25 seconds, the Falcons survived their fourth consecutive close call, 58-55, preserving their unblemished record.

While the press focused on Miami-Dade's brushes with defeat and Cinderella Midland with its tourney "darling," Spud Webb, Henderson County quietly established itself as the team to beat. Henderson *did* look beatable through the first 19 minutes of the nightcap when Volunteer State played the Cardinals to a 45-all tie. Then Henderson ripped off 11 straight points and was never threatened again.

The Cardinals dominated in all areas, particularly on the boards, outrebounding Volunteer State, 47-33, led by Stan Cloudy and Pat Marshall with 11 and 10 caroms, respectively. Five Cardinals hit double figures with running mates Cloudy and Niles Dockery pacing the others with 21 apiece. Henderson County became the first to break the century mark, winning convincingly, 102-88.

FRIDAY — JUST ONE MORE TIME

The day's consolation action was filled with outstanding individual efforts.

In the opener, Chris Crockett fired in a game-high 30, all from the field and many from long distance, and James Williams added 26, giving him the scoring title with 96 in just three games, but no other Ferrum player tallied more than four. Mercer County controlled the tempo and the middle, placed five players in double figures, and eliminated the Panthers, 89-76.

Reserve Greg Edwards hit a 10-foot jumper with 44 seconds left, giving Jamestown a 51-50 lead over Calhoun State in the matinee feature. Then, after regaining possession with six seconds to go on a Calhoun miscue, Edwards made back-to-back heady plays on the attempted inbounds pass to keep from having a five-second count, first calling time, then bouncing the ball off an opponent's leg. Finally, he spotted Jon Lamar Johnson open. Johnson was intentionally fouled, hit one, and sealed the Jayhawk victory. A 70-foot desperation shot by Calhoun's Greg Andrews hit off the top of the glass and nearly in at the buzzer.

In the afternoon finale, Malcolm Thomas (34), Jerome Clayton (31), and Gerald Wilkins (30) combined for 95 points and led Moberly's 56-40 domination of the boards as the Greyhounds raced past Volunteer State, 118-103. It was the first time in tourney history that three players from the same team scored 30 or more in a game.

* * *

Said a Midland sportswriter, "I took everything Spud did pretty much in stride until he got called for goaltending one night." Said another scribe, "He looks like a 9-year-old who has wandered onto the court by mistake."

Gerald Wilkins, brother of Georgia All-American and later NBA star Dominique, was one of Moberly's trio of 30-point scorers in the 1982 consolation contest versus Volunteer State. Wilkins finished his collegiate career at Tennessee-Chattanooga before entering the pro ranks with the New York Knicks. (Photo courtesy of the **Moberly Monitor-Index**)

The "darling" of the 1982 tournament, 5-6 Anthony "Spud" Webb later starred for North Carolina State University, then became an overnight sensation as a rookie with the Atlanta Hawks, winning the NBA's 1986 slam-dunk competition at the All-Star Game in Dallas. (Photo courtesy of Midland College, photo taken by Paul Gilbert, Midland Reporter-Telegram)

The charm of a talented 5-6 star in a big man's game was irresistible. In Midland, the Spud Webb phenomenon developed into hot-selling "I'm a Spud nut" buttons. By the end of tournament week, nearly every fan at the Sports Arena had jumped on the bandwagon. Said the *Midland Reporter-Telegram*, "Spud Webb could be elected mayor of Hutchinson."

Naturally, the Midland team reaped the benefits in terms of fan support. The city was enthralled with the underdog Chaparrals and fervently hoped they would go all the way. However, bad news on Friday further lengthened their already long odds.

During the Chaparrals' off day, a trainer in the stands noticed forward Lance McCain was sitting awkwardly. When told that he had injured his back in practice two weeks earlier, but had been pronounced well, the trainer suggested to Coach Jerry Stone that he be rechecked — this time with an x-ray. The results showed McCain had a fractured vertebrae in his neck.

According to Stone, if Midland had to lose a starter, McCain was the best choice. Reserve Rodney McChriston, who had hit four straight jumpers to key a comeback rally in the regionals, could adequately fill McCain's shoes.

Instead, the loss of McCain presented more an emotional problem than a strategic one. To combat the bowed heads and long faces he saw in practice later, Stone called the team together. "If anybody's going to think one second about Lance not playing, you're crazy. We're going to win this thing anyway. Rodney will come in and do the job." To himself, however, "I was crossing my fingers, my legs, my eyes, and saying, 'God, please don't let Rodney be too nervous.'"

Midland was not the same team at the start of the opening semifinal. After taking early leads in their previous two outings, the Chaparrals quickly fell behind Vincennes, 17-12.

Then, in the next 6½ minutes Webb, Chester Smith, and Puntus Wilson combined for 17 as Midland swamped the Trailblazers, 20-2. Courtney Witte hit three long bombs to ignite a 9-point spurt, pulling Vincennes within four, but by halftime Midland was in charge, 40-30.

The Chaparrals were still on top 53-44 with 15:11 remaining when, as had happened in their previous two outings, they appeared to tire. With McCain unavailable and the bench unproved, Stone could not afford to rest his stars. "If Spud made a mistake," explained Stone, "I didn't have the luxury to take him out. Because when I took Spud out, anybody in America could press us and beat us."

Midland struggled, missing six consecutive opportunities to score on four turnovers and two missed shots. Vincennes surged from behind, outscoring the Chaparrals, 14-2, building a three-point margin with 6:52 to go.

But, Midland gained second wind. A three-point play by Smith tied the game, 58-all, with 6:42 remaining. With 5:08 left, Wilson hit an 18-footer to regain the lead for Midland.

Then came the most electrifying moment of the contest.

At the 4:02 mark, Webb stole the ball and broke away for a spectacular slam dunk, bringing Stone and the whole Arena out of their seats.

"I knew that was very likely the turning point in the game," said Stone. "The guys had been flat and I decided I had to be a cheerleader. I don't usually do that, but they couldn't hear me [he was gravel-voiced from repeated yelling] so I had to jump."

Led by Wilson's 24 and Webb's 21, Midland downed Vincennes, 71-66, extending its winning streak to 23, one away from a miracle title.

The other semifinal, pitting No. 1 Miami-Dade North and No. 3 Henderson County, was expected to be equally exciting. However, as they had all week, the Henderson Cardinals completely dominated, shooting 63 percent from the field, building a 34-22 margin at intermission.

With 9:30 remaining the difference was 56-43. Miami-Dade was in the worst position yet to lose its first game.

Up to that point, Falcon Coach Bill Alheim had foregone pressing in fear of Henderson's superior quickness. Now there was no choice.

To his surprise, Miami-Dade forced six turnovers and converted them into 12 unanswered points. Suddenly, the Falcons were in their fifth thriller in a row.

Miami-Dade gained the advantage on an easy bucket by Yvon Joseph with three minutes left, then maintained it with free throws until the 11-second mark. Then, with the Falcons leading 67-66, Joseph missed the front end of one-and-one, giving Henderson a chance for a game-winner.

With five seconds showing, Cardinal center Carey Stewart shot, hitting the front of the rim. The rebound went directly into the hands of Joseph. He was immediately fouled and converted one of two free throws, lifting Miami-Dade and its undefeated record into the championship game, 68-66.

Afterwards in the Arena hallway, Coach Alheim collapsed against the wall and told reporters, "Just one more time."

SATURDAY — DOUBLE OVERTIME

The consolation trophy parade began with a battle for bragging rights in the East. Dubbed "the championship of the Super 8 Motel" (where both teams were housed), Jamestown downed Mercer County, 76-68, for seventh.

Using an aggressive defense, Moberly overcame a 42-35 halftime deficit and Chris McMullin's game-high 27 to top Dixie, 80-73, for fifth.

In the third-place contest, Henderson County scored the first 10 points of the final period, going from five down to five up. Then Stan Cloudy hit five of his game-high 25 from the line down the stretch to preserve the Cardinal win over Vincennes, 72-64.

The championship game drew a full house, including 300 standing-room-only ticketholders, the largest overflow crowd since Hutchinson's title try in 1973. Most were there to see if Cinderella Midland could accomplish what, at the beginning of the week, looked impossible. There were many, however, who were just as interested in seeing the persistent, do-or-die Falcons from Miami-Dade North who protectively clung to their unblemished record.

Midland had received more attention. But the stories about the top-rated Falcons were just as compelling.

Sophomore forward Emery Atkinson, a Region 8 all-star and the Falcons' leading scorer, had not received a single major college offer out of high school, mostly because Miami was not a mecca for college recruiters. Coach Bill Alheim had recruited the team's other forward, freshman Malcolm Williams, off a garbage truck, convincing him to give up the job, "or at least only work it part-time." The most fascinating individual, however, was the Falcons' center — Yvon Joseph.

Alheim first heard about Joseph through his assistant Clarence Strong who played in a summer league which toured Haiti. Joseph was an intelligent young man, spoke four languages, and was a member of Haiti's national volleyball team. At the time, he was working for Rawlings' baseball production plant in the accounting office, making $10 a day.

Later that summer, Joseph went to Miami with a desire to continue his education in America. His selection of Miami-Dade North was primarily due to having two aunts in Miami, one living just 15 blocks from the school and the other only five blocks from Alheim.

Because volleyball was not a varsity collegiate sport, Joseph decided to learn basketball. His skills on the court left much to be desired. "It was terrible, his passing," described Alheim. "His dribbling was ridiculous. It's indescribable. In fact, I cussed Strong out, 'Why did you bring this guy?' He was so terrible.

"[However], one of the joys of getting a person like that," continued Alheim, "is the fact they don't have any bad habits. If you teach him right, they'll learn right. He was smart enough to know and accept the coaching and apply what we were teaching him."

Alheim had a cement court in his backyard with porch lights so it could be used at night. He and his son Billy worked with Joseph on low post moves and left a basketball outside so he could practice anytime he wanted. "I had an outdoor [light] switch we left on for him. We'd hear the ball bouncing. That would be Yvon outside."

Joseph's progress was rocky. Because of his awkwardness, he constantly received jibes from other players. "You know how cruel kids can be," said Alheim. "I had to keep bolstering his ego, talk to him about his intelligence, and that one day he would be in a major university and they would be collecting garbage. Now he makes all of them look silly like we said he would."

When Coach Jerry Stone and his Midland squad first drove up to the Holiday Inn where both teams were staying, the first person they saw was Joseph. Said Stone, "It was almost enough to make you get back in the van and go to another motel." Joseph was an imposing 6-10, 235 pounds compared to Spud Webb's slight 5-6, 135 pounds.

The contrast in size was only one of the differences between the two championship game opponents. Both had also taken opposite approaches toward winning a crown: the pattern of Midland during the week was get a quick lead, then hold on for dear life; for Miami-Dade it was dig a hole, then barely climb out by the final buzzer.

The title tilt was no different. Miami-Dade trailed most of the game, by as many as eight in each half. The Falcons first lead of the final period did not come until the 1:54 mark when point guard Tracy Stringer hit a jumper from the lane, giving Miami-Dade a 74-73 edge.

Then the Falcons fell back in the hole.

First, Webb returned the lead to Midland with two free throws, his 15th and 16th from the line in 18 tries. Second, Stringer, the Falcon floor leader, fouled out. Third, with Stringer no longer controlling the ball out front, Midland's Puntus Wilson stole the ball and drove for an easy lay-up. Finally, after a Miami-Dade miss, the Falcons tied the ball up. Unfortunately, the possession arrow pointed toward Midland. The Chaparrals had the ball and a 77-74 cushion with 25 seconds to go.

Miami-Dade pressured. Webb, the fastest man on the floor, broke through creating a three-on-one situation. Throughout the night the popular guard had alternated brilliant play with errors a freshman often makes. He now reverted to the latter. Instead of passing off or holding the ball to run out the clock, Webb challenged the lone Falcon — Joseph. The shot missed. Miami-Dade grabbed the rebound with 17 seconds remaining.

The Falcons quickly worked it upcourt and inside. With 11 seconds showing, Joseph scored and was fouled by Wilson. For Wilson it was his fifth. He left the game with 25 points to his credit. For Joseph it was a chance to give the Falcons new life. His free throw swished, sending the game into overtime.

With Wilson on the bench, Midland played cautiously, keeping scoring at a minimum. Chester Smith gave the Chaparrals the lead with 3:30 remaining on a jumper from right of the circle. Atkinson tied it back up with 1:40 left, scoring on his own missed turnaround jumper.

Then the Falcons turned the tables. With 48 seconds to go, Craig Jay stole the ball out front and went all the way for an easy two. Miami-Dade was on top, 81-79.

After a Midland time-out, the Chaparrals slowly worked the ball out front. Suddenly, Webb broke through the key and into the lane. Off balance he put up a 10-footer, in among the long arms of Joseph and Atkinson. The ball went through, tying it again.

A potential game-winner by Williams bounced away at the other end at the three-second mark. For only the second time in tourney history, the championship game went to double overtime.

Webb continued his heroics by immediately canning a jumper from the line. After a Jerome Crowe free throw with 3:36 remaining, Midland held an 84-81 edge.

Atkinson responded for Miami-Dade by faking once, then scoring off the glass, reducing the margin to one.

Then came the play of the game.

After considerable confusion as to what they were supposed to do, the Chaparrals cleared everyone to the left side of the lane, creating a clear path to the basket on the right for Webb. With a lightning-quick move, he broke past his man, then past Joseph who had sluffed off, and finally jumped, arching the ball over the outstretched fingertips of Atkinson, the Falcons last line of defense. The ball banked high off the glass and in. The Arena exploded.

Moments later it rocked again when Webb picked up a loose ball at the other end and scooted past everyone for a lay-up, prudently passing up a chance to dunk. With 2:25 to go, Midland was in charge, 88-83.

Miami-Dade was also a team of heart, however, and not about to fold. Another clutch basket by Atkinson and a free throw by Jay reduced the deficit to two with 1:21 to play.

The Falcons applied terrific pressure against Midland's stall, but could not force a turnover. In desperation, Atkinson intentionally fouled Justin Morett with 32 seconds left. The Chaparral sub missed the first, hit the second, giving Midland a comfortable 89-86 edge.

Though Webb fouled out, receiving a standing ovation after a game-high 36-point performance, third-highest in a title game, Miami-Dade could not find another foothold out of the pit. Four free throws by Smith clinched it for Midland.

In one of the greatest games in tourney history, the Chaparrals defied the odds, winning 93-88.

Overshadowed by teammates Puntus Wilson and Spud Webb, Midland center Chester Smith was a consistent factor in the middle during the 1982 tournament, averaging 18.8 points and 10.0 rebounds per game. Smith was later an NAIA All-American at Wisconsin-Eau Claire. (Photo courtesy of Midland College)

THE AFTERMATH — IT'S A DREAM

With four seconds left, Midland ahead by three and in possession out of bounds, Jerry Stone gathered his players around him during a time-out. "Spud's out. Puntus is out. There's only one guy I want to catch the ball and that's Chester," related Stone. "I'm describing this play — we've never run it before — and I'm telling everybody exactly what to do. And I look up and say 'Do you have that Chester? Do you understand that?' Chester's not even in the huddle. He's down at the end of the bench putting scissors in his socks so that he can cut the net down."

Smith's show of confidence was typical of the Midland squad. Though predominately freshmen (only Wilson and injured Lance McCain were sophomores), the Chaparrals displayed sober, mature presence on the court and were rarely rattled. Not so their coach. "We were making up plays as we came down the floor," said Stone of the final minutes. "I was playing three post men and one guy who hadn't played in a game since Christmas. I'm not sure some of the people we had out there had ever seen each other before."

The magnificent performance by both sides drew standing ovations when each team received its trophy. Yvon Joseph and Emery Atkinson, the latter leading Miami-Dade North in the championship game with 29, many in clutch situations, picked up All-Tournament plaques to hearty applause. But, the biggest response was saved for the smallest.

In his presentation of the Obee Small Player Award, Tournament Director Al Wagler stated, "Probably in all the years of this award, this is the most *difficult* decision we've had to make." The whole Arena laughed. "But, after long consultation, the winner of this year's award is 5-6 from Midland, Texas — Spud Webb!"

After a week's exhibition of his many abilities and his championship courage, Webb had carved a special place in the hearts of tourney fans. Few players have ever received a warmer reception. Many felt that he was not only the best small player but the best player overall.

The French Most Valuable Player Award, however, went to teammate Puntus Wilson. Webb — who later starred for North Carolina State and became an overnight national sensation after winning the dunk contest at the NBA All-Star game his rookie season with the Atlanta Hawks — described Wilson as "the ideal player. He could do it all. He had the sweetest left-handed jump shot I've ever seen. I think he should be in the pros right now."

Wilson was also special for Coach Stone. Earlier in the season Stone had placed the team under curfew. If a player came in one minute late, he would be immediately asked to put on his gear and head for the gym to run line drills (sprinting back-and-forth between lines on the court).

But, toward the end of the season Stone dropped the curfew. "The only reason I did that was because I was tired of catching Puntus," said Stone. "Puntus would run line drills so hard that he would temporarily pass out. I thought that I was literally wearing that kid out. That kid had more guts and I admired him so much that when that [championship] game was over, I didn't go to Spud, I didn't go to my mama, I went to Puntus Wilson."

For Stone, the Coach of the Tournament, winning a national title was particularly meaningful. A native of Arkansas City, Kansas, Stone had played in the Arena in high school. "Hutchinson and that tournament are a part of me. Ever since I was a little kid we'd go up and watch that tournament. [Later after seeing the tournament as a coach] I remember going to a bar with some guys and I slammed my fist on the table. They thought I was crazy. I was almost in tears. I said, 'I'm bringing a team up here.' I wasn't just talking. It was something I knew was going to happen."

Yet, even with a first-place trophy in hand, it was all hard to believe. Said Stone to the Arena audience, "I appreciate everything that's happened this week. It's a dream. I hope we don't wake up in the morning and realize it didn't come true."

---

[2]Smith exhibited even more confident exuberance during the Region 5 final against Cisco Junior College. With eight seconds left, Midland on top by two, Cisco started a potential tying fast break. Described Jerry Stone, "On film, I've got him [Smith] going to the opposing bench, picking up a folding chair, and taking it out on the court so he can get the net down. And that's the god's truth!"

The French MVP and 1st Team All-American, Puntus Wilson (white uniform) tied teammate Spud Webb with 94 points, third-high for 1982. Wilson completed his collegiate career at the Universities of Arizona and Lamar. (Photo courtesy of Midland College)

Tournament Results

Tuesday: Game

1	Tunxis — 90 Ferrum — 75
2	Vincennes — 77 Nebraska Western — 55
3	Moberly — 77 Jamestown — 73
4	Dixie — 90 Mercer County — 82
5	Midland — 71 Westark — 70
6	Miami-Dade North — 50 Southern Idaho — 49

Wednesday: Game

7	Volunteer St. — 97 Allegany — 74
8	Henderson County — 86 Calhoun St. — 57
9	Ferrum — 99 Nebraska Western — 87
10	Vincennes — 94 Tunxis — 78
11	Midland — 85 Dixie — 82

Thursday: Game

12	Mercer County — 66 Westark — 57
13	Jamestown — 68 Southern Idaho — 66
14	Calhoun St. — 67 Allegany — 64
15	Dixie — 86 Tunxis — 82 OT
16	Miami-Dade North — 58 Moberly — 55
17	Henderson County — 102 Volunteer St. — 88

Friday: Game

18	Mercer County — 89 Ferrum — 76
19	Jamestown — 52 Calhoun St. — 50
20	Moberly — 118 Volunteer St. — 103
21	Midland — 71 Vincennes — 66
22	Miami-Dade North — 68 Henderson County — 66

Saturday: Game

23	Jamestown — 76 Mercer County — 68
24	Moberly — 80 Dixie — 73
25	Henderson County — 72 Vincennes — 64
26	Midland — 93 Miami-Dade North — 88 2OT

How They Finished in 1982

1. Midland College
2. Miami-Dade Community College, North Campus
3. Henderson County Junior College
4. Vincennes University
5. Moberly Junior College
6. Dixie College
7. Jamestown Community College
8. Mercer County Community College

All-Tournament Team

Emery Atkinson — Miami-Dade Community College, North Campus
Jerome Clayton — Moberly Junior College
Niles Dockery — Henderson County Junior College
Carl Jeter — Jamestown Community College
Yvon Joseph — Miami-Dade Community College, North Campus
Chris McMullin — Dixie College
Anthony "Spud" Webb — Midland College
James Williams — Ferrum College
Puntus Wilson — Midland College
Courtney Witte — Vincennes University

Coach of the Tournament

Jerry Stone — Midland College

French Most Valuable Player Award

Puntus Wilson — Midland College

Sesher Sportsmanship Award

Brent Wade — Dixie College

Bud Obee Outstanding Small Player Award

Anthony "Spud" Webb — Midland College

1983:

SPOON-SIZED

After playing only one year at Wabash Valley College, Ken Norman became an All-American at the University of Illinois before moving into the pro ranks with the Los Angeles Clippers. (Photo courtesy of the University of Illinois)

The National Juco Tournament had seen numero sellouts of season tickets in the past, but never since every se in the Sports Arena was reserved.

However, one week before its 36th anniversary, there w not a seat to be had. Except for 500 standing-room-only ticke to be sold each evening, the tournament was a complete se out.

There were two reasons for this first.

One was the good possibility Spud Webb and defendi champ Midland College, which was 31-4, ranked 20th, a undefeated since Christmas, would return.

The other was that the No. 13 Hutchinson Blue Dragons we one win away from their first appearance in 10 years.

Unfortunately, many of the ticketholders who had specul ed were disappointed. First, in one of the best Region 6 fin ever, Hutchinson fell to Independence Community Colle 70-68. Then, four days later, San Jacinto College shot dov Webb and the Chaparrals, 82-69.

THE PARTICIPANTS

Region	Team
1	Mesa Community College — Mesa, Arizona
2	Seminole Junior College —Seminole, Oklahoma
3	Jamestown Community College — Jamestown, New York
6	Independence Community College — Independence, Kansas
8	Florida College — Temple Terrace, Florida
9	Southeast Community College — Fairbury, Nebraska
11	Clinton Community College — Clinton, Iowa
12	Vincennes University — Vincennes, Indiana
13	North Dakota State School of Science — Wahpeton, North Dakota
14	San Jacinto College, Central Campus — Pasadena, Texas
16	Moberly Area Junior College — Moberly, Missouri
17	DeKalb Community College, South Campus — Decatur, Georgia
19	Mercer County Community College — Trenton, New Jerse
20	Community College of Allegheny County, Allegheny Campus — Pittsburgh, Pennsylvania
22	Walker College — Jasper, Alabama
24	Wabash Valley College — Mt. Carmel, Illinois
Lost in First-Round Play-Offs:	
4	Kankakee Community College — Kankakee, Illinois
5	Midland College — Midland, Texas
7	Shelby State Community College — Memphis, Tennessee
10	Spartanburg Methodist College — Spartanburg, South Carolina
15	Fashion Institute of Technology — New York, New York
18	Chemeketa Community College — Salem, Oregon
21	Mattatuck Community College — Waterbury, Connecticut
23	Copiah-Lincoln Junior College — Wesson, Mississippi

"It wasn't a fluke," Midland Coach Jerry Stone told the pre: "They are a very, very good team. Nobody we played in t tournament last year was quite as good as they are."

Based on Stone's testimonial and the sound thrashing t Chaparrals received in the first-round play-off, No. 6 San Jacin (31-2) was instantly installed as pre-tourney favorite. The fc mer champion Ravens were big and from Region 14. Nothi more needed to be said.

San Jacinto would not have a walk-through, however. The 6-team field not only included the top team in the nation, but our other champs with 12 titles between them.

First, there was No. 1 Jamestown Community College (33-1). Led by 1982 All-Tourney selection Carl Jeter, the team's leading scorer (22.0), Nick Creola's Jayhawks were making their third straight appearance, having finished seventh the year before, and had just held Mattatuck Community College, the top offensive squad in the nation (102.7), 23 points under its average in the Region 3 final.

Next followed two-time champ Mercer County Community College (27-1) whose only loss came during semester break. In a scheduled game against Brookdale Community College of Lincroft, New Jersey, Mercer County Coach Howie Landa found himself short-handed with several players unavailable because of make-up work, one in the hospital, and one at a funeral. Then, on game day, a 6-8 sub slipped trying to catch the bus and had his foot run over, bruising it severely. With only four players left, Landa was forced to forfeit. Now, Landa's Vikings were in peak form, tied for No. 4 in the rankings and leading the nation in defense, holding opponents to 55 points a game.

Then came No. 8 Vincennes University (34-2), a three-time champ, returning with All-Tourney selection Courtney Witte from a team that earned fourth the year before.

No. 11 Independence (31-3), another three-time champ, was also a definite threat, particularly with an almost homecourt advantage.

Finally, there was Moberly Area Junior College (28-6). The four-time champion returned for the 20th time, bringing three starters from its 1982 fifth-place squad, including All-Tourney selection Jerome Clayton and All-American candidate Malcolm Thomas, a top-10 performer nationally in rebounds and field goal percentage. In Region 16 play-off action, the Greyhounds had downed No. 9 Three Rivers Community College — the only team to beat top-rated Jamestown during the season — in two straight, 96-75 and 78-74. Though unranked, Moberly was a certain contender.

Other teams with an outside shot at the crown were Pittsburgh's Community College of Allegheny County (35-2), tied for No. 4 with Mercer County, and No. 16 Walker College (27-2). Their exclusion from the elite was based on it being Allegheny County's first appearance in the tournament and Walker's first in 19 years.

Also not discounted were unranked Seminole Junior College (32-4), Wabash Valley Community College (31-4), and Mesa Community College (25-8). Seminole had the distinction of splitting with Independence during the year. Wabash Valley owned a win over Vincennes. And Mesa upset No. 3 Scottsdale Community College in the Region 1 final, before being given a free pass to Hutchinson when Region 18 winner Chemeketa Community College abided by its policy of not playing past the regionals.

The long shots were Florida College (30-3) and Clinton Community College (26-6), because they were unheralded newcomers; DeKalb Community College, South (18-13), because of its season record; and Southeast Community College of Fairbury (26-5) and North Dakota State School of Science from Wahpeton (23-6), because of their tourney record. Fairbury squads had not won in six tries; Wahpeton crews, only once in nine.

TUESDAY — PLAYING ABOVE THE RIMS

On January 22, Clinton center Quinton Dale underwent orthoscopic knee surgery. One month later, he was out of the cast and practicing. He saw limited action during the regionals, but did hit 32 in the final. The 6-6 sophomore came into the tournament carrying a 25.9 average, tops of anyone participating at Hutchinson.

In the tourney opener, Dale looked back to normal, scoring 18 first-half points, leading Clinton to a 38-37 advantage.

Then fatigue and fouls limited his playing time and his output to two in the final frame. The Huskers fell behind Florida College, 58-48, with 11:55 remaining.

Teammate Vic Couch took over, scoring 18 second-half points as smaller, slower Clinton outhustled the Hustling Falcons, winning 82-75, avenging an earlier loss to the Floridians.

The only size on Dana Altman's Southeast Community College Bombers was Neil Wake, a 6-7 skeleton with skin, all elbows, hips, and knees.

"All the coaches in our regional said, 'Well, Mercer's going to be an awfully good team. You probably don't have a chance to win the game,'" stated Altman.

It was hard to tell who was better in the first 10 minutes of the matinee feature since street ball reigned. Finally, the game settled into a defensive struggle with the Fairbury squad surprisingly matching Mercer County's tough zone. At the 2:21 mark, Mercer's lead was only, 56-52.

Then, in the final two minutes, the Vikings missed two critical short jumpers. A pair of free throws by Leo "B.B." McGainey and a beautiful reverse lay-up by Charles Howell pulled the Nebraskans even, sending the contest into overtime.

After Wake gave the Bombers a cushion with the first five points, the extra period was all SECC. The Fairbury five protected the lead with 13 of 14 foul shots, upsetting Mercer County, 71-64.

Another close defensive battle followed, both Mesa and Seminole slowing the tempo and forcing poor shooting. Leads were minimal and switched back and forth.

Down the stretch, a turnaround jumper by Chuck Walheim gave Mesa a 42-40 edge. Then, after a Seminole miss, the Thunderbirds spread it out.

With 2:11 remaining, Trojan Ray Alford stole the ball in backcourt and drove for a tying slam dunk.

Mesa continued to hold the ball, again with no success. With 1:35 left, Seminole's tight man-to-man defense forced a five-second count. At the 45-second mark, the Trojan's Win Case was fouled and hit one of two free throws.

Despite now trailing by one, Mesa still held the ball, choosing to go for the last shot. With 22 seconds remaining, the Thunderbirds called time. When they returned to the court, Seminole had switched from its game-long man-to-man to a zone. Confused, Mesa called time again with 10 seconds left.

Finally, the Thunderbirds worked it into 6-5 forward Pete Murphy. The sophomore's shot was blocked out of bounds by Alford with five seconds showing. Bobby Jenkins took a 12-footer off the inbounds pass with two seconds left, but the ball rimmed in and out.

Seminole won, 43-42, the lowest tourney score in 32 years.

In the evening opener, 5-9 Larry Hamilton hit 20 points, leading the Wahpeton Wildcats to an eye-opening 36-31 lead over top-rated Jamestown with 2:11 left in the first half.

Then the sophomore guard picked up his third foul and sat down. Jamestown rallied, taking a 40-37 advantage at intermission, destroying any ideas of an upset.

Hamilton managed nine second-half points for a game-high 29, but the intimidation of 6-10½ Jon Taylor — who blocked 13 NDSSS shots, forced several air balls, and nabbed 17 rebounds — proved too much. Jamestown advanced, 78-70.

The evening feature also started out as a major upset in the making. To the dismay of the predominately pro-Independence crowd, DeKalb-South gained control early, building a 29-22 margin with 3:50 remaining in the half.

Then the quick-handed trio of Darren Brunson, Anthony White, and Todd Gandy pressured the Eagles into six turnovers. Independence scored the final 10 points of the period.

With the momentum all theirs, the Pirates increased the tempo in the final stanza, racing to an 84-65 victory.

The most anticipated game of the opening-round capped the first day's activities: San Jacinto versus Moberly.

The only previous match-ups of the two former champs were in the 1967 championship game and in the first-round of 1974. Both times Moberly won.

This time San Jacinto was favored. The Ravens possessed an imposing front line: 6-9 Andre Ross and 6-7½ Carey Holland, a pair of agile Mac trucks, plus versatile 6-8 swing man Frank "Spoon" James.

However, if any team had a chance of knocking off the pre-tourney pick, it was Moberly. Greyhound front-liners 6-6 Robert Pittman, 6-7 Malcolm Thomas, and 6-5 Jerome Clayton were somewhat smaller than their counterparts, but just as bulky.

San Jacinto took the threat seriously. During pre-game warm-ups, the Ravens ignited the crowd and themselves with an awesome dunking display.

If the exhibition was meant to intimidate Moberly, it apparently worked. San Jacinto fired ahead, opening a 21-7 lead in less than seven minutes.

Then a superb Greyhound man-to-man forced the Texans into poor shot selection. Behind Jeff Strong's 18, Moberly rallied, taking a 36-35 edge with 4:41 left, before losing the half-time advantage to the Ravens, 47-43.

Both squads continued to play way above the rims in the final frame, particularly Moberly which won the board battle convincingly, 45 to 35. However, an eight-point spurt with 7½ minutes remaining gave San Jacinto a comfortable 70-60 barrier the Greyhounds could not surmount. The Ravens won, 84-76.

Because of the heavy traffic in the middle, scoring honors went to guards. San Jacinto was led by floor general Nolan Gibson with 22, 14 in the first half. Moberly's Strong topped all scorers with 27.

WEDNESDAY — COLORFUL DEBUT

The Allegheny County Cougars made sure their first trip to Hutchinson was memorable.

As soon as the Arena doors opened for Wednesday's afternoon session, Allegheny cheerleaders accosted fans, handing out buttons, stickers, T-shirts, and hats, the biggest goodwill give-a-way the tourney had seen in many years.

Fans were also intrigued by the Cougars' attire. The school colors were described as "rainbow" or "many and varied." The team had 10 sets of uniforms, all with different color combinations. It was anybody's guess what motif they would appear in next.

Allegheny oddities did not stop there. After building a small 36-33 halftime lead, Cougar Coach Bill Shay introduced an unusual stack offense — one ballhandler and four men in a row parallel to the free throw line — in order to draw Wabash Valley's superior size away from the basket. The tactic kept the game close to the finish.

After Wabash Valley missed a crucial one-and-one, the Cougars held for one. With three seconds left, Earl Minor, the ballhandler in the stack, drove the lane and was fouled. His two free throws gave Allegheny County-Pittsburgh a 66-64 win.

"Nationally speaking, we did not have the respect or notoriety of a Vincennes, or an Independence, or a San Jacinto," said Walker Coach Glen Clem. "I'm sure that everyone expected Vincennes to send us into the consolation bracket."

Therefore, it came as a major surprise when Walker jumped out to a 30-19 lead in the final opening-round contest.

Then the Rebels were jolted back to reality. Four consecutive turnovers allowed Vincennes to mount a rally. At intermission, Walker's advantage was down to a mere basket, 32-30.

Again the Alabamans bolted ahead, building a 60-44 margin with 5:04 remaining. Again Rebel errors let Vincennes come back.

But, with the Trailblazers only hitting 33 percent from the field — Vincennes' leading scorer Bernard Campbell (20.8 average) was held to six points, hitting only 3 of 21 shots — Walker's cushion was sufficient. Led by the game-high 22 points of Mark Atkinson (ironically a native of Indiana), the Rebels upended Vincennes, 67-63.

The opening-round had been thoroughly entertaining for fans. There were two upsets and all but two of the games had been hotly contested throughout. Though many were saying that San Jacinto and Moberly, the two most physically dominate teams in the field, had already played for the championship, there was plenty of excitement yet to follow.

In the opening quarterfinal, the Clinton Huskers displayed the same hustle that had led them past Florida College, controlling action from the beginning, building a 52-45 advantage over SECC of Fairbury midway in the final period.

Then, utilizing similar hustle, the Bombers rallied, pulling within one, 65-64, with 1:45 to go.

"I guess the best way to put it, I begged him all summer to come back," said SECC Coach Dana Altman of center Neil Wake, the Bombers' only returning starter. "When he decided on the last day to come back to Fairbury and be a part of our ball club, that was the thing that probably made our entire year. Without Neil, we weren't a very good team."

Wake's importance had been felt in the Bombers' upset outing against Mercer County and was again felt now in the waning minutes of an uphill struggle.

With 1:30 left, Wake rejected Jeff Rock's shot and, on the ensuing possession, tallied a three-point play giving the Nebraskans their first lead of the game.

Tom Sweeney rescued Clinton with a bucket at the 50-second mark. At the end of regulation, the game was a 67-all draw.

It was the second straight overtime for the Fairbury squad. And for the second straight time, free throws played a part in the outcome. Up until that point, SECC charity shooting had been hit-or-miss. Now, as in their opener, the Bombers were deadly accurate. A pair of free tosses by Scott Harris and another pair by Kenny Fields in the final 1:30 lifted SECC over Clinton, 75-74.

In the evening's other quarterfinal, underdog Seminole got things started on a positive note with a stuff.

Talented No. 1 Jamestown appeared able to turn it on at will, however. The Jayhawks quickly gained control, forging a 45-32 halftime advantage.

Generally in the past, whenever a favored team was far ahead at intermission of the nightcap early in the tournament, fans made a mass exit, hoping to rest up for later in the week.

But, with Jamestown in obvious command, the crowd uncharacteristically remained seated, as though expecting something to happen.

Sure enough, Seminole came out pumped up, committed only two second-period turnovers, and crawled back into contention. With 25 seconds left, William Childs hit a free throw, giving the Trojans a 71-70 edge.

Jamestown's last chance at avoiding upset came inside the 10-second mark when guard Tyrone Scott drove toward the middle. At the free throw line he met two Trojan defenders. One, Anthony Bowie, stripped the ball, drove the length of the court, and slammed it. Though the basket came after the final buzzer, it was a fitting exclamation mark on an unexpected Seminole victory.

THURSDAY — END OF A STREAK

In afternoon consolation action:

Mesa held on against a furious NDSSS-Wahpeton rally, eliminating the Wildcats, 55-54;

Malcolm Thomas scored a tourney-high 42 and Jerome Clayton added another 24, combining for 80 percent of Moberly's output, as the Greyhounds downed DeKalb-South, 84-77, despite 64 percent shooting by the Georgians;

And Wabash Valley evened its season series with rival Vincennes (only 30 miles from Mt. Carmel) at two apiece with a hard-fought 89-88 overtime victory.

For the second year in a row, officials tinkered with the tourney's long-established schedule. Instead of introducing Thursday evening action with a consolation preliminary, the remaining two quarterfinals were moved up, the first starting promptly at 6 p.m.

In the past fans usually grabbed a bite to eat after work before heading for the Arena. The stands normally did not start filling until halftime of the opener.

But, with local favorite Independence versus pre-tourney pick San Jacinto on tap, empty stomachs won out. By 6:15 three-quarters of the Arena was full.

The predominately pro-Independence audience had little to cheer though. The first Pirate point, a free throw by Armon Gilliam, did not come until the 15:36 mark. It took another two minutes before the first Pirate field goal. By then, San Jacinto was firmly in control, 16-3.

Independence made two runs, one in each half, but the Raven defense proved too much. San Jacinto's zone forced the Pirates outside where Anthony White, Curtis Moore, and Joe McAdoo were only able to hit 6 for 20, 6 for 23, and 0 for 12, respectively.

Though Independence's defense matched the Ravens at times, it was unable to cool the hot hands of Spoon James (23) and Nolan Gibson (19).

"What really hurt us in the last seven or eight minutes," said Pirate Coach Bob Kivisto, who wore an eye-catching light green tux in honor of St. Patrick's Day, "they moved [James] from a rward to the point guard. We were playing a zone at that time nd he just killed us from the point. He just picked us apart."

San Jacinto won convincingly, 75-62, ending Independence's 14-game tourney win streak (going back to 1963), an ll-time record.

The remaining quarterfinal was not the first meeting for the wo opposing coaches. "[Allegheny County Coach] Bill Shay nd I were in the Sports Festival in Indianapolis the summer efore," explained Walker's Glen Clem. "I was the team manager for the South team and Bill was the team manager for the ast team. We talked about getting our teams to Hutch the folwing year. In fact, the last thing we said when we left Indiaapolis was, 'Well, I'll see you in Hutch.' Lo and behold . . .''

The Walker-Allegheny County quarterfinal was a confrontaon of styles. Walker was conservative; the colorful Cougars, p-tempo. The early moments were a battle to see which pace ould prevail.

With a 15-3 beginning spurt, Walker won the choice and dicated restraint. Both sides put up only 41 shots. Committing just ine turnovers, the disciplined Rebels defeated Allegheny ounty-Pittsburgh, 60-48.

Though the change of schedule meant less time for supper, did allow more time for sleep if one chose. With swift, talentd, top-rated Jamestown against slow Clinton in the nightcap, ans took advantage of the latter. Following the quarterfinals, he Arena cleared quickly, leaving only a few pockets of spectaors dotting the stands.

With eight minutes to go, Jamestown in total command, 71-3, those who had left early appeared to have made a judicious ecision. Said one diehard, who had not been to the tournaent in nearly 20 years, "The only people still here are either asketball junkies or those of us who were given a ticket for onight and want to get full use of it.''

Then St. Patrick's Day leprechauns began playing a joke on he green-clad Jayhawks from New York.

Clinton's scrappy press was principally responsible for the urnaround, but Jamestown helped with sloppy passing and omical turnovers. Once guard Tyrone Scott dribbled the ball ff a teammate's leg out of bounds. Another time, in the crucial nal seconds, a perfect pass went right through a Jayhawk playr's legs and out of play.

With 18 seconds left, Clinton's Vic Couch drove, scored, and vas fouled. His free throw tied the score, 83-all, sending the ame into overtime.

Jamestown survived further embarrassment thanks to nine xtra-period points by Carl Jeter, boosting his game-high total o 26. However, the 96-92 final was not reflected in the postame reactions at courtside. The few remaining spectators conratulated the losing Clinton players who were all smiles. The vinning Jayhawks exited the court without fanfare, frowning in lisgruntlement.

FRIDAY — CINDERELLA, CINDERELLA, CINDERELLA

Mercer County opened the day's consolation play by buildng a comfortable 50-38 advantage with 7:45 to go, then withtanding a determined Mesa rally to eke out a 61-60 win.

In the matinee feature, Moberly fell behind early, trailing Wabash Valley by as much as 19. With 2:37 remaining, the defiit was still 96-83.

Then the Greyhounds awoke from lethargy, tying the game at 01-all. Paced by Jerome Clayton's overtime heroics and Malolm Thomas' game-high 31 points and 25 rebounds, Moberly lowned Wabash Valley, 110-106.

There was no furious comeback in the afternoon finale. Led oy Armon Gilliam (30) and Curtis Moore (22), Independence cored 38 points during a 13-minute stretch in the final period o run away from Allegheny County-Pittsburgh, 81-66.

For the many underdog lovers in the crowd, the evening's emifinals were a special treat. Cinderellas were coming out of he woodwork. The later contest featured Walker, which had ashioned upsets over two top-10 teams. In the curtain raiser, here was a choice — Seminole, which had downed No. 1 amestown, and the most Cinderella of them all, SECC of Fairury, winner of two overtime close calls.

Fans were particularly taken by the Fairbury Bombers. They vere a motley crew with a kid at the helm. Rookie coach Dana Altman — who had once played at Fairbury under Hutchinson

Community College Coach Gary Bargen — was blond, goodlooking and 24, only a couple weeks older than his oldest player, Neil Wake.

Altman's youthful appearance often caused problems at game meals. When asked who was paying, the players would answer, "The coach." Invariably, the next question would be, "Well, which one is he?"

Since half the team had agreed to shave their heads if they won the region, there was little confusion as to who was coach when the Fairbury squad arrived at Hutchinson. "Everybody would kind of look at us and maybe chuckle a little bit," said Altman. "Talent-wise we probably weren't considered that good of a ballclub."

SECC did not look particularly good to start the opening semifinal, turning the ball over several times. However, because of Wake's board work and numerous blocked shots, the Bombers stayed in contention. At intermission, Seminole led by only one, 36-35.

Because of foul problems, Wake was less effective in the second half. He sat down at the 11:55 mark with his fourth and remained seated for nearly six minutes.

Point guard Leo McGainey kept SECC from faltering in Wake's absence, his three-point play with 6:20 remaining cutting Seminole's six-point edge in half. Two subsequent free throws by Joel Clark reduced it to one.

For the next three minutes, Seminole's advantage wavered between one and three. Then, with 1:58 to go, Wake stole the ball and drove the length of the court for a swooping dunk. The Bombers took the lead, 71-70, their first since the opening moments.

With 1:18 remaining, guard Adam Frank recaptured the lead for Seminole with an 18-footer. A Frank free throw shortly thereafter gave the Trojans a 73-71 margin with 57 seconds left.

Clark continued the Fairbury squad's clutch free throw exhibition with two at the 43-second mark.

Frank missed with 24 seconds showing, but SECC was called for traveling after the rebound.

As the clock wound down inside 10 seconds, the ball ended in the hands of 5-10 Win Case. The sophomore guard drove the lane, at the last moment, kicking it off to reserve Kenneth Bullard on the baseline. Taking what many observers felt were too many steps, Ballard laid in the apparent game-winner with seven seconds left.

No violation was called, however. In the confusion, the clock ran down to four seconds before the Bomber's anxious plea for time-out was acknowledged. A last-second shot by McGainey hit the heel of the rim and bounced away. Seminole advanced to the title game, 75-73.

Said SECC's Altman afterwards, "I think it was obvious from the replays that he [Bullard] did [walk]. The refs had called a great game, so that one play wasn't the difference. But, just at that particular time, it sticks out in your mind so much more. It was one of those things."

For Coach Glen Clem, in his 24th year at Walker, playing in the national tournament, let alone having a shot at the title game, were far beyond his expectations — particularly earlier in the season. On November 22, in a game against Lawson State Community College, Clem suffered a heart attack and was immediately flown to Birmingham for bypass surgery.

"It was a sobering feeling. That kind of things makes you realize that basketball is just a game," Clem related to the press. "I told Gene Bartow (head coach at Alabama-Birmingham) when he came to visit me at the hospital that when you go through an ordeal like I went through, that making the Final Four or the final 16 is of little significance."

Clem's recuperation was miraculously quick. He returned to the team January 12. Now his Rebels were two games away from a national crown. The next obstacle — San Jacinto.

Said Clem, "I felt if we really got a break, things went well, we played to our capabilities, and we could frustrate San Jacinto, I thought we had a chance against them."

There were others who agreed. Like Moberly, Walker had size to match the Ravens. Though shorter than their counterparts on San Jacinto, the Rebel front-liners — 6-4 Willie "Sam" Ervin, 6-6 Robert Epps, and 6-7 Mark Atkinson — were equally bulky. Given their penchant for slow deliberate play, if the Alabamans gained an early lead, San Jacinto might have a tough time.

"Our guys knew that we had to get the lead or we were going to be chasing them around the gymnasium the whole night," stated Raven Coach Ronnie Arrow, reflecting how seriously San Jacinto viewed the Walker threat.

Accordingly, the course of the game was established early. San Jacinto's first two shots were lay-ups; Walker's first two were from far outside.

San Jacinto's height and long reach made its zone impenetrable. Instead of gaining the lead as planned, Walker fell behind. Rebel frustration reached an acme when Coach Clem collected a technical for disputing a tip he felt was offensive goaltending against the Texans. San Jacinto built a 15-point lead and was comfortably in command, 35-25, at halftime.

Walker might have been even further behind had Floyd Calhoun not hit a last-second 20-footer, stirring the Arena audience. During intermission, the Rebel cheerleaders fanned the crowd's growing leanings toward Walker with an acrobatic display at center court. When Walker returned to the floor, hitting the first two baskets of the final period, the crowd was fully rooting for a comeback.

Then a three-point play by Carey Holland and a slam dunk by Spoon James put a damper on the rally. San Jacinto took a 42-29 lead and was never threatened again, winning 72-57.

Coach Clem's final comments echoed those of other San Jacinto opponents. "We couldn't handle them. They were too big for us."

SATURDAY — OVERPOWERING

At the outset of their two consolation outings, the Moberly Greyhounds had shown a lackadaisical spirit, apparently needing to be behind before their competitive juices flowed.

In the contest for seventh, it happened again. Mercer County built a 39-23 lead before Moberly' man-to-man defense became serious. The Greyhounds finished the half with a 13-1 spurt, then continued it in the final frame, winning 85-80.

While Moberly's Jeff Strong topped everyone with 26, teammate Malcolm Thomas, who had been the tournament's leading scorer coming into the game was held to six. Thomas did grab the rebounding title, however, with 55 for the week.

Jamestown was another team with a reputation of playing only hard enough to win. But, unlike Moberly, the Jayhawks

With 177 points in 1982 and 1983 combined, Moberly's Malcolm Thomas is tied for 19th in career tourney scoring. Thomas later starred at the University of Missouri. (Photo courtesy of the **Moberly Monitor-Index**)

took a different approach toward making their contests interesting.

As in its earlier outings, Jamestown built a convincing 58-margin with 13:55 remaining in the fifth-place game. Then before, the Jayhawks frittered away the lead. With 4:43 to g Independence had drawn within one, 70-69.

Led by Carl Jeter, who hit half of the Jayhawks' final 18 point giving him a game-high 35, Jamestown weathered the rall winning 88-79.

Armon Gilliam paced Independence with 26, giving him th tourney scoring title with 99.

The outcome of the third-place contest was reflected in th post-game statements of the opposing coaches —

The leading scorer of the 1983 tournament with 99 points, Independence's Armon Gilliam later starred for the UNLV Runnin' Rebels and the NBA's Phoenix Suns. (Photo courtesy of Nevada-Las Vegas)

Dana Altman: "We showed a great deal of pride. We'll neve forget that loss last night, but [we] did do a pretty good job o putting it behind [us]."

Glen Clem: "The season ended against San Jacinto."

The hustling Fairbury Bombers dominated Walker through out, outrebounding the taller Rebels with quick leaps an excellent positioning, outscoring them, 102-84. The only brigh spots for Walker were Sam Ervin's 31 and Mark Atkinson's 20 All SECC players scored, six making double figures.

Fans did not expect the championship game to be any closer San Jacinto's size had already proven too much for the only oth er big teams in the tourney field. Against Seminole and its trio o lean 6-5 front-liners — Ray Alford, Anthony Bowie, and Wil liams Childs, nicknamed the "ABC Gang" by the Seminol press — the Ravens appeared a sure bet.

However, Jim Kerwin's Trojans showed no intimidation Using their superior quickness to advantage, they put on a fin display of passing and shooting, jumping out to a quick nine point lead.

In its three previous outings, San Jacinto had been the team which had built the early big lead. Having the tables turned wa clearly frustrating. Raven Coach Ronnie Arrow was forced t call time.

A more intense San Jacinto squad returned to the floor. Fol lowing Arrow's instructions, the Ravens pressed and whittle the lead. Back-to-back baskets by Spoon James, the latter off hi own steal, finally gave San Jacinto its first lead, 34-33, with 1:2 left in the half.

Seminole played for the last shot. Capping a brilliant 19-poin period, Bowie drilled a 25-footer at the buzzer, giving the Tro jans a 35-34 halftime edge and hope for the final frame.

With 13:12 remaining Seminole still led by one, 46-45.

Then the Raven big men began to assert themselves. Andr Ross scored. James tallied a three-point play. Carey Holland hi two consecutive baskets. Ross ended the spree he had started with another two. With nine minutes remaining, San Jacinto was in charge, 56-46.

Though Bowie topped all scorers with 31, the ABC Gang was no match for the San Jacinto front line. Holland anchored the middle with 22 points, 11 rebounds, and four blocked shots in the final period. James and Ross tallied 17 and 10, respectively, and 6-6½, 210-pound Keith Berry came off the bench to nab 10 rebounds.

San Jacinto's superior size and strength netted an overwhelming 40-29 board advantage and gradually wore down Seminole. The closest the Trojans could get thereafter was five, the final difference.

San Jacinto won its second crown, 73-68.

THE AFTERMATH — JUST A MATTER OF TIME

With the early season ticket sellout, the 1983 Juco Tournament was destined to be the most financially successful to date. With superior height and depth, San Jacinto was equally destined to win the championship.

"We had size, but more than anything else, we had bulk," described Raven Coach Ronnie Arrow. "When it got down to the nitty gritty, I think in a lot of instances it wore some people down physically inside."

It also did not hurt that part of that size possessed extreme versatility. Whenever Arrow needed someone to create action out front, whether offensively or defensively, he had the ability to play a wild card — Frank "Spoon" James.

"In 95 percent of the junior colleges in the country, they would have put him at the post, because of being 6-8," explained Arrow. "We like to pride ourselves on playing them in the position they're going to play in major college. Spoon played the point, the next guard, [and] the three spot for us at one time or another."

James' all-around importance to the Ravens made him the obvious choice for tourney MVP.

The 1983 French MVP, Frank "Spoon" James later starred at the University of Nevada-Las Vegas. (Photo courtesy of Nevada-Las Vegas)

At the beginning of the week, Arrow had told his players, "We've got a week to win the national championship, something that you'll remember all your life. Put everything out of your mind except doing everything that you can to bring back a national championship to Pasadena, Texas."

Saying and doing are two different things. However, "when that bunch went up there and got the first game under their belt," said Arrow, "it was almost as if they knew it [the championship] was going to be theirs.

"It was just a matter of time."

Tournament Results

Tuesday:	Game		
	1	Clinton — 82	Florida College — 75
	2	SECC-Fairbury — 71	Mercer County — 64 OT
	3	Seminole — 43	Mesa — 42
	4	Jamestown — 78	NDSSS-Wahpeton — 70
	5	Independence — 84	DeKalb-South — 65
	6	San Jacinto — 84	Moberly — 76
Wednesday:	Game		
	7	CCAC-Pittsburgh — 66	Wabash Valley — 64
	8	Walker — 67	Vincennes — 63
	9	Mercer County — 99	Florida College — 68
	10	SECC-Fairbury — 75	Clinton — 74 OT
	11	Seminole — 71	Jamestown — 70
Thursday:	Game		
	12	Mesa — 55	NDSSS-Wahpeton — 54
	13	Moberly — 84	DeKalb-South — 77
	14	Wabash Valley — 89	Vincennes — 88 OT
	15	San Jacinto — 75	Independence — 62
	16	Walker — 60	CCAC-Pittsburgh — 48
	17	Jamestown — 96	Clinton — 92 OT
Friday:	Game		
	18	Mercer County — 61	Mesa — 60
	19	Moberly — 110	Wabash Valley — 106 OT
	20	Independence — 81	CCAC-Pittsburgh — 66
	21	Seminole — 75	SECC-Fairbury — 73
	22	San Jacinto — 72	Walker — 57
Saturday:	Game		
	23	Moberly — 85	Mercer County — 80
	24	Jamestown — 88	Independence — 79
	25	SECC-Fairbury — 103	Walker — 84
	26	San Jacinto — 73	Seminole — 68

How They Finished in 1983

1. San Jacinto College, Central Campus
2. Seminole Junior College
3. Southeast Community College
4. Walker College
5. Jamestown Community College
6. Independence Community College
7. Moberly Area Junior College
8. Mercer County Community College

All-Tournament Team

Anthony Bowie — Seminole Junior College
William Childs — Seminole Junior College
Willie "Sam" Ervin — Walker College
Nolan Gibson — San Jacinto College, Central Campus
Armon Gilliam — Independence Community College
Frank "Spoon" James — San Jacinto College, Central Campus
Carl Jeter — Jamestown Community College
Jeff Strong — Moberly Area Junior College
Malcolm Thomas — Moberly Area Junior College
Neil Wake — Southeast Community College

Coach of the Tournament

Ronnie Arrow — San Jacinto College, Central Campus

French Most Valuable Player Award

Frank "Spoon" James — San Jacinto College, Central Campus

Sesher Sportsmanship Award

Vic Couch — Clinton Community College

Bud Obee Outstanding Small Player Award

Winfred Case — Seminole Junior College

The No. 2 scorer in the 1984 tournament with 97 points, Harvey Marshall (No. 13) later played for the University of Nebraska. (Photo courtesy of the University of Nebraska)

Walter Berry was a living legend from the playground of New York City. His 6-8, 210-pound body was described by *Boston Globe* sportswriter Bob Ryan as "a sinful marriage of grace and power." He was destined for great accomplishment on the collegiate basketball court.

Unfortunately, due to family problems, Berry fell behind in his studies. In June 1982, the high school All-American dropped out of Benjamin Franklin High.

To the rescue came St. John's University. Through the institution's Queens campus, Berry took a 24-unit program designed to provide GED equivalency.

However, though sufficient to attain athletic eligibility in New York State, the program was not acceptable to the NCAA. St. John's fought the judgment, seeking an injunction which would allow Berry to play. In September 1983, a federal court sided with the NCAA ruling that the state equivalency work was not the same as the national GED standard.

Walter Berry was left out in the cold.

One course remained. That fall Berry enrolled at San Jacinto College. Immediately the Ravens became the odds-on favorite to defend their national title.

THE PARTICIPANTS

Walter Berry was by far the most celebrated player to come into the National Juco Tournament. His battle with the NCAA gained national attention, including a *Sports Illustrated* feature. Newspapers tracked his progress at San Jacinto throughout the year, making fans everywhere aware of his talent. His participation in Hutchinson alone was enough to attract many sports writers and four-year coaches to the event for the first time.

Still, Berry's performance in the junior college ranks had not been as overpowering as expected. True, he was in the top 10 statistically in scoring (28.9), rebounding (14.1), and field goal percentage (67 percent). But, there were those, including San Jacinto Coach Ronnie Arrow, who felt he could do even better.

"Walter was up and down as far as intensity," stated Arrow. There were the times when he scored 38 points and grabbed 30 rebounds as he did against St. Phillips College of San Antonio. There were also the times when playing a dinky Texas junior college failed to compare to playing a Georgetown and he appeared to coast.

"If Walter Berry comes ready to play," Arrow told the press, "they'll see the best player ever to take the court in that Hutchinson Arena."

Because of Berry, the No. 4 Ravens (31-2) were instantly installed as the team to beat. The defending champs were the top offensive squad coming into the tournament with a 101-point average and had confirmed their potential by beating No. 1 Laredo Junior College in the finals of Region 14's south zone tournament.

However, as was often the case with the NJCAA's out-of-the-hat bracket selections, San Jacinto did not have a clear track to a crown. Four of the other five top-20 squads were in the Ravens' path, including No. 2 Miami-Dade Community College North (33-1), No. 3 Three Rivers Community College (35-2) and No. 5 Westchester Community College (33-1). Two-time former champ Western Texas College (24-10) and 1983 participant Wabash Valley College (31-5) also obstructed the way

Region	Team
1	Eastern Arizona College — Thatcher, Arizona
3	Erie Community College — Buffalo, New York
5	Western Texas College — Snyder, Texas
6	Independence Community College — Independence, Kansas
8	Miami-Dade Community College, North Campus — Miami, Florida
9	Northeastern Junior College — Sterling, Colorado
10	Chowan College — Murfreesboro, North Carolina
12	Vincennes University — Vincennes, Indiana
14	San Jacinto College, Central Campus — Pasadena, Texas
15	Westchester Community College — Valhalla, New York
16	Three Rivers Community College — Poplar Bluff, Missouri
18	Ricks College — Rexburg, Idaho
19	Essex County College — Newark, New Jersey
21	Springfield Technical Community College — Springfield, Massachusetts
23	Delgado Community College — New Orleans, Louisiana
24	Wabash Valley College — Mt. Carmel, Illinois
	Lost in First-Round Play-Offs:
2	Seminole Junior College — Seminole, Oklahoma
4	Malcolm X College — Chicago, Illinois
7	Hiwassee College — Madisonville, Tennessee
11	Southeastern Community College — West Burlington, Iowa
13	Fergus Falls Community College — Fergus Falls, Minnesota
17	Brunswick Junior College — Brunswick, Georgia
20	Community College of Allegheny County, Allegheny Campus — Pittsburgh, Pennsylvania
22	Walker College — Jasper, Alabama

Only Eastern Arizona College (26-4), making its first appearance in 20 years, and Erie Community College (29-4), 14th-ranked but from traditionally weak Region 3, seemed the only easy opponents in the lower flight.

The upper bracket was wide open. The top contenders looked to be: No. 11 Essex County College, at 21-0 the only undefeated squad in the field; Northeastern of Sterling, 33-3 with a 17-game win streak; and three-time champs Vincennes University (30-7) and Independence Community College (27-8). All were tourney veterans with the latter two having winning traditions which offset their lack of ranking. For example, Vincennes upset No. 17 Malcolm X College, 106-104, in a first-round play-off on a last-second shot. And Independence topped No. 14 Seminole Junior College, which returned the "ABC Gang" from the previous year's national runner-up, 70-64, ending the Trojans 24-game homecourt string.

Then there were the four newcomers, one of which was assured of gaining the semifinals: Springfield Technical Community College (31-1), featuring Foster Jacobs, the leading scorer coming into the tournament with a 31.3 average; Chowan College (28-7), with starting point guard Nate McMillan and center David Burgess having already signed letters-of-intent to North Carolina State and Virginia Tech, respectively; Ricks College (25-7), the largest privately owned junior college in the country; and Delgado Community College (24-10), led by 1983 All-American Marcus Hamilton.

Besides being able to see one of the brightest stars at any level of the collegiate ranks, fans were guaranteed an interesting week of competition.

TUESDAY — 1000

On Monday, the day before the official start of spring, Old Man Winter left a final remembrance. Snow thunderstorms created blizzard conditions across Kansas, dumping 12 inches of snow on Hutchison.

Most of the tourney participants had anticipated the bad weather, arriving a day earlier. Only three were caught unawares.

Springfield Tech, which edged out Miami-Dade North as the team traveling the farthest, encountered no problems at all until landing at Wichita. "I've never seen so many cars in the ditch," said Coach Steve Athas of the drive to Hutchinson. "I saw a car every 25 feet."

The eight-hour trip that Northeastern of Colorado expected turned into a 13½-hour endurance run due to road crews clearing 20-foot drifts off I-70 and to a Good-Samaritan stop to push *Hutchinson News* sports editor Bob Lyster out of a ditch. The Plainsmen arrived Monday night, but too late to attend the player banquet.

Western Texas, like guest speaker Norm Stewart of Missouri, also failed to make the banquet. However, the Texans' absence was planned since they did not play until Wednesday.

By Tuesday's noon tip-off, however, the sun was out and well on its way to melting Monday's excess. Thoughts shifted from the weather to the basketball court.

For Wayne McGrath, the Director of Community Colleges in Arizona, it was the third time in the Hutchinson Sports Arena. In 1956, he was a starting guard for Eastern Arizona. In 1964, he coached the school's tourney representative. Now, he was in attendance to see his son Phil, a starting forward for the Gila Monsters.

In the Eastern Arizona-Three Rivers opener, featuring the two top defenses in the field, McGrath's biggest tourney thrill to date came when the younger McGrath banked a shot off the glass with eight seconds left, knotting the score, 48-all.

The Gila Monsters quickly gained control in overtime with a delay game which forced Three Rivers into numerous fouls. Eastern Arizona hit 9 of 12 free shots, upsetting the No. 3 Raiders, 59-54.

Another rated squad bit the dust in the matinee feature. Tyress Carter hit a 25-footer to start the game, but it was Essex County's only lead. Behind Jerome Brewer's 28 and Mark Harris' 24, Vincennes built a 23-point lead, then thwarted a last ditch Essex rally, handing the Wolverines their first loss of the year, 88-76.

Because of the length of the opener, the afternoon finale started late. As soon as Delgado jumped out to a 20-2 lead, taking advantage of a bad case of Chowan jitters, fans began leaving, hoping to catch a quick bite before the evening session. By halftime, with the Dolphins comfortably in front, 38-26, the stands were virtually cleared.

During the season the Chowan Braves had played a preliminary before a Duke-North Carolina State contest in Reynolds Coliseum. "I knew our team wasn't scared of anything because of having played before that crowd of 12,000," said Chowan Coach Bob Burke.

When Delgado became overly cautious in the second half, the Braves took charge. Led by Nate McMillan, who hit 21 of his game-high 23 after intermission, Chowan went from 10 down with 14 minutes remaining to three up with 3:50 left.

Suddenly the game was up for grabs. Fans quickly returned to the Arena.

With 10 seconds left, Earl Robinson returned the lead to Delgado with two free throws.

At the three-second mark, Chowan reserve Todd Wright hit a 15-footer, his first basket of the game. Just as fans began arriving for the night session, the contest went into overtime.

With more people in the Arena parking lot listening to the game on the radio than watching it inside, substitutes continued to carry the Chowan flag in the extra period. In place of Brave stars McMillan and David Burgess who were on the bench with five fouls each, Clifton Lynch and Tracy Battle combined for six clutch free throws in the final minute, giving Chowan a 91-88 win.

Of the four newcomers, only Ricks showed no signs of debutitis. With a large fan contingent cheering their every move, the Vikings could do no wrong. Though big and not particularly quick, Ricks created excellent offensive movement. Behind the long-distance pokes of Alan Campbell, who hit 20 of his game-high 26, the Vikings grabbed an imposing 46-28 halftime margin in the evening opener.

The Springfield Tech Rams did not know what hit them. "It was a big surprise that they could be that big and shoot that well from outside," Coach Steve Athas told the press. "We were not getting any rebounding and we were in awe of their size."

In the final period, the Vikings continued their outside shooting exhibition and their domination of the boards (55-35), bombing Springfield, 96-58.

In the evening feature, favored Independence never maintained the intensity of its regional win over Barton County Community College or its unexpected victory over Seminole in the first-round play-off. Though they hit 64 percent from the field, the Pirates managed a maximum margin of eight and were unable to put away the Plainsmen from Sterling.

Center Dennis Jenkins (26 points, including 10 of 11 from the field) and guard Harvey Marshall (25 points, most from long range) kept Northeastern in contention until the end. Trailing by one with 1:47 remaining, the Plainsmen called time. An upset was a definite possibility.

When play resumed, however, Independence scored six straight points, putting the game out of reach. Behind Brad Underwood's 30 and Carliss Jeter's 22, the Pirates eked out an 80-76 win.

The nightcap, recognized as the 1000th game played in the NJCAA Tournament,[1] was a seesaw contest for 25 minutes. Then a momentary lapse by Wabash Valley resulted in six quick Westchester points. The contest was never the same afterwards. Utilizing the superior overall quickness, Westchester downed the Warriors, 95-76.

WEDNESDAY — HARD-EARNED VICTORY

With all the advance hoopla about Walter Berry, it was ironic that in his team's first appearance the public address announcer almost forgot to introduce him.

But, once San Jacinto hit the floor, there was little question who the star was. Anchoring an obviously taller and more talented squad, Berry led the Ravens to an easy 23-9 advantage over Erie.

Then things went awry. San Jacinto began picking up fouls — especially Berry, who promptly sat down. The Ravens were forced to drop their press and fell back into a zone. Said Coach Ronnie Arrow, "That's when we started sleepwalking, standing around."

While San Jacinto played as though the game was a snap, Don Silveri's Kats clawed for dear life. By intermission, Erie had tied the score, 37-all, surprising the large afternoon crowd.

Buoyed by their first-half success against the defending national champs, the Kats came out confident, quickly establishing a 45-39 margin. If Erie could hold on, it would be the greatest upset in tourney history.

With San Jacinto now aroused, it was a struggle for the Kats to remain on top. At the 7:26 mark, their chances were hurt when 1983 1st Team All-American John McNulty — who had faced Berry in high school — joined the Raven big man with four fouls. Then, for the next three minutes, the two sides traded baskets. Finally, with Erie clinging to a 70-69 edge, San Jacinto's Willie Jennings swished one from the top of the key.

In the battle for the potential rebound, Erie's Ray Swogger was whistled for pushing Berry, who had just reentered the line-up after having spent most of the half on the bench. Swogger protested the call and was slapped with a technical.

Berry made both ends of one-and-one, missed the technical, then downed a short hook with 4:22 remaining. The six-point swing gave San Jacinto control of the game.

During Berry's long absences from the floor, Linwood Moye and Jennings had carried the Raven load, contributing 25 and 21, respectively. Now Berry took over, picking up the pace, ending the game with 21 points and 10 rebounds. Though Erie's Tyrone Thomas led everyone with 28, including 13 of 16 from the field, San Jacinto grabbed a hard-earned victory, 89-82.

In the final opening-round contest, unranked and unheralded Western Texas proved that the Western Texas Juco Conference, where the Westerners finished fourth, was indeed a competitive league. During a nine-minute span, the Texans outscored No. 2 Miami-Dade North, 26-7, taking a 28-13 lead with eight minutes left in the first period.

Miami-Dade made a nine-point run at the Westerners in the final frame, but could come no closer than 63-59 with 5:17 remaining. Richie Fells and Larry Banks kept Western Texas on top, combining for 11 free throws down the stretch, protecting the Westerners' 81-74 upset win.

With only one other top-20 team left after the surprises of the opening round, San Jacinto went from "favorite" to "heavy favorite." However, two serious threats were brewing in the upper bracket.

In the opening quarterfinal pitting two three-time champs, Vincennes fell behind Independence, 53-36, with 17:13 to go. Then, led by Jerome Brewer, reserve Darnell Glenn, and especially Mark Harris, who fired 18 of his game-high 28 in the final period, the Trailblazers pressed, mounted a valiant rally, and eventually knotted the score, 71-all, with 6:30 remaining.

From then on, the heavily pro-Independence crowd was treated to a tense basket-trading affair.

With six seconds left, Vincennes ahead, 80-79, Harris stepped to the line for one-and-one. He was a perfect 4-for-4 for the evening. The Trailblazers were going to cinch it.

Instead, Harris missed and Pirate Ron Roberts grabbed the rebound. Carliss Jeter received the outlet, raced for a last-ditch effort from 15 feet, and missed. At the last moment, Roberts and Darrell Davis jumped. Though Roberts got the credit — a year later he admitted "I went up, but I don't think I tipped it" — Davis tipped it in. Independence grabbed an 81-80 victory at the buzzer.

While the Arena rocked with jubilant noise, the basketball bounced over in front of the Vincennes bench. Coach Dan Sparks dropped kicked it, sending the ball and his loafer soaring to the ceiling.

Sparks' frustration was twofold. First, the Trailblazers had missed six key free throws in the final four minutes, including three one-and-ones. Second, in the hectic moments following Harris' final miss from the line, there was an apparent delay in the start of the clock.

"I know if we hit the free throws we win," reflected Sparks. "But, the guy didn't turn the clock on. He was watching the game. It still said five seconds when they [Independence] crossed midcourt."

Though happy with the win, Pirate Coach Bob Kivisto shared Sparks' doubt. "It was close. Maybe it [Davis' final tip] shouldn't have counted."

Nonetheless, Independence, with its large following from southeastern Kansas plus the solid support of local Hutchonians — a rarity given the intense rivalry between the two towns — would be a difficult opponent from now on out.

So would Chowan.

The Braves possessed a strong front line — John Thomas (6-5, 215 pounds), David Burgess (6-8, 225), and Jerome Cooper (6-7, 195) — plus a do-everything point guard — 6-5 Nate McMillan, who topped everyone with 14 rebounds and six assists — and no longer showed opening-night butterflies. In a turnaround from its previous come-from-behind performance, Chowan shot ahead of Ricks, 20-10.

Then the Vikings cranked up their long-range guns. "Ricks has the finest shooting team I've ever seen," Chowan Coach Bob Burke later told the press. "We played near-perfect basketball for nine minutes or so but we couldn't put them away."

Though a coatless Burke nervously paced, never sitting down, actively helping his shooters with body-English along the sidelines, the Braves held firm. Ricks reduced the deficit to six on numerous occasions, but could never break the barrier. Chowan won the battle between the only private institutions in the tournament, advancing 86-80.

THURSDAY — THE WALTER BERRY SHOW

Delgado opened the day's consolation action with five consecutive baskets, including a blind reverse two-handed overhead bank by 6-4 freshman John Ray. Using the quick start to advantage, the Dolphins upped the margin to 25, then coasted, eliminating Springfield Tech, 74-66.

Springfield's Foster Jacobs topped all scorers, matching his 31-point average. However, it was Delgado's Willie Bland who stole the limelight. The 6-5 sophomore led the Dolphins with 25, including a half-dozen stirring dunks.

In the afternoon feature, Ivan Stone's game-high 28 paced Three Rivers as the Raiders led virtually from beginning to end, downing Wabash Valley, 85-80.

Then came an almost exact replay of the Erie-San Jacinto opening-round game. As before, Erie fell behind, this time to No. 2 Miami-Dade, rallied to take the lead, 40-39, with 18 minutes left, then struggled to remain in contention. Miami-Dade

---

[1]Officially, the 1000-game total included extra games played in the 1963 tournament because of an ineligible player incident, the extra games in the tourney's expanded format in 1976 and 1977, and all first-round play-off games played at various regional sites since 1978.

had its hands full until the final minute when the Falcons scored the last seven points. The Kats fell again, 85-74.

Considering Eastern Arizona's proven ability to control the ball and the tempo, the Gila Monsters' 30-23 halftime margin over Westchester, a team with a 97.1 scoring average, looked comfortable in the evening's first quarterfinal.

But, according to Westchester Coach Ralph Arietta, the Westcos "never played well the first half." In the Region 15 tournament, Westchester trailed by four at intermission of the opener and won by 40, trailed by a pair in the next contest and won by 30, then was even at halftime of the final and won by 27.

"I think basketball is a game of quickness," explained Arietta. "When you've got good overall quickness, are playing with athletes, I think you can go a long way."

There were few arguments the Westcos were the quickest team in the tournament. Led by guards Wendell Owens and Alex Agudio, Westchester applied defensive pressure and immediately upped the tempo. Running and gunning all the way, the Westcos outscored Eastern Arizona, 42-17, in the second half, downing the Monsters, 65-47. No Eastern Arizona player hit double figures, while all Westco starters cracked that mark, paced by Owens' 21.

The remaining quarterfinal was the "Walter Berry Show" all the way.

Claiming that his uninspired performance against Erie was possibly due to the noon starting time — "I like to sleep late," he told the press — the big freshman swept away any doubts that he was the best player in the tournament, definite Division I material, and a potential pro. Berry dominated the court scoring a tourney-high 39 points, grabbing 14 rebounds, and blocking 12 shots, the latter a San Jacinto school record, breaking the mark held by then Milwaukee Buck Alton Lister.

Though Western Texas stayed with San Jacinto early, the Ravens, like Berry, were more intense than in their opener. A 10-point spurt in the first half and a 12-point spree in the final frame erased any Western Texas hopes of an upset. San Jacinto advanced to the semifinals, 91-82.

The consolation nightcap was the best game of the day. The contest featured a battle between the tournament's two best cheering squads who had plenty to cheer about. Though the one-two punch of Vincennes reserve Darnell Glenn (24) and leading scorer Jerome Brewer (23) did not compare to the dynamic Ricks duo of Roland Smith (31 points, 14 rebounds) and Brian Fink (30 points, 15 rebounds), the Trailblazers still managed to force an overtime. Then, Alan Campbell's four free throws in the final 34 seconds tipped the scale toward Ricks, 92-89.

FRIDAY — SIX-SECOND WONDERS

The ever-changing Kansas weather did another flip-flop on Friday. While ice and snow plagued western portions of the state, with some places still contending with four-foot drifts from earlier in the week, rain drenched Hutchinson. Nearly 1½ inches fell at the same time Northeastern of Sterling downed Delgado, 74-65, leading wire-to-wire; No. 3 Three Rivers edged No. 2 Miami-Dade North, 61-58, on free throws by Brad Phillips with 11 seconds left; and Western Texas outmuscled Eastern Arizona, 68-52, controlling the boards, 37 to 25.

By game time of the opening semifinal that evening, the temperature had dipped to 33 degrees with the rain containing an occasional spit of snow.

However, back in Murfreesboro, North Carolina — population less than 5,000 — Milton's Pizza, the only pizza restaurant in town, was anything but cold and damp. Throughout the tournament, the owner piped in the Chowan games on the radio and the response was overwhelming. Related Chowan Coach Bob Burke, "The guy sold more pizza during that particular week than he sold the previous year. They had so many people trying to get in there, they were piping it [the radio broadcast] back out into the streets."

Milton's patrons were forgiving of the Kansas announcer's many stabs at pronouncing the school name [shaWAN], especially since the Braves sounded so unstoppable. Utilizing its superior front-line size, Chowan dominated the boards (49-33 for the game), building a 51-39 cushion over hometown favorite Independence early in the second half.

Independence chipped at the lead, but was still down, 75-69, with three minutes remaining.

Then two Chowan turnovers and a pair of missed one-and-ones allowed the Pirates to tie the game on a Carliss Jeter tip with 47 seconds left.

Chowan held the ball for one. With eight seconds to go, the Braves called time. When play resumed, Nate McMillan hit John Thomas — the game's leading scorer with 28 — who tried to get off a turnaround jumper. Independence reserve Ron Barnes blocked the attempt, forcing a jump ball.

On the alternate possession rule, the Pirates took over. There were six seconds left, the exact amount of time Independence had had on its final possession in the last-second victory over Vincennes.

After both teams called time, the Pirates inbounded the ball to Jeter. As he had against Vincennes, the sophomore guard drove the length of the floor, stopped to the right of the key, and fired.

Unlike the previous night's miss, this Jeter shot swished. Independence won its second six-second wonder in a row, 77-75.

"When Carliss got the ball inbounds without much trouble," described Independence Coach Bob Kivisto, "I knew we were going to get off a good shot. He's the best pressure shooter on the team. I'm not surprised he made it. What we can't believe is that he missed the one against Vincennes."

Jeter was one of the reasons that the 1984 Juco Tournament was being labeled "the year of the transfer." The previous year he had made an appearance on the Arena floor as a member of fifth-place finisher, Jamestown Community College. Then the New York school suddenly dropped its basketball program. Jeter was one of several Jayhawk freshmen who were picked up by junior colleges all over the nation. Another was 6-7 forward Linwood Moye, now a starter with San Jacinto.

A third player who was making his second appearance in Hutchinson, but in a different uniform, was Westchester's Wendell Owens. Oddly enough, however, Owens had transferred from a solid winning program.

As a member of San Jacinto's 1983 national champion squad, Owens was used in reserve roles at guard. Frustrated with his lack of playing time, he asked Raven Coach Ronnie Arrow if his PT would increase the following year. Arrow was unable to promise it. "Wendell was more a driving scorer," stated Arrow, not an outside-shooting floor general he needed to feed the big men, handling the bulk of Raven scoring.

Since Owens was from Queens, New York, Arrow contacted Westchester Coach Ralph Arietta. Both coaches encouraged Owens to transfer. The 6-1 sophomore agreed.

The No. 3 scorer (96 points) and the Obee Small Player for 1984, Wendell Owens (No. 15) finished his collegiate career at Texas Tech University. (Photo courtesy of Westchester Community College)

At the first Westco practice, Owens began to doubt his decision. "Wendell looked at me and basically said, 'Coach, what the hell did you get me into?'" recalled Arietta. "We looked so bad. Wendell was used to having all that talent coming out of San Jac. It looked like the whole season was going to be a disaster."

The semester addition of guard Alex Agudio, a transfer from Penn State, helped improve the team outlook. In his first appearance in a Westco uniform during a January tournament in New Jersey, Agudio hit his first nine shots. He was selected the tourney MVP.

With Agudio and Owens, a two-pronged buzz saw chewing up defenses with aggressive drives, Westchester lost only once. The Westcos were currently riding a 29-game win streak, one away from a title game. The remaining obstacle — San Jacinto. Wendell Owens could not have asked for more.

Though Arietta told the press, "We'll have to play the greatest game of our life to beat San Jacinto," Westchester showed no intimidation. After falling behind, 4-0, the smaller quicker Westcos scored six straight, then built an eight-point margin. They did not trail again until three minutes remained in the half when a Willie Jennings free throw returned the advantage to San Jacinto, 37-36. Westchester held the ball for the rest of the period, but failed to make a last-second attempt. As a noted second-half ballclub, the Westcos were in perfect position for an upset.

Then a sleeping giant awakened.

After scoring a quiet 10 points in the first period, Walter Berry hit 12 of San Jacinto's first 19 in the second half. The Ravens pulled away, 57-46, with 13:05 remaining.

Westchester responded with 10 unanswered points. The Westcos stayed close for another three minutes before San Jacinto upped the difference to nine.

Westchester made a final run at the Ravens, pulling within three, 81-78, with just under two minutes left. Then two misses and an authoritative rebound by Berry halted the rally.

Though all five Westco starters tallied double figures, they were no match for San Jacinto's star forward. Behind another man-sized performance by Berry — 35 points, 10 rebounds, and 6 blocked shots — San Jacinto advanced to the title match, winning 91-82.

SATURDAY — HOT HANDS IN THE BERRY PATCH

Three Rivers' aggressive man-to-man defense and superior quickness forced 24 Northeastern turnovers, limited the Plainsmen to 42 shots, and held Harvey Marshall, the second-leading scorer in the tournament, to 13. The Raiders grabbed seventh-place with ease, 74-51, giving them a remarkable 22-6 tourney record in seven appearances.

In the fifth-place contest, a questionable no-call after a Western Texas player appeared to hang on the rim following a missed dunk, effectively halted a Ricks rally which had erased an 11-point deficit midway in the second half. Then 12 for 17 free throw shooting in the final frame salvaged a 74-71 Western Texas victory.

Two very popular teams matched up in the third-place game with Westchester taking a backseat to Chowan throughout the contest. Then, with 1:53 remaining, Alex Agudio converted a three-point play, tying the score, 74-all.

After a miss at the Chowan end of the court, Westchester held for one. With 10 seconds left, Brave reserve Jim Dillard blocked center Keith Malone's tie-breaking attempt, picked up the loose ball, and — thinking time was almost up — threw it the length of the court, missing the basket out of bounds, Westchester had another chance to break the deadlock.

The Westcos missed, sending the game into overtime.

The extra period, however, was all Westchester and, in fact, almost all Alex Agudio. The 6-1 guard scored the Westcos' first four points, all from the line, made a steal and a crucial rebound, then added a basket at the buzzer.

Led by the clutch performances of Agudio and Wendell Owens, Agudio's defensive partner in crime in the second half and the game's top scorer with 30, Westchester took third, 84-78, the highest finish for a Region 15 representative in tourney history.

The title game drew one of the largest sellout crowds in tourney history. On one side was favored San Jacinto, featuring one of the event's greatest players, Walter Berry. On the other side, cast in the uncommon role of underdog, was local favorite Independence, a three-time former champ with a chance to tie Moberly for most national titles. It was the first rematch of a previous championship-game pairing.

Decked out in a yellow tux, navy blue cummerbund and bow tie — formal attire in various color schemes of gold and blue, the Pirate colors, had been a tourney tradition for him since the regionals of 1983 — Coach Bob Kivisto stated in a pre-game interview on radio station KWBW that there were two requirements for an Independence victory. "Number one, we're going to have to contain their physical brute strength on the boards. And number two, we're going to have to have a great shooting night."

The latter condition did not appear to be a problem. Independence had the best shooting team in the tournament. Freshman guard Barry Fields was excellent from outside, averaging 12 points a game. So was freshman center Ron Roberts, averaging 17 points a game, despite the fact that the coaching staff at the University of Colorado, where Roberts had been red-shirted the year before, had indicated the contrary. Kivisto's best shooters, however, were sophomores Brad Underwood and Carliss Jeter, averaging 16 and 17, respectively.

Underwood, a transfer from Hardin-Simmons, but at home on the Arena floor, having been a stand-out at McPherson High, just 30 miles from Hutchinson, was a perfectionist regarding his shot. Any time he missed more than once, he would start analyzing what went wrong, often causing problems that did not exist. Consequently, his confidence needed constant bolstering.

During the post-warm-up team meetings before each tourney game, Kivisto made a point to comment to him, "Boy, Brad, your shot looks as good as it ever has."

Underwood frequently replied, "Well, I didn't think I shot the ball that good in the warm-ups, Coach."

Kivisto' response: "Brad, your form looks great. It just looks great."

"The funny thing about it," Kivisto related later, "I never watched one shot he took in the warm-ups."

Jeter was the complete opposite. According to Kivisto, "Carliss was as loose as a goose. Carliss could miss five shots [and say], 'Coach, I'll make the next 10.'"

In the Region 6 final against Barton County Community College, Jeter experienced one of his few poor shooting nights of the year, hitting 3 for 20. Not wanting the performance to discourage the sophomore forward in the upcoming first-round play-off with highly-regarded Seminole, Kivisto talked to Jeter afterwards, telling him he had a week to find his shooting eye again.

"Find it, Coach?" reacted Jeter. "The way I shot tonight that means I'm going to make every shot I shoot against Seminole. I'm due."

"And the first play of the game," recalled Kivisto, "we got the ball to Carliss and, hell, he takes a bad shot, off balance, a guy on him — and it goes in."

Having such excellent outside shooters with corresponding egos posed a morale problem early in the season for Kivisto. "I thought one time we were going to have to play with two basketballs to keep everybody happy." But, by season's end, the two sharpshooters were best buddies. "They said they wanted to go and play together somewhere [the next year] so nobody could double-team them."

The duo was a definite factor in the title game. Complying with Kivisto's requirements for victory, Independence hit its first five shots from the field, Underwood and Jeter supplying a pair apiece. The Pirates jumped on top, 12-4, further igniting the crowd which was into the game from the start. With Underwood and Jeter unstoppable — each scored 12 in the first half — Independence could do no wrong.

Unfortunately for the Pirates, neither could Walter Berry.

Berry scored San Jacinto's first eight points, ending the period with 18, virtually carrying the Ravens on his broad back. He blocked shots, stole the ball, and slam dunked, putting on an awesome display of power. On one occasion he blocked a Roberts tip try, leading KWBW announcer Jerry Kershaw to declare

The No. 4 scorer in the 1984 tournament with 94 points, Independence's Carliss Jeter (No. 22) continued his collegiate career at the University of Tennessee-Chattanooga. (Photo courtesy of Independence Community College)

in amazement, "Berry simply wiped it out of the sky and out of bounds." Another time he scored with his back to the basket, without even looking where he was shooting.

With Berry opening mouths with his feats, San Jacinto remained in contention. On a successful tip off a Berry-led fast break with six minutes remaining, the Ravens took their first lead, 34-32.

Hungry for another crown, Independence quickly regained the advantage, taking a 42-40 halftime edge. In the first seven minutes of the final period, the Pirates upped the margin to seven.

Then a three-point play by Linwood Moye, a basket by Lew Hill, and another by Moye tied the game at 62-all. From then on, the lead repeatedly changed hands, neither side willing to give in.

During a one-minute stretch, Independence reserve Ron Barnes blocked three Raven shots, one of them Berry's. Though Underwood and Jeter continued to contribute offensively (10 apiece in the second half, all from the field) it was Roberts who shouldered most of the Pirate load, ending the contest with 24 points and 13 rebounds.

On the San Jacinto side of the ledger, firepower came from an unexpected source — the Raven guards. Hill and Ron Singleton were outstanding from outside, hitting 12 each for the period, ending with 20 and 18, respectively. Hill also offered 10 assists.

But, the man of the hour, if not the week, was Berry. Playing the entire second half with three fouls, Berry compiled a final tally of 28 points, 18 rebounds, and six blocked shots. Given such credentials, it could be assumed he was involved in the key sequence of the contest.

With under four minutes remaining, the Ravens down two, Berry swiped a lob pass out of the air, initiated a fast break, then received a lob from Hill, slamming it home one-handed. Said Independence's Kivisto, "He stole our dunk and then slammed one that Wilt Chamberlain couldn't have stopped." San Jacinto went on top, 80-78, never to trail again.

Though Independence pressured until the end, especially when Roberts' two-hand stuff pulled the Pirates within one, 81-80, with 55 seconds left, San Jacinto would not succumb. Fittingly, Berry extinguished the Pirates' last flicker of hope, blocking an Underwood shot with 21 seconds left.

The Ravens won their second straight title, 86-82, oddly enough holding all four opponents to the same total.

Often overlooked because of the scoring prowess of teammates Carliss Jeter and Brad Underwood, center Ron Roberts (No. 32) led Independence with 24 points and 13 rebounds in the 1984 championship game against San Jacinto. Roberts finished his collegiate career at the University of Oklahoma. (Photo courtesy of Independence Community College)

THE AFTERMATH — NOBODY BETTER

After viewing the championship game from the bleachers, St. John's University head coach Lou Carnesecca, Walter Berry's future collegiate mentor, commented about the NJCAA Tournament. "I was dazzled. I was really dazzled. The intensity of play, the intensity of the coaches, the hoopla — and the *fans*. What really got me going were the fans. The Hutchinson people and the people who came in to back their clubs are unbelievable."

The week had been a memorable treat for all involved.

Even though he failed to take home another championship souvenir, Westchester's Wendell Owens would never forget the hardware he did accumulate — an All-Tournament Team plaque and the Obee Small Player Award.

Fans would also not forget the courage of the Sesher Sportsmanship Award-winner, Larry Banks, Western Texas' leading scorer, despite missing the thumb and index finger of his left hand because of a childhood accident.

For Westchester's Ralph Arietta, the surprise Coach of the Tournament recipient, the awards ceremony was the highlight moment of his career. Besides having his daughter in the audience to witness the crowd's affectionate approval of the award, Arietta remembered, "One of the nicest things was, after the presentation was made, Ronnie Arrow's wife came over and gave me a big hug and kiss. That made me feel even better."

But, if the 1984 Juco Tournament was to be remembered by fans 30 years in the future, it would be because of one individual — Walter Berry.

Stated St. John's Carnesecca, "He has things that you can't coach. He's able to adjust his shot according to the defense. This is a gift. And two things he does very well: he can score and rebound."

Despite confirming the "man-among-boys" hype of the press, winning the scoring (123) and rebounding (52) titles and the French Most Valuable Player Award hands down, Berry was often criticized for appearing to glide through the motions as though on automatic pilot.

When Berry was relegated to the Texas League instead of the majors, it created a motivational challenge for San Jacinto Coach Ronnie Arrow. "Walter just tried to get by all his life by being the big kid on the block," explained Arrow. "He could half-step it and still be the best. We tried to explain to him, 'Walt, a lot of the stuff you're doing, you're doing just because you're bigger and stronger. But, there's going to come a time, even at this level, that you're going to have to have technique.'"

Arrow often joked with Berry that his intensity level was associated with the presence of a full moon. Prior to coming to Hutchinson, Arrow told him, "Walt, for the first time I hope there's five days of full moon."

However, Arrow found out he had nothing to worry about. During Region 14 tourney action, Arrow showed his squad the game film for the Ravens' 1983 championship. "Most of the time Walter would sit back there, picking his nose, sleeping or something. All of a sudden from the background in the dark I heard Walt say, 'You mean *that's* where we're going to be playing?' When I heard him say that, that sort of got *me* fired up.

"Walt was a good kid," insisted Arrow. It was team policy that anyone missing a class, regardless of the reason, was required to run a mile at six o'clock the following morning. "Walter ran three mornings the whole year. He knew that, for him to get back to the big time, he had to go to class."

"That's like most great players," said Independence's Bob Kivisto about Berry's playing his best when the chips were on the table. "The way I look at it, Berry didn't want to get every rebound, take every shot. He had other players out there and let them do their thing until it was time to take over."

When it counted, there was nobody better than Walter Berry.

One of the most dominate players to participate in the Juco Tournament, French MVP Walter Berry led 1984 tourney stats with 123 points and 52 rebounds. Berry was later the 1986 College Player of the Year at St. John's University before entering the pro ranks. (Photo courtesy of San Jacinto College)

Tournament Results

Tuesday:	Game	
	1	Eastern Arizona — 59 Three Rivers — 54 OT
	2	Vincennes — 88 Essex County — 76
	3	Chowan — 91 Delgado — 88 OT
	4	Ricks — 96 Springfield Tech — 58
	5	Independence — 80 Northeastern — 76
	6	Westchester — 95 Wabash Valley — 76
Wednesday:	Game	
	7	San Jacinto — 89 Erie — 82
	8	Western Texas — 81 Miami-Dade North — 74
	9	Northeastern — 80 Essex County — 71
	10	Independence — 81 Vincennes — 80
	11	Chowan — 86 Ricks — 80
Thursday:	Game	
	12	Delgado — 74 Springfield Tech — 66
	13	Three Rivers — 85 Wabash Valley — 80
	14	Miami-Dade North — 85 Erie — 74
	15	Westchester — 65 Eastern Arizona — 47
	16	San Jacinto — 91 Western Texas — 82
	17	Ricks — 92 Vincennes — 89 OT
Friday:	Game	
	18	Northeastern — 74 Delgado — 65
	19	Three Rivers — 61 Miami-Dade North — 58
	20	Western Texas — 68 Eastern Arizona — 52
	21	Independence — 77 Chowan — 75
	22	San Jacinto — 91 Westchester — 82
Saturday:	Game	
	23	Three Rivers — 74 Northeastern — 51
	24	Western Texas — 74 Ricks — 71
	25	Westchester — 84 Chowan — 78 OT
	26	San Jacinto — 86 Independence — 82

How They Finished in 1984

1. San Jacinto College, Central Campus
2. Independence Community College
3. Westchester Community College
4. Chowan College
5. Western Texas College
6. Ricks College
7. Three Rivers Community College
8. Northeastern Junior College

All-Tournament Team

Larry Banks — Western Texas College
Walter Berry — San Jacinto College, Central Campus
Jerome Brewer — Vincennes University
Bryan Fink — Ricks College
Chuck Glass — Three Rivers Community College
Carliss Jeter — Independence Community College
Harvey Marshall — Northeastern Junior College
Nate McMillan — Chowan College
Linwood Moye — San Jacinto College, Central Campus
Wendell Owens — Westchester Community College
John Thomas — Chowan College
Brad Underwood — Independence Community College

Coach of the Tournament

Ralph Arietta — Westchester Community College

French Most Valuable Player Award

Walter Berry — San Jacinto College, Central Campus

Sesher Sportsmanship Award

Larry Banks — Western Texas College

Bud Obee Most Outstanding Small Player Award

Wendell Owens — Westchester Community College

he 1985 National Juco Tournament opened on a down note. After 16 years in Hutchinson, the NJCAA planned to move its headquarters to Colorado Springs. The NJCAA executive board had already okayed the change. All that was left was the rubber-stamp approval of the full organization the following week at its annual convention.

Though the move was being made for strategic reasons — Colorado Springs was also the site of many other sports organizations with which the NJCAA was closely associated — Hutchonians feared the worst.

Their beloved basketball tournament would be the next to leave.

When asked the question by *Hutchinson News* sports editor Dana McBratney, Executive Director George Killian said, "For the 1,000th time, there are no plans now or forever of moving the basketball tournament."

The Juco Tournament was the NJCAA's biggest money-maker. It had reached the position because of the faithful community service of Lysle Rishel Post No. 68 of the American Legion, co-sponsors of the event.

In recognition of the Legion's effort, the NJCAA Basketball Coaches Association selected a Hutchonian as the first Hall of Fame inductee in the contributor category.

Guy Holt symbolized the Legion's hard work and dedication. He had been a member of the tournament committee for 37 years, 35 as its chairman.

Said Holt on receipt of the award at Monday's player banquet, "I accept this honor for all the people who deserve it."

He also added that he had two wishes. "First of all, I want to wish all of you teams out there the best of luck.

"My second wish is a little broader in scope. As you may or may not know, to be a member of the American Legion you have to have served your country in time of war in the armed forces. My second wish is to all the young people in the United States:

"May you never become eligible for the American Legion."

THE PARTICIPANTS

For the first time in three years, San Jacinto College was not the name on everybody's lips at tourney time. The No. 14 Ravens failed to win Region 14's south zone play-off, losing to Laredo Junior College, 84-83, at Alvin, Texas, a long way from Hutchinson.

Instead, the honor of favorite fell to No. 1 Highland Park Community College. Glen Donahue's Panthers were undefeated in 38 games, were one of the top offensive squads in the nation (97.5 average), and were led by a highly recruited All-American, Vernon Carr.

But, because it was Highland Park's first trip to Hutchinson, most observers were hedging their bets. The competition was sufficient to make the 38th Juco Tournament a wide open event.

Leading the list of Highland Park's challengers was No. 3 Allegany Community College (31-3). Bob Kirk's Trojans were an up-and-coming name in the juco world, having amassed 152 wins over the past five years. Early in the season they became the first team in 18 years to beat host Vincennes University in the annual Trailblazer Invitational. Allegany also made history by topping Casper College's home win record of 75, on the final night of

In the high-flying quarterfinal between Moberly and No. 1 Highland Park, Greyhound Bernard Day had his shot blocked by another All-Tourney performer, Vernon Carr. Day later played at Nebraska and Carr at Michigan State. (Photo courtesy of the **Hutchinson News***)*

the Trojans' Kiwanis Christmas Classic. By season's end, Allegany had extended the mark to 85.

No. 4 Dixie College (31-1) was also a threat with top-10 stats in offense (94.1), field goal percentage (55.4 percent), and free throw percentage (73.3 percent). The Rebels also boasted an All-American in Averian Parrish who during the season surpassed pro Lionel Hollins as the school's all-time leading scorer.

DeKalb Community College-South was another serious contender despite having a 14-20 record as listed in the program. After Region 17 action started, it was discovered that an Eagle reserve was ineligible. Under the current NJCAA by-laws, DeKalb-South forfeited the games the reserve had played in, was placed on probation for the following year, but was allowed to continue in national competition. The Eagles' status as a top contender was based on a No. 7 ranking and a 33-1 record before the ineligible player adjustment.

Two squads were included in the elite not only because of their ranking, but also because of their recent experience. No. 11 Westchester Community College (32-3), which took third, and No. 12 Erie Community College (32-4), which almost upset eventual champion San Jacinto, were the only returning schools from the previous year's tournament.

Region	Team
2	Westark Community College — Fort Smith, Arkansas
3	Erie Community College — Buffalo, New York
4	Kankakee Community College — Kankakee, Illinois
5	Midland College — Midland, Texas
7	Shelby State Community College — Memphis, Tennessee
9	Casper College — Casper, Wyoming
10	Ferrum College — Ferrum, Virginia
12	Highland Park Community College — Highland Park, Michigan
15	Westchester Community College — Valhalla, New York
16	Moberly Area Junior College — Moberly, Missouri
17	DeKalb Community College, South Campus — Decatur, Georgia
18	Dixie College — St. George, Utah
20	Allegany Community College — Cumberland, Maryland
22	Chattahoochee Valley Community College — Phenix City, Alabama
23	Hinds Junior College — Raymond, Mississippi
24	Kaskaskia College — Centralia, Illinois
	Lost in First-Round Play-Offs:
1	Eastern Arizona College — Thatcher, Arizona
6	Seward County Community College — Liberal, Kansas
8	Manatee Community College — Bradenton, Florida
11	Southeastern Community College — West Burlington, Iowa
13	Worthington Community College — Worthington, Minnesota
14	Laredo Junior College — Laredo, Texas
19	Gloucester Community College — Sewell, New Jersey
21	Middlesex Community College — Middletown, Connecticut

Still, No. 16 Kaskaskia College (33-2) was also considered a top threat despite having not appeared in Hutchinson since 1964 as Centralia Junior College.

Also feared were former champs Westark Community College (33-3) and Midland College (29-5). Though unranked, Gayle Kaundart's Westark Lions were again a top-10 defensive crew (56.5) and Jerry Stone's Midland Chaparrals had dumped No. 19 Laredo in a first-round play-off.

However, the name which drew the most respect in the list of competitors was Moberly Area Junior College. During the year the 20th-ranked Greyhounds had won the 1000th game in the school's history. Moberly had made more tourney appearances (21) and had earned more national championships (4) than any other junior college. Since many deemed the Greyhounds the best aggregate of talent in the field, another Moberly crown was a definite possibility.

The remaining six teams posed the least threat to Highland Park's unblemished record.

Casper College (29-7), a sentimental favorite because Coach Swede Erickson, in his 26th year, was one of the most recent inductees into the NJCAA Basketball Hall of Fame, Ferrum College (26-4), with Norwood "Pee Wee" Barber, the leading scorer (28) coming into the tournament, and Shelby State Community College (23-4), a top offensive squad (97.5), possessed only marginal potential.

Newcomers Hinds Junior College (25-6), Kankakee Community College (28-8), and Chattahoochee Valley Community College (21-8) were discounted as long shots.

TUESDAY — PEE WEE POWER

Since accepting the head coaching job at Kankakee, Denny Lehnus had compiled 302 wins in 11 years. The Cavaliers were routinely listed in the NJCAA poll, finishing in the top-10 four of the past six years. In the same span, Lehnus squads produced five All-Americans. But none were able to guide the team to Hutchinson, twice missing the opportunity by one game.

The current Cavalier crew contained no All-American. No one even rated inclusion on the Region 4 all-star squad. There were no starters taller than 6-3 and the leading scorer averaged a meager 8.7 points per contest. During the season Kankakee ended a 61-game home win streak, then later suffered its worst defeat in five years, losing to Vincennes, 76-59. It was the first time in five years the Cavaliers had not won 30 games.

Yet, unaccountably, this Kankakee squad appeared charmed. With two starters on the bench, the Cavaliers upended Kennedy-King Community College by 25, avenging the previous week's loss on Kankakee's own floor. Then the Cavaliers survived a one-point win over Thornton Community College when a last-second finger-roll rimmed out. Finally, against Carl Sandburg College, which possessed a 23-game win streak including a decisive win over No. 17 College of DuPage, Kankakee overcame a five-point halftime deficit, shot almost 80 percent from the field in the final 20 minutes, and won the regional title, 77-73.

If a first-time trip to the nationals was not enough, then the irony of the Cavaliers' opening opponent was the topper. Said Lehnus, "It's something that we have come all the way to Kansas to play another Illinois team."

By luck of the draw, Kankakee's tip-off-game match-up was Kaskaskia, from Centralia. The pairing brought immediate confusion to the Arena patrons and a sore throat to any broadcaster who continuously repeated the school names over the course of 40 minutes. Public address announcer Terry Messing avoided the latter by simply referring to the teams as the Cavaliers and the Blue Devils.

Fan curiosity quickly evaporated once the game started, however. Kankakee's aggressive, pressing defense slowed the tempo creating what many called "the most boring game" they had seen in years.

Though Kankakee held usually high-scoring Kaskaskia in check, the Cavaliers trailed most of the first half.

Then Tracy Nicholson — out of action since the regional semifinal when he suffered a concussion — stole a cross-court pass and broke away for a slam. He immediately duplicated the theft, fed Cleo Foster on another break away, then scored, following Foster's miss. The bang, bang plays gave underdog Kankakee a 21-16 halftime edge.

Kankakee's relentless pressure and use of 10 players gradually took its toll. Despite excellent outside shooting by Mike McCraeven, who finished with a game-high 14 after being held to a pair of free throws in the opening frame, Kaskaskia was unable to pull any closer than two. Kankakee scored its last field goal with 4:35 remaining, then rode 15 of 22 free throw shooting to the wire, upsetting the Blue Devils, 53-47.

The pace of the second contest was the complete opposite waking up the afternoon audience. Ferrum's run-and-gun style broke the game open early as the Panthers scooted to a 37-19 advantage with 7:09 remaining in the first half.

Then Westchester rallied, pulling within one, 80-79, with 6:14 left in the game.

The Westcos could not make it over the hump, however. Westchester set an all-time tourney record with 43 fouls. The combined total fouls of 68 was also an all-time mark. With a record 49 free throws in 66 attempts, Ferrum downed Westchester, 115-107.

Ferrum's Pee Wee Barber became an instant hit with the fans, scoring a tourney-high 45, 25 coming from the line, including 19 in a row. Though impressed with his scoring ability, most were more taken by Barber's assists, especially when he purposely missed an easy lay-up, banking the ball off the glass, right into the waiting hands of teammate Delano Jackson for a stuff.

The Ferrum-Westchester hack-and-chop shoot-out was the high-water mark in terms of the day's excitement.

In the afternoon finale, Highland Park did not look like a No. 1 team, blowing 10-point leads in both halves. With 3:30 remaining, the Panthers had to spread their offense and rely on fouls and free throws to hold on to an 83-80 victory over unheralded Chattahoochee Valley.

After Moberly scored the first four points and Ronnie Sims, Shelby State's best player, picked up three personals in four minutes, the writing was already on the wall for the evening opener. Six powerful Greyhound dunks punctuated it in the second half. Moberly routed the Saluqis, 94-76, placing six players in double figures.

If the performance of No. 4 Dixie looked lacklaster, it was forgivable. After defeating North Idaho College, 78-74, in Coeur d'Alene (80 miles from the Canadian border), the Rebels flew immediately to Thatcher, Arizona (120 miles from the Mexican border), downing Eastern Arizona College, 84-71, in a first-round play-off. Then, with only four hours sleep, they caught a flight out of Phoenix for Wichita and the nationals.

Though Dixie jumped out to a 20-6 lead in the evening feature, the jet-set Rebel offense sputtered. Casper gradually worked itself back into contention, taking its first lead, 38-37, with 18:34 remaining.

A 15-footer by Robert Maxwell returned the advantage to Dixie and restored Rebel dominance. With excellent 22-for-25 free throw shooting, Dixie never trailed again, downing the Thunderbirds, 74-61.

The only other surprise of the day came in the nightcap.

Though holding a 41-37 halftime edge, No. 12 Erie trailed No. 7 DeKalb-South most of the game. Led by Ray Salters' game-high 25, the Kats rallied in both halves, the final time from a 64-59 deficit with 6:45 remaining, as Erie upended DeKalb, 79-72.

"They looked like an NFL football team," stated Erie Coach Don Silveri. "But, we were too quick for them. Our pressure wore them down."

WEDNESDAY — UNLOADING THE ARTILLERY

None of Tuesday's contests were especially well-played and the remaining opening-round games followed suit.

Underdog Hinds did give No. 3 Allegany a tough time in the first period of the tip-off match, gaining the lead twice before falling behind, 36-33, at intermission.

But, the final period was all Allegany. Paced by Darrin Mosley's 21 and J.P. Warner's 20, the Trojans gradually pulled away, easily downing Hinds, 85-60.

The last opening-round game was an interesting rematch of two former titleholders, their first meeting since soon-to-be champion Midland upset then defending champion Westark four years prior.

However, action here also lagged, both teams showing first-game jitters in the spacious Arena, shooting poorly from the field. By hitting 11 of 16 free throws, Westark took a 27-23 half-time edge.

Then Midland's balanced attack took over. Five Chaparrals hit double figures while the team as a whole dominated the boards, 40 to 29. Midland again upended Westark in opening-round action, 70-61.

In the afternoon finale, Kaskaskia's high-powered offense finally got untracked after three periods of frustration. The Blue Devils exploded for 71 points in the final frame of the opening consolation game, demolishing Westchester, 105-73. The Westcos went home, having committed 78 fouls and given up 220 points in two games, one of the more ignominious appearances in tourney history.

The intensity level, as well as the quality of play, picked up once the quarterfinals got under way.

Ferrum won the battle of quickness at the outset of the evening opener, jumping in front, 5-0.

Kankakee was equally quick, however, frustrating the Panthers with its swarming zone trap. Ferrum Coach Grant Hudson called two time-outs in a two-minute span amid a 20-2 Kankakee spree, but was unable to counteract the surge.

Star guard Pee Wee Barber took game honors with 24, but his effort epitomized Panther frustrations. The 6-1 sophomore was never able to penetrate effectively as he had when he scored 45 against Westchester and, even though considered one of the quickest players in the tournament, one time had the ball stripped from his hands for an embarrassingly easy Kankakee basket. Barber was held to seven first-half points and only attained his game-high total with 10 points in the final 10 minutes after the game had already been decided.

Though team-oriented Kankakee did not have a star of Barber's brilliance, several individual efforts shown bright.

Forward LeRoy Parnell was perfect in eight tries from the line in the final period to share team-scoring honors with center Allen Eaton, each netting 16.

Point guard Mike Murff contributed 11 plus was the primary thorn in Barber's side throughout the game.

However, the most impressive performance was turned in by Jeff Thurman. Though only 6-3 and 180 pounds, the sophomore forward dominated the boards during Kankakee's early surge, particularly at the offensive end. He scored 12 of his total 14 points and pulled down 6 of his 10 rebounds in the opening frame, leading the Cavaliers to a convincing 41-30 advantage at intermission.

Ferrum never recovered, falling to the fairy tale team from Illinois, 87-70. The unexpected victory gave Kankakee its fifth consecutive 30-win season. .

Kankakee's outstanding Cinderella effort was forgotten, though, after the toe-to-toe blasting which followed.

Crowd enthusiasm was ignited even before action began when Highland Park finished its warm-ups with a dive drill, each player hitting the floor like heavily padded tackles diving for a loose football.

The all-out display continued after the tip with both Highland Park and Moberly unloading the artillery, hitting 57 percent and 69 percent, respectively, for the game.

Highland Park got hot first, scoring the opening eight points. Then Moberly warmed up, rolling to a 24-15 lead with 11:23 remaining.

The Panthers responded in kind, reducing the difference to 47-45 at intermission.

The contest continued to be played way above the rims in the second half. Vernon Carr, Highland Park's leading scorer with 18, set the example for all, when he swooped in for a spectacular dunk after leaving the floor at the free throw line.

The biggest lead of the final period came at the midpoint, Moberly on top, 71-66. But, the Panthers battled back, taking a 74-73 advantage with 5:52 to go.

From then on, it was a coaching chess match between Highland Park's Glen Donahue and Moberly's Dana Altman.

With Moberly leading, 79-78, with under four minutes to play, Highland Park spread its offense, looking for a sure two. The Panthers' go-ahead bucket was nullified, however, by an over-the-back foul. Moberly took possession and stalled.

Then, at the 40-second mark, Greyhound Bernard Day, the game's top scorer with 21, missed an easy basket, giving the ball back to Highland Park.

Day immediately redeemed himself by blocking Robert Alexander's sure lay-up. Moberly acquired the loose ball and held again.

With 22 seconds left, Highland Park fouled. Unfortunately, the Panthers were three fouls shy of creating a bonus situation for Moberly. It required an intentional foul with 15 seconds left to send Mitch Richmond to the line for the Greyhounds.

Richmond hit both charities and, after Highland Park missed at its end, rammed home a clinching dunk with four seconds showing. Moberly handed the Panthers their first defeat of the year, 83-78.

THURSDAY — NO UPSET

The excellent play of Wednesday night's quarterfinals appeared infectious. With the exception of Westark's wire-to-wire dispatch of Hinds, 76-69, in the finale, Thursday afternoon's consolation matches were close hard-fought barn-burners.

In the opener, Chattahoochee Valley's Ben Powell, who was already playing with a broken ring finger with a pin in it, suffered a cut under the left eye requiring three stitches. The 6-4, 205-pound sophomore forward remained on the bench just long enough to be mended, then promptly scored 25 of his game-high 35, leading the Pirates to a 49-46 halftime advantage.

Shelby State claimed the lead three minutes into the final period, however, and held on, eliminating CVCC, 96-93.

With 24 seconds remaining in the matinee feature, the game tied, DeKalb-South played the ball in under its own basket only to have it bounce out of bounds off one of the closely guarded Eagles.

Taking no time-out, Casper quickly brought the ball upcourt and worked it to top scorer Tony Gulley. The sophomore guard's shot from the right wing banged off the rim. Fortunately for the Thunderbirds, the shot was ruled to have followed an official's whistle signaling a Casper time-out with eight seconds left.

When play resumed, Casper had a hard time getting the ball in bounds and an even harder time finding Gulley open. Peter Lock finally saw reserve Rick Domonkos open underneath and fed him for the winning lay-up with three seconds showing. Casper downed DeKalb-South, 65-63.

In the evening's first quarterfinal, Erie had two brief leads in the first half, but the rest of the time played catch-up to Dixie's running offense and keep-away from the Rebel pressure defense. Paced by Brent Stephenson's 16, Dixie built a 45-37 halftime margin and was on the verge of breaking the game open.

Erie might have been overmatched in the size department, but not when it came to heart. The scrappy Kats fought back with a press which eventually netted a 50-49 lead with 15:15 remaining.

According to Erie Coach Don Silveri, "To win the national title, you've got to make your own breaks."

The previous year, Erie had been on the precipice of a major upset only to have a foul and a technical lead to a six-point swing and loss of momentum.

With 7:25 to go, on top 67-63, Erie again failed to make its own break. The Kats' spread offense backfired, turning the ball over twice. Dixie scored both times, tying the game.

In the final three minutes, Dixie outscored Erie, 11-3, all but four coming from the line. With 23-of-27 free throw shooting, the Rebels advanced to the semifinals, 83-75.

The last quarterfinal was summed up in the opening moments:

Teviin Binns slammed home a Zeak Williams alley-oop to open scoring for Midland;

At the other end of the court, Darrin Mosely missed a dunk for Allegany.

Midland charged to an 11-2 advantage which Allegany was never able to overcome. Two authoritative stuffs in the final minutes — one by Williams, the other by Eddie Frazier with a man hanging on him — emphasized the fact that Midland's victory over the No. 3 Trojans was no upset. Led by Binns' 27 points (13 for 16 from the field) and nine rebounds, the Chaparrals downed Allegany convincingly, 79-63.

Offense highlighted the nightcap. Behind Vernon Carr's 33 and Lenith Cotton's 21, Highland Park won its 40th game of the year, outlasting Ferrum, 106-104. Pee Wee Barber, who led Ferrum with 32 before fouling out, secured the tourney scoring title with 101 after only three games.

FRIDAY — POOL TALK

The poolside celebration in the Hutchinson Holidome Thursday night started early and extended late. So late that the hotel management had to move it to a secluded meeting room so other guests could sleep.

The participants were primarily fans from Moberly and Midland who were certain they would face each other for the crown Saturday night. Winning the semifinals was taken for granted.

Though the display might have appeared to be unwise counting of chickens before the eggs hatched, most impartial observers agreed. Moberly and Midland had each defeated top-rated teams with impressive aplomb. They were powerful and deep, a perfect pairing for the championship game.

The disparity in the semifinal match-ups was no better illustrated than in the opener. Moberly starters topped Kankakee starters an average three inches and 25 pounds per man. No less than seven Greyhounds were touted as Division I prospects. Add to that the fact flu had suddenly struck the Kankakee camp Friday morning and there seemed no question Moberly would triumph.

Kankakee Coach Danny Lehnus — suffering from a touch of the bug himself — tried to rouse support by telling the press he felt Moberly's confidence after downing No. 1 Highland Park "will be to our advantage. They have to think they've played their toughest game."

Few bought the argument. Most thought Moberly's Dana Altman, who had barely missed a title try two years earlier with

Southeast Community College of Fairbury, would finally reach his goal.

All were surprised when Kankakee opened the game, hitting its first eight baskets, taking a 20-14 lead. They were further dumbfounded when, after a Moberly bucket, the Cavaliers reeled off eight more unanswered points, upping the margin to 28-16.

The quick deficit promoted a more serious Moberly attitude. Behind Mitch Richmond's 12 and reserve Cecil Estes' 13, the Greyhounds rallied, grabbing a five-point cushion just before intermission.

The Cavaliers did not scare, however. A long jumper by Mike Nowlin, a pair of free throws by LeRoy Parnell, and another charity by Cedric Bell allowed Kankakee to tie the game 41-all at halftime.

If there was a Rodney Dangerfield in the 16-team field, it was Kankakee. The undermanned Cavaliers had been given little credit for their first two victories. Few recognized that in the opener Kankakee had held Kaskaskia 38 points below its average, following that by curbing Ferrum to a total 45 points below the Panthers' opening romp. Both should have been expected. Kankakee possessed a top-10 defense (55.5) — a regular occurrence for Lehnus squads.

In the second half, fans finally took notice. With their press working at full tilt, the Cavaliers scored the first two baskets and eventually built a nine-point margin. With 4:30 remaining, Kankakee was in complete control of the tempo, leading 69-63.

However, the poor health of the Cavalier crew was beginning to show. Lehnus had little choice but to spread his offense and hope to hold on.

Two Kankakee turnovers followed, allowing Moberly to score five unanswered points, the Greyhounds' longest spree of the second half. At the 2:29 mark, the Cavalier lead was a slim 69-68.

Moberly missed extending its unanswered string to seven and taking the lead when a Richmond bucket was disallowed because the 6-5 freshman went over the back of Kankakee forward Jeff Thurman.

With 1:40 left, Thurman upped the margin to three with both ends of one-and-one.

Moberly again cut the difference to one and quickly regained possession. At the 53-second mark, Estes stepped to the line in a bonus situation and another chance to put the Greyhounds in front.

His first opportunity missed.

Fortunately, 6-7 center Charles Bledsoe saved the rebound allowing Moberly another try at the lead. With 20 seconds remaining, Richmond fired from 15 and missed.

Thurman grabbed the rebound for Kankakee and was fouled. Two more free throws made it 73-70.

A hurried shot from the corner by Richmond reduced the margin to one again. The result now depended upon whether underdog Kankakee could continue sinking pressure free throws.

Mike Murff and Andre Bryson proved they could, hitting a pair apiece.

Little Kankakee stunned mighty Moberly, 77-72.

Considering all of Moberly's advantages, including outshooting the Cavaliers 63 percent to 58 percent, the Kankakee win was remarkable. The keys to the upset were the Cavaliers' overlooked quickness on defense, precise execution of fundamentals such as blocking out on the boards, disciplined passing which secured great shots instead of good ones, and determined unwillingness to fold down the stretch. Despite the tremendous height disadvantage, Kankakee held its own on the board, topping the Greyhounds 26 to 25 in caroms retrieved. Moberly captured only eight offensive boards. The Cavaliers hit 19 of 25 free throws, including 8 of 9 when it counted most.

"There was no real reason for us to win this game," Lehnus told reporters afterwards. "You have to give the kids credit, especially those who were sick but still played. They had the courage to reach down and get it done."

In the other semifinal, No. 4 Dixie was also a heavy underdog in spite of its ranking. That is, to everyone but its fans. The Rebel contingent had grown daily throughout the week so that it now rivaled the fanatical mass of Moberly supporters.

With its backers in full voice, the Confederate flag waving prominently — the southern Utah school's name was in remembrance of the early Mormon settlers of the St. George area who migrated from homes south of the Mason-Dixon line, bringing with them all the trappings of the Deep South — Dixie struck early, taking a 14-4 lead. The tough Rebel 3-2 zone stymied Midland attempts to catch up, forcing numerous turnovers. Frustrated, Midland pressed and quickly found itself in foul trouble. Hitting 30 of 37 free throws, compared to the Chaparrals' 7 of 9, Dixie won with impressive ease, 72-57.

As predicted at poolside the night before, Midland would face Moberly Saturday night — but not for the championship.

SATURDAY — THE CONFEDERACY VERSUS THE SMURFS

Kaskaskia recorded its third straight impressive victory, tipping off trophy day with a 70-57 win over Westark. After being held to the lowest point total of the week in the tourney opener, the Blue Devils averaged nearly 90 points per game while their opponents averaged 21 points less. The statistics were further proof that Kankakee, Kaskaskia's opening-round nemesis, might be better than everyone originally thought.

The battle between the No. 1 and No. 3 teams coming into the week was not what it could have been had it been for the championship. Hurt by ankle injuries to starter Robert Alexander (who did not play) and star Vernon Carr (who played, but was slowed by the injury), Highland Park displayed none of its previous tourney form. Allegany forced 17 first-half turnovers, took a 39-33 lead at intermission, then went on a 60-point rampage, claiming fifth, 99-65.

The evening session opened with a close 13 minutes. Then Moberly scored seven straight, opening a 29-22 gap. Midland never threatened thereafter.

In a typical uninspired third-place contest, Moberly won, 67-58.

For longtime tourney fans, the championship tilt was a no lose proposition. Throughout the years, Dixie had always been popular with the local crowd. And no one could remain unaffected by Kankakee's Cinderella climb.

Though many courtside touts were again saying that the shorter, starless Cavaliers had no business playing for a national title — one reporter referred to the Kankakee squad as the "Smurfs," a reference to its size and a corruption of its floor leader's name, Mike Murff — no one could doubt their due once the action began.

Winner or loser, neither team had reason for shame after the game's conclusion. It was one of the most flawless contests in tourney history, one of the tightest championship bouts ever.

The two squads matched each other bucket for bucket through the first 14 points. From then on, neither team gained control for more than a brief period. The largest lead either held was five points, each forcing the other to prove its mettle.

Kankakee's rally came in the first half, making the Cavalier deficit at intermission, 31-30.

Kankakee's quickness continued to bother Dixie in the final period, forcing seven Rebel miscues in a five-minute period. The Cavaliers gained their five-point advantage at 38-33 with 15:21 to play.

Then it was Dixie's turn to show heart. Seven consecutive baskets by Brent Stephenson, including two dunks, propelled the Rebels back into the lead.

The score was tied at 46 and 55.

The only truly bad plays of the game came in the final two minutes. When pressure was at its peak, both sides committed a costly error. The final turnover, an intercepted Cavalier pass by Steve Schreiner, came with 1:46 remaining.

Dixie worked for a good shot. When none materialized, forward Averian Parrish drove into traffic and lofted a short jumper. The basketball bounced on the rim — then through, putting the Rebels on top, 57-55, with 45 seconds left.

Kankakee labored for a tie, taking time-outs at the 29- and 5-second marks. The Cavaliers' only shot came with two ticks showing. Like Parrish's shot, Murff's baseline jumper bounced on the rim. But, unlike the Parrish basket, the ball bounced away, no good.

The Confederacy downed the Smurfs for the crown.

THE AFTERMATH — THE MORMON EXPERIENCE

There was no better illustration of the philosophy that "the whole is greater than the sum of its parts" than the undersized Cavaliers and their oversized coach.

"I was so impressed with the intensity they played with," said Dixie's Neil Roberts, Coach of the Tournament. "They were not a spectator's team. They were a great coach's team. In other words, we in the profession really appreciated what was going on there. As a coach, I loved watching them play."

However, the Rebels were just as team-oriented.

"Had we played anybody but Dixie, we might have won the thing," reflected Kankakee Coach Denny Lehnus. "They played in a manner that was almost a mirror [of us]."

With such unselfish units in the championship contest, doling out the top awards was difficult.

For example, the Obee Small Player and Sesher Sportsmanship Awards could easily have been flip-flopped.

Kankakee's quiet Mike Murff, a steady floor general who had been cut from the squad as a freshman, won the Obee while Robert Maxwell, the aggressive floor leader for Dixie, took the Sesher.

Sesher Sportsmanship Award winner Robert Maxwell drives on Obee Small Player Award winner Mike Murff in the 1985 championship game. Maxwell later attended Weber State while Murff went to Northwestern Oklahoma State. (Photo courtesy of the **Hutchinson News**)

The French Most Valuable Player Award might have gone to mild-mannered center Brent Stephenson, whose second-half basket barrage rescued the Rebels.

Instead it went to teammate Averian Parrish, Dixie's leading scorer. It was a piece of ironic justice for the man who fired the winning bucket, considering he had missed the shot which would have put Dixie in the tournament the year before.

Stated Coach Roberts, "Every JC coach should have the experience once in his life of coaching a group of kids like that."

The Rebels were atypical champions. Most junior college squads were manned with individuals who were unable to finance their education at the four-year level or lacked academic achievement. In contrast, many of Dixie's players came from affluent homes. Seven Rebels were honor-roll students. In fact, the team's overall GPA was 3.4, an unheard of figure in a typical junior college environment.

When someone asked Parrish — along with starting guard Ricky Henry, the only other black on the Dixie squad, both hailing from the same northwest Las Vegas ghetto — why he chose to attend a small Mormon school, he responded, "My mother wouldn't let me go anywhere else. She wanted me to live in that kind of environment."

The Mormon religion played a major role in Dixie's success, particularly as applied to the maturity level of Roberts' players.

"If it wasn't for the Mormon religion, those kids wouldn't have had that experience of going on a mission," explained Roberts. "When they do that, they go out on their own for two years. They become more independent. When they come back, they have a better direction of which way to go, what they want to accomplish, and how to accomplish it."

(Above, left) Brent Stephenson's (No. 32) seven consecutive baskets saved Dixie's chances for the 1985 crown in the title match with Kankakee. Stephenson later played for Brigham Young University. (Photo courtesy of the **Hutchinson News***)*

(Above, right) French MVP Averian Parrish (No. 44) led Dixie to a 1985 national title with 14 points and 9 rebounds in the final against Kankakee. (Photo courtesy of the **Hutchinson News***)*

Reserve guard Brent Wade, the Sesher Sportsmanship-winner of 1982, was one of those who had interrupted a college education to go on an LDS mission. Another was All-Tournament selection, Brent Stephenson.

Stephenson also served as an example of what two years could do to a young body. When he tried out for Dixie as a freshman walk-on, he stated his height as 6-4, his listed height in high school. Since the gangly young man had to duck to enter his office, Roberts was skeptical. They measured and sure enough he had grown five inches. Said Stephenson, "Well when I was on my mission I noticed my pants kept getting shorter." It also explained why he had scraped his head on ceilings and broke light bulbs with his forehead in what he had thought were smaller rooms in Brazil.

The influence of the Mormon religion was also reflected by Dixie fans.

Loyal Rebel followers made the nearly 900-mile journey to Hutchinson in "every way possible," said Roberts. "After the first two wins, they just got in their cars and came. They didn't have a place to stay. They didn't have a ticket to the game or anything. They just came."

Remembered Stephenson. "Every game we won, it seemed like the next day a new plane-load of fans would arrive. If we'd played two more games, we'd probably have had half of St. George there."

In spite of their numbers the Dixie rooting section was always at its best behavior; loud, but never rowdy.

The best illustration of Rebel fan comportment was at the celebration in the Holidome following the championship. Despite the non-alcoholic punch served, the gathering was just as boisterous as any group of people experiencing the heady emotions associated with wearing a national crown.

However, when silence was asked for, it was immediately granted. There were appropriate times for enthusiastic demonstrations.

And the greatest display of appreciation was saved until the Rebels' homecoming. The Dixie players were provided a Roman-chariot, fire-engine-ride entrance to the city of St. George where fans lined the streets to greet their conquering heroes. Signs read, "Welcome back Rebels" and "You've made us proud."

At the Dixie College Gymnasium, Athletic Director Doug Allred, himself a former player and coach in the Juco Tournament, summarized the feelings of all in attendance. "Ladies and gentlemen this is incredible. This is probably the greatest thing in the history of Dixie College and St. George."

Tournament Results

	Game	
Tuesday:	1	Kankakee — 53 Kaskaskia — 47
	2	Ferrum — 115 Westchester — 107
	3	Highland Park — 83 Chattahoochee Valley — 80
	4	Moberly — 94 Shelby St. — 76
	5	Dixie — 74 Casper — 61
	6	Erie — 79 DeKalb-South — 72
Wednesday:	7	Allegany — 85 Hinds — 60
	8	Midland — 70 Westark — 61
	9	Kaskaskia — 105 Westchester — 73
	10	Kankakee — 87 Ferrum — 70
	11	Moberly — 83 Highland Park — 78
Thursday:	12	Shelby St. — 96 Chattahoochee Valley — 93
	13	Casper — 65 DeKalb-South — 63
	14	Westark — 76 Hinds — 69
	15	Dixie — 83 Erie — 75
	16	Midland — 79 Allegany — 63
	17	Highland Park — 106 Ferrum — 104
Friday:	18	Kaskaskia — 94 Shelby St. — 76
	19	Westark — 65 Casper — 49
	20	Allegany — 77 Erie — 72
	21	Kankakee — 77 Moberly — 72
	22	Dixie — 72 Midland — 57
Saturday:	23	Kaskaskia — 70 Westark — 57
	24	Allegany — 99 Highland Park — 65
	25	Moberly — 67 Midland — 58
	26	Dixie — 57 Kankakee — 55

How They Finished in 1985

1. Dixie College
2. Kankakee Community College
3. Moberly Area Junior College
4. Midland College
5. Allegany Community College
6. Highland Park Community College
7. Kaskaskia College
8. Westark Community College

All-Tournament Team

Norwood "Pee Wee" Barber — Ferrum College
Teviin Binns — Midland College
Vernon Carr — Highland Park Community College
Louis Cook — Westark Community College
Bernard Day — Moberly Area Junior College
Allen Eaton — Kankakee Community College
Danny Johnson — Kaskaskia College
Averian Parrish — Dixie College
Brent Stephenson — Dixie College
William Stuart — Allegany Community College
Ray Swogger — Erie Community College
Jeff Thurman — Kankakee Community College

Coach of the Tournament

Neil Roberts — Dixie College

French Most Valuable Player

Averian Parrish — Dixie College

Sesher Sportsmanship Award

Robert Maxwell — Dixie College

Bud Obee Most Outstanding Small Player Award

Mike Murff — Kankakee Community College

A coach who averaged 24 wins a year and whose teams had tied or won their conference five out of seven times would normally be considered "successful." However, in Hutchinson, Kansas, success was measured on getting to the Juco Tournament.

In seven previous seasons at the Hutchinson Community College helm, Gary Bargen had qualified for the nationals only once and then failed to make it to the Arena, losing a first-round play-off to Westark Community College.

After the 1983-84 season, Bargen most likely would have lost his job had a public outcry not won him another year. After the 1984-85 season, his contract was renewed without fanfare. But, he received no salary increase and it was understood through the community gossip line that it was "get to the Tournament or else."

In June of 1985, Bargen was offered the head coaching job at Pittsburg State University in southeastern Kansas. It was a lucrative step up, a nice, supportive environment, good facilities, and the competition of a league which usually produced one of the top teams in the NAIA national tournament each year in Kansas City.

Given the uncertain climate of the Hutchinson position, most men would have quickly opted for the Pittsburg job. For Bargen, it was a tough family decision. In the end, however, there was one overriding factor which decided the issue.

"The only thing that kept me here was this team," explained Bargen. "I had built it. I didn't want somebody coming in here, going to the national tournament, and have all the dogs saying, 'I told you so. All we had to do was get rid of him.' "

The squad Bargen put together was one of the best ever assembled at Hutchinson. It was certainly the biggest with twin towers in Sean Alvarado, a 6-10 product from famous Dunbar High School in Washington, D.C. and Ben Gillery, the first seven-foot Blue Dragon. There was plenty of experience with seven returning sophomores. The lone freshman to crack the starting lineup was a high school All-American, Tyrone Jones, also a Dunbar graduate. Everyone shared Bargen's optimism.

Then the season began.

Hutchinson's first loss came on a last-second, 25-footer by Gerald Paddio of Seminole Junior College in the Dragons' own Classic. Two days later they suffered defeat again in the event, this time to Moberly Area Junior College. In a little more than a week, the Dragons lost a second time to Moberly in the State Fair Classic. Bargen critics mounted their soap boxes.

In Hutchinson's last game before the Christmas break, Sean Alvarado tripped over his discarded jersey while entering the game. The result was a broken left foot, the second injury in two years to sideline the big man for most of the season.

In the first-round of the Mesa Rotary Shootout in January, the Blue Dragons fell to Ricks College, 93-92, in overtime when the officials allowed a Ricks tip-in that had been scored after time ran out on the clock, but before a delayed buzzer sounded.

Considered the overwhelming favorite at the start of the year, Hutchinson did not win the Western Division of the Jayhawk Juco Conference until the last game, rallying from an 11-point halftime deficit to top Barton County Community College, 68-66.

*Moberly All-Tourney selection Mitch Richmond later starred for the Kansas State Wildcats. (Photo courtesy of the **Moberly Monitor-Index**)*

Still, despite all the adversity, the Blue Dragons downed Pratt Community College, 83-64, in the first round of the Region 6 play-offs and were only two steps away from a berth in the nationals.

The next step, however, was against rival Independence Community College. With 52 seconds left, the Pirates leading, 62-58, and at the line for one-and-one, it appeared the same old story for Hutchinson fans. Bargen's dream was over.

Then Independence started missing charities, hitting only once in four tries. Meanwhile, Henry "T" Buchanan scored a lay-up and a free throw and Jones added three free throws, the last two coming with eight seconds left. Miraculously Hutchinson pulled out a 64-63 victory.

The Arena went berserk.

Though the Blue Dragons needed one more win over Cloud County Community College — which they accomplished with ease, 93-75 — the celebration was already on.

For the first time in 11 years, Hutchinson was in the Juco Tournament.

Region	Team
2	Westark Community College — Fort Smith, Arkansas
3	Erie Community College — Buffalo, New York
6	Hutchinson Community College — Hutchinson, Kansas
8	Pensacola Junior College — Pensacola, Florida
9	Trinidad State Junior College — Trinidad, Colorado
11	Ellsworth Community College — Iowa Falls, Iowa
12	Vincennes University — Vincennes, Indiana
13	Madison Area Technical College — Madison, Wisconsin
14	San Jacinto College, Central Campus — Pasadena, Texas
16	Moberly Area Junior College — Moberly, Missouri
17	Brunswick Junior College — Brunswick, Georgia
18	College of Southern Idaho — Twin Falls, Idaho
19	Gloucester County College — Sewell, New Jersey
20	Allegany Community College — Cumberland, Maryland
23	Copiah-Lincoln Junior College — Wesson, Mississippi
24	Wabash Valley College — Mt. Carmel, Illinois
	Lost in First-Round Play-Offs:
1	Arizona Western College — Yuma, Arizona
4	Triton College — River Grove, Illinois
5	Midland College — Midland, Texas
7	Paducah Community College — Paducah, Kentucky
10	Anderson College — Anderson, South Carolina
15	Fashion Institute of Technology — New York, New York
21	Mattatuck Community College — Waterbury, Connecticut
22	Walker College — Jasper, Alabama

The Blue Dragon return to Hutchinson's most cherished event could not have been more untimely. The participants in the 39th Juco Tournament included 10 of the 20 ranked teams, 7 of the top 10, and featured six former champs who had amassed one-third of all the national titles awarded to date.

Topping the list was perennial powerhouse San Jacinto College. The No. 2 Ravens were 33-0, possessed the second-best offense in the country (102.2), and had already upended previously unbeaten No. 3 Midland College, 107-96, in a first-round play-off. On the strength of the latter, many considered San Jacinto a shoo-in to win its third title in four years.

Raven Coach Ronnie Arrow bought none of the hype. "If that was the championship game, then why don't they just send the championship trophy to us and we won't have to have a tournament."

To win a crown, San Jacinto would have to get past:

No. 4 Moberly Area Junior College (32-2), the senior tourney participant in terms of appearances and titles and ranked No. 1 for most of the season;

No. 5 College of Southern Idaho (33-1), the top offensive squad in the nation (103.0);

No. 6 Allegany Community College (36-2), the country's second-best defense (56.7);

No. 7 Trinidad State Junior College (33-2), whose only loss, outside an end-of-season upset, had been to Midland;

No. 8 Erie Community College (31-1), making its fourth straight trip to Hutchinson, its sole defeat in the current campaign at the hands of Allegany;

No. 10 Copiah-Lincoln Junior College (32-2), which had knocked off top-rated Delgado Community College, 72-65, in the Region 23 semifinals;

No. 11 Gloucester County Community College (32-2), which beat No. 20 Fashion Institute of Technology, 105-104, in overtime in first-round action;

No. 12 Vincennes University (30-4), which owned a win over Allegany and only one true loss;[1] and

No. 16 Ellsworth Community College (29-2), which had only been defeated once in two previous tourney appearances.

A small group of unranked tourney veterans also showed potential: Pensacola Junior College (26-6) owned a win over Copiah-Lincoln; Wabash Valley Community College (28-8) handed Vincennes its only on-court loss; and Westark Community College (25-9) brought another stingy Gayle Kaundart club which could be counted on to be competitive regardless of its record.

Only newcomers Brunswick Junior College (22-7) and Madison Area Technical College (21-12) were discounted.

One team, however, would have a distinct advantage over San Jacinto and all the rest. Seven-thousand screaming, title-hungry fans would be in the corner of the unranked, 28-6 Hutchinson Blue Dragons all week long.

TUESDAY — WE WON'T TAKE THEM LIGHTLY

Gloucester County featured two of the better players in the country in 6-6 Rico Washington, the MVP of the Dapper Dan Classic his senior year in high school, and 6-2 Jody Johnson, the school's first 1,000-point career scorer.

In the tourney opener, Washington and Johnson were again the Roadrunner mainstays, netting 26 and 23, respectively.

However, freshman-dominated Pensacola was more balanced and deeper. The Pirates also hit two-thirds of their shots, mostly off well-executed plays, featuring precise passing. Pensacola broke on top, 42-34, at halftime, then picked up steam. When Kelvin Ardister — the Pirate top gun with 26 — hammered home the tourney's first dunk with 1:52 remaining, then immediately followed it with another, Pensacola was in complete charge. The unranked Pirates tipped off the week, downing No. 11 Gloucester, 106-83.

With the tasty hors d'oeuvre of an upset whetting their appetites, fans were ready for the entrees — three consecutive contests matching ranked opponents.

Unfortunately, the first turned out to be bland. Neither team looked spectacular, but Trinidad State looked particularly sluggish. The Trojans hit only 15 of 27 free throws and a cold 33 percent from the field. Led by Perry Smith and Cal Foster, both with game-high totals of 24, Vincennes won easily, 78-61.

The start of the afternoon finale looked to follow suit. Copiah-Lincoln, making its first tourney appearance in 12 years, showed a case of Arena nerves, experiencing a five-minute drought. Southern Idaho opened an 18-6 gap and quickly built it to 35-18.

Then the Co-Lin Wolves settled down, reducing the margin to 51-41 by intermission. Led by freshman standout Johnny Steptoe, who tallied 30 for the game, the Mississipians steadily closed the gap in the next 12 minutes. After Bernard Chatman hit three straight baskets in a 47-second span, Southern Idaho's margin was cut to one, 72-71.

Free throws proved the difference. After hitting only 7 of 14 from the line in the opening frame, CSI hit 18 of 20 to finish the game, at one point nailing 18 in a row. Paced by the crowd-pleasing performances of Chris Blocker (37) and Joey Johnson (26), the Golden Eagles held off Copiah-Lincoln, 99-89.

With five ties in the early going, the evening opener appeared the meatiest meal of the day. Then Moberly cut loose with 15 unanswered points, opening a 49-39 halftime lead over Erie.

To the Kats' credit, a full-court press and excellent outside shooting brought Erie back to within four, 77-73, with 3:07 to go. However, a baseline drive by David Knight and a slam by Mitch Richmond settled matters. Six Greyhounds hit double figures as Moberly downed Erie, 97-78.

The evening feature was one of the greatest mismatches in tourney history, yet, oddly enough, attracted an SRO audience.

The chances of first-time participant Madison Tech winning its opener was equivalent to the proverbial chances of a snowball surviving an afternoon in Hell. The Trojans owned the worst record in the field, had finished fourth in the Wisconsin Technical College Conference with a 5-7 mark, and were reduced to only seven members after losing six players at the semester to grades and their leading scorer before the regionals to a broken wrist. To top it off, the Trojans faced everyone's favorite to win the tournament — San Jacinto.

Asked to describe his expectations, Madison Tech Coach Jack Brenegan quipped, "Well, we're not going to take them lightly."

Madison Tech's opening 4-2 lead was the only Trojan hurrah. San Jacinto unleashed a ferocious attack, featuring three Ledell Eackles three-point plays, three Greg "Boo" Harvey lay-ups after steals, plus a pair of slams by Eackles and one each by John

---

[1] The last player to join the Trailblazers was a walk-on from the student body who had supposedly attended Lake Land Community College less than the NJCAA's prescribed 15 days before withdrawing. Vincennes immediately requested a transcript to verify the circumstances. When the records finally came in December, it showed he had actually attended Lake Land 28 days. The Trailblazers were forced to forfeit the only three games the walk-on made it into. The three victories — over Cuyahoga Community College, 114-66; Shawnee State College, 96-39; and Sinclair Community College, 109-77 — were won by a grand total of 137 points.

ludson and Tom Grant. During a 27-2 Raven string, Madison turned the ball over eight times, each leading to a San Jacinto bucket. Led by Eackles' 30 points and 11 rebounds, the Ravens romped, 88-53.

The nightcap was the most exciting opening-round contest with nine ties and 11 lead changes. With less than 10 seconds remaining, the score knotted 83-all, Wabash Valley's Norton "Skip" Ellison forced Brunswick's leading scorer, Gary Campbell (28), into a turnover. Then, for the last-second climax, Ellison was the intended shooter. Instead, he fumbled the ball and was forced to pass off to Arthur Goodwin. Goodwin's 25-foot desperation heave, his only shot of the game, gave Wabash Valley the win at the buzzer.

WEDNESDAY — FILLING THE HOUSE

The inclusion of Hutchinson in the tourney field always represented good news and bad news for the local American Legion sponsors.

The good news in 1986 was that the event completely sold out in February, the earliest ever.

The bad news was how to seat all the Hutchinson faithful and still remain impartial to all teams in the competition.

The Legion's first dilemma came with the Hutchinson opener Wednesday. Since season ticketholders were admitted free for afternoon sessions, there was no way to estimate how many general admission tickets to sell.

The problem was solved by opening the doors at 11 a.m. for season ticketholders. Then at 11:30, the normal opening time, "We will sell general admission tickets until we are full," stated Tournament Chairman Guy Holt. If a season ticketholder could not get off work in time to be in the doors before 11:30, there was no guarantee of a seat.

The lineup for general admission tickets began before midnight Tuesday. However, the crunch did not become heavy until mid-morning Wednesday. Even then the crowd was made up mostly of season ticketholders more concerned about finding a good place to park than about getting a seat inside.

In fact, the anticipated huge crowd never materialized. Though the Arena was packed to the brim, everyone who wanted in got in.

And everyone included some very big names in college basketball — Larry Brown of Kansas, Bobby Knight of Indiana, and Ted Owens of Oral Roberts to name a few. Most prominent of all was Georgetown's John Thompson who sat front row center on the sidelines munching nachos.

The attraction for all the four-year coaches in attendance were the Hutchinson big men — Ben Gillery and Sean Alvarado. Coach Gary Bargen rarely used the two together, choosing to always have one in reserve, particularly since Alvarado was still not in peak condition after his broken foot. But, for only the second time that season, he started the twin towers.

The imposing height had an immediate impact on much smaller Westark. Hutchinson intimidated inside, hit seven of its first eight shots, and jumped out to a 14-4 advantage.

The Lion's scrambling 2-1-2 zone tightened. Todd Christian, Hutchinson's leading scorer and best outside shooter, could only find the range 3 out of 10 times in the first period. Westark caught up, took the lead briefly, and trailed by a mere 27-25 at intermission.

After tying the score at 29-all, the Lions fell behind by four and came no closer until the 11:53 mark when they pulled within one, 39-38.

Then Hutchinson lowered the boom, reeling off eight unanswered points. Hitting only 8 of 20 free throws, Westark was never able to crack the four-point barrier again. Despite a pair of imprudent shots in the final minute which almost gave the Lions second life, Hutchinson held on, winning 65-56.

Combining a soft outside shot with brute strength in the middle, Ellsworth's Mike Flory dominated the final opening-round contest. After trailing Allegany most of the period, the Panthers pulled within one, 38-37, at halftime, Flory scoring 10 of his game-high 28 to lead the way.

Then Craig Jenkins followed Flory's outside shooting example and Caldin Rogers joined him on the boards to take control. After Ellsworth moved in front, 60-53, at the 7:23 mark, Allegany gambled on defense and fell further behind. With 45-32

command of the boards — paced by Flory's game-high 17 rebounds — Ellsworth downed Allegany convincingly, 82-68.

The surprise team of the opening round was Pensacola. Despite having 11 freshmen on the roster, the Pirates had displayed the composure of veterans in upsetting Gloucester County.

In the first 10 minutes of the opening quarterfinal, Pensacola was again impressive, playing favored Vincennes even or a little better.

Then Trailblazer Coach Dan Sparks called time and put in four substitutes. The Vincennes intensity level immediately increased.

Sparked by Reggie Kirk's two lay-ups and a dunk, the Trailblazers went from down 16-15 to ahead 27-20 in four minutes. During the final four minutes, Pensacola managed only four field goals. At intermission Vincennes was in charge, 43-28.

The Pirates never recovered. Recalled Pensacola Coach Bobby Stinnett the next day, "When we were down last night 12 or 13 points, we weren't running anything. They just flat wouldn't let us. That was very alarming to our kids. And, of course, it was super alarming to the coach." Pensacola fell to Vincennes, 90-72, the widest margin of defeat for the Pirates all year.

For Moberly, the second quarterfinal was a repeat of the Greyhounds' 1985 quarterfinal with Highland Park. Most of the slam-bang action took place above the rims and spectacular physical feats were the norm.

Southern Idaho countered the Greyhounds' size and strength advantage with a disciplined defense and a super leaper. Joey Johnson, whose 48-inch vertical leap even topped brother Dennis Johnson of the Boston Celtics, canned 12 of his total 20 and made three out-of-nowhere blocks, to lead the Golden Eagles to a 31-25 halftime edge, becoming a crowd favorite in the process.

Then Chris Blocker finished it off with 14 of his 15 in the final eight minutes after sitting out nearly 18 minutes because of fouls. CSI hit 58 percent from the field, converted 21 of 27 from the line, and downed Moberly, 83-76.

THURSDAY — FEELING THE PRESSURE

By winning its opening-round game at the last second, Wabash Valley earned the dubious honor of facing the firing squad in the quarterfinals — San Jacinto. The Warriors responded by hitting a cool 39 percent from the field and committing 14 turnovers in the first half.

Led by Ledell Eackles' 22 and Michael Porter's 10, including a fabulous dunk over two Wabash Valley players, San Jacinto looked near perfect, building a 24-point margin before settling for a 54-32 advantage at intermission.

Perfection faded in the final frame, as the Ravens reciprocated with 18 miscues. However, even playing poorly by their standards was better than most teams playing at their best.

Wabash Valley rallied, but could edge no closer than 11. San Jacinto's fast-paced offense — featuring 14 fast-break baskets and seven dunks (five by Eackles, netting him a game-high 35) — raced to a 102-79 victory. It was the Ravens' 21st 100-point game and 35th consecutive win of the year, both school records.

As the quarterfinals neared completion, tension mounted for local fans. Before the largest crowd of the season, Hutchinson kept its title hopes alive, building a 67-58 advantage over Ellsworth with 4:54 to go.

Then the pressure of the moment caught up with the Blue Dragons. Hutchinson did not score another field goal and also failed to protect the ball. Ellsworth steadily closed ground, pulling within one, 67-66, with 2:55 remaining.

One of Hutchinson's most overlooked strengths was free throw shooting. Stressing concentration and rhythm, Coach Gary Bargen had watched his charges improve from a mid-60s rate early in the year to a season-ending 72 percent. Pressure only improved the percentage.

With nothing else working for them, the Blue Dragons relied on a pair of free throws by Todd Christian and six by "T" Buchanan, his final four coming within the last 24 seconds, to preserve a 75-72 win.

FRIDAY — LIVE OR DIE

The afternoon consolation fare provided some of the top excitement of the week.

In the opener, Trinidad State survived its second straight one-point thriller, edging Copiah-Lincoln, 98-97, despite a tourney-high 39 by the Wolves' Johnny Steptoe.

The turning point in the matinee feature came with 1:15 remaining when Allegany's sensational freshman guard Rudy Archer blocked Gene Durden's lay-up, setting up an easy fast break the other way. The Trojans overcame Vernon Zimmerman's game-high 28 to defeat Brunswick, 75-67.

Copiah-Lincoln freshman Johnny Steptoe (No. 22) was an All-Tourney selection based on 88 points in three games, including a tourney-high 39 points versus Trinidad State. The following year he was a first-team NJCAA All-American before attending Southern University. (Photo courtesy of the **Hutchinson News***)*

Finally, using an effective press, Wabash Valley overcame an 11-point deficit before squeezing by Ellsworth, 69-65.

Though some considered Moberly on the same plateau as the semifinalists, the Greyhounds were not the same team as they had been before losing 6-7 sophomore center Charles Bledsoe in mid-February to a broken wrist.[2] Consequently Ronnie Arrow's statement that "the best four teams made it to the final four this year" reflected the feelings of most observers. Everyone expected the day's already exciting start to continue through the evening.

The first semifinal match-up was particularly intriguing, pitting Vincennes' tenacious defense versus Southern Idaho's top-rated offense. Unfortunately, the game failed to live up to expectations.

The repeated sound of the referees' whistles marred action, accounting for 59 personal infractions. Key players spent much of the game on the bench: centers Cal Foster and Antone Gallishaw fouled out for Vincennes; Southern Idaho stars Chris Blocker and Joey Johnson each acquired their fourth fouls within the first two minutes of the second half.

Though the Golden Eagles made an heroic attempt to catch up, a 10-point spree by Vincennes in the first period and CSI's mediocre 21-of-36 free throw shooting proved obstacles too great to overcome. With 27 of 34 from the line, Vincennes advanced to the title game, 95-91.

Then came the showdown everyone had been waiting for. Many considered it the championship game.

The pairing was already on San Jacinto Coach Ronnie Arrow's mind even before the tournament started. When asked his expectations, considering seven of the top-20 teams were in the opposite bracket, Arrow replied, "The upper bracket's got some real nice teams in it. But, we've got a team in this bracket that sort of brings a few people with them."

He was equally concerned about Hutchinson's personnel. After the *Hutchinson News* cited Blue Dragon Coach Gary Bargen' statement that "there are a lot of Division I schools that don't have the talent that San Jacinto has," Arrow accused the paper of downplaying the caliber of players on the local squad. "John Thompson didn't just drive down here for the hell of it," countered Arrow. "They've got six legitimate major college players. They're bigger than probably 90 percent of the major colleges. I think this will be the first time that we play a team that's overall bigger [than we are]."

There were several keys to the contest.

San Jacinto's problem was containing Todd Christian and Tyrone Jones on the perimeter while protecting the middle against the Hutchinson big men, Ben Gillery, Sean Alvarado, and Derrick Vick.

For Hutchinson, it was the Raven press and the tempo it entailed. Against Ellsworth pressure, the Blue Dragons turned the ball over 18 times. A repeat performance against San Jacinto would mean a foot race and early defeat.

Hutchinson also had to guard against fouls. Throughout the year giants Gillery and Alvarado had been prone to personals. Said San Jacinto forward Tyrone Shaw, a high school rival of Alvarado, "If they both foul out, they can cancel Christmas."

For fans who had supported a tournament for 38 years without seeing their own team in the winner's circle, the first half was a poorly written scenario. San Jacinto dictated the tempo from the start, forcing 16 Hutchinson turnovers. To add to the Blue Dragon frustrations, inside men Gillery, Alvarado, and Vick picked up three fouls apiece. The Ravens hit 14 of 19 free throws, gaining a 48-40 halftime lead and control of the game.

The second half was a different matter.

More patient and deliberate, committing just three turnovers, slowing the pace to its advantage, the Blue Dragons gradually crept back.

Then, after a jumper by "T" Buchanan, two free throws by Vick, and a dunk by Gillery, the score was tied, 73-all, with 5:32 remaining, bringing the crowd into the game, a factor Arrow had not wanted. Arrow had not helped matters by questioning an official's call, stepping on the playing floor, and acquiring a technical.

Despite the Arena's full-house enthusiasm, Hutchinson could not get over the hump. After a Boo Harvey three-point play with 1:01 to go, San Jacinto was back in the driver's seat.

Two free throws by Buchanan reduced the difference to one with 56 seconds left.

At the 20-second mark, San Jacinto called time.

In the Raven huddle, the plan was to go inside.

Hutchinson's strategy was to foul center Tom Grant — a 3-for-7 foul shooter so far in the tournament — no matter the situation.

Neither ploy materialized. Hutchinson's defense, a major factor in its second-half comeback, held strong, forcing the Ravens outside. With three seconds left on the shot clock and 15 seconds in the game, Ledell Eackles was forced to fire from 25, the shot the Blue Dragons wanted him to take.

Unfortunately, it swished.

A last-second basket by Christian was immaterial. The San Jacinto Ravens survived the hometown threat, 82-81.

Said Vincennes Coach Dan Sparks of Eackles' game-winner, "That was a live or die shot — and they lived."

SATURDAY — TV FIRST

When Trinidad State won its 76th straight home game, the Trojans celebrated, thinking they had just set a new junior college mark, breaking the record of Region 9 rival Casper College.

---

[2]The Greyhounds were also emotionally distressed by the condition of Moberly's No. 1 fan — Dr. W.H. "Harold" McCormick.

"Doc" was more than just the team physician and Mabel more than just the scorekeeper; together they were affectionately known as "the Parents of Greyhound Basketball."

Ask any former Greyhound player what they most remember about their stay in Moberly and one of the first things they will say is "Doc and Mabel." For more than 40 years, starting with Maury Johns' rebuilding of the Moberly program after World War II, the McCormicks followed the Greyhounds wherever they went. Said Mabel, "We never took any vacation. Traveling with the Greyhounds was our vacation."

During the 1985-86 season, Doc slipped on ice and fell, breaking five ribs. When x-rays were taken, something more serious was discovered. On February 2, Doc's cancerous right lung was removed. He made rapid recovery and was able to attend the tournament in Hutchinson, giving the Moberly squad a much-needed boost. But, everyone feared the worst. On December 29, Doc died and with him went a great measure of Moberly tradition.

Then they found out their string was nowhere close to the record. Another group of Trojans on the East Coast had topped Casper's mark much earlier, but kept quiet about the feat until extending the string to 100. At the end of the season, Allegany's skein was still intact, standing at 104.

Ironically, the two sets of Trojans faced each other to tip off trophy day action. And, again the Trinidad Trojans fell short. After a close start, Allegany applied pressure, outdistanced Trinidad 15-1 to finish the first half, and spread the gap to 24 in the final frame, eventually grabbing seventh-place, 100-78.

In the fifth-place contest, Skip Ellison scored a game-high 26 points, pulled down 10 rebounds, and made four steals, three in crucial situations, leading Wabash Valley's trapping defense as the Warriors undermined Moberly's brute strength, 82-73.

For the first time in tourney history, the third-place and championship games were televised live. Besides giving south central Kansas a unique glimpse of Hutchinson's yearly passion, Wichita's KSNW-TV3 beamed the telecasts via satellite to Twin Falls, Idaho, and Vincennes, Indiana.

Unfortunately, transmission problems prevented viewers from seeing the first half of the evening opener.

But, by the time the problems were rectified, few cared. Usually a tepid affair between disappointed participants, the battle for third proved to be one of the best barn-burners of the week.

Part of the reason for the increased intensity level for the contest was that the local Hutchinson squad was involved. Gary Bargen's Blue Dragons were determined to show that the previous night's near miss against San Jacinto was no fluke.

Consequently, the Dragons put on their best team effort of the tournament. Tyrone Jones hit his first 10 shots, missing two all night, for a team-leading 24 points. Sean Alvarado played his best game of the week, adding 23. Derrick Vick continued his strong work inside, grabbing a game-high 13 rebounds. And "T" Buchanan provided steady leadership out front despite near immobility of his left leg because of ligament problems which had bothered him the final two games.

Still, the competitive spirit of Southern Idaho was such that it took a 15-foot jumper by Todd Christian at the seven-second mark to give Hutchinson its second-most successful season ever.

Even then the Blue Dragons had to suffer through visions of another Ledell Eackles last-second saving bomb. Fortunately, All-Tournament selection Jones dogged Chris Blocker — the game's top scorer with 26 — three-quarters of the floor, forcing the CSI sophomore to put up an off-balance 15-footer with two seconds left.

Hutchinson escaped with an 80-79 victory. It was not the championship the town yearned for, but it was a satisfying second-best and vindication for Bargen, the second-winningest coach in Blue Dragon history.

The title match was noteworthy for several reasons.

First, regardless whether it was San Jacinto or Vincennes, the winner would tie Moberly for the most championships ever.

For the Ravens' Ronnie Arrow, a win also meant tying recent Hall of Fame inductee Allen Bradfield for the most titles by a coach.

And for Vincennes' Dan Sparks, a member of the Trailblazers' first title team in 1965, a win would duplicate the feat of Hall of Famer Jim Carey who played on and coached tourney champs.

But, despite the stakes, the final game of the week lacked the sparkle of previous championship tilts.

The fact that San Jacinto was an overwhelming favorite had much to do with the ho-hum attitude of the crowd. Even Vincennes' Sparks had no illusions about the task ahead. "It's going to be hard for us to match up with them with their talent and their quickness. We're just going to have to come out and play hard aggressive defense like we have all year."

The title game was also anticlimactic after the exciting San Jacinto-Hutchinson semifinal the previous night and, particularly, coming on the heels of Hutchinson's exhilarating third-place triumph. It did not help that San Jacinto dominated Vincennes from the start, taking a 48-34 halftime lead. Though the Trailblazers bravely rallied, pulling within five, 58-53, with 11:53 remaining, there was none of the electricity normally associated with a battle for the crown.

Showing its most balanced attack of the tournament, San Jacinto topped Vincennes, 84-78, winning the title for an unprecedented third time in four years.

High-flying brother of NBA pro Dennis Johnson, Southern Idaho's Joey Johnson set an NJCAA meet record in the high jump after helping the Golden Eagles place fourth in the 1986 Juco Tournament. (Photo courtesy of the Hutchinson News)

All-American at Dunbar High School in Washington, D.C., Tyrone Jones (30) was later an NJCAA first-team All-American for 1986-87 while being Hutchinson's all-time leading scorer. He later played for the University of Oklahoma. (Photo courtesy of the Hutchinson News)

THE AFTERMATH — BEST EVER

"There is no question that this was the biggest tournament we've ever had," stated Guy Holt at the week's conclusion. "Arena ticket sales were up 55 percent. That is the most tickets we've sold at the Arena."

"I guarantee you there's not one person who'll go away from these games saying they didn't get their money's worth," said San Jacinto Coach Ronnie Arrow. "I'm very happy that I was down there coaching. But, I would have liked to have been somewhere relaxed and seen these good games here."

Those who had been able to do what Arrow had not agreed and showed their gratification during the awards ceremony.

The selection of Hutchinson's Henry "T" Buchanan as the Outstanding Small Player drew roaring approval from the local crowd. It was a fitting tribute to the tourney's assist leader (27) and the Blue Dragons' Most Inspirational Player. He had spent three sessions in the training room Saturday in order to play that night. Said Coach Gary Bargen, "There are a lot of players who would not have been able to go ahead and compete and do the things that he did for us tonight."

Another popular award went to Southern Idaho's Joey Johnson. The tourney's Sesher Sportsman had literally jumped into the hearts of fans. His high-flying leaping ability was destined for notice and later that spring he added to his lengthening list of legendary feats. In a 35 mile-per-hour windstorm in Odessa, Texas, the 6-3½ freshman set a new NJCAA national meet record in the high jump at 2.23 meters (just under 7-feet 3⅞-inches).

Ledell Eackles was the obvious choice for MVP. "You've got to have money players," said Eackles' mentor Arrow, "And he's one of those." Though San Jacinto was loaded with talented bodies, the 6-5 sophomore was repeatedly the Ravens' most potent force on the floor, leading tourney scoring with 103 (sharing the honor with Southern Idaho's Chris Blocker), not to mention being San Jacinto's savior against Hutchinson. Without him the Ravens would not have finished 37-0, only the fourth squad in NJCAA history to achieve an undefeated season.

According to Arrow, in order to win a national championship without a loss, "you've got to have a lot of things going for you on a lot of given nights. People just don't realize what it takes, getting them [the players] in the classrooms, fighting colds, getting to gymnasiums and playing, other teams shooting for you because you are one of the top teams in the country. You've got to be good and you've got to be lucky."

At the beginning of the week, Arrow stated, "It would really be good to win a national championship with these guys. I hope we can for their sake. There's been a hell of a lot of these guys come a long way and it would be important in their life to see that all the b.s. we put them through [was worth it].

"That's what it's all about at this level. If they didn't have a problem, whatever it be, academics, or whatever, then they wouldn't be at San Jacinto anyway. They'd be at a major college program. So, the farther that we can get them to develop — and I'm not talking about shooting jump shots on the court, I'm talking about as a person — then the closer they'll be to doing something with their lives."

With his third championship trophy in four years and his second Coach of the Tournament award at his side, Arrow reflected, "All the individual honor is nice. Somebody would have to be a complete fool to tell you it wouldn't be nice.

"But, these guys have really worked hard. All those days of hard work paid off tonight. I couldn't be prouder or happier. This is the best team I've ever coached."

*San Jacinto Coach Ronnie Arrow — only the second coach to win three NJCAA basketball titles and the first to do it in a four year span — gives French MVP Ledell Eackles a word of encouragement during the championship game. (Photo courtesy of the **Hutchinson News**)*

Tournament Results

	Game			
Tuesday:				
		1	Pensacola — 106 Gloucester County — 83	
		2	Vincennes — 78 Trinidad St. — 61	
		3	Southern Idaho — 99 Copiah-Lincoln — 89	
		4	Moberly — 95 Erie — 78	
		5	San Jacinto — 88 Madison Area Tech — 53	
		6	Wabash Valley — 85 Brunswick — 83	
Wednesday:	Game			
		7	Hutchinson — 65 Westark — 56	
		8	Ellsworth — 82 Allegany — 68	
		9	Trinidad St. — 93 Gloucester County — 92	
		10	Vincennes — 90 Pensacola — 72	
		11	Southern Idaho — 83 Moberly — 76	
Thursday:	Game			
		12	Copiah-Lincoln — 68 Erie — 65	
		13	Brunswick — 95 Madison Area Tech — 65	
		14	Allegany — 86 Westark — 85 OT	
		15	San Jacinto — 102 Wabash Valley — 79	
		16	Hutchinson — 75 Ellsworth — 72	
		17	Moberly — 102 Pensacola — 96	
Friday:	Game			
		18	Trinidad St. — 98 Copiah-Lincoln — 97	
		19	Allegany — 75 Brunswick — 67	
		20	Wabash Valley — 69 Ellsworth — 65	
		21	Vincennes — 95 Southern Idaho — 91	
		22	San Jacinto — 82 Hutchinson — 81	
Saturday:	Game			
		23	Allegany — 100 Trinidad St. — 78	
		24	Wabash Valley — 82 Moberly — 73	
		25	Hutchinson — 80 Southern Idaho — 79	
		26	San Jacinto — 84 Vincennes — 78	

How They Finished in 1986

1. San Jacinto College, Central Campus
2. Vincennes University
3. Hutchinson Community College
4. College of Southern Idaho
5. Wabash Valley College
6. Moberly Area Junior College
7. Allegany Community College
8. Trinidad State Junior College

All-Tournament Team

Rudy Archer — Allegany Community College
Chris Blocker — College of Southern Idaho
Ledell Eackles — San Jacinto College, Central Campus
Mike Flory — Ellsworth Community College
Tyrone Jones — Hutchinson Community College
Ed Louden — Vincennes University
Michael Porter — San Jacinto College, Central Campus
Mitch Richmond — Moberly Area Junior College
Tyrone Shaw — San Jacinto College, Central Campus
Perry Smith — Vincennes University
Johnny Steptoe — Copiah-Lincoln Junior College
Derrick Vick — Hutchinson Community College

Coach of the Tournament

Ronnie Arrow — San Jacinto College, Central Campus

French Most Valuable Player

Ledell Eackles — San Jacinto College, Central Campus

Sesher Sportsmanship Award

Joey Johnson — College of Southern Idaho

Bud Obee Most Outstanding Small Player Award

Henry "T" Buchanan — Hutchinson Community College

EPILOGUE:
WILL THE DRAGONS EVER WIN IT?

riginally, this 40-year history of the NJCAA Basketball Tournament was to be completed shortly after the 1987 event and ready for the public by the beginning of the 1987-88 basketball season. Unfortunately, "the best laid plans . . ."

Another year passed.

Though 39 unsuccessful years had come and gone since the city's first try at the title, the people of Hutchinson were ever optimistic; another year meant another chance for the Blue Dragons to win the national crown.

There was good reason for Hutch fans to be excited about the upcoming basketball season, however.

The previous year had supposedly been one of rebuilding for the Dragons. Hutchinson returned only one sophomore with experience, from a squad that placed third in the nation, and was guided by a new coach, Dave Farrar, formerly an assistant at Western Kentucky.

But, instead of being also-rans, the Blue Dragons lost only one game in the Jayhawk Juco Conference Western Division, then won the Region 6 title. Only a first-round regional play-off loss to Westark Community College, prevented them from participating in the Juco Tournament's "Sweet Sixteen."

The 1987-88 season augured an even better conclusion. Though Hutchinson lost 1st-Team All-American Tyrone Jones — the school's all-time leading scorer — to the University of Oklahoma, the Dragons returned six sophomores; 6-9 Maurice Brittian, who started every game as a freshman, had been a member of the gold-medal North team in the past summer's U.S. Olympic Festival, and was considered one of the top uncommitted big men in junior college ranks; 6-6 William Davis, the team's top returning rebounder and scorer; 6-1 Reggie Morton, the team's floor leader; 6-3 Steve Fritz, though only a role player in basketball, one of the top junior college decathletes in the nation; 6-7 Rowdy Meeks, another unselfish role player; and 6-10 Shaun Vandiver, a sophomore academically, but a freshman in eligibility, having spent the prior season off the court with a knee injury. Add to them two recent Proposition 48 casualties, 6-4 Kevin Howard, who originally signed with Georgia, and 6-0 Antoine Lewis, who originally signed with Kansas, and two local freshmen, 6-6 Cody Walters from Hutch High, and 6-4 Cornell Bell from Wichita, and the Dragons were again a top contender.

Just before the season began, Farrar told the press, "I'm really excited about starting practice . . . We will have good balance as we have 10 players we can play and not miss much. We have the opportunity to be a good defensive team and we should be able to play with basketball smarts."

The Jayhawk Juco coaches agreed, tabbing Hutchinson to win the conference. Another Region 6 title and a chance at a coveted national crown was definitely within the realm of possibility.

The expectations of Hutchinson fans soared once the season began. The Blue Dragons downed their first 16 opponents by an average 26 points per game. Going into the Christmas break, Hutchinson was ranked No. 2 in the NJCAA basketball poll and the city full of joy and hope for the coming New Year.

Then the holiday cheer was shattered by a double dose of tragedy.

William Howard "Hod" Humiston, a former mayor and radio personality, was a pillar of the Hutchinson community who was noted most for two things: he was the city's most popular Christmas Santa Claus; and he was its biggest cheerleader of junior college basketball. He was a fixture of the Juco Tournament as its awards ceremony emcee for 35 years. Fittingly, the offices of the Hutchinson Community College athletic department in the Sports Arena were named after him. During the early games of the season, fans had missed his ever-cheerful demeanor at Blue Dragon games. Likewise, many children missed the kindly, silver-haired man who handed them gifts with a rosy smile. On December 28, after a period of deteriorating health and a 10-day hospital stay, Hod Humiston died of heart failure at the age of 76.

At 4:30 p.m. of the same day, on an icy stretch of highway K-96 three miles east of Haven and 12 miles southeast of Hutchinson, five vehicles — including a semi fully loaded with rock salt — were involved in a chain-reaction crash. After trying to avoid a skidding car coming its way, the semi, in turn, skidded into the oncoming lane, smashing into a Toyota, killing two of its four occupants, a two-year old boy and his grandfather. The semi then hit a Camaro and a Lincoln Continental before overturning in a ditch. The occupants of the Lincoln Continental were uninjured. However, the critically hurt driver of the Camaro was flown by LifeWatch helicopters to Wesley Medical Center in Wichita. At 8 p.m., at approximately the same time Humiston was passing away in another Wichita hospital, Hutchinson Blue Dragon freshman Cornell Bell was pronounced clinically dead, though kept on a life-support system for purposes of organ donation.

REBOUNDING FROM LOSS

Losses of such dramatic proportions can be particularly hard on a small community, let alone the young men the town idolize, many of whom have never faced the loss of someone close to them.

"I laid in bed last night thinking about a lot of things," said Reggie Morton who, at the last minute, changed his mind about going home to Wichita for Christmas. "I would have been in the car with him [Cornell Bell] if I had gone home for Christmas . . . I counted my blessings last night."

"I'm very hurt," said Cody Walters who had first gotten to know Bell at all-star games in high school. "We were pretty close and awfully good friends. He was the type of kid you wanted your son to be like. He was always polite and a great inspiration to the team. . .If he were here today, he would want us to go out and play."

Could the Dragons rebound from the loss of one of their own?

There were those who did not think they would go far — but, not because of the effect Hutchinson's terrible off-court losses would have on the team. Stated Tony Jimenez in his *Basketball Weekly* column, "Don't look for this year's team to be [in the Juco Tournament.] The pros and cons of having 16 consecutive home games to open the campaign and 25-of-31 in a season, which Hutchinson has in 1987-88, have been cussed and discussed. A lack of road experience will slay the Dragons down the stretch."

Others also criticized the Dragons schedule for not being very competitive. A vast majority of the teams Hutchinson faced before Christmas had losing records. It was hard to measure how good the squad was when they slaughtered teams like Southeast Nebraska twice, 98-28 and 114-51.

The Blue Dragons quickly quieted their critics by winning their first six battles in the Jayhawk Juco West, including wins at

Dodge City (97-64), Barton County (73-68), and Garden City (81-75). They had won 23 straight, one away from tying a school record, before they suffered their first defeat to Butler County at El Dorado, 93-88. Hutchinson fell again four games later, this time to Pratt, 65-60, the first time the Beavers had beaten the Dragons at Pratt in 17 years. But, by then, Hutchinson had easily sewed up the division title. Entering Region 6 championship play, the Blue Dragons were 29-2, ranked No. 5, and the top seed in the Western Division.

Then matters turned serious.

The week before, Hutchinson had run away from a troubled Garden City team, 79-42, in the final regular season game for both squads. But, in their Region 6 opener at Hutch, the Dragons could not shake the Broncbusters. At the end of regulation, the score was tied, 49-all.

Fortunately for Hutchinson, Garden City then went cold, missing all six attempts from the field, failing to score in overtime. The Blue Dragons escaped with a 62-49 victory and the realization that the road to the national tournament was not a Sunday stroll.

Against Barton County, Hutchinson's nearest rival, the Dragons were all business, hitting 60 percent from the field, winning the board war, 39 to 19, and canning 14 of 18 free throws. Hutchinson beat the Cougars for the third time that year, 78-65.

Only one game remained for the region title. It would be Hutchinson's toughest test of the season. Not only would the Blue Dragons be facing their arch-rival, Independence Community College, they would be facing the former national champs on the Pirates' home floor where Hutchinson had never won. Suddenly, Tony Jimenez's earlier prediction seemed not so farfetched.

When Independence scored first, the court was showered with debris from the SRO crowd. The celebration continued when the Pirates made it 4-0.

Then Hutchinson tied the score, 6-all. From then on, the Blue Dragons never trailed. Hutchinson outscored Independence, 11-2, in the final four minutes of the first half to take a 42-28 lead at intermission, then went on a 12-point run in the final frame to blow the game open. The Blue Dragons turned the ball over only nine times, hit 26 of 32 free throws, shot 60 percent from the field, and held Indy to only 36 percent. The result was a stunning 100-70 masterpiece.

"This win proves that a group of kids can still set goals, practice hard, compete, and win," said Coach Farrar. "There is not a better example of team basketball around. Everybody did something to contribute in this game."

Now all that stood in the way of the Dragons' 14th appearance in the nationals at Hutch was a first-round region play-off game in the Sports Arena with Region 2 winner, Seminole Junior College. Since Hutchinson had previously beaten the Trojans, 106-65, in the Dragons' Thanksgiving Classic, few doubted the outcome.

Though the Blue Dragons lacked the intensity of their magnificent win against Independence, there were sufficient moments of brilliance. It was not impressive, but Hutch's 84-68 victory earned a ticket to the nationals, giving the community another shot at a dream.

HUTCH'S TO WIN OR LOSE

At the same time Hutchinson was trying to secure a birth in the nationals, providence was making the path to the national title less cluttered for the Dragons once they got there: No. 4 and defending champion College of Southern Idaho fell to No. 19 Arizona Western College, in a first-round play-off game; No. 3 and previously undefeated Northeast Mississippi Junior College fell to No. 8 Copiah-Lincoln Junior College in the Region 23 final; No. 2 and previously undefeated Miami-Dade Community College, North was upset by Chipola Junior College in the Region 8 final; and No. 1, former champion, and previously undefeated San Jacinto College, Central lost two out of three to Jacksonville College for the Region 14 title.

Consequently, Hutchinson entered the 41st NJCAA Basketball Tournament as the highest ranked squad in the 16-team field. With 41 consecutive victories on the Sports Arena floor, the No. 5 Blue Dragons were quickly installed as the team to beat.

But, Hutchinson fans had trod the mine fields of tournament competition before with no success. Nothing was a given. The first game, in particular, was often the key.

The Blue Dragons' first opponent had already humbled one of the top teams in the country. Chipola Coach Milt Johnson was a veteran with six previous tourney appearances spanning 26 years, the longest span of experience in the event's history. Plus, the Indian backcourt combo of Karl Brown and Derrick Forrest was one of the best in the tournament and would be a stern test for Hutchinson's guards, considered by many to be the Dragons' weakest attribute.

When top rebounders Maurice Brittian and William Davis and floor leader Reggie Morton sat down with two fouls each, reserves were forced to carry the load for Hutchinson in the first half of the opening-day evening feature. However, Chipola failed to take advantage of Blue Dragon fouls, hitting only 6 of 16 from the line for the period. Hutchinson led at intermission, 34-28.

Then the Dragons returned to the form that had devastated Independence, rolling to a comfortable 58-40 advantage with 6:33 to go. Brown and Forrest ignited a Chipola rally which pulled the Indians within four, 63-59, with 1:32 remaining, but Hutchinson either made free throws or secured the rebound to preserve a 70-64 win.

With the always tough first game under their belts, Dragon fans could now relax — particularly since destiny seemed to be bending over backward to insure Hutchinson had an easy road to the final. In the day's previous games: Shelby State Community College connected on nine three-pointers in downing No. 12 Westchester Community College, 97-81; Todd Dunnings canned a three-pointer from the corner with time running out in overtime as Vincennes University dumped No. 8 Copiah-Lincoln, 82-79; and, after rallying from an initial 17-2 deficit, Belleville Area College survived two potential tying shots in the final 10 seconds to stun No. 13 Chowan College, 61-59.

Finally, in the nightcap following Hutchinson's victory over Chipola, Jacksonville missed three shots in the final seconds before falling to No. 20 Casper College, 72-71. Though unranked, Jacksonville had been considered the Dragons' eventual title-game foe since the Jaguar's had already defeated No. 1 San Jacinto and No. 7 Laredo Junior College to get to Hutch. Scouting four-year coaches also labelled Jacksonville the best aggregation of talent in the tourney field.

As one visiting reporter stated after leaving press row at the end of the first day's action, "This tournament is Hutch's to win or lose."

The Blue Dragons solidified their role as team-to-beat in the Wednesday evening quarterfinals. Hutchinson dominated Shelby State, handling the Saluqis full-court pressure with aplomb while dismantling their high-scoring offense (101 points per game), holding them to 38 percent from the field. The Dragons hit 69 percent from the field and canned 14 of 17 free throws in building a 50-29 lead with 1:26 remaining, before settling for a 50-32 halftime advantage. Shelby State heated up after intermission, but could not overcome Hutchinson's big lead and 20-of-27 Dragon free throw shooting in the final period. A three-point goal by Paul Wooten with eight seconds left brought the Saluqis as close as they could get, 97-90, the final.

There were very few who needed further convincing that this would finally be Hutchinson's year. Even Tony Jimenez had jumped on the band wagon. In the weekly juco rankings he prepared for *USA Today*, which came out Thursday of tournament week, Jimenez tabbed the Blue Dragons No. 1.

Hutchinson's first two tourney outings had been Arena sellouts. But, they were nothing compared to the semifinals turnout Friday night. General admission ticket holders stood two-deep along the outer walls upstairs and were packed three-deep downstairs on the floor around the court. Three-quarters of the building was dressed in traditional Blue Dragon red.

For its semifinal opponent, the massive opposition was overwhelming. Counting the players themselves, Mattatuck Community College had a grand total of 19 people that were totally behind the Connecticut squad. Said Coach Bob Ruderman later, "They [his players] said they weren't bothered by the people, but I think they were a little bit intimidated."

Behind Rufus Freeman's 38 and Brent Dabbs' 30, Mattatuck had surprised Arizona Western with its offense, hitting 68 percent from the field, downing the Matadors, 107-95, in the open-ng round. The following night, the Chiefs' Anthony Johnson picked up a loose ball with three seconds left, shot from 18-feet out on the baseline, and banked in the game-winner from an improbable angle to down Vincennes, 71-69.

But, against Hutchinson, fate no longer sided with Mattatuck. Every break, roll, and bounce appeared to favor the hometown Blue Dragons as though destiny was cooperating at its fullest. Hutchinson jumped out to an 8-0 lead over the obviously nervous Chiefs and never looked back. The Dragons opened a 41-25 advantage with a little more than two minutes left in the first period, then coasted the rest of the way, winning 86-63.

"I was happy the kids were having the opportunity to play [in the semifinals]," said Ruderman after Mattatuck's loss to Hutchinson. "I was hoping they would make it a good game." But, he was realistic about his chances against a well-coached Dragon squad that was "so organized and so team-like."

What about Hutchinson's chances in the final?

"This place is going to be packed with Hutch fans," said Ruderman. "Let's face it. Kankakee is going to have 200 people here — which is better than none, but it's still not like 9,000."

40 YEARS OF PRESSURE

Earlier in the season, Blue Dragon Coach Dave Farrar stated, "Our team last year wasn't very good chemistry-wise. . . If the chemistry had been very, very good, it could have won a national championship as silly as that sounds . . . This year's team has the capability chemistry-wise to be as good as anybody in the country."

The squad seemed to have grown even closer after the death of their comrade, Cornell Bell. Under Farrar's guidance, Hutchinson was a well-disciplined machine whose nine parts functioned as a unit. The Dragon style was concentrate on defense, keep the opponent from getting a good shot, then, on offense, pass the ball, run the patterns over and over until a good shot prevailed. When the final NJCAA statistics were released, Hutchinson was No. 3 in defense (63.0), No. 2 in field goal percentage (56.6), and No. 1 in free throw percentage (74.9). The Blue Dragons rarely made mistakes. For once, Hutchinson fans were backing a squad which displayed the character to overcome the pressure that had jinxed Dragon teams of the past.

Still, the pressure was there — 40 years of it.

"We don't have many advantages," said Kankakee Coach Denny Lehnus. "But, if we have one, I think [Hutch's having come close before without winning] is the biggest one. I feel like the media has taken a shovel and heaped pressure on them. I can't imagine what the general public has done to them."

As for the Cavaliers, they had nothing to lose. No. 14 Kankakee had entered the tournament without fanfare, downed Moberly Area Junior College, 77-61, forcing the Greyhounds into 23 turnovers and 44-percent shooting from the field, edged No. 6 Allegany Community College, 74-73, in overtime in a game many thought was the best of the week, then handled Belleville easily, 81-69, in the semifinals.

It was the second Lehnus squad to reach the title game in four years. But, though Lehnus rated this Cavalier team better than its 1985 version — "they're probably the most talented team I've had at Kankakee in terms of sheer physical talent" — it was also very young. The Cavaliers' leading scorers, Andre Tate and Julius Denton, and forward Cass White were the squad's only sophomores.

"There's no pressure on us," said Lehnus. "There's no one who expects us to come within 20 points. I don't know if we have a chance, but we'll try."

Kankakee's biggest disadvantage was in the support they would receive in the Sports Arena. Lehnus guessed that between 75 and 100 Cavalier followers had made the trip to Hutchinson. But, "If we have 70 people there tonight, it's still long odds."

In 1985, the Cavaliers were the Cinderella favorite of the crowd. "Now, not only are we not going to have the Hutch people on our side," said Lehnus, "now we're the enemy. We're standing in the way of something that these people have dreamed about achieving since they've been Hutch fans."

The key for Kankakee was to take the 7,500-plus Blue Dragon supporters out of the game.

In its three previous outings, Hutchinson had never trailed or been tied after the opening tip. The Cavaliers quickly ended that string by scoring the first six points, putting the crowd on edge.

Reggie Morton eased the tension for Dragon fans with a three-pointer.

Then Kankakee scored four more.

Though Morton hit a second three-pointer, memories of past Hutchinson title failures were already being evoked. The play was not following the script. The Dragons, who disdained 20-foot shots, let alone three-pointers, were not working the ball inside, mainly because Kankakee's persistent 1-3-1 defense disrupted Hutchinson's offensive flow. By monitoring the passing lanes, the Cavaliers forced the Blue Dragons into 14 first-half turnovers. Kankakee built a 23-11 lead with 12:32 remaining in the opening period, accomplishing Lehnus' goal of quieting the crowd.

Behind Morton's 14 points, Hutchinson managed to pull within five, 39-34, at halftime, but the intensity needed to win a national title was still not there.

The second half was a different matter. The Dragons came out obviously more determined. After a William Davis steal, Maurice Brittian slammed home a dunk which put Hutch on top for the first time, 44-43, with 16:55 to go. Though Lehnus immediately called time-out to dampen the crowd's growing enthusiasm, the complexion of the game had already changed.

From then on, the contest was a toss-up. There were 12 lead changes and five ties to the finish. Hutchinson was in the driver's seat most of the time, taking its biggest lead, 52-47, with 12:47 left. However, Kankakee gained control down the stretch, taking a 71-68 advantage with 2:29 remaining on a basket by Andy Kpedi.

With 1:47 to go, Blue Dragon Steve Fritz stole the ball and dunked it.

Kpedi answered with the front end of one-and-one, putting the Cavaliers on top, 72-70.

At the 1:09 mark, Morton's fourth three-pointer of the game gave Hutchinson the lead, 73-72.

Reserve Maurice Lamar returned the edge to Kankakee with a bucket at the 55-second mark.

Hutchinson worked cautiously on offense. When an opening in the Cavaliers' tough zone finally appeared, Fritz drove left of the lane and put up a bank shot. The basket was good and Fritz was fouled by Kankakee's top player, Julius Denton, his fifth. An 80-percent foul shooter during the year, Fritz calmly put the Dragons up by two, 76-74.

Kankakee still had 22 seconds to tie or win it. The Cavaliers called time at the 18- and 8-second marks. With his best outside shooter on the bench and facing a fired-up, overwhelmingly pro-Hutchinson crowd, Lehnus overruled his assistants, electing to go for the game-winner, even though, like Hutchinson, the Cavaliers rarely opted for the three-pointer.

Kankakee quickly set up its offense, putting two men wide at the wings. The ball went to Andre Tate on the left and, with time almost out, he launched from behind the line. The trajectory was on target. But, the shot was too hard. The ball hit the heel of the rim and bounded over the backboard out of bounds.

The Arena erupted.

Thinking they had finally won a title, several fans tossed rolls of toilet paper on the court in celebration. However, there was still one second left on the clock.

During Kankakee's ensuing time-out, the referees were questioned about the debris on the floor. After a referees' conference at center court, Manny Reynoso stepped forward and formed his hands in a "T."

Suddenly, Hutchinson's certain victory was in question. The same thought crossed every fan's mind: "Are the Blue Dragons going to lose it again, after coming so close?"

From the Hutchinson bench, Coach Farrar charged the scorer's table. As his assistant tried to restrain him, Farrar yelled, "But, this is a neutral site. You can't call a technical."

Again the referees conferred. Finally, they summoned Tournament Director Al Wagler to the scorer's table. Asked if the Sports Arena was officially considered a neutral site, Wagler replied, "Yes. The NJCAA rents this facility for the week."

After more than five minutes of delay, play resumed with no technical assessed. Hutchinson successfully inbounded the ball and the game was over.

For 40 years, the people of Hutchinson had opened their doors for junior colleges from across the nation who came to participate in the NJCAA Basketball Tournament. For 39 years, they had applauded the successes of others, never able t experience the sensation of winning first hand. Now, th moment was theirs.

The Hutchinson Blue Dragons were finally national champ ons.

Hutchinson's first national championship team: back row (right to left) William Davis, Shaun Vandiver, Maurice Brittian, Rowdy Meeks, Cody Walters, and Manager Glenn McKeon; front row — Assistant Coach Steve McClain, Head Coach Dave Farrar, Steve Fritz, Reggie Morton, Antoine Lewis, and Kevin Howard. (Photo courtesy of the **Hutchinson News**)

Name	Symbol	Atomic number	Atomic Mass*	Notes
Actinium	Ac	89	[227]	5
Aluminum	Al	13	26.9815386(8)	
Americium	Am	95	[243]	5
Antimony	Sb	51	121.760(1)	1
Argon	Ar	18	39.948(1)	1, 2
Arsenic	As	33	74.92160(2)	
Astatine	At	85	[210]	5
Barium	Ba	56	137.327(7)	
Berkelium	Bk	97	[247]	5
Beryllium	Be	4	9.012182(3)	
Bismuth	Bi	83	208.98040(1)	
Bohrium	Bh	107	[272]	5
Boron	B	5	10.811(7)	1, 2, 3
Bromine	Br	35	79.904(1)	
Cadmium	Cd	48	112.411(8)	1
Calcium	Ca	20	40.078(4)	1
Californium	Cf	98	[251]	5
Carbon	C	6	12.0107(8)	1, 2
Cerium	Ce	58	140.116(1)	1
Cesium	Cs	55	132.9054519(2)	
Chlorine	Cl	17	35.453(2)	3
Chromium	Cr	24	51.9961(6)	
Cobalt	Co	27	58.933195(5)	
Copper	Cu	29	63.546(3)	2
Curium	Cm	96	[247]	5
Darmstadtium	Ds	110	[281]	5
Dubnium	Db	105	[268]	5
Dysprosium	Dy	66	162.500(1)	1
Einsteinium	Es	99	[252]	5
Erbium	Er	68	167.259(3)	1
Europium	Eu	63	151.964(1)	1
Fermium	Fm	100	[257]	5
Fluorine	F	9	18.9984032(5)	
Francium	Fr	87	[223]	5
Gadolinium	Gd	64	157.25(3)	1
Gallium	Ga	31	69.723(1)	
Germanium	Ge	32	72.64(1)	
Gold	Au	79	196.966569(4)	
Hafnium	Hf	72	178.49(2)	
Hassium	Hs	108	[270]	5
Helium	He	2	4.002602(2)	1, 2
Holmium	Ho	67	164.93032(2)	
Hydrogen	H	1	1.00794(7)	1, 2, 3
Indium	In	49	114.818(3)	
Iodine	I	53	126.90447(3)	
Iridium	Ir	77	192.217(3)	
Iron	Fe	26	55.845(2)	
Krypton	Kr	36	83.798(2)	1, 3
Lanthanum	La	57	138.90547(7)	1
Lawrencium	Lr	103	[262]	5
Lead	Pb	82	207.2(1)	1, 2
Lithium	Li	3	6.941(2)	1, 2, 3, 4
Lutetium	Lu	71	174.967(1)	1
Magnesium	Mg	12	24.3050(6)	
Manganese	Mn	25	54.938045(5)	
Meitnerium	Mt	109	[276]	5
Mendelevium	Md	101	[258]	5
Mercury	Hg	80	200.59(2)	
Molybdenum	Mo	42	95.94(2)	1

Name	Symbol	Atomic number	Atomic Mass*	Notes
Neodymium	Nd	60	144.242(3)	1
Neon	Ne	10	20.1797(6)	1, 3
Neptunium	Np	93	[237]	5
Nickel	Ni	28	58.6934(2)	
Niobium	Nb	41	92.90638(2)	
Nitrogen	N	7	14.0067(2)	1, 2
Nobelium	No	102	[259]	5
Osmium	Os	76	190.23(3)	1
Oxygen	O	8	15.9994(3)	1, 2
Palladium	Pd	46	106.42(1)	1
Phosphorus	P	15	30.973762(2)	
Platinum	Pt	78	195.084(9)	
Plutonium	Pu	94	[244]	5
Polonium	Po	84	[209]	5
Potassium	K	19	39.0983(1)	1
Praseodymium	Pr	59	140.90765(2)	
Promethium	Pm	61	[145]	5
Protactinium	Pa	91	231.03588(2)	5
Radium	Ra	88	[226]	5
Radon	Rn	86	[222]	5
Rhenium	Re	75	186.207(1)	
Rhodium	Rh	45	102.90550(2)	
Roentgenium	Rg	111	[280]	5
Rubidium	Rb	37	85.4678(3)	1
Ruthenium	Ru	44	101.07(2)	1
Rutherfordium	Rf	104	[267]	5
Samarium	Sm	62	150.36(2)	1
Scandium	Sc	21	44.955912(6)	
Seaborgium	Sg	106	[271]	5
Selenium	Se	34	78.96(3)	
Silicon	Si	14	28.0855(3)	2
Silver	Ag	47	107.8682(2)	1
Sodium	Na	11	22.98976928(2)	
Strontium	Sr	38	87.62(1)	1, 2
Sulfur	S	16	32.065(5)	1, 2
Tantalum	Ta	73	180.94788(2)	
Technetium	Tc	43	[98]	5
Tellurium	Te	52	127.60(3)	1
Terbium	Tb	65	158.92535(2)	
Thallium	Tl	81	204.3833(2)	
Thorium	Th	90	232.03806(2)	1, 5
Thulium	Tm	69	168.93421(2)	
Tin	Sn	50	118.710(7)	1
Titanium	Ti	22	47.867(1)	
Tungsten	W	74	183.84(1)	
Ununbium	Uub	112	[285]	5, 6
Ununhexium	Uuh	116	[293]	5, 6
Ununoctium	Uuo	118	[294]	5, 6
Ununpentium	Uup	115	[288]	5, 6 .
Ununquadium	Uuq	114	[289]	5, 6
Ununtrium	Uut	113	[284]	5, 6
Uranium	U	92	238.02891(3)	1, 3, 5
Vanadium	V	23	50.9415(1)	
Xenon	Xe	54	131.293(6)	1, 3
Ytterbium	Yb	70	173.04(3)	1
Yttrium	Y	39	88.90585(2)	
Zinc	Zn	30	65.409(4)	
Zirconium	Zr	40	91.224(2)	1

* A number in parentheses at the end of an atomic mass is the uncertainty in the preceding digit.

NOTES

1 Geological specimens are known in which the element has an isotopic composition outside the limits for normal material. The difference between the atomic mass of the element in such specimens and that given in the Table may exceed the stated uncertainty.

2 Range in isotopic composition of normal terrestrial material prevents a more precise value being given; the tabulated value should be applicable to any normal material.

3 Modified isotopic compositions may be found in commercially available material because it has been subject to an undisclosed or inadvertent isotopic fractionation. Substantial deviations in atomic mass of the element from that given in the Table can occur.

4 Commercially available Li materials have atomic masses that range between 6.939 and 6.996; if a more accurate value is required, it must be determined for the specific material.

5 Element has no stable nuclides. The value enclosed in brackets, e.g. [209], indicates the mass number of the longest-lived isotope of the element. However three such elements (Th, Pa, and U) do have a characteristic terrestrial isotopic composition, and for these an atomic mass is tabulated.

6 The names and symbols for elements 112-118 are under review. The temporary system recommended by J Chatt, *Pure Appl. Chem.*, 51, 381-384 (1979) is used above.

The 5th Edition of CHEMISTRY: MATTER AND ITS CHANGES

by James E. Brady and Fred Senese, is supported by an extensive array of multimedia teaching and learning aids. These resources can be accessed in the WileyPLUS course **www.wiley.com/wileyplus** and selected resources can also be accessed at the book's web site **www.wiley.com/college/brady.**

This booklet contains brief overviews of each chapter written by the Instructor's Manual author, Mark Benvenuto, plus extensive information regarding the web and multimedia resources available to instructors with this edition of the text, including:

CATALYST

On-line assignments that teach students how to think their way through a problem by placing a strong emphasis on developing problem-solving skills and conceptual understanding. CATALYST assignments use multiple representations (visual, graphic, and numeric) of core concepts to facilitate a deeper understanding of concepts.

Office Hours Videos

Videos of a chemistry instructor working step-by-step through end-of-chapter exercises.

Skill-Building Tutorials

Animated presentations of key concepts, problem-solving strategies, and fundamental tools for approaching general chemistry.

Interactive LearningWare

Interactive exercises that lead students, stepwise, through the solutions to key end-of-chapter problems.

Video Demonstrations

Short video clips illustrating chemical principles and laboratory procedures.

ChemFAQs

Alternate presentations for topics in the book using interactive examples, virtual experiments, animations, and learning games that help guide students to construct knowledge themselves through a series of questions.

At the end of this booklet, you will find additional information regarding each of these resources. In the following pages, you will find a brief sample of the resources available for each chapter of the text.

Chapter 1

Fundamental Concepts and Units of Measurement

The first chapter introduces the student to the field of chemistry and to the scientific method. A discussion of materials and their classifications is included, as is an introduction to measurement systems, such as the SI. The factor-label method and density computations conclude the chapter. *One area in which students often have problems, and need several practice examples, is the area of SI terminology.*

Media Resources

WILEYPLUS ASSESSMENT

CATALYST

Significant Figures
Precision
Applied Precision
SI Units and Prefixes
Mole Applications

Selected End-of-Chapter Problems

CLASSROOM PRESENTATION

PPT Lecture Slides

Personal Response System Content

PROBLEM-SOLVING ASSISTANCE FOR STUDENTS

Office Hours Videos

Prob. 1.4, page 29
Prob. 1.7, page 30
Prob. 1.17, page 30
Prob. 1.38, page 31
Prob. 1.58, page 31
Prob. 1.66, page 32
Prob. 1.77, page 32

Sampling of ChemFAQs

- Why are units essential in scientific calculations?
- How can I tell whether a number is exact or not?
- What's the difference between a number and a measurement?

- What does SI stand for?
- What units are used for volume measurements in the laboratory?
- How do I convert Celsius temperatures to Kelvin (and vice versa)?
- How do I convert Fahrenheit temperatures to Celsius (and vice versa)?
- How do I count significant digits in a single measurement?
- How do I write a number in scientific notation?
- How are measurements rounded to the correct number of significant digits?
- How do I convert units?
- What is a conversion factor?
- How do I compute the volume of an object, given its mass and density?

TUTORIAL ASSISTANCE FOR STUDENTS

Skill-Building Tutorials

Significant Figures and Scientific Notation
Scientific Notation to Decimal Notation
Scientific Notation to SI Notation
SI Notation to Scientific Notation
Introduction to Conversion Ratios
Models: Phase Diagram
Models: Heating/Cooling Curve
Density

Interactive LearningWare

Prob. 1.48, page 31
Prob. 1.62, page 31

Chapter 2
Elements, Compounds, and Chemical Reactions

In this chapter, the student is introduced to the division of matter into the categories of elements, compounds, and mixtures. Dalton's atomic theory is discussed, and molecular compounds as well as ionic compounds are presented. The chapter ends with sections detailing how ionic and molecular compounds are named. *The nomenclature section is very often the most challenging part for students.*

Media Resources

WILEYPLUS ASSESSMENT

CATALYST

Elements and the Periodic Table
Formula Information
Introductory Nomenclature
Periodic Table Introduction
Periodic Trends
Chemical Equations

Selected End-of-Chapter Problems

CLASSROOM PRESENTATION

Video Demonstration

Sodium and Chloride

PPT Lecture Slides

Personal Response System Content

PROBLEM-SOLVING ASSISTANCE FOR STUDENTS

Office Hours Videos

Prob. 2.76, page 82
Prob. 2.83, page 83
Prob. 2.99, page 83
Prob. 2.104, page 84
Prob. 2.120, page 84
Prob. 2.129, page 85
Prob. 2.130, page 85
Prob. 2.132, page 85
Prob. 2.138, page 85

Sampling of ChemFAQs

- What is the law of conservation of mass?
- How can I use the law of definite proportions to recognize a compound?
- What is the law of multiple proportions?
- What is an atomic mass unit?
- How do I calculate an average atomic mass from isotopic masses and abundances?
- How do I calculate isotopic masses or abundances using average atomic mass?
- How do I write symbols for isotopes?
- How do I classify elements according to group or family?
- How do I classify elements as metals, nonmetals, or metalloids?
- How do I classify an element as a metal or nonmetal based on its properties?
- How do I count the atoms of elements in a chemical formula?
- How do I count the number of electrons present in an atom or elemental ion?
- How do I name an ionic compound, given its formula?

TUTORIAL ASSISTANCE FOR STUDENTS

Interactive LearningWare

Prob. 2.86, page 83
Prob. 2.88, page 83

Chapter 3
The Mole: Relating the Microscopic World of Atoms to Laboratory Measurements

The third chapter discusses the mole and how to compute moles of substance when mass of a material is known. Empirical formulas and mass percentage are also presented. Later in the chapter the idea of balanced chemical equations and stoichiometry as a means to compute an amount of product or reactant is treated in detail. The chapter concludes with a very clear treatment of limiting reactants, as well as theoretical yield, actual yield, and competing reactions. *The entire chapter is somewhat more challenging than the previous two and poses more problems from the student point of view. The subject of limiting reactants seems to present students with a number of difficulties.*

Media Resources

WILEYPLUS ASSESSMENT

CATALYST

Formula Information
Chemical Equations
Mole Calculations
Mole Applications
Mole and Mass Mixtures
Basic Calculations
Empirical Formulas
Formula Calculations
Introduction to Stoichiometry
Applied Stoichiometry

Selected End-of-Chapter Problems

CLASSROOM PRESENTATION

Video Demonstration

Thermite Reaction

PPT Lecture Slides

Personal Response System Content

PROBLEM-SOLVING ASSISTANCE FOR STUDENTS

Office Hours Videos

Prob. 3.46, page 119
Prob. 3.60, page 119
Prob. 3.71, page 120
Prob. 3.99, page 121
Prob. 3.110, page 121
Prob. 3.128, page 123

Sampling of ChemFAQs

- What is a mole?
- What is molar mass?
- What is Avogadro's number?
- How do I convert masses into moles?
- How can I compute the percentage composition of a compound from element masses?
- How can I compute the percentage composition of a compound from its formula?
- How can I calculate an empirical formula, given the masses of elements within a compound?
- How can I calculate an empirical formula from percent composition?
- How can I calculate an empirical formula from a combustion analysis?
- How can I obtain mole-to-mole conversion factors from a chemical equation?
- How do I balance a chemical equation?
- How do I determine which reactant is limiting?
- How do I compute grams of product when I have grams of more than one reactant?
- How do I compute the percent yield of a reaction?

TUTORIAL ASSISTANCE FOR STUDENTS

Skill-Building Tutorials

Introduction to Stoichiometry
Limiting Reagent

Interactive LearningWare

Prob. 3.39, page 119
Prob. 3.59, page 119
Prob. 3.85, page 120
Prob. 3.93, page 120
Prob. 3.113, page 122
Prob. 3.119, page 122
Prob. 3.125, page 122

Chapter 4
Reactions of Ions and Molecules in Aqueous Solutions

The chapter introduces the idea of how ions conduct electricity when they are aqueous, and offers a first treatment of acids and bases. *The chapter also has a clear discussion of how the products of ionic, aqueous reactions can be predicted, although student comments indicate that this is the hardest subject matter within the chapter.* Concentration and concentration units, specifically molarity, are introduced. The chapter concludes with several problems dealing with titrations as an application of the stoichiometry of solutions.

Media Resources

WILEYPLUS ASSESSMENT

CATALYST

Solubility and Nature of Compounds in Solution
Introductory Nomenclature
Basic Nomenclature
Mole and Mass Mixtures
Molarity
Mole Applications
Solution Stoichiometry
Applied Stoichiometry
Analysis
Precipitation
Acid/Base Reactivity
Basic Calculations

Selected End-of-Chapter Problems

CLASSROOM PRESENTATION

Video Demonstrations

Supersaturated Solution
Electrical Conductivity Apparatus
Orange Tornado

PPT Lecture Slides

Personal Response System Content

PROBLEM-SOLVING ASSISTANCE FOR STUDENTS

Office Hours Videos

Prob. 4.50, page 171
Prob. 4.53, page 171
Prob. 4.72, page 172
Prob. 4.79, page 172
Prob. 4.97, page 172
Prob. 4.113, page 173
Prob. 4.122, page 174
Prob. 4.123, page 174

Sampling of ChemFAQs

- What is concentration?
- How do I write an ionic equation for an ionic reaction?
- How can I tell whether an ionic equation is correctly balanced?
- How do I use solubility rules to predict the solubility of an ionic compound?
- How do I predict whether a precipitate will form when two ionic compounds are mixed?
- How do I write an equation to describe the dissociation of an acid in water?
- How do I write an equation to describe the ionization of a weak base in water?
- How do I classify acids as strong or weak?
- How do I write equations to describe the dynamic equilibrium that exists in solutions of weak acids and bases?
- How can I relate moles of solute to volume of solution, given the solution's molarity?
- How much solute do I have to weigh out to prepare a solution of known molarity?
- How do I determine the concentration of a solution using titration?

TUTORIAL ASSISTANCE FOR STUDENTS

Skill-Building Tutorials

Models: Water
Types of Chemical Reactions
Density Percent and Molarity

Interactive LearningWare

Prob. 4.75, page 172
Prob. 4.83, page 172
Prob. 4.87, page 172
Prob. 4.105, page 173
Prob. 4.113, page 173

Chapter 5
Oxidation–Reduction Reactions

The chapter is a broad treatment and introduction to oxidation–reduction reactions. The oxidation of metals and the displacement of one ion in solution by another is treated in detail. *This displacement, and how it can be predicted, presents challenges for many students.* A further section is dedicated to the understanding of oxygen as an oxidizing agent. The chapter finishes by combining redox chemistry with the stoichiometry presented in earlier chapters.

Media Resources

WILEYPLUS ASSESSMENT

CATALYST

Combustion Reactivity
Redox Principles
Redox Reactivity

Selected End-of-Chapter Problems

CLASSROOM PRESENTATION

Video Demonstrations

Magnesium/Dry Ice
Dichromate Volcano
Aluminum and Bromine
Liquid Oxygen
Silver Mirror
Reduction of Permanganate

PPT Lecture Slides

Personal Response System Content

PROBLEM-SOLVING ASSISTANCE FOR STUDENTS

Office Hours Videos

Prob. 5.26, page 201
Prob. 5.40, page 202
Prob. 5.46, page 202
Prob. 5.48, page 202
Prob. 5.58, page 203
Prob. 5.65, page 203

Sampling of ChemFAQs

- What is an oxidation–reduction reaction?
- How can I recognize oxidizing and reducing agents in a redox equation?
- How do I assign oxidation numbers to elements within a compound?
- How do I write equations describing metal displacement reactions?
- How do I determine which of two metals is more easily oxidized?
- How do I determine the percent of metal in an ore using a redox titration?

TUTORIAL ASSISTANCE FOR STUDENTS

Skill-Building Tutorial

Types of Chemical Reactions

Interactive LearningWare

Prob. 5.35, page 201
Prob. 5.71, page 204

Chapter 6
Energy and Chemical Change

The chapter presents a broad overview of thermochemistry. The topic of thermochemical equations is treated in detail. The use of standard heats of reaction is also presented, along with several good examples. *Students sometimes have difficulty understanding how to use the tabulated enthalpies of formation, especially when dealing with substances that are listed in two different physical states.*

Media Resources

WILEYPLUS ASSESSMENT

CATALYST

Thermochemistry
Born-Haber Calculations

Selected End-of-Chapter Problems

CLASSROOM PRESENTATION

Video Demonstrations

Endothermic Reaction
Thermite Reaction

PPT Lecture Slides

Personal Response System Content

PROBLEM-SOLVING ASSISTANCE FOR STUDENTS

Office Hours Videos

Prob. 6.46, page 243
Prob. 6.49, page 243
Prob. 6.53, page 243
Prob. 6.58, page 244
Prob. 6.70, page 245
Prob. 6.73, page 245
Prob. 6.83, page 246

Sampling of ChemFAQs

- What is energy?
- What is heat?
- What is a joule?
- What is a calorie?
- What is a dietary calorie?
- How is heat capacity calculated from experimental data?
- How can we predict whether reactions involving atoms will absorb or release energy?
- What is the first law of thermodynamics?
- How do I write an equation for a standard heat of combustion?
- How do I write an equation for a standard heat of formation?

Chapter 7
The Quantum Mechanical Atom

This chapter introduces the idea of the electromagnetic spectrum and discusses line spectra and how they are related to electrons. Quantum numbers, electron configurations, and the shapes of the atomic orbitals are also discussed, with numerous examples given. *Students appear to find it difficult to understand quantum numbers, how they are determined, and what they represent.*

Media Resources

WILEYPLUS ASSESSMENT

CATALYST

Electron Configurations
Valence Electrons
Periodic Table Structure
Periodic Trends
Light and Matter

Selected End-of-Chapter Problems

CLASSROOM PRESENTATION

Video Demonstrations

Chemiluminescence / Luminol Spiral
Flame Colors

PPT Lecture Slides

Personal Response System Content

PROBLEM-SOLVING ASSISTANCE FOR STUDENTS

Office Hours Videos

Prob. 7.74, page 295
Prob. 7.87, page 295
Prob. 7.101, page 296
Prob. 7.109, page 296
Prob. 7.130, page 296
Prob. 7.143, page 297
Prob. 7.144, page 297
Prob. 7.146, page 297

Sampling of ChemFAQs

- How do I calculate frequency from wavelength?
- How do I calculate wavelength from frequency?
- What patterns exist in the line spectrum for hydrogen?
- How are wavelike and particlelike properties of electrons in atoms connected?
- What is an orbital?
- What is the principal quantum number?
- What is the significance of the spin quantum number, m_s?
- What is the Pauli exclusion principle?
- How do I distinguish ground state from excited state electron configurations?
- What is effective nuclear charge?

TUTORIAL ASSISTANCE FOR STUDENTS

Skill-Building Tutorial

Models: Atomic Orbitals

Interactive LearningWare

Prob. 7.109, page 296

Chapter 8
Chemical Bonding: General Concepts

Ionic and covalent bonding are the main focus of this chapter. There is extensive coverage of Lewis structures, including how they are drawn, how dipoles are produced, and what resonance structures are. In addition, the chapter covers trends in elemental reactivity. *Students often find the greatest challenge of this chapter to be section 8.6, drawing Lewis structures.*

Media Resources

WILEYPLUS ASSESSMENT

CATALYST

Formula Information
Electron Configurations
Valence Electrons
Bonding Quiz
Organic Structure

Selected End-of-Chapter Problems

CLASSROOM PRESENTATION

Video Demonstration

Thermite Reaction

PPT Lecture Slides

Personal Response System Content

PROBLEM-SOLVING ASSISTANCE FOR STUDENTS

Office Hours Videos

Prob. 8.57, page 334
Prob. 8.64, page 334
Prob. 8.68, page 334
Prob. 8.74, page 335
Prob. 8.77, page 335
Prob. 8.92, page 335
Prob. 8.103, page 336

Sampling of ChemFAQs

- How can I predict the charges of many elemental ions?
- How do I write the ground state electron configurations of elemental ions?
- How do I recognize the positive and negative ends of a polar bond?
- How do I select the most stable Lewis structure for a molecule when several are possible?
- What is resonance?
- What is a coordinate covalent bond?

TUTORIAL ASSISTANCE FOR STUDENTS

Sampling of Skill-Building Tutorials

Bonding Tutorials (Main Group Hydrides):
Beryllium Hydride: Lewis Structure, VSEPR, Valence Bond
Methane: Lewis Structure, VSEPR, Valence Bond
Ammonia: Lewis Structure, VSEPR, Valence Bond
Water: Lewis Structure, VSEPR, Valence Bond
Ammonium(+) Ion: Lewis Structure, VSEPR, Valence Bond
Hydronium(+) Ion: Lewis Structure, VSEPR, Valence Bond
Beryllium Fluoride: Lewis Structure, VSEPR, Valence Bond
Carbon Tetrachloride: Lewis Structure, VSEPR, Valence Bond
Sulfur Dichloride: Lewis Structure, VSEPR, Valence Bond
Iodine Trifluoride: Lewis Structure, VSEPR, Valence Bond
Xenon Difluoride: Lewis Structure, VSEPR, Valence Bond
Silicon Hexafluoride (2-) Ion: Lewis Structure, VSEPR, Valence Bond

Interactive LearningWare

Prob. 8.57, page 334
Prob. 8.85, page 335
Prob. 8.97, page 335
Prob. 8.102, page 336

Chapter 9
Chemical Bonding and Molecular Structure

This chapter is a logical next step to the topics of Chapter 8, specifically Lewis structures. The discussion broadens to include the three-dimensional shapes of molecules, and hybrid orbitals. Multiple bonding and molecular orbital theory (MO theory) are the latter sections of the chapter. *Many students have difficulty understanding the three-dimensional shapes of molecules and how they are determined.*

Media Resources

WILEYPLUS ASSESSMENT

CATALYST

Intro to Structure
Formula and Structure
Molecular Orbitals
Bonding Quiz
Organic Structure

Selected End-of-Chapter Problems

CLASSROOM PRESENTATION

Video Demonstration

Chemiluminescence/Singlet Oxygen Reaction

PPT Lecture Slides

Personal Response System Content

PROBLEM-SOLVING ASSISTANCE FOR STUDENTS

Office Hours Videos

Prob. 9.59, page 383
Prob. 9.66, page 384
Prob. 9.69, page 384
Prob. 9.72, page 384
Prob. 9.83, page 384
Prob. 9.84, page 384
Prob. 9.90, page 385
Prob. 9.95, page 385

Sampling of ChemFAQs

- What is an electron domain?
- How do I identify domains in a molecule?
- How do I predict whether a molecule is polar or non-polar?
- What are hybrid orbitals?

- What is a molecular orbital?
- What are bonding and antibonding molecular orbitals?
- How do I compute bond orders from an MO diagram?

TUTORIAL ASSISTANCE FOR STUDENTS

Sample of Skill-Building Tutorials

Bonding Tutorials (Main Group Hydrides):
Beryllium Hydride: Lewis Structure, VSEPR, Valence Bond
Borane: Lewis Structure, VSEPR, Valence Bond
Methane: Lewis Structure, VSEPR, Valence Bond
Water: Lewis Structure, VSEPR, Valence Bond
Tetrahydroborate(-) Ion: Lewis Structure, VSEPR, Valence Bond

Bonding Tutorials (Main Group Acids, Anions and Oxygen Compounds):
Chlorine Dioxide: Lewis Structure, VSEPR, Valence Bond
Perchlorate Ion: Lewis Structure, VSEPR, Valence Bond
Carbon Dioxide: Lewis Structure, VSEPR, Valence Bond
Sulfuric Acid: Lewis Structure, VSEPR, Valence Bond
Phosphoric Acid: Lewis Structure, VSEPR, Valence Bond

Molecular Orbitals Exploration (Diatomic Molecules):
Carbon Monoxide: Lewis Structure, Valence Bond/Molecular Orbital
Difluorine: Lewis Structure, Valence Bond/Molecular Orbital
Dinitrogen: Lewis Structure, Valence Bond/Molecular Orbital
Hydrogen Fluoride: Lewis Structure, Valence Bond/Molecular Orbital
Nitrogen Oxide: Lewis Structure, Valence Bond/Molecular Orbital

Interactive LearningWare

Prob. 9.52, page 383
Prob. 9.62, page 383
Prob. 9.84, page 384

Chapter 10
Properties of Gases

The chapter begins with a discussion of gas behavior and why there are numerous similarities in behavior between completely different gases. Boyle's, Charles', Gay-Lussac's, and the combined gas law are introduced and discussed, as is the ideal gas law. Partial pressures and gas effusion are also treated; and kinetic molecular theory is treated qualitatively. The section concludes with a brief treatment of the van der Waals gas law. *Students seem to have the most difficulty with connecting two gas laws, such as Dalton's law of partial pressure and the ideal gas law.* The chapter has some very good examples of this, which helps in understanding.

Media Resources

WILEYPLUS ASSESSMENT

CATALYST

Gas Law Calculations
Gas Phase Stoichiometry
Kinetic Molecular Theory
Applied Stoichiometry
Solution Stoichiometry

Selected End-of-Chapter Problems

CLASSROOM PRESENTATION

Video Demonstrations

Kinetic Molecular Theory
Graham's Law of Effusion

PPT Lecture Slides

Personal Response System Content

PROBLEM-SOLVING ASSISTANCE FOR STUDENTS

Office Hours Videos

Prob. 10.25, page 427
Prob. 10.38, page 428
Prob. 10.57, page 429
Prob. 10.64, page 429
Prob. 10.71, page 429
Prob. 10.82, page 430
Prob. 10.88, page 430
Prob. 10.91, page 430
Prob. 10.96, page 431

Sampling of ChemFAQs

- What pressure units are commonly used in chemistry?
- How can the pressure exerted by a fluid column be calculated?
- What is the law of combining volumes?
- How can changes in pressure, temperature, volume, and moles of gas be predicted using the ideal gas law?
- How can gas densities be estimated using molecular mass, pressure, and temperature?
- How can the molecular mass of a gas be estimated from its density?
- What is a mole fraction?
- How can the partial pressure of a gas collected over water be estimated?
- How can partial pressures of gas be used to compute mole fractions?
- How can the molar volume of a gas be computed from its pressure and temperature?

TUTORIAL ASSISTANCE FOR STUDENTS

Skill-Building Tutorial

Models: Boltzman Distribution

Interactive LearningWare

Prob. 10.41, page 428
Prob. 10.59, page 429
Prob. 10.65, page 429
Prob. 10.73, page 429

Chapter 11
Intermolecular Attractions and the Properties of Liquids and Solids

The chapter begins with a discussion of how the properties of gases differ from those of liquids and solids, and of the intermolecular forces between particles. It progresses to a discussion of phase changes, then introduces the energy changes that accompany changes of state. Le Chatelier's principle is treated, as are X-ray diffraction and the physical properties associated with crystal types. *Students often find it difficult to visualize the three-dimensional crystal structures and thus find the latter sections of the chapter to be a challenge.*

Media Resources

WILEYPLUS ASSESSMENT

CATALYST

Formula Information
Solids, Liquids, and Gases
Solid State Structure

Selected End-of-Chapter Problems

CLASSROOM PRESENTATION

Video Demonstration

Liquid Nitrogen

PPT Lecture Slides

Personal Response System Content

PROBLEM-SOLVING ASSISTANCE FOR STUDENTS

Office Hours Videos

Prob. 11.79, page 477
Prob. 11.82, page 477
Prob. 11.86, page 477
Prob. 11.88, page 477
Prob. 11.94, page 477
Prob. 11.98, page 478
Prob. 11.111, page 478
Prob. 11.113, page 478
Prob. 11.115, page 478
Prob. 11.118, page 478

ChemFAQs

- How can I predict boiling point trends from the relative strengths of intermolecular forces?
- What is a boiling point?
- What is Le Chatelier's principle?
- What is position of equilibrium?
- Explain how temperature affects phase equilibria using Le Chatelier's principle.
- Explain how pressure affects phase equilibria using Le Chatelier's principle.
- How can I determine what phase will be present at a given pressure and temperature using a phase diagram?

TUTORIAL ASSISTANCE FOR STUDENTS

Interactive LearningWare

Prob. 11.94, page 477

Chapter 12
Properties of Solutions; Mixtures of Substances at the Molecular Level

The behavior of solutions and the particles within them are the main theme of this chapter. The chapter progresses from a qualitative treatment of the subject to quantitative presentations of freezing point depression and boiling point elevation. The chapter concludes with a presentation of osmosis and how ionic and non-ionic particles affect colligative properties. *One area that students generally have difficulty with is figuring out what particles move, and in what direction, in both osmosis and reverse osmosis.*

Media Resources

WILEYPLUS ASSESSMENT

CATALYST

Mole Applications
Ions Charge and Number
Solution Concentration
Colligative Properties
Basic Calculations

Selected End-of-Chapter Problems

CLASSROOM PRESENTATION

Video Demonstrations

Solvated Electron
Ammonia Fountain

PPT Lecture Slides

Personal Response System Content

PROBLEM-SOLVING ASSISTANCE FOR STUDENTS

Office Hours Videos

Prob. 12.39, page 514
Prob. 12.40, page 514
Prob. 12.50, page 514
Prob. 12.54, page 514
Prob. 12.64, page 515
Prob. 12.69, page 515
Prob. 12.72, page 515
Prob. 12.81, page 516
Prob. 12.83, page 516

Sampling of ChemFAQs

- Why do gases mix spontaneously?
- What is a heat of solution?
- How can the solution of one liquid into another be modeled?
- What is an ideal solution?
- How does pressure affect the solubility of gases?
- How do I estimate vapor pressures with Raoult's Law?
- Why does adding a solute lower the freezing point of a solution?
- What is percent ionization?

TUTORIAL ASSISTANCE FOR STUDENTS

Skill-Building Tutorial

Density Percent and Molarity

Interactive LearningWare

Prob. 12.52, page 514
Prob. 12.66, page 515
Prob. 12.68, page 515

Chapter 13
Kinetics: The Study of Rates of Reaction

The study of kinetics begins with the factors that affect rates of reaction, and progresses to a mathematical treatment of first- and second-order rate laws. Activation energies are presented, as is the Arrhenius equation, and how it is used. The chapter concludes with a discussion of how experimentally determined rate laws support a mechanism, or reject it, and a brief overview of catalysis. *Students who struggle with math tend to have difficulty with the Arrhenius equation. The idea of how an experimental rate law relates to a proposed mechanism (discussed in section 13.7) can also be a problem for students.*

Media Resources

WILEYPLUS ASSESSMENT

Selected End-of-Chapter Problems

CLASSROOM PRESENTATION

Video Demonstrations

Liquid Oxygen
The Mock Sun (Red Phosphorous)
Giant's Toothpaste
Reversible Blue and Gold
Iodine Clock
Four-Color Oscillation

PPT Lecture Slides

Personal Response System Content

PROBLEM-SOLVING ASSISTANCE FOR STUDENTS

Office Hours Videos

Prob. 13.50, page 563
Prob. 13.55, page 563
Prob. 13.65, page 564
Prob. 13.81, page 565
Prob. 13.87, page 565
Prob. 13.90, page 566
Prob. 13.91, page 566
Prob. 13.93, page 566

ChemFAQs

- Estimate the initial rate of a reaction from experimental data.
- How do I calculate reaction rate using a rate law?
- What is the order of a reaction?
- How does concentration vary with time in a first-order reaction?
- How does concentration vary with time in a second-order reaction?
- What is the half-life of a first-order reaction?
- Calculate k at a selected temperature, given E_a and k at another temperature.
- Test a mechanism by comparing the predicted rate law with the experimental rate law.

TUTORIAL ASSISTANCE FOR STUDENTS

Interactive LearningWare

Prob. 13.61, page 564
Prob. 13.65, page 564
Prob. 13.81, page 565

Chapter 14
Chemical Equilibrium: General Concepts

This chapter begins a very detailed, multi-chapter discussion of rate laws and rate constants, Ks, of various aqueous systems. The chapter starts with an understanding of equilibria, then progresses to a mathematical treatment of K, then moves to an understanding of the meaning of the value of K. The chapter also looks at Le Chatelier's principle, and how an equilibrium responds to changes in conditions. *Students often have problems determining how rate law expressions are actually set up and tend to need the idea of "products over reactants" presented more than once.*

Media Resources

WILEYPLUS ASSESSMENT

CATALYST

Chemical Equilibrium

Selected End-of-Chapter Problems

CLASSROOM PRESENTATION

Video Demonstration

Le Chatelier's Principle

PPT Lecture Slides

Personal Response System Content

PROBLEM-SOLVING ASSISTANCE FOR STUDENTS

Office Hours Videos

Prob. 14.23, page 600
Prob. 14.32, page 600
Prob. 14.43, page 601
Prob. 14.46, page 601
Prob. 14.51, page 601
Prob. 14.75, page 603
Prob. 14.86, page 603

ChemFAQs

- How do changes in the way a chemical equation is written change mass action expressions and equilibrium constants?
- How does the size of the equilibrium constant affect the position of equilibrium?
- How can pressure-based and concentration-based equilibrium constants be related?
- How do I write equilibrium laws for heterogeneous reactions?
- How can K be computed from equilibrium concentrations and gas pressures?

TUTORIAL ASSISTANCE FOR STUDENTS

Interactive LearningWare

Prob. 14.33, page 600
Prob. 14.55, page 601
Prob. 14.65, page 602
Prob. 14.67, page 602

Chapter 15
Acids and Bases: A Second Look

Both Brønsted acids and bases, as well as Lewis acids and bases, are the topic of this chapter. Acid strengths are discussed, as are the comparisons that can be made among acids based on elemental positions on the periodic table. The concept of pH is also introduced, and the chapter ends with a treatment of what defines an acid in solution as strong or weak. *Students usually understand Brønsted acids well, but have some difficulty seeing an electron acceptor, such as a metal ion, as a Lewis acid.*

Media Resources

WILEYPLUS ASSESSMENT

Selected End-of-Chapter Problems

CLASSROOM PRESENTATION

Video Demonstration

Rainbow Connection

PPT Lecture Slides

Personal Response System Content

PROBLEM-SOLVING ASSISTANCE FOR STUDENTS

Office Hours Videos

Prob. 15.41, page 639
Prob. 15.49, page 639
Prob. 15.55, page 640
Prob. 15.58, page 640
Prob. 15.63, page 640
Prob. 15.72, page 640

Sampling of ChemFAQs

- How do I find the conjugate base for a given acid?
- How do I find the conjugate acid for a given base?
- How do I recognize conjugate acid-base pairs in a reaction?
- How do I write net ionic equations to show that a given substance is amphoteric?
- How can I compare acid and base strengths?
- How can I use the periodic table to compare the strengths of binary acids?
- How can I compare the strengths of two oxoacids using their formulas?
- What is pH?
- How do I estimate pH from hydrogen ion molarities?
- How do I estimate pOH from hydrogen ion molarities?
- How do I estimate pH from hydroxide ion molarities?
- How do I estimate hydrogen ion molarity from pH?
- How do I estimate pH for a strong acid solution?
- How do I estimate pH for a strong base solution?

TUTORIAL ASSISTANCE FOR STUDENTS

Interactive LearningWare

Prob. 15.71, page 640

Chapter 16
Equilibria in Solutions of Weak Acids and Bases

The chapter focuses exclusively on weak acids and bases, and introduces K_a, K_b, pK_a, and pK_b very early. The treatment of the subject matter then moves to buffers and buffer capacity, and discusses polyprotic acids as well. The chapter concludes with a discussion of pH changes in titrations. *In many cases, students find the understanding of buffers and buffer capacity to be more difficult than other subjects within this chapter.*

Media Resources

WILEYPLUS ASSESSMENT

CATALYST

Acid/Base Equilibrium
Acid/Base Equilibria

Selected End-of-Chapter Problems

CLASSROOM PRESENTATION

PPT Lecture Slides

Personal Response System Content

PROBLEM-SOLVING ASSISTANCE FOR STUDENTS

Office Hours Videos

Prob. 16.35, page 688
Prob. 16.38, page 688
Prob. 16.58, page 689
Prob. 16.62, page 689
Prob. 16.76, page 689
Prob. 16.87, page 690

TUTORIAL ASSISTANCE FOR STUDENTS

Interactive LearningWare

Prob. 16.40, page 688
Prob. 16.42, page 688
Prob. 16.54, page 689
Prob. 16.74, page 689

Chapter 17
Solubility and Simultaneous Equilibria

Insoluble salts and the idea of K_{sp} are introduced at the outset of this chapter. Selective metal ion precipitation is discussed next, with worked examples. The chapter concludes with a treatment of complex ions and how they alter solution solubility. *Invariably, the selective precipitation of metal ions from solutions, and the understanding of the basic concept of it, confuses some students.*

Media Resources

WILEYPLUS ASSESSMENT

CATALYST

Solubility Products

Selected End-of-Chapter Problems

CLASSROOM PRESENTATION

PPT Lecture Slides

Personal Response System Content

PROBLEM-SOLVING ASSISTANCE FOR STUDENTS

Office Hours Videos

Prob. 17.19, page 719
Prob. 17.58, page 720
Prob. 17.64, page 720
Prob. 17.75, page 721
Prob. 17.81, page 721

TUTORIAL ASSISTANCE FOR STUDENTS

Interactive LearningWare

Prob. 17.36, page 719
Prob. 17.58, page 720

Chapter 18
Thermodynamics

This chapter begins its treatment of thermodynamics with a discussion of spontaneous change and progresses to a quantitative treatment of entropy. Gibbs free energy is also discussed, with numerous worked examples. Gibbs free energy is defined when a system is at equilibrium, and the chapter concludes by relating equilibrium constants and free energy changes. *Students sometimes consider the math involved in relating free energies to equilibrium constants to be a considerable challenge.*

Media Resources

WILEYPLUS ASSESSMENT

CATALYST

Bond Energy
Free Energy and Entropy

Selected End-of-Chapter Problems

CLASSROOM PRESENTATION

PPT Lecture Slides

Personal Response System Content

PROBLEM-SOLVING ASSISTANCE FOR STUDENTS

Office Hours Videos

Prob. 18.49, page 764
Prob. 18.59, page 765
Prob. 18.62, page 765
Prob. 18.67, page 765
Prob. 18.72, page 766
Prob. 18.75, page 766
Prob. 18.80, page 766
Prob. 18.90, page 766
Prob. 18.109, page 767

Sampling of ChemFAQs

- How do I write chemical equations and equilibrium laws for the ionization of a weak acid?
- How do I write chemical equations and equilibrium laws for the hydrolysis of a weak base?
- How do I calculate K_a from pK_a?
- How can I compute K_a from K_b for any acid-base conjugate pair?
- How are pK_a and pK_b related?
- How do I compute percent ionization, given the equilibrium concentrations of substances in a weak electrolyte solution?
- How do I use successive approximations to solve an equilibrium law that contains a power of x?
- How do I rearrange the expression for K_a in order to solve for the hydrogen ion concentration?
- What is a buffer solution?
- How do I select an indicator for a particular acid-base titration?

TUTORIAL ASSISTANCE FOR STUDENTS

Interactive LearningWare

Prob. 18.66, page 765
Prob. 18.78, page 766
Prob. 18.82, page 766
Prob. 18.92, page 767

Chapter 19
Electrochemistry

This chapter discusses galvanic cells and the use of electrolysis to drive reactions. Cell potentials are presented and treated quantitatively. The chapter also relates stoichiometry to cell potential and electrolysis. Finally, the chapter concludes with a series of examples of practical, large-scale applications of electrochemical processes. *One area in which students struggle is in determining how to use standard reduction potential tables properly in quantitative problems relating to electrochemistry.*

Media Resources

WILEYPLUS ASSESSMENT

CATALYST

Electrochemistry

Selected End-of-Chapter Problems

CLASSROOM PRESENTATION

Video Demonstrations

Silver One Pot
Orange Tornado

PPT Lecture Slides

Personal Response System Content

PROBLEM-SOLVING ASSISTANCE FOR STUDENTS

Office Hours Videos

Prob. 19.51, page 816
Prob. 19.56, page 817
Prob. 19.62, page 817
Prob. 19.67, page 817
Prob. 19.74, page 818
Prob. 19.86, page 818
Prob. 19.90, page 818
Prob. 19.94, page 819

ChemFAQs

- How does the equilibrium law relate to the reaction?
- Compute K_{sp} from solubility data.
- Compute solubility from K_{sp}.
- Compute K_{sp} from solubility data in a solution where one of the ions is already present.
- Compute solubility from K_{sp} in a solution where one of the ions is already present.
- Estimate the solubility of a metal salt in the presence of a ligand.

TUTORIAL ASSISTANCE FOR STUDENTS

Interactive LearningWare

Prob. 19.60, page 817
Prob. 19.66, page 817
Prob. 19.82, page 818
Prob. 19.84, page 818

Chapter 20
Nuclear Reactions and Their Role in Chemistry

This chapter introduces the basics of nuclear decay reactions, as well as nuclear transmutation. The discussion includes the nuclear band of stability as well as the ways in which radiation is measured. The chapter concludes with a presentation of medical and other applications of radionuclides, as well as of the heat released in fission and fusion reactions. *Because the subject matter of this chapter comes after several chapters in which there was a heavy emphasis on the mathematics involved in various topics, students tend to have difficulty switching back to a certain amount of memorization of the new material and terminology that is presented here.*

Media Resources

WILEYPLUS ASSESSMENT

Selected End-of-Chapter Problems

CLASSROOM PRESENTATION

PPT Lecture Slides

Personal Response System Content

PROBLEM-SOLVING ASSISTANCE FOR STUDENTS

Office Hours Videos

Prob. 20.47, page 850
Prob. 20.49, page 850
Prob. 20.59, page 850
Prob. 20.65, page 850
Prob. 20.73, page 851
Prob. 20.79, page 851
Prob. 20.87, page 851

Sampling of ChemFAQs
- What is a spontaneous change?
- How can the Gibbs free energy change for a process indicate whether the process is spontaneous, non-spontaneous, or at equilibrium?
- How can I calculate the standard Gibbs free energy change for a reaction from free energies of formation of the components?
- How can I classify processes as thermodynamically reversible or thermodynamically nonreversible?

- How can we use the fact that $G = 0$ at equilibrium to predict melting points?
- How can we use the fact that $G = 0$ at equilibrium to predict boiling points?
- How can we use the sign of $G°$ to predict whether a reaction is spontaneous under standard conditions?
- How are G and $G°$ related?
- How can we use the sign of G to predict whether a reaction is spontaneous when we are NOT at standard conditions?
- How can I compute a thermodynamic equilibrium constant from $G°$?

TUTORIAL ASSISTANCE FOR STUDENTS

Interactive LearningWare

Prob. 20.49, page 850

Chapter 21
Nonmetals, Metalloids, Metals, and Metal Complexes

This chapter begins with a survey of the nonmetal elements and the means by which they are produced. It then progresses to the formation of complexes and complex ions. The discussion includes coordination number in metal complexes and the basics of ligand field theory, and concludes with some bio-inorganic chemical examples of such complexes. *Perhaps the most challenging aspect of this chapter for students is the visualization of numerous three-dimensional structures, such as the complex ions.*

Media Resources

WILEYPLUS ASSESSMENT

Selected End-of-Chapter Problems

CLASSROOM PRESENTATION

Video Demonstration

Cathodic Protection

PPT Lecture Slides

Personal Response System Content

PROBLEM-SOLVING ASSISTANCE FOR STUDENTS

Office Hours Videos

Prob. 21.102, page 897
Prob. 21.103, page 897
Prob. 21.107, page 897
Prob. 21.109, page 897
Prob. 21.115, page 897
Prob. 21.123, page 898
Prob. 21.126, page 898
Prob. 21.134, page 898
Prob. 21.135, page 898
Prob. 21.138, page 899

Sampling of ChemFAQs

- How can we compute the cell potential from reduction and oxidation potentials at the electrodes?
- How can I predict whether a redox reaction occurs spontaneously as written, using reduction potentials?
- How can I predict the cell potential of a galvanic cell?
- How can I predict whether a redox reaction is spontaneous, using the calculated cell potential?
- How can I compute G from a cell potential?
- How can I compute the thermodynamic equilibrium constant from the cell potential?
- How can I predict the products in an electrolysis reaction?

Chapter 22
Organic Compounds, Polymers, and Biochemicals

The chapter presents a broad treatment of organic chemistry, including polymers. It then connects organic chemistry to biochemistry with an emphasis on nucleic acids. Students consider the large number of new structures they must learn to be a major challenge within this chapter.

Media Resources

WILEYPLUS ASSESSMENT

CATALYST

Organic Structure

Selected End-of-Chapter Problems

CLASSROOM PRESENTATION

Video Demonstration

Geiger On It

PPT Lecture Slides

Personal Response System Content

PROBLEM-SOLVING ASSISTANCE FOR STUDENTS

ChemFAQs

- Write a balanced nuclear equation to represent a nuclear decay.
- Use the law of radioactive decay to compute the activity of a radioactive sample.
- Predict the intensity of radiation at various distances from a radioactive source.

TUTORIAL ASSISTANCE FOR STUDENTS

Skill-Building Tutorials

Bonding Tutorials (Organic Compounds):
Allene: Lewis Structure, VSEPR, Valence Bond
Ethyne (acetylene): Lewis Structure, VSEPR, Valence Bond
Acetate Ion: Lewis Structure, VSEPR, Valence Bond
Ethyene (ethylene): Lewis Structure, VSEPR, Valence Bond
Ethanol: Lewis Structure, VSEPR, Valence Bond
Ethane: Lewis Structure, VSEPR, Valence Bond
Formaldehyde: Lewis Structure, VSEPR, Valence Bond
Acetaldehyde: Lewis Structure, VSEPR, Valence Bond
Methylamine: Lewis Structure, VSEPR, Valence Bond
Formate Ion: Lewis Structure, VSEPR, Valence Bond
Acetic Acid: Lewis Structure, VSEPR, Valence Bond
Formic Acid: Lewis Structure, VSEPR, Valence Bond
Methanol: Lewis Structure, VSEPR, Valence Bond
Hydrazine: Lewis Structure, VSEPR, Valence Bond
Propyne: Lewis Structure, VSEPR, Valence Bond

Multiple representations challenge conceptual understanding.

Each time students access a CATALYST assignment, they are given a set of problems where a concept is represented symbolically, numerically or visually. These multiple representations challenge students' conceptual understanding, requiring them to make connections and solve the problems, regardless of the presentation.

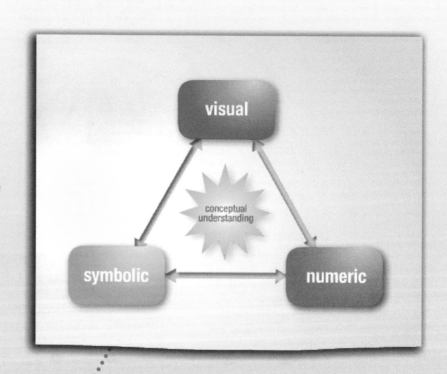

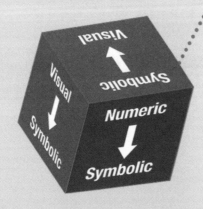

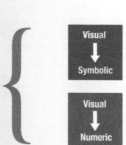

EARNING SYSTEM IN CHEMISTRY

CATALYST students are better conceptual problem-solvers.

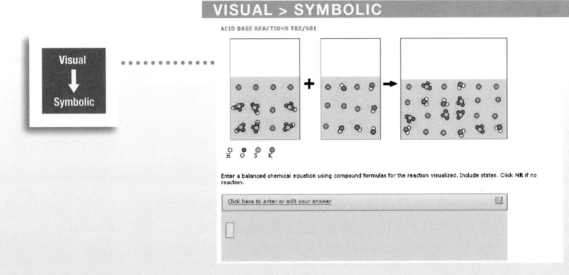

Insures concept mastery.

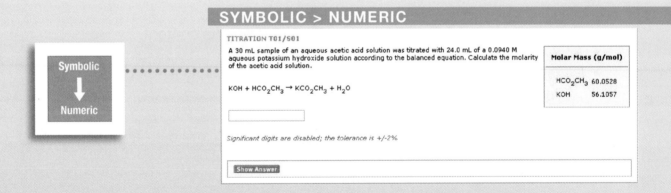

Never simply the same questions with different variables.

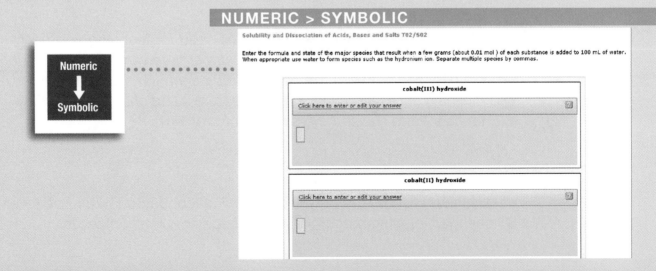

Designed for the Unique Challenges of Teaching Chemistry

 *" I created CATALYST to assist student learning. Particularly in science, students must fully understand how to do homework problems and practice them in order to master the course content. Normally it is very difficult to determine if students are doing their homework if only a static or algorithmic set of problems (end of chapter) is assigned from the book. Students typically have too many opportunities to get answers, but not understanding or mastery. "*

CATALYST was developed by Dr. Patrick Wegner (California State University, Fullerton) to promote conceptual understanding and visualization of chemical phenomena.

True understanding requires a student to:

- Examine a completely different question on the same content
- Analyze what is requested
- Recall the skills needed to solve the problem (frequently learned earlier in the course)

CATALYST is highly effective in developing true learning and deeper understanding because it consistently requires this process throughout.

 *" Our results strongly suggested the need for teaching approaches that paid more attention to guiding students towards making the logical connections between the different representations (and the underlying meaning associated with specific features) and showing how they functioned to support the solution of problems. "*

Dr. Ramesh D. Arasasingham (University of California, Irvine) conducted extensive research on how CATALYST changed learning outcomes in very large enrollment classes.

Proven Student Learning Gains at University of California, Irvine

Data over a six-year research period from University of California, Irvine[1] proved students using CATALYST had more learning gains and had significantly higher retention of chemistry concepts when tested one year later, than a control group using graded paper-and-pencil homework. Ramesh Arasasingham of University of California at Irvine compared the effect of CATALYST and textbook homework on student achievement as measured by exam performance.

What the University of California, Irvine Study Found

- CATALYST-based homework improved instruction and learning outcomes.
- CATALYST students were better conceptual problem-solvers than the non-CATALYST students.
- CATALYST students performed better on tests than students who did textbook homework that was individually graded.
- Because CATALYST homework is both individualized and automatically graded, instruction in large classes (about 400-500 students per class) is substantially more efficient.
- With CATALYST, students focused on the "mastery of the material" and individualization allowed them to spend the time needed to do so compared to "one time use only" textbook problems.

What University of California, Irvine Students Have to Say

- All students were asked to estimate how well the homework helped them learn, how well they felt they understood the material, how much the course activities added to their skills, and the degree to which they made gains in the course.
- Non-CATALYST students believed they were better-served by the textbook in their learning than the Catalyst students.
- CATALYST students felt that the homework better helped their learning

" The electronic homework was essential to my understanding of the concepts reviewed in class. "

" I found that the electronic homework was a great tool for learning. It provided a weekly (at least) practice of chemistry and forced me to actually do the work. It also forced me to learn concepts until I could prove that I really understood the material (via posttest). "

" This was an excellent class. Even though I despise electronic homework, and would prefer to do pages of book homework, I believe the hours I put into each assignment helped me tremendously. I understand how electronic homework can force us to spend quality time with the material. "

1. You can read more about this research in the *Journal of Chemical Education,* "Assessing the Effect of Web-Based Learning Tools on Student Understanding of Stoichiometry Using Knowledge Space Theory," by Ramesh D. Arasasingham, Mare Taagepera, Frank Potter, Ingrid Martorell, and Stacy Lonjers, Vol. 82., No. 8, Aug. 2005.

WileyPLUS for Chemistry is a proven, easy-to-use,

The problem types and rich resources are designed to support problem-solving skill development and conceptual understanding. WileyPLUS offers online grading, progress tracking, integrated eBook, and media in a complete course-management system.

- **Easy to use and reliable: over 1 million students have used WileyPLUS**
- **Unsurpassed training and technical support through the Wiley Faculty Network and Account Managers**

Assignable GO(TM) Tutorial Problems

show students how to break down complex problems into simpler steps; feedback is provided for each step.

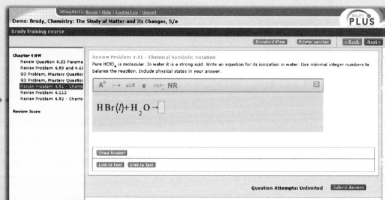

Extensive problem banks

include chemically parameterized end-of-chapter problems, symbolic answer problems, and tutorial problems.

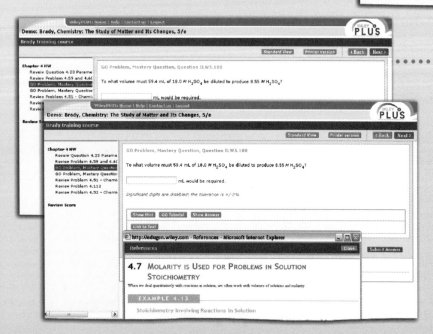

Instructor-controlled problem-solving assistance

within problems links students to hints, additional examples, videos, and specific sections of the eBook.

online learning and assessment system.

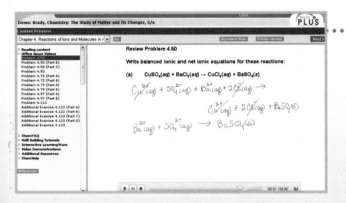

Office Hours Videos

allow students to see and hear a chemistry professor solve select end-of-chapter problems. Students can view these video-worked examples anytime and replay them as needed for a consistent presentation. Office Hours Videos are also downloadable into video players for content on the go.

ChemFAQs

guide students to construct knowledge themselves through a series of "Frequently Asked Questions" using interactive examples, virtual experiments, animations, and learning games

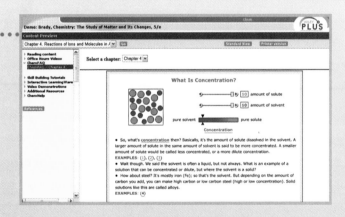

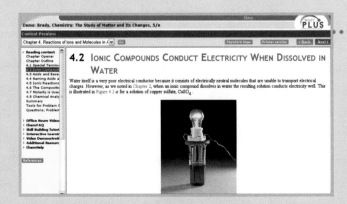

Interactive eBook

provides students with hyperlinks to interactive resources such as animations, simulations, audio/video, tutorials and more. Our HTML book allows students to print any section they need, and gives the online flexibility students want for anytime access.

www.wiley.com/college/brady

ISBN 978-0-470-28643-2

90000

9 780470 286432

cover photo: ©Chris Ewels

Every one of your students has the potential to make a difference. And realizing that potential starts right here, in your course.

When students succeed in your course—when they stay on-task and make the breakthrough that turns confusion into confidence—they are empowered to build the skill and confidence they need to succeed. We know your goal is to create a positively charged learning environment where students reach their full potential to become active engaged learners. *WileyPLUS* can help you reach that goal.

Wiley**PLUS** is a suite of resources—including the complete, online text—that will help your students:

- come to class better prepared for your lectures
- get immediate feedback and context-sensitive help on assignments and quizzes
- track their progress throughout the course

www.wileyplus.com

88% of students surveyed said it improved their understanding of the material.*

WileyPLUS is built around the activities you perform

Prepare & Present

Create outstanding class presentations using a wealth of resources, such as PowerPoint™ slides, image galleries, interactive learningware, and more. Plus you can easily upload any materials you have created into your course, and combine them with the resources *WileyPLUS* provides.

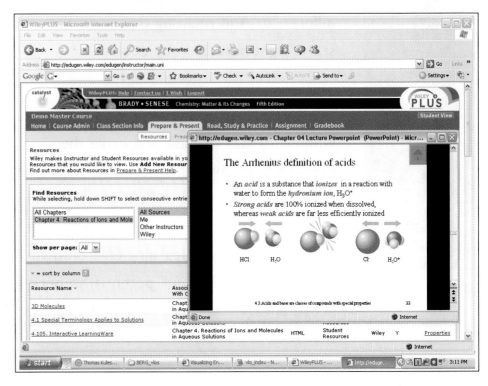

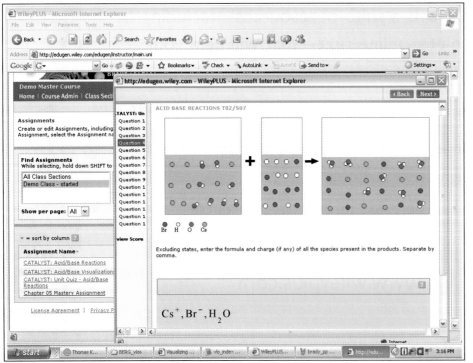

catalyst CATALYST

With the 5th edition of Brady/Senese, we are introducing an innovative on-line learning program called CATALYST. The CATALYST assignments ask students to consider the key concepts and topics at hand from different perspectives; with different givens and desired responses required each time a new question is presented.

Create Assignments

Automate the assigning and grading of homework or quizzes by using the provided question banks. Student results will be automatically graded and recorded in your gradebook. *WileyPLUS* also links homework problems to relevant sections of the online text, hints, or solutions—context-sensitive help where students need it most!

*Based upon 7,000 survey responses from student users of *WileyPLUS* in academic year 2006-2007.

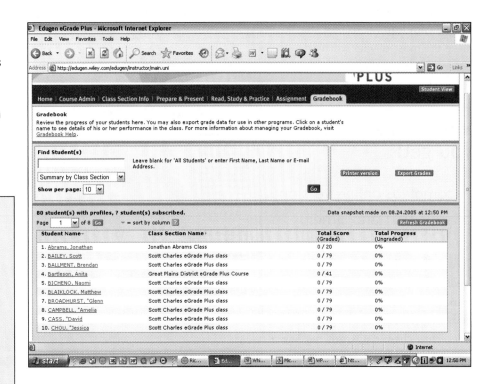

TO THE STUDENT

You have the potential to make a difference!

WileyPLUS is a powerful online system packed with features to help you make the most of your learning potential, and get the best grade you can!

With WileyPLUS you get:

A complete online version of your text and other study resources

Study more effectively and get instant feedback when you practice on your own. Resources like self-assessment quizzes, interactive learningware, video clips, chem FAQs, skill building tutorials, and office hours videos bring the subject to life, and help you master the material.

Problem-solving help, instant grading, and feedback on your homework and quizzes

You can keep all of your assigned work in one location, making it easy for you to stay on task. Plus, many homework problems contain direct links to the relevant portion of your text to help you deal with problem-solving obstacles at the moment they come up.

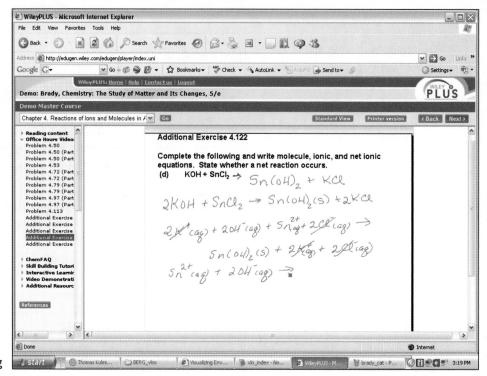

The ability to track your progress and grades throughout the term.

A personal gradebook allows you to monitor your results from past assignments at any time. You'll always know exactly where you stand.

If your instructor uses *WileyPLUS*, you will receive a URL for your class. If not, your instructor can get more information about *WileyPLUS* by visiting www.wileyplus.com

"It has been a great help, and I believe it has helped me to achieve a better grade."

Michael Morris, *Columbia Basin College*

74% of students surveyed said it helped them get a better grade.*

5th EDITION

CHEMISTRY
MATTER AND
ITS CHANGES

JAMES E. BRADY

St. John's University, New York

FRED SENESE

Frostburg State University, Maryland

In collaboration with

NEIL D. JESPERSEN

St. John's University, New York

WILEY

JOHN WILEY & SONS, INC.

EXECUTIVE EDITOR Stuart Johnson
PROJECT EDITOR Jennifer Yee
EXECUTIVE MARKETING MANAGER Amanda Wainer
SENIOR PRODUCTION EDITOR Elizabeth Swain
SENIOR MEDIA EDITOR Thomas Kulesa
SENIOR DESIGNER Madelyn Lesure
SENIOR ILLUSTRATION EDITOR Anna Melhorn
SENIOR PHOTO EDITOR Jennifer MacMillan

FRONT COVER PHOTO: © Chris Ewels
BACK COVER PHOTOS: (from top to bottom): Laguna Design/Photo Researchers, Inc.; Courtesy Dr. Ernst Richter; Courtesy Dr. Mark McClure, University of North Carolina at Pembroke; Courtesy Wikimedia Commons.

This book was set in 10.5/12 Adobe Garamond by Prepare and printed and bound by Courier Kendallville. The cover was printed by Courier Kendallville.

This book is printed on acid free paper. ∞

To order books or for customer service please, call 1-800-CALL WILEY (225-5945).

Library of Congress Cataloging-in-Publication Data:
Brady, James E.
   Chemistry: matter and its changes.—5th ed./James E. Brady, Fred Senese.
      p. cm.
   Includes index.
   ISBN 978-0-470-12094-1 (cloth)
   Instructor's edition: ISBN 978-0-470-28644-9
   1. Chemistry. I. Senese, Frederick. II. Title.
   QD33.2.B73 2009
   540—dc22
                                                              2007033355

Printed in the United States of America
10 9 8 7 6 5 4 3 2 1

PREFACE

The goal of this textbook and its supporting material is to address the needs within the entire range of student ability in the general chemistry course. Our approach provides tutorial help and instruction precisely when students need it - without burdening them when they do not. This format has reached its present form through a process of evolution. Over the course of numerous editions, we have responded to suggestions by instructors and students who have used the text. Their responses to the innovations that we have introduced over time have allowed us to polish our approach, each time making this text a more effective teaching tool.

REFINING THE PROBLEM-SOLVING APPROACH

We are among those who firmly believe that problem solving reinforces concepts, and that learning to become a good problem solver is essential for anyone studying the sciences. This belief has served as a guiding principle through previous editions and for this edition as well.

One of the strengths of the 4th edition teaching package was its integrated system of support, and our intent in this edition was to refine our approach to make it even more effective. Toward this end, we've made the following changes, refinements, and additions.

- We have thoroughly reviewed and edited the worked examples to be sure they follow our three-step approach to solving problems: *Analysis*, in which the nature of the problem is analyzed and the method of solution is developed; *Solution*, in which the actual solution to the problem is reached; and *Is the Answer Reasonable?*, in which we describe how we check to be sure the answer makes sense.

- We've added more examples in the *Is the Answer Reasonable?* discussions that illustrate how simple chemical logic and/or approximate arithmetic can be used to judge whether an answer is "in the right ballpark."

- We've increased the number of Practice Exercises following the worked examples. The first Practice Exercise in a set includes a hint designed to get the student's thinking started in the right direction.

- We've retained the Chemical Tools concept and reorganized the summary of the Tools at the end of each chapter to make it easier for students to see how they are applied to problem solving. Where appropriate, we include equations or figures.

- In the worked examples, we've made an effort to improve the connection between the problem solving "Tools" described in the body of the text and their application to solving problems.

- In addition to the end-of-chapter Review Questions, Review Problems, and Additional Exercises, we've added a new set of exercises called Exercises in Critical Thinking, which offer more open-ended problems for students with advanced problem-solving skills. These have been thoroughly reviewed.

- As part of our Web-based support, we offer a new feature called Office Hours, in which an experienced teacher provides detailed explanations for the solution of problems chosen from among the Review Problems and Exercises in each chapter. Using screen capture technology with accompanying voiceover instruction, our Office Hours videos offer students a virtual tutorial session with a chemistry instructor.

- We've expanded the number of questions and problems in the periodic review segments previously called *Test of Facts and Concepts*, now more aptly named *Bringing it Together*.

Significant changes in this edition

In addition to fine tuning our already robust approach to teaching problem solving, a principal goal in this revision was to produce a shorter textbook that focused on topics most often taught by chemistry teachers.

Chemistry textbooks, including ours, have grown by a process of accretion to the point where it has become very difficult to cover their contents within a two-semester course. To address this issue, we carefully reviewed the topics included in the last edition and selected for removal content that we - and our reviewers - felt was not essential. We also rewrote some discussions to both reduce their length and to improve their clarity. For example,

- As part of a reorganization and streamlining of the beginning chapters in the text, we moved the topics of measurement, units, and the factor label method to Chapter 1. They are no longer in a separate chapter. We also eliminated the discussion of specific gravity.

- We rewrote, shortened, and clarified topics in the chapter dealing with stoichiometry.

- We rewrote and shortened somewhat the chapters dealing with reactions in aqueous solutions and oxidation-reduction.

- Topics in the thermochemistry chapter have been rewritten to improve clarity and decrease length.

- We returned the discussion of crystal structures to the chapter dealing with the properties of solids, liquids, and changes of state.

- We removed discussions of liquid crystals and high-tech ceramics. Although these topics are interesting, few instructors felt they had enough time to teach or assign them.

- The discussion of polymers has been moved to the chapter on organic chemistry.

- Carbon-14 dating is now included as a topic in the chapter on kinetics.

- The nuclear chemistry chapter has been shortened somewhat. Nuclear fusion has been added to the chapter.

- Descriptive chemistry chapters have been condensed and some topics have been removed.

Organization and content development

For those looking at our text for the first time, we provide here a more detailed overview of the book. As noted earlier, it is designed for a mainstream university-level general chemistry course for science majors (e.g., chemistry, biology, pre-med). As in previous editions, we employ a relaxed writing style and student-friendly attitude while providing clear and thorough explanations of difficult concepts. So as not to lose the less-prepared student, we do not assume students have had a previous course in chemistry, and mastery of only basic algebra is expected.

In structuring the text we have sought to provide a logical progression of topics arranged to yield the maximum flexibility for the teacher in organizing his or her course. As much as possible, chapters have been written so they can easily be presented out of order if the instructor wishes to alter the topic sequence to suit his or her course. For example, the chapter dealing with the properties of gases could easily be moved to an earlier point if so desired.

Chapter content is based on our conviction that a general chemistry course serves a variety of goals in the education of a student. First, of course, it must provide a sound foundation in the basic facts and concepts of chemistry upon which theoretical models can be constructed. The general chemistry course should also give the student an appreciation of the central role that chemistry plays among the sciences as well as the importance of chemistry in society and day-to-day living. In addition, it should enable the student to develop skills in analytical thinking and problem solving.

To assist students in previewing chapter contents and in reviewing key concepts, we use descriptive phrases both for section headings as well as subheadings. This enables us to use the **Chapter Outline** at the start of each chapter to provide a meaningful overview of the chapter contents. This is followed by a section titled **This Chapter in Context** where we describe the nature of the chapter contents and where they fit within the broad scope of the course. The sequence of chapters described below gives an overview of the development of concepts in the text.

Foundations in reaction chemistry and stoichiometry

Chapters 1 through 6 develop a foundation in reaction chemistry, the importance of measurement and units, stoichiometry, and thermochemistry, along with a basic introduction to the structure of matter and the periodic table.

To enable students from the outset to obtain a feel for the nature of chemistry, Chapters 1 and 2 cover the basic concepts of atoms, molecules, elements, and compounds, with a brief treatment of the nature of chemical reactions. These chapters include discussions of measurement, units, significant figures, and unit conversions and introduce the periodic table and the nature of ionic and molecular compounds. The naming of chemical compounds is presented on an "as needed" basis. In Chapter 2, methods of naming ionic and molecular compounds are discussed, while naming acids and bases is postponed until Chapter 4 when these compounds are introduced.

Chapter 3 provides a careful and thorough discussion of the mole concept and chemical stoichiometry. Chapter 4 deals with simple acid-base chemistry, metathesis reactions, and solution stoichiometry. Chapter 5 focuses on redox reactions and includes discussions of the activity series of metals and oxidation reactions involving oxygen. Chapters 4 and 5 provide students with a foundation in the basic descriptive chemistry of solution reactions and gives them a knowledge base that serves as a foundation for theoretical concepts developed in Chapters 7–9 (which deal with atomic structure and bonding).

Chapter 6 has been partially rewritten to give students a better understanding of the nature of heat and how it is measured. The kinetic molecular theory is presented here as well as the first law of thermodynamics.

Electronic structure and bonding

Chapters 7 through 9 cover electronic structures of atoms and bonding in compounds. In Chapter 7 (The Quantum Mechanical Atom), the introduction to quantum theory has been improved. We show with minimal mathematics how the concept of standing waves and the de Broglie hypothesis can be combined to yield the energy levels for a confined electron. Discussions of irregularities in periodic trends in ionization energy and electron affinity are covered as a special topic ("Facets of Chemistry"). This enables teachers who do not wish to dwell on these finer details to easily omit them. Yet they are available for teachers who wish to discuss them.

The discussion of bonding is divided between two chapters. The first treats the topic at a relatively elementary level, describing the principal features of ionic and covalent bonds using Lewis structures. The second bonding chapter deals with molecular structure (VSEPR theory) and the valence bond and molecular orbital theories (including some simple heteronuclear diatomic molecules).

Physical properties and the states of matter

Chapters 10 through 12 focus on the properties of the states of matter and solutions. In Chapter 10, dealing with gases, we have expanded the discussion of real gases to include an explanation of the origin of the correction terms in the van der Waals equation.

Chapter 12 examines the physical properties of solutions and presents students with a preview of the concept of entropy in the discussion of the factors that influence the solubilities of substances in various solvents.

Kinetics and equilibrium

Chapters 13 and 14 examine rates of chemical reactions and chemical equilibrium. In the kinetics chapter we include calculations involving carbon-14 dating so that teachers who find it difficult to find time to discuss nuclear reactions can include some treatment of this important subject in their course. Chapter 15 (Acids and Bases: A Second Look) brings together the various views of acids and bases, including the Brønsted-Lowry and Lewis acid-base concepts. The pH concept is introduced in Chapter 15 and applied to solutions of strong acids and bases.

Chapters 16 and 17 cover equilibria in aqueous solutions. Equilibria involving weak acids and bases, including polyprotic acids and their salts, are discussed in Chapter 16. As in the last edition, treatment of problems requiring the quadratic equation or the method of successive approximations are placed in a separate section. Chapter 17 deals with solubility and complex ion equilibria.

Thermodynamics and electrochemistry

The discussion of thermodynamics in Chapter 18 places this topic after the chapters on equilibria, so we are able to incorporate the treatment of thermodynamic equilibrium constants. We also include a discussion of the calculation of bond energies from thermodynamic data.

Chapter 19 (Electrochemistry) ties together concepts of thermodynamics and equilibrium as well as practical applications of electrolysis and galvanic cells. We begin with the discussion of galvanic cells, including standard reduction potentials and the Nernst equation. We have an up-to-date treatment of practical galvanic cells that includes nickel-metal hydride and lithium ion batteries, which are used extensively in modern electronics, and we have updated our treatment of fuel cells. By placing galvanic cells at the beginning of the chapter, discussion of electrolysis reactions proceeds with less mystery.

Nuclear, inorganic, and organic chemistry

Chapter 20 presents an overview of nuclear reactions and the role they play in chemistry and society. This chapter, which could actually be presented earlier in the course should the teacher elect to do so, has been revised to keep it up to date. Nuclear fission and fusion reactions are included in our discussions.

Recognizing the fact that most teachers do not have time to teach a great deal of descriptive chemistry, we provide one chapter that deals with highlights or this material. Here we take a unique approach that looks at trends in properties that can be explained using the principles of bonding, thermodynamics, and kinetics developed in earlier chapters. We also examine trends in properties and structure that extend across periods and down groups in the periodic table. Included in Chapter 21 are discussions of the structures, nomenclature, and bonding involving complex ions, particularly those of the transition metals.

Chapter 22, the final chapter of the text, serves as an introduction to organic and biochemistry. In this chapter we include a discussion of some important organic polymers.

LEARNING FEATURES THAT ENHANCE PROBLEM-SOLVING AND CRITICAL THINKING SKILLS

Aware of possible student difficulties with problem solving and analytical thinking, we have adopted a unique approach to developing thinking skills. We distinguish three types of learning aids: those that enhance problem-solving skills; those that further comprehension and learning; and those that extend the breadth and knowledge of the student.

Many students entering college today lack experience in analytical thinking. A course in chemistry should provide an ideal opportunity to help students sharpen their reasoning skills because problem solving in chemistry operates on two levels. Because of the nature of the subject, in addition to mathematics, many problems also involve the application of theoretical concepts. Students often have difficulty at both levels, and one of the goals of this text has been to develop a unified approach that addresses each level.

Chemical tools approach to problem analysis

Students are taught a variety of basic skills, such as finding the number of grams in a mole of a substance or writing the Lewis structure of a molecule. Problem solving often involves bringing together a sequence of such simple tasks. Therefore, if we are to teach problem solving, we must teach students how to seek out the necessary relationships required to obtain solutions to problems.

We use an innovative approach to problem solving that makes an analogy between the abstract tools of chemistry and the concrete tools of a mechanic. Students are encouraged to think of simple skills as tools that can be used to solve more complex problems. When faced with a new problem, the student is urged to examine the tools that have been taught and to select those that bear on the problem at hand.

To foster this approach to thinking through problems, we present a comprehensive program of reinforcement and review:

TOOLS FOR PROBLEM SOLVING

In this chapter you learned to apply the following concepts as tools in solving problems dealing with reactions in aqueous solutions. Study each one carefully so that you know what each is used for. When faced with solving a problem, recall what each tool does and consider whether it will be helpful in finding a solution. This will aid you in selecting the tools you need.

Criteria for a balanced ionic or net ionic equation *(page 135)* For an equation that includes the formulas of ions to be balanced, it must satisfy two criteria. The number of atoms of each kind must be the same on both sides, and the total net electrical charge shown on both sides must be the same.

Equation for the ionization of an acid in water *(page 137)* Equation 4.2 describes how acids react with water to form hydronium ion plus an anion.

$$HA + H_2O \longrightarrow H_3O^+ + A^-$$

Use this tool to write equations for ionizations of acids and to determine the formula of the anion formed when the acid molecule loses an H^+. The equation also applies to acid anions such as HSO_4^- which gives SO_4^{2-} when it loses an H^+. Often H_2O is omitted from the equation and the hydronium ion is abbreviated as H^+.

Equation for the ionization of a molecular base in water *(page 139)* Equation 4.3 describes how molecules of molecular bases acquire H^+ from H_2O to form a cation plus a hydroxide ion.

$$B + H_2O \longrightarrow BH^+ + OH^-$$

Use this tool to write equations for ionizations of bases and to determine the formula of the cation formed when the base molecule gains an H^+. *Molecular bases are weak and are not completely ionized.*

Table of strong acids *(page 140)* Formulas of the most common strong acids are given here. If you learn this list and encounter an acid that's *not* on the list, you can assume it to be a weak acid. The most common strong acids are HCl, HNO_3, and H_2SO_4. *Remember that strong acids are completely ionized in water.*

Predicting the existence of a net ionic equation *(page 146)* A net ionic equation will exist and a reaction will occur when:

- A precipitate is formed from a mixture of soluble reactants.
- An acid reacts with a base. *This includes strong or weak acids reacting with strong or weak bases or insoluble metal hydroxides or oxides.*
- A weak electrolyte is formed from a mixture of strong electrolytes.
- A gas is formed from a mixture of reactants.

These criteria are tools to determine whether or not a net reaction will occur in a solution.

Solubility rules *(page 147)* The rules in Table 4.1 are the tool we use to determine whether a particular salt is soluble in water. (If a salt is soluble, it's completely dissociated into ions.) They also serve as a tool to help predict the course of metathesis reactions.

Substances that form gases in metathesis reactions *(page 152)* Use Table 4.2 as a tool to help predict the outcome of metathesis reactions. The most common gas formed in such reactions is CO_2, which comes from the reaction of an acid with a carbonate or bicarbonate.

Molarity *(page 154)* Molarity provides the connection between moles of a solute and the volume of its solution. The definition

---

TOOLS ICON. The Tools icon in the margin calls attention to each chemical tool when it is first introduced and is accompanied by a brief statement that identifies the tool. Following the Summary at the end of the chapter, the tools are reviewed under the heading **Tools for Problem Solving,** preparing students for the exercises that follow.

WORKED EXAMPLES, as noted earlier, follow a three-step process. Each begins with an Analysis that describes the thought processes and critical links involved in selecting the tools needed to solve the problem, as well as how information will be assembled to achieve the solution. In many of the example problems in this edition, the analysis step has been expanded to include greater detail. Next comes the *Solution* step in which the problem is solved according to the plan developed in the *Analysis.* Examples conclude with a section titled *Is the Answer Reasonable?* in which the answer is studied to see whether it "makes sense." Here, students are taught to perform approximate arithmetic to get ballpark estimates of the answers to numerical problems. They are also warned of common errors and other ways to check their work.

EXAMPLE 4.2
Writing Molecular, Ionic, and Net Ionic Equations

☐ If necessary, review Section 2.9, which discusses naming ionic compounds.

Write the molecular, ionic, and net ionic equations for the reaction of aqueous solutions of lead acetate and sodium iodide, which yields a precipitate of lead iodide and leaves the compound sodium acetate in solution.

ANALYSIS: To write a chemical equation, we must begin with the correct formulas of the reactants and products. If only the names of the reactants and products are given, we have to translate them into chemical formulas. Following the rules we discussed in Chapter 2, we have

Reactants		Products	
lead acetate	$Pb(C_2H_3O_2)_2$	lead iodide	PbI_2
sodium iodide	NaI	sodium acetate	$NaC_2H_3O_2$

We arrange the formulas to form the molecular equation, which we then balance. To obtain the ionic equation, we write soluble ionic compounds in dissociated form and the formula of the precipitate in "molecular" form. Finally, we look for spectator ions and eliminate them from the ionic equation to obtain the net ionic equation.

SOLUTION:

The Molecular Equation   We assemble the chemical formulas into the molecular equation.

$$Pb(C_2H_3O_2)_2(aq) + 2NaI(aq) \longrightarrow PbI_2(s) + 2NaC_2H_3O_2(aq)$$

Notice that we've indicated which substances are in solution and which is a precipitate, and we've balanced the equation. This is the *balanced molecular equation.*

The Ionic Equation   To write the ionic equation, we write the formulas of all soluble salts in dissociated form and the formulas of precipitates in "molecular" form. We are careful to use the subscripts and coefficients in the molecular equation to properly obtain the coefficients of the ions in the ionic equation.

$$Pb(C_2H_3O_2)_2(aq) \qquad 2NaI(aq) \qquad 2NaC_2H_3O_2(aq)$$

$$Pb^{2+}(aq) + 2C_2H_3O_2^-(aq) + 2Na^+(aq) + 2I^-(aq) \longrightarrow PbI_2(s) + 2Na^+(aq) + 2C_2H_3O_2^-(aq)$$

This is the *balanced ionic equation.* Notice that to properly write the ionic equation it is necessary to know both the formulas and charges of the ions.

The Net Ionic Equation   We obtain the net ionic equation from the ionic equation by eliminating spectator ions, which are Na^+ and $C_2H_3O_2^-$ (they're the same on both sides of the arrow). Let's cross them out.

$$Pb^{2+}(aq) + 2C_2H_3O_2^-(aq) + 2Na^+(aq) + 2I^-(aq) \longrightarrow$$
$$PbI_2(s) + 2Na^+(aq) + 2C_2H_3O_2^-(aq)$$

What's left is the *net ionic equation.*

$$Pb^{2+}(aq) + 2I^-(aq) \longrightarrow PbI_2(s)$$

Notice this is the same net ionic equation as in the reaction of lead nitrate with potassium iodide.

ARE THE ANSWERS REASONABLE?   When you look back over a problem such as this, things to ask yourself are (1) "Have I written the correct formulas for the reactants and products?", (2) "Is the molecular equation balanced correctly?", (3) "Have I divided the soluble ionic compounds into their ions correctly, being careful to properly apply the subscripts of the ions and the coefficients in the molecular equation?", and (4) "Have I identified and eliminated the correct ions from the ionic equation to obtain the net ionic equation?" If each of these questions can be answered in the affirmative, as they can here, the problem has been solved correctly.

Practice Exercise 3: When solutions of $(NH_4)_2SO_4$ and $Ba(NO_3)_2$ are mixed, a precipitate of $BaSO_4$ forms, leaving soluble NH_4NO_3 in the solution. Write the molecular, ionic, and net ionic equations for the reaction. (Hint: Remember that polyatomic ions do not break apart when ionic compounds dissolve in water.)

Practice Exercise 4: Write molecular, ionic, and net ionic equations for the reaction of aqueous solutions of cadmium chloride and sodium sulfide to give a precipitate of cadmium sulfide and a solution of sodium chloride.

PRACTICE EXERCISES follow most worked examples to enable the student to apply what has just been studied to a similar problem. The first member of each Practice Exercise set includes a hint designed to focus the student's thinking in the right direction. All of the Practice Exercises have answers in Appendix B at the back of the book.

END-OF-CHAPTER EXERCISES are divided into four sections. **Review Questions,** classified according to topic, enable students to gauge their progress in learning concepts presented in a chapter. **Review Problems,** also classified according to topic, are presented in pairs of similar problems, with the first member of each pair having its answer in Appendix B. These problems provide routine practice in the use of basic tools as well as opportunities to incorporate the tools in the solution of more complex problems. **Additional Exercises** at the end of the problem sets are unclassified. Many problems are cumulative, requiring two or more concepts, and several in later chapters require skills learned in earlier chapters. The range of problem difficulty provides the instructor flexibility is assigning homework. **Exercises in Critical Thinking** are sets of questions that require students to "think outside the box" and often go beyond explanations provided in the text, frequently requiring exploration on the internet. Many are quite open ended.

BRINGING IT TOGETHER are problem sets placed between chapters at strategic intervals. These enable the student to review and gauge their progress. Many of the problems in these sets incorporate concepts developed over two or more chapters.

CHAPTERS 4–6

BRINGING IT TOGETHER

We pause again to allow you to test your understanding of concepts, your knowledge of scientific terms, and your skills at solving chemistry problems. Read through the following questions carefully, and answer each as fully as possible. When necessary, review topics you are uncertain of. If you can answer these questions correctly, you are ready to go on to the next group of chapters.

1. What is the difference between a strong electrolyte and a weak electrolyte? Formic acid, $HCHO_2$, is a weak acid. Write a chemical equation showing its reaction with water.
2. Write an equation showing the reaction of water with itself to form ions.
3. Methylamine, CH_3NH_2, is a weak base. Write a chemical equation showing its reaction with water.
4. Write molecular, ionic, and net ionic equations for the reaction that occurs when a solution containing hydrochloric acid is added to a solution of the weak base methylamine (CH_3NH_2).
5. According to the solubility rules, which of the following salts would be classified as soluble?
   (a) $Ca_3(PO_4)_2$ (f) $Au(ClO_4)_3$ (k) $ZnSO_4$
   (b) $Ni(OH)_2$ (g) $Cu(C_2H_3O_2)_2$ (l) Na_2S
   (c) $(NH_4)_2HPO_4$ (h) $AgBr$ (m) $CoCO_3$
   (d) $SnCl_2$ (i) KOH (n) $BaSO_3$
   (e) $Sr(NO_3)_2$ (j) Hg_2Cl_2 (o) MnS
6. What are the two criteria that must be met for an ionic equation to be balanced correctly?
7. Write molecular, ionic, and net ionic equations for any reactions that would occur between the following pairs of compounds. If no reaction occurs, write "N.R."
   (a) $CuCl_2(aq)$ and $(NH_4)_2CO_3(aq)$
   (b) $HCl(aq)$ and $MgCO_3(s)$
   (c) $ZnCl_2(aq)$ and $AgC_2H_3O_2(aq)$
   (d) $HClO_4(aq)$ and $NaCHO_2(aq)$
   (e) $MnO(s)$ and $H_2SO_4(aq)$
   (f) $FeS(s)$ and $HCl(aq)$
8. Write a chemical equation for the complete neutralization of H_3PO_4 by NaOH.
9. Which ion exists in abundance in all solutions of strong acids?
10. Which ion makes a solution basic?
11. Define *monoprotic acid, diprotic acid,* and *polyprotic acid.* What is the general definition of a *salt*?
12. Which of the following oxides are acidic and which are basic: P_4O_6, Na_2O, SeO_3, CaO, PbO, and SO_2?
13. Write the formulas of any acid salts that could be formed by the reaction of the following acids with potassium hydroxide.
    (a) sulfurous acid

(d) lithium hydrogen sulfate
(e) bromic acid
16. How many milliliters of 0.200 M $BaCl_2$ must be added to 27.0 mL of 0.600 M Na_2SO_4 to give a complete reaction between their solutes?
17. What mass of $Mg(OH)_2$ will be formed when 30.0 mL of 0.200 M $MgCl_2$ solution is mixed with 25.0 mL of 0.420 M NaOH solution? What will be the molar concentrations of the ions remaining in solution?
18. How many milliliters of 6.00 M HNO_3 must be added to 200 mL of water to give 0.150 M HNO_3?
19. How many grams of CO_2 must be dissolved in 300 mL of 0.100 M Na_2CO_3 solution to change the solute entirely into $NaHCO_3$?
20. A certain toilet cleaner uses $NaHSO_4$ as its active ingredient. In an analysis, 0.500 g of the cleaner was dissolved in 30.0 mL of distilled water and required 24.60 mL of 0.105 M NaOH for complete neutralization in a titration. What was the percentage by weight of $NaHSO_4$ in the cleaner?
21. A volume of 28.50 mL of a freshly prepared solution of KOH was required to titrate 50.00 mL of 0.0922 M HCl solution. What was the molarity of the KOH solution?
22. To neutralize the acid in 10.0 mL of 18.0 M H_2SO_4 that was accidentally spilled on a laboratory bench top, solid sodium bicarbonate was used. The container of sodium bicarbonate was known to weigh 155.0 g before this use and out of curiosity its mass was measured as 144.5 g afterward. The reaction forms sodium sulfate. Was sufficient sodium bicarbonate used? Determine the limiting reactant and calculate the maximum yield in grams of sodium sulfate.
23. How many milliliters of concentrated sulfuric acid (18.0 M) are needed to prepare 125 mL of 0.144 M H_2SO_4?
24. The density of concentrated phosphoric acid is 1.689 g solution/mL solution at 20 °C. It contains 144 g H_3PO_4 per 1.00×10^2 mL of solution.
    (a) Calculate the molar concentration of H_3PO_4 in this solution.
    (b) Calculate the number of grams of this solution required to hold 50.0 g H_3PO_4.
25. A mixture consists of lithium carbonate (Li_2CO_3) and potassium carbonate (K_2CO_3). These react with hydrochloric acid

---

FEATURES THAT FURTHER COMPREHENSION AND LEARNING

MACRO-TO-MICRO ILLUSTRATIONS. To help students make the connection between the macroscopic world we see and events that take place at the molecular level, we have a substantial number of illustrations that combine both views. A photograph, for example, will show a chemical reaction as well as an artist's rendition of the chemical interpretation of what is taking place between the atoms, molecules, or ions involved. We include a variety of illustrations that visualize reactions at the molecular level. The goal is to show how models of nature enable chemists to better understand their observations and to get students to visualize events at the molecular level.

MARGIN COMMENTS make it easy to enrich a discussion, without carrying the aura of being essential. Some margin comments jog the student's memory concerning a definition of a term.

PERIODIC TABLE CORRELATIONS One of our goals was to call particular attention to the usefulness of the periodic table in correlating chemical and physical properties of the elements.

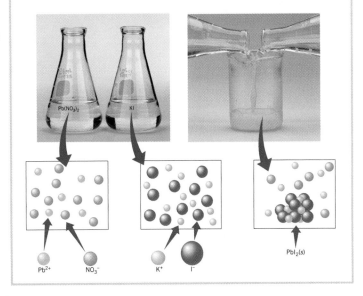

BOLDFACE TERMS alert the student to "must-learn" items. Especially important equations are highlighted with a beige background. Definitions of boldfaced terms are included in the Glossary.

PROBLEM ANALYSIS AT A GLANCE Where appropriate, figures contain flow-charts that summarize the relationships involved in solving problems, the approach used to analyze the method of attack on problems, or the approach to applying rules of chemical nomenclature.

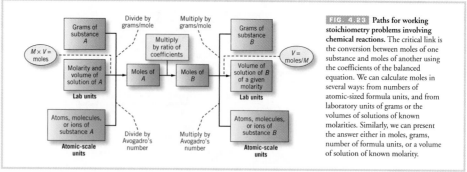

FIG. 4.23 Paths for working stoichiometry problems involving chemical reactions. The critical link is the conversion between moles of one substance and moles of another using the coefficients of the balanced equation. We can calculate moles in several ways: from numbers of atomic-sized formula units, and from laboratory units of grams or the volumes of solutions of known molarities. Similarly, we can present the answer either in moles, grams, number of formula units, or a volume of solution of known molarity.

CHAPTER SUMMARIES use the boldface terms to show how the terms fit into statements that summarize concepts.

FEATURES THAT EXTEND THE BREADTH OF KNOWLEDGE OF THE STUDENT

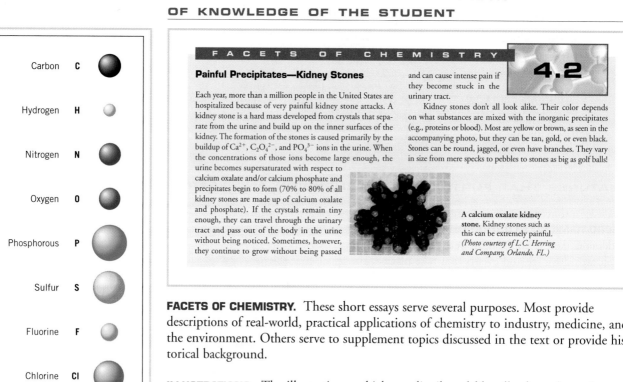

FACETS OF CHEMISTRY

4.2

Painful Precipitates—Kidney Stones

Each year, more than a million people in the United States are hospitalized because of very painful kidney stone attacks. A kidney stone is a hard mass developed from crystals that separate from the urine and build up on the inner surfaces of the kidney. The formation of the stones is caused primarily by the buildup of Ca^{2+}, $C_2O_4^{2-}$, and PO_4^{3-} ions in the urine. When the concentrations of those ions become large enough, the urine becomes supersaturated with respect to calcium oxalate and/or calcium phosphate and precipitates begin to form (70% to 80% of all kidney stones are made up of calcium oxalate and phosphate). If the crystals remain tiny enough, they can travel through the urinary tract and pass out of the body in the urine without being noticed. Sometimes, however, they continue to grow without being passed and can cause intense pain if they become stuck in the urinary tract.

Kidney stones don't all look alike. Their color depends on what substances are mixed with the inorganic precipitates (e.g., proteins or blood). Most are yellow or brown, as seen in the accompanying photo, but they can be tan, gold, or even black. Stones can be round, jagged, or even have branches. They vary in size from mere specks to pebbles to stones as big as golf balls!

A calcium oxalate kidney stone. Kidney stones such as this can be extremely painful. (Photo courtesy of L.C. Herring and Company, Orlando, FL.)

FACETS OF CHEMISTRY. These short essays serve several purposes. Most provide descriptions of real-world, practical applications of chemistry to industry, medicine, and the environment. Others serve to supplement topics discussed in the text or provide historical background.

ILLUSTRATIONS. The illustrations, which are distributed liberally throughout the text, have been drawn using modern computer techniques to provide accurate, eye-appealing complements to discussions. Color is used constructively rather than for its own sake. For example, a consistent set of colors is used to identify atoms of the elements in drawings that illustrate molecular structures. These are shown in the margin.

PHOTOGRAPHS. The many striking photographs in the book serve two purposes. One is to provide a sense of reality and color to the chemical and physical phenomena described in the text. Toward this end, many photographs of chemicals and chemical reactions are included. The photographs also serve to illustrate how chemistry relates to the world outside of the laboratory. The chapter-opening photos, for example, call the students' attention to the relationship between the chapter's content and common (and often notso-common) things. Similar photos within the chapters illustrate practical examples and applications of chemical reactions and physical phenomena.

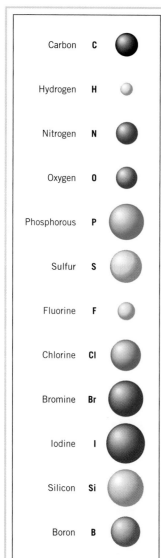

Carbon	C
Hydrogen	H
Nitrogen	N
Oxygen	O
Phosphorous	P
Sulfur	S
Fluorine	F
Chlorine	Cl
Bromine	Br
Iodine	I
Silicon	Si
Boron	B

SUPPLEMENTS

A comprehensive package of supplements has been created to assist both the teacher and the student and includes the following:

Study Guide by Neil Jespersen of St. John's University. This guide has been written to further enhance understanding of concepts. It is an invaluable tool for students and contains chapter overviews, additional worked-out problems giving detailed steps involved in solving them, alternate problem-solving approaches, as well as extensive review exercises.

Solutions Manual by Alison Hyslop of St. John's University. The manual contains worked-out solutions for text problems whose answers appear in Appendix B.

Laboratory Manual for Principles of General Chemistry, Eighth Edition by Jo Beran of Texas A&M University, Kingsville. This comprehensive laboratory manual is for use in the general chemistry course. This manual is known for its broad selection of topics and experiments, and for its clear layout and design. Contai-ning enough material for two or three terms, this lab manual emphasizes techniques, helping students learn the time and situation for their correct use. The accompanying Instructor's Manual (IM) presents the details of each experiment, including overviews, an instructor's lecture outline, and teaching hints. The IM also contains answers to the pre-lab assignment and laboratory questions.

Office Hours Videos by Dixie Goss, of Hunter College. These video clips with accompanying audio voiceover walk students through the problem solving process and provide students with a virtual office hour experience with a chemistry instructor. The videos focus on selected end of chapter problems from the text.

Instructor's Manual by Mark A. Benvenuto of University of Detroit–Mercy. In addition to lecture outlines, alternate syllabi, and chapter overviews, this manual contains suggestions for small group active-learning projects, class discussions, and short writing projects, and contains relevant web links for each chapter.

Test Bank by Jason D'Acchioli of the University of Wisconsin – Stevens Point. The Test Bank contains over 1,800 questions including; multiple choice, true-false, short answer questions, and critical thinking problems.

Computerized Test Bank IBM and Macintosh versions of the entire Test Bank are available with full editing features to help the instructor customize tests.

Instructor's Solutions Manual by Alison Hyslop of St. John's University. Contains worked-out solutions to all end of chapter problems.

Digital Image Archive Text web site includes downloadable files of text images in JPG format. Instructors may use these images to customize their presentations and to provide additional visual support for quizzes and exams.

Power Point Lecture Slides by Nancy Mullins of Jacksonville Community College. Featuring images from the text, the slides are customizable to fit your course.

Personal Response Systems/"Clicker" Questions. A bank of questions is available for anyone using personal response systems technology in their classroom.

WileyPLUS with CATALYST

WileyPlus with CATALYST partners with the instructor to teach students how to think their way through a problem, rather than rely on a list of memorized equations, by placing a strong emphasis on developing problem-solving skills and conceptual understanding. *WileyPlus* with CATALYST incorporates an online learning system designed to facilitate dynamic learning and retention of learned concepts. CATALYST was developed by Dr. Patrick Wegner (California State University, Fullerton) to promote conceptual understanding and visualization of chemical phenomena in undergraduate chemistry courses.

CATALYST assignments have multiple levels of parameterization and test on key concepts from multiple points of view (visual, symbolic, graphical, quantitative). Hundreds of end-of-chapter problems are available for assignment, and all are available with multiple forms of problem-solving support.

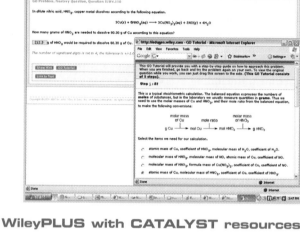

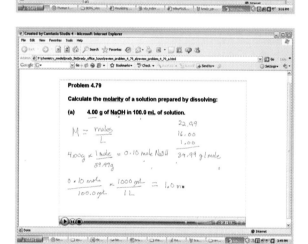

WileyPLUS with CATALYST resources

For Students

Office Hours Videos are video worked examples based on end-of-chapter problems.

Chem FAQs give alternate presentations for topics in the book using interactive examples, virtual experiments, animations, and learning games. They guide students to construct knowledge themselves through a series of questions.

Skill Building Tutorials are animated presentations of key concepts, problem-solving strategies, and fundamental tools for approaching general chemistry

Interactive LearningWare are interactive exercises that allow students to work through the solutions to key end of chapter problems

Study Guide. The Study Guide further enhances understanding of text concepts and contains additional worked examples giving detailed steps involved in solving them, additional problems and questions, chapter overviews, alternate problem-solving approaches, and extensive review exercises.

Video Demonstrations are short video clips illustrating chemical principles and laboratory procedures.

Conceptual Self Quizzes feature detailed feedback based on common errors students make.

Additional Resources • 3D Molecules • Audio Pronunciation Guide • Key Tables

For Instructors

A description of each of the following resources can be found on page xv.

- Instructor's Solutions Manual
- Test Bank
- Digital Image Archive
- PowerPoint Lecture Slides

ACKNOWLEDGMENTS

We begin with words of welcome to Neil Jespersen, a respected analytical chemist, colleague at St. John's University, and close friend for many years. Neil's collaboration on this edition has added a fresh perspective on teaching general chemistry. His contributions have enhanced the quality of presentations in many places throughout the book.

We express our fond thanks to our wives, June Brady, Marilyn Jespersen, and Lori Senese, and our children, Mark and Karen Brady, Lisa Fico and Kristen Pierce, and Kai and Keiran Senese, for their constant support, understanding, and patience. They have been, and continue to be a constant source of inspiration for us all.

We deeply appreciate the contributions of others who have helped in preparing materials for this edition, in particular Alison Hyslop of St. John's University for her diligence in preparing the Answer Appendix, and Conrad Bergo of East Stroudsburg University for checking the answers for accuracy. We thank Mike Borut for his thoughtful suggestions regarding various aspects of the text. We thank Dixie Goss, of Hunter College, for her skillful creation of the Office Hours videos.

It is with particular pleasure that we thank the staff at Wiley for their careful work, encouragement, and sense of humor, particularly our editors, Jennifer Yee and Stuart Johnson. We are also grateful for the efforts of Marketing Manager Amanda Wainer, our Editorial Program Assistant, Catherine Donovan, Senior Media Editor, Thomas Kulesa, our Photo Editor, Jennifer MacMillan, our Designer, Madelyn Lesure, our Illustration Editor, Anna Melhorn, the entire production team, and especially Elizabeth Swain for her tireless attention to getting things right. Our thanks also go to Pietro Paolo Adinolfi and others at Preparé (the Compositor) for their unflagging efforts toward changing a manuscript into a book.

We express gratitude to the colleagues whose careful reviews, helpful suggestions, and thoughtful criticism of previous editions as well as the current edition manuscript have been so important in the development of this book. Additional thanks go to those who participated in the media development by creating content and reviewing extensively. Our thanks go out to the reviewers of previous editions and of the current edition, and to authors and reviewers of the supporting media package:

Hugh Akers
Lamar University

Robert D. Allendoerfer
State University of New York, Buffalo

Patricia Amateis
Virginia Polytechnic Institute

Mark Amman
Alfred State College

David Anderson
University of Colorado

Dale Arlington
South Dakota School of Mines and Technology

George C. Bandik
University of Pittsburgh

Wesley Bentz
Alfred University

Conrad Bergo
East Stroudsburg University

Mark A. Benvenuto
University of Detroit–Mercy

Keith O. Berry
Oklahoma State University

William Bitner
Alvin Community College

Neal Boehnke
Jacksonville University

Simon Bott
University of North Texas

Donald Brandvold
New Mexico Institute of Mining and Technology

Timothy Brewer
Eastern Michigan University

Brian P. Buffin
University of Michigan, Flint

Robert F. Bryan
University of Virginia

Steven W. Buckner
Columbus State University

C. Eugene Burchill
University of Manitoba

Barbara A. Burke
California State Polytechnic University-Pomona

Jerry Burns
Pellissippi State Technical College

Jidhyt Burstyn
University of Wisconsin

Sheila Cancella
Raritan Valley Community College

Deborah Carey
Stark Learning Center

Tara S. Carpenter
University of Maryland, Baltimore County

Charles Carraher
Florida Atlantic University

Jefferson D. Cavalieri
Dutchess Community College

Laura Chaudhury
Broward Community College

Michael Chetcuti
University of Notre Dame

Ronald J. Clark
Florida State University

Wendy Clevenger
University of Tennessee at Chattanooga

Paul S. Cohen
The College of New Jersey

Kathleen Crago
Loyola University

Jason D'Acchioli
University of Wisconsin, Stevens Point

Henry Daley
Bridgewater State College

Diana Daniel
General Motors Institute

John E. Davidson
Eastern Kentucky University

William Davies
Emporia State University

William Deese
Louisiana Tech University

David F. Dever
Macon College

Gregg R. Diekmann
University of Texas at Dallas

Bonnie Dixon
University of Maryland

David Dobberpuhl
Creighton University

Joseph Dreisbach
University of Scranton

Barbara Drescher
Middlesex County College

Wendy Elcesser
Indiana University of Pennsylvania

William B. Euler
University of Rhode Island

James Farrar
University of Rochester

Dongling Fei
Manatee Community College

John H. Forsberg
St. Louis University

David Frank
Ferris State University

Donna Jean A. Fredeen
Southern Connecticut State University

Donna Friedman
Florrisant Valley Community College

Linda Galang
Madison Area Technical College

Ronald A. Garber
California State University, Long Beach

Paul Gaus
College of Wooster

John I. Gelder
Oklahoma State University

Jim Giles
Mesa Community College

David B. Green
Pepperdine University

Thomas Greenbowe
Iowa State University

Tammy S. Gummersheimer
Schenectady County Community College

Michael Guttman
Miami-Dade Community College

Peter Hambright
Howard University

Paul Hanson
University of New Orleans

Henry Harris
Armstrong State College

Mark Harris
Lebanon Valley College

Daniel T. Haworth
Marquette University

Harlon J. Hawthorne
Broward Community College

Sherell Hickman
Brevard Community College

Craig Hoag
SUNY Plattsburgh

Carl A. Hoeger
University of California, San Diego

Jason Hofstein
Sienna College

Paul A. Horton
Indian River Community College

Thomas Huang
East Tennessee State University

Dan Huchital
Florida Atlantic University

Alison Hyslop
St. John's University

Peter Iyere
Tennessee State University

Denley Jacobson
Purdue University

Andrew Jorgensen
University of Toledo

George Kaminski
Central Michigan University

Wendy L. Keeney-Kennicutt
Texas A & M University

Janice Kelland
Memorial University of Newfoundland

Henry C. Kelly
Texas Christian University

Reynold Kero
Saddleback College

Ernest Kho
University of Hawaii-Hilo

Laura Kibler-Herzog
Georgia State University

Louis Kirschenbaum
University of Rhode Island

Nina Klein
Montana Tech

Larry Krannich
University of Alabama-Birmingham

Robert M. Kren
University of Michigan-Flint

Chandrika Kulatilleke
Baruch College

Russell D. Larsen
Texas Technical University

Gerald Lesley
Southern Connecticut State University

Melvin Lesley
Southern Connecticut University

Shari J. Lillard
California State University, Northridge

Patrick Lloyd
Kingsborough Community College

Ken Loach
SUNY-Plattsburgh

Glen Loppnow
University of Alberta

Steve Lower-Simon
Fraser University

Sunil Malapati
Ferris State University

David Marten
Westmont College

Barbara McGoldrick
Union County College

Cathy MacGowan
Armstrong Atlanta State University

Garrett J. McGowan
Alfred University

Michael McIntire
University of Wisconsin, Green Bay

Sara Leslie McIntosh
Rensselaer Polytechnic Institute

Jeanette Medina
SUNY-Geneseo

William A. Meena
Rock Valley College

Patrick Meyer
Grand Valley State University

Stephen Mezyk
California State, Long Beach

Jalal U. Mondal
University of Texas, Pan American

Chad Morris
University of Vermont

Barbara Mowery
Thomas Nelson Community College

Patricia Moyer
Phoenix College

Nancy Mullins
Florida Community College, Jacksonville

Robert Nakon
West Virginia University

Alex Nazarenko
Buffalo State University

Edward Neth
University of Connecticut

Anne-Marie Nickel
Milwaukee School of Engineering

James Niewahner
Northern Kentucky University

Brian Nordstrom
Embry-Riddle Aeronautical University

Sabrina Godfrey Novick
Hofstra University

Robert H. Paine
Rochester Institute of Technology

Naresh Pandya
Kapiolani Community College

Cynthia Peck
Delta College

Lee Pedersen
University of North Carolina, Chapel Hill

James Penner Hahn
University of Michigan

Les Pesterfield
Western Kentucky University

Giuseppe Petrucci
University of Vermont

Casey Raymond
SUNY Oswego

Jason Ribbett
Ball State University

Michelle Richards-Babb
West Virginia University

Nina Rokainen
Benedictine University

Richard J. Rosso
St. John's University

Alan Sadurski
Ohio Northern University

Jerry L. Sarquis
Miami University

Lisa Seagraves
Broward Community College

Paula Secondo
Western Connecticut State University

Ronald See
St. Louis University

Karl Seff
University of Hawaii

Edward Senkbeil
Salisbury State University

Venkatesh Shanbhag
Mississippi State University

Ralph W. Sheets
Southwest Missouri State University

John Sheriden
Rutgers University – Newark

David Shinn
University of Hawaii

Anton Shurpik
U.S. Merchant Marine Academy

John W. Sibert
University of Texas at Dallas

Reuben Simoyi
West Virginia University

Mary Sohn
Florida Institute of Technology

Thomas E. Sorensen
University of Wisconsin, Milwaukee

S. Paul Steed
Sacramento City College

Darel Straub
University of Pittsburgh

Agnes Tenney
University of Portland

Wayne Tikkanen
California State, Los Angeles

Roselin Wagner
Hofstra University

David White
State University of New York, New Paltz

S.D. Worley
Auburn University

Warren Yeakel
Henry Ford Community College

David Young
Ohio University

Jose Zambrana
Queens College

E. Peter Zurbach
St. Joseph's University

The college level course in chemistry that you are about to begin will be one of the most challenging in your academic career. Successfully meeting this challenge will have its own rewards. One of these rewards is that you will have earned an essential foundation for any one of a large selection of technical career paths including art conservation, basic chemical research, environmental science, medicine, and veterinary science. Another will be the confidence you gain as you understand the chemical world around you and learn how you can make informed decisions. Finally, the discipline you gain in the study of chemistry, regular reading before class, working problems in a logical manner and thinking through the larger concepts, will carry over and have a positive effect on all of your studies and beyond. Let's take a look at some of the specific attributes of this book so that you can utilize them fully.

THE LANGUAGE OF CHEMISTRY

Every job description, from plumber to pharmacist, comes with its own vocabulary that helps the practitioner communicate with colleagues quickly and efficiently. Chemistry is no different. There is a large body of new words and phrases that need to be remembered. This will make it easier to learn the concepts of chemistry. To help all users of the text, even those who have never had a previous chemistry course, we highlight in bold text the first appearance of all new terms. These terms are defined in the glossary and can be accessed on-line by clicking on the word or phrase. Looking up a term in the glossary will lead you to the section(s) that use the term in a significant way. Learning the vocabulary of chemistry and using it appropriately is an important step in understanding and applying the ideas and concepts of this fundamental science.

PROBLEM SOLVING REINFORCES CONCEPTS

You may hear that chemistry involves solving many problems, and that is true. The reason for all of the problem solving is that chemistry is built on certain fundamental concepts describing how the physical world works. Problems are designed to reinforce these concepts and to illustrate how, in many instances, several concepts can be combined to obtain useful results. As a modern student you have a calculator and access to a computer to do mathematical calculations. Some of these take mere seconds to perform compared to hours that students previously spent on the same calculations. This just emphasizes the fact that problem solving in chemistry is NOT just mathematical calculation. In fact, we present the calculation part of a problem as a small segment of an overall thought process.

The thought process involves three steps, ***analysis, solution,*** and deciding ***is the answer reasonable?***. The first step is an ***analysis*** of the problem. What specifically does the problem ask us to do? What concepts and laws are involved in the question? If a calculation is involved, what data is given, and where can additional facts be found? What tools for problem solving have we learned that can help us? What sequence of logical steps are needed for our calculation? Then there is the ***solution*** step, where the information in the analysis step is put together in a logical fashion to develop an answer. A reasoned solution includes understanding how you arrived at the answer. For math problems it includes the correct use of significant figures. Finally, it is important to ask ***is the answer reasonable?*** By the time you finish with the solution, it is a natural tendency to feel that the problem is finished. However, if you start with one drop of reactant and end up with a swimming pool of product, something is obviously wrong. That is a much different error from one where you calculate 2.65 g of product and the actual answer is 2.68 g. Each problem in this book illustrates how you can check your answers to avoid large errors that will take you off course. We provide a variety of ways to check your answers as illustrations throughout the book so that you can see which method might be best for you. The three-step method of *analysis, solution,* and *is the answer reasonable?* works well in chemistry and also in many other subjects.

TOOLS FOR PROBLEM SOLVING

Earlier we mentioned that within the plumbing profession there is a specialized vocabulary. Plumbers also have specialized tools used to perform their jobs. In developing proficiency in their craft, the professional plumber must learn to use the proper tool for the job at hand. We can visualize the concepts, laws, and equivalencies of chemistry as tools to do our job of solving problems.

Throughout this book we point out (with a tool symbol as shown in the margin) the tools that should be thoroughly understood in order to solve problems. These tools will be especially helpful for problems within the chapter and will often pop up again in additional problems in the rest of the book. To help with the tools, we collect them at the end of each chapter so you can review them quickly to determine which tools will apply to your problem. If you don't find a tool in a chapter, look in previous chapters. We have made a special effort to never ask questions before you have all of the needed information to solve the problem.

We place special emphasis on problem solving in this text. Along with laboratory work, it is the preferred method for learning and applying the concepts of chemistry. By applying concepts to a variety of situations and often combining two or more concepts in a single problem we see the true richness of the science of chemistry.

Problem solving is a skill that needs to be developed in a logical progression. Each chapter has many *Examples* that give detailed solutions using our three-step process. Often, the step-by-step algebraic process is given and the cancellation of units is clearly shown in color. Immediately after the examples are the *Practice Exercises.* These reinforce the just-solved example and the first practice exercise usually includes a hint to help you get started. You will find answers to all the Practice Exercises in Appendix B at the back of the book. Finally, we have the end-of-chapter *Questions, Problems, and Exercises.* The questions often ask non-numerical questions about the material in the chapter. The problems tend to be numerical and they are presented in pairs of similar problems, one of which has the answer in Appendix B. Finally, the exercises present more difficult problems and open-ended *Critical Thinking* questions that often require use of reference material outside this book or on the internet.

Certain end-of-chapter problems are designated with an asterisk (*) to indicate that they are more difficult. Other questions have the symbol **ILW**, indicating that they are available as an Interactive Learningware problem, which can be analyzed and solved on-line within a stepped-out tutorial. Other questions are marked with the symbol **OH**, to indicate that they are available with an Office Hours video to help guide you through the problem. Within Office Hours, problems are solved by an instructor giving details and insights that are not possible in the printed text. Finally, we hope that your instructor will set up on-line problem sets using the WileyPlus with CATALYST system. Here you will be able to solve end-of-chapter problems and get instant feedback on whether or not your answers are correct. Problem-solving assistance and support is available with each question. With WileyPlus with CATALYST, you will be able to test your problem-solving skills by tackling a variety of unique questions each time you access the system.

FACETS OF CHEMISTRY

BRIEF CONTENTS

CONTENTS

1 FUNDAMENTAL CONCEPTS AND UNITS OF MEASUREMENT

Mike Peterson #54 of the Jacksonville Jaguars sacks Houston quarterback David Carr #8. Athletes such as these find their sports safer than ever before thanks to high tech materials made possible through chemical research. Most of the materials used in their uniforms, helmets, and protective pads do not occur naturally in our world and would not exist without discoveries made by observant chemists. The fruits of chemical science touch all our lives every day in ways most of us rarely think of. (Lisa Blumenfeld/ Getty Images/NewsCom.)

CHAPTER OUTLINE

1.1 Chemistry is important for anyone studying the sciences

1.2 The scientific method helps us build models of nature

1.3 Matter is composed of elements, compounds, and mixtures

1.4 Properties of matter can be classified in different ways

1.5 Measurements are essential to describe properties

1.6 Measurements always contain some uncertainty

1.7 Units can be converted using the factor-label method

1.8 Density is a useful intensive property

Chemistry is a science that has impacted every aspect of our lives. We have come to take for granted so many of the materials, discovered by chemists, that make us comfortable, provide for our entertainment, and ensure that the foods we place on our tables are fresh and wholesome. Most of the medicines to cure disease and relieve pain, and nearly all of the objects used by doctors in hospitals, would not exist if chemists had not synthesized the materials from which they are made. As we guide you through the study of chemistry, we will provide numerous examples of how this subject relates to the world in which we live. Our aim is to give you an appreciation of the significant role that chemistry plays in modern society.

This chapter has three principal goals. The first is to provide you with an appreciation of the central role that chemistry plays among the sciences. The second is to have you understand the way scientists approach the study of nature and how they construct mental pictures of the microscopic world to explain the results of experimental observations. And third, we will begin to discuss the principal substances that serve as building blocks for all the materials we encounter in our daily lives.

If you've had a prior course in chemistry, perhaps in high school, you're likely to be familiar with many of the topics that we cover in this chapter. Nevertheless, it is important to be sure you have a mastery of these subjects, because if you don't start this course with a firm understanding of the basics, you may find yourself in trouble later on.

1.1 | CHEMISTRY IS IMPORTANT FOR ANYONE STUDYING THE SCIENCES

☐ In our discussions, we do not assume that you have had a prior course in chemistry. However, we do urge you to study this chapter thoroughly, because the concepts developed here will be used in later chapters.

Chemistry[1] is the study of the composition and properties of matter, which includes all of the chemicals that make up tangible things, from rocks to people to pizza. Chemists search for answers to fundamental questions about the effect of a substance's composition on its properties. They also seek to learn the way substances change, often dramatically, when they interact with each other in *chemical reactions*. And permeating all of this is a search for knowledge about the basic underlying structure of matter and the forces that determine the properties we observe through our senses. From these studies has come the ability to create materials never before found on earth, materials with especially desirable properties that fulfill specific needs of society. This knowledge has also enabled biologists to develop a fundamental understanding of many of the processes taking place in living organisms.

Although you may not plan to be a chemist, some knowledge of chemistry will surely be valuable to you. In fact, the involvement of chemistry among the various branches of science is evidenced by the names of some of the divisions of the American Chemical Society, the largest scientific organization in the world (see Table 1.1).

TABLE 1.1	Names of Some of the Divisions of the American Chemical Society
Agricultural & Food Chemistry	Computers in Chemistry
Agrochemicals	Environmental Chemistry
Biochemical Technology	Fuel Chemistry
Biological Chemistry	Geochemistry
Business Development & Management	Industrial & Engineering Chemistry
Carbohydrate Chemistry	Medicinal Chemistry
Cellulose and Renewable Materials	Nuclear Chemistry & Technology
Chemical Health & Safety	Petroleum Chemistry
Chemical Toxicology	Polymer Chemistry
Chemistry & the Law	Polymeric Materials: Science & Engineering
Colloid & Surface Chemistry	Rubber

[1] Important terms will be set in bold type to call them to your attention. Be sure you learn their meanings.

1.2 | THE SCIENTIFIC METHOD HELPS US BUILD MODELS OF NATURE

Scientists who work in university, industrial, and government laboratories follow a general approach to their work called the **scientific method.** In very simple terms, it is a cyclical process in which we gather and assemble information about nature, formulate explanations for what we've observed, and then test the explanations with new experiments.

In the sciences, we usually gather information by performing experiments in laboratories under controlled conditions so observations we make are reproducible (Figure 1.1). An **observation** *is a statement that accurately describes something we see, hear, taste, feel, or smell.*

Observations gathered during an experiment often lead us to make conclusions. A **conclusion** *is a statement that's based on what we think about a series of observations.* For example, consider the following statements about the fermentation of grape juice to make wine:

1. Before fermentation, grape juice is very sweet and contains no alcohol.
2. After fermentation, the grape juice is no longer as sweet and it contains a great deal of alcohol.
3. In fermentation, sugar is converted into alcohol.

Statements 1 and 2 are observations because they describe properties of the grape juice that can be tasted and smelled. Statement 3 is a conclusion because it *interprets* the observations that are available.

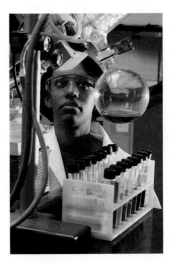

FIG. 1.1 A scientist working in a chemical research laboratory. Reproducible conditions in a laboratory permit experiments to yield reliable results. *(Index Stock.)*

Experimental observations lead to scientific laws

Observations we make while performing experiments are referred to as **data.** For example, if we study the behavior of gases, such as the air we breathe, we soon discover that the volume of a gas depends on a number of factors, including the mass of the gas, its temperature, and its pressure. The observations we record relating these factors are our data.

One of the goals of science is to organize facts so that relationships or generalizations among the data can be established. For instance, one generalization we would make from our observations is that when the temperature of a gas is held constant, squeezing the gas into half its original volume causes the pressure of the gas to double. If we were to repeat our experiments many times with numerous different gases, we would find that this generalization is uniformly applicable to all of them. Such a broad generalization, based on the results of many experiments, is called a **law** or **scientific law.**

We often express laws in the form of mathematical equations. For example, if we represent the pressure of a gas by the symbol P and its volume by V, the inverse relationship between pressure and volume can be written as

$$P = \frac{C}{V}$$

where C is a proportionality constant. (We will discuss gases and the laws relating to them in greater detail in Chapter 10.)

☐ We would say that the pressure of the gas is inversely proportional to its volume; the smaller the volume, the larger the pressure.

Hypotheses and theories are models of nature

As useful as they may be, laws only state what happens; they do not provide explanations. *Why,* for example, are gases so easily compressed to a smaller volume? More specifically, *what must gases be like at the most basic, elementary level for them to behave as they do*? Answering such questions when they first arise is no simple task and requires much speculation. But over time scientists build mental pictures, called **theoretical models,** that enable them to explain observed laws.

In the development of a theoretical model, researchers form tentative explanations called **hypotheses** (Figure 1.2). They then perform experiments that test predictions derived from the model. Sometimes the results show the model is wrong. When this happens, the model must be abandoned or modified to account for the new data. Eventually, if the model

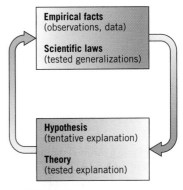

FIG. 1.2 The scientific method is cyclical. Observations suggest explanations, which suggest new experiments, which suggest new explanations, and so on.

survives repeated testing, it achieves the status of a theory. *A* **theory** *is a tested explanation of the behavior of nature.* You should keep in mind, however, that it is impossible to perform every test that might show a theory to be wrong, so we can never prove *absolutely* that a theory is correct.

Science doesn't always proceed in the orderly stepwise fashion described above. Luck sometimes plays an important role. For example, in 1828 Frederick Wöhler, a German chemist, was testing one of his theories and obtained an unexpected material when he heated a substance called ammonium cyanate. Out of curiosity he analyzed it and found it to be urea (a component of urine). This was exciting because it was the first time anyone had knowingly made a substance produced only by living creatures from a chemical not having a life origin. The fact that this could be done led to the beginning of a whole branch of chemistry called *organic chemistry.* Yet, had it not been for Wöhler's curiosity and his application of the scientific method to his unexpected results, the importance of his experiment might have gone unnoticed.

As a final note, it is significant that the most spectacular and dramatic changes in science occur when major theories are proved to be wrong. Although this happens only rarely, when it occurs, scientists are sent scrambling to develop new theories, and exciting new frontiers are opened.

□ Many breakthrough discoveries in science have come about by accident.

The atomic theory is a model of nature

Virtually every scientist would agree that the most significant theoretical model of nature ever formulated is the atomic theory. According to this theory, which we will discuss further in Chapter 2, all chemical substances are composed of tiny particles that we call **atoms.** Individual atoms combine in diverse ways to form more complex particles called **molecules.** Consider, for example, the substance water. Experimental evidence suggests that water molecules are each composed of two atoms of hydrogen and one of oxygen. To aid in our understanding and to help visualize how atoms combine, we often use drawings such as Figure 1.3. According to what we wish to emphasize, a variety of ways are used to describe the structures of molecules, as illustrated in Figure 1.4 for molecules of methane (the combustible fuel in natural gas).

Today we know a great deal about atoms and how they combine to form more complex materials. In coming chapters you will learn how we've come to apply this knowledge to making connections between what we physically observe in our large, *macroscopic* world and what we believe takes place in the tiny, submicroscopic world of atoms and molecules.

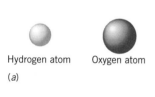

FIG. 1.3 **Atoms combine to form molecules.** Illustrated here is a molecule of water, which consists of one atom of oxygen and two atoms of hydrogen. (*a*) Colored spheres are used to represent individual atoms, white for hydrogen and red for oxygen. (*b*) A drawing that illustrates the shape of a water molecule.

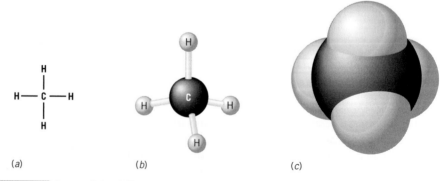

FIG. 1.4 **Some of the different ways that the structures of molecules are represented.** (*a*) A structure using chemical symbols to stand for atoms and dashes to indicate how the atoms are connected to each other. The molecule is methane, the substance present in natural gas that fuels stoves and Bunsen burners. A methane molecule is composed of one atom of carbon (C) and four atoms of hydrogen (H). (*b*) A *ball-and-stick model* of methane. The black ball is the carbon atom and the white balls are hydrogen atoms. (*c*) A *space-filling model* of methane that shows the relative sizes of the C and H atoms. Ball-and-stick and space-filling models are used to illustrate the three-dimensional shapes of molecules.

Learning to appreciate how chemists interpret behavior on a macroscopic level in terms of the composition of substances on an atomic scale should be one of your major goals in studying this course.

☐ Macroscopic refers to objects large enough to be observed with the naked eye. Here we use the term to mean the things we observe with our senses, whether it be in the laboratory or in the world we encounter in our day-to-day living.

1.3 | MATTER IS COMPOSED OF ELEMENTS, COMPOUNDS, AND MIXTURES

Earlier we described chemistry as being concerned with the properties and transformations of matter. **Matter** is *anything that occupies space and has mass.* It is the stuff our universe is made of, and all of the chemicals that make up tangible things, from rocks to pizza to people, are examples of matter.

In this definition, we've used the term *mass* rather than *weight*. The words mass and weight are often used interchangeably even though they refer to different things. **Mass** *refers to how much matter there is in a given object,[2] whereas* **weight** *refers to the force with which the object is attracted by gravity.* For example, a golf ball contains a certain amount of matter and has a certain mass, which is the same regardless of the golf ball's location. However, a golf ball on earth weighs about six times more than on the moon because the gravitational attraction of the earth is six times that of the moon. Because mass does not vary from place to place, we use mass rather than weight when we specify the amount of matter in an object. Mass is measured with an instrument called a balance, which we will discuss in Section 1.5.

Elements cannot be decomposed into simpler substances by chemical reactions

Chemistry is especially concerned with **chemical reactions,** which are *transformations that alter the chemical compositions of substances.* An important type of chemical reaction is **decomposition** in which one substance is changed into two or more others. For example, if we pass electricity through molten (melted) sodium chloride (salt), the silvery metal sodium and the pale green gas, chlorine, are formed. This change has decomposed sodium chloride into two simpler substances. No matter how we try, however, sodium and chlorine cannot be decomposed further by chemical reactions into still simpler substances that can be stored and studied.

In chemistry, *substances that cannot be decomposed into simpler materials by chemical reactions are called* **elements.** Sodium and chlorine are two examples. Others you may be familiar with include iron, aluminum, sulfur, and carbon (as in charcoal). Some elements are gases at room temperature. Examples include chlorine, oxygen, hydrogen, nitrogen, and helium. Elements are the simplest forms of matter that chemists work with directly. All more complex substances are composed of elements in various combinations.

Chemical symbols are used to identify elements

So far, scientists have discovered 90 existing elements in nature and have made 27 more, for a total of 117. Each element is assigned a unique **chemical symbol,** which can be used as an abbreviation for the name of the element. Chemical symbols are also used to stand for atoms of elements when we write *chemical formulas* such as H_2O (water) and CO_2 (carbon dioxide). We will have a lot more to say about formulas later.

In most cases, an element's chemical symbol is formed from one or two letters of its English name. For instance, the symbol for carbon is C, for bromine it is Br, and for silicon it is Si. For some elements, the symbols are derived from the non-English names given to those elements long ago. Table 1.2 contains a list of elements whose symbols come to us in that way.[3] Regardless of the origin of the symbol, the first letter is always capitalized and the second letter, if there is one, is always written lowercase. The names and chemical symbols of the elements are given on the inside front cover of the book.

---

[2] Mass is a measure of an object's momentum, or resistance to a change in motion. Something with a large mass, such as a truck, contains a lot of matter and is difficult to stop once it's moving. An object with less mass, such as a baseball, is much easier to stop.

[3] The symbol for tungsten is W, from the German name *wolfram.* This is the only element whose symbol is neither related to its English name nor derived from its Latin name.

TABLE 1.2		Elements That Have Symbols Derived from Their Latin Names			
Element	Symbol	Latin Name	Element	Symbol	Latin Name
Sodium	Na	Natrium	Gold	Au	Aurum
Potassium	K	Kalium	Mercury	Hg	Hydrargyrum
Iron	Fe	Ferrum	Antimony	Sb	Stibium
Copper	Cu	Cuprum	Tin	Sn	Stannum
Silver	Ag	Argentum	Lead	Pb	Plumbum

Compounds are composed of two or more elements in fixed proportions

By means of chemical reactions, elements combine in various *specific proportions* to give all of the more complex substances in nature. Thus, hydrogen and oxygen combine to form water (H_2O), and sodium and chlorine combine to form sodium chloride (NaCl, common table salt). Water and sodium chloride are examples of compounds. A **compound** *is a substance formed from two or more **different elements** in which the elements are always combined in the same fixed (i.e., constant) proportions by mass.* For example, if any sample of pure water is decomposed, the mass of oxygen obtained is *always* eight times the mass of hydrogen. Similarly, when hydrogen and oxygen react to form water, the mass of oxygen consumed is always eight times the mass of hydrogen, never more and never less.

Mixtures can have variable compositions

Elements and compounds are examples of **pure substances.**[4] The composition of a pure substance is always the same, regardless of its source. Pure substances are rare, however. Usually, we encounter mixtures of compounds or elements. Unlike elements and compounds, **mixtures** *can have variable compositions.* For example, Figure 1.5 shows three mixtures that contain sugar. They have different degrees of sweetness because the amount of sugar in a given size sample varies from one to the other.

Mixtures can be either homogeneous or heterogeneous. A **homogeneous mixture** *has the same properties throughout the sample.* An example is a thoroughly stirred mixture of sugar in water. We call such a homogeneous mixture a **solution.** Solutions need not be liquids, just homogeneous. For example, the alloy used in the U.S. 5 cent coin is a solid solution of copper and nickel, and clean air is a gaseous solution of oxygen, nitrogen, and a number of other gases.

FIG. 1.5 Orange juice, Coca-Cola, and pancake syrup are mixtures that contain sugar. The amount of sugar varies from one to another because mixtures can have variable compositions. *(Thomas Brase/Stone/Getty Images; Andy Washnik; Andy Washnik.)*

[4] We have used the term *substance* rather loosely until now. Strictly speaking, **substance** really means *pure substance.* Each unique chemical element and compound is a *substance;* a mixture consists of two or more substances.

A **heterogeneous mixture** *consists of two or more regions, called* **phases,** *that differ in properties.* A mixture of olive oil and vinegar in a salad dressing, for example, is a two-phase mixture in which the oil floats on the vinegar as a separate layer (Figure 1.6). The phases in a mixture don't have to be chemically different substances like oil and vinegar, however. A mixture of ice and liquid water is a two-phase heterogeneous mixture in which the phases have the same chemical composition but occur in different *physical states* (a term we will discuss further in the next section).

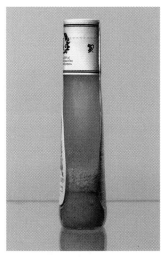

FIG. 1.6 **A heterogeneous mixture.** The salad dressing shown here contains vinegar and vegetable oil (plus assorted other flavorings). Vinegar and oil do not dissolve in each other; instead, they form two layers. The mixture is heterogeneous because each of the separate phases (oil, vinegar, and other solids) has its own set of properties that differ from the properties of the other phases. *(Andy Washnik.)*

(a)   *(b)*

FIG. 1.7 **Formation of a mixture of iron and sulfur.** (*a*) Samples of powdered sulfur and powdered iron. (*b*) A mixture of sulfur and iron is made by stirring the two powders together. *(Michael Watson.)*

The process we use to create a mixture is said to involve a **physical change,** because *no new chemical substances form.* This is illustrated in Figure 1.7 for powdered samples of the elements iron and sulfur. By simply dumping them together and stirring, the mixture forms, but both elements retain their original properties. To separate the mixture, we could similarly use just physical changes. For example, we could remove the iron by stirring the mixture with a magnet—a physical operation. The iron powder sticks to the magnet as we pull it out, leaving the sulfur behind (Figure 1.8). The mixture also could be separated by treating it with a liquid called carbon disulfide, which is able to dissolve the sulfur but not the iron. Filtering the sulfur solution from the solid iron, followed by evaporation of the liquid carbon disulfide from the sulfur solution, gives the original components, iron and sulfur, separated from each other.

The formation of a compound involves a **chemical change** (chemical reaction) because *the chemical makeup of the substances involved are changed.* Iron and sulfur, for example, combine to form a compound often called "fool's gold" because of its appearance (Figure 1.9). In this compound the elements no longer have the same properties they had before they combined, and they cannot be separated by physical means. The decomposition of fool's gold into iron and sulfur is also a chemical reaction.

The relationships among elements, compounds, and mixtures are shown in Figure 1.10.

FIG. 1.8 **Formation of a mixture is a physical change.** Here we see that forming the mixture has not changed the iron and sulfur into a compound of the two elements. The mixture can be separated by pulling the iron out with a magnet. *(Michael Watson.)*

FIG. 1.9 **"Fool's gold."** The mineral pyrite (also called iron pyrite) has an appearance that caused some miners to mistake it for real gold. *(D. Harms/ Peter Arnold, Inc.)*

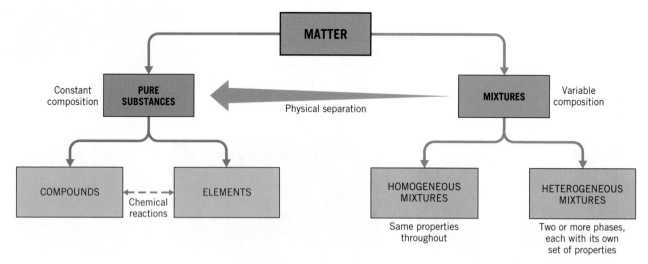

FIG. 1.10 Classification of matter.

PROPERTIES OF MATTER CAN BE CLASSIFIED IN DIFFERENT WAYS

In chemistry we use **properties** (characteristics) of materials to identify them and to distinguish one kind from another. To help organize our thinking, we classify properties into different types.

Properties can be classified as physical or chemical

One way to classify properties is based on whether or not the chemical composition of an object is changed by the act of observing the property. *A* **physical property** *is one that can be observed without changing the chemical makeup of a substance.* For example, a physical property of gold is that it is yellow. The act of observing this property (color) doesn't change the chemical makeup of the gold. Neither does observing that gold conducts electricity, so color and electrical conductivity are physical properties.

Sometimes, observing a physical property does lead to a physical change. To measure the melting point of ice, for example, we observe the temperature at which the solid begins to melt (Figure 1.11). This is a physical change because it does not lead to a change in chemical composition; both ice and liquid water are composed of water molecules.

FIG. 1.11 Liquid water and ice are both composed of water molecules. Melting the ice cube doesn't change the chemical composition of the molecules. *(Susumu Sato/Corbis Images.)*

Solids, liquids, and gases are physical states of matter

Although ice, liquid water, and steam have quite different appearances and physical properties, they are just different forms of the same substance, water. **Solid, liquid,** and **gas** are the most common **states of matter.** As with water, most substances are able to exist in all three of these states, and the state we observe generally depends on the temperature. The obvious properties of solids, liquids, and gases can be interpreted at a submicroscopic level according to the different ways the individual atomic-size particles are organized (Figure 1.12). For a given substance, a change from one state to another is a physical change.

A chemical property describes a chemical change

A **chemical property** *describes a chemical change (chemical reaction) that a substance undergoes.* When a chemical reaction takes place, chemicals interact to form entirely *different* substances with different properties. An example is the rusting of iron, which involves a chemical reaction between iron, oxygen, and water. When the substances react, the product, rust, no longer looks like iron, oxygen, or water. It's a brown solid that isn't at all like a metal and it is not attracted by a magnet (Figure 1.13).

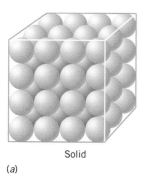 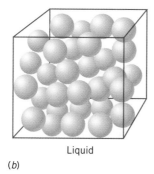 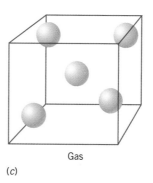

Solid (a) Liquid (b) Gas (c)

FIG. 1.12 Solid, liquid and gaseous states of matter as viewed by the atomic model of matter. (*a*) In a solid, the particles are tightly packed and cannot move easily. (*b*) In a liquid, the particles are still close together but can move past one another. (*c*) In a gas, the particles are far apart with much empty space between them.

The ability of iron to form rust in the presence of oxygen and moisture is a chemical property of iron. When we observe this property, the reaction changes the iron, oxygen, and water into rust, so after we've made the observation we no longer have the same substances as before.

Properties can also be classified as intensive or extensive

Another way of classifying a property is according to whether or not it depends on the size of the sample under study. For example, two different pieces of gold can have different volumes, but both have the same characteristic shiny yellow color and both will begin to melt if heated to the same temperature. Volume is said to be an **extensive property**—*a property that depends on sample size.* Color and melting point (and boiling point, too) are examples of **intensive properties**—*properties that are independent of sample size.*

Some kinds of properties are better than others for identifying substances

A job chemists often perform is *chemical analysis.* They're asked, "What is a particular sample composed of?" To answer such a question, the chemist relies on the properties of the chemicals that make up the sample. For identification purposes, intensive properties are more useful than extensive ones because every sample of a given substance exhibits the same set of intensive properties.

Color, freezing point, and boiling point are examples of intensive physical properties that can help us identify substances. Chemical properties are also intensive properties and also can be used for identification. For example, gold miners were able to distinguish between real gold and fool's gold, a mineral also called pyrite (Figure 1.9, page 7), by heating the material in a flame. Nothing happens to the gold, but the pyrite sputters, smokes, and releases bad-smelling fumes because of its ability, when heated, to react chemically with oxygen in the air.

FIG. 1.13 Chemical reactions cause changes in composition. Here we see a coating of rust that has formed on an iron object. The properties and chemical composition of the rust are entirely different from those of the iron. (*George B. Diebold/ Corbis Images.*)

| 1.5 | **MEASUREMENTS ARE ESSENTIAL TO DESCRIBE PROPERTIES** |

Observations can be qualitative or quantitative

Earlier you learned that an important step in the scientific method is observation. In general, observations fall into two categories, qualitative and quantitative. **Qualitative observations,** such as the color of a chemical or that a mixture becomes hot when a reaction occurs, do not involve numerical information and are usually of limited value. More important are **quantitative observations,** or **measurements,** which do yield numerical data. You make such observations in everyday life, for example, when you glance at your watch, or step onto a bathroom scale. In chemistry, we make various measurements that aid us in describing both chemical and physical properties.

Measurements always include units

Measurements involve numbers, but they differ from the numbers used in mathematics in two crucial ways.

First, measurements always involve a comparison. When you say that a person is six feet tall, you're really saying that the person is six times taller than a reference object that is 1 foot high, where *foot* is an example of a **unit.** Both the number and the unit are essential parts of the measurement, because the unit gives the reported value a sense of size. For example, if you were told that the distance between two points is 25, you would naturally ask "25 what?" The distance could be 25 inches, 25 feet, 25 miles, or 25 of any other unit that's used to express distance. A number without a unit is really meaningless. *Writing down a measurement without a unit is a common and serious mistake, and one you should avoid.*

The second important difference is that measurements always involve uncertainty; they are *inexact.* The act of measurement involves an estimation of one sort or another, and both the observer and the instruments used to make the measurement have inherent physical limitations. As a result, measurements always include some uncertainty, which can be minimized but never entirely eliminated. We will say more about this topic in Section 1.6.

SI units are standard in science

A standard system of units is essential if measurements are to be made consistently. In the sciences, and in every industrialized nation on earth, metric-based units are used. The advantage of working with metric units is that converting to larger or smaller units can be done simply by moving a decimal point, because metric units are related to each other by simple multiples of ten.

In 1960, a simplification of the original metric system was adopted by the General Conference on Weights and Measures (an international body). It is called the **International System of Units,** abbreviated **SI** from the French name, *Le Système International d'Unités.* The SI is now the dominant system of units in science and engineering, although there is still some usage of older metric units.

The SI has as its foundation a set of **base units** (Table 1.3) for seven measured quantities. For now, we will focus on the base units for length, mass, time, and temperature. We will discuss the unit for amount of substance, the mole, at length in Chapter 3. The unit for electrical current, the ampere, will be discussed briefly when we study electrochemistry in Chapter 19. The unit for luminous intensity, the candela, will not be important to us in this book.

Most of the base units are defined in terms of reproducible physical phenomena. For instance, the meter is defined as exactly the distance light travels in a vacuum in 1/299,792,458 of a second. Everyone has access to this standard because light and a vacuum are available to all. Only the base unit for mass is defined by an object made by human hands—a carefully preserved platinum–iridium alloy block stored at the International Bureau of Weights and Measures in France (Figure 1.14). This block serves indirectly as the calibrating standard for all "weights" used for scales and balances in the world.[5]

FIG. 1.14 The international standard kilogram. This standard for mass in the SI is made of a platinum–iridium alloy and is kept at the International Bureau of Weights and Measures in France. Other nations such as the United States maintain their own standard masses that have been carefully calibrated against this international standard. *(Courtesy Bureau International des Poids et Mesures.)*

TABLE 1.3	The SI Base Units	
Measurement	Unit	Symbol
Length	meter	m
Mass	kilogram	kg
Time	second	s
Electric current	ampere	A
Temperature	kelvin	K
Amount of substance	mole	mol
Luminous intensity	candela	cd

[5] Scientists are working on a method of accurately counting atoms whose masses are accurately known. Their goal is to develop a new definition of the kilogram that doesn't depend on an object that can be stolen, lost, or destroyed.

All SI units are built from the base units

The SI units for *any* physical quantity can be built from these seven base units. For example, there is no SI base unit for area, but we know that to calculate the area of a rectangular room we multiply its length by its width. Therefore, the *unit* for area is derived by multiplying the *unit* for length by the *unit* for width. Length (or width) is a base measured quantity in the SI and has the *meter* (m) as its base unit.

$$\text{length} \times \text{width} = \text{area}$$
$$(\text{meter}) \times (\text{meter}) = (\text{meter})^2$$
$$\text{m} \times \text{m} = \text{m}^2$$

The SI **derived unit** for area is therefore m^2 (read as *meters squared*, or *square meter*).

In deriving SI units, we employ a very important concept that we will use repeatedly throughout this book when we perform calculations: *Units undergo the same kinds of mathematical operations that numbers do.* We will see how this fact can be used to convert from one unit to another in Section 1.7.

EXAMPLE 1.1
Deriving SI Units

Linear momentum is a measure of the "push" a moving object has, equal to the object's mass times its velocity. What is the SI derived unit for linear momentum?

> *A Word about Problem Solving*   This is the first of many encounters you will have with solving problems in chemistry. Helping you learn how to approach and solve problems is one of the major goals of this textbook. We view problem solving as a three-step process. The first step is figuring out what has to be done to solve the problem, which is the function of the *Analysis* step described below. The second is actually performing whatever is required to obtain the answer (the *Solution* step). And finally, we examine the answer to determine whether it seems to be *reasonable*. For more information on the aids that are available to assist you in problem solving, we recommend that you read the "To the Student" section at the beginning of the book.

ANALYSIS: To derive a unit for a quantity we must first express it in terms of simpler quantities. We're told that linear momentum is mass times velocity. Therefore, the SI unit for linear momentum will be the SI unit for mass times the SI unit for velocity. The SI unit for mass is the kilogram (kg). Velocity is distance traveled (length) per unit time, so it has derived SI units of meters per second, m/s. Multiplying these units should give the derived unit for linear momentum.

SOLUTION:

$$\text{mass} \times \text{velocity} = \text{linear momentum}$$
$$\text{mass} \times \text{length/time} = \text{linear momentum}$$
$$\text{kilogram} \times \text{meter/second} = \text{kilogram meter/second}$$
$$\text{kg} \times \text{m/s} = \text{kg m/s}$$

IS THE ANSWER REASONABLE?   *Before leaving a problem, it is always wise to examine the answer to see whether it makes sense.* For numerical calculations, ask yourself, "Is the answer too large, or too small?" Judging the answers to such questions serves as a check on the arithmetic as well as on the method of obtaining the answer and can help you find obvious errors. In this problem, the check is simple. The derived unit for linear momentum should be the product of units for mass and velocity, and this is obviously true. Therefore, our answer is correct.

Practice Exercise 1:[6] The volume of a sphere is given by the formula $V = \frac{4}{3}\pi r^3$, where r is the radius of the sphere. From this equation, determine the SI unit for volume. (Hint: r is a distance, so it must have a distance unit.)

---

[6] Answers to the Practice Exercises are found at the back of the book.

Practice Exercise 2: When you "step hard on the gas" in a car you feel an invisible force pushing you back in your seat. This force equals the product of your mass, m, times the acceleration, a, of the car. In equation form, this is $F = ma$. Acceleration is the change in velocity, v, with time, t:

$$a = \frac{\text{change in } v}{\text{change in } t}$$

Therefore, the units of acceleration are those of velocity divided by time. Velocity is a ratio of distance divided by time, $v = d/t$, so the units of velocity are those of distance divided by time. What is the SI derived unit for force expressed in SI base units?

We can construct SI units of any convenient size using decimal multipliers

Sometimes the basic units are either too large or too small to be used conveniently. For example, the meter is inconvenient for expressing the size of very small things such as bacteria. The SI solves this problem by forming larger or smaller units by applying **decimal multipliers** to the base units. Table 1.4 lists the most commonly used decimal multipliers and the prefixes used to identify them.

When the name of a unit is preceded by one of these prefixes, the size of the unit is modified by the corresponding decimal multiplier. For instance, the prefix *kilo-* indicates a multiplying factor of 10^3, or 1000. Therefore, a *kilo*meter is a unit of length equal to 1000 meters.[7] The symbol for kilometer (km) is formed by applying the symbol meaning kilo (k) as a prefix to the symbol for meter (m). Thus 1 km = 1000 m (or alternatively, 1 km = 10^3 m). Similarly a decimeter (dm) is 1/10 of a meter, so 1 dm = 0.1 m (1 dm = 10^{-1} m).

The symbols and multipliers listed in colored, boldface type in Table 1.4 are the ones most commonly encountered in chemistry.

TOOLS
SI prefixes

TABLE 1.4	Decimal Multipliers That Serve as SI Prefixes[a]			
Prefix	Meaning	Symbol	Multiplication factor (fraction)	Multiplication factor (power of ten)
exa		E		10^{18}
peta		P		10^{15}
tera		T		10^{12}
giga		G		10^{9}
mega	millions of	M	1,000,000	10^{6}
kilo	thousands of	k	1000	10^{3}
hecto		h		10^{2}
deka		da		10^{1}
deci	tenths of	d	0.1	10^{-1}
centi	hundredths of	c	0.01	10^{-2}
milli	thousandths of	m	0.001	10^{-3}
micro	millionths of	μ	0.000001	10^{-6}
nano	billionths of	n	0.000000001	10^{-9}
pico	trillionths of	p	0.000000000001	10^{-12}
femto		f		10^{-15}
atto		a		10^{-18}

[a]Be sure you learn the prefixes shown in bold colored type.

[7] In the sciences, powers of 10 are often used to express large and small numbers. The quantity 10^3 means $10 \times 10 \times 10 = 1000$. Similarly, the quantity $6.5 \times 10^2 = 6.5 \times 100 = 650$. Numbers less than 1 have negative exponents when expressed as powers of 10. Thus, the fraction $\frac{1}{10}$ is expressed as 10^{-1}, so the quantity 10^{-3} means $\frac{1}{10} \times \frac{1}{10} \times \frac{1}{10} = \frac{1}{1000} = 0.001$. A value of $6.5 \times 10^{-3} = 6.5 \times 0.001 = 0.0065$. Numbers written as 6.5×10^2 and 6.5×10^{-3}, with the decimal point between the first and second digit, are said to be expressed in **standard scientific notation.**

Non-SI units are still in common use

Some older metric units that are not part of the SI system are still used in the laboratory and in the scientific literature. Some of these units are listed in Table 1.5; others will be introduced as needed in upcoming chapters.

The United States is the only large nation still using the *English system* of units, which measures distance in inches, feet, and miles; volume in ounces, quarts, and gallons; and mass in ounces and pounds. However, a gradual transition to metric units is occurring. Beverages, food packages, tools, and machine parts are often labeled in both English and metric units (Figure 1.15). Common conversions between the English system and the SI are given in Table 1.6 and inside the rear cover of the book.[8]

355mL   454g   1 liter
454g

FIG. 1.15 Metric units are becoming commonplace on many consumer products. *(Michael Watson.)*

TABLE 1.5	Some Non-SI Metric Units Commonly Used in Chemistry		
Measurement	Name	Symbol	Value in SI units
Length	angstrom	Å	$1\ \text{Å} = 0.1\ \text{nm} = 10^{-10}\ \text{m}$
Mass	atomic mass unit	u (amu)	$1\ \text{u} = 1.66054 \times 10^{-27}\ \text{kg}$, approximately
	metric ton	t	$1\ \text{t} = 10^3\ \text{kg}$
Time	minute	min	$1\ \text{min} = 60\ \text{s}$
	hour	h (hr)	$1\ \text{h} = 60\ \text{min} = 3600\ \text{s}$
Temperature	degree Celsius	°C	Add 273.15 to obtain the Kelvin temperature
Volume	liter	L	$1\ \text{L} = 1000\ \text{cm}^3$

TABLE 1.6	Some Useful Conversions	
Measurement	English to Metric	Metric to English
Length	1 in. = 2.54 cm	1 m = 39.37 in.
	1 yd = 0.9144 m	1 km = 0.6215 mi
	1 mi = 1.609 km	
Mass	1 lb = 453.6 g	1 kg = 2.205 lb
	1 oz = 28.35 g	
Volume	1 gal = 3.785 L	1 L = 1.057 qt
	1 qt = 946.4 mL	
	1 oz (fluid) = 29.6 mL	

We use several common units in laboratory measurements

The most common measurements you will make in the laboratory will be those of length, volume, mass, and temperature.

Length

The SI base unit for length, the **meter (m),** is too large for most laboratory purposes. More convenient units are the **centimeter (cm)** and the **millimeter (mm).** They are related to the meter as follows.

$$1\ \text{cm} = 10^{-2}\ \text{m} = 0.01\ \text{m}$$
$$1\ \text{mm} = 10^{-3}\ \text{m} = 0.001\ \text{m}$$

It is also useful to know the relationships

$$1\ \text{m} = 100\ \text{cm} = 1000\ \text{mm}$$
$$1\ \text{cm} = 10\ \text{mm}$$

TOOLS

Units for laboratory measurements

☐ An older non-SI unit called the angstrom (Å) is often used to describe the dimensions of atomic and molecular sized particles: $1\ \text{Å} = 0.1\ \text{nm} = 10^{-10}\ \text{m}$

---

[8] Originally, these conversions were established by measurement. For example, if a metric ruler is used to measure the length of an inch, it is found that 1 in. equals 2.54 cm. Later, to avoid confusion about the accuracy of such measurements, it was agreed that these relationships would be taken to be exact. For instance, 1 in. is now defined as *exactly* 2.54 cm. Exact relationships also exist for the other quantities, but for simplicity many have been rounded off. For example, 1 lb = 453.59237 g, *exactly*.

FIG. 1.16 Common laboratory glassware used for measuring volumes. Graduated cylinders are used to measure volumes to the nearest milliliter. Precise measurements of volume are made using burets, pipets, and volumetric flasks. *(Andy Washnik.)*

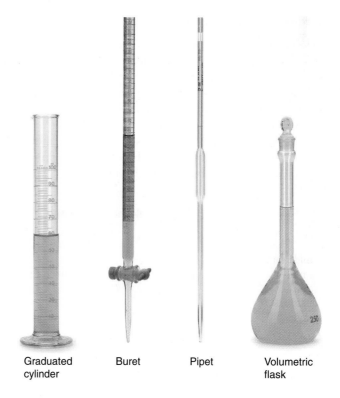

Graduated cylinder   Buret   Pipet   Volumetric flask

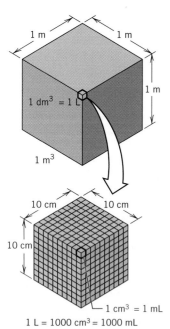

FIG. 1.17 Comparing volume units. A cubic meter (m^3) is approximately equal to a cubic yard, 1000 cm^3 is approximately a quart, and 1 cm^3 is approximately $\frac{1}{30}$ of a fluid ounce.

Volume

Volume is a derived unit with dimensions of (length)^3. With these dimensions expressed in meters, the derived SI unit for volume is the **cubic meter, m^3.**

In chemistry, measurements of volume usually arise when we measure amounts of liquids. The traditional metric unit of volume used for this is the **liter (L).** In SI terms, a liter is defined as exactly 1 cubic decimeter.

$$1 \text{ L} = 1 \text{ dm}^3$$

However, even the liter is too large to conveniently express most volumes measured in the lab. The glassware we normally use, such as that illustrated in Figure 1.16, is marked in **milliliters (mL).**[9]

$$1 \text{ L} = 1000 \text{ mL}$$

Because 1 dm = 10 cm, then 1 dm^3 = 1000 cm^3. Therefore, 1 mL is exactly the same as 1 cm^3.

$$1 \text{ cm}^3 = 1 \text{ mL}$$
$$1 \text{ L} = 1000 \text{ cm}^3 = 1000 \text{ mL}$$

Sometimes you may see cm^3 abbreviated cc (especially in medical applications), although the SI frowns on this symbol. Figure 1.17 compares the cubic meter, liter, and milliliter.

Mass

In the SI, the base unit for mass is the **kilogram (kg),** although the **gram (g)** is a more conveniently sized unit for most laboratory measurements. One gram, of course, is $\frac{1}{1000}$ of a kilogram (1 kilogram = 1000 g, so 1 g must equal 0.001 kg).

Mass is measured by comparing the weight of a sample with the weights of known standard masses. The operation is called **weighing,** and the apparatus used is called a **balance** (Figure 1.18). For the balance in Figure 1.18*a*, we would place our sample on the left pan and then add standard masses to the other. When the weight of the sample and the total weight of the standards are in balance (when they match), their masses are then equal. Figure 1.19 gives the masses of some common objects in SI units.

[9] Use of the abbreviations L for liter and mL for milliliter is rather recent. Confusion between the printed letter l and the number 1 prompted the change from l for liter and ml for milliliter. You may encounter the abbreviation ml in other books or on older laboratory glassware.

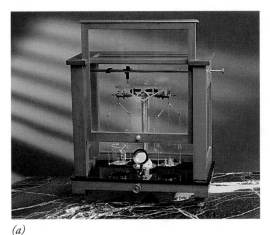

(a)

(b)

(c)

FIG. 1.18 **Typical laboratory balances.** (*a*) A traditional two-pan analytical balance capable of measurements to the nearest 0.0001 g. (*b*) A modern top-loading balance capable of mass measurements to the nearest 0.001 g (fitted with a cover to reduce the effects of air currents and thereby improve precision). (*c*) A modern analytical balance capable of measurements to the nearest 0.0001 g. *(Michael Watson; Courtesy Central Scientific Co.; Courtesy Cole-Parmer Instrument Co.)*

Paper clip  0.4 g

Penny  3.1 g

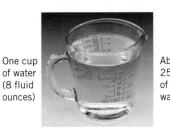

One cup of water (8 fluid ounces)

About 250 g of water

A 220 lb football player

100 kg

FIG. 1.19 Masses of several common objects in metric and English units.
(Coco McCoy/Rainbow; Coco McCoy/Rainbow; Andy Washnik; Jim Cummins/Taxi/Getty Images.)

Temperature

Temperature is usually measured with a thermometer (Figure 1.20). Thermometers are graduated in *degrees* according to one of two temperature scales. Both scales use as reference

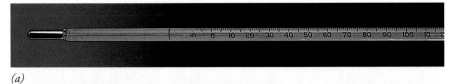

(a)

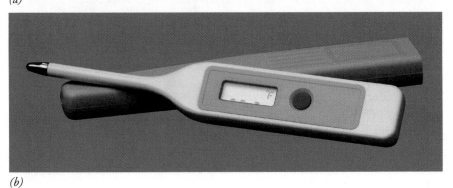

(b)

FIG. 1.20 Typical laboratory thermometers. (*a*) A traditional mercury thermometer. (*b*) An electronic thermometer. *(Michael Watson/ Corbis Images.)*

□ In chemistry, reference data are commonly tabulated at 25 °C, which is close to room temperature. Biologists often carry out their experiments at 37 °C because that is normal human body temperature.

TOOLS
Celsius to Fahrenheit conversions

□ We will use a capital T to stand for the Kelvin temperature and a lowercase t (as in t_C) to stand for the Celsius temperature. This conforms to usage described by the International Bureau of Weights and Measures in Sèvres, France, and the National Institute of Standards and Technology (NIST) in Gaithersburg, MD.

points the temperature at which water freezes[10] and the temperature at which it boils. On the **Fahrenheit scale** water freezes at 32 °F and boils at 212 °F. If you've been raised in the United States, this is probably the scale you're most familiar with. In recent times, however, you have probably noticed an increased use of the Celsius scale, especially in weather broadcasts. This is the scale we use most often in the sciences. On the **Celsius scale** water freezes at 0 °C and boils at 100 °C. (See Figure 1.21.)

As you can see in Figure 1.21, on the Celsius scale there are 100 degree units between the freezing and boiling points of water, while on the Fahrenheit scale this same temperature range is spanned by 180 degree units. Consequently, 5 Celsius degrees are the same as 9 Fahrenheit degrees. We can use the following equation as a tool to convert between these temperature scales.

$$t_F = \left(\frac{9\ °F}{5\ °C}\right)t_C + 32\ °F \tag{1.1}$$

In this equation, t_F is the Fahrenheit temperature and t_C is the Celsius temperature. As noted earlier, units behave like numbers in calculations, and we see in Equation 1.1 that °C "cancels out" to leave only °F. The 32 °F is added to account for the fact that the freezing point of water (0 °C) occurs at 32 °F on the Fahrenheit scale. Equation 1.1 can easily be rearranged to permit calculating °C from °F.

The SI unit of temperature is the **kelvin (K),** which is the degree unit on the **Kelvin temperature scale.** Notice that the temperature unit is K, not °K (the degree symbol, °, is omitted). Also notice that the name of the unit, kelvin, is not capitalized. Equations that include temperature as a variable sometimes take on a simpler form when Kelvin temperatures are used. We will encounter this situation many times throughout the book.

□ The name of the temperature scale, the Kelvin scale, is capitalized, but the name of the unit, the kelvin, is not. However, the symbol for the kelvin is the capital letter K.

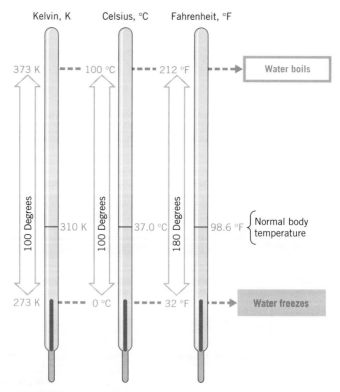

FIG. 1.21 Comparison among Kelvin, Celsius, and Fahrenheit temperature scales.

[10] Water freezes and ice melts at the same temperature, and a mixture of ice and liquid water will maintain a constant temperature of 32 °F or 0 °C. If heat is added, some ice melts; if heat is removed, some liquid water freezes, but the temperature doesn't change. This constancy of temperature is what makes the "ice point" convenient for calibrating thermometers.

Figure 1.21 shows how the Kelvin, Celsius, and Fahrenheit temperature scales relate to each other. Notice that the kelvin is *exactly* the same size as the Celsius degree. *The only difference between these two temperature scales is the zero point.* The zero point on the Kelvin scale is called **absolute zero** and corresponds to nature's coldest temperature. It is 273.15 degree units below the zero point on the Celsius scale, which means that 0 °C equals 273.15 K, and 0 K equals −273.15 °C. Thermometers are never marked with the Kelvin scale, so to convert from Celsius to Kelvin temperatures the following equation applies.

$$T_K = (t_C + 273.15\ °C)\left(\frac{1\ K}{1\ °C}\right) \qquad (1.2)$$

TOOLS
Celsius to Kelvin conversions

This amounts to simply adding 273.15 to the Celsius temperature to obtain the Kelvin temperature. Often we are given Celsius temperatures rounded to the nearest degree, in which case we round 273.15 to 273. Thus, 25 °C equals (25 + 273) K or 298 K.

EXAMPLE 1.2
Converting among
Temperature Scales

Thermal pollution, the release of large amounts of heat into rivers and other bodies of water, is a serious problem near power plants and can affect the survival of some species of fish. For example, trout will die if the temperature of the water rises above approximately 25 °C. (a) What is this temperature in °F? (b) Rounded to the nearest whole degree unit, what is this temperature in kelvins?

ANALYSIS: *Usually, the first job in solving a problem is determining which tools are required to do the work.* Both parts of the problem here deal with temperature conversions. Therefore, we ask ourselves, "What tools do we have that relate temperature scales to each other?" Let's write them:

Equation 1.1 $$t_F = \left(\frac{9\ °F}{5\ °C}\right) t_C + 32\ °F$$

Equation 1.2 $$T_K = (t_C + 273.15\ °C)\left(\frac{1\ K}{1\ °C}\right)$$

Equation 1.1 relates Fahrenheit temperatures to Celsius temperatures, so this is the tool we need to answer part (a). Equation 1.2 relates Kelvin temperatures to Celsius temperatures, and this is the tool we need for part (b). Now that we have what we need, the rest follows.

SOLUTION:

(*a*) We substitute the value of the Celsius temperature (25 °C) for t_C.

$$t_F = \left(\frac{9\ °F}{5\ °C}\right)(25\ °C) + 32\ °F$$
$$= 77\ °F$$

Therefore, 25 °C = 77 °F. (Notice that we have canceled the unit °C in the equation above. As noted earlier, units behave the same as numbers do in calculations.)

(*b*) Once again, we have a simple substitution. Since $t_C = 25\ °C$, the Kelvin temperature (rounded) is

$$T_K = (25\ °C + 273\ °C)\left(\frac{1\ K}{1\ °C}\right)$$

$$= 298\ °C\left(\frac{1\ K}{1\ °C}\right) = 298\ K$$

Thus, 25 °C = 298 K.

ARE THE ANSWERS REASONABLE? For part (a), we know that a Fahrenheit degree is about half the size of a Celsius degree, so 25 Celsius degrees should be about 50 Fahrenheit degrees. The positive value for the Celsius temperature tells us we have a temperature *above* the freezing point of water. Since water freezes at 32 °F, the Fahrenheit temperature should be approximately 32 °F + 50 °F = 82 °F. The answer of 77 °F is quite close.

For part (b), we recall that 0 °C = 273 K. A temperature above 0 °C must be higher than 273 K. Our calculation, therefore, appears to be correct.

Practice Exercise 3: What Fahrenheit temperature corresponds to a Celsius temperature of 86 °C? (Hint: What tool relates the two temperature scales?)

Practice Exercise 4: What Celsius temperature corresponds to 50 °F? What Kelvin temperature corresponds to 68 °F (expressed to the nearest whole kelvin unit)?

1.6 | MEASUREMENTS ALWAYS CONTAIN SOME UNCERTAINTY

We noted in the preceding section that measurements are inexact; they contain **uncertainties** (also called **errors**). One source of uncertainty is associated with limitations in our ability to read the scale of the measuring instrument. Uncontrollably changing conditions at the time of the measurement can also cause errors that are more important than scale reading errors. For example, if you are measuring a length of wire with a ruler, you may not be holding the wire perfectly straight every time.

If we were to take an enormous number of measurements using appropriately adjusted instruments, statistically half of the measurements should be larger and half smaller than the true value of the measured quantity. And, in fact, we do observe that a series of measurements tend to cluster around some central value, which we generally assume is close to the true value. We can estimate the central value quite simply by reporting the **average,** or **mean,** of the series of measurements. This is done by summing the measurements and then dividing by the number of measurements we made. Although making repeated measurements is tedious, the more measurements we make, the more confident we can be that the average is close to the true value that all measurements would be grouped around.

Uncertainties in measurements are a natural part of reading a scale

One kind of error that can't be eliminated arises when we attempt to obtain a measurement by reading the scale on an instrument. Consider, for example, reading the same temperature from each of the two thermometers in Figure 1.22.

The marks on the left thermometer are one degree apart, and we can see that the temperature lies between 24 °C and 25 °C. When reading a scale, we always record the last digit to the nearest tenth of the smallest scale division. Looking closely, therefore, we might estimate that the fluid column falls about 3/10 of the way between the marks for 24 and 25 degrees, so we can report the temperature to be 24.3 °C. However, it would be foolish to say that the temperature is *exactly* 24.3 °C. The last digit is only an estimate, and the left thermometer might be read as 24.2 °C by one observer or 24.4 °C by another. Because different observers might obtain values that differ by 0.1 °C, there is an uncertainty of ±0.1 °C in the measured temperature. We can express this, if we wish, by writing the temperature as 24.3 ± 0.1 °C.

The thermometer on the right has marks that are 1/10 of a degree apart, which allows us to estimate the temperature as 24.32 °C. In this case, we are estimating the hundredths place and the uncertainty is ±0.01 °C. We could write the temperature as 24.32 ± 0.01 °C. Notice that because the thermometer on the right is more finely graduated, we are able to obtain measurements with smaller uncertainties. We would have more confidence in temperatures read from the thermometer on the right in Figure 1.22 because it has more digits and a smaller amount of uncertainty. *The reliability of a piece of data is indicated by the number of digits used to represent it.*

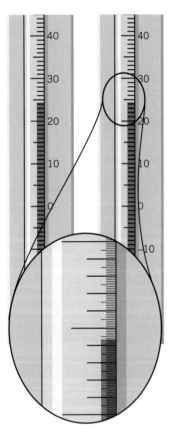

FIG. 1.22 **Thermometers with different scales give readings with different precision.** The thermometer on the left has marks that are one degree apart, allowing the temperature to be estimated to the nearest tenth of a degree. The thermometer on the right has marks every 0.1 °C. This scale permits estimation of the hundredths place.

By convention in science, *all digits in a measurement up to and including the first estimated digit are recorded.* If a reading measured with the thermometer on the right seemed exactly on the 24 °C mark, we would record the temperature as 24.00 °C, not 24 °C, to show that the thermometer can be read to the nearest 1/100 of a degree.

Measurements are written using the significant figures convention

The concepts discussed above are so important that we have special terminology to describe numbers that come from measurements.

> *Digits that result from measurement such that only the digit farthest to the right is not known with certainty are called* **significant figures** *(or* **significant digits***).*

The number of significant figures in a measurement is equal to the number of digits known for sure *plus* one that is estimated. Let's look at our two temperature measurements.

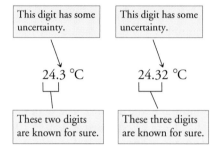

The first measurement, 24.3 °C, has three significant figures; the second, 24.32 °C, has four significant figures.

Accuracy is correctness; precision is reproducibility

Two words often used in reference to measurements are *accuracy* and *precision*. **Accuracy** refers to how close a measurement is to the true or correct value. **Precision** refers to how closely repeated measurements of a quantity come to each other and to the average. Notice that the two terms are not equivalent, because the average doesn't always correspond to the true or correct value. A practical example of how accuracy and precision differ is illustrated in Figure 1.23.

For measurements to be **accurate,** the measuring device must be carefully calibrated (adjusted) so it gives correct values when a standard reference is used with it. For example, to calibrate an electronic balance, a known reference mass is placed on the balance and a calibration routine within the balance is initiated. Once calibrated, the balance will give correct readings, the accuracy of which is determined by the accuracy of the standard mass used. Standard reference masses (also called "weights") can be purchased from scientific supply companies.

Precision refers to how closely repeated measurements of the same quantity come to each other. In general, the smaller the uncertainty (i.e., the "plus or minus" part of the measurement), the more precise the measurement. This translates as: *the more significant figures in a measured quantity, the more precise the measurement.*

We usually assume that a very precise measurement is also of high accuracy. We can be wrong, however, if our instruments are improperly calibrated. For example, the improperly marked ruler in Figure 1.24 might yield measurements which vary by a hundredth of a centimeter (±0.01 cm), but all the measurements would be too large by 1 cm—a case of good precision but poor accuracy.

When are zeros significant digits?

Usually, it is simple to determine the number of significant figures in a measurement; we just count the digits. Thus 3.25 has three significant figures and 56.205 has five of them. When zeros come at the beginning or the end of a number, however, they sometimes cause confusion.

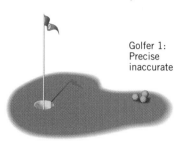

Golfer 1:
Precise
inaccurate

Golfer 2:
Imprecise
inaccurate

Golfer 3:
Accurate
precise

FIG. 1.23 **The difference between precision and accuracy in the game of golf.** Golfer 1 hits shots that are precise (because they are tightly grouped) but the accuracy is poor because the balls are not near the target (the "true" value). Golfer 2 needs help. His shots are neither precise nor accurate. Golfer 3 wins the prize with shots that are precise (tightly grouped) and accurate (in the hole).

How accurate would measurements be with this ruler?

FIG. 1.24 **An improperly marked ruler.** This improperly marked ruler will yield measurements that are each wrong by one whole unit. The measurements might be precise, but the accuracy would be very poor.

TOOLS
Counting significant figures

Zeros to the right of a decimal point are always counted as significant. Thus, 4.500 m has four significant figures because the zeros would not be written unless those digits were known to be zeros.

Zeros to the left of the first nonzero digit are never counted as significant. For instance, a length of 2.3 mm is the same as 0.0023 m. Since we are dealing with the same measured value, its number of significant figures cannot change when we change the units. Both quantities have two significant figures.

Zeros on the end of a number without a decimal point are assumed not to be significant. For example, suppose you were told that a protest march was attended by 45,000 people. If this was just a rough estimate, it might be uncertain by as much as several thousand, in which case the value 45,000 represents just two significant figures, since the "5" is the uncertain digit. None of the zeros would then count as significant figures. On the other hand, suppose the protesters were carefully counted using an aerial photograph, so that the count could be reported to be 45,000 give or take about 100 people. In this case, the value represents 45,000 ± 100 protesters and contains three significant figures, with the uncertain digit being the zero in the hundreds place. So a simple statement such as "there were 45,000 people attending the march" is ambiguous. We can't tell how many significant digits the number has from the number alone. We can be sure that the nonzero digits are significant, though. The best we can do is to say, "45,000 has *at least* two significant figures."

We can avoid confusion by using *scientific notation* when we report a measurement. For example, if we want to report the number of protesters as 45,000 give or take a thousand, we can write the rough estimate as 4.5×10^4. The 4.5 shows the number of significant figures and the 10^4 tells us the location of the decimal. The value obtained from the aerial photograph count, on the other hand, can be expressed as 4.50×10^4. This time the 4.50 shows three significant figures and an uncertainty of ±100 people.

Measurements limit the precision of results calculated from them

When several measurements are obtained in an experiment they are usually combined in some way to calculate a desired quantity. For example, to determine the area of a rectangular carpet we require two measurements, length and width, which are then multiplied to give the answer we want. To get some idea of how precise the area really is, we need a way to take into account the precision of the various values used in the calculation. To make sure this happens, we follow certain rules according to the kinds of arithmetic being performed.

Multiplication and division

Significant figures: multiplication and division

For multiplication and division, the number of significant figures in the answer should not be greater than the number of significant figures in the least precise measurement. Let's look at a typical problem involving some measured quantities.

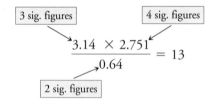

The result displayed on a calculator[11] is 13.49709375. However, the least precise factor, 0.64, has only two significant figures, so the answer should have only two. The correct answer, 13, is obtained by rounding off the calculator answer.[12]

---

[11] Calculators usually give too many significant figures. An exception is when the answer has zeros at the right that are significant figures. For example, an answer of 1.200 would be displayed on most calculators as 1.2. If the zeros belong in the answer, be sure to write them down.

[12] When we wish to round off a number at a certain point, we simply drop the digits that follow if the first of them is less than 5. Thus, 8.1634 rounds to 8.16, if we wish to have only two decimal places. If the first digit after the point of round off is larger than 5, or if it is 5 followed by other nonzero digits, then we add 1 to the preceding digit. Thus 8.167 and 8.1653 both round to 8.17. Finally, when the digit after the point of round off is a 5 and no other digits follow the 5, then we drop the 5 if the preceding digit is even and add 1 if it is odd. Thus, 8.165 rounds to 8.16 and 8.175 rounds to 8.18.

Addition and subtraction

For addition and subtraction, the answer should have the same number of decimal places as the quantity with the fewest number of decimal places. As an example, consider the following addition of measured quantities.

$$
\begin{array}{r}
3.247 \\
41.36 \\
+ \, 125.2 \\
\hline
169.8
\end{array}
$$

+ 125.2 ← (This number has only 1 decimal place.)

169.8 ← (The answer has been rounded to 1 decimal place.)

In this calculation, the digits beneath the 6 and the 7 are unknown; they could be anything. (They're not necessarily zeros because if we *knew* they were zeros, then zeros would have been written there.) Adding an unknown digit to the 6 or 7 will give an answer that's also unknown, so for this sum we are not justified in writing digits in the second and third places after the decimal point. Therefore, we round the answer to the nearest tenth.

Exact numbers contain no uncertainty

Numbers that come from definitions, such as 12 in. = 1 ft, and those that come from a direct count, such as the number of people in a room, have no uncertainty. We can assume that such **exact numbers** have an infinite number of significant figures. Therefore, we ignore exact numbers when applying the rules described above.

Practice Exercise 5: Perform the following calculations involving measurements and round the results so they have the correct number of significant figures and proper units. (Hint: Apply the rules for significant figures described in this section and keep in mind that units behave like numbers do in calculations.)

(a) 21.0233 g + 21.0 g

(b) 10.0324 g/11.7 mL

(c) $\dfrac{14.25 \text{ cm} \times 12.334 \text{ cm}}{(2.223 \text{ cm} - 1.04 \text{ cm})}$

Practice Exercise 6: Perform the following calculations involving measurements and round the results so that they are written to the correct number of significant figures and have the correct units.

(a) 32.02 mL − 2.0 mL

(b) 54.183 g − 0.0278 g

(c) 10.0 g + 1.03 g + 0.243 g

(d) $43.4 \text{ in.} \times \dfrac{1 \text{ ft}}{12 \text{ in.}}$

(e) $\dfrac{1.03 \text{ m} \times 2.074 \text{ m} \times 3.9 \text{ m}}{12.46 \text{ m} + 4.778 \text{ m}}$

1.7 | UNITS CAN BE CONVERTED USING THE FACTOR-LABEL METHOD

After analyzing a problem and assembling the necessary information to solve it, the next step is working the problem to obtain an answer. For numerical problems, scientists usually use a system called the **factor-label method** (also called **dimensional analysis**) to help them perform the correct arithmetic. As you will see, often this method also helps in analyzing the problem and selecting the tools needed to solve it.

In the factor-label method we treat a numerical problem as one involving a conversion of units from one kind to another. To do this we use one or more *conversion factors* to change the units of the given quantity to the units of the answer.

(Given quantity) × (conversion factor) = (desired quantity)

A **conversion factor** *is a fraction formed from a valid relationship or equality between units and is used to switch from one system of measurement and units to another.* To illustrate, suppose we want to express a person's height of 72.0 inches in centimeters. To do this we need the relationship between the inch and the centimeter. We can obtain this from Table 1.6.

$$2.54 \text{ cm} = 1 \text{ in. (exactly)} \qquad (1.3)$$

□ To construct a valid conversion factor, the relationship between the units must be true. For example, the statement

3 ft = 41 in.

is false. Although you might make a conversion factor out of it, any answers you would calculate are sure to be incorrect. *Correct answers require correct relationships between units.*

If we divide both sides of this equation by 1 in., we obtain a conversion factor.

$$\frac{2.54 \text{ cm}}{1 \text{ in.}} = \frac{\cancel{1 \text{ in.}}}{\cancel{1 \text{ in.}}} = 1$$

Notice that we have canceled the units from both the numerator and denominator of the center fraction, leaving the first fraction equaling 1. As mentioned earlier, *units behave just as numbers do in mathematical operations;* this is a key part of the factor-label method. Let's see what happens if we multiply 72.0 inches, the height that we mentioned, by this fraction.

☐ The relationship between the inch and the centimeter is exact, so the numbers in 1 in. = 2.54 cm have an infinite number of significant figures.

$$72.0 \; \cancel{\text{in.}} \times \frac{2.54 \text{ cm}}{1 \; \cancel{\text{in.}}} = 183 \text{ cm}$$

$$\left(\begin{array}{c} \text{given} \\ \text{quantity} \end{array} \right) \times \left(\begin{array}{c} \text{conversion} \\ \text{factor} \end{array} \right) = \left(\begin{array}{c} \text{desired} \\ \text{quantity} \end{array} \right)$$

Because we have multiplied 72.0 in. by something that is equal to 1, we know we haven't changed the magnitude of the person's height. We have, however, changed the units. Notice that we have canceled the unit inches. The only unit left is centimeters, which is the unit we want for the answer. The result, therefore, is the person's height in centimeters.

One of the benefits of the factor-label method is that it often lets you know when you have done the *wrong* arithmetic. From the relationship in Equation 1.3, we can actually construct two conversion factors:

$$\frac{2.54 \text{ cm}}{1 \text{ in.}} \quad \text{and} \quad \frac{1 \text{ in.}}{2.54 \text{ cm}}$$

We used the first one correctly, but what would have happened if we had used the second by mistake?

$$72.0 \text{ in.} \times \frac{1 \text{ in.}}{2.54 \text{ cm}} = 28.3 \text{ in.}^2/\text{cm}$$

In this case, none of the units cancel. We get units of in.^{2}/cm because inches times inches is inches squared. Even though our calculator may be very good at arithmetic, we've got the wrong answer. *The factor-label method lets us know we have the wrong answer because the units are wrong!*

We will use the factor-label method extensively throughout this book to aid us in setting up the proper arithmetic in problems. In fact, we will see that it also helps us assemble the information we need to solve the problem. The following examples illustrate the method.

EXAMPLE 1.3
Applying the Factor-Label Method

Convert 3.25 m to millimeters (mm).

ANALYSIS: To clearly identify the problem, let's write the given quantity (with its units) on the left and the *units* of the desired answer on the right.

$$3.25 \text{ m} = ? \text{ mm}$$

To solve this problem our tool will be a conversion factor that relates the unit meter to the unit millimeter. From the table of decimal multipliers, the prefix "milli" means "$\times 10^{-3}$," so we can write

$$1 \text{ mm} = 10^{-3} \text{ m}$$

Notice that this relationship connects the units given to the units desired.

We now have all the information we need to solve the problem.

SOLUTION: From the relationship above, we can form two conversion factors.

$$\frac{1 \text{ mm}}{10^{-3} \text{ m}} \quad \text{and} \quad \frac{10^{-3} \text{ m}}{1 \text{ mm}}$$

We know we have to cancel the unit meter, so we need to multiply by a conversion factor with this unit in the denominator. Therefore, we select the one on the left as our tool. This gives

$$3.25 \text{ m} \times \frac{1 \text{ mm}}{10^{-3} \text{ m}} = 3.25 \times 10^3 \text{ mm}$$

Notice we have expressed the answer to three significant figures because that is how many there are in the given quantity, 3.25 m.

IS THE ANSWER REASONABLE? We know that millimeters are much smaller than meters, so 3.25 m must represent a lot of millimeters. Our answer, therefore, makes sense.

EXAMPLE 1.4
Applying the Factor-Label Method

A liter, which is slightly larger than a quart, is defined as 1 cubic decimeter (1 dm³). How many liters are there in 1 cubic meter (1 m³)?

ANALYSIS: Let's begin once again by stating the problem in equation form.

$$1 \text{ m}^3 = ? \text{ L}$$

Next, we assemble the tools. What relationships do we know that relate these various units? We are given the relationship between liters and cubic decimeters,

$$1 \text{ L} = 1 \text{ dm}^3 \qquad (1.4)$$

From the table of decimal multipliers, we also know the relationship between decimeters and meters,

$$1 \text{ dm} = 0.1 \text{ m}$$

but we need a relationship between cubic units. Since units undergo the same kinds of operations numbers do, we simply cube each side of this equation (being careful to cube *both* the numbers and the units).

$$(1 \text{ dm})^3 = (0.1 \text{ m})^3$$
$$1 \text{ dm}^3 = 0.001 \text{ m}^3 \qquad (1.5)$$

Notice how Equations 1.4 and 1.5 provide a path from the given units to those we seek. Such a path is always a necessary condition when we apply the factor-label method.

$$\text{m}^3 \xrightarrow[\text{Equation 1.5}]{} \text{dm}^3 \xrightarrow{\text{Equation 1.4}} \text{L}$$

Now we are ready to solve the problem.

SOLUTION: The first step is to eliminate the units m³. We use Equation 1.5.

$$1 \text{ m}^3 \times \frac{1 \text{ dm}^3}{0.001 \text{ m}^3} = 1000 \text{ dm}^3$$

Then we use Equation 1.4 to take us from dm³ to L.

$$1000 \text{ dm}^3 \times \frac{1 \text{ L}}{1 \text{ dm}^3} = 1000 \text{ L}$$

Thus, 1 m³ = 1000 L.

Usually, when a problem involves the use of two or more conversion factors, they can be "strung together" in a "chain calculation" to avoid having to compute intermediate results. For example, this problem can be set up as follows.

$$1 \text{ m}^3 \times \frac{1 \text{ dm}^3}{0.001 \text{ m}^3} \times \frac{1 \text{ L}}{1 \text{ dm}^3} = 1000 \text{ L}$$

IS THE ANSWER REASONABLE?   One liter is about a quart. A cubic meter is about a cubic yard. Therefore, we expect a large number of liters in a cubic meter, so our answer seems reasonable. (Notice here that in our analysis we have approximated the quantities in the calculation in units of quarts and cubic yards, which may be more familiar than liters and cubic meters if you've been raised in the United States. We get a feel for the approximate magnitude of the answer using our familiar units and then relate this to the actual units of the problem.)

EXAMPLE 1.5
Applying the Factor-Label Method

Some mountain climbers are susceptible to high altitude pulmonary edema (HAPE), a life-threatening condition that causes fluid retention in the lungs. It can develop when a person climbs rapidly to heights greater than 2,500 meters (2.5×10^3 m). What is this distance expressed in feet?

ANALYSIS: The problem can be stated as

$$2500 \text{ m} = ? \text{ ft}$$

We are converting a metric unit of length (the meter) into an English unit of length (the foot). The critical link between the two will be a metric-to-English length conversion. One of several sets of tools we can use is

$$1 \text{ cm} = 10^{-2} \text{ m} \qquad \text{(from Table 1.4)}$$
$$1 \text{ in.} = 2.54 \text{ cm} \qquad \text{(from Table 1.6)}$$
$$1 \text{ ft} = 12 \text{ in.}$$

Notice how they provide a path from meters to centimeters to inches to feet.

SOLUTION: Now we apply the factor-label method by eliminating unwanted units to bring us to the units of the answer.

$$2.5 \times 10^3 \text{ m} \times \frac{1 \text{ cm}}{10^{-2} \text{ m}} \times \frac{1 \text{ in.}}{2.54 \text{ cm}} \times \frac{1 \text{ ft}}{12 \text{ in.}} = 8.2 \times 10^3 \text{ ft}$$

Notice that if we were to stop after the first conversion factor, the units of the answer would be centimeters; if we stop after the second, the units would be inches, and after the third we get feet—the units we want. This time the answer has been rounded to two significant figures because that's how many there were in the measured distance. Notice that the numbers 12 and 2.54 do not affect the number of significant figures in the answer because they are exact numbers derived from definitions.

This is not the only way we could have solved this problem. Other sets of conversion factors could have been chosen. For example, we could have used 1 yd = 0.9144 m and 3 ft = 1 yd. Then the problem would have been set up as

$$2500 \text{ m} \times \frac{1 \text{ yd}}{0.9144 \text{ m}} \times \frac{3 \text{ ft}}{1 \text{ yd}} = 8200 \text{ ft} \qquad \text{(rounded correctly)}$$

Many problems that you meet, just like this one, have more than one path to the answer. There isn't necessarily any *one* correct way to set up the solution. *The important thing is for you to be able to reason your way through a problem and find some set of relationships that can take you from the given information to the answer.* The factor-label method can help you search for these relationships if you keep in mind the units that must be eliminated by cancellation.

IS THE ANSWER REASONABLE? Let's do some approximate arithmetic to get a feel for the size of the answer. A meter is slightly longer than a yard, so let's approximate the given distance, 2500 m, as 2500 yd. In 2500 yd, there are $3 \times 2500 = 7500$ ft. Since the meter is a bit longer than a yard, our answer should be a bit longer than 7500 ft, so the answer of 8200 ft seems to be reasonable.

Practice Exercise 7: Use the factor-label method to convert an area of 124 ft² to square meters. (Hint: What relationships would be required to convert feet to meters?)

Practice Exercise 8: Use the factor-label method to perform the following conversions: (a) 3.00 yd to inches, (b) 1.25 km to centimeters, (c) 3.27 mm to feet, and (d) 20.2 miles/gallon to kilometers/liter.

1.8 | DENSITY IS A USEFUL INTENSIVE PROPERTY

In our earlier discussion of properties we noted that intensive properties are useful for identifying substances. One of the interesting things about extensive properties is that if you take the ratio of two of them, the resulting quantity is usually independent of sample size. In effect, the sample size cancels out and the calculated quantity becomes an intensive property. A useful property obtained this way is **density,** *which is defined as the ratio of an object's mass to its volume.* Using the symbols d for density, m for mass, and V for volume, we can express this mathematically as

$$d = \frac{m}{V} \tag{1.6}$$

TOOLS
Density

Notice that to determine an object's density we make two measurements, mass and volume.

> **EXAMPLE 1.6**
> **Calculating Density**

A sample of blood completely fills an 8.20 cm³ vial. The empty vial has a mass of 10.30 g. The vial has a mass of 18.91 g after being filled with blood. What is the density of blood?

ANALYSIS: This problem asks you to connect the mass and volume of blood with its density. The critical link between these quantities is the definition of density, given by Equation 1.6. (Without knowing this definition, you cannot solve the problem.) Equation 1.6 becomes the tool we'll use to obtain the answer.

SOLUTION: The volume of the blood equals the volume of the vial, 8.20 cm³. The mass of the blood is the difference between the masses of the full and empty vials:

$$\text{Mass of blood} = 18.91 \text{ g} - 10.30 \text{ g} = 8.61 \text{ g}$$

To determine the density we simply take the ratio of mass to volume.

$$\text{Density} = \frac{m}{V} = \frac{8.61 \text{ g}}{8.20 \text{ cm}^3} = 1.05 \text{ g/cm}^3$$

This could also be written as

$$\text{Density} = 1.05 \text{ g/mL}$$

because 1 cm³ = 1 mL.

IS THE ANSWER REASONABLE? First, the answer has the correct units, so that's encouraging. In the calculation we are dividing 8.61 by 8.20, a number that is slightly smaller. The answer should be slightly larger than one, which it is, so a density of 1.05 g/cm³ seems reasonable.

☐ There is more mass in 1 cm³ of gold than in 1 cm³ of iron.

☐ Although the density of water varies slightly with temperature, it is useful to remember the value 1.00 g/cm³. It can be used if the water is near room temperature and only three (or fewer) significant figures are required.

Each pure substance has its own characteristic density (Table 1.7). Gold, for instance, is much more dense than iron. Each cubic centimeter of gold has a mass of 19.3 g, so its density is 19.3 g/cm³. By comparison, the density of water is 1.00 g/cm³ and the density of air at room temperature is about 0.0012 g/cm³.

Most substances, such as the mercury in the bulb of a thermometer, expand slightly when they are heated, so the amount of matter packed into each cubic centimeter is less. Therefore, density usually decreases slightly with increasing temperature.[13] For solids and liquids the size of this change is small, as you can see from the data for water in Table 1.8. When only two or three significant figures are required, we can often ignore the variation of density with temperature.

TABLE 1.7

Densities of Some Common Substances in g/cm³ at Room Temperature

Water	1.00
Aluminum	2.70
Iron	7.86
Silver	10.5
Gold	19.3
Glass	2.2
Air	0.0012

TABLE 1.8 Density of Water as a Function of Temperature

Temperature (°C)	Density (g/cm³)
10	0.999700
15	0.999099
20	0.998203
25	0.997044
30	0.995646

Use density to relate a material's mass to its volume

A useful property of density is that it provides a way to convert between the mass and volume of a substance. It defines a relationship, which we will call an **equivalence**, between the amount of mass and its volume. For instance, the density of gold (19.3 g/cm³) tells us that 19.3 g of the metal is equivalent to a volume of 1.00 cm³. We express this relationship symbolically as

$$19.3 \text{ g gold} \Leftrightarrow 1.00 \text{ cm}^3 \text{ gold}$$

where we have used the symbol $\Leftrightarrow$ to mean "is equivalent to." (We can't really use an equals sign in this expression because grams can't *equal* cubic centimeters; one is a unit of mass and the other is a unit of volume.)

In setting up calculations by the factor-label method, an equivalence can be used to construct conversion factors just as equalities can. From the equivalence we have just written we can form two conversion factors:

$$\frac{19.3 \text{ g gold}}{1.00 \text{ cm}^3 \text{ gold}} \quad \text{and} \quad \frac{1.00 \text{ cm}^3 \text{ gold}}{19.3 \text{ g gold}}$$

The following example illustrates how we use density in calculations.

EXAMPLE 1.7
Calculations Using Density

Seawater has a density of about 1.03 g/mL. (a) What mass of seawater would fill a sampling vessel to a volume of 225 mL? (b) What is the volume, in milliliters, of 45.0 g of seawater?

ANALYSIS: For both parts of this problem, we are relating the mass of a material to its volume. Density is the critical link that we need between these two quantities. The given density tells us that *1.03 g of seawater is equivalent to 1.00 mL of seawater*, which we write as

$$1.03 \text{ g seawater} \Leftrightarrow 1.00 \text{ mL seawater}$$

[13] Liquid water behaves oddly. Its maximum density is at 4 °C, so when water at 0 °C is warmed, its density increases until the temperature reaches 4 °C. As the temperature is increased further the density of water gradually decreases.

From this relationship we can construct two conversion factors. These will be the tools we use to obtain the answers.

$$\frac{1.03 \text{ g seawater}}{1.00 \text{ mL seawater}} \quad \text{and} \quad \frac{1.00 \text{ mL seawater}}{1.03 \text{ g seawater}}$$

SOLUTION: (a) The question can be restated as 225 mL seawater ⟺ ? g seawater. We need to eliminate the unit *mL seawater*, so we choose the conversion factor on the left as our tool.

$$225 \ \cancel{\text{mL seawater}} \ \times \ \frac{1.03 \text{ g seawater}}{1.00 \ \cancel{\text{mL seawater}}} \Longleftrightarrow 232 \text{ g seawater}$$

Thus, 225 mL of seawater has a mass of 232 g.

(b) The question is, 45.0 g seawater ⟺ ? mL seawater. This time we need to eliminate the unit *g seawater*, so we use the conversion factor on the right as our tool.

$$45.0 \ \cancel{\text{g seawater}} \ \times \ \frac{1.00 \text{ mL seawater}}{1.03 \ \cancel{\text{g seawater}}} \Longleftrightarrow 43.7 \text{ mL seawater}$$

Thus, 45.0 g of seawater has a volume of 43.7 mL.

ARE THE ANSWERS REASONABLE?   Notice that the density tells us that 1 mL of seawater has a mass of slightly more than 1 g. So for part (a), we might expect that 225 mL of seawater should have a mass slightly more than 225 g. Our answer, 232 g, is reasonable. For part (b), 45 g of seawater should have a volume not too far from 45 mL, so our answer of 43.7 mL is the right size.

Practice Exercise 9: A gold-colored metal object has a mass of 365 g and a volume of 22.12 cm³. Is the object composed of pure gold? (Hint: How does the density of the object compare with that of pure gold?)

Practice Exercise 10: A certain metal alloy has a density of 12.6 g/cm³. How many pounds would 0.822 ft³ of this alloy weigh? (Hint: What is the density of the alloy in units of lb/ft³?)

Practice Exercise 11: An ocean-dwelling dinosaur was estimated to have had a body volume of 1.38×10^6 cm³. The animal's mass when alive was estimated at 1.24×10^6 g. What is its density?

Practice Exercise 12: The density of diamond is 3.52 g/cm³. What is the volume in cubic centimeters of a 1 carat diamond, which has a mass of 200 mg? (Assume three significant figures.)

Conclusions must be drawn from reliable measurements

We saw earlier that substances can be identified by their properties. If we are to rely on properties such as density for identification of substances, it is very important that our measurements be reliable. We must have some idea of what the measurement's accuracy and precision are.

The importance of accuracy is obvious. If we have no confidence that our measured values are close to the true values, we certainly cannot trust any conclusions that are based on the data we have collected.

Precision of measurements can be equally important. For example, suppose we had a gold wedding ring and we wanted to determine whether or not the gold was 24 carat. We could determine the mass of the ring, and then its volume, and compute the density of the ring. We could then compare our experimental density with the density of 24 carat gold (which is 19.3 g/mL). Suppose the ring had a volume of 1.0 mL and the ring had a mass of 18 g, as measured using a graduated cup measure and a kitchen scale. The density of the ring would then be 18 g/mL, to the correct number of significant figures. Could we conclude that the ring was made of 24 carat gold? We know the density to only two significant figures. The experimental density could be as low as 17 g/mL or as high as 19 g/mL, which means the ring *could* be 24 carat gold—or it could be 22 carat gold (which has a density of around 17.7 to 17.8 g/mL) or maybe even 18 carat gold (which has a density up to 16.9 g/mL).

Suppose we now measure the mass of the ring with a laboratory balance capable of measurements to the nearest ± 0.001 g and obtain a mass of 18.153 g. We measure the volume using volumetric glassware and find a volume of 1.03 mL. The density is 17.6 g/mL to the correct number of significant figures. The difference between this density and the density of 24 carat gold is 19.3 g/mL $-$ 17.6 g/mL = 1.7 g/mL. This is considerably larger than the uncertainty in the experimental density (which is about ± 0.1 g/mL). We can be reasonably confident that the ring is not 24 carat gold, and in fact the measurements point toward the ring being composed of 22 carat gold.

To trust conclusions drawn from measurements, we must be sure the measurements are accurate and that they are of sufficient precision to be meaningful. This is a key consideration in designing experiments.

SUMMARY

Chemistry and the Scientific Method. Chemistry is a science that studies the properties and composition of **matter,** which is anything that has **mass** and occupies space. It employs the **scientific method** in which **observations** are used to collect **empirical facts,** or **data,** that can be summarized in **scientific laws. Models** of nature begin as **hypotheses** that mature into **theories** when they survive repeated testing. According to the **atomic theory,** matter is composed of **atoms** that combine to form more complex substances, many of which consist of **molecules** composed of two or more atoms.

Elements, Compounds, and Mixtures. An **element,** which is identified by its **chemical symbol,** cannot be decomposed into something simpler by a **chemical reaction.** Elements combine in fixed proportions to form **compounds.** Elements and compounds are **pure substances** that may be combined in *varying* proportions to give **mixtures.** If a mixture has two or more **phases,** it is **heterogeneous.** A one-phase **homogeneous** mixture is called a **solution.** Formation or separation of a mixture into its components can be accomplished by a **physical change,** which doesn't alter the chemical composition of the substances involved. Formation or decomposition of a compound takes place by a **chemical change** that changes the chemical makeup of the substances involved.

Properties of Materials. Physical properties are measured without changing the chemical composition of a sample. **Solid, liquid,** and **gas** are the most common **states of matter.** Their properties can be related to the different ways the individual atomic-size particles are organized. A **chemical property** describes a chemical reaction a substance undergoes. **Intensive properties** are independent of sample size; **extensive properties** depend on sample size.

Units of Measurement. Qualitative observations lack numerical information, whereas **quantitative observations** require numerical measurements. The units used for scientific measurements are based on the set of seven **SI base units** which

can be combined to give various **derived units.** These all can be scaled to larger or smaller sized units by applying **decimal multiplying factors.** In the laboratory we routinely measure length, volume, mass, and temperature. Convenient units for length and volume are, respectively, **centimeters** or **millimeters,** and **liters** or **milliliters. Mass** is a measure of the amount of matter in an object and differs from weight. Mass is measured with a **balance** and is expressed in units of **kilograms** or **grams.** Temperature is measured in units of **degrees Celsius** (or **Fahrenheit**) using a thermometer. For many calculations, temperature must be expressed in **kelvins (K).** The zero point on the **Kelvin temperature scale** is called **absolute zero.**

Significant Figures. The **precision** of a measured quantity is revealed by the number of **significant figures** that it contains, which equals the number of digits known for sure plus the first one that possesses some uncertainty. Measured values are **precise** if they contain many significant figures and therefore differ from each other by small amounts. A measurement is **accurate** if its value lies very close to the true value. When measurements are combined in calculations, rules help us determine the correct number of significant figures in the answer (see below). **Exact numbers** are considered to have an infinite number of significant figures.

Factor-Label Method. The **factor-label method** is based on the ability of units to undergo the same mathematical operations as numbers. **Conversion factors** are constructed from *valid relationships* between units. These relationships can be either equalities or **equivalencies** (indicated by the symbol $\Leftrightarrow$) between units. Unit cancellation serves as a guide to the use of conversion factors and aids us in correctly setting up the arithmetic for a problem.

Density. Density is an intensive property equal to the ratio of a sample's mass to its volume. Besides serving as a means for identifying substances, density provides a conversion factor that relates mass to volume.

TOOLS FOR PROBLEM SOLVING

In this chapter you learned to apply the following concepts as tools in solving problems. Study each one carefully so that you know what each is used for. When faced with solving a problem, recall what each tool does and consider whether it will be helpful in finding a solution. This will aid you in selecting the tools you need.

SI Prefixes *(Table 1.4, page 12)* We use the prefixes to create larger and smaller units. They are also used to create conversion factors for converting between differently sized units. Be sure you are familiar with the ones in bold colored type in Table 1.4.

Units in laboratory measurements *(pages 13-17)* Often we must convert among units commonly used for laboratory measurements.

$$\text{Length:} \quad 1 \text{ m} = 100 \text{ cm} = 1000 \text{ mm}$$
$$\text{Volume:} \quad 1 \text{ L} = 1000 \text{ mL} = 1000 \text{ cm}^3$$

Temperature conversions *(pages 16-17)* Use Equations 1.1 and 1.2 to convert between temperature scales.

$$t_F = \left(\frac{9\,^\circ\text{F}}{5\,^\circ\text{C}}\right)t_C + 32\,^\circ\text{F} \qquad T_K = (t_C + 273.15\,^\circ\text{C})\left(\frac{1\text{ K}}{1\,^\circ\text{C}}\right)$$

Add 273.15 to Celsius temperature
to obtain the Kelvin temperature.

Rules for counting significant figures in a number *(page 19)* To gauge the quality of a measurement, we must know the number of significant figures it contains:

- All nonzero digits are significant.
- Zeros to the right of the decimal are significant if they follow a nonzero digit.
- Zeros between significant digits are significant.
- Zeros that are to the *left* of the first nonzero digit are not significant.
- Zeros on the end of a number without a decimal point are assumed not to be significant. (To avoid confusion, scientific notation should be used.)

Rules for arithmetic and significant figures *(pages 20-21)* We use these rules in almost every numerical problem to obtain the correct number of significant figures in the answer.

Multiplication and division: Round the answer to the same number of significant figures as the least precise factor.

Addition and subtraction: Round the answer to match the same number of decimal places as the quantity with the fewest number of decimal places.

Exact numbers: Exact numbers, such as those that arise from definitions, do not affect the number of significant figures in the result of a calculation.

Density *(page 25)* The density, *d*, relates mass, *m*, and volume, *V*, for a substance.

$$d = \frac{m}{V}$$

Density provides an equivalence between mass and volume, from which we can construct conversion factors to convert between mass and volume for a substance.

QUESTIONS, PROBLEMS, AND EXERCISES

Answers to problems whose numbers are printed in color are given in Appendix B. More challenging problems are marked with asterisks. ILW = Interactive Learningware solution is available at *www.wiley.com/college/brady*. OH = an Office Hours video is available for this problem.

REVIEW QUESTIONS

Introduction; The Scientific Method

1.1 After some thought, give two reasons why a course in chemistry will benefit *you* in the pursuit of your particular major.

1.2 What steps are involved in the scientific method?

1.3 What is the difference between (a) a law and a theory, (b) an observation and a conclusion, (c) an observation and data?

Properties of Substances

OH **1.4** Define *matter*. Which of the following are examples of matter? (a) air, (b) a pencil, (c) a cheese sandwich, (d) a squirrel, (e) your mother

1.5 What is *a physical property?* What is *a chemical property?* What is the chief distinction between physical and chemical properties? Define the terms *intensive property* and *extensive property.* Give two examples of each.

1.6 "A sample of calcium (an electrically conducting white metal that is shiny, relatively soft, melts at 850 °C, and boils at 1440 °C) was placed into liquid water that was at 25 °C. The calcium reacted slowly with the water to give bubbles of gaseous hydrogen and a solution of the substance calcium hydroxide." In this description, what physical properties and what chemical properties are described?

OH 1.7 In places like Saudi Arabia, freshwater is scarce and is recovered from seawater. When seawater is boiled, the water evaporates and the steam can be condensed to give pure water that people can drink. If all the water is evaporated, solid salt is left behind. Are the changes described here chemical or physical?

1.8 Name the three states of matter.

Elements, Compounds, and Mixtures

1.9 Define (a) element, (b) compound, (c) mixture, (d) homogeneous, (e) heterogeneous, (f) phase, and (g) solution.

1.10 What is the chemical symbol for each of the following elements? (a) chlorine, (b) sulfur, (c) iron, (d) silver, (e) sodium, (f) phosphorus, (g) iodine, (h) copper, (i) mercury, (j) calcium

1.11 What is the name of each of the following elements? (a) K, (b) Zn, (c) Si, (d) Sn, (e) Mn, (f) Mg, (g) Ni, (h) Al, (i) C, (j) N

SI Units

1.12 Why must measurements always be written with units?

1.13 What is the only SI base unit that includes a decimal prefix?

1.14 What is the meaning of each of the following prefixes? (a) centi-, (b) milli-, (c) kilo-, (d) micro-, (e) nano-, (f) pico-, (g) mega-

1.15 What abbreviation is used for each of the prefixes named in Question 1.14?

1.16 What reference points do we use in calibrating the scale of a thermometer? What temperature on the Celsius scale do we assign to each of these reference points?

OH 1.17 In each pair, which is larger: (a) A Fahrenheit degree or a Celsius degree? (b) A Celsius degree or a kelvin? (c) A Fahrenheit degree or a kelvin?

Significant Figures; the Factor-Label Method

1.18 Define the term *significant figures.*

1.19 What is the difference between *accuracy* and *precision?*

1.20 Suppose a length had been reported to be 31.24 cm. What is the minimum uncertainty implied in this measurement?

1.21 Suppose someone suggested using the fraction $\frac{3 \text{ yd}}{1 \text{ ft}}$ as a conversion factor to change a length expressed in feet to its equivalent in yards. What is wrong with this conversion factor? Can we construct a valid conversion factor relating centimeters to meters from the equation 1 cm = 1000 m? Explain your answer.

1.22 In 1 hour there are 3600 seconds. By what conversion factor would you multiply 250 seconds to convert it to hours? By what conversion factor would you multiply 3.84 hours to convert it to seconds?

1.23 If you were to convert the measured length 4.165 ft to yards by multiplying by the conversion factor (1 yd/3 ft), how many significant figures should the answer contain? Why?

Density

1.24 Write the equation that defines density. Identify the symbols in the equation.

1.25 Silver has a density of 10.5 g cm^{-3}. Express this as an equivalence between mass and volume for silver. Write two conversion factors that can be formed from this equivalence for use in calculations.

REVIEW PROBLEMS

SI Prefixes

1.26 What number should replace the question mark in each of the following?
(a) 1 cm = ? m
(b) 1 km = ? m
(c) 1 m = ? pm
(d) 1 dm = ? m
(e) 1 g = ? kg
(f) 1 cg = ? g

1.27 What numbers should replace the question marks below?
(a) 1 nm = ? m
(b) 1 μg = ? g
(c) 1 kg = ? g
(d) 1 Mg = ? g
(e) 1 mg = ? g
(f) 1 dg = ? g

Temperature Conversions

1.28 Perform the following conversions.
(a) 50 °C to °F
(b) 10 °C to °F
(c) 25.5 °F to °C
(d) 49 °F to °C
(e) 60 °C to K
(f) −30 °C to K

1.29 Perform the following conversions.
(a) 96 °F to °C
(b) −6 °F to °C
(c) −55 °C to °F
(d) 273 K to °C
(e) 299 K to °C
(f) 40 °C to K

1.30 A healthy dog has a temperature ranging from 37.2 to 39.2 °C. Is a dog with a temperature of 103.5 °F within normal range?

1.31 The coldest permanently inhabited place on earth is the Siberian village of Oymyakon in Russia. In 1964 the temperature reached a shivering −96 °F! What is this temperature in °C?

1.32 Estimates of the temperature at the core of the sun range from 10 megakelvins to 25 megakelvins. What is this range in °C and °F?

1.33 Natural gas is mostly methane, a substance that boils at a temperature of 111 K. What is its boiling point in °C and °F?

1.34 Helium has the lowest boiling point of any liquid. It boils at 4 K. What is its boiling point in °C?

1.35 The atomic bomb detonated over Hiroshima, Japan, at the end of World War II raised the temperature on the ground below to about 6000 K. Is this hot enough to melt concrete? (Concrete melts at 2000 °C.)

Significant Figures

1.36 How many significant figures do the following measured quantities have?
(a) 37.53 cm
(b) 37.240 cm
(c) 202.0 g
(d) 0.00024 kg
(e) 0.07080 m
(f) 2400 mL

1.37 How many significant figures do the following measured quantities have?
(a) 0.0230 g
(b) 105.303 m
(c) 0.007 kg
(d) 614.00 mg
(e) 10 L
(f) 3.8105 mm

OH 1.38 Perform the following arithmetic and round off the answers to the correct number of significant figures. Include the correct units with the answers.
(a) 0.0023 m × 315 m
(b) 84.25 kg − 0.01075 kg
(c) (184.45 g − 94.45 g)/(31.4 mL − 9.9 mL)
(d) (23.4 g + 102.4 g + 0.003 g)/(6.478 mL)
(e) (313.44 cm − 209.1 cm) × 8.2234 cm

1.39 Perform the following arithmetic and round off the answers to the correct number of significant figures. Include the correct units with the answers.
(a) 3.58 g/1.739 mL
(b) 4.02 mL + 0.001 mL
(c) (22.4 g − 8.3 g)/(1.142 mL − 0.002 mL)
(d) (1.345 g + 0.022 g)/(13.36 mL − 8.4115 mL)
(e) (74.335 m − 74.332 m)/(4.75 s × 1.114 s)

Unit Conversions by the Factor-Label Method

OH 1.40 Perform the following conversions.
(a) 32.0 dm/s to km/hr   (d) 137.5 mL to L
(b) 8.2 mg/mL to μg/L   (e) 0.025 L to mL
(c) 75.3 mg to kg   (f) 342 pm^2 to dm^2

1.41 Perform the following conversions.
(a) 92 dL to μm^3 (d) 230 km^3 to m^3
(b) 22 ng to μg   (e) 87.3 cm s^{-2} to km hr^{-2}
(c) 83 pL to nL   (f) 238 mm^2 to nm^2

1.42 Perform the following conversions. If necessary, refer to Tables 1.4 and 1.6.
(a) 36 in. to cm   (d) 1 cup (8 oz) to mL
(b) 5.0 lb to kg   (e) 55 mi/hr to km/hr
(c) 3.0 qt to mL   (f) 50.0 mi to km

1.43 Perform the following conversions. If necessary, refer to Tables 1.4 and 1.6.
(a) 250 mL to qt   (d) 1.75 L to fluid oz
(b) 3.0 ft to m   (e) 35 km/hr to mi/hr
(c) 1.62 kg to lb   (f) 80.0 km to mi

1.44 Perform the following conversions.
(a) 8.4 ft^2 to cm^2 (b) 223 mi^2 to km^2 (c) 231 ft^3 to cm^3

1.45 Perform the following conversions.
(a) 2.4 yd^2 to m^2 (b) 8.3 in.^{2} to mm^2 (c) 9.1 ft^3 to L

1.46 The human stomach can expand to hold up to 4.2 quarts of food. A pistachio nut has a volume of about 0.9 mL. Use this information to estimate the maximum number of pistachios that can be eaten in one sitting.

1.47 In the movie *Cool Hand Luke* (1967), Luke wagers that he can eat 50 eggs in one hour. The prisoners and guards bet against him, saying, "Fifty eggs gotta weigh a good six pounds. A man's gut can't hold that." A chewed, peeled chicken egg has a volume of approximately 53 mL. If Luke's stomach has a volume of 4.2 quarts, does he have any chance of winning the bet?

ILW 1.48 The winds in a hurricane can reach almost 200 miles per hour. What is this speed in meters per second? (Assume three significant figures.)

1.49 A bullet is fired at a speed of 2435 ft/s. What is this speed expressed in kilometers per hour?

1.50 A bullet leaving the muzzle of a pistol was traveling at a speed of 2230 feet per second. What is this speed in miles per hour?

1.51 On average, water flows over Niagara Falls at a rate of 2.05 × 10^5 cubic feet per second. One cubic foot of water weighs 62.4 lb. Calculate the rate of water flow in tons of water per day. (1 ton = 2000 lb.)

1.52 The brightest star in the night sky in the northern hemisphere is Sirius. Its distance from earth is estimated to be 8.7 light-years. A light-year is the distance light travels in one year. Light travels at a speed of 3.00 × 10^8 m/s. Calculate the distance from earth to Sirius in miles. (1 mi = 5280 ft.)

1.53 One degree of latitude on the earth's surface equals 60.0 nautical miles. One nautical mile equals 1.151 statute miles. (A *statute mile* is the distance over land that we normally associate with the unit mile.) Calculate the circumference of the earth in statute miles.

1.54 The deepest point in the earth's oceans is found in the Mariana Trench, a deep crevasse located about 1000 miles southeast of Japan beneath the Pacific Ocean. Its maximum depth is 6033.5 fathoms. One fathom is defined as 6 feet. Calculate the depth of the Mariana Trench in meters.

1.55 At sea level, our atmosphere exerts a pressure of about 14.7 lb/in.^{2}, which means that each square inch of your body experiences a force of 14.7 lb from the air that surrounds you. As you descend below the surface of the ocean, the pressure produced by the seawater increases by about 14.7 lb/in.^{2} for every 10 meters of depth. In the preceding problem you calculated the maximum depth of the Mariana Trench, located in the Pacific Ocean. What is the approximate pressure in pounds per square inch and in tons per square inch exerted by the sea at the deepest point of the trench? (1 ton = 2000 lb.)

Density

1.56 A sample of kerosene weighs 36.4 g. Its volume was measured to be 45.6 mL. What is the density of the kerosene?

1.57 A block of magnesium has a mass of 14.3 g and a volume of 8.46 cm^3. What is the density of magnesium in g/cm^3?

OH 1.58 Acetone, the solvent in some nail polish removers, has a density of 0.791 g/mL. What is the volume of 25.0 g of acetone?

1.59 A glass apparatus contains 26.223 g of water when filled at 25 °C. At this temperature, water has a density of 0.99704 g/mL. What is the volume of this apparatus?

1.60 Chloroform, a chemical once used as an anesthetic, has a density of 1.492 g/mL. What is the mass in grams of 185 mL of chloroform?

1.61 Gasoline has a density of about 0.65 g/mL. How much does 34 L (approximately 18 gallons) weigh in kilograms? In pounds?

ILW 1.62 A graduated cylinder was filled with water to the 15.0 mL mark and weighed on a balance. Its mass was 27.35 g. An object made of silver was placed in the cylinder and completely submerged in the water. The water level rose to 18.3 mL. When reweighed, the cylinder, water, and silver object had a total mass of 62.00 g. Calculate the density of silver.

1.63 Titanium is a metal used to make golf clubs. A rectangular bar of this metal measuring 1.84 cm × 2.24 cm × 2.44 cm was found to have a mass of 45.7 g. What is the density of titanium?

1.64 The space shuttle uses liquid hydrogen as its fuel. The external fuel tank used during takeoff carries 227,641 lb of hydrogen with a volume of 385,265 gallons. Calculate the density of liquid hydrogen in units of g/mL. (Express your answer to three significant figures.)

1.65 Some time ago, a U.S. citizen traveling in Canada observed that the price of regular gasoline was 0.959 Canadian dollars per liter. The exchange rate at the time was 1.142 Canadian dollars per one U.S. dollar. Calculate the price of the Canadian gasoline in units of U.S. dollars per gallon. (Just the week before, the traveler had paid $2.249 per gallon in the United States.)

ADDITIONAL EXERCISES

OH 1.66 You are the science reporter for a daily newspaper and your editor asks you to write a story based on a report in the scientific literature. The report states that analysis of the sediments in Hausberg Tarn (elevation 4350 m) on the side of Mount Kenya (elevation 4600–4700 m) shows that the average temperature of the water rose by 4.0 °C between 350 BC and AD 450. Your editor tells you that she wants all the data expressed in the English system of units. Make the appropriate conversions.

1.67 An astronomy website states that neutron stars have a density of 1.00×10^8 tons per cubic centimeter. The site does not specify whether "tons" means metric tons (1 metric ton = 1000 kg) or English tons (1 English ton = 2000 pounds). How many grams would one teaspoon of a neutron star weigh, if the density were in metric tons per cm³? How many grams would the teaspoon weigh if the density were in English tons per cm³? (One teaspoon is approximately 4.93 mL.)

1.68 The star Arcturus is 3.50×10^{14} km from the earth. How many days does it take for light to travel from Arcturus to earth? What is the distance to Arcturus in light-years? One light-year is the distance light travels in one year (365 days); light travels at a speed of 3.00×10^8 m/s.

1.69 A pycnometer is a glass apparatus used for accurately determining the density of a liquid. When dry and empty, a certain pycnometer had a mass of 27.314 g. When filled with distilled water at 25.0 °C, it weighed 36.842 g. When filled with chloroform (a liquid once used as an anesthetic before its toxic properties were known), the apparatus weighed 41.428 g. At 25.0 °C, the density of water is 0.99704 g/mL. (a) What is the volume of the pycnometer? (b) What is the density of chloroform?

1.70 Radio waves travel at the speed of light, 3.00×10^8 m/s. If you were to broadcast a question to an astronaut on the moon, which is 239,000 miles from earth, what is the minimum time that you would have to wait to receive a reply?

1.71 Suppose you have a job in which you earn $4.50 for each 30 minutes that you work.
(a) Express this information in the form of an equivalence between dollars earned and minutes worked.
(b) Use the equivalence defined in (a) to calculate the number of dollars earned in 1 hr 45 min.
(c) Use the equivalence defined in (a) to calculate the number of minutes you would have to work to earn $17.35.

1.72 When an object floats in water, it displaces a volume of water that has a weight equal to the weight of the object. If a ship has a weight of 4255 tons, how many cubic feet of seawater will it displace? Seawater has a density of 1.025 g cm⁻³; 1 ton = 2000 lb.

1.73 Aerogel or "solid smoke" is a novel material that is made of silicon dioxide, like glass, but is a thousand times less dense than glass because it is extremely porous. Material scientists at NASA's Jet Propulsion Laboratory created the lightest aerogel ever in 2002, with a density of 0.00011 pounds per cubic inch. The material was used for thermal insulation in the 2003 Mars Exploration Rover. If the maximum space for insulation in the spacecraft's hull was 2510 cm³, what mass (in grams) did the aerogel insulation add to the spacecraft?

Aerogel. *(NASA/JPL.)*

1.74 A liquid known to be either ethanol (ethyl alcohol) or methanol (methyl alcohol) was found to have a density of 0.798 ± 0.001 g/mL. Consult the *Handbook of Chemistry and Physics* to determine which liquid it is. What other measurements could help to confirm the identity of the liquid?

1.75 An unknown liquid was found to have a density of 69.22 lb/ft³. The density of ethylene glycol (the liquid used in antifreeze) is 1.1088 g/mL. Could the unknown liquid be ethylene glycol?

1.76 When an object is heated to a high temperature, it glows and gives off light. The color balance of this light depends on the temperature of the glowing object. Photographic lighting is described, in terms of its color balance, as a temperature in kelvins. For example, a certain electronic flash gives a color balance (called color temperature) rated at 5800 K. What is this temperature expressed in °C?

OH *1.77 There exists a single temperature at which the value reported in °F is numerically the same as the value reported in °C. What is that temperature?

***1.78** In the text, the Kelvin scale of temperature is defined as an absolute scale in which one Kelvin degree unit is the same size as one Celsius degree unit. A second absolute temperature scale exists called the Rankine scale. On this scale, one Rankine degree unit (°R) is the same size as one Fahrenheit degree unit. (a) What is the only temperature at which the Kelvin and Rankine scales possess the same numerical value? Explain your answer. (b) What is the boiling point of water expressed in °R?

***1.79** Density measurements can be used to analyze mixtures. For example, the density of solid sand (without air spaces) is about 2.84 g/mL. The density of gold is 19.3 g/mL. If a 1.00 kg sample of sand containing some gold has a density of 3.10 g/mL (without air spaces), what is the percentage of gold in the sample?

***1.80** An artist's statue has a surface area of 14.6 ft². The artist plans to apply gold plate to the statue and wants the coating to be 2.50 μm thick. If the price of gold were $625.10 per troy ounce, how much would it cost to give the statue its gold coating? (1 troy ounce = 31.1035 g; the density of gold is 19.3 g/mL.)

***1.81** A cylindrical metal bar has a diameter of 0.753 cm and a length of 2.33 cm. It has a mass of 8.423 g. Calculate the density of the metal in the units lb/ft³.

1.82 What is the volume in cubic millimeters of a 3.54 carat diamond, given that the density of the diamond is 3.51 g/mL? (1 carat = 200 mg.)

1.83 Because of the serious consequences of lead poisoning, the Federal Centers for Disease Control in Atlanta has set a threshold of concern for lead levels in children's blood. This threshold was based on a study that suggested that lead levels in blood as low as *10 micrograms of lead per deciliter of blood* can result in subtle effects of lead toxicity. Suppose a child had a lead level in her blood of 2.5×10^{-4} grams of lead per liter of blood. Is this person in danger of exhibiting the effects of lead poisoning?

*__1.84__ Gold has a density of 19.31 g cm^{-3}. How many grams of gold are required to provide a gold coating 0.500 mm thick on a ball bearing having a diameter of 2.000 mm?

*__1.85__ A Boeing 747 jet airliner carrying 568 people burns about 5.0 gallons of jet fuel per mile. What is the rate of fuel consumption in units of miles per gallon per person? Is this better or worse than the rate of fuel consumption in an automobile carrying two people that gets 21.5 miles per gallon? If the airliner were making the 3470 mile trip from New York to London, how many pounds of jet fuel would be consumed? (Jet fuel has a density of 0.803 g/mL.)

EXERCISES IN CRITICAL THINKING

1.86 A homogeneous solution is defined as a uniform mixture consisting of a single phase. With our vastly improved abilities to "see" smaller and smaller particles, down to the atomic level, present an argument for the proposition that all mixtures are heterogeneous. Present the argument that the ability to observe objects as small as an atom has no effect on the definitions of heterogeneous and homogeneous.

1.87 Find two or more websites that give the values for each of the seven base SI units. Keeping in mind that not all websites provide reliable information, which website do you believe provides the most reliable values? Justify your answer.

1.88 Reference books such as the *Handbook of Chemistry and Physics* report the specific gravities of substances instead of their densities. Find the definition of specific gravity and discuss the relative merits of specific gravity and density in terms of their usefulness as a physical property.

1.89 A student used a graduated cylinder having volume markings every 2 mL to carefully measure 100 mL of water for an experiment. A fellow student said that by reporting the volume as "100 mL" in her lab notebook, she was only entitled to one significant figure. She disagreed. Why did her fellow student say the reported volume had only one significant figure? Considering the circumstances, how many significant figures are in her measured volume? Justify your answer.

1.90 Download a table of data for the density of water between its freezing and boiling points. Use a spreadsheet program to plot (a) the density of water versus temperature and (b) the volume of a kilogram of water versus temperature. Interpret the significance of these plots.

1.91 List the physical and chemical properties mentioned in this chapter. What additional physical and chemical properties can you think of to extend the list?

ELEMENTS, COMPOUNDS, AND CHEMICAL REACTIONS

2

From a safe distance lightning illuminates the sky and puts on a splendid show in a springtime thunderstorm. In addition to the dazzling show, lightning has the energy to cause chemical reactions to occur between the atmosphere's oxygen and nitrogen molecules. Some of these compounds are fertilizers, essential for life below, and others are compounds that we call pollutants. In this chapter we see how to use chemical reactions to summarize the interactions of elements and compounds.

(Scott Stulberg/Corbis.)

Students sometimes say that to them "chemistry is a foreign language." The statement is not far from the truth. We can consider the elements in the periodic table to be our new alphabet; the formulas for compounds are the words of chemistry; and balanced equations that show how those compounds react with each other are the sentences of this new language. Learning the language of chemistry will help you succeed because you will be able to concentrate on new concepts that depend on being fluent in our new language.

In Chapter 1 we learned about the broad scope and nature of the subject of chemistry. Importantly we learned that precise and accurate measurements and calculations are central to all sciences, especially chemistry. Now that you've learned these introductory concepts we turn our attention to atoms, elements, chemical compounds, and chemical reactions.

Our study begins with *Dalton's atomic theory*, a theory that has its roots in two basic laws of nature. The law of conservation of mass and the law of definite proportions are the foundation of one of the most important scientific theories.

The atomic theory leads us to the study of the atom's basic parts, *electrons, protons*, and *neutrons*, and how one atom and its isotopes differ from another. *Mendeleev's periodic table* on the other hand is a storehouse of relationships, trends, and similarities between the elements. When elements combine to form a compound, they do so in two broad general ways, either by the sharing of electrons between atoms to make *molecular compounds* or by the transfer of one or more electrons from one atom to another forming *ions* and *ionic compounds*. Compounds are described by *chemical formulas* and their corresponding names. How compounds and elements react with each other is described by a *balanced chemical equation*.

This chapter has three principal goals. The first is to teach you about the atomic theory so you develop an appreciation of scientific theories in general. The second is to help you understand the nature of ionic and molecular substances, how they are formed, and some of their properties. This includes understanding how to interpret chemical formulas and the basics of balancing equations. The third is to introduce you to *chemical nomenclature*—the system used to name chemical compounds. Being able to describe compounds by name is essential for communication among scientists. Therefore, we urge you to make the effort to learn how to name compounds and how to translate chemical names into chemical formulas.

As with the preceding chapter, you may already be familiar with some of the topics we discuss here. Nevertheless, be sure to study them thoroughly. By doing so you begin to build your store of factual knowledge that will enable you to more easily interpret and understand advanced topics as we get to them in later chapters.

2.1 | ELEMENTS AND ATOMS ARE DESCRIBED BY DALTON'S ATOMIC THEORY

In our discussion of elements in the preceding chapter, no reference was made to the atomic nature of matter. In fact, the distinction between elements and compounds had been made even before the atomic theory of matter was formulated. In this section we will examine how the atomic theory began and take a closer look at elements in terms of our modern view of atomic structure.

Dalton's atomic theory explained chemical laws

In modern science, we have come to take for granted the existence of atoms and molecules. In fact, we've already used the atomic theory to explain some of the properties of materials. However, scientific evidence for the existence of atoms is relatively recent, and chemistry did not progress very far until that evidence was found.

The concept of atoms began nearly 2500 years ago when certain Greek philosophers expressed the belief that matter is ultimately composed of tiny indivisible particles, and it is from the Greek word *atomos*, meaning "not cut," that the word *atom* is derived. The philosophers' conclusions, however, were not supported by any evidence; they were derived simply from philosophical reasoning.

Laws of chemical combination evolved from experimental observations

The concept of atoms remained a philosophical belief, having limited scientific usefulness, until the discovery of two quantitative laws of chemical combination: the *law of conservation of mass* and the *law of definite proportions*. The evidence that led to the discovery of these laws came from the experimental observations of many scientists in the eighteenth and early nineteenth centuries.

TOOLS

Law of conservation of mass and law of definite proportions

> **Law of Conservation of Mass.** No detectable gain or loss of mass occurs in chemical reactions. Mass is *conserved*.
>
> **Law of Definite Proportions.** In a given chemical compound, the elements are always combined in the same proportions by mass.

Notice that both of these laws refer to the masses of substances because the balance was one of the few chemical instruments in those times. Earlier, in our definition of matter, we noted that mass is a measure of the amount of matter in an object. Recall that mass and weight are not the same and you should be careful to use these terms correctly.

The **law of conservation of mass** means that if a chemical reaction takes place in a sealed vessel that permits no matter to enter or escape, the mass of the vessel and its contents after the reaction will be identical to its mass before. Although this may seem quite obvious to us now, it wasn't quite so clear in the early history of modern chemistry when colorless gases could easily be overlooked. When scientists were able to make sure that *all* substances, including any gaseous reactants and/or products, were included when masses were measured, the law of conservation of mass could be truly tested.

We actually used the **law of definite proportions** on page 6 when we defined a compound as a substance in which two or more elements are chemically combined in a *definite fixed proportion by mass*. Thus, if we decompose samples of water (a compound) into the elements oxygen and hydrogen, we always find that the ratio of oxygen to hydrogen, *by mass*, is 8 to 1. In other words, the mass of oxygen obtained is always eight times the mass of hydrogen.

In any sample of water, the mass of oxygen is always
eight times the mass of hydrogen.

Similarly, if we form water from oxygen and hydrogen, the mass of oxygen consumed will always be eight times the mass of hydrogen that reacts. This is true even if there's a large excess of one of them. For instance, if 100 g of oxygen is mixed with 1 g of hydrogen and the reaction to form water is initiated, all the hydrogen would react but only 8 g of oxygen would be consumed; there would be 92 g of oxygen left over. No matter how we try, we can't alter the chemical composition of the water formed in the reaction.

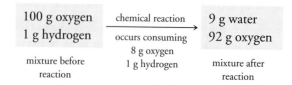

Let's look at a sample calculation that shows how we might use the law of definite proportions.

EXAMPLE 2.1
Applying the Law
of Definite Proportions

The element molybdenum (Mo) combines with sulfur (S) to form a compound commonly called molybdenum disulfide that is useful as a dry lubricant, similar to graphite. It is also used in specialized lithium batteries. A sample of this compound contains 1.50 g of Mo for each 1.00 g of S. If a different sample of the compound contains 2.50 g of S, how many grams of Mo does it contain?

ANALYSIS: As you learned in Chapter 1, much of the effort in solving a chemistry problem is devoted to determining which concepts have to be applied. We view these concepts as *tools*, each with its specific uses when applied to problem solving. Our goal in this Analysis step is to identify which tools we need and how we will apply them.

Let's begin by examining the problem and asking a question: What have we learned that relates the masses of elements in two samples of the same compound? We've described two tools relating to masses, the laws of conservation of mass and definite proportions. The law of conservation of mass concerns only the total mass of the chemicals in a reaction, so it doesn't seem to help us here. The law of definite proportions does seem to apply since it concerns the mathematical relationships of elements within a compound no matter where the sample came from. It states that the proportions of the elements by mass must be the same in both samples; so the law of definite proportions is the tool we need to apply. The law tells us that the ratio of grams of Mo to grams of S must be the same in both samples. To solve the problem, then, we will set up the mass ratios for the two samples. In the ratio for the second sample, the mass of molybdenum will be an unknown quantity. We'll equate the two ratios and solve for the unknown quantity.

SOLUTION: Now that we've determined what we need to do to solve the problem, the rest is pretty easy. The first sample has a Mo to S mass ratio of

$$\frac{1.50 \text{ g Mo}}{1.00 \text{ g S}}$$

In the second sample, we know the mass of S (2.50 g) and we want to find the mass of Mo (the unknown is *mass of Mo*). The mass ratio of Mo to S in the second sample is therefore

$$\frac{mass\ of\ Mo}{2.50 \text{ g S}}$$

Now we equate them, because the two ratios must be equal.

$$\frac{mass\ of\ Mo}{2.50 \text{ g S}} = \frac{1.50 \text{ g Mo}}{1.00 \text{ g S}}$$

Solving for the *mass of Mo* gives

$$Mass\ of\ Mo = 2.50 \text{ g S} \times \frac{1.50 \text{ g Mo}}{1.00 \text{ g S}} = 3.75 \text{ g Mo}$$

IS THE ANSWER REASONABLE? To avoid errors, it's always wise to do a rough check of the answer. Usually, some simple reasoning is all we need to see if the answer is "in the right ball park." This is how we might do such a check here: Notice that the amount of sulfur in the second sample is more than twice the amount in the first sample. Therefore, we should expect the amount of Mo in the second sample to be somewhat more than twice what it is in the first. The answer we obtained, 3.75 g Mo, is more than twice 1.50 g Mo, so our answer seems to be reasonable. In addition we can check that the units "g S" cancel, as shown, to leave the desired units "g Mo."

Practice Exercise 1: Cadmium sulfide is a yellow compound that is used as a pigment in artist's oil colors. A sample of this compound is composed of 1.25 g of cadmium and 0.357 g of sulfur. If a second sample of the same compound contains 3.50 g of sulfur, how many grams of cadmium does it contain? (Hint: Identify the law and write its mathematical form as it applies to this problem.)

Practice Exercise 2: Several samples of compounds containing only iron and sulfur were analyzed by taking the sample and heating it strongly to produce gaseous sulfur oxides and metallic iron. Which of the following compounds are the same and which are different?

Sample	Mass of compound before heating	Mass of iron after heating
A	25.36 g	16.11 g
B	15.42 g	8.28 g
C	7.85 g	4.22 g
D	11.87 g	7.54 g

The atomic theory was proposed by John Dalton

The laws of conservation of mass and definite proportions served as the *experimental foundation* for the atomic theory. They prompted the question: "What must be true about the nature of matter, given the truth of these laws?" In other words, what is matter made of?

At the beginning of the nineteenth century, John Dalton (1766–1844), an English scientist, used the Greek concept of atoms to make sense out of the laws of conservation of mass and definite proportions. Dalton reasoned that if atoms really exist, they must have certain properties to account for these laws. He described such properties, and the list constitutes what we now call **Dalton's atomic theory.**

Dalton's Atomic Theory

1. *Matter consists of tiny particles called atoms.*
2. *Atoms are indestructible. In chemical reactions, the atoms rearrange but they do not themselves break apart.*
3. *In any sample of a pure element, all the atoms are identical in mass and other properties.*
4. *The atoms of different elements differ in mass and other properties.*
5. *When atoms of different elements combine to form compounds, new and more complex particles form. However, in a given compound the constituent atoms are always present in the same fixed **numerical** ratio.*

Dalton's theory easily explained the law of conservation of mass. According to the theory, a chemical reaction is simply a reordering of atoms from one combination to another. If no atoms are gained or lost and if the masses of the atoms can't change, then the mass after the reaction must be the same as the mass before. This explanation of the law of conservation of mass works so well that it serves as the reason for balancing chemical equations, which we will discuss in the next chapter.

The law of definite proportions is also easy to explain. According to the theory, a given compound always has atoms of the same elements in the same numerical ratio. Suppose, for example, that two elements, *A* and *B*, combine to form a compound in which the number of atoms of *A* equals the number of atoms of *B* (i.e., the *atom ratio* is 1 to 1). If the mass of a *B* atom is twice that of an *A* atom, then every time we encounter a sample of this compound, the mass ratio (*A* to *B*) would be 1 to 2. This same mass ratio would exist regardless of the size of the sample, so in samples of this compound the elements *A* and *B* are always present in the same proportion by mass.

The atomic theory led to the discovery of the law of multiple proportions

Strong support for Dalton's theory came when Dalton and other scientists studied elements that are able to combine to give two (or more) compounds. For example, sulfur and oxygen form two different compounds, which we call sulfur dioxide and sulfur trioxide. If we decompose a 2.00 g sample of sulfur dioxide, we find it contains 1.00 g of S and 1.00 g of O. If we decompose a 2.50 g sample of sulfur trioxide, we find it also contains 1.00 g of S, but this time the mass of O is 1.50 g. This is summarized in the following table.

Compound	Sample Size	Mass of Sulfur	Mass of Oxygen
Sulfur dioxide	2.00 g	1.00 g	1.00 g
Sulfur trioxide	2.50 g	1.00 g	1.50 g

First, notice that sample sizes aren't the same; they were chosen so that each has the *same mass of sulfur.* Second, the ratio of the masses of oxygen in the two samples is one of small whole numbers.

$$\frac{\text{mass of oxygen in sulfur trioxide}}{\text{mass of oxygen in sulfur dioxide}} = \frac{1.50 \text{ g}}{1.00 \text{ g}} = \frac{3}{2}$$

Similar observations are made when we study other elements that form more than one compound with each other, and these observations form the basis of the **law of multiple proportions**.

> **Law of Multiple Proportions.** Whenever two elements form more than one compound, the different masses of one element that combine with the same mass of the other element are in the ratio of small whole numbers.

Dalton's theory explains the law of multiple proportions in a very simple way. Suppose a molecule of sulfur trioxide contains one sulfur and three oxygen atoms, and a molecule of sulfur dioxide contains one sulfur and two oxygen atoms (Figure 2.1). If we had just one molecule of each, then our samples each would have one sulfur atom and therefore the same mass of sulfur. Then, comparing the oxygen atoms, we find they are in a numerical ratio of 3 to 2. But because oxygen atoms all have the same mass, the mass ratio must also be 3 to 2.

The law of multiple proportions was not known before Dalton presented his theory, and its discovery demonstrates the scientific method in action. Experimental data suggested to Dalton the existence of atoms, and the atomic theory suggested the relationships that we now call the law of multiple proportions. Repeated experimental tests have uncovered no instances where the law of multiple proportions fails. These successful tests added great support to the atomic theory. In fact, for many years the law was one of the strongest arguments in favor of the existence of atoms.

Modern experimental evidence exists for atoms

Atoms are so incredibly tiny that even the most powerful optical microscopes are unable to detect them. In recent times, though, scientists have developed very sensitive instruments that are able to map the surfaces of solids with remarkable resolution. One such instrument is called a **scanning tunneling microscope.** It was invented in the early 1980s by Gerd Binnig and Heinrich Rohrer and earned them the 1986 Nobel Prize in Physics. With this instrument, the tip of a sharp metal probe is brought very close to an electrically conducting surface and an electric current bridging the gap is begun. The flow of current is extremely sensitive to the distance between the tip of the probe and the sample. As the tip is moved across the surface, the height of the tip is continually adjusted to keep the current flow constant. By accurately recording the height fluctuations of the tip, a map of the hills and valleys on the surface is obtained. The data are processed using a computer to reveal images such as that shown in Figure 2.2.

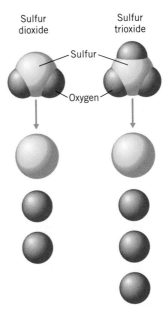

FIG. 2.1 Oxygen compounds of sulfur demonstrate the law of multiple proportions. Illustrated here are molecules of sulfur trioxide and sulfur dioxide. Each has one sulfur atom, and therefore the same mass of sulfur. The oxygen ratio is 3 to 2, both by atoms and by mass.

FIG. 2.2 Individual atoms can be imaged using a scanning tunneling microscope. This STM micrograph reveals the pattern of individual atoms of palladium deposited on a graphite surface. Palladium is a silvery white metal used in alloys such as white gold and dental crowns. *(Eurelios/Phototake.)*

2.2 ATOMS ARE COMPOSED OF SUBATOMIC PARTICLES

The earliest theories about atoms imagined them to be indestructible and totally unable to be broken into smaller pieces. However, as you probably know, atoms are not quite as indestructible as Dalton had thought. During the late 1800s and early 1900s, experiments were performed that demonstrated that atoms are composed of **subatomic particles.** (For some of the details about these experiments, see Facets of Chemistry 2.1.) From this work the current theoretical model of atomic structure evolved. We will examine it in general terms in this chapter. A more detailed discussion of atomic structure will follow in Chapter 7.

Protons, neutrons, and electrons are subatomic particles

☐ Physicists have discovered a large number of subatomic particles, but protons, neutrons, and electrons are the only ones that will concern us at this time.

☐ Protons are in all nuclei. Except for ordinary hydrogen, all nuclei also contain neutrons.

Experiments have shown that atoms are composed of three principal kinds of subatomic particles: **protons, neutrons,** and **electrons.** Experiments also revealed that at the center of an atom there exists a very tiny, extremely dense core called the **nucleus,** which is where an atom's protons and neutrons are found. Because they are found in nuclei, protons and neutrons are sometimes called **nucleons.** The electrons in an atom surround the nucleus and fill the remaining volume of the atom. (*How* the electrons are distributed around the nucleus is the subject of Chapter 7.) The properties of the subatomic particles are summarized in Table 2.1, and the general structure of the atom is illustrated in Figure 2.3.

Notice that two of the subatomic particles carry electrical charges. Protons carry a single unit of **positive charge** and electrons carry one unit of the opposite charge, a **negative charge.** Two particles that have the same electrical charge repel each other and two particles that have opposite charges will experience an attractive force. In an atom the negatively charged electrons are attracted to positively charged protons. In fact, it is this attraction that holds the electrons around the nucleus. Neutrons have no charge and are said to be electrically neutral (hence the name *neutron*).

Because of their identical charges, electrons repel each other. The repulsions between the electrons keep them spread out throughout the volume of the atom, and it is the *balance* between the attractions the electrons feel toward the nucleus and the repulsions they feel toward each other that controls the sizes of atoms.

Protons also repel each other, but they are able to stay together in the small volume of the nucleus because their repulsions are apparently offset by powerful nuclear forces that involve other subatomic particles we will not study.

☐ The binding energy of nucleons is discussed in Chapter 20.

Matter as we generally find it in nature appears to be electrically neutral, which means that it contains equal numbers of positive and negative charges. Therefore, *in a neutral atom, the number of electrons must equal the number of protons.*

The proton and neutron are much more massive than the electron, so in any atom almost all of the atomic mass is contributed by the particles that are found in the nucleus. (The mass of an electron is only about 1/1800 of that of a proton or neutron.) It is also interesting to note, however, that the diameter of an atom is approximately 10,000 times the diameter of its nucleus, so almost all the *volume* of an atom is occupied by its electrons, which fill the space around the nucleus. (To place this on a more meaningful scale, if the nucleus were 1 ft in diameter, it would lie at the center of an atom with a diameter of approximately 1.9 miles!)

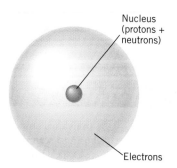

Nucleus (protons + neutrons)

Electrons

FIG. 2.3 **The internal structure of an atom.** An atom is composed of a tiny nucleus that holds all the protons and neutrons; the electrons fill the space outside the nucleus.

TABLE 2.1	Properties of Subatomic Particles		
Particle	Mass (g)	Electrical Charge	Symbol
Electron	9.109383×10^{-28}	$1-$	$_{-1}^{0}e$
Proton	$1.6726217 \times 10^{-24}$	$1+$	$_{1}^{1}H^{+}, _{1}^{1}p$
Neutron	$1.6749273 \times 10^{-24}$	0	$_{0}^{1}n$

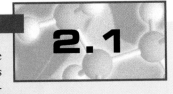

Experiments Leading to the Discovery of Subatomic Particles

Our current knowledge of atomic structure was pieced together from facts obtained from experiments by scientists that began in the nineteenth century. In 1834, Michael Faraday discovered that the passage of electricity through aqueous solutions could cause chemical changes, which was the first hint that matter was electrical in nature. Later in that century, scientists began to experiment with *gas discharge tubes* in which a high-voltage electric current was passed through a gas at low pressure in a glass tube (Figure 1). Such a tube is fitted with a pair of metal *electrodes* and when the electricity begins to flow between them, the gas in the tube glows. This flow of electricity is called an *electric discharge*, which is how the tubes got their names. (Modern neon signs work this way.)

The physicists who first studied this phenomenon did not know what caused the tube to glow, but tests soon revealed that negatively charged particles were moving from the negative electrode (the *cathode*) to the positive electrode (the *anode*). According to legend, it was Benjamin Franklin who decided which electrode was positive and which was negative. The physicists called these emissions *rays,* and because the rays came from the cathode, they were called *cathode rays*.

In 1897, the British physicist J. J. Thomson constructed a special gas discharge tube to make quantitative measurements of the properties of cathode rays. In some ways, the *cathode ray tube* he used was similar to a TV picture tube, as Figure 2 shows. In Thomson's tube, a beam of cathode rays was focused on a glass surface coated with a phosphor that glows when the cathode rays strike it (point 1). The cathode ray beam passed between the poles of a magnet and between a pair of metal electrodes that could be given electrical charges. The magnetic field tends to bend the beam in one direction (to point 2) whereas the charged electrodes bend the beam in the opposite direction (to point 3). By adjusting the charge on the electrodes, the two effects can be made to cancel, and from the amount of charge on the electrodes required to balance the effect of the magnetic field, Thomson was able to calculate the first bit of quantitative

information about a cathode ray particle—the ratio of its charge to its mass (often expressed as *e/m,* where *e* stands for charge and *m* stands for mass). The charge-to-mass ratio has a value of -1.76×10^8 coulombs/gram, where the coulomb (C) is a standard unit of electrical charge and the negative sign reflects the negative charge on the particle.

Many experiments were performed using the cathode ray tube and they demonstrated that cathode ray particles are in all matter. They are, in fact, *electrons.*

Measuring the Charge and Mass of the Electron. In 1909, a researcher at the University of Chicago, Robert Millikan, designed a clever experiment that enabled him to measure the electron's charge (Figure 3). During an experiment he would spray a fine mist of oil droplets above a pair of parallel metal plates, the top one of which had a small hole in it. As the oil drops settled, some would pass through this hole into the space between the plates, where he would irradiate them briefly with X rays. The X rays knocked electrons off molecules in the air, and the electrons became attached to the oil drops, which thereby were given an electrical charge. By observing the rate of fall of the charged drops both when the metal plates were electrically charged and when they were not, Millikan was able to calculate the amount of charge carried by each drop. When he examined his results, he found that all the values he obtained were whole-number multiples of -1.60×10^{-19} C. He reasoned that since a drop could only pick up whole numbers of electrons, this value must be the charge carried by each individual electron.

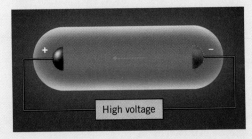

FIG. 1 A gas discharge tube. Cathode rays flow from the negatively charged cathode to the positively charged anode.

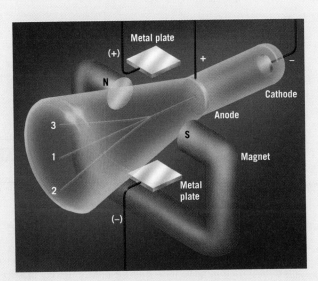

FIG. 2 Thomson's cathode ray tube. This device was used to measure the charge-to-mass ratio for the electron.

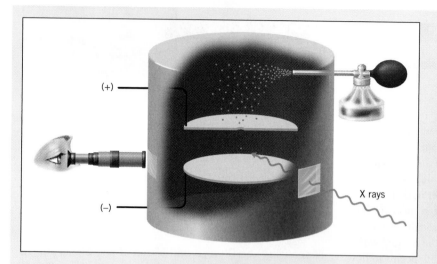

FIG. 3 Millikan's oil drop experiment. Electrons, which are ejected from air molecules by the X rays, are picked up by very small drops of oil falling through the tiny hole in the upper metal plate. By observing the rate of fall of the charged oil drops, with and without electrical charges on the metal plates, Millikan was able to calculate the charge carried by an electron.

Once Millikan had measured the electron's charge, its mass could then be calculated from Thomson's charge-to-mass ratio. This mass was calculated to be 9.09×10^{-28} g. More precise measurements have since been made, and the mass of the electron is currently reported to be 9.109383×10^{-28} g.

Discovery of the Proton. The removal of electrons from an atom gives a positively charged particle (called an *ion*). To study these, a modification was made in the construction of the cathode ray tube to produce a new device called a *mass spectrometer*. This apparatus is described in Facets of Chemistry 2.2 on page 47 and was used to measure the charge-to-mass ratios of positive ions. These ratios were found to vary, depending on the chemical nature of the gas in the discharge tube, showing that their masses also varied. The lightest positive particle observed was produced when hydrogen was in the tube, and its mass was about 1800 times as heavy as an electron. When other gases were used, their masses always seemed to be whole-number multiples of the mass observed for hydrogen atoms. This suggested the possibility that clusters of the positively charged particles made from hydrogen atoms made up the positively charged particles of other gases. The hydrogen atom, minus an electron, thus seemed to be a fundamental particle in all matter and was named the *proton*, after the Greek word *proteios*, meaning "of first importance."

Discovery of the Atomic Nucleus

Early in the twentieth century, Hans Geiger and Ernest Marsden, working under Ernest Rutherford at Great Britain's Manchester University, studied what happened when *alpha rays* hit thin metal foils. Alpha rays are composed of particles having masses four times those of the proton and bearing two positive charges; they are emitted by certain unstable atoms in a phenomenon called *radioactivity*. Most of the alpha particles sailed right on through as if the foils were virtually empty space (Figure 4). A significant number of alpha particles,

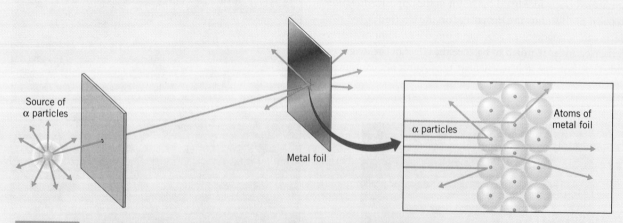

FIG. 4 Rutherford's alpha-particle experiment. Alpha particles are scattered in all directions by a thin metal foil. Some hit something very massive head-on and are deflected backward. Many sail through. Some, making near misses with the massive "cores" (nuclei), are still deflected, because alpha particles have the same kind of charge (+) as these cores.

however, were deflected at very large angles. Some were even deflected backward, as if they had hit stone walls. Rutherford was so astounded that he compared the effect to that of firing a 15 in. artillery shell at a piece of tissue paper and having it come back and hit the gunner! From studying the angles of deflection of the particles, Rutherford reasoned that only something extraordinarily massive and positively charged could cause such an occurrence. Since most of the alpha particles went straight through, he further reasoned that the metal atoms in the foils must be mostly empty space. Rutherford's ultimate conclusion was that virtually all of the mass of an atom must be concentrated in a particle having a very small volume located in the center of the atom. He called this massive particle the atom's *nucleus*.

Discovery of the Neutron

From the way alpha particles were scattered by a metal foil, Rutherford and his students were able to estimate the number of positive charges on the nucleus of an atom of the metal. This had to be equal to the number of protons in the nucleus, of course. But when they computed the nuclear mass based on this number of protons, the value always fell short of the actual mass. In fact, Rutherford found that only about half of the nuclear mass could be accounted for by protons. This led him to suggest that there were other particles in the nucleus that had a mass close to or equal to that of a proton, but with no electrical charge. This suggestion initiated a search that finally ended in 1932 with the discovery of the *neutron* by Sir James Chadwick, a British physicist.

Atomic numbers define elements and mass numbers describe isotopes

What distinguishes one element from another is the number of protons in the nuclei of its atoms, because *all the atoms of a particular element have an identical number of protons*. In fact, this allows us to redefine an **element** as *a substance whose atoms all contain the identical number of protons*. Thus, each element has associated with it a unique number, which we call its **atomic number** (Z), that equals the number of protons in the nuclei of any of its atoms.

TOOLS
The number of electrons, protons, and neutrons in atoms

$$\text{Atomic number } (Z) = \text{number of protons}$$

Most elements exist in nature as mixtures of similar atoms called *isotopes* that differ only in mass. What makes isotopes of the same element different are the numbers of neutrons in their nuclei. *The* **isotopes** *of a given element have atoms with the same number of protons but different numbers of neutrons*. The numerical sum of the protons and neutrons in the atoms of a particular isotope is called the **mass number** (A) of the isotope.

$$\text{Isotope mass number } (A) = (\text{number of protons}) + (\text{number of neutrons})$$

Therefore, every isotope is fully defined by two numbers, its atomic number and its mass number. Sometimes these numbers are added to the left of the chemical symbol as a subscript and a superscript, respectively. Thus, if X stands for the chemical symbol for the element, an isotope of X is represented as

$$_{Z}^{A}X$$

The isotope of uranium used in nuclear reactors, for example, can be symbolized as follows:

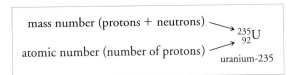

TOOLS
Atomic symbols for isotopes

As indicated, the name of this isotope is uranium-235 or U-235. Each neutral atom contains 92 protons and $(235 - 92) = 143$ neutrons as well as 92 electrons. In writing the symbol for the isotope, the atomic number is often omitted because it is redundant. Every atom of uranium has 92 protons, and every atom that has 92 protons is an atom of uranium. Therefore, this uranium isotope can be represented simply as ^{235}U.

☐ It is useful to remember that for a neutral atom, the atomic number equals both the number of protons and the number of electrons.

In naturally occurring uranium, a more abundant isotope is ^{238}U. Atoms of this isotope also have 92 protons, but the number of neutrons is 146. Thus, atoms of ^{235}U and ^{238}U have the identical number of protons but differ in the numbers of neutrons.

EXAMPLE 2.2
Counting Protons, Neutrons, and Electrons

How many electrons, protons, and neutrons does the Cr-52 isotope have?

ANALYSIS: This problem asks for all three of the major subatomic particles in the chromium isotope that has a nominal mass of 52. Therefore, all three of the tools for subatomic particles must be used:

$$\text{Protons} = \text{atomic number} = Z$$
$$\text{Electrons} = \text{atomic number} = Z$$
$$\text{Neutrons} = \text{mass number} - \text{atomic number} = A - Z$$

SOLUTION: Applying the tools we find that $Z = 24$ and $A = 52$ and we conclude

$$\text{Protons} = 24 \qquad \text{Electrons} = 24 \qquad \text{Neutrons} = 52 - 24 = 28$$

IS THE ANSWER REASONABLE? One check is to be sure that the sum of the number of protons and neutrons is the mass number. A second check is that the number of any of the particles is not larger than the mass (the largest number given in the problem) and in most cases the number of electrons, protons, or neutrons is usually close to half of the mass. Our answers fulfill these conditions.

Practice Exercise 3: Write the symbol for the isotope of plutonium (Pu) that contains 146 neutrons. How many electrons does it have? (Hint: Review the tools for writing isotope symbols and counting electrons.)

Practice Exercise 4: How many protons, neutrons, and electrons are in each atom of $^{35}_{17}Cl$?

Practice Exercise 5: In the previous exercise, can we discard the 35 or the 17 or both from the symbol without losing the ability to solve the problem? Explain your reasoning.

Relative atomic masses of elements can be found

One of the most useful concepts to come from Dalton's atomic theory is that atoms of an element have a constant, characteristic **atomic mass** (or **atomic weight**). This concept opened the door to the determination of chemical formulas and ultimately to one of the most useful devices chemists have for organizing chemical information, the periodic table of the elements. But how can the masses of atoms be measured?

Individual atoms are much too small to weigh in the traditional manner. However, the *relative masses* of the atoms of elements can be determined *provided we know the ratio in which the atoms occur in a compound.* Let's look at an example to see how this could work.

Hydrogen (H) combines with the element fluorine (F) to form the compound hydrogen fluoride. Each molecule of this compound contains one atom of hydrogen and one atom of fluorine, which means that in *any* sample of this substance the fluorine-to-hydrogen *atom ratio* is always 1 to 1. It is also found that when a sample of hydrogen fluoride is decomposed, the mass of fluorine obtained is always 19.0 times larger than the mass of hydrogen, so the fluorine-to-hydrogen *mass ratio* is always 19.0 to 1.00.

F-to-H atom ratio: 1 to 1
F-to-H mass ratio: 19.0 to 1.00

How could a 1-to-1 atom ratio give a 19.0-to-1.00 mass ratio? *Only if each fluorine atom is 19.0 times heavier than each H atom.*

Notice that even though we haven't found the actual masses of F and H atoms, we do now know how their masses compare (i.e., we know their *relative masses*). Similar procedures with other elements in other compounds are able to establish relative mass relationships among the other elements as well. What we need next is a way to place all these masses on the same mass scale.

Carbon-12 is the standard on the atomic mass scale

To establish a uniform mass scale for atoms it is necessary to select a standard against which the relative masses can be compared. Currently, the agreed-upon reference is the most abundant isotope of carbon, called carbon-12 and symbolized ^{12}C. One atom of this isotope is assigned *exactly* 12 units of mass, which are called **atomic mass units.** Some prefer to use the symbol **amu** for the atomic mass unit. The internationally accepted symbol is **u,** which is the symbol we will use throughout the rest of the book. By assigning 12 u to the mass of one atom of ^{12}C, the size of the atomic mass unit is established to be $\frac{1}{12}$ of the mass of a single carbon-12 atom:

TOOLS
*Atomic masses
are relative*

> 1 atom of ^{12}C has a mass of 12 u (exactly)
> 1 u equals $\frac{1}{12}$ the mass of 1 atom of ^{12}C (exactly)

☐ The atomic mass unit is sometimes called a dalton, 1 u = 1 dalton.

In modern terms, the atomic mass of an element is the average mass of the element's atoms (as they occur in nature) relative to an atom of carbon-12, which is assigned a mass of 12 units. Thus, if an average atom of an element has a mass twice that of a ^{12}C atom, its atomic mass would be 24 u.

The definition of the size of the atomic mass unit is really quite arbitrary. It could just as easily have been selected to be $\frac{1}{24}$ of the mass of a carbon atom, or $\frac{1}{10}$ of the mass of an iron atom, or any other value. Why $\frac{1}{12}$ of the mass of a ^{12}C atom? First, carbon is a very common element, available to any scientist. Second, and most important, by choosing the atomic mass unit of this size, the atomic masses of nearly all the other elements are almost whole numbers, with the lightest atom (hydrogen) having a mass of approximately 1 u.

Chemists generally work with whatever *mixture* of isotopes comes with a given element as it occurs naturally. Because the composition of this isotopic mixture is very nearly constant regardless of the source of the element, we can speak of an *average atom* of the element—average in terms of mass. For example, naturally occurring hydrogen is a mixture of two isotopes in the relative proportions given in the margin. The "average atom" of the element hydrogen, as it occurs in nature, has a mass that is 0.083992 times that of a ^{12}C atom. Since $0.083992 \times 12.000 \text{ u} = 1.0079 \text{ u}$, the average atomic mass of hydrogen is 1.0079 u. Notice that this average value is just a little larger than the atomic mass of ^{1}H because naturally occurring hydrogen also contains a little ^{2}H as shown in Table 2.2.

☐ Even the smallest laboratory sample of an element has so many atoms that the relative proportions of the isotopes is constant.

In general, the mass number of an isotope differs slightly from the atomic mass of the isotope. For instance, the isotope ^{35}Cl has an atomic mass of 34.968852 u. In fact, the *only* isotope that has an atomic mass equal to its mass number is ^{12}C; *by definition* the mass of this atom is exactly 12 u.

TABLE 2.2	Abundance of Hydrogen Isotopes	
Hydrogen Isotope	Mass	Percentage Abundance
^{1}H	1.007825 u	99.985
^{2}H	2.0140 u	0.015

Average atomic masses can be calculated from isotopic abundances

Originally, the relative atomic masses of the elements were determined in a way similar to that described for hydrogen and fluorine in our earlier discussion. A sample of a compound was analyzed and from the formula of the substance the relative atomic masses were calculated. These were then adjusted to place them on the unified atomic mass scale. In modern times, methods have been developed to measure very precisely both the relative abundances of the isotopes of the elements and their atomic masses. (See Facets of Chemistry 2.2.) This kind of information has permitted the calculation of more precise values of the average atomic masses, which are found in the table on the inside front cover of the book. Example 2.3 illustrates how this calculation is done.

EXAMPLE 2.3
Calculating Average Atomic
Masses from Isotopic Abundances

Naturally occurring chlorine is a mixture of two isotopes. In every sample of this element, 75.77% of the atoms are ^{35}Cl and 24.23% are atoms of ^{37}Cl. The accurately measured atomic mass of ^{35}Cl is 34.9689 u and that of ^{37}Cl is 36.9659 u. From these data, calculate the average atomic mass of chlorine.

ANALYSIS: In any natural sample containing many atoms of chlorine, 75.77% of the mass is contributed by atoms of ^{35}Cl and 24.23% is contributed by atoms of ^{37}Cl. This means that when we calculate the mass of the "average atom," we have to proportion it according to both the masses of the isotopes and their relative abundances. It is convenient to imagine an "average atom" to be composed of 75.77% of ^{35}Cl and 24.23% of ^{37}Cl. (Keep in mind, of course, that such an atom doesn't really exist.) We also recall that when we need to use percentages in calculations, we must divide the percentage by 100 to obtain a decimal number. This decimal number, when multiplied by the isotope mass, will tell us how much of the average mass is contributed by that isotope. All we need to do is add the contributions for all isotopes to obtain the average mass.

SOLUTION: We will calculate 75.77% of the mass of an atom of ^{35}Cl, which is the contribution of this isotope to the "average atom":

$$\text{contribution of } ^{35}Cl = \frac{75.77\% \ ^{35}Cl \times 34.9689 \text{ u}}{100 \%} = 26.496 \text{ u}$$

and for the ^{37}Cl, its contribution is

$$\text{contribution of } ^{37}Cl = \frac{24.23\% \ ^{37}Cl \times 36.9659 \text{ u}}{100\%} = 8.9568 \text{ u}$$

Then we add these contributions to give us the total mass of the "average atom."

$$26.496 \text{ u} + 8.957 \text{ u} = 35.453 \text{ u rounded to } 35.45 \text{ u}$$

Notice that in a two-step problem we kept one extra significant figure until the final rounding to four significant figures.

IS THE ANSWER REASONABLE? Once again, the final step is a check to see if the answer makes sense. Here is how we might do such a check: First, from the masses of the isotopes, we know the average atomic mass is somewhere between approximately 35 and 37. If the abundances of the two isotopes were equal, the average would be nearly 36. But there is more ^{35}Cl than ^{37}Cl, so a value closer to 35 than 37 seems reasonable; therefore, we can feel pretty confident our answer is correct.

Practice Exercise 6: Aluminum atoms have a mass that is 2.24845 times that of an atom of ^{12}C. What is the atomic mass of aluminum? (Hint: Recall that we have a tool that gives the relationship between the atomic mass unit and ^{12}C.)

Practice Exercise 7: How much heavier than an atom of ^{12}C is the average atom of naturally occurring copper? Refer to the table inside the front cover of the book for the necessary data.

Practice Exercise 8: Naturally occurring boron is composed of 19.8% of ^{10}B and 80.2% of ^{11}B. Atoms of ^{10}B have a mass of 10.0129 u and those of ^{11}B have a mass of 11.0093 u. Calculate the average atomic mass of boron.

FACETS OF CHEMISTRY

2.2

The Mass Spectrometer and the Experimental Measurement of Atomic Masses

When a spark is passed through a gas, electrons are knocked off the gas molecules. Because electrons are negatively charged, the particles left behind carry positive charges; they are called *positive ions*. These positive ions have different masses, depending on the masses of the molecules from which they are formed. Thus, some molecules have large masses and give heavy ions, while others have small masses and give light ions.

The device that is used to study the positive ions produced from gas molecules is called a *mass spectrometer* (illustrated in the figure at the right). In a mass spectrometer, positive ions are created by passing an electrical spark (called an *electric discharge*) through a sample of the particular gas being studied. As the positive ions are formed, they are attracted to a negatively charged metal plate that has a small hole in its center. Some of the positive ions pass through this hole and travel onward through a tube that passes between the poles of a powerful magnet.

One of the properties of charged particles, both positive and negative, is that their paths become curved as they pass through a magnetic field. This is exactly what happens to the positive ions in the mass spectrometer as they pass between the poles of the magnet. However, the extent to which their paths are bent depends on the masses of the ions. This is because the path of a heavy ion, like that of a speeding cement truck, is difficult to change, but the path of a light ion, like that of a motorcycle, is influenced more easily. As a result, heavy ions emerge from between the magnet's poles along different lines than the lighter ions. In effect, an entering beam containing ions of

different masses is sorted by the magnet into a number of beams, each containing ions of the same mass. This spreading out of the ion beam thus produces an array of different beams called a *mass spectrum*.

In practice, the strength of the magnetic field is gradually changed, which sweeps the beams of ions across a detector located at the end of the tube. As a beam of ions strikes the detector, its intensity is measured and the masses of the particles in the beam are computed based on the strength of the magnetic field and the geometry of the apparatus.

Among the benefits derived from measurements using the mass spectrometer are very accurate isotopic masses and relative isotopic abundances. These serve as the basis for the very precise values of the atomic masses that you find in the periodic table.

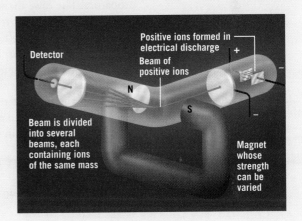

Detector

Positive ions formed in electrical discharge

Beam of positive ions

N

S

Beam is divided into several beams, each containing ions of the same mass

Magnet whose strength can be varied

2.3 | THE PERIODIC TABLE IS USED TO ORGANIZE AND CORRELATE FACTS

When we study different kinds of substances, we find that some are elements and others are compounds. Among compounds, some are composed of discrete molecules. Others, as you will learn, are made up of atoms that have acquired electrical charges. For elements such as sodium and iron we mentioned their metallic properties. On the other hand, chlorine and oxygen are not classified as metals. If we were to continue on this way, without attempting to build our subject around some central organizing structure, it would not be long before we became buried beneath a mountain of information in the form of seemingly unconnected facts.

The need for organization was recognized by many early chemists, and there were numerous attempts to discover relationships among the chemical and physical properties of the elements. A number of different sequences of elements were tried in the search for some sort of order or pattern. A few of these arrangements came quite close, at least in some respects, to our current periodic table, but either they were flawed in some way or they were presented to the scientific community in a manner that did not lead to their acceptance.

Mendeleev created the first periodic table

The periodic table we use today is based primarily on the efforts of a Russian chemist, Dmitri Ivanovich Mendeleev (1834–1907), and a German physicist, Julius Lothar Meyer (1830–1895). Working independently, these scientists developed similar periodic tables only a few months apart in 1869. Mendeleev is usually given the credit, however, because he had the good fortune to publish first.

Mendeleev was preparing a chemistry textbook for his students at the University of St. Petersburg. Looking for some pattern among the properties of the elements, he found that when he arranged them in order of increasing atomic mass, similar chemical properties were repeated over and over again at regular intervals. For instance, the elements lithium (Li), sodium (Na), potassium (K), rubidium (Rb), and cesium (Cs) are soft metals that are very reactive toward water. They form compounds with chlorine that have a 1-to-1 ratio of metal to chlorine. Similarly, the elements that immediately follow each of these also constitute a set with similar chemical properties. Thus, beryllium (Be) follows lithium, magnesium (Mg) follows sodium, calcium (Ca) follows potassium, strontium (Sr) follows rubidium, and barium (Ba) follows cesium. All of these elements form a water-soluble chlorine compound with a 1-to-2 metal to chlorine atom ratio. Mendeleev used such observations to construct his **periodic table,** which is illustrated in Figure 2.4.

▢ Periodic refers to the recurrence of properties at regular intervals.

The elements in Mendeleev's table are arranged in order of increasing atomic mass. When the sequence is broken at the right places and stacked, the elements fall naturally into columns, called *groups*, in which the elements of a given group have similar chemical properties. The rows themselves are called *periods*.

Mendeleev's genius rested on his placing elements with similar properties in the same group even when this left occasional gaps in the table. For example, he placed arsenic (As) in Group V under phosphorus because its chemical properties were similar to those of phosphorus, even though this left gaps in Groups III and IV. Mendeleev reasoned, correctly, that the elements that belonged in these gaps had simply not yet been discovered. In fact, on the basis of the location of these gaps Mendeleev was able to predict with remarkable accuracy the properties of these yet-to-be-found substances. His predictions helped serve as a guide in the search for the missing elements.

FIG. 2.4 **The first periodic table.** Mendeleev's periodic table roughly as it appeared in 1871. The numbers next to the symbols are atomic masses.

		Group I	Group II	Group III	Group IV	Group V	Group VI	Group VII	Group VIII
	1	H 1							
	2	Li 7	Be 9.4	B 11	C 12	N 14	O 16	F 19	
	3	Na 23	Mg 24	Al 27.3	Si 28	P 31	S 32	Cl 35.5	
	4	K 39	Ca 40	— 44	Ti 48	V 51	Cr 52	Mn 55	Fe 56, Co 59 Ni 59, Cu 63
	5	(Cu 63)	Zn 65	— 68	— 72	As 75	Se 78	Br 80	
Periods	6	Rb 85	Sr 87	?Yt 88	Zr 90	Nb 94	Mo 96	— 100	Ru 104, Rh 104 Pd 105, Ag 108
	7	(Ag 108)	Cd 112	In 113	Sn 118	Sb 122	Te 128	I 127	
	8	Cs 133	Ba 137	?Di 138	?Ce 140	—	—	—	— —
	9	—	—	—	—	—			
	10	—	—	?Er 178	?La 180	Ta 182	W 184	—	Os 195, Ir 197 Pt 198, Au 199
	11	(Au 199)	Hg 200	Tl 204	Pb 207	Bi 208	—		
	12	—	—	—	Th 231	—	U 240	—	— — — —

The elements tellurium (Te) and iodine (I) caused Mendeleev some problems. According to the best estimates at that time, the atomic mass of tellurium was greater than that of iodine. Yet if these elements were placed in the table according to their atomic masses, they would not fall into the proper groups required by their properties. Therefore, Mendeleev switched their order and in so doing violated his ordering sequence. (Actually, he believed that the atomic mass of tellurium had been incorrectly measured, but this wasn't so.)

The table that Mendeleev developed is in many ways similar to the one we use today. One of the main differences, though, is that Mendeleev's table lacks the column containing the elements helium (He) through radon (Rn). In Mendeleev's time, none of these elements had yet been found because they are relatively rare and because they have virtually no tendency to undergo chemical reactions. When these elements were finally discovered, beginning in 1894, another problem arose. Two more elements, argon (Ar) and potassium (K), did not fall into the groups required by their properties if they were placed in the table in the order required by their atomic masses. Another switch was necessary and another exception had been found. It became apparent that atomic mass was not the true basis for the periodic repetition of the properties of the elements. To determine what the true basis was, however, scientists had to await the discoveries of the atomic nucleus, the proton, and atomic numbers.

The modern periodic table arranges elements by atomic number

When atomic numbers were discovered, it was soon realized that the elements in Mendeleev's table are arranged in precisely the order of increasing atomic number. In other words, if we take atomic numbers as the basis for arranging the elements in sequence, no annoying switches are required and the elements Te and I or Ar and K are no longer a problem. The fact that it is the atomic number—the number of protons in the nucleus of an atom—that determines the order of elements in the table is very significant. We will see later that this has important implications with regard to the relationship between the number of electrons in an atom and the atom's chemical properties.

The modern periodic table is shown in Figure 2.5 and also appears on the inside front cover of the book. We will refer to the table frequently, so it is important for you to become familiar with it and with some of the terminology applied to it.

Special terminology is associated with the periodic table

As in Mendeleev's table, the elements are arranged in rows that we call **periods**, but here they are arranged in order of increasing atomic number. For identification purposes the periods are numbered. We will find these numbers useful later on. Below the main body of the table are two long rows of 14 elements each. These actually belong in the main body of the table following La ($Z = 57$) and Ac ($Z = 89$), as shown in Figure 2.6. They are almost always placed below the table simply to conserve space. If the fully spread-out table is printed on one page, the type is so small that it's difficult to read. Notice that in the fully extended form of the table, with all the elements arranged in their proper locations, there is a great deal of empty space. An important requirement of a detailed atomic theory, which we will get to in Chapter 7, is that it must explain not only the repetition of properties, but also why there is so much empty space in the table.

Again, as in Mendeleev's table, the vertical columns are called **groups.** However, there is not uniform agreement among chemists on how they should be numbered. In an attempt to standardize the table, the International Union of Pure and Applied Chemistry (the IUPAC), an international body of scientists responsible for setting standards in chemistry, officially adopted a system in which the groups are simply numbered sequentially, 1 through 18, from left to right using Arabic numerals. Chemists in North America favor the system where the longer groups are labeled IA to VIIIA and the shorter groups are labeled IB to VIIIB in the sequence depicted in Figure 2.5. Note that Group VIIIB encompasses three columns; moreover, the sequence of the B-group elements is unique and will make sense when we learn more about the structure of the atom in Chapter 7. European chemists favor a third numbering system with roman numerals and the designation of A and B groups but with a different sequence from the North American table. In Figure 2.5 and on the

TOOLS
Rows are periods

☐ Recall that the symbol Z stands for atomic number.

TOOLS
Columns are groups or families

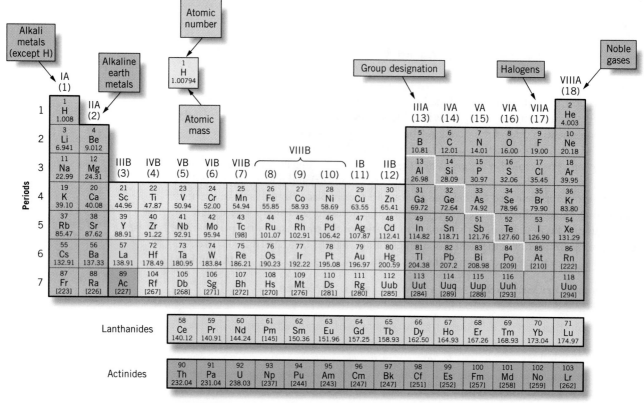

FIG. 2.5 **The modern periodic table.** At room temperature, mercury and bromine are liquids. Eleven elements are gases including the noble gases and the diatomic gases of hydrogen, oxygen, nitrogen, fluorine, and chlorine. The remaining elements are solids.

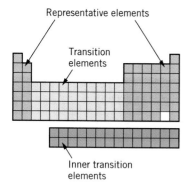

Representative elements

Transition elements

Inner transition elements

inside front cover of the book, we have used both the North American labels as well as those preferred by the IUPAC. Because of the lack of uniform agreement among chemists on how the groups should be specified, we will use the North American A-group/B-group designations in Figure 2.5 when we wish to specify a particular group.

As we have already noted, the elements in a given group bear similarities to each other. Because of such similarities, groups are sometimes referred to as **families of elements.** The elements in the longer columns (the A groups) are known as the **representative elements** or **main group elements.** Those that fall into the B groups in the center of the table are called **transition elements.** The elements in the two long rows below the main body of the table are the **inner transition elements,** and each row is named after the element that it follows in the main body of the table. Thus, elements 58–71 are called the **lanthanide elements** because they follow lanthanum ($Z = 57$), and elements 90–103 are called the **actinide elements** because they follow actinium ($Z = 89$). The lanthanides are also called **rare earth metals.**

Some of the groups have acquired common names. For example, except for hydrogen, the Group IA elements are metals. They form compounds with oxygen that dissolve in water to give solutions that are strongly alkaline, or caustic. As a result, they are called the **alkali metals** or simply the *alkalis.* The Group IIA elements are also metals. Their oxygen compounds are alkaline, too, but many compounds of the Group IIA elements are unable to dissolve in water and are found in deposits in the ground. Because of their properties and where they occur in nature, the Group IIA elements became known as the **alkaline earth metals.**

On the right side of the table, in Group VIIIA, are the **noble gases.** They used to be called the **inert gases** until it was discovered that the heavier members of the group show a small degree of chemical reactivity. The term *noble* is used when we wish to suggest a very limited degree of chemical reactivity. Gold, for instance, is often referred to as a noble metal because so few chemicals are capable of reacting with it.

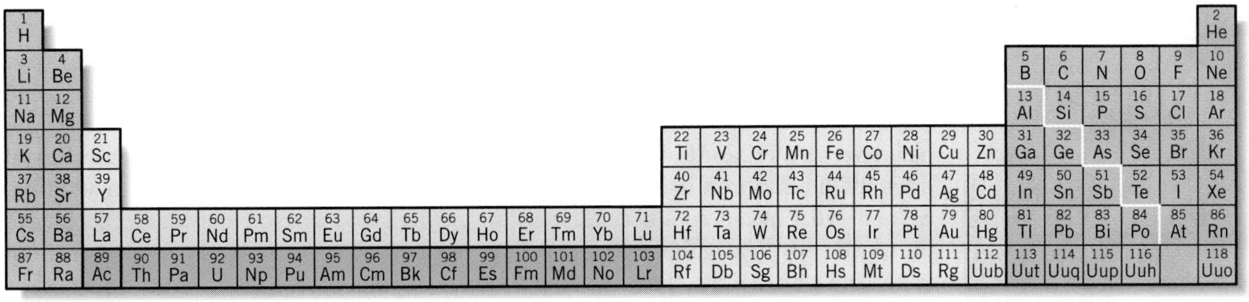

FIG. 2.6 Extended form of the periodic table. The two long rows of elements below the main body of the table in Figure 2.5 are placed in their proper places in this table.

Finally, the elements of Group VIIA are called the **halogens,** derived from the Greek word meaning "sea" or "salt." Chlorine (Cl), for example, is found in familiar table salt, a compound that accounts in large measure for the salty taste of seawater. The other groups of the representative elements have less frequently used names and we will name those groups based on the first element in the family; for example, Group VA is the **nitrogen family** and Group VIA is the **oxygen family.**

2.4 ELEMENTS CAN BE METALS, NONMETALS, OR METALLOIDS

The periodic table organizes all sorts of chemical and physical information about the elements and their compounds. It allows us to study systematically the way properties vary with an element's position within the table and, in turn, makes the similarities and differences among the elements easier to understand and remember.

Even a casual inspection of samples of the elements reveals that some are familiar metals and that others, equally well known, are not metals. Most of us recognize metals such as lead, iron, or gold and nonmetals such as oxygen or nitrogen. A closer look at the non-metallic elements, though, reveals that some of them, silicon and arsenic to name two, have properties that lie between those of true metals and true nonmetals. These elements are called **metalloids.** The elements are not evenly divided into the categories of metals, nonmetals, and metalloids. (See Figure 2.7.) Most elements are metals, slightly over a dozen are nonmetals, and only a handful are metalloids.

TOOLS
Periodic table metals, nonmetals, and metalloids

☐ Notice that the metalloids are grouped around the bold stair-step line that is drawn diagonally from boron (B) to astatine (At).

FIG. 2.7 Distribution of metals, nonmetals, and metalloids among the elements in the periodic table.

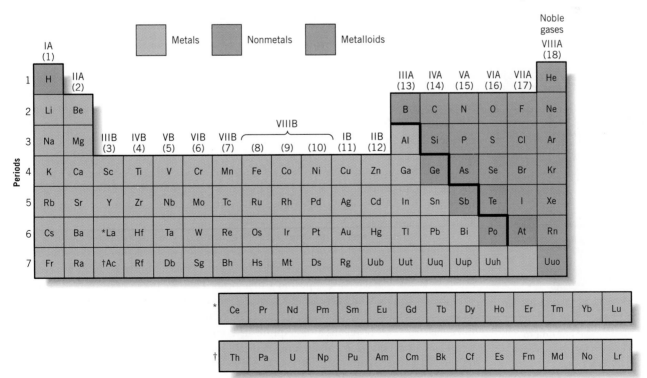

Metals have distinctive physical properties

You probably know a **metal** when you see one. Metals tend to have a shine so unique that it's called a *metallic luster*. For example, the silvery sheen of the freshly exposed surface of sodium in Figure 2.8 would most likely lead you to identify sodium as a metal even if you had never seen or heard of it before. We also know that metals conduct electricity. Few of us would hold an iron nail in our hand and poke it into an electrical outlet. In addition, we know that metals conduct heat very well. On a cool day, metals always feel colder to the touch than do neighboring nonmetallic objects because metals conduct heat away from your hand very rapidly. Nonmetals seem less cold because they can't conduct heat away as quickly and therefore their surfaces warm up faster.

Other properties that metals possess, to varying degrees, are **malleability**—the ability to be hammered or rolled into thin sheets—and **ductility**—the ability to be drawn into wire. The ability of a blacksmith to fashion horseshoes from a bar of iron (Figure 2.9) depends on the malleability of iron and steel, and the manufacture of electrical wire is based on the ductility of copper.

Hardness is another physical property that we usually think of for metals. Some, such as chromium or iron, are indeed quite hard; but others, like copper and lead, are rather soft. The alkali metals such as sodium (Figure 2.8) are so soft they can be cut with a knife, but they are also so chemically reactive that we rarely get to see them as free elements.

All the metallic elements, except mercury, are solids at room temperature (Figure 2.10). Mercury's low freezing point (−39 °C) and fairly high boiling point (357 °C) make it useful as a fluid in thermometers. Most of the other metals have much higher melting points, and some are used primarily because of this. Tungsten, for example, has the highest melting point of any metal (3400 °C, or 6150 °F), which explains its use as filaments that glow white-hot in electric lightbulbs.

The chemical properties of metals vary tremendously. Some, such as gold and platinum, are very unreactive toward almost all chemical agents. This property, plus their natural beauty and rarity, makes them highly prized for use in jewelry. Other metals, however, are so reactive that few people except chemists and chemistry students ever get to see them in their "free" states. For instance, the metal sodium reacts very quickly with oxygen or moisture in the air, and its bright metallic surface tarnishes almost immediately. In contrast, compounds of sodium, such as table salt and baking soda, are quite stable and very common.

Nonmetals lack the properties of metals

Substances such as plastics, wood, and glass that lack the properties of metals are said to be *nonmetallic*, and an element that has nonmetallic properties is called a **nonmetal** or **nonmetallic element.** Most often, we encounter the nonmetals in the form of compounds or mixtures of compounds. There are some nonmetals, however, that are very important to us in their elemental forms. The air we breathe, for instance, contains mostly nitrogen and oxygen. Both are gaseous, colorless, and odorless nonmetals. Since we can't see, taste, or smell them, however, it's difficult to experience their existence. (Although if you step into an atmosphere without oxygen, your body will soon tell you that something is missing!) Probably the most commonly *observed* nonmetallic element is carbon. We find it as the graphite in pencils, as coal, and as the charcoal used for barbecues. It also occurs in a more valuable form as diamond (Figure 2.11). Although diamond and graphite differ in appearance, each is a form of elemental carbon.

Many of the nonmetals are solids at room temperature and atmospheric pressure, while many others are gases. Photographs of some of the nonmetallic elements appear in Figure 2.12. Their properties are almost completely opposite those of metals. Each of these elements lacks the characteristic appearance of a metal. They are poor conductors of heat and, with the exception of the graphite form of carbon, are also poor conductors of electricity. The electrical conductivity of graphite appears to be an accident of molecular structure, since the structures of metals and graphite are completely different.

The nonmetallic elements lack the malleability and ductility of metals. A lump of sulfur crumbles when hammered and breaks apart when pulled on. Diamond cutters rely on

FIG. 2.8 **Sodium is a metal.** The freshly exposed surface of a bar of sodium reveals its shiny metallic luster. The metal reacts quickly with moisture and oxygen to form a white coating. Its high reactivity makes it dangerous to touch with bare skin. *(Michael Watson.)*

☐ Thin lead sheets are used for sound-deadening because the easily deformed lead absorbs the sound vibrations.

☐ We use the term *free element* to mean an element that is not chemically combined with any other element.

FIG. 2.9 Malleability of iron. A blacksmith uses the malleability of hot iron to fashion horseshoes from an iron bar. *(Stone/Getty Images.)*

FIG. 2.10 **Mercury droplet.** The metal mercury (once known as quicksilver) is a liquid at room temperature, unlike other metals, which are solids. *(OPC, Inc.)*

FIG. 2.11 **Diamond.** This gem is simply another form of the element carbon. *(Charles D. Winters/ Photo Researchers, Inc.)*

FIG. 2.12 **Some nonmetallic elements.** In the bottle on the left is dark-red liquid bromine, which vaporizes easily to give a deeply colored orange vapor. Pale green chlorine fills the round flask in the center. Solid iodine lines the bottom of the flask on the right and gives off a violet vapor. Powdered red phosphorus occupies the dish in front of the flask of chlorine, and black powdered graphite is in the watch glass. Also shown are lumps of yellow sulfur. *(Michael Watson.)*

the brittle nature of carbon when they split a gem-quality stone by carefully striking a quick blow with a sharp blade.

As with metals, nonmetals exhibit a broad range of chemical reactivity. Fluorine, for instance, is extremely reactive. It reacts readily with almost all the other elements. At the other extreme is helium, the gas used to inflate children's balloons and the blimps seen at major sporting events. This element does not react with anything, a fact that chemists find useful when they want to provide a totally *inert* (unreactive) atmosphere inside some apparatus.

Metalloids have physical properties between metals and nonmetals

The properties of metalloids lie between those of metals and nonmetals. This shouldn't surprise us since the metalloids are located between the metals and the nonmetals in the periodic table. In most respects, metalloids behave as nonmetals, both chemically and physically. However, in their most important physical property, electrical conductivity, they somewhat resemble metals. Metalloids tend to be **semiconductors;** they conduct electricity, but not nearly so well as metals. This property, particularly as found in silicon and germanium, is responsible for the remarkable progress made during the last five decades in the field of solid-state electronics. The operation of every computer, audio system, TV receiver, DVD or CD player, and AM–FM radio relies on transistors made from semiconductors. Perhaps the most amazing advance of all has been the fantastic reduction in the size of electronic components that semiconductors have allowed (Figure 2.13). To it, we owe the development of small and versatile cell phones, cameras, MP3 players, handheld calculators,

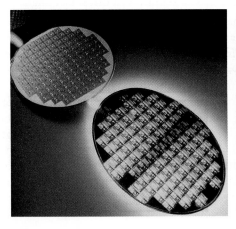

FIG. 2.13 **Modern electronic circuits rely on the semiconductor properties of silicon.** The silicon wafer shown here contains more electronic components (10 billion) than there are people on our entire planet (about 6.5 billion)! *(Courtesy Sematech; Courtesy NASA)*

and microcomputers. The heart of these devices is an integrated circuit that begins as a wafer of extremely pure silicon (or germanium) that is etched and chemically modified into specialized arrays of thousands of transistors.

Metallic and nonmetallic character is related to an element's position in the periodic table

The occurrence of the metalloids between the metals and the nonmetals is our first example of trends in properties within the periodic table. We will frequently see that as we move from position to position across a period or down a group, chemical and physical properties change in a more or less regular way. There are few abrupt changes in the characteristics of the elements as we scan across a period or down a group. The location of the metalloids can be seen, then, as an example of the gradual transition between metallic and nonmetallic properties. From left to right across Period 3, we go from aluminum, an element that has every appearance of a metal; to silicon, a semiconductor; to phosphorus, an element with clearly nonmetallic properties. A similar gradual change is seen going down Group IVA. Carbon is certainly a nonmetal, silicon and germanium are metalloids, and tin and lead are metals. Trends such as these are useful to spot because they help us remember properties.

2.5 FORMULAS AND EQUATIONS DESCRIBE SUBSTANCES AND THEIR REACTIONS

A property possessed by nearly every element is the ability to combine with other elements to form compounds, although not all combinations appear to be possible. For example, iron reacts with oxygen to form a compound that we commonly call rust, but no compound is formed between sodium and iron.

In Chapter 1 we noted that during chemical reactions, the properties of the substances change, often dramatically, when a reaction takes place. This is certainly true in the reactions of elements to form compounds. An example is the reaction between hydrogen and oxygen to form ordinary water.

At room temperature both hydrogen and oxygen are clear colorless gases. When they are mixed and ignited, these elements combine explosively to form the familiar compound water, which of course is a liquid at room temperature. As with nearly all chemical reactions, the properties of the substances present prior to the reaction differ quite a lot from the properties of those present afterwards.

The reaction between hydrogen and oxygen is not one we would expect to encounter in our daily lives, but it does have applications. When hydrogen and oxygen are cooled to sufficiently low temperatures, they condense to form liquids that serve as the fuel for the main rocket engines of the space shuttle (Figure 2.14). Hydrogen has also been used to power nonpolluting vehicles in which its reaction with oxygen (from air) yields an exhaust containing only water vapor.

A chemical formula describes the composition of a substance

TOOLS
Chemical formulas

To describe chemical substances, both elements and compounds, we commonly use **chemical formulas,** in which chemical symbols are used to represent atoms of the elements that are present. For a **free element** (*one that is not combined with another element in a compound*) we often simply use the chemical symbol. Thus, the element sodium is represented by its symbol, Na, which is interpreted to mean one atom of sodium.

Except for the noble gases, all the free nonmetallic elements exist as molecules that contain two or more atoms. Many of those we encounter frequently occur as **diatomic molecules** (molecules composed of two atoms each). Among them are the gases hydrogen, oxygen, and nitrogen and the halogens (fluorine, chlorine, bromine, and iodine). We represent these elements with chemical formulas in which subscripts indicate the number of atoms in a molecule. Thus, the **formula** for molecular hydrogen is H_2, and those for oxygen, nitrogen, and chlorine are O_2, N_2, and Cl_2, respectively. (See Figure 2.15.) The elements that occur as diatomic molecules are listed in Table 2.3. This would be a good time to learn them because

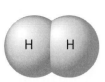
Hydrogen molecule, H_2

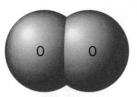
Oxygen molecule, O_2

Nitrogen molecule, N_2

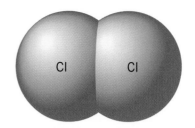
Chlorine molecule, Cl_2

FIG. 2.15 **Models that depict the diatomic molecules of hydrogen, oxygen, nitrogen, and chlorine.** Each contains two atoms per molecule; their different sizes reflect differences in the sizes of the atoms that make up the molecules. The atoms are shaded by color to indicate the element (hydrogen, white; oxygen, red; nitrogen, blue; and chlorine, green).

TABLE 2.3	**Elements That Occur Naturally as Diatomic Molecules**		
Hydrogen	H_2	Fluorine	F_2
Nitrogen	N_2	Chlorine	Cl_2
Oxygen	O_2	Bromine	Br_2
		Iodine	I_2

you will come upon them often throughout the course. Other nonmetals have their atoms arranged in even more complex combinations. Elemental sulfur, for example, contains molecules of S_8 and one form of phosphorus has molecules of P_4.

Just as chemical symbols can be used as shorthand notations for the names of elements, a chemical formula is a shorthand way of writing the name for a compound. However, *the most important characteristic of a compound's formula is that it specifies the composition of the substance.*

In the formula of a compound, each element present is identified by its chemical symbol. Table salt, for example, has the chemical formula NaCl which indicates it is composed of the elements sodium (Na) and chlorine (Cl). When more than one atom of an element is present, the number of atoms is given by a **subscript** after the symbol. For instance, the iron oxide in rust has the formula Fe_2O_3, which tells us that the compound is composed of iron (Fe) and oxygen (O), and that in this compound there are two atoms of iron for every three atoms of oxygen. When no subscript is written, we assume it to be 1, so in NaCl we find one atom of sodium (Na) for each atom of chlorine (Cl). Similarly, the formula H_2O tells us that in water there are two hydrogen atoms for every one oxygen atom, and the formula for chloroform, $CHCl_3$, indicates that one atom of carbon, one atom of hydrogen, and three atoms of chlorine have combined (Figure 2.16).

For more complicated compounds, we sometimes find formulas that contain parentheses. An example is the formula for urea, $CO(NH_2)_2$, which tells us that the group of atoms within the parentheses, NH_2, occurs twice. (The formula for urea also could be written as CON_2H_4, but there are good reasons for writing certain formulas with parentheses, as you will see later.)

Hydrates are crystals that contain water in fixed proportions

Certain compounds form crystals that contain water molecules. An example is ordinary plaster—the material often used to coat the interior walls of buildings. Plaster consists of crystals of calcium sulfate, $CaSO_4$, that contain two molecules of water for each $CaSO_4$. These water molecules are not held very tightly and can be driven off by heating the crystals. The dried crystals absorb water again if exposed to moisture, and the amount of water absorbed always gives crystals in which the H_2O-to-$CaSO_4$ ratio is 2 to 1. Compounds whose crystals contain water molecules in fixed ratios are quite common and are called **hydrates**. The formula for this hydrate of calcium sulfate is written $CaSO_4 \cdot 2H_2O$ to show that there are two molecules of water per $CaSO_4$. The raised dot is used to indicate that the water molecules are not bound too tightly in the crystal and can be removed.

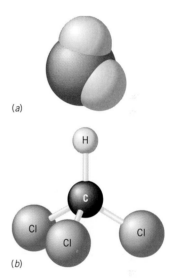
(a)

(b)

FIG. 2.16 **Molecules of water and chloroform.** (*a*) A space-filling model of H_2O. (*b*) A ball-and-stick model of $CHCl_3$. (Hydrogen, white; oxygen, red; carbon, black; and chlorine, green.)

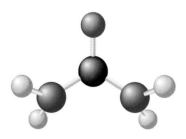
Ball-and-stick model of the urea molecule, $CO(NH_2)_2$.

 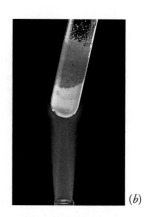

FIG. 2.17 Water can be driven from hydrates by heating. (*a*) Blue crystals of copper sulfate pentahydrate, $CuSO_4 \cdot 5H_2O$, about to be heated. (*b*) The hydrate readily loses water when heated. The light colored solid observed in the lower half of the test tube is pure $CuSO_4$. (*Richard Megna/Fundamental Photographs; Michael Watson*)

(*a*)   (*b*)

Sometimes the *dehydration* (removal of water) of hydrate crystals produces changes in color. An example is copper sulfate, which is sometimes used as an agricultural fungicide. Copper sulfate forms blue crystals with the formula $CuSO_4 \cdot 5H_2O$ in which there are five water molecules for each $CuSO_4$. When these blue crystals are heated, most of the water is driven off and the solid that remains, now nearly pure $CuSO_4$, is almost white (Figure 2.17). If left exposed to the air, the $CuSO_4$ will absorb moisture and form blue $CuSO_4 \cdot 5H_2O$ again.

☐ When all the water is removed, the solid is said to be **anhydrous**, meaning "without water."

Counting atoms in formulas is a necessary skill

Counting the number of atoms of the elements in a chemical formula is an operation you will have to perform many times, so let's look at an example.

EXAMPLE 2.4
Counting Atoms in Formulas

How many atoms of each element are represented by the formulas (a) $Al_2(SO_4)_3$ and (b) $CoCl_2 \cdot 6H_2O$?

ANALYSIS: The essential tool to use here is the set of principles governing how we count atoms in a chemical formula in the preceding section. To review, the subscript following an element indicates how many of that element are part of the formula; a subscript of 1 is implied if there is no subscript. We also must recall that a quantity within parentheses is repeated a number of times equal to the subscript that follows, and a raised dot in a formula indicates the substance is a hydrate in which the number preceding H_2O specifies how many water molecules are present.

SOLUTION: (a) Here we must recognize that all the atoms within the parentheses occur three times.

Subscript 3 indicates three SO_4 units.

$$Al_2(SO_4)_3$$

Each SO_4 contains one S and four O atoms, so three of them contain three S and twelve O atoms. The subscript for Al tells us there are two Al atoms. Therefore, the formula $Al_2(SO_4)_3$ shows

2   Al   3   S   12   O

(b) This is a formula for a hydrate, as indicated by the raised dot. It contains six water molecules, each with two H and one O, for every $CoCl_2$.

The 6 indicates there are six molecules of H_2O.

$$CoCl_2 \cdot 6H_2O$$

Dot indicates the compound is a hydrate.

Therefore, the formula $CoCl_2 \cdot 6H_2O$ represents

$$1 \quad Co \qquad 2 \quad Cl \qquad 12 \quad H \qquad 6 \quad O$$

ARE THE ANSWERS REASONABLE? The only way to check the answer here is to perform a recount.

Practice Exercise 9: How many atoms of each element are expressed by the formulas below? (Hint: Pay special attention to counting elements within parentheses.)

(a) $NiCl_2$ (b) $FeSO_4$ (c) $Ca_3(PO_4)_2$ (d) $Co(NO_3)_2 \cdot 6H_2O$

Practice Exercise 10: How many atoms of each element are present in each of the formulas that follow? Consult the table inside the front cover to write the full name of each element as well as its symbol.

(a) NH_4NO_3 (b) $FeNH_4(SO_4)_2$ (c) $Mo(NO_3)_2 \cdot 5H_2O$ (d) $C_6H_4ClNO_2$

Chemical equations describe what happens in chemical reactions

A **chemical equation** *describes what happens when a chemical reaction occurs.* It uses chemical formulas to provide a before-and-after picture of the chemical substances involved. Consider, for example, the reaction between hydrogen and oxygen to give water. The chemical equation that describes this reaction is

$$2H_2 + O_2 \longrightarrow 2H_2O$$

The two substances that appear to the left of the arrow are the **reactants;** they are the substances present before the reaction begins. To the right of the arrow we find the formula for the **product** of the reaction, water. In this example, only one substance is formed in the reaction, so there is only one product. As we will see, however, in most chemical reactions there is more than one product. The products are the substances that are formed and that exist after the reaction is over. The arrow means "reacts to yield." Thus, this equation tells us that *hydrogen and oxygen react to yield water.*

Coefficients are written in front of formulas to satisfy the law of conservation of mass

In the equation for the reaction of hydrogen and oxygen, you'll notice that the number 2 precedes the formulas of hydrogen and water. Numbers in front of the formulas are called **coefficients,** and they indicate the number of molecules of each kind among the reactants and products. Thus, $2H_2$ means two molecules of H_2, and $2H_2O$ means two molecules of H_2O. When no number is written, the coefficient is assumed to be 1 (so the coefficient of O_2 equals 1).

Coefficients are needed to have the equation conform to the law of conservation of mass, as illustrated in Figure 2.18. Because atoms cannot be created or destroyed in a chemical reaction, we must have the same number of atoms of each kind present before and after the reaction (that is, on both sides of the arrow). When this condition is met, we say the equation is **balanced.** Another example is the equation for the combustion of butane, C_4H_{10}, the fluid in disposable cigarette lighters (Figure 2.19).

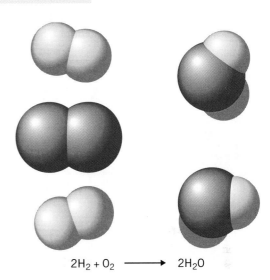

$$2H_2 + O_2 \longrightarrow 2H_2O$$

FIG. 2.18 The reaction between molecules of hydrogen and oxygen. The reaction between two molecules of hydrogen and one molecule of oxygen gives two molecules of water.

FIG. 2.19 The combustion of butane, C_4H_{10}. The products are carbon dioxide and water vapor. *(Robert Capece.)*

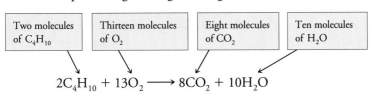

| Two molecules of C_4H_{10} | Thirteen molecules of O_2 | Eight molecules of CO_2 | Ten molecules of H_2O |

$$2C_4H_{10} + 13O_2 \longrightarrow 8CO_2 + 10H_2O$$

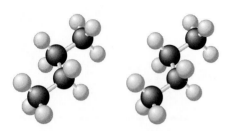

Two molecules of butane contain 8 atoms of C and 20 atoms of H.

FIG. 2.20 **Understanding coefficients in an equation.** The expression $2C_4H_{10}$ describes two molecules of butane, each of which contains 4 carbon and 10 hydrogen atoms. This gives a total of 8 carbon and 20 hydrogen atoms.

☐ Remember:

s = solid
l = liquid
g = gas
aq = aqueous

The 2 before the C_4H_{10} tells us that two molecules of butane react. This involves a total of 8 carbon atoms and 20 hydrogen atoms, as we see in Figure 2.20. Notice we have multiplied the numbers of atoms of C and H in one molecule of C_4H_{10} by the coefficient 2. On the right we find 8 molecules of CO_2, which contain a total of 8 carbon atoms. Similarly, 10 water molecules contain 20 hydrogen atoms. Finally, we can count 26 oxygen atoms on both sides of the equation. You will learn to balance equations such as this in Chapter 3.

The states of the reactants and products can be specified in a chemical equation

In a chemical equation we sometimes find it useful to specify the physical states of the reactants and products, that is, whether they are solids, liquids, or gases. This is done by writing s for solid, l for liquid, or g for gas in parentheses after the chemical formulas. For example, the equation for the combustion of the carbon in a charcoal briquette can be written as

$$C(s) + O_2(g) \longrightarrow CO_2(g)$$

At times we will also find it useful to indicate that a particular substance is dissolved in water. We do this by writing aq, meaning "*aqueous* solution," in parentheses after the formula. For instance, the reaction between stomach acid (an aqueous solution of HCl) and the active ingredient in Tums, $CaCO_3$, is

$$2HCl(aq) + CaCO_3(s) \longrightarrow CaCl_2(aq) + H_2O(l) + CO_2(g)$$

EXAMPLE 2.5
Determining if an Equation Is Balanced

Determine whether or not the following chemical equations are balanced. Support your conclusions by writing how many atoms of each element are on each side of the arrow.

(a) $Fe(OH)_3 + 2HNO_3 \longrightarrow Fe(NO_3)_3 + 2H_2O$

(b) $BaCl_2 + H_2SO_4 \longrightarrow BaSO_4 + 2HCl$

(c) $C_6H_{12}O_6 + 6O_2 \longrightarrow 6CO_2 + 6H_2O$

ANALYSIS: The statement of the problem asks if the equations are balanced. You can prove an equation is balanced if each element has the same number of atoms on each side of the arrow. Again, in this example, we use the tool that tells us how to use subscripts to count atoms in each formula. Also, a given atom, such as oxygen, in these equations may appear in both reactants or both products and we need to be sure to account for all of them.

SOLUTION: (a) Reactants: 1 Fe, 9 O, 5 H, 2 N. Products: 1 Fe, 11 O, 4 H, 3 N. Only Fe has the same number of atoms on each side of the arrow. This is *not* balanced.
(b) Reactants: 1 Ba, 2 Cl, 2 H, 1 S, 4 O. Products: 1 Ba, 2 Cl, 2 H, 1 S, 4 O. This equation *is* balanced.
(c) Reactants: 6 C, 12 H, 18 O. Products: 6 C, 18 O, 12 H. This equation *is* balanced.

ARE THE ANSWERS REASONABLE? The appropriate way to check this is to recount the atoms. Try counting the atoms in the reverse direction this time.

Practice Exercise 11: How many atoms of each element appear on each side of the arrow in the following equation? (Hint: Recall that coefficients multiply the elements in the entire formula.)

$$Mg(OH)_2 + 2HCl \longrightarrow MgCl_2 + 2H_2O$$

Practice Exercise 12: Rewrite the equation in Practice Exercise 11 to show that $Mg(OH)_2$ is a solid, HCl and $MgCl_2$ are dissolved in water, and H_2O is a liquid.

Practice Exercise 13: Count each of the atoms in the following equation to determine if it is balanced.

$$2(NH_4)_3PO_4 + 3Ba(C_2H_3O_2)_2 \longrightarrow Ba_3(PO_4)_2 + 6NH_4C_2H_3O_2$$

2.6 | MOLECULAR COMPOUNDS CONTAIN NEUTRAL PARTICLES CALLED MOLECULES

The concept of molecules dates to the time of Dalton's atomic theory, where a part of his theory was that atoms of elements combine in fixed numerical ratios to form "molecules" of a compound. By our modern definition *a* **molecule** *is an electrically neutral particle consisting to two or more atoms.* Accordingly, the term molecule applies to many elements such as H_2 and O_2 as well as to **molecular compounds**.

Experimental evidence exists for molecules

One phenomenon that points to the existence of molecules is called **Brownian motion** [named after Robert Brown (1773–1858), the Scottish botanist who first observed it]. When very small particles such as tiny grains of pollen are suspended in a liquid and observed under a microscope, the tiny particles are seen to be constantly jumping and jiggling about. It appears as though they are continually being knocked back and forth by collisions with something. An explanation is that this "something" is *molecules* of the liquid. The microscopic particles are constantly bombarded by molecules of the liquid, but because the suspended particles are so small, the collisions are not occurring equally on all sides. The unequal numbers of collisions cause the lightweight particles to jerk about.

There is additional evidence for molecules, and today scientists accept the existence of molecules as fact. Looking more closely, within molecules atoms are held to each other by attractions called **chemical bonds,** which are electrical in nature. In molecular compounds chemical bonds arise from the sharing of electrons between one atom and another. We will discuss such bonds at considerable length in Chapters 8 and 9. What is important to know about molecules now is that *the group of atoms that make up a molecule move about together and behave as a single particle,* just as the various parts that make up a car move about as one unit. The chemical formulas that we write to describe the compositions of molecules are called **molecular formulas,** which specify the actual numbers of atoms of each kind that make up a single molecule.

Molecular compounds form when nonmetals combine

As a general rule, *molecular compounds are formed when nonmetallic elements combine.* For example, you learned that H_2 and O_2 combine to form molecules of water. Similarly, carbon and oxygen combine to form either carbon monoxide, CO, or carbon dioxide, CO_2. (Both are gases that are formed in various amounts as products in the combustion of fuels such as gasoline and charcoal.) Although molecular compounds can be formed by the direct combination of elements, often they are the products of reactions between compounds. You will encounter many such reactions in your study of chemistry.

Although there are relatively few nonmetals, the number of molecular substances formed by them is huge. This is because of the variety of ways in which they combine as well as the varying degrees of complexity of their molecules. Variety and complexity reach a maximum with compounds in which carbon is combined with a handful of other elements such as hydrogen, oxygen, and nitrogen. There are so many of these compounds, in fact, that their study encompasses the chemical specialties called organic chemistry and biochemistry.

Molecules vary in size from small to very large. Some contain as few as two atoms (diatomic molecules). Most molecules are more complex, however, and contain more atoms.

□ Carbon monoxide is a poisonous gas found in the exhaust of automobiles.

Molecules of water (H_2O), for example, have three atoms and those of ordinary table sugar ($C_{12}H_{22}O_{11}$) have 45. There also are molecules that are very large, such as those that occur in plastics and in living organisms, some of which contain millions of atoms.

At this early stage we can only begin to look for signs of order among the vast number of nonmetal–nonmetal compounds. To give you a taste of the subject, we will look briefly at some simple compounds that the nonmetals form with hydrogen, as well as some simple compounds of carbon.

Hydrogen forms compounds with many nonmetals

Compounds that elements form with hydrogen are often called **hydrides,** and the formulas of the simple hydrides of the nonmetals are given in Table 2.4.[1] These compounds provide an opportunity to observe how we can use the periodic table as an aid in remembering factual information, in this case, the formulas of the hydrides. Notice that the number of hydrogen atoms combined with the nonmetal atom equals *the number of spaces to the right that we have to move in the periodic table to get to a noble gas.* (You will learn *why* this is so in Chapter 8, but for now we can just use the periodic table to help us remember the formulas.)

Predicting hydride formulas

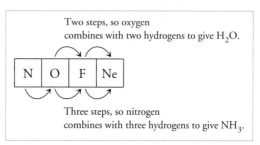

Two steps, so oxygen combines with two hydrogens to give H_2O.

| N | O | F | Ne |

Three steps, so nitrogen combines with three hydrogens to give NH_3.

▢ Many of the nonmetals form more complex compounds with hydrogen, but we will not discuss them here.

Also note in Table 2.4 that the formulas of the simple hydrides are similar for nonmetals within a given group of the periodic table. If you know the formula for the hydride of the top member of the group, then you know the formulas of all of them in that group.

We live in a three-dimensional world, and this is reflected in the three-dimensional shapes of molecules. The shapes of the simple nonmetal hydrides of nitrogen, oxygen, and fluorine are illustrated as space-filling models in Figure 2.21. Our understanding of the geometric shapes of molecules is described in Chapter 9.

TABLE 2.4	Simple Hydrogen Compounds of the Nonmetallic Elements			
	Group			
Period	IVA	VA	VIA	VIIA
2	CH_4	NH_3	H_2O	HF
3	SiH_4	PH_3	H_2S	HCl
4	GeH_4	AsH_3	H_2Se	HBr
5		SbH_3	H_2Te	HI

Ammonia, NH_3

Water, H_2O

Hydrogen fluoride, HF

FIG. 2.21 Nonmetal hydrides of nitrogen, oxygen, and fluorine.

[1] Table 2.4 shows how the formulas are normally written. The order in which the hydrogens appear in the formula is not of concern to us now. Instead, we are interested in the *number* of hydrogens that combine with a given nonmetal.

Compounds of carbon form the basis for organic chemistry

Among all the elements, carbon is unique in the variety of compounds it forms with elements such as hydrogen, oxygen, and nitrogen. As a consequence, the number and complexity of such **organic compounds** is enormous, and their study constitutes the major specialty called **organic chemistry**. The term *organic* here comes from an early belief that these compounds could only be made by living organisms. We now know this isn't true, but the name organic chemistry persists nonetheless.

Organic compounds are around us everywhere and we will frequently use such substances as examples in our discussions. Therefore, it will be helpful if you can begin to learn some of them now.

The study of organic chemistry begins with **hydrocarbons** (compounds of carbon and hydrogen). The simplest hydrocarbon is methane, CH_4, which is a member of a series of hydrocarbons with the general formula C_nH_{2n+2}, where n is an integer (i.e., a whole number). The first six members of this series, called the **alkane** series, are given in Table 2.5 along with their boiling points. Notice that as the molecules become larger, their boiling points increase.

□ Our goal at this time is to acquaint you with some of the important kinds of organic compounds we encounter regularly, so our discussion here is brief.

TABLE 2.5	Hydrocarbons Belonging to the Alkane Series	
Compound	Name	Boiling Point (°C)
CH_4	Methane[a]	−161.5
C_2H_6	Ethane[a]	−88.6
C_3H_8	Propane[a]	−42.1
C_4H_{10}	Butane[a]	−0.5
C_5H_{12}	Pentane	36.1
C_6H_{14}	Hexane	68.7

[a] Gases at room temperature (25 °C) and atmospheric pressure.

Molecular formulas can be written in different ways depending on what information is needed. A condensed formula such as C_2H_6 for ethane or C_3H_8 for propane simply indicates the number of each type of atom in the molecule. Structural formulas indicate how the carbon atoms are connected. Ethane is written as CH_3CH_3 and propane is $CH_3CH_2CH_3$ in the structural format. Line structures and a ball-and-stick representation are illustrated in Figure 1.3 for methane, while Figure 2.22. illustrates ethane and propane in space-filling models.

The alkanes are common substances. They are the principal constituents of petroleum from which most of our useful fuels are produced. Methane itself is the major component of natural gas that is often used for home heating and cooking. Gas-fired barbecues and some homes use propane as a fuel, and butane is the fuel in inexpensive cigarette lighters.[2] Hydrocarbons with higher boiling points are found in gasoline, kerosene, paint thinners, diesel fuel, and even candle wax.

Methane, CH_4

Ethane, C_2H_6

Propane, C_3H_8

FIG. 2.22 The first three members of the alkane series of hydrocarbons. White atoms represent hydrogen and black atoms represent carbon in these space-filling models that demonstrate the shapes of the molecules.

[2] Propane and butane are gases when they're at the pressure of the air around us, but they become liquids when compressed. When you purchase these substances, they are liquids with pressurized gas above them. The gas can be drawn off and used by opening a valve to the container.

□ The chemically correct names for ethylene and acetylene are ethene and ethyne, respectively.

□ Methanol is also known as wood alcohol because it was originally made by distilling wood. It is quite poisonous. Ethanol in high doses is also a poison.

Methane

Methanol

FIG. 2.23 Relationship between an alkane and an alcohol. The alcohol methanol is derived from methane by replacing one H by OH. (Color code: carbon is black, hydrogen is white, and oxygen is red.)

Alkanes are not the only class of hydrocarbons. For example, there are three two-carbon hydrocarbons. In addition to ethane, C_2H_6, there are ethylene, C_2H_4 (an alkene from which polyethylene is made), and acetylene, C_2H_2 (an alkyne, which is the fuel used in *acetylene* welding torches).

The hydrocarbons serve as the foundation for organic chemistry. Derived from them are various other classes of organic compounds. An example is the class of compounds called **alcohols,** in which the atoms OH replace a hydrogen in the hydrocarbon. Thus, *methanol*, CH_3OH (also called *methyl alcohol*), is related to methane, CH_4, by removing one H and replacing it with OH (Figure 2.23). Methanol is used as a fuel and as a raw material for making other organic chemicals. Another familiar alcohol is *ethanol* (also called *ethyl alcohol*), C_2H_5OH. Ethanol, known as grain alcohol because it is obtained from the fermentation of grains, is in alcoholic beverages. It is also mixed with gasoline to reduce petroleum consumption. A 10% ethanol/90% gasoline mixture is known as gasohol; an 85% mixture of ethanol and gasoline is called E85.

Alcohols constitute just one class of compounds derived from hydrocarbons. We will discuss some others after you've learned more about how atoms bond to each other and about the structures of molecules.

Practice Exercise 14: Gasoline used in modern cars is a complex mixture of hundreds of different organic compounds. Less than 1% of gasoline is actually octane. Write the formula for octane using the condensed and structural format. (Hint: The prefix "octa-" stands for the number 8.)

Practice Exercise 15: What is the formula of the alkane hydrocarbon having 10 carbon atoms, decane? Write the formula in the condensed form and in the structural form. Download the space-filling molecule from the Internet.

Practice Exercise 16: On the basis of the discussions in this section, what are the formulas of (a) propanol and (b) butanol? Write the formula in the condensed form and in the structural form. Download the space-filling molecules from the Internet.

2.7 **IONIC COMPOUNDS ARE COMPOSED OF CHARGED PARTICLES CALLED IONS**

Formation of an ionic compound from its elements involves electron transfer

Under appropriate conditions, atoms are able to transfer electrons between one another when they react. This is what happens, for example, when the metal sodium combines with the nonmetal chlorine. As shown in Figure 2.24, sodium is a typical shiny metal and chlorine is

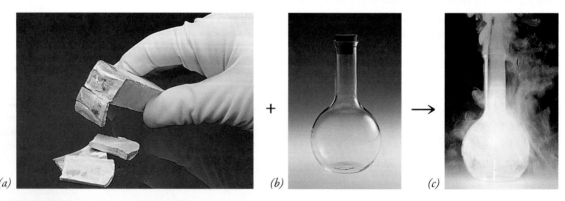

(a)   +   *(b)*   →   *(c)*

FIG. 2.24 **Sodium reacts with chlorine to give the ionic compound sodium chloride.** (*a*) Freshly cut sodium has a shiny metallic surface. The metal reacts with oxygen and moisture, so it cannot be touched with bare fingers. (*b*) Chlorine is a pale green gas. (*c*) When a small piece of sodium is melted in a metal spoon and thrust into the flask of chlorine, it burns brightly as the two elements react to form sodium chloride. The smoke coming from the flask is composed of fine crystals of salt. (*Michael Watson; Richard Megna/Fundamental Photographs; Richard Megna/Fundamental Photographs.*)

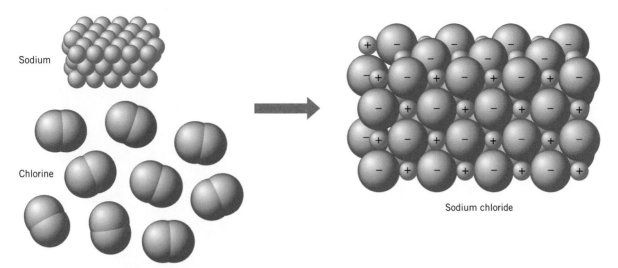

FIG. 2.25 **The reaction of sodium with chlorine viewed at the atomic level.** Electrically neutral atoms and molecules react to yield positive and negative ions which are held to each other by electrostatic attractions (attractions between opposite electrical charges).

a pale green gas. When a piece of heated sodium is thrust into the chlorine, a vigorous reaction takes place yielding a white powder, salt (NaCl). The equation for the reaction is

$$2Na(s) + Cl_2(g) \longrightarrow 2NaCl(s)$$

The changes that take place at the atomic level are illustrated in Figure 2.25.

The formation of the **ions** in salt results from the transfer of electrons between the reacting atoms. Specifically, each sodium atom gives up one electron to a chlorine atom. We can diagram the changes in equation form by using the symbol e^- to stand for an electron.

$$Na + Cl \longrightarrow Na^+ + Cl^-$$

The electrically charged particles formed in this reaction are a sodium ion (Na^+) and a chloride ion (Cl^-). The sodium ion has a positive 1+ charge, indicated by the superscript plus sign, because the loss of an electron leaves it with one more proton in its nucleus than there are electrons outside. Similarly, by gaining one electron the chlorine atom has added one more negative charge, so the chloride ion has a single negative charge indicated by the minus sign. Solid sodium chloride is composed of these charged sodium and chloride ions and is said to be an **ionic compound.**

As a general rule, *ionic compounds are formed when metals react with nonmetals.* In the electron transfer, however, not all atoms gain or lose just one electron; some gain or lose more. For example, when calcium atoms react, they lose two electrons to form Ca^{2+} ions and when oxygen atoms form ions they each gain two electrons to give O^{2-} ions. (We will have to wait until a later chapter to study the reasons why certain atoms gain or lose one electron each, whereas other atoms gain or lose two or more electrons.)

▢ Here we are concentrating on what happens to the individual atoms, so we have not shown chlorine as diatomic Cl_2 molecules.

▢ A neutral sodium atom has 11 protons and 11 electrons; a sodium ion has 11 protons and 10 electrons, so it carries a unit positive charge. A neutral chlorine atom has 17 protons and 17 electrons; a chloride ion has 17 protons and 18 electrons, so it carries a unit negative charge.

Practice Exercise 17: For each of the following atoms or ions, give the number of protons and the number of electrons in one particle. (a) an Fe atom, (b) an Fe^{3+} ion, (c) an N^{3-} ion, (d) an N atom. (Hint: Recall that electrons have a negative charge and ions that have a negative charge are atoms must have gained electrons.)

Practice Exercise 18: For each of the following atoms or ions, give the number of protons and the number of electrons in one particle. (a) an O atom, (b) an O^{2-} ion, (c) an Al^{3+} ion, (d) an Al atom.

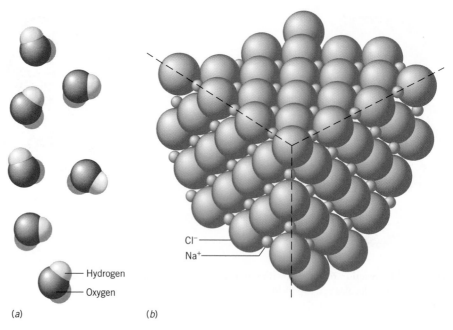

Hydrogen
Oxygen

(a)   (b)

Cl⁻
Na⁺

FIG. 2.26 **Molecular and ionic substances.** (*a*) In water there are discrete molecules that each consist of one atom of oxygen and two atoms of hydrogen. Each particle has the formula H_2O. (*b*) In sodium chloride, ions are packed in the most efficient way. Each Na^+ is surrounded by six Cl^-, and each Cl^- is surrounded by six Na^+. Because individual molecules do not exist, we simply specify the ratio of ions as NaCl.

☐ Notice that the charges on the ions are omitted when writing formulas for compounds. This is because compounds are electrically neutral overall.

Figure 2.26 compares the structures of water and sodium chloride and demonstrates an important difference between molecular and ionic compounds. In water it is safe to say that two hydrogen atoms "belong" to each oxygen atom in a particle having the formula H_2O. However, in NaCl it is impossible to say that a particular Na^+ ion belongs to a particular Cl^- ion. The ions in a crystal of NaCl are simply packed in the most efficient way, so that positive ions and negative ions can be as close to each other as possible. In this way, the attractions between oppositely charged ions, which are responsible for holding the compound together, can be as strong as possible.

Because molecules don't exist in ionic compounds, the subscripts in their formulas are always chosen to specify the smallest whole-number ratio of the ions. This is why the formula of sodium chloride is given as NaCl rather than Na_2Cl_2 or Na_3Cl_3. Although the smallest unit of an ionic compound can't be called a molecule, the idea of "smallest unit" is still quite often useful. Therefore, we take the smallest unit of an ionic compound to be whatever is represented in its formula and call this unit a **formula unit.** Thus, one formula unit of NaCl consists of one Na^+ and one Cl^-, whereas one formula unit of the ionic compound $CaCl_2$ consists of one Ca^{2+} and two Cl^- ions. (In a broader sense, we can use the term *formula unit* to refer to whatever is represented by a formula. Sometimes the formula specifies a set of ions, as in NaCl; sometimes it is a molecule, as in O_2 or H_2O; sometimes it can be just an ion, as in Cl^- or Ca^{2+}; and sometimes it might be just an atom, as in Na.)

Experimental evidence exists for ions in compounds

We know that metals conduct electricity because electrons can move from one atom to the next in a wire when connected to a battery. Solid ionic compounds are poor conductors of electricity as are molecular substances such as water. However, if an ionic compound is dissolved in water or is heated to a high temperature, so that it melts, the resulting liquids are able to conduct electricity easily. These observations suggest that ionic compounds are composed of charged ions rather than neutral molecules and these ions when made mobile by dissolving or melting can conduct electricity. Figure 2.27 illustrates how the electrical conductivity can be tested.

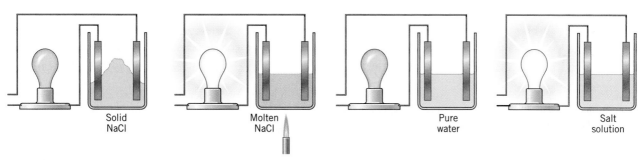

Solid
NaCl

Molten
NaCl

Pure
water

Salt
solution

FIG. 2.27 **An apparatus to test for electrical conductivity.** The electrodes are dipped into the substance to be tested. If the lightbulb glows when electricity is applied, the sample is an electrical conductor. Here we see that solid sodium chloride does not conduct electricity, but when the solid is melted it does conduct. Liquid water, a molecular compound, is not a conductor of electricity because it does not contain electrically charged particles. An aqueous salt solution contains ions of the salt and will conduct electricity.

2.8 THE FORMULAS OF MANY IONIC COMPOUNDS CAN BE PREDICTED

In the preceding section we noted that metals combine with nonmetals to form ionic compounds. In such reactions, metal atoms lose one or more electrons to become positively charged ions and nonmetal atoms gain one or more electrons to become negatively charged ions. In referring to these particles, we will frequently call a positively charged ion a **cation** (pronounced *CAT-i-on*) and a negatively charged ion an **anion** (pronounced *AN-i-on*).[3] Thus, solid NaCl is composed of sodium cations and chloride anions.

Ions formed by representative metals and nonmetals can be remembered using the periodic table

In Section 2.6 you saw that the periodic table can be helpful in remembering the formulas of the nonmetal hydrides. It can also help us remember the kinds of ions formed by many of the representative elements (elements in the A groups of the periodic table). For example, except for hydrogen, the neutral atoms of the Group IA elements always lose one electron each when they react, thereby becoming ions with a charge of $1+$. Similarly, atoms of the Group IIA elements always lose two electrons when they react; so these elements always form ions with a charge of $2+$. In Group IIIA, the only important positive ion we need consider now is that of aluminum, Al^{3+}; an aluminum atom loses three electrons when it reacts to form the ion.

All these ions are listed in Table 2.6. *Notice that the number of positive charges on each of the cations is the same as the group number when we use the North American numbering of groups in the periodic table.* Thus, sodium is in Group IA and forms an ion with a $1+$

☐ Positive ions, called **cations**, are usually metals that have lost one or more electrons.

TOOLS
Predicting cation charge

TABLE 2.6	Some Ions Formed from the Representative Elements					
Group Number						
IA	IIA	IIIA	IVA	VA	VIA	VIIA
Li^+	Be^{2+}		C^{4-}	N^{3-}	O^{2-}	F^-
Na^+	Mg^{2+}	Al^{3+}	Si^{4-}	P^{3-}	S^{2-}	Cl^-
K^+	Ca^{2+}				Se^{2-}	Br^-
Rb^+	Sr^{2+}				Te^{2-}	I^-
Cs^+	Ba^{2+}					

[3] The names *cation* and *anion* come from the way the ions behave when electrically charged metal plates called electrodes are dipped into a solution that contains them. We will discuss this in detail in Chapter 19.

charge, barium (Ba) is in Group IIA and forms an ion with a 2+ charge, and aluminum is in Group IIIA and forms an ion with a 3+ charge. Although this generalization doesn't work for all the metallic elements (it doesn't work for the transition elements, for instance), it does help us remember what happens to the metallic elements of Groups IA and IIA and aluminum when they react.

Among the nonmetals on the right side of the periodic table we also find some useful generalizations. For example, when they combine with metals, the halogens (Group VIIA) form ions with one negative charge (written as 1−) and the nonmetals in Group VIA form ions with two negative charges (written as 2−). Notice that *the number of negative charges on the anion is equal to the number of spaces to the right that we have to move in the periodic table to get to a noble gas.*

□ Negative ions, called **anions**, are monatomic nonmetals that have gained one or more electrons.

TOOLS
Predicting anion charge

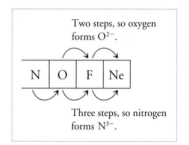

You've probably also noticed that the number of negative charges on an anion is the same as the number of hydrogens in the simple nonmetal hydride of the element, as shown in Table 2.4.

Writing formulas for ionic compounds follows certain rules

All chemical compounds are electrically neutral, so the ions in an ionic compound always occur in a ratio such that the total positive charge is equal to the total negative charge. This is why the formula for sodium chloride is NaCl; the 1-to-1 ratio of Na^+ to Cl^- gives electrical neutrality. In addition, as we've already mentioned, discrete molecules do not exist in ionic compounds, so we always use the smallest set of subscripts that specify the correct ratio of the ions. The following, therefore, are the rules we use in writing the formulas of ionic compounds.

TOOLS
Formulas for ionic compounds

□ A substance is electrically neutral, with a net charge of zero, if the total positive charge equals the total negative charge.

Rules for Writing Formulas of Ionic Compounds

1. The positive ion is given first in the formula. (This isn't required by nature, but it is a custom we always follow.)
2. The subscripts in the formula must produce an electrically neutral formula unit. (Nature *does* require electrical neutrality.)
3. The subscripts should be the smallest set of whole numbers possible. For instance, if all subscripts are even, divide them by 2. (You may have to repeat this simplification step several times.)
4. The charges on the ions are not included in the finished formula for the substance. When a subscript is 1 it is left off; no subscript implies a subscript of 1.

EXAMPLE 2.6
Writing Formulas for Ionic Compounds

Write the formulas for the ionic compounds formed from (a) Ba and S, (b) Al and Cl, and (c) Al and O.

ANALYSIS: To correctly write the formula, we have to apply our tool that summarizes the rules for ionic compounds listed above. First, we need to figure out the charges of the ions and since we're working with representative elements, we can use the periodic table to do this. Then we need to assemble the ions so that the formula unit is electrically neutral.

SOLUTION: (a) The element Ba is in Group IIA, so the charge on its ion is 2+. Sulfur is in Group VIA, so its ion has a charge of 2−. Therefore, the ions are Ba^{2+} and S^{2-}. Since the charges are equal but opposite, a 1-to-1 ratio will give a neutral formula unit. Therefore, the formula is BaS. Notice that we have not included the charges on the ions in the finished formula.

(b) By using the periodic table, the ions of these elements are Al^{3+} and Cl^-. We can obtain a neutral formula unit by combining one Al^{3+} with three Cl^-. (The charge on Cl^- is 1−; the 1 is understood.)

$$1(3+) + 3(1-) = 0$$

The formula is $AlCl_3$.

(c) For these elements, the ions are Al^{3+} and O^{2-}. In the formula we seek there must be the same number of positive charges as negative charges. This number must be a whole-number multiple of both 3 and 2. The smallest number that satisfies this condition is 6, so there must be two Al^{3+} and three O^{2-} in the formula.

$$
\begin{array}{ll}
2Al^{3+} & 2(3+) = 6+ \\
3O^{2-} & \underline{3(2-) = 6-} \\
& \text{sum} = 0
\end{array}
$$

The formula is Al_2O_3.

A "trick" you may have seen before is to use the *number* of positive charges for the subscript of the anion and the *number* of negative charges as the subscript for the cation as shown in the diagram.

$$Al\overset{\frown}{\underset{\smile}{\text{③}}}^{+}\quad\times\quad O\overset{\frown}{\underset{\smile}{\text{②}}}^{-}$$

When using this method, always be sure to check that the subscripts cannot be reduced to smaller numbers.

ARE THE ANSWERS REASONABLE? In writing a formula, there are two things to check. First, be sure you've correctly written the formulas of the ions. (This is where students make a lot of mistakes.) Then check that you've combined them in a ratio that gives electrical neutrality.

Practice Exercise 19: Write formulas for ionic compounds formed from (a) Na and F, (b) Na and O, (c) Mg and F, and (d) Al and C. (Hint: One element must form a cation and the other will form an anion based on its position in the periodic table.)

Practice Exercise 20: Write the formulas for the compounds made from (a) Ca and N, (b) Al and Br, (c) Na and P, and (d) Cs and Cl.

Many of our most important chemicals are ionic compounds. We have mentioned NaCl, common table salt, and $CaCl_2$, which is a substance often used to melt ice on walkways in the winter. Other examples are sodium fluoride, NaF, used by dentists to give fluoride treatments to teeth, and calcium oxide, CaO, an important ingredient in cement.

Transition and post-transition metals form more than one cation

The transition elements are located in the center of the periodic table, from Group IIIB on the left to Group IIB on the right (Groups 3 to 12 using the IUPAC system). All of them lie to the left of the metalloids, and they all are metals. Included here are some of our most familiar metals, including iron, chromium, copper, silver, and gold.

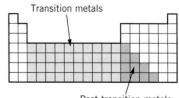

Distribution of transition and post-transition metals in the periodic table.

TABLE 2.7	Ions of Some Transition Metals and Post-transition Metals
Transition Metals	
Chromium	Cr^{2+}, Cr^{3+}
Manganese	Mn^{2+}, Mn^{3+}
Iron	Fe^{2+}, Fe^{3+}
Cobalt	Co^{2+}, Co^{3+}
Nickel	Ni^{2+}
Copper	Cu^{+}, Cu^{2+}
Zinc	Zn^{2+}
Silver	Ag^{+}
Cadmium	Cd^{2+}
Gold	Au^{+}, Au^{3+}
Mercury	Hg_2^{2+}, Hg^{2+}
Post-transition Metals	
Tin	Sn^{2+}, Sn^{4+}
Lead	Pb^{2+}, Pb^{4+}
Bismuth	Bi^{3+}

Most of the transition metals are much less reactive than the metals of Groups IA and IIA, but when they react they also transfer electrons to nonmetal atoms to form ionic compounds. However, the charges on the ions of the transition metals do not follow as straightforward a pattern as do those of the alkali and alkaline earth metals. One of the characteristic features of the transition metals is the ability of many of them to form more than one positive ion. Iron, for example, can form two different ions, Fe^{2+} and Fe^{3+}. This means that iron can form more than one compound with a given nonmetal. For example, with the chloride ion, Cl^-, iron forms two compounds, with the formulas $FeCl_2$ and $FeCl_3$. With oxygen, we find the compounds FeO and Fe_2O_3.

As usual, we see that the formulas contain the ions in a ratio that gives electrical neutrality. Some of the most common ions of the transition metals are given in Table 2.7. Notice that one of the ions of mercury is diatomic Hg_2^{2+}. It consists of two Hg^+ ions joined by the same kind of bond found in molecular substances. The simple Hg^+ ion does not exist.

☐ The prefix *post* means "after."

The **post-transition metals** are those metals that occur in the periodic table immediately following a row of transition metals. The two most common and important ones are tin (Sn) and lead (Pb). Except for bismuth, post-transition metals have the ability to form two different ions, and therefore two different compounds with a given nonmetal. For example, tin forms two oxides, SnO and SnO_2. Lead also forms two oxides that have similar formulas (PbO and PbO_2). The ions that these metals form are also included in Table 2.7.

Practice Exercise 21: Write formulas for the chlorides and oxides formed by (a) chromium and (b) copper. (Hint: There are more than one chloride and oxide for each of these transition metals.)

Practice Exercise 22: Write the formulas for the sulfides and nitrides of (a) gold and (b) tin.

Ions may be composed of more than one element

☐ A substance is **diatomic** if it is composed of molecules that contain only two atoms. It is a **binary compound** if it contains two different elements, regardless of the number of each. Thus, BrCl is a binary compound and is also diatomic; CH_4 is a binary compound but is not diatomic.

The metal compounds that we have discussed so far have been **binary compounds**—compounds formed from *two* different elements. There are many other ionic compounds that contain more than two elements. These substances usually contain **polyatomic ions,** which are ions that are themselves composed of two or more atoms linked by the same kinds of bonds that hold molecules together. Polyatomic ions differ from molecules, however, in that they contain either too many or too few electrons to make them electrically neutral. Table 2.8 lists some important polyatomic ions. It is very important that you learn the formulas, charges, and names of all of these ions.

The formulas of compounds formed from polyatomic ions are determined in the same way as are those of binary ionic compounds; the ratio of the ions must be such that the formula unit is electrically neutral, and the smallest set of whole-number subscripts is used. One difference in writing formulas with polyatomic ions is that parentheses are needed around the polyatomic ion if a subscript is required.

TABLE 2.8	Formulas and Names of Some Polyatomic Ions
Ion	Name (Alternate Name in Parentheses)
NH_4^+	ammonium ion
H_3O^+	hydronium ion[a]
OH^-	hydroxide ion
CN^-	cyanide ion
NO_2^-	nitrite ion
NO_3^-	nitrate ion
ClO^- or OCl^-	hypochlorite ion
ClO_2^-	chlorite ion
ClO_3^-	chlorate ion
ClO_4^-	perchlorate ion
MnO_4^-	permanganate ion
$C_2H_3O_2^-$	acetate ion
$C_2O_4^{2-}$	oxalate ion
CO_3^{2-}	carbonate ion
HCO_3^-	hydrogen carbonate ion (bicarbonate ion)[b]
SO_3^{2-}	sulfite ion
HSO_3^-	hydrogen sulfite ion (bisulfite ion)[b]
SO_4^{2-}	sulfate ion
HSO_4^-	hydrogen sulfate ion (bisulfate ion)[b]
SCN^-	thiocyanate ion
$S_2O_3^{2-}$	thiosulfate ion
CrO_4^{2-}	chromate ion
$Cr_2O_7^{2-}$	dichromate ion
PO_4^{3-}	phosphate ion
HPO_4^{2-}	monohydrogen phosphate ion
$H_2PO_4^-$	dihydrogen phosphate ion

[a]You will encounter this ion only in aqueous solutions.
[b]You will often see and hear the alternate names for these ions.

TOOLS
Polyatomic ions

☐ In general, polyatomic ions are not formed by the direct combination of elements. They are the products of reactions between compounds.

EXAMPLE 2.7
Formulas That Contain Polyatomic Ions

One of the minerals responsible for the strength of bones is the ionic compound calcium phosphate, which is formed from Ca^{2+} and PO_4^{3-}. Write the formula for this compound.

ANALYSIS: The essential tool for solving this problem is the identity of the formula, including the charge, of the polyatomic ion. We have related much information about ions to the periodic table. Unfortunately, the polyatomic ions must be memorized. Knowledge of the polyatomic ions is required for this problem.

SOLUTION: As before, if the number of positive charges on the cation is equal to the number of negative of charges on the anion, the formula unit will contain one of each. If the number of charges are not equal then we use the number of positive charges as the subscript for the anion and the number of negative charges as the subscript for the cation. We will need three calcium ions to give a total charge of 6+ and two phosphate ions to give a charge of 6− so that the total charge is $+6 - 6 = 0$. The formula is written with parentheses to show that the PO_4^{3-} ion occurs two times in the formula unit.

$$Ca_3(PO_4)_2$$

IS THE ANSWER REASONABLE? We double-check to see that electrical neutrality is achieved for the compound. We have six positive charges from the three Ca^{2+} ions and six negative charges from the two PO_4^{3-} ions. The sum is zero and our compound is electrically neutral as required.

Practice Exercise 23: Write the formula for the ionic compound formed from (a) potassium ion and acetate ion, (b) strontium ion and nitrate ion, and (c) Fe^{3+} and acetate ion. (Hint: See if you remember these polyatomic ions before looking at the table.)

Practice Exercise 24: Write the formula for the ionic compound formed from (a) Na^+ and CO_3^{2-}, (b) NH_4^+ and SO_4^{2-}.

Polyatomic ions are found in a large number of very important compounds. Examples include $CaSO_4$ (calcium sulfate, in plaster of Paris), $NaHCO_3$ (sodium bicarbonate, also called baking soda), $NaOCl$ (sodium hypochlorite, in liquid laundry bleach), $NaNO_2$ (sodium nitrite, a meat preservative), $MgSO_4$ (magnesium sulfate, also known as Epsom salts), and $NH_4H_2PO_4$ (ammonium dihydrogen phosphate, a fertilizer).

2.9 | MOLECULAR AND IONIC COMPOUNDS ARE NAMED FOLLOWING A SYSTEM

In conversation, chemists rarely use formulas to describe compounds. Instead, names are used. For example, you already know that water is the name for the compound having the formula H_2O and that sodium chloride is the name of NaCl.

At one time there was no uniform procedure for assigning names to compounds, and those who discovered compounds used whatever method they wished. Today, we know of more than 15 million different chemical compounds, and it is necessary to have a logical system for naming them. Chemists around the world now agree on a systematic method for naming substances that is overseen by the International Union of Pure and Applied Chemistry, IUPAC. By using the **IUPAC rules** we are able to write the correct formula given the name for the many compounds we will encounter. Additionally we will be able to take a formula and correctly name it.

In this section we discuss the **nomenclature** (naming) of simple molecular and ionic inorganic compounds. In general, **inorganic compounds** are substances that would *not* be considered to be derived from hydrocarbons such as methane (CH_4), ethane (C_2H_6), and other carbon–hydrogen compounds. As we noted earlier, the hydrocarbons and compounds that can be thought of as coming from them are called organic compounds. We will have more to say about naming organic compounds later.

Even if we exclude organic compounds, the number and variety of molecular substances is quite enormous. To introduce you to the naming of them, we will restrict ourselves to binary compounds.

Binary compounds composed of two nonmetals are named using Greek prefixes

Our goal is to be able to translate a chemical formula into a name that contains information that would enable someone else, just looking at the name, to reconstruct the formula. For a binary molecular compound, therefore, we must indicate which two elements are present and the number of atoms of each in a molecule of the substance.

To identify the first element in a formula, we just specify its English name. Thus, for HCl the first word in the name is "hydrogen" and for PCl_5 the first word is "phosphorus." To identify the second element, we append the suffix *-ide* to the stem of the element's English name. Here are some examples:

Element	Stem	Name as second element
oxygen	ox-	oxide
sulfur	sulf-	sulfide
nitrogen	nitr-	nitride
phosphorus	phosph-	phosphide
fluorine	fluor-	fluoride
chlorine	chlor-	chloride
bromine	brom-	bromide
iodine	iod-	iodide

To form the name of the compound, we place the two parts of the name one after another. Therefore, the name of HCl is hydrogen chloride. However, to name PCl_5, we need a way to specify the number of Cl atoms bound to the phosphorus in the molecule. This is done using the following Greek prefixes:

mono-	= 1 (often omitted)	hexa-	= 6
di-	= 2	hepta-	= 7
tri-	= 3	octa-	= 8
tetra-	= 4	nona-	= 9
penta-	= 5	deca-	= 10

To name PCl_5, therefore, we add the prefix *penta-* to chloride to give the name phosphorus pentachloride. Notice how easily this allows us to translate the name back into the formula.

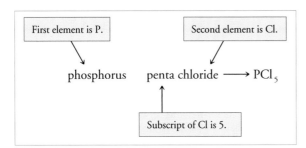

TOOLS

Naming binary molecular compounds

The prefix *mono-* is used when we want to emphasize that only one atom of a particular element is present. For instance, carbon forms two compounds with oxygen, CO and CO_2. To clearly distinguish between them, the first is called carbon monoxide (one of the o's is omitted to make the name easier to pronounce) and the second is carbon dioxide.

As indicated above, the prefix *mono-* is often omitted from a name. Therefore, in general, if there is no prefix before the name of an element, we take it to mean there is only one atom of that element in the molecule. An exception to this is in the names of binary compounds of nonmetals with hydrogen. An example is hydrogen sulfide. The name tells us the compound contains the two elements hydrogen and sulfur. We don't have to be told how many hydrogens are in the molecule because, as you learned earlier, we can use the periodic table to determine the number of hydrogen atoms in molecules of the simple nonmetal hydrides. Sulfur is in Group VIA, so to get to the noble gas column we have to move two steps to the right; the number of hydrogens combined with the atom of sulfur is two. The formula for hydrogen sulfide is therefore H_2S.

EXAMPLE 2.8
Naming Compounds and Writing Formulas

(1) What is the name of $AsCl_3$? (2) What is the formula for dinitrogen tetraoxide?

ANALYSIS: (1) In naming compounds, the first step is to determine what type of compound is involved. Looking at the periodic table, we see that $AsCl_3$ is made up of two nonmetals, so we conclude that it is a molecular compound. Once we've done this, we apply the tool for naming molecular compounds described above.

(2) To write the formula from the name, we convert the prefixes to numbers and apply them as subscripts to the chemical symbols of the elements.

☐ After we've discussed ionic compounds this first step in the analysis will be particularly important, because different rules apply depending on the type of compound being named.

SOLUTION: (1) In $AsCl_3$, As is the symbol for arsenic and, of course, Cl is the symbol for chlorine. The first word in the name is just arsenic and the second will contain chloride with an appropriate prefix to indicate number. There are three Cl atoms, so the prefix is tri-. Therefore, the name of the compound is arsenic trichloride.

(2) As we did earlier for phosphorus pentachloride, we convert the prefixes to numbers and apply them as subscripts.

☐ Sometimes we drop the *a* before an *o* for ease of pronunciation. N_2O_4 would then be named dinitrogen tetroxide.

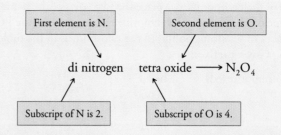

ARE THE ANSWERS REASONABLE? To feel comfortable with the answers, be sure to double-check for careless errors. Next, take your answers and reverse the process. Does arsenic trichloride result in the original formula, $AsCl_3$? Does N_2O_4 have a name of dinitrogen tetraoxide? We can say yes to both and have confidence in our work.

Practice Exercise 25: Name the following compounds using Greek prefixes when needed: (a) PCl_3, (b) SO_2, and (c) Cl_2O_7. (Hint: See the list of prefixes above.)

Practice Exercise 26: Write formulas for the following compounds: (a) arsenic pentachloride, (b) sulfur hexachloride, and (c) disulfur dichloride.

Common names exist for many molecular compounds

Not every compound is named according to the systematic procedure described above. Many familiar substances were discovered long before a systematic method for naming them had been developed, and they acquired common names that are so well known that no attempt has been made to rename them. For example, following the scheme described above we might expect that H_2O would have the name hydrogen oxide (or even dihydrogen monoxide). Although this isn't wrong, the common name water is so well known that it is always used. Another example is ammonia, NH_3, whose odor you have no doubt experienced while using household ammonia solutions or the glass cleaner Windex. Common names are used for the other hydrides of the nonmetals in Group VA as well. The compound PH_3 is called phosphine and AsH_3 is called arsine.

Common names are also used for very complex substances. An example is sucrose, which is the chemical name for table sugar, $C_{12}H_{22}O_{11}$. The structure of this compound is pretty complex, and its name assigned following the systematic method is equally complex. It is much easier to say the simple name sucrose, and be understood, than to struggle with the cumbersome systematic name for this common compound.

For ionic compounds, the name of the cation precedes that of the anion

TOOLS

Naming ionic compounds

In naming ionic compounds, our goal is the same as in naming molecular substances—we want a name that someone else could use to reconstruct the formula. The system we use here, however, is somewhat different than for molecular compounds.

For ionic compounds, the name of the cation is given first, followed by the name of the anion. This is the same as the sequence in which the ions appear in the formula. If the metal in the compound forms only one cation, such as Na^+ or Ca^{2+}, the cation is specified by just giving the English name of the metal. The anion in a binary compound is formed from a nonmetal and its name is created by adding the suffix *-ide* to the stem of the name for the nonmetal just as we did for molecular compounds. An example is KBr, potassium bromide. Table 2.9 lists some common **monatomic** (one-atom) negative ions and their names. It is also useful to know that the *-ide* suffix is usually used only for monatomic ions, with just two common exceptions—*hydroxide ion* (OH^-) and *cyanide ion* (CN^-).[4]

---

[4] If the name of a compound ends in *-ide* and it isn't either a hydroxide or a cyanide, you can feel confident the substance is a binary compound.

TABLE 2.9	Monatomic Negative Ions						
H^-	hydride	N^{3-}	nitride	O^{2-}	oxide	F^-	fluoride
C^{4-}	carbide	P^{3-}	phosphide	S^{2-}	sulfide	Cl^-	chloride
Si^{4-}	silicide	As^{3-}	arsenide	Se^{2-}	selenide	Br^-	bromide
				Te^{2-}	telluride	I^-	iodide

To form the name of an ionic compound, we simply specify the names of the cation and anion. *Use of prefixes to identify the number of cations and anions would be redundant and therefore prefixes are never used when naming ionic compounds.* The reason is that once we know what the ions are, we can assemble the formula correctly just by taking them in a ratio that gives electrical neutrality.

□ To keep the name as simple as possible, we give the minimum amount of information necessary to be able to reconstruct the formula. To write the formula of an ionic compound, we only need the formulas of the ions.

EXAMPLE 2.9
Naming Compounds and Writing Formulas

(a) What is the name of $SrBr_2$? (b) What is the formula for aluminum selenide?

ANALYSIS: The first step in naming a compound is to determine the type of compound it is. As you've already seen, there are slightly different rules for ionic and molecular substances. What clues do we have there that these are ionic?

(a) The element Sr is a metal and Br is a nonmetal. Compounds of a metal and nonmetal are ionic, so we use the rules for naming ionic compounds.

(b) Aluminum is a metal. The only compounds of metals that we've discussed are ionic, so we'll proceed on that assumption. The *-ide* ending of selenide suggests the anion is composed of a single atom of a nonmetal. The only one that begins with the letters "selen-" is selenium, Se. (See the table inside the front cover.)

SOLUTION: (a) The compound is composed of the ions Sr^{2+} (an element from Group IIA) and Br^- (an element from Group VIIA). The cation simply takes the name of the metal, which is strontium. The anion's name is derived from bromine by replacing *-ine* with *-ide*; it is the bromide ion. The name of the compound is strontium bromide.

(b) The name tells us that the cation is the aluminum ion, Al^{3+}. The anion is formed from selenium (Group VIA), and its formula is Se^{2-}. The correct formula must represent an electrically neutral formula unit. Using the number of charges on one ion as the subscript of the other, the formula is Al_2Se_3.

ARE THE ANSWERS REASONABLE? First, we review the analysis and check to be sure we've applied the correct rules, which we have. Next we can reverse the process to be sure our name strontium bromide does mean $SrBr_2$, and that it is reasonable to call Al_2Se_3 aluminum selenide.

Practice Exercise 27: Give the correct formulas for (a) potassium oxide, (b) barium bromide, (c) sodium nitride, and (d) aluminum sulfide. (Hint: Recall what the ending *-ide* means.)

Practice Exercise 28: Give the correct names for (a) $AlCl_3$, (b) BaS, (c) NaBr, and (d) CaF_2.

When a metal can form more than one ion, the charge is indicated with a Roman numeral

Many of the transition metals and post-transition metals are able to form more than one positive ion. Iron, a typical example, forms ions with either a 2+ or a 3+ charge (Fe^{2+} or Fe^{3+}). Compounds that contain these different iron ions have different formulas, so in their names it is necessary to specify which iron ion is present.

2.3

Another System for Naming Ionic Compounds

The Stock system, which we use when naming compounds of metals able to form more than one positive ion, is a relatively recent development in inorganic nomenclature. A slightly different method existed before it.

In the older system, the suffix *-ous* is used to specify the ion with the lower charge and the suffix *-ic* is used to specify the ion with the higher charge. With this method, we also use the Latin stem for elements whose symbols are derived from their Latin names. Some examples are

Fe^{2+}	ferrous ion	$FeCl_2$	ferrous chloride
Fe^{3+}	ferric ion	$FeCl_3$	ferric chloride
Cu^{+}	cuprous ion	$CuCl$	cuprous chloride
Cu^{2+}	cupric ion	$CuCl_2$	cupric chloride

One difficulty with this method is that it does not specify what the charges on the metal ions are, so it becomes necessary to memorize the ions formed by the metals. Additional examples are given in the table below. Notice that mercury is an exception; we use the English stem when naming its ions.

Even though the Stock system is now preferred, some chemical companies still label bottles of chemicals using the old system. These old names also appear in the older scientific literature, which still holds much excellent data. This means that you may need to learn both systems.

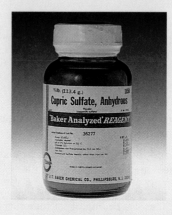

The older system of nomenclature is still found on the labels of many laboratory chemicals. This bottle contains copper(II) sulfate, which according to the older system of nomenclature is called cupric sulfate. *(Michael Watson.)*

Cr^{2+}	chromous	Mn^{2+}	manganous	Fe^{2+}	ferrous	Co^{2+}	cobaltous
Cr^{3+}	chromic	Mn^{3+}	manganic	Fe^{3+}	ferric	Co^{3+}	cobaltic
Au^{+}	aurous	Hg_2^{2+}	mercurous	Sn^{2+}	stannous	Pb^{2+}	plumbous
Au^{3+}	auric	Hg^{2+}	mercuric	Sn^{4+}	stannic	Pb^{4+}	plumbic

☐ Alfred Stock (1876–1946), a German inorganic chemist, was one of the first scientists to warn the public of the dangers of mercury poisoning.

Originally the cations with different charges were given names that distinguished the higher charge from the lower one. That system is described in Facets of Chemistry 2.3 for those who are interested.

The currently preferred method for naming ions of metals that can have more than one charge in compounds is called the **Stock system.** Here we use the English name followed, *without a space*, by the numerical value of the charge written as a Roman numeral in parentheses.[5] Examples of using the Stock system are shown below.

Fe^{2+}	iron(II)	$FeCl_2$	iron(II) chloride
Fe^{3+}	iron(III)	$FeCl_3$	iron(III) chloride
Cr^{2+}	chromium(II)	CrS	chromium(II) sulfide
Cr^{3+}	chromium(III)	Cr_2S_3	chromium(III) sulfide

TOOLS

Using the Stock system

Remember that *the Roman numeral equals the positive charge on the metal ion*; it is not necessarily a subscript in the formula. For example, copper forms two oxides, one containing the Cu^{+} ion and the other containing the Cu^{2+} ion. Their formulas are Cu_2O and CuO and their names are as follows[6]:

---

[5] Silver and nickel are almost always found in compounds as Ag^{+} and Ni^{2+}, respectively. Therefore, $AgCl$ and $NiCl_2$ are almost always called simply silver chloride and nickel chloride.

[6] For some metals, such as copper and lead, one of their ions is much more commonly found in compounds than any of their others. For example, most common copper compounds contain Cu^{2+} and most common lead compounds contain Pb^{2+}. For compounds of these metals, if the charge is not indicated by a Roman numeral, we assume the ion present has a $2+$ charge. Thus, it not unusual to find $PbCl_2$ called lead chloride, or for $CuCl_2$ to be called copper chloride.

Cu^+ copper(I) Cu_2O copper(I) oxide
Cu^{2+} copper(II) CuO copper(II) oxide

These copper compounds illustrate that in deriving the formula from the name, you must figure out the formula from the ionic charges, as discussed in Section 2.8 and illustrated in the preceding example.

EXAMPLE 2.10
Naming Compounds and Writing Formulas

The compound $MnCl_2$ has a number of commercial uses, including disinfecting, the manufacture of batteries, and purifying natural gas. What is the name of the compound?

ANALYSIS: The first step is to determine the kind of compound involved so we can apply the appropriate rules. The compound here is made up of a metal and a nonmetal, so we use the rules for naming ionic compounds.

To name the cation, we need to know whether the metal is one that forms more than one positive ion. Manganese (Mn) is a transition element, and transition elements often do form more than one cation, so we should apply the Stock method as our tool. To do this, we need to determine the charge on the manganese cation. We can figure this out because the sum of the charges on the Mn and Cl ions must equal zero, and because the only ion chlorine forms has a single negative charge.

SOLUTION: The anion of chlorine (the chloride ion) is Cl^-, so a total of two negative charges are supplied by the two Cl^- ions. Therefore, for $MnCl_2$ to be electrically neutral, the Mn ion must carry two positive charges, 2+. The cation is named as manganese(II), and the name of the compound is manganese(II) chloride.

IS THE ANSWER REASONABLE? Performing a quick check of the arithmetic assures us we've got the correct charges on the ions. Everything appears to be okay.

EXAMPLE 2.11
Naming Compounds and Writing Formulas

What is the formula for cobalt(III) fluoride?

ANALYSIS: To answer this question, we first need to determine the charges on the two ions using the tool above. Then we assemble them into a chemical formula being sure to achieve an electrically neutral formula unit.

SOLUTION: Cobalt(III) corresponds to Co^{3+}. The fluoride ion is F^-. To obtain an electrically neutral substance, we must have three F^- ions for each Co^{3+} ion, so the formula is CoF_3.

IS THE ANSWER REASONABLE? We can check to see that we have the correct formulas of the ions and that we've combined them to achieve an electrically neutral formula unit. This will tell us we've obtained the correct answer.

Practice Exercise 29: Name the compounds (a) K_2S, (b) Mg_3P_2, (c) $NiCl_2$, and (d) Fe_2O_3. Use the Stock system where appropriate. (Hint: Determine which metals can have more than one charge.)

Practice Exercise 30: Write formulas for (a) aluminum sulfide, (b) strontium fluoride, (c) titanium(IV) oxide, and (d) gold(III) oxide.

Similar rules apply to naming ionic compounds that contain polyatomic ions

Naming with polyatomic ions

☐ It is important that you learn the formulas (including charges) and the names of the polyatomic ions in Table 2.8. You will encounter them frequently throughout your chemistry course.

The extension of the nomenclature system to include ionic compounds containing polyatomic ions is straightforward. Most of the polyatomic ions listed in Table 2.8 are anions and their names are used as the second word in the name of the compound. For example, Na_2SO_4 contains the sulfate ion, SO_4^{2-}, and is called sodium sulfate. Similarly, $Cr(NO_3)_3$ contains the nitrate ion, NO_3^-. Chromium is a transition element, and in this compound its charge must be 3+ to balance the negative charges of three NO_3^- ions. Therefore, $Cr(NO_3)_3$ is called chromium(III) nitrate.

Among the ions in Table 2.8, the only cation that forms compounds which can be isolated is ammonium ion, NH_4^+. It forms ionic compounds such as NH_4Cl (ammonium chloride) and $(NH_4)_2SO_4$ (ammonium sulfate), even though NH_4^+ is not a metal cation. Notice that the latter compound is composed of two polyatomic ions.

EXAMPLE 2.12
Naming Compounds and Writing Formulas

What is the name of $Mg(ClO_4)_2$, a compound used commercially for removing moisture from gases?

ANALYSIS: To answer this question, it is essential that you recognize that the compound contains a polyatomic ion. If you've learned the contents of Table 2.8, you know that "ClO_4" is the formula (without the charge) of the perchlorate ion. With the charge, the ion's formula is ClO_4^-. We also have to decide whether we need to apply the Stock system in naming the metal Mg. We use the naming tool for polyatomic ion compounds to complete the exercise.

SOLUTION: Magnesium is in Group IIA, and forms only the ion Mg^{2+}. Therefore, we don't need to use the Stock system in naming the cation; it is named simply as "magnesium." The anion is perchlorate, so the name of $Mg(ClO_4)_2$ is magnesium perchlorate.

IS THE ANSWER REASONABLE? We can check to be sure we've named the anion correctly, and we have. The metal is magnesium, which only forms Mg^{2+}. Therefore, the answer seems to be correct.

Practice Exercise 31: What are the names of (a) Li_2CO_3 and (b) $Fe(OH)_3$? (Hint: Recall the names of the polyatomic ions and the positions of Li and Fe in the periodic table.)

Practice Exercise 32: Write the formulas for (a) potassium chlorate and (b) nickel(II) phosphate.

Hydrates are named using Greek prefixes

Earlier we discussed compounds called hydrates, such as $CuSO_4 \cdot 5H_2O$. Usually, hydrates are ionic compounds whose crystals contain water molecules in fixed proportions relative to the ionic substance. To name them, we provide two pieces of information: the name of the ionic compound and the number of water molecules in the formula. The number of water molecules is specified using the Greek prefixes mentioned earlier (mono-, di-, tri-, etc.), which precede the word "hydrate." Thus, $CuSO_4 \cdot 5H_2O$ is named as "copper sulfate *pentahydrate*." Similarly, $CaSO_4 \cdot 2H_2O$ is named calcium sulfate dihydrate, and $FeCl_3 \cdot 6H_2O$ is iron(III) chloride hexahydrate.[7]

---

[7] Chemical suppliers (who do not always follow current rules of nomenclature) sometimes indicate the number of water molecules using a number and a dash. For example, one supplier lists $Ca(NO_3)_2 \cdot 4H_2O$ as "Calcium nitrate, 4-hydrate."

Naming a compound requires that we select the rules that apply

In this chapter we've discussed how to name two classes of compounds, molecular and ionic, and you saw that slightly different rules apply to each. To name chemical compounds successfully we need to make a series of decisions based on the rules we just covered. At this point we can summarize this decision process in a flowchart such as the one shown in Figure 2.28. The example below illustrates how to use the flowchart, and when working on the Review Problems, you may want to refer to Figure 2.28 until you are able to develop the skills that will enable you to work without it.

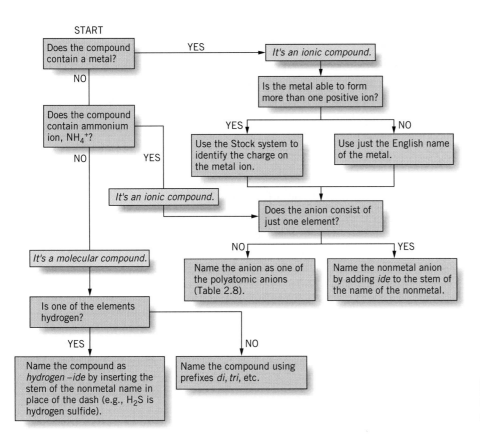

FIG. 2.28 Flowchart for naming molecular and ionic compounds.

What is the name of (a) $CrCl_3$, (b) P_4S_3, and (c) NH_4NO_3?

ANALYSIS: For each compound, we use the tools summarized in Figure 2.28 and proceed through the decision processes to arrive at the way to name the compound. As you read through the solution below, be sure to refer to Figure 2.28 so you can see how we decide which rules we need to apply.

SOLUTION: (a) Starting at the top of Figure 2.28, we first determine that the compound contains a metal (Cr), so it's an ionic compound. Next, we see that the metal is a transition element, and chromium is one of those that forms more than one cation, so we have to apply the Stock method. To do this, we need to know what the charge is on the metal ion. We can figure this out using the charge on the anion and the fact that the compound must be electrically neutral overall. The anion is formed from chlorine, so its charge must be 1− (the anion is Cl^-). Therefore, the metal ion must be Cr^{3+}; we name the metal as *chromium(III)*. Next, we see that there is only one nonmetallic element in the compound, Cl, so the name of the anion ends in *-ide*; it's the *chloride* ion. The compound $CrCl_3$ is therefore named *chromium(III) chloride*.

(b) Once again, we start at the top. First we determine that the compound doesn't contain a metal. It also doesn't contain NH_4, so the compound is molecular. It doesn't contain hydrogen, so we are led to the decision that we must use Greek prefixes to specify the numbers of atoms of each element. Applying the procedure on page 71, the name of the compound P_4S_3 is *tetraphosphorus trisulfide*.

(c) We begin at the top. Studying the formula, we see that it does not contain the symbol for a metal, so we proceed down the left side of the figure. The formula does contain NH_4 which indicates the compound contains the *ammonium* ion, NH_4^+ (it's an ionic compound). The rest of the formula is NO_3, which consists of more than one atom. This suggests the polyatomic anion, NO_3^- (*nitrate* ion). The name of the compound NH_4NO_3 is *ammonium nitrate*.

ARE THE ANSWERS REASONABLE? To check the answers in a problem of this kind, review the decision processes which led you to the names. In part (a), you can check to be sure you've calculated the charge on the chromium ion correctly. Also, check to be sure you've used the correct names of any polyatomic ions. Doing these things will show we've named the compounds correctly.

Practice Exercise 33: The compound I_2O_5 is used in respirators where it serves to react with highly toxic carbon monoxide to give the much less toxic gas, carbon dioxide. What is the name of I_2O_5? (Hint: Is this a molecular or ionic compound?)

Practice Exercise 34: The compound $Cr(C_2H_3O_2)_3$ is used in the tanning of leather. What is the name for this compound?

SUMMARY

Elements and Atoms. When accurate masses of all the reactants and products in a reaction are measured and compared, no observable changes in mass accompany chemical reactions (the **law of conservation of mass**). The mass ratios of the elements in any compound are constant regardless of the source of the compound or how it is prepared (the **law of definite proportions**). **Dalton's atomic theory** explained the laws of chemical combination by proposing that matter consists of indestructible atoms with masses that do not change during chemical reactions. During a chemical reaction, atoms may change partners, but they are neither created nor destroyed. After Dalton had proposed his theory, it was discovered that whenever two elements form more than one compound, the different masses of one element that combine with a fixed mass of the other are in a ratio of small whole numbers (the **law of multiple proportions**). Using modern instruments such as the **scanning tunneling microscope,** scientists are able to "see" atoms on the surfaces of solids.

Atomic Mass. An element's **atomic mass (atomic weight)** is the relative mass of its atoms on a scale in which atoms of carbon-12 have a mass of exactly 12 u (**atomic mass units**). Most elements occur in nature as uniform mixtures of a small number of **isotopes,** whose masses differ slightly. However, all isotopes of an element have very nearly identical chemical properties and the percentages of the isotopes that make up an element are generally so constant throughout the world that we can say that the average mass of their atoms is a constant.

Atomic Structure. Atoms can be split into **subatomic particles,** such as **electrons, protons,** and **neutrons. Nucleons** are particles that make up the atomic **nucleus** and include the protons, each of which carries a single unit of **positive charge** (charge $= 1+$), and neutrons (no charge). The number of protons is called the **atomic number (Z)** of the element. Each element has a different atomic number. The electrons, each with a unit of **negative charge** (charge $= 1-$) are found outside the nucleus; their number equals the atomic number in a neutral atom. Isotopes of an element have identical atomic numbers but different numbers of neutrons. In more modern terms, an **element** can be defined as a substance whose atoms all have the same number of protons in their nuclei.

The Periodic Table. The search for similarities and differences among the properties of the elements led Mendeleev to discover that when the elements are placed in (approximate) order of increasing atomic mass, similar properties recur at regular, repeating intervals. In the modern **periodic table** the elements are arranged in rows, called **periods,** in order of increasing atomic number. The rows are stacked so that elements in the columns, called **groups** or **families,** have similar chemical and physical properties. The A-group elements (IUPAC Groups 1, 2, and 13–18) are called **representative elements;** the B-group elements (IUPAC Groups 3–12) are called **transition elements.** The two long rows of **inner transition elements** located below the main body of the table consist of the **lanthanides,** which follow La ($Z = 57$), and the **actinides,** which follow Ac ($Z = 89$). Certain groups are given family names: Group IA (Group 1), except for hydrogen, are the **alkali metals** (the alkalis); Group IIA (Group 2), the **alkaline earth metals;** Group VIIA (Group 17), the **halogens;** Group VIIIA (Group 18), the **noble gases.**

Metals, Nonmetals, and Metalloids. Most elements are **metals;** they occupy the lower left-hand region of the periodic table (to the left of a line drawn approximately from boron, B, to astatine, At). **Nonmetals** are found in the upper right-hand region of the table. **Metalloids** occupy a narrow band between the metals and nonmetals.

Metals exhibit a **metallic luster,** tend to be **ductile** and **malleable,** and conduct electricity. Nonmetals tend to be brittle, lack metallic luster, and are nonconductors of electricity. Many nonmetals are gases. Bromine (a nonmetal) and mercury (a metal) are the two elements that are liquids at ordinary room temperature. Metalloids have properties intermediate between those of metals and nonmetals and are **semiconductors** of electricity.

Reactions of Elements to Form Compounds. Nearly every element has the ability to form compounds, although not all combinations are possible. When a chemical reaction takes place, the properties of the substances present at the start disappear and are replaced by the properties of the substances formed in the reaction. Chemical symbols are used to write **chemical formulas,** both for **free elements** that occur as molecules (e.g., **diatomic molecules** of elements such as H_2, O_2, N_2, and Cl_2) and for chemical compounds. **Subscripts** are used to specify how many atoms of each element are present. Some compounds form solids called **hydrates,** which contain water molecules in definite proportions. Heating a hydrate usually drives off the water.

Chemical Equations. A **chemical equation** presents a before-and-after description of a chemical reaction. When **balanced,** an equation contains **coefficients** that make the number of atoms of each kind the same among the **reactants** and the **products.** In this way, the equation conforms to the law of conservation of mass. The physical states of the reactants and products can be specified in an equation by placing the following symbols within parentheses following the chemical formulas: *s, l, g,* and *aq,* which stand for solid, liquid, gas, and aqueous solution (dissolved in water), respectively.

Molecules and Molecular Compounds. Molecules are electrically neutral particles consisting of two or more atoms. The erratic movements of microscopic particles suspended in a liquid (**Brownian motion**) can be interpreted to be caused by collisions with molecules of the liquid. Molecules are held together by

chemical bonds that arise from the sharing of electrons between atoms. Formulas we write for molecules are **molecular formulas.** Molecular compounds are formed when nonmetals combine with each other. The simple nonmetal hydrides have formulas that can be remembered by the position of the nonmetal in the periodic table. **Organic compounds** are **hydrocarbons,** or compounds considered to be derived from hydrocarbons by replacing H atoms with other atoms.

Ions and Ionic Compounds. Binary ionic compounds are formed when metals react with nonmetals. In the reaction, electrons are transferred from a metal to a nonmetal. The metal atom becomes a positive ion (a **cation**); the nonmetal atom becomes a negative ion (an **anion**). The formula of an ionic compound specifies the smallest whole-number ratio of the ions. The smallest unit of an ionic compound is called a **formula unit,** which specifies the smallest whole-number ratio of the ions that produces electrical neutrality. Many ionic compounds also contain **polyatomic ions**—ions that are composed of two or more atoms.

Naming Molecular Compounds. The system of **nomenclature** for **binary** molecular **inorganic compounds** uses a set of **Greek prefixes** to specify the numbers of atoms of each kind in the formula of the compound. The first element in the formula is specified by its English name; the second element takes the suffix *-ide,* which is added to the stem of the English name. For simple nonmetal hydrides, it is not necessary to specify the number of hydrogens in the formula. Many familiar substances as well as very complex molecules are usually identified by **common names.**

Naming Ionic Compounds. In naming an ionic compound, the cation is specified first, followed by the anion. Metal cations take the English name of the element, and when more than one positive ion can be formed by the metal, the **Stock system** is used to identify the amount of positive charge on the cation. This is done by placing a Roman numeral equal to the positive charge in parentheses following the name of the metal. Simple **monatomic** anions are formed by nonmetals and their names are formed by adding the suffix *-ide* to the stem of the nonmetal's name. Only two common polyatomic anions (cyanide and hydroxide) end in the suffix *-ide.*

Properties of Molecular and Ionic Compounds. We found that it is often possible to distinguish ionic compounds from molecular compounds by their ability to **conduct electricity.** Molecular compounds are generally poor electrical conductors, whereas ionic compounds when melted into the liquid state or dissolved in water will conduct electricity readily.

TOOLS FOR PROBLEM SOLVING

We have learned the following concepts which can be applied as tools in solving problems. Study each one carefully so that you know what each is used for. When faced with solving a problem, recall what each tool does and consider whether it will be helpful in finding a solution. This will aid you in selecting the tools you need. If necessary, refer to these tools when working on the exercises in the chapter and the review questions and problems that follow. Remember that tools from Chapter 1 may be needed at times to solve problems in this chapter.

Law of definite proportions *(page 36)* If we know the **mass ratio** of the elements in one sample of a compound, we know the ratio will be the same in a different sample of the same compound.

Law of conservation of mass *(page 36)* The total mass of chemicals present before a reaction starts equals the total mass after the reaction is finished. We can use this law to check whether we have accounted for all the substances formed in a reaction.

Subatomic particles *(page 43* There are three important relationships between the numbers of **protons, neutrons (nucleons)**, and **electrons.** These relationships are

> For a neutral atom: number of electrons = number of protons
> Atomic number (Z) = number of protons
> Mass number (A) = number of protons + number of neutrons

Relative atomic masses *(page 45)* Atomic masses are relative to the mass of a ^{12}C atom that has a mass of exactly 12 atomic mass units (u). Therefore the atomic mass of ^{12}C is exactly 12 u.

Chemical formula *(page 54)* **Subscripts** in a formula specify the number of atoms of each element in one formula unit of the substance. This gives us *atom ratios* that we will find useful when we deal with the compositions of compounds in Chapter 3.

Rules for writing formulas of ionic compounds *(page 66)* The rules permit us to write correct chemical formulas for ionic compounds. You will need to learn to use the periodic table (see below) to remember the charges on the cations and anions of the representative metals and nonmetals.

Polyatomic ions *(page 69)* Certain groups of atoms arrange themselves into stable configurations that we call polyatomic ions. It is very important that you commit to memory the names, formulas, and charges of these ions (which are given in Table 2.8).

Monatomic anion names *(page 73)* The list on this page gives the common names of anions that must be remembered.

Greek prefixes *(page 71)* This page has a list of the Greek prefixes from one to ten that you should know for naming molecular compounds and hydrates.

Rules for naming molecular compounds *(page 71)* These rules give us a logical system for naming binary molecular compounds by specifying the number of each type of atom using Greek prefixes.

Rules for naming ionic compounds *(page 72)* These rules give us a systematic method for naming ionic compounds. The name of the cation is combined with the name of a monatomic anion as given on page 73. These rules are used with slight modification for cations that can have more than one possible charge (see using the **Stock system** below) and for situations where a polyatomic ion is involved (see naming with **polyatomic ions** below)

Using the Stock system *(page 74)* The Stock system specifies the charge of a cation by placing a Roman numeral in parentheses just after the name of the cation. The Stock system and its Roman numerals are only used for cations that can have more than one possible charge.

Naming with polyatomic ions *(page 76)* Naming compounds that contain polyatomic anions is done by specifying the cation name, using the Stock system if needed, and then specifying the polyatomic anion name as given in Table 2.8. The one polyatomic cation, the ammonium ion (NH_4^+), uses its name and then the appropriate name of the anion.

Periodic table The periodic table has several tool icons in this chapter illustrating its use in a variety of different ways. The periodic table is used to find group numbers and period numbers of the elements *(page 49)*. The table will help us recall group names and we can obtain atomic numbers and average masses of the elements *(page 50)*. From an element's position in the periodic table, we can tell whether it's a metal, nonmetal, or metalloid *(page 51)*. From a nonmetal's position in the periodic table we can write the formula of its simple hydride *(page 60)* and predict the charge of monatomic anions *(page 65)*. For the metals in Groups IA and IIA, we can use the elements' positions in the periodic table to obtain the charges on their ions *(page 65)*.

QUESTIONS, PROBLEMS, AND EXERCISES

Answers to problems whose numbers are printed in color are given in Appendix B. More challenging problems are marked with asterisks. ILW = Interactive Learningware solution is available at www.wiley.com/college/brady. OH = an Office Hours video is available for this problem.

REVIEW QUESTIONS

Laws of Chemical Combination and Dalton's Theory

2.1 Name and state the two laws of chemical combination discussed in this chapter.

2.2 Why didn't the existence of isotopes affect the apparent validity of the atomic theory?

2.3 In your own words, describe how Dalton's theory explains the law of conservation of mass and the law of definite proportions.

2.4 Which of the laws of chemical combination is used to define the term *compound*?

2.5 Describe what you need to do in the laboratory to test (a) the law of conservation of mass, (b) the law of definite proportions, and (c) the law of multiple proportions.

Atomic Masses and Atomic Structure

2.6 What are the names, symbols, and electrical charges of the three subatomic particles introduced in this chapter?

2.7 Where in an atom is nearly all of its mass concentrated? Explain your answer in terms of the particles that contribute to this mass.

2.8 What is a *nucleon*? Which ones have we studied?

2.9 Define the terms *atomic number* and *mass number*. What symbols are used to designate these terms?

2.10 Consider the symbol $_b^a X$, where X stands for the chemical symbol for an element. What information is given in locations (a) *a* and (b) *b*?

2.11 Write the symbols of the isotopes that contain the following. (Use the table of atomic masses and numbers printed inside the front cover for additional information, as needed.)
(a) An isotope of iodine whose atoms have 78 neutrons.
(b) An isotope of strontium whose atoms have 52 neutrons.
(c) An isotope of cesium whose atoms have 82 neutrons.
(d) An isotope of fluorine whose atoms have 9 neutrons.

The Periodic Table

2.12 In the compounds formed by Li, Na, K, Rb, and Cs with chlorine, how many atoms of Cl are there per atom of the metal? In the compounds formed by Be, Mg, Ca, Sr, and Ba with chlorine, how many atoms of Cl are there per atom of metal? How did this kind of information lead Mendeleev to develop his periodic table?

2.13 On what basis did Mendeleev construct his periodic table? On what basis are the elements arranged in the modern periodic table?

2.14 On the basis of their positions in the periodic table, why is it not surprising that strontium-90, a dangerous radioactive isotope of strontium, replaces calcium in newly formed bones?

2.15 In the refining of copper, sizable amounts of silver and gold are recovered. Why is this not surprising?

2.16 Why would you reasonably expect cadmium to be a contaminant in zinc but not in silver?

2.17 Using the symbol for nitrogen, N, indicate what information is conveyed by the superscripts before and after the symbol and by subscripts before and after the symbol.

2.18 Make a rough sketch of the periodic table and mark off those areas where you would find (a) the representative elements, (b) the transition elements, and (c) the inner transition elements.

2.19 Which of the following is
(a) an alkali metal: Ca, Cu, In, Li, S?
(b) a halogen: Ce, Hg, Si, O, I?
(c) a transition element: Pb, W, Ca, Cs, P?
(d) a noble gas: Xe, Se, H, Sr, Zr?
(e) a lanthanide element: Th, Sm, Ba, F, Sb?
(f) an actinide element: Ho, Mn, Pu, At, Na?
(g) an alkaline earth metal: Mg, Fe, K, Cl, Ni?

Physical Properties of Metals, Nonmetals, and Metalloids

2.20 Name five physical properties that we usually observe for metals.

2.21 Why is mercury used in thermometers? Why is tungsten used in lightbulbs?

2.22 Which nonmetals occur as monatomic gases (gases whose particles consist of single atoms)?

2.23 Which two elements exist as liquids at room temperature and pressure?

2.24 Which physical property of metalloids distinguishes them from metals and nonmetals?

2.25 Sketch the shape of the periodic table and mark off those areas where we find (a) metals, (b) nonmetals, and (c) metalloids.

2.26 Most periodic tables have a heavy line that looks like a staircase starting from boron down to polonium. What information does this line convey?

2.27 Which metals can you think of that are commonly used to make jewelry? Why isn't iron used to make jewelry? Why isn't potassium used?

2.28 What trends (regular changes in physical or chemical properties) in the periodic table have been mentioned in this chapter?

2.29 Find a periodic table on the Internet that lists physical properties of the elements. Can you distinguish trends in the periodic table based on (a) melting point, (b) boiling point, or (c) density?

Chemical Formulas

2.30 What are two ways to interpret a chemical symbol?

2.31 What is the difference between an atom and a molecule?

2.32 Write the formulas and names of the nonmetallic elements that exist in nature as diatomic molecules.

Chemical Equations

2.33 What do we mean when we say a chemical equation is *balanced*? Why do we balance chemical equations?

2.34 For a chemical reaction, what do we mean by the term *reactants*? What do we mean by the term *products*?

2.35 The combustion of a thin wire of magnesium metal (Mg) in an atmosphere of pure oxygen produces the brilliant light of a flashbulb, once commonly used in photography. After the reaction, a thin film of magnesium oxide is seen on the inside of the bulb. The equation for the reaction is

$$2Mg + O_2 \longrightarrow 2MgO$$

(a) State in words how this equation is read.
(b) Give the formula(s) of the reactants.
(c) Give the formula(s) of the products.
(d) Rewrite the equation to show that Mg and MgO are solids and O_2 is a gas.

2.36 The chemical equation for the combustion of octane (C_8H_{18}), a component of gasoline, is

$$2C_8H_{18} + 25O_2 \longrightarrow 16CO_2 + 18H_2O$$

Rewrite the equation so that it specifies octane and water as liquids and oxygen and carbon dioxide (CO_2) as gases.

Molecular Compounds of Nonmetals

2.37 Which are the only elements that exist as free, individual atoms when not chemically combined with other elements?

2.38 Write chemical formulas for molecules of elemental sulfur and phosphorus mentioned in this chapter.

2.39 Which kind of elements normally combine to form molecular compounds?

2.40 Without referring to Table 2.4, but using the periodic table, write chemical formulas for the simplest hydrogen compounds of (a) carbon, (b) nitrogen, (c) tellurium, and (d) iodine.

2.41 The simplest hydrogen compound of phosphorus is phosphine, a highly flammable and poisonous compound with an odor of decaying fish. What is the formula for phosphine?

2.42 Astatine, a radioactive member of the halogen family, forms a compound with hydrogen. Predict its chemical formula.

2.43 Under appropriate conditions, tin can be made to form a simple molecular compound with hydrogen. Predict its formula.

2.44 Write the chemical formulas for (a) methane, (b) ethane, (c) propane, and (d) butane. Give one practical use for each of these hydrocarbons.

2.45 What are the formulas of (a) methanol and (b) ethanol?

2.46 What is the formula for the alkane that has 10 carbon atoms?

2.47 Candle wax is a mixture of hydrocarbons, one of which is an alkane with 23 carbon atoms. What is the formula for this hydrocarbon?

2.48 The formula for a compound is correctly given as $C_6H_{12}O_6$. State two reasons why we expect this to be a molecular compound, rather than an ionic compound.

2.49 Explore the Internet and find a reliable source of structures for molecular compounds. For questions 44 to 47 print out the ball-and-stick and space-filling models of the compounds mentioned.

Ionic Compounds

2.50 Describe what kind of event must occur (involving electrons) if the atoms of two different elements are to react to form (a) an ionic compound or (b) a molecular compound.

2.51 With what kind of elements do metals react?

2.52 With what kind of elements do nonmetals react?

2.53 Why are nonmetals found in more compounds than are metals, even though there are fewer nonmetals than metals?

2.54 What is an ion? How does it differ from an atom or a molecule?

2.55 Why do we use the term *formula unit* for ionic compounds instead of the term *molecule*?

2.56 Most compounds of aluminum are ionic, but a few are molecular. How do we know that Al_2Cl_6 is molecular?

2.57 Consider the sodium atom and the sodium ion.
(a) Write the chemical symbol of each.
(b) Do these particles have the same number of nuclei?
(c) Do they have the same number of protons?
(d) Could they have different numbers of neutrons?
(e) Do they have the same number of electrons?

2.58 Define *cation, anion,* and *polyatomic ion.*

2.59 How many electrons has a titanium atom lost if it has formed the ion Ti^{4+}? What are the total numbers of protons and electrons in a Ti^{4+} ion?

2.60 If an atom gains an electron to become an ion, what kind of electrical charge does the ion have?

2.61 How many electrons has a nitrogen atom gained if it has formed the ion N^{3-}? How many protons and electrons are in an N^{3-} ion?

2.62 What is wrong with the formula $RbCl_3$? What is wrong with the formula SNa_2?

2.63 A student wrote the formula for an ionic compound of titanium as Ti_2O_4. What is wrong with this formula? What should the formula be?

2.64 What are the formulas of the ions formed by (a) iron, (b) cobalt, (c) mercury, (d) chromium, (e) tin, and (f) copper?

2.65 Which of the following formulas are incorrect? (a) NaN_2, (b) $RbCl$, (c) K_2S, (d) Al_2Cl_3, (e) MgO_2

2.66 What are the formulas (including charges) for (a) cyanide ion, (b) ammonium ion, (c) nitrate ion, (d) sulfite ion, (e) chlorate ion, and (f) sulfate ion?

2.67 What are the formulas (including charges) for (a) hypochlorite ion, (b) bisulfate ion, (c) phosphate ion, (d) dihydrogen phosphate ion, (e) permanganate ion, and (f) oxalate ion?

2.68 What are the names of the following ions? (a) $Cr_2O_7^{2-}$, (b) OH^-, (c) $C_2H_3O_2^-$, (d) CO_3^{2-}, (e) CN^-, (f) ClO_4^-

2.69 From what you have learned in Section 2.8, write correct balanced equations for the reactions between (a) calcium and chlorine, (b) magnesium and oxygen, (c) aluminum and oxygen, and (d) sodium and sulfur.

2.70 Write the balanced equations (including phases) for the reactions described below: (a) Solid iron(III) hydroxide reacts with gaseous hydrogen chloride forming water and iron(III) chloride. (b) Aqueous silver nitrate is reacted with aqueous barium chloride to form solid silver chloride and aqueous barium nitrate.

2.71 Write the balanced equations (including phases) for the reactions described below: (a) Gaseous propane reacts with gaseous oxygen to form carbon dioxide and water. (b) Sodium metal is added to water and the products are aqueous sodium hydroxide and hydrogen gas.

Naming Compounds

2.72 What is the difference between a binary compound and one that is diatomic? Give examples that illustrate this difference.

2.73 In naming the compounds discussed in this chapter, why is it important to know whether a compound is molecular or ionic?

2.74 In naming ionic compounds of the transition elements, why is it essential to know the charge on the anion?

2.75 Describe (a) the three situations in which Greek prefixes are used and (b) when Roman numerals are used.

REVIEW PROBLEMS

Laws of Chemical Combination

OH **2.76** Ammonia is composed of hydrogen and nitrogen in a ratio of 9.33 g of nitrogen to 2.00 g of hydrogen. If a sample of ammonia contains 6.28 g of hydrogen, how many grams of nitrogen does it contain?

2.77 A compound of phosphorus and chlorine used in the manufacture of a flame retardant treatment for fabrics contains 1.20 grams of phosphorus for every 4.12 g of chlorine. Suppose a sample of this compound contains 6.22 g of chlorine. How many grams of phosphorus does it contain?

2.78 Refer to the data about ammonia in Problem 2.76. If 4.56 g of nitrogen combined completely with hydrogen to form ammonia, how many grams of ammonia would be formed?

2.79 Refer to the data about the phosphorus–chlorine compound in Problem 2.77. If 12.5 g of phosphorus combined completely with chlorine to form this compound, how many grams of the compound would be formed?

2.80 Molecules of a certain compound of nitrogen and oxygen contain one atom each of N and O. In this compound there are 1.143 g of oxygen for each 1.000 g of nitrogen. Molecules of a different compound of nitrogen and oxygen contain one atom of N and two atoms of O. How many grams of oxygen would be combined with each 1.000 g of nitrogen in the second compound?

2.81 Tin forms two compounds with chlorine. In one of them (compound 1), there are two Cl atoms for each Sn atom; in the other (compound 2), there are four Cl atoms for each Sn atom. When combined with the same mass of tin, what would be the ratio of the masses of chlorine in the two compounds? In compound 1, 0.597 g of chlorine is combined with each 1.000 g of tin. How many grams of chlorine would be combined with 1.000 g of tin in compound 2?

Atomic Masses and Isotopes

2.82 The chemical substance in natural gas is a compound called methane. Its molecules are composed of carbon and hydrogen, and each molecule contains four atoms of hydrogen and one atom of carbon. In this compound, 0.33597 g of hydrogen is combined with 1.0000 g of carbon-12. Use this information to calculate the atomic mass of the element hydrogen.

OH 2.83 A certain element X forms a compound with oxygen in which there are two atoms of X for every three atoms of O. In this compound, 1.125 g of X is combined with 1.000 g of oxygen. Use the average atomic mass of oxygen to calculate the average atomic mass of X. Use your calculated atomic mass to identify the element X.

2.84 If an atom of carbon-12 had been assigned a relative mass of 24.0000 u, what would be the average atomic mass of hydrogen relative to this mass?

2.85 One atom of ^{109}Ag has a mass that is 9.0754 times that of a ^{12}C atom. What is the atomic mass of this isotope of silver expressed in atomic mass units?

Atomic Structure

ILW 2.86 Naturally occurring copper is composed of 69.17% of ^{63}Cu, with an atomic mass of 62.9396 u, and 30.83% of ^{65}Cu, with an atomic mass of 64.9278 u. Use these data to calculate the average atomic mass of copper.

2.87 Naturally occurring magnesium (one of the elements in milk of magnesia) is composed of 78.99% of ^{24}Mg (atomic mass, 23.9850 u), 10.00% of ^{25}Mg (atomic mass, 24.9858 u), and 11.01% of ^{26}Mg (atomic mass, 25.9826 u). Use these data to calculate the average atomic mass of magnesium.

ILW 2.88 Give the numbers of neutrons, protons, and electrons in the atoms of each of the following isotopes. (Use the table of atomic masses and numbers printed inside the front cover for additional information, as needed.) (a) radium-226, (b) ^{206}Pb, (c) carbon-14, (d) ^{23}Na

2.89 Give the numbers of electrons, protons, and neutrons in the atoms of each of the following isotopes. (As necessary, consult the table of atomic masses and numbers printed inside the front cover.) (a) cesium-137, (b) ^{238}U, (c) iodine-131, (d) ^{197}Au

Chemical Formulas

2.90 The compound $Cr(C_2H_3O_2)_3$ is used in the tanning of leather. How many atoms of each element are given in this formula?

2.91 Asbestos, a known cancer-causing agent, has as a typical formula, $Ca_3Mg_5(Si_4O_{11})_2(OH)_2$. How many atoms of each element are given in this formula?

2.92 Epsom salts is a hydrate of magnesium sulfate, $MgSO_4 \cdot 7H_2O$. What is the formula of the substance that remains when Epsom salts is completely dehydrated?

2.93 Rochelle salt is the tetrahydrate of $KNaC_4H_4O_6$. Write the formula for Rochelle salt.

2.94 How many atoms of each element are represented in each of the following formulas? (a) $K_2C_2O_4$, (b) H_2SO_3, (c) $C_{12}H_{26}$, (d) $HC_2H_3O_2$, (e) $(NH_4)_2HPO_4$

2.95 How many atoms of each kind are represented in the following formulas? (a) Na_3PO_4, (b) $Ca(H_2PO_4)_2$, (c) C_4H_{10}, (d) $Fe_3(AsO_4)_2$, (e) $C_3H_5(OH)_3$

2.96 How many atoms of each kind are represented in the following formulas? (a) $Ni(ClO_4)_2$, (b) $CuCO_3$, (c) $K_2Cr_2O_7$, (d) CH_3CO_2H, (e) $(NH_4)_2HPO_4$

2.97 How many atoms of each kind are represented in the following formulas? (a) $CH_3CH_2CO_2C_3H_7$, (b) $MgSO_4 \cdot 7H_2O$, (c) $KAl(SO_4)_2 \cdot 12H_2O$, (d) $Cu(NO_3)_2$, (e) $(CH_3)_3COH$

2.98 How many atoms of each element are represented in each of the following expressions? (a) $3N_2O$, (b) $4NaHCO_3$, (c) $2CuSO_4 \cdot 5H_2O$

OH 2.99 How many atoms of each element are represented in each of the following expressions? (a) $7CH_3CO_2H$, (b) $2(NH_2)_2CO$, (c) $5K_2Cr_2O_7$

Chemical Equations

2.100 Consider the balanced equation

$$2Fe(NO_3)_3 + 3Na_2CO_3 \longrightarrow Fe_2(CO_3)_3 + 6NaNO_3$$

(a) How many atoms of Na are on each side of the equation?
(b) How many atoms of C are on each side of the equation?
(c) How many atoms of O are on each side of the equation?

2.101 Consider the balanced equation for the combustion of octane, a component of gasoline:

$$2C_8H_{18} + 25O_2 \longrightarrow 16CO_2 + 18H_2O$$

(a) How many atoms of C are on each side of the equation?
(b) How many atoms of H are on each side of the equation?
(c) How many atoms of O are on each side of the equation?

Ionic Compounds

2.102 Use the periodic table, but not Table 2.6, to write the symbols for the ions of (a) K, (b) Br, (c) Mg, (d) S, and (e) Al.

2.103 Use the periodic table, but not Table 2.6, to write the symbols for ions of (a) barium, (b) oxygen, (c) fluorine, (d) strontium, and (e) rubidium.

OH 2.104 Write formulas for ionic compounds formed between (a) Na and Br, (b) K and I, (c) Ba and O, (d) Mg and Br, and (e) Ba and F.

2.105 Write the formulas for the ionic compounds formed by the following transition metals with the chloride ion, Cl^-: (a) chromium, (b) iron, (c) manganese, (d) copper, and (e) zinc.

2.106 Write formulas for the ionic compounds formed from (a) K^+ and nitrate ion, (b) Ca^{2+} and acetate ion, (c) ammonium ion and Cl^-, (d) Fe^{3+} and carbonate ion, and (e) Mg^{2+} and phosphate ion.

2.107 Write formulas for the ionic compounds formed from (a) Zn^{2+} and hydroxide ion, (b) Ag^+ and chromate ion, (c) Ba^{2+} and sulfite ion, (d) Rb^+ and sulfate ion, and (e) Li^+ and bicarbonate ion.

2.108 Write formulas for two compounds formed between O^{2-} and (a) lead, (b) tin, (c) manganese, (d) iron, and (e) copper.

2.109 Write formulas for the ionic compounds formed from Cl^- and (a) cadmium ion, (b) silver ion, (c) zinc ion, and (d) nickel ion.

Naming Compounds

2.110 Name the following molecular compounds.
(a) SiO_2 (b) XeF_4 (c) P_4O_{10} (d) Cl_2O_7

2.111 Name the following molecular compounds.
(a) ClF_3 (b) S_2Cl_2 (c) N_2O_5 (d) $AsCl_5$

2.112 Name the following ionic compounds.
(a) CaS   (b) $AlBr_3$ (c) Na_3P (d) Ba_3As_2 (e) Rb_2S

2.113 Name the following ionic compounds.
(a) NaF   (b) Mg_2C (c) Li_3N (d) Al_2O_3 (e) K_2Se

2.114 Name the following ionic compounds using the Stock system.
(a) FeS   (b) CuO   (c) SnO_2 (d) $CoCl_2 \cdot 6H_2O$

2.115 Name the following ionic compounds using the Stock system.
(a) Mn_2O_3 (b) Hg_2Cl_2 (c) PbS   (d) $CrCl_3 \cdot 4H_2O$

2.116 Name the following. If necessary, refer to Table 2.8 on page 69.
(a) $NaNO_2$ (b) $KMnO_4$ (c) $MgSO_4 \cdot 7H_2O$ (d) KSCN

2.117 Name the following. If necessary, refer to Table 2.8 on page 69.
(a) K_3PO_4 (c) $Fe_2(CO_3)_3$
(b) $NH_4C_2H_3O_2$ (d) $Na_2S_2O_3 \cdot 5H_2O$

2.118 Identify each of the following as molecular or ionic and give its name:
(a) $CrCl_2$ (f) P_4O_6
(b) S_2Cl_2 (g) $CaSO_3$
(c) $NH_4C_2H_3O_2$ (h) AgCN
(d) SO_3 (i) $ZnBr_2$
(e) KIO_3 (j) H_2Se

2.119 Identify each of the following as molecular or ionic and give its name:
(a) $V(NO_3)_3$ (f) K_2CrO_4
(b) $Co(C_2H_3O_2)_2$ (g) $Fe(OH)_2$
(c) Au_2S_3 (h) I_2O_4
(d) Au_2S (i) I_4O_9
(e) $GeBr_4$ (j) P_4Se_3

OH 2.120 Write formulas for the following.
(a) sodium monohydrogen phosphate
(b) lithium selenide
(c) chromium(III) acetate
(d) disulfur decafluoride
(e) nickel(II) cyanide
(f) iron(III) oxide
(g) antimony pentafluoride

2.121 Write formulas for the following.
(a) dialuminum hexachloride
(b) tetraarsenic decaoxide
(c) magnesium hydroxide
(d) copper(II) bisulfate
(e) ammonium thiocyanate
(f) potassium thiosulfate
(g) diiodine pentaoxide

2.122 Write formulas for the following.
(a) ammonium sulfide
(b) chromium(III) sulfate hexahydrate
(c) silicon tetrafluoride
(d) molybdenum(IV) sulfide
(e) tin(IV) chloride
(f) hydrogen selenide
(g) tetraphosphorus heptasulfide

2.123 Write formulas for the following.
(a) mercury(II) acetate
(b) barium hydrogen sulfite
(c) boron trichloride
(d) calcium phosphide
(e) magnesium dihydrogen phosphate
(f) calcium oxalate
(g) xenon tetrafluoride

2.124 The compounds Se_2S_6 and Se_2S_4 have been shown to be antidandruff agents. What are their names?

2.125 The compound P_2S_5 is used to manufacture safety matches. What is the name of this compound?

ADDITIONAL EXERCISES

2.126 An element has 25 protons in its nucleus.
(a) Is the element a metal, a nonmetal, or a metalloid?
(b) On the basis of the average atomic mass, write the symbol for the element's most abundant isotope.
(c) How many neutrons are in the isotope you described in part (b)?
(d) How many electrons are in atoms of this element?
(e) How many times heavier than ^{12}C is the average atom of this element?

*2.127 Elements X and Y form a compound in which there is one atom of X for every four atoms of Y. When these elements react, it is found that 1.00 g of X combines with 5.07 g of Y. When 1.00 g of X combines with 1.14 g of O, it forms a compound containing two atoms of O for each atom of X. Calculate the atomic mass of Y.

2.128 An iron nail is composed of four isotopes with the percentage abundances and atomic masses given in the following table. Calculate the average atomic mass of iron.

Isotope	Percentage Abundance	Atomic Mass (u)
^{54}Fe	5.80	53.9396
^{56}Fe	91.72	55.9349
^{57}Fe	2.20	56.9354
^{58}Fe	0.28	57.9333

*2.129 OH Bromine (shown in Figure 2.12, page 53) is a dark red liquid that vaporizes easily and is very corrosive to the skin. It is used commercially as a bleach for fibers and silk. Naturally occurring bromine is composed of two isotopes: ^{79}Br, with a mass of 78.9183 u, and ^{81}Br, with a mass of 80.9163 u. Use this information and the average atomic mass of bromine given in the table on the inside front cover of the book to calculate the percentage abundances of the two isotopes.

*2.130 OH Rust contains an iron–oxygen compound in which there are three oxygen atoms for each two iron atoms. In this compound, the iron to oxygen mass ratio is 2.325 g Fe to 1.000 g O. Another compound of iron and oxygen contains these elements in the ratio of 2.616 g Fe to 1.000 g O. What is the ratio of iron to oxygen atoms in this other iron–oxygen compound?

2.131 One atomic mass unit has a mass of $1.6605389 \times 10^{-24}$ g. Calculate the mass, in grams, of one atom of magnesium. What is the mass of one atom of iron, expressed in grams? Use these two answers to determine how many atoms of Mg are in 24.31 g of magnesium and how many atoms of Fe are in 55.85 g of iron. Compare your answers. What conclusions can you draw from the results of these calculations? Without actually performing any calculations, how many atoms do you think would be in 40.08 g of calcium?

OH 2.132 What are the formulas for mercury(I) nitrate dihydrate and mercury(II) nitrate monohydrate?

2.133 Consider the following substances: Cl_2, CaO, HBr, $CuCl_2$, AsH_3, $NaNO_3$, and NO_2.
(a) Which are binary substances?
(b) Which is a triatomic molecule?
(c) In which do we find only electron sharing?
(d) Which are diatomic?
(e) In which do we find only attractions between ions?
(f) Which are molecular?
(g) Which are ionic?

2.134 Using the old system of nomenclature, write the names for the following compounds. (See Facets of Chemistry 2.3.)
(a) gold(III) sulfate
(b) gold(III) nitrate
(c) lead(IV) oxide
(d) mercury(I) chloride
(e) copper(II) sulfate
(f) mercury(II) chloride
(g) cobalt(II) hydroxide
(h) tin(II) chloride
(i) tin(IV) sulfide

2.135 Write the names of the following compounds using the Stock system of nomenclature. Also write their formulas. (See Facets of Chemistry 2.3.)
(a) cupric bromide
(b) cuprous iodide
(c) ferrous sulfate
(d) chromous chloride
(e) mercurous nitrate
(f) manganous sulfate
(g) plumbous acetate

2.136 A student needed a sample of $Fe(NO_3)_3 \cdot 9H_2O$, but when she went to the latest edition of the catalog of a major chemical supplier, she could not find it listed alphabetically under "iron." Knowing that suppliers of laboratory chemicals still often list chemicals under their older names, what name should she look for in the catalog?

2.137 Write the balanced chemical equation for the reaction between elements with atomic numbers of (a) 20 and 35, (b) 6 and 17, (c) 13 and 16. For each of these determine the ratio of the mass of the heavier element to the lighter element in the compound.

OH 2.138 Write the balanced gas phase chemical equation for the reaction of dinitrogen pentoxide with sulfur dioxide to form sulfur trioxide and nitrogen oxide. What small, whole-number ratios are expected for oxygen in the nitrogen oxides and the sulfur oxides?

EXERCISES IN CRITICAL THINKING

2.139 Imagine a world where, for some reason, hydrogen and helium have not been discovered. Would Mendeleev have had enough information to predict their existence?

2.140 Around 1750 Benjamin Franklin knew of two opposite types of electric charge, produced by rubbing a glass rod or amber rod with fur. He decided that the charge developed on the glass rod should be the "positive" charge and from there on charges were defined. What would have changed if Franklin decided the amber rod acquired the positive charge?

2.141 Explore the Internet and find for yourself a reliable source of physical properties of elements and compounds. Justify how you decided the site was reliable.

2.142 Spreadsheet applications such as Microsoft Excel can display data in a variety of ways; some of these are shown throughout this book. What method of displaying periodic trends (line graphs, tables, bar graphs, 3-D views, etc.) is most effective for your learning style? Explain your answer by stating why your chosen display is better than the others.

2.143 Scientists often validate measurements such as measuring the circumference of the earth by using two independent methods to measure the same value. Describe two independent methods for determining the atomic mass of an element. Explain how these methods are truly independent.

THE MOLE: RELATING THE MICROSCOPIC WORLD OF ATOMS TO LABORATORY MEASUREMENTS

3

The rich and famous often fly to exotic vacation spots using private airplanes such as this. Even now you may be dreaming about your upcoming vacation after the final exam. Here, the plane is prepared for takeoff with the necessary mass (weight) of aviation fuel to reach the planned destination with some excess to spare. Professionals use complex calculations that include the mole concept described in this chapter to determine the mass of fuel needed to transport vacationers safely to their next destination. [Alice M. Prescott/Unicorn Stock Photos]

THIS CHAPTER IN CONTEXT   In Chapters 1 and 2 we reviewed the basics of the mathemat language of chemistry. In this chapter we combine the material from Chapters 1 and 2 to learn the fundame chemical calculations. These calculations are important for success in laboratory work in this course. You find this chapter to be important for future courses in organic chemistry, biochemistry, and almost any other ac laboratory course in the sciences.

Our chemical calculations are called **stoichiometry** (stoy-kee-AH-meh-tree), which loosely translates as "the ure of the elements." Stoichiometry involves converting chemical formulas and equations that represent in atoms, molecules, and formula units to the laboratory scale that uses milligrams, grams, and even kilograms substances. To do this we introduce the *mole concept*. The mole concept allows the chemist to scale up fr atomic and molecular level to the laboratory scale much as the baker in Figure 3.1 scales up the amount of ingr

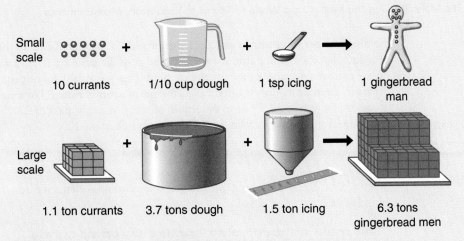

Small scale

10 currants + 1/10 cup dough + 1 tsp icing → 1 gingerbread man

Large scale

1.1 ton currants + 3.7 tons dough + 1.5 ton icing → 6.3 tons gingerbread men

FIG. 3.1 **Manufacture on small and large scales.** Making a single gingerbread man requires 10 currants for eyes and buttons, 1/10 of a cup of spiced cookie dough, and a teaspoon of glacé icing. To manufacture gingerbread men by the million, you will have to order raw materials by the ton. To scale up the recipe, you will need to know the masses of raw materials required to manufacture some fixed number of gingerbread men.

from a single gingerbread man to a mass-production scale. Chemical conversions are similar in nature to the gingerbread man example but of course they answer different questions. Some of these questions are

How many grams of product can be made if we react *x* grams of *A* and *y* grams of *B*?

How can we be sure to get the most product from an expensive reactant?

If a reaction has a 70% yield, how many grams of reactants are needed to produce the amount of product needed?

How many grams of each reactant are needed so that there will be no reactants left over (i.e., no waste)?

Our stoichiometric calculations are almost always factor-label conversions from one set of units to another as we saw in Chapter 1. To be successful at factor-label calculations we need two things, a knowledge of the equalities that can be made into conversion factors and a logical sequence of steps to apply the conversion factors to our problem. Figure 3.6 at the end of this chapter organizes the equalities and sequence of steps in a simple flowchart. As you read this chapter, you might want to look at Figure 3.6 to see how all the parts fit together neatly.

3.1 | THE MOLE CONVENIENTLY LINKS MASS TO NUMBER OF ATOMS OR MOLECULES

We can tell from the fundamental measurements of the mass of the proton, neutron, and electron that even the largest of the atoms must have extremely small masses and correspondingly small sizes. Any sample of matter that is observable by the naked eye must have very large numbers of atoms or molecules. The methods of calculation developed in Chapter 1 and the mole concept allow us to count by weighing and then use that information to solve some very interesting problems.

Counting by weighing is familiar to everyone even if you are not aware of it. A pound of chocolate chips counts out the needed number of chocolate chips for your cookies. A quarter pound of rice counts out the correct number of rice grains to accompany your meal. Weighing a bag of dimes, knowing that each dime weighs 2.27 grams, will allow you to calculate the number of coins. Similarly, the mass of a chemical substance can be used to determine the number of atoms or molecules in the sample. This last conversion is possible because of the mole concept.

The SI unit for the *amount of substance* is the mole

The **mole** (abbreviated as mol) is the SI unit for the amount of substance. The amount of substance does not refer to the mass or volume of your sample but it does refer to the number of atoms, molecules, or formula units, etc., in your sample. **One mole is defined**

☐ *Mole* is a Latin word with several meanings, including: a shapeless mass; a large number; or trouble or difficulty.

as the number of atoms in exactly 12 grams of ^{12}C atoms. Based on this definition and the fact that the average atomic masses in the periodic table are relative values, we can deduce that we will have a mole of any element if we weigh an amount equal to the atomic mass in gram units (this is often called the **gram atomic mass**). For example, the atomic mass of sodium is 22.99 u, so one mole of sodium has a mass of 22.99 g and contains as many atoms as there are in a 12.00 g sample of carbon-12.

TOOLS

One mole of any element is equal to the atomic mass with gram units

$$1 \text{ mole of element } X = \text{gram atomic mass of } X$$

Figure 3.2 is a photo showing one mole of some common elements: iron, mercury, copper, and sulfur.

The mole concept also applies to compounds

☐ Many chemists use the terms *molecular weight* and *atomic weight* for molecular mass and atomic mass.

Molecules and ionic compounds discussed in Chapter 2 have definite formulas. For molecular compounds and elements, adding the atomic masses of all atoms in the formula results in the **molecular mass (molecular weight)**. The gram molecular mass of a molecular substance (a mass in grams numerically equal to the molecular mass) is also equal to one mole.

$$1 \text{ mole of molecule } X = \text{gram molecular mass of } X$$

For example, a molecule of H_2O consists of 2 atoms of H (with a total mass of 2×1.00 u = 2.00 u) and one atom of O (with a mass of 16.00 u) for a total of 18.00 u. Therefore, the molecular mass of H_2O is 18.00 u. The gram molecular mass of H_2O is 18.00 g, so 1 mol $H_2O = 18.00$ g H_2O.

TOOLS

Molecular mass or **formula mass** *is the sum of the masses of all atoms in a chemical formula*

Similarly, the **formula mass** of an ionic compound is the sum of the masses of all the atoms in the formula of an ionic compound.

$$1 \text{ mole of ionic compound } X = \text{gram formula mass of } X$$

For example, the ionic compound calcium chloride, $CaCl_2$, has a formula mass that is the sum of the atomic masses of one calcium atom and two chlorine atoms. One calcium atom has an atomic mass of 40.08 u. Two chlorine atoms each with an atomic mass of 35.45 u have a total mass of 70.90 u. Adding these together gives us 110.98 u for the formula mass of $CaCl_2$. Therefore, 1 mol $CaCl_2$ has a mass of 110.98 g. There is a distinct similarity between all three equations above. To simplify discussions we will often use the following relationship between moles and mass unless one of the other, equivalent, definitions provides more clarity.

TOOLS

Molar mass *is the mass in grams of one mole of any substance*

$$1 \text{ mole of } X = \text{gram molar mass of } X$$

The gram **molar mass** is simply the mass of one mole of the substance under consideration. Figure 3.3 depicts one mole of four different compounds.

FIG. 3.2 **Moles of elements.** Each sample of these elements contains the same number of atoms. *(Michael Watson.)*

FIG. 3.3 **Moles of compounds.** One mole of four different compounds: water, sodium chloride, copper sulfate pentahydrate, and sodium chromate. Each sample contains the identical number of formula units or molecules. *(Michael Watson.)*

Convert mass to moles and moles to mass using molar masses

At this point we recognize the above relationships or equalities as the necessary information for doing conversion problems similar to those in Chapter 1. Now, however, the problems will be couched in chemical terms. We will also use all of the principles in Section 1.6 to end up with the maximum, and correct, number of significant figures in our answers. To do this we will need to round our atomic or molar masses to at least one more significant figure than the data given in the example.

☐ The term *molar mass* has been coined as a general term to cover all items previously called atomic masses, atomic weights, molecular masses, molecular weights, formula masses, and formula weights.

EXAMPLE 3.1
Converting from Grams to Moles

How many moles of sulfur are there in a 23.5 g sample of sulfur?

ANALYSIS: We see that the problem starts with a certain mass of sulfur and asks us to convert it to moles. This uses the tool we just described that equates moles and grams of an element. The equality shows that there is a one-step conversion possible using 1 mol S = 32.06 g S.

SOLUTION: Let's begin by expressing the question in the form of an equation.

$$23.5 \text{ g S} = ? \text{ mol S}$$

$$\underset{\text{start}}{\nearrow} \qquad \underset{\text{end}}{\nwarrow}$$

Now use the equality to cancel the grams of sulfur as shown below.

$$23.5 \text{ g S} \times \left(\frac{1 \text{ mol S}}{32.06 \text{ g S}} \right) = 0.733 \text{ mol S}$$

IS THE ANSWER REASONABLE? First review the math to be sure that the units cancel properly, and they do. Second, round off all numbers to one significant figure and calculate an estimated answer. This gives 20/30 = 2/3, and our answer is not very different (very different is a factor of 10 or more) from 2/3. We are justified in being confident in our answer.

☐ Solving a stoichiometry problem is much like giving directions to get from your house to your college. You need to know both the starting and ending points. Setting up the problem in this way gives you those reference points. The factor-label ratios get us from one to the other.

EXAMPLE 3.2
Converting from Moles to Grams

We need 0.254 mol of iron(III) chloride for a certain experiment. How many grams do we need to weigh?

ANALYSIS: The formula for iron(III) chloride is $FeCl_3$. As in the last example we need the tool for the conversion between mass and moles. We write the equality as

$$1 \text{ mol FeCl}_3 = \text{gram molar mass FeCl}_3$$

This tells us we need the gram molar mass of $FeCl_3$ that is the sum of the gram atomic masses of one iron atom and three chlorine atoms.

$$\text{gram molar mass} = 55.85 \text{ g Fe mol}^{-1} + (3 \times 35.45 \text{ g Cl mol}^{-1}) = 162.20 \text{ g FeCl}_3 \text{ mol}^{-1}$$

The equality can be written as 1 mol $FeCl_3$ = 162.20 g $FeCl_3$.

SOLUTION: The problem starts with

$$0.254 \text{ mol FeCl}_3 = ? \text{ g FeCl}_3$$

Use the factor label to perform the conversion:

$$0.254 \text{ mol FeCl}_3 \left(\frac{162.20 \text{ g FeCl}_3}{1 \text{ mol FeCl}_3} \right) = 41.2 \text{ g FeCl}_3$$

IS THE ANSWER REASONABLE? First we verify that the units cancel properly, and they do. Next we do an approximate calculation. If we round 0.254 to 0.25 and 162.20 to 160, the arithmetic becomes 0.25 × 160 = 40, which gives a result that is very close to the calculated value. We also could have estimated the answer by rounding to one significant figure, which gives 0.3 × 200 = 60, and still have concluded that the math was correct. Remember, this is just an estimate, but it tells us our more precise answer is correct.

Practice Exercise 1: How many moles of aluminum are there in a 3.47 gram sheet of aluminum foil used to wrap your sandwich for lunch today? (Hint: Recall the tool that relates the mass of an element to moles of that element.)

Practice Exercise 2: Your laboratory balance can weigh samples to three decimal places. If the uncertainty in your weighing is ±0.002 g, what is the uncertainty in moles if the sample being weighed is pure silicon?

The number of particles in a mole is called Avogadro's number

□ Avogadro's number was named for Amedeo Avogadro (1776–1856), an Italian scientist who was one of the pioneers of stoichiometry.

TOOLS

Avogadro's number

□ Avogadro's number is a link between moles of substance and elementary units of substance in a stoichiometry problem. If a problem does not mention atoms or molecules at all, you don't need to use Avogadro's number in the calculation!

The definition of the mole refers to a number equal to the number of atoms in exactly 12 g of ^{12}C. Just what is that number? After much experimentation the scientific community agrees that the value, to four significant figures, is 6.022×10^{23}. In honor of Amedeo Avogadro, this value has been named **Avogadro's number.** Now we can write a very important relationship between the atomic scale and the laboratory scale as

$$1 \text{ mole of } X = 6.022 \times 10^{23} \text{ units of } X$$

The units of our chemicals can be atoms, molecules, formula units, etc.

We use Avogadro's number to relate the macroscopic and microscopic worlds

The relationships developed above allow us to connect the laboratory scale with the atomic scale using our standard factor-label calculations as shown in the next two examples.

EXAMPLE 3.3
Converting from the Laboratory Scale to the Atomic Scale

How many atoms of copper are there in a piece of pure copper wire that weighs 14.3 grams?

ANALYSIS: Here we do not have any tool that directly converts grams of copper to atoms of copper. However, we do have one tool that relates mass to moles (the atomic mass of copper) and another tool that relates moles to atoms (Avogadro's number). We need to start with the grams of copper and use the appropriate conversion factors derived from these tools in sequence.

grams copper → moles copper → atoms copper

SOLUTION: We start by mathematically stating the problem:

14.3 g Cu = ? atoms Cu

The first step will be to convert grams of copper to moles of copper. The atomic mass gives us

1 mol Cu = 63.546 g Cu

□ Estimates are done without calculators. For exponential numbers the numerical part of the calculation is separated from the exponents. The numerical part, to one significant figure, is usually easy to evaluate. The exponent is easier since it involves simple addition and subtraction.

This will allow us to construct a conversion factor to take us from grams to moles. To go from moles of copper to the number of copper atoms, we need Avogadro's number, which gives the relationship

1 mol Cu = 6.02×10^{23} atom Cu

This will provide a conversion factor to take us from moles to atoms.

To assemble the solution, we begin with the given amount of copper (14.3 g) and apply conversion factors that eliminate units we don't want and take us to the units of the answer. This could be done in two steps or in one complete step as shown here. Note how the units cancel.

$$14.3 \text{ g Cu} \times \left(\frac{1 \text{ mol Cu}}{63.546 \text{ g Cu}} \right) \times \left(\frac{6.022 \times 10^{23} \text{ atoms Cu}}{1 \text{ mol Cu}} \right) = 1.35 \times 10^{23} \text{ atoms Cu}$$

Also notice that the first factor converts grams of copper to moles of copper and the second takes us from moles of copper to atoms of copper.

IS THE ANSWER REASONABLE? The most common mistake students make in this kind of calculation is using Avogadro's number incorrectly, or not using it at all. Think about the answer for a moment. We know copper atoms are very small, so in 14.3 g Cu there will be an enormous number of atoms. Our answer is a very large number, so it appears to be reasonable.

EXAMPLE 3.4
Calculating the Mass
of a Molecule

What is the mass in grams of one molecule of carbon tetrachloride?

ANALYSIS: Using the nomenclature tools of Chapter 2, the formula of the molecule in question is CCl_4. In this problem we're asked to express the mass of a single CCl_4 molecule (composed of just 5 atoms) in a laboratory sized unit, grams. This tells us we need to use Avogadro's number, which is a tool that relates molecules to moles. Then we can use the molecular mass as a tool to relate moles to grams.

SOLUTION: Let's begin by expressing the question in the form of an equation.

$$1 \text{ molecule } CCl_4 = ? \text{ g } CCl_4$$

Avogadro's number lets us write

$$1 \text{ mol } CCl_4 = 6.02 \times 10^{23} \text{ molecules } CCl_4$$

This allows us to calculate the number of moles of CCl_4

$$1 \text{ molecule } CCl_4 \times \left(\frac{1 \text{ mol } CCl_4}{6.02 \times 10^{23} \text{ molecules } CCl_4} \right) = 1.661 \times 10^{-24} \text{ mol } CCl_4$$

To find grams, we need the molecular mass of CCl_4, which is 153.823. Therefore, 1 mol CCl_4 = 153.823 g CCl_4. Now we can calculate grams of CCl_4.

$$1.661 \times 10^{-24} \text{ mol } CCl_4 \times \left(\frac{153.823 \text{ g } CCl_4}{1 \text{ mol } CCl_4} \right) = 2.56 \times 10^{-22} \text{ g } CCl_4$$

In stepwise calculations such as this we normally keep at least one extra significant figure until the final result is determined. The calculated mass of one molecule of CCl_4 is 2.56×10^{-22} g.

IS THE ANSWER REASONABLE? We expect a single molecule to have a very small mass. Our answer is a very small number, so it appears to be reasonable.

Practice Exercise 3: Would you be able to use a balance capable of weighing to the nearest 0.001 g to weigh 5.64×10^{18} formula units of calcium nitrate? [Hint: What is the mass of this amount of $Ca(NO_3)_2$?]

Practice Exercise 4: If the uncertainty in weighing a sample in the lab is ± 0.002 g, what is this uncertainty in terms of molecules of sucrose, $C_{12}H_{22}O_{11}$?

3.2 | **CHEMICAL FORMULAS RELATE AMOUNTS OF SUBSTANCES IN A COMPOUND**

Consider the chemical formula for water, H_2O:

- One molecule of water contains 2 H atoms and 1 O atom.
- Two molecules of water contain 4 H atoms and 2 O atoms.
- A dozen molecules of water contain 2 dozen H atoms and 1 dozen O atoms.
- A mole of molecules of water contains 2 moles of H atoms and 1 mole of O atoms.

Whether we're dealing with atoms, dozens of atoms, or moles of atoms, the chemical formula tells us that the ratio of H atoms to O atoms is always 2 to 1. In addition we can write the following **Stoichiometric equivalencies** concerning the water molecule:

$$1 \text{ mol } H_2O \Leftrightarrow 2 \text{ mol } H \qquad 1 \text{ mol } H_2O \Leftrightarrow 1 \text{ mol } O \qquad 1 \text{ mol } O \Leftrightarrow 2 \text{ mol } H$$

We recall that the symbol ⟺ means "is chemically equivalent to" and it is treated mathematically as an equal sign (see page 26 in Chapter 1).

TOOLS

Subscripts tell us the number of atoms in a formula

Within chemical compounds, moles of atoms always combine in the same ratio as the individual atoms themselves.

This fact lets us prepare mole-to-mole conversion factors involving elements in compounds as we need them. For example, in the formula P_4O_{10}, the subscripts mean that there are 4 moles of P for every 10 moles of O in this compound. We can relate P and O within the compound using the following conversion factors.

$$4 \text{ mol P} \Leftrightarrow 10 \text{ mol O} \qquad \text{from which we write} \qquad \frac{4 \text{ mol P}}{10 \text{ mol O}} \quad \text{or} \quad \frac{10 \text{ mol O}}{4 \text{ mol P}}$$

The formula P_4O_{10} also implies other equivalencies, each with its two associated conversion factors.

$$1 \text{ mol } P_4O_{10} \Leftrightarrow 4 \text{ mol P} \qquad \text{or} \qquad \frac{1 \text{ mol } P_4O_{10}}{4 \text{ mol P}} \quad \text{and} \quad \frac{4 \text{ mol P}}{1 \text{ mol } P_4O_{10}}$$

$$1 \text{ mol } P_4O_{10} \Leftrightarrow 10 \text{ mol O} \qquad \text{or} \qquad \frac{1 \text{ mol } P_4O_{10}}{10 \text{ mol O}} \quad \text{and} \quad \frac{10 \text{ mol O}}{1 \text{ mol } P_4O_{10}}$$

EXAMPLE 3.5

Calculating Amount of a Compound by Analyzing One Element

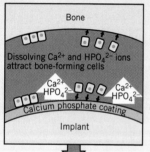

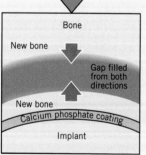

Some surfaces on bone implants are coated with calcium phosphate to permit bone to actually bond to the surface.

Calcium phosphate is widely found in nature in the form of natural minerals. It is also found in bones and some kidney stones. In many instances if we determine one element in a compound we can find out how much of the compound is present. In one case a sample is found to contain 0.864 mole of phosphorus. How many moles of $Ca_3(PO_4)_2$ will that represent?

ANALYSIS: We need to use the mole ratio tool that gives the relationships between the compound's formula and the individual elements in that formula. Specifically we need to use the equivalence 2 mol P ⟺ 1 mol $Ca_3(PO_4)_2$ to construct the conversion factor needed to convert moles of P into moles of $Ca_3(PO_4)_2$.

SOLUTION: The initial question is written as an equation:

$$0.864 \text{ mol P} = ? \text{ mol } Ca_3(PO_4)_2$$

Seeing that mol P must cancel and mol $Ca_3(PO_4)_2$ must remain, the correct conversion factor must be 1 mol $Ca_3(PO_4)_2$/2 mol P and we solve the equation as

$$0.864 \text{ mol P} \left(\frac{1 \text{ mol } Ca_3(PO_4)_2}{2 \text{ mol P}} \right) = 0.432 \text{ mol } Ca_3(PO_4)_2$$

IS THE ANSWER REASONABLE? For a quick check, you can round 0.864 to 1 and divide by 2 to get 0.5. There is little difference between our estimate, 0.5, and the calculated answer, 0.432.

☐ Whenever a problem asks you to convert an amount of one substance into an amount of a different substance, the most important conversion factor in the problem is usually a mole-to-mole relationship between the two substances.

Practice Exercise 5: Aluminum sulfate is analyzed and it is determined that the sample contains 0.0774 mole of sulfate ions. How many moles of aluminum does the sample contain? (Hint: Construct the correct formula for aluminum sulfate, then use the tool in this section.)

Practice Exercise 6: How many moles of nitrogen atoms are combined with 8.60 mol of oxygen atoms in dinitrogen pentoxide, N_2O_5?

One common use of stoichiometry in the lab occurs when we must relate the masses of two raw materials that are needed to make a compound. These calculations are summarized by the following sequence of steps to convert the mass of compound A to the mass of compound B.

$$\text{mass of } A \longrightarrow \text{moles of } A \longrightarrow \text{moles of } B \longrightarrow \text{mass of } B$$

In the following example we see how this is applied.

TOOLS

Sequence of steps for mass-to-mass conversions

EXAMPLE 3.6
Calculating Amounts of One Element from Amounts of Another in a Compound

Chlorophyll a, the green pigment in leaves, has the formula $C_{55}H_{72}MgN_4O_5$. If 0.0011 g of Mg is available to a plant cell for chlorophyll a synthesis, how many grams of carbon will be required to completely use up the magnesium?

ANALYSIS: Let's begin, as usual, by restating the problem as follows.

$$0.0011 \text{ g Mg} \Longleftrightarrow ? \text{ g C} \qquad \text{(for chlorophyll a only)}$$

A mole-to-mole ratio is the tool to use in problems that convert the moles of one substance into the moles of another. The formula of chlorophyll a, $C_{55}H_{72}MgN_4O_5$, relates Mg to C within the compound. We use the formula's subscripts as the tool we need to establish the relationship between moles of Mg and moles of C.

$$1 \text{ mol Mg} \Longleftrightarrow 55 \text{ mol C}$$

We know we'll need to use this relationship to solve the problem. Let's drop it into the middle of our calculation sequence:

$$\boxed{1 \text{ mol Mg} \Longleftrightarrow 55 \text{ mol C}}$$

$$0.0011 \text{ g Mg} \longrightarrow \text{mol Mg} \longrightarrow \text{mol C} \longrightarrow ? \text{ g C}$$

By placing this tool between our given information (0.0011 g Mg) and our desired units (g C) sequence, we've cut a difficult problem into two simpler ones. All we have to do now to complete the conversion of units is relate grams of Mg to moles of Mg, and moles of C to grams of C. The atomic mass of C links moles of C to grams of C, and the atomic mass of Mg links moles of Mg to grams of Mg. Rounding them to three significant figures, we can write

$$1 \text{ mol Mg} = 24.3 \text{ g Mg}$$
$$1 \text{ mol C} = 12.0 \text{ g C}$$

Our complete sequence for the problem is

$$\boxed{1 \text{ mol Mg} = 24.31 \text{ g Mg}} \qquad \boxed{1 \text{ mol Mg} \Longleftrightarrow 55 \text{ mol C}} \qquad \boxed{1 \text{ mol C} = 12.0 \text{ g C}}$$

$$0.0011 \text{ g Mg} \longrightarrow \text{mol Mg} \longrightarrow \text{mol C} \longrightarrow \text{g C}$$

SOLUTION: We now set up the solution by forming conversion factors so the units cancel:

$$0.0011 \text{ g Mg} \times \left(\frac{1 \text{ mol Mg}}{24.3 \text{ g Mg}} \right) \times \left(\frac{55 \text{ mol C}}{1 \text{ mol Mg}} \right) \times \left(\frac{12.0 \text{ g C}}{1 \text{ mol C}} \right) = 0.030 \text{ g C}$$

A plant cell must supply 0.030 g C for every 0.0011 g Mg to completely use up the magnesium in the synthesis of chlorophyll a.

IS THE ANSWER REASONABLE? After checking that our units cancel properly, a quick estimate of the answer can be made by rounding all numbers to one significant figure. One way to do this results in the following expression (without units):

$$\frac{0.001 \times 1 \times 50 \times 10}{20 \times 1 \times 1} = \frac{0.5}{20} = \frac{0.05}{2} = 0.025$$

This value is close to the answer we got and gives us confidence that it is correct. (Note that if we rounded the 55 up to 60 our estimate would have been 0.030, which would still confirm our conclusion.)

Our answer was 0.030 g C from 0.0011 g Mg, so the mass of carbon we obtained is about 30 times the mass of the magnesium we started with. This seems reasonable because there are 55 times as many C atoms as Mg but a Mg atom weighs twice as much as a carbon atom.

Practice Exercise 7: How many grams of iron are needed to combine with 25.6 g of O to make Fe_2O_3? (Hint: Determine the mole ratios that the formula provides.)

Practice Exercise 8: An important iron ore called hematite contains iron(III) oxide. How many grams of iron are in a 15.0 g sample of hematite?

Practice Exercise 9: How many grams of iron will combine with 12.0 g of oxygen to form iron(III) oxide? Hematite, mentioned above, is often highly polished and used as a semiprecious gemstone.

3.3 | CHEMICAL FORMULAS CAN BE DETERMINED FROM EXPERIMENTAL MASS MEASUREMENTS

In pharmaceutical research, chemists often synthesize entirely new compounds, or isolate new compounds from plant and animal tissues. They must then determine the formula and structure of the new compound. This is usually accomplished using mass spectroscopy, which gives an experimental value for the molecular mass. The compound can also be decomposed chemically to find the masses of elements within a given amount of compound. Let's see how experimental mass measurements can be used to determine a compound's formula.

Percentage composition describes the relative masses of the elements in a compound

The usual form for describing the relative masses of the elements in a compound is a list of *percentages by mass* called the compound's **percentage composition.** The **percentage by mass** of an element is the number of grams of the element present in 100 g of the compound. In general, a percentage by mass is found by using the following equation.

TOOLS
Percentage composition

$$\% \text{ by mass of element} = \frac{\text{mass of element}}{\text{mass of whole sample}} \times 100\% \qquad (3.1)$$

EXAMPLE 3.7
Calculating a Percentage Composition from Chemical Analysis

A sample of a liquid with a mass of 8.657 g was decomposed into its elements and gave 5.217 g of carbon, 0.9620 g of hydrogen, and 2.478 g of oxygen. What is the percentage composition of this compound?

ANALYSIS: We must use the tool expressed in Equation 3.1 and apply it to each element. The "mass of whole sample" here is 8.657 g, so we take each element in turn and perform the calculations.

SOLUTION:

For C: $\dfrac{5.217 \text{ g C}}{8.657 \text{ g sample}} \times 100\% = 60.26\% \text{ C}$

For H: $\dfrac{0.9620 \text{ g H}}{8.657 \text{ g sample}} \times 100\% = 11.11\% \text{ H}$

For O: $\dfrac{2.478 \text{ g O}}{8.657 \text{ g sample}} \times 100\% = \underline{28.62\% \text{ O}}$

Sum of percentages: 99.99%

One of the useful things about a percentage composition is that it tells us the mass of each of the elements in 100 g of the substance. For example, the results in this problem tell us that in 100.00 g of the liquid there are 60.26 g of carbon, 11.11 g of hydrogen, and 28.62 g of oxygen.

IS THE ANSWER REASONABLE? The "check" is that the percentages must add up to 100%, allowing for small differences caused by rounding. We can also check the individual results by rounding all the numbers to one significant figure to estimate the results. For example, the percentage C would be estimated as 5/9 × 100, which is a little over 50% and agrees with our answer.

Practice Exercise 10: An organic compound weighing 0.6672 g is decomposed giving 0.3481 g carbon and 0.0870 g hydrogen. What are the percentages of hydrogen and carbon in this compound? Is it likely that this compound contains another element? (Hint: Recall the tool concerning the conservation of mass.)

Practice Exercise 11: From 0.5462 g of a compound there was isolated 0.2012 g of nitrogen and 0.3450 g of oxygen. What is the percentage composition of this compound? Are any other elements present?

Experimental percentage compositions can help identify an unknown compound

Elements can combine in many different ways. Nitrogen and oxygen, for example, form all of the following compounds: N_2O, NO, NO_2, N_2O_3, N_2O_4, and N_2O_5. To identify an unknown sample of a compound of nitrogen and oxygen, one might compare the percentage composition found by experiment with the calculated, or theoretical, percentages for each possible formula. Which formula, for example, fits the percentage composition calculated in Practice Exercise 11? A strategy for matching empirical formulas with mass percentages is outlined in the following example.

> **EXAMPLE 3.8**
> Calculating a Theoretical Percentage Composition from a Chemical Formula

Do the mass percentages of 25.94% N and 74.06% O match the formula N_2O_5?

ANALYSIS: To calculate the theoretical percentages by mass of N and O in N_2O_5, we need the masses of N and O in a specific sample of N_2O_5. *If we choose 1 mol of the given compound to be this sample, calculating the percentages will be simple using the tool in Equation 3.1.*

SOLUTION: We know that 1 mol of N_2O_5 must contain 2 mol N and 5 mol O. The corresponding number of grams of N and O are found as follows.

$$2 \text{ N:}\quad 2 \text{ mol N} \times \dfrac{14.01 \text{ g N}}{1 \text{ mol N}} = 28.02 \text{ g N}$$

$$5 \text{ O:}\quad 5 \text{ mol O} \times \dfrac{16.00 \text{ g O}}{1 \text{ mol O}} = \underline{80.00 \text{ g O}}$$

$$1 \text{ mol } N_2O_5 = 108.02 \text{ g } N_2O_5$$

Now we can calculate the percentages.

For % N: $\dfrac{28.02 \text{ g N}}{108.02 \text{ g sample}} \times 100\% = 25.94\%$ N in N_2O_5

For % O: $\dfrac{80.00 \text{ g O}}{108.02 \text{ g sample}} \times 100\% = 74.06\%$ O in N_2O_5

Thus the experimental values do match the theoretical percentages for the formula N_2O_5.

IS THE ANSWER REASONABLE? We can easily check our math. Since the denominator in each fraction is close to 100, the numerator is a simple estimate of the percentage. For nitrogen the numerator of 28 compares well to our 25.94% answer to satisfy us that the calculation was done correctly.

Practice Exercise 12: Calculate the theoretical percentage composition of N_2O_4. (Hint: Recall the definition of percentage composition.)

Practice Exercise 13: Calculate the theoretical percentage compositions for N_2O, NO, NO_2, N_2O_3, N_2O_4, and N_2O_5. Which of these compounds produced the data in Practice Exercise 11?

An empirical formula can be determined from the masses of the different elements in a sample of a compound

The compound that forms when phosphorus burns in oxygen consists of molecules with the formula P_4O_{10}. When a formula gives the composition of one *molecule*, it is called a **molecular formula.** Notice, however, that both the subscripts 4 and 10 are divisible by 2, so the *smallest* numbers that tell us the *ratio* of P to O are 2 and 5. We can write a simpler (but less informative) formula that expresses this ratio, P_2O_5. This is called the **empirical formula** because it can be obtained from an experimental analysis of the compound.

TOOLS
Empirical formula

> The empirical formula expresses the simplest whole number ratio of the atoms of each element in a compound.

We already know that the ratio of atoms in a compound is the same as a ratio of the moles of those atoms in the compound. We will determine the simplest ratio of moles from experimental data. The experimental data we need is any information that allows us to determine the moles of each element in the compound. We will investigate three types of data that can be used to determine empirical formulas. They are (a) masses of the elements, (b) percentage composition, and (c) combustion data. In all three, the goal is to obtain the simplest ratio of moles of each element in the formula.

The next four examples illustrate how we can calculate empirical formulas. We will then look at what additional data are required to obtain a compound's molecular formula.

EXAMPLE 3.9
Calculating an Empirical Formula from Mass Data

A 2.57 g sample of a compound composed of only tin and chlorine was found to contain 1.17 g of tin. What is the compound's empirical formula?

ANALYSIS: The subscripts in an empirical formula give the relative number of moles of elements in a compound. If we can find the *mole* ratio of Sn to Cl, we will have the empirical formula. The first step, therefore, is to convert the numbers of grams of Sn and Cl to the numbers of moles of Sn and Cl using the tool that relates mass to moles. Then we convert these numbers into their simplest *whole-number* ratio.

The problem did not give the mass of chlorine in the 2.57 g sample. But there are only two elements present in the compound, tin and chlorine. We know the mass of the tin, and we know the total mass of compound. The law of conservation of mass, one of our tools from the previous chapter, requires that the mass of Cl is the difference between 2.57 g of compound and 1.17 g of Sn.

SOLUTION: First, we find the mass of Cl in 2.57 g of compound:

$$\text{Mass of Cl} = 2.57 \text{ g compound} - 1.17 \text{ g Sn} = 1.40 \text{ g Cl}$$

Now we use the atomic masses to convert the mass data for tin and chlorine into moles.

$$1.17 \text{ g Sn} \times \frac{1 \text{ mol Sn}}{118.71 \text{ g Sn}} = 0.00986 \text{ mol Sn}$$

$$1.40 \text{ g Cl} \times \frac{1 \text{ mol Cl}}{35.45 \text{ g Cl}} = 0.0395 \text{ mol Cl}$$

We could now write a formula: $Sn_{0.00986}Cl_{0.0395}$, which does express the mole ratio, but subscripts also represent atom ratios and need to be integers. To convert the decimal subscripts to integers we begin by dividing each by the smallest number in the set. *This is always the way to begin the search for whole-number subscripts; pick the smallest number of the set as the divisor.* It's guaranteed to make at least one subscript a whole number, namely, 1. Here, we divide both numbers by 0.00986.

$$Sn_{\frac{0.00986}{0.00986}} Cl_{\frac{0.0395}{0.00986}} = Sn_{1.00}Cl_{4.01}$$

We may round 4.01 to 4, because even if the third significant digit is uncertain, we do know the second significant digit, the zero, with certainty; so the empirical formula is $SnCl_4$.

IS THE ANSWER REASONABLE? If $SnCl_4$ is the right formula, one mole of the compound contains 118.7 grams of tin and 142 grams of chlorine, or a little more chlorine than tin. The statement of the problem also gives us slightly more chlorine than tin. You should also recall from Chapter 2 that tin forms either the Sn^{2+} or the Sn^{4+} ion and that chlorine forms only the Cl^- ion. Therefore either $SnCl_2$ or $SnCl_4$ are reasonable compounds and one of them was our answer.

□ We cannot forget that we now have a storehouse of reasonable chemical formulas that were developed in Chapter 2.

Practice Exercise 14: A 1.525 g sample of a compound between nitrogen and oxygen contains 0.712 g of nitrogen. Calculate its empirical formula. (Hint: How many grams of oxygen are there?)

Practice Exercise 15: A 1.525 g sample of a compound between sulfur and oxygen was prepared by burning 0.7625 g of sulfur in air and collecting the product. What is the empirical formula for the compound formed?

Sometimes our strategy of using the lowest common divisor does not give whole numbers. Let's see how to handle such a situation.

EXAMPLE 3.10
Calculating an Empirical Formula from Mass Composition

One of the compounds of iron and oxygen, "black iron oxide," occurs naturally in the mineral magnetite. When a 2.448 g sample was analyzed it was found to have 1.771 g of Fe. Calculate the empirical formula of this compound.

ANALYSIS: To calculate the empirical formula, we need to know the masses of both iron and oxygen, but we've only been given the mass of iron. We use the law of conservation of mass as a tool (page 36) to calculate the mass of oxygen. Next we will use our tools for converting masses to moles, recalling that one mole of an element is equal to its atomic mass in gram units.

The mineral magnetite, like any magnet, is able to affect the orientation of a compass needle. *(Paul Silverman/Fundamental Photographs.)*

Then we'll write a trial formula and see whether we can adjust the subscripts to their smallest whole numbers by the strategy learned in Example 3.9.

SOLUTION: The mass of O is, as we said, found by difference.

$$2.448 \text{ g compound} - 1.771 \text{ g Fe} = 0.677 \text{ g O}$$

The moles of Fe and O in the sample can now be calculated.

$$1.771 \ \cancel{\text{g Fe}} \times \frac{1 \text{ mol Fe}}{55.845 \ \cancel{\text{g Fe}}} = 0.03171 \text{ mol Fe}$$

$$0.677 \ \cancel{\text{g O}} \times \frac{1 \text{ mol O}}{16.00 \ \cancel{\text{g O}}} = 0.0423 \text{ mol O}$$

These results let us write the formula as $Fe_{0.03171}O_{0.0423}$.

Our first effort to change the ratio of 0.03171 to 0.0423 into whole numbers is to divide both by the smaller, 0.03171.

$$Fe_{\frac{0.03171}{0.03171}}O_{\frac{0.0423}{0.03171}} = Fe_{1.000}O_{1.33}$$

This time we cannot round 1.33 to 1.0. The subscript for oxygen has three significant figures, so we can be sure that the digits 1.3 in 1.33 are known with certainty. Therefore the subscript for O, 1.33, is much too far from a whole number to round off and retain the required precision. In a *mole* sense, the ratio of 1 to 1.33 is correct; we just need a way to restate this ratio in whole numbers. Let's look at a simple strategy that will give us whole-number subscripts.

Trial and error is an easy way to obtain integer subscripts. We try multiplying the subscripts by 2, then 3, 4, 5, 6, and so on. The lowest multiplier that results in integer subscripts is the correct one to use. For example, let's multiply each subscript in $Fe_{1.000}O_{1.33}$ by a whole number, 2. *Since we multiply all subscripts by 2 we do not change the ratio;* it changes only the size of the numbers used to state it.

$$Fe_{(1.000 \times 2)}O_{(1.33 \times 2)} = Fe_{2.000}O_{2.66}$$

This didn't work either; 2.66 is also too far from a whole number (based on the allowed precision) to be rounded off. Let's try using 3 instead of 2 *on the original ratio of 1.000 to 1.33.*

$$Fe_{(1.000 \times 3)}O_{(1.33 \times 3)} = Fe_{3.000}O_{3.99}$$

We are now justified in rounding; 3.99 is acceptably close to 4. The empirical formula of the oxide of iron is Fe_3O_4. A different method is noted in the margin, where Table 3.1 shows us which whole number multiplier should be used to convert a decimal that cannot be rounded to a whole number.

IS THE ANSWER REASONABLE? First, the fact that our calculation gives whole number subscripts is a good indicator that we've solved the problem correctly. Second, another way to check our answer is to estimate the percentage of iron from the given data and from our result. The given data are 1.771 g Fe and 2.448 g of sample and the percentage iron is estimated as

$$\frac{1.771 \text{ g}}{2.448 \text{ g}} \times 100 \approx \frac{\mathbf{1.8 \text{ g}}}{\mathbf{2.4 \text{ g}}} \times \mathbf{100} = \frac{3}{4} \times 100 = \text{approximately } 75\%$$

In one mole of the compound Fe_3O_4, the mass of iron is $3 \times 55.8 = 167.4$ and the molar mass is 231.4. The percentage of iron is estimated as

$$\frac{167.4 \text{ g}}{231.4 \text{ g}} \times 100 \approx \frac{170 \text{ g}}{230 \text{ g}} \times 100 = \frac{\mathbf{1.7 \text{ g}}}{\mathbf{2.3 \text{ g}}} \times \mathbf{100} = \text{approximately } 75\%$$

TOOLS

Techniques for finding whole-number subscripts for empirical formulas

TABLE 3.1

Decimal Numbers and Their Rational Fractions

Decimal	Fraction[a]
0.20	1/5
0.25	1/4
0.33	1/3
0.40	2/5
0.50	1/2
0.60	3/5
0.66	2/3
0.75	3/4
0.80	4/5

[a]Use the denominator of the fraction as a multiplier to create whole-number subscripts in empirical formulas.

We don't have to do any calculations because we can see that mathematical expressions from both calculations are almost the same, and the answers will be very close to each other. Let's compare the bold term from each equation,

$$\frac{1.8\ g}{2.4\ g} \times 100 \approx \frac{1.7\ g}{2.3\ g} \times 100$$

We are able to conclude that our percentages of iron are the same and our empirical formula is reasonable.

Practice Exercise 16: When aluminum is produced on an industrial scale 5.68 tons of aluminum and 5.04 tons of oxygen are obtained. What is the empirical formula of the compound used to produce aluminum? (Hint: 1 ton = 2000 lb and 1 lb = 454 g.)

Practice Exercise 17: A 2.012 g sample of a compound of nitrogen and oxygen has 0.522 g of nitrogen. Calculate its empirical formula.

Empirical formulas can be determined from mass percentages

Only rarely is it possible to obtain the masses of every element in a compound by the use of just one weighed sample. Two or more analyses carried out on different samples are often needed. For example, suppose an analyst is given a compound known to consist exclusively of calcium, chlorine, and oxygen. The mass of calcium in one weighed sample and the mass of chlorine in another sample would be determined in separate experiments. Then the mass data for calcium and chlorine would be converted to percentages by mass *so that the data from different samples relate to the same sample size, namely, 100 g of the compound.* The percentage of oxygen would be calculated by difference because % Ca + % Cl + % O = 100%. Each mass percentage represents a certain number of grams of the element, which is next converted into the corresponding number of moles of the element. The mole proportions are converted to whole numbers in the way we just studied, giving us the subscripts for the empirical formula. Let's see how this works.

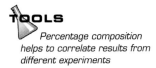

TOOLS

Percentage composition helps to correlate results from different experiments

EXAMPLE 3.11
Calculating an Empirical Formula from Percentage Composition

A white powder used in paints, enamels, and ceramics has the following percentage composition: Ba, 69.6%; C, 6.09%; and O, 24.3%. What is its empirical formula? What is the name of this compound?

ANALYSIS: Consider having 100 grams of this compound. The percentages of the elements given in the problem are numerically the same as the masses of these elements in our 100 g sample. We see a general principle that by assuming a 100 g sample, all percent signs can be changed to gram units. Now that we have the masses of the elements we can use the procedures and tools used in Examples 3.9 and 3.10.

SOLUTION: Assuming a 100 g sample of the compound we quickly convert 69.6% Ba to 69.6 g Ba, 6.09% C to 6.09 g C, and 24.3% O to 24.3 g O. Now we convert these to moles.

$$\text{Ba:} \quad 69.6\ \text{g Ba} \times \frac{1\ \text{mol Ba}}{137.33\ \text{g Ba}} = 0.507\ \text{mol Ba}$$

$$\text{C:} \quad 6.09\ \text{g C} \times \frac{1\ \text{mol C}}{12.01\ \text{g C}} = 0.507\ \text{mol C}$$

$$\text{O:} \quad 24.3\ \text{g O} \times \frac{1\ \text{mol O}}{16.00\ \text{g O}} = 1.52\ \text{mol O}$$

Our preliminary empirical formula is then

$$Ba_{0.507}C_{0.507}O_{1.52}$$

We next divide each subscript by the smallest, 0.507.

$$Ba_{\frac{0.507}{0.507}}C_{\frac{0.507}{0.507}}O_{\frac{1.52}{0.507}} = Ba_{1.00}C_{1.00}O_{3.00}$$

The subscripts are whole numbers, so the empirical formula is $BaCO_3$, representing barium carbonate.

IS THE ANSWER REASONABLE? The fact that our calculations led to whole number subscripts is a strong clue that the answer is correct. In addition, our knowledge of ionic compounds and the polyatomic carbonate ion from Chapter 2 tell us that the barium ion is Ba^{2+} and the carbonate ion is CO_3^{2-}; $BaCO_3$ is a reasonable formula.

Practice Exercise 18: A white solid used to whiten paper has the following percentage composition: Na, 32.4%; S, 22.6%. The unanalyzed element is oxygen. What is the compound's empirical formula? (Hint: What law allows you to calculate the % oxygen?)

Practice Exercise 19: Cinnamon gets some of its flavor from cinnamaldehyde that is 81.79% C, 6.10% H, and the rest oxygen. Determine the empirical formula for this compound.

Percentage composition is important since it allowed us to determine the amount of three substances using only two experiments. This in itself is a considerable saving in time and effort. Additionally, it is often difficult to analyze a sample for certain elements, oxygen for example, and using percentage measurements helps avoid this problem.

Empirical formulas can be determined from indirect analyses

In practice, a compound is seldom broken down completely to its *elements* in a quantitative analysis. Instead, the compound is changed into other *compounds*. The reactions separate the elements by capturing each one entirely (quantitatively) in a *separate* compound *whose formula is known*.

In the following example, we illustrate the indirect analysis of a compound made entirely of carbon, hydrogen, and oxygen. Such compounds burn completely in pure oxygen—it is called a *combustion reaction*—and the sole products are carbon dioxide and water. (This particular kind of indirect analysis is sometimes called a *combustion analysis*.) The complete combustion of methyl alcohol (CH_3OH), for example, occurs according to the following equation.

$$2CH_3OH + 3O_2 \longrightarrow 2CO_2 + 4H_2O$$

The carbon dioxide and water can be separated and are individually weighed. Notice that all of the carbon atoms in the original compound end up among the CO_2 molecules, and all of the hydrogen atoms are in H_2O molecules. In this way at least two of the original elements, C and H, are quantitatively measured.

We will calculate the mass of carbon in the CO_2 collected, which equals the mass of carbon in the original sample. Similarly, we will calculate the mass of hydrogen in the H_2O collected, which equals the mass of hydrogen in the original sample. When added together, the mass of C and mass of H are less than the total mass of the sample because part of the sample is composed of oxygen. The law of conservation of mass allows us to subtract the sum of the C and H masses from the original sample mass to obtain the mass of oxygen in the sample of the compound.

◻ Organic compounds react with a stream of pure oxygen to give CO_2 and H_2O. The flowing gases pass through a preweighed tube of $CaSO_4$ to absorb the water and then through a tube of NaOH deposited on a binder to absorb the carbon dioxide. The increase in mass of the $CaSO_4$ and NaOH tubes represents the mass of water and CO_2, respectively.

EXAMPLE 3.12
Empirical Formula from
Indirect Analysis

A 0.5438 g sample of a liquid consisting of only C, H, and O was burned in pure oxygen, and 1.039 g of CO_2 and 0.6369 g of H_2O were obtained. What is the empirical formula of the compound?

ANALYSIS: There are two parts to this problem. First we need to calculate the mass of the elements, C and H, by determining the number of grams of C in the CO_2 and the number of grams of H in the H_2O. (This kind of calculation was illustrated in Example 3.6 and uses the tools that tell us how to create conversion factors from grams to moles and from moles of one substance to moles of another.) These values represent the number of grams of C and H in the original sample. Adding them together and subtracting the sum from the mass of the original sample will give us the mass of oxygen in the sample.

In the second half of the solution, we use the masses of C, H, and O to calculate the empirical formula as in Example 3.9.

SOLUTION: First we find the number of grams of C in the CO_2 and of H in the H_2O. We use the normal conversion sequence from grams of compound, to moles of compound, to moles of element, and then to grams of element as shown in the next two equations.

$$1.039 \text{ g } CO_2 \times \frac{1 \text{ mol } CO_2}{44.009 \text{ g } CO_2} \times \frac{1 \text{ mol C}}{1 \text{ mol } CO_2} \times \frac{12.011 \text{ g C}}{1 \text{ mol C}} = 0.2836 \text{ g C}$$

$$0.6369 \text{ g } H_2O \times \frac{1 \text{ mol } H_2O}{18.015 \text{ g } H_2O} \times \frac{2 \text{ mol H}}{1 \text{ mol } H_2O} \times \frac{1.0079 \text{ g H}}{1 \text{ mol H}} = 0.07125 \text{ g H}$$

The total mass of C and H is therefore the sum of these two quantities.

Total mass of C and H = 0.2836 g C + 0.07125 g H = 0.3548 g

The difference between this total and the 0.5438 g in the original sample is the mass of oxygen (the only other element).

Mass of O = 0.5438 g − 0.3548 g = 0.1890 g O

Now we can convert the masses of the elements to an empirical formula.

For C: $0.2836 \text{ g C} \times \dfrac{1 \text{ mol C}}{12.011 \text{ g C}} = 0.02361 \text{ mol C}$

For H: $0.07125 \text{ g H} \times \dfrac{1 \text{ mol H}}{1.0079 \text{ g H}} = 0.07068 \text{ mol H}$

For O: $0.1890 \text{ g O} \times \dfrac{1 \text{ mol O}}{15.999 \text{ g O}} = 0.01181 \text{ mol O}$

Our preliminary empirical formula is thus $C_{0.02361}H_{0.07068}O_{0.01181}$. We divide all of these subscripts by the smallest number, 0.01181.

$$C_{\frac{0.02361}{0.01181}} H_{\frac{0.07068}{0.01181}} O_{\frac{0.01181}{0.01181}} = C_{1.998}H_{5.985}O_1$$

The results are acceptably close to integers to say that the empirical formula is C_2H_6O.

IS THE ANSWER REASONABLE? Our checks on problems need to be quick and efficient. In previous examples we have been able to use our knowledge of ionic compounds to see if formulas are reasonable. In the future, with some knowledge of organic chemistry you will know that the formula C_2H_6O is reasonable. Beyond that, the fact that we obtained whole number subscripts after all these calculations is also a good indicator that we've solved the problem correctly.

Practice Exercise 20: A sample containing only sulfur and carbon is completely burned in air. The analysis produced 0.640 g SO_2 and 0.220 g of CO_2. What is the empirical formula? (Hint: Use the tools for relating grams of a compound to grams of an element.)

Practice Exercise 21: The combustion of a 5.048 g sample of a compound of C, H, and O gave 7.406 g CO_2 and 3.027 g H_2O. Calculate the empirical formula of the compound.

As we said earlier, more than one sample of a substance must be analyzed whenever more than one reaction is necessary to separate the elements. This is also true in indirect analyses. For example, if a compound contains C, H, N, and O, combustion converts the C and H to CO_2 and H_2O, which are separated by special techniques and weighed. The mass of C in the CO_2 sample and the mass of H in the H_2O sample are then calculated in the usual way. A second reaction with a different sample of the compound can be used to obtain the nitrogen, either as N_2 or as NH_3. Because different size samples are used, the masses of C and H from one sample and the mass of N from another cannot be used to calculate the empirical formula. So we convert the masses of the elements found in their respective samples into percentages of the element by mass in the compound. We add up the percentages, subtract from 100 to get the percentage of O, and then calculate the empirical formula from the percentage composition as described earlier.

Molecular formulas are determined from empirical formulas and molecular masses

The empirical formula is the accepted formula unit for ionic compounds. For molecular compounds, however, chemists prefer *molecular* formulas because they give the number of atoms of each type in a molecule.

□ Molecular masses can sometimes be obtained using mass spectroscopy, discussed in Chapter 1. Other methods will be discussed in Chapters 10, 11, and 12.

Sometimes an empirical formula and a molecular formula are the same. Two examples are H_2O and NH_3. Usually, however, the subscripts of a molecular formula are whole-number multiples of those in the empirical formula. The subscripts of the molecular formula P_4O_{10}, for example, are each two times those in the empirical formula, P_2O_5, as you saw earlier. The molecular mass of P_4O_{10} is likewise two times the formula mass of P_2O_5. This observation provides us with a way to find out the molecular formula for a compound provided we have a way of determining experimentally the molecular mass of the compound. If the experimental molecular mass *equals* the calculated empirical formula mass, the empirical formula itself is also a molecular formula. Otherwise, the experimental molecular mass will be some whole-number multiple of the value calculated from the empirical formula. Whatever the whole number is, it's a common multiplier for the subscripts of the empirical formula.

EXAMPLE 3.13
Determining a Molecular Formula from an Empirical Formula and a Molecular Mass

Styrene, the raw material for polystyrene foam plastics, has an empirical formula of CH. Its molecular mass is 104 g mol^{-1}. What is its molecular formula?

ANALYSIS: The molecular mass of styrene, 104 g mol^{-1}, is some simple multiple of the formula mass of the empirical formula, CH. When we compute that multiple it will tell us how many CH units make up the styrene molecule. We can compute this multiple by dividing the molecular mass by the empirical formula mass.

SOLUTION: For the empirical formula, CH, the formula mass is

$$12.01 + 1.008 = 13.02$$

To find how many CH units weighing 13.02 are in a mass of 104, we divide.

$$\frac{104}{13.02} = 7.99$$

Rounding this to 8, we see that 104 is 8 times larger than 13.02, so the correct molecular formula of styrene must have subscripts 8 times those in CH. Styrene, therefore, is C_8H_8.

IS THE ANSWER REASONABLE? The molecular mass of C_8H_8 is approximately $(8 \times 12) + (8 \times 1) = 104$ g mol^{-1}, which is consistent with the molecular mass we started with.

Practice Exercise 22: After determining that the empirical formulas of two different compounds were CH_2Cl and $CHCl$ a student mixed up the data for the molecular masses. However, the student knew that one compound had a molecular mass of 100 and the other had a molecular mass of 289 g mol^{-1}. What are the likely molecular formulas of the two compounds? (Hint: Recall the relationship between the molecular and empirical formula.)

Practice Exercise 23: The empirical formula of hydrazine is NH_2, and its molecular mass is 32.0 g mol^{-1}. What is its molecular formula?

3.4 CHEMICAL EQUATIONS LINK AMOUNTS OF SUBSTANCES IN A REACTION

Balancing an equation involves adjusting coefficients

We learned in Chapter 2 that a *chemical equation* is a shorthand, quantitative description of a chemical reaction. An equation is *balanced* when all atoms present among the reactants are also somewhere among the products. As we learned, coefficients, the numbers in front of formulas, are multiplier numbers for their respective formulas, and the values of the coefficients determine whether an equation is balanced.

Always approach the balancing of an equation as a two-step process.

Step 1. *Write the unbalanced "equation."* Organize the formulas in the pattern of an equation with plus signs and an arrow. Use *correct* formulas. (You learned to write many of them in Chapter 2, but until we have studied more chemistry, you will usually be given formulas.)

Step 2. *Adjust the coefficients to get equal numbers of each kind of atom on both sides of the arrow.* When doing step 2, make no changes in the formulas, either in the atomic symbols or their subscripts. If you do, the equation will involve different substances from those intended. You may still be able to balance it, but the equation will not be for the reaction you want.

We'll begin with simple equations that can be balanced easily by inspection. An example is the reaction of zinc metal with hydrochloric acid (margin photo). First, we need the correct formulas, and this time we'll include the physical states because they are different. The reactants are zinc, $Zn(s)$, and hydrochloric acid, an aqueous solution of the gas hydrogen chloride, HCl, symbolized as $HCl(aq)$. We also need formulas for the products. Zn changes to a water-soluble compound, zinc chloride, $ZnCl_2(aq)$, and hydrogen gas, $H_2(g)$, bubbles out as the other product. (Recall that hydrogen occurs naturally as a *diatomic molecule*, not as an atom.)

Zinc metal reacts with hydrochloric acid. *(Richard Megna/Fundamental Photographs.)*

Step 1. Write an unbalanced equation.

$$Zn(s) + HCl(aq) \longrightarrow ZnCl_2(aq) + H_2(g) \qquad \text{(unbalanced)}$$

Step 2. Adjust the coefficients to get equal numbers of each kind of atom on both sides of the arrow.

There is no simple set of rules for adjusting coefficients. Experience is the greatest help, and experience has taught chemists that the following guidelines often get to the solution most directly when they are applied in the order given.

TOOLS

Guidelines for balancing chemical equations

> **Some Guidelines for Balancing Equations**
>
> 1. Balance elements other than H and O first.
> 2. Elements should be balanced last (e.g., Zn and H_2 in our example).
> 3. Balance as a group those polyatomic ions that appear unchanged on both sides of the arrow.

Using the guidelines given here, we'll look at Cl first in our example. Because there are two Cl to the right of the arrow but only one to the left, we put a 2 in front of the HCl on the left side. The result is

$$Zn(s) + 2HCl(aq) \longrightarrow ZnCl_2(aq) + H_2(g)$$

We then balance the hydrogen and zinc and find that no additional coefficient changes are needed. Everything is now balanced. On each side we find 1 Zn, 2 H, and 2 Cl. One complication is that an infinite number of *balanced* equations can be written for any given reaction! We might, for example, have adjusted the coefficients so that our equation came out as follows.

$$2Zn(s) + 4HCl(aq) \longrightarrow 2ZnCl_2(aq) + 2H_2(g)$$

This equation is also correctly balanced. For simplicity, we prefer the *smallest* whole-number coefficients when writing balanced equations.

EXAMPLE 3.14
Writing a Balanced Equation

Sodium hydroxide and phosphoric acid, H_3PO_4, react as aqueous solutions to give sodium phosphate and water. The sodium phosphate remains in solution. Write the balanced equation for this reaction.

ANALYSIS: First, we need to write an unbalanced equation that includes the reactant formulas on the left-hand side and the product formulas on the right. We are given the formula only for phosphoric acid. We need to use the tools in Chapter 2 to determine that sodium hydroxide is NaOH, water is H_2O, and sodium phosphate has a formula of Na_3PO_4. Next we write the unbalanced equation placing all the reactants to the left of the arrow and all products to the right. Finally we use the procedures suggested in the tool for balancing equations to adjust stoichiometric coefficients (*never change subscripts!*) until there are the same number of each type of atom on the left and right sides of the equation.

SOLUTION: We include the designation (*aq*) for all substances dissolved in water (except H_2O itself; we'll usually not give it any designation when it is in its liquid state).

$$NaOH(aq) + H_3PO_4(aq) \longrightarrow Na_3PO_4(aq) + H_2O \qquad \text{(unbalanced)}$$

There are several things not in balance, but our guidelines suggest that we work with Na first rather than with O, H, or PO_4. There are 3 Na on the right side, so we put a 3 in front of NaOH on the left, as a trial.

$$3NaOH(aq) + H_3PO_4(aq) \longrightarrow Na_3PO_4(aq) + H_2O \qquad \text{(unbalanced)}$$

Now the Na are in balance. The unit of PO_4 is balanced also. Not counting the PO_4, we have on the left 3 O and 3 H in 3NaOH plus 3 H in H_3PO_4, for a net of 3 O and 6 H on the left. On the right, in H_2O, we have 1 O and 2 H. The ratio of 3 O to 6 H on the left is equivalent to the ratio of 1 O to 2 H on the right, so we write the multiplier (coefficient) 3 in front of H_2O.

$$3NaOH(aq) + H_3PO_4(aq) \longrightarrow Na_3PO_4(aq) + 3H_2O \qquad \text{(balanced)}$$

We now have a balanced equation.

IS THE ANSWER REASONABLE? On each side we have 3 Na, 1 PO_4, 6 H, and 3 O besides those in PO_4, and since the coefficients for $H_3PO_4(aq)$ and $Na_3PO_4(aq)$ are 1 our coefficients cannot be reduced to smaller whole numbers.

Practice Exercise 24: Write the balanced chemical equation that describes what happens when a solution containing aluminum chloride is mixed with a solution containing sodium phosphate and the product of the reaction is solid aluminum phosphate and a solution of sodium chloride. (Hint: Write the correct formulas based on information in Chapter 2.)

Practice Exercise 25: When aqueous solutions of calcium chloride, $CaCl_2$, and potassium phosphate, K_3PO_4, are mixed, a reaction occurs in which solid calcium phosphate, $Ca_3(PO_4)_2$, separates from the solution. The other product is $KCl(aq)$. Write the balanced equation.

The strategy of balancing whole units of polyatomic ions, like PO_4, as a group is extremely useful. Using this method we have less atom counting to do and balancing equations is often easier.

Coefficients in a balanced equation provide mole-to-mole ratios among reactants and products

So far we have focused on relationships between elements within a single compound. We have seen that the essential conversion factor between substances within a compound is the mole-to-mole ratio obtained from the compound's formula. In this section, we'll see that the same techniques can be used to relate substances involved in a chemical reaction. The critical link between substances involved in a reaction is a mole-to-mole ratio obtained from the coefficients in the chemical equation that describes the reaction.

To see how chemical equations can be used to obtain mole-to-mole relationships, consider the equation that describes the burning of octane (C_8H_{18}) in oxygen (O_2) to give carbon dioxide and steam:

$$2C_8H_{18}(l) + 25O_2(g) \longrightarrow 16CO_2(g) + 18H_2O(g)$$

This equation can be interpreted on a *microscopic* (molecular) scale as follows:

For every two molecules of liquid octane that react with twenty-five molecules of oxygen gas, sixteen molecules of carbon dioxide gas and eighteen molecules of steam are produced.

This statement immediately suggests many equivalence relationships that can be used to build conversion factors in stoichiometry problems:

$$2 \text{ molecules } C_8H_{18} \Leftrightarrow 25 \text{ molecules } O_2$$

$$2 \text{ molecules } C_8H_{18} \Leftrightarrow 16 \text{ molecules } CO_2$$

$$2 \text{ molecules } C_8H_{18} \Leftrightarrow 18 \text{ molecules } H_2O$$

$$25 \text{ molecules } O_2 \Leftrightarrow 16 \text{ molecules } CO_2$$

$$25 \text{ molecules } O_2 \Leftrightarrow 18 \text{ molecules } H_2O$$

$$16 \text{ molecules } CO_2 \Leftrightarrow 18 \text{ molecules } H_2O$$

◻ The chemical equation gives relative amounts of molecules of each type that participate in the reaction. It does *not* mean that 2 octane molecules actually collide with 25 O_2 molecules. The reaction occurs in many steps, which the chemical equation does not show.

Any of these microscopic relationships can be scaled up to the macroscopic level by multiplying both sides of the equivalency by Avogadro's number, which effectively allows us to replace "molecules" with "moles" or "mol":

$$2 \text{ mol } C_8H_{18} \Leftrightarrow 25 \text{ mol } O_2$$

$$2 \text{ mol } C_8H_{18} \Leftrightarrow 16 \text{ mol } CO_2$$

$$2 \text{ mol } C_8H_{18} \Leftrightarrow 18 \text{ mol } H_2O$$

$$25 \text{ mol } O_2 \Leftrightarrow 16 \text{ mol } CO_2$$

$$25 \text{ mol } O_2 \Leftrightarrow 18 \text{ mol } H_2O$$

$$16 \text{ mol } CO_2 \Leftrightarrow 18 \text{ mol } H_2O$$

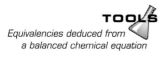

TOOLS
Equivalencies deduced from a balanced chemical equation

We can interpret the equation on a macroscopic (mole) scale as follows:

Two moles of liquid octane react with twenty-five moles of oxygen gas to produce sixteen moles of carbon dioxide gas and eighteen moles of steam.

To use these equivalencies in a stoichiometry problem, the equation must be **balanced.** That means that every atom found in the reactants must also be found somewhere in the products. You must always check to see whether this is so for a given equation before you can use the coefficients in the equation to build equivalencies and conversion factors.

First, let's see how mole-to-mole relationships obtained from a balanced chemical equation can be used to convert moles of one substance to moles of another when both substances are involved in a chemical reaction.

EXAMPLE 3.15
Stoichiometry of Chemical Reactions

How many moles of sodium phosphate can be made from 0.240 mol of sodium hydroxide by the following unbalanced reaction?

$$NaOH(aq) + H_3PO_4(aq) \longrightarrow Na_3PO_4(aq) + H_2O$$

ANALYSIS: The question asks us to relate amounts of two different substances. *A mole-to-mole relationship is the tool that defines the relationship between two different substances in a stoichiometry problem.* The balanced equation is the tool to use because it gives the coefficients we need. We are given an unbalanced equation and need to balance this equation to use this tool.

$$3NaOH(aq) + H_3PO_4(aq) \longrightarrow Na_3PO_4(aq) + 3H_2O$$

From the coefficients, we now know that

$$3 \text{ mol NaOH} \Leftrightarrow 1 \text{ mol } Na_3PO_4$$

This enables us to prepare the conversion factor that we need.

SOLUTION: We write the question in equation form as

$$0.240 \text{ mol NaOH} \Leftrightarrow ? \text{ mol } Na_3PO_4$$

and convert 0.240 mol NaOH to the numbers of moles of Na_3PO_4 equivalent to it in the reaction as follows:

$$0.240 \text{ mol NaOH} \times \frac{1 \text{ mol } Na_3PO_4}{3 \text{ mol NaOH}} = 0.0800 \text{ mol } Na_3PO_4$$

Thus we can make 0.0800 mol Na_3PO_4 from 0.240 mol NaOH.

IS THE ANSWER REASONABLE? The equation tells us that 3 mol NaOH $\Leftrightarrow$ 1 mol Na_3PO_4, so the actual number of moles of Na_3PO_4 (0.0800 mol) should be one-third the actual number of moles of NaOH (0.240 mol), and it is. We can also check that the units cancel correctly.

Practice Exercise 26: In the reaction $2SO_2(g) + O_2(g) \longrightarrow 2SO_3(g)$ how many moles of O_2 are needed to produce 6.76 moles of SO_3? (Hint: Write the equivalence that relates O_2 to SO_3.)

Practice Exercise 27: How many moles of sulfuric acid, H_2SO_4, are needed to react with 0.366 mol of NaOH by the following reaction?

$$2NaOH(aq) + H_2SO_4(aq) \longrightarrow Na_2SO_4(aq) + 2H_2O$$

Mole-to-mole ratios link masses of different substances in chemical reactions

The most common stoichiometric calculation the chemist does is to relate grams of one substance with grams of another in a chemical reaction. For example, glucose ($C_6H_{12}O_6$) is one of the body's primary energy sources. The body combines glucose and oxygen to give carbon dioxide and water. The balanced equation for the overall reaction is

$$C_6H_{12}O_6(aq) + 6O_2(aq) \longrightarrow 6CO_2(aq) + 6H_2O(l)$$

How many grams of oxygen must the body take in to completely process 1.00 g of glucose? The problem can be expressed as

$$1.00 \text{ g } C_6H_{12}O_6 \Leftrightarrow ? \text{ g } O_2$$

The first thing we should notice about this problem is that we're relating *two different substances* in a reaction. The equivalence that relates the substances is the mole-to-mole relationship between glucose and O_2 given by the chemical equation. In this case, the equation tells us that

$$1 \text{ mol } C_6H_{12}O_6 \Leftrightarrow 6 \text{ mol } O_2$$

If we insert that mole-to-mole conversion between our starting point (1.00 g $C_6H_{12}O_6$) and the desired quantity (g O_2) we have cut the problem into three simple steps:

$$\boxed{1 \text{ mol } C_6H_{12}O_6 \Leftrightarrow 6 \text{ mol } O_2}$$

$$1.00 \text{ g } C_6H_{12}O_6 \longrightarrow \text{mol } C_6H_{12}O_6 \longrightarrow \text{mol } O_2 \longrightarrow \text{g } O_2$$

TOOLS

Sequence of steps for mass-to-mass calculations using balanced chemical equations

We convert grams of $C_6H_{12}O_6$ to moles of $C_6H_{12}O_6$ (using the molecular mass of $C_6H_{12}O_6$). We then convert mol $C_6H_{12}O_6$ to mol O_2 using the equivalence relationship from the balanced equation. Finally, we convert mol O_2 into g O_2 using the molecular mass of O_2.

Figure 3.4 outlines this flow for *any* stoichiometry problem that relates reactant or product masses. If we know the *balanced equation* for a reaction and the *mass* of any reactant or product, we can calculate the required or expected mass of *any* other substance in the equation. Example 3.16 shows how it works.

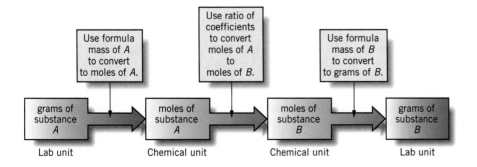

FIG. 3.4 The sequence of calculations for solving stoichiometry problems. This sequence applies to all calculations that start with the mass of one substance (*A*) and require the mass of a second substance (*B*) as the answer.

EXAMPLE 3.16
Stoichiometric Mass Calculations

Portland cement is a mixture of the oxides of calcium, aluminum, and silicon. The raw material for its calcium oxide is calcium carbonate, which occurs as the chief component of a natural rock, limestone. When calcium carbonate is strongly heated it decomposes. One product, carbon dioxide, is driven off to leave the desired calcium oxide as the only other product.

A chemistry student is to prepare 1.50×10^2 g of calcium oxide in order to test a particular "recipe" for Portland cement. How many grams of calcium carbonate should be used, assuming that all will be converted?

ANALYSIS: We begin by obtaining a balanced chemical reaction. From the nomenclature tools we find that calcium carbonate is $CaCO_3$. Using the tools from Chapter 2, the formulas for carbon dioxide and calcium oxide are CO_2 and CaO, respectively. Our balanced equation must be

$$CaCO_3(s) \xrightarrow{\text{heat}} CaO(s) + CO_2(g)$$

Now we can state the problem in mathematical form as

$$1.50 \times 10^2 \text{ g CaO} \Leftrightarrow ? \text{ g CaCO}_3$$

In problems that convert an amount of one substance to amount of a different substance in a chemical reaction, the tool we use is a mole-to-mole conversion factor. From the balanced chemical equation, we have

$$1 \text{ mol CaO} \Leftrightarrow 1 \text{ mol CaCO}_3$$

☐ Special reaction conditions are often indicated with words or symbols above the arrow. In this reaction temperatures above 2000 °C are needed and this is indicated with the word, *heat*, above the arrow.

In our road map, this is the central conversion between CaO and $CaCO_3$ as shown below.

$$\boxed{1 \text{ mol CaO} \Leftrightarrow 1 \text{ mol CaCO}_3}$$

$$1.50 \times 10^2 \text{ g CaO} \longrightarrow \text{mol CaO} \longrightarrow \text{mol CaCO}_3 \longrightarrow \text{g CaCO}_3$$

For the complete calculation we must convert g CaO to mol CaO. *The equality tool relating mass and moles uses the molar mass:*

$$56.08 \text{ g CaO} = 1 \text{ mol CaO}$$

Next, the mole ratio tool converts moles of CaO to moles of $CaCO_3$. Finally, we must also convert mol $CaCO_3$ to g $CaCO_3$. Again, the tool defining the equality between mass and moles uses the molar mass:

$$100.09 \text{ g CaCO}_3 = 1 \text{ mol CaCO}_3$$

Putting this all together, our overall strategy will be as follows.

$$\boxed{1 \text{ mol CaO} \Leftrightarrow 1 \text{ mol CaCO}_3}$$

$$1.50 \times 10^2 \text{ g CaO} \longrightarrow \text{mol CaO} \longrightarrow \text{mol CaCO}_3 \longrightarrow \text{g CaCO}_3$$

$$\boxed{56.08 \text{ g CaO} = 1 \text{ mol CaO}} \qquad \boxed{1 \text{ mol CaCO}_3 = 100.09 \text{ g CaCO}_3}$$

SOLUTION: We assemble conversion factors so the units cancel correctly:

$$1.50 \times 10^2 \text{ g CaO} \times \left(\frac{1 \text{ mol CaO}}{56.08 \text{ g CaO}} \right) \times \left(\frac{1 \text{ mol CaCO}_3}{1 \text{ mol CaO}} \right) \times \left(\frac{100.09 \text{ g CaCO}_3}{1 \text{ mol CaCO}_3} \right)$$
$$= 268 \text{ g CaCO}_3$$

Notice how the calculation flows from grams of CaO to moles of CaO, then to moles of $CaCO_3$ (using the equation), and finally to grams of $CaCO_3$. We cannot emphasize too much that *the key step in all calculations of reaction stoichiometry is the use of the balanced equation.*

IS THE ANSWER REASONABLE? In a mass-to-mass calculation like this the first check is the magnitude of the answer compared to the starting mass. In the majority of reactions the calculated mass is not less than 1/5 of the starting mass nor is it larger than five times the starting mass. Our result is reasonable on this criterion. We can make a more detailed check by first making sure that the units cancel properly. We can also round all numbers to one or two significant figures and estimate the answer. We would estimate $\frac{150 \times 100}{50} = 300$ and this value is close to our answer of 268, giving us confidence in the calculation. Alternately we may round the denominator to 60 instead of 50 to get an equally good estimate of 250.

EXAMPLE 3.17
Stoichiometric Mass Calculations

The thermite reaction is one of the most spectacular reactions of aluminum with iron(III) oxide by which metallic iron and aluminum oxide are made. So much heat is generated that the iron forms in the liquid state (Figure 3.5).

A certain welding operation requires at least 86.0 g of iron each time a weld is made. What is the minimum mass, in grams, of iron(III) oxide that must be used for each weld? Also calculate how many grams of aluminum are needed.

ANALYSIS: First we need to write a balanced chemical equation. From the information given and our nomenclature tools (Chapter 2) we determine that Al and Fe_2O_3 are the reactants and that Fe and Al_2O_3 are the products. The equation is written and then balanced to obtain

$$2Al(s) + Fe_2O_3(s) \longrightarrow Al_2O_3(s) + 2Fe(l)$$

Now, we state the problem in mathematical form:

$$86.0 \text{ g Fe} \Leftrightarrow ? \text{ g Fe}_2O_3$$

Remember that all problems in reaction stoichiometry must be solved at the mole level because an equation's coefficients disclose *mole* ratios, not mass ratios. So we use our tool that relates mass to moles to convert the number of grams of Fe to moles. Then we can use the tool that gives us the mole-to-mole relationship indicated by the coefficients in the balanced equation,

$$1 \text{ mol Fe}_2O_3 \Leftrightarrow 2 \text{ mol Fe}$$

to see how many *moles* of Fe_2O_3 are needed. Finally we use our tools to convert this answer into grams of Fe_2O_3. The other calculations follow the same pattern.

SOLUTION: We'll set up the first calculation as a chain; the steps are summarized below the conversion factors.

$$86.0 \text{ g Fe} \times \frac{1 \text{ mol Fe}}{55.85 \text{ g Fe}} \times \frac{1 \text{ mol Fe}_2O_3}{2 \text{ mol Fe}} \times \frac{159.70 \text{ g Fe}_2O_3}{1 \text{ mol Fe}_2O_3} = 123 \text{ g Fe}_2O_3$$

grams Fe → moles Fe → moles Fe_2O_3 → grams Fe_2O_3

A minimum of 123 g of Fe_2O_3 is required to make 86.0 g of Fe.

Next, we calculate the number of grams of Al needed, but we know that we must first find the number of *moles* of Al required. Only from this can the grams of Al be calculated. The relevant mole-to-mole relationship, again using the balanced equation, is

$$2 \text{ mol Al} \Leftrightarrow 2 \text{ mol Fe}$$

Employing another chain calculation to find the mass of Al needed to make 86.0 g of Fe, we have (using 26.98 as the atomic mass of Al)

$$86.0 \text{ g Fe} \times \frac{1 \text{ mol Fe}}{55.85 \text{ g Fe}} \times \frac{2 \text{ mol Al}}{2 \text{ mol Fe}} \times \frac{26.98 \text{ g Al}}{1 \text{ mol Al}} = 41.5 \text{ g Al}$$

grams Fe → moles Fe → moles Al → grams Al

FIG. 3.5 **The thermite reaction.** Pictured here is a device for making white-hot iron by the reaction of aluminum with iron oxide and letting the molten iron run down into a mold between the ends of two steel railroad rails. The rails are thereby welded together. *(Courtesy Orgo-Thermit.)*

☐ We could simplify the mole ratio to 1 mol Al ⇔ 1 mol Fe. Leaving the 2-to-2 ratio maintains the relationship with the balanced equation coefficients.

ARE THE ANSWERS REASONABLE? The estimate that our answers in a mass-to-mass calculation should be within 1/5 to 5 times the initial mass is true for both Al and Fe_2O_3. Rounding the numbers to one or two significant figures and estimating the answer (after rechecking that the units cancel properly) results in

$$\frac{90 \times 160}{60 \times 2} = 120 \text{ g } Fe_2O_3 \quad \text{and} \quad \frac{90 \times 30}{60} = 45 \text{ g Al}$$

Both estimates are close to our calculated values and give us confidence that we calculated correctly.

Practice Exercise 28: Using the information in Example 3.17 calculate the mass of Al_2O_3 formed under the conditions specified. (Hint: Recall the law of conservation of mass.)

Practice Exercise 29: How many grams of carbon dioxide are also produced by the reaction described in Example 3.16?

3.5 | THE REACTANT IN SHORTEST SUPPLY LIMITS THE AMOUNT OF PRODUCT THAT CAN FORM

We've seen that balanced chemical equations can tell us how to mix reactants together in just the right proportions to get a certain amount of product. For example, ethanol, C_2H_5OH, is prepared industrially as follows:

$$\underset{\text{ethylene}}{C_2H_4} + H_2O \longrightarrow \underset{\text{ethanol}}{C_2H_5OH}$$

The equation tells us that one mole of ethylene will react with one mole of water to give one mole of ethanol. We can also interpret the equation on a molecular level: Every molecule of ethylene that reacts requires one molecule of water to produce one molecule of ethanol:

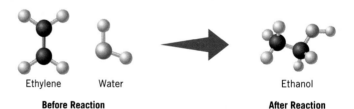

Ethylene   Water   Ethanol
Before Reaction   **After Reaction**

☐ Notice that in both the "before" and "after" views of the reaction, the numbers of carbon, hydrogen, and oxygen atoms are the same.

If we have three molecules of ethylene reacting with three molecules of water, then three ethanol molecules are produced:

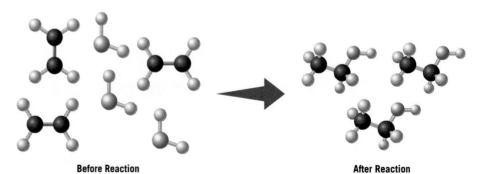

Before Reaction   **After Reaction**

What happens if we mix 3 molecules of ethylene with 5 molecules of water? The ethylene will be completely used up before all the water is, and the product will contain two unreacted water molecules:

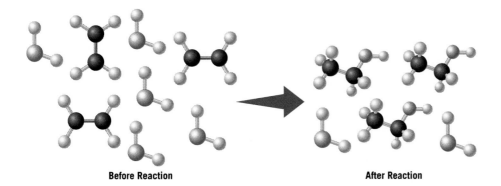

Before Reaction   **After Reaction**

We don't have enough ethylene to use up all the water. The excess water remains after the reaction stops. This situation can be a problem in the manufacture of chemicals because not only do we waste one of our reactants (water, in this case), but we also obtain a product that is contaminated with unused reactant.

In this reaction mixture, ethylene is called the **limiting reactant** because it limits the amount of product (ethanol) that forms. The water is called an **excess reactant,** because we have more of it than is needed to completely consume all the ethylene.

TOOLS
Limiting reactants

To predict the amount of product we'll actually obtain in a reaction, we need to know which of the reactants is the limiting reactant. In the last example above, we saw that we needed only 3 H_2O molecules to react with 3 C_2H_4 molecules, but we had 5 H_2O molecules, so H_2O is present in excess and C_2H_4 is the limiting reactant. We could also have reasoned that 5 molecules of H_2O would require 5 molecules of C_2H_4, and since we have only 3 molecules of C_2H_4, it must be the limiting reactant.

Once we have identified the limiting reactant, it is possible to compute the amount of product that will actually form, and the amount of excess reactant that will be left over after the reaction stops. We must use the amount of the limiting reactant given in the problem for these calculations.

Example 3.18 shows how to solve a typical limiting reactant problem when the amounts of the reactants are given in mass units.

EXAMPLE 3.18
Limiting Reactant Calculation

Gold(III) hydroxide is used for electroplating gold onto other metals. It can be made by the following reaction.

$$2KAuCl_4(aq) + 3Na_2CO_3(aq) + 3H_2O \longrightarrow 2Au(OH)_3(aq) +$$
$$6 NaCl(aq) + 2KCl(aq) + 3CO_2(g)$$

To prepare a fresh supply of $Au(OH)_3$, a chemist at an electroplating plant has mixed 20.00 g of $KAuCl_4$ with 25.00 g of Na_2CO_3 (both dissolved in a large excess of water). What is the maximum number of grams of $Au(OH)_3$ that can form?

ANALYSIS: The clue that tells us this is a limiting reactant question is that *the quantities of two reactants are given.* Once we determine which reactant limits the product, we use its mass in our calculation. We will need to use a combination of our stoichiometry tools to solve this problem.

To find the limiting reactant, we arbitrarily pick one of the reactants ($KAuCl_4$ or Na_2CO_3) and calculate whether it would all be used up. If so, we've found the limiting reactant. If not, the other reactant limits. (We were told that water is in excess, so we know that it does not limit the reaction.)

SOLUTION: We will show, in the two boxes below, the calculations needed to determine which is the limiting reactant. In solving a limiting reactant problem you will need to do only one of these calculations.

We start with $KAuCl_4$ as the reactant to work with and calculate how many grams of Na_2CO_3 *should* be provided to react with 20.00 g of $KAuCl_4$. The formula masses are 377.88 for $KAuCl_4$ and 105.99 for Na_2CO_3. We'll set up a chain calculation using the following mole- to-mole relationship.

$$2 \text{ mol } KAuCl_4 \Leftrightarrow 3 \text{ mol } Na_2CO_3$$

$$\text{grams } KAuCl_4 \quad \rightarrow \quad \text{moles } KAuCl_4 \quad \rightarrow \quad \text{moles } Na_2CO_3 \quad \rightarrow \quad \text{grams } Na_2CO_3$$

$$20.00 \text{ g } KAuCl_4 \times \frac{1 \text{ mol } KAuCl_4}{377.88 \text{ g } KAuCl_4} \times \frac{3 \text{ mol } Na_2CO_3}{2 \text{ mol } KAuCl_4} \times \frac{105.99 \text{ g } Na_2CO_3}{1 \text{ mol } Na_2CO_3}$$

$$= 8.415 \text{ g } Na_2CO_3$$

We find that 20.00 g of $KAuCl_4$ needs 8.415 g of Na_2CO_3. The 25.00 g of Na_2CO_3 taken is therefore more than enough to let the $KAuCl_4$ react completely. The Na_2CO_3 is the excess reactant, so **$KAuCl_4$ is the limiting reactant.**

We start with Na_2CO_3 as the reactant to work with and calculate how many grams of $KAuCl_4$ *should* be provided to react with 25.00 g of Na_2CO_3. The formula masses are 377.88 for $KAuCl_4$ and 105.99 for Na_2CO_3. We'll set up a chain calculation using the following mole-to-mole relationship.

$$3 \text{ mol } Na_2CO_3 \Leftrightarrow 2 \text{ mol } KAuCl_4$$

$$\text{grams } Na_2CO_3 \quad \rightarrow \quad \text{moles } Na_2CO_3 \quad \rightarrow \quad \text{moles } KAuCl_4 \quad \rightarrow \quad \text{grams } KAuCl_4$$

$$25.00 \text{ g } Na_2CO_3 \times \frac{1 \text{ mol } Na_2CO_3}{105.99 \text{ g } Na_2CO_3} \times \frac{2 \text{ mol } KAuCl_4}{3 \text{ mol } Na_2CO_3} \times \frac{377.88 \text{ g } KAuCl_4}{1 \text{ mol } KAuCl_4}$$

$$= 59.42 \text{ g } KAuCl_4$$

We find that 25.00 g Na_2CO_3 would require much more $KAuCl_4$ than provided, so we conclude that **$KAuCl_4$ is the limiting reactant.**

■ After determining which reactant is the limiting reactant, return to the statement of the problem and use the amount of the limiting reactant stated in the problem to perform further calculations.

The result from either calculation above is sufficient to designate $KAuCl_4$ as the limiting reactant. From here on, we have a routine calculation converting the mass of the limiting reactant, $KAuCl_4$, to mass of product, $Au(OH)_3$. We know from the equation's coefficients that

$$1 \text{ mol } KAuCl_4 \Leftrightarrow 1 \text{ mol } Au(OH)_3$$

Using this, and the conversion factors constructed from the formula masses, we set up the following chain calculation.

$$\text{grams } KAuCl_4 \quad \rightarrow \quad \text{moles } KAuCl_4 \quad \rightarrow \quad \text{moles } Au(OH)_3 \quad \rightarrow \quad \text{grams } Au(OH)_3$$

$$20.00 \text{ g } KAuCl_4 \times \left(\frac{1 \text{ mol } KAuCl_4}{377.88 \text{ g } KAuCl_4} \right) \times \left(\frac{1 \text{ mol } Au(OH)_3}{1 \text{ mol } KAuCl_4} \right) \times \left(\frac{247.99 \text{ g } Au(OH)_3}{1 \text{ mol } Au(OH)_3} \right)$$

$$= 13.13 \text{ g } Au(OH)_3$$

Thus from 20.00 g of $KAuCl_4$ we can make a maximum of 13.13 g of $Au(OH)_3$.

In this synthesis, some of the initial 25.00 g of Na_2CO_3 is left over. Since one of our calculations showed that 20.00 g of $KAuCl_4$ requires only 8.415 g of Na_2CO_3 out of 25.00 g Na_2CO_3, the difference, (25.00 g − 8.415 g) = 16.58 g of Na_2CO_3, remains unreacted. It is possible that the chemist used an excess to ensure that every last bit of the very expensive $KAuCl_4$ would be changed to $Au(OH)_3$.

IS THE ANSWER REASONABLE? First, the resulting mass is within the range of 1/5 to 5 times the starting mass and is not unreasonable. Again, we check that our units cancel properly and then we estimate the answer as $\frac{20 \times 250}{400} = 12.5$ g $Au(OH)_3$. That estimate is close to our answer, which assures us the calculation was done correctly.

Practice Exercise 30: A Kipp generator is an old device for making carbon dioxide as needed. It consists of an enclosed flask that contains limestone, $CaCO_3$, and has a valve to add hydrochloric acid, $HCl(aq)$, as needed. The reaction between the limestone and hydrochloric acid produces carbon dioxide as shown in the reaction

$$CaCO_3(s) + 2HCl(aq) \longrightarrow CO_2(g) + CaCl_2(aq) + H_2O$$

How many grams of CO_2 can be made by reacting 125 g of $CaCO_3$ with 125 g of HCl? How many grams of which reactant are left over? (Hint: Find the limiting reactant.)

Practice Exercise 31: In an industrial process for making nitric acid, the first step is the reaction of ammonia with oxygen at high temperature in the presence of a platinum gauze. Nitrogen monoxide forms as follows.

$$4NH_3 + 5O_2 \longrightarrow 4NO + 6H_2O$$

How many grams of nitrogen monoxide can form if a mixture initially contains 30.00 g of NH_3 and 40.00 g of O_2?

3.6 | THE PREDICTED AMOUNT OF PRODUCT IS NOT ALWAYS OBTAINED EXPERIMENTALLY

In most experiments designed for chemical synthesis, the amount of a product actually isolated falls short of the calculated maximum amount. Losses occur for several reasons. Some are mechanical, such as materials sticking to glassware. In some reactions, losses occur by the evaporation of a volatile product. In others, a product is a solid that separates from the solution as it forms because it is largely insoluble. The solid is removed by filtration. What stays in solution, although relatively small, contributes to some loss of product.

One of the common causes of obtaining less than the stoichiometric amount of a product is the occurrence of a **competing reaction** (or **side reaction**). It produces a **by-product,** a substance made by a reaction that competes with the **main reaction.** The synthesis of phosphorus trichloride, for example, gives some phosphorus pentachloride as well, because PCl_3 can react further with Cl_2.

Main reaction:	$2P(s) + 3Cl_2(g) \longrightarrow 2PCl_3(l)$
Competing reaction:	$PCl_3(l) + Cl_2(g) \longrightarrow PCl_5(s)$

The competition is between newly formed PCl_3 and still unreacted phosphorus for still unchanged chlorine.

The **actual yield** of desired product is simply how much is isolated, stated in mass units or moles. The **theoretical yield** of the product is what must be obtained if no losses occur. When less than the theoretical yield of product is obtained, chemists generally calculate the *percentage yield* of product to describe how well the preparation went. The **percentage yield** is the actual yield calculated as a percentage of the theoretical yield.

$$\text{Percentage yield} = \frac{\text{actual yield}}{\text{theoretical yield}} \times 100\%$$

TOOLS

Theoretical, actual, and percentage yields

Both the actual and theoretical yields must be in the same units, of course.

It is important to realize that the actual yield is an experimentally determined quantity. It cannot be calculated. The theoretical yield is always a calculated quantity based on a chemical equation and the amounts of the reactants available.

Let's now work an example that combines the determination of the limiting reactant with a calculation of percentage yield.

EXAMPLE 3.19
Calculating a Percentage Yield

A chemist set up a synthesis of phosphorus trichloride by mixing 12.0 g of phosphorus with 35.0 g of chlorine gas and obtained 42.4 g of liquid phosphorus trichloride. Calculate the percentage yield of this compound.

ANALYSIS: We start by determining the formulas for the reactants and products and then balancing the chemical equation. Phosphorus is represented as $P(s)$, chlorine gas is $Cl_2(g)$, and the product is $PCl_3(l)$. The balanced equation is

$$2P(s) + 3Cl_2(g) \longrightarrow 2PCl_3(l)$$

Now we notice that the masses of *both* reactants are given, so this must be a limiting reactant problem. The first step is to figure out which reactant, P or Cl_2, is the limiting reactant, because we must base all calculations on the limiting reactant. Our basic tools to use are the mass-to-moles relationship and the mole ratio expressed by the balanced equation.

SOLUTION: In any limiting reactant problem, we can arbitrarily pick one reactant and do a calculation to see whether it can be entirely used up. We'll choose phosphorus and see whether there is enough to react with 35.0 g of chlorine. The following calculation gives us the answer.

$$12.0 \text{ g P} \times \frac{1 \text{ mol P}}{30.97 \text{ g P}} \times \frac{3 \text{ mol Cl}_2}{2 \text{ mol P}} \times \frac{70.90 \text{ g Cl}_2}{1 \text{ mol Cl}_2} = 41.2 \text{ g Cl}_2$$

Thus, with 35.0 g of Cl_2 provided but 41.2 g of Cl_2 needed, there is not enough Cl_2 to react with all 12.0 g of P. The Cl_2 will be all used up before the P is used up, so Cl_2 is the limiting reactant. We therefore base the calculation of the theoretical yield of PCl_3 on Cl_2. (Be careful to use the 35.0 g of Cl_2 given in the problem, *not* the 41.2 g calculated while we determined the limiting reactant.)

To find the *theoretical yield* of PCl_3, we calculate how many grams of PCl_3 could be made from 35.0 g of Cl_2 if everything went perfectly according to the equation given.

$$35.0 \text{ g Cl}_2 \times \frac{1 \text{ mol Cl}_2}{70.90 \text{ g Cl}_2} \times \frac{2 \text{ mol PCl}_3}{3 \text{ mol Cl}_2} \times \frac{137.32 \text{ g PCl}_3}{1 \text{ mol PCl}_3} = 45.2 \text{ g PCl}_3$$

$$\text{grams Cl} \rightarrow \text{moles Cl}_2 \rightarrow \text{moles PCl}_3 \rightarrow \text{grams PCl}_3$$

The actual yield was 42.4 g of PCl_3, not 45.2 g, so the percentage yield is calculated as follows.

$$\text{Percentage yield} = \frac{42.4 \text{ g PCl}_3}{45.2 \text{ g PCl}_3} \times 100\% = 93.8\%$$

Thus 93.8% of the theoretical yield of PCl_3 was obtained.

IS THE ANSWER REASONABLE? The obvious check is that the calculated or theoretical yield can never be *less* than the actual yield. Second, our answer is within the range of 1/5 to 5 times the starting amount. Finally an estimated answer, after checking that all units cancel properly, is $\frac{35 \times 2 \times 140}{70 \times 3} \approx 50 \text{ g PCl}_3$, which is close to the 45.2 g we calculated.

Practice Exercise 32: In the synthesis of aspirin we react salicylic acid with acetic anhydride. The balanced chemical equation is

$$2HOOCC_6H_4OH + C_4H_6O_3 \longrightarrow 2HOOCC_6H_4O_2C_2H_3 + H_2O$$

salicylic acid   acetic anhydride   acetyl salicylic acid   water

If we mix together 28.2 grams of salicylic acid with 15.6 grams of acetic anhydride in this reaction we obtain 30.7 grams of aspirin. What are the theoretical and percentage yields of our experiment? (Hint: What is the limiting reactant?)

Practice Exercise 33: Ethanol, C_2H_5OH, can be converted to acetic acid (the acid in vinegar), $HC_2H_3O_2$, by the action of sodium dichromate in aqueous sulfuric acid according to the following equation.

$$3C_2H_5OH(aq) + 2Na_2Cr_2O_7(aq) + 8H_2SO_4(aq) \longrightarrow 3HC_2H_3O_2(aq) + 2Cr_2(SO_4)_3(aq)$$
$$+ 2Na_2SO_4(aq) + 11H_2O$$

In one experiment, 24.0 g of C_2H_5OH, 90.0 g of $Na_2Cr_2O_7$, and an excess of sulfuric acid were mixed, and 26.6 g of acetic acid ($HC_2H_3O_2$) was isolated. Calculate the theoretical and percentage yields of $HC_2H_3O_2$.

SUMMARY

Mole Concept and Formula Mass or Molecular Mass. In the SI definition, one mole of any substance is an amount with the same number, **Avogadro's number** (6.022×10^{23}), of atoms, molecules, or formula units as there are atoms in 12 g (exactly) of carbon-12. For monatomic elements, the **atomic mass** in grams is one mole of that element. The sum of the atomic masses of all of the atoms appearing in a chemical formula gives the **formula mass** or the **molecular mass.**

Molar Mass. This is a general term for the mass in grams numerically equal to the atomic mass, molecular mass, or formula mass. Like an atomic mass, a formula mass, or a molecular mass, the **molar mass** is a tool for grams-to-moles or moles-to-grams conversions.

Chemical Formulas. The actual composition of a molecule is given by its **molecular formula.** An **empirical formula** gives the ratio of atoms, but in the smallest whole numbers, and it is generally the *only* formula we write for ionic compounds. In the case of a molecular compound, the molecular mass is a small whole-number multiple of the empirical formula mass.

Empirical Formulas. An empirical formula may be experimentally determined if there is some way to determine the small whole-number ratio of the atoms in the substance. This calculation can be done if we know the mass or percentage of each element in the compound.

Formula Stoichiometry. A chemical formula is a tool for stoichiometric calculations, because its subscripts tell us the mole ratios in which the various elements are combined.

Balanced Equations and Reaction Stoichiometry. A balanced equation is a tool for reaction stoichiometry because its coefficients disclose the stoichiometric equivalencies. When balancing an equation, only the coefficients can be adjusted, never the subscripts. All problems of reaction stoichiometry must be solved by first converting to moles.

Yields of Products. A reactant taken in a quantity less than required by another reactant, as determined by the reaction's stoichiometry, is called the **limiting reactant.** The **theoretical yield** of a product can be no more than permitted by the limiting reactant. Sometimes **competing reactions** (side reactions) producing by-products reduce the **actual yield.** The ratio of the actual to the theoretical yields, expressed as a percentage, is the **percentage yield.**

Stoichiometric Calculations. These are generally problems where units are converted. The sequence of steps typically used in stoichiometric calculations is shown in Figure 3.6. Conversion factors in this sequence are found in the molar mass, Avogadro's number, the chemical formula, or the balanced chemical reaction.

FIG. 3.6 **Stoichiometry pathways.** This summarizes all of the possible stoichiometric calculations encountered in this chapter. The boxes represent either grams, moles, or elementary units (atoms, molecules, formula units, or ions). Problems will give starting information representing one of the boxes. The question asked will tell you where to end. Perform conversions as noted in the instructions between each box.

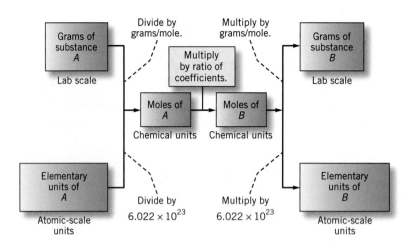

TOOLS FOR PROBLEM SOLVING

In this chapter you learned to apply the following concepts as tools in solving problems. Study each one carefully so that you know what each is used for. When faced with solving a problem, recall what each tool does and consider whether it will be helpful in finding a solution. This will aid you in selecting the tools you need. In this chapter we see that many of the tools from Chapters 1 and 2 must be used with the new tools from this chapter.

Atomic mass *(page 88)* Atomic masses are used to form a conversion factor to calculate mass from moles of an element, or moles from the mass of an element.

$$\text{Gram atomic mass of } X = 1 \text{ mole } X$$

Formula mass, molecular mass *(page 88)* The formula mass or molecular mass is used to form a conversion factor to calculate mass from moles of a compound, or moles from the mass of a compound.

$$\text{Gram molecular mass of } X = 1 \text{ mole } X$$
$$\text{Gram formula mass of } X = 1 \text{ mole } X$$

Molar mass *(page 88)* This is a general term encompassing atomic, molecular, and formula masses. All are the sum of the masses of the elements in the chemical formula.

$$\text{Gram molar mass of } X = 1 \text{ mole of } X$$

Avogadro's number *(page 90)* This relates macroscopic lab-sized quantities (e.g., moles) to numbers of individual atomic-sized particles such as atoms, molecules, or ions.

$$1 \text{ mole } X = 6.022 \times 10^{23} \text{ particles of } X$$

Chemical formula, subscripts *(page 92)* Subscripts in a formula establish atom ratios and mole ratios between the elements in the substance.

Conversion sequence *(page 93)* This is the logical sequence of steps required for a mass-to-mass conversion problem using a chemical formula; also see Figure 3.6.

Percentage composition *(page 94 and 99)* The percentage composition is used to represent the composition of a compound and can be the basis for computing the empirical formula. Comparing experimental and theoretical percentage compositions can help establish the identity of a compound. Percentage composition also helps correlate information from different experiments.

$$\text{Percentage of } X = \frac{\text{mass of } X \text{ in the sample}}{\text{mass of the entire sample}} \times 100\%$$

Determination of an empirical formula *(page 96)* The simplest ratio of elements in a molecule or in the formula for an ionic compound can be calculated when the mass of each element of a compound is experimentally determined.

Methods for finding integer subscripts *(page 98)* Dividing all molar amounts by the smallest value often normalizes subscripts to integers. If decimals remain, multiplication by a small whole number can result in integer subscripts.

Guidelines for balancing chemical equations *(page 104)* Balancing equations means setting coefficients so that equal numbers of each atom will be reactants as well as products. A logical sequence for balancing equations by inspection is presented.

Equivalencies obtained from balanced equations *(page 106)* Balanced chemical equations give us relationships between all reactants and products that can be used in factor-label calculations.

Sequence of conversions using balanced equations *(page 107)* As with chemical formulas, a logical sequence of conversions allows calculation of amounts of all components of a chemical reaction. See Figure 3.6.

Limiting reactant calculations *(page 111)* When the amounts of at least two reactants are known, solution of problems requires identifying the limiting reactant. All calculations must be based only on the amount of the limiting reactant available.

Theoretical, actual, and percentage yields *(page 113)* The theoretical yield is calculated from the limiting reactant. The actual yield must be determined by experiment, and the percentage yield relates the magnitude of the actual yield to the percentage yield.

$$\text{Percentage yield} = \frac{\text{actual mass by experiment}}{\text{theoretical mass by calculation}} \times 100\%$$

QUESTIONS, PROBLEMS, AND EXERCISES

Answers to problems whose numbers are printed in color are given in Appendix B. More challenging problems are marked with asterisks. ILW = Interactive Learningware solution is available at www.wiley.com/college/brady. OH = an Office Hours video is available for this problem.

REVIEW QUESTIONS

Mole Concept

3.1 How would you estimate the number of atoms in a gram of iron, using the mass in grams of an atomic mass unit?

3.2 What is the definition of the mole?

3.3 Why are moles used when all stoichiometry problems could be done using only the mass in grams of an atomic mass unit?

3.4 Which contains more molecules: 2.5 mol of H_2O or 2.5 mol of H_2?

Chemical Formulas

3.5 How many moles of iron atoms are in one mole of Fe_2O_3? How many iron atoms are in one mole of Fe_2O_3?

3.6 Write all the mole-to-mole conversion factors that can be written based on the following chemical formulas.
(a) SO_2 (b) As_2O_3 (c) K_2SO_4 (d) Na_2HPO_4

3.7 Write all the mole-to-mole conversion factors that can be written based on the following chemical formulas.
(a) Mn_3O_4 (b) Sb_2S_5 (c) $(NH_4)_2SO_4$ (d) Hg_2Cl_2

3.8 What information is required to convert grams of a substance into moles of that same substance?

3.9 Why is the expression "1.0 mol of oxygen" ambiguous? Why doesn't a similar ambiguity exist in the expression "64 g of oxygen?"

3.10 The atomic mass of aluminum is 26.98. What specific conversion factors does this value make available for relating a mass of aluminum (in grams) and a quantity of aluminum given in moles?

Empirical Formulas

3.11 In general, what fundamental information, obtained from experimental measurements, is required to calculate the empirical formula of a compound?

3.12 Why is the changing of subscripts not allowed when balancing a chemical equation?

3.13 Under what circumstances can we change, or assign, subscripts in a chemical formula?

3.14 How many distinct empirical formulas are shown by the following models for compounds formed between elements *A* and *B*? Explain. (Element *A* is represented by a black sphere and element *B* by a light gray sphere.)

Avogadro's Number

3.15 How would Avogadro's number change if the atomic mass unit were to be redefined as 2×10^{-27} kg, exactly?

3.16 What information is required to convert grams of a substance into molecules of that same substance?

Stoichiometry with Balanced Equations

3.17 When given the *unbalanced* equation

$$Na(s) + Cl_2(g) \longrightarrow NaCl(s)$$

and asked to balance it, student *A* wrote

$$Na(s) + Cl_2(g) \longrightarrow NaCl_2(s)$$

and student *B* wrote

$$2Na(s) + Cl_2(g) \longrightarrow 2NaCl(s)$$

Both equations are balanced, but which student is correct? Explain why the other student's answer is incorrect.

3.18 Give a step-by-step procedure for estimating the number grams of *A* required to completely react with 10 moles of *B*, given the following information:
   A and *B* react to form A_5B_2.
   A has a molecular mass of 100.0.
   B has a molecular mass of 200.0.
   There are 6.022×10^{23} molecules of *A* in a mole of *A*.
Which of these pieces of information weren't needed?

3.19 If two substances react completely in a 1-to-1 ratio *both* by mass and by moles, what must be true about these substances?

3.20 What information is required to determine how many grams of sulfur would react with a gram of arsenic?

3.21 A mixture of 0.020 mol of Mg and 0.020 mol of Cl_2 reacted completely to form $MgCl_2$ according to the equation

$$Mg + Cl_2 \longrightarrow MgCl_2$$

What information describes the *stoichiometry* of this reaction? What information gives the *scale* of the reaction?

3.22 In a report to a supervisor, a chemist described an experiment in the following way: "0.0800 mol of H_2O_2 decomposed into 0.0800 mol of H_2O and 0.0400 mol of O_2." Express the chemistry and stoichiometry of this reaction by a conventional chemical equation.

3.23 On April 16, 1947, in Texas City, Texas, two cargo ships, the *Grandcamp* and the *High Flier,* were each loaded with approximately 2000 tons of ammonium nitrate fertilizer. The *Grandcamp* caught fire and exploded, followed by the *High Flier.* Over 600 people were killed and one-third of the city was destroyed. Considering a much smaller mass, how would you calculate the number of N_2 molecules that could be produced after the explosion of 1.00 kg of NH_4NO_3?

3.24 Molecules containing *A* and *B* react to form *AB* as shown at the top of the next column. Based on the equations and the contents of the boxes labeled "Initial," sketch for each reaction the molecular models of what is present after the reaction is over. (In both cases, the species *B* exists as B_2. In reaction 1, *A* is monatomic; in reaction 2, *A* exists as diatomic molecules A_2.)

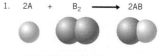

1. $2A$ + B_2 ⟶ $2AB$

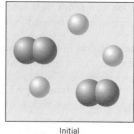

Initial

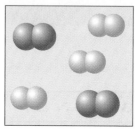

2. A_2 + B_2 ⟶ $2AB$

Initial

REVIEW PROBLEMS

The Mole Concept and Stoichiometric Equivalencies

3.25 In what smallest whole-number ratio must N and O atoms combine to make dinitrogen tetroxide, N_2O_4? What is the mole ratio of the elements in this compound?

3.26 In what atom ratio are the elements present in methane, CH_4 (the chief component of natural gas)? In what mole ratio are the atoms of the elements present in this compound?

3.27 How many moles of tantalum atoms correspond to 1.56×10^{21} atoms of tantalum?

3.28 How many moles of iodine molecules correspond to 1.80×10^{24} molecules of I_2?

3.29 Sucrose (table sugar) has the formula $C_{12}H_{22}O_{11}$. In this compound, what is the
(a) atom ratio of C to H?
(b) mole ratio of C to O?
(c) atom ratio of H to O?
(d) mole ratio of H to O?

3.30 Nail polish remover is sometimes the volatile liquid ethyl acetate, $CH_3COOC_2H_5$. In this compound, what is the
(a) atom ratio of C to O?
(b) mole ratio of C to O?
(c) atom ratio of C to H?
(d) mole ratio of C to H?

3.31 How many moles of Bi atoms are needed to combine with 1.58 mol of O atoms to make bismuth oxide, Bi_2O_3?

3.32 How many moles of vanadium atoms, V, are needed to combine with 0.565 mol of O atoms to make vanadium pentoxide, V_2O_5?

3.33 How many moles of Cr are in 2.16 mol of Cr_2O_3?

3.34 How many moles of O atoms are in 4.25 mol of calcium carbonate, $CaCO_3$, the chief constituent of seashells?

3.35 Aluminum sulfate, $Al_2(SO_4)_3$, is a compound used in sewage treatment plants.
(a) Construct a pair of conversion factors that relate moles of aluminum to moles of sulfur for this compound.
(b) Construct a pair of conversion factors that relate moles of sulfur to moles of $Al_2(SO_4)_3$.
(c) How many moles of Al are in a sample of this compound if the sample also contains 0.900 mol S?
(d) How many moles of S are in 1.16 mol $Al_2(SO_4)_3$?

3.36 Magnetite is a magnetic iron ore. Its formula is Fe_3O_4.
(a) Construct a pair of conversion factors that relate moles of Fe to moles of Fe_3O_4.
(b) Construct a pair of conversion factors that relate moles of Fe to moles of O in Fe_3O_4.
(c) How many moles of Fe are in 2.75 mol of Fe_3O_4?
(d) If this compound could be prepared from Fe_2O_3 and O_2, how many moles of Fe_2O_3 would be needed to prepare 4.50 mol Fe_3O_4?

3.37 How many moles of H_2 and N_2 can be formed by the decomposition of 0.145 mol of ammonia, NH_3?

3.38 How many moles of S are needed to combine with 0.225 mol Al to give Al_2S_3?

ILW **3.39** How many moles of UF_6 would have to be decomposed to provide enough fluorine to prepare 1.25 mol of CF_4? (Assume sufficient carbon is available.)

3.40 How many moles of Fe_3O_4 are required to supply enough iron to prepare 0.260 mol Fe_2O_3? (Assume sufficient oxygen is available.)

3.41 How many atoms of carbon are combined with 4.13 moles of hydrogen in a sample of the compound propane, C_3H_8? (Propane is used as the fuel in gas barbecues.)

3.42 How many atoms of hydrogen are found in 2.31 mol of propane, C_3H_8?

3.43 What is the total number of C, H, and O atoms in 0.260 moles of glucose, $C_6H_{12}O_6$?

3.44 What is the total number of N, H, and O atoms in 0.356 mol of ammonium nitrate, NH_4NO_3, an important fertilizer?

Measuring Moles of Elements and Compounds

3.45 How many atoms are in 6.00 g of carbon-12?

OH **3.46** How many atoms are in 1.50 mol of carbon-12? How many grams does this much carbon-12 weigh?

3.47 Determine the mass in grams of each of the following:
(a) 1.35 mol Fe   (b) 24.5 mol O   (c) 0.876 mol Ca

3.48 Determine the mass in grams of each of the following:
(a) 0.546 mol S   (b) 3.29 mol N   (c) 8.11 mol Al

3.49 What is the mass, in grams, of 2×10^{12} atoms of potassium?

3.50 What is the mass, in grams, of 4×10^{17} atoms of sodium?

3.51 How many moles of nickel are in 17.7 g of Ni?

3.52 How many moles of chromium are in 85.7 g of Cr?

3.53 Calculate the formula mass of each of the following to the maximum number of significant figures possible using the periodic table inside the front cover.
(a) $NaHCO_3$ (d) potassium dichromate
(b) $(NH_4)_2CO_3$ (e) aluminum sulfate
(c) $CuSO_4 \cdot 5H_2O$

3.54 Calculate the formula mass of each of the following to the maximum number of significant figures possible using the periodic table inside the front cover.
(a) calcium nitrate   (d) $Fe_4[Fe(CN)_6]_3$
(b) $Pb(C_2H_5)_4$ (e) magnesium phosphate
(c) $Na_2SO_4 \cdot 10H_2O$

3.55 Calculate the mass in grams of the following.
(a) 1.25 mol $Ca_3(PO_4)_2$
(b) 0.625 mmol iron(III) nitrate
(c) 0.600 μmol C_4H_{10}
(d) 1.45 mol ammonium carbonate

3.56 What is the mass in grams of the following?
(a) 0.754 mol zinc chloride
(b) 0.194 μmol potassium chlorate
(c) 0.322 mmol $POCl_3$
(d) 4.31×10^{-3} mol $(NH_4)_2HPO_4$

3.57 Calculate the number of moles of each compound in the following samples.
(a) 21.5 g calcium carbonate
(b) 1.56 ng NH_3
(c) 16.8 g strontium nitrate
(d) 6.98 μg Na_2CrO_4

3.58 Calculate the number of moles of each compound in the following samples.
(a) 9.36 g calcium hydroxide
(b) 38.2 kg lead(II)sulfate
(c) 4.29 g H_2O_2
(d) 4.65 mg $NaAuCl_4$

ILW **3.59** One sample of CaC_2 contains 0.150 mol of carbon. How many moles and how many grams of calcium are also in the sample? [Calcium carbide, CaC_2, was once used to make signal flares for ships. Water dripped onto CaC_2 reacts to give acetylene (C_2H_2), which burns brightly.]

OH **3.60** How many moles of iodine are in 0.500 mol of $Ca(IO_3)_2$? How many grams of calcium iodate are needed to supply this much iodine? [Iodized salt contains a trace amount of calcium iodate, $Ca(IO_3)_2$, to help prevent a thyroid condition called goiter.]

3.61 How many moles of nitrogen, N, are in 0.650 mol of ammonium carbonate? How many grams of this compound supply this much nitrogen?

3.62 How many moles of nitrogen, N, are in 0.556 mol of ammonium nitrate? How many grams of this compound supply this much nitrogen?

3.63 How many kilograms of a fertilizer made of pure $(NH_4)_2CO_3$ would be required to supply 1.00 kilogram of nitrogen to the soil?

3.64 How many kilograms of a fertilizer made of pure P_2O_5 would be required to supply 1.00 kilogram of phosphorus to the soil?

Percentage Composition

3.65 Calculate the percentage composition by mass for each of the following:
(a) sodium dihydrogenphosphate
(b) $NH_4H_2PO_4$
(c) $(CH_3)_2CO$
(d) calcium sulfate dihydrate
(e) $CaSO_4 \cdot 2H_2O$

3.66 Calculate the percentage composition by mass of each of the following:
(a) $(CH_3)_2N_2H_2$ (d) C_3H_8
(b) $CaCO_3$ (e) aluminum sulfate
(c) iron(III) nitrate

3.67 Which has a higher percentage of oxygen: morphine ($C_{17}H_{19}NO_3$) or heroin ($C_{21}H_{23}NO_5$)?

3.68 Which has a higher percentage of nitrogen: carbamazepine ($C_{15}H_{12}N_2O$) or carbetapentane ($C_{20}H_{31}NO_3$)?

3.69 Freon is a trade name for a group of gaseous compounds once used as propellants in aerosol cans. Which has a higher percentage of chlorine: Freon-12 (CCl_2F_2) or Freon-141b ($C_2H_3Cl_2F$)?

3.70 Which has a higher percentage of fluorine: Freon-12 (CCl_2F_2) or Freon 113 ($C_2Cl_3F_3$)?

OH 3.71 It was found that 2.35 g of a compound of phosphorus and chlorine contained 0.539 g of phosphorus. What are the percentages by mass of phosphorus and chlorine in this compound?

3.72 An analysis revealed that 5.67 g of a compound of nitrogen and oxygen contained 1.47 g of nitrogen. What are the percentages by mass of nitrogen and oxygen in this compound?

3.73 Phencyclidine ("angel dust") is $C_{17}H_{25}N$. A sample suspected of being this illicit drug was found to have a percentage composition of 84.71% C, 10.42% H, and 5.61% N. Do these data acceptably match the theoretical data for phencyclidine?

3.74 The hallucinogenic drug LSD has the molecular formula $C_{20}H_{25}N_3O$. One suspected sample contained 74.07% C, 7.95% H, and 9.99% N.
(a) What is the percentage O in the sample?
(b) Are these data consistent for LSD?

3.75 How many grams of O are combined with 7.14×10^{21} atoms of N in the compound dinitrogen pentoxide?

3.76 How many grams of C are combined with 4.25×10^{23} atoms of H in the compound C_5H_{12}?

Empirical Formulas

3.77 Write empirical formulas for the following compounds.
(a) S_2Cl_2 (b) $C_6H_{12}O_6$ (c) NH_3 (d) As_2O_6 (e) H_2O_2

3.78 What are the empirical formulas of the following compounds?
(a) $C_2H_4(OH)_2$ (d) B_2H_6
(b) $H_2S_2O_8$ (e) C_2H_5OH
(c) C_4H_{10}

3.79 Quantitative analysis of a sample of sodium pertechnetate with a mass of 0.896 g found 0.111 g of sodium and 0.477 g of technetium. The remainder was oxygen. Calculate the empirical formula of sodium pertechnetate. (Radioactive sodium pertechnetate is used as a brain-scanning agent in medicine.)

3.80 A sample of Freon was found to contain 0.423 g C, 2.50 g Cl, and 1.34 g F. What is the empirical formula of this compound?

3.81 A dry-cleaning fluid composed of only carbon and chlorine was found to be composed of 14.5% C and 85.5% Cl (by mass). What is the empirical formula of this compound?

3.82 One compound of mercury with a formula mass of 519 g mol^{-1} contains 77.26% Hg, 9.25% C, and 1.17% H (with the balance being O). Calculate the empirical and molecular formulas.

3.83 Cinnamic acid, a compound related to the flavor component of cinnamon, is 72.96% carbon, 5.40% hydrogen, and the rest is oxygen. What is the empirical formula of this acid?

3.84 Vanillin, a compound used as a flavoring agent in food products, has the following percentage composition: 63.2% C, 5.26% H, and 31.6% O. What is the empirical formula of vanillin?

ILW 3.85 When 0.684 g of an organic compound containing only carbon, hydrogen, and oxygen was burned in oxygen, 1.312 g CO_2 and 0.805 g H_2O were obtained. What is the empirical formula of the compound?

3.86 Methyl ethyl ketone (often abbreviated MEK) is a powerful solvent with many commercial uses. A sample of this compound (which contains only C, H, and O) weighing 0.822 g was burned in oxygen to give 2.01 g CO_2 and 0.827 g H_2O. What is the empirical formula for MEK?

3.87 When 6.853 mg of a sex hormone was burned in a combustion analysis, 19.73 mg of CO_2 and 6.391 mg of H_2O were obtained. What is the empirical formula of the compound?

3.88 When a sample of a compound in the vitamin D family was burned in a combustion analysis, 5.983 mg of the compound gave 18.490 mg of CO_2 and 6.232 mg of H_2O. What is the empirical formula of the compound?

Molecular Formulas

3.89 The following are empirical formulas and the masses per mole for three compounds. What are their molecular formulas?
(a) NaS_2O_3;   270.4 g/mol
(b) C_3H_2Cl;   147.0 g/mol
(c) C_2HCl;   181.4 g/mol

3.90 The following are empirical formulas and the masses per mole for three compounds. What are their molecular formulas?
(a) Na_2SiO_3;   732.6 g/mol
(b) $NaPO_3$;   305.9 g/mol
(c) CH_3O;   62.1 g/mol

3.91 The compound described in Problem 3.87 was found to have a molecular mass of 290. What is its molecular formula?

3.92 The compound described in Problem 3.88 was found to have a molecular mass of 399 g mol^{-1}. What is the molecular formula of this compound?

ILW 3.93 A sample of a compound of mercury and bromine with a mass of 0.389 g was found to contain 0.111 g bromine. Its molecular mass was found to be 561 g mol^{-1}. What are its empirical and molecular formulas?

3.94 A 0.6662 g sample of "antimonal saffron" was found to contain 0.4017 g of antimony. The remainder was sulfur. The formula mass of this compound is 404 g mol^{-1}. What are the empirical and molecular formulas of this pigment? (This compound is a red pigment used in painting.)

3.95 A sample of a compound of C, H, N, and O, with a mass of 0.6216 g was found to contain 0.1735 g C, 0.01455 g H, and 0.2024 g N. Its formula mass is 129 g mol^{-1}. Calculate its empirical and molecular formulas.

3.96 Strychnine, a deadly poison, has a formula mass of 334 g mol^{-1} and a percentage composition of 75.42% C, 6.63% H, 8.38% N, and the balance oxygen. Calculate the empirical and molecular formulas of strychnine.

Balancing Chemical Equations

3.97 How many moles of hydrogen are part of the expression "$2Ba(OH)_2 \cdot 8H_2O$," taken from a balanced equation?

3.98 How many moles of oxygen are part of the expression "$3Ca_3(PO_4)_2$," taken from a balanced equation?

OH 3.99 Write the equation that expresses in acceptable chemical shorthand the following statement: "Iron can be made to react with molecular oxygen to give iron(III) oxide."

3.100 The conversion of one air pollutant, nitrogen monoxide, produced in vehicle engines, into another, nitrogen dioxide, occurs when nitrogen monoxide reacts with molecular oxygen in the air. Write the balanced equation for this reaction.

3.101 Balance the following equations.
(a) Calcium hydroxide reacts with hydrogen chloride to form calcium chloride and water.
(b) Silver nitrate and calcium chloride react to form calcium nitrate and silver chloride.
(c) Lead nitrate reacts with sodium sulfate to form lead sulfate and sodium nitrate.
(d) Iron(III) oxide and carbon react to form iron and carbon dioxide.
(e) Butane reacts with oxygen to form carbon dioxide and water.

3.102 Balance the following equations.
(a) $SO_2 + O_2 \longrightarrow SO_3$
(b) $NaHCO_3 + H_2SO_4 \longrightarrow Na_2SO_4 + H_2O + CO_2$
(c) $P_4O_{10} + H_2O \longrightarrow H_3PO_4$
(d) $Fe_2O_3 + H_2 \longrightarrow Fe + H_2O$
(e) $Al + H_2SO_4 \longrightarrow Al_2(SO_4)_3 + H_2$

3.103 Balance the following equations.
(a) $Mg(OH)_2 + HBr \longrightarrow MgBr_2 + H_2O$
(b) $HCl + Ca(OH)_2 \longrightarrow CaCl_2 + H_2O$
(c) $Al_2O_3 + H_2SO_4 \longrightarrow Al_2(SO_4)_3 + H_2O$
(d) $KHCO_3 + H_3PO_4 \longrightarrow K_2HPO_4 + H_2O + CO_2$
(e) $C_9H_{20} + O_2 \longrightarrow CO_2 + H_2O$

3.104 Balance the following equations.
(a) $CaO + HNO_3 \longrightarrow Ca(NO_3)_2 + H_2O$
(b) $Na_2CO_3 + Mg(NO_3)_2 \longrightarrow MgCO_3 + NaNO_3$
(c) $(NH_4)_3PO_4 + NaOH \longrightarrow Na_3PO_4 + NH_3 + H_2O$
(d) $LiHCO_3 + H_2SO_4 \longrightarrow Li_2SO_4 + H_2O + CO_2$
(e) $C_4H_{10}O + O_2 \longrightarrow CO_2 + H_2O$

3.105 Chemical reactions can be used to change the charge of ions. Fe^{3+} is converted to Fe^{2+} when iron(III) chloride reacts with tin(II) chloride to make iron(II) chloride and tin(IV) chloride. Write and balance the equation that represents this reaction.

3.106 A precipitation reaction is one where soluble reactants form an insoluble product. A common precipitation reaction involves the reaction of the soluble salt aluminum chloride with soluble silver nitrate to form the insoluble silver chloride and soluble aluminum nitrate. Write and balance the equation for this reaction along with the appropriate states indicated in parentheses.

Stoichiometry Based on Chemical Equations

3.107 Chlorine is used by textile manufacturers to bleach cloth. Excess chlorine is destroyed by its reaction with sodium thiosulfate, $Na_2S_2O_3$, as follows.

$$Na_2S_2O_3(aq) + 4Cl_2(g) + 5H_2O \longrightarrow$$
$$2NaHSO_4(aq) + 8HCl(aq)$$

(a) How many moles of $Na_2S_2O_3$ are needed to react with 0.12 mol of Cl_2?
(b) How many moles of HCl can form from 0.12 mol of Cl_2?
(c) How many moles of H_2O are required for the reaction of 0.12 mol of Cl_2?
(d) How many moles of H_2O react if 0.24 mol HCl is formed?

3.108 The octane in gasoline burns according to the following equation.

$$2C_8H_{18} + 25O_2 \longrightarrow 16CO_2 + 18H_2O$$

(a) How many moles of O_2 are needed to react fully with 6 mol of octane?
(b) How many moles of CO_2 can form from 0.5 mol of octane?
(c) How many moles of water are produced by the combustion of 8 mol of octane?
(d) If this reaction is used to synthesize 6.00 mol of CO_2, how many moles of oxygen are needed? How many moles of octane?

3.109 The following reaction is used to extract gold from pretreated gold ore:

$$2Au(CN)_2^-(aq) + Zn(s) \longrightarrow 2Au(s) + Zn(CN)_4^{2-}(aq)$$

(a) How many grams of Zn are needed to react with 0.11 mol of $Au(CN)_2^-$?
(b) How many grams of Au can form from 0.11 mol of $Au(CN)_2^-$?
(c) How many grams of $Au(CN)_2^-$ are required for the reaction of 0.11 mol of Zn?

OH 3.110 Propane burns according to the following equation.

$$C_3H_8 + 5O_2 \longrightarrow 3CO_2 + 4H_2O$$

(a) How many grams of O_2 are needed to react fully with 3 mol of propane?
(b) How many grams of CO_2 can form from 0.1 mol of propane?
(c) How many grams of water are produced by the combustion of 4 mol of propane?

3.111 The incandescent white of a fireworks display is caused by the reaction of phosphorus with O_2 to give P_4O_{10}.
(a) Write the balanced chemical equation for the reaction.
(b) How many grams of O_2 are needed to combine with 6.85 g of P?
(c) How many grams of P_4O_{10} can be made from 8.00 g of O_2?
(d) How many grams of P are needed to make 7.46 g of P_4O_{10}?

3.112 The combustion of butane, C_4H_{10}, produces carbon dioxide and water. When one sample of C_4H_{10} was burned, 4.46 g of water was formed.
(a) Write the balanced chemical equation for the reaction.
(b) How many grams of butane were burned?
(c) How many grams of O_2 were consumed?
(d) How many grams of CO_2 were formed?

ILW 3.113 In *dilute* nitric acid, HNO_3, copper metal dissolves according to the following equation.

$$3Cu(s) + 8HNO_3(aq) \longrightarrow$$
$$3Cu(NO_3)_2(aq) + 2NO(g) + 4H_2O$$

How many grams of HNO_3 are needed to dissolve 11.45 g of Cu according to this equation?

3.114 The reaction of hydrazine, N_2H_4, with hydrogen peroxide, H_2O_2, has been used in rocket engines. One way these compounds react is described by the equation

$$N_2H_4 + 7H_2O_2 \longrightarrow 2HNO_3 + 8H_2O$$

According to this equation, how many grams of H_2O_2 are needed to react completely with 852 g of N_2H_4?

3.115 Oxygen gas can be produced in the laboratory by decomposition of hydrogen peroxide (H_2O_2):

$$2H_2O_2(aq) \longrightarrow 2H_2O + O_2(g)$$

How many kilograms of O_2 can be produced from 1.0 kg of H_2O_2?

3.116 Oxygen gas can be produced in the laboratory by decomposition of potassium chlorate ($KClO_3$):

$$2KClO_3(s) \longrightarrow 2KCl(s) + 3O_2(g)$$

How many kilograms of O_2 can be produced from 1.0 kg of $KClO_3$?

Limiting Reactant Calculations

3.117 The reaction of powdered aluminum and iron(III) oxide,

$$2Al + Fe_2O_3 \longrightarrow Al_2O_3 + 2Fe$$

produces so much heat the iron that forms is molten. Because of this, railroads use the reaction to provide molten steel to weld steel rails together when laying track. Suppose that in one batch of reactants 4.20 mol of Al was mixed with 1.75 mol of Fe_2O_3.
(a) Which reactant, if either, was the limiting reactant?
(b) Calculate the number of grams of iron that can be formed from this mixture of reactants.

3.118 Ethanol (C_2H_5OH) is synthesized for industrial use by the following reaction, carried out at very high pressure:

$$C_2H_4(g) + H_2O(g) \longrightarrow C_2H_5OH(l)$$

What is the maximum amount of ethanol that can be produced when 1.0 kg of ethylene (C_2H_4) and 0.010 kg of steam are placed into the reaction vessel?

ILW 3.119 Silver nitrate, $AgNO_3$, reacts with iron(III) chloride, $FeCl_3$, to give silver chloride, $AgCl$, and iron(III) nitrate, $Fe(NO_3)_3$. A solution containing 18.0 g of $AgNO_3$ was mixed with a solution containing 32.4 g of $FeCl_3$. How many grams of which reactant remains after the reaction is over?

3.120 Chlorine dioxide, ClO_2, has been used as a disinfectant in air-conditioning systems. It reacts with water according to the equation

$$6ClO_2 + 3H_2O \longrightarrow 5HClO_3 + HCl$$

If 142.0 g of ClO_2 is mixed with 38.0 g of H_2O, how many grams of which reactant remain if the reaction is complete?

3.121 Some of the acid in acid rain is produced by the following reaction:

$$3NO_2(g) + H_2O(l) \longrightarrow 2HNO_3(aq) + NO(g)$$

If a falling raindrop weighing 0.050 g comes into contact with 1.0 mg of $NO_2(g)$, how much HNO_3 can be produced?

3.122 Phosphorus pentachloride reacts with water to give phosphoric acid and hydrogen chloride according to the following equation.

$$PCl_5 + 4H_2O \longrightarrow H_3PO_4 + 5HCl$$

In one experiment, 0.360 mol of PCl_5 was slowly added to 2.88 mol of water.
(a) Which reactant, if either, was the limiting reactant?
(b) How many grams of HCl were formed in the reaction?

Theoretical Yield and Percentage Yield

3.123 Barium sulfate, $BaSO_4$, is made by the following reaction.

$$Ba(NO_3)_2(aq) + Na_2SO_4(aq) \longrightarrow BaSO_4(s) + 2NaNO_3(aq)$$

An experiment was begun with 75.00 g of $Ba(NO_3)_2$ and an excess of Na_2SO_4. After collecting and drying the product, 64.45 g of $BaSO_4$ was obtained. Calculate the theoretical yield and percentage yield of $BaSO_4$.

3.124 The Solvay process for the manufacture of sodium carbonate begins by passing ammonia and carbon dioxide through a solution of sodium chloride to make sodium bicarbonate and ammonium chloride. The equation for the overall reaction is

$$H_2O + NaCl + NH_3 + CO_2 \longrightarrow NH_4Cl + NaHCO_3$$

In the next step, sodium bicarbonate is heated to give sodium carbonate and two gases, carbon dioxide and steam.

$$2NaHCO_3 \longrightarrow Na_2CO_3 + CO_2 + H_2O$$

What is the theoretical yield of sodium carbonate, expressed in grams, if 120 g NaCl was used in the first reaction? If 85.4 g of Na_2CO_3 was obtained, what was the percentage yield?

ILW 3.125 Aluminum sulfate can be made by the following reaction.

$$2AlCl_3(aq) + 3H_2SO_4(aq) \longrightarrow Al_2(SO_4)_3(aq) + 6HCl(aq)$$

It is quite soluble in water, so to isolate it the solution has to be evaporated to dryness. This drives off the volatile HCl, but the residual solid has to be heated to a little over 200 °C to drive off all of the water. In one experiment, 25.0 g of $AlCl_3$ was mixed with 30.0 g of H_2SO_4. Eventually, 28.46 g of pure $Al_2(SO_4)_3$ was isolated. Calculate the percentage yield.

3.126 The combustion of methyl alcohol in an abundant excess of oxygen follows the equation

$$2CH_3OH + 3O_2 \longrightarrow 2CO_2 + 4H_2O$$

When 6.40 g of CH_3OH was mixed with 10.2 g of O_2 and ignited, 6.12 g of CO_2 was obtained. What was the percentage yield of CO_2?

*3.127 The potassium salt of benzoic acid, potassium benzoate ($KC_7H_5O_2$), can be made by the action of potassium permanganate on toluene (C_7H_8) as follows.

$$C_7H_8 + 2KMnO_4 \longrightarrow KC_7H_5O_2 + 2MnO_2 + KOH + H_2O$$

If the yield of potassium benzoate cannot realistically be expected to be more than 71%, what is the minimum number of grams of toluene needed to produce 11.5 g of potassium benzoate?

*3.128 Manganese trifluoride, MnF_3, can be prepared by the following reaction.

$$2MnI_2(s) + 13F_2(g) \longrightarrow 2MnF_3(s) + 4IF_5(l)$$

If the percentage yield of MnF_3 is always approximately 56%, how many grams of MnF_3 can be expected if 10.0 grams of each reactant is used in an experiment?

ADDITIONAL EXERCISES

3.129 Mercury is an environmental pollutant because it can be converted by certain bacteria into the very poisonous substance methyl mercury, $(CH_3)_2Hg$. This compound ends up in the food chain and accumulates in the tissues of aquatic organisms, particularly fish, which renders them unsafe to eat. It is estimated that in the United States 263 tons of mercury are released into the atmosphere each year. If only 1.0 percent of this mercury is changed to $(CH_3)_2Hg$, how many pounds of this compound are formed annually?

*3.130 Lead compounds are often highly colored and are toxic to mold, mildew, and bacteria, properties that in the past were useful for paints used before 1960. Today we know lead is very hazardous and it is not used in paint; however, old paint is still a problem. If a certain lead-based paint contains 14.5% $PbCr_2O_7$ and 73% of the paint evaporates as it dries, what mass of lead will be in a paint chip that weighs 0.15 g?

3.131 A superconductor is a substance that is able to conduct electricity without resistance, a property that is very desirable in the construction of large electromagnets. Metals have this property if cooled to temperatures a few degrees above absolute zero, but this requires the use of expensive liquid helium (boiling point 4 K). Scientists have discovered materials that become superconductors at higher temperatures, but they are ceramics. Their brittle nature has so far prevented them from being made into long wires. A recently discovered compound of magnesium and boron, which consists of 52.9% Mg and 47.1% B, shows special promise as a high-temperature superconductor because it is inexpensive to make and can be fabricated into wire relatively easily. What is the formula of the compound?

*3.132 A 0.1246 g sample of a compound of chromium and chlorine was dissolved in water. All of the chloride ion was then captured by silver ion in the form of AgCl. A mass of 0.3383 g of AgCl was obtained. Calculate the empirical formula of the compound of Cr and Cl.

*3.133 A compound of Ca, C, N, and S was subjected to quantitative analysis and formula mass determination, and the following data were obtained. A 0.250 g sample was mixed with Na_2CO_3 to convert all of the Ca to 0.160 g of $CaCO_3$. A 0.115 g sample of the compound was carried through a series of reactions until all of its S was changed to 0.344 g of $BaSO_4$. A 0.712 g sample was processed to liberate all of its N as NH_3, and 0.155 g NH_3 was obtained. The formula mass was found to be 156. Determine the empirical and molecular formulas of the compound.

3.134 Ammonium nitrate will detonate if ignited in the presence of certain impurities. The equation for this reaction at a high temperature is

$$2NH_4NO_3(s) \xrightarrow{>300\,°C} 2N_2(g) + O_2(g) + 4H_2O(g)$$

Notice that all of the products are gases and so must occupy a vastly greater volume than the solid reactant.
(a) How many moles of *all* gases are produced from 1 mol of NH_4NO_3?
(b) If 1.00 ton of NH_4NO_3 exploded according to this equation, how many moles of *all* gases would be produced? (1 ton = 2000 lb.)

3.135 A lawn fertilizer is rated as 6.00% nitrogen, meaning 6.00 g of N in 100 g of fertilizer. The nitrogen is present in the form of urea, $(NH_2)_2CO$. How many grams of urea are present in 100 g of the fertilizer to supply the rated amount of nitrogen?

*3.136 Nitrogen is the "active ingredient" in many quick acting fertilizers. You are operating a farm of 1500 acres to produce soybeans. Which of the following fertilizers will you choose as the most economical for your farm? (a) NH_4NO_3 at $625 for 25 kg, (b) $(NH_4)_2HPO_4$ at $55 for 1 kg, (c) urea, CH_4ON_2, at $60 for 5 kg, (d) ammonia, NH_3, at $128 for 50 kg

3.137 Based solely on the amount of available carbon, how many grams of sodium oxalate, $Na_2C_2O_4$, could be obtained from 125 g of C_6H_6? (Assume that no loss of carbon occurs in any of the reactions needed to produce the $Na_2C_2O_4$.)

3.138 According to NASA, the space shuttle's external fuel tank for the main propulsion system carries 1,361,936 lb of liquid oxygen and 227,641 lb of liquid hydrogen. During takeoff, these chemicals are consumed as they react to form water. If the reaction is continued until all of one reactant is gone, how many pounds of which reactant are left over?

*3.139 For a research project, a student decided to test the effect of the lead(II) ion (Pb^{2+}) on the ability of salmon eggs to hatch. This ion was obtainable from the water-soluble salt, lead(II) nitrate, $Pb(NO_3)_2$, which the student decided to make by the following reaction. (The desired product was to be isolated by the slow evaporation of the water.)

$$PbO(s) + 2HNO_3(aq) \longrightarrow Pb(NO_3)_2(aq) + H_2O$$

Losses of product for various reasons were anticipated, and a yield of 86.0% was expected. In order to have 5.00 g of product at this yield, how many grams of PbO should be taken? (Assume that sufficient nitric acid, HNO_3, would be used.)

3.140 Chlorine atoms cause chain reactions in the stratosphere that destroy ozone that protects the earth's surface from ultraviolet radiation. The chlorine atoms come from chlorofluorocarbons, compounds that contain carbon, fluorine, and chlorine, which were used for many years as refrigerants. One of these compounds is Freon-12, CF_2Cl_2. If a sample contains 1.0×10^{-9} g of Cl, how many grams of F should be present if all of the F and Cl atoms in the sample came from CF_2Cl_2 molecules?

*3.141 Lime, CaO, can be produced in two steps shown in the equations below. If the percentage yield of the first step is 83.5% and the percentage yield of the second step is 71.4%, what is the expected overall percentage yield for producing CaO from $CaCl_2$?

$$CaCl_2(aq) + CO_2(g) + H_2O \longrightarrow CaCO_3(s) + 2HCl(aq)$$

$$CaCO_3(s) \xrightarrow{heat} CaO + H_2O$$

EXERCISES IN CRITICAL THINKING

3.142 A newspaper story describing the local celebration of Mole Day on October 23 (selected for Avogadro's number, 6.022×10^{23}) attempted to give the readers a sense of the size of the number by stating that a mole of M&Ms would be equal to 18 tractor trailers full. Assuming that an M&M occupies a volume of about 0.5 cm^3, calculate the dimensions of a cube required to hold one mole of M&Ms. Would 18 tractor trailers be sufficient?

3.143 Suppose you had one mole of pennies and that you were going to spend 500 million dollars each and every second until you spent your entire fortune. How many years would it take you to spend all this cash? (Assume 1 year = 365 days.)

3.144 Using the above two exercises as examples, devise a creative way to demonstrate the size of the mole, or Avogadro's number.

3.145 List the different ways in which a chemist could use the information used to determine empirical formulas.

3.146 Calculate the percentage carbon in $C_{20}H_{42}$ and $C_{21}H_{44}$. If you were to burn one gram of each compound and quantitatively collect the carbon dioxide and water produced, would you be able to discern the difference between these two compounds with the equipment in your laboratory? In your evaluation consider the difference in masses expected from each sample and the number of decimal places your balance must read to. Also, list, in order of importance, all factors that can create error in this experiment.

Many of the fundamental concepts and problem-solving skills that were developed in the preceding chapters will carry forward into the rest of this book. Therefore, we recommend that you pause here to see how well you have grasped the concepts, how familiar you are with important terms, and how able you are at working chemical problems. Don't be discouraged if some of the problems seem to be difficult at first. Where necessary, take some time to review the concepts and problem-solving tools required.

Some of the problems here require data or other information found in tables in this book, including those inside the covers. Freely use these tables as needed. For problems that require mathematical solutions, we recommend that you first assemble the necessary information in the form of equivalencies and then use them to set up appropriate conversion factors needed to obtain the answers.

1. A rectangular box was found to be 24.6 cm wide, 0.35140 m high, and 7,424 mm deep.
   (a) How many significant figures are in each measurement?
   (b) Calculate the volume of the box in units of cm^3. Be sure to express your answer to the correct number of significant figures.
   (c) Use the answer in part (b) to calculate the volume of the box in cubic feet.
   (d) Suppose the box was solid and composed entirely of zinc, which has a density of 7.140 g/cm^3. What would be the mass of the box in kilograms?

2. What is the difference between an atom and a molecule? What is the difference between a molecule and a mole?

3. If a 10 g sample of element X contains twice as many atoms as a 10 g sample of element Y, how does the atomic mass of X compare with the atomic mass of Y?

4. How did Dalton's atomic theory account for the law of conservation of mass? How did it explain the law of definite proportions?

5. If atom A has the same number of neutrons as atom B, must A and B be atoms of the same element? Explain.

6. Construct a conversion factor that would enable you to convert a volume of 3.14 ft^3 into cubic centimeters (cm^3).

7. The atoms of an isotope of plutonium, Pu, each contain 94 protons, 150 neutrons, and 94 electrons. Write a symbol for this element that incorporates its mass number and atomic number. Write the symbol for a different isotope of plutonium.

8. An atom of an isotope of nickel has a mass number of 60. How many protons, neutrons, and electrons are in this atom?

9. A solution was found to contain particles consisting of 12 neutrons, 10 electrons, and 11 protons. Write the chemical symbol for this particle, consulting the periodic table as needed.

10. For each of the following, indicate whether it is possible to see the item specified with the naked eye. If not, explain.
    (a) A molar mass of iron
    (b) An atom of iron
    (c) A molecule of water
    (d) A mole of water
    (e) An ion of sodium
    (f) A formula unit of sodium chloride

11. Make a sketch of the general shape of the modern periodic table and mark off those areas where we find the metals, metalloids, and nonmetals.

12. Which of the following elements would most likely be found together in nature: Ca, Hf, Sn, Cu, Zr?

13. Match an element on the left with a description on the right.

    | Calcium | Halogen |
    | Iron | Noble gas |
    | Helium | Alkali metal |
    | Gadolinium | Alkaline earth metal |
    | Iodine | Transition metal |
    | Sodium | Inner transition metal |

14. Define *ductile* and *malleable*.

15. Which metal is a liquid at room temperature? Which metal has the highest melting point?

16. What is the most important property that distinguishes a metalloid from a metal or a nonmetal?

17. Give the symbols of the post-transition metals.

18. Give chemical formulas for the following.
    (a) potassium nitrate
    (b) calcium carbonate
    (c) cobalt(II) phosphate
    (d) magnesium sulfite
    (e) iron(III) bromide
    (f) magnesium nitride
    (g) aluminum selenide
    (h) copper(II) perchlorate
    (i) bromine pentafluoride
    (j) dinitrogen pentaoxide
    (k) strontium acetate
    (l) ammonium dichromate
    (m) copper(I) sulfide

19. Give chemical names for the following.
    (a) $NaClO_3$ (g) K_2CrO_4
    (b) $Ca_3(PO_4)_2$ (h) $Ca(CN)_2$
    (c) $NaMnO_4$ (i) $MnCl_2$
    (d) AlP (j) $NaNO_2$
    (e) ICl_3 (k) $Fe(NO_3)_2$
    (f) PCl_3

20. Why do we always write empirical formulas for ionic compounds?

21. Which of the following are binary substances: Al_2O_3, Cl_2, MgO, NO_2, $NaClO_4$?

22. A sample of a compound with a mass of 204 g consists of 1.00×10^{23} molecules. What is its molar mass?

23. Calculate the mass in grams of one formula unit of $K_4Fe(CN)_6$.

24. How many grams of copper(II) nitrate trihydrate, $Cu(NO_3)_2 \cdot 3H_2O$, are present in 0.118 mol of this compound?

25. A sample of 0.5866 g of nicotine was analyzed and found to consist of 0.4343 g C, 0.05103 g H, and 0.1013 g N. Calculate the percentage composition of nicotine.

26. A compound of potassium had the following percentage composition: K, 37.56%; H, 1.940%; P, 29.79%. The rest was oxygen. Calculate the empirical formula of this compound (arranging the atomic symbols in the order K H P O).

27. How many molecules of ethyl alcohol, C_2H_5OH, are in 1.00 fluid ounce of the liquid? The density of ethyl alcohol is 0.798 g/mL (1 oz = 29.6 mL).

28. What volume in liters is occupied by a sample of ethylene glycol, $C_2H_6O_2$, that consists of 5.00×10^{24} molecules. The density of ethylene glycol is 1.11 g/mL.

29. If 2.56 g of chlorine, Cl_2, will be used to prepare dichlorine heptoxide, how many moles and how many grams of molecular oxygen are needed?

30. Balance the following equations.
    (a) $Fe_2O_3 + HNO_3 \longrightarrow Fe(NO_3)_3 + H_2O$
    (b) $C_{21}H_{30}O_2 + O_2 \longrightarrow CO_2 + H_2O$

31. How many moles of nitric acid, HNO_3, are needed to react with 2.56 mol of Cu in the following reaction?

    $$3Cu + 8HNO_3 \longrightarrow 3Cu(NO_3)_2 + 2NO + 4H_2O$$

32. Under the right conditions, ammonia can be converted to nitrogen monoxide, NO, by the following reaction.

    $$4NH_3 + 5O_2 \longrightarrow 4NO + 6H_2O$$

    How many moles and how many grams of O_2 are needed to react with 56.8 g of ammonia by this reaction?

33. Dolomite is a mineral consisting of calcium carbonate and magnesium carbonate. When dolomite is strongly heated, its carbonates decompose to their oxides (CaO and MgO) and carbon dioxide is expelled.
    (a) Write separate equations for the decompositions of calcium carbonate and magnesium carbonate.
    (b) When a dolomite sample with a mass of 5.78 g was heated strongly, the residue had a mass of 3.02 g. Calculate the masses in grams and the percentages of calcium carbonate and magnesium carbonate in this sample of dolomite.

34. Adipic acid, $C_6H_{10}O_4$, is a raw material for making nylon, and it can be prepared in the laboratory by the following reaction between cyclohexene, C_6H_{10}, and sodium dichromate, $Na_2Cr_2O_7$, in sulfuric acid, H_2SO_4.

    $3C_6H_{10}(l) + 4Na_2Cr_2O_7(aq) + 16H_2SO_4\ (aq) \longrightarrow$
    $3C_6H_{10}O_4(s) + 4Cr_2(SO_4)_3\ (aq) + 4Na_2SO_4(aq) + 16H_2O$

    There are side reactions. These plus losses of product during its purification reduce the overall yield. A typical yield of purified adipic acid is 68.6%.

    (a) To prepare 12.5 g of adipic acid in 68.6% yield requires how many grams of cyclohexene?
    (b) The only available supply of sodium dichromate is its dihydrate, $Na_2Cr_2O_7 \cdot 2H_2O$. (Since the reaction occurs in an aqueous medium, the water in the dihydrate causes no problems, but it does contribute to the mass of what is taken of this reactant.) How many grams of this dihydrate are also required in the preparation of 12.5 g of adipic acid in a yield of 68.6%?

35. One of the ores of iron is hematite, Fe_2O_3, mixed with other rock. One sample of this ore is 31.4% hematite. How many tons of this ore are needed to make 1.00 ton of iron if the percentage recovery of iron from the ore is 91.5% (1 ton = 2000 lb)?

36. Gold occurs in the ocean in a range of concentration of 0.1 to 2 mg of gold per ton of seawater. Near one coastal city the gold concentration of the ocean is 1.5 mg/ton.
    (a) How many tons of seawater have to be processed to obtain 1.0 troy ounce of gold if the recovery is 65% successful? (The troy ounce, 31.1 g, is the standard "ounce" in the gold trade.)
    (b) If gold can be sold for $625.10 per troy ounce, what is the breakeven point in the dollar-cost per ton of processed seawater for extracting gold from the ocean at this location?

37. *C.I. Pigment Yellow 45* ("sideran yellow") is a pigment used in ceramics, glass, and enamel. When analyzed, a 2.164 g sample of this substance was found to contain 0.5259 g of Fe and 0.7345 g of Cr. The remainder was oxygen. Calculate the empirical formula of this pigment. What additional data are needed to calculate the molecular mass of this compound?

38. When 6.584 g of one of the hydrates of sodium sulfate was heated so as to drive off all of its water of hydration, the residue of anhydrous sodium sulfate had a mass of 2.889 g. What is the formula of the hydrate?

39. In an earlier problem we described the reaction of ammonia with oxygen to form nitrogen monoxide, NO.

    $$4NH_3 + 5O_2 \longrightarrow 4NO + 6H_2O$$

    How many moles and how many grams of NO could be formed from a mixture of 45.0 g of NH_3 and 58.0 g of O_2? How many grams of which reactant would remain unreacted?

40. A sample of 14.0 cm³ of aluminum, in powdered form, was mixed with an excess of iron(III) oxide. A reaction between them was initiated that formed aluminum oxide and metallic iron. How many cubic centimeters of metallic iron were formed?

4 REACTIONS OF IONS AND MOLECULES IN AQUEOUS SOLUTIONS

The ability of molecules and ions to come into intimate contact when a substance is dissolved in a liquid forms the basis for the chemical reaction that takes place when Alka-Seltzer tablets are dropped into a glass of water. In this chapter we explore a variety of types of chemical reactions that occur in aqueous solutions. *(Gusto Productions/ Photo Researchers, Inc.)*

CHAPTER OUTLINE

4.1 Special terminology applies to solutions

4.2 Ionic compounds conduct electricity when dissolved in water

4.3 Acids and bases are classes of compounds with special properties

4.4 Naming acids and bases follows a system

4.5 Ionic reactions can often be predicted

4.6 The composition of a solution is described by its concentration

4.7 Molarity is used for problems in solution stoichiometry

4.8 Chemical analysis and titration are applications of solution stoichiometry

Ionic compounds are common, and many of them are soluble in water where they break apart into individual ions. Examples of such solutions include seawater and the fluids that surround cells in our bodies. In this chapter our goal is to teach you what happens when ionic substances dissolve in water, the nature of the chemical reactions they undergo, and the products that form.

We will also introduce you to another important class of compounds called acids and bases. These are also common substances that include many household products as well as compounds found in all living creatures. In this chapter we will examine the kinds of substances that are acids and bases and their reactions in aqueous solutions.

In the laboratory, liquid solutions in general (and aqueous solutions in particular) serve as a medium for many chemical reactions. This is because, for a reaction to occur, the particles of the reactants must make physical contact. The particles need freedom of motion, which is made possible when all of the reactants are in one fluid phase. When possible, therefore, solutions of reactants are combined to give a fluid reaction mixture in which chemical changes can occur swiftly and smoothly. To deal quantitatively with such reactions, we will extend the principles of stoichiometry you learned in Chapter 3 to deal with chemical reactions in solution.

| 4.1 | SPECIAL TERMINOLOGY APPLIES TO SOLUTIONS |

Before we get to the meat of our subject, we first must define some terms. A **solution** is a homogeneous mixture in which the molecules or ions of the components freely intermingle. When a solution forms, at least two substances are involved. One is the *solvent* and all of the others are *solutes*. The **solvent** is the medium into which the solutes are mixed or dissolved. In this chapter we deal with *aqueous solutions*, so the solvent will be liquid water.[1] A **solute** is any substance dissolved in the solvent. It might be a gas, like the carbon dioxide dissolved in carbonated beverages. Some solutes are liquids, like ethylene glycol dissolved in water to protect a vehicle's radiator against freezing. Solids, of course, can be solutes, like the sugar dissolved in lemonade or the salt dissolved in seawater.

☐ When water is a component of a solution, it is usually considered to be the solvent even when it is present in small amounts.

To describe the composition of a solution, we often specify a **concentration,** which is the *ratio* of the amount of solute either to the amount of solvent or to the amount of solution. A **percentage concentration,** for example, is the number of grams of solute per 100 g of *solution*, a "solute-to-solution" ratio. Thus, the concentration of salt in seawater is often given as 3 g salt/100 g seawater.

The *relative* amounts of solute and solvent are often loosely given without specifying actual quantities. In a **dilute solution** the ratio of solute to solvent is small, for example, a few crystals of salt in a glass of water. In a **concentrated solution,** the ratio of solute to solvent is large. Syrup, for example, is a very concentrated solution of sugar in water.

Concentrated and dilute are relative terms. For example, a solution of 100 g of sugar in 100 mL of water is concentrated compared to one with just 10 g of sugar in 100 mL of water, but the latter solution is more concentrated than one that has 1 g of sugar in 100 mL of water.

Usually there is a limit to the amount of a solute that can dissolve in a given amount of solvent at a given temperature. When this limit is reached, we have a **saturated solution** and any excess solute that's added simply sits at the bottom of the solution. The **solubility** of a solute is the amount required to give a saturated solution, usually expressed as grams dissolved in 100 g of *solvent* at a given temperature. The temperature must be specified because solubilities vary with temperature. A solution having less solute than required for saturation is called an **unsaturated solution.** It is able to dissolve more solute.

In most cases, the solubility of a solute increases with temperature, so more solute can be dissolved by heating a saturated solution in the presence of excess solute. If the temperature of such a warm, saturated solution is subsequently lowered, the additional solute should separate from the solution, and indeed, this tends to happen spontaneously.

[1] Liquid water is a typical and very common solvent, but the solvent can actually be in any physical state, solid, liquid, or gas.

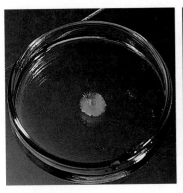

FIG. 4.1 **Crystallization.** When a small seed crystal of sodium acetate is added to a supersaturated solution of the compound, excess solute crystallizes rapidly until the solution is just saturated. The crystallization shown in this sequence took less than 10 seconds! *(Andy Washnik.)*

However, sometimes the solute doesn't separate, leaving us with a **supersaturated solution,** a solution that actually contains more solute than required for saturation. Supersaturated solutions are unstable and can only be prepared if there are no traces of undissolved solute. If even a tiny crystal of the solute is present or is added, the extra solute crystallizes (Figure 4.1). A solid that forms in a solution is called a **precipitate,** and a chemical reaction that produces a precipitate is called a **precipitation reaction.**

4.2 | IONIC COMPOUNDS CONDUCT ELECTRICITY WHEN DISSOLVED IN WATER

Water itself is a very poor electrical conductor because it consists of electrically neutral molecules that are unable to transport electrical charges. However, as we noted in Chapter 2, when an ionic compound dissolves in water the resulting solution conducts electricity well. This is illustrated in Figure 4.2*a* for a solution of copper sulfate, $CuSO_4$.

Solutes such as $CuSO_4$, which yield electrically conducting aqueous solutions, are called **electrolytes.** Their ability to conduct electricity suggests the presence of electrically charged particles that are able to move through the solution. The generally accepted reason is that when an ionic compound dissolves in water, the ions separate from each other and enter the solution as more or less independent particles that are surrounded by molecules of the solvent. This change is called the **dissociation** of the ionic compound, and is

☐ Solutions of electrolytes conduct electricity in a way that's different from metals. This is discussed more completely in Chapter 19.

(a)   *(b)*

FIG. 4.2 **Electrical conductivity of solutions of electrolytes versus nonelectrolytes.** *(a)* The copper sulfate solution is a strong conductor of electricity, and $CuSO_4$ is a strong electrolyte. *(b)* Neither sugar nor water is an electrolyte, and this sugar solution is a nonconductor. *(Michael Watson.)*

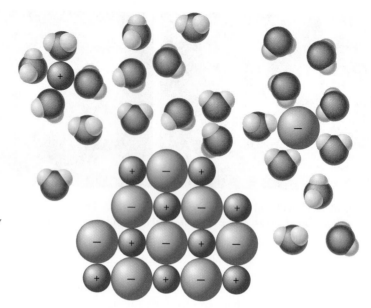

FIG. 4.3 Dissociation of an ionic compound as it dissolves in water. Ions separate from the solid and become surrounded by molecules of water. The ions are said to be hydrated. In the solution, the ions are able to move freely and the solution is able to conduct electricity.

illustrated in Figure 4.3. In general, *we will assume that in water the dissociation of any salt (i.e., ionic compound) is complete* and that the solution contains no undissociated formula units of the salt. Thus, an aqueous solution of $CuSO_4$ is really a solution that contains Cu^{2+} and SO_4^{2-} ions, with virtually no undissociated formula units of $CuSO_4$. Because these solutions contain so many ions, they are strong conductors of electricity, and salts are said to be **strong electrolytes.**

☐ Keep in mind that a strong electrolyte is 100% dissociated in an aqueous solution.

Many ionic compounds have low solubilities in water. An example is AgBr, the light sensitive compound in most photographic film. Although only a tiny amount of this compound dissolves in water, all of it that does dissolve is completely dissociated. However, because of the extremely low solubility, the number of ions in the solution is extremely small and the solution doesn't conduct electricity well. Nevertheless, it is still convenient to think of AgBr as a strong electrolyte because it serves to remind us that salts are completely dissociated in aqueous solution.

☐ Ethylene glycol, $C_2H_4(OH)_2$, is a type of alcohol. Other alcohols, such as ethanol and methanol, are also nonelectrolytes.

Aqueous solutions of most molecular compounds do not conduct electricity, and such solutes are called **nonelectrolytes.** Examples are sugar (Figure 4.2*b*) and ethylene glycol (the solute in antifreeze solutions). Both consist of uncharged molecules that stay intact and simply intermingle with water molecules when they dissolve.

Equations for dissociation reactions show the ions

A convenient way to describe the dissociation of an ionic compound is with a chemical equation. Thus, for the dissociation of calcium chloride in water we write

$$CaCl_2(s) \longrightarrow Ca^{2+}(aq) + 2Cl^-(aq)$$

We use the symbol *aq* after a charged particle to mean that it is surrounded by water molecules in the solution. We say it is **hydrated.** By writing the formulas of the ions separately, we mean that they are essentially independent of each other in the solution. Notice that each formula unit of $CaCl_2(s)$ releases three ions, one $Ca^{2+}(aq)$ and two $Cl^-(aq)$.

Often, when the context is clear that the system is aqueous, the symbols (*s*) and (*aq*) are omitted. They are "understood." You should not be disturbed, therefore, when you see an equation such as

$$CaCl_2 \longrightarrow Ca^{2+} + 2Cl^-$$

☐ Be sure you know the formulas and charges on the polyatomic ions listed in Table 2.8 on page 69.

Polyatomic ions generally remain intact as dissociation occurs. When copper sulfate dissolves, for example, both Cu^{2+} and SO_4^{2-} ions are released.

$$CuSO_4(s) \longrightarrow Cu^{2+}(aq) + SO_4^{2-}(aq)$$

EXAMPLE 4.1
Writing the Equation for the
Dissociation of an Ionic Compound

Ammonium sulfate is used as a fertilizer to supply nitrogen to crops. Write the equation for the dissociation of this compound when it dissolves in water.

ANALYSIS: To write the equation correctly, we need to know the formulas of the ions that make up the compound. In this case, the cation is NH_4^+ (ammonium ion) and the anion is SO_4^{2-} (sulfate ion). The correct formula of the compound is therefore $(NH_4)_2SO_4$, which means there are *two* NH_4^+ ions for each SO_4^{2-} ion. We have to be sure to indicate this in the equation.

SOLUTION: We write the formula for the solid on the left of the equation and indicate its state by (s). The ions are written on the right side of the equation and are shown to be in aqueous solution by the symbol (aq) following their formulas.

$$(NH_4)_2SO_4(s) \longrightarrow 2NH_4^+(aq) + SO_4^{2-}(aq)$$

The subscript 2 becomes the coefficient for NH_4^+.

IS THE ANSWER REASONABLE? There are two things to check when writing equations such as this. First, be sure you have the correct formulas for the ions, including their charges. Second, be sure you've indicated the number of ions of each kind that comes from one formula unit when the compound dissociates. Performing these checks here confirms we've solved the problem correctly.

Practice Exercise 1: Write equations that show the dissociation of the following compounds in water: (a) $FeCl_3$ and (b) potassium phosphate. (Hint: Identify the ions present in each compound.)

Practice Exercise 2: Write equations that show what happens when the following solid ionic compounds dissolve in water: (a) $MgCl_2$, (b) $Al(NO_3)_3$, and (c) sodium carbonate.

Equations for ionic reactions can be written in different ways

Often, ionic compounds react with each other when their aqueous solutions are combined. For example, when solutions of lead nitrate, $Pb(NO_3)_2$, and potassium iodide, KI, are mixed, a bright yellow precipitate of lead iodide, PbI_2, forms (Figure 4.4). The chemical equation for the reaction is

$$Pb(NO_3)_2(aq) + 2KI(aq) \longrightarrow PbI_2(s) + 2KNO_3(aq) \qquad (4.1)$$

where we have noted the insolubility of PbI_2 by writing (s) following its formula. This is called a **molecular equation** because all the formulas are written with the ions together, as if the substances in solution consist of neutral "molecules." Equation 4.1 is fine for performing stoichiometric calculations, but let's look at other ways that we might write the chemical equation.

Soluble ionic compounds are fully dissociated in solution, so $Pb(NO_3)_2$, KI, and KNO_3 are not present in the solution as intact units or "molecules." To show this, we can write the formulas of all soluble strong electrolytes in "dissociated" form to give the **ionic equation** for the reaction.

$$Pb(NO_3)_2(aq) \quad + \quad 2KI(aq) \quad \longrightarrow \quad PbI_2(s) + 2KNO_3(aq)$$

$$Pb^{2+}(aq) + 2NO_3^-(aq) + 2K^+(aq) + 2I^-(aq) \longrightarrow PbI_2(s) + 2K^+(aq) + 2NO_3^-(aq)$$

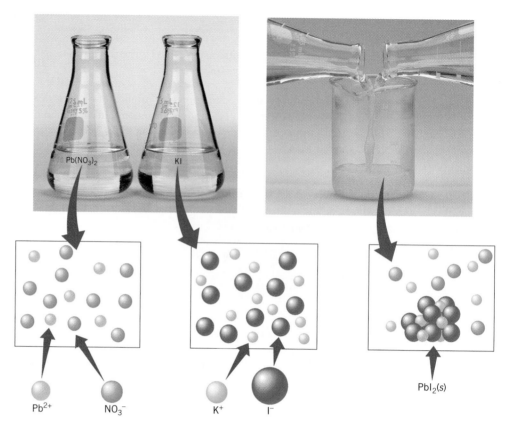

FIG. 4.4 **The reaction of $Pb(NO_3)_2$ with KI.** On the left are flasks containing solutions of lead nitrate and potassium iodide. These solutes exist as separated ions in their respective solutions. On the right, we observe that when the solutions of the ions are combined, there is an immediate reaction as the Pb^{2+} ions join with the I^- ions to give a precipitate of small crystals of solid, yellow PbI_2. The reaction is so rapid that the yellow color develops where the two streams of liquid come together. If the $Pb(NO_3)_2$ and KI are combined in a 1-to-2 mole ratio, the solution would now contain only K^+ and NO_3^- ions (the ions of KNO_3). *(Andy Washnik.)*

Notice that we have *not* separated PbI_2 into its ions in this equation. This is because PbI_2 has an extremely low solubility in water; it is essentially insoluble. When the Pb^{2+} and I^- ions meet in the solution, insoluble PbI_2 forms and separates as a precipitate. Therefore, after the reaction is over, the Pb^{2+} and I^- ions are no longer able to move independently. They are trapped in the insoluble product.

The ionic equation gives a clearer picture of what is actually going on in the solution during the reaction. The Pb^{2+} and I^- ions come together to form the product, while the other ions, K^+ and NO_3^-, are unchanged by the reaction. *Ions that do not actually take part in a reaction are sometimes called* **spectator ions;** in a sense, they just "stand by and watch the action."

To emphasize the actual reaction that occurs, we can write the **net ionic equation,** *which is obtained by eliminating spectator ions from the ionic equation.* Let's cross out the spectator ions, K^+ and NO_3^-.

$$Pb^{2+}(aq) \,+\, \cancel{2NO_3^-(aq)} \,+\, \cancel{2K^+(aq)} \,+\, 2I^-(aq) \longrightarrow$$
$$PbI_2(s) \,+\, \cancel{2K^+(aq)} \,+\, \cancel{2NO_3^-(aq)}$$

What remains is the net ionic equation,

$$Pb^{2+}(aq) \,+\, 2I^-(aq) \longrightarrow PbI_2(s)$$

Notice how it calls our attention to the ions that are actually participating in the reaction as well as the change that occurs.

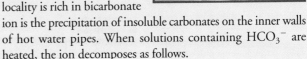

FACETS OF CHEMISTRY   4.1

Boiler Scale and Hard Water

Precipitation reactions occur around us all the time and we hardly ever take notice until they cause a problem. One common problem is caused by **hard water**—groundwater that contains the "hardness ions," Ca^{2+}, Mg^{2+}, Fe^{2+}, or Fe^{3+}, in concentrations high enough to form precipitates with ordinary soap. Soap normally consists of the sodium salts of organic acids derived from animal fats or oils (so-called *fatty acids*). An example is sodium stearate, $NaC_{18}H_{35}O_2$. The negative ion of the soap forms an insoluble "scum" with hardness ions, which reduces the effectiveness of the soap for removing dirt and grease.

Hardness ions can be removed from water in a number of ways. One way is to add hydrated sodium carbonate, $Na_2CO_3 \cdot 10H_2O$, often called washing soda, to the water. The carbonate ion forms insoluble precipitates with the hardness ions; an example is $CaCO_3$.

$$Ca^{2+}(aq) + CO_3^{2-}(aq) \longrightarrow CaCO_3(s)$$

Once precipitated, the hardness ions are not available to interfere with the soap.

Another problem when the hard water of a particular locality is rich in bicarbonate ion is the precipitation of insoluble carbonates on the inner walls of hot water pipes. When solutions containing HCO_3^- are heated, the ion decomposes as follows.

$$2HCO_3^-(aq) \longrightarrow H_2O + CO_2(g) + CO_3^{2-}(aq)$$

Like most gases, carbon dioxide becomes less soluble as the temperature is raised, so CO_2 is driven from the hot solution and the HCO_3^- is gradually converted to CO_3^{2-}. As the carbonate ions form, they are able to precipitate the hardness ions. This precipitate, which sticks to the inner walls of pipes and hot water boilers, is called *boiler scale*. In locations that have high concentrations of Ca^{2+} and HCO_3^- in the water supply, boiler scale is a very serious problem, as illustrated in the accompanying photograph.

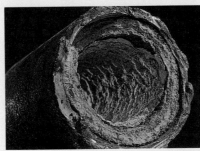

Boiler scale built up on the inside of a water pipe. *(Courtesy of Betz Company.)*

The net ionic equation is especially useful because it permits us to *generalize*. It tells us that if we combine *any* solution that contains Pb^{2+} with *any* other solution that contains I^-, we ought to expect a precipitate of PbI_2. And this is exactly what happens if we mix aqueous solutions of lead acetate, $Pb(C_2H_3O_2)_2$, and sodium iodide, NaI. A yellow precipitate of PbI_2 forms immediately (Figure 4.5). Example 4.2 demonstrates how we construct the molecular, ionic, and net ionic equations for the reaction.

FIG. 4.5 Another reaction that forms lead iodide. The net ionic equation tells us that any soluble lead compound will react with any soluble iodide compound to give lead iodide. This prediction is borne out here as a precipitate of lead iodide is formed when a solution of sodium iodide is added to a solution of lead acetate. *(Andy Washnik.)*

EXAMPLE 4.2
Writing Molecular, Ionic, and Net Ionic Equations

Write the molecular, ionic, and net ionic equations for the reaction of aqueous solutions of lead acetate and sodium iodide, which yields a precipitate of lead iodide and leaves the compound sodium acetate in solution.

ANALYSIS: To write a chemical equation, we must begin with the correct formulas of the reactants and products. If only the names of the reactants and products are given, we have to translate them into chemical formulas. Following the rules we discussed in Chapter 2, we have

☐ If necessary, review Section 2.9, which discusses naming ionic compounds.

Reactants		*Products*	
lead acetate	$Pb(C_2H_3O_2)_2$	lead iodide	PbI_2
sodium iodide	NaI	sodium acetate	$NaC_2H_3O_2$

We arrange the formulas to form the molecular equation, which we then balance. To obtain the ionic equation, we write soluble ionic compounds in dissociated form and the formula of the precipitate in "molecular" form. Finally, we look for spectator ions and eliminate them from the ionic equation to obtain the net ionic equation.

SOLUTION:

The Molecular Equation We assemble the chemical formulas into the molecular equation.

$$Pb(C_2H_3O_2)_2(aq) + 2NaI(aq) \longrightarrow PbI_2(s) + 2NaC_2H_3O_2(aq)$$

Notice that we've indicated which substances are in solution and which is a precipitate, and we've balanced the equation. This is the *balanced molecular equation*.

The Ionic Equation To write the ionic equation, we write the formulas of all soluble salts in dissociated form and the formulas of precipitates in "molecular" form. We are careful to use the subscripts and coefficients in the molecular equation to properly obtain the coefficients of the ions in the ionic equation.

$$Pb(C_2H_3O_2)_2(aq) \qquad 2NaI(aq) \qquad 2NaC_2H_3O_2(aq)$$

$$Pb^{2+}(aq) + 2C_2H_3O_2^-(aq) + 2Na^+(aq) + 2I^-(aq) \longrightarrow PbI_2(s) + 2Na^+(aq) + 2C_2H_3O_2^-(aq)$$

This is the *balanced ionic equation*. Notice that to properly write the ionic equation it is necessary to know both the formulas and charges of the ions.

The Net Ionic Equation We obtain the net ionic equation from the ionic equation by eliminating spectator ions, which are Na^+ and $C_2H_3O_2^-$ (they're the same on both sides of the arrow). Let's cross them out.

$$Pb^{2+}(aq) + 2C_2H_3O_2^-(aq) + 2Na^+(aq) + 2I^-(aq) \longrightarrow$$
$$PbI_2(s) + 2Na^+(aq) + 2C_2H_3O_2^-(aq)$$

What's left is the *net ionic equation*.

$$Pb^{2+}(aq) + 2I^-(aq) \longrightarrow PbI_2(s)$$

Notice this is the same net ionic equation as in the reaction of lead nitrate with potassium iodide.

ARE THE ANSWERS REASONABLE? When you look back over a problem such as this, things to ask yourself are (1) "Have I written the correct formulas for the reactants and products?", (2) "Is the molecular equation balanced correctly?", (3) "Have I divided the soluble ionic compounds into their ions correctly, being careful to properly apply the subscripts of the ions and the coefficients in the molecular equation?", and (4) "Have I identified and eliminated the correct ions from the ionic equation to obtain the net ionic equation?" If each of these questions can be answered in the affirmative, as they can here, the problem has been solved correctly.

Practice Exercise 3: When solutions of $(NH_4)_2SO_4$ and $Ba(NO_3)_2$ are mixed, a precipitate of $BaSO_4$ forms, leaving soluble NH_4NO_3 in the solution. Write the molecular, ionic, and net ionic equations for the reaction. (Hint: Remember that polyatomic ions do not break apart when ionic compounds dissolve in water.)

Practice Exercise 4: Write molecular, ionic, and net ionic equations for the reaction of aqueous solutions of cadmium chloride and sodium sulfide to give a precipitate of cadmium sulfide and a solution of sodium chloride.

FIG. 4.6 **An acid–base indicator.** Litmus paper, a strip of paper impregnated with the dye litmus, becomes blue in aqueous ammonia (a base) and pink in lemon juice (which contains citric acid). *(Ken Karp.)*

In a balanced ionic or net ionic equation, both atoms and charge must balance

In the ionic and net ionic equations we've written, not only are the atoms in balance, but so is the net electrical charge, which is the same on both sides of the equation. Thus, in the ionic equation for the reaction of lead nitrate with potassium iodide, the sum of the charges of the ions on the left (Pb^{2+}, $2NO_3^-$, $2K^+$, and $2I^-$) is zero, which matches the sum of the charges on all of the formulas of the products (PbI_2, $2K^+$, and $2NO_3^-$).[2] In the net ionic equation the charges on both sides are also the same: on the left we have Pb^{2+} and $2I^-$, with a net charge of zero, and on the right we have PbI_2, also with a charge of zero. We now have an additional requirement for an ionic equation or net ionic equation to be balanced: *the net electrical charge on both sides of the equation must be the same.*

Criteria for Balanced Ionic and Net Ionic Equations

1. **Material balance.** There must be the same number of atoms of each kind on both sides of the arrow.
2. **Electrical balance.** The *net* electrical charge on the left must equal the *net* electrical charge on the right (although this charge does not necessarily have to be zero).

TOOLS
Criteria for a balanced ionic equation

4.3 ACIDS AND BASES ARE CLASSES OF COMPOUNDS WITH SPECIAL PROPERTIES

Acids and bases constitute a class of compounds that include some of our most familiar chemicals and important laboratory reagents. Vinegar, lemon juice, and the liquid in an automobile battery contain acids. The white crystals of lye in some drain cleaners, the white substance that makes milk of magnesia opaque, and household ammonia are all bases.

There are some general properties that are common to aqueous solutions of acids and bases. For example, **acids** generally have a tart (sour) taste, whereas **bases** have a somewhat bitter taste and have a soapy "feel." (However, taste is *never* used as a laboratory test for acids or bases; some are extremely corrosive to animal tissue. *Never taste chemicals in the laboratory!*)

Acids and bases also affect the colors of certain dyes we call **acid–base indicators.** An example is litmus (Figure 4.6), which has a pink or red color in an acidic solution and a blue color in a basic solution.[3]

One of the most important properties of acids and bases is their reaction with each other, a reaction referred to as **neutralization.** For example, when solutions of hydrochloric acid, $HCl(aq)$, and the base sodium hydroxide, $NaOH(aq)$, are mixed the following reaction occurs.

$$HCl(aq) + NaOH(aq) \longrightarrow NaCl(aq) + H_2O$$

□ Acids and bases should be treated with respect because of their potential for causing bodily injury if spilled on the skin. If you spill an acid or base on yourself in the lab, be sure to wash it off immediately and notify your instructor at once.

---

[2] There is no charge written for the formula of a compound such as PbI_2, so as we add up charges, we take the charge on PbI_2 to be zero.

[3] Litmus paper, commonly found among the items in a locker in the general chemistry lab, consists of strips of absorbent paper that have been soaked in a solution of litmus and dried. Red litmus paper is used to test if a solution is basic. A basic solution turns red litmus blue. To test if the solution is acidic, blue litmus paper is used. Acidic solutions turn blue litmus red.

When the reactants are combined in a 1-to-1 ratio by moles, the acidic and basic properties of the solutes disappear and the resulting solution is neither acidic nor basic. We say an *acid–base neutralization* has occurred. Svante Arrhenius,[4] a Swedish chemist, was the first to suggest that an acid–base neutralization is simply the combination of a hydrogen ion with a hydroxide ion to produce a water molecule, thus making H^+ ions and OH^- ions disappear.

Today we know that in aqueous solutions hydrogen ions, H^+, attach themselves to water molecules to form **hydronium ions,** H_3O^+. However, for the sake of convenience, we often use the term *hydrogen ion* as a substitute for *hydronium ion*, and in many equations, we use $H^+(aq)$ to stand for $H_3O^+(aq)$. In fact, whenever you see the symbol $H^+(aq)$, you should realize that we are actually referring to $H_3O^+(aq)$.

For most purposes, we find that the following modified versions of Arrhenius' definitions work satisfactorily when we deal with aqueous solutions.

□ Even the formula H_3O^+ is something of a simplification. In water the H^+ ion is associated with more than one molecule of water, but we use the formula H_3O^+ as a simple representation.

Arrhenius Definition of Acids and Bases

An **acid** is a substance that reacts with water to produce hydronium ion, H_3O^+.

A **base** is a substance that produces hydroxide ion in water.

In general, the reaction of an acid with a base produces an ionic compound as one of the products. In the reaction of $HCl(aq)$ with $NaOH(aq)$, the compound is sodium chloride, or salt. This reaction is so general, in fact, that *we use the word* **salt** *to mean any ionic compound that doesn't contain either hydroxide ion, OH^-, or oxide ion, O^{2-}*. (Ionic compounds that contain OH^- or O^{2-} are bases, as described below.)

In aqueous solutions, acids give H_3O^+

In general, **acids** are molecular substances that react with water to produce ions, one of which is the hydronium ion, H_3O^+. Thus, when gaseous molecular HCl dissolves in water, a hydrogen ion (H^+) transfers from the HCl molecule to a water molecule. The reaction is depicted in Figure 4.7 using space-filling models, and is represented by the chemical equation

$$HCl(g) + H_2O \longrightarrow H_3O^+(aq) + Cl^-(aq)$$

This is an **ionization reaction** because ions form where none existed before. Because the solution contains ions, it conducts electricity, so acids are electrolytes.

Sometimes acids also contain hydrogen atoms that are not able to form H_3O^+. An example is acetic acid, $HC_2H_3O_2$, the acid that gives vinegar its sour taste. This acid reacts with water as follows.

$$HC_2H_3O_2(aq) + H_2O \longrightarrow H_3O^+(aq) + C_2H_3O_2^-(aq)$$

□ If gaseous HCl is cooled to about $-85\ °C$, it condenses to a liquid that doesn't conduct electricity. No ions are present in pure liquid HCl.

HCl H_2O Cl^- H_3O^+

FIG. 4.7 **Ionization of HCl in water.** Collisions between HCl molecules and water molecules lead to a transfer of H^+ from HCl to H_2O, giving Cl^- and H_3O^+ as products.

---

[4] Arrhenius proposed his theory of acids and bases in 1884 in his Ph.D. thesis. He won the Nobel Prize in Chemistry for his work in 1903.

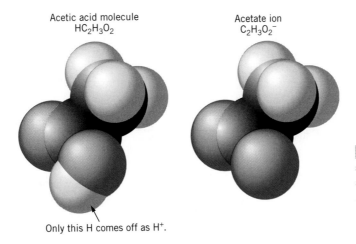

Acetic acid molecule
$HC_2H_3O_2$

Acetate ion
$C_2H_3O_2^-$

Only this H comes off as H^+.

FIG. 4.8 **Acetic acid and acetate ion.** The structures of acetic acid and acetate ion are illustrated here. In acetic acid, only the hydrogen attached to an oxygen can come off as H^+.

Notice that only the hydrogen written first in the formula is able to transfer to H_2O to give hydronium ions. The structures of the acetic acid molecule and the acetate ion are shown in Figure 4.8, with the hydrogen that can be lost by the acetic acid molecule indicated.

As noted earlier, the "active ingredient" in the hydronium ion is H^+, which is why $H^+(aq)$ is often used in place of $H_3O^+(aq)$ in equations. Using this simplification, the ionization of HCl and $HC_2H_3O_2$ in water can be represented as

$$HCl(g) \xrightarrow{H_2O} H^+(aq) + Cl^-(aq)$$

and

$$HC_2H_3O_2(aq) \xrightarrow{H_2O} H^+(aq) + C_2H_3O_2^-(aq)$$

In the ionization reactions of HCl and $HC_2H_3O_2$, an anion is formed when the acid transfers an H^+ to the water molecule. If we represent the acid molecule by the general formula HA, we might represent the ionization of an acid in general terms by the equation

$$HA + H_2O \longrightarrow H_3O^+ + A^- \tag{4.2}$$

> ☐ Hydrogens that are able to be transferred to water molecules to form hydronium ions are usually written first in the formula for the acid.

TOOLS
Ionization of an acid in water

The molecules HCl and $HC_2H_3O_2$ are said to be **monoprotic acids** because they are capable of furnishing only *one* H^+ per molecule of acid. **Polyprotic acids** can furnish more than one H^+ per molecule. They undergo reactions similar to those of HCl and $HC_2H_3O_2$, except that the loss of H^+ by the acid occurs in two or more steps. Thus, the ionization of sulfuric acid, a **diprotic acid,** takes place by two successive steps.

$$H_2SO_4(aq) + H_2O \longrightarrow H_3O^+(aq) + HSO_4^-(aq)$$

$$HSO_4^-(aq) + H_2O \longrightarrow H_3O^+(aq) + SO_4^{2-}(aq)$$

Triprotic acids ionize in three steps, as illustrated in Example 4.3.

EXAMPLE 4.3
Writing Equations for Ionization Reactions of Acids

Phosphoric acid, H_3PO_4, is a triprotic acid found in some soft drinks such as Coca-Cola where it adds a touch of tartness to the beverage. Write equations for its stepwise ionization in water.

ANALYSIS: We are told that H_3PO_4 is a triprotic acid, which is also indicated by the three hydrogens at the beginning of the formula. Because there are three hydrogens to come off the molecule, we expect there to be three steps in the ionization. Each step removes one H^+, and we can use that knowledge to deduce the formulas of the products. Let's line them up so we can see the progression.

$$H_3PO_4 \xrightarrow{-H^+} H_2PO_4^- \xrightarrow{-H^+} HPO_4^{2-} \xrightarrow{-H^+} PO_4^{3-}$$

Notice that loss of H^+ decreases the number of hydrogens by one and increases the negative charge by one unit. Also, the product of one step serves as the reactant in the next step. We'll use Equation 4.2 for the ionization of an acid as a tool in writing the chemical equation for each step.

SOLUTION: The first step is the reaction of H_3PO_4 with water to give H_3O^+ and $H_2PO_4^-$.

$$H_3PO_4(aq) + H_2O \longrightarrow H_3O^+(aq) + H_2PO_4^-(aq)$$

The second and third steps are similar to the first.

$$H_2PO_4^-(aq) + H_2O \longrightarrow H_3O^+(aq) + HPO_4^{2-}(aq)$$
$$HPO_4^{2-}(aq) + H_2O \longrightarrow H_3O^+(aq) + PO_4^{3-}(aq)$$

IS THE ANSWER REASONABLE? Check to see whether the equations are balanced in terms of atoms and charge. If any mistakes were made, something would be out of balance and we would discover the error. In this case, all the equations are balanced, so we can feel confident we've written them correctly.

Practice Exercise 5: Write the equation for the ionization of $HCHO_2$ (formic acid) in water. Formic acid is used industrially to remove hair from animal skins prior to tanning. (Hint: Formic acid and acetic acid are both examples of organic acids.)

Practice Exercise 6: Write equations for the stepwise ionization in water of citric acid, $H_3C_6H_5O_7$, the acid in citrus fruits.

Nonmetal oxides can be acids

The acids we've discussed so far have been molecules containing hydrogen atoms that can be transferred to water molecules. Nonmetal oxides form another class of compounds that yield acidic solutions in water. Examples are SO_3, CO_2, and N_2O_5 whose aqueous solutions contain H_3O^+ and turn litmus red. These oxides are called **acidic anhydrides,** where *anhydride* means "without water." They react with water to form molecular acids containing hydrogen, which are then able to undergo reaction with water to yield H_3O^+.

$$SO_3(g) + H_2O \longrightarrow H_2SO_4(aq) \qquad \text{sulfuric acid}$$
$$N_2O_5(g) + H_2O \longrightarrow 2HNO_3(aq) \qquad \text{nitric acid}$$
$$CO_2(g) + H_2O \longrightarrow H_2CO_3(aq) \qquad \text{carbonic acid}$$

Although carbonic acid is too unstable to be isolated as a pure compound, its solutions in water are quite common. Carbon dioxide from the atmosphere dissolves in rainwater and the waters of lakes and streams where it exists partly as carbonic acid and its ions (HCO_3^- and CO_3^{2-}). This makes these waters naturally slightly acidic. Carbonic acid is also present in carbonated beverages.

Not all nonmetal oxides are acidic anhydrides, only those that are able to react with water. For example, carbon monoxide doesn't react with water, so its solutions in water are not acidic; carbon monoxide, therefore, is not classified as an acidic anhydride.

Bases are substances that give OH^- in water

Bases fall into two categories: ionic compounds that contain OH^- or O^{2-}, and molecular compounds that react with water to give hydroxide ions. Because solutions of bases contain ions, they conduct electricity. Therefore, bases are electrolytes.

Ionic bases are metal hydroxides and oxides

Ionic bases include metal hydroxides, such as NaOH and $Ca(OH)_2$. When dissolved in water, they dissociate just like other soluble ionic compounds.

$$NaOH(s) \longrightarrow Na^+(aq) + OH^-(aq)$$

$$Ca(OH)_2(s) \longrightarrow Ca^{2+}(aq) + 2OH^-(aq)$$

Soluble metal oxides are **basic anhydrides** because they react with water to form the hydroxide ion as one of the products. Calcium oxide is typical.

$$CaO(s) + H_2O \longrightarrow Ca(OH)_2(aq)$$

This reaction occurs when water is added to dry cement or concrete because calcium oxide or "quicklime" is an ingredient in those materials. In this case it is the oxide ion, O^{2-}, that actually forms the OH^-.

$$O^{2-} + H_2O \longrightarrow 2OH^-$$

◻ Continual contact of your hands with fresh Portland cement can lead to irritation because the mixture is quite basic.

Even insoluble metal hydroxides and oxides are basic because they are able to neutralize acids. We will study these reactions in Section 4.5.

Many nitrogen compounds are molecular bases

The most common molecular base is the gas ammonia, NH_3, which dissolves in water and reacts to give a basic solution by an ionization reaction.

$$NH_3(aq) + H_2O \longrightarrow NH_4^+(aq) + OH^-(aq)$$

Organic compounds called amines, in which fragments of hydrocarbons are attached to nitrogen in place of hydrogen, are similar to ammonia in their behavior toward water. An example is methylamine, CH_3NH_2, in which a **methyl group,** CH_3, replaces a hydrogen in ammonia.

$$CH_3NH_2(aq) + H_2O \longrightarrow CH_3NH_3^+(aq) + OH^-(aq)$$

The hydrogen taken from the H_2O molecule becomes attached to the nitrogen atom of the amine. This is how nitrogen-containing bases behave, which is why we've included the H^+ with the other two hydrogens on the nitrogen.

Notice that when a molecular base reacts with water, an H^+ is lost by the water molecule and gained by the base. (See Figure 4.9.) One product is a cation that has one more H and one more positive charge than the reactant base. Loss of H^+ by the water gives the other product, the OH^- ion, which is why the solution is basic. We might represent this by the general equation

$$base + H_2O \longrightarrow baseH^+ + OH^-$$

If we signify the base by the symbol B, this becomes

$$B + H_2O \longrightarrow BH^+ + OH^- \tag{4.3}$$

TOOLS
Ionization of a base in water

FIG. 4.9 **Ionization of ammonia in water.** Collisions between NH_3 molecules and water molecules lead to a transfer of H^+ from H_2O to NH_3, giving NH_4^+ and OH^- ions.

NH₃   H₂O   NH₄⁺   OH⁻

EXAMPLE 4.4
Writing the Equation
for the Ionization of a Base

Dimethylamine, $(CH_3)_2NH$, is used as an attractant for boll weevils so they can be destroyed. This insect has caused more than a $14 billion loss to the yield of cotton in the United States since it arrived from Mexico in 1892. The compound is a base in water. Write an equation for its ionization.

ANALYSIS: The reactants in the equation are $(CH_3)_2NH$ and H_2O. To write the equation, we need to know the formulas of the products. We've been told that $(CH_3)_2NH$ is a base, so Equation 4.3 is the tool we will use to write the chemical equation.

SOLUTION: When a base reacts with water, it takes an H^+ from H_2O, leaving OH^- behind. Therefore, when an H^+ is picked up by $(CH_3)_2NH$, the product will be $(CH_3)_2NH_2^+$. The equation for the reaction is

$$(CH_3)_2NH(aq) + H_2O \longrightarrow (CH_3)_2NH_2^+(aq) + OH^-(aq)$$

IS THE ANSWER REASONABLE? Compare the equation we've written with the general equation for reaction of a base with water. Notice that the formula for the product has one more H and a positive charge, and that the H^+ has been added to the nitrogen. Also, notice that the water has become OH^- when it loses H^+. The equation is therefore correct.

Practice Exercise 7: Triethylamine, $(C_2H_5)_3N$, is a base in water. Write an equation for its reaction with the solvent. (Hint: How do nitrogen-containing bases react toward water?)

Practice Exercise 8: Hydroxylamine, $HONH_2$, is a base in water. Write an equation for its reaction with the solvent.

Acids and bases are classified as strong or weak

Ionic compounds such as NaCl and $CaCl_2$ break up essentially 100% into ions in water. No "molecules" of either NaCl or $CaCl_2$ are detectable in their aqueous solutions. Because these solutions contain so many ions, they are strong conductors of electricity, so ionic compounds are said to be **strong electrolytes.**

□ All strong acids are strong electrolytes.

Hydrochloric acid is also a strong electrolyte. Its ionization in water is essentially complete; its solutions are strongly acidic, and it is said to be a *strong acid*. In general, *acids that are strong electrolytes are called* **strong acids.** There are relatively few strong acids; the most common ones are listed below.

TOOLS
List of strong acids

Strong Acids

$HClO_4(aq)$	perchloric acid
$HCl(aq)$	hydrochloric acid
$HBr(aq)$	hydrobromic acid
$HI(aq)$	hydroiodic acid[5]
$HNO_3(aq)$	nitric acid
$H_2SO_4(aq)$	sulfuric acid

Metal hydroxides are ionic compounds, so they are also strong electrolytes. Those that are soluble are the hydroxides of Group IA and the hydroxides of calcium, strontium, and barium of Group IIA. Solutions of these compounds are strongly basic, so these substances are considered to be **strong bases.** The hydroxides of other metals have very low solubilities in water. They are strong electrolytes in the sense that the small amounts of them that dissolve in solution are completely dissociated. However, because of their low solubility in water, their solutions are very weakly basic.

[5] Sometimes the first "o" in the name of $HI(aq)$ is dropped for ease of pronunciation to give *hydriodic acid.*

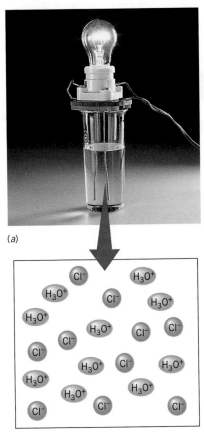

(a)

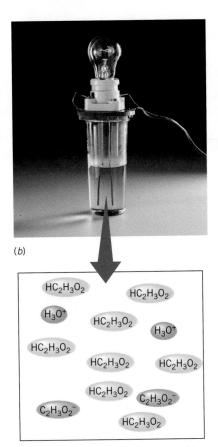

(b)

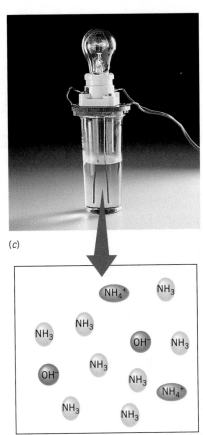

(c)

All the HCl is ionized in the solution, so there are many ions present.

Only a small fraction of the acetic acid is ionized, so there are few ions to conduct electricity. Most of the acetic acid is present as neutral molecules of $HC_2H_3O_2$.

Only a small fraction of the ammonia is ionized, so few ions are present to conduct electricity. Most of the ammonia is present as neutral molecules of NH_3.

FIG. 4.10 Electrical conductivity of solutions of strong and weak acids and bases at equal concentrations. *(a)* HCl is 100% ionized and is a strong conductor, enabling the light to glow brightly. *(b)* $HC_2H_3O_2$ is a weaker conductor than HCl because the extent of its ionization is far less, so the light is dimmer. *(c)* NH_3 also is a weaker conductor than HCl because the extent of its ionization is low, and the light remains dim. *(Michael Watson.)*

Weak acids and bases are weak electrolytes

Most acids are not completely ionized in water. For instance, a solution of acetic acid, $HC_2H_3O_2$, is a relatively poor conductor of electricity compared to a solution of HCl with the same concentration (Figure 4.10), so acetic acid is classified as a **weak electrolyte** and is a **weak acid.**

The reason an acetic acid solution is a poor conductor is because in the solution only a small fraction of the acid exists as H_3O^+ and $C_2H_3O_2^-$ ions. The rest is present as molecules of $HC_2H_3O_2$. This is because $C_2H_3O_2^-$ ions have a strong tendency to react with H_3O^+ when the ions meet in the solution. As a result, there are two opposing reactions occurring simultaneously (Figure 4.11). One involves the formation of the ions,

$$HC_2H_3O_2(aq) + H_2O \longrightarrow H_3O^+(aq) + C_2H_3O_2^-(aq)$$

and the other removes ions

$$H_3O^+(aq) + C_2H_3O_2^-(aq) \longrightarrow HC_2H_3O_2(aq) + H_2O$$

A balance is reached when ions form and disappear at the same rate, and for acetic acid this happens when only a small percentage of the $HC_2H_3O_2$ is ionized.

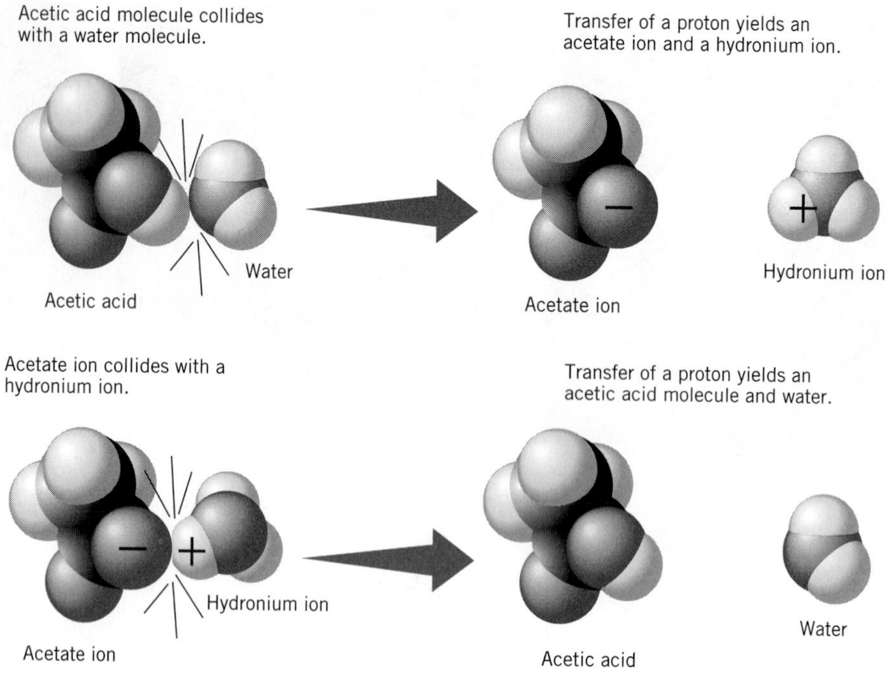

Acetic acid molecule collides with a water molecule.

Transfer of a proton yields an acetate ion and a hydronium ion.

Water

Acetic acid

Hydronium ion

Acetate ion

Acetate ion collides with a hydronium ion.

Transfer of a proton yields an acetic acid molecule and water.

Hydronium ion

Water

Acetate ion

Acetic acid

FIG. 4.11 Equilibrium in a solution of acetic acid. Two opposing reactions take place simultaneously in a solution of acetic acid. Molecules of acid collide with molecules of water and form acetate ions and H_3O^+ ions. Meanwhile, acetate ions collide with H_3O^+ ions to give acetic acid molecules and water molecules. (The usual colors are used: white = H, red = O, black = C.)

The condition we've just described, with two opposing reactions occurring at the same rate, is called a **chemical equilibrium** or **dynamic equilibrium**. It is an *equilibrium* because the concentrations of the substances present in the solution do not change with time; it is *dynamic* because the opposing reactions continue endlessly.

The two opposing processes in a dynamic equilibrium are usually represented in a single equation by using double arrows, $\rightleftharpoons$. For acetic acid, we write

$$HC_2H_3O_2(aq) + H_2O \rightleftharpoons H_3O^+(aq) + C_2H_3O_2^-(aq)$$

The **forward reaction** (read from left to right) forms the ions; the **reverse reaction** (from right to left) removes them from the solution.

Molecular bases, such as ammonia and methylamine, are also weak electrolytes and have a low percentage ionization. They are classified as **weak bases.** (See Figure 4.10c.) In a solution of ammonia, only a small fraction of the solute is ionized to give NH_4^+ and OH^- because the ions have a strong tendency to react with each other. This leads to the dynamic equilibrium (Figure 4.12)

$$NH_3(aq) + H_2O \rightleftharpoons NH_4^+(aq) + OH^-(aq)$$

in which most of the base is present as NH_3 molecules.

Let's briefly summarize the results of our discussion.

Weak acids and weak bases are weak electrolytes.

Strong acids and strong bases are strong electrolytes.

In describing equilibria such as those above, we will often talk about the **position of equilibrium.** By this we mean the extent to which the forward reaction proceeds toward completion. If very little of the products are present at equilibrium, the forward reaction has not gone far toward completion and we say "the position of equilibrium lies to the left," toward the reactants. On the other hand, if large amounts of the products are present at equilibrium, we say "the position of equilibrium lies to the right."

For any weak electrolyte, only a small percentage of the solute is actually ionized at any instant after equilibrium is reached, so the position of equilibrium lies to the left. To call acetic acid a *weak* acid, for example, is just another way of saying that the forward reaction in this equilibrium is far from completion.

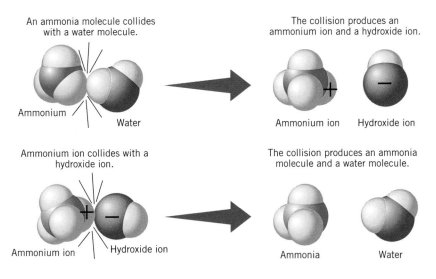

An ammonia molecule collides with a water molecule.

The collision produces an ammonium ion and a hydroxide ion.

Ammonium   Water

Ammonium ion   Hydroxide ion

Ammonium ion collides with a hydroxide ion.

The collision produces an ammonia molecule and a water molecule.

Ammonium ion   Hydroxide ion

Ammonia   Water

FIG. 4.12 Equilibrium in a solution of the weak base ammonia. Collisions between water and ammonia molecules produce ammonium and hydroxide ions. The reverse process, which involves collisions between ammonium ions and hydroxide ions, removes ions from the solution and forms ammonia and water molecules.

Strong acids do not participate in equilibria because they are fully ionized

With molecular compounds that are strong electrolytes, the tendency of the forward ionization reaction to occur is very large, while the tendency of the reverse reaction to occur is extremely small. In aqueous HCl, for example, there is little tendency for Cl^- and H_3O^+ to react to form molecules of HCl and H_2O. As a result, all of the HCl molecules dissolved in water become converted to ions—the acid becomes 100% ionized. For this reason, *we do not use double arrows in describing what happens when HCl(g) or any other strong electrolyte undergoes ionization or dissociation.*

Practice Exercise 9: Earlier you learned that methylamine, CH_3NH_2 (a fishy smelling substance found in herring brine), is a base in water. Write the equation that shows that methylamine is a weak base. (Hint: How do we show an equilibrium exists in the solution?)

Practice Exercise 10: Nitrous acid, HNO_2, is a weak acid thought to be responsible for certain cancers of the intestinal system. Write the chemical equation that shows that HNO_2 is a weak acid in water.

4.4 NAMING ACIDS AND BASES FOLLOWS A SYSTEM

Although at first there seems to be little order in the naming of acids, there are patterns that help organize names of acids and the anions that come from them when the acids are neutralized.

Hydrogen compounds of nonmetals can be acids

The binary compounds of hydrogen with many of the nonmetals are acidic, and in their aqueous solutions they are referred to as **binary acids.** Some examples are HCl, HBr, and H_2S. In naming these substances as acids, we add the prefix *hydro-* and the suffix *-ic* to the stem of the nonmetal name, followed by the word *acid*. For example, aqueous solutions of hydrogen chloride and hydrogen sulfide are named as follows:

Name of the molecular compound		Name of the binary acid in water	
HCl(*g*)	hydrogen chloride	HCl(*aq*)	*hydro*chlor*ic acid*
H_2S(*g*)	hydrogen sulfide	H_2S(*aq*)	*hydro*sulfur*ic acid*

Notice that the gaseous molecular substances are named in the usual way as binary compounds. *It is their aqueous solutions that are named as acids.*

When an acid is neutralized, the salt that is produced contains the anion formed by removing a hydrogen ion, H^+, from the acid molecule. Thus HCl yields salts containing the chloride ion, Cl^-. Similarly, HBr gives salts containing the bromide ion, Br^-. In general, then, neutralization of a binary acid yields the simple anion of the nonmetal.

Oxoacids contain hydrogen, oxygen, and another element

□ In the name of an acid, the prefix *hydro-* tells us it is a binary acid. If the prefix *hydro-* is absent, it tells us the substance is not a binary acid.

Acids that contain hydrogen, oxygen, plus another element are called **oxoacids.** Examples are H_2SO_4 and HNO_3. These acids do not take the prefix *hydro-*. Many nonmetals form two or more oxoacids that differ in the number of oxygen atoms in their formulas. When there are two oxoacids, the one with the larger number of oxygens takes the suffix *-ic* and the one with the fewer number of oxygens takes the suffix *-ous.*

H_2SO_4	sulfur*ic acid*		HNO_3	nit*ric acid*
H_2SO_3	sulfur*ous acid*		HNO_2	nit*rous acid*

The halogens can occur in as many as four different oxoacids. The oxoacid with the most oxygens has the prefix *per-*, and the one with the least has the prefix *hypo-*.

$HClO_4$	*perchloric acid*		$HClO_2$	chlor*ous acid*
$HClO_3$	chlor*ic acid*		$HClO$	*hypochlorous acid* (usually written HOCl)

□ This relationship between name of the acid and name of the anion carries over to other acids that end in the suffix *-ic*. For example, acetic acid gives the anion acetate, and citric acid gives the anion citrate.

The neutralization of oxoacids produces negative polyatomic ions. The name of the polyatomic ion is related to that of its parent acid.

(1) *-ic* acids give *-ate* anions: HNO_3 (nit*ric acid*) $\longrightarrow$ NO_3^- (nit*rate* ion)

(2) *-ous* acids give *-ite* anions: H_2SO_3 (sulfur*ous acid*) $\longrightarrow$ SO_3^{2-} (sulf*ite* ion)

In naming polyatomic anions, the prefixes *per-* and *hypo-* carry over from the name of the parent acid. Thus perchloric acid, $HClO_4$, gives perchlorate ion, ClO_4^-, and hypochlorous acid, $HClO$, gives hypochlorite ion, ClO^-.

EXAMPLE 4.5
Naming Acids and Their Salts

Bromine forms four oxoacids, similar to those of chlorine. What is the name of the acid $HBrO_2$ and what is the name of the salt $NaBrO_3$?

ANALYSIS AND SOLUTION: Let's review the acids formed by chlorine and then reason by analogy. For chlorine we have

$HClO_4$	perchloric acid		$HClO_2$	chlorous acid
$HClO_3$	chloric acid		$HClO$	hypochlorous acid

The acid $HBrO_2$ is similar to chlorous acid, so to name it we will use the stem of the element name bromine (brom-) in place of chlor-. Therefore, the name of $HBrO_2$ is *bromous acid.*

To find the name of $NaBrO_3$, let's begin by asking "What acid would give this salt by neutralization?" Neutralization involves removing an H^+ from the acid molecule and replacing it with a cation, in this case Na^+. Therefore, the salt $NaBrO_3$ would be obtained by neutralizing the acid $HBrO_3$. This acid has one more oxygen than bromous acid, $HBrO_2$, so it would have the ending *-ic*. Thus, $HBrO_3$ is named bromic acid. Neutralizing an acid that has a name that ends in *-ic* gives an anion with a name that ends in *-ate*, so the anion BrO_3^- is the bromate ion. Therefore, the salt $NaBrO_3$ is *sodium bromate.*

ARE THE ANSWERS REASONABLE? There's really not much we can do to check the answers here. For the salt, if $HClO_3$ is chloric acid, then it seems reasonable that $HBrO_3$ would be bromic acid, which would mean that BrO_3^- is the bromate ion and $NaBrO_3$ is sodium bromate.

Practice Exercise 11: The formula for arsenic acid is H_3AsO_4. What is the name of the salt Na_3AsO_4? (Hint: Recall how the name of the anion is related to the name of the acid.)

Practice Exercise 12: Formic acid is $HCHO_2$. What is the name of the salt $Ca(CHO_2)_2$?

Practice Exercise 13: Name the water solutions of the following acids: HF, HBr. Name the sodium salts formed by neutralizing the acids with NaOH.

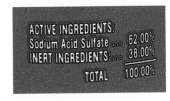

Acid salts can be formed by polyprotic acids

Monoprotic acids such as HCl and $HC_2H_3O_2$ have only one hydrogen that can be removed by neutralization and these acids form only one anion. However, polyprotic acids can be neutralized stepwise and the neutralization can be halted before all the hydrogens have been removed. For example, partial neutralization of H_2SO_4 gives the HSO_4^- ion, which forms salts such as $NaHSO_4$. This compound is called an **acid salt** because its anion, HSO_4^-, is capable of furnishing additional H^+.

In naming ions such as HSO_4^-, we specify the number of hydrogens that can still be neutralized if the anion were to be treated with additional base. Thus, HSO_4^- is called the hydrogen sulfate ion; it's the active ingredient in Sani-Flush (Figure 4.13). Similarly, $H_2PO_4^-$ is named as the dihydrogen phosphate ion. These anions give the following salts with Na^+:

> $NaHSO_4$ sodium hydrogen sulfate
> NaH_2PO_4 sodium dihydrogen phosphate

For acid salts of diprotic acids, the prefix *bi-* is still often used.

> $NaHCO_3$ sodium bicarbonate
>   or
>   sodium hydrogen carbonate

Notice that the prefix bi- does *not* mean "two"; it means that there is an acidic hydrogen in the compound.

FIG. 4.13 Many acid salts have useful applications. As its active ingredient, this familiar product contains sodium hydrogen sulfate (sodium bisulfate), which the manufacturer calls "sodium acid sulfate." (*Robert Capece.*)

Practice Exercise 14: What is the formula for sodium bisulfite? What is the chemically correct name for this compound? (Hint: What information do we get from the prefix bi- and the suffix -ite?)

Practice Exercise 15: Write molecular equations for the stepwise neutralization of phosphoric acid by sodium hydroxide. What are the names of the salts that are formed?

Bases are named as hydroxides or molecules

Metal compounds that contain the ions OH^- or O^{2-}, such as NaOH and Na_2O, are ionic and are named just like any other ionic compound. Thus, NaOH is sodium hydroxide and Na_2O is sodium oxide.

Molecular bases such as NH_3 (ammonia) and CH_3NH_2 (methylamine) are specified by just giving the name of the molecule.[6] There is nothing special in their names that tells us they are bases.

---

[6] Solutions of ammonia are sometimes called *ammonium hydroxide*, although there is no evidence that the species NH_4OH actually exists.

4.5 | IONIC REACTIONS CAN OFTEN BE PREDICTED

In our discussion of the reaction of KI with $Pb(NO_3)_2$ (page 132), you saw that the net ionic equation reveals a change in the number of ions in solution when the reaction takes place. Such changes characterize ionic reactions in general. In this section you will learn how we can use the existence or nonexistence of a net ionic equation as a criterion to determine whether or not an ionic reaction occurs in a solution of mixed solutes.

TOOLS
Predicting net ionic equations

> In general, a net ionic equation will exist (and a reaction will occur) under the following conditions:
>
> A precipitate is formed from a mixture of soluble reactants.
>
> An acid reacts with a base.
>
> A weak electrolyte is formed from a mixture of strong electrolytes.
>
> A gas is formed from a mixture of reactants.

It is also important to note that *no net reaction will occur if all the substances in the ionic equation cancel.* There will be no net ionic equation, and therefore no net reaction!

Predicting precipitation reactions

The reaction between $Pb(NO_3)_2$ and KI,

$$Pb(NO_3)_2(aq) + 2KI(aq) \longrightarrow PbI_2(s) + 2KNO_3(aq)$$

is just one example of a large class of ionic reactions in which cations and anions change partners. The technical term we use to describe them is **metathesis,** but they are also sometimes called **double replacement reactions.** (In the formation of the products, PbI_2 and KNO_3, the I^- replaces NO_3^- in the lead compound and NO_3^- replaces I^- in the potassium compound.) Metathesis reactions in which a precipitate forms are sometimes called **precipitation reactions.**

FACETS OF CHEMISTRY

4.2

Painful Precipitates—Kidney Stones

Each year, more than a million people in the United States are hospitalized because of very painful kidney stone attacks. A kidney stone is a hard mass developed from crystals that separate from the urine and build up on the inner surfaces of the kidney. The formation of the stones is caused primarily by the buildup of Ca^{2+}, $C_2O_4^{2-}$, and PO_4^{3-} ions in the urine. When the concentrations of those ions become large enough, the urine becomes supersaturated with respect to calcium oxalate and/or calcium phosphate and precipitates begin to form (70% to 80% of all kidney stones are made up of calcium oxalate and phosphate). If the crystals remain tiny enough, they can travel through the urinary tract and pass out of the body in the urine without being noticed. Sometimes, however, they continue to grow without being passed

and can cause intense pain if they become stuck in the urinary tract.

Kidney stones don't all look alike. Their color depends on what substances are mixed with the inorganic precipitates (e.g., proteins or blood). Most are yellow or brown, as seen in the accompanying photo, but they can be tan, gold, or even black. Stones can be round, jagged, or even have branches. They vary in size from mere specks to pebbles to stones as big as golf balls!

A calcium oxalate kidney stone. Kidney stones such as this can be extremely painful. *(Photo courtesy of L.C. Herring and Company, Orlando, FL.)*

TABLE 4.1	Solubility Rules for Ionic Compounds in Water

Soluble Compounds

1. All compounds of the alkali metals (Group IA) are soluble.
2. All salts containing NH_4^+, NO_3^-, ClO_4^-, and ClO_3^-, and $C_2H_3O_2^-$ are soluble.
3. All chlorides, bromides, and iodides (salts containing Cl^-, Br^-, or I^-) are soluble *except* when combined with Ag^+, Pb^{2+}, and Hg_2^{2+} (note the subscript "2").
4. All sulfates (salts containing SO_4^{2-}) are soluble *except* those of Pb^{2+}, Ca^{2+}, Sr^{2+}, Hg_2^{2+}, and Ba^{2+}.

Insoluble Compounds

5. All metal hydroxides (ionic compounds containing OH^-) and all metal oxides (ionic compounds containing O^{2-}) are insoluble *except* those of Group IA and those of Ca^{2+}, Sr^{2+}, and Ba^{2+}.

    When metal oxides do dissolve, they react with water to form hydroxides. The oxide ion, O^{2-}, does not exist in water. For example,

$$Na_2O(s) + H_2O \longrightarrow 2NaOH(aq)$$

6. All salts that contain PO_4^{3-}, CO_3^{2-}, SO_3^{2-}, and S^{2-} are insoluble *except* those of Group IA and NH_4^+.

Lead nitrate and potassium iodide react because one of the products is insoluble. This is what leads to a net ionic equation. Such reactions can be predicted if we know which substances are soluble and which are insoluble. To help us, we can use a set of **solubility rules** (Table 4.1) to tell us, in many cases, whether an ionic compound is soluble or insoluble. To make the rules easier to remember, they are divided into two categories. The first includes compounds that are soluble, with some exceptions. The second describes compounds that are generally insoluble, with some exceptions. Some examples will help clarify their use.

Rule 1 states that all compounds of the alkali metals are soluble in water. This means that you can expect *any* compound containing Na^+ or K^+, or any of the Group IA metal ions, *regardless of the anion*, to be soluble. If one of the reactants in a metathesis is Na_3PO_4, you now know from Rule 1 that it is soluble. Therefore, you would write it in *dissociated* form in the ionic equation. Similarly, Rule 6 states, in part, that all carbonate compounds are *insoluble* except those of the alkali metals and the ammonium ion. If one of the products in a metathesis reaction is $CaCO_3$, you'd expect it to be insoluble, because the cation is not an alkali metal or NH_4^+. Therefore, you would write its formula in undissociated form as $CaCO_3(s)$ in the ionic equation.

Let's look at an example that illustrates how we can use the rules to predict the outcome of a reaction.

EXAMPLE 4.6
Predicting Reactions and Writing Their Equations

Predict whether a reaction will occur when aqueous solutions of $Fe_2(SO_4)_3$ and $Pb(NO_3)_2$ are mixed. Write molecular, ionic, and net ionic equations for it.

ANALYSIS: We know the molecular equation will take the form

$$Fe_2(SO_4)_3 + Pb(NO_3)_2 \longrightarrow$$

To complete the equation we have to determine the makeup of the products. We begin, therefore, by predicting what a double replacement (metathesis) might produce. Then we proceed to expand the molecular equation into an ionic equation, and finally we drop spectator ions to obtain the net ionic equation. The existence of a net ionic equation tells us that a reaction does indeed take place. To accomplish all of this we need to know solubilities, and here our tool is the solubility rules.

☐ The critical step in determining whether a reaction occurs is obtaining a net ionic equation.

SOLUTION: The reactants, $Pb(NO_3)_2$ and $Fe_2(SO_4)_3$, contain the ions Pb^{2+} and NO_3^-, and Fe^{3+} and SO_4^{2-}, respectively. To write the formulas of the products, we interchange anions. We combine Pb^{2+} with SO_4^{2-}, and for electrical neutrality, we must use one ion of each. Therefore, we write $PbSO_4$ as one possible product. For the other product, we combine Fe^{3+} with NO_3^-. Electrical neutrality now demands that we use *three* NO_3^- to *one* Fe^{3+} to make $Fe(NO_3)_3$. The correct formulas of the products, then, are $PbSO_4$ and $Fe(NO_3)_3$. The unbalanced molecular equation at this point is

$$Fe_2(SO_4)_3 + Pb(NO_3)_2 \longrightarrow Fe(NO_3)_3 + PbSO_4 \qquad \text{(unbalanced)}$$

□ Always write equations in two steps: First write correct formulas for the reactants and products, then adjust the coefficients to balance the equation.

Next, let's determine solubilities. The reactants are ionic compounds and we are told that they are in solution, so we know they are water soluble. Solubility Rules 2 and 4 tell us this also. For the products, we find that Rule 2 says that all nitrates are soluble, so $Fe(NO_3)_3$ is soluble; Rule 4 tells us that the sulfate of Pb^{2+} is insoluble. This means that a precipitate of $PbSO_4$ will form. Writing (*aq*) and (*s*) following appropriate formulas, the unbalanced molecular equation is

$$Fe_2(SO_4)_3(aq) + Pb(NO_3)_2(aq) \longrightarrow Fe(NO_3)_3(aq) + PbSO_4(s) \qquad \text{(unbalanced)}$$

When balanced, we obtain the *molecular equation*.

$$Fe_2(SO_4)_3(aq) + 3Pb(NO_3)_2(aq) \longrightarrow 2Fe(NO_3)_3(aq) + 3PbSO_4(s)$$

Next, we expand this to give the *ionic equation* in which soluble compounds are written in dissociated (separated) form as ions, and insoluble compounds are written in "molecular" form. Once again, we are careful to apply the subscripts of the ions and the coefficients.

$$2Fe^{3+}(aq) + 3SO_4^{2-}(aq) + 3Pb^{2+}(aq) + 6NO_3^-(aq) \longrightarrow$$
$$2Fe^{3+}(aq) + 6NO_3^-(aq) + 3PbSO_4(s)$$

By removing spectator ions (Fe^{3+} and NO_3^-), we obtain

$$3Pb^{2+}(aq) + 3SO_4^{2-}(aq) \longrightarrow 3PbSO_4(s)$$

Finally, we reduce the coefficients to give us the correct *net ionic equation*.

$$Pb^{2+}(aq) + SO_4^{2-}(aq) \longrightarrow PbSO_4(s)$$

The existence of the net ionic equation confirms that a reaction does take place between lead nitrate and iron(III) sulfate.

IS THE ANSWER REASONABLE? One of the main things we have to check in solving a problem such as this is that we've written the correct formulas of the products. For example, in this problem some students might be tempted (without thinking) to write $Pb(SO_4)_2$ and $Fe_2(NO_3)_3$, or even $Pb(SO_4)_3$ and $Fe_2(NO_3)_2$. *This is a common error.* Always be careful to figure out the charges on the ions that must be combined in the formula. Then take the ions in a ratio that gives an electrically neutral formula unit.

Once we're sure the formulas of the products are right, we check that we've applied the solubility rules correctly, which we have. Then we check that we've properly balanced the equation (We have.), that we've correctly divided the soluble compounds into their ions (We have.), and that we've eliminated the spectator ions to obtain the net ionic equation (We have.).

Practice Exercise 16: Show that in aqueous solutions there is no net reaction between $Zn(NO_3)_2$ and $Ca(C_2H_3O_2)_2$. (Hint: Write molecular, ionic, and net ionic equations.)

Practice Exercise 17: Predict the reaction that occurs on mixing the following solutions. Write molecular, ionic, and net ionic equations for the reactions that take place. (a) $AgNO_3$ and NH_4Cl, (b) sodium sulfide and lead acetate.

Predicting acid-base reactions

Earlier we discussed neutralization as one of the key properties of acids and bases. Many such reactions can be viewed as metathesis. An example is the reaction between HCl and NaOH.

$$HCl(aq) + NaOH(aq) \longrightarrow NaCl(aq) + H_2O$$

Writing this as an ionic equation gives

$$H^+(aq) + Cl^-(aq) + Na^+(aq) + OH^-(aq) \longrightarrow Na^+(aq) + Cl^-(aq) + H_2O$$

where we have used H^+ as shorthand for H_3O^+. The net ionic equation is obtained by removing spectator ions.

$$H^+(aq) + OH^-(aq) \longrightarrow H_2O$$

In this case, a net ionic equation exists because of the formation of a very weak electrolyte, H_2O, instead of a precipitate. In fact, we find this same net ionic equation for any reaction between a strong acid and a soluble strong base.

The formation of water in a neutralization reaction is such a strong driving force for reaction that it will form even if the acid is weak or if the base is insoluble, or both. Here are some examples.

Reaction of a weak acid with a strong base

Molecular equation:

$$\underset{\text{weak acid}}{HC_2H_3O_2(aq)} + \underset{\text{strong base}}{NaOH(aq)} \longrightarrow NaC_2H_3O_2(aq) + H_2O$$

Net ionic equation:

$$HC_2H_3O_2(aq) + OH^-(aq) \longrightarrow C_2H_3O_2^-(aq) + H_2O$$

This reaction is illustrated in Figure 4.14.

Reaction of a strong acid with an insoluble base

Figure 4.15 shows the reaction of hydrochloric acid with milk of magnesia, which contains $Mg(OH)_2$.

Molecular equation:

$$\underset{\text{strong acid}}{2HCl(aq)} + \underset{\text{insoluble base}}{Mg(OH)_2(s)} \longrightarrow MgCl_2(aq) + 2H_2O$$

Net ionic equation:

$$2H^+(aq) + Mg(OH)_2(s) \longrightarrow Mg^{2+}(aq) + 2H_2O$$

FIG. 4.15 **Hydrochloric acid is neutralized by milk of magnesia.** A solution of hydrochloric acid is added to a beaker containing milk of magnesia. The thick white solid in milk of magnesia is magnesium hydroxide, $Mg(OH)_2$, which is able to neutralize the acid. The mixture is clear where some of the solid $Mg(OH)_2$ has already reacted and dissolved. (*Andy Washnik.*)

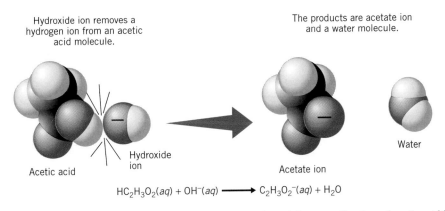

Hydroxide ion removes a hydrogen ion from an acetic acid molecule.

The products are acetate ion and a water molecule.

Acetic acid

Hydroxide ion

Acetate ion

Water

$$HC_2H_3O_2(aq) + OH^-(aq) \longrightarrow C_2H_3O_2^-(aq) + H_2O$$

FIG. 4.14 **Net reaction of acetic acid with a strong base.** The neutralization of acetic acid by hydroxide ion occurs primarily by the removal of H^+ from acetic acid molecules by OH^- ions.

Reaction of a weak acid with an insoluble base

Molecular equation:

$$2HC_2H_3O_2(aq) + Mg(OH)_2(s) \longrightarrow Mg(C_2H_3O_2)_2(aq) + 2H_2O$$

Net ionic equation:

$$2HC_2H_3O_2(aq) + Mg(OH)_2(s) \longrightarrow Mg^{2+}(aq) + 2C_2H_3O_2^-(aq) + 2H_2O$$

Notice that in the last two examples, the formation of water drives the reaction, even though one of the reactants is insoluble. To correctly write the ionic and net ionic equations, it is important to know both the solubility rules and which acids are strong and weak. If you've learned the list of strong acids, you can expect that any acid *not* on the list will be a weak acid. (Unless specifically told otherwise, you should assume weak acids to be water soluble.)

Reaction of an acid with a weak base

Acid–base neutralization doesn't always involve the formation of water. We see this in the reaction of an acid with a weak base such as NH_3. For a strong acid such as HCl, we have

Molecular equation:

$$HCl(aq) + NH_3(aq) \longrightarrow NH_4Cl(aq)$$

Net ionic equation (using H^+ as shorthand for H_3O^+):

$$H^+(aq) + NH_3(aq) \longrightarrow NH_4^+(aq)$$

Figure 4.16 depicts the transfer of H^+ from H_3O^+ to NH_3.
With a weak acid such as $HC_2H_3O_2$, we have

Molecular equation:

$$HC_2H_3O_2(aq) + NH_3(aq) \longrightarrow NH_4C_2H_3O_2(aq)$$

Ionic and net ionic equation:

$$HC_2H_3O_2(aq) + NH_3(aq) \longrightarrow NH_4^+(aq) + C_2H_3O_2^-(aq)$$

Even though solutions of $HC_2H_3O_2$ contain some H^+, and solutions of NH_3 contain some OH^-, when these solutions are mixed the predominant reaction is between molecules of acid and base. This is illustrated in Figure 4.17.

Practice Exercise 18: Write the molecular, ionic, and net ionic equations for the neutralization of $HNO_3(aq)$ by $Ca(OH)_2(aq)$. (Hint: First determine whether the acid and base are strong or weak.)

Practice Exercise 19: Write molecular, ionic, and net ionic equations for the reaction of (a) HCl with KOH, (b) $HCHO_2$ with LiOH, and (c) N_2H_4 with HCl.

Practice Exercise 20: Write molecular, ionic, and net ionic equations for the reaction of the weak base methylamine, CH_3NH_2, with formic acid, $HCHO_2$ (a weak acid).

FIG. 4.16 **Reaction of ammonia with a strong acid.** The reaction occurs primarily by the direct attack of H_3O^+ on NH_3 molecules. Transfer of a proton to the ammonia molecule produces an ammonium ion and a water molecule.

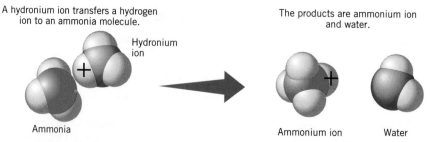

A hydronium ion transfers a hydrogen ion to an ammonia molecule.

The products are ammonium ion and water.

Hydronium ion

Ammonia

Ammonium ion

Water

$$NH_3(aq) + H_3O^+(aq) \longrightarrow NH_4^+(aq) + H_2O$$

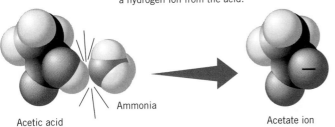

Ammonia molecule collides with an acetic acid molecule and extracts a hydrogen ion from the acid.

Acetic acid   Ammonia   Acetate ion   Ammonium ion

$$HC_2H_3O_2(aq) + NH_3(aq) \longrightarrow C_2H_3O_2^-(aq) + NH_4^+(aq)$$

FIG. 4.17 Reaction of acetic acid with ammonia. The collision of an ammonia molecule with an acetic acid molecule leads to a transfer of H^+ from the acetic acid to ammonia and the formation of ions.

Predicting reactions in which a gas is formed

Sometimes a product of a metathesis reaction is a substance that normally is a gas at room temperature and is not very soluble in water. The most common example is carbon dioxide. This product forms when an acid reacts with either a bicarbonate or carbonate. For example, as a sodium bicarbonate solution is added to hydrochloric acid, bubbles of carbon dioxide are released (Figure 4.18). This is the same reaction that occurs if you take sodium bicarbonate to soothe an upset stomach. Stomach acid is HCl and its reaction with the $NaHCO_3$ both neutralizes the acid and produces CO_2 gas (burp!). The molecular equation for the metathesis reaction is

$$HCl(aq) + NaHCO_3(aq) \longrightarrow NaCl(aq) + H_2CO_3(aq)$$

Carbonic acid, H_2CO_3, is too unstable to be isolated in pure form. When it forms in appreciable amounts as a product in a metathesis reaction, it decomposes into its anhydride (the gas CO_2) and water. Carbon dioxide is only slightly soluble in water, so most of the CO_2 bubbles out of the solution. The decomposition reaction is

$$H_2CO_3(aq) \longrightarrow H_2O + CO_2(g)$$

Therefore, the overall molecular equation for the reaction is

$$HCl(aq) + NaHCO_3(aq) \longrightarrow NaCl(aq) + H_2O + CO_2(g)$$

The ionic equation is

$$H^+(aq) + Cl^-(aq) + Na^+(aq) + HCO_3^-(aq) \longrightarrow$$
$$Na^+(aq) + Cl^-(aq) + H_2O + CO_2(g)$$

and the net ionic equation is

$$H^+(aq) + HCO_3^-(aq) \longrightarrow H_2O + CO_2(g)$$

Similar results are obtained if we begin with a carbonate instead of a bicarbonate. In this case, hydrogen ions combine with carbonate ions to give H_2CO_3, which subsequently decomposes to water and CO_2.

$$2H^+(aq) + CO_3^{2-}(aq) \longrightarrow H_2CO_3(aq) \longrightarrow H_2O + CO_2(g)$$

The net reaction is

$$2H^+(aq) + CO_3^{2-}(aq) \longrightarrow H_2O + CO_2(g)$$

The release of CO_2 by the reaction of a carbonate with an acid is such a strong driving force for reaction that it enables insoluble carbonates to dissolve in acids (strong and weak). The reaction of limestone, $CaCO_3$, with hydrochloric acid is shown in Figure 4.19. The molecular and net ionic equations for the reaction are as follows:

$$CaCO_3(s) + 2HCl(aq) \longrightarrow CaCl_2(aq) + CO_2(g) + H_2O$$
$$CaCO_3(s) + 2H^+(aq) \longrightarrow Ca^{2+}(aq) + CO_2(g) + H_2O$$

Carbon dioxide is not the only gas formed in metathesis reactions. Table 4.2 lists others and the reactions that form them.

FIG. 4.18 The reaction of sodium bicarbonate with hydrochloric acid. The bubbles contain the gas carbon dioxide. *(Michael Watson.)*

FIG. 4.19 Limestone reacts with acid. Bubbles of CO_2 are formed in the reaction of limestone ($CaCO_3$) with hydrochloric acid. *(Andy Washnik.)*

TOOLS

Gases formed in metathesis reactions

TABLE 4.2 Gases Formed in Metathesis Reactions

Gas	Formed by Reaction of Acids with:	Equation for Formation[a]
H_2S	Sulfides	$2H^+ + S^{2-} \longrightarrow H_2S$
HCN	Cyanides	$H^+ + CN^- \longrightarrow HCN$
CO_2	Carbonates	$2H^+ + CO_3^{2-} \longrightarrow (H_2CO_3) \longrightarrow H_2O + CO_2$
	Bicarbonates (hydrogen carbonates)	$H^+ + HCO_3^- \longrightarrow (H_2CO_3) \longrightarrow H_2O + CO_2$
SO_2	Sulfites	$2H^+ + SO_3^{2-} \longrightarrow (H_2SO_3) \longrightarrow H_2O + SO_2$
	Bisulfites (hydrogen sulfites)	$H^+ + HSO_3^- \longrightarrow (H_2SO_3) \longrightarrow H_2O + SO_2$

Gas	Formed by Reaction of Bases with:	Equation for Formation
NH_3	Ammonium salts[b]	$NH_4^+ + OH^- \longrightarrow NH_3 + H_2O$

[a]Formulas in parentheses are of unstable compounds that break down according to the continuation of the sequence.
[b]In writing a metathesis reaction, you may be tempted sometimes to write NH_4OH as a formula for "ammonium hydroxide." That compound does not exist. In water, it is nothing more than a solution of NH_3.

EXAMPLE 4.7
Predicting Reactions and Writing Their Equations

What reaction (if any) occurs when solutions of ammonium carbonate, $(NH_4)_2CO_3$, and propionic acid, $HC_3H_5O_2$, are mixed?

ANALYSIS: Our tools for working a problem such as this are the list of strong acids (page 140), the solubility rules (Table 4.1, page 147), and the list of gases formed in metathesis reactions (Table 4.2). We begin by writing a potential metathesis equation in molecular form. Then we examine the reactants and products to see if any are weak electrolytes or substances that give gases. We also look for soluble or insoluble ionic compounds. Then we form the ionic equation and search for spectator ions which we eliminate to obtain the net ionic equation.

SOLUTION: We begin by constructing a molecular equation, treating the reaction as a metathesis. For the acid, we take the cation to be H^+ and the anion to be $C_3H_5O_2^-$. Therefore, after exchanging cations between the two anions we can obtain the following balanced molecular equation.

$$(NH_4)_2CO_3 + 2HC_3H_5O_2 \longrightarrow 2NH_4C_3H_5O_2 + H_2CO_3$$

In the statement of the problem we are told that we are working with a *solution* of $HC_3H_5O_2$, so we know it's soluble. Also, it is not on the list of strong acids, so we expect it to be a weak acid; we will write it in molecular form in the ionic equation.

Next, we recognize that H_2CO_3 decomposes into $CO_2(g)$ and H_2O. (This information is also found in Table 4.2.) Let's rewrite the molecular equation taking this into account.

$$(NH_4)_2CO_3 + 2HC_3H_5O_2 \longrightarrow 2NH_4C_3H_5O_2 + CO_2(g) + H_2O$$

Next, we need to determine which of the ionic substances are soluble. The solubility rules tell us that all ammonium salts are soluble, and we know that all salts are strong electrolytes. Therefore, we will write $(NH_4)_2CO_3$ and $NH_4C_3H_5O_2$ in dissociated form. Now we are ready to expand the molecular equation into the ionic equation.

$$2NH_4^+(aq) + CO_3^{2-}(aq) + 2HC_3H_5O_2(aq) \longrightarrow$$
$$2NH_4^+(aq) + 2C_3H_5O_2^-(aq) + CO_2(g) + H_2O$$

The only spectator ion is NH_4^+. Dropping this gives the net ionic equation.

$$CO_3^{2-}(aq) + 2HC_3H_5O_2(aq) \longrightarrow 2C_3H_5O_2^-(aq) + CO_2(g) + H_2O$$

IS THE ANSWER REASONABLE? There are some common errors that people make in working problems of this kind, so it is important to double-check. First, *proceed carefully*. Be sure you've written the formulas of the products correctly. (If you need review, you might look at Example 4.6 on page 147.) Look for weak acids. (You need to know the list of strong ones; if an acid isn't on the list, it's a weak acid.) Look for gases, or substances that decompose into gases. (Be sure you've studied Table 4.2.) Check for insoluble compounds. (You need to know the solubility rules in Table 4.1.) If you've learned what is expected of you, and checked each step, it is likely your result is correct.

EXAMPLE 4.8
Predicting Reactions
and Writing Their Equations

What reaction (if any) occurs in water between potassium nitrate and ammonium chloride?

ANALYSIS: First, we have to convert the names of the compounds into chemical formulas. Here we use the principles of nomenclature rules from Chapter 2. The ions in potassium nitrate are K^+ and NO_3^-, so the salt has the formula KNO_3. In ammonium chloride, the ions are NH_4^+ and Cl^-, so the salt is NH_4Cl. Now we can proceed to writing molecular, ionic, and net ionic equations as in the preceding example.

SOLUTION: First we write the molecular equation, being sure to construct correct formulas for the products.

$$KNO_3 + NH_4Cl \longrightarrow KCl + NH_4NO_3$$

Looking over the substances in the equation, we don't find any that are weak acids or that decompose to give gases. Next, we check solubilities.

Solubility Rule 2 tells us that both KNO_3 and NH_4Cl are soluble. By solubility Rules 1 and 2, both products are also soluble in water. The anticipated molecular equation is therefore

$$\underset{\text{soluble}}{KNO_3(aq)} + \underset{\text{soluble}}{NH_4Cl(aq)} \longrightarrow \underset{\text{soluble}}{KCl(aq)} + \underset{\text{soluble}}{NH_4NO_3(aq)}$$

and the ionic equation is

$$K^+(aq) + NO_3^-(aq) + NH_4^+(aq) + Cl^-(aq) \longrightarrow$$
$$K^+(aq) + Cl^-(aq) + NH_4^+(aq) + NO_3^-(aq)$$

Notice that the right side of the equation is the same as the left side except for the order in which the ions are written. When we eliminate spectator ions, everything goes. There is no net ionic equation, which means there is no net reaction.

IS THE ANSWER REASONABLE? Once again, we perform the same checks here as in Example 4.7, and they tell us our answer is right.

Practice Exercise 21: Knowing that salts of the formate ion, CHO_2^-, are water soluble, predict the reaction between $Co(OH)_2$ and formic acid, $HCHO_2$. Write molecular, ionic, and net ionic equations. (Hint: Apply the tools we used in Example 4.7.)

Practice Exercise 22: Predict whether a reaction will occur in aqueous solution between the following pairs of substances. Write molecular, ionic, and net ionic equations. (a) $KCHO_2$ and HCl, (b) $CuCO_3$ and $HC_2H_3O_2$, (c) calcium acetate and silver nitrate, and (d) sodium hydroxide and nickel(II) chloride.

<table>
<tr><td>**4.6**</td><td>**THE COMPOSITION OF A SOLUTION IS DESCRIBED BY ITS CONCENTRATION**</td></tr>
</table>

As you learned earlier, the composition of a solution is specified by giving its *concentration*. Percentage concentration (grams of solute per 100 g of solution) was used as an example. To deal with the stoichiometry of reactions in solution, however, percentage concentration is not a convenient way to express concentrations of solutes. Instead, we express the amount of solute in moles and the amount of solution in liters.

The **molar concentration,** or **molarity** (abbreviated *M*), of a solution is defined as *the number of moles of solute per liter of solution.* It is a ratio of moles of solute to the volume of the solution expressed in liters.

TOOLS
Molarity

$$\text{Molarity } (M) = \frac{\text{moles of solute}}{\text{liters of solution}} \qquad (4.4)$$

Thus, a solution that contains 0.100 mol of NaCl in 1.00 L has a molarity of 0.100 *M*, and we would refer to the solution as 0.100 *molar* NaCl or as 0.100 *M* NaCl. The same concentration would result if we dissolved 0.0100 mol of NaCl in 0.100 L (100 mL) of solution, because the *ratio* of moles of solute to volume of solution is the same.

$$\frac{0.100 \text{ mol NaCl}}{1.00 \text{ L NaCl soln}} = \frac{0.0100 \text{ mol NaCl}}{0.100 \text{ L NaCl soln}} = 0.100 \; M \text{ NaCl}$$

Molarity is a conversion factor relating moles of solute and volume of a solution

Whenever we have to deal with a problem that involves an amount of a chemical and a volume of a solution of that substance, you can expect that solving the problem will involve molarity.

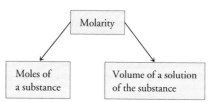

Molarity is a tool that provides the conversion factors we need to convert between moles and volume (either in liters or milliliters). Consider, for example, a solution labeled 0.100 *M* NaCl. The unit *M* always translates to mean "moles per liter," so we can write

$$0.100 \; M \text{ NaCl} = \frac{0.100 \text{ mol NaCl}}{1.00 \text{ L soln}}$$

This gives us an equivalence relationship between "mol NaCl" and "L soln" that we can use to form two conversion factors.[7]

$$0.100 \text{ mol NaCl} \Longleftrightarrow 1.00 \text{ L soln}$$

$$\frac{0.100 \text{ mol NaCl}}{1.00 \text{ L NaCl soln}} \qquad \frac{1.00 \text{ L NaCl soln}}{0.100 \text{ mol NaCl}}$$

[7] Some students find it easier to translate the "1.00 L" part of these factors into the equivalent 1000 mL here rather than convert between liters and milliliters at some other stage of the calculation. Factors such as the two above, therefore, can be rewritten as follows whenever it is convenient. (Remember that "1000") in the following is regarded as having an infinite number of significant figures because, standing as it does for 1 L, it is part of the definition of molarity and is an exact number.)

$$\frac{0.100 \text{ mol NaCl}}{1000 \text{ mL NaCl soln}} \quad \text{and} \quad \frac{1000 \text{ mL NaCl soln}}{0.100 \text{ mol NaCl}}$$

EXAMPLE 4.9
Calculating the Molarity
of a Solution

To study the effect of dissolved salt on the rusting of an iron sample, a student prepared a solution of NaCl by dissolving 1.461 g of NaCl in a total volume of 250.0 mL. What is the molarity of this solution?

ANALYSIS: The tool we'll use to solve this problem is Equation 4.4, which defines molarity as the ratio of *moles of solute* to *liters of solution*. If we can find these two pieces of information, we can arrange them as a ratio:

$$\text{Molarity} = \frac{? \text{ mol NaCl}}{? \text{ L soln}}$$

Therefore, we have to convert 1.461 g of NaCl to moles of NaCl and 250.0 mL to liters. Then we simply divide one by the other to find the molarity.

SOLUTION: The number of moles of NaCl is found using the formula mass of NaCl, 58.443 g mol^{-1}.

$$1.461 \text{ g NaCl} \times \frac{1 \text{ mol NaCl}}{58.443 \text{ g NaCl}} = 0.02500 \text{ mol NaCl}$$

To find the volume of the solution in liters, we move the decimal three places to the left, so 250.0 mL equals 0.2500 L.

The ratio of moles to liters, therefore, is

$$\frac{0.02500 \text{ mol NaCl}}{0.2500 \text{ L}} = 0.1000 \ M \text{ NaCl}$$

☐ If necessary, practice converting between liters and milliliters. It's a task you will have to perform frequently.

IS THE ANSWER REASONABLE? Let's use our answer to do a rough calculation of the amount of NaCl in the solution. If our answer is right, we should find a value not too far from the amount given in the problem (1.461 g). If we round the formula mass of NaCl to 60, and use 0.1 *M* as an approximate concentration, then one liter of the solution contains 0.1 mol of NaCl, or approximately 6 g of NaCl (one-tenth of 60 g). But 250 mL is only 1/4 of a liter, so the mass of NaCl will be approximately 1/4 of 6 g, or about 1.5 g. This is pretty close to the amount that was given in the problem, so our answer is probably correct.

Practice Exercise 23: A certain solution contains 16.9 g of HNO$_3$ dissolved in 125 mL of solution. Water is added until the volume is 175 mL. What is the molarity of HNO$_3$ in the final solution? (Hint: Does the amount of HNO$_3$ change when the water is added?)

Practice Exercise 24: Suppose 1.223 g of NaCl is added to the 250.0 mL of NaCl solution described in Example 4.9. If there is no change in the total volume of the solution, what is the molarity of the new NaCl solution?

EXAMPLE 4.10
Using Molar Concentrations

How many milliliters of 0.250 *M* NaCl solution must be measured to obtain 0.100 mol of NaCl?

ANALYSIS: We can restate the problem as follows:

$$0.100 \text{ mol NaCl} \Leftrightarrow ? \text{ mL soln}$$

To relate moles and volume, the tool we use is the molarity.

$$0.250 \ M \text{ NaCl} = \frac{0.250 \text{ mol NaCl}}{1 \text{ L NaCl soln}}$$

The fraction on the right relates moles of NaCl to liters of the solution, which we can express as an equivalence.

$$0.250 \text{ mol NaCl} \Leftrightarrow 1 \text{ L NaCl soln}$$

The equivalence allows us to construct two conversion factors.

$$\frac{0.250 \text{ mol NaCl}}{1 \text{ L NaCl soln}} \quad \text{and} \quad \frac{1.00 \text{ L NaCl soln}}{0.250 \text{ mol NaCl}}$$

To obtain the answer, we select the one that will allow us to cancel the unit "mol NaCl."

SOLUTION: We operate with the second factor on 0.100 mol NaCl.

$$0.100 \text{ mol NaCl} \times \frac{1.00 \text{ L NaCl soln}}{0.250 \text{ mol NaCl}} = 0.400 \text{ L of } 0.250 \, M \text{ NaCl}$$

Because 0.400 L corresponds to 400 mL, 400 mL of 0.250 M NaCl provides 0.100 mol of NaCl.

IS THE ANSWER REASONABLE? The molarity tells us one liter contains 0.250 mol NaCl, so we need somewhat less than half of a liter (500 mL) to obtain just 0.100 mol. The answer, 400 mL, is reasonable.

Practice Exercise 25: A student measured 175 mL of 0.250 M HCl solution into a beaker. How many moles of HCl were in the beaker? (Hint: Molarity gives the equivalence between moles of solute and volume of solution in liters.)

Practice Exercise 26: How many milliliters of 0.250 M HCl solution contain 1.30 g of HCl?

Moles of solute can always be obtained from the volume and molarity of a solution

If you worked Practice Exercise 25 you learned that we can use the volume and molarity of a solution to calculate the number of moles of solute in it. This is such a useful relationship that it warrants special attention. Solving Equation 4.4 for *moles of solute* gives

TOOLS
Molarity times volume gives moles

$$\text{molarity} \times \text{volume (L)} = \text{moles of solute} \tag{4.5}$$

$$\frac{\text{mol solute}}{\text{L soln}} \times \text{L soln} = \text{mol solute}$$

Thus, *any time you know both the molarity and volume of a solution, you can easily calculate the number of moles of solute in it.* As you will see, this concept will be very useful in solving a variety of problems.

One situation in which Equation 4.5 is useful is when we must prepare some specific volume of a solution having a desired molarity (for example, 250 mL of 0.0800 M Na_2CrO_4). To proceed, we have to calculate the amount of solute that will be in the solution after it's made. Thus, in 250 mL of 0.0800 M Na_2CrO_4 there are

◻ In the laboratory, 250 mL is easily measured to a precision equal to or greater than ±1 mL, so we will take 250 mL to have three significant figures.

$$\frac{0.0800 \text{ mol } Na_2CrO_4}{1 \text{ L soln}} \times 0.250 \text{ L soln} = 0.0200 \text{ mol } Na_2CrO_4$$

Figure 4.20 shows how we would use a 250 mL volumetric flask to prepare such a solution. (A *volumetric flask* is a narrow-necked flask having an etched mark high on its neck. When filled to the mark, the flask contains precisely the volume given by the flask's label.)

(a)   *(b)*   *(c)*   *(d)*   *(e)*

FIG. 4.20 **The preparation of a solution having a known molarity.** *(a)* A 250 mL volumetric flask, one of a number of sizes available for preparing solutions. When filled to the line etched around its neck, this flask contains exactly 250 mL of solution. The flask here already contains a weighed amount of solute. *(b)* Water is being added. *(c)* The solute is brought completely into solution before the level is brought up to the narrow neck of the flask. *(d)* More water is added to bring the level of the solution to the etched line. *(e)* The flask is stoppered and then inverted several times to mix its contents thoroughly. *(Michael Watson.)*

EXAMPLE 4.11
Preparing a Solution with a Known Molarity

Strontium nitrate, $Sr(NO_3)_2$, is used in fireworks to produce brilliant red colors. Suppose we need to prepare 250.0 mL of 0.100 M $Sr(NO_3)_2$ solution. How many grams of strontium nitrate are required?

ANALYSIS: The critical link in solving this problem is realizing that we know both the volume and molarity of the final solution, which permits us to calculate the number of moles of $Sr(NO_3)_2$ that will be in it. Once we know the number of moles of $Sr(NO_3)_2$, we can calculate its mass using the molar mass of the salt.

SOLUTION: You've learned that the product of molarity and volume equals moles of solute, so Equation 4.5 is the tool we need. The volume 250.0 mL converts to 0.2500 L. Therefore, multiplying the molarity by the volume in liters takes the following form.

$$\underbrace{\frac{0.100 \text{ mol } Sr(NO_3)_2}{1.00 \text{ L } Sr(NO_3)_2 \text{ soln}}}_{\text{molarity}} \times \underbrace{0.2500 \text{ L } Sr(NO_3)_2 \text{ soln}}_{\text{volume (L)}} = \underbrace{0.0250 \text{ mol } Sr(NO_3)_2}_{\text{moles of solute}}$$

Finally, we convert from moles to grams using the molar mass of $Sr(NO_3)_2$, which is 211.63 g mol^{-1}.

$$0.0250 \text{ mol } Sr(NO_3)_2 \times \frac{211.63 \text{ g } Sr(NO_3)_2}{1 \text{ mol } Sr(NO_3)_2} = 5.29 \text{ g } Sr(NO_3)_2$$

Thus, to prepare the solution we need to dissolve 5.29 g of $Sr(NO_3)_2$ in a total volume of 250.0 mL.

We could also have set this up as a chain calculation as follows, with the conversion factors strung together.

$$0.2500 \text{ L } Sr(NO_3)_2 \text{ soln} \times \frac{0.100 \text{ mol } Sr(NO_3)_2}{1.00 \text{ L } Sr(NO_3)_2 \text{ soln}} \times \frac{211.63 \text{ g } Sr(NO_3)_2}{1 \text{ mol } Sr(NO_3)_2} = 5.29 \text{ g } Sr(NO_3)_2$$

IS THE ANSWER REASONABLE? If we were working with a full liter of this solution, it would contain 0.1 mol of $Sr(NO_3)_2$. The molar mass of the salt is 211.63 g mol^{-1}, so 0.1 mol is slightly more than 20 g. However, we are working with just a quarter of a liter (250 mL), so the amount of $Sr(NO_3)_2$ needed is slightly more than a quarter of 20 g, or 5 g. The answer, 5.29 g, is close to this, so it makes sense.

Practice Exercise 27: Suppose you wished to prepare 50 mL of 0.2 M $Sr(NO_3)_2$ solution. Using the kind of approximate arithmetic we employed in the Is the Answer Reasonable step in the preceding example, estimate the number of grams of $Sr(NO_3)_2$ required. [Hint: How many moles of $Sr(NO_3)_2$ would be in one liter of the solution?]

Practice Exercise 28: How many grams of $AgNO_3$ are needed to prepare 250.0 mL of 0.0125 M $AgNO_3$ solution?

Diluting a solution reduces the concentration

Laboratory chemicals are usually purchased in concentrated form and must be *diluted* (made less concentrated) before being used. This is accomplished by adding more solvent to the solution, which spreads the solute through a larger volume and causes the concentration (the amount per unit volume) to decrease.

During dilution, the amount of solute remains constant. This means that the product of molarity and volume, which equals the moles of solute, must be the same for both the concentrated and diluted solution.

$$\left(\begin{array}{c} \text{Volume of} \\ \text{dilute solution} \\ \textit{to be prepared} \end{array}\right) \times M_{\text{dilute}} = \left(\begin{array}{c} \text{Volume of} \\ \text{concentrated solution} \\ \textit{to be used} \end{array}\right) \times M_{\text{conc}}$$

moles of solute in
the dilute solution

moles of solute in the
concentrated solution

Or,

TOOLS
Dilution of solutions

$$V_{\text{dil}} \cdot M_{\text{dil}} = V_{\text{conc}} \cdot M_{\text{conc}} \tag{4.6}$$

Any units can be used for volume in Equation 4.6 provided that the volume units are the same on both sides of the equation. We thus normally solve dilution problems using *milliliters* directly in Equation 4.6.

EXAMPLE 4.12

Preparing a Solution of Known
Molarity by Dilution

How can we prepare 100.0 mL of 0.0400 M $K_2Cr_2O_7$ from 0.200 M $K_2Cr_2O_7$?

ANALYSIS: This is the way such a question comes up in the lab, but what it is really asking is, "How many milliliters of 0.200 M $K_2Cr_2O_7$ (the more concentrated solution) must be diluted to give a solution with a final volume of 100.0 mL and a final molarity of 0.0400 M?" Once we see the question this way, we realize that Equation 4.6 is the tool we need to solve the problem.

SOLUTION: It's a good idea to assemble the data first, noting what is missing (and therefore what has to be calculated).

$$V_{\text{dil}} = 100.0 \text{ mL} \qquad M_{\text{dil}} = 0.0400 \ M$$
$$V_{\text{conc}} = ? \qquad M_{\text{conc}} = 0.200 \ M$$

Next, we use Equation 4.6 ($V_{dil} \times M_{dil} = V_{conc} \times M_{conc}$):

$$100.0 \text{ mL} \times 0.0400 \ M = V_{conc} \times 0.200 \ M$$

Solving for V_{conc} gives

$$V_{conc} = \frac{100.0 \text{ mL} \times 0.0400 \ M}{0.200 \ M}$$

$$= 20.0 \text{ mL}$$

Therefore, the answer to the question as asked is, We would withdraw 20.0 mL of 0.200 M $K_2Cr_2O_7$, place it in a 100 mL volumetric flask, and then add water until the final volume is exactly 100 mL. (See Figure 4.21.)

IS THE ANSWER REASONABLE? Notice that the concentrated solution is 5 times as concentrated as the dilute solution ($5 \times 0.04 = 0.2$). To reduce the concentration by a factor of 5 requires that we increase the volume by a factor of 5, and we see that 100 mL is 5 times 20 mL. The answer appears to be correct.

FIG. 4.21 Preparing a solution by dilution. *(a)* The calculated volume of the more concentrated solution is withdrawn from the stock solution by means of a volumetric pipet. *(b)* The solution is allowed to drain entirely from the pipet into the volumetric flask. *(c)* Water is added to the flask, the contents are mixed, and the final volume is brought up to the etch mark on the narrow neck of the flask. *(d)* The new solution is put into a labeled container. *(OPC, Inc.)*

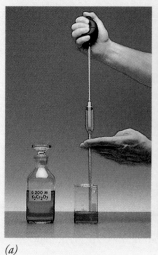
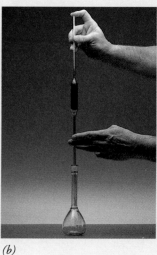

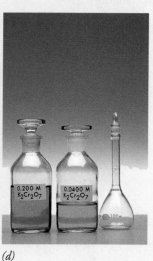

(a) *(b)* *(c)* *(d)*

Practice Exercise 29: To what final volume must 100.0 mL of 0.125 M H_2SO_4 solution be diluted to give a 0.0500 M H_2SO_4 solution? (Hint: Write the equation we used for dilution problems.)

Practice Exercise 30: How many milliliters of water have to be *added* to 150 mL of 0.50 M HCl to reduce the concentration to 0.10 M HCl?

4.7 MOLARITY IS USED FOR PROBLEMS IN SOLUTION STOICHIOMETRY

When we deal quantitatively with reactions in solution, we often work with volumes of solutions and molarity.

EXAMPLE 4.13
Stoichiometry Involving Reactions in Solution

One of the solids present in photographic film is silver bromide, AgBr. One way to prepare it is to mix solutions of silver nitrate and calcium bromide. Suppose we wished to prepare AgBr by the following precipitation reaction.

$$2AgNO_3(aq) + CaBr_2(aq) \longrightarrow 2AgBr(s) + Ca(NO_3)_2(aq)$$

How many milliliters of 0.125 M $CaBr_2$ solution must be used to react with the solute in 50.0 mL of 0.115 M $AgNO_3$?

Silver bromide (AgBr) precipitates when solutions of calcium bromide and silver nitrate are mixed. (*Michael Watson.*)

ANALYSIS: As you've learned, when we have a stoichiometry problem dealing with a chemical reaction, the tool that relates the amounts of the substances is their coefficients in the equation. For this problem, therefore, we can write

$$2 \text{ mol AgNO}_3 \Leftrightarrow 1 \text{ mol CaBr}_2$$

However, we're not given moles directly. Instead we have molarities and the volume of the $AgNO_3$ solution. The critical link in solving the problem is recognizing that the molarity and volume of the $AgNO_3$ solution provides a path to finding the number of moles of $AgNO_3$.

Knowing that we will use molarity as a tool in working the problem, let's outline the path to the answer. We can calculate the moles of $AgNO_3$ by multiplying the volume and molarity of the $AgNO_3$ solution. We then use the coefficients in the equation to translate to moles of $CaBr_2$. Finally, we use the molarity of the $CaBr_2$ solution as a conversion factor to find the volume of the solution needed. The calculation flow will look like the following.

$$\text{mol AgNO}_3 \xrightarrow[\text{balanced equation}]{\text{coefficients of}} \text{mol CaBr}_2$$

volume and molarity of $AgNO_3$ solution

moles of $CaBr_2$ and molarity of $CaBr_2$ solution

$AgNO_3$ soln   **$CaBr_2$ soln**

Given: 50.0 mL of   To find: ? mL of
0.115 M $AgNO_3$ 0.125 M $CaBr_2$

SOLUTION: First, we find the moles of $AgNO_3$ taken. Changing 50.0 mL to 0.0500 L,

volume (L)   molarity

$$0.0500 \text{ L AgNO}_3 \text{ soln} \times \frac{0.115 \text{ mol AgNO}_3}{1.00 \text{ L AgNO}_3 \text{ soln}} = 5.75 \times 10^{-3} \text{ mol AgNO}_3$$

Next, we use the coefficients of the equation to calculate the amount of $CaBr_2$ required.

$$5.75 \times 10^{-3} \text{ mol AgNO}_3 \times \frac{1 \text{ mol CaBr}_2}{2 \text{ mol AgNO}_3} = 2.88 \times 10^{-3} \text{ mol CaBr}_2$$

Finally we calculate the volume (mL) of 0.125 M $CaBr_2$ that contains this many moles of $CaBr_2$. Here we use the fact that the molarity of the $CaBr_2$ solution, 0.125 M, gives two possible conversion factors:

$$\frac{0.125 \text{ mol CaBr}_2}{1.00 \text{ L CaBr}_2 \text{ soln}} \quad \text{and} \quad \frac{1.00 \text{ L CaBr}_2 \text{ soln}}{0.125 \text{ mol CaBr}_2}$$

We use the one that cancels the unit "mol $CaBr_2$."

$$2.88 \times 10^{-3} \text{ mol CaBr}_2 \times \frac{1.00 \text{ L CaBr}_2 \text{ soln}}{0.125 \text{ mol CaBr}_2} = 0.0230 \text{ L CaBr}_2 \text{ soln}$$

Thus 0.0230 L, or 23.0 mL, of 0.125 M $CaBr_2$ has enough solute to combine with the $AgNO_3$ in 50.0 mL of 0.115 M $AgNO_3$.

IS THE ANSWER REASONABLE? The molarities of the two solutions are about the same, but only 1 mol of $CaBr_2$ is needed for each 2 mol $AgNO_3$. Therefore, the volume of $CaBr_2$ solution needed (23.0 mL) should be about half the volume of $AgNO_3$ solution taken (50.0 mL), which it is.

Practice Exercise 31: How many milliliters of 0.0475 M H_3PO_4 could be completely neutralized by 45.0 mL of 0.100 M KOH? The balanced equation for the reaction is

$$H_3PO_4(aq) + 3KOH(aq) \longrightarrow K_3PO_4(aq) + 3H_2O$$

(Hint: Outline the path of the calculations as in the preceding example.)

Practice Exercise 32: How many milliliters of 0.124 M NaOH contain enough NaOH to react with the H_2SO_4 in 15.4 mL of 0.108 M H_2SO_4 according to the following equation?

$$2NaOH(aq) + H_2SO_4(aq) \longrightarrow Na_2SO_4(aq) + 2H_2O$$

Net ionic equations can be used in stoichiometric calculations

In the preceding problem, we worked with a molecular equation in solving a stoichiometry problem. Ionic and net ionic equations can also be used, but this requires that we work with the concentrations of the ions in solution.

Calculating concentrations of ions in solutions of electrolytes

The concentrations of the ions in a solution of an electrolyte are obtained from the formula and molar concentration of the solute. For example, suppose we are working with a solution labeled "0.10 M $CaCl_2$." In 1.0 L of this solution there is 0.10 mol of $CaCl_2$, which is fully dissociated into Ca^{2+} and Cl^- ions.

$$CaCl_2 \longrightarrow Ca^{2+} + 2Cl^-$$

From the stoichiometry of the dissociation, we see that 1 mol Ca^{2+} and 2 mol Cl^- are formed from each 1 mol of $CaCl_2$. Therefore, 0.10 mol $CaCl_2$ will yield 0.10 mol Ca^{2+} and 0.20 mol Cl^-. In 0.10 M $CaCl_2$, then, the concentration of Ca^{2+} is 0.10 M and the concentration of Cl^- is 0.20 M. Thus,

> *The concentration of a particular ion equals the concentration of the salt multiplied by the number of ions of that kind in one formula unit of the salt.*

◻ The solution doesn't actually contain any $CaCl_2$, even though this is the solute used to prepare the solution. Instead, the solution contains Ca^{2+} and Cl^- ions.

TOOLS
Molarity of ions in a salt solution

EXAMPLE 4.14
Calculating the Concentrations of Ions in a Solution

What are the molar concentrations of the ions in 0.20 M aluminum sulfate?

ANALYSIS: First, we need the formula for the solute. Aluminum forms the Al^{3+} ion and sulfate ion is SO_4^{2-}. For electrical neutrality, the formula of the salt must be $Al_2(SO_4)_3$. In the solution, the concentrations of the ions are determined by the stoichiometry of the salt. Therefore, we determine the number of ions of each kind formed from one formula unit of $Al_2(SO_4)_3$. These values are then used along with the given concentration of the salt to calculate the ion concentrations.

SOLUTION: When $Al_2(SO_4)_3$ dissolves, it dissociates as follows:

$$Al_2(SO_4)_3(s) \longrightarrow 2Al^{3+}(aq) + 3SO_4^{2-}(aq)$$

Each formula unit of $Al_2(SO_4)_3$ yields two Al^{3+} ions and three SO_4^{2-} ions. Therefore, 0.20 mol $Al_2(SO_4)_3$ yields 0.40 mol Al^{3+} and 0.60 mol SO_4^{2-}, and we conclude that the solution contains 0.40 M Al^{3+} and 0.60 M SO_4^{2-}.

IS THE ANSWER REASONABLE? The answers here have been obtained by simple mole reasoning. We could have found the answers in a more formal manner using the factor-label method. For example, for Al^{3+}, we have

$$\frac{0.20 \text{ mol } Al_2(SO_4)_3}{1.0 \text{ L soln}} \times \frac{2 \text{ mol } Al^{3+}}{1 \text{ mol } Al_2(SO_4)_3} = \frac{0.40 \text{ mol } Al^{3+}}{1.0 \text{ L soln}} = 0.40 \ M \ Al^{3+}$$

A similar calculation would give the concentration of SO_4^{2-} as 0.60 M. Study both methods. With just a little practice, you will have little difficulty with the reasoning approach we used first.

EXAMPLE 4.15
Calculating the Concentration of a Salt from the Concentration of One of Its Ions

A student found that the sulfate ion concentration in a solution of $Al_2(SO_4)_3$ was 0.90 M. What was the concentration of $Al_2(SO_4)_3$ in the solution?

ANALYSIS: Once again, we use the formula of the salt to determine the number of ions released when it dissociates. This time we use the information to work backward to find the salt concentration.

SOLUTION: Let's set up the problem using the factor label method to be sure of our procedure. We will use the fact that 1 mol $Al_2(SO_4)_3$ yields 3 mol SO_4^{2-} in solution.

$$1 \text{ mol } Al_2(SO_4)_3 \Leftrightarrow 3 \text{ mol } SO_4^{2-}$$

Therefore,

$$\frac{0.90 \text{ mol } SO_4^{2-}}{1.0 \text{ L soln}} \times \frac{1 \text{ mol } Al_2(SO_4)_3}{3 \text{ mol } SO_4^{2-}} = \frac{0.30 \text{ mol } Al_2(SO_4)_3}{1.0 \text{ L soln}} = 0.30 \ M \ Al_2(SO_4)_3$$

The concentration of $Al_2(SO_4)_3$ is 0.30 M.

IS THE ANSWER REASONABLE? We'll use the reasoning approach to check our answer. We know that 1 mol $Al_2(SO_4)_3$ yields 3 mol SO_4^{2-} in solution. Therefore, the number of moles of $Al_2(SO_4)_3$ is only one-third the number of moles of SO_4^{2-}. So the concentration of $Al_2(SO_4)_3$ must be one-third of 0.90 M, or 0.30 M.

Practice Exercise 33: What are the molar concentrations of the ions in 0.40 M $FeCl_3$? (Hint: How many ions of each kind are formed when $FeCl_3$ dissociates?)

Practice Exercise 34: In a solution of Na_3PO_4, the PO_4^{3-} concentration was determined to be 0.250 M. What was the sodium ion concentration in the solution?

Net ionic equations can be used in stoichiometry calculations

You have seen that a net ionic equation is convenient for describing the net chemical change in an ionic reaction. Let's study an example that illustrates how such equations can be used in stoichiometric calculations.

EXAMPLE 4.16
Stoichiometric Calculations Using a Net Ionic Equation

How many milliliters of 0.100 M $AgNO_3$ solution are needed to react completely with 25.0 mL of 0.400 M $CaCl_2$ solution? The net ionic equation for the reaction is

$$Ag^+(aq) + Cl^-(aq) \longrightarrow AgCl(s)$$

ANALYSIS: In many ways, this problem is similar to Example 4.13. However, to use the net ionic equation, we will need to work with the concentrations of the ions. Therefore, the tools we will use to solve this problem are the formulas of the salts (to find the molar concentrations of the ions) and the coefficients of the equation (to relate moles of Ag^+ and Cl^-).

To solve the problem, the first step will be to calculate the molarities of the ions in the solutions being mixed. Next, using the volume and molarity of the Cl^- solution, we will calculate the moles of Cl^- available. Then we'll use the coefficients of the equation to find the moles of Ag^+ that react. Finally, we'll use the molarity of the Ag^+ solution to determine the volume of the 0.100 M $AgNO_3$ solution needed.

SOLUTION: We begin by finding the concentrations of the ions in the reacting solutions:

0.100 M $AgNO_3$ contains 0.100 M Ag^+ and 0.100 M NO_3^-

0.400 M $CaCl_2$ contains 0.400 M Ca^{2+} and 0.800 M Cl^-

We're only interested in the Ag^+ and Cl^-; the Ca^{2+} and NO_3^- are spectator ions. For our purposes, then, the solution concentrations are 0.100 M Ag^+ and 0.800 M Cl^-. Having these values, we can now restate the problem: How many milliliters of 0.100 M Ag^+ solution are needed to react completely with 25.0 mL of 0.800 M Cl^- solution?

$$25.0 \text{ mL } Cl^- \text{ soln} \Leftrightarrow ? \text{ mL } Ag^+ \text{ soln}$$

The moles of Cl^- available for reaction are obtained from the molarity and volume (0.0250 L) of the Cl^- solution.

$$0.0250 \text{ L } Cl^- \text{ soln} \times \frac{0.800 \text{ mol } Cl^-}{1.00 \text{ L } Cl^- \text{ soln}} = 0.0200 \text{ mol } Cl^-$$

The coefficients of the equation tell us the Ag^+ and Cl^- combine in a 1-to-1 mole ratio, so 0.0200 mol $Cl^- \Leftrightarrow$ 0.0200 mol Ag^+. Finally, we calculate the volume of the Ag^+ solution using its molarity as a conversion factor. As we've done earlier, we use the factor that makes the units cancel correctly.

$$0.0200 \text{ mol } Ag^+ \times \frac{1.00 \text{ L } Ag^+ \text{ soln}}{0.100 \text{ mol } Ag^+} = 0.200 \text{ L } Ag^+ \text{ soln}$$

Our calculations tell us that we must use 0.200 L or 200 mL of the $AgNO_3$ solution. We could also have used the following chain calculation, of course.

$$0.0250 \text{ L } Cl^- \text{ soln} \times \frac{0.800 \text{ mol } Cl^-}{1.00 \text{ L } Cl^- \text{ soln}} \times \frac{1 \text{ mol } Ag^+}{1 \text{ mol } Cl^-} \times \frac{1.00 \text{ L } Ag^+ \text{ soln}}{0.100 \text{ mol } Ag^+} = 0.200 \text{ L } Ag^+ \text{ soln}$$

IS THE ANSWER REASONABLE? The silver ion concentration is one-eighth as large as the chloride ion concentration. Since the ions react one-for-one, we will need eight times as much silver ion solution as chloride solution. Eight times the amount of chloride solution, 25 mL, is 200 mL, which is the answer we obtained. Therefore, the answer appears to be correct.

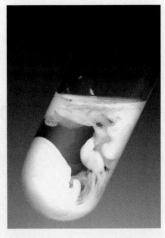

A solution of $AgNO_3$ is added to a solution of $CaCl_2$, producing a precipitate of AgCl. *(Andy Washnik.)*

□ Simple reasoning works well here. Since the coefficients of Ag^+ and Cl^- are the same, the numbers of moles that react must be equal.

Practice Exercise 35: Suppose 18.4 mL of 0.100 M $AgNO_3$ solution was needed to react completely with 20.5 mL of $CaCl_2$ solution. What is the molarity of the $CaCl_2$ solution? Use the net ionic equation in the preceding example to work the problem. (Hint: How can you calculate molarity from moles and volume, and how can you calculate the molarity of the $CaCl_2$ solution from the molarity of Cl^-?)

Practice Exercise 36: How many milliliters of 0.500 M KOH are needed to react completely with 60.0 mL of 0.250 M $FeCl_2$ solution to precipitate $Fe(OH)_2$? The net ionic equation is $Fe^{2+}(aq) + 2OH^-(aq) \longrightarrow Fe(OH)_2(s)$.

4.8 | CHEMICAL ANALYSIS AND TITRATION ARE APPLICATIONS OF SOLUTION STOICHIOMETRY

Chemical analyses fall into two categories. In a **qualitative analysis** we simply determine which substances are present in a sample without measuring their amounts. In a **quantitative analysis,** our goal is to measure the amounts of the various substances in a sample.

When chemical reactions are used in a quantitative analysis, a useful strategy is to capture *all* of a desired chemical species in a compound with a known formula. From the amount of this compound obtained, we can determine how much of the desired chemical species was present in the original sample. The calculations required for these kinds of problems are not new; they are simply applications of the stoichiometric calculations you've already learned.

EXAMPLE 4.17
Calculation Involving a Quantitative Analysis

A certain insecticide is a compound known to contain carbon, hydrogen, and chlorine. Reactions were carried out on a 0.134 g sample of the compound that converted all of its chlorine to chloride ion dissolved in water. This aqueous solution required 37.80 mL of 0.0500 M AgNO$_3$ to precipitate all the chloride ion as AgCl. What was the percentage by mass of Cl in the original insecticide sample? The precipitation reaction was

$$Ag^+(aq) + Cl^-(aq) \longrightarrow AgCl(s)$$

ANALYSIS: The percentage Cl in the sample will be calculated as follows:

$$\% \text{ Cl by mass} = \frac{\text{mass of Cl in sample}}{\text{mass of sample}} \times 100\%$$

So, we need to determine the mass of Cl. We can use Equation 4.5 (page 156) and the volume and molarity of the AgNO$_3$ solution to find the number of moles of Ag$^+$ that reacts with the Cl$^-$ in the solution. The ionic equation tells us Ag$^+$ and Cl$^-$ react in a 1-to-1 mole ratio, so the moles of Ag$^+$ equals the moles of Cl$^-$ that react. This is the same as the number of moles of Cl in the sample. Then we'll use the molar mass of Cl as a tool to change moles of Cl to grams of Cl.

□ The molar mass of a chlorine atom and a chloride ion differ by such a small amount that we can use them interchangeably.

SOLUTION: In 0.0500 M AgNO$_3$, the molarity of Ag$^+$ is 0.0500 M. Applying Equation 4.5,

$$0.03780 \text{ L Ag}^+ \text{ soln} \times \frac{0.0500 \text{ mol Ag}^+}{1.00 \text{ L Ag}^+ \text{ soln}} = 1.89 \times 10^{-3} \text{ mol Ag}^+$$

From the stoichiometry of the equation, when 1.89×10^{-3} mol Ag$^+$ reacts, 1.89×10^{-3} mol Cl$^-$ reacts. This is the amount of Cl$^-$ that came from the sample, so the sample must have contained 1.89×10^{-3} mol Cl. The atomic mass of Cl is 35.45, so 1 mol Cl = 35.45 g Cl. Therefore, the mass of Cl in the sample was

$$1.89 \times 10^{-3} \text{ mol Cl} \times \frac{35.45 \text{ g Cl}}{1 \text{ mol Cl}} = 6.70 \times 10^{-2} \text{ g Cl}$$

The percentage by mass of Cl in the sample is

$$\% \text{ Cl} = \frac{6.70 \times 10^{-2} \text{ g Cl}}{0.134 \text{ g sample}} \times 100\%$$

$$= 50.0\%$$

The insecticide was 50.0% Cl by mass.

IS THE ANSWER REASONABLE? Although we could do some approximate arithmetic to check our calculation, that's more easily done with the calculator. Therefore, let's look over the reasoning and calculations to see if they make sense. We've used the molarity and volume of the AgNO$_3$ solution to calculate the number of moles of Ag$^+$ that reacted (1.89×10^{-3} mol Ag$^+$). This has to be the same as the moles of Cl$^-$ that reacted, and because the Cl$^-$ came from the sample, the sample must have contained 1.89×10^{-3} mol of Cl. The mass of this Cl was calculated in the usual way using the molar mass of Cl. The value we obtained, 0.067 g, is half the sample weight of 0.134 g, so half (50%) of the sample weight was Cl. The answer, therefore, seems to be correct.

Practice Exercise 37: A solution containing Na_2SO_4 was treated with 0.150 M $BaCl_2$ solution until all the sulfate ion had reacted to form $BaSO_4$. The net reaction

$$Ba^{2+}(aq) + SO_4{}^{2-}(aq) \longrightarrow BaSO_4(s)$$

required 28.40 mL of the $BaCl_2$ solution. How many grams of Na_2SO_4 were in the solution? (Hint: How do moles of $SO_4{}^{2-}$ relate to moles of Na_2SO_4?)

Practice Exercise 38: A sample of a mixture containing $CaCl_2$ and $MgCl_2$ weighed 2.000 g. The sample was dissolved in water and H_2SO_4 was added until the precipitation of $CaSO_4$ was complete.

$$CaCl_2(aq) + H_2SO_4(aq) \longrightarrow CaSO_4(s) + 2HCl(aq)$$

The $CaSO_4$ was filtered, dried completely, and weighed. A total of 0.736 g of $CaSO_4$ was obtained.

   (a) How many moles of Ca^{2+} were in the $CaSO_4$?
   (b) How many moles of Ca^{2+} were in the original 2.000 g sample?
   (c) How many moles of $CaCl_2$ were in the 2.000 g sample?
   (d) How many grams of $CaCl_2$ were in the 2.000 g sample?
   (e) What was the percentage by mass of $CaCl_2$ in the original mixture?

Acid–base titrations are useful in chemical analyses

Titration is an important laboratory procedure used in performing chemical analyses. The apparatus is shown in Figure 4.22. The long tube is called a **buret**, which is marked for volumes, usually in increments of 0.10 mL. The valve at the bottom of the buret is called a **stopcock**, and it permits the analyst to control the amount of **titrant** (the solution in the buret) that is delivered to the receiving vessel (the beaker shown in the drawing).

In a typical titration, a solution containing one reactant is placed in the receiving vessel. Carefully measured volumes of a solution of the other reactant are then added from the buret. (One of the two solutions is of a precisely known concentration and is called a **standard solution**.) This addition is continued until something (usually a visual effect, like a color change) signals that the two reactants have been combined in just the right proportions to give a complete reaction.

In acid–base titrations, an **acid–base indicator** is used to detect the completion of the reaction by a change in color. Indicators are dyes that have one color in an acidic solution and a different color in a basic solution. Litmus was mentioned earlier. Phenolphthalein is

◻ The theory of acid–base indicators is discussed in Chapter 16.

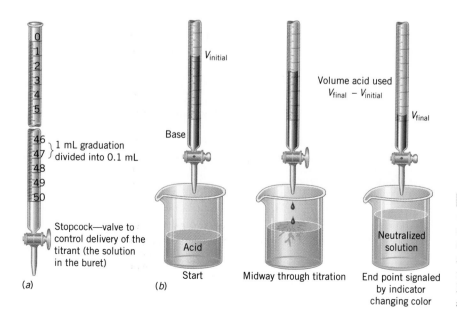

FIG. 4.22 **Titration.** (*a*) A buret. (*b*) The titration of an acid by a base in which an acid–base indicator is used to signal the end point, which is the point at which all of the acid has been neutralized and addition of the base is halted.

a common indicator for titrations; it changes from colorless to pink when a solution changes from acidic to basic. This color change is very abrupt, and occurs with the addition of only one final drop of the titrant just as the end of the reaction is reached. When we observe the color change, the **end point** has been reached and the addition of titrant is stopped. We then record the total volume of the titrant that's been added to the receiving flask.

EXAMPLE 4.18
Calculation Involving Acid–Base Titration

A student prepares a solution of hydrochloric acid that is approximately 0.1 M and wishes to determine its precise concentration. A 25.00 mL portion of the HCl solution is transferred to a flask, and after a few drops of indicator are added, the HCl solution is titrated with 0.0775 M NaOH solution. The titration requires exactly 37.46 mL of the standard NaOH solution to reach the end point. What is the molarity of the HCl solution?

ANALYSIS: This is really a straightforward stoichiometry calculation involving a chemical reaction. The first step in solving it is to write the balanced equation, which will give us the stoichiometric equivalency between HCl and NaOH. The reaction is an acid–base neutralization, so the product is a salt plus water. Following the procedures developed earlier, the reaction is

$$HCl(aq) + NaOH(aq) \longrightarrow NaCl(aq) + H_2O$$

Solving the problem will follow the same route as in Example 4.13. Our tools will be the molarity and volume of the NaOH solution (to calculate moles of NaOH that react), the coefficients of the equation (to obtain moles of HCl), and the definition of molarity (to calculate the molarity of the HCl solution from moles HCl and the volume of the HCl sample taken).

A solution of HCl is titrated with a solution of NaOH using phenolphthalein as the acid–base indicator. The pink color that phenolphthalein has in a basic solution can be seen where a drop of the NaOH solution has entered the HCl solution, to which a few drops of the indicator had been added. *(Michael Watson.)*

SOLUTION: From the molarity and volume of the NaOH solution, we calculate the number of moles of NaOH consumed in the titration.

$$0.03746 \text{ L NaOH soln} \times \frac{0.0775 \text{ mol NaOH}}{1.00 \text{ L NaOH soln}} = 2.90 \times 10^{-3} \text{ mol NaOH}$$

The coefficients in the equation tell us that NaOH and HCl react in a 1-to-1 mole ratio,

$$2.90 \times 10^{-3} \text{ mol NaOH} \times \frac{1 \text{ mol HCl}}{1 \text{ mol NaOH}} = 2.90 \times 10^{-3} \text{ mol HCl}$$

so in this titration, 2.90×10^{-3} mol HCl was in the flask. To calculate the molarity of the HCl, we simply apply the definition of molarity. We take the ratio of the number of moles of HCl that reacted (2.90×10^{-3} mol HCl) to the volume (in liters) of the HCl solution used (25.00 mL, or 0.02500 L).

$$\text{Molarity of HCl soln} = \frac{2.90 \times 10^{-3} \text{ mol HCl}}{0.02500 \text{ L HCl soln}}$$

$$= 0.116 \, M \text{ HCl}$$

The molarity of the hydrochloric acid is 0.116 M.

IS THE ANSWER REASONABLE? If the concentrations of the NaOH and HCl were the same, the volumes used would have been equal. However, the volume of the NaOH solution used is larger than the volume of HCl solution. This must mean that the HCl solution is more concentrated than the NaOH solution. The value we obtained, 0.116 M, is larger than 0.0775 M, so our answer makes sense.

Practice Exercise 39: In a titration, a sample of H_2SO_4 solution having a volume of 15.00 mL required 36.42 mL of 0.147 M NaOH solution for *complete* neutralization. What is the molarity of the H_2SO_4 solution? (Hint: Check to be sure your chemical equation is written correctly and balanced.)

Practice Exercise 40: "Stomach acid" is hydrochloric acid. A sample of gastric juice having a volume of 5.00 mL required 11.00 mL of 0.0100 M KOH solution for neutralization in a titration. What was the molar concentration of HCl in this fluid? If we assume a density of 1.00 g mL^{-1} for the fluid, what was the percentage by weight of HCl?

SUMMARY

Solution Vocabulary. A **solution** is a homogeneous mixture in which one or more **solutes** are dissolved in a **solvent.** A solution may be **dilute** or **concentrated,** depending on the amount of solute dissolved in a given amount of solvent. **Concentration** (e.g., **percentage concentration**) is a ratio of the amount of solute to either the amount of solvent or the amount of solution. The amount of solute required to give a **saturated** solution at a given temperature is called the solute's **solubility. Unsaturated** solutions will dissolve more solute, but **supersaturated** solutions are unstable and tend to give a **precipitate.**

Electrolytes. Substances that **dissociate** or **ionize** in water to produce cations and anions are **electrolytes;** those that do not are called **nonelectrolytes.** Electrolytes include salts and metal hydroxides as well as molecular acids and bases that ionize by reaction with water. In water, ionic compounds are completely dissociated into ions and are **strong electrolytes.**

Ionic and Net Ionic Equations. Reactions that occur in solution between ions and are called **ionic reactions.** Solutions of soluble strong electrolytes often yield an insoluble product which appears as a **precipitate.** Equations for these reactions can be written in three different ways. In **molecular equations,** complete formulas for all reactants and products are used. In an **ionic equation,** soluble strong electrolytes are written in dissociated (ionized) form; "molecular" formulas are used for solids and weak electrolytes. A **net ionic equation** is obtained by eliminating **spectator ions** from the ionic equation, and such an equation allows us to identify other combinations of reactants that give the same net reaction. An ionic or net ionic equation is balanced only if both atoms *and* net charge are balanced.

Acids and Bases as Electrolytes. An **acid** is a substance that produces hydronium ions, H_3O^+, when dissolved in water, and a **base** produces hydroxide ions, OH^-, when dissolved in water. The oxides of nonmetals are generally **acidic anhydrides** and react with water to give acids. Metal oxides are usually **basic anhydrides** because they tend to react with water to give metal hydroxides or bases.

Strong acids and bases are also strong electrolytes. **Weak acids and bases** are **weak electrolytes,** which are incompletely ionized in water. In a solution of a weak electrolyte there is a **chemical equilibrium (dynamic equilibrium)** between the non-ionized molecules of the solute and the ions formed by the reaction of the solute with water.

Predicting Metathesis Reactions. Metathesis or **double replacement** reactions take place when anions and cations of two salts change partners. A metathesis reaction will occur if there is a net ionic equation. This happens if (1) a precipitate forms from soluble reactants, (2) an acid–base neutralization occurs, (3) a gas is formed, or (4) a weak electrolyte forms from soluble strong electrolytes. You should learn the **solubility rules** (Table 4.1), and remember that all salts are strong electrolytes. Remember that all strong acids and bases are strong electrolytes, too. Strong acids react with strong bases in neutralization reactions to produce a salt and water. Acids react with insoluble oxides and hydroxides to form water and the corresponding salt. Many **acid–base neutralization** reactions can be viewed as a type of metathesis reaction in which one product is water. Be sure to learn the reactions that produce gases in metathesis reactions, which are found in Table 4.2.

Molar Concentration, Dilution, and Solution Stoichiometry. Molarity is the ratio of moles of solute to liters of solution. Molarity provides two conversion factors relating moles of solute and the volume of a solution.

$$\frac{\text{mol solute}}{\text{1 L soln}} \quad \text{and} \quad \frac{\text{1 L soln}}{\text{mol solute}}$$

Concentrated solutions of known molarity can be diluted quantitatively using volumetric glassware such as pipets and volumetric flasks. When a solution is diluted by adding solvent, the amount of solute doesn't change but the concentration decreases.

In ionic reactions, the concentrations of the ions in a solution of a salt can be derived from the molar concentration of the salt, taking into account the number of ions formed per formula unit of the salt.

Titration is a technique used to make quantitative measurements of the amounts of solutions needed to obtain a complete reaction. The apparatus is a long tube called a **buret** that has a **stopcock** at one end, which is used to control the flow of **titrant.** In an acid–base titration, the **end point** is normally detected visually using an **acid–base indicator.** A color change indicates complete reaction, at which time addition of titrant is stopped and the volume added is recorded.

TOOLS FOR PROBLEM SOLVING

In this chapter you learned to apply the following concepts as tools in solving problems dealing with reactions in aqueous solutions. Study each one carefully so that you know what each is used for. When faced with solving a problem, recall what each tool does and consider whether it will be helpful in finding a solution. This will aid you in selecting the tools you need.

Criteria for a balanced ionic or net ionic equation *(page 135)* For an equation that includes the formulas of ions to be balanced, it must satisfy two criteria. The number of atoms of each kind must be the same on both sides, and the total net electrical charge shown on both sides must be the same.

Equation for the ionization of an acid in water *(page 137)* Equation 4.2 describes how acids react with water to form hydronium ion plus an anion.

$$HA + H_2O \longrightarrow H_3O^+ + A^-$$

Use this tool to write equations for ionizations of acids and to determine the formula of the anion formed when the acid molecule loses an H^+. The equation also applies to acid anions such as HSO_4^- which gives SO_4^{2-} when it loses an H^+. Often H_2O is omitted from the equation and the hydronium ion is abbreviated as H^+.

Equation for the ionization of a molecular base in water *(page 139)* Equation 4.3 describes how molecules of molecular bases acquire H^+ from H_2O to form a cation plus a hydroxide ion.

$$B + H_2O \longrightarrow BH^+ + OH^-$$

Use this tool to write equations for ionizations of bases and to determine the formula of the cation formed when the base molecule gains an H^+. *Molecular bases are weak and are not completely ionized.*

Table of strong acids *(page 140)* Formulas of the most common strong acids are given here. If you learn this list and encounter an acid that's *not* on the list, you can assume it to be a weak acid. The most common strong acids are HCl, HNO_3, and H_2SO_4. *Remember that strong acids are completely ionized in water.*

Predicting the existence of a net ionic equation *(page 146)* A net ionic equation will exist and a reaction will occur when:

- A precipitate is formed from a mixture of soluble reactants.
- An acid reacts with a base. *This includes strong or weak acids reacting with strong or weak bases or insoluble metal hydroxides or oxides.*
- A weak electrolyte is formed from a mixture of strong electrolytes.
- A gas is formed from a mixture of reactants.

These criteria are tools to determine whether or not a net reaction will occur in a solution.

Solubility rules *(page 147)* The rules in Table 4.1 are the tool we use to determine whether a particular salt is soluble in water. (If a salt is soluble, it's completely dissociated into ions.) They also serve as a tool to help predict the course of metathesis reactions.

Substances that form gases in metathesis reactions *(page 152)* Use Table 4.2 as a tool to help predict the outcome of metathesis reactions. The most common gas formed in such reactions is CO_2, which comes from the reaction of an acid with a carbonate or bicarbonate.

Molarity *(page 154)* Molarity provides the connection between moles of a solute and the volume of its solution. The definition provided by Equation 4.4 serves as a tool for calculating molarity from values of moles of solute and volume of solution (in liters).

$$\text{Molarity } (M) = \frac{\text{moles of solute}}{\text{liters of solution}}$$

Molarity is the tool we use to write an equivalence between moles of solute and volume of solution, from which appropriate conversion factors can be formed.

Product of molarity and volume gives moles *(page 156)* For any problem in which you're given both molarity and volume of a solution of a substance, you can always calculate the number of moles of the substance using Equation 4.5.

$$\text{Molarity} \times \text{volume (L)} = \text{moles of solute}$$

Recognizing this relationship is very important when working stoichiometry problems involving solutions.

Dilution problems *(page 158)* Equation 4.6 is the tool we use for working dilution problems.

$$V_{dil} \cdot M_{dil} = V_{conc} \cdot M_{conc}$$

The volume units must be the same on both sides of the equation.

Concentrations of ions in a solution of a salt *(page 161)* When using a net ionic equation to work stoichiometry problems, we need the concentrations of the ions in the solutions. *The concentration of a particular ion equals the concentration of the salt multiplied by the number of ions of that kind in one formula unit of the salt.*

Overview of stoichiometry problems In this chapter you encountered another way that the data in stoichiometry problems are presented. Figure 4.23 gives an overview of the various paths through problems that involve chemical reactions. All funnel through the coefficients of the equation as the means to convert from moles of one substance to moles of another. The starting and finishing quantities can be moles, grams, or volumes of solutions of known molarity.

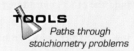

TOOLS
Paths through stoichiometry problems

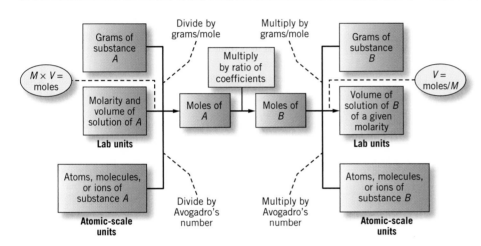

FIG. 4.23 **Paths for working stoichiometry problems involving chemical reactions.** The critical link is the conversion between moles of one substance and moles of another using the coefficients of the balanced equation. We can calculate moles in several ways: from numbers of atomic-sized formula units, and from laboratory units of grams or the volumes of solutions of known molarities. Similarly, we can present the answer either in moles, grams, number of formula units, or a volume of solution of known molarity.

QUESTIONS, PROBLEMS, AND EXERCISES

Answers to problems whose numbers are printed in color are given in Appendix B. More challenging problems are marked with asterisks. ILW = Interactive Learningware solution is available at *www.wiley.com/college/brady*. OH = an Office Hours video is available for this problem.

REVIEW QUESTIONS

Solution Terminology

4.1 Define the following: (a) solvent, (b) solute, (c) concentration.

4.2 Define the following: (a) concentrated, (b) dilute, (c) saturated, (d) unsaturated, (e) supersaturated, (f) solubility.

4.3 Why are chemical reactions often carried out using solutions?

4.4 Describe what will happen if a crystal of sugar is added to (a) a saturated sugar solution, (b) a supersaturated solution of sugar, and (c) an unsaturated solution of sugar.

4.5 What is the meaning of the term *precipitate*? What condition must exist for a precipitate to form spontaneously in a solution?

Electrolytes

4.6 What is an *electrolyte*? What is a *nonelectrolyte*?

4.7 Why is an electrolyte able to conduct electricity while a nonelectrolyte cannot? What does it mean when we say that an ion is "hydrated?"

4.8 Define *dissociation* as it applies to ionic compounds that dissolve in water.

4.9 Write equations for the dissociation of the following in water: (a) $CaCl_2$, (b) $(NH_4)_2SO_4$, (c) $NaC_2H_3O_2$.

Ionic Reactions

4.10 How do molecular, ionic, and net ionic equations differ? What are spectator ions?

4.11 The following equation shows the formation of cobalt(II) hydroxide, a compound used to improve the drying properties of lithographic inks.

$$Co^{2+}(aq) + 2Cl^-(aq) + 2Na^+(aq) + 2OH^-(aq) \longrightarrow$$
$$Co(OH)_2(s) + 2Na^+(aq) + 2Cl^-(aq)$$

Which are the spectator ions? Write the net ionic equation.

4.12 What two conditions must be fulfilled by a balanced ionic equation? The following equation is not balanced. How do we know? Find the errors and fix them.

$$3Co^{3+}(aq) + 2HPO_4^{2-}(aq) \longrightarrow Co_3(PO_4)_2(s) + 2H^+(aq)$$

Acids, Bases, and Their Reactions

4.13 Give two general properties of an acid. Give two general properties of a base.

4.14 If you believed a solution was basic, which color litmus paper (blue or pink) would you use to test the solution to see if you were correct? What would you observe if you've selected correctly? Why would the other color litmus paper not lead to a conclusive result?

4.15 How did Arrhenius define an acid and a base?

4.16 Which of the following undergo dissociation in water? Which undergo ionization? (a) NaOH, (b) HNO_3, (c) NH_3, (d) H_2SO_4.

4.17 Which of the following would yield an acidic solution when they react with water? Which would give a basic solution? (a) P_4O_{10}, (b) K_2O, (c) SeO_3, (d) Cl_2O_7.

4.18 What is a *dynamic equilibrium*? Using acetic acid as an example, describe why all the $HC_2H_3O_2$ molecules are not ionized in water.

4.19 Why don't we use double arrows in the equation for the reaction of a strong acid with water?

4.20 Which of the following are strong acids? (a) HCN, (b) HNO_3, (c) H_2SO_3, (d) HCl, (e) $HCHO_2$, (f) HNO_2.

4.21 Which of the following produce a strongly basic solution when dissolved in water? (a) C_5H_5N, (b) $Ba(OH)_2$, (c) KOH, (d) $C_6H_5NH_2$, (e) Cs_2O, (f) N_2O_5.

4.22 Methylamine, CH_3NH_2, reacts with hydronium ion in very much the same manner as ammonia.

$$CH_3NH_2(aq) + H_3O^+(aq) \longrightarrow CH_3NH_3^+(aq) + H_2O$$

On the basis of what you have learned so far in this course, sketch the molecular structures of CH_3NH_2 and $CH_3NH_3^+$ (the methylammonium ion).

Nomenclature of Acids and Bases

4.23 Name the following: (a) $H_2Se(g)$, (b) $H_2Se(aq)$

4.24 Iodine, like chlorine, forms several acids. What are the names of the following? (a) HIO_4, (b) HIO_3, (c) HIO_2, (d) HIO, (e) HI.

4.25 For the acids in the preceding question, (a) write the formulas and (b) name the ions formed by removing a hydrogen ion (H^+) from each acid.

4.26 Write the formula for (a) chromic acid, (b) carbonic acid, and (c) oxalic acid. (Hint: Check the table of polyatomic ions.)

4.27 Name the following acid salts: (a) $NaHCO_3$, (b) KH_2PO_4, (c) $(NH_4)_2HPO_4$.

4.28 Write the formulas for all the acid salts that could be formed from the reaction of NaOH with the acid H_3PO_4.

4.29 Name the following oxoacids and give the names and formulas of the salts formed from them by neutralization with NaOH: (a) HOCl, (b) HIO_2, (c) $HBrO_3$, (d) $HClO_4$.

4.30 The formula for the arsenate ion is AsO_4^{3-}. What is the formula for arsenous acid?

4.31 Butyric acid, $HC_4H_7O_2$, gives rancid butter is bad odor. What is the name of the salt $NaC_4H_7O_2$?

4.32 Calcium propionate, $Ca(C_3H_5O_2)_2$ is used in baked foods as a preservative and to prevent the growth of mold. What is the name of the acid $HC_3H_5O_2$?

Predicting Ionic Reactions

4.33 What factors lead to the existence of a net ionic equation in a reaction between ions?

4.34 What is another name for *metathesis reaction*?

4.35 Silver bromide is "insoluble." What does this mean about the concentrations of Ag^+ and Br^- in a saturated solution of AgBr? Explain why a precipitate of AgBr forms when solutions of the soluble salts $AgNO_3$ and NaBr are mixed.

4.36 If a solution of trisodium phosphate, Na_3PO_4, is poured into seawater, precipitates of calcium phosphate and magnesium phosphate are formed. (Magnesium and calcium ions are among the principal ions found in seawater.) Write net ionic equations for the reactions.

4.37 Washing soda is $Na_2CO_3 \cdot 10H_2O$. Explain, using chemical equations, how this substance is able to remove Ca^{2+} ions from "hard water."

4.38 With which of the following will the weak acid $HCHO_2$ react? Where there is a reaction, write the formulas of the products. (a) KOH, (b) MgO, (c) NH_3

4.39 Suppose you suspected that a certain solution contained ammonium ions. What simple chemical test could you perform that would tell you whether your suspicion was correct?

4.40 What gas is formed if HCl is added to (a) $NaHCO_3$, (b) Na_2S, and (c) K_2SO_3?

Molarity and Dilution

4.41 What is the definition of molarity? Show that the ratio of millimoles (mmol) to milliliters (mL) is equivalent to the ratio of moles to liters.

4.42 A solution is labeled 0.25 *M* HCl. Construct two conversion factors that relate moles of HCl to the volume of solution expressed in liters.

4.43 When the units *molarity* and *liter* are multiplied, what are the resulting units?

4.44 When a solution labeled 0.50 *M* HNO_3 is diluted with water to give 0.25 *M* HNO_3, what happens to the number of moles of HNO_3 in the solution?

4.45 Two solutions, A and B, are labeled "0.10 *M* $CaCl_2$" and "0.20 *M* $CaCl_2$," respectively. Both solutions contain the same number of moles of $CaCl_2$. If solution A has a volume of 50 mL, what is the volume of solution B?

Chemical Analyses and Titrations

4.46 What is the difference between a qualitative analysis and a quantitative analysis?

4.47 Describe each of the following: (a) buret, (b) titration, (c) titrant, and (d) end point.

4.48 What is the function of an indicator in a titration? What color is phenolphthalein in (a) an acidic solution and (b) a basic solution?

REVIEW PROBLEMS

Ionic Reactions

4.49 Write ionic and net ionic equations for these reactions.
(a) $(NH_4)_2CO_3(aq) + MgCl_2(aq) \longrightarrow$
$$2NH_4Cl(aq) + MgCO_3(s)$$
(b) $CuCl_2(aq) + 2NaOH(aq) \longrightarrow$
$$Cu(OH)_2(s) + 2NaCl(aq)$$
(c) $3FeSO_4(aq) + 2Na_3PO_4(aq) \longrightarrow$
$$Fe_3(PO_4)_2(s) + 3Na_2SO_4(aq)$$
(d) $2AgC_2H_3O_2(aq) + NiCl_2(aq) \longrightarrow$
$$2AgCl(s) + Ni(C_2H_3O_2)_2(aq)$$

OH 4.50 Write balanced ionic and net ionic equations for these reactions.
(a) $CuSO_4(aq) + BaCl_2(aq) \longrightarrow CuCl_2(aq) + BaSO_4(s)$
(b) $Fe(NO_3)_3(aq) + LiOH(aq) \longrightarrow$
$$LiNO_3(aq) + Fe(OH)_3(s)$$
(c) $Na_3PO_4(aq) + CaCl_2(aq) \longrightarrow$
$$Ca_3(PO_4)_2(s) + NaCl(aq)$$
(d) $Na_2S(aq) + AgC_2H_3O_2(aq) \longrightarrow$
$$NaC_2H_3O_2(aq) + Ag_2S(s)$$

Acids and Bases as Electrolytes

4.51 Pure $HClO_4$ is molecular. In water it is a strong acid. Write an equation for its ionization in water.

4.52 HBr is a molecular substance that is a strong acid in water. Write an equation for its ionization in water.

OH 4.53 Hydrazine is a toxic substance that can form when household ammonia is mixed with a bleach such as Clorox. Its formula is N_2H_4, and it is a weak base. Write a chemical equation showing the reaction of hydrazine with water.

4.54 Pyridine, C_5H_5N, is a fishy smelling compound used as an intermediate in making insecticides. It is a weak base. Write a chemical equation showing its reaction with water.

4.55 Nitrous acid, HNO_2, is a weak acid that can form when sodium nitrite, a meat preservative, reacts with stomach acid (HCl). Write an equation showing the ionization of HNO_2 in water.

4.56 Pentanoic acid, $HC_5H_9O_2$, is found in a plant called valerian, which cats seem to like almost as much as catnip. Also called valeric acid, it is a weak acid. Write an equation showing its reaction with water.

4.57 Carbonic acid, H_2CO_3, is a weak diprotic acid formed in rainwater as it passes through the atmosphere and dissolves carbon dioxide. Write chemical equations for the equilibria involved in the stepwise ionization of H_2CO_3 in water.

4.58 Phosphoric acid, H_3PO_4, is a weak acid found in some soft drinks. It undergoes ionization in three steps. Write chemical equations for the equilibria involved in each of these reactions.

Metathesis Reactions

4.59 Write *balanced* ionic and net ionic equations for these reactions.
(a) $FeSO_4(aq) + K_3PO_4(aq) \longrightarrow Fe_3(PO_4)_2(s) + K_2SO_4(aq)$
(b) $AgC_2H_3O_2(aq) + AlCl_3(aq) \longrightarrow$
$$AgCl(s) + Al(C_2H_3O_2)_3(aq)$$

4.60 Write *balanced* ionic and net ionic equations for these reactions.
(a) $Fe(NO_3)_3(aq) + KOH(aq) \longrightarrow KNO_3(aq) + Fe(OH)_3(s)$
(b) $Na_3PO_4(aq) + SrCl_2(aq) \longrightarrow Sr_3(PO_4)_2(s) + NaCl(aq)$

4.61 Aqueous solutions of sodium sulfide and copper(II) nitrate are mixed. A precipitate of copper(II) sulfide forms at once. The solution that remains contains sodium nitrate. Write the molecular, ionic, and net ionic equations for this reaction.

4.62 If an aqueous solution of iron(III) sulfate (a compound used in dyeing textiles and also for etching aluminum) is mixed with a solution of barium chloride, a precipitate of barium sulfate forms and the solution that remains contains iron(III) chloride. Write the molecular, ionic, and net ionic equations for this reaction.

4.63 Use the solubility rules to decide which of the following compounds are *soluble* in water.
(a) $Ca(NO_3)_2$ (d) silver nitrate
(b) $FeCl_2$ (e) barium sulfate
(c) $Ni(OH)_2$ (f) copper(II) carbonate

4.64 Predict which of the following compounds are *soluble* in water.
(a) $HgBr_2$ (d) ammonium phosphate
(b) $Sr(NO_3)_2$ (e) lead(II) iodide
(c) Hg_2Br_2 (f) lead(II) acetate

Acid–Base Neutralization Reactions

4.65 Complete and balance the following equations. For each, write the molecular, ionic, and net ionic equations. (All the products are soluble in water.)
(a) $Ca(OH)_2(aq) + HNO_3(aq) \longrightarrow$
(b) $Al_2O_3(s) + HCl(aq) \longrightarrow$
(c) $Zn(OH)_2(s) + H_2SO_4(aq) \longrightarrow$

4.66 Complete and balance the following equations. For each, write the molecular, ionic, and net ionic equations. (All the products are soluble in water.)
(a) $HC_2H_3O_2(aq) + Mg(OH)_2(s) \longrightarrow$
(b) $HClO_4(aq) + NH_3(aq) \longrightarrow$
(c) $H_2CO_3(aq) + NH_3(aq) \longrightarrow$

4.67 How would the electrical conductivity of a solution of $Ba(OH)_2$ change as a solution of H_2SO_4 is added slowly to it? Use a net ionic equation to justify your answer.

4.68 How would the electrical conductivity of a solution of $HC_2H_3O_2$ change as a solution of NH_3 is added slowly to it? Use a net ionic equation to justify your answer.

Ionic Reactions That Produce Gases

4.69 Write balanced net ionic equations for these reactions:
(a) $HNO_3(aq) + K_2CO_3(aq)$
(b) $Ca(OH)_2(aq) + NH_4NO_3(aq)$

4.70 Write balanced net ionic equations for these reactions:
(a) $H_2SO_4(aq) + NaHSO_3(aq)$
(b) $HNO_3(aq) + (NH_4)_2CO_3(aq)$

Predicting Ionic Reactions

4.71 Explain why the following reactions take place.
(a) $CrCl_3 + 3NaOH \longrightarrow Cr(OH)_3 + 3NaCl$
(b) $ZnO + 2HBr \longrightarrow ZnBr_2 + H_2O$

OH **4.72** Explain why the following reactions take place.
(a) $MnCO_3 + H_2SO_4 \longrightarrow MnSO_4 + H_2O + CO_2$
(b) $Na_2C_2O_4 + 2HNO_3 \longrightarrow 2NaNO_3 + H_2C_2O_4$

4.73 Complete and balance the molecular, ionic, and net ionic equations for the following reactions.
(a) $HNO_3 + Cr(OH)_3 \longrightarrow$
(b) $HClO_4 + NaOH \longrightarrow$
(c) $Cu(OH)_2 + HC_2H_3O_2 \longrightarrow$
(d) $ZnO + H_2SO_4 \longrightarrow$

4.74 Complete and balance molecular, ionic, and net ionic equations for the following reactions.
(a) $NaHSO_3 + HBr \longrightarrow$
(b) $(NH_4)_2CO_3 + NaOH \longrightarrow$
(c) $(NH_4)_2CO_3 + Ba(OH)_2 \longrightarrow$
(d) $FeS + HCl \longrightarrow$

ILW **4.75** Write balanced molecular, ionic, and net ionic equations for the following pairs of reactants. If all ions cancel, indicate that no reaction (N.R.) takes place.
(a) sodium sulfite and barium nitrate
(b) formic acid ($HCHO_2$) and potassium carbonate
(c) ammonium bromide and lead(II) acetate
(d) ammonium perchlorate and copper(II) nitrate

4.76 Write balanced molecular, ionic, and net ionic equations for the following pairs of reactants. If all ions cancel, indicate that no reaction (N.R.) takes place.
(a) ammonium sulfide and sodium hydroxide
(b) chromium(III) sulfate and potassium carbonate
(c) silver nitrate and chromium(III) acetate
(d) strontium hydroxide and magnesium chloride

***4.77** Choose reactants that would yield the following net ionic equations. Write molecular equations for each.
(a) $HCO_3^-(aq) + H^+(aq) \longrightarrow H_2O + CO_2(g)$
(b) $Fe^{2+}(aq) + 2OH^-(aq) \longrightarrow Fe(OH)_2(s)$
(c) $Ba^{2+}(aq) + SO_3^{2-}(aq) \longrightarrow BaSO_3(s)$
(d) $2Ag^+(aq) + S^{2-}(aq) \longrightarrow Ag_2S(s)$
(e) $ZnO(s) + 2H^+(aq) \longrightarrow Zn^{2+}(aq) + H_2O$

***4.78** Suppose that you wished to prepare copper(II) carbonate by a precipitation reaction involving Cu^{2+} and CO_3^{2-}. Which of the following pairs of reactants could you use as solutes?
(a) $Cu(OH)_2 + Na_2CO_3$ (d) $CuCl_2 + K_2CO_3$
(b) $CuSO_4 + (NH_4)_2CO_3$ (e) $CuS + NiCO_3$
(c) $Cu(NO_3)_2 + CaCO_3$

Molar Concentration

OH **4.79** Calculate the molarity of a solution prepared by dissolving
(a) 4.00 g of sodium hydroxide in 100.0 mL of solution
(b) 16.0 g of calcium chloride in 250.0 mL of solution

4.80 Calculate the molarity of a solution that contains
(a) 3.60 g of sulfuric acid in 450.0 mL of solution
(b) 2.0×10^{-3} mol iron(II) nitrate in 12.0 mL of solution

4.81 How many milliliters of 0.265 M $NaC_2H_3O_2$ are needed to supply 14.3 g $NaC_2H_3O_2$?

4.82 How many milliliters of 0.615 M HNO_3 contain 1.67 g HNO_3?

ILW **4.83** Calculate the number of grams of each solute that has to be taken to make each of the following solutions.

(a) 125 mL of 0.200 M NaCl
(b) 250.0 mL of 0.360 M $C_6H_{12}O_6$ (glucose)
(c) 250.0 mL of 0.250 M H_2SO_4

4.84 How many grams of solute are needed to make each of the following solutions?
(a) 250.0 mL of 0.100 M potassium sulfate
(b) 100.0 mL of 0.250 M iron(III) chloride
(c) 500.0 mL of 0.400 M barium acetate

Dilution of Solutions

4.85 If 25.0 mL of 0.56 M H_2SO_4 is diluted to a volume of 125 mL, what is the molarity of the resulting solution?

4.86 A 150 mL sample of 0.45 M HNO_3 is diluted to 450 mL. What is the molarity of the resulting solution?

ILW **4.87** To what volume must 25.0 mL of 18.0 M H_2SO_4 be diluted to produce 1.50 M H_2SO_4?

4.88 To what volume must 50.0 mL of 1.50 M HCl be diluted to produce 0.200 M HCl?

4.89 How many milliliters of water must be added to 150.0 mL of 2.50 M KOH to give a 1.00 M solution? (Assume volumes are additive.)

4.90 How many milliliters of water must be added to 120.0 mL of 1.50 M HCl to give 1.00 M HCl?

Concentrations of Ions in Solutions of Electrolytes

4.91 Calculate the number of moles of each of the ions in the following solutions.
(a) 32.3 mL of 0.45 M $CaCl_2$
(b) 50.0 mL of 0.40 M $AlCl_3$

4.92 Calculate the number of moles of each of the ions in the following solutions.
(a) 18.5 mL of 0.40 M $(NH_4)_2CO_3$
(b) 30.0 mL of 0.35 M $Al_2(SO_4)_3$

4.93 Calculate the concentrations of each of the ions in (a) 0.25 M $Cr(NO_3)_2$, (b) 0.10 M $CuSO_4$, (c) 0.16 M Na_3PO_4, and (d) 0.075 M $Al_2(SO_4)_3$.

4.94 Calculate the concentrations of each of the ions in (a) 0.060 M $Ca(OH)_2$, (b) 0.15 M $FeCl_3$, (c) 0.22 M $Cr_2(SO_4)_3$, and (d) 0.60 M $(NH_4)_2SO_4$.

4.95 In a solution of $Al_2(SO_4)_3$ the Al^{3+} concentration is 0.12 M. How many grams of $Al_2(SO_4)_3$ are in 50.0 mL of this solution?

4.96 In a solution of $NiCl_2$, the Cl^- concentration is 0.055 M. How many grams of $NiCl_2$ are in 250 mL of this solution?

Solution Stoichiometry

OH **4.97** How many milliliters of 0.25 M $NiCl_2$ solution are needed to react completely with 20.0 mL of 0.15 M Na_2CO_3 solution? How many grams of $NiCO_3$ will be formed? The reaction is

$$Na_2CO_3(aq) + NiCl_2(aq) \longrightarrow NiCO_3(s) + 2NaCl(aq)$$

4.98 How many milliliters of 0.100 M NaOH are needed to completely neutralize 25.0 mL of 0.250 M $H_2C_4H_4O_6$? The reaction is

$$2NaOH(aq) + H_2C_4H_4O_6(aq) \longrightarrow Na_2C_4H_4O_6(aq) + 2H_2O$$

4.99 What is the molarity of an aqueous solution of potassium hydroxide if 21.34 mL is exactly neutralized by 20.78 mL of 0.116 M HCl? Write and balance the molecular equation for the reaction.

4.100 What is the molarity of an aqueous phosphoric acid solution if 12.88 mL is completely neutralized by 26.04 mL of 0.1024 M NaOH? Write and balance the molecular equation for the reaction.

4.101 Aluminum sulfate, $Al_2(SO_4)_3$, is used in water treatment to remove fine particles suspended in the water. When made basic, a gel-like precipitate forms that removes the fine particles as it settles. In an experiment, a student planned to react $Al_2(SO_4)_3$ with $Ba(OH)_2$. How many grams of $Al_2(SO_4)_3$ are needed to react with 85.0 mL of 0.0500 M $Ba(OH)_2$?

4.102 How many grams of baking soda, $NaHCO_3$, are needed to react with 162 mL of stomach acid having an HCl concentration of 0.052 M?

4.103 How many milliliters of 0.150 M $FeCl_3$ solution are needed to react completely with 20.0 mL of 0.0450 M $AgNO_3$ solution? How many grams of AgCl will be formed? The net ionic equation for the reaction is

$$Ag^+(aq) + Cl^-(aq) \longrightarrow AgCl(s)$$

4.104 How many grams of cobalt(II) chloride are needed to react completely with 60.0 mL of 0.200 M KOH solution? The net ionic equation for the reaction is

$$Co^{2+}(aq) + 2OH^-(aq) \longrightarrow Co(OH)_2(s)$$

ILW 4.105 Consider the reaction of aluminum chloride with silver acetate. How many milliliters of 0.250 M aluminum chloride would be needed to react completely with 20.0 mL of 0.500 M silver acetate solution? The net ionic equation for the reaction is

$$Ag^+(aq) + Cl^-(aq) \longrightarrow AgCl(s)$$

4.106 How many milliliters of ammonium sulfate solution having a concentration of 0.250 M are needed to react completely with 50.0 mL of 1.00 M sodium hydroxide solution? The net ionic equation for the reaction is

$$NH_4^+(aq) + OH^-(aq) \longrightarrow NH_3(g) + H_2O$$

***4.107** Suppose that 4.00 g of solid Fe_2O_3 is added to 25.0 mL of 0.500 M HCl solution. What will the concentration of the Fe^{3+} be when all the HCl has reacted? What mass of Fe_2O_3 will not have reacted?

***4.108** Suppose 3.50 g of solid $Mg(OH)_2$ is added to 30.0 mL of 0.500 M H_2SO_4 solution. What will the concentration of Mg^{2+} be when all of the acid has been neutralized? How many grams of $Mg(OH)_2$ will not have dissolved?

***4.109** Suppose that 25.0 mL of 0.440 M NaCl is added to 25.0 mL of 0.320 M $AgNO_3$.
(a) How many moles of AgCl would precipitate?
(b) What would be the concentrations of each of the ions in the reaction mixture after the reaction?

***4.110** A mixture is prepared by adding 25.0 mL of 0.185 M Na_3PO_4 to 34.0 mL of 0.140 M $Ca(NO_3)_2$.
(a) What mass of $Ca_3(PO_4)_2$ will be formed?
(b) What will be the concentrations of each of the ions in the mixture after the reaction?

Titrations and Chemical Analyses

4.111 In a titration, 23.25 mL of 0.105 M NaOH was needed to react with 21.45 mL of HCl solution. What is the molarity of the acid?

4.112 A 12.5 mL sample of vinegar, containing acetic acid, was titrated using 0.504 M NaOH solution. The titration required 20.65 mL of the base.
(a) What was the molar concentration of acetic acid in the vinegar?
(b) Assuming the density of the vinegar to be 1.0 g mL^{-1}, what was the percentage (by mass) of acetic acid in the vinegar?

ILW
OH **4.113** Lactic acid, $HC_3H_5O_3$, is a monoprotic acid that forms when milk sours. An 18.5 mL sample of a solution of lactic acid required 17.25 mL of 0.155 M NaOH to reach an end point in a titration. How many moles of lactic acid were in the sample?

4.114 Ascorbic acid (vitamin C) is a diprotic acid having the formula $H_2C_6H_6O_6$. A sample of a vitamin supplement was analyzed by titrating a 0.1000 g sample dissolved in water with 0.0200 M NaOH. A volume of 15.20 mL of the base was required to completely neutralize the ascorbic acid. What was the percentage by mass of ascorbic acid in the sample?

4.115 Magnesium sulfate forms a hydrate known as *Epsom salts*. A student dissolved 1.24 g of this hydrate in water and added a barium chloride solution until the precipitation reaction was complete. The precipitate was filtered, dried, and found to weigh 1.174 g. Determine the formula for Epsom salts.

4.116 A sample of iron chloride weighing 0.300 g was dissolved in water and the solution was treated with $AgNO_3$ solution to precipitate the chloride as AgCl. After precipitation was complete, the AgCl was filtered, dried, and found to weigh 0.678 g. Determine the empirical formula of the iron chloride.

4.117 A certain lead ore contains the compound $PbCO_3$. A sample of the ore weighing 1.526 g was treated with nitric acid, which dissolved the $PbCO_3$. The resulting solution was filtered from undissolved rock and required 29.22 mL of 0.122 M Na_2SO_4 to completely precipitate all the lead as $PbSO_4$. What is the percentage by mass of lead in the ore?

4.118 An ore of barium contains $BaCO_3$. A 1.542 g sample of the ore was treated with HCl to dissolve the $BaCO_3$. The resulting solution was filtered to remove insoluble material and then treated with H_2SO_4 to precipitate $BaSO_4$. The precipitate was filtered, dried, and found to weigh 1.159 g. What is the percentage by mass of barium in the ore? (Assume all the barium is precipitated as $BaSO_4$.)

4.119 To a mixture of NaCl and Na_2CO_3 with a mass of 1.243 g was added 50.00 mL of 0.240 M HCl (an excess of HCl). The mixture was warmed to expel all of the CO_2 and then the unreacted HCl was titrated with 0.100 M NaOH. The titration required 22.90 mL of the NaOH solution. What was the percentage by mass of NaCl in the original mixture of NaCl and Na_2CO_3?

4.120 A mixture was known to contain both KNO_3 and K_2SO_3. To 0.486 g of the mixture, dissolved in enough water to give 50.00 mL of solution, was added 50.00 mL of 0.150 M HCl (an excess of HCl). The reaction mixture was heated to drive off all of the SO_2, and then 25.00 mL of the reaction mixture was titrated with 0.100 M KOH. The titration required 13.11 mL of the KOH solution to reach an end point. What was the percentage by mass of K_2SO_3 in the original mixture of KNO_3 and K_2SO_3?

ADDITIONAL EXERCISES

4.121 Classify each of the following as a strong electrolyte, weak electrolyte, or nonelectrolyte.
(a) KCl
(b) $C_3H_5(OH)_3$ (glycerin)
(c) NaOH
(d) $C_{12}H_{22}O_{11}$ (sucrose, or table sugar)
(e) $HC_2H_3O_2$ (acetic acid)
(f) CH_3OH (methyl alcohol)
(g) H_2SO_4
(h) NH_3

OH 4.122 Complete the following and write molecular, ionic, and net ionic equations. State whether a net reaction occurs in each case.
(a) $CaCO_3 + HNO_3 \longrightarrow$
(b) $CaCO_3 + H_2SO_4 \longrightarrow$
(c) $FeS + HBr \longrightarrow$
(d) $KOH + SnCl_2 \longrightarrow$

OH *4.123 Aspirin is a monoprotic acid called acetylsalicylic acid. Its formula is $HC_9H_7O_4$. A certain pain reliever was analyzed for aspirin by dissolving 0.250 g of it in water and titrating it with 0.0300 M KOH solution. The titration required 29.40 mL of base. What is the percentage by weight of aspirin in the drug?

***4.124** In an experiment, 40.0 mL of 0.270 M barium hydroxide was mixed with 25.0 mL of 0.330 M aluminum sulfate.
(a) Write the net ionic equation for the reaction that takes place.
(b) What is the total mass of precipitate that forms?
(c) What are the molar concentrations of the ions that remain in the solution after the reaction is complete?

***4.125** Qualitative analysis of an unknown acid found only carbon, hydrogen, and oxygen. In a quantitative analysis, a 10.46 mg sample was burned in oxygen and gave 22.17 mg CO_2 and 3.40 mg H_2O. The molecular mass was determined to be 166 g mol^{-1}. When a 0.1680 g sample of the acid was titrated with 0.1250 M NaOH, the end point was reached after 16.18 mL of the base had been added.
(a) Calculate the percentage composition of the acid.
(b) What is its empirical formula?
(c) What is its molecular formula?
(d) Is the acid mono-, di-, or triprotic?

***4.126** How many milliliters of 0.10 M HCl must be added to 50.0 mL of 0.40 M HCl to give a final solution that has a molarity of 0.25 M?

EXERCISES IN CRITICAL THINKING

4.127 Compare the advantages and disadvantages of performing a titration using the mass of the sample and titrant rather than the volume.

4.128 What kinds of experiments could you perform to measure the solubility of a substance in water? Describe the procedure you would use and the measurements you would make. What factors would limit the precision of your measurements?

4.129 Describe experiments, both qualitative and quantitative, that you could perform to show that lead chloride is more soluble in water than lead iodide.

4.130 How could you check the accuracy of a 100 mL volumetric flask?

4.131 Suppose a classmate doubted that an equilibrium really exists between acetic acid and its ions in an aqueous solution. What argument would you use to convince that person that such an equilibrium does exist?

4.132 When Arrhenius originally proposed that ions exist in solution, his idea was not well received. Propose another explanation for the conduction of electricity in molten salts and aqueous salt solutions.

4.133 Carbon dioxide is one obvious contributor to excessive global warming. What is your plan for controlling CO_2 emissions? What are the advantages and disadvantages of your plan?

5 OXIDATION-REDUCTION REACTIONS

This athlete is able to perform because her body derives energy from food she consumed. The metabolism of foods provides the energy we need for all sorts of activities, from simply thinking to participating in sports. The chemical reactions involved can be viewed as occurring by electron transfer. In this chapter we study such reactions, how to balance equations that describe them, and how these reactions are useful for laboratory work. *(Tim Pannell/Corbis)*

CHAPTER OUTLINE

5.1 Oxidation–reduction reactions involve electron transfer

5.2 The ion–electron method creates balanced net ionic equations for redox reactions

5.3 Metals are oxidized when they react with acids

5.4 A more active metal will displace a less active one from its compounds

5.5 Molecular oxygen is a powerful oxidizing agent

5.6 Redox reactions follow the same stoichiometric principles as other reactions

THIS CHAPTER IN CONTEXT In the preceding chapter you learned about some important reactions that take place in aqueous solutions. This chapter expands on that knowledge with a discussion of a class of reactions that can be viewed as involving the transfer of one or more electrons from one reactant to another. Our goal is to teach you how to recognize and analyze the changes that occur in these reactions and how to balance equations for reactions that involve electron transfer. You will also learn how to apply the principles of stoichiometry to these reactions and how to predict a type of reaction called single replacement. The reactions discussed here constitute a very broad class with many practical examples that range from combustion to batteries to the metabolism of foods by our bodies. Although we will introduce you to some of those reactions in this chapter, we will have to wait until a later time to discuss some of the others.

5.1 OXIDATION-REDUCTION REACTIONS INVOLVE ELECTRON TRANSFER

Among the first reactions studied by early scientists were those that involved oxygen. The combustion of fuels and the reactions of metals with oxygen to give oxides were described by the word *oxidation*. The removal of oxygen from metal oxides to give the metals in their elemental forms was described as *reduction*.

In 1789, the French chemist Antoine Lavoisier discovered that *combustion* involves the reaction of chemicals in various fuels, like wood and coal, not just with air but specifically with the oxygen in air. Over time, scientists came to realize that such reactions were actually special cases of a much more general phenomenon, one in which electrons are transferred from one substance to another. Collectively, electron transfer reactions came to be called **oxidation–reduction reactions,** or simply **redox reactions.** The term **oxidation** was used to describe the loss of electrons by one reactant, and **reduction** was used to describe the gain of electrons by another. For example, the reaction between sodium and chlorine to yield sodium chloride involves a loss of electrons by sodium (*oxidation* of sodium) and a gain of electrons by chlorine (*reduction* of chlorine). We can write these changes in equation form including the electrons, which we represent by the symbol e^-.

$$Na \longrightarrow Na^+ + e^- \qquad \text{(oxidation)}$$
$$Cl_2 + 2e^- \longrightarrow 2Cl^- \qquad \text{(reduction)}$$

☐ Notice that when we write equations of this type, the electron appears as a "product" if the process is oxidation and as a "reactant" if the process is reduction.

We say that sodium (Na) is oxidized and chlorine (Cl_2) is reduced.

Oxidation and reduction always occur together. No substance is ever oxidized unless something else is reduced, and the total number of electrons lost by one substance is always the same as the total number gained by the other. If this were not true, electrons would appear as a product of the overall reaction, and this is never observed.[1] In the reaction of sodium with chlorine, for example, the overall reaction is

$$2Na + Cl_2 \longrightarrow 2NaCl$$

When two sodium atoms are oxidized, two electrons are lost, which is exactly the number of electrons gained when one Cl_2 molecule is reduced.

☐ The *oxidizing agent* causes oxidation to occur by accepting electrons (it gets reduced). The *reducing agent* causes reduction by supplying electrons (it gets oxidized).

For a redox reaction to occur, one substance must accept electrons from the other. The substance that accepts the electrons is called the **oxidizing agent;** it is the agent that allows the other substance to lose electrons and be oxidized. Similarly, the substance that supplies the electrons is called the **reducing agent** because it helps something else to be reduced. In our example above, sodium is serving as a reducing agent when it supplies electrons to chlorine. In the process, sodium is oxidized. Chlorine is an oxidizing agent when it accepts electrons from the sodium, and when that happens, chlorine is reduced to chloride ion. One way to remember this is by the following summary:

TOOLS
Oxidizing and reducing agents

> The reducing agent is the substance that is oxidized.
> The oxidizing agent is the substance that is reduced.

Redox reactions are very common. They occur in batteries, which are built so that the electrons transferred can pass through some external circuit where they are able to light a flashlight or power an iPod. The metabolism of foods, which supplies our bodies with energy, also occurs by a series of redox reactions. And ordinary household bleach works by oxidizing substances that stain fabrics, making them colorless or easier to remove from the fabric (see Figure 5.1).

---

[1] If electron loss didn't equal electron gain, it would also violate the law of conservation of mass, and that doesn't happen in chemical reactions.

FIG. 5.1 "Chlorine" bleach. This common household product is a dilute aqueous solution of sodium hypochlorite, NaOCl, which destroys fabric stains by oxidizing them to colorless products. *(OPC, Inc.)*

EXAMPLE 5.1
Identifying Oxidation–Reduction

The bright light produced by the reaction between magnesium and oxygen often is used in fireworks displays. The product of the reaction is magnesium oxide, an ionic compound. Which element is oxidized and which is reduced? What are the oxidizing and reducing agents?

ANALYSIS: This example asks us to apply the definitions presented above, so we need to know how the electrons are transferred in the reaction. As a first step, let's write the chemical equation for the reaction.

Magnesium oxide is a compound of a metal and a nonmetal, so it's an ionic substance. The locations of the elements in the periodic table tell us that the ions are Mg^{2+} and O^{2-}, so the formula for magnesium oxide is MgO. (You probably already knew the formulas of these ions, but we're showing how you can apply previous knowledge to the problem at hand.) The reactants are magnesium, Mg, and molecular oxygen, O_2. The equation for the reaction is therefore

$$2Mg + O_2 \longrightarrow 2MgO$$

Now that we have the equation and the formulas of the ions we can determine how electrons are exchanged.

SOLUTION: When a magnesium atom becomes a magnesium ion, it must lose two electrons. Because electrons are lost in this process, they appear on the right when we express it as an equation.

$$Mg \longrightarrow Mg^{2+} + 2e^-$$

By losing electrons, *magnesium is oxidized*. This also means that *Mg must be the reducing agent*.

When oxygen reacts to yield O^{2-} ions, each oxygen atom must gain two electrons, so an O_2 molecule must gain four electrons. Because electrons are gained, they appear on the left in the equation.

$$O_2 + 4e^- \longrightarrow 2O^{2-}$$

By gaining electrons, O_2 *is reduced and must be the oxidizing agent*.

ARE THE ANSWERS REASONABLE? There are two things we can do to check our answers. First, we can check to be sure that we've placed electrons on the correct sides of the equations. As with ionic equations, *the number of atoms of each kind and the net charge must be the same on both sides*. We see that this is true for both equations. (If we had placed the electrons on the wrong side, the charges would not balance.) By observing the locations of the electrons in the equations (on the right for oxidation; on the left for reduction), we come to the same conclusions that Mg is oxidized and O_2 is reduced.

Another check is noting that we've identified one substance as being oxidized and the other as being reduced. If we had made a mistake, we might have concluded that both were oxidized, or both were reduced. But that's impossible, because in every reaction in which there is oxidation, there must also be reduction.

Fireworks display over Washington, D.C. *(Pete Saloutos/Corbis Images.)*

Practice Exercise 1: When sodium reacts with molecular oxygen, O_2, the product is sodium peroxide, Na_2O_2, which contains the peroxide ion, O_2^{2-}. In this reaction, is O_2 oxidized or reduced? (Hint: Which reactant gains electrons, and which loses electrons?)

Practice Exercise 2: Identify the substances oxidized and reduced and the oxidizing and reducing agents in the reaction of aluminum and chlorine to form aluminum chloride.

Oxidation numbers are used to follow redox changes

Unlike the reaction of magnesium with oxygen, not all reactions with oxygen produce ionic products. For example, sulfur reacts with oxygen to give sulfur dioxide, SO_2, which is molecular. Nevertheless, it is convenient to also view this as a redox reaction, but this requires that we change the way we define oxidation and reduction. To do this, chemists developed a bookkeeping system called **oxidation numbers,** which provides a way to keep tabs on electron transfers.

The oxidation number of an element in a particular compound is assigned according to a set of rules, which are described below. For simple, monatomic ions in a compound such as NaCl, the oxidation numbers are the same as the charges on the ions, so in NaCl the oxidation number of Na^+ is $+1$ and the oxidation number of Cl^- is -1. The real value of oxidation numbers is that they can also be assigned to atoms in molecular compounds. In such cases, it is important to realize that the oxidation number does not actually equal a charge on an atom. To be sure to differentiate oxidation numbers from actual electrical charges, we will specify the sign *before* the number when writing oxidation numbers, and *after* the number when writing electrical charges. Thus, a sodium ion has a charge of $1+$ and an oxidation number of $+1$.

A term that is frequently used interchangeably with *oxidation number* is **oxidation state**. In NaCl, sodium has an oxidation number of $+1$ and is said to be "in the $+1$ oxidation state." Similarly, the chlorine in NaCl is said to be in the -1 oxidation state. There are times when it is convenient to specify the oxidation state of an element when its name is written out. This is done by writing the oxidation number as a Roman numeral in parentheses after the name of the element. For example, "iron(III)" means iron in the $+3$ oxidation state.

We can use these new terms now to redefine a redox reaction.

☐ Oxidation numbers are sometimes written as a superscript using Roman numerals. Thus S^{VI} stands for sulfur in the $+6$ oxidation state.

> A **redox reaction** is a chemical reaction in which changes in oxidation numbers occur.

We will find it easy to follow redox reactions by taking note of the changes in oxidation numbers. To do this, however, we must be able to assign oxidation numbers to atoms in a quick and simple way.

Rules permit assignment of oxidation numbers to almost any atom

We can use some basic knowledge learned earlier plus the set of rules below to determine the oxidation numbers of the atoms in almost any compound.

TOOLS

Assigning oxidation numbers

Rules for Assigning Oxidation Numbers

1. The oxidation number of any *free element* (an element not combined chemically with a different element) is zero, regardless of how complex its molecules are.
2. The oxidation number for any simple, monatomic ion (e.g., Na^+ or Cl^-) is equal to the charge on the ion. The charge on a polyatomic ion can be viewed as the *net* oxidation number of the ion.
3. The sum of all the oxidation numbers of the atoms in a molecule or polyatomic ion must equal the charge on the particle.
4. In its compounds, fluorine has an oxidation number of -1.
5. In its compounds, hydrogen has an oxidation number of $+1$.
6. In its compounds, oxygen has an oxidation number of -2.

☐ Rule 1 means that O in O_2, P in P_4, and S in S_8 all have oxidation numbers of zero.

As you will see shortly, occasionally there is a conflict between two of these rules. When this happens, *we apply the rule with the lower number and ignore the conflicting rule.*

In addition to these basic rules, there is some other chemical knowledge you will need to remember. Recall that we can use the periodic table to help us remember the charges on certain ions of the elements. For instance, all the metals in Group IA form ions with a 1+ charge, and all those in Group IIA form ions with a 2+ charge. This means that when we find sodium in a compound, we can assign it an oxidation number of +1 because its simple ion, Na^+, has a charge of 1+. (We have applied Rule 2.) Similarly, calcium in a compound exists as Ca^{2+} and has an oxidation number of +2.

In binary ionic compounds with metals, the nonmetals have oxidation numbers equal to the charges on their anions (Table 2.6 on page 65). For example, the compound Fe_2O_3 contains the oxide ion, O^{2-}, which is assigned an oxidation number of −2. Similarly, Mg_3P_2 contains the phosphide ion, P^{3-}, which has an oxidation number of −3.

The numbered rules given above usually come into play when an element is capable of having more than one oxidation state. For example, you learned that transition metals can form more than one ion. Iron, for example, forms Fe^{2+} and Fe^{3+} ions, so in an iron compound we have to use the rules to figure out which iron ion is present. Similarly, when nonmetals are combined with hydrogen and oxygen in compounds or polyatomic ions, their oxidation numbers can vary and must be calculated using the rules.

With this as background, let's look at some examples that illustrate how we apply the rules, especially when they don't explicitly cover all the atoms in a formula.

EXAMPLE 5.2
Assigning Oxidation Numbers

Titanium dioxide, TiO_2, is a white pigment used in making paint. A now outmoded process of making TiO_2 from its ore involved $Ti(SO_4)_2$ as an intermediate. What is the oxidation number of titanium in $Ti(SO_4)_2$?

ANALYSIS: The key here is recognizing SO_4 as the sulfate ion, SO_4^{2-}. Once we know this, the rest is straightforward. Because we're only interested in the oxidation number of titanium, we use the charge on SO_4^{2-} to equal the net oxidation number of the ion (Rule 2).

SOLUTION: The sulfate ion has a charge of 2−, which we can take to be its net oxidation number. Then we apply the summation rule (Rule 3) to find the oxidation number of titanium, which we will represent by x.

$$
\begin{array}{lll}
Ti & (1 \text{ atom}) \times (x) = & x \\
SO_4^{2-} & (2 \text{ ions}) \times (-2) = & -4 \\
\hline
& \text{Sum} = 0 & (\text{Rule 3})
\end{array}
$$

Obviously, the oxidation number of titanium is +4 so that the sum can be zero.

IS THE ANSWER REASONABLE? We have the sum of oxidation numbers adding up to zero, the charge on $Ti(SO_4)_2$, so our answer is okay.

EXAMPLE 5.3
Assigning Oxidation Numbers

Determine the oxidation numbers of the atoms in hydrogen peroxide, H_2O_2, a common antiseptic purchased in pharmacies.

ANALYSIS: The compound is molecular, so there are no ions to work with. Scanning the rules, we see we have one for hydrogen and another for oxygen. However, we begin to see we have a conflict between two of the rules. Rule 5 tells us to assign an oxidation number of +1

Hydrogen peroxide destroys bacteria by oxidizing them. *(Robert Capece.)*

to hydrogen, and Rule 6 tells us to give oxygen an oxidation number of -2. Both of these can't be correct because the sum must be zero (Rule 3).

$$
\begin{array}{lll}
\text{H} & (2 \text{ atoms}) \times (+1) = +2 & (\text{Rule 5}) \\
\text{O} & (2 \text{ atoms}) \times (-2) = -4 & (\text{Rule 6}) \\
\hline
& \text{Sum} \neq 0 & (\text{violates Rule 3})
\end{array}
$$

As mentioned above, when there is a conflict between the rules, we ignore the higher numbered rule that causes the conflict.

SOLUTION: Rule 6 is the higher numbered rule causing the conflict, so we have to ignore it this time and just apply Rules 3 (the sum rule) and 5 (the rule that tells us the oxidation number of hydrogen is $+1$). Because we don't have a rule that applies to oxygen in this case, we'll represent the oxidation number of O by x.

$$
\begin{array}{lll}
\text{H} & (2 \text{ atoms}) \times (+1) = +2 & (\text{Rule 5}) \\
\text{O} & (2 \text{ atoms}) \times (x) = 2x & \\
\hline
& \text{Sum} = 0 & (\text{Rule 3})
\end{array}
$$

For the sum to be zero, $2x = -2$, so $x = -1$. Therefore, in this compound, oxygen has an oxidation number of -1.

$$
\text{H} = +1 \qquad \text{O} = -1
$$

IS THE ANSWER REASONABLE? A conflict between the rules occurs only rarely, but when it happens the conflict becomes apparent because it causes a violation of the sum rule. However, *the sum rule always applies,* so the answer is reasonable.

Sometimes, oxidation numbers calculated by the rules have fractional values, as illustrated in the next example.

EXAMPLE 5.4
Assigning Oxidation Numbers

The air bags used as safety devices in modern autos are inflated by the very rapid decomposition of the ionic compound sodium azide, NaN_3. The reaction gives elemental sodium and gaseous nitrogen. What is the average oxidation number of the nitrogen in sodium azide?

ANALYSIS: We're told that NaN_3 is ionic, so we know there is a cation and an anion. The cation is the sodium ion, Na^+, which means that the remainder of the formula unit, "N_3," must carry one unit of negative charge. However, there could not be three nitrogen anions each with a charge of $-\frac{1}{3}$ because it would mean that each nitrogen atom had acquired one-third of an electron. Whole numbers of electrons are always involved in electron transfers. Therefore, the anion must be a single particle with a negative one charge, namely, N_3^-. For this anion, the sum of the oxidation numbers of the three nitrogens must be -1. We can use this information, now, to solve the problem.

The explosive decomposition of sodium azide releases nitrogen gas, which rapidly inflates an air bag during a crash. *(Corbis-Bettmann.)*

SOLUTION: The sum of the oxidation numbers of the nitrogen must be equal to -1. If we let x stand for the oxidation number of just one of the nitrogens, then

$$
(3 \text{ atoms}) \times (x) = 3x = -1
$$
$$
x = -\frac{1}{3}
$$

We could have also tackled the problem just using the rules for assigning oxidation numbers. We know that sodium exists as the ion Na^+ and that the compound is neutral overall. Therefore,

$$
\begin{array}{lll}
\text{Na} & (1 \text{ atom}) \times (+1) = +1 & (\text{Rule 2}) \\
\text{N} & (3 \text{ atoms}) \times (x) = 3x & \\
\hline
& \text{Sum} = 0 & (\text{Rule 3})
\end{array}
$$

The sum of the oxidation numbers of the three nitrogen atoms in this ion must add up to -1, so each nitrogen must have an oxidation number of $-\frac{1}{3}$.

IS THE ANSWER REASONABLE? We've solved this example two ways, so we can certainly feel confident the answer is correct.

Practice Exercise 3: Chlorite ion, ClO_2^-, has been shown to be a potent disinfectant, and solutions of it are sometimes used to disinfect air-conditioning systems in cars. What is the oxidation number of chlorine in this ion? (Hint: The sum of the oxidation numbers is not zero.)

Practice Exercise 4: Assign oxidation numbers to each atom in (a) $NiCl_2$, (b) Mg_2TiO_4, (c) $K_2Cr_2O_7$, (d) HPO_4^{2-}, and (e) $V(C_2H_3O_2)_3$.

Practice Exercise 5: Iron forms a magnetic oxide with the formula Fe_3O_4 that contains both Fe^{2+} and Fe^{3+} ions. What is the *average* oxidation number of iron in this oxide?

Oxidation numbers are used to identify oxidation and reduction

Oxidation numbers can be used in several ways. One is to define oxidation and reduction in the most comprehensive manner, as follows:

Oxidation is an increase in oxidation number.
Reduction is a decrease in oxidation number.

Let's see how these definitions apply to the reaction of hydrogen with chlorine. To avoid ever confusing oxidation numbers with actual electrical charges, we will write oxidation numbers directly above the chemical symbols of the elements.

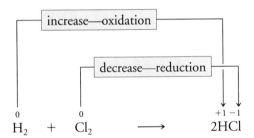

Notice that we have assigned the atoms in H_2 and Cl_2 oxidation numbers of zero, in accord with Rule 1. The changes in oxidation number tell us that hydrogen is oxidized and chlorine is reduced.

EXAMPLE 5.5
Using Oxidation Numbers to
Follow Redox Reactions

Is the following a redox reaction? If so, identify the substance oxidized and the substance reduced as well as the oxidizing and reducing agents.

$$2KCl + MnO_2 + 2H_2SO_4 \longrightarrow K_2SO_4 + MnSO_4 + Cl_2 + 2H_2O$$

ANALYSIS: To determine whether the reaction is redox and to give the specific answers requested, our tools will be the rules for assigning oxidation numbers and the revised definitions of oxidation and reduction. This will tell us whether redox is occurring, and if so, what is oxidized and reduced. Then we recall that the substance oxidized is the reducing agent, and the substance reduced is the oxidizing agent.

SOLUTION: To determine whether redox is occurring here, we first must assign oxidation numbers to each atom on both sides of the equation. Following the rules, we get

$$\overset{+1-1}{2KCl} + \overset{+4\ -2}{MnO_2} + \overset{+1+6-2}{2H_2SO_4} \longrightarrow \overset{+1+6-2}{K_2SO_4} + \overset{+2+6-2}{MnSO_4} + \overset{0}{Cl_2} + \overset{+1\ -2}{2H_2O}$$

Next we look for changes, keeping in mind that an increase in oxidation number is oxidation and a decrease is reduction.

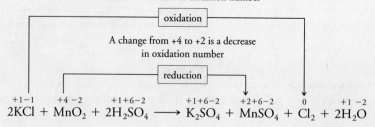

A change from −1 to 0 is going up the number scale, so it's an increase in oxidation number

oxidation

A change from +4 to +2 is a decrease in oxidation number

reduction

$$\overset{+1-1}{2KCl} + \overset{+4\ -2}{MnO_2} + \overset{+1+6-2}{2H_2SO_4} \longrightarrow \overset{+1+6-2}{K_2SO_4} + \overset{+2+6-2}{MnSO_4} + \overset{0}{Cl_2} + \overset{+1\ -2}{2H_2O}$$

Thus the Cl in KCl is oxidized and the Mn in MnO_2 is reduced. The reducing agent is KCl and the oxidizing agent is MnO_2. (Notice that when we identify the oxidizing and reducing agents, we give the entire formulas for the substances that contain the atoms with oxidation numbers that change.)

IS THE ANSWER REASONABLE? There are lots of things we could check here. We have found changes that lead us to conclude that redox is happening. Assigning oxidation numbers also allows us to identify one change as oxidation and the other as reduction, which gives us confidence that we've done the rest of the work correctly.

Practice Exercise 6: Consider the following reactions:

$$N_2O_5 + 2NaHCO_3 \longrightarrow 2NaNO_3 + 2CO_2 + H_2O$$
$$KClO_3 + 3HNO_2 \longrightarrow KCl + 3HNO_3$$

Which one is a redox reaction? For the redox reaction, which compound is oxidized and which is reduced? (Hint: How is redox defined using oxidation numbers?)

Practice Exercise 7: Chlorine dioxide, ClO_2, is used to kill bacteria in the dairy industry, meat industry, and other food and beverage industry applications. It is unstable, but can be made by the following reaction.

$$Cl_2 + 2NaClO_2 \longrightarrow 2ClO_2 + 2NaCl$$

Identify the substances oxidized and reduced as well as the oxidizing and reducing agents in the reaction.

Practice Exercise 8: When hydrogen peroxide is used as an antiseptic, it kills bacteria by oxidizing them. When the H_2O_2 serves as an oxidizing agent, which product might be formed from it, O_2 or H_2O? Why?

5.2 | THE ION-ELECTRON METHOD CREATES BALANCED NET IONIC EQUATIONS FOR REDOX REACTIONS

Many redox reactions take place in aqueous solution and many of these involve ions; they are ionic reactions. An example is the reaction of laundry bleach with substances in the wash water. The active ingredient in the bleach is hypochlorite ion, OCl^-, which is the oxidizing agent in these reactions. To study redox reactions, it is often helpful to write ionic and net ionic equations, just as we did in our analysis of metathesis reactions earlier in Chapter 4. Balancing net ionic equations for redox reactions is especially easy if we follow a procedure called the ion–electron method.

The ion–electron method uses a divide and conquer approach

In the **ion–electron method,** we divide the oxidation and reduction processes into individual equations called **half-reactions** that are balanced separately. Each half-reaction is made to obey *both* criteria for a balanced ionic equation: *both atoms and charge have to balance.* Then we combine the balanced half-reactions to obtain the fully balanced net ionic equation.

In balancing the half-reactions, we must take into account that for many redox reactions in aqueous solutions, H^+ or OH^- ions play an important role, as do water molecules. For example, when solutions of $K_2Cr_2O_7$ and $FeSO_4$ are mixed, the acidity of the mixture decreases as dichromate ion, $Cr_2O_7^{2-}$, oxidizes Fe^{2+} (Figure 5.2). This is because the reaction uses up H^+ as a reactant and produces H_2O as a product. In other reactions, OH^- is consumed, while in still others H_2O is a reactant. Another fact is that in many cases the products (or even the reactants) of a redox reaction will differ depending on the acidity of the solution. For example, in an acidic solution MnO_4^- is reduced to Mn^{2+} ion, but in a neutral or slightly basic solution, the reduction product is insoluble MnO_2.

Because of these factors, redox reactions are generally carried out in solutions containing a substantial excess of either acid or base, so before we can apply the ion–electron method, we have to know whether the reaction occurs in an acidic or a basic solution. (This information will always be given to you in this book.)

H$^+$ and H$_2$O help balance redox equations for acidic solutions

As you just learned, $Cr_2O_7^{2-}$ reacts with Fe^{2+} in an acidic solution to give Cr^{3+} and Fe^{3+} as products. This information permits us to write the **skeleton equation,** which shows only the ions (or sometimes molecules, too) involved in the redox changes.

$$Cr_2O_7^{2-} + Fe^{2+} \longrightarrow Cr^{3+} + Fe^{3+}$$

We then proceed through the steps described below to find the balanced equation. As you will see, the ion–electron method will tell us how H^+ and H_2O are involved in the reaction; we don't need to know this in advance.

Step 1. Divide the skeleton equation into half-reactions. We choose one of the reactants, let's say $Cr_2O_7^{2-}$, and write it at the left of an arrow. On the right, we write what $Cr_2O_7^{2-}$ changes to, which is Cr^{3+}. This gives us the beginnings of one half-reaction. For the second half-reaction, we write the other reactant, Fe^{2+}, on the left and the other product, Fe^{3+}, on the right. *Notice we are careful to use the complete formulas for the ions that appear in the skeleton equation.* Except for hydrogen and oxygen, the same elements must appear on both sides of a given half-reaction.

$$Cr_2O_7^{2-} \longrightarrow Cr^{3+}$$
$$Fe^{2+} \longrightarrow Fe^{3+}$$

Step 2. Balance atoms other than H and O. There are two Cr atoms on the left and only one on the right, so we place a coefficient of 2 in front of Cr^{3+}. The second half-reaction is already balanced in terms of atoms, so we leave it "as is."

$$Cr_2O_7^{2-} \longrightarrow 2Cr^{3+}$$
$$Fe^{2+} \longrightarrow Fe^{3+}$$

Step 3. Balance oxygen by adding H$_2$O to the side that needs O. There are seven oxygen atoms on the left of the first half-reaction and none on the right. Therefore, we add $7H_2O$ to the right side of the first half-reaction to balance the oxygens. (There is no oxygen imbalance in the second half-reaction, so there's nothing to do there.)

$$Cr_2O_7^{2-} \longrightarrow 2Cr^{3+} + 7H_2O$$
$$Fe^{2+} \longrightarrow Fe^{3+}$$

The oxygen atoms now balance, but we've created an imbalance in hydrogen. That issue is addressed next.

□ Equations for redox reactions are often more complex than those for metathesis reactions and can be difficult to balance by inspection. The ion–electron method is a systematic procedure for balancing redox equations.

FIG. 5.2 A redox reaction taking place in an acidic solution. A solution of $K_2Cr_2O_7$ oxidizes Fe^{2+} to Fe^{3+} in an acidic solution. At the same time, the orange dichromate ion is reduced to Cr^{3+}. (*Peter Lerman.*)

□ Many students tend to forget this step. If you do, you may end up in trouble later on.

□ We use H_2O, not O or O_2, to balance oxygen atoms because H_2O is what is actually present in the solution.

Step 4. Balance hydrogen by adding H⁺ to the side that needs H. After adding the water, we see that the first half-reaction has 14 hydrogens on the right and none on the left. To balance hydrogen, we add $14H^+$ to the left side of the half-reaction. When you do this step (or others) *be careful to write the charges on the ions.* If they are omitted, you will not obtain a balanced equation in the end.

$$14H^+ + Cr_2O_7^{2-} \longrightarrow 2Cr^{3+} + 7H_2O$$

$$Fe^{2+} \longrightarrow Fe^{3+}$$

Now each half-reaction is balanced in terms of atoms. Next we will balance the charge.

Step 5. Balance the charge by adding electrons. First we compute the net electrical charge on each side. For the first half-reaction we have

$$\underbrace{14H^+ + Cr_2O_7^{2-}}_{\text{Net charge} = (14+) + (2-) = 12+} \longrightarrow \underbrace{2Cr^{3+} + 7H_2O}_{\text{Net charge} = 2(3+) + 0 = 6+}$$

The algebraic difference between the net charges on the two sides equals the number of electrons that must be added to the more positive (or less negative) side. In this instance, we must add $6e^-$ to the left side of the half-reaction.

$$6e^- + 14H^+ + Cr_2O_7^{2-} \longrightarrow 2Cr^{3+} + 7H_2O$$

This half-reaction is now complete; it is balanced in terms of both atoms and charge. (We can check this by recalculating the charge on both sides.)

To balance the other half-reaction, we add one electron to the right.

$$Fe^{2+} \longrightarrow Fe^{3+} + e^-$$

Step 6. Make the number of electrons gained equal to the number lost and then add the two half-reactions. At this point we have the two balanced half-reactions

$$6e^- + 14H^+ + Cr_2O_7^{2-} \longrightarrow 2Cr^{3+} + 7H_2O$$

$$Fe^{2+} \longrightarrow Fe^{3+} + e^-$$

Six electrons are gained in the first, but only one is lost in the second. Therefore, before combining the two equations we multiply all of the coefficients of the second half-reaction by 6.

□ Because we know the electrons will cancel, we really don't have to carry them down into the combined equation. We've done so here just for emphasis.

$$6e^- + 14H^+ + Cr_2O_7^{2-} \longrightarrow 2Cr^{3+} + 7H_2O$$
$$6(Fe^{2+} \longrightarrow Fe^{3+} + e^-)$$
$$\overline{\text{(Sum)} \quad 6e^- + 14H^+ + Cr_2O_7^{2-} + 6Fe^{2+} \longrightarrow 2Cr^{3+} + 7H_2O + 6Fe^{3+} + 6e^-}$$

Step 7. Cancel anything that is the same on both sides. This is the final step. Six electrons cancel from both sides to give the final balanced equation.

$$14H^+ + Cr_2O_7^{2-} + 6Fe^{2+} \longrightarrow 2Cr^{3+} + 7H_2O + 6Fe^{3+}$$

Notice that both the charge and the atoms balance.

In some reactions, after adding the two half-reactions you may have H_2O or H^+ on both sides—for example, $6H_2O$ on the left and $2H_2O$ on the right. Cancel as many as you can. Thus,

$$\ldots + 6H_2O \ldots \longrightarrow \ldots + 2H_2O \ldots$$

reduces to

$$\ldots + 4H_2O \ldots \longrightarrow \ldots$$

The following is a summary of the steps we've followed for balancing an equation for a redox reaction in an acidic solution. If you don't skip any steps and you perform them in the order given, you will always obtain a properly balanced equation.

Ion–Electron Method—Acidic Solution

Step 1. Divide the equation into two half-reactions.
Step 2. Balance atoms other than H and O.
Step 3. Balance O by adding H_2O.
Step 4. Balance H by adding H^+.
Step 5. Balance net charge by adding e^-.
Step 6. Make e^- gain equal e^- loss; then add half-reactions.
Step 7. Cancel anything that's the same on both sides.

TOOLS

Ion–electron method for acidic solutions

EXAMPLE 5.6
Using the Ion–Electron Method

Balance the following equation. The reaction occurs in an acidic solution.

$$MnO_4^- + H_2SO_3 \longrightarrow SO_4^{2-} + Mn^{2+}$$

ANALYSIS: In using the ion–electron method, there's not much to analyze. It's necessary to know the steps and to follow them in sequence.

SOLUTION: We follow the steps given above.

Step 1. Divide the skeleton equation into half-reactions.

$$MnO_4^- \longrightarrow Mn^{2+}$$
$$H_2SO_3 \longrightarrow SO_4^{2-}$$

Step 2. There is nothing to do for this step. All the atoms except H and O are already in balance.

Step 3. Add H_2O to balance oxygens.

$$MnO_4^- \longrightarrow Mn^{2+} + 4H_2O$$
$$H_2O + H_2SO_3 \longrightarrow SO_4^{2-}$$

Step 4. Add H^+ to balance H.

$$8H^+ + MnO_4^- \longrightarrow Mn^{2+} + 4H_2O$$
$$H_2O + H_2SO_3 \longrightarrow SO_4^{2-} + 4H^+$$

Step 5. Balance charge by adding electrons to the more positive side.

$$5e^- + 8H^+ + MnO_4^- \longrightarrow Mn^{2+} + 4H_2O$$
$$H_2O + H_2SO_3 \longrightarrow SO_4^{2-} + 4H^+ + 2e^-$$

Step 6. Make electron loss equal to electron gain, then add half-reactions

$$2(5e^- + 8H^+ + MnO_4^- \longrightarrow Mn^{2+} + 4H_2O)$$
$$5(H_2O + H_2SO_3 \longrightarrow SO_4^{2-} + 4H^+ + 2e^-)$$
$$\overline{10e^- + 16H^+ + 2MnO_4^- + 5H_2O + 5H_2SO_3 \longrightarrow}$$
$$2Mn^{2+} + 8H_2O + 5SO_4^{2-} + 20H^+ + 10e^-$$

Step 7. Cancel $10e^-$, $16H^+$, and $5H_2O$ from both sides. The final equation is

$$2MnO_4^- + 5H_2SO_3 \longrightarrow 2Mn^{2+} + 3H_2O + 5SO_4^{2-} + 4H^+$$

IS THE ANSWER REASONABLE? The check involves *two* steps. First, we check that each side of the equation has the same number of atoms of each element, which it does. Second, we check to be sure that the net charge is the same on both sides. On the left we have $2MnO_4^-$ with a net charge of $2-$. On the right we have $2Mn^{2+}$ and $4H^+$ (total charge = $8+$) along with $5SO_4^{2-}$ (total charge = $10-$), so the net charge is also $2-$. Having both atoms *and* charge in balance makes it a balanced equation and confirms that we've worked the problem correctly.

Practice Exercise 9: Explain why the following equation is not balanced. Balance it using the ion–electron method. (Hint: What are the criteria for a balanced ionic equation?)

$$Al(s) + Cu^{2+}(aq) \longrightarrow Al^{3+}(aq) + Cu(s)$$

Practice Exercise 10: The element technetium (atomic number 43) is radioactive and one of its isotopes, ^{99}Tc, is used in medicine for diagnostic imaging. The isotope is usually obtained in the form of the pertechnetate anion, TcO_4^-, but its use sometimes requires the technetium to be in a lower oxidation state. Reduction can be carried out using Sn^{2+} in an acidic solution. The skeleton equation is

$$TcO_4^- + Sn^{2+} \longrightarrow Tc^{4+} + Sn^{4+} \qquad \text{(acidic solution)}$$

Balance the equation by the ion–electron method.

Practice Exercise 11: What is the balanced net ionic equation for the following reaction in an acidic solution?

$$Cu + NO_3^- \longrightarrow Cu^{2+} + N_2O$$

Additional steps produce balanced equations for basic solutions

In a basic solution, the concentration of H^+ is very small; the dominant species are H_2O and OH^-. Strictly speaking, these should be used to balance the half-reactions. However, the simplest way to obtain a balanced equation for a basic solution is to first *pretend* that the solution is acidic. We balance the equation using the seven steps just described, and then we use a simple three-step procedure described below to convert the equation to the correct form for a basic solution. The conversion uses the fact that H^+ and OH^- react in a 1-to-1 ratio to give H_2O.

TOOLS

Ion–electron method for basic solutions

Additional Steps in the Ion–Electron Method for Basic Solutions

Step 8. Add to *both* sides of the equation the same number of OH^- as there are H^+.
Step 9. Combine H^+ and OH^- to form H_2O.
Step 10. Cancel any H_2O that you can.

As an example, suppose we wanted to balance the following equation for a basic solution.

$$SO_3^{2-} + MnO_4^- \longrightarrow SO_4^{2-} + MnO_2$$

Following Steps 1 through 7 for acidic solutions gives

$$2H^+ + 3SO_3^{2-} + 2MnO_4^- \longrightarrow 3SO_4^{2-} + 2MnO_2 + H_2O$$

Conversion of this equation to one appropriate for a basic solution proceeds as follows.

Step 8. Add to *both* sides of the equation the same number of OH^- as there are H^+. The equation for acidic solution has $2H^+$ on the left, so we add $2OH^-$ to *each* side. This gives

$$2OH^- + 2H^+ + 3SO_3^{2-} + 2MnO_4^- \longrightarrow 3SO_4^{2-} + 2MnO_2 + H_2O + 2OH^-$$

Step 9. Combine H^+ and OH^- to form H_2O. The left side has $2OH^-$ and $2H^+$, which become $2H_2O$. So in place of $2OH^- + 2H^+$ we write $2H_2O$.

$$2OH^- + 2H^+ + 3SO_3^{2-} + 2MnO_4^- \longrightarrow 3SO_4^{2-} + 2MnO_2 + H_2O + 2OH^-$$

$$2H_2O + 3SO_3^{2-} + 2MnO_4^- \longrightarrow 3SO_4^{2-} + 2MnO_2 + H_2O + 2OH^-$$

Step 10. Cancel any H_2O that you can. In this equation, one H_2O can be eliminated from both sides. The final equation, balanced for basic solution, is

$$H_2O + 3SO_3^{2-} + 2MnO_4^- \longrightarrow 3SO_4^{2-} + 2MnO_2 + 2OH^-$$

Consider the following half-reaction balanced for an acidic solution:

$$2H_2O + SO_2 \longrightarrow SO_4^{2-} + 4H^+ + 2e^-$$

What is the balanced half-reaction for a basic solution? (Hint: Remember that H^+ and OH^- react to form H_2O.)

Practice Exercise 13: Balance the following equation for a basic solution.

$$MnO_4^- + C_2O_4^{2-} \longrightarrow MnO_2 + CO_3^{2-}$$

5.3 | METALS ARE OXIDIZED WHEN THEY REACT WITH ACIDS

Earlier you learned that one of the properties of acids is that they react with bases. Another important property is their ability to react with certain metals. These are redox reactions in which the metal is oxidized and the acid is reduced. But in these reactions, the part of the acid that's reduced depends on the composition of the acid itself as well as on the metal.

When a piece of zinc is placed into a solution of hydrochloric acid, bubbling is observed and the zinc gradually dissolves (Figure 5.3). The chemical reaction is

$$Zn(s) + 2HCl(aq) \longrightarrow ZnCl_2(aq) + H_2(g)$$

for which the net ionic equation is

$$Zn(s) + 2H^+(aq) \longrightarrow Zn^{2+}(aq) + H_2(g)$$

In this reaction, zinc is oxidized and hydrogen ions are reduced. Stated another way, *the H^+ of the acid is the oxidizing agent.*

Many metals react with acids just as zinc does—by being oxidized by hydrogen ions. In these reactions a metal salt and gaseous hydrogen are the products.

Metals that are able to react with acids such as HCl and H_2SO_4 to give hydrogen gas are said to be *more active* than hydrogen (H_2). For other metals, however, hydrogen ions are not powerful enough to cause their oxidation. Copper, for example, is significantly less reactive than zinc or iron, and H^+ cannot oxidize it. Copper is an example of a metal that is *less active* than H_2.

The oxidizing power of an acid depends on the nature of the anion

Hydrochloric acid contains H_3O^+ ions (which we abbreviate as H^+) and Cl^- ions. The hydrogen ion in hydrochloric acid is able to be an oxidizing agent by being reduced to H_2. However, the Cl^- ion in the solution has no tendency at all to be an oxidizing agent, so in a solution of HCl the only oxidizing agent is H^+. The same applies to dilute solutions of sulfuric acid, H_2SO_4.

The hydrogen ion in water is actually a rather poor oxidizing agent, so hydrochloric acid and sulfuric acid have rather poor oxidizing abilities. They are often called **nonoxidizing acids,** even though their hydrogen ions are able to oxidize certain metals. (When we call something a nonoxidizing acid, we mean the *anion* of the acid is a weaker oxidizing agent than H^+ and that the anion of the acid is more difficult to reduce than H^+.) Some acids contain anions that are stronger oxidizing agents than H^+ and are called **oxidizing acids.** (See Table 5.1.)

☐ The strongest oxidizing agent in a solution of a "nonoxidizing" acid is H^+.

Nitric acid is a powerful oxidizing agent

Nitric acid, HNO_3, ionizes in water to give H^+ and NO_3^- ions. In this solution the nitrate ion is a more powerful oxidizing agent than the hydrogen ion. This makes it able to oxidize metals that H^+ cannot, such as copper and silver. For example, the molecular equation for the reaction of concentrated HNO_3 with copper, shown in Figure 5.4, is

$$Cu(s) + 4HNO_3(aq) \longrightarrow Cu(NO_3)_2(aq) + 2NO_2(g) + 2H_2O$$

Oxidizing and nonoxidizing acids

TABLE 5.1	Nonoxidizing and Oxidizing Acids
Nonoxidizing Acids	
$HCl(aq)$	
$H_2SO_4(aq)^a$	
$H_3PO_4(aq)$	
Most organic acids (e.g., $HC_2H_3O_2$)	

Oxidizing Acids	Reduction reaction
HNO_3	(conc.) $NO_3^- + 2H^+ + e^- \longrightarrow NO_2(g) + H_2O$
	(dilute) $NO_3^- + 4H^+ + 3e^- \longrightarrow NO(g) + 2H_2O$
	(very dilute, with strong reducing agent)
	$NO_3^- + 10H^+ + 8e^- \longrightarrow NH_4^+ + 3H_2O$
H_2SO_4	(hot, conc.) $SO_4^{2-} + 4H^+ + 2e^- \longrightarrow SO_2(g) + 2H_2O$
	(hot, conc., with strong reducing agent)
	$SO_4^{2-} + 10H^+ + 8e^- \longrightarrow H_2S(g) + 4H_2O$

$^a H_2SO_4$ is a nonoxidizing acid when cold and dilute.

$$Cu + 4HNO_3 \longrightarrow Cu(NO_3)_2 + 2NO_2 + 2H_2O$$

FIG. 5.4 **The reaction of copper with concentrated nitric acid.** A copper penny reacts vigorously with concentrated nitric acid, as this sequence of photographs shows. The dark red brown vapors are nitrogen dioxide, the same gas that gives smog its characteristic color. *(Michael Watson.)*

If we convert this to a net ionic equation and then assign oxidation numbers, we can see that NO_3^- is the oxidizing agent and Cu is the reducing agent.

$$\underset{\substack{\text{reducing} \\ \text{agent}}}{\overset{0}{Cu(s)}} + \underset{\substack{\text{oxidizing} \\ \text{agent}}}{\overset{+5}{2NO_3^-}(aq)} + 4H^+(aq) \longrightarrow \overset{+2}{Cu^{2+}}(aq) + \overset{+4}{2NO_2}(g) + 2H_2O$$

Notice that in this reaction, *no hydrogen gas is formed.* The H^+ ions of the HNO_3 are an essential part of the reaction, but they just become part of water molecules without a change in oxidation number.

The nitrogen-containing product formed in the reduction of nitric acid depends on the concentration of the acid and the reducing power of the metal. With *concentrated* nitric acid, nitrogen dioxide, NO_2, is often the reduction product. With *dilute* nitric acid the product is often nitrogen monoxide (also called nitric oxide), NO, instead. Copper, for example, reacts as follows:

Concentrated HNO₃

$$Cu(s) + 4H^+(aq) + 2NO_3^-(aq) \longrightarrow Cu^{2+}(aq) + 2NO_2(g) + 2H_2O$$

Dilute HNO₃

$$3Cu(s) + 8H^+(aq) + 2NO_3^-(aq) \longrightarrow 3Cu^{2+}(aq) + 2NO(g) + 4H_2O$$

Nitric acid is a very effective oxidizing acid. All metals except the most unreactive ones, such as platinum and gold, are attacked by it. Nitric acid also does a good job of oxidizing organic compounds, so it is wise to be especially careful when working with this acid in the laboratory. Very serious accidents have occurred when inexperienced people have used concentrated nitric acid around organic substances.

☐ Nitric acid causes severe skin burns, so be careful when you work with it in the laboratory. If you spill any on your skin, wash it off immediately and seek the help of your lab teacher.

Hot concentrated sulfuric acid is an oxidizing acid

In a dilute solution, the sulfate ion of sulfuric acid has little tendency to serve as an oxidizing agent. However, if the sulfuric acid is both concentrated and hot, it becomes a fairly potent oxidizer. For example, copper is not bothered by cool dilute H_2SO_4, but it is attacked by hot concentrated H_2SO_4 according to the following equation:

$$Cu + 2H_2SO_4(\text{hot, conc.}) \longrightarrow CuSO_4 + SO_2 + 2H_2O$$

Because of this oxidizing ability, hot concentrated sulfuric acid can be very dangerous. The liquid is viscous and can stick to the skin, causing severe burns.

> **Practice Exercise 14:** Write the balanced half-reactions for the reaction of zinc with hydrogen ions. (Hint: Be sure to place the electrons on the correct sides of the half-reactions.)
>
> **Practice Exercise 15:** When very dilute nitric acid reacts with a strong oxidizing agent such as magnesium, the nitrate ion is reduced to ammonium ion. Write a balanced net ionic equation for the reaction.
>
> **Practice Exercise 16:** Write balanced molecular, ionic, and net ionic equations for the reaction of hydrochloric acid with (a) magnesium and (b) aluminum. (Both metals are oxidized by hydrogen ions.)

5.4 | A MORE ACTIVE METAL WILL DISPLACE A LESS ACTIVE ONE FROM ITS COMPOUNDS

The formation of hydrogen gas in the reaction of a metal with an acid is a special case of a more general phenomenon—one element displacing (pushing out) another element from a compound by means of a redox reaction. In the case of a metal–acid reaction, it is the metal that displaces hydrogen from the acid, changing $2H^+$ to H_2.

Another reaction of this same general type occurs when one metal displaces another metal from its compounds, and is illustrated by the experiment shown in Figure 5.5. Here we see a brightly polished strip of metallic zinc that is dipped into a solution of copper sulfate. After the zinc is in the solution for a while, a reddish brown deposit of metallic copper forms on the zinc, and if the solution were analyzed, we would find that it now contains zinc ions, as well as some remaining unreacted copper ions.

The results of this experiment can be summarized by the following net ionic equation.

$$Zn(s) + Cu^{2+}(aq) \longrightarrow Cu(s) + Zn^{2+}(aq)$$

☐ Sulfate ion is a spectator ion in this reaction.

Metallic zinc is oxidized as copper ion is reduced. In the process, Zn^{2+} ions have taken the place of the Cu^{2+} ions, so a solution of copper sulfate is changed to a solution of zinc sulfate. An atomic-level view of what's happening at the surface of the zinc during the reaction is depicted in Figure 5.6. A reaction such as this, in which one element replaces another in a compound, is sometimes called a **single replacement reaction.**

The activity series arranges metals according to their ease of oxidation

In the reaction of zinc with copper ion, the more "active" zinc displaces the less "active" copper in a compound, where we have used the word *active* to mean "easily oxidized." This is actually a general phenomenon: *an element that is more easily oxidized will displace one that is less*

FIG. 5.5 **The reaction of zinc with copper ion.** (*Left*) A piece of shiny zinc next to a beaker containing a copper sulfate solution. (*Center*) When the zinc is placed in the solution, copper ions are reduced to the free metal while the zinc dissolves. (*Right*) After a while the zinc becomes coated with a red-brown layer of copper. Notice that the solution is a lighter blue than before, showing that some of the copper ions have left the solution. (*Michael Watson.*)

FIG. 5.6 **The reaction of copper ions with zinc, viewed at the atomic level.** (*a*) Copper ions (blue) collide with the zinc surface where they pick up electrons from zinc atoms (gray). The zinc atoms become zinc ions (yellow) and enter the solution. The copper ions become copper atoms (red-brown) and stick to the surface of the zinc. (For clarity, the water molecules of the solution and the sulfate ions are not shown.) (*b*) A close-up view of the exchange of electrons that leads to the reaction.

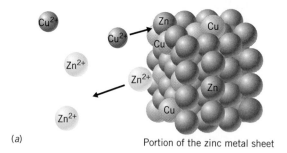

(a) Portion of the zinc metal sheet

Two electrons are transferred from the zinc atom to the copper ion. The result is a zinc ion and a copper atom.

(b)

easily oxidized from its compounds. By comparing the relative ease of oxidation of various metals using experiments like the one pictured in Figure 5.5, we can arrange metals in order of their ease of oxidation. This yields the **activity series** shown in Table 5.2. In this table, metals at the bottom are more easily oxidized (are more active) than those at the top. *This means that a given element will be displaced from its compounds by any metal below it in the table.*

Notice that we have included hydrogen in the activity series. Metals below hydrogen in the series can displace hydrogen from solutions containing H^+. These are the metals that are capable of reacting with nonoxidizing acids. On the other hand, metals above hydrogen in the table do not react with acids having H^+ as the strongest oxidizing agent.

Metals at the very bottom of the table are very easily oxidized and are extremely strong reducing agents. They are so reactive, in fact, that they are able to reduce the hydrogen in water molecules. Sodium, for example, reacts vigorously (see Figure 5.7).

$$2Na(s) + 2H_2O \longrightarrow H_2(g) + 2NaOH(aq)$$

For metals below hydrogen in the activity series, there's a parallel between the ease of oxidation of the metal and the speed with which it reacts with H^+. For example, in

TABLE 5.2	Activity Series for Some Metals (and Hydrogen)

	Element	Oxidation Product
Least Active	Gold	Au³⁺
	Mercury	Hg²⁺
	Silver	Ag⁺
	Copper	Cu²⁺
	HYDROGEN	H⁺
	Lead	Pb²⁺
	Tin	Sn²⁺
	Cobalt	Co²⁺
	Cadmium	Cd²⁺
	Iron	Fe²⁺
	Chromium	Cr³⁺
	Zinc	Zn²⁺
	Manganese	Mn²⁺
	Aluminum	Al³⁺
	Magnesium	Mg²⁺
	Sodium	Na⁺
	Calcium	Ca²⁺
	Strontium	Sr²⁺
	Barium	Ba²⁺
	Potassium	K⁺
	Rubidium	Rb⁺
Most Active	Cesium	Cs⁺

Increasing ease of oxidation of the metal →
Increasing ease of reduction of the ion →

FIG. 5.7 **Metallic sodium reacts violently with water.** The heat of the reaction ignites the sodium metal, which can be seen burning and sending sparks from the surface of the water. In the reaction, sodium is oxidized to Na⁺ and water molecules are reduced to give hydrogen gas and hydroxide ions. When the reaction is over, the solution contains sodium hydroxide. *(OPC, Inc.)*

Figure 5.8, we see samples of iron, zinc, and magnesium reacting with solutions of hydrochloric acid. In each test tube the initial HCl concentration is the same, but we see that the magnesium reacts more rapidly than zinc, which reacts more rapidly than iron. You can see that the order of reactivity in Table 5.2 is the same; magnesium is more easily oxidized than zinc, which is more easily oxidized than iron.

The activity series can be used to predict reactions

The activity series in Table 5.2 permits us to make predictions of the outcome of single replacement redox reactions, as illustrated in the following examples.

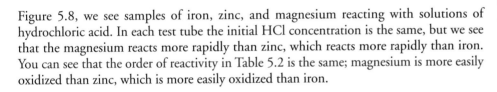

$2HCl(aq) + Fe(s) \longrightarrow$
$FeCl_2(aq) + H_2(g)$

$2HCl(aq) + Zn(s) \longrightarrow$
$ZnCl_2(aq) + H_2(g)$

$2HCl(aq) + Mg(s) \longrightarrow$
$MgCl_2(aq) + H_2(g)$

FIG. 5.8 **The relative ease of oxidation of metals parallels their rates of reaction with hydrogen ions of an acid.** The products are hydrogen gas and the metal ion in solution. All three test tubes contain HCl(*aq*) at the same concentration. The first also contains pieces of iron, the second, pieces of zinc, and the third, pieces of magnesium. Among these three metals, the ease of oxidation increases from iron to zinc to magnesium. *(OPC, Inc.)*

EXAMPLE 5.7
Using the Activity Series

What will happen if an iron nail is dipped into a solution containing copper(II) sulfate? If a reaction occurs, write its molecular equation.

ANALYSIS: Reading the question, we have to ask, what *could* happen? If a chemical reaction were to occur, iron would have to react with the copper sulfate. A *metal* possibly reacting with the *salt of another metal?* This suggests the possibility of a single replacement reaction. The tool we use to predict such reactions is the activity series.

Examining Table 5.2 we see that iron is below copper. This means iron is more easily oxidized than copper, so we expect metallic iron to displace copper ions from the solution. *A reaction will occur.* (We've answered one part of the question.) The formula for copper(II) sulfate is $CuSO_4$. To write an equation for the reaction, we have to know the final oxidation state of the iron. In the table, this is indicated as $+2$, so the Fe atoms change to Fe^{2+} ions. To write the formula of the salt in the solution we pair Fe^{2+} with SO_4^{2-} to give $FeSO_4$. Copper(II) ions are reduced to copper atoms.

SOLUTION: Our analysis told us that a reaction *will* occur and it also gave us the products, so the equation is

$$Fe(s) + CuSO_4(aq) \longrightarrow Cu(s) + FeSO_4(aq)$$

IS THE ANSWER REASONABLE? We can check the activity series again to be sure we've reached the correct conclusion, and we can check to be sure the equation we've written has the correct formulas and is balanced correctly. Doing this confirms that we've got the right answers.

EXAMPLE 5.8
Using the Activity Series

What happens if an iron nail is dipped into a solution of aluminum sulfate? If a reaction occurs, write the molecular equation.

ANALYSIS: Once again, we have to realize that we're looking for a potential single replacement reaction. Scanning the activity series, we see that aluminum metal is *more* easily oxidized than iron metal. This means that aluminum atoms would be able to displace iron ions from an iron compound. But it also means that iron atoms cannot displace aluminum ions from its compounds, and iron *atoms* plus aluminum *ions* are what we're given.

SOLUTION: Our analysis has told us that iron atoms will not reduce aluminum ions, so we must conclude that no reaction can occur.

$$Fe(s) + Al_2(SO_4)_3(aq) \longrightarrow \text{no reaction}$$

IS THE ANSWER REASONABLE? Checking the activity series again, we are confident we've come to the correct answer. In writing the equation, we've also been careful to correctly write the formula of aluminum sulfate.

Practice Exercise 17: Suppose a mixture is prepared containing magnesium sulfate ($MgSO_4$), copper(II) sulfate ($CuSO_4$), metallic magnesium, and metallic copper. What reaction, if any, will occur? (Hint: What reactions could occur?)

Practice Exercise 18: Write a chemical equation for the reaction that will occur, if any, when (a) aluminum metal is added to a solution of copper(II) chloride and (b) silver metal is added to a solution of magnesium sulfate. If no reaction will occur, write "no reaction" in place of the products.

5.5 | MOLECULAR OXYGEN IS A POWERFUL OXIDIZING AGENT

Oxygen is a plentiful chemical; it's in the air and available to anyone who wants to use it, chemist or not. Furthermore, O_2 is a very reactive oxidizing agent, so its reactions have been well studied. When they are rapid, with the evolution of light and heat, we call them **combustion**. The products of reactions with oxygen are generally oxides, *molecular oxides* when oxygen reacts with nonmetals and *ionic oxides* when oxygen reacts with metals.

Organic compounds burn in oxygen

Experience has taught you that certain materials burn. For example, if you had to build a fire to keep warm, you no doubt would look for combustible materials like twigs, logs, or other pieces of wood to use as fuel. When you drive a car, it is probably powered by the combustion of gasoline. Wood and gasoline are examples of substances or mixtures of substances that chemists call *organic compounds*—compounds whose structures are determined primarily by the linking together of carbon atoms. When organic compounds burn, the products of the reactions are usually easy to predict.

Hydrocarbons are important fuels

Fuels such as natural gas, gasoline, kerosene, heating oil, and diesel fuel are examples of *hydrocarbons*—compounds containing only the elements carbon and hydrogen. Natural gas is composed principally of methane, CH_4. Gasoline is a mixture of hydrocarbons, the most familiar of which is octane, C_8H_{18}. Kerosene, heating oil, and diesel fuel are mixtures of hydrocarbons in which the molecules contain even more atoms of carbon and hydrogen.

TOOLS

Hydrocarbon combustion with plentiful supply of O_2

*When hydrocarbons burn in a **plentiful** supply of oxygen, the products of combustion are always carbon dioxide and water.* Thus, methane and octane combine with oxygen according to the equations

$$CH_4 + 2O_2 \longrightarrow CO_2 + 2H_2O$$

$$2C_8H_{18} + 25O_2 \longrightarrow 16CO_2 + 18H_2O$$

Many people don't realize that water is one of the products of the combustion of hydrocarbons, even though they have seen evidence for it. Perhaps you've seen clouds of condensed water vapor coming from the exhaust pipes of automobiles on cold winter days, or you may have noticed that shortly after you first start a car, drops of water fall from the exhaust pipe. This is water that has been formed during the combustion of the gasoline. Similarly, the "smokestacks" of power stations release clouds of condensed water vapor (Figure 5.9), which is often mistaken for smoke from fires used to generate power to make electricity. Actually, many of today's power stations produce very little smoke because they burn clean natural gas instead of coal.

FIG. 5.9 **Water is a product of the combustion of hydrocarbons.** Here we see clouds of condensed water vapor coming from the stacks of an oil-fired electric generating plant during the winter. *(Sandra Baker/Liaison Agency, Inc./ Getty Images.)*

TOOLS

Hydrocarbon combustion with limited supply of O_2

TOOLS

Hydrocarbon combustion with extremely limited supply of O_2

When the supply of oxygen is somewhat restricted during the combustion of a hydrocarbon, some of the carbon is converted to carbon monoxide. The formation of CO is a pollution problem associated with the use of gasoline engines, as you may know.

$$2CH_4 + 3O_2 \longrightarrow 2CO + 4H_2O \qquad \text{(in a limited oxygen supply)}$$

When the oxygen supply is extremely limited, only the hydrogen of a hydrocarbon mixture is converted to the oxide (water). The carbon atoms emerge as elemental carbon. For example, when a candle burns, the fuel is a high-molecular-weight hydrocarbon (e.g., $C_{20}H_{42}$) and incomplete combustion forms tiny particles of carbon that glow brightly. If a cold surface is held in the flame, the unburned carbon deposits, as seen in Figure 5.10.

An important commercial reaction is the incomplete combustion of methane in a very limited oxygen supply, which follows the equation

$$CH_4 + O_2 \longrightarrow C + 2H_2O \qquad \text{(in a very limited oxygen supply)}$$

◻ This finely divided form of carbon is also called *carbon black.*

The carbon that forms is very finely divided and would be called *soot* by almost anyone observing the reaction. Nevertheless, such soot has considerable commercial value when collected and marketed under the name *lampblack.* This sooty form of carbon is used to manufacture inks and much of it is used in the production of rubber tires, where it serves as a binder and a filler. When soot from incomplete combustion is released into air, its tiny particles constitute a component of air pollution referred to as *particulates,* which contribute to the haziness of smog.

Combustion of organic compounds that contain oxygen also produces CO_2 and H_2O

◻ The formula for cellulose can be expressed as $(C_6H_{10}O_5)n$, which indicates that the molecule contains the $C_6H_{10}O_5$ unit repeated some large number *n* times.

Earlier we mentioned that you might choose wood to build a fire. The chief combustible ingredient in wood is cellulose, a fibrous material that gives plants their structural strength. Cellulose is composed of the elements carbon, hydrogen, and oxygen. Each cellulose molecule consists of many small, identical groups of atoms that are linked together to form a very long molecule, although the lengths of the molecules differ. For this reason we cannot specify a molecular formula for cellulose. Instead, we use the empirical formula, $C_6H_{10}O_5$, which represents the small, repeating "building block" units in large cellulose molecules. When cellulose burns, the products are also carbon dioxide and water. The only difference between its reaction and the reaction of a hydrocarbon with oxygen is that some of the oxygen in the products comes from the cellulose.

$$C_6H_{10}O_5 + 6O_2 \longrightarrow 6CO_2 + 5H_2O$$

TOOLS

Combustion of organic compounds containing C, H, and O

The complete combustion of all other organic compounds containing only carbon, hydrogen, and oxygen produces the same products, CO_2 and H_2O, and follows similar equations.

Burning organic compounds that contain sulfur gives SO_2 as one of the products

TOOLS

Combustion of organic compounds containing sulfur

A major pollution problem in industrialized countries is caused by the release into the atmosphere of sulfur dioxide formed by the combustion of fuels that contain sulfur or its compounds. *The products of the combustion of organic compounds of sulfur are carbon dioxide, water, and sulfur dioxide.* A typical reaction is

$$2C_2H_5SH + 9O_2 \longrightarrow 4CO_2 + 6H_2O + 2SO_2$$

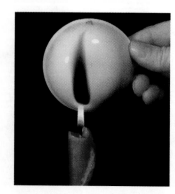

FIG. 5.10 Incomplete **combustion of a hydrocarbon.** The bright yellow color of a candle flame is caused by glowing particles of elemental carbon. Here we see that a black deposit of carbon is formed when the flame contacts a cold porcelain surface. *(Andy Washnik.)*

A solution of sulfur dioxide in water is acidic, and when rain falls through polluted air it picks up SO_2 and becomes "acid rain." Some SO_2 is also oxidized to SO_3, which reacts with moisture to give H_2SO_4, making the acid rain even more acidic.

Practice Exercise 19: Write a balanced chemical equation for the combustion of candle wax, $C_{20}H_{42}$, in a very limited supply of oxygen. (Hint: What happens to methane under these conditions?)

Practice Exercise 20: Write a balanced equation for the combustion of butane, C_4H_{10}, in an abundant supply of oxygen. Butane is the fuel used in disposable cigarette lighters.

Practice Exercise 21: Ethanol, C_2H_5OH, is now mixed with gasoline, and the mixture is sold under the name *gasohol*. Write a chemical equation for the combustion of ethanol.

Many metals react with oxygen

We don't often think of metals as undergoing combustion, but have you ever seen an old-fashioned flashbulb fired to take a photograph? The source of light is the reaction of the metal magnesium with oxygen (see Figure 5.11). A close look at a fresh flashbulb reveals a fine web of thin magnesium wire within the glass envelope. The wire is surrounded by an atmosphere of oxygen, a colorless gas. When the flashbulb is used, a small electric current surges through the thin wire, causing it to become hot enough to ignite, and it burns rapidly in the oxygen atmosphere. The equation for the reaction is

$$2Mg + O_2 \longrightarrow 2MgO$$

Most metals react directly with oxygen, although not so spectacularly, and usually we refer to the reaction as **corrosion** or **tarnishing** because the oxidation products dull the shiny metal surface. Iron, for example, is oxidized fairly easily, especially in the presence of moisture. As you know, under these conditions the iron corrodes—it rusts. Rust is a form of iron(III) oxide, Fe_2O_3, that also contains an appreciable amount of absorbed water. The formula for rust is therefore normally given as $Fe_2O_3 \cdot xH_2O$ to indicate its somewhat variable composition. Although the rusting of iron is a slow reaction, the combination of iron with oxygen can be speeded up if the metal is heated to a very high temperature under a stream of pure O_2 (see Figure 5.12).

An aluminum surface, unlike that of iron, is not noticeably dulled by the reaction of aluminum with oxygen. Aluminum is a common metal found around the home in uses ranging from aluminum foil to aluminum window frames, and it surely appears shiny. Yet, aluminum is a rather easily oxidized metal, as can be seen from its position in the activity series (Table 5.2). A *freshly* exposed surface of the metal does react very quickly with oxygen and becomes coated with a very thin film of aluminum oxide, Al_2O_3, so thin that it doesn't obscure the shininess of the metal beneath. Fortunately, the oxide coating adheres very tightly to the surface of the metal and makes it very difficult for additional oxygen to combine with the aluminum. Therefore, further oxidation of aluminum occurs very slowly.

Practice Exercise 22: Write a balanced chemical equation for the reaction of molecular oxygen with strontium metal to form the oxide. (Hint: Strontium, Sr, is in the same group in the periodic table as calcium.)

Practice Exercise 23: The oxide formed in the reaction shown in Figure 5.12 is iron(III) oxide. Write a balanced chemical equation for the reaction.

Most nonmetals react with oxygen directly

Most nonmetals combine as readily with oxygen as do the metals, and their reactions usually occur rapidly enough to be described as combustion. To most people, the most important nonmetal combustion reaction is that of carbon because the reaction is a source of heat. Coal and charcoal, for example, are common carbon fuels. Coal is used worldwide in large amounts to generate electricity, and charcoal is a popular fuel for broiling hamburgers. If plenty of oxygen is available, the combustion of carbon gives CO_2, but when the supply

FIG. 5.11 **A flashbulb, before and after firing.** Fine magnesium wire in an atmosphere of oxygen fills the flashbulb at the left. After being used (*right*), the interior of the bulb is coated with a white film of magnesium oxide. (*Robert Capece.*)

FIG. 5.12 **Cutting steel with an oxyacetylene torch.** An oxygen–acetylene flame is used to heat steel until its glowing red hot. Then the acetylene is turned off and the steel is cut by a stream of pure oxygen whose reaction with the hot metal produces enough heat to melt the steel and send a shower of burning steel sparks flying. (*Scott T. Smith/Corbis Images.*)

The label on a bag of charcoal displays a warning about carbon monoxide. *(Andy Washnik.)*

of O_2 is limited, some CO forms as well. Manufacturers that package charcoal briquettes, therefore, print a warning on the bag that the charcoal shouldn't be used indoors for cooking or heating.

Sulfur is another nonmetal that burns readily in oxygen. In the manufacture of sulfuric acid, the first step is the combustion of sulfur to produce sulfur dioxide. As mentioned earlier, sulfur dioxide also forms when sulfur compounds burn, and the presence of sulfur and sulfur compounds as impurities in coal and petroleum is a major source of air pollution. Power plants that burn coal are making strides to remove the SO_2 from their exhausts and it is being used to make sulfuric acid. As we noted earlier, when SO_2 does enter the atmosphere, it can dissolve in rainwater and become one of the components of acid rain. Some SO_2 is also oxidized slowly to SO_3, which gives the strong acid H_2SO_4 when it dissolves in rainwater.

5.6 | REDOX REACTIONS FOLLOW THE SAME STOICHIOMETRIC PRINCIPLES AS OTHER REACTIONS

In general, working stoichiometry problems involving redox reactions follows the same principles we've applied to other reactions. The principal difference is that the chemical equations are more complex. Nevertheless, once we have a balanced equation, moles of substances involved in the reaction are related by the coefficients in the balanced equation.

Because so many reactions involve oxidation and reduction, it should not be surprising that they have useful applications in the lab. Some redox reactions are especially useful in chemical analyses, particularly in titrations. Unlike in acid–base titrations, however, there are no simple indicators that can be used to conveniently detect the end points in redox titrations, so we have to rely on color changes among the reactants themselves.

One of the most useful reactants for redox titrations is potassium permanganate, $KMnO_4$, especially when the reaction can be carried out in an acidic solution. Permanganate ion is a powerful oxidizing agent, so it oxidizes most substances that are capable of being oxidized. That's one reason why it is used. Especially important, though, is the fact that the MnO_4^- ion has an intense purple color and its reduction product in acidic solution is the almost colorless Mn^{2+} ion. Therefore, when a solution of $KMnO_4$ is added from a buret to a solution of a reducing agent, the chemical reaction that occurs forms a nearly colorless product. This is illustrated in Figure 5.13, where we see a solution of $KMnO_4$ being poured into an acidic solution containing Fe^{2+}. As the $KMnO_4$ solution is added, the purple color continues to be destroyed as long as there is any reducing agent left. In a titration, after the last trace of the reducing agent has been consumed, the MnO_4^- ion in the next drop of titrant has nothing to react with, so it colors the solution pink. This signals the end of the titration. In this way, permanganate ion serves as its own indicator in redox titrations. The next example illustrates a typical analysis using $KMnO_4$ in a redox titration.

☐ In concentrated solutions, MnO_4^- is purple, but dilute solutions of the ion appear pink.

FIG. 5.13 **Reduction of MnO_4^- by Fe^{2+}.** A solution of $KMnO_4$ is added to a stirred acidic solution containing Fe^{2+}. The reaction oxidizes the pale blue-green Fe^{2+} to Fe^{3+} while the MnO_4^- is reduced to the almost colorless Mn^{2+} ion. The purple color of the permanganate will continue to be destroyed until all of the Fe^{2+} has reacted. Only then will the iron-containing solution take on a pink or purple color. This ability of MnO_4^- to signal the completion of the reaction makes it especially useful in redox titrations, where it serves as its own indicator. *(Andy Washnik.)*

EXAMPLE 5.9
Redox Titrations in Chemical Analysis

All the iron in a 2.000 g sample of an iron ore was dissolved in an acidic solution and converted to Fe^{2+}, which was then titrated with 0.1000 M $KMnO_4$ solution. In the titration the iron was oxidized to Fe^{3+}. The titration required 27.45 mL of the $KMnO_4$ solution to reach the end point.

(a) How many grams of iron were in the sample?

(b) What was the percentage iron in the sample?

(c) If the iron was present in the sample as Fe_2O_3, what was the percentage by mass of Fe_2O_3 in the sample?

ANALYSIS: We're dealing with a chemical reaction, so the first step will be to write the balanced equation using the ion–electron method covered earlier in this chapter. With this as a start, let's look over the tools we'll use to answer the first two questions. We'll tackle the last part afterward.

- Molarity and volume of the $KMnO_4$: These will give us moles of $KMnO_4$ used in the titration (remember: volume (L) $\times$ molarity = moles).
- Coefficients of the equation: These permit us to find moles of iron from the moles of $KMnO_4$ used.
- Molar mass of iron: This lets us calculate the mass of iron in the sample from moles of iron.
- Equation to calculate the percentage of iron: % Fe $= \dfrac{\text{g Fe}}{\text{g sample}} \times 100\%$.

SOLUTION: The skeleton equation for the reaction is

$$Fe^{2+} + MnO_4^- \longrightarrow Fe^{3+} + Mn^{2+}$$

Balancing it by the ion–electron method for acidic solutions gives

$$5Fe^{2+} + MnO_4^- + 8H^+ \longrightarrow 5Fe^{3+} + Mn^{2+} + 4H_2O$$

The number of moles of $KMnO_4$ consumed in the reaction is calculated from the volume of the solution used in the titration and its concentration.

$$0.02745 \text{ L } KMnO_4 \text{ soln} \times \frac{0.1000 \text{ mol } KMnO_4}{1.000 \text{ L } KMnO_4 \text{ soln}} \Leftrightarrow 0.002745 \text{ mol } KMnO_4$$

Next, we use the coefficients of the equation to calculate the number of moles of Fe^{2+} that reacted. The chemical equation tells us five moles of Fe^{2+} react per mole of MnO_4^- consumed.

$$0.002745 \text{ mol } KMnO_4 \times \frac{5 \text{ mol } Fe^{2+}}{1 \text{ mol } KMnO_4} \Leftrightarrow 0.01372 \text{ mol } Fe^{2+}$$

This is the number of moles of iron in the ore sample, so the mass of iron in the sample is

$$0.01372 \text{ mol Fe} \times \frac{55.845 \text{ g Fe}}{1 \text{ mol Fe}} = 0.7662 \text{ g Fe}$$

This is the answer to part (a) of the problem. Next we calculate the percentage of iron in the sample, which is the mass of iron divided by the mass of the sample, all multiplied by 100%.

$$\% \text{ Fe} = \frac{\text{mass of Fe}}{\text{mass of sample}} \times 100\%$$

Substituting gives

$$\% \text{ Fe} = \frac{0.7662 \text{ g Fe}}{2.000 \text{ g sample}} \times 100\% = 38.31\% \text{ Fe}$$

The answer to part (b) is that the sample is 38.31% iron.

ARE THE ANSWERS REASONABLE? We can use some approximate arithmetic to estimate the answer. In the titration we used approximately 30 mL, or 0.030 L, of the $KMnO_4$ solution, which is 0.10 M. Multiplying these tells us we've used approximately 0.003 mol of $KMnO_4$. From the coefficients of the equation, five times as many moles of Fe^{2+} react, so the amount of Fe in the sample is approximately $5 \times 0.003 = 0.015$ mol. The atomic mass of Fe is about 55 g/mol, so the mass of Fe in the sample is approximately $0.015 \times 55 \approx 0.8$ g. Our answer (0.7662 g) is reasonable. Calculating % Fe is then straightforward.

ANALYSIS CONTINUED: Now we can work on the last part of the question. Earlier in the problem we determined the number of moles of iron that reacted, 0.01372 mol Fe. How many moles of Fe_2O_3 would have contained that number of moles of iron? That's the critical question we have to answer. Once we know this, we can calculate the mass of the Fe_2O_3 and the percentage of Fe_2O_3 in the original sample. The tools we'll use in solving this part of the problem are

- The chemical formula, Fe_2O_3: The formula relates moles of iron to moles Fe_2O_3.
- Molar mass of Fe_2O_3: This lets us calculate the mass of Fe_2O_3.
- Formula for calculating percentage of Fe_2O_3: % $Fe_2O_3 = \dfrac{g\ Fe_2O_3}{g\ sample} \times 100\%$.

SOLUTION CONTINUED: The chemical formula for the iron oxide gives us

$$1\ mol\ Fe_2O_3 \Leftrightarrow 2\ mol\ Fe$$

This provides the conversion factor we need to determine how many moles of Fe_2O_3 were present in the sample. Working with the number of moles of Fe,

$$0.01372\ \text{mol Fe} \times \frac{1\ mol\ Fe_2O_3}{2\ \text{mol Fe}} \Leftrightarrow 0.006860\ mol\ Fe_2O_3$$

This is the number of moles of Fe_2O_3 in the sample. The formula mass of Fe_2O_3 is 159.69 g mol^{-1}, so the mass of Fe_2O_3 in the sample was

$$0.006860\ \text{mol Fe}_2\text{O}_3 \times \frac{159.69\ g\ Fe_2O_3}{1\ \text{mol Fe}_2\text{O}_3} = 1.095\ g\ Fe_2O_3$$

Finally, the percentage of Fe_2O_3 in the sample was

$$\%\ Fe_2O_3 = \frac{1.095\ g\ Fe_2O_3}{2.000\ g\ sample} \times 100\% = 54.75\%\ Fe_2O_3$$

The ore sample contained 54.75% Fe_2O_3.

IS THE ANSWER REASONABLE? We've noted that the amount of Fe in the sample is approximately 0.015 mol. The amount of Fe_2O_3 that contains this much Fe is 0.0075 mol. The formula mass of Fe_2O_3 is about 160, so the mass of Fe_2O_3 in the sample was approximately $0.0075 \times 160 = 1.2$ g, which isn't too far from the mass we obtained (1.095 g). Since 1.095 g is about half of the total sample mass of 2.000 g, the sample was approximately 50% Fe_2O_3, in agreement with the answer we obtained.

Practice Exercise 24: A 15.00 mL sample of a solution containing oxalic acid, $H_2C_2O_4$, was titrated with 0.02000 M $KMnO_4$. The titration required 18.30 mL of the $KMnO_4$ solution. What was the molarity of the $H_2C_2O_4$ solution? In the reaction, oxalate ion $(C_2O_4^{2-})$ is oxidized to CO_2 and MnO_4^- is reduced to Mn^{2+}. (Hint: You will need to calculate number of moles of $H_2C_2O_4$ in the sample and then apply the definition of molarity.)

Practice Exercise 25: A researcher planned to use chlorine gas in an experiment and wished to trap excess chlorine to prevent it from escaping into the atmosphere. To accomplish this, the reaction of sodium thiosulfate ($Na_2S_2O_3$) with chlorine gas in an acidic aqueous solution to give sulfate ion and chloride ion would be used. How many grams of $Na_2S_2O_3$ are needed to trap 4.25 g of chlorine?

Practice Exercise 26: A sample of a tin ore weighing 0.3000 g was dissolved in an acid solution and all the tin in the sample was changed to tin(II). In a titration, 8.08 mL of 0.0500 M $KMnO_4$ solution was required to oxidize the tin(II) to tin(IV).
(a) What is the balanced equation for the reaction in the titration?
(b) How many grams of tin were in the sample?
(c) What was the percentage by mass of tin in the sample?
(d) If the tin in the sample had been present in the compound SnO_2, what would have been the percentage by mass of SnO_2 in the sample?

SUMMARY

Oxidation–Reduction. **Oxidation** is the loss of electrons or an algebraic increase in oxidation number; **reduction** is the gain of electrons or an algebraic decrease in oxidation number. Both always occur together in **redox reactions.** The substance oxidized is the **reducing agent;** the substance reduced is the **oxidizing agent.** **Oxidation numbers** are a bookkeeping device that we use to follow changes in redox reactions. They are assigned according to the rules on page 178. The term **oxidation state** is equivalent to oxidation number.

Ion–Electron Method. In a balanced redox equation, the number of electrons gained by one substance is always equal to the number lost by another substance. This fact forms the basis for the **ion–electron method** (page **183**), which provides a systematic method for deriving a net ionic equation for a redox reaction in aqueous solution. According to this method the *skeleton* net ionic equation is divided into two **half-reactions,** which are balanced separately before being recombined to give the final balanced net ionic equation. For reactions in basic solution, the equation is balanced as if it occurred in an acidic solution, and then the balanced equation is converted to its proper form for basic solution by adding an appropriate number of OH^-.

Metal–Acid Reactions. In **nonoxidizing acids,** the strongest oxidizing agent is H^+ (Table 5.1). The reaction of a metal with a nonoxidizing acid gives hydrogen gas and a salt of the acid. Only metals more active than hydrogen react this way. These are metals that are located below hydrogen in the **activity series** (Table 5.2). **Oxidizing acids,** like HNO_3, contain an anion that is a stronger oxidizing agent than H^+, and they are able to oxidize many metals that nonoxidizing acids cannot.

Metal-Displacement Reactions. If one metal is more easily oxidized than another, it can displace the other metal from its compounds by a redox reaction. Such reactions are sometimes called **single replacement reactions.** Atoms of the more active metal become ions; ions of the less active metal generally become atoms. In this manner, any metal in the **activity series** can displace any of the others above it in the series from their compounds.

Oxidations by Molecular Oxygen. **Combustion** is the rapid reaction of a substance with oxygen accompanied by the evolution of heat and light. Combustion of a hydrocarbon in the presence of excess oxygen gives CO_2 and H_2O, two molecular oxides. When the supply of oxygen is limited, some CO also forms, and in a very limited supply of oxygen the products are H_2O and very finely divided, elemental carbon (as soot or lampblack). The combustion of organic compounds containing only carbon, hydrogen, and oxygen also gives the same products, CO_2 and H_2O. Sulfur burns to give SO_2, which also forms when sulfur-containing fuels burn. Most nonmetals also burn in oxygen to give molecular oxides.

Many metals combine with oxygen in a process often called **corrosion,** but only sometimes is the reaction rapid enough to be considered combustion. The products are ionic metal oxides.

Redox Titrations. Potassium permanganate is often used in redox titrations because it is a powerful oxidizing agent and serves as its own indicator. In acidic solutions, the purple MnO_4^- ion is reduced to the nearly colorless Mn^{2+} ion.

TOOLS FOR PROBLEM SOLVING

In this chapter you learned to apply the following concepts as tools in solving problems. Study each one carefully so that you know what each is used for. When faced with solving a problem, recall what each tool does and consider whether it will be helpful in finding a solution. This will aid you in selecting the tools you need.

Identifying oxidizing and reducing agents *(page 176)* The substance reduced is the oxidizing agent; the substance oxidized is the reducing agent.

Rules for assigning oxidation numbers *(page 178)* The rules permit us to assign oxidation numbers to elements in compounds and ions. You use changes in oxidation numbers to identify oxidation and reduction. Remember that when there is a conflict between two rules, the rule with the lower number is followed and the rule with the higher number is ignored.

Ion–electron method *(For acidic solutions, page 185; for basic solutions, page 186)* Use this method when you need to obtain a balanced net ionic equation for a redox reaction. Be sure to follow the steps in the order given and do not skip steps. Also, be sure to include charges on all ions.

Table of oxidizing and nonoxidizing acids *(Table 5.1, page 188)* Refer to this table to identify oxidizing and nonoxidizing acids, which enables you to anticipate the products of reactions of metals with acids. Nonoxidizing acids will react with metals below hydrogen in Table 5.2 to give H_2 and the metal ion.

Activity series of metals *(Table 5.2, page 191)* When a question deals with the possible reaction of one metal with the salt of another, refer to the activity series to determine the outcome. A metal in the table will reduce the ion of any metal above it in the table, leading to a single replacement reaction.

Combustion reactions of hydrocarbons with oxygen *(pages 193 and 194)* The products of the reaction do not depend on the identity of the hydrocarbon, but they do depend on the availability of oxygen.

$$\text{hydrocarbon} + O_2 \longrightarrow CO_2 + H_2O \quad \text{(plentiful supply of } O_2)$$

$$\text{hydrocarbon} + O_2 \longrightarrow CO + H_2O \quad \text{(limited supply of } O_2)$$

$$\text{hydrocarbon} + O_2 \longrightarrow C + H_2O \quad \text{(very limited supply of } O_2)$$

Combustion of compounds containing C, H, and O *(page 194)* Complete combustion gives CO_2 and H_2O.

$$(\text{C,H,O compound}) + O_2 \longrightarrow CO_2 + H_2O \quad \text{(complete combustion)}$$

Organic compounds containing sulfur give SO₂ when burned *(page 194)* If an organic compound contains sulfur, SO_2 is formed in addition to CO_2 and H_2O when the compound is burned.

QUESTIONS, PROBLEMS, AND EXERCISES

Answers to problems whose numbers are printed in color are given in Appendix B. More challenging problems are marked with asterisks. ILW = Interactive Learningware solution is available at www.wiley.com/college/brady. OH = an Office Hours video is available for this problem.

REVIEW QUESTIONS

Oxidation–Reduction

5.1 Define *oxidation* and *reduction* (a) in terms of electron transfer and (b) in terms of oxidation numbers.

5.2 In the reaction $2Mg + O_2 \longrightarrow 2MgO$, which substance is the oxidizing agent and which is the reducing agent? Which substance is oxidized and which is reduced?

5.3 Why must both oxidation and reduction occur simultaneously during a redox reaction? What is an oxidizing agent? What happens to it in a redox reaction? What is a reducing agent? What happens to it in a redox reaction?

5.4 In the compound As_4O_6, arsenic has an *oxidation number* of +3. What is the *oxidation state* of arsenic in this compound?

5.5 Is the following a redox reaction? Explain.

$$2NO_2 \longrightarrow N_2O_4$$

5.6 Is the following a redox reaction? Explain.

$$2CrO_4^{2-} + 2H^+ \longrightarrow Cr_2O_7^{2-} + H_2O$$

5.7 If the oxidation number of nitrogen in a certain molecule changes from +3 to −2 during a reaction, is the nitrogen oxidized or reduced? How many electrons are gained (or lost) by each nitrogen atom?

Ion–Electron Method

5.8 The following equation is not balanced. Why? Use the ion–electron method to balance it.

$$Ag + Fe^{2+} \longrightarrow Ag^+ + Fe$$

5.9 Use the ion–electron method to balance the following equation.

$$Cr^{3+} + Zn \longrightarrow Cr + Zn^{2+}$$

5.10 What are the net charges on the left and right sides of the following equations? Add electrons as necessary to make each of them a balanced half-reaction.
(a) $NO_3^- + 10H^+ \longrightarrow NH_4^+ + 3H_2O$
(b) $Cl_2 + 4H_2O \longrightarrow 2ClO_2^- + 8H^+$

5.11 In the preceding question, which half-reaction represents oxidation? Which represents reduction?

Reactions of Metals with Acids and the Activity Series

5.12 What is a *single replacement reaction*?

5.13 What is a nonoxidizing acid? Give two examples. What is the oxidizing agent in a nonoxidizing acid?

5.14 What is the strongest oxidizing agent in an aqueous solution of nitric acid?

5.15 If a metal is able to react with a solution of HCl, where must the metal stand relative to hydrogen in the activity series?

5.16 Where in the activity series (Table 5.2) do we find the best reducing agents? Where do we find the best oxidizing agents?

5.17 Which metals in Table 5.2 will not react with nonoxidizing acids?

5.18 Which metals in Table 5.2 will react with water? Write chemical equations for each of these reactions.

5.19 When manganese reacts with silver ion, is manganese oxidized or reduced? Is it an oxidizing agent or a reducing agent?

Oxygen as an Oxidizing Agent

5.20 Define *combustion*.

5.21 Why is "loss of electrons" described as oxidation?

5.22 What products are produced in the combustion of $C_{10}H_{22}$ (a) if there is an excess of oxygen available? (b) If there is a slightly limited oxygen supply? (c) If there is a very limited supply of oxygen?

5.23 If one of the impurities in diesel fuel has the formula C_2H_6S, what products will be formed when it burns? Write a balanced chemical equation for the reaction.

5.24 Burning ammonia in an atmosphere of oxygen produces stable N_2 molecules as one of the products. What is the other product? Write the balanced equation for the reaction.

REVIEW PROBLEMS

Oxidation–Reduction; Oxidation Numbers

5.25 Assign oxidation numbers to the atoms in the following:
(a) S^{2-}, (b) SO_2, (c) P_4, and (d) PH_3.

OH 5.26 Assign oxidation numbers to the atoms in the following:
(a) ClO_4^-, (b) $CrCl_3$, (c) SnS_2, and (d) $Au(NO_3)_3$.

5.27 Assign oxidation numbers to each atom in the following:
(a) $NaOCl$, (b) $NaClO_2$, (c) $NaClO_3$, and (d) $NaClO_4$.

5.28 Assign oxidation numbers to the elements in the following.
(a) $Ca(VO_3)_2$, (b) $SnCl_4$, (c) MnO_4^{2-}, (d) MnO_2

5.29 Assign oxidation numbers to the elements in the following.
(a) PbS, (b) $TiCl_4$, (c) CsO_2, (d) O_2F_2

5.30 Assign oxidation numbers to the elements in the following.
(a) $Sr(IO_3)_2$, (b) Cr_2S_3, (c) OF_2, (d) HOF

5.31 When chlorine is added to drinking water to kill bacteria, some of the chlorine is changed into ions by the following equilibrium:

$$Cl_2(aq) + H_2O \rightleftharpoons H^+(aq) + Cl^-(aq) + HOCl(aq)$$

In the forward reaction (the reaction going from left to right), which substance is oxidized and which is reduced? In the reverse reaction, which is the oxidizing agent and which is the reducing agent?

5.32 A pollutant in smog is nitrogen dioxide, NO_2. The gas has a reddish brown color and is responsible for the red-brown color associated with this type of air pollution. Nitrogen dioxide is also a contributor to acid rain because when rain passes through air contaminated with NO_2, it dissolves and undergoes the following reaction:

$$3NO_2(g) + H_2O \longrightarrow NO(g) + 2H^+(aq) + 2NO_3^-(aq)$$

In this reaction, which element is reduced and which is oxidized?

5.33 For the following reactions, identify the substance oxidized, the substance reduced, the oxidizing agent, and the reducing agent.
(a) $2HNO_3 + 3H_3AsO_3 \longrightarrow 2NO + 3H_3AsO_4 + H_2O$
(b) $NaI + 3HOCl \longrightarrow NaIO_3 + 3HCl$
(c) $2KMnO_4 + 5H_2C_2O_4 + 3H_2SO_4 \longrightarrow 10CO_2 + K_2SO_4 + 2MnSO_4 + 8H_2O$
(d) $6H_2SO_4 + 2Al \longrightarrow Al_2(SO_4)_3 + 3SO_2 + 6H_2O$

5.34 For the following reactions, identify the substance oxidized, the substance reduced, the oxidizing agent, and the reducing agent.
(a) $Cu + 2H_2SO_4 \longrightarrow CuSO_4 + SO_2 + 2H_2O$
(b) $3SO_2 + 2HNO_3 + 2H_2O \longrightarrow 3H_2SO_4 + 2NO$
(c) $5H_2SO_4 + 4Zn \longrightarrow 4ZnSO_4 + H_2S + 4H_2O$
(d) $I_2 + 10HNO_3 \longrightarrow 2HIO_3 + 10NO_2 + 4H_2O$

Ion–Electron Method

ILW 5.35 Balance the following equations for reactions occurring in an acidic solution.
(a) $S_2O_3^{2-} + OCl^- \longrightarrow Cl^- + S_4O_6^{2-}$
(b) $NO_3^- + Cu \longrightarrow NO_2 + Cu^{2+}$
(c) $IO_3^- + AsO_3^{3-} \longrightarrow I^- + AsO_4^{3-}$
(d) $SO_4^{2-} + Zn \longrightarrow Zn^{2+} + SO_2$
(e) $NO_3^- + Zn \longrightarrow NH_4^+ + Zn^{2+}$
(f) $Cr^{3+} + BiO_3^- \longrightarrow Cr_2O_7^{2-} + Bi^{3+}$
(g) $I_2 + OCl^- \longrightarrow IO_3^- + Cl^-$
(h) $Mn^{2+} + BiO_3^- \longrightarrow MnO_4^- + Bi^{3+}$
(i) $H_3AsO_3 + Cr_2O_7^{2-} \longrightarrow H_3AsO_4 + Cr^{3+}$
(j) $I^- + HSO_4^- \longrightarrow I_2 + SO_2$

5.36 Balance these equations for reactions occurring in an acidic solution.
(a) $Sn + NO_3^- \longrightarrow SnO_2 + NO$
(b) $PbO_2 + Cl^- \longrightarrow PbCl_2 + Cl_2$
(c) $Ag + NO_3^- \longrightarrow NO_2 + Ag^+$

(d) $Fe^{3+} + NH_3OH^+ \longrightarrow Fe^{2+} + N_2O$
(e) $HNO_2 + I^- \longrightarrow I_2 + NO$
(f) $C_2O_4^{2-} + HNO_2 \longrightarrow CO_2 + NO$
(g) $HNO_2 + MnO_4^- \longrightarrow Mn^{2+} + NO_3^-$
(h) $H_3PO_2 + Cr_2O_7^{2-} \longrightarrow H_3PO_4 + Cr^{3+}$
(i) $VO_2^+ + Sn^{2+} \longrightarrow VO^{2+} + Sn^{4+}$
(j) $XeF_2 + Cl^- \longrightarrow Xe + F^- + Cl_2$

5.37 Balance equations for these reactions occurring in a basic solution.
(a) $CrO_4^{2-} + S^{2-} \longrightarrow S + CrO_2^-$
(b) $MnO_4^- + C_2O_4^{2-} \longrightarrow CO_2 + MnO_2$
(c) $ClO_3^- + N_2H_4 \longrightarrow NO + Cl^-$
(d) $NiO_2 + Mn(OH)_2 \longrightarrow Mn_2O_3 + Ni(OH)_2$
(e) $SO_3^{2-} + MnO_4^- \longrightarrow SO_4^{2-} + MnO_2$

5.38 Balance equations for these reactions occurring in a basic solution.
(a) $CrO_2^- + S_2O_8^{2-} \longrightarrow CrO_4^{2-} + SO_4^{2-}$
(b) $SO_3^{2-} + CrO_4^{2-} \longrightarrow SO_4^{2-} + CrO_2^-$
(c) $O_2 + N_2H_4 \longrightarrow H_2O_2 + N_2$
(d) $Fe(OH)_2 + O_2 \longrightarrow Fe(OH)_3 + OH^-$
(e) $Au + CN^- + O_2 \longrightarrow Au(CN)_4^- + OH^-$

5.39 Laundry bleach such as Clorox is a dilute solution of sodium hypochlorite, NaOCl. Write a balanced net ionic equation for the reaction of NaOCl with $Na_2S_2O_3$. The OCl^- is reduced to chloride ion and the $S_2O_3^{2-}$ is oxidized to sulfate ion.

OH 5.40 Calcium oxalate is one of the minerals found in kidney stones. If a strong acid is added to calcium oxalate, the compound will dissolve and the oxalate ion will be changed to oxalic acid (a weak acid). Oxalate ion is a moderately strong reducing agent. Write a balanced net ionic equation for the oxidation of $H_2C_2O_4$ by $K_2Cr_2O_7$ in an acidic solution. The reaction yields Cr^{3+} and CO_2 among the products.

5.41 Ozone, O_3, is a very powerful oxidizing agent, and in some places ozone is used to treat water to kill bacteria and make it safe to drink. One of the problems with this method of purifying water is that if there is any bromide ion in the water, it becomes oxidized to bromate ion, which has shown evidence of causing cancer in test animals. Assuming that ozone is reduced to water, write a balanced chemical equation for the reaction. (Assume an acidic solution.)

5.42 Chlorine is a good bleaching agent because it is able to oxidize substances that are colored to give colorless reaction products. It is used in the pulp and paper industry as a bleach, but after it has done its work, residual chlorine must be removed. This is accomplished using sodium thiosulfate, $Na_2S_2O_3$, which reacts with the chlorine, reducing it to chloride ion. The thiosulfate ion is changed to sulfate ion, which is easily removed by washing with water. Write a balanced chemical equation for the reaction of chlorine with thiosulfate ion, assuming an acidic solution.

Reactions of Metals with Acids

5.43 Write balanced molecular, ionic, and net ionic equations for the reactions of the following metals with hydrochloric acid to give hydrogen plus the metal ion in solution.
(a) Manganese (gives Mn^{2+})
(b) Cadmium (gives Cd^{2+})
(c) Tin (gives Sn^{2+})

5.44 Write balanced molecular, ionic, and net ionic equations for the reaction of each of the following metals with dilute sulfuric acid.
(a) Nickel (gives Ni^{2+})
(b) Chromium (gives Cr^{3+})
(c) Aluminum (gives Al^{3+})

5.45 On the basis of the discussions in this chapter, suggest chemical equations for the oxidation of metallic silver to Ag^+ ion with (a) dilute HNO_3 and (b) concentrated HNO_3.

OH 5.46 When hot and concentrated, sulfuric acid is a fairly strong oxidizing agent. Write a balanced net ionic equation for the oxidation of metallic copper to copper(II) ion by hot concentrated H_2SO_4, in which the sulfur is reduced to SO_2. Write a balanced molecular equation for the reaction.

Single Replacement Reactions and the Activity Series

5.47 Use Table 5.2 to predict the outcome of the following reactions. If no reaction occurs, write N.R. If a reaction occurs, write a balanced chemical equation for it.
(a) $Fe + Mg^{2+} \longrightarrow$
(b) $Cr + Pb^{2+} \longrightarrow$
(c) $Ag^+ + Fe \longrightarrow$
(d) $Ag + Au^{3+} \longrightarrow$

OH 5.48 Use Table 5.2 to predict the outcome of the following reactions. If no reaction occurs, write N.R. If a reaction occurs, write a balanced chemical equation for it.
(a) $Mn + Fe^{2+} \longrightarrow$
(b) $Cd + Zn^{2+} \longrightarrow$
(c) $Mg + Co^{2+} \longrightarrow$
(d) $Cr + Sn^{2+} \longrightarrow$

5.49 The following reactions occur spontaneously.

$$Pu + 3Tl^+ \longrightarrow Pu^{3+} + 3Tl$$

$$Ru + Pt^{2+} \longrightarrow Ru^{2+} + Pt$$

$$2Tl + Ru^{2+} \longrightarrow 2Tl^+ + Ru$$

List the metals Pu, Pt, and Tl in order of increasing ease of oxidation.

5.50 The following reactions occur spontaneously.

$$2Y + 3Ni^{2+} \longrightarrow 2Y^{3+} + 3Ni$$

$$2Mo + 3Ni^{2+} \longrightarrow 2Mo^{3+} + 3Ni$$

$$Y^{3+} + Mo \longrightarrow Y + Mo^{3+}$$

List the metals Y, Ni, and Mo in order of increasing ease of oxidation.

5.51 It is found that the following reaction occurs spontaneously.

$$Ru^{2+}(aq) + Cd(s) \longrightarrow Ru(s) + Cd^{2+}(aq)$$

What reaction will occur if a mixture is prepared containing the following: $Cd(s)$, $Cd(NO_3)_2(aq)$, $Tl(s)$, $TlCl(aq)$? (Refer to the information in Problem 5.49 above.)

5.52 It is observed that when magnesium metal is dipped into a solution of nickel(II) chloride, some of the magnesium dissolves and nickel metal is deposited on the surface of the magnesium. Referring to Problem 5.50, can you tell which of the following reactions will occur spontaneously? Explain the reason for your answer.
(a) $2Mo^{3+} + 3Mg \longrightarrow 3Mg^{2+} + 2Mo$
(b) $2Mo + 3Mg^{2+} \longrightarrow 2Mo^{3+} + 3Mg$

Reactions of Oxygen

5.53 Write balanced chemical equations for the complete combustion (in the presence of excess oxygen) of the following:
(a) C_6H_6 (benzene, an important industrial chemical and solvent)
(b) C_3H_8 (propane, a gaseous fuel used in many stoves)
(c) $C_{21}H_{44}$ (a component of paraffin wax)

5.54 Write balanced chemical equations for the complete combustion (in the presence of excess oxygen) of the following:
(a) $C_{12}H_{26}$ (a component of kerosene)
(b) $C_{18}H_{36}$ (a component of diesel fuel)
(c) C_7H_8 (toluene, a raw material in the production of TNT)

5.55 Write balanced equations for the combustion of the hydrocarbons in Problem 5.53 in (a) a slightly limited supply of oxygen and (b) a very limited supply of oxygen.

5.56 Write balanced equations for the combustion of the hydrocarbons in Problem 5.54 in (a) a slightly limited supply of oxygen and (b) a very limited supply of oxygen.

5.57 Methanol, CH_3OH, has been suggested as an alternative to gasoline as an automotive fuel. Write a balanced chemical equation for its complete combustion.

OH 5.58 Metabolism of carbohydrates such as glucose, $C_6H_{12}O_6$, produces the same products as complete combustion. Write a chemical equation representing the metabolism (combustion) of glucose.

5.59 Write the balanced equation for the combustion of dimethylsulfide, $(CH_3)_2S$, in an abundant supply of oxygen.

5.60 Thiophene, C_4H_4S, is an impurity in crude oil and is a source of pollution if not removed. Write an equation for the combustion of thiophene.

5.61 Write chemical equations for the reaction of oxygen with (a) zinc, (b) aluminum, (c) magnesium, and (d) iron to form iron(III) oxide.

5.62 Write chemical equations for the reaction of oxygen with (a) beryllium, (b) lithium, (c) barium, and (d) bismuth to form bismuth(III) oxide.

Redox Reactions and Stoichiometry

5.63 Iodate ion reacts with sulfite ion to give sulfate ion and iodide ion.
(a) Write a balanced net ionic equation for the reaction.
(b) How many grams of sodium sulfite are needed to react with 5.00 g of sodium iodate?

5.64 Potable water (drinking water) should not have manganese concentrations in excess of 0.05 mg/mL. If the manganese concentration is greater than 0.1 mg/mL, it imparts a foul taste to the water and discolors laundry and porcelain surfaces. Manganese(II) ion is oxidized to permanganate ion by bismuthate ion, BiO_3^-, in an acidic solution. In the reaction, BiO_3^- is reduced to Bi^{3+}.
(a) Write a balanced net ionic equation for the reaction.
(b) How many milligrams of $NaBiO_3$ are needed to oxidize the manganese in 18.5 mg of manganese(II) sulfate?

OH 5.65 How many grams of copper must react to displace 12.0 g of silver from a solution of silver nitrate?

5.66 How many grams of aluminum must react to displace all the silver from 25.0 g of silver nitrate? The reaction occurs in aqueous solution.

5.67 In an acidic solution, permanganate ion reacts with tin(II) ion to give manganese(II) ion and tin(IV) ion.
(a) Write a balanced net ionic equation for the reaction.
(b) How many milliliters of 0.230 M potassium permanganate solution are needed to react completely with 40.0 mL of 0.250 M tin(II) chloride solution?

5.68 In an acidic solution, bisulfite ion reacts with chlorate ion to give sulfate ion and chloride ion.
(a) Write a balanced net ionic equation for the reaction.
(b) How many milliliters of 0.150 M sodium chlorate solution are needed to react completely with 30.0 mL of 0.450 M sodium bisulfite solution?

5.69 Sulfites are used worldwide in the wine industry as antioxidant and antimicrobial agents. However, sulfites have also been identified as causing certain allergic reactions suffered by asthmatics, and the FDA mandates that sulfites be identified on the label if they are present at levels of 10 ppm (parts per million) or higher. The analysis of sulfites in wine uses the "Ripper method" in which a standard iodine solution, prepared by the reaction of iodate and iodide ions, is used to titrate a sample of the wine. The iodine is formed in the reaction

$$IO_3^- + 5I^- + 6H^+ \longrightarrow 3I_2 + 3H_2O$$

The iodine is held in solution by adding an excess of I^- which combines with I_2 to give I_3^-. In the titration, the SO_3^{2-} is converted to SO_2 by acidification and the reaction during the titration is

$$SO_2 + I_3^- + 2H_2O \longrightarrow SO_4^{2-} + 3I^- + 4H^+$$

Starch is added to the wine sample to detect the end point, which is signaled by the formation of a dark blue color when excess iodine binds to the starch molecules. In a certain analysis, 0.0421 g of $NaIO_3$ was dissolved in dilute acid and excess NaI was added to the solution, which was then diluted to a total volume of 100.0 mL. A 50.0 mL sample of wine was then acidified and titrated with the iodine-containing solution. In the titration, 2.47 mL of the iodine solution was required.
(a) What was the molarity of the iodine (actually, I_3^-) in the standard solution?
(b) How many grams of SO_2 were in the wine sample?
(c) If the density of the wine was 0.96 g/mL, what was the percentage of SO_2 in the wine?
(d) Parts per million (ppm) is calculated in a manner similar to percent (which is equivalent to *parts per hundred*).

$$ppm = \frac{\text{grams of component}}{\text{grams of sample}} \times 10^6 \text{ ppm}$$

What was the concentration of sulfite in the wine, expressed as parts per million SO_2?

5.70 Methylbromide, CH_3Br, is used in agriculture to fumigate soil to rid it of pests such as nematodes. It is injected directly into the soil, but over time it has a tendency to escape before it can undergo natural degradation to innocuous products. Soil chemists have found that ammonium thiosulfate, $(NH_4)_2S_2O_3$, a nitrogen and sulfur fertilizer, drastically reduces methylbromide emissions by causing it to degrade.

In a chemical analysis to determine the purity of a batch of commercial ammonium thiosulfate, a chemist first prepared a standard solution of iodine following the procedure in the preceding problem. First, 0.462 g of KIO_3 was dissolved in 100 mL of water. The solution was made acidic and treated with excess potassium iodide, which caused the following reaction to take place:

$$IO_3^- + 8I^- + 6H^+ \longrightarrow 3I_3^- + 3H_2O$$

The solution containing the I_3^- was then diluted to exactly 250 mL in a volumetric flask. Next, the chemist dissolved 0.218 g of the fertilizer in water, added starch indicator, and titrated it with the standard I_3^- solution. The reaction was

$$2S_2O_3^{2-} + I_3^- \longrightarrow S_4O_6^{2-} + 3I^-$$

The titration required 27.99 mL of the I_3^- solution.
(a) What was the molarity of the I_3^- solution used in the titration?
(b) How many grams of $(NH_4)_2S_2O_3$ were in the fertilizer sample?
(c) What was the percentage by mass of $(NH_4)_2S_2O_3$ in the fertilizer?

ILW 5.71 A sample of a copper ore with a mass of 0.4225 g was dissolved in acid. A solution of potassium iodide was added, which caused the reaction

$$2Cu^{2+}(aq) + 5I^-(aq) \longrightarrow I_3^-(aq) + 2CuI(s)$$

The I_3^- that formed reacted quantitatively with exactly 29.96 mL of 0.02100 M $Na_2S_2O_3$ according to the following equation.

$$I_3^-(aq) + 2S_2O_3^{2-}(aq) \longrightarrow 3I^-(aq) + S_4O_6^{2-}(aq)$$

(a) What was the percentage by mass of copper in the ore?
(b) If the ore contained $CuCO_3$, what was the percentage by mass of $CuCO_3$ in the ore?

5.72 A 1.362 g sample of an iron ore that contained Fe_3O_4 was dissolved in acid and all the iron was reduced to Fe^{2+}. The solution was then acidified with H_2SO_4 and titrated with 39.42 mL of 0.0281 M $KMnO_4$, which oxidized the iron to Fe^{3+}. The net ionic equation for the reaction is

$$5Fe^{2+} + MnO_4^- + 8H^+ \longrightarrow 5Fe^{3+} + Mn^{2+} + 4H_2O$$

(a) What was the percentage by mass of iron in the ore?
(b) What was the percentage by mass of Fe_3O_4 in the ore?

5.73 Hydrogen peroxide (H_2O_2) solution can be purchased in drug stores for use as an antiseptic. A sample of such a solution weighing 1.000 g was acidified with H_2SO_4 and titrated with a 0.02000 M solution of $KMnO_4$. The net ionic equation for the reaction is

$$6H^+ + 5H_2O_2 + 2MnO_4^- \longrightarrow 5O_2 + 2Mn^{2+} + 8H_2O$$

The titration required 17.60 mL of $KMnO_4$ solution.
(a) How many grams of H_2O_2 reacted?
(b) What is the percentage by mass of the H_2O_2 in the original antiseptic solution?

5.74 Sodium nitrite, $NaNO_2$, is used as a preservative in meat products such as frankfurters and bologna. In an acidic solution, nitrite ion is converted to nitrous acid, HNO_2, which reacts with permanganate ion according to the equation

$$H^+ + 5HNO_2 + 2MnO_4^- \longrightarrow 5NO_3^- + 2Mn^{2+} + 3H_2O$$

A 1.000 g sample of a water-soluble solid containing $NaNO_2$ was dissolved in dilute H_2SO_4 and titrated with 0.01000 M $KMnO_4$

solution. The titration required 12.15 mL of the $KMnO_4$ solution. What was the percentage by mass of $NaNO_2$ in the original 1.000 g sample?

5.75 A sample of a chromium-containing alloy weighing 3.450 g was dissolved in acid, and all the chromium in the sample was oxidized to CrO_4^{2-}. It was then found that 3.18 g of Na_2SO_3 was required to reduce the CrO_4^{2-} to CrO_2^- in a basic solution, with the SO_3^{2-} being oxidized to SO_4^{2-}.
(a) Write a balanced equation for the reaction of CrO_4^{2-} with SO_3^{2-} in a basic solution.
(b) How many grams of chromium were in the alloy sample?
(c) What was the percentage by mass of chromium in the alloy?

5.76 Solder is an alloy containing the metals tin and lead. A particular sample of the alloy weighing 1.50 g was dissolved in acid. All the tin was then converted to the +2 oxidation state. Next, it was found that 0.368 g of $Na_2Cr_2O_7$ was required to oxidize the Sn^{2+} to Sn^{4+} in an acidic solution. In the reaction the chromium was reduced to Cr^{3+} ion.
(a) Write a balanced net ionic equation for the reaction between Sn^{2+} and $Cr_2O_7^{2-}$ in an acidic solution.
(b) Calculate the number of grams of tin that were in the sample of solder.
(c) What was the percentage by mass of tin in the solder?

5.77 Both calcium chloride and sodium chloride are used to melt ice and snow on roads in the winter. A certain company was marketing a mixture of these two compounds for this purpose. A chemist, wishing to analyze the mixture, dissolved 2.463 g of it in water and precipitated calcium oxalate by adding sodium oxalate, $Na_2C_2O_4$. The calcium oxalate was carefully filtered from the solution, dissolved in sulfuric acid, and titrated with 0.1000 M $KMnO_4$ solution. The reaction that occurred was

$$6H^+ + 5H_2C_2O_4 + 2MnO_4^- \longrightarrow 10CO_2 + 2Mn^{2+} + 8H_2O$$

The titration required 21.62 mL of the $KMnO_4$ solution.
(a) How many moles of $C_2O_4^{2-}$ were present in the calcium oxalate precipitate?
(b) How many grams of calcium chloride were in the original 2.463 g sample?
(c) What was the percentage by mass of calcium chloride in the sample?

5.78 A way to analyze a sample for nitrite ion is to acidify a solution containing NO_2^- and then allow the HNO_2 that is formed to react with iodide ion in the presence of excess I^-. The reaction is

$$2HNO_2 + 2H^+ + 3I^- \longrightarrow 2NO + 2H_2O + I_3^-$$

Then the I_3^- is titrated with $Na_2S_2O_3$ solution using starch as an indicator.

$$I_3^- + 2S_2O_3^{2-} \longrightarrow 3I^- + S_4O_6^{2-}$$

In a typical analysis, a 1.104 g sample that was known to contain $NaNO_2$ was treated as described above. The titration required 29.25 mL of 0.3000 M $Na_2S_2O_3$ solution to reach the end point.
(a) How many moles of I_3^- had been produced in the first reaction?
(b) How many moles of NO_2^- had been in the original 1.104 g sample?
(c) What was the percentage by mass of $NaNO_2$ in the original sample?

ADDITIONAL EXERCISES

5.79 What is the oxidation number of sulfur in the tetrathionate ion, $S_4O_6^{2-}$?

*5.80 In Practice Exercise 7 (page 182), some of the uses of chlorine dioxide were described along with a reaction that could be used to make ClO_2. Another reaction that is used to make this substance is

$$HCl + NaOCl + 2NaClO_2 \longrightarrow 2ClO_2 + 2NaCl + NaOH$$

Which element is oxidized? Which element is reduced? Which substance is the oxidizing agent and which is the reducing agent?

5.81 What is the average oxidation number of carbon in (a) C_2H_5OH (grain alcohol), (b) $C_{12}H_{22}O_{11}$ (sucrose—table sugar), (c) $CaCO_3$ (limestone), and (d) $NaHCO_3$ (baking soda)?

5.82 The following chemical reactions are *observed to occur* in aqueous solution.

$$2Al + 3Cu^{2+} \longrightarrow 2Al^{3+} + 3Cu$$

$$2Al + 3Fe^{2+} \longrightarrow 3Fe + 2Al^{3+}$$

$$Pb^{2+} + Fe \longrightarrow Pb + Fe^{2+}$$

$$Fe + Cu^{2+} \longrightarrow Fe^{2+} + Cu$$

$$2Al + 3Pb^{2+} \longrightarrow 3Pb + 2Al^{3+}$$

$$Pb + Cu^{2+} \longrightarrow Pb^{2+} + Cu$$

Arrange the metals Al, Pb, Fe, and Cu in order of increasing ease of oxidation.

5.83 In the preceding problem, were all the experiments described actually necessary to establish the order?

5.84 According to the activity series in Table 5.2, which of the following metals react with nonoxidizing acids? (a) silver, (b) gold, (c) zinc, (d) magnesium

5.85 In each pair below, choose the metal that would most likely react more rapidly with a nonoxidizing acid such as HCl. (a) aluminum or iron, (b) zinc or nickel, (c) cadmium or magnesium

5.86 In June 2002, the Department of Health and Children in Ireland began a program to distribute tablets of potassium iodate to households as part of Ireland's National Emergency Plan for Nuclear Accidents. Potassium iodate provides iodine, which when taken during a nuclear emergency, works by "topping off" the thyroid gland to prevent the uptake of radioactive iodine that might be released into the environment by a nuclear accident.

To test the potency of the tablets, a chemist dissolved one in 100 mL of water, made the solution acidic, and then added excess potassium iodide, which caused the following reaction to occur.

$$IO_3^- + 8I^- + 6H^+ \longrightarrow 3I_3^- + 3H_2O$$

The resulting solution containing I_3^- was titrated with 0.0500 M $Na_2S_2O_3$ solution, using starch indicator to detect the end point. (In the presence of iodine, starch turns dark blue. When the $S_2O_3^{2-}$ has consumed all the iodine, the solution becomes colorless.) The titration required 22.61 mL of the thiosulfate solution to reach the end point. The reaction during the titration was

$$I_3^- + 2S_2O_3^{2-} \longrightarrow 3I^- + S_4O_6^{2-}$$

How many milligrams of KIO_3 were in the tablet?

5.87 Use Table 5.2 to predict whether the following displacement reactions should occur. If no reaction occurs, write N.R. If a reaction does occur, write a balanced chemical equation for it.
(a) $Zn + Sn^{2+} \longrightarrow$ (d) $Zn + Co^{2+} \longrightarrow$
(b) $Cr + H^+ \longrightarrow$ (e) $Mn + Pb^{2+} \longrightarrow$
(c) $Pb + Cd^{2+} \longrightarrow$

5.88 Sucrose, $C_{12}H_{22}O_{11}$, is ordinary table sugar. Write a balanced chemical equation representing the metabolism of sucrose. (See Review Problem 5.58.)

*5.89 Balance the following equations by the ion–electron method.
(a) $NBr_3 \longrightarrow N_2 + Br^- + HOBr$ (basic solution)
(b) $Cl_2 \longrightarrow Cl^- + ClO_3^-$ (basic solution)
(c) $H_2SeO_3 + H_2S \longrightarrow S + Se$ (acidic solution)
(d) $MnO_2 + SO_3^{2-} \longrightarrow Mn^{2+} + S_2O_6^{2-}$ (acidic solution)
(e) $XeO_3 + I^- \longrightarrow Xe + I_2$ (acidic solution)
(f) $(CN)_2 \longrightarrow CN^- + OCN^-$ (basic solution)

5.90 Lead(IV) oxide reacts with hydrochloric acid to give chlorine. The unbalanced equation for the reaction is

$$PbO_2 + Cl^- \longrightarrow PbCl_2 + Cl_2$$

How many grams of PbO_2 must react to give 15.0 g of Cl_2?

*5.91 A solution contains $Ce(SO_4)_3^{2-}$ at a concentration of 0.0150 M. It was found that in a titration, 25.00 mL of this solution reacted completely with 23.44 mL of 0.032 M $FeSO_4$ solution. The reaction gave Fe^{3+} as a product in the solution. In this reaction, what is the final oxidation state of the Ce?

*5.92 A copper bar with a mass of 12.340 g is dipped into 255 mL of 0.125 M $AgNO_3$ solution. When the reaction that occurs has finally ceased, what will be the mass of unreacted copper in the bar? If all the silver that forms adheres to the copper bar, what will be the total mass of the bar after the reaction?

5.93 A solution containing 0.1244 g of $K_2C_2O_4$ was acidified, changing the $C_2O_4^{2-}$ ions to $H_2C_2O_4$. The solution was then titrated with 13.93 mL of a $KMnO_4$ solution to reach a faint pink end point. In the reaction, $H_2C_2O_4$ was oxidized to CO_2 and MnO_4^- was reduced to Mn^{2+}. What was the molarity of the $KMnO_4$ solution used in the titration?

*5.94 It was found that a 20.0 mL portion of a solution of oxalic acid, $H_2C_2O_4$, requires 6.25 mL of 0.200 M $K_2Cr_2O_7$ for complete reaction in an acidic solution. In the reaction, the oxidation product is CO_2 and the reduction product is Cr^{3+}. How many milliliters of 0.450 M NaOH are required to completely neutralize the $H_2C_2O_4$ in a separate 20.00 mL sample of the same oxalic acid solution?

*5.95 A mixture is made by combining 300 mL of 0.0200 M $Na_2Cr_2O_7$ with 400 mL of 0.060 M $Fe(NO_3)_2$. Initially, the H^+ concentration in the mixture is 0.400 M. Dichromate ion oxidizes Fe^{2+} to Fe^{3+} and is reduced to Cr^{3+}. After the reaction in the mixture has ceased, how many milliliters of 0.0100 M NaOH will be required to neutralize the remaining H^+?

*5.96 A solution with a volume of 500.0 mL contained a mixture of SO_3^{2-} and $S_2O_3^{2-}$. A 100.0 mL portion of the solution was found to react with 80.00 mL of 0.0500 M CrO_4^{2-} in a basic solution to give CrO_2^-. The only sulfur-containing product was SO_4^{2-}. After the reaction, the solution was treated with excess 0.200 M $BaCl_2$ solution, which precipitated $BaSO_4$. This solid was filtered from the solution, dried, and found to weigh 0.9336 g.

Explain in detail how you can determine the molar concentrations of SO_3^{2-} and $S_2O_3^{2-}$ in the original solution.

*5.97 An organic compound contains carbon, hydrogen, and sulfur. A sample of it with a mass of 1.045 g was burned in oxygen to give gaseous CO_2, H_2O, and SO_2. These gases were passed through 500.0 mL of an acidified 0.0200 M $KMnO_4$ solution, which caused the SO_2 to be oxidized to SO_4^{2-}. Only part of the available $KMnO_4$ was reduced to Mn^{2+}. Next, 50.00 mL of 0.0300 M $SnCl_2$ was added to a 50.00 mL portion of this solution, which still contained unreduced $KMnO_4$. There was more than enough added $SnCl_2$ to cause all of the remaining MnO_4^- in the 50 mL portion to be reduced to Mn^{2+}. The excess Sn^{2+} that still remained after the reaction was then titrated with 0.0100 M $KMnO_4$, requiring 27.28 mL of the $KMnO_4$ solution to reach the end point. What was the percentage of sulfur in the original sample of the organic compound that had been burned?

*5.98 A bar of copper weighing 32.00 g was dipped into 50.0 mL of 0.250 M $AgNO_3$ solution. If all the silver that deposits adheres to the copper bar, how much will the bar weigh after the reaction is complete? Write and balance any necessary chemical equations.

EXERCISES IN CRITICAL THINKING

5.99 The ion $OSCN^-$ is found in human saliva. Discuss the problems in assigning oxidation numbers to the atoms in this ion. Suggest a reasonable set of oxidation numbers for the atoms in $OSCN^-$.

5.100 We described the ion–electron method for balancing redox equations. Can you devise an alternate method using oxidation numbers?

5.101 Assuming that a chemical reaction with DNA could lead to damage causing cancer, would a very strong or a weak oxidizing agent have a better chance of being a carcinogen? Justify your answer.

5.102 Would you expect atomic oxygen and chlorine to be better or worse oxidizing agents than molecular oxygen and molecular chlorine? Justify your answer.

5.103 Do we live in an oxidizing or reducing environment? What effect might our environment have on chemistry we do in the laboratory? What effect might the environment have on the nature of the chemicals (minerals, etc.) we find on earth?

6 ENERGY AND CHEMICAL CHANGE

The power for this "top fuel dragster" comes from the combustion of fuel, but the amount of energy produced depends on the type of fuel and what is used to burn it. In this chapter we study the nature of energy, how it is measured, and how it relates to chemical reactions. *(© 2006 Jason Ellis)*

CHAPTER OUTLINE

6.1 An object has energy if it is capable of doing work

6.2 Internal energy is the total energy of an object's molecules

6.3 Heat can be determined by measuring temperature changes

6.4 Energy is absorbed or released during most chemical reactions

6.5 Heats of reaction are measured at constant volume or constant pressure

6.6 Thermochemical equations are chemical equations that quantitatively include heat

6.7 Thermochemical equations can be combined because enthalpy is a state function

6.8 Tabulated standard heats of reaction can be used to predict any heat of reaction using Hess's law

THIS CHAPTER IN CONTEXT Energy is a term we often see in the news. We hear reports on the cost of energy and what's happening to the world's energy supplies. One might come away with the notion that energy is something you can hold in your hands and place in a bottle. Energy is not like matter, however. Rather, it is something that matter can possess, something that enables objects to move or cause other objects to move. Understanding what energy *really* is should be one of your goals in studying this chapter.

Nearly every chemical and physical change is accompanied by a *change* in energy. The energy changes associated with the evaporation and condensation of water drive global weather systems. The combustion of fuels produces energy changes we use to power cars and generate electricity, and our bodies use energy released in the metabolism of foods to drive biochemical processes. In this chapter we study **thermochemistry,** the branch of chemistry that deals specifically with the energy absorbed or released by chemical reactions. Thermochemistry has many practical applications, but it is also of great theoretical importance, because it provides an important link between laboratory measurements (such as temperature changes) and events on the molecular level that occur when molecules form or break apart.

Thermochemistry is part of the science of **thermodynamics,** the study of energy transfer and energy transformation. Thermodynamics allows scientists to predict whether a proposed physical change or chemical reaction can occur under a given set of conditions. It is an essential part of chemistry (and all the natural sciences). We'll continue our study of thermodynamics in Chapter 18.

6.1 AN OBJECT HAS ENERGY IF IT IS CAPABLE OF DOING WORK

☐ Work is done by an object when it causes something to move. A moving car has energy because it can move another car in a collision.

As mentioned in the introduction above, energy is intangible; you can't hold it in your hand to study it and you can't put it in a bottle. **Energy** *is something an object has if the object is able to do work.* It can be possessed by the object in two different ways, as kinetic energy and as potential energy.

Kinetic energy (KE) *is the energy an object has when it is moving.* It depends on the object's mass and velocity; the larger its mass and the greater its velocity, the more kinetic energy it has. A simple equation relates kinetic energy (KE) to these quantities:

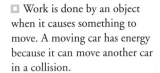

$$ KE = \frac{1}{2}mv^2 \tag{6.1} $$

Kinetic energy

where m is the mass and v is the velocity.

Potential energy (PE) *is energy an object has that can be changed to kinetic energy; it can be thought of as* **stored energy.** For example, when you wind an alarm clock, you transfer energy to a spring. The spring holds this stored energy (potential energy) and gradually releases it, in the form of kinetic energy, to make the clock's mechanism work.

☐ Unlike kinetic energy, there is no single, simple equation that can be used to calculate the amount of potential energy an object has.

Chemicals also possess potential energy, which is sometimes called **chemical energy.** When chemical reactions occur, the chemical energy possessed by the substances involved changes, leading to either an absorption or release of energy (as heat or light, for instance). For example, the explosive reaction between hydrogen and oxygen in the main engines of the space shuttle, shown in Figure 6.1, produces light, heat, and the expanding gases that help lift the space vehicle from its launchpad. One of the practical uses of chemical reactions such as this is to satisfy the energy needs of society.

Potential energy depends on position

An important aspect of potential energy is the way it depends on the positions of objects that experience attractions or repulsions toward other objects. For example, a book has potential energy because it experiences a gravitational attraction toward the earth. Lifting the book, which changes its position, increases the potential energy. This energy is supplied by the person doing the lifting. Letting the book fall allows the potential energy to decrease. The lost potential energy is changed to kinetic energy as the book gains speed during its descent.

How potential energy varies with position for objects that attract or repel is illustrated in Figure 6.2 for two balls connected by a spring. In the center we see the spring in its relaxed state and the two balls have the minimum potential energy. Stretching the spring, illustrated in the top two drawings, opposes a force that tends to pull the balls toward each other. This requires work and the energy supplied is stored as potential energy in the stretched spring. Similarly, compressing the spring as illustrated in the bottom two drawings also requires work, and the energy supplied is stored as potential energy in the compressed spring. These observations lead to two very important relationships we will use often.

Factors that affect potential energy

• Potential energy increases when objects that attract move apart, and decreases when they move toward each other.

• Potential energy increases when objects that repel move toward each other, and decreases when they move apart.

If you ever have trouble remembering this, think back to the balls connected by a spring.

In chemical systems we don't have springs between particles, but we do have attractions and repulsions between electrical charges. Electrons are attracted to protons because of their opposite electrical charges. Electrons repel electrons and nuclei repel other nuclei because they have the same kind of electrical charge. Changes in the relative positions of these particles as atoms join to form molecules or break apart when molecules decompose lead to changes in potential energy. These are the kinds of potential energy changes that lead to the release or absorption of energy by chemical systems during chemical reactions.

Energy cannot be created or destroyed

One of the most important facts about energy is that *it cannot be created or destroyed; it can only be changed from one form to another.* This fact was established by many experiments and observations, and is known today as the **law of conservation of energy.** (Recall that when we say in science that something is "conserved," we mean that it is unchanged or remains constant.) You observe this law whenever you toss something—a ball, for instance—into the air. You give the ball some initial amount of kinetic energy when you throw it. As it rises, its potential energy increases. Because energy cannot come from nothing, the rise in potential energy comes at the expense of the ball's kinetic energy. Therefore, the ball's $\frac{1}{2}mv^2$ becomes smaller, and because the mass of the ball cannot change, the

TOOLS
Potential energy changes

FIG. 6.1 Liquid hydrogen and oxygen serve as fuel for the space shuttle. Almost invisible points of blue flame come from the main engines of the space shuttle, which consume hydrogen and oxygen in the formation of water. *(Corbis Images.)*

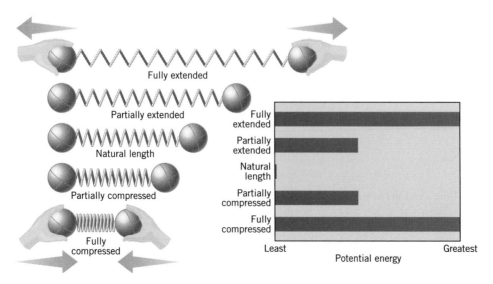

FIG. 6.2 The potential energy of a spring depends on its length. Either stretching or squeezing the spring raises the potential energy. The potential energy is at its lowest when the spring is at its natural length.

velocity (*v*) becomes less—the ball slows down. When all the kinetic energy has changed to potential energy, the ball can go no higher; it has stopped moving and its potential energy is at a maximum. The ball then begins to fall, and its potential energy is changed back to kinetic energy.

Heat and temperature are not the same

In any object, the atoms, molecules, or ions are constantly moving and colliding with each other, which gives them varying amounts of kinetic energy. *The temperature of an object is proportional to the* **average** *kinetic energy of its particles—the higher the average kinetic energy, the higher the temperature.* What this means is that when the temperature of an object is raised, the molecules move faster. (Recall that KE = $\frac{1}{2}mv^2$. Increasing the average kinetic energy doesn't increase the masses of the atoms, so it must increase their speeds.)

Heat is energy (also called **thermal energy**) that is transferred between objects caused by differences in their temperatures, and as you know, heat always passes spontaneously from a warmer object to a cooler one. This energy transfer continues until both objects come to the same temperature.

When a hot object is placed in contact with a cold one, the faster atoms of the hot object collide with and lose kinetic energy to the slower atoms of the cold object (Figure 6.3). This decreases the average kinetic energy of the particles of the hot object, causing its temperature to drop. At the same time, the average kinetic energy of the particles in the cold object is raised, causing the temperature of the cold object to rise. Eventually, the average kinetic energies of the atoms in both objects become the same and the objects reach the same temperature. Thus, the transfer of heat is interpreted as a transfer of kinetic energy between two objects.

All forms of energy (potential and kinetic) can be transformed to heat energy. For example, when you "step on the brakes" to stop your car, the kinetic energy of the car is changed to heat energy by friction between the brake shoes and the wheels.

The SI derived unit for energy is the joule

The SI unit of energy is a derived unit called the **joule** (symbol **J**) and corresponds to the amount of kinetic energy possessed by a 2 kilogram object moving at a speed of 1 meter per second. Using the equation for kinetic energy, KE = $\frac{1}{2}mv^2$,

$$1\,J = \frac{1}{2}(2\,\text{kg})\left(\frac{1\,\text{m}}{1\,\text{s}}\right)^2$$

$$1\,J = 1\,\text{kg m}^2\,\text{s}^{-2}$$

The joule is actually a rather small amount of energy and in most cases we will use the larger unit, the **kilojoule (kJ);** 1 kJ = 1000 J = 10^3 J.

 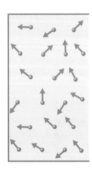 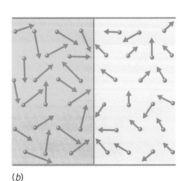 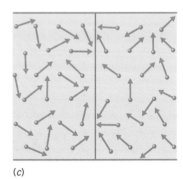

(a)   (b)   (c)

FIG. 6.3   **Energy transfer from a warmer to a cooler object.** (*a*) The longer arrows on the left denote higher kinetic energies and so something warmer, like hot water just before it's poured into a cooler coffee cup. (*b*) The hot water and the cup's inner surface are now in thermal contact. Collisions between the fast moving water molecules and the slower molecules in the cup's material cause the water molecules to slow down and the cup's molecules to speed up. In this way, kinetic energy is transferred from the water to the cup. (*c*) Thermal equilibrium is established: the temperatures of the water and the cup wall are now equal.

Another energy unit you may be familiar with is called the **calorie (cal).** Originally, it was defined as the energy needed to raise the temperature of 1 gram of water by 1 degree Celsius. (Temperature units are discussed below.) With the introduction of the SI, the calorie has been redefined as follows:

$$1 \text{ cal} = 4.184 \text{ J (exactly)} \qquad (6.2)$$

The larger unit **kilocalorie (kcal),** which equals 1000 calories, can also be related to the kilojoule.

$$1 \text{ kcal} = 4.184 \text{ kJ}$$

The nutritional or dietary Calorie (note the capital), Cal, is actually one kilocalorie.

$$1 \text{ Cal} = 1 \text{ kcal} = 4.184 \text{ kJ}$$

While joules and kilojoules have been accepted worldwide as the standard units of energy, calories and kilocalories are still in common use, so you will need to be able to convert joules into calories and vice versa.

6.2 INTERNAL ENERGY IS THE TOTAL ENERGY OF AN OBJECT'S MOLECULES

In the preceding section we introduced *heat* as a transfer of energy that occurs between objects with different temperatures. For example, heat will flow from a hot cup of coffee into the cooler surroundings. Eventually the coffee and surroundings come to the same temperature and we say they are in **thermal equilibrium** with each other. The temperature of the coffee has dropped and the temperature of the surroundings has increased a bit.

Energy that is transferred as heat comes from an object's fund of internal energy. **Internal energy (E)** is the sum of energies for all of the individual particles in a sample of matter. All of the particles within any object are in constant motion. For example, in a sample of air at room temperature, oxygen and nitrogen molecules travel faster than rifle bullets, constantly colliding with each other and with the walls of their container. The molecules spin as they move, and the atoms within the molecules jiggle and vibrate; these internal molecular motions also contribute to the kinetic energy of the molecule and so to the internal energy of the sample. We'll use the term **molecular kinetic energy** for the energy associated with such motions. Each particle has a certain value of molecular kinetic energy at any given moment. Molecules are continually exchanging energy with each other during collisions, but as long as the sample is isolated, the total kinetic energy of all the molecules remains constant.

☐ Recall that kinetic energy is energy of motion and is given by KE = $1/2\ mv^2$, where m is the mass of an object and v is its velocity.

Internal energy is often given the symbol E.[1] In studying both chemical and physical changes, we will be interested in the *change* in internal energy that accompanies the process. This is defined as the **internal energy change (ΔE),** where the symbol Δ (Greek letter delta) signifies a change.

$$\Delta E = E_{\text{final}} - E_{\text{initial}}$$

☐ The symbol Δ denotes a *change between some initial and final state.*

For a chemical reaction, E_{final} corresponds to the internal energy of the products, so we'll write it as E_{products}. Similarly, we'll use the symbol $E_{\text{reactants}}$ for E_{initial}. So for a chemical reaction the change in internal energy is given by

$$\Delta E = E_{\text{products}} - E_{\text{reactants}} \qquad (6.3)$$

Notice carefully an important convention illustrated by this equation. Changes in something like temperature (Δt) or in internal energy (ΔE) are always figured by taking "final minus initial" or "products minus reactants." This means that if a system *absorbs* energy from its surroundings during a change, its final energy is greater than its initial energy and ΔE is positive. This is what happens, for example, when photosynthesis occurs or when something in the surroundings supplies energy to charge a battery. As the system (the battery) absorbs the energy, its internal energy increases and is then available for later use elsewhere.

[1] Sometimes the symbol U is used for internal energy.

Temperature is related to average molecular kinetic energy

☐ Temperature is related to average molecular kinetic energy, but it is not equal to it. Temperature is *not* an energy.

The notion, introduced in Section 6.1, that atoms and molecules are in constant random motion forms the basis for the **kinetic molecular theory.** It is this theory that tells us in part that *temperature* is related to the *average kinetic energy* of the atoms and molecules of an object. Be sure to keep in mind the distinction between temperature and internal energy; the two are quite different. Temperature is related to the *average* molecular kinetic energy, whereas internal energy is related to the *total* molecular kinetic energy.[2]

The concept of an *average* kinetic energy implies that there is a distribution of kinetic energies among the molecules in an object. Let's examine this further. At any particular moment, the individual particles in an object are moving at different velocities, which gives them a broad range of kinetic energies. An extremely small number of particles will be standing still as a result of balanced collisions, so their kinetic energies will be zero. Another small number will have very large velocities acquired through successive "rear end" collisions; these will have very large kinetic energies. Between these extremes there will be many molecules with intermediate amounts of kinetic energy.

Figure 6.4 shows graphs that describe the kinetic energy distributions among molecules in a sample at two different temperatures. The vertical axis represents the *fraction* of molecules with a given kinetic energy (i.e., the number of molecules with a given KE divided by the total number of molecules in the sample). Each curve in Figure 6.4 describes how the fraction of molecules with a given KE varies with KE.

Each curve starts out with a fraction equal to zero when KE equals zero. This is because the fraction of molecules with zero KE (corresponding to molecules that are motionless) is essentially zero, regardless of the temperature. Moving to higher values of KE, we find greater fractions. For very large values of KE, the fraction drops off again because very few molecules have very large velocities.

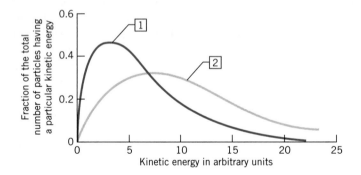

FIG. 6.4 **The distribution of kinetic energies among gas particles.** The distribution of individual kinetic energies changes in going from a lower temperature, curve 1, to a higher temperature, curve 2. The highest point on each curve is the most probable value of kinetic energy for that temperature. It's the value of the molecular kinetic energy that we would most frequently find, if we could get inside the system and observe and measure the kinetic energy of each molecule. The most probable value of molecular kinetic energy is less at the lower temperature. At the higher temperature, more molecules have high speeds and fewer molecules have low speeds, so the maximum shifts to the right and the curve flattens.

---

[2] When we're looking at heat flow, the total molecular kinetic energy is the part of the internal energy we're most interested in. However, internal energy is the total energy of all the particles in the object, so molecular potential energies (from forces of attraction and repulsion that operate between and within molecules) can and do make a large contribution to the internal energy. This is especially true in liquids and solids.

Each curve in Figure 6.4 has a characteristic peak or maximum corresponding to the most frequently experienced values for molecular KE. Because the curves are not symmetrical, the *average* values of molecular KE lie slightly to the right of the maxima. Notice that when the temperature increases (going from curve 1 to 2), the curve flattens and the maximum shifts to a higher value, as does the average molecular KE. In fact, *if we double the Kelvin temperature, the average KE also doubles, so the Kelvin temperature is directly proportional to the average KE.* The reason the curve flattens is because the area under each curve corresponds to the *sum* of all the fractions, and when all the fractions are added, they must equal one. (No matter how you cut up a pie, if you add all the fractions, you must end up with *one* pie!)

We will find the graphs illustrated in Figure 6.4 very useful later when we discuss the effect of temperature on such properties as the rates of evaporation of liquids and the rates of chemical reactions.

Internal energy is a state function

Equation 6.3 defines what we mean by a change in the internal energy of a chemical system during a reaction. This energy change can be made to appear entirely as heat, and as you will learn soon, we can measure heat. However, there is no way to actually measure either $E_{products}$ or $E_{reactants}$. Fortunately, we are more interested in ΔE than we are in the absolute amounts of energy that the reactants or products have.

If we can measure heat, but not internal energy itself, why talk about energy at all? It turns out that *the energy of an object depends only on the object's current condition.* It doesn't matter how the object acquired that energy, or how it will lose it. This simple fact vastly simplifies thermochemical calculations.

The complete list of properties that specify an object's current condition is known as the **state** of the object. In chemistry, it is usually enough to specify the object's pressure, temperature, volume, and chemical composition (numbers of moles of all substances present).

Any property that, like energy, depends *only* on an object's current state is called a **state function.** Pressure, temperature, and volume are themselves examples of state functions and it's easy to understand why. A system's current temperature, for example, does not depend on what it was yesterday. Nor does it matter *how* the system acquired it, that is, the path to its current value. If it's now 25 °C, we know all we can or need to know about its temperature. We do not have to specify how it got there or where it's going. Also, if the temperature were to increase, say, to 35 °C, the change in temperature, Δt, is simply the difference between the final and the initial temperatures.

$$\Delta t = t_{final} - t_{initial} \qquad (6.4)$$

To make the calculation of Δt, we do not have to know what caused the temperature change—exposure to sunlight, heating by an open flame, or any other mechanism. All we need are the initial and final values. *This independence from the method or mechanism by which a change occurs is the important feature of all state functions.* As we'll see later, the advantage of recognizing that some property is a state function is that many calculations are then much, much easier.

> ☐ "State," as used in thermochemistry, doesn't have the same meaning as when it's used in terms such as "solid state" or "liquid state."

6.3 | HEAT CAN BE DETERMINED BY MEASURING TEMPERATURE CHANGES

By measuring the amount of heat that is absorbed or released by an object, we are able to quantitatively study nearly any type of energy transfer. For example, if we want to measure the energy transferred by an electrical current, we can force the current through something with high electrical resistance, like the heating element in a toaster, and the energy transferred by the current becomes heat.

In our study it is very important to specify the **boundary** across which heat flows. The boundary might be visible (like the walls of a beaker) or invisible (like the boundary that separates warm air from cold air along a weather front). The boundary encloses the **system,** which is the object we are interested in studying. Everything outside the system is called the **surroundings.** The system and the surroundings together are called the **universe.**

Three types of systems are possible, depending on whether matter or energy can cross the boundary.

- **Open systems** can gain or lose mass and energy across their boundaries. The human body is an example of an open system.
- **Closed systems** can absorb or release energy, but not mass, across the boundary. The mass of a closed system is constant, no matter what happens inside. A lightbulb is an example of a closed system.
- **Isolated systems** cannot exchange matter or energy with their surroundings. Because energy cannot be created or destroyed, the energy of an isolated system is constant, no matter what happens inside. Processes that occur within an isolated system are called **adiabatic,** from the Greek *a* + *diabatos*, meaning "not passable." A stoppered Thermos bottle is a good approximation of an isolated system.

The heat an object gains or loses is directly proportional to its temperature change

There is no instrument available that directly measures heat. Instead, we measure temperature changes, and then use them to calculate heat. Common sense and experience tell you that the more heat you add to an object, the more its temperature will rise. In fact, experiments show that the temperature change, Δt, is *directly proportional* to the amount of heat absorbed, which we will identify by the symbol q. This can be expressed in the form of an equation as

TOOLS
Heat capacity

$$q = C\,\Delta t \qquad\qquad (6.5)$$

where C is a proportionality constant called the **heat capacity.** The units of heat capacity are usually $J\,°C^{-1}$, expressing the amount of energy needed to raise the temperature of an object by 1 °C.

Heat capacity depends on two factors. One is the size of the sample; if we double the size of the sample, we need twice as much heat to cause the same temperature increase. Heat capacity also depends on what the sample is made of. For example, it's found that it takes more heat to raise the temperature of one gram of water by 1 °C than to cause the same temperature change in one gram of iron.

Specific heat is an intensive property related to heat capacity

From the preceding discussion, we expect that different samples of a given substance will have different heat capacities, and this is what is observed. For example, if we have 10.0 g of water, it must absorb 41.8 J of heat energy to raise its temperature by 1.00 °C. The heat capacity of the sample is found by solving Equation 6.5 for C.

$$C = \frac{q}{\Delta t} = \frac{41.8\ J}{1.00\ °C} = 41.8\ J/°C$$

On the other hand, a 100 g sample of water must absorb 418 J of heat to have its temperature raised by 1.00 °C. The heat capacity of this sample is

$$C = \frac{q}{\Delta t} = \frac{418\ J}{1.00\ °C} = 418\ J/°C$$

Notice that a 10-fold increase in sample size has produced a 10-fold increase in the heat capacity. This indicates that the heat capacity is directly proportional to the mass of the sample,

$$C = m \times s \tag{6.6}$$

where m is the mass of the sample and s is a constant called the **specific heat capacity** (or simply the **specific heat**). If the heat capacity has units of J/°C, and if the mass is in grams, the specific heat capacity has units of (J/g °C) or $J\ g^{-1}\ °C^{-1}$. The units tell us that the specific heat capacity is the amount of heat required to raise the temperature of 1 gram of a substance by 1 °C.

Because C depends on the size of the sample, *heat capacity is an extensive property*. When we discussed density in Section 1.8 you learned that if we take the ratio of two extensive properties, we can obtain an intensive property—one that is independent of the size of the sample. Because heat capacity and mass both depend on sample size, their ratio obtained by solving Equation 6.6 for s yields a property that is the same for any sample of a substance.

If we substitute Equation 6.6 into Equation 6.5, we can obtain an equation for q in terms of specific heat.

$$q = ms\,\Delta t \tag{6.7}$$

TOOLS
Specific heat

We can use this equation to calculate the specific heat of water from the information given above, which states that 10.0 g of water requires 41.8 J to have its temperature raised by 1.00 °C. Solving for s and substituting gives

$$s = \frac{q}{m\,\Delta t} = \frac{41.8\ \text{J}}{10.0\ \text{g} \times 1.00\,°\text{C}}$$

$$= 4.18\ \text{J}\ \text{g}^{-1}\ °\text{C}^{-1}$$

Recall that the older energy unit calorie (cal) is currently defined as 1 cal = 4.184 J. Therefore, the specific heat of water expressed in calories is

$$s = 1.00\ \text{cal}\ \text{g}^{-1}\ °\text{C}^{-1} \qquad \text{(for H}_2\text{O)}$$

In measuring heat, we often use an apparatus containing water, so the specific heat of water is a quantity we will use in working problems. Every substance has its own characteristic specific heat, and some are given in Table 6.1.

☐ You should learn these values for water:

$s = 1.00\ \text{cal}\ \text{g}^{-1}\ °\text{C}^{-1}$
$s = 4.18\ \text{J}\ \text{g}^{-1}\ °\text{C}^{-1}$

TABLE 6.1	**Specific Heats**
Substance	Specific Heat, $J\ g^{-1}\ °C^{-1}$ (25 °C)
Carbon (graphite)	0.711
Copper	0.387
Ethyl alcohol	2.45
Gold	0.129
Granite	0.803
Iron	0.4498
Lead	0.128
Olive oil	2.0
Silver	0.235
Water (liquid)	4.18

When comparing or working with mole-sized quantities of substances, we can use the **molar heat capacity,** which is the amount of heat needed to raise the temperature of 1 mol of a substance by 1 °C. Molar heat capacity equals the specific heat times the molar mass and has units of $J\ \text{mol}^{-1}\ °C^{-1}$.

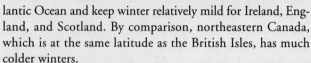

FACETS OF CHEMISTRY

6.1

Water, Climate, and the Body's "Thermal Cushion"

Compared with most substances, water has a very high specific heat. A body of water can therefore gain or lose a substantial amount of heat without undergoing a large change in temperature. Because of this, the oceans of the world have a very significant moderating effect on climate. This is particularly apparent when we compare temperature extremes of locales near the oceans with those inland away from the sea and away from large lakes (such as the Great Lakes in the upper United States). Places near the sea tend to have cooler summers and milder winters than places located inland because the ocean serves as a thermal "cushion," absorbing heat in the summer and giving some of it back during the winter.

Warm and cool ocean currents also have global effects on climate. For example, the warm waters of the Gulf of Mexico are carried by the Gulf Stream across the Atlantic Ocean and keep winter relatively mild for Ireland, England, and Scotland. By comparison, northeastern Canada, which is at the same latitude as the British Isles, has much colder winters.

Water also serves as a thermal cushion for the human body. The adult body is about 60% water by mass, so it has a high heat capacity. This makes it relatively easy for the body to maintain a steady temperature of 37 °C, which is vital to survival. In other words, the body can exchange considerable energy with the environment but experience only a small change in temperature. With a substantial thermal cushion, the body adjusts to large and sudden changes in outside temperature while experiencing very small fluctuations of its core temperature.

The algebraic sign of q is used to indicate the direction of heat flow

Heat is energy that's transferred from one object to another. This means that heat is lost by one object and the same amount of heat is gained by the other. To indicate the direction of heat flow, we assign a positive sign to q if the heat is gained and a negative sign if the heat is lost. For example, if a piece of warm iron is placed into a beaker of cool water and the iron loses 10.0 J of heat, the water gains 10.0 J of heat. For the iron, $q = -10.0$ J and for the water, $q = +10.0$ J.

The relationship between the algebraic signs of q in a transfer of heat can be stated in a general way by the equation

TOOLS
Heat transfer

$$q_1 = -q_2 \qquad (6.8)$$

where 1 and 2 refer to the objects between which the heat is transferred.

EXAMPLE 6.1
Determining the Heat Capacity of an Object

Central processing chips in computers generate a tremendous amount of heat—enough to damage themselves permanently if the chip is not cooled somehow. Aluminum "heat sinks" are often attached to the chips to carry away excess heat. Suppose that a heat sink at 71.3 °C is dropped into a Styrofoam cup containing 100.0 g of water at 25.0 °C. The temperature of the water rises to 27.4 °C. What is the heat capacity of the heat sink, in J/°C?

ANALYSIS: Heat capacity is related to temperature change by Equation 6.5, so that's the tool we need to solve the problem. To find C, we divide both sides by the temperature change, Δt:

$$C = q/\Delta t$$

Let's find q first, *being very careful about algebraic signs.* We can assume that the heat lost by the heat sink, $q_{(\text{heat sink})}$, will be gained by the much cooler water, q_{H_2O}. Because the water is gaining heat, q_{H_2O} will be a positive quantity, and because the heat sink loses heat, $q_{(\text{heat sink})}$ will be a negative quantity *equal in size* to q_{H_2O}. This lets us apply Equation 6.8 and write

$$q_{(\text{heat sink})} = -q_{H_2O}$$

The negative sign on the right assures us that when we substitute the positive value for q_{H_2O} the sign of $q_{(\text{heat sink})}$ will be negative.

To calculate q_{H_2O}, our tool will be Equation 6.7, which enables us to use the specific heat of water (4.18 J g^{-1} °C^{-1}), the mass of water, and the temperature change for water. Once we've found q_{H_2O}, we change its algebraic sign to obtain $q_{(heat\ sink)}$. Then we use the temperature change for the heat sink to calculate C for the heat sink.

SOLUTION: The temperature of the water rises from 25.0 °C to 27.4 °C, so for the water,

$$\Delta t_{H_2O} = t_{final} - t_{initial} = 27.4\ °C - 25.0\ °C = 2.4\ °C$$

The specific heat of water is 4.18 J g^{-1} °C^{-1} and its mass is 100.0 g. Therefore, for water, the heat absorbed is

$$q_{H_2O} = ms\,\Delta t = 100.0\ g \times 4.18\ J\,g^{-1}\,°C^{-1} \times 2.4\ °C$$

$$= +1.0 \times 10^3\ J$$

Therefore, $q_{(heat\ sink)} = -1.0 \times 10^3\ J$

The temperature of the heat sink decreases from 71.3 °C to 27.4 °C, so

$$\Delta t_{(heat\ sink)} = t_{final} - t_{initial} = 27.4\ °C - 71.3\ °C = -43.9\ °C$$

The heat capacity of the heat sink is then

$$C = \frac{q_{(heat\ sink)}}{\Delta t} = \frac{-1.0 \times 10^3\ J}{-43.9\ °C} = 23\ J/°C$$

IS THE ANSWER REASONABLE? In any calculation involving energy transfer, we first check to see that all quantities have the correct signs. Heat capacities are positive for common objects, so the fact that we've obtained a positive value for C tells us we've handled the signs correctly.

For the transfer of a given amount of heat, the larger the heat capacity, the smaller the temperature change. The heat capacity of the water is $C = ms = 100\ g \times 4.18\ J\,g^{-1}\,°C^{-1} = 418\ J\,°C^{-1}$ and the water changes temperature by 2.4 °C. The size of the temperature change for the heat sink, 43.9 °C, is almost 20 times as large as that for the water, so the heat capacity should be about 1/20 that of the water. Dividing 418 J °C^{-1} by 20 gives 20.9 J °C^{-1}, which is not too far from our answer, so our calculations seem to be reasonable.

If a gold ring with a mass of 5.50 g changes in temperature from 25.00 to 28.00 °C, how much heat has it absorbed?

ANALYSIS: The question asks us to connect the heat absorbed by the ring with its temperature change, Δt. Equations 6.5 or 6.7 could provide this connection. However, we don't know the heat capacity of the ring. We do know the mass of the ring, and the fact that it is made of gold, so we can look up the specific heat and use Equation 6.7 as our tool to solve the problem. Table 6.1 gives the specific heat of gold as 0.129 J g^{-1} °C^{-1}.

SOLUTION: The mass m of the ring is 5.50 g, the specific heat s is 0.129 J g^{-1} °C^{-1}, and the temperature increases from 25.00 to 28.00 °C, so Δt is 3.00 °C. Using these values in Equation 6.7 gives

$$q = ms\,\Delta t$$

$$= (5.50\ g) \times (0.129\ J\,g^{-1}°C^{-1}) \times (3.00\ °C)$$

$$= 2.13\ J$$

☐ The sign of Δt will determine the sign of the heat exchanged. Δt is positive because ($t_{final} - t_{initial}$) is positive.

Thus, only 2.13 J raises the temperature of 5.50 g of gold by 3.00 °C. Because Δt is positive, so is q, 2.13 J. Thus the *sign* of the energy change is in agreement with the fact that the ring *absorbs* heat.

IS THE ANSWER REASONABLE? If the ring had a mass of only 1 g and its temperature increased by 1 °C, we'd know from the specific heat of gold (let's round it to 0.13 J g^{-1} °C^{-1}) that the ring would absorb 0.13 J. For a 3 °C increase, the answer would be three times as much, or 0.39 J, nearly 0.4 J. For a ring a little heavier than 5 g, the heat absorbed would be five times as much, or about 2.0 J. So our answer (2.13 J) is clearly reasonable.

Practice Exercise 1: A ball bearing at 220 °C is dropped into a cup containing 250 g of water at 20.0 °C. The water and ball bearing come to a temperature of 30.0 °C. What is the heat capacity of the ball bearing, in J/°C? (Hint: How are the algebraic signs of q related for the ball bearing and the water?)

Practice Exercise 2: The temperature of 250 g of water is changed from 25.0 to 30.0 °C. How much energy was transferred into the water? Calculate your answer in joules, kilojoules, calories, and kilocalories.

6.4 | ENERGY IS ABSORBED OR RELEASED DURING MOST CHEMICAL REACTIONS

Almost every chemical reaction involves the absorption or release of energy. When this happens, the potential energy (also called chemical energy) of the substances involved in the reaction changes. To understand the origin of this energy change we need to explore the origin of potential energy in chemical systems.

In Chapter 2 we introduced you to the concept of *chemical bonds*, which are the attractive forces that bind atoms to each other in molecules, or ions to each other in ionic compounds. In this chapter you learned that when particles experience attractions or repulsions, potential energy changes occur when the particles come together or move apart. We can now bring these concepts together to understand the origin of energy changes in reactions.

Exothermic reactions release heat; endothermic reactions absorb heat

Chemical reactions generally involve *both* the breaking and making of chemical bonds. In most reactions, when bonds *form*, things that attract each other move closer together, which tends to decrease the potential energy of the reacting system. When bonds *break*, on the other hand, things that normally attract each other are forced apart, which increases the potential energy of the reacting system. Every reaction, therefore, has a certain net overall potential energy change, a net balance between the "costs" of breaking bonds and the "profits" from making them.

In many reactions, the products have *less* potential energy (chemical energy) than the reactants. When the gas methane burns in a Bunsen burner, for example, molecules of CH_4 and O_2 with large amounts of chemical energy but relatively low amounts of molecular kinetic energy change into products (CO_2 and H_2O) that have less chemical energy but much more molecular kinetic energy. Thus some chemical energy changes into molecular *kinetic* energy. The increase in molecular kinetic energy leads to a temperature increase in the reaction mixture, and if the reaction is occurring in an uninsulated system, some of this energy can be transferred to the surroundings as heat. The net result, then, is that the drop in chemical energy appears as heat that's transferred to the surroundings. In the chemical equation, therefore, we can write heat as a product.

$$CH_4(g) + 2O_2(g) \longrightarrow CO_2(g) + 2H_2O(g) + \text{heat}$$

☐ *exo* means "out" *endo* means "in" *therm* means "heat"

Any reaction in which heat is a product is said to be **exothermic.**

In some reactions the products have *more* chemical energy than the reactants. For example, green plants make energy-rich molecules of glucose ($C_6H_{12}O_6$) and oxygen from carbon dioxide and water by a multistep process called *photosynthesis*. It requires a continuous supply of energy, which is provided by the sun. The plant's green pigment, chlorophyll, is the solar energy absorber for photosynthesis.

$$6CO_2 + 6H_2O + \text{solar energy} \xrightarrow[\text{many steps}]{\text{chlorophyll}} C_6H_{12}O_6 + 6O_2$$

Reactions that consume energy are said to be **endothermic.** Usually such reactions change kinetic energy into potential energy (chemical energy), so the temperature of the system tends to drop as the reaction proceeds. If the reaction is occurring in an uninsulated vessel, the temperature of the surroundings will drop as heat flows into the system.

By an endothermic reaction, photosynthesis converts solar energy, trapped by the green pigment chlorophyll, into plant compounds that are rich in chemical energy. *(© Index Stock.)*

Energy can be released by breaking weak bonds to form stronger ones

The strength of a chemical bond is measured by how much energy is needed to separate the atoms that the bond holds together, or by how much energy is released when the bond forms. The larger this amount of energy, the stronger the bond.

Breaking weak bonds requires relatively little energy compared to the amount of energy released when strong bonds form. This is key to understanding why burning fuels such as CH_4 produce heat. Weaker bonds between carbon and hydrogen within the fuel break so that stronger bonds in the water and carbon dioxide molecules can form. Burning a hydrocarbon fuel produces one molecule of carbon dioxide for each carbon atom and one molecule of water for each pair of hydrogen atoms in the fuel. Generally, the more carbon and hydrogen atoms a molecule of the fuel contains, the more strong bonds can form when it burns—and the more heat it will produce, per molecule.

We will have a lot more to say about chemical bonds and their strengths in later chapters.

6.5 HEATS OF REACTION ARE MEASURED AT CONSTANT VOLUME OR CONSTANT PRESSURE

The amount of heat absorbed or released in a chemical reaction is called the **heat of reaction.** Heats of reaction are determined by measuring the change in temperature they cause in their surroundings, using an apparatus called a **calorimeter.** The calorimeter is often just a container with a known heat capacity in which the reaction is carried out. We can calculate the heat of reaction by measuring the temperature change the reaction causes in the calorimeter. The science of using a calorimeter for determining heats of reaction is called **calorimetry.**

Calorimeter design is not standard, varying according to the kind of reaction and the precision desired. Calorimeters are usually designed to measure heats of reaction under conditions of either constant volume or constant pressure. We have constant-volume conditions if we run the reaction in a closed, rigid container. Running the reaction in an open container imposes constant-pressure conditions.

Pressure is an important variable in calorimetry, as we'll see in a moment. If you have ever blown up a balloon or worked with an auto or bicycle tire, you have already learned something about *pressure*. You know that when a tire holds air at a relatively high pressure, it is hard to dent or push in its sides because "something" is pushing back. That something is the air pressure inside the tire.

Pressure is the amount of *force* acting on a unit of area; it's the ratio of force to area.

$$\text{Pressure} = \frac{\text{force}}{\text{area}}$$

You can increase the pressure in a tire by pushing or forcing air into it. Its pressure, when you quit, is whatever pressure you have added *above the initial pressure,* namely, the atmospheric pressure. We describe the air in the tire as being *compressed,* meaning that it's at a higher pressure than the atmospheric pressure.

☐ There is no instrument that *directly* measures energy. A calorimeter does not do this; its thermometer is the only part to provide raw data, the temperature change. We *calculate* the energy change.

Atmospheric pressure is the pressure exerted by the mixture of gases in our atmosphere. In English units this ratio of force to area is approximately 14.7 lb in.$^{-2}$ at sea level. The ratio does vary a bit with temperature and weather, and it varies a lot with altitude. The value of 14.7 lb in.$^{-2}$ is very close to two other common pressure units, the **standard atmosphere** (abbreviated **atm**), and the **bar,** which will be discussed in Chapter 10. A container that is open to the atmosphere is under a constant pressure of about 14.7 lb in.$^{-2}$, which is approximately 1 bar or 1 atm.

◻ More precisely, 14.696 lb in.$^{-2}$ = 1.0000 atm = 1.0133 bar.

We've used the symbol q for heat; the symbols q_v and q_p are often used to show heats measured at constant volume or constant pressure, respectively. We must distinguish q_v from q_p. For reactions that involve big changes in volume (such as consumption or production of a gas) the difference between the two can be quite large.

EXAMPLE 6.3
Computing q_v and q_p Using Calorimetry

A gas-phase chemical reaction occurs inside an apparatus similar to that shown in Figure 6.5. The reaction vessel is a cylinder topped by a piston. The piston can be locked in place with a pin. The cylinder is immersed in an insulated bucket containing a precisely weighed amount of water. A separate experiment determined that the calorimeter (which includes the piston, cylinder, bucket, and water) has a heat capacity of 8.101 kJ/°C. The reaction was run twice with identical amounts of reactants each time. The following data were collected.

Run	Pin position	Initial bucket temperature (°C)	Final bucket temperature (°C)
1	a (piston locked)	24.00	28.91
2	b (piston unlocked)	27.32	31.54

Determine q_v and q_p for this reaction.

ANALYSIS: The key to solving the problem is realizing that from the heat capacity and temperature change, we can calculate the heat absorbed by the calorimeter. The tool is Equation 6.5. Run 1 will give the heat at constant volume, q_v, since the piston cannot move. Run 2 will give the heat at constant pressure, q_p, because with the piston unlocked the entire reaction will run under atmospheric pressure.

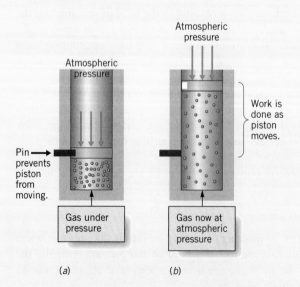

(a)   (b)

FIG. 6.5 **Pressure–volume work.** (*a*) A gas is confined under pressure in a cylinder fitted with a piston that is held in place by a sliding pin. (*b*) When the piston is released, the gas inside the cylinder expands and pushes the piston upward against the opposing pressure of the atmosphere. As it does so, the gas does some pressure–volume work on the surroundings.

SOLUTION: For Run 1, Equation 6.5 gives the heat absorbed by the calorimeter as

$$q = C\Delta t = (8.101 \text{ kJ/°C}) \times (28.91 \text{ °C} - 24.00 \text{ °C}) = 39.8 \text{ kJ}$$

Because the calorimeter gains heat, this amount of heat is released by the reaction, so *q for the reaction* must be negative. Therefore, $q_v = -39.8$ kJ.
For Run 2,

$$q = C\Delta t = (8.101 \text{ kJ/°C}) \times (31.54 \text{ °C} - 27.32 \text{ °C}) = 34.2 \text{ kJ}$$

so $q_p = -34.2$ kJ.

IS THE ANSWER REASONABLE? The arithmetic is straightforward, but in any calculation involving heat, always check to see that the signs of the heats in the problem make sense. The calorimeter absorbs heat, so its heats are positive. The reaction releases heat, so its heats must be negative.

Why are q_v and q_p different for reactions that involve a significant volume change? The system in this case is the reacting mixture. If the system expands against atmospheric pressure, it is doing work. Some of the energy that would otherwise appear as heat is used up when the system pushes back the atmosphere. In the example, the work done to expand the system against atmospheric pressure is equal to amount of "missing" heat in the constant-pressure case:

$$\text{Work} = (-39.8 \text{ kJ}) - (-34.2 \text{ kJ}) = -5.6 \text{ kJ}.$$

The minus sign indicates that energy is leaving the system. This is called **expansion work** (or, more precisely, **pressure–volume work** or **P–V work**). A common example of pressure–volume work is the work done by the expanding gases in a cylinder of a car engine as they move a piston. Another example is the work done by expanding gases to lift a rocket from the ground. The amount of expansion work w done can be computed from atmospheric pressure and the volume change that the system undergoes[3]:

$$w = -P\Delta V \tag{6.9}$$

▢ The sign of w confirms that the system loses energy by doing work pushing back the atmosphere.

P is the *opposing pressure* against which the piston pushes, and ΔV is the change in the volume of the system (the gas) during the expansion, i.e., $\Delta V = V_{final} - V_{initial}$. Because V_{final} is greater than $V_{initial}$, ΔV must be positive. This makes the expansion work negative.

Heat and work are both ways to transfer energy

In chemistry, *a minus sign on an energy transfer always means that the system loses energy.* Consider what happens whenever work can be done or heat can flow in the system shown in Figure 6.5b. If work is negative (as in an expansion) the system loses energy and the surroundings gain it. We say work is done *by* the system. If heat is negative (as in an

---

[3] $P\Delta V$ must have units of energy if it is referred to as work. Work is accomplished when an opposing force, F, is pushed through some distance or length, L. The amount of work done is equal to the strength of the opposing force multiplied by the distance the force is moved.

$$\text{Work} = F \times L$$

Because pressure is force (F) per unit area, and area is simply length squared, L^2, we can write the following equation for pressure.

$$P = \frac{F}{L^2}$$

Volume (or a volume change) has dimensions of length cubed, L^3, so pressure times volume change is

$$P\Delta V = \frac{F}{L^2} \times L^3 = F \times L$$

But, from above, $F \times L$ also equals work.

exothermic reaction) the system loses energy and the surroundings gain it. Either event should cause a drop in internal energy. On the other hand, if work is positive (as in a compression), the system gains energy and the surroundings lose it. We say that work is done *on* the system. If heat is positive (as in an endothermic reaction), again, the system will gain energy and the surroundings will lose it. Either positive work or positive heat should cause a positive change in internal energy.

Work and heat are simply alternative ways to transfer energy. Using this sign convention, we can relate the work w and the heat q that go into the system to the internal energy change (ΔE) the system undergoes:

TOOLS

First law of thermodynamics

$$\Delta E = q + w \qquad (6.10)$$

In Section 6.2 we pointed out that the internal energy depends only on the current state of the system; we said that *internal energy is a state function.* This statement (together with Equation 6.10, which is a definition of internal energy change) is a statement of the **first law of thermodynamics.** The first law is one of the most subtle and most powerful principles ever devised by science. It implies that we can move energy around in various ways, but we cannot create energy, or destroy it.

ΔE is independent of how a change takes place; it depends only on the state of the system at the beginning and the end of the change. But the values of q and w depend on what happens *between* the initial and final states. Thus, neither q nor w is a state function. Their values depend on the *path* of the change. For example, consider the discharge of an automobile battery by two different paths (see Figure 6.6). Both paths take us between the same two states, one being the fully charged state and the other the fully discharged state. Because ΔE is a state function and because both paths have the same initial and final states, ΔE *must be the same for both paths.* But how about q and w?

In path 1, we simply short the battery by placing a heavy wrench across the terminals. If you have ever done this, even by accident, you know how violent the result can be. Sparks fly and the wrench becomes very hot as the battery quickly discharges. Lots of heat is given off, but *the system does no work* ($w = 0$). All of ΔE appears as heat.

In path 2, we discharge the battery more slowly by using it to operate a motor. Along this path, much of the energy represented by ΔE appears as work (running the motor) and

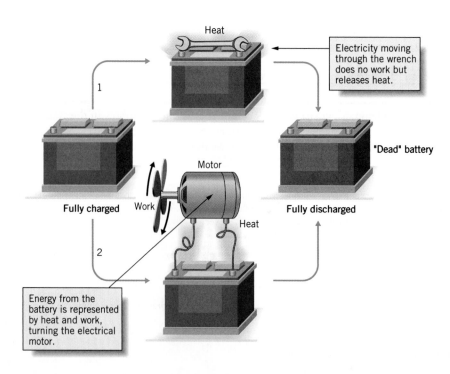

FIG. 6.6 **Energy, heat, and work.** The complete discharge of a battery along two different paths yields the same total amount of energy, ΔE. However, if the battery is simply shorted with a heavy wrench, as shown in path 1, this energy appears entirely as heat. Path 2 gives part of the total energy as heat, but much of the energy appears as work done by the motor.

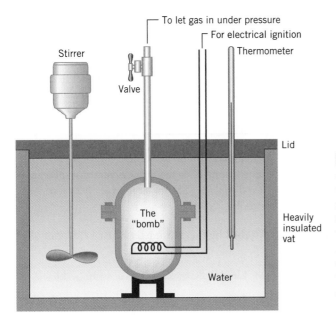

FIG. 6.7 A bomb calorimeter. The water bath is usually equipped with devices for adding or removing heat from the water, thus keeping its temperature constant up to the moment when the reaction occurs in the bomb. The reaction chamber is of fixed volume, so $P \Delta V$ must equal zero for reactions in this apparatus.

only a relatively small amount appears as heat (from the friction within the motor and the electrical resistance of the wires).

There are two vital lessons here. The first is that neither q nor w is a state function. Their values depend *entirely* on the path between the initial and final states. Yet, their sum, ΔE, as we said, *is* a state function.

Heats of combustion are determined using constant-volume calorimetry

The heat produced by a combustion reaction is called a **heat of combustion.** Because combustion reactions require oxygen and produce gaseous products, we have to measure heats of combustion in a closed container. Figure 6.7 shows the apparatus that is usually used to determine heats of combustion. The instrument is called a *bomb calorimeter* because the vessel holding the reaction itself resembles a small bomb. The "bomb" has rigid walls, so the change in volume, ΔV, is zero when the reaction occurs. This means, of course, that $P \Delta V$ must also be zero, and no expansion work is done, so w in Equation 6.10 is zero. Therefore, the heat of reaction measured in a bomb calorimeter is the **heat of reaction at constant volume, q_v,** and corresponds to ΔE.

$$\Delta E = q_v$$

Food scientists determine dietary calories in foods and food ingredients by burning them in a bomb calorimeter. The reactions that break down foods in the body are complex, but they have the same initial and final states as the combustion reaction for the food.

EXAMPLE 6.4
Bomb Calorimetry

(a) When 1.000 g of olive oil was completely burned in pure oxygen in a bomb calorimeter like the one shown in Figure 6.7, the temperature of the water bath increased from 22.000 °C to 26.049 °C. How many dietary Calories are in olive oil, per gram? The heat capacity of the calorimeter is 9.032 kJ/°C.

(b) Olive oil is almost pure glyceryl trioleate, $C_{57}H_{104}O_6$. The equation for its combustion is

$$C_{57}H_{104}O_6 + 80O_2 \longrightarrow 57CO_2 + 52H_2O$$

What is the change in internal energy, ΔE, for the combustion of one mole of glyceryl trioleate? Assume the olive oil burned in part (a) was pure glyceryl trioleate.

ANALYSIS: In part (a), Equation 6.5 is the tool to compute the heat absorbed by the calorimeter from its temperature change and heat capacity. Then we place a minus sign in front of the result to get the heat released by the combustion reaction.

Since the heat capacity is in kilojoules, the heat released will be in kilojoules, too. We'll need to convert kilojoules to dietary Calories, which are actually kilocalories (kcal). We can use the relationship

$$1 \text{ kcal} = 4.184 \text{ kJ}$$

Part (b) asks for the change in internal energy, ΔE. Bomb calorimetry measures q_v, which is equal to the internal energy change for the reaction. Thus the heat calculated in part (a) is equal to ΔE for combustion of 1.000 g of glyceryl trioleate. The molar mass of glyceryl trioleate is the tool to convert ΔE per gram to ΔE per mole.

SOLUTION: First, let's compute the heat absorbed by the calorimeter when 1.000 g of olive oil is burned, using Equation 6.5:

$$q_{\text{calorimeter}} = C \, \Delta t = (9.032 \text{ kJ/°C}) \times (26.049 \text{ °C} - 22.000 \text{ °C}) = 36.57 \text{ kJ}$$

Changing the algebraic sign gives the heat of combustion of 1.000 g of olive oil, $q_v = -36.57$ kJ. Part (a) asks for the heat in dietary Calories. We convert to kilocalories (kcal), which are equivalent to dietary Calories (Cal):

$$\frac{-36.57 \text{ kJ}}{1.000 \text{ g oil}} \times \frac{1 \text{ kcal}}{4.184 \text{ kJ}} \times \frac{1 \text{ Cal}}{1 \text{ kcal}} = -8.740 \text{ Cal/g oil}$$

We can say "8.740 dietary Calories are released when one gram of olive oil is burned." For part (b), we'll convert the heat produced per gram to the heat produced per mole, using the molar mass of $C_{57}H_{104}O_6$, 885.39 g/mol:

$$\frac{-36.57 \text{ kJ}}{1.000 \text{ g } C_{57}H_{104}O_6} \times \frac{885.39 \text{ g } C_{57}H_{104}O_6}{1 \text{ mol } C_{57}H_{104}O_6} = -3.238 \times 10^4 \text{ kJ/mol}$$

Since this is heat at constant volume, we have $\Delta E = q_v = -3.238 \times 10^4$ kJ for the combustion of 1 mol of $C_{57}H_{104}O_6$.

ARE THE ANSWERS REASONABLE? Let's do some simple approximate arithmetic. In part (a) the temperature change is about 4 °C, so the product $C \, \Delta t$ is about 9 kJ/°C $\times$ 4 °C $\approx$ 36 kJ. We must be careful to give q a negative sign to show that heat is released, so $q_v \approx -36$ kJ. To find q_v in kcal, we have to divide -36 kJ by about 4 (1 kcal $\approx$ 4 kJ), so q_v is approximately -9 kcal or -9 Cal. The answer obtained above, -8.740 Cal/g, is close to this, so we can be confident it is correct.

For part (b), to calculate q_v in units of kJ/mol we multiply q_v per gram (about -36 kJ) by the molar mass, which is somewhat smaller than 1000 g mol^{-1}. The answer should be somewhat smaller than $-36{,}000$ kJ/mol or -3.6×10^4 kJ/mol. Our answer, -3.238×10^4 kJ/mol, agrees with this analysis, so we can be confident it is correct.

Practice Exercise 3: The heat of combustion of methyl alcohol, CH_3OH, is -715 kJ mol^{-1}. When 2.85 g of CH_3OH was burned in a bomb calorimeter, the temperature of the calorimeter changed from 24.05 °C to 29.19 °C. What is the heat capacity of the calorimeter in units of kJ/°C? (Hint: Which equation relates temperature change, energy, and heat capacity?)

Practice Exercise 4: A 1.50 g sample of carbon is burned in a bomb calorimeter which has a heat capacity of 8.930 kJ/°C. The temperature of the water jacket rises from 20.00 °C to 25.51 °C. What is ΔE for the combustion of 1 mole of carbon?

Heats of reactions in solution are determined by constant-pressure calorimetry

Most reactions that are of interest to us do not occur at constant volume. Instead, they run in open containers like test tubes, beakers, and flasks, where they experience the constant pressure of the atmosphere. When reactions run under constant pressure, they may transfer energy as the **heat of reaction at constant pressure, q_p,** and as expansion work, w, so to calculate ΔE we need the equation

$$\Delta E = q_p + w \tag{6.11}$$

This is inconvenient. If we want to calculate the internal energy change for the reaction, we'll have to measure its volume change and then use Equation 6.9. To avoid this problem, scientists have defined a "corrected" internal energy called **enthalpy,** or **H.** Enthalpy is defied by the equation

$$H = E + PV$$

At constant pressure,

$$\Delta H = \Delta E + P\,\Delta V$$

$$= (q_p + w) + P\,\Delta V$$

From Equation 6.9, $P\,\Delta V = -w$, so

$$\Delta H = (q_p + w) + (-w)$$

$$\Delta H = q_p \tag{6.12}$$

Like E, H is a state function.

As with internal energy, an **enthalpy change, ΔH,** is defined by the equation

$$\Delta H = H_{\text{final}} - H_{\text{initial}}$$

For a chemical reaction, this can be rewritten as follows.

$$\Delta H = H_{\text{products}} - H_{\text{reactants}} \tag{6.13}$$

Positive and negative values of ΔH have the same interpretation as positive and negative values of ΔE.

Significance of the sign of ΔH:

For an endothermic change, ΔH is positive.

For an exothermic change, ΔH is negative.

The difference between ΔH and ΔE for a reaction equals $P\,\Delta V$. This difference can be fairly large for reactions that produce or consume gases, because these reactions can have very large volume changes. For reactions that involve only solids and liquids, though, the values of ΔV are tiny, so ΔE and ΔH for these reactions are nearly identical.

A very simple constant-pressure calorimeter, dubbed the coffee cup calorimeter, is made of two nested and capped cups made of Styrofoam, a very good insulator (Figure 6.8). A reaction occurring in such a calorimeter exchanges very little heat with the surroundings, particularly if the reaction is fast. The temperature change is rapid and easily measured. We can use Equation 6.5 to find the heat of reaction, if we have determined the heat capacity of the calorimeter and its contents before the reaction. The Styrofoam cup and the thermometer absorb only a tiny amount of heat, and we can usually ignore them in our calculations.

◻ Biochemical reactions also occur at constant pressure.

◻ From the Greek *en* + *thalpein*, meaning "to heat" or "to warm."

FIG. 6.8 A coffee cup calorimeter used to measure heats of reaction at constant pressure.

T▽OLS

Algebraic sign of ΔH

◻ Research-grade calorimeters have greater accuracy and precision than the coffee cup calorimeter.

EXAMPLE 6.5
Constant-Pressure Calorimetry

The reaction of hydrochloric acid and sodium hydroxide is very rapid and exothermic. The equation is

$$HCl(aq) + NaOH(aq) \longrightarrow NaCl(aq) + H_2O$$

In one experiment, a student placed 50.0 mL of 1.00 M HCl at 25.5 °C in a coffee cup calorimeter. To this was added 50.0 mL of 1.00 M NaOH solution also at 25.5 °C. The mixture was stirred, and the temperature quickly increased to a maximum of 32.2 °C. What is ΔH expressed in kJ per mole of HCl? Because the solutions are relatively dilute, we can assume that their specific heats are close to that of water, 4.18 J g^{-1} °C^{-1}. The density of 1.00 M HCl is 1.02 g mL^{-1} and that of 1.00 M NaOH is 1.04 g mL^{-1}. (We will neglect the heat lost to the Styrofoam itself, to the thermometer, or to the surrounding air.)

ANALYSIS: The reaction is taking place at constant pressure, so the heat we're calculating is q_p, which equals ΔH. We're given the specific heat of the solutions, so to calculate q_p we also need the system's total mass and the temperature change. (The tool used here will be Equation 6.7, $q = ms\,\Delta t$.) The mass here refers to the *total* grams of the combined solutions, but we've been given volumes. So we have to use their densities as a tool to calculate their masses, which you learned to do in Chapter 1.

SOLUTION: For the HCl solution, the density is 1.02 g mL^{-1} and we have

$$\text{Mass (HCl)} = \frac{1.02 \text{ g}}{1.00 \text{ mL}} \times 50.0 \text{ mL} = 51.0 \text{ g}$$

Similarly, for the NaOH solution, the density is 1.04 g mL^{-1} and

$$\text{Mass (NaOH)} = \frac{1.04 \text{ g}}{1.00 \text{ mL}} \times 50.0 \text{ mL} = 52.0 \text{ g}$$

The mass of the final solution is thus the sum, 103.0 g.

The reaction changes the system's temperature by $(t_{\text{final}} - t_{\text{initial}})$, so

$$\Delta t = 32.2 \text{ °C} - 25.5 \text{ °C} = 6.7 \text{ °C}$$

Now we can calculate the heat absorbed by the solution using Equation 6.7.

$$\text{Heat absorbed by the solution} = \text{mass} \times \text{specific heat} \times \Delta t$$

$$= 103.0 \text{ g} \times 4.18 \text{ J g}^{-1} \text{ °C}^{-1} \times 6.7 \text{ °C}$$

$$= 2.9 \times 10^3 \text{ J} = 2.9 \text{ kJ}$$

Changing the sign gives the heat evolved by the reaction, $q_p = -2.9$ kJ. But this is q_p specifically for the mixture prepared; the problem calls for kilojoules *per mole* of HCl. The tool we use to calculate the number of moles of HCl is the molarity, which provides a conversion factor connecting volume and moles. In 50.0 mL of HCl solution (0.0500 L) we have

$$0.0500 \text{ L HCl soln} \times \frac{1.00 \text{ mol HCl}}{1.00 \text{ L HCl soln}} = 0.0500 \text{ mol HCl}$$

The neutralization of 0.0500 mol of acid has $q_p = -2.9$ kJ. To calculate the heat released per mole, ΔH, we simply take the ratio of joules to moles.

$$\Delta H \text{ per mole of HCl} = \frac{-2.9 \text{ kJ}}{0.0500 \text{ mol HCl}} = -58 \text{ kJ mol}^{-1} \text{ HCl}$$

Thus, ΔH for neutralizing HCl by NaOH is -58 kJ mol^{-1} HCl.

IS THE ANSWER REASONABLE? Let's first review the logic of the steps we used. *Notice how the logic is driven by definitions, which carry specific units.* Working backward, knowing that we want units of kilojoules per mole in the answer, we must calculate separately the number of moles of acid neutralized and the number of kilojoules that evolved. The latter will emerge when we multiply the solution's mass (g) and specific heat ($J\ g^{-1}\ ^{\circ}C^{-1}$) by the degrees of temperature increase (°C). A simple change from joules to kilojoules is also required.

We can check the answer with some simplified arithmetic. Let's start with the mass of the solution. Because the densities are close to 1 g mL^{-1}, each solution has a mass of about 50 g, so the mixture weighs about 100 g.

The heat evolved will equal the specific heat times the mass times the temperature change. The specific heat is around $4\ J\ g^{-1}\ ^{\circ}C^{-1}$, the mass is about 100 g, and the temperature change is about 7 °C. The heat evolved will be approximately 4×700, or 2800 J. That's equal to 2.8×10^3 J or 2.8 kJ so $q_p \approx -2.8$ kJ. Our answer of -2.9 kJ is certainly reasonable. This much heat is associated with neutralizing 0.05 mol HCl, so the heat per mole is -2.9 kJ divided by 0.05 mol, or -58 kJ mol^{-1}.

Practice Exercise 5: For the preceding worked example, calculate ΔH per mole of NaOH. (Hint: How many moles of NaOH were neutralized in the reaction?)

Practice Exercise 6: When pure sulfuric acid dissolves in water, much heat is given off. To measure it, 175 g of water was placed in a coffee cup calorimeter and chilled to 10.0 °C. Then 4.90 g of sulfuric acid (H_2SO_4), also at 10.0 °C, was added, and the mixture was quickly stirred with a thermometer. The temperature rose rapidly to 14.9 °C. Assume that the value of the specific heat of the solution is $4.18\ J\ g^{-1}\ ^{\circ}C^{-1}$, and that the solution absorbs all the heat evolved. Calculate the heat evolved in kilojoules by the formation of this solution. (Remember to use the *total* mass of the solution, the water plus the solute.) Calculate also the heat evolved *per mole* of sulfuric acid.

6.6 THERMOCHEMICAL EQUATIONS ARE CHEMICAL EQUATIONS THAT QUANTITATIVELY INCLUDE HEAT

The amount of heat a reaction produces or absorbs depends on the number of moles of reactants we combine. It makes sense that if we burn two moles of carbon, we're going to get twice as much heat as we would if we had burned one mole. For heats of reaction to have meaning, we must describe the **system** completely. Our description must include amounts and concentrations of reactants, amounts and concentrations of products, temperature, and pressure, because all of these things can influence heats of reaction.

◻ Unless we specify otherwise, whenever we write ΔH we mean ΔH for the *system*, not the surroundings.

Chemists have agreed to a set of **standard states** to make it easier to report and compare heats of reaction. Most thermochemical data are reported for a pressure of 1 bar, or (for substances in aqueous solution) a concentration of 1 M. A temperature of 25 °C (298 K) is often specified as well, although temperature is not part of the definition of standard states in thermochemistry.

ΔH° is the enthalpy change for a reaction with all reactants and products at standard state

The **standard heat of reaction (ΔH°)** is the value of ΔH for a reaction occurring under standard conditions and involving the actual numbers of *moles* specified by the coefficients of the equation. To show that ΔH is for *standard* conditions, a degree sign is added to ΔH to make ΔH° (pronounced "delta H naught" or "delta H zero"). The units of ΔH° are normally kilojoules.

To illustrate clearly what we mean by ΔH°, let us use the reaction between gaseous nitrogen and hydrogen that produces gaseous ammonia.

$$N_2(g) + 3H_2(g) \longrightarrow 2NH_3(g)$$

When specifically 1.000 mol of N_2 and 3.000 mol of H_2 react to form 2.000 mol of NH_3 at 25 °C and 1 bar, the reaction releases 92.38 kJ. Hence, for the reaction *as given by the above equation,* $\Delta H^\circ = -92.38$ kJ. Often the enthalpy change is given immediately after the equation; for example,

$$N_2(g) + 3H_2(g) \longrightarrow 2NH_3(g) \qquad \Delta H^\circ = -92.38 \text{ kJ}$$

TOOLS

Thermochemical equations

An equation that also shows the value of ΔH° is called a **thermochemical equation.** It always gives the physical states of the reactants and products, and *its ΔH° value is true only when the coefficients of the reactants and products are taken to mean moles of the corresponding substances.* The above equation, for example, shows a release of 92.38 kJ if *two* moles of NH_3 form. If we were to make twice as much or 4.000 mol of NH_3 (from 2.000 mol of N_2 and 6.000 mol of H_2), then twice as much heat (184.8 kJ) would be released. On the other hand, if only 0.5000 mol of N_2 and 1.500 mol of H_2 were to react to form 1.000 mole of NH_3, then only half as much heat (46.19 kJ) would be released. To describe the various *sizes* of the reactions just described, we write the following thermochemical equations.

$$N_2(g) + 3H_2(g) \longrightarrow 2NH_3(g) \qquad \Delta H^\circ = -92.38 \text{ kJ}$$

$$2N_2(g) + 6H_2(g) \longrightarrow 4NH_3(g) \qquad \Delta H^\circ = -184.8 \text{ kJ}$$

$$\tfrac{1}{2}N_2(g) + \tfrac{3}{2}H_2(g) \longrightarrow NH_3(g) \qquad \Delta H^\circ = -46.19 \text{ kJ}$$

Because the coefficients of a thermochemical equation always mean *moles*, not molecules, we may use fractional coefficients. (In the kinds of equations you've seen up till now, fractional coefficients were not allowed because we cannot have fractions of *molecules*, but we can have fractions of moles in a thermochemical equation.)

You must write down physical states for all reactants and products in thermochemical equations. The combustion of 1 mol of methane, for example, has different values of ΔH° if the water produced is in its liquid or its gaseous state.

$$CH_4(g) + 2O_2(g) \longrightarrow CO_2(g) + 2H_2O(l) \qquad \Delta H^\circ = -890.5 \text{ kJ}$$

$$CH_4(g) + 2O_2(g) \longrightarrow CO_2(g) + 2H_2O(g) \qquad \Delta H^\circ = -802.3 \text{ kJ}$$

(The difference in ΔH° values for these two reactions is the amount of energy that would be released by the physical change of 2 mol of water vapor at 25 °C to 2 mol of liquid water at 25 °C.)

EXAMPLE 6.6

Writing a Thermochemical Equation

The following thermochemical equation is for the exothermic reaction of hydrogen and oxygen that produces water.

$$2H_2(g) + O_2(g) \longrightarrow 2H_2O(l) \qquad \Delta H^\circ = -571.8 \text{ kJ}$$

What is the thermochemical equation for this reaction when it is conducted to produce 1.000 mol H_2O?

ANALYSIS: The given equation is for 2.000 mol of H_2O, and any changes in the coefficient for water must be made identically to all other coefficients, *as well as to the value of ΔH°.*

SOLUTION: We divide everything by 2, to obtain

$$H_2(g) + \tfrac{1}{2}O_2(g) \longrightarrow H_2O(l) \qquad \Delta H^\circ = -285.9 \text{ kJ}$$

IS THE ANSWER REASONABLE? Compare the equation just found with the initial equation to see that the coefficients and the value of ΔH° are all divided by 2.

Practice Exercise 7: The combustion of methane follows the thermochemical equation

$$CH_4(g) + 2O_2(g) \longrightarrow CO_2(g) + 2H_2O(l) \qquad \Delta H° = -890.5 \text{ kJ}$$

Write the thermochemical equation for the combustion of methane when 1/2 mol of $H_2O(l)$ is formed. [Hint: What do you have to do to the coefficient of $H_2O(l)$ to give $\frac{1}{2}H_2O(l)$?]

Practice Exercise 8: What is the thermochemical equation for the formation of 2.500 mol of $H_2O(l)$ from $H_2(g)$ and $O_2(g)$?

6.7 THERMOCHEMICAL EQUATIONS CAN BE COMBINED BECAUSE ENTHALPY IS A STATE FUNCTION

We mentioned earlier that enthalpy is a state function. This important fact permits us to calculate heats of reaction for reactions we cannot actually carry out in the laboratory. You will see soon that to accomplish this, we will combine known thermochemical equations, which usually requires that we manipulate them in some way.

Both the coefficients and direction of thermochemical equations can be adjusted

In the last section you learned that if we change the size of a reaction by multiplying or dividing the coefficients of a thermochemical equation by some factor, the value of $\Delta H°$ is multiplied by the same factor. Another way to manipulate a thermochemical equation is to change its direction. For example, the thermochemical equation for the combustion of carbon in oxygen to give carbon dioxide is

$$C(s) + O_2(g) \longrightarrow CO_2(g) \qquad \Delta H° = -393.5 \text{ kJ}$$

The reverse reaction, which is extremely difficult to carry out, would be the decomposition of carbon dioxide to carbon and oxygen. The law of conservation of energy requires that its value of $\Delta H°$ equals +393.5 kJ.

$$CO_2(g) \longrightarrow C(s) + O_2(g) \qquad \Delta H° = +393.5 \text{ kJ}$$

In effect, these two thermochemical equations tell us that the combustion of carbon is exothermic (as indicated by the negative sign of $\Delta H°$) and that the reverse reaction is endothermic. The same amount of energy is involved in both reactions; it is just the direction of energy flow that is different. The lesson to learn here is that *we can reverse any thermochemical equation as long as we change the sign of its $\Delta H°$.*

Enthalpy changes depend only on initial and final states, not on the path between them

What we're leading up to is a method for combining known thermochemical equations in a way that will allow us to calculate an unknown $\Delta H°$ for some other reaction. Let's revisit the combustion of carbon to see how this works.

We can imagine two paths leading from 1 mole each of carbon and oxygen to 1 mol of carbon dioxide.

One-Step Path. Let C and O_2 react to give CO_2 directly.

$$C(s) + O_2(g) \longrightarrow CO_2(g) \qquad \Delta H° = -393.5 \text{ kJ}$$

Two-Step Path. Let C and O_2 react to give CO, and then let CO react with more O_2 to give CO_2.

$$\text{Step 1:} \quad C(s) + \tfrac{1}{2}O_2(g) \longrightarrow CO(g) \qquad \Delta H° = -110.5 \text{ kJ}$$

$$\text{Step 2:} \ CO(g) + \tfrac{1}{2}O_2(g) \longrightarrow CO_2(g) \qquad \Delta H° = -283.0 \text{ kJ}$$

Overall, the two-step path consumes 1 mol each of C and O_2 to make 1 mol of CO_2, just like the one-step path. The initial and final states for the two routes to CO_2, in other words, are identical.

Because $\Delta H°$ is a state function dependent only on the initial and final states and is independent of path, the values of $\Delta H°$ for both routes should be identical. We can see that this is exactly true simply by adding the equations for the two-step path and comparing the result with the equation for the single step.

Step 1: $C(s) + \frac{1}{2}O_2(g) \longrightarrow CO(g)$ $\Delta H° = -110.5 \text{ kJ}$

Step 2: $CO(g) + \frac{1}{2}O_2(g) \longrightarrow CO_2(g)$ $\Delta H° = -283.0 \text{ kJ}$

$CO(g) + C(s) + O_2(g) \longrightarrow CO_2(g) + CO(g)$ $\Delta H° = -110.5 \text{ kJ} + (-283.0 \text{ kJ})$

$\Delta H° = -393.5 \text{ kJ}$

The equation resulting from adding Steps 1 and 2 has "$CO(g)$" appearing *identically* on opposite sides of the arrow. We can cancel them to obtain the net equation. *Such a cancellation is permitted only when both the formula and the physical state of a species are identical on opposite sides of the arrow.* The net thermochemical equation for the two-step process, therefore, is

$$C(s) + O_2(g) \longrightarrow CO_2(g) \qquad \Delta H° = -393.5 \text{ kJ}$$

The results, chemically and thermochemically, are thus identical for both routes to CO_2.

Enthalpy diagrams show alternative pathways between initial and final states

TOOLS
Enthalpy diagram

The energy relationships among the alternative pathways for the same overall reaction are clearly seen using a graphical construction called an **enthalpy diagram.** Figure 6.9 is an enthalpy diagram for the formation of CO_2 from C and O_2. Each horizontal line corresponds to a certain total amount of enthalpy, which we can't actually measure. We *can* measure differences in enthalpy, however, and that's what we use the diagram for. Lines higher up the enthalpy scale represent larger amounts of enthalpy, so going from a lower line to a higher line corresponds to an increase in enthalpy and a positive value for $\Delta H°$ (an endothermic change). The size of $\Delta H°$ is represented by the vertical distance between the two lines. Likewise, going from a higher line to a lower one represents a decrease in enthalpy and a negative value for $\Delta H°$ (an exothermic change).

Notice in Figure 6.9 that the line for the absolute enthalpy of $C(s) + O_2(g)$, taken as the sum, is above the line for the final product, CO_2. A horizontal line represents the *sum*

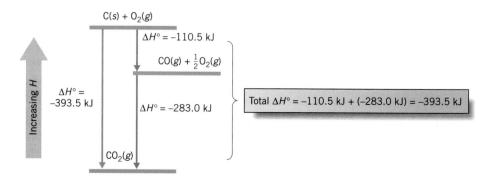

FIG. 6.9   **An enthalpy diagram for the formation of $CO_2(g)$ from its elements by two different paths.** On the left is path 1, the direct conversion of $C(s)$ and $O_2(g)$ to $CO_2(g)$. On the right, path 2 shows two shorter, downward pointing arrows. The first step of path 2 takes the elements to $CO(g)$, and the second step takes $CO(g)$ to $CO_2(g)$. The overall enthalpy change is identical for both paths, as it must be, because enthalpy is a state function.

of the enthalpies of all of the substances on the line, *in the physical states specified.* Near the left side of Figure 6.9, we see a long downward arrow that connects the enthalpy level for the reactants, $C(s) + O_2(g)$, to that of the final product, $CO_2(g)$. This is for the one-step path, the direct path.

On the right we have the two-step path. Here, Step 1 brings us to an intermediate enthalpy level corresponding to the intermediate products, $CO(g) + \frac{1}{2}O_2(g)$. These include the mole of $CO(g)$ made in the first step plus $\frac{1}{2}$ mol of O_2 which has not reacted. Then Step 2 occurs to give the final product. What the enthalpy diagram shows is that the total decrease in enthalpy is the same regardless of the path.

EXAMPLE 6.7
Preparing an Enthalpy Diagram

Hydrogen peroxide, H_2O_2, decomposes into water and oxygen by the following equation.

$$H_2O_2(l) \longrightarrow H_2O(l) + \tfrac{1}{2}O_2(g)$$

Construct an enthalpy diagram for the following two reactions of hydrogen and oxygen, and use the diagram to determine the value of $\Delta H°$ for the decomposition of hydrogen peroxide.

$$H_2(g) + O_2(g) \longrightarrow H_2O_2(l) \qquad \Delta H° = -188 \text{ kJ}$$
$$H_2(g) + \tfrac{1}{2}O_2(g) \longrightarrow H_2O_2(l) \qquad \Delta H° = -286 \text{ kJ}$$

ANALYSIS: The two given reactions are exothermic, so their values of $\Delta H°$ will be associated with downward pointing arrows. The highest enthalpy level, therefore, must be for the elements themselves. The lowest level must be for the product of the reaction with the largest negative $\Delta H°$, the formation of water by the second equation. The enthalpy level for the H_2O_2, formed by a reaction with the less negative $\Delta H°$, must be in between.

SOLUTION: First, let's diagram the two reactions having known values of $\Delta H°$. Notice that the first reaction requires an entire mole of O_2, whereas the second needs only 1/2 mol of O_2. On the top line we'll include enough O_2 for the first reaction. This leaves $\frac{1}{2}O_2(g)$ unreacted when we form $H_2O(l)$, as indicated on the bottom line.

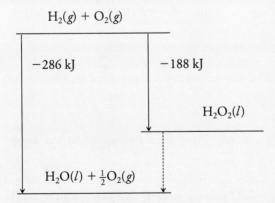

Notice that the gap on the right side (represented by the dotted arrow) corresponds exactly to the change of $H_2O_2(l)$ into $H_2O(l) + \frac{1}{2}O_2(g)$, the reaction for which $\Delta H°$ is sought. This enthalpy separation corresponds to the difference between the enthalpy changes -286 kJ and -188 kJ. Thus for the decomposition of $H_2O_2(l)$ into $H_2O(l)$ and $\frac{1}{2}O_2(g)$,

$$\Delta H° = [-286 \text{ kJ} - (-188 \text{ kJ})] = -98 \text{ kJ}$$

Our completed enthalpy diagram is shown on the next page, indicating that $\Delta H°$ for the decomposition of 1 mol of $H_2O_2(l)$ is -98 kJ.

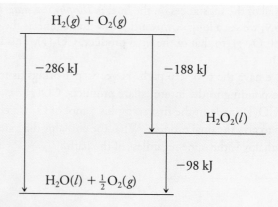

IS THE ANSWER REASONABLE? First be sure that the chemical formulas are arrayed properly on the horizontal lines in the enthalpy diagram. The arrows pointing downward should indicate negative values of $\Delta H°$. These arrows must be consistent *in direction* with the given equations (in other words, they must point from reactants to products). Finally, notice that the total amount of energy associated with the two-step process, namely, (-188 kJ) plus (-98 kJ) equals -286 kJ, the energy for the one-step process.

Practice Exercise 9: Two oxides of copper can be made from copper by the following reactions.

$$2Cu(s) + O_2(g) \longrightarrow 2CuO(s) \qquad \Delta H° = -310 \text{ kJ}$$

$$2Cu(s) + \tfrac{1}{2}O_2(g) \longrightarrow Cu_2O(s) \qquad \Delta H° = -169 \text{ kJ}$$

Using these data, construct an enthalpy diagram that can be used to find $\Delta H°$ for the reaction $Cu_2O(s) + \tfrac{1}{2}O_2(g) \rightarrow 2CuO(s)$. Is the reaction endothermic or exothermic? (Hint: Remember, an arrow points down for a negative $\Delta H°$ and up for a positive $\Delta H°$.)

Practice Exercise 10: Consider the following thermochemical equations:

$$\tfrac{1}{2}N_2(g) + \tfrac{1}{2}O_2(g) \longrightarrow NO(g) \qquad \Delta H° = +90.4 \text{ kJ}$$

$$NO(g) + \tfrac{1}{2}O_2(g) \longrightarrow NO_2(g) \qquad \Delta H° = -56.6 \text{ kJ}$$

Using these data, construct an enthalpy diagram that can be used to find $\Delta H°$ for the reaction $\tfrac{1}{2}N_2(g) + O_2(g) \longrightarrow NO_2(g)$. Is the reaction endothermic or exothermic?

Predict any heat of reaction using Hess's law

☐ Germain Henri Hess (1802–1850) anticipated the law of conservation of energy in the law named after him.

Enthalpy diagrams, while instructive, are not necessary to calculate $\Delta H°$ for a reaction from known thermochemical equations. Using the tools for manipulating equations, we ought to be able to calculate $\Delta H°$ values simply by algebraic summing. G. H. Hess was the first to realize this, so the associated law is called **Hess's law of heat summation** or, simply, **Hess's law.**

TOOLS
Hess's law

Hess's Law. The value of $\Delta H°$ for any reaction that can be written in steps equals the sum of the values of $\Delta H°$ of each of the individual steps.

For example, suppose we add the two equations in Practice Exercise 10 and then cancel anything that's the same on both sides.

$$\tfrac{1}{2}N_2(g) + \tfrac{1}{2}O_2(g) \longrightarrow NO(g)$$

$$NO(g) + \tfrac{1}{2}O_2(g) \longrightarrow NO_2(g)$$

$$\tfrac{1}{2}N_2(g) + \cancel{NO(g)} + \tfrac{1}{2}O_2(g) + \tfrac{1}{2}O_2(g) \longrightarrow \cancel{NO(g)} + NO_2(g)$$

$$\underbrace{\phantom{\tfrac{1}{2}O_2(g) + \tfrac{1}{2}O_2(g)}}_{O_2(g)}$$

Notice that we've combined the two $\tfrac{1}{2}O_2(g)$ to give $O_2(g)$. Rewriting the equation gives

$$\tfrac{1}{2}N_2(g) + O_2(g) \longrightarrow NO_2(g)$$

This is the equation for which we were asked to determine $\Delta H°$. According to Hess's law, we should be able to obtain $\Delta H°$ for this reaction by simply adding the $\Delta H°$ values for the equations we've added.

$$\Delta H° = (+90.4\ \text{kJ}) + (-56.6\ \text{kJ}) = +33.8\ \text{kJ}$$

This was the answer to Practice Exercise 10. Thus, we've added the two given equations to obtain the desired equation and we've added their $\Delta H°$ values to obtain the desired $\Delta H°$.

The chief use of Hess's law is to calculate the enthalpy change for a reaction for which such data cannot be determined experimentally or are otherwise unavailable. Often this requires that we manipulate equations, so let's recapitulate the few rules that govern these operations.

Rules for Manipulating Thermochemical Equations

1. When an equation is reversed—written in the opposite direction—the sign of $\Delta H°$ must also be reversed.[4]
2. Formulas canceled from both sides of an equation must be for the substance in identical physical states.
3. If all the coefficients of an equation are multiplied or divided by the same factor, the value of $\Delta H°$ must likewise be multiplied or divided by that factor.

TOOLS

Manipulating thermochemical equations

EXAMPLE 6.8
Using Hess's Law

Carbon monoxide is often used in metallurgy to remove oxygen from metal oxides and thereby give the free metal. The thermochemical equation for the reaction of CO with iron(III) oxide, Fe_2O_3, is

$$Fe_2O_3(s) + 3CO(g) \longrightarrow 2Fe(s) + 3CO_2(g) \qquad \Delta H° = -26.7\ \text{kJ}$$

Use this equation and the equation for the combustion of CO,

$$CO(g) + \tfrac{1}{2}O_2(g) \longrightarrow CO_2(g) \qquad \Delta H° = -283.0\ \text{kJ}$$

to calculate the value of $\Delta H°$ for the following reaction.

$$2Fe(s) + \tfrac{3}{2}O_2(g) \longrightarrow Fe_2O_3(s)$$

ANALYSIS: The tools will be Hess's law and the rules for manipulating thermochemical equations. In this problem, we cannot simply add the two given equations, because this will not produce the equation we want. We first have to manipulate the equations so that when we add them we will get the target equation. In performing these adjustments, we have to keep our eye

---

[4] To illustrate, the reverse of the equation

$$C(s) + O_2(g) \longrightarrow CO_2(g) \qquad \Delta H° = -394\ \text{kJ}$$

is the following equation:

$$CO_2(g) \longrightarrow C(s) + O_2(g) \qquad \Delta H° = +394\ \text{kJ}$$

on our target—the final desired equation. When we've done this, we can then add the adjusted $\Delta H°$ values to obtain the desired $\Delta H°$.

SOLUTION: We can manipulate the two given equations as follows.

Step 1. We begin by trying to get the iron atoms to come out right. The target equation must have 2Fe on the *left*, but the first equation above has 2Fe to the *right* of the arrow. To move it to the left, we reverse the *entire* equation, remembering also to reverse the sign of $\Delta H°$. This puts Fe_2O_3 to the right of the arrow, which is where it has to be after we add the adjusted equations. After these manipulations, and reversing the sign of $\Delta H°$, we have

$$2Fe(s) + 3CO_2(g) \longrightarrow Fe_2O_3(s) + 3CO(g) \qquad \Delta H° = +26.7 \text{ kJ}$$

Step 2. There must be $\frac{3}{2}O_2$ on the left, and we must be able to cancel *three* CO and *three* CO_2 when the equations are added. If we multiply the second of the equations given above by 3, we will obtain the necessary coefficients. We must also multiply the value of $\Delta H°$ of this equation by 3, because three times as many moles of substances are now involved in the reaction. When we have done this, we have

$$3CO(g) + \tfrac{3}{2}O_2(g) \longrightarrow 3CO_2(g) \qquad \Delta H° = 3 \times (-283.0 \text{ kJ}) = -849.0 \text{ kJ}$$

Let's now put our two equations together and find the answer.

$$2Fe(s) + \cancel{3CO_2(g)} \longrightarrow Fe_2O_3(s) + \cancel{3CO(g)} \qquad \Delta H° = +26.7 \text{ kJ}$$

$$\cancel{3CO(g)} + \tfrac{3}{2}O_2(g) \longrightarrow \cancel{3CO_2(g)} \qquad \Delta H° = -849.0 \text{ kJ}$$

Sum $\qquad 2Fe(s) + \tfrac{3}{2}O_2(g) \longrightarrow Fe_2O_3(s) \qquad \Delta H° = -822.3 \text{ kJ}$

Thus, the value of $\Delta H°$ for the oxidation of 2 mol Fe(s) to 1 mol $Fe_2O_3(s)$ is -822.3 kJ. (The reaction is *very* exothermic.)

IS THE ANSWER REASONABLE? There is no quick "head check." But for each step, double-check that you have heeded the rules for manipulating thermochemical equations. Also, be careful with the algebraic signs when adding the $\Delta H°$ values.

Practice Exercise 11: Consider the thermochemical equation

$$H_2(g) + \tfrac{1}{2}O_2(g) \longrightarrow H_2O(l) \qquad \Delta H° = -285.9 \text{ kJ}$$

What is the value of $\Delta H°$ for the following reaction? (Hint: How does altering the coefficients and changing direction change $\Delta H°$?)

$$3H_2O(l) \longrightarrow 3H_2(g) + \tfrac{3}{2}O_2(g)$$

Practice Exercise 12: Given the following thermochemical equations:

$$2NO(g) + O_2(g) \longrightarrow 2NO_2(g) \qquad \Delta H° = -113.2 \text{ kJ}$$

$$2N_2O(g) + 3O_2(g) \longrightarrow 4NO_2(g) \qquad \Delta H° = -28.0 \text{ kJ}$$

calculate $\Delta H°$ for this reaction: $N_2O(g) + \tfrac{1}{2}O_2(g) \longrightarrow 2NO(g)$

Practice Exercise 13: Ethanol, C_2H_5OH, is made industrially by the reaction of water with ethylene, C_2H_4. Calculate the value of $\Delta H°$ for the reaction

$$C_2H_4(g) + H_2O(l) \longrightarrow C_2H_5OH(l)$$

given the following thermochemical equations.

$$C_2H_4(g) + 3O_2(g) \longrightarrow 2CO_2(g) + 2H_2O(l) \qquad \Delta H° = -1411.1 \text{ kJ}$$

$$C_2H_5OH(l) + 3O_2(g) \longrightarrow 2CO_2(g) + 3H_2O(l) \qquad \Delta H° = -1367.1 \text{ kJ}$$

6.8 | TABULATED STANDARD HEATS OF REACTION CAN BE USED TO PREDICT ANY HEAT OF REACTION USING HESS'S LAW

Enormous databases of thermochemical equations have been compiled to allow the calculation of any heat of reaction, using Hess's law. The most frequently tabulated reactions are combustion reactions, phase changes, and formation reactions. We'll discuss the enthalpy changes that accompany phase changes in Chapter 11.

The **standard heat of combustion, ΔH_c°**, of a substance is the amount of heat released when one mole of a fuel substance is completely burned in pure oxygen gas, with all reactants and products brought to 25 °C and 1 bar of pressure. All carbon in the fuel becomes carbon dioxide gas, and all the fuel's hydrogen becomes liquid water. *Combustion reactions are always exothermic*, so ΔH_c° is always negative.

EXAMPLE 6.9
Writing an Equation for a Standard Heat of Combustion

How many moles of carbon dioxide gas are produced by a gas-fired power plant for every 1.00 MJ (megajoule) of energy it produces? The plant burns methane, $CH_4(g)$, for which ΔH_c° is -890 kJ/mol.

ANALYSIS: We can restate the problem as an equivalency relation:

$$1.00 \text{ MJ released} \iff ? \text{ mol } CO_2(g)$$

We need to link moles of carbon dioxide with megajoules of heat produced. The tool we will use is the balanced thermochemical equation. This is a combustion reaction, and you learned in Chapter 5 that when a hydrocarbon burns, the products are CO_2 and H_2O. The first step in the solution will be to write a balanced chemical equation for the reaction of CH_4 with O_2. Because ΔH_c° gives the heat evolved *per mole* of CH_4, we will have to be sure the coefficient of CH_4 is one. In the equation CH_4, O_2, and CO_2 will be gases and H_2O will be a liquid (because that's the standard form of H_2O at 25 °C.)

Once we have the thermochemical equation, the coefficients will let us relate moles of CO_2 to kilojoules of heat released. To relate megajoules with kilojoules, our tools will be the SI prefixes *kilo-* and *mega-*.

$$1 \text{ MJ} = 10^6 \text{ J}$$

$$1 \text{ kJ} = 10^3 \text{ J}$$

SOLUTION: First, we write and balance the thermochemical equation, remembering that ΔH° is ΔH_c°.

$$CH_4(g) + 2O_2(g) \longrightarrow CO_2(g) + 2H_2O(l) \qquad \Delta H_c^\circ = -890 \text{ kJ}$$

So, 1 mol CO_2 is formed for every 890 kJ of heat that is released. The number of moles of CO_2 released for production of 1.0 MJ of energy is

$$1.00 \cancel{\text{ MJ}} \times \frac{10^6 \cancel{\text{ J}}}{1 \cancel{\text{ MJ}}} \times \frac{1 \cancel{\text{ kJ}}}{10^3 \cancel{\text{ J}}} \times \frac{1 \text{ mol } CO_2}{890 \cancel{\text{ kJ}}} = 1.12 \text{ mol } CO_2$$

IS THE ANSWER REASONABLE? When 1 mol CH_4 burns, 890 kJ is released. This is just a little less than 1000 kJ (or 1 MJ), so the amount of CH_4 needed to release 1 MJ should be a bit larger than 1 mol. Because 1 mol $CH_4 \iff 1$ mol CO_2, our answer, 1.12 mol CO_2, is reasonable.

Practice Exercise 14: The heat of combustion, ΔH_c°, of acetone, C_3H_6O, is 1790.4 kJ/mol. How many kilojoules of heat are evolved in the combustion of 12.5 g of acetone? (Hint: Calculate the molar mass of acetone.)

Practice Exercise 15: n-Octane, $C_8H_{18}(l)$, has a standard heat of combustion of 5450.5 kJ/mol. A 15 gallon automobile fuel tank could hold about 480 moles of n-octane. How much heat could be produced by burning a full tank of n-octane?

Forming one mole of a compound from its elements involves the heat of formation

The **standard enthalpy of formation, ΔH_f°,** of a substance, also called its **standard heat of formation,** is the amount of heat absorbed or evolved when specifically *one mole* of the substance is formed at 25 °C and 1 bar from its elements in their *standard states.* An element is in its **standard state** when it is at 25 °C and 1 bar and in its most stable form and physical state (solid, liquid, or gas). Oxygen, for example, is in its standard state only as a gas at 25 °C and 1 bar and only as O_2 molecules, not as O atoms or O_3 (ozone) molecules. Carbon must be in the form of graphite, not diamond, to be in its standard state, because the graphite form of carbon is the more stable form under standard conditions.

Standard enthalpies of formation for a variety of substances are given in Table 6.2, and a more extensive table of standard heats of formation can be found in Appendix C. Notice in particular that *all values of ΔH_f° for the elements in their standard states are zero.* (Forming

☐ Older thermochemical data used a standard pressure of 1 atm, not 1 bar. Because 1 atm = 1.01325 bar, the new definition made little difference in tabulated heats of reaction.

TABLE 6.2	**Standard Enthalpies of Formation of Typical Substances**		
Substance	ΔH_f° (kJ mol^{-1})	Substance	ΔH_f° (kJ mol^{-1})
Ag(s)	0	$H_2O_2(l)$	−187.6
AgBr(s)	−100.4	HBr(g)	−36
AgCl(s)	−127.0	HCl(g)	−92.30
Al(s)	0	HI(g)	26.6
$Al_2O_3(s)$	−1669.8	$HNO_3(l)$	−173.2
C(s, graphite)	0	$H_2SO_4(l)$	−811.32
CO(g)	−110.5	$HC_2H_3O_2(l)$	−487.0
$CO_2(g)$	−393.5	Hg(l)	0
$CH_4(g)$	−74.848	Hg(g)	60.84
$CH_3Cl(g)$	−82.0	$I_2(s)$	0
$CH_3I(g)$	14.2	K(s)	0
$CH_3OH(l)$	−238.6	KCl(s)	−435.89
$CO(NH_2)_2(s)$ (urea)	−333.19	$K_2SO_4(s)$	−1433.7
$CO(NH_2)_2(aq)$	−391.2	$N_2(g)$	0
$C_2H_2(g)$	226.75	$NH_3(g)$	−46.19
$C_2H_4(g)$	52.284	$NH_4Cl(s)$	−315.4
$C_2H_6(g)$	−84.667	NO(g)	90.37
$C_2H_5OH(l)$	−277.63	$NO_2(g)$	33.8
Ca(s)	0	$N_2O(g)$	81.57
$CaBr_2(s)$	−682.8	$N_2O_4(g)$	9.67
$CaCO_3(s)$	−1207	$N_2O_5(g)$	11
$CaCl_2(s)$	−795.0	Na(s)	0
CaO(s)	−635.5	$NaHCO_3(s)$	−947.7
$Ca(OH)_2(s)$	−986.59	$Na_2CO_3(s)$	−1131
$CaSO_4(s)$	−1432.7	NaCl(s)	−411.0
$CaSO_4 \cdot \frac{1}{2}H_2O(s)$	−1575.2	NaOH(s)	−426.8
$CaSO_4 \cdot 2H_2O(s)$	−2021.1	$Na_2SO_4(s)$	−1384.5
$Cl_2(g)$	0	$O_2(g)$	0
Fe(s)	0	Pb(s)	0
$Fe_2O_3(s)$	−822.2	PbO(s)	−219.2
$H_2(g)$	0	S(s)	0
$H_2O(g)$	−241.8	$SO_2(g)$	−296.9
$H_2O(l)$	−285.9	$SO_3(g)$	−395.2

an element *from itself*, of course, would yield no change in enthalpy.) In most tables, values of ΔH_f° for the elements are not included for this reason.

It is important to remember the meaning of the subscript f in the symbol ΔH_f°. It is applied to a value of ΔH° only when *one mole* of the substance is formed *from its elements in their standard states.* Consider, for example, the following four thermochemical equations and their corresponding values of ΔH°.

$$H_2(g) + \tfrac{1}{2}O_2(g) \longrightarrow H_2O(l) \qquad \Delta H_f^\circ = -285.9 \text{ kJ/mol}$$

$$2H_2(g) + O_2(g) \longrightarrow 2H_2O(l) \qquad \Delta H^\circ = -571.8 \text{ kJ}$$

$$CO(g) + \tfrac{1}{2}O_2(g) \longrightarrow CO_2(g) \qquad \Delta H^\circ = -283.0 \text{ kJ}$$

$$2H(g) + O(g) \longrightarrow H_2O(l) \qquad \Delta H^\circ = -971.1 \text{ kJ}$$

Only in the first equation is ΔH° given the subscript f. It is the only reaction that satisfies both of the conditions specified above for standard enthalpies of formation. The second equation shows the formation of *two* moles of water, not one. The third involves a *compound* as one of the reactants. The fourth involves the elements as *atoms*, which are *not standard states* for these elements. Also notice that the units of ΔH_f° are kilojoules *per mole*, not just kilojoules, because the value is for the formation of 1 mol of the compound (from its elements). We can obtain the enthalpy of formation of two moles of water (ΔH° for the second equation) simply by multiplying the ΔH_f° value for 1 mol of H_2O by the factor, 2 mol $H_2O(l)$.

$$\left(\frac{-285.9 \text{ kJ}}{\text{mol } H_2O(l)} \right) \times 2 \text{ mol } H_2O(l) = -571.8 \text{ kJ}$$

EXAMPLE 6.10
Writing an Equation for a Standard Heat of Formation

What equation must be used to represent the formation of nitric acid, $HNO_3(l)$, when we want to include its value of ΔH_f°?

ANALYSIS: Answering the question requires that we know the definition of ΔH_f°, which demands that the equation must show only *one mole* of the product. We begin with its formula and take whatever fractions of moles of the elements are required to make it. We must also be careful to include the physical states. Table 6.2 gives the value of ΔH_f° for $HNO_3(l)$, $-173.2 \text{ kJ mol}^{-1}$.

SOLUTION: The three elements, H, N, and O, all occur as diatomic molecules in the gaseous state, so the following fractions of moles supply exactly enough of each to make one mole of HNO_3.

$$\tfrac{1}{2}H_2(g) + \tfrac{1}{2}N_2(g) + \tfrac{3}{2}O_2(g) \longrightarrow HNO_3(l) \qquad \Delta H_f^\circ = -173.2 \text{ kJ mol}^{-1}$$

IS THE ANSWER REASONABLE? The answer correctly shows only 1 mol of HNO_3, and this governs the coefficients for the reactants. So simply check to be sure everything is balanced.

Practice Exercise 16: Write the thermochemical equation that would be used to represent the standard heat of formation of $NH_4Cl(s)$. (Hint: Be sure you show substances in their standard states.)

Practice Exercise 17: Write the thermochemical equation that would be used to represent the standard heat of formation of sodium bicarbonate, $NaHCO_3(s)$.

Standard enthalpies of formation are useful because they provide a convenient method for applying Hess's law without having to manipulate thermochemical equations. To see how this works, let's look again at Example 6.7 where we calculated $\Delta H°$ for the decomposition of H_2O_2.

$$H_2O_2(l) \longrightarrow H_2O(l) + \tfrac{1}{2}O_2(g)$$

The two equations we used were

(1) $\quad H_2(g) + O_2(g) \longrightarrow H_2O_2(l) \qquad \Delta H_f°\,(1) = -188\ kJ$

(2) $\quad H_2(g) + \tfrac{1}{2}O_2(g) \longrightarrow H_2O(l) \qquad \Delta H_f°\,(2) = -286\ kJ$

This time we have numbered the equations and identified the enthalpy changes as $\Delta H_f°$ because in each case we're forming one mole of the compound from elements in their standard states. To combine these equations to find $\Delta H°$ for the decomposition of H_2O_2, we have to reverse equation (1), which means we change the sign of its ΔH.

(1 reversed) $\qquad H_2O_2(l) \longrightarrow H_2(g) + O_2(g) \qquad \Delta H° = -\Delta H_f°(1) = +188\ kJ$

(2) $\qquad H_2(g) + \tfrac{1}{2}O_2(g) \longrightarrow H_2O(l) \qquad \Delta H_f°\,(2) = -286\ kJ$

Sum $\qquad H_2O_2(l) \longrightarrow H_2O(l) + \tfrac{1}{2}O_2(g) \qquad \Delta H° = \Delta H_f°(2) + \left[-\Delta H_f°(1)\right]$

$$= -286\ kJ + (+188\ kJ)$$

$$= -98\ kJ$$

▢ We can use either heats of combustion or heats of formation for the reactants and products in Hess's law, but don't mix them. Use heats of combustion for all reactants and all products, *or* use heats of formation for all reactants and all products.

Thus, the desired $\Delta H°$ was obtained by subtracting the $\Delta H_f°$ for the reactant (H_2O_2) from the $\Delta H_f°$ for the product (H_2O). In fact, this works for *any* reaction where we know the heats of formation of all the reactants and products. So if we're working with heats of formation, Hess's law can be restated as follows: the net $\Delta H°_{reaction}$ equals the sum of the heats of formation of the products minus the sum of the heats of formation of the reactants, each $\Delta H_f°$ value multiplied by the appropriate coefficient given by the thermochemical equation. In other words, we can express Hess's law in the form of the **Hess's law equation.**

TOOLS

Hess's law equation

$$\Delta H°_{reaction} = \left(\begin{array}{c} \text{sum of } \Delta H_f° \text{ of all} \\ \text{of the products} \end{array}\right) - \left(\begin{array}{c} \text{sum of } \Delta H_f° \text{ of all} \\ \text{of the reactants} \end{array}\right) \qquad (6.14)$$

As long as we have access to a table of standard heats of formation, using Equation 6.14 avoids having to manipulate a series of thermochemical equations. Finding $\Delta H°_{reaction}$ reduces to performing arithmetic, as we see in the next example.

EXAMPLE 6.11
Using Hess's Law and Standard Enthalpies of Formation

Some chefs keep baking soda, $NaHCO_3$, handy to put out grease fires. When thrown on the fire, baking soda partly smothers the fire and the heat decomposes it to give CO_2, which further smothers the flame. The equation for the decomposition of $NaHCO_3$ is

$$2NaHCO_3(s) \longrightarrow Na_2CO_3(s) + H_2O(l) + CO_2(g)$$

Use the data in Table 6.2 to calculate the $\Delta H°$ for this reaction in kilojoules.

ANALYSIS: When values of $\Delta H_f°$ are available, Hess's law equation (Equation 6.14) is our basic tool for computing values of $\Delta H°$. We will calculate the sum of $\Delta H_f°$ for the products, and then the sum of $\Delta H_f°$ for the reactants. Then we will subtract the total $\Delta H_f°$ for the reactants from the total $\Delta H_f°$ for the products to calculate $\Delta H°_{reaction}$. For each of the reactants and products, we compute its $\Delta H°$ by multiplying its $\Delta H_f°$ (from Table 6.2) by its coefficient in the balanced chemical equation.

SOLUTION: First, let's set up the calculation using symbols for the quantities we will use.

$$\Delta H° = [1 \text{ mol } Na_2CO_3(s) \times \Delta H°_{f\,Na_2CO_3(s)} + 1 \text{ mol } H_2O(l) \times \Delta H°_{f\,H_2O(l)}$$
$$+ 1 \text{ mol } CO_2(g) \times \Delta H°_{f\,CO_2(g)}] - [2 \text{ mol } NaHCO_3(s) \times \Delta H°_{f\,NaHCO_3(s)}]$$

We now go to Table 6.2 to find the values of $\Delta H°_f$ for each substance *in its proper physical state*.

$$\Delta H° = \left[1 \text{ mol } Na_2CO_3 \times \left(\frac{-1131 \text{ kJ}}{\text{mol } Na_2CO_3} \right) + 1 \text{ mol } H_2O \times \left(\frac{-285.9 \text{ kJ}}{\text{mol } H_2O} \right) \right.$$
$$\left. + 1 \text{ mol } CO_2 \times \left(\frac{-393.5 \text{ kJ}}{\text{mol } CO_2} \right) \right] - \left[2 \text{ mol } NaHCO_3 \times \left(\frac{-947.7 \text{ kJ}}{\text{mol } NaHCO_3} \right) \right]$$

This reduces to

$$\Delta H° = (-1810 \text{ kJ}) - (-1895 \text{ kJ})$$
$$= +85 \text{ kJ}$$

Thus, under standard conditions, the reaction is endothermic by 85 kJ. (Notice that we did not have to manipulate any equations.)

IS THE ANSWER REASONABLE? Double-check that all of the coefficients found in the chemical equation are correctly applied as multipliers on the $\Delta H°_f$ quantities. Be sure that the *signs* of the values of $\Delta H°_f$ have all been carefully used. Keeping track of the algebraic signs requires particular care and is the greatest source of error in these calculations. Also check to be sure you've followed the correct order of subtraction specified in Equation 6.14. In other words, have you subtracted the $\Delta H°$ of the *reactants* from the $\Delta H°$ of the *products*?

Practice Exercise 18: Use heats of formation data from Table 6.2 to calculate $\Delta H°$ for this reaction: $CaCl_2(s) + H_2SO_4(l) \longrightarrow CaSO_4(s) + 2HCl(g)$. (Hint: Be sure to follow the correct order of subtraction.)

Practice Exercise 19: Write thermochemical equations corresponding to $\Delta H°_f$ for $SO_3(g)$ and $SO_2(g)$ and show how they can be manipulated to calculate $\Delta H°$ for the following reaction:

$$SO_3(g) \longrightarrow SO_2(g) + \tfrac{1}{2}O_2(g) \qquad \Delta H° = ?$$

Use Equation 6.14 to calculate $\Delta H°$ for the reaction using the heats of formation of $SO_3(g)$ and $SO_2(g)$. How do the answers compare?

Practice Exercise 20: Calculate $\Delta H°$ for the following reactions.
(a) $2NO(g) + O_2(g) \longrightarrow 2NO_2(g)$
(b) $NaOH(s) + HCl(g) \longrightarrow NaCl(s) + H_2O(l)$

SUMMARY

Introduction. Thermochemistry, which deals with energy absorbed or released in chemical reactions, is a part of **thermodynamics,** the study of energy transfer and energy transformation. **Heat** is energy **(thermal energy)** that transfers between objects having different temperatures. Heat continues to flow until the two objects come to the same temperature and **thermal equilibrium** is established.

Energy Is the Ability to Do Work or Supply Heat. An object has **kinetic energy (KE)** if it is moving ($KE = \frac{1}{2}mv^2$) and

potential energy (PE) when it experiences attractions or repulsions toward other objects. When objects that attract are moved apart, PE increases. Similarly, when objects that repel are pushed together, PE increases. Because electrical attractions and repulsions occur within atoms, molecules, and ions, substances have **chemical energy,** a form of **potential energy.** The particles that make up matter are in constant random motion, so they also possess kinetic energy, specifically, **molecular kinetic energy.** According to the **kinetic molecular theory,** the average molecular kinetic energy is directly proportional to the Kelvin temperature. The **law**

of conservation of energy states that energy can be neither created nor destroyed, but only changed from one form to another. The SI unit of energy is the **joule**; 4.184 J = 1 cal (calorie). Larger units are the **kilojoule (kJ)** and **kilocalorie (kcal,** which is the same as the nutritional Calorie).

Internal Energy and Temperature. The **state** of a system is the list of properties that describe its current condition. The **internal energy** of a system, E, is a **state function,** which is a property that depends only on the current state of the system. E equals the sum of the system's molecular kinetic and potential energies. A change in E is defined as $\Delta E = E_{final} - E_{initial}$, although absolute amounts of E cannot be measured or calculated. For a chemical reaction, the definition translates to $\Delta E = E_{products} - E_{reactants}$. A positive value for ΔE, which can be measured, means a system absorbs energy from its surroundings during a change.

Measuring Heat. The boundary across which heat is transferred encloses the **system** (the object we're interested in). Everything else in the universe is the system's **surroundings.** The heat flow q is related to the temperature change Δt by $q = C \Delta t$, where C is the **heat capacity** of the system (the heat needed to change the temperature of the system by one degree Celsius). The heat capacity for a pure substance can be computed from its mass, m, using the equation $C = ms$, where s is the **specific heat** of the material (the heat needed to change the temperature of 1 g of a substance by 1 °C). Water has an unusually high specific heat. We can compute a heat flow when we know the mass and specific heat of an object using the equation $q = ms \Delta t$. The heat, q, is given a positive sign when it flows into a system and a negative sign when it flows out.

Energy Changes when Bonds Are Formed or Broken. Bond breaking increases potential energy (chemical energy); bond formation decreases potential energy (chemical energy). In an **exothermic** reaction, chemical energy is changed to molecular kinetic energy. If the system is **adiabatic** (no heat leaves it), the internal temperature increases. Otherwise, the heat has a tendency to leave the system. In **endothermic** reactions, molecular kinetic energy of the reactants is converted into potential energy of the products. This tends to lower the system's temperature and lead to a flow of heat into the system.

Heats of Reaction. The change in chemical potential energy in a reaction is the **heat of reaction, q,** which can be measured at constant volume or constant pressure. Pressure is the ratio of force to the area over which the force is applied. **Atmospheric pressure** is the pressure exerted by the mixture of gases in our atmosphere. When a volume change, ΔV, occurs at constant opposing pressure, P, the associated **pressure–volume work (expansion work)** is given by $w = -P \Delta V$. The energy expended in doing this pressure–volume work causes heats of reaction measured at constant

volume (q_v) to differ numerically from heats measured at constant pressure (q_p).

The **first law of thermodynamics** says that no matter how the change in energy accompanying a reaction may be allocated between q and w, their sum, ΔE, is the same: $\Delta E = q + w$. The algebraic sign for q and w is negative when the system gives off heat to or does work on the surroundings. The sign is positive when the system absorbs heat or receives work energy done to it. When the volume of a system cannot change, as in a **bomb calorimeter,** w is zero, and q_v is the **heat of reaction at constant volume, ΔE.**

When the system is under conditions of constant pressure, the energy of the system is called its **enthalpy, H.** At constant pressure, $\Delta H = \Delta E + P \Delta V$. The **heat of reaction at constant pressure, q_p,** is the **enthalpy change, ΔH.** ΔH is a state function. Its value differs from that of ΔE by the work involved in interacting with the atmosphere when the change occurs at constant atmospheric pressure. In general, the difference between ΔE and ΔH is quite small. Exothermic reactions have negative values of ΔH; endothermic changes have positive values.

Thermochemical Equations. A balanced chemical equation that includes both the enthalpy change and the physical states of the substances is called a **thermochemical equation.** Coefficients in a thermochemical equation represent mole quantities of reactants and products. Such equations can be added, reversed (reversing also the sign of ΔH), or multiplied by a constant multiplier (doing the same to ΔH). If formulas are canceled or added, they must be of substances in identical physical states.

The reference conditions for thermochemistry, called **standard conditions,** are 25 °C and 1 bar of pressure. An enthalpy change measured under those conditions is called the **standard enthalpy of reaction** or the **standard heat of reaction,** given the symbol $\Delta H°$.

Hess's law of heat summation is possible because enthalpy is a state function. Values of $\Delta H°$ can be determined *by the manipulation of any combination of thermochemical equations that add up to the final net equation. The units for $\Delta H°$ are generally joules or kilojoules.* An **enthalpy diagram** provides a graphical description of the enthalpy changes for alternative paths from reactants to products.

When the enthalpy change is for the complete combustion of one mole of a pure substance under standard conditions in pure oxygen, $\Delta H°$ is called the **standard heat of combustion** of the compound, symbolized as $\Delta H°_c$.

When the enthalpy change is for the formation of *one* mole of a substance under standard conditions from its *elements in their standard states,* $\Delta H°$ is called the **standard heat of formation** of the compound, symbolized as $\Delta H°_f$ (usually in units of kilojoules per mole, kJ mol^{-1}). The value of $\Delta H°$ for a reaction can be calculated from tabulated values of $\Delta H°_f$ using the **Hess's law equation.**

TOOLS FOR PROBLEM SOLVING

In this chapter you learned to apply the following concepts as tools in solving problems. Study each one carefully so that you know what each is used for. When faced with solving a problem, recall what each tool does and consider whether it will be helpful in finding a solution. This will aid you in selecting the tools you need.

Kinetic energy *(page 208)* Kinetic energy (KE) can be calculated from an object's mass, m, and its speed or velocity, v, using Equation 6.1: $KE = \frac{1}{2}mv^2$.

Factors that affect potential energy *(page 209)* You should know how potential energy varies when the distance changes between objects that attract or repel.

Heat capacity *(page 214)* Heat capacity, C, provides a way of determining heat by measuring a temperature change. Its units are energy divided by temperature (e.g., $J\ °C^{-1}$).

$$q = C\,\Delta t$$

The value of C depends on sample size.

Specific heat capacity *(page 215)* Also called specific heat, s, specific heat capacity is an intensive property. When mass, m, and temperature change, Δt, are known, q is calculated by the equation

$$q = ms\,\Delta t$$

Heat transfer *(page 216)* When heat is transferred between two objects, the *size* of q is identical for both objects, but the algebraic signs of q are opposite.

$$q_1 = -q_2$$

First law of thermodynamics *(page 222)* This law relates energy transfer in the forms of heat, q, and work, w, to the internal energy change, ΔE.

$$\Delta E = q + w$$

The algebraic sign of ΔH *(page 225)* The sign of ΔH indicates the direction of energy flow.

For an endothermic change, ΔH is positive.

For an exothermic change, ΔH is negative.

Thermochemical equations *(page 228)* Thermochemical equations show enthalpy changes for reactions where the amounts of reactants and products in moles are represented by the coefficients. They can be manipulated and combined to determine heats of reactions for other reactions.

Enthalpy diagrams *(page 230)* We use enthalpy diagrams to provide a graphical picture of the enthalpy changes associated with a set of thermochemical equations that are combined to give some net reaction.

Hess's law *(page 232)* This law allows us to combine thermochemical equations to give a final desired equation and its associated $\Delta H°$. We adjust the coefficients and directions of the given equations, and make appropriate adjustments to their $\Delta H°$ values, so the equations add to give the desired equation. Adding the adjusted $\Delta H°$ values gives the $\Delta H°$ for the desired equation.

Manipulating thermochemical equations *(page 233)* Changing the direction of a reaction changes the sign of $\Delta H°$. When the coefficients are multiplied by a factor, the value of $\Delta H°$ is multiplied by the same factor. Formulas can be canceled only when the substances are in the same physical state. These rules are used in applying Hess's law.

Hess's law equation *(page 238)* We use this equation with standard heats of formation, $\Delta H_f°$, to calculate $\Delta H°$ for some desired equation.

$$\Delta H°_{reaction} = \left(\begin{array}{c} \text{sum of } \Delta H_f° \text{ of all} \\ \text{of the products} \end{array} \right) - \left(\begin{array}{c} \text{sum of } \Delta H_f° \text{ of all} \\ \text{of the reactants} \end{array} \right)$$

QUESTIONS, PROBLEMS, AND EXERCISES

Answers to problems whose numbers are printed in color are given in Appendix B. More challenging problems are marked with asterisks. ILW = Interactive Learningware solution is available at www.wiley.com/college/brady. OH = an Office Hours video is available for this problem.

REVIEW QUESTIONS

Kinetic and Potential Energy

6.1 Give definitions for (a) *energy* and (b) *work*.

6.2 Define (a) *kinetic energy* and (b) *potential energy*.

6.3 State the equation used to calculate an object's kinetic energy. Define the symbols used in the equation.

6.4 If a car increases its speed from 30 mph to 60 mph, by what factor does the kinetic energy of the car increase?

6.5 What is meant by the term *chemical energy*?

6.6 How does the potential energy change (increase, decrease, or no change) for each of the following?
(a) Two electrons come closer together.
(b) An electron and a proton become farther apart.
(c) Two atomic nuclei approach each other.
(d) A ball rolls downhill.

6.7 State the *law of conservation of energy*. Describe how it explains the motion of a child on a swing.

6.8 Define *heat*. How do *heat* and *temperature* differ?

6.9 On a molecular level, how is thermal equilibrium achieved when a hot object is placed in contact with a cold object?

6.10 What is the SI unit of energy? How much energy (in joules and in calories) does a 75 kg object have if it's moving at 45 m s^{-1}?

Internal Energy and the Kinetic Theory of Matter

6.11 How is internal energy related to molecular kinetic and potential energy? How is a *change* in internal energy defined for a chemical reaction?

6.12 Consider the distribution of molecular kinetic energies shown in the diagram below for a gas at 25 °C.

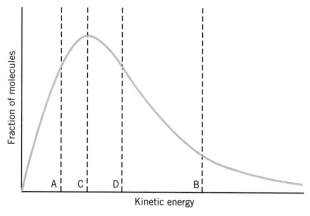

(a) Which point corresponds to the most frequently occurring (also called the most probable) molecular kinetic energy?
(b) Which point corresponds to the average molecular kinetic energy?
(c) If the temperature of the gas is raised to 50 °C, how will the height of the curve at B change?

(d) If the temperature of the gas is raised to 50 °C, how will the height of the curve at A change? How will the maximum height of the curve change?

6.13 Suppose the temperature of an object is raised from 100 °C to 200 °C by heating it with a Bunsen burner. Which of the following will be true?
(a) The average molecular kinetic energy will increase.
(b) The total kinetic energy of all the molecules will increase.
(c) The number of fast-moving molecules will increase.
(d) The number of slow-moving molecules will increase.
(e) The chemical potential energy will decrease.

6.14 A quart of boiling water will cause a more severe burn if it's spilled on you than just a drop of boiling water. Explain this in terms of the amounts of kinetic energy possessed by the water molecules in the two samples.

6.15 How can the *state* of a system be specified? What is a *state function*?

Experimental Measurement of Heat

6.16 What do the terms *system* and *surroundings* mean? What is the difference between an isolated system and a closed system?

6.17 What is the name of the thermal property whose values can have the following units?
(a) J g^{-1} °C^{-1} (b) J mol^{-1} °C^{-1} (c) J °C^{-1}

6.18 For samples with the same mass, which kind of substance needs more energy to undergo an increase of 5 °C, something with a *large* or with a *small* specific heat? Explain.

6.19 How do heat capacity and specific heat differ?

6.20 What is the meaning of a negative value for q?

6.21 Suppose object A has twice the specific heat and twice the mass of object B. If the same amount of heat is applied to both objects, how will the temperature change of A be related to the temperature change in B?

Energy Changes in Chemical Reactions

6.22 In a certain chemical reaction, there is a decrease in the potential energy (chemical energy) as the reaction proceeds.
(a) How does the total kinetic energy of the particles change?
(b) How does the temperature of the reaction mixture change?

6.23 What term do we use to describe a reaction that liberates heat to its surroundings? How does the chemical energy change during such a reaction? What is the algebraic sign of q for such a reaction?

6.24 What term is used to describe a reaction that absorbs heat from the surroundings? How does the chemical energy change during such a reaction? What is the algebraic sign of q for such a reaction?

6.25 Some instant cold packs sold in pharmacies contain a bag of water inside a pouch of ammonium nitrate, NH_4NO_3. When the bag of water is broken and the two substances mixed, the ammonium nitrate dissolves and the solution becomes quite cold. What happens to the average kinetic energy of the substances in the cold pack? What happens to the chemical energy of the water and ammonium nitrate?

6.26 When gasoline burns, it reacts with oxygen in the air and forms hot gases consisting of carbon dioxide and water vapor. How does the potential energy of the gasoline and oxygen compare with the potential energy of the carbon dioxide and water vapor?

6.27 Describe how the potential energy of the system of atomic-sized particles changes when each of the following events occurs.
(a) The wax of a candle burns in air, giving a yellow flame. (The system consists of the wax and O_2 in the air.)
(b) Ammonium nitrate dissolves in water to produce a cooling effect.

Internal Energy and Enthalpy

6.28 Write the equation that states the first law of thermodynamics. In your own words, what does this statement mean in terms of energy exchanges between a system and its surroundings?

6.29 How is *enthalpy* defined?

6.30 What is the *sign* of ΔH for an exothermic change?

6.31 If the enthalpy of a system increases by 100 kJ, what must be true about the enthalpy of the surroundings? Why?

6.32 When we measure the heat of combustion of glucose, $C_6H_{12}O_6$, in a bomb calorimeter, what products are formed in the reaction? Is the heat we measure equal to ΔE or ΔH?

6.33 If a system containing gases expands and pushes back a piston against a constant opposing pressure, what equation describes the work done on the system?

6.34 Consider the reaction

$$C_{12}H_{22}O_{11}(s) + 12O_2(g) \longrightarrow 12CO_2(g) + 11H_2O(l)$$

Are the values of ΔE and ΔH expected to be appreciably different?

Enthalpy and Heats of Reaction

6.35 Why do standard reference values for temperature and pressure have to be selected when we consider and compare heats of reaction for various reactions? What are the values for the standard temperature and standard pressure?

6.36 What distinguishes a *thermochemical* equation from an ordinary chemical equation?

6.37 Why are fractional coefficients permitted in a balanced thermochemical equation? If a formula in a thermochemical equation has a coefficient of $\frac{1}{2}$, what does it signify?

Hess's Law

6.38 What fundamental fact about ΔH makes Hess's law possible?

6.39 What *two* conditions must be met by a thermochemical equation so that its standard enthalpy change can be given the symbol ΔH_f°?

6.40 What is Hess's law expressed in terms of standard heats of formation?

REVIEW PROBLEMS

First Law of Thermodynamics

6.41 If a system does 45 J of work and receives 28 J of heat, what is the value of ΔE for this change?

6.42 If a system absorbs 48 J of heat and does 22 J of work, what is the value of ΔE for this change?

6.43 An automobile engine converts heat into work via a cycle. The cycle must finish exactly where it started, so the energy at the start of the cycle must be exactly the same as the energy at the end of the cycle. If the engine is to do 100 J of work per cycle, how much heat must it absorb?

6.44 If the engine in the previous problem absorbs 250 joules of heat per cycle, how much work can it do per cycle?

Thermal Properties, Measuring Energy Changes

6.45 How much heat, in joules and in calories, must be removed from 1.75 mol of water to lower its temperature from 25.0 to 15.0 °C?

OH **6.46** How many grams of water can be heated from 25.0 °C to 35.0 °C by the heat released from 85.0 g of iron that cools from 85.0 °C to 30.0 °C?

6.47 A 5.00 g mass of a metal was heated to 100.0 °C and then plunged into 100.0 g of water at 24.0 °C. The temperature of the resulting mixture became 28.0 °C.
(a) How many joules did the water absorb?
(b) How many joules did the metal lose?
(c) What is the heat capacity of the metal sample?
(d) What is the specific heat of the metal?

6.48 A sample of copper was heated to 120.00 °C and then thrust into 200.0 g of water at 25.00 °C. The temperature of the mixture became 26.50 °C.
(a) How much heat in joules was absorbed by the water?
(b) The copper sample lost how many joules?
(c) What was the mass in grams of the copper sample?

OH **6.49** Calculate the molar heat capacity of iron in J mol^{-1} °C^{-1}. Its specific heat is 0.4498 J g^{-1} °C^{-1}.

6.50 What is the molar heat capacity of ethyl alcohol, C_2H_5OH, in units of J mol^{-1} °C^{-1}, if its specific heat is 0.586 cal g^{-1} °C^{-1}?

Calorimetry

6.51 A vat of 4.54 kg of water underwent a decrease in temperature from 60.25 to 58.65 °C. How much energy in kilojoules left the water? (For this range of temperature, use a value of 4.18 J g^{-1} °C^{-1} for the specific heat of water.)

6.52 A container filled with 2.46 kg of water underwent a temperature change from 25.24 °C to 27.31 °C. How much heat, measured in kilojoules, did the water absorb? (The specific heat of water is 4.18 J g^{-1} °C^{-1}.)

OH **6.53** Nitric acid neutralizes potassium hydroxide. To determine the heat of reaction, a student placed 55.0 mL of 1.3 M HNO$_3$ in a coffee cup calorimeter, noted that the temperature was 23.5 °C, and added 55.0 mL of 1.3 M KOH, also at 23.5 °C. The mixture was stirred quickly with a thermometer, and its temperature rose to 31.8 °C. Write the balanced equation for the reaction. Calculate the heat of reaction in joules. Assume that the specific heats of all solutions are 4.18 J g^{-1} °C^{-1} and that all densities are 1.00 g mL^{-1}. Calculate the heat of reaction per mole of acid (in units of kJ mol^{-1}).

6.54 A dilute solution of hydrochloric acid with a mass of 610.29 g and containing 0.33183 mol of HCl was exactly neutralized in a calorimeter by the sodium hydroxide in 615.31 g of a dilute NaOH solution. The temperature increased from 16.784 to 20.610 °C. The specific heat of the HCl solution was 4.031 J g^{-1} °C^{-1}; that of the NaOH solution was 4.046 J g^{-1} °C^{-1}. The heat capacity of the calorimeter was 77.99 J °C^{-1}. Write the balanced equation for the reaction. Use the data above to calculate the heat evolved. What is the heat of neutralization per mole of HCl? Assume that the original solutions made independent contributions to the total heat capacity of the system following their mixing.

6.55 A 1.00 mol sample of propane, a gas used for cooking in many rural areas, was placed in a bomb calorimeter with excess oxygen and ignited. The initial temperature of the calorimeter was 25.000 °C and its total heat capacity was 97.1 kJ °C^{-1}. The reaction raised the temperature of the calorimeter to 27.282 °C.
(a) Write the balanced chemical equation for the reaction in the calorimeter.
(b) How many joules were liberated in this reaction?
(c) What is the heat of reaction of propane with oxygen expressed in kilojoules per mole of C_3H_8 burned?

6.56 Toluene, C_7H_8, is used in the manufacture of explosives such as TNT (trinitrotoluene). A 1.500 g sample of liquid toluene was placed in a bomb calorimeter along with excess oxygen. When the combustion of the toluene was initiated, the temperature of the calorimeter rose from 25.000 °C to 26.413 °C. The products of the combustion are $CO_2(g)$ and $H_2O(l)$, and the heat capacity of the calorimeter was 45.06 kJ °C^{-1}.
(a) Write the balanced chemical equation for the reaction in the calorimeter.
(b) How many joules were liberated by the reaction?
(c) How many joules would be liberated under similar conditions if 1.00 mol of toluene were burned?

Enthalpy Changes and Heats of Reaction

6.57 One thermochemical equation for the reaction of carbon monoxide with oxygen is

$$3CO(g) + \tfrac{3}{2}O_2(g) \longrightarrow 3CO_2(g) \qquad \Delta H° = -849 \text{ kJ}$$

(a) Write the thermochemical equation for the reaction using 2 mol of CO.
(b) What is $\Delta H°$ for the formation of 1 mol of CO_2 by this reaction?

OH 6.58 Ammonia reacts with oxygen as follows.

$$4NH_3(g) + 7O_2(g) \longrightarrow 4NO_2(g) + 6H_2O(g)$$
$$\Delta H° = -1132 \text{ kJ}$$

(a) Calculate the enthalpy change for the combustion of 1 mol of NH_3.
(b) Write the thermochemical equation for the reaction in which one mole of H_2O is formed.

6.59 Magnesium burns in air to produce a bright light and is often used in fireworks displays. The combustion of magnesium follows the thermochemical equation

$$2Mg(s) + O_2(g) \longrightarrow 2MgO(s) \qquad \Delta H° = -1203 \text{ kJ}$$

How much heat (in kilojoules) is liberated by the combustion of 6.54 g of magnesium?

6.60 Methanol is the fuel in "canned heat" containers (e.g., Sterno) that are used to heat foods at cocktail parties. The combustion of methanol follows the thermochemical equation

$$2CH_3OH(l) + 3O_2(g) \longrightarrow 2CO_2(g) + 4H_2O(g)$$
$$\Delta H° = -1199 \text{ kJ}$$

How many kilojoules are liberated by the combustion of 46.0 g of methanol?

Hess's Law

6.61 Construct an enthalpy diagram that shows the enthalpy changes for a one-step conversion of germanium, Ge(s), into $GeO_2(s)$, the dioxide. On the same diagram, show the two-step process, first to the monoxide, GeO(s), and then its conversion to the dioxide. The relevant thermochemical equations are the following.

$$Ge(s) + \tfrac{1}{2}O_2(g) \longrightarrow GeO(s) \qquad \Delta H° = -255 \text{ kJ}$$

$$Ge(s) + O_2(g) \longrightarrow GeO_2(s) \qquad \Delta H° = -534.7 \text{ kJ}$$

Using this diagram, determine $\Delta H°$ for the following reaction.

$$GeO(s) + \tfrac{1}{2}O_2(g) \longrightarrow GeO(s)$$

6.62 Construct an enthalpy diagram for the formation of $NO_2(g)$ from its elements by two pathways: first, from its elements and, second, by a two-step process, also from the elements. The relevant thermochemical equations are

$$\tfrac{1}{2}N_2(g) + O_2(g) \longrightarrow NO_2(g) \qquad \Delta H° = +33.8 \text{ kJ}$$

$$\tfrac{1}{2}N_2(g) + \tfrac{1}{2}O_2(g) \longrightarrow NO(g) \qquad \Delta H° = +90.37 \text{ kJ}$$

$$NO(g) + \tfrac{1}{2}O_2(g) \longrightarrow NO_2(g) \qquad \Delta H° = ?$$

Be sure to note the signs of the values of $\Delta H°$ associated with arrows pointing up or down. Using the diagram, determine the value of $\Delta H°$ for the third equation.

6.63 Show how the equations

$$N_2O_4(g) \longrightarrow 2NO_2(g) \qquad \Delta H° = +57.93 \text{ kJ}$$

$$2NO(g) + O_2(g) \longrightarrow 2NO_2(g) \qquad \Delta H° = -113.14 \text{ kJ}$$

can be manipulated to give $\Delta H°$ for the following reaction.

$$2NO(g) + O_2(g) \longrightarrow N_2O_4(g)$$

6.64 We can generate hydrogen chloride by heating a mixture of sulfuric acid and potassium chloride according to the equation

$$2KCl(s) + H_2SO_4(l) \longrightarrow 2HCl(g) + K_2SO_4(s)$$

Calculate $\Delta H°$ in kilojoules for this reaction from the following thermochemical equations.

$$HCl(g) + KOH(s) \longrightarrow KCl(s) + H_2O(l) \quad \Delta H° = -203.6 \text{ kJ}$$

$$H_2SO_4(l) + 2KOH(s) \longrightarrow K_2SO_4(s) + 2H_2O(l)$$
$$\Delta H° = -342.4 \text{ kJ}$$

6.65 Calculate $\Delta H°$ in kilojoules for the following reaction, the preparation of the unstable acid nitrous acid, HNO_2.

$$HCl(g) + NaNO_2(s) \longrightarrow HNO_2(l) + NaCl(s)$$

Use the following thermochemical equations.

$$2NaCl(s) + H_2O(l) \longrightarrow 2HCl(g) + Na_2O(s)$$
$$\Delta H° = +507.31 \text{ kJ}$$

$NO(g) + NO_2(g) + Na_2O(s) \longrightarrow 2NaNO_2(s)$
$$\Delta H° = -427.14 \text{ kJ}$$

$NO(g) + NO_2(g) \longrightarrow N_2O(g) + O_2(g)$
$$\Delta H° = -42.68 \text{ kJ}$$

$2HNO_2(l) \longrightarrow N_2O(g) + O_2(g) + H_2O(l)$
$$\Delta H° = +34.35 \text{ kJ}$$

6.66 Calcium hydroxide reacts with hydrochloric acid by the following equation.

$$Ca(OH)_2(aq) + 2HCl(aq) \longrightarrow CaCl_2(aq) + 2H_2O(l)$$

Calculate $\Delta H°$ in kilojoules for this reaction, using the following equations as needed.

$CaO(s) + 2HCl(aq) \longrightarrow CaCl_2(aq) + H_2O(l)$
$$\Delta H° = -186 \text{ kJ}$$

$CaO(s) + H_2O(l) \longrightarrow Ca(OH)_2(s)$ $\quad \Delta H° = -65.1 \text{ kJ}$

$Ca(OH)_2(s) \xrightarrow{\text{dissolving in water}} Ca(OH)_2(aq)$ $\quad \Delta H° = -12.6 \text{ kJ}$

6.67 Given the following thermochemical equations:

$CaO(s) + Cl_2(g) \longrightarrow CaOCl_2(s)$ $\quad \Delta H° = -110.9 \text{ kJ}$

$H_2O(l) + CaOCl_2(s) + 2NaBr(s) \longrightarrow$
$2NaCl(s) + Ca(OH)_2(s) + Br_2(l)$ $\quad \Delta H° = -60.2 \text{ kJ}$

$Ca(OH)_2(s) \longrightarrow CaO(s) + H_2O(l)$ $\quad \Delta H° = +65.1 \text{ kJ}$

calculate the value of $\Delta H°$ (in kilojoules) for the reaction

$$\tfrac{1}{2}Cl_2(g) + NaBr(s) \longrightarrow NaCl(s) + \tfrac{1}{2}Br_2(l)$$

6.68 Given the following thermochemical equations:

$2Cu(s) + S(s) \longrightarrow Cu_2S(s)$ $\quad \Delta H° = -79.5 \text{ kJ}$

$S(s) + O_2(g) \longrightarrow SO_2(g)$ $\quad \Delta H° = -297 \text{ kJ}$

$Cu_2S(s) + 2O_2(g) \longrightarrow 2CuO(s) + SO_2(g)$ $\quad \Delta H° = -527.5 \text{ kJ}$

calculate the standard enthalpy of formation (in kilojoules per mole) of $CuO(s)$.

6.69 Given the following thermochemical equations:

$4NH_3(g) + 7O_2(g) \longrightarrow 4NO_2(g) + 6H_2O(g)$
$$\Delta H° = -1132 \text{ kJ}$$

$6NO_2(g) + 8NH_3(g) \longrightarrow 7N_2(g) + 12H_2O(g)$
$$\Delta H° = -2740 \text{ kJ}$$

calculate the value of $\Delta H°$ (in kilojoules) for the reaction

$$4NH_3(g) + 3O_2(g) \longrightarrow 2N_2(g) + 6H_2O(g)$$

OH 6.70 Given the following thermochemical equations:

$3Mg(s) + 2NH_3(g) \longrightarrow Mg_3N_2(s) + 3H_2(g)$
$$\Delta H° = -371 \text{ kJ}$$

$\tfrac{1}{2}N_2(g) + \tfrac{3}{2}H_2(g) \longrightarrow NH_3(g)$ $\quad \Delta H° = -46 \text{ kJ}$

calculate $\Delta H°$ (in kilojoules) for the following reaction.

$$3Mg(s) + N_2(g) \longrightarrow Mg_3N_2(s)$$

Hess's Law and Standard Heats of Formation

6.71 Write the thermochemical equations, including values of $\Delta H_f°$ in kilojoules per mole (from Table 6.2), for the formation of

each of the following compounds from their elements, everything in standard states.
(a) $HC_2H_3O_2(l)$, acetic acid
(b) $C_2H_5OH(l)$, ethyl alcohol
(c) $CaSO_4 \cdot 2H_2O(s)$, gypsum

6.72 Write the thermochemical equations, including values of $\Delta H_f°$ in kilojoules per mole (from Appendix C), for the formation of each of the following compounds from their elements, everything in standard states.
(a) $MgCl_2 \cdot 2H_2O(s)$
(b) $(NH_4)_2Cr_2O_7(s)$
(c) $POCl_3(g)$

OH 6.73 Using data in Table 6.2, calculate $\Delta H°$ in kilojoules for the following reactions.
(a) $2H_2O_2(l) \longrightarrow 2H_2O(l) + O_2(g)$
(b) $HCl(g) + NaOH(s) \longrightarrow NaCl(s) + H_2O(l)$

6.74 Using data in Table 6.2, calculate $\Delta H°$ in kilojoules for the following reactions.
(a) $CH_4(g) + Cl_2(g) \longrightarrow CH_3Cl(g) + HCl(g)$
(b) $2NH_3(g) + CO_2(g) \longrightarrow CO(NH_2)_2(s) + H_2O(l)$

6.75 The enthalpy change for the combustion of *one* mole of a compound under standard conditions is called the standard heat of combustion, and its symbol is $\Delta H_c°$. The value for sucrose, $C_{12}H_{22}O_{11}$, is $-5.65 \times 10^3 \text{ kJ mol}^{-1}$. Write the thermochemical equation for the combustion of 1 mol of sucrose and calculate the value of $\Delta H_f°$ for this compound. The sole products of combustion are $CO_2(g)$ and $H_2O(l)$. Use data in Table 6.2 as necessary.

6.76 The thermochemical equation for the combustion of acetylene gas, $C_2H_2(g)$, is

$2C_2H_2(g) + 5O_2(g) \longrightarrow 4CO_2(g) + 2H_2O(l)$
$$\Delta H° = -2599.3 \text{ kJ}$$

Using data in Table 6.2, determine the value of $\Delta H_f°$ for acetylene gas.

ADDITIONAL EXERCISES

*__6.77__ A 2.00 kg piece of granite with a specific heat of $0.803 \text{ J g}^{-1} °C^{-1}$ and a temperature of 95.0 °C is placed into 2.00 L of water at 22.0 °C. When the granite and water come to the same temperature, what will that temperature be?

6.78 In the recovery of iron from iron ore, the reduction of the ore is actually accomplished by reactions involving carbon monoxide. Use the following thermochemical equations:

$Fe_2O_3(s) + 3CO(g) \longrightarrow 2Fe(s) + 3CO_2(g)$ $\quad \Delta H° = -28 \text{ kJ}$

$3Fe_2O_3(s) + CO(g) \longrightarrow 2Fe_3O_4(s) + CO_2(g)$
$$\Delta H° = -59 \text{ kJ}$$

$Fe_3O_4(s) + CO(g) \longrightarrow 3FeO(s) + CO_2(g)$ $\quad \Delta H° = +38 \text{ kJ}$

to calculate $\Delta H°$ for the reaction

$$FeO(s) + CO(g) \longrightarrow Fe(s) + CO_2(g)$$

6.79 Use the results of Problem 6.78 and data in Table 6.2 to calculate the value of $\Delta H_f°$ for FeO. Express the answer in units of kilojoules per mole.

6.80 The amino acid glycine, $C_2H_5NO_2$, is one of the compounds used by the body to make proteins. The equation for its combustion is

$$4C_2H_5NO_2(s) + 9O_2(g) \longrightarrow 8CO_2(g) + 10H_2O(l) + 2N_2(g)$$

For each mole of glycine that burns, 973.49 kJ of heat is liberated. Use this information plus values of ΔH_f° for the products of combustion to calculate ΔH_f° for glycine.

6.81 The value of ΔH_f° for HBr(g) was first evaluated using the following standard enthalpy values obtained experimentally. Use these data to calculate the value of ΔH_f° for HBr(g).

$$Cl_2(g) + 2KBr(aq) \longrightarrow Br_2(aq) + 2KCl(aq)$$
$$\Delta H^\circ = -96.2 \text{ kJ}$$

$$H_2(g) + Cl_2(g) \longrightarrow 2HCl(g) \qquad \Delta H^\circ = -184 \text{ kJ}$$

$$HCl(aq) + KOH(aq) \longrightarrow KCl(aq) + H_2O(l)$$
$$\Delta H^\circ = -57.3 \text{ kJ}$$

$$HBr(aq) + KOH(aq) \longrightarrow KBr(aq) + H_2O(l)$$
$$\Delta H^\circ = -57.3 \text{ kJ}$$

$$HCl(g) \xrightarrow[\text{dissolving in water}]{} HCl(aq) \qquad \Delta H^\circ = -77.0 \text{ kJ}$$

$$Br_2(l) \xrightarrow[\text{dissolving in water}]{} Br_2(aq) \qquad \Delta H^\circ = -4.2 \text{ kJ}$$

$$HBr(g) \xrightarrow[\text{dissolving in water}]{} HBr(aq) \qquad \Delta H^\circ = -79.9 \text{ kJ}$$

*6.82 Acetylene, C_2H_2, is a gas commonly used in welding. It is formed in the reaction of calcium carbide, CaC_2, with water. Given the thermochemical equations below, calculate the value of ΔH_f° for acetylene in units of kilojoules per mole.

$$CaO(s) + H_2O(l) \longrightarrow Ca(OH)_2(s) \qquad \Delta H^\circ = -65.3 \text{ kJ}$$

$$CaO(s) + 3C(s) \longrightarrow CaC_2(s) + CO(g) \qquad \Delta H^\circ = +462.3 \text{ kJ}$$

$$CaCO_3(s) \longrightarrow CaO(s) + CO_2(g) \qquad \Delta H^\circ = +178 \text{ kJ}$$

$$CaC_2(s) + 2H_2O(l) \longrightarrow Ca(OH)_2(s) + C_2H_2(g)$$
$$\Delta H^\circ = -126 \text{ kJ}$$

$$2C(s) + O_2(g) \longrightarrow 2CO(g) \qquad \Delta H^\circ = -220 \text{ kJ}$$

$$2H_2O(l) \longrightarrow 2H_2(g) + O_2(g) \qquad \Delta H^\circ = +572 \text{ kJ}$$

OH 6.83 The reaction for the metabolism of sucrose, $C_{12}H_{22}O_{11}$, is the same as for its combustion in oxygen to yield $CO_2(g)$ and $H_2O(l)$. The standard heat of formation of sucrose is $-2230 \text{ kJ mol}^{-1}$. Use data in Table 6.2 to compute the amount of energy (in kJ) released by metabolizing 1 oz (28.3 g) of sucrose.

*6.84 For ethanol, C_2H_5OH, which is mixed with gasoline to make the fuel gasohol, $\Delta H_f^\circ = -277.63 \text{ kJ/mol}$. Calculate the number of kilojoules released by burning completely 1 gallon of ethanol. The density of ethanol is 0.787 g cm^{-3}. Use data in Table 6.2 to help in the computation.

6.85 Consider the following thermochemical equations:

$$\text{(1) } CH_3OH(l) + O_2(g) \longrightarrow HCHO_2(l) + H_2O(l)$$
$$\Delta H^\circ = -411 \text{ kJ}$$

$$\text{(2) } CO(g) + 2H_2(g) \longrightarrow CH_3OH(l) \qquad \Delta H^\circ = -128 \text{ kJ}$$

$$\text{(3) } HCHO_2(l) \longrightarrow CO(g) + H_2O(l) \qquad \Delta H^\circ = -33 \text{ kJ}$$

Suppose Equation (1) is reversed and divided by 2, Equations (2) and (3) are multiplied by $\frac{1}{2}$, and then the three adjusted equations are added. What is the net reaction, and what is the value of ΔH° for the net reaction?

6.86 Chlorofluoromethanes (CFMs) are carbon compounds of chlorine and fluorine and are also known as Freons. Examples are Freon-11 ($CFCl_3$) and Freon-12 (CF_2Cl_2), which have been used as aerosol propellants. Freons have also been used in refrigeration and air-conditioning systems. It is feared that as these Freons escape into the atmosphere they will lead to a significant depletion of ozone from the upper atmosphere where ozone protects the earth's inhabitants from harmful ultraviolet radiation. In the stratosphere CFMs absorb high-energy radiation from the sun and split off chlorine atoms that hasten the decomposition of ozone, O_3. Possible reactions are

$$\text{(1) } O_3(g) + Cl(g) \longrightarrow O_2(g) + ClO(g)$$
$$\Delta H^\circ = -126 \text{ kJ}$$

$$\text{(2) } ClO(g) + O(g) \longrightarrow Cl(g) + O_2(g)$$
$$\Delta H^\circ = -268 \text{ kJ}$$

$$\text{(3) } O_3(g) + O(g) \longrightarrow 2O_2(g)$$

The O atoms in Equation 2 come from the breaking apart of O_2 molecules caused by radiation from the sun. Use Equations 1 and 2 to calculate the value of ΔH° (in kilojoules) for Equation 3, the net reaction for the removal of O_3 from the atmosphere.

6.87 Suppose a truck with a mass of 14.0 tons (1 ton = 2000 lb) is traveling at a speed of 45.0 mi/hr. If the truck driver slams on the brakes, the kinetic energy of the truck is changed to heat as the brakes slow the truck to a stop. How much would the temperature of 5.00 gallons of water increase if all the heat could be absorbed by the water?

EXERCISES IN CRITICAL THINKING

6.88 Suppose we compress a spring, tie it up tightly, and then dissolve the spring in acid. What happens to the potential energy contained in the compressed spring? How could you measure it?

6.89 Carefully and precisely describe the difference between H, ΔH, and ΔH°.

6.90 Why do we usually use ΔH° rather than ΔE° when we discuss energies of reaction? Develop an argument for using ΔE° instead.

6.91 Explain why we can never determine values for E or H. Make a list of the factors we would need to know to determine E or H.

6.92 Find the heats of formation of some compounds that are explosives. What do they have in common? Compare them to the ΔH_f° values of stable compounds such as H_2O, $NaCl$, and $CaCO_3$. Formulate a generalization to summarize your observations.

We pause again to allow you to test your understanding of concepts, your knowledge of scientific terms, and your skills at solving chemistry problems. Read through the following questions carefully, and answer each as fully as possible. When necessary, review topics you are uncertain of. If you can answer these questions correctly, you are ready to go on to the next group of chapters.

1. What is the difference between a strong electrolyte and a weak electrolyte? Formic acid, $HCHO_2$, is a weak acid. Write a chemical equation showing its reaction with water.

2. Write an equation showing the reaction of water with itself to form ions.

3. Methylamine, CH_3NH_2, is a weak base. Write a chemical equation showing its reaction with water.

4. Write molecular, ionic, and net ionic equations for the reaction that occurs when a solution containing hydrochloric acid is added to a solution of the weak base methylamine (CH_3NH_2).

5. According to the solubility rules, which of the following salts would be classified as soluble?
    (a) $Ca_3(PO_4)_2$ (f) $Au(ClO_4)_3$ (k) $ZnSO_4$
    (b) $Ni(OH)_2$ (g) $Cu(C_2H_3O_2)_2$ (l) Na_2S
    (c) $(NH_4)_2HPO_4$ (h) $AgBr$ (m) $CoCO_3$
    (d) $SnCl_2$ (i) KOH (n) $BaSO_3$
    (e) $Sr(NO_3)_2$ (j) Hg_2Cl_2 (o) MnS

6. What are the two criteria that must be met for an ionic equation to be balanced correctly?

7. Write molecular, ionic, and net ionic equations for any reactions that would occur between the following pairs of compounds. If no reaction occurs, write "N.R."
    (a) $CuCl_2(aq)$ and $(NH_4)_2CO_3(aq)$
    (b) $HCl(aq)$ and $MgCO_3(s)$
    (c) $ZnCl_2(aq)$ and $AgC_2H_3O_2(aq)$
    (d) $HClO_4(aq)$ and $NaCHO_2(aq)$
    (e) $MnO(s)$ and $H_2SO_4(aq)$
    (f) $FeS(s)$ and $HCl(aq)$

8. Write a chemical equation for the complete neutralization of H_3PO_4 by $NaOH$.

9. Which ion exists in abundance in all solutions of strong acids?

10. Which ion makes a solution basic?

11. Define *monoprotic acid, diprotic acid,* and *polyprotic acid.* What is the general definition of a *salt*?

12. Which of the following oxides are acidic and which are basic: P_4O_6, Na_2O, SeO_3, CaO, PbO, and SO_2?

13. Write the formulas of any acid salts that could be formed by the reaction of the following acids with potassium hydroxide.
    (a) sulfurous acid
    (b) nitric acid
    (c) hypochlorous acid
    (d) phosphoric acid
    (e) carbonic acid

14. Name the following
    (a) HIO_3 (d) $Ca(H_2PO_4)_2$
    (b) $HOBr$ (e) $Fe(HSO_4)_3$
    (c) HNO_2

15. Write formulas for the following:
    (a) bromous acid
    (b) hypoiodous acid
    (c) sodium dihydrogen phosphate

    (d) lithium hydrogen sulfate
    (e) bromic acid

16. How many milliliters of $0.200\ M$ $BaCl_2$ must be added to 27.0 mL of $0.600\ M$ Na_2SO_4 to give a complete reaction between their solutes?

17. What mass of $Mg(OH)_2$ will be formed when 30.0 mL of $0.200\ M$ $MgCl_2$ solution is mixed with 25.0 mL of $0.420\ M$ $NaOH$ solution? What will be the molar concentrations of the ions remaining in solution?

18. How many milliliters of $6.00\ M$ HNO_3 must be added to 200 mL of water to give $0.150\ M$ HNO_3?

19. How many grams of CO_2 must be dissolved in 300 mL of $0.100\ M$ Na_2CO_3 solution to change the solute entirely into $NaHCO_3$?

20. A certain toilet cleaner uses $NaHSO_4$ as its active ingredient. In an analysis, 0.500 g of the cleaner was dissolved in 30.0 mL of distilled water and required 24.60 mL of $0.105\ M$ $NaOH$ for complete neutralization in a titration. What was the percentage by weight of $NaHSO_4$ in the cleaner?

21. A volume of 28.50 mL of a freshly prepared solution of KOH was required to titrate 50.00 mL of $0.0922\ M$ HCl solution. What was the molarity of the KOH solution?

22. To neutralize the acid in 10.0 mL of $18.0\ M$ H_2SO_4 that was accidentally spilled on a laboratory bench top, solid sodium bicarbonate was used. The container of sodium bicarbonate was known to weigh 155.0 g before this use and out of curiosity its mass was measured as 144.5 g afterward. The reaction forms sodium sulfate. Was sufficient sodium bicarbonate used? Determine the limiting reactant and calculate the maximum yield in grams of sodium sulfate.

23. How many milliliters of concentrated sulfuric acid $(18.0\ M)$ are needed to prepare 125 mL of $0.144\ M$ H_2SO_4?

24. The density of concentrated phosphoric acid solution is 1.689 g solution/mL solution at 20 °C. It contains 144 g H_3PO_4 per 1.00×10^2 mL of solution.
    (a) Calculate the molar concentration of H_3PO_4 in this solution.
    (b) Calculate the number of grams of this solution required to hold 50.0 g H_3PO_4.

25. A mixture consists of lithium carbonate (Li_2CO_3) and potassium carbonate (K_2CO_3). These react with hydrochloric acid as follows.

$$Li_2CO_3(s) + 2HCl(aq) \longrightarrow 2LiCl(aq) + H_2O + CO_2(g)$$

$$K_2CO_3(s) + 2HCl(aq) \longrightarrow 2KCl(aq) + H_2O + CO_2(g)$$

When 4.43 g of this mixture was analyzed, it consumed 53.2 mL of $1.48\ M$ HCl. Calculate the number of grams of each carbonate and their percentages.

26. One way to prepare iodine is to react sodium iodate, $NaIO_3$, with hydroiodic acid, HI. The following reaction occurs.

$$NaIO_3 + 6HI \longrightarrow 3I_2 + NaI + 3H_2O$$

Calculate the number of moles and the number of grams of iodine that can be made this way from 16.4 g of $NaIO_3$.

27. A white solid was known to be the anhydrous form of either sodium carbonate or sodium bicarbonate. Both react with hydrochloric acid to give sodium chloride, water, and carbon dioxide, but the mole proportions are not the same.
    (a) Write the balanced equation for each reaction.
    (b) It was found that 0.5128 g of the solid reacted with 47.80 mL of 0.2024 M HCl, and that the addition of more acid caused the formation of no more carbon dioxide. Perform the calculations that establish which substance the unknown solid was.

28. Assign oxidation numbers to the atoms in the following formulas: (a) As_4, (b) $HClO_2$, (c) $MnCl_2$, and (d) $V_2(SO_3)_3$.

29. For the following unbalanced equations, write the reactants and products in the form they should appear in an ionic equation. Then write balanced net ionic equations by applying the ion–electron method.
    (a) $K_2Cr_2O_7 + HCl \longrightarrow KCl + Cl_2 + H_2O + CrCl_3$
    (b) $KOH + SO_2(aq) + KMnO_4 \longrightarrow$
    $$K_2SO_4 + MnO_2 + H_2O$$

30. Balance the following equations by the ion–electron method for *acidic solutions*.
    (a) $Cr_2O_7^{2-} + Br^- \longrightarrow Br_2 + Cr^{3+}$
    (b) $H_3AsO_3 + MnO_4^- \longrightarrow H_2AsO_4^- + Mn^{2+}$

31. Balance the following equations by the ion–electron method for *basic solutions*.
    (a) $I^- + CrO_4^{2-} \longrightarrow CrO_2^- + IO_3^-$
    (b) $SO_2 + MnO_4^- \longrightarrow MnO_2 + SO_4^{2-}$

32. In the previous two questions, identify the oxidizing agents and reducing agents.

33. Complete and balance the following equations if a reaction occurs.
    (a) $Sn(s) + HCl(aq) \longrightarrow$
    (b) $Cu(s) + HNO_3$ (conc.) $\longrightarrow$
    (c) $Zn(s) + Cu^{2+}(aq) \longrightarrow$
    (d) $Ag(s) + Cu^{2+}(aq) \longrightarrow$

34. Write a balanced chemical equation for the combustion of cetane, $C_{16}H_{34}$, a hydrocarbon present in diesel fuel, (a) in the presence of excess oxygen, (b) in a somewhat limited supply of oxygen, and (c) in a severely limited supply of oxygen.

35. Stearic acid, $C_{17}H_{35}CO_2H$, is derived from animal fat. Write a balanced chemical equation for the combustion of stearic acid in an abundant supply of oxygen.

36. Methanethiol, CH_3SH, is a foul-smelling gas produced in the intestinal tract by bacteria acting on albumin in the absence of air. Write a chemical equation for the combustion of CH_3SH in an excess supply of oxygen.

37. Why is $KMnO_4$ such a useful laboratory oxidizing agent? Write half-reactions for the reduction of MnO_4^- in (a) acidic solution and (b) basic solution.

38. Write molecular equations for the reaction of O_2 with (a) magnesium, (b) aluminum, (c) phosphorus, and (d) sulfur.

39. *Bordeaux mixture* is traditionally prepared by mixing copper sulfate and calcium hydroxide in water. The resulting suspension of copper hydroxide is sprayed on trees and shrubs to fight fungus diseases. This fungicide is also available in commercial preparations. In an analysis of one such product, a sample weighing 0.238 g was dissolved in hydrochloric acid. Excess KI solution was then added, forming copper (I) iodide

and iodine, and the iodine that was formed was titrated with 0.01669 M $Na_2S_2O_3$ solution using starch as an indicator. The titration required 28.62 mL of the thiosulfate solution. What was the percentage by weight of copper in the sample of Bordeaux mixture?

40. An aluminum ball 0.500 cm in diameter is to be dissolved in hydrochloric acid. What is the minimum volume of 0.500 M HCl needed to dissolve the aluminum?

41. Suppose we have a system that consists of 225 g of pure water at 25.00 °C and 1 atm of pressure. What value do we use for the heat capacity of this system? What value do we use for the specific heat of the water? (For the energy part of the unit, use the joule.)

42. In what specific ways do a standard enthalpy of reaction and a standard enthalpy of formation differ?

43. Write the chemical equation for which the $\Delta H°$ is equal to the standard heat of formation of nitric acid.

44. Why was the concept of a *standard state* introduced into chemistry?

45. Under what conditions is an element in its standard state? Which form of oxygen can exist in the standard state of oxygen?

46. Why isn't the value of $\Delta H_f°$ equal to zero for ozone, O_3?

47. The specific heat of helium is 5.19 J/g °C and that of nitrogen is 1.04 J/g °C. How many joules can one mole of each gas absorb when its temperature increases by 1.00 °C?

48. A calorimeter vat in which a stirring motor, a thermometer, and a "bomb" are immersed absorbed the heat released by the combustion of 0.514 g of benzoic acid. The thermochemical equation for its combustion is as follows.
    $$2C_7H_6O_2(s) + 15O_2(g) \longrightarrow 14CO_2(g) + 6H_2O(l)$$
    $$\Delta H° = -7048 \text{ kJ}$$
    The temperature of the calorimeter rose from 24.112 °C to 24.866 °C. What is the heat capacity of this calorimeter in kJ/°C?

49. A sample of 10.1 g of ammonium nitrate, NH_4NO_3, was dissolved in 125 g of water in a coffee cup calorimeter. The temperature changed from 24.5 °C to 18.8 °C. Calculate the *heat of solution* of ammonium nitrate in kJ/mol. Assume that the energy exchange involves only the solution and that the specific heat of the solution is 4.18 J/g °C.

50. When 0.6484 g of cetyl palmitate, $C_{32}H_{64}O_2$ (a fruit wax), was burned in a bomb calorimeter with a heat capacity of 11.99 kJ/°C, the temperature of the calorimeter rose from 24.518 °C to 26.746 °C. Calculate the molar heat of combustion of cetyl palmitate in kJ/mol.

51. When we say that the value of ΔH for a chemical reaction is a *state function*, what do we mean?

52. The combustion of methane (the chief component of natural gas) follows the equation
    $$CH_4(g) + 2O_2(g) \longrightarrow CO_2(g) + 2H_2O(g)$$
    $\Delta H°$ for this reaction is −802.3 kJ. How many grams of methane must be burned to provide enough heat to raise the temperature of 250 mL of water from 25.0 °C to 50.0 °C?

53. Label the following thermal properties as intensive or extensive.
    (a) specific heat   (d) $\Delta H°$
    (b) heat capacity   (e) molar heat capacity
    (c) $\Delta H_f°$

54. What is the definition of *internal energy*? State the first law of thermodynamics.

55. What is *pressure–volume work*? Give the equation that could be used to calculate it.

56. The change in the internal energy, ΔE, is equal to the "heat of reaction at constant volume." Explain the reason for this.

57. Suppose that a gas is produced in an exothermic chemical reaction between two reactants in an aqueous solution. Which quantity will have the larger magnitude, ΔE or ΔH?

58. The thermochemical equation for the combustion reaction of half a mole of carbon monoxide is as follows.

$$\tfrac{1}{2}CO(g) + \tfrac{1}{4}O_2(g) \longrightarrow \tfrac{1}{2}CO_2(g) \quad \Delta H° = -141.49 \text{ kJ}$$

Write the thermochemical equation for
(a) the combustion of 2 mol of $CO(g)$
(b) the decomposition of 1 mol of $CO_2(g)$ to $O_2(g)$ and $CO(g)$

59. The standard heat of combustion of eicosane, $C_{20}H_{42}(s)$, a typical component of candle wax, is 1.332×10^4 kJ/mol, when it burns in pure oxygen and the products are cooled to 25 °C. The only products are $CO_2(g)$ and $H_2O(l)$. Calculate the value of the standard heat of formation of eicosane (in kJ/mol) and write the corresponding thermochemical equation.

60. Using data in Table 6.2 calculate values for the standard heats of reaction (in kilojoules) for the following reactions.
(a) $H_2SO_4(l) \longrightarrow SO_3(g) + H_2O(l)$
(b) $C_2H_6(g) \longrightarrow C_2H_4(g) + H_2(g)$

61. Calculate the standard heat of formation of calcium carbide, $CaC_2(s)$, in kJ/mol using the following thermochemical equations.

$$Ca(s) + 2H_2O(l) \longrightarrow Ca(OH)_2(s) + H_2(g)$$
$$\Delta H° = -414.79 \text{ kJ}$$
$$2C(s) + O_2(g) \longrightarrow 2CO(g) \qquad \Delta H° = -221.0 \text{ kJ}$$
$$CaO(s) + H_2O(l) \longrightarrow Ca(OH)_2(s) \qquad \Delta H° = -65.19 \text{ kJ}$$
$$2H_2(g) + O_2(g) \longrightarrow 2H_2O(l) \qquad \Delta H° = -571.8 \text{ kJ}$$
$$CaO(s) + 3C(s) \longrightarrow CaC_2(s) + CO(g)$$
$$\Delta H° = +462.3 \text{ kJ}$$

THE QUANTUM MECHANICAL ATOM

7

Colorful fireworks such as this in Washington, D.C., on the fourth of July are popular events worldwide. Many of the fireworks displays resemble the flowers they are named after, such as chrysanthemum, peony, and palm. Each display is the result of two or more carefully timed chemical explosions. In this chapter we will see that the colors in a fireworks display are easily explained by modern quantum mechanics.
(Bill Ross/Corbis)

CHAPTER OUTLINE

7.1 Electromagnetic radiation provides the clue to the electronic structures of atoms

7.2 Atomic line spectra are evidence that electrons in atoms have quantized energies

7.3 Electrons have properties of both particles and waves

7.4 Electron spin affects the distribution of electrons among orbitals in atoms

7.5 The ground state electron configuration is the lowest energy distribution of electrons among orbitals

7.6 Electron configurations explain the structure of the periodic table

7.7 Quantum theory predicts the shapes of atomic orbitals

7.8 Atomic properties correlate with an atom's electron configuration

Nature presents the observer with very complex and often large chemical structures that are essential for life and also make up the nonliving world around us. Understanding these structures starts at the atomic level. If we know how the atoms are put together and their properties we can understand how they bond to each other (Chapter 8) and then we will understand the basic three-dimensional geometries (Chapter 9) that then allow us to understand the larger structures and the interactions of matter. This chapter introduces us to the most modern concepts of the atom itself.

In previous chapters we have described how the structure of the atom was deduced from a variety of experimental evidence. Each experiment added more detail to the make-up of the atom. It started with the indivisible atom and grew to the nuclear model proposed by Rutherford where negatively charged electrons surrounded an extremely dense positively charged nucleus composed of protons and neutrons. This model explained the mass relationships between the elements and the nature of isotopes. However, there were many unanswered questions. Why do metals tend to form cations and why do nonmetals tend to form anions? Why are certain combinations of elements very common while other combinations are never observed? Why do two nonmetals combine to form compounds while no similar process exists for two metals to form a compound? Why are the noble gases virtually inert? Why does the periodic table have the arrangement and shape it has? Many more questions could also be posed, but there was one major question.

This fundamental question concerned the fact that classical physics predicted that atoms simply could not exist. The physics of the late 1800s predicted that electrons surrounding the nucleus must quickly lose energy and crash into the nucleus. We call this the **collapsing atom paradox.** At the same time other unsolvable problems arose for classical physics. Heated objects should have emitted vast quantities of ultraviolet (UV) light. In fact they emit very little UV radiation. This was known as the **ultraviolet catastrophe.** In addition, emerging studies of particles, such as electrons, passing through very small openings gave results (diffraction patterns) that could only be explained if we regarded particles as waves. This led to the concept of the **wave/particle duality** of matter and energy.

The above problems with classical physics made it clear that an entirely new set of concepts would be needed to define modern physics and chemistry. These concepts are commonly called **wave mechanics, quantum mechanics,** or **quantum theory** and they are now a cornerstone of modern chemistry.

Light emitted from atoms gives us clues about how electrons are arranged within an atom. At the same time an understanding of standing waves develops insights to explain why atoms do not collapse. Therefore we must begin our introduction to quantum mechanics by describing the nature of electromagnetic radiation.

| 7.1 | **ELECTROMAGNETIC RADIATION PROVIDES THE CLUE TO THE ELECTRONIC STRUCTURES OF ATOMS** |

Electromagnetic radiation can be described as a wave or as a stream of photons

You've learned that objects can have energy in only two ways, as kinetic energy and as potential energy. You also learned that energy can be transferred between things, and in Chapter 6 our principal focus was on the transfer of heat. Energy can also be transferred between atoms and molecules in the form of light or electromagnetic energy. This is a very important form of energy in chemistry. For example, many chemical systems emit visible light as they react (see Figure 7.1).

Many experiments show that electromagnetic radiation carries energy through space by means of **waves.** Waves are an oscillation that moves outward from a disturbance (think of ripples moving away from a pebble dropped into a pond). In the case of electromagnetic radiation, the disturbance can be a vibrating electric charge. When the charge oscillates, it produces a pulse in the electric field around it. As the electric field pulses, it creates a pulse in the magnetic field. The magnetic field pulse gives rise to yet another electric field pulse

□ Electricity and magnetism are closely related to each other. A moving charge creates an electric current, which in turn creates a magnetic field around it. This is the fundamental idea behind electric motors. A moving magnetic field creates an electric field or current. This is the idea behind electrical generators and turbines.

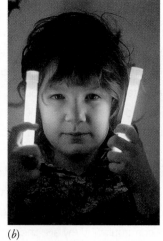

(a)　　　　　　　　　(b)　　　　　　　　　(c)

FIG. 7.1 **Light is given off in a variety of chemical reactions.** (*a*) Combustion. (*b*) Cyalume light sticks. (*c*) A lightning bug. *(Peter Arnold, Inc.; IPA/The Image Works; Edward Degginger/Bruce Coleman, Inc.)*

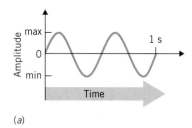
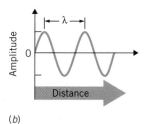

(a)　　　　　　　　　(b)

FIG. 7.2 **Two views of electromagnetic radiation.** (*a*) The frequency, ν, of a light wave is the number of complete oscillations each second. Here two cycles span a one-second time interval, so the frequency is 2 cycles per second, or 2 Hz. (*b*) Electromagnetic radiation frozen in time. This curve shows how the amplitude varies along the direction of travel. The distance between two peaks is the wavelength, λ, of the electromagnetic radiation.

☐ Electromagnetic waves don't need a medium to travel through, as water and sound waves do. They can cross empty space. The speed of the electromagnetic wave in a vacuum is the same no matter how the radiation is created (about 3.00×10^8 m/s).

further away from the disturbance. The process continues, with a pulse in one field giving rise to a pulse in the other, and the resulting train of pulses in the electric and magnetic fields is called an **electromagnetic wave.** This wave ripples away from the source at extremely high speeds.

An electromagnetic wave is often depicted as a sine wave that has an amplitude, wavelength, and frequency. Figure 7.2 shows how the amplitude or intensity of the wave varies with time and with distance as the wave travels through space. **Amplitude** of the wave is related to the intensity or brightness of the radiation. In Figure 7.2*a*, we see two complete oscillations or *cycles* of the wave during a one-second interval. The number of cycles per second is called the **frequency** of the electromagnetic radiation, and its symbol is ν (the Greek letter *nu*, pronounced "new"). In the SI, the unit of time is the second (s), so frequency is given the unit "per second," which is $\frac{1}{\text{second}}$, or (second)$^{-1}$. This unit is given the special name **hertz (Hz).**

$$1 \text{ Hz} = 1 \text{ s}^{-1}$$

☐ The SI symbol for the second is s.

$$\text{s}^{-1} = \frac{1}{\text{s}}$$

As electromagnetic radiation moves away from its source, the positions of maximum and minimum amplitude (peaks and troughs) are regularly spaced. The peak-to-peak distance is called the radiation's **wavelength,** symbolized by λ (the Greek letter *lambda*). See Figure 7.2*b*. Because wavelength is a distance, it has distance units (for example, meters).

If we multiply the wavelength by frequency, the result is the speed of the wave. We can see this if we analyze the units.

□ For any wave, the product of its wavelength and its frequency equals the speed of the wave.

(In SI units)

$$\text{meters} \times \frac{1}{\text{second}} = \frac{\text{meters}}{\text{second}} = \text{speed}$$

$$\text{m} \times \frac{1}{\text{s}} = \frac{\text{m}}{\text{s}} = \text{m s}^{-1}$$

The speed of electromagnetic radiation in a vacuum is a constant and is commonly called the **speed of light.** Its value to three significant figures is 3.00×10^8 m/s (or m s^{-1}). This important physical constant is given the symbol c.

$$c = 3.00 \times 10^8 \text{ m s}^{-1}$$

From the preceding discussion we obtain a very important relationship that allows us to convert between wavelength, λ and frequency, ν.

$$\lambda \times \nu = c = 3.00 \times 10^8 \text{ m s}^{-1} \tag{7.1}$$

□ The speed of light is one of our most carefully measured constants, because the meter is defined in terms of it. The precise value of the speed of light in a vacuum is 2.99792458×10^8 m/s, and a meter is defined as exactly the distance traveled by light in 1/299,792,458 of a second.

TOOLS

Wavelength–frequency relationship

EXAMPLE 7.1
Calculating Frequency from Wavelength

Mycobacterium tuberculosis, the organism that causes tuberculosis, can be completely destroyed by irradiation with ultraviolet light with a wavelength of 254 nm. What is the frequency of this radiation?

ANALYSIS: To convert between wavelength and frequency we use the tool expressed by Equation 7.1. However, we must be careful about the units.

SOLUTION: To calculate the frequency, we solve Equation 7.1 for ν.

$$\nu = \frac{c}{\lambda}$$

Next, we substitute for c (3.00×10^8 m s^{-1}) and use 254 nm for the wavelength. However, to cancel units correctly, we must have the wavelength in meters. Recall from Chapter 1 that nm means nanometer and the prefix nano implies the factor "$\times 10^{-9}$."

$$1 \text{ nm} = 1 \times 10^{-9} \text{ m}$$

Therefore, 254 nm equals 254×10^{-9} m. Substituting gives

$$\nu = \frac{3.00 \times 10^8 \text{ m s}^{-1}}{254 \times 10^{-9} \text{ m}}$$
$$= 1.18 \times 10^{15} \text{ s}^{-1}$$
$$= 1.18 \times 10^{15} \text{ Hz}$$

IS THE ANSWER REASONABLE? One way to test if our answer is correct is to see if the given wavelength, multiplied by our calculated frequency, gives us the speed of light. We will round the 254 nm to 250×10^{-9} m and round our answer to 1×10^{15} s^{-1}

$$(250 \times 10^{-9} \text{ m}) \times (1 \times 10^{15} \text{ s}^{-1}) = 250 \times 10^6 \text{ m s}^{-1} = 2.5 \times 10^8 \text{ m s}^{-1}$$

which is close to the actual speed of light, within one significant figure. Using the actual data and a calculator gives us the exact value for the speed of light.

EXAMPLE 7.2
Calculating Wavelength from Frequency

Radio station WGBB on Long Island, New York, broadcasts its AM signal, a form of electromagnetic radiation, at a frequency of 1240 kHz. What is the wavelength of the radio waves expressed in meters?

ANALYSIS: This question will utilize the same equation as Example 7.1. This time we solve for wavelength in the units asked for in the problem.

SOLUTION: Solving Equation 7.1 for the wavelength gives

$$\lambda = \frac{c}{\nu} = \frac{3.00 \times 10^8 \text{ m s}^{-1}}{1240 \text{ kHz}}$$

In order for the units to work out we recall that the prefix "k" in kHz means kilo and stands for "$\times 10^3$" and Hz means s^{-1}. Replacing k with $\times 10^3$ and Hz with s^{-1} results in the frequency written as $1240 \times 10^3 \text{ s}^{-1}$. Substituting gives

$$\lambda = \frac{3.00 \times 10^8 \text{ m s}^{-1}}{1240 \times 10^3 \text{ s}^{-1}}$$

$$= 242 \text{ m}$$

IS THE ANSWER REASONABLE? If this wavelength is correct, we should be able to multiply it by the original frequency (in Hz) and get the speed of light, as we did in the previous example. Another approach is to test our answer by dividing the speed of light by the wavelength to get back the frequency. Rounding to one significant figure we get

$$\frac{3 \times 10^8 \text{ m/s}}{2 \times 10^2 \text{ m}} = 1.5 \times 10^6 \text{ Hz} = 1500 \text{ kHz}$$

which is reasonably close to the original frequency of 1240 kHz.

Practice Exercise 1: Helium derives it name from the Latin name for the sun. Helium was discovered when spectroscopists found that the 588 nm wavelength (among others) was missing from the sun's spectrum. What is the frequency of this radiation? (Hint: Recall the metric prefixes so units will cancel correctly.)

Practice Exercise 2: The most intense radiation emitted by the earth has a wavelength of about 10.0 μm. What is the frequency of this radiation in hertz?

Practice Exercise 3: An FM radio station in West Palm Beach, Florida, broadcasts electromagnetic radiation at a frequency of 104.3 MHz (megahertz). What is the wavelength of the radio waves, expressed in meters?

Electromagnetic waves are categorized by frequency

Electromagnetic radiation comes in a broad range of frequencies called the **electromagnetic spectrum,** illustrated in Figure 7.3. Some portions of the spectrum have popular names. For example, radio waves are electromagnetic radiations having very low frequencies (and therefore very long wavelengths). Microwaves, which also have low frequencies, are emitted by radar instruments such as those the police use to monitor the speeds of cars. In microwave ovens, similar radiation is used to heat water in foods, causing the food to cook quickly. Infrared radiation is emitted by hot objects and consists of the range of frequencies that can make molecules of most substances vibrate internally. You can't see infrared radiation, but you can feel how your body absorbs it by holding your hand near a hot radiator; the absorbed radiation makes your hand warm. Gamma rays (γ rays) are at the high-frequency end of the electromagnetic spectrum. They are produced by certain

☐ Remember that there is an inverse relationship between wavelength and frequency. The lower the frequency, the longer the wavelength.

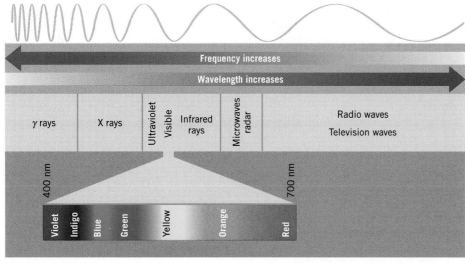

(a)

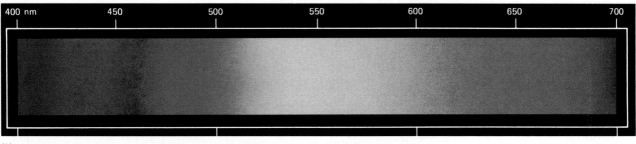

(b)

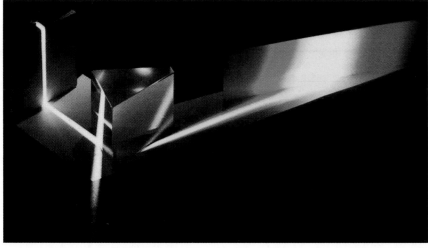

(c)

FIG. 7.3 **The electromagnetic spectrum.** (*a*) The electromagnetic spectrum is divided into regions according to the wavelengths of the radiation. (*b*) The visible spectrum is composed of wavelengths that range from about 400 to 700 nm. (*c*) The production of a visible spectrum by splitting white light into its rainbow of colors. (*From "The Gift of Color," Eastman Kodak Company.*)

elements that are radioactive. X rays are very much like gamma rays, but they are usually made by special equipment. Both X rays and gamma rays penetrate living things easily.

Most of the time, you are bombarded with electromagnetic radiation from all portions of the electromagnetic spectrum. Radio and TV signals pass through you; you feel infrared radiation when you sense the warmth of a radiator; X rays and gamma rays fall on you from space; and light from a lamp reflects into your eyes from the page you're reading. Of all these radiations, your eyes are able to sense only a very narrow band of wavelengths ranging from about 400 to 700 nm. This band is called the **visible spectrum** and consists of all the colors you can see, from red through orange, yellow, green, blue, and violet. White light is composed of all these colors and it can be separated into them by focusing a beam of white light through a prism, which spreads the various wavelengths apart. This is illustrated in Figure 7.3*b*. A photograph showing the production of a visible spectrum is given in Figure 7.3*c*.

The way substances absorb electromagnetic radiation often can help us characterize them. For example, each substance absorbs a uniquely different set of infrared frequencies. A plot of the wavelengths absorbed versus the intensities of absorption is called an infrared absorption spectrum. It can be used to identify a compound, because each infrared spectrum is as unique as a set of fingerprints. (See Figure 7.4.) Many substances absorb visible and ultraviolet radiations in unique ways, too, and they have visible and ultraviolet spectra (Figure 7.5).

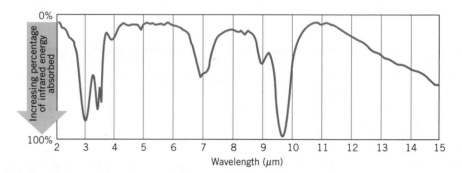

FIG. 7.4   **Infrared absorption spectrum of methyl alcohol (also called wood alcohol), the fuel in "canned heat" products such as Sterno.** In an infrared spectrum, the usual practice is to show the amount of light absorbed increasing from top to bottom in the graph. Thus, there is a peak in the percentage of light absorbed at about 3 μm. (Spectrum courtesy Sadtler Research Laboratories, Inc., Philadelphia, Pa.)

(*a*)

(*b*)

FIG. 7.5   **Absorption of light by chlorophyll.** (*a*) Chlorophyll is the green pigment plants use to harvest solar energy for photosynthesis. (*b*) In this visible absorption spectrum of chlorophyll, the percentage of light absorbed increases from bottom to top. Thus, there is a peak in the light absorbed at about 420 nm and another at about 660 nm. This means the pigment strongly absorbs blue-violet and red light. The green color we *see* is the light that's *not* absorbed. It's composed of the wavelengths of visible light that are reflected. (Our eyes are most sensitive to green, so we don't notice the yellow components of the reflected light.) (*(a) Gary Braasch/Stone/Getty Images.*)

Electromagnetic radiation can be viewed as a stream of photons

When an electromagnetic wave passes an object, the oscillating electric and magnetic fields may interact with it, as ocean waves interact with a buoy in a harbor. A tiny charged particle placed in the path of the wave will be yanked back and forth by the oscillating electric and magnetic fields. For example, when a radio wave strikes an antenna, electrons within the antenna begin to bounce up and down, creating an alternating current which can be detected and decoded electronically. Because the wave exerts a force on the antenna's electrons and moves them through a distance, work is done. Thus, as energy is lost by the source of the wave (the radio transmitter) energy is gained by the electrons in the antenna.

A series of groundbreaking experiments showed that classical physics does not correctly describe energy transfer by electromagnetic radiation. In 1900 a German physicist named Max Planck (1858–1947) proposed that electromagnetic radiation can be viewed as a stream of tiny packets or **quanta** of energy that were later called **photons.** Each photon travels at the speed of light. Planck proposed, and Albert Einstein (1879–1955) confirmed, that *the energy of a photon of electromagnetic radiation is proportional to the radiation's frequency,* not to its intensity or brightness as had been believed up to that time. (See Facets of Chemistry 7.1.)

$$\text{Energy of a photon} = E = h\nu \qquad (7.2)$$

In this expression, h is a proportionality constant that we now call **Planck's constant.** Note that Equation 7.2 relates two representations of electromagnetic radiation. The left-hand side of the equation deals with a property of particles (energy per photon); the right-hand side deals with a property of waves (the frequency). Quantum theory unites the two representations, so we can use whichever representation of electromagnetic radiation is convenient for describing experimental results. For example, in describing the photoelectric effect (Facets of Chemistry 7.1), we represent radiation as a stream of particles. When describing

☐ The energy of one photon is called one **quantum** of energy.

TOOLS
Energy of a photon

☐ The value of Planck's constant is 6.626×10^{-34} J s. It has units of energy (joules) multiplied by time (seconds).

FACETS OF CHEMISTRY 7.1

Photoelectricity and Its Applications

One of the earliest clues to the relationship between the frequency of light and its energy was the discovery of the photoelectric effect. In the latter part of the nineteenth century, it was found that certain metals acquired a positive charge when they were illuminated by light. Apparently, light is capable of kicking electrons out of the surface of the metal.

When this phenomenon was studied in detail, it was discovered that electrons could be made to leave a metal's surface only if the frequency of the incident radiation was above some minimum value, which was named the threshold frequency. This threshold frequency differs for different metals, depending on how tightly the metal atom holds onto electrons. Above the threshold frequency, the kinetic energy of the emitted electron increases with increasing frequency of the light. Interestingly, however, its kinetic energy does not depend on the intensity of the light. In fact, if the frequency of the light is below the minimum frequency, no electrons are observed at all, no matter how bright the light is. To physicists of that time, this was very perplexing because they believed the energy of light was related to its brightness. The explanation of the phenomenon was finally given by Albert Einstein in the form of a very simple equation.

$$\text{KE} = h\nu - w$$

where KE is the kinetic energy of the electron that is emitted, $h\nu$ is the energy of the photon of frequency ν, and w is the minimum energy needed to eject the electron from the metal's surface. Stated another way, part of the energy of the photon is needed just to get the electron off the surface of the metal. This amount is w. Any energy left over ($h\nu - w$) appears as the electron's kinetic energy.

Besides its important theoretical implications, the photoelectric effect has many practical applications. For example, automatic "electric eye" door openers use this phenomenon by sensing the interruption of a light beam caused by the person wishing to use the door. The phenomenon is also responsible for photoconduction by certain substances that are used in light meters in cameras and other devices. The production of sound in motion pictures was first made possible by incorporating a strip along the edge of the film (called the sound track) that causes the light passing through it to fluctuate in intensity according to the frequency of the sound that's been recorded. A photocell converts this light to a varying electric current that is amplified and played through speakers in the theater. Even the sensitivity of photographic film to light is related to the release of photoelectrons within tiny grains of silver bromide that are suspended in a coating on the surface of the film.

7.2

Electromagnetic Fields and Their Possible Physiological Effects

Over the past few years you may have heard reports of possible dangers associated with living near high-voltage power lines or operating electrical equipment. What has caused public concern is the fear that 60 Hz electromagnetic radiation emitted by electricity passing through wires might be affecting the health of those nearby. Such fears have been fueled by news media reports of increased cancer rates among groups receiving strong exposure to this radiation, although the actual evidence supporting a relationship between exposure and cancer is weak and even partly contradictory.

When an oscillating electric current with a certain frequency passes through a wire it emits radiation with that same frequency. In fact, that's how radio and TV stations broadcast their signals—by pulsing an electric current through a transmitting antenna. Ordinary household AC (alternating current) electricity has a frequency of 60 Hz, and weak electromagnetic signals are emitted by all wires that carry it. This radiation is most intense when the voltage is highest, as in the lines that carry electricity over long distances between power plants and cities.

The energy possessed by photons of 60 Hz electromagnetic

radiation is extremely small (you might try the calculation), so small that it cannot affect the bonds that hold molecules together or even cause heating effects the way microwaves do. How, then, can they affect the activities of cells? The answer might be in the weak pulsating electric and magnetic fields induced in the body by this radiation.

Strong electromagnetic fields have been shown to affect the rate of bone growth as well as the amounts of various proteins produced in cells. Experiments have also revealed that cells exposed to an electric field hold onto calcium ions more than cells not exposed. Other experiments have demonstrated that weak magnetic fields increase the uptake of calcium ions in cells that have been exposed to a substance

High-voltage power lines such as these emit low levels of 60 Hz electromagnetic radiation (also called *ultralow frequency*, or ULF, radiation). *(Martin Heitner/Stock Connection Worldwide/NewsCom.)*

that triggers cell division. It is believed that this additional calcium increases the tendency of these cells to divide. Since cancer growth depends on the rate of cell division, these results suggest one way cancers might be promoted by such radiation.

Despite laboratory evidence, the connection between electromagnetic radiation and cancer remains inconclusive. Although it is at least *possible* that cancer can be induced by electromagnetic fields, a lot of additional research will be necessary to pin down the answer.

---

how radiation can bend around small obstacles and fan out after passing through pinholes, we represent radiation as a wave phenomenon. Electromagnetic radiation is not a stream of particles, and it is not a wave, it's a combination of both that is difficult to describe. However, we can say that in some experiments radiation is best described as a wave and in other experiments the particle explanation works best.

Planck's and Einstein's discovery was really quite surprising. If a particular event requiring energy, such as photosynthesis in green plants, is initiated by the absorption of light, it is the frequency of the light that is important, not its intensity or brightness. This makes sense when we view light as a stream of photons, since "high frequency" is associated with higher energy of the photons, while higher intensity is associated with greater numbers of photons. But it makes no sense at all when we view radiation as a wave phenomenon.

☐ Brighter light delivers more photons; higher frequency light delivers more energetic photons.

The idea that electromagnetic radiation can be represented as either a stream of photons or a wave is a cornerstone of the quantum theory. Physicists were able to use the concept of photons to understand many experimental results that classical physics simply had no explanation for. The success of the quantum theory in describing radiation paved the way for a second startling realization: electrons, like radiation, could be represented as either waves or particles. We now turn our attention to the first experimental evidence that led to our modern quantum mechanical model of atomic structure: the existence of discrete lines in atomic spectra.

7.2 | ATOMIC LINE SPECTRA ARE EVIDENCE THAT ELECTRONS IN ATOMS HAVE QUANTIZED ENERGIES

Each spectrum described in Figure 7.3 is called a **continuous spectrum** because it contains a continuous unbroken distribution of light of *all* colors. It is formed when the light from an object that's been heated to a very high temperature (such as the filament in an electric lightbulb) is split by a prism and displayed on a screen. A rainbow after a summer shower appears as a continuous spectrum that most people have seen. In this case, tiny water droplets in the air spread out the colors contained in sunlight.

A rather different kind of spectrum is observed if we examine the light that is given off when an *electric discharge*, or spark, passes through a gas such as hydrogen. The electric discharge is an electric current that *excites*, or energizes, the atoms of the gas. More specifically, the electric current transfers energy to the electrons in the atoms raising them to **excited states.** The atoms then emit the absorbed energy in the form of light as the electrons return to lower energy states. When a narrow beam of this light is passed through a prism, as shown in Figure 7.6, we do *not* see a continuous spectrum. Instead, only a few colors are observed, displayed as a series of individual lines. This series of lines is called the element's **atomic spectrum** or **emission spectrum.** Figure 7.7 shows the visible portions of the atomic spectra of two common elements, sodium and hydrogen, and how they compare with a continuous spectrum. Notice that the spectra of these elements are quite different. In fact, each element has its own unique atomic spectrum that is as characteristic as a fingerprint, and can be used to produce fireworks as in the photo on page 250.

☐ Atoms of an element can also be excited by adding them to the flame of a Bunsen burner.

☐ An emission spectrum is also called a **line spectrum** because the light corresponding to the individual emissions appears as lines on the screen.

☐ Characteristic emissions from these substances add the color to modern fireworks: strontium for red; sodium for yellow; barium for green; copper for blue; charcoal for gold and burning titanium, aluminum or magnesium for silver and white.

A simple pattern of lines in the spectrum of hydrogen suggests a simple explanation for atomic spectra

The first success in explaining atomic spectra quantitatively came with the study of the spectrum of hydrogen. This is the simplest element, since its atoms have only one electron, and it produces the simplest spectrum with the fewest lines.

The atomic spectrum of hydrogen actually consists of several series of lines. One series is in the visible region of the electromagnetic spectrum and is shown in Figure 7.7c. Another series is in the ultraviolet region, and the rest are in the infrared. In 1885, J. J. Balmer found an equation that was able to give the wavelengths of the lines in the visible portion of the spectrum. This was soon extended to a more general equation, called the **Rydberg equation,** that could be used to calculate the wavelengths of *all* the spectral lines of hydrogen.

$$\text{Rydberg equation:} \quad \frac{1}{\lambda} = R_H\left(\frac{1}{n_1^2} - \frac{1}{n_2^2}\right)$$

The symbol λ stands for the wavelength, R_H is the Rydberg constant (109,678 cm^{-1}), and n_1 and n_2 are variables whose values are whole numbers that range from 1 to ∞. The only

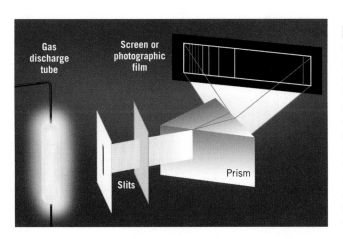

FIG. 7.6 **Production and observation of an atomic spectrum.** Light emitted by excited atoms is formed into a narrow beam by the slits. It then passes through a prism, which divides the light into relatively few narrow beams with frequencies that are characteristic of the particular element that's emitting the light. When these beams fall on a screen, a series of lines is observed, which is why the spectrum is also called a *line spectrum.*

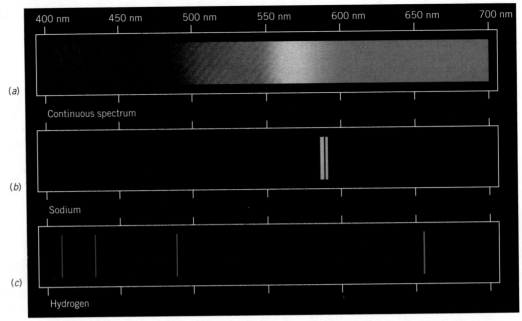

FIG. 7.7 **Continuous and atomic emission spectra.** (*a*) The continuous visible spectrum produced by the sun or an incandescent lamp. (*b*) The atomic spectrum emission produced by sodium. The emission spectrum of sodium actually contains more than 90 lines in the visible region. The two brightest lines are shown here. All the others are less than 1% as bright as these. (*c*) The atomic spectrum (line spectrum) produced by hydrogen. There are only four lines in this visible spectrum. They vary in brightness by only a factor of five, so they are all shown.

restriction is that the value of n_2 must be larger than n_1. (This assures that the calculated wavelength has a positive value.) Thus, if $n_1 = 1$, acceptable values of n_2 are 2, 3, 4, ..., ∞. The Rydberg constant is an *empirical constant*, which means its value was chosen so that the equation gives values for λ that match the ones determined experimentally. The use of the Rydberg equation is straightforward, as illustrated in the following example.

EXAMPLE 7.3
Calculating the Wavelength of a
Line in the Hydrogen Spectrum

The lines in the visible portion of the hydrogen spectrum are called the Balmer series, for which $n_1 = 2$ in the Rydberg equation. Calculate, to four significant figures, the wavelength in nanometers of the spectral line in this series for which $n_2 = 4$.

ANALYSIS: The Rydberg equation will be used for this calculation. The values for n_1 and n_2 are clearly given and the answer is calculated.

SOLUTION: To solve this problem, we substitute values into the Rydberg equation, which will give us $1/\lambda$. Taking the reciprocal will then give the wavelength. As usual, we must be careful with the units.

Substituting $n_1 = 2$ and $n_2 = 4$ into the Rydberg equation gives

$$\frac{1}{\lambda} = 109{,}678 \text{ cm}^{-1}\left(\frac{1}{2^2} - \frac{1}{4^2}\right)$$

$$= 109{,}678 \text{ cm}^{-1}\left(\frac{1}{4} - \frac{1}{16}\right)$$

$$= 109{,}678 \text{ cm}^{-1}(0.2500 - 0.0625)$$

$$= 109{,}678 \text{ cm}^{-1}(0.1875)$$

$$= 2.0565 \times 10^4 \text{ cm}^{-1}$$

Taking the reciprocal gives the wavelength in centimeters.

$$\lambda = \frac{1}{2.0565 \times 10^4 \text{ cm}^{-1}}$$

$$= 4.8626 \times 10^{-5} \text{ cm}$$

Finally, we convert to nanometers.

$$\lambda = 4.8626 \times 10^{-5} \text{ cm} \times \frac{10^{-2} \text{ m}}{1 \text{ cm}} \times \frac{1 \text{ nm}}{10^{-9} \text{ m}}$$

$$= 486.3 \text{ nm}$$

Note that we kept one extra significant figure until the end and then rounded to the desired four significant figures.

IS THE ANSWER REASONABLE? Besides double-checking the arithmetic, we can note that the wavelength falls within the visible region of the spectrum, 400 to 700 nm. We can also check the answer against the experimental spectrum of hydrogen in Figure 7.7c. This wavelength corresponds to the turquoise line in the hydrogen spectrum.

Practice Exercise 4: Calculate the wavelength in micrometers, μm, of radiation expected when $n_1 = 4$ and $n_2 = 6$. Report your result to three significant figures. (Hint: The values of n_1 and n_2 are used to calculate the term in parentheses first.)

Practice Exercise 5: Calculate the wavelength in nanometers of the spectral line in the visible spectrum of hydrogen for which $n_1 = 2$ and $n_2 = 3$. What color is this line?

The discovery of the Rydberg equation was both exciting and perplexing. The fact that the wavelength of any line in the hydrogen spectrum can be calculated by a simple equation involving just one constant and the reciprocals of the squares of two whole numbers is remarkable. What is there about the behavior of the electron in the atom that could account for such simplicity?

The energy of electrons in atoms is quantized

Earlier you saw that there is a simple relationship between the frequency of light and its energy, $E = h\nu$. Because excited atoms emit light of only certain specific frequencies, it must be true that only certain characteristic energy changes are able to take place within the atoms. For instance, in the spectrum of hydrogen there is a red line (see Figure 7.7c) that has a wavelength of 656.4 nm and a frequency of 4.567×10^{14} Hz. The energy of a photon of this light is 3.026×10^{-19} J. Whenever a hydrogen atom emits red light, the frequency of the light is always precisely 4.567×10^{14} Hz and the energy of the atom decreases by *exactly* 3.026×10^{-19} J, never more and never less. Atomic spectra, then, tell us that *when an excited atom loses energy, not just any arbitrary amount can be lost.* The same is true if the atom gains energy.

How is it that atoms of a given element always undergo exactly the same specific energy changes? The answer seems to be that in an atom an electron can have only certain definite amounts of energy and no others. We say that the electron is restricted to certain **energy levels,** and that the energy of the electron is **quantized.**

The energy of an electron in an atom might be compared to the energy of the tortoise in the exhibit shown in Figure 7.8b. The tortoise trapped inside the zoo exhibit can only be "stable" on one of the ledges, so it has certain specific amounts of potential energy as determined by the "energy levels" of the various ledges. If the tortoise is raised to a higher ledge, its potential energy is increased. When it drops to a lower ledge, its potential energy decreases. If the tortoise tries to occupy heights between the ledges, it immediately falls to the lower ledge. Therefore, the energy changes for the tortoise are restricted to the differences in potential energy between the ledges.

Any potential energy allowed: energy values are *continuous*

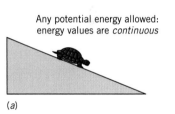

(a)

Potential energy restricted: energy values are *discrete*

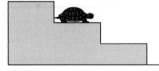

(b)

FIG. 7.8 **Continuous and discrete energies.** (a) The tortoise is free to move to any height less than the height of the hill. Its potential energy can take on any value between the maximum (at the hill top) and the minimum (at the bottom). Similarly, the energy of a free electron can take on any value. (b) The tortoise trapped inside a zoo exhibit is found only at three heights: at the bottom (the lowest, or *ground state*), middle, or top ledges. The potential energy of the tortoise at rest is quantized. Similarly, the energy of the electron trapped inside an atom is restricted to certain values, which correspond to the various energy levels in an atom.

So it is with an electron in an atom. The electron can only have energies corresponding to the set of electron energy levels in the atom. When the atom is supplied with energy (by an electric discharge, for example), an electron is raised from a low-energy level to a higher one. When the electron drops back, energy equal to the difference between the two levels is released and emitted as a photon. Because only certain energy jumps can occur, only certain frequencies of light can appear in the spectrum.

The existence of specific energy levels in atoms, as implied by atomic spectra, forms the foundation of all theories about electronic structure. Any model of the atom that attempts to describe the positions or motions of electrons must also account for atomic spectra.

The Bohr model explains the simple pattern of lines seen in the spectrum of hydrogen

☐ Niels Bohr won the 1922 Nobel Prize in Physics for his work on atomic structure.

☐ Classical physical laws, such as those discovered by Isaac Newton, place no restrictions on the sizes or energies of orbits.

The first theoretical model of the hydrogen atom that successfully accounted for the Rydberg equation was proposed in 1913 by Niels Bohr (1885–1962), a Danish physicist. In his model, Bohr likened the electron moving around the nucleus to a planet circling the sun. He suggested that the electron moves around the nucleus along fixed paths, or orbits. His model broke with the classical laws of physics by placing restrictions on the sizes of the orbits and the energy that the electron could have in a given orbit. This ultimately led Bohr to an equation that described the energy of the electron in the atom. The equation includes a number of physical constants such as the mass of the electron, its charge, and Planck's constant. It also contains an integer, n, that Bohr called a **quantum number.** Each of the orbits is identified by its value of n. When all the constants are combined, Bohr's equation becomes

☐ Bohr's equation for the energy actually is

$$E = -\frac{2\pi^2 m e^4}{n^2 h^2}$$

where m is the mass of the electron, e is the charge on the electron, n is the quantum number, and h is Planck's constant. Therefore, in Equation 7.3,

$$b = -\frac{2\pi^2 m e^4}{h^2} = 2.18 \times 10^{-18} \text{ J}.$$

$$E = \frac{-b}{n^2} \tag{7.3}$$

where E is the energy of the electron and b is the combined constant (its value is 2.18×10^{-18} J). The allowed values of n are whole numbers that range from 1 to ∞ (i.e., n could equal 1, 2, 3, 4, . . ., ∞). From this equation the energy of the electron in any particular orbit could be calculated.

Because of the negative sign in Equation 7.3, the lowest (most negative) energy value occurs when $n = 1$, which corresponds to the *first Bohr orbit*. The lowest energy state of an atom is the most stable one and is called the **ground state.** For hydrogen, the ground state occurs when its electron has $n = 1$. According to Bohr's theory, this orbit brings the electron closest to the nucleus. Conversely, an atom with $n = \infty$ would correspond to an "unbound" electron that had escaped from the nucleus. Such an electron has an energy of zero in Bohr's theory. The negative sign in Equation 7.3 ensures that any electron with a finite value of n has a lower energy than an unbound electron. Thus, energy is released when a free electron is bound to a proton to form a hydrogen atom.

When a hydrogen atom absorbs energy, as it does when an electric discharge passes through it, the electron is raised from the orbit having $n = 1$ to a higher orbit, to $n = 2$ or $n = 3$ or even higher. The hydrogen atom is now in an excited state. These higher orbits are less stable than the lower ones, so the electron quickly drops to a lower orbit. When this happens, energy is emitted in the form of light (see Figure 7.9). Since the energy of the electron in a given orbit is fixed, a drop from one particular orbit to another, say, from $n = 2$ to $n = 1$, always releases the same amount of energy, and the frequency of the light emitted because of this change is always precisely the same.

The success of Bohr's theory was in its ability to account for the Rydberg equation. When the atom emits a photon, an electron drops from a higher initial energy E_{high} to a lower final energy E_{low}. If the initial quantum number of the electron is n_{high} and the final quantum number is n_{low}, then the energy change, calculated as a positive quantity, is

$$\Delta E = E_{\text{high}} - E_{\text{low}} = \left(\frac{-b}{n_{\text{high}}^2}\right) - \left(\frac{-b}{n_{\text{low}}^2}\right)$$

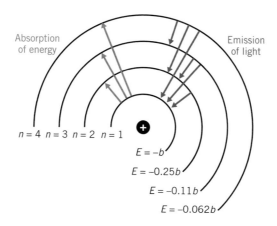

$n = 4 \ n = 3 \ n = 2 \ n = 1$

$E = -b$

$E = -0.25b$

$E = -0.11b$

$E = -0.062b$

FIG. 7.9 **Absorption of energy and emission of light by the hydrogen atom.** When the atom absorbs energy, the electron is raised to a higher energy level. When the electron falls to a lower energy level, light of a particular energy and frequency is emitted.

This can be rearranged to give

$$\Delta E = b\left(\frac{1}{n_{\text{low}}^2} - \frac{1}{n_{\text{high}}^2}\right) \quad \text{with } n_{\text{high}} > n_{\text{low}}$$

By combining Equations 7.1 and 7.2, the relationship between the energy "ΔE" of a photon and its wavelength λ is

$$\Delta E = \frac{hc}{\lambda} = hc\left(\frac{1}{\lambda}\right)$$

Substituting and solving for $1/\lambda$ give

$$\frac{1}{\lambda} = \frac{b}{hc}\left(\frac{1}{n_{\text{low}}^2} - \frac{1}{n_{\text{high}}^2}\right) \quad \text{with } n_{\text{high}} > n_{\text{low}}$$

Notice how closely this equation derived from Bohr's theory matches the Rydberg equation, which was obtained solely from the experimentally measured atomic spectrum of hydrogen. Equally satisfying is that the combination of constants, b/hc, has a value of $109,730 \text{ cm}^{-1}$, which differs by only 0.05% from the experimentally derived value of R_{H} in the Rydberg equation.

The Bohr model fails for atoms with more than one electron

Bohr's model of the atom was both a success and a failure. By calculating the energy changes that occur between energy levels, Bohr was able to account for the Rydberg equation and, therefore, for the atomic spectrum of hydrogen. However, the theory was not able to explain quantitatively the spectra of atoms with more than one electron, and all attempts to modify the theory to make it work met with failure. Gradually, it became clear that Bohr's picture of the atom was flawed and that another theory would have to be found. Nevertheless, the concepts of quantum numbers and fixed energy levels were important steps forward.

7.3 ELECTRONS HAVE PROPERTIES OF BOTH PARTICLES AND WAVES

Bohr's efforts to develop a theory of electronic structure were doomed from the very beginning because the classical laws of physics—those known in his day—simply do not apply to objects as small as the electron. Classical physics fails for atomic particles because matter is not really as our physical senses perceive it. When bound inside an atom, electrons behave not like solid particles, but instead like waves. This idea was proposed in 1924 by a young French graduate student, Louis de Broglie.

The solar system model of the atom was the way that Niels Bohr's model was presented to the public. Today this simple picture of the atom makes a nice corporate logo, but the idea of an atom with electrons orbiting a nucleus as planets orbit a sun has been replaced by the wave mechanical model.

☐ All the objects that had been studied by scientists until the time of Bohr were large and massive in comparison with the electron, so no one had detected the limits of classical physics.

☐ De Broglie was awarded a Nobel prize in 1929.

In Section 7.1 you learned that light waves are characterized by their wavelengths and their frequencies. The same is true of matter waves. De Broglie suggested that the wavelength of a matter wave, λ is given by the equation

$$\lambda = \frac{h}{mv} \tag{7.4}$$

where h is Planck's constant, m is the particle's mass, and v is its velocity. Notice that this equation allows us to connect a wave property, wavelength, with particle properties, mass and velocity. We may describe the electron either as a particle or a wave, and the de Broglie relationship provides a link between the two descriptions.

When first encountered, the concept of a particle of matter behaving as a wave rather than as a solid object is difficult to comprehend. This book certainly seems solid enough, especially if you drop it on your toe! The reason for the book's apparent solidity is that in de Broglie's equation (Equation 7.4) the mass appears in the denominator. This means that heavy objects have extremely short wavelengths. The peaks of the matter waves for heavy objects are so close together that the wave properties go unnoticed and can't even be measured experimentally. But tiny particles with very small masses have much longer wavelengths, so their wave properties become an important part of their overall behavior.

Diffraction provides evidence that electrons have wave properties

Perhaps by now you've begun to wonder if there is any way to *prove* that matter has wave properties. Actually, these properties can be demonstrated by a phenomenon that you have probably witnessed. When raindrops fall on a quiet pond, ripples spread out from where the drops strike the water, as shown in Figure 7.10. When two sets of ripples cross, there are places where the waves are *in phase*, which means that the peak of one wave coincides with the peak of the other. At these points the intensities of the waves add and the height of the water is equal to the sum of the heights of the two crossing waves. At other places the crossing waves are *out of phase*, which means the peak of one wave occurs at the trough of the other. In these places the intensities of the waves cancel. This reinforcement and cancellation of wave intensities, referred to, respectively, as *constructive* and *destructive interference*, is a phenomenon called **diffraction.** It is examined more closely in Figure 7.11. Note how diffraction creates characteristic **interference fringes** when waves pass through adjacent pinholes or reflect off closely spaced grooves. You have seen interference fringes yourself if you've ever noticed the rainbow of colors that shine from the surface of a compact disc (Figure 7.12). When white light, which contains all the visible wavelengths,

FIG. 7.10 **Diffraction of water waves on the surface of a pond.** As the waves cross, the amplitudes increase where the waves are in phase and cancel where they are out of phase. *(Mandy Collins/Alamy Images.)*

☐ Gigantic waves, called rogue waves, with heights up to 100 ft have been observed in the ocean and are believed to be formed when a number of wave sets moving across the sea become in phase simultaneously.

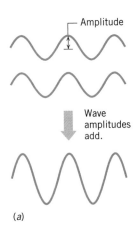

(a)

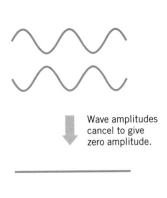

(b)

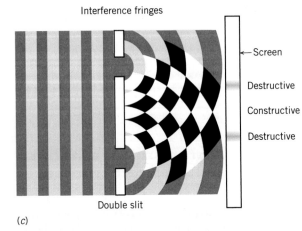

(c)

FIG. 7.11 **Constructive and destructive interference.** (*a*) Waves in phase produce constructive interference and an increase in intensity. (*b*) Waves out of phase produce destructive interference and yield cancellation of intensity. (*c*) Light waves passing through two pinholes fan out and interfere with each other, producing an interference pattern characteristic of waves.

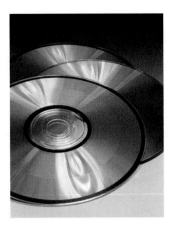

FIG. 7.12 **Diffraction of light from a compact disc.** Colored interference fringes are produced by the diffraction of reflected light from the closely spaced grooves on the surface of a compact disc. *(John Paul Endress/Corbis Stock Market.)*

is reflected from the closely spaced "grooves" on the CD, it is divided into many individual light beams. For a given angle between the incoming and reflected light, the light waves experience interference with each other for all wavelengths (colors) except for one wavelength which is reinforced. Our eye sees the wavelength of light that is reinforced and as the angle changes the wavelengths that are reinforced change. The result is a rainbow of colors reflected from the CD.

Diffraction is a phenomenon that can only be explained as a property of waves, and we have seen how it can be demonstrated with water waves and light waves. Experiments can also be done to show that electrons, protons, and neutrons experience diffraction, which demonstrates their wave nature (see Figure 7.13). In fact, electron diffraction is the principle on which the electron microscope is based (see Facets of Chemistry 7.3).

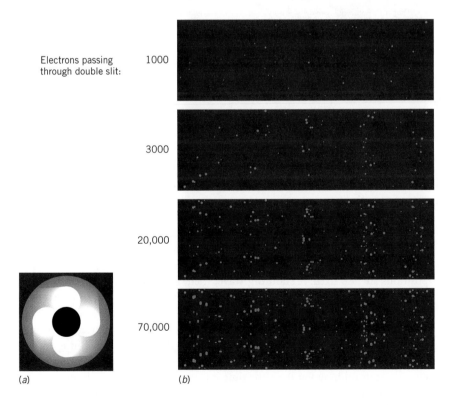

Electrons passing through double slit:

1000

3000

20,000

70,000

(a)

(b)

FIG. 7.13 **Experimental evidence of wave behavior in electrons.** (*a*) An electron diffraction pattern collected by reflecting a beam of electrons from crystalline silicon. (Semiconductor Surface Physics Group, Queens University.) (*b*) Electrons passing *one at a time* through a double slit. Each spot shows an electron impact on a detector. As more and more electrons are passed through the slits, interference fringes are observed.

Bound electrons have quantized energies because they behave like standing waves

Before we can discuss how electron waves behave in atoms, we need to know a little more about waves in general. There are basically two kinds of waves, **traveling waves** and **standing waves**. On a lake or ocean the wind produces waves whose crests and troughs

7.3

The Electron Microscope

The usefulness of a microscope in studying small specimens is limited by its ability to distinguish between closely spaced objects. We call this ability the *resolving power* of the microscope. Through optics, it is possible to increase the magnification and thereby increase the resolving power, but only within limits. These limits depend on the wavelength of the light that is used. Objects with diameters less than the wavelength of the light cannot be seen in detail. Since the smallest wavelength of visible light is about 400 nm, objects smaller than this can't be clearly seen with a microscope that uses visible light.

The electron microscope uses electron waves to "see" very small objects.

De Broglie's equation, $\lambda = h/mv$, suggests that if an electron, proton, or neutron has a very high velocity, its wavelength will be very small. In the electron microscope, electrons are accelerated to high speeds across high-voltage electrodes. This gives electron waves with typical wavelengths of about 0.006 to 0.001 nm that strike the sample and are then focused magnetically (using "magnetic lenses") onto a fluorescent screen where they form a visible image. Because of certain difficulties, the actual resolving power of the instrument is quite a bit less than the wavelength of the electron waves—generally on the order of 6 to 1 nm. Some high resolution electron microscopes, however, are able to reveal the shadows of individual atoms in very thin specimens through which the electron beam passes.

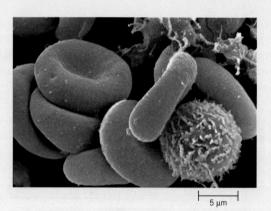

5 μm

A modern electron microscope operated by trained technicians is used to obtain electron-micrographs such as the one shown here depicting red and white blood cells. (*Brand X/Superstock; Yorgos Nikas/Stone/Getty Images.*)

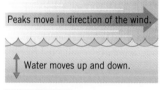

Peaks move in direction of the wind.

Water moves up and down.

FIG. 7.14 Traveling waves.

□ Notes played this way are called harmonics.

move across the water's surface, as shown in Figure 7.14. The water moves up and down while the crests and troughs travel horizontally in the direction of the wind. These are examples of **traveling waves.**

A more important kind of wave for us is the standing wave. An example is the vibrating string of a guitar. When the string is plucked, its center vibrates up and down while the ends, of course, remain fixed. The crest, or point of maximum amplitude of the wave, occurs at one position. At the ends of the string are points of zero amplitude, called **nodes,** and their positions are also fixed. A **standing wave,** then, is one in which the crests and nodes do not change position. One of the interesting things about standing waves is that they lead naturally to "quantum numbers." Let's see how this works using the guitar as an example.

As you know, many notes can be played on a guitar string by shortening its effective length with a finger placed at frets along the neck of the instrument. But even without shortening the string, we can play a variety of notes. For instance, if the string is touched momentarily at its midpoint at the same time it is plucked, the string vibrates as shown in Figure 7.15 and produces a tone an octave higher. The wave that produces this higher tone has a wavelength exactly half of that formed when the untouched string is plucked. In Figure 7.15 we see that other wavelengths are possible, too, and each gives a different note.

If you examine Figure 7.15, you will see that there are some restrictions on the wavelengths that can exist. Not just any wavelength is possible because the nodes at either end of the string are in fixed positions. The only waves that can occur are those for which a half-wavelength is repeated *exactly* a whole number of times. Expressed another way, the

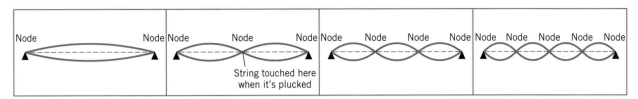

FIG. 7.15 Standing waves on a guitar string.

length of the string is a whole-number multiple of half-wavelengths. In a mathematical form we could write this as

$$L = n\left(\frac{\lambda}{2}\right)$$

where L is the length of the string, λ is a wavelength (therefore, $\lambda/2$ is half the wavelength), and n is an integer. Rearranging this to solve for the wavelength gives

$$\lambda = \frac{2L}{n} \tag{7.5}$$

We see that the waves that are possible are determined quite naturally by a set of whole numbers (similar to quantum numbers).

We are now in a position to demonstrate how quantum theory unites wave and particle descriptions to build a simple but accurate model of a bound electron. Let's look at an electron that is confined to a wire of length L. To keep things simple, let's assume that the wire is infinitely thin, so that the electron can only move in straight lines along the wire. The wire is clamped in place at either end, and its ends cannot move up or down.

First, let's consider a classical particle model: the "bead on a wire" model shown in Figure 7.16a. The bead can slide in either direction along the wire, like a bead on an abacus. If the electron's mass is m and its velocity is v, its kinetic energy is given by

$$E = \frac{1}{2}mv^2$$

The bead can have any velocity, even zero, so the energy E can have any value, even zero. No position on the wire is any more favorable than any other, and the bead is equally likely to be found anywhere on the wire. There is no reason why the bead's position and velocity cannot be known simultaneously.

Now consider a classical wave along the wire, Figure 7.16b. It is exactly like the guitar string we looked at in Figure 7.15. The ends of the wire are clamped in place, so there *must* be a whole number of peaks and troughs along the wire. The wavelength is restricted to values calculated by Equation 7.5. We can see that the quantum number, n, is just the number of peaks and troughs along the wave. It has integer values (1, 2, 3, . . .) because you can't have half a peak or half a trough.

Notes played on a guitar rely on standing waves. The ends of the strings correspond to nodes of the standing waves. Different notes can be played by shortening the effective lengths of the strings with fingers placed along the neck of the instrument. *(© Index Stock.)*

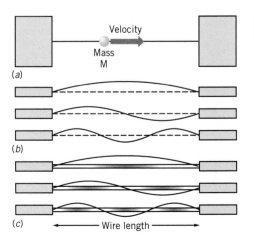

FIG. 7.16 **Three models of an electron on an infinitely thin wire of length L.** (*a*) A classical model of the electron as a bead that can slide along the wire. Any energy is possible, even zero, and the exact position and velocity of the bead can be known simultaneously. (*b*) A classical model of the electron as a standing wave on a wire. An integer number of peaks and troughs (*n*) is required. The wavelength is restricted to values given by Equation 7.5. (*c*) A quantum mechanical model of the electron on a wire obtained by uniting model (*a*) with model (*b*), using the de Broglie relationship (Equation 7.4). The shaded areas indicate most probable positions for the electron. Energy is quantized and is never zero.

Now let's use the de Broglie relation, Equation 7.4, to unite these two classical models. Our goal is to derive an expression for the energy of an electron trapped on the wire. Notice that to calculate the kinetic energy of the bead on a wire, we need to know its velocity, a particle property. The de Broglie relation lets us relate particle velocities with wavelengths. Rearranging Equation 7.4, we have

$$v = \frac{h}{m\lambda}$$

and inserting this into the equation for kinetic energy gives

$$E = \frac{1}{2} m \left(\frac{h}{m\lambda} \right)^2$$
$$= \frac{h^2}{2m\lambda^2}$$

This equation will give us the energy of the electron from its wavelength. If we substitute in Equation 7.5, which gives the wavelength of the standing wave in terms of the wire length L and the quantum number n, we have

$$E = \frac{n^2 h^2}{8mL^2} \qquad (7.6)$$

This equation has a number of profound implications. The fact that the electron's energy depends on an integer, n, means that *only certain energy states are allowed*. The allowed states are plotted on the energy level diagram shown in Figure 7.17. The lowest value of n is 1, so the lowest energy level (the ground state) is $E_1 = h^2/8mL^2$. Energies lower than this are not allowed, so the energy cannot be zero! This indicates that the electron will always have some residual kinetic energy. The electron is never at rest. This is true for the electron trapped in a wire and it is also true for an electron trapped in an atom. Thus, *quantum theory resolves the collapsing atom paradox*.

Note that the spacing between energy levels is proportional to $1/L^2$. This means that when the wire is made longer, the energy levels become more closely spaced. In general, *the more room an electron has to move in, the smaller the spacings between its energy levels*. Chemical reactions sometimes change the way that electrons are confined in molecules. This causes changes in the wavelengths of light the reacting mixture absorbs. This is why color changes sometimes occur during chemical changes.

Electron waves are represented by wave functions

The wave that corresponds to the electron is called a **wave function**. The wave function is usually represented by the symbol ψ (Greek letter psi). The wave function can be used to describe the shape of the electron wave and its energy. The wave function is not an

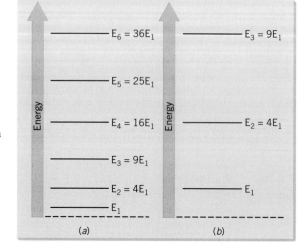

FIG. 7.17 Energy level diagram for the electron on a wire model. (*a*) A long wire, with $L = 2$ nm, and (*b*) a short wire, with $L = 1$ nm. Notice how the energy levels become more closely spaced when the electron has more room to move. Also notice that the energy in the ground state is not zero.

$E_6 = 36E_1$ $E_3 = 9E_1$

$E_5 = 25E_1$

$E_4 = 16E_1$ $E_2 = 4E_1$

$E_3 = 9E_1$

$E_2 = 4E_1$ E_1

E_1

Energy

Energy

(*a*) (*b*)

oscillation of the wire, like a guitar wave, nor is it an electromagnetic wave. The wave's amplitude at any given point can be related to the probability of finding the electron there.

The electron waves shown in Figure 7.16c show that, unlike the bead on a wire model, the electron is more likely to be found at some places on the wire than others. For the ground state, with $n = 1$, the electron is most likely to be found in the center of the wire. Where the amplitude is zero, for example, at the ends of the wire or the center of the wire in the $n = 2$ state, there is a zero probability of finding the electron! Points where the amplitude of the electron wave is zero are called **nodes.** Notice that the higher the quantum number n, the more nodes the electron wave has and, from Equation 7.6, the more energy the electron has. It is generally true that *the more nodes an electron wave has, the higher its energy.*

Electron waves in atoms are called orbitals

In 1926 Erwin Schrödinger (1887–1961), an Austrian physicist, became the first scientist to successfully apply the concept of the wave nature of matter to an explanation of electronic structure. His work and the theory that developed from it are highly mathematical. Fortunately, we need only a qualitative understanding of electronic structure, and the main points of the theory can be understood without all the math.

Schrödinger developed an equation that can be solved to give wave functions and energy levels for electrons trapped inside atoms. Wave functions for electrons in atoms are called **orbitals.** Not all of the energies of the waves are different, but most are. *Energy changes within an atom are simply the result of an electron changing from a wave pattern with one energy to a wave pattern with a different energy.*

We will be interested in two properties of orbitals, their energies and their shapes. Their energies are important because when an atom is in its most stable state (its *ground state*), the atom's electrons have waveforms with the lowest possible energies. The shapes of the wave patterns (i.e., where their amplitudes are large and where they are small) are important because the theory tells us that the amplitude of a wave at any particular place is related to the likelihood of finding the electron there. This will be important when we study how and why atoms form chemical bonds to each other.

In much the same way that the characteristics of a wave on a one-dimensional guitar string can be related to a single integer, wave mechanics tells us that the three-dimensional electron waves (orbitals) can be characterized by a set of *three* integer quantum numbers, n, ℓ, and m_ℓ. In discussing the energies of the orbitals, it is usually most convenient to sort the orbitals into groups according to these quantum numbers.

The principal quantum number, *n*
The quantum number *n* is called the **principal quantum number,** and all orbitals that have the same value of *n* are said to be in the same **shell.** The values of *n* can range from $n = 1$ to $n = \infty$. The shell with $n = 1$ is called the *first shell,* the shell with $n = 2$ is the *second shell,* and so forth. The various shells are also sometimes identified by letters, beginning (for no significant reason) with K for the first shell ($n = 1$).

The principal quantum number is related to the size of the electron wave (i.e., how far the wave effectively extends from the nucleus). The higher the value of *n,* the larger is the electron's average distance from the nucleus. This quantum number is also related to the energy of the orbital. As *n* increases, the energies of the orbitals also increase.

Bohr's theory took into account only the principal quantum number *n*. His theory worked fine for hydrogen because hydrogen just happens to be the one element in which all orbitals having the same value of *n* also have the same energy. Bohr's theory failed for atoms other than hydrogen, however, because when the atom has more than one electron, orbitals with the same value of *n* can have different energies.

The secondary quantum number, *ℓ*
The **secondary quantum number, ℓ,** divides the shells into smaller groups of orbitals called **subshells.** The value of *n* determines which values of ℓ are allowed. For a given *n*, ℓ can range from $\ell = 0$ to $\ell = (n - 1)$. Thus, when $n = 1$, $(n - 1) = 0$, so the only value of ℓ that's allowed is zero. This means that when $n = 1$, there is only one subshell (the shell and subshell are really identical). When $n = 2$, ℓ can have values of 0 or 1. (The maximum value

□ The probability of finding an electron at a given point is proportional to the amplitude of the electron wave squared. Thus, peaks and troughs in the electron wave indicate places where there is the greatest buildup of negative charge.

□ Schrödinger won a Nobel prize in 1933 for his work. The equation he developed that gives electronic wave functions and energies is known as *Schrödinger's equation.* The equation is extremely difficult to solve. Even an approximate solution of the equation for large molecules can require hours or days of supercomputer time.

□ Electron waves are described by the term *orbital* to differentiate them from the notion of *orbits,* which was part of the Bohr model of the atom.

□ "Most stable" almost always means "lowest energy."

□ The term shell comes from an early notion that atoms could be thought of as similar to onions, with the electrons being arranged in layers around the nucleus.

□ Bohr was fortunate to have used the element hydrogen to develop his model of the atom. If he had chosen a different element, his model would not have worked.

□ ℓ is also called the **azimuthal quantum number** and the **orbital angular momentum number.**

Relationship between *n* and ℓ

Value of *n*	Values of ℓ
1	0
2	0, 1
3	0, 1, 2
4	0, 1, 2, 3
5	0, 1, 2, 3, 4
n	0, 1, 2, ..., (*n* − 1)

▢ The number of subshells in a given shell equals the value of *n* for that shell. For example, when *n* = 3, there are three subshells.

of $\ell = n - 1 = 2 - 1 = 1$.) This means that when $n = 2$, there are two subshells. One has $n = 2$ and $\ell = 0$, and the other has $n = 2$ and $\ell = 1$. The relationship between n and the allowed values of ℓ are summarized in the table in the margin.

Subshells could be identified by their value of ℓ. However, to avoid confusing numerical values of n with those of ℓ, a letter code is normally used to specify the value of ℓ.

Value of ℓ	0	1	2	3	4	5	...
Letter designation	*s*	*p*	*d*	*f*	*g*	*h*	...

To designate a particular subshell, we write the value of its principal quantum number followed by the letter code for the subshell. For example, the subshell with $n = 2$ and $\ell = 1$ is the 2*p* subshell; the subshell with $n = 4$ and $\ell = 0$ is the 4*s* subshell. Notice that because of the relationship between n and ℓ, every shell has an *s* subshell (1*s*, 2*s*, 3*s*, etc.). All the shells except the first have a *p* subshell (2*p*, 3*p*, 4*p*, etc.). All but the first and second shells have a *d* subshell (3*d*, 4*d*, etc.); and so forth.

> **Practice Exercise 6:** How many subshells are there in each of the first six shells of an atom? (Hint: Count the subshells based on sets of groups representing *s*, *p*, *d*, and *f* orbitals.)
>
> **Practice Exercise 7:** What subshells would be found in the shells with $n = 3$ and $n = 4$?

The secondary quantum number determines the shape of the orbital, which we will examine more closely later. Except for the special case of hydrogen, which has only one electron, the value of ℓ also affects the energy. This means that in atoms with two or more electrons, the subshells within a given shell differ slightly in energy, with the energy of the subshell increasing with increasing ℓ. Therefore, within a given shell, the *s* subshell is lowest in energy, *p* is the next lowest, followed by *d*, then *f*, and so on. For example,

$$4s < 4p < 4d < 4f$$
— increasing energy →

The magnetic quantum number, m_ℓ

The third quantum number, m_ℓ, is known as the **magnetic quantum number.** Its value indicates individual orbitals within a subshell. Also, its values are related to the way the individual orbitals are oriented relative to each other in space. As with ℓ, there are restrictions as to the possible values of m_ℓ, which can range from $+\ell$ to $-\ell$. When $\ell = 0$, m_ℓ can have only the value 0 because $+0$ and -0 are the same. An *s* subshell, then, has just a single orbital. When $\ell = 1$, the possible values of m_ℓ are $+1$, 0, and -1. A *p* subshell therefore has three orbitals: one with $\ell = 1$ and $m_\ell = 1$, another with $\ell = 1$ and $m_\ell = 0$, and a third with $\ell = 1$ and $m_\ell = -1$. Similarly, we find that a *d* subshell has five orbitals and an *f* subshell has seven orbitals. The numbers of orbitals in the subshells are easy to remember because they follow a simple arithmetic progression.

s	*p*	*d*	*f*	...
1	3	5	7	...

▢ Spectroscopists used m_ℓ to explain additional lines that appear in atomic spectra when atoms emit light while in a magnetic field, which explains how this quantum number got its name.

The whole picture

The relationships among all three quantum numbers are summarized in Table 7.1. In addition, the relative energies of the subshells in an atom containing two or more electrons are depicted in Figure 7.18. Several important features should be noted. First, observe that each orbital on this energy diagram is indicated by a separate circle—one for an *s* subshell, three for a *p* subshell, and so forth. Second, notice that all the orbitals of a given subshell have the *same* energy. Third, note that, in going upward on the energy scale, the spacing between successive shells decreases as the number of subshells increases. This leads to some overlapping of shells having different values of n. For instance, the 4*s* subshell is lower in energy than the 3*d* subshell, 5*s* is lower than 4*d*, and 6*s* is lower than 5*d*. In addition, the 4*f* subshell is below the 5*d* subshell and 5*f* is below 6*d*.

TABLE 7.1	Summary of Relationships among the Quantum Numbers n, ℓ, and m_ℓ			
Value of n	Value of ℓ	Values of m_ℓ	Subshell	Number of Orbitals
1	0	0	$1s$	1
2	0	0	$2s$	1
	1	$-1, 0, 1$	$2p$	3
3	0	0	$3s$	1
	1	$-1, 0, 1$	$3p$	3
	2	$-2, -1, 0, 1, 2$	$3d$	5
4	0	0	$4s$	1
	1	$-1, 0, 1$	$4p$	3
	2	$-2, -1, 0, 1, 2$	$4d$	5
	3	$-3, -2, -1, 0, 1, 2, 3$	$4f$	7

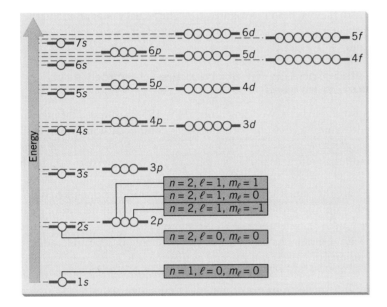

FIG. 7.18 Approximate energy level diagram for atoms with two or more electrons. The quantum numbers associated with the orbitals in the first two shells are also shown.

We will see shortly that Figure 7.18 is very useful for predicting the electronic structures of atoms. Before discussing this, however, we must study another very important property of the electron, a property called spin. Electron spin gives rise to a fourth quantum number.

<table>
<tr><td>

7.4

</td><td>

ELECTRON SPIN AFFECTS THE DISTRIBUTION OF ELECTRONS AMONG ORBITALS IN ATOMS

</td></tr>
</table>

Earlier it was stated that an atom is in its most stable state (its ground state) when its electrons have the lowest possible energies. This occurs when the electrons "occupy" the lowest energy orbitals that are available. But what determines how the electrons "fill" these orbitals? Fortunately, there are some simple rules that can help. These govern both the maximum number of electrons that can be in a particular orbital and how orbitals with the same energy become filled. One important factor that influences the distribution of electrons is the phenomenon known as *electron spin*.

Electrons behave like tiny charges that can spin in one of two directions

When a beam of atoms with an odd number of electrons is passed through an uneven magnetic field, the beam is split in two, as shown in Figure 7.19. The splitting occurs because the electrons within the atoms interact with the magnetic field in two different ways. The electrons behave like tiny magnets, and they are attracted to one or the other of the poles depending on their orientation. This can be explained by imagining that an electron spins around its axis, like a toy top. A moving charge creates a moving electric field, which in

☐ In an atom, an electron can take on many different energies and waveshapes, each of which is called an orbital that is identified by a set of values for n, ℓ, and m_ℓ. When the electron wave possesses a given set of n, ℓ, and m_ℓ, we say the electron "occupies the orbital" with that set of quantum numbers.

FIG. 7.19 **The discovery of electron spin.** In this classic experiment by Stern and Gerlach, a beam of atoms with an odd number of electrons is passed through an uneven magnetic field, created by magnet pole faces of different shapes. The beam splits in two, indicating that the electrons in the atoms behave as tiny magnets, which are attracted to one or the other of the poles depending on their orientation. "Electron spin" was proposed to account for the two possible orientations for the electron's magnetic field.

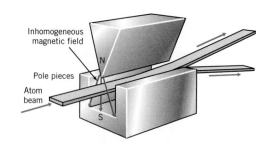

Inhomogeneous magnetic field

Pole pieces

Atom beam

☐ Electrons don't actually spin. We've seen that electrons are not simply particles. But the magnetic properties of electrons are just what we'd see if the electron were a spinning charged particle, and it is useful to picture the electron as spinning.

turn creates a magnetic field. The spinning electrical charge of the electron creates its own magnetic field. This **electron spin** could occur in two possible directions, which accounted for the two beams.

Electron spin gives us a fourth quantum number for the electron, called the **spin quantum number, m_s,** which can take on two possible values: $m_s = +\frac{1}{2}$ or $m_s = -\frac{1}{2}$, corresponding to the two beams in Figure 7.19. The actual values of m_s and the reason they are not integers aren't very important to us, but the fact that there are *only* two values is very significant.

No two electrons in an atom have identical sets of quantum numbers

☐ Pauli received the 1945 Nobel Prize in Physics for his discovery of the exclusion principle.

In 1925 an Austrian physicist, Wolfgang Pauli (1900–1958), expressed the importance of electron spin in determining electronic structure. The **Pauli exclusion principle** states that *no two electrons in the same atom can have identical values for all four of their quantum numbers.* To understand the significance of this, suppose two electrons were to occupy the 1s orbital of an atom. Each electron would have $n = 1$, $\ell = 0$, and $m_\ell = 0$. Since these three quantum numbers are the same for both electrons, the exclusion principle requires that their fourth quantum numbers (their spin quantum numbers) be different; one electron must have $m_s = +\frac{1}{2}$ and the other, $m_s = -\frac{1}{2}$. No more than two electrons can occupy the 1s orbital of the atom simultaneously because there are only two possible values of m_s. Thus the Pauli exclusion principle is really telling us that *the maximum number of electrons in any orbital is two,* and that *when two electrons are in the same orbital, they must have opposite spins.*

The limit of two electrons per orbital also limits the maximum electron populations of the shells and subshells. For the subshells we have

☐ Remember that a shell is a group of orbitals with the same value of n. A subshell is a group of orbitals with the same values of n and ℓ.

Subshell	Number of Orbitals	Maximum Number of Electrons
s	1	2
p	3	6
d	5	10
f	7	14

The maximum electron population per shell is shown below.

Shell	Subshells	Maximum Shell Population	
1	1s	2	
2	2s 2p	8	(2 + 6)
3	3s 3p 3d	18	(2 + 6 + 10)
4	4s 4p 4d 4f	32	(2 + 6 + 10 + 14)

This trend shows that the maximum electron population of a shell is $2n^2$.

Atoms with unpaired electrons are weakly attracted to magnets

The electron can spin in either of two directions in the presence of an external magnetic field.

We have seen that when two electrons occupy the same orbital they must have different values of m_s. When this occurs, we say that the spins of the electrons are *paired,* or simply that the electrons are *paired.* Such pairing leads to the cancellation of the magnetic effects of the electrons because the north pole of one electron magnet is opposite the south pole of the other. Atoms with more electrons that spin in one direction than in the other are said to contain *unpaired* electrons. For these atoms, the magnetic effects do not cancel and the atoms themselves become tiny magnets that can be attracted to an external magnetic field. This weak attraction of a substance containing unpaired electrons to a magnet indicates that the material is **paramagnetic.** Substances in which all the electrons are paired are not attracted to a magnet and are said to be **diamagnetic.**

□ Diamagnetic substances are actually weakly repelled by a magnetic field.

Paramagnetism and diamagnetism are measurable properties that provide experimental verification of the presence or absence of unpaired electrons in substances. In addition, the quantitative measurement of the strength of the attraction of a paramagnetic substance toward a magnetic field permits the calculation of the number of unpaired electrons in its atoms, molecules, or ions.

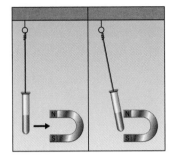

A paramagnetic substance is attracted to a magnetic field.

7.5 THE GROUND STATE ELECTRON CONFIGURATION IS THE LOWEST ENERGY DISTRIBUTION OF ELECTRONS AMONG ORBITALS

The distribution of electrons among the orbitals of an atom is called the atom's **electronic structure** or **electron configuration.** This is something very useful to know about an element because the arrangement of electrons in the outer parts of an atom, which is determined by its electron configuration, controls the chemical properties of the element.

We are interested in the ground state electron configurations of the elements. This is the configuration that yields the lowest energy for an atom and can be predicted for many of the elements by the use of the energy level diagram in Figure 7.18 and application of the Pauli exclusion principle. To see how we go about this, let's begin with the simplest atom of all, hydrogen.

Hydrogen has an atomic number, Z, equal to 1, so a neutral hydrogen atom has one electron. In its ground state this electron occupies the lowest energy orbital that's available, which is the $1s$ orbital. To indicate symbolically the electron configuration we list the subshells that contain electrons and indicate their electron populations by appropriate superscripts. Thus the electron configuration of hydrogen is written as

$$\text{H} \qquad 1s^1$$

Another way of expressing electron configurations that we will sometimes find useful is the **orbital diagram.** In it, a circle will represent each orbital and arrows will be used to indicate the individual electrons, head up for spin in one direction and head down for spin in the other. The orbital diagram for hydrogen is simply

$$\text{H} \qquad \textcircled{\uparrow}$$
$$1s$$

□ It doesn't matter whether the arrow points up or down. The energy of the electron is the same whether it has one spin or the other. For consistency, when an orbital is half-filled, we will show the electron with an arrow that points up.

Electron configurations are built up by filling lowest energy orbitals first

To arrive at the electron configuration of an atom of another element, we imagine that we begin with a hydrogen atom and then add one proton after another (plus whatever neutrons are also needed) until we obtain the nucleus of the atom of interest. As we proceed, we also must add electrons, one at a time to the lowest available orbital, until we have added enough electrons to give the neutral atom of the element in question. This process for obtaining the electronic structure of an atom is known as the **aufbau principle,** the word *aufbau* being German for "building up."

How *s* orbitals fill

Let's look at the way this works for helium, which has $Z = 2$. This atom has two electrons, both of which are permitted to occupy the $1s$ orbital. The electron configuration and orbital diagram of helium can now be written as

$$\text{He} \quad 1s^2 \qquad \text{or} \qquad \text{He} \quad \textcircled{\uparrow\downarrow}$$
$$1s$$

Notice that the orbital diagram shows that both electrons in the $1s$ orbital are paired.

We can proceed in the same fashion to predict successfully the electron configurations of most of the elements in the periodic table. For example, the next two elements in the table are lithium, Li ($Z = 3$), and beryllium, Be ($Z = 4$), which have three and four electrons, respectively. For each of these, the first two electrons enter the $1s$ orbital with their spins paired. The Pauli exclusion principle tells us that the $1s$ subshell is filled with two electrons, and Figure 7.18 shows that the orbital of next lowest energy is the $2s$, which can also hold up to two electrons. Therefore, the third electron of lithium and the third and fourth electrons of beryllium enter the $2s$. We can represent the electronic structures of lithium and beryllium as

Li $\quad 1s^22s^1 \quad$ or $\quad$ Li $\quad$ ⚛ ⚛
$\qquad\qquad\qquad\qquad\qquad\qquad\qquad\; 1s \quad\; 2s$

Be $\quad 1s^22s^2 \quad$ or $\quad$ Be $\quad$ ⚛ ⚛
$\qquad\qquad\qquad\qquad\qquad\qquad\qquad\; 1s \quad\; 2s$

Filling p orbitals

After beryllium comes boron, B ($Z = 5$). Referring to Figure 7.18, we see that the first four electrons of this atom complete the $1s$ and $2s$ subshells, so the fifth electron must be placed into the $2p$ subshell.

$$\text{B} \qquad 1s^22s^22p^1$$

In the orbital diagram for boron, the fifth electron can be put into any one of the $2p$ orbitals—which one doesn't matter because they are all of equal energy.

B $\quad$ ⚛ ⚛ ⚛ ○ ○
$\qquad\quad 1s \quad 2s \qquad 2p$

Notice, however, that when we give this orbital diagram we show *all* of the orbitals of the $2p$ subshell even though two of them are empty.

Next we come to carbon, which has six electrons. As before, the first four electrons complete the $1s$ and $2s$ orbitals. The remaining two electrons go in the $2p$ subshell to give

$$\text{C} \qquad 1s^2\,2s^2\,2p^2$$

■ Spread them out and then line them up.

Now, however, to write the orbital diagram we have to make a decision as to where to put the two p electrons. (At this point you may have an unprintable suggestion! But try to bear up. It's really not all that bad.) To make this decision, we apply **Hund's rule,** which states that *when electrons are placed in a set of orbitals of equal energy, they are spread out as much as possible to give as few paired electrons as possible.* Both theory and experiment have shown that if we follow this rule, we obtain the electron configuration with the lowest energy. For carbon, it means that the two p electrons are in separate orbitals and their spins are in the same direction.[1]

■ It doesn't matter which two orbitals are shown as occupied. Any of these are okay for the ground state of carbon.

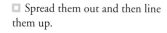

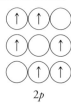

$2p$

C $\quad$ ⚛ ⚛ ↑ ↑ ○
$\qquad\quad 1s \quad 2s \qquad 2p$

Applying the Pauli exclusion principle and Hund's rule, we can now complete the electron configurations and orbital diagrams for the rest of the elements of the second period.

[1] Hund's rule gives us the *lowest* energy (ground state) distribution of electrons among the orbitals. However, configurations such as

C $\quad$ ⚛ ⚛ ↑ ↓ ○

C $\quad$ ⚛ ⚛ ⚛ ○ ○
$\qquad\quad 1s \quad 2s \qquad 2p$

are not impossible; it is just that neither of them corresponds to the lowest energy distribution of electrons in the carbon atom.

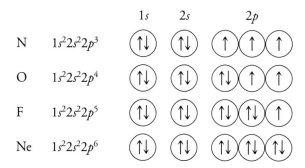

We can continue to predict electron configurations in this way, using Figure 7.18 as a guide to tell us which subshells become occupied and in what order. For instance, after completing the $2p$ subshell at neon, Figure 7.18 predicts that the next two electrons enter the $3s$, followed by the filling of the $3p$. Then we find the $4s$ is lower in energy than the $3d$, so it is filled first. Next, the $3d$ is completed before we go on to fill the $4p$, and so forth.

You might be thinking that you'll have to consult Figure 7.18 whenever you need to write down the ground state electron configuration of an element. However, as you will see in the next section, all the information contained in that figure is also contained in the periodic table.

7.6 | ELECTRON CONFIGURATIONS EXPLAIN THE STRUCTURE OF THE PERIODIC TABLE

In Chapter 2 you learned that when Mendeleev constructed his periodic table, elements with similar chemical properties were arranged in vertical columns called groups. Later work led to the expanded version of the periodic table we use today. The basic structure of this table is one of the strongest empirical supports for the quantum theory, which we have been using to predict electron configurations, and it also permits us to use the periodic table itself as a device for predicting electron configurations.

The periodic table is a guide for predicting electron configurations

Consider, for example, the way the table is laid out (Figure 7.20). On the left there is a block of *two* columns shown in blue; on the right there is a block of *six* columns shown in pink; in the center there is a block of *ten* columns shown in yellow, and below the table there are two rows consisting of *fourteen* elements each shown in gray. These numbers—2, 6, 10, and 14—are *precisely* the numbers of electrons that the quantum theory tells us can occupy s, p, d, and f subshells, respectively. In fact, *we can use the structure of the periodic table to predict the filling order of the subshells when we write the electron configuration of an element.*

To use the periodic table to predict electron configurations, we follow the aufbau principle as before. We start with hydrogen and then move through the table row after row

TOOLS
Periodic table and electron configurations

☐ This would be an amazing coincidence if the theory were wrong!

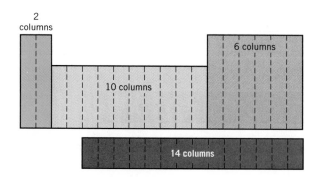

FIG. 7.20 The overall column structure of the periodic table. The table is naturally divided into regions of 2, 6, 10, and 14 columns, which are the numbers of electrons that can occupy s, p, d, and f subshells.

until we reach the element of interest, noting as we go along which regions of the table we pass through. For example, consider the element calcium. Using Figure 7.20, we obtain the electron configuration

$$\text{Ca} \qquad 1s^2 2s^2 2p^6 3s^2 3p^6 4s^2$$

To see how this configuration relates to the periodic table, refer to the inside front cover of the book.

Filling periods 1, 2, and 3

Notice that the first period has just two elements, H and He. Starting with hydrogen and passing through this period, two electrons are added to the atom. These enter the $1s$ subshell and are written as $1s^2$. Next we move across the second period, where the first two elements, Li and Be, are in the block of two columns. The two electrons for Li and Be enter the $2s$ subshell and are written as $2s^2$. Then we move to the block of six columns, and as we move across this region in the second row we fill the $2p$ subshell with six electrons, writing $2p^6$. Now we go to the third period where we first pass through the block of two columns, filling the $3s$ subshell with two electrons ($3s^2$), and then through the block of six columns, filling the $3p$ with six electrons ($3p^6$).

Filling periods 4 and 5

Next, we move to the fourth period. To get to calcium in the example above we step through two elements in the two-column block, filling the $4s$ subshell with two more electrons. Up to calcium we have only filled s and p subshells. Figure 7.21 shows that after calcium the $3d$ subshell will be filled. Ten electrons are then added for the ten elements in the first row of the transition elements. After the $3d$ subshell we complete the fourth period by filling the $4p$ subshell with six electrons. The fifth period fills the $5s$, $4d$, and $5p$ subshells in sequence with 2, 10, and 6 electrons, respectively.

Filling periods 6 and 7

The inner transition elements (f subshells) begin to fill in the sixth and seventh periods. Period 6 fills the $6s$, $4f$, $5d$, and $6p$ subshells with 2, 14, 10, and 6 electrons, respectively. The reason for this sequence is that, in general, the $6s$ subshell has the lowest energy. Subshells $4f$, $5d$, and $6p$ have increasingly greater energies in this period. There are many irregularities in this sequence, however, and Appendix A should be consulted for the correct electron configurations. The seventh period fills the $7s$, $5f$, $6d$, and $7p$ subshells. Once again, the sequence is based on the energies of the subshells and there are many irregularities that make it advisable to consult Appendix A for the correct electron configurations.

Notice that in the above patterns the s and p subshells always have the same number as the period they are in. The d subshells always have a number that is one less than the period they are in. Finally, the f subshells are always two less than the period in which they reside.

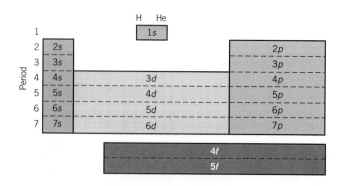

FIG. 7.21 **Arrangement of subshells in the periodic table.** This format illustrates the sequence for filling subshells.

EXAMPLE 7.4
Predicting Electron Configurations

What is the electron configuration of (a) Mn and (b) Bi?

ANALYSIS: We use the periodic table as a tool to tell us which subshells become filled. It is best if you can do this without referring to Figure 7.21.

SOLUTION: (a) To get to manganese, we cross the following regions of the table, with the results indicated.

Period 1   Fill the $1s$ subshell

Period 2   Fill the $2s$ and $2p$ subshells

Period 3   Fill the $3s$ and $3p$ subshells

Period 4   Fill the $4s$ and then move five places in the $3d$ region

The electron configuration of Mn is therefore

$$\text{Mn} \qquad 1s^2 2s^2 2p^6 3s^2 3p^6 4s^2 3d^5$$

This configuration is correct as is. In elements with electrons in d and f orbitals, we can also group all subshells of the same shell together. For manganese, this gives

$$\text{Mn} \qquad 1s^2 2s^2 2p^6 3s^2 3p^6 3d^5 4s^2$$

We'll see later that writing the configuration with this way is convenient when working out ground state electronic configurations for ions.

(b) To get to bismuth, we fill the following subshells:

Period 1   Fill the $1s$

Period 2   Fill the $2s$ and $2p$

Period 3   Fill the $3s$ and $3p$

Period 4   Fill the $4s$, $3d$, and $4p$

Period 5   Fill the $5s$, $4d$, and $5p$

Period 6   Fill the $6s$, $4f$, $5d$, and then add three electrons to the $6p$

This gives

$$\text{Bi} \qquad 1s^2 2s^2 2p^6 3s^2 3p^6 4s^2 3d^{10} 4p^6 5s^2 4d^{10} 5p^6 6s^2 4f^{14} 5d^{10} 6p^3$$

Grouping subshells with the same value of n gives

$$\text{Bi} \qquad 1s^2 2s^2 2p^6 3s^2 3p^6 3d^{10} 4s^2 4p^6 4d^{10} 4f^{14} 5s^2 5p^6 5d^{10} 6s^2 6p^3$$

Again, either of these configurations is correct.

IS THE ANSWER REASONABLE? We can count the number of electrons to be sure we have 25 for Mn and 83 for Bi and none have been left out or added. If the textbook is available we can look at Appendix A to check our configurations.

Practice Exercise 8: Use the periodic table to predict the electron configurations of (a) Mg, (b) Ge, (c) Cd, and (d) Gd. Group subshells of the same shell together. (Hint: Recall which areas of the periodic table represent s, p, d, and f electrons.)

Practice Exercise 9: Describe in your own words how to use the periodic table to write the electron configuration of an element.

Practice Exercise 10: Use the periodic table to predict the electron configurations of (a) O, S, Se and (b) P, N, Sb. What is the same about all the elements in part (a), and the elements in part (b)?

Practice Exercise 11: Draw orbital diagrams for (a) Na, (b) S, and (c) Fe. (Hint: Recall how we indicate paired electron spins.)

Practice Exercise 12: Use orbital diagrams to determine how many unpaired electrons are in each of these elements: (a) Mg, (b) Ge, (c) Cd, and (d) Gd.

Electron configurations can be abbreviated using noble gas core configurations

When we consider the chemical reactions of atoms, our attention is usually focused on the distribution of electrons in the **outer shell** of the atom (the occupied shell with the largest value of *n*). This is because the **outer electrons** (those in the outer shell) are the ones that are exposed to other atoms when the atoms react. The inner electrons of an atom, called the **core electrons,** are buried deep within the atom and normally do not play a role when chemical bonds are formed.

Because we are interested primarily in the electrons of the outer shell, we often write electron configurations in an abbreviated, or shorthand, form. To illustrate, let's consider the elements sodium and magnesium. Their full electron configurations are

$$\text{Na} \qquad 1s^2 2s^2 2p^6 3s^1$$
$$\text{Mg} \qquad 1s^2 2s^2 2p^6 3s^2$$

The outer electrons of both atoms are in the 3*s* subshell and each has the core configuration $1s^2 2s^2 2p^6$, which is the same as that of the noble gas neon.

To write the *shorthand configuration* for an element we indicate what the core is by placing in brackets the symbol of the noble gas whose electron configuration is the same as the core configuration. This is followed by the configuration of the outer electrons for the particular element. The noble gas used is almost always the one that occurs at the end of the period preceding the period containing the element whose configuration we wish to represent. Thus, for sodium and magnesium we write

$$\text{Na} \qquad [\text{Ne}]\, 3s^1$$
$$\text{Mg} \qquad [\text{Ne}]\, 3s^2$$

Even with the transition elements, we need only concern ourselves with the outermost shell and the *d* subshell just below. For example, iron has the configuration

$$\text{Fe} \qquad 1s^2 2s^2 2p^6 3s^2 3p^6 3d^6 4s^2$$

Only the 4*s* and 3*d* electrons play a role in the chemistry of iron. In general, the electrons below the outer *s* and *d* subshells of a transition element—the *core* electrons—are relatively unimportant. In every case these core electrons have the electron configuration of a noble gas. Therefore, for iron the core is $1s^2 2s^2 2p^6 3s^2 3p^6$, which is the same as the electron configuration of argon. The abbreviated configuration of iron is therefore written as

$$\text{Fe} \qquad [\text{Ar}]\, 3d^6 4s^2$$

EXAMPLE 7.5
Writing Shorthand Electron Configurations

What is the shorthand electron configuration of manganese? Draw the orbital diagram for manganese using the shorthand configuration.

ANALYSIS: As usual, the periodic table serves as our tool for deriving the electron configuration. For the shorthand configuration of an element, we write, in brackets, the symbol for the noble gas that is at the end of the preceding period, followed by the electron configuration of the occupied subshells that exist beyond the noble gas core. For the orbital diagram, we use a circle to represent each of the orbitals in a populated subshell. The orbitals are then populated with the required number of electrons, using arrows as appropriate, following Hund's rule.

SOLUTION: Manganese is in Period 4. The preceding noble gas is argon, Ar, so to write the abbreviated configuration we write the symbol for argon in brackets followed by the electron configuration that exists beyond the argon core. We can obtain this by noting that to get to Mn in Period 4, we first cross the "s region" by adding two electrons to the $4s$ subshell, and then go five steps into the "d region" where we add five electrons to the $3d$ subshell. Therefore, the short-hand electron configuration for Mn is

$$\text{Mn} \qquad [\text{Ar}]\ 4s^2 3d^5$$

Placing the electrons that are in the highest shell farthest to the right gives

$$\text{Mn} \qquad [\text{Ar}]\ 3d^5 4s^2$$

To draw the orbital diagram, we simply distribute the electrons in the $3d$ and $4s$ orbitals following Hund's rule. This gives

Mn   [Ar]   ⟨↑⟩ ⟨↑⟩ ⟨↑⟩ ⟨↑⟩ ⟨↑⟩   ⟨↑↓⟩
                         $3d$ $4s$

Notice that each of the $3d$ orbitals is half-filled. The atom contains five unpaired electrons and is paramagnetic.

IS THE ANSWER REASONABLE? From the left, count the groups needed to reach Mn. These should equal seven, the number of electrons in the orbitals beyond Ar as written above. The orbital diagram must have seven electrons and must obey Hund's rule.

Practice Exercise 13: Can an element with an even atomic number be paramagnetic? (Hint: Try writing the orbital diagrams of a few of the transition elements in Period 4.)

Practice Exercise 14: Write shorthand configurations and abbreviated orbital diagrams for (a) P and (b) Sn. Where appropriate, place the electrons that are in the highest shell farthest to the right. How many unpaired electrons does each of these atoms have?

Chemical properties of the representative elements depend on valence shell electron configurations

You learned that Mendeleev constructed the periodic table by placing elements with similar properties in the same group. We are now ready to understand the reason for these similarities in terms of the electronic structures of atoms. It seems reasonable, therefore, that elements with similar properties should have similar outer shell electron configurations. This is, in fact, exactly what we observe. For example, let's look at the alkali metals of Group IA. Going by our rules, we obtain the following configurations.

Li	[He] $2s^1$	or	$1s^2 2s^1$
Na	[Ne] $3s^1$	or	$1s^2 2s^2 2p^6 3s^1$
K	[Ar] $4s^1$	or	$1s^2 2s^2 2p^6 3s^2 3p^6 4s^1$
Rb	[Kr] $5s^1$	or	$1s^2 2s^2 2p^6 3s^2 3p^6 3d^{10} 4s^2 4p^6 5s^1$
Cs	[Xe] $6s^1$	or	$1s^2 2s^2 2p^6 3s^2 3p^6 3d^{10} 4s^2 4p^6 4d^{10} 5s^2 5p^6 6s^1$

Each of these elements has just one outer shell electron that is in an s subshell. We know that when they react, the alkali metals each lose one electron to form ions with a charge of $1+$. For each, the electron that is lost is this outer s electron, and the electron configuration of the ion that is formed is the same as that of the preceding noble gas.

Li$^+$	$1s^2$		He	$1s^2$
Na$^+$	$1s^2 2s^2 2p^6$		Ne	$1s^2 2s^2 2p^6$
K$^+$	$1s^2 2s^2 2p^6 3s^2 3p^6$		Ar	$1s^2 2s^2 2p^6 3s^2 3p^6$
		etc.		

If you write the electron configurations of the members of any of the groups in the periodic table, you will find the same kind of similarity among the configurations of the outer shell electrons. The differences are in the value of the principal quantum number of the outer electrons.

For the representative elements (those in the longer columns), the only electrons that are normally important in controlling chemical properties are the ones in the outer shell. This outer shell is known as the **valence shell,** and it is always the occupied shell with the largest value of n. The electrons in the valence shell are called **valence electrons.** (The term *valence* comes from the study of chemical bonding and relates to the combining capacity of an element, but that's not important here.)

For the representative elements it is very easy to determine the electron configuration of the valence shell by using the periodic table. *The valence shell always consists of just the s and p subshells that we encounter crossing the period that contains the element in question.* Thus, to determine the valence shell configuration of sulfur, a Period 3 element, we note that to reach sulfur in Period 3 we place two electrons into the 3s and four electrons into the 3p. The valence shell configuration of sulfur is therefore

$$S \qquad 3s^2 3p^4$$

EXAMPLE 7.6

Writing Valence Shell Configurations

Predict the electron configuration of the valence shell of arsenic ($Z = 33$).

ANALYSIS: To determine the number of s and p electrons in the highest shell we write the electron configuration grouping the subshells in each shell together. The last subshell must be either an s or p subshell. If it is an s subshell, the valence shell consists of the s electrons. If the last subshell is a p subshell, the valence shell includes both the s and p electrons in that shell.

SOLUTION: To reach arsenic in Period 4, we add electrons to the 4s, 3d, and 4p subshells. But the 3d is not part of the fourth shell and therefore not part of the valence shell, so all we need be concerned with are the electrons in the 4s and 4p subshells. This gives us the valence shell configuration of arsenic,

$$As \qquad 4s^2 4p^3$$

IS THE ANSWER REASONABLE? First of all, only s and p electrons can be valence electrons. We can then count backward from As to the start of the period counting only the p and then s electrons. These add up to the numbers above, indicating the answer is correct.

Practice Exercise 15: Give an example of a valence shell with more than eight electrons. If that is not possible, explain why. (Hint: Are there any elements where d shell electrons are valence shell electrons?)

Practice Exercise 16: What is the valence shell electron configuration of (a) Se, (b) Sn, and (c) I?

Configurations for transition and rare earth elements are sometimes unexpected

The rules you've learned for predicting electron configurations work most of the time, but not always. Appendix A gives the electron configurations of all of the elements as determined experimentally. Close examination reveals that there are quite a few exceptions to the rules. Some of these exceptions are significant for us because they occur with common elements.

Two important exceptions are for chromium and copper. Following the rules, we would expect the configurations to be

$$Cr \qquad [Ar]\, 3d^4 4s^2$$
$$Cu \qquad [Ar]\, 3d^9 4s^2$$

However, the actual electron configurations, determined experimentally, are

$$Cr \quad [Ar]\ 3d^54s^1$$
$$Cu \quad [Ar]\ 3d^{10}4s^1$$

The corresponding orbital diagrams are

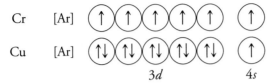

Notice that for chromium, an electron is "borrowed" from the 4s subshell to give a 3d subshell that is exactly half-filled. For copper the 4s electron is borrowed to give a completely filled 3d subshell. A similar thing happens with silver and gold, which have filled 4d and 5d subshells, respectively.

$$Ag \quad [Kr]\ 4d^{10}5s^1$$
$$Au \quad [Xe]\ 4f^{14}5d^{10}6s^1$$

Apparently, half-filled and filled subshells (particularly the latter) have some special stability that makes such borrowing energetically favorable. This subtle but nevertheless important phenomenon affects not only the ground state configurations of atoms but also the relative stabilities of some of the ions formed by the transition elements. Similar irregularities occur among the lanthanide and the actinide elements.

7.7 QUANTUM THEORY PREDICTS THE SHAPES OF ATOMIC ORBITALS

To picture what electrons are doing within the atom, we are faced with imagining an object that behaves like a particle in some experiments and like a wave in others. There is nothing in our experience that is comparable. Fortunately we can still think of the electron as a particle in the usual sense by using the statistical probability of the electron being found at a particular place. We can then use quantum mechanics to mathematically connect the particle and wave representations of the electron. Even though we may have trouble imagining an object that can be represented both ways, mathematics describes its behavior very accurately.

Describing the electron's position in terms of statistical probability is based on more than simple convenience. The German physicist Werner Heisenberg showed mathematically that it is impossible to measure with complete precision both a particle's velocity and position at the same instant. To measure an electron's position or velocity, we have to bounce another particle off it. Thus, the very act of making the measurement changes the electron's position and velocity. We cannot determine both exact position and exact velocity simultaneously, no matter how cleverly we make the measurements. This was Heisenberg's famous **uncertainty principle.** The theoretical limitations on measuring speed and position are not significant for large objects. For small particles such as the electron, however, these limitations prevent us from ever knowing or predicting where in an atom an electron will be at a particular instant, so we speak of probabilities instead.

Wave mechanics views the probability of finding an electron at a given point in space as equal to the square of the amplitude of the electron wave (given by the square of the wave function, ψ^2) at that point. It seems quite reasonable to relate probability to amplitude, or intensity, because where a wave is intense its presence is strongly felt. The amplitude is squared because, mathematically, the amplitude can be either positive or negative, but probability only makes sense if it is positive. Squaring the amplitude assures us that the probabilities will be positive. We need not be very concerned about this point, however.

The notion of electron probability leads to two very important and frequently used concepts. One is that an electron behaves as if it were spread out around the nucleus in a sort of **electron cloud.** Figure 7.22a is a *dot-density diagram* that illustrates the way

☐ The uncertainty principle is often stated mathematically as

$$\Delta x = \frac{h}{4\pi m}\left(\frac{1}{\Delta v}\right)$$

where Δx is the minimum uncertainty in the particle's location, h is Planck's constant, m is the mass of the particle, and Δv is the minimum uncertainty in the particle's velocity. Notice that we can generally measure the particle's location more precisely if the particle is heavier. Notice also that the greater the uncertainty in the velocity, the smaller the uncertainty in the particle's location.

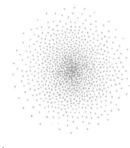
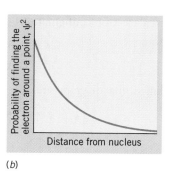

(a)   (b)

FIG. 7.22 Electron distribution in a 1s orbital. (a) A dot-density diagram that illustrates the electron probability distribution for a 1s electron. (b) A graph that shows how the probability of finding the 1s electron around a given point, ψ^2, decreases as the distance from the nucleus increases.

☐ The amplitude of an electron wave is described by a *wave function,* which is usually given the symbol ψ (the Greek letter psi). The probability of finding the electron in a given location is given by ψ^2.

the probability of finding the electron varies in space for a 1s orbital. In those places where the dot density is large (i.e., where there are large numbers of dots per unit volume), the amplitude of the wave is large and the probability of finding the electron is also large. Figure 7.22b shows how the electron probability for a 1s orbital varies as we move away from the nucleus. As you might expect, the probability of finding the electron close to the nucleus is large and decreases with increasing distance from the nucleus.

The other important concept that stems from the notion that the electron probability varies from place to place is **electron density,** which relates to how much of the electron's charge is packed into a given volume. In regions of high probability there is a high concentration of electrical charge (and mass) and the electron density is large; in regions of low probability, the electron density is small.

Remember that an electron confined to a tiny space no longer behaves much like a particle. It's more like a cloud of negative charge. Like clouds made of water vapor, the density of the cloud varies from place to place. In some places the cloud is dense; in others the cloud is thinner and may be entirely absent. This is a useful picture to keep in mind as you try to visualize the shapes of atomic orbitals.

s orbitals are spherical; *p* orbitals have two lobes

In looking at the way the electron density distributes itself in atomic orbitals, we are interested in three things: the *shape* of the orbital, its *size,* and its *orientation* in space relative to other orbitals.

The electron density in an orbital doesn't end abruptly at some particular distance from the nucleus. It gradually fades away. Therefore, to define the size and shape of an orbital, it is useful to picture some imaginary surface enclosing, say, 90% of the electron density of the orbital, and on which the probability of finding the electron is everywhere the same. For the 1s orbital in Figure 7.22, we find that if we go out a given distance from the nucleus in *any* direction, the probability of finding the electron is the same. This means that all the points of equal probability lie on the surface of a sphere, so we can say that the shape of the orbital is spherical. In fact, all *s* orbitals are spherical. As suggested earlier, their sizes increase with increasing *n*. This is illustrated in Figure 7.23. Notice that beginning with the 2s orbital, there are certain places where the electron density drops to zero. These are spherical shaped nodes of the *s* orbital electron waves. It is interesting that electron waves have nodes just like the waves on a guitar string. For *s* orbital electron waves, however, the nodes consist of imaginary spherical *surfaces* on which the electron density is zero.

The *p* orbitals are quite different from *s* orbitals, as shown in Figure 7.24. Notice that the electron density is equally distributed in two regions on opposite sides of the nucleus. Figure 7.24a illustrates the two "lobes" of *one* 2p orbital. Between the lobes is a **nodal plane**—an imaginary flat surface on which every point has an electron density of zero. The size of the *p* orbitals also increases with increasing *n* as illustrated by the cross section

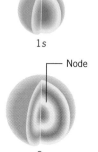

1s

— Node

2s

— Nodes

3s

FIG. 7.23 Size variations among *s* orbitals. The orbitals become larger as the principal quantum number, *n*, becomes larger.

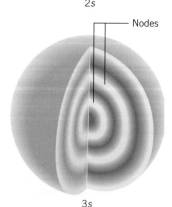

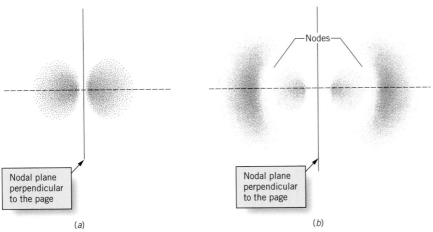

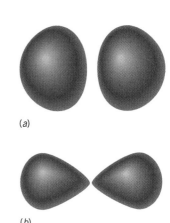

FIG. 7.24 Distribution of electron density in *p* orbitals. (*a*) Dot-density diagram that represents a cross section of the probability distribution in a 2*p* orbital. There is a nodal plane between the two lobes of the orbital. (*b*) Cross section of a 3*p* orbital. Note the nodes in the electron density that are in addition to the nodal plane passing through the nucleus.

of a 3*p* orbital in Figure 7.24*b*. The 3*p* and higher *p* orbitals have additional nodes besides the nodal plane that passes through the nucleus.

Figure 7.25*a* illustrates the shape of a surface of constant probability for a 2*p* orbital. Often chemists will simplify this shape by drawing two "balloons" connected at the nucleus and pointing in opposite directions as shown in Figure 7.25*b*. Both representations emphasize the point that a *p* orbital has two equal-sized lobes that extend in opposite directions along a line that passes through the nucleus.

Orbitals in a *p* subshell are oriented at 90° to each other
As you've learned, a *p* subshell consists of three orbitals of equal energy. Wave mechanics tells us that the lines along which the orbitals have their maximum electron densities are oriented at 90° angles to each other, corresponding to the axes of an imaginary *xyz* coordinate system (Figure 7.26). For convenience in referring to the individual *p* orbitals they are often labeled according to the axis along which they lie. The *p* orbital concentrated along the *x* axis is labeled *p*$_x$, and so forth.

Four of the five *d* orbitals in a *d* subshell have the same shape

The shapes of the *d* orbitals, illustrated in Figure 7.27, are a bit more complex than are those of the *p* orbitals. Because of this, and because there are five orbitals in a *d* subshell, we haven't attempted to draw all of them at the same time on the same set of coordinate axes. Notice that four of the five *d* orbitals have the same shape and consist of four lobes

FIG. 7.25 Representations of the shapes of *p* orbitals. (*a*) Shape of a surface of constant probability for a 2*p* orbital. (*b*) A simplified representation of a *p* orbital that emphasizes the directional nature of the orbital.

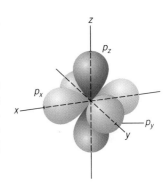

FIG. 7.26 The orientations of the three *p* orbitals in a *p* subshell. Because the directions of maximum electron density lie along lines that are mutually perpendicular, like the axes of an *xyz* coordinate system, it is convenient to label the orbitals *p*$_x$, *p*$_y$, and *p*$_z$.

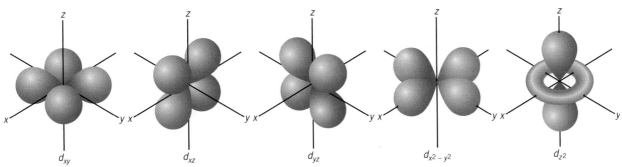

FIG. 7.27 The shapes and directional properties of the five *d* orbitals of a *d* subshell.

☐ The *f* orbitals are even more complex than the *d* orbitals, but we will have no need to discuss their shapes.

of electron density. These four *d* orbitals each have two perpendicular nodal planes that intersect the nucleus. These orbitals differ only in their orientations around the nucleus (their labels come from the mathematics of wave mechanics). The fifth *d* orbital, labeled d_{z^2}, has two lobes that point in opposite directions along the *z* axis plus a doughnut-shaped ring of electron density around the center that lies in the *x–y* plane. The two nodes for the d_{z^2} orbital are conic surfaces whose peaks meet at the nucleus. We will see that the *d* orbitals are important in the formation of chemical bonds in certain molecules, and that their shapes and orientations are important in understanding the properties of the transition metals, which will be discussed in Chapter 21.

The shapes of the *f* orbitals are more complex than those of the *d* orbitals, having more lobes and a variety of shapes. Use of *f* orbitals for bonding is not important for this course. However, we should note that each *f* orbital has three nodal planes or surfaces.

7.8 | ATOMIC PROPERTIES CORRELATE WITH AN ATOM'S ELECTRON CONFIGURATION

There are many chemical and physical properties that vary in a more or less systematic way according to an element's position in the periodic table. For example, in Chapter 2 we noted that the metallic character of the elements increases from top to bottom in a group and decreases from left to right across a period. In this section we discuss several physical properties of the elements that have an important influence on chemical properties. We will see how these properties correlate with an atom's electron configuration, and because electron configuration is also related to the location of an element in the periodic table, we will study their periodic variations as well.

Effective nuclear charge is the positive charge "felt" by outer electrons

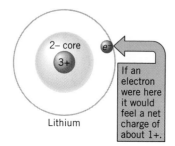

FIG. 7.28 **Effective nuclear charge.** If the 2− charge of the $1s^2$ core of lithium were 100% effective at shielding the 2*s* electron from the nucleus, the valence electron would feel an effective nuclear charge of only about 1+.

Many of an atom's properties are determined by the amount of positive charge felt by the atom's outer electrons. Except for hydrogen, this positive charge is always *less* than the full nuclear charge, because the negative charge of the electrons in inner shells partially offsets, or "neutralizes," the positive charge of the nucleus.

To gain a better understanding of this, consider the element lithium, which has the electron configuration $1s^2 2s^1$. The core electrons ($1s^2$), which lie beneath the valence shell ($2s^1$), are tightly packed around the nucleus and for the most part lie between the nucleus and the electron in the outer shell. This core has a charge of 2− and it surrounds a nucleus that has a charge of 3+. When the outer 2*s* electron "looks toward" the center of the atom, it "sees" the 3+ charge of the nucleus reduced to only about 1+ because of the intervening 2− charge of the core. In other words, the 2− charge of the core effectively neutralizes two of the positive charges of the nucleus, so the net charge that the outer electron feels, which we call the **effective nuclear charge,** is only about 1+. This is illustrated in an overly simplified way in Figure 7.28.

Although electrons in inner shells shield the electrons in outer shells quite effectively from the nuclear charge, electrons in the *same* shell are much less effective at shielding each other. For example, in the element beryllium ($1s^2 2s^2$) each of the electrons in the outer 2*s* orbital is shielded quite well from the nuclear charge by the inner $1s^2$ core, but one 2*s* electron doesn't shield the other 2*s* electron very well at all. This is because electrons in the same shell are at about the same average distance from the nucleus, and in attempting to stay away from each other they only spend a very small amount of time one below the other, which is what's needed to provide shielding. Since electrons in the same shell hardly shield each other at all from the nuclear charge, *the effective nuclear charge felt by the outer electrons is determined primarily by the difference between the charge on the nucleus and the charge on the core.* With this as background, let's examine some properties controlled by the effective nuclear charge.

☐ An electron spends very little time between the nucleus and another electron in the same shell, so it shields that other electron poorly.

Atomic and ionic sizes increase with increasing *n* and decreasing effective nuclear charge

The wave nature of the electron makes it difficult to define exactly what we mean by the "size" of an atom or ion. As we've seen, the electron cloud doesn't simply stop at some particular distance from the nucleus; instead it gradually fades away. Nevertheless, atoms and ions do behave in many ways as though they have characteristic sizes. For example, in a whole host of hydrocarbons, ranging from methane (CH_4, natural gas) to octane (C_8H_{18}, in gasoline) to many others, the distance between the nuclei of carbon and hydrogen atoms is virtually the same. This would suggest that carbon and hydrogen have the same relative sizes in each of these compounds.

☐ The C—H distance in most hydrocarbons is about 110 pm (110×10^{-12} m).

Experimental measurements reveal that the diameters of atoms range from about 1.4×10^{-10} to 5.7×10^{-10} m. Their radii, which is the usual way that size is specified, range from about 7.0×10^{-11} to 2.9×10^{-10} m. Such small numbers are difficult to comprehend. A million carbon atoms placed side by side in a line would extend a little less than 0.2 mm, or about the diameter of the period at the end of this sentence.

The sizes of atoms and ions are rarely expressed in meters because the numbers are so cumbersome. Instead, a unit is chosen that makes the values easier to comprehend. A unit that scientists have traditionally used is called the **angstrom** (symbolized **Å**), which is defined as

$$1 \text{ Å} = 1 \times 10^{-10} \text{ m}$$

☐ The angstrom is named after Anders Jonas Ångström (1814–1874), a Swedish physicist who was the first to measure the wavelengths of the four most prominent lines of the hydrogen spectrum.

However, the angstrom is not an SI unit, and in many current scientific journals, atomic dimensions are in picometers, or sometimes in nanometers (1 pm = 10^{-12} m and 1 nm = 10^{-9} m). In this book, we will normally express atomic dimensions in picometers, but because much of the scientific literature has these quantities in angstroms, you may someday find it useful to remember the conversions:

$$1 \text{ Å} = 100 \text{ pm}$$

$$1 \text{ Å} = 0.1 \text{ nm}$$

Atomic size varies periodically

The variations in atomic radii within the periodic table are illustrated in Figure 7.29. Here we see that atoms generally become larger going from top to bottom in a group, and they become smaller going from left to right across a period. To understand these variations we must consider two factors. One is the value of the principal quantum number of the valence electrons, and the other is the effective nuclear charge felt by the valence electrons.

☐ Large atoms are found in the lower left of the periodic table, and small atoms are found in the upper right.

TOOLS
Periodic trends in atomic size

Going from top to bottom within a group, the effective nuclear charge felt by the outer electrons remains nearly constant, while the principal quantum number of the valence shell increases. For example, consider the elements of Group IA. For lithium, the valence shell configuration is $2s^1$; for sodium, it is $3s^1$; for potassium, it is $4s^1$; and so forth. For each of these elements, the core has a negative charge that is one less than the nuclear charge, so the valence electron of each experiences a nearly constant effective nuclear charge of about 1+. However, as we descend the group, the value of *n* for the valence shell increases, and as you learned earlier, the larger the value of *n*, the larger is the orbital. Therefore, the atoms become larger as we go down a group simply because the orbitals containing the valence electrons become larger. This same argument applies whether the valence shell orbitals are *s* or *p*.

Moving from left to right across a period, electrons are added to the same shell. The orbitals holding the valence electrons all have the *same* value of *n*. In this case we have to examine the variation in the effective nuclear charge felt by the valence electrons.

As we move from left to right across a period, the nuclear charge increases; the outer shells of the atoms become more populated, but the inner core remains the same. For example, from lithium to fluorine the nuclear charge increases from 3+ to 9+. The core ($1s^2$) stays the same, however. As a result, the outer electrons feel an increase in positive charge (i.e., effective nuclear charge) that causes them to be drawn inward, and thereby causes the sizes of the atoms to decrease.

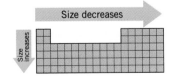

Across a row of transition elements or inner transition elements, the size variations are less pronounced than among the representative elements. This is because the outer shell

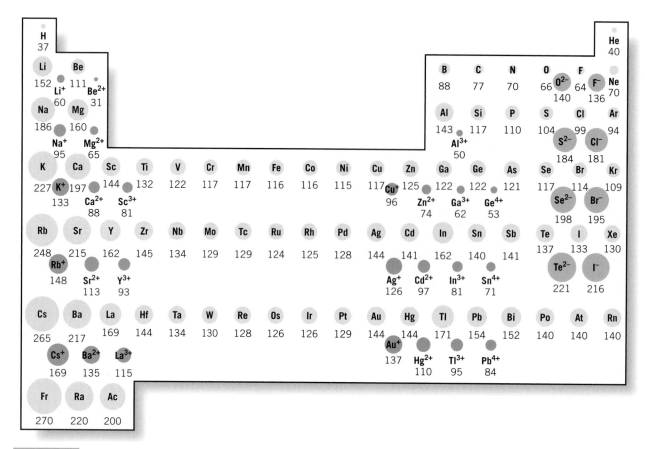

FIG. 7.29 Variation in atomic and ionic radii in the periodic table. Values are in picometers.

configuration remains essentially the same while an inner shell is filled. From atomic numbers 21 to 30, for example, the outer electrons occupy the $4s$ subshell while the underlying $3d$ subshell is gradually completed. The amount of shielding provided by the addition of electrons to this inner $3d$ level is greater than the amount of shielding that would occur if the electrons were added to the outer shell, so the effective nuclear charge felt by the outer electrons increases more gradually. As a result, the decrease in size with increasing atomic number is also more gradual.

Ion sizes show the same trends as atom sizes, but anions are larger and cations are smaller than their parent atoms

TOOLS
Trends in ionic size

Figure 7.29 also illustrates how sizes of the ions compare with those of the neutral atoms. As you can see, when atoms gain or lose electrons to form ions, rather significant size changes take place. The reasons are easy to understand and remember.

When electrons are added to an atom, the mutual repulsions between them increase. This causes the electrons to push apart and occupy a larger volume. Therefore, *negative ions are always about 1.5 to 2 times larger than the atoms from which they are formed* (Figure 7.30).

When electrons are removed from an atom, the electron–electron repulsions decrease, which allows the remaining electrons to be pulled closer together around the nucleus. Therefore, *positive ions are always smaller than the atoms from which they are formed.* As Figure 7.29 shows, cations often are only 1/2 to 2/3 the size of their parent atom. This is also illustrated in Figure 7.30 for the elements lithium and iron. For lithium, removal of the outer $2s$ electron completely empties the valence shell and exposes the smaller $1s^2$ core. When a metal is able to form more than one positive ion, the sizes of the ions decrease as the amount of positive charge on the ion increases. To form the Fe^{2+} ion, an iron atom loses its outer $4s$ electrons. To form the Fe^{3+} ion, an additional electron is lost from the $3d$ subshell that lies beneath the $4s$. Comparing sizes, we see that the radius of an iron atom

□ Adding electrons creates an ion that is larger than the neutral atom; removing electrons produces an ion that is smaller than the neutral atom.

□ Li $1s^2 2s^1$
   Li^+ $1s^2$

□ Fe   [Ar] $3d^6 4s^2$
   Fe^{2+} [Ar] $3d^6$
   Fe^{3+} [Ar] $3d^5$

is 116 pm whereas the radius of the Fe^{2+} ion is 76 pm. Removing yet another electron to give Fe^{3+} decreases electron–electron repulsions in the d subshell and gives the Fe^{3+} ion a radius of 64 pm.

Practice Exercise 17: Use the periodic table to choose the largest atom or ion in each set. (Hint: Recall that electrons repel each other.)
(a) Ge, Te, Se, Sn   (c) Cr, Cr^{2+}, Cr^{3+}
(b) C, F, Br, Ga   (d) O, O^{2-}, S, S^{2-}

Practice Exercise 18: Use the periodic table to determine the smallest atom or ion in each group.
(a) Si, Ge, As, P   (c) Db, W, Tc, Fe
(b) Fe^{2+}, Fe^{3+}, Fe   (d) Br^-, I^-, Cl^-

Energy changes are associated with the gain or loss of electrons by atoms

The ionization energy is the energy required to remove an electron from an atom or ion

The **ionization energy** (abbreviated **IE**) *is the energy required to remove an electron from an isolated, gaseous atom or ion in its ground state.* For an atom of an element X, it is the increase in potential energy associated with the change

$$X(g) \longrightarrow X^+(g) + e^-$$

In effect, the ionization energy is a measure of how much work is required to pull an electron from an atom, so it reflects how tightly the electron is held by the atom. Usually, the ionization energy is expressed in units of kilojoules per mole (kJ/mol), so we can also view it as the energy needed to remove one mole of electrons from one mole of gaseous atoms.

Table 7.2 gives the ionization energies of the first 12 elements. As you can see, atoms with more than one electron have more than one ionization energy. These correspond to the stepwise removal of electrons, one after the other. Lithium, for example, has three ionization energies because it has three electrons. Removing the outer 2s electrons from

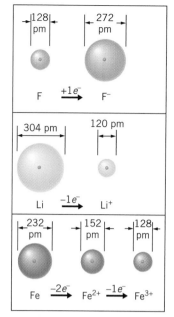

FIG. 7.30 Changes in size when atoms gain or lose electrons to form ions. Adding electrons leads to an increase in the size of the particle, as illustrated for fluorine. Removing electrons leads to a decrease in the size of the particle, as shown for lithium and iron.

TABLE 7.2	Successive Ionization Energies for Hydrogen through Magnesium (kJ/mol)[a]							
	1st	2nd	3rd	4th	5th	6th	7th	8th
H	1312							
He	2372	5250						
Li	520	7297	11,810					
Be	899	1757	14,845	21,000				
B	800	2426	3659	25,020	32,820			
C	1086	2352	4619	6221	37,820	47,260		
N	1402	2855	4576	7473	9442	53,250	64,340	
O	1314	3388	5296	7467	10,987	13,320	71,320	84,070
F	1680	3375	6045	8408	11,020	15,160	17,860	92,010
Ne	2080	3963	6130	9361	12,180	15,240	—	—
Na	496	4563	6913	9541	13,350	16,600	20,113	25,666
Mg	737	1450	7731	10,545	13,627	17,995	21,700	25,662

[a]Note the sharp increase in ionization energy when crossing the "staircase," indicating that the last of the valence electrons has been removed.

☐ Ionization energies are additive. For example,

$$Li(g) \longrightarrow Li^+(g) + e^-$$
$$IE_1 = 520 \text{ kJ}$$
$$Li^+(g) \longrightarrow Li^{2+}(g) + e^-$$
$$IE_2 = 7297 \text{ kJ}$$

$$Li(g) \longrightarrow Li^{2+}(g) + 2e^-$$
$$IE_{total} = IE_1 + IE_2 = 7817 \text{ kJ}$$

☐ It is often helpful to remember that the trends in IE are just the opposite of the trends in atomic size within the periodic table; when size increases, IE decreases.

one mole of isolated lithium atoms to give one mole of gaseous lithium ions, Li^+, requires 520 kJ; so the *first ionization energy* of lithium is 520 kJ/mol. The second IE of lithium is 7297 kJ/mol, and corresponds to the process

$$Li^+(g) \longrightarrow Li^{2+}(g) + e^-$$

This involves the removal of an electron from the now-exposed $1s$ core of lithium. Removal of the third (and last) electron requires the third IE, which is 11,810 kJ/mol. In general, successive ionization energies always increase because each subsequent electron is being pulled away from an increasingly more positive ion, and that requires more work.

Larger atoms have lower ionization energies

Within the periodic table there are trends in the way IE varies that are useful to know and to which we will refer in later discussions. We can see these by examining a graph that shows how the first ionization energy varies with an element's position in the table, which is shown in Figure 7.31. Notice that the elements with the largest ionization energies are the nonmetals in the upper right of the periodic table, and that those with the smallest ionization energies are the metals in the lower left of the table. In general, then, the following trends are observed.

TOOLS
Periodic trends in ionization energy

Ionization energy generally increases from bottom to top within a group and increases from left to right within a period. Overall the ionization energy increases from the lower left corner of the periodic table to the upper right corner. This is usually referred to as a **diagonal relationship.**

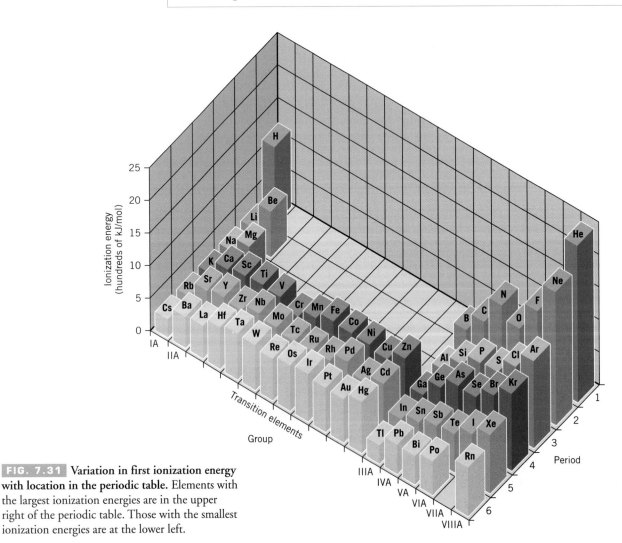

FIG. 7.31 Variation in first ionization energy with location in the periodic table. Elements with the largest ionization energies are in the upper right of the periodic table. Those with the smallest ionization energies are at the lower left.

The same factors that affect atomic size also affect ionization energy. As the value of n increases going down a group, the orbitals become larger and the outer electrons are farther from the nucleus. Electrons farther from the nucleus are bound less tightly, so IE decreases from top to bottom. Of course, this is just the same as saying that it increases from bottom to top.

As you can see, there is a gradual overall increase in IE as we move from left to right across a period, although the horizontal variation of IE is somewhat irregular (see Facets of Chemistry 7.4). The reason for the overall trend is the increase in effective nuclear charge felt by the valence electrons as we move across a period. As we've seen, this draws the valence electrons closer to the nucleus and leads to a decrease in atomic size as we move from left to right. But the increasing effective nuclear charge also causes the valence electrons to be held more tightly, which makes it more difficult to remove them.

The results of these trends place elements with the largest IE in the upper right-hand corner of the periodic table. It is very difficult to cause these atoms to lose electrons. In the lower left-hand corner of the table are elements that have loosely held valence electrons. These elements form positive ions relatively easily, as you learned in Chapter 2.

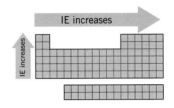

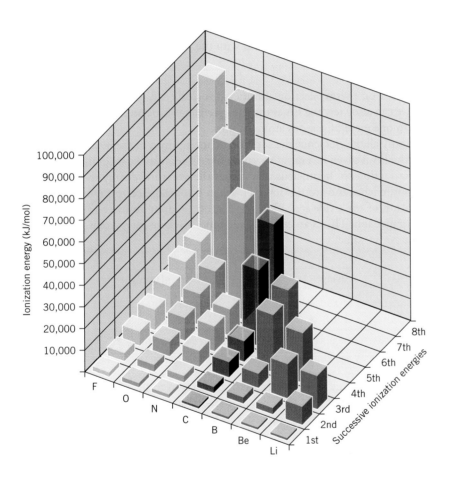

FIG. 7.32 Variations in successive ionization energies for the elements lithium through fluorine.

Noble gas configurations are extremely stable

Table 7.2 shows that, for a given element, successive ionization energies increase gradually until the valence shell is emptied. Then a very much larger increase in IE occurs when core electrons are removed. This is illustrated graphically in Figure 7.32 for the Period 2 elements lithium through fluorine. For lithium, we see that the first electron (the $2s$ electron) is removed rather easily, but the second and third electrons, which come from the $1s$ core, are much more difficult to dislodge. For beryllium, the large jump in IE occurs after two electrons (the two $2s$ electrons) are removed. In fact, for all of these elements, the big jump in IE happens when the core electrons are removed.

The data displayed in Figure 7.32 suggest that although it may be moderately difficult to empty the valence shell of an atom, it is *extremely* difficult to remove the core electrons that have the noble gas configuration. As you will learn, this is one of the factors that influences the number of positive charges on ions formed by the representative metals.

Practice Exercise 19: Use the periodic table to select the atom with the most positive value for its first ionization energy, IE: (a) Na, Sr, Be, Rb; (b) B, Al, C, Si. (Hint: Use the diagonal relationships of the IE values within the periodic table.)

Practice Exercise 20: Use Table 7.2 to determine which of the following is expected to have the most positive ionization energy, IE: (a) Na^+, Mg^+, H, C^{2+}; (b) Ne, F, Mg^{2+}, Li^+.

Electron affinity is energy released or absorbed when a particle gains an electron

The **electron affinity** (abbreviated **EA**) *is the potential energy change associated with the addition of an electron to a gaseous atom or ion in its ground state.* For an element X, it is the change in potential energy associated with the process

$$X(g) + e^- \longrightarrow X^-(g)$$

As with ionization energy, electron affinities are usually expressed in units of kilojoules per mole, so we can also view the EA as the energy change associated with adding one mole of electrons to one mole of gaseous atoms or ions.

For nearly all the elements, the addition of one electron to the neutral atom is exothermic, and the EA is given as a negative value. This is because the incoming electron experiences an attraction to the nucleus that causes the potential energy to be lowered as the electron approaches the atom. However, when a second electron must be added, as in the formation of the oxide ion, O^{2-}, work must be done to force the electron into an already negative ion. This is an endothermic process where energy must be added and the EA has a positive value.

Change	EA (kJ/mol)
$O(g) + e^- \longrightarrow O^-(g)$	-141
$O^-(g) + e^- \longrightarrow O^{2-}(g)$	$+844$
$O(g) + 2e^- \longrightarrow O^{2-}(g)$	$+703$ (net)

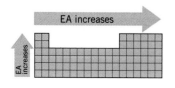

FIG. 7.33 Variation of electron affinity (as an exothermic quantity) within the periodic table.

Notice that more energy is absorbed adding an electron to the O^- ion than is released by adding an electron to the O atom. Overall, the formation of an isolated oxide ion leads to a net increase in potential energy (so we say its formation is *endothermic*). The same applies to the formation of *any* negative ion with a charge larger than $1-$.

The electron affinities of the representative elements are given in Table 7.3, and we see that periodic trends in electron affinity roughly parallel those for ionization energy. (See Facets of Chemistry 7.4 for a discussion of some of the irregularities in the trends.)

TOOLS
Periodic trends in electron affinity

> Although there are some irregularities, overall, the electron affinities of the elements become more *exothermic* going from left to right across a period and from bottom to top in a group (Figure 7.33).

This shouldn't be surprising, because a valence shell that loses electrons easily (low IE) will have little attraction for additional electrons (small EA). On the other hand, a valence shell that holds its electrons tightly will also tend to bind an additional electron tightly.

TABLE 7.3	Electron Affinities of the Representative Elements (kJ/mol)					
IA	IIA	IIIA	IVA	VA	VIA	VIIA
H −73						
Li −60	Be +238	B −27	C −122	N ~ +9	O −141	F −328
Na −53	Mg +230	Al −44	Si −134	P −72	S −200	Cl −348
K −48	Ca +155	Ga −30	Ge −120	As −77	Se −195	Br −325
Rb −47	Sr +167	In −30	Sn −121	Sb −101	Te −190	I −295
Cs −45	Ba +50	Tl −30	Pb −110	Bi −110	Po −183	At −270

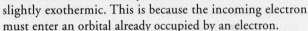

FACETS OF CHEMISTRY

7.4

Irregularities in the Periodic Variations in Ionization Energy and Electron Affinity

The variation in first ionization energy across a period is not a smooth one, as seen in the graph for the elements in period 2. The first irregularity occurs between Be and B, where the IE increases from Li to Be but then decreases from Be to B. This happens because there is a change in the nature of the subshell from which the electron is being removed. For Li and Be, the electron is removed from the 2s subshell, but at boron the first electron comes from the higher energy 2p subshell where it is not bound so tightly.

Another irregularity occurs between nitrogen and oxygen. For nitrogen, the electron that's removed comes from a singly occupied orbital. For oxygen, the electron is taken from an orbital that already contains an electron. We can diagram this as follows:

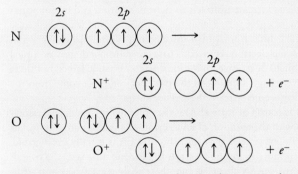

For oxygen, repulsions between the two electrons in the p orbital that's about to lose an electron help the electron leave. This "help" is absent for the electron that's about to leave the p orbital of nitrogen. As a result, it is not as difficult to remove one electron from an oxygen atom as it is to remove one electron from a nitrogen atom.

As with ionization energy, there are irregularities in the periodic trends for electron affinity. For example, the Group IIA elements have little tendency to acquire electrons because their outer shell s orbitals are filled. The incoming electron must enter a higher energy p orbital.

We also see that the EA for elements in Group VA are either endothermic or only slightly exothermic. This is because the incoming electron must enter an orbital already occupied by an electron.

One of the most interesting irregularities occurs between periods 2 and 3 among the nonmetals. In any group, the element in period 2 has a less exothermic electron affinity than the element below it. The reason seems to be the small size of the nonmetal atoms of period 2, which are among the smallest elements in the periodic table. Repulsions between the many electrons in the small valence shells of these atoms leads to a lower than expected attraction for an incoming electron and a less exothermic electron affinity than the element below in period 3.

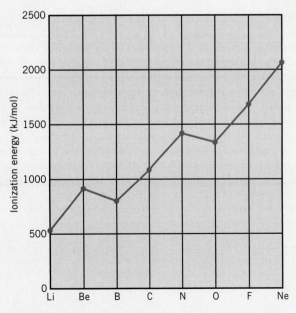

Variation in IE for the Period 2 elements, Li through Ne.

SUMMARY

Electromagnetic Radiation. Electromagnetic radiation, or light energy, travels through space at a constant speed of 3.00×10^8 m s^{-1} in the form of waves. The **wavelength,** λ, and **frequency,** ν, of the wave are related by the equation $\lambda\nu = c$, where c is the **speed of light.** The SI unit for frequency is the **hertz (Hz,** 1 Hz $= 1$ s^{-1}). Light also behaves as if it consists of small packets of energy called **photons** or **quanta.** The energy delivered by a photon is proportional to the frequency of the light, and is given by the equation $E = h\nu$, where h is **Planck's constant.** White light is composed of all the frequencies visible to the eye and can be split into a **continuous spectrum.** Visible light represents only a small portion of the entire **electromagnetic spectrum,** which also includes **X rays, ultraviolet, infrared, microwaves,** and **radio** and **TV** waves.

Atomic Spectra. The occurrence of **line spectra** tells us that atoms can emit energy only in discrete amounts and suggests that the energy of the electron is **quantized;** that is, the electron is restricted to certain specific **energy levels** in an atom. Niels Bohr recognized this and, although his theory was later shown to be incorrect, he was the first to propose a model that was able to account for the **Rydberg equation.** Bohr was the first to introduce the idea of **quantum numbers.**

Matter Waves. The wave behavior of electrons and other tiny particles, which can be demonstrated by **diffraction** experiments, was suggested by de Broglie. Schrödinger applied wave theory to the atom and launched the theory we call **wave mechanics** or **quantum mechanics.** This theory tells us that electron waves in atoms are **standing waves** whose crests and **nodes** are stationary. Each standing wave, or **orbital,** is characterized by three quantum numbers, n, ℓ, and m_ℓ (**principal, secondary,** and **magnetic quantum numbers,** respectively). **Shells** are designated by n (which can range from 1 to ∞), **subshells** by ℓ (which can range from 0 to $n - 1$), and orbitals within subshells by m_ℓ (which can range from $-\ell$ to $+\ell$).

Electron Configurations. The electron has magnetic properties that are explained in terms of spin. The **spin quantum number,** m_s, can have values of $+\frac{1}{2}$ or $-\frac{1}{2}$. The **Pauli exclusion principle** limits orbitals to a maximum population of two electrons with **paired spins.** Substances with unpaired electrons are **paramagnetic** and are attracted weakly to a magnetic field. Substances with only paired electrons are **diamagnetic** and are slightly repelled by a magnetic field. The **electron configuration** of an element in its **ground state** is obtained by filling orbitals beginning with the $1s$ subshell and following the Pauli exclusion principle and **Hund's rule** (which states that electrons spread out as much as possible in orbitals of equal energy). The periodic table serves as a guide in predicting electron configurations. **Abbreviated configurations** show subshell populations outside a noble gas **core.** **Valence shell configurations** show the populations of subshells in the **outer shell** of an atom of the representative elements. Sometimes we represent electron configurations using **orbital diagrams.** Unexpected configurations occur for chromium and copper because of the extra stability of half-filled and filled subshells, respectively.

Orbital Shapes. The **Heisenberg uncertainty principle** says we cannot know exactly the position and velocity of an electron both at the same instant. Consequently, wave mechanics describes the probable locations of electrons in atoms. In each orbital the electron is conveniently viewed as an **electron cloud** with a varying **electron density.** All s orbitals are spherical; each p orbital consists of two lobes with a **nodal plane** between them. A p subshell has three p orbitals whose axes are mutually perpendicular and point along the x, y, and z axes of an imaginary coordinate system centered at the nucleus. Four of the five d orbitals in a d subshell have the same shape, with four lobes of electron density each. The fifth has two lobes of electron density pointing in opposite directions along the z axis and a ring of electron density in the x–y plane.

Atomic Properties. The amount of positive charge felt by the valence electrons of an atom is the **effective nuclear charge.** This is less than the actual nuclear charge because core electrons partially shield the valence electrons from the full positive charge of the nucleus. **Atomic radii** depend on the value of n of the valence shell orbitals and the effective nuclear charge experienced by the valence electrons. These radii are expressed in units of picometers or nanometers, or an older unit called the **angstrom (Å),** where 1 Å $= 100$ pm $= 0.1$ nm. Atomic radii decrease from left to right in a period and from bottom to top in a group in the periodic table. Negative ions are larger than the atoms from which they are formed; positive ions are smaller than the atoms from which they are formed.

Ionization energy (IE) is the energy needed to remove an electron from an isolated gaseous atom, molecule, or ion in its ground state; it is endothermic. The first ionization energies of the elements increase from left to right in a period and from bottom to top in a group. (Irregularities occur in a period when the nature of the orbital from which the electron is removed changes and when the electron removed is first taken from a doubly occupied p orbital.) Successive ionization energies become larger, but there is a very large jump when the next electron must come from the noble gas core beneath the valence shell.

Electron affinity (EA) is the potential energy change associated with the addition of an electron to a gaseous atom or ion in its ground state. For atoms, the first EA is usually exothermic. When more than one electron is added to an atom, the overall potential energy change is endothermic. In general, electron affinity becomes more exothermic from left to right in a period and from bottom to top in a group. (However, the EA of second period nonmetals is less exothermic than for the nonmetals of the third period. Irregularities across a period occur when the electron being added must enter the next higher energy subshell and when it must enter a half-filled p subshell.)

TOOLS FOR PROBLEM SOLVING

Below we list the tools you have learned in this chapter. Notice that only two of them are related to numerical calculations. The others are conceptual tools that we use in analyzing properties of substances in terms of the underlying structure of matter. Review all these tools and refer to them, if necessary, when working on the Review Questions and Problems that follow.

Wavelength–frequency relationship (*page 253*) Use this equation to convert between frequency and wavelength.

$$c = \frac{\lambda}{\nu}$$

Energy of a photon (*page 257*) Use the following equation to calculate the energy carried by a photon of frequency ν. Also, ν can be calculated if E is known.

$$E = h\nu = h\frac{c}{\lambda}$$

Periodic table We will use the periodic table as a tool for many purposes. In this chapter you learned to use the periodic table as an aid in writing electron configurations (page 275) of the elements and as a tool to correlate an element's location in the table to similarities in chemical properties (page 280).

Periodic trends in atomic and ionic size (*pages 285, 286*) The periodic table helps us predict relative sizes of atoms and ions.

Periodic trends in ionization energy (*page 288*) Trends are used to compare the ease with which atoms of the elements lose electrons.

Periodic trends in electron affinity (*page 290*) Trends help to compare the tendency of atoms or ions to gain electrons.

QUESTIONS, PROBLEMS, AND EXERCISES

Answers to problems whose numbers are printed in color are given in Appendix B. More challenging problems are marked with asterisks. ILW = Interactive Learningware solution is available at www.wiley.com/college/brady. OH = an Office Hours video is available for this problem.

REVIEW QUESTIONS

Electromagnetic Radiation

7.1 In general terms, why do we call light *electromagnetic radiation*?

7.2 In general, what does the term *frequency* imply? What is meant by the term *frequency of light*? What symbol is used for it, and what is the SI unit (and symbol) for frequency?

7.3 What is meant by the term *wavelength* of light? What symbol is used for it?

7.4 Sketch a picture of a wave and label its wavelength and its amplitude.

7.5 Which property of light waves is a measure of the brightness of the light? Which specifies the color of the light? Which is related to the energy of the light?

7.6 Arrange the following regions of the electromagnetic spectrum in order of increasing wavelength (i.e., shortest wavelength → longest wavelength): microwaves, TV, X rays, ultraviolet, visible, infrared, gamma rays.

7.7 What wavelength range is covered by the *visible spectrum*?

7.8 Arrange the following colors of visible light in order of increasing wavelength: orange, green, blue, yellow, violet, red.

7.9 Write the equation that relates the wavelength and frequency of a light wave. (Define all symbols used.)

7.10 How is the frequency of a particular type of radiation related to the energy associated with it? (Give an equation, defining all symbols.)

7.11 What is a photon?

7.12 Show that the energy of a photon is given by the equation $E = hc/\lambda$.

7.13 Examine each of the following pairs and state which of the two has the higher *energy*.
(a) microwaves and infrared
(b) visible light and infrared
(c) ultraviolet light and X rays
(d) visible light and ultraviolet light

7.14 What is a quantum of energy?

Atomic Spectra

7.15 What is an atomic spectrum? How does it differ from a continuous spectrum?

7.16 What fundamental fact is implied by the existence of atomic spectra?

Bohr Atom and the Hydrogen Spectrum

7.17 Describe Niels Bohr's model of the structure of the hydrogen atom.

7.18 In qualitative terms, how did Bohr's model account for the atomic spectrum of hydrogen?

7.19 What is the "ground state"?

7.20 In what way was Bohr's theory a success? How was it a failure?

Wave Nature of Matter

7.21 How does the behavior of very small particles differ from that of the larger, more massive objects that we meet in everyday life? Why don't we notice this same behavior for the larger, more massive objects?

7.22 Describe the phenomenon called diffraction. How can this be used to demonstrate that de Broglie's theory was correct?

7.23 What experiment could you perform to determine whether a beam was behaving as a wave or as a stream of particles?

7.24 What is *wave/particle duality*?

7.25 What is the difference between a *traveling wave* and a *standing wave*?

7.26 What is the collapsing atom paradox?

7.27 How does quantum mechanics resolve the collapsing atom paradox?

Electron Waves in Atoms

7.28 What are the names used to refer to the theories that apply the matter–wave concept to electrons in atoms?

7.29 What is the term used to describe a particular waveform of a standing wave for an electron?

7.30 What are the two properties of orbitals in which we are most interested? Why?

Quantum Numbers

7.31 What are the allowed values of the principal quantum number?

7.32 What is the value for n for (a) the K shell and (b) the M shell?

7.33 Why does every shell contain an s subshell?

7.34 How many orbitals are found in (a) an s subshell, (b) a p subshell, (c) a d subshell, and (d) an f subshell?

7.35 If the value of m_ℓ for an electron in an atom is 2, could another electron in the same subshell have $m_\ell = -3$?

7.36 Suppose an electron in an atom has the following set of quantum numbers: $n = 2$, $\ell = 1$, $m_\ell = 1$, $m_s = +\frac{1}{2}$. What set of quantum numbers is impossible for another electron in this same atom?

Electron Spin

7.37 What physical property of electrons leads us to propose that they spin like a toy top?

7.38 What is the name of the magnetic property exhibited by atoms that contain unpaired electrons?

7.39 What is the Pauli exclusion principle? What effect does it have on the populating of orbitals by electrons?

7.40 What are the possible values of the spin quantum number?

Electron Configuration of Atoms

7.41 What do we mean by the term *electronic structure?*

7.42 Within any given shell, how do the energies of the s, p, d, and f subshells compare?

7.43 What fact about the energies of subshells was responsible for the apparent success of Bohr's theory about electronic structure?

7.44 How do the energies of the orbitals belonging to a given subshell compare?

7.45 Give the electron configurations of the elements in Period 2 of the periodic table.

7.46 Give the correct electron configurations of (a) Cr and (b) Cu.

7.47 What is the correct electron configuration of silver?

7.48 How are the electron configurations of the elements in a given group similar? Illustrate your answer by writing shorthand configurations for the elements in Group VIA.

7.49 Define the terms *valence shell* and *valence electrons.*

Shapes of Atomic Orbitals

7.50 Why do we use probabilities when we discuss the position of an electron in the space surrounding the nucleus of an atom?

7.51 Sketch the approximate shape of (a) a $1s$ orbital and (b) a $2p$ orbital.

7.52 How does the size of a given type of orbital vary with n?

7.53 How are the p orbitals of a given p subshell oriented relative to each other?

7.54 What is a *nodal plane*?

7.55 What is a spherical node?

7.56 How many nodal planes does a p orbital have? How many does a d orbital have?

7.57 On appropriate coordinate axes, sketch the shape of the following d orbitals: (a) d_{xy}, (b) $d_{x^2-y^2}$, and (c) d_{z^2}.

Atomic and Ionic Size

7.58 What is the meaning of *effective nuclear charge?* How does the effective nuclear charge felt by the outer electrons vary going down a group? How does it change as we go from left to right across a period?

7.59 In what region of the periodic table are the largest atoms found? Where are the smallest atoms found?

7.60 Going from left to right in the periodic table, why are the size changes among the transition elements more gradual than those among the representative elements?

Ionization Energy

7.61 Define ionization energy. Why are ionization energies of atoms and positive ions endothermic quantities?

7.62 For oxygen, write a reaction for the change associated with (a) its first ionization energy and (b) its third ionization energy.

7.63 Explain why ionization energy increases from left to right in a period and decreases from top to bottom in a group.

7.64 Why is an atom's second ionization energy always larger than its first ionization energy?

7.65 Why is the fifth ionization energy of carbon so much larger than its fourth?

7.66 Why is the first ionization energy of aluminum less than the first ionization energy of magnesium?

7.67 Why does phosphorus have a larger first ionization energy than sulfur?

Electron Affinity

7.68 Define *electron affinity*.

7.69 For sulfur, write an equation for the change associated with (a) its first electron affinity and (b) its second electron affinity. How should they compare?

7.70 Why does Cl have a more exothermic electron affinity than F? Why does Br have a less exothermic electron affinity than Cl?

7.71 Why is the second electron affinity of an atom always endothermic?

7.72 How is electron affinity related to effective nuclear charge? On this basis, explain the relative magnitudes of the electron affinities of oxygen and fluorine.

REVIEW PROBLEMS

Electromagnetic Radiation

7.73 What is the frequency in hertz of blue light having a wavelength of 430 nm?

OH 7.74 Ultraviolet light with a wavelength of more than 280 nm has little germicidal value. What is the frequency that corresponds to this wavelength?

7.75 A certain substance strongly absorbs infrared light having a wavelength of 6.85 μm. What is the frequency of this light in hertz?

7.76 The sun emits many wavelengths of light. The brightest light is emitted at about 0.48 μm. What frequency does this correspond to?

7.77 Ozone protects the earth's inhabitants from the harmful effects of ultraviolet light arriving from the sun. This shielding is a maximum for UV light having a wavelength of 295 nm. What is the frequency in hertz of this light?

7.78 The meter is defined as the length of the path light travels in a vacuum during the time interval of 1/299,792,458 of a second. The standards body recommends use of light from a helium–neon laser for realizing the meter. The light from the laser has a wavelength of 632.99139822 nm. What is the frequency of this light, in hertz?

7.79 In New York City, radio station WCBS broadcasts its FM signal at a frequency of 101.1 megahertz (MHz). What is the wavelength of this signal in meters?

7.80 Sodium vapor lamps are often used in residential street lighting. They give off a yellow light having a frequency of 5.09×10^{14} Hz. What is the wavelength of this light in nanometers?

7.81 There has been some concern in recent times about possible hazards to people who live very close to high-voltage electric power lines. The electricity in these wires oscillates at a frequency of 60 Hz, which is the frequency of any electromagnetic radiation that they emit. What is the wavelength of this radiation in meters? What is it in kilometers?

7.82 An X-ray beam has a frequency of 1.50×10^{18} Hz. What is the wavelength of this light in nanometers and in picometers?

7.83 Calculate the energy in joules of a photon of red light having a frequency of 4.0×10^{14} Hz. What is the energy of one mole of these photons?

7.84 Calculate the energy in joules of a photon of green light having a wavelength of 560 nm.

Atomic Spectra

7.85 In the spectrum of hydrogen, there is a line with a wavelength of 410.3 nm. (a) What color is this line? (b) What is its frequency? (c) What is the energy of each of its photons?

7.86 In the spectrum of sodium, there is a line with a wavelength of 589 nm. (a) What color is this line? (b) What is its frequency? (c) What is the energy of each of its photons?

OH 7.87 Use the Rydberg equation to calculate the wavelength in nanometers of the spectral line of hydrogen for which $n_2 = 6$ and $n_1 = 3$. Would we be expected to see the light corresponding to this spectral line? Explain your answer.

7.88 Use the Rydberg equation to calculate the wavelength in nanometers of the spectral line of hydrogen for which $n_2 = 5$ and $n_1 = 2$. Would we be expected to see the light corresponding to this spectral line? Explain your answer.

7.89 Calculate the wavelength of the spectral line produced in the hydrogen spectrum when an electron falls from the tenth Bohr orbit to the fourth. In which region of the electromagnetic spectrum (UV, visible, or infrared) is the line?

7.90 Calculate the energy in joules and the wavelength in nanometers of the spectral line produced in the hydrogen spectrum when an electron falls from the fourth Bohr orbit to the first. In which region of the electromagnetic spectrum (UV, visible, or infrared) is the line?

Quantum Numbers

7.91 What is the letter code for a subshell with (a) $\ell = 1$ and (b) $\ell = 3$?

7.92 What is the value of ℓ for (a) an f orbital and (b) a d orbital?

7.93 Give the values of n and ℓ for the following subshells: (a) $3s$ and (b) $5d$.

7.94 Give the values of n and ℓ for the following subshells: (a) $4p$ and (b) $6f$.

7.95 For the shell with $n = 6$, what are the possible values of ℓ?

7.96 In a particular shell, the largest value of ℓ is 7. What is the value of n for this shell?

7.97 What are the possible values of m_ℓ for a subshell with (a) $\ell = 1$ and (b) $\ell = 3$?

7.98 If the value of ℓ for an electron in an atom is 5, what are the possible values of m_ℓ that this electron could have?

7.99 If the value of m_ℓ for an electron in an atom is -4, what is the smallest value of ℓ that the electron could have? What is the smallest value of n that the electron could have?

7.100 How many orbitals are there in an h subshell ($\ell = 5$)? What are their values of m_ℓ?

OH 7.101 Give the complete set of quantum numbers for all of the electrons that could populate the $2p$ subshell of an atom.

7.102 Give the complete set of quantum numbers for all of the electrons that could populate the $3d$ subshell of an atom.

7.103 In an antimony atom, how many electrons have $\ell = 1$? How many electrons have $\ell = 2$ in an antimony atom?

7.104 In an atom of barium, how many electrons have (a) $\ell = 0$ and (b) $m_\ell = 1$?

Electron Configurations of Atoms

7.105 Give the electron configurations of (a) S, (b) K, (c) Ti, and (d) Sn.

7.106 Write the electron configurations of (a) As, (b) Cl, (c) Ni, and (d) Si.

7.107 Which of the following atoms in their ground states are expected to be paramagnetic: (a) Mn, (b) As, (c) S, (d) Sr, and (e) Ar?

7.108 Which of the following atoms in their ground states are expected to be diamagnetic: (a) Ba, (b) Se, (c) Zn, and (d) Si?

ILW OH 7.109 How many unpaired electrons would be found in the ground state of (a) Mg, (b) P, and (c) V?

7.110 How many unpaired electrons would be found in the ground state of (a) Cs, (b) S, and (c) Ni?

7.111 Write the shorthand electron configurations for (a) Ni, (b) Cs, (c) Ge, (d) Br, and (e) Bi.

7.112 Write the shorthand electron configurations for (a) Al, (b) Se, (c) Ba, (d) Sb, and (e) Gd.

7.113 Draw complete orbital diagrams for (a) Mg and (b) Ti.

7.114 Draw complete orbital diagrams for (a) As and (b) Ni.

7.115 Draw orbital diagrams for the shorthand configurations of (a) Ni, (b) Cs, (c) Ge, and (d) Br.

7.116 Draw orbital diagrams for the shorthand configurations of (a) Al, (b) Se, (c) Ba, and (d) Sb.

7.117 What is the value of n for the valence shells of (a) Sn, (b) K, (c) Br, and (d) Bi?

7.118 What is the value of n for the valence shells of (a) Al, (b) Se, (c) Ba, and (d) Sb?

7.119 Give the configuration of the valence shell for (a) Na, (b) Al, (c) Ge, and (d) P.

7.120 Give the configuration of the valence shell for (a) Mg, (b) Br, (c) Ga, and (d) Pb.

7.121 Draw the orbital diagram for the valence shell for (a) Na, (b) Al, (c) Ge, and (d) P.

7.122 Draw the orbital diagram for the valence shell of (a) Mg, (b) Br, (c) Ga, and (d) Pb.

Atomic Properties

7.123 If the core electrons were 100% effective at shielding the valence electrons from the nuclear charge and the valence electrons

provided no shielding for each other, what would be the effective nuclear charge felt by a valence electron in (a) Na, (b) S, and (c) Cl?

7.124 If the core electrons were 100% effective at shielding the valence electrons from the nuclear charge and the valence electrons provided no shielding for each other, what would be the effective nuclear charge felt by a valence electron in (a) Mg, (b) Si, and (c) Br?

7.125 Choose the larger atom in each pair: (a) Mg or S; (b) As or Bi.

7.126 Choose the larger atom in each pair: (a) Al or Ar; (b) Tl or In.

7.127 Choose the largest atom among the following: Ge, As, Sn, and Sb.

7.128 Place the following in order of increasing size: N^{3-}, Mg^{2+}, Na^+, Ne, F^-, and O^{2-}.

7.129 Choose the larger particle in each pair: (a) Na or Na^+; (b) Co^{3+} or Co^{2+}; (c) Cl or Cl^-.

OH 7.130 Choose the larger particle in each pair: (a) S or S^{2-}; (b) Al^{3+} or Al; (c) Au^+ or Au^{3+}.

7.131 Choose the atom with the larger first ionization energy in each pair: (a) B or N; (b) Se or S; (c) Cl or Ge.

7.132 Choose the atom with the larger first ionization energy in each pair: (a) Li or Rb ; (b) Al or F; (c) F or C.

7.133 Choose the atom with the more exothermic electron affinity in each pair: (a) I or Br; (b) Ga or As.

7.134 Choose the atom with the more exothermic electron affinity in each pair: (a) S or As; (b) Si or N.

7.135 Use the periodic table to select the element in the following list for which there is the largest difference between the second and third ionization energies: Na, Mg, Al, Si, P, Se, and Cl.

7.136 Use the periodic table to select the element in the following list for which there is the largest difference between the fourth and fifth ionization energies: Na, Mg, Al, Si, P, Se, and Cl.

ADDITIONAL EXERCISES

7.137 The human ear is sensitive to sound ranging from 20 to 20,000 Hz. The speed of sound is 330 m/s in air, and 1500 m/s under water. What is the longest and the shortest wavelength that can be heard (a) in air and (b) under water?

7.138 Microwaves are used to heat food in microwave ovens. The microwave radiation is absorbed by moisture in the food. This heats the water, and as the water becomes hot, so does the food. How many photons having a wavelength of 3.00 mm would have to be absorbed by 1.00 g of water to raise its temperature by 1.00 °C?

7.139 In the spectrum of hydrogen, there is a line with a wavelength of 410.3 nm. Use the Rydberg equation to calculate the value of n for the higher energy Bohr orbit involved in the emission of this light. Assume the value of n for the lower energy orbit equals 2.

7.140 Calculate the wavelength in nanometers of the shortest wavelength of light emitted by a hydrogen atom.

7.141 Which of the following electronic transitions could lead to the emission of light from an atom?

$$1s \longrightarrow 4p \longrightarrow 3d \longrightarrow 5f \longrightarrow 4d \longrightarrow 2p$$

7.142 A neon sign is a gas discharge tube in which electrons traveling from the cathode to the anode collide with neon atoms in the tube and knock electrons off of them. As electrons return to the neon ions and drop to lower energy levels, light is given off. How fast would an electron have to be moving to eject an electron from an atom of neon, which has a first ionization energy equal to 2080 kJ mol^{-1}?

OH *7.143** How many grams of water could have its temperature raised by 5.0 °C by a mole of photons that have a wavelength of (a) 600 nm and (b) 300 nm?

OH *7.144** It has been found that when the chemical bond between chlorine atoms in Cl_2 is formed, 328 kJ is released per mole of Cl_2 formed. What is the wavelength of light that would be required to break chemical bonds between chlorine atoms?

7.145 Calculate the wavelengths of the lines in the spectrum of hydrogen that result when an electron falls from a Bohr orbit with (a) $n = 5$ to $n = 1$, (b) $n = 4$ to $n = 2$, and (c) $n = 6$ to $n = 4$. In which regions of the electromagnetic spectrum are these lines?

OH 7.146 What, if anything, is wrong with the following electron configurations for atoms in their ground states?

(a) $1s^2 2s^1 2p^3$ (c) $1s^2 2s^2 2p^4$
(b) [Kr] $3d^7 4s^2$ (d) [Xe] $4f^{14} 5d^8 6s^1$

7.147 Suppose students gave the following orbital diagrams for the $2s$ and $2p$ subshell in the ground state of an atom. What, if anything, is wrong with them? Are any of these electron distributions impossible?

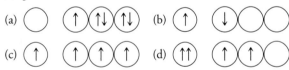

7.148 How many electrons are in p orbitals in an atom of germanium?

7.149 What are the quantum numbers of the electrons that are lost by an atom of iron when it forms the ion Fe^{2+}?

*7.150 The removal of an electron from the hydrogen atom corresponds to raising the electron to the Bohr orbit that has $n = \infty$. On the basis of this statement, calculate the ionization energy of

hydrogen in units of (a) joules per atom and (b) kilojoules per mole.

7.151 Use orbital diagrams to illustrate what happens when an oxygen atom gains two electrons. On the basis of what you have learned about electron affinities and electron configurations, why is it extremely difficult to place a third electron on the oxygen atom?

7.152 From the data available in this chapter, determine the ionization energy of (a) F^-, (b) O^-, and (c) O^{2-}. Are any of these energies exothermic?

7.153 For an oxygen atom, which requires more energy, the addition of two electrons or the removal of one electron?

EXERCISES IN CRITICAL THINKING

7.154 Our understanding of the quantum mechanical atom has been developing since the early 1900s. Has quantum mechanics had any effect on the daily lives of people?

7.155 When a copper atom loses an electron to become a Cu^+ ion, what are the possible quantum numbers of the electron that was lost?

7.156 The "red shift" of spectral features of distant stars is used to estimate their relative velocity compared to the earth. Using the information in this chapter, and other reference sources, explain how this is done.

7.157 Placing a small piece of an element from Group IA in water results in increasingly rapid and violently spectacular reactions as we progress from lithium down to cesium. What information in this chapter makes this behavior understandable?

7.158 In this chapter we saw that atoms in an excited state emit light when their electrons relax to lower energy levels. Lasers also emit certain wavelengths of light. What are the similarities and differences in how laser light is produced compared to atomic spectra?

7.159 In this chapter we saw that atoms in an excited state emit light when their electrons relax to lower energy levels. Light emitting diodes, LEDs, can be designed to emit light of different colors. How does the way light is produced in an LED differ from an excited state atom?

CHEMICAL BONDING: GENERAL CONCEPTS

8

Children learn that they can build complex structures by linking together blocks such as these. Molecules in chemical compounds are likewise built by linking together atoms of various kinds. In this chapter we begin our study of the nature of the forces, called chemical bonds, that bind atoms to each other in compounds. Such knowledge is important because the kinds and strengths of chemical bonds determine the chemical properties of substances. *(Ted Horowitz/Corbis)*

CHAPTER OUTLINE

8.1 Electron transfer leads to the formation of ionic compounds

8.2 Lewis symbols help keep track of valence electrons

8.3 Covalent bonds are formed by electron sharing

8.4 Covalent bonds can have partial charges at opposite ends

8.5 The reactivities of metals and nonmetals can be related to their electronegativities

8.6 Drawing Lewis structures is a necessary skill

8.7 Resonance applies when a single Lewis structure fails

THIS CHAPTER IN CONTEXT In earlier chapters we examined the nature of some ionic and molecular substances. For example, you learned that ionic compounds, such as ordinary table salt, consist of electrically charged particles (ions) that bind to each other by electrostatic forces. In water, ionic compounds dissociate and undergo the kinds of reactions we discussed in Chapter 4. Molecular compounds, on the other hand, are composed of atoms that bind to each other by sharing electrons, which causes them to undergo different kinds of reactions. To understand such differences in chemical properties, we need to know more about the nature of the attractions, which we call **chemical bonds,** that exist between atoms in compounds. Therefore, our principal goal in this chapter is to gain some insight into the reasons why certain combinations of atoms prefer electron transfer and the formation of ions (leading to *ionic bonding*) while other combinations bind by electron sharing (leading to *covalent bonding*).

As with electronic structure, models of chemical bonding have evolved, and in this chapter we introduce you to relatively simple theories. Although more complex theories exist (some of which we will explore in Chapter 9), the basic concepts you will study in this chapter still find many useful applications in modern chemical thought.

8.1 | ELECTRON TRANSFER LEADS TO THE FORMATION OF IONIC COMPOUNDS

In Chapter 2 you learned that ionic compounds are formed when metals react with non-metals. Among the examples discussed was sodium chloride, table salt. You learned that when this compound is formed from its elements, each sodium atom loses one electron to form a sodium ion, Na^+, and each chlorine atom gains one electron to become a chloride ion, Cl^-.

$$Na \longrightarrow Na^+ + e^-$$
$$Cl + e^- \longrightarrow Cl^-$$

Once formed, these ions become tightly packed together, as illustrated in Figure 8.1, because their opposite charges attract. *This attraction between positive and negative ions in an ionic compound is what we call an* **ionic bond.**

The reason Na^+ and Cl^- ions attract each other is easy to understand. But *why* are electrons transferred between these and other atoms? *Why* does sodium form Na^+ and not Na^- or Na^{2+}? And *why* does chlorine form Cl^- instead of Cl^+ or Cl^{2-}? To answer such questions we have to consider factors that are related to the potential energy of the system of reactants and products. This is because *for any stable compound to form from its elements, there must be a net lowering of the potential energy.* In other words, the reaction must be exothermic.

☐ Keep in mind the relationship between potential energy changes and endothermic and exothermic processes:

endothermic ⟺ increase in PE
exothermic ⟺ decrease in PE

The lattice energy enables ionic compounds to form

Let's begin by examining the energy change associated with the exchange of electrons between sodium atoms and chlorine atoms. If we deal with a collection of gaseous atoms, we can use the ionization energy (IE) and electron affinity (EA) of sodium and chlorine, respectively. Working on a mole basis, we have

$Na(g) \longrightarrow Na^+(g) + e^-$	$+495.4$ kJ	(IE of sodium)
$Cl(g) + e^- \longrightarrow Cl^-(g)$	-348.8 kJ	(EA of chlorine)
Net	$+146.6$ kJ	

This calculation tells us that forming gaseous sodium and chloride ions from gaseous sodium and chlorine atoms requires a substantial increase in the potential energy. In fact, if the IE and EA were the only energy changes involved, ionic sodium chloride would not form from sodium and chlorine. So where does the stability of the compound come from? The answer is seen if we examine a quantity called the lattice energy.

In the calculation above, we looked at the formation of gaseous ions, but salt is not a gas; it's a solid in which the ions are packed together in a way that maximizes the attractions between oppositely charged ions. Imagine, now, pulling these ions away from each other to form a gas of ions. This process would require a lot of work and would lead to a large increase in the potential energies of the ions. The **lattice energy** *is the energy required to completely separate the ions in one mole of a solid compound from each other to form a cloud of gaseous ions.* For sodium chloride, the process associated with the lattice energy is pictured in Figure 8.2 and in equation form can be represented as

$$NaCl(s) \longrightarrow Na^+(g) + Cl^-(g)$$

The energy associated with this change (the *lattice energy* of sodium chloride) has been both measured and calculated to be $+787.0$ kJ mol^{-1}. The positive sign means that it takes 787.0 kJ to separate the ions of one mole of NaCl. *It also means that if we bring together a mole of Na^+ and Cl^- ions from the gaseous state into one mole of crystalline NaCl, 787 kJ will be released.* If we now include the lattice energy (with its sign reversed because we're changing the direction of the change) along with the IE and EA, we have

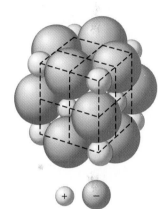

FIG. 8.1 **Packing of ions in NaCl.** In NaCl electrostatic forces hold the ions in place in the solid. Those forces constitute ionic bonds.

☐ The name lattice energy comes from the word *lattice*, which is used to describe the regular pattern of ions or atoms in a crystal. Lattice energies are endothermic and so are given positive signs.

	$Na(g) \longrightarrow Na^+(g) + e^-$	$+495.4$ kJ	(IE of sodium)
	$Cl(g) + e^- \longrightarrow Cl^-(g)$	-348.8 kJ	(EA of chlorine)
	$Na^+(g) + Cl^-(g) \longrightarrow NaCl(s)$	-787.0 kJ	($-$lattice energy)
Net	$Na(g) + Cl(g) \longrightarrow NaCl(s)$	-640.4 kJ	

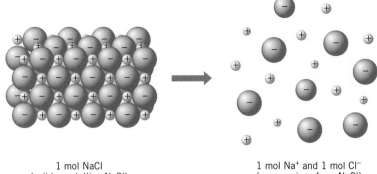

1 mol NaCl
(solid, crystalline NaCl)

1 mol Na^+ and 1 mol Cl^-
(gaseous ions from NaCl)

FIG. 8.2 **Lattice energy of NaCl.** The lattice energy is equal to the amount of energy needed to separate the ions in one mole of an ionic compound. For NaCl, the process requires converting a mole of crystalline NaCl into two moles of ions (1 mol Na^+ and 1 mol Cl^-). The amount of energy absorbed equals 787 kJ.

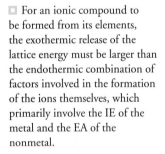

☐ For an ionic compound to be formed from its elements, the exothermic release of the lattice energy must be larger than the endothermic combination of factors involved in the formation of the ions themselves, which primarily involve the IE of the metal and the EA of the nonmetal.

Thus, the release of energy equivalent to the lattice energy provides a large net lowering of the potential energy as solid NaCl is formed. We can also say that *it is the lattice energy that provides the stabilization necessary for the formation of NaCl.* Without it, the solid compound could not exist.

At this point, you may be wondering about our starting point in these energy calculations, gaseous sodium atoms and chlorine atoms. In nature, sodium is a solid metal and chlorine consists of gaseous Cl_2 molecules. A complete analysis of the energy changes has to take this into account, and we do this in Facets of Chemistry 8.1. Our overall conclusion doesn't change, however. *For any ionic compound, the chief stabilizing influence is the lattice energy, which when released is large enough to overcome the net energy input required to form the ions from the elements.*

Lattice energy depends on ionic size and charge

The lattice energies of some ionic compounds are given in Table 8.1. As you can see, they are all very large endothermic quantities. Their magnitudes depend on a number of factors, including the sizes of the ions and their charges.[1] In general, as the ions become smaller, the lattice energy increases; smaller ions allow the charges to get closer together

TABLE 8.1	Lattice Energies of Some Ionic Compounds	
Compound	Ions	Lattice Energy (kJ mol^{-1})
LiCl	Li^+ and Cl^-	845
NaCl	Na^+ and Cl^-	787
KCl	K^+ and Cl^-	709
LiF	Li^+ and F^-	1033
$CaCl_2$	Ca^{2+} and Cl^-	2258
$AlCl_3$	Al^{3+} and Cl^-	5492
CaO	Ca^{2+} and O^{2-}	3401
Al_2O_3	Al^{3+} and O^{2-}	15,916

[1] The potential energy of two particles with charges q_1 and q_2 separated by a distance r is

$$E = \frac{q_1 q_2}{kr}$$

where k is a proportionality constant. In an ionic solid, q_1 and q_2 have opposite signs, so E is calculated to be a negative quantity. If r increases, E becomes smaller and therefore less negative. As r approaches infinity, corresponding to complete separation of the ions, E approaches zero. Therefore, the more negative the value of E for a pair of ions in the solid, the larger is the amount of energy needed to separate the ions. In a rough way, the size of the lattice energy parallels the magnitude of E. When the charges q_1 and q_2 become larger, E becomes more negative and the lattice energy becomes larger. Similarly, when r becomes smaller, corresponding to smaller ions, E also becomes more negative and the lattice energy becomes larger.

8.1

Calculating the Lattice Energy

In the main body of the text, we described the pivotal role played by the lattice energy in the formation of an ionic compound. But how can we possibly measure the amount of energy required to completely vaporize an ionic compound to give gaseous ions? Actually, we can't measure the lattice energy directly, but we can use Hess's law and some other experimental data to calculate the lattice energy indirectly.

In Chapter 6 you learned that the enthalpy change for a process is the same regardless of the path we follow from start to finish. With this in mind, we can construct a set of alternate paths from the free elements to the solid ionic compound. This is called a Born–Haber cycle after the scientists who were the first to use it to calculate lattice energies, and is shown in the accompanying figure for the formation of sodium chloride.

You may recognize the figure as an enthalpy diagram.

We begin with the free elements, sodium and chlorine. The direct path at the bottom left has as its enthalpy change the heat of formation of NaCl, ΔH_f°.

$$\text{Na}(s) + \tfrac{1}{2}\text{Cl}_2(g) \longrightarrow \text{NaCl}(s) \qquad \Delta H_f^\circ = -411.3 \text{ kJ}$$

The alternative path is divided into a number of steps. The first two steps, both of which have ΔH° values that can be measured experimentally, are endothermic. They change $\text{Na}(s)$ and $\text{Cl}_2(g)$ into gaseous atoms, $\text{Na}(g)$ and $\text{Cl}(g)$. The next two steps change these atoms to ions, first by the endothermic ionization energy (IE) of Na followed by the exothermic electron affinity (EA) of Cl. This brings us to the gaseous ions, $\text{Na}^+(g)$ and $\text{Cl}^-(g)$. Notice that at this point, if we add all the energy changes, the ions are at a considerably higher energy than the reactants. If these were the only energy terms involved in the formation of NaCl, the heat of formation would be endothermic and the compound would be unstable; it could not be formed by direct combination of the elements.

The last step on the right finally brings us to solid NaCl and corresponds the negative of the lattice energy. (Remember, the lattice energy is defined as the energy needed to *separate* the ions; in the last step, we are *bringing the ions together* to form the solid.) To make the net energy changes the same along both paths, the energy released when the ions condense to form the solid must equal -787.0 kJ. Therefore, the calculated lattice energy of NaCl must be $+787.0$ kJ mol^{-1}.

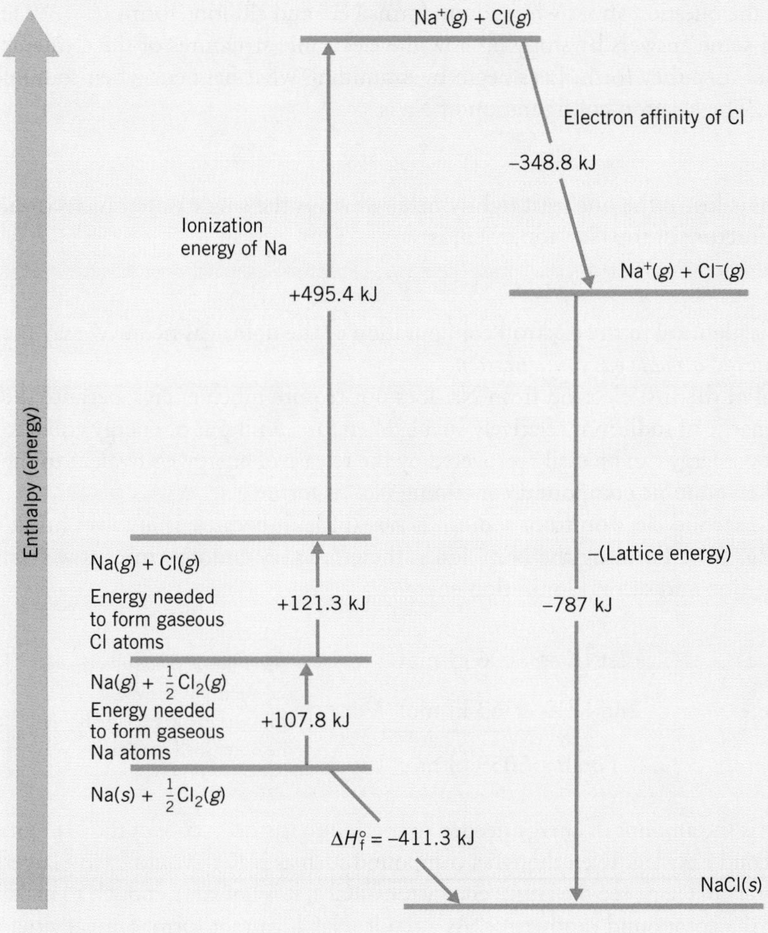

Enthalpy (energy)

$\text{Na}^+(g) + \text{Cl}(g)$

Electron affinity of Cl

-348.8 kJ

Ionization energy of Na

$+495.4$ kJ

$\text{Na}^+(g) + \text{Cl}^-(g)$

$\text{Na}(g) + \text{Cl}(g)$

Energy needed to form gaseous Cl atoms

$+121.3$ kJ

$-$(Lattice energy)

-787 kJ

$\text{Na}(g) + \tfrac{1}{2}\text{Cl}_2(g)$

Energy needed to form gaseous Na atoms

$+107.8$ kJ

$\text{Na}(s) + \tfrac{1}{2}\text{Cl}_2(g)$

$\Delta H_f^\circ = -411.3$ kJ

$\text{NaCl}(s)$

Born–Haber cycle for sodium chloride. The path at the lower left labeled ΔH_f° leads directly to NaCl(s). The upper path involves the formation of gaseous atoms from the elements, then the formation of gaseous ions from the atoms, and finally the condensation of Na$^+$ and Cl$^-$ ions to give solid NaCl. The final step releases energy equivalent to the lattice energy. Both the upper and lower paths lead from the elements to solid NaCl and yield the same net energy change.

which makes them more difficult to pull apart. For example, the lattice energy for LiCl is larger than that for NaCl, reflecting the smaller size of the lithium ion.

The lattice energy also becomes larger as the amount of charge on the ions increases, because more highly charged ions attract each other more strongly. Thus, salts of Ca^{2+} have larger lattice energies than comparable salts of Na^+, and those containing Al^{3+} have even larger lattice energies.

Besides affecting the ability of ionic compounds to form, lattice energies are also important in determining the solubilities of ionic compounds in water and other solvent. We will explore this topic in Chapter 12.

Energy factors determine that metals form cations and nonmetals form anions

We are now in a position to understand why metals tend to form positive ions and nonmetals tend to form negative ions. Metals, at the left of the periodic table, are elements with small ionization energies and electron affinities. Relatively little energy is needed to remove electrons from them to produce positive ions. Nonmetals, at the upper right of the periodic table, have large ionization energies and generally exothermic electron affinities. It is quite difficult to remove electrons from these elements, but sizable amounts of energy are released when they gain electrons. On an energy basis, therefore, it is least "expensive" to form a cation from a metal and an anion from a nonmetal, so it is relatively easy for the energy-lowering effect of the lattice energy to exceed the net energy-raising effect of the ionization energy and electron affinity. In fact, metals combine with nonmetals to form ionic compounds simply because ionic bonding is favored energetically over other types whenever atoms with small ionization energies combine with atoms that have large exothermic electron affinities.

The stability of the noble gas configuration can control which ions are possible

Earlier we raised the question about why sodium forms Na^+ and chlorine forms Cl^-. We're now able to find some answers by studying how the electronic structures of the elements affect the kinds of ions they form. Let's begin by examining what happens when sodium loses an electron. The electron configuration of Na is

$$\text{Na} \qquad 1s^2 2s^2 2p^6 3s^1$$

The electron that is lost is the one least tightly held, which is the single outer $3s$ electron. The electronic structure of the Na^+ ion, then, is

$$Na^+ \qquad 1s^2 2s^2 2p^6$$

Notice that this is identical to the electron configuration of the noble gas neon. We say the Na^+ ion has achieved a *noble gas configuration*.

The removal of the first electron from Na does not require much energy because the first ionization energy of sodium is relatively small. Therefore, an input of energy equal to the first ionization energy can be easily recovered by the release of energy equivalent to the lattice energy when an ionic compound containing Na^+ is formed.

Removal of a second electron from sodium is *very* difficult because it involves breaking into the $2s^2 2p^6$ core. Forming the Na^{2+} ion is therefore very endothermic, as we can see by adding the first and second ionization energies.

$Na(g) \longrightarrow Na^+(g) + e^-$	1st IE =	496 kJ mol^{-1}
$Na^+(g) \longrightarrow Na^{2+}(g) + e^-$	2nd IE =	$\underline{4563 \text{ kJ mol}^{-1}}$
	Total	5059 kJ mol^{-1}

This value is so large because the electron removed is from the noble gas core beneath the outer shell of sodium.

Notice how large is the amount of energy needed to break into the neon core of the Na^+ ion to remove the second electron. Even though a compound such as $NaCl_2$ would have a larger lattice energy than NaCl (e.g., see the lattice energy for $CaCl_2$), it is not large enough to make the formation of the compound exothermic. As a result, $NaCl_2$ cannot form. Similar situations exist for other compounds of sodium, so when sodium forms a cation, electron loss stops once the Na^+ ion is formed and a noble gas electron configuration is reached.

Similar situations exist for other metals, too. For example, the first two electrons to be removed from a calcium atom come from the $4s$ valence shell.

$$\text{Ca} \qquad 1s^2 2s^2 2p^6 3s^2 3p^6 4s^2$$

$$Ca^{2+} \qquad 1s^2 2s^2 2p^6 3s^2 3p^6$$

The energy needed to accomplish this can be recovered by the release of energy equivalent to the lattice energy when a calcium compound forms.[2] Electron loss ceases at this point, however, because of the huge amount of energy needed to break into the noble gas core. As a result, a calcium atom loses just two electrons when it reacts.

In the case of sodium and calcium, we find that the large ionization energy of the noble gas core just below their outer shells limits the number of electrons they lose, so the ions that are formed have noble gas electron configurations.

Nonmetals also tend to have noble gas configurations when they form anions. For example, when a chlorine atom reacts, it gains one electron.

$$Cl \quad 1s^2 2s^2 2p^6 3s^2 3p^5$$
$$Cl^- \quad 1s^2 2s^2 2p^6 3s^2 3p^6$$

At this point, we have a noble gas configuration (that of argon). Electron gain ceases, because if another electron were to be added, it would have to enter an orbital in the next higher shell, which is very energetically unfavorable. Similar arguments apply to the other nonmetals as well.

The octet rule can sometimes provide a guide to the ions formed by elements

In the preceding discussion you learned that a balance of energy factors causes many atoms to form ions that have a noble gas electron configuration. Historically, this is expressed in the form of a generalization: *When they form ions, atoms of most of the representative elements tend to gain or lose electrons until they have obtained a configuration identical to that of the nearest noble gas.* Because all the noble gases except helium have outer shells with eight electrons, this rule has become known as the **octet rule,** which can be stated as follows: *Atoms tend to gain or lose electrons until they have achieved an outer shell that contains an* **octet of electrons** *(eight electrons).*

Many cations do not obey the octet rule

The octet rule, as applied to ionic compounds, really works well only for the cations of the Group IA and IIA metals and for the anions of the nonmetals. It does not work so well for the transition metals and post-transition metals (the metals that follow a row of transition metals).

To obtain the correct electron configurations of the cations of these metals, we apply the following rules:

Obtaining the electron configuration of an ion

1. The first electrons to be lost by an atom or ion are always those from the shell with the largest value of n (i.e., the outer shell).

2. As electrons are removed from a given shell, they come from the highest-energy occupied subshell first, before any are removed from a lower-energy subshell. Within a given shell, the energies of the subshells vary as follows: $s < p < d < f$. This means that f is emptied before d, which is emptied before p, which is emptied before s.

Let's look at two examples.

Tin (a post-transition metal) forms two ions, Sn^{2+} and Sn^{4+}. The electron configurations are

$$Sn \quad [Kr]\, 4d^{10} 5s^2 5p^2$$
$$Sn^{2+} \quad [Kr]\, 4d^{10} 5s^2$$
$$Sn^{4+} \quad [Kr]\, 4d^{10}$$

□ For calcium:

> 1st IE = 590 kJ/mol
> 2nd IE = 1146 kJ/mol
> 3rd IE = 4940 kJ/mol

Because it is so difficult to break into the noble gas core, it's convenient to think of it as being very stable.

TOOLS
Electron configurations of ions of the representative elements

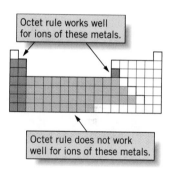

Octet rule works well for ions of these metals.

Octet rule does not work well for ions of these metals.

TOOLS
Order in which electrons are lost from an atom

□ Applying these rules to the metals of Groups IA and IIA also gives the correct electron configurations.

---

[2] Compounds of Ca^+ don't exist because the lattice energies of compounds containing Ca^{2+} are so large that they drive the loss of another electron from the Ca^+ ion. In other words, $CaCl_2$ is more stable than $CaCl$, so the latter never forms.

Notice that the Sn^{2+} ion is formed by the loss of the higher energy $5p$ electrons first. Then, further loss of the two $5s$ electrons gives the Sn^{4+} ion. However, neither of these ions has a noble gas configuration.

For the transition elements, the first electrons lost are the s electrons of the outer shell. Then, if additional electrons are lost, they come from the underlying d subshell. An example is iron, which forms the ions Fe^{2+} and Fe^{3+}. The element iron has the electron configuration

$$Fe \qquad [Ar]\ 3d^6 4s^2$$

Iron loses its $4s$ electrons fairly easily to give Fe^{2+}, which has the electron configuration

$$Fe^{2+} \qquad [Ar]\ 3d^6$$

The Fe^{3+} ion results when another electron is removed, this time from the $3d$ subshell.

$$Fe^{3+} \qquad [Ar]\ 3d^5$$

Iron is able to form Fe^{3+} because the $3d$ subshell is close in energy to the $4s$, so it is not very difficult to remove the third electron. Notice once again that the first electrons to be removed come from the shell with the largest value of n (the $4s$ subshell). Then, after this shell is emptied, the next electrons are removed from the shell below.

Because so many of the transition elements are able to form ions in a way similar to that of iron, the ability to form more than one positive ion is usually cited as one of the characteristic properties of the transition elements. Frequently, one of the ions formed has a 2+ charge, which arises from the loss of the two outer s electrons. Ions with larger positive charges result when additional d electrons are lost. Unfortunately, it is not easy to predict exactly which ions can form for a given transition metal, nor is it simple to predict their relative stabilities with respect to oxidation or reduction.

EXAMPLE 8.1

Writing Electron Configurations of Ions

How do the electron configurations change (a) when a nitrogen atom forms the N^{3-} ion and (b) when an antimony atom forms the Sb^{3+} ion?

ANALYSIS: For the nonmetals, you've learned that the octet rule does work, so the ion that is formed by nitrogen will have a noble gas configuration.

Antimony is a post-transition element, so we don't expect its cation to obey the octet rule. To determine the electron configuration of Sb^{3+}, our tool will be the rules describing the order in which electrons are lost. The rules tell us that when a cation is formed, electrons are removed first from the outer shell of the atom (the shell with the largest value of the principal quantum number, n). Within a given shell, electrons are always removed first from the subshell highest in energy.

SOLUTION: (a) The electron configuration for nitrogen is

$$N \qquad [He]\ 2s^2 2p^3$$

To form N^{3-}, three electrons are gained. These enter the $2p$ subshell because it is the lowest available energy level. Filling the $2p$ subshell completes the octet; the configuration for the ion is therefore

$$N^{3-} \qquad [He]\ 2s^2 2p^6$$

(b) Let's begin with the ground state electron configuration for antimony.

$$Sb \qquad [Kr]\ 4d^{10} 5s^2 5p^3$$

To form the Sb^{3+} ion, three electrons must be removed. These will come from the outer shell, which has $n = 5$. Within this shell, the energies of the subshells increase in the order $s < p < d < f$. Therefore, the $5p$ subshell is higher in energy than the $5s$, so all three electrons are removed from the $5p$. This gives

$$Sb^{3+} \qquad [Kr]\, 4d^{10}5s^2$$

ARE THE ANSWERS REASONABLE?   In Chapter 2 you learned to use the periodic table to figure out the charges on anions of the nonmetals. For nitrogen, we would take three steps to the right to get to the nearest noble gas, neon. The electron configuration we obtained for N^{3-} is that of neon, so our answer should be correct.

For antimony, we had to remove three electrons, which completely emptied the $5p$ subshell. That's also good news, because ions do not tend to have partially filled s or p subshells (although partially filled d subshells are not uncommon for the transition metals). If we had taken the electrons from any other subshells, the Sb^{3+} ion would have had a partially filled $5p$ subshell.

EXAMPLE 8.2
Writing Electron Configurations of Ions

What is the electron configuration of the V^{3+} ion? Give the orbital diagram for the ion.

ANALYSIS: To obtain the electron configuration of an ion, always begin with the electron configuration of the neutral atom. In this case we will then remove three electrons to obtain the electron configuration of the ion. We have to keep in mind that the electrons are lost first from the occupied shell with highest n.

SOLUTION: The electron configuration of vanadium is

$$V \qquad \underbrace{1s^2 2s^2 2p^6 3s^2 3p^6 3d^3 4s^2}_{\text{argon core}}$$

Notice that we've written the configuration showing the outer shell $4s$ electrons farthest to the right. To form the V^{3+} cation, three electrons must be removed from the neutral atom. The first two come from the $4s$ subshell and the third comes from the $3d$. This means we won't have to take any from the $3s$ or $3p$ subshells, so the argon core will remain intact. Therefore, let's rewrite the electron configuration in abbreviated form.

$$V \qquad [Ar]\, 3d^3 4s^2$$

Removing the three electrons gives

$$V^{3+} \qquad [Ar]\, 3d^2$$

To form the orbital diagram, we show all five orbitals of the $3d$ subshell and then spread the two electrons out with spins unpaired. This gives

$$V^{3+} \qquad [Ar] \quad \text{↑} \; \text{↑} \; \bigcirc \; \bigcirc \; \bigcirc$$
$$3d$$

IS THE ANSWER REASONABLE? First, we check that we've written the correct electron configuration of vanadium, which we have. (A quick count of the electrons gives 23, which is the atomic number of vanadium.) We've also taken electrons away from the atom following the rules, so the electron configuration of the ion seems okay. Finally, we remembered to show all five orbitals of the $3d$ subshell, even though only two of the them are occupied.

Practice Exercise 1: What is wrong with the following electron configuration of the In^+ ion? What should the electron configuration be?

$$In^+ \qquad 1s^2 2s^2 2p^6 3s^2 3p^6 3d^{10} 4s^2 4p^6 4d^{10} 5s^1 5p^1$$

(Hint: Check the rules that tell us the order in which electrons are lost by an atom or ion.)

Practice Exercise 2: How do the electron configurations change when a chromium atom forms the following ions: (a) Cr^{2+}, (b) Cr^{3+}, and (c) Cr^{6+}?

Practice Exercise 3: How are the electron configurations of S^{2-} and Cl^- related?

Gilbert N. Lewis, chemistry professor at the University of California, helped develop theories of chemical bonding. In 1916, he proposed that atoms form bonds by sharing pairs of electrons between them. (*Lawrence Berkeley National/ Photo Researchers.*)

TOOLS

Lewis symbols

☐ This is one of the advantages of the North American convention for numbering groups in the periodic table.

8.2 | LEWIS SYMBOLS HELP KEEP TRACK OF VALENCE ELECTRONS

In the last section you saw how the valence shells of atoms change when electrons are transferred during the formation of ions. We will soon study how many atoms share their valence electrons with each other when they form covalent bonds. In these discussions it is useful to be able to keep track of valence electrons. To help us do this, we use a simple bookkeeping device called Lewis symbols, named after their inventor, a famous American chemist, G. N. Lewis (1875–1946).

To draw the **Lewis symbol** for an element, we write its chemical symbol surrounded by a number of dots (or some other similar mark), which represent the atom's valence electrons. For example, the element lithium, which has one valence electron in its $2s$ subshell, has the Lewis symbol

$$Li \cdot$$

In fact, each element in Group IA has a similar Lewis symbol, because each has only one valence electron. The Lewis symbols for all of the Group IA metals are

$$Li \cdot \quad Na \cdot \quad K \cdot \quad Rb \cdot \quad Cs \cdot$$

The Lewis symbols for the eight A group elements of Period 2 are[3]

Group	IA	IIA	IIIA	IVA	VA	VIA	VIIA	VIIIA
Symbol	Li·	·Be·	·Ḃ·	·Ċ·	·N̈:	·Ö:	·F̈:	:N̈e:

The elements below each of these in their respective groups have identical Lewis symbols except, of course, for the chemical symbol of the element. Notice that when an atom has more than four valence electrons, the additional electrons are shown to be paired with others. Also notice that *for the representative elements, the group number is equal to the number of valence electrons* when the North American convention for numbering groups in the periodic table is followed.

EXAMPLE 8.3
Writing Lewis Symbols

What is the Lewis symbol for arsenic?

ANALYSIS: We need to know the number of valence electrons, which we can obtain from the group number. Then we distribute the electrons (dots) around the chemical symbol.

SOLUTION: The symbol for arsenic is As and we find it in Group VA. The element therefore has five valence electrons. The first four are placed around the symbol for arsenic as follows:

$$\cdot \overset{\cdot}{As} \cdot$$

---

[3] For beryllium, boron, and carbon, the number of unpaired electrons in the Lewis symbol doesn't agree with the number predicted from the atom's electron configuration. Boron, for example, has two electrons paired in its $2s$ orbital and a third electron in one of its $2p$ orbitals; therefore, there is actually only one unpaired electron in a boron atom. The Lewis symbols are drawn as shown, however, because when beryllium, boron, and carbon form bonds, they *behave* as if they have two, three, and four unpaired electrons, respectively.

The fifth electron is paired with one of the first four. This gives

$$\cdot \overset{\textstyle\cdot}{\underset{\textstyle\cdot}{As}} :$$

The location of the fifth electron doesn't really matter, so equally valid Lewis symbols are

$$\cdot \overset{\textstyle\cdot\cdot}{As} \cdot \quad \text{or} \quad : \overset{\textstyle\cdot}{As} \cdot \quad \text{or} \quad \cdot \overset{\textstyle\cdot}{\underset{\textstyle\cdot\cdot}{As}} \cdot$$

IS THE ANSWER REASONABLE? There's not much to check here. Have we got the correct chemical symbol? Yes. Do we have the right number of dots? Yes.

Although we will use Lewis symbols mostly to follow the fate of valence electrons in covalent bonds, they can also be used to describe what happens during the formation of ions. For example, when a sodium atom reacts with a chlorine atom, the electron transfer can be depicted as

$$Na\,\overset{\frown}{\circ}+\!\overset{\cdot\cdot}{\underset{\cdot\cdot}{Cl}}: \longrightarrow Na^+ + \left[:\overset{\cdot\cdot}{\underset{\cdot\cdot}{Cl}}:\right]^-$$

The valence shell of the sodium atom is emptied, so no dots remain. The outer shell of chlorine, which formerly had seven electrons, gains one to give a total of eight. The brackets are drawn around the chloride ion to show that all eight electrons are the exclusive property of the Cl^- ion.

We can diagram a similar reaction between calcium and chlorine atoms.

$$:\overset{\cdot\cdot}{\underset{\cdot\cdot}{Cl}}\cdot \overset{\curvearrowleft}{} \,\circ\, Ca \,\circ\, \overset{\curvearrowright}{} \cdot\overset{\cdot\cdot}{\underset{\cdot\cdot}{Cl}}: \longrightarrow Ca^{2+} + 2\left[:\overset{\cdot\cdot}{\underset{\cdot\cdot}{Cl}}:\right]^-$$

EXAMPLE 8.4
Using Lewis Symbols

Use Lewis symbols to diagram the reaction that occurs between sodium and oxygen atoms to give Na^+ and O^{2-} ions.

ANALYSIS: For electrical neutrality, the formula will be Na_2O, so we know we will use two sodium atoms and one oxygen atom. The sodiums will lose one electron each to give Na^+ and the oxygen will gain two electrons to give O^{2-}.

SOLUTION: First let's draw the Lewis symbols for Na and O.

$$Na\cdot \quad \cdot\overset{\cdot\cdot}{O}:$$

It takes two electrons to complete the octet around oxygen. Each Na supplies one. Therefore,

$$Na\,\overset{\curvearrowright}{}\,\cdot\overset{\cdot\cdot}{O}:\,\overset{\curvearrowleft}{}\,Na \longrightarrow 2Na^+ + \left[:\overset{\cdot\cdot}{\underset{\cdot\cdot}{O}}:\right]^{2-}$$

Notice that we have put brackets around the oxide ion.

IS THE ANSWER REASONABLE? We have accounted for all the valence electrons (an important check), the net charge is the same on both sides of the arrow (the equation is balanced), and we've placed the brackets around the oxide ion to emphasize that the octet belongs exclusively to that ion.

Practice Exercise 4: Use Lewis symbols to diagram the formation of CaI_2 from Ca and I atoms. (Hint: Begin by determining how many electrons are gained or lost by each atom.)

Practice Exercise 5: Diagram the reaction between magnesium and oxygen atoms to give Mg^{2+} and O^{2-} ions.

Most of the substances we encounter in our daily lives are not ionic. Instead, they are composed of electrically neutral molecules. The chemical bonds that bind the atoms to each other in such molecules are electrical in nature, but they arise from the sharing of electrons rather than by electron transfer.

Forming a covalent bond lowers the potential energy

Earlier we saw that for ionic bonding to occur, the energy-lowering effect of the lattice energy must be greater than the combined net energy-raising effects of the ionization energy (IE) and electron affinity (EA). Many times this is not possible, particularly when the ionization energies of all the atoms involved are large. This happens, for example, when nonmetals combine with each other to form molecules. In such cases, nature uses a different way to lower the energy—electron sharing.

Let's look at what happens when two hydrogen atoms join to form an H_2 molecule (Figure 8.3). As the two atoms approach each other, the electron of each atom begins to feel the attraction of both nuclei. This causes the electron density around each nucleus to shift toward the region between the two atoms. Therefore, as the distance between the nuclei decreases, there is an increase in the probability of finding either electron near either nucleus. In effect, as the molecule is formed, each of the hydrogen atoms in the H_2 molecule acquires a share of two electrons.

In the H_2 molecule, the buildup of electron density between the two atoms attracts both nuclei and pulls them together. Being of the same charge, however, the two nuclei also repel each other, as do the two electrons. In the molecule that forms, therefore, the atoms are held at a distance at which all these attractions and repulsions are balanced. Overall, the nuclei are kept from separating, and the net force of attraction produced by sharing the pair of electrons is called a **covalent bond.**

Every covalent bond is characterized by two quantities, the average distance between the nuclei held together by the bond, and the amount of energy needed to separate the two atoms to produce neutral atoms again. In the hydrogen molecule, the attractive forces pull the nuclei to a distance of 75 pm, and this distance is called the **bond length** (or sometimes the **bond distance**). Because a covalent bond holds atoms together, work must be done (energy must be supplied) to separate them. The amount of energy needed to "break" the bond (or the energy released when the bond is formed) is called the **bond energy.**

Figure 8.4 shows how the potential energy changes when two hydrogen atoms come together to form H_2. We see that the minimum potential energy occurs at a bond distance of 75 pm, and that 1 mol of hydrogen molecules is more stable than 2 mol of hydrogen atoms by 435 kJ. In other words, the bond energy of H_2 is 435 kJ/mol.

Pairing of electrons occurs when a covalent bond forms

Before joining, each of the separate hydrogen atoms has one electron in a $1s$ orbital. When these electrons are shared, the $1s$ orbital of each atom is, in a sense, filled. Because the electrons now share the same space, they become paired as required by the Pauli exclusion

☐ As the distance between the nuclei and the electron cloud that lies between them decreases, the potential energy decreases.

FIG. 8.3 Formation of a covalent bond between two hydrogen atoms. (*a*) Two H atoms separated by a large distance. (*b*) As the atoms approach each other, their electron densities are pulled into the region between the two nuclei. (*c*) In the H_2 molecule, the electron density is concentrated between the nuclei. Both electrons in the bond are distributed over both nuclei.

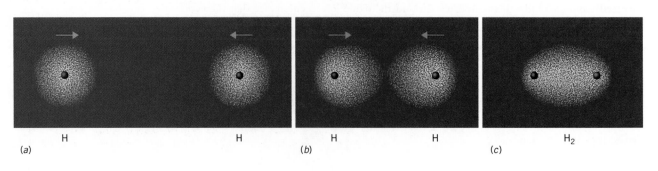

(*a*) H   (*b*) H   H   (*c*) H_2

8.2

Sunlight and Skin Cancer

The ability of light to provide the energy for chemical reactions enables life to exist on our planet. Green plants absorb sunlight and, with the help of chlorophyll, convert carbon dioxide and water into carbohydrates (e.g., sugars and cellulose), which are essential constituents of the food chain. However, not all effects of sunlight are so beneficial.

As you know, light packs energy that's proportional to its frequency, and if the photons that are absorbed by a substance have enough energy, they can rupture chemical bonds and initiate chemical reactions. Light that is able to do this has frequencies in the UV region of the electromagnetic spectrum, and the sunlight bombarding the earth contains substantial amounts of UV radiation. Fortunately, a layer of ozone (O_3) in the stratosphere, a region of the atmosphere extending from about 45 to 55 km altitude, absorbs most of the incoming UV, protecting life on the surface. However, some UV radiation does get through, and the part of the spectrum of most concern is called "UV-B" with wavelengths between 280 and 320 nm.

What makes UV-B so dangerous is its ability to affect the DNA in our cells. (The structure of DNA and its replication are discussed in Chapter 22.) Absorption of UV radiation causes constituents of the DNA, called *pyrimidine bases*, to undergo reactions that form bonds between them. This causes transcription errors when the

DNA replicates during cell division, giving rise to genetic mutations that can lead to skin cancers. These skin cancers fall into three classes: basal cell carcinomas, squamous cell carcinomas, and melanomas (the last being the most dangerous). Recent estimates indicate that in the United States there were about 500,000 cases of the first, 100,000 cases of the second, and 27,600 cases of the third. It has also been estimated that more than 90% of the skin cancers are due to absorption of UV-B radiation.

In recent years concern has grown over the apparent depletion of the ozone layer in the stratosphere caused by the release of gases called chlorofluorocarbons (CFCs), which have been widely used in refrigerators and air conditioners. Some scientists have estimated a substantial increase in the rate of skin cancer caused by increased amounts of UV-B reaching the earth's surface due to this ozone depletion.

Dawn of a new day brings the risk of skin cancer to those particularly susceptible. Fortunately, understanding the risk allows us to protect ourselves with clothing and sunblock creams. *(Taxi/Getty Images.)*

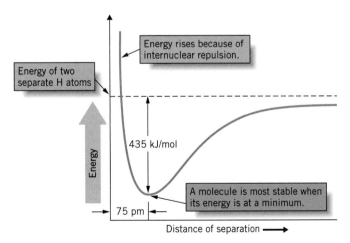

FIG. 8.4 Changes in the potential energies of two hydrogen atoms as they form H_2. The energy of the molecule reaches a minimum when there is a balance between the attractions and repulsions.

principle; that is, m_s is $+\frac{1}{2}$ for one of the electrons and $-\frac{1}{2}$ for the other. In general, the electrons involved almost always become paired when atoms form covalent bonds. In fact, a covalent bond is sometimes referred to as an **electron pair bond.**

Lewis symbols are often used to keep track of electrons in covalent bonds. The electrons that are shared between two atoms are shown as a pair of dots placed between the symbols for the bonded atoms. The formation of H_2 from hydrogen atoms, for example, can be depicted as

$$H \cdot + H \cdot \longrightarrow H : H$$

☐ In Chapter 7 you learned that when two electrons occupy the same orbital, and therefore share the same space, their spins must be paired. The pairing of electrons is an important part of the formation of a covalent bond.

Because the electrons are shared, each H atom is considered to have two electrons.

$$\text{H} : \text{H}$$

(Colored circles emphasize that two electrons can be counted around each of the H atoms.)

For simplicity, the electron pair in a covalent bond is usually depicted as a single dash. Thus, the hydrogen molecule is represented as

$$\text{H} - \text{H}$$

A formula such as this, which is drawn with Lewis symbols, is called a **Lewis formula** or **Lewis structure.** It is also called a **structural formula** because it shows which atoms are present in the molecule *and* how they are attached to each other.

Covalent bonding often follows the octet rule

You have seen that when a nonmetal atom forms an anion, electrons are gained until the *s* and *p* subshells of its valence shell are completed. The tendency of a nonmetal atom to finish with a completed valence shell, usually consisting of eight electrons, also influences the number of electrons the atom tends to acquire by sharing, and it thereby affects the number of covalent bonds the atom forms.

Hydrogen, with just one electron in its $1s$ orbital, completes its valence shell by obtaining a share of just one electron from another atom, so a hydrogen atom forms just one covalent bond. When this other atom is hydrogen, the H_2 molecule is formed.

Many atoms form covalent bonds by sharing enough electrons to give them complete *s* and *p* subshells in their outer shells. This is the noble gas configuration mentioned earlier and is the basis of the octet rule described in Section 8.1. As applied to covalent bonding, the **octet rule** can be stated as follows: *When atoms form covalent bonds, they tend to share sufficient electrons so as to achieve an outer shell having eight electrons.*

Often, the octet rule can be used to explain the number of covalent bonds an atom forms. This number normally equals the number of electrons the atom must acquire to have a total of eight (an octet) in its outer shell. For instance, the halogens (Group VIIA) all have seven valence electrons. The Lewis symbol for a typical member of this group, chlorine, is

$$\cdot \ddot{\text{Cl}} :$$

We can see that only one electron is needed to complete its octet. Of course, chlorine can actually gain this electron and become a chloride ion. This is what it does when it forms an ionic compound such as sodium chloride (NaCl). But when chlorine combines with another nonmetal, the complete transfer of an electron is not energetically favorable. Therefore, in forming such compounds as HCl or Cl_2, chlorine gets the one electron it needs by forming a covalent bond.

$$\text{H} \cdot + \cdot \ddot{\text{Cl}} : \longrightarrow \text{H} : \ddot{\text{Cl}} :$$

$$: \ddot{\text{Cl}} \cdot + \cdot \ddot{\text{Cl}} : \longrightarrow : \ddot{\text{Cl}} : \ddot{\text{Cl}} :$$

The HCl and Cl_2 molecules can also be represented using dashes for the bonds.

$$\text{H} - \ddot{\text{Cl}} : \quad \text{and} \quad : \ddot{\text{Cl}} - \ddot{\text{Cl}} :$$

There are many nonmetals that form more than one covalent bond. For example, the three most important elements in biochemical systems are carbon, nitrogen, and oxygen.

$$\cdot \dot{\text{C}} \cdot \qquad \cdot \dot{\text{N}} \cdot \qquad \cdot \ddot{\text{O}} :$$

The simplest hydrogen compounds of these elements are methane, CH_4, ammonia, NH_3, and water, H_2O. Their Lewis structures are

□ As you will see, it is useful to remember that hydrogen atoms form only one covalent bond.

TOOLS

Octet rule and covalent bonding

$$\begin{array}{ccc}
H & H & H \\
H\!:\!\overset{\cdot\cdot}{C}\!:\!H & H\!:\!\overset{\cdot\cdot}{N}\!:\!H & H\!:\!\overset{\cdot\cdot}{\underset{\cdot\cdot}{O}}\!: \\
H & & \\
\end{array}$$

$$\begin{array}{ccc}
\text{or} & \text{or} & \text{or} \\
\end{array}$$

$$\begin{array}{ccc}
H & H & H \\
| & | & | \\
H\!-\!C\!-\!H & H\!-\!N\!-\!H & H\!-\!\overset{\cdot\cdot}{\underset{\cdot\cdot}{O}}\!: \\
| & | & \\
H & & \\
\text{methane} & \text{ammonia} & \text{water}
\end{array}$$

Multiple bonds consist of two or more pairs of electrons

The bond produced by the sharing of *one* pair of electrons between two atoms is called a **single bond.** So far, these have been the only kind we've discussed. There are, however, many molecules in which more than a single pair of electrons are shared between two atoms. For example, we can diagram the formation of the bonds in CO_2 as follows.

$$:\overset{\cdot\cdot}{\underset{\cdot\cdot}{O}}\cdot \rightleftharpoons \cdot\overset{\cdot\cdot}{C}\cdot \rightleftharpoons \cdot\overset{\cdot\cdot}{\underset{\cdot\cdot}{O}}: \longrightarrow :\overset{\cdot\cdot}{\underset{\cdot\cdot}{O}}::C::\overset{\cdot\cdot}{\underset{\cdot\cdot}{O}}:$$

The central carbon atom shares two of its electrons with each of the oxygen atoms, and each oxygen shares two electrons with carbon. The result is the formation of two **double bonds.** Notice that in the Lewis formula, both of the shared electron pairs are placed between the symbols for the two atoms joined by the double bond. Once again, if we circle the valence shell electrons that "belong" to each atom, we see that each has an octet.

8 electrons

The Lewis structure for CO_2, using dashes, is

$$:\overset{}{O}\!=\!C\!=\!\overset{\cdot\cdot}{\underset{\cdot\cdot}{O}}:$$

Sometimes three pairs of electrons are shared between two atoms. The most abundant gas in the atmosphere, nitrogen, occurs in the form of diatomic molecules, N_2. As we've just seen, the Lewis symbol for nitrogen is

$$\cdot\overset{\cdot}{\underset{\cdot}{N}}:$$

and each nitrogen atom needs three electrons to complete its octet. When the N_2 molecule is formed, each of the nitrogen atoms shares three electrons with the other.

$$:\overset{\cdot}{N}\cdot \rightleftharpoons \cdot\overset{\cdot}{N}: \longrightarrow :N\!:::\!N:$$

The result is called a **triple bond.** Again, notice that we place all three electron pairs of the bond between the two atoms. We count all of these electrons as though they belong to both of the atoms. Each nitrogen therefore has an octet.

8 electrons   8 electrons

$$(:\!N\!:::\!N\!:)$$

The triple bond is usually represented by three dashes, so the bonding in the N_2 molecule is normally shown as

$$:N\!\equiv\!N:$$

□ The locations of the unshared pairs of electrons around the oxygen are unimportant. Two equally valid Lewis structures for CO_2 are

$$:\overset{}{O}\!=\!C\!=\!\overset{\cdot\cdot}{\underset{\cdot\cdot}{O}}: \quad \text{and} \quad \overset{\cdot\cdot}{\underset{\cdot\cdot}{O}}\!=\!C\!=\!\overset{\cdot\cdot}{\underset{\cdot\cdot}{O}}$$

More complex molecules can contain single, double, and/or triple bonds

All of the bonds in a molecule don't have to be of the same kind. Often we find single, double, and even triple bonds in the same molecule. For example, consider propylene, the raw material in the manufacture of polypropylene, a plastic used to form containers and in making fibers for textiles, carpet, and rope.

$$\begin{array}{ccc} & \text{H} & \\ & | & \\ \text{H}-\text{C}-\text{C}=&\text{C}-\text{H} \\ & | \quad | \quad | & \\ & \text{H} \;\; \text{H} \;\; \text{H} & \end{array}$$

In this molecule there are both single and double bonds between carbon atoms, as well as the C—H single bonds. Notice that each carbon atom forms four covalent bonds to neighboring atoms, thereby completing its octet. The formation of four covalent bonds is a characteristic property of carbon and is a feature of almost all organic compounds.

Another example is acetic acid, $HC_2H_3O_2$. The shape of the molecule was illustrated in Figure 4.8 (page 137), showing the single hydrogen atom that is capable of ionizing in the formation of H_3O^+. The Lewis structures of acetic acid and the acetate ion are

acetic acid   acetate ion

Acetic acid is but one of a large number of substances known as **organic acids** or **carboxylic acids.** In general, their structures are characterized by the presence of the **carboxyl group,** —CO_2H.

carboxyl group

All of the organic acids you will encounter in this course are weak acids.

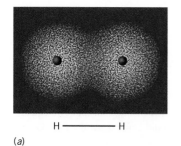

H ———— H

(a)

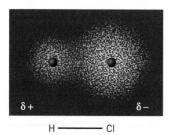

δ+   δ−

H ———— Cl

(b)

FIG. 8.5   Nonpolar and polar covalent bonds. (*a*) The electron density of the electron pair in the bond is spread evenly between the two H atoms in H_2, which gives a nonpolar covalent bond. (*b*) In HCl, the electron density of the bond is pulled more tightly around the Cl end of the molecule, causing that end of the bond to become slightly negative. At the same time, the opposite end of the bond becomes slightly positive. The result is a polar covalent bond.

8.4   COVALENT BONDS CAN HAVE PARTIAL CHARGES AT OPPOSITE ENDS

When two identical atoms form a covalent bond, as in H_2 or Cl_2, each atom has an equal share of the bond's electron pair. The electron density at both ends of the bond is the same, because the electrons are equally attracted to both nuclei. However, when different kinds of atoms combine, as in HCl, one nucleus usually attracts the electrons in the bond more strongly than the other.

The result of unequal attractions for the bonding electrons is an unbalanced distribution of electron density within the bond. For example, chlorine attracts electrons in a bond more strongly than hydrogen does. In the HCl molecule, therefore, the electron cloud is pulled more tightly around the Cl, and that end of the molecule experiences a slight buildup of negative charge. The electron density that shifts toward the chlorine is removed from the hydrogen, which causes the hydrogen end to acquire a slight positive charge. These charges are less than full 1+ and 1− charges and are called **partial charges,** which are usually indicated by the lowercase Greek letter delta, δ (see Figure 8.5). Partial charges can also be indicated on Lewis structures. For example,

$$\text{H}-\ddot{\underset{..}{\text{Cl}}}:$$
δ+   δ−

A bond that carries partial positive and negative charges on opposite ends is called a **polar covalent bond,** or often simply a **polar bond** (the word *covalent* is understood). The term *polar* comes from the notion of *poles* of equal but opposite charge at either end of the bond. Because *two poles* of electric charge are involved, the bond is said to be an **electric dipole.**

The polar bond in HCl causes the molecule as a whole to have opposite charges on either end, so the HCl molecule as a whole is an electric dipole. We say that HCl is a **polar molecule.** The magnitude of its polarity is expressed quantitatively by its **dipole moment** (symbol μ), which is equal to the amount of charge on either end of the molecule, q, multiplied by the distance between the charges, r.

$$\mu = q \times r \qquad (8.1)^4$$

TOOLS
Dipole moment

Table 8.2 lists the dipole moments and bond lengths for some diatomic molecules. The dipole moments are reported in *debye* units (symbol D), where 1 D = 3.34 × 10⁻³⁰ C m (coulomb × meter).

By separate experiments, it is possible to measure both μ and r (which corresponds to the bond length in a diatomic molecule such as HCl). Knowledge of μ and r allows calculation of the amount of charge on opposite ends of the dipole. For HCl, such calculations show that q equals 0.17 electronic charge units, which means the hydrogen carries a charge of $+0.17e$ and the chlorine a charge of $-0.17e$.

☐ The electronic charge unit is represented by the symbol e. We use the symbol e^- to stand for an electron.

One of the main reasons we are concerned about whether a molecule is polar or not is because many physical properties, such as melting point and boiling point, are affected by it. This is because polar molecules attract each other more strongly than do nonpolar molecules. The positive end of one polar molecule attracts the negative end of another. The strength of the attraction depends both on the amount of charge on either end of the molecule and on the distance between the charges; in other words, it depends on the molecule's dipole moment.

TABLE 8.2	Dipole Moments and Bond Lengths for Some Diatomic Molecules[a]	
Compound	Dipole Moment (D)	Bond Length (pm)
HF	1.83	91.7
HCl	1.09	127
HBr	0.82	141
HI	0.45	161
CO	0.11	113
NO	0.16	115

[a]*Source*: National Institute of Standards and Technology.

EXAMPLE 8.5
Calculating the Charge on the End of a Polar Molecule

The HF molecule has a dipole moment of 1.83 D and a bond length of 91.7 pm. What is the amount of charge, in electronic charge units, on either end of the bond?

ANALYSIS: The tool that relates the quantities in this problem is Equation 8.1. To answer the problem correctly, we will have to be especially careful of the units.

SOLUTION: We will solve Equation 8.1 for q.

$$q = \frac{\mu}{r}$$

The debye unit, D, equals 3.34 × 10⁻³⁰ C m, so the dipole moment of HF is

$$\mu = 1.83 \times (3.34 \times 10^{-30} \text{ C m}) = 6.11 \times 10^{-30} \text{ C m}$$

The SI prefix p (pico) means × 10⁻¹², so the bond length r = 91.7 × 10⁻¹² m. Substituting in the equation above gives

$$q = \frac{6.11 \times 10^{-30} \text{ C m}}{91.7 \times 10^{-12} \text{ m}} = 6.66 \times 10^{-20} \text{ C}$$

[4] In this case, we're using the symbol q to mean electric charge, not heat as in the preceding chapter. Because the number of letters in the alphabet is limited, it's not uncommon in science for the same letter to be used to stand for different quantities. This usually doesn't present a problem as long as the symbol is defined in the context in which it is used.

The amount of charge on an electron (i.e., an electronic charge unit) equals 1.602×10^{-19} C, which we can express as

$$1\ e = 1.602 \times 10^{-19}\ \text{C}$$

The value of q in electronic charge units is therefore

$$q = 6.66 \times 10^{-20}\ \cancel{C} \left(\frac{1\ e}{1.602 \times 10^{-19}\ \cancel{C}} \right) = 0.416e$$

As in HCl, the hydrogen carries the positive charge, so the charge on the hydrogen end of the molecule is $+0.416e$ and the charge on the fluorine end is $-0.416e$.

IS THE ANSWER REASONABLE? If we look over the units, we see they cancel correctly, so that gives us confidence we've done the calculation correctly. The fact that our answer is between zero and one electronic charge unit, and therefore a partial electrical charge, further suggests we've solved the problem correctly.

Practice Exercise 6: The chlorine end of the chlorine monoxide molecule carries a charge of $+0.167e$. The bond length is 154.6 pm. Calculate the dipole moment of the molecule in debye units. (Hint: Be sure to convert the charge to coulombs.)

Practice Exercise 7: Although isolated Na^+ and Cl^- ions are unstable, these ions can exist in the gaseous state as *ion pairs*. An ion pair consists of an NaCl unit in which the bond length is 236 pm. The dipole moment of the ion pair is 9.00 D. What are the actual amounts of charge on the sodium and chlorine atoms in this NaCl pair? What percentage of full 1+ and 1− charges are these? (This is the *percentage ionic character* in the NaCl pair.)

Electronegativity expresses an atom's attraction for electrons in a bond

The degree to which a covalent bond is polar depends on the difference in the abilities of the bonded atoms to attract electrons. The greater the difference, the more polar the bond, and the more the electron density is shifted toward the atom that attracts electrons more.

The term that we use to describe the attraction an atom has for the electrons in a bond is called **electronegativity.** In HCl, for example, chlorine is *more electronegative* than hydrogen. This causes the electron pair of the covalent bond to spend more of its time around the more electronegative atom, which is why the Cl end of the bond acquires a partial negative charge.

The first scientist to develop numerical values for electronegativity was Linus Pauling (1901–1994). He observed that polar bonds have a bond energy larger than would be expected if the opposite ends of the bonds were electrically neutral. Pauling reasoned that the extra bond energy arises because of the attraction between the partial charges on opposite ends of the bond. By estimating the extra bond energy, he was able to develop a scale of electronegativities for the elements. Other scientists have used different approaches to measuring electronegativities, with similar results.

A set of numerical values for the electronegativities of the elements is shown in Figure 8.6. These data are useful because the *difference* in electronegativity provides an estimate of the degree of polarity of a bond. For instance, the data tell us fluorine is more electronegative than chlorine, so we expect HF to be more polar than HCl. (This is confirmed by the larger dipole moment of the HF molecule.) In addition, the relative magnitudes of the electronegativities indicate which ends of a bond carry the partial positive and negative charges. Thus, hydrogen is less electronegative than either fluorine or chlorine, so in both of these molecules the hydrogen bears the partial positive charge.

Linus Pauling contributed greatly to our understanding of chemical bonding. He was the winner of two Nobel prizes, in 1954 for Chemistry and in 1962 for Peace. *(Roger Ressmeyer/Corbis Images.)*

☐ The noble gases are assigned electronegativities of zero and are omitted from the figure.

$$\underset{\delta+ \quad \delta-}{\text{H}—\overset{\cdot\cdot}{\underset{\cdot\cdot}{\text{F}}}\text{:}} \qquad \underset{\delta+ \quad \delta-}{\text{H}—\overset{\cdot\cdot}{\underset{\cdot\cdot}{\text{Cl}}}\text{:}}$$

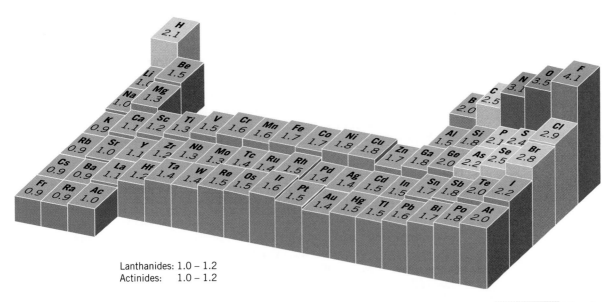

Lanthanides: 1.0 – 1.2
Actinides: 1.0 – 1.2

FIG. 8.6 The electronegativities of the elements.

Practice Exercise 8: Bromine and chlorine form a molecular substance with the formula BrCl. Is the bond polar? If so, which atom carries the negative charge? (Hint: Compare electronegativities.)

Practice Exercise 9: For each of the following bonds, choose the atom that carries the partial negative charge: (a) P—Br, (b) Si—Cl, and (c) S—Cl.

By studying electronegativity values and their differences we find that there is no sharp dividing line between ionic and covalent bonding. Ionic bonding and *nonpolar covalent bonding* simply represent the two extremes. A bond is mostly ionic when the difference in electronegativity between two atoms is very large; the more electronegative atom acquires essentially complete control of the bonding electrons. In a **nonpolar covalent bond,** there is no difference in electronegativity, so the pair of bonding electrons is shared equally.

$$Cs^+ \left[:\overset{..}{\underset{..}{F}}: \right]^- \qquad\qquad :\overset{..}{\underset{..}{F}}:\overset{..}{\underset{..}{F}}:$$

"bonding pair" held   bonding pair
exclusively by fluorine   shared equally

The degree to which the bond is polar, which we might think of as the amount of **ionic character** of the bond, varies in a continuous way with changes in the electronegativity difference (Figure 8.7). The bond becomes more than 50% ionic when the electronegativity difference exceeds approximately 1.7.

Electronegativity follows trends within the periodic table

An examination of Figure 8.6 reveals trends in electronegativity within the periodic table; *electronegativity increases from bottom to top in a group, and from left to right in a period.* Notice that the trends follow those for ionization energy (IE). This is because an atom that has a small IE will lose an electron more easily than an atom with a large IE, just as an atom with a small electronegativity will lose its share of an electron pair more readily than an atom with a large electronegativity.

Elements located in the same region of the table (for example, the nonmetals) have similar electronegativities, which means that if they form bonds with each other, the electronegativity differences will be small and the bonds will be more covalent than ionic. On the other hand, if elements from widely separated regions of the table combine, large electronegativity differences occur and the bonds will be predominantly ionic. This is what happens, for example, when an element from Group IA or Group IIA reacts with a nonmetal from the upper right-hand corner of the periodic table.

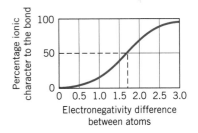

FIG. 8.7 Variation in the percentage ionic character of a bond with electronegativity difference. The bond becomes about 50% ionic when the electronegativity difference equals 1.7, which means that the atoms in the bond carry a partial charge of approximately ±0.5 units.

TOOLS
Periodic trends in electronegativity

☐ It is found that the electronegativity is proportional to the average of the ionization energy and the electron affinity of an element.

8.5 THE REACTIVITIES OF METALS AND NONMETALS CAN BE RELATED TO THEIR ELECTRONEGATIVITIES

In addition to enabling us to determine the polarity of covalent bonds, electronegativities can also help us understand chemical properties, particularly those that involve an atom's tendency to gain or lose electrons. Thus, there are parallels between an element's electronegativity and its **reactivity**—its tendency to undergo redox reactions. In this section we will examine some of these trends.

Reactivities of metals relate to their ease of oxidation

□ *Reactivity* refers in general to the tendency of a substance to react with something. The *reactivity of a metal* refers to its tendency specifically to undergo *oxidation.*

In nearly every compound containing a metal, the metal exists in a positive oxidation state. Therefore, for a metal, *reactivity* relates to how easily the metal is oxidized. For example, a metal like sodium, which is very easily oxidized, is said to be very reactive, whereas a metal like platinum, which is very difficult to oxidize, is said to be unreactive.

There are several ways to compare how easily metals are oxidized. In Chapter 5 we saw that by comparing the abilities of metals to displace each other from compounds we are able to establish their relative ease of oxidation. This was the basis for the activity series (Table 5.2).

As useful as the activity series is in predicting the outcome of certain redox reactions, it is difficult to remember in detail. Furthermore, often it is sufficient just to know approximately where an element stands in relation to others in a broad range of reactivity. This is where the periodic table can be especially useful to us once again, because there are trends and variations in reactivity within the periodic table that are simple to identify and remember.

Figure 8.8 illustrates how the ease of oxidation (reactivity) of metals varies in the periodic table. In general, these trends roughly follow the variations in electronegativity, with the metal being less easily oxidized as its electronegativity increases. You might expect this, because electronegativity is a measure of how strongly the atom of an element attracts electrons when combining with an atom of a different element. The more strongly the atom attracts electrons, the more difficult it is to oxidize. This relationship between reactivity and electronegativity is only approximate, however, because many other factors affect the stability of the compounds that are formed.

In Figure 8.8, we see that the metals that are most easily oxidized are found at the far left in the periodic table. These are elements with very low electronegativities. The metals in Group IA, for example, are so easily oxidized that all of them react with water to liberate hydrogen. Because of their reactivity toward moisture and oxygen, they have no useful applications that require exposure to the atmosphere, so we rarely encounter them as free metals. The same is true of the heavier metals in Group IIA, calcium through barium. These elements also react with water to liberate hydrogen. In Figure 8.6 we see that electronegativity decreases going down a group, which explains why the heavier elements in Group IIA are more reactive than those at the top of the group.

TOOLS

Trends in the reactivity of metals in the periodic table

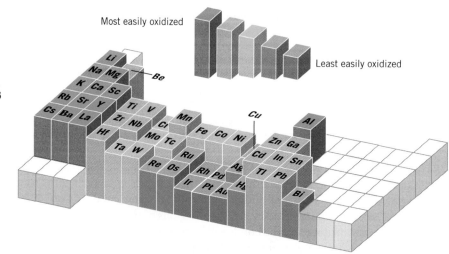

FIG. 8.8 The variation of the ease of oxidation of metals with position in the periodic table.

In Figure 8.8 we can also locate the metals that are the most difficult to oxidize. They occur for the most part among the heavier transition elements in the center of the periodic table, where we find the very unreactive elements platinum and gold—metals used to make fine jewelry. Their bright luster and lack of any tendency to corrode in air or water combine to make them particularly attractive for this purpose. This same lack of reactivity also is responsible for their industrial uses. Gold, for example, is used to coat the electrical contacts in low-voltage circuits found in microcomputers, because even small amounts of corrosion on more reactive metals would be sufficient to impede the flow of electricity so much as to make the devices unreliable.

The funeral mask of Tut'ankhamun, almost 3,300 years old, shows no sign of age. It is made of gold with glass eyes and lapis lazuli eyebrows and eyelashes. (*Roger Wood/Corbis Images.*)

The oxidizing power of nonmetals is related to their electronegativities

The reactivity of a metal is determined by its ease of oxidation, and therefore its ability to serve as a reducing agent. *For a nonmetal, reactivity is usually gauged by its ability to serve as an oxidizing agent.* This ability also varies according to the element's electronegativity. Nonmetals with high electronegativities have strong tendencies to acquire electrons and are therefore strong oxidizing agents. In parallel with changes in electronegativities in the periodic table, *the oxidizing abilities of nonmetals increase from left to right across a period and from bottom to top in a group.* Thus, the most powerful oxidizing agent is fluorine, followed closely by oxygen, both in the upper right-hand corner of the periodic table.

Single replacement reactions occur among the nonmetals, just as with the metals (which you studied in Chapter 5). For example, heating a metal sulfide in oxygen causes the sulfur to be replaced by oxygen. The displaced sulfur then combines with additional oxygen to give sulfur dioxide. The equation for a typical reaction is

$$2CuS(s) + 3O_2(g) \longrightarrow 2CuO(s) + 2SO_2(g)$$

Displacement reactions are especially evident among the halogens, where a particular halogen in its elemental form will oxidize the *anion* of any halogen below it in Group VIIA, as illustrated in the margin. Thus, F_2 will oxidize Cl^-, Br^-, and I^-. However, Cl_2 will only oxidize Br^- and I^-, and Br_2 will only oxidize I^-.

🛠️ **TOOLS**
Trends in the reactivity of nonmetals in the periodic table

□ Fluorine:

$$F_2 + 2Cl^- \longrightarrow 2F^- + Cl_2$$
$$F_2 + 2Br^- \longrightarrow 2F^- + Br_2$$
$$F_2 + 2I^- \longrightarrow 2F^- + I_2$$

Chlorine:

$$Cl_2 + 2Br^- \longrightarrow 2Cl^- + Br_2$$
$$Cl_2 + 2I^- \longrightarrow 2Cl^- + I_2$$

Bromine:

$$Br_2 + 2I^- \longrightarrow 2Br^- + I_2$$

8.6 DRAWING LEWIS STRUCTURES IS A NECESSARY SKILL

Lewis structures are very useful in chemistry because they give us a relatively simple way to describe the structures of molecules. As a result, much chemical reasoning is based on them. Also, as you will learn in the next chapter, we can use the Lewis structure to make reasonably accurate predictions about the shape of a molecule.

In Section 8.3 you saw Lewis structures for a variety of molecules that obey the octet rule. Examples included CO_2, Cl_2, and N_2. The octet rule is not always obeyed, however. For instance, there are some molecules in which one or more atoms must have more than an octet in the valence shell. Examples are PCl_5 and SF_6, whose Lewis structures are

□ Lewis structures just describe which atoms are bonded to each other and the kinds of bonds involved. Thus, the Lewis structure for water can be drawn as H—Ö—H, but it does not mean the water molecule is linear, with all the atoms in a straight line. Actually, water isn't linear; the two O—H bonds form an angle of about 104°.

In these molecules the formation of more than four bonds to the central atom requires that the central atom have a share of more than eight electrons. With the exception of Period 2 elements like carbon and nitrogen, most nonmetals can have more than an octet of electrons in the outer shell.

There are also some molecules (but not many) in which the central atom behaves as though it has less than an octet. The most common examples involve compounds of beryllium and boron.

$$\cdot \ddot{Be} \cdot + 2 \cdot \ddot{\underset{\cdot\cdot}{Cl}}: \longrightarrow :\ddot{\underset{\cdot\cdot}{Cl}} - Be - \ddot{\underset{\cdot\cdot}{Cl}}:$$

four electrons around Be

$$\cdot \dot{B} \cdot + 3 \cdot \ddot{\underset{\cdot\cdot}{Cl}}: \longrightarrow :\ddot{\underset{\cdot\cdot}{Cl}} - \overset{\overset{\displaystyle :\ddot{Cl}:}{\displaystyle |}}{B} - \ddot{\underset{\cdot\cdot}{Cl}}:$$

six electrons around B

Although Be and B sometimes have less than an octet, the elements in Period 2 never *exceed* an octet. The reason is because their valence shells, having $n = 2$, can hold a maximum of only 8 electrons. (This explains why the octet rule works so well for atoms of carbon, nitrogen, and oxygen.) However, elements in periods below Period 2, such as phosphorus and sulfur, sometimes do exceed an octet, because their valence shells can hold more than 8 electrons. For example, the valence shell for elements in Period 3, for which $n = 3$, can hold a maximum of 18 electrons, and the valence shell for Period 4 elements, which have s, p, d, and f subshells, can hold as many as 32 electrons.

TOOLS
Method for drawing Lewis structures

A simple procedure enables us to draw Lewis structures

Figure 8.9 outlines a series of steps that provides a systematic method for writing Lewis structures. The first is to decide which atoms are bonded to each other, so that we know where to put the dots or dashes. This is not always a simple matter. Many times the formula suggests the way the atoms are arranged because the central atom, which is usually the least electronegative one, is usually written first. Examples are CO_2 and ClO_4^-, which have the following *skeletal structures* (i.e., arrangements of atoms):

$$
\begin{array}{ccc}
 & & O \\
O \quad C \quad O & \quad & O \quad Cl \quad O \\
 & & O
\end{array}
$$

Sometimes, obtaining the skeletal structure is not quite so simple, especially when more than two elements are present. Some generalizations are possible, however. For example, the skeletal structure of nitric acid, HNO_3, is

$$
\begin{array}{cccc}
 & & O & \\
H & O & N & O \qquad \text{(correct)}
\end{array}
$$

rather than one of the following.

$$
\begin{array}{cccccc}
O & & & & & \\
O \quad N \quad O & \text{or} & H & O & O & N & O \qquad \text{(incorrect)} \\
H & & & & &
\end{array}
$$

Nitric acid is an oxoacid (Section 4.4), and it happens that the hydrogen atoms that can be released from molecules of oxoacids are always bonded to oxygen atoms, which are in turn bonded to the third nonmetal atom. Therefore, recognizing HNO_3 as the formula of an oxoacid allows us to predict that the three oxygen atoms are bonded to the nitrogen, and the hydrogen is bonded to one of the oxygens. (It is also useful to remember that hydrogen forms only one bond, so we would not choose it to be a central atom.)

There are times when no reasonable basis can be found for choosing a particular skeletal structure. If you must make a guess, choose the most symmetrical arrangement of atoms, because it has the greatest chance of being correct.

After you've decided on the skeletal structure, the next step is to count all of the *valence electrons* to find out how many dots must appear in the final formula. Using the periodic table, locate the groups in which the elements in the formula occur to determine the

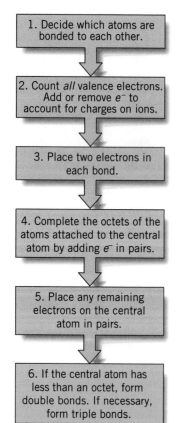

1. Decide which atoms are bonded to each other.

2. Count *all* valence electrons. Add or remove e^- to account for charges on ions.

3. Place two electrons in each bond.

4. Complete the octets of the atoms attached to the central atom by adding e^- in pairs.

5. Place any remaining electrons on the central atom in pairs.

6. If the central atom has less than an octet, form double bonds. If necessary, form triple bonds.

FIG. 8.9 **Summary of steps in writing a Lewis structure.** If you follow these steps, you will obtain a Lewis structure in which the octet rule is obeyed by the maximum number of atoms.

number of valence electrons contributed by each atom. If the structure you wish to draw is that of an ion, *add one additional valence electron for each negative charge or remove a valence electron for each positive charge*. Some examples are

SO_3	Sulfur (Group VIA) contributes $6e^-$.	$1 \times 6 =\ \ 6e^-$
	Each oxygen (Group VIA) contributes $6e^-$.	$3 \times 6 = 18e^-$
		Total $\quad 24e^-$

ClO_4^-	Chlorine (Group VIIA) contributes $7e^-$.	$1 \times 7 =\ \ 7e^-$
	Each oxygen (Group VIA) contributes $6e^-$.	$4 \times 6 = 24e^-$
	Add $1e^-$ for the $1-$ charge.	$+1e^-$
		Total $\quad 32e^-$

NH_4^+	Nitrogen (Group VA) contributes $5e^-$.	$1 \times 5 = 5e^-$
	Each hydrogen (Group IA) contributes $1e^-$.	$4 \times 1 = 4e^-$
	Subtract $1e^-$ for the $1+$ charge.	$-1e^-$
		Total $\quad 8e^-$

After we have determined the number of valence electrons, we place them into the skeletal structure in pairs following the steps outlined in Figure 8.9. Let's look at some examples of how we go about this.

EXAMPLE 8.6
Drawing Lewis Structures

What is the Lewis structure of the chloric acid molecule, $HClO_3$?

ANALYSIS: The first step is to select a reasonable skeletal structure. Because the substance is an oxoacid, we can expect the hydrogen to be bonded to an oxygen, which in turn is bonded to the chlorine. The other two oxygens would also be bonded to the chlorine. This gives

$$\begin{array}{c} O \\ H\ O\ Cl\ O \end{array}$$

After this, we follow the procedure outlined in Figure 8.9.

SOLUTION: The total number of valence electrons is 26 ($1e^-$ from H, $6e^-$ from each O, and $7e^-$ from Cl). To distribute the electrons, we start by placing a pair of electrons in each bond, because we know that there must be at least one pair of electrons between each pair of atoms.

$$\begin{array}{c} O \\ H:O:\overset{..}{Cl}:O \end{array}$$

This has used $8e^-$, so we still have $18e^-$ to go. Next, we work on the atoms surrounding the chlorine (which is the central atom in this structure). No additional electrons are needed around the H, because $2e^-$ are all that can occupy its valence shell. Therefore, we next complete the octets of the oxygens, which uses 16 more electrons.

$$\begin{array}{c} :\overset{..}{O}: \\ H:\overset{..}{O}:\overset{..}{Cl}:\overset{..}{O}: \end{array}$$

We have now used a total of $24e^-$, so there are two electrons left. "Leftover" electrons are always placed on the central atom in pairs (the Cl atom, in this case). This gives

$$\begin{array}{c} :\overset{..}{O}: \\ H:\overset{..}{O}:\overset{..}{\underset{..}{Cl}}:\overset{..}{O}: \end{array}$$

□ The valence shell of hydrogen contains only the $1s$ subshell, which can hold a maximum of two electrons. This means hydrogen can have a share of only two electrons and can form just one covalent bond.

which we can also write as follows, using dashes for the electron pairs in the bonds.

$$:\ddot{O}:$$
$$|$$
$$H—\ddot{O}—Cl—\ddot{O}:$$

The chlorine and the three oxygens have octets, and the valence shell of hydrogen is complete with $2e^-$, so we are finished.

IS THE ANSWER REASONABLE? The most common error is to have either too many or too few valence electrons in the structure, so that's always the best place to begin your check. Doing this will confirm that the number of e^- is correct.

EXAMPLE 8.7
Drawing Lewis Structures

Draw the Lewis structure for the SO_3 molecule.

ANALYSIS: Sulfur is less electronegative than oxygen and it is written first in the formula, so we expect it to be the central atom, surrounded by the three O atoms. This gives the skeletal structure

$$O$$
$$O \; S \; O$$

From here we proceed to count valence electrons and follow the appropriate steps in entering them into the structure.

SOLUTION: The total number of electrons in the formula is 24 ($6e^-$ from the sulfur, plus $6e^-$ from each oxygen). We begin to distribute the electrons by placing a pair in each bond. This gives

$$O$$
$$O:\ddot{S}:O$$

We have used $6e^-$, so there are $18e^-$ left. We next complete the octets around the oxygens, which uses the remaining electrons.

$$:\ddot{O}:$$
$$:\ddot{O}:\ddot{S}:\ddot{O}:$$

At this point all the electrons have been placed into the structure, but we see that the sulfur still lacks an octet. We cannot simply add more dots because the total must be 24. Therefore, according to the last step of the procedure in Figure 8.9, we have to create a multiple bond. To do this we move a pair of electrons that we have shown to belong solely to an oxygen into a sulfur–oxygen bond so that it can be counted as belonging to both the oxygen *and* the sulfur. In other words, we place a double bond between sulfur and one of the oxygens. It doesn't matter which oxygen we choose for this honor.

$$:\ddot{O}: \qquad\qquad :\ddot{O}: \qquad\qquad :\ddot{O}:$$
$$:\ddot{O}:\ddot{S}:\ddot{O}: \quad \text{gives} \quad :\ddot{O}::\ddot{S}:\ddot{O}: \quad \text{or} \quad :\ddot{O}=S—\ddot{O}:$$

Notice that each atom has an octet.

IS THE ANSWER REASONABLE? The key step in completing the structure is recognizing what we have to do to obtain an octet around the sulfur. We have to add more electrons to the valence shell of sulfur, but without removing them from any of the oxygen atoms. By forming the double bond, we accomplish this. A quick check also confirms that we've placed exactly the correct number of valence electrons into the structure.

EXAMPLE 8.8
Drawing Lewis Structures

What is the Lewis structure for the ion IF_4^-?

ANALYSIS: We can anticipate that iodine will be the central atom, so our skeletal structure is

$$\begin{array}{c} \text{F} \\ \text{F I F} \\ \text{F} \end{array}$$

Next, we count valence electrons, remembering to add an extra electron to account for the negative charge. Then we distribute the electrons in pairs following the usual procedure.

SOLUTION: The iodine and fluorine atoms are in Group VIIA and each contribute 7 electrons, for a total of $35e^-$. The negative charge requires one additional electron to give a total of $36e^-$.

First we place $2e^-$ into each bond, and then we complete the octets of the fluorine atoms. This uses 32 electrons.

$$\begin{array}{cc} & :\!\overset{..}{\underset{..}{F}}\!: \\ :\!\overset{..}{\underset{..}{F}}\!:\!\overset{..}{\underset{..}{I}}\!:\!\overset{..}{\underset{..}{F}}\!: & \text{or} \quad :\!\overset{..}{\underset{..}{F}}\!-\!I\!-\!\overset{..}{\underset{..}{F}}\!: \\ :\!\overset{..}{\underset{..}{F}}\!: & :\!\overset{..}{\underset{..}{F}}\!: \end{array}$$

There are four electrons left, and according to step 5 in Figure 8.9 they are placed on the central atom as *pairs* of electrons. This gives

$$:\!\overset{..}{\underset{..}{F}}\!:$$
$$:\!\overset{..}{\underset{..}{F}}\!-\!\overset{..}{\underset{..}{I}}\!-\!\overset{..}{\underset{..}{F}}\!:$$
$$:\!\overset{..}{\underset{..}{F}}\!:$$

The last step is to add brackets around the formula and write the charge outside as a superscript.

$$\left[\begin{array}{c} :\!\overset{..}{\underset{..}{F}}\!: \\ :\!\overset{..}{\underset{..}{F}}\!-\!\overset{..}{\underset{..}{I}}\!-\!\overset{..}{\underset{..}{F}}\!: \\ :\!\overset{..}{\underset{..}{F}}\!: \end{array}\right]^-$$

IS THE ANSWER REASONABLE? We can recount the valence electrons, which tells us we have the right number of them, and all are in the Lewis structure. Each fluorine atom has an octet, which is proper. Notice that we have placed the "leftover" electrons onto the central atom. This gives iodine more than an octet, but that's okay because iodine is not a Period 2 element.

Practice Exercise 10: Predict a reasonable skeletal structure for $H_2PO_4^-$ and determine the number of valence electrons that should be in its Lewis structure. (Hint: It's an ion derived from an oxoacid.)

Practice Exercise 11: Predict reasonable skeletal structures for SO_2, NO_3^-, $HBrO_3$, and H_3AsO_4.

Practice Exercise 12: How many valence electrons should appear in the Lewis structures of SO_2, SeO_4^{2-}, and NO^+?

Practice Exercise 13: Draw Lewis structures for OF_2, NH_4^+, SO_2, NO_3^-, ClF_3, and $HClO_4$.

Formal charges help select correct Lewis structures

Lewis structures are meant to describe how atoms share electrons in chemical bonds. Such descriptions are theoretical explanations or predictions that relate to the forces that hold molecules and polyatomic ions together. But, as you learned in Chapter 1, a theory is only as good as the observations on which it is based, so to have confidence in a theory about chemical bonding, we need to have a way to check it. We need experimental observations that relate to the description of bonding.

Two properties that are related to the number of electron pairs shared between two atoms are *bond length,* the distance between the nuclei of the bonded atoms, and *bond energy,* the energy required to separate the bonded atoms to give neutral particles. For example, we mentioned in Section 8.3 that measurements have shown the H_2 molecule has a bond length of 75 pm and a bond energy of 435 kJ/mol, which means that it takes 435 kJ to break the bonds of 1 mol of H_2 molecules to give 2 mol of hydrogen atoms.

Comparing bonds between the same elements, the bond length and bond energy depend on the **bond order,** which is defined as *the number of pairs of electrons shared between two atoms.* The bond order is a measure of the amount of electron density in the bond, and the greater the electron density, the more tightly the nuclei are held and the more closely they are drawn together. This is illustrated by the data in Table 8.3, which gives typical bond lengths and bond energies for single, double, and triple bonds between carbon atoms. In summary:

☐ A single bond has a bond order of 1, a double bond a bond order of 2, and a triple bond a bond order of 3.

> As the bond order increases, the bond length decreases and the bond energy increases, provided we are comparing bonds between the same elements.

TOOLS

Correlation between bond properties and bond order

With this as background, let's examine the Lewis structure of sulfuric acid, drawn according to the procedure given in Figure 8.9.

$$H-\ddot{\underset{..}{O}}-\underset{\underset{\ddot{\ddot{O}}:}{|}}{\overset{\overset{\ddot{\ddot{O}}:}{|}}{S}}-\ddot{\underset{..}{O}}-H \qquad \text{(Structure I)}$$

It obeys the octet rule, and there doesn't seem to be any need to attempt to write any other structures for it. But a problem arises if we compare the predicted bond lengths with those found experimentally. In our Lewis structure, all four sulfur-oxygen bonds are single bonds, which means they should have about the same bond lengths. However, experimentally it has been found that the bonds are not of equal length, as illustrated in Figure 8.10. The S—O bonds are shorter than the S—OH bonds, which means they must have a larger bond order. Therefore, we need to modify our Lewis structure to make it conform to reality.

Because sulfur is in Period 3, its valence shell has 3s, 3p, and 3d subshells, which together can accommodate more than eight electrons. Therefore, sulfur is able to form more than four bonds, so we are allowed to increase the bond order in the S—O bonds by moving electron pairs to create sulfur–oxygen double bonds as shown below.

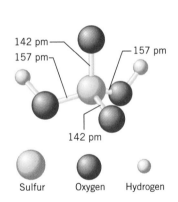

142 pm
157 pm
157 pm
142 pm

Sulfur   Oxygen   Hydrogen

FIG. 8.10 **The structure of sulfuric acid in the vapor state.** Notice the difference in the sulfur–oxygen bond lengths.

$$H-\ddot{\underset{..}{O}}-\underset{\underset{:\overset{..}{\underset{..}{O}}{\scriptstyle\ominus}}{\Big\uparrow}}{\overset{\overset{:\overset{..}{O}{\scriptstyle\oplus}}{\Big\downarrow}}{S}}-\ddot{\underset{..}{O}}-H \quad \text{gives} \quad H-\ddot{\underset{..}{O}}-\underset{\underset{:\overset{..}{\underset{..}{O}}}{\|}}{\overset{\overset{:\overset{..}{O}}{\|}}{S}}-\ddot{\underset{..}{O}}-H \quad \text{(Structure II)}$$

TABLE 8.3	Average Bond Lengths and Bond Energies Measured for Carbon–Carbon Bonds	
Bond	Bond Length (pm)	Bond Energy (kJ/mol)
C—C	154	348
C=C	134	615
C≡C	120	812

Now we have a Lewis structure that better fits experimental observations because the sulfur–oxygen double bonds are expected to be shorter than the sulfur–oxygen single bonds. Because this second Lewis structure agrees better with the actual structure of the molecule, it is the *preferred* Lewis structure, even though it violates the octet rule.

Formal charges are apparent charges on atoms

Are there any criteria that we could have applied that would have allowed us to predict that the second Lewis structure for H_2SO_4 is better than the one with only single bonds, even though it seems to violate the octet rule unnecessarily? To answer this question, let's take a closer look at the two Lewis structures we've drawn.

In Structure I, there are only single bonds between the sulfur and oxygen atoms. If the electrons in the bonds are shared equally by S and O, then each atom "owns" half of the electron pair, or the equivalent of one electron. In other words, the four single bonds place the equivalent of four electrons in the valence shell of the sulfur. An isolated single atom of sulfur, however, has six valence electrons, so in Structure I the sulfur has two electrons *less* than it does as just an isolated atom. Thus, at least in a bookkeeping sense, it would appear that if sulfur obeyed the octet rule in H_2SO_4, it would have a charge of $2+$. This *apparent* charge on the sulfur atom is called its **formal charge.**

Notice that in defining formal charge, we've stressed the word "apparent." *The formal charge arises because of the bookkeeping we've done and should not be confused with whatever the actual charge is on an atom in the molecule.* (The situation is somewhat similar to the oxidation numbers you learned to assign in Chapter 5, which are artificial charges assigned according to a set of rules.) Here's how formal charges are assigned.

☐ The actual charges on the atoms in a molecule are determined by the relative electronegativities of the atoms.

Calculating the formal charge on an atom

Step 1. Write down the number of valence electrons in an isolated atom of the element.

Step 2. Using the Lewis structure, add up the valence electrons that "belong to" the atom in the molecule or ion, and then subtract this total from the value in Step 1.

In performing the calculation in Step 2, electrons in bonds are divided equally between the two atoms, while unshared electrons are assigned exclusively to the atom on which they reside. For example, for Structure I above, we have

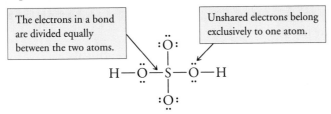

Therefore, the calculation of formal charge is summarized by the following equation:

Calculated number of electrons in the valence shell of the atom in the Lewis structure

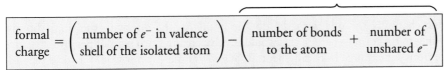

$$\text{formal charge} = \left(\begin{array}{c} \text{number of } e^- \text{ in valence} \\ \text{shell of the isolated atom} \end{array} \right) - \left(\begin{array}{c} \text{number of bonds} \\ \text{to the atom} \end{array} + \begin{array}{c} \text{number of} \\ \text{unshared } e^- \end{array} \right) \quad (8.2)$$

TOOLS
Formal charges

For example, for the sulfur in Structure I, we get

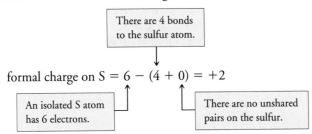

$$\text{formal charge on S} = 6 - (4 + 0) = +2$$

Let's also calculate the formal charges on the hydrogen and oxygen atoms in Structure I. An isolated H atom has one electron. In Structure I each H has one bond and no unshared electrons. Therefore,

$$\text{Formal charge on H} = 1 - (1 + 0) = 0$$

In Structure I, we also see that there are two kinds of oxygens to consider. An isolated oxygen atom has six electrons, so we have, for the oxygens also bonded to hydrogen,

$$\text{Formal charge} = 6 - (2 + 4) = 0$$

and for the oxygens not bonded to hydrogen,

$$\text{Formal charge} = 6 - (1 + 6) = -1$$

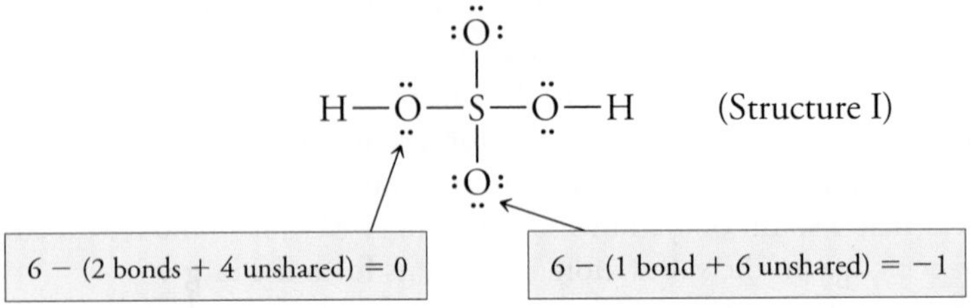

| 6 − (2 bonds + 4 unshared) = 0 | | 6 − (1 bond + 6 unshared) = −1 |

Nonzero formal charges are indicated in a Lewis structure by placing them in circles alongside the atoms, as shown below.

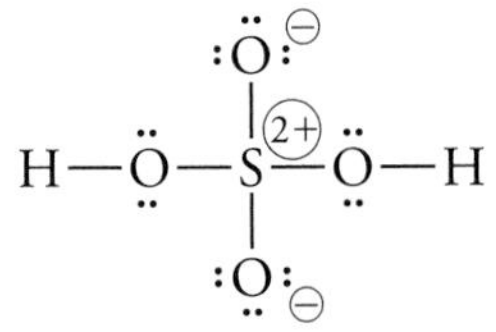

Notice that the sum of the formal charges in the molecule is zero. It is useful to remember that, in general, *the formal charges in any Lewis structure add up to the charge on the particle.*

Now let's look at the formal charges in Structure II. For sulfur we have

$$\text{Formal charge on S} = 6 - (6 + 0) = 0$$

so the sulfur has no formal charge. The hydrogens and the oxygens that are also bonded to H are the same in this structure as before, so they have no formal charges. And finally, the oxygens that are not bonded to hydrogen have

$$\text{Formal charge} = 6 - (2 + 4) = 0$$

These oxygens also have no formal charges.

Now let's compare the two structures side by side.

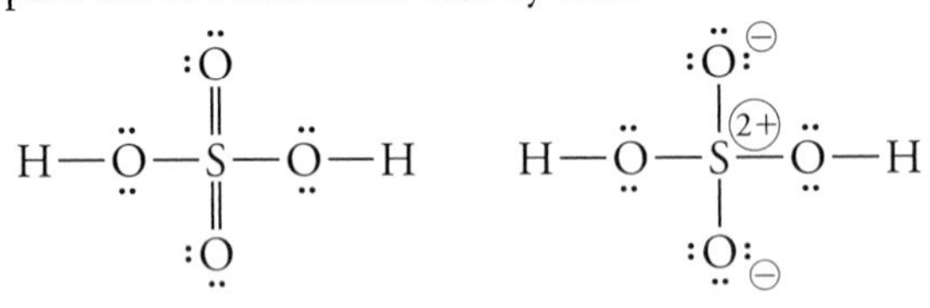

Imagine changing the one with the double bonds to the one with the single bonds. According to the formal charges, this would involve creating two pairs of positive–negative charge from something electrically neutral. Stated another way, it would involve separating negative charges from positive charges, and this would require an increase in the potential energy. Our conclusion is that the singly bonded structure on the right has a higher potential energy than the one with the double bonds. In general, the lower the potential energy of a molecule, the more stable it is. Therefore, the lower energy structure with the double bonds is, in principle, the more stable structure, so it is preferred over the one with only single bonds. This now gives us a rule that we can use in selecting the best Lewis structures for a molecule or ion:

TOOLS

Selecting the best Lewis structure

When several Lewis structures are possible, the one with formal charges closest to zero is the most stable and is preferred.

EXAMPLE 8.9
Selecting Lewis Structures Based
on Formal Charges

A student drew three Lewis structures for the nitric acid molecule:

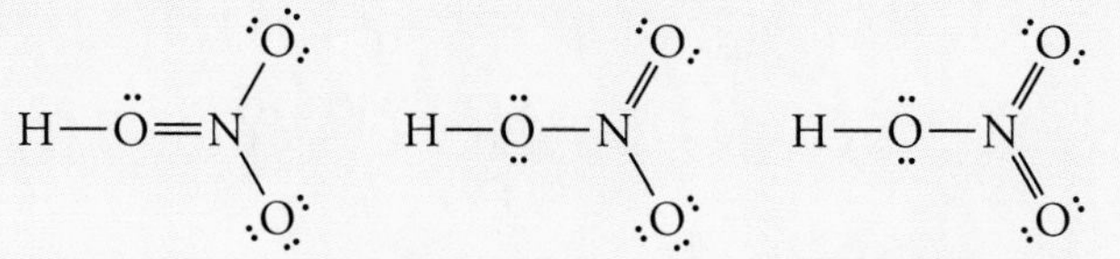

(I)   (II)   (III)

Which one is preferred?

ANALYSIS: When we have to select among several Lewis structures to find the best one, the tool is the procedure for assigning formal charges. As a rule, the structure with the fewest formal charges will be the best structure. We have to be careful, however, that we don't select a structure in which an atom is assigned more electrons than its valence shell can actually hold. Such a structure must be eliminated from consideration.

SOLUTION: Except for hydrogen, all the atoms in the molecule are from Period 2, and therefore can have a maximum of eight electrons in their valence shells. (Period 2 elements *never* exceed an octet because their valence shells have only s and p subshells and can accommodate a maximum of eight electrons.) Scanning the structures, we see that I and II show octets around both N and O. However, the nitrogen in Structure III has 5 bonds to it, which require 10 electrons. Therefore, this structure is not acceptable and can be eliminated immediately. Our choice is then between Structures I and II. Let's calculate formal charges on the atoms in each of them.

▫ In Structure III, the formal charges are zero on each of the atoms, but this cannot be the "preferred structure" because the nitrogen atom has too many electrons in its valence shell.

Structure I

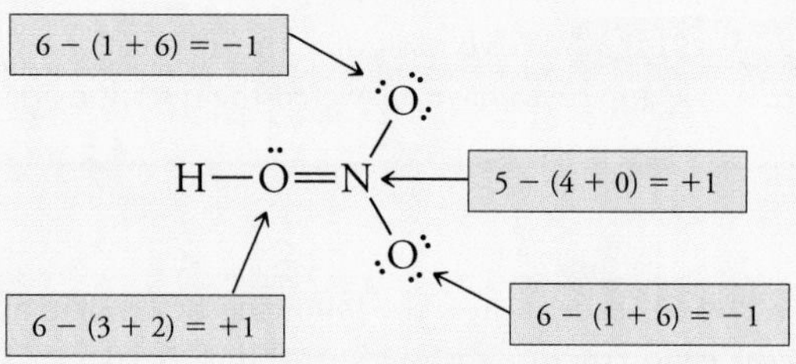

$6 - (1 + 6) = -1$

$5 - (4 + 0) = +1$

$6 - (3 + 2) = +1$

$6 - (1 + 6) = -1$

Structure II

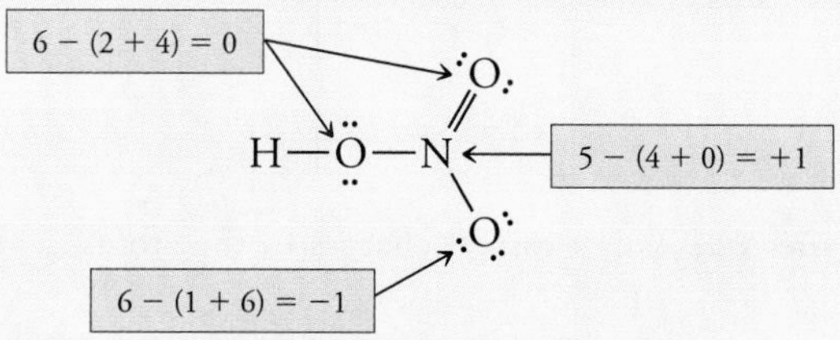

$6 - (2 + 4) = 0$

$5 - (4 + 0) = +1$

$6 - (1 + 6) = -1$

Next, we place the formal charges on the atoms in the structures.

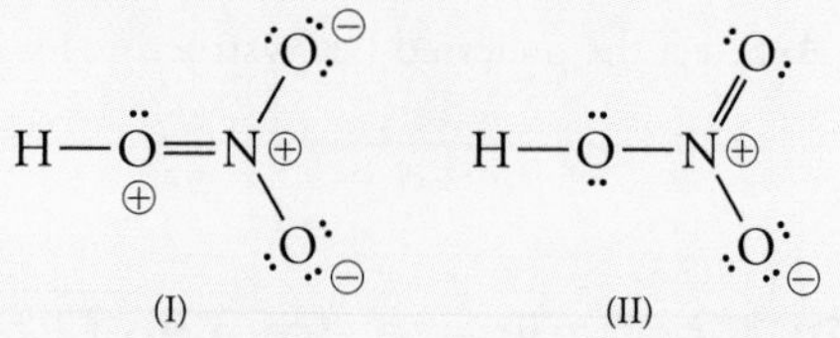

(I)   (II)

Because Structure II has fewer formal charges than Structure I, it is the lower-energy, preferred Lewis structure for HNO_3.

IS THE ANSWER REASONABLE? One simple check we can do is to add up the formal charges in each structure. The sum must equal the net charge on the particle, which is zero for HNO_3. Adding formal charges gives zero for each structure, so we can be confident we've assigned them correctly. This gives us confidence in our answer, too.

EXAMPLE 8.10
Selecting Lewis Structures Based on Formal Charges

Two structures can be drawn for BCl_3, as shown below

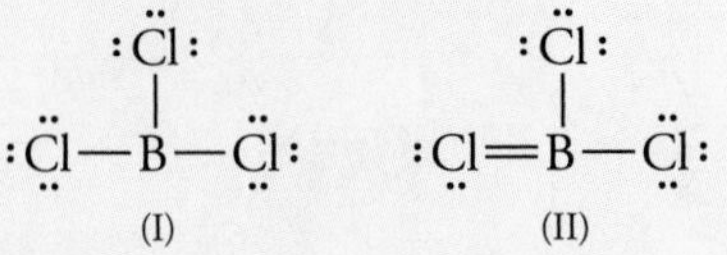

$$:\overset{..}{\underset{..}{Cl}}-B-\overset{..}{\underset{..}{Cl}}: \qquad :\overset{..}{\underset{..}{Cl}}=B-\overset{..}{\underset{..}{Cl}}:$$

(I)   (II)

Why is the one that violates the octet rule preferred?

ANALYSIS: We're asked to select between Lewis structures, which tells us that we have to consider formal charges. We'll assign them and then see if we can answer the question.

SOLUTION: Assigning formal charges gives

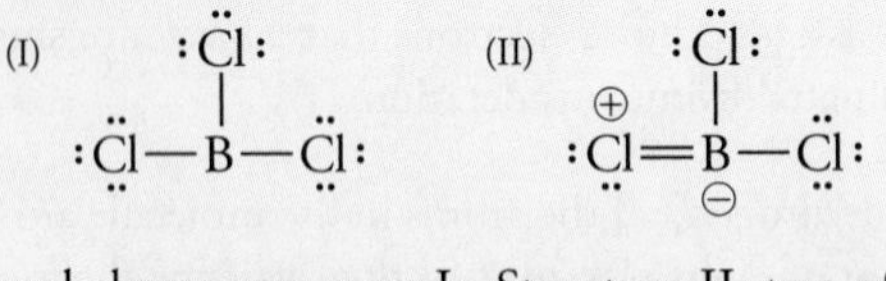

(I)   (II)

$$:\overset{..}{\underset{..}{Cl}}-B-\overset{..}{\underset{..}{Cl}}: \qquad \overset{\oplus}{:\overset{..}{\underset{..}{Cl}}}=\underset{\ominus}{B}-\overset{..}{\underset{..}{Cl}}:$$

In Structure I all the formal charges are zero. In Structure II, two of the atoms have formal charges, so this alone would argue in favor of Structure I. There is another argument in favor as well. Notice that the formal charges in Structure II place the positive charge on the more electronegative chlorine atom and the negative charge on the less electronegative boron. If charges could form in the molecule, they certainly would not be expected to form in this way. Therefore, there are two factors that make the structure with the double bond unfavorable, so we usually write the Lewis structure for BCl_3 as shown in Structure I.

IS THE ANSWER REASONABLE? We've assigned the formal charges correctly, and our reasoning seems sound, so we appear to have answered the question adequately.

Practice Exercise 14: A student drew the following Lewis structure for the sulfite ion, SO_3^{2-}. Is this the best Lewis structure for the ion? (Hint: Negative formal charges should be on the more electronegative atoms.)

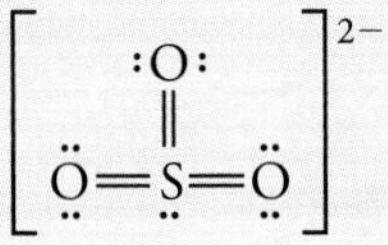

$$\left[\overset{\overset{\displaystyle :O:}{\|}}{\overset{..}{\underset{..}{O}}=S=\overset{..}{\underset{..}{O}}} \right]^{2-}$$

Practice Exercise 15: Assign formal charges to the atoms in the following Lewis structures.

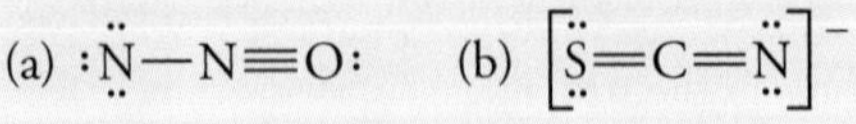

(a) $:\overset{..}{\underset{..}{N}}-N\equiv O:$ (b) $\left[\overset{..}{\underset{..}{S}}=C=\overset{..}{\underset{..}{N}} \right]^{-}$

Practice Exercise 16: Select the preferred Lewis structure for (a) SO_2, (b) $HClO_3$, and (c) H_3PO_4.

Both electrons in a coordinate covalent bond come from the same atom

Often we use Lewis structures to follow the course of chemical reactions. For example, we can diagram the reaction of hydrogen ion combining with a water molecule to form the hydronium ion, which occurs in aqueous solutions of acids.

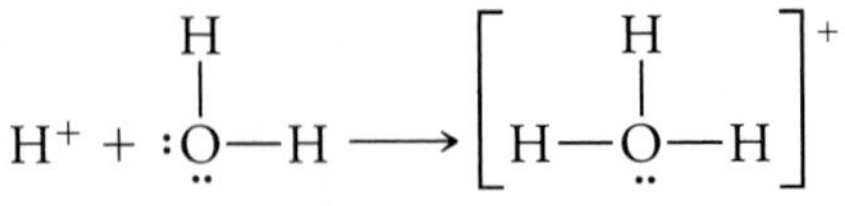

$$H^+ + \overset{\textstyle H}{\underset{..}{:O}}-H \longrightarrow \left[H-\overset{\textstyle H}{\underset{..}{O}}-H \right]^+$$

The formation of the bond between H^+ and H_2O follows a different path than the covalent bonds we discussed earlier in this chapter. For instance, when two H atoms combine to form H_2, each atom brings one electron to the bond.

$$H\cdot\ +\ \cdot H\ \longrightarrow\ H{-}H$$

But in the formation of H_3O^+, both of the electrons that become shared between the H^+ and the O originate on the oxygen atom of the water molecule. *This type of bond, in which both electrons of the shared pair come from just one of the two atoms, is called a* **coordinate covalent bond.**

Although we can make a distinction about the origin of the electrons shared in the bond, once the bond is formed a coordinate covalent bond is really the same as any other covalent bond. In other words, we can't tell where the electrons in the bond came from *after* the bond has been formed. In the H_3O^+ ion, for example, all three O—H bonds are identical once they've been formed.

The concept of a coordinate covalent bond is helpful in explaining what happens to atoms in a chemical reaction. For example, when ammonia is mixed with boron trichloride, an exothermic reaction takes place and the compound NH_3BCl_3 is formed in which there is a boron–nitrogen bond. Using Lewis structures, we can diagram this reaction as follows.

□ All electrons are alike, of course. We are using different colors for them so we can see where the electrons in the bond came from.

In the reaction, we might say that "the boron forms a coordinate covalent bond with the nitrogen of the ammonia molecule."

An arrow sometimes is used to represent the donated pair of electrons in a coordinate covalent bond. The direction of the arrow indicates the direction in which the electron pair is donated, in this case from the nitrogen to the boron.

□ Compounds like BCl_3NH_3, which are formed by simply joining two smaller molecules, are sometimes called **addition compounds.**

Practice Exercise 17: Use Lewis structures to show how the formation of NH_4^+ from NH_3 and H^+ involves formation of a coordinate covalent bond. How does this bond differ from the other NH bonds in NH_4^+? (Hint: You need to keep in mind the definition of a coordinate covalent bond.)

Practice Exercise 18: Use Lewis structures to explain how the reaction between hydroxide ion and hydrogen ion involves the formation of a coordinate covalent bond.

8.7 | RESONANCE APPLIES WHEN A SINGLE LEWIS STRUCTURE FAILS

There are some molecules and ions for which we cannot write Lewis structures that agree with experimental measurements of bond length and bond energy. An example is the formate ion, CHO_2^-. Following the usual steps, we would write its Lewis structure as

□ Formate ion is formed by neutralizing formic acid, an organic acid with the structure

The name formic acid comes from *formica*, the Latin word for ant. The one shown here is a fire ant. Formic acid is the substance that causes the stinging sensation in bites from this creature. *(J. H. Robinson/Photo Researchers.)*

This structure suggests that one carbon–oxygen bond should be longer than the other, but experiment shows that they are identical with lengths that are about halfway between the expected values for a single bond and a double bond. The Lewis structure doesn't match the experimental evidence, and there's no way to write one that does. It would require showing all of the electrons in pairs and, at the same time, showing 1.5 pairs of electrons in each carbon–oxygen bond.

The way we get around problems like this is through the use of a concept called **resonance.** We view the actual structure of the molecule or ion, which we cannot draw satisfactorily, as a composite, or average, of a number of Lewis structures that we can draw. For example, for formate we write

☐ No atoms have been moved; the electrons have just been redistributed.

where we have simply shifted electrons around in going from one structure to the other. The bond between the carbon and a particular oxygen is depicted as a single bond in one structure and as a double bond in the other. The average of these is 1.5 bonds (halfway between a single and a double bond), which is in agreement with the experimental bond lengths. These two Lewis structures are called **resonance structures** or **contributing structures.** The actual structure of the ion, which we can't draw, is called a **resonance hybrid** of these two resonance structures. The double-ended arrow is used to show that we are drawing resonance structures and implies that the true hybrid structure is a composite of the two resonance structures.[5]

Equivalent choices for double bond locations lead to resonance structures

TOOLS

Determining resonance structures

There is a simple way to determine when resonance should be applied to Lewis structures. If you find that you must move electrons to create one or more double bonds while following the procedures developed in the previous section, the number of resonance structures is equal to the number of equivalent choices for the locations of the double bonds. For example, in drawing the Lewis structure for the NO_3^- ion, we reach the stage

A double bond must be created to give the nitrogen an octet. Since it can be placed in any one of three locations, there are three resonance structures for this ion.

☐ The three oxygens in NO_3^- are said to be equivalent; that is, they are all alike in their chemical environment. Each oxygen is bonded to a nitrogen atom that's attached to two other oxygen atoms.

Notice that each structure is the same, except for the location of the double bond.

---

[5] The term *resonance* is often misleading to the beginning student. The word itself suggests that the actual structure flip-flops back and forth between the two structures shown. This is *not* the case! A mule, which is the *hybrid* offspring of a donkey and a horse, isn't a donkey one minute and a horse the next! Although it may have characteristics of both parents, a mule is a mule. A *resonance hybrid* also has characteristics of its "parents," but it never has the exact structure of any of them.

In the nitrate ion, the extra bond that moves around from one structure to another is divided among all three bond locations. Therefore, the average bond order in the N—O bonds is expected to be $1\frac{1}{3}$, or 1.33.[6]

EXAMPLE 8.11
Drawing Resonance Structures

Use formal charges to show that resonance applies to the preferred Lewis structure for the sulfite ion, SO_3^{2-}. Draw the resonance structures and determine the average bond order of the S—O bonds.

ANALYSIS: Following our usual procedure we obtain the Lewis structure

$$
\left[\begin{array}{c} :\ddot{O}: \\ | \\ :\ddot{O}-S-\ddot{O}: \end{array}\right]^{2-}
$$

All of the valence electrons have been placed into the structure and we have octets around all of the atoms, so it doesn't seem that we need the concept of resonance. However, the question refers to the "preferred" structure, which suggests that we are going to have to assign formal charges and determine what the preferred structure is. Then we can decide whether the concept of resonance will apply.

SOLUTION: When we assign formal charges, we get

$$
\left[\begin{array}{c} \overset{\ominus}{:}\ddot{O}: \\ | \\ \overset{\ominus}{:}\ddot{O}-\underset{\oplus}{S}-\ddot{O}:\overset{\ominus}{} \end{array}\right]^{2-}
$$

We can obtain a better Lewis structure if we can reduce the number of formal charges. This can be accomplished by moving an unshared pair from one of the oxygens into an S—O bond, thereby forming a double bond. Let's do this using the oxygen at the left.

$$
\left[\begin{array}{c} \overset{\ominus}{:}\ddot{O}: \\ | \\ :\ddot{O}-S-\ddot{O}:\overset{\ominus}{} \end{array}\right]^{2-} \xrightarrow{\text{gives}} \left[\begin{array}{c} \overset{\ominus}{:}\ddot{O}: \\ | \\ :O=S-\ddot{O}:\overset{\ominus}{} \end{array}\right]^{2-}
$$

However, we could have done this with any of the three S—O bonds, so there are three equivalent choices for the location of the double bond. Therefore, there are three resonance structures.

$$
\left[\begin{array}{c} :\ddot{O}: \\ | \\ :O=S-\ddot{O}: \end{array}\right]^{2-} \longleftrightarrow \left[\begin{array}{c} :\ddot{O} \\ \| \\ :\ddot{O}-S-\ddot{O}: \end{array}\right]^{2-} \longleftrightarrow \left[\begin{array}{c} :\ddot{O}: \\ | \\ :\ddot{O}-S=O: \end{array}\right]^{2-}
$$

As with the nitrate ion, we expect an average bond order of 1.33.

IS THE ANSWER REASONABLE? If we can answer "yes" to the following questions, the problem is solved correctly: Have we counted valence electrons correctly? Have we properly placed the electrons into the skeletal structure? Do the formal charges we've calculated add up to the charge on the SO_3^{2-} ion? Have we correctly determined the number of equivalent positions for the double bond? Have we computed the average bond order correctly?

---

[6] For resonance structures, the average bond order can be calculated by adding up the total number of bonds and dividing by the number of equivalent positions. In the NO_3^- ion, we have a total of four bonds (two single bonds and a double bond) distributed over three equivalent positions, so the bond order is $4/3 = 1\ 1/3$.

Practice Exercise 19: The phosphate ion has the following Lewis structure, where we've used formal charges to obtain the best structure.

$$\left[\begin{array}{c} :\!\ddot{O}\!: \\ \| \\ :\!\ddot{O}\!-\!P\!-\!\ddot{O}\!: \\ | \\ :\!\ddot{O}\!: \end{array} \right]^{3-}$$

How many resonance structures are there for this ion? (Hint: How many equivalent positions are there for the double bond?)

Practice Exercise 20: Draw the resonance structures for HCO_3^-.

Practice Exercise 21: Determine the preferred Lewis structure for the bromate ion, BrO_3^-, and, if appropriate, draw resonance structures.

Resonance is used to explain the stability of some molecules and ions

One of the benefits that a molecule or ion derives from existing as a resonance hybrid is that its total energy is lower than that of any one of its resonance structures. A particularly important example of this occurs with the compound benzene, C_6H_6. This is a flat, hexagonal ring-shaped molecule (Figure 8.11) with a basic structure that appears in many important organic molecules, ranging from plastics to amino acids.

Two resonance structures are usually drawn for benzene.

FIG. 8.11 Benzene. The molecule has a planar hexagonal structure.

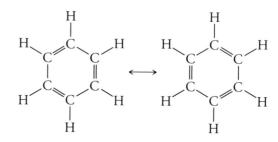

These are generally represented as hexagons with dashes showing the locations of the double bonds. It is assumed that at each apex of the hexagon there is a carbon bonded to a hydrogen as well as to the adjacent carbon atoms.

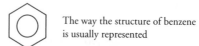

Usually, the actual structure of benzene (that of its resonance hybrid) is represented as a hexagon with a circle in the center. This is intended to show that the electron density of the three extra bonds is evenly distributed around the ring.

The way the structure of benzene is usually represented

Polystyrene plastic, a common polymer, contains benzene rings joined to alternating carbon atoms in a long hydrocarbon chain. When a gas is blown into melted polystyrene, the lightweight product called Styrofoam is formed. Styrofoam is used to make a wide variety of packaging products for consumer goods. *(Courtesy Polystyrene Packaging Council.)*

Although the individual resonance structures for benzene show double bonds, the molecule does not react like other organic molecules that have true carbon–carbon double bonds. The reason appears to be that the resonance hybrid is considerably more stable than either of the resonance forms. In fact, it has been calculated that the actual structure of the benzene molecule is more stable than either of its resonance structures by approximately 146 kJ/mol. This extra stability achieved through resonance is called the **resonance energy.**

SUMMARY

Ionic Bonding. In ionic compounds, the forces of attraction between positive and negative ions are called **ionic bonds.** The formation of ionic compounds by electron transfer is favored when atoms of low ionization energy react with atoms of high electron affinity. The chief stabilizing influence in the formation of ionic compounds is the release of the **lattice energy,** which is the energy required to completely separate the ions of an ionic compound. When atoms of the elements in Groups IA and IIA as well as the nonmetals form ions, they usually gain or lose enough electrons to achieve a noble gas electron configuration. Transition elements lose their outer *s* electrons first, followed by loss of *d* electrons from the shell below the outer shell. Post-transition metals lose electrons from their outer *p* subshell first, followed by electrons from the outer *s* subshell.

Covalent Bonding. Electron sharing between atoms occurs when electron transfer is energetically too "expensive." Shared electrons attract the positive nuclei, and this leads to a lowering of the potential energy of the atoms as a covalent bond forms. Electrons generally become paired when they are shared. An atom tends to share enough electrons to complete its valence shell. Except for hydrogen, the valence shell usually holds eight electrons, which forms the basis of the octet rule. The **octet rule** states that atoms of the representative elements tend to acquire eight electrons in their outer shells when they form bonds. **Single, double,** and **triple bonds** involve the sharing of one, two, and three pairs of electrons, respectively, between two atoms. Boron and beryllium often have less than an octet in their compounds. Atoms of the elements of Period 2 cannot have more than an octet because their outer shells can hold only eight electrons. Elements in Periods 3, 4, 5, and 6 can exceed an octet if they form more than four bonds.

   Bond energy (the energy needed to separate the bonded atoms) and **bond length** (the distance between the nuclei of the atoms connected by the bond) are two experimentally measurable quantities that can be related to the number of pairs of electrons in the bond. For bonds between atoms of the same elements, bond energy increases and bond length decreases as the **bond order** increases.

Electronegativity and Polar Bonds. The attraction an atom has for the electrons in a bond is called the atom's **electronegativity.** When atoms of different electronegativities form a bond, the electrons are shared unequally and the bond is **polar,** with **partial positive** and **partial negative** charges at opposite ends. This causes the bond to be an electric **dipole.** In a **polar molecule,** such as HCl, the product of the charge at either end multiplied by the distance between the charges gives the **dipole moment, μ.** When the two atoms have the same electronegativity, the bond is **nonpolar.** The extent of polarity of the bond depends on the electronegativity difference between the two bonded atoms. When the electronegativity difference is very large, ionic bonding results. A bond is approximately 50% ionic when the electronegativity difference is 1.7. In the periodic table, electronegativity increases from left to right across a period and from bottom to top in a group.

Reactivity and Electronegativity. The **reactivity** of metals is related to the ease with which they are oxidized (lose electrons); for nonmetals it is related to the ease with which they are reduced (gain electrons). Metals with low electronegativities lose electrons easily, are good reducing agents, and tend to be very reactive. The most reactive metals are located in Groups IA and IIA, and their ease of oxidation increases going down the group. For nonmetals, the higher the electronegativity, the stronger is their ability to serve as oxidizing agents. The strongest oxidizing agent is fluorine. Among the halogens, oxidizing strength decreases from fluorine to iodine.

Lewis Symbols and Lewis Structures. Lewis symbols are a bookkeeping device used to keep track of valence electrons in ionic and covalent bonds. The **Lewis symbol** of an element consists of the element's chemical symbol surrounded by a number of dots equal to the number of valence electrons. In the **Lewis structure** for an ionic compound, the Lewis symbol for the anion is enclosed in brackets (with the charge written outside) to show that all the electrons belong entirely to the ion. The Lewis structure for a molecule or polyatomic ion uses pairs of dots between chemical symbols to represent shared pairs of electrons. The electron pairs in covalent bonds usually are represented by dashes; one dash equals two electrons. The following procedure is used to draw the Lewis structure: (1) decide on the skeletal structure (remember that the least electronegative atom is usually the central atom and is usually first in the formula); (2) count all the valence electrons, taking into account the charge, if any; (3) place a pair of electrons in each bond; (4) complete the octets of atoms other than the central atom (but remember that hydrogen can only have two electrons); (5) place any leftover electrons on the central atom in pairs; (6) if the central atom still has *less than* an octet, move electron pairs to make double or triple bonds.

Formal Charges. The **formal charge** assigned to an atom in a Lewis structure (which usually differs from the actual charge on the atom) is calculated as the difference between the number of valence electrons of an isolated atom of the element and the number of electrons that "belong" to the atom because of its bonds to other atoms and its unshared valence electrons. The sum of the formal charges always equals the net charge on the molecule or ion. The most stable (lowest energy) Lewis structure for a molecule or ion is the one with formal charges closest to zero. This is usually the preferred Lewis structure for the particle.

Coordinate Covalent Bonding. For bookkeeping purposes, we sometimes single out a covalent bond whose electron pair originated from one of the two bonded atoms. An arrow is sometimes used to indicate the donated pair of electrons. Once formed, a coordinate covalent bond is no different from any other covalent bond.

Resonance. Two or more atoms in a molecule or polyatomic ion are *chemically equivalent* if they are attached to the same kinds of atoms or groups of atoms. Bonds to chemically equivalent atoms must be the same; they must have the same bond length and the same bond energy, which means they must involve the sharing of the same number of electron pairs. Sometimes the Lewis structures we draw suggest that the bonds to chemically equivalent atoms are not the same. Typically, this occurs when it is necessary to form multiple bonds during the drawing of a Lewis structure. When alternatives exist for the location of a multiple bond among two or more equivalent atoms, then each possible Lewis structure is actually a **resonance structure** or **contributing structure,** and we draw them all. In drawing resonance structures, the relative locations of the nuclei must be identical in all. Remember that none of the resonance structures corresponds to a real molecule, but their composite—the **resonance hybrid**—does approximate the actual structure of the molecule or ion.

TOOLS FOR PROBLEM SOLVING

In this chapter you learned to apply the following concepts as tools in solving problems. Study each one carefully so that you know what each is used for. When faced with solving a problem, recall what each tool does and consider whether it will be helpful in finding a solution. This will aid you in selecting the tools you need.

Electron configurations of ions of representative elements *(page 303)* Metals in Groups IA and IIA and the nonmetals obey the octet rule when they form ions. Use this knowledge to derive the electron configurations of ions of these elements.

Order in which electrons are lost from an atom *(page 303)* Electrons are lost first from the shell with largest n. For a given shell, electrons are lost from subshells in the following order: f before d before p before s. Use this knowledge to obtain electron configurations of ions of the transition and post-transition metals.

Lewis symbols *(page 306)* Lewis symbols are a bookkeeping device that we use to keep track of valence electrons in atoms and ions. For a neutral atom of the representative elements, the Lewis symbol consists of the atomic symbol surrounded by dots equal in number to the group number.

Octet rule and covalent bonding *(page 310)* The octet rule helps us construct Lewis structures for covalently bonded molecules. Elements in Period 2 never exceed an octet in their valence shells.

Dipole moment *(page 313)* Dipole moments are a measure of the polarity of molecules, so they can be used to compare molecular polarity. The dipole moment (μ) of a diatomic molecule is calculated as the charge on an end of the molecule, q, multiplied by the bond length, r. Dipole moments are expressed in debye units.

$$\mu = q \times r$$

Periodic trends in electronegativity *(page 315)* The trends revealed in Figure 8.6 allow us to use the locations of elements in the periodic table to estimate the degree of polarity of bonds and to estimate which of two atoms in a bond is the most electronegative.

Trends in the reactivity of metals in the periodic table *(page 316)* A knowledge of where the most reactive and least reactive metals are located in the periodic table gives a qualitative feel for how reactive a metal is by locating it in the periodic table.

Trends in the reactivity of nonmetals in the periodic table *(page 317)* The periodic table correlates the position of a non-metal with its strength as an oxidizing agent. Oxidizing ability increases from left to right across a period and from bottom to top in a group.

Method for drawing Lewis structures *(page 318)* The method described in Figure 8.9 yields Lewis structures in which the maximum number of atoms obey the octet rule.

Correlation between bond properties and bond order *(page 322)* The correlations allow us to compare experimental covalent bond properties (bond energy and bond length) with those predicted by theory.

Formal charges *(page 323)* Use formal charges to select the best Lewis structure for a molecule or polyatomic ion. The best structure is usually the one with the fewest formal charges. Assign formal charges to atoms as follows.

$$\text{Formal charge} = \left(\begin{array}{c} \text{number of } e^- \text{ in valence} \\ \text{shell of the isolated atom} \end{array} \right) - \left(\begin{array}{c} \text{number of bonds} \\ \text{to the atom} \end{array} + \begin{array}{c} \text{number of} \\ \text{unshared } e^- \end{array} \right)$$

Selecting the best Lewis structure *(page 324)* The structure having the smallest formal charges is preferred. Be sure none of the atoms in the structure appears to have more electrons than permitted by its location in the periodic table.

Method for determining resonance structures *(page 328)* By distributing multiple bonds over equivalent atoms in a molecule we obtain a better description of the bonding in the molecule. We also know that when resonance structures can be drawn, a molecule or ion will be more stable than any of the individual resonance structures. Expect resonance structures when there is more than one option for assigning the location of a double bond.

QUESTIONS, PROBLEMS, AND EXERCISES

Answers to problems whose numbers are printed in color are given in Appendix B. More challenging problems are marked with asterisks. ILW = Interactive Learningware solution is available at www.wiley.com/college/brady. OH = an Office Hours video is available for this problem.

REVIEW QUESTIONS

Ionic Bonding

8.1 What must be true about the change in the total potential energy of a collection of atoms for a stable compound to be formed from the elements?

8.2 What is an *ionic bond?*

8.3 How is the tendency to form ionic bonds related to the IE and EA of the atoms involved?

8.4 Define the term *lattice energy.* In what ways does the lattice energy contribute to the stability of ionic compounds?

8.5 Magnesium forms the ion Mg^{2+}, but not the ion Mg^{3+}. Why?

8.6 Why doesn't chlorine form the ion Cl^{2-}?

8.7 Why do many of the transition elements in Period 4 form ions with a 2+ charge?

8.8 If we were to compare the first, second, third, and fourth ionization energies of aluminum, between which pair of successive ionization energies would there be the largest difference? (Refer to the periodic table in answering this question.)

8.9 In each of the following pairs of compounds, which would have the larger lattice energy? (a) CaO or Al_2O_3, (b) BeO or SrO, (c) NaCl or NaBr.

Lewis Symbols

8.10 The Lewis symbol for an atom only accounts for electrons in the valence shell of the atom. Why are we not concerned with the other electrons?

8.11 Which of these Lewis symbols is incorrect?

(a) $:\!\overset{\cdot}{\underset{\cdot\cdot}{O}}\!:$ (b) $\cdot\overset{\cdot\cdot}{\underset{\cdot\cdot}{Cl}}\cdot$ (c) $:\!\overset{\cdot\cdot}{\underset{\cdot\cdot}{Ne}}\!:$ (d) $:\!\overset{\cdot\cdot}{Sb}\!\cdot$

Electron Sharing

8.12 In terms of the potential energy change, why doesn't ionic bonding occur when two nonmetals react with each other?

8.13 Describe what happens to the electron density around two hydrogen atoms as they come together to form an H_2 molecule.

8.14 What happens to the energy of two hydrogen atoms as they approach each other? What happens to the spins of the electrons?

8.15 Is the formation of a covalent bond endothermic or exothermic?

8.16 What factors control the bond length in a covalent bond?

Covalent Bonding and the Octet Rule

8.17 What is the *octet rule?* What is responsible for it?

8.18 How many covalent bonds are normally formed by (a) hydrogen, (b) carbon, (c) oxygen, (d) nitrogen, and (e) chlorine?

8.19 Why do Period 2 elements never form more than four covalent bonds? Why are Period 3 elements able to exceed an octet?

8.20 Define (a) *single bond,* (b) *double bond,* and (c) *triple bond.*

8.21 The Lewis structure for hydrogen cyanide is $H\!-\!C\!\equiv\!N\!:$. Draw circles enclosing electrons to show that carbon and nitrogen obey the octet rule.

8.22 Why doesn't hydrogen obey the octet rule? How many covalent bonds does a hydrogen atom form?

8.23 Use Lewis structures to show the ionization of the following organic acid (a weak acid) in water. If necessary, refer to Figure 4.11 on page 142.

$$CH_3\!-\!CH_2\!-\!\overset{\displaystyle :\overset{\cdot\cdot}{O}:}{\overset{\|}{C}}\!-\!\overset{\cdot\cdot}{O}H$$

8.24 The compound below is called an amine. It is a weak base and undergoes ionization in water following a path similar to that of ammonia. Use Lewis structures to diagram the reaction of this amine with water. If necessary, refer to Figure 4.12 on page 143.

$$CH_3\!-\!\overset{\displaystyle H}{\underset{\displaystyle \cdot\cdot}{N}}\!-\!CH_2\!-\!CH_3$$

8.25 Use Lewis structures to diagram the reaction between the acid in Question 8.23 and the base in Question 8.24. If necessary, refer to Figure 4.17 on page 151.

Polar Bonds and Electronegativity

8.26 What is a polar covalent bond?

8.27 Define *dipole moment* in the form of an equation. What is the value of the *debye* (with appropriate units)?

8.28 Define *electronegativity.* On what basis did Pauling develop his scale of electronegativities?

8.29 Which element has the highest electronegativity? Which is the second most electronegative element?

8.30 Which elements are assigned electronegativities of zero? Why?

8.31 Among the following bonds, which are more ionic than covalent?

(a) Si—O, (b) Ba—O, (c) Se—Cl, (d) K—Br

8.32 If an element has a low electronegativity, is it likely to be a metal or a nonmetal? Explain your answer.

Electronegativity and the Reactivities of the Elements

8.33 When we say that aluminum is more *reactive* than iron, which kind of reaction of these elements are we describing?

8.34 In what groups in the periodic table are the most reactive metals found? Where do we find the least reactive metals?

8.35 How is the electronegativity of a metal related to its reactivity?

8.36 Arrange the following metals in their approximate order of reactivity (most reactive first, least reactive last) based on their locations in the periodic table: (a) iridium, (b) silver, (c) calcium, and (d) iron.

8.37 Complete and balance equations for the following. If no reaction occurs, write "N.R."
(a) $KCl + Br_2 \longrightarrow$
(b) $NaI + Cl_2 \longrightarrow$
(c) $KCl + F_2 \longrightarrow$
(d) $CaBr_2 + Cl_2 \longrightarrow$
(e) $AlBr_3 + F_2 \longrightarrow$
(f) $ZnBr_2 + I_2 \longrightarrow$

8.38 In each pair, choose the better oxidizing agent.
(a) O_2 or F_2
(b) As_4 or P_4
(c) Br_2 or I_2
(d) P_4 or S_8
(e) Se_8 or Cl_2
(f) As_4 or S_8

Failure of the Octet Rule

8.39 How many electrons are in the valence shells of (a) Be in $BeCl_2$, (b) B in BCl_3, and (c) H in H_2O?

8.40 What is the minimum number of electrons that would be expected to be in the valence shell of As in $AsCl_5$?

8.41 Nitrogen and arsenic are in the same group in the periodic table. Arsenic forms both $AsCl_3$ and $AsCl_5$, but with chlorine, nitrogen only forms NCl_3. On the basis of the electronic structures of N and As, explain why this is so.

Bond Length and Bond Energy

8.42 Define *bond length* and *bond energy*.

8.43 Define *bond order*. How are bond energy and bond length related to bond order? Why are there these relationships?

8.44 The energy required to break the H—Cl bond to give H^+ and Cl^- ions would not be called the H—Cl bond energy. Why?

Formal Charge

8.45 What is the definition of *formal charge*?

8.46 How are formal charges used to select the best Lewis structure for a molecule? What is the basis for this method of selection?

8.47 What are the formal charges on the atoms in the HCl molecule? What are the actual charges on the atoms in this molecule? (Hint: See Section 8.4.) Are formal charges the same as actual charges?

Resonance

8.48 Why is the concept of resonance needed?

8.49 What is a *resonance hybrid*? How does it differ from the resonance structures drawn for a molecule?

8.50 Draw the resonance structures of the benzene molecule. Why is benzene more stable than one would expect if the ring contained three carbon–carbon double bonds?

8.51 Polystyrene plastic consists of a long chain of carbon atoms in which every other carbon is attached to a benzene ring. The ring is attached by replacing a hydrogen of benzene with a bond to the carbon chain. In the chain, carbons not attached to other carbons are bonded to hydrogen atoms. Sketch a portion of a polystyrene molecule that contains five benzene rings.

Coordinate Covalent Bonds

8.52 What is a *coordinate covalent bond*?

8.53 Once formed, how (if at all) does a coordinate covalent bond differ from an ordinary covalent bond?

8.54 BCl_3 has an incomplete valence shell. Use Lewis structures to show how it could form a coordinate covalent bond with a water molecule.

REVIEW PROBLEMS

Electron Configurations of Ions

8.55 Explain what happens to the electron configurations of Mg and Br when they react to form magnesium bromide.

8.56 Describe what happens to the electron configurations of lithium and nitrogen when they react to form lithium nitride.

8.57 What are the electron configurations of the Pb^{2+} and Pb^{4+} ions?

8.58 What are the electron configurations of the Bi^{3+} and Bi^{5+} ions?

8.59 Write the abbreviated electron configuration of the Mn^{3+} ion. How many unpaired electrons does the ion contain?

8.60 Write the abbreviated electron configuration of the Co^{3+} ion. How many unpaired electrons does the ion contain?

Lewis Symbols

8.61 Write Lewis symbols for the following atoms: (a) Si, (b) Sb, (c) Ba, (d) Al, and (e) S.

8.62 Write Lewis symbols for the following atoms: (a) K, (b) Ge, (c) As, (d) Br, and (e) Se.

8.63 Use Lewis symbols to diagram the reactions between (a) Ca and Br, (b) Al and O, and (c) K and S.

8.64 Use Lewis symbols to diagram the reactions between (a) Mg and S, (b) Mg and Cl, and (c) Mg and N.

Dipole Moments:

8.65 Use the data in Table 8.2 (page 313) to calculate the amount of charge on the oxygen and nitrogen in the nitrogen monoxide molecule, expressed in electronic charge units ($e = 1.60 \times 10^{-19}$ C). Which atom carries the positive charge?

8.66 The molecule bromine monofluoride has a dipole moment of 1.42 D and a bond length of 176 pm. Calculate the charge on the ends of the molecule, expressed in electronic charge units ($e = 1.60 \times 10^{-19}$ C). Which atom carries the positive charge?

8.67 The dipole moment of HF is 1.83 D and the bond length is 91.7 pm. Calculate the amount of charge (in electronic charge units) on the hydrogen and the fluorine atoms in the HF molecule.

8.68 In the vapor state, cesium and fluoride ions pair to give CsF formula units that have a bond length of 0.255 nm and a dipole moment of 7.88 D. What is the actual charge on the cesium and fluorine atoms in CsF? What percentage of full 1+ and 1− charges is this?

Bond Energy

8.69 How many grams of water could have its temperature raised from 25 °C (room temperature) to 100 °C (the boiling point of water) by the amount of energy released in the formation of 1 mol of H_2 from hydrogen atoms? The bond energy of H_2 is 435 kJ/mol.

8.70 How much energy, in joules, is required to break the bond in *one* chlorine molecule? The bond energy of Cl_2 is 242.6 kJ/mol.

8.71 The reason there is danger in exposure to high-energy radiation (e.g., ultraviolet and X rays) is that the radiation can rupture chemical bonds. In some cases, cancer can be caused by it. A carbon–carbon single bond has a bond energy of approximately 348 kJ per mole. What wavelength of light is required to provide sufficient energy to break the C—C bond? In which region of the electromagnetic spectrum is this wavelength located?

8.72 A mixture of H_2 and Cl_2 is stable, but a bright flash of light passing through it can cause the mixture to explode. The light causes Cl_2 molecules to split into Cl atoms, which are highly reactive. What wavelength of light is necessary to cause the Cl_2 molecules to split? The bond energy of Cl_2 is 242.6 kJ per mole.

Covalent Bonds and the Octet Rule

8.73 Use Lewis structures to diagram the formation of (a) Br_2, (b) H_2O, and (c) NH_3 from neutral atoms.

OH 8.74 Chlorine tends to form only one covalent bond because it needs just one electron to complete its octet. What are the Lewis structures for the simplest compound formed by chlorine with (a) nitrogen, (b) carbon, (c) sulfur, and (d) bromine?

8.75 Use the octet rule to predict the formula of the simplest compound formed from hydrogen and (a) selenium, (b) arsenic, and (c) silicon. (Remember, however, that the valence shell of hydrogen can hold only two electrons.)

8.76 What would be the formula for the simplest compound formed from (a) phosphorus and chlorine, (b) carbon and fluorine, and (c) iodine and chlorine?

Electronegativity

OH 8.77 Use Figure 8.6 to choose the atom in each of the following bonds that carries the partial positive charge: (a) N—S, (b) Si—I, (c) N—Br, and (d) C—Cl.

8.78 Use Figure 8.6 to choose the atom that carries the partial negative charge in each of the following bonds: (a) Hg—I, (b) P—I, (c) Si—F, and (d) Mg—N.

8.79 Which of the bonds in Problem 8.77 is the most polar?

8.80 Which of the bonds in Problem 8.78 is the least polar?

Drawing Lewis Structures

8.81 What are the expected skeletal structures for (a) $SiCl_4$, (b) PF_3, (c) PH_3, and (d) SCl_2?

8.82 What are the expected skeletal structures for (a) HIO_3, (b) H_2CO_3, (c) HCO_3^-, and (d) PCl_4^+?

8.83 How many dots must appear in the Lewis structures of (a) $SiCl_4$, (b) PF_3, (c) PH_3, and (d) SCl_2?

8.84 How many dots must appear in the Lewis structures of (a) HIO_3, (b) H_2CO_3, (c) HCO_3^-, and (d) PCl_4^+?

ILW 8.85 Draw Lewis structures for (a) $AsCl_4^+$, (b) ClO_2^-, (c) HNO_2, and (d) XeF_2.

8.86 Draw Lewis structures for (a) TeF_4, (b) ClF_5, (c) PF_6^-, and (d) XeF_4.

8.87 Draw Lewis structures for (a) $SiCl_4$, (b) PF_3, (c) PH_3, and (d) SCl_2.

8.88 Draw Lewis structures for (a) HIO_3, (b) H_2CO_3, (c) HCO_3^-, and (d) PCl_4^+.

8.89 Draw Lewis structures for (a) carbon disulfide and (b) cyanide ion.

8.90 Draw Lewis structures for (a) selenium trioxide and (b) selenium dioxide.

8.91 Draw Lewis structures for (a) AsH_3, (b) $HClO_2$, (c) H_2SeO_3, and (d) H_3AsO_4.

OH 8.92 Draw Lewis structures for (a) NO^+, (b) NO_2^-, (c) $SbCl_6^-$, and (d) IO_3^-.

8.93 Draw the Lewis structure for (a) CH_2O (the central atom is carbon, which is attached to two hydrogens and an oxygen) and (b) $SOCl_2$ (the central atom is sulfur, which is attached to an oxygen and two chlorines).

8.94 Draw Lewis structures for (a) $GeCl_4$, (b) CO_3^{2-}, (c) PO_4^{3-}, and (d) O_2^{2-}.

Formal Charge

8.95 Assign formal charges to each atom in the following structures:

(a) $H\!-\!\ddot{O}\!-\!\ddot{C}l\!-\!\ddot{O}\!:$

(b) $\ddot{O}\!=\!S\!-\!\ddot{O}\!:$ with $:\!\ddot{O}\!:$ below S

(c) $\ddot{O}\!=\!S\!-\!\ddot{O}\!:$

8.96 Assign formal charges to each atom in the following structures:

(a) $:\!\ddot{C}l\!-\!N\!-\!\ddot{O}\!:$ with $:\!O\!:$ (double bond) above N

(b) $:\!\ddot{F}\!-\!N\!-\!\ddot{O}\!:$ with $:\!\ddot{F}\!:$ above and $:\!\ddot{F}\!:$ below N

(c) $:\!\ddot{F}\!-\!S\!-\!\ddot{F}\!:$ with $:\!\ddot{O}\!:$ above and $:\!\ddot{O}\!:$ below S

ILW 8.97 Draw the Lewis structure for $HClO_4$ according to the procedure described in Figure 8.9. Assign formal charges to each atom in the formula. Determine the preferred Lewis structure for this compound.

8.98 Draw the Lewis structure for SO_2Cl (sulfur bonded to two Cl and one O). Assign formal charges to each atom. Determine the preferred Lewis structure for this molecule.

8.99 Below are two structures for $BeCl_2$. Give two reasons why the one on the left is the preferred structure.

$:\!\ddot{C}l\!-\!Be\!-\!\ddot{C}l\!:$ $:\!\ddot{C}l\!-\!Be\!=\!\ddot{C}l\!:$

8.100 The following are two Lewis structures that can be drawn for phosgene, a substance that has been used as a war gas.

$$:\overset{..}{\underset{}{O}}: \qquad \overset{..}{\underset{}{O}}:$$
$$:\overset{..}{\underset{..}{Cl}}-C=\overset{..}{\underset{..}{Cl}}: \qquad :\overset{..}{\underset{..}{Cl}}-C-\overset{..}{\underset{..}{Cl}}:$$

Which is the better Lewis structure? Why?

Resonance

8.101 Draw the resonance structures for CO_3^{2-}. Calculate the average C—O bond order.

ILW 8.102 Draw all the resonance structures for the N_2O_4 molecule and determine the average N—O bond order. The skeletal structure of the molecule is

$$\begin{array}{ccc} O & & O \\ & N \; N & \\ O & & O \end{array}$$

OH 8.103 How should the N—O bond lengths compare in the NO_3^- and NO_2^- ions?

8.104 Arrange the following in order of increasing C—O bond length: CO, CO_3^{2-}, CO_2, and HCO_2^- (formate ion, page 327).

8.105 The Lewis structure of CO_2 was given as

$$\overset{..}{O}=C=\overset{..}{O}$$

but two other resonance structures can also be drawn for it. What are they? On the basis of formal charges, why are they not preferred structures?

8.106 Use formal charges to establish the preferred Lewis structures for the ClO_3^- and ClO_4^- ions. Draw resonance structures for both ions and determine the average Cl—O bond order in each. Which of these ions would be expected to have the shorter Cl—O bond length?

Coordinate Covalent Bonds

8.107 Use Lewis structures to show that the hydronium ion, H_3O^+, can be considered to be formed by the creation of a coordinate covalent bond between H_2O and H^+.

8.108 Use Lewis structures to show that the reaction

$$BF_3 + F^- \longrightarrow BF_4^-$$

involves the formation of a coordinate covalent bond.

ADDITIONAL EXERCISES

8.109 Use data from the tables of ionization energies and electron affinities on pages 287 and 291 to calculate the energy changes for the following reactions.

$$Na(g) + Cl(g) \longrightarrow Na^+(g) + Cl^-(g)$$
$$Na(g) + 2Cl(g) \longrightarrow Na^{2+}(g) + 2Cl^-(g)$$

Approximately how many times larger would the lattice energy of $NaCl_2$ have to be compared to the lattice energy of NaCl for $NaCl_2$ to be more stable than NaCl?

8.110 Changing 1 mol of Mg(s) and 1/2 mol of $O_2(g)$ to gaseous atoms requires a total of approximately 150 kJ of energy. The first and second ionization energies of magnesium are 737 and 1450 kJ/mol, respectively; the first and second electron affinities of oxygen are −141 and +844 kJ/mol, respectively, and the standard heat of formation of MgO(s) is −602 kJ/mol. Construct an enthalpy diagram similar to the one in Facets of Chemistry 8.1 and use it to calculate the lattice energy of magnesium oxide. How does the lattice energy of MgO compare with that of NaCl? What might account for the difference?

*8.111 Use an enthalpy diagram to calculate the lattice energy of $CaCl_2$ from the following information. Energy needed to vaporize one mole of Ca(s) is 192 kJ. For calcium, 1st IE = 589.5 kJ mol^{-1}, 2nd IE = 1146 kJ mol^{-1}. Electron affinity of Cl is −348 kJ mol^{-1}. Bond energy of Cl_2 is 242.6 kJ per mole of Cl—Cl bonds. Standard heat of formation of $CaCl_2$ is −795 kJ mol^{-1}.

*8.112 Use an enthalpy diagram and the following data to calculate the electron affinity of bromine. Standard heat of formation of NaBr is −360 kJ mol^{-1}. Energy needed to vaporize one mole of $Br_2(l)$ to give $Br_2(g)$ is 31 kJ mol^{-1}. The energy needed to change 1 mol Na(s) to 1 mol Na(g) is 107.8 kJ. The first ionization energy of Na is 495.4 kJ mol^{-1}. The bond energy of Br_2 is 192 kJ per mole of Br—Br bonds. The lattice energy of NaBr is 743.3 kJ mol^{-1}.

8.113 In many ways, tin(IV) chloride behaves more like a covalent molecular species than as a typical ionic chloride. Draw the Lewis structure for the tin(IV) chloride molecule.

8.114 In each pair, choose the one with more polar bonds. (Use the periodic table to answer the question.)
(a) PCl_3 or $AsCl_3$ (c) $SiCl_4$ or SCl_2
(b) SF_2 or GeF_4 (d) SrO or SnO

8.115 How many electrons are in the outer shell of the Zn^{2+} ion?

8.116 The Lewis structure for carbonic acid (formed when CO_2 dissolves in water) is usually given as

$$H-\overset{..}{\underset{..}{O}}-\overset{\overset{\displaystyle \overset{..}{O}:}{\|}}{C}-\overset{..}{\underset{..}{O}}-H$$

What is wrong with the following structures?

(a) $H-\overset{..}{\underset{..}{O}}-\overset{..}{C}-\overset{..}{\underset{..}{O}}-H$ (b) $H-\overset{..}{\underset{.}{O}}=C-\overset{..}{\underset{..}{O}}-H$

(c) $H-\overset{..}{\underset{}{O}}=C=\overset{..}{\underset{}{O}}-H$

8.117 Are the following Lewis structures considered to be resonance structures? Explain. Which is the more likely structure for $POCl_3$?

$$:\overset{..}{\underset{..}{Cl}}-\overset{\overset{\displaystyle :\overset{..}{Cl}:}{|}}{\underset{\underset{\displaystyle :\overset{..}{Cl}:}{|}}{P}}=\overset{..}{\underset{..}{O}} \qquad :\overset{..}{\underset{..}{Cl}}-\overset{\overset{\displaystyle :\overset{..}{Cl}:}{|}}{\underset{\underset{\displaystyle :\overset{..}{Cl}:}{|}}{O}}=\overset{..}{\underset{..}{P}}$$

8.118 Assign formal charges to all the atoms in the following Lewis structure of hydrazoic acid, HN_3.

$$H-N\equiv N-\overset{..}{\underset{..}{N}}:$$

Suggest a lower energy resonance structure for this molecule.

8.119 Assign formal charges to all the atoms in the Lewis structure

$$:\overset{..}{\underset{..}{O}}-\overset{\overset{\displaystyle :\overset{..}{O}-H}{|}}{\underset{\underset{\displaystyle H-\overset{..}{O}:}{|}}{As}}-\overset{..}{\underset{}{O}}-H$$

Suggest a lower energy Lewis structure for this molecule.

8.120 The inflation of an "air bag" when a car experiences a collision occurs by the explosive decomposition of sodium azide, NaN_3, which yields nitrogen gas that inflates the bag. The following resonance structures can be drawn for the azide ion, N_3^-. Identify the best and worst of them.

$$\left[:\ddot{N}=N=\ddot{N}: \right]^- \longleftrightarrow \left[\ddot{N}\equiv N-\ddot{N}: \right]^-$$

$$\updownarrow \qquad\qquad \updownarrow$$

$$\left[:N\equiv N=\ddot{N}: \right]^- \longleftrightarrow \left[:\ddot{N}-N-\ddot{N}: \right]^-$$

8.121 How should the sulfur–oxygen bond lengths compare for the species SO_3, SO_2, SO_3^{2-}, and SO_4^{2-}?

8.122 What is the most reasonable Lewis structure for S_2Cl_2?

*__8.123__ There are two acids that have the formula HCNO. Which of the following skeletal structures are most likely for them? Justify your answer.

H C O N   H N O C   H O C N
H C N O   H N C O   H O N C

*__8.124__ What wavelength of light, if absorbed by a hydrogen molecule, could cause the molecule to split into the ions H^+ and H^-? (The data required are available in this and previous chapters.)

8.125 In the vapor state, ion pairs of KF can be identified. The dipole moment of such a pair is measured to be 8.59 D and the K—F bond length is found to be 217 pm. Is the K—F bond 100% ionic? If not, what percent of full 1+ and 1− charges do the K and F atoms carry, respectively?

EXERCISES IN CRITICAL THINKING

8.126 What is the average bond energy of a C—C covalent bond? What wavelength of light provides enough energy to break such a bond? Using this information, explain why unfiltered sunlight is damaging to the skin.

8.127 One way of estimating the electronegativity of an atom is to use an average of its ionization energy and electron affinity. Why would these two quantities be related to electronegativity?

8.128 The attractions between molecules of a substance can be associated with the size of the molecule's dipole moment. Explain why this is so.

8.129 The positive end of the dipole in a water molecule is not located on an atom. Explain why this happens and suggest other simple molecules that show the same effect.

8.130 In describing the structures of molecules we use Lewis structures, formal charges, and experimental evidence. Rank these in terms of importance in deciding on the true structure of a molecule, and defend your choice.

CHEMICAL BONDING AND MOLECULAR STRUCTURE

9

All of the variety of living things found in this rain forest, and elsewhere on earth, depends on the three-dimensional shapes of molecules and the requirement that certain molecules fit precisely together for biochemical reactions to occur. In this chapter we will study the kinds of shapes that molecules have and the way the electronic structures of atoms influence the chemical bonds that determine molecular geometry. *(Steve Satushek/ Iconica/Getty Images)*

The structure of an ionic compound, such as NaCl, is controlled primarily by the sizes of the ions and their charges. The attractions between the ions have no preferred directions, so if an ionic compound is melted, this structure is lost and the array of ions collapses into a jumbled liquid state. Molecular substances are quite different, however. Molecules have three-dimensional shapes that are determined by the relative orientations of their covalent bonds, and this structure is maintained regardless of whether the substance is a solid, a liquid, or a gas.

Many of the properties of a molecule depend on the three-dimensional arrangement of its atoms. For example, the functioning of enzymes, which are substances that affect how fast biochemical reactions occur, requires that there be a very precise fit between one molecule and another. Even slight alterations in molecular geometry can destroy this fit and deactivate the enzyme, which in turn prevents the biochemical reaction involved from occurring. Similarly, the structures of polymer molecules in plastics have a strong influence on the properties of materials made from them.

In this chapter we will explore the topic of molecular geometry and study theoretical models that allow us to explain, and in some cases predict, the shapes of molecules. We will also examine theories that explain, in terms of wave mechanics and the electronic structures of atoms, *why* covalent bonds form and *why* they are so highly directional in nature. You will find the knowledge gained here helpful in later discussions of physical properties of substances such as melting points and boiling points.

9.1 | MOLECULES ARE THREE-DIMENSIONAL WITH SHAPES THAT ARE BUILT FROM FIVE BASIC ARRANGEMENTS

We live in a three-dimensional world made up of three-dimensional molecules. However, the Lewis structures we've been using to describe the bonding in molecules do not convey any information about the shapes of molecules; they simply describe which atoms are bonded to each other. Our goal now is to examine theories that predict molecular shapes and explain covalent structures in terms of quantum theory. We'll begin by studying some of the kinds of shapes molecules have.

Molecular shape only becomes a question when there are at least three atoms present. If there are only two, there is no doubt as to how they are arranged; one is just alongside the other. But when there are three or more atoms in a molecule we find that its shape is often built from just one or another of five basic geometrical structures.

TOOLS

Basic molecular shapes

Linear molecules

In a **linear molecule** the atoms lie in a straight line. When the molecule has three atoms, the angle formed by the covalent bonds, which we call the **bond angle,** equals 180° as illustrated below.

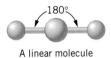

A linear molecule

Planar triangular molecules

A **planar triangular molecule** is one in which three atoms are located at the corners of a triangle and are bonded to a fourth atom that lies in the center of the triangle.

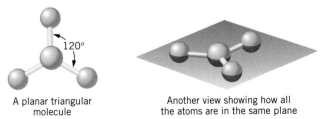

A planar triangular molecule

Another view showing how all the atoms are in the same plane

In this molecule, all four atoms lie in the same plane and the bond angles are all equal to 120°.

Tetrahedral molecules

□ As you study these structures, you should try hard to visualize them in three dimensions. You should also learn how to sketch them in a way that conveys the three-dimensional information.

A **tetrahedron** is a four-sided geometric figure shaped like a pyramid with triangular faces. A **tetrahedral molecule** is one in which four atoms, located at the vertices of a tetrahedron, are bonded to a fifth atom in the center of the structure.

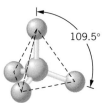

109.5°

A tetrahedron   A tetrahedral molecule

All the bond angles in a tetrahedral molecule are the same and are equal to 109.5°.

Trigonal bipyramidal molecules

A **trigonal bipyramid** consists of two *trigonal pyramids* (pyramids with triangular faces) that share a common base. In a **trigonal bipyramidal molecule,** the central atom is located in the middle of the triangular plane shared by the upper and lower trigonal pyramids and is bonded to five atoms that are at the vertices of the figure.

An axial bond

An equatorial bond

FIG. 9.1 Axial and equatorial bonds in a trigonal bipyramidal molecule.

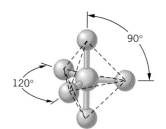

90°

120°

A trigonal bipyramid   A trigonal bipyramidal molecule

In this type of molecule, not all the bonds are equivalent. If we imagine the trigonal bipyramid centered inside a sphere similar to the earth, as illustrated in Figure 9.1, the atoms in the triangular plane are located around the equator. The bonds to these atoms are called **equatorial bonds.** The angle between two equatorial bonds is 120°. The two vertical bonds pointing along the north and south axis of the sphere are 180° apart and are called **axial bonds.** The bond angle between an axial bond and an equatorial bond is 90°.

A simplified representation of a trigonal bipyramid is illustrated in Figure 9.2. The equatorial triangular plane is sketched as it would look tilted, so we're looking at it from its edge. The axial bonds are represented as lines pointing up and down. To add more three-dimensional character, notice that the bond pointing down appears to be partially hidden by the triangular plane in the center.

FIG. 9.2 A simplified way of drawing a trigonal bipyramid. To form a trigonal bipyramidal molecule, atoms would be attached at the corners of the triangle in the center and at the ends of the bonds that extend vertically up and down.

Octahedral molecules

An **octahedron** is an eight-sided figure, which you might think of as two *square pyramids* sharing a common square base. The octahedron has only six vertices, and in an **octahedral molecule** we find an atom in the center of the octahedron bonded to six other atoms at the vertices.

All the bonds in an octahedral molecule are equivalent, with angles between adjacent bonds equal to 90°.

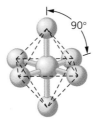

An octahedron

An octahedral molecule

A simplified representation of an octahedron is shown in Figure 9.3. The square plane in the center of the octahedron, when drawn in perspective and viewed from its edge, looks like a parallelogram. The bonds to the top and bottom of the octahedron are shown as vertical lines. Once again, the bond pointing down is drawn so it appears to be partially hidden by the square plane in the center.

 **A simplified way of drawing an octahedron.** To form an octahedral molecule, atoms would be attached at the corners of the square in the center and at the ends of the bonds that extend vertically up and down.

9.2 | MOLECULAR SHAPES ARE PREDICTED USING THE VSEPR MODEL

A useful theoretical model should explain known facts, and it should be capable of making accurate predictions. The **valence shell electron pair repulsion model** (called the **VSEPR model,** for short) is remarkably successful at both and is also conceptually simple. The model is based on the following idea:

> Groups of electrons in the valence shell of an atom repel each other and will position themselves in the valence shell so that they are as far apart as possible.

We will use the term **electron domain** to describe regions in space where groups of valence shell electrons can be found. We will consider two types of domains:

- **Bonding domains** contain electron pairs that are involved in bonds between pairs of atoms. *All of the electrons within a given single, double, or triple bond are considered to be in the same bonding domain.* A double bond (containing 4 electrons) will occupy more space than a single bond (with only 2 electrons) but all electrons in a bond occupy the same region in space, so they all belong to the same bonding domain.

- **Nonbonding domains** contain valence electrons that are associated with *a single atom.* A nonbonding domain is either an unshared pair of valence electrons (called a **lone pair)** or a single unpaired electron (found in molecules with an odd number of valence electrons).

Figure 9.4 shows the orientations assumed by different numbers of electron domains which permit them to minimize repulsions by remaining as far apart as possible. Notice that when atoms are attached to these electron domains, molecules are formed having the shapes described in the preceding section.

TOOLS

VSEPR model

☐ An *electron domain* can be a bond, a lone pair, or an unpaired electron. Some prefer to call the VSEPR model (or VSEPR theory) the *electron domain model.*

Lewis structures permit us to apply the VSEPR model

When we speak of the shape of a molecule, we are referring to the arrangement of some number of atoms around a central atom. To apply the VSEPR model in predicting shape, we have to know how many electron domains are in the valence shell of the central atom. This is where Lewis structures are helpful.

Consider the $BeCl_2$ molecule. On page 318 we gave its Lewis structure as

$$:\ddot{C}l - Be - \ddot{C}l:$$

Because there are three atoms, the molecule is either linear or nonlinear; that is, the atoms lie in a straight line, or they form some angle less than 180°.

$$Cl - Be - Cl \qquad or \qquad \underset{Cl}{\overset{Be}{\diagdown}} \, Cl$$
$$180° \qquad\qquad\qquad <180°$$

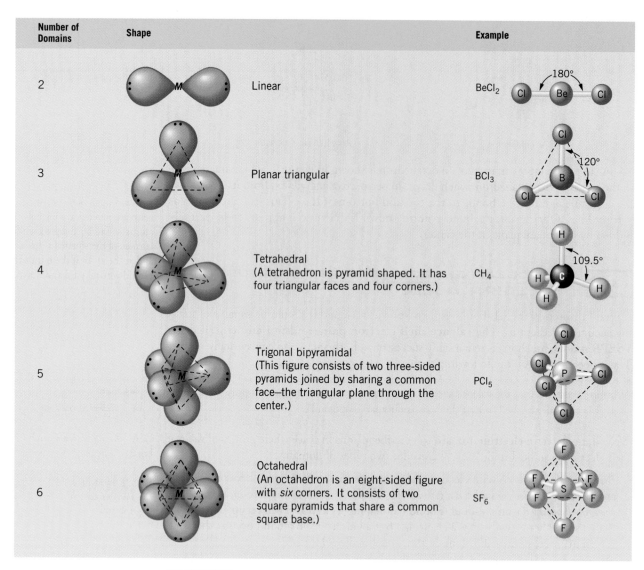

Number of Domains	Shape		Example
2		Linear	BeCl₂
3		Planar triangular	BCl₃
4		Tetrahedral (A tetrahedron is pyramid shaped. It has four triangular faces and four corners.)	CH₄
5		Trigonal bipyramidal (This figure consists of two three-sided pyramids joined by sharing a common face—the triangular plane through the center.)	PCl₅
6		Octahedral (An octahedron is an eight-sided figure with *six* corners. It consists of two square pyramids that share a common square base.)	SF₆

FIG. 9.4 Shapes expected for different numbers of electron domains around a central atom, **M**. Each lobe represents an electron domain.

☐ electron domains

To decide on the structure, we begin by counting the number of electron domains in the valence shell of the Be atom. In this molecule Be forms two single bonds to Cl atoms, each of which corresponds to a domain, so Be has two bonding domains in its valence shell. In Figure 9.4, we see that when there are two electron domains in the valence shell of an atom, minimum repulsion occurs if they are on opposite sides of the nucleus, pointing in opposite directions. We can represent this as

to suggest the approximate locations of the electron clouds of the valence shell electron pairs. In order for the electrons to be in the Be—Cl bonds, the Cl atoms must be placed where the electrons are; the result is that we predict that a BeCl₂ molecule should be linear.

$$Cl—Be—Cl$$

In fact, this is the shape of BeCl₂ molecules in the vapor state.

EXAMPLE 9.1
Predicting Molecular Shapes

Carbon tetrachloride was once used as a cleaning fluid until it was discovered that it causes liver damage if absorbed by the body. What is the shape of the molecule?

ANALYSIS: The primary tool for solving this kind of problem is the Lewis structure, which we will draw following the procedure in Chapter 8. First, however, we need the chemical formula. Applying the rules of nomenclature in Chapter 2 gives CCl_4. After we draw the Lewis structure, we can count the number of electron domains around the central atom. Finally, we'll use the VSEPR model as a tool to deduce the structure of the molecule.

SOLUTION: Following the procedure in Figure 8.9, the Lewis structure of CCl_4 is

$$:\overset{\cdot\cdot}{\underset{\cdot\cdot}{Cl}}:$$
$$:\overset{\cdot\cdot}{\underset{\cdot\cdot}{Cl}}-C-\overset{\cdot\cdot}{\underset{\cdot\cdot}{Cl}}:$$
$$:\overset{\cdot\cdot}{\underset{\cdot\cdot}{Cl}}:$$

There are four bonds, each corresponding to a bonding domain around the carbon. According to Figure 9.4, the domains can be farthest apart when arranged tetrahedrally, so the molecule is expected to be tetrahedral. (This is, in fact, its structure.)

IS THE ANSWER REASONABLE? The answer depends critically on the Lewis structure, so be sure to check that you've constructed it correctly. Once we're confident in the Lewis structure the rest is straightforward. The arrangement of domains gives us the arrangement of Cl atoms around the C atom.

Practice Exercise 1: What is the shape of the SeF_6 molecule? (Hint: If necessary, refer to Figure 8.9 on page 318.)

Practice Exercise 2: What shape is expected for the $SbCl_5$ molecule?

Nonbonding domains affect the shape of a molecule

Some molecules have a central atom with one or more nonbonding domains, consisting of unshared electron pairs (lone pairs) or unpaired valence electrons. These nonbonding domains affect the geometry of the molecule. An example is $SnCl_2$.

$$:\overset{\cdot\cdot}{Cl}-\overset{\cdot\cdot}{Sn}-\overset{\cdot\cdot}{Cl}:$$

There are *three* domains around the tin atom, two bonding domains plus a nonbonding domain (the lone pair). According to Figure 9.4, the domains are farthest apart when at the corners of a triangle. For the moment, let's ignore the chlorine atoms and concentrate on how the electron domains are arranged.

☐ The electronegativity difference between tin and chlorine is only 1.1, which means tin–chlorine bonds have a significant degree of covalent character. Many compounds of tin are molecular, especially those of Sn^{IV}. $SnCl_2$ is another example of a molecule that behaves as though it has less than an octet around the central atom.

We can see the shape of the molecule, now, by placing the two Cl atoms where two of the domains are.

We can't describe this molecule as triangular, even though that is how the domains are arranged. *Molecular shape describes the arrangement of atoms, not the arrangement of domains.* Therefore, we describe the shape of the $SnCl_2$ molecule as being **nonlinear** or **bent** or **V-shaped.**

Notice that when there are three domains around the central atom, *two* different molecular shapes are possible. If all three are bonding domains, a molecule with a planar triangular shape is formed, as shown for BCl_3 in Figure 9.4. If one of the domains is nonbonding, as in $SnCl_2$, the arrangement of the atoms in the molecule is said to be nonlinear. The predicted shapes of both, however, are *derived* by first noting the triangular arrangement of domains around the central atom and *then* adding the necessary number of atoms.

Molecules with four domains have shapes derived from a tetrahedron

There are many molecules with four electron pairs (an octet) in the valence shell of the central atom. When these electron pairs are used to form four bonds, as in methane (CH_4), the resulting molecule is tetrahedral (Figure 9.4). There are many examples, however, where nonbonding domains are also present. For example,

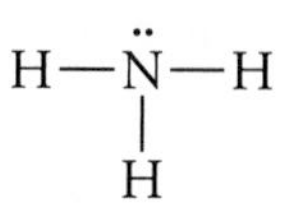

$$H - \overset{\cdot\cdot}{N} - H \qquad H - \overset{\cdot\cdot}{\underset{\cdot\cdot}{O}} - H$$
$$\underset{\text{one lone pair}}{\overset{|}{H}} \qquad \underset{\text{two lone pairs}}{}$$

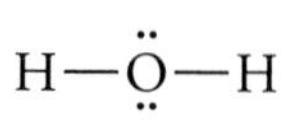

Figure 9.5 shows how the nonbonding domains affect the shapes of molecules of this type.

With one nonbonding domain, the central atom is at the top of a pyramid with three atoms at the corners of the triangular base. The resulting structure is said to be **trigonal pyramidal.** When there are two nonbonding domains in the tetrahedron, the three atoms of the molecule (the central atom plus the two atoms bonded to it) do not lie in a straight line, so the structure is described as nonlinear or bent.

☐ Note once again that in describing the shape of the molecule, we look at how the atoms are arranged and ignore the nonbonding domains.

Number of Bonding Domains	Number of Nonbonding Domains	Structure	
4	0	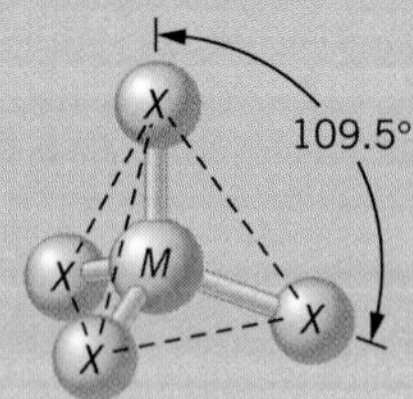 109.5°	**Tetrahedral** (example, CH_4) All bond angles are 109.5°.
3	1	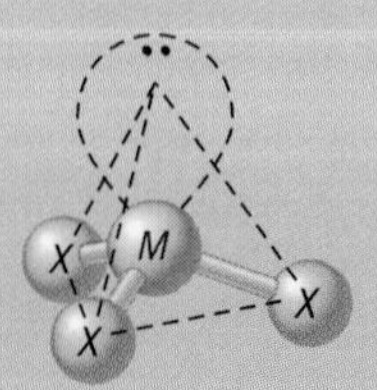	**Trigonal pyramidal** (pyramid shaped) (example, NH_3)
2	2	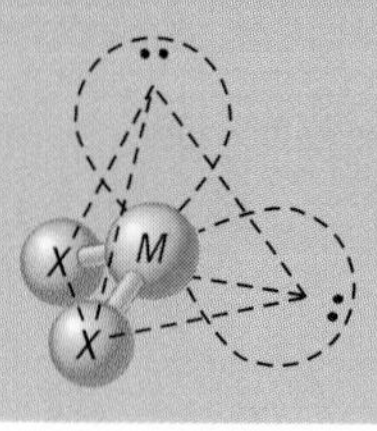	**Nonlinear, bent** (example, H_2O)

FIG. 9.5 Molecular shapes with four domains around the central atom. The molecules MX_4, MX_3, and MX_2 shown here all have four domains arranged tetrahedrally around the central atom. The shapes of the molecules and their descriptions are derived from the way the X atoms are arranged around M, ignoring the nonbonding domains.

Number of Bonding Domains	Number of Nonbonding Domains	Structure	
5	0	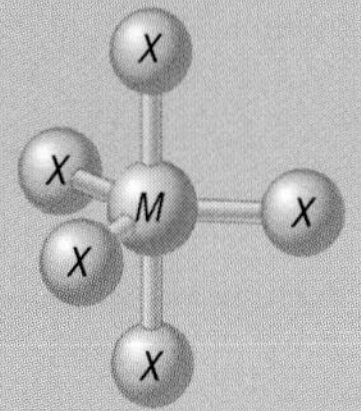	**Trigonal bipyramidal** (example, PCl_5)
4	1	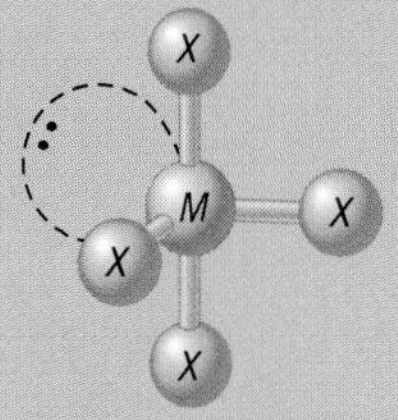	**Distorted tetrahedral** 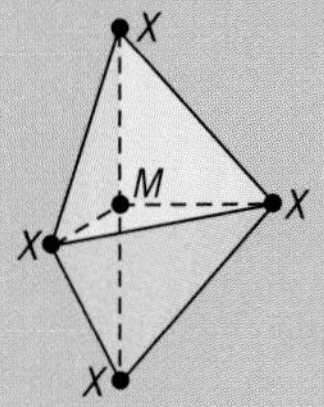 (example, SF_4)
3	2	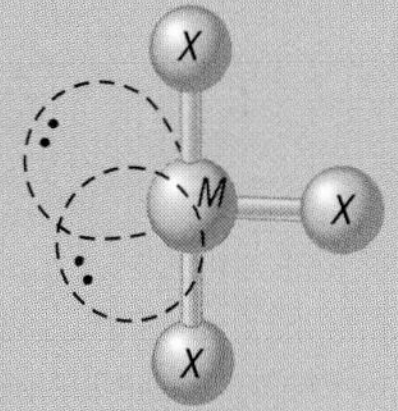	**T-shaped** 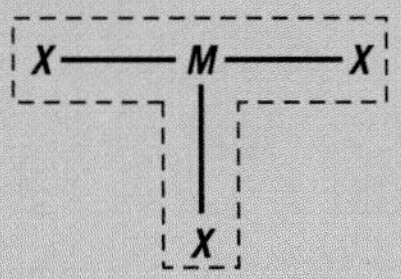 (example, ClF_3)
2	3	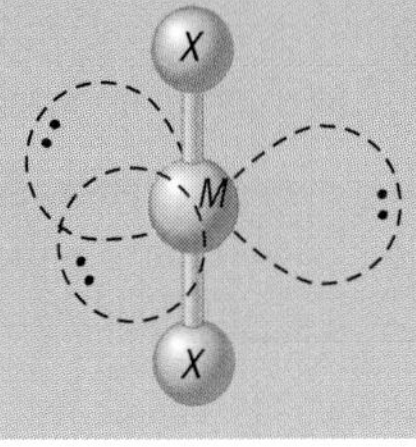	**Linear** (example, I_3^-)

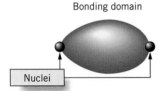

FIG. 9.6 Relative sizes of bonding and nonbonding domains.

FIG. 9.7 Molecular shapes with five domains around the central atom. Four different molecular structures are possible, depending on the number of nonbonding domains around the central atom *M*.

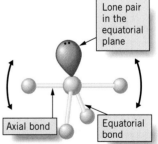

FIG. 9.8 This distorted tetrahedron is sometimes described as a *seesaw structure*. The origin of this description can be seen if we tip the structure over so it stands on the two atoms in the equatorial plane, with the nonbonding domain pointing up.

Molecules with five domains have shapes derived from a trigonal bipyramid

When five domains are present around the central atom, they are directed toward the vertices of a trigonal bipyramid. Molecules such as PCl_5 have this geometry, as shown in Figure 9.4, and are said to have a **trigonal bipyramidal** shape.

In the trigonal bipyramid, nonbonding domains always occupy positions in the *equatorial plane* (the triangular plane through the center of the molecule). This is because nonbonding domains, which have a positive nucleus only at one end, are larger than bonding domains, as illustrated in Figure 9.6. The larger nonbonding domains are less crowded in the equatorial plane, where they have just two closest neighbors at 90°, than they would be in an axial position, where they would have three closest neighbors at 90°.

Figure 9.7 shows the kinds of geometries that we find for different numbers of nonbonding domains in the trigonal bipyramid. When there is only one nonbonding domain, as in SF_4, the structure is described as a **distorted tetrahedron** or **seesaw** in which the central atom lies along one edge of a four-sided figure (Figure 9.8).

Number of Bonding Domains	Number of Nonbonding Domains	Structure	
6	0	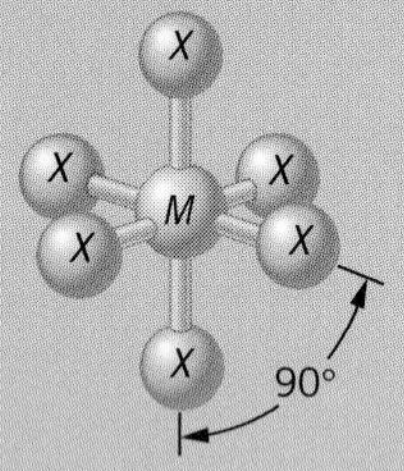	**Octahedral** (example, SF_6) All bond angles are 90°.
5	1	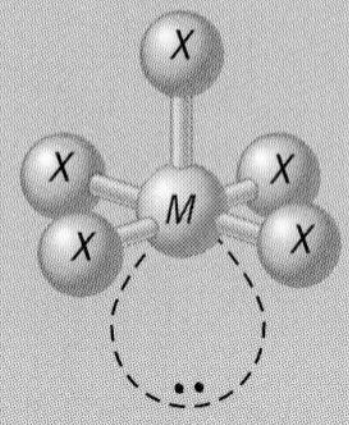	**Square pyramidal** 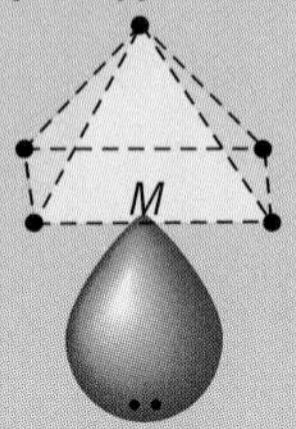 (example, BrF_5)
4	2	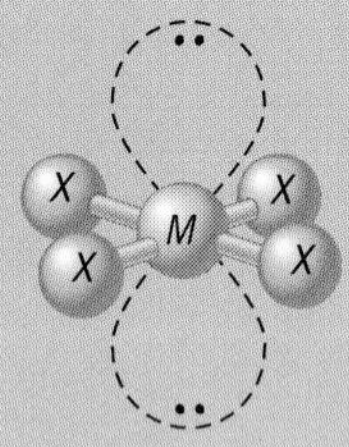	**Square planar** (example, XeF_4)

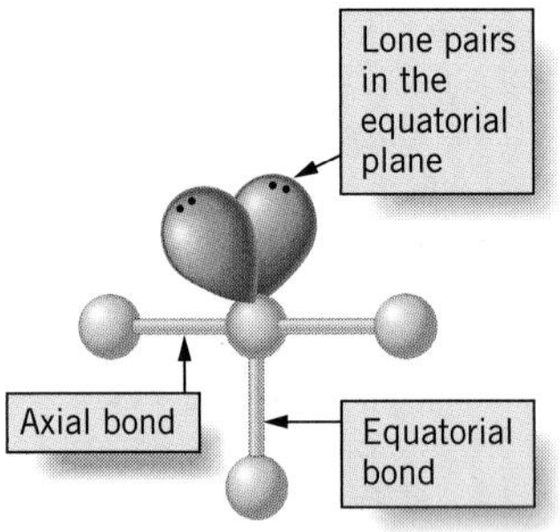

FIG. 9.9 A molecule with two nonbonding domains in the equatorial plane of the trigonal bipyramid. When tipped over, the molecule looks like a T, so it is called *T-shaped.*

FIG. 9.10 Molecular shapes with six domains around the central atom. Although more are theoretically possible, only three different molecular shapes are observed, depending on the number of nonbonding domains around the central atom.

With two nonbonding domains in the equatorial plane, the molecule is **T-shaped** (shaped like the letter T, Figure 9.9), and when there are three nonbonding domains in the equatorial plane, the molecule is **linear.**

Molecules with six domains have shapes derived from an octahedron
Finally, we come to molecules or ions that have six domains around the central atom. When all are in bonds, as in SF_6, the molecule is octahedral (Figure 9.4). When one nonbonding domain is present the molecule or ion has the shape of a **square pyramid,** and when two nonbonding domains are present they take positions on opposite sides of the nucleus and the molecule or ion has a **square planar** structure. These shapes are shown in Figure 9.10.

◻ No common molecule or ion with six domains around the central atom has more than two nonbonding domains.

EXAMPLE 9.2
Predicting the Shapes of Molecules and Ions

Do we expect the ClO_2^- ion to be linear?

ANALYSIS: To predict the shape, the first step is to draw the Lewis structure for the ClO_2^- ion. Then we can count the number of domains around the central atom. This will determine which of the basic geometries describes the orientations of the domains. We sketch this shape and then attach the two oxygens. Finally, we ignore any nonbonding domains to arrive at the description of the shape of the ion. In other words, in this last step we note how the *atoms* are arranged, not how the domains are arranged.

SOLUTION: Following the usual procedure, we obtain

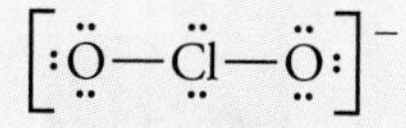

$$\left[:\overset{..}{\underset{..}{O}} - \overset{..}{\underset{..}{Cl}} - \overset{..}{\underset{..}{O}}: \right]^{-}$$

There are four domains around the chlorine: two bonding and two nonbonding. Four domains (according to the theory) are always arranged tetrahedrally. This gives

Now we add the two oxygens. It doesn't matter which locations in the tetrahedron we choose because all the bond angles are equal.

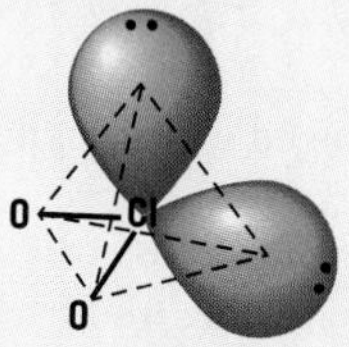

We see that the O—Cl—O angle is less than 180°, so the ion is expected to be nonlinear.

□ For a molecule with three atoms, there are only two ways they can be arranged, either in a straight line (linear) or in a nonlinear arrangement.

IS THE ANSWER REASONABLE? Here are questions we have to answer to check our work. First, has the Lewis structure been drawn correctly? Have we counted the domains correctly? Have we selected the correct orientation of the domains? And finally, have we correctly described the structure obtained by adding the two oxygen atoms? Our answer to each of these questions is "Yes," so we can be confident our answer is right.

EXAMPLE 9.3
Predicting the Shapes of
Molecules and Ions

Xenon is one of the noble gases, and is generally quite unreactive. In fact, it was long believed that all the noble gases were totally unable to form compounds. It came as quite a surprise, therefore, when it was discovered that some compounds could be made. One of these is xenon difluoride. What would you expect the geometry of xenon difluoride to be, linear or nonlinear?

ANALYSIS: First, we use the rules of nomenclature from Chapter 2 to obtain the formula, which is XeF_2. From here, the procedure is the same as before. First we write the compound's Lewis structure. Then we count domains around the central atom to determine which of the basic geometries forms the basis for the structure. Next, we sketch the structure and attach the fluorine atoms to two of the domains. Finally, we ignore any nonbonding domains and observe how the atoms are arranged to describe the shape of the molecule.

SOLUTION: The outer shell of xenon, of course, has a noble gas configuration, which contains 8 electrons. Each fluorine has 7 valence electrons. Using this information we obtain the following Lewis structure for XeF_2.

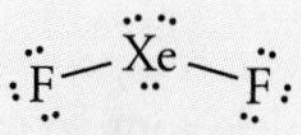

$$:\overset{..}{\underset{..}{F}} - \overset{..}{\underset{..}{Xe}} - \overset{..}{\underset{..}{F}}:$$

Next we count domains around xenon; there are five of them, three nonbonding and two bonding domains. When there are five domains, they are arranged in a trigonal bipyramid.

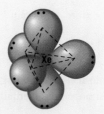

Now we must add the fluorine atoms. In a trigonal bipyramid, the nonbonding domains always occur in the equatorial plane through the center, so the fluorines go on the top and bottom. This gives

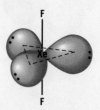

The three atoms, F—Xe—F, are arranged in a straight line, so the molecule is linear.

IS THE ANSWER REASONABLE? Is the Lewis structure correct? Yes. Have we selected the correct basic geometry? Yes. Have we attached the F atoms to the Xe correctly? Yes. All is in order, so the answer is correct.

EXAMPLE 9.4
Predicting the Shapes of Molecules and Ions

The Lewis structure for the very poisonous gas hydrogen cyanide, HCN, is

$$H—C≡N:$$

Is the HCN molecule linear or nonlinear?

ANALYSIS: We already have the Lewis structure, so we count electron domains and proceed as before. The critical link in this problem is remembering that *all the electron pairs in a given bond belong to the same bonding domain.*

SOLUTION: There are two bonding domains around the carbon, one for the triple bond with nitrogen, and one for the single bond with hydrogen.

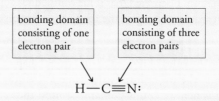

Therefore, we expect the two bonds to locate themselves 180° apart, yielding a linear HCN molecule.

IS THE ANSWER REASONABLE? Have we correctly counted bonding domains? Yes. We can expect our answer to be correct.

Practice Exercise 3: The first known compound of the noble gas argon is HArF. What shape is expected for the HArF molecule? (Hint: Remember, argon is a noble gas with eight electrons in its valence shell.)

Practice Exercise 4: What shape is expected for the I_3^- ion?

Practice Exercise 5: What shape is expected for the XeF_4 molecule?

Practice Exercise 6: Predict the shapes of SO_3^{2-}, CO_3^{2-}, XeO_4, and OF_2.

9.3 | MOLECULAR SYMMETRY AFFECTS THE POLARITY OF MOLECULES

The dipole moment of a molecule is a property that can be determined experimentally, and when this is done, an interesting observation is made. There are many molecules that have no dipole moment even though they contain bonds that are polar. Stated differently, they are nonpolar molecules, even though they have polar bonds. The reason for this can be seen if we examine the key role that molecular structure plays in determining molecular polarity.

For a diatomic molecule such as HCl, the polar bond causes the molecule as a whole to be polar. Similarly, H_2 is nonpolar because the H—H bond is nonpolar. For molecules that contain more than two atoms, however, we have to consider the combined effects of all the bonds. Sometimes, when all the atoms attached to the central atom are the same, the effects of the individual polar bonds cancel and the molecule as a whole is nonpolar. Some examples are shown in Figure 9.11. In this figure the dipoles associated with the bonds themselves—the **bond dipoles**—are shown as arrows crossed at one end, ⟶. The arrowhead indicates the negative end of the bond dipole and the crossed end corresponds to the positive end.

☐ Any molecule composed of just two atoms that differ in electronegativity must be polar because the bond is polar.

The CO_2 molecule is symmetric. Both bonds are identical, so each bond dipole is of the same magnitude. Because CO_2 is a linear molecule, these bond dipoles point in opposite directions and work against each other. The net result is that their effects cancel, and CO_2 is nonpolar. Although it isn't so easy to visualize, the same thing also happens in BCl_3 and CCl_4. In each of these molecules, the influence of one bond dipole is canceled by the effects of the others.

☐ Bond dipoles can be treated as vectors, and the polarity of a molecule is predicted by taking the vector sum of the bond dipoles. If you've studied vectors before, this may help your understanding.

Perhaps you've noticed that the structures of the molecules in Figure 9.11 correspond to three of the basic shapes that we used to derive the shapes of molecules. Molecules with the remaining two structures, trigonal bipyramidal and octahedral, also are nonpolar if all the atoms attached to the central atom are the same. All of the basic shapes are "balanced," or **symmetric**,[1] if all of the domains and groups attached to them are identical. Examples

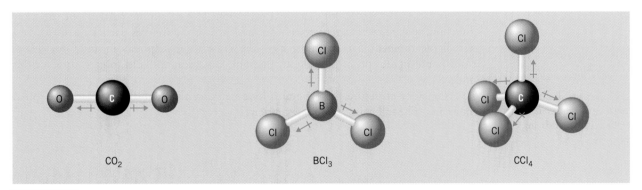

CO_2 BCl_3 CCl_4

FIG. 9.11 In symmetric molecules such as these, the bond dipoles cancel to give nonpolar molecules.

[1] Symmetry is a more complex subject than we present it here. When we describe the symmetry properties of a molecule, we are specifying the various ways the molecule can be turned and otherwise manipulated while leaving the molecule looking exactly as it appeared before the manipulation. For example, imagine the BCl_3 molecule in Figure 9.11 being rotated 120° around an axis, perpendicular to the page, that passes through the B atom. Performing this rotation leaves the molecule looking just as it did before the rotation. This rotation axis is a symmetry property of BCl_3.

Intuitively, we can recognize when an object possesses symmetry elements such as rotation axes (as well as other symmetry properties we haven't mentioned). Comparing objects, we can usually tell when one is more symmetric than another, and in our discussions in this chapter we rely on this qualitative sense of symmetry.

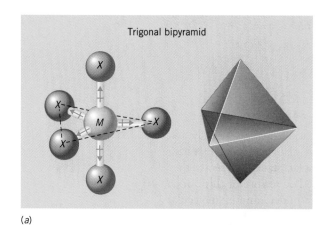

Trigonal bipyramid

(a)

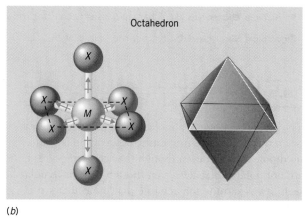

Octahedron

(b)

FIG. 9.12 **Cancellation of bond dipoles in trigonal bipyramidal and octahedral molecules.** (a) A trigonal bipyramidal molecule, MX_5, in which the central atom M is bonded to five identical atoms X. The set of three bond dipoles in the triangular plane in the center (in blue) cancel, as do the linear set of dipoles (red). Overall, the molecule is nonpolar. (b) An octahedral molecule MX_6 in which the central atom is bonded to six identical atoms. This molecule contains three linear sets of bond dipoles. Cancellation occurs for each set, so the molecule is nonpolar overall.

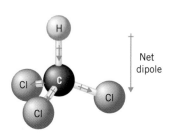

Net dipole

FIG. 9.13 **Bond dipoles in the chloroform molecule, $CHCl_3$.** Because C is slightly more electronegative than H, the C—H bond dipole points toward the carbon. The small C—H bond dipole actually adds to the effects of the C—Cl bond dipoles. All the bond dipoles are additive, and this causes $CHCl_3$ to be a polar molecule.

☐ The lone pairs also influence the polarity of a molecule, but we will not explore this any further here.

are shown in Figure 9.12. The trigonal bipyramidal structure can be viewed as a planar triangular set of atoms (shown in blue) plus a pair of atoms arranged linearly (shown in red). All the bond dipoles in the planar triangle cancel, as do the two dipoles of the bonds arranged linearly, so the molecule is nonpolar overall. Similarly, we can look at the octahedral molecule as consisting of three linear sets of bond dipoles. Cancellation of bond dipoles occurs in each set, so overall the octahedral molecule is also nonpolar.

*If all the atoms attached to the central atom are not the same, or if there are lone pairs in the valence shell of the central atom, the molecule is **usually** polar.* For example, in $CHCl_3$, one of the atoms in the tetrahedral structure is different from the others. The C—H bond is less polar than the C—Cl bonds, and the bond dipoles do not cancel (Figure 9.13). An "unbalanced" structure such as this is said to be **dissymmetric.**

Two familiar molecules that have lone pairs in the valence shells of their central atoms are shown in Figure 9.14. Here the bond dipoles are oriented in such a way that their effects do not cancel. In water, for example, each bond dipole points partially in the same direction, toward the oxygen atom. As a result, the bond dipoles partially add to give a net dipole moment for the molecule. The same thing happens in ammonia where three bond dipoles point partially in the same direction and add to give a polar NH_3 molecule.

Not every structure that contains lone pairs on the central atom produces polar molecules. The following are two exceptions.

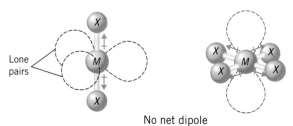

Lone pairs

No net dipole

In the first case, we have a pair of bond dipoles arranged linearly, just as they are in CO_2. In the second, the bonded atoms lie at the corners of a square, which can be viewed as two linear sets of bond dipoles. *If the atoms attached to the central atom are the same,* cancellation of bond dipoles is bound to occur and produce nonpolar molecules. This means that molecules such as linear XeF_2 and square planar XeF_4 are nonpolar.

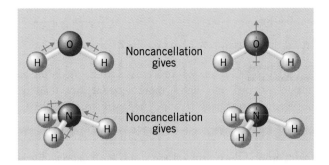

FIG. 9.14 When nonbonding domains occur on the central atom, the bond dipoles usually do not cancel, and polar molecules result.

In Summary
- A molecule will be nonpolar if (a) the bonds are nonpolar or (b) there are no lone pairs in the valence shell of the central atom and all the atoms attached to the central atom are the same.
- A molecule in which the central atom has lone pairs of electrons will usually be polar, with the two exceptions described above.

TOOLS
Molecular shape and molecular polarity

On the basis of the preceding discussions, let's see how we can predict whether molecules are expected to be polar or nonpolar.

EXAMPLE 9.5
Predicting Molecular Polarity

Do we expect the phosphorus trichloride molecule to be polar or nonpolar?

ANALYSIS: As before, the first step is to convert the name of the compound into a chemical formula. Our tool is the set of rules given in Chapter 2, which gives the formula PCl_3. Next, we'll use electronegativities as a tool to determine whether the bonds in the molecule are polar. If they're not, the molecule will be nonpolar regardless of its structure. If the bonds are polar, we then need to determine the molecular structure. Our tools will be the procedure for drawing the Lewis structure and the VSEPR model. On the basis of the molecular structure, we can then decide whether the bond dipoles cancel.

SOLUTION: The electronegativities of the atoms (P = 2.1, Cl = 2.9) tell us that the individual P—Cl bonds will be polar. Therefore, to predict whether or not the molecule is polar, we need to know its shape. First we draw the Lewis structure following our usual procedure.

$$:\ddot{Cl}:$$
$$|$$
$$:\ddot{Cl}—\underset{..}{P}—\ddot{Cl}:$$

There are four domains around the phosphorus, so they should be arranged tetrahedrally. This means that the PCl_3 molecule should have a trigonal pyramidal shape, as shown in the margin. Because of the structure, the bond dipoles do not cancel, and we expect the molecule to be polar.

Net dipole

IS THE ANSWER REASONABLE? There's not much to do here except to carefully check the Lewis structure to be sure it's correct and to check that we've applied the VSEPR theory correctly.

EXAMPLE 9.6
Predicting Molecular Polarity

Would you expect the molecule HCN to be polar or nonpolar?

ANALYSIS AND SOLUTION: Our analysis proceeds as in the preceding example. To begin, we have polar bonds because carbon is slightly more electronegative than hydrogen and nitrogen is slightly more electronegative than carbon. The Lewis structure of HCN is

$$H—C≡N:$$

There are two domains around the central carbon atom, so we expect a linear shape. However, the two bond dipoles do not cancel. One reason is that they are not of equal magnitude, which we know because the difference in electronegativity between C and H is 0.4, whereas the difference in electronegativity between C and N is 0.6. The other reason is because both bond dipoles point in the same direction, from the atom of low electronegativity to the one of high electronegativity. This is illustrated in the margin. Notice that the bond dipoles add to give a net dipole moment for the molecule.

Bond dipoles

Net dipole

IS THE ANSWER REASONABLE? As in the preceding example, we can check that we've obtained the correct Lewis structure and applied the VSEPR theory correctly, which we have. We can also check to see whether we've used the electronegativities to reach the right conclusions, which we have. We can be confident in our conclusions.

Practice Exercise 7: Is the sulfur tetrafluoride molecule polar or nonpolar? (Hint: Use the VSEPR model to sketch the shape of the molecule.)

Practice Exercise 8: Which of the following molecules would you expect to be polar? (a) SF_6, (b) SO_2, (c) BrCl, (d) AsH_3, (e) CF_2Cl_2

9.4 | VALENCE BOND THEORY EXPLAINS BONDING AS AN OVERLAP OF ATOMIC ORBITALS

So far we have described the bonding in molecules using Lewis structures. Lewis structures, however, tell us nothing about *why* covalent bonds are formed or *how* electrons manage to be shared between atoms. Nor does the VSEPR model explain *why* electrons group themselves into domains as they do. Thus, we must look beyond these simple models to understand more fully the covalent bond and the factors that determine molecular geometry.

There are fundamentally two theories of covalent bonding that have evolved based on quantum theory, the **valence bond theory** (or **VB theory,** for short) and the **molecular orbital theory (MO theory).** They differ principally in the way they construct a theoretical model of the bonding in a molecule. The valence bond theory imagines individual atoms, each with its own orbitals and electrons, coming together to form the covalent bonds of the molecule. The molecular orbital theory doesn't concern itself with *how* the molecule is formed. It just views a molecule as a collection of positively charged nuclei surrounded in some way by electrons that occupy a set of *molecular orbitals*, in much the same way that the electrons in an atom occupy *atomic orbitals*. (In a sense, MO theory would look at an atom as if it were a special case—a molecule having only one positive center, instead of many.)

TOOLS
VB criteria for bond formation

According to VB theory, *a bond between two atoms is formed when **two electrons** with their **spins paired** are shared by two **overlapping** atomic orbitals, one orbital from each of the atoms joined by the bond.* By **overlap of orbitals** we mean that portions of two atomic orbitals from different atoms share the same space.

An important part of the theory, as suggested by the bold italic type above, is that only *one* pair of electrons, with paired spins, can be shared by two overlapping orbitals. This

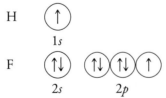

FIG. 9.15 The formation of the hydrogen molecule according to valence bond theory.

electron pair becomes concentrated in the region of overlap and helps "cement" the nuclei together, so the amount that the potential energy is lowered when the bond is formed is determined in part by the extent to which the orbitals overlap. Therefore, *atoms tend to position themselves so that the maximum amount of orbital overlap occurs because this yields the minimum potential energy and therefore the strongest bonds.*

The way VB theory views the formation of a hydrogen molecule is shown in Figure 9.15. As the two atoms approach each other, their $1s$ orbitals begin to overlap and merge as the electron pair spreads out over both orbitals, thereby giving the H—H bond. The description of the bond in H_2 provided by VB theory is essentially the same as that discussed in Chapter 8.

Now let's look at the HF molecule, which is a bit more complex than H_2. Following the usual rules we can write its Lewis structure as

$$H-\ddot{\underset{..}{F}}:$$

and we can diagram the formation of the bond as

$$H\cdot + \cdot\ddot{\underset{..}{F}}: \longrightarrow H-\ddot{\underset{..}{F}}:$$

Our Lewis symbols suggest that the H—F bond is formed by the pairing of electrons, one from hydrogen and one from fluorine. To explain this according to VB theory, we must have two half-filled orbitals, one from each atom, that can be joined by overlap. (They must be half-filled, because we can't place more than two electrons into the bond.) To see clearly what must happen, it is best to look at the orbital diagrams of the valence shells of hydrogen and fluorine.

The requirements for bond formation are met by overlapping the half-filled $1s$ orbital of hydrogen with the half-filled $2p$ orbital of fluorine; there are then two orbitals plus two electrons whose spins can adjust so they are paired. The formation of the bond is illustrated in Figure 9.16.

The overlap of orbitals provides a means for sharing electrons, thereby allowing each atom to complete its valence shell. It is sometimes convenient to indicate this using orbital diagrams. For example, the diagram below shows how the fluorine atom completes its $2p$ subshell by acquiring a share of an electron from hydrogen.

Notice that in both the Lewis and VB descriptions of the formation of the H—F bond, the atoms' valence shells are completed.

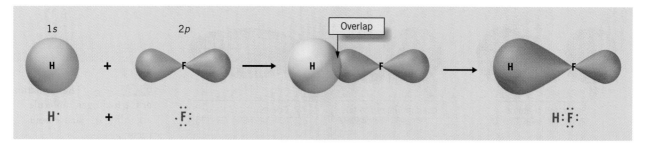

FIG. 9.16 **The formation of the hydrogen fluoride molecule according to valence bond theory.** For clarity, only the half-filled $2p$ orbital of fluorine is shown. The other $2p$ orbitals of fluorine are filled and cannot participate in bonding.

Valence bond theory can explain bond angles

☐ H₂S is the compound that gives rotten eggs their foul odor.

Let's look now at a more complex molecule, hydrogen sulfide, H₂S. Experiments have shown that it is a nonlinear molecule in which the H—S—H bond angle is about 92°.

$$
\begin{array}{c}
\text{S} \\
\text{H} \diagup \diagdown \text{H} \\
92°
\end{array}
$$

Using Lewis symbols, we would diagram the formation of H₂S as

$$2\,\text{H}\cdot \; + \; \cdot \ddot{\text{S}}\cdot \; \longrightarrow \; \text{H}-\ddot{\text{S}}-\text{H}$$

☐ If necessary, review the procedure for drawing orbital diagrams on page 273–275 in Chapter 7.

Our Lewis symbols suggest that each H—S bond is formed by the pairing of two electrons, one from H and one from S. Applying this to VB theory, each bond requires the overlap of two half-filled orbitals, one on H and one on S. Therefore, forming *two* H—S bonds in H₂S will require *two* half-filled orbitals on sulfur to form bonds to two separate H atoms. To clearly see what happens, let's look at the orbital diagrams of the valence shells of hydrogen and sulfur.

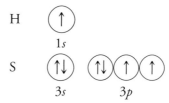

Sulfur has two $3p$ orbitals that each contain only one electron. Each of these can overlap with the $1s$ orbital of a hydrogen atom, as shown in Figure 9.17. This overlap completes the $3p$ subshell of sulfur because each hydrogen provides one electron.

S (in H₂S) (↑↓) (↑↓)(↑↓)(↑↓)   (Colored arrows are H electrons.)
　　　　　　　3s　　3p

☐ In VB theory, two orbitals from different atoms never overlap simultaneously with opposite ends of the same p orbital.

In Figure 9.17, notice that when the $1s$ orbital of a hydrogen atom overlaps with a p orbital of sulfur, the best overlap occurs when the hydrogen atom lies along the axis of the p orbital. Because p orbitals are oriented at 90° to each other, the H—S bonds are expected to be at this angle, too. Therefore, the predicted bond angle is 90°. This is very close to the actual bond angle of 92° found by experiment. Thus, the VB theory requirement for maximum overlap quite nicely explains the geometry of the hydrogen sulfide molecule. Also, notice that both the Lewis and VB descriptions of the formation of the H—S bonds account for the completion of the atoms' valence shells. Therefore, *a Lewis structure can be viewed, in a very qualitative sense, as a shorthand notation for the valence bond description of a molecule.*

Other kinds of orbital overlaps are also possible. For example, according to VB theory the bonding in the fluorine molecule, F₂, occurs by the overlap of two $2p$ orbitals, as shown

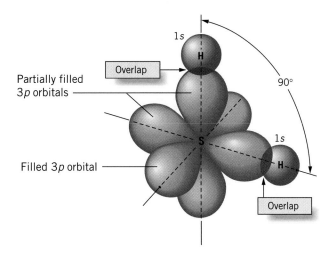

FIG. 9.17 Bonding in H$_2$S. We expect the hydrogen 1s orbitals to position themselves so that they can best overlap with the two partially filled 3p orbitals of sulfur, which gives a predicted bond angle of 90°. The experimentally measured bond angle of 92° is very close to the predicted angle.

in Figure 9.18. The formation of the other diatomic molecules of the halogens, all of which are held together by single bonds, could be similarly described.

Practice Exercise 9: Use the principles of VB theory to explain the bonding in HCl. Give the orbital diagram for chlorine in the HCl molecule and indicate the orbital that shares the electron with one from hydrogen. Sketch the orbital overlap that gives rise to the H—Cl bond. (Hint: Remember that a half-filled orbital on each atom is required to form the covalent bond.)

Practice Exercise 10: The phosphine molecule, PH$_3$, has a trigonal pyramidal shape with H—P—H bond angles equal to 93.7°. Give the orbital diagram for phosphorus in the PH$_3$ molecule and indicate the orbitals that share electrons with those from hydrogen. On a set of *xyz* coordinate axes, sketch the orbital overlaps that give rise to the P—H bonds.

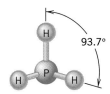

9.5 HYBRID ORBITALS ARE USED TO EXPLAIN EXPERIMENTAL MOLECULAR GEOMETRIES

There are many molecules for which the simple VB theory described above fails to account for the correct shape. For example, there are no simple atomic orbitals that are oriented so they point toward the corners of a tetrahedron, yet there are many tetrahedral molecules. Therefore, to explain the bonds in molecules such as CH$_4$ we must study the way atomic

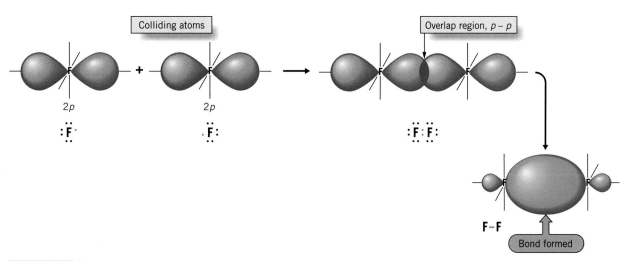

FIG. 9.18 Bonding in the fluorine molecule according to valence bond theory. The two completely filled p orbitals on each fluorine atom are omitted, for clarity.

TOOLS

Orientations of hybrid orbitals

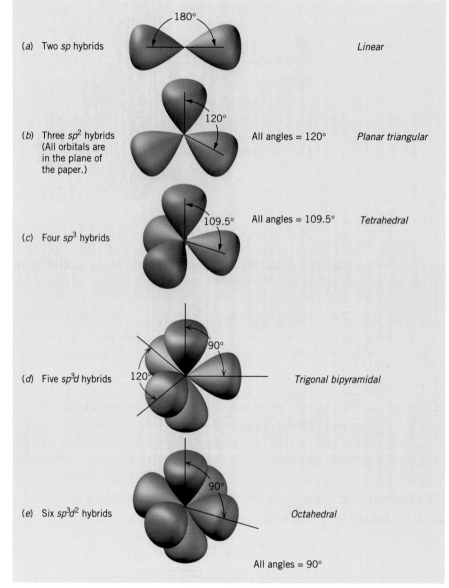

(a) Two *sp* hybrids — 180° — Linear

(b) Three *sp²* hybrids (All orbitals are in the plane of the paper.) — 120° — All angles = 120° — Planar triangular

(c) Four *sp³* hybrids — 109.5° — All angles = 109.5° — Tetrahedral

(d) Five *sp³d* hybrids — 90° — 120° — Trigonal bipyramidal

(e) Six *sp³d²* hybrids — 90° — Octahedral

All angles = 90°

FIG. 9.19 Directional properties of hybrid orbitals formed from *s*, *p*, and *d* atomic orbitals. (*a*) *sp* hybrid orbitals oriented at 180° to each other. (*b*) *sp²* hybrid orbitals formed from an *s* orbital and two *p* orbitals. The angle between them is 120°. (*c*) *sp³* hybrid orbitals formed from an *s* orbital and three *p* orbitals. The angle between them is 109.5°. (*d*) *sp³d* hybrid orbitals formed from an *s* orbital, three *p* orbitals, and a *d* orbital. The orbitals point toward the vertices of a trigonal bipyramid. (*e*) *sp³d²* hybrid orbitals formed from an *s* orbital, three *p* orbitals, and two *d* orbitals. The orbitals point toward the vertices of an octahedron.

orbitals *of the same atom* combine with each other to produce new orbitals with the correct orientations when bonds are formed.

Atomic orbitals (*s*, *p*, and *d*) are the basic building blocks of chemical bonds. To account for the variety of molecular shapes, we often must blend two or more of these basic building blocks to form **hybrid atomic orbitals.**[2] The new orbitals have new shapes and new directional properties, and they can be overlapped to give structures that have bond angles that match those found by experiment. It's important to realize that hybrid orbitals are part of the valence bond *theory.* They can't be directly observed in an experiment. We use them to describe molecular structures that have been determined experimentally.

Figure 9.19 shows the approximate shapes and orientations of five important kinds of hybrid orbitals. You may recognize them as being the same as the orientations of electron domains predicted by the VSEPR model. This is as it should be, of course, because both theories are used to describe the same molecular structures; if they didn't agree with each other, we would have to discard the one that gave incorrect results.

---

[2] Mathematically, hybrid orbitals are formed by the addition and subtraction of the wave functions for the basic atomic orbitals. This process produces a new set of wave functions corresponding to the hybrid orbitals. The hybrid orbital wave functions describe the shape and directional properties of the orbitals.

In identifying hybrid orbitals, we specify which kinds of pure atomic orbitals, as well as the number of each, that are mixed to form the hybrids. Thus, hybrid orbitals labeled sp^3d^2 are formed by blending one s orbital, three p orbitals, and two d orbitals. *The total number of hybrid orbitals in a set is equal to the number of basic atomic orbitals used to form them.* Therefore, a set of sp^3d^2 hybrids consists of six orbitals, whereas a set of sp^3 orbitals consists of four orbitals.

Figure 9.20 illustrates how an s and p orbital mix to form a set of two sp hybrid orbitals. Notice that each of the hybrid orbitals has the same shape; each has one large lobe and another much smaller one. The large lobe extends farther from the nucleus than either the s or p orbital from which the hybrid was formed. This allows the hybrid orbital to overlap more effectively with an orbital on another atom when a bond is formed. Therefore, hybrid orbitals form stronger, more stable bonds than would be possible if just simple atomic orbitals were used. In fact, the strength of these bonds is in good agreement with bond strengths that are determined experimentally.

Another point to notice in Figure 9.20 is that the large lobes of the two sp hybrid orbitals point in opposite directions; that is, they are 180° apart. If bonds are formed by the overlap of these hybrids with orbitals of other atoms, the other atoms will occupy positions on opposite sides of this central atom. Let's look at a specific example, the linear beryllium hydride molecule, BeH_2, as it would be formed in the gas phase.[3]

The orbital diagram for the valence shell of beryllium is

> ☐ In general, the greater the overlap of two orbitals, the stronger is the bond. At a given distance between nuclei, the greater "reach" of a hybrid orbital gives better overlap than either an s or p orbital.

Be   (↑↓) ◯◯◯

        2s   2p

Notice that the 2s orbital is filled and the three 2p orbitals are empty. For bonds to form at a 180° angle between beryllium and the two hydrogen atoms, two conditions must be met: (1) the two orbitals that beryllium uses to form the Be—H bonds must point in opposite directions, and (2) each of the beryllium orbitals must contain only one electron. In satisfying these requirements, the electrons of the beryllium atom become unpaired and the resulting half-filled s and p atomic orbitals become hybridized.

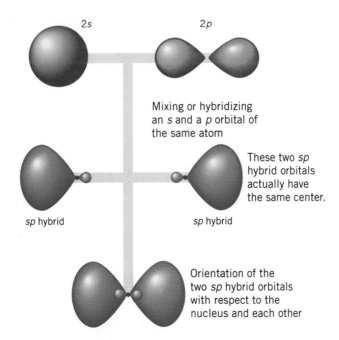

2s   2p

Mixing or hybridizing an s and a p orbital of the same atom

These two sp hybrid orbitals actually have the same center.

sp hybrid sp hybrid

Orientation of the two sp hybrid orbitals with respect to the nucleus and each other

FIG. 9.20 **Formation of** sp **hybrid orbitals.** Mixing of the 2s and 2p atomic orbitals produces a pair of sp hybrid orbitals. The large lobes of these orbitals point in opposite directions.

[3] In the solid state, BeH_2 has a complex structure not consisting of simple BeH_2 molecules.

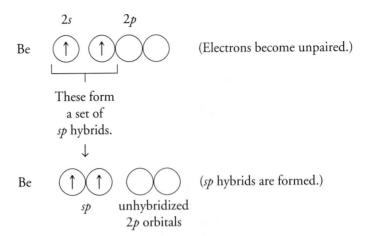

Now the $1s$ orbitals of the hydrogen atoms can overlap with the sp hybrids of beryllium to form the bonds, as shown in Figure 9.21. Because the two sp hybrid orbitals of beryllium are identical in shape and energy, the two Be—H bonds are alike except for the directions in which they point, and we say that the bonds are *equivalent*. Since the bonds point in opposite directions, the linear geometry of the molecule is also explained. The orbital diagram for beryllium in this molecule is

Be (in BeH₂)   ⬆⬇ ⬆⬇ ◯◯   (Colored arrows are H electrons.)
                sp unhybridized
                         $2p$ orbitals

Even if we had not known the shape of the BeH₂ molecule, we could have obtained the same bonding picture by applying the VSEPR model first. The Lewis structure for BeH₂ is H:Be:H, with two bonding domains around the central atom, so the molecule is linear. Once the shape is known, we can apply the VB theory to explain the bonding in

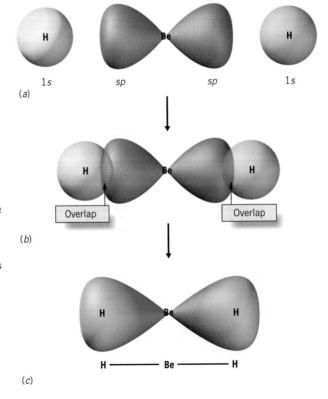

FIG. 9.21 Bonding in BeH₂ according to valence bond theory. Only the larger lobe of each sp hybrid orbital is shown. (*a*) The two hydrogen $1s$ orbitals approach the pair of sp hybrid orbitals of beryllium. (*b*) Overlap of the hydrogen $1s$ orbitals with the sp hybrid orbitals. (*c*) A representation of the distribution of electron density in the two Be—H bonds after they have been formed.

terms of orbital overlaps. Thus, the VB theory and VSEPR model complement each other well. The VSEPR model allows us to predict geometry in a simple way, and once the geometry is known, it is relatively easy to analyze the bonding in terms of VB theory.

EXAMPLE 9.7
Explaining Bonding with Hybrid Orbitals

Methane, CH_4, is a tetrahedral molecule. How is this explained in terms of valence bond theory?

ANALYSIS: No pure atomic orbitals have the correct orientations to form a tetrahedral molecule, so we expect hybrid orbitals will be used. Our tool is Figure 9.19, which permits us to select which hybrids are appropriate based on the geometry of the molecule. Then we can use the orbital diagram of carbon to follow the changes leading to bond formation.

SOLUTION: The tetrahedral structure of the molecule suggests that sp^3 hybrid orbitals are involved in bonding. Let's examine the valence shell of carbon.

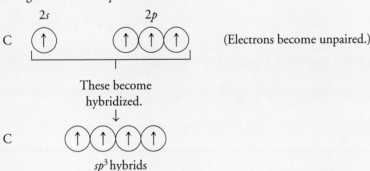

To form four C—H bonds, we need four half-filled orbitals. Unpairing the electrons in the $2s$ and moving one to the vacant $2p$ orbital satisfies this requirement. Then we can hybridize all the orbitals to give the desired sp^3 set.

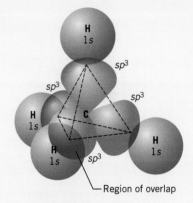

FIG. 9.22 **Formation of the bonds in methane.** Each bond results from the overlap of a hydrogen $1s$ orbital with an sp^3 hybrid orbital on the carbon atom.

Then we form the four bonds to hydrogen $1s$ orbitals.

This is illustrated in Figure 9.22.

IS THE ANSWER REASONABLE? The positions of the hydrogen atoms around the carbon give the correct tetrahedral shape for the molecule. The Lewis structure for CH_4 shows four bonding domains around the carbon atom, which is consistent with the idea of four sp^3 orbitals overlapping with hydrogen $1s$ orbitals to form four bonds.

Practice Exercise 11: The BCl_3 molecule has a planar triangular shape. What kind of hybrid orbitals does boron use in this molecule? Use orbital diagrams to explain how the bonds are formed. (Hint: Which kind of hybrid orbitals are oriented correctly to give this molecular shape?)

Practice Exercise 12: In the gas phase, beryllium fluoride exists as linear molecules. Which kind of hybrid orbitals does Be use in this compound? Use orbital diagrams to explain how the bonds are formed.

In methane, carbon forms four single bonds with hydrogen atoms by using sp^3 hybrid orbitals. In fact, carbon uses these same kinds of orbitals in all of its compounds in which it is bonded to four other atoms by single bonds. This makes the tetrahedral orientation of atoms around carbon one of the primary structural features of organic compounds, and organic chemists routinely think in terms of "tetrahedral carbon."

In the alkane series of hydrocarbons (compounds with the general formula C_nH_{2n+2}, page 61), carbon atoms are bonded to other carbon atoms. An example is ethane, C_2H_6.

$$\begin{array}{ccc} & H & H \\ & | & | \\ H- & C-C & -H \\ & | & | \\ & H & H \end{array}$$

ethane

In this molecule, the carbons are bonded together by the overlap of sp^3 hybrid orbitals (Figure 9.23). One of the most important characteristics of this bond is that the overlap of the orbitals in the C—C bond is hardly affected at all if one portion of the molecule rotates relative to the other around the bond axis. Such rotation, therefore, is said to occur freely and permits different possible relative orientations of the atoms in the molecule. These different relative orientations are called **conformations.** With complex molecules, the number of possible conformations is enormous. For example, Figure 9.24 illustrates three of the large number of possible conformations of the pentane molecule, C_5H_{12}, one of the low molecular weight organic compounds in gasoline.

TOOLS

VSEPR model and hybridization

We can use the VSEPR model to predict hybridization

We've seen that if we know the structure of a molecule, we can make a reasonable guess as to the kind of hybrid orbitals that the central atom uses to form its bonds. Because the VSEPR model works so well in predicting geometry, we can use it to help us obtain VB descriptions of bonding. This is illustrated in the following example.

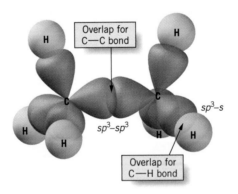

(a)

FIG. 9.23 The bonds in the ethane molecule. (*a*) Overlap of orbitals. (*b*) The degree of overlap of the sp^3 orbitals in the carbon–carbon bond is not appreciably affected by the rotation of the two CH₃— groups relative to each other around the bond.

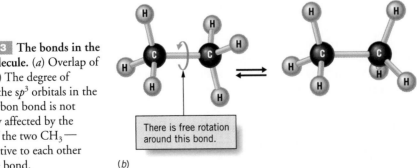

(b)

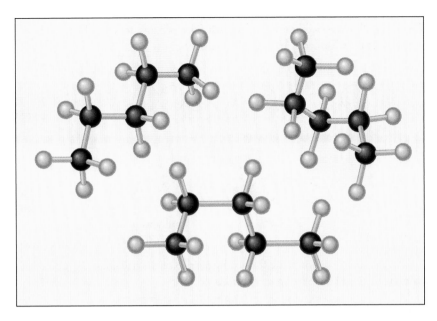

FIG. 9.24 Three of the many conformations of the atoms in the pentane molecule, C_5H_{12}. Free rotation around single bonds makes these different conformations possible.

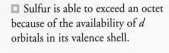

EXAMPLE 9.8
Using the VSEPR Model to Predict Hybridization

Predict the shape of the sulfur hexafluoride molecule and describe the bonding in the molecule in terms of valence bond theory.

ANALYSIS: The rules of nomenclature tell us the chemical formula is SF_6. Based on the formula, we will write a Lewis structure for the molecule. This will permit us to determine its geometry. Then we will examine Figure 9.19 to select the hybrid orbitals that fit this geometry. Finally, we will write the orbital diagram for sulfur to determine which orbitals are used to form the hybrids.

SOLUTION: Following the procedure discussed earlier, the Lewis structure for SF_6 is

$$
\begin{array}{c}
\ddot{F} \\
\ddot{F} \diagdown \, | \diagup \ddot{F} \\
S \\
\ddot{F} \diagup \, | \diagdown \ddot{F} \\
\ddot{F}
\end{array}
$$

The VSEPR model tells us the molecule should be octahedral, and referring to Figure 9.19, we find that the hybrid set that fits this structure is sp^3d^2.

As before, let's examine the valence shell of sulfur.

    S   ⟨↑↓⟩ ⟨↑↓⟩⟨↑⟩⟨↑⟩
         3s   3p

To form six bonds to fluorine atoms we need six half-filled orbitals, but we show only four orbitals altogether. However, sp^3d^2 orbitals tell us we need to look for d orbitals to include in the set of hybrids.

An isolated sulfur atom has electrons only in its $3s$ and $3p$ subshells, so these are the only ones we usually show in the orbital diagram. But the third shell also has a d subshell, which is empty in a sulfur atom. Therefore, let's rewrite the orbital diagram to show the vacant $3d$ subshell.

□ Sulfur is able to exceed an octet because of the availability of d orbitals in its valence shell.

   S   ⟨↑↓⟩ ⟨↑↓⟩⟨↑⟩⟨↑⟩ ◯◯◯◯◯
         3s   3p   3d

Unpairing all of the electrons to give six half-filled orbitals, followed by hybridization, gives the required set of half-filled sp^3d^2 orbitals (Figure 9.25).

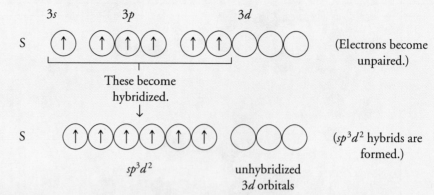

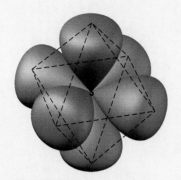

FIG. 9.25 The sp^3d^2 hybrid orbitals of sulfur in SF_6.

Finally, the six S—F bonds are formed by overlap of the half-filled $2p$ orbitals of the fluorine atoms with these half-filled sp^3d^2 hybrids.

S (in SF_6) (Colored arrows are F electrons.)

sp^3d^2 unhybridized $3d$ orbitals

IS THE ANSWER REASONABLE? The fact that all the parts fit together so well to account for the structure of SF_6 makes us feel that our explanation of the bonding is reasonable.

Practice Exercise 13: What kind of hybrid orbitals are expected to be used by the central atom in PCl_5? (Hint: Which hybrid orbitals have the same geometry as the molecule?)

Practice Exercise 14: What kind of hybrid orbitals are expected to be used by the central atom in SiH_4? Use orbital diagrams to describe the bonding in the molecule.

Practice Exercise 15: Use the VSEPR model to predict the shape of the $AsCl_5$ molecule and then describe the bonding in the molecule using valence bond theory.

Hybrid orbitals can be used to describe molecules with nonbonding domains

Methane is a tetrahedral molecule with sp^3 hybridization of the orbitals of carbon and H—C—H bond angles that are each equal to 109.5°. In ammonia, NH_3, the H—N—H bond angles are 107°, and in water the H—O—H bond angle is 104.5°. Both NH_3 and H_2O have H—X—H bond angles that are close to the bond angles expected for a molecule whose central atom has sp^3 hybrids. The use of sp^3 hybrids by oxygen and nitrogen, therefore, is often used to explain the geometry of H_2O and NH_3.

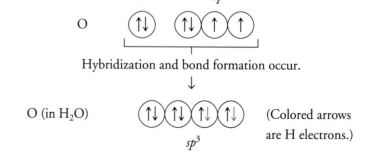

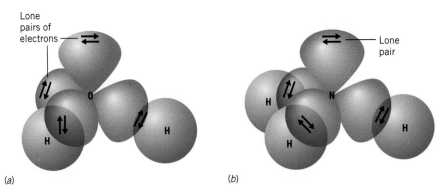

FIG. 9.26 **Hybrid orbitals can hold lone pairs of electrons.** (*a*) In water, two lone pairs on oxygen are held in *sp³* hybrid orbitals. (*b*) Ammonia has one lone pair in an *sp³* hybrid orbital.

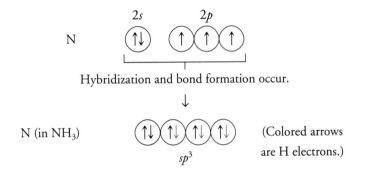

According to these descriptions, not all of the hybrid orbitals of the central atom must be used for bonding. Lone pairs of electrons can be accommodated in them too, as illustrated in Figure 9.26. In fact, putting the lone pair on the nitrogen in an *sp³* hybrid orbital gives a geometry that agrees well with the experimentally determined structure of the ammonia molecule.

EXAMPLE 9.9
Explaining Bonding with
Hybrid Orbitals

Use valence bond theory to explain the bonding in the SF₄ molecule.

ANALYSIS: Once again, our primary tool in answering the question is the Lewis structure, which will tell us the number of electron domains around the central atom. We'll use this information to select the kinds of hybrid orbitals used by sulfur in the molecule. Then we can construct the orbital diagrams as before.

SOLUTION: Let's begin by constructing the Lewis structure for the molecule. Following the usual procedure, we obtain

$$
\begin{array}{c}
:\ddot{F}: \\
| \\
:\ddot{F}-\overset{..}{S}-\ddot{F}: \\
| \\
:\ddot{F}: \\
\end{array}
$$

The VSEPR model predicts that the electron pairs around the sulfur should be in a trigonal bipyramidal arrangement, and the only hybrids that fit this geometry are *sp³d*. To see how they are formed, we look at the valence shell of sulfur, including the vacant *3d* subshell.

To form the four bonds to fluorine atoms, we need four half-filled orbitals, so we unpair the electrons in one of the filled orbitals. This gives

Next, we form the hybrid orbitals. In doing this, we use all the valence shell orbitals that have electrons in them.

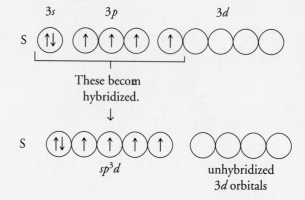

The structure of SF₄

Lone pair

Now, four S—F bonds can be formed by overlap of half-filled $2p$ orbitals of fluorine with the sp^3d hybrid orbitals of sulfur.

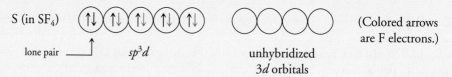

IS THE ANSWER REASONABLE? Counting electrons in the Lewis structure gives a total of 34, which is how many electrons are in the valence shells of one sulfur and four fluorine atoms, so the Lewis structure appears to be correct. The rest of the answer flows smoothly, so the bonding description appears to be reasonable.

Practice Exercise 16: What kind of orbitals are used by Xe in the XeF₄ molecule? (Hint: An Xe atom has eight valence electrons.)

Practice Exercise 17: What kind of hybrid orbitals would we expect the central atom to use for bonding in (a) PCl₃ and (b) ClF₃?

Hybrid orbitals can be used to explain the formation of coordinate covalent bonds

In Section 8.6 we defined a coordinate covalent bond as one in which both of the shared electrons are provided by just one of the joined atoms. Such a bond is formed when boron trifluoride, BF_3, combines with an additional fluoride ion to form the tetrafluoroborate ion, BF_4^-.

$$BF_3 + F^- \longrightarrow BF_4^-$$
tetrafluoroborate ion

We can diagram this reaction as follows:

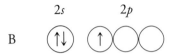

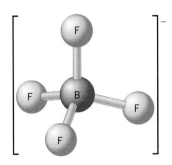

FIG. 9.27 The tetrahedral structure of the BF_4^- ion.

As we mentioned previously, the coordinate covalent bond is really no different from any other covalent bond once it has formed. The distinction is made *only* for bookkeeping purposes. One place where such bookkeeping is useful is in keeping track of the orbitals and electrons used when atoms bond together.

The VB theory requirements for bond formation—two overlapping orbitals sharing two paired electrons—can be satisfied in two ways. One, as we have already seen, is by the overlapping of two half-filled orbitals. This gives an "ordinary" covalent bond. The other is by overlapping one filled orbital with one empty orbital. The atom with the filled orbital donates the shared pair of electrons, and a coordinate covalent bond is formed.

The structure of the BF_4^- ion, which the VSEPR model predicts to be tetrahedral (Figure 9.27), can be explained as follows. First we examine the orbital diagram for boron.

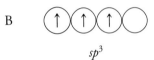

To form four bonds, we need four hybrid orbitals arranged tetrahedrally around the boron, so we expect boron to use sp^3 hybrids. Notice we spread the electrons out over the hybrid orbitals as much as possible.

Boron forms three ordinary covalent bonds with fluorine atoms plus one coordinate covalent bond with a fluoride ion.

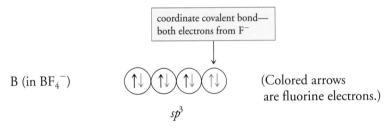

Practice Exercise 18: If we assume nitrogen uses sp^3 hybrid orbitals in NH_3, use valence bond theory to account for the formation of NH_4^+ from NH_3 and H^+. (Hint: Which atom donates the pair of electrons in the formation of the bond between H^+ and NH_3?)

Practice Exercise 19: What is the shape of the PCl_6^- ion? What hybrid orbitals are used by phosphorus in PCl_6^-? Draw the orbital diagram for phosphorus in PCl_6^-.

9.6 HYBRID ORBITALS CAN BE USED TO DESCRIBE MULTIPLE BONDS

The types of orbital overlap that we have described so far produce bonds in which the electron density is concentrated most heavily between the nuclei of the two atoms along an imaginary line that joins their centers. Any bond of this kind, whether formed from the overlap of *s* orbitals, *p* orbitals, or hybrid orbitals (Figure 9.28), is called a **sigma bond** (or **σ bond**).

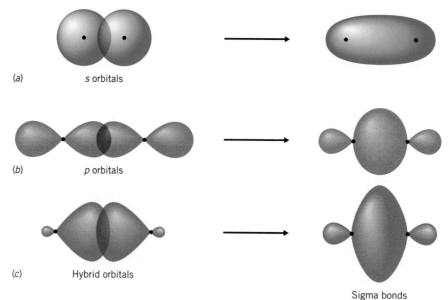

FIG. 9.28 Formation of σ bonds. Sigma bonds concentrate electron density along the line between the two atoms joined by the bond. (*a*) From the overlap of *s* orbitals. (*b*) From the end-to-end overlap of *p* orbitals. (*c*) From the overlap of hybrid orbitals.

(*a*)   *s* orbitals

(*b*)   *p* orbitals

(*c*)   Hybrid orbitals

Sigma bonds

Another way that *p* orbitals can overlap is shown in Figure 9.29. This produces a bond in which the electron density is divided between two separate regions that lie on opposite sides of an imaginary line joining the two nuclei. This kind of bond is called a **pi bond** (or **π bond**). Notice that a π bond, like a *p* orbital, consists of two parts, and each part makes up just half of the π bond; it takes *both* of them to equal *one* π bond. The formation of π bonds allows atoms to form double and triple bonds.

A double bond consists of a sigma bond and a pi bond

A hydrocarbon that contains a double bond is ethylene (also called ethene), C_2H_4. It has the Lewis structure

$$\begin{array}{ccc} H & & H \\ & C{=}C & \\ H & & H \end{array}$$

ethylene

The molecule is planar and each carbon atom lies in the center of a triangle surrounded by three other atoms (two H and one C atom). A planar triangular arrangement of bonds suggests that carbon uses sp^2 hybrid orbitals. Therefore, let's look at the distribution of electrons among the orbitals that carbon has available in its valence shell, assuming sp^2 hybridization.

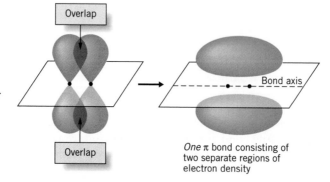

FIG. 9.29 Formation of a π bond. Two *p* orbitals overlap sideways instead of end-to-end. The electron density is concentrated in two regions on opposite sides of the bond axis.

Overlap

Overlap

Bond axis

One π bond consisting of two separate regions of electron density

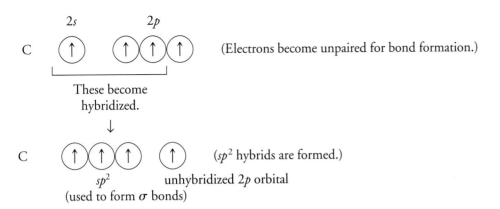

(Electrons become unpaired for bond formation.)

Notice that the carbon atom has an unpaired electron in an unhybridized $2p$ orbital. This p orbital is oriented perpendicular to the triangular plane of the sp^2 hybrid orbitals, as shown in Figure 9.30. Now we can see how the molecule goes together.

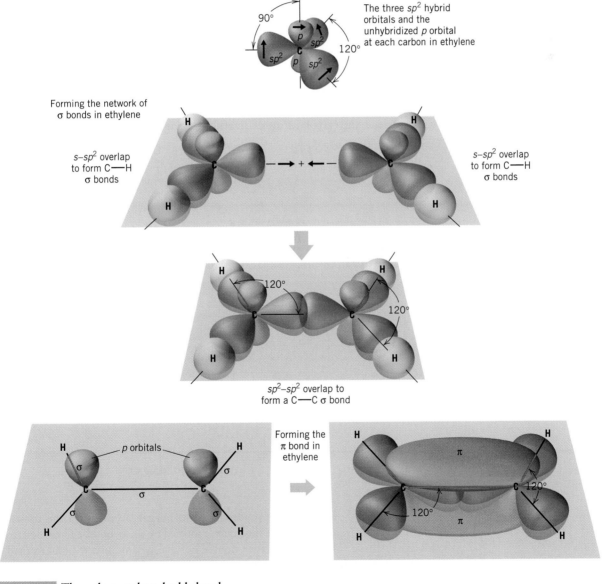

FIG. 9.30 The carbon–carbon double bond.

□ The double bond is a little like a hot dog on a bun.
The sigma bond is like the hot dog, and the π bond is like the two parts of the bun.

□ Restricted rotation around double bonds affects the properties of organic and biochemical molecules.

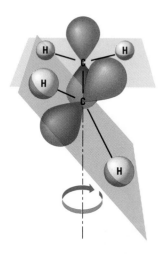

FIG. 9.31 Restricted rotation around a double bond. As the CH_2 group closest to us rotates relative to the one at the rear, the unhybridized p orbitals become misaligned, as shown here. This destroys the overlap and breaks the π bond. Bond breaking requires a lot of energy, more than is available to the molecule through the normal bending and stretching of its bonds at room temperature. Because of this, rotation about the double bond axis is hindered or "restricted."

□ The two filled sp^2 hybrids on the oxygen become lone pairs on the oxygen atom in the molecule.

The basic framework of the molecule is determined by the formation of σ bonds. Each carbon uses two of its sp^2 hybrids to form σ bonds to hydrogen atoms. The third sp^2 hybrid on each carbon is used to form a σ bond between the two carbon atoms, thereby accounting for one of the two bonds of the double bond. Finally, the remaining unhybridized 2p orbitals, one from each carbon atom, overlap to produce a π bond, which accounts for the second bond of the double bond.

This description of the bonding in C_2H_4 accounts for one of the most important properties of double bonds: rotation of one portion of the molecule relative to the rest around the axis of the double bond occurs only with great difficulty. The reason for this is illustrated in Figure 9.31. We see that as one CH_2 group is rotated relative to the other around the carbon–carbon bond, the unhybridized p orbitals become misaligned and can no longer overlap effectively. This destroys the π bond. In effect, then, rotation around a double bond involves bond breaking, which requires more energy than is normally available to molecules at room temperature. As a result, rotation around the axis of a double bond usually doesn't take place.

In almost every instance, a double bond consists of a σ bond and a π bond. Another example is the compound formaldehyde (the substance used as a preservative for biological specimens and as an embalming fluid). The Lewis structure of this compound is

$$\begin{array}{c} H \\ \diagdown \\ C=\ddot{O} \\ \diagup \quad \ddot{} \\ H \end{array}$$

formaldehyde

As with ethylene, the carbon forms sp^2 hybrids, leaving an unpaired electron in an unhybridized p orbital.

C ⬆ ⬆ ⬆   ⬆

sp^2 unhybridized 2p orbital

The oxygen can also form sp^2 hybrids, with electron pairs in two of them and an unpaired electron in the third. This means that the remaining unhybridized p orbital also has an unpaired electron.

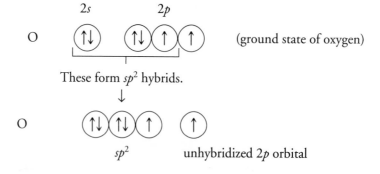

Figure 9.32 shows how the carbon, hydrogen, and oxygen atoms form the molecule. As before, the basic framework of the molecule is formed by the σ bonds. These determine the molecular shape. The carbon–oxygen double bond also contains a π bond formed by the overlap of the unhybridized p orbitals.

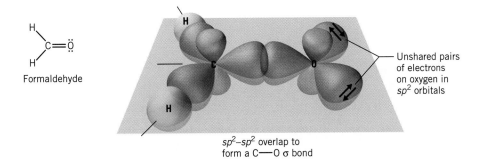

Formaldehyde

sp^2–sp^2 overlap to form a C—O σ bond

Unshared pairs of electrons on oxygen in sp^2 orbitals

Forming the π bond in formaldehyde

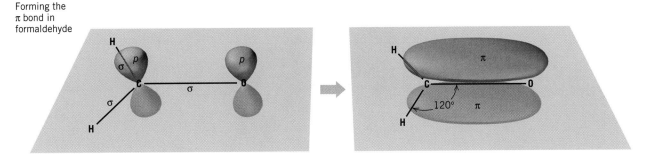

FIG. 9.32 Bonding in formaldehyde. The carbon–oxygen double bond consists of a σ bond and a π bond. The σ bond is formed by overlap of sp^2 hybrid orbitals. Overlap of unhybridized p orbitals on the two atoms gives the π bond.

A triple bond consists of a sigma bond and two pi bonds

An example of a molecule containing a triple bond is ethyne, also known as acetylene, C_2H_2 (a gas used as a fuel for welding torches).

$$H—C≡C—H$$
ethyne
(acetylene)

In the linear acetylene molecule, each carbon needs two hybrid orbitals to form two σ bonds—one to a hydrogen atom and one to the other carbon atom. These can be provided by mixing the $2s$ and one of the $2p$ orbitals to form sp hybrids. To help us visualize the bonding, we will imagine that there is an xyz coordinate system centered at each carbon atom and that it is the $2p_z$ orbital that becomes mixed in the hybrid orbitals.

☐ We label the orbitals p_x, p_y, and p_z just for convenience; they are really all equivalent.

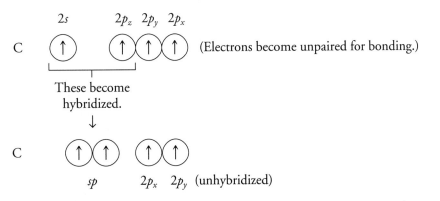

Figure 9.33 shows how the molecule is formed. The sp orbitals point in opposite directions and are used to form the σ bonds. The unhybridized $2p_x$ and $2p_y$ orbitals are perpendicular to the C—C bond axis and overlap sideways to form two separate π bonds that surround the C—C σ bond. Notice that we now have three pairs of electrons in three bonds—one σ bond and two π bonds—whose electron densities are concentrated in different places. Also notice that the use of sp hybrid orbitals for the σ bonds allows us to explain the linear arrangement of atoms in the molecule.

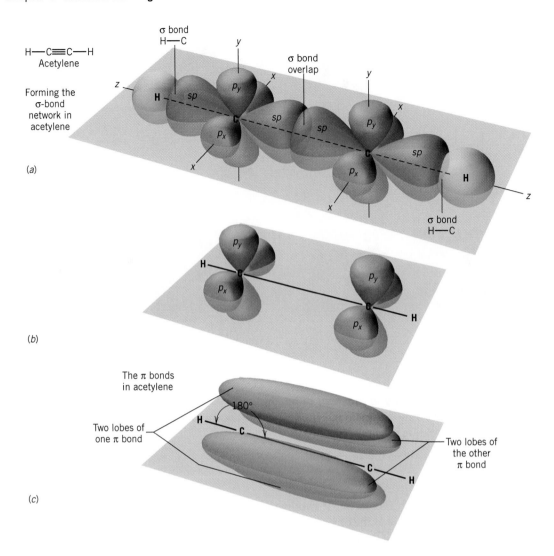

FIG. 9.33 The carbon–carbon triple bond in acetylene. (*a*) The *sp* hybrid orbitals on the carbon atoms are used to form sigma bonds to the hydrogen atoms and to each other. This accounts for one of the three bonds between the carbon atoms. (*b*) Sideways overlap of unhybridized $2p_x$ and $2p_y$ orbitals of the carbon atoms produces two π bonds. (*c*) The two π bonds in acetylene after they've formed surround the σ bond.

Similar descriptions can be used to explain the bonding in other molecules that have triple bonds. Figure 9.34, for example, shows how the nitrogen molecule, N_2, is formed. In it, too, the triple bond is composed of one σ bond and two π bonds.

TOOLS

Analyzing bonding in molecules

A Brief Summary

On the basis of the preceding discussion, we can make some observations that are helpful in applying the valence bond theory to a variety of molecules.

1. The basic molecular framework of a molecule is determined by the arrangement of its σ bonds.
2. Hybrid orbitals are used by an atom to form its σ bonds and to hold lone pairs of electrons.
3. The number of hybrid orbitals needed by an atom in a structure equals the number of atoms to which it is bonded *plus* the number of lone pairs of electrons in its valence shell.
4. When there is a double bond in a molecule, it consists of one σ bond and one π bond.
5. When there is a triple bond in a molecule, it consists of one σ bond and two π bonds.

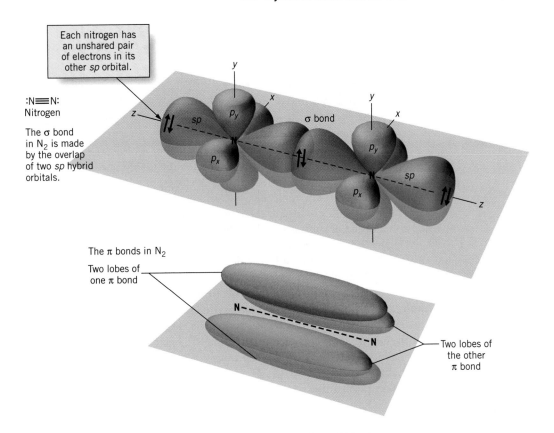

FIG. 9.34 **Bonding in nitrogen.** The triple bond in nitrogen, N_2, is formed like the triple bond in acetylene. A sigma bond is formed by overlap of *sp* hybrid orbitals. The two unhybridized 2*p* orbitals on each nitrogen atom overlap to give the two π bonds. On each nitrogen, there is a lone pair of electrons in the *sp* hybrid orbital that's not used to form the sigma bond.

Practice Exercise 20: Consider the molecule below. What kind of hybrid orbitals are used by atoms 1, 2, and 3? How many sigma bonds and pi bonds are in the molecule? (Hint: Study the brief summary above.)

Practice Exercise 21: Consider the molecule below. What kind of hybrid orbitals are used by atoms 1, 2, and 3? How many sigma bonds and pi bonds are in the molecule?

9.7 MOLECULAR ORBITAL THEORY EXPLAINS BONDING AS CONSTRUCTIVE INTERFERENCE OF ATOMIC ORBITALS

Molecular orbital theory takes the view that a molecule is similar to an atom in one important respect. Both have energy levels that correspond to various orbitals that can be populated by electrons. In atoms, these orbitals are called atomic orbitals; in molecules, they are called **molecular orbitals.** (We shall frequently call them **MOs.**)

In most cases, the actual shapes and energies of molecular orbitals cannot be determined exactly. Nevertheless, reasonably good estimates of their shapes and energies can be obtained by combining the electron waves corresponding to the atomic orbitals of the atoms that make up the molecule. In forming molecular orbitals, these waves interact by constructive and destructive interference just like other waves we've seen. Their intensities are either added or subtracted when the atomic orbitals overlap.

The number of MOs formed is always equal to the number of atomic orbitals that are combined.

Figure 9.35 illustrates the formation of molecular orbitals by the overlap of two 1*s* orbitals. Notice that the *two* 1*s* atomic orbitals combine to give *two* MOs. In one MO, the intensities of the electron waves add between the nuclei, which gives a buildup of electron density that helps hold the nuclei near each other. Such an MO is called a **bonding molecular orbital.** *Electrons in bonding MOs tend to stabilize a molecule.* In the other MO, cancellation of the electron waves reduces the electron density between the nuclei, which allows the nuclei to repel each other strongly. This is an **antibonding molecular orbital.** *Antibonding MOs tend to destabilize a molecule when occupied by electrons.*

Both MOs in Figure 9.35 have their maximum electron density on an imaginary line that passes through the two nuclei, giving them properties of sigma bonds. MOs like this are also designated as sigma (σ), with a subscript showing which atomic orbitals make up the MO. An asterisk indicates which is an antibonding MO. Thus, the bonding and antibonding MOs formed by overlap of 1*s* orbitals are symbolized as σ_{1s} and σ^*_{1s} respectively.

Bonding MOs are lower in energy than antibonding MOs formed from the same atomic orbitals, as shown in Figure 9.35. When electrons populate molecular orbitals, they fill the lower energy, bonding MOs first. The rules that apply to filling MOs are the same as those for filling atomic orbitals: *Electrons spread out over molecular orbitals of equal energy (Hund's rule) and two electrons can only occupy the same orbital if their spins are paired.* When filling the MOs, we also have to be sure we've accounted for all of the valence electrons of the separate atoms.

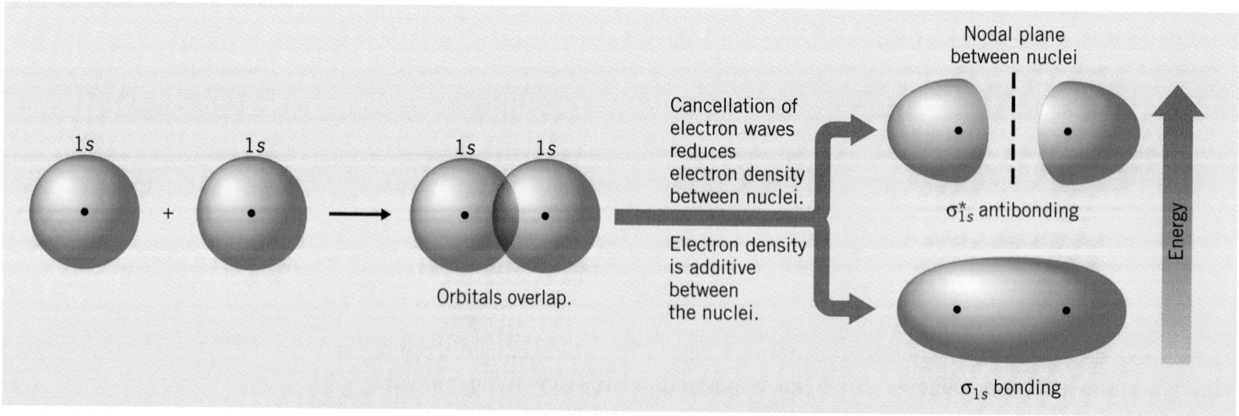

FIG. 9.35 Interaction of 1*s* atomic orbitals to produce bonding and antibonding molecular orbitals. These are σ-type orbitals because the electron density is concentrated along the imaginary line that passes through both nuclei. The antibonding orbital has a nodal plane between the nuclei where the electron density drops to zero.

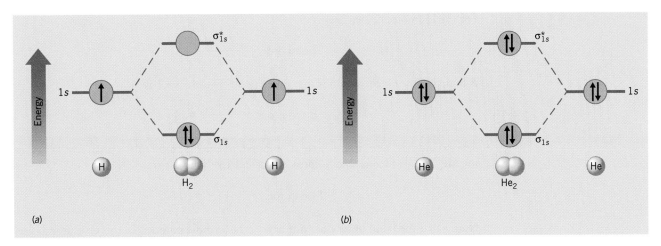

FIG. 9.36 Molecular orbital descriptions of H_2 and He_2. (*a*) Molecular orbital energy level diagram for H_2. (*b*) Molecular orbital energy level diagram for He_2.

Molecular orbital theory can explain why some molecules exist and others do not

Figure 9.36*a* is an MO energy level diagram for H_2. The energies of the separate $1s$ atomic orbitals are indicated at the left and right; those of the molecular orbitals are shown in the center. The H_2 molecule has two electrons, and both can be placed in the σ_{1s} orbital. The shape of this bonding orbital, shown in Figure 9.35, should be familiar. It's the same as the shape of the electron cloud that we described using the valence bond theory.

Next, let's consider what happens when two helium atoms come together. Why can't a stable molecule of He_2 be formed? Figure 9.36*b* is the energy diagram for He_2. Notice that both bonding and antibonding orbitals are filled. In situations such as this there is a net destabilization because the antibonding MO is raised in energy more than the bonding MO is lowered, relative to the orbitals of the separated atoms. This means the total energy of He_2 is larger than that of two separate He atoms, so the "molecule" is unstable and immediately comes apart.

In general, the effects of **antibonding electrons** (those in antibonding MOs) cancel the effects of an equal number of bonding electrons, and molecules with equal numbers of bonding and antibonding electrons are unstable. If we remove an antibonding electron from He_2 to give He_2^+, there is a net excess of bonding electrons, and the ion should be capable of existence. In fact, the emission spectrum of He_2^+ can be observed when an electric discharge is passed through a helium-filled tube, which shows that He_2^+ is present during the electric discharge. However, the ion is not very stable and cannot be isolated.

Bond order is related to the difference in the number of electron pairs in bonding and antibonding orbitals

The concept of **bond order** was introduced in Section 8.6 where it was defined as the number of pairs of electrons shared between two atoms. To translate the MO description into these terms, we compute the bond order as follows:

$$\text{Bond order} = \frac{(\text{number of bonding } e^-) - (\text{number of antibonding } e^-)}{2 \text{ electrons/bond}}$$

TOOLS

MO bond order

For the H_2 molecule, we have

$$\text{Bond order} = \frac{2 - 0}{2} = 1$$

A bond order of 1 corresponds to a single bond. For He_2 we have

$$\text{Bond order} = \frac{2 - 2}{2} = 0$$

A bond order of zero means there is no bond, so the He_2 molecule is unable to exist. For the He_2^+ ion, which is able to form, the calculated bond order is

$$\text{Bond order} = \frac{2 - 1}{2} = 0.5$$

Notice that the bond order does not have to be a whole number. In this case, it indicates a bond character equivalent to about half a bond.

Molecular orbital theory successfully predicts the properties of second period diatomics

The outer shell of a Period 2 element (Li through Ne) consists of $2s$ and $2p$ subshells. When atoms of this period bond to each other, the atomic orbitals of these subshells interact strongly to produce molecular orbitals. The $2s$ orbitals, for example, overlap to form σ_{2s} and σ_{2s}^* molecular orbitals having essentially the same shapes as the σ_{1s} and σ_{1s}^* MOs, respectively. Figure 9.37 shows the shapes of the bonding and antibonding MOs produced

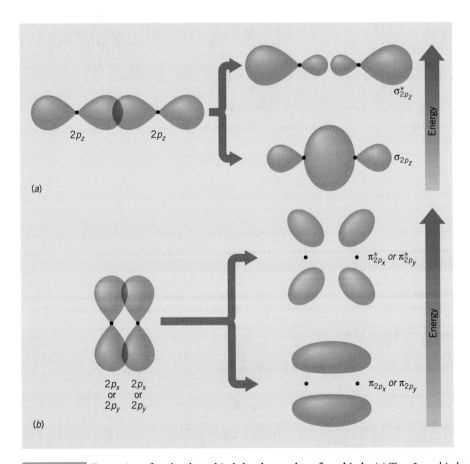

FIG. 9.37 Formation of molecular orbitals by the overlap of *p* orbitals. (*a*) Two $2p_z$ orbitals that point at each other give bonding and antibonding σ-type MOs. (*b*) Perpendicular to the $2p_z$ orbitals are $2p_x$ and $2p_y$ orbitals that overlap to give two sets of bonding and antibonding π-type MOs.

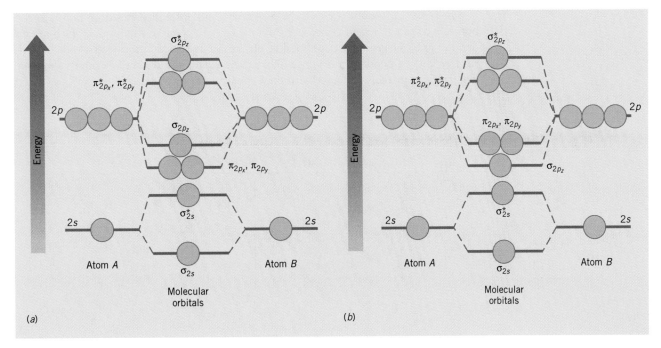

FIG. 9.38 Approximate relative energies of molecular orbitals in second period diatomic molecules. (*a*) Li_2 through N_2. (*b*) O_2 through Ne_2.

when the $2p$ orbitals overlap. If we label those that point toward each other as $2p_z$, a set of bonding and antibonding MOs are formed that we can label as σ_{2p_z} and $\sigma^*_{2p_z}$. The $2p_x$ and $2p_y$ orbitals, which are perpendicular to the $2p_z$ orbitals, overlap sideways to give π-type molecular orbitals. They are labeled π_{2p_x} and $\pi^*_{2p_x}$, and π_{2p_y} and $\pi^*_{2p_y}$, respectively.

The approximate relative energies of the MOs formed from the second shell atomic orbitals are shown in Figure 9.38. Notice that from Li to N, the energies of the π_{2p_x} and π_{2p_y} orbitals are lower than the energy of the σ_{2p_z}. Then from O to Ne, the energies of the two levels are reversed. The reasons for this are complex and beyond the scope of this book.

Using Figure 9.38, we can predict the electronic structures of diatomic molecules of Period 2. These *MO electron configurations* are obtained using the same rules that are applied to the filling of atomic orbitals in atoms.

How Electrons Fill Molecular Orbitals

1. Electrons fill the lowest energy orbitals that are available.
2. No more than two electrons, with spins paired, can occupy any orbital.
3. Electrons spread out as much as possible, with spins unpaired, over orbitals that have the same energy.

TOOLS

How electrons fill MOs

Applying these rules to the valence electrons of Period 2 atoms gives the MO electron configurations shown in Table 9.1. Let's see how well MO theory performs by examining data that are available for these molecules.

According to Table 9.1, MO theory predicts that molecules of Be_2 and Ne_2 should not exist at all because they have bond orders of zero. In beryllium vapor and in gaseous neon, no evidence of Be_2 or Ne_2 has ever been found. MO theory also predicts that diatomic molecules of the other Period 2 elements should exist because they all have bond orders greater than zero. These molecules have, in fact, been observed. Although lithium, boron, and carbon are complex solids under ordinary conditions, they can be vaporized. In the vapor, molecules of Li_2, B_2, and C_2 can be detected. Nitrogen, oxygen, and fluorine, as you know, are gaseous elements that exist as N_2, O_2, and F_2.

In Table 9.1, we also see that the predicted bond order increases from boron to carbon to nitrogen and then decreases from nitrogen to oxygen to fluorine. As the bond order increases, the *net* number of bonding electrons increases, so the bonds should become stronger and the bond lengths shorter. The *experimentally measured* bond energies and bond lengths given in Table 9.1 agree with these predictions quite nicely.

TABLE 9.1 Molecular Orbital Populations and Bond Orders for Period 2 Diatomic Molecules[a]

Left-side energy ordering (Energy increasing upward): $\sigma^*_{2p_z}$; $\pi^*_{2p_x}, \pi^*_{2p_y}$; σ_{2p_z}; π_{2p_x}, π_{2p_y}; σ^*_{2s}; σ_{2s} — for Li_2, Be_2, B_2, C_2, N_2.

Right-side energy ordering (Energy increasing upward): $\sigma^*_{2p_z}$; $\pi^*_{2p_x}, \pi^*_{2p_y}$; π_{2p_x}, π_{2p_y}; σ_{2p_z}; σ^*_{2s}; σ_{2s} — for O_2, F_2, Ne_2.

	Li_2	Be_2	B_2	C_2	N_2		O_2	F_2	Ne_2
Number of Bonding Electrons	2	2	4	6	8		8	8	8
Number of Antibonding Electrons	0	2	2	2	2		4	6	8
Bond Order	1	0	1	2	3		2	1	0
Bond Energy (kJ/mol)	110	—	300	612	953		501	129	—
Bond Length (pm)	267	—	158	124	109		121	144	—

[a] Although the order of the energy levels corresponding to the σ_{2p_z}, and the π bonding MOs become reversed at oxygen, either sequence would yield the same result—a triple bond for N_2, a double bond for O_2, and a single bond for F_2.

Molecular orbital theory is particularly successful in explaining the electronic structure of the oxygen molecule. Experiments show that O_2 is paramagnetic (it's weakly attracted to a magnet) and that the molecule contains two unpaired electrons. In addition, the bond length in O_2 is about what is expected for an oxygen–oxygen double bond. These data cannot be explained by valence bond theory. For example, if we write a Lewis structure for O_2 that shows a double bond and also obeys the octet rule, all the electrons appear in pairs.

$$:\ddot{O}::\ddot{O}:$$ 　　(not acceptable based on experimental evidence because all electrons are paired)

On the other hand, if we show the unpaired electrons, the structure has only a single bond and doesn't obey the octet rule.

$$:\ddot{O}:\dot{\underset{.}{O}}:$$ 　　(not acceptable based on experimental evidence because of the O—O single bond)

☐ Although MO theory handles easily the bonding situations that VB theory has trouble with, MO theory loses the simplicity of VB theory. For even quite simple molecules, MO theory is too complicated to make predictions without extensive calculations.

With MO theory, we don't have any of these difficulties. By applying Hund's rule, the two electrons in the π^* orbitals of O_2 spread out over these orbitals with their spins unpaired because both orbitals have the same energy (see Table 9.1). The electrons in the two antibonding π^* orbitals cancel the effects of two electrons in the two bonding π orbitals, so the net bond order is 2 and the bond is effectively a double bond.

Bonding of heteronuclear diatomic molecules is also explained by MO theory

As molecules become more complex, the simple application of MO theory becomes much more difficult. This is because it is necessary to consider the relative energies of the individual atomic orbitals as well as the orientations of the orbitals relative to those on other atoms. Nevertheless, we can take a brief look at the MO descriptions of a couple of diatomic molecules to see what happens when both atoms in the molecule are not the same. Such molecules are said to be **heteronuclear**.

The MO description of HF is similar to that of valence bond theory

When we consider the possible interaction of the orbitals of different atoms to form molecular orbitals, the first factor we have to consider is the relative energies of the orbitals. This is because orbitals interact most effectively when they are of about equal energy; the greater the difference in energy between the orbitals, the less the orbitals interact, and the more the orbitals behave like simple atomic orbitals.

In HF, the $1s$ orbital of hydrogen is higher in energy than either the $2s$ or $2p$ subshell of fluorine, but it is closest in energy to the $2p$ subshell (Figure 9.39). Taking the z axis as the internuclear axis, the hydrogen $1s$ orbital overlaps with the $2p_z$ orbital of fluorine to give bonding and antibonding σ type orbitals, as illustrated in Figure 9.40. The $2p_x$ and $2p_y$ orbitals of fluorine, however, have no orbitals on hydrogen with which to interact, so they are unchanged when the molecule is formed. These two orbitals are said to be **nonbonding orbitals** because they are neither bonding nor antibonding; they have no effect on the stability of the molecule.

In the MO description of HF, we have a pair of electrons in the bonding MO formed by the overlap of the hydrogen $1s$ orbital with the fluorine $2p_z$ orbital. Earlier we saw that valence bond theory explains the bond in HF in the same way, as a pair of electrons shared between the hydrogen $1s$ orbital and a fluorine $2p$ orbital.

The MO energy diagram for CO is similar to that of Period 2 homonuclear diatomics

A **homonuclear diatomic molecule** is one in which both atoms are of the same element. Examples are N_2 and O_2. Carbon monoxide is a heteronuclear molecule, but both atoms are from Period 2 and we expect the orbitals of the second shell to be the ones used to form

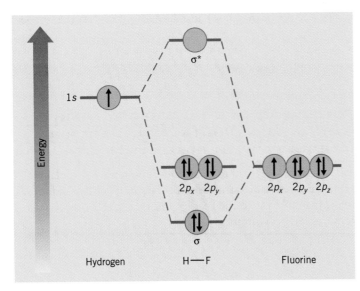

□ The $2s$ orbital of fluorine is so much lower in energy than the $2p$ subshell that we don't need to consider its interaction with the hydrogen $1s$ orbital. That's why it isn't shown in the energy diagram.

FIG. 9.39 Molecular orbital energy diagram for HF. Only the $1s$ orbital of hydrogen and the $2p$ orbitals of fluorine are shown.

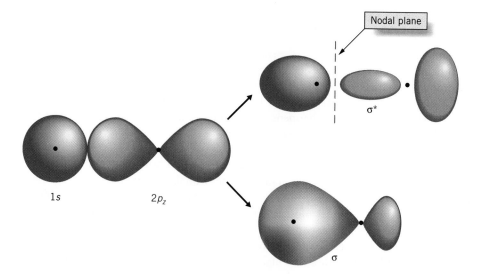

FIG. 9.40 **Formation of σ and σ^* orbitals in HF.** Notice that the antibonding σ^* orbital has a nodal plane between the nuclei, which effectively removes electron density from the region between the nuclei and, if occupied, leads to destabilization of the molecule.

the MOs. The orbital overlaps are similar to those of the homonuclear diatomics of Period 2, so the energy diagram resembles the one shown in Figure 9.38*a*.

Because the outer shell electrons of oxygen experience a larger effective nuclear charge than those of carbon, the oxygen orbitals will be somewhat lower in energy. This is shown in Figure 9.41. There's a total of 10 valence electrons (4 from carbon and 6 from oxygen) to distribute among the MOs of the molecule. When we do this, there are 8 bonding electrons and 2 antibonding electrons, so the net bond order is 3, corresponding to a triple bond. As expected, it consists of a σ bond and two π bonds.

Practice Exercise 22: The molecular orbital energy level diagram for the cyanide ion, CN^-, is similar to that of the Period 2 homonuclear diatomics. Sketch the energy diagram for the ion and indicate the electron population of the MOs. What is the bond order in the ion? How does this agree with the bond order predicted from the Lewis structure of the ion? (Hint: How many valence electrons are there in the ion?)

Practice Exercise 23: The MO energy level diagram for the nitrogen monoxide molecule is essentially the same as that shown in Table 9.1 for O_2, except the oxygen orbitals are slightly lower in energy than the corresponding nitrogen orbitals. Sketch the energy diagram for nitrogen monoxide and indicate which MOs are populated. Calculate the bond order for the molecule. (Hint: Make adjustments to Figure 9.38*b*.)

9.8 MOLECULAR ORBITAL THEORY USES DELOCALIZED ORBITALS TO DESCRIBE MOLECULES WITH RESONANCE STRUCTURES

One of the least satisfying aspects of the way valence bond theory explains chemical bonding is the need to write resonance structures for certain molecules and ions. For example, consider benzene, C_6H_6. As you learned earlier, this molecule has the shape of a ring whose resonance structures can be written as

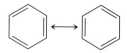

The MO description of bonding in this molecule is as follows: The basic structure of the molecule is determined by the sigma-bond framework, which requires that the carbon atoms use sp^2 hybrid orbitals. This allows each carbon to form three σ bonds (two to other C atoms and one to an H atom). Each carbon atom is left with a half-filled unhybridized p orbital perpendicular to the plane of the ring. These p orbitals overlap to give

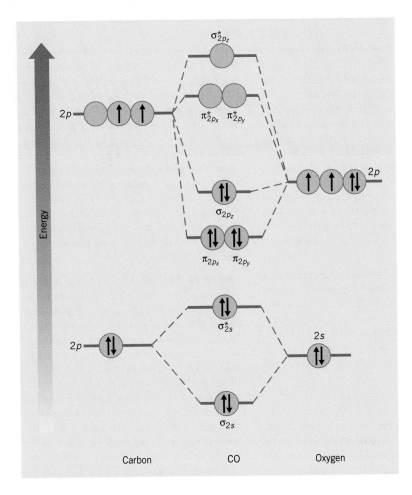

FIG. 9.41 Approximate molecular orbital energy diagram for carbon monoxide. The oxygen orbitals are lower in energy than the corresponding carbon orbitals. The net bond order for CO is 3.

a delocalized π-electron cloud (a **delocalized molecular orbital**) that looks something like two doughnuts with the sigma-bond framework sandwiched between them (Figure 9.42). The delocalized nature of the pi electrons is the reason we usually represent the structure of benzene as

One of the special characteristics of delocalized bonds is that they make a molecule or ion more stable than it would be if it had localized bonds. In Section 8.7 this was described in terms of *resonance energy*. In the molecular orbital theory, we no longer speak of resonance; instead, we refer to the electrons as being delocalized. The extra stability that is associated with this delocalization is therefore described, in the language of MO theory, as the **delocalization energy.**

☐ Functionally, the terms *resonance energy* and *delocalization energy* are the same; they just come from different approaches to bonding theory.

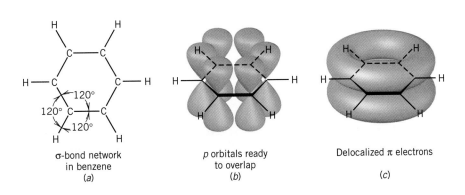

FIG. 9.42 Benzene. (*a*) The σ-bond framework. All atoms lie in the same plane. (*b*) The unhybridized *p* orbitals at each carbon prior to side-to-side overlap. (*c*) The double doughnut-shaped electron cloud formed by the delocalized π electrons.

SUMMARY

Molecular Shapes and VSEPR Theory. The structures of most molecules can be described in terms of one or another of five basic geometries: **linear, planar triangular, tetrahedral, trigonal bipyramidal,** and **octahedral.** The **VSEPR theory** predicts molecular geometry by assuming that **electron domains**—regions of space that contain bonding electrons, unpaired valence electrons, or lone pairs—stay as far apart as possible from each other, while staying as close as possible to the central atom. Figures 9.4, 9.5, 9.7, and 9.10 illustrate the structures obtained with different numbers of groups of electrons in the valence shell of the central atom in a molecule or ion and with different numbers of lone pairs and attached atoms. The correct shape of a molecule or polyatomic ion can usually be predicted from the Lewis structure.

Molecular Shape and Molecular Polarity. A molecule that contains identical atoms attached to a central atom will be nonpolar if there are no lone pairs of electrons in the central atom's valence shell. It will be polar if lone pairs are present, except in two cases: (1) when there are three lone pairs and two attached atoms, and (2) when there are two lone pairs and four attached atoms. If all the atoms attached to the central atom are not alike, the molecule will usually be polar.

Valence Bond (VB) Theory. According to VB theory, a covalent bond is formed between two atoms when an atomic orbital on one atom **overlaps** with an atomic orbital on the other and a pair of electrons with paired spins is shared between the overlapping orbitals. In general, the better the overlap of the orbitals, the stronger the bond. A given atomic orbital can only overlap with one other orbital on a different atom, so a given atomic orbital can only form one bond with an orbital on one other atom.

Hybrid Atomic Orbitals. **Hybrid orbitals** are formed by mixing pure s, p, and d orbitals. Hybrid orbitals overlap better with other orbitals than the pure atomic orbitals from which they are formed, so bonds formed by hybrid orbitals are stronger than those formed by ordinary atomic orbitals. **Sigma bonds** (σ bonds) are formed by the following kinds of orbital overlap: s–s, s–p, end-to-end p–p, and overlap of hybrid orbitals. Sigma bonds allow free rotation around the bond axis. The side-by-side overlap of p orbitals produces a **pi bond** (π bond). Pi bonds do not permit free rotation around the bond axis because such a rotation involves bond breaking. In complex molecules, the basic molecular framework is built with σ bonds. A double bond consists of one σ bond and one π bond. A triple bond consists of one σ bond and two π bonds.

Molecular Orbital (MO) Theory. This theory begins with the supposition that molecules are similar to atoms, except they have more than one positive center. They are treated as collections of nuclei and electrons, with the electrons of the molecule distributed among **molecular orbitals** of different energies. Molecular orbitals can spread over two or more nuclei, and can be considered to be formed by the constructive and destructive interference of the overlapping electron waves corresponding to the atomic orbitals of the atoms in the molecule. **Bonding MOs** concentrate electron density between nuclei; **antibonding MOs** remove electron density from between nuclei. **Nonbonding MOs** do not affect the energy of the molecule. The rules for the filling of MOs are the same as those for atomic orbitals. The ability of MO theory to describe **delocalized orbitals** avoids the need for resonance theory. Delocalization of bonds leads to a lowering of the energy by an amount called the **delocalization energy** and produces more stable molecular structures.

TOOLS FOR PROBLEM SOLVING

In this chapter you learned to apply the following concepts as tools in solving problems related to chemical bonding and molecular structure. Study each one carefully so that you know what each is used for. When faced with solving a problem, recall what each tool does and consider whether it will be helpful in finding a solution. This will aid you in selecting the tools you need.

Basic molecular shapes *(pages 339–341)* You need an understanding of the five basic geometries discussed. Practice drawing them and be sure you know their names.

VSEPR model *(page 341)* Electron groups repel each other and arrange themselves in the valence shell of an atom to yield minimum repulsions, which is what determines the shape of the molecule. This tool serves as the foundation for understanding the VSEPR model.

Molecular shape and polarity *(page 351)* We can use molecular shape to determine whether a molecule will be polar or nonpolar. Refer to the summary on page 351.

Criteria for bond formation according to VB theory *(page 352)* A bond requires overlap of two orbitals sharing two electrons with paired spins. Both orbitals can be half-filled, or one can be filled and the other empty. We use these criteria to establish which orbitals atoms use when bonds are formed.

The VSEPR model *(page 341)* **and orientations of hybrid orbitals** *(page 356)* These tools are interrelated. Lewis structures permit us to use the VSEPR model to predict molecular shape, which then allows us to select the correct hybrid orbitals for the valence bond description of bonding. After forming the Lewis structure, we determine the number of domains, from which we derive the structure of the molecule or ion. A convenient way of doing this is to describe the VSEPR structure symbolically. In doing this we represent the central atom by M, the atoms attached to the central atom by X, and lone pairs by E. We can then signify the number of bonding and nonbonding domains around M as a formula MX_nE_m, where n is the number of bonding domains and m is the number of nonbonding domains. The resulting formula is related to the structure of the molecule or ion, and to the hybrid orbitals used by the central atom, as shown below. Practice sketching the structures, associating them with the appropriate generalized formula MX_nE_m, and using the structures to select the appropriate set of hybrid orbitals.

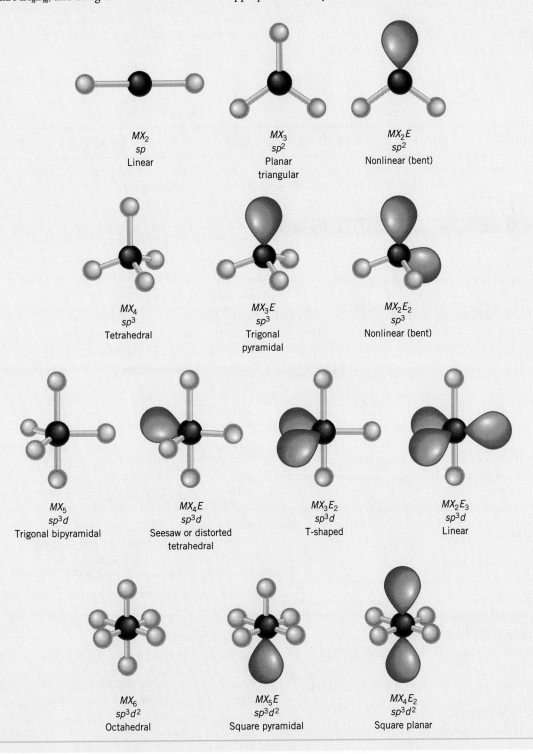

MX_2
sp
Linear

MX_3
sp^2
Planar
triangular

MX_2E
sp^2
Nonlinear (bent)

MX_4
sp^3
Tetrahedral

MX_3E
sp^3
Trigonal
pyramidal

MX_2E_2
sp^3
Nonlinear (bent)

MX_5
sp^3d
Trigonal bipyramidal

MX_4E
sp^3d
Seesaw or distorted
tetrahedral

MX_3E_2
sp^3d
T-shaped

MX_2E_3
sp^3d
Linear

MX_6
sp^3d^2
Octahedral

MX_5E
sp^3d^2
Square pyramidal

MX_4E_2
sp^3d^2
Square planar

Criteria for determining numbers of σ and π bonds and hybridization *(page 370)* The Lewis structure for a polyatomic molecule lets us apply these criteria to determine how many σ and π bonds are between atoms and the kind of hybrid orbitals each atom uses. Remember that the shape of the molecule is determined by the framework of σ bonds, with π bonds used in double and triple bonds.

Calculating bond order in MO theory *(page 373)*

$$\text{Bond order} = \frac{(\text{number of bonding } e^-) - (\text{number of antibonding } e^-)}{2 \text{ electrons/bond}}$$

How electrons fill molecular orbitals *(page 375)* Electrons populate MOs following the same rules that apply to atomic orbitals in an atom. Use this tool to obtain the correct distribution of electrons over the MOs of a molecule or ion.

QUESTIONS, PROBLEMS, AND EXERCISES

Answers to problems whose numbers are printed in color are given in Appendix B. More challenging problems are marked with asterisks. ILW = Interactive Learningware solution is available at www.wiley.com/college/brady. OH = an Office Hours video is available for this problem.

REVIEW QUESTIONS

Shapes of Molecules

9.1 Sketch the following molecular shapes and give the various bond angles in the structure: (a) planar triangular, (b) tetrahedral, and (c) octahedral.

9.2 Sketch the following molecular shapes and give the bond angles in the structure: (a) linear, and (b) trigonal bipyramidal.

VSEPR Theory

9.3 What is the underlying principle on which the VSEPR model is based?

9.4 What is an *electron domain?*

9.5 How many bonding domains and how many nonbonding domains are there in a molecule of formaldehyde, HCHO?

9.6 Sketch the following molecular shapes and give the various bond angles in the structures: (a) T-shaped, (b) seesaw-shaped, and (c) square pyramidal.

9.7 What arrangements of domains around an atom are expected when there are (a) three domains, (b) six domains, (c) four domains, or (d) five domains?

Predicting Molecular Polarity

9.8 Why is it useful to know the polarities of molecules?

9.9 How do we indicate a bond dipole when we draw the structure of a molecule?

9.10 Are all dissymmetric molecules polar?

9.11 What condition must be met if a molecule having polar bonds is to be nonpolar?

9.12 Use a drawing to show why the SO_2 molecule is polar.

Modern Bonding Theories

9.13 What is the theoretical basis of both valence bond (VB) theory and molecular orbital (MO) theory?

9.14 What shortcomings of Lewis structures and VSEPR theory do VB and MO theories attempt to overcome?

9.15 What is the main difference in the way VB and MO theories view the bonds in a molecule?

Valence Bond Theory

9.16 What is meant by *orbital overlap?*

9.17 What are the main principles of the valence bond theory?

9.18 Use sketches of orbitals to describe how VB theory would explain the formation of the H—Br bond in hydrogen bromide.

Hybrid Orbitals

9.19 Why do atoms usually prefer to use hybrid orbitals for bonding rather than pure atomic orbitals?

9.20 Sketch figures that illustrate the directional properties of the following hybrid orbitals: (a) sp, (b) sp^2, (c) sp^3, (d) sp^3d, and (e) sp^3d^2.

9.21 Why do Period 2 elements never use sp^3d or sp^3d^2 hybrid orbitals for bond formation?

9.22 What relationship is there, if any, between Lewis structures and the valence bond descriptions of molecules?

9.23 How can the VSEPR model be used to predict the hybridization of an atom in a molecule?

9.24 If the central oxygen in the water molecule did not use sp^3 hybridized orbitals (or orbitals of any other kind of hybridization), what would be the expected bond angle in H_2O (assuming no angle-spreading force)?

9.25 Using orbital diagrams, describe how sp^3 hybridization occurs in each atom: (a) carbon, (b) nitrogen, and (c) oxygen. If these elements use sp^3 hybrid orbitals to form bonds, how many lone pairs of electrons would be found on each?

9.26 Sketch the way the orbitals overlap to form the bonds in each of the following: (a) CH_4, (b) NH_3, and (c) H_2O. (Assume the central atom uses hybrid orbitals.)

9.27 We explained the bond angles of 107° in NH_3 by using sp^3 hybridization of the central nitrogen atom. Had the original unhybridized p orbitals of the nitrogen been used to overlap with $1s$ orbitals of each hydrogen, what would have been the H—N—H bond angles? Explain.

9.28 Using sketches of orbitals and orbital diagrams, describe sp^2 hybridization at (a) boron and (b) carbon.

9.29 What two basic shapes have hybridizations that include d orbitals?

Coordinate Covalent Bonds and VB Theory

9.30 The ammonia molecule, NH_3, can combine with a hydrogen ion, H^+ (which has an empty $1s$ orbital), to form the ammonium ion, NH_4^+. (This is how ammonia can neutralize an acid and therefore function as a base.) Sketch the geometry of the ammonium ion, indicating the bond angles.

9.31 How does the geometry around B and O change in the following reaction? How does the hybridization of each atom change?

$$\text{H} \quad :\ddot{\text{C}}\text{l}: \qquad\qquad \text{H} \quad :\ddot{\text{C}}\text{l}:$$
$$\text{H}-\ddot{\text{O}}: \ + \ \text{B}-\ddot{\text{C}}\text{l}: \ \longrightarrow \ \text{H}-\ddot{\text{O}}-\text{B}-\ddot{\text{C}}\text{l}:$$
$$\qquad\qquad :\ddot{\text{C}}\text{l}: \qquad\qquad\qquad :\ddot{\text{C}}\text{l}:$$

Multiple Bonds and Hybrid Orbitals

9.32 How do σ and π bonds differ?

9.33 Why can free rotation occur easily around a σ-bond axis but not around a π-bond axis?

9.34 Using sketches, describe the bonds and bond angles in ethylene, C_2H_4.

9.35 Sketch the way the bonds form in acetylene, C_2H_2.

9.36 How does VB theory treat the benzene molecule? (Draw sketches describing the orbital overlaps and the bond angles.)

Molecular Orbital Theory

9.37 Why is the higher-energy MO in H_2 called an antibonding orbital?

9.38 Using a sketch, describe the two lowest energy MOs of H_2 and their relationship to their parent atomic orbitals.

9.39 Explain why He_2 does not exist but H_2 does.

9.40 How does MO theory account for the paramagnetism of O_2?

9.41 On the basis of MO theory, explain why Li_2 molecules can exist but Be_2 molecules cannot. Could the ion Be_2^+ exist?

9.42 What are the bond orders in (a) O_2^+, (b) O_2^-, and (c) C_2^+?

9.43 What relationship is there between bond order and bond energy?

9.44 Sketch the shapes of the π_{2p_y} and $\pi_{2p_y}^*$ MOs.

9.45 What is a *delocalized MO*?

9.46 What problem encountered by VB theory does MO theory avoid by delocalized bonding?

9.47 Draw the representation of the benzene molecule that indicates its delocalized π system.

9.48 What effect does delocalization have on the stability of the electronic structure of a molecule?

9.49 What is delocalization energy? How is it related to resonance energy?

REVIEW PROBLEMS

9.50 Predict the shapes (a) NH_2^-, (b) CO_3^{2-}, (c) IF_3, (d) Br_3^-, and (e) GaH_3.

9.51 Predict the shapes of (a) SF_3^+, (b) NO_3^-, (c) SO_4^{2-}, (d) O_3, and (e) N_2O.

ILW 9.52 Predict the shapes of (a) FCl_2^+, (b) AsF_5, (c) AsF_3, (d) SbH_3, and (e) SeO_2.

9.53 Predict the shapes of (a) TeF_4, (b) $SbCl_6^-$, (c) NO_2^-, (d) PCl_4^+, and (e) PO_4^{3-}.

9.54 Predict the shapes of (a) IO_4^-, (b) ICl_4^-, (c) TeF_6, (d) SiO_4^{4-}, and (e) ICl_2^-.

9.55 Predict the shapes of (a) CS_2, (b) BrF_4^-, (c) ICl_3, (d) ClO_3^-, and (e) SeO_3.

9.56 Which of the following has a shape described by the figure below? (a) IO_4^-, (b) ICl_4^-, (c) $SnCl_4$, (d) BrF_4^+

9.57 Which of the following has a shape described by the figure below? (a) BrF_3, (b) PF_3, (c) NO_3^-, (d) SCl_3^-

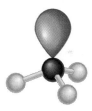

9.58 Acetylene, a gas used in welding torches, has the Lewis structure H—C≡C—H. What would you expect the H—C—C bond angle to be in this molecule?

OH 9.59 Ethylene, a gas used to ripen tomatoes artificially, has the Lewis structure

$$\begin{array}{cc} \text{H} & \text{H} \\ | & | \\ \text{H}-\text{C} & =\text{C}-\text{H} \end{array}$$

What would you expect the H—C—H and H—C—C bond angles to be in this molecule? (Caution: Don't be fooled by the way the structure is drawn here.)

9.60 Predict the bond angle for each of the following. (a) Cl_2O, (b) H_2O, (c) SO_2, (d) I_3^-, (e) NH_2^-

9.61 Predict the bond angle for each of the following. (a) HOCl, (b) PH_2^-, (c) OCN^-, (d) O_3, (e) SnF_2

Predicting Molecular Polarity

ILW 9.62 Which of the following molecules would be expected to be polar? (a) HBr, (b) $POCl_3$, (c) CH_2O, (d) $SnCl_4$, (e) $SbCl_5$

9.63 Which of the following molecules would be expected to be polar? (a) PBr_3, (b) SO_3, (c) $AsCl_3$, (d) ClF_3, (e) BCl_3

9.64 Which of the following molecules or ions would be expected to have a net dipole moment? (a) ClNO, (b) XeF_3^+, (c) $SeBr_4$, (d) NO, (e) NO_2

9.65 Which of the following molecules or ions would be expected to have a net dipole moment? (a) H_2S, (b) BeH_2, (c) SCN^-, (d) CN^-, (e) $BrCl_3$

OH 9.66 Explain why SF_6 is nonpolar, but SF_5Br is polar.

9.67 Explain why CH_3Cl is polar, but CCl_4 is not.

Valence Bond Theory

9.68 Hydrogen selenide is one of nature's most foul-smelling substances. Molecules of H_2Se have H—Se—H bond angles very close to 90°. How would VB theory explain the bonding in H_2Se? Use sketches of orbitals to show how the bonds are formed. Illustrate with appropriate orbital diagrams as well.

OH 9.69 Use sketches of orbitals to show how VB theory explains the bonding in the F_2 molecule. Illustrate with appropriate orbital diagrams as well.

Hybrid Orbitals

9.70 Use orbital diagrams to explain how the beryllium chloride molecule is formed. What kind of hybrid orbitals does beryllium use in this molecule?

9.71 Use orbital diagrams to describe the bonding in (a) tin tetrachloride and (b) antimony pentachloride. Be sure to indicate hybrid orbital formation.

OH 9.72 Draw Lewis structures for the following and use the geometry predicted by the VSEPR model to determine what kind of hybrid orbitals the central atom uses in bond formation: (a) ClO_3^-, (b) SO_3, and (c) OF_2.

9.73 Draw Lewis structures for the following and use the geometry predicted by the VSEPR model to determine what kind of hybrid orbitals the central atom uses in bond formation: (a) $SbCl_6^-$, (b) $BrCl_3$, and (c) XeF_4.

9.74 Use the VSEPR model to help you describe the bonding in the following molecules according to VB theory: (a) arsenic trichloride and (b) chlorine trifluoride. Use orbital diagrams for the central atom to show how hybridization occurs.

9.75 Use the VSEPR model to help you describe the bonding in the following molecules according to VB theory: (a) antimony pentafluoride and (b) selenium dichloride. Use orbital diagrams for the central atom to show how hybridization occurs.

Coordinate Covalent Bonds and VB Theory

9.76 Use orbital diagrams to show that the bonding in SbF_6^- involves the formation of a coordinate covalent bond.

9.77 What kind of hybrid orbitals are used by tin in $SnCl_6^{2-}$? Draw the orbital diagram for Sn in $SnCl_6^{2-}$. What is the geometry of $SnCl_6^{2-}$?

Multiple Bonding and Valence Bond Theory

9.78 A nitrogen atom can undergo sp^2 hybridization when it becomes part of a carbon–nitrogen double bond, as in H_2C=NH.

(a) Using a sketch, show the electron configuration of sp^2 hybridized nitrogen just before the overlapping occurs to make the double bond.
(b) Using sketches (and the analogy to the double bond in C_2H_4), describe the two bonds of the carbon–nitrogen double bond.
(c) Describe the geometry of H_2C=NH (using a sketch that shows all expected bond angles).

9.79 A nitrogen atom can undergo sp hybridization and then become joined to carbon by a triple bond to give the structural unit —C≡N:. This triple bond consists of one σ bond and two π bonds.

(a) Write the orbital diagram for sp hybridized nitrogen as it would look before any bonds form.
(b) Using the carbon–carbon triple bond as the analogy, and drawing pictures to show which atomic orbitals overlap with which, show how the three bonds of the triple bond in —C≡N: form.
(c) Again using sketches, describe all the bonds in hydrogen cyanide, H—C≡N:.
(d) What is the likeliest H—C—N bond angle in HCN?

9.80 Tetrachloroethylene, a common dry-cleaning solvent, has the formula C_2Cl_4. Its structure is

Use the electron domain and VB theories to describe the bonding in this molecule. What are the expected bond angles?

9.81 Phosgene, $COCl_2$, was used as a war gas during World War I. It reacts with moisture in the lungs of its victims to form CO_2 and gaseous HCl, which cause the lungs to fill with fluid. Phosgene is a simple molecule having the structure

Describe the bonding in this molecule using VB theory.

9.82 What kind of hybrid orbitals do the numbered atoms use in the following molecule?

OH 9.83 What kinds of bonds (σ, π) are found in the numbered bonds in the following molecule?

Molecular Orbital Theory

ILW 9.84 Use the MO energy diagram to predict which in each pair
OH has the greater bond energy: (a) O_2 or O_2^+, (b) O_2 or O_2^-, and (c) N_2 or N_2^+.

9.85 Assume that in the NO molecule the molecular orbital energy level sequence is similar to that for O_2. What happens to the NO bond length when an electron is removed from NO to give NO^+?

9.86 In each of the following pairs, which substance has the longer bond length? (a) N_2 or N_2^+, (b) NO or NO^+, (c) O_2 or O_2^-

9.87 Which of the following molecules or ions are paramagnetic? (a) O_2^+, (b) O_2, (c) O_2^-, (d) NO, (e) N_2.

9.88 Construct the MO energy level diagram for the OH molecule assuming it is similar to that for HF. How many electrons are in (a) bonding MOs and (b) nonbonding MOs? What is the net bond order in the molecule?

9.89 If boron and nitrogen were to form a molecule with the formula BN, what would its MO energy level diagram look like, given that the energies of the $2p$ orbitals of nitrogen are lower than those of boron? If Figure 9.38*a* applies, would the molecule be paramagnetic or diamagnetic? What is the net bond order in the molecule?

ADDITIONAL EXERCISES

OH 9.90 Formaldehyde has the Lewis structure

$$H-\overset{\overset{\displaystyle H}{|}}{C}=\overset{..}{\underset{..}{O}}$$

What would you predict its shape to be?

9.91 The molecule XCl_3 is pyramidal. In which group in the periodic table is element X found? If the molecule were planar triangular, in which group would X be found? If the molecule were T-shaped, in which group would X be found? Why is it unlikely that element X is in Group VI?

9.92 Antimony forms a compound with hydrogen that is called stibine. Its formula is SbH_3 and the $H-Sb-H$ bond angles are 91.3°. Which kinds of orbitals does Sb most likely use to form the Sb—H bonds, pure p orbitals or hybrid orbitals? Explain your reasoning.

9.93 Describe the changes in molecular geometry and hybridization that take place during the following reactions:
(a) $BF_3 + F^- \longrightarrow BF_4^-$
(b) $PCl_5 + Cl^- \longrightarrow PCl_6^-$
(c) $ICl_3 + Cl^- \longrightarrow ICl_4^-$
(d) $PCl_3 + Cl_2 \longrightarrow PCl_5$
(e) $C_2H_2 + H_2 \longrightarrow C_2H_4$

9.94 Which one of the following five diagrams best represents the structure of $BrCl_4^+$?

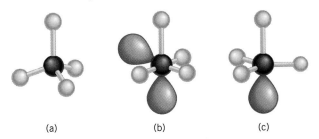

(a)   (b)   (c)

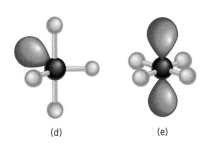

(d)   (e)

OH 9.95 Cyclopropane is a triangular molecule with C—C—C bond angles of 60°. Explain why the σ bonds joining carbon atoms in cyclopropane are weaker than the carbon–carbon σ bonds in the noncyclic propane.

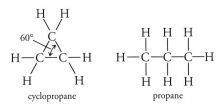

cyclopropane   propane

9.96 Phosphorus trifluoride, PF_3, has $F-P-F$ bond angles of 97.8°.
(a) How would VB theory use hybrid orbitals to explain these data?
(b) How would VB theory use unhybridized orbitals to account for these data?
(c) Do either of these models work very well?

9.97 A six-membered ring of carbons can hold a double bond but not a triple bond. Explain.

cyclohexene (exists)   cyclohexyne (unknown)

*9.98 There exists a hydrocarbon called butadiene, which has the molecular formula C_4H_6 and the structure

$$\underset{\underset{H}{|}}{\overset{\overset{H}{|}}{\underset{H}{\underset{|}{C}}}}=\underset{H}{\overset{H}{C}}$$

The $C=C$ bond lengths are 134 pm (about what is expected for a carbon–carbon double bond), but the $C-C$ bond length in this molecule is 147 pm, which is shorter than a normal $C-C$ single bond. The molecule is planar (i.e., all the atoms lie in the same plane).
(a) What kind of hybrid orbitals do the carbon atoms use in this molecule to form the carbon–carbon bonds?
(b) Between which pairs of carbon atoms do we expect to find sideways overlap of p orbitals (i.e., π-type p–p overlap)?
(c) On the basis of your answer to part (b), do you expect to find localized or delocalized π bonding in the carbon chain in this molecule?
(d) Based on your answer to part (c), explain why the center carbon–carbon bond is shorter than a carbon–carbon single bond.

*9.99 *The more electronegative are the atoms bonded to the central atom, the less are the repulsions between the electron pairs in the bonds.* On the basis of this statement, predict the most probable structure for the molecule PCl_3F_2. Do we expect the molecule to be polar or nonpolar?

*9.100 *A lone pair of electrons in the valence shell of an atom has a larger effective volume than a bonding electron pair. Lone pairs therefore repel other electron pairs more strongly than do bonding pairs.* On the basis of these statements, describe how the bond angles in TeF_4 and BrF_4^- deviate from those found in a trigonal bipyramid and an octahedron, respectively. Sketch the molecular shapes of TeF_4 and BrF_4^- and indicate these deviations on your drawing.

*9.101 *The two electron pairs in a double bond repel other electron pairs more than the single pair of electrons in a single bond.* On the basis of this statement, which bond angles should be larger in SO_2Cl_2, the $O-S-O$ bond angles or the $Cl-S-Cl$ bond angles? (In the molecule, sulfur is bonded to two oxygen atoms and two chlorine atoms. *Hint:* Assign formal charges and work with the best Lewis structure for the molecule.)

*9.102 *A hybrid orbital does not distribute electron density symmetrically around the nucleus of an atom. Therefore, a lone pair in a hybrid orbital contributes to the overall polarity of a molecule.* On the basis of these statements and the fact that NH_3 is a very polar molecule and NF_3 is a nearly nonpolar molecule, justify the notion that the lone pair of electrons in each of these molecules is held in an sp^3 hybrid orbital.

9.103 In a certain molecule, a p orbital overlaps with a d orbital as shown below. Which kind of bond is formed, σ or π? Explain your choice.

9.104 If we take the internuclear axis in a diatomic molecule to be the z axis, what kind of p orbital (p_x, p_y, or p_z) on one atom would have to overlap with a d_{xz} orbital on the other atom to give a pi bond?

9.105 The peroxynitrite ion, $OONO^-$, is a potent toxin formed in cells affected by diseases such as diabetes or atherosclerosis. Peroxynitrite ion can oxidize and destroy biomolecules crucial for the survival of the cell.

(a) Give the $O-O-N$ and $O-N-O$ bond angles in peroxynitrite ion.
(b) What is the hybridization of the N atom in peroxynitrite ion?
(c) Suggest why the peroxynitrite ion is expected to be much less stable than the nitrate ion, NO_3^-.

EXERCISES IN CRITICAL THINKING

9.106 Five basic molecular shapes were described for simple molecular structures containing a central atom bonded to various numbers of surrounding atoms. Can you suggest additional possible structures? Provide arguments about the likelihood that these other structures might actually exist.

9.107 Compare and contrast the concepts of *delocalization* and *resonance*.

9.108 Why doesn't a carbon–carbon quadruple bond exist?

9.109 What might the structure of the iodine heptafluoride molecule be? If you can think of more than one possible structure, which is likely to be of lowest energy based on the VSEPR model?

9.110 The $F-F$ bond is weaker than the $Cl-Cl$ bond. How might the lone pairs on the atoms in the molecules be responsible for this?

9.111 Molecular orbital theory predicts the existence of antibonding molecular orbitals. How do antibonding electrons affect the stability in a molecule?

9.112 The structure of the diborane molecule, B_2H_6, is sometimes drawn as

There are not enough valence electrons in the molecule to form eight single bonds, which is what the structure implies. Assuming that the boron atoms use sp^3 hybrid orbitals, suggest a way that hydrogen $1s$ orbitals can be involved in forming delocalized molecular orbitals that bridge the two boron atoms. Use diagrams to illustrate your answer. What would be the average bond order in the bridging bonds?

Once again you have an opportunity to test your understanding of concepts, your knowledge of scientific terms, and your problem-solving skills. Read through the following questions carefully, and answer each as fully as possible. When necessary, review topics that give you difficulty. When you are able to answer these questions correctly, you are ready to study the next group of chapters.

1. What are the three principal particles that make up the atom? On the atomic mass scale, what are their approximate masses? What are their electrical charges?

2. A beam of green light has a wavelength of 500 nm. What is the frequency of this light? What is the energy, in joules, of one photon of this light? What is the energy, in joules, of one mole of photons of this light? Would blue light have more or less energy per photon than this light?

3. Arrange the following kinds of electromagnetic radiation in order of increasing frequency: X rays, blue light, radio waves, gamma rays, microwaves, red light, infrared light, ultraviolet light.

4. What is a *continuous spectrum*? How does it differ from an *atomic spectrum*?

5. What experimental evidence is there that matter has wavelike properties?

6. What is the difference between a *traveling wave* and a *standing wave*? What is a *node*?

7. How is the energy of an electron related to the number of nodes in its electron wave?

8. What is a *wave function*? What Greek letter is usually used to represent a wave function? What word do we use to refer to an electron wave in an atom?

9. What are the quantum numbers of the electrons in the valence shells of (a) sulfur, (b) strontium, (c) lead, (d) bromine, and (e) boron?

10. If a given shell has $n = 4$, which kinds of subshells (*s*, *p*, etc.) does it have? What is the maximum number of electrons that could populate this shell?

11. Use the periodic table to predict the electron configurations of (a) tin, (b) germanium, (c) silicon, (d) lead, and (e) nickel.

12. Give the electron configurations of the ions (a) Pb^{2+}, (b) Pb^{4+}, (c) S^{2-}, (d) Fe^{3+}, and (e) Zn^{2+}.

13. What causes an atom, molecule, or ion to be paramagnetic? Which of the ions in the preceding question are paramagnetic? What term describes the magnetic properties of the others?

14. Give the shorthand electron configurations of (a) Ni, (b) Cr, (c) Sr, (d) Sb, and (e) Po.

15. Define *ionization energy* and *electron affinity*. In terms of these properties, which kinds of elements tend to react to form ionic compounds?

16. In general, the second ionization energy of an atom is larger than the first, the third is larger than the second, and so on. Why?

17. Which of the following elements has the largest difference between its second and third ionization energy? Explain your choice.
    (a) Li   (b) Be   (c) B   (d) C

18. Which of the following processes are endothermic?
    (a) $P^-(g) + e^- \longrightarrow P^{2-}(g)$
    (b) $Fe^{3+}(g) + e^- \longrightarrow Fe^{2+}(g)$

(c) $Cl(g) + e^- \longrightarrow Cl^-(g)$
(d) $S(g) + 2e^- \longrightarrow S^{2-}(g)$

19. Sketch the shape of (a) an *s* orbital, (b) a *p* orbital, and (c) the $3d_{xz}$ orbital.

20. What is meant by the term *electron density*?

21. Give orbital diagrams for the valence shells of selenium and thallium.

22. Which ion would be larger? (a) Fe^{2+} or Fe^{3+}, (b) O^- or O^{2-}

23. Which of the following pairs of elements would be expected to form ionic compounds? (a) Br and F, (b) H and P, (c) Ca and F.

24. Use Lewis symbols to diagram the reaction of calcium with sulfur to form CaS.

25. Draw Lewis structures for (a) SbH_3, (b) IF_3, (c) $HClO_2$, (d) C_2^{2-}, (e) AsF_5, (f) O_2^{2-}, (g) HCO_3^-, (h) TeF_6, and (i) HNO_3.

26. Use the VSEPR theory to predict the shapes of (a) $SbCl_3$, (b) IF_5, (c) AsH_3, (d) BrF_2, and (e) OF_2.

27. What kinds of hybrid orbitals are used by the central atom in each of the species in the preceding question?

28. Referring to your answers to Questions 25 and 26, which of the following molecules would be nonpolar? SbH_3, IF_3, AsF_5, $SbCl_3$, OF_2

29. The oxalate ion has the following arrangement of atoms.

$$
\begin{array}{cc}
O & O \\
C & C \\
O & O \\
\end{array}
$$

Draw all of its resonance structures.

30. What is meant by the term *overlap of orbitals*?

31. What are *sigma bonds*? What are *pi bonds*? How are sigma and pi bonds used to explain the formation of double and triple bonds?

32. Some resonance structures that can be drawn for carbon dioxide are shown below.

$$\ddot{O}=C=\ddot{O} \quad \quad :O\equiv C-\ddot{O}: \quad \quad :\ddot{O}-C\equiv O:$$
$$\text{I} \quad \quad \quad \text{II} \quad \quad \quad \text{III}$$

Assign formal charges to the atoms in these structures. Explain why Structure I is the preferred structure.

33. Ozone, O_3, consists of a chain of three oxygen atoms.
    (a) Draw the two resonance structures for ozone that obey the octet rule.
    (b) Based on your answer to (a), is the molecule linear or nonlinear?
    (c) Assign formal charges to the atoms in the resonance structures you have drawn in part (a).
    (d) On the basis of your answers to (b) and (c), explain why ozone is a polar molecule even though it is composed of three atoms that have identical electronegativities.

34. Why, on the basis of formal charges and relative electronegativities, is it more reasonable to expect the structure of $POCl_3$ to be the one on the left rather than the one on the right?

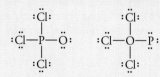

Is either of these the "best" Lewis structure that can be drawn for this molecule?

35. A certain element X was found to form three compounds with chlorine having the formulas XCl_2, XCl_4, and XCl_6. One of its oxides has the formula XO_3, and X reacts with sodium to form the compound Na_2X.

(a) Is X a metal or a nonmetal?

(b) In which group in the periodic table is X located?

(c) In which periods in the periodic table could X possibly be located?

(d) Draw Lewis structures for XCl_2, XCl_4, XCl_6, and XO_3. (Where possible, follow the octet rule.) Which has multiple bonding?

(e) What do we expect the molecular structures of XCl_2, XCl_4, XCl_6, and XO_3 to be? Which are polar molecules?

(f) The element X also forms the oxide XO_2. Draw a Lewis structure for XO_2 that obeys the octet rule.

(g) Assign formal charges to the atoms in the Lewis structures for XO_2 and XO_3 drawn for parts (d) and (f).

(h) What kinds of hybrid orbitals would X use for bonding in XCl_4 and XCl_6?

(i) If X were to form a compound with aluminum, what would be its formula?

(j) Which compound of X would have the more ionic bonds, Na_2X or MgX?

(k) If X were in Period 5, what would be the electron configuration of its valence shell?

36. Where in the periodic table are the very reactive metals located? Where are the least reactive ones located?

37. What are bonding and antibonding molecular orbitals? How do they differ in shape and energy?

38. What is a *delocalized molecular orbital*? How does molecular orbital theory avoid the concept of resonance?

39. Predict the shapes of the following molecules and ions:

(a) PF_3 (c) PF_6^-

(b) PF_4^+ (d) PF_5

40. Which of the substances in the preceding question have a net dipole moment?

41. According to the VSEPR model, which of the following best illustrates the structure of the $AsCl_3^{2-}$ ion?

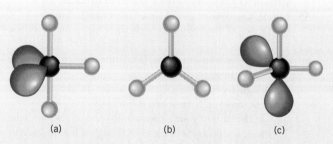

(a)   (b)   (c)

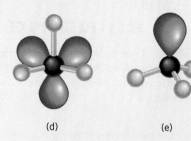

(d)   (e)

42. Describe how molecular orbital theory explains the bonding in the oxygen molecule.

43. Consider the following statements: (1) Fe^{2+} is easily oxidized to Fe^{3+}, and (2) Mn^{2+} is difficult to oxidize to Mn^{3+}. On the basis of the electron configurations of the ions, explain the difference in ease of oxidation.

44. For each of the following pairs of compounds, which has the larger lattice energy: (a) MgO or NaCl, (b) MgO or BeO, (c) NaI or NaF, and (d) MgO or CaS? Explain your choices.

45. The melting point of Al_2O_3 is much higher than the melting point of NaCl. On the basis of lattice energies, explain why this is so.

46. Why is the change in atomic size, going from one element to the next in a period, smaller among the transition elements than among the representative elements?

47. The VSEPR model predicts the structure below for a certain molecule. Which kind of hybrid orbitals does the central atom in the molecule use to form its covalent bonds?

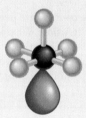

48. Which kind of bond, σ or π, is produced by the overlap of d orbitals pictured below?

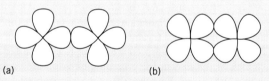

(a)   (b)

49. The following is the chemical structure of acetaminophen, the painkiller in Tylenol.

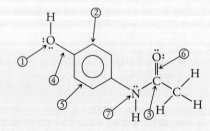

What kinds of hybrid orbitals are used by atoms 1, 2, 3, and 7? How many σ and π bonds are in bonds 4 and 6? What is the average bond order of bond 5?

10 PROPERTIES OF GASES

A cool summer morning provides the ideal conditions for hot-air balloon enthusiasts. Propane heaters inflate each balloon, no matter what shape the creative designers choose. Balloonists then control these brightly colored craft using the properties of gases introduced in this chapter. *(Raymond Watt/ Albuquerque International Balloon Fiesta, Inc.)*

CHAPTER OUTLINE

THIS CHAPTER IN CONTEXT In the preceding chapters we've discussed the chemical properties of a variety of different substances. We've also studied the kinds of forces (chemical bonds) that hold molecular and ionic substances together and their three-dimensional structures. In fact, it is the nature of the chemical bonds that dictates chemical properties and it is the five simple structures that are used repeatedly to create fantastic molecules such as DNA and modern plastics. But this is only part of the description of matter as we know it. Another important topic concerns the interaction of one molecule with another without a chemical reaction occurring. These interactions are *physical properties* that are macroscopic manifestations of atomic-scale interactions between molecules, atoms, and ions. These interactions cause phospholipids to arrange themselves into a cell membrane. They also hold DNA together in the famous double helix while allowing the DNA to "unzip" to replicate in the life process. These interactions also explain something as simple as why your pancake syrup is thick when cold but thins out when warmed. The next few chapters will reveal the scientific principles behind why matter acts as it does, even in the absence of a chemical reaction. With this chapter we begin a systematic study of the physical properties of materials, including the factors that govern the behavior of gases, liquids, and solids. We study gases first because they are the easiest to understand and their behavior will help explain some of the properties of liquids and solids in the next chapter.

We live in a mixture of gases called the earth's atmosphere. Through everyday experience, you have become familiar with many of the properties that gases have. Our goal in this chapter is to refine this understanding in terms of the physical laws that govern the way gases behave. You will also learn how this behavior is interpreted in terms of the way we view gases at a molecular level. In our discussions we will describe how the energy concepts, first introduced to you in Chapter 6, provide an explanation of the gas laws. Finally, you will learn how a close examination of gas properties furnishes clues about molecular size and the attractions that exist between molecules.

10.1 | FAMILIAR PROPERTIES OF GASES CAN BE EXPLAINED AT THE MOLECULAR LEVEL

For a long time, early scientists didn't recognize the existence of gases as examples of matter. Of course, we now understand that gases are composed of chemical substances that exist in one of the three common states of matter. The reason for the early confusion is that the physical properties of gases differ so much from those of liquids and solids. Consider water, for example. We can see and feel it as a liquid, but it seems to disappear when it evaporates and surrounds us as water vapor. With this in mind, let's examine some of the properties of gaseous substances to look for clues that suggest the nature of gases when viewed at a molecular level.

The most common gas familiar to people is air. (Actually, air is a mixture, but that doesn't matter much when it comes to the physical properties of gases.) Because you've grown up surrounded by gas, you already are aware of many properties that gases have. Let's look at two of them.

☐ Air is roughly 21% O_2 and 79% N_2, but it has traces of several other gases.

Because air has so little weight for a given volume, it makes things filled with air float, much to the relief of the occupants of an inflatable life raft. (*Courtesy U.S. Air Force photo by K.L. Kibrell.*)

- You can wave your hand through air with little resistance. (Compare that with waving your hand through a tub filled with water.)
- The air in a bottle has little weight to it, so if a bottle of air is submerged under water and released, it quickly bobs to the surface.

Both of these observations suggest that a given volume of air doesn't have much matter in it. (We can express this by saying that air has a low density.) What else do you know about gases?

- Gases can be compressed. Inflating a tire involves pushing more and more air into the same container (the tire). This behavior is a lot different from liquids; you can't squeeze more water into an already filled bottle.
- Gases exert a pressure. Whenever you inflate a balloon you have an experience with gas pressure, and the "feel" of a balloon suggests that the pressure acts equally in all directions.
- The pressure of a gas depends on *how much* gas is confined. The *more air* you pump into a tire, the greater the pressure.
- Gases fill completely any container into which they're placed. You've never heard of half a bottle of air. If you put air in a container, it expands and fills the container's entire volume. (This is certainly a lot different than the behavior of liquids and solids.)
- Gases mix freely and quickly with each other. You've experienced this when you've smelled the perfume of someone passing by. The vapors of the person's perfume mix with and spread through the air.

- The pressure of a gas rises when its temperature is increased. That's why there's the warning "Do Not Incinerate" printed on aerosol cans. A sealed can, if made too hot, is in danger of exploding from the increased pressure.

Properties suggest a molecular model

The simple qualitative observations about gases described above suggest what gases must be like when viewed at a molecular level (Figure 10.1). The fact that there's so little matter in a given volume suggests that there is a lot of space between the individual molecules, especially when compared to liquids or solids. This would also explain why gases can be so easily compressed—squeezing a gas simply removes some of the empty space.

It also seems reasonable to believe that the molecules of a gas are moving around fairly rapidly. How else could we explain the travel of the molecules of a perfume so quickly through the air? Furthermore, if gas molecules didn't move, gravity would cause them to settle to the bottom of a container (which they don't do). And if gas molecules are moving, some must be colliding with the walls of the container, and the force of these tiny collisions would explain the pressure a gas exerts. It also explains why adding more gas increases the pressure; the more gas in the container, the more collisions with the walls, and the higher the pressure.

Finally, the fact that gas pressure rises with increasing temperature suggests that the molecules move faster with increasing temperature, because faster molecules would exert greater forces when they collide with the walls.

10.2 | PRESSURE IS A MEASURED PROPERTY OF GASES

As we discussed in Chapter 6, **pressure** *is force per unit area*, calculated by dividing the force by the area over which the force acts.

$$\text{Pressure} = \frac{\text{force}}{\text{area}}$$

The earth exerts a gravitational force on everything with mass that is on it or near it. What we call the *weight* of an object, like a book, is simply our measure of the force it exerts because gravity acts on it.

The pressure of the atmosphere is measured with a barometer

Earth's gravity pulls on the air mass of the atmosphere, causing it to cover the earth's surface like an invisible blanket. The molecules in the air collide with every object the air contacts, and by doing so, produce a pressure we call the *atmospheric pressure.*

At any particular location on the earth, the atmospheric pressure acts equally in all directions—up, down, and sideways. In fact, it presses against our bodies with a surprising amount of force, but we don't really feel it because the fluids in our bodies push back with equal pressure. We can observe atmospheric pressure, however, if we pump the air from a collapsible container such as the can in Figure 10.2. Before air is removed, the walls of the can experience atmospheric pressure equally inside and out. When some air is pumped out, however, the pressure inside decreases, making the atmospheric pressure outside of the can greater than the pressure inside. The net inward pressure is sufficiently great to make the can crumple.

To measure atmospheric pressure we use a device called a **barometer**. The simplest type is the *Torricelli barometer*[1] (Figure 10.3), which consists of a glass tube sealed at one end, 80 cm or more in length. To set up the apparatus, the tube is filled with mercury, capped,

Aerosol cans carry a warning about subjecting them to high temperatures because the internal pressure can become large enough to cause them to explode. *(Andy Washnik.)*

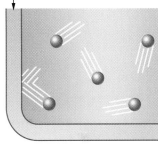

Container wall

Gas molecule = ●

FIG. 10.1 A gas viewed at the molecular level. Simple qualitative observations of the properties of gases lead us to conclude that a gas is composed of widely spaced molecules that are in constant motion. Collisions of molecules with the walls produce tiny forces that, when taken all together, are responsible for the gas pressure.

---

[1] In 1643 Evangelista Torricelli, an Italian mathematician, suggested an experiment, later performed by a colleague, that demonstrated that atmospheric pressure determines the height to which a fluid will rise in a tube inverted over the same liquid. This concept led to the development of the Torricelli barometer, which is named in his honor.

FIG. 10.2 The effect of an unbalanced pressure. (*a*) The pressure inside the can, P_{inside}, is the same as the atmospheric pressure outside, P_{atm}. The pressures are balanced; $P_{inside} = P_{atm}$. (*b*) When a vacuum pump reduces the pressure inside the can, P_{inside} is made less than P_{atm}, and the unbalanced outside pressure quickly and violently makes the can collapse. (*(a), (b) OPC, Inc.*)

(a)

(b)

FIG. 10.3 A Torricelli barometer. The apparatus is also called a mercury barometer. The height of the mercury column inside the tube is directly proportional to the atmospheric pressure. In the United States, weather reports often give the height of the mercury column in inches.

inverted, and then its capped end is immersed in a dish of mercury. When the cap is removed, some mercury runs out, but not all.[2] Atmospheric pressure, pushing on the surface of the mercury in the dish, holds most of the mercury in the tube. Opposing the atmosphere is the downward pressure caused by the weight of the mercury still inside the tube. When the two pressures become equal, no more mercury can run out, but a space inside the tube above the mercury level has been created having essentially no atmosphere; it's a *vacuum*.

The height of the mercury column, measured from the surface of the mercury in the dish, is directly proportional to atmospheric pressure. On days when the atmospheric pressure is high, more mercury is forced from the dish into the tube and the height of

[2] Today, mercury is kept as much as possible in closed containers. Although atoms of mercury do not readily escape into the gaseous state, mercury vapor is a dangerous poison.

the column increases. When the atmospheric pressure drops, during an approaching storm, for example, some mercury flows out of the tube and the height of the column decreases. Most people live where this height fluctuates between 730 and 760 mm.

Units of pressure include the pascal, atmosphere, and torr

At sea level, the height of the mercury column in a barometer fluctuates around a value of 760 mm. Some days it's a little higher, some a little lower, depending on the weather. The average pressure at sea level has long been used by scientists as a standard unit of pressure. The **standard atmosphere (atm)** was originally defined as the pressure needed to support a column of mercury 760 mm high measured at 0 °C.[3]

In the SI, the unit of pressure is the **pascal,** symbolized **Pa.** In SI units, the pascal is the ratio of force in *newtons* (N, the SI unit of force) to area in meters squared,

$$1 \ Pa = \frac{1 \ N}{1 \ m^2} = 1 \ N \ m^{-2}$$

It's a very small pressure; 1 Pa is approximately the pressure exerted by the weight of a lemon spread over an area of 1 m².

To bring the standard atmosphere unit in line with other SI units, it has been redefined in terms of the pascal as follows.

$$1 \ atm = 101{,}325 \ Pa \ (exactly)$$

A unit of pressure related to the pascal is the **bar,** which is defined as 100 kPa. Consequently, one bar is slightly smaller than one standard atmosphere (1 bar = 0.9869 atm). You may have heard the **millibar** unit (1 mb = 10^{-3} bar) used in weather reports describing pressures inside storms such as hurricanes. For example, the lowest atmospheric pressure at sea level ever observed in the Atlantic basin was 882 mb during Hurricane Wilma on October 19, 2005. The storm later weakened but still caused extensive damage as it crossed Florida.

For ordinary laboratory work, the pascal (or kilopascal) is not a conveniently measured unit. Usually we use a unit of pressure called the **torr** (named after Torricelli). The torr is defined as 1/760th of 1 atm.

$$1 \ torr = \tfrac{1}{760} \ atm$$

$$1 \ atm = 760 \ torr \ (exactly)$$

The torr is very close to the pressure that is able to support a column of mercury 1 mm high. In fact, the *millimeter of mercury* (abbreviated *mm Hg*) is often itself used as a pressure unit. Except when the most exacting measurements are being made, it is safe to use the relationship

$$1 \ torr = 1 \ mm \ Hg$$

Practice Exercise 1: Using the margin table above, determine the atmospheric pressure in pounds per square inch and inches of mercury when the barometer reads 730 mm Hg. (Hint: Recall your tools for converting units.)

Practice Exercise 2: The second lowest barometric pressure ever recorded at sea level in the western hemisphere was 888 mb during Hurricane Gilbert in 1988. What was the pressure in pascals and in torr?

[3] Because any metal, including mercury, expands or contracts as the temperature increases or decreases, the height of the mercury column varies with temperature (just like in a thermometer). Therefore, the definition of the standard atmosphere required that the temperature at which the mercury height is measured be specified.

■ In English units, one atmosphere of pressure is 14.7 lb in.$^{-2}$. This means that at sea level, each square inch of your body is experiencing a force of nearly 15 pounds.

■ Below are values of the standard atmosphere (atm) expressed in different pressure units. Studying the table will give you a feel for the sizes of the different units.

760 torr
101,325 Pa
101.325 kPa
1.013 bar
1013 mb
14.7 lb in.$^{-2}$
1.034 kg cm^{-2}

A satellite photo of Hurricane Wilma when it reached Category 5 strength, with sustained winds of 175 miles per hour in the eye wall. (*Terra MODIS data acquired by direct broadcast at the University of South Florida [Judd Taylor] Image processed at the "University of Wisconsin-Madison [Liam Gumley]".*)

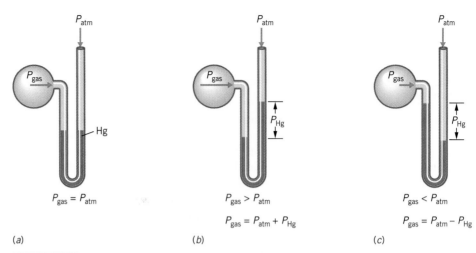

FIG. 10.4 **An open-end manometer.** The difference in the heights of the mercury in the two arms equals the pressure difference, in torr, between the atmospheric pressure, P_{atm}, and the pressure of the trapped gas, P_{gas}.

Manometers measure the pressures of trapped gas samples

Gases used as reactants or formed as products in chemical reactions are kept from escaping by using closed glassware. To measure pressures inside such vessels, a **manometer** is used. Two types are common, open-end and closed-end manometers.

☐ Advantages of mercury over other liquids are its low reactivity, its low melting point, and particularly its very high density, which permits short manometer tubes.

An **open-end manometer** consists of a U-tube partly filled with a liquid, usually mercury (see Figure 10.4). One arm of the U-tube is open to the atmosphere; the other is exposed to a container of some trapped gas. In Figure 10.4*a* the pressure in the flask is equal to the atmospheric pressure and the mercury levels are equal. Figure 10.4*b* illustrates a flask containing a gas at a pressure that is greater than the atmospheric pressure. In Figure 10.4*c*, the mercury level is higher in the arm connected to the container of gas, indicating that the pressure of the atmosphere must be higher than the gas pressure. When mercury is the liquid in the tube, the difference in the heights in the two arms, represented here as P_{Hg}, is equal to the difference between the pressure of the gas and the pressure of the atmosphere. By measuring P_{Hg} in millimeters, the value equals the pressure difference in torr. For the situation shown in Figure 10.4*b*, we would calculate the pressure of the trapped gas as

$$P_{gas} = P_{atm} + P_{Hg} \qquad (\text{when } P_{gas} > P_{Hg})$$

For the situation shown in Figure 10.4*c* we note that the pressure in the flask must be less than the atmospheric pressure or

$$P_{gas} = P_{atm} - P_{Hg} \qquad (\text{when } P_{gas} < P_{Hg})$$

Example 10.1 illustrates how the open-end manometer is used.

EXAMPLE 10.1
Measuring the Pressure of a Gas Using a Manometer

A student collected a gas in an apparatus connected to an open-end manometer, as illustrated in the figure in the margin. The difference in the heights of the mercury in the two columns was 10.2 cm and the atmospheric pressure was measured to be 756 torr. What was the pressure of the gas in the apparatus?

ANALYSIS: From the preceding discussion, we know we will use the atmospheric pressure and either add to it or subtract from it the difference in heights of the mercury columns, expressed in pressure units of torr. But which should we do? In a problem of this type, it is best to use some common sense (something that will help a lot in working problems involving gases).

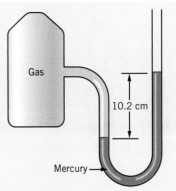

When we look at the diagram of the apparatus, we see that the mercury is pushed up into the arm of the manometer that's open to the air. Common sense tells us that the pressure of the gas inside must be larger than the pressure of the air outside. Therefore, we will add the pressure difference to the atmospheric pressure.

Finally, before we can do the arithmetic, we must be sure the pressure difference is calculated in torr. We know that 1 torr is equivalent to 1 mm Hg, but the difference in heights was measured in centimeters. Therefore, we have to convert 10.2 cm to millimeters.

SOLUTION: You probably know that 1 cm equals 10 mm. If so, that makes the conversion of the pressure difference easy:

$$10.2 \text{ cm Hg} = 102 \text{ mm Hg}$$

If you weren't sure of the conversion, you could always go back to the definitions of the SI prefixes. The two equalities we need are: $1 \text{ cm} = 10^{-2} \text{ m}$ and $1 \text{ mm} = 10^{-3} \text{ m}$. Ratios of these equalities provide the factor labels for the conversion as shown next.

$$10.2 \text{ cm} \times \frac{10^{-2} \text{ m}}{1 \text{ cm}} \times \frac{1 \text{ mm}}{10^{-3} \text{ m}} = 102 \text{ mm}$$

Either way, we find the difference in pressures to be 102 mm Hg, which is equivalent to 102 torr. To find the gas pressure, we add 102 torr to the atmospheric pressure.

$$\begin{aligned} P_{gas} &= P_{atm} + P_{Hg} \\ &= 756 \text{ torr} + 102 \text{ torr} \\ &= 858 \text{ torr} \end{aligned}$$

The gas pressure is 858 torr.

IS THE ANSWER REASONABLE? We can check our conversion of cm to mm by recalling that for the same measurement, the number of millimeters should always be larger than the measurement expressed in centimeters. We can also double-check that we've done the right *kind* of arithmetic (adding or subtracting). Look at the apparatus again. If the gas pressure were lower than atmospheric pressure, it would appear as though the atmosphere was pushing the mercury higher in the same way that the heavier child on a seesaw pushes his lighter friend higher. That's not what we see here. It almost looks like the gas is trying to push the mercury out of the manometer, so we conclude that the gas pressure must be higher than atmospheric pressure. That's exactly what we've found in our calculation, so we can feel confident we've solved the problem correctly.

Practice Exercise 3: A 55 cm high open-end manometer is filled with mercury so that each side has a height equal to 25 cm. If the atmospheric pressure is 770 torr on a given day, what are the approximate maximum and minimum pressures that this manometer can measure? (Hint: What is the maximum difference in mercury height for this manometer?)

Practice Exercise 4: In another experiment, it was found that the mercury level in the arm of the manometer attached to the container of gas was 10.7 cm higher than in the arm open to the air ($P_{atm} = 770$ torr). What was the pressure of the gas?

A closed-end manometer avoids the need to measure atmospheric pressure
A **closed-end manometer** (Figure 10.5) is made by sealing the arm that will be farthest from the gas sample and then filling the closed arm completely with mercury. When the gas pressures to be measured are expected to be small, the filled arm can be made short, making the entire apparatus compact. In this design, the mercury is pushed to the top of the closed arm when the open arm of the manometer is exposed to the atmosphere. When connected to a gas at a low pressure, however, the mercury level in the sealed arm will drop,

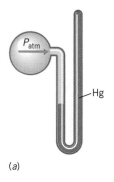

(a)

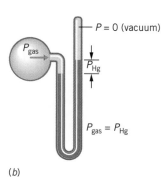

(b)

FIG. 10.5 A closed-end manometer for measuring gas pressures less than 1 atm or 760 torr. (a) When constructed, the tube is fully evacuated and then mercury is allowed to enter the tube to completely fill the closed arm. (b) When the tube is connected to a bulb containing a gas at low pressure, the difference in the mercury heights (P_{Hg}) equals the pressure, in torr, of the trapped gas, P_{gas}.

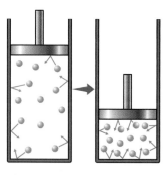

FIG. 10.6 Compressing a gas increases its pressure. A molecular view of what happens when a gas is squeezed into a smaller volume. By crowding the molecules together, the number of collisions with a given area of the walls increases, which causes the pressure to rise.

leaving a vacuum above it. The pressure of the gas can then be measured just by reading the difference in heights of the mercury in the two arms, P_{Hg}. No separate measurement of the atmospheric pressure is required.

10.3 THE GAS LAWS SUMMARIZE EXPERIMENTAL OBSERVATIONS

Earlier, we examined some properties of gases that are familiar to you. Our discussion was only qualitative, however, and now that we've discussed pressure and its units, we are ready to examine gas behavior quantitatively.

There are four variables that affect the properties of a gas—pressure, volume, temperature, and the amount of gas. In this section, we will study situations in which the amount of gas (measured by either grams or moles) remains constant and observe how gas samples respond to changes in pressure, volume, and temperature.

At constant temperature for a fixed amount of gas, the volume is inversely proportional to the pressure

When you inflate a bicycle tire with a hand pump, you squeeze air into a smaller volume and increase its pressure. Packing molecules into a smaller space causes an increased number of collisions with the walls, and because these collisions are responsible for the pressure, the pressure increases (Figure 10.6).

Robert Boyle, an English scientist (1627–1691), performed experiments to determine quantitatively how the volume of a fixed amount of gas varies with pressure. Because the volume is also affected by the temperature, he held that variable constant. A graph of typical data collected in his experiments is shown in Figure 10.7a and demonstrates that *the volume of a given amount of gas held at constant temperature varies inversely with the applied pressure.* Mathematically, this can be expressed as

$$V \propto \frac{1}{P} \qquad \text{(temperature and amount of gas held constant)}$$

where V is the volume and P is the pressure. This relationship between pressure and volume is now called **Boyle's law** or the **pressure–volume law.**

In the expression above, the proportionality sign, $\propto$, can be removed by introducing a proportionality constant, C.

$$V = \frac{1}{P} \times C$$

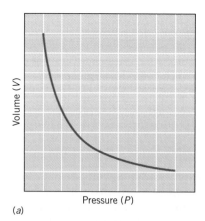

(a)

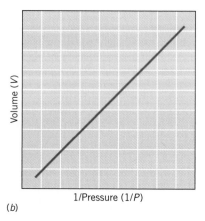

(b)

FIG. 10.7 The variation of volume with pressure at constant temperature for a fixed amount of gas. (a) A typical graph of volume versus pressure, showing that as the pressure increases, the volume decreases. (b) A straight line is obtained when volume is plotted against $1/P$, which shows that $V \propto 1/P$.

Rearranging gives

$$PV = C$$

This equation tells us, for example, that if at constant temperature the gas pressure is doubled the gas volume must be cut in half so that the product $P \times V$ doesn't change.

What is remarkable about Boyle's discovery is that *this relationship is essentially the same for all gases at temperatures and pressures usually found in the laboratory.*

An ideal gas would obey Boyle's law perfectly

When very precise measurements are made, it's found that Boyle's law doesn't quite work. This is especially a problem when the pressure of the gas is very high or when the gas is at a temperature where it's on the verge of changing to a liquid. Although real gases do not *exactly* obey Boyle's law, or any of the other gas laws that we'll study, it is often useful to imagine a hypothetical gas that would. We call such a hypothetical gas an *ideal gas*. An **ideal gas** *would obey the gas laws exactly over all temperatures and pressures.* A real gas behaves more and more like an ideal gas as its pressure decreases and its temperature increases. Most gases we work with in the lab can be treated as ideal gases unless we're dealing with extremely precise measurements.

At constant pressure for a fixed amount of gas, the volume increases with increasing temperature

In 1787 a French chemist and mathematician named Jacques Alexandre Charles became interested in hot-air ballooning, which at the time was becoming popular in France. His new interest led him to study what happens to the volume of a sample of gas when the temperature is varied, keeping the pressure constant.

When data from experiments such as his are plotted, a graph like that shown in Figure 10.8 is obtained. Here the volume of the gas is plotted against the temperature in degrees Celsius. The colored points correspond to typical data, and the lines are drawn to most closely fit the data. Each line represents data collected for a different sample. Because all gases eventually become liquids if cooled sufficiently, the solid portions of the lines correspond to temperatures at which measurements are possible; at lower temperatures the gas liquefies. However, if the lines are extrapolated (reasonably extended) back to a point where the volume of the gas would become zero if it didn't condense, all the lines meet at the same temperature, −273.15 °C. Especially significant is the fact that this exact same behavior is exhibited by all gases; when plots of volume versus temperature are extrapolated to zero volume, the temperature axis is always crossed at −273.15 °C. This point represents the temperature at which all gases, if they did not condense, would have a volume of zero, and below which they would have a negative volume. Negative volumes are impossible,

☐ Jacques Alexandre César Charles (1746–1823), a French scientist, had a keen interest in hot air balloons. He was the first to inflate a balloon with hydrogen.

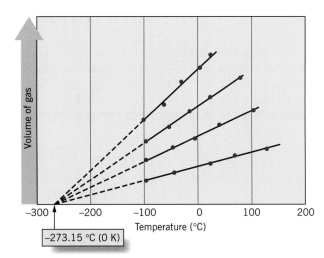

FIG. 10.8 **Charles' law plots.** Each line shows how the gas volume changes with temperature for a different size sample of the same gas.

of course, so it was reasoned that $-273.15\ °C$ must be nature's coldest temperature, and it was called **absolute zero.**

As you learned earlier, absolute zero corresponds to the zero point on the Kelvin temperature scale, and to obtain a Kelvin temperature, we add $273.15\ °C$ to the Celsius temperature.[4]

$$T_K = t_C + 273.15$$

For most purposes, we will need only three significant figures, so we can use the following approximate relationship.

$$T_K = t_C + 273$$

The straight lines in Figure 10.8 suggest that at constant pressure, the volume of a gas is directly proportional to its temperature, provided the temperature is expressed in kelvins. This became known as **Charles' law** (or the **temperature–volume law**) and is expressed mathematically as

$$V \propto T \qquad \text{(pressure and amount of gas held constant)}$$

☐ The value of C' depends on the size and pressure of the gas sample.

Using a different proportionality constant, C', we can write

$$V = C'T \qquad \text{(pressure and amount of gas held constant)}$$

At constant volume for a fixed amount of gas, the pressure is proportional to the absolute temperature

☐ Joseph Louis Gay-Lussac (1778–1850), a French scientist, was a codiscoverer of the element boron.

The French scientist Joseph Louis Gay-Lussac studied how the pressure and temperature of a fixed amount of gas at constant volume are related. (Such conditions exist, for example, when a gas is confined in a vessel with rigid walls, like an aerosol can.) The relationship that he established, called **Gay-Lussac's law** or the **pressure–temperature law,** states that *the pressure of a fixed amount of gas held at constant volume is directly proportional to the Kelvin temperature.* Thus,

$$P \propto T \qquad \text{(volume and amount of gas held constant)}$$

Using still another constant of proportionality, Gay-Lussac's law becomes

$$P = C''T \qquad \text{(volume and amount of gas held constant)}$$

☐ We're using different symbols for the various gas law constants because they are different for each law.

The combined gas law brings together the other gas laws we've studied

The three gas laws we've just examined can be brought together into a single equation known as the **combined gas law,** which states that *the ratio PV/T is a constant for a fixed amount of gas.*

$$\frac{PV}{T} = \text{constant} \qquad \text{(for a fixed amount of gas)}$$

Usually, we use the combined gas law in problems where we know some given set of conditions of temperature, pressure, and volume (for a fixed amount of gas), and wish to find out how one of these variables will change when the others are changed. If we label the initial conditions of P, V, and T with the subscript 1 and the final conditions with the subscript 2, the combined gas law can be written in the following useful form.

TOOLS
Combined gas law

$$\frac{P_1 V_1}{T_1} = \frac{P_2 V_2}{T_2} \qquad (10.1)$$

---

[4]In Chapter 1 we presented this equation as $T_K = (t_C + 273.15\ °C)\,(1\ K/1\ °C)$ to emphasize unit cancellation. Operationally, however, we just add 273.15 to the Celsius temperature to obtain the Kelvin temperature (or we just add 273 if three significant figures are sufficient).

In applying this equation, T must always be in kelvins. The pressure and volume can have any units, but whatever the units are on one side of the equation, they must be the same on the other side.

It is simple to show that Equation 10.1 contains each of the other gas laws as special cases. Boyle's law, for example, applies when the temperature is constant. Under these conditions, T_1 equals T_2 and temperature cancels from the equation. This leaves us with

$$P_1 V_1 = P_2 V_2 \qquad \text{(when } T_1 \text{ equals } T_2\text{)}$$

which is one way to write Boyle's law. Similarly, under conditions of constant pressure, P_1 equals P_2 and the pressure cancels, so Equation 10.1 reduces to

$$V_1 / T_1 = V_2 / T_2 \qquad \text{(when } P_1 \text{ equals } P_2\text{)}$$

This, of course, is another way of writing Charles' law. Under the constant-volume conditions required by Gay-Lussac's law, V_1 equals V_2, and Equation 10.1 reduces to

$$P_1 / T_1 = P_2 / T_2 \qquad \text{(when } V_1 \text{ equals } V_2\text{)}$$

EXAMPLE 10.2
Using the Combined Gas Law

(PhotoDisc, Inc./Getty Images.)

An ordinary incandescent lightbulb contains a tungsten filament, which becomes white hot (about 2500 °C) when electricity is passed through it. To prevent the filament from rapidly vaporizing, the bulb is filled to a low pressure with the inert (unreactive) gas argon. Suppose a 12.0 L cylinder containing compressed argon at a pressure of 57.8 atm measured at 25 °C is to be used to fill electric lightbulbs, each with a volume of 158 mL, to a pressure of 3.00 torr at 20 °C. How many of these lightbulbs could be filled by the argon in the cylinder?

ANALYSIS: What do we need to know to figure out how many lightbulbs can be filled? If we knew the total volume of gas with a pressure of 3.00 torr at 20 °C, we could just divide by the volume of one lightbulb; the result is the number of lightbulbs that can be filled. So, our main problem is determining what volume the argon in the cylinder will occupy when its pressure is reduced to 3.00 torr and its temperature is lowered to 20 °C. Because the total amount of argon isn't changing, we can use the combined gas law for the calculation.

The initial conditions will be 12.0 L of argon at 57.8 atm and 25 °C. The final pressure and temperature will be 3.00 torr and 20 °C. To apply the combined gas law, the pressure units will have to be the same, so we can convert 57.8 atm to torr. The temperatures will have to be in kelvins, so we add 273 to the Celsius temperatures. We're now ready to perform the math.

SOLUTION: We'll begin by converting 57.8 atm to torr. We know that 1 atm = 760 torr, so

$$57.8 \text{ atm} \times \frac{760 \text{ torr}}{1 \text{ atm}} = 4.39 \times 10^4 \text{ torr}$$

Now we can assemble the data, again using "1" for the initial conditions and "2" for the final ones.

	Initial (1)	Final (2)
P	4.39×10^4 torr	3.00 torr
V	12.0 L	?
T	298 K (25 + 273)	293 K (20 + 273)

Now we have to use the combined gas law.

$$\frac{P_1 V_1}{T_1} = \frac{P_2 V_2}{T_2}$$

To obtain the final volume, we solve for V_2. We'll do this and then rearrange the equation slightly.

ratio of temperatures

$$V_2 = V_1 \times \frac{P_1}{P_2} \times \frac{T_2}{T_1}$$

ratio of pressures

Notice that for V_2 to have the same units as V_1, the units in numerator and denominator of both ratios must cancel. That's the reason we had to convert atmospheres to torr for P_1. Let's now substitute values from our table of data.

$$V_2 = 12.0 \text{ L} \times \frac{4.39 \times 10^4 \text{ torr}}{3.00 \text{ torr}} \times \frac{293 \text{ K}}{298 \text{ K}}$$

$$= 1.73 \times 10^5 \text{ L}$$

Before we can divide by the volume of one lightbulb (158 mL), we have to convert the total volume to milliliters.

$$1.73 \times 10^5 \text{ L} \times \frac{1000 \text{ mL}}{1 \text{ L}} = 1.73 \times 10^8 \text{ mL}$$

The volume per lightbulb gives us the relationship

$$1 \text{ lightbulb} \Leftrightarrow 158 \text{ mL argon}$$

which we can use to find the number of lightbulbs that can be filled.

$$1.73 \times 10^8 \text{ mL argon} \times \frac{1 \text{ lightbulb}}{158 \text{ mL argon}} = 1.09 \times 10^6 \text{ lightbulbs}$$

That's 1.09 million lightbulbs! As you can see, there's not much argon in each one.

IS THE ANSWER REASONABLE? Looking at our setup, one way we can round the numbers to estimate the answer is

$$V_2 = 12.0 \text{ L} \times \frac{4.5 \times 10^4 \text{ torr}}{3 \text{ torr}} \times \frac{300 \text{ K}}{300 \text{ K}}$$

The estimated answer is $V_2 = 18 \times 10^4$ L, which is very close to our calculator answer. We can multiply the liters by 10^3 to get 18×10^7 mL and then we will "round" the 158 mL/bulb to 18×10^1 mL/bulb. Dividing the two gives us 1×10^6 bulbs. This again agrees quite well with the calculated answer.

▢ Notice that we use our knowledge of how gases behave to determine whether we've done the correct arithmetic. If you learn to do this, you can catch your mistakes.

To determine whether we've set up the combined gas law properly, we check to see if the pressure and temperature ratios move the volume in the right direction. Going from the initial to final conditions, the pressure *decreases* from 4.39×10^4 torr to 3.00 torr, so the volume should *increase* a lot. The pressure ratio we used is much larger than 1, so multiplying by it should increase the volume, which agrees with what we expect. Next, look at the temperature change; a *drop in temperature* should tend to *decrease* the volume, so we should be multiplying by a ratio that's less than 1. The ratio 293/298 is less than one, so that ratio is correct, too.

(An observant student might note that in the end 12 L of argon must remain in the cylinder. However, we can divide 12,000 mL by 158 to get an answer of approximately 75 bulbs. Subtracting 75 from 1.09×10^6 still leaves us, when rounded, with 1.09×10^6 lightbulbs.)

Practice Exercise 5: Use the combined gas law to determine by what factor the pressure of an ideal gas must change if the Kelvin temperature is doubled and the volume is tripled. (Hint: Sometimes it is easier to assume a starting set of temperature, volume, and pressure readings and then apply the conditions of the problem.)

Practice Exercise 6: A sample of nitrogen has a volume of 880 mL and a pressure of 740 torr. What pressure will change the volume to 870 mL at the same temperature?

Practice Exercise 7: What will be the final pressure of a sample of nitrogen with a volume of 950 m^3 at 745 torr and 25.0 °C if it is heated to 60.0 °C and given a final volume of 1150 m^3?

10.4 | GAS VOLUMES CAN BE USED IN SOLVING STOICHIOMETRY PROBLEMS

At constant *T* and *P*, gas volumes are in whole-number ratios in a gas-phase reaction

When scientists studied reactions between gases quantitatively, they made an interesting discovery. If the volumes of the reacting gases, as well as the volumes of gaseous products, are measured under the same conditions of temperature and pressure, the volumes are in simple whole-number ratios. For example, hydrogen gas reacts with chlorine gas to give gaseous hydrogen chloride. Beneath the names in the following equation are the relative volumes with which these gases interact (at the same *T* and *P*).

$$\text{hydrogen} + \text{chlorine} \longrightarrow \text{hydrogen chloride}$$
$$\quad\ \text{1 volume}\qquad \text{1 volume}\qquad\qquad\quad \text{2 volumes}$$

What this means is that if we were to use 1.0 L of hydrogen, it would react with 1.0 L of chlorine and produce 2.0 L of hydrogen chloride. If we were to use 10.0 L of hydrogen, all the other volumes would be multiplied by 10 as well.

Similar simple, whole-number ratios by volume are observed when hydrogen combines with oxygen to give water, which is a gas above 100 °C.

$$\text{hydrogen} + \text{oxygen} \longrightarrow \text{water (gaseous)}$$
$$\quad\ \text{2 volumes}\qquad \text{1 volume}\qquad\qquad \text{2 volumes}$$

Notice that the reacting volumes, *measured under identical temperatures and pressures*, are in ratios of simple, whole numbers.[5]

Observations such as those above led Gay-Lussac to formulate his **law of combining volumes,** which states that *when gases react at the same temperature and pressure, their combining volumes are in ratios of simple whole numbers.* Much later, it was learned that these "simple whole numbers" are the coefficients of the balanced equations for the reactions.

At a given temperature and pressure, equal volumes of gas contain the same number of molecules

The observation that gases react in whole-number volume ratios led Amedeo Avogadro to conclude that, at the same *T* and *P*, equal volumes of gases must have identical numbers of molecules. Today, we know that "equal numbers of *molecules*" is the same as "equal numbers of *moles*," so Avogadro's insight, now called **Avogadro's principle,** is expressed as follows. *When measured at the same temperature and pressure, equal volumes of gases contain equal numbers of moles.* A corollary to Avogadro's principle is that *the volume of a gas is directly proportional to its number of moles, n.*

$$V \propto n \qquad \text{(at constant } T \text{ and } P)$$

□ Amedeo Avogadro (1776–1856), an Italian scientist, helped to put chemistry on a quantitative basis.

The standard molar volume is the volume occupied by one mole of gas at STP

Avogadro's principle implies that the volume occupied by one mole of *any* gas—its *molar volume*—must be identical for all gases under the same conditions of pressure and temperature. To compare the molar volumes of different gases, scientists agreed to use 1 atm and 273.15 K (0 °C) as the **standard conditions of temperature and pressure,** or **STP** for short.

---

[5] The great French chemist Antoine Laurent Lavoisier (1743–1794) was the first to observe the volume relationships of this particular reaction. In his 1789 textbook, *Elements of Chemistry,* he wrote that the formation of water from hydrogen and oxygen requires that two volumes of hydrogen be used for every volume of oxygen. Lavoisier was unable to extend the study of this behavior of hydrogen and oxygen to other gas reactions because he was beheaded during the French Revolution. (See Michael Laing, *The Journal of Chemical Education,* February 1998, page 177.)

TABLE 10.1	Molar Volumes of Some Gases	
Gas	Formula	Molar Volume (L)
Helium	He	22.398
Argon	Ar	22.401
Hydrogen	H_2	22.410
Nitrogen	N_2	22.413
Oxygen	O_2	22.414
Carbon dioxide	CO_2	22.414

If we measure the molar volumes for a variety of gases at STP, we find that the values fluctuate somewhat because the gases are not "ideal." Some typical values are shown in Table 10.1 and if we were to examine the data for many gases, we would find, an average of around 22.4 L per mole. This value is taken to be the molar volume of an *ideal gas* at STP and is now called the **standard molar volume** of a gas.

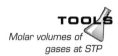

TOOLS
Molar volumes of gases at STP

> *For an ideal gas at STP:*
>
> $$1 \text{ mol gas} \Leftrightarrow 22.4 \text{ L gas}$$

Avogadro's principle was a remarkable advance in our understanding of gases. His insight enabled chemists for the first time to determine the formulas of gaseous elements.[6]

Gas volumes can be used in solving stoichiometry problems

For reactions involving gases, Avogadro's principle lets us use a new kind of stoichiometric equivalency, one between *volumes* of gases. Earlier, for example, we noted the following reaction and its gas volume relationships.

$$2H_2(g) + O_2(g) \longrightarrow 2H_2O(g)$$
2 volumes   1 volume   2 volumes

Provided we are dealing with gas volumes measured at the same temperature and pressure, we can write the following stoichiometric equivalencies.

□ The recognition that equivalencies in gas *volumes* are numerically the same as those for numbers of moles of gas in reactions involving gases simplifies many calculations.

2 volumes $H_2(g) \Leftrightarrow$ 1 volume $O_2(g)$	just as	2 mol $H_2 \Leftrightarrow$ 1 mol O_2
2 volumes $H_2(g) \Leftrightarrow$ 2 volumes $H_2O(g)$	just as	2 mol $H_2 \Leftrightarrow$ 2 mol H_2O
1 volume $O_2(g) \Leftrightarrow$ 2 volumes $H_2O(g)$	just as	1 mol $O_2 \Leftrightarrow$ 2 mol H_2O

Relationships such as these can greatly simplify stoichiometry problems, as we see in Example 10.3.

EXAMPLE 10.3
Stoichiometry of Reactions of Gases

How many liters of hydrogen, measured at STP, are needed to combine exactly with 1.50 L of nitrogen, also measured at STP, to form ammonia?

ANALYSIS: The problem states that the reactants are at STP, standard temperature (273 K) and pressure (760 torr). Therefore all the gases in this example are at the same temperature and

---

[6]Suppose that hydrogen chloride, for example, is correctly formulated as HCl, not as H_2Cl_2 or H_3Cl_3 or higher, and certainly not as $H_{0.5}Cl_{0.5}$. Then the only way that *two* volumes of hydrogen chloride could come from just *one* volume of hydrogen and *one* of chlorine is if each particle of hydrogen and each of chlorine were to consist of *two* atoms of H and Cl, respectively, H_2 and Cl_2. If these particles were single-atom particles, H and Cl, then one volume of H and one volume of Cl could give only *one* volume of HCl, not two. Of course, if the initial assumption were incorrect so that hydrogen chloride is, say, H_2Cl_2 instead of HCl, then hydrogen would be H_4 and chlorine would be Cl_4. The extension to larger subscripts works in the same way.

pressure. That makes the ratios by volume the same as the ratio by moles, which means that the ratios by volume are the same as the ratios of the coefficients of the balanced equation.

We can restate the problem as

$$1.50 \text{ L N}_2 \Longleftrightarrow ? \text{ L H}_2$$

We're dealing with a chemical reaction, so we need the chemical equation.

$$3H_2(g) + N_2(g) \longrightarrow 2NH_3(g)$$

Avogadro's principle gives us the equivalency we need to perform the calculation.

$$3 \text{ volumes H}_2 \Longleftrightarrow 1 \text{ volume N}_2$$

SOLUTION: The volume of hydrogen is given in liters, so we need to express the volume equivalency in those units as well.

$$3 \text{ L H}_2 \Longleftrightarrow 1 \text{ L N}_2$$

We then multiply the given amount, 1.50 L N$_2$, by a conversion factor made from the equivalency above:

$$\text{Volume of H}_2 = 1.50 \text{ L N}_2 \times \frac{3 \text{ L H}_2}{1 \text{ L N}_2}$$

$$= 4.50 \text{ L H}_2$$

IS THE ANSWER REASONABLE? The volume of H$_2$ needed is three times the volume of N$_2$, and 3 × 1.5 equals 4.5, so the answer is correct. Remember, however, that the simplicity of this problem arises because the volumes are at the same temperature and pressure.

EXAMPLE 10.4
Stoichiometry Calculations when Gases Are Not at the Same T and P

Nitrogen monoxide, a pollutant released by automobile engines, is oxidized by molecular oxygen to give the reddish-brown gas nitrogen dioxide, which gives smog its characteristic color. The equation is

$$2NO(g) + O_2(g) \longrightarrow 2NO_2(g)$$

How many milliliters of O$_2$, measured at 20 °C and 755 torr, are needed to react with 180 mL of NO, measured at 45 °C and 720 torr?

ANALYSIS: Once again, we have a stoichiometry problem, but this one is more complicated than in the preceding example because the gases are not at the same temperature and pressure. The way to resolve this difficulty is to make the temperature and pressure the same for both gases.

We can use the combined gas law to find what volume the NO would occupy if it were at the same temperature and pressure as the O$_2$. Then we can use the coefficients of the equation to find the volume of O$_2$.

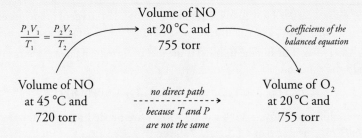

SOLUTION: The first step is to use the combined gas law applied to the given volume of NO, so let's set up the data as usual.

	Initial (1)	Final (2)
P	720 torr	755 torr
V	180 mL	?
T	318 K (45 °C + 273)	293 K (20 °C + 273)

Solving the combined gas law for V_2 gives

$$V_2 = V_1 \times \left(\frac{P_1}{P_2}\right) \times \left(\frac{T_2}{T_1}\right)$$

Next we substitute values.

$$V_2 = 180 \text{ mL} \times \left(\frac{720 \text{ torr}}{755 \text{ torr}}\right) \times \left(\frac{293 \text{ K}}{318 \text{ K}}\right)$$

$$= 158 \text{ mL NO}$$

Now we have the volume of NO *at the same temperature and pressure as the oxygen*. This lets us use the coefficients of the equation to establish the equivalency

$$2 \text{ mL NO} \Leftrightarrow 1 \text{ mL O}_2$$

and apply it to find the volume of O_2 required for the reaction.

$$158 \text{ mL NO} \times \frac{1 \text{ mL O}_2}{2 \text{ mL NO}} = 79.0 \text{ mL O}_2$$

IS THE ANSWER REASONABLE? For the first part of the calculation, we can check to see whether the pressure and temperature ratios move the volume in the right direction. The pressure is increasing (702 torr → 755 torr), so that should have a lowering effect on the volume. The pressure ratio is smaller than 1, so it is having the proper effect. The temperature is dropping (318 K → 293 K), so this change should also have a volume lowering effect. The temperature ratio is smaller than 1, so it is also having the correct effect. The volume of NO at 20 °C and 755 torr is probably correct. We can also observe that the two ratios are only slightly less than 1.0 and we expect the answer to be close to the given volume, which it is.

The check of the second part of the calculation is simple. According to the equation, the volume of O_2 required should be half the volume of NO, which it is, so the final answer seems to be okay.

Practice Exercise 8: Methane burns according to the following equation.

$$CH_4(g) + 2O_2(g) \longrightarrow CO_2(g) + 2H_2O(g)$$

The combustion of 4.50 L of CH_4 consumes how many liters of O_2, both volumes measured at 25 °C and 740 torr? (Hint: Recall Avogadro's principle concerning the number of molecules in a fixed volume of gas at a given temperature and pressure.)

Practice Exercise 9: How many liters of air (air is 21% oxygen) are required for the combustion of 6.75 L of CH_4? (Assume air and CH_4 are at the same T and P.)

Practice Exercise 10: Butane (C_4H_{10}) is the fuel in cigarette lighters. It burns in oxygen according to the equation

$$2C_4H_{10}(g) + 13O_2(g) \longrightarrow 8CO_2(g) + 10H_2O(g)$$

How many milliliters of O_2 at 35 °C and 725 torr are needed to react completely with 75.0 mL of C_4H_{10} measured at 45 °C and 760 torr?

10.5 | THE IDEAL GAS LAW RELATES *P*, *V*, *T*, AND THE NUMBER OF MOLES OF GAS, *n*

In our discussion of the combined gas law, we noted that the ratio PV/T equals a constant for a fixed amount of gas. However, the value of this "constant" is actually proportional to the number of moles of gas, *n*, in the sample.[7]

To create an equation even more general than the combined gas law, therefore, we can write

$$\frac{PV}{T} \propto n$$

We can replace the proportionality symbol with an equals sign by including another proportionality constant.

$$\frac{PV}{T} = n \times \text{constant}$$

This new constant is given the symbol **R** and is called the **universal gas constant.** We can now write the combined gas law in a still more general form called the **ideal gas law.**

$$\frac{PV}{T} = nR$$

An ideal gas would obey this law exactly over all ranges of the gas variables. The equation, sometimes called the **equation of state for an ideal gas,** is usually rearranged and written as follows.

□ Sometimes this equation is called the *universal gas law.*

> ### Ideal Gas Law (Equation of State for an Ideal Gas)
> $$PV = nRT \qquad (10.2)$$

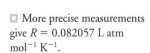

TOOLS

Ideal gas law

Equation 10.2 tells us how the four important variables for a gas, *P*, *V*, *n*, and *T*, are related. If we know the values of three, we can calculate the fourth. In fact, Equation 10.2 tells us that if values for three of the four variables are fixed for a given gas, *the fourth can only have one value.* We can define the *state* of a given gas simply by specifying any three of the four variables.

□ If *n*, *P*, and *T* in Equation 10.2 are known, for example, then *V* can have *only one value.*

To use the ideal gas law, we have to know the value of the universal gas constant, *R*. To calculate it, we use the standard conditions of pressure and temperature, and we use the standard molar volume, which sets *n* equal to 1 mol, the number of moles of the sample. We still have to decide what units to use for pressure and volume, and the value of *R* differs with these choices. Our choices for this chapter are to express volumes in *liters* and pressures in *atmospheres*. Thus for one molar volume at STP, $n = 1$ mol, $V = 22.4$ L, $P = 1.00$ atm, and $T = 273$ K. Using these values lets us calculate *R* as follows.

$$R = \frac{PV}{nT} = \frac{(1.00 \text{ atm})(22.4 \text{ L})}{(1.00 \text{ mol})(273 \text{ K})}$$

$$= 0.0821 \frac{\text{atm L}}{\text{mol K}}$$

Or, arranging the units in a commonly used order,

$$R = 0.0821 \text{ L atm mol}^{-1} \text{ K}^{-1}$$

□ More precise measurements give $R = 0.082057$ L atm mol^{-1} K^{-1}.

To use this value of *R* in working problems, we have to be sure to express volumes in liters and pressures in atmospheres. And, of course, temperatures must be expressed in kelvins.

---

[7] In the problems we worked earlier, we were able to use the combined gas law expressed as

$$\frac{P_1 V_1}{T_1} = \frac{P_2 V_2}{T_2}$$

because the amount of gas remained fixed.

EXAMPLE 10.5
Using the Ideal Gas Law

In Example 10.2, we described filling a 158 mL lightbulb with argon at a temperature of 20 °C and a pressure of 3.00 torr. How many grams of argon are in the lightbulb under these conditions?

ANALYSIS: In gas law calculations we usually have the possibility of either using the combined gas law equation (used if we are changing from one set of P, V, and T to another set of P, V, and T) or the ideal gas law equation (used if we know three of the four variables P, V, n, and T). In this case we see that the tool to accomplish this is the ideal gas law equation, $PV = nRT$. We will solve it for n and substitute values for P, V, R, and T. Once we have the number of moles of argon, a simple moles-to-grams conversion using the atomic mass will give us the mass of Ar in grams.

In performing the calculation, we will have to be sure to convert the volume to liters, pressure to atmospheres, and the temperature to kelvins so the units will cancel correctly.

SOLUTION: To use $R = 0.0821$ L atm mol^{-1} K^{-1}, we must have V in liters, P in atmospheres, and T in kelvins. Gathering the data and making the necessary unit conversions as we go, we have

$$P = 3.95 \times 10^{-3} \text{ atm} \qquad \text{from } 3.00 \text{ torr} \times \frac{1 \text{ atm}}{760 \text{ torr}}$$

$$V = 0.158 \text{ L} \qquad \text{from 158 mL}$$

$$T = 293 \text{ K} \qquad \text{from } (20 \text{ °C} + 273)$$

Solving the ideal gas law for n gives us

$$n = \frac{PV}{RT}$$

Substituting the proper values of P, V, R, and T into this equation gives

$$n = \frac{(3.95 \times 10^{-3} \text{ atm})(0.158 \text{ L})}{(0.0821 \text{ L atm mol}^{-1}\text{K}^{-1})(293 \text{ K})}$$

$$= 2.59 \times 10^{-5} \text{ mol Ar}$$

The atomic mass of Ar is 39.95, so 1 mol Ar = 39.95 g Ar. A conversion factor made from this relationship lets us convert "mol Ar" into "g Ar."

$$2.59 \times 10^{-5} \text{ mol Ar} \times \frac{39.95 \text{ g Ar}}{1 \text{ mol Ar}} = 1.04 \times 10^{-3} \text{ g Ar}$$

Thus, the lightbulb contains only about one-thousandth of a gram of argon.

IS THE ANSWER REASONABLE? As in other problems we approximate the answer by rounding all values to one significant figure to get:

$$n = \frac{(4 \times 10^{-3} \text{ atm})(0.2 \text{ L})}{(0.1 \text{ L atm mol}^{-1} \text{ K}^{-1})(300 \text{ K})} = \frac{0.8 \times 10^{-3} \text{ mol}}{30} = 2.66 \times 10^{-5} \text{ mol}$$

For ease of calculation we round this answer to 2.5×10^{-5} mol and multiply by 40 g Ar per mol Ar to get 1×10^{-3} grams, very close to our calculated value. An alternate rounding of the moles to 3×10^{-5} will give an answer of 1.2×10^{-3} grams, equally close to our original answer.

Another view tells us we can also expect that the amount of argon in the bulb will also be quite small, since one mole occupies 22.4 L at STP; the 158 mL bulb has a much smaller volume than 22.4 L so our final answer also makes sense. As a final check, we can look to be sure the units cancel correctly, and we see that they do. (Whenever you're working a problem where there is unit cancellation, be sure to check to be sure the units do cancel as they are supposed to.)

Practice Exercise 11: Dry ice, $CO_2(s)$, can be made by allowing pressurized $CO_2(g)$ to expand rapidly. If 35% of the expanding $CO_2(g)$ ends up as $CO_2(s)$, how many grams of dry ice can be made from a tank of $CO_2(g)$ that has a volume of 6.0 cubic feet with a gauge pressure of 2000 pounds per square inch (PSIG) at 22 °C? (Hint: The information in the margin table on page 393 will help set up the conversions needed. PSIG is the pressure above the prevailing atmospheric pressure.)

Practice Exercise 12: How many grams of argon were in the 12.0 L cylinder of argon used to fill the lightbulbs described in Example 10.2? The pressure of the argon was 57.8 atm and the temperature was 25 °C.

Molar mass can be calculated from measurements of *P*, *V*, *T*, and mass

When a chemist makes a new compound, its molar mass is usually determined to help establish its chemical identity. In general, *to determine the molar mass of a compound experimentally, we need to find two pieces of information about a given sample: the mass of the sample and the number of moles of the substance in the sample.* Once we have mass and moles for the same sample, we simply divide the number of grams by the number of moles to find the molar mass. For instance, if we had a sample weighing 6.40 g and found that it also contained 0.100 mol of the substance, the molar mass would be

$$\frac{6.40 \text{ g}}{0.100 \text{ mol}} = 64.0 \text{ g mol}^{-1}$$

If the compound is a gas, its molar mass can be found using experimental values of pressure, volume, temperature, and sample mass. The *P*, *V*, *T* data allow us to calculate the number of moles using the ideal gas law (as in Example 10.5). Once we know the number of moles of gas and the mass of the gas sample, the molar mass is obtained by taking the ratio of *grams to moles*.

TOOLS
Determination of molar mass from ideal gas law

☐ Recall that when the molecular mass of a substance is expressed in units of grams per mole, the quantity is called the *molar mass*.

EXAMPLE 10.6
Determining the Molar Mass of a Gas

As part of a rock analysis, a student added hydrochloric acid to a rock sample and observed a fizzing action, indicating a gas was being evolved (see the figure in the margin). The student collected a sample of the gas in a 0.220 L gas bulb until its pressure reached 0.757 atm at a temperature of 25.0 °C. The sample weighed 0.299 g. What is the molar mass of the gas? What kind of compound was the likely source of the gas?

ANALYSIS: The strategy for finding the molar mass was described above. We use the *P*, *V*, *T* data to calculate the number of moles of gas in the sample. To do this, we solve the ideal gas law for *n* and then substitute values, being sure the units will cancel correctly. Then we divide the given mass by the number of moles to find the molar mass.

SOLUTION: Pressure is already in atmospheres and the volume is in liters, but we must convert degrees Celsius into kelvins. Gathering our data, we have

$$P = 0.757 \text{ atm} \quad V = 0.220 \text{ L} \quad T = 298 \text{ K} \quad (25.0 \text{ °C} + 273)$$

Next, we solve the ideal gas law ($PV = nRT$) for the number of moles, *n*.

$$n = \frac{PV}{RT}$$

Now we can substitute the data for *P*, *V*, and *T*, along with the value of *R*. This gives

$$n = \frac{(0.757 \text{ atm})(0.220 \text{ L})}{(0.0821 \text{ L atm mol}^{-1} \text{ K}^{-1})(298 \text{ K})}$$

$$= 6.81 \times 10^{-3} \text{ mol}$$

Hydrochloric acid reacting with a rock sample. (*Andy Washnik.*)

The molar mass is obtained from the ratio of grams to moles.

$$\text{Molar mass} = \frac{0.299 \text{ g}}{6.81 \times 10^{-3} \text{ mol}} = 43.9 \text{ g mol}^{-1}$$

We now know the measured molar mass is 43.9, but what gas could this be? Looking back on our discussions in Chapter 4, what gases do we know are given off when a substance reacts with acids? On page 152 we find some options; the gas might be H_2S, HCN, CO_2, or SO_2. Using atomic masses to calculate their molar masses we get

H_2S	34 g mol^{-1}	CO_2	44 g mol^{-1}
HCN	27 g mol^{-1}	SO_2	64 g mol^{-1}

The only gas with a molar mass close to 43.9 is CO_2, and that gas would be evolved if we treat a carbonate with an acid. The rock probably contains a carbonate compound. (Limestone and marble are examples of such minerals.)

ARE THE ANSWERS REASONABLE? If our value for n is correct, then the rest of the calculation is most likely okay too. Let's round the data and estimate n as

$$n = \frac{(3/4 \text{ atm})(0.2 \text{ L})}{(0.1 \text{ L atm mol}^{-1} \text{ K}^{-1})(300 \text{ K})} = \frac{0.15 \text{ atm L}}{30 \text{ L atm mol}^{-1}} = 0.005 \text{ mol}$$

This is reasonably close to the 6.81×10^{-3} mol calculated above. Therefore our molar mass is most likely correct. The rest of the reasoning seems sound and CO_2 from a carbonate compound seems to be reasonable.

Practice Exercise 13: A glass bulb is found to have a volume of 544.23 mL. The mass of the glass bulb filled with air is 735.6898 g. The bulb is then flushed with a gaseous organic compound. The bulb, now filled with the organic gas, weighs 735.6220 g. The measurements were made at STP. What is the molar mass of the organic gas? (Hint: Calculate the difference in molar masses. The average molar mass of air is 28.8 g/mol air.)

Practice Exercise 14: The label on a cylinder of a noble gas became illegible, so a student allowed some of the gas to flow into an evacuated glass bulb with a volume of 300.0 mL until the pressure was 685 torr. The mass of the glass bulb increased by 1.45 g; its temperature was 27.0 °C. What is the molar mass of this gas? Which of the Group VIIIA gases was it?

Gas densities depend on molar masses

Because one mole of any gas occupies the same volume at a particular pressure and temperature, the mass contained in that volume depends on the molar mass of the gas. Consider, for example, one-mole samples of O_2 and CO_2 at STP (Figure 10.9). Each sample occupies a volume of 22.4 L. The oxygen sample has a mass of 32.0 g while the carbon dioxide sample has a mass of 44.0 g. If we calculate the densities of the gases, we find the density of CO_2 is larger than that of O_2.

$$d_{O_2} = \frac{32.0 \text{ g}}{22.4 \text{ L}} = 1.43 \text{ g L}^{-1} \qquad d_{CO_2} = \frac{44.0 \text{ g}}{22.4 \text{ L}} = 1.96 \text{ g L}^{-1}$$

☐ Recall from Chapter 1 that density is the ratio of mass to volume. For liquids and solids, we usually use units of g mL^{-1} (or g cm^{-3}), but because gases have such low densities, units of g L^{-1} give numbers that are easier to comprehend.

FIG. 10.9 **One-mole samples of O_2 and CO_2 at STP.** Each sample occupies 22.4 L, but the O_2 weighs 32.0 g whereas the CO_2 weighs 44.0 g. The CO_2 has more mass per unit volume than the O_2 and has the higher density.

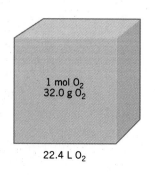
1 mol O₂
32.0 g O₂
22.4 L O₂

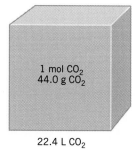
1 mol CO₂
44.0 g CO₂
22.4 L CO₂

Because the volume of a gas is affected by temperature and pressure, the density of a gas changes as these variables change. Gases become less dense as their temperatures rise, which is why hot air balloons are able to float (see chapter opening photo); the less dense hot air inside the balloon floats in the more dense cool air that surrounds it. Gases also become more dense as their pressures increase because increasing the pressure packs more molecules into the same space. To calculate the density of a gas at conditions other than STP, we use the ideal gas law, as illustrated in Example 10.7.

EXAMPLE 10.7
Calculating the Density of a Gas

One procedure used to separate the isotopes of uranium to obtain material to construct a nuclear weapon employs a uranium compound with the formula UF_6. The compound boils at about 56 °C, so at 100 °C it is a gas. What is the density of UF_6 at 100 °C if the pressure of the gas is 740 torr? (Assume the gas contains the mix of uranium isotopes commonly found in nature.)

ANALYSIS: In our discussion above, you learned that if the gas were at STP, we could calculate the density by dividing the mass of one mole of the gas by its molar volume, 22.4 L. We can do a similar calculation here if we first calculate the molar volume at 100 °C and 740 torr. To do this, we can use the ideal gas law, setting n equal to 1.00 mol and converting the pressure to atmospheres and the temperature to kelvins.

SOLUTION: The pressure is 740 torr, so to convert to atmospheres, we use the relationship between the atmosphere and torr.

$$740 \text{ torr} \times \frac{1 \text{ atm}}{760 \text{ torr}} = 0.974 \text{ atm}$$

The temperature is 100 °C, which converts to 373 K, and we said we would use $n = 1.00$ mol. To find the molar volume, we solve the ideal gas law for V.

$$V = \frac{nRT}{P}$$

Now we substitute values.

$$V = \frac{1.00 \text{ mol} \times 0.0821 \text{ L atm mol}^{-1} \text{K}^{-1} \times 373 \text{ K}}{0.974 \text{ atm}} = 31.4 \text{ L}$$

At these conditions of temperature and pressure, the molar volume is 31.4 L per mole. To calculate the density, we need one more piece of data, the molar mass of UF_6. Adding up the atomic masses, we get a molar mass of 352.0 g mol^{-1}. The density is therefore

$$d_{UF_6} = \frac{352.0 \text{ g}}{31.4 \text{ L}} = 11.2 \text{ g L}^{-1}$$

IS THE ANSWER REASONABLE? At STP, the density would be equal to 352 g ÷ 22.4 L = 15.7 g L^{-1}. The pressure is almost 1 atm, but the temperature is quite a bit larger than 273 K. Gases expand when heated, so a liter of the gas at the higher temperature will have less UF_6 in it. That means the density will be lower at the higher temperature, and our answer agrees with this analysis. It is probably correct.

Practice Exercise 15: Radon, a radioactive gas, is formed in one step of the natural radioactive decay sequence of U-235 to Pb-207. Radon usually escapes harmlessly through the soil to the atmosphere. When the soil is frozen or saturated with water the only escape route is through cracks in the basements of houses and other buildings. In order to detect radon in a residence, would you place the sensor in the attic, ground floor living area, or the basement? Justify your answer. (Hint: Compare the approximate density of air from data given in Practice Exercise 13 to the density of radon.)

Practice Exercise 16: Sulfur dioxide is a gas that has been used in commercial refrigeration, but not in residential refrigeration because it is toxic. If your refrigerator used SO_2, you could be injured if it developed a leak. What is the density of SO_2 gas measured at $-20\ °C$ and a pressure of 96.5 kPa?

Gas densities can be used to calculate molar masses

One of the ways we can use the density of a gas is to determine the molar mass. To do this, we also need to know the temperature and pressure at which the density was measured. Example 10.8 illustrates the reasoning and calculation involved.[8]

EXAMPLE 10.8

Calculating the Molar Mass from Gas Density

A liquid sold under the name Perclene is used as a dry cleaning solvent. It has an empirical formula CCl_2 and a boiling point of 121 °C. When vaporized, the gaseous compound has a density of 4.93 g L^{-1} at 785 torr and 150 °C. What is the molar mass of the compound and what is its molecular formula?

ANALYSIS: Earlier you saw that for gases, we can calculate the molar mass if we have P, V, and T data for a weighed sample of the substance. We use the P, V, T data with the ideal gas law to calculate n, and then divide the number of grams by the number of moles. But in this problem we seem to be given values only for P and T. How will we obtain the other data we need (V and grams of gas)? The answer comes from what the density tells us. A value of 4.93 g L^{-1} translates to 4.93 g per liter, which means that if we had 1.00 L of the gas, it would have a mass of 4.93 g. Thus, the density gives the other two data items we need.

$$1.00\ \text{L gas} \Longleftrightarrow 4.93\ \text{g gas}$$

After we've calculated the molar mass, we find the molecular formula following the procedure discussed in Chapter 3. We divide the molar mass by the empirical formula mass to find the factor by which we multiply the subscripts in the empirical formula to obtain the molecular formula.

SOLUTION: To calculate the number of moles of gas in 1.00 L, we use the ideal gas law, making unit conversions as needed. The data are

$$T = 423\ \text{K} \qquad \text{From (150 °C + 273)}$$

$$P = 1.03\ \text{atm} \qquad \text{From 785 torr} \times \frac{1\ \text{atm}}{760\ \text{torr}}$$

$$V = 1.00\ \text{L}$$

---

[8] From the ideal gas law we can derive an equation from which we could calculate the molar mass directly from the density. If we let the mass of gas equal g, we could calculate the number of moles, n, by the ratio

$$n = \frac{g}{\text{molar mass}}$$

Substituting into the ideal gas law gives

$$PV = nRT = \frac{gRT}{\text{molar mass}}$$

Solving for molar mass, we have

$$\text{Molar mass} = \frac{gRT}{PV} = \left(\frac{g}{V}\right) \times \frac{RT}{P}$$

The quantity g/V is the ratio of mass to volume, which is the density d, so making this substitution gives

$$\text{Molar mass} = \frac{dRT}{P}$$

This equation could also be used to solve the problem in Example 10.8 by substituting values for d, R, T, and P.

Solving the ideal gas law for *n* and substituting values, we have

$$n = \frac{PV}{RT} = \frac{(1.03 \text{ atm})(1.00 \text{ L})}{(0.0821 \text{ L atm mol}^{-1}\text{K}^{-1})(423 \text{ K})}$$

$$= 2.97 \times 10^{-2} \text{ mol}$$

Now we can calculate the molar mass by dividing the mass, 4.93 g, by the number of moles, 2.97×10^{-2} mol.

$$\frac{4.93 \text{ g}}{2.97 \times 10^{-2} \text{ mol}} = 166 \text{ g mol}^{-1}$$

The molar mass of the compound is thus 166 g mol^{-1}.

The empirical formula mass that we calculate from the empirical formula, CCl_2, is 82.9. We now divide the molar mass by this value to see how many times CCl_2 occurs in the molecular formula.

$$\frac{166}{82.9} = 2.00$$

To find the molecular formula, we multiply the subscripts of the empirical formula by 2.

$$\text{Molecular formula} = C_{1\times2}Cl_{2\times2} = C_2Cl_4$$

(This is the formula for a compound commonly called tetrachloroethylene, which is indeed used as a dry cleaning fluid.)

ARE THE ANSWERS REASONABLE? Sometimes we don't have to do any arithmetic to see that an answer is almost surely correct. The fact that the molar mass we calculated from the gas density is evenly divisible by the empirical formula mass suggests we've worked the problem correctly.

Practice Exercise 17: A gaseous compound of phosphorus and fluorine with an empirical formula of PF_2 has a density of 5.60 g L^{-1} at 23.0 °C and 750 torr. Determine the molecular formula of this compound. (Hint: Calculate the molar mass from the density.)

Practice Exercise 18: A compound composed of only carbon and hydrogen has a density of 5.55 g/L at 40.0 °C and 1.25 atm. What is the molar mass of the compound? What are the possible combinations of C and H that add up to that molar mass? Using the information in Section 2.6, determine which of your formulas is most likely the correct one.

The ideal gas law can be used in stoichiometry calculations

Many chemical reactions either consume or give off gases. The ideal gas law can be used to relate the volumes of such gases to the amounts of other substances involved in the reaction, as illustrated by the following example.

EXAMPLE 10.9
Calculating the Volume of a Gaseous Product Using the Ideal Gas Law

An important chemical reaction in the manufacture of Portland cement is the high temperature decomposition of calcium carbonate to give calcium oxide and carbon dioxide. Suppose a 1.25 g sample of calcium carbonate is decomposed by heating. How many milliliters of carbon dioxide gas will be evolved if the volume will be measured at 740 torr and 25 °C?

ANALYSIS: The first thing to do is determine the reactants and products of the reaction and to balance the equation. Using our rules for naming compounds we can determine that calcium carbonate is $CaCO_3$, carbon dioxide is CO_2, and calcium oxide is CaO. The balanced equation is

$$CaCO_3(s) \longrightarrow CaO(s) + CO_2(g)$$

This balanced equation tells us

$$1 \text{ mol CaCO}_3 \Leftrightarrow 1 \text{ mol CO}_2$$

Now, we will calculate the *moles* of $CaCO_3$, which equals the number of moles of CO_2. We will use this value for n in the ideal gas law equation to find the volume of CO_2.

SOLUTION: The formula mass of $CaCO_3$ is 100.1, so

$$\text{moles of CaCO}_3 = 1.25 \text{ g CaCO}_3 \times \frac{1 \text{ mol CaCO}_3}{100.1 \text{ g CaCO}_3}$$

$$= 1.25 \times 10^{-2} \text{ mol CaCO}_3$$

Because $1 \text{ mol CaCO}_3 \Leftrightarrow 1 \text{ mol CO}_2$,

$$n = 1.25 \times 10^{-2} \text{ mol CO}_2$$

Before we use n in the ideal gas law equation, we must convert the given pressure and temperature into the units required by R.

$$P = 740 \text{ torr} \times \frac{1 \text{ atm}}{760 \text{ torr}} = 0.974 \text{ atm} \qquad T = 298 \text{ K} \ (25.0 \ ^\circ\text{C} + 273)$$

By rearranging the ideal gas law equation we obtain

$$V = \frac{nRT}{P}$$

$$= \frac{(1.25 \times 10^{-2} \text{ mol})(0.0821 \text{ L atm mol}^{-1} \text{ K}^{-1})(298 \text{ K})}{0.974 \text{ atm}}$$

$$= 0.314 \text{ L} = 314 \text{ mL}$$

The reaction will yield 314 mL of CO_2 at the conditions specified.

IS THE ANSWER REASONABLE? We round all of the numbers in our calculation to one significant figure to get

$$V = \frac{(1 \times 10^{-2} \text{ mol})(0.1 \text{ L atm mol}^{-1} \text{ K}^{-1})(300 \text{ K})}{1 \text{ atm}} = 0.3 \text{ L} \quad \text{or} \quad 300 \text{ mL}$$

This answer is close to what we calculated above and we may assume the calculation is correct. We also note that all units cancel to leave the desired liter units for volume.

Practice Exercise 19: Carbon disulfide is an extremely flammable substance. It can be ignited by any small spark or even a very hot surface such as a steam pipe. When 10.0 g of CS_2 is burned in excess oxygen, how many liters of CO_2 and of SO_2 are formed at 28 °C and 880 torr? (Hint: Treat this as an ordinary stoichiometry problem but write the balanced equation first.)

Practice Exercise 20: In one lab, the gas collecting apparatus used a glass bulb with a volume of 250 mL. How many grams of $CaCO_3(s)$ need to be heated to prepare enough $CO_2(g)$ to fill this bulb to a pressure of 738 torr at a temperature of 23 °C?

10.6 IN A MIXTURE EACH GAS EXERTS ITS OWN PARTIAL PRESSURE

So far in our discussions we've dealt with only pure gases. However, gas mixtures, such as the air we breathe, are quite common. In general, gas mixtures obey the same laws as pure gases, so Boyle's law applies equally to both pure oxygen and to air. There are times, though, when we must be concerned with the composition of a gas mixture, such as when we are concerned with a pollutant in the atmosphere. In these cases, the variables affected by the composition of a gas mixture are the numbers of moles of each component and the contribution each component makes to the total observed pressure. Because gases mix completely, all the components of the mixture occupy the same volume—that of the container holding them. Furthermore, the temperature of each gaseous component is the same as the temperature of the entire mixture. Therefore, in a gas mixture, each of the components has the same volume and the same temperature.

Each gas in a mixture exerts its own pressure which contributes to the total pressure

In a mixture of nonreacting gases such as air, each gas contributes to the total pressure in proportion to the fraction (by moles) in which it is present (see Figure 10.10). This contribution to the total pressure is called the **partial pressure** of the gas. It is the pressure the gas would exert if it were the only gas in a container of the same size at the same temperature.

The general symbol we will use for the partial pressure of gas A is P_A. For a particular gas, the formula of the gas may be put into the subscript, as in P_{O_2}. What John Dalton discovered about partial pressures is now called **Dalton's law of partial pressures:** *The total pressure of a mixture of gases is the sum of their individual partial pressures.* In equation form, the law is

$$P_{\text{total}} = P_A + P_B + P_C + \cdots \qquad (10.3)$$

In dry CO_2-free air at STP, for example, P_{O_2} is 159.12 torr, P_{N_2} is 593.44 torr, and P_{Ar} is 7.10 torr. These partial pressures add up to 759.66 torr, just 0.34 torr less than 760 torr or 1.00 atm. The remaining 0.34 torr is contributed by several trace gases, including other noble gases.

> **Practice Exercise 21:** At 20 °C a 1.00 liter flask is filled with 10.0 g of Ar, 10.0 g of N_2, and 10.0 g of O_2. What are the partial pressures of each gas and what is the total pressure in the flask? (Hint: Start by calculating the moles of each gas present.)
>
> **Practice Exercise 22:** Suppose a tank of oxygen-enriched air prepared for scuba diving has a volume of 17.00 L and a pressure of 237.0 atm at 25 °C. How many grams of oxygen are present if all the other gases in the tank exert a combined partial pressure of 115.0 atm?

Collecting gases over water

When gases that do not react with water are prepared in the laboratory, they can be trapped over water by an apparatus like that shown in Figure 10.11. Because of the way the gas is collected, it is saturated with water vapor. (We say the gas is "wet.") Water vapor in a mixture of gases has a partial pressure like that of any other gas.

The vapor present in the space above *any* liquid always contains some of the liquid's vapor, which exerts its own pressure called the liquid's **vapor pressure**. Its value for any given

☐ Under ordinary temperatures and pressures, nitrogen and oxygen in air do not react.

TOOLS
Dalton's law of partial pressures

Container wall
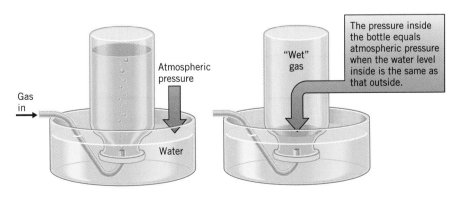
Gas A ●   Gas B ○

FIG. 10.10 Partial pressures viewed at the molecular level. In a mixture of two gases, A and B, both collide with the walls of the container and thereby contribute their partial pressures to the total pressure.

☐ Even the mercury in a barometer has a tiny vapor pressure—0.0012 torr at 20 °C, which is much too small to affect readings of barometers and the manometers studied in this chapter.

Gas in →   Atmospheric pressure   "Wet" gas   The pressure inside the bottle equals atmospheric pressure when the water level inside is the same as that outside.

Water

FIG. 10.11 Collecting a gas over water. As the gas bubbles through the water, water vapor goes into the gas, so the total pressure inside the bottle includes the partial pressure of the water vapor at the temperature of the water.

TABLE 10.2	Vapor Pressure of Water at Various Temperatures		
Temperature (°C)	Vapor Pressure (torr)	Temperature (°C)	Vapor Pressure (torr)
0	4.579	50	92.51
5	6.543	55	118.0
10	9.209	60	149.4
15	12.79	65	187.5
20	17.54	70	233.7
25	23.76	75	289.1
30	31.82	80	355.1
35	41.18	85	433.6
37[a]	47.07	90	525.8
40	55.32	95	633.9
45	71.88	100	760.0

[a] Human body temperature.

substance depends only on the temperature. The vapor pressures of water at different temperatures, for example, are given in Table 10.2. A more complete table is in Appendix C.4.

If we have adjusted the height of the collecting jar so the water level inside matches that outside, the total pressure of the trapped gas equals the atmospheric pressure, so the value for P_{total} is obtained from the laboratory barometer. We thus calculate P_{gas}, which is the pressure that the gas would exert if it were dry (i.e., without water vapor in it) and inside the same volume that was used to collect it.[9]

EXAMPLE 10.10
Collecting a Gas over Water

A sample of oxygen is collected over water at 20 °C and a pressure of 738 torr. Its volume is 310 mL. (a) What is the partial pressure of the oxygen? (b) What would be its volume when dry at STP?

ANALYSIS: There are two parts to this problem, so before we get started, let's determine which of the gas laws will be our tools for solving them. It seems pretty clear that for part (a) we will need Dalton's law of partial pressures. We have O_2 collected over water, so we know the container holds both O_2 and $H_2O(g)$. For part (b), we have to determine how the volume of the O_2 collected will change when the conditions change to those of STP. We're not changing the amount of O_2. The amount of O_2 is fixed (constant); it just undergoes changes in P, V, and T. To work problems of this kind, our tool is the combined gas law.

To solve part (a), we will have to subtract the vapor pressure of water from the total pressure of the gas mixture (738 torr). That's all there is to it.

To solve part (b), we substitute into the combined gas law after solving it for V_2. Our starting conditions will be 310 mL, 20 °C, and the pressure obtained in part (a). The final conditions will have a temperature of 0 °C and a pressure of 760 torr.

SOLUTION: To calculate the partial pressure of the oxygen, we use Dalton's law. We will need the vapor pressure of water at 20 °C, which we find in Table 10.2 to be 17.5 torr.

$$P_{O_2} = P_{total} - P_{water\ vapor}$$

$$= 738\ torr - 17.5\ torr = 720\ torr$$

The answer to part (a) is that the partial pressure of O_2 is 720 torr.

---

[9] If the water levels are not the same inside the flask and outside, a correction has to be calculated and applied to the room pressure to obtain the true pressure in the flask. For example, if the water level is higher inside the flask than outside, the pressure in the flask is lower than atmospheric pressure. The difference in levels is in millimeters of *water*, so this has to be converted to the equivalent in millimeters of mercury using the fact that the pressure exerted by a column of fluid is inversely proportional to the fluid's density.

For part (b), we'll begin by assembling the data.

	Initial (1)	Final (2)
P	720 torr (which is P_{O_2})	760 torr (standard pressure)
V	310 mL	?
T	293 K (20.0 °C + 273)	273 K (standard temperature)

We use these in the combined gas law equation:

$$\frac{P_1 V_1}{T_1} = \frac{P_2 V_2}{T_2}$$

Solving for V_2 and rearranging the equation a bit we have

$$V_2 = V_1 \times \left(\frac{P_1}{P_2}\right) \times \left(\frac{T_2}{T_1}\right)$$

Now we can substitute values and calculate V_2.

$$V_2 = 310 \text{ mL} \times \left(\frac{720 \text{ torr}}{760 \text{ torr}}\right) \times \left(\frac{273 \text{ K}}{293 \text{ K}}\right)$$

$$= 274 \text{ mL}$$

Thus, when the water vapor is removed from the gas sample, the dry oxygen will occupy a volume of 274 mL at STP.

ARE THE ANSWERS REASONABLE? We know the pressure of the dry O_2 will be less than that of the wet gas, so the answer to part (a) seems reasonable. To check part (b), we can see if the pressure and temperature ratios move the volume in the right direction. The pressure is increasing (720 torr → 760 torr), which should tend to lower the volume. The pressure ratio above will do that. The temperature change (293 K → 273 K) should also lower the volume, and once again, the temperature ratio above will have that effect. Our answer to part (b) is probably okay.

Practice Exercise 23: A 2.50 L sample of methane was collected over water at 30 °C until the pressure in the flask was 775 torr. A small amount of $CaSO_4(s)$ was then added to the flask to absorb the water vapor [forming $CaSO_4 \cdot 2H_2O(s)$]. What is the pressure inside the flask once all the water is absorbed? Assume that the addition of $CaSO_4(s)$ absorbed all the water and did not change the volume of the flask. How many moles of $CH_4(g)$ have been collected? (Hint: Find the partial pressure of water at 30 °C.)

Practice Exercise 24: Suppose you prepared a sample of nitrogen and collected it over water at 15 °C at a total pressure of 745 torr and a volume of 310 mL. Find the partial pressure of the nitrogen and the volume it would occupy at STP.

The composition of a mixture can be expressed in mole fractions or mole percents

One of the useful ways of describing the composition of a mixture is in terms of the *mole fractions* of the components. The **mole fraction** *is the ratio of the number of moles of a given component to the total number of moles of all components.* Expressed mathematically, the mole fraction of substance *A* in a mixture of *A, B, C, ..., Z* substances is

$$X_A = \frac{n_A}{n_A + n_B + n_C + n_D + \cdots + n_Z} \qquad (10.4)$$

where X_A is the mole fraction of component *A*, and n_A, n_B, n_C, ..., n_Z are the numbers of moles of each component, *A, B, C, ..., Z*, respectively. The sum of all mole fractions for a mixture must always equal 1.

☐ The concept of mole fraction applies to any uniform mixture in any physical state—gas, liquid, or solid.

TOOLS Mole fractions

You can see in Equation 10.4 both numerator and denominator have the same units (moles), so they cancel. As a result, a mole fraction has no units. Nevertheless, always remember the definition: a mole fraction stands for the ratio of *moles* of one component to the total number of *moles* of all components.

Sometimes the mole fraction composition of a mixture is expressed on a percentage basis; we call it a **mole percent (mol%).** The mole percent is obtained by multiplying the mole fraction by 100 mol%.

Mole fractions of gases are related to partial pressures

Partial pressure data can be used to calculate the mole fractions of individual gases in a gas mixture because the number of *moles* of each gas is directly proportional to its partial pressure. We can demonstrate this as follows. The partial pressure, P_A, for any one gas, A, in a gas mixture with a total volume V at a temperature T is found by the ideal gas law equation, $PV = nRT$. So to calculate the number of moles of A present, we have

$$n_A = \frac{P_A V}{RT}$$

For any particular gas mixture at a given temperature, the values of V, R, and T are all constants, making the ratio V/RT a constant, too. We can therefore simplify the previous equation by using C to stand for V/RT. In other words, we can write

$$n_A = P_A C$$

The result is the same as saying that *the number of moles of a gas in a mixture of gases is directly proportional to the partial pressure of the gas.* The constant C is the same for all gases in the mixture. So by using different letters to identify individual gases, we can let $P_B C$ stand for n_B, $P_C C$ stand for n_C, and so on in Equation 10.4. Thus,

$$X_A = \frac{P_A C}{P_A C + P_B C + P_C C + \cdots + P_Z C}$$

The constant, C, can be factored out and canceled, so

$$X_A = \frac{P_A}{P_A + P_B + P_C + \cdots + P_Z}$$

The denominator is the sum of the partial pressures of all the gases in the mixture, but this sum equals the total pressure of the mixture (Dalton's law of partial pressures). Therefore, the previous equation simplifies to

TOOLS
Mole fraction and partial pressure.

$$X_A = \frac{P_A}{P_{\text{total}}} \qquad (10.5)$$

Thus, the mole fraction of a gas in a gas mixture is simply the ratio of its partial pressure to the total pressure. Equation 10.5 also gives us a simple way to calculate the partial pressure of a gas in a gas mixture when we know its mole fraction.

EXAMPLE 10.11
Using Mole Fractions to Calculate Partial Pressures

Suppose a mixture of oxygen and nitrogen is prepared in which there are 0.200 mol O_2 and 0.500 mol N_2. If the total pressure of the mixture is 745 torr, what are the partial pressures of the two gases in the mixture?

ANALYSIS: In this problem we know the composition of the mixture and the total pressure. It is important to remember that we can calculate the partial pressure of a gas if we know its mole fraction in the mixture and the total pressure. To solve the problem we will first calculate the mole fraction of each gas and then apply Equation 10.5.

SOLUTION: The mole fractions are calculated as follows:

$$X_{O_2} = \frac{\text{moles of } O_2}{\text{moles of } O_2 + \text{moles of } N_2}$$

$$= \frac{0.200 \text{ mol}}{0.200 \text{ mol} + 0.500 \text{ mol}}$$

$$= \frac{0.200 \text{ mol}}{0.700 \text{ mol}} = 0.286$$

Similarly, for N_2 we have[10]

$$X_{N_2} = \frac{0.500 \text{ mol}}{0.200 \text{ mol} + 0.500 \text{ mol}} = 0.714$$

We can now use Equation 10.5 to calculate the partial pressure. Solving the equation for partial pressure, we have

$$P_{O_2} = X_{O_2} P_{total}$$

$$= 0.286 \times 745 \text{ torr}$$

$$= 213 \text{ torr}$$

$$P_{N_2} = X_{N_2} P_{total}$$

$$= 0.714 \times 745 \text{ torr}$$

$$= 532 \text{ torr}$$

Thus, the partial pressure of O_2 is 213 torr and the partial pressure of N_2 is 532 torr.

ARE THE ANSWERS REASONABLE? There are three things we can check here. First, the mole fractions add up to 1.000, which they must. Second, the partial pressures add up to 745 torr, which equals the given total pressure. Third, the mole fraction of N_2 is somewhat more than twice that for O_2, so its partial pressure should be somewhat more than twice that of O_2. Examining the answers, we see this is true, so our answers should be correct.

Practice Exercise 25: Sulfur dioxide and oxygen react according to the equation

$$2SO_2(g) + O_2(g) \longrightarrow 2SO_3(g)$$

If 50.0 g of $SO_2(g)$ is added to a flask resulting in a pressure of 0.750 atm, what will be the total pressure in the flask when a stoichiometric amount of oxygen is added? (Hint: This problem gives you more information than is needed.)

Practice Exercise 26: Suppose a mixture containing 2.15 g H_2 and 34.0 g NO has a total pressure of 2.05 atm. What are the partial pressures of both gases in the mixture?

Practice Exercise 27: What is the mole fraction and the mole percent of oxygen in exhaled air if P_{O_2} is 116 torr and P_{total} is 760 torr?

10.7 | EFFUSION AND DIFFUSION IN GASES LEADS TO GRAHAM'S LAW

If you've ever walked past a restaurant and found your mouth watering after smelling the aroma of food, you've learned firsthand about diffusion! **Diffusion** is the spontaneous mixing of the molecules of one gas, like those of the food aromas, with molecules of another gas, like the air outside the restaurant. (See Figure 10.12a.) **Effusion,** on the other hand,

---

[10]Notice that the sum of the mole fractions (0.286 + 0.714) equals 1.000. In fact, we could have obtained the mole fraction of nitrogen with less calculation by subtracting the mole fraction of oxygen from 1.00.

$$X_{O_2} + X_{N_2} = 1.000$$
$$X_{N_2} = 1.000 - X_{O_2}$$
$$= 1.000 - 0.286 = 0.714$$

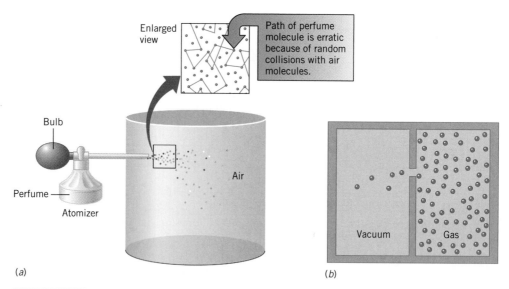

FIG. 10.12 Spontaneous movements of gases. (a) Diffusion. (b) Effusion.

is the gradual movement of gas molecules through a very tiny hole into a vacuum (Figure 10.12*b*). The rates at which both of these processes occur depends on the speeds of gas molecules; the faster the molecules move, the more rapidly diffusion and effusion occur.

The Scottish chemist Thomas Graham (1805–1869) studied the rates of diffusion and effusion of a variety of gases through porous clay pots and through small apertures. Comparing different gases at the same temperature and pressure, Graham found that their rates of effusion were inversely proportional to the square roots of their densities. This relationship is now called **Graham's law.**

Graham's law of effusion

□ By taking the ratio, the proportionality constant, *k*, cancels from numerator and denominator.

$$\text{Effusion rate} = \frac{k}{\sqrt{d}} \quad \left(\begin{array}{c}\text{when compared at the} \\ \text{same } T \text{ and } P\end{array}\right)$$

Graham's law is usually used in comparing the rates of effusion of different gases, so the proportionality constant can be eliminated and an equation can be formed by writing the ratio of effusion rates.

$$\frac{\text{effusion rate } (A)}{\text{effusion rate } (B)} = \frac{\sqrt{d_B}}{\sqrt{d_A}} = \sqrt{\frac{d_B}{d_A}} \qquad (10.6)$$

Earlier you saw that the density of a gas is directly proportional to its molar mass. Therefore, we can re-express Equation 10.6 as follows.

$$\frac{\text{effusion rate } (A)}{\text{effusion rate } (B)} = \frac{\sqrt{d_B}}{\sqrt{d_A}} = \sqrt{\frac{M_B}{M_A}} \qquad (10.7)$$

where M_A and M_B are the molar masses of gases A and B.

Molar masses also affect the rates at which gases undergo diffusion. Gases with low molar masses diffuse (and effuse) more rapidly than gases with high molar masses. Thus, hydrogen with a molar mass of 2 will diffuse more rapidly than methane, CH_4, with a molar mass of 16.

EXAMPLE 10.12
Using Graham's Law

At a given temperature and pressure, which effuses more rapidly and by what factor, ammonia or hydrogen chloride?

ANALYSIS: A gas effusion problem requires the use of Graham's law, which says that the gas with the smaller molar mass will effuse more rapidly. So we need to find the molar masses. Then the relative rates of effusion are found by using them in Equation 10.7.

FACETS OF CHEMISTRY

Effusion and Nuclear Energy

The fuel used in almost all nuclear reactors is uranium, but only one of its naturally occurring isotopes, ^{235}U, can be easily split to yield energy. Unfortunately, this isotope is present in a very low concentration (about 0.72%) in naturally occurring uranium. Most of the element as it is mined consists of the more abundant isotope ^{238}U. Therefore, before uranium can be fabricated into fuel elements, it must be enriched to a ^{235}U concentration of about 2 to 5 percent. Enrichment requires that the isotopes be separated, at least to some degree.

Separating the uranium isotopes is not feasible by chemical means because the chemical properties of both isotopes are essentially identical. Instead, a method is required that is based on the very small difference in the masses of the isotopes. As it happens, uranium forms a compound with fluorine, UF_6, that is easily vaporized at a relatively low temperature. The UF_6 gas thus formed consists of two kinds of molecules, $^{235}UF_6$ and $^{238}UF_6$, with molecular masses of 349 and 352, respectively. Because of their different masses, their rates of effusion are slightly different; $^{235}UF_6$ effuses 1.0043 times faster than $^{238}UF_6$. Although the difference is small, it is sufficient to enable enrichment, provided the effusion is carried out over and over again enough times. In fact, it takes over 1400 separate effusion chambers arranged one after another to achieve the necessary level of enrichment.

SOLUTION: The molar masses are 17.03 for NH_3 and 36.46 for HCl, so we know that NH_3, with its smaller molar mass, effuses more rapidly than HCl. The ratio of the effusion rates is given by

$$\frac{\text{effusion rate (NH}_3)}{\text{effusion rate (HCl)}} = \sqrt{\frac{M_{HCl}}{M_{NH_3}}}$$

$$= \sqrt{\frac{36.46}{17.03}} = 1.463$$

We can rearrange the result as

$$\text{Effusion rate (NH}_3) = 1.463 \times \text{effusion rate (HCl)}$$

Thus, ammonia effuses 1.463 times more rapidly than HCl under the same conditions.

IS THE ANSWER REASONABLE? The only quick check is to be sure that the arithmetic tells us ammonia with its lower molar mass effuses more rapidly than the HCl, and that's what our result tells us.

Practice Exercise 28: Bromine has two isotopes with masses of 78.9 and 80.9 (to three significant figures), respectively. What is the expected ratio of the rate of effusion of Br-81 compared to Br-79? (Hint: Note that the example above gives the equation for the rate of effusion of ammonia compared to hydrogen chloride.)

Practice Exercise 29: The hydrogen halide gases all have the same general formula, HX, where X can be F, Cl, Br, or I. If HCl(g) effuses 1.88 times more rapidly than one of the others, which hydrogen halide is the other, HF, HBr, or HI?

10.8 | THE KINETIC MOLECULAR THEORY EXPLAINS THE GAS LAWS

Scientists in the nineteenth century, who already knew the gas laws, wondered what had to be true about all gases to account for their conformity to a common set of gas laws. The **kinetic molecular theory of gases** provided an answer. We introduced some of its ideas in Chapter 6, and at the beginning of this chapter we described a number of observations that suggest what gases must be like when viewed at a molecular level. Let's look more closely now at the kinetic molecular theory to see how well it explains the behavior of gases.

The theory, often called simply the kinetic theory of gases, consisted of a set of postulates that describe the makeup of an ideal gas. Then the laws of physics and statistics were applied to see whether the observed gas laws could be predicted from the model. The results were splendidly successful.

> ### Postulates of the Kinetic Theory of Gases
>
> 1. A gas consists of an extremely large number of very tiny particles that are in constant, random motion.
> 2. The gas particles themselves occupy a net volume so small in relation to the volume of their container that their contribution to the total volume can be ignored.
> 3. The particles often collide in perfectly elastic collisions[11] with themselves and with the walls of the container, and they move in straight lines between collisions neither attracting nor repelling each other.

☐ The particles are assumed to be so small that they have no dimensions at all. They are essentially points in space.

In summary, the model pictures an ideal gas as a collection of constantly moving, extremely small, billiard balls that continually bounce off each other and the walls of their container, and so exert a net pressure on the walls (as described in Figure 10.1, page 391). The gas particles are assumed to be so small that their individual volumes can be ignored, so an ideal gas is effectively all empty space.

The gas laws are predicted by the kinetic theory

According to the model, gases are mostly empty space. As we noted earlier, this explains why gases, unlike liquids and solids, can be compressed so much (squeezed to smaller volumes). It also explains why we have gas laws for gases, and *the same laws for all gases*, but not comparable laws for liquids or solids. The chemical identity of the gas does not matter, because gas molecules do not touch each other except when they collide, and there are extremely weak interactions, if any, between them.

We cannot go over the mathematical details, but we can describe some of the ways in which the laws of physics and the model of an ideal gas account for the gas laws.

Kinetic molecular theory relates temperature to average kinetic energy

The greatest triumph of the kinetic theory came with its explanation of gas temperature, which we discussed in Section 6.2. What the calculations showed was that the product of gas pressure and volume, PV, is proportional to the average kinetic energy of the gas molecules.

$$PV \propto \text{average molecular KE}$$

But from the experimental study of gases, culminating in the equation of state for an ideal gas, we have another term to which PV is proportional, namely, the Kelvin temperature of the gas.

$$PV \propto T$$

(We know what the proportionality constant here is, namely, nR, because by the ideal gas law, PV equals nRT.) With PV proportional *both* to T and to the "average molecular KE," then it must be true that the temperature of a gas is proportional to the average molecular KE.

$$T \propto \text{average molecular KE}$$

Kinetic theory explains the pressure–volume law (Boyle's law)

Using the model of an ideal gas, physicists were able to demonstrate that gas pressure is the net effect of innumerable collisions made by gas particles with the walls of the container. Let's imagine that one wall of a gas container is a movable piston that we can push in (or pull out) and so change the volume (see Figure 10.13). If we reduce the volume by one-half, we double the number of molecules per unit volume. This would double the number of collisions per second with each unit area of the wall and therefore double the pressure.

Lower pressure

1 kg

(a)

Higher pressure

1 kg   1 kg

(b)

FIG. 10.13 The kinetic theory and the pressure–volume law (Boyle's law). When the gas volume is made smaller in going from (a) to (b), the number of collisions per second with each unit area of the container's walls increases. Therefore, the pressure increases.

---

[11]In *perfectly elastic* collisions, no energy is lost by friction as the colliding objects deform momentarily.

Thus, cutting the volume in half forces the pressure to double, which is exactly what Boyle discovered:

$$P \propto \frac{1}{V} \quad \text{or} \quad V \propto \frac{1}{P}$$

Kinetic theory explains the pressure–temperature law (Gay-Lussac's law)

As you learned earlier, the kinetic theory tells us that increasing the temperature increases the average velocity of gas particles. At higher velocities, the particles strike the container's walls more frequently and with greater force. If we don't change the volume, the *area* being struck remains the same, so the force per unit area (the pressure) must increase. Thus, the kinetic theory explains how the pressure of a fixed amount of gas is proportional to temperature (at constant volume), which is the pressure–temperature law of Gay-Lussac.

Kinetic theory explains the temperature–volume law (Charles' law)

We've just seen that the kinetic theory predicts that increasing the temperature of a gas should increase the pressure if the volume doesn't change. But suppose we wished to keep the pressure constant when we raised the temperature. We could only do this if we allowed the gas to expand. Therefore, a gas expands with increasing T in order to keep P constant, which is another way of saying that V is proportional to T at constant P. Thus, the kinetic theory explains Charles' law.

Kinetic theory explains Dalton's law of partial pressures

The law of partial pressures is actually evidence for that part of the third postulate in the kinetic theory that pictures particles of an ideal gas moving in straight lines between collisions, neither attracting nor repelling each other (see Figure 10.14). By not interacting with each other, the molecules act *independently*, so each gas behaves as though it were alone in the container. Only if the particles of each gas do act independently can the partial pressures of the gases add up in a simple way to give the total pressure.

Kinetic theory explains Graham's law of effusion

The key conditions of Graham's law are that the rates of effusion of two gases with different molecular masses must be compared at the same pressure and temperature and under conditions where the gas molecules do not hinder each other. When two gases have the same temperature, their particles have identical average molecular kinetic energies. Using subscripts 1 and 2 to identify two gases with molecules having different masses m_1 and m_2, we can write that at a given temperature

$$\overline{KE_1} = \overline{KE_2}$$

where the bar over KE signifies "average."

For a single molecule, its kinetic energy is $KE = \frac{1}{2}mv^2$. For a large collection of molecules of the same substance, the average kinetic energy is $\overline{KE} = \frac{1}{2}m\overline{v^2}$, where $\overline{v^2}$ is the *average of the velocities squared* (called the *mean square* velocity). We have not extended the "average" notation (the bar) over the mass because all the molecules of a given substance have the same mass (the average of their masses is just the mass).

Once again comparing two gases, 1 and 2, we take $\overline{v_1^2}$ and $\overline{v_2^2}$ to be the average of the velocities squared of their molecules. If both gases are at the same temperature, we have

$$\overline{KE_1} = \frac{1}{2}m_1\overline{v_1^2} = \frac{1}{2}m_2\overline{v_2^2} = \overline{KE_2}$$

Now let's rearrange the previous equation to get the ratio of $\overline{v^2}$ terms.

$$\frac{\overline{v_1^2}}{\overline{v_2^2}} = \frac{m_2}{m_1}$$

Next, we'll take the square root of both sides. When we do this, we obtain a ratio of quantities called the **root mean square** (abbreviated **rms**) **speeds**, which we will represent as $(\overline{v_1})_{rms}$ and $(\overline{v_2})_{rms}$.

$$\frac{(\overline{v_1})_{rms}}{(\overline{v_2})_{rms}} = \sqrt{\frac{m_2}{m_1}}$$

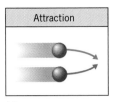

(a)

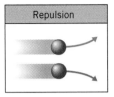

(b)

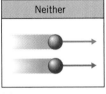

(c)

FIG. 10.14 **Gas molecules act independently when they neither attract nor repel each other.** Gas molecules would not travel in straight lines if they attracted each other as in (*a*) or repelled each other as in (*b*). They would have to travel farther between collisions with the walls and, therefore, would collide with the walls less frequently. This would affect the pressure. Only if the molecules traveled in straight lines with no attractions or repulsions, as in (*c*), would their individual pressures not be influenced by near misses or by collisions between the molecules.

□ Suppose we have two molecules with speeds of 6 and 10 m s^{-1}. The average speed is $\frac{1}{2}(6 + 10) = 8$ m s^{-1}. The rms speed is obtained by squaring each speed, averaging the squared values, and then taking the square root of the result. Thus,

$$\overline{v_{\text{rms}}} = \sqrt{\tfrac{1}{2}(6^2 + 10^2)}$$
$$= 8.2 \text{ m s}^{-1}$$

The rms speed, $(\overline{v})_{\text{rms}}$, is not actually the same as the average speed of the gas molecules, but instead represents the speed of a molecule that would have the average kinetic energy. (The difference is subtle, and the two averages do not differ by much, as noted in the margin.)

For any substance, the mass of an individual molecule is proportional to the molecular mass. Representing a molecular mass of a gas by M, we can restate this as $m \propto M$. The proportionality constant is the same for all gases. (It's in grams per atomic mass unit when we express m in atomic mass units.) When we take a ratio of two molecular masses, the constant cancels anyway, so we can write

$$\frac{(\overline{v_1})_{\text{rms}}}{(\overline{v_2})_{\text{rms}}} = \sqrt{\frac{m_2}{m_1}} = \sqrt{\frac{M_2}{M_1}}$$

Notice that the preceding equation tells us that the rms speed of the molecules is inversely proportional to the square root of the molecular mass. This means that *at a given temperature, molecules of a gas with a high molecular mass move more slowly, on average, than molecules of a gas with a low molecular mass.*

As you might expect, fast moving molecules will find an opening in the wall of a container more often than slow moving molecules, so they will effuse faster. Therefore, the rate of effusion of a gas is proportional to the average speed of its molecules, and it is also proportional to $1/\sqrt{M}$.

$$\text{Effusion rate} \propto (\overline{v})_{\text{rms}} \propto \frac{1}{\sqrt{M}}$$

Let's use k as the proportionality constant. This gives

$$\text{Effusion rate} = \frac{k}{\sqrt{M}}$$

Comparing two gases, 1 and 2, and taking a ratio of effusion rates to cause k to cancel, we have

$$\frac{\text{effusion rate (gas 1)}}{\text{effusion rate (gas 2)}} = \sqrt{\frac{M_2}{M_1}}$$

This is the way we expressed Graham's law in Equation 10.7. Thus, still another gas law supports the model of an ideal gas.

Kinetic theory predicts an absolute zero

The kinetic theory found that the temperature is proportional to the average kinetic energy of the molecules.

$$T \propto \text{average molecular KE} \propto \tfrac{1}{2}m\overline{v^2}$$

If the average molecular KE becomes zero, the temperature must also become zero. But mass (m) cannot become zero, so the only way that the average molecular KE can be zero is if v goes to zero. A particle cannot move any slower that it does at a dead standstill, so if the particles stop moving entirely, the substance is as cold as anything can get. It's at absolute zero.[12]

---

[12]Actually, even at 0 K, there must be some slight motion. It's required by the Heisenberg uncertainty principle, which says (in one form) that it's impossible to know precisely both the speed and the location of a particle simultaneously. (If one knows the speed, then there's uncertainty in the location, for example.) If the molecules were actually dead still at absolute zero, there would be no uncertainty in their speed. But then the uncertainty in their *position* would be infinitely great. We would not know where they were! But we do know; they're in this or that container. Thus some uncertainty in speed must exist to have less uncertainty in position and so locate the sample!

10.9 | REAL GASES DON'T OBEY THE IDEAL GAS LAW PERFECTLY

According to the ideal gas law, the ratio PV/T equals a product of two constants, nR. But, experimentally, for real gases PV/T is actually not quite a constant. When we use experimental values of P, V, and T for a real gas, such as O_2, to plot actual values of PV/T as a function of P, we get the curve shown in Figure 10.15. The *horizontal* line at $PV/T = 1$ in Figure 10.15 is what we should see if PV/T were truly constant over all values of P, as it would be for an ideal gas.

A real gas, like oxygen, deviates from ideal behavior for two important reasons. First, the model of an ideal gas assumes that gas molecules are infinitesimally small—that the individual molecules have no volume. But real molecules do take up some space. (If all of the kinetic motions of the gas molecules ceased and the molecules settled, you could imagine the net space that the molecules would occupy in and of themselves.) Second, in an ideal gas there would be no attractions between molecules, but in a real gas molecules do experience weak attractions toward each other.

At room temperature and atmospheric pressure, most gases behave nearly like an ideal gas, also for two reasons. First, the space between the molecules is so large that the volume occupied by the molecules themselves is insignificant. By doubling the pressure, we are able to squeeze the gas into very nearly half the volume. Second, the molecules are moving so rapidly and are so far apart that the attractions between them are hardly felt. As a result, the gas behaves almost as though there are no attractions.

Deviations from ideal behavior are felt most when the gas is at very high pressure and when the temperature is low. Raising the pressure can reduce only the empty space between the molecules, not the volume of the individual particles themselves. At high pressure, the space taken by the molecules themselves is a significant part of the total volume, so doubling the pressure cannot halve the total volume. As a result, the actual volume of a real gas is larger than expected for an ideal gas, and the ratio PV/T is larger than if the gas were ideal. We see this for O_2 at the right side of the graph in Figure 10.15.

The attractive forces between molecules reveal themselves by causing the pressure of a real gas to be slightly lower than that expected for an ideal gas. The attractions cause the paths of the molecules to bend whenever they pass near each other (Figure 10.16). Because the molecules are not traveling in straight lines, as they would in an ideal gas, they have to travel farther between collisions with the walls. As a result, the molecules of a real gas don't strike the walls as frequently as they would if the gas were ideal, and this reduced frequency of collision translates to a reduced pressure. Thus, the ratio PV/T is *less* than that for an ideal gas, particularly where the problem of particle volume is least, at lower pressures. The curve for O_2 in Figure 10.15, therefore, dips at lower pressures.

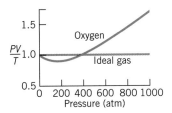

FIG. 10.15 **Deviation from the ideal gas law.** A graph of PV/T versus P for an ideal gas is equivalent to plotting a constant versus P. The graph must be a straight line, as shown, because the ideal gas law equation tells us that $PV/T = nR$ (a product of constants). The same plot for oxygen, a real gas, is not a straight line, showing that O_2 is not "ideal."

The van der Waals equation corrects for deviations from ideal behavior

Many attempts have been made to modify the equation of state of an ideal gas to get an equation that better fits the experimental data for individual real gases. One of the more successful efforts was that of J. D. van der Waals. He found ways to correct the measured values of P and V to give better fits of the data to the general gas law equation. The result of his derivation is called the *van der Waals equation of state for a real gas*. Let's take a brief look at how van der Waals made corrections to measured values of P and V to obtain expressions that fit the ideal gas law.

As you know, if a gas were ideal, it would obey the equation

$$P_{ideal}V_{ideal} = nRT$$

But for a real gas, using the measured pressure, P_{meas}, and measured volume, V_{meas},

$$P_{meas}V_{meas} \neq nRT$$

The reason is because P_{meas} is smaller than P_{ideal} (as a result of attractive forces between real gas molecules), and because V_{meas} is larger than V_{ideal} (because real molecules do take up

J. D. van der Waals (1837–1923), a Dutch scientist, won the 1910 Nobel Prize in Physics.

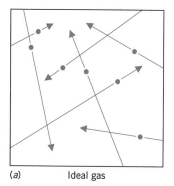

(a)   Ideal gas

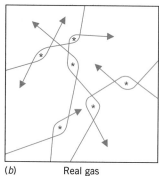

(b)   Real gas

FIG. 10.16 **The effect of attractive forces on the pressure of a real gas.** (*a*) In an ideal gas, the molecules would travel in straight lines. (*b*) In a real gas, the paths curve as one molecule passes close to another because the molecules attract each other. Asterisks indicate the points at which molecules come close to each other. Because of the curved paths, molecules of a real gas take longer to reach the walls between collisions, which reduces the collision frequency and so slightly lowers the pressure.

some space). Therefore, to get the pressure and volume to obey the ideal gas law, we have to *add* something to the measured pressure and *subtract* something from the measured volume. That's exactly what van der Waals did. Here's his equation.

the measured pressure

the measured volume

$$\left(P_{\text{meas}} + \frac{n^2 a}{V^2}\right)(V_{\text{meas}} - nb) = nRT \tag{10.8}$$

correction to bring measured P up to the pressure an ideal gas would exert

correction to reduce measured V to the volume an ideal gas would have

The constants a and b are called *van der Waals constants* (see Table 10.3). They are determined for each real gas by carefully measuring P, V, and T under varying conditions. Then trial calculations are made to figure out what values of the constants give the best matches between the observed data and the van der Waals equation.

Notice that the constant a involves a correction to the pressure term of the ideal gas law, so the size of a would indicate something about attractions between molecules. Larger values of a mean stronger attractive forces between molecules. Thus, the most easily liquefied substances, like water and ethyl alcohol, have the largest values of the van der Waals constant a, suggesting relatively strong attractive forces between their molecules.

The constant b helps to correct for the volume occupied by the molecules themselves, so the size of b indicates something about the sizes of particles in the gas. Larger values of b mean larger molecular sizes. Looking at data for the noble gases in Table 10.3, we see that as the atoms become larger from helium through xenon, the values of b also become larger. In the next chapter we'll continue the study of factors that control the physical state of a substance, particularly attractive forces and their origins.

TABLE 10.3	Van der Waals Constants	
Substance	a (L^2 atm mol^{-2})	b (L mol^{-1})
Noble Gases		
Helium, He	0.03421	0.02370
Neon, Ne	0.2107	0.01709
Argon, Ar	1.345	0.03219
Krypton, Kr	2.318	0.03978
Xenon, Xe	4.194	0.05105
Other Gases		
Hydrogen, H_2	0.02444	0.02661
Oxygen, O_2	1.360	0.03183
Nitrogen, N_2	1.390	0.03913
Methane, CH_4	2.253	0.04278
Carbon dioxide, CO_2	3.592	0.04267
Ammonia, NH_3	4.170	0.03707
Water, H_2O	5.464	0.03049
Ethyl alcohol, C_2H_5OH	12.02	0.08407

SUMMARY

Barometers, Manometers, and Pressure Units. Atmospheric pressure is measured with a **barometer** in which a pressure of one **standard atmosphere** (1 **atm**) will support a column of mercury 760 mm high. This is a pressure of 760 **torr**. By definition, 1 atm = 101,325 **pascals (Pa)** and 1 **bar** = 100 kPa. **Manometers,** both open end and closed end, are used to measure the pressure of trapped gases.

Gas Laws. An **ideal gas** is a hypothetical gas that obeys the gas laws exactly over all ranges of pressure and temperature. Real gases exhibit ideal gas behavior most closely at low pressures and high temperatures, which are conditions remote from those that liquefy a gas.

Boyle's Law (Pressure–Volume Law). For a fixed amount of gas at constant temperature, volume varies inversely with pressure: $V \propto 1/P$. A useful form of the equation is $P_1 V_1 = P_2 V_2$.

Charles' Law (Temperature–Volume Law). For a fixed amount of gas at constant pressure, volume varies directly with the Kelvin temperature: $V \propto T$, or $V_1/V_2 = T_1/T_2$.

Gay-Lussac's Law (Temperature–Pressure Law). For a fixed amount of gas at constant volume, pressure varies directly with Kelvin temperature: $P \propto T$, or $P_1/P_2 = T_1/T_2$.

Avogadro's Principle. Equal volumes of gases contain equal numbers of moles when compared at the same temperature and pressure. At **STP**, 1 mol of an ideal gas occupies a volume of 22.4 L.

Combined Gas Law. PV divided by *T* for a given gas sample is a constant: $PV/T = C$, or $P_1 V_1/T_1 = P_2 V_2/T_2$.

Ideal Gas Law. $PV = nRT$. When *P* is in atmospheres and *V* is in liters, the value of *R* is 0.0821 L atm mol^{-1} K^{-1} (*T* being, as usual, in kelvins).

Gay-Lussac's Law of Combining Volumes. When measured at the same temperature and pressure, the volumes of gases consumed and produced in chemical reactions are in the same ratios as their coefficients.

Mole Fraction. The mole fraction X_A of a substance *A* equals the ratio of the number of moles of *A*, n_A, to the total number of moles, n_{total}, of all the components of a mixture:

$$X_A = \frac{n_A}{n_{total}}$$

Dalton's Law of Partial Pressures. The total pressure of a mixture of gases is the sum of the partial pressures of the individual gases:

$$P_{total} = P_A + P_B + P_C + \cdots$$

In terms of mole fractions, $P_A = X_A P_{total}$ and $X_A = P_A/P_{total}$.

Graham's Law of Effusion. The rate of effusion of a gas varies inversely with the square root of its density (or the square root of its molecular mass) at constant pressure and temperature. Comparing different gases at the same temperature and pressure,

$$\frac{\text{effusion rate } (A)}{\text{effusion rate } (B)} = \sqrt{\frac{d_B}{d_A}} = \sqrt{\frac{M_B}{M_A}}$$

Kinetic Theory of Gases. An ideal gas consists of a large number of particles, each having essentially zero volume, that are in constant, chaotic, random motion, traveling in straight lines with no attractions or repulsions between them. When the laws of physics and statistics are applied to this model, and the results compared with the ideal gas law, the Kelvin temperature of a gas is found to be proportional to the average kinetic energy of the gas particles. Pressure is the result of forces of collision of the particles with the container's walls.

Real Gases. Because individual gas particles do have real volumes and because small forces of attraction do exist between them, real gases do not exactly obey the gas laws. The van der Waals equation of state for a real gas makes corrections for the volume of the gas molecules and for the attractive forces between gas molecules. The van der Waals constant *a* provides a measure of the attractive forces between molecules, whereas the constant *b* gives a measure of the relative size of the gas molecules.

Reaction Stoichiometry: A Summary. With the study in this chapter of the stoichiometry of reactions involving gases, we have completed our study of the tools needed for the calculations of all variations of reaction stoichiometry. The critical link in all such calculations is the set of coefficients given by the balanced equation, which provides the stoichiometric equivalencies needed to convert from the number of moles of one substance to the numbers of moles of any of the others in the reaction. To use the coefficients requires that all the calculations must funnel through *moles.* Whether we start with grams of some compound in a reaction, with the molarity of its solution plus a volume, or with *P–V–T* data for a gas in the reaction, *we must get the essential calculation into moles.* After applying the coefficients, we can then move back to any other kind of unit we wish. The flowchart below summarizes what we have been doing.

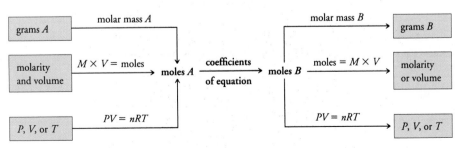

The labels on the arrows of the flowchart suggest the basic tools. Formula masses or molecular masses get us from grams to moles or from moles to grams. Molarity and volume data move us from concentration to moles or back. With *P–V–T* data we can find moles or, knowing moles of a gas, we can calculate *P, V,* or *T,* as long as the other two are known.

TOOLS FOR PROBLEM SOLVING

The compilation below lists the concepts that you've learned in this chapter which can be applied as tools in solving problems. Study each one carefully so that you know what each is used for. When faced with solving a problem, recall what each tool does and consider whether it will be helpful in finding a solution. This will aid you in selecting the tools you need. If necessary, refer to this table when working on the Review Exercises that follow.

Combined gas law *(page 398)*,

$$\frac{P_1 V_1}{T_1} = \frac{P_2 V_2}{T_2}$$

This law applies when the amount of gas is constant and we are asked how one of the variables (P, V, or T) changes when we change two of the others. When the amount of gas and one of the variables (P, V, or T) are constant, the problem reduces to one involving Boyle's, Charles', or Gay-Lussac's law.

Molar volumes *(page 402)*. For one mole of any gas at STP

$$1 \text{ mol} \Leftrightarrow 22.4 \text{ L}$$

Ideal gas law *(page 405)*,

$$PV = nRT$$

This law applies when any three of the four variables P, V, T, or n, are known and we wish to calculate the value of the fourth.

Determination of molar mass: Molar mass M can be determined in a variety of ways from equations used in this chapter.

From ideal gas law *(page 407)*,

$$\text{molar mass} = \frac{g}{V} \frac{RT}{P} = d \frac{RT}{P}$$

From effusion rates *(Rearrangement of Equation 10.7 page 418)*,

$$M_B = M_A \left(\frac{\text{effusion rate } (A)}{\text{effusion rate } (B)} \right)^2$$

From mole fractions *(Rearrangement of Equation 10.4 page 415)*,

$$M_A = \frac{g_A}{X_A \times n_{\text{total}}}$$

Dalton's law of partial pressures *(page 413)*,

$$P_{\text{total}} = P_A + P_B + P_C + \cdots$$

We use this law to calculate the partial pressure of one gas in a mixture of gases. This requires the total pressure and either the partial pressures of the other gases or their mole fractions. If the partial pressures are known, their sum is the total pressure. When a gas is collected over water, this law is used to obtain the partial pressure of the collected gas in the "wet" gas mixture: $P_{\text{total}} = P_{water} + P_{gas}$.

Mole fractions *(pages 415 and 416)*,

$$X_A = \frac{n_A}{n_{\text{total}}} = \frac{P_A}{P_{\text{total}}}$$

Given the composition of a gas mixture, we can calculate the mole fraction of a component. The mole fraction can then be used to find the partial pressure of the component given the total pressure. If the total pressure and partial pressure of a component are known, we can calculate the mole fraction of the component.

Graham's law of effusion *(page 418)*,

$$\frac{\text{effusion rate } (A)}{\text{effusion rate } (B)} = \sqrt{\frac{d_B}{d_A}} = \sqrt{\frac{M_B}{M_A}}$$

This law allows us to calculate relative rates of effusion of gases (A and B in this equation). It also allows us to calculate molecular masses from relative rates of effusion.

QUESTIONS, PROBLEMS, AND EXERCISES

Answers to problems whose numbers are printed in color are given in Appendix B. More challenging problems are marked with asterisks. ILW = Interactive Learningware solution is available at www.wiley.com/college/brady. OH = an Office Hours video is available for this problem.

REVIEW QUESTIONS

Concept of Pressure; Manometers and Barometers

10.1 If you get jabbed by a pencil, why does is hurt so much more if it's with the sharp point rather than the eraser? Explain in terms of the concepts of force and pressure.

10.2 Write expressions that could be used to form conversion factors to convert between:
(a) kilopascal and atm (d) torr and pascal
(b) torr and mm Hg (e) bar and pascal
(c) torr and atm (f) bar and atm

10.3 At 20 °C the density of mercury is 13.6 g mL^{-1} and that of water is 1.00 g mL^{-1}. At 20 °C, the vapor pressure of mercury is 0.0012 torr and that of water is 18 torr. Give and explain two reasons why water would be an inconvenient fluid to use in a Torricelli barometer.

10.4 What is the advantage of using a closed-end manometer, rather than an open-end one, when measuring the pressure of a trapped gas?

Gas Laws

10.5 Express the following gas laws in equation form: (a) temperature–volume law (Charles' law), (b) temperature–pressure law (Gay-Lussac's law), (c) pressure–volume law (Boyle's law), and (d) combined gas law.

10.6 Which of the four important variables in the study of the physical properties of gases are assumed to be held constant in each of the following laws? (a) Boyle's law, (b) Charles' law, (c) Gay-Lussac's law, (d) combined gas law

10.7 What is meant by an *ideal gas*? Under what conditions does a real gas behave most like an ideal gas?

10.8 State the ideal gas law in the form of an equation. What is the value of the gas constant in units of L atm mol^{-1} K^{-1}?

10.9 State Dalton's law of partial pressures in the form of an equation.

10.10 Define *mole fraction*. How is the partial pressure of a gas related to its mole fraction and the total pressure?

10.11 Consider the diagrams below that illustrate three mixtures of gases A and B. If the total pressure of each mixture is 1.00 atm, which of the drawings corresponds to a mixture in which the partial pressure of A equals 0.600 atm? What are the partial pressures of A in the other mixtures? What are the partial pressures of B?

Gas A ●   Gas B ●

10.12 What is the difference between *diffusion* and *effusion*? State Graham's law in the form of an equation.

Kinetic Theory of Gases

10.13 Describe the model of a gas proposed by the kinetic theory of gases.

10.14 If the molecules of a gas at constant volume are somehow given a lower average kinetic energy, what two measurable properties of the gas will change and in what direction?

10.15 Explain *how* raising the temperature of a gas causes it to expand at constant pressure. (Describe how the model of an ideal gas connects the increase in temperature to the gas expansion.)

10.16 Explain in terms of the kinetic theory *how* raising the temperature of a confined gas makes its pressure increase.

10.17 How does the kinetic theory explain the existence of an absolute zero, 0 K?

10.18 Which of the following gases has the largest value of $(\bar{v})_{rms}$ at 25 °C? (a) N$_2$, (b) CO$_2$, (c) NH$_3$, or (d) HBr

10.19 How would you expect the rate of effusion of a gas to depend on (a) the pressure of the gas and (b) the temperature of the gas?

Real Gases

10.20 Which postulates of the kinetic theory are not strictly true, and why?

10.21 A small value for the van der Waals constant a suggests something about the molecules of the gas. What?

10.22 Which of the molecules below has the larger value of the van der Waals constant b? Explain your choice.

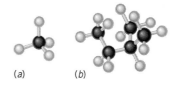

(a)   (b)

10.23 Under the same conditions of T and V, why is the pressure of a real gas less than the pressure the gas would exert if it were ideal? At a given T and P, why is the volume of a real gas larger than it would be if the gas were ideal?

10.24 Suppose we have a mixture of helium and argon. On average, which atoms are moving faster at 25 °C, and why?

REVIEW PROBLEMS

Pressure Unit Conversions

OH 10.25 Carry out the following unit conversions: (a) 1.26 atm to torr, (b) 740 torr to atm, (c) 738 torr to mm Hg, and (d) 1.45 × 10^3 Pa to torr.

10.26 Carry out the following unit conversions: (a) 0.625 atm to torr, (b) 825 torr to atm, (c) 62 mm Hg to torr, and (d) 1.22 kPa to bar.

10.27 What is the pressure in torr of each of the following?
(a) 0.329 atm (summit of Mt. Everest, the world's highest mountain)
(b) 0.460 atm (summit of Mt. Denali, the highest mountain in the United States)

10.28 What is the pressure in atm of each of the following? (These are the values of the pressures exerted individually by N_2, O_2, and CO_2, respectively, in typical inhaled air.)
(a) 595 torr   (b) 160 torr   (c) 0.300 torr

Manometers and Barometers

10.29 An open-end manometer containing mercury was connected to a vessel holding a gas at a pressure of 720 torr. The atmospheric pressure was 765 torr. Sketch a diagram of the apparatus showing the relative heights of the mercury in the two arms of the manometer. What is the difference in the heights of the mercury expressed in centimeters?

10.30 An open-end manometer containing mercury was connected to a vessel holding a gas at a pressure of 820 torr. The atmospheric pressure was 750 torr. Sketch a diagram of the apparatus showing the relative heights of the mercury in the two arms of the manometer. What is the difference in the heights of the mercury expressed in centimeters?

10.31 An open-end mercury manometer was connected to a flask containing a gas at an unknown pressure. The mercury in the arm open to the atmosphere was 65 mm higher than the mercury in the arm connected to the flask. The atmospheric pressure was 748 torr. What was the pressure of the gas in the flask (in torr)?

10.32 An open-end mercury manometer was connected to a flask containing a gas at an unknown pressure. The mercury in the arm open to the atmosphere was 82 mm lower than the mercury in the arm connected to the flask. The atmospheric pressure was 752 torr. What was the pressure of the gas in the flask (in torr)?

10.33 Suppose that in a closed-end manometer the mercury in the closed arm was 12.5 cm higher than the mercury in the arm connected to a vessel containing a gas. What is the pressure of the gas expressed in torr?

10.34 Suppose a gas is in a vessel connected to both an open-end and a closed-end manometer. The difference in heights of the mercury in the closed-end manometer was 236 mm, while in the open-end manometer the mercury level in the arm open to the atmosphere was 512 mm below the level in the arm connected to the vessel. Calculate the atmospheric pressure and sketch a diagram of the apparatus.

Gas Laws for a Fixed Amount of Gas

10.35 A gas has a volume of 255 mL at 725 torr. What volume will the gas occupy at 365 torr if the temperature of the gas doesn't change?

10.36 A bicycle pump has a barrel that is 75.0 cm long (about 30 in.). If air is drawn into the pump at a pressure of 1.00 atm during the upstroke, how long must the downstroke be, in centimeters, to raise the pressure of the air to 5.50 atm (approximately the pressure in the tire of a 10-speed bike)? Assume no change in the temperature of the air.

10.37 A gas has a volume of 3.86 L at a temperature of 45 °C. What will the volume of the gas be if its temperature is raised to 80 °C while its pressure is kept constant?

OH 10.38 A balloon has a volume of 2.50 L indoors at a temperature of 22 °C. If the balloon is taken outdoors on a cold day when the air temperature is −15 °C (5 °F), what will its volume be in liters? Assume constant air pressure within the balloon.

10.39 A sample of a gas has a pressure of 850 torr at 285 °C. To what Celsius temperature must the gas be heated to double its pressure if there is no change in the volume of the gas?

10.40 Before taking a trip, you check the air in a tire of your automobile and find it has a pressure of 45 lb in.$^{-2}$ on a day when the air temperature is 10 °C (50 °F). After traveling some distance, you find that the temperature of the air in the tire has risen to 43 °C (approximately 110 °F). What is the air pressure in the tire at this higher temperature, expressed in units of lb in.$^{-2}$?

ILW 10.41 A sample of helium at a pressure of 740 torr and in a volume of 2.58 L was heated from 24.0 to 75.0 °C. The volume of the container expanded to 2.81 L. What was the final pressure (in torr) of the helium?

10.42 When a sample of neon with a volume of 648 mL and a pressure of 0.985 atm was heated from 16.0 to 63.0 °C, its volume became 689 mL. What was its final pressure (in atm)?

10.43 What must be the new volume of a sample of nitrogen (in L) if 2.68 L at 745 torr and 24.0 °C is heated to 375.0 °C under conditions that let the pressure change to 760 torr?

10.44 When 280 mL of oxygen at 741 torr and 18.0 °C was warmed to 33.0 °C, the pressure became 760 torr. What was the final volume (in mL)?

10.45 A sample of argon with a volume of 6.18 L, a pressure of 761 torr, and a temperature of 20.0 °C expanded to a volume of 9.45 L and a pressure of 373 torr. What was its final temperature in °C?

10.46 A sample of a refrigeration gas in a volume of 455 mL, at a pressure of 1.51 atm, and at a temperature of 25.0 °C was compressed into a volume of 220 mL with a pressure of 2.00 atm. To what temperature (in °C) did it have to change?

Ideal Gas Law

10.47 What would be the value of the gas constant R in units of $mL\ torr\ mol^{-1}\ K^{-1}$?

10.48 The SI generally uses its base units to compute constants involving derived units. The SI unit for volume, for example, is the cubic meter, called the *stere*, because the meter is the base unit of length. We learned about the SI unit of pressure, the pascal, in this chapter. The temperature unit is the kelvin. Calculate the value of the gas constant in the SI units $m^3\ Pa\ mol^{-1}\ K^{-1}$.

10.49 What volume in liters does 0.136 g of O_2 occupy at 20.0 °C and 748 torr?

10.50 What volume in liters does 1.67 g of N_2 occupy at 22.0 °C and 756 torr?

10.51 What pressure (in torr) is exerted by 10.0 g of O_2 in a 2.50 L container at a temperature of 27 °C?

10.52 If 12.0 g of water is converted to steam in a 3.60 L pressure cooker held at a temperature of 108 °C, what pressure would be produced?

10.53 A sample of carbon dioxide has a volume of 26.5 mL at 20.0 °C and 624 torr. How many grams of CO_2 are in the sample?

10.54 Methane is formed in landfills by the action of certain bacteria on buried organic matter. If a sample of methane collected from a landfill has a volume of 250 mL at 750 torr and 27 °C, how many grams of methane are in the sample?

10.55 To three significant figures, calculate the density in g L^{-1} of the following gases at STP: (a) C_2H_6 (ethane), (b) N_2, (c) Cl_2, and (d) Ar.

10.56 To three significant figures, calculate the density in g L^{-1} of the following gases at STP: (a) Ne, (b) O_2, (c) CH_4 (methane), and (d) CF_4.

OH **10.57** What density (in g L^{-1}) does oxygen have at 24.0 °C and 742 torr?

10.58 At 748.0 torr and 20.65 °C, what is the density of argon (in g L^{-1})?

ILW **10.59** A chemist isolated a gas in a glass bulb with a volume of 255 mL at a temperature of 25.0 °C and a pressure (in the bulb) of 10.0 torr. The gas weighed 12.1 mg. What is the molecular mass of the gas?

10.60 Boron forms a variety of unusual compounds with hydrogen. A chemist isolated 6.3 mg of one of the boron hydrides in a glass bulb with a volume of 385 mL at 25.0 °C and a bulb pressure of 11 torr.
(a) What is the molecular mass of this hydride?
(b) Which of the following is likely to be its molecular formula, BH_3, B_2H_6, or B_4H_{10}?

10.61 At 22.0 °C and a pressure of 755 torr, a gas was found to have a density of 1.13 g L^{-1}. Calculate its molecular mass.

10.62 A gas was found to have a density of 0.08747 mg mL^{-1} at 17.0 °C and a pressure of 760 torr. What is its molecular mass? Can you tell what the gas most likely is?

Stoichiometry of Reactions of Gases

10.63 How many milliliters of oxygen are required to react completely with 175 mL of butane if the volumes of both gases are measured at the same temperature and pressure?

OH **10.64** How many milliliters of O_2 are consumed in the complete combustion of a sample of hexane if the reaction produces 855 mL of CO_2? Assume all gas volumes are measured at the same temperature and pressure.

ILW **10.65** Propylene, C_3H_6, reacts with hydrogen under pressure to give propane, C_3H_8:

$$C_3H_6(g) + H_2(g) \longrightarrow C_3H_8(g)$$

How many liters of hydrogen (at 740 torr and 24 °C) react with 18.0 g of propylene?

10.66 Nitric acid is formed when NO_2 is dissolved in water.

$$3NO_2(g) + H_2O(l) \longrightarrow 2HNO_3(aq) + NO(g)$$

How many milliliters of NO_2 at 25 °C and 752 torr are needed to form 12.0 g of HNO_3?

10.67 How many milliliters of O_2 measured at 27 °C and 654 torr are needed to react completely with 16.8 mL of CH_4 measured at 35 °C and 725 torr?

10.68 How many milliliters of H_2O vapor, measured at 318 °C and 735 torr, are formed when 33.6 mL of NH_3 at 825 torr and 127 °C react with oxygen according to the following equation?

$$4NH_3(g) + 3O_2(g) \longrightarrow 2N_2(g) + 6H_2O(g)$$

10.69 Calculate the maximum number of milliliters of CO_2, at 745 torr and 27 °C, that could be formed in the combustion of carbon monoxide if 300 mL of CO at 683 torr and 25 °C is mixed with 150 mL of O_2 at 715 torr and 125 °C.

10.70 A mixture of ammonia and oxygen is prepared by combining 300 mL of NH_3 (measured at 750 torr and 28 °C) with 220 mL of O_2 (measured at 780 torr and 50 °C). How many milliliters of N_2 (measured at 740 torr and 100 °C) could be formed if the following reaction occurs?

$$4NH_3(g) + 3O_2(g) \longrightarrow 2N_2(g) + 6H_2O(g)$$

Dalton's Law of Partial Pressures

OH **10.71** A 1.00 L container was filled by pumping into it 1.00 L of N_2 at 200 torr, 1.00 L of O_2 at 150 torr, and 1.00 L of He at 300 torr. All volumes and pressures were measured at the same temperature. What was the total pressure inside the container after the mixture was made?

10.72 A mixture of N_2, O_2, and CO_2 has a total pressure of 740 torr. In this mixture the partial pressure of N_2 is 120 torr and the partial pressure of O_2 is 400 torr. What is the partial pressure of the CO_2?

ILW **10.73** A 22.4 L container at 0 °C contains 0.30 mol N_2, 0.20 mol O_2, 0.40 mol He, and 0.10 mol CO_2. What are the partial pressures of each of the gases?

10.74 A 0.200 mol sample of a mixture of nitrogen and carbon dioxide with a total pressure of 840 torr is exposed to solid calcium oxide which reacts with the carbon dioxide to form solid calcium carbonate. Assume the reaction goes to completion. After the reaction was complete, the pressure of the gas had dropped to 320 torr. How many moles of CO_2 were in the original mixture? (Assume no change in volume or temperature.)

10.75 A sample of carbon monoxide was prepared and collected over water at a temperature of 20 °C and a total pressure of 754 torr. It occupied a volume of 268 mL. Calculate the partial pressure of the CO in torr as well as its dry volume (in mL) under a pressure of 1.00 atm and 20 °C.

10.76 A sample of hydrogen was prepared and collected over water at 25 °C and a total pressure of 742 torr. It occupied a volume of 288 mL. Calculate its partial pressure (in torr) and what its dry volume would be (in mL) under a pressure of 1.00 atm at 25 °C.

10.77 What volume of "wet" methane would you have to collect at 20.0 °C and 742 torr to be sure that the sample contains 244 mL of dry methane (also at 742 torr)?

10.78 What volume of "wet" oxygen would you have to collect if you need the equivalent of 275 mL of dry oxygen at 1.00 atm?

The atmospheric pressure in the lab is 746 torr, and the oxygen is to be collected over water at 15.0 °C.

Graham's Law

10.79 Under conditions in which the density of CO_2 is 1.96 g L^{-1} and that of N_2 is 1.25 g L^{-1}, which gas will effuse more rapidly? What will be the ratio of the rates of effusion of N_2 to CO_2?

10.80 Arrange the following gases in order of increasing rate of diffusion at 25 °C: Cl_2, C_2H_4, SO_2.

10.81 Uranium hexafluoride is a white solid that readily passes directly into the vapor state. (Its vapor pressure at 20.0 °C is 120 torr.) A trace of the uranium in this compound—about 0.7%—is uranium-235, which can be used in a nuclear power plant. The rest of the uranium is essentially uranium-238, and its presence interferes with these applications for uranium-235. Gas effusion of UF_6 can be used to separate the fluoride made from uranium-235 and the fluoride made from uranium-238. Which hexafluoride effuses more rapidly? By how much? (You can check your answer by reading Facets of Chemistry 10.1 on page 419.)

OH 10.82 An unknown gas X effuses 1.65 times faster than C_3H_8. What is the molecular mass of gas X?

ADDITIONAL EXERCISES

10.83 One of the oldest units for atmospheric pressure is lb in.$^{-2}$ (pounds per square inch, or *psi*). Calculate the numerical value of the standard atmosphere in these units to three significant figures. Calculate the mass in pounds of a uniform column of water 33.9 ft high having an area of 1.00 in.^{2} at its base. (Use the following data: density of mercury = 13.6 g mL^{-1}; density of water = 1.00 g mL^{-1}; 1 mL = 1 cm^3; 1 lb = 454 g; 1 in. = 2.54 cm.)

***10.84** A typical automobile has a weight of approximately 3500 lb. If the vehicle is to be equipped with tires, each of which will contact the pavement with a "footprint" that is 6.0 in. wide by 3.2 in. long, what must the gauge pressure of the air be in each tire? (Gauge pressure is the amount that the gas pressure exceeds atmospheric pressure. Assume that atmospheric pressure is 14.7 lb in.$^{-2}$.)

10.85 Suppose you were planning to move a house by transporting it on a large trailer. The house has an estimated weight of 45.6 tons (1 ton = 2000 lb). The trailer is expected to weigh 8.3 tons. Each wheel of the trailer will have tires inflated to a gauge pressure of 85 psi (which is actually 85 psi above atmospheric pressure). If the area of contact between a tire and the pavement can be no larger than 100 in.^{2} (10 in. × 10 in.), what is the minimum number of wheels the trailer must have? (Remember, tires are mounted in multiples of two on a trailer. Assume that atmospheric pressure is 14.7 psi.)

***10.86** The motion picture *Titanic* described the tragedy of the collision of the ocean liner of the same name with an iceberg in the North Atlantic. The ship sank soon after the collision on April 14, 1912, and now rests on the sea floor at a depth of 12,468 ft. Recently, the wreck was explored by the research vessel *Nautile*, which has successfully recovered a variety of items from the debris field surrounding the sunken ship. Calculate the pressure in atmospheres and pounds per square inch exerted on the hull of the *Nautile* as it explores the seabed surrounding the *Titanic*. (Hint:

The height of a column of liquid required to exert a given pressure is inversely proportional to the liquid's density. Seawater has a density of approximately 1.025 g mL^{-1}; mercury has a density of 13.6 g mL^{-1}; 1 atm = 14.7 lb in.$^{-2}$.)

***10.87** Two flasks (which we will refer to as Flask 1 and Flask 2) are connected to each other by a U-shaped tube filled with an oil having a density of 0.826 g mL^{-1}. The oil level in the arm connected to Flask 2 is 16.24 cm higher than in the arm connected to Flask 1. Flask 1 is also connected to an open-end mercury manometer. The mercury level in the arm open to the atmosphere is 12.26 cm higher than the level in the arm connected to Flask 1. The atmospheric pressure is 0.827 atm. What is the pressure of the gas in Flask 2 expressed in torr? (See the hint given in the preceding exercise.)

***10.88** OH A bubble of air escaping from a diver's mask rises from a depth of 100 ft to the surface where the pressure is 1.00 atm. Initially, the bubble has a volume of 10.0 mL. Assuming none of the air dissolves in the water, how many times larger is the bubble just as it reaches the surface. Use your answer to explain why scuba divers constantly exhale as they slowly rise from a deep dive. (The density of seawater is approximately 1.025 g mL^{-1}; the density of mercury is 13.6 g mL^{-1}.)

***10.89** In a diesel engine, the fuel is ignited when it is injected into hot compressed air, heated by the compression itself. In a typical high-speed diesel engine, the chamber in the cylinder has a diameter of 10.7 cm and a length of 13.4 cm. On compression, the length of the chamber is shortened by 12.7 cm (a "5-inch stroke"). The compression of the air changes its pressure from 1.00 to 34.0 atm. The temperature of the air before compression is 364 K. As a result of the compression, what will be the final air temperature (in K and °C) just before the fuel injection?

***10.90** Early one cool (60.0 °F) morning you start on a bike ride with the atmospheric pressure at 14.7 lb in.$^{-2}$ and the tire gauge pressure at 50.0 lb in.$^{-2}$. (Gauge pressure is the amount that the pressure exceeds atmospheric pressure.) By late afternoon, the air had warmed up considerably, and this plus the heat generated by tire friction sent the temperature inside the tire to 104 °F. What will the tire gauge now read, assuming that the volume of the air in the tire and the atmospheric pressure have not changed?

OH 10.91 The range of temperatures over which an automobile tire must be able to withstand pressure changes is roughly −50 to 120 °F. If a tire is filled to 35 lb in.$^{-2}$ at −50 °F (on a cold day in Alaska, for example), what will be the pressure in the tire (in the same pressure units) on a hot day in Death Valley when the temperature is 120 °F? (Assume that the volume of the tire does not change.)

10.92 Chlorine reacts with sulfite ion to give sulfate ion and chloride ion. How many milliliters of Cl_2 gas measured at 25 °C and 734 torr are required to react with all the SO_3^{2-} in 50.0 mL of 0.200 M Na_2SO_3 solution?

10.93 A common laboratory preparation of hydrogen on a small scale uses the reaction of zinc with hydrochloric acid. Zinc chloride is the other product.
(a) Write the balanced equation for the reaction.
(b) If 12.0 L of H_2 at 760 torr and 20.0 °C is wanted, how many grams of zinc are needed, in theory?
(c) If the acid is available as 8.00 M HCl, what is the minimum volume of this solution (in milliliters) required to produce the amount of H_2 described in part (b)?

***10.94** In an experiment designed to prepare a small amount of hydrogen by the method described in the preceding exercise, a student was limited to using a gas-collecting bottle with a maximum capacity of 335 mL. The method involved collecting the hydrogen over water. What are the minimum number of grams of Zn and the minimum number of milliliters of 6.00 M HCl needed to produce the *wet* hydrogen that can exactly fit this collecting bottle at 740 torr and 25.0 °C?

10.95 Carbon dioxide can be made in the lab by the reaction of hydrochloric acid with calcium carbonate.

$$CaCO_3(s) + 2HCl(aq) \longrightarrow CaCl_2(aq) + H_2O(l) + CO_2(g)$$

How many milliliters of dry CO_2 at 20.0 °C and 745 torr can be prepared from a mixture of 12.3 g of $CaCO_3$ and 185 mL of 0.250 M HCl?

OH 10.96 A mixture was prepared in a 500 mL reaction vessel from 300 mL of O_2 (measured at 25 °C and 740 torr) and 400 mL of H_2 (measured at 45 °C and 1250 torr). The mixture was ignited and the H_2 and O_2 reacted to form water. What was the final pressure inside the reaction vessel after the reaction was over if the temperature was held at 120 °C?

10.97 A student collected 18.45 mL of H_2 over water at 24 °C. The water level inside the collection apparatus was 8.5 cm higher than the water level outside. The barometric pressure was 746 torr. How many grams of zinc had to react with $HCl(aq)$ to produce the H_2 that was collected?

10.98 A mixture of gases is prepared from 87.5 g of O_2 and 12.7 g of H_2. After the reaction of O_2 and H_2 is complete, what is the total pressure of the mixture if its temperature is 160 °C and its volume is 12.0 L? What are the partial pressures of the gases remaining in the mixture?

10.99 A sample of an unknown gas with a mass of 3.620 g was made to decompose into 2.172 g of O_2 and 1.448 g of S. Prior to the decomposition, this sample occupied a volume of 1120 mL at 750 torr and 25.0 °C.
(a) What is the percentage composition of the elements in this gas?
(b) What is the empirical formula of the gas?
(c) What is its molecular formula?

*****10.100** A sample of a new antimalarial drug with a mass of 0.2394 g was made to undergo a series of reactions that changed all of the nitrogen in the compound into N_2. This gas had a volume of 18.90 mL when collected over water at 23.80 °C and a pressure of 746.0 torr. At 23.80 °C, the vapor pressure of water is 22.110 torr.
(a) Calculate the percentage of nitrogen in the sample.
(b) When 6.478 mg of the compound was burned in pure oxygen, 17.57 mg of CO_2 and 4.319 mg of H_2O were obtained. What are the percentages of C and H in this compound? Assuming that any undetermined element is oxygen, write an empirical formula for the compound.
(c) The molecular mass of the compound was found to be 324. What is its molecular formula?

*****10.101** In one analytical procedure for determining the percentage of nitrogen in unknown compounds, weighed samples are made to decompose to N_2, which is collected over water at known temperatures and pressures. The volumes of N_2 are then translated into grams and then into percentages.
(a) Show that the following equation can be used to calculate the percentage of nitrogen in a sample having a mass of W grams when the N_2 has a volume of V mL and is collected over water at t_C °C at a total pressure of P torr. The vapor pressure of water occurs in the equation as $P^\circ_{H_2O}$

$$\text{Percentage N} = 0.04489 \times \frac{V(P - P^\circ_{H_2O})}{W(273 + t_C)}$$

(b) Use this equation to calculate the percentage of nitrogen in the sample described in the preceding exercise.

10.102 The odor of a rotten egg is caused by hydrogen sulfide, H_2S. Most people can detect it at a concentration of 0.15 ppb (parts per billion), meaning 0.15 L of H_2S in 10^9 L of space. A typical student lab is $40 \times 20 \times 8$ ft.
(a) At STP, how many liters of H_2S could be present in a typical lab to have a concentration of 0.15 ppb?
(b) How many milliliters of 0.100 M Na_2S would be needed to generate the amount of H_2S in part (a) by the following reaction with hydrochloric acid?

$$Na_2S(aq) + 2HCl(aq) \longrightarrow H_2S(g) + 2NaCl(aq)$$

EXERCISES IN CRITICAL THINKING

10.103 Firefighters advise that you get out of a burning building by keeping close to the floor. We learned that carbon dioxide and most other hazardous compounds are more dense than air and they should settle to the floor. What other facts do we know that make the firefighter's advice correct?

10.104 Carbon dioxide is implicated in global warming. Propose ways to control or perhaps decrease the carbon dioxide content in our air. Rank each proposal based on its feasibility.

10.105 Methane is another gas implicated in the global warming problem. It has been proposed that much of the methane in the atmosphere is from ruminating cows. Evaluate that suggestion and come up with other possible sources of methane.

10.106 Why does the barometric pressure decrease when a rainstorm approaches? What was the lowest barometric pressure ever measured on the earth?

10.107 What gases are responsible for photochemical smog? What chemical reactions are involved? Propose a solution to the problem and estimate the cost to implement it.

10.108 The ozone hole is caused by gases released from ice crystals that melt as spring returns to the south pole. What issues are involved with the ozone hole and how does that affect you?

INTERMOLECULAR ATTRACTIONS AND THE PROPERTIES OF LIQUIDS AND SOLIDS

11

Heated to high temperatures within the earth, lava bursts forth from a volcano's caldera on Hawaii. In addition to the lava, high temperatures and pressures inside the earth contribute to the formation of important minerals such as diamonds. The extreme properties of molten lava and diamond formation can be understood based on the principles in this chapter. *(Joanna McCarthy/Photographers Choice/Getty Images.)*

CHAPTER OUTLINE

11.1 Gases, liquids, and solids differ because intermolecular forces depend on the distances between molecules

11.2 Intermolecular attractions involve electrical charges

11.3 Intermolecular forces and tightness of packing affect the physical properties of liquids and solids

11.4 Changes of state lead to dynamic equilibria

11.5 Vapor pressures of liquids and solids are controlled by temperature and intermolecular attractions

11.6 Boiling occurs when a liquid's vapor pressure equals atmospheric pressure

11.7 Energy changes occur during changes of state

11.8 Changes in a dynamic equilibrium can be analyzed using Le Châtelier's principle

11.9 Crystalline solids have an ordered internal structure

11.10 X-Ray diffraction is used to study crystal structures

11.11 Physical properties of solids are related to their crystal types

11.12 Phase diagrams graphically represent pressure–temperature relationships

In the preceding chapter we studied the physical properties of gases, and we observed that all gases behave pretty much alike, regardless of their chemical composition. This is especially so at low pressures and high temperatures, which allows us to use one set of gas laws to describe the behavior of *any* gas. However, when we compare substances in their liquid or solid states (their *condensed states*), the situation is quite different. When a substance is a liquid or a solid, its particles are packed closely together and the forces between them, which we call *intermolecular forces*, are quite strong. Chemical composition and molecular structure play an important role in determining the strengths of such forces, and this causes different substances to behave quite differently from each other when they are liquids or solids.

In this chapter, we focus our attention on the properties of liquids and solids. We begin our study by looking at the basic differences among the states of matter in terms of both common observable properties and the way the states of matter differ at the molecular level. In this chapter we will also examine the different kinds and relative strengths of intermolecular forces. You will learn how they are related to molecular composition and structure, and how intermolecular forces influence a variety of familiar physical properties of liquids, such as boiling points and ease of evaporation. And by studying the energy changes associated with changes of states (for example, evaporation or condensation), you will become familiar with the forces that affect practical applications ranging from evaporative air-conditioning to weather prediction.

11.1 | GASES, LIQUIDS, AND SOLIDS DIFFER BECAUSE INTERMOLECULAR FORCES DEPEND ON THE DISTANCES BETWEEN MOLECULES

There are differences among gases, liquids, and solids that are immediately obvious and familiar to everyone. For example, any gas will expand to fill whatever volume is available to it, even if it has to mix with other gases to do so. Liquids and solids, however, retain a constant volume when transferred from one container to another. A solid, such as an ice cube, also keeps its shape, but a liquid such as soda conforms to the shape of whatever bottle or glass we put it in.

In Chapter 10 you learned that gases are easily compressed. Liquids and solids, on the other hand, are nearly *incompressible*, which means their volumes change very little when they are subjected to high pressures. Properties such as the ones we've described can be understood in terms of the way the particles are distributed in the three states of matter, which is summarized in Figure 11.1.

Intermolecular forces depend on distance

If you've ever played with magnets you know that their mutual attraction weakens rapidly as the distance between them increases. Intermolecular attractions are similarly affected by the distance between molecules, rapidly becoming weaker as the distance between the molecules increases.

In gases, the molecules are so far apart that intermolecular attractions are almost negligible, so differences between the attractive forces hardly matter. As a result, chemical composition has little effect on the properties of a gas. But in a liquid or a solid, the molecules are close together and the attractions are strong. Differences among these attractions caused by differences in chemical makeup are greatly amplified, so the properties of liquids and solids depend quite heavily on chemical composition.

□ The closer two molecules are, the more strongly they attract each other.

11.2 | INTERMOLECULAR ATTRACTIONS INVOLVE ELECTRICAL CHARGES

Intermolecular forces (the attractions *between* molecules) are always much weaker than the attractions between atoms *within* molecules (***intramolecular forces,*** which are the *chemical bonds* that hold molecules together). In a molecule of HCl, for example,

Observable Properties

Gases are easily compressed, but expand spontaneously to fill whatever container they are in.

Liquids retain their volume when placed into a container, but conform to the shape of the container. They are fluid and are able to flow. Liquids are nearly incompressible.

Solids keep their shape and volume *and* are virtually incompressible. They often have crystalline shapes.

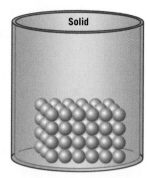

Molecular View

Widely spaced molecules with much empty space between them. Motion is random and with very weak attractions between the molecules.

Molecules tightly packed but with little order. They are able to move past each other with little difficulty. Intermolecular attractive forces are relatively strong.

Molecules tightly packed and highly ordered. Very strong attractions between molecules hold them in place so they are effectively locked in position.

FIG. 11.1 General properties of gases, liquids, and solids. Properties can be understood in terms of how tightly the molecules are packed together and the strengths of the intermolecular attractions between them.

the H and Cl atoms are held very tightly to each other by a covalent bond, and it is the strength of this bond that affects the *chemical properties* of HCl. The strength of the chemical bond also keeps the molecule intact as it moves about. When a particular chlorine atom moves, the hydrogen atom bonded to it is forced to follow along (see Figure 11.2). Attractions between neighboring HCl molecules, in contrast, are much weaker. In fact, they are only about 4% as strong as the covalent bond in HCl. These weaker attractions are what determine the *physical properties* of liquid and solid HCl.

There are several kinds of intermolecular attractions, which are discussed in this section. They all have something in common; *they arise from attractions between opposite electrical charges.* Collectively, they are called **van der Waals forces,** after J. D. van der Waals who studied the nonideal behavior of real gases.

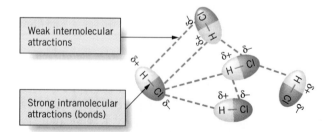

Weak intermolecular attractions

Strong intramolecular attractions (bonds)

FIG. 11.2 Attractions within and between hydrogen chloride molecules. Strong *intramolecular* attractions (chemical bonds) exist between H and Cl atoms within HCl molecules. These attractions control the chemical properties of HCl. Weaker *intermolecular* attractions exist between neighboring HCl molecules. The intermolecular attractions control the physical properties of this substance.

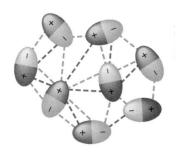

Attractions (– –) are greater than repulsions (– –), so the molecules feel a net attraction to each other.

FIG. 11.3 Dipole–dipole attractions. Attractions between polar molecules occur because the molecules tend to align themselves so that opposite charges are near each other and like charges are as far apart as possible. The alignment is not perfect because the molecules are constantly moving and colliding.

Dipole–dipole attractions

Polar molecules, such as HCl, have a partial positive charge at one end and a partial negative charge at the other. Because unlike charges attract, polar molecules tend to line up so the positive end of one dipole is near the negative end of another. Thermal energy (molecular kinetic energy), however, causes the molecules to collide and become disoriented, so the alignment isn't perfect. Nevertheless, there is still a net attraction between them (see Figure 11.3). We call this kind of intermolecular force a **dipole–dipole attraction.** Because collisions lead to substantial misalignment of the dipoles and because the attractions are only between partial charges, dipole–dipole forces are much weaker than covalent bonds, being only about 1–4% as strong. Dipole–dipole attractions fall off rapidly with distance, with the energy required to separate a pair of dipoles being proportional to $1/d^3$, where d is the distance between the dipoles.

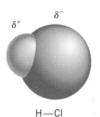

δ^+ δ^-

H—Cl

Hydrogen bonds

When hydrogen is covalently bonded to a very small, highly electronegative atom (principally, fluorine, oxygen, or nitrogen), a particularly strong type of dipole–dipole attraction occurs that's called **hydrogen bonding.** Hydrogen bonds are exceptionally strong because F—H, O—H, and N—H bonds are very polar, and because the partial charges can get quite close because they are concentrated on very small atoms. Typically, a hydrogen bond is about five to ten times stronger than other dipole–dipole attractions.

Hydrogen bonds in water and biological systems

Most substances become more dense when they change from a liquid to a solid. Not so with water. In liquid water, the molecules experience hydrogen bonds that continually break and re-form as the molecules move around (Figure 11.4b). As water begins to freeze, however, the molecules become locked in place, and each water molecule participates in four hydrogen bonds (Figure 11.4c). The resulting structure occupies a larger volume than the same amount of liquid water, so ice is less dense than the liquid. Because of this, ice cubes and icebergs float in the more dense liquid. The expansion of freezing water is capable of cracking a car's engine block, which is one reason we add antifreeze to a car's cooling system. Ice formation is also responsible for erosion, causing rocks to split where water has seeped into cracks. And in northern cities, freezing water breaks up pavement, creating potholes in the streets.

Hydrogen bonding is especially important in biological systems because many molecules in our bodies contain N—H and O—H bonds. Examples are proteins and DNA. Proteins are made up mostly (in some cases, entirely) of long chains of amino acids, linked head to tail to form polypeptides.

☐ A hydrogen bond is not a covalent bond. In water there are oxygen–hydrogen covalent bonds within H_2O molecules and hydrogen bonds between H_2O molecules.

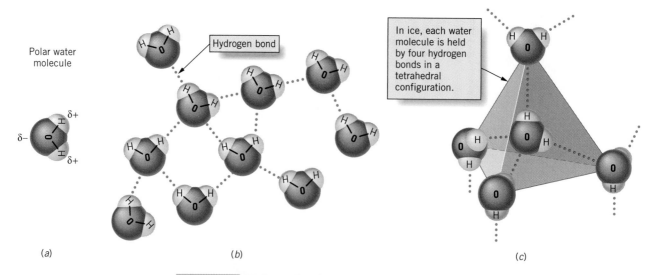

Polar water molecule

Hydrogen bond

In ice, each water molecule is held by four hydrogen bonds in a tetrahedral configuration.

(a)   (b)   (c)

FIG. 11.4 **Hydrogen bonding in water.** (*a*) The polar water molecule. (*b*) Hydrogen bonding (dotted lines) produces strong attractions between water molecules in the liquid. (*c*) Hydrogen bonding between water molecules in ice, where each water molecule is held by four hydrogen bonds in a tetrahedral configuration.

☐ Polypeptides are examples of *polymers*, which are large molecules made by linking together many smaller units called *monomers* (in this case, amino acids). An amino acid contains both a carboxyl group and an amine group, NH_2. An example is glycine, NH_2CH_2COOH.

Part of a polypeptide chain is shown below.

$$---N—CHC---N—CHC---N—CHC—N—CHC---$$

One amino acid segment of a polypeptide

Hydrogen bonding between N—H units in one part of the chain and polar C=O groups in another part help determine the shape of the protein, which greatly influences its biological function. Hydrogen bonding is also responsible for the double helix structure of DNA, which carries our genetic information. This structure is illustrated in Figure 11.5.

London forces

Even nonpolar substances experience intermolecular attractions, as evidenced by the ability of the noble gases and nonpolar molecules such as Cl_2 and CH_4 to condense to liquids, and then crystallize into solids, when cooled to very low temperatures. In such liquids or solids attractions between their particles must exist to cause them to cling together.

In 1930 Fritz London, a German physicist, explained how the particles in even nonpolar substances can experience intermolecular attractions. He noted that in any atom or molecule the electrons are constantly moving. If we could examine such motions in two neighboring particles, we would find that the movement of electrons in one influences the movement of electrons in the other. Because electrons repel each other, as an electron of one particle gets near the other particle, electrons on the second particle are pushed away. This happens continually as the electrons move around, so to some extent, the electron density in both particles flickers back and forth in a synchronous fashion. This is illustrated in Figure 11.6, which depicts a series of instantaneous views of the electron density. Notice that *at any given moment the electron density of a particle can be unsymmetrical,* with more negative charge on one side than on the other. For that particular instant, the particle is a dipole, and we call it a momentary dipole or **instantaneous dipole.**

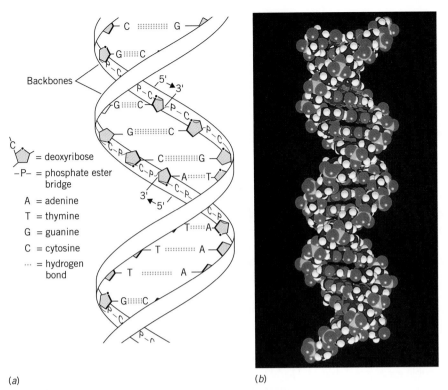

(a)   (b)

FIG. 11.5 **Hydrogen bonding holds the DNA double helix together.** (a) A schematic drawing in which the hydrogen bonds between the two strands are indicated by dotted lines. The legend to the left of the structure describes the various components of the DNA molecule. (b) Phosphorous atoms are shown in blue and they help us trace the DNA "backbone" in this short section of the double helix. *(Nelson Max/Peter Arnold, Inc.)*

As an instantaneous dipole forms in one particle, it causes the electron density in its neighbor to become unsymmetrical, too. As a result, this second particle also becomes a dipole. We call it an **induced dipole** because it is caused by, or *induced* by, the formation of the first dipole. Because of the way the dipoles are formed, they always have the positive end of one near the negative end of the other, so there is a dipole–dipole attraction between them. It is a very short-lived attraction, however, because the electrons keep moving; the dipoles vanish as quickly as they form. But, in another moment, the dipoles will reappear in a different orientation and there will be another brief dipole–dipole attraction. In this way the short-lived dipoles cause momentary tugs between the particles. When averaged over a period of time, there is a net, overall attraction. It tends to be relatively weak, however, because the attractive forces are only "turned on" part of the time.

The momentary dipole–dipole attractions that we've just discussed are called *instantaneous dipole–induced dipole attractions*, to distinguish them from the kind of permanent dipole–dipole attractions that exist without interruption in polar substances like HCl. They are also called **London dispersion forces** (or simply **London forces** or **dispersion forces**).

London forces exist between all molecules and ions. Although they are the only kind of attraction possible between nonpolar molecules, London forces also contribute significantly to the total intermolecular attraction between polar molecules, where they are present in addition to the regular dipole–dipole attractions. London forces even occur between oppositely charged ions, but their effects are relatively weak compared to ionic attractions. London forces contribute little to the net overall attractions between ions and are often ignored.

The strengths of London forces

To compare the strengths of intermolecular attractions, a property we can use is boiling point. As we will explain in more detail later in this chapter, the higher the boiling point, the stronger are the attractions between molecules in the liquid.

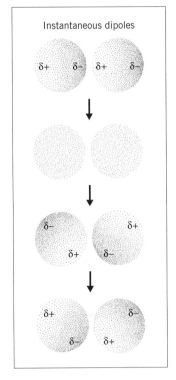

FIG. 11.6 **Instantaneous "frozen" views of the electron density in two neighboring particles.** Attractions occur between the instantaneous dipoles while they exist.

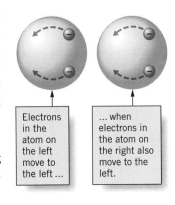

Electrons in the atom on the left move to the left …

… when electrons in the atom on the right also move to the left.

TABLE 11.1	Boiling Points of the Halogens and Noble Gases		
Group VIIA	Boiling Point (°C)	Group VIIIA	Boiling Point (°C)
F_2	−188.1	He	−268.6
Cl_2	−34.6	Ne	−245.9
Br_2	58.8	Ar	−185.7
I_2	184.4	Kr	−152.3
		Xe	−107.1
		Rn	−61.8

◻ London forces decrease very rapidly as the distance between particles increases. The energy required to separate particles held by London forces varies as $1/d^6$, where d is the distance between the particles.

The strengths of London forces are found to depend chiefly on three factors. One is the **polarizability** of the electron cloud of a particle, which is a measure of the ease with which the electron cloud is distorted, and thus is a measure of the ease with which the instantaneous and induced dipoles can form. In general, *as the volume of the electron cloud increases, its polarizability also increases.* When an electron cloud is large, the outer electrons are generally not held very tightly by the nucleus (or nuclei, if the particle is a molecule). This causes the electron cloud to be "mushy" and rather easily deformed, so instantaneous dipoles and induced dipoles form without much difficulty (see Figure 11.7). As a result, particles with large electron clouds experience stronger London forces than do similar particles with small electron clouds.

The effects of size can be seen if we compare the boiling points of the halogens and the noble gases (see Table 11.1). As the atoms become larger, the boiling points increase, reflecting increasingly stronger intermolecular attractions (stronger London forces).

A second factor that affects the strengths of London forces is the number of atoms in a molecule. For molecules containing the same elements, London forces increase with the number of atoms, as illustrated by the hydrocarbons (see Table 11.2). As the number of atoms increases, there are more places along their lengths where instantaneous dipoles can develop and lead to London attractions (Figure 11.8). Even if the strength of attraction at each location is about the same, the *total* attraction experienced between the longer molecules is greater.[1]

The third factor that affects the strengths of London forces is molecular shape. Even with molecules that have the same number of the same kinds of atoms, those that have compact shapes experience weaker London forces than long, chainlike molecules (Figure 11.9). Presumably, because of the compact shape of the $(CH_3)_4C$ molecule, the individual hydrogens on neighboring molecules cannot interact with each other as effectively as those on the chainlike molecule.

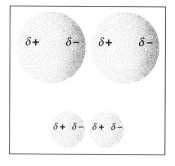

δ+ δ− δ+ δ−

δ+ δ− δ+ δ−

FIG. 11.7 Effect of molecular size on the strengths of London dispersion forces. A large electron cloud is more easily deformed than a small one, so in a large molecule the charges on opposite ends of an instantaneous dipole are larger than in a small molecule. Large molecules therefore experience stronger London forces than small molecules.

TABLE 11.2	Boiling Points of Some Hydrocarbons[a]
Molecular Formula	Boiling Point at 1 atm (°C)
CH_4	−161.5
C_2H_6	−88.6
C_3H_8	−42.1
C_4H_{10}	−0.5
C_5H_{12}	36.1
C_6H_{14}	68.7
⋮	⋮
$C_{10}H_{22}$	174.1
⋮	⋮
$C_{22}H_{46}$	327

[a] The molecules of each hydrocarbon in this table have carbon chains of the type C—C—C—C— etc.; that is, one carbon follows another.

[1] The effect of large numbers of atoms on the total strengths of London forces can be compared to the bond between loop and hook layers of the familiar product Velcro. Each loop-to-hook attachment is not very strong, but when large numbers of them are involved, the overall bond between Velcro layers is quite strong.

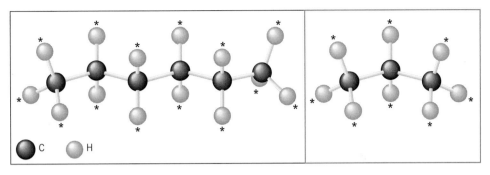

FIG. 11.8 **The number of atoms in a molecule affects London forces.** The C_6H_{14} molecule, left, has more sites (indicated by asterisks, *) along its chain where it can be attracted to other molecules nearby than does the shorter C_3H_8 molecule, right. As a result, the boiling point of C_6H_{14} (hexane, 68.7 °C) is higher than that of C_3H_8 (propane, −42.1 °C).

neopentane, $(CH_3)_4C$
bp = 9.5 °C

n-pentane, $CH_3CH_2CH_2CH_2CH_3$
bp = 36.1 °C

FIG. 11.9 **Molecular shape affects the strengths of London forces.** Shown are two molecules with the formula C_5H_{12}. Not all hydrogen atoms can be seen in these space-filling models. The neopentane molecule, $(CH_3)_4C$, has a more compact shape than the *n*-pentane molecule, $CH_3CH_2CH_2CH_2CH_3$. In the more compact structure, the H atoms cannot interact with those on neighboring molecules as well as the H atoms in the long chainlike structure, so overall the intermolecular attractions are weaker between the more compact molecules

Ion–dipole and ion–induced dipole forces of attraction

In addition to the attractions that exist between neutral molecules, which we discussed above, there are also forces that arise when ions interact with molecules. For example, ions are able to attract the charged ends of polar molecules to give **ion–dipole attractions.** This occurs in water, for example, when ionic compounds dissolve to give hydrated ions. Cations become surrounded by water molecules that are oriented with the negative ends of their dipoles pointing toward the cation. Similarly, anions attract the positive ends of water dipoles. This is illustrated in Figure 11.10. These same interactions can persist into the solid state as well. For example, aluminum chloride crystallizes from water as a hydrate with the formula $AlCl_3 \cdot 6H_2O$. In it the Al^{3+} ion is surrounded by water molecules at the vertices of an octahedron, as illustrated in Figure 11.11. They are held there by ion–dipole attractions.

Ions are also capable of distorting nearby electron clouds, thereby creating dipoles in neighboring particles (like molecules of a solvent, or even other ions). This leads to **ion–induced dipole** attractions, which can be quite strong because the charge on the ion doesn't flicker on and off like the instantaneous charges responsible for ordinary London dispersion forces.

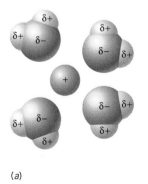

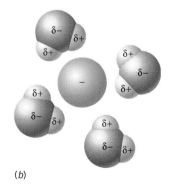

(a)

(b)

FIG. 11.10 **Ion–dipole attractions.** Here we see the attractions between water molecules and positive and negative ions. (*a*) The negative ends of water dipoles surround a cation and are attracted to the ion. (*b*) The positive ends of water molecules surround an anion, which gives a net attraction.

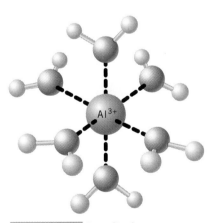

FIG. 11.11 **Ion–dipole attractions hold water molecules in a hydrate.** Water molecules are arranged at the vertices of an octahedron around an aluminum ion in $AlCl_3 \cdot 6H_2O$.

TOOLS

Intermolecular attractions: Hydrogen bonding, dipole–dipole forces, and London forces

TABLE 11.3	Summary of Intermolecular Attractions	
Intermolecular Attraction	Types of Substances That Exhibit Attraction	Strength Relative to a Covalent Bond
Dipole–dipole attractions	Occurs between molecules that have permanent dipoles (i.e., polar molecules)	1–5%
Hydrogen bonding	Occurs when molecules contain N—H and O—H bonds	5–10%
London dispersion forces	All atoms, molecules, and ions experience these kinds of attractions. They are present in all substances.	Depends on sizes and shapes of molecules. For large molecules, the cumulative effect of many weak attractions can lead to a large net attraction.
Ion–dipole attractions	Occurs when ions interact with polar molecules	~10%; depends on ion charge and polarity of molecule
Ion–induced dipole attractions	Occurs when an ion creates a dipole in a neighboring particle, which may be a molecule or another ion	Variable, depends on the charge on the ion and the polarizability of its neighbor

Estimating the effects of intermolecular forces

In this section we have described a number of different types of intermolecular attractive forces and the kinds of substances in which they occur (see the summary in Table 11.3). With this knowledge, you should now be able to make some estimate of the nature and relative strengths of intermolecular attractions if you know the molecular structure of a substance. This will enable you to understand and sometimes predict how the physical properties of different substances compare. For example, we've already mentioned that boiling point is a property that depends on the strengths of intermolecular attractions. By being able to compare intermolecular forces in different substances, we can sometimes predict how their boiling points compare. This is illustrated in Example 11.1.

EXAMPLE 11.1
Using Relative Attractive Forces to Predict Properties

Below are structural formulas of ethanol (ethyl alcohol) and propylene glycol (a compound used as a nontoxic antifreeze). Which of these compounds would be expected to have the higher boiling point?

$$\begin{array}{ccc} & H & H \\ & | & | \\ H- & C- & C-OH \\ & | & | \\ & H & H \end{array} \qquad \begin{array}{cccc} & H & H & H \\ & | & | & | \\ H- & C- & C- & C-OH \\ & | & | & | \\ & H & OH & H \end{array}$$

ethanol   propylene glycol

ANALYSIS: We know that boiling points are related to the strengths of intermolecular attractions—the stronger the attractions, the higher the boiling point. Therefore, if we can determine which compound has the stronger intermolecular attractions, we can answer the question. Let's decide which kinds of attractions are present and then try to determine their relative strengths.

SOLUTION: We know that both substances will experience London forces, because they are present between *all* molecules. London forces become stronger as molecules become larger, so the London forces should be stronger in propylene glycol.

Looking at the structures, we see that both contain —OH groups (one in ethanol and two in propylene glycol). This means we can expect that there will be hydrogen bonding in both liquids. Because there are more —OH groups per molecule in propylene glycol than in ethanol, we might reasonably expect that there are more opportunities for the ethylene glycol molecules to participate in hydrogen bonding. This would make the hydrogen bonding forces greater in propylene glycol.

Our analysis tells us that both kinds of attractions are stronger in propylene glycol than in ethanol, so propylene glycol should have the higher boiling point.

IS THE ANSWER REASONABLE? There's not much we can do to check our answer other than to review the reasoning, which is sound. (We could also check a reference book, where we would find that the boiling point of ethanol is 78.5 °C and the boiling point of propylene glycol is 188.2 °C!)

Practice Exercise 1: List the following in order of their boiling points from lowest to highest. (a) $Ca(OH)_2$, $CH_3CH_2CH_2CH_2CH_3$, CH_3CH_2OH; (b) $CH_3CH_2NH_2$, $CH_3—O—CH_3$, $HOCH_2CH_2CH_2CH_2OH$. (Hint: Determine what types of intermolecular attractive forces are important for each molecule.)

Practice Exercise 2: Propylamine and trimethylamine have the same molecular formula, C_3H_9N, but quite different structures, as shown below. Which of these substances is expected to have the higher boiling point? Why?

$$CH_3—CH_2—CH_2—NH_2 \qquad H_3C—\overset{\overset{\displaystyle CH_3}{|}}{N}—CH_3$$
propylamine   trimethylamine

11.3 INTERMOLECULAR FORCES AND TIGHTNESS OF PACKING AFFECT THE PHYSICAL PROPERTIES OF LIQUIDS AND SOLIDS

Earlier we briefly described some properties of liquids and solids. We continue here with a more in-depth discussion, and we'll start by examining two properties that depend mostly on how tightly packed the molecules are, namely, *compressibility* and *diffusion*. Other properties depend much more on the strengths of intermolecular attractive forces, properties such as *retention of volume or shape, surface tension*, the ability of a liquid to *wet* a surface, the *viscosity* of a liquid, and a solid's or liquid's *tendency to evaporate*.

Compressibility and diffusion depend primarily on tightness of packing

Compressibility

The **compressibility** of a substance is a measure of its ability to be forced into a smaller volume. Gases are highly compressible because the molecules are far apart. However, in a liquid or solid most of the space is taken up by the molecules, and there is very little empty space into which to crowd other molecules. As a result, it is very difficult to compress liquids or solids to a smaller volume by applying pressure, so we say that these states of matter are nearly **incompressible.** This is a useful property. When you "step on the brakes" of a car, for example, you rely on the incompressibility of the brake fluid to transmit the pressure you apply with your foot to the brake shoes on the wheels. The incompressibility of liquids is also the foundation of the engineering science of *hydraulics*, which uses fluids to transmit forces that lift or move heavy objects.

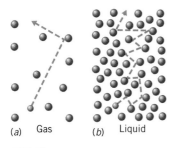

(a)   Gas   (b)   Liquid

FIG. 11.12 Diffusion in a gas and a liquid viewed at the molecular level. (*a*) Diffusion in a gas is rapid because relatively few collisions occur between widely spaced molecules. (*b*) Diffusion in a liquid is slow because of many collisions between closely spaced particles.

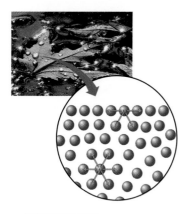

FIG. 11.13 Surface tension and intermolecular attractions. In water, as in other liquids, molecules at the surface are surrounded by fewer molecules than those below the surface. As a result, surface molecules experience fewer attractions than molecules within the liquid. (*Pat O'Hara/Stone/Getty Images.*)

An insect called a *water strider*, shown here, is able to walk on water because of the liquid's surface tension, which causes the water to behave as though it has a skin that resists piercing by the insect's legs. (*Hermann Eisenbeiss/Photo Researchers.*)

Diffusion

Diffusion occurs much more rapidly in gases than in liquids, and hardly at all in solids. In gases, molecules diffuse rapidly because they travel relatively long distances between collisions, as illustrated in Figure 11.12. In liquids, however, a given molecule suffers many collisions as it moves about, so it takes longer to move from place to place and diffusion is much slower. Diffusion in solids is almost nonexistent at room temperature because the particles of a solid are held tightly in place. At high temperatures, though, the particles of a solid sometimes have enough kinetic energy to jiggle their way past each other, and diffusion can occur slowly. Such high temperature solid-state diffusion is used to make electronic devices, like transistors.

Most physical properties depend primarily on the strengths of intermolecular attractions

Retention of volume and shape

In gases, intermolecular attractions are too weak to prevent the molecules from moving apart to fill an entire vessel, so a gas will conform to the shape and volume of its container. In liquids and solids, however, the attractions are much stronger and are able to hold the particles closely together. As a result, liquids and solids keep the same volume regardless of the size of their container. In a solid, the attractions are even stronger than in a liquid. They hold the particles more or less rigidly in place, so a solid retains its shape when moved from one container to another.

Surface tension

A property that is especially evident for liquids is *surface tension*, which is related to the tendency of a liquid to seek a shape that yields the minimum surface area. For a given volume, the shape with the minimum surface area is a sphere—it's a principle of solid geometry. This is why raindrops tend to be little spheres.

To understand surface tension, we need to examine why molecules would prefer to be within a liquid rather than at its surface. In Figure 11.13 we see that a molecule *within* the liquid is surrounded by densely packed molecules on all sides, whereas one at the *surface* has neighbors beside and below it, but none above. As a result, a surface molecule is attracted to fewer neighbors than one within the liquid. With this in mind, let's imagine how we might change an interior molecule to one at the surface. To accomplish this, we would have to pull away some of the surrounding molecules. Because there are intermolecular attractions, removing neighbors requires work; so there's an increase in potential energy involved. This leads to the conclusion that *a molecule at the surface has a higher potential energy than a molecule in the bulk of the liquid.*

In general, a system becomes more stable when its potential energy decreases. For a liquid, reducing its surface area (and thereby reducing the number of molecules at the surface) lowers its potential energy. The lowest energy is achieved when the liquid has the smallest surface area possible (namely, a spherical shape). In more accurate terms, then, *the **surface tension** of a liquid is proportional to the energy needed to expand its surface area.*

The tendency of a liquid to spontaneously acquire a minimum surface area explains many common observations. For example, surface tension causes the sharp edges of glass tubing to become rounded when the glass is softened in a flame, an operation called "fire polishing." Surface tension is also what allows us to fill a water glass above the rim, giving the surface a rounded appearance (Figure 11.14). The surface behaves as if it has a thin, invisible "skin" that lets the water in the glass pile up, trying to assume a spherical shape. Gravity, of course, works in opposition, tending to pull the water down. If too much water is added to the glass, the gravitational force finally wins and the skin breaks; the water overflows. If you push on the surface of a liquid, it resists expansion and pushes back, so the surface "skin" appears to resist penetration. This is what enables certain insects to "walk on water," as illustrated in the photo in the margin.

Surface tension is a property that varies with the strengths of intermolecular attractions. Liquids with strong intermolecular attractive forces have large differences in potential energy between their interior and surface molecules, and have large surface tensions.

Not surprisingly, water's surface tension is among the highest known (comparisons being at the same temperature); its intermolecular forces are hydrogen bonds, the strongest kind of dipole–dipole attraction. In fact, the surface tension of water is roughly three times that of gasoline, which consists of relatively nonpolar hydrocarbon molecules able to experience only London forces.

Wetting of a surface by a liquid

A property we associate with liquids, especially water, is their ability to wet things. **Wetting** is the spreading of a liquid across a surface to form a thin film. Water wets clean glass, such as the windshield of a car, by forming a thin film over the surface of the glass (see Figure 11.15*a*). Water won't wet a greasy windshield, however. Instead, on greasy glass water forms tiny beads (see Figure 11.15*b*).

For wetting to occur, the intermolecular attractions between the liquid and the surface must be of about the same strength as the attractions within the liquid itself. Such a rough equality exists when water touches clean glass. This is because the glass surface contains lots of oxygen atoms to which water molecules can form hydrogen bonds. As a result, part of the energy needed to expand the water's surface area when wetting occurs is recovered by the formation of hydrogen bonds to the glass surface.

FIG. 11.14 **Surface tension in a liquid.** Surface tension allows a glass to be filled with water above the rim. *(Michael Watson.)*

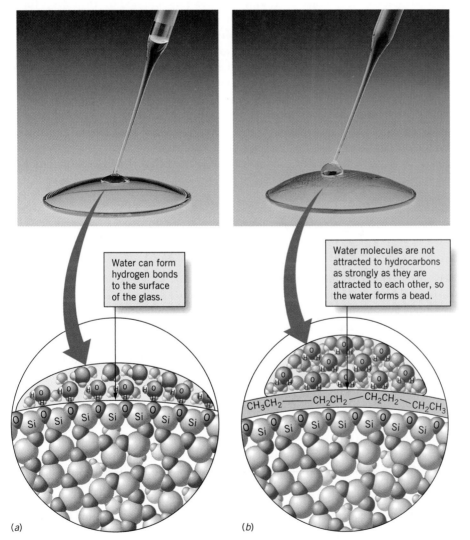

Water can form hydrogen bonds to the surface of the glass.

Water molecules are not attracted to hydrocarbons as strongly as they are attracted to each other, so the water forms a bead.

(a)   (b)

☐ Glass is characterized by a vast network of silicon–oxygen bonds.

FIG. 11.15 **Intermolecular attractions affect the ability of water to wet a surface.** (*a*) Water wets a clean glass surface because the surface contains many oxygen atoms to which water molecules can form hydrogen bonds. (*b*) If the surface has a layer of grease, to which water molecules are only weakly attracted, the water doesn't wet it. The water resists spreading and forms a bead instead. *((a), (b) Michael Watson.)*

When the glass is coated by a film of oil or grease, the surface exposed to the water drop becomes oil and grease and is now composed of relatively nonpolar molecules (Figure 11.15b). These attract other molecules (including water) largely by London forces, which are weak compared with hydrogen bonds. Therefore, the attractions *within* liquid water are much stronger than the attractions *between* water molecules and the greasy surface. The weak water-to-grease London forces can't overcome the hydrogen bonding within liquid water, so the water doesn't spread out; it forms beads instead.

One of the reasons why detergents are used for such chores as doing laundry or washing floors is that detergents contain chemicals called **surfactants** that drastically lower the surface tension of water. This makes the water "wetter," which allows the detergent solution to spread more easily across the surface to be cleaned.

When a liquid has a low surface tension, like gasoline, we know that it has weak intermolecular attractions, and such a liquid easily wets solid surfaces. The weak attractions between molecules in gasoline, for example, are readily replaced by attractions to almost any surface, so gasoline easily spreads to a thin film. If you've ever spilled a little gasoline, you have experienced firsthand that it doesn't bead.

Viscosity

As everybody knows, syrup flows less readily or is more resistant to flow than water (both at the same temperature). Flowing is a change in the *form* of the liquid, and such resistance to a change in form is called the liquid's **viscosity.** We say that syrup is more *viscous* than water. The concept of viscosity is not confined to liquids, however, although it is with liquids that the property is most commonly associated. Solid things, even rock, also yield to forces acting to change their shapes, but normally do so only gradually and imperceptibly. Gases also have viscosity, but they respond almost instantly to form-changing forces.

Viscosity has been called the "internal friction" of a material. It is influenced both by intermolecular attractions and by molecular shape and size. For molecules of similar size, we find that as the strengths of the intermolecular attractions increase, so does the viscosity. For example, consider acetone (nail polish remover) and ethylene glycol (automotive antifreeze), each of which contains 10 atoms.

$$\underset{\text{acetone}}{\text{H}_3\text{C}-\overset{\overset{\displaystyle \text{O}}{\|}}{\text{C}}-\text{CH}_3} \qquad \underset{\text{ethylene glycol}}{\text{HO}-\text{CH}_2-\text{CH}_2-\text{OH}}$$

☐ If you've ever spilled a little acetone, you know that it flows very easily. In contrast, ethylene glycol has an "oily" thickness to it and flows more slowly.

Ethylene glycol is more viscous than acetone, and looking at the molecular structures, it's easy to see why. Acetone contains a polar carbonyl group ($>\text{C}=\text{O}$), so it experiences dipole–dipole attractions as well as London forces. Ethylene glycol, on the other hand, contains two —OH groups, so in addition to London forces, ethylene glycol molecules also participate in hydrogen bonding (a much stronger interaction than ordinary dipole–dipole forces). Strong hydrogen bonding in ethylene glycol makes it more viscous than acetone.

Molecular size and the ability of molecules to tangle with each other is another major factor in determining viscosity. The long, floppy, entangling molecules in heavy machine oil (almost entirely a mixture of long chain, nonpolar hydrocarbons), plus the London forces in the material, give it a viscosity roughly 600 times that of water at 15 °C. Vegetable oils, like the olive oil or corn oil used to prepare salad dressings, consist of molecules that are also large but generally nonpolar. Olive oil is roughly 100 times more viscous than water.

☐ As the temperature drops, molecules move more slowly and intermolecular forces become more effective at restraining flow.

Viscosity also depends on temperature; as the temperature drops, the viscosity increases. When water, for example, is cooled from its boiling point to room temperature, its viscosity increases by over a factor of three. The increase in viscosity with cooling is why operators of vehicles use a "light," thin (meaning less viscous) motor oil during subzero weather.

Evaporation and sublimation are affected by intermolecular attractions

One of the most important physical properties of liquids and solids is their tendency to undergo a change of state from liquid to gas or from solid to gas. For liquids, the change is called **evaporation.** For solids, which can also change directly to the gaseous state by evaporation without going through the liquid state, we use a special term, **sublimation.** Solid carbon dioxide is commonly called *dry ice* because it doesn't melt. Instead, at atmospheric pressure it *sublimes*, changing directly to gaseous CO_2. Naphthalene, the ingredient in some brands of moth flakes, is another substance that can sublime and seemingly disappear.

To understand evaporation and sublimation, we have to examine the motions of molecules. In a solid or liquid, molecules are not stationary; they bounce around, colliding with their neighbors. At a given temperature, there is *exactly the same* distribution of kinetic energies in a liquid or a solid as there is in a gas, which means that Figure 6.4 on page 212 applies to liquids and solids, too. This figure tells us that at a given temperature a small fraction of the molecules have very large kinetic energies and therefore very high velocities. When one of these high velocity molecules is at the surface and is moving outward fast enough, it can escape the attractions of its neighbors and enter the vapor state. We say the molecule has left by evaporation (or by sublimation, if the substance is a solid).

Evaporation produces a cooling effect

One of the things we notice about the evaporation of a liquid is that it produces a cooling effect. You've experienced this if you've stepped out of a shower and been chilled by the air. The evaporation of water from your body produced this effect. In fact, our bodies use the evaporation of perspiration to maintain a constant body temperature.

We can see why liquids become cool during evaporation by examining Figure 11.16, which illustrates the kinetic energy distribution in a liquid at a particular temperature. A marker along the horizontal axis shows the minimum kinetic energy needed by a molecule to escape the attractions of its neighbors. Only molecules with kinetic energies equal to or greater than the minimum can leave the liquid. Others may begin to leave, but before they can escape they slow to a stop and then fall back. Notice in Figure 11.16 that the minimum kinetic energy needed to escape is much larger than the average, which means that when molecules evaporate they carry with them large amounts of kinetic energy. As a result, the average kinetic energy of the molecules left behind decreases. (You might think of this as being similar to removing people taller than 6 ft from a large class of students. When this is done, the average height of those who are left is less.) Because the Kelvin temperature of the remaining liquid is directly proportional to the now lower average kinetic energy, the temperature is lower; in other words, evaporation causes the liquid that remains to be cooler.

The rate of evaporation depends on surface area, temperature, and strengths of intermolecular attractions

Later in this chapter we are going to be concerned about the *rate of evaporation* of a liquid. There are several factors that control this. You are probably already aware of one of them—the surface area of the liquid. Because evaporation occurs from the liquid's surface and not from within, it makes sense that as the surface area is increased, more molecules are able to escape

Naphthalene sublimes when heated and the vapor condenses directly to a solid when it encounters a cool surface. Here, beautiful flaky naphthalene crystals have been formed on the bottom of a flask containing ice water. *(Michael Watson.)*

□ To understand how temperature and intermolecular forces affect the rate of evaporation, we must compare evaporation rates from the same size surface area. In this discussion, therefore, "rate of evaporation" means "rate of evaporation *per unit surface area.*"

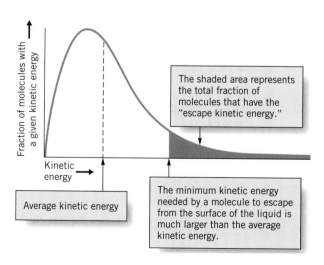

The shaded area represents the total fraction of molecules that have the "escape kinetic energy."

Average kinetic energy

The minimum kinetic energy needed by a molecule to escape from the surface of the liquid is much larger than the average kinetic energy.

FIG. 11.16 **Cooling of a liquid by evaporation.**
Molecules that are able to escape from the liquid have kinetic energies larger than the average. When they leave, the average kinetic energy of the molecules left behind is less, so the temperature is lower.

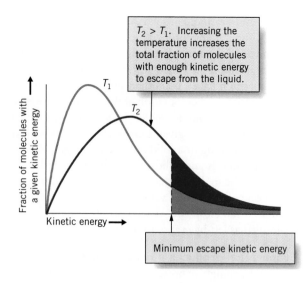

$T_2 > T_1$. Increasing the temperature increases the total fraction of molecules with enough kinetic energy to escape from the liquid.

FIG. 11.17 **Effect of increasing the temperature on the rate of evaporation of a liquid.** At the higher temperature, the total fraction of molecules with enough kinetic energy to escape is larger, so the rate of evaporation is larger.

Minimum escape kinetic energy

and the liquid evaporates more quickly. For liquids having the same surface area, the rate of evaporation depends on two factors, namely, temperature and the strengths of intermolecular attractions. Let's examine each of them separately.

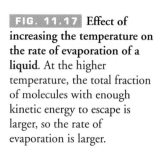

TOOLS

Effect of temperature on rate of evaporation

The influence of temperature on evaporation rate is no surprise; you already know that hot water evaporates faster than cold water. The reason can be seen by studying Figure 11.17, which shows kinetic energy distributions for the *same* liquid at two temperatures. Notice two important features of the figure. First, the same minimum kinetic energy is needed for the escape of molecules at both temperatures. This minimum is determined by the kinds of attractive forces between the molecules, and is independent of temperature. Second, the shaded area of the curve represents the *total* fraction of molecules having kinetic energies equal to or greater than the minimum. At the higher temperature, the total fraction is larger, which means that at the higher temperature a greater total fraction has the ability to evaporate. As you might expect, when more molecules have the needed energy, more evaporate in a unit of time. Therefore, *the rate of evaporation per unit surface area of a given liquid is greater at a higher temperature.*

The effect of intermolecular attractions on evaporation rate can be seen by studying Figure 11.18. Here we have kinetic energy distributions for two *different* liquids—call them

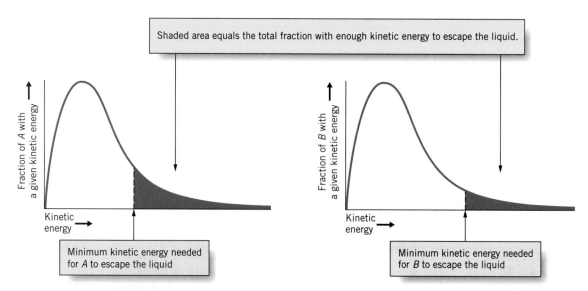

Shaded area equals the total fraction with enough kinetic energy to escape the liquid.

Minimum kinetic energy needed for *A* to escape the liquid

Minimum kinetic energy needed for *B* to escape the liquid

FIG. 11.18 **Kinetic energy distribution in two different liquids, *A* and *B*, at the same temperature.** The minimum kinetic energy required by molecules of *A* to escape is less than that for *B* because the intermolecular attractions in *A* are weaker than in *B*. This causes *A* to evaporate faster than *B*.

A and *B*—both at the same temperature. In liquid *A*, the attractive forces are weak; they might be of the London type, for example. As we see, the minimum kinetic energy needed by *A* molecules to escape is not very large because they are not attracted very strongly to each other. In liquid *B*, the intermolecular attractive forces are much stronger; they might be hydrogen bonds, for instance. Molecules of *B*, therefore, are held more tightly to each other at the liquid's surface and must have a higher kinetic energy to evaporate. As you can see from the figure, the total fraction of molecules with enough energy to evaporate is greater for *A* than for *B*, which means that *A* evaporates faster than *B*. In general, then, *the weaker the intermolecular attractive forces, the faster is the rate of evaporation at a given temperature*. You are probably also aware of this phenomenon. At room temperature, for example, nail polish remover [acetone, $(CH_3)_2CO$], whose molecules experience weak dipole–dipole and London forces of attraction, evaporates faster than water, whose molecules feel the effects of much stronger hydrogen bonds.

TOOLS
Intermolecular forces and rate of evaporation

11.4 | CHANGES OF STATE LEAD TO DYNAMIC EQUILIBRIA

A **change of state** occurs when a substance is transformed from one physical state to another. Evaporation of a liquid and sublimation of a solid are two examples. Others are the melting of a solid such as ice and the freezing of a liquid such as water.

One of the important features about changes of state is that, at any particular temperature, they always tend toward a condition of *dynamic equilibrium*. We introduced the concept of dynamic equilibrium on page 142 with an example of a system at chemical equilibrium. The same general principles apply to a physical equilibrium, such as that between a liquid and its vapor. Let's see how such an equilibrium is established.

When a liquid is placed in an empty container, it immediately begins to evaporate and molecules of the substance begin to collect in the space above the liquid (see Figure 11.19*a*). As they fly around in the vapor, the molecules collide with each other, with the walls of the container, and with the surface of the liquid itself. Those that strike the liquid's surface tend to stick because their kinetic energies become scattered among the surface molecules. This change, which involves vapor molecules changing to the liquid state, is called **condensation.**

Initially, when the liquid is first introduced into the container, the rate of evaporation is high, but the rate of condensation is very low because there are few molecules in the vapor state. As vapor molecules accumulate, the rate of condensation increases. This continues until the rate at which molecules are condensing becomes equal to the rate at which they are evaporating (Figure 11.19*b*). From that moment on, the number of molecules in the vapor will remain constant, because over a given period of time the

☐ In chemistry (unless otherwise indicated), when we use the term *equilibrium*, we always mean *dynamic equilibrium*.

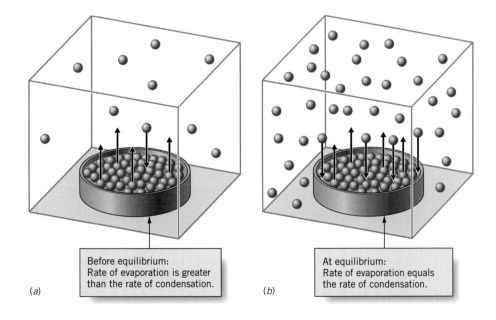

Before equilibrium:
Rate of evaporation is greater than the rate of condensation.

At equilibrium:
Rate of evaporation equals the rate of condensation.

(*a*)   (*b*)

FIG. 11.19 **Evaporation of a liquid into a sealed container.** (*a*) The liquid has just begun to evaporate into the container. The rate of evaporation is greater than the rate of condensation. (*b*) A dynamic equilibrium is reached when the rate of evaporation equals the rate of condensation. In a given time period, the number of molecules entering the vapor equals the number that leave, so there is no net change in the number of gaseous molecules.

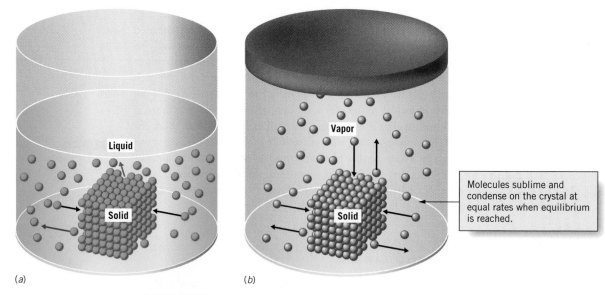

Molecules sublime and condense on the crystal at equal rates when equilibrium is reached.

(a)   (b)

FIG. 11.20 Solid–liquid and solid–vapor equilibria. (*a*) As long as no heat is added or removed, melting (red arrows) and freezing (black arrows) occur at equal rates and the number of particles in the solid remains constant. (*b*) Equilibrium is established when molecules evaporate from the solid at the same rate as they condense from the vapor.

☐ A vapor–liquid equilibrium is possible only in a closed container. When the container is open, vapor molecules drift away and the liquid might completely evaporate.

number that enters the vapor is the same as the number that leaves. At this point we have a condition of *dynamic equilibrium,* one in which two opposing effects, evaporation and condensation, are occurring at equal rates.

Similar equilibria are also reached in melting and sublimation. At a temperature called the **melting point,** a solid begins to change to a liquid as heat is added. At this temperature a dynamic equilibrium can exist between molecules in the solid and those in the liquid. Molecules leave the solid and enter the liquid at the same rate as molecules leave the liquid and join the solid (Figure 11.20*a*). As long as no heat is added or removed from such a solid–liquid equilibrium mixture, melting and freezing occur at equal rates. For sublimation, the situation is exactly the same as in the evaporation of a liquid into a sealed container (see Figure 11.20*b*). After a few moments, the rates of sublimation and condensation become the same and equilibrium is established.

| 11.5 | VAPOR PRESSURES OF LIQUIDS AND SOLIDS ARE CONTROLLED BY TEMPERATURE AND INTERMOLECULAR ATTRACTIONS |

☐ A liquid with a high vapor pressure at a given temperature is said to be **volatile.**

When a liquid evaporates, the molecules that enter the vapor exert a pressure called the **vapor pressure.** From the very moment a liquid begins to evaporate into the vapor space above it, there is a vapor pressure. If the evaporation is taking place inside a sealed container, this pressure grows until finally equilibrium is reached. Once the rates of evaporation and condensation become equal, the concentration of molecules in the vapor remains constant and the vapor exerts a constant pressure. This final pressure is called the **equilibrium vapor pressure of the liquid.** In general, when we refer to the *vapor pressure,* we really mean the equilibrium vapor pressure.

Two factors determine the equilibrium vapor pressure

TOOLS
Factors that affect vapor pressure

Figure 11.21 shows plots of equilibrium vapor pressure versus temperature for a few liquids. From these graphs we see that both a liquid's temperature and its chemical composition are the major factors affecting its vapor pressure. Once we have selected a particular liquid, however, only the temperature matters. The reason is that the vapor pressure of a given liquid is a function solely of its rate of evaporation *per unit area of the liquid's surface.* When this rate is large, a large concentration of molecules in the vapor state is necessary to establish

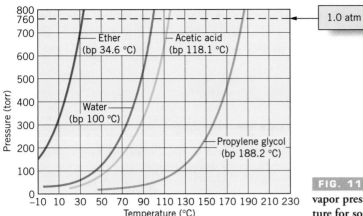

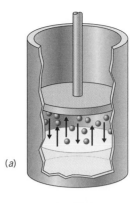

(a)

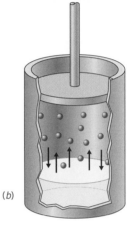

(b)

FIG. 11.21 Variation of vapor pressure with temperature for some common liquids.

equilibrium, which is another way of saying that the vapor pressure is relatively high when the evaporation rate is high. As the temperature of a given liquid increases, so does its rate of evaporation and so does its equilibrium vapor pressure.

As chemical composition changes in going from one liquid to another, the strengths of intermolecular attractions change. If the attractions increase, the rates of evaporation at a given temperature decrease, and the vapor pressures decrease. These data on relative vapor pressures tell us that, of the four liquids in Figure 11.21, intermolecular attractions are strongest in propylene glycol, next strongest in acetic acid, third strongest in water, and weakest in ether. Thus, *we can use vapor pressures as indications of relative strengths of the attractive forces in liquids.*

Some factors do not affect the vapor pressure

An important fact about vapor pressure is that *its magnitude doesn't depend on the **total** surface area of the liquid, nor on the volume of the liquid in the container, nor on the volume of the container itself, just as long as some liquid remains when equilibrium is reached.* The reason is because none of these factors affects the rate of evaporation *per unit surface area.*

Increasing the *total* surface area does increase the *total* rate of evaporation, but the larger area is also available for condensation; so the rate at which molecules return to the liquid also increases. The rates of both evaporation and condensation are thus affected equally, and no change occurs to the equilibrium vapor pressure.

Adding more liquid to the container can't affect the equilibrium either because evaporation occurs from the *surface*. Having more molecules in the bulk of the liquid does not change what is going on at the surface.

To understand why the vapor pressure doesn't depend on the *size* of the vapor space, consider a liquid in equilibrium with its vapor in a cylinder with a movable piston, as illustrated in Figure 11.22*a*. Withdrawing the piston (Figure 11.22*b*) increases the volume of the vapor space; as the vapor expands, the pressure it exerts becomes less, so there's a momentary drop in the pressure. The molecules of the vapor, being more spread out now, no longer strike the surface as frequently, so the rate of condensation also decreases. The rate of evaporation hasn't changed, however, so for a moment the system is not at equilibrium and the substance is evaporating faster than it is condensing (Figure 11.22*b*). This condition prevails, changing more liquid into vapor, until the concentration of molecules in the vapor has risen enough to make the condensation rate again equal to the evaporation rate (Figure 11.22*c*). At this point the vapor pressure has returned to its original value. Therefore, the net result of expanding the space above the liquid is to change more liquid into vapor, but it does not affect the equilibrium vapor pressure. Similarly, we expect that reducing the volume of the vapor space above the liquid will also not affect the equilibrium vapor pressure.

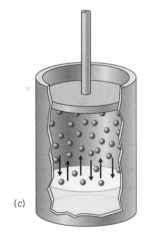

(c)

FIG. 11.22 Effect of a volume change on the vapor pressure of a liquid. (*a*) Equilibrium exists between liquid and vapor. (*b*) The volume is increased, which upsets the equilibrium and causes the pressure to drop. The rate of condensation is now less than the rate of evaporation, which hasn't changed. (*c*) After more liquid has evaporated, equilibrium is restored and the rates of condensation and evaporation are again equal and the vapor pressure has returned to its initial value.

Practice Exercise 3: Considering Figure 11.22, in which direction should the piston be moved to decrease the number of molecules in the gas phase? (Hint: Consider what must happen to re-establish equilibrium after the piston is moved.)

Practice Exercise 4: Suppose a liquid is in equilibrium with its vapor in a piston–cylinder apparatus like that in Figure 11.22. If the piston is pushed in a short way and the system is allowed to return to equilibrium, what will have happened to the *total number* of molecules in both the liquid and the vapor?

Solids also have vapor pressures

◻ In many solids, such as NaCl, the attractive forces are so strong that virtually no particles have enough kinetic energy to escape at room temperature, so essentially no evaporation occurs. Their vapor pressures at room temperature are virtually zero.

Solids have vapor pressures just as liquids do. In a crystal, the particles are constantly jiggling around, bumping into their neighbors. At a given temperature there is a distribution of kinetic energies, so some particles at the surface have large enough kinetic energies to break away from their neighbors and enter the vapor state. When particles in the vapor collide with the crystal, they can be recaptured, so condensation can occur too. Eventually, the concentration of particles in the vapor reaches a point where the rate of sublimation equals the rate of condensation, and a dynamic equilibrium is established. The pressure of the vapor that is in equilibrium with the solid is called the **equilibrium vapor pressure of the solid.** As with liquids, this equilibrium vapor pressure is usually referred to simply as the vapor pressure. Like that of a liquid, the vapor pressure of a solid is determined by the strengths of the attractive forces between the particles and by the temperature.

11.6 | BOILING OCCURS WHEN A LIQUID'S VAPOR PRESSURE EQUALS ATMOSPHERIC PRESSURE

If you were asked to check whether a pot of water was boiling, what would you look for? The answer, of course, is *bubbles*. When a liquid boils, large bubbles usually form at many places on the inner surface of the container and rise to the top. If you were to place a thermometer into the boiling water, you would find that the temperature remains constant, regardless of how you adjust the flame under the pot. A hotter flame just makes the water bubble faster, but it doesn't raise the temperature. *Any pure liquid remains at a constant temperature while it is boiling,* a temperature that's called the liquid's *boiling point.*

◻ On the top of Mt. Everest, the world's tallest peak, water boils at only 69 °C.

If you measure the boiling point of water in Philadelphia, New York, or any place else that is nearly at sea level, your thermometer will read 100 °C or very close to it. However, if you try this experiment in Denver, Colorado, you will find that water boils at about 95 °C. Denver, at a mile above sea level, has a lower atmospheric pressure, so we find that the boiling point depends on the atmospheric pressure.

These observations raise some interesting questions. Why do liquids boil? And why does the boiling point depend on the pressure of the atmosphere? The answers become apparent when we realize that inside the bubbles of a boiling liquid is the *liquid's vapor*, not air. When water boils, the bubbles contain water vapor (steam); when alcohol boils, the bubbles contain alcohol vapor. As a bubble grows, liquid evaporates into it, and the pressure of the vapor pushes the liquid aside, making the size of the bubble increase (see Figure 11.23). Opposing the bubble's internal vapor pressure, however, is the pressure of the atmosphere pushing down on the top of the liquid, attempting to collapse the bubble. The only way the bubble can exist and grow is for the vapor pressure within it to equal (maybe just slightly exceed) the pressure exerted by the atmosphere. In other words, bubbles of vapor cannot even form until the temperature of the liquid rises to a point at which the liquid's vapor pressure equals the atmospheric pressure. Thus, in scientific terms, the **boiling point** is defined as *the temperature at which the vapor pressure of the liquid is equal to the prevailing atmospheric pressure.*

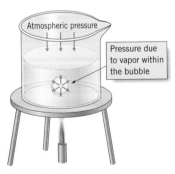

FIG. 11.23 **A liquid at its boiling point.** The pressure of the vapor within a bubble in a boiling liquid pushes the liquid aside against the opposing pressure of the atmosphere. Bubbles can't form unless the vapor pressure of the liquid is at least equal to the pressure of the atmosphere.

Now we can easily understand why water boils at a lower temperature in Denver than it does in New York City. Because the atmospheric pressure is lower in Denver, the water there doesn't have to be heated to as high a temperature to make its vapor pressure equal to the atmospheric pressure. The lower temperature of boiling water at places with high altitudes, like Denver, makes it necessary to cook foods longer. At the other extreme, a pressure cooker is a device that increases the pressure over the boiling water and thereby raises the boiling point. At the higher temperature, foods cook more quickly.

To make it possible to compare the boiling points of different liquids, chemists have chosen 1 atm as the reference pressure. The boiling point of a liquid at 1 atm is called its **normal boiling point.** (If a boiling point is reported without also mentioning the pressure at which it was measured, we assume it to be the normal boiling point.) Notice in Figure 11.21, page 449, that we can find the normal boiling points of ether, water, acetic acid, and propylene glycol by noting the temperatures at which their vapor pressure curves cross the 1 atm pressure line.

Boiling point is affected by intermolecular attractions

Earlier we mentioned that the boiling point is a property whose value depends on the strengths of the intermolecular attractions in a liquid. When the attractive forces are strong, the liquid has a low vapor pressure at a given temperature, so it must be heated to a high temperature to bring its vapor pressure up to atmospheric pressure. High boiling points therefore result from strong intermolecular attractions, so we often use normal boiling point data to assess relative intermolecular attractions among different liquids. (In fact, we did this in solving Example 11.1.)

The effects of intermolecular attractions on boiling point are easily seen by examining Figure 11.24, which gives the plots of the boiling points versus period numbers for some families of binary hydrogen compounds. Notice, first, the gradual increase in boiling point for the hydrogen compounds of the Group IVA elements (CH_4 through GeH_4). These compounds are composed of nonpolar tetrahedral molecules. The boiling points increase from CH_4 to GeH_4 simply because the molecules become larger and their electron clouds become more polarizable, which leads to an increase in the strengths of the London forces.

When we look at the hydrogen compounds of the other nonmetals, we find the same trend from Period 3 through Period 5. Thus, for three compounds of the Group VA series, PH_3, AsH_3, and SbH_3, there is a gradual increase in boiling point, corresponding again to the increasing strengths of London forces. Similar increases occur for the three Group VIA compounds (H_2S, H_2Se, and H_2Te) and for the three Group VIIA compounds (HCl, HBr, and HI). Significantly, however, the Period 2 members of each of these series (NH_3, H_2O, and HF) have much higher boiling points than might otherwise be expected. The reason is that each is involved in hydrogen bonding, which is a much stronger attraction than London forces.

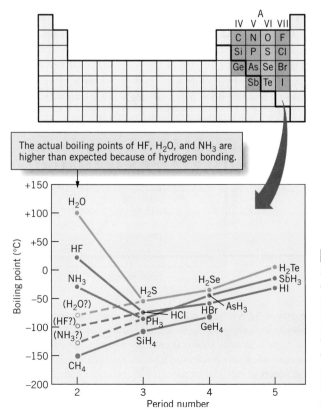

The actual boiling points of HF, H_2O, and NH_3 are higher than expected because of hydrogen bonding.

TOOLS

Boiling ponts are related to intermolecular attractive forces

FIG. 11.24 **Effects of intermolecular attractions on boiling point.** Boiling points of the hydrogen compounds of elements of Groups IVA, VA, VIA, and VIIA of the periodic table. The dashed lines lead to hypothetical boiling points, if hydrogen bonding did not exist, for HF, H_2O, and NH_3.

One of the most interesting and far-reaching consequences of hydrogen bonding is that it causes water to be a liquid, rather than a gas, at temperatures near 25 °C. If it were not for hydrogen bonding, water would have a boiling point somewhere near −80 °C and could not exist as a liquid except at still lower temperatures. At such low temperatures it is unlikely that life as we know it could have developed.

Practice Exercise 5: The Dead Sea is approximately 1300 ft below sea level and its barometric pressure is approximately 830 torr. Will the boiling point of water be elevated from 100 °C by (a) less than 10 °C, (b) 10 °C to 25 °C, (c) 25 °C to 50 °C, or (d) above 50 °C? (Hint: Extrapolate from Figure 11.21.)

Practice Exercise 6: The atmospheric pressure at the top of Mt. McKinley in Alaska, 3.85 miles above sea level, is 330 torr. Use Figure 11.21 to estimate the boiling point of water at the top of the mountain.

11.7 | ENERGY CHANGES OCCUR DURING CHANGES OF STATE

When a liquid or solid evaporates or a solid melts, there are increases in the distances between the particles of the substance. Particles that normally attract each other are forced apart, increasing their potential energies. Such energy changes affect our daily lives in many ways, especially the energy changes associated with the changes in state of water, changes which even control the weather on our planet. To study these energy changes, let's begin by examining how the temperature of a substance varies as it is heated.

Heating curves and cooling curves reveal changes in kinetic and potential energy

☐ When a solid or liquid is heated, the volume expands only slightly, so there are only small changes in the average distance between the particles. This means that very small changes in potential energy take place, so almost all the heat added goes to increasing the kinetic energy.

Figure 11.25a illustrates the way the temperature of a substance changes as we add heat to it *at a constant rate*, starting with the solid and finishing with the gaseous state of the substance. The graph is sometimes called a **heating curve** for the substance.

First, let's look at the portions of the graph that slope upward. These occur where we are increasing the temperature of the solid, liquid, and gas phases. Because temperature is related to average kinetic energy, nearly all of the heat we add in these regions of the heating curve goes to increasing the average kinetic energies of the particles. In other words, the added heat makes the particles go faster and collide with each other with more force. In addition, the slopes of the rising portions have units of degrees Celsius per joule.

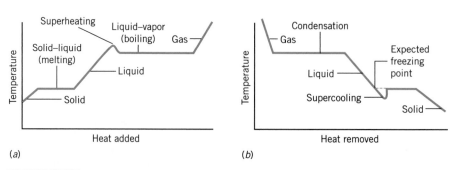

FIG. 11.25 Heating and cooling curves. (*a*) A heating curve observed when heat is added to a substance at a constant rate. The temperatures corresponding to the flat portions of the curve occur at the melting point and boiling point. Superheating in shown as continued heating beyond the boiling point. (*b*) A cooling curve observed when heat is removed from a substance at a constant rate. Condensation of vapor to a liquid occurs at the same temperature as the liquid boils. Supercooling is seen here as the temperature of the liquid dips below its freezing point (the same temperature as its melting point). Once a tiny crystal forms, the temperature rises to the freezing point.

This is the reciprocal of the heat capacity, meaning that the greater the slope, the lower the heat capacity. Gases have lower heat capacities than liquids and solids, therefore the heating of the gas phase has the largest slope.

In those portions of the heating curve where the temperature remains constant, the average kinetic energy of the particles is not changing. This means that all the heat being added must go to increase the *potential energies* of the particles. During melting, the particles held rigidly in the solid begin to separate slightly as they form the mobile liquid phase. The potential energy increase accompanying this process equals the amount of heat input during the melting process. During boiling, there is an even greater increase in the distance between the molecules. Here they go from the relatively tight packing in the liquid to the widely spaced distribution of molecules in the gas. This gives rise to an even larger increase in the potential energy, which we see as a longer flat region on the heating curve during the boiling of the liquid.

The opposite of a heating curve is a **cooling curve** (see Figure 11.25*b*). Here we start with a gas and gradually cool it—remove heat from it at a constant rate—until we have reached a solid.

Superheating and supercooling

Looking at Figure 11.25 again we notice two unusual features, one on each curve. There is a small "blip" on the heating curve near the transition from the liquid to a gas. A similar feature occurs when a liquid is cooled to a solid. These "blips" represent the phenomena of superheating and supercooling. Superheating occurs when the liquid is heated above the boiling point without boiling. If disturbed, a **superheated liquid** will erupt with a shower of vapor and liquid. Many people have discovered this effect when heating their favorite beverage in a microwave oven. When cooling a liquid it is possible to decrease the temperature below the freezing point without solidification occurring, creating a supercooled liquid. Once again if the supercooled liquid is disturbed, very rapid crystallization occurs. Some commercial products take advantage of supercooling to provide an instant heat source for minor injuries since the crystallization process often evolves large quantities of heat.

◻ Supercooling of a vapor is also possible. Condensation of supercooled water vapor onto solid surfaces leads to dew in warm weather and frost in freezing weather.

Molar heats of fusion, vaporization, and sublimation

Because phase changes occur at constant temperature and pressure, the potential energy changes associated with melting and vaporization can be expressed as enthalpy changes. Usually, enthalpy changes are expressed on a "per mole" basis and are given special names to identify the kind of change involved. For example, using the word **fusion** instead of "melting," *the* **molar heat of fusion**, ΔH_{fusion}, *is the heat absorbed by one mole of a solid when it melts to give a liquid at the same temperature and pressure.* Similarly, *the* **molar heat of vaporization**, $\Delta H_{vaporization}$, *is the heat absorbed when one mole of a liquid is changed to one mole of vapor at a constant temperature and pressure.* Finally, *the* **molar heat of sublimation**, $\Delta H_{sublimation}$, *is the heat absorbed by one mole of a solid when it sublimes to give one mole of vapor, once again at a constant temperature and pressure.* The values of ΔH for fusion, vaporization, and sublimation are all positive because the phase change in each case is endothermic, being accompanied by a net increase in potential energy.

TOOLS
Enthalpy changes in phase change

◻ These are also called *enthalpies* of fusion, vaporization, and sublimation.

Examples of the influence of these energy changes on our daily lives abound. For example, you've added ice to a drink to keep it cool because as the ice melts, it absorbs heat (its heat of fusion). Your body uses the heat of vaporization of water to cool itself through the evaporation of perspiration. During the summer, ice cream trucks carry dry ice because the sublimation of CO_2 absorbs its heat of sublimation and keeps the ice cream cold. And perhaps most importantly, weather on our planet is driven by the heat of vaporization of water which serves to convert solar energy into the energy of winds and storms. For example, over oceans large storms such as hurricanes rely on a continued supply of warm moist air produced by rapid evaporation of H_2O from tropical waters. Continual condensation in the high clouds forms rain and supplies the energy needed to feed the storm's winds.

Solidification of a liquid to a crystal, condensation of a gas to a liquid, or deposition of a gas as a solid are simply the reverse of fusion, vaporization, and sublimation processes. Therefore the heat of crystallization is equal to the heat of fusion but it has the opposite

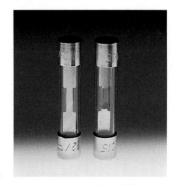

Fusion means melting. The thin metal band in an electrical fuse becomes hot as electricity passes through it. It protects a circuit by melting if too much current is drawn. On the right we see a fuse that has done its job. *(Michael Watson.)*

algebraic sign. Similarly the heats of condensation and deposition have the opposite signs of their counterparts.

Since heat is released when liquids condense or when gases become solids or liquids, that heat can be put to practical use. For example, a supersaturated solution of ammonium nitrate can be caused to crystallize inside a plastic bag. The heat liberated is used to treat some sports injuries with this "heat pack." Similarly, meteorologists can often use the "dew point" of the atmosphere to predict overnight low temperatures. The dew point is the temperature at which moisture in the air begins to condense. If the nighttime temperature decreases to the dew point, the heat released by the condensation of water keeps the temperature from falling much further.

FACETS OF CHEMISTRY
11.1

Determining Heats of Vaporization

The way the vapor pressure varies with temperature, which was described in Section 11.5 and Figure 11.21, depends on the heat of vaporization of a substance. The relationship, however, is not a simple proportionality. Instead, it involves *natural logarithms*, which are logarithms to the base e as compared to the more familiar base-10 logarithms. With modern calculators the logarithm function can be applied with the press of the *ln* key for natural logarithms and the *log* key for base-10 logarithms. The reverse process of taking an "antilogarithm" uses an *inv* or *2nd* function key with the *ln* or *log* keys on most calculators.

Rudolf Clausius (1822–1888), a German physicist, and Benoit Clapeyron (1799–1864), a French engineer, used the principles of thermodynamics (a subject that's discussed in Chapter 18) to derive the following equation that relates the vapor pressure, heat of vaporization (ΔH_{vap}), and temperature

$$\ln P = \frac{-\Delta H_{vap}}{RT} + C \qquad (1)$$

The quantity $\ln P$ is the natural logarithm of the vapor pressure, R is the gas constant expressed in energy units ($R = 8.314$ J mol^{-1} K^{-1}), T is the absolute temperature, and C is a constant. Scientists call this the **Clausius–Clapeyron equation.**

The Clausius–Clapeyron equation provides a convenient graphical method for determining heats of vaporization from experimentally measured vapor pressure–temperature data. To see this, let's rewrite the equation as follows.

$$\ln P = \left(\frac{-\Delta H_{vap}}{R}\right)\frac{1}{T} + C$$

Recall from algebra that a straight line is represented by the general equation

$$y = mx + b$$

where x and y are variables, m is the slope, and b is the intercept of the line with the y axis. In this case, we can make the substitutions

$$y = \ln P \qquad x = \frac{1}{T} \qquad m = \frac{-\Delta H_{vap}}{R} \qquad b = C$$

Therefore, we have

$$\ln P = \left(\frac{-\Delta H_{vap}}{R}\right)\frac{1}{T} + C$$
$$\updownarrow \qquad\qquad \updownarrow \quad\ \updownarrow \quad \updownarrow$$
$$y = \qquad\quad m \quad\ x + b$$

Thus, a graph of $\ln P$ versus $1/T$ should give a straight line that has a slope equal to $-\Delta H_{vap}/R$. Such straight line relationships are illustrated in Figure 1 in which experimental data are plotted for water, acetone, and ethanol. From the graphs in Figure 1, the calculated values of ΔH_{vap} are as follows: for water, 43.9 kJ mol^{-1}; for acetone, 32.0 kJ mol^{-1}; and for ethanol, 40.5 kJ mol^{-1}.

Using Equation 1 above, a "two point" form of the Clausius–Clapeyron equation can be derived that can be used to calculate ΔH_{vap} if the vapor pressure is known at two different temperatures. This equation is

$$\ln \frac{P_1}{P_2} = \frac{\Delta H_{vap}}{R}\left(\frac{1}{T_2} - \frac{1}{T_1}\right) \qquad (2)$$

If we know the value of the heat of vaporization, Equation 2 can also be used to calculate the vapor pressure at some particular temperature (say, P_2 at a temperature T_2) if we already know the vapor pressure P_1 at a temperature T_1.

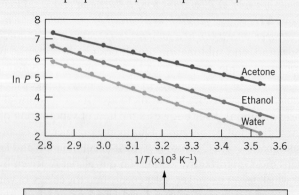

The numbers along the horizontal axis are equal to $1/T$ values multiplied by 1000 to make the axis easier to label.

Figure 1 A graph showing plots of $\ln P$ versus $1/T$ for acetone, ethanol, and water.

TABLE 11.4	Some Typical Heats of Vaporization	
Substance	$\Delta H_{vaporization}$(kJ mol^{-1})	Type of Attractive Force
H_2O	+43.9	Hydrogen bonding and London
NH_3	+21.7	Hydrogen bonding and London
HCl	+15.6	Dipole–dipole and London
SO_2	+24.3	Dipole–dipole and London
F_2	+5.9	London
Cl_2	+10.0	London
Br_2	+15.0	London
I_2	+22.0	London
CH_4	+8.16	London
C_2H_6	+15.1	London
C_3H_8	+16.9	London
C_6H_{14}	+30.1	London

Energy changes are related to intermolecular attractions

When a liquid evaporates or a solid sublimes, the particles go from a situation in which the attractive forces are very strong to one in which the attractive forces are so small they can almost be ignored. Therefore, the values of $\Delta H_{vaporization}$ and $\Delta H_{sublimation}$ give us directly the energy needed to separate molecules from each other. We can examine such values to obtain reliable comparisons of the strengths of intermolecular attractions.

In Table 11.4, notice that the heats of vaporization of water and ammonia are very large, which is just what we would expect for hydrogen-bonded substances. By comparison, CH_4, a nonpolar substance composed of atoms of similar size, has a very small heat of vaporization. Note also that polar substances such as HCl and SO_2 have fairly large heats of vaporization compared with nonpolar substances. For example, compare HCl with Cl_2. Even though Cl_2 contains two relatively large atoms, and therefore would be expected to have larger London forces than HCl, the HCl has the larger $\Delta H_{vaporization}$. This must be due to dipole–dipole attractions between polar HCl molecules—attractions that are absent in nonpolar Cl_2.

Heats of vaporization also reflect the factors that control the strengths of London forces. For example, the data in Table 11.4 show the effect of chain length on the intermolecular attractions between hydrocarbons; as the chain length increases from one carbon in CH_4 to six carbons in C_6H_{14}, the heat of vaporization also increases, showing that the London forces also increase. Similarly, the heats of vaporization of the halogens in Table 11.4 show that the strengths of London forces increase as the electron clouds of the particles become larger.

TOOLS
Intermolecular attractive forces are related to heats of vaporization and sublimation

☐ The stronger the attractions, the more the potential energy will increase when the molecules become separated, and the larger will be the value of ΔH.

11.8 | CHANGES IN A DYNAMIC EQUILIBRIUM CAN BE ANALYZED USING LE CHÂTELIER'S PRINCIPLE

Throughout this chapter, we have studied various dynamic equilibria. One example was the equilibrium that exists between a liquid and its vapor in a closed container. You learned that when the temperature of the liquid is increased in this system, its vapor pressure also increases. Let's briefly review why this occurs.

Initially, the liquid is in equilibrium with its vapor, which exerts a certain pressure. When the temperature is increased, equilibrium no longer exists because evaporation occurs more rapidly than condensation. Eventually, as the concentration of molecules in the vapor increases, *the system reaches a new equilibrium* in which there is more vapor and a little less liquid. The greater concentration of molecules in the vapor causes a larger pressure.

The way a liquid's equilibrium vapor pressure responds to a temperature change is an example of a general phenomenon. *Whenever a dynamic equilibrium is upset by some disturbance, the system changes in a way that will, if possible, bring the system back to equilibrium again.* It's also important to understand that in the process of regaining equilibrium, the system undergoes a net change. Thus, when the temperature of a liquid is raised, there is some net conversion of liquid into vapor as the system returns to equilibrium. When the new equilibrium is reached, the amount of liquid and the amount of vapor are not the same as they were before.

Throughout the remainder of this book, we will deal with many kinds of equilibria, both chemical and physical. It would be very time-consuming and sometimes very difficult to carry out a detailed analysis each time we wish to know the effects of some disturbance on an equilibrium system. Fortunately, there is a relatively simple and fast method for predicting the effect of a disturbance, one based on a principle proposed in 1888 by a brilliant French chemist, Henry Le Châtelier (1850–1936).

TOOLS

Le Châtelier's principle

> **Le Châtelier's Principle.** When a dynamic equilibrium in a system is upset by a disturbance, the system responds in a *direction* that tends to counteract the disturbance and, if possible, restore equilibrium.

Let's see how we can apply Le Châtelier's principle to a liquid–vapor equilibrium that is subjected to a temperature increase. We cannot increase a temperature, of course, without adding heat. Thus, *the addition of heat is really the disturbing influence when a temperature is increased.* So let's incorporate "heat" as a member of the equation used to represent the liquid–vapor equilibrium.

$$\text{Heat} + \text{liquid} \rightleftharpoons \text{vapor} \tag{11.1}$$

Recall that we use double arrows, $\rightleftharpoons$, to indicate a dynamic equilibrium in an equation. They imply opposing changes happening at equal rates. Evaporation is endothermic, so the heat is placed on the left side of Equation 11.1 to show that heat is absorbed by the liquid when it changes to the vapor, and that heat is released when the vapor condenses to a liquid.

Le Châtelier's principle tells us that when we add heat to raise the temperature of the equilibrium system, the system will try to adjust in a way that absorbs some of the added heat. This can happen if some liquid evaporates, because vaporization is endothermic. When liquid evaporates, the amount of vapor increases and causes the pressure to rise. Thus, we have reached the correct conclusion in a very simple way, namely, that heating a liquid must increase its vapor pressure.

We often use the term **position of equilibrium** to refer to the relative amounts of the substances on opposite sides of the double arrows in an equilibrium expression such as Equation 11.1. Thus, we can think of how a disturbance affects the position of equilibrium. For example, increasing the temperature increases the amount of vapor and decreases the amount of liquid, and we say *the position of equilibrium has shifted*; in this case, it has shifted in the direction of the vapor, or it has *shifted to the right*. In using Le Châtelier's principle, it is often convenient to think of a disturbance as "shifting the position of equilibrium" in one direction or another in the equilibrium equation.

Practice Exercise 7: Use Le Châtelier's principle to predict how a temperature increase will affect the vapor pressure of a solid. (Hint: Solid + heat $\rightleftharpoons$ vapor.)

Practice Exercise 8: Designate whether each of the following physical processes is exothermic or endothermic. Can any of them be exothermic for some substances and endothermic for others? Boiling, melting, condensing, subliming, freezing

11.9 CRYSTALLINE SOLIDS HAVE AN ORDERED INTERNAL STRUCTURE

When many substances freeze, or when they separate as a solid from a solution, they tend to form crystals that have highly regular features. For example, Figure 11.26 is a photograph of crystals of sodium chloride—ordinary table salt. Notice that each particle is very nearly a perfect little cube. Whenever a solution of NaCl is evaporated, the crystals that form have edges that intersect at 90° angles. Thus, cubes are the norm for NaCl.

Crystals in general tend to have flat surfaces that meet at angles that are characteristic of the substance. The regularity of these surface features reflects the high degree of order

FIG. 11.26 **Crystals of table salt.** The size of the tiny cubic sodium chloride crystals can be seen in comparison with a penny. *(The Photo Works.)*

among the particles that lie within the crystal. This is true whether the particles are atoms, molecules, or ions.

Crystal structures are described by lattices and unit cells

Any repetitive pattern has a symmetrical aspect about it, whether it be a wallpaper design or the orderly packing of particles in a crystal (Figure 11.27). For example, we can easily recognize certain repeating distances between the elements of the pattern, and we can see that the lines along which the elements of the pattern repeat are at certain angles to each other.

To concentrate on the symmetrical features of a repeating structure, it is convenient to describe it in terms of a set of points that have the same repeat distances as the structure, arranged along lines oriented at the same angles. Such a pattern of points is called a **lattice,** and when we apply it to describe the packing of particles in a solid, we often call it a **crystal lattice.**

In a crystal, the number of particles is enormous. If you could imagine being at the center of even the tiniest crystal, you would find that the particles go on as far as you can see in every direction. Describing the positions of all these particles or their lattice points is impossible and, fortunately, unnecessary. All we need to do is describe the repeating unit of the lattice, which we call the *unit cell*. To see this, and to gain an insight into the usefulness of the lattice concept, let's begin in two dimensions.

In Figure 11.28 we see a two-dimensional *square lattice*, which means the lattice points lie at the corners of squares. The repeating unit of the lattice, its **unit cell,** is indicated in the drawing. If we began with this unit cell, we could produce the entire lattice by moving it repeatedly left and right and up and down by distances equal to its edge length. In this sense, all the properties of a lattice are contained in the properties of its unit cell.

An important fact about lattices is that the same lattice can be used to describe many different designs or structures. For example, in Figure 11.28*b*, we see a design formed by associating a pink heart with each lattice point. Using a square lattice, we could form any number of designs just by using different design elements (for example, a rose or a diamond) or by changing the lengths of the edges of the unit cell. *The only requirement is that the same design element must be associated with each lattice point.* In other words, if there is a rose at one lattice point, then there must be a rose at all the other lattice points.

Extending the lattice concept to three dimensions is straightforward. Illustrated in Figure 11.29 is a *simple cubic* (also called a **primitive cubic**) lattice, the simplest and most symmetrical three-dimensional lattice. Its unit cell, the **simple cubic unit cell,** is a cube with lattice points only at its eight corners. Figure 11.29*c* shows the packing of atoms in a crystal

☐ A high degree of regularity is the principal feature that makes solids different from liquids. A liquid lacks this long-range repetition of structure because the particles in a liquid are jumbled and disorganized as they move about.

A wallpaper design

Packing of atoms in a crystal

FIG. 11.27 **Symmetry among repetitive patterns.** A wallpaper design and particles arranged in a crystal each show a repeating pattern of structural units. The pattern can be described by the distances between the repeating units and the angles along which the repetition of structure occurs.

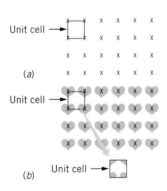

FIG. 11.28 A two-dimensional lattice. (*a*) A simple square lattice, for which the unit cell is a square with lattice points at the corners. (*b*) A wallpaper pattern formed by associating a design element (pink heart) with each lattice point. The X centered on each heart corresponds to a lattice point. The unit cell contains portions of a heart at each corner.

FIG. 11.29 **A three-dimensional simple cubic lattice.** (*a*) A simple cubic unit cell showing the locations of the lattice points. (*b*) A portion of a simple cubic lattice built by stacking simple cubic unit cells. (*c*) The crystal structure of polonium having a simple cubic lattice with identical atoms at the lattice points. Only a portion of each atom lies within this particular unit cell.

of polonium that crystallizes in a simple cubic lattice as well as the unit cell for that substance.[2] Notice that when the unit cell is "carved out" of the crystal, we find only part of an atom (1/8th of an atom, actually) at each corner. The rest of each atom resides in adjacent unit cells. Because the unit cell has eight corners, if we put all the corner pieces together we would obtain one complete atom. Thus, we conclude that this unit cell contains just one atom.

$$8 \; \text{corners} \times \frac{1/8 \; \text{atom}}{\text{corner}} = 1 \; \text{atom}$$

As with the two-dimensional lattice, we could use the same simple cubic lattice to describe the structures of many different substances. The *sizes* of the unit cells would vary because the sizes of atoms vary, but the essential symmetry of the stacking would be the same in them all. This fact about lattices makes it possible to describe limitless numbers of different compounds with just a small set of three-dimensional lattices. In fact, it has been shown mathematically that there are only 14 different three-dimensional lattices possible, which means that all the chemical substances that can exist must form crystals with one or another of these 14 lattice types.

Cubic unit cells

There are three cubic lattices

In addition to simple cubic, two other cubic lattices are possible: face-centered cubic and body-centered cubic. The **face-centered cubic** (abbreviated **fcc**) **unit cell** has lattice points (and therefore, identical particles) at each of its eight corners plus another in the center of each face, as shown in Figure 11.30. Many common metals—copper, silver, gold, aluminum, and lead, for example—form crystals that have face-centered cubic lattices. Each of these metals has the same *kind* of lattice, but the *sizes* of their unit cells differ because the sizes of the atoms differ (see Figure 11.31).

The **body-centered cubic (bcc) unit cell** has lattice points at each corner plus one in the center of the cell, as illustrated in Figure 11.32. The body-centered cubic lattice is also common among a number of metals; examples are chromium, iron, and platinum. Again, these are substances with the same *kind* of lattice, but the dimensions of the lattices vary because of the *different sizes* of the particular atoms.

Not all unit cells are cubic. Some have edges of different lengths or edges that intersect at angles other than 90°. Although you should be aware of the existence of other unit cells and lattices, we will limit the remainder of our discussion to cubic lattices and their unit cells.

Many compounds crystallize with cubic lattices

We have seen that a number of metals have cubic lattices. The same is true for many compounds. Figure 11.33, for example, is a view of a portion of a sodium chloride crystal.

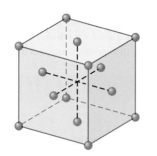

FIG. 11.30 A face-centered cubic unit cell. Lattice points are found at each of the eight corners and in the center of each face.

FIG. 11.31 Unit cells for copper and gold. These metals both crystallize in a face-centered cubic structure with similar face centered cubic unit cells. The atoms are arranged in the same way, but their unit cells have edges of different lengths because the atoms are of different sizes (1 Å = 1 × 10⁻¹⁰ m).

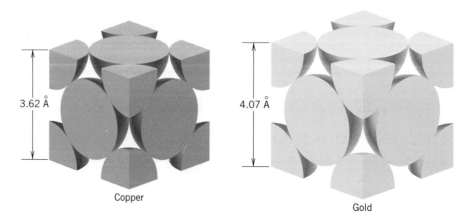

3.62 Å

Copper

4.07 Å

Gold

[2] Polonium is the only element known to crystallize with a simple cubic lattice. Some compounds also form simple cubic lattices.

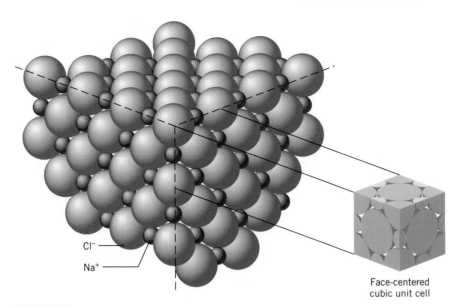

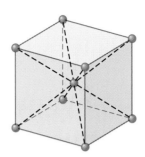

FIG. 11.32 A body-centered cubic unit cell. Lattice points are located at each of the eight corners and in the center of the unit cell.

FIG. 11.33 **The packing of ions in a sodium chloride crystal.** Chloride ions are shown here to be associated with the lattice points of a face-centered cubic unit cell, with the sodium ions placed between the chloride ions.

The Cl^- ions (green) are shown at the lattice points that correspond to a face-centered cubic unit cell. The smaller gray spheres represent Na^+ ions. Notice that they fill the spaces between the Cl^- ions. If we look at the locations of identical particles (Cl^-, for example) we find them at lattice points that describe a face-centered cubic structure. Thus, sodium chloride is said to have a face-centered cubic lattice, and the cubic shape of this lattice is what accounts for the cubic shape of a sodium chloride crystal.

Many of the alkali halides (Group IA–VIIA compounds), such as NaBr and KCl, crystallize with fcc lattices that have the same arrangement of ions as found in NaCl. In fact, this arrangement of ions is so common that it's called the **rock salt structure** (rock salt is the mineral name of NaCl). Because sodium bromide and potassium chloride both have the same kind of lattice as sodium chloride, Figure 11.33 also could be used to describe their unit cells. The *sizes* of their unit cells are different, however, because K^+ is a larger ion than Na^+, and Br^- is larger than Cl^-.

Other examples of cubic unit cells are shown in Figures 11.34 and 11.35. The structure of cesium chloride in Figure 11.34 is simple cubic, although at first glance it may appear to be body centered. This is because in a crystal lattice, identical chemical units must be at each lattice point. In CsCl, Cs^+ ions are found at the corners, but not in the center, so the Cs^+ ions describe a simple cubic unit cell.

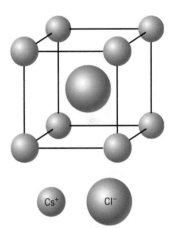

FIG. 11.34 **The unit cell for cesium chloride, CsCl.** The chloride ion is located in the center of the unit cell. The ions are not shown full-size to make it easier to see their locations in the unit cell.

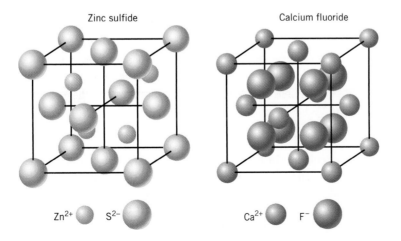

Zinc sulfide   Calcium fluoride

Zn^{2+} S^{2-} Ca^{2+} F^-

FIG. 11.35 **Crystal structures based on the face-centered cubic lattice.** Both zinc sulfide, ZnS, and calcium fluoride, CaF_2, have crystal structures that fit a face-centered cubic lattice. In ZnS, the sulfide ions are shown at the fcc lattice sites with the four zinc ions entirely within the unit cell. In CaF_2, the calcium ions are at the lattice points with the eight fluorides entirely within the unit cell. The ions are not shown full-size to make it easier to see their locations in the unit cells.

Both zinc sulfide and calcium fluoride in Figure 11.35 have face-centered cubic unit cells that differ from that for sodium chloride, which illustrates once again how the same basic kind of lattice can be used to describe a variety of chemical structures.

Stoichiometry affects the packing of atoms in a unit cell

At this point, you may wonder why a compound crystallizes with a particular structure. Although this is a complex issue, at least one factor is the stoichiometry of the substance. Because the crystal is made up of a huge number of identical unit cells, the stoichiometry within the unit cell must match the overall stoichiometry of the compound. Let's see how this applies to sodium chloride.

EXAMPLE 11.2
Counting Atoms or Ions
in a Unit Cell

How many sodium and chloride ions are there in the unit cell of sodium chloride?

ANALYSIS: To answer this question, we have to look closely at the unit cell of sodium chloride. The critical link is realizing that when the unit cell is carved out of the crystal, it encloses *parts of ions*, so we have to determine how many *whole* sodium and chloride ions can be constructed from the pieces within a given unit cell.

SOLUTION: Let's look at an "exploded" view of the NaCl unit cell, shown in Figure 11.36. We see that we have parts of chloride ions at the corners and in the center of each face. Let's add the parts. For chloride:

$$8 \text{ corners} \times \tfrac{1}{8} \text{Cl}^- \text{per corner} = 1 \text{ Cl}^-$$

$$6 \text{ faces} \times \tfrac{1}{2} \text{Cl}^- \text{ per face} = 3 \text{ Cl}^-$$

For the sodium ions, we have parts along each of the 12 edges plus one whole Na^+ ion in the center of the unit cell. Let's add them. For sodium:

$$12 \text{ edges} \times \tfrac{1}{4} \text{Na}^+ \text{ per edge} = 3 \text{ Na}^+$$

$$1 \text{ Na}^+ \text{ in the center } = 1 \text{ Na}^+$$

$$\text{Total } = 4 \text{ Na}^+$$

Thus, in one unit cell, there are four chloride ions and four sodium ions.

IS THE ANSWER REASONABLE? The ratio of the ions is 4 to 4, which is the same as 1 to 1. That's the ratio of the ions in NaCl, so the answer is correct.

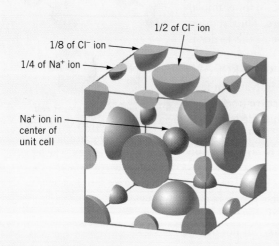

1/2 of Cl⁻ ion
1/8 of Cl⁻ ion
1/4 of Na⁺ ion
Na⁺ ion in
center of
unit cell

FIG. 11.36 An exploded view of the unit cell of sodium chloride.

Practice Exercise 9: How many calcium ions and how many fluoride ions are in the unit cell of calcium fluoride, CaF_2? (Hint: see Figure 11.35.)

Practice Exercise 10: What is the ratio of the ions in the unit cell of cesium chloride? See Figure 11.34.

The calculation in Example 11.2 shows why NaCl can have the crystal structure it does; the unit cell has the proper ratio of cations to anions. It also shows why a compound such as $CaCl_2$ could *not* crystallize with the same kind of unit cell as NaCl. The sodium chloride structure demands a 1-to-1 ratio of cation to anion, so it could not be used by $CaCl_2$ (which has a 1-to-2 cation-to-anion ratio).

Efficiency of packing also can affect how atoms are arranged in a solid

For many solids, particularly metals, the type of crystal structure formed is controlled by max-imizing the number of neighbors that surround a given atom. The more neighbors an atom has, the greater are the number of interatomic attractions and the greater is the energy low-ering when the solid forms. Structures that achieve the maximum density of packing are known as **closest-packed structures,** and there are two of them that are only slightly differ-ent. To visualize how these are produced, let's look at ways to pack spheres of identical size.

Figure 11.37*a* illustrates a layer of blue spheres packed as tightly as possible. Notice that each sphere is touched by six others in this layer. When we add a second layer, each sphere (red) rests in a depression formed by three spheres in the first layer, as illustrated in Figures 11.37*b* and *c*.

The difference between the two closest-packed structures lies in the relative orientations of the spheres in the first layer and those that form the third layer. In Figure 11.38*a* the green spheres in the third layer each lie in a depression between red spheres that is directly above a depression between blue spheres in the first layer. This kind of packing is called **cubic clos-est packing,** abbreviated **ccp,** because when viewed from a different perspective, the atoms are located at positions corresponding to a face-centered cubic lattice. Figure 11.38*b* describes the other closest-packed structure in which a green sphere in the third layer rests in a de-pression between red spheres and directly above a blue sphere in the first layer. This arrange-ment of spheres is called **hexagonal closest packing,** abbreviated **hcp.**

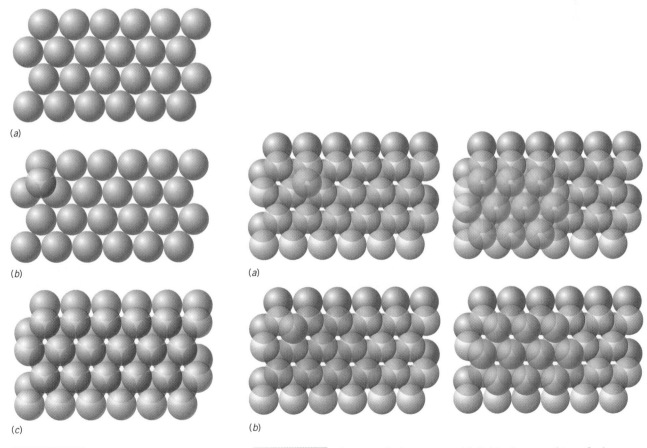

(a)

(b)

(c)

(a)

(b)

FIG. 11.37 Packing of spheres. (*a*) One layer of closely packed spheres. (*b*) A second layer is started by placing a sphere (colored red) in a depression formed between three spheres in the first layer. (*c*) A second layer of spheres shown slightly transparent so we can see how the atoms are stacked over the first layer.

FIG. 11.38 Closest-packed structures. (*a*) Cubic closest packing of spheres. (*b*) Hexagonal closest packing of spheres. In both (*a*) and (*b*) the left diagram illustrates the position of one atom on the third layer and the right diagram shows the third layer partially complete. Notice that there are subtle differences between the two modes of packing.

FIG. 11.39 Glass is a **noncrystalline solid**. When glass breaks, the pieces have sharp edges, but their surfaces are not flat planes. This is because in an amorphous solid like glass, long molecules (much simplified here for clarity) are tangled and disorganized, so there is no long-range order characteristic of a crystal. *(Robert Capece.)*

Within this solid, long molecules become tangled. Solid lacks the long-range order found in crystals.

In the hcp structure, the layers alternate in an A-B-A-B. . . pattern, where A stands for the orientations of the first, third, fifth, etc. layers, and B stands for the orientations of the second, fourth, sixth, etc. layers. Thus, the spheres in the third, fifth, seventh, etc. layers are directly above those in the first, while spheres in the fourth, sixth, eighth, etc. layers are directly above those in the second. In the ccp structure, there is an A-B-C-A-B-C. . . pattern. The first layer is oriented like the fourth, the second like the fifth, and the third like the sixth.

Both the ccp and hcp structures yield very efficient packing of identically sized atoms. In both structures, each atom is in contact with 12 neighboring atoms: 6 atoms in its own layer, 3 atoms in the layer below, and 3 atoms in the layer above. Metals that crystallize with the ccp structure include copper, silver, gold, aluminum, and lead. Metals with the hcp structure include titanium, zinc, cadmium, and magnesium.

Not all solids are crystalline

If a cubic salt crystal is broken, the pieces still have flat faces that intersect at 90° angles. If you shatter a piece of glass, on the other hand, the pieces often have surfaces that are not flat. Instead, they tend to be smooth and curved (see Figure 11.39). This behavior illustrates a major difference between crystalline solids, such as NaCl, and noncrystalline solids, also called **amorphous solids,** such as glass.

The word *amorphous* is derived from the Greek word *amorphos,* which means "without form." Amorphous solids do not have the kinds of long-range repetitive internal structures that are found in crystals. In some ways their structures, being jumbled, are more like liquids than solids. Examples of amorphous solids are ordinary glass and many plastics. In fact, the word **glass** is often used as a general term to refer to any amorphous solid.

As suggested in Figure 11.39, substances that form amorphous solids often consist of long, chainlike molecules that are intertwined in the liquid state somewhat like long strands of cooked spaghetti. To form a crystal from the melted material, these long molecules would have to become untangled and line up in specific patterns. But as the liquid cools, the molecules slow down. Unless the liquid is cooled extremely slowly, the molecular motion decreases too rapidly for the untangling to take place, and the substance solidifies with the molecules still intertwined. As a result, amorphous solids are sometimes described as **supercooled liquids,** a term suggesting the kind of structural disorder found in liquids.

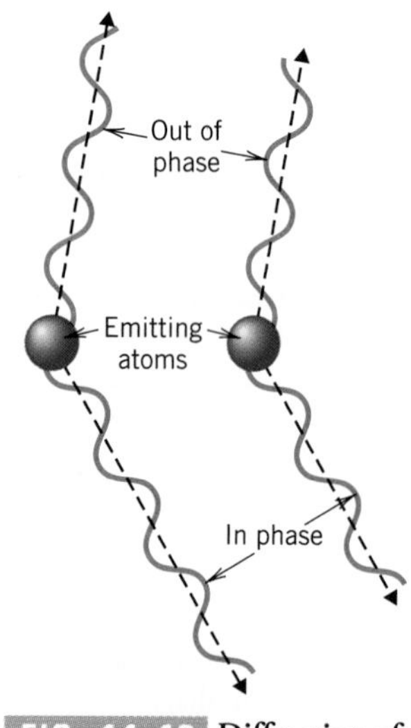

11.10 | X-RAY DIFFRACTION IS USED TO STUDY CRYSTAL STRUCTURES

Out of phase

Emitting atoms

In phase

FIG. 11.40 Diffraction of X rays from atoms in a crystal. X rays emitted from atoms are in phase in some directions and out of phase in other directions.

When atoms in a crystal are bathed in X rays, they absorb some of the radiation and then emit it again in all directions. In effect, each atom becomes a tiny X-ray source. If we look at radiation from two such atoms (Figure 11.40), we find that the X rays emitted are in phase in some directions but out of phase in others. In Chapter 7 you learned that constructive (in-phase) and destructive (out-of-phase) interferences create a phenomenon called *diffraction*. X-Ray diffraction by crystals has enabled many scientists to win Nobel prizes by determining the structures of extremely complex compounds in a particularly elegant way.

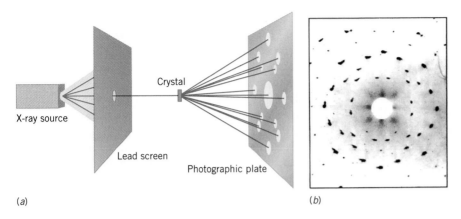

(a)   (b)

FIG. 11.41 X-Ray diffraction. (*a*) The production of an X-ray diffraction pattern. (*b*) An X-ray diffraction pattern produced by sodium chloride recorded on photographic film. *(Visuals Unlimited.)*

In a crystal, there are enormous numbers of atoms, evenly spaced throughout the lattice. When the crystal is bathed in X rays, intense beams are diffracted because of constructive interference, and they appear only in specific directions. In other directions, no X rays appear because of destructive interference. When the X rays coming from the crystal fall on photographic film, the diffracted beams form a **diffraction pattern** (see Figure 11.41). The film is darkened only where the X rays strike.[3]

In 1913, the British physicist William Henry Bragg and his son William Lawrence Bragg discovered that just a few variables control the appearance of an X-ray diffraction pattern. These are shown in Figure 11.42, which illustrates the conditions necessary to obtain constructive interference of the X rays from successive layers of atoms (planes of atoms) in a crystal. A beam of X rays having a wavelength λ strikes the layers at an angle θ. Constructive interference causes an intense diffracted beam to emerge at the same angle θ. The Braggs derived an equation, now called the **Bragg equation,** relating λ, θ, and the distance between the planes of atoms, d,

$$n\lambda = 2d \sin \theta \qquad (11.2)$$

TOOLS
Bragg equation

where n is a whole number. The Bragg equation is the basic tool used by scientists in the study of solid structures.

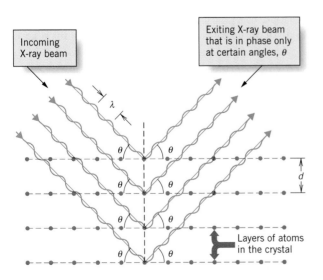

Incoming X-ray beam

Exiting X-ray beam that is in phase only at certain angles, θ

Layers of atoms in the crystal

FIG. 11.42 Diffraction of X rays from successive layers of atoms in a crystal. The layers of atoms are separated by a distance d. The X rays of wavelength λ enter and emerge at an angle θ relative to the layers of the atoms. For the emerging beam of X rays to have any intensity, the condition $n\lambda = 2d \sin \theta$ must be fulfilled, where n is a whole number.

---

[3] Modern X-ray diffraction instruments use electronic devices to detect and measure the angles and intensities of the diffracted X rays.

To determine the structure of a crystal, the angles θ at which diffracted X-ray beams emerge from a crystal are measured. These angles are used to calculate the distances between the various planes of atoms in the crystal. The calculated interplanar distances are then used to work backward to deduce where the atoms in the crystal must be located so that layers of atoms are indeed separated by these distances. This is not a simple task, and some sophisticated mathematics as well as computers are needed to accomplish it. The efforts, however, are well rewarded because the calculations give the locations of atoms within the unit cell and the distances between them. This information, plus a lot of chemical "common sense," is used by chemists to arrive at the shapes and sizes of the molecules in the crystal. Example 11.3 below provides a very simple illustration of how such data are used.

X-Ray diffraction has had a profound impact on the study of biochemical molecules. For example, the general shape of DNA molecules, the chemicals of genes, was deduced by using X-ray diffraction. Today, X-ray diffraction continues to be one of the tools used by biochemists to determine the structures of complex proteins and enzymes.

EXAMPLE 11.3
Using Crystal Structure Data to Calculate Atomic Sizes

X-Ray diffraction measurements reveal that copper crystallizes with a face-centered cubic lattice in which the unit cell length is 3.62 Å (see Figure 11.31). What is the radius of a copper atom expressed in angstroms and in picometers?

ANALYSIS: In Figure 11.31, we see that copper atoms are in contact along a diagonal (the dashed line below) that runs from one corner of a face to another corner.

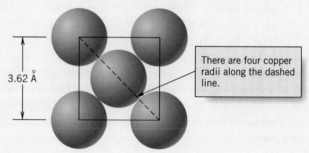

3.62 Å

There are four copper radii along the dashed line.

By geometry, we can calculate the length of this diagonal, which equals four times the radius of a copper atom. Once we calculate the radius in angstrom units we can convert to picometers using the relationships

$$1 \text{ Å} = 1 \times 10^{-10} \text{ m}$$
$$1 \text{ pm} = 1 \times 10^{-12} \text{ m}$$

SOLUTION: From geometry, the length of the diagonal is $\sqrt{2}$ times the length of the edge of the unit cell.

$$\text{Diagonal} = \sqrt{2} \times (3.62 \text{ Å}) = 5.12 \text{ Å}$$

If we call the radius of the copper atom r_{Cu}, then the diagonal equals $4 \times r_{Cu}$. Therefore,

$$4 \times r_{Cu} = 5.12 \text{ Å}$$
$$r_{Cu} = 1.28 \text{ Å}$$

The calculated radius of the copper atom is 1.28 Å.

Next we convert this to picometers.

$$1.28 \text{ Å} \times \frac{1 \times 10^{-10} \text{ m}}{1 \text{ Å}} \times \frac{1 \text{ pm}}{1 \times 10^{-12} \text{ m}} = 128 \text{ pm}$$

IS THE ANSWER REASONABLE? It's difficult to get an intuitive feel for the sizes of atoms, so we should be careful to check the calculation. The length of the diagonal seems about right; it is longer than the edge of the unit cell. If we look again at the diagram above, we can see that along the diagonal there are four copper radii. The rest of the arithmetic is okay, so our answer is correct.

11.11 PHYSICAL PROPERTIES OF SOLIDS ARE RELATED TO THEIR CRYSTAL TYPES

Solids exhibit a wide range of properties. Some, such as diamond, are very hard whereas others, such as ice and naphthalene (moth flakes), are relatively soft. Some, such as salt crystals, have high melting points, whereas others, such as candle wax, melt at low temperatures. And some conduct electricity but others are nonconducting. Physical properties such as these depend on the kinds of particles in the solid as well as on the strengths of attractive forces holding the solid together. Even though we can't make exact predictions about such properties, some generalizations do exist. In discussing them, it is convenient to divide crystals into four types: ionic, molecular, covalent, and metallic.

Ionic crystals have cations and anions at lattice sites

Ionic crystals have ions at the lattice sites and the binding between them is mainly electrostatic, which is essentially nondirectional. As a result, the kind of lattice formed is determined mostly by the relative sizes of the ions and their charges. When the crystal forms, the ions arrange themselves to maximize attractions and minimize repulsions.

Because electrostatic forces are strong, ionic crystals tend to be hard. They also tend to have high melting points because the ions have to be given a lot of kinetic energy to enable them to break free of the lattice and enter the liquid state. The forces between ions can also be used to explain the brittle nature of many ionic compounds. For example, when struck by a hammer, a salt crystal shatters into many small pieces. A view at the atomic level reveals how this could occur (Figure 11.43). The slight movement of a layer of ions within an ionic crystal suddenly places ions of the *same* charge next to each other, and for that instant there are large repulsive forces that split the solid.

In the solid state, ionic compounds do not conduct electricity because the charges present are not able to move. When melted, however, ionic compounds are good conductors of electricity. Melting frees the electrically charged ions to move.

Molecular crystals have neutral molecules at lattice sites

Molecular crystals are solids in which the lattice sites are occupied either by atoms (as in solid argon or krypton) or by molecules (as in solid CO_2, SO_2, or H_2O). If the molecules of such solids are relatively small, the crystals tend to be soft and have low melting points because the particles in the solid experience relatively weak intermolecular attractions. In crystals of argon, for example, the attractive forces are exclusively London forces. In SO_2, which is composed of polar molecules, there are dipole–dipole attractions as well as London forces. And in water crystals (ice) the molecules are held in place primarily by strong hydrogen bonds. Molecular compounds do not conduct electricity in either the solid or liquid state because they are unable to transport electrical charges.

☐ Molecular crystals are soft because little effort is needed to separate the particles or cause them to move past each other.

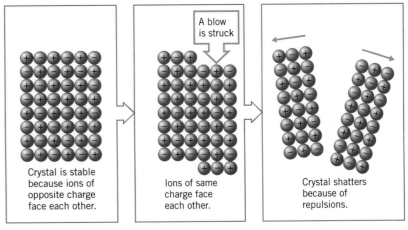

Crystal is stable because ions of opposite charge face each other.

A blow is struck

Ions of same charge face each other.

Crystal shatters because of repulsions.

FIG. 11.43 **An ionic crystal shatters when struck.** In this microview we see that striking an ionic crystal causes some of the layers to shift. This can bring ions of like charge face-to-face. The repulsions between the ions can then force parts of the crystal apart, causing the crystal to shatter. *(Andy Washnik.)*

FIG. 11.44 **The structure of diamond.** Each carbon atom is covalently bonded to four others at the corners of a tetrahedron. This is just a tiny portion of a diamond, of course; the structure extends throughout the entire diamond crystal.

Covalent crystals have atoms at lattice sites covalently bonded to other atoms

Covalent crystals are solids in which lattice positions are occupied by atoms that are covalently bonded to other atoms at neighboring lattice sites. The result is a crystal that is essentially one gigantic molecule. These solids are sometimes called **network solids** because of the interlocking network of covalent bonds extending throughout the crystal in all directions. A typical example is diamond (see Figure 11.44). Covalent crystals tend to be very hard and to have very high melting points because of the strong attractions between covalently bonded atoms. Other examples of covalent crystals are quartz (SiO_2, found in some types of sand) and silicon carbide (SiC, a common abrasive used in sandpaper). Covalent crystals are poor conductors of electricity, although some, such as silicon, are semiconductors.

Metallic crystals have cations at lattice sites surrounded by mobile electrons

Metallic crystals have properties that are quite different from those of the other three types. Metallic crystals conduct heat and electricity well, and they have the luster characteristically associated with metals. A number of different models have been developed to explain metallic crystals. One of the simplest models views the lattice positions of a metallic crystal as being occupied by *positive ions* (nuclei plus core electrons). Surrounding them is a "cloud" of electrons formed by the valence electrons, which extends throughout the entire solid (see Figure 11.45). The electrons in this cloud belong to no single positive ion,

TOOLS
Physical properties relate to crystal type

Positive ions from the metal

Electron cloud that doesn't belong to any one metal ion

FIG. 11.45 **The "electron sea" model of a metallic crystal.** In this highly simplified view of a metallic solid, metal atoms lose valence electrons to the solid as a whole and exist as positive ions surrounded by a mobile "cloud" of electrons.

Crystal Type	Particles Occupying Lattice Sites	Type of Attractive Force	Typical Examples	Typical Properties
		TABLE 11.5 Types of Crystals		
Ionic	Positive and negative ions	Attractions between ions of opposite charge	NaCl, CaCl$_2$, NaNO$_3$	Relatively hard; brittle; high melting points; nonconductors of electricity as solids, but conduct when melted
Molecular	Atoms or molecules	Dipole–dipole attractions, London forces, hydrogen bonding	HCl, SO$_2$, N$_2$, Ar, CH$_4$, H$_2$O	Soft; low melting points; nonconductors of electricity in both solid and liquid states
Covalent (network)	Atoms	Covalent bonds between atoms	Diamond, SiC, (silicon carbide), SiO$_2$ (sand, quartz)	Very hard; very high melting points; nonconductors of electricity
Metallic	Positive ions	Attractions between positive ions and an electron cloud that extends throughout the crystal	Cu, Ag, Fe, Na, Hg	Range from very hard to very soft; melting points range from high to low; conduct electricity in both solid and liquid states; have characteristic luster

but rather to the crystal as a whole. Because the electrons aren't localized on any one atom, they are free to move easily, which accounts for the high electrical conductivity of metals. The electrons can also carry kinetic energy rapidly through the solid, so metals are also good conductors of heat. This model explains the luster of metals, too. When light shines on the metal, the loosely held electrons vibrate easily and readily re-emit the light with essentially the same frequency and intensity.

Some metals, like tungsten, have very high melting points (mp = 3422 °C). Others, such as sodium (mp = 97.8 °C) and mercury, which is a liquid at room temperature, have quite low melting points. To some extent, the melting point depends on the charge of the positive ions in the metallic crystal. The Group IA metals have just one valence electron, so their cores are cations with a 1+ charge, which are only weakly attracted to the "electron cloud" that surrounds them. Atoms of the Group IIA metals, however, form ions with a 2+ charge. These are attracted more strongly to the surrounding electron sea, so the Group IIA metals have higher melting points than their neighbors in Group IA. Metals with very high melting points, like tungsten, must have very strong attractions between their atoms, which suggests that there probably is some covalent bonding between them as well.

The different ways of classifying crystals and a summary of their general properties are given in Table 11.5.

EXAMPLE 11.4
Identifying Crystal Types from Physical Properties

The metal osmium, Os, forms an oxide with the formula OsO_4. The soft crystals of OsO_4 melt at 40 °C, and the resulting liquid does not conduct electricity. To which crystal type does solid OsO_4 probably belong?

ANALYSIS: You might be tempted to suggest that the compound is ionic simply because it is formed from a metal and a nonmetal. However, the properties of the compound are inconsistent with its being ionic. Therefore, we have to consider that there may be exceptions to the generalization discussed earlier about metal–nonmetal compounds. If so, what do the properties of OsO_4 suggest about its crystal type?

SOLUTION: The characteristics of the OsO_4 crystals—softness and low melting point—suggest that solid OsO_4 is a molecular solid and that it contains molecules of OsO_4. This is further supported by the fact that liquid OsO_4 does not conduct electricity, which is evidence for the lack of ions in the liquid.

IS THE ANSWER REASONABLE? There's not much we can do to check ourselves here except to review our analysis.

Practice Exercise 11: Stearic acid is an organic acid that has a chain of 18 carbon atoms. It is a soft solid with a melting point of 70 °C. What crystal type best describes this compound? (Hint: Determine the dominant attractive forces that cause stearic acid to be a solid at room temperature.)

Practice Exercise 12: Boron nitride, which has the empirical formula BN, melts at 2730 °C and is almost as hard as a diamond. What is the probable crystal type for this compound?

Practice Exercise 13: Crystals of elemental sulfur are easily crushed and melt at 113 °C to give a clear yellow liquid that does not conduct electricity. What is the probable crystal type for solid sulfur?

11.12 | PHASE DIAGRAMS GRAPHICALLY REPRESENT PRESSURE–TEMPERATURE RELATIONSHIPS

TOOLS
Phase diagram

Sometimes it is useful to know under what combinations of temperature and pressure a substance will be a liquid, a solid, or a gas, or the conditions of temperature and pressure that produce an equilibrium between any two phases. A simple way to determine this is to

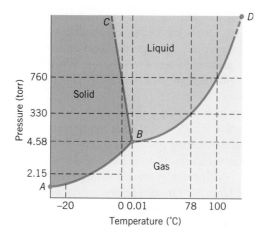

FIG. 11.46 The phase diagram for water, distorted to emphasize certain features. Temperatures and pressures corresponding to the dashed lines on the diagram are referred to in the text discussion.

use a **phase diagram**—a graphical representation of the pressure–temperature relationships that apply to the equilibria between the phases of the substance.

Figure 11.46 is the phase diagram for water. On it, there are three lines that intersect at a common point. Points on these lines correspond to temperatures and pressures at which equilibria between phases can exist. For example, line *AB* is the vapor pressure curve for the solid (ice). Every point on this line gives a temperature and a pressure at which ice and its vapor are able to coexist in equilibrium.

Line *BD* is the vapor pressure curve for liquid water. It gives the temperatures and pressures at which the liquid and vapor are able to coexist in equilibrium. Notice that when the temperature is 100 °C, the vapor pressure is 760 torr. Therefore, this diagram also tells us that water boils at 100 °C when the pressure is 1 atm (760 torr), because that is the temperature at which the vapor pressure equals 1 atm.

The solid–vapor equilibrium line, *AB*, and the liquid–vapor line, *BD*, intersect at a common point, *B*. Because this point is on both lines, there is equilibrium between all three phases at the same time.

☐ The melting point and boiling point can be read directly from the phase diagram.

vapor

liquid ⇌ solid

☐ In the SI, the triple point of water is used to define the Kelvin temperature of 273.16 K.

The temperature and pressure at which this triple equilibrium occurs define the **triple point** of the substance. For water, the triple point occurs at 0.01 °C and 4.58 torr. Every known chemical substance except helium has its own characteristic triple point, which is controlled by the balance of intermolecular forces in the solid, liquid, and vapor.

Line *BC*, which extends upward from the triple point, is the solid–liquid equilibrium line or *melting point line*. It gives temperatures and pressures at which the solid and the liquid are able to be in equilibrium. At the triple point, the melting of ice occurs at +0.01 °C (and 4.58 torr); at 760 torr, melting occurs very slightly lower, at 0 °C. Thus, we can tell that *increasing the pressure on ice lowers its melting point*.

The effect of pressure on the melting point of ice can be predicted using Le Châtelier's principle and the knowledge that a given mass of liquid water occupies *less volume* than the same mass of ice (i.e., liquid water is more dense than ice). Consider an equilibrium that is established between ice and liquid water at 0 °C and 1 atm in an apparatus like that shown in Figure 11.47,

$$H_2O(s) \rightleftharpoons H_2O(l)$$

If the piston is forced in slightly, the pressure increases. According to Le Châtelier's principle the system should respond, if possible, in a way that reduces the pressure. This can happen if some of the ice melts, so the ice–liquid mixture won't require as much space. Then the molecules won't push as hard against each other and the walls, and the pressure

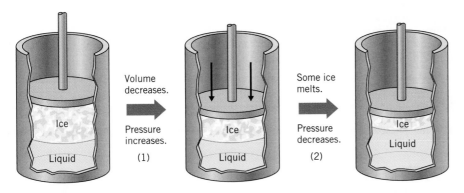

FIG. 11.47 The effect of pressure on the equilibrium $H_2O(s) \rightleftharpoons H_2O(l)$.
(1) Pushing down on the piston decreases the volume of both the ice and liquid water by a small amount and increases the pressure. (2) Some of the ice melts, producing the more dense liquid. As the total volume of ice and liquid water decreases, the pressure drops and equilibrium is restored.

will drop. Thus, a pressure increasing disturbance to the system favors a volume decreasing change, which corresponds to the melting of some ice.

Now, suppose we have ice at a pressure just below the solid–liquid line, *BC.* If, *at constant temperature,* we raise the pressure to a point just above the line, the ice will melt and become a liquid. This could only happen if the melting point becomes lower as the pressure is raised.

Water is very unusual. Almost all other substances have melting points that increase with increasing pressure as illustrated by the phase diagram for carbon dioxide (see Figure 11.48). For CO_2 the solid–liquid line slants to the right (it slanted to the left for water). Also notice that carbon dioxide has a triple point that's above 1 atm. At atmospheric pressure, the only equilibrium that can be established is between solid carbon dioxide and its vapor. At a pressure of 1 atm, this equilibrium occurs at a temperature of $-78\,°C$. This is the temperature of dry ice, which sublimes at atmospheric pressure at $-78\,°C$.

Single phase regions can be identified in a phase diagram

Besides specifying phase equilibria, the three intersecting lines on a phase diagram serve to define regions of temperature and pressure at which only a single phase can exist. For example, between lines *BC* and *BD* in Figure 11.46 are temperatures and pressures at which water exists as a liquid without being in equilibrium with either vapor or ice. At 760 torr, water is a liquid anywhere between 0 °C and 100 °C. For instance, we are told by the diagram that we can't have ice with a temperature of 25 °C if the pressure is 760 torr (which, of course, you already knew; ice never has a temperature of 25 °C). The diagram also says that we can't have water vapor with a pressure of 760 torr when the temperature is 25 °C (which, again, you already knew; the temperature has to be taken to 100 °C for the vapor pressure to reach 760 torr). Instead, we are told by the phase diagram that the *only* phase for pure water at 25 °C and 1 atm is the liquid. Below 0 °C at 760 torr, water is a solid; above 100 °C at 760 torr, water is a vapor. On the phase diagram for water, the phases that can exist in the different temperature–pressure regions are marked.

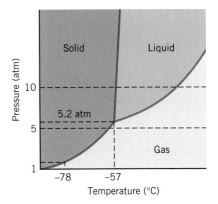

FIG. 11.48 The phase diagram for carbon dioxide.

EXAMPLE 11.5
Interpreting a Phase Diagram

What phase would we expect for water at 0 °C and 4.58 torr?

ANALYSIS: The words, "What phase. . .," as well as the specified temperature and pressure suggest that we refer to the phase diagram of water (Figure 11.46).

SOLUTION: First we find 0 °C on the temperature axis of the phase diagram of water. Then we move upward until we intersect a line corresponding to 4.58 torr. This intersection occurs in the "Solid" region of the diagram. At 0 °C and 4.58 torr, then, water exists as a solid.

IS THE ANSWER REASONABLE? We've seen that the freezing point of water increases slightly when we lower the pressure, so below 1 atm, water should still be a solid at 0 °C. That agrees with the answer we obtained from the phase diagram.

EXAMPLE 11.6
Interpreting a Phase Diagram

What phase changes occur if water at 0 °C is gradually compressed from a pressure of 2.15 torr to 800 torr?

ANALYSIS: Asking about "what phase changes occur" suggests once again that we use the phase diagram of water (Figure 11.46).

SOLUTION: According to the phase diagram, at 0 °C and 2.15 torr, water exists as a gas (water vapor). As the vapor is compressed, we move upward along the 0 °C line until we encounter the solid–vapor line. Here, an equilibrium will exist as compression gradually transforms the gas into solid ice. Once all the vapor has frozen, further compression raises the pressure and we continue the climb along the 0 °C line until we next encounter the solid–liquid line at 760 torr. As further compression takes place, the solid will gradually melt. After all the ice has melted, the pressure will continue to climb while the water remains a liquid. At 800 torr and 0 °C, the water will be liquid.

IS THE ANSWER REASONABLE? There's not too much we can do to check all this except to take a fresh look at the phase diagram. We do expect that above 760 torr the melting point of ice will be less than 0 °C, so at 0 °C and 800 torr we can anticipate that water will be a liquid.

Practice Exercise 14: The equilibrium line from point B to D in Figure 11.46 is present in another figure in this chapter. Identify what that line represents. (Hint: A review of the other figures will reveal the nature of the line.)

Practice Exercise 15: What phase changes will occur if water at −20 °C and 2.15 torr is heated to 50 °C under constant pressure?

Practice Exercise 16: What phase will water be in if it is at a pressure of 330 torr and a temperature of 50 °C?

Above the critical temperature only one phase is possible

For water (Figure 11.46), the vapor pressure line for the liquid, which begins at point B, terminates at point D, which is known as the **critical point.** The temperature and pressure at D are called the **critical temperature, T_c,** and **critical pressure, P_c.** Above the critical temperature, a distinct liquid phase cannot exist, *regardless of the pressure.*

Figure 11.49 illustrates what happens to a substance as it approaches its critical point. In Figure 11.49a, we see a liquid in a container with some vapor above it. We can distinguish

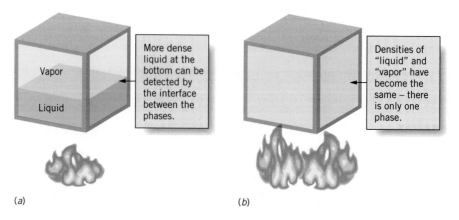

FIG. 11.49 Changes that are observed when a liquid is heated in a sealed container. (*a*) Below the critical temperature. (*b*) Above the critical temperature.

More dense liquid at the bottom can be detected by the interface between the phases.

Densities of "liquid" and "vapor" have become the same – there is only one phase.

Vapor

Liquid

(*a*)

(*b*)

11.2

Decaffeinated Coffee and Supercritical Carbon Dioxide

Many people prefer to avoid caffeine, yet still enjoy a cup of coffee. For them, decaffeinated coffee is just the thing. To satisfy this demand, coffee producers remove caffeine from the coffee beans before roasting them. Several methods have been used, some of which use solvents such as methylene chloride (CH_2Cl_2) or ethyl acetate ($CH_3CO_2C_2H_5$) to dissolve the caffeine. Even though only trace amounts of these solvents remain after the coffee beans are dried, there are those who would prefer not to have any such chemicals in their coffee. And that's where carbon dioxide comes into the picture.

It turns out that supercritical carbon dioxide is an excellent solvent for many organic substances, including caffeine. To make it, gaseous CO_2 is heated to a temperature above its critical temperature of 31 °C, typically to about 80 °C. It is then compressed to about 200 atm. This gives it a density near that of a liquid, but with

(Andy Washnik.)

some properties of a gas. The fluid has a very low viscosity and readily penetrates coffee beans that have been softened with steam, drawing out the water and caffeine. After several hours, the CO_2 has removed as much as 97% of the caffeine, and the fluid containing the water and caffeine is then drawn off. When the pressure of the supercritical CO_2 solution is reduced, the CO_2 turns to a gas and the water and caffeine separate. The caffeine is recovered and sold to beverage or pharmaceutical companies. Meanwhile, the pressure over the coffee beans is also reduced and the beans are warmed to about 120 °C, causing residual CO_2 to evaporate. Because CO_2 is not a toxic gas, any small traces of CO_2 that remain are totally harmless.

Decaffeination of coffee is not the only use of supercritical CO_2. It is also used to extract the essential flavor ingredients in spices and herbs for use in a variety of products. As with coffee, using supercritical CO_2 as a solvent completely avoids any potential harm that might be caused by small residual amounts of other solvents.

---

between the two phases because they have different densities, which causes them to bend light differently. This allows us to see the interface, or surface, between the more dense liquid and the less dense vapor. If this liquid is now heated, two things happen. First, more liquid evaporates. This causes an increase in the number of molecules per cubic centimeter of vapor which, in turn, causes the density of the vapor to increase. Second, the liquid expands (just like mercury does in a thermometer). This means that a given mass of liquid occupies more volume, so its density decreases. As the temperature of the liquid and vapor continue to increase, the vapor density rises and the liquid density falls; they approach each other. Eventually the densities become equal, and a separate liquid phase no longer exists; everything is the same (see Figure 11.49*b*). The highest temperature at which a liquid phase still exists is the critical temperature, and the pressure of the vapor at this temperature is the critical pressure. A substance that has a temperature above its critical temperature and a density near its liquid density is described as a **supercritical fluid.** Supercritical fluids have some unique properties that make them excellent solvents, and one that is particularly useful is supercritical carbon dioxide, which is used as a solvent to decaffeinate coffee.

The values of the critical temperature and critical pressure are unique for every chemical substance and are controlled by the intermolecular attractions (see Table 11.6). Notice

☐ This interface between liquid and gas is called the **meniscus.**

TABLE 11.6	Some Critical Temperatures and Pressures	
Compound	T_c (°C)	P_c (atm)
Water	374.1	217.7
Ammonia	132.5	112.5
Carbon dioxide	31	72.9
Ethane (C_2H_6)	32.2	48.2
Methane (CH_4)	−82.1	45.8
Helium	−267.8	2.3

that liquids with strong intermolecular attractions, like water, tend to have high critical temperatures. Under pressure, the strong attractions between the molecules are able to hold them together in a liquid state even when the molecules are jiggling about violently at an elevated temperature. In contrast, substances with weak intermolecular attractions, such as methane and helium, have low critical temperatures. For these substances, even the small amounts of kinetic energy possessed by the molecules at low temperatures is sufficient to overcome the intermolecular attractions and prevent the molecules from sticking together as a liquid, despite being held close together under high pressure.

At room temperature, some gases will liquefy and others will not

When a gaseous substance has a temperature below its critical temperature, it is capable of being liquefied by compressing it. For example, carbon dioxide is a gas at room temperature (approximately 25 °C). This is below its critical temperature of 31 °C. If the $CO_2(g)$ is gradually compressed, a pressure will eventually be reached that lies on the liquid–vapor curve for CO_2, and further compression will cause the CO_2 to liquefy. In fact, that's what happens when a CO_2 fire extinguisher is filled; the CO_2 that's pumped in is a liquid under a high pressure. If you shake a filled CO_2 fire extinguisher, you can feel the liquid sloshing around inside, provided the temperature of the fire extinguisher is below 31 °C (88 °F). When the fire extinguisher is used, a valve releases the pressurized CO_2, which rushes out to extinguish the fire.

□ On a very hot day, when the temperature is in the 90s, a filled CO_2 fire extinguisher won't give the sensation that it's filled with a liquid. At such temperatures, the CO_2 is in a supercritical state and no separate liquid phase exists.

Gases such as O_2 and N_2, which have critical temperatures far below 0 °C, can never be liquids at room temperature. When they are compressed, they simply become high-pressure gases. To make liquid N_2 or O_2, the gases must be made very cold as well as being compressed to high pressures.

SUMMARY

Physical Properties: Gases, Liquids, and Solids. Gases expand to fill the entire volume of a container. Liquids and solids retain a constant volume if transferred from one container to another. Solids also retain a constant shape. These characteristics are related to how tightly packed the particles are and to the relative strengths of the intermolecular attractions in the different states of matter. Most physical properties depend primarily on intermolecular attractions. In gases, these attractions are weak because the molecules are so far apart. They are much stronger in liquids and solids, where the particles are packed together tightly.

Intermolecular Attractions. Polar molecules attract each other by **dipole–dipole attractions,** which arise because the positive end of one dipole attracts the negative end of another. Nonpolar molecules are attracted to each other by **London dispersion forces,** which are **instantaneous dipole–induced dipole attractions.** London forces are present between all particles, including atoms, polar and nonpolar molecules, and ions. Among different substances, London forces increase with an increase in size of a particle's electron cloud; they also increase with increasing chain length among molecules such as the hydrocarbons. Compact molecules experience weaker London forces than similar long chain molecules. For large molecules, the cumulative effect of large numbers of weak London force interactions can be quite strong and outweigh other intermolecular attractions. **Hydrogen bonding,** a special case of dipole–dipole attractions, occurs between molecules in which hydrogen is covalently bonded to a small, very electronegative atom—principally, nitrogen, oxygen, or fluorine. Hydrogen bonding is much stronger than the other types of intermolecular attractions. **Ion–dipole attractions** occur when ions interact with polar substances. **Ion–induced dipole attractions** result when an ion creates a dipole in a neighboring molecule or ion.

General Properties of Liquids and Solids. Properties that depend mostly on closeness of packing of particles are **compressibility** (or the opposite, incompressibility) and **diffusion.** Diffusion is slow in liquids and almost nonexistent in solids at room temperature. Properties that depend mostly on the strengths of intermolecular attractions are **retention of volume and shape, surface tension,** and **ease of evaporation. Surface tension** is related to the energy needed to expand a liquid's surface area. A liquid can **wet** a surface if its molecules are attracted to the surface about as strongly as they are attracted to each other. **Evaporation** of liquids and solids is endothermic and produces a cooling effect. The overall rate of evaporation increases with increasing surface area. The rate of evaporation from a given surface area of a liquid increases with increasing temperature, and with decreasing intermolecular attractions. Evaporation of a solid is called **sublimation.**

Changes of State. Changes from one physical state to another, such as melting, vaporization, or sublimation, can occur as dynamic equilibria. In a **dynamic equilibrium,** opposing processes occur continually at equal rates, so over time there is no apparent change in the composition of the system. For liquids and solids, equilibria are established when vaporization occurs in a sealed container. A solid is in equilibrium with its liquid at the melting point.

Vapor Pressures. When the rates of evaporation and condensation of a liquid are equal, the vapor above the liquid exerts a pressure called the **equilibrium vapor pressure** (or more commonly, just the **vapor pressure**). The vapor pressure is controlled by the rate of evaporation *per unit surface area*. When the intermolecular attractive forces are large, the rate of evaporation is small and the vapor pressure is small. Vapor pressure increases with increasing temperature because the rate of evaporation increases as the temperature rises. The vapor pressure is independent of the *total* surface area of the liquid. Solids have vapor pressures just as liquids do.

Boiling Point. A substance boils when its vapor pressure equals the prevailing atmospheric pressure. The **normal boiling point** of a liquid is the temperature at which its vapor pressure equals 1 atm. Substances with high boiling points have strong intermolecular attractions.

Energy Changes Associated with Changes of State. On a **heating curve,** flat portions correspond to phase changes in which the heat added changes the potential energies of the particles without changing their average kinetic energy. **Superheating** sometimes occurs when a liquid is heated above its boiling point. On a **cooling curve, supercooling** sometimes occurs when the temperature of the liquid drops below the freezing point of the substance. The enthalpy changes for melting, vaporization of a liquid, and sublimation are the **molar heat of fusion,** ΔH_{fusion}, the **molar heat of vaporization,** $\Delta H_{\text{vaporization}}$, and the **molar heat of sublimation,** $\Delta H_{\text{sublimation}}$, respectively. They are all endothermic and are related in size as follows: $\Delta H_{\text{fusion}} < \Delta H_{\text{vaporization}} < \Delta H_{\text{sublimation}}$. The sizes of these enthalpy changes are large for substances with strong intermolecular attractive forces.

Le Châtelier's Principle. When the equilibrium in a system is upset by a disturbance, the system changes in a direction that minimizes the disturbance and, if possible, brings the system back to equilibrium. By this principle, we find that raising the temperature favors an endothermic change. Decreasing the volume favors a change toward a more dense phase.

Crystalline Solids. Crystalline solids have highly ordered arrangements of particles within them, which can be described in terms of repeating three-dimensional arrays of points called **lattices.** The simplest portion of a lattice is its **unit cell.** Many structures can be described with the same lattice by associating different units (atoms, molecules, or ions) to lattice points and by changing the dimensions of the unit cell. Three cubic unit cells are possible—**simple cubic, face-centered cubic,** and **body-centered cubic.** Sodium chloride and many other alkali metal halides crystallize in the **rock salt structure,** which contains four formula units per unit cell. Two modes of closest packing of atoms are **cubic closest packing (ccp)** and **hexagonal closest packing (hcp).** The ccp structure has an A-B-C-A-B-C. . . alternating stacking of layers of spheres; the hcp structure has an A-B-A-B-. . . stacking of layers. **Amorphous** solids lack the internal structure of crystalline solids. Glass is an amorphous solid and is sometimes called a **supercooled liquid.**

X-Ray Diffraction. Information about crystal structures is obtained experimentally from **X-ray diffraction patterns** produced by constructive and destructive interference of X rays scattered by atoms. Distances between planes of atoms in a crystal can be calculated by the Bragg equation, $n\lambda = 2d \sin \theta$, where n is a whole number, λ is the wavelength of the X rays, d is the distance between planes of atoms producing the diffracted beam, and θ is the angle at which the diffracted X-ray beam emerges relative to the planes of atoms producing the diffracted beam.

Crystal Types. Crystals can be divided into four general types: **ionic, molecular, covalent,** and **metallic.** Their properties depend on the kinds of particles within the lattice and on the attractions between the particles, as summarized in Table 11.5.

Phase Diagrams. Temperatures and pressures at which equilibria can exist between phases are given graphically in a **phase diagram.** The three equilibrium lines intersect at the **triple point.** The liquid–vapor line terminates at the **critical point.** At the **critical temperature,** a liquid has a vapor pressure equal to its **critical pressure.** Above the critical temperature a liquid phase cannot be formed; the single phase that exists is called a **supercritical fluid.** The equilibrium lines also divide a phase diagram into temperature–pressure regions in which a substance can exist in just a single phase. Water is different from most substances in that its melting point decreases with increasing pressure.

T**OOLS FOR PROBLEM SOLVING**

The concepts that you've learned in this chapter are collected below. They can be applied as tools in solving problems. Study each one carefully so that you know what each is used for. When faced with solving a problem, recall what each tool does and consider whether it will be helpful in finding a solution. This will aid you in selecting the tools you need. If necessary, refer to this table when working on the Review Problems that follow.

Relationship between intermolecular forces and molecular structure *(page 433)* From molecular structure, we can determine whether a molecule is polar or not and whether it has N—H or O—H bonds. This lets us predict and compare the strengths of intermolecular attractions. You should be able to identify when dipole–dipole, London, and hydrogen bonding occurs. See the summary Table 11.3 on page *440*.

Factors that affect rates of evaporation and vapor pressure *(pages 446, 447, and 448)* They allow us to compare the relative rates of evaporation based on temperature and the strengths of intermolecular forces in substances. They also allow us to compare the strengths of intermolecular forces based on the relative magnitudes of vapor pressures at a given temperature.

Boiling points of substances *(page 451)* They allow us to compare the strengths of intermolecular forces in substances based on their boiling points.

Enthalpy changes during phase changes *(pages 453 and 455)* They allow us to compare the strengths of intermolecular forces in substances based on relative values of $\Delta H_{\text{vaporization}}$ and $\Delta H_{\text{sublimation}}$.

Le Châtelier's principle *(page 456)* Le Châtelier's principle enables us to predict the direction in which the position of equilibrium is shifted when a dynamic equilibrium is upset by a disturbance. You should be able to predict how the position of equilibrium between phases is affected by temperature and pressure changes.

Bragg equation *(page 463)*

$$n\lambda = 2d \sin \theta$$

Using the wavelength of X rays and angles at which X rays are diffracted from a crystal, the distances between planes of atoms can be calculated.

Unit cell structures for simple cubic, face-centered cubic, and body-centered cubic lattices *(page 458)* By knowing the arrangements of atoms in these unit cells, we can use the dimensions of the unit cell to calculate atomic radii and other properties.

Properties of crystal types *(page 466)* By examining certain physical properties of a solid (hardness, melting point, electrical conductivity in the solid and liquid state), we can often predict the nature of the particles that occupy lattice sites in the solid and the kinds of attractive forces between them.

Phase diagram *(page 467)* We use a phase diagram to identify temperatures and pressures at which equilibrium can exist between phases of a substance, and to identify conditions under which only a single phase can exist.

QUESTIONS, PROBLEMS, AND EXERCISES

Answers to problems whose numbers are printed in color are given in Appendix B. More challenging problems are marked with asterisks. ILW = Interactive Learningware solution is available at www.wiley.com/college/brady. OH = an Office Hours video is available for this problem.

REVIEW QUESTIONS

Comparisons among the States of Matter

11.1 Why are the intermolecular attractive forces stronger in liquids and solids than they are in gases?

11.2 Compare the behavior of gases, liquids, and solids when they are transferred from one container to another.

11.3 For a given substance, how do the intermolecular attractive forces compare in its gaseous, liquid, and solid states?

Intermolecular Attractions

11.4 Which kinds of attractive forces, intermolecular or intramolecular, are responsible for chemical properties? Which kind are responsible for physical properties?

11.5 Describe *dipole–dipole attractions*.

11.6 What are *London forces*? How are they affected by the sizes of the atoms in a molecule? How are they affected by the number of atoms in a molecule? How are they affected by the shape of a molecule?

11.7 Define *polarizability*. How does this property affect the strengths of London forces?

11.8 Which nonmetals, besides hydrogen, are most often involved in hydrogen bonding? Why these and not others?

11.9 Which is expected to have the higher boiling point, C_8H_{18} or C_4H_{10}? Explain your choice.

11.10 Ethanol and dimethyl ether have the same molecular formula, C_2H_6O. Ethanol boils at 78.4 °C, whereas dimethyl ether boils at −23.7 °C. Their structural formulas are

$$CH_3CH_2OH \qquad\qquad CH_3OCH_3$$
ethanol   dimethyl ether

Explain why the boiling point of the ether is so much lower than the boiling point of ethanol.

11.11 How do the strengths of covalent bonds and dipole–dipole attractions compare? How do the strengths of ordinary dipole–dipole attractions compare with the strengths of hydrogen bonds?

11.12 For each pair, in which compound are the ion–induced dipole attractions stronger? (a) CaO or CaS, (b) MgO or Al_2O_3

General Properties of Liquids and Solids

11.13 Name two physical properties of liquids and solids that are controlled primarily by how tightly packed the particles are. Name three that are controlled mostly by the strengths of the intermolecular attractions.

11.14 Why does diffusion occur more slowly in liquids than in gases? Why does diffusion occur extremely slowly in solids?

11.15 On the basis of kinetic theory, would you expect the rate of diffusion in a liquid to increase or decrease as the temperature is increased? Explain your answer.

11.16 What is *surface tension?* Why do molecules at the surface of a liquid behave differently from those within the interior?

11.17 Which liquid is expected to have the larger surface tension at a given temperature, CCl_4 or H_2O? Explain your answer.

11.18 What does *wetting* of a surface mean? What is a *surfactant?* What is its purpose and how does it function?

11.19 Polyethylene plastic consists of long chains of carbon atoms, each of which is also bonded to hydrogens, as shown below:

$$\cdots-\overset{\displaystyle \underset{|}{H}\;\,\underset{|}{H}\;\,\underset{|}{H}\;\,\underset{|}{H}\;\,\underset{|}{H}\;\,\underset{|}{H}\;\,\underset{|}{H}\;\,\underset{|}{H}}{\underset{\displaystyle \overset{|}{H}\;\,\overset{|}{H}\;\,\overset{|}{H}\;\,\overset{|}{H}\;\,\overset{|}{H}\;\,\overset{|}{H}\;\,\overset{|}{H}\;\,\overset{|}{H}}{C-C-C-C-C-C-C-C}}-\cdots$$

Water forms beads when placed on a polyethylene surface. Why?

11.20 The structural formula for glycerol is

$$H-\overset{\displaystyle \overset{|}{H}}{\underset{\displaystyle \underset{|}{OH}}{C}}-\overset{\displaystyle \overset{|}{H}}{\underset{\displaystyle \underset{|}{OH}}{C}}-\overset{\displaystyle \overset{|}{H}}{\underset{\displaystyle \underset{|}{OH}}{C}}-H$$

Would you expect this liquid to wet glass surfaces? Explain your answer.

11.21 On the basis of what happens on a molecular level, why does evaporation lower the temperature of a liquid?

11.22 On the basis of the distribution of kinetic energies of the molecules of a liquid, explain why increasing the liquid's temperature increases the rate of evaporation.

11.23 How is the rate of evaporation of a liquid affected by increasing the surface area of the liquid? How is the rate of evaporation affected by the strengths of intermolecular attractive forces?

11.24 During the cold winter months, snow often disappears gradually without melting. How is this possible? What is the name of the process responsible for this phenomenon?

Changes of State and Equilibrium

11.25 What terms do we use to describe the following changes of state?
(a) solid → gas, (b) liquid → gas, (c) gas → liquid,
(d) solid → liquid, (e) liquid → solid

11.26 When a molecule escapes from the surface of a liquid by evaporation, it has a kinetic energy that's much larger than the average KE. Why is it likely that after being in the vapor for a while its kinetic energy will be much less? If this molecule collides with the surface of the liquid, is it likely to bounce out again?

11.27 Why does a molecule of a vapor that collides with the surface of a liquid tend to be captured by the liquid, even if the incoming molecule has a large kinetic energy?

11.28 When an equilibrium is established in the evaporation of a liquid into a sealed container, we refer to it as a *dynamic equilibrium*. Why?

11.29 Viewed at a molecular level, what is happening when a dynamic equilibrium is established between the liquid and solid forms of a substance? What is the temperature called at which there is an equilibrium between a liquid and a solid?

11.30 Is it possible to establish an equilibrium between a solid and its vapor? Explain.

Vapor Pressure

11.31 Define *equilibrium vapor pressure*. Why do we call the equilibrium involved a *dynamic equilibrium*?

11.32 Explain why changing the volume of a container in which there is a liquid–vapor equilibrium has no effect on the equilibrium vapor pressure.

11.33 Why doesn't a change in the surface area of a liquid cause a change in the equilibrium vapor pressure?

11.34 What effect does increasing the temperature have on the equilibrium vapor pressure of a liquid? Why?

11.35 Why does moisture condense on the outside of a cool glass of water in the summertime?

11.36 Why do we feel more uncomfortable in humid air at 90 °F than in dry air at 90 °F?

Boiling Points of Liquids

11.37 Define *boiling point* and *normal boiling point*.

11.38 Why does the boiling point vary with atmospheric pressure?

11.39 Mt. Kilimanjaro in Tanzania is the tallest peak in Africa (19,340 ft). The normal barometric pressure at the top of this mountain is about 345 torr. At what Celsius temperature would water be expected to boil there? (See Figure 11.21.)

11.40 When liquid ethanol begins to boil, what is present inside the bubbles that form?

11.41 The radiator cap of an automobile engine is designed to maintain a pressure of approximately 15 lb/in.^{2} above normal atmospheric pressure. How does this help prevent the engine from "boiling over" in hot weather?

11.42 Butane, C_4H_{10}, has a boiling point of −0.5 °C (which is 31 °F). Despite this, liquid butane can be seen sloshing about inside a typical butane lighter, even at room temperature. Why isn't the butane boiling inside the lighter at room temperature?

11.43 Why does H_2S have a lower boiling point than H_2Se? Why does H_2O have a much higher boiling point than H_2S?

11.44 An H—F bond is more polar than an O—H bond, so HF forms stronger hydrogen bonds than H_2O. Nevertheless, HF has a lower boiling point than H_2O. Explain why this is so.

Energy Changes That Accompany Changes of State

11.45 Below is a cooling curve for one mole of a substance.

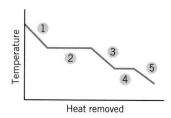

(a) On which portions of this graph do we find the average kinetic energy of the molecules of the substance changing?

(b) On which portions of this graph is the amount of heat removed related primarily to a lowering of the potential energy of the molecules?

(c) Which portion of the graph corresponds to the release of the heat of vaporization?

(d) Which portion of the graph corresponds to the release of the heat of fusion?

(e) Which is larger, the heat of fusion or the heat of vaporization?

(f) On the graph, indicate the melting point of the solid.

(g) On the graph, indicate the boiling point of the liquid.

(h) On the drawing, indicate how supercooling of the liquid would affect the graph.

11.46 Why is $\Delta H_{\text{vaporization}}$ larger than ΔH_{fusion}? How does $\Delta H_{\text{sublimation}}$ compare with $\Delta H_{\text{vaporization}}$? Explain your answer.

11.47 Would the "heat of condensation," $\Delta H_{\text{condensation}}$, be exothermic or endothermic?

11.48 Hurricanes can travel for thousands of miles over warm water, but they rapidly lose their strength when they move over a large land mass or over cold water. Why?

11.49 Ethanol (grain alcohol) has a molar heat of vaporization of 39.3 kJ mol^{-1}. Ethyl acetate, a common solvent, has a molar heat of vaporization of 32.5 kJ mol^{-1}. Which of these substances has the larger intermolecular attractions?

11.50 A burn caused by steam is much more serious than one caused by the same amount of boiling water. Why?

11.51 Arrange the following substances in order of their increasing values of $\Delta H_{\text{vaporization}}$: (a) HF, (b) CH$_4$, (c) CF$_4$, and (d) HCl.

Le Châtelier's Principle

11.52 State Le Châtelier's principle in your own words.

11.53 What do we mean by the *position of equilibrium*?

11.54 Use Le Châtelier's principle to predict the effect of adding heat in the equilibrium: solid + heat $\rightleftharpoons$ liquid.

11.55 Use Le Châtelier's principle to explain why lowering the temperature lowers the vapor pressure of a solid.

Crystalline Solids and X-Ray Diffraction

11.56 What is the difference between a crystalline solid and an amorphous solid?

11.57 What is a *lattice*? What is a *unit cell*?

11.58 What relationship is there between a crystal lattice and its unit cell?

11.59 The diagrams below illustrate typical arrangements of paving bricks in a patio or driveway. Sketch the unit cells that correspond to these patterns of bricks.

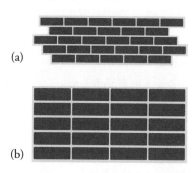

11.60 Below is illustrated the way the atoms of two different elements are packed in a certain solid. The nuclei occupy positions at the corners of a cube. Is this cube the unit cell for this substance? Explain your answer.

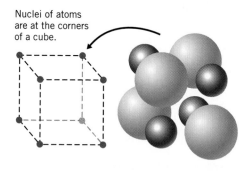

Nuclei of atoms are at the corners of a cube.

11.61 Make a sketch of a layer of sodium ions and chloride ions in a NaCl crystal. Indicate how the ions are arranged in a face-centered cubic pattern, regardless of whether we place lattice points at the Cl$^-$ ions or Na$^+$ ions.

11.62 How do the crystal structures of copper and gold differ? In what way are they similar? On the basis of the locations of the elements in the periodic table, what kind of crystal structure would you expect for silver?

11.63 What kind of lattice does zinc sulfide have? What kind of lattice does calcium fluoride have?

11.64 Only 14 different kinds of crystal lattices are possible. How can this be true, considering the fact that there are millions of different chemical compounds that are able to form crystals?

11.65 Write the Bragg equation and define the symbols.

11.66 Why can't CaCl$_2$ or AlCl$_3$ form crystals with the same structure as NaCl?

Crystal Types

11.67 What kinds of particles are located at the lattice sites in a metallic crystal?

11.68 What kinds of attractive forces exist between particles in (a) molecular crystals, (b) ionic crystals, and (c) covalent crystals?

11.69 Why are covalent crystals sometimes called *network solids*?

Amorphous Solids

11.70 What does the word *amorphous* mean?

11.71 What is an *amorphous solid*? Compare what happens when crystalline and amorphous solids are broken into pieces.

Phase Diagrams

11.72 For most substances, the solid is more dense than the liquid. Use Le Châtelier's principle to explain why the melting point of such substances should *increase* with increasing pressure. Sketch the phase diagram for such a substance, being sure to have the solid–liquid equilibrium line slope in the correct direction.

11.73 Define *critical temperature* and *critical pressure*.

11.74 What is a *supercritical fluid*? Why is supercritical CO_2 used to decaffeinate coffee?

11.75 What phases of a substance are in equilibrium at the triple point?

11.76 Why doesn't CO_2 have a normal boiling point?

11.77 At room temperature, hydrogen can be compressed to very high pressures without liquefying. On the other hand, butane becomes a liquid at high pressure (at room temperature). What does this tell us about the critical temperatures of hydrogen and butane?

REVIEW PROBLEMS

Intermolecular Attractions and Molecular Structure

11.78 Which liquid evaporates faster at 25 °C, diethyl ether (an anesthetic) or butanol (a solvent used in the preparation of shellac and varnishes)? Both have the molecular formula $C_4H_{10}O$, but their structural formulas are different, as shown below.

$$CH_3CH_2CH_2CH_2OH \qquad CH_3CH_2-O-CH_2CH_3$$
$$\text{butanol} \qquad\qquad\qquad \text{diethyl ether}$$

OH 11.79 Which compound should have the higher vapor pressure at 25 °C, butanol or diethyl ether? Which should have the higher boiling point?

11.80 What kinds of intermolecular attractive forces (dipole–dipole, London, hydrogen bonding) are present in the following substances?
(a) HF   (b) PCl_3 (c) SF_6 (d) SO_2

11.81 What kinds of intermolecular attractive forces are present in the following substances?

(a) $CH_3-\overset{\displaystyle O}{\overset{\|}{C}}-OH$ (b) H_2S (c) SO_3 (d) CH_3NH_2

OH 11.82 Consider the compounds $CHCl_3$ (chloroform, an important solvent that was once used as an anesthetic) and $CHBr_3$ (bromoform, which has been used as a sedative). Compare the strengths of their dipole–dipole attractions and the strengths of their London forces. Their boiling points are 61 °C and 149 °C, respectively. For these compounds, which kinds of attractive forces (dipole–dipole or London) are more important in determining their boiling points? Justify your answer.

11.83 Carbon dioxide does not liquefy at atmospheric pressure, but instead forms a solid that sublimes at −78 °C. Nitrogen dioxide forms a liquid that boils at 21 °C at atmospheric pressure.

How do these data support the statement that CO_2 is a linear molecule whereas NO_2 is nonlinear?

11.84 Which should have the higher boiling point, ethanol (CH_3CH_2OH, found in alcoholic beverages) or ethanethiol (CH_3CH_2SH, a foul-smelling liquid found in the urine of rabbits that have feasted on cabbage)?

11.85 How do the strengths of London forces compare in $CO_2(l)$ and $CS_2(l)$? Which of these is expected to have the higher boiling point? (Check your answer by referring to the *Handbook of Chemistry and Physics*, which is available in your school library.)

OH 11.86 Below are the vapor pressures of some relatively common chemicals measured at 20 °C. Arrange these substances in order of increasing intermolecular attractive forces.

Benzene, C_6H_6	80 torr
Acetic acid, $HC_2H_3O_2$	11.7 torr
Acetone, C_3H_6O	184.8 torr
Diethyl ether, $C_4H_{10}O$	442.2 torr
Water	17.5 torr

11.87 The boiling points of some common substances are given here. Arrange these substances in order of increasing strengths of intermolecular attractions.

Ethanol, C_2H_5OH	78.4 °C
Ethylene glycol, $C_2H_4(OH)_2$	197.2 °C
Water	100 °C
Diethyl ether, $C_4H_{10}O$	34.5 °C

Energy Changes That Accompany Changes of State

OH 11.88 The molar heat of vaporization of water at 25 °C is +43.9 kJ mol⁻¹. How many kilojoules of heat would be required to vaporize 125 mL (0.125 kg) of water?

11.89 The molar heat of vaporization of acetone, C_3H_6O, is 30.3 kJ mol⁻¹ at its boiling point. How many kilojoules of heat would be liberated by the condensation of 5.00 g of acetone?

11.90 Suppose 45.0 g of water at 85 °C is added to 105.0 g of ice at 0 °C. The molar heat of fusion of water is 6.01 kJ mol⁻¹, and the specific heat of water is 4.18 J/g °C. On the basis of these data, (a) what will be the final temperature of the mixture and (b) how many grams of ice will melt?

11.91 A cube of solid benzene (C_6H_6) at its melting point and weighing 10.0 g is placed in 10.0 g of water at 30 °C. Given that the heat of fusion of benzene is 9.92 kJ mol⁻¹, to what temperature will the water have cooled by the time all of the benzene has melted?

Crystalline Solids and X-Ray Diffraction

11.92 How many zinc and sulfide ions are present in the unit cell of zinc sulfide? (See Figure 11.35.)

11.93 How many copper atoms are within the face-centered cubic unit cell of copper? (Hint: See Figure 11.31 and add up all the *parts* of atoms in the fcc unit cell.)

OH ILW 11.94 The atomic radius of nickel is 1.24 Å. Nickel crystallizes in a face-centered cubic lattice. What is the length of the edge of the unit cell expressed in angstroms and in picometers?

11.95 Silver forms face-centered cubic crystals. The atomic radius of a silver atom is 144 pm. Draw the face of a unit cell with the nuclei of the silver atoms at the lattice points. The atoms are in contact along the diagonal. Calculate the length of an edge of this unit cell.

11.96 Potassium ions have a radius of 133 pm, and bromide ions have a radius of 195 pm. The crystal structure of potassium bromide is the same as for sodium chloride. Estimate the length of the edge of the unit cell in potassium bromide.

11.97 The unit cell edge in sodium chloride has a length of 564.0 pm. The sodium ion has a radius of 95 pm. What is the *diameter* of a chloride ion?

OH 11.98 Calculate the angles at which X rays of wavelength 229 pm will be observed to be defracted from crystal planes spaced (a) 1000 pm apart and (b) 250 pm apart. Assume $n = 1$ for both calculations.

11.99 Calculate the interplanar spacings (in picometers) that correspond to defracted beams of X rays at $\theta = 20.0°$, $27.4°$, and $35.8°$, if the X rays have a wavelength of 141 pm. Assume that $n = 1$.

11.100 Cesium chloride forms a simple cubic lattice in which Cs^+ ions are at the corners and a Cl^- ion is in the center (see Figure 11.34). The cation–anion contact occurs along the *body diagonal* of the unit cell. (The body diagonal starts at one corner and then runs through the center of the cell to the opposite corner.) The length of the edge of the unit cell is 412.3 pm. The Cl^- ion has a radius of 181 pm. Calculate the radius of the Cs^+ ion.

11.101 Rubidium chloride has the rock salt structure. Cations and anions are in contact along the edge of the unit cell, which is 658 pm long. The radius of the chloride ion is 181 pm. What is the radius of the Rb^+ ion?

Crystal Types

11.102 Tin(IV) chloride, $SnCl_4$, has soft crystals with a melting point of -30.2 °C. The liquid is nonconducting. What type of crystal is formed by $SnCl_4$?

11.103 Elemental boron is a semiconductor, is very hard, and has a melting point of about 2250 °C. What type of crystal is formed by boron?

11.104 Columbium is another name for one of the elements. This element is shiny, soft, and ductile. It melts at 2468 °C, and the solid conducts electricity. What kind of solid does columbium form?

11.105 Elemental phosphorus consists of soft white "waxy" crystals that are easily crushed and melt at 44 °C. The solid does not conduct electricity. What type of crystal does phosphorus form?

11.106 Indicate which type of crystal (ionic, molecular, covalent, metallic) each of the following would form when it solidifies. (a) Br_2, (b) LiF, (c) MgO, (d) Mo, (e) Si, (f) PH_3, (g) NaOH

11.107 Indicate which type of crystal (ionic, molecular, covalent, metallic) each of the following would form when it solidifies: (a) O_2, (b) H_2S, (c) Pt, (d) KCl, (e) Ge, (f) $Al_2(SO_4)_3$, (g) Ne

Phase Diagrams

11.108 Sketch the phase diagram for a substance that has a triple point at -15.0 °C and 0.30 atm, melts at -10.0 °C at 1 atm, and has a normal boiling point of 90 °C.

11.109 Based on the phase diagram of the preceding problem, below what pressure will the substance undergo sublimation? How does the density of the liquid compare with the density of the solid?

11.110 According to Figure 11.48, what phase(s) should exist for CO_2 at (a) -60 °C and 6 atm, (b) -60 °C and 2 atm, (c) -40 °C and 10 atm, and (d) -57 °C and 5.2 atm?

OH 11.111 Looking at the phase diagram for CO_2 (Figure 11.48), how can we tell that solid CO_2 is more dense than liquid CO_2?

ADDITIONAL EXERCISES

11.112 Make a list of *all* of the attractive forces that exist in solid Na_2SO_3.

OH 11.113 Calculate the mass of water vapor present in 10.0 L of air at 20 °C if the relative humidity is 75%.

11.114 Should acetone molecules be attracted to water molecules more strongly than to other acetone molecules? Explain your answer. The structure of acetone is shown below.

$$
\begin{array}{ccccc}
& H & O & H & \\
& | & \| & | & \\
H- & C & -C & -C & -H \\
& | & & | & \\
& H & & H &
\end{array}
$$

OH 11.115 Acetic acid has a heat of fusion of 10.8 kJ mol^{-1} and a heat of vaporization of 24.3 kJ mol^{-1}.

$$HC_2H_3O_2(s) \longrightarrow HC_2H_3O_2(l) \quad \Delta H_{fusion} = 10.8 \text{ kJ mol}^{-1}$$

$$HC_2H_3O_2(l) \longrightarrow HC_2H_3O_2(g) \quad \Delta H_{vaporization} = 24.3 \text{ kJ mol}^{-1}$$

Use Hess's law to estimate the value for the heat of sublimation of acetic acid, in kilojoules per mole.

*11.116 Melting point is sometimes used as an indication of the extent of covalent bonding in a compound—the higher the melting point, the more ionic the substance. On this basis, oxides of metals seem to become less ionic as the charge on the metal ion increases. Thus, Cr_2O_3 has a melting point of 2266 °C whereas CrO_3 has a melting point of only 196 °C. The explanation often given is similar in some respects to explanations of the variations in the strengths of certain intermolecular attractions given in this chapter. Provide an explanation for the greater degree of electron sharing in CrO_3 as compared with Cr_2O_3.

*11.117 When warm moist air sweeps in from the ocean and rises over a mountain range, it expands and cools. Explain how this cooling is related to the attractive forces between gas molecules. Why does this cause rain to form? When the air drops down the far side of the range, its pressure rises as it is compressed. Explain why this causes the air temperature to rise. How does the humidity of this air compare with the air that originally came in off the ocean? Now, explain why the coast of California is lush farmland, whereas valleys (such as Death Valley) that lie to the east of the tall Sierra Nevada are arid and dry.

OH *11.118 Gold crystallizes in a face-centered cubic lattice. The edge of the unit cell has a length of 407.86 pm. The density of gold is 19.31 g cm^{-3}. Use these data and the atomic mass of gold to calculate the value of Avogadro's number.

11.119 Gold crystallizes with a face-centered cubic unit cell with an edge length of 407.86 pm. Calculate the atomic radius of gold in units of picometers.

*__11.120__ Calculate the amount of empty space (in pm^3) in simple cubic, body-centered cubic, and face-centered cubic unit cells if the lattice points are occupied by identical atoms with a diameter of 1.00 pm. Which of these structures gives the most efficient packing of atoms.

__11.121__ Silver has an atomic radius of 144 pm. What would be the density of silver (in $g\ cm^{-3}$) if it were to crystallize in (a) a simple cubic lattice, (b) a body-centered cubic lattice, and (c) a face-centered cubic lattice? The actual density of silver is $10.6\ g\ cm^{-3}$. Which cubic lattice does silver have?

*__11.122__ Potassium chloride crystallizes with the rock salt structure. When bathed in X rays, the layers of atoms corresponding to the surfaces of the unit cell produce a diffracted beam of X rays at an angle of 12.8°. Calculate the density of KCl.

__11.123__ Why do clouds form when the humid air of a weather system called a *warm front* encounters the cool, relatively dry air of a *cold front*?

EXERCISES IN CRITICAL THINKING

__11.124__ Supercritical CO_2 is used to decaffeinate coffee. Propose other uses for supercritical fluids.

__11.125__ Freshly precipitated crystals are usually very small. Over time the crystals tend to grow larger. How can we use the concept of dynamic equilibrium to explain this phenomenon?

__11.126__ What are some "everyday" applications of Le Châtelier's principle? For example, we turn up the heat in an oven to cook a meal faster.

__11.127__ Lubricants, oils, greases, etc. are very important in everyday life. Explain how a lubricant works in terms of intermolecular forces.

__11.128__ Galileo's thermometer is a tube of liquid that has brightly colored glass spheres that float or sink depending on the temperature. Using your knowledge from the past two chapters, explain all of the processes that are involved in this thermometer.

__11.129__ Use the Clausius–Clapeyron equation to plot the vapor pressure curve of a gas that has a heat of vaporization of $21.7\ kJ\ mol^{-1}$ and a boiling point of 48 °C. Compare your results to the other vapor pressure curves in this chapter.

__11.130__ Will the near weightless environment of the international space station have any effect on intermolecular forces and chemical reactions? What types of chemical reactions may benefit from a weightless environment?

PROPERTIES OF SOLUTIONS; MIXTURES OF SUBSTANCES AT THE MOLECULAR LEVEL

12

Life-saving intravenous fluids are as indispensable to modern medicine as the rapid helecopter transport to the hospital. An I.V. helps maintain body fluids and also provides a quick way to administer drug solutions to a patient. These solutions are critical to patient care and are best understood by looking at the molecular level of the solution process presented in this chapter. *(Mike Powell/ Riser/Getty Images)*

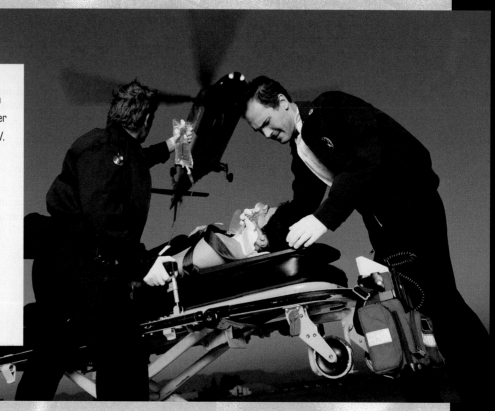

CHAPTER OUTLINE

12.1 Substances mix spontaneously when there is no energy barrier to mixing

12.2 Heats of solution come from unbalanced intermolecular attractions

12.3 A substance's solubility changes with temperature

12.4 Gases become more soluble at higher pressures

12.5 Molarity changes with temperature; molality, weight percentages, and mole fractions do not

12.6 Solutes lower the vapor pressure of a solvent

12.7 Solutions have lower melting points and higher boiling points than pure solvents

12.8 Osmosis is a flow of solvent through a semipermeable membrane due to unequal concentrations

12.9 Ionic solutes affect colligative properties differently from nonionic solutes

THIS CHAPTER IN CONTEXT   In Chapter 4 we discussed solutions as a medium for carrying out chemical reactions. Our focus at that time was the kinds of reactions that take place in aqueous solution. In this chapter we will examine how the addition of a solute affects the *physical properties* of the mixture. For the chemist we will see that changes in these physical properties can be used to determine molar masses. The experienced chemist uses the properties of various mixtures to dissolve or precipitate substances in order to purify them. In our daily lives we add ethylene glycol (antifreeze) to a car's radiator to protect it against freezing and overheating since water has a lower freezing point and a higher boiling point when such a solute is dissolved in it.

Here we will study not only aqueous solutions, but solutions involving other solvents as well. We will concentrate on liquid solutions, although solutions can also be gaseous or solid. In fact, all gases mix completely at the molecular level, so the gas mixtures we studied in Chapter 10 were gaseous solutions. Solid solutions of metals are called alloys and include such materials as brass and bronze.

12.1 | SUBSTANCES MIX SPONTANEOUSLY WHEN THERE IS NO ENERGY BARRIER TO MIXING

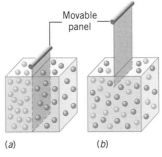

FIG. 12.1 **Mixing of gases.** When two gases, initially in separate compartments (*a*), suddenly find themselves in the same container (*b*), they mix spontaneously.

There is a wide variation in the ability of liquids to dissolve different solutes. For example, water and gasoline do not dissolve in each other, but water and alcohol do. Similarly, salt will dissolve in water, but not in liquid hydrocarbons such as paint thinner. To understand the reasons for these differences, we must examine the factors that drive solution formation as well as those that inhibit it.

In Chapter 10 you learned that all gases mix spontaneously to form homogeneous mixtures (i.e., solutions). If two gases are placed in separate compartments of a container such as that in Figure 12.1, and the movable partition between them is removed, the molecules will begin to intermingle. The random motions of the molecules will cause them to diffuse one into the other until a uniform mixture is achieved.

The spontaneous mixing of gases illustrates one of nature's strong "driving forces" for change. *A system, left to itself, will tend toward the most probable state.*[1] At the instant we remove the partition, the container holds two separate gas samples, in contact but unmixed. This represents a highly improbable state because of the natural motions of the molecules. The vastly more probable distribution is one in which the molecules are thoroughly mixed, so formation of the gaseous solution involves a transition from a highly improbable state to a highly probable one.

Attractive forces affect the ability of solutions to form

The drive to attain the most probable state favors the formation of *any* solution. What limits the ability of most substances to mix completely, however, are intermolecular forces of attraction. Such attractions are negligible in gases, so regardless of the chemical makeup of the molecules, the forces are unable to prevent them from mixing. That's why all gases spontaneously form solutions with each other. In liquids and solids, however, the situation is much different because intermolecular attractions are so much stronger.

For a liquid solution to form, there must be a balance among the attractive forces so the natural tendency of particles to intermingle can proceed. In other words, the attractive forces between molecules within the solvent and between molecules within the solute must be about as strong as attractions between solute and solvent molecules. Let's look at two examples, mixtures of water with benzene and with ethanol.

benzene
(nonpolar)

ethanol
(contains a polar OH group)

Water and benzene (C_6H_6) are insoluble in each other. In water, there are strong hydrogen bonds between the molecules; in benzene the molecules attract each other by relatively weak London forces and are not able to form hydrogen bonds. Suppose that we

---

[1] In Chapter 18 this driving force will be called *entropy.*

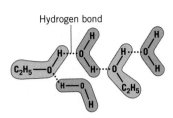

FIG. 12.2 **Hydrogen bonds in aqueous ethanol.** Ethanol molecules form hydrogen bonds (···) to water molecules.

TOOLS

"Like dissolves like" rule

did manage to disperse water molecules in benzene. As they move about, the water molecules would occasionally encounter each other. Because the water molecules attract each other so much more strongly than they attract benzene molecules, hydrogen bonds would cause water molecules to stick together at each such encounter. This would continue to happen until all the water was in a separate phase. Thus, a solution of water in benzene would not be stable and would gradually separate into two phases. We say water and benzene are **immiscible,** meaning they are mutually insoluble.

Water and ethanol (C_2H_5OH), on the other hand, are **miscible;** they are soluble in all proportions. This is because water and ethanol molecules can form hydrogen bonds with each other that are nearly equivalent to those in the separate pure liquids (Figure 12.2). Mixing these molecules offers little resistance, so they are able to mingle relatively freely.

Like dissolves like rule

Observations like those for benzene–water and ethanol–water mixtures led to a generalization often called the **"like dissolves like" rule:** when solute and solvent have molecules "like" each other in polarity, they tend to form a solution. When solute and solvent molecules are quite different in polarity, solutions of any appreciable concentration do not form. The rule has long enabled chemists to use chemical composition and molecular structure to predict the likelihood of two substances dissolving in each other.

The solubility of solids depends on the relative strengths of intermolecular attractions

The "like dissolves like" principle also applies to the solubility of solids in liquid solvents. Polar solvents tend to dissolve polar and ionic compounds, whereas nonpolar solvents tend to dissolve nonpolar compounds.

Figure 12.3 depicts a section of a crystal of NaCl in contact with water. The dipoles of water molecules orient themselves so that the negative ends of some point toward Na^+ ions and the positive ends of others point at Cl^- ions. In other words, *ion–dipole* attractions

FIG. 12.3 **Hydration of ions.** Hydration involves a complex redirection of forces of attraction and repulsion. Before this solution forms, water molecules are attracted only to each other, and Na^+ and Cl^- ions have only each other in the crystal to be attracted to. In the solution, the ions have water molecules to take the places of their oppositely charged counterparts; in addition, water molecules are attracted to ions even more than they are to other water molecules.

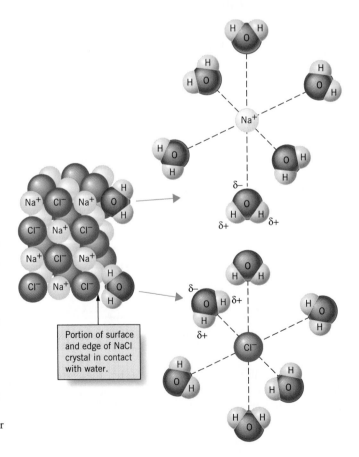

Portion of surface and edge of NaCl crystal in contact with water.

occur that tend to tug and pull ions from the crystal. At the corners and edges of the crystal, ions are held by fewer neighbors within the solid and so are more readily dislodged than those elsewhere on the crystal's surface. As water molecules dislodge these ions, new corners and edges are exposed, and the crystal continues to dissolve.

As they become free, the ions become completely surrounded by water molecules (also shown in Figure 12.3). The phenomenon is called the **hydration** of ions. The *general* term for the surrounding of a solute particle by solvent molecules is **solvation,** so hydration is just a special case of solvation. Ionic compounds are able to dissolve in water when the attractions between water dipoles and ions overcome the attractions of the ions for each other within the crystal.

Similar events explain why solids composed of polar molecules, like those of sugar, dissolve in water (see Figure 12.4). Attractions between the solvent and solute dipoles help to dislodge molecules from the crystal and bring them into solution. Again we see that "like dissolves like"; a polar solute dissolves in a polar solvent.

The same reasoning explains why nonpolar solids like wax are soluble in nonpolar solvents such as benzene. Wax is a solid mixture of long chain hydrocarbons, held together by London forces. The attractions between benzene molecules are also London forces, of comparable strength, so molecules of the wax can easily be dispersed among those of the solvent.

When intermolecular attractive forces within solute and solvent are sufficiently different, the two do not form a solution. For example, ionic solids or very polar molecular solids (like sugar) have strong attractions between their particles which cannot be overcome by attractions to molecules of a nonpolar solvent such as benzene.

◻ Water molecules collide everywhere along the crystal surface, but *successful* collisions—those that dislodge ions—are more likely to occur at corners and edges.

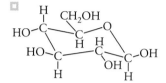

Sugar molecules such as this have polar OH groups that interact with water by hydrogen bonding.

12.2 | HEATS OF SOLUTION COME FROM UNBALANCED INTERMOLECULAR ATTRACTIONS

Because intermolecular attractive forces are important when liquids and solids are involved, the formation of a solution is inevitably associated with energy exchanges. The total energy absorbed or released when a solute dissolves in a solvent at constant pressure to make a solution is called the **molar enthalpy of solution,** or usually just the **heat of solution,** ΔH_{soln}.

Energy is required to separate the particles of solute and also those of the solvent and make them spread out to make room for each other. This step is *endothermic,* because we must overcome the attractions between molecules to spread the particles out. But once the particles come back together as a *solution,* the attractive forces between approaching solute and solvent particles yield a decrease in the system's potential energy, and this is an *exothermic* change. The enthalpy of solution, ΔH_{soln}, is simply the net result of these two opposing enthalpy contributions.

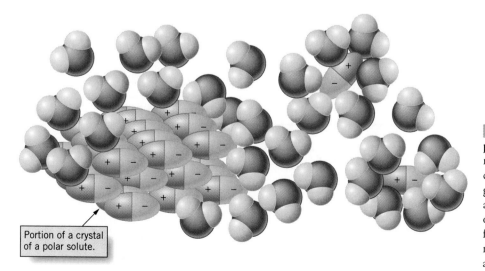

Portion of a crystal of a polar solute.

FIG. 12.4 **Hydration of a polar molecule.** A polar molecule of a molecular compound (such as the sugar glucose) can trade the forces of attraction it experiences for other molecules of its own kind for forces of attraction to molecules of water in an aqueous solution.

The heat of solution for a solid is the lattice energy plus the solvation energy

Because enthalpy is a state function, the magnitude of ΔH_{soln} doesn't depend on the path we take from the separated solute and solvent to the solution. For a solid dissolving in a liquid, it is convenient to imagine a two-step path.

Step 1. *Vaporize the solid to form individual solute particles.* The particles are molecules for molecular substances and ions for ionic compounds. The energy absorbed is the lattice energy of the solid.

Step 2. *Bring the separated gaseous solute particles into the solvent to form the solution.* This step is exothermic, and the enthalpy change when the particles from one mole of solute are dissolved in the solvent is called the **solvation energy.** If the solvent is water, the solvation energy can also be called the **hydration energy.**

The enthalpy diagram showing these steps for potassium iodide is given in Figure 12.5. Step 1 corresponds to the lattice energy of KI, which is represented by the thermochemical equation

$$KI(s) \longrightarrow K^+(g) + I^-(g) \qquad \Delta H = +632 \text{ kJ}$$

Step 2 corresponds to the hydration energy of gaseous K^+ and I^- ions.

$$K^+(g) + I^-(g) \longrightarrow K^+(aq) + I^-(aq) \qquad \Delta H = -619 \text{ kJ}$$

The *enthalpy of solution* is obtained from the sum of the equations for Steps 1 and 2 and is the enthalpy change when one mole of crystalline KI dissolves in water (corresponding to the direct path in Figure 12.5).

$$KI(s) \longrightarrow K^+(aq) + I^-(aq) \qquad \Delta H_{\text{soln}} = +13 \text{ kJ}$$

The value of ΔH_{soln} indicates that the solution process is endothermic for KI, in agreement with the observation that when KI is added to water and the mixture is stirred, it becomes cool as the KI dissolves.

Table 12.1 provides a comparison between values of ΔH_{soln} obtained by the method described above and values obtained by direct measurements. The agreement between calculated and measured values doesn't seem particularly impressive, but this is partly because lattice and hydration energies are not precisely known and partly because the model used in our analysis is evidently too simple. Notice, however, that when "theory" predicts

☐ Small percentage errors in very large numbers can cause huge percentage changes in the *differences* between such numbers.

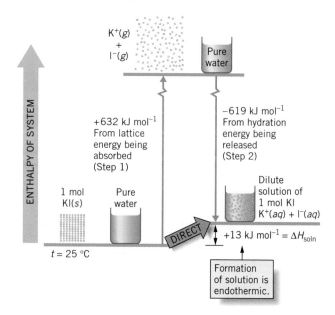

FIG. 12.5 Enthalpy diagram for the heat of solution of one mole of potassium iodide. Adding the lattice energy to the hydration energy gives a positive value for ΔH_{soln}, indicating the solution process is endothermic.

Lattice energy:	$KI(s) \longrightarrow K^+(g) + I^-(g)$		$\Delta H = +632 \text{ kJ}$
Hydration energy:	$K^+(g) + I^-(g) \longrightarrow K^+(aq) + I^-(aq)$		$\Delta H = -619 \text{ kJ}$
Total:	$KI(s) \longrightarrow K^+(aq) + I^-(aq)$		$\Delta H_{\text{soln}} = +13 \text{ kJ}$

TABLE 12.1	Lattice Energies, Hydration Energies, and Heats of Solution for Some Group IA Metal Halides			
			$\Delta H_{soln}{}^{a}$	
Compound	Lattice Energy (kJ mol^{-1})	Hydration Energy (kJ mol^{-1})	Calculated^{b} ΔH_{soln} (kJ mol^{-1})	Measured ΔH_{soln} (kJ mol^{-1})
LiCl	+833	−883	−50	−37.0
NaCl	+766	−770	−4	+3.9
KCl	+690	−686	+4	+17.2
LiBr	+787	−854	−67	−49.0
NaBr	+728	−741	−13	−0.602
KBr	+665	−657	+8	+19.9
KI	+632	−619	+13	+20.33

^{a} Heats of solution refer to the formation of extremely dilute solutions.
^{b} Calculated ΔH_{soln} = lattice energy + hydration energy.

relatively large heats of solution, the experimental values are also relatively large, and that both values have the same sign (except for NaCl). Notice also that the variations among the values follow the same trends when we compare the three chloride salts—LiCl, NaCl, and KCl—or the three bromide salts—LiBr, NaBr, and KBr.

Solution of a liquid in another liquid can be modeled as a three-step process

To consider heats of solution when liquids dissolve in liquids, it's useful to imagine a three-step path going from the initial to the final state (see Figure 12.6). We will designate one liquid as the solute and the other as the solvent.

Step 1. *Expand the solute liquid.* First, we imagine that the molecules of one liquid are moved apart just far enough to make room for molecules of the other liquid. Because we have to overcome forces of attraction, this step increases the system's potential energy and so is *endothermic*.

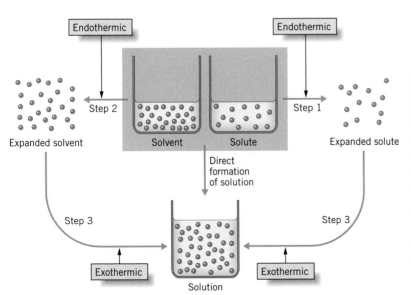

FIG. 12.6 **Enthalpy of solution for the mixing of two liquids.** To analyze the enthalpy change for the formation of a solution of two liquids, we can imagine the hypothetical steps shown here. **Step 1.** The molecules of the liquid designated as the solute move apart slightly to make room for the solvent molecules, an endothermic process. **Step 2.** The molecules of the solvent are made to take up a larger volume to make room for the solute molecules, which is also an endothermic change. **Step 3.** The expanded samples of solute and solvent spontaneously intermingle, their molecules also attracting each other making the step exothermic.

Step 2. *Expand the solvent liquid.* The second step is like the first, but is done to the other liquid (solvent). On an enthalpy diagram (Figure 12.7) we have climbed two energy steps and have both the solvent and the solute in their slightly "expanded" conditions.

Step 3. *Mix the expanded liquids.* The third step brings the molecules of the expanded solvent and solute together to form the solution. Because the molecules of the two liquids experience mutual forces of attraction, bringing them together lowers the system's potential energy, so Step 3 is exothermic. The value of ΔH_{soln} will, again, be the net energy change for these steps.

Ideal solutions have ΔH_{soln} equal to zero

The enthalpy diagram in Figure 12.7 shows the case when the sum of the energy inputs for Steps 1 and 2 is equal to the energy released in Step 3, so the overall value of ΔH_{soln} is zero. This is very nearly the case when we make a solution of benzene and carbon tetrachloride. Attractive forces between molecules of benzene are almost exactly the same as those between molecules of CCl_4, or between molecules of benzene and those of CCl_4. If all such intermolecular forces were identical, the net ΔH_{soln} would be exactly zero, and the resulting solution would be called an **ideal solution.** Be sure to notice the difference between an *ideal solution* and an *ideal gas.* In an ideal gas, there are no attractive forces. In an ideal solution, there are attractive forces, but they all have the same magnitude.

For most liquids that are mutually soluble, ΔH_{soln} is not zero. Instead, heat is either given off or absorbed. For example, acetone and water are liquids that form a solution exothermically (ΔH_{soln} is negative). With these liquids, the third step releases more energy than the sum of the first two chiefly because molecules of water and acetone attract each other more strongly than acetone molecules attract each other. This is because water molecules can form hydrogen bonds to acetone molecules in the solution, but acetone molecules cannot form hydrogen bonds to other acetone molecules in the pure liquid.

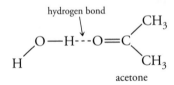

acetone

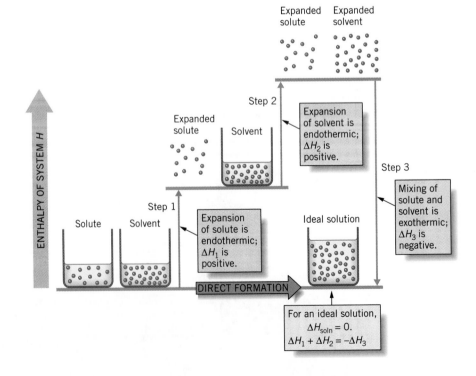

FIG. 12.7 **Enthalpy changes in the formation of an ideal solution.** The three-step and the direct-formation paths both start and end at the same place with the same enthalpy outcome. The sum of the positive ΔH values for the two endothermic steps, 1 and 2, numerically equals the negative ΔH value for the exothermic step, 3. The net ΔH for the formation of an ideal solution is therefore zero.

Ethanol and hexane form a solution endothermically. In this case, the release of energy in the third step is not enough to compensate for the energy demands of Steps 1 and 2, and the solution cools as it forms. Ethanol molecules attract each other more strongly than they can attract hexane molecules. Hexane molecules cannot push their way into ethanol without breaking up some of the hydrogen bonding between ethanol molecules.

□ $CH_3CH_2CH_2CH_2CH_2CH_3$
hexane

Gas solubility can be understood using a simple molecular model

Unlike the case for solid and liquid solutes, only very weak attractions exist between gas molecules, so the energy required to "expand the solute" is negligible. The heat absorbed or released when a gas dissolves in a liquid has essentially two contributions, as shown in Figure 12.8:

1. *Energy is absorbed to open "pockets" in the solvent that can hold gas molecules.* The solvent must be expanded slightly to accommodate the molecules of the gas. This requires a small energy input since attractions between solvent molecules must be overcome. Water is a special case; it already contains open holes in its network of loose hydrogen bonds around room temperature. For water, very little energy is required to create pockets that can hold gas molecules.

2. *Energy is released when gas molecules enter the pockets.* Intermolecular attractions between the gas molecules and the surrounding solvent molecules lower the total energy, and energy is released as heat. The stronger the attractions are, the more heat is released. Water is capable of forming hydrogen bonds with some gases, while organic solvents often can't. A larger amount of heat is released when a gas molecule is placed in the pocket in water than in organic solvents.

These factors lead to two generalizations. *Heats of solution for gases in organic solvents are often endothermic* because the energy required to open up pockets is greater than the energy released by attractions formed between the gas and solvent molecules. *Heats of solution for gases in water are often exothermic* because water already contains pockets to hold the gas molecules, and energy is released when water and gas molecules attract each other.

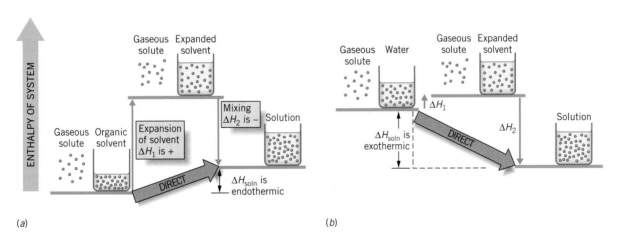

(a)

(b)

FIG. 12.8 **A molecular model of gas solubility.** (*a*) A gas dissolves in an organic solvent. Energy is absorbed to open "pockets" in the solvent that can hold the gas molecules. In the second step, energy is released when the gas molecules enter the pockets where they are attracted to the solvent molecules. Here the solution process is shown to be endothermic. (*b*) At room temperature, water's loose network of hydrogen bonds already contains pockets that can accommodate gas molecules, so little energy is needed to prepare the solvent to accept the gas. In the second step, energy is released as the gas molecules take their places in the pockets where they experience attractions to the water molecules. In this case, the solution process is exothermic.

12.3 A SUBSTANCE'S SOLUBILITY CHANGES WITH TEMPERATURE

By "solubility" we mean the mass of solute that forms a *saturated* solution with a given mass of solvent at a specified temperature. The units often are grams of solute per 100 g of solvent. In such a solution there is an equilibrium between the undissolved solute and the solute dissolved in the solution.

$$\text{Solute}_{\text{undissolved}} \rightleftharpoons \text{Solute}_{\text{dissolved}}$$

(Solute contacts the   (Solute is in the
saturated solution.)   saturated solution.)

As long as the temperature is held constant, the concentration of the solute in the solution remains the same. If the temperature of the mixture changes, however, this equilibrium tends to be upset and either more solute will dissolve or some will precipitate. To analyze how temperature affects solubility we can use Le Châtelier's principle, which we introduced in Chapter 11. Recall that this principle tells us that if a system at equilibrium is disturbed, the system will change in a direction that counteracts the disturbance and returns the system to equilibrium (if it can).

To increase the temperature of a solution, heat (energy) is added. When solute dissolves in a solvent, heat is absorbed or evolved. As in Section 11.8, heat is the factor through which Le Châtelier's principle is applied. Let's consider a common situation in which energy is absorbed when additional solute is dissolved in an already saturated solution.

$$\text{Solute}_{\text{undissolved}} + \text{energy} \rightleftharpoons \text{Solute}_{\text{dissolved}}$$

According to Le Châtelier's principle, when we add heat energy to raise the temperature, the system responds by consuming some of the energy we've added. This causes the equilibrium to "shift to the right." In other words, more solute dissolves and when equilibrium is re-established, there is more solute dissolved in the solution. Thus, *when dissolving more solute in a saturated solution is endothermic, raising the temperature increases the solubility of the solute.* This is a common situation for solids dissolving in liquid solvents. How much the solubility is affected by temperature varies widely, as seen in Figure 12.9

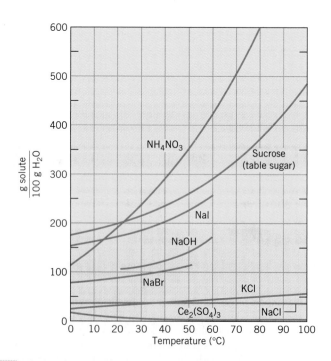

FIG. 12.9 Solubility in water versus temperature for several substances. Most substances become more soluble when the temperature of the solution is increased, but the amount of this increased solubility varies considerably.

TABLE 12.2	Solubilities of Common Gases in Water[a]			
		Temperature		
Gas	0 °C	20 °C	50 °C	100 °C
Nitrogen, N_2	0.0029	0.0019	0.0012	0
Oxygen, O_2	0.0069	0.0043	0.0027	0
Carbon dioxide, CO_2	0.335	0.169	0.076	0
Sulfur dioxide, SO_2	22.8	10.6	4.3	1.8[b]
Ammonia, NH_3	89.9	51.8	28.4	7.4[c]

[a] Solubilities are in grams of solute per 100 g of water when the gaseous space over the liquid is saturated with the gas and the total pressure is 1 atm.
[b] Solubility at 90 °C.
[c] Solubility at 96 °C.

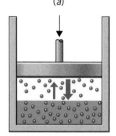

Some solutes, such as cerium(III) sulfate, $Ce_2(SO_4)_3$, become *less* soluble with increasing temperature (Figure 12.9). Energy must be *released* from a saturated solution of $Ce_2(SO_4)_3$ to make more solute dissolve. For its equilibrium equation, we must show "energy" on the right side because heat is released when more of the solute dissolves into a saturated solution.

$$\text{Solute}_{\text{undissolved}} \rightleftharpoons \text{Solute}_{\text{dissolved}} + \text{energy}$$

Temperature affects the solubility of a gas in a liquid

Table 12.2 gives data for the solubilities of several common gases in water at different temperatures, but all under 1 atm of pressure. In water, gases are usually more soluble at colder temperatures. But the solubility of gases, like other solubilities, can increase or decrease with temperature, depending on the gas and the solvent. For example, the solubilities of H_2, N_2, CO, He, and Ne actually rise with rising temperature in common organic solvents like carbon tetrachloride, toluene, and acetone.

FIG. 12.10 How pressure increases the solubility of a gas in a liquid. (*a*) At some specific pressure, equilibrium exists between the vapor phase and the solution. (*b*) An increase in pressure upsets the equilibrium. More gas molecules are dissolving than are leaving the solution. (*c*) More gas has dissolved and equilibrium is restored.

12.4 GASES BECOME MORE SOLUBLE AT HIGHER PRESSURES

The solubility of a gas in a liquid increases with increasing pressure. To understand this at the molecular level, imagine the following equilibrium established in a closed container fitted with a movable piston (Figure 12.10*a*).

$$\text{gas} + \text{solvent} \rightleftharpoons \text{solution} \qquad (12.1)$$

If the piston is pushed down (Figure 12.10*b*), the gas is compressed and its pressure increases. This causes the concentration of the gas molecules over the solution to increase, so the rate at which the gas dissolves is now greater than the rate at which it leaves the solution. Eventually, equilibrium is re-established when the concentration of the gas in the solution has increased enough to make the rate of escape equal to the rate at which the gas dissolves (Figure 12.10*c*). At this point, the concentration of the gas in the solution is larger than before.

The effect of pressure on the solubility of a gas can also be explained by Le Châtelier's principle. In this case, the disturbance is an increase in the pressure of the gas above the solution. How could the system counteract the pressure increase? The answer is, by having more gas dissolve in the solution. In this way, the pressure of the gas is reduced and the concentration of the gas in the solution is increased. In other words, increasing the pressure of the gas will cause the gas to become more soluble.

Bottled carbonated beverages fizz when the cap is opened because the sudden drop in pressure causes a sudden drop in gas solubility. (*Andy Washnik.*)

Henry's law relates gas solubility to pressure

□ William Henry (1774–1836), an English chemist, first reported the relationship between gas solubility and pressure.

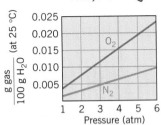

FIG. 12.11 Solubility in water versus pressure for two gases.

Figure 12.11 shows how the solubility in water of oxygen and nitrogen vary with pressure. The straight lines on the graph indicate that the concentration of the gas is directly proportional to its pressure above the solution. This is expressed quantitatively by **Henry's law** (also called the **Pressure-Solubility law**) which states that *the concentration of a gas in a liquid at any given temperature is directly proportional to the partial pressure of the gas over the solution.*

$$C_{gas} = k_H P_{gas} \qquad (T \text{ is constant})$$

where C_{gas} is the concentration of the gas and P_{gas} is the partial pressure of the gas above the solution. The proportionality constant, k_H, called the Henry's law constant, is unique to each gas. The equation is true only at low concentrations and pressures and for gases that do not react with the solvent.

An alternate (and commonly used) form of Henry's law is

$$\frac{C_1}{P_1} = \frac{C_2}{P_2} \qquad (12.2)$$

where the subscripts 1 and 2 refer to initial and final conditions, respectively. By taking the ratio, the Henry's law constant cancels.

EXAMPLE 12.1
Using Henry's Law

At 20 °C the solubility of N_2 in water is 0.0150 g L^{-1} when the partial pressure of nitrogen is 580 torr. What will be the solubility of N_2 in water at 20 °C when its partial pressure is 800 torr? Calculate your answer to three significant figures.

ANALYSIS: This problem deals with the effect of gas pressure on gas solubility, so Henry's law applies. We use this law in its form given by Equation 12.2 because it lets us avoid having to know or calculate the Henry's law constant.

SOLUTION: Let's gather the data first.

$$C_1 = 0.0150 \text{ g L}^{-1} \qquad C_2 = ?$$
$$P_1 = 580 \text{ torr} \qquad P_2 = 800 \text{ torr}$$

Using Equation 12.2, we have

$$\frac{0.0150 \text{ g L}^{-1}}{580 \text{ torr}} = \frac{C_2}{800 \text{ torr}}$$

Solving for C_2,

$$C_2 = 0.0207 \text{ g L}^{-1}$$

The solubility under the higher pressure is 0.0207 g L^{-1}.

IS THE ANSWER REASONABLE? In relationship to the initial concentration, the size of the answer makes sense because Henry's law tells us to expect a greater solubility at the higher pressure.

Practice Exercise 1: At room temperature and pressure a hydrogen sulfide solution can be made by bubbling $H_2S(g)$ into water; the result is a 0.1 molar solution. Since $H_2S(g)$ is more dense than air we can assume that a layer of pure $H_2S(g)$ at atmospheric pressure covers the solution. What is the value of Henry's law constant, and is the solubility of $H_2S(g)$ much greater or smaller than other gases mentioned in this section? If so, suggest a reason for the difference. (Hint: Assume 20 °C and 1.0 atm for room temperature and pressure.)

Practice Exercise 2: How many grams of nitrogen and oxygen are dissolved in 100 g of water at 20 °C when the water is saturated with air? At 1 atm pressure, the solubility of oxygen in water is 0.00430 g O_2/100 g H_2O, and the solubility of nitrogen in water is 0.00190 g N_2/100 g H_2O. In pure, dry air, P_{N_2} equals 593 torr and P_{O_2} equals 159 torr. Calculate your answers to three significant figures.

Gases with polar molecules or that react with the solvent are more soluble in water

The gases sulfur dioxide, ammonia, and, to a lesser extent, carbon dioxide are far more soluble in water than are oxygen or nitrogen (see Table 12.2). Part of the reason is that SO_2, NH_3, and CO_2 molecules have polar bonds and sites of partial charge that attract water molecules, forming hydrogen bonds to help hold the gases in solution. Ammonia molecules, in addition, not only can accept hydrogen bonds from water ($O-H\cdots N$) but also can donate them through their $N-H$ bonds ($N-H\cdots O$).

The more soluble gases also react with water to some extent as the following chemical equilibria show.

$$CO_2(aq) + H_2O \rightleftharpoons H_2CO_3(aq) \rightleftharpoons H^+(aq) + HCO_3^-(aq)$$

$$SO_2(aq) + H_2O \rightleftharpoons H^+(aq) + HSO_3^-(aq)$$

$$NH_3(aq) + H_2O \rightleftharpoons NH_4^+(aq) + OH^-(aq)$$

The forward reactions contribute to the higher concentrations of the gases in solution, as compared to gases such as O_2 and N_2 that do not react with water at all. Gaseous sulfur trioxide is very soluble in water because it reacts *quantitatively* (i.e., completely) with water to form sulfuric acid.[2]

$$SO_3(g) + H_2O \longrightarrow H_2SO_4(aq)$$

12.5 MOLARITY CHANGES WITH TEMPERATURE; MOLALITY, WEIGHT PERCENTAGES, AND MOLE FRACTIONS DO NOT

In Section 4.6 you learned that for stoichiometry *molar concentration* or *molarity*, mol L^{-1}, is a convenient unit of concentration because it lets us measure out moles of a solute simply by measuring volumes of solution. For studying physical properties, however, molarity is not preferred because the molarity of a solution varies slightly with temperature. Most liquids expand slightly when heated, so a given solution will have a larger volume, and therefore a lower ratio of moles to volume, as its temperature is raised. For this reason, temperature-insensitive concentration units are used. The most common are *percentage by mass, molality,* and *mole fraction* (or *mole percent*).

Percent concentration

Concentrations of solutions are often expressed as a **percentage by mass** (sometimes called a *percent by weight*), which gives grams of solute per 100 grams of solution. Percentage by

---

[2] The "concentrated sulfuric acid" of commerce has a concentration of 93 to 98% H_2SO_4, or roughly 18 *M*. This solution takes up water avidly and very exothermically, removing moisture even out of humid air itself (and so must be kept in stoppered bottles). Because it is dense, oily, sticky, and highly corrosive, it must be handled with extreme care. Safety goggles and gloves must be worn when dispensing concentrated sulfuric acid. When making a more dilute solution, *always pour (slowly with stirring) the concentrated acid into the water.* If water is poured onto concentrated sulfuric acid, it can layer on the acid's surface, because the density of the acid is so much higher than water's (1.8 g mL^{-1} vs. 1.0 g mL^{-1} for water). At the interface, such intense heat can be generated that the steam thereby created could explode from the container, spattering acid around.

mass is indicated by % (w/w), where the "w" stands for "weight." To calculate a percentage by mass from solute and solution masses, we can use the following formula:

TOOLS

Percentage by mass

$$\text{Percentage by mass} = \frac{\text{mass of solute}}{\text{mass of solution}} \times 100\%$$

For example, a solution labeled "0.85% (w/w) NaCl," is one in which the ratio of solute to solution is 0.85 g of NaCl to 100 g of NaCl solution. Often, the "(w/w)" is omitted.[3]

Percentages could also be called *parts per hundred*. Other similar expressions of concentration are *parts per million* (ppm) and *parts per billion* (ppb), where 1 ppm equals 1 g of component in 10^6 g of the mixture and 1 ppb equals 1 g of component in 10^9 g of the mixture.

EXAMPLE 12.2
Using Percent Concentrations

Seawater is typically 3.5% sea salt and has a density of about 1.03 g mL^{-1}. How many grams of sea salt would be needed to prepare enough seawater solution to completely fill a 62.5 L aquarium?

ANALYSIS: We need the number of grams of sea salt in 62.5 L of seawater solution. We can write the problem as

$$62.5 \text{ L soln} \Leftrightarrow ? \text{ g sea salt}$$

To solve the problem, we'll need a relationship that links seawater and sea salt. The percent concentration is the link we need. If we assume that the percent is a percentage by mass, we can write "3.5% sea salt" as follows:

$$3.5 \text{ g sea salt} \Leftrightarrow 100 \text{ g soln}$$

We now need a link between grams of solution and liters of solution. Density relates the mass of a substance to its volume, so we can write a density of 1.03 g mL^{-1} as

$$1.03 \text{ g soln} \Leftrightarrow 1.00 \text{ mL soln}$$

If we convert 62.5 L solution into milliliters of solution, we can use this relationship to obtain the grams of solution. We can then use the percent to convert grams of solution into grams of sea salt.

SOLUTION: The hard work has been done. We just need to assemble the information so that the units cancel properly.

$$62.5 \text{ L soln} \times \frac{1000 \text{ mL soln}}{1 \text{ L soln}} \times \frac{1.03 \text{ g soln}}{1.00 \text{ mL soln}} \times \frac{3.5 \text{ g sea salt}}{100 \text{ g soln}} = 2.2 \times 10^3 \text{ g sea salt}$$

IS THE ANSWER REASONABLE? If seawater is about 4% sea salt, 100 g of seawater should contain about 4 g of salt. A liter of seawater weighs about 1000 g, so it would contain about 40 g of salt. We have about 60 L of seawater, which would contain 60 × 40 g of salt, or 2400 g of salt. This is not too far from our answer, so the answer seems reasonable.

---

[3] Clinical laboratories sometimes report concentrations as percent by mass/volume, using the symbol "% (w/v)":

$$\text{Percentage by mass/volume} = \frac{\text{mass of solute (g)}}{\text{volume of solution (mL)}} \times 100\%$$

For example, a solution that is 4% (w/v) SrCl$_2$ contains 4 g of SrCl$_2$ dissolved in 100 mL of solution. Notice that with a percentage by mass, we can use any units for the mass of the solute and mass of the solution, as long as they are the same for both. With percentage by mass/volume, we *must* use grams for the mass of solute and milliliters for the volume of solution. If a percent concentration does not include a (w/v) or (w/w) designation, we assume that it is a percentage by mass.

Practice Exercise 3: What volume of water at 20 °C ($d = 0.9982$ g cm^{-3}) is needed to dissolve 45.0 g of sucrose to make a 10% (w/w) solution? (Hint: you need the mass of water to solve this problem.)

Practice Exercise 4: How many grams of NaBr are needed to prepare 250 g of 1.00% (w/w) NaBr solution in water? How many grams of water are needed? How many milliliters are needed, given that the density of water at room temperature is 0.988 g mL^{-1}?

Practice Exercise 5: Hydrochloric acid can be purchased from chemical supply houses as a solution that is 37% (w/w) HCl. What mass of this solution contains 7.5 g of HCl?

Molal concentration

The number of moles of solute per kilogram of *solvent* is called the **molal concentration** or the **molality** of a solution. The usual symbol for molality is ***m***.

$$\text{Molality} = m = \frac{\text{mol of solute}}{\text{kg of solvent}}$$

TOOLS
Molal concentration

For example, if we dissolve 0.500 mol of sugar in 1.00 kg of water, we have a 0.500 *m* solution of sugar. We would not need a volumetric flask to prepare the solution, because we weigh the solvent. Some important physical properties of a solution are related in a simple way to its molality, as we'll soon see.

It is important not to confuse *molarity* with *molality*.

$$\text{Molality} = m = \frac{\text{mol of solute}}{\text{kg of } solvent} \qquad \text{Molarity} = M = \frac{\text{mol of solute}}{\text{L of } solution}$$

☐ Be sure to notice that molality is defined per kilogram of *solvent*, not kilogram of solution.

As we pointed out at the beginning of this section, the molarity of a solution changes slightly with temperature, but molality does not. Therefore, molality is more convenient in experiments involving temperature changes.

When water is the solvent, a solution's molarity approaches its molality as the solution becomes more dilute. In very dilute solutions, 1 L of *solution* is nearly 1 L of water, which has a mass close to 1 kg. Under these conditions, the ratio of moles per liter (molarity) is very nearly the same as the ratio of moles per kilogram (molality).

☐ This only applies when the solvent is water. For other solvents molarity and molality have quite different values for the same solution.

EXAMPLE 12.3
Calculation to Prepare a Solution of a Given Molality

An experiment calls for a 0.150 *m* solution of sodium chloride in water. How many grams of NaCl would have to be dissolved in 500.0 g of water to prepare a solution of this molality?

ANALYSIS: *Molality* means moles of solute per kilogram of solvent. The concentration 0.150 *m* means that the solution must contain 0.150 mol of NaCl for every 1.000 kg (1000 g) of water. We can write

$$0.150 \text{ mol NaCl} \Leftrightarrow 1000 \text{ g H}_2\text{O}$$

To calculate the number of moles of NaCl needed for 500.0 g of H$_2$O, we use this relationship as a conversion factor. We can then use the molar mass of NaCl to convert moles of NaCl into grams of NaCl.

SOLUTION:

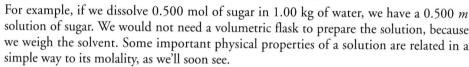

$$500.0 \text{ g H}_2\text{O} \times \frac{0.150 \text{ mol NaCl}}{1000 \text{ g H}_2\text{O}} \times \frac{58.44 \text{ g NaCl}}{1 \text{ mol NaCl}} = 4.38 \text{ g NaCl}$$

When 4.38 g of NaCl is dissolved in 500 g of H$_2$O, the concentration is 0.150 *m* NaCl.

IS THE ANSWER REASONABLE? We'll round the formula mass of NaCl to 60, so 0.15 mol would weigh about 9 g. A 0.15 *m* solution would contain about 9 g NaCl in 1000 g of water. If we used only 500 g of water, we would need half as much salt, or about 4.5 g. Our answer is close to this, so it seems reasonable.

Practice Exercise 6: If you prepare a solution by dissolving 44.00 g of Na_2SO_4 in 250.0 g of water, what is the molality of the solution? Is the molarity of this solution numerically larger or smaller than its molality? [Hint: Recall the definition of molality and molarity (see above and Section 4.6).]

Practice Exercise 7: Water freezes at a lower temperature when it contains solutes. To study the effect of methanol on the freezing point of water, we might begin by preparing a series of solutions of known molalities. Calculate the number of grams of methanol (CH_3OH) needed to prepare a 0.250 *m* solution, using 2.000 kg of water.

Practice Exercise 8: What mass of a 0.853 molal solution of $Fe(NO_3)_3$ is needed to obtain (a) 0.0200 mol of $Fe(NO_3)_3$, (b) 0.0500 mol of Fe^{3+} ions, and (c) 0.00300 mol of nitrate ions?

Mole fraction (mole percent)

Mole fraction and mole percent are important tools that were discussed in Chapter 10 (page 415), so for the sake of completeness we will just review the definitions. The mole fraction X_A of a substance *A* is given by

TOOLS
Mole fraction

$$X_A = \frac{n_A}{n_A + n_B + n_C + n_D + \cdots + n_Z}$$

where n_A, n_B, n_C, ..., n_Z are the numbers of moles of each component, *A, B, C, ..., Z*, respectively. The sum of all mole fractions for a mixture must always equal 1. The mole percent is obtained by multiplying the mole fraction by 100%.

Conversions among concentration units

There are times when we need to relate concentrations expressed in different units. The following example shows that all we need to convert concentrations are the definitions of the units.

EXAMPLE 12.4
Finding Molality from Mass Percent

What is the molality of 10.0% (w/w) aqueous NaCl?

ANALYSIS: The main tools used in performing conversions among concentration units are the definitions of molality and mass percent. The question asks us to go from

$$\frac{10.0 \text{ g NaCl}}{100.0 \text{ g NaCl soln}} \quad \text{to} \quad \frac{? \text{ mol NaCl}}{1 \text{ kg water}}$$

We have two conversions to perform:
- In the numerator, we must convert 10.0 g of NaCl into moles of NaCl. The conversion equality is 58.44 g NaCl = 1 mol NaCl.
- In the denominator, we must convert 100.0 grams of NaCl *solution* to kilograms of *water*. If we subtract the mass of NaCl (10.0 g) from the mass of the NaCl solution (100.0 g), we see that 100.0 g of NaCl solution contains 90.0 g of water. We can write

$$100.0 \text{ g NaCl soln} \Leftrightarrow 90.0 \text{ g water}$$

- We can then convert grams of water to kilograms.

SOLUTION: We write the linking relationships as conversion factors, arranging them so that units cancel properly:

$$\frac{10.0 \text{ g NaCl}}{100.0 \text{ g NaCl soln}} \times \frac{1 \text{ mol NaCl}}{58.44 \text{ g NaCl}} \times \frac{100.0 \text{ g NaCl soln}}{90.0 \text{ g water}} \times \frac{1000 \text{ g water}}{1 \text{ kg water}} = 1.90 \ m \text{ NaCl}$$

A 10.0% NaCl solution is also 1.90 molal.

IS THE ANSWER REASONABLE? A convenient rounding of the numbers in our calculation to one significant figure might be:

$$\frac{10 \text{ g NaCl}}{100 \text{ g NaCl soln}} \times \frac{1 \text{ mol NaCl}}{50 \text{ g NaCl}} \times \frac{100 \text{ g NaCl soln}}{100 \text{ g water}} \times \frac{1000 \text{ g water}}{1 \text{ kg water}} = 2 \ m \text{ NaCl}$$

This is close to our calculated value and we conclude we were correct. Notice that rounding the 58.44 down to 50 compensates for rounding 90 up to 100 so that our estimate is closer to the correct number. We do not need a calculator for this estimate. First cancel five zeros from the numerator numbers and five zeros from the denominator numbers. This leaves you with 10 divided by 5, which equals 2.

Practice Exercise 9: A bottle on the stockroom shelf reads 50% sodium hydroxide solution. What is the molality of this solution? [Hint: Recall that the % means (w/w) percentage.]

Practice Exercise 10: A certain sample of concentrated hydrochloric acid is 37.0% HCl. Calculate the molality of this solution.

Another kind of calculation is to find the molarity of a solution from its mass percent. This cannot be done without the density of the solution, as the next example shows.

EXAMPLE 12.5
Finding Molarity from
Mass Percent

A certain supply of concentrated hydrochloric acid has a concentration of 36.0% HCl. The density of the solution is 1.19 g mL^{-1}. Calculate the molar concentration of HCl.

ANALYSIS: Recall the definitions of percentage by mass and molarity. We must perform the following conversion:

$$\frac{36.0 \text{ g HCl}}{100 \text{ g HCl soln}} \quad \text{to} \quad \frac{? \text{ mol HCl}}{1 \text{ L HCl soln}}$$

We have two conversions to perform:
- The numerators show that we need a grams-to-moles conversion for the solute, HCl. The link between grams and moles is the molar mass (36.46 g mol^{-1} for HCl).
- The denominators tell us that we must carry out a grams-to-liters conversion for the HCl solution, which is why we need the solution's density. Remember from Chapter 1 that *density is the link between a substance's mass and volume.* We can write

$$1.19 \text{ g HCl soln} \Leftrightarrow 1.00 \text{ mL HCl soln}$$

To complete the conversion we'll have to change milliliters to liters.

SOLUTION: We can do the conversions in either order. Here, we've converted the numerator first:

$$\frac{36.0 \text{ g HCl}}{100 \text{ g HCl soln}} \times \frac{1 \text{ mol HCl}}{36.46 \text{ g HCl}} \times \frac{1.19 \text{ g HCl soln}}{1.00 \text{ mL HCl soln}} \times \frac{1000 \text{ mL HCl soln}}{1 \text{ L HCl soln}} = 11.7 \, M \text{ HCl}$$

So 36.0% HCl is also 11.8 *M* HCl.

IS THE ANSWER REASONABLE? We can estimate the answer in our head. First cancel the 36 g HCl in the numerator and the 36.46 g HCl in the denominator to give 1.0 (shown in red below). Now we divide 1000 in the numerator by 100 in the denominator to get 10 (shown in blue). All that is left is $1.19 \times 10 = 11.9$ *M* as shown below.

$$\frac{36.0 \text{ g HCl}}{100 \text{ g HCl soln}} \times \frac{1 \text{ mol HCl}}{36.46 \text{ g HCl}} \times \frac{1.19 \text{ g HCl soln}}{1.00 \text{ mL HCl soln}} \times \frac{1000 \text{ mL HCl soln}}{1 \text{ L HCl soln}} = 11.9 \, M \text{ HCl}$$

This is very close to our calculator answer and we can assume we did the calculation correctly.

Practice Exercise 11: Hydrobromic acid can be purchased as 40.0% HBr. The density of this solution is 1.38 g mL^{-1}. What is the molar concentration of HBr in this solution?

Practice Exercise 12: One gram of $Al(NO_3)_3$ is dissolved in 1.00 liter of water at 20 °C. The density of water at this temperature is 0.9982 g cm^{-3} and the density of the resulting solution is 0.9989 g cm^{-3}. Calculate the molarity and molality of this solution. (Hint: remember that density can be used to convert mass to volume.)

Practice Exercise 12 illustrated that when the concentration of an aqueous solution is very low, one gram per liter for example, the molality and the molarity are very close to the same numerical value. As a result we can conveniently interchange molality and molarity when aqueous solutions are very dilute.

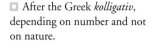

12.6 SOLUTES LOWER THE VAPOR PRESSURE OF A SOLVENT

□ After the Greek *kolligativ*, depending on number and not on nature.

The physical properties of solutions to be studied in this and succeeding sections are called **colligative properties,** because they depend mostly on the relative *populations* of particles in mixtures, not on their chemical identities. In this section, we examine the effects of solutes on the vapor pressures of solvents in liquid solutions.

All liquid solutions of **nonvolatile** solutes (solutes that have no tendency to evaporate) have lower vapor pressures than their pure solvents. The vapor pressure of such a solution is proportional to how much of the solution actually consists of the solvent. This proportionality is given by **Raoult's law** (also known as the **Vapor Pressure–Concentration law**) which says that the vapor pressure of the solution, P_{solution}, equals the mole fraction of the solvent, X_{solvent}, multiplied by its vapor pressure when pure, $P^{\circ}_{\text{solvent}}$. In equation form, Raoult's law is expressed as follows.

□ Francois Marie Raoult (1830–1901) was a French scientist.

TOOLS
Raoult's law

> **Raoult's law equation**
>
> $$P_{\text{solution}} = X_{\text{solvent}} P^{\circ}_{\text{solvent}}$$

Because of the form of this equation, a plot of P_{solution} versus X_{solvent} should be *linear* at all concentrations when the system obeys Raoult's law (see Figure 12.12).

Notice that the mole fraction in Raoult's law refers to the solvent, not the solute. Usually we're more interested in the effect of the *solute's* mole fraction concentration, X_{solute}, on the vapor pressure. We can show that the change in vapor pressure, ΔP, is directly proportional to the mole fraction of solute, X_{solute}, as follows.[4]

$$\Delta P = X_{solute} P^\circ_{solvent} \qquad (12.3)$$

The change in vapor pressure equals the mole fraction of the solute times the solvent's vapor pressure when pure.

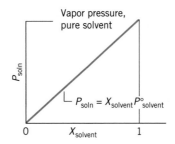

FIG. 12.12 A Raoult's law plot. When the vapor pressure of a solution is plotted against the mole fraction of the solvent, the result is a straight line.

EXAMPLE 12.6
Calculating with Raoult's Law

Carbon tetrachloride has a vapor pressure of 100 torr at 23 °C. This solvent can dissolve candle wax, which is essentially nonvolatile. Although candle wax is a mixture, we can take its molecular formula to be $C_{22}H_{46}$ (molar mass 311 g mol^{-1}). What is the vapor pressure at 23 °C of a solution prepared by dissolving 10.0 g of wax in 40.0 g of CCl_4 (molar mass 154 g mol^{-1})?

ANALYSIS: This problem involves the vapor pressure of a solution and so we need Equation 12.3. We need the mole fraction of the *solute* to use the equation, so we must first calculate the total number of moles of solute and solvent.

SOLUTION: First we calculate the moles of each component.

For CCl_4 $\qquad 40.0 \text{ g CCl}_4 \times \dfrac{1 \text{ mol CCl}_4}{154 \text{ g CCl}_4} = 0.260 \text{ mol CCl}_4$

For $C_{22}H_{46}$ $\qquad 10.0 \text{ g C}_{22}\text{H}_{46} \times \dfrac{1 \text{ mol C}_{22}\text{H}_{46}}{311 \text{ g C}_{22}\text{H}_{46}} = 0.0322 \text{ mol C}_{22}\text{H}_{46}$

The total number of moles = 0.292 mol

Now, we can calculate the mole fraction of the solute, $C_{22}H_{46}$.

$$X_{C_{22}H_{46}} = \frac{0.0322 \text{ mol}}{0.292 \text{ mol}} = 0.110$$

The amount that the vapor pressure is lowered, ΔP, will be this particular mole fraction, 0.110, times the vapor pressure of pure CCl_4 (100 torr), calculated by Equation 12.3.

$$\Delta P = 0.110 \times 100 \text{ torr} = 11.0 \text{ torr}$$

The presence of the wax in the CCl_4 lowers the vapor pressure of the CCl_4 by 11.0 torr from 100 to 89 torr.

---

[4] To derive Equation 12.3, note that the value of ΔP is simply the following difference.

$$\Delta P = P^\circ_{solvent} - P_{solution}$$

The mole fractions for our two-component system, $X_{solvent}$ and X_{solute}, must add up to 1; it's the nature of mole fractions.

$$X_{solvent} = 1 - X_{solute}$$

We now insert this expression for $X_{solvent}$ into the Raoult's law equation.

$$P_{solution} = X_{solvent} P^\circ_{solvent}$$
$$P_{solution} = (1 - X_{solute})P^\circ_{solvent} = P^\circ_{solvent} - X_{solute} P^\circ_{solvent}$$

So, by rearranging terms,

$$X_{solute} P^\circ_{solvent} = P^\circ_{solvent} - P_{solution} = \Delta P$$

This result can be rearranged again to give Equation 12.3.

IS THE ANSWER REASONABLE? Raoult's law implies that *the vapor pressure of a solvent in a solution must be less than that of the pure solvent.* Our answer does show a lowering of the vapor pressure of CCl_4 in the wax solution. We could also apply the Raoult's law equation directly; we multiply the mole fraction of the *solvent* by the vapor pressure of the solvent. The mole fraction of the solvent must be 1 minus 0.11 (the other mole fraction) or 0.89. Taking 0.89 times 100 torr gives 89 torr, which is our answer.

Practice Exercise 13: Dibutyl phthalate, $C_{16}H_{22}O_4$ (molecular mass 278 g mol^{-1}), is an oil sometimes used to soften plastic articles. Its vapor pressure is negligible around room temperature. What is the vapor pressure, at 20 °C, of a solution of 20.0 g of dibutyl phthalate in 50.0 g of octane, C_8H_{18} (molecular mass 114 g mol^{-1})? The vapor pressure of pure octane at 20 °C is 10.5 torr. (Hint: Calculate mole fractions first.)

Practice Exercise 14: Acetone (molar mass 58.1 g mol^{-1}) has a vapor pressure at a given temperature of 162 torr. How many grams of the nonvolatile stearic acid (molar mass 284.5 g mol^{-1}) must be added to 156 g of acetone to decrease its vapor pressure to 150 torr?

A molecular explanation can be provided for Raoult's law

How does a nonvolatile solute lower the vapor pressure of the solvent in a solution? Consider the following analogy. Imagine a crowded stadium, filled to capacity. The stadium has separate restrooms for men and women. Men will be entering and leaving the men's restrooms at a certain rate. The rate will depend on the number of men in the stadium. If 50% of the people in the stadium are men, we expect the men's restrooms to be twice as busy as it would be if only 25% of the people were men. In other words, increasing the concentration of women in the stadium lowers the amount of traffic in and out of the men's rooms. Increasing the number of women in the stadium also lowers the number of men occupying the men's restrooms, on average.

In our analogy, the stadium and the men's restrooms represent the solution and vapor phases. The men represent the solvent molecules and the women represent nonvolatile solute. Adding a nonvolatile solute to a solution will lower the evaporation rate of the solvent, just as increasing the fraction of women in the stadium will decrease traffic to the men's restrooms. Increasing the concentration of solute lowers the number of solvent molecules in the vapor phase, on average, just as increasing the fraction of women in the stadium lowers the number of men occupying the men's rooms. If the number of solvent molecules in the vapor phase is lowered, the partial pressure of the solvent above the solution is lowered, as well. The effect is shown in Figure 12.13.

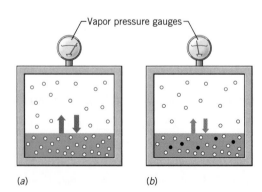

FIG. 12.13 **Effect of a nonvolatile solute on the vapor pressure of a solvent.** (*a*) Equilibrium between a pure solvent and its vapor. With a high number of solvent molecules in the liquid phase, the rates of evaporation and condensation are relatively high. (*b*) In the solution, some of the solvent molecules have been replaced with solute molecules. There are fewer solvent molecules available to evaporate from solution. The evaporation rate is lower. When equilibrium is established, there are fewer molecules in the vapor. The vapor pressure of the solution is less than that of the pure solvent.

How can we predict the vapor pressure of a solution that contains more than one volatile component?

When two (or more) components of a liquid solution can evaporate, the vapor contains molecules of each substance. Each volatile component contributes its own partial pressure to the total pressure. By Raoult's law, the partial pressure of a particular component is directly proportional to the component's mole fraction in the solution. By Dalton's law of partial pressures, the total vapor pressure will be the sum of the partial pressures. To calculate these partial pressures, we use the Raoult's law equation for each component. When component A is present in a mole fraction of X_A, its partial pressure (P_A) is this fraction of its vapor pressure when pure, namely, P_A°.

$$P_A = X_A P_A^\circ$$

And, by the same argument, P_B, the partial pressure of component B, is

$$P_B = X_B P_B^\circ$$

☐ Remember, P_A and P_B here are the *partial* pressures as calculated by Raoult's law.

The total vapor pressure of the solution of liquids A and B is then, by Dalton's law of partial pressures, the sum of P_A and P_B.

$$P_{\text{total}} = X_A P_A^\circ + X_B P_B^\circ$$

Notice that this equation contains the Raoult's law equation as a special case. If one component, say, component B, is nonvolatile, it has no vapor pressure (P_B° is zero) so the $X_B P_B^\circ$ term drops out, leaving the Raoult's law equation.

EXAMPLE 12.7
Calculating the Vapor Pressure of a Solution of Two Volatile Liquids

Acetone is a solvent for both water and molecular liquids that do not dissolve in water, like benzene. At 20 °C, acetone has a vapor pressure of 162 torr. The vapor pressure of water at 20 °C is 17.5 torr. Assuming that the mixture obeys Raoult's law, what would be the vapor pressure of a solution of acetone and water with 50.0 mol% of each?

ANALYSIS: To find P_{total} we need to calculate the individual partial pressures and then add them.

SOLUTION: A concentration of 50.0 mol% corresponds to a mole fraction of 0.500, so

$$P_{\text{acetone}} = 0.500 \times 162 \text{ torr} = 81.0 \text{ torr}$$

$$P_{\text{water}} = 0.500 \times 17.5 \text{ torr} = \underline{8.75 \text{ torr}}$$

$$P_{\text{total}} = 89.8 \text{ torr}$$

IS THE ANSWER REASONABLE? The vapor pressure of the solution (89.8 torr) has to be much higher than that of pure water (17.5 torr), because of the volatile acetone, but much less than that of pure acetone (162 torr), because of the high mole fraction of water. The answer seems reasonable.

Practice Exercise 15: At 20 °C, the vapor pressure of cyclohexane, a hydrocarbon solvent, is 66.9 torr and that of toluene (another solvent) is 21.1 torr. What is the vapor pressure of a solution of the two at 20 °C when the mole fraction of toluene is 0.250? (Hint: Recall that the sum of the all mole fractions in a mixture must add up to 1.00.)

Practice Exercise 16: Using the information from the exercise above, calculate the expected vapor pressure of a mixture of cyclohexane and toluene that consists of 100.0 grams of each solvent.

Only ideal solutions obey Raoult's law exactly. The vapor pressures of components over real solutions are sometimes higher or sometimes lower than Raoult's law would predict. These differences between ideal and real solution behavior are quite useful. They can tell us whether the attractive forces in the pure solvents, before mixing, are stronger or weaker than the attractive forces in the mixture. Comparing experimental vapor pressures with the predictions of Raoult's law provides a simple way to compare the relative strengths of attractions between molecules in solution. When the attractions between unlike molecules in the mixture are strongest, the experimental vapor pressure will be lower than calculated with Raoult's law. Conversely, when the attractions between identical molecules in the pure solvents are strongest, the experimental vapor pressure is higher than Raoult's law would predict.

12.7 | SOLUTIONS HAVE LOWER MELTING POINTS AND HIGHER BOILING POINTS THAN PURE SOLVENTS

The lowering of the vapor pressure produced by the presence of a nonvolatile solute affects both the boiling and freezing points of a solution. This is illustrated for water in Figure 12.14.

The solid blue lines in the figure correspond to the three equilibrium lines in the phase diagram for pure water, which we discussed in Section 11.12. Adding a nonvolatile solute lowers the vapor pressure of the solution, giving a new liquid–vapor equilibrium line for the solution, which is shown as the red line connecting points A and B.

When the solution freezes, the solid that forms is pure ice; there is no solute within the ice crystals. This is because the highly ordered structure of the solid doesn't allow solute molecules to take the place of water molecules. As a result, both pure water and the solution

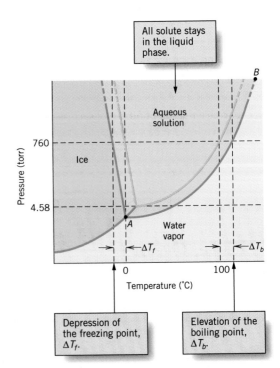

FIG. 12.14 Phase diagram for water and an aqueous solution. Phase diagram for pure water (blue curves) and for an aqueous solution of a nonvolatile solute (red curves).

TABLE 12.3	**Molal Boiling Point Elevation and Freezing Point Depression Constants**			
Solvent	BP (°C)	K_b (°C m^{-1})	MP (°C)	K_f (°C m^{-1})
Water	100	0.51	0	1.86
Acetic acid	118.3	3.07	16.6	3.57
Benzene	80.2	2.53	5.45	5.07
Chloroform	61.2	3.63	—	—
Camphor	—	—	178.4	37.7
Cyclohexane	80.7	2.69	6.5	20.0

BP = normal boiling point; MP = normal melting point.

have the same solid–vapor equilibrium line on the phase diagram. Point A on the diagram is at the intersection of the liquid–vapor and solid–vapor equilibrium lines for the solution and represents the new triple point for the solution. Rising from this triple point is the solid–liquid equilibrium line for the solution, shown in red.

If we look at where the solid–liquid and liquid–vapor lines cross the 1 atm (760 torr) pressure line, we can find the normal freezing and boiling points. For water (the blue lines), the freezing point is 0 °C and the boiling point is 100 °C. Notice that the solid–liquid line for the solution meets the 760 torr line at a temperature *below* 0 °C. In other words, the freezing point of the solution is below that of pure water. The amount by which the freezing point is lowered is called the **freezing point depression,** and is given the symbol ΔT_f. Similarly, we can see that the liquid–vapor line for the solution crosses the 760 torr line at a temperature *above* 100 °C, so the solution boils at a higher temperature than pure water. The amount by which the boiling point is raised is called the **boiling point elevation.** It is given the symbol ΔT_b.

□ Recall that the normal boiling and freezing points are those at a pressure of 1 atm.

ΔT_f and ΔT_b are related to the molality of the solute

Freezing point depression and boiling point elevation are both colligative properties. The magnitudes of ΔT_f and ΔT_b are proportional to the relative populations of solute and solvent molecules. Molality (m) is the preferred concentration expression (rather than mole fraction or percent by mass) because of the resulting simplicity of the equations relating ΔT to concentration. The following equations work reasonably well only for dilute solutions, however.

□ There are many practical applications of freezing point depression and boiling point elevation. For example, antifreeze solutions are added to the radiator of a car to prevent freezing in winter and boiling over in summer. Similarly, salt is spread on icy roads to cause the ice to melt and salt is mixed with ice to decrease the temperature in home ice cream machines.

$$\Delta T_f = K_f m \qquad (12.4)$$

$$\Delta T_b = K_b m \qquad (12.5)$$

TOOLS
Freezing point depression, boiling point elevation, determination of molar mass

K_f and K_b are proportionality constants and are called, respectively, the **molal freezing point depression constant** and the **molal boiling point elevation constant.** The values of both K_f and K_b are characteristic of each solvent (see Table 12.3). The units of each constant are °C m^{-1}. Thus, the value of K_f for a given solvent corresponds to the number of degrees of freezing point lowering for each molal unit of concentration. The K_f for water is 1.86 °C m^{-1}. A 1.00 m solution in water freezes at 1.86 °C *below* the normal freezing point of 0 °C, or at −1.86 °C. A 2.00 m solution should freeze at −3.72 °C. (We say "should" but systems are seldom this ideal.) Similarly, because K_b for water is 0.51 °C m^{-1}, a 1.00 m aqueous solution at 1 atm pressure boils at (100 + 0.51) °C or 100.51 °C, and a 2.00 m solution should boil at 101.02 °C.

EXAMPLE 12.8
Estimating a Freezing Point Using a Colligative Property

Estimate the freezing point of a solution made from 10.0 g of urea, $CO(NH_2)_2$ (molar mass 60.06 g mol^{-1}), and 125 g of water.

ANALYSIS: Equation 12.4 relates concentration to freezing point depression. To use the equation, we must first calculate the molality of the solution.

SOLUTION: Molality is the ratio of moles of solute to kilograms of solvent, so we'll convert grams of urea to moles.

$$10.0 \ \cancel{g \ CO(NH_2)_2} \times \frac{1 \ mol \ CO(NH_2)_2}{60.06 \ \cancel{g \ CO(NH_2)_2}} = 0.166 \ mol \ CO(NH_2)_2$$

This is the number of moles of $CO(NH_2)_2$ in 125 g or 0.125 kg of water, so the molality is given by

$$Molality = \frac{0.166 \ mol}{0.125 \ kg} = 1.33 \ m$$

For our estimate we must next use Equation 12.4 although it is most reliably used only for dilute solutions. Table 12.3 tells us that K_f for water is $1.86 \ °C \ m^{-1}$.

$$\Delta T_f = K_f m = (1.86 \ °C \ \cancel{m^{-1}})(1.33 \ \cancel{m})$$

$$= 2.47 \ °C$$

The solution should freeze at 2.47 °C below 0 °C, or at −2.47 °C.

IS THE ANSWER REASONABLE? For every unit of molality, the freezing point must be depressed by about 2 °C. The molality of this solution is between 1 m and 2 m, so we expect the freezing point depression to be between about 2 °C and 4 °C. It is.

Practice Exercise 17: At what temperature will a 10% aqueous solution of sugar ($C_{12}H_{22}O_{11}$) boil? (Hint: Recall that the boiling point elevation is a change in temperature.)

Practice Exercise 18: How many grams of glucose (molar mass 180.2 g mol^{-1}) must be dissolved in 250 g of water to raise the boiling point to 102.36 °C?

Freezing point depression and boiling point elevation can be used to determine molar masses

We have described freezing point depression and boiling point elevation as *colligative* properties; they depend on the relative *numbers* of particles, not on their kinds. Because the effects are proportional to molal concentrations, experimentally measured values of ΔT_f or ΔT_b can be useful for calculating the molar masses of unknown solutes, as illustrated in the following example.

EXAMPLE 12.9

Calculating a Molar Mass from Freezing Point Depression Data

A solution made by dissolving 5.65 g of an unknown molecular compound in 110.0 g of benzene froze at 4.39 °C. What is the molar mass of the solute?

ANALYSIS: *To calculate the molar mass, we need to know two things about the same sample, the number of moles and the number of grams.* Dividing grams by moles gives the number of grams per mole, which is the molar mass. In this example, we've been given the number of grams, and we have to use the remaining data to calculate the number of moles.

We can use the value of ΔT_f (the difference between the freezing point of pure benzene and that of the solution) along with the value of K_f for benzene from Table 12.3 to calculate the molality of the solution. This gives the ratio of moles of solute to kilograms of benzene, which we can then use as a conversion factor to calculate the number of moles dissolved in the 110.0 g of benzene.

SOLUTION: Table 12.3 tells us that the melting point of benzene is 5.45 °C and that the value of K_f for benzene is $5.07 \ °C \ m^{-1}$. The amount of freezing point depression is

$$\Delta T_f = 5.45\ ^\circ C - 4.39\ ^\circ C = 1.06\ ^\circ C$$

We now use Equation 12.4 to find the molality of the solution.

$$\Delta T_f = K_f m$$

$$\text{Molality} = \frac{\Delta T_f}{K_f} = \frac{1.06\ ^\circ\!\!\!\!\!\diagup C}{5.07\ ^\circ\!\!\!\!\!\diagup C\ m^{-1}} = 0.209\ m$$

This means that for every kilogram of benzene in the solution, there are 0.209 mol of solute. But we have only 110.0 g or 0.1100 kg of benzene. So the actual number of moles of solute in the given solution is found by

$$0.1100\ \text{kg benzene} \times \frac{0.209\ \text{mol solute}}{1\ \text{kg benzene}} = 0.0230\ \text{mol solute}$$

We can now obtain the molar mass. There are 5.65 g of solute per 0.0230 mol of solute:

$$\frac{5.65\ g}{0.0230\ mol} = 246\ g\ mol^{-1}$$

The mass of one mole of the solute is 246 g.

IS THE ANSWER REASONABLE? A common mistake to avoid is using the given value of the freezing point, 4.39 °C, in Equation 12.4, instead of calculating ΔT_f. A check shows that we *have* calculated ΔT_f correctly. The ratio of ΔT_f to K_f is about 1/5, or 0.2 *m*, which corresponds to a ratio of 0.2 mol solute per 1 kg of benzene. The solution prepared has only 0.1 kg of solvent, so to have the same ratio, the amount of solute must be about 0.02 mol (2×10^{-2} mol). The sample weighs about 5 g, and dividing 5 g by 2×10^{-2} mol gives 2.5×10^2 g/mol, or 250 g/mol. This is very close to the answer we obtained, so we can feel confident it's correct.

Practice Exercise 19: A solution made by dissolving 3.46 g of an unknown compound in 85.0 g of benzene froze at 4.13 °C. What is the molar mass of the compound? (Hint: Recall the equation for calculating moles of a substance to find the key relationship.)

Practice Exercise 20: A mixture is prepared that is 5.0% (w/w) of an unknown substance mixed with naphthalene (molar mass 128.2 g mol^{-1}). The freezing point of the mixture is found to be 77.3 °C. What is the molar mass of the unknown substance? (The melting point of naphthalene is 80.2 °C and $K_f = 6.9\ ^\circ C$.)

12.8 OSMOSIS IS A FLOW OF SOLVENT THROUGH A SEMIPERMEABLE MEMBRANE DUE TO UNEQUAL CONCENTRATIONS

In living things, membranes of various kinds keep mixtures and solutions organized and separated. Yet some substances have to be able to pass through membranes in order that nutrients and products of chemical work can be distributed correctly. These membranes, in other words, must have a selective *permeability*. They must keep some substances from going through while letting others pass. Such membranes are said to be *semipermeable*.

The degree of permeability varies with the kind of membrane. Cellophane, for example, is permeable to water and small solute particles—ions or molecules—but impermeable to very large molecules, like those of starch or proteins. Special membranes can even be prepared that are permeable only to water, not to any solutes.

Depending on the kind of membrane separating solutions of different concentration, two similar phenomena, *dialysis* and *osmosis*, can be observed. Both are functions of the relative populations of the particles of the dissolved materials, so they are colligative properties.

When a membrane is able to let both water and *small* solute particles through, such as the membranes in living systems, the process is called **dialysis,** and the membrane is called a *dialyzing membrane.* It does not permit huge molecules through, like those of proteins and starch. Artificial kidney machines use dialyzing membranes to help remove the smaller molecules of wastes from the blood while letting the blood retain its large protein molecules.

Osmosis involves the movement of solvent across a membrane

When a semipermeable membrane will let only solvent molecules get through, this movement is called *osmosis*, and the special membrane needed to observe it is called an **osmotic membrane.**

When **osmosis** occurs, there's a net shift of solvent across the membrane from the more dilute solution (or pure solvent) into the more concentrated solution. This happens because there is a tendency toward the equalization of concentrations between the two solutions in contact with one another across the membrane. The rate of passage of solvent molecules through the membrane into the more concentrated solution is greater than their rate of passage in the opposite direction, presumably because at the surface of the membrane the solvent concentration is greater in the more dilute solution (Figure 12.15*a*). This leads to a gradual net flow of water through the membrane into the more concentrated solution.

We observe an effect similar to osmosis if two solutions with unequal concentrations of a nonvolatile solute are placed in a sealed container (Figure 12.15*b*). The rate of evaporation from the more dilute solution is greater than that of the more concentrated solution, but the rate of return to each is the same because both solutions are in contact with the same gas phase. As a result, neither solution is in equilibrium with the vapor. In the dilute solution, molecules of solvent are evaporating faster than they're condensing. But in the concentrated solution, just the opposite occurs; more water molecules return to the solution than leave it. Therefore, over time there is a gradual net transfer of solvent from the dilute solution into the more concentrated one until they both achieve the same concentration.

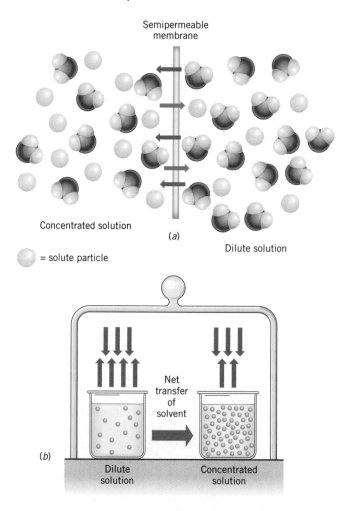

FIG. 12.15 **Principles at work in osmosis.** (*a*) Osmosis. Solvent molecules pass more frequently from the more dilute solution into the more concentrated one, as indicated by the arrows. This leads to a gradual transfer of solvent from the less concentrated solution into the more concentrated one. (*b*) Because the two solutions have unequal vapor pressures, there is a gradual net transfer of solvent from the more dilute solution into the more concentrated one.

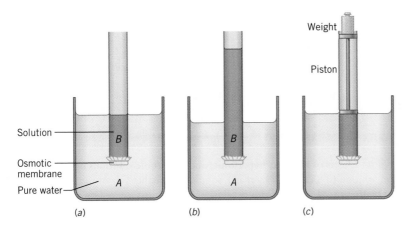

FIG. 12.16 Osmosis and osmotic pressure. (*a*) Initial conditions. A solution, *B*, is separated from pure water, *A*, by an osmotic membrane; no osmosis has yet occurred. (*b*) After a while, the volume of fluid in the tube has increased visibly. Osmosis has taken place. (*c*) A back-pressure is needed to prevent osmosis. The amount of back-pressure is the osmotic pressure of the solution.

Applying pressure to a solution can prevent osmosis

An osmosis experiment is illustrated in Figure 12.16. Initially, we have a solution (*B*) in a tube fitted with an osmotic membrane that dips into a container of pure water (*A*). As time passes, the volume of liquid in the tube increases as solvent molecules transfer into the solution. In Figure 12.16*b*, the net transport of water into the solution has visibly increased the volume.

The weight of the rising fluid column in Figure 12.16*b* provides a push or opposing pressure that makes it increasingly more difficult for molecules of water to enter the solution. Eventually, this pressure becomes sufficient to stop the osmosis. If we apply further pressure, as illustrated in Figure 12.16*c*, we can force enough water back through the membrane to restore the system to its original condition. The exact opposing pressure needed to prevent any osmotic flow *when one of the liquids is pure solvent* is called the **osmotic pressure** of the solution.

Notice that the term "osmotic pressure" uses the word *pressure* in a novel way. Apart from osmosis, a solution does not "have" a special pressure called osmotic pressure. What the solution has is a *concentration* that can generate the occurrence of osmosis and the associated osmotic pressure under the right circumstances. Then, in proportion to the solution's concentration, a specific back-pressure is required to prevent osmosis. By *exceeding* this back-pressure, osmosis can be reversed. *Reverse osmosis* is widely used to purify seawater, both on ocean-going ships and in remote locations where fresh water is unavailable.

The symbol for osmotic pressure is the Greek capital pi, Π. In a dilute aqueous solution, Π is proportional both to temperature, *T*, and molar concentration of the solute in the solution, *M*:

$$\Pi \propto MT$$

The proportionality constant turns out to be the gas constant, *R*, so for a *dilute* aqueous solution we can write

$$\Pi = MRT \qquad (12.6)$$

Of course, *M* is the ratio mol/L, which we can write as n/V, where *n* is the number of moles and *V* is the volume in liters. If we replace *M* with n/V in Equation 12.6, and rearrange terms, we have an equation for osmotic pressure identical in form to the ideal gas law.

$$\Pi V = nRT \qquad (12.7)$$

Equation 12.7 is the *van't Hoff equation for osmotic pressure*.

Osmotic pressure is of tremendous importance in biology and medicine. Cells are surrounded with membranes that restrict the flow of salts but allow water to pass through freely. To maintain a constant amount of water, the osmotic pressure of solutions on either side of the cell membrane must be identical. For example, a solution that is 0.9% (w/v) NaCl has the same osmotic pressure as the contents of red blood cells, and red blood cells bathed in this solution can maintain their normal water content. The solution is said to be isotonic with red blood cells. Blood plasma is an **isotonic solution.**

☐ Reverse osmosis systems are available at home centers for home use. They can be installed to remove impurities and foul tastes from drinking water. Some bottled water available on supermarket shelves contains water that's been purified by reverse osmosis.

TOOLS
Osmotic pressure, determination of molar mass

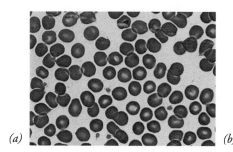

(a)

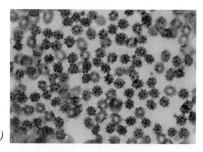

(b)

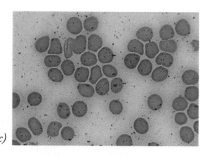

(c)

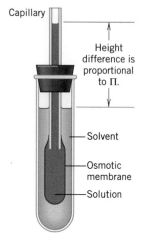

FIG. 12.18 Simple osmometer. When solvent moves into the solution by osmosis, the level of the solution in the capillary rises. The height reached can be related to the osmotic pressure of the solution.

FIG. 12.17 **Effects of isotonic, hypertonic, and hypotonic solutions on red blood cells.** (*a*) In an isotonic solution (0.85% NaCl by mass), solutions on either side of the membrane have the same osmotic pressure, and there is no net flow of water across the cell membrane. (*b*) In this hypertonic solution (5.0% NaCl by mass), water flows from areas of lower salt concentration (inside the cell) to higher concentration (the hypertonic solution), causing the cell to dehydrate. (*c*) In this hypotonic solution (0.1% NaCl by mass), water flows from areas of lower salt concentration (the hypotonic solution) to higher concentration (inside the cell). The cells swell and burst. (*(a), (b),* and *(c) Dennis Strete/Fundamental Photographs.*)

If the cell is placed in a solution with a salt concentration higher than the concentration within the cell, osmosis causes water to flow out of the cell. Such a solution is said to be **hypertonic.** The cell shrinks and dehydrates, and eventually dies. This process kills freshwater fish and plants that are washed out to sea.

On the other hand, water will flow into the cell if it is placed into a solution with an osmotic pressure that is much lower than the osmotic pressure of the cell's contents. Such a solution is called a **hypotonic solution.** A cell placed in distilled water, for example, will swell and burst. If you've ever tried to put in a pair of contact lenses with tap water instead of an isotonic saline solution, you've experienced cell damage from a hypotonic solution. The effects of isotonic, hypotonic, and hypertonic solutions on cells are shown in Figure 12.17.

Obviously, the measurement of osmotic pressure can be very important in preparing solutions that will be used to culture tissues or to administer medicines intravenously. Osmotic pressures can be measured by an instrument called an *osmometer,* illustrated and explained in Figure 12.18. Osmotic pressures can be very high, even in dilute solutions, as Example 12.10 shows.

EXAMPLE 12.10
Calculating an Osmotic Pressure

A very dilute solution, 0.00100 *M* sugar in water, is separated from pure water by an osmotic membrane. What osmotic pressure in torr develops at 25 °C?

ANALYSIS: This is nothing more than an application of Equation 12.6. However, we must be sure to use $R = 0.0821$ L atm mol^{-1} K^{-1}, otherwise the units won't work out correctly.

SOLUTION: Substituting into Equation 12.6, being sure to use the temperature in kelvins so the units cancel correctly,

$$\Pi = (0.00100 \text{ mol L}^{-1})(0.0821 \text{ L atm mol}^{-1} \text{ K}^{-1})(298 \text{ K})$$
$$= 0.0245 \text{ atm}$$

In torr we have

$$\Pi = 0.0245 \text{ atm} \times \frac{760 \text{ torr}}{1 \text{ atm}} = 18.6 \text{ torr}$$

The osmotic pressure of 0.00100 *M* sugar in water is 18.6 torr.

IS THE ANSWER REASONABLE? A 1 *M* solution should have an osmotic pressure of *RT.* Rounding the gas law constant to 0.08 and the temperature to 300, the osmotic pressure of a 1 *M* solution should be about 24 atm. The osmotic pressure of an 0.001 *M* solution should be 1/1000 of this, or about 0.024 atm, which is fairly close to what we got before we converted to torr.

Practice Exercise 21: What is the osmotic pressure, in mm Hg and mm water, of a protein solution when 5.00 g of the protein (molar mass 230,000 g mol^{-1}) is used to prepare 100.0 mL of an aqueous solution at 4.0 °C? (Hint: The height of a column of liquid supported by any pressure is inversely proportional to the density of the liquid. The equivalence to use is 1 torr = 13.6 mm H$_2$O.)

Practice Exercise 22: An aqueous solution of glucose (C$_6$H$_{12}$O$_6$) has an osmotic pressure of 42.5 torr at 25 °C. How many grams of glucose are in 125 mL of this solution?

In the preceding example, you saw that a 0.00100 M solution of sugar has an osmotic pressure of 18.6 torr, which is equivalent to 18.6 mm Hg. This pressure is sufficient to support a column of the solution (which is mostly water) roughly 25 cm or 10 in. high. If the solution had been 100 times as concentrated, 0.100 M sugar—still relatively dilute—the height of the column supported would be roughly 25 m or over 80 ft!

Molar mass can be estimated from osmotic pressure measurements

An osmotic pressure measurement taken of a dilute solution can be used to determine the molar concentration of the solute, regardless of its chemical composition. Such data along with the mass of the solute in the solution permits us to calculate the molar mass.

Determination of molar mass by osmotic pressure is much more sensitive than determination by freezing point depression or boiling point elevation. The following example illustrates the method.

> **EXAMPLE 12.11**
> Calculating Molar Mass from Osmotic Pressure

An aqueous solution with a volume of 100 mL and containing 0.122 g of an unknown molecular compound has an osmotic pressure of 16.0 torr at 21.0 °C. What is the molar mass of the solute?

ANALYSIS: As we noted in Example 12.9, to determine a molar mass we need to measure two quantities for the same sample, its mass and the number of moles. Then, the molar mass is the ratio of grams to moles. We're given the number of *grams* of the solute, so we need to find the number of *moles* equivalent to this mass in order to compute the ratio.

We can use Equation 12.6 to find the molarity of the solute from the osmotic pressure and the temperature. In the calculation, we have to remember to use $R = 0.0821$ L atm mol^{-1} K^{-1}. Then we can use the given volume of the solution (in liters) and the molarity to calculate the number of moles of solute. This is how many moles are in the 0.122 g of solute. Finally, we can calculate the molar mass by dividing grams of solute by moles of solute.

SOLUTION: First, the solution's molarity, M, is calculated using the osmotic pressure. This pressure (Π), 16.0 torr, corresponds to 0.0211 atm. The temperature, 20.1 °C, corresponds to 294 K (273 + 21). Using Equation 12.6,

$$\Pi = MRT$$
$$0.0211 \text{ atm} = (M)(0.0821 \text{ L atm mol}^{-1} \text{ K}^{-1})(294 \text{ K})$$
$$M = 8.74 \times 10^{-4} \text{ mol L}^{-1}$$

$$16.0 \text{ torr} \times \frac{1 \text{ atm}}{760 \text{ torr}}$$
$$= 0.0211 \text{ atm}$$

The 0.122 g of solute is in 100 mL or 0.100 L of solution, not in a whole liter. So the number of moles of solute corresponding to 0.122 g is found by

$$\text{Moles of solute} = 0.100 \text{ L soln} \times \frac{8.74 \times 10^{-4} \text{ mol}}{1 \text{ L soln}}$$
$$= 8.74 \times 10^{-5} \text{ mol}$$

The molar mass of the solute is the number of grams of solute per mole of solute:

$$\text{Molar mass} = \frac{0.122 \text{ g}}{8.74 \times 10^{-5} \text{ mol}} = 1.40 \times 10^3 \text{ g mol}^{-1}$$

IS THE ANSWER REASONABLE? In using Equation 12.6, it is essential that the pressure be in atmospheres when using $R = 0.0821$ L atm mol^{-1} K^{-1}. If all the units cancel correctly (and they do), we've computed the molarity correctly. We've also changed the volume of the solution to liters, so calculating the moles of solute seems to be okay. The moles of solute is approximately 10×10^{-5}, or 1×10^{-4}. Dividing the mass, roughly 0.12 g, by 1×10^{-4} mol gives 0.12×10^{4} g per mol or 1.2×10^{3} g per mol, which is close to the value we found.

Practice Exercise 23: Estimate the molecular mass of a protein when 0.137 g of the protein, dissolved in 100.0 mL of water at 4 °C, supports a column of water that is 6.45 cm high. The density of mercury is 13.6 g ml^{-1} (Hint: The answer should be very large. Don't forget to convert centimeters of water to atmospheres of pressure.)

Practice Exercise 24: A solution of a carbohydrate prepared by dissolving 72.4 mg in 100 mL of solution has an osmotic pressure of 25.0 torr at 25.0 °C. What is the molecular mass of the compound?

12.9 IONIC SOLUTES AFFECT COLLIGATIVE PROPERTIES DIFFERENTLY FROM NONIONIC SOLUTES

The molal freezing point depression constant for water is 1.86 °C m^{-1}. So you might think that a 1.00 m solution of NaCl would freeze at -1.86 °C. Instead, it freezes at -3.37 °C. This greater depression of the freezing point by the salt, which is almost twice 1.86 °C, is not hard to understand if we remember that colligative properties depend on the concentrations of *particles*. We know that NaCl(*s*) dissociates into two ions in water.

$$NaCl(s) \longrightarrow Na^+(aq) + Cl^-(aq)$$

If the ions are truly separated, 1.00 m NaCl actually has a concentration of dissolved solute particles of 2.00 m, twice the given molal concentration. Theoretically, 1.00 m NaCl should freeze at $2 \times (-1.86 °C)$ or -3.72 °C. (Why it actually freezes a little higher than this, at -3.37 °C, will be discussed shortly.)

If we made up a solution of 1.00 m $(NH_4)_2SO_4$, we would have to consider the following dissociation.

$$(NH_4)_2SO_4(s) \longrightarrow 2NH_4^+(aq) + SO_4^{2-}(aq)$$

One mole of $(NH_4)_2SO_4$ can give a total of 3 mol of ions (2 mol of NH_4^+ and 1 mol of SO_4^{2-}). We would expect the freezing point of a 1 m solution of $(NH_4)_2SO_4$ to be $3 \times (-1.86 °C) = -5.58$ °C.

When we want to roughly *estimate* a colligative property of a solution of an electrolyte, we recalculate the solution's molality using an assumption about the way the solute dissociates or ionizes.

EXAMPLE 12.12
Estimating the Freezing Point of a Salt Solution

Estimate the freezing point of aqueous 0.106 m $MgCl_2$, assuming that it dissociates completely.

ANALYSIS: The equation that relates a change in freezing temperature to molality is Equation 12.4.

$$\Delta T_f = K_f m$$

From Table 12.3, K_f for water is 1.86 °C m^{-1}. We cannot simply use 0.106 m as the molality because $MgCl_2$ is an ionic compound that dissociates in water. We must use the total molality of ions calculated from the equation for the dissociation.

SOLUTION: When $MgCl_2$ dissolves in water it breaks up as follows.

$$MgCl_2(s) \longrightarrow Mg^{2+}(aq) + 2Cl^-(aq)$$

Because 1 mol of $MgCl_2$ gives 3 mol of ions, the effective (assumed) molality of ions in the solution is three times 0.106 m.

$$\text{Effective molality} = (3)(0.106 \ m) = 0.318 \ m$$

Now we can use Equation 12.4.

$$\Delta T_f = (1.86 \ ^\circ C \ m^{-1})(0.318 \ m)$$

$$= 0.591 \ ^\circ C$$

The freezing point is depressed below 0.000 °C by 0.591 °C, so we calculate that this solution freezes at −0.591 °C.

IS THE ANSWER REASONABLE? The molality, as recalculated, is roughly 0.3, so 3/10th of 1.86 (call it 2) is 0.6. After we add the unit, °C, and subtract from 0 °C we get −0.6 °C, which is close to the answer.

Practice Exercise 25: Calculate the freezing point of aqueous 0.237 m LiCl on the assumption that it is 100% dissociated. Calculate what its freezing point would be if the percent dissociation were 0%. (Hint: Recall the relationship developed in Section 12.7.)

Practice Exercise 26: Determine the freezing point depression of aqueous solutions of $MgSO_4$ that are (a) 0.1 m, (b) 0.01 m, and (c) 0.001 m. Which of these could be measured with a laboratory thermometer that has markings at one °C intervals?

Percent ionization can be estimated from colligative property measurements

Experiments show that neither the 1.00 m NaCl nor the 1.00 m $(NH_4)_2SO_4$ solutions described earlier in this section freeze quite as low as calculated. Our assumption that an electrolyte separates *completely* into its ions is incorrect. Some oppositely charged ions exist as very closely associated pairs, called **ion pairs,** which behave as single "molecules" (Figure 12.19). Clusters larger than two ions probably also exist. The formation of ion pairs and clusters makes the actual *particle* concentration in a 1.00 m NaCl solution somewhat less than 2.00 m. As a result, the freezing point depression of 1.00 m NaCl is not quite as large as calculated on the basis of 100% dissociation.

As solutions of electrolytes are made more and more *dilute,* the observed and calculated freezing points come closer and closer together. At greater dilutions, the **association** (coming together) of ions is less a complication because the ions can be farther apart. So the solutes behave increasingly as if they were 100% separated into their ions at ever higher dilutions.

□ "Association" is the opposite of dissociation. It is the coming together of particles to form larger particles.

(a) 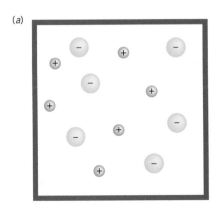 (b)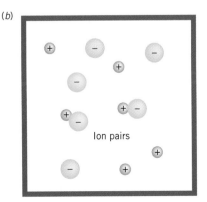

Ion pairs

FIG. 12.19 Ion pairs in a solution of NaCl. (*a*) If NaCl were completely dissociated in water, the Na^+ and Cl^- ions would be totally independent. (*b*) Interionic attractions cause some ions to group together as ion pairs, which reduces the total number of independent particles in the solution. In this diagram, two ion pairs are shown.

Chemists compare the degrees of dissociation of electrolytes at different dilutions by a quantity called the **van't Hoff factor, *i*.** It is the ratio of the observed freezing point depression to the value calculated on the assumption that the solute dissolves as a nonelectrolyte.

$$i = \frac{(\Delta T_f)_{\text{measured}}}{(\Delta T_f)_{\text{calculated as a nonelectrolyte}}}$$

The hypothetical van't Hoff factor, *i*, is 2 for NaCl, KCl, and $MgSO_4$, which break up into two ions on 100% dissociation. For K_2SO_4, the theoretical value of *i* is 3 because one K_2SO_4 unit gives 3 ions. The actual van't Hoff factors for several electrolytes at different dilutions are given in Table 12.4. Notice that with decreasing concentration (that is, at higher dilutions) the experimental van't Hoff factors agree better with their corresponding hypothetical van't Hoff factors.

TABLE 12.4 **Van't Hoff Factors versus Concentration**

| | Van't Hoff Factor, *i* | | | |
| | Molal Concentration $(mol_{\text{salt}}\ kg_{\text{water}}^{-1})$ | | | Value of *i* if 100% Dissociation Occurred |
Salt	0.1	0.01	0.001	
NaCl	1.87	1.94	1.97	2.00
KCl	1.85	1.94	1.98	2.00
K_2SO_4	2.32	2.70	2.84	3.00
$MgSO_4$	1.21	1.53	1.82	2.00

The increase in the percentage dissociation that comes with greater dilution is not the same for all salts. In going from concentrations of 0.1 to 0.001 *m*, the increase in percentage dissociation of KCl, as measured by the change in *i*, is only about 7%. But for K_2SO_4, the increase for the same dilution is about 22%, a difference caused by the anion, SO_4^{2-}. It has twice the charge as the anion in KCl and so the SO_4^{2-} ion attracts K^+ more strongly than can Cl^-. Hence, letting an ion of $2-$ charge and an ion of $1+$ charge get farther apart by dilution has a greater effect on their acting independently than giving ions of $1-$ and $1+$ charge more room. When *both* cation and anion are doubly charged, the improvement in percent dissociation with dilution is even greater. We can see from Table 12.4 that there is an almost 50% increase in the value of *i* for $MgSO_4$ as we go from a 0.1 to a 0.001 *m* solution.

Colligative properties provide evidence for clustering of solute particles

Some molecular solutes produce *weaker* colligative effects than their molal concentrations would lead us to predict. These unexpectedly weak colligative properties are often evidence that solute molecules are clustering or associating in solution. For example, when dissolved in benzene, benzoic acid molecules associate as **dimers.** They are held together by hydrogen bonds, indicated by the dotted lines in the following.

□ *Di*-signifies two, so a dimer is the result of the combination of two single molecules.

benzoic acid   benzoic acid dimer

□ C_6H_5 — means

Because of association, the depression of the freezing point of a 1.00 *m* solution of benzoic acid in benzene is only about one-half the calculated value. By forming a dimer, benzoic acid has an effective molecular mass that is twice as much as normally calculated. The larger effective molecular mass reduces the molal concentration of particles by half, and the effect on the freezing point depression is reduced by one-half.

SUMMARY

Solutions. Polar or ionic solutes generally dissolve well in polar solvents such as water. Nonpolar, molecular solutes dissolve well in nonpolar solvents. These observations are behind the **"like dissolves like" rule.** Nature's driving force for establishing the more statistically probable mixed state plus intermolecular attractions are the major factors in the formation of a solution. When both solute and solvent are nonpolar, nature's tendency toward the more probable mixed state dominates because intermolecular attractive forces are weak. Ion–dipole attractions and the **solvation** or **hydration** of dissolved species are major factors in forming solutions of ionic or polar solutes in something polar, like water.

Heats of Solution.
The **molar enthalpy of solution** of a solid in a liquid, also called the **heat of solution,** is the net of the **lattice energy** and the **solvation energy** (or, when water is the solvent, the **hydration energy**). The lattice energy is the increase in the potential energy of the system required to separate the molecules or ions of the solute from each other. The solvation energy corresponds to the potential energy lowering that occurs in the system from the subsequent attractions of those particles to the solvent molecules as intermingling occurs.

When liquids dissolve in liquids, an **ideal solution** forms if the potential energy increase needed to separate the molecules equals the energy lowering as the separated molecules come together. Usually, some net energy exchange occurs, however, and few solutions are ideal.

When a gas dissolves in a gas, the energy cost to separate the particles is virtually zero, because they're already separated. They remain separated in the gas mixture, so the net enthalpy of solution is very small if not zero. When a gas dissolves in an organic solvent, the solution process is often endothermic. When a gas dissolves in water, the solution process is often exothermic.

Pressure and Gas Solubility.
At pressures not too much different from atmospheric pressure, the solubility of a gas in a liquid is directly proportional to the partial pressure of the gas— **Henry's law.**

Concentration Expressions.
To study and use colligative properties, a solution's concentration ideally is expressed either in mole fractions or as a **molal concentration,** or **molality.** The **molality** of a solution, *m*, is the ratio of the number of moles of solute to the kilograms of *solvent* (not solution, but solvent). **Mass fractions** and **mass percents** are concentration expressions used often for reagents when direct information about number of moles of solutes is not considered important. Mole fraction, molality, and mass percent are temperature-independent concentration expressions.

Colligative Properties.
Colligative properties are those that depend on the ratio of the particles of the solute to the molecules of the solvent. These properties include the **lowering of the vapor pressure,** the **depression of a freezing point,** the **elevation of a boiling point,** and the **osmotic pressure** of a solution.

According to **Raoult's law,** the vapor pressure of a solution of a nonvolatile (molecular) solute is the vapor pressure of the pure solvent times the mole fraction of the solvent. An alternative expression of this law is that the *change* in vapor pressure caused by the solute equals the mole fraction of the solute times the pure solvent's vapor pressure. When the components of a solution are volatile liquids, then Raoult's law calculations find the *partial pressures* of the vapors of the individual liquids. The sum of the partial pressures equals the total vapor pressure of the solution.

An *ideal solution* is one that would obey Raoult's law exactly and in which all attractions between molecules are equal. An ideal solution has $\Delta H_{soln} = 0$. Solutions of liquids that form exothermically usually have vapor pressures lower than predicted by Raoult's law. Those that form endothermically have vapor pressures higher than predicted.

In proportion to its molal concentration, a solute causes a **freezing point depression** and a **boiling point elevation.** The proportionality constants are the **molal freezing point depression constant** and the **molal boiling point elevation constant,** and they differ from solvent to solvent. Freezing point and boiling point data from a solution made from known masses of both solute and solvent can be used to calculate the molecular mass of a solute.

When a solution is separated from the pure solvent (or from a less concentrated solution) by an *osmotic membrane*, **osmosis** occurs, which is the net flow of solvent into the more concentrated solution. The back-pressure required to prevent osmosis is called the solution's **osmotic pressure,** which, in a dilute aqueous solution, is proportional to the product of the Kelvin temperature and the molar concentration. The proportionality constant is *R*, the ideal gas constant, and the equation relating these variables is $\Pi = MRT$.

When the membrane separating two different solutions is a *dialyzing membrane*, it permits **dialysis,** the passage not only of solvent molecules but also of small solute molecules or ions. Only very large molecules are denied passage.

Colligative Properties of Electrolytes.
Because an electrolyte releases more ions in solution than indicated by the molal (or molar) concentration, a solution of an electrolyte has more pronounced colligative properties than a solution of a molecular compound at the same concentration. The dissociation of a strong electrolyte approaches 100% in very dilute solutions, particularly when both ions are singly charged.

The ratio of the value of a particular colligative property (e.g., ΔT_f) to the value expected if there were no dissociation is the **van't Hoff factor, *i*.** A solute whose formula unit breaks into two ions, like NaCl or $MgSO_4$, would have a van't Hoff factor of 2 if it were 100% dissociated. Observed van't Hoff factors are less than the theoretical values because of formation of **ion pairs,** brought about by **association** of ions in solution. The van't Hoff factors approach those corresponding to 100% dissociation only as the solutions are made more and more dilute.

TOOLS FOR PROBLEM SOLVING

The compilation below lists the tools you have learned in this chapter that are applicable to problem solving. Review them if necessary, and refer to them when working on the Review Problems that follow.

"Like dissolves like" rule *(page 482)* This rule uses the polarity and strengths of attractive forces along with chemical composition and structure to predict whether two substances can form a solution.

Henry's law *(page 490)* The solubility of a gas at a given pressure can be determined from its solubility at another pressure by using the Henry's law equation.

$$C_{gas} = k_H P_{gas}$$

Mass fraction; mass percent *(page 492)* These concentration terms are one way to express concentration and they can be used as conversion factors to calculate the mass of solution needed to deliver a desired mass of solute.

$$\text{mass fraction} = \frac{\text{mass of solute}}{\text{mass of solution}}$$

$$\text{mass percent} = \%(w/w) = \frac{\text{mass of solute}}{\text{mass of solution}} \times 100\%$$

Molal concentration *(page 493)* This is a temperature-independent concentration unit that is used in experiments where temperature may be varied.

$$\text{molality} = \frac{\text{moles of solute}}{\text{kg of solvent}}$$

This equation also relates the mass of solvent to the moles of solute. Molality is also used in freezing point depression and boiling point elevation experiments to determine molar masses.

Mole fraction; mole percent *(page 494)* This is a temperature-independent concentration unit used with Raoult's law.

$$\text{mole fraction} = X_A = \frac{n_A}{n_{total}}$$

$$\text{mole percent} = \frac{n_A}{n_{total}} \times 100\%$$

Raoult's law *(page 496)* This law summarizes the effect of a non-volatile solute on the vapor pressure of a solution.

$$P_{solution} = X_{solvent} P^\circ_{solvent}$$

Raoult's law for a mixture of two volatile solvents, A and B, is

$$P_{solution} = X_A P^\circ_A + X_B P^\circ_B$$

Equations for freezing point depression and boiling point elevation *(page 501)*

$$\Delta T_f = K_f m \qquad \Delta T_b = K_b m$$

These equations are used to estimate the decrease in freezing point and increase in boiling point of solutions. These equations are also used to estimate the molar mass of non-dissociating solutes.

Equation for osmotic pressure *(page 505)*

$$\Pi V = nRT \qquad \Pi = MRT$$

The osmotic pressure equation is similar to the ideal gas law equation. It is used to calculate molecular masses from osmotic pressure and concentration data. In this form, remember that R must be 0.0821 L atm mol^{-1} K^{-1}.

QUESTIONS, PROBLEMS, AND EXERCISES

Answers to problems whose numbers are printed in color are given in Appendix B. More challenging problems are marked with asterisks. ILW = Interactive Learningware solution is available at www.wiley.com/college/brady. OH = an Office Hours video is available for this problem.

REVIEW QUESTIONS

Why Solutions Form

12.1 Why do two gases spontaneously mix when they are brought into contact?

12.2 When substances form liquid solutions, what two factors are involved in determining the solubility of the solute in the solvent?

12.3 Methanol, CH_3—O—H, and water are miscible in all proportions. What does this mean? Explain how the O—H unit in methanol contributes to this.

12.4 Hexane (C_6H_{12}) and water are immiscible. What does this mean? Explain why they are immiscible in terms of structural features of their molecules and the forces of attraction between them.

12.5 Explain how ion–dipole forces help to bring potassium chloride into solution in water.

12.6 Explain why potassium chloride will not dissolve in carbon tetrachloride, CCl_4.

Heat of Solution

12.7 The value of ΔH_{soln} for a soluble compound is, say, $+26$ kJ mol^{-1}, and a nearly saturated solution is prepared in an insulated container (e.g., a coffee cup calorimeter). Will the system's temperature increase or decrease as the solute dissolves?

12.8 Referring to the preceding question, which value for this compound would be numerically larger, its lattice energy or its hydration energy?

12.9 Which would be expected to have the larger hydration energy, Al^{3+} or Li^+? Why? (Both ions are about the same size.)

12.10 Suggest a reason why the value of ΔH_{soln} for a gas such as CO_2, dissolving in water, is negative.

12.11 The value of ΔH_{soln} for the formation of an acetone–water solution is negative. Explain this in general terms that discuss intermolecular forces of attraction.

12.12 The value of ΔH_{soln} for the formation of an ethanol–hexane solution is positive. Explain this in general terms that involve intermolecular forces of attraction.

12.13 When a certain solid dissolves in water, the solution becomes cool. Is ΔH_{soln} for this solute positive or negative? Explain your reasoning. Is the solubility of this substance likely to increase or decrease with increasing temperature? Explain your answer using Le Châtelier's principle.

12.14 If the value of ΔH_{soln} for the formation of a mixture of two liquids A and B is zero, what does this imply about the relative strengths of A–A, B–B, and A–B intermolecular attractions?

Temperature and Solubility

12.15 If a saturated solution of NH_4NO_3 at 70 °C is cooled to 10 °C, how many grams of solute will separate if the quantity of the solvent is 100 g? (Use data in Figure 12.9.)

12.16 Anglers know that on hot summer days, the largest fish will be found in deep sinks in lake bottoms, where the water is coolest. Use the temperature dependence of oxygen solubility in water to explain why.

Pressure and Solubility

12.17 What is Henry's law?

12.18 Mountain streams often contain fewer living things than equivalent streams at sea level. Give one reason why this might be true in terms of oxygen solubilities at different pressures.

12.19 Why is ammonia so much more soluble in water than is nitrogen? Would you expect hydrogen chloride gas to have a high or low solubility in water? Explain your answers to both questions.

12.20 Why does a bottled carbonated beverage fizz when you take the cap off?

Expressions of Concentration

12.21 Write the definition for each of the following concentration units: mole fraction, mole percent, molality, percent by mass.

12.22 How does the molality of a solution vary with increasing temperature? How does the molarity of a solution vary with increasing temperature?

12.23 Suppose a 1.0 m solution of a solute is made using a solvent with a density of 1.15 g/mL. Will the molarity of this solution be numerically larger or smaller than 1.0? Explain.

Colligative Properties

12.24 What specific fact about a physical property of a solution must be true to call it a colligative property?

12.25 What kinds of data would have to be obtained to find out if a solution of two miscible liquids is almost exactly an ideal solution?

12.26 When octane is mixed with methanol, the vapor pressure of the octane over the solution is higher than what we would calculate using Raoult's law. Why? Explain the discrepancy in terms of intermolecular attractions.

12.27 Explain why a nonvolatile solute dissolved in water makes the system have (a) a higher boiling point than water and (b) a lower freezing point than water.

12.28 Why do we call dialyzing and osmotic membranes *semipermeable*? What is the opposite of *permeable*?

12.29 What is the key difference between dialyzing and osmotic membranes?

12.30 At a molecular level, explain why in osmosis there is a net migration of solvent from the side of the membrane less concentrated in solute to the side more concentrated in solute.

12.31 Two glucose solutions of unequal molarity are separated by an osmotic membrane. Which solution will *lose* water, the one with the higher or the lower molarity?

12.32 Which aqueous solution has the higher osmotic pressure, 10% glucose, $C_6H_{12}O_6$, or 10% sucrose, $C_{12}H_{22}O_{11}$? (Both are molecular compounds.)

12.33 When a solid is *associated* in a solution, what does this mean? What difference does it make to expected colligative properties?

12.34 What is the difference between a *hypertonic* solution and a *hypotonic* solution?

Colligative Properties of Electrolytes

12.35 Why are colligative properties of solutions of ionic compounds usually more pronounced than those of solutions of molecular compounds of the same molalities?

12.36 What is the van't Hoff factor? What is its expected value for all nondissociating molecular solutes? If its measured value is slightly larger than 1.0, what does this suggest about the solute? What is suggested by a van't Hoff factor of approximately 0.5?

12.37 Which aqueous solution, if either, is likely to have the higher boiling point, 0.50 *m* NaI or 0.50 *m* Na_2CO_3?

REVIEW PROBLEMS

Heat of Solution

12.38 Consider the formation of a solution of aqueous potassium chloride. Write the thermochemical equations for (a) the conversion of solid KCl into its gaseous ions and (b) the subsequent formation of the solution by hydration of the ions. The lattice energy of KCl is -690 kJ mol^{-1}, and the hydration energy of the ions is -686 kJ mol^{-1}. Calculate the enthalpy of solution of KCl in kJ mol^{-1}.

OH 12.39 For an ionic compound dissolving in water, $\Delta H_{soln} = -50$ kJ mol^{-1} and the hydration energy is -890 kJ mol^{-1}. Estimate the lattice energy of the ionic compound.

Henry's Law

OH 12.40 The solubility of methane, the chief component of natural gas, in water at 20 °C and 1.0 atm pressure is 0.025 g L^{-1}. What is its solubility in water at 1.5 atm and 20 °C?

12.41 At 740 torr and 20 °C, nitrogen has a solubility in water of 0.018 g L^{-1}. At 620 torr and 20 °C, its solubility is 0.015 g L^{-1}. Show that nitrogen obeys Henry's law.

12.42 If the solubility of a gas in water is 0.010 g L^{-1} at 25 °C with the partial pressure of the gas over the solution at 1.0 atm, predict the solubility of the gas at the same temperature but at double the pressure.

12.43 If 100.0 mL of water is shaken with oxygen gas at 1.0 atm, it will dissolve 0.0039 g O_2. Estimate the Henry's law constant for oxygen gas in water.

Expressions of Concentration

12.44 What is the molality of NaCl in a solution that is 3.000 *M* NaCl, with a density of 1.07 g mL^{-1}?

12.45 A solution of acetic acid, CH_3COOH, has a concentration of 0.143 *M* and a density of 1.00 g mL^{-1}. What is the molality of this solution?

12.46 What is the molal concentration of glucose, $C_6H_{12}O_6$, a sugar found in many fruits, in a solution made by dissolving 24.0 g of glucose in 1.00 kg of water? What is the mole fraction of glucose in the solution? What is the mass percent of glucose in the solution?

12.47 If you dissolved 11.5 g of NaCl in 1.00 kg of water, what would be its molal concentration? What are the mass percent NaCl and the mole percent NaCl in the solution? The volume of this solution is virtually identical to the original volume of the 1.00 kg of water. What is the molar concentration of NaCl in this solution? What would have to be true about any solvent for one of its dilute solutions to have essentially the same molar and molal concentrations?

12.48 A solution of ethanol, CH_3CH_2OH, in water has a concentration of 1.25 *m*. Calculate the mass percent of ethanol.

12.49 A solution of NaCl in water has a concentration of 19.5%. Calculate the molality of the solution.

OH 12.50 A solution of NH_3 in water is at a concentration of 7.50% by mass. Calculate the mole percent NH_3 in the solution. What is the molal concentration of the NH_3?

12.51 An aqueous solution of isopropyl alcohol, C_3H_8O, rubbing alcohol, has a mole fraction of alcohol equal to 0.250. What is the percent by mass of alcohol in the solution? What is the molality of the alcohol?

ILW 12.52 Sodium nitrate, $NaNO_3$, is sometimes added to tobacco to improve its burning characteristics. An aqueous solution of $NaNO_3$ has a concentration of 0.363 *m*. Its density is 1.0185 g mL^{-1}. Calculate the molar concentration of $NaNO_3$ and the mass percent of $NaNO_3$ in the solution. What is the mole fraction of $NaNO_3$ in the solution?

12.53 In an aqueous solution of sulfuric acid, the concentration is 1.89 mol% of acid. The density of the solution is 1.0645 g mL^{-1}. Calculate the following: (a) the molal concentration of H_2SO_4, (b) the mass percent of the acid, and (c) the molarity of the solution.

Raoult's Law

OH 12.54 At 25 °C, the vapor pressure of water is 23.8 torr. What is the vapor pressure of a solution prepared by dissolving 65.0 g of $C_6H_{12}O_6$ (a nonvolatile solute) in 150 g of water? (Assume the solution is ideal.)

12.55 The vapor pressure of water at 20 °C is 17.5 torr. A 35% solution of the nonvolatile solute ethylene glycol, $C_2H_4(OH)_2$, in water is prepared. Estimate the vapor pressure of the solution.

12.56 At 25 °C the vapor pressures of benzene (C_6H_6) and toluene (C_7H_8) are 93.4 and 26.9 torr, respectively. A solution is made by mixing 35.0 g of benzene and 65.0 g of toluene. At what applied pressure, in torr, will this solution boil at 25 °C?

12.57 Pentane (C_5H_{12}) and heptane (C_7H_{16}) are two hydrocarbon liquids present in gasoline. At 20 °C, the vapor pressure of pentane is 420 torr and the vapor pressure of heptane is 36.0 torr. What will be the total vapor pressure (in torr) of a solution prepared by mixing equal masses of the two liquids?

*12.58 Benzene and toluene help get good engine performance from lead-free gasoline. At 40 °C, the vapor pressure of benzene is 180 torr and that of toluene is 60 torr. Suppose you wished to prepare a solution of these liquids that will have a total vapor pressure of 96 torr at 40 °C. What must be the mole percent concentrations of each in the solution?

*12.59 The vapor pressure of pure methanol, CH_3OH, at 30 °C is 160 torr. How many grams of the nonvolatile solute glycerol, $C_3H_5(OH)_3$, must be added to 100 g of methanol to obtain a solution with a vapor pressure of 140 torr?

12.60 A solution containing 8.3 g of a nonvolatile nondissociating substance dissolved in 1 mol of chloroform, $CHCl_3$, has a vapor pressure of 511 torr. The vapor pressure of pure $CHCl_3$ at the same temperature is 526 torr. Calculate (a) the mole fraction of the solute, (b) the number of moles of solute in the solution, and (c) the molecular mass of the solute.

12.61 At 21.0 °C, a solution of 18.26 g of a nonvolatile, nonpolar compound in 33.25 g of ethyl bromide, C_2H_5Br, had a vapor pressure of 336.0 torr. The vapor pressure of pure ethyl bromide at this temperature is 400.0 torr. What is the molecular mass of the compound?

Freezing Point Depression and Boiling Point Elevation

12.62 How many grams of sucrose ($C_{12}H_{22}O_{11}$) are needed to lower the freezing point of 100 g of water by 3.00 °C?

12.63 To make sugar candy a concentrated sucrose solution is boiled until the temperature reaches 270 °F. What is the molality and what is the mole fraction of sucrose in this mixture?

OH 12.64 A solution of 12.00 g of an unknown nondissociating compound dissolved in 200.0 g of benzene freezes at 3.45 °C. Calculate the molecular mass of the unknown.

12.65 A solution of 14 g of a nonvolatile, nondissociating compound in 1.0 kg of benzene boils at 81.7 °C. Calculate the molecular mass of the unknown.

ILW 12.66 What are the molecular mass and molecular formula of a nondissociating molecular compound whose empirical formula is C_4H_2N if 3.84 g of the compound in 500 g of benzene gives a freezing point depression of 0.307 °C?

12.67 Benzene reacts with hot concentrated nitric acid dissolved in sulfuric acid to give chiefly nitrobenzene, $C_6H_5NO_2$. A by-product is often obtained, which consists of 42.86% C, 2.40% H, and 16.67% N (by mass). The boiling point of a solution of 5.5 g of the by-product in 45 g of benzene was 1.84 °C higher than that of benzene. (a) Calculate the empirical formula of the by-product. (b) Calculate a molecular mass of the by-product and determine its molecular formula.

Osmotic Pressure

ILW 12.68

(a) Show that the following equation is true.

$$\text{Molar mass of solute} = \frac{(\text{grams of solute})RT}{\Pi V}$$

(b) An aqueous solution of a compound with a very high molecular mass was prepared in a concentration of 2.0 g L^{-1} at 25 °C. Its osmotic pressure was 0.021 torr. Calculate the molecular mass of the compound.

OH 12.69 A saturated solution is made by dissolving 0.400 g of a polypeptide (a substance formed by joining together in a chainlike fashion some number of amino acids) in water to give 1.00 L of solution. The solution has an osmotic pressure of 3.74 torr at 27 °C. What is the approximate molecular mass of the polypeptide?

Colligative Properties of Electrolyte Solutions

12.70 The vapor pressure of water at 20 °C is 17.5 torr. What would be the vapor pressure at 20 °C of a solution made by dissolving 23.0 g of NaCl in 100 g of water? (Assume complete dissociation of the solute and an ideal solution.)

12.71 How many grams of $AlCl_3$ would have to be dissolved in 150 mL of water to give a solution that has a vapor pressure of 38.7 torr at 35 °C? Assume complete dissociation of the solute and ideal solution behavior. (At 35 °C, the vapor pressure of pure water is 42.2 torr.)

OH 12.72 What is the osmotic pressure, in torr, of a 2.0% solution of NaCl in water when the temperature of the solution is 25 °C?

12.73 Below are the concentrations of the most abundant ions in seawater.

Ion	Molality
Chloride	0.566
Sodium	0.486
Magnesium	0.055
Sulfate	0.029
Calcium	0.011
Potassium	0.011
Bicarbonate	0.002

Use these data to estimate the osmotic pressure of seawater at 25 °C in units of atmospheres. What is the minimum pressure in atm needed to desalinate seawater by reverse osmosis?

12.74 What is the expected freezing point of a 0.20 m solution of $CaCl_2$? (Assume complete dissociation.)

12.75 The freezing point of a 0.10 m solution of mercury(I) nitrate is approximately −0.27 °C. Show that these data suggest that the formula of the mercury(I) ion is Hg_2^{2+}.

Interionic Attractions and Colligative Properties

12.76 The van't Hoff factor for the solute in 0.100 m $NiSO_4$ is 1.19. What would this factor be if the solution behaved as if it were 100% dissociated?

12.77 What is the expected van't Hoff factor for K_2SO_4 in an aqueous solution, assuming 100% dissociation?

12.78 A 0.118 m solution of LiCl has a freezing point of −0.415 °C. What is the van't Hoff factor for this solute at this concentration?

12.79 What is the approximate osmotic pressure of a 0.118 m solution of LiCl at 10 °C? Express the answer in torr. (Use the data in the preceding problem.)

ADDITIONAL EXERCISES

*12.80 The "bends" is a medical emergency caused by the formation of tiny bubbles in the blood vessels of divers who rise too quickly to the surface from a deep dive. The origin of the problem is seen in the calculations in this problem. At 37 °C (normal body temperature), the solubility of N_2 in water is 0.015 g L^{-1} when its pressure over the solution is 1 atm. Air is approximately 78 mol% N_2. How many moles of N_2 are dissolved per liter of blood (essentially an aqueous solution) when a diver inhales air at a pressure of 1 atm? How many moles of N_2 dissolve per liter of blood when the diver is submerged to a depth of approximately 100 ft, where the total pressure of the air being breathed is 4 atm? If the diver suddenly surfaces, how many milliliters of N_2 gas, in the form of tiny bubbles, are released into the bloodstream from each liter of blood (at 37 °C and 1 atm)?

OH 12.81 The vapor pressure of a mixture of 400 g of carbon tetrachloride and 43.3 g of an unknown compound is 137 torr at 30 °C. The vapor pressure of pure carbon tetrachloride at 30 °C is 143 torr, while that of the pure unknown is 85 torr. What is the approximate molecular mass of the unknown?

*12.82 An experiment calls for the use of the dichromate ion, $Cr_2O_7^{2-}$, in sulfuric acid as an oxidizing agent for isopropyl alcohol, C_3H_8O. The chief product is acetone, C_3H_6O, which forms according to the following equation.

$$3C_3H_8O + Na_2Cr_2O_7 + 4H_2SO_4 \longrightarrow$$
$$3C_3H_6O + Cr_2(SO_4)_3 + Na_2SO_4 + 7H_2O$$

(a) The oxidizing agent is available only as sodium dichromate dihydrate. What is the minimum number of grams of sodium dichromate dihydrate needed to oxidize 21.4 g of isopropyl alcohol according to the balanced equation?

(b) The amount of acetone actually isolated was 12.4 g. Calculate the percentage yield of acetone.

(c) The reaction produces a volatile by-product. When a sample of it with a mass of 8.654 mg was burned in oxygen, it was converted into 22.368 mg of carbon dioxide and 10.655 mg of water, the sole products. (Assume that any unaccounted for element is oxygen.) Calculate the percentage composition of the by-product and determine its empirical formula.

(d) A solution prepared by dissolving 1.338 g of the by-product in 115.0 g of benzene had a freezing point of 4.87 °C. Calculate the molecular mass of the by-product and write its molecular formula.

OH 12.83 What is the osmotic pressure in torr of a 0.010 M aqueous solution of a molecular compound at 25 °C?

*12.84 Ethylene glycol, $C_2H_6O_2$, is used in some antifreeze mixtures. Protection against freezing to as low as −40 °F is sought.

(a) How many moles of solute are needed per kilogram of water to ensure this protection?

(b) The density of ethylene glycol is 1.11 g mL^{-1}. To how many milliliters of solute does your answer to part (a) correspond?

(c) Calculate the number of quarts of ethylene glycol that should be mixed with each quart of water to get the desired protection.

12.85 The osmotic pressure of a dilute solution of a slightly soluble *polymer* (a compound composed of large molecules formed by linking many smaller molecules together) in water was measured using the osmometer in Figure 12.18. The difference in the heights of the liquid levels was determined to be 1.26 cm at 25 °C. Assume the solution has a density of 1.00 g mL^{-1}. (a) What is the osmotic pressure of the solution in torr? (b) What is the molarity of the solution? (c) At what temperature would the solution be expected to freeze? (d) On the basis of the results of these calculations, explain why freezing point depression cannot be used to determine the molecular masses of compounds composed of very large molecules.

12.86 A solution of ethanol, C_2H_5OH, in water has a concentration of 4.613 mol L^{-1}. At 20 °C, its density is 0.9677 g mL^{-1}. Calculate the following: (a) the molality of the solution and (b) the percent concentration of the alcohol. The density of ethanol is 0.7893 g mL^{-1} and the density of water is 0.9982 g mL^{-1} at 20 °C.

12.87 Consider an aqueous 1.00 m solution of Na_3PO_4, a compound with useful detergent properties.

(a) Calculate the boiling point of the solution on the assumption that Na_3PO_4 does not ionize at all in solution.

(b) Do the same calculation assuming that the van't Hoff factor for Na_3PO_4 reflects 100% dissociation into its ions.

(c) The 1.00 m solution boils at 100.183 °C at 1 atm. Calculate the van't Hoff factor for the solute in this solution.

EXERCISES IN CRITICAL THINKING

12.88 A certain organic substance is soluble in solvent A but it is insoluble in solvent B. If solvents A and B are miscible, will the organic compound be soluble in a mixture of A and B? What additional information is needed to answer this question?

12.89 The situation described in the previous exercise is actually quite common. How might it be used to purify the organic compound?

12.90 Compile and review all of the methods discussed for the determination of molecular masses. Assess which methods are the most reliable, which are the most sensitive, and which are the most convenient to use.

12.91 Having had some laboratory experience by now, evaluate whether preparation of a 0.25 *molar* solution is easier or more difficult than preparing a 0.25 *molal* solution. What experiments require the use of *molal* concentrations?

12.92 This chapter focused on the physical description of osmosis and its use in determining molar masses. What other practical uses are there for osmosis?

12.93 What are the chemical and physical processes that lead to oxygen depletion and the possibility of large-scale fish kills?

12.94 Some gases exhibit an effect that can be described as dissolving in a solid. What gases "dissolve" to a significant extent in what metals? Why is this property of practical interest?

Here is another chance for you to test your understanding of concepts, your knowledge of scientific terms, and your skills at problem solving. Read through the following questions carefully, and answer each as fully as possible. Review topics when necessary. When you are able to answer these questions correctly, you are ready to go on to the next group of chapters.

1. A 15.5 L sample of neon at 25.0 °C and a pressure of 748 torr is kept at 25.0 °C as it is allowed to expand to a final volume of 25.4 L. What is the final pressure?

2. An 8.95 L sample of nitrogen at 25.0 °C and 1.00 atm is compressed to a volume of 0.895 L and a pressure of 5.56 atm. What must its final temperature be?

3. A mixture of propane and air will explode if it is heated to 466 °C. If a 20.0 L sample of such a mixture originally at 25.0 °C and 1.00 atm is to be detonated by the heat that is generated by compression alone, what will the pressure of the mixture be at 466 °C if its volume is to be 1.00 L?

4. A sample of oxygen-enriched air with a volume of 12.5 L at 25.0 °C and 1.00 atm consists of 45.0% (v/v) oxygen and 55.0% (v/v) nitrogen What are the partial pressures of oxygen and nitrogen (in torr) in this sample after it has been warmed to a temperature of 37.0 °C and is still at a final volume of 12.5 L?

5. If a gas in a cylinder pushes back a piston against a constant opposing pressure of 3.0×10^5 pascals and undergoes a volume change of 0.50 m^3, how much work will the gas do, expressed in joules?

6. What is the formula mass of a gaseous element if 6.45 g occupies 1.92 L at 745 torr and 25.0 °C? Which element is it?

7. What is the formula mass of a gaseous element if at room temperature it effuses through a pinhole 2.16 times as rapidly as xenon? Which element is it?

8. Briefly and qualitatively explain how the model of an ideal gas, as described by the kinetic theory of gases, explains the following.
   (a) Boyle's law   (d) the meaning of gas temperature
   (b) Graham's law   (e) pressure–temperature law
   (c) Charles' law   (f) absolute zero

9. Which has a higher value of the van der Waals constant a, a gas whose molecules are polar or one whose molecules are nonpolar? Explain.

10. What is the van der Waals constant b used to correct for, and in what way is this correction accomplished?

11. How many milliliters of dry CO_2, measured at STP, could be evolved in the reaction between 20.0 mL of 0.100 M $NaHCO_3$ and 30.0 mL of 0.0800 M HCl?

12. How many milliliters of Cl_2 gas, measured at 25 °C and 740 torr, are needed to react with 10.0 mL of 0.10 M NaI if the I^- is oxidized to IO_3^- and Cl_2 is reduced to Cl^-?

13. Potassium hypobromite, KOBr, converts ammonia to nitrogen by the following reaction.

$$3KOBr + 2NH_3 \longrightarrow N_2 + 3KBr + 3H_2O$$

To prepare 475 mL of dry N_2, when measured at 24.0 °C and 738 torr, what is the minimum number of grams of KOBr required?

14. Hydrogen peroxide, H_2O_2, is decomposed by potassium permanganate according to the following reaction.

$$5H_2O_2 + 2KMnO_4 + 3H_2SO_4 \longrightarrow$$
$$5O_2 + 2MnSO_4 + K_2SO_4 + 8H_2O$$

What is the minimum number of milliliters of 0.125 M $KMnO_4$ required to prepare 375 mL of dry O_2 when the gas volume is measured at 22.0 °C and 738 torr?

15. One way to make chlorine is to let manganese dioxide, MnO_2, react with hydrochloric acid according to the following equation.

$$4HCl + MnO_2 \longrightarrow Cl_2 + MnCl_2 + 2H_2O$$

What is the minimum volume (in mL) of 6.44 M HCl needed to prepare 525 mL of dry chlorine when the gas is obtained at 24.0 °C and 742 torr?

16. A sample of 248 mL of wet nitrogen gas was collected over water at a total gas pressure of 736 torr and a temperature of 21.0 °C. (The vapor pressure of water at 21.0 °C is 18.7 torr.) The nitrogen was produced by the reaction of sulfamic acid, HNH_2SO_3, with 425 mL of a solution of sodium nitrite according to the following equation.

$$NaNO_2 + HNH_2SO_3 \longrightarrow N_2 + NaHSO_4 + H_2O$$

Calculate what must have been the molar concentration of the sodium nitrite.

17. What two factors are principally responsible for the differences in the behavior of gases and liquids?

18. If the ideal gas law worked well for all substances at all temperatures and pressures, what volume would 1.00 mol of water vapor occupy at 25 °C and 1.00 atm? What volume does 1.00 mol of water actually occupy under these conditions?

19. Which properties of liquids and solids are controlled chiefly by the closeness of the packing of molecules in these states? Which properties are determined chiefly by the strengths of the intermolecular attractions?

20. Consider the molecule $POCl_3$, in which phosphorus is the central atom and is bonded to an oxygen atom and three chlorine atoms.
   (a) Draw the Lewis structure of $POCl_3$ and predict its geometry.
   (b) Is the molecule polar or nonpolar? Explain.
   (c) What kinds of attractive forces would be present between $POCl_3$ molecules in the liquid?

21. What kinds of attractive forces, including chemical bonds, would be present between the particles in the following?
   (a) $H_2O(l)$ (c) $CH_3OH(l)$ (e) $NaCl(s)$
   (b) $CCl_4(l)$ (d) $BrCl(l)$ (f) $Na_2SO_4(s)$

22. What is a change of state? What terms are used to describe the energy changes associated with the change (a) solid $\rightarrow$ liquid, (b) solid $\rightarrow$ gas, and (c) liquid $\rightarrow$ gas?

23. What is a *dynamic equilibrium*? In terms of Le Châtelier's principle and the "equation"

$$\text{Liquid} + \text{heat} \rightleftharpoons \text{vapor}$$

explain why raising the temperature of a liquid increases the liquid's equilibrium vapor pressure.

24. Can a solid have a vapor pressure? How would the vapor pressure of a solid vary with temperature?

25. Trimethylamine, $(CH_3)_3N$, is a substance responsible in part for the smell of fish. It has a boiling point of 3.5 °C and a molecular weight of 59.1. Dimethylamine, $(CH_3)_2NH$, has a similar odor and boils at a slightly higher temperature, 7 °C, even though it has a somewhat lower molecular mass (45.1). How can this be explained in terms of the kinds of attractive forces between their molecules?

26. Methanol, CH_3OH, commonly known as wood alcohol, has a boiling point of 64.7 °C. Methylamine, a fishy-smelling chemical found in herring brine, has a boiling point of −6.3 °C. Ethane, a hydrocarbon present in petroleum, has a boiling point of −88 °C.

```
      H                 H   H              H   H
      |                 |   |              |   |
  H — C — O — H     H — C — N — H      H — C — C — H
      |                 |                  |   |
      H                 H                  H   H
   methanol         methylamine          ethane
   b.p. 64.7 °C     b.p. −6.3 °C      b.p. −88 °C
```

Each has nearly the same molecular mass. Account for the large differences in their boiling points in terms of the attractive forces between their molecules.

27. Based on what you've learned in these chapters, explain the following.
(a) A breeze cools you when you're perspiring.
(b) Droplets of water form on the outside of a glass of cold soda on a warm, humid day.
(c) You feel more uncomfortable on a warm, humid day than on a warm, dry day.
(d) The origin of the energy in a violent thunderstorm.
(e) Clouds form as warm, moist air flows over a mountain range.

28. How do the magnitudes of ΔH_{fusion}, $\Delta H_{vaporization}$, and $\Delta H_{sublimation}$ compare for a given substance?

29. Make sketches of (a) a face-centered cubic unit cell, (b) a body-centered cubic unit cell, and (c) a simple cubic unit cell. Which type of unit cell does NaCl have?

30. Aluminum has a density of 2.70 g cm^{-3} and crystallizes in a face-centered cubic lattice. Use these and other data to calculate the atomic radius of an aluminum atom.

31. What is the difference between the closest packed structures identified as ccp and hcp? In each of these structures, how many atoms are in contact with any given atom?

32. Tin tetraiodide (stannic iodide) has the formula SnI_4. It forms soft, yellow to reddish crystals that melt at about 143 °C. What kind of solid does SnI_4 form? What kind of bonding occurs in SnI_4?

33. A certain compound has the formula MCl_2. Crystals of the compound melt at 772 °C and give a liquid that is electrically conducting. What kind of crystal does this compound form?

34. What general properties are expected of covalent crystals?

35. Silicon dioxide, SiO_2, forms very hard crystals that melt at 1610 °C to yield a liquid that does not conduct electricity. What crystal type does SiO_2 form?

36. Sketch the phase diagram for a substance that has a triple point at 25 °C and 100 torr, a normal boiling point of 150 °C, and a melting point at 1 atm of 27 °C. Is the solid more dense or less dense than the liquid? Where on the curve would the critical temperature and critical pressure be? What phase would exist at 30 °C and 10.0 torr?

37. How many grams of 4.00% (w/w) solution of KOH in water are needed to neutralize completely the acid in 10.0 mL $0.256 M H_2SO_4$?

38. Calculate the molar concentration of 15.00% (w/w) Na_2CO_3 solution at 20.0 °C given that its density is 1.160 g mL^{-1}.

39. The solubility of pure oxygen in water at 20.0 °C and 760 torr is 4.30×10^{-2} g O_2 per liter of H_2O. When air is in contact with water and the air pressure is 585 torr at 20 °C, how many grams of oxygen from the air dissolve in 1.00 L of water? The average concentration of oxygen in the air is 21.1% (v/v).

40. Compound A is a white solid with a high melting point. When it melts, it conducts electricity. In which solvent is it likely to be more soluble, water or gasoline? Explain.

41. Compound XY is an ionic compound that dissociates as it dissolves in water. The lattice energy of XY is −600 kJ mol^{-1}. The hydration energy of its ions is −610 kJ mol^{-1}.
(a) Write the thermochemical equations for the two steps in the formation of a solution of XY in water.
(b) Write the sum of these two equations in the form of a thermochemical equation, showing the net ΔH.
(c) Draw an enthalpy diagram for the formation of this solution.

42. A 0.270 M KOH solution has a density of 1.01 g mL^{-1}. Calculate the percent concentration (w/w) of KOH.

43. A 5.30 M solution of glycerol in water has a density of 1.11 g mL^{-1}. Calculate the percent concentration by mass of glycerol ($C_3H_8O_3$) and the mole fraction of glycerol present.

44. At 20 °C a 40.00% (v/v) solution of ethyl alcohol, C_2H_5OH, in water, has a density of 0.9369 g mL^{-1}. The density of pure ethyl alcohol at this temperature is 0.7907 g mL^{-1} and that of water is 0.9982 g mL^{-1}.
(a) Calculate the molar concentration and the molal concentration of C_2H_5OH in this solution.
(b) Calculate the mole fraction and mole percent of C_2H_5OH in this solution.
(c) The vapor pressure of ethyl alcohol at 20 °C is 41.0 torr and that of water is 17.5 torr. If the 40.00% (v/v) solution were ideal, what would be the vapor pressure of each component over the solution?

45. Estimate the boiling point of 1.0 molal $Al(NO_3)_3$, assuming that it dissociates entirely into Al^{3+} and NO_3^- ions in solution.

46. Squalene is an oil found chiefly in shark liver oil but also present in low concentrations in olive oil, wheat germ oil, and yeast. A qualitative analysis disclosed that its molecules consist entirely of carbon and hydrogen. When a sample of squalene with a mass of 0.5680 g was burned in pure oxygen, there was obtained 1.8260 g of carbon dioxide and 0.6230 g of water.
(a) Calculate the empirical formula of squalene.
(b) When 0.1268 g of squalene was dissolved in 10.50 g of molten camphor, the freezing point of this solution was 177.3 °C. (The melting point of pure camphor is 178.4 °C, and its molal freezing point depression constant is 37.7 °C kg camphor^{-1}). Calculate the molar mass of squalene and determine its molecular formula.

13 KINETICS: THE STUDY OF RATES OF REACTION

This photo shows how speed adds excitement to the movie *Mission Impossible III*. Wreckage of a high-speed chase and the explosion that the hero, Tom Cruise, barely escapes as he dashes to safety are evidence of fast chemical reactions. Kinetics is the name that describes studies of fast (and slow) chemical reactions that we will learn about in this chapter. *(Stephen Vaughan/ Paramount Pictures/The Kobal Collection, Ltd.)*

CHAPTER OUTLINE

13.1 Five factors affect reaction rates

13.2 Rates of reaction are measured by monitoring change in concentration over time

13.3 Rate laws give reaction rate as a function of reactant concentrations

13.4 Integrated rate laws give concentration as a function of time

13.5 Reaction rate theories explain experimental rate laws in terms of molecular collisions

13.6 Activation energies are measured by fitting experimental data to the Arrhenius equation

13.7 Experimental rate laws can be used to support or reject proposed mechanisms for a reaction

13.8 Catalysts change reaction rates by providing alternative paths between reactants and products

THIS CHAPTER IN CONTEXT

Chemical reactions run at many different speeds. Some, such as the rusting of iron or the breakdown of plastics in the environment, take place very slowly. Others, like the combustion of gasoline or the explosion of gunpowder, occur very quickly. **Chemical kinetics** is the study of the speeds (or *rates*) of chemical reactions. On a practical level, it is concerned with factors that affect the speeds of reactions and how reaction speeds can be controlled. This is essential in industry, where synthetic reactions must take place at controlled speeds. If a reaction takes weeks or months to occur, it may not be economically feasible; if it occurs too quickly or uncontrollably, it may not be safe to carry out. For the consumer, studies on rates of decomposition allow a manufacturer to reliably determine the shelf life, or expiration date, of a product or drug. At a more fundamental level, a study of the speed of a reaction often gives clues that lead to an understanding about *how*, at a molecular level, reactants change into products. Understanding the reaction at this level of detail often allows even finer control of the reaction's speed, and suggests ways to modify the reaction to produce new types of products, or to improve the reaction's yield by preventing undesirable side reactions from occurring.

13.1 | FIVE FACTORS AFFECT REACTION RATES

The **rate of reaction** for a given chemical change is the speed with which the reactants disappear and the products form. It is measured by the amount of products produced or reactants consumed per unit time. Usually this is done by monitoring the concentrations of the reactants or products over time, as the reaction runs (see Figure 13.1).

Before we take up the quantitative aspects of reaction rates, let's look qualitatively at factors that can make a reaction run faster or slower. There are five principal factors that influence reaction rates.

1. Chemical nature of the reactants
2. Ability of the reactants to come in contact with each other
3. Concentrations of the reactants
4. Temperature
5. Availability of rate-accelerating agents called *catalysts*

Chemical nature of the reactants

Bonds break and new bonds form during reactions. The most fundamental differences among reaction rates, therefore, lie in the reactants themselves, in the inherent tendencies of their atoms, molecules, or ions to undergo changes in chemical bonds. Some reactions are fast by nature and others are slow (Figure 13.2). Because sodium atoms lose electrons so easily, for example, a freshly exposed surface of metallic sodium tarnishes almost instantly when exposed to air and moisture. Under identical conditions, potassium also reacts with air and moisture, but the reaction is much faster because potassium atoms lose electrons more easily than sodium atoms.

FIG. 13.1 Reaction rates are measured by monitoring concentration changes over time. The progress of the reaction $A \rightarrow B$. Note that the number of A molecules (in red) decreases with time, as the number of B molecules (in blue) increases. The steeper the concentration versus time curves are, the faster the rate of reaction is. The filmstrip represents the relative numbers of molecules of A and B at each time.

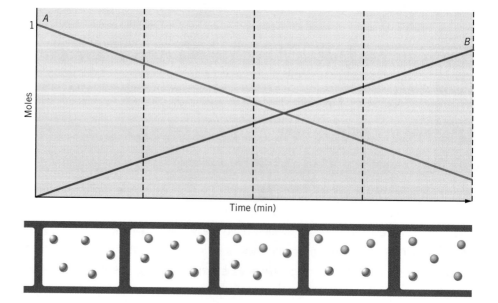

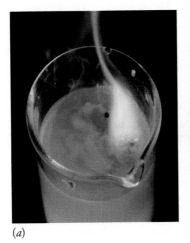

(a)   (b)

FIG. 13.2 **The chemical nature of reactants affects reaction rates.** (*a*) Sodium loses electrons easily, so it reacts quickly with water. (*b*) Potassium loses electrons even more easily than sodium, so its reaction with water is explosively fast. (*Fundamental Photographs*)

Ability of the reactants to meet

Most reactions involve two or more reactants whose particles (atoms, ions, or molecules) must collide with each other for the reaction to occur. This is why reactions are so often carried out in liquid solutions or in the gas phase, states in which the particles are able to intermingle at a molecular level and collide with each other easily.

Reactions in which all the reactants are in the same phase are called **homogeneous reactions.** Examples include the neutralization of sodium hydroxide by hydrochloric acid when both are dissolved in water, and the explosive gas-phase reaction of gasoline vapor with oxygen that can occur when the two are mixed in the right proportions. (An *explosion* is an extremely rapid reaction that quickly generates hot expanding gases.)

When the reactants are present in different phases—for example, when one is a gas and the other a liquid or a solid—the reaction is called a **heterogeneous reaction.** An example is the combustion of coal, in which solid carbon combines with gaseous oxygen. In a heterogeneous reaction, the reactants are able to meet only at the interface between the phases, so *the area of contact between the phases is a major factor in determining the rate of the reaction.* This area is controlled by the sizes of the particles of the reactants. By pulverizing a solid, the total surface area can be hugely increased (Figure 13.3). This maximizes contact between the atoms, ions, or molecules in the solid state with those in a different phase.

Although heterogeneous reactions are important, they are very complex and difficult to analyze. In this chapter, therefore, we'll focus mostly on homogeneous systems.

Concentrations of the reactants

The rates of both homogeneous and heterogeneous reactions are affected by the concentrations of the reactants. For example, wood burns relatively quickly in air but extremely rapidly in pure oxygen. It has been estimated that if air were 30% oxygen instead of 20%, it would not be possible to put out forest fires. Even red hot steel wool, which only sputters and glows in air, bursts into flame when thrust into pure oxygen (see Figure 13.4).

Temperature of the system

Almost all chemical reactions occur faster at higher temperatures than they do at lower temperatures. You may have noticed, for example, that insects move more slowly when the air is cool. An insect is a cold-blooded creature, which means that its body temperature is determined by the temperature of its surroundings. As the air cools, insects cool, and so the rates of their chemical metabolism slow down, making insects sluggish.

Presence of catalysts

Catalysts are substances that increase the rates of chemical reactions without being used up. They affect every moment of our lives. Catalysts are used in the chemical industry to make

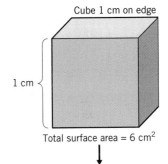

Cube 1 cm on edge

1 cm

Total surface area = 6 cm^2

Dividing into cubes 0.01 cm on an edge gives 1,000,000 cubes.

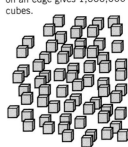

0.01 cm

Total surface area of all cubes = 600 cm^2

FIG. 13.3 **Effect of crushing a solid.** When a single solid is subdivided into much smaller pieces, the total surface area on all of the pieces becomes very large.

FIG. 13.4 **Effect of concentration on rate.** Steel wool, after being heated to redness in a flame, burns spectacularly when dropped into pure oxygen. *(OPC, Inc.)*

gasoline, plastics, fertilizers, and other products that have become virtual necessities in our lives. In our bodies, substances called enzymes serve as catalysts for biochemical reactions. By making enzymes available or not, a cell is able to direct our body chemistry by controlling which chemical reactions can occur rapidly.

<table>
<tr><td>**13.2**</td><td>**RATES OF REACTION ARE MEASURED BY MONITORING CHANGE IN CONCENTRATION OVER TIME**</td></tr>
</table>

The qualitative factors we covered in the previous section can also be described quantitatively. To do this we need to express reaction rates in mathematical terms. Let's start with the concept of **rate,** which always implies a ratio in which a unit of time is in the denominator. Suppose, for example, that you have a job with a pay rate of ten dollars per hour. Because *per* can be translated as *divided by*, your rate of pay can be written as a fraction (abbreviating hour as hr).

$$\text{Rate of pay} = 10 \text{ dollars per hour} = \frac{10 \text{ dollars}}{1 \text{ hr}} = 10 \text{ dollars hr}^{-1}$$

where we've expressed 1/hr as hr^{-1}.

When chemical reactions occur, the concentrations of reactants decrease as they are used up, while the concentrations of the products increase as they form. So one way to describe a reaction's rate is to pick one substance in the reaction's equation and describe its change in concentration per unit of time. The result is the rate of the reaction *with respect to that substance.* Remembering that we always take "final minus initial," the rate of reaction with respect, say, to substance X is

$$\text{Rate with respect to } X = \frac{(\text{conc. of } X \text{ at time } t_{final} - \text{conc. of } X \text{ at time } t_{initial})}{(t_{final} - t_{initial})}$$

$$= \frac{\Delta(\text{conc. of } X)}{\Delta t}$$

Molarity (mol/L) is normally the concentration unit, and the second (s) is the most often used unit of time. Therefore, the units for reaction rates are most frequently the following.

$$\frac{\text{mol/L}}{\text{s}}$$

Because 1/L and 1/s can also be written as L^{-1} and s^{-1}, the units for a reaction rate can be expressed as $mol \, L^{-1} \, s^{-1}$. For instance, if the concentration of one product of a reaction increases by 0.50 mol/L each second, the rate of its formation is $0.50 \, mol \, L^{-1} \, s^{-1}$. Similarly, if the concentration of a reactant decreases by 0.20 mol/L per second, its rate of reaction is $0.20 \, mol \, L^{-1} \, s^{-1}$. By convention, reaction rate is reported as a positive value whether something increases or decreases in concentration.

Relative rates of reaction depend on the coefficients in the equation

When we know the value of a reaction rate with respect to one substance, the coefficients of the reaction's balanced equation can be used to find the rates with respect to the other substances. For example, in the combustion of propane,

$$C_3H_8(g) + 5O_2(g) \longrightarrow 3CO_2(g) + 4H_2O(g)$$

five moles of O_2 *must* be consumed per unit of time for each mole of C_3H_8 used in the same time. Therefore, in this reaction oxygen *must* react five times faster than propane in units of $mol \, L^{-1} \, s^{-1}$. Similarly, CO_2 forms three times faster than C_3H_8 reacts and H_2O four times faster. The magnitudes of the rates relative to each other are thus in the same relationship as the coefficients in the balanced equation.

EXAMPLE 13.1
Relationships of Rates within
a Reaction

Butane, the fuel in cigarette lighters, burns in oxygen to give carbon dioxide and water. If, in a certain experiment, the butane concentration is decreasing at a rate of 0.20 mol L^{-1} s^{-1}, what is the rate at which the oxygen concentration is decreasing, and what are the rates at which the product concentrations are increasing?

ANALYSIS: As always we need a balanced chemical equation. Butane, C_4H_{10}, burns in oxygen to give CO_2 and H_2O according to the equation

$$2C_4H_{10}(g) + 13O_2(g) \longrightarrow 8CO_2(g) + 10H_2O(g)$$

We now need to relate the rate in terms of oxygen and the products to the given rate in terms of butane. The chemical equation is the tool that links amounts of these substances to the amount of butane. The magnitudes of the rates relative to each other are in the same relationship as the coefficients in the balanced equation.

SOLUTION: For oxygen

$$\frac{0.20 \text{ mol } C_4H_{10}}{L \text{ s}} \times \frac{13 \text{ mol } O_2}{2 \text{ mol } C_4H_{10}} = \frac{1.3 \text{ mol } O_2}{L \text{ s}}$$

Oxygen is reacting at a rate of 1.3 mol L^{-1} s^{-1}. For CO_2 and H_2O, we have similar calculations.

$$\frac{0.20 \text{ mol } C_4H_{10}}{L \text{ s}} \times \frac{8 \text{ mol } CO_2}{2 \text{ mol } C_4H_{10}} = \frac{0.80 \text{ mol } CO_2}{L \text{ s}}$$

$$\frac{0.20 \text{ mol } C_4H_{10}}{L \text{ s}} \times \frac{10 \text{ mol } H_2O}{2 \text{ mol } C_4H_{10}} = \frac{1.0 \text{ mol } H_2O}{L \text{ s}}$$

Therefore,

$$\text{Rate of formation of } CO_2 = 0.80 \text{ mol L}^{-1}\text{s}^{-1}$$
$$\text{Rate of formation of } H_2O = 1.0 \text{ mol L}^{-1}\text{s}^{-1}$$

ARE THE ANSWERS REASONABLE? If what we've calculated is correct, then the ratio of the numerical values of the last two rates, namely 0.80 to 1.0, should check out to be the same as the ratio of the corresponding coefficients in the chemical equation, namely, 8 to 10 (the same as 0.8 to 1.0).

Practice Exercise 1: The iodate ion reacts with sulfite ions in the reaction

$$IO_3^- + 3SO_3^{2-} \longrightarrow I^- + 3SO_4^{2-}$$

At what rate are the iodide and sulfate ions being produced if the sulfite ion is disappearing at a rate of 2.4×10^{-4} mol L^{-1} s^{-1}? (Hint: Recall the names of polyatomic ions.)

Practice Exercise 2: Hydrogen sulfide burns in oxygen to form sulfur dioxide and water. If sulfur dioxide is being formed at a rate of 0.30 mol L^{-1} s^{-1}, what are the rates of disappearance of hydrogen sulfide and oxygen?

Because the rates of reaction of reactants and products are all related, it doesn't matter which species we pick to follow concentration changes over time. For example, to study the decomposition of hydrogen iodide, HI, into H_2 and I_2,

$$2HI(g) \longrightarrow H_2(g) + I_2(g)$$

it is easiest to monitor the I_2 concentration because it is the only colored substance in the reaction. As the reaction proceeds, purple iodine vapor forms, and there are instruments that

TABLE 13.1	Data, at 508 °C, for the Reaction $2HI(g) \rightarrow H_2(g) + I_2(g)$
Concentration of HI (mol L^{-1})	Time (s)
0.100	0
0.0716	50
0.0558	100
0.0457	150
0.0387	200
0.0336	250
0.0296	300
0.0265	350

allow us to relate the intensity of the color to the iodine concentration. Then, once we know the rate of formation of iodine, we also know the rate of formation of hydrogen. It's the same because the coefficients of H_2 and I_2 are the same. And the rate of disappearance of HI, which has a coefficient of 2 in the equation, is twice as fast as the rate of formation of I_2.

Most reactions slow down as reactants are used up

A reaction rate is generally not constant throughout the reaction but commonly changes as the reactants are used up. This is because the rate usually depends on the concentrations of the reactants, and these change as the reaction proceeds. For example, Table 13.1 contains data for the decomposition of hydrogen iodide at a temperature of 508 °C. The data, which show the changes in molar HI concentration over time, are plotted in Figure 13.5. Notice that the molar HI concentration drops fairly rapidly during the first 50 seconds of the reaction, which means that the initial rate is relatively fast. However, later, in the interval between 300 s and 350 s, the concentration changes by only a small amount, so the rate has slowed considerably. Thus, the steepness of the curve at any moment reflects the rate of the reaction; the steeper the curve, the higher is the rate.

□ When we use the term "reaction rate" we mean the instantaneous rate, unless we state otherwise.

The rate at which the HI is being consumed at any particular moment is called the **instantaneous rate.** The instantaneous rate can be determined from the slope (or tangent) of the curve measured at the time we have chosen. The slope, which can be read off the graph, is the ratio (expressed positively) of the change in concentration to the change in time. In Figure 13.5, for example, the rate of the decomposition of hydrogen iodide is determined for a time 100 seconds from the start of the reaction. After the tangent to the

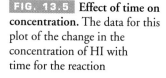

FIG. 13.5 Effect of time on concentration. The data for this plot of the change in the concentration of HI with time for the reaction

$$2HI(g) \longrightarrow H_2(g) + I_2(g)$$

at 508 °C are taken from Table 13.1. The slope is negative because we're measuring the *disappearance* of HI. But when its value is used as a rate of reaction, we express the rate as positive, as we do all rates of reaction.

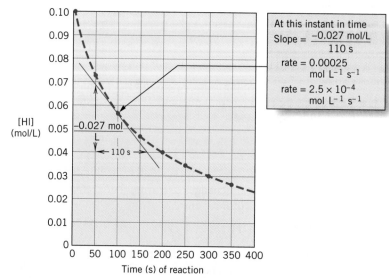

At this instant in time

Slope = $\dfrac{-0.027 \text{ mol/L}}{110 \text{ s}}$

rate = 0.00025 mol L^{-1} s^{-1}

rate = 2.5×10^{-4} mol L^{-1} s^{-1}

[HI] (mol/L)

−0.027 mol L

← 110 s →

Time (s) of reaction

curve is drawn, we measure the concentration change (a decrease of 0.027 mol/L) and the time change (110 s) from the graph. Because the rate is based on a *decreasing* concentration, we use a minus sign for the *equation* that describes this rate so that the rate itself will be a positive quantity. We use square brackets to signify concentrations specifically in moles per liter; [HI] thus means the molar concentration of HI.

$$\text{Rate}_{\text{(with respect to HI)}} = -\left(\frac{[HI]_{\text{final}} - [HI]_{\text{initial}}}{t_{\text{final}} - t_{\text{initial}}}\right) = -\left(\frac{-0.027 \text{ mol/L}}{110 \text{ s}}\right)$$

$$\text{Rate}_{\text{(with respect to HI)}} = 2.5 \times 10^{-4} \text{ mol L}^{-1}\text{s}^{-1}$$

Thus, at this moment in the reaction, the rate with respect to HI is $2.5 \times 10^{-4} \text{ mol L}^{-1}\text{s}^{-1}$. In the following example, we'll use this technique to obtain the *initial instantaneous rate* of the reaction, that is, the instantaneous rate of reaction at time zero.

EXAMPLE 13.2
Estimating the Initial Rate
of a Reaction

For the experimental data shown in Figure 13.5, what is the initial rate of the reaction

$$2HI(g) \longrightarrow H_2(g) + I_2(g)$$

at 508 °C, with respect to HI?

ANALYSIS: The question asks about the initial rate, which is the instantaneous rate of the reaction at time zero. Using Figure 13.5, we can draw a tangent line to the curve showing HI concentration as a function of time at time zero. The instantaneous rate will be the slope of the tangent line. Remember that the slope of a straight line can be calculated from the coordinates of any two points (x_1, y_1) and (x_2, y_2) using the equation

$$\text{Slope} = \frac{y_2 - y_1}{x_2 - x_1}$$

SOLUTION: Remembering that a tangent line to a curve touches the curve at only one point, we can draw the line as shown in the graph below. To more precisely determine the slope of the tangent line, we should choose two points that are as far apart as possible. The point on the curve (0 s, 0.10 mol/L) and the intersection of the tangent line with the time axis (130 s, 0 mol/L) are widely separated:

$$\text{Slope} = \frac{0.10 \text{ mol/L} - 0.00 \text{ mol/L}}{0 \text{ s} - 130 \text{ s}} = -7.7 \times 10^{-4} \text{ mol L}^{-1}\text{s}^{-1}$$

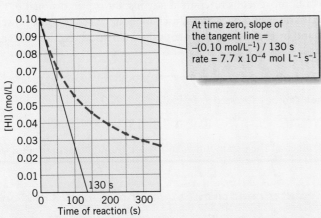

At time zero, slope of the tangent line = $-(0.10 \text{ mol/L}^{-1}) / 130 \text{ s}$ rate = $7.7 \times 10^{-4} \text{ mol L}^{-1}\text{s}^{-1}$

The slope is negative because the concentration of HI is decreasing as time increases. Rates are positive quantities, so we can report the initial rate of reaction as $7.7 \times 10^{-4} \text{ mol L}^{-1}\text{s}^{-1}$. Since the tangent line might be drawn a number of different ways, the time difference is uncertain by more than ten seconds and the rate can be reported simply as $8 \times 10^{-4} \text{ mol L}^{-1}\text{s}^{-1}$.

☐ The average rate is the slope of a line connecting two points on a concentration versus time graph. The instantaneous rate is the slope of a tangent line at a single point. The average and instantaneous rates are quite different from each other.

IS THE ANSWER REASONABLE? The instantaneous rate at time zero ought to be slightly larger than the *average rate* between zero and 50 seconds. We can compute the average rate directly from data in Table 13.1 by selecting a pair of concentrations at two different times.

$$\text{Slope} = \frac{0.0716 \text{ mol/L} - 0.100 \text{ mol/L}}{50 \text{ s} - 0 \text{ s}} = -5.7 \times 10^{-4} \text{ mol L}^{-1} \text{ s}^{-1}$$

Thus, the average rate from 0 to 50 s is 5.7×10^{-4} mol L^{-1} s^{-1}. As expected, this is slightly less than the instantaneous rate at time zero, 8×10^{-4} mol L^{-1} s^{-1}.

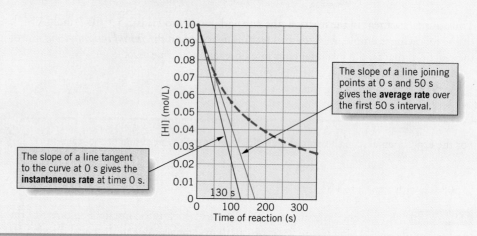

The slope of a line joining points at 0 s and 50 s gives the **average rate** over the first 50 s interval.

The slope of a line tangent to the curve at 0 s gives the **instantaneous rate** at time 0 s.

Practice Exercise 3: Use the graph in Figure 13.5 to estimate the rate of reaction with respect to HI 2.00 minutes after the start of the reaction. (Hint: You need to have time in seconds units to find the point where the tangent should be drawn.)

Practice Exercise 4: Use the graph in Figure 13.5 to estimate the rate of reaction with respect to HI 250 seconds after the start of the reaction.

13.3 RATE LAWS GIVE REACTION RATE AS A FUNCTION OF REACTANT CONCENTRATIONS

Thus far we have focused on a rate with respect to *one* component of a reaction. We'll now broaden our focus to consider a rate expression that includes all reactants.

The rate of a homogeneous reaction at any instant is proportional to the product of the molar concentrations of the reactants, each molarity raised to some power or exponent that has to be found by experiment. Let's consider a chemical reaction with an equation of the following form.

$$A + B \longrightarrow \text{products}$$

Its rate of reaction can be expressed as follows.

$$\text{Rate} \propto [A]^m[B]^n \tag{13.1}$$

As we said, the values of the exponents n and m are found by experiment, which we'll go into shortly.

Rate laws relate reaction rates and concentrations

The proportionality symbol, $\propto$, in Equation 13.1 can be replaced by an equals sign if we introduce a proportionality constant, **k**, which is called the **rate constant** for the reaction. This gives Equation 13.2.

TOOLS

Rate law of a reaction

$$\text{Rate} = k[A]^m[B]^n \tag{13.2}$$

Equation 13.2 is called the **rate law** for the reaction of A with B. Once we have found values for k, n, and m, the rate law allows us to calculate the rate of the reaction at any set of known values of concentrations. Consider, for example, the following reaction.

$$H_2SeO_3 + 6I^- + 4H^+ \longrightarrow Se + 2I_3^- + 3H_2O$$

Its rate law is of the form

$$\text{Rate} = k[H_2SeO_3]^x[I^-]^y[H^+]^z$$

The exponents have been found experimentally to be the following for the initial rate of this reaction (i.e., the rate when the reactants are first combined).

$$x = 1, y = 3, \text{ and } z = 2$$

At 0 °C, k equals $5.0 \times 10^5 \text{ L}^5 \text{ mol}^{-5} \text{ s}^{-1}$. (We have to specify the temperature because k varies with it.) Substituting the exponents and the value of k into the rate law equation gives the rate law for the reaction.

$$\text{Rate} = (5.0 \times 10^5 \text{ L}^5 \text{ mol}^{-5} \text{ s}^{-1})[H_2SeO_3][I^-]^3[H^+]^2 \quad \text{(at 0 °C)}$$

We can calculate the rate of the reaction at 0 °C for any set of concentrations of H_2SeO_3, I^-, and H^+ using this rate law.

☐ The value of k depends on the particular reaction being studied as well as the temperature at which the reaction occurs.

☐ The units of the rate constant are such that the calculated rate will have the units $\text{mol L}^{-1} \text{ s}^{-1}$.

EXAMPLE 13.3
Calculating Reaction Rate from the Rate Law

In the stratosphere, molecular oxygen (O_2) can be broken into two oxygen atoms by ultraviolet radiation from the sun. When one of these oxygen atoms strikes an ozone (O_3) molecule in the stratosphere, the ozone molecule is destroyed, and two oxygen molecules are created:

$$O(g) + O_3(g) \longrightarrow 2O_2(g)$$

This reaction is part of the natural cycle of ozone destruction and creation in the stratosphere. What is the rate of ozone destruction *for this reaction alone* at an altitude of 25 km, if the rate law for the reaction is

$$\text{Rate} = 4.15 \times 10^5 \text{ L mol}^{-1} \text{ s}^{-1}[O_3][O]$$

and the reactant concentrations at 25 km are the following: $[O_3] = 1.2 \times 10^{-8} M$ and $[O] = 1.7 \times 10^{-14} M$?

ANALYSIS: The tool we use for calculating the rate is the rate law. Because we already know the rate law, the answer to this question is merely a matter of substituting the given molar concentrations into this law.

SOLUTION: To see how the units work out, let's write all of the concentration values as well as the rate constant's units in fraction form.

$$\text{Rate} = \frac{4.15 \times 10^5 \text{ L}}{\text{mol s}} \times \left(\frac{1.2 \times 10^{-8} \text{ mol}}{\text{L}} \right) \times \left(\frac{1.7 \times 10^{-14} \text{ mol}}{\text{L}} \right)$$

Performing the arithmetic and canceling the units, we see that

$$\text{Rate} = \frac{8.5 \times 10^{-17} \text{ mol}}{\text{L s}} = 8.5 \times 10^{-17} \text{ mol L}^{-1} \text{ s}^{-1}$$

IS THE ANSWER REASONABLE? There's obviously no simple check. Multiplying the powers of ten for the rate constant and the concentrations together reassures us that the rate is of the correct order of magnitude, and we can see that at least the answer has the correct units for a reaction rate.

Practice Exercise 5: The rate law for the reaction $2NO(g) + 2H_2(g) \longrightarrow N_2(g) + 2H_2O(g)$ is

$$\text{Rate} = k[NO]^2[H_2]$$

If the rate of reaction is 7.86×10^{-3} mol L^{-1} s^{-1} when the concentrations of NO and H_2 are both 2×10^{-6} mol L^{-1} (a) what is the value of the rate constant and (b) what are the units for the rate constant? (Hint: Note the units of the reaction rate.)

Practice Exercise 6: The rate law for the decomposition of HI to I_2 and H_2 is

$$\text{Rate} = k[HI]^2$$

Figure 13.5 shows that at 508 °C, the rate of the reaction of HI was found to be 2.5×10^{-4} mol L^{-1} s^{-1} when the HI concentration was 0.0558 M (see Figure 13.5). (a) What is the value of k? (b) What are the units of k?

You cannot predict the rate law for a reaction from the overall balanced equation for the reaction

Although a rate law's exponents are generally unrelated to the chemical equation's coefficients, they sometimes are the same by coincidence, as is the case in the decomposition of hydrogen iodide.

$$2HI(g) \longrightarrow H_2(g) + I_2(g)$$

The rate law, as we've said, is

$$\text{Rate} = k[HI]^2$$

The exponent of [HI] in the rate law, namely 2, happens to match the coefficient of HI in the overall chemical equation, but *there is no way we could have predicted this match without experimental data.* Therefore, *never* simply assume the exponents and the coefficients are the same; it's a trap that many students fall into.

An exponent in a rate law is called the **order of the reaction**[1] with respect to the corresponding reactant. For instance, the decomposition of gaseous N_2O_5 into NO_2 and O_2,

$$2N_2O_5(g) \longrightarrow 4NO_2(g) + O_2(g)$$

has the rate law

$$\text{Rate} = k[N_2O_5]$$

☐ When the exponent on a concentration term is equal to 1, it is usually omitted.

The exponent of $[N_2O_5]$ is 1, so the reaction rate is said to be *first order* in N_2O_5. The rate law for the decomposition of HI has an exponent of 2 for the HI concentration, so its reaction rate is *second order* in HI. The rate law

$$\text{Rate} = k[H_2SeO_3][I^-]^3[H^+]^2$$

describes a reaction rate that is first order with respect to H_2SeO_3, third order with respect to I^-, and second order with respect to H^+.

The **overall order of reaction** is the sum of the orders with respect to each reactant in the rate law. The decomposition of N_2O_5 is a **first-order reaction,** and the decomposition of HI is a **second-order reaction.** The overall order for the reaction with H_2SeO_3 above is $1 + 3 + 2 = 6$.

The exponents in a rate law are usually small whole numbers, but fractional and negative exponents are occasionally found. A negative exponent means that the concentration term really belongs in the denominator, which means that as the concentration of the species increases, the rate of reaction decreases.

[1] The reason for describing the *order* of a reaction is to take advantage of a great convenience; namely, the mathematics involved in the treatment of the data is the same for all reactions having the same order. We will not go into this very deeply, but you should be familiar with this terminology; it's often used to describe the effects of concentration on reaction rates.

There are even **zero-order reactions.** They have reaction rates that are independent of the concentration of any reactant. Zero-order reactions usually involve a small amount of a catalyst that is saturated with reactants. This is rather like the situation in a crowded supermarket with only a single checkout lane open. It doesn't matter how many people join the line; the line will move at the same rate no matter how many people are standing in it. An example of a zero-order reaction is the elimination of ethyl alcohol in the liver. Regardless of the blood alcohol level, the rate of alcohol removal by the body is constant, because the number of available catalyst molecules present in the liver is constant. Another zero-order reaction is the decomposition of gaseous ammonia into H_2 and N_2 on a hot platinum surface. The rate at which ammonia decomposes is the same, regardless of its concentration in the gas. The rate law for a zero-order reaction is simply

$$\text{Rate} = k$$

where the rate constant k has units of mol L^{-1} s^{-1}. The rate constant depends on the amount, quality, and available surface area of the catalyst. For example, forcing ammonia through hot platinum powder (with a high surface area) would cause it to decompose faster than simply passing it over a hot platinum surface.

Practice Exercise 7: The following reaction

$$\text{BrO}_3^- + 3\text{SO}_3^{2-} \longrightarrow \text{Br}^- + 3\text{SO}_4^{2-}$$

has the rate law

$$\text{Rate} = k[\text{BrO}_3^-][\text{SO}_3^{2-}]$$

What is the order of the reaction with respect to each reactant? What is the overall order of the reaction? (Hint: Recall that a concentration with no exponent has, in effect, an exponent of 1.)

Practice Exercise 8: A certain reaction has an experimental rate law that is found to be second order in Cl_2 and first order in NO. Write the rate law for this reaction.

The order of a reaction must be determined experimentally

We've mentioned several times that the exponents in the rate law of an overall reaction must be determined experimentally. *This is the only way to know for sure what the exponents are.* To determine the exponents, we study how changes in concentration affect the rate of the reaction. For example, consider again the following hypothetical reaction.

$$A + B \longrightarrow \text{products}$$

Suppose, further, that the data in Table 13.2 have been obtained in a series of five experiments. We know the form of the rate law for the reaction will be

$$\text{Rate} = k[A]^m[B]^n$$

TABLE 13.2	Concentration–Rate Data for the Hypothetical Reaction $A + B \longrightarrow$ products		
	Initial Concentrations		Initial Rate of Formation of Products
Experiment	$[A]$ (mol L^{-1})	$[B]$ (mol L^{-1})	(mol L^{-1} s^{-1})
1	0.10	0.10	0.20
2	0.20	0.10	0.40
3	0.30	0.10	0.60
4	0.30	0.20	2.40
5	0.30	0.30	5.40

The values of m and n can be discovered by looking for patterns in the rate data given in the table. *One of the easiest ways to reveal patterns in data is to form ratios of results using different sets of conditions.* Because this technique is quite generally useful, let's look in some detail at how it is applied to the problem of finding the rate law exponents.

For experiments 1, 2, and 3 in Table 13.2, the concentration of B has been held constant at 0.10 M. Any change in the rate for these first three experiments must be due to the change in $[A]$. The rate law tells us that when the concentration of B is held constant, the rate must be proportional to $[A]^m$, so if we take the ratio of rate laws for experiments 2 and 1, we obtain

$$\frac{\text{Rate}_2}{\text{Rate}_1} = \frac{k[A]_2^m [B]_2^n}{k[A]_1^m [B]_1^n} = \frac{k}{k}\left(\frac{[A]_2}{[A]_1}\right)^m \left(\frac{[B]_2}{[B]_1}\right)^n$$

For experiments 1 and 2, the left side of this equation is

$$\frac{\text{Rate}_2}{\text{Rate}_1} = \frac{0.40 \ \text{mol L}^{-1}\text{s}^{-1}}{0.20 \ \text{mol L}^{-1}\text{s}^{-1}} = 2.0$$

and on the right side of the equation the identical concentrations of B and the rate constant k cancel to give

$$\left(\frac{[A]_2}{[A]_1}\right)^m = \left(\frac{0.20 \ \text{mol L}^{-1}}{0.10 \ \text{mol L}^{-1}}\right)^m = 2.0^m$$

so doubling $[A]$ in going from experiment 1 to experiment 2 doubles the rate, and the relationship reduces to $2.0 = 2.0^m$. For each unique combination of experiments 1, 2, and 3, we have

$$2.0 = 2.0^m \quad \text{(for experiments 2 and 1)}$$
$$3.0 = 3.0^m \quad \text{(for experiments 3 and 1)}$$
$$1.5 = 1.5^m \quad \text{(for experiments 3 and 2)}$$

The only value of m that makes all of these equations true is $m = 1$. Therefore, this reaction must be first order with respect to A.

A similar method will give us the exponent on $[B]$. In the final three experiments, the concentration of B changes while the concentration of A is held constant. This time it is the concentration of B that affects the rate. Taking the ratio of rate laws for experiments 4 and 3, we have

$$\frac{\text{Rate}_4}{\text{Rate}_3} = \frac{k\,[A]_4^m\,[B]_4^n}{k\,[A]_3^m\,[B]_3^n}$$

that, after cancelling the identical concentrations of A and the rate constant, k, becomes

$$\frac{\text{Rate}_4}{\text{Rate}_3} = \left(\frac{[B]_4}{[B]_3}\right)^n$$

For each unique combination of experiments 3, 4, and 5, we have

$$4.0 = 2.0^n \quad \text{(for experiments 4 and 3)}$$
$$9.0 = 3.0^n \quad \text{(for experiments 5 and 3)}$$
$$2.25 = 1.5^n \quad \text{(for experiments 5 and 4)}$$

The only value of n that makes all of these equations true is $n = 2$, so the reaction must be second order with respect to B.

Having determined the exponents for the concentration terms, we now know that the rate law for the reaction must be

$$\text{Rate} = k[A]^1[B]^2$$

To calculate the value of k, we substitute rate and concentration data into the rate law for any one of the sets of data.

		Exponent on the Concentration
Factor by Which the Concentration Is Changed	Factor by Which the Rate Changes	Term in the Rate Law
2	Rate	0
3	is	0
4	unchanged	0
2	$2 = 2^1$	1
3	$3 = 3^1$	1
4	$4 = 4^1$	1
2	$4 = 2^2$	2
3	$9 = 3^2$	2
4	$16 = 4^2$	2
2	$8 = 2^3$	3
3	$27 = 3^3$	3
4	$64 = 4^3$	3

TABLE 13.3 Relationship between the Order of a Reaction and Changes in Concentration and Rate

$$k = \frac{\text{rate}}{[A]^1[B]^2}$$

Using the data from the first set in Table 13.2,

$$k = \frac{0.20 \text{ mol L}^{-1} \text{ s}^{-1}}{(0.10 \text{ mol L}^{-1})(0.10 \text{ mol L}^{-1})^2}$$

$$= \frac{0.20 \text{ mol L}^{-1} \text{ s}^{-1}}{0.0010 \text{ mol}^3 \text{ L}^{-3}}$$

After canceling such units as we can, the value of k with the net units is

$$k = 2.0 \times 10^2 \text{ L}^2 \text{ mol}^{-2} \text{ s}^{-1}$$

Practice Exercise 9: Use the data from the other four experiments (Table 13.2) to calculate k for this reaction. What do you notice about the values of k? (Hint: Don't forget the exponents in the rate law.)

Practice Exercise 10: Use the rate law determined above to describe what will happen to the reaction rate under the following conditions: (a) the concentration of B is tripled, (b) the concentration of A is tripled, (c) the concentration of A is tripled and the concentration of B is halved.

Table 13.3 summarizes the reasoning used to determine the order with respect to each reactant from experimental data.

EXAMPLE 13.4
Determining the Exponents of a Rate Law

Sulfuryl chloride, SO_2Cl_2, is used to manufacture the antiseptic chlorophenol. The following data were collected on the decomposition of SO_2Cl_2 at a certain temperature.

$$SO_2Cl_2(g) \longrightarrow SO_2(g) + Cl_2(g)$$

Initial Concentration of SO_2Cl_2 (mol L^{-1})	Initial Rate of Formation of SO_2 (mol L^{-1} s^{-1})
0.100	2.2×10^{-6}
0.200	4.4×10^{-6}
0.300	6.6×10^{-6}

What are the rate law and the value of the rate constant for this reaction?

ANALYSIS: The first step is to write the general form of the expected rate law so we can see which exponents have to be determined. Then we study the data to see how the rate changes when the concentration is changed by a certain factor.

SOLUTION: We expect the rate law to have the form

$$\text{Rate} = k[SO_2Cl_2]^x$$

Let's examine the data from the first two experiments. Notice that when we double the concentration from 0.100 M to 0.200 M, the initial rate doubles (from 2.2×10^{-6} mol L^{-1} s^{-1} to 4.4×10^{-6} mol L^{-1} s^{-1}). If we look at the first and third, we see that when the concentration triples (from 0.100 M to 0.300 M), the rate also triples (from 2.2×10^{-6} mol L^{-1} s^{-1} to 6.6×10^{-6} mol L^{-1} s^{-1}). This behavior tells us that the reaction must be first order in the SO_2Cl_2 concentration. The rate law is therefore

$$\text{Rate} = k[SO_2Cl_2]^1$$

☐ We could also use experiments 2 and 3. From the second to the third, the rate increases by the same factor, 1.5, as the concentration, so by these data, too, the reaction must be first order.

To evaluate k, we can use any of the three sets of data. Choosing the first,

$$k = \frac{\text{rate}}{[SO_2Cl_2]^1}$$

$$= \frac{2.2 \times 10^{-6} \;\cancel{\text{mol L}^{-1}}\; s^{-1}}{0.100 \;\cancel{\text{mol L}^{-1}}}$$

$$= 2.2 \times 10^{-5} \; s^{-1}$$

IS THE ANSWER REASONABLE? We should get the same value of k by picking any other pair of values. With the last pair of data, at an initial molar concentration of SO_2Cl_2 of 0.300 mol L^{-1} and an initial rate of 6.6×10^{-6} mol L^{-1} s^{-1}, we calculate k again to be 2.2×10^{-5} s^{-1}.

EXAMPLE 13.5
Determining the Exponents of a Rate Law

The following data were measured for the reduction of nitric oxide with hydrogen.

$$2NO(g) + 2H_2(g) \longrightarrow N_2(g) + 2H_2O(g)$$

Initial Concentrations (mol L^{-1})		Initial Rate of Formation of H$_2$O (mol L^{-1} s^{-1})
[NO]	[H$_2$]	
0.10	0.10	1.23×10^{-3}
0.10	0.20	2.46×10^{-3}
0.20	0.10	4.92×10^{-3}

What is the rate law for the reaction?

ANALYSIS: This time we have two reactants. To see how their concentrations affect the rate we must vary only one concentration at a time. Therefore, we choose two experiments in which the concentration of one reactant doesn't change and examine the effect of a change in the concentration of the other reactant. Then we repeat the procedure for the second reactant.

SOLUTION: We expect the rate law to have the form

$$\text{Rate} = k[NO]^m[H_2]^n$$

Let's look at the first two experiments. Here the concentration of NO remains the same, so the rate is being affected by the change in the H_2 concentration. When we double the H_2 concentration, the rate doubles, so the reaction is first order with respect to H_2. This means $n = 1$.

Next, we need to pick two experiments in which the H_2 concentration doesn't change. Working with the first and third, we see that [NO] doubles and the rate increases by a factor of $4.92/1.23 = 4.00$. When doubling the concentration of a species quadruples the rate, the reaction is second order in that species, so $m = 2$.

Therefore, the rate law for the reaction is

$$\text{Rate} = k[NO]^2[H_2]$$

IS THE ANSWER REASONABLE? The only data that we haven't used as a pair are the data for the second and third reactions. The value of [NO] increases by 2 in going from the second to the third set of data, so this should multiply the rate by 2^2 or 4, if we've found the right exponents. But the value for $[H_2]$ halves at the same time, so this should take a rate that is otherwise four times as large and cut it by a factor of $(1/2)^1$ or in half. The net effect, then, is to make the rate of the third reaction two times as large as that of the second reaction, which is the observed rate change.

Practice Exercise 11: The following reaction is investigated to determine its rate law.

$$2NO(g) + 2H_2(g) \longrightarrow N_2(g) + 2H_2O(g)$$

Experiments yielded the following results.

Initial Concentrations (mol L^{-1})		Initial Rate of Formation of N_2 (mol L^{-1} s^{-1})
[NO]	[H$_2$]	
0.40×10^{-4}	0.30×10^{-4}	1.0×10^{-8}
0.80×10^{-4}	0.30×10^{-4}	4.0×10^{-8}
0.80×10^{-4}	0.60×10^{-4}	8.0×10^{-8}

(a) Show that these data yield the same rate law as in the preceding Example. (b) What is the value of the rate constant? (c) What are the units for the rate constant? (Hint: Identify the two experiments where only the [NO] changes and the two experiments where only the $[H_2]$ varies.)

Practice Exercise 12: Ordinary sucrose (table sugar) reacts with water in an acidic solution to produce two simpler sugars, glucose and fructose, that have the same molecular formulas.

$$\underset{\text{sucrose}}{C_{12}H_{22}O_{11}} + H_2O \longrightarrow \underset{\text{glucose}}{C_6H_{12}O_6} + \underset{\text{fructose}}{C_6H_{12}O_6}$$

In a series of experiments, the following data were obtained.

Initial Sucrose Concentration (mol L^{-1})	Rate of Formation of Glucose (mol L^{-1} s^{-1})
0.10	6.17×10^{-5}
0.20	1.23×10^{-4}
0.50	3.09×10^{-4}

(a) What is the order of the reaction with respect to sucrose? (b) What is the value of the rate constant, with its units?

Practice Exercise 13: A certain reaction has the following equation: $A + B \longrightarrow C + D$. Experiments yielded the following results.

Initial Concentrations (mol L^{-1})		Initial Rate of Formation of C (mol L^{-1} s^{-1})
$[A]$	$[B]$	
0.40	0.30	1.00×10^{-4}
0.60	0.30	2.25×10^{-4}
0.80	0.60	1.60×10^{-3}

(a) What is the rate law for the reaction? (b) What is the value of the rate constant? (c) What are the units for the rate constant? (d) What is the overall order of this reaction?

13.4 | INTEGRATED RATE LAWS GIVE CONCENTRATION AS A FUNCTION OF TIME

The rate law tells us how the speed of a reaction varies with the concentrations of the reactants. Often, however, we are more interested in how the concentrations change over time. For instance, if we were preparing some compound, we might want to know how long it will take for the reactant concentrations to drop to some particular value, so we can decide when to isolate the products.

The relationship between the concentration of a reactant and time can be derived from a rate law using calculus. By summing or "integrating" the instantaneous rates of a reaction from the start of the reaction until some specified time t, we can obtain **integrated rate laws** that quantitatively give concentration as a function of time. The form of the integrated rate law depends on the order of the reaction. The mathematical expressions that relate concentration and time in complex reactions can be complicated, so we will concentrate on using integrated rate laws for a few simple first- and second-order reactions.

The natural logarithm of concentration is related linearly with time for first-order reactions

A reaction that is first order has a rate law of the type

$$\text{Rate} = k[A]$$

Using calculus[2] the following equation can be derived that relates the concentration of A and time.

TOOLS
Integrated rate law, first-order reaction

$$\ln \frac{[A]_0}{[A]_t} = kt \tag{13.3}$$

---

[2] For a first-order reaction, the integrated rate law is obtained by calculus as follows. The instantaneous rate of change of the reactant A is given as

$$\text{Rate} = \frac{-d[A]}{dt} = k[A]$$

This can be rearranged to

$$\frac{d[A]}{[A]} = -k\,dt$$

Next, we integrate between $t = 0$ and $t = t$ as the concentration of A changes from $[A]_0$ to $[A]_t$.

$$\int_{[A]_0}^{[A]_t} \frac{d[A]}{[A]} = \int_0^t -k\,dt$$

$$\ln[A]_t - \ln[A]_0 = -kt$$

Using the properties of logarithms, this can be rearranged to give

$$\ln \frac{[A]_0}{[A]_t} = kt$$

The symbol "ln" means natural logarithm. The expression to the left of the equals sign is the natural logarithm of the ratio of $[A]_0$ (the initial concentration of A at $t = 0$) to $[A]_t$ (the concentration of A at a time t after the start of the reaction). We take advantage of a property of logarithms that allows us to write the ratio as a difference in logarithms.

$$\ln[A]_0 - \ln[A]_t = kt$$

We can take the antilogarithm of both sides of Equation 13.3 and rearrange it to obtain the concentration at time t directly as a function of time. Taking the antilogarithm and rearranging algebraically gives[3]

$$[A]_t = [A]_0\, e^{-kt} \qquad (13.4)$$

where e is the base of the system of natural logarithms ($e = 2.718\ldots$). Equation 13.4 shows that the concentration of A decays (decreases) exponentially with time. Calculations can use Equation 13.3 or 13.4. When both of the concentrations are known, it is easiest to use Equation 13.3; when we wish to calculate either $[A]_0$ or $[A]_t$ it may be easier to use Equation 13.4.

☐ $[A]_t$ decreases exponentially because the product kt increases with time, but its negative value becomes more negative with time. As the exponent of e becomes a larger negative number the value of the expression becomes smaller.

EXAMPLE 13.6
Concentration–Time Calculations for First-Order Reactions

Dinitrogen pentoxide is not very stable. In the gas phase or dissolved in a nonaqueous solvent, like carbon tetrachloride, it decomposes by a first-order reaction into dinitrogen tetroxide and molecular oxygen.

$$2N_2O_5 \longrightarrow 2N_2O_4 + O_2$$

The rate law is

$$\text{Rate} = k[N_2O_5]$$

At 45 °C, the rate constant for the reaction in carbon tetrachloride is $6.22 \times 10^{-4}\ s^{-1}$. If the initial concentration of N_2O_5 in a carbon tetrachloride solution at 45 °C is 0.500 M, what will its concentration be after exactly one hour?

ANALYSIS: We're dealing with a first-order reaction and the relationship between concentration and time, so the tool we have to apply is either Equation 13.3 or 13.4. Specifically, we have to solve for an unknown concentration. The easiest form of the equation to use when one of the unknowns is a concentration term is Equation 13.4. In performing the calculation, we have to remember that the unit of k involves seconds, not hours, so we must convert the given 1 hr into seconds (1 hr = 3600 s).

SOLUTION: Let's begin by listing the data.

$$[N_2O_5]_0 = 0.500\,M \qquad [N_2O_5]_t = ?\,M$$
$$k = 6.22 \times 10^{-4}\,s^{-1} \qquad t = 3600\,s$$

Using Equation 13.4,[4]

$$[N_2O_5]_t = [N_2O_5]_0\, e^{-kt}$$
$$= (0.500\,M) \times e^{-(6.22\times10^{-4}s^{-1}) \times 3600\,s}$$
$$= (0.500\,M) \times e^{-2.24}$$
$$= (0.500\,M) \times 0.11$$
$$= 0.055\,M$$

☐ Calculating $e^{-2.24}$ is a simple operation using a scientific calculator. In most cases it is the inverse of the ln function.

[3] Because of the nature of logarithms, if $\ln x = y$, then $e^{\ln x} = e^y$. But $e^{\ln x} = x$, so $x = e^y$. A similar relationship exists for common (base 10) logarithms. If $\log x = y$, then $10^{\log x} = x = 10^y$.

[4] There are special rules for significant figures for logarithms and antilogarithms. In writing the logarithm of a quantity, the number of digits written *after the decimal point* equals the number of significant figures in the quantity. Raising e to the -2.24 power is the same as taking the antilogarithm of -2.24. Because the quantity -2.24 has two digits after the decimal, the antilogarithm, $0.1064\ldots$, must be rounded to 0.11 to show just two significant figures.

After one hour, the concentration of N_2O_5 will have dropped to 0.055 M.

The calculation could also have been done using Equation 13.3. We would begin by solving for the concentration ratio, substituting values for k and t.

$$\ln\left(\frac{[N_2O_5]_0}{[N_2O_5]_t}\right) = (6.22 \times 10^{-4}\, s^{-1}) \times 3600\, s$$

To take the antilogarithm (antiln), we raise e to the 2.24 power.

$$\text{antiln}\left[\ln\left(\frac{[N_2O_5]_0}{[N_2O_5]_t}\right)\right] = \frac{[N_2O_5]_0}{[N_2O_5]_t}$$

$$\text{antiln}\,(2.24) = e^{2.24}$$

$$= 9.4 \text{ (rounding to 2 significant figures)}$$

This means that

$$\frac{[N_2O_5]_0}{[N_2O_5]_t} = 9.4$$

Now we can substitute the known concentration, $[N_2O_5]_0 = 0.500\ M$. This gives

$$\frac{0.500\ M}{[N_2O_5]_t} = 9.4$$

Solving for $[N_2O_5]_t$ gives

$$[N_2O_5]_t = \frac{0.500\ M}{9.4}$$

$$= 0.053\ M$$

The answers obtained by the two methods differ slightly because of "rounding errors." You can see that using Equation 13.4 is much easier for working this particular problem.

IS THE ANSWER REASONABLE? Notice that the final concentration of N_2O_5 is *less* than its initial concentration. You'd know that you made a huge mistake if the calculated final concentration was larger than the initial 0.500 M because reactants are used up by reactions. Also, we obtained essentially the same answer using both equations, so we can be confident it's correct. (If you're faced with a problem like this, you don't have to do it both ways; we just wanted to show that either equation could be used.)

Practice Exercise 14: When designing a consumer product it is desirable that it have a two year shelf life. Often this means that the active ingredient in the product should not decrease by more than 5% in two years. If the reaction is first order, what rate constant must the decomposition reaction of the active ingredient have? (Hint: What are the initial and final percentages of active ingredient?)

Practice Exercise 15: In Practice Exercise 12, the reaction of sucrose with water in an acidic solution was described.

$$\underset{\text{sucrose}}{C_{12}H_{22}O_{11}} + H_2O \longrightarrow \underset{\text{glucose}}{C_6H_{12}O_6} + \underset{\text{fructose}}{C_6H_{12}O_6}$$

The reaction is first order with a rate constant of $6.2 \times 10^{-5}\ s^{-1}$ at 35 °C, when the H^+ concentration is 0.10 M. Suppose, in an experiment, the initial sucrose concentration was 0.40 M. (a) What will its concentration be after exactly 2 hours? (b) How many minutes will it take for the concentration of sucrose to drop to 0.30 M?

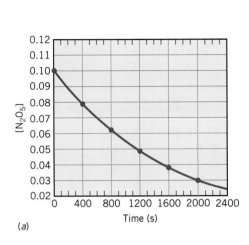
(a)

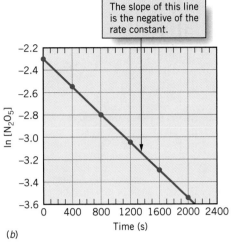
(b)

The slope of this line is the negative of the rate constant.

FIG. 13.6 The decomposition of N_2O_5. (*a*) A graph of concentration versus time for the decomposition at 45 °C. (*b*) A straight line is obtained if the logarithm of the concentration is plotted versus time. The slope of this line equals the negative of the rate constant for the reaction.

The rate constant can be determined graphically

Using the properties of logarithms,[5] Equation 13.3 can be rewritten in a form that corresponds to the equation for a straight line.

$$\ln[A]_t = -kt + \ln[A]_0$$
$$\updownarrow \qquad \updownarrow\updownarrow \qquad \updownarrow$$
$$y = mx + b$$

A plot of the values of $\ln[A]_t$ (vertical axis) versus values of t (horizontal axis) should give a straight line that has a slope equal to $-k$. Such a plot is illustrated in Figure 13.6 for the decomposition of N_2O_5 into N_2O_4 and O_2 in the solvent carbon tetrachloride.

□ The equation for a straight line is usually written
$$y = mx + b$$
where x and y are variables, m is the slope, and b is the intercept of the line with the y axis.

The half-life of a reactant is a measure of its speed of reaction

The *half-life* of a reactant is a convenient way to describe how fast it reacts, particularly for a first-order process. A reactant's **half-life, $t_{1/2}$,** is the amount of time required for half of the reactant to disappear. A rapid reaction has a short half-life because half of the reactant disappears quickly. The equations for half-lives depend on the order of the reaction.

When a reaction, overall, is first order, the half-life of the reactant can be obtained from Equation 13.3 by setting $[A]_t$ equal to one-half of $[A]_0$.

$$[A]_t = \tfrac{1}{2}[A]_0$$

Substituting $\tfrac{1}{2}[A]_0$ for $[A]_t$ and $t_{1/2}$ for t in Equation 13.3, we have

$$\ln \frac{[A]_0}{\tfrac{1}{2}[A]_0} = kt_{1/2}$$

Noting that the left-hand side of the equation simplifies to $\ln 2$, and solving the equation for $t_{1/2}$, we have

$$t_{1/2} = \frac{\ln 2}{k} \qquad (13.5)$$

□ Because $\ln 2$ equals 0.693, Equation 13.5 is sometimes written
$$t_{1/2} = \frac{0.693}{k}$$

TOOLS
Half-life

Because k is a constant for a given reaction, the half-life is also a constant for any particular first-order reaction (at any given temperature). Remarkably, in other words, *the half-life of a first-order reaction is not affected by the initial concentration of the reactant.* This can be illustrated by one of the most common first-order events in nature, the change that radioactive isotopes undergo during radioactive "decay." In fact, you have probably heard the term *half-life* used in reference to the life spans of radioactive substances.

[5] The logarithm of a quotient, $\ln \dfrac{a}{b}$, can be written as the difference, $\ln a - \ln b$.

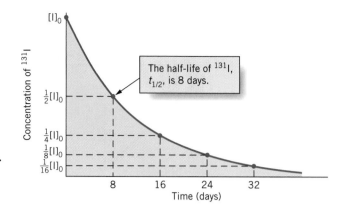

FIG. 13.7 First-order radioactive decay of iodine-131. The initial concentration of the isotope is represented by $[I]_0$.

☐ $^{131}_{53}I \rightarrow ^{131}_{54}Xe + ^{0}_{-1}e$

Iodine-131, an unstable, radioactive isotope of iodine, undergoes a nuclear reaction whereby it emits a beta particle ($^{0}_{-1}e$) and changes into a stable isotope of xenon.[6] The intensity of the radiation decreases, or *decays,* with time (see Figure 13.7). Notice that the time it takes for the first half of the ^{131}I to disappear is 8 days. Then, during the next 8 days half of the remaining ^{131}I disappears, and so on. Regardless of the initial amount, it takes 8 days for half of that amount of ^{131}I to disappear, which means that the half-life of ^{131}I is a constant.

EXAMPLE 13.7
Half–life Calculations

Suppose a patient is given a certain amount of iodine-131 as part of a diagnostic procedure for a thyroid disorder. Given that the half-life of radioactive iodine-131 is 8.0 days, what fraction of the initial iodine-131 would be present in a patient after 24 days if none of it were eliminated through natural body processes?

ANALYSIS: We've learned that radioactive iodine-131 decays by a first-order process with a constant half-life. A period of 24 days is exactly three 8.0 day half-lives. Therefore, let's apply the half-life concept three times.

SOLUTION: If we take the fraction initially present to be 1, we can set up a table

☐ The fraction remaining after n half-lives is $\left(\frac{1}{2}\right)^n$, or simply $\frac{1}{2^n}$.

Half-life	0	1	2	3
Fraction	1	$\frac{1}{2}$	$\frac{1}{4}$	$\frac{1}{8}$

Half of the iodine-131 is lost in the first half-life, half of that disappears in the second half-life, and so on. Therefore, the fraction remaining after three half-lives is $\frac{1}{8}$.

IS THE ANSWER REASONABLE? We could also have solved the problem using the integrated first-order rate law, Equation 13.3. We'll need the first order rate constant, k, which we can obtain from the half-life by rearranging Equation 13.5:

$$k = \frac{\ln 2}{t_{1/2}} = \frac{0.693}{8.0 \text{ days}} = 0.0866 \text{ day}^{-1}$$

Then we can use Equation 13.3 to compute the fraction $\frac{[A]_0}{[A]_t}$

$$\ln \frac{[A]_0}{[A]_t} = kt = (0.0866 \text{ day}^{-1})(24.0 \text{ day}) = 2.08$$

---

[6] Iodine-131 is used in the diagnosis of thyroid disorders. The thyroid gland is a small organ located just below the Adam's apple and astride the windpipe. It uses iodide ion to make a hormone, so when a patient is given a dose of $^{131}I^-$ mixed with nonradioactive I^-, both ions are taken up by the thyroid gland. The change in (temporary) radioactivity of the gland is a measure of thyroid activity.

Taking the antilogarithm of both sides, we have

$$\frac{[A]_0}{[A]_t} = e^{2.08} = 8.0$$

The initial concentration, $[A]_0$, is 8.0 times as large as the concentration after 24.0 days, so the fraction remaining after 24 days is $\frac{1}{8}$, which is exactly what we obtained much more simply above.

Practice Exercise 16: In Practice Exercise 12, the reaction of sucrose with water was found to be first order with respect to sucrose. The rate constant under the conditions of the experiments was 6.17×10^{-4} s^{-1}. Calculate the value of $t_{1/2}$ for this reaction in minutes. How many minutes would it take for three-quarters of the sucrose to react? (Hint: What fraction of the sucrose remains?)

Practice Exercise 17: From the answer to Practice Exercise 14, determine the half-life of an active ingredient that has a shelf life of 2.00 years.

Carbon-14 dating determines the age of organic substances

Carbon-14 is a radioactive isotope that is formed in small amounts in the upper atmosphere by the action of cosmic rays on nitrogen atoms. Once formed, the carbon-14 diffuses into the lower atmosphere. It becomes oxidized to carbon dioxide and enters the earth's biosphere by means of photosynthesis. Carbon-14 thus becomes incorporated into plant substances and into the materials of animals that eat plants. As the carbon-14 decays, more is ingested by the living thing. The net effect is an overall equilibrium involving carbon-14 in the global system. As long as the plant or animal is alive, its ratio of carbon-14 atoms to carbon-12 atoms is constant. At death, an organism's remains have as much carbon-14 as they can ever have, and they now slowly lose this carbon-14 by decay. The decay is a first-order process with a rate independent of the *number* of original carbon atoms. The ratio of carbon-14 to carbon-12, therefore, can be related to the years that have elapsed between the time of death and the time of the measurement. The critical assumption in carbon-14 dating is that the steady-state availability of carbon-14 from the atmosphere has remained largely unchanged over the period for which measurements are valid.[7]

In contemporary biological samples the ratio $^{14}C/^{12}C$ is about 1.2×10^{-12}. Thus, each fresh 1.0 g sample of biological carbon in equilibrium with the $^{14}CO_2$ of the atmosphere has a ratio of 5.8×10^{10} atoms of carbon-14 to 4.8×10^{22} atoms of carbon-12. The ratio decreases by a factor of 2 for each half-life period of ^{14}C (5730 years).

The dating of an object makes use of the fact that radioactive decay is a first-order process. If we let r_0 stand for the $^{14}C/^{12}C$ ratio at the time of death of the carbon-containing species and r_t stand for the $^{14}C/^{12}C$ ratio now, after the elapse of t years, we can substitute into Equation 13.3 to obtain

$$\ln \frac{r_0}{r_t} = kt \tag{13.6}$$

where k is the rate constant for the decay (the *decay constant* for ^{14}C) and t is the elapsed time. We can obtain the rate constant from the half-life of ^{14}C using Equation 13.5.

$$\ln 2 = kt_{1/2}$$

◻ In all dating experiments the amounts of sample are extremely small and extraordinary precautions must be taken to avoid contaminating specimens with "modern" materials.

◻ Willard F. Libby won the Nobel Prize in Chemistry in 1960 for his discovery of the carbon-14 method for dating ancient objects.

---

[7] The available atmospheric pool of carbon-14 atoms fluctuates somewhat with the intensities of cosmic ray showers, with slow, long-term changes in the earth's magnetic field, and with the huge injections of carbon-12 into the atmosphere from the large-scale burning of coal and petroleum in the 1900s. To reduce the uncertainties in carbon-14 dating, results of the method have been corrected against dates made by tree-ring counting. For example, an uncorrected carbon-14 dating of a Viking site at L'anse aux Meadows, Newfoundland, gave a date of AD 895 ± 30. When corrected, the date of the settlement became AD 997, almost exactly the time indicated in Icelandic sagas for Leif Eriksson's landing at "Vinland," now believed to be the L'anse aux Meadows site.

Substituting 5730 yr for $t_{1/2}$ and solving for k gives $k = 1.21 \times 10^{-4}$ yr^{-1}. We can now substitute this value into Equation 13.6 to give

$$\ln \frac{r_0}{r_t} = (1.21 \times 10^{-4} \text{ yr}^{-1})t \tag{13.7}$$

Equation 13.7 can be used to calculate the age of a once-living object if its current $^{14}C/^{12}C$ ratio can be measured.

EXAMPLE 13.8
Calculating the Age of an Object by ^{14}C Dating

Using a device similar to a mass spectrometer, a sample of an ancient wooden object was found to have a ratio of ^{14}C to ^{12}C equal to 3.3×10^{-13}. What is the age of the object?

ANALYSIS: This is a straightforward calculation that involves using Equation 13.7. We simply substitute values.

SOLUTION: The contemporary ratio of ^{14}C to ^{12}C was given earlier as 1.2×10^{-12}. This corresponds to r_0 in Equation 13.7. Substituting into Equation 13.7 gives

$$\ln \frac{1.2 \times 10^{-12}}{3.3 \times 10^{-13}} = (1.21 \times 10^{-4} \text{ yr}^{-1})t$$

$$\ln(3.6) = (1.21 \times 10^{-4} \text{ yr}^{-1})t$$

Solving for t gives an age of 1.1×10^4 years (11,000 years).

IS THE ANSWER REASONABLE? We've been told that the object is ancient, so 11,000 years old seems to make sense. (Also, if you had substituted incorrectly into Equation 13.7, the answer would have been negative, and that certainly doesn't make sense!)

Practice Exercise 18: The ^{14}C content of an ancient piece of wood was found to be one-eighth of that in living trees. How many years old is this piece of wood ($t_{1/2} = 5730$ for ^{14}C)? (Hint: Recall the relationship between the integrated rate equation and half-life.)

Practice Exercise 19: When using carbon-14 dating, samples that have decayed less than 5% and those that have decayed more than 95% may have unacceptably large uncertainties. With that information, what are the upper and lower limits of dates before present, BP, that can be determined?

The reciprocal of the concentration is related linearly to time for second-order reactions

For simplicity, we will only consider a second-order reaction with a rate law of the following type.

$$\text{Rate} = k[B]^2$$

The relationship between concentration and time for a reaction with such a rate law is given by Equation 13.8, an equation that is quite different from that for a first-order reaction.

TOOLS
Integrated rate law, second-order reaction

$$\frac{1}{[B]_t} - \frac{1}{[B]_0} = kt \tag{13.8}$$

$[B]_0$ is the initial concentration of B and $[B]_t$ is the concentration at time t. The next example illustrates how Equation 13.8 is applied to calculations.

EXAMPLE 13.9
Concentration–Time Calculations for Second-Order Reactions

Nitrosyl chloride, NOCl, decomposes slowly to NO and Cl_2.

$$2NOCl \longrightarrow 2NO + Cl_2$$

The rate law shows that the rate is second order in NOCl.

$$\text{Rate} = k[NOCl]^2$$

The rate constant k equals 0.020 L mol^{-1} s^{-1} at a certain temperature. If the initial concentration of NOCl in a closed reaction vessel is 0.050 M, what will the concentration be after 30 minutes?

ANALYSIS: We're given a rate law and so can see that it is for a second-order reaction and has the simple form to which our study is limited. We must calculate [NOCl]$_t$, the molar concentration of NOCl, after 30 minutes (1800 s). Our tool for doing this is Equation 13.8.

SOLUTION: Let's begin by tabulating the data.

$$[\text{NOCl}]_0 = 0.050\ M \qquad [\text{NOCl}]_t = ?\ M$$
$$k = 0.020\ \text{L mol}^{-1}\text{s}^{-1} \qquad t = 1800\ s$$

The equation we wish to substitute into is

$$\frac{1}{[\text{NOCl}]_t} - \frac{1}{[\text{NOCl}]_0} = kt$$

Making the substitutions gives

$$\frac{1}{[\text{NOCl}]_t} - \frac{1}{0.050\ \text{mol L}^{-1}} = (0.020\ \text{L mol}^{-1}\text{s}^{-1}) \times (1800\ s)$$

Solving for 1/[NOCl]$_t$ gives

$$\frac{1}{[\text{NOCl}]_t} - 20\ \text{L mol}^{-1} = 36\ \text{L mol}^{-1}$$

$$\frac{1}{[\text{NOCl}]_t} = 56\ \text{L mol}^{-1}$$

Taking the reciprocals of both sides gives us the value of [NOCl]$_t$.

$$[\text{NOCl}]_t = \frac{1}{56\ \text{L mol}^{-1}} = 0.018\ \text{mol L}^{-1} = 0.018\ M$$

The molar concentration of NOCl has decreased from 0.050 M to 0.018 M after 30 minutes.

IS THE ANSWER REASONABLE? The concentration of NOCl has decreased, so the answer appears to be reasonable.

Practice Exercise 20: For the reaction in the preceding example, determine how many minutes it would take for the NOCl concentration to drop from 0.040 M to 0.010 M. (Hint: In solving Equation 13.8 time must be a positive value.)

Practice Exercise 21: A sample of nitrosyl chloride was collected for analysis at 10:35 am. At 3:15 pm the same day the sample was analyzed and was found to contain 0.00035 M NOCl. What was the concentration of NOCl at the time the sample was collected?

The second-order rate constant also can be determined graphically

The rate constant k for a second-order reaction, one with a rate following Equation 13.8, can be determined graphically by a method similar to that used for a first-order reaction. We can rearrange Equation 13.8 so that it corresponds to an equation for a straight line.

$$\frac{1}{[B]_t} = kt + \frac{1}{[B]_0}$$
$$\updownarrow \qquad \updownarrow\updownarrow \qquad \updownarrow$$
$$y = \quad mx + \quad b$$

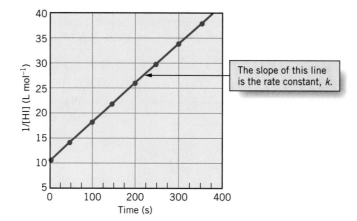

FIG. 13.8 Second-order kinetics. A graph of 1/[HI] versus time for the data in Table 13.1.

When a reaction is second order, then, a plot of $1/[B]_t$ versus t should yield a straight line having a slope k. This is illustrated in Figure 13.8 for the decomposition of HI, using data in Table 13.1.

Half-lives of second-order reactions depend on concentration

The half-life of a second-order reaction *does* depend on initial reactant concentrations. We can see this by examining Figure 13.5 (page 524), which follows the decomposition of gaseous HI, a second-order reaction. The reaction begins with a hydrogen iodide concentration of 0.10 *M*. After 125 seconds, the concentration of HI drops to 0.050 *M*, so 125 s is the observed half-life when the initial concentration of HI is 0.10 *M*. If we then take 0.050 *M* as the next "initial" concentration, we find that it takes 250 seconds (at a *total* elapsed time of 375 seconds) to drop to 0.025 *M*. If we cut the initial concentration in half, from 0.10 *M* to 0.05 *M*, the half-life doubles, from 125 to 250 seconds.

It can be shown that for a second-order reaction of the type we're studying, the half-life is inversely proportional to the initial concentration of the reactant. The half-life is related to the rate constant by Equation 13.9.

$$t_{1/2} = \frac{1}{k \times \text{(initial concentration of reactant)}} \tag{13.9}$$

EXAMPLE 13.10
Half–life Calculations

The reaction $2HI(g) \longrightarrow H_2(g) + I_2(g)$ has the rate law, Rate $= k[HI]^2$, with $k = 0.079$ L mol^{-1} s^{-1} at 508 °C. What is the half-life for this reaction at this temperature when the initial HI concentration is 0.10 *M*?

ANALYSIS: The rate law tells us that the reaction is second order. To calculate the half-life, we need to use Equation 13.9.

SOLUTION: The initial concentration is 0.10 mol L^{-1}; $k = 0.079$ L mol^{-1} s^{-1}. Substituting these values into Equation 13.9 gives

$$t_{1/2} = \frac{1}{(0.079 \text{ L mol}^{-1} \text{ s}^{-1})(0.10 \text{ mol L}^{-1})}$$

$$= 1.3 \times 10^2 \text{ s}$$

IS THE ANSWER REASONABLE? To estimate the answer we round the 0.079 to 0.1. The estimated answer is $\frac{1}{0.1 \times 0.1} = 100$. This is close to our calculated value. In addition we check that the units cancel to leave only the seconds units. Both of these checks support our answer.

Practice Exercise 22: The reaction $2NO_2 \longrightarrow 2NO + O_2$ is second order with respect to NO_2. If the initial concentration of $NO_2(g)$ is 6.54×10^{-4} mol L^{-1}, what is the rate constant if the initial reaction rate is 4.42×10^{-7} mol L^{-1} s^{-1}? What is the half-life of this system? (Hint: Start by setting up and solving the rate law before the integrated equation.)

Practice Exercise 23: Suppose that the value of $t_{1/2}$ for a certain reaction was found to be independent of the initial concentration of the reactants. What could you say about the order of the reaction? Justify your answer.

13.5 | REACTION RATE THEORIES EXPLAIN EXPERIMENTAL RATE LAWS IN TERMS OF MOLECULAR COLLISIONS

In Section 13.1 we mentioned that nearly all reactions proceed faster at higher temperatures. As a rule, the reaction rate increases by a factor of about 2 or 3 for each 10 °C increase in temperature, although the actual amount of increase differs from one reaction to another. Temperature evidently has a strong effect on reaction rate. To understand why, we need to develop theoretical models that explain our observations. One of the simplest models is called *collision theory.*

Reaction rate is related to the number of effective collisions per second between reactant molecules

The basic postulate of **collision theory** is that the rate of a reaction is proportional to the number of *effective* collisions per second among the reactant molecules. An *effective collision* is one that actually gives product molecules. Anything that can increase the frequency of effective collisions should, therefore, increase the rate.

☐ The kinetic theory provides insights for reaction rate theory.

One of the several factors that influences the number of effective collisions per second is *concentration.* As reactant concentrations increase, the number of collisions per second of all types, including effective collisions, cannot help but increase. We'll return to the significance of concentration in Section 13.7.

Not *every* collision between reactant molecules actually results in a chemical change. We know this because the reactant atoms or molecules in a gas or a liquid undergo an enormous number of collisions per second with each other. If every collision were effective, all reactions would be over in an instant. *Only a very small fraction of all the collisions can really lead to a net change.* Why is this so?

Molecular orientation is important

In most reactions, when two reactant molecules collide they must be oriented correctly for a reaction to occur. For example, the reaction represented by the following equation.

$$2NO_2Cl \longrightarrow 2NO_2 + Cl_2$$

appears to proceed by a two-step mechanism. One step involves the collision of an NO_2Cl molecule with a chlorine atom.

$$NO_2Cl + Cl \longrightarrow NO_2 + Cl_2$$

The orientation of the NO_2Cl molecule when hit by the Cl atom is important (see Figure 13.9). The poor orientation shown in Figure 13.9*a* cannot result in the formation of Cl_2 because the two Cl atoms are not being brought close enough together for a new Cl—Cl bond to form as an N—Cl bond breaks. Figure 13.9*b* shows the necessary orientation if the collision of NO_2Cl and Cl is to effectively lead to products.

A minimum molecular kinetic energy is required

Not all collisions, even those correctly oriented, are energetic enough to result in products, and this is the major reason that only a small percentage of all collisions actually lead to chemical change. The colliding particles must carry into the collision a certain minimum combined molecular kinetic energy, called the **activation energy, E_a.** In a successful collision, activation energy changes over to potential energy as the particles hit each other

☐ At the start of the reaction described by Figure 13.5, only about one of every billion billion (10^{18}) collisions leads to a net chemical reaction. In each of the other collisions, the reactant molecules just bounce off each other.

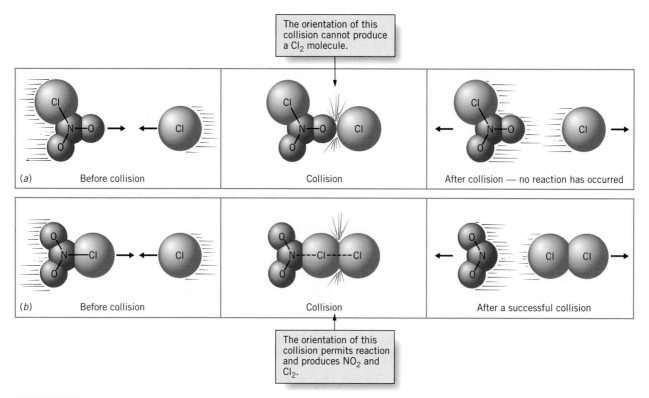

The orientation of this collision cannot produce a Cl_2 molecule.

(a) Before collision | Collision | After collision — no reaction has occurred

(b) Before collision | Collision | After a successful collision

The orientation of this collision permits reaction and produces NO_2 and Cl_2.

FIG. 13.9 **The importance of molecular orientation during a collision in a reaction.** The key step in the decomposition of NO_2Cl to NO_2 and Cl_2 is the collision of a Cl atom with a NO_2Cl molecule. (*a*) A poorly oriented collision. (*b*) An effectively oriented collision.

and chemical bonds become reorganized into those of the products. For most chemical reactions, the activation energy is quite large, and only a small fraction of all well-oriented, colliding molecules have it.

We can understand the existence of activation energy by studying in detail what actually takes place during a collision. For old bonds to break and new bonds to form, the atomic nuclei within the colliding particles must get close enough together. The molecules on a collision course must, therefore, be moving with a combined kinetic energy great enough to overcome the natural repulsions between electron clouds. Otherwise, the molecules simply veer away or bounce apart. Only fast molecules with large kinetic energies can collide with enough collision energy to enable their nuclei and electrons to overcome repulsions and thereby reach the positions required for the bond breaking and bond making that the chemical change demands.

Rising temperature increases reaction rates

With the concept of activation energy, we can now explain why the rate of a reaction increases so much with increasing temperature. We'll use the two curves in Figure 13.10, each corresponding to a different temperature for the same mixture of reactants. Each curve is a plot of the different *fractions* of all collisions (vertical axis) that have particular values of kinetic energy of collision (horizontal axis). (The total area under a curve then represents the total number of collisions, because all of the fractions must add up to this total.) Notice what happens to the plots when the temperature is increased; the maximum point shifts to the right and the curve flattens somewhat. However, *a modest increase in temperature generally does not affect the reaction's activation energy.* Within reason, the activation energy of a reaction is not affected by a change in temperature. In other words, as the curve flattens and shifts to the right with an increase in temperature, the value of E_a stays the same.

The shaded areas under the curves in Figure 13.10 represent the sum of all those fractions of the total collisions that equal or exceed the activation energy. This sum—we could call it the *reacting fraction*—is relatively much greater at the higher temperature than at the lower temperature because a significant fraction of the curve shifts beyond the activation

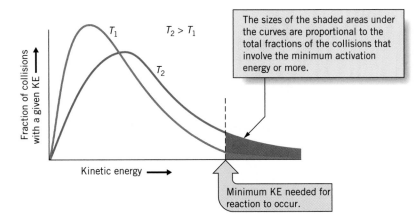

Minimum KE needed for reaction to occur.

FIG. 13.10 Kinetic energy distributions for a reaction mixture at two different temperatures.

energy in even a modest change to a higher temperature. In other words, at the higher temperature, a much greater fraction of the collisions occurring each second results in a chemical change, so the reactants disappear faster at the higher temperature.

On the molecular scale we can write an equation that summarizes the three factors involved in the collision theory as

$$\text{Reaction rate (molecules L}^{-1}\text{ s}^{-1}) = N \times f_{\text{orientation}} \times f_{\text{KE}}$$

where N represents the collisions per second per liter of the mixture, approximately 10^{27} s^{-1}. The two other terms represent the fraction of collisions with the correct orientation, $f_{\text{orientation}}$, and the fraction of collisions with the required total kinetic energy, f_{KE}. To convert this to the laboratory scale rate of mol $L^{-1}\text{ s}^{-1}$, we divide the equation by Avogadro's number.

$$\text{Reaction rate (mol L}^{-1}\text{ s}^{-1}) = \frac{\text{reaction rate (molecules L}^{-1}\text{ s}^{-1})}{6.02 \times 10^{23} \text{ (molecules mol}^{-1})}$$

□ The fraction of molecules, f_{KE}, having or exceeding the activation energy, E_a, is given by the expression

$$\ln f_{\text{KE}} = \frac{-E_a}{RT}$$

The transition state is the arrangement of atoms at the top of the activation energy "hill"

Transition state theory is used to explain in detail what happens when reactant molecules come together in a collision. Most often, those in a head-on collision slow down, stop, and then fly apart unchanged. When a collision does cause a reaction, the particles that separate are those of the products. Regardless of what happens to them, however, as the molecules on a collision course slow down, their total kinetic energy decreases as it changes into potential energy (PE). It's like the momentary disappearance of the kinetic energy of a tennis ball when it hits the racket. In the deformed racket and ball, this energy becomes potential energy, which soon changes back to kinetic energy as the ball takes off in a new direction.

Potential energy diagrams summarize energy changes during the course of a reaction

To visualize the relationship between activation energy and the development of total potential energy we sometimes use a *potential energy diagram* (see Figure 13.11). The vertical axis represents changes in *potential* energy as the kinetic energy of the colliding particles changes over to this form. The horizontal axis is called the **reaction coordinate,** and it represents the extent to which the reactants have changed to the products. It helps us follow the path taken by the reaction as reactant molecules come together and change into product molecules. Activation energy appears as a potential energy "hill" or barrier between the reactants and products. Only colliding molecules, properly oriented, that can deliver kinetic energy into potential energy at least as large as E_a are able to climb over the hill and produce products.

We can use a potential energy diagram to follow the progress of both an unsuccessful and a successful collision (see Figure 13.12). As two reactant molecules collide, we say that they begin to climb the potential energy barrier as they slow down and experience the

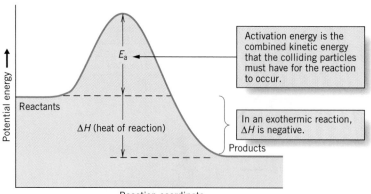

Activation energy is the combined kinetic energy that the colliding particles must have for the reaction to occur.

In an exothermic reaction, ΔH is negative.

FIG. 13.11 Potential energy diagram for an exothermic reaction.

conversion of their kinetic energy into potential energy. But if their combined initial kinetic energies are equivalent to a potential energy that is less than E_a, the molecules are unable to reach the top of the hill (Figure 13.12a). Instead, they fall back toward the reactants. They bounce apart chemically unchanged with their original total kinetic energy; no net reaction has occurred. On the other hand, if the combined kinetic energy of the colliding molecules equals or exceeds E_a, and if the molecules are oriented properly, they are able to pass over the activation energy barrier and form product molecules (Figure 13.12b).

Potential energy diagrams also show the heat of reaction

A reaction's potential energy diagram, such as that of Figure 13.11, helps us to visualize the *heat of reaction*, ΔH, a concept introduced in Chapter 6. It's the difference between the potential energy of the products and the potential energy of the reactants. Figure 13.11 is for an *exothermic* reaction because the products have a *lower* potential energy than the reactants. In such a system, the net decrease in potential energy appears as an increase in the molecular kinetic energy of the emerging product molecules. The temperature of the system increases during an exothermic reaction because the average molecular kinetic energy of the system increases.

A potential energy diagram for an endothermic reaction is shown in Figure 13.13. Now the products have a *higher* potential energy than the reactants and, in terms of the heat of reaction, a net input of energy is needed to form the products. Endothermic reactions produce a cooling effect as they proceed because there is a net conversion of molecular kinetic energy to potential energy. As the *total* molecular kinetic energy decreases, the *average* molecular kinetic energy decreases as well, and the temperature drops.

Notice that E_a for an endothermic process is invariably greater than (or it might be equal to) the heat of reaction. If ΔH is both positive and *high*, E_a must also be high, making such reactions very slow. However, for an exothermic reaction (ΔH is negative) we cannot tell from ΔH how large E_a is. It could be high, making for a slow reaction despite its being exothermic. If E_a is low, the reaction would be rapid and all its heat would appear quickly.

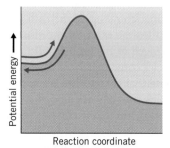

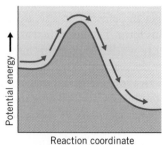

FIG. 13.12 The difference between an unsuccessful and a successful collision.

(a) An unsuccessful collision; the colliding molecules separate unchanged.

(b) A successful collision; the activation energy barrier is crossed and the products are formed.

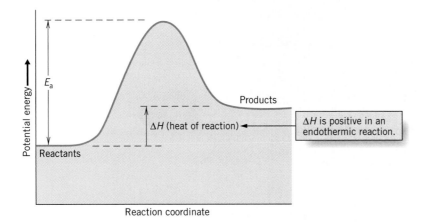

FIG. 13.13 A potential energy diagram for an endothermic reaction.

In Chapter 6 we saw that when the direction of a reaction is reversed, the sign given to the enthalpy change, ΔH, is reversed. In other words, a reaction that is exothermic in the forward direction *must* be endothermic in the reverse direction, and vice versa. This might seem to suggest that reactions are generally reversible. Many are, but if we look again at the energy diagram for a reaction that is exothermic in the forward direction (Figure 13.11), it is obvious that in the opposite direction the reaction is endothermic *and must have a significantly higher activation energy* than the forward reaction. What differs most for the forward and reverse directions is the relative height of the activation energy barrier (see Figure 13.14).

One of the main reasons for studying activation energies is that they provide information about what actually occurs during an effective collision. For example, in Figure 13.9*b* on page 544, we described a way that NO_2Cl could react successfully with a Cl atom during a collision. During this collision, there is a moment when the N—Cl bond is partially broken and the new Cl—Cl bond is partially formed. This brief moment during a successful collision is called the reaction's **transition state.** The potential energy of the transition state corresponds to the high point on the potential energy diagram (see Figure 13.15). The unstable chemical species that momentarily exists at this instant, O_2N---Cl---Cl, with its partially formed and partially broken bonds, is called the **activated complex.**

The size of the activation energy tells us about the relative importance of bond breaking and bond making during the formation of the activated complex. A very high activation energy suggests, for instance, that bond *breaking* contributes very heavily to the formation of the activated complex because bond breaking is an energy-absorbing process. On the other hand, a low activation energy may mean that bonds of about equal strength are being both broken and formed simultaneously.

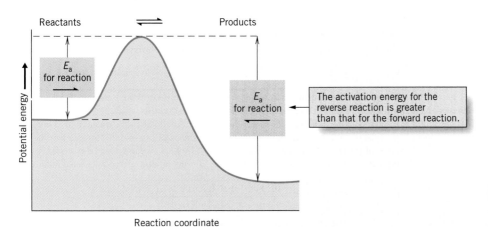

FIG. 13.14 Activation energy barrier for the forward and reverse reactions.

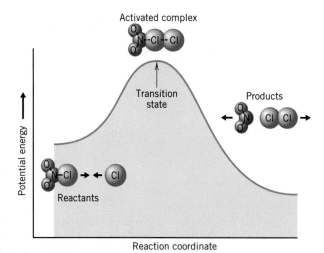

Activated complex

Transition state

Products

Reactants

Reaction coordinate

Potential energy →

FIG. 13.15 **Transition state and the activated complex.** Formation of an activated complex in the reaction between NO_2Cl and Cl.

$$NO_2Cl + Cl \longrightarrow NO + Cl_2$$

13.6 | ACTIVATION ENERGIES ARE MEASURED BY FITTING EXPERIMENTAL DATA TO THE ARRHENIUS EQUATION

We've noted that the activation energy is a useful quantity to know because its value can provide clues to the relative importance of bond breaking and bond making during the formation of the activated complex. Determining the value of E_a is accomplished by observing how temperature affects the value of the rate constant, k.

The activation energy is linked to the rate constant by a relationship discovered in 1889 by Svante Arrhenius, whose name you may recall from our discussion of electrolytes and acids and bases in Chapter 4. The usual form of the **Arrhenius equation** is

TOOLS
Arrhenius equation

$$k = A\,e^{-E_a/RT} \tag{13.10}$$

where k is the rate constant, e is the base of the natural logarithm system, and T is the Kelvin temperature. A is a proportionality constant sometimes called the **frequency factor** or the **pre-exponential factor.** R is the gas constant, which we'll express in our study of kinetics in energy units, namely, R equals 8.314 J mol^{-1} K^{-1}.[8]

The activation energy can be determined graphically

Equation 13.10 is normally used in its logarithmic form. If we take the natural logarithm of both sides, we obtain

$$\ln k = \ln A - E_a/RT$$

Let's rewrite the equation as

$$\ln k = \ln A - (E_a/R) \times (1/T) \tag{13.11}$$

[8] The units of R given here are actually SI units, namely, the joule (J), the mole (n), and the kelvin (K). To calculate R in these units we need to go back to the defining equation for the universal gas law, rearranging terms.

$$R = PV/nT$$

In Chapter 10 we learned that the standard conditions of pressure and temperature are 1 atm and 273.15 K; we expressed the standard molar volume in liters, namely 22.414 L. But 1 atm equals 1.01325×10^5 N m^{-2}, where N is the SI unit of force, the newton, and m is the meter, the SI unit of length. So m^2 is area given in SI units. From Chapter 10, the ratio of force to area given by N m^{-2} is called the pascal, Pa, and that force times distance or N m defines one unit of energy in the SI and is called the joule, J. In the SI, volume must be expressed as m^3, to employ the SI unit of length to define volume, and 1 L equals 10^{-3} m^3. So now we can calculate R in SI units.

$$R = \frac{(1.01325 \times 10^5 \text{ N m}^{-2}) \times (22.414 \times 10^{-3} \text{ m}^3)}{(1 \text{ mol} \times 273.15 \text{ K})}$$

$$= 8.314 \text{ N m mol}^{-1} \text{ K}^{-1} = 8.314 \text{ J mol}^{-1} \text{ K}^{-1}$$

We know that the rate constant k varies with the temperature T, which also means that the quantity $\ln k$ varies with the quantity $(1/T)$. These two quantities, namely, $\ln k$ and $1/T$, are variables, so Equation 13.11 is in the form of an equation for a straight line.

$$\ln k = \ln A + (-E_a/R) \times (1/T)$$
$$\updownarrow \quad\quad \updownarrow \quad\quad\quad \updownarrow \quad\quad\quad \updownarrow$$
$$y = b + m \quad x$$

To determine the activation energy, we can make a graph of $\ln k$ versus $1/T$, measure the slope of the line, and then use the relationship

$$\text{Slope} = -E_a/R$$

to calculate E_a. Example 13.11 illustrates how this is done.

> **EXAMPLE 13.11**
> Determining Energy of Activation Graphically

Consider again the decomposition of NO_2 into NO and O_2. The equation is

$$2NO_2(g) \longrightarrow 2NO(g) + O_2(g)$$

The following data were collected for the reaction.

Rate Constant, k (L mol^{-1} s^{-1})	Temperature (°C)
7.8	400
10	410
14	420
18	430
24	440

Use the graphical method to determine the activation energy for the reaction in kilojoules per mole.

ANALYSIS: Equation 13.11 is the tool that applies. However, the use of rate data to determine the activation energy graphically requires that we plot $\ln k$, not k, versus the *reciprocal* of the *Kelvin* temperature, so we have to convert the given data into $\ln k$ and $1/T$ before we can construct the graph.

SOLUTION: To illustrate, using the first set of data, the conversions are

$$\ln k = \ln (7.8) = 2.05$$

$$\frac{1}{T} = \frac{1}{(400 + 273)\ K} = \frac{1}{673\ K}$$

$$= 1.486 \times 10^{-3}\ K^{-1}$$

We are carrying extra "significant figures" for the purpose of graphing the data. The remaining conversions give the table below. Then we plot $\ln k$ versus $1/T$ as shown on the next page.

$\ln k$	$1/T$ (K^{-1})
2.05	1.486×10^{-3}
2.30	1.464×10^{-3}
2.64	1.443×10^{-3}
2.89	1.422×10^{-3}
3.18	1.403×10^{-3}

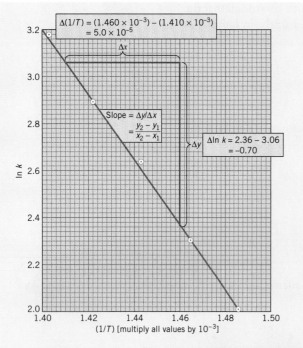

The slope of the curve is obtained as the ratio

$$\text{Slope} = \frac{\Delta(\ln k)}{\Delta(1/T)}$$

$$= \frac{-0.70}{5.0 \times 10^{-5}\,\text{K}^{-1}}$$

$$= -1.4 \times 10^4\,\text{K} = -E_a/R$$

After changing signs and solving for E_a we have

$$E_a = (8.314\,\text{J mol}^{-1}\,\text{K}^{-1})(1.4 \times 10^4\,\text{K})$$

$$= 1.2 \times 10^5\,\text{J mol}^{-1}$$

$$= 1.2 \times 10^2\,\text{kJ mol}^{-1}$$

IS THE ANSWER REASONABLE? Activation energies must always have a positive sign and our result is positive. In addition, a check of the units shows that they cancel to give us the correct kJ mol^{-1}. We could try a different pair of points on the same graph to check our work.

The activation energy can be calculated from rate constants measured at two temperatures

If the activation energy and the rate constant at a particular temperature are known, the rate constant at another temperature can be calculated using the following relationship, which can be derived from Equation 13.11,

TOOLS
Arrhenius equation, alternate form

$$\ln\left(\frac{k_2}{k_1}\right) = \frac{-E_a}{R}\left(\frac{1}{T_2} - \frac{1}{T_1}\right) \tag{13.12}$$

This equation can also be used to calculate the activation energy from rate constants measured at two different temperatures. However, the graphical method discussed earlier gives more precise values of E_a.

EXAMPLE 13.12

Calculating the Rate Constant at a Particular Temperature

The reaction $2NO_2 \longrightarrow 2NO + O_2$ has an activation energy of 111 kJ mol^{-1}. At 400 °C, $k = 7.8$ L mol^{-1} s^{-1}. What is the value of k at 430 °C?

ANALYSIS: We know the activation energy and k at one temperature. We will need to use Equation 13.12 as our tool to obtain k at the other temperature. Since the logarithm term contains the ratio of the rate constants, we will solve for the value of this ratio, substitute the known value of k, and then solve for the unknown k.

SOLUTION: Let's begin by writing Equation 13.12.

$$\ln\left(\frac{k_2}{k_1}\right) = \frac{-E_a}{R}\left(\frac{1}{T_2} - \frac{1}{T_1}\right)$$

Organizing the data gives us the following table.

	k (L mol^{-1} s^{-1})	T (K)
1	7.8	400 + 273 = 673 K
2	?	430 + 273 = 703 K

We must use $R = 8.314$ J mol^{-1} K^{-1} and express E_a in joules ($E_a = 1.11 \times 10^5$ J mol^{-1}). Next, we substitute values into the right side of the equation and solve for $\ln(k_2/k_1)$.

$$\ln\left(\frac{k_2}{k_1}\right) = \frac{-1.11 \times 10^5 \text{ J mol}^{-1}}{8.314 \text{ J mol}^{-1}\text{ K}^{-1}}\left(\frac{1}{703 \text{ K}} - \frac{1}{673 \text{ K}}\right)$$

$$= (-1.34 \times 10^4 \text{ K})(-6.34 \times 10^{-5} \text{ K}^{-1})$$

Therefore,

$$\ln\left(\frac{k_2}{k_1}\right) = 0.850$$

Taking the antilog gives the ratio of k_2 to k_1.

$$\frac{k_2}{k_1} = e^{0.850} = 2.34$$

Solving for k_2,

$$k_2 = 2.34k_1$$

Substituting the value of k_1 from the data table gives

$$k_2 = 2.34 \, (7.8 \text{ L mol}^{-1}\text{ s}^{-1})$$

$$= 18 \text{ L mol}^{-1}\text{ s}^{-1}$$

IS THE ANSWER REASONABLE? Although no simple check exists, we have at least found that the value of k for the higher temperature is greater than it is for the lower temperature, as it should be.

Practice Exercise 24: The rate constant is directly proportional to the reaction rate if the same reactant concentrations are used. When determining the stability of a consumer product, less than 5% should decompose in two years at 25 °C. What temperature should we set our oven to if we want to see that same 5% decomposition in one week? Assume the activation energy was previously determined to be 154 kJ mol^{-1}. (Hint: All the information is here to apply the Arrhenius equation.)

Practice Exercise 25: The reaction $CH_3I + HI \longrightarrow CH_4 + I_2$ was observed to have rate constants $k = 3.2$ L mol^{-1} s^{-1} at 350 °C and $k = 23$ L mol^{-1} s^{-1} at 400 °C. (a) What is the value of E_a expressed in kJ mol^{-1}? (b) What would be the rate constant at 300 °C?

13.7 EXPERIMENTAL RATE LAWS CAN BE USED TO SUPPORT OR REJECT PROPOSED MECHANISMS FOR A REACTION

A balanced equation generally describes only a net overall change. Usually, however, the net change is the result of a series of simple reactions that are not at all evident from the equation. Consider, for example, the combustion of propane, C_3H_8.

$$C_3H_8(g) + 5O_2(g) \longrightarrow 3CO_2(g) + 4H_2O(g)$$

Anyone who has ever played billiards knows that this reaction simply cannot occur in a single, simultaneous collision between one propane molecule and five oxygen molecules. Just getting only three balls to come together with but one "click" on a flat, two-dimensional surface is extremely improbable. How unlikely it must be, then, for the *simultaneous* collision in three-dimensional space of six reactant molecules, one of which must be C_3H_8 and the other five O_2. Instead, the combustion of propane proceeds very rapidly by a series of much more probable steps, involving colliding chemical species of fleeting existence. *The series of individual steps that add up to the overall observed reaction is called the* **mechanism of a reaction.** Information about reaction mechanisms is one of the dividends paid by the study of rates.

Each individual step in a reaction mechanism is a simple chemical reaction called an *elementary process.* An **elementary process** is a reaction involving collisions between molecules. As you will soon see, its rate law can be written from its own chemical equation, using coefficients as exponents for the concentration terms without requiring experiments to determine the exponents. For most reactions, the individual elementary processes cannot actually be observed; instead, we only see the net reaction. Therefore, the mechanism a chemist writes is really a *theory* about what occurs step by step as the reactants are changed to the products.

Because the individual steps in a mechanism usually cannot be observed directly, devising a mechanism for a reaction requires some ingenuity. However, we can immediately tell whether a proposed mechanism is feasible. *The overall rate law derived from the mechanism must agree with the observed rate law for the overall reaction.*

The rate law for an elementary process can be predicted from the chemical equation for the process

Consider the following elementary process that involves collisions between two identical molecules leading directly to the products shown.

$$2NO_2 \longrightarrow NO_3 + NO \tag{13.13}$$
$$\text{Rate} = k[NO_2]^x$$

How can we predict the value of the exponent x? Suppose the NO_2 concentration were doubled. There would now be *twice* as many individual NO_2 molecules and *each* would have *twice* as many neighbors with which to collide. The number of NO_2-to-NO_2 collisions per second would doubly double—in other words, increase by a factor of 4. This would cause the rate to increase by a factor of 4, which is 2^2. Earlier we saw that when doubling a concentration leads to a fourfold increase in the rate, the concentration of that reactant is raised to the second power in the rate law. Thus, if Equation 13.13 represents an elementary process, its rate law should be

$$\text{Rate} = k[NO_2]^2$$

□ We double the number of NO_2 molecules and double the number each can collide with, so the collision frequency increases by a factor of 4.

Notice that the exponent in the rate law for this elementary process is the same as the coefficient in the chemical equation. Similar analyses for other types of elementary processes lead to similar observations and the following statement:

> The exponents in the rate law for an elementary process are equal to the coefficients of the reactants in the chemical equation for that elementary process.

Remember that this rule applies only to *elementary processes.* If all we know is the balanced equation for the overall reaction, the only way we can find the exponents of the rate law is by doing experiments.

The rate law for the slowest step in a mechanism should agree with the experimental rate law

How does the ability to predict the rate law of an elementary process help chemists predict reaction mechanisms? To answer this question, let's look at two reactions and what are believed to be their mechanisms. (There are many other, more complicated systems, and Facets of Chemistry 13.1 describes one type, the free radical chain reaction, that is particularly important.)

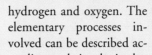

Free Radicals, Explosions, Octane Ratings, Aging and Health

A **free radical** is a very reactive species that contains one or more unpaired electrons. Examples are chlorine atoms formed when a Cl_2 molecule absorbs a photon (light) of the appropriate energy:

$$Cl_2 + \text{light energy } (h\nu) \longrightarrow 2Cl\cdot$$

(A dot placed next to the symbol of an atom or molecule represents an unpaired electron and indicates that the particle is a free radical.) The reason free radicals are so reactive is because of the tendency of electrons to become paired through the formation of either ions or covalent bonds.

Free radicals are important in many gaseous reactions, including those responsible for the production of photochemical smog in urban areas. Reactions involving free radicals have useful applications, too. For example, many plastics are made by reactions that take place by mechanisms that involve free radicals. In addition, free radicals play a part in one of the most important processes in the petroleum industry, *thermal cracking*. This reaction is used to break $C-C$ and $C-H$ bonds in long chain hydrocarbons to produce the smaller molecules that give gasoline a higher octane rating. An example is the formation of free radicals in the thermal cracking reaction of butane. When butane is heated to 700–800 °C, one of the major reactions that occurs is

$$CH_3-CH_2:CH_2-CH_3 \xrightarrow{\text{heat}} CH_3CH_2\cdot + CH_3CH_2\cdot$$

The central $C-C$ bond of butane is shown here as a pair of dots, :, rather than the usual dash. When the bond is broken, the electron pair is divided between the two free radicals that are formed. This reaction produces two ethyl radicals, $CH_3CH_2\cdot$.

Free radical reactions tend to have high initial activation energies because chemical bonds must be broken to form the radicals. Once the free radicals are formed, however, reactions in which they are involved tend to be very rapid.

Free Radical Chain Reactions

In many cases, a free radical reacts with a reactant molecule to give a product molecule plus another free radical. Reactions that involve such a step are called **chain reactions.**

Many explosive reactions are chain reactions involving free radical mechanisms. One of the most studied reactions of this type is the formation of water from

hydrogen and oxygen. The elementary processes involved can be described according to their roles in the mechanism.

The reaction begins with an **initiation step** that gives free radicals.

$$H_2 + O_2 \xrightarrow{\text{hot surface}} 2OH\cdot \quad \text{(initiation)}$$

The chain continues with a **propagation step,** which produces the product plus another free radical.

$$OH\cdot + H_2 \longrightarrow H_2O + H\cdot \quad \text{(propagation)}$$

The reaction of H_2 and O_2 is explosive because the mechanism also contains **branching steps.**

$$\left.\begin{array}{l} H\cdot + O_2 \longrightarrow OH\cdot + O\cdot \\ O\cdot + H_2 \longrightarrow OH\cdot + H\cdot \end{array}\right\} \quad \text{branching}$$

Thus, the reaction of one $H\cdot$ with O_2 leads to the net production of two $OH\cdot$ plus an $O\cdot$. Every time an $H\cdot$ reacts with oxygen, then, there is an increase in the number of free radicals in the system. The free radical concentration grows rapidly, and the reaction rate becomes explosively fast.

Chain mechanisms also contain **termination steps,** which remove free radicals from the system. In the reaction of H_2 and O_2, the wall of the reaction vessel serves to remove $H\cdot$, which tends to halt the chain process.

$$2H\cdot \xrightarrow{\text{wall}} H_2$$

Free Radicals and Aging

Direct experimental evidence also exists for the presence of free radicals in functioning biological systems. These highly reactive species play many roles, but one of the most interesting is their apparent involvement in the aging process. One theory suggests that free radicals attack protein molecules in collagen. Collagen is composed of long strands of fibers of proteins and is found throughout the body, especially in the flexible tissues of the lungs, skin, muscles, and blood vessels. Attack by free radicals seems to lead to cross-linking between these fibers, which stiffens them and makes them less flexible. The most readily observable result of this is the stiffening and hardening of the skin that accompanies aging or too much sunbathing.

People exposed to sunlight over long periods, like this woman from Nepal (a small country between India and Tibet), tend to develop wrinkles because ultraviolet radiation causes changes in their skin. *(Alison Wright/Corbis)*

Free Radicals and Health

Around 1987 evidence began to surface identifying a stable free radical, nitrogen monoxide (nitric oxide, NO), as a key inorganic molecule controlling a variety of biological functions, from the chemiluminescent flash of a firefly to beneficial effects in the human body. Amyl nitrate and nitroglycerine have been used medicinally since the early 1900s, and NO is apparently the metabolic product that makes these substances effective drugs. Currently, at an estimated rate of 3000 research papers per year, the discoveries of the functions of NO have become major medical milestones of the 21st century. For example, this very simple, diatomic molecule can be used to treat high blood pressure, angina, pulmonary hypertension, breathing problems in newborn babies, erectile dysfunction, and even Alzheimer's and Parkinson's disease. Discovery of the effects of NO and its possible therapeutic applications led to the 1998 Nobel Prize in Medicine honoring Robert Furchgott, Louis Ignarro, and Ferid Murad.

First, consider the gaseous reaction

$$2NO_2Cl \longrightarrow 2NO_2 + Cl_2 \qquad (13.14)$$

Experimentally, the rate is first order in NO_2Cl, so the rate law is

$$Rate = k[NO_2Cl] \qquad (\textit{experimental})$$

The first question we might ask is, Could the overall reaction (Equation 13.14) occur in a single step by the collision of two NO_2Cl molecules? The answer is no, because then it would be an elementary process and the rate law predicted for it would include a squared term, $[NO_2Cl]^2$. But the experimental rate law is first order in NO_2Cl. So the predicted and experimental rate laws don't agree, and we must look further to find the mechanism of the reaction.

On the basis of chemical intuition and other information that we won't discuss here, chemists believe the actual mechanism of the reaction in Equation 13.14 is the following two-step sequence of elementary processes.

$$NO_2Cl \longrightarrow NO_2 + Cl$$
$$NO_2Cl + Cl \longrightarrow NO_2 + Cl_2$$

□ The Cl atom formed here is called a *reactive intermediate*. We never actually observe the Cl because it reacts so quickly.

Notice that when the two reactions are added, the *intermediate*, Cl, drops out and we obtain the net overall reaction given in Equation 13.14. *Being able to add the elementary processes and thus to obtain the overall reaction is another major test of a mechanism.*

In any multistep mechanism, one step is usually much slower than the others. In this mechanism, for example, it is believed that the first step is slow and that once a Cl atom forms, it reacts very rapidly with another NO_2Cl molecule to give the final products.

The final products of a multistep reaction cannot appear faster than the products of the slow step, so the slow step in a mechanism is called the **rate-determining step** or the **rate-limiting step.** In the two-step mechanism above, then, the first reaction is the rate-determining step because the final products can't be formed faster than the rate at which Cl atoms form.

The rate-determining step is similar to a slow worker on an assembly line. The production rate depends on how quickly the slow worker works, regardless of how fast the other workers are. The factors that control the speed of the rate-determining step therefore also control the overall rate of the reaction. This means that *the rate law for the rate-determining step is directly related to the rate law for the overall reaction.*

Because the rate-determining step is an elementary process, we can predict its rate law from the coefficients of its reactants. The coefficient of NO_2Cl in its relatively slow breakdown to NO_2 and Cl is 1. Therefore, the rate law predicted for the first step is

$$Rate = k[NO_2Cl] \qquad (\textit{predicted})$$

Notice that the predicted rate law derived for the two-step mechanism agrees with the experimentally measured rate law. Although this doesn't *prove* that the mechanism is correct, it does provide considerable support for it. From the standpoint of kinetics, therefore, the mechanism is reasonable.

The second reaction mechanism that we will study is that of the following gas-phase reaction.

$$2NO + 2H_2 \longrightarrow N_2 + 2H_2O \qquad (13.15)$$

The experimentally determined rate law is

$$Rate = k[NO]^2[H_2] \qquad (experimental)$$

We can quickly tell from this rate law that Equation 13.15 could *not* itself be an elementary process. If it were, the exponent for $[H_2]$ would have to be 2. Obviously, a mechanism involving two or more steps must be involved.

A chemically reasonable mechanism that yields the correct form for the rate law consists of the following two steps.

$$2NO + H_2 \longrightarrow N_2O + H_2O \qquad (slow)$$
$$N_2O + H_2 \longrightarrow N_2 + H_2O \qquad (fast)$$

One test of the mechanism, as we said, is that the two equations must add to give the correct overall equation; and they do. Further, the chemistry of the second step has actually been observed in separate experiments. N_2O is a known compound, and it does react with H_2 to give N_2 and H_2O. Another test of the mechanism involves the coefficients of NO and H_2 in the predicted rate law for the first step, the supposed rate-determining step.

$$Rate = k[NO]^2[H_2] \qquad (predicted)$$

This rate equation does match the experimental rate law, but there is still a serious flaw in the proposed mechanism. If the postulated slow step actually describes an elementary process, it would involve the simultaneous collision between three molecules, two NO and one H_2. A three-way collision is so unlikely that if it were really involved in the mechanism, the overall reaction would be extremely slow. Reaction mechanisms seldom include elementary processes that involve more than two-body or **bimolecular collisions.**

Chemists believe the reaction in Equation 13.15 proceeds by the following three-step sequence of bimolecular elementary processes.

$$2NO \rightleftharpoons N_2O_2 \qquad (fast)$$
$$N_2O_2 + H_2 \longrightarrow N_2O + H_2O \qquad (slow)$$
$$N_2O + H_2 \longrightarrow N_2 + H_2O \qquad (fast)$$

In this mechanism the first step is proposed to be a rapidly established equilibrium in which the unstable intermediate N_2O_2 forms in the forward reaction and then quickly decomposes into NO by the reverse reaction. The rate-determining step is the reaction of N_2O_2 with H_2 to give N_2O and a water molecule. The third step is the reaction mentioned above. Once again, notice that the three steps add to give the net overall change.

□ The occurrence of N_2O_2 as an intermediate in the proposed mechanism can only be surmised. The compound is never present at a detectable concentration because, as supposed, it's too unstable.

Since the second step is rate determining, the rate law for the reaction should match the rate law for this step. We predict this to be

$$Rate = k[N_2O_2][H_2] \qquad (13.16)$$

However, the experimental rate law does not contain the species N_2O_2. Therefore, we must find a way to express the concentration of N_2O_2 in terms of the reactants in the overall reaction. To do this, let's look closely at the first step of the mechanism, which we view as a reversible reaction.

The rate in the forward direction, in which NO is the reactant, is

$$Rate \ (forward) = k_f[NO]^2$$

The rate of the reverse reaction, in which N_2O_2 is the reactant, is

$$Rate \ (reverse) = k_r[N_2O_2]$$

☐ Recall that in a dynamic equilibrium forward and reverse reactions occur at equal rates.

If we view this as a dynamic equilibrium, then the rate of the forward and reverse reactions are equal, which means that

$$k_f[NO]^2 = k_r[N_2O_2] \tag{13.17}$$

Since we would like to eliminate N_2O_2 from the rate law in Equation 13.16, let's solve Equation 13.17 for $[N_2O_2]$.

$$[N_2O_2] = \frac{k_f}{k_r}[NO]^2$$

Substituting into the rate law in Equation 13.16 yields

$$\text{Rate} = k\left(\frac{k_f}{k_r}\right)[NO]^2[H_2]$$

Combining all the constants into one (k') gives

$$\text{Rate} = k'[NO]^2[H_2] \quad (\textit{predicted})$$

☐ There are many reactions that do not follow simple first- or second-order rate laws and have mechanisms far more complex than those studied in this section. Even so, their more complex kinetics still serve as clues to their complex set of elementary processes.

Now the rate law derived from the mechanism matches the rate law obtained experimentally. The three-step mechanism does appear to be reasonable on the basis of kinetics.

The procedure we have worked through here applies to many reactions that proceed by mechanisms involving sequential steps. Steps that precede the rate-determining step are considered to be rapidly established equilibria involving unstable intermediates.

A proposed mechanism must always account for the experimental rate law
Although chemists may devise other experiments to help prove or disprove the correctness of a mechanism, one of the strongest pieces of evidence is the experimentally measured rate law for the overall reaction. No matter how reasonable a particular mechanism may appear, if its elementary processes cannot yield a predicted rate law that matches the experimental one, the mechanism is wrong and must be discarded.

Practice Exercise 26: Select the reactions below that may be elementary processes. For those not selected explain why they are not likely to be elementary processes.

(a) $2N_2O_5 \longrightarrow 2N_2O_4 + O_2$
(b) $NO + O_3 \longrightarrow NO_2 + O_2$
(c) $2NO + H_2 \longrightarrow N_2O + H_2O$
(d) $C_3H_8(g) + 5O_2(g) \longrightarrow 3CO_2(g) + 4H_2O(g)$
(e) $C_{12}H_{22}O_{11} + H_2O \longrightarrow C_6H_{12}O_6 + C_6H_{12}O_6$
(f) $3H_2 + N_2 \longrightarrow 2NH_3$

(Hint: How many molecules are likely to collide at exactly the same time?)

Practice Exercise 27: Ozone, O_3, reacts with nitric oxide, NO, to form nitrogen dioxide and oxygen.

$$NO + O_3 \longrightarrow NO_2 + O_2$$

This is one of the reactions involved in the formation of photochemical smog. If this reaction occurs in a single step, what is the expected rate law for the reaction?

Practice Exercise 28: The mechanism for the decomposition of NO_2Cl is

$$NO_2Cl \longrightarrow NO_2 + Cl$$
$$NO_2Cl + Cl \longrightarrow NO_2 + Cl_2$$

What would the predicted rate law be if the second step in the mechanism were the rate-determining step?

13.8 CATALYSTS CHANGE REACTION RATES BY PROVIDING ALTERNATIVE PATHS BETWEEN REACTANTS AND PRODUCTS

A **catalyst** is a substance that changes the rate of a chemical reaction without itself being used up. In other words, all of the catalyst added at the start of a reaction is present chemically unchanged after the reaction has gone to completion. The action caused by a catalyst is called **catalysis.** Broadly speaking, there are two kinds of catalysts. *Positive catalysts* speed up reactions, and *negative catalysts,* usually called *inhibitors,* slow reactions down. After this, when we use "catalyst" we'll mean positive catalyst, the usual connotation.

Although the catalyst is not part of the overall reaction, it does participate by changing the mechanism of the reaction. The catalyst provides a path to the products that has a rate-determining step with a lower activation energy than that of the uncatalyzed reaction (see Figure 13.16). Because the activation energy along this new route is lower, a greater fraction of the collisions of the reactant molecules have the minimum energy needed to react, so the reaction proceeds faster.

Catalysts can be divided into two groups—**homogeneous catalysts**, which exist in the same phase as the reactants, and **heterogeneous catalysts,** which exist in a separate phase.

Homogeneous catalysts are in the same phase as the reactants

An example of homogeneous catalysis is found in the now outdated *lead chamber process* for manufacturing sulfuric acid. To make sulfuric acid by this process, sulfur is burned to give SO_2, which is then oxidized to SO_3. The SO_3 is dissolved in water as it forms to give H_2SO_4.

□ In the modern process for making sulfuric acid, the contact process, vanadium(V) oxide, V_2O_5, is a heterogeneous catalyst that promotes the oxidation of sulfur dioxide to sulfur trioxide.

$$S + O_2 \longrightarrow SO_2$$

$$SO_2 + \tfrac{1}{2} O_2 \longrightarrow SO_3$$

$$SO_3 + H_2O \longrightarrow H_2SO_4$$

Unassisted, the second reaction, oxidation of SO_2 to SO_3, occurs slowly. In the lead chamber process, the SO_2 is combined with a mixture of NO, NO_2, air, and steam in large lead-lined reaction chambers. The NO_2 readily oxidizes the SO_2 to give NO and SO_3. The NO is then reoxidized to NO_2 by oxygen.

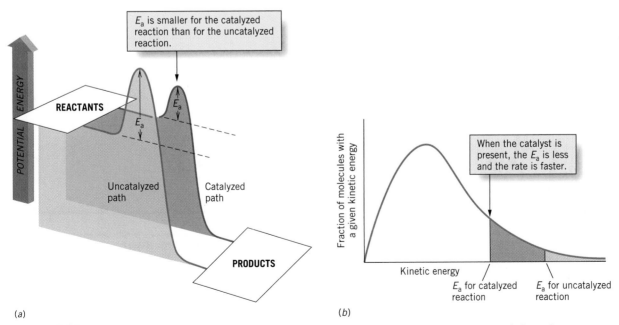

(a) (b)

FIG. 13.16 **Effect of a catalyst on a reaction.** (*a*) The catalyst provides an alternative, low-energy path from the reactants to the products. (*b*) A larger fraction of molecules have sufficient energy to react when the catalyzed path is available.

□ The NO_2 is regenerated in the second reaction and so is recycled over and over. Thus, only small amounts of it are needed in the reaction mixture to do an effective catalytic job.

$$NO_2 + SO_2 \longrightarrow NO + SO_3$$

$$NO + \tfrac{1}{2}O_2 \longrightarrow NO_2$$

The NO_2 serves as a catalyst by being an oxygen carrier and by providing a low-energy path for the oxidation of SO_2 to SO_3. Notice, as must be true for any catalyst, the NO_2 is regenerated; it has not been permanently changed.

Heterogeneous catalysts are in a separate phase from the reactants

□ **Adsorption** means that molecules bind to a surface.

A heterogeneous catalyst is commonly a solid, and it usually functions by promoting a reaction on its surface. One or more of the reactant molecules are adsorbed onto the surface of the catalyst where an interaction with the surface increases their reactivity. An example is the synthesis of ammonia from hydrogen and nitrogen by the Haber process.

$$3H_2 + N_2 \longrightarrow 2NH_3$$

The reaction takes place on the surface of an iron catalyst that contains traces of aluminum and potassium oxides. It is thought that hydrogen molecules and nitrogen molecules dissociate while being held on the catalytic surface. The hydrogen atoms then combine with the nitrogen atoms to form ammonia. Finally, the completed ammonia molecule breaks away, freeing the surface of the catalyst for further reaction. This sequence of steps is illustrated in Figure 13.17.

Heterogeneous catalysts are used in many important commercial processes. The petroleum industry uses heterogeneous catalysts to crack hydrocarbons into smaller fragments and then re-form them into the useful components of gasoline (see Figure 13.18). The availability of such catalysts allows refineries to produce gasoline, jet fuel, or heating oil from crude oil in any ratio necessary to meet the demands of the marketplace.

A vehicle that uses unleaded gasoline is equipped with a catalytic converter (Figure 13.19) designed to lower the concentrations of exhaust gas pollutants, such as carbon monoxide, unburned hydrocarbons, and nitrogen oxides. The catalysts are nanometer size particles of platinum, ruthenium, and rhodium dispersed in a honeycomb of a high temperature ceramic. The large ratio of surface area to mass enables the catalytic converter to react large volumes of exhaust efficiently. Air is introduced into the exhaust stream that then passes over a catalyst that adsorbs CO, NO, and O_2. The NO dissociates into N and O atoms, and the O_2 also dissociates into atoms. Pairing of nitrogen

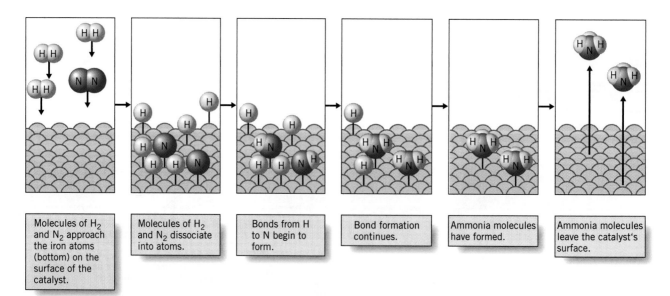

| Molecules of H_2 and N_2 approach the iron atoms (bottom) on the surface of the catalyst. | Molecules of H_2 and N_2 dissociate into atoms. | Bonds from H to N begin to form. | Bond formation continues. | Ammonia molecules have formed. | Ammonia molecules leave the catalyst's surface. |

FIG. 13.17 **The Haber process.** Catalytic formation of ammonia molecules from hydrogen and nitrogen occurs on the surface of a catalyst.

(a)

(b)

atoms then produces N_2, and oxidation of CO by oxygen atoms produces CO_2. Unburned hydrocarbons are also oxidized to CO_2 and H_2O. The catalysts in catalytic converters are deactivated or "poisoned" by lead-based octane boosters like tetraethyl lead [$Pb(C_2H_5)_4$]. "Leaded" gasoline was finally banned in 1995. Leaded gasoline also posed an environmental hazard from the lead emitted in automobile exhaust.

The poisoning of catalysts is also a major problem in many industrial processes. Methyl alcohol (methanol, CH_3OH), for example, is a promising fuel that can be made from coal and steam by the reaction

$$C \text{ (from coal)} + H_2O \longrightarrow CO + H_2$$

followed by

$$CO + 2H_2 \longrightarrow CH_3OH$$

A catalyst for the second step is copper(I) ion held in solid solution with zinc oxide. However, traces of sulfur, a contaminant in coal, must be avoided because sulfur reacts with the catalyst and destroys its catalytic activity.

Enzymes are biological catalysts

In living systems, complex protein-based molecules called **enzymes** catalyze almost every reaction that occurs in living cells. Enzymes contain a specially shaped area called an active site that lowers the energy of the transition state of the reaction being catalyzed. This causes the reaction rate to increase significantly. Many poisons have been shown to work by blocking important enzyme systems. Heavy metals bind to sulfur-containing groups and distort the active site. Molecular modeling is used to design drug molecules to have optimum shapes to fit enzymatic active sites.

SUMMARY

Reaction Rates. The speeds or **rates** of reactions are controlled by five factors: (1) the nature of the reactants, (2) the ability of reactants to meet, (3) the concentrations of the reactants, (4) the temperature, and (5) the presence of catalysts. The rates of **heterogeneous reactions** are determined largely by the area of contact between the phases; the rates of **homogeneous reactions** are determined by the concentrations of the reactants. The rate is measured by monitoring the change in reactant or product concentrations with time.

$$\text{Rate} = \Delta(\text{concentration})/\Delta(\text{time})$$

In any chemical reaction, the rates of formation of products and the rates of disappearance of reactants are related by the coefficients of the balanced overall chemical equation.

Rate Laws. The **rate law** for a reaction relates the reaction rate to the molar concentrations of the reactants. The rate is proportional to the product of the molar concentrations of the reactants, each raised to an appropriate power. These exponents must be determined by experiments in which the concentrations are varied and the effects of the variations on the rate are measured. The proportionality constant, *k*, is called the **rate constant.** Its value depends on temperature but not on the concentrations of the reactants. The sum of the exponents in the rate law is the **order** (or overall order) of the reaction.

Concentration and Time. Equations exist that relate the concentration of a reactant at a given time *t* to the initial concentration and the rate constant. The time required for half of a reactant to disappear is the **half-life,** $t_{1/2}$. For a first-order reaction, the half-life is a constant that depends only on the rate constant for the reaction; it is independent of the initial concentration. The half-life for a second-order reaction is inversely proportional both to the initial concentration of the reactant and to the rate constant.

Theories of Reaction Rate. According to **collision theory,** the rate of a reaction depends on the number per second of **effective collisions** of the reactant particles, which is only an extremely small fraction of the total number of collisions per second. This fraction is so small partly because the reactant molecules must be suitably oriented, but mostly because the colliding molecules must jointly possess a minimum molecular kinetic energy called the **activation energy,** E_a. As the temperature increases, a larger fraction of the collisions have this necessary energy, making more collisions effective each second and the reaction faster.

Transition state theory visualizes how the energies of molecules and the orientations of their nuclei interact as they collide. In this theory, the energy of activation is viewed as an energy barrier on the reaction's potential energy diagram. The *heat of reaction* is the net potential energy difference between the reactants and the products. In reversible reactions, the values of E_a for both the forward and reverse reactions can be identified on an energy diagram. The species at the high point on an energy diagram is the **activated complex** and is said to be in the **transition state.**

Determining the Activation Energy. The **Arrhenius equation** lets us see how changes in activation energy and temperature affect a rate constant. The Arrhenius equation also lets us determine E_a either graphically or by a calculation using the appropriate form of the Arrhenius equation. The calculation requires two rate constants determined at two temperatures. The graphical method uses more values of rate constants at more temperatures and thus usually yields more accurate results. The activation energy and the rate constant at one temperature can be used to calculate the rate constant at another temperature.

Reaction Mechanisms. The detailed sequence of elementary processes that lead to the net chemical change is the **mechanism** of the reaction. Since intermediates usually cannot be detected, the mechanism is a theory. Support for a mechanism comes from matching the predicted rate law for the mechanism with the rate law obtained from experimental data. For the **rate-determining step** or for any **elementary process** the corresponding rate law has exponents equal to the coefficients in the balanced equation for the elementary process.

Catalysts. **Catalysts** are substances that change a reaction rate but are not consumed by the reaction. Negative catalysts inhibit reactions. Positive catalysts provide alternative paths for reactions for which at least one step has a smaller activation energy than the uncatalyzed reaction. **Homogeneous catalysts** are in the same phase as the reactants. **Heterogeneous catalysts** provide a path of lower activation energy by having a surface on which the reactants are adsorbed and react. Catalysts in living systems are called **enzymes.**

T🧪OLS FOR PROBLEM SOLVING

In this chapter you learned to apply the following concepts as tools in solving problems dealing with aspects of chemical kinetics. Study each tool carefully so that you know what each is used for. When faced with solving a problem, recall what each tool does and consider whether it will be helpful in finding a solution. This will aid you in selecting the tools you need. Remember that at times tools from previous chapters will be needed along with the new ones in this chapter.

Rate law of a reaction (*page 526*) A rate law allows us to calculate the rate of reaction for a given set of reactant concentrations. It also serves as a guide in devising reasonable reaction mechanisms. Exponents for the concentrations in the rate law are always determined experimentally as described on page 529. Rate constants determined at different temperatures are used in the Arrhenius equation described below.

$$\text{Rate} = k[A]^n[B]^m$$

Integrated first-order rate law (*page 534*) For a first-order reaction with known *k*, this equation is used when we need to calculate the concentration of a reactant at some specified time after the start of the reaction. We could also calculate the time required for the concentration to drop to some specified value. This equation is also used for carbon-14 dating of organic materials.

$$\ln \frac{[A]_0}{[A]_t} = kt$$

Integrated second-order rate law (*page 540*) For a second-order reaction of the form, Rate = $k[B]^2$, with known *k*, this equation is used to calculate the concentration of a reactant at some specified time after the start of the reaction, or the time required for the concentration to drop to some specified value.

$$\frac{1}{[B]_t} - \frac{1}{[B]_0} = kt$$

Half-lives of a first-order reaction *(page 537)* This equation relates the rate constant to the half-life, $t_{1/2}$, for first-order reactions. Use of half-lives can be a convenient alternative to the integrated first-order rate law to determine the concentration of a reactant after it has reacted for a whole number of number of half-lives. The amount of reactant left after n half-lives is equal to $(1/2)^n$.

$$\ln 2 = kt_{1/2}$$

Arrhenius equation *(pages 548 and 550)* This equation relates the rate constant, k, to the activation energy, E_a, and temperature. Activation energies are determined by measuring rate constants at a variety of temperatures and graphically analyzing the data (see page 549). This equation is also used to determine the shelf life of a wide variety of consumer products.

$$k = A\,e^{-E_a/RT} \qquad \ln\left(\frac{k_2}{k_1}\right) = \frac{-E_a}{R}\left(\frac{1}{T_2} - \frac{1}{T_1}\right)$$

QUESTIONS, PROBLEMS, AND EXERCISES

Answers to problems whose numbers are printed in color are given in Appendix B. More challenging problems are marked with asterisks. ILW = Interactive Learningware solution is available at www.wiley.com/college/brady. OH = an Office Hours video is available for this problem.

REVIEW QUESTIONS

Factors That Affect Reaction Rate

13.1 Give an example from everyday experience of (a) a very fast reaction, (b) a moderately fast reaction, and (c) a slow reaction.

13.2 Suppose we compared two reactions, one requiring the simultaneous collision of three molecules and the other requiring a collision between two molecules. From the standpoint of statistics, and all other factors being equal, which reaction should be faster? Explain your answer.

13.3 How does an instantaneous rate of reaction differ from an average rate of reaction?

13.4 Explain how the initial instantaneous rate of reaction can be determined from experimental concentration versus time data.

13.5 What is a *homogeneous reaction*? What is a *heterogeneous reaction*? Give examples.

13.6 Why are chemical reactions usually carried out in solution?

13.7 What is the major factor that affects the rate of a heterogeneous reaction?

13.8 How does particle size affect the rate of a heterogeneous reaction? Why?

13.9 The rate of hardening of epoxy glue depends on the amount of hardener that is mixed into the glue. What factor affecting reaction rates does this illustrate?

13.10 A Polaroid instant photograph develops faster if it's kept warm than if it is exposed to cold. Why?

13.11 Insects have no way of controlling their body temperatures like mammals do. In cool weather, they become sluggish and move less quickly. How can this be explained using the principles developed in this chapter?

13.12 On the basis of what you learned in Chapter 11, why do foods cook faster in a pressure cooker than in an open pot of boiling water?

13.13 Persons who have been submerged in very cold water and who are believed to have drowned sometimes can be revived. On the other hand, persons who have been submerged in warmer water for the same length of time have died. Explain this in terms of factors that affect the rates of chemical reactions.

Concentration and Rate; Rate Laws

13.14 What are the units of reaction rate?

13.15 What are the units of the rate constant for (a) a first-order reaction, (b) a second-order reaction, and (c) a zero-order reaction?

13.16 How does the dependence of reaction rate on concentration differ between a zero-order and a first-order reaction?

13.17 Is there any way of using the coefficients in the balanced overall equation for a reaction to predict with certainty what the exponents are in the rate law?

13.18 If the concentration of a reactant is doubled and the reaction rate is unchanged, what must be the order of the reaction with respect to that reactant?

13.19 If the concentration of a reactant is doubled and the reaction rate doubles, what must be the order of the reaction with respect to that reactant?

13.20 If the concentration of a reactant is doubled, by what factor will the rate increase if the reaction is second order with respect to that reactant?

13.21 In an experiment, the concentration of a reactant was tripled. The rate increased by a factor of 27. What is the order of the reaction with respect to that reactant?

13.22 Biological reactions usually involve the interaction of an enzyme with a *substrate*, the substance that actually undergoes the chemical change. In many cases, the rate of reaction depends on the concentration of the enzyme but is independent of the substrate concentration. What is the order of the reaction with respect to the substrate in such instances?

13.23 A reaction has the following rate law:

$$\text{Rate} = k[A]^2[B][C]$$

What are the units of the rate constant, k?

Concentration and Time, Half-lives

13.24 How is the half-life of a first-order reaction affected by the initial concentration of the reactant?

13.25 How is the half-life of a second-order reaction affected by the initial reactant concentration?

13.26 Derive the equations for $t_{1/2}$ for first- and second-order reactions from Equations 13.3 and 13.8, respectively.

13.27 The integrated rate law for a zero-order reaction is

$$[A]_t - [A]_0 = -kt$$

Derive an equation for the half-life of a zero-order reaction.

Effect of Temperature on Rate

13.28 What is the basic postulate of collision theory?

13.29 What two factors influence the effectiveness of molecular collisions in producing chemical change?

13.30 In terms of the kinetic theory, why does an increase in temperature increase the reaction rate?

13.31 Draw the potential energy diagram for an endothermic reaction. Indicate on the diagram the activation energy for both the forward and reverse reactions. Also indicate the heat of reaction.

13.32 Explain, in terms of the law of conservation of energy, why an endothermic reaction leads to a cooling of the reaction mixture (provided heat cannot enter from outside the system).

13.33 Draw a potential energy diagram for an exothermic reaction and indicate on the diagram the location of the transition state.

13.34 The decomposition of carbon dioxide,

$$CO_2 \longrightarrow CO + O$$

has a very large activation energy of approximately 460 kJ mol^{-1}. Explain why this is consistent with a mechanism that involves the breaking of a C$=$O bond.

Reaction Mechanisms

13.35 What is the definition of an *elementary process?* How are elementary processes related to the mechanism of a reaction?

13.36 What is a *rate-determining step?*

13.37 In what way is the rate law for a reaction related to the rate-determining step?

13.38 A reaction has the following mechanism.

$$2NO \longrightarrow N_2O_2$$
$$N_2O_2 + H_2 \longrightarrow N_2O + H_2O$$
$$N_2O + H_2 \longrightarrow N_2 + H_2O$$

What is the net overall change that occurs in this reaction? Identify any intermediates in the reaction.

13.39 If the reaction $NO_2 + CO \longrightarrow NO + CO_2$ occurs by a one-step collision process, what would be the expected rate law

for the reaction? The actual rate law is Rate $= k[NO_2]^2$. Could the reaction actually occur by a one-step collision between NO_2 and CO? Explain.

13.40 Oxidation of NO to NO_2—one of the reactions in the production of smog—appears to involve carbon monoxide. A possible mechanism is

$$CO + \cdot OH \longrightarrow CO_2 + H\cdot$$
$$H\cdot + O_2 \longrightarrow HOO\cdot$$
$$HOO\cdot + NO \longrightarrow \cdot OH + NO_2$$

(The formulas with dots represent extremely reactive species with unpaired electrons and are called *free radicals.*) Write the net chemical equation for the reaction.

13.41 Show that the following two mechanisms give the same net overall reaction.

Mechanism 1

$$OCl^- + H_2O \longrightarrow HOCl + OH^-$$
$$HOCl + I^- \longrightarrow HOI + Cl^-$$
$$HOI + OH^- \longrightarrow H_2O + OI^-$$

Mechanism 2

$$OCl^- + H_2O \longrightarrow HOCl + OH^-$$
$$I^- + HOCl \longrightarrow ICl + OH^-$$
$$ICl + 2OH^- \longrightarrow OI^- + Cl^- + H_2O$$

13.42 The experimental rate law for the reaction

$$NO_2 + CO \longrightarrow CO_2 + NO$$

is rate $= k[NO_2]^2$. If the mechanism is

$$2NO_2 \longrightarrow NO_3 + NO \quad \text{(slow)}$$
$$NO_3 + CO \longrightarrow NO_2 + CO_2 \quad \text{(fast)}$$

show that the predicted rate law is the same as the experimental rate law.

Catalysts

13.43 How does a catalyst increase the rate of a chemical reaction?

13.44 What is a *homogeneous catalyst?* How does it function, in general terms?

13.45 What is the difference in meaning between the terms *adsorption* and *absorption?* (If necessary, use a dictionary.) Which one applies to heterogeneous catalysts?

13.46 What does the catalytic converter do in the exhaust system of an automobile? Why should leaded gasoline not be used in cars equipped with catalytic converters?

REVIEW PROBLEMS

Measuring Rates of Reaction

13.47 The following data were collected at a certain temperature for the decomposition of sulfuryl chloride, SO_2Cl_2, a chemical used in a variety of organic syntheses.

$$SO_2Cl_2 \longrightarrow SO_2 + Cl_2$$

Time (min)	$[SO_2Cl_2]$ (mol L^{-1})
0	0.1000
100	0.0876
200	0.0768
300	0.0673
400	0.0590
500	0.0517
600	0.0453
700	0.0397
800	0.0348
900	0.0305
1000	0.0267
1100	0.0234

Make a graph of concentration versus time and determine the rate of formation of SO_2 at $t = 200$ minutes and $t = 600$ minutes.

13.48 The following data were collected for the decomposition of acetaldehyde, CH_3CHO (used in the manufacture of a variety of chemicals including perfumes, dyes, and plastics), into methane and carbon monoxide. The data were collected at a temperature of 530 °C.

$$CH_3CHO \longrightarrow CH_4 + CO$$

$[CH_3CHO]$ (mol L^{-1})	Time (s)
0.200	0
0.153	20
0.124	40
0.104	60
0.090	80
0.079	100
0.070	120
0.063	140
0.058	160
0.053	180
0.049	200

Make a graph of concentration versus time and determine the rate of reaction of CH_3CHO after 60 seconds and after 120 seconds.

13.49 In the reaction $3H_2 + N_2 \longrightarrow 2NH_3$, how does the rate of disappearance of hydrogen compare to the rate of disappearance of nitrogen? How does the rate of appearance of NH_3 compare to the rate of disappearance of nitrogen?

OH 13.50 For the reaction $2A + B \longrightarrow 3C$, it was found that the rate of disappearance of B was 0.30 mol L^{-1} s^{-1}. What were the rate of disappearance of A and the rate of appearance of C?

13.51 In the combustion of hexane (a low-boiling component of gasoline),

$$2C_6H_{14}(g) + 19O_2(g) \longrightarrow 12CO_2(g) + 14H_2O(g)$$

it was found that the rate of reaction of C_6H_{14} was 1.20 mol L^{-1} s^{-1}.
(a) What was the rate of reaction of O_2?
(b) What was the rate of formation of CO_2?
(c) What was the rate of formation of H_2O?

13.52 At a certain moment in the reaction

$$2N_2O_5 \longrightarrow 4NO_2 + O_2$$

N_2O_5 is decomposing at a rate of 2.5×10^{-6} mol L^{-1} s^{-1}. What are the rates of formation of NO_2 and O_2?

Rate Laws for Reactions

13.53 Estimate the rate of the reaction

$$H_2SeO_3 + 6I^- + 4H^+ \longrightarrow Se + 2I_3^- + 3H_2O$$

given the rate law for the reaction at 0 °C is

$$Rate = (5.0 \times 10^5 \text{ L}^5 \text{ mol}^{-5} \text{ s}^{-1})[H_2SeO_3][I^-]^3[H^+]^2$$

and the reactant concentrations are $[H_2SeO_3] = 2.0 \times 10^{-2}$ M, $[I^-] = 2.0 \times 10^{-3}$ M, and $[H^+] = 1.0 \times 10^{-3}$ M.

13.54 Estimate the rate of the reaction

$$H^+(aq) + OH^-(aq) \longrightarrow H_2O(l)$$

given that the rate law for the reaction is

$$Rate = (1.3 \times 10^{11} \text{ L mol}^{-1} \text{ s}^{-1})[OH^-][H^+]$$

for neutral water where $[H^+] = 1.0 \times 10^{-7}$ M and $[OH^-] = 1.0 \times 10^{-7}$ M.

OH 13.55 The oxidation of NO (released in small amounts in the exhaust of automobiles) produces the brownish-red gas NO_2, which is a component of urban air pollution.

$$2NO + O_2 \longrightarrow 2NO_2$$

The rate law for the reaction is Rate = $k[NO]^2[O_2]$. At 25 °C, $k = 7.1 \times 10^9$ L^2 mol^{-2} s^{-1}. What would be the rate of the reaction if [NO] = 0.0010 mol L^{-1} and $[O_2]$ = 0.034 mol L^{-1}?

13.56 The rate law for the decomposition of N_2O_5 is

$$Rate = k[N_2O_5]$$

If $k = 1.0 \times 10^{-5}$ s^{-1}, what is the reaction rate when the N_2O_5 concentration is 0.0010 mol L^{-1}?

13.57 The following data were collected for the reaction

$$M + N \longrightarrow P + Q$$

Initial Concentrations (mol L^{-1})		Initial rate of reaction
$[M]$	$[N]$	(mol L^{-1} s^{-1})
0.010	0.010	2.5×10^{-3}
0.020	0.010	5.0×10^{-3}
0.020	0.030	4.5×10^{-2}

What is the rate law for the reaction? What is the value of the rate constant (with correct units)?

13.58 Cyclopropane, C_3H_6, is a gas used as a general anesthetic. It undergoes a slow molecular rearrangement to propylene.

cyclopropane   propylene

At a certain temperature, the following data were obtained relating concentration and rate.

Initial Concentration of C_3H_6 (mol L^{-1})	Rate of Formation of Propylene (mol L^{-1} s^{-1})
0.050	2.95×10^{-5}
0.100	5.90×10^{-5}
0.150	8.85×10^{-5}

What is the rate law for the reaction? What is the value of the rate constant, with correct units?

13.59 The reaction of iodide ion with hypochlorite ion, OCl^- (the active ingredient in a "chlorine bleach" such as Clorox), follows the equation $OCl^- + I^- \longrightarrow OI^- + Cl^-$. It is a rapid reaction that gives the following rate data.

Initial Concentrations (mol L^{-1})		Rate of Formation of Cl^- (mol L^{-1} s^{-1})
[OCl^-]	[I^-]	
1.7×10^{-3}	1.7×10^{-3}	1.75×10^4
3.4×10^{-3}	1.7×10^{-3}	3.50×10^4
1.7×10^{-3}	3.4×10^{-3}	3.50×10^4

What is the rate law for the reaction? Determine the value of the rate constant with its correct units.

13.60 The formation of small amounts of nitric oxide, NO, in automobile engines is the first step in the formation of smog. As noted in Problem 13.55, nitric oxide is readily oxidized to nitrogen dioxide by the reaction

$$2NO(g) + O_2(g) \longrightarrow 2NO_2(g)$$

The following data were collected in a study of the rate of this reaction.

Initial Concentrations (mol L^{-1})		Rate of Formation of of NO_2 (mol L^{-1} s^{-1})
[O_2]	[NO]	
0.0010	0.0010	7.10
0.0040	0.0010	28.4
0.0040	0.0030	255.6

What is the rate law for the reaction? What is the rate constant with its correct units?

ILW 13.61 At a certain temperature the following data were collected for the reaction $2ICl + H_2 \longrightarrow I_2 + 2HCl$

Initial Concentrations (mol L^{-1})		Initial Rate of Formation of I_2 (mol L^{-1} s^{-1})
[ICl]	[H_2]	
0.10	0.10	0.0015
0.20	0.10	0.0030
0.10	0.0500	0.00075

Determine the rate law and the rate constant (with correct units) for the reaction.

13.62 The following data were obtained for the reaction of $(CH_3)_3CBr$ with hydroxide ion at 55 °C.

$$(CH_3)_3CBr + OH^- \longrightarrow (CH_3)_3COH + Br^-$$

Initial Concentrations (mol L^{-1})		Initial Rate of Formation of $(CH_3)_3COH$ (mol L^{-1} s^{-1})
[$(CH_3)_3CBr$]	[OH^-]	
0.10	0.10	1.0×10^{-3}
0.20	0.10	2.0×10^{-3}
0.30	0.10	3.0×10^{-3}
0.10	0.20	1.0×10^{-3}
0.10	0.30	1.0×10^{-3}

What is the rate law for the reaction? What is the value of the rate constant (with correct units) at this temperature?

Concentration and Time

13.63 Data for the decomposition of SO_2Cl_2 according to the equation $SO_2Cl_2(g) \longrightarrow SO_2(g) + Cl_2(g)$ were given in Problem 13.47. Show graphically that these data fit a first-order rate law. Graphically determine the rate constant for the reaction.

13.64 For the data in Problem 13.48, decide graphically whether the reaction is first or second order. Determine the rate constant for the reaction described in that problem.

ILW OH 13.65 The decomposition of SO_2Cl_2 described in Problem 13.47 has a first-order rate constant $k = 2.2 \times 10^{-5}$ s^{-1} at 320 °C. If the initial SO_2Cl_2 concentration in a container is 0.0040 M, what will its concentration be (a) after 1.00 hour and (b) after 1.00 day?

13.66 If it takes 75.0 min for the concentration of a reactant to drop to 20% of its initial value in a first-order reaction, what is the rate constant for the reaction in the units min^{-1}?

13.67 The concentration of a drug in the body is often expressed in units of milligrams per kilogram of body weight. The initial dose of a drug in an animal was 25.0 mg/kg body weight. After 2.00 hours, this concentration had dropped to 15.0 mg/kg body weight. If the drug is eliminated metabolically by a first-order process, what is the rate constant for the process in units of min^{-1}?

13.68 In the preceding problem, what must the initial dose of the drug be in order for the drug concentration 3.00 hours afterward to be 5.0 mg/kg body weight?

13.69 The decomposition of hydrogen iodide follows the equation $2HI(g) \longrightarrow H_2(g) + I_2(g)$. The reaction is second order and has a rate constant equal to 1.6×10^{-3} L mol^{-1} s^{-1} at 700 °C. If the initial concentration of HI in a container is 3.4×10^{-2} M, how many minutes will it take for the concentration to be reduced to 8.0×10^{-4} M?

13.70 The second-order rate constant for the decomposition of HI at 700 °C was given in the preceding problem. At 2.5×10^3 minutes after a particular experiment had begun, the HI concentration was equal to 4.5×10^{-4} mol L^{-1}. What was the initial molar concentration of HI in the reaction vessel?

Half-lives

13.71 The half-life of a certain first-order reaction is 15 minutes. What fraction of the original reactant concentration will remain after 2.0 hours?

13.72 Strontium-90 has a half-life of 28 years. How long will it take for all of the strontium-90 presently on the earth to be reduced to 1/32nd of its present amount?

13.73 Using the graph from Problem 13.47, determine the time required for the SO_2Cl_2 concentration to drop from 0.100 mol L^{-1} to 0.050 mol L^{-1}. How long does it take for the concentration to drop from 0.050 mol L^{-1} to 0.025 mol L^{-1}? What is the order of this reaction? (Hint: How is the half-life related to concentration?)

13.74 Using the graph from Problem 13.48, determine how long it takes for the CH_3CHO concentration to decrease from 0.200 mol L^{-1} to 0.100 mol L^{-1}. How long does it take the concentration to drop from 0.100 mol L^{-1} to 0.050 mol L^{-1}? What is the order of this reaction? (Hint: How is the half-life related to concentration?)

Radiological Dating

****13.75** A 500 mg sample of rock was found to have 2.45×10^{-6} mol of potassium-40 ($t_{1/2} = 1.3 \times 10^9$ yr) and 2.45×10^{-6} mol of argon-40. How old was the rock? (What assumption is made about the origin of the argon-40?)

****13.76** If a rock sample was found to contain 1.16×10^{-7} mol of argon-40, how much potassium-40 would also have to be present for the rock to be 1.3×10^9 years old?

ILW 13.77 A tree killed by being buried under volcanic ash was found to have a ratio of carbon-14 atoms to carbon-12 atoms of 4.8×10^{-14}. How long ago did the eruption occur?

13.78 A wooden door lintel from an excavated site in Mexico would be expected to have what ratio of carbon-14 to carbon-12 atoms if the lintel is 9.0×10^3 yr old?

Calculations Involving the Activation Energy

13.79 The following data were collected for a reaction.

Rate Constant (L mol^{-1} s^{-1})	Temperature (°C)
2.88×10^{-4}	320
4.87×10^{-4}	340
7.96×10^{-4}	360
1.26×10^{-3}	380
1.94×10^{-3}	400

Determine the activation energy for the reaction in kJ mol^{-1} both graphically and by calculation using Equation 13.12. For the calculation of E_a, use the first and last sets of data in the table above.

13.80 Rate constants were measured at various temperatures for the reaction $HI(g) + CH_3I(g) \longrightarrow CH_4(g) + I_2(g)$. The following data were obtained.

Rate Constant (L mol^{-1} s^{-1})	Temperature (°C)
1.91×10^{-2}	205
2.74×10^{-2}	210
3.90×10^{-2}	215
5.51×10^{-2}	220
7.73×10^{-2}	225
1.08×10^{-1}	230

Determine the activation energy in kJ mol^{-1} both graphically and by calculation using Equation 13.12. For the calculation of E_a, use the first and last sets of data in the table above.

ILW OH 13.81 The decomposition of NOCl, $2NOCl \longrightarrow 2NO + Cl_2$ has $k = 9.3 \times 10^{-5}$ L mol^{-1} s^{-1} at 100 °C and $k = 1.0 \times 10^{-3}$ L mol^{-1} s^{-1} at 130 °C. What is E_a for this reaction in kJ mol^{-1}? Use the data at 100 °C to calculate the frequency factor.

13.82 The conversion of cyclopropane, an anesthetic, to propylene (see Problem 13.58) has a rate constant $k = 1.3 \times 10^{-6}$ s^{-1} at 400 °C and $k = 1.1 \times 10^{-5}$ s^{-1} at 430 °C.
(a) What is the activation energy in kJ mol^{-1}?
(b) What is the value of the frequency factor, A, for this reaction?
(c) What is the rate constant for the reaction at 350 °C?

13.83 The decomposition of N_2O_5 has an activation energy of 103 kJ mol^{-1} and a frequency factor of 4.3×10^{13} s^{-1}. What is the rate constant for this decomposition at (a) 20 °C and (b) 100 °C?

13.84 At 35 °C, the rate constant for the reaction

$$C_{12}H_{22}O_{11} + H_2O \longrightarrow C_6H_{12}O_6 + C_6H_{12}O_6$$
$$\text{sucrose} \qquad\qquad \text{glucose} \qquad \text{fructose}$$

is $k = 6.2 \times 10^{-5}$ s^{-1}. The activation energy for the reaction is 108 kJ mol^{-1}. What is the rate constant for the reaction at 45 °C?

ADDITIONAL EXERCISES

13.85 For the reaction and data given in Problem 13.48, make a graph of concentration versus time for the *formation* of CH_4. What are the rates of formation of CH_4 at $t = 40$ s and $t = 100$ s?

13.86 The age of wine can be determined by measuring the trace amount of radioactive tritium, ^3H, present in a sample. Tritium is formed from hydrogen in water vapor in the upper atmosphere by cosmic bombardment, so all naturally occurring water contains a small amount of this isotope. Once the water is in a bottle of wine, however, the formation of additional tritium from the water is negligible, so the tritium initially present gradually diminishes by a first-order radioactive decay with a half-life of 12.5 years. If a bottle of wine is found to have a tritium concentration that is 0.100 that of freshly bottled wine (i.e., $[^3H]_t = 0.100[^3H]_0$), what is the age of the wine?

OH 13.87 Carbon-14 dating can be used to estimate the age of formerly living materials because the uptake of carbon-14 from carbon dioxide in the atmosphere stops once the organism dies. If tissue samples from a mummy contain about 81.0% of the carbon-14 expected in living tissue, how old is the mummy? The half-life for decay of carbon-14 is 5730 years.

OH **13.88** What percentage of cesium chloride made from cesium-137 ($t_{1/2}=30$ yr; beta emitter) remains after 150 yr? What *chemical* product forms?

13.89 One of the reactions that occurs in polluted air in urban areas is $2NO_2(g) + O_3(g) \longrightarrow N_2O_5(g) + O_2(g)$. It is believed that a species with the formula NO_3 is involved in the mechanism, and the observed rate law for the overall reaction is Rate $= k[NO_2][O_3]$. Propose a mechanism for this reaction that includes the species NO_3 and is consistent with the observed rate law.

OH **13.90** Suppose a reaction occurs with the mechanism

(1) $2A \rightleftharpoons A_2$ (fast)

(2) $A_2 + E \longrightarrow B + C$ (slow)

in which the first step is a very rapid reversible reaction that can be considered to be essentially an equilibrium (forward and reverse reactions occurring at the same rate) and the second is a slow step.
(a) Write the rate law for the forward reaction in step (1).
(b) Write the rate law for the reverse reaction in step (1).
(c) Write the rate law for the rate-determining step.
(d) What is the chemical equation for the net reaction that occurs in this chemical change?
(e) Use the results of parts (a) and (b) to rewrite the rate law of the rate-determining step in terms of the concentrations of the reactants in the overall balanced equation for the reaction.

OH **13.91** The decomposition of urea, $(NH_2)_2CO$, in 0.10 M HCl follows the equation

$$(NH_2)_2CO(aq) + 2H^+(aq) + H_2O \longrightarrow$$
$$2NH_4^+(aq) + CO_2(g)$$

At 60 °C, $k = 5.84 \times 10^{-6}$ min^{-1} and at 70 °C, $k = 2.25 \times 10^{-5}$ min^{-1}. If this reaction is run at 80 °C starting with a urea concentration of 0.0020 M, how many minutes will it take for the urea concentration to drop to 0.0012 M?

13.92 Show that for a reaction that obeys the general rate law

$$\text{Rate} = k[A]^n$$

a graph of log(rate) versus log[A] should yield a straight line with a slope equal to the order of the reaction. For the reaction in Problem 13.47, measure the rate of the reaction at $t = 150, 300, 450$, and 600 s. Then graph log(rate) versus log[SO_2Cl_2] and determine the order of the reaction with respect to SO_2Cl_2.

OH **13.93** It was mentioned that the rates of many reactions approximately double for each 10 °C rise in temperature. Assuming a starting temperature of 25 °C, what would the activation energy be, in kJ mol^{-1}, if the rate of a reaction were to be twice as large at 35 °C?

13.94 The development of a photographic image on film is a process controlled by the kinetics of the reduction of silver halide by a developer. The time required for development at a particular temperature is inversely proportional to the rate constant for the process. Below are published data on development times for Kodak's Tri-X film using Kodak D-76 developer. From these data, estimate the activation energy (in units of kJ mol^{-1}) for the development process. Also estimate the development time at 15 °C.

Temperature (°C)	Development Time (minutes)
18	10
20	9
21	8
22	7
24	6

13.95 The rate at which crickets chirp depends on the ambient temperature, because crickets are cold-blooded insects whose body temperature follows the temperature of their environment. It has been found that the Celsius temperature can be estimated by counting the number of chirps in 8 seconds and then adding 4. In other words, $t_C =$ (number of chirps in 8 seconds) + 4.
(a) Calculate the number of chirps in 8 seconds for temperatures of 20, 25, 30, and 35 °C.
(b) The number of chirps per unit of time is directly proportional to the rate constant for a biochemical reaction involved in the cricket's chirp. On the basis of this assumption, make a graph of ln(chirps in 8 s) versus $(1/T)$. Calculate the activation energy for the biochemical reaction involved.
(c) How many chirps would a cricket make in 8 seconds at a temperature of 40 °C?

*13.96 The cooking of an egg involves the denaturation of a protein called albumen. The time required to achieve a particular degree of denaturation is inversely proportional to the rate constant for the process. This reaction has a high activation energy, $E_a = 418$ kJ mol^{-1}. Calculate how long it would take to cook a traditional three-minute egg on top of Mt. McKinley in Alaska on a day when the atmospheric pressure there is 355 torr.

*13.97 The following question is based on Facets of Chemistry 13.1. The reaction of hydrogen and bromine appears to follow the mechanism

$$Br_2 \xrightarrow{h\nu} 2Br\cdot$$

$$Br\cdot + H_2 \longrightarrow HBr + H\cdot$$

$$H\cdot + Br_2 \longrightarrow HBr + Br\cdot$$

$$2Br\cdot \longrightarrow Br_2$$

(a) Identify the initiation step in the mechanism.
(b) Identify any propagation steps.
(c) Identify the termination step.
(d) The mechanism also contains the reaction

$$H\cdot + HBr \longrightarrow H_2 + Br\cdot$$

How does this reaction affect the rate of formation of HBr?

EXERCISES IN CRITICAL THINKING

13.98 Provide three examples of ordinary occurrences that mimic a reaction mechanism and have a rate-limiting step.

13.99 Can a reaction have a negative activation energy? Explain your response.

13.100 Assume you have a three-step mechanism. Would the potential energy diagram have three peaks? If so, how would you distinguish the rate-limiting step?

13.101 What range of ages can C-14 dating reliably determine?

13.102 Why are initial reaction rates used to determine rate laws?

13.103 If a reaction is reversible (i.e., the products can react to re-form the reactants) what would the rate law look like?

*13.104 The ozone layer protects us from high energy radiation. Description of the ozone layer is a kinetics problem concerning the formation and destruction of ozone to produce a steady state. How can we write this mathematically assuming that the processes are elementary reactions?

*13.105 How would you measure an extremely fast reaction?

CHEMICAL EQUILIBRIUM: GENERAL CONCEPTS

14

One of the chemicals used in a dry chemical fire extinguisher, like the one being used here to extinguish a car fire, is sodium bicarbonate, $NaHCO_3$. Its decomposition when heated produces carbon dioxide, which helps to smother the flames. The decomposition of sodium bicarbonate involves a heterogeneous chemical equilibrium and is one of the reactions discussed in this chapter. (Sean Murphy/ Stone/Getty Images, Inc)

In Chapter 13 you learned that most chemical reactions slow down as the reactants are consumed and the products form. The focus there was learning about the factors that affect how *fast* the reactant and product concentrations change. In this and the following four chapters we will turn our attention to the ultimate fate of chemical systems, *dynamic chemical equilibrium*—the situation that exists when the concentrations cease to change.

You have already encountered the concept of a dynamic equilibrium several times earlier in this book. Recall that such an equilibrium is established when two opposing processes occur at equal rates. In a liquid–vapor equilibrium, for example, the processes are evaporation and condensation. In a chemical equilibrium, such as the ionization of a weak acid, they are the forward and reverse reactions represented by the chemical equation.

In this chapter we will study the equilibrium condition both qualitatively and quantitatively. Understanding the factors that affect equilibrium systems is important not only in chemistry but in other sciences as well. They apply to biology because living cells must control the concentrations of substances within them in order to survive. And they are fundamental in understanding chemical reactions that affect many current environmental problems, including global warming, acid rain, and stratospheric ozone depletion.

We begin our discussion of equilibrium here by examining principles that apply to chemical systems in general. In Chapters 15 through 17 we will focus on equilibria in aqueous solutions. Then, in Chapter 18 we will tie together the concept of chemical equilibrium with the energetics of chemical change and the drive toward the most probable state.

14.1 | DYNAMIC EQUILIBRIUM IS ACHIEVED WHEN THE RATES OF FORWARD AND REVERSE PROCESSES BECOME EQUAL

Let's review the process by which a system reaches equilibrium. For this purpose, we'll examine the reaction for the decomposition of gaseous N_2O_4 into NO_2.

$$N_2O_4(g) \longrightarrow 2NO_2(g)$$

When we first begin, there are no molecules of NO_2, so the only reaction taking place is the decomposition of N_2O_4. As the concentration of N_2O_4 decreases, its rate of decomposition slows, as illustrated in Figure 14.1. At the same time, the concentration of NO_2 rises, which is also shown in Figure 14.1. When NO_2 molecules collide, they are able to re-form N_2O_4, so while the rate of decomposition of N_2O_4 slows, the rate at which NO_2 molecules combine increases. This corresponds to the reverse reaction in the equation above. Eventually, the rate of the reverse reaction becomes equal to the rate of the forward reaction, at which point the concentrations cease to change. N_2O_4 is

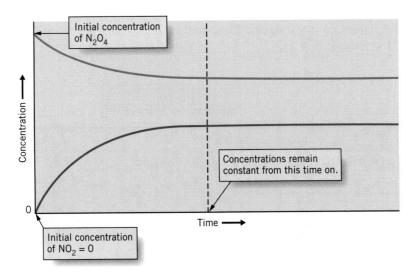

Initial concentration of N_2O_4

Concentrations remain constant from this time on.

Concentration

Time

Initial concentration of $NO_2 = 0$

FIG. 14.1 **The approach to equilibrium.** In the decomposition of $N_2O_4(g)$ into $NO_2(g)$,

$$N_2O_4(g) \rightleftharpoons 2NO_2(g)$$

the concentrations of the N_2O_4 and NO_2 change relatively fast at first. As time passes, the concentrations change more and more slowly. When equilibrium is reached, the concentrations of N_2O_4 and NO_2 no longer change with time; they remain constant.

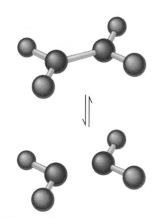

The equilibrium between N_2O_4 and NO_2.

decomposing as fast as it's being formed, and we've reached *dynamic equilibrium*. As you learned earlier, when we write the equation to describe the equilibrium, we use double arrows ($\rightleftharpoons$).

$$N_2O_4(g) \rightleftharpoons 2NO_2(g) \tag{14.1}$$

Most chemical systems reach a state of dynamic equilibrium, given enough time. Sometimes, though, this equilibrium is extremely difficult (or even impossible) to detect, because in some reactions the amounts of either the reactants or products present at equilibrium are virtually zero. For instance, in water vapor at room temperature there are no detectable amounts of either H_2 or O_2 from the equilibrium

$$2H_2O(g) \rightleftharpoons 2H_2(g) + O_2(g)$$

Water molecules are so stable that we can't detect whether any of them decompose. Even in cases such as this, however, it is often *convenient* to assume that an equilibrium does exist.

The meaning of reactants and products in a chemical equilibrium

☐ For the equilibrium $A \rightleftharpoons B$, the reaction read from left to right is the *forward reaction*; the reaction read from right to left is the *reverse reaction*.

$A \longrightarrow B$ (forward reaction)
$A \longleftarrow B$ (reverse reaction)

Remember, even after equilibrium has been reached, both the forward and reverse reactions continue to occur.

For the forward reaction in Equation 14.1, N_2O_4 is the reactant and NO_2 is the product. But the reverse reaction is also occurring, where NO_2 is the reactant and N_2O_4 is the product. When the system is at equilibrium, the usual definitions of reactant and product don't make a lot of sense. In these situations, when we use the term *reactants*, we simply mean those substances written to the left of the double arrows. Similarly, we use the term *products* to mean the substances to the right of the double arrows.

Closed systems reach the same equilibrium concentrations whether we start with reactants or with products

The composition of an equilibrium mixture is found to be independent of whether we begin the reaction from the "reactant side" or the "product side." For example, suppose we set up the two experiments shown in Figure 14.2. In the first one-liter flask we place 0.0350 mol N_2O_4. Since no NO_2 is present, some N_2O_4 must decompose for the mixture to reach equilibrium, so the reaction in Equation 14.1 will proceed in the forward direction (i.e., from left to right). When equilibrium is reached, we find the concentration of N_2O_4 has dropped to 0.0292 mol L^{-1} and the concentration of NO_2 has become 0.0116 mol L^{-1}.

☐ Stoichiometrically, 0.0700 mol of NO_2 could be formed from 0.0350 mol of N_2O_4, since the ratio of NO_2 to N_2O_4 is 2:1.

In the second one-liter flask we place 0.0700 mol of NO_2 (*precisely* the amount of NO_2 that would form if 0.0350 mol of N_2O_4—the amount placed in the first flask—decomposed completely). In this second flask there is no N_2O_4 present initially, so NO_2 molecules must combine, following the reverse reaction (right to left) in Equation 14.1, to give enough N_2O_4 for equilibrium. When we measure the concentrations at equilibrium in the second flask, we find, once again, 0.0292 mol L^{-1} of N_2O_4 and 0.0116 mol L^{-1} of NO_2.

FIG. 14.2 **Reaction reversibility for the equilibrium $N_2O_4(g) \rightleftharpoons 2NO_2(g)$.** The same equilibrium composition is reached from either the forward or reverse direction, provided the overall system composition is the same. Because pure NO_2 is brown, and pure N_2O_4 is colorless, the amber color of the equilibrium mixture indicates that both species are present at equilibrium.

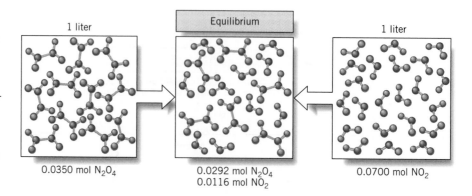

1 liter | Equilibrium | 1 liter

0.0350 mol N_2O_4

0.0292 mol N_2O_4
0.0116 mol NO_2

0.0700 mol NO_2

We see here that the same equilibrium composition is reached whether we begin with pure NO_2 or pure N_2O_4, as long as the *total* amount of nitrogen and oxygen to be divided between these two substances is the same. Similar observations apply to other chemical systems as well, which leads to the following generalization.

> For a given *overall* system composition, we always reach the same equilibrium concentrations whether equilibrium is approached from the forward or reverse direction.

TOOLS
Approach to equilibrium

There are times when it is very convenient to be able to imagine the approach to equilibrium starting from the product side of the equation.

14.2 A LAW RELATING EQUILIBRIUM CONCENTRATIONS CAN BE DERIVED FROM THE BALANCED CHEMICAL EQUATION FOR A REACTION

For any chemical system at equilibrium, there exists a simple relationship among the molar concentrations of the reactants and products. To see this, let's consider the gaseous reaction of hydrogen with iodine to form hydrogen iodide.

$$H_2(g) + I_2(g) \rightleftharpoons 2HI(g)$$

Figure 14.3 shows the results of several experiments measuring equilibrium amounts of each gas, starting with different amounts of the reactants and product in a 10.0 L reaction vessel. When equilibrium is reached, the amounts of H_2, I_2, and HI are different for each experiment, as are their molar concentrations. This isn't particularly surprising, but what is amazing is that the relationship among the concentrations is very simple and can actually be predicted (once we've learned how) from the balanced equation for the reaction.

For each experiment in Figure 14.3, if we square the molar concentration of HI at equilibrium and then divide this by the product of the equilibrium molar

☐ The molar concentrations are obtained by dividing the number of moles of each substance by the volume, 10.0 L.

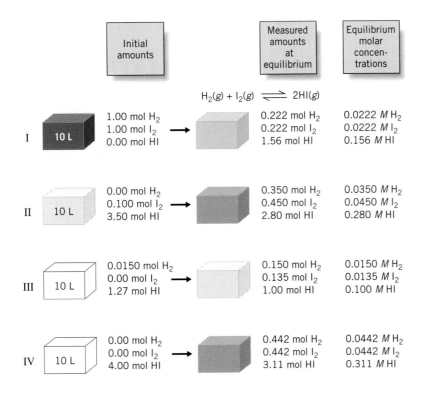

FIG. 14.3 **Four experiments to study the equilibrium among H_2, I_2, and HI gases.** Different amounts of the reactants and product are placed in a 10.0 L reaction vessel at 440 °C where the gases established the equilibrium

$$H_2(g) + I_2(g) \rightleftharpoons 2HI(g)$$

When equilibrium is reached, different amounts of reactants and products remain in each experiment, which gives different equilibrium concentrations.

concentrations of H_2 and I_2, we obtain the same numerical value. This is shown in Table 14.1 where we have once again used square brackets around formulas as symbols for molar concentrations.

The fraction used to calculate the values in the last column of Table 14.1,

$$\frac{[HI]^2}{[H_2][I_2]}$$

is called the **mass action expression.**[1] The origin of this term isn't important; just consider it a name we use to refer to this fraction. The numerical value of the mass action expression is called the **reaction quotient,** and is often symbolized by the letter **Q.** For this reaction, we can write

$$Q = \frac{[HI]^2}{[H_2][I_2]}$$

This equation applies for any set of H_2, I_2, and HI concentrations, whether we are at equilibrium or not.

In Table 14.1, notice that when H_2, I_2, and HI are in dynamic equilibrium at 440 °C, Q is equal to essentially the same constant value of 49.5. In fact, if we repeated the experiments in Figure 14.3 over and over again starting with different amounts of H_2, I_2, and HI, we would still obtain the same reaction quotient, provided the systems had reached equilibrium and the temperature was 440 °C. Therefore, for this reaction at equilibrium we can write

$$\frac{[HI]^2}{[H_2][I_2]} = 49.5 \qquad \text{(at equilibrium at 440 °C)} \qquad (14.2)$$

This relationship is called the **equilibrium law** for the system. Significantly, it tells us that for a mixture of these three gases to be at equilibrium at 440 °C, the value of the mass action expression (the reaction quotient) must equal 49.5. If the reaction quotient has any other value, then the gases are not in equilibrium at this temperature. The constant 49.5, which characterizes this equilibrium system, is called the **equilibrium constant.** The equilibrium constant is usually symbolized by K_c (the subscript c because we write the mass action expression using molar concentrations). Thus, we can state the equilibrium law as follows:

$$\frac{[HI]^2}{[H_2][I_2]} = K_c = 49.5 \qquad \text{(at 440 °C)} \qquad (14.3)$$

TABLE 14.1	Equilibrium Concentrations and the Mass Action Expression			
	Equilibrium Concentrations (mol L^{-1})			$\dfrac{[HI]^2}{[H_2][I_2]}$
Experiment	$[H_2]$	$[I_2]$	$[HI]$	
I	0.0222	0.0222	0.156	$(0.156)^2/(0.0222)(0.0222) = 49.4$
II	0.0350	0.0450	0.280	$(0.280)^2/(0.0350)(0.0450) = 49.8$
III	0.0150	0.0135	0.100	$(0.100)^2/(0.0150)(0.0135) = 49.4$
IV	0.0442	0.0442	0.311	$(0.311)^2/(0.0442)(0.0442) = 49.5$
				Average = 49.5

[1] The mass action expression is derived using thermodynamics, which we'll discuss in Chapter 18. Technically, each concentration in the mass action expression should be divided by its standard state value before inserting it into the expression. This makes the value of any mass action expression unitless. *For substances in solution,* the standard state is an effective molar concentration of 1 *M;* so we would have to divide each concentration by 1 *M* (1 mol L^{-1}) which makes no difference in the numerical value of the mass action expression as long as all concentrations are molarities. *For gases,* the standard state is 1 bar, so we would have to divide each gas concentration by its concentration at that pressure, or each gas partial pressure by 1 bar. For simplicity, we'll leave the standard state values out of our mass action expressions. Later we'll see that these values are lumped into the numerical value of the expression.

It is often useful to think of an equilibrium law such as Equation 14.3 as a *condition* that must be met for equilibrium to exist.

> For chemical equilibrium to exist in a reaction mixture, the reaction quotient Q must be equal to the equilibrium constant, K_c.

As you've probably noticed, we have repeatedly mentioned the temperature when referring to the value of K_c. This is because the value of the equilibrium constant changes when the temperature changes. Thus, if we had performed the experiments in Figure 14.3 at a temperature other than 440 °C, we would have obtained a different value for K_c.

An important fact about the mass action expression and the equilibrium law is that it can *always* be predicted from the balanced chemical equation for the reaction. For example, for the general chemical equation

$$dD + eE \rightleftharpoons fF + gG$$

where D, E, F, and G represent chemical formulas and d, e, f, and g are their coefficients, the mass action expression is

$$\frac{[F]^f [G]^g}{[D]^d [E]^e}$$

The exponents in the mass action expression are the same as the stoichiometric coefficients in the balanced equation.

The condition for equilibrium in this reaction is given by the equation

$$\frac{[F]^f [G]^g}{[D]^d [E]^e} = K_c$$

where the only concentrations that satisfy the equation are *equilibrium concentrations*.

Notice that in writing the mass action expression the molar concentrations of the products are always placed in the numerator and those of the reactants appear in the denominator. Also note that after being raised to appropriate powers the concentration terms are *multiplied*, not added.

□ In general, it is necessary to specify the temperature when giving a value of K_c, because K_c changes when the temperature changes. For example,

$$CH_4(g) + H_2O(g) \rightleftharpoons CO(g) + 3H_2(g)$$

$K_c = 1.78 \times 10^{-3}$ at 800 °C
$K_c = 4.68 \times 10^{-2}$ at 1000 °C
$K_c = 5.67$ at 1500 °C

□ Notice that even though we cannot predict the *rate law* from the balanced overall equation, we can predict the *equilibrium law*.

 **TOOLS**
The equilibrium law

EXAMPLE 14.1
Writing the Equilibrium Law

Most of the hydrogen produced in the United States is derived from methane in natural gas, using the forward reaction of the equilibrium

$$CH_4(g) + H_2O(g) \rightleftharpoons CO(g) + 3H_2(g)$$

What is the equilibrium law for this reaction?

ANALYSIS: The equilibrium law sets the mass action expression equal to the equilibrium constant. To form the mass action expression, we place the concentrations of the products in the numerator and the concentrations of the reactants in the denominator. The coefficients in the equation become exponents on the concentrations.

SOLUTION: The equilibrium law is

$$\frac{[CO][H_2]^3}{[CH_4][H_2O]} = K_c$$

IS THE ANSWER REASONABLE? Check to see that the products are on top of the fraction and that the reactants are on the bottom. Also check the exponents and be sure they are the same as the coefficients in the balanced chemical equation. Notice that we omit writing the exponent when it is equal to 1.

Practice Exercise 1: The equilibrium law for a reaction is

$$\frac{[NO_2]^4}{[N_2O_3]^2[O_2]} = K_c$$

Write the chemical equation for the equilibrium. (Hint: In the equilibrium law, remember where the reactant and product concentrations go and what the exponents mean.)

Practice Exercise 2: Write the equilibrium law for each of the following:
(a) $2H_2(g) + O_2(g) \rightleftharpoons 2H_2O(g)$
(b) $CH_4(g) + 2O_2(g) \rightleftharpoons CO_2(g) + 2H_2O(g)$

The rule that we always write the concentrations of the products in the numerator of the mass action expression and the concentrations of the reactants in the denominator is not required by nature. It is simply a convention chemists have agreed on. Certainly, if the mass action expression is equal to a constant, its reciprocal is also equal to a constant (let's call it K_c')

$$\frac{[HI]^2}{[H_2][I_2]} = K_c \qquad \frac{[H_2][I_2]}{[HI]^2} = \frac{1}{K_c} = K_c'$$

The value in having a set rule for constructing the mass action expression is that we don't have to specify the mass action expression when we give the equilibrium constant for a reaction. For example, suppose we're told that at a particular temperature $K_c = 10.0$ for the reaction

$$2NO_2(g) \rightleftharpoons N_2O_4(g)$$

From the chemical equation, we can write the correct mass action expression and the correct equilibrium law.

$$K_c = \frac{[N_2O_4]}{[NO_2]^2} = 10.0$$

The balanced chemical equation contains all the information we need to write the equilibrium law.

Equilibrium laws can be combined, scaled, and reversed

TOOLS

Manipulating equilibrium equations

Sometimes it is useful to be able to combine chemical equilibria to obtain the equation for some other reaction of interest. In doing this, we perform various operations such as reversing an equation, multiplying the coefficients by some factor, and adding the equations to give the desired equation. In our discussion of thermochemistry, you learned how such manipulations affect ΔH values. Some different rules apply to changes in the mass action expressions and equilibrium constants.

Changing the Direction of an Equilibrium
When the direction of an equation is reversed, the new equilibrium constant is the reciprocal of the original. You have just seen this in the discussion above. As another example, when we reverse the equilibrium

$$PCl_3 + Cl_2 \rightleftharpoons PCl_5 \qquad K_c = \frac{[PCl_5]}{[PCl_3][Cl_2]}$$

we obtain

$$PCl_5 \rightleftharpoons PCl_3 + Cl_2 \qquad K_c' = \frac{[PCl_3][Cl_2]}{[PCl_5]}$$

The mass action expression for the second reaction is the reciprocal of that for the first, so K_c' equals $1/K_c$.

Multiplying the Coefficients by a Factor
When the coefficients in an equation are multiplied by a factor, the equilibrium constant is raised to a power equal to that factor. For example, suppose we multiply the coefficients of the equation

$$PCl_3 + Cl_2 \rightleftharpoons PCl_5 \qquad K_c = \frac{[PCl_5]}{[PCl_3][Cl_2]}$$

by 2. This gives

$$2PCl_3 + 2Cl_2 \rightleftharpoons 2PCl_5 \qquad K_c'' = \frac{[PCl_5]^2}{[PCl_3]^2[Cl_2]^2}$$

Comparing mass action expressions, we see that $K_c'' = K_c^2$.

Adding Chemical Equilibria

When chemical equilibria are added, their equilibrium constants are multiplied. For example, suppose we add the following two equations.

$$2N_2 + O_2 \rightleftharpoons 2N_2O \qquad K_{c1} = \frac{[N_2O]^2}{[N_2]^2[O_2]}$$

$$2N_2O + 3O_2 \rightleftharpoons 4NO_2 \qquad K_{c2} = \frac{[NO_2]^4}{[N_2O]^2[O_2]^3}$$

$$2N_2 + 4O_2 \rightleftharpoons 4NO_2 \qquad K_{c3} = \frac{[NO_2]^4}{[N_2]^2[O_2]^4}$$

◻ We have numbered the equilibrium constants just to distinguish one from the other.

If we multiply the mass action expression for K_{c1} by that for K_{c2}, we obtain the mass action expression for K_{c3}.

$$\frac{\cancel{[N_2O]^2}}{[N_2]^2[O_2]} \times \frac{[NO_2]^4}{\cancel{[N_2O]^2}[O_2]^3} = \frac{[NO_2]^4}{[N_2]^2[O_2]^4}$$

Therefore, $K_{c1} \times K_{c2} = K_{c3}$.

Practice Exercise 3: At 25 °C, $K_c = 7.0 \times 10^{25}$ for the reaction

$$2SO_2(g) + O_2(g) \rightleftharpoons 2SO_3(g)$$

What is the value of K_c for the reaction $SO_3(g) \rightleftharpoons SO_2(g) + \frac{1}{2}O_2(g)$?
(Hint: What do you have to do with the original equation to obtain the new equation?)

Practice Exercise 4: At 25 °C, the following reactions have the equilibrium constants noted to the right of their equations.

$$2CO(g) + O_2(g) \rightleftharpoons 2CO_2(g) \qquad K_c = 3.3 \times 10^{91}$$
$$2H_2(g) + O_2(g) \rightleftharpoons 2H_2O(g) \qquad K_c = 9.1 \times 10^{80}$$

Use these data to calculate K_c for the reaction

$$H_2O(g) + CO(g) \rightleftharpoons CO_2(g) + H_2(g)$$

14.3 **EQUILIBRIUM LAWS FOR GASEOUS REACTIONS CAN BE WRITTEN IN TERMS OF EITHER CONCENTRATIONS OR PRESSURES**

When all the reactants and products are gases, we can formulate mass action expressions in terms of partial pressures as well as molar concentrations. This is possible because the molar concentration of a gas is proportional to its partial pressure. This comes from the ideal gas law,

$$PV = nRT$$

Solving for P gives

$$P = \left(\frac{n}{V}\right)RT$$

The quantity n/V has units of mol/L and is simply the molar concentration. Therefore, we can write

$$P = (\text{molar concentration}) \times RT \qquad (14.4)$$

◻ If you double the molar concentration of a gas without changing its temperature or volume, you double its pressure.

This equation applies whether the gas is by itself in a container or part of a mixture. In the case of a gas mixture, P is the partial pressure of the gas.

The relationship expressed in Equation 14.4 lets us write the mass action expression for reactions between gases either in terms of molarities or partial pressures. However, when we make a switch we can't expect the numerical values of the equilibrium constants to be the same, so we use two different symbols for K. When molar concentrations are used, we use the symbol K_c. When partial pressures are used, then K_P is the symbol. For example, the equilibrium law for the reaction of nitrogen with hydrogen to form ammonia

$$N_2(g) + 3H_2(g) \rightleftharpoons 2NH_3(g)$$

can be written in either of the following two ways

$$\frac{[NH_3]^2}{[N_2][H_2]^3} = K_c \quad \left(\begin{array}{l} \text{because molar concentrations} \\ \text{are used in the mass action} \\ \text{expression} \end{array} \right)$$

$$\frac{P_{NH_3}^2}{P_{N_2}P_{H_2}^3} = K_P \quad \left(\begin{array}{l} \text{because partial pressures are} \\ \text{used in the mass action} \\ \text{expression} \end{array} \right)$$

The equilibrium molar concentrations can be used to calculate K_c, whereas the equilibrium partial pressures can be used to calculate K_P.

EXAMPLE 14.2
Writing Expressions for K_P

Most of the world's supply of methanol, CH_3OH, is produced by the following reaction.

$$CO(g) + 2H_2(g) \rightleftharpoons CH_3OH(g)$$

What is the expression for K_P for this equilibrium?

ANALYSIS: For K_P we use partial pressures in the mass action expression. We put the equilibrium partial pressures of the products in the numerator and the equilibrium partial pressures of the reactants in the denominator. The coefficients in the equation become exponents on the pressures.

SOLUTION: The expression for K_P for the reaction is

$$K_P = \frac{P_{CH_3OH}}{(P_{CO})(P_{H_2})^2}$$

IS THE ANSWER REASONABLE? Check to see that the mass action expression gives products over reactants, and not the other way around. Check each exponent against the coefficients in the balanced chemical equation.

Practice Exercise 5: Write the equilibrium law in terms of partial pressures for the following reaction. (Hint: Keep in mind how the mass action expression is written.)

$$2N_2(g) + O_2(g) \rightleftharpoons 2N_2O(g)$$

Practice Exercise 6: Using partial pressures, write the equilibrium law for the reaction

$$H_2(g) + I_2(g) \rightleftharpoons 2HI(g)$$

A simple expression relates K_P and K_c

For some reactions K_P is equal to K_c, but for many others the two constants have different values. It is therefore desirable to have a way to calculate one from the other.

Converting between K_P and K_c uses the relationship between partial pressure and molarity. Equation 14.4 can be used to change K_P to K_c by substituting

$$\text{(molar concentration)} \times RT$$

for the partial pressure of each gas in the mass action expression for K_P. Similarly, K_c can be changed to K_P by solving Equation 14.4 for the molar concentrations, and then substituting the result, P/RT, into the appropriate expression for K_c. This sounds like a lot of work, and it is. Fortunately, there is a general equation, which can be derived from these relationships, that we can use to make these conversions simply.

$$K_P = K_c (RT)^{\Delta n_g} \tag{14.5}$$

TOOLS

Converting between K_P and K_c

In this equation, the value of Δn_g is equal to the change in the *number of moles of gas* in going from the reactants to the products.

$$\Delta n_g = \text{(moles of } gaseous \text{ products)} - \text{(moles of } gaseous \text{ reactants)}$$

We use the coefficients of the balanced equation for the reaction to calculate the numerical value of Δn_g. For example, the equation

$$N_2(g) + 3H_2(g) \rightleftharpoons 2NH_3(g) \tag{14.6}$$

tells us that two moles of NH_3 are formed when one mole of N_2 and three moles of H_2 react. In other words, two moles of gaseous product are formed from a total of four moles of gaseous reactants. That's a decrease of two moles of gas, so Δn_g for this reaction equals -2.

For some reactions, the value of Δn_g is equal to zero. An example is the decomposition of HI.

$$2HI(g) \rightleftharpoons H_2(g) + I_2(g)$$

If we take the coefficients to mean moles, there are two moles of gas on each side of the equation, so $\Delta n_g = 0$. Because (RT) raised to the zero power is equal to 1, $K_P = K_c$.

EXAMPLE 14.3
Converting between K_P and K_c

At 500 °C, the reaction between N_2 and H_2 to form ammonia

$$N_2(g) + 3H_2(g) \rightleftharpoons 2NH_3(g)$$

has $K_c = 6.0 \times 10^{-2}$. What is the numerical value of K_P for this reaction?

ANALYSIS: The tool we need to convert between K_P and K_c is Equation 14.5.

$$K_P = K_c (RT)^{\Delta n_g}$$

In the discussion above, we saw that $\Delta n_g = -2$ for this reaction. All we need now are appropriate values of R and T. The temperature, T, must be expressed in kelvins. (When used to stand for temperature, a capital letter T in an equation always means the absolute temperature.) Next we must choose an appropriate value for R. Referring back to Equation 14.4, if the partial pressures are expressed in atm and the concentration in mol L^{-1}, the only value of R that includes all of these units (L, mol, atm, and K) is $R = 0.0821$ L atm mol^{-1} K^{-1}, and this is the *only* value of R that can be used in Equation 14.5.

SOLUTION: Assembling the data, then, we have

$$K_c = 6.0 \times 10^{-2} \qquad \Delta n_g = -2$$
$$T = (500 + 273) \text{ K} = 773 \text{ K} \qquad R = 0.0821 \text{ L atm mol}^{-1} \text{ K}^{-1}$$

Substituting these into the equation for K_P gives

$$K_P = (6.0 \times 10^{-2}) \times [(0.0821) \times (773)]^{-2}$$
$$= (6.0 \times 10^{-2})/(63.5)^2$$
$$= 1.5 \times 10^{-5}$$

In this case, K_P has a numerical value quite different from that of K_c.

IS THE ANSWER REASONABLE? In working these problems, check to be sure you have used the correct value of R and that the temperature is expressed in kelvins. Notice that if Δn_g is negative, as it is in this reaction, the expression $(RT)^{\Delta n_g}$ will be less than one. That should make K_p smaller than K_c, which is consistent with our results.

1 mol NaHCO₃

38.9 cm³

Molarity $= \dfrac{1 \text{ mol NaHCO}_3}{0.0389 \text{ L}}$

$= 25.7$ mol/L

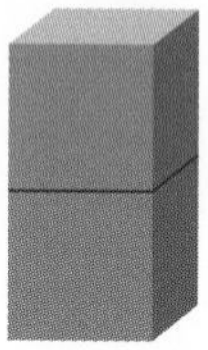

2 mol NaHCO₃

77.8 cm³

Molarity $= \dfrac{2 \text{ mol NaHCO}_3}{0.0778 \text{ L}}$

$= 25.7$ mol/L

FIG. 14.4 **The concentration of a substance in the solid state is a constant.** Doubling the number of moles also doubles the volume, but the *ratio* of moles to volume remains the same.

☐ Safety-minded cooks keep a box of baking soda nearby because this reaction makes it an excellent fire extinguisher for fats or oils that have caught fire. The fire is smothered by the products of the reaction.

Practice Exercise 7: Nitrous oxide, N_2O, is a gas used as an anesthetic; it is sometimes called "laughing gas." This compound has a strong tendency to decompose into nitrogen and oxygen following the equation

$$2N_2O(g) \rightleftharpoons 2N_2(g) + O_2(g)$$

but the reaction is so slow that the gas appears to be stable at room temperature (25 °C). The decomposition reaction has $K_c = 7.3 \times 10^{34}$. What is the value of K_p for this reaction at 25 °C? (Hint: Be careful in calculating Δn_g.)

Practice Exercise 8: Methanol, CH_3OH, is a promising fuel that can be synthesized from carbon monoxide and hydrogen according to the reaction

$$CO(g) + 2H_2(g) \rightleftharpoons CH_3OH(g)$$

For this reaction at 200 °C, $K_p = 3.8 \times 10^{-2}$. Do you expect K_p to be larger or smaller than K_c? Calculate the value of K_c at this temperature.

14.4 HETEROGENEOUS EQUILIBRIA INVOLVE REACTION MIXTURES WITH MORE THAN ONE PHASE

In a **homogeneous reaction**—or a **homogeneous equilibrium**—all of the reactants and products are in the same phase. Equilibria among gases are homogeneous because all gases mix freely with each other, so a single phase exists. There are also many equilibria in which reactants and products are dissolved in the same liquid phase.

When more than one phase exists in a reaction mixture, we call it a **heterogeneous reaction.** A common example is the combustion of wood, in which a solid fuel reacts with gaseous oxygen. Another is the thermal decomposition of sodium bicarbonate (baking soda), which occurs when the compound is sprinkled on a fire.

$$2NaHCO_3(s) \longrightarrow Na_2CO_3(s) + H_2O(g) + CO_2(g)$$

If $NaHCO_3$ is placed in a sealed container so that no CO_2 or H_2O can escape, the gases and solids come to a heterogeneous equilibrium.

$$2NaHCO_3(s) \rightleftharpoons Na_2CO_3(s) + H_2O(g) + CO_2(g)$$

Following our usual procedure, we can write the equilibrium law for this reaction as

$$\frac{[Na_2CO_3(s)][H_2O(g)][CO_2(g)]}{[NaHCO_3(s)]^2} = K$$

However, the equilibrium law for reactions involving pure liquids and solids can be written in an even simpler form. This is because the concentration of a pure liquid or solid is unchangeable at a given temperature. *For any pure liquid or solid, the ratio of amount of substance to volume of substance is a constant.* For example, if we had a 1 mole crystal of $NaHCO_3$, it would occupy a volume of 38.9 cm³. Two moles of $NaHCO_3$ would occupy twice this volume, 77.8 cm³ (Figure 14.4), but the *ratio* of moles to liters (i.e., the molar concentration) remains the same.

Similar reasoning shows that the concentration of Na_2CO_3 in pure solid Na_2CO_3 is a constant, too. This means that the equilibrium law now has three constants, K plus two of the concentration terms. It makes sense to combine all of the numerical constants together.

$$[H_2O(g)][CO_2(g)] = \frac{K[NaHCO_3(s)]^2}{[Na_2CO_3(s)]} = K_c$$

The equilibrium law for a heterogeneous reaction is written without concentration terms for pure solids or liquids.

Equilibrium constants that are given in tables represent all of the constants combined.[2]

> **EXAMPLE 14.4**
> Writing the Equilibrium Law for a Heterogeneous Reaction

The air pollutant sulfur dioxide can be removed from a gas mixture by passing the gases over calcium oxide. The equation is

$$CaO(s) + SO_2(g) \rightleftharpoons CaSO_3(s)$$

Write the equilibrium law for the reaction.

ANALYSIS: For a heterogeneous equilibrium, we do not include solids or pure liquids in the mass action expression. Therefore, we exclude CaO and $CaSO_3$ and include only SO_2.

SOLUTION: The equilibrium law is simply

$$\frac{1}{[SO_2(g)]} = K_c$$

IS THE ANSWER REASONABLE? There's not much to check here except to review the reasoning, which appears to be okay.

Practice Exercise 9: Write the equilibrium law for the following reaction. (Hint: Follow the reasoning above.)

$$NH_3(g) + HCl(g) \rightleftharpoons NH_4Cl(s)$$

Practice Exercise 10: Write the equilibrium law for the following heterogeneous reactions.
(a) $2Hg(l) + Cl_2(g) \rightleftharpoons Hg_2Cl_2(s)$
(b) $Na(s) + H_2O(l) \rightleftharpoons NaOH(aq) + H_2(g)$
(c) Dissolving solid Ag_2CrO_4 in water: $Ag_2CrO_4(s) \rightleftharpoons 2Ag^+(aq) + CrO_4^{2-}(aq)$
(d) $CaCO_3(s) + H_2O(l) + CO_2(aq) \rightleftharpoons Ca^{2+}(aq) + 2HCO_3^-(aq)$

14.5 | WHEN *K* IS LARGE, THE POSITION OF EQUILIBRIUM LIES TOWARD THE PRODUCTS

Whether we work with K_P or K_c, a bonus of always writing the mass action expression with the product concentrations in the numerator is that the size of the equilibrium constant gives us a measure of the *position of equilibrium* (how far the reaction proceeds toward completion when equilibrium is reached). For example, the reaction

$$2H_2(g) + O_2(g) \rightleftharpoons 2H_2O(g)$$

has $K_c = 9.1 \times 10^{80}$ at 25 °C. For an equilibrium between these gases,

$$K_c = \frac{[H_2O]^2}{[H_2]^2[O_2]} = \frac{9.1 \times 10^{80}}{1}$$

---

[2] Thermodynamics handles heterogeneous equilibria in a more elegant way by expressing the mass action expression in terms of "effective concentrations," or **activities.** In doing this, thermodynamics *defines* the *activity* of any pure liquid or solid as equal to 1, which means terms involving such substances drop out of the mass action expression.

By writing K_c as a fraction, $(9.1 \times 10^{80})/1$, we see that the numerator of the mass action expression must be enormous compared with the denominator, which means that the concentration of H_2O is huge compared with the concentrations of H_2 and O_2. At equilibrium, therefore, almost all of the hydrogen and oxygen atoms in the system are found in H_2O molecules and very few are present in H_2 and O_2. Thus, the enormous value of K_c tells us that the position of equilibrium in this reaction lies far toward the right and that the reaction of H_2 and O_2 goes essentially to completion.

 Actually, you would need about 200,000 L of water vapor at 25 °C just to find one molecule of O_2 and two molecules of H_2.

The reaction between N_2 and O_2 to give NO

$$N_2(g) + O_2(g) \rightleftharpoons 2NO(g)$$

has a very small equilibrium constant; $K_c = 4.8 \times 10^{-31}$ at 25 °C. The equilibrium law for the reaction is

$$\frac{[NO]^2}{[N_2][O_2]} = 4.8 \times 10^{-31} = \frac{4.8}{10^{31}}$$

In air at 25 °C, the equilibrium concentration of NO *should be* about 10^{-17} mol/L. It is usually higher because NO is formed in various reactions, such as those responsible for air pollution caused by automobiles.

Here the denominator is huge compared with the numerator, so the concentrations of N_2 and O_2 must be very much larger than the concentration of NO. This means that in a mixture of N_2 and O_2 at this temperature, the amount of NO that is formed is negligible. The reaction hardly proceeds at all toward completion before equilibrium is reached, and the position of equilibrium lies far toward the left.

The relationship between the equilibrium constant and the position of equilibrium can thus be summarized as follow (also see Figure 14.5):

TOOLS

Significance of the magnitude of K

When K is very large	The reaction proceeds far toward completion. The position of equilibrium lies far to the right, toward the products.
When $K \approx 1$	The concentrations of reactants and products are nearly the same at equilibrium. The position of equilibrium lies approximately midway between reactants and products.
When K is very small	Extremely small amounts of products are formed. The position of equilibrium lies far to the left, toward the reactants.

Notice that we have omitted the subscript for K in this summary. The same qualitative predictions about the extent of reaction apply whether we use K_P or K_c.

One of the ways that we can use equilibrium constants is to compare the extents to which two or more reactions proceed to completion. Take care in making such

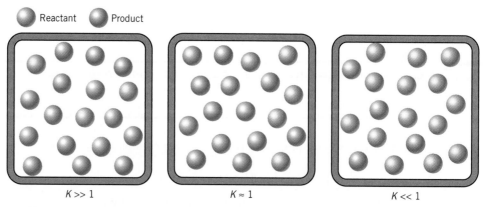

Reactant   Product

$K \gg 1$ $K \approx 1$ $K \ll 1$

FIG. 14.5 **The magnitude of K and the position of equilibrium.** For the reaction

Reactant $\rightleftharpoons$ Product

a large amount of product and very little reactant are in the reaction mixture at equilibrium when K is very large ($K \gg 1$), so we say *the position of equilibrium lies to the right*. When $K \approx 1$, approximately equal amounts of reactant and product are present at equilibrium. When $K \ll 1$, the reaction mixture contains a large amount of reactant at equilibrium and very little product, so we say *the position of equilibrium lies to the left*.

comparisons, however, because unless the values of K are greatly different, the comparison is valid only if both reactions have the same number of reactant and product molecules appearing in their balanced chemical equations.

Practice Exercise 11: Suppose a mixture contained equal concentrations of H_2, Br_2, and HBr. Given that the reaction $H_2(g) + Br_2(g) \rightleftharpoons 2HBr(g)$ has $K_c = 1.4 \times 10^{-21}$, will the reaction proceed to the left or right in order to reach equilibrium? (Hint: In the mass action expression for this reaction, how should the size of the numerator compare with that of the denominator when the system reaches equilibrium?)

Practice Exercise 12: Which of the following reactions will tend to proceed farthest toward completion?
(a) $H_2(g) + Br_2(g) \rightleftharpoons 2HBr(g)$ $K_c = 1.4 \times 10^{-21}$
(b) $2NO(g) \rightleftharpoons N_2(g) + O_2(g)$ $K_c = 2.1 \times 10^{30}$
(c) $2BrCl \rightleftharpoons Br_2 + Cl_2$ (in CCl_4 solution) $K_c = 0.145$

14.6 LE CHÂTELIER'S PRINCIPLE TELLS US HOW A CHEMICAL EQUILIBRIUM RESPONDS WHEN DISTURBED

In Section 14.7 you will see that it is possible to perform calculations that tell us what the composition of an equilibrium system is. However, many times we really don't need to know exactly what the equilibrium concentrations are. Instead, we may want to know what actions we should take to control the relative amounts of the reactants or products at equilibrium. For instance, if we were designing gasoline engines, we would like to know what could be done to minimize the formation of nitrogen oxide pollutants. Or, if we were preparing ammonia, NH_3, by the reaction of N_2 with H_2, we might want to know how to maximize the yield of NH_3.

Le Châtelier's principle, introduced in Chapter 11, provides us with the means for making qualitative predictions about changes in chemical equilibria. It does this in much the same way that it allows us to predict the effects of outside influences on equilibria that involve physical changes, such as liquid–vapor equilibria. Recall that **Le Châtelier's principle** states that *if an outside influence upsets an equilibrium, the system undergoes a change in a direction that counteracts the disturbing influence and, if possible, returns the system to equilibrium.* Let's examine the kinds of "outside influences" that affect chemical equilibria.

Adding a reactant or product changes *Q*
For a homogeneous system at equilibrium, adding or removing a reactant or product changes the value of Q so that it no longer equals K. The equilibrium is upset, and according to Le Châtelier's principle the system should change in a direction that opposes the disturbance we've introduced. If we've added a substance, the reaction should proceed in a direction to remove some of it; if we've removed a substance, the reaction should proceed in a direction to replace it.

As an example, let's study the equilibrium between two ions of copper.

$$Cu(H_2O)_4{}^{2+}(aq) + 4Cl^-(aq) \rightleftharpoons CuCl_4{}^{2-}(aq) + 4H_2O(l)$$
     blue   yellow

As noted, $Cu(H_2O)_4{}^{2+}$ is blue and $CuCl_4{}^{2-}$ is yellow. Mixtures of the two have an intermediate color and therefore appear blue-green, as illustrated in Figure 14.6, center.

Suppose we add chloride ion to an equilibrium mixture of these copper ions. The system can remove some Cl^- by reacting it with $Cu(H_2O)_4{}^{2+}$. This gives more $CuCl_4{}^{2-}$ (Figure 14.6, right), and we say that the equilibrium has "shifted to the right" or "shifted toward the products." In the new position of equilibrium, there is less $Cu(H_2O)_4{}^{2+}$ and more $CuCl_4{}^{2-}$ and uncombined H_2O. There is also more Cl^-, because not all that we add reacts. In other words, in this new position of equilibrium, *all* the concentrations have changed in a way that causes Q to become equal to K_c. Similarly, the position of equilibrium is shifted to the left when we add water to the mixture (Figure 14.6, left). The system is able to get rid of some of the H_2O by reaction with $CuCl_4{}^{2-}$, so more of the blue $Cu(H_2O)_4{}^{2+}$ is formed.

FIG. 14.6 **The effect of concentration changes on the position of equilibrium.** The solution in the center contains a mixture of blue $Cu(H_2O)_4{}^{2+}$ and yellow $CuCl_4{}^{2-}$, so it has a blue-green color. At the right is some of the same solution after the addition of concentrated HCl. It has a more pronounced green color because the equilibrium is shifted toward $CuCl_4{}^{2-}$. At the left is some of the original solution after the addition of water. It is blue because the equilibrium has shifted toward $Cu(H_2O)_4{}^{2+}$. *(Michael Watson.)*

☐ $Cu(H_2O)_4{}^{2+}$ and $CuCl_4{}^{2-}$ are called *complex ions*. Some of the interesting properties of complex ions of metals are discussed in Chapter 21.

If we were able to remove a reactant or product, the position of equilibrium would also be changed. For example, if we add Ag^+ to a solution that contains both copper ions in equilibrium, we see an enhancement of the blue color.

$$Cu(H_2O)_4{}^{2+}(aq) + 4Cl^-(aq) \rightleftharpoons CuCl_4{}^{2-}(aq) + 4H_2O$$

blue   yellow

$$\Downarrow +Ag^+$$

$$Ag^+(aq) + Cl^-(aq) \rightleftharpoons AgCl(s)$$

As the Ag^+ reacts with Cl^- to form insoluble AgCl in the second reaction, the equilibrium in the first reaction shifts to the left to replace some of the Cl^-, which also produces more blue $Cu(H_2O)_4{}^{2+}$. The position of equilibrium shifts to replace the substance that is removed.

TOOLS

Le Châtelier's principle; adding or removing a reactant or product

> The position of equilibrium shifts in a way to remove reactants or products that have been added, or to replace reactants or products that have been removed.

Changing the volume in gaseous reactions will sometimes upset the equilibrium

Changing the volume of a mixture of reacting gases changes molar concentrations and partial pressures, so we expect volume to have some effect on the position of equilibrium. Let's consider the equilibrium:

$$3H_2(g) + N_2(g) \rightleftharpoons 2NH_3(g)$$

If we reduce the volume of the reaction mixture, we expect the pressure to increase. The system can oppose the pressure change if it is able to reduce the number of molecules of gas, because fewer molecules of gas exert a lower pressure. If the reaction proceeds to the right, two NH_3 molecules appear when four molecules (one N_2 and three H_2) disappear. Therefore, this equilibrium is shifted to the right when the volume of the reaction mixture is reduced.

Now let's look at the equilibrium:

$$H_2(g) + I_2(g) \rightleftharpoons 2HI(g)$$

If this reaction proceeds in either direction, there is no change in the number of molecules of gas. This reaction, then, cannot respond to pressure changes, so changing the volume of the reaction vessel has virtually no effect on the equilibrium.

The simplest way to analyze the effects of a volume change on an equilibrium system involving gases is to count the number of molecules of gaseous substances on both sides of the equation.

TOOLS

Le Châtelier's principle; changing the volume of a gaseous reaction

> Reducing the volume of a gaseous reaction mixture causes the position of equilibrium to shift in a direction that decreases the number of molecules of gas. No change in the equilibrium will occur if a volume change cannot affect the number of molecules of gas.

As a final note here, *moderate pressure changes have negligible effects on reactions involving only liquids or solids.* Substances in these states are virtually incompressible, and reactions involving them have no way to counteract pressure changes.

Changing the temperature involves adding or removing heat

When the system is heated, the reaction will shift in the direction that absorbs heat. If the reaction is endothermic, it will run in the forward direction to remove the added energy. For example, the melting of ice absorbs heat and is endothermic:

$$H_2O(s) \rightleftharpoons H_2O(l) \qquad \Delta H° = +6 \text{ kJ (at 0 °C)}$$

If you cup your hands around a glass of ice and water at 0 °C, the heat you've added to the system shifts the equilibrium to the right, and some of the ice melts. If we include energy as a reactant in the equation, we could write

$$\text{heat} + H_2O(s) \rightleftharpoons H_2O(l)$$

Adding a reactant drives the reaction in the forward direction, with energy behaving like any other reactant in this case.

Removing some amount of reactant should shift the equilibrium to the left. We expect that removing energy from this system would have the same effect. Putting the glass in the freezer causes some of the water to freeze. Some of the energy is removed, so the equilibrium shifts toward the reactant side of the equation.

The same arguments can be used for equations that describe chemical changes. For instance, the reaction to produce NH_3 from N_2 and H_2 is exothermic; heat is released when NH_3 molecules are formed ($\Delta H_f^\circ = -46.19$ kJ/mol from Table 6.2). Since the reaction releases energy, we can include energy as a product in the equilibrium equation:

$$3H_2(g) + N_2(g) \rightleftharpoons 2NH_3(g) + \text{heat}$$

It is easy to predict what will happen when the reaction mixture is heated or cooled. Heating the mixture adds energy, so the system will counter by shifting to the left. The added energy will be absorbed, and at the same time NH_3 will decompose to produce more H_2 and N_2. Cooling the mixture removes energy, so the equilibrium shifts to the right. H_2 and N_2 will react to produce more NH_3, and energy will be released to compensate for energy removed by cooling.

□ This same kind of analysis was used in Chapter 12 to predict how solubility changes with temperature.

Increasing the temperature shifts a reaction in a direction that produces an endothermic (heat-absorbing) change.

Decreasing the temperature shifts a reaction in a direction that produces an exothermic (heat-releasing) change.

TOOLS

Le Châtelier's principle; raising or lowering the temperature

This gives us a way to experimentally determine whether a reaction is exothermic or endothermic, without using a thermometer. Earlier we described the equilibrium involving complex ions of copper. The effect of temperature on this equilibrium is demonstrated in Figure 14.7. When the reaction mixture is heated, we see from the color change that the equilibrium shifts toward the products. Therefore, the reaction must be endothermic.

□ When heat is added to an equilibrium mixture, it is added to all of the substances present (reactants *and* products). As the system returns to equilibrium, the net reaction that occurs is the one that is endothermic.

□ Temperature is the only factor that can change K for a given reaction.

Changing the temperature changes *K* for a reaction

Changes in concentrations or volume can shift the position of equilibrium, but *they do not change the equilibrium constant*. However, changing the temperature causes the position of equilibrium to shift because it changes the value of K. The enthalpy change of the reaction is the critical factor. Let's look once again at the equilibrium law for the industrial synthesis of ammonia.

$$3H_2(g) + N_2(g) \rightleftharpoons 2NH_3(g) \qquad \Delta H^\circ = -46.19 \text{ kJ}$$

$$\frac{[NH_3]^2}{[H_2]^3[N_2]} = K_c$$

FIG. 14.7 **The effect of temperature on the equilibrium** $Cu(H_2O)_4^{2+} + 4Cl^- \rightleftharpoons CuCl_4^{2-} + 4H_2O.$ In the center is an equilibrium mixture of the two complexes. When the solution is cooled in ice (left), the equilibrium shifts toward the blue $Cu(H_2O)_4^{2+}$. When heated in boiling water (right), the equilibrium shifts toward $CuCl_4^{2-}$. This behavior indicates that the reaction is endothermic in the forward direction. (*Michael Watson.*)

☐ We'll see how to quantitatively relate K and temperature in Chapter 18.

Because the reaction is exothermic, increasing the temperature shifts the equilibrium to the left. The concentration of NH_3 decreases while the concentrations of N_2 and H_2 increase. Therefore, the numerator of the mass action expression becomes *smaller* and the denominator becomes *larger*. This gives a smaller reaction quotient and therefore a smaller value of K_c.

TOOLS

Le Châtelier's principle; changing temperature changes K

> Increasing the temperature of an exothermic reaction makes its equilibrium constant smaller.
>
> Increasing the temperature of an endothermic reaction makes its equilibrium constant larger.

Catalysts have no effect on the position of equilibrium

☐ Catalysts don't appear in the chemical equation for a reaction, so they don't appear in the mass action expression, either.

Recall that catalysts are substances that affect the speeds of chemical reactions without actually being used up. Catalysts do not, however, affect the position of equilibrium in a system. The reason is that a catalyst affects both the forward and reverse reactions equally. Both are speeded up to the same degree, so adding a catalyst to a system has no net effect on the system's equilibrium composition. The catalyst's only effect is to bring the system to equilibrium faster.

Adding an inert gas at constant volume has no effect on the position of equilibrium

A change in volume is not the only way to change the pressure in an equilibrium system of gaseous reactants and products. The pressure can also be changed by keeping the volume the same and adding another gas. If this gas cannot react with any of the gases already present (i.e., if the added gas is *inert* toward the substances in equilibrium), the concentrations of the reactants and products won't change. The concentrations will continue to satisfy the equilibrium law and the reaction quotient will continue to equal K_c, so there will be no change in the position of equilibrium.

EXAMPLE 14.5
Application of Le Châtelier's Principle

The reaction $N_2O_4(g) \rightleftharpoons 2NO_2(g)$ is endothermic, with $\Delta H° = +56.9$ kJ. How will the amount of NO_2 at equilibrium be affected by (a) adding N_2O_4, (b) lowering the pressure by increasing the volume of the container, (c) raising the temperature, and (d) adding a catalyst to the system? Which of these changes will alter the value of K_c?

ANALYSIS: We are applying various types of disturbances to an equilibrium mixture of NO_2 and N_2O_4. The tool we use to judge the effects of such disturbances is Le Châtelier's principle. As we discussed above, we expect the equilibrium to shift to the left or right to counteract the disturbance in most cases.

SOLUTION: (a) Adding N_2O_4 will cause the equilibrium to shift to the right—in a direction that will consume some of the added N_2O_4. The amount of NO_2 will increase.

(b) When the pressure in the system drops, the system responds by producing more molecules of gas, which will tend to raise the pressure and partially offset the change. Since more gas molecules are formed if some N_2O_4 decomposes, the amount of NO_2 at equilibrium will increase.

(c) Because the reaction is endothermic, we write the equation showing heat as a reactant:

$$\text{heat} + N_2O_4(g) \rightleftharpoons 2NO_2(g)$$

Raising the temperature is accomplished by adding heat, so the system will respond by absorbing heat. This means that the equilibrium will shift to the right and the amount of NO_2 at equilibrium will increase.

(d) A catalyst causes a reaction to reach equilibrium more quickly, but it has no effect on the position of chemical equilibrium. Therefore, the amount of NO_2 at equilibrium will not be affected.

Finally, the *only* change that alters K is the temperature change. Raising the temperature (adding heat) will increase K_c for this endothermic reaction.

ARE THE ANSWERS REASONABLE? There's not much we can do here other than review our reasoning. Doing so will reveal we've answered the questions correctly.

Practice Exercise 13: Consider the equilibrium $PCl_5(g) + 4H_2O(g) \rightleftharpoons H_3PO_4(l) + 5HCl(g)$. How will the amount of H_3PO_4 at equilibrium be affected by decreasing the volume of the container holding the reaction mixture? (Hint: Notice that this is a heterogeneous equilibrium.)

Practice Exercise 14: Consider the equilibrium $PCl_3(g) + Cl_2(g) \rightleftharpoons PCl_5(g)$, for which $\Delta H° = -88$ kJ. How will the amount of Cl_2 at equilibrium be affected by (a) adding PCl_3, (b) adding PCl_5, (c) raising the temperature, and (d) decreasing the volume of the container? How (if at all) will each of these changes affect K_P for the reaction?

14.7 | EQUILIBRIUM CONCENTRATIONS CAN BE USED TO DETERMINE EQUILIBRIUM CONSTANTS, AND VICE VERSA

You have seen that the magnitude of an equilibrium constant gives us some feel for the extent to which the reaction proceeds at equilibrium. Sometimes, however, it is necessary to have more than merely a qualitative knowledge of equilibrium concentrations. This requires that we be able to use the equilibrium law for purposes of calculation.

Equilibrium calculations for gaseous reactions can be performed using either K_P or K_c, but for reactions in solution we must use K_c. Whether we deal with concentrations or partial pressures, however, the same basic principles apply.

Overall, we can divide equilibrium calculations into two main categories:

1. Calculating equilibrium constants from known equilibrium concentrations or partial pressures.
2. Calculating one or more equilibrium concentrations or partial pressures using the known value of K_c or K_P.

Equilibrium concentrations can be used to calculate K_c

One way to determine the value of K_c is to carry out the reaction, measure the concentrations of reactants and products after equilibrium has been reached, and then use the equilibrium values in the equilibrium law to compute K_c. As an example, let's look again at the decomposition of N_2O_4.

$$N_2O_4(g) \rightleftharpoons 2NO_2(g)$$

In Section 14.1, we saw that if 0.0350 mol of N_2O_4 is placed into a 1 liter flask at 25 °C, the concentrations of N_2O_4 and NO_2 at equilibrium are

$$[N_2O_4] = 0.0292 \text{ mol/L}$$

$$[NO_2] = 0.0116 \text{ mol/L}$$

To calculate K_c for the reaction, we substitute the equilibrium concentrations into the mass action expression of the equilibrium law.

$$\frac{[NO_2]^2}{[N_2O_4]} = K_c$$

$$\frac{(0.0116)^2}{(0.0292)} = K_c$$

Performing the arithmetic gives

$$K_c = 4.61 \times 10^{-3}$$

Concentration tables are an aid in analyzing and solving equilibrium problems

Only rarely are we given all the equilibrium concentrations required to calculate the equilibrium constant. Usually, we have information about the composition of a reaction mixture when it is first prepared, as well as some additional data that we can use to figure out what the equilibrium concentrations are. To help organize our thinking, we will set up a **concentration table** beneath the chemical equation in which we keep track of the concentrations of the substances involved in the reaction as it proceeds toward equilibrium. The table has three rows, which we label *Initial Concentrations, Changes in Concentrations*, and *Equilibrium Concentrations*. To be useful, all entries in the table *must* have units of molar concentration (mol L^{-1}). Let's look at how the data for each row is obtained.

TOOLS

Concentration table

☐ Remember, all entries in the concentration table must be molarities. If you use moles instead, you may end up with incorrect answers.

Initial Concentrations

The initial concentrations are those present in the reaction mixture when it's prepared; *we imagine that no reaction occurs until everything is mixed.* Often, the statement of a problem will give the initial molar concentrations, and these are then entered into the table under the appropriate formulas. In other cases, the number of moles of reactants or products dissolved in a specified volume are given and we must then calculate the molar concentrations. If the amount or concentration of a reactant or product is not mentioned in the problem, we will assume none was added to the reaction mixture initially, so its initial concentration is entered as zero.

Changes in Concentrations

If the reaction mixture is not at equilibrium when it's prepared, the chemical reaction must occur (either to the left or right) to bring the system to equilibrium. When this happens, the concentrations change. We will use a positive sign to indicate that a concentration increases and a negative sign to show a decrease in concentration.

The changes in concentrations *always* occur in the same ratio as the coefficients in the balanced equation. For example, if we were dealing with the equilibrium

$$3H_2(g) + N_2(g) \rightleftharpoons 2NH_3(g)$$

and found that the $N_2(g)$ concentration decreases by 0.10 *M* during the approach to equilibrium, the entries in the "change" row would be as follows:

$$3H_2(g) \quad + \quad N_2(g) \quad \rightleftharpoons \quad 2NH_3(g)$$
Changes in Concentrations: $-3 \times (0.10\ M) \quad -1 \times (0.10\ M) \quad +2 \times (0.10\ M)$
$$\downarrow \qquad\qquad \downarrow \qquad\qquad \downarrow$$
$$-0.30\ M \qquad\quad -0.10\ M \qquad\quad +0.20\ M$$

In constructing the "change" row, be sure the reactant concentrations all change in the same direction, and that the product concentrations all change in the opposite direction. If the concentrations of the reactants decrease, all the entries for the reactants in the "change" row should have a minus sign, and all the entries for the products should be positive. In this example, N_2 reacts with H_2 (so their concentrations both decrease) and form NH_3 (so its concentration increases).

Equilibrium Concentrations

These are the concentrations of the reactants and products when the system finally reaches equilibrium. We obtain them by adding the changes in concentrations to the initial concentrations.

$$\left(\begin{array}{c}\text{Initial} \\ \text{concentration}\end{array}\right) + \left(\begin{array}{c}\text{change in} \\ \text{concentration}\end{array}\right) = \left(\begin{array}{c}\text{equilibrium} \\ \text{concentration}\end{array}\right)$$

The equilibrium concentrations are the only quantities that satisfy the equilibrium law.

The concentration table is one of our most useful tools for analyzing and setting up equilibrium problems. As you will see, we will use it in almost every problem. The following example illustrates how we can use it in calculating an equilibrium constant.

EXAMPLE 14.6
Calculating K_c from Equilibrium Concentrations

At a certain temperature, a mixture of H_2 and I_2 was prepared by placing 0.200 mol of H_2 and 0.200 mol of I_2 into a 2.00 liter flask. After a period of time the equilibrium

$$H_2(g) + I_2(g) \rightleftharpoons 2HI(g)$$

was established. The purple color of the I_2 vapor was used to monitor the reaction, and from the decreased intensity of the purple color it was determined that, at equilibrium, the I_2 concentration had dropped to 0.020 mol L^{-1}. What is the value of K_c for this reaction at this temperature?

ANALYSIS: The first step in any equilibrium problem is to write the balanced chemical equation and the related equilibrium law. The equation is already given, and the equilibrium law corresponding to it is

$$\frac{[HI]^2}{[H_2][I_2]} = K_c$$

To calculate the value of K_c we must substitute the *equilibrium concentrations* of H_2, I_2, and HI into the mass action expression. But what are they? We have been given only one directly, the value of $[I_2]$. To obtain the others, we have to do some reasoning. Our tool for this will be a concentration table, constructed following the procedure described above. Once we've filled in the last row of the table, we can substitute the values for the equilibrium concentrations into the equilibrium law and calculate K_c.

SOLUTION: To construct the concentration table, we begin by entering the data given in the statement of the problem. For the initial concentrations, we have to calculate the ratio of moles to liters for both the H_2 and I_2, (0.200 mol/2.00 L) = 0.100 M. Because no HI was placed into the reaction mixture, its initial concentration is set to zero. These quantities are shown in colored type in the first row. The problem statement also gives us the equilibrium concentration of I_2, so we enter this in the table in the last row (also shown in colored type). The values in regular type are then derived as described below.

	$H_2(g)$ +	$I_2(g)$ $\rightleftharpoons$	$2HI(g)$
Initial concentrations (M)	0.100	0.100	0.000
Changes in concentrations (M)	−0.080	−0.080	+2(0.080)
Equilibrium concentrations (M)	0.020	0.020	0.160

Changes in Concentrations. We have been given both the initial and equilibrium concentrations of I_2, so by difference we can calculate the change for I_2 (−0.080 M). The other changes are then calculated from the mole ratios specified in the chemical equation. Because H_2 and I_2 have the same coefficients (i.e., 1), their changes are equal. The coefficient of HI is 2, so its change must be twice that of I_2. Reactant concentrations are decreasing, so their changes are negative; the product concentration increases, so its change is positive.

□ The changes in concentrations are controlled by the stoichiometry of the reaction. If we can find one of the changes, we can calculate the others from it by using the coefficients of the balanced equation.

Equilibrium Concentrations. For H_2 and HI, we just add the change to the initial value.

Now we can substitute the equilibrium concentrations into the mass action expression and calculate K_c.

$$K_c = \frac{(0.160)^2}{(0.020)(0.020)}$$

$$= 64$$

IS THE ANSWER REASONABLE? First, carefully examine the equilibrium law. As always, products must be placed in the numerator and reactants in the denominator. Be sure that each exponent corresponds to the correct coefficient in the balanced chemical equation.

Next, check the concentration table to be sure all entries are molar concentrations. Note that the initial concentration of HI is zero. The change for HI must be positive, because the HI concentration cannot become smaller than zero. The positive value in the table agrees with this assessment. Notice, also, that the changes for both reactants have the same sign, which is opposite that of the product. *This relationship among the signs of the changes is always true and serves as a useful check when you construct a concentration table.*

Finally, we can check to be sure we've entered each of the equilibrium concentrations into the mass action expression correctly. At this point we can be confident we've set up the problem correctly. To be sure of the answer, redo the calculation on your calculator.

Practice Exercise 15: In a particular experiment, it was found that when $O_2(g)$ and $CO(g)$ were mixed and reacted according to the equation

$$2CO(g) + O_2(g) \rightleftharpoons 2CO_2(g)$$

the O_2 concentration had decreased by 0.030 mol L^{-1} when the reaction reached equilibrium. How had the concentrations of CO and CO_2 changed? (Hint: How are the changes in concentrations related to one another as the reaction approaches equilibrium?)

Practice Exercise 16: An equilibrium was established for the reaction

$$CO(g) + H_2O(g) \rightleftharpoons CO_2(g) + H_2(g)$$

at 500 °C. (This is an industrially important reaction for the preparation of hydrogen.) At equilibrium, the following concentrations were found in the reaction vessel: $[CO] = 0.180\ M$, $[H_2O] = 0.0411\ M$, $[CO_2] = 0.150\ M$, and $[H_2] = 0.200\ M$. What is the value of K_c for this reaction?

Practice Exercise 17: A student placed 0.200 mol of $PCl_3(g)$ and 0.100 mol of $Cl_2(g)$ into a 1.00 liter container at 250 °C. After the reaction

$$PCl_3(g) + Cl_2(g) \rightleftharpoons PCl_5(g)$$

came to equilibrium it was found that the flask contained 0.120 mol of PCl_3.
(a) What were the initial concentrations of the reactants and product?
(b) By how much had the concentrations changed when the reaction reached equilibrium?
(c) What were the equilibrium concentrations?
(d) What is the value of K_c for the reaction at that temperature?

Equilibrium concentrations can be calculated using K_c

In the simplest calculation of this type, all but one of the equilibrium concentrations are known, as illustrated in Example 14.7.

EXAMPLE 14.7

Using K_c to Calculate Concentrations at Equilibrium

The reversible reaction

$$CH_4(g) + H_2O(g) \rightleftharpoons CO(g) + 3H_2(g)$$

has been used as a commercial source of hydrogen. At 1500 °C, an equilibrium mixture of the gases was found to have the following concentrations: $[CO] = 0.300\ M$, $[H_2] = 0.800\ M$, and $[CH_4] = 0.400\ M$. At 1500 °C, $K_c = 5.67$ for the reaction. What was the equilibrium concentration of $H_2O(g)$ in the mixture?

ANALYSIS AND SOLUTION: This is really a very simple problem. The first step, once we have the chemical equation for the equilibrium, is to write the equilibrium law for the reaction.

$$K_c = \frac{[CO][H_2]^3}{[CH_4][H_2O]}$$

The equilibrium constant and all of the equilibrium concentrations except that for H_2O are known, so we substitute these values into the equilibrium law and solve for the unknown quantity.

$$5.67 = \frac{(0.300)(0.800)^3}{(0.400)[H_2O]}$$

Solving for $[H_2O]$ gives

$$[H_2O] = \frac{(0.300)(0.800)^3}{(0.400)(5.67)}$$

$$= \frac{0.154}{2.27}$$

$$= 0.0678 \; M$$

IS THE ANSWER REASONABLE? We can always check problems of this kind by substituting all of the equilibrium concentrations into the mass action expression to see if we get the original equilibrium constant back. We have

$$K_c = \frac{[CO][H_2]^3}{[CH_4][H_2O]} = \frac{(0.300)(0.800)^3}{(0.400)(0.0678)} = 5.66$$

Rounding off the H_2O concentration caused a slight error in K_c, but it is consistent with the equilibrium constant given in the problem.

Practice Exercise 18: The decomposition of N_2O_4 at 25 °C,

$$N_2O_4(g) \rightleftharpoons 2NO_2(g)$$

has $K_c = 4.61 \times 10^{-3}$. A 2.00 L vessel contained 0.0466 mol N_2O_4 at equilibrium. What was the concentration of NO_2 in the vessel? (Hint: What was the concentration of N_2O_4 in the container at equilibrium?)

Practice Exercise 19: Ethyl acetate, $CH_3CO_2C_2H_5$, is an important solvent used in lacquers, adhesives, the manufacture of plastics, and even as a food flavoring. It is produced from acetic acid and ethanol by the reaction

$$\underset{\text{acetic acid}}{CH_3CO_2H(l)} + \underset{\text{ethanol}}{C_2H_5OH(l)} \rightleftharpoons CH_3CO_2C_2H_5(l) + H_2O(l)$$

At 25 °C, $K_c = 4.10$ for this reaction. In a reaction mixture, the following equilibrium concentrations were observed: $[CH_3CO_2H] = 0.210 \; M$, $[H_2O] = 0.00850 \; M$, and $[CH_3CO_2C_2H_5] = 0.910 \; M$. What was the concentration of C_2H_5OH in the mixture?

□ Acetic acid has the structure

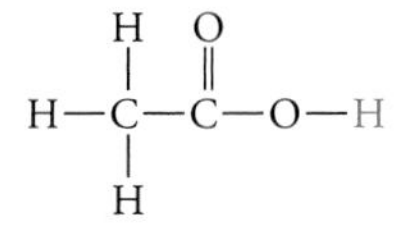

$$H-\overset{\overset{\displaystyle H}{|}}{\underset{\underset{\displaystyle H}{|}}{C}}-\overset{\overset{\displaystyle O}{\|}}{C}-O-H$$

where the hydrogen released by ionization is indicated in red. The formula of the acid is written either as CH_3CO_2H (which emphasizes its molecular structure) or as $HC_2H_3O_2$ (which emphasizes that the acid is monoprotic).

Equilibrium concentrations can be calculated using K_c and initial concentrations

A more complex type of calculation involves the use of initial concentrations and K_c to compute equilibrium concentrations. Although some of these problems can be so complicated that a computer is needed to solve them, we can learn the general principles involved by working on simple calculations. Even these, however, require a little applied algebra. This is where the concentration table can be especially helpful.

EXAMPLE 14.8
Using K_c to Calculate Equilibrium Concentrations

The reaction

$$CO(g) + H_2O(g) \rightleftharpoons CO_2(g) + H_2(g)$$

has $K_c = 4.06$ at 500 °C. If 0.100 mol of CO and 0.100 mol of $H_2O(g)$ are placed in a 1.00 liter reaction vessel at this temperature, what are the concentrations of the reactants and products when the system reaches equilibrium?

ANALYSIS: The key to solving this kind of problem is recognizing that at equilibrium the mass action expression must equal K_c.

$$\frac{[CO_2][H_2]}{[CO][H_2O]} = 4.06 \quad \text{(at equilibrium)}$$

We must find values for the concentrations that satisfy this condition. Our tool in setting up the calculation will be the concentration table.

The problem gives us information about the initial concentrations, which we'll use to establish values for the first line of the table. If we knew how much the concentrations change, we could calculate the equilibrium concentrations. There are no data that lets us calculate directly what any of the changes are, so we will represent them algebraically as unknowns. Combining the changes with the initial concentrations will give us algebraic expressions for the equilibrium concentrations. The relationship among the equilibrium concentrations is established by substituting them into the mass action expression.

☐ The quantities representing the equilibrium concentrations must satisfy the equation given by the equilibrium law.

To see how all this works, let's begin by building the concentration table.

SOLUTION: To build the table, we need quantities to enter into the "initial concentrations," "changes in concentrations," and "equilibrium concentrations" rows.

Initial Concentrations. The initial concentrations of CO and H_2O are each 0.100 mol/1.00 L = 0.100 *M*. Since no CO_2 or H_2 are initially placed into the reaction vessel, their initial concentrations both are zero.

Changes in Concentrations. Some CO_2 and H_2 must form for the reaction to reach equilibrium. This also means that some CO and H_2O must react. But how much? If we knew the answer, we could calculate the equilibrium concentrations. Therefore, the changes in concentration are our unknown quantities.

Let us allow x to be equal to the number of moles per liter of CO that react. The change in the concentration of CO is then $-x$ (it is negative because the change decreases the CO concentration). Because CO and H_2O react in a 1:1 mole ratio, the change in the H_2O concentration is also $-x$. Since one mole each of CO_2 and H_2 are formed when one mole of CO reacts, the CO_2 and H_2O concentrations each increase by x (their changes are $+x$).

☐ We could just as easily have chosen x to be the number of mol/L of H_2O that reacts or the number of mol/L of CO_2 or H_2 that forms. There's nothing special about having chosen CO to define x.

Equilibrium Concentrations. We obtain the equilibrium concentrations as

$$\left(\begin{array}{c}\text{Equilibrium} \\ \text{concentration}\end{array}\right) = \left(\begin{array}{c}\text{initial} \\ \text{concentration}\end{array}\right) + \left(\begin{array}{c}\text{change in} \\ \text{concentration}\end{array}\right)$$

☐ The last line in the table tells us the equilibrium CO and H_2O concentrations are equal to the number of moles per liter that were present initially minus the number of moles per liter that react. The equilibrium concentrations of CO_2 and H_2 equal the number of moles per liter of each that forms, since no CO_2 or H_2 is present initially.

Here is the completed concentration table.

	CO(*g*)	+ H₂O(*g*) ⇌	CO₂(*g*)	+ H₂(*g*)
Initial concentrations (*M*)	0.100	0.100	0.0	0.0
Changes in concentrations (*M*)	$-x$	$-x$	$+x$	$+x$
Equilibrium concentrations (*M*)	$0.100 - x$	$0.100 - x$	x	x

Next, we substitute the quantities from the "equilibrium concentrations" row into the mass action expression and solve for x.

$$\frac{(x)(x)}{(0.100 - x)(0.100 - x)} = 4.06$$

which we can write as

$$\frac{x^2}{(0.100 - x)^2} = 4.06$$

In this example we can solve the equation for x most easily by taking the square root of both sides.

$$\sqrt{\frac{x^2}{(0.100 - x)^2}} = \frac{x}{(0.100 - x)} = \sqrt{4.06} = 2.01$$

Clearing fractions gives

$$x = 2.01(0.100 - x)$$
$$x = 0.201 - 2.01x$$

Collecting terms in x gives

$$x + 2.01x = 0.201$$
$$3.01x = 0.201$$
$$x = 0.0668$$

☐ Taking the square root of 4.06 actually gives two values, $+2.01$ and -2.01. However, the negative root leads to a negative concentration, which doesn't make sense. Therefore, the remainder of the calculation is performed using the positive root.

Now that we know the value of x, we can calculate the equilibrium concentrations from the last row of the table.

$$[CO] = 0.100 - x = 0.100 - 0.0668 = 0.033 \ M$$
$$[H_2O] = 0.100 - x = 0.100 - 0.0668 = 0.033 \ M$$
$$[CO_2] = x = 0.0668 \ M$$
$$[H_2] = x = 0.0668 \ M$$

IS THE ANSWER REASONABLE? First, we should check to see that all concentrations are positive numbers. They are. As in the preceding example, we can check the answer by substituting the equilibrium concentrations we've found into the mass action expression and evaluate the reaction quotient. If our answers are correct, Q should equal K_c. Let's do this.

$$Q = \frac{(0.0668)^2}{(0.033)^2} = 4.1$$

Rounding K_c to two significant figures gives 4.1, so the calculated concentrations satisfy the equilibrium law.

EXAMPLE 14.9
Using K_c to Calculate Equilibrium Concentrations

In the preceding example it was stated that the reaction

$$CO(g) + H_2O(g) \rightleftharpoons CO_2(g) + H_2(g)$$

has $K_c = 4.06$ at 500 °C. Suppose 0.0600 mol each of CO and H_2O are mixed with 0.100 mol each of CO_2 and H_2 in a 1.00 L reaction vessel. What will the concentrations of all the substances be when the mixture reaches equilibrium at that temperature?

ANALYSIS: We will proceed in much the same way as in the preceding example. However, this time determining the algebraic signs of x will not be quite so simple because none of the initial concentrations is zero. The best way to determine the algebraic signs is to use the initial concentrations to calculate the initial reaction quotient. Then we can compare Q to K_c. By reasoning we will figure out which way the reaction must proceed to make Q equal to K_c.

SOLUTION: The equilibrium law for the reaction is

$$\frac{[CO_2][H_2]}{[CO][H_2O]} = K_c$$

Let's use the initial concentrations, shown in the first row of the concentration table below, to determine the initial value of the reaction quotient.

$$Q_{initial} = \frac{(0.100)(0.100)}{(0.0600)(0.0600)} = 2.78 < K_c$$

As indicated, $Q_{initial}$ is less than K_c, so the system is not at equilibrium. To reach equilibrium Q must become larger, which requires an increase in the concentrations of CO_2 and H_2 as the reaction proceeds. This means that for CO_2 and H_2, the change must be positive, and, for CO and H_2O, the change must be negative.

Here is the completed concentration table.

	CO(g) +	H$_2$O(g) $\rightleftharpoons$	CO$_2$(g) +	H$_2$(g)
Initial concentrations (M)	0.0600	0.0600	0.100	0.100
Change in concentrations (M)	$-x$	$-x$	$+x$	$+x$
Equilibrium concentrations (M)	$0.0600 - x$	$0.0600 - x$	$0.100 + x$	$0.100 + x$

Substituting equilibrium quantities into the mass action expression in the equilibrium law gives us

$$\frac{(0.100 + x)^2}{(0.0600 - x)^2} = 4.06$$

Taking the square root of both sides yields

$$\frac{0.100 + x}{0.0600 - x} = 2.01$$

To solve for x we first multiply each side by $(0.0600 - x)$ to obtain

$$0.100 + x = 2.01(0.0600 - x)$$
$$0.100 + x = 0.121 - 2.01x$$

Collecting terms in x to one side and the constants to the other gives

$$x + 2.01x = 0.121 - 0.100$$
$$3.01x = 0.021$$
$$x = 0.0070$$

Now we can calculate the equilibrium concentrations:

$$[CO] = [H_2O] = (0.0600 - x) = 0.0600 - 0.0070 = 0.0530 \ M$$
$$[CO_2] = [H_2] = (0.100 + x) = 0.100 + 0.0070 = 0.107 \ M$$

IS THE ANSWER REASONABLE? As a check, let's evaluate the reaction quotient using the calculated equilibrium concentrations.

$$Q = \frac{(0.107)^2}{(0.0530)^2} = 4.08$$

This is acceptably close to the value of K_c. (That it is not *exactly* equal to K_c is because of the rounding of answers during the calculations.)

In each of the preceding two examples, we were able to calculate the answer directly by taking the square root of both sides of the algebraic equation obtained by substituting equilibrium concentrations into the mass action expression. Such direct calculations are not always possible, however, as illustrated in the next example.

EXAMPLE 14.10
Using K_c to Calculate Equilibrium Concentrations

At a certain temperature, $K_c = 4.50$ for the reaction

$$N_2O_4(g) \rightleftharpoons 2NO_2(g)$$

If 0.300 mol of N_2O_4 is placed into a 2.00 L container at that temperature, what will be the equilibrium concentrations of both gases?

ANALYSIS: As in the preceding example, at equilibrium the mass action expression must be equal to K_c.

$$\frac{[NO_2]^2}{[N_2O_4]} = 4.50$$

We will need to find algebraic expressions for the equilibrium concentrations and substitute them into the mass action expression. To obtain these, we set up the concentration table for the reaction.

SOLUTION:

Initial Concentrations. The initial concentration of N_2O_4 is 0.300 mol/2.00 L = 0.150 M. Since no NO_2 was placed in the reaction vessel, its initial concentration is 0.000 M.

Changes in Concentrations. There is no NO_2 in the reaction mixture, so we know its concentration must increase. This means the N_2O_4 concentration must decrease as some of the NO_2 is formed. Let's allow x to be the number of moles per liter of N_2O_4 that reacts, so the change in the N_2O_4 concentration is $-x$. Because of the stoichiometry of the reaction, the NO_2 concentration must increase by $2x$, so its change in concentration is $+2x$.

Equilibrium Concentrations. As before, we add the change to the initial concentration in each column to obtain expressions for the equilibrium concentrations.

Here is the completed concentration table.

	$N_2O_4(g) \rightleftharpoons$	$2NO_2(g)$
Initial concentrations (M)	0.150	0.000
Changes in concentrations (M)	$-x$	$+2x$
Equilibrium concentrations (M)	$0.150 - x$	$2x$

Now we substitute the equilibrium quantities into the mass action expression.

$$\frac{(2x)^2}{(0.150 - x)} = 4.50$$

or

$$\frac{4x^2}{(0.150 - x)} = 4.50 \qquad (14.7)$$

This time the left side of the equation is not a perfect square, so we cannot just take the square root of both sides as in Example 14.9. However, because the equation involves terms in x^2, x, and a constant, we can use the quadratic formula to obtain the value of x. Recall that for a quadratic equation of the form

$$ax^2 + bx + c = 0$$

$$x = \frac{-b \pm \sqrt{b^2 - 4ac}}{2a}$$

Expanding Equation 14.7 above gives

$$4x^2 = 4.50(0.150 - x)$$

$$= 0.675 - 4.50x$$

☐ Where the changes in concentrations are unknown, it is convenient to let the coefficients of x be the same as the coefficients in the balanced equation. This ensures they are in the correct ratio.

Arranging terms in the standard order gives

$$4x^2 + 4.50x - 0.675 = 0$$

Therefore, the quantities we will substitute into the quadratic formula are as follows: $a = 4$, $b = 4.50$, and $c = -0.675$. Making these substitutions gives

$$x = \frac{-4.50 \pm \sqrt{(4.50)^2 - 4(4)(-0.675)}}{2(4)}$$

$$= \frac{-4.50 \pm \sqrt{31.05}}{8}$$

$$= \frac{-4.50 \pm 5.57}{8}$$

Because of the $\pm$ term, there are two values of x that satisfy the equation, $x = 0.134$ and $x = -1.26$. However, only the first value, $x = 0.134$, makes any sense chemically. Using this value, the equilibrium concentrations are

$$[N_2O_4] = 0.150 - 0.134 = 0.016 \; M$$

$$[NO_2] = 2(0.134) = 0.268 \; M$$

Notice that if we had used the negative root, -1.26, the equilibrium concentration of NO_2 would be negative. Negative concentrations are impossible, so $x = -1.26$ is not acceptable *for chemical reasons*. In general, whenever you use the quadratic equation in a chemical calculation, one root will be satisfactory and the other will lead to answers that are nonsense.

IS THE ANSWER REASONABLE? Once again, we can evaluate the reaction quotient using the calculated equilibrium values. When we do this, we obtain $Q = 4.49$, which is acceptably close to the value of K_c given.

Practice Exercise 20: During an experiment, 0.200 mol of H_2 and 0.200 mol of I_2 were placed into a 1.00 liter vessel where the reaction

$$H_2(g) + I_2(g) \rightleftharpoons 2HI(g)$$

came to equilibrium. For this reaction, $K_c = 49.5$ at the temperature of the experiment. What were the equilibrium concentrations of H_2, I_2, and HI? (Hint: The quadratic formula will not be necessary.)

Practice Exercise 21: In an experiment, 0.200 mol H_2 and 0.100 mol I_2 were placed in a 1.00 L vessel where the following equilibrium was established:

$$H_2(g) + I_2(g) \rightleftharpoons 2HI(g)$$

For this reaction, $K_c = 49.5$ at the temperature of the experiment. What were the equilibrium concentrations of H_2, I_2, and HI?

Equilibrium problems can be much more complex than the ones we have just discussed. However, sometimes you can make assumptions that simplify the problem so that an approximate solution can be obtained.

Equilibrium calculations can usually be simplified when K_c is very small

Many chemical reactions have equilibrium constants that are either very large or very small. For example, most weak acids have very small values for K_c. Therefore, only very tiny amounts of products form when these weak acids react with water.

When the K_c for a reaction is very small, the position of equilibrium lies far to the left, toward the reactants. Usually this permits us to simplify the calculations considerably, as shown in the next example.

Hydrogen, a potential fuel, is found in great abundance in water. Before the hydrogen can be used as a fuel, however, it must be separated from the oxygen; the water must be split into H_2 and O_2. One possibility is thermal decomposition, but this requires very high temperatures. Even at 1000 °C, $K_c = 7.3 \times 10^{-18}$ for the reaction

$$2H_2O(g) \rightleftharpoons 2H_2(g) + O_2(g)$$

If at 1000 °C the H_2O concentration in a reaction vessel is set initially at 0.100 M, what will the H_2 concentration be when the reaction reaches equilibrium?

ANALYSIS: We know that at equilibrium

$$\frac{[H_2]^2[O_2]}{[H_2O]^2} = 7.3 \times 10^{-18}$$

As usual, our tool is the concentration table. After we've set up the table, we substitute equilibrium concentrations into the equilibrium law. The equilibrium concentrations will be expressions that contain the unknown quantity x. We can solve the equilibrium law for x and use the concentration table to relate x to the H_2 concentration that we're trying to calculate.

SOLUTION:

Initial Concentrations. The initial concentration of H_2O is 0.100 M; those of H_2 and O_2 are both 0.0 M.

Changes in Concentrations. We know the changes must be in the same ratio as the coefficients in the balanced equation, so we place x's in this row with coefficients equal to those in the chemical equation. Because there are no products present initially, their changes must be positive and the change for the water must be negative.

The complete concentration table is

	$2H_2O(g) \rightleftharpoons$	$2H_2(g) +$	$O_2(g)$
Initial concentrations (M)	0.100	0.0	0.0
Changes in concentrations (M)	$-2x$	$+2x$	$+x$
Equilibrium concentrations (M)	$0.100 - 2x$	$2x$	x

When we substitute the equilibrium quantities into the mass action expression we get

$$\frac{(2x)^2x}{(0.100 - 2x)^2} = 7.3 \times 10^{-18}$$

☐ $(2x)^2x = (4x^2)x = 4x^3$

or

$$\frac{4x^3}{(0.100 - 2x)^2} = 7.3 \times 10^{-18}$$

This is a *cubic equation* (one term involves x^3) and can be rather difficult to solve unless we can simplify it. In this instance we are able to do so because the very small value of K_c tells us that hardly any of the H_2O will decompose. Whatever the actual value of x, we know *in advance* that it is going to be very small. This means that $2x$ will also be small, so when this tiny value is subtracted from 0.100, the result will still be very, very close to 0.100. We will make the assumption, then, that the term in the denominator will be essentially unchanged from 0.100 by subtracting $2x$ from it; that is, we will assume that $0.100 - 2x \approx 0.100$.

☐ Even before we solve the problem, we know that hardly any H_2 and O_2 will be formed, because K_c is so small.

This assumption greatly simplifies the math. We now have

$$\frac{4x^3}{(0.100 - 2x)^2} \approx \frac{4x^3}{(0.100)^2} = 7.3 \times 10^{-18}$$

$$4x^3 = (0.0100)(7.3 \times 10^{-18}) = 7.3 \times 10^{-20}$$

$$x^3 = 1.8 \times 10^{-20}$$

$$x = \sqrt[3]{1.8 \times 10^{-20}}$$

$$= 2.6 \times 10^{-7}$$

Notice that the value of x that we've obtained is indeed very small. If we double it and subtract the answer from 0.100, we still get 0.100 when we round to the correct number of significant figures (the third decimal place).

☐ Always be sure to check your assumptions when solving a problem of this kind.

$$0.100 - 2x = 0.100 - 2(2.6 \times 10^{-7}) = 0.09999948$$

$$= 0.100 \qquad \text{(rounded correctly)}$$

This check verifies that our assumption was valid. Finally, we have to obtain the H_2 concentration. Our table gives

$$[H_2] = 2x$$

Therefore,

$$[H_2] = 2(2.6 \times 10^{-7}) = 5.2 \times 10^{-7} M$$

IS THE ANSWER REASONABLE? The equilibrium constant is very small for this reaction (7.3×10^{-18}), so we expect the amount of product at equilibrium to be small as well. The very low concentration of H_2 seems reasonable. The value of x was positive, which means that there was a decrease in reactant concentrations and an increase in product concentrations as we would expect if only reactants were originally present. Finally, we can check the calculation by seeing if the mass action expression is equal to the equilibrium constant:

$$\frac{[H_2]^2[O_2]}{[H_2O]^2} = \frac{(5.2 \times 10^{-7})^2(2.6 \times 10^{-7})}{0.100^2} = 7.0 \times 10^{-18}$$

The calculated value differs from the original equilibrium constant only because the value of x was rounded off when we took the cube root.

Certain situations suggest that simplification of the math will work

The simplifying assumption made in the preceding example is valid because a very small number is subtracted from a much larger one. We could also have neglected x (or $2x$) if it were a very small number that was being added to a much larger one. Remember that you can only neglect an x that's *added* or *subtracted*; you can never drop an x that occurs as a multiplying or dividing factor. Some examples are

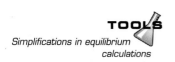

TOOLS

Simplifications in equilibrium calculations

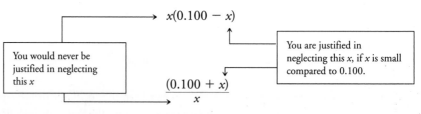

As a rule of thumb, you can expect that these simplifying assumptions will be valid if the concentration from which x is subtracted, or to which x is added, is at least 1000 times greater than K. For instance, in the preceding example, $2x$ was subtracted from 0.100. Since 0.100 is much larger than $1000 \times (7.3 \times 10^{-18})$ we expect the assumption $0.100 - 2x \approx 0.100$ to be valid. However, even though the simplifying assumption is expected to be valid, always check to see if it really is after finishing the calculation. If the assumption proves invalid, then some other way to solve the algebra must be found.

Practice Exercise 22: At 25 °C, the reaction $2NH_3(g) \rightleftharpoons N_2(g) + 3H_2(g)$ has $K_c = 2.3 \times 10^{-9}$. If 0.041 mol NH_3 is placed in a 1.00 L container, what will the concentrations of N_2 and H_2 be when equilibrium is established? (Hint: Review the math beneath the concentration table in the preceding example.)

Practice Exercise 23: In air at 25 °C and 1 atm, the N_2 concentration is 0.033 M and the O_2 concentration is 0.00810 M. The reaction

$$N_2(g) + O_2(g) \rightleftharpoons 2NO(g)$$

has $K_c = 4.8 \times 10^{-31}$ at 25 °C. Taking the N_2 and O_2 concentrations given above as initial values, calculate the equilibrium NO concentration that should exist in our atmosphere from this reaction at 25 °C.

SUMMARY

Dynamic Equilibrium. When the forward and reverse reactions in a chemical system occur at equal rates, a dynamic equilibrium exists and the concentrations of the reactants and products remain constant. For a given overall chemical composition, the amounts of reactants and products that are present at equilibrium are the same regardless of whether the equilibrium is approached from the direction of pure "reactants," pure "products," or any mixture of them. (In a chemical equilibrium, the terms *reactants* and *products* do not have the usual significance because the reaction is proceeding in both directions simultaneously. Instead, we use *reactants* and *products* simply to identify the substances on the left- and right-hand sides, respectively, of the equation for the equilibrium.)

The Equilibrium Law. The **mass action expression** is a fraction. The concentrations of the products, raised to powers equal to their coefficients in the chemical equation, are multiplied together in the numerator. The denominator is constructed in the same way from the concentrations of the reactants raised to powers equal to their coefficients. The numerical value of the mass action expression is the **reaction quotient, Q**. At equilibrium, the reaction quotient is equal to the **equilibrium constant, K_c**. If partial pressures of gases are used in the mass action expression, K_P is obtained. The magnitude of the equilibrium constant is roughly proportional to the extent to which the reaction proceeds to completion when equilibrium is reached. Equilibrium equations can be manipulated by multiplying the coefficients by a common factor, by changing the direction of the reaction, and by adding two or more equilibria. The rules given in the description of the *Tools for Problem Solving* below apply.

Relating K_P to K_c. The values of K_P and K_c are only equal if the same number of moles of gas are represented on both sides of the chemical equation. When the number of moles of gas are different, K_P is related to K_c by the equation $K_P = K_c(RT)^{\Delta n_g}$. Remember to use $R = 0.0821$ L atm mol^{-1} K^{-1} and $T =$ absolute

temperature. Also, be careful to calculate Δn_g as the difference between the number of moles of *gaseous* products and the number of moles of *gaseous* reactants in the balanced equation.

Heterogeneous Equilibria. An equilibrium involving substances in more than one phase is a **heterogeneous equilibrium.** The mass action expression for a heterogeneous equilibrium omits concentration terms for pure liquids and/or pure solids.

Le Châtelier's Principle. This principle states that *when an equilibrium is upset, a chemical change occurs in a direction that opposes the disturbing influence and brings the system to equilibrium again.* Adding a reactant or a product causes a reaction to occur that uses up part of what has been added. Removing a reactant or a product causes a reaction that replaces part of what has been removed. Increasing the pressure (by reducing the volume) drives a reaction in the direction of the fewer number of moles of gas. Pressure changes have virtually no effect on equilibria involving only solids and liquids. Raising the temperature causes an equilibrium to shift in an endothermic direction. The value of K increases with increasing temperature for reactions that are endothermic in the forward direction. A change in temperature is the only factor that changes K. Addition of a catalyst or an inert gas has no effect on an equilibrium.

Equilibrium Calculations. The initial concentrations in a chemical system are controlled by the person who combines the chemicals at the start of the reaction. The changes in concentration are determined by the stoichiometry of the reaction. Only equilibrium concentrations satisfy the equilibrium law. When these are used, the value of the mass action expression, Q, is equal to K_c. When a change in concentration is expected to be very small compared to the initial concentration, the change may be neglected and the algebraic equation derived from the equilibrium law can be simplified. In general, this simplification is valid if the initial concentration is at least 1000 times larger than K.

TOOLS FOR PROBLEM SOLVING

In this chapter you learned to apply the following concepts as tools in solving problems dealing with aspects of chemical equilibrium. Study each tool carefully so that you know what each is used for. When faced with solving a problem, recall what each tool does and consider whether it will be helpful in finding a solution. This will aid you in selecting the tools you need.

The approach to equilibrium *(page 571)* There are times when it is very helpful to remember that the same equilibrium composition is reached regardless of whether it is approached from the direction of the reactants or from the direction of the products. Some equilibrium problems can be greatly simplified if we first imagine the reaction going to completion (converting all the reactants to products) and then approach the equilibrium from the direction of the products.

The equilibrium law *(page 573)* To solve most chemical equilibrium problems we need the equation for the equilibrium and the equilibrium law. The knowledge of how to construct the equilibrium law from the chemical equation is an essential tool for dealing with such problems. An equation of the form

$$dD + eE \rightleftharpoons fF + gG$$

has the equilibrium law

$$\frac{[F]^f [G]^g}{[D]^d [E]^e} = K_c$$

Remember that for gaseous reactions, partial pressures can be used in place of concentrations, in which case the mass action expression equals K_P. In general, K_P does not equal K_c.

Manipulating equilibrium equations *(pages 574 through 575)* There are occasions when it is necessary to modify an equation for an equilibrium, or combine two or more chemical equilibria. The tools discussed here are used to obtain the new equilibrium constants for the new equations.

- When two equations are added, we multiply their Ks to obtain the new K.
- When an equation is multiplied by a factor n to obtain a new equation, we raise its K to the power n to obtain the K for the new equation.
- When an equation is reversed, we take the reciprocal of its K to obtain the new K.

Converting between K_P and K_c *(page 577)* In Chapter 18 you will learn how to calculate equilibrium constants from thermodynamic data. These calculations give K_P for gaseous reactions. To change to K_c values, we use the equation

$$K_P = K_c(RT)^{\Delta n_g}$$

Remember to use $R = 0.0821$ L atm mol^{-1} K^{-1}.

Equilibrium laws for heterogeneous reactions *(page 579)* Being able to write the equilibrium law for a heterogeneous reaction is a tool you will need in later chapters when we deal with solubility equilibria. Remember that pure solids and liquids do not appear in the mass action expression.

Magnitude of K *(page 580)* Use this tool to gain a rough estimate of the position of equilibrium.

- When K is very large, the position of equilibrium lies far to the right (toward the products).
- When K is very small, the position of equilibrium lies far to the left (toward the reactants).

Le Châtelier's principle This tool lets us predict how disturbing influences shift the position of equilibrium. Factors to consider are as follows:

- Adding or removing a reactant or product *(page 582)*
- Changing the volume for gaseous reactions *(page 582)*
- Changing the temperature *(pages 583, 584)*

Catalysts or inert gases have no effect on the position of equilibrium.

Concentration table *(page 586)* This is a tool you will use in almost all equilibrium calculations. Remember the following points when constructing the table:

- All entries in the table must have units of molarity (mol L^{-1}).
- Any reactant or product for which an initial concentration or amount is not given in the statement of the problem is assigned an initial concentration of zero.

- Any substance with an initial concentration of zero must have a positive change in concentration when the reaction proceeds to equilibrium.
- The changes in concentration are in the same ratio as the coefficients in the balanced equation. When the changes are unknown, the coefficients of x can be the same as the coefficients in the balanced equation.
- Only quantities in the last row (Equilibrium Concentrations) satisfy the equilibrium law.

Simplifications in equilibrium calculations *(page 596)* When the initial reactant concentrations are larger than $1000 \times K$, they will change only slightly as the reaction approaches equilibrium. You can therefore expect to be able to neglect the change when it is being added to or subtracted from an initial concentration. This tool is especially useful when working problems in which K is very small and the initial conditions are not far from the final position of equilibrium. *If you use these simplifying approximations, be sure to check their validity after obtaining an answer.*

QUESTIONS, PROBLEMS, AND EXERCISES

Answers to problems whose numbers are printed in color are given in Appendix B. More challenging problems are marked with asterisks. ILW = Interactive Learningware solution is available at www.wiley.com/college/brady. OH = an Office Hours video is available for this problem.

REVIEW QUESTIONS

General

14.1 Sketch a graph showing how the concentrations of the reactants and products of a typical chemical reaction vary with time during the course of the reaction. Assume no products are present at the start of the reaction. Indicate on the graph where the system has reached equilibrium.

14.2 What meanings do the terms *reactants* and *products* have when describing a chemical equilibrium?

Mass Action Expression, K_P, and K_c

14.3 What is an *equilibrium law*? How is the term *reaction quotient* defined?

14.4 Under what conditions does the reaction quotient equal K_c?

14.5 Suppose for the reaction $A \longrightarrow B$ the value of Q is less than K_c. Which way does the reaction have to proceed to reach equilibrium, in the forward or reverse direction?

14.6 When a chemical equation and its equilibrium constant are given, why is it not necessary to also specify the form of the mass action expression?

14.7 At 225 °C, $K_P = 6.3 \times 10^{-3}$ for the reaction

$$CO(g) + 2H_2(g) \rightleftharpoons CH_3OH(g)$$

Would we expect this reaction to go nearly to completion?

14.8 Here are some reactions and their equilibrium constants.
(a) $2CH_4(g) \rightleftharpoons C_2H_6(g) + H_2(g)$ $K_c = 9.5 \times 10^{-13}$
(b) $CH_3OH(g) + H_2(g) \rightleftharpoons CH_4(g) + H_2O(g)$
  $K_c = 3.6 \times 10^{20}$
(c) $H_2(g) + Br_2(g) \rightleftharpoons 2HBr(g)$ $K_c = 2.0 \times 10^9$
Arrange these reactions in order of their increasing tendency to go toward completion.

Converting between K_P and K_c

14.9 State the equation relating K_P to K_c and define all terms. Which is the only value of R that can be properly used in the equation?

14.10 Use the ideal gas law to show that the partial pressure of a gas is directly proportional to its molar concentration. What is the proportionality constant?

Heterogeneous Equilibria

14.11 What is the difference between a *heterogeneous equilibrium* and a *homogeneous equilibrium*?

14.12 Why do we omit the concentrations of pure liquids and solids from the mass action expression of heterogeneous reactions?

14.13 Consider the following equilibrium.

$$2NaHCO_3(s) \rightleftharpoons Na_2CO_3(s) + CO_2(g) + H_2O(g)$$

If you were converting between K_P and K_c, what value of Δn_g would you use?

Le Châtelier's Principle

14.14 State Le Châtelier's principle in your own words.

14.15 Explain, using its effect on the reaction quotient, why adding a reactant to the following equilibrium shifts the position of equilibrium to the right.

$$PCl_3(g) + Cl_2(g) \rightleftharpoons PCl_5(g)$$

14.16 Halving the volume of a gas doubles its pressure. Using the reaction quotient corresponding to K_P, explain why halving the volume shifts the following equilibrium to the left.

$$N_2O_4(g) \rightleftharpoons 2NO_2(g)$$

14.17 How will the value of K_P for the following reactions be affected by an increase in temperature?
(a) $CO(g) + 2H_2(g) \rightleftharpoons CH_3OH(g)$ $\Delta H° = -18$ kJ
(b) $N_2O(g) + NO_2(g) \rightleftharpoons 3NO(g)$ $\Delta H° = +155.7$ kJ
(c) $2NO(g) + Cl_2(g) \rightleftharpoons 2NOCl(g)$ $\Delta H° = -77.07$ kJ

14.18 Why doesn't a catalyst affect the position of equilibrium in a chemical reaction?

REVIEW PROBLEMS

Equilibrium Laws for K_P and K_c

14.19 Write the equilibrium law for each of the following reactions in terms of molar concentrations:

(a) $2PCl_3(g) + O_2(g) \rightleftharpoons 2POCl_3(g)$

(b) $2SO_3(g) \rightleftharpoons 2SO_2(g) + O_2(g)$

(c) $N_2H_4(g) + 2O_2(g) \rightleftharpoons 2NO(g) + 2H_2O(g)$

(d) $N_2H_4(g) + 6H_2O_2(g) \rightleftharpoons 2NO_2(g) + 8H_2O(g)$

(e) $SOCl_2(g) + H_2O(g) \rightleftharpoons SO_2(g) + 2HCl(g)$

14.20 Write the equilibrium law for each of the following gaseous reactions in terms of molar concentrations.

(a) $3Cl_2(g) + NH_3(g) \rightleftharpoons NCl_3(g) + 3HCl(g)$

(b) $PCl_3(g) + PBr_3(g) \rightleftharpoons PCl_2Br(g) + PClBr_2(g)$

(c) $NO(g) + NO_2(g) + H_2O(g) \rightleftharpoons 2HNO_2(g)$

(d) $H_2O(g) + Cl_2O(g) \rightleftharpoons 2HOCl(g)$

(e) $Br_2(g) + 5F_2(g) \rightleftharpoons 2BrF_5(g)$

14.21 Write the equilibrium law for the reactions in Problem 14.19 in terms of partial pressures.

14.22 Write the equilibrium law for the reactions in Problem 14.20 in terms of partial pressures.

OH 14.23 Write the equilibrium law for each of the following reactions in aqueous solution.

(a) $Ag^+(aq) + 2NH_3(aq) \rightleftharpoons Ag(NH_3)_2^+(aq)$

(b) $Cd^{2+}(aq) + 4SCN^-(aq) \rightleftharpoons Cd(SCN)_4^{2-}(aq)$

14.24 Write the equilibrium law for each of the following reactions in aqueous solution.

(a) $HClO(aq) + H_2O \rightleftharpoons H_3O^+(aq) + ClO^-(aq)$

(b) $CO_3^{2-}(aq) + HSO_4^-(aq) \rightleftharpoons HCO_3^-(aq) + SO_4^{2-}(aq)$

Manipulating Equilibrium Equations

14.25 At 25 °C, $K_c = 1 \times 10^{-85}$ for the reaction

$$7IO_3^-(aq) + 9H_2O + 7H^+(aq) \rightleftharpoons I_2(aq) + 5H_5IO_6(aq)$$

What is the value of K_c for the following reaction?

$$I_2(aq) + 5H_5IO_6(aq) \rightleftharpoons 7IO_3^-(aq) + 9H_2O + 7H^+(aq)$$

14.26 Use the following equilibria

$$2CH_4(g) \rightleftharpoons C_2H_6(g) + H_2(g) \qquad K_c = 9.5 \times 10^{-13}$$
$$CH_4(g) + H_2O(g) \rightleftharpoons CH_3OH(g) + H_2(g)$$
$$K_c = 2.8 \times 10^{-21}$$

to calculate K_c for the reaction

$$2CH_3OH(g) + H_2(g) \rightleftharpoons C_2H_6(g) + 2H_2O(g)$$

14.27 Write the equilibrium law for each of the following reactions in terms of molar concentrations:

(a) $H_2(g) + Cl_2(g) \rightleftharpoons 2HCl(g)$

(b) $\frac{1}{2}H_2(g) + \frac{1}{2}Cl_2(g) \rightleftharpoons HCl(g)$

How does K_c for reaction (a) compare with K_c for reaction (b)?

14.28 Write the equilibrium law for the reaction

$$2HCl(g) \rightleftharpoons H_2(g) + Cl_2(g)$$

How does K_c for this reaction compare with K_c for reaction (a) in the preceding problem?

Converting between K_P and K_c

14.29 A 345 mL container holds NH_3 at a pressure of 745 torr and a temperature of 45 °C. What is the molar concentration of ammonia in the container?

14.30 In a certain container at 145 °C the concentration of water vapor is 0.0200 M. What is the partial pressure of H_2O in the container?

14.31 For which of the following reactions does $K_P = K_c$?

(a) $2H_2(g) + C_2H_2(g) \rightleftharpoons C_2H_6(g)$

(b) $N_2(g) + O_2(g) \rightleftharpoons 2NO(g)$

(c) $2NO(g) + O_2(g) \rightleftharpoons 2NO_2(g)$

OH 14.32 For which of the following reactions does $K_P = K_c$?

(a) $CO_2(g) + H_2(g) \rightleftharpoons CO(g) + H_2O(g)$

(b) $PCl_3(g) + Cl_2(g) \rightleftharpoons PCl_5(g)$

(c) $N_2O_4(g) \rightleftharpoons 2NO_2(g)$

ILW 14.33 The reaction $CO(g) + 2H_2(g) \rightleftharpoons CH_3OH(g)$ has $K_P = 6.3 \times 10^{-3}$ at 225 °C. What is the value of K_c at that temperature?

14.34 The reaction $HCO_2H(g) \rightleftharpoons CO(g) + H_2O(g)$ has $K_P = 1.6 \times 10^6$ at 400 °C. What is the value of K_c for the reaction at that temperature?

14.35 The reaction $N_2O(g) + NO_2(g) \rightleftharpoons 3NO(g)$ has $K_c = 4.2 \times 10^{-4}$ at 500 °C. What is the value of K_P at this temperature?

14.36 One possible way of removing NO from the exhaust of a gasoline engine is to cause it to react with CO in the presence of a suitable catalyst.

$$2NO(g) + 2CO(g) \rightleftharpoons N_2(g) + 2CO_2(g)$$

At 300 °C, the reaction has $K_c = 2.2 \times 10^{59}$. What is K_P at 300 °C?

14.37 At 773 °C the reaction

$$CO(g) + 2H_2(g) \rightleftharpoons CH_3OH(g)$$

has $K_c = 0.40$. What is K_P at that temperature?

14.38 The reaction $COCl_2(g) \rightleftharpoons CO(g) + Cl_2(g)$ has $K_P = 4.6 \times 10^{-2}$ at 395 °C. What is K_c at that temperature?

Heterogeneous Equilibria

14.39 Calculate the molar concentration of water in (a) 18.0 mL of H_2O, (b) 100.0 mL of H_2O, and (c) 1.00 L of H_2O. Assume that the density of water is 1.00 g/mL.

14.40 The density of sodium chloride is 2.164 g cm^{-3}. What is the molar concentration of NaCl in a 12.0 cm^3 sample of pure NaCl? What is the molar concentration of NaCl in a 25.0 g sample of pure NaCl?

14.41 Write the equilibrium law corresponding to K_c for each of the following heterogeneous reactions.

(a) $2C(s) + O_2(g) \rightleftharpoons 2CO(g)$

(b) $2NaHSO_3(s) \rightleftharpoons Na_2SO_3(s) + H_2O(g) + SO_2(g)$

(c) $2C(s) + 2H_2O(g) \rightleftharpoons CH_4(g) + CO_2(g)$

(d) $CaCO_3(s) + 2HF(g) \rightleftharpoons CaF_2(s) + H_2O(g) + CO_2(g)$

(e) $CuSO_4 \cdot 5H_2O(s) \rightleftharpoons CuSO_4(s) + 5H_2O(g)$

14.42 Write the equilibrium law corresponding to K_c for each of the following heterogeneous reactions.

(a) $CaCO_3(s) + SO_2(g) \rightleftharpoons CaSO_3(s) + CO_2(g)$

(b) $AgCl(s) + Br^-(aq) \rightleftharpoons AgBr(s) + Cl^-(aq)$

(c) $Cu(OH)_2(s) \rightleftharpoons Cu^{2+}(aq) + 2OH^-(aq)$

(d) $Mg(OH)_2(s) \rightleftharpoons MgO(s) + H_2O(g)$

(e) $3CuO(s) + 2NH_3(g) \rightleftharpoons 3Cu(s) + N_2(g) + 3H_2O(g)$

OH 14.43 The heterogeneous reaction

$$2HCl(g) + I_2(s) \rightleftharpoons 2HI(g) + Cl_2(g)$$

has $K_c = 1.6 \times 10^{-34}$ at 25 °C. Suppose 0.100 mol of HCl and solid I_2 is placed in a 1.00 L container. What will be the equilibrium concentrations of HI and Cl_2 in the container?

14.44 At 25 °C, $K_c = 360$ for the reaction

$$AgCl(s) + Br^-(aq) \rightleftharpoons AgBr(s) + Cl^-(aq)$$

If solid AgCl is added to a solution containing 0.10 M Br^-, what will be the equilibrium concentrations of Br^- and Cl^-?

Le Châtelier's Principle

14.45 How will the position of equilibrium in the following reaction

$$heat + CH_4(g) + 2H_2S(g) \rightleftharpoons CS_2(g) + 4H_2(g)$$

be affected by:
(a) Adding $CH_4(g)$?
(b) Adding $H_2(g)$?
(c) Removing $CS_2(g)$?
(d) Decreasing the volume of the container?
(e) Increasing the temperature?

OH 14.46 The reaction $CO(g) + 2H_2(g) \rightleftharpoons CH_3OH(g)$ has $\Delta H° = -18$ kJ. How will the amount of CH_3OH present at equilibrium be affected by the following?
(a) Adding $CO(g)$.
(b) Removing $H_2(g)$.
(c) Decreasing the volume of the container.
(d) Adding a catalyst.
(e) Increasing the temperature.

14.47 Consider the equilibrium

$$N_2O(g) + NO_2(g) \rightleftharpoons 3NO(g) \qquad \Delta H° = +155.7 \text{ kJ}$$

In which direction will this equilibrium be shifted by the following changes?
(a) Adding N_2O.
(b) Removing NO_2.
(c) Adding NO.
(d) Increasing the temperature of the reaction mixture.
(e) Adding helium gas to the reaction mixture at constant volume.
(f) Decreasing the volume of the container at constant temperature.

14.48 Consider the equilibrium

$$2NO(g) + Cl_2(g) \rightleftharpoons 2NOCl(g)$$

for which $\Delta H° = -77.07$ kJ. How will the amount of Cl_2 at equilibrium be affected by the following?
(a) Removing $NO(g)$.
(b) Adding $NOCl(g)$.
(c) Raising the temperature.
(d) Decreasing the volume of the container.

Equilibrium Calculations

14.49 At a certain temperature, $K_c = 0.18$ for the equilibrium

$$PCl_3(g) + Cl_2(g) \rightleftharpoons PCl_5(g)$$

Suppose a reaction vessel at that temperature contained these three gases at the following concentrations: $[PCl_3] = 0.0420$ M, $[Cl_2] = 0.0240$ M, $[PCl_5] = 0.00500$ M.
(a) Is the system in a state of equilibrium?
(b) If not, in which direction will the reaction have to proceed to get to equilibrium?

14.50 At 460 °C, the reaction

$$SO_2(g) + NO_2(g) \rightleftharpoons NO(g) + SO_3(g)$$

has $K_c = 85.0$. A reaction flask at 460 °C contains these gases at the following concentrations: $[SO_2] = 0.00250$ M, $[NO_2] = 0.00350$ M, $[NO] = 0.0250$ M, $[SO_3] = 0.0400$ M.
(a) Is the reaction at equilibrium?
(b) If not, in which way will the reaction have to proceed to arrive at equilibrium?

OH 14.51 At a certain temperature, the reaction

$$CO(g) + 2H_2(g) \rightleftharpoons CH_3OH(g)$$

has $K_c = 0.500$. If a reaction mixture at equilibrium contains 0.180 M CO and 0.220 M H_2, what is the concentration of CH_3OH?

14.52 At a certain temperature $K_c = 64$ for the reaction

$$N_2(g) + 3H_2(g) \rightleftharpoons 2NH_3(g)$$

Suppose it was found that an equilibrium mixture of these gases contained 0.360 M NH_3 and 0.0192 M N_2. What was the concentration of H_2 in the mixture?

14.53 At 773 °C, a mixture of $CO(g)$, $H_2(g)$, and $CH_3OH(g)$ was allowed to come to equilibrium. The following equilibrium concentrations were then measured: $[CO] = 0.105$ M, $[H_2] = 0.250$ M, $[CH_3OH] = 0.00261$ M. Calculate K_c for the reaction

$$CO(g) + 2H_2(g) \rightleftharpoons CH_3OH(g)$$

14.54 Ethylene, C_2H_4, and water react under appropriate conditions to give ethanol. The reaction is

$$C_2H_4(g) + H_2O(g) \rightleftharpoons C_2H_5OH(g)$$

An equilibrium mixture of these gases at a certain temperature had the following concentrations: $[C_2H_4] = 0.0148$ M, $[H_2O] = 0.0336$ M, and $[C_2H_5OH] = 0.180$ M. What is the value of K_c?

ILW 14.55 At high temperature, 2.00 mol of HBr was placed in a 4.00 L container where it decomposed to give the equilibrium

$$2HBr(g) \rightleftharpoons H_2(g) + Br_2(g)$$

At equilibrium the concentration of Br_2 was measured to be 0.0955 M. What is K_c for the reaction at that temperature?

14.56 A 0.050 mol sample of formaldehyde vapor, CH_2O, was placed in a heated 500 mL vessel and some of it decomposed. The reaction is

$$CH_2O(g) \rightleftharpoons H_2(g) + CO(g)$$

At equilibrium, the $CH_2O(g)$ concentration was 0.066 mol L^{-1}. Calculate the value of K_c for this reaction.

14.57 The reaction $NO_2(g) + NO(g) \rightleftharpoons N_2O(g) + O_2(g)$ reached equilibrium at a certain high temperature. Originally, the reaction vessel contained the following initial concentrations: $[N_2O] = 0.184\ M$, $[O_2] = 0.377\ M$, $[NO_2] = 0.0560\ M$, and $[NO] = 0.294\ M$. The concentration of the NO_2, the only colored gas in the mixture, was monitored by following the intensity of the color. At equilibrium, the NO_2 concentration had become 0.118 M. What is the value of K_c for the reaction at that temperature?

14.58 At 25 °C, 0.0560 mol O_2 and 0.020 mol N_2O were placed in a 1.00 L container where the following equilibrium was then established.

$$2N_2O(g) + 3O_2(g) \rightleftharpoons 4NO_2(g)$$

At equilibrium, the NO_2 concentration was 0.020 M. What is the value of K_c for this reaction?

14.59 At 25 °C, $K_c = 0.145$ for the following reaction in the solvent CCl_4.

$$2BrCl \rightleftharpoons Br_2 + Cl_2$$

If the initial concentration of BrCl in the solution is 0.050 M, what will the equilibrium concentrations of Br_2 and Cl_2 be?

14.60 At 25 °C, $K_c = 0.145$ for the following reaction in the solvent CCl_4.

$$2BrCl \rightleftharpoons Br_2 + Cl_2$$

If the initial concentrations of Br_2 and Cl_2 are each 0.0250 M, what will their equilibrium concentrations be?

14.61 The equilibrium constant, K_c, for the reaction

$$SO_3(g) + NO(g) \rightleftharpoons NO_2(g) + SO_2(g)$$

was found to be 0.500 at a certain temperature. If 0.240 mol of SO_3 and 0.240 mol of NO are placed in a 2.00 L container and allowed to react, what will be the equilibrium concentration of each gas?

14.62 For the reaction in the preceding problem, a reaction mixture is prepared in which 0.120 mol NO_2 and 0.120 mol of SO_2 are placed in a 1.00 L vessel. After the system reaches equilibrium, what will be the equilibrium concentrations of all four gases? How do these equilibrium values compare to those calculated in Problem 14.61? Account for your observation.

14.63 At a certain temperature the reaction

$$CO(g) + H_2O(g) \rightleftharpoons CO_2(g) + H_2(g)$$

has $K_c = 0.400$. Exactly 1.00 mol of each gas was placed in a 100.0 L vessel and the mixture underwent reaction. What was the equilibrium concentration of each gas?

14.64 At 25 °C, $K_c = 0.145$ for the following reaction in the solvent CCl_4.

$$2BrCl \rightleftharpoons Br_2 + Cl_2$$

If the initial concentrations of each substance in a solution are 0.0400 M, what will their equilibrium concentrations be?

ILW 14.65 The reaction $2HCl(g) \rightleftharpoons H_2(g) + Cl_2(g)$ has $K_c = 3.2 \times 10^{-34}$ at 25 °C. If a reaction vessel contains initially 0.0500 mol L^{-1} of HCl and then reacts to reach equilibrium, what will be the concentrations of H_2 and Cl_2?

14.66 At 200 °C, $K_c = 1.4 \times 10^{-10}$ for the reaction

$$N_2O(g) + NO_2(g) \rightleftharpoons 3NO(g)$$

If 0.200 mol of N_2O and 0.400 mol NO_2 are placed in a 4.00 L container, what would the NO concentration be if this equilibrium were established?

ILW 14.67 At 2000 °C, the decomposition of CO_2,

$$2CO_2(g) \rightleftharpoons 2CO(g) + O_2(g)$$

has $K_c = 6.4 \times 10^{-7}$. If a 1.00 L container holding 1.0×10^{-2} mol of CO_2 is heated to 2000 °C, what will be the concentration of CO at equilibrium?

14.68 At 500 °C, the decomposition of water into hydrogen and oxygen,

$$2H_2O(g) \rightleftharpoons 2H_2(g) + O_2(g)$$

has $K_c = 6.0 \times 10^{-28}$. How many moles of H_2 and O_2 are present at equilibrium in a 5.00 L reaction vessel at that temperature if the container originally held 0.015 mol H_2O?

14.69 At a certain temperature, $K_c = 0.18$ for the equilibrium

$$PCl_3(g) + Cl_2(g) \rightleftharpoons PCl_5(g)$$

If 0.026 mol of PCl_5 is placed in a 2.00 L vessel at that temperature, what will the concentration of PCl_3 be at equilibrium?

14.70 At 460 °C, the reaction

$$SO_2(g) + NO_2(g) \rightleftharpoons NO(g) + SO_3(g)$$

has $K_c = 85.0$. Suppose 0.100 mol of SO_2, 0.0600 mol of NO_2, 0.0800 mol of NO, and 0.120 mol of SO_3 are placed in a 10.0 L container at that temperature. What will the concentrations of all the gases be when the system reaches equilibrium?

14.71 At a certain temperature, $K_c = 0.500$ for the reaction

$$SO_3(g) + NO(g) \rightleftharpoons NO_2(g) + SO_2(g)$$

If 0.100 mol SO_3 and 0.200 mol NO are placed in a 2.00 L container and allowed to come to equilibrium, what will the NO_2 and SO_2 concentrations be?

14.72 At 25 °C, $K_c = 0.145$ for the following reaction in the solvent CCl_4.

$$2BrCl \rightleftharpoons Br_2 + Cl_2$$

A solution was prepared with the following initial concentrations: $[BrCl] = 0.0400\ M$, $[Br_2] = 0.0300\ M$, and $[Cl_2] = 0.0200\ M$. What will their equilibrium concentrations be?

****14.73** At a certain temperature, $K_c = 4.3 \times 10^5$ for the reaction

$$HCO_2H(g) \rightleftharpoons CO(g) + H_2O(g)$$

If 0.200 mol of HCO_2H is placed in a 1.00 L vessel, what will be the concentrations of CO and H_2O when the system reaches equilibrium? (Hint: The same equilibrium concentrations are reached whether equilibrium is approached from the left or the right.)

*14.74 The reaction $H_2(g) + Br_2(g) \rightleftharpoons 2HBr(g)$ has $K_c = 2.0 \times 10^9$ at 25 °C. If 0.100 mol of H_2 and 0.200 mol of Br_2 are placed in a 10.0 L container, what will all the equilibrium concentrations be at 25 °C? (Hint: The same equilibrium concentrations are reached whether equilibrium is approached from the left or the right.)

ADDITIONAL EXERCISES

OH **14.75** The reaction $N_2O_4(g) \rightleftharpoons 2NO_2(g)$ has $K_P = 0.140$ at 25 °C. In a reaction vessel containing the gases in equilibrium at that temperature, the partial pressure of N_2O_4 was 0.250 atm.
(a) What was the partial pressure of the NO_2 in the reaction mixture?
(b) What was the total pressure of the mixture of gases?

14.76 At 25 °C, the following concentrations were found for the gases in an equilibrium mixture for the reaction

$$N_2O(g) + NO_2(g) \rightleftharpoons 3NO(g)$$

$[NO_2] = 0.24\ M$, $[NO] = 4.7 \times 10^{-8}\ M$, and $[N_2O] = 0.023\ M$. What is the value of K_P for this reaction?

14.77 The following reaction in aqueous solution has $K_c = 1 \times 10^{-85}$ at a temperature of 25 °C.

$$7IO_3^-(aq) + 9H_2O + 7H^+(aq) \rightleftharpoons I_2(aq) + 5H_5IO_6(aq)$$

What is the equilibrium law for this reaction?

*14.78 At a certain temperature, $K_c = 0.914$ for the reaction

$$NO_2(g) + NO(g) \rightleftharpoons N_2O(g) + O_2(g)$$

A mixture was prepared containing 0.200 mol NO_2, 0.300 mol NO, 0.150 mol N_2O, and 0.250 mol O_2 in a 4.00 L container. What will be the equilibrium concentrations of each gas?

*14.79 At 400 °C, $K_c = 2.9 \times 10^4$ for the reaction

$$HCHO_2(g) \rightleftharpoons CO(g) + H_2O(g)$$

A mixture was prepared with the following initial concentrations: $[CO] = 0.20\ M$ and $[H_2O] = 0.30\ M$. No formic acid, $HCHO_2$, was initially present. What was the equilibrium concentration of $HCHO_2$?

*14.80 At 27 °C, $K_P = 1.5 \times 10^{18}$ for the reaction

$$3NO(g) \rightleftharpoons N_2O(g) + NO_2(g)$$

If 0.030 mol of NO were placed in a 1.00 L vessel and equilibrium were established, what would be the equilibrium concentrations of NO, N_2O, and NO_2?

14.81 Consider the equilibrium

$$2NaHSO_3(s) \rightleftharpoons Na_2SO_3(s) + H_2O(g) + SO_2(g)$$

How will the position of equilibrium be affected by the following?
(a) Adding $NaHSO_3$ to the reaction vessel.
(b) Removing Na_2SO_3 from the reaction vessel.
(c) Adding H_2O to the reaction vessel.
(d) Increasing the volume of the reaction vessel.

*14.82 For the reaction below, $K_P = 1.6 \times 10^6$ at 400 °C.

$$HCHO_2(g) \rightleftharpoons CO(g) + H_2O(g)$$

A mixture of $CO(g)$ and $H_2O(l)$ was prepared in a 2.00 L reaction vessel at 25 °C in which the pressure of CO was 0.177 atm.

The mixture also contained 0.391 g of H_2O. The vessel was sealed and heated to 400 °C. When equilibrium was reached, what was the partial pressure of the $HCHO_2$?

*14.83 At a certain temperature, $K_c = 0.914$ for the reaction

$$NO_2(g) + NO(g) \rightleftharpoons N_2O(g) + O_2(g)$$

A mixture was prepared containing 0.200 mol of each gas in a 5.00 L container. What will be the equilibrium concentration of each gas? How will the concentrations then change if 0.050 mol of NO_2 is added to the equilibrium mixture?

*14.84 At a certain temperature, $K_c = 0.914$ for the reaction

$$NO_2(g) + NO(g) \rightleftharpoons N_2O(g) + O_2(g)$$

Equal amounts of NO and NO_2 are to be placed in a 5.00 L container until the N_2O concentration at equilibrium is 0.050 M. How many moles of NO and NO_2 must be placed in the container?

14.85 Two 1.00 L bulbs are filled with 0.500 atm of $F_2(g)$ and $PF_3(g)$, as illustrated in the figure below. At a particular temperature, $K_P = 4.0$ for the reaction of the gases to form $PF_5(g)$:

$$F_2(g) + PF_3(g) \rightleftharpoons PF_5(g)$$

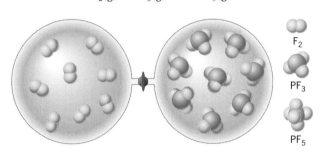

(a) The stopcock between the bulbs is opened and the pressure falls. Make a sketch of this apparatus showing the gas composition once the pressure is stable.
(b) List any chemical reactions that continue to occur once the pressure is stable.
(c) Suppose all the gas in the left bulb is forced into the bulb on the right and then the stopcock is closed. Make a second sketch to show the composition of the gas mixture after equilibrium is reached. Comment on how the composition of the one-bulb system differs from that for the two-bulb system.

OH **14.86** For the equilibrium

$$3NO_2(g) \rightleftharpoons N_2O_5(g) + NO(g)$$

$K_c = 1.0 \times 10^{-11}$. If a 4.00 L container initially holds 0.20 mol of NO_2, how many moles of N_2O_5 will be present when this system reaches equilibrium?

14.87 To study the following reaction at 20°C,

$$NO(g) + NO_2(g) + H_2O(g) \rightleftharpoons 2HNO_2(g)$$

a mixture of $NO(g)$, $NO_2(g)$, and $H_2O(g)$ was prepared in a 10.0 L glass bulb. For NO, NO_2, and HNO_2, the initial concentrations were as follows: $[NO] = [NO_2] = 2.59 \times 10^{-3}\ M$ and $[HNO_2] = 0.0\ M$. The initial partial pressure of $H_2O(g)$ was 17.5 torr. When equilibrium was reached, the HNO_2 concentration was $4.0 \times 10^{-4}\ M$. Calculate the equilibrium constant, K_c, for the reaction.

14.88 At 100 °C, $K_c = 0.135$ for the reaction

$$3H_2(g) + N_2(g) \rightleftharpoons 2NH_3(g)$$

In a reaction mixture at equilibrium at that temperature, $[NH_3] = 0.030\ M$ and $[N_2] = 0.50\ M$. What are the partial pressures of all of the gases in the mixture? Use them to calculate K_P and compare the result with K_P calculated using Equation 14.5.

EXERCISES IN CRITICAL THINKING

14.89 In an equilibrium law, coefficients in the balanced equation appear as exponents on concentrations. Why, in general, does this not also apply for rate laws?

14.90 Why are equilibrium concentrations useful to know?

14.91 Suppose we set up a system in which water is poured into a vessel having a hole in the bottom. If the rate of water inflow is adjusted so that it matches the rate at which water drains through the hole, the amount of water in the vessel remains constant over time. Is this an equilibrium system? Explain.

14.92 Do equilibrium laws apply to other systems outside of chemistry? Give examples.

14.93 What might prevent a system from reaching dynamic equilibrium? Illustrate your answer with examples.

14.94 After many centuries the earth's atmosphere still has not come to equilibrium with the oceans and land. What factors are responsible for this?

14.95 If a mixture consisting of many small crystals in contact with a saturated solution is studied for a period of time, the smallest of the crystals are observed to dissolve while the larger ones grow even larger. Explain this phenomenon in terms of equilibrium.

15 ACIDS AND BASES: A SECOND LOOK

The economic health of a country is often reflected in the activity of the stock and commodity exchanges. Chemicals, including pharmaceuticals, agrochemicals and home-care products, make up a large component of the economic activity of many countries. Acids and bases described in this chapter are a major component of the chemical industry.
(© AP/Wide World Photos)

CHAPTER OUTLINE

THIS CHAPTER IN CONTEXT In Chapter 4 we introduced you to compounds that we call acids and bases. Many common substances, from household products such as vinegar and ammonia, to biologically important compounds such as amino acids, are conveniently classified as either an acid or a base. The significant property that makes such classifications useful is that *acids react with bases*. In fact, this is such a useful relationship that the acid–base concept has been expanded far beyond the limited Arrhenius definition we discussed in Chapter 4. We now return to acid–base chemistry to learn about these broader and often more useful views.

At the same time, we will study how trends in the strengths of acids and bases correlate with the periodic table. We will use the principles developed in previous chapters to explain why one acid should be stronger than another. The ability to judge relative acid strengths is an important skill to bring to the study of organic chemistry. In the next chapter we will assign a numerical value that helps us more precisely compare strengths of acids and bases.

BRØNSTED-LOWRY ACIDS AND BASES EXCHANGE PROTONS

In our earlier discussion, an acid was described as a substance that produces H_3O^+ in water, whereas a base gives OH^-. An acid–base neutralization, according to Arrhenius, is a reaction in which an acid and a base combine to produce water and a salt. However, many reactions resemble neutralizations without involving H_3O^+, OH^-, or even H_2O. For example, when open bottles of concentrated hydrochloric acid and concentrated aqueous ammonia are placed side by side, a white cloud forms when the vapors from the two bottles mix (see Figure 15.1). The cloud consists of tiny crystals of ammonium chloride which form when ammonia and hydrogen chloride gases, escaping from the open bottles, mix in air and react.

$$NH_3(g) + HCl(g) \longrightarrow NH_4Cl(s)$$

What's interesting is that this is the same net reaction that occurs when an aqueous solution of ammonia (a base) is neutralized by an aqueous solution of hydrogen chloride (an acid). Yet, the gaseous reaction doesn't fit the description of an acid–base neutralization according to the Arrhenius definition because there's no water involved.

If we look at both the aqueous and gaseous reactions, they do have something in common. Both involve the transfer of a *proton* (a hydrogen ion, H^+) from one particle to another.[1] In water, where HCl is completely ionized, the transfer is from H_3O^+ to NH_3, as we discussed on page 150. The ionic equation is

$$NH_3(aq) + H_3O^+(aq) + Cl^-(aq) \longrightarrow \underbrace{NH_4^+(aq) + Cl^-(aq)}_{\text{The ions of } NH_4Cl} + H_2O$$

In the gas phase, the proton is transferred directly from the HCl molecule to the NH_3 molecule.

FIG. 15.1 **The reaction of gaseous HCl with gaseous NH₃.** As each gas escapes from its concentrated aqueous solution and mingles with the other, a cloud of microcrystals of NH_4Cl forms above the bottles. *(Andy Washnik.)*

☐ We are using arrows to show how electrons shift and rearrange during the formation of the ions. The electron pair on the nitrogen atom of the NH_3 molecule binds to H^+ as it is removed from the electron pair in the H—Cl bond. The electron pair in the H—Cl bond shifts entirely to the Cl as the Cl^- ion is formed.

Electron pair in the bond becomes a lone pair on Cl as the chloride ion is formed.

Electron pair on N binds to a proton (H^+) as the proton separates from the electron pair of the H—Cl bond.

As ammonium ions and chloride ions form, they attract each other, gather, and settle as crystals of ammonium chloride.

The Brønsted-Lowry concept views acid–base reactions as proton transfers

Johannes Brønsted (1879–1947), a Danish chemist, and Thomas Lowry (1874–1936), a British scientist, realized that the important event in most acid–base reactions is simply the transfer of a proton from one species to another. Therefore, they redefined *acids* as species that donate protons and *bases* as species that accept protons. The heart of the *Brønsted–Lowry concept of acids and bases* is that *acid–base reactions are proton transfer reactions*. The definitions are therefore very simple.

---

[1] When the single electron is removed from a hydrogen atom, what remains is just the nucleus of the atom, which is a proton. Therefore, a hydrogen ion, H^+, consists of a proton, and the terms *proton* and *hydrogen ion* are often used interchangeably.

> **Brønsted–Lowry Definitions of Acids and Bases**[2]
>
> An **acid** is a proton donor.
>
> A **base** is a proton acceptor.

TOOLS
Brønsted-Lowry acids and bases

Accordingly, hydrogen chloride is an acid because when it reacts with ammonia, HCl molecules donate protons to NH_3 molecules. Similarly, ammonia is a base because NH_3 molecules accept protons.

Even when water is the solvent, chemists use the Brønsted–Lowry definitions more often than those of Arrhenius. Thus, the reaction between hydrogen chloride and water to form hydronium ion (H_3O^+) and chloride ion (Cl^-), which is another proton transfer reaction, is clearly a Brønsted–Lowry acid–base reaction. Molecules of HCl are the acid in this reaction, and water molecules are the base. HCl molecules collide with water molecules and protons transfer during the collisions.

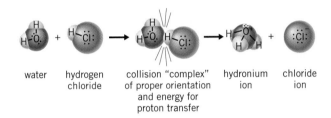

water   hydrogen   collision "complex"   hydronium   chloride
          chloride   of proper orientation   ion   ion
                      and energy for
                      proton transfer

Conjugate acids and bases differ by a single proton

Under the Brønsted–Lowry view, it is useful to consider any acid–base reaction as a chemical equilibrium, having both a forward and a reverse reaction. We first encountered a chemical equilibrium in a discussion of weak acids on page 142. Let's examine it again in the light of the Brønsted–Lowry definitions, using formic acid, $HCHO_2$, as an example. Formic acid is a weak acid, so we represent its ionization as a chemical equilibrium in which water is not just a solvent but also a chemical reactant, a proton acceptor.[3]

$$HCHO_2(aq) + H_2O \rightleftharpoons H_3O^+(aq) + CHO_2{}^-(aq)$$

In the forward reaction, a formic acid molecule donates a proton to the water molecule and changes to a formate ion, $CHO_2{}^-$ (see Figure 15.2a). Thus $HCHO_2$ behaves as a **Brønsted acid**, a **proton donor.** Because water accepts this proton from $HCHO_2$, water behaves as a **Brønsted base**, a **proton acceptor.**

Now let's look at the reverse reaction (see Figure 15.2b). In it, H_3O^+ behaves as a Brønsted acid because it donates a proton to the $CHO_2{}^-$ ion. The $CHO_2{}^-$ ion behaves as a Brønsted base by accepting the proton.

The equilibrium involving $HCHO_2$, H_2O, H_3O^+, and $CHO_2{}^-$ is typical of proton transfer equilibria in general, in that we can identify *two* acids (e.g., $HCHO_2$ and H_3O^+) and *two* bases (e.g., H_2O and $CHO_2{}^-$). Notice that in the aqueous formic acid equilibrium, the acid on the right of the arrows (H_3O^+) is formed from the base on the left (H_2O), and the base on the right ($CHO_2{}^-$) is formed from the acid on the left ($HCHO_2$).

$$\begin{array}{c} O \\ \parallel \\ H-O-C-H \end{array}$$

formic acid ($HCHO_2$)

Only the H in red is available
in an acid–base reaction.

$$\begin{array}{c} O \\ \parallel \\ {}^-O-C-H \end{array}$$

formate ion ($CHO_2{}^-$)

---

[2] Although Brønsted and Lowry are both credited with defining acids and bases in terms of proton transfer, Brønsted carried the concepts further. For the sake of brevity, we will often use the terms *Brønsted acid* and *Brønsted base* when referring to the substances involved in proton transfer reactions.

[3] Just as we have represented acetic acid as $HC_2H_3O_2$, placing the ionizable or acidic hydrogen first (as we do in HCl or HNO_3), so we give the formula of formic acid as $HCHO_2$ and the formula of the formate ion as $CHO_2{}^-$. As the chemical structure shows, however, the acidic hydrogen in formic acid resides on O, not on C. Many chemists prefer to write formic acid as HCO_2H or $HCOOH$.

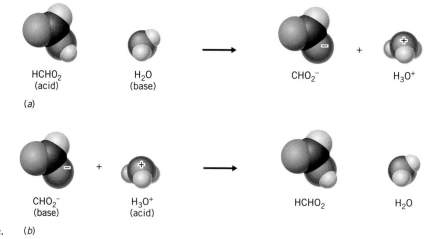

(a)

(b)

FIG. 15.2 **Brønsted acids and bases in aqueous formic acid.** (*a*) Formic acid transfers a proton to a water molecule. HCHO₂ is the acid and H₂O is the base. (*b*) When hydronium ion transfers a proton to the CHO₂⁻ ion, H₃O⁺ is the acid and CHO₂⁻ is the base.

Conjugate acids and bases differ by one proton, H⁺

☐ Notice how the conjugate acid always has one more H⁺ than the conjugate base.

A Brønsted–Lowry acid–base equilibrium has two acid–base pairs

Two substances that differ from each other only by one proton are referred to as a **conjugate acid–base pair.** Thus, H_3O^+ and H_2O are such a pair; they are alike except that H_3O^+ has one more proton than H_2O. One member of the pair is called the **conjugate acid** because it is the proton donor of the two. The other member is the **conjugate base,** because it is the pair's proton acceptor. We say that *H_3O^+ is the conjugate acid of H_2O, and H_2O is the conjugate base of H_3O^+.* Notice that *the acid member of the pair has one more H^+ than the base member.*

The pair $HCHO_2$ and CHO_2^- is the other conjugate acid–base pair in the aqueous formic acid equilibrium. $HCHO_2$ has one more H^+ than CHO_2^-, so the conjugate acid of CHO_2^- is $HCHO_2$; the conjugate base of $HCHO_2$ is CHO_2^-. One way to highlight the two members of a conjugate acid–base pair in an equilibrium equation is to connect them by a line.

$$\overbrace{HCHO_2}^{} \ + \ H_2O \ \rightleftharpoons \ H_3O^+ \ + \ CHO_2^-$$

conjugate pair

$$\underset{\text{acid}}{HCHO_2} \ + \ \underset{\text{base}}{H_2O} \ \rightleftharpoons \ \underset{\text{acid}}{H_3O^+} \ + \ \underset{\text{base}}{CHO_2^-}$$

conjugate pair

In any Brønsted–Lowry acid–base equilibrium, there are invariably *two* conjugate acid–base pairs. It is important that you learn how to pick them out of an equation by inspection and to write them from formulas.

EXAMPLE 15.1
Determining the Formulas of Conjugate Acids and Bases

What is the conjugate base of nitric acid, HNO_3, and what is the conjugate acid of the hydrogen sulfate ion, HSO_4^-?

ANALYSIS: The first tool in this chapter says that members of any conjugate acid–base pair differ by one H^+, with the member having the greater number of hydrogens being the acid. We are asked to find the conjugate base of HNO_3, so HNO_3 must be the acid member of the pair. To find the formula of the base, we remove one H^+ from the acid, HNO_3. This is equivalent to removing one hydrogen from the acid and decreasing its positive charge by one unit (or, increasing the negative charge by one unit).

We are also asked to find the conjugate acid of HSO_4^-, so HSO_4^- must be the base member of an acid–base pair. To find the formula of the acid, we add one H^+ to the base, which is equivalent to adding one hydrogen to the formula of the base and increasing its positive charge (or decreasing its negative charge) by one unit.

SOLUTION: Removing one H^+ (both the atom and the charge) from HNO_3 leaves NO_3^-. The nitrate ion, NO_3^-, is thus the conjugate base of HNO_3. Adding an H^+ to HSO_4^- gives its conjugate acid, H_2SO_4. (Notice that the charge goes from $1-$ to zero because we've added the positively charged H^+.)

ARE THE ANSWERS REASONABLE? As a check, we can quickly compare the two formulas in each pair.

$$HNO_3 \quad NO_3^-$$
$$H_2SO_4 \quad HSO_4^-$$

In each case, the formula on the right has one less H^+ than the one on the left, so it is the conjugate base. We've answered the question correctly.

Practice Exercise 1: Which of the following are conjugate acid–base pairs? Describe why the others are not true conjugate acid–base pairs. (a) H_3PO_4 and $H_2PO_4^-$, (b) HI and H^+, (c) NH_2^- and NH_3, (d) HNO_2 and NH_4^+, (e) CO_3^{2-} and CN^-, (f) HPO_4^{2-} and $H_2PO_4^-$ (Hint: Recall that conjugate acid–base pairs must differ by one H^+.)

Practice Exercise 2: Write the formula of the conjugate base for each of the following Brønsted acids. (a) H_2O, (b) HI, (c) HNO_2, (d) H_3PO_4, (e) $H_2PO_4^-$, (f) HPO_4^{2-}, (g) H_2S, (h) NH_4^+

Practice Exercise 3: Write the formula of the conjugate acid for each of the following Brønsted bases. (a) HO_2^-, (b) SO_4^{2-}, (c) CO_3^{2-}, (d) CN^-, (e) NH_2^-, (f) NH_3, (g) $H_2PO_4^-$, (h) HPO_4^{2-}

EXAMPLE 15.2

Identifying Conjugate Acid–Base Pairs in a Brønsted–Lowry Acid–Base Reaction

The anion of sodium hydrogen sulfate, HSO_4^-, reacts as follows with the phosphate ion, PO_4^{3-}.

$$HSO_4^-(aq) + PO_4^{3-}(aq) \longrightarrow SO_4^{2-}(aq) + HPO_4^{2-}(aq)$$

Identify the two conjugate acid–base pairs.

ANALYSIS: There are two things to look for in identifying the conjugate acid–base pairs in an equation. One is our tool that reminds us that the members of a conjugate pair are alike except for the number of hydrogens and charge. The second is the tool that the members of each pair must be on opposite sides of the arrow in the Brønsted–Lowry acid–base equation. In each pair, of course, the acid is the one with the greater number of hydrogens.

SOLUTION: Two of the formulas in the equation contain "PO_4," so they must belong to the same conjugate pair. The one with the greater number of hydrogens, HPO_4^{2-}, must be the Brønsted acid, and the other, PO_4^{3-}, must be the Brønsted base. Therefore, one conjugate acid–base pair is HPO_4^{2-} and PO_4^{3-}. The other two ions, HSO_4^- and SO_4^{2-}, belong to the second conjugate acid–base pair; HSO_4^- is the conjugate acid and SO_4^{2-} is the conjugate base.

$$\overbrace{HSO_4^-(aq)}^{\text{acid}} + \overbrace{PO_4^{3-}(aq)}^{\text{base}} \longrightarrow \overbrace{SO_4^{2-}(aq)}^{\text{base}} + \overbrace{HPO_4^{2-}(aq)}^{\text{acid}}$$

conjugate pair

□ Sodium hydrogen sulfate (also called sodium bisulfate) is used in the manufacture of certain kinds of cement and to clean oxide coatings from metals.

IS THE ANSWER REASONABLE? A check satisfies us that we have fulfilled the requirements that each conjugate pair has one member on one side of the arrow and the other member on the opposite side of the arrow and that the members of each pair differ from each other by one (and *only* one) H^+.

Practice Exercise 4: Sodium cyanide solution, when poured into excess hydrochloric acid, releases hydrogen cyanide as a gas. The reaction is

$$NaCN(aq) + HCl(aq) \longrightarrow HCN(g) + NaCl(aq)$$

Identify the conjugate acid–base pairs in this reaction. (Hint: It may be more obvious if the spectator ions are removed.)

Practice Exercise 5: One kind of baking powder contains sodium bicarbonate and calcium dihydrogen phosphate. When water is added, a reaction occurs by the following net ionic equation.

$$HCO_3^-(aq) + H_2PO_4^-(aq) \longrightarrow H_2CO_3(aq) + HPO_4^{2-}(aq)$$

Identify the two Brønsted acids and the two Brønsted bases in this reaction. (The H_2CO_3 decomposes to release CO_2, which causes the cake batter to rise.)

Practice Exercise 6: When some of the strong cleaning agent "trisodium phosphate" is mixed with household vinegar, which contains acetic acid, the following equilibrium is one of the many that are established. (The position of equilibrium lies to the right.) Identify the pairs of conjugate acids and bases.

$$PO_4^{3-}(aq) + HC_2H_3O_2(aq) \rightleftharpoons HPO_4^{2-}(aq) + C_2H_3O_2^-(aq)$$

Amphoteric substances can behave as either acids or bases

Some molecules or ions are able to function either as an acid or as a base, depending on the kind of substance mixed with them. For example, in its reaction with hydrogen chloride, water behaves as a *base* because it *accepts* a proton from the HCl molecule.

$$\underset{\text{base}}{H_2O} + \underset{\text{acid}}{HCl(g)} \longrightarrow H_3O^+(aq) + Cl^-(aq)$$

On the other hand, water behaves as an *acid* when it reacts with the weak base ammonia.

$$\underset{\text{acid}}{H_2O} + \underset{\text{base}}{NH_3(aq)} \rightleftharpoons NH_4^+(aq) + OH^-(aq)$$

Here, H_2O *donates* a proton to NH_3 in the forward reaction.

A substance that can be either an acid or a base depending on the other substance present is said to be **amphoteric.** Another term is **amphiprotic** to stress that the *proton* donating or accepting ability is of central concern.

□ From the Greek *amphoteros,* "partly one and partly the other."

Amphoteric or amphiprotic substances may be either molecules or ions. For example, anions of acid salts, such as the bicarbonate ion of baking soda, are amphoteric. The HCO_3^- ion can either donate a proton to a base or accept a proton from an acid. Thus, toward the hydroxide ion, the bicarbonate ion is an acid; it donates its proton to OH^-.

$$\underset{\text{acid}}{HCO_3^-(aq)} + \underset{\text{base}}{OH^-(aq)} \longrightarrow CO_3^{2-}(aq) + H_2O$$

Toward hydronium ion, however, HCO_3^- is a base; it accepts a proton from H_3O^+.

$$\underset{\text{base}}{HCO_3^-(aq)} + \underset{\text{acid}}{H_3O^+(aq)} \longrightarrow H_2CO_3(aq) + H_2O$$

[Recall that H_2CO_3 (carbonic acid) almost entirely decomposes to $CO_2(g)$ and water as it forms.]

Practice Exercise 7: Which of the following are amphoteric and which are not? Provide reasons for your decisions. (a) $H_2PO_4^-$, (b) HPO_4^{2-}, (c) H_2S, (d) H_3PO_4, (e) NH_4^+, (f) H_2O, (g) HI, (h) HNO_2 (Hint: Amphoteric substances must be able to provide an H^+ and also react with an H^+.)

Practice Exercise 8: The anion of sodium monohydrogen phosphate, Na_2HPO_4, is amphoteric. Using H_3O^+ and OH^-, write net ionic equations that illustrate this property.

15.2 | STRENGTHS OF BRØNSTED ACIDS AND BASES FOLLOW PERIODIC TRENDS

Brønsted acids and bases have differing abilities to lose or gain protons. In this section we examine how these abilities can be compared and how we can anticipate differences according to the locations of key elements in the periodic table.

Acid and base strengths are measured relative to a standard

When we speak of the strength of a Brønsted acid, we are referring to its ability to donate a proton to a base. We measure this by determining the extent to which the reaction of the acid with the base proceeds toward completion—the more complete the reaction, the stronger the acid. To compare the strengths of a series of acids, we have to select some reference base, and because we are interested most in reactions in aqueous media, that base is usually water (although other reference bases could be chosen).

In Chapter 4 we discussed strong and weak acids from the Arrhenius point of view, and much of what we said there applies when the same acids are studied using the Brønsted–Lowry concept. Thus, acids such as HCl and HNO_3 react completely with water to give H_3O^+ because they are strong proton donors. Hence, we classify them as *strong Brønsted acids*. On the other hand, acids such as HNO_2 (nitrous acid) and $HC_2H_3O_2$ (acetic acid) are much weaker proton donors. Their reactions with water are far from complete and we classify them as *weak acids*.

In a similar manner, the relative strengths of Brønsted *bases* are assigned according to their abilities to accept and bind protons. Once again, to compare strengths, we have to choose a standard acid. Because water is amphiprotic, it can also serve as the standard acid. Substances that are powerful proton acceptors, such as the oxide ion, react completely and are considered to be *strong Brønsted bases*.

$$O^{2-} + H_2O \xrightarrow{100\%} 2OH^-$$

Weaker proton acceptors, such as ammonia, undergo incomplete reactions with water; we classify them *weak bases*.

Hydronium ion and hydroxide ion are the strongest acid and base that can exist in the presence of water

Both HCl and HNO_3 are very powerful proton donors. When placed in water they react completely, losing their protons to water molecules to yield H_3O^+ ions. Representing them by the general formula HA, we have

$$\underset{\text{acid}}{HA} + \underset{\text{base}}{H_2O} \xrightarrow{100\%} \underset{\text{acid}}{H_3O^+} + \underset{\text{base}}{A^-}$$

Because both reactions go to completion, we really can't tell which of the two, HCl or HNO_3, is actually the better proton donor (stronger acid). This would require a reference base less willing than water to accept protons. In water, both HCl and HNO_3 are converted quantitatively to another acid, H_3O^+. The conclusion, therefore, is that *H_3O^+ is the strongest acid we will ever find in an aqueous solution*, because stronger acids react completely with water to give H_3O^+.

A similar conclusion is reached regarding hydroxide ion. We noted that the strong Brønsted base O^{2-} reacts completely with water to give OH^-. Another very powerful proton acceptor is the amide ion, NH_2^-, which also reacts completely with water.

$$NH_2^- + H_2O \xrightarrow{100\%} NH_3 + OH^-$$

$$\text{base} \qquad \text{acid} \qquad\qquad \text{acid} \qquad \text{base}$$

Using water as the reference acid, we can't tell which is the better proton acceptor, O^{2-} or NH_2^-, because both react completely, being replaced by another base, OH^-. Therefore, we can say that *OH^- is the strongest base we will ever find in an aqueous solution*, because stronger bases react completely with water to give OH^-.

Comparing the acid–base strengths of conjugate pairs

As we noted earlier, the chemical equation for the equilibrium present in an aqueous solution of a weak acid actually shows two acids. One is almost always stronger than the other, and the position of the equilibrium tells us which of the two acids is stronger. Let's see how this works using the acetic acid equilibrium, in which the position of equilibrium lies to the left.

$$HC_2H_3O_2(aq) + H_2O \rightleftharpoons H_3O^+(aq) + C_2H_3O_2^-(aq)$$

$$\text{acid} \qquad\qquad \text{base} \qquad\qquad \text{acid} \qquad\qquad \text{base}$$

The two Brønsted acids in this equilibrium are $HC_2H_3O_2$ and H_3O^+, and it's helpful to think of them as competing with each other in donating protons to acceptors. The fact that nearly all potential protons stay on the $HC_2H_3O_2$ molecules, and only a relative few spend their time on the H_3O^+ ions, means that the *hydronium ion is a better proton donor than the acetic acid molecule.* Thus, the hydronium ion is a stronger Brønsted acid than acetic acid, and we inferred this relative acidity from the position of equilibrium.

The acetic acid equilibrium also has two bases, $C_2H_3O_2^-$ and H_2O. Both compete for any available protons. But at equilibrium, most of the protons originally carried by acetic acid are still found on $HC_2H_3O_2$ molecules; relatively few are joined to H_2O in the form of H_3O^+ ions. This means that *acetate ions must be more effective than water molecules at obtaining and holding protons from proton donors.* This is the same as saying that the acetate ion is a stronger base than the water molecule. So this illustrates a relative basicity that we are able to infer from the position of the acetic acid equilibrium.

Notice what our discussion of the two conjugate pairs in the acetic acid equilibrium has brought out. Both the weaker of the two acids and the weaker of the two bases are found on the same side of the equation, which is the side favored by the position of equilibrium.

TOOLS

Relative strengths of conjugate acids and bases are related to the position of equilibrium

> *The position of an acid–base equilibrium favors the weaker acid and base.*

$$HC_2H_3O_2(aq) + H_2O \rightleftharpoons H_3O^+(aq) + C_2H_3O_2^-(aq)$$

$$\text{weaker acid} \qquad \text{weaker base} \qquad \text{stronger acid} \qquad \text{stronger base}$$

$\longleftarrow$ | *Position of equilibrium lies to the left, in favor of the weaker acid and base.*

There's a reciprocal relationship within a conjugate acid–base pair

One aid in predicting the relative strengths of acids and bases is the existence of a reciprocal relationship.

TOOLS

A strong Brønsted acid has a weak conjugate base

> *The stronger a Brønsted acid is, the weaker is its conjugate base.*

To illustrate, recall that $HCl(g)$ is a very strong Brønsted acid; it's 100% ionized in a dilute aqueous solution.

$$HCl(g) + H_2O \xrightarrow{100\%} H_3O^+(aq) + Cl^-(aq)$$

As we explained in Chapter 4, we don't write double equilibrium arrows for the ionization of a strong acid. Not doing so with HCl is another way of saying that the chloride ion, the conjugate base of HCl, must be a very weak Brønsted base. Even in the presence of H_3O^+, a very strong proton donor, chloride ions aren't able to win protons. So HCl, the strong acid, has a particularly weak conjugate base, Cl^-.

There's a matching reciprocal relationship.

> *The weaker a Brønsted acid is, the stronger is its conjugate base.*

TOOLS

A strong Brønsted base has a weak conjugate acid

Consider, for example, the conjugate pair OH^- and O^{2-}. The hydroxide ion is the conjugate acid and the oxide ion is the conjugate base. But the hydroxide ion must be an *extremely* weak Brønsted acid; in fact, we've known it so far only as a base. Given the extraordinary weakness of OH^- as an acid, its conjugate base, the oxide ion, must be an exceptionally strong base. And as you've already learned, oxide ion is such a strong base that its reaction with water is 100% complete. That's why we don't write double equilibrium arrows in the equation for the reaction.

$$O^{2-} + H_2O \xrightarrow{100\%} OH^- + OH^-$$

base acid   acid base

The very strong base O^{2-} has
a very weak conjugate acid, OH^-.

An amphoteric substance will act as a base if reacted with an acid but it will act as an acid if mixed with a base. You might ask, if two amphoteric substances are mixed together which will act as the acid and which as the base? The obvious answer is that the stronger acid will act as the acid and the other will be the base. To discover the stronger acid, consider the following reaction

$$H_2S(aq) + HCO_3^-(aq) \rightleftharpoons HS^-(aq) + H_2CO_3(aq)$$

where the position of equilibrium lies to the left (with the reactants). This is interpreted as meaning that $HCO_3^-(aq)$ is a weaker base than $HS^-(aq)$. Therefore, when we mix the two together the reaction will be

$$HS^-(aq) + HCO_3^-(aq) \longrightarrow H_2S(aq) + CO_3^{2-}(aq)$$

because the stronger base, $HS^-(aq)$, will remove the H^+ from the weaker base HCO_3^-.

EXAMPLE 15.3

Using Reciprocal Relationships to Predict Equilibrium Positions

In the reaction below, will the position of equilibrium lie to the left or to the right, given the fact that acetic acid is known to be a stronger acid than the hydrogen sulfite ion?

$$HSO_3^-(aq) + C_2H_3O_2^-(aq) \rightleftharpoons HC_2H_3O_2(aq) + SO_3^{2-}(aq)$$

ANALYSIS: We just learned that the position of an acid–base equilibrium favors the weaker acid and base. That's the tool we need to solve this problem. We have to identify which acid and base make up the weaker set. When we do this, we'll have discovered which substances make up the stronger set, and we can then predict where the position of equilibrium will lie.

SOLUTION: We'll write the equilibrium equation using the given fact about the relative strengths of acetic acid and the hydrogen sulfite ion to start writing labels.

$$HSO_3^-(aq) + C_2H_3O_2^-(aq) \rightleftharpoons HC_2H_3O_2(aq) + SO_3^{2-}(aq)$$

weaker acid   stronger acid

Now we'll use our tool about the reciprocal relationships to label the two bases. The stronger acid must have the weaker conjugate base; the weaker acid must have the stronger conjugate base.

$$HSO_3^-(aq) + C_2H_3O_2^-(aq) \rightleftharpoons HC_2H_3O_2(aq) + SO_3^{2-}(aq)$$

weaker acid   weaker base   stronger acid   stronger base

Finally, because the position of equilibrium favors the weaker acid and base, the position of equilibrium lies to the left.

IS THE ANSWER REASONABLE? There are two things we can check. First, both of the weaker conjugates should be on the same side of the equation. They are, so that suggests we've made the correct assignments. Second, the reaction will proceed farther in the direction of the weaker acid and base, so that places the position of equilibrium on the left, which agrees with our answer.

Practice Exercise 9: Given that HSO_4^- is a stronger acid than HPO_4^{2-}, what is the chemical reaction if solutions containing those ions are mixed together? (Hint: One of these must be an acid and the other a base.)

Practice Exercise 10: Given that HSO_4^- is a stronger acid than HPO_4^{2-}, determine whether the substances on the left of the arrows or those on the right are favored in the following equilibrium.

$$HSO_4^-(aq) + PO_4^{3-}(aq) \rightleftharpoons SO_4^{2-}(aq) + HPO_4^{2-}(aq)$$

Periodic trends exist in the strengths of binary acids

Many of the binary compounds between hydrogen and nonmetals, which we may represent by HX, H_2X, H_3X, etc., are acidic and are called **binary acids.** HCl is a common example, but Table 15.1 lists the others that are acids in water. The strong acids are marked by asterisks.

TABLE 15.1	**Acidic Binary Compounds of Hydrogen and Nonmetals**[a]
Group VIA	
(H_2O)	
H_2S	Hydrosulfuric acid
H_2Se	Hydroselenic acid
H_2Te	Hydrotelluric acid
Group VIIA	
HF	Hydrofluoric acid
*HCl	Hydrochloric acid
*HBr	Hydrobromic acid
*HI	Hydriodic acid

[a] The *names* are for the aqueous solutions of these compounds. Strong acids are marked with asterisks.

The relative strengths of binary acids correlate with the periodic table in two ways.

> The strengths of the binary acids increase from left to right within the same period.
>
> The strengths of binary acids increase from top to bottom within the same group.

TOOLS

Strengths of binary acids correlate to the periodic table

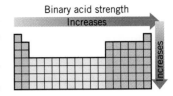

First, as we go left to right within a period, the increase in electronegativities causes the corresponding H—X bonds to become more polar, making the partial positive charge ($\delta+$) on H greater. This makes it easier for the hydrogen to separate as H$^+$, so the molecule becomes a better proton donor. For example, as we go from S to Cl in Period 3, the electronegativity increases and we find that HCl is a stronger acid than H$_2$S. A similar increase in electronegativity occurs going left to right in Period 2, from O to F, and HF is a stronger acid than H$_2$O.

Second, binary acids become stronger from the top of a group to the bottom. Among the binary acids of the halogens, for example, the following is the order of relative acidity.[4]

$$HF \;<\; HCl \;<\; HBr \;<\; HI$$

Thus, HF is the weakest acid in the series, and HI is the strongest. The identical trend occurs in the series of the binary acids of Group VIA elements, having formulas of the general type H$_2$X. These trends in acidity are opposite what we would expect on the basis of trends in electronegativities, which tell us that the H—F bond is more polar than the H—I bond and that the O—H bond is more polar than the H—S bond.

In understanding the proton donating ability of an acid, one of the most important factors to consider is the strength of the H—X bond. Breaking this bond is essential for the hydrogen to separate as an H$^+$ ion, so anything that contributes to variations in bond strength will also impact variations in acid strength.

In general, small atoms tend to form stronger bonds than large atoms. Moving horizontally within a period, atomic size varies relatively little, so the strengths of the H—X bonds are nearly the same. As a result, the most significant influence on acid strength is variations in the polarity of the H—X bonds. Descending a group, however, there is a significant increase in atomic size from one element to the next, which is accompanied by a rapid decrease in the H—X bond strength. Apparently, this more than compensates for the decrease in the polarity of the H—X bonds, and the molecules become better able to release protons as we go down a group. The net effect of the two opposing factors, therefore, is an increase in the strengths of the binary acids as we go from top to bottom in a group.

Practice Exercise 11: Order the following groups of acids from the weakest to the strongest. (a) HI, HF, HBr, (b) HCl, PH$_3$, H$_2$S, (c) H$_2$Te, H$_2$O, H$_2$Se, (d) AsH$_3$, HBr, H$_2$Se, (e) HI, PH$_3$, H$_2$Se (Hint: These are all binary acids.)

Practice Exercise 12: Using *only* the periodic table, choose the stronger acid of each pair. (a) H$_2$Se or HBr, (b) H$_2$Se or H$_2$Te, (c) H$_2$O or H$_2$S

Trends exist in the strengths of oxoacids

Acids composed of hydrogen, oxygen, and some other element are called **oxoacids** (see Table 15.2). Those that are strong acids in water are marked in the table by asterisks.

---

[4] We compare acid strengths by the acid's ability to donate a proton to a particular base. As we noted earlier, for strong acids such as HCl, HBr, and HI, water is too strong a proton acceptor to permit us to see differences among their proton-donating abilities. All three of these acids are completely ionized in water and so appear to be of equal strength, a phenomenon called the *leveling effect* (the differences are obscured or *leveled* out). To compare the acidities of these acids, a solvent that is a weaker proton acceptor than water (HF or HC$_2$H$_3$O$_2$, for example) has to be used.

TABLE 15.2	Some Oxoacids of Nonmetals and Metalloids[a]		
Group IVA	Group VA	Group VIA	Group VIIA
H_2CO_3 Carbonic acid	*HNO_3 Nitric acid		HFO Hypofluorous acid
	HNO_2 Nitrous acid		
	H_3PO_4 Phosphoric acid	*H_2SO_4 Sulfuric acid	*$HClO_4$ Perchloric acid
	H_3PO_3 Phosphorous acid[b]	H_2SO_3 Sulfurous acid[c]	*$HClO_3$ Chloric acid
			$HClO_2$ Chlorous acid
			HClO Hypochlorous acid
	H_3AsO_4 Arsenic acid	*H_2SeO_4 Selenic acid	*$HBrO_4$ Perbromic acid[d]
	H_3AsO_3 Arsenous acid	H_2SeO_3 Selenous acid	*$HBrO_3$ Bromic acid
			HIO_4 Periodic acid (H_5IO_6)[e]
			HIO_3 Iodic acid

[a]Strong acids are marked with asterisks.
[b]Phosphorous acid, despite its formula, is only a diprotic acid.
[c]Hypothetical. An aqueous solution actually contains just dissolved sulfur dioxide, $SO_2(aq)$.
[d]Pure perbromic acid is unstable; a dihydrate is known.
[e]H_5IO_6 is formed from $HIO_4 + 2H_2O$.

A feature common to the structures of all oxoacids is the presence of O—H groups bonded to some central atom. For example, the structures of two oxoacids of the Group VIA elements are

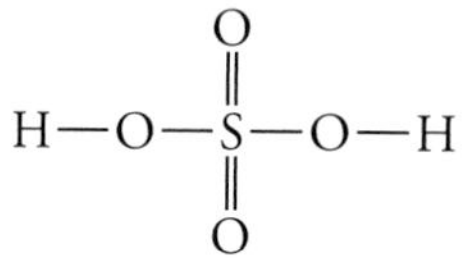

H_2SO_4
sulfuric acid

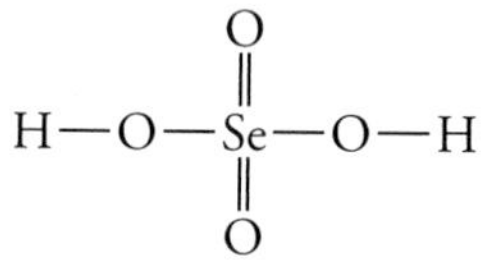

H_2SeO_4
selenic acid

When an oxoacid ionizes, the hydrogen that's lost as an H^+ comes from the same kind of bond in every instance, specifically, an O—H bond. The "acidity" of such a hydrogen, meaning the ease with which it's released as H^+, is determined by how the group of atoms attached to the oxygen affects the polarity of the O—H bond. If this group of atoms makes the O—H bond more polar, it will cause the H to come off more easily as H^+ and thereby increase the acidity of the molecule.

$$G—O—H$$

If the group of atoms, G, attached to the O—H group is able to draw electron density from the O atom, the O will pull electron density from the O—H bond, thereby making the bond more polar.

It turns out that there are two principal factors that determine how the polarity of the O—H bond is affected. One is the electronegativity of the central atom in the oxoacid and the other is the number of oxygens attached to the central atom.

The electronegativity of the central atom affects the acidity of an oxoacid
To study the effects of the electronegativity of the central atom, we must compare oxoacids having the same number of oxygens. When we do this, we find that as the electronegativity

of the central atom increases, the oxoacid becomes a better proton donor (i.e., a stronger acid). The following diagram illustrates the effect.

$$-\overset{|}{\underset{|}{X}}-\overset{\delta-}{O}-\overset{\delta+}{H}$$

As the electronegativity of X increases, electron density is drawn away from O, which draws electron density away from the O—H bond. This makes the bond more polar and makes the molecule a better proton donor.

Because electronegativity increases from bottom to top within a group and from left to right within a period, we can make the following generalization.

When the central atoms of oxoacids hold the same number of oxygen atoms, the acid strength increases from bottom to top within a group and from left to right within a period.

In Group VIA, for example, H_2SO_4 is a stronger acid than H_2SeO_4 because sulfur is more electronegative than selenium. Similarly, among the halogens, acid strength increases for acids with the formula HXO_4 as follows

$$HIO_4 \; < \; HBrO_4 \; < \; HClO_4$$

Going from left to right within Period 3, we can compare the acids H_3PO_4, H_2SO_4, and $HClO_4$, where we find the following order of acidities.

$$H_3PO_4 \; < \; H_2SO_4 \; < \; HClO_4$$

TOOLS

Strengths of oxoacids correlate to the periodic table

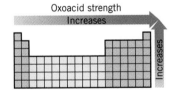

Practice Exercise 13: Which is the stronger acid? (a) $HClO_3$ or $HBrO_3$, (b) H_3PO_4 or H_2SO_4 (Hint: Note that each pair has the same number of oxygen atoms.)

Practice Exercise 14: In each pair indicate the weaker acid. (a) H_3PO_4 or H_3AsO_4, (b) HIO_4 or H_2TeO_4

The number of oxygens affects the acidity of an oxoacid

Comparing oxoacids with the same central atom, we find that as the number of *lone oxygens* increases, the oxoacid becomes a better proton donor. (A *lone oxygen* is one that is bonded only to the central atom and not to a hydrogen.) Thus, comparing HNO_3 with HNO_2, we find that HNO_3 is the stronger acid. To understand why, let's look at their molecular structures.

nitrous acid   nitric acid

In an oxoacid, lone oxygens pull electron density away from the central atom, which increases the central atom's ability to draw electron density away from the O—H bond. It's as though the lone oxygens make the central atom more electronegative. Therefore, the more lone oxygens that are attached to a central atom, the more polar will be the O—H bonds of the acid and the stronger will be the acid. Thus, the two lone oxygens in HNO_3 produce a greater effect than the one lone oxygen in HNO_2, so HNO_3 is the stronger acid.

Similar effects are seen among other oxoacids, as well. For the oxoacids of chlorine, for instance, we find this trend.

$$HClO \; < \; HClO_2 \; < \; HClO_3 \; < \; HClO_4$$

☐ Oxygen is a very electronegative element and has a strong tendency to pull electron density away from any atom to which it is attached in an oxoacid.

Comparing their structures, we have

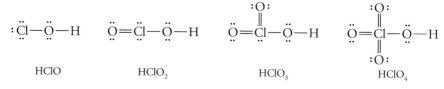

$\quad$ HClO $\qquad\qquad$ HClO$_2$ $\qquad\qquad\qquad$ HClO$_3$ $\qquad\qquad\qquad$ HClO$_4$

☐ Usually, the formula for hypochlorous acid is written HOCl. We've written it as HClO here to make it easier to follow the trend in acid strengths among the oxoacids of chlorine.

This leads to another generalization.

TOOLS

Strengths of oxo acids depend on lone oxygens

> For a given central atom, the acid strength of an oxoacid increases with the number of oxygens held by the central atom.

$\quad$ The ability of lone oxygens to affect acid strength extends to organic compounds as well. For example, compare the molecules below.

$$
\underset{\text{ethanol}}{\text{H}-\overset{\overset{\displaystyle\text{H}}{|}}{\underset{\underset{\displaystyle\text{H}}{|}}{\text{C}}}-\overset{\overset{\displaystyle\text{H}}{|}}{\underset{\underset{\displaystyle\text{H}}{|}}{\text{C}}}-\text{O}-\text{H}}
\qquad\qquad
\underset{\text{acetic acid}}{\text{H}-\overset{\overset{\displaystyle\text{H}}{|}}{\underset{\underset{\displaystyle\text{H}}{|}}{\text{C}}}-\overset{\overset{\displaystyle\text{O}}{\|}}{\text{C}}-\text{O}-\text{H}}
$$

In water, ethanol (ethyl alcohol) is not acidic at all. Replacing the two hydrogens on the carbon adjacent to the OH group with an oxygen, however, yields acetic acid. The greater ability of oxygen to pull electron density from the carbon produces a greater polarity of the O—H bond, which is one factor that causes acetic acid to be a better proton donor than ethanol.

Delocalization of negative charge to the lone oxygens affects the basicity of the anion of an oxoacid

Earlier we noted the reciprocal relationship between the strength of an acid and that of its conjugate base. For oxoacids, the lone oxygens play a part in determining the basicity of the anion formed in the ionization reaction. Consider the acids HClO$_3$ and HClO$_4$.

$$
\underset{\text{HClO}_3}{\text{H}-\text{O}-\overset{\overset{\displaystyle\text{O}}{\|}}{\text{Cl}}=\text{O}}
\qquad\qquad
\underset{\text{HClO}_4}{\text{H}-\text{O}-\overset{\overset{\displaystyle\text{O}}{\|}}{\underset{\underset{\displaystyle\text{O}}{\|}}{\text{Cl}}}=\text{O}}
$$

From our earlier discussion, we expect HClO$_4$ to be a stronger acid than HClO$_3$, which it is. Ionizations of their protons yield the anions ClO$_3^-$ and ClO$_4^-$.

$$
\underset{\text{ClO}_3^-}{\left[\text{O}-\overset{\overset{\displaystyle\text{O}}{\|}}{\text{Cl}}=\text{O}\right]^-}
\qquad\qquad
\underset{\text{ClO}_4^-}{\left[\text{O}-\overset{\overset{\displaystyle\text{O}}{\|}}{\underset{\underset{\displaystyle\text{O}}{\|}}{\text{Cl}}}=\text{O}\right]^-}
$$

☐ The concept of delocalization of electrons to provide stability was presented in Section 9.8.

In an **oxoanion** (an anion formed from an oxoacid) the negative charge is delocalized over the oxygens. In the ClO$_3^-$ ion, the single negative charge is spread over three oxygens, so each carries a charge of about $\frac{1}{3}-$. This is not a *formal* charge obtained by the rules on page 322. We're only saying that the charge of 1$-$ is delocalized over three oxygens to give each a charge of $\frac{1}{3}-$. By the same reasoning, in the ClO$_4^-$ ion each oxygen carries a charge of about $\frac{1}{4}-$. The smaller negative charge on the oxygens in ClO$_4^-$ makes this ion less able than ClO$_3^-$ to attract H$^+$ ions from H$_3$O$^+$, so ClO$_4^-$ is a weaker base than ClO$_3^-$. Thus, the anion of the stronger acid is the weaker base.

Practice Exercise 15: In each pair, select the stronger acid: (a) HIO_3 or HIO_4, (b) H_2TeO_3 or H_2TeO_4, (c) H_3AsO_3 or H_3AsO_4. (Hint: This problem focuses on the effect of oxygen atoms in acids.)

Practice Exercise 16: In each pair select the weaker acid: (a) H_2SO_4 or $HClO_4$, (b) H_3AsO_4 or H_2SO_4.

Other groups also affect the strength of organic acids

Acetic acid and most organic acids are characterized by the $-COOH$ functional group. The delocalization of the electron on the $-COO^-$ stabilizes the anion after the H^+ ionizes. If other electronegative groups such as halogens are bonded to carbon atoms near the $-COOH$ group, they increase the strength of the acid. As a result, chloroacetic acid is a stronger acid than acetic acid. Dichloroacetic acid and trichloroacetic acids are increasingly stronger acids.

$$CH_3COOH \ < \ CH_2ClCOOH \ < \ CHCl_2COOH \ < \ CCl_3COOH$$

Addition of each chlorine effectively withdraws more electron density from the $-O-H$ bond, resulting in a weaker bond and a stronger acid.

15.3 | LEWIS ACIDS AND BASES INVOLVE COORDINATE COVALENT BONDS

In our preceding discussions, acids and bases have been characterized by their tendency to lose or gain protons. However, there are many reactions not involving proton transfer that have properties we associate with acid–base reactions. For example, if gaseous SO_3 is passed over solid CaO, a reaction occurs in which $CaSO_4$ forms.

$$CaO(s) + SO_3(g) \longrightarrow CaSO_4(s) \qquad (15.1)$$

If these reactants are dissolved in water first, they react to form $Ca(OH)_2$ and H_2SO_4, and when their solutions are mixed the following reaction takes place.

$$Ca(OH)_2(aq) + H_2SO_4(aq) \longrightarrow CaSO_4(s) + 2H_2O \qquad (15.2)$$

The same two initial reactants, CaO and SO_3, form the same ultimate product, $CaSO_4$. It certainly seems that if Reaction 15.2 is an acid–base reaction, we should be able to consider Reaction 15.1 to be an acid–base reaction, too. But there are no protons being transferred, so our definitions require further generalizations. These were provided by G. N. Lewis, after whom Lewis symbols are named.

▢ Remember, a coordinate covalent bond is just like any other covalent bond once it has formed. By using this term, we are following the origin of the electron pair that forms the bond.

Lewis Definitions of Acids and Bases

1. A **Lewis acid** is any ionic or molecular species that can accept a pair of electrons in the formation of a coordinate covalent bond.
2. A **Lewis base** is any ionic or molecular species that can donate a pair of electrons in the formation of a coordinate covalent bond.
3. **Neutralization** is the formation of a coordinate covalent bond between the donor (base) and the acceptor (acid).

TOOLS

Lewis acids and bases

Examples of Lewis acid–base reactions

The reaction between BF_3 and NH_3 illustrates a Lewis acid–base neutralization. The reaction is exothermic because a bond is formed between N and B, with the nitrogen donating an electron pair and the boron accepting it.

▢ A similar reaction was described in Section 8.6 between BCl_3 and ammonia.

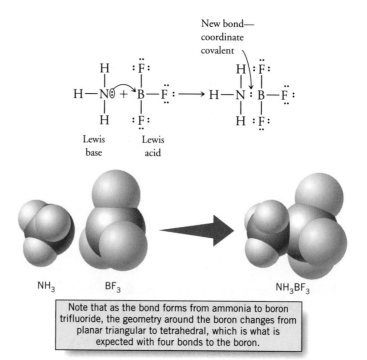

The ammonia molecule thus acts as a *Lewis base*. The boron atom in BF_3, having only six electrons in its valence shell and needing two more to achieve an octet, accepts the pair of electrons from the ammonia molecule. Hence, BF_3 is functioning as a *Lewis acid*.

As this example illustrates, Lewis bases are substances that have completed valence shells *and unshared pairs of electrons* (e.g., NH_3, H_2O, and O^{2-}). A Lewis acid, on the other hand, can be a substance with an incomplete valence shell, such as BF_3 or H^+.

A substance can also be a Lewis acid even when it has a central atom with a complete valence shell. This works when the central atom has a double bond that, by the shifting of an electron pair to an adjacent atom, can make room for an incoming pair of electrons from a Lewis base. Carbon dioxide is an example. When carbon dioxide is bubbled into aqueous sodium hydroxide, the gas is instantly trapped as the bicarbonate ion.

$$CO_2(g) + OH^-(aq) \longrightarrow HCO_3^-(aq)$$

Lewis acid–base theory represents the movement of electrons in this reaction as follows.

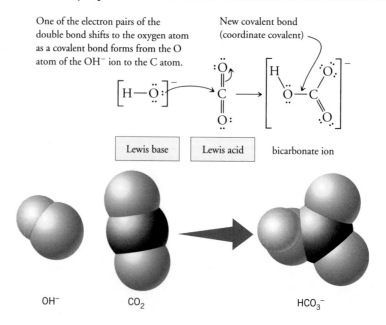

The donation of an electron pair *from* the oxygen of the OH^- ion produces a bond, so the OH^- ion is the Lewis base. The carbon atom of the CO_2 accepts the electron pair, so CO_2 is the Lewis acid.

Lewis acids can also be substances that have valence shells capable of holding more electrons. For example, consider the reaction of sulfur dioxide as a Lewis acid with oxide ion as a Lewis base to make the sulfite ion. This reaction occurs when gaseous sulfur dioxide, an acidic anhydride, mingles with solid calcium oxide, a basic anhydride, to give calcium sulfite, $CaSO_3$.

$$SO_2(g) + CaO(s) \longrightarrow CaSO_3(s)$$

Let's see how electrons relocate as the sulfite ion forms. We use one of the two resonance structures of SO_2 and one of the three such structures for the sulfite ion.

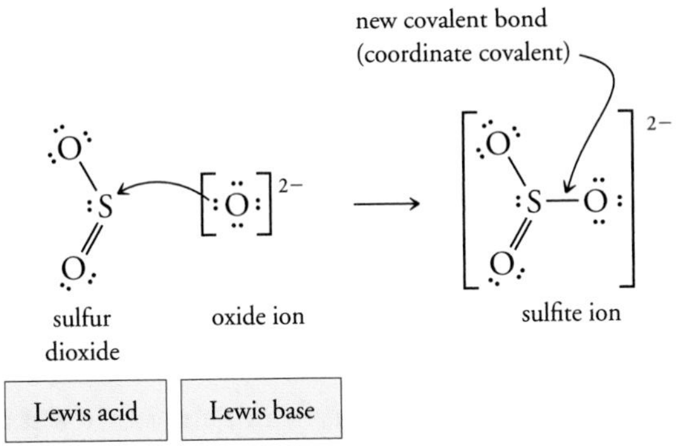

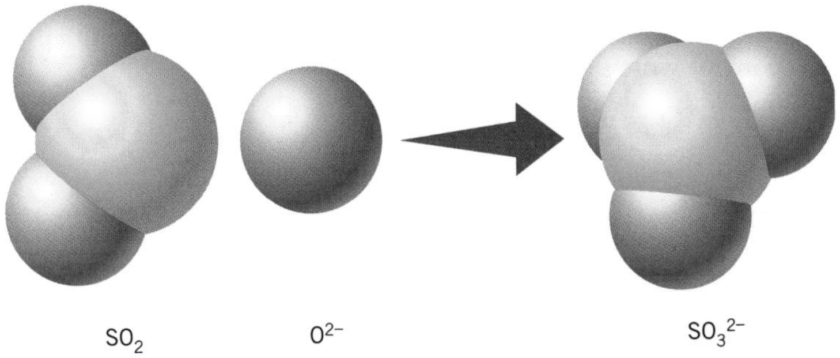

The two very electronegative oxygens attached to the sulfur in SO_2 give the sulfur a substantial positive partial charge, which induces the formation of the coordinate covalent bond from the oxide ion to the sulfur. In this case, sulfur can accommodate more than an octet in its valence shell, so relocation of electron pairs is not necessary.

Table 15.3 summarizes the kinds of substances that behave as Lewis acids and bases. Study it and then work on the practice exercises on the next page.

TABLE 15.3   **Types of Substances That Are Lewis Acids and Bases**

Lewis Acids

Molecules or ions with incomplete valence shells (e.g., BF_3, H^+)

Molecules or ions with complete valence shells, but with multiple bonds that can be shifted to make room for more electrons (e.g., CO_2)

Molecules or ions that have central atoms capable of holding additional electrons (usually, atoms of elements in Period 3 and below) (e.g., SO_2)

Lewis Bases

Molecules or ions that have unshared pairs of electrons and that have complete valence shells (e.g., O^{2-}, NH_3)

Practice Exercise 17: Identify the Lewis acids and bases in each aqueous reaction.

(a) $NH_3 + H^+ \rightleftharpoons NH_4^+$

(b) $(CH_3)_2O + BCl_3 \rightleftharpoons (CH_3)_2OBCl_3$

(c) $Ag^+ + 2NH_3 \rightleftharpoons Ag(NH_3)_2^+$

(Hint: Draw Lewis structures of the reactants.)

Practice Exercise 18: (a) Is the fluoride ion more likely to behave as a Lewis acid or a Lewis base? Explain. (b) Is the $BeCl_2$ molecule more likely to behave as a Lewis acid or a Lewis base? Explain. (c) Is the SO_3 molecule more likely to behave as a Lewis acid or a Lewis base? Explain.

A Brønsted acid–base reaction is an exchange of a Lewis acid between two Lewis bases

Reactions involving the transfer of a proton can be analyzed by either the Brønsted or Lewis definitions of acids and bases. Consider, for example, the reaction between hydronium ion and ammonia in aqueous solution.

$$H_3O^+ + NH_3 \longrightarrow H_2O + NH_4^+$$

Applying the Brønsted definitions, we have an acid, H_3O^+, reacting with a base, NH_3, to give the corresponding conjugates: H_2O being the conjugate base of H_3O^+ and NH_4^+ being the conjugate acid of NH_3.

To interpret this reaction using the Lewis definitions, we view it as the movement of a Lewis acid (the proton, H^+) from a weaker Lewis base (H_2O) to a stronger Lewis base (NH_3). In other words, we view the hydronium ion as the "neutralization" product of the Lewis base H_2O with the Lewis acid H^+. To emphasize that it is the proton that is transferring, we might write the equation as

$$H_2O—H^+ + NH_3 \longrightarrow H_2O + H^+—NH_3$$

We can diagram this as follows using Lewis structures:

Electron pair in the OH bond shifts to the oxygen as the water molecule is formed.

The electron pair of the nitrogen captures H^+ (a Lewis acid) from the oxygen of the hydronium ion.

The molecular view of the reaction is

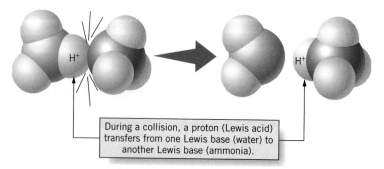

During a collision, a proton (Lewis acid) transfers from one Lewis base (water) to another Lewis base (ammonia).

In general, all Brønsted–Lowry acid–base reactions can be analyzed from the Lewis point of view following this same pattern, with the position of equilibrium favoring the proton being attached to the stronger Lewis base.

A word of caution is in order here. In analyzing proton transfer reactions, it is wise to stick to one interpretation or the other (Brønsted–Lowry or Lewis). Usually we will use the Brønsted–Lowry approach because it is useful to think in terms of conjugate acid–base pairs. However, if you switch to the Lewis interpretation, don't try to apply Brønsted–Lowry terminology at the same time; it won't work and you'll only get confused.

15.4 | ELEMENTS AND THEIR OXIDES DEMONSTRATE ACID–BASE PROPERTIES

The elements most likely to form acids are the nonmetals in the upper right-hand corner of the periodic table. Those most likely to form basic hydroxides are similarly grouped in one general location in the table, among the metals, particularly those in Groups IA (alkali metals) and IIA (alkaline earth metals). Thus, elements can themselves be classified according to their abilities to be involved in acids or bases.

In general, the experimental basis for classifying an element according to its abilities to form an acid or base depends on how its *oxide* behaves toward water. Earlier you learned that metal oxides like Na_2O and CaO are called *basic anhydrides* ("anhydride" means "without water") because they react with water to form hydroxides.

$$Na_2O + H_2O \longrightarrow 2NaOH \qquad \text{sodium hydroxide}$$

$$CaO + H_2O \longrightarrow Ca(OH)_2 \qquad \text{calcium hydroxide}$$

The reactions of metal oxides with water are really reactions of their oxide ions, which take H^+ from molecules of H_2O, leaving ions of OH^-.

Many metal oxides are insoluble in water, so their oxide ions are unable to take H^+ ions from H_2O molecules. Many are able to react with acids, which attack the oxide ions in the solid. Iron(III) oxide, for example, reacts with acid as follows.

$$Fe_2O_3(s) + 6H^+(aq) \longrightarrow 2Fe^{3+}(aq) + 3H_2O$$

This is a common method for removing rust from iron in industrial processes.

Nonmetal oxides are usually *acidic anhydrides;* those that react with water give acidic solutions. Typical examples of the formation of acids from nonmetal oxides are the following reactions.

$$SO_3(g) + H_2O \longrightarrow H_2SO_4(aq) \qquad \text{sulfuric acid}$$
$$N_2O_5(g) + H_2O \longrightarrow 2HNO_3(aq) \qquad \text{nitric acid}$$
$$CO_2(g) + H_2O \longrightarrow H_2CO_3(aq) \qquad \text{carbonic acid}$$

Hydrated metal ions can behave as weak acids

When an ionic compound dissolves in water, molecules of the solute gather around the ions and we say the ions are *hydrated*. Within a hydrated cation, the metal ion behaves as a Lewis acid, binding to the partial negative charge on the oxygens of the surrounding water molecules, which serve as Lewis bases. Hydrated metal ions themselves tend to be Brønsted acids because of the equilibrium shown below. For simplicity, the equation represents a metal ion as a *mono*hydrate, namely, $M(H_2O)^{n+}$ with a net positive charge of $n+$ (n being 1, 2, or 3, depending on M).

$$M(H_2O)^{n+} + H_2O \rightleftharpoons MOH^{(n-1)+} + H_3O^+$$

In other words, hydrated metal ions tend to be proton donors in water. Let's see why.

The positive charge on the metal ion attracts the water molecule and draws electron density from the O—H bonds, causing them to become more polar as shown in the margin. This increases the partial positive charge on H and weakens the O—H bond with respect to the transfer of H^+ to another nearby water molecule in the formation of a hydronium ion, which we can illustrate as follows.

□ The force of attraction between an ion and water molecules is often strong enough to persist when the solvent water evaporates. Solid *hydrates* crystallize from solution, for example, $CuSO_4 \cdot 5H_2O$ (page 56).

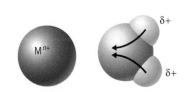

The positive charge on the metal ion pulls electron density away from the H atoms of the water molecule.

Electron density is reduced in the O—H bonds of water (indicated by the curved arrows) by the positive charge of the metal ion, thereby increasing the partial positive charge on the hydrogens. This promotes the transfer of H^+ to a water molecule.

The degree to which metal ions produce acidic solutions depends on the amount of charge on the cation and the cation's size. As the cation's charge increases, the polarizing effect is increased, which thereby favors the release of H^+. This means that highly charged metal ions ought to produce more acidic solutions than ions of low charge, and that is generally the case.

The reason the size of the cation also affects its acidity is that when the cation is small, the positive charge is highly concentrated. A highly concentrated positive charge is better able to pull electrons from an O—H bond than a positive charge that is more spread out. Therefore, for a given positive charge, the smaller the cation, the more acidic are its solutions.

Both size and amount of charge can be considered together by referring to a metal ion's *positive charge density*, the ratio of the positive charge to the volume of the cation (its ionic volume).

$$\text{Charge density} = \frac{\text{ionic charge}}{\text{ionic volume}}$$

The higher the positive charge density, the more effective the metal ion is at drawing electron density from the O—H bond and the more acidic is the hydrated cation.

Very small cations with large positive charges have large positive charge densities and tend to be quite acidic. An example is the hydrated aluminum ion, Al^{3+}. The hexahydrate, $Al(H_2O)_6^{3+}$, is one of several of this cation's hydrated forms that are present in an aqueous solution of an aluminum salt. This ion is acidic in water because of the equilibrium

$$[Al(H_2O)_6]^{3+}(aq) + H_2O \rightleftharpoons [Al(H_2O)_5(OH)]^{2+}(aq) + H_3O^+(aq)$$

The equilibrium, while not actually *strongly* favoring the products, does produce enough hydronium ion so that a 0.1 M solution of $AlCl_3$ in water has about the same concentration of hydronium ions as a 0.1 M solution of acetic acid, roughly 1×10^{-3} M.

The acidities of metal ions follow periodic trends

Within the periodic table, atomic size increases down a group and decreases from left to right in a period. Cation sizes follow these same trends, so within a given group, the cation of the metal at the top of the group has the smallest volume and the largest charge density. Therefore, hydrated metal ions at the top of a group in the periodic table are the most acidic within the group.

The cations of the Group IA metals (Li^+, Na^+, K^+, Rb^+, or Cs^+), with charges of just 1+, have little tendency to increase the H_3O^+ concentration in an aqueous solution.

Within Group IIA, the Be^{2+} cation is very small and has sufficient charge density to cause the hydrated ion to be a weak acid. The other cations of Group IIA (Mg^{2+}, Ca^{2+}, Sr^{2+}, Ba^{2+}) have charge densities that become progressively smaller as we go down the group. Although their hydrated ions all generate some hydronium ion in water, the amount is negligible.

Some transition metal ions are also acidic, especially those with charges of 3+. For example, solutions containing salts of Fe^{3+} and Cr^{3+} tend to be acidic because their ions in solution exist as $Fe(H_2O)_6^{3+}$ and $Cr(H_2O)_6^{3+}$, respectively, and undergo the same ionization reaction as does the $Al(H_2O)_6^{3+}$ ion discussed above.

Acid-base properties of metal oxides are influenced by the oxidation number of the metal

Not all metal oxides are basic. As the oxidation number (or charge) on a metal ion increases, the metal ion becomes more *acidic*; it becomes a better electron pair acceptor. For metal hydrates, we've seen that this causes electron density to be pulled from the OH bonds of water molecules, causing the hydrate itself to become a weak proton donor. The increasing acidity of metal ions with increasing charge also affects the basicity of their oxides.

When the positive charge on a metal is small, the oxide tends to be basic, as we've seen for oxides such as Na_2O and CaO. With ions having a 3+ charge, the oxides are less basic and begin to take on acidic properties as well; they become amphoteric. (Recall that a substance is *amphoteric* if it is capable of reacting as either an acid or a base.) Aluminum oxide is an example; it is able to react with both acids and bases. It has basic properties when it dissolves in acid.

$$Al_2O_3(s) + 6H^+(aq) \longrightarrow 2Al^{3+}(aq) + 3H_2O$$

As noted earlier, the hydrated aluminum ion has six water molecules surrounding it, so in an acidic solution the aluminum exists primarily as $Al(H_2O)_6^{3+}$.

Aluminum oxide exhibits acidic properties when it dissolves in a base. One way to write the equation for the reaction is

$$Al_2O_3(s) + 2OH^-(aq) \longrightarrow 2AlO_2^-(aq) + H_2O$$

Actually, in basic solution the formula of the aluminum-containing species is more complex than this and is better approximated by $Al(H_2O)_2(OH)_4^-$. Note that the difference between the two formulas is just the number of water molecules involved in the formation of the ion.

$$Al(H_2O)_2(OH)_4^- \quad \text{is equivalent to} \quad AlO_2^- + 4H_2O$$

However we write the formula for the aluminum-containing ion, it is an anion, not a cation.

When the metal is in a very high oxidation state, the oxide becomes acidic. Chromium(VI) oxide, CrO_3, is an example. When dissolved in water, the resulting solution is quite acidic and is called chromic acid. One of the principal species in the solution is H_2CrO_4, which is a strong acid that is more than 95% ionized. The acid forms salts containing the chromate ion, CrO_4^{2-}.

15.5 | pH IS A MEASURE OF THE ACIDITY OF A SOLUTION

There are literally thousands of weak acids and bases, and they vary widely in how weak they are. Both the acetic acid in vinegar and the carbonic acid in pressurized soda water, for example, are classified as weak. Yet carbonic acid is only about 3% as strong an acid as acetic acid. To study such differences quantitatively, we need to explore acid–base equilibria in greater depth. This requires that we first discuss a particularly important equilibrium that exists in *all* aqueous solutions, namely, the ionization of water itself.

Water is a very weak electrolyte

Using sensitive instruments, pure water is observed to weakly conduct electricity, indicating the presence of very small concentrations of ions. They arise from the very slight self-ionization, or *autoionization,* of water itself, represented by the following equilibrium equation.

$$H_2O + H_2O \rightleftharpoons H_3O^+ + OH^-$$

The forward reaction requires a collision of two H_2O molecules.

☐ We've omitted the usual (*aq*) following the symbols for ions in water for the sake of simplicity.

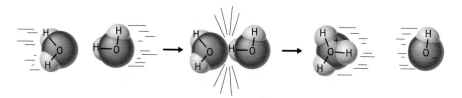

Its equilibrium law, following the procedures developed in Chapter 14, is

$$\frac{[H_3O^+][OH^-]}{[H_2O]^2} = K_c$$

In pure water, and even in dilute aqueous solutions, the molar concentration of water is essentially a constant, with a value of 55.6 M. Therefore, the term $[H_2O]^2$ in the denominator is a constant which we can combine with K_c.

$$[H_3O^+][OH^-] = K_c \times [H_2O]^2$$

The product of the two constants, $K_c \times [H_2O]^2$, must also be a constant. Because of the importance of the autoionization equilibrium, it is given the special symbol $\boldsymbol{K_w}$ and is called the **ion product constant of water.**

$$[H_3O^+][OH^-] = K_w$$

Often, for convenience, we omit the water molecule that carries the hydrogen ion and write H^+ in place of H_3O^+. The equilibrium equation for the autoionization of water then simplifies as follows.

$$H_2O \rightleftharpoons H^+ + OH^-$$

The equation for K_w based on this is likewise simplified.

$$[H^+][OH^-] = K_w \tag{15.3}$$

In pure water, the concentrations of H^+ and OH^- produced by the autoionization are equal because the ions are formed in equal numbers. It's been found that the concentrations have the following values at 25 °C.

$$[H^+] = [OH^-] = 1.0 \times 1.0^{-7} \text{ mol L}^{-1}$$

Therefore, at 25 °C,

$$K_w = (1.0 \times 10^{-7}) \times (1.0 \times 10^{-7})$$

$$K_w = 1.0 \times 10^{-14} \qquad \text{(at 25 °C)} \tag{15.4}$$

As with other equilibrium constants, the value of K_w varies with temperature (see Table 15.4). But, for simplicity, we will generally deal with systems at 25 °C, so we'll usually not specify the temperature each time. The value of K_w at 25 °C ($K_w = 1.0 \times 10^{-14}$) is so important that it should be learned (memorized).

Solutes can affect [H⁺] and [OH⁻], but they can't alter K_w

Water's autoionization takes place in *any* aqueous solution, but because of the effects of other solutes, the molar concentrations of H^+ and OH^- may not be equal. Nevertheless, their product, K_w, is the same. Thus, although Equations 15.3 and 15.4 were derived for pure water, they also apply to dilute aqueous solutions. The significance of this must be emphasized. *In any aqueous solution, the product of* [H⁺] *and* [OH⁻] *equals K_w, although the two molar concentrations may not actually equal each other.*

TABLE 15.4	K_w at Various Temperatures
Temperature (°C)	K_w
0	1.5×10^{-15}
10	3.0×10^{-15}
20	6.8×10^{-15}
25	1.0×10^{-14}
30	1.5×10^{-14}
37^a	2.5×10^{-14}
40	3.0×10^{-14}
50	5.5×10^{-14}
60	9.5×10^{-14}

^{a} Normal body temperature 98.6°F

Criteria for acidic, basic, and neutral solutions

One of the consequences of the autoionization of water is that *in any aqueous solution, there are always both H_3O^+ and OH^- ions, regardless of what solutes are present.* This means that in a solution of the acid HCl there is some OH^-, and in a solution of the base NaOH, there is some H_3O^+. So what criteria do we use to determine whether a solution is neutral, acidic, or basic?

A **neutral solution** is one in which the molar concentrations of H_3O^+ and OH^- are equal; neither ion is present in a greater concentration than the other. An **acidic solution** is one in which some solute has made the molar concentration of H_3O^+ greater than that of OH^-. On the other hand, a **basic solution** exists when the molar concentration of OH^- exceeds that of H_3O^+. We therefore define acidic and basic solutions in terms of the *relative* molarities of H_3O^+ and OH^-.

☐ Because of the autoionization of water, even the most acidic solution has some OH^-, and even the most basic solution has some H_3O^+.

Neutral solution	$[H_3O^+] = [OH^-]$
Acidic solution	$[H_3O^+] > [OH^-]$
Basic solution	$[H_3O^+] < [OH^-]$

EXAMPLE 15.4
Finding [H⁺] from [OH⁻] or Finding [OH⁻] from [H⁺]

In a sample of blood at 25 °C, $[H^+] = 4.6 \times 10^{-8}\ M$. Find the molar concentration of OH^-, and decide if the sample is acidic, basic, or neutral.

ANALYSIS: To reach a decision, we need to know how $[H^+]$ and $[OH^-]$ compare. The tool to use is the relationship between the concentrations of $[H^+]$ and $[OH^-]$. We know that the values of $[H^+]$ and $[OH^-]$ are *always* related to each other and to K_w at 25 °C as follows.

$$1.0 \times 10^{-14} = [H^+][OH^-]$$

If we know one concentration, we can *always* find the other.

SOLUTION: We substitute the given value of $[H^+]$ into this equation and solve for $[OH^-]$.

$$1.0 \times 10^{-14} = (4.6 \times 10^{-8})[OH^-]$$

Solving for $[OH^-]$, and remembering that its units are mol L^{-1} or M,

$$[OH^-] = \frac{1.0 \times 10^{-14}}{4.6 \times 10^{-8}}\ M = 2.2 \times 10^{-7}\ M$$

When we compare $[H^+]$ equaling $4.6 \times 10^{-8}\ M$ with $[OH^-]$ equaling $2.2 \times 10^{-7}\ M$, we see that $[OH^-] > [H^+]$. Our answer, then, is that the blood is slightly basic.

ARE THE ANSWERS REASONABLE? We know $K_w = 1.0 \times 10^{-14} = [H^+][OH^-]$. So one check is to note that if $[H^+]$ is slightly *less* than 1×10^{-7}, $[OH^-]$ will have to be slightly *more* than 1×10^{-7}, as it is. (Be careful in comparing numbers when the exponent on 10 is negative. A value of 10^{-7} is larger than 10^{-8}.)

Practice Exercise 19: Commercial, concentrated, hydrochloric acid has a concentration of 12 moles per liter. If the molarity of hydronium ions is assumed to also be 12 M, what is the concentration of hydroxide ions? (Hint: Use the relationships just discussed.)

Practice Exercise 20: An aqueous solution of sodium bicarbonate, $NaHCO_3$, has a molar concentration of hydroxide ion of 7.8×10^{-6} M. What is the molar concentration of hydrogen ion? Is the solution acidic, basic, or neutral?

The pH concept provides a logarithmic scale of acidity

In most solutions of weak acids and bases, the molar concentrations of H^+ and OH^- are very small, like those in Example 15.4. When you tried to compare the two values in that example, namely, 4.6×10^{-8} M and 2.2×10^{-7} M, you had to look in four places, two before the multiplication symbol and the two negative exponents. There's an easier approach involving only one number. A Danish chemist, S. P. L. Sørenson (1868–1939), suggested it.

To make comparisons of small values of $[H^+]$ easier, Sørenson defined a quantity that he called the **pH** of the solution as follows.

Definition of pH

$$pH = -\log [H^+] \qquad (15.5)^5$$

The properties of logarithms let us rearrange Equation 15.5 as follows.

☐ The expression $[H^+] = 10^{-pH}$ corresponds to taking the antilogarithm of the negative of the pH, i.e., $[H^+] = antilog(-pH)$

$$[H^+] = 10^{-pH} \qquad (15.6)$$

Equation 15.5 can be used to calculate the pH of a solution if its molar concentration of H^+ is known. On the other hand, if the pH is known and we wish to calculate the molar concentration of hydrogen ion, we apply Equation 15.6. We will illustrate these calculations with examples shortly.

The logarithmic definition of pH, Equation 15.5, has proved to be so useful that it has been adapted to quantities other than $[H^+]$. Thus, for any quantity X, we may define a term, pX, in the following way.

Defining the p-function, pX

$$pX = -\log X \qquad (15.7)$$

For example, to express small concentrations of hydroxide ion, we can define the **pOH** of a solution as

$$pOH = -\log [OH^-]$$

Similarly, for K_w we can define **pK_w** as follows.

$$pK_w = -\log K_w$$

The numerical value of pK_w at 25 °C equals $-\log (1.0 \times 10^{-14})$ or $-(-14.00)$. Thus,

$$pK_w = 14.00 \qquad \text{(at 25 °C)}$$

---

[5] In this equation and similar ones, like Equation 15.7, the logarithm of only the numerical part of the bracketed term is taken. The physical units must be mol L^{-1}, but they are set aside for the calculation.

A useful relationship among pH, pOH, and pK_w can be derived from Equation 15.3 that defines K_w.

$$[H^+][OH^-] = K_w \qquad \text{(Equation 15.3)}$$

By the properties of logarithms,

$$\log [H^+] + \log [OH^-] = \log K_w$$

We next multiply the terms on both sides by -1.

$$-\log [H^+] + -\log [OH^-] = -\log K_w$$

But each of these terms is in the form of pX (Equation 15.7), so

$$pH + pOH = pK_w = 14.00 \qquad \text{(at 25 °C)} \qquad (15.8)$$

This tells us that in an aqueous solution of any solute at 25 °C, the sum of pH and pOH is 14.00.

Acidic, basic, and neutral solutions are identified by their pH

One meaning attached to pH is that it is a measure of the acidity of a solution. Hence, we may define *acidic*, *basic*, and *neutral* in terms of pH values. In pure water, or in any solution that is *neutral*,

$$[H^+] = [OH^-] = 1.0 \times 10^{-7}\ M$$

Therefore, by Equation 15.5, *the pH of a neutral solution at 25 °C is 7.00.*[6]

An *acidic solution* is one in which $[H^+]$ is larger than $10^{-7}\ M$ and so has a pH *less* than 7.00. Thus, *as a solution's acidity increases, its pH decreases.*

A *basic solution* is one in which the value of $[H^+]$ is less than $10^{-7}\ M$ and so has a pH that is *greater* than 7.00. *As a solution's acidity decreases, its pH increases.* These simple relationships may be summarized as follows. At 25 °C:

pH < 7.00	**Acidic solution**
pH > 7.00	**Basic solution**
pH = 7.00	**Neutral solution**

The pH values for some common substances are given on a pH scale in Figure 15.3.

One of the deceptive features of pH is how much the hydrogen ion concentration changes with a relatively small change in pH. Thus, a change of one pH unit corresponds to a 10-fold change in the hydrogen ion concentration. For example, by Equation 15.5, at pH 6.0 the hydrogen ion concentration is 1×10^{-6} mol L^{-1}. At pH 5.0, it's 1×10^{-5} mol L^{-1}, or 10 times greater. That's a major difference.

The pH concept is almost never used when a pH value would be a negative number, namely, with solutions having hydrogen ion concentrations greater than $1\ M$. For example, in a solution where the value of $[H^+]$ is $2\ M$, the "2" is a simple enough number; we can't simplify it further by using its corresponding pH value. When $[H^+]$ is $2.00\ M$, the pH, calculated by Equation 15.5, would be $-\log (2.00)$ or -0.301. There is nothing wrong with negative pH values, but they offer no advantage over the actual value of $[H^+]$.

[6] Recall that the rule for significant figures in logarithms is that *the number of **decimal places** in the logarithm of a number equals the number of significant figures in the number.* For example, 3.2×10^{-5} has just two significant figures. The logarithm of that number, displayed on a pocket calculator, is -4.494850022. We write the logarithm, when correctly rounded, as -4.49.

TOOLS

Relationship of pH and pOH to pK$_w$

Neutral pH is 7.00 only for 25 °C. At other temperatures a neutral solution still has $[H^+] = [OH^-]$, but because K_w changes with temperature, so do the values of $[H^+]$ and $[OH^-]$. This causes the pH of the neutral solution to differ from 7.00. For example, at normal body temperature (37 °C), a neutral solution has $[H^+] = [OH^-] = 1.6 \times 10^{-7}$, so pH = 6.80.

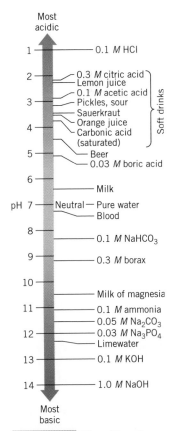

FIG. 15.3 The pH scale.

pH 3.2   pH 4.4
Methyl orange

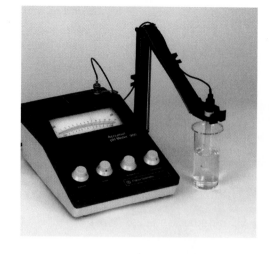

FIG. 15.4 **A pH meter.**
A special combination electrode
that is sensitive to hydrogen ion
concentration is dipped into the
solution to be tested. After the
instrument has been calibrated
using a solution of known pH,
the electrode is dipped into the
solution to be tested and the pH
is read from the meter. *(Courtesy
Hanna Instruments.)*

pH 4.8   pH 5.4
Methyl purple

pH 6.0   pH 7.6
Bromothymol blue

pH can be measured or estimated

One of the remarkable things about pH is that it can be easily measured using an instrument called a pH meter (Figure 15.4). An electrode system sensitive to the hydrogen ion concentration in a solution is first dipped into a solution of known pH to calibrate the instrument. Once calibrated, the apparatus can then be used to measure the pH of any other solution simply by immersing the electrode into it. Most modern pH meters are able to determine pH values to within ±0.01 pH units, and research-grade instruments are capable of even greater precision in the pH range of 0.0 to 14.0.

Another less precise method of obtaining the pH uses acid–base indicators. As you learned in Chapter 4, these are dyes whose colors in aqueous solution depend on the acidity of the solution. Table 15.5 gives several examples. Indicators change color over a narrow range of pH values, and Figure 15.5 shows the colors of some indicators at opposite ends of their color change ranges. Facets of Chemistry 15.1 describes some applications of indicators to measuring pH.

pH 8.2   pH 10.0
Phenolphthalein

FIG. 15.5 **Colors of some common acid–base indicators.** *(Andy Washnik.)*

TABLE 15.5 **Common Acid–Base Indicators**

Indicator	Approximate pH Range over Which the Color Changes	Color Change (Lower to Higher pH)
Methyl green	0.2–1.8	Yellow to blue
Thymol blue	1.2–2.8	Yellow to blue
Methyl orange	3.2–4.4	Red to yellow
Ethyl red	4.0–5.8	Colorless to red
Methyl purple	4.8–5.4	Purple to green
Bromocresol purple	5.2–6.8	Yellow to purple
Bromothymol blue	6.0–7.6	Yellow to blue
Phenol red	6.4–8.2	Yellow to red/violet
Litmus	4.7–8.3	Red to blue
Cresol red	7.0–8.8	Yellow to red
Thymol blue	8.0–9.6	Yellow to blue
Phenolphthalein	8.2–10.0	Colorless to pink
Thymolphthalein	9.4–10.6	Colorless to blue
Alizarin yellow R	10.1–12.0	Yellow to red
Clayton yellow	12.2–13.2	Yellow to amber

Swimming Pools, Aquariums, and Flowers

Something these have in common is the need for a proper pH. The water in swimming pools is more than just water; its a dilute mix of chemicals that prevent the growth of bacteria and stabilize the pool lining. For the pool chemistry to be properly balanced, the optimum pH range is between 7.2 and 7.6. Aquariums have to have their pH controlled because fish are very sensitive to how acidic or basic the water is. Depending on the species of fish in the tank, the pH should be between 6.0 and 7.6, and if it drifts much outside this range, the fish will die.

The pH can also affect the availability of substances that plants need to grow. A pH of from 6 to 7 is best for most plants because most nutrients are more soluble when the soil is slightly acidic than when it is neutral or slightly basic. If the soil pH is too high, metal ions such as iron, manganese, and boron that plants need will precipitate and not be available in the groundwater. A very low pH is not good either. If the pH drops to between 4 and 5, metal ions that are toxic to many plants become released as their compounds become more soluble. A low pH also inhibits the growth of certain beneficial bacteria that are needed to decompose organic matter in the soil and release nutrients, especially nitrogen.

There are chemicals that can be added to swimming pools, aquariums, and soil that will raise or lower the pH, but to know how to use them, it's necessary to measure the pH. Commercial test kits are available to enable you to do this, and they involve the use of acid–base indicators. Kits for testing the pH of pool water (Figure 1) use *phenol red* indicator, which changes color over the pH range 6.4–8.2. This places the intermediate color of the indicator right in the middle of the desired range of 7.0–7.6. To use the kit, a sample of pool water is placed into the plastic cylinder and 5 drops of the indicator solution are added. After shaking the mixture to ensure uniform mixing, the color is compared to the standards to gauge the pH. It can then be decided whether chemicals have to be added to either raise or lower the pH.

Similar test kits are available to test the water in an aquarium, except that the indicator used is bromothymol blue, which changes color over a pH range of 6.0–7.6. This generally matches the desired pH range for the water in the aquarium. Soil test kits, such as that shown in Figure 2, use a "universal indicator," which is a mixture of indicators that enable estimation of the pH over a wider range. A sample of the soil to be tested is placed in the plastic apparatus that comes with the kit. Water is added along with a tablet of the

indicator. The mixture is shaken and then the color of the water is compared with the color chart. The color that most closely matches the color of the solution gives the estimated pH.

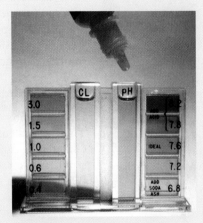

FIG. 1 **Swimming pool test kit.** This apparatus is used to test for both pH and chlorine concentration. The color of the indicator on the right tells us the pH of the pool water is approximately 7.6, which is slightly basic. *(Larry Stepanowicz/ Fundamental Photographs.)*

FIG. 2 **Testing soil pH.** The indicator reveals that the soil sample being tested has a pH of approximately 6.5, which is slightly acidic. *(Andy Washnik.)*

FIG. 15.6 **Using a pH test paper.** The color of this Hydrion test strip changed to orange when a drop of the lemon juice solution in the beaker was placed on it. According to the color code, the pH of the solution is closer to 3 than to 5. *(Andy Washnik.)*

pH test papers are available that are impregnated with one or more indicator dyes. To obtain a rough idea of the pH, a drop of the solution to be tested is touched to a strip of the test paper and the resulting color is compared with a color code. Some commercial test papers (e.g., Hydrion) are impregnated with several dyes, with their vials carrying the color code (see Figure 15.6).

Litmus paper, commonly found in chemistry labs, is often used qualitatively to test whether a solution is acidic or basic. It consists of porous paper impregnated with litmus dye, made either red or blue by exposure to acid or base, and then dried. Below pH 4.7, litmus is red and above pH 8.3 it is blue. The transition for the color change occurs over a pH range of 4.7 to 8.3 with the center of the change at about 6.5, very nearly a neutral pH. To test whether a solution is acidic, a drop of it is placed on blue litmus paper. If the dye turns pink, the solution is acidic. Similarly, to test if the solution is basic, a drop is touched to red litmus paper. If the dye turns blue, the solution is basic.

pH calculations

Let's now look at some examples of pH calculations using Equations 15.5 and 15.6. These are calculations you will be performing often in Section 15.6 and throughout Chapter 16, so be sure you become proficient at them. The first example calculates a pH from a value either of $[H^+]$ or of $[OH^-]$. Another finds the value of $[H^+]$ or $[OH^-]$ given a pH.

EXAMPLE 15.5
Calculating pH and pOH from $[H^+]$

Because rain washes pollutants out of the air, the lakes in many parts of the world have undergone pH changes. In a New England state, the water in one lake was found to have a hydrogen ion concentration of 3.2×10^{-5} mol L^{-1}. What are the calculated pH and pOH values of the lake's water? Is the water acidic or basic?

ANALYSIS: If we know the value of $[H^+]$, Equation 15.5 is the tool we use to find the pH. The calculation is straightforward.

SOLUTION: First, let's write the equation we will use.

$$pH = -\log [H^+] \qquad \text{(Equation 15.5)}$$

□ Be sure to notice that *common* logs (base 10 logs) are used in pH calculations. Don't use the *natural* log function on your scientific calculator by mistake.

Next, we simply make the substitution for $[H^+]$.

$$pH = -\log (3.2 \times 10^{-5})$$

Using a calculator to find the logarithm of 3.2×10^{-5} gives the value -4.49 (note the negative sign). To find the pH, we change its algebraic sign.

$$pH = -(-4.49) = 4.49$$

The pH is less than 7.00, so the lake's water is acidic (too acidic, in fact, for game fish to survive).

Once we know the pH, finding the pOH is most easily done by using the fact that the sum of pH and pOH equals 14.00. Therefore, the pOH of the lake water is

$$pOH = 14.00 - 4.49$$
$$= 9.51$$

ARE THE ANSWERS REASONABLE? The value of $[H^+]$ is between 1×10^{-5} and 1×10^{-4}. Using these in Equation 15.5 yields pH values of 5 and 4, respectively, so the pH has to be between 5 and 4, which it is. Therefore, the pOH must be between 9 and 10, as it is.

Practice Exercise 21: Water draining from old coal and mineral mines often has pH values of 4.0 or lower. The cause is thought to stem from reactions of ground water and oxygen with iron pyrite, FeS. What is the pOH, $[H^+]$, and $[OH^-]$ concentrations in an acid mine drainage sample that has a pH of 4.25? (Hint: Recall that pH, pOH, $[H^+]$, and $[OH^-]$ are all interrelated using K_w and pK_w.)

Practice Exercise 22: A carbonated beverage was found to have a hydrogen ion concentration of 3.67×10^{-4} mol L^{-1}. What are the calculated pH and pOH values of the beverage? Is it acidic, basic, or neutral?

EXAMPLE 15.6
Calculating pH from $[OH^-]$

What is the pH of a sodium hydroxide solution at 25 °C in which the hydroxide ion concentration equals 0.0026 *M*?

ANALYSIS: There are two ways to solve this problem. We could use the tool concerning the K_w expression ($K_w = [H^+][OH^-] = 1 \times 10^{-14}$) and the given value of the hydroxide ion concentration to find $[H^+]$, and then calculate the pH using Equation 15.5. The second way would be to use the tool defining pOH to calculate the pOH from the hydroxide ion concentration (pOH = $-\log [OH^-]$) and then subtract the pOH from 14.00 to find the pH. The second path requires less effort, so let's proceed that way.

SOLUTION: First, we substitute the $[OH^-]$, which equals 0.0026 *M*, into the equation for pOH.

$$pOH = -\log [OH^-]$$
$$= -\log (0.0026)$$
$$= -(-2.59) = 2.59$$

Then we subtract this pOH value from 14.00 to find the pH.

$$pH = 14.00 - 2.59$$
$$= 11.41$$

Notice that the pH in this basic solution is well above 7.

IS THE ANSWER REASONABLE? The molar concentration of hydroxide ion is between 0.001 (or 10^{-3}) and 0.01 (or 10^{-2}), so the pOH must be between 3 and 2, which it is. Thus, the pH ought to be between 11 and 12.

Practice Exercise 23: The molarity of OH^- in the water in which a soil sample has soaked overnight is 1.47×10^{-9} mol L^{-1}. What is the pH of the solution? (Hint: Recall the relationships between pH, pOH, $[H^+]$, and $[OH^-]$.)

Practice Exercise 24: Soil that is close to neutral is often best for growing plants. Based on the above exercise would you recommend adding lime (CaO) or aluminum sulfate $[Al_2(SO_4)_3]$? Recall the discussion in Section 15.4 concerning metal ions.

EXAMPLE 15.7
Calculating $[H^+]$ from pH

"Calcareous soil" is soil rich in calcium carbonate. The pH of the moisture in such soil generally ranges from just over 7 to as high as 8.3. After one particular soil sample was soaked in water, the pH of the water was measured to be 8.14. What value of $[H^+]$ corresponds to a pH of 8.14? Is the soil acidic or basic?

ANALYSIS: The tool we use to calculate $[H^+]$ from pH is Equation 15.6.

$$[H^+] = 10^{-pH}$$

☐ To convert pH into $[H^+]$ we use the 10^x function on the calculator. This is often the inverse or 2nd function of the log key.

SOLUTION: We substitute the pH value, 8.14, into the equation above, which gives

$$[H^+] = 10^{-8.14}$$

Because the pH has two digits following the decimal point, we obtain two significant figures in the hydrogen ion concentration. Therefore, the answer, correctly rounded is

$$[H^+] = 7.2 \times 10^{-9} M$$

Because the pH > 7 and $[H^+] < 1 \times 10^{-7} M$, the soil is basic.

IS THE ANSWER REASONABLE? The given value of 8.14 is between 8 and 9, so at a pH of 8.14, the hydrogen ion concentration must lie between 10^{-8} and 10^{-9} mol L^{-1}. And that's what we found.

Practice Exercise 25: What are the pH and pOH values of the concentrated hydrochloric acid mentioned in Practice Exercise 19? (Hint: The correct answers may be surprising.)

Practice Exercise 26: Find the values of $[H^+]$ and $[OH^-]$ that correspond to each of the following values of pH. State whether each solution is acidic or basic.

(a) 2.90 (the approximate pH of lemon juice)
(b) 3.85 (the approximate pH of sauerkraut)
(c) 10.81 (the pH of milk of magnesia, a laxative)
(d) 4.11 (the pH of orange juice, on the average)
(e) 11.61 (the pH of dilute, household ammonia)

15.6 | STRONG ACIDS AND BASES ARE FULLY DISSOCIATED IN SOLUTION

Many solutes affect the pH of an aqueous solution. In this section we examine how strong acids and bases behave and how to calculate the pH of their solutions. Weak acids and bases have similar effects, which we will discuss in the next chapter.

Calculating the pH of dilute solutions of strong acids and bases takes into account their complete dissociation

☐ If necessary, review the list of strong acids on page 140.

By now you know that strong acids and bases are considered to be 100% dissociated in an aqueous solution. This makes calculating the concentrations of H^+ and OH^- in their solutions a relatively simple task.

When the solute in a solution is a strong monoprotic acid, such as HCl or HNO_3, we expect to obtain one mole of H^+ for every mole of the acid in the solution. Thus, a 0.010 M solution of HCl contains 0.010 mol L^{-1} of H^+ and a 0.0020 M solution of HNO_3 contains 0.0020 mol L^{-1} of H^+. (In this chapter we will not consider strong diprotic acids, such as H_2SO_4, because only the first step in their ionization is complete. In solutions of H_2SO_4, for example, only about 10% of the HSO_4^- ions are further ionized to SO_4^{2-} ions and hydrogen ions.)

To calculate the pH of a solution of a strong monoprotic acid, we use the molarity of the H^+ obtained from the stated molar concentration of the acid. Thus, the 0.010 M HCl solution mentioned above has $[H^+] = 0.010 M$, from which we calculate the pH to be equal to 2.00.

For strong bases, calculating the OH^- concentration is similarly straightforward. A 0.050 M solution of NaOH contains 0.050 mol L^{-1} of OH^- because the base is fully dissociated and each mole of NaOH releases one mole of OH^- when it dissociates. For bases such as $Ba(OH)_2$ we have to recognize that two moles of OH^- are released by each mole of the base.

$$Ba(OH)_2(s) \longrightarrow Ba^{2+}(aq) + 2OH^-(aq)$$

Therefore, if a solution contained 0.010 mol $Ba(OH)_2$ per liter, the concentration of OH^- would be 0.020 *M*. Of course, once we know the OH^- concentration we can calculate pOH, from which we can calculate the pH. The following example illustrates the kinds of calculations we've just described.

EXAMPLE 15.8

Calculating the pH, pOH, and $[OH^-]$ for Solutions of Strong Acids or Strong Bases

Calculate the values of pH, pOH, and $[OH^-]$ for the following solutions: (a) 0.020 *M* HCl, (b) 0.00035 *M* $Ba(OH)_2$.

ANALYSIS: The first step in calculating the pH of a solution is an examination of the solute (or solutes) that are present. There are several questions you need to ask yourself. Are they strong or weak electrolytes? Are they acids or bases? How will they affect the pH? The answers to these questions will determine how you proceed next.

In this example, we expect the solutes to be strong electrolytes because that's what we've been discussing. However, let's take a look at them. The solute in part (a) is HCl, which you should recognize as one of the strong acids. Therefore, we expect it to be 100% ionized. From each mole of HCl, we expect one mole of H^+, so we will use the molar concentration of HCl to obtain $[H^+]$, from which we can calculate the pH, pOH, and $[OH^-]$.

The solute in part (b), $Ba(OH)_2$, is a soluble metal hydroxide, which is also a strong electrolyte. From each mole of $Ba(OH)_2$, there are *two* moles of OH^- liberated. We'll use the molarity of the $Ba(OH)_2$ to calculate the hydroxide ion concentration. From $[OH^-]$, we can calculate pOH and then pH.

SOLUTION: (a) In 0.020 *M* HCl, $[H^+] = 0.020\ M$. Therefore,

$$\begin{aligned} pH &= -\log(0.020) \\ &= 1.70 \end{aligned}$$

Thus in 0.020 *M* HCl, the pH is 1.70. The pOH is $(14.00 - 1.70) = 12.30$. To find $[OH^-]$, we can use this value of pOH.

$$\begin{aligned} [OH^-] &= 10^{-pOH} \\ &= 10^{-12.30} \\ &= 5.0 \times 10^{-13}\ M \end{aligned}$$

Notice how much smaller $[OH^-]$ is in this acidic solution than it is in pure water. This makes sense, because the solution is quite acidic.

(b) As noted, for each mole of $Ba(OH)_2$ we obtain two moles of OH^-. Therefore,

$$\begin{aligned} [OH^-] &= 2 \times 0.00035\ M \\ &= 0.00070\ M \\ pOH &= -\log(0.00070) \\ &= 3.15 \end{aligned}$$

Thus the pOH of this solution is 3.15, and the pH = $(14.00 - 3.15) = 10.85$.

ARE THE ANSWERS REASONABLE? In part (a), the molarity of H^+ is between 0.01 *M* and 0.1 *M*, or between 10^{-2} *M* and 10^{-1} *M*. So the pH must be between 1 and 2, as we found. In part (b), the molarity of OH^- is between 0.0001 and 0.001, or between 10^{-4} and 10^{-3}. Hence, the pOH must be between 3 and 4, which it is.

Practice Exercise 27: Calculate the $[H^+]$, pH, and pOH in 0.0050 *M* HNO_3. (Hint: HNO_3 is a strong acid.)

Practice Exercise 28: Calculate the pOH, $[H^+]$, and pH in a solution made by weighing 1.20 g of KOH and dissolving it in sufficient water to make 250.0 mL of solution.

Practice Exercise 29: Rhododendrons are shrubs that produce beautiful flowers in the springtime. They only grow well in soil that has a pH that is 5.5 or slightly lower. What is the hydrogen ion concentration in the soil moisture if the pH is 5.5?

Acidic or basic solutes suppress the ionization of water

In the preceding calculations, we have made a critical and correct assumption, namely, that the autoionization of water contributes negligibly to the total $[H^+]$ in a solution of an acid and to the total $[OH^-]$ in a solution of a base.[7] Let's take a closer look at this.

In a solution of an acid, there are actually *two* sources of H^+. One is from the ionization of the acid solute itself and the other is from the autoionization of water. Thus,

$$[H^+]_{total} = [H^+]_{from\ solute} + [H^+]_{from\ H_2O}$$

Except in very dilute solutions of acids, the amount of H^+ contributed by the water ($[H^+]_{from\ H_2O}$) is small compared to the amount of H^+ contributed by the solute ($[H^+]_{from\ solute}$). For instance, in Example 15.8 we saw that in 0.020 *M* HCl the molarity of OH^- was 5.0×10^{-13} *M*. The only source of OH^- in this acidic solution is from the autoionization of water, and the amounts of OH^- and H^+ *formed by the autoionization of water* must be equal. Therefore, $[H^+]_{from\ H_2O}$ also equals 5.0×10^{-13} *M*. If we now look at the total $[H^+]$ for this solution, we have

$$[H^+]_{total} = 0.020\ M + 5.0 \times 10^{-13}\ M$$
$$\text{(from HCl)} \qquad \text{(from H}_2\text{O)}$$

$$= 0.020\ M \qquad \text{(rounded correctly)}$$

In any solution of an acid, the autoionization of water is suppressed by the H^+ furnished by the solute. It's simply an example of Le Châtelier's principle. If we look at the autoionization reaction, we can see that if some H^+ is provided by an external source (an acidic solute, for example), the position of equilibrium will be shifted to the left.

$$H_2O \rightleftharpoons H^+ + OH^-$$

Adding H^+ from a solute causes the position of equilibrium to shift to the left.

As the results of our calculation have shown, the concentrations of H^+ and OH^- *from the autoionization reaction* are reduced well below their values in a neutral solution (1.0×10^{-7} *M*). Therefore, except for *very* dilute solutions (10^{-6} *M* or less), we will assume that all of the H^+ in the solution of an acid comes from the solute. Similarly, *we'll assume that in a solution of a base, all the OH^- comes from the dissociation of the solute.*

☐ A similar equation applies to the total OH^- concentration in a solution of a base.

$$[OH^-]_{total} = [OH^-]_{from\ solute} + [OH^-]_{from\ H_2O}$$

SUMMARY

Brønsted–Lowry Acids and Bases. A **Brønsted–Lowry acid** (or more simply a **Brønsted acid**) is a proton donor; a **Brønsted base** is a proton acceptor. According to the Brønsted–Lowry approach, an acid–base reaction is a proton transfer event. In an equilibrium involving a Brønsted acid and base, there are two **conjugate acid–base pairs.** The members of any given pair differ from each other by only one H^+. A substance that can

be either an acid or a base, depending on the nature of the other reactant, is **amphoteric** or, with emphasis on proton transfer reactions, **amphiprotic.**

Lewis Acids and Bases. A **Lewis acid** accepts a pair of electrons from a **Lewis base** in the formation of a coordinate covalent bond. Lewis bases often have filled valence shells and must have at least one unshared electron pair. Lewis acids have an incomplete valence shell that can accept an electron pair, have double bonds that allow electron pairs to be moved to make room for an incoming electron pair from a Lewis base, or have valence shells that can accept more than an octet of electrons.

Relative Acidities and the Periodic Table.

Binary acids contain only hydrogen and another nonmetal. Their strengths increase from top to bottom within a group and from left to right across a period. **Oxoacids,** which contain oxygen atoms in addition to hydrogen and another element, increase in strength as the number of oxygen atoms on the same central atom increases. Delocalization of negative charge enhances the stability of oxoacid anions, making them weaker bases, and as a result, their conjugate acids are correspondingly stronger. Oxoacids having the same number of oxygens generally increase in strength as the central atom moves from bottom to top within a group and from left to right across a period.

Acid–Base Properties of the Elements and Their Oxides.

Oxides of metals are basic anhydrides when the charge on the ion is small. Those of the Group IA and IIA metals neutralize acids and tend to react with water to form soluble metal hydroxides. The hydrates of metal ions tend to be proton donors when the positive charge density of the metal ion is itself sufficiently high, as it is when the ion has a $3+$ charge. The small beryllium ion, Be^{2+}, forms a weakly acidic hydrated ion. Metal oxides become more acidic as the oxidation number of the metal becomes larger. Aluminum oxide is amphoteric, dissolving in both acids and bases. Chromium(VI) oxide is acidic, forming chromic acid when it dissolves in water.

The Autoionization of Water and the pH Concept.

Water reacts with itself to produce small amounts of H_3O^+ (often abbreviated H^+) and OH^- ions. The concentrations of these ions both in pure water *and* in dilute aqueous solutions are related by the expression

$$[H^+][OH^-] = K_w = 1.0 \times 10^{-14} \qquad \text{(at 25 °C)}$$

K_w is the **ion product constant of water.** In pure water,

$$[H^+] = [OH^-] = 1.0 \times 10^{-7}\ M$$

The **pH** of a solution is a measure of the acidity of a solution and is normally measured with a pH meter. As the pH decreases, the acidity increases. The defining equation for pH is $pH = -\log[H^+]$. In exponential form, this relationship between $[H^+]$ and pH is given by $[H^+] = 10^{-pH}$.

Comparable expressions can be used to describe low OH^- ion concentrations in terms of **pOH** values: $pOH = -\log[OH^-]$ and $[OH^-] = 10^{-pOH}$. At 25 °C, $pH + pOH = 14.00$. A solution is acidic if its pH is less than 7.00 and basic if its pH is greater than 7.00. A neutral solution has a pH of 7.00.

Solutions of Strong Acids and Strong Bases.

In calculating the pH of solutions of strong acids and bases, we assume that they are 100% ionized. The autoionization of water contributes a negligible amount to the $[H^+]$ in a solution of an acid. It also contributes a negligible amount to the $[OH^-]$ in a solution of a base.

TOOLS FOR PROBLEM SOLVING

In this chapter you learned to apply the following concepts as tools in solving problems dealing with aspects of acid–base properties and equilibria. Study each tool carefully so that you know what each is used for. When faced with solving a problem, recall what each tool does and consider whether it will be helpful in finding a solution. This will aid you in selecting the tools you need. Remember that at times tools from previous chapters will be needed along with the new ones in this chapter.

Brønsted–Lowry conjugate acids and bases *(page 607)* The Brønsted–Lowry acid–base equilibrium is based on conjugate acid–base pairs. Every conjugate acid–base pair consists of an acid and a base that has lost one proton (H^+) *(page 608)* The conjugate acid is always on the opposite side of an equation from its conjugate base, and the Brønsted–Lowry acid–base equilibrium is typically written with two sets of conjugate acid–base pairs *(page 608)*. Finally we can use the position of equilibrium to determine the relative strengths of conjugate acids and bases *(pages 612 and 613)*.

Periodic trends in strengths of binary acids *(page 615)* You can use the trends to predict the relative acidities of X—H bonds, both for the binary hydrides themselves and for molecules that contain X—H bonds. In general these acids increase in strength going from left to right in a period and from top to bottom of a group in the periodic table.

Periodic trends in strengths of oxoacids *(pages 617, 618)* You can use the trends to predict the relative acidities of oxoacids according to the nature of the central nonmetal as well as the number of oxygens attached to a given nonmetal. The principles involved also let you compare acidities of compounds containing different electronegative elements.

Lewis acids and bases *(page 619)* A Lewis acid is an electron pair acceptor and a Lewis base is an electron pair donor.

Ion product constant for water *(page 626)* Use this equation to calculate $[H^+]$ if you know $[OH^-]$, and vice versa. Be sure you have learned the value of K_w.

$$[H^+][OH^-] = K_w$$

Defining equations for pX *(page 628)* Use the equations of this type to calculate pH and pOH from $[H^+]$ and $[OH^-]$, respectively. You also use them to calculate $[H^+]$ and $[OH^-]$ from pH and pOH, respectively.

$$pX = -\log X \quad \text{and} \quad X = 10^{-pX}$$

Relationship between pH and pOH *(page 629)* This relationship is used to calculate pH if you know pOH, and vice versa.

$$pH + pOH = pK_w = 14.00 \quad \text{(at 25°C)}$$

QUESTIONS, PROBLEMS, AND EXERCISES

Answers to problems whose numbers are printed in color are given in Appendix B. More challenging problems are marked with asterisks. ILW = Interactive Learningware solution is available at www.wiley.com/college/brady. OH = an Office Hours video is available for this problem.

REVIEW QUESTIONS

Brønsted–Lowry Acids and Bases

15.1 How is a *Brønsted acid* defined? How is a *Brønsted base* defined?

15.2 How are the formulas of the members of a conjugate acid–base pair related to each other? Within the pair, how can you tell which is the acid?

15.3 Is H_2SO_4 the conjugate acid of SO_4^{2-}? Explain your answer.

15.4 What is meant by the term *amphoteric*? Give two chemical equations that illustrate the amphoteric nature of water.

15.5 Define the term *amphiprotic*.

Trends in Acid–Base Strengths

15.6 Within the periodic table, how do the strengths of the binary acids vary from left to right across a period? How do they vary from top to bottom within a group?

15.7 Astatine, atomic number 85, is radioactive and does not occur in appreciable amounts in nature. On the basis of what you have learned in this chapter, answer the following.
(a) How would the acidity of HAt compare to HI?
(b) How would the acidity of $HAtO_3$ compare with $HBrO_3$?

15.8 Explain why nitric acid is a stronger acid than nitrous acid.

$$\begin{array}{cc} HO-NO_2 & HO-NO \\ \text{nitric acid} & \text{nitrous acid} \end{array}$$

15.9 Explain why H_2S is a stronger acid than H_2O.

15.10 Which is the stronger Brønsted base, $CH_3CH_2O^-$ or $CH_3CH_2S^-$? What is the basis for your selection?

15.11 Explain why $HClO_4$ is a stronger acid than H_2SeO_4.

15.12 The position of equilibrium in the equation below lies far to the left. Identify the conjugate acid–base pairs. Which of the two acids is stronger?

$$HOCl(aq) + H_2O \rightleftharpoons H_3O^+(aq) + OCl^-(aq)$$

15.13 Consider the following: CO_3^{2-} is a weaker base than hydroxide ion, and HCO_3^- is a stronger acid than water. In the equation below, would the position of equilibrium lie to the left or to the right? Justify your answer.

$$CO_3^{2-}(aq) + H_2O \rightleftharpoons HCO_3^-(aq) + OH^-(aq)$$

15.14 Acetic acid, $HC_2H_3O_2$, is a weaker acid than nitrous acid, HNO_2. How do the strengths of the bases $C_2H_3O_2^-$ and NO_2^- compare?

15.15 Nitric acid, HNO_3, is a very strong acid. It is 100% ionized in water. In the reaction below, would the position of equilibrium lie to the left or to the right?

$$NO_3^-(aq) + H_2O \rightleftharpoons HNO_3(aq) + OH^-(aq)$$

15.16 $HClO_4$ is a stronger proton donor than HNO_3, but in water both acids appear to be of equal strength; they are both 100% ionized. Why is this so? What solvent property would be necessary in order to distinguish between the acidities of these two Brønsted acids?

15.17 Formic acid, $HCHO_2$, and acetic acid, $HC_2H_3O_2$, are classified as weak acids, but in water $HCHO_2$ is more fully ionized than $HC_2H_3O_2$. However, if we use liquid ammonia as a solvent for these acids, they both appear to be of equal strengths; both are 100% ionized in liquid ammonia. Explain why this is so.

15.18 Which of the molecules below is expected to be the stronger Brønsted acid? Why?

15.19 In which of the molecules below is the hydrogen printed in color the more acidic hydrogen? Explain your choice.

Lewis Acids and Bases

15.20 Define *Lewis acid* and *Lewis base*.

15.21 Explain why the addition of a proton to a water molecule to give H_3O^+ is a Lewis acid–base reaction.

15.22 Methylamine has the formula CH_3NH_2 and the structure

Use Lewis structures to illustrate the reaction of methylamine with boron trifluoride.

15.23 Use Lewis structures to show the Lewis acid–base reaction between CO_2 and H_2O to give H_2CO_3. Identify the Lewis acid and the Lewis base in the reaction.

15.24 Explain why the oxide ion, O^{2-}, can function as a Lewis base but not as a Lewis acid.

15.25 The molecule SbF_5 is able to function as a Lewis acid. Explain why it is able to be a Lewis acid.

15.26 In the reaction of calcium with oxygen to form calcium oxide, each calcium gives a pair of electrons to an oxygen atom. Why isn't this viewed as a Lewis acid–base reaction?

15.27 Boric acid is very poisonous and is used in ant bait (to kill ant colonies) and to poison cockroaches. It is a weak acid with a formula often written as H_3BO_3, although it is better written as $B(OH)_3$. It functions not as a Brønsted acid, but as a Lewis acid. Using Lewis structures, show how $B(OH)_3$ can bind to a water molecule and cause the resulting product to be a weak Brønsted acid.

Acid–Base Properties of the Elements and Their Oxides

15.28 Suppose that a new element was discovered. Based on the discussions in this chapter, what properties (both physical and chemical) might be used to classify the element as a metal or a nonmetal?

15.29 If the oxide of an element dissolves in water to give an acidic solution, is the element more likely to be a metal or a nonmetal?

15.30 Many chromium salts crystallize as hydrates containing the ion $Cr(H_2O)_6^{3+}$. Solutions of these salts tend to be acidic. Explain why.

15.31 Which ion is expected to give the more acidic solution, Fe^{2+} or Fe^{3+}? Why?

15.32 Ions of the alkali metals have little effect on the acidity of a solution. Why?

15.33 What acid is formed when the following oxides react with water?
(a) SO_3, (b) CO_2, (c) P_4O_{10}

15.34 Consider the following oxides: CrO, Cr_2O_3, and CrO_3.
(a) Which is most acidic?
(b) Which is most basic?
(c) Which is most likely to be amphoteric?

15.35 Write equations for the reaction of Al_2O_3 with (a) a strong acid, and (b) a strong base.

Ionization of Water and the pH Concept

15.36 Write the chemical equation for the autoionization of water and the equilibrium law for K_w.

15.37 How are acidic, basic, and neutral solutions in water defined (a) in terms of $[H^+]$ and $[OH^-]$ and (b) in terms of pH?

15.38 At 25 °C, how are the pH and pOH of a solution related to each other?

15.39 Explain how acids and bases suppress the ionization of water, often called the common ion effect.

15.40 Explain the leveling effect of water.

REVIEW PROBLEMS

Brønsted Acids and Bases

OH 15.41 Write the formula for the conjugate acid of each of the following.
(a) F^- (d) O_2^{2-}
(b) N_2H_4 (e) $HCrO_4^-$
(c) C_5H_5N

15.42 Write the formula for the conjugate base of each of the following.
(a) NH_2OH (d) H_5IO_6
(b) HSO_3^- (e) HNO_2
(c) HCN

15.43 Identify the conjugate acid–base pairs in the following reactions.
(a) $HNO_3 + N_2H_4 \rightleftharpoons NO_3^- + N_2H_5^+$
(b) $NH_3 + N_2H_5^+ \rightleftharpoons NH_4^+ + N_2H_4$
(c) $H_2PO_4^- + CO_3^{2-} \rightleftharpoons HPO_4^{2-} + HCO_3^-$
(d) $HIO_3 + HC_2O_4^- \rightleftharpoons IO_3^- + H_2C_2O_4$

15.44 Identify the conjugate acid–base pairs in the following reactions.
(a) $HSO_4^- + SO_3^{2-} \rightleftharpoons HSO_3^- + SO_4^{2-}$
(b) $S^{2-} + H_2O \rightleftharpoons HS^- + OH^-$
(c) $CN^- + H_3O^+ \rightleftharpoons HCN + H_2O$
(d) $H_2Se + H_2O \rightleftharpoons HSe^- + H_3O^+$

Trends in Acid–Base Strengths

15.45 Choose the stronger acid: (a) HBr or HCl; (b) H_2O or HF; (c) H_2S or HBr. Give your reasons.

15.46 Choose the stronger acid: (a) H_2S or H_2Se; (b) H_2Te or HI; (c) PH_3 or NH_3. Give your reasons.

15.47 Choose the stronger acid: (a) HOCl or $HClO_2$; (b) H_2SeO_4 or H_2SeO_3. Give your reasons.

15.48 Choose the stronger acid: (a) HIO_3 or HIO_4; (b) H_3AsO_4 or H_3AsO_3. Give your reasons.

OH 15.49 Choose the stronger acid: (a) $HClO_3$ or HIO_3; (b) HIO_2 or $HClO_3$; (c) H_2SeO_3 or $HBrO_4$. Give your reasons.

15.50 Choose the stronger acid: (a) H_3AsO_4 or H_3PO_4; (b) H_2CO_3 or HNO_3; (c) H_2SeO_4 or $HClO_4$. Give your reasons.

Lewis Acids and Bases

15.51 Use Lewis symbols to diagram the reaction

$$NH_2^- + H^+ \longrightarrow NH_3$$

Identify the Lewis acid and Lewis base in the reaction.

15.52 Use Lewis symbols to diagram the reaction

$$BF_3 + F^- \longrightarrow BF_4^-$$

Identify the Lewis acid and Lewis base in the reaction.

15.53 Beryllium chloride, $BeCl_2$, exists in the solid as a polymer composed of long chains of $BeCl_2$ units arranged as indicated on p. 640. The formula of the chain can be represented as $(BeCl_2)_n$, where n is a large number. Use Lewis structures to show how the reaction $n\text{BeCl}_2 \longrightarrow (\text{BeCl}_2)_n$ is a Lewis acid–base reaction.

15.54 Aluminum chloride, AlCl_3, forms molecules with itself with the formula Al_2Cl_6. Its structure is

Use Lewis structures to show how the reaction $2\text{AlCl}_3 \longrightarrow \text{Al}_2\text{Cl}_6$ is a Lewis acid–base reaction.

OH 15.55 Use Lewis structures to diagram the reaction

$$\text{CO}_2 + \text{H}_2\text{O} \longrightarrow \text{H}_2\text{CO}_3$$

Identify the Lewis acid and Lewis base in this reaction.

15.56 Use Lewis structures to diagram the reaction

$$\text{CO}_2 + \text{O}^{2-} \longrightarrow \text{CO}_3^{2-}$$

Identify the Lewis acid and Lewis base in this reaction.

15.57 Use Lewis structures to show how the following reaction can be viewed as the displacement of one Lewis base by another Lewis base from a Lewis acid. Identify the two Lewis bases and the Lewis acid.

$$\text{NH}_2^- + \text{H}_2\text{O} \longrightarrow \text{NH}_3 + \text{OH}^-$$

OH 15.58 Use Lewis structures to show how the following reaction involves the transfer of a Lewis base from one Lewis acid to another. Identify the two Lewis acids and the two Lewis bases.

$$\text{CO}_3^{2-} + \text{SO}_2 \longrightarrow \text{CO}_2 + \text{SO}_3^{2-}$$

Autoionization of Water and pH

15.59 Deuterium oxide, D_2O, ionizes like water. At 20 °C its K_w or ion product constant, analogous to that of water, is 8.9×10^{-16}. Calculate $[\text{D}^+]$ and $[\text{OD}^-]$ in deuterium oxide at 20 °C. Calculate also the pD and the pOD.

15.60 At the temperature of the human body, 37 °C, the value of K_w is 2.5×10^{-14}. Calculate $[\text{H}^+]$, $[\text{OH}^-]$, pH, and pOH of pure water at that temperature. What is the relationship between pH, pOH, and K_w at that temperature? Is water neutral at that temperature?

15.61 Calculate the $[\text{H}^+]$, pH, and pOH in each of the following solutions in which the hydroxide ion concentrations are
(a) 0.0068 M (c) 1.6×10^{-8} M
(b) 6.4×10^{-5} M (d) 8.2×10^{-12} M

15.62 Calculate the $[\text{OH}^-]$, pH, and pOH in each of the following solutions in which the H^+ concentrations are
(a) 3.5×10^{-7} M (c) 2.5×10^{-11} M
(b) 0.0017 M (d) 7.9×10^{-2} M

OH 15.63 A certain brand of beer had a H^+ concentration equal to 1.9×10^{-5} mol L^{-1}. What is the pH of the beer?

15.64 A soft drink was put on the market with $[\text{H}^+] = 1.4 \times 10^{-5}$ mol L^{-1}. What is its pH?

15.65 Calculate the molar concentrations of H^+ and OH^- in solutions that have the following pH values.
(a) 8.14   (d) 13.28
(b) 2.56   (e) 6.70
(c) 11.25

15.66 Calculate the molar concentrations of H^+ and OH^- in solutions that have the following pOH values.
(a) 12.27   (d) 4.28
(b) 6.14   (e) 3.76
(c) 10.65

15.67 The interaction of water droplets in rain with carbon dioxide that is naturally present in the atmosphere causes rainwater to be slightly acidic because CO_2 is an acidic anhydride. As a result, pure clean rain has a pH of about 5.7. What are the hydrogen ion and hydroxide ion concentrations in this rainwater?

15.68 "Acid rain" forms when rain falls through air polluted by oxides of sulfur and nitrogen, which dissolve to form acids such as H_2SO_3, H_2SO_4, and HNO_3. Trees and plants are affected if the acid rain has a pH of 3.5 or lower. What is the hydrogen ion concentration in acid rain that has a pH of 3.16? What is the pH of a solution having twice your calculated hydrogen ion concentration?

Solutions of Strong Acids and Bases

15.69 What is the concentration of H^+ in 0.00065 M HNO_3? What is the pH of the solution? What is the OH^- concentration in the solution?

15.70 What is the concentration of H^+ in 0.031 M HClO_4? What is the pH of the solution? What is the OH^- concentration in the solution? By how much does the pH change if the concentration of H^+ is doubled?

ILW 15.71 A sodium hydroxide solution is prepared by dissolving 6.0 g NaOH in 1.00 L of solution. What is the molar concentration of OH^- in the solution? What is the pOH and the pH of the solution? What is the hydrogen ion concentration in the solution?

OH 15.72 A solution was made by dissolving 0.837 g Ba(OH)_2 in 100 mL final volume. What is the molar concentration of OH^- in the solution? What are the pOH and the pH? What is the hydrogen ion concentration in the solution?

15.73 A solution of Ca(OH)_2 has a measured pH of 11.60. What is the molar concentration of the Ca(OH)_2 in the solution? What is the molar concentration of Ca(OH)_2 if the solution is diluted so that the pH is 10.60?

15.74 A solution of HCl has a pH of 2.50. How many grams of HCl are there in 250 mL of this solution? How many grams of HCl are in 250 mL of an HCl solution that has twice the pH?

15.75 How many milliliters of 0.0100 M KOH are needed to completely neutralize the HCl in 300 mL of a hydrochloric acid solution that has a pH of 2.25?

15.76 It was found that 25.20 mL of an HNO_3 solution is needed to react completely with 300 mL of a LiOH solution that has a pH of 12.05. What is the molarity of the HNO_3 solution?

15.77 In a 0.0020 M solution of NaOH, how many moles per liter of OH^- come from the ionization of water?

15.78 In a certain solution of HCl, the ionization of water contributes 3.4×10^{-11} moles per liter to the H^+ concentration. What is the total H^+ concentration in the solution?

ADDITIONAL EXERCISES

15.79 What is the formula of the conjugate acid of dimethylamine, $(CH_3)_2NH$? What is the formula of its conjugate base?

15.80 Suppose 10.0 mL of HCl gas at 25 °C and 734 torr is bubbled into 250 mL of pure water. What will be the pH of the resulting solution, assuming all the HCl dissolves in the water?

15.81 Suppose the HCl described in the preceding exercise is bubbled into 200 mL of a solution of NaOH that has a pH of 10.50. What will the pH of the resulting solution be?

15.82 Write equations that illustrate the amphiprotic nature of the bicarbonate ion.

15.83 Hydrogen peroxide is a stronger Brønsted acid than water. (a) Explain why this is so. (b) Is an aqueous solution of hydrogen peroxide acidic or basic?

15.84 Hydrazine, N_2H_4, is a weaker Brønsted base than ammonia. In the following reaction, would the position of equilibrium lie to the left or to the right? Justify your answer.

$$N_2H_5^+ + NH_3 \rightleftharpoons N_2H_4 + NH_4^+$$

15.85 Identify the two Brønsted acids and two Brønsted bases in the reaction

$$NH_2OH + CH_3NH_3^+ \rightleftharpoons NH_3OH^+ + CH_3NH_2$$

15.86 In the reaction in the preceding exercise, the position of equilibrium lies to left. Identify the stronger acid in each of the conjugate pairs in the reaction.

*15.87 How would you expect the degree of ionization of $HClO_3$ to compare in the solvents $H_2O(l)$ and $HF(l)$? The reactions are

$$HClO_3 + H_2O \rightleftharpoons H_3O^+ + ClO_3^-$$
$$HClO_3 + HF \rightleftharpoons H_2F^+ + ClO_3^-$$

Justify your answer.

*15.88 Suppose 38.0 mL of 0.000200 M HCl is added to 40.0 mL of 0.000180 M NaOH. What will be the pH of the final mixture?

*15.89 What is the pH of a 3.0×10^{-7} M solution of HCl?

*15.90 How many milliliters of 0.10 M NaOH must be added to 200 mL of 0.010 M HCl to give a mixture with a pH of 3.00?

15.91 Milk of magnesia is a suspension of magnesium hydroxide in water. Although $Mg(OH)_2$ is relatively insoluble, a small amount does dissolve in the water, which makes the mixture slightly basic and gives it a pH of 10.08. How many grams of $Mg(OH)_2$ are actually dissolved in 100 mL of milk of magnesia?

*15.92 A 1.0 M solution of acetic acid has a pH of 2.37. What percentage of the acetic acid is ionized in the solution?

EXERCISES IN CRITICAL THINKING

15.93 Are all Arrhenius acids Brønsted acids? Lewis acids? Give examples if they are not. Give a reasoned explanation if they are.

15.94 How could you determine whether HBr is a stronger acid than HI?

15.95 What happens to the pH of a solution as it is heated? Does that mean that the autoionization of water is exothermic or endothermic?

15.96 Can the pH of a solution ever have a negative value? If so give an example of a situation where the pH has a negative value.

15.97 Alcohols are organic compounds that have an —OH group. Are alcohols acids or bases? Sugars have an —OH group on almost every carbon atom. Are sugars acids or bases? Phenol is a benzene ring with an —OH group. Is phenol an acid or base?

15.98 Acid rain, acid mine drainage, and acid leaching of metals from soils are important environmental considerations. What do these topics refer to and how do they affect you as a person?

EQUILIBRIA IN SOLUTIONS OF WEAK ACIDS AND BASES

16

Interesting gardens often have flowering plants with different colors. In this photo all of the plants are hydrangias but they are growing in soils with differing levels of acidity. In this chapter we will find methods chemists use to precisely control the acidity of solutions and soils. *(age fotostock/SUPERSTOCK)*

CHAPTER OUTLINE

THIS CHAPTER IN CONTEXT   In Chapters 14 and 15 we discussed the general principles of c equilibrium and how to deal with calculating the hydrogen and hydroxide ion concentrations and pH of solu strong acids and bases. Our goal in this chapter is to bring these concepts together as we examine the c equilibria that exist in solutions of weak acids and bases. There are literally thousands of such substances, r which are found in the environment or in biological systems as a consequence of the natural acidity or basicity of biological molecules.

The principles we develop here have applications not only in traditional chemistry labs, but also in labs that investigate environmental, forensic, and biochemical problems. High-technology laboratories interested in materials science and nanotechnology often use the principles of acid–base equilibria. The consumer oriented industries that make products such as cosmetics, foods, beverages, and cleaning chemicals all employ chemists who are aware that control of pH is very important in safe and effective consumer products.

16.1 | IONIZATION CONSTANTS CAN BE DEFINED FOR WEAK ACIDS AND BASES

As you've learned, weak acids and bases are incompletely ionized in water and exist in solution as molecules that are in equilibria with the ions formed by their reactions with water. To deal quantitatively with these equilibria it is essential that you be able to write correct chemical equations for the equilibrium reactions, from which you can then obtain the corresponding correct equilibrium laws. Fortunately, there is a pattern that applies to the way these substances react. *Once you've learned how to write the correct equation for one acid or base, you can write the correct equation for any other.*

A weak acid reacts with water to give its conjugate base and hydronium ion

In aqueous solutions, all weak acids behave the same way. They are Brønsted acids and, therefore, proton donors. Some examples are $HC_2H_3O_2$, HSO_4^-, and NH_4^+. In water, these participate in the following equilibria.

$$HC_2H_3O_2 + H_2O \rightleftharpoons H_3O^+ + C_2H_3O_2^-$$

$$HSO_4^- + H_2O \rightleftharpoons H_3O^+ + SO_4^{2-}$$

$$NH_4^+ + H_2O \rightleftharpoons H_3O^+ + NH_3$$

Notice that, in each case, the acid reacts with water to give H_3O^+ and the corresponding conjugate base. We can represent these reactions in a general way using HA to stand for the formula of the acid.

$$HA + H_2O \rightleftharpoons H_3O^+ + A^- \qquad (16.1)$$

As you can see from the equations above, HA does not have to be electrically neutral; it can be a molecule such as $HC_2H_3O_2$, a negative ion such as HSO_4^-, or a positive ion such as NH_4^+. (Of course, the actual charge on the conjugate base will then depend on the charge on the parent acid.)

Following the procedure developed in Chapter 14, we can also write a general equation for the equilibrium law for Reaction 16.1, using K_c' to stand for the equilibrium constant.

$$K_c' = \frac{[H_3O^+][A^-]}{[HA][H_2O]}$$

In our discussion of the autoionization of water in Chapter 15, we noted that in dilute aqueous solutions $[H_2O]$ can be considered a constant, so it can be combined with K_c' to give a new equilibrium constant. Doing this gives

$$K_c' \times [H_2O] = \frac{[H_3O^+][A^-]}{[HA]} = K_a$$

The new constant K_a is called an **acid ionization constant.** Abbreviating H_3O^+ as H^+, the equation for the ionization of the acid can be simplified as

$$HA \rightleftharpoons H^+ + A^-$$

from which the expression for K_a is obtained directly.

TOOLS

General equation for the ionization of a weak acid

☐ Some call K_a the *acid dissociation constant.*

$$K_a = \frac{[H^+][A^-]}{[HA]} \qquad (16.2)$$

You should learn how to write the chemical equation for the ionization of a weak acid and be able to write the equilibrium law corresponding to its K_a. This is illustrated in Example 16.1.

EXAMPLE 16.1
Writing the K_a Expression for a Weak Acid

Nitrous acid, HNO_2, is a weak acid that's formed in the stomach when nitrite food preservatives encounter stomach acid. There has been some concern that this acid may form carcinogenic products by reacting with proteins. Write the chemical equation for the equilibrium ionization of HNO_2 in water and the appropriate K_a expression.

ANALYSIS: To solve this problem, we have to think about what happens when the acid reacts with water so we can construct the chemical equation. Once we have the equation, we use it to construct the equilibrium law, which will consist of the mass action expression set equal to K_a.

SOLUTION: When HNO_2 reacts with water, the products will be hydronium ion, H_3O^+, and the conjugate base. The conjugate base of HNO_2 is NO_2^-, so the equation for the ionization reaction is

$$HNO_2 + H_2O \rightleftharpoons H_3O^+ + NO_2^-$$

In the K_a expression, we leave out the H_2O that appears on the left:

$$K_a = \frac{[H_3O^+][NO_2^-]}{[HNO_2]}$$

For simplicity, we usually represent H_3O^+ as H^+, so we can write the expression as

$$K_a = \frac{[H^+][NO_2^-]}{[HNO_2]}$$

Alternatively, we could have written the simplified equation for the ionization reaction, from which the K_a expression above is obtained directly.

$$HNO_2 \rightleftharpoons H^+ + NO_2^-$$

IS THE ANSWER REASONABLE? Our K_a expression has products multiplied in the numerator and reactants in the denominator as required. Also required is that terms within brackets must be multiplied or divided and they are (there are no addition, $+$, or subtraction, $-$, signs where they don't belong). We are now confident we have solved the problem correctly.

The meat products shown here contain nitrite ion as a preservative. *(Andy Washnik.)*

Practice Exercise 1: For each of the following acids, write the equation for its ionization in water and the appropriate expression for K_a: (a) $HC_2H_3O_2$, (b) $(CH_3)_3NH^+$, and (c) H_3PO_4. (Hint: Determine the conjugate base for each of these acids.)

Practice Exercise 2: For each of the following acids, write the equation for its ionization in water and the appropriate expression for K_a: (a) $HCHO_2$, (b) $(CH_3)_2NH_2^+$, and (c) $H_2PO_4^-$.

For weak acids, values of K_a are usually quite small and can be conveniently represented in a logarithmic form similar to pH. Thus, we can define the **pK_a** of an acid as

☐ Also, $K_a = $ antilog$(-pK_a)$ or $K_a = 10^{-pK_a}$.

$$pK_a = -\log K_a$$

The strength of a weak acid is determined by its value of K_a; the larger the K_a, the stronger and more fully ionized the acid. Because of the negative sign in the defining equation for pK_a, the stronger the acid, the *smaller* is its value of pK_a. The values of K_a and pK_a for some typical weak acids are given in Table 16.1. A more complete list is located in Appendix C.7.

TABLE 16.1	K_a and pK_a Values for Weak Monoprotic Acids at 25 °C		
Name of Acid	Formula	K_a	pK_a
Iodic acid	HIO_3	1.7×10^{-1}	0.77
Chloroacetic acid	$HC_2H_2O_2Cl$	1.36×10^{-3}	2.87
Nitrous acid	HNO_2	7.1×10^{-4}	3.15
Hydrofluoric acid	HF	6.8×10^{-4}	3.17
Cyanic acid	$HOCN$	3.5×10^{-4}	3.46
Formic acid	$HCHO_2$	1.8×10^{-4}	3.74
Barbituric acid	$HC_4H_3N_2O_3$	9.8×10^{-5}	4.01
Acetic acid	$HC_2H_3O_2$	1.8×10^{-5}	4.74
Hydrazoic acid	HN_3	1.8×10^{-5}	4.74
Butanoic acid	$HC_4H_7O_2$	1.52×10^{-5}	4.82
Propanoic acid	$HC_3H_5O_2$	1.34×10^{-5}	4.87
Hypochlorous acid	$HOCl$	3.0×10^{-8}	7.52
Hydrocyanic acid (*aq*)	HCN	6.2×10^{-10}	9.21
Phenol	HC_6H_5O	1.3×10^{-10}	9.89
Hydrogen peroxide	H_2O_2	1.8×10^{-12}	11.74

☐ The values of K_a for strong acids are very large and are not tabulated. For many strong acids, K_a values have not been measured.

EXAMPLE 16.2
Interpreting pK_a and Finding K_a

A certain acid was found to have a pK_a equal to 4.88. Is this acid stronger or weaker than acetic acid? What is the value of K_a for the acid?

ANALYSIS: We can compare the acid strengths by comparing their pK_a values. The larger the pK_a, the weaker the acid. Finding K_a from pK_a involves the same kind of calculation as finding $[H^+]$ from pH, which you learned to do in Chapter 15.

SOLUTION: From Table 16.1, the pK_a of acetic acid equals 4.74. The acid referred to in the problem has pK_a equal to 4.88. Because the acid has a larger pK_a than acetic acid, it is a weaker acid.

To find K_a from pK_a, we use an equation similar to that for finding $[H^+]$ from pH, namely

$$K_a = 10^{-pK_a}$$

Substituting,

$$K_a = 10^{-4.88} = 1.3 \times 10^{-5}$$

☐ On most calculators this is the inverse (or 2nd) operation of the *log* function.

IS THE ANSWER REASONABLE? As a quick check, we can compare the K_a values. For acetic acid, $K_a = 1.8 \times 10^{-5}$. This is larger than 1.3×10^{-5}, which tells us that acetic acid is the stronger acid. That agrees with our conclusion based on the pK_a values.

Practice Exercise 3: Use Table 16.1 to find all the acids that are stronger than acetic acid and weaker than formic acid. (Hint: It may be easier to focus on the K_a values since they are directly related to acid strength.)

Practice Exercise 4: Two acids, HA and HB, have pK_a values of 3.16 and 4.14, respectively. Which is the stronger acid? What are the K_a values for the acids?

A weak base reacts with water to give its conjugate acid and hydroxide ion

As with weak acids, all weak bases behave in a similar manner in water. They are weak Brønsted bases and are therefore proton acceptors. Examples are ammonia, NH_3, and acetate ion, $C_2H_3O_2^-$. Their reactions with water are

$$NH_3 + H_2O \rightleftharpoons NH_4^+ + OH^-$$

$$C_2H_3O_2^- + H_2O \rightleftharpoons HC_2H_3O_2 + OH^-$$

Notice that, in each instance, the base reacts with water to give OH^- and the corresponding conjugate acid. We can also represent these reactions by a general equation. If we represent the base by the symbol B, the reaction is

TOOLS

General equation for the ionization of a weak base

$$B + H_2O \rightleftharpoons BH^+ + OH^- \tag{16.3}$$

(As with weak acids, B does not have to be electrically neutral.) This yields the equilibrium law

$$K'_c = \frac{[BH^+][OH^-]}{[B][H_2O]}$$

As with solutions of weak acids, the quantity $[H_2O]$ in the denominator is effectively a constant that can be combined with K_c' to give a new constant that we call the **base ionization constant, K_b.**

☐ K_b is also called the *base dissociation constant.*

$$K_b = \frac{[BH^+][OH^-]}{[B]} \tag{16.4}$$

EXAMPLE 16.3
Writing the K_b Expression for a Weak Base

☐ Hydrazine is a rocket fuel and is used in the manufacture of semiconductor devices.

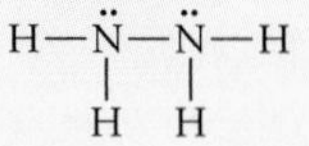

H—N̈—N̈—H   hydrazine
  | | N_2H_4
  H   H

[H—N̈—N—H]⁺   hydrazinium ion
    | | $N_2H_5^+$
    H   H

Hydrazine, N_2H_4, is a weak base. It is a poisonous substance that's sometimes formed when a "chlorine bleach," which contains hypochlorite ion, is added to an aqueous solution of ammonia. Write the equation for the reaction of hydrazine with water and write the expression for its K_b.

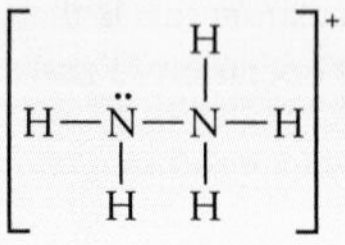

ANALYSIS: To solve this problem, we have to think about what happens when the base reacts with water so we can correctly construct the chemical equation. Once we have the equation, we use it to construct the equilibrium law, which will consist of the mass action expression set equal to K_b.

SOLUTION: When N_2H_4 reacts with water, the products will be OH^- and the conjugate acid. The conjugate acid of N_2H_4 is $N_2H_5^+$, which we obtain by adding a proton (H^+) to N_2H_4. Therefore, the equation for the ionization reaction in water is[1]

$$N_2H_4 + H_2O \rightleftharpoons N_2H_5^+ + OH^-$$

[1] When a proton is accepted by a weak base that contains a nitrogen atom, such as NH_3, N_2H_4, or $(CH_3)_2NH$, the proton binds to a lone pair of electrons on a nitrogen atom of the base. With water serving as a Brønsted acid, we can diagram the reactions of these bases as follows. (The curved arrows indicate how a lone pair extracts the H^+ from the H_2O molecule and how the electron pair in the O—H bond becomes a lone pair in the OH^- ion.)

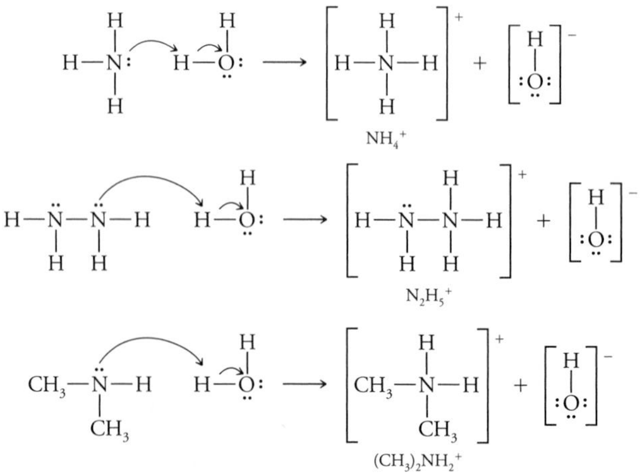

In the expression for K_b we omit the H_2O, so the equilibrium law is

$$K_b = \frac{[N_2H_5^+][OH^-]}{[N_2H_4]}$$

IS THE ANSWER REASONABLE? The most important test is to be sure that products are in the numerator and reactants in the denominator and that all operations are multiplication or division (no addition or subtraction should appear here). Comparing our answer to Equations 16.3 and 16.4, we see they fit the correct pattern for a weak base, so our answers are correct.

EXAMPLE 16.4
Writing the K_b Expression for a Weak Base

Solutions of chlorine bleach such as Clorox contain the hypochlorite ion, OCl^-, which is a weak base. Write the chemical equation for the reaction of OCl^- with water and the appropriate expression for K_b for this anion.

ANALYSIS: This is similar to the preceding example. We have to be sure we have the correct formulas for the reactants and products of the equation.

SOLUTION: The reaction of hypochlorite ion as a base will yield its conjugate acid plus OH^-. We obtain the formula for the conjugate acid of OCl^- by adding one H^+ to the anion, which gives HOCl. Therefore, the equation for the equilibrium is

$$OCl^- + H_2O \rightleftharpoons HOCl + OH^-$$

As before, we omit H_2O from the expression for K_b.

$$K_b = \frac{[HOCl][OH^-]}{[OCl^-]}$$

IS THE ANSWER REASONABLE? We can check that we followed the rules for writing equilibrium constants, with the reactants in the denominator and products in the numerator. We also can compare our answers to Equations 16.3 and 16.4. The answers are okay.

Practice Exercise 5: For each of the following bases, write the equation for its ionization in water and the appropriate expression for K_b. (Hint: See footnote 1.) (a) $(CH_3)_3N$ (trimethylamine), (b) SO_3^{2-} (sulfite ion), (c) NH_2OH (hydroxylamine)

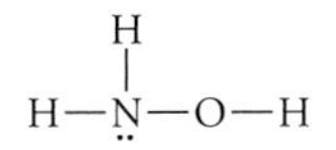

Practice Exercise 6: Write the ionization reaction, and the K_b expression, when each of the following amphiprotic substances acts as a base. (a) HSO_4^-, (b) $H_2PO_4^-$, (c) HPO_4^{2-}, (d) HCO_3^-, (e) HSO_3^-

H
|
H—N—O—H

hydroxylamine, NH_2OH

Because the K_b values for weak bases are usually small numbers, the same kind of logarithmic notation is often used to represent their equilibrium constants. Thus, **pK_b** is defined as

$$pK_b = -\log K_b$$

Table 16.2 lists some molecular bases and their corresponding values of K_b and pK_b. A more complete list is located in Appendix C.7.

Also, $K_b = $ antilog$(-pK_b)$ or $K_b = 10^{-pK_b}$.

The product of K_a and K_b equals K_w for an acid–base conjugate pair

Formic acid, $HCHO_2$ (a substance partly responsible for the sting of a fire ant), is a typical weak acid that ionizes according to the equation

$$HCHO_2 + H_2O \rightleftharpoons H_3O^+ + CHO_2^-$$

TABLE 16.2	K_b and pK_b Values for Weak Molecular Bases at 25 °C		
Name of Base	Formula	K_b	pK_b
Butylamine	$C_4H_9NH_2$	5.9×10^{-4}	3.23
Methylamine	CH_3NH_2	4.4×10^{-4}	3.36
Ammonia	NH_3	1.8×10^{-5}	4.74
Strychnine	$C_{21}H_{22}N_2O_2$	1.0×10^{-6}	6.00
Hydrazine	N_2H_4	9.6×10^{-7}	6.02
Morphine	$C_{17}H_{19}NO_3$	7.5×10^{-7}	6.13
Hydroxylamine	$HONH_2$	6.6×10^{-9}	8.18
Pyridine	C_5H_5N	1.5×10^{-9}	8.82
Aniline	$C_6H_5NH_2$	4.1×10^{-10}	9.39

◻ Formic acid and formate ion have the structures

formic acid, $HCHO_2$
(Acidic hydrogen shown in red.)

formate ion, CHO_2^-

Often the formula for formic acid is written HCOOH to emphasize its molecular structure. In this chapter we will write the formulas for acids with the acidic hydrogens first in the formula, which is why we've given the formula for formic acid as $HCHO_2$.

As you've seen, we write its K_a expression as

$$K_a = \frac{[H^+][CHO_2^-]}{[HCHO_2]}$$

The conjugate base of formic acid is the formate ion, CHO_2^-, and when a solute that contains this ion (e.g., $NaCHO_2$) is dissolved in water, the solution is slightly basic. In other words, the formate ion is a weak base in water and participates in the equilibrium

$$CHO_2^- + H_2O \rightleftharpoons HCHO_2 + OH^-$$

The K_b expression for this base is

$$K_b = \frac{[HCHO_2][OH^-]}{[CHO_2^-]}$$

There is an important relationship between the equilibrium constants for this acid–base pair: the product of K_a times K_b equals K_w. We can see this by multiplying the mass action expressions.

$$K_a \times K_b = \frac{[H^+][\cancel{CHO_2^-}]}{[\cancel{HCHO_2}]} \times \frac{[\cancel{HCHO_2}][OH^-]}{[\cancel{CHO_2^-}]} = [H^+][OH^-] = K_w$$

In fact, this same relationship exists for *any* acid–base conjugate pair.

For *any* acid–base conjugate pair:

Relationship between K_a and K_b

$$K_a \times K_b = K_w \qquad (16.5)$$

Another useful relationship, which can be derived by taking the negative logarithm of each side of Equation 16.5, is

Relationship between pK_a and pK_b

$$pK_a + pK_b = pK_w = 14.00 \qquad \text{(at 25 °C)} \qquad (16.6)$$

There are some important consequences of the relationship expressed in Equation 16.5. One is that it is not necessary to tabulate both K_a and K_b for the members of an acid–base pair; if one K is known, the other can be calculated. For example, the K_a for $HCHO_2$ and the K_b for NH_3 will be found in most tables of acid–base equilibrium constants, but these tables usually will not contain the equilibrium constants for the ions that are the conjugates. Thus, tables usually will not contain the K_b for CHO_2^- or the K_a for NH_4^+. If we need them for a calculation, we can calculate them using Equation 16.5.

◻ Tables of ionization constants usually give values for only the molecular member of an acid–base pair.

Practice Exercise 7: The methylammonium ion $CH_3NH_3^+$ has a K_a of 2.3×10^{-11}. What is the K_b for the base methylamine? (Hint: Recall that K_a and K_b are inversely proportional to each other.)

Practice Exercise 8: The value of K_a for $HCHO_2$ is 1.8×10^{-4}. What is the value of K_b for the CHO_2^- ion?

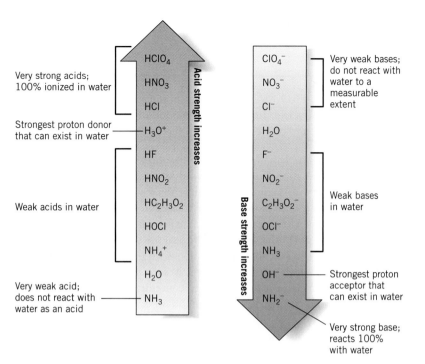

FIG. 16.1 **The relative strengths of conjugate acid–base pairs.** The stronger the acid, the weaker is its conjugate base. The weaker the acid, the stronger is its conjugate base. Very strong acids are 100% ionized and their conjugate bases do not react with water to any measurable extent.

Another interesting and useful observation is that *there is an inverse relationship between the strengths of the acid and base members of a conjugate pair.* This is illustrated graphically in Figure 16.1. Because the product of K_a and K_b is a constant, the larger the value of K_a is, the smaller is the value of K_b. In other words, *the stronger the conjugate acid, the weaker is its conjugate base* (a fact that we noted in Chapter 15 in our discussion of the strengths of Brønsted acids and bases). We will say more about this relationship in Section 16.3.

16.2 CALCULATIONS CAN INVOLVE FINDING OR USING K_a AND K_b

Our goal in this section is to develop a general strategy for dealing quantitatively with the equilibria of weak acids and bases in water. Generally, these calculations fall into two categories. The first involves calculating the value of K_a or K_b from the initial concentration of the acid or base and the measured pH of the solution (or some other data about the equilibrium composition of the solution). The second involves calculating equilibrium concentrations given K_a or K_b and initial concentrations.

Initial concentrations and equilibrium data can be used to calculate K_a or K_b

In problems of this type, our *first* goal is to obtain numerical values for *all* the equilibrium concentrations that are needed to evaluate the mass action expression in the definition of K_a or K_b. (The reason, of course, is that at equilibrium the reaction quotient, Q, equals the equilibrium constant.) We are usually given the molar concentration of the acid or base as it would appear on the label of a bottle containing the solution. Also provided is information from which we can obtain directly at least one of the equilibrium concentrations. Thus, we might be given the measured pH of the solution, which provides an estimate of the equilibrium concentration of H^+. (Equilibrium is achieved rapidly in these solutions, so when we measure the pH, the value obtained can be used to calculate the equilibrium concentration of H^+.) Alternatively, we might be given the **percentage ionization** of the acid or base, which we define as follows:

$$\text{Percentage ionization} = \frac{\text{moles ionized per liter}}{\text{moles available per liter}} \times 100\% \qquad (16.7)$$

TOOLS

Percentage ionization

Let's look at some examples that illustrate how to determine K_a and K_b from the kind of data mentioned.

EXAMPLE 16.5
Calculating K_a and pK_a from pH

For some, nothing goes better on a hot dog than sauerkraut and mustard. Lactic acid gives sauerkraut its sour taste. *(Coco McCoy/Rainbow.)*

Lactic acid ($HC_3H_5O_3$), which is present in sour milk, also gives sauerkraut its tartness. It is a monoprotic acid. In a 0.100 M solution of lactic acid, the pH is 2.44 at 25 °C. Calculate the K_a and pK_a for lactic acid at that temperature.

ANALYSIS: In any problem involving the ionization of a weak acid or base, the first step is to write the chemical equation. From the equation we can write the correct equilibrium law and perform any necessary stoichiometric reasoning. You've learned how to write equations for such reactions, so all we need to know is whether the solute is an acid or a base. We're told it's an acid, so we'll begin by writing the equilibrium equation, and then the K_a expression.

We're given the pH of the solution, so we can use this to calculate the H^+ concentration. This will be the *equilibrium* [H^+]; as noted above, equilibrium is reached rapidly in solutions of acids and bases, so when a pH is measured, it is the pH at equilibrium. Once we know the [H^+], we will perform some reasoning using a concentration table of the type we developed in Chapter 14 to figure out the rest of the equilibrium concentrations. After we know them all, we will substitute them into the mass action expression to calculate K_a. (It's important to remember that values that satisfy the K_a expression are *equilibrium* values only.)

SOLUTION: We know the solute is an acid, and we know the general equation for the ionization of an acid, which we apply to the solute in question.

$$HC_3H_5O_3 \rightleftharpoons H^+ + C_3H_5O_3^- \qquad K_a = \frac{[H^+][C_3H_5O_3^-]}{[HC_3H_5O_3]}$$

At this point it will help to set up an equilibrium table as introduced in Chapter 14. To obtain the initial concentrations we see that the only solute is the weak acid (0.100 M), so the only source of the ions, H^+ and $C_3H_5O_3^-$, is the ionization of the acid. Their concentrations are listed initially as zero. (Remember, in a solution of an acid, it is safe to ignore the small amount of H^+ contributed by the autoionization of water.) These entries are shown in black.

We now find the [H^+] from pH. This gives us the *equilibrium* value of [H^+].

$$[H^+] = 10^{-2.44}$$
$$= 0.0036 \ M$$

☐ Remember, the measured pH *always* gives the equilibrium concentration of H^+.

Because the ions are formed in a 1 to 1 ratio, [$C_3H_5O_3^-$] = [H^+], so we now know that [$C_3H_5O_3^-$] = 0.0036 M. These concentrations are equilibrium values and are entered as the red numbers in the table. Since the initial concentration added to the corresponding change gives us the equilibrium concentration, we can deduce that changes for H^+ and $C_3H_5O_3^-$ are 0.0036 and the change for $HC_3H_5O_3$ must be −0.0036. Finally we can calculate the equilibrium concentration of $HC_3H_5O_3$ as shown in boldface in the table.

	$HC_3H_5O_3$ $\rightleftharpoons$	H^+ +	$C_3H_5O_3^-$
Initial concentrations (M)	0.100	0	0
Changes in concentrations caused by the ionization (M)	−0.0036	+0.0036	+0.0036
Final concentrations at equilibrium (M)	**(0.100 − 0.0036) = 0.096 (correctly rounded)**	0.0036	0.0036

The last row of data contains the equilibrium concentrations that we now use to calculate K_a. We simply substitute them into the K_a expression.

$$K_a = \frac{(3.6 \times 10^{-3})(3.6 \times 10^{-3})}{0.096} = 1.4 \times 10^{-4}$$

Thus the acid ionization constant for lactic acid is 1.4×10^{-4}. To find pK_a, we take the negative logarithm of K_a.

$$pK_a = -\log K_a = -\log (1.4 \times 10^{-4}) = 3.85$$

IS THE ANSWER REASONABLE? Weak acids have small ionization constants, so the value we obtained for K_a seems to be reasonable. *We should also check the entries in the concentration table to be sure they are reasonable.* For example, the "changes" for the ions are both positive, meaning both of their concentrations are increasing. This is the way it *must* be because neither ion can have a concentration less than zero. The changes are caused by the ionization reaction, so they both have to change in the same direction and must be equal to each other. Also, we have the concentration of the molecular acid decreasing, as it should if the ions are being formed by the ionization.

EXAMPLE 16.6
Calculating K_b and pK_b from pH

Methylamine, CH_3NH_2, is a weak base and one of several substances that give herring brine its pungent odor. In 0.100 M CH_3NH_2, only 6.4% of the base is ionized. What are K_b and pK_b of methylamine?

ANALYSIS: In this problem we've been given the percentage ionization of the base. We will use this to calculate the equilibrium concentrations of the ions in the solution. After we know these, solving the problem follows the same path as in the preceding example.

SOLUTION: The first step is to write the chemical equation for the equilibrium and the equilibrium law. To write the chemical equation we need the formula for the conjugate acid of CH_3NH_2, which is $CH_3NH_3^+$ (we've added one H^+ to the nitrogen atom of the base to obtain the conjugate acid). Therefore, applying the general equation for the ionization of a weak base given on page 646, the chemical equation and equilibrium law are

$$CH_3NH_2(aq) + H_2O \rightleftharpoons CH_3NH_3^+(aq) + OH^-(aq)$$

$$K_b = \frac{[CH_3NH_3^+][OH^-]}{[CH_3NH_2]}$$

We can start constructing the equilibrium table at this point with the chemical equation and the appropriate rows and columns. We also enter the initial concentrations as shown in black. The initial concentration means those concentrations before any reaction takes place. Therefore the ions are listed as zeros.

The percentage ionization tells us that 6.4% of the CH_3NH_2 has reacted. Therefore, the number of moles per liter of the base that has ionized at equilibrium in this solution is:

$$\text{Moles per liter of } CH_3NH_2 \text{ ionized} = 0.064 \times 0.100 \, M = 0.0064 \, M$$

This value represents the *decrease* in the concentration of CH_3NH_2, which we record in the "change" row of the concentration table as -0.0064. We can now use the change in $[CH_3NH_2]$ to determine the concentrations of the other species. These are entered in red. The final equilibrium concentrations are calculated from the initial concentrations and the changes we calculated. They are shown in boldface in the table.

Methylamine is responsible in part for the fishy aroma of pickled herring. (*Andy Washnik.*)

☐ To find 6.4% of 0.100 M the percentage must be converted to the fraction 0.064 first, as shown.

	H_2O + CH_3NH_2 $\rightleftharpoons$ $CH_3NH_3^+$ + OH^-		
Initial concentrations (M)	0.100	0	0
Changes in concentrations caused by the ionization (M)	-0.0064	$+0.0064$	$+0.0064$
Final concentrations at equilibrium (M)	**(0.100 − 0.0064)** **= 0.094 (properly rounded)**	**0.0064**	**0.0064**

Now we can calculate K_b by substituting equilibrium quantities into the mass action expression.

$$K_b = \frac{(0.0064)(0.0064)}{(0.094)} = 4.4 \times 10^{-4}$$

and

$$pK_b = -\log(4.4 \times 10^{-4}) = 3.36$$

IS THE ANSWER REASONABLE? First, the value of K_b is small, so that suggests we've probably worked the problem correctly. We can also check the "Change" row to be sure the algebraic signs are correct. Both ions' initial concentrations start out at zero, so they must both increase, which they do. The change for the CH_3NH_2 is opposite in sign to that for the ions, and that's as it should be. Therefore, we appear to have set up the problem correctly.

Practice Exercise 9: Salicylic acid reacts with acetic acid to form aspirin, acetylsalicylic acid. A 0.200 molar solution of salicylic acid has a pH of 1.836. Calculate the K_a and pK_a of salicylic acid. (Hint: Convert the pH to $[H^+]$ first.)

☐
$$CH_3-CH_2-CH_2-\overset{\overset{\textstyle O}{\|}}{C}-O-H$$
butyric acid
$HC_4H_7O_2$

Practice Exercise 10: When butter turns rancid, its foul odor is mostly that of butyric acid, $HC_4H_7O_2$, a weak monoprotic acid similar to acetic acid in structure. In a 0.0100 M solution of butyric acid at 20 °C, the acid is 4.0% ionized. Calculate the K_a and pK_a of butyric acid at that temperature.

Practice Exercise 11: Few substances are more effective in relieving intense pain than morphine. Morphine is an alkaloid—an alkali-like compound obtained from plants—and alkaloids are all weak bases. In 0.010 M morphine, the pOH is 3.90. Calculate the K_b and pK_b for morphine. (You don't need to know the formula for morphine, just that it's a base. Use whatever symbol you want to write the equation.)

Equilibrium concentrations can be calculated from K_a (or K_b) and initial concentrations

These calculations are not especially difficult providing you start off on the right foot. The key to success is examining the statement of the problem carefully so you can construct the correct chemical equation, which will then lead you to write the equilibrium law that's required to obtain the solution. With this in mind, let's take an overview of the "landscape" to develop a method for selecting the correct approach to the problem.

Almost any problem in which you are given a value of K_a or K_b falls into one of three categories: (1) the aqueous solution contains a weak acid as its *only* solute, (2) the solution contains a weak base as its *only* solute, or (3) the solution contains *both* a weak acid and its conjugate base. The approach we take for each of these conditions is described below and is summarized in Figure 16.2.

1. If the solution contains only a weak acid as the solute, then the problem *must* be solved using K_a. This means that the correct chemical equation for the problem is the ionization of the weak acid. It also means that if you are given the K_b for the acid's conjugate base, you will have to calculate the K_a in order to solve the problem.

☐ Conditions 1 and 2 apply to solutions of weak molecular acids and bases and to solutions of salts that contain an ion that is an acid or a base. Condition 3 applies to solutions called buffers, which are discussed in Section 16.5.

2. If the solution contains only a weak base, the problem *must* be solved using K_b. The correct chemical equation is for the ionization of the weak base. If the problem gives you K_a for the base's conjugate acid, then you must calculate K_b to solve the problem.

3. Solutions that contain two solutes, one a weak acid and the other its conjugate base, have some special properties that we will discuss later. (Such solutions are called buffers.) To work problems for these kinds of mixtures, we can use *either* K_a or K_b—it doesn't matter which we use, because we will obtain the same answers either way. However, if we elect to use K_a, then the chemical equation we use must be for the ionization of

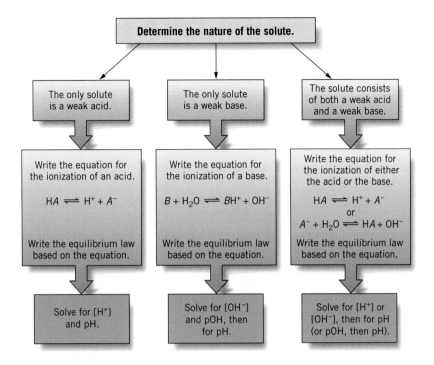

FIG. 16.2 Determining how to proceed in acid–base equilibrium problems. The nature of the solute species determines how the problem is approached. Following this diagram will get you started in the right direction.

the acid. If we decide to use K_b, then the correct chemical equation is for the ionization of the base. Usually, the choice of whether to use K_a or K_b is made on the basis of which constant is most readily available.

When you begin to solve a problem, decide which of the three conditions above applies. If necessary, keep Figure 16.2 handy to guide you in your decision, so that you select the correct path to follow.

Simplifications can usually be made in acid–base equilibrium calculations

In Chapter 14 you learned that when the equilibrium constant is small, it is frequently possible to make simplifying assumptions that greatly reduce the algebraic effort in obtaining equilibrium concentrations. For many acid–base equilibrium problems such simplifications are particularly useful.

Let's consider a solution of 1.0 M acetic acid, $HC_2H_3O_2$, for which $K_a = 1.8 \times 10^{-5}$. What is involved in determining the equilibrium concentrations in the solution?

To answer this question, we begin with the chemical equation for the equilibrium. Because the only solute in the solution is the weak acid, we must use K_a and therefore write the equation for the ionization of the acid. Let's use the simplified version.

$$HC_2H_3O_2 \rightleftharpoons H^+ + C_2H_3O_2^-$$

The equilibrium law is

$$K_a = \frac{[H^+][C_2H_3O_2^-]}{[HC_2H_3O_2]} = 1.8 \times 10^{-5}$$

We will take the given concentration, 1.0 M, to be the initial concentration of $HC_2H_3O_2$ (i.e., the concentration of the acid before any ionization has occurred). This concentration will drop slightly as the acid ionizes and the ions form. If we let x be the amount of acetic acid that ionizes per liter, then the $HC_2H_3O_2$ concentration will decrease by x (its change will be $-x$) and the H^+ and $C_2H_3O_2^-$ concentrations will each increase by x (their changes will be $+x$). We can now construct the following concentration table.

□

$$CH_3-\overset{\overset{\displaystyle O}{\|}}{C}-O-H$$
acetic acid
$HC_2H_3O_2$

□ The initial concentrations of the ions are set equal to zero because none of them have been supplied by a solute.

	HC$_2$H$_3$O$_2$ $\rightleftharpoons$ H$^+$ + C$_2$H$_3$O$_2^-$		
Initial concentrations (M)	1.0	0	0
Changes in concentrations caused by the ionization (M)	$-x$	$+x$	$+x$
Concentrations at equilibrium (M)	$1.0 - x$	x	x

The values in the last row of the table should satisfy the equilibrium law. When they are substituted into the mass action expression we obtain

$$\frac{(x)(x)}{1.0 - x} = 1.8 \times 10^{-5}$$

This equation involves a term in x^2, and it could be solved using the quadratic formula. However, this and many other similar calculations involving weak acids and bases can be simplified. Let's look at the reasoning.

The equilibrium constant, 1.8×10^{-5}, is quite small, so we can anticipate that very little of the acetic acid will be ionized at equilibrium. This means x will be very small, so we make the approximation $(1.0 - x) \approx 1.0$. Replacing $1.0 - x$ with 1.0 yields the equation

☐ We are assuming that when x is subtracted from 1.0 and *the result is rounded to the correct number of significant figures*, the answer will round to 1.0.

$$\frac{x^2}{1.0} = 1.8 \times 10^{-5}$$

Solving for x gives $x = 0.0042\ M$. We see that the value of x is indeed negligible compared to $1.0\ M$ (i.e., if we subtract $0.0042\ M$ from $1.0\ M$ and round correctly, we obtain $1.0\ M$).

Notice that when we make this approximation, *the initial concentration of the acid is used as if it were the equilibrium concentration.* The approximation is valid when the equilibrium constant is small and the concentrations of the solutes are reasonably high—conditions that will apply to most situations you will encounter in this chapter. In Section 16.4 we will discuss the conditions under which the approximation is not valid.

Let's look at some examples that illustrate typical acid–base equilibrium problems.

EXAMPLE 16.7

Calculating the Values of [H$^+$] and pH for a Solution of a Weak Acid from Its K_a Value

The calcium salt of propionic acid, calcium propionate, is used as a preservative in baked products. *(Andy Washnik.)*

A student planned an experiment that would use $0.10\ M$ propionic acid, HC$_3$H$_5$O$_2$. Calculate the value of [H$^+$] and the pH for this solution. For propionic acid, $K_a = 1.34 \times 10^{-5}$.

ANALYSIS: First, we note that the only solute in the solution is a weak acid, so we know we will have to use K_a and write the equation for the ionization of the acid.

$$HC_3H_5O_2 \rightleftharpoons H^+ + C_3H_5O_2^-$$

$$K_a = \frac{[H^+][C_3H_5O_2^-]}{[HC_3H_5O_2]}$$

The initial concentration of the acid is $0.10\ M$, and the initial concentrations of the ions are both $0\ M$. Then we construct the concentration table.

SOLUTION: All concentrations in the table are in moles per liter.

	HC$_3$H$_5$O$_2$ $\rightleftharpoons$ H$^+$ + C$_3$H$_5$O$_2^-$		
Initial concentrations (M)	0.10	0	0
Changes in concentrations caused by the ionization (M)	$-x$	$+x$	$+x$
Final concentrations at equilibrium (M)	$(0.10 - x)$ ≈ 0.10	x	x

Notice that the equilibrium concentrations of H^+ and $C_3H_5O_2^-$ are the same; they are represented by x. Anticipating that x will be very small, we make the simplifying approximation $(0.10 - x) \approx 0.10$, so we take the equilibrium concentration of $HC_3H_5O_2$ to be $0.10\ M$. Substituting these quantities into the K_a expression gives

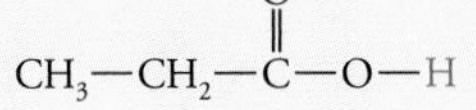

$$K_a = \frac{[H^+][C_3H_5O_2^-]}{[HC_3H_5O_2]} = \frac{(x)(x)}{(0.10 - x)} \approx \frac{(x)(x)}{(0.10)} = 1.34 \times 10^{-5}$$

Solving for x yields

$$x = 1.2 \times 10^{-3}$$

Because $x = [H^+]$,

$$[H^+] = 1.2 \times 10^{-3}\ M$$

Finally, we calculate the pH

$$pH = -\log (1.2 \times 10^{-3})$$
$$= 2.92$$

IS THE ANSWER REASONABLE? First, we check to be sure our assumption was reasonable, and it is $(0.10 - 0.0012 = 0.10$ when rounded correctly). Also we see that the calculated pH is less than 7. This tells us that the solution is acidic, which it should be for a solution of an acid. Also, the pH is higher than it would be if the acid were strong. (A $0.10\ M$ solution of a strong acid would have $[H^+] = 0.10\ M$ and $pH = 1.0$). If we wish to further check the accuracy of the calculation, we can substitute the calculated equilibrium concentrations into the mass action expression. If the calculated quantities are correct, the reaction quotient should equal K_a. Let's do the calculation.

$$\frac{[H^+][C_3H_5O_2^-]}{[HC_3H_5O_2]} = \frac{(x)(x)}{(0.10)} = \frac{(1.2 \times 10^{-3})^2}{0.10} = 1.4 \times 10^{-5} \approx K_a$$

The check works, so we know we have done the calculation correctly.

propionic acid
$HC_3H_5O_2$

Practice Exercise 12: Boric acid, H_3BO_3, behaves as a monoprotic acid with a $K_a = 5.8 \times 10^{-10}$. Calculate $[H^+]$ and the pH of a $0.050\ M$ solution of H_3BO_3. (Hint: Consider using an assumption to solve this problem.)

Practice Exercise 13: Nicotinic acid, $HC_2H_4NO_2$, is a B vitamin. It is also a weak acid with $K_a = 1.4 \times 10^{-5}$. Calculate $[H^+]$ and the pH of a $0.050\ M$ solution of $HC_2H_4NO_2$.

EXAMPLE 16.8
Calculating the pH of a Solution and the Percentage Ionization of the Solute

A solution of hydrazine, N_2H_4, has a concentration of $0.25\ M$. What is the pH of the solution, and what is the percentage ionization of the hydrazine? Hydrazine has $K_b = 9.6 \times 10^{-7}$.

ANALYSIS: Hydrazine must be a weak base, because we have its value of K_b (the "b" in K_b tells us this is a *base* ionization constant). Since hydrazine is the only solute in the solution, we will have to write the equation for the ionization of a weak base and then set up the K_b expression. The conjugate acid of N_2H_4 has one additional H^+, so its formula is $N_2H_5^+$. We need this formula so we can write the correct chemical equation.

SOLUTION: We begin with the chemical equation and the K_b expression.

$$N_2H_4 + H_2O \rightleftharpoons N_2H_5^+ + OH^-$$
$$K_b = \frac{[N_2H_5^+][OH^-]}{[N_2H_4]}$$

Let's once again construct the concentration table. The only sources of $N_2H_5^+$ and OH^- are the ionization of the N_2H_4, so their initial concentrations are both zero. They will form in equal amounts, so we let their changes in concentration equal $+x$. The concentration of N_2H_4 will decrease by x, so its change is $-x$.

	H_2O +	N_2H_4	$\rightleftharpoons$	$N_2H_5^+$ +	OH^-
Initial concentrations (M)		0.25		0	0
Changes in concentrations caused by the ionization (M)		$-x$		$+x$	$+x$
Final concentrations at equilibrium (M)		$(0.25 - x)$ ≈ 0.25		x	x

Because K_b is so small, $[N_2H_4] \approx 0.25$ M. (As before, we assume the initial concentration will be effectively the same as the equilibrium concentration, an approximation that we expect to be valid.) Substituting into the K_b expression,

$$\frac{(x)(x)}{0.25 - x} \approx \frac{(x)(x)}{0.25} = 9.6 \times 10^{-7}$$

Solving for x gives $x = 4.9 \times 10^{-4}$. This value represents the hydroxide ion concentration, from which we can calculate the pOH.

$$pOH = -\log(4.9 \times 10^{-4}) = 3.31$$

The pH of the solution can then be obtained from the relationship

$$pH + pOH = 14.00$$

Thus,

$$pH = 14.00 - 3.31 = 10.69$$

To calculate the percentage ionization, we need to use Equation 16.7 on page 649. This requires that we know the number of moles per liter of the base that has ionized. From the concentration table, we see that this value is also equal to x, the amount of N_2H_4 that ionizes per liter (i.e., the change in the N_2H_4 concentration). Therefore,

$$\text{Percentage ionization} = \frac{4.9 \times 10^{-4} \, M}{0.25 \, M} \times 100\%$$
$$= 0.20\%$$

The base is 0.20% ionized.

IS THE ANSWER REASONABLE? First, we can quickly check to see whether the value of x satisfies our assumption, and it does $(0.25 - 0.00049 = 0.25)$. The value of the hydroxide ion concentration is small and the pH indicates a basic solution. Additionally the small concentration of hydroxide ions agrees with the small percentage ionization we calculated. We could also use our equilibrium concentrations to calculate K_b as in the previous example.

Practice Exercise 14: Aniline, $C_6H_5NH_2$, is a precursor for many dyes used to color fabrics, known as aniline dyes. Aniline has a K_b of 4.1×10^{-10}. What is the pOH of a 0.025 molar solution of aniline? (Hint: Calculate the OH^- concentration.)

Practice Exercise 15: Pyridine, C_5H_5N, is a foul-smelling liquid for which $K_b = 1.5 \times 10^{-9}$. What is the pH of a 0.010 M aqueous solution of pyridine?

Practice Exercise 16: Phenol is an acidic organic compound for which $K_a = 1.3 \times 10^{-10}$. What is the pH of a 0.15 M solution of phenol in water?

16.3 | SALT SOLUTIONS ARE NOT NEUTRAL IF THE IONS ARE WEAK ACIDS OR BASES

When we study solutions of salts, we find that many have a neutral pH. Examples are NaCl or KNO_3. However, not all salt solutions behave this way. Some, such as $NaC_2H_3O_2$, are slightly basic while others, such as NH_4Cl, are slightly acidic. To understand this behavior, we have to examine how the ions of a salt can affect the pH of a solution.

In Section 16.1 you saw that weak acids and bases are not limited to molecular substances. For instance, on page 643 NH_4^+ was given as an example of a weak acid, and on page 645 $C_2H_3O_2^-$ was cited as an example of a weak base. Ions such as these always come to us in compounds in which there is both a cation *and* an anion. Therefore, to place NH_4^+ in water, we need a salt such as NH_4Cl, and to place $C_2H_3O_2^-$ in water, we need a salt such as $NaC_2H_3O_2$.

Because a salt contains two ions, the pH of its solution can potentially be affected by either the cation or the anion, or perhaps even both. Therefore, we have to consider *both* ions if we wish to predict the effect of a salt on the pH of a solution.

Cations can be acids

If the cation of a salt is able to influence the pH of a solution, it does so by behaving as a weak acid. Not all cations are acidic, however, so let's look at the possibilities.

Conjugate acids of molecular bases are weak acids

The ammonium ion, NH_4^+, is the conjugate acid of the molecular base, NH_3. We have already learned that NH_4^+, supplied for example by NH_4Cl, is a weak acid. As seen in Figure 16.3, solutions of this salt have a pH lower than 7. The equation for the reaction as an acid is

$$NH_4^+(aq) + H_2O \rightleftharpoons NH_3(aq) + H_3O^+(aq)$$

Writing this in a simplified form, along with the K_a expression, we have

$$NH_4^+(aq) \rightleftharpoons NH_3(aq) + H^+(aq) \qquad K_a = \frac{[NH_3][H^+]}{[NH_4^+]}$$

☐ The reaction of a salt with water to give either an acidic or basic solution is sometimes called **hydrolysis.** Hydrolysis means *reaction with water.*

Because the K_a values for ions are seldom tabulated, we would usually expect to calculate the K_a value using the relationship: $K_a \times K_b = K_w$. In Table 16.2 the K_b for NH_3 is given as 1.8×10^{-5}. Therefore,

$$K_a = \frac{K_w}{K_b} = \frac{1.0 \times 10^{-14}}{1.8 \times 10^{-5}} = 5.6 \times 10^{-10}$$

Another example is the hydrazinium ion, $N_2H_5^+$, which is also a weak acid.

$$N_2H_5^+(aq) \rightleftharpoons N_2H_4(aq) + H^+(aq) \qquad K_a = \frac{[N_2H_4][H^+]}{[N_2H_5^+]}$$

The tabulated K_b for N_2H_4 is 1.7×10^{-6}. From this, the calculated value of K_a equals 5.9×10^{-9}.

These examples illustrate a general phenomenon:

> Cations that are the conjugate acids of molecular bases tend to be weakly acidic.

Cations that are not conjugate acids of molecular bases are generally metal ions such as Na^+, K^+, and Ca^{2+}. In Chapter 15 we learned that the cations of the Group IA metals are very weak acids and are unable to affect the pH of a solution. Except for Be^{2+}, the cations of Group IIA also do not affect pH.

Anions can be bases

When a Brønsted acid loses a proton, its conjugate base is formed. Thus Cl^- is the conjugate base of HCl, and $C_2H_3O_2^-$ is the conjugate base of $HC_2H_3O_2$.

TOOLS

Identification of acidic cations

FIG. 16.4 **Acetate ion is a weak base in water.** The pH of a solution of $KC_2H_3O_2$ is greater than 7, which shows that the solution is basic. Acetate ion reacts with water to yield small amounts of hydroxide ion.

$$C_2H_3O_2^- + H_2O \rightleftharpoons$$
$$HC_2H_3O_2 + OH^-$$

(Andy Washnik.)

Acid	Base
HCl	Cl^-
$HC_2H_3O_2$	$C_2H_3O_2^-$

Although both Cl^- and $C_2H_3O_2^-$ are bases, only the latter affects the pH of an aqueous solution. Why?

Earlier you learned that there is an inverse relationship between the strengths of an acid and its conjugate base—the stronger the acid, the weaker is the conjugate base. Therefore, when an acid is *extremely strong*, as in the case of HCl or other "strong" acids that are 100% ionized (such as HNO_3), the conjugate base is *extremely weak* — too weak to affect in a measurable way the pH of a solution. Consequently, we have the following generalization:

> The anion of a strong acid is too weak a base to influence the pH of a solution.

Acetic acid is much weaker than HCl, as evidenced by its value of K_a (1.8×10^{-5}). Because acetic acid is a weak acid, its conjugate base is much stronger than Cl^- and we can expect it to affect the pH (Figure 16.4). We can calculate the value of K_b for $C_2H_3O_2^-$ from the K_a for $HC_2H_3O_2$, also with the equation $K_a \times K_b = K_w$.

$$K_b = \frac{1.0 \times 10^{-14}}{1.8 \times 10^{-5}} = 5.6 \times 10^{-10}$$

This leads to another conclusion:

TOOLS

Identification of basic anions

> The anion of a weak acid is a weak base and can influence the pH of a solution. It will tend to make the solution basic.

Acid-base properties of a salt can be predicted

To decide if any given salt will affect the pH of an aqueous solution, we must examine each of its ions and see what it alone might do. There are four possibilities:

1. If neither the cation nor the anion can affect the pH, the solution should be neutral.
2. If only the cation of the salt is acidic, the solution will be acidic.
3. If only the anion of the salt is basic, the solution will be basic.
4. If a salt has a cation that is acidic and an anion that is basic, the pH of the solution is determined by the *relative* strengths of the acid and base based on the K_a and K_b of the ions.

Let's work some examples to show how we use these generalizations.

EXAMPLE 16.9
Predicting the Effect of a Salt on the pH of a Solution

Will a solution of NaOCl, an ingredient in many common bleaching and disinfecting agents, be acidic, basic, or neutral? Will a solution of $Ca(NO_3)_2$, a compound used in fireworks and fertilizers, be acidic, basic, or neutral?

ANALYSIS: Each solute is a salt, so we assume it to be 100% dissociated in water.

$$NaOCl(s) \xrightarrow{H_2O} Na^+(aq) + OCl^-(aq)$$

$$Ca(NO_3)_2(s) \xrightarrow{H_2O} Ca^{2+}(aq) + 2NO_3^-(aq)$$

To answer the question for each solution, we take each ion, in turn, and examine its effect on the acidity of the solution.

SOLUTION: *For NaOCl:* The Na^+ ion is an ion of a Group IA metal and is *not* acidic. Therefore, it does not affect the pH of the solution. We might say Na^+ has a "neutral" effect on the pH. Next, we need to determine whether the anion might be basic. To decide, we need to know about the strength of its conjugate acid, which we obtain by adding H^+ to OCl^- to give $HOCl$. The list of strong acids is short, and $HOCl$ is not on it, so we can expect that it is a weak acid. If $HOCl$ is a weak acid, then OCl^- is a weak base and its presence should tend to make the solution basic.

Of the two ions in the salt, one is basic and the other is neutral. Therefore, a solution of $NaOCl$ will be basic.

For Ca(NO₃)₂: The Ca^{2+} ion is an ion of a Group IIA metal, so it is not acidic. It will have no effect on the pH. The anion, NO_3^-, comes from the acid HNO_3, which is on our list of strong acids. Therefore, NO_3^- is an extremely weak base and will also have no effect on the pH. Our conclusion, therefore, is that a solution of $Ca(NO_3)_2$ will be neutral.

ARE THE ANSWERS REASONABLE? All we can do here is check our reasoning, which appears to be sound.

□ The only time an anion might be acidic is if it is from a partially neutralized polyprotic acid, e.g., HSO_4^-. Because OCl^- doesn't have a hydrogen, it can't be a Brønsted acid.

Practice Exercise 17: Are solutions of (a) $NaNO_2$, (b) KCl, and (c) NH_4Br acidic, basic, or neutral? (Hint: Write the ions for these compounds. What are the conjugate acids and bases of these ions?)

Practice Exercise 18: Are solutions of (a) $NaNO_3$, (b) $KOCl$, and (c) NH_4NO_3 acidic, basic, or neutral?

What is the pH of a 0.10 M solution of NaOCl? For HOCl, $K_a = 3.0 \times 10^{-8}$.

EXAMPLE 16.10
Calculating the pH of a Salt Solution

ANALYSIS: Problems such as this are just like the other acid–base equilibrium problems you have learned to solve. We proceed as follows: (1) We determine the nature of the solute: Is it a weak acid, is it a weak base, or are both a weak acid and weak base present? (2) We write the appropriate chemical equation and equilibrium law. (3) We proceed with the solution.

The solute is a salt, which is dissociated into the ions Na^+ and OCl^-. The analysis we performed in Example 16.9 tells us that only OCl^- can affect the pH. It is the conjugate *base* of HOCl, so for the purposes of problem solving, the active solute species is a weak base. On page 652 you learned that when the *only* solute is a weak base, we must use the K_b expression to solve the problem. This is where we begin the solution to the problem.

SOLUTION: We write the chemical equation for the equilibrium ionization of the base, OCl^-, and its K_b expression.

□ If you had trouble writing the correct chemical equation for this equilibrium, you should review Section 16.1.

$$OCl^- + H_2O \rightleftharpoons HOCl + OH^- \qquad K_b = \frac{[HOCl][OH^-]}{[OCl^-]}$$

The data provided in the problem gives the K_a for HOCl. But we can easily calculate K_b because $K_a \times K_b = K_w$.

$$K_b = \frac{K_w}{K_a} = \frac{1.0 \times 10^{-14}}{3.0 \times 10^{-8}} = 3.3 \times 10^{-7}$$

Now let's set up the concentration table. The only sources of HOCl and OH^- are the reaction of the OCl^-, so their concentrations will each increase by x and the concentration of OCl^- will decrease by x.

	H_2O	$+$	OCl^-	$\rightleftharpoons$	$HOCl$	$+$	OH^-
Initial concentrations (M)			0.10		0		0
Changes in concentrations caused by the ionization (M)			$-x$		$+x$		$+x$
Final concentrations at equilibrium (M)			$(0.10 - x)$ ≈ 0.10		x		x

At equilibrium, the concentrations of HOCl and OH^- are the same, x.

$$[HOCl] = [OH^-] = x$$

Because K_b is so small, $[OCl^-] \approx 0.10\ M$. (Once again, we expect x to be so small that we are able to use the initial concentration of the base as if it were the equilibrium concentration.) Substituting into the K_b expression gives

$$\frac{(x)(x)}{0.10-x} \approx \frac{(x)(x)}{0.10} = 3.3 \times 10^{-7}$$

$$x = 1.8 \times 10^{-4}\ M$$

This value of x represents the OH^- concentration, from which we can calculate the pOH and then the pH.

$$[OH^-] = 1.8 \times 10^{-4}\ M$$
$$pOH = -\log(1.8 \times 10^{-4}) = 3.74$$
$$pH = 14.00 - pOH$$
$$= 14.00 - 3.74$$
$$= 10.26$$

The pH of this solution is 10.26.

IS THE ANSWER REASONABLE? First we check our assumption and find it is correct $(0.10 - 0.00018 = 0.10)$. Also, from the nature of the salt, we expect the solution to be basic. The calculated pH corresponds to a basic solution, so the answer seems to be reasonable. You've also seen that we can check the accuracy of the answer by substituting the calculated equilibrium concentrations into the mass action expression.

$$\frac{[HOCl][OH^-]}{[OCl^-]} = \frac{(x)(x)}{0.10} = \frac{(1.8 \times 10^{-4})^2}{0.10} = 3.2 \times 10^{-7}$$

The result is quite close to the given value of K_a, so our answers are correct.

EXAMPLE 16.11

Calculating the pH of a Salt Solution

What is the pH of a 0.20 M solution of hydrazinium chloride, N_2H_5Cl? Hydrazine, N_2H_4, is a weak base with $K_b = 9.6 \times 10^{-7}$.

ANALYSIS: This problem is quite similar to the preceding one. Looking over the statement of the problem, we should realize that N_2H_5Cl is a salt composed of $N_2H_5^+$ (the conjugate acid of N_2H_4) and Cl^-. Since N_2H_4 is a weak base, we expect the $N_2H_5^+$ ion to be a weak acid and thereby affect the pH of the solution. On the other hand, Cl^- is the conjugate base of HCl (a strong acid) and is too weak to influence the pH. Therefore, the only active solute species is the acid, $N_2H_5^+$, which means that to solve the problem we must write the equation for the ionization of the acid and use the K_a expression.

SOLUTION: We will begin with the simplified chemical equation for the equilibrium and write the K_a expression.

$$N_2H_5^+ \rightleftharpoons H^+ + N_2H_4 \qquad K_a = \frac{[H^+][N_2H_4]}{[N_2H_5^+]}$$

The problem has given us K_b for N_2H_4, but we need K_a for $N_2H_5^+$. We obtain this by solving the equation $K_a \times K_b = K_w$ for K_a.

$$K_a = \frac{K_w}{K_b} = \frac{1.0 \times 10^{-14}}{9.6 \times 10^{-7}} = 1.0 \times 10^{-8}$$

Now we set up the concentration table. The initial concentrations of H^+ and N_2H_4 are both set equal to zero; there is no strong acid to give H^+ in the solution and no N_2H_4 is present before the reaction of water with $N_2H_5^+$. Next, we indicate that the concentration of $N_2H_5^+$ decreases by x and the concentrations of H^+ and N_2H_4 both increase by x.

	$N_2H_5^+ \rightleftharpoons H^+ + N_2H_4$		
Initial concentrations (M)	0.20	0	0
Changes in concentrations caused by the ionization (M)	$-x$	$+x$	$+x$
Final concentrations at equilibrium (M)	$(0.20 - x)$ ≈ 0.20	x	x

At equilibrium, equal amounts of H^+ and N_2H_4 are present, and their equilibrium concentrations are each equal to x.

$$[H^+] = [N_2H_4] = x$$

We also assume that $[N_2H_5^+] \approx 0.20\ M$ and then substitute quantities into the mass action expression.

$$\frac{(x)(x)}{(0.20 - x)} = \frac{(x)(x)}{0.20} = 1.0 \times 10^{-8}$$

$$x = 4.5 \times 10^{-5}\ M$$

Since $x = [H^+]$, the pH of the solution is

$$pH = -\log (4.5 \times 10^{-5})$$
$$= 4.35$$

IS THE ANSWER REASONABLE? The assumption holds true $(0.20 - 0.000045 = 0.20)$. The active solute species in the solution is a weak acid and the calculated pH is less than 7, so the answer seems reasonable. Check the accuracy yourself by substituting equilibrium concentrations into the mass action expression.

Practice Exercise 19: What is the pH of a solution when 25.0 g of methylammonium chloride, CH_3NH_3Cl, is dissolved in enough water to make 500 mL of solution? (Hint: What is the molarity of the CH_3NH_3Cl solution?)

Practice Exercise 20: What is the pH of a 0.10 M solution of $NaNO_2$?

Practice Exercise 21: If 500 mL of a 0.20 M solution of ammonia is mixed with 500 mL of a 0.20 M solution of HBr, what is the pH of the resulting solution of NH_4Br?

Acidity of solutions that contain both the salt of a weak acid and a weak base can be predicted

There are many salts whose ions are both able to affect the pH of the salt solution. Whether or not the salt has a net effect on the pH now depends on the relative strengths of its ions in functioning one as an acid and the other as a base. If they are matched in their respective strengths, the salt has no net effect on pH. In ammonium acetate, for example, the ammonium ion is an acidic cation and the acetate ion is a basic anion. However, the K_a of NH_4^+ is 5.6×10^{-10} and the K_b of $C_2H_3O_2^-$ just happens to be the same,

☐ If *neither* the cation nor anion are able to affect the pH, the salt solution will be neutral (provided no other acidic or basic solutes are present).

5.6×10^{-10}. The cation tends to produce H^+ ions to the same extent that the anion tends to produce OH^-. So in aqueous ammonium acetate, $[H^+] = [OH^-]$, and the solution has a pH of 7.

Consider, now, ammonium formate, NH_4CHO_2. The formate ion, CHO_2^-, is the conjugate base of the weak acid, formic acid, so it is a Brønsted base. Its K_b is 5.6×10^{-11}. Comparing this value to the (slightly larger) K_a of the ammonium ion, 5.6×10^{-10}, we see that NH_4^+ is slightly stronger as an acid than the formate ion is as a base. As a result, a solution of ammonium formate is slightly acidic. We are not concerned here about calculating a pH, only in predicting if the solution is acidic, basic, or neutral.

EXAMPLE 16.12
Predicting How a Salt Affects the pH of Its Solution

Will an aqueous solution that is 0.20 M NH_4F be acidic, basic, or neutral?

ANALYSIS: This is a salt in which the cation is a weak acid (it's the conjugate acid of a weak base, NH_3) and the anion is a weak base (it's the conjugate base of a weak acid, HF). The question, then, is, "How do the two ions compare in their abilities to affect the pH of the solution?" We have to calculate their respective K_a and K_b to compare their strengths.

SOLUTION: The K_a of NH_4^+ (calculated from the K_b for NH_3) is 5.6×10^{-10}. Similarly, the K_b of F^- is 1.5×10^{-11} (calculated from the K_a for HF, 6.8×10^{-4}). Comparing the two equilibrium constants, we see that the acid (NH_4^+) is stronger than the base (F^-), so we expect the solution to be slightly acidic.

IS THE ANSWER REASONABLE? We can use the reciprocal relationship between the strengths of the members of conjugate acid–base pairs as a qualitative check. From their respective ionization constants, HF is more fully ionized than NH_3. Therefore, the extent to which F^- reacts with water is *less* than NH_4^+. In other words, F^- is weaker as a base than NH_4^+ is as an acid, so the solution should be slightly acidic.

Practice Exercise 22: Will an aqueous solution of ammonium cyanide, NH_4CN, be acidic, basic, or neutral? (Hint: These anions and cations are conjugates of an acid and a base listed in Tables 16.1 and 16.2.)

Practice Exercise 23: In the discussion above it was shown that an aqueous solution of ammonium acetate, $NH_4C_2H_3O_2$, will be neutral. Will a solution containing an equal number of moles of potassium acetate, $KC_2H_3O_2$, and ammonium nitrate, NH_4NO_3, also be neutral? Justify your answer.

16.4 | **SIMPLIFICATIONS FAIL FOR SOME EQUILIBRIUM CALCULATIONS**

In the preceding two sections we used initial concentrations of solutes as though they were equilibrium concentrations when we performed calculations. This is only an approximation, as we discussed on page 654, but it is one that works most of the time. Unfortunately, it does not work in all cases, so now that you have learned the basic approach to solving equilibrium problems, we will examine those conditions under which simplifying approximations do and do not work. We will also study how to solve problems when the approximations cannot be used.

When simplifying assumptions fail other methods work

When a weak acid, HA, ionizes in water, its concentration is reduced as the ions form. If we let x represent the amount of acid that ionizes per liter, the equilibrium concentration becomes

$$[HA]_{equilib} = [HA]_{initial} - x$$

and because the equilibrium constants are small we can often assume that x is very small and

$$[HA]_{equilib} \approx [HA]_{initial}$$

Even when x is up to 5% (or one twentieth) of the initial concentration of HA our assumption will still work very well[2]. It is not difficult to show that for x to be less than or equal to ± 5% of $[HA]_{initial}$, $[HA]_{initial}$ must be greater than or equal to 400 times the value of K_a.

Simplifications work when $[HA]_{initial} \geq 400 \times K_a$.

TOOLS
When simplifications work

For the equilibrium problems in the preceding sections, this condition was fulfilled, so our simplifications were valid. We now want to study what to do when $[HA]_{initial} < 400 \times K_a$ (i.e., when we cannot justify simplifying the algebra).

The quadratic equation is one solution

When the algebraic equation obtained by substituting quantities into the equilibrium law is a quadratic equation, we can use the quadratic formula to obtain the solution. This is illustrated by the following example.

EXAMPLE 16.13
Using the Quadratic Formula in Equilibrium Problems

Chloroacetic acid, $HC_2H_2O_2Cl$, is used as an herbicide and in the manufacture of dyes and other organic chemicals. It is a weak acid with $K_a = 1.4 \times 10^{-3}$. What is the pH of a 0.010 M solution of $HC_2H_2O_2Cl$?

ANALYSIS: Before we begin the solution, we check to see whether we can use our usual simplifying approximation. For the simplification to work, the initial concentration of the acid (0.010 M) must be larger than $400 \times K_a$, so let's compute this quantity first.

$$400 \times K_a = 400 (1.4 \times 10^{-3}) = 0.56 \, M$$

The initial concentration of $HC_2H_2O_2Cl$ is *less than* 0.56 M so we know the simplification does not work.

chloroacetic acid

SOLUTION: Let's begin by writing the chemical equation and the K_a expression. (We know we must use K_a because the only solute is the acid.)

$$HC_2H_2O_2Cl \rightleftharpoons H^+ + C_2H_2O_2Cl^-$$

$$K_a = \frac{[H^+][C_2H_2O_2Cl^-]}{[HC_2H_2O_2Cl]} = 1.4 \times 10^{-3}$$

The initial concentration of the acid will be reduced by an amount x as it undergoes ionization to form the ions. From this, let's build the concentration table.

---

[2] Neglecting x if it is within 5% of the initial concentration of the acid or base will introduce some error into our results. However, there is a similar or greater error introduced by using molar concentrations rather than activities (effective concentrations of ions in solution) in our calculations. Activities are generally covered in higher level chemistry courses. The overall effect is that our calculated pH results are not exact and can be in error by as much as 0.02 pH units..

	$HC_2H_2O_2Cl \rightleftharpoons$	$H^+ +$	$C_2H_2O_2Cl^-$
Initial concentrations (M)	0.010	0	0
Changes in concentrations (M)	$-x$	$+x$	$+x$
Equilibrium concentrations (M)	$0.010 - x$	x	x

Substituting equilibrium concentrations into the equilibrium law gives

$$\frac{(x)(x)}{(0.010 - x)} = 1.4 \times 10^{-3}$$

We solved a quadratic equation almost exactly the same as this in Section 14.7 so we need only show an abbreviated solution here. The quadratic formula is

$$x = \frac{-b \pm \sqrt{b^2 - 4ac}}{2a}$$

Rearranging our equation to follow the general form gives

$$x^2 + (1.4 \times 10^{-3})x - (1.4 \times 10^{-5}) = 0$$

and we make the substitutions $a = 1$, $b = 1.4 \times 10^{-3}$, and $c = -1.4 \times 10^{-5}$. Entering these into the quadratic formula gives

$$x = \frac{-1.4 \times 10^{-3} \pm \sqrt{(1.4 \times 10^{-3})^2 - 4(1)(-1.4 \times 10^{-5})}}{2(1)}$$

Because of the $\pm$ sign we obtain two values for x, but as you saw in Chapter 14, only one of them makes any sense. Here are the two values:

$$x = 3.1 \times 10^{-3}\, M \quad \text{and} \quad x = -4.5 \times 10^{-3}\, M$$

We know that x cannot be negative because that would give negative concentrations for the ions (which is impossible), so we must choose the first value as the correct one. This yields the following equilibrium concentrations.

$$[H^+] = 3.1 \times 10^{-3}\, M$$
$$[C_2H_2O_2Cl^-] = 3.1 \times 10^{-3}\, M$$
$$[HC_2H_2O_2Cl] = 0.010 - 0.0031 = 0.007\, M$$

Finally, we calculate the pH of the solution.

$$pH = -\log(3.1 \times 10^{-3}) = 2.51$$

IS THE ANSWER REASONABLE? We have no assumptions to check. Our concentrations are small and the pH represents an acidic solution expected of an acid. As before, a quick check can be performed by substituting the calculated equilibrium concentrations into the mass action expression.

☐ Notice that, indeed, x is not negligible compared to the initial concentration, so the simplifying approximation would not have been valid.

(Note: If we made the usual assumption, the result would have been $[H^+] = 3.7 \times 10^{-3}\, M$ which is a 20% error in the hydrogen ion concentration!)

Practice Exercise 24: Calculate the pH of a 0.0010 M solution of dimethylamine, $(CH_3)_2NH$, for which $K_b = 9.6 \times 10^{-4}$. (Hint: Check to see if you can use any simplifications to solve this problem.)

Practice Exercise 25: Calculate, using the quadratic equation and the usual simplification, the pH of a 0.030 M solution of hydrofluoric acid, HF, for which $K_a = 6.8 \times 10^{-4}$. Is there a significant difference between the results?

Practice Exercise 26: Calculate the pH of a 0.0010 M solution of methylamine, CH_3NH_2, for which $K_b = 4.4 \times 10^{-4}$.

Another solution is the successive approximations method

If you worked your way through the discussion of the use of the quadratic equation, you'll surely be better able to appreciate the *method of successive approximations*. It's not only much faster, particularly with a scientific calculator, but just as accurate. The procedure is outlined in Figure 16.5; follow the diagram as we apply the method below.

If we were to attempt to use the simplifying approximation in the preceding Example, we would obtain the following:

$$\frac{x^2}{0.010} = 1.4 \times 10^{-3}$$

for which we obtain the solution $x = 3.7 \times 10^{-3}$. We will call this our *first approximation* to a solution to the equation

$$\frac{(x)(x)}{(0.010 - x)} = 1.4 \times 10^{-3}$$

Let's put $x = 3.7 \times 10^{-3}$ into the term in the denominator, $(0.010 - x)$, and recalculate x. This gives us

$$\frac{x^2}{(0.010 - 0.0037)} = 1.4 \times 10^{-3}$$

or,

$$x^2 = (0.006) \times 1.4 \times 10^{-3}$$

Taking only the positive root,

$$x = 2.9 \times 10^{-3}$$

Notice that this value of x is much closer to the value calculated using the quadratic equation (which gave $x = 3.1 \times 10^{-3}$). Now we'll call $x = 2.9 \times 10^{-3}$ our *second approximation*, and repeat the process. This gives

$$\frac{x^2}{(0.010 - 0.0029)} = 1.4 \times 10^{-3}$$

$$x^2 = (0.007) \times 1.4 \times 10^{-3}$$

$$x = 3.1 \times 10^{-3}$$

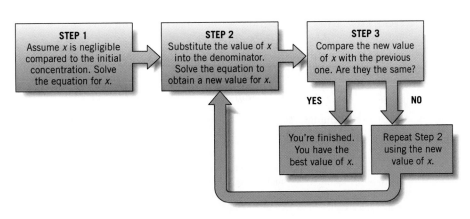

STEP 1	STEP 2	STEP 3
Assume x is negligible compared to the initial concentration. Solve the equation for x.	Substitute the value of x into the denominator. Solve the equation to obtain a new value for x.	Compare the new value of x with the previous one. Are they the same?

YES   NO

| You're finished. You have the best value of x. | Repeat Step 2 using the new value of x. |

TOOLS
Method of successive approximations

FIG. 16.5 **The method of successive approximations.** Following the steps outlined here leads to a rapid solution of equilibrium problems when the usual simplifications fail.

This is the identical value obtained using the quadratic equation. Notice also that the *change* in x between the two approximations grew smaller. The second approximation gave a smaller correction than the first. Each succeeding approximation differs from the preceding one by smaller and smaller amounts. We stop the calculation when the difference between two approximations is insignificant. Try this approach by reworking Practice Exercise 26 and solving for $[OH^-]$ in the 0.0010 M CH_3NH_2 solution using the method of successive approximations.[3]

16.5 BUFFERS ENABLE THE CONTROL OF pH

Many chemical and biological systems are quite sensitive to pH. For example, if the pH of your blood were to change from what it should be, within the range of 7.35 to 7.42, either to 7.00 or to 8.00, you would die. Thus, a change in pH can produce unwanted effects, and systems that are sensitive to pH must be protected from the H^+ or OH^- that might be formed or consumed by some reaction. *Buffers* are mixtures of solutes that accomplish this. The solution containing this mix of solutes is said to be *buffered* or it is described as a *buffer solution*.

Buffers contain a weak acid and a weak base

A **buffer** contains solutes that enable it to resist large changes in pH when small amounts of either strong acid or strong base are added to it. Ordinarily, the buffer consists of two solutes, one providing a weak Brønsted acid and the other a weak Brønsted base. Usually, the acid and base represent a conjugate pair. If the acid is molecular, then the conjugate base is *supplied by a soluble salt of the acid*. For example, a common buffer system consists of acetic acid plus sodium acetate, with the salt's acetate ion serving as the Brønsted base. In your blood, carbonic acid (H_2CO_3, a weak diprotic acid) and the bicarbonate ion (HCO_3^-, its conjugate base) serve as one of the buffer systems used to maintain a remarkably constant pH in the face of the body's production of organic acids by metabolism. Another common buffer consists of the weakly acidic cation, NH_4^+, supplied by a salt like NH_4Cl, and its conjugate base, NH_3.

One important point about buffers is the distinction between keeping a solution at a particular pH and keeping it neutral—at a pH of 7. Although it is certainly possible to prepare a buffer to work at pH 7, buffers can be made that will work around any pH value throughout the pH scale.

A buffer works by neutralizing small additions of strong acid or base

TOOLS

Reactions in a buffer when H^+ or OH^- is added

To work, a buffer must be able to neutralize either a strong acid or strong base that is added to it. This is precisely what the weak base and weak acid components of the buffer do. Consider, for example, a buffer composed of acetic acid, $HC_2H_3O_2$, and acetate ion, $C_2H_3O_2^-$, supplied by a salt such as $NaC_2H_3O_2$. If we add extra H^+ to the buffer (from a strong acid) the acetate ion (the weak conjugate base) can react with it as follows.

$$H^+(aq) + C_2H_3O_2^-(aq) \longrightarrow HC_2H_3O_2(aq)$$

Thus, the added H^+ changes some of the buffer's Brønsted base, $C_2H_3O_2^-$, to its conjugate (weak) acid, $HC_2H_3O_2$. This reaction prevents a large buildup of H^+ that would otherwise be caused by the addition of the strong acid.

☐ Not all the added H^+ is neutralized, so the pH is lowered a little. Soon we'll see how much it changes.

A similar response occurs when a strong base is added to the buffer. The OH^- from the strong base will react with some $HC_2H_3O_2$.

$$HC_2H_3O_2(aq) + OH^-(aq) \longrightarrow C_2H_3O_2^-(aq) + H_2O$$

Here the added OH^- changes some of the buffer's Brønsted acid, $HC_2H_3O_2$, into its conjugate base, $C_2H_3O_2^-$. This prevents a buildup of OH^-, which would otherwise cause

[3] Many modern handheld calculators have "solver" functions that enable the user to solve equilibrium problems such as those discussed here without having to make approximations. You might wish to check the instruction manual for your calculator to see if it has these capabilities. You should also check with your instructor to be sure you are allowed to use this kind of calculator on an exam.

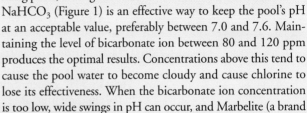

FACETS OF CHEMISTRY

16.1

Swimming Pools and Buffers

The water in a swimming pool is a highly dilute solution of chemicals that prevent the growth of bacteria and help stabilize the pool lining. These substances can affect the pH of the pool water, making it unpleasant for swimmers. Therefore, the pH must be monitored and controlled, and control of pH is what buffers do.

Although most buffer systems consist of two separate species that react with H^+ or OH^-, the bicarbonate ion is an example of a single ion that is able to serve both functions. The reactions are

$$HCO_3^-(aq) + H^+(aq) \longrightarrow H_2CO_3(aq)$$

$$HCO_3^-(aq) + OH^-(aq) \longrightarrow H_2O + CO_3^{2-}(aq)$$

Because sodium bicarbonate is nontoxic and because the pH of a solution of the salt is close to 7.0, there are many practical applications of the HCO_3^- buffer. For swimming pools, adding nontoxic $NaHCO_3$ (Figure 1) is an effective way to keep the pool's pH at an acceptable value, preferably between 7.0 and 7.6. Maintaining the level of bicarbonate ion between 80 and 120 ppm produces the optimal results. Concentrations above this tend to cause the pool water to become cloudy and cause chlorine to lose its effectiveness. When the bicarbonate ion concentration is too low, wide swings in pH can occur, and Marbelite (a brand of high-strength polymer cement) and plaster walls will become etched, metals can corrode, the pool's walls and floor can stain, the water can turn green, and the water can cause eyes to burn.

FIG. 1 **A practical application of a buffer.** Baking soda, which is sodium bicarbonate, is sometimes added to swimming pools to control the pH of the water. *(Courtesy Chris Stocker.)*

a large change in the pH. Thus, one member of a buffer team neutralizes H^+ that might get into the solution, and the other member neutralizes OH^-. *Understanding buffers is an important tool for chemists to use in applications ranging from the protocols of a research project to designing a consumer product.*

Practice Exercise 27: Acetic acid, $HC_2H_3O_2$, and sodium acetate, $NaC_2H_3O_2$ (this provides the acetate ion, $C_2H_3O_2^-$), can be used to make an "acetate" buffer. Does the acetate ion or the acetic acid concentration increase when a strong acid is added to the buffer? Is it the acetate ion or acetic acid that decreases when a strong base is added to the buffer? Explain your answers. (Hint: Which of the buffer components will react with HCl? Which will react with NaOH?)

Practice Exercise 28: For a buffer composed of NH_3 and NH_4^+ (from NH_4Cl), write chemical equations that show what happens when (a) a small amount of strong acid is added, and (b) a small amount of strong base is added.

Calculating the pH of a buffer solution

Calculating the pH of a buffer mixture follows the same procedures we employed in Section 16.2 with a few small changes. The following example illustrates the principles involved.

EXAMPLE 16.14
Calculating the pH of a Buffer

To study the effects of a weakly acidic medium on the rate of corrosion of a metal alloy, a student prepared a buffer solution containing both 0.11 *M* $NaC_2H_3O_2$ and 0.090 *M* $HC_2H_3O_2$. What is the pH of the solution?

ANALYSIS: The buffer solution contains *both* the weak acid $HC_2H_3O_2$ and its conjugate base $C_2H_3O_2^-$. Earlier we noted that when both solute species are present we can use *either* K_a or K_b to perform calculations, whichever is handy. In our tables we find $K_a = 1.8 \times 10^{-5}$ for

$HC_2H_3O_2$, so the simplest approach is to use the equation for the ionization of the acid. We will also be able to use the simplifying approximations developed earlier; these always work for buffers.

SOLUTION: As usual, we begin with the chemical equation and the expression for K_a.

$$HC_2H_3O_2 \rightleftharpoons H^+ + C_2H_3O_2^- \qquad K_a = \frac{[H^+][C_2H_3O_2^-]}{[HC_2H_3O_2]} = 1.8 \times 10^{-5}$$

Let's set up the concentration table so we can proceed carefully. We will take the initial concentrations of $HC_2H_3O_2$ and $C_2H_3O_2^-$ to be the values given in the problem statement. There's no H^+ present from a strong acid, so we set that concentration equal to zero. If the initial concentration of H^+ is zero, its concentration must increase on the way to equilibrium, so under H^+ in the change row we enter $+x$. The other changes follow from that. Here's the completed table.

	$HC_2H_3O_2$	$\rightleftharpoons$	H^+	$+$	$C_2H_3O_2^-$
Initial concentrations (M)	0.090		0		0.11
Changes in concentrations (M)	$-x$		$+x$		$+x$
Equilibrium concentrations (M)	$(0.090 - x) \approx 0.090$		x		$(0.11 + x) \approx 0.11$

For buffer solutions the quantity x will be very small, so it is safe to make the simplifying approximations. What remains, then, is to substitute the quantities from the last row of the table into the K_a expression.

$$\frac{(x)(0.11 + x)}{(0.090 - x)} \approx \frac{(x)(0.11)}{(0.090)} = 1.8 \times 10^{-5}$$

Solving for x gives us

$$x = \frac{(0.090) \times 1.8 \times 10^{-5}}{(0.11)} = 1.5 \times 10^{-5}$$

Because x equals $[H^+]$, we now have $[H^+] = 1.5 \times 10^{-5}\ M$. Then we calculate pH:

$$pH = -\log(1.5 \times 10^{-5}) = 4.82$$

Thus, the pH of the buffer is 4.82.

☐ Notice how small x is compared to the initial concentrations. The simplification was valid.

IS THE ANSWER REASONABLE? Again, we check our assumptions and find they worked $(0.090 - 0.000015 = 0.090$ and $0.11 + 0.000015 = 0.11)$. The pK_a of acetic acid is 4.74 and our pH is within one pH unit of that value. In fact, the ratio of the conjugate acid and conjugate base concentrations is close to 1.0 and our pH is similarly close to the pK_a. Also, we can check the answer in the usual way by substituting our calculated equilibrium values into the mass action expression. Let's do it.

$$\frac{[H^+][C_2H_3O_2^-]}{[HC_2H_3O_2]} = \frac{(1.5 \times 10^{-5})(0.11)}{(0.090)} = 1.8 \times 10^{-5}$$

The reaction quotient equals K_a, so the values we've obtained are correct equilibrium concentrations.

Practice Exercise 29: Calculate the pH of the buffer solution in the preceding example by using the K_b for $C_2H_3O_2^-$. Be sure to write the chemical equation for the equilibrium as the reaction of $C_2H_3O_2^-$ with water. Then use the chemical equation as a guide in setting up the equilibrium expression for K_b. (Hint: If you work the problem correctly, you should obtain the same answer as above.)

Practice Exercise 30: One liter of buffer is made by dissolving 100.0 grams of acetic acid, $HC_2H_3O_2$, and 100.0 grams of sodium acetate, $NaC_2H_3O_2$, in enough water to make one liter. What is the pH of the solution?

Le Châtelier's principle explains the "common ion effect"

If the solution in the preceding example had contained only acetic acid with a concentration of 0.090 M, the calculated $[H^+]$ would have been 1.3×10^{-3} M, considerably higher than that of the buffer which also contains 0.11 M $C_2H_3O_2^-$. The effect of adding sodium acetate, a substance containing $C_2H_3O_2^-$ ion, to a solution of acetic acid is to suppress the ionization of the acid—it's an example of Le Châtelier's principle. Suppose, for example, we had established the equilibrium

$$HC_2H_3O_2 \rightleftharpoons H^+ + C_2H_3O_2^-$$

According to Le Châtelier's principle, if we add $C_2H_3O_2^-$, the reaction will proceed in a direction to remove some of it. This will shift the equilibrium to the left, thereby reducing the concentration of H^+.

In this example, acetate ion is said to be a **common ion,** in the sense that it is *common* to both the acetic acid equilibrium and to the salt we added, sodium acetate. The suppression of the ionization of acetic acid by addition of the common ion is referred to as the **common ion effect.** We will encounter this phenomenon again in Chapter 17 when we consider the solubilities of salts.

Simplifications are permitted in buffer calculations

There are two useful simplifications that we can use in working buffer calculations. The first is the one we made in Example 16.14:

> Because the initial concentrations are so close to the equilibrium concentrations in the buffer mixture, we can use *initial* concentrations of both the weak acid and its conjugate base as though they were equilibrium values.

A further simplification can be made because the mass action expression contains the ratio of the molar concentrations (in units of moles per liter) of the acid and conjugate base. Let's enter these units for the acid and its conjugate base into the mass action expression. For an acid HA,

$$K_a = \frac{[H^+][A^-]}{[HA]} = \frac{[H^+](\text{mol } A^- \, \cancel{L^{-1}})}{(\text{mol } HA \, \cancel{L^{-1}})} = \frac{[H^+](\text{mol } A^-)}{(\text{mol } HA)} \tag{16.8}$$

Notice that the units L^{-1} cancel from the numerator and denominator. This means that for a given acid–base pair, $[H^+]$ is determined by the *mole* ratio of conjugate base to conjugate acid; we don't *have* to use molar concentrations.

> *For buffer solutions* **only,** we can use either molar concentrations or moles in the K_a (or K_b) expression to express the amounts of the members of the conjugate acid–base pair (but we must use the same units for each member of the pair).

A further consequence of the relationship derived above is that the pH of a buffer should not change if the buffer is diluted. Dilution changes the volume of a solution but it does not change the number of moles of the solutes, so their mole *ratio* remains constant and so does $[H^+]$.

Buffers can be prepared having a desired pH

The hydrogen ion concentration of a buffer is controlled by both K_a and the ratio of concentrations (or ratio of moles) of the members of the acid–base pair. This can be seen by rearranging Equation 16.8 to solve for $[H^+]$:

$$[H^+] = K_a \frac{[HA]}{[A^-]} \qquad (16.9)$$

or

$$[H^+] = K_a \frac{\text{mol } HA}{\text{mol } A^-} \qquad (16.10)$$

Buffers are most effective when the mole ratio of acid to base is nearly one, in other words, when $[H^+] = K_a$. Therefore, if we want to prepare a buffer that works well near some specified pH, we look for an acid with a K_a as close to the desired pH as possible. Usually, this means selecting an acid with a pK_a within ± 1 of the desired pH. For experiments in biology, the toxicity of the members of the acid–base pair must also be considered, and that often narrows the choices considerably.

EXAMPLE 16.15

Preparing a Buffer Solution to Have a Predetermined pH

A solution buffered at a pH of 5.00 is needed in an experiment. Can we use acetic acid and sodium acetate to make it? If so, how many moles of $NaC_2H_3O_2$ must be added to 1.0 L of a solution that contains 1.0 mol $HC_2H_3O_2$ to prepare the buffer?

ANALYSIS: There are two parts to this problem. To answer the first, we must check the pK_a of acetic acid to see if it is in the desired range of pH = $pK_a \pm 1$. If it is, we can convert pH to $[H^+]$ and then use Equation 16.10 to calculate the necessary mole ratio. Once we have this, we can proceed to calculate the number of moles of $C_2H_3O_2^-$ needed, and then the number of moles of $NaC_2H_3O_2$.

SOLUTION: Because we want the pH to be 5.00, the pK_a of the selected acid should be 5.00 ± 1, meaning the pK_a should be between 4.00 and 6.00. Because $K_a = 1.8 \times 10^{-5}$ for acetic acid, $pK_a = -\log(1.8 \times 10^{-5}) = 4.74$. So the pK_a of acetic acid falls in the desired range, and acetic acid can be used together with the acetate ion to make the buffer.

Next, we use Equation 16.10 to find the mole ratio of solutes.

$$[H^+] = K_a \times \frac{\text{mol } HC_2H_3O_2}{\text{mol } C_2H_3O_2^-}$$

First, let's solve for the mole ratio.

$$\frac{\text{mol } HC_2H_3O_2}{\text{mol } C_2H_3O_2^-} = \frac{[H^+]}{K_a}$$

The desired pH = 5.00, so $[H^+] = 1.0 \times 10^{-5}$; also $K_a = 1.8 \times 10^{-5}$. Substituting gives

$$\frac{\text{mol } HC_2H_3O_2}{\text{mol } C_2H_3O_2^-} = \frac{1.0 \times 10^{-5}}{1.8 \times 10^{-5}} = 0.56$$

This is the *mole* ratio of the buffer components we want. The solution we are preparing contains 1.0 mol $HC_2H_3O_2$, so the number of moles of acetate ion required is

$$\text{moles } C_2H_3O_2^- = \frac{1.0 \text{ mol } HC_2H_3O_2}{0.56}$$

$$= 1.8 \text{ moles } C_2H_3O_2^-$$

For each mole of $NaC_2H_3O_2$ there is one mole of $C_2H_3O_2^-$, so to prepare the solution we need 1.8 mol $NaC_2H_3O_2$.

IS THE ANSWER REASONABLE? A 1-to-1 mole ratio of $C_2H_3O_2^-$ to $HC_2H_3O_2$ would give pH = pK_a = 4.74. The desired pH of 5.00 is slightly more basic than 4.74, so we can expect that the amount of conjugate base needed should be larger than the amount of conjugate acid. Our answer of 1.8 mol of $NaC_2H_3O_2$ appears to be reasonable.

Practice Exercise 31: From Table 16.1 select an acid that, along with its sodium salt, can be used to make a buffer that has a pH of 5.25. If you have 500.0 mL of a 0.200 M solution of that acid, how many grams of the corresponding sodium salt do you have to dissolve to obtain the desired pH? (Hint: There is more than one correct answer to this problem. The first step is to determine the ratio of molarities of the conjugate acid and conjugate base.)

Practice Exercise 32: A chemist needed an aqueous buffer with a pH of 3.90. Would formic acid and its salt, sodium formate, make a good pair for this purpose? If so, what mole ratio of the acid, $HCHO_2$, to the anion of this salt, CHO_2^-, is needed? How many grams of $NaCHO_2$ would have to be added to a solution that contains 0.10 mol $HCHO_2$?

If you take a biology course, you're likely to run into a logarithmic form of Equation 16.9 called the **Henderson–Hasselbalch equation.** This is obtained by taking the negative logarithm of both sides of Equation 16.9 and rearranging the term involving the concentrations.

$$pH = pK_a + \log \frac{[A^-]}{[HA]} \qquad (16.11)$$

In most buffers used in the life sciences, the anion A^- comes from a salt in which the cation has a charge of 1+, such as NaA, and the acid is monoprotic. With these as conditions, the equation is sometimes written

$$pH = pK_a + \log \frac{[\text{salt}]}{[\text{acid}]} \qquad (16.12)$$

For practice, you may wish to apply this equation to buffer problems at the end of the chapter.

We can calculate the change in pH when strong acid or base is added to a buffer

Earlier we described how a buffer is able to neutralize small amounts of either strong acid or base. We can use this knowledge now to calculate how much the pH will change.

EXAMPLE 16.16
Calculating How a Buffer Resists Changes in pH

How much will the pH change if 0.020 mol of HCl is added to a buffer solution that was made by dissolving 0.12 mol of NH_3 and 0.095 mol of NH_4Cl in 250 mL of water?

ANALYSIS: This problem will require two calculations. The first is the pH of the original buffer. The second is the pH of the mixture after the HCl has been added. For the second calculation, we have to determine how the acid changes the amounts of NH_3 and NH_4^+. This requires that we examine how the buffer functions. In this case, the HCl (a strong acid) will supply H^+ that will react completely with NH_3 (the conjugate base of the buffer pair), changing it to NH_4^+.

For both calculations, the pH is determined by the mole ratio of the members of the acid–base pair. To calculate the pH we will be able to use the moles of NH_3 and NH_4^+ directly in the mass action expression. To set up the equilibrium law we can use either the K_a for NH_4^+ or the K_b for NH_3. Since K_b is tabulated, we will use it and write the equation for the ionization of the base.

SOLUTION: We begin with the chemical equation and the K_b expression.

$$NH_3 + H_2O \rightleftharpoons NH_4^+ + OH^- \qquad K_b = \frac{[NH_4^+][OH^-]}{[NH_3]} = 1.8 \times 10^{-5}$$

☐ The solution also contains 0.095 mol of Cl^-, of course, but this ion is not involved in the equilibrium.

The solution contains 0.12 mol of NH_3 and 0.095 mol of NH_4^+ from the complete dissociation of the salt NH_4Cl. We can enter these quantities into the mass action expression in place of concentrations and solve for $[OH^-]$.

$$1.8 \times 10^{-5} = \frac{\text{mol } NH_4^+ \times [OH^-]}{\text{mol } NH_3} = \frac{(0.095)[OH^-]}{0.12}$$

solving for $[OH^-]$ gives

$$[OH^-] = 2.3 \times 10^{-5}$$

To calculate the pH, we obtain pOH and subtract it from 14.00.

$$pOH = -\log(2.3 \times 10^{-5}) = 4.64$$
$$pH = 14.00 - 4.64 = 9.36$$

This is the pH before we add any HCl.

Next, we consider the reaction that takes place when we add the HCl to the buffer. The 0.020 mol of HCl is completely ionized, so we're adding 0.020 mol H^+. This will react as follows.

☐ The equilibrium constant for this reaction is 1.8×10^{10}, so the reaction goes almost to completion. Nearly all the added H^+ reacts with NH_3.

$$NH_3(aq) + H^+(aq) \longrightarrow NH_4^+(aq)$$

The 0.020 mol of H^+ will react with 0.020 mol of NH_3 to form 0.020 mol of NH_4^+. This causes the number of moles of NH_3 to *decrease* by 0.020 mol and the number of moles of NH_4^+ to *increase* by 0.020 mol. After addition of the acid, we have

Number of moles in the original buffer mixture	Change in the number of moles because of reaction

Moles of NH_3 = 0.12 mol − 0.020 mol = 0.10 mol NH_3

Moles of NH_4^+ = 0.095 mol + 0.020 mol = 0.115 mol NH_4^+

We now use these new amounts of NH_3 and NH_4^+ to calculate the new pH of the buffer solution. First we calculate $[OH^-]$.

$$1.8 \times 10^{-5} = \frac{(0.115)[OH^-]}{0.10}$$

Solving for $[OH^-]$ gives

$$[OH^-] = 1.6 \times 10^{-5}$$

To calculate the pH, we obtain pOH and subtract it from 14.00.

$$pOH = -\log(1.6 \times 10^{-5}) = 4.80$$
$$pH = 14.00 - 4.80 = 9.20$$

This is the pH after addition of the acid. We're asked for the change in pH, so we take the difference between the two values.

$$\text{Change in pH} = 9.36 - 9.20 = 0.16$$

Thus, the pH has dropped by 0.16 pH units.

IS THE ANSWER REASONABLE? In general, we can assume that changes in pH should be small (less than 1.0 pH unit); otherwise, there's no simple way to estimate how *much* the pH will change when H^+ or OH^- is added to the buffer. However, we can anticipate the *direction* of the change. Adding H^+ to a buffer will lower the pH somewhat and adding OH^- will raise it. In this example, the buffer is absorbing H^+, so its pH should drop, and our calculations agree. If our calculated pH had been higher than the original, we might expect to find errors in the calculation of the final values for the number of moles of NH_3 and NH_4^+.

Practice Exercise 33: How much will the pH change if we add 0.15 mol NaOH to 1.00 L of a buffer that contains 1.00 mol $HC_2H_3O_2$ and 1.00 mol $NaC_2H_3O_2$? (Hint: Will the NaOH react with $HC_2H_3O_2$ or $NaC_2H_3O_2$? Write the equation for the reaction.)

Practice Exercise 34: A buffer is prepared by mixing 50.0 g of NH_3 and 50.0 g of NH_4Cl in 500 mL of solution. What is the pH of this buffer and what will the pH change to if 5.00 g of HCl is then added to the mixture?

If you look back over the calculations in the preceding example, you can get some feel for how effective buffers can be at preventing large swings in pH. Notice that we've added enough HCl to react with approximately 20% of the NH_3 in the solution, but the pH changed by only 0.16 pH units. If we were to add this same amount of HCl to 250 mL of pure water, it would give a solution with $[H^+] = 0.080$ *M*. Such a solution would have a pH of 1.10, which is quite acidic. However, the buffer mixture was still basic, with a pH of 9.20, even after addition of the acid. That's pretty remarkable!

16.6 POLYPROTIC ACIDS IONIZE IN TWO OR MORE STEPS

Until now our discussion of weak acids has focused entirely on equilibria involving monoprotic acids. There are, of course, many acids capable of supplying more than one H^+ per molecule. Recall that these are called polyprotic acids. Examples include sulfuric acid, H_2SO_4, carbonic acid, H_2CO_3, and phosphoric acid, H_3PO_4. These acids undergo ionization in a series of steps, each of which releases one proton. For weak polyprotic acids, such as H_2CO_3 and H_3PO_4, each step is an equilibrium. Even sulfuric acid, which we consider a strong acid, is not completely ionized. Loss of the first proton to yield the HSO_4^- ion is complete, but the loss of the second proton is incomplete and involves an equilibrium. In this section, we will focus our attention on weak polyprotic acids as well as solutions of their salts.

Let's begin with the weak diprotic acid H_2CO_3. In water, the acid ionizes in two steps, each of which is an equilibrium that transfers an H^+ ion to a water molecule.

$$H_2CO_3 + H_2O \rightleftharpoons H_3O^+ + HCO_3^-$$
$$HCO_3^- + H_2O \rightleftharpoons H_3O^+ + CO_3^{2-}$$

As usual, we can use H^+ in place of H_3O^+ and simplify these equations to give

$$H_2CO_3 \rightleftharpoons H^+ + HCO_3^-$$
$$HCO_3^- \rightleftharpoons H^+ + CO_3^{2-}$$

Each step has its own ionization constant, K_a, which we identify as K_{a_1} for the first step and K_{a_2} for the second. For carbonic acid,

$$K_{a_1} = \frac{[H^+][HCO_3^-]}{[H_2CO_3]} = 4.5 \times 10^{-7}$$

$$K_{a_2} = \frac{[H^+][CO_3^{2-}]}{[HCO_3^-]} = 4.7 \times 10^{-11}$$

Notice that each ionization makes a contribution to the total molar concentration of H^+, and one of our goals here is to relate the K_a values and the concentration of the acid to $[H^+]$. At first glance, this seems to be a formidable task, but certain simplifications are justified that make the problem relatively simple to solve.

TOOLS
Polyprotic acids ionize stepwise

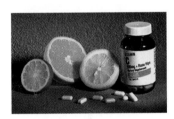
Vitamin C. Many fruits and vegetables contain ascorbic acid (vitamin C), a weak diprotic acid with the formula $H_2C_6H_6O_6$. *(Andy Washnik.)*

Simplifications in calculations involving polyprotic acids

The principal factor that simplifies calculations involving many polyprotic acids is the large differences between successive ionization constants. Notice that for H_2CO_3, K_{a_1} is much larger than K_{a_2} (they differ by a factor of nearly 10,000). Similar differences between K_{a_1} and K_{a_2} are observed for many diprotic acids. One reason is that an H^+ is lost much more easily from the neutral H_2A molecule than from the HA^- ion. The stronger attraction of the opposite charges inhibits the second ionization. Typically, K_{a_1} is greater than K_{a_2} by a factor of between 10^4 and 10^5, as the data in Table 16.3 show. For a triprotic acid, such as phosphoric acid, H_3PO_4, the second acid ionization constant is similarly greater than the third.

Because K_{a_1} is so much larger than K_{a_2}, virtually all the H^+ in a solution of the acid comes from the first step in the ionization. In other words,

$$[H^+]_{total} = [H^+]_{first\ step} + [H^+]_{second\ step}$$

$$[H^+]_{first\ step} \gg [H^+]_{second\ step}$$

Therefore, we make the approximation that

$$[H^+]_{total} \approx [H^+]_{first\ step}$$

This means that as far as calculating the H^+ concentration is concerned, we can treat the acid as though it were a monoprotic acid and ignore the second step in the ionization. In addition we have

$$[HCO_3^-]_{total} = [HCO_3^-]_{first\ step} - [CO_3^{2-}]_{second\ step}$$

However, since $[CO_3^{2-}]_{second\ step} = [H^+]_{second\ step}$ and $[H^+]_{second\ step}$ is very small we can say that

$$[HCO_3^-]_{total} \approx [HCO_3^-]_{first\ step}$$

It is therefore reasonable to conclude that

$$[H^+]_{first\ step} = [HCO_3^-]_{first\ step}$$

Example 16.17 illustrates how these relationships are applied.

□ Additional K_a values of polyprotic acids are located in Appendix C.7.

TABLE 16.3	Acid Ionization Constants for Polyprotic Acids			
		Acid Ionization Constant for Successive Ionizations (25 °C)		
Name	Formula	K_{a_1}	K_{a_2}	K_{a_3}
Carbonic acid	H_2CO_3	4.5×10^{-7}	4.7×10^{-11}	
Hydrosulfuric acid	$H_2S(aq)$	9.5×10^{-8}	1×10^{-19}	
Phosphoric acid	H_3PO_4	7.1×10^{-3}	6.3×10^{-8}	4.5×10^{-13}
Arsenic acid	H_3AsO_4	5.6×10^{-3}	1.7×10^{-7}	4.0×10^{-12}
Sulfuric acid	H_2SO_4	Large	1.0×10^{-2}	
Selenic acid	H_2SeO_4	Large	1.2×10^{-2}	
Telluric acid	H_6TeO_6	2×10^{-8}	1×10^{-11}	
Sulfurous acid	H_2SO_3	1.2×10^{-2}	6.6×10^{-8}	
Selenous acid	H_2SeO_3	4.5×10^{-3}	1.1×10^{-8}	
Tellurous acid	H_2TeO_3	3.3×10^{-3}	2.0×10^{-8}	
Ascorbic acid (vitamin C)	$H_2C_6H_6O_6$	6.8×10^{-5}	2.7×10^{-12}	
Oxalic acid	$H_2C_2O_4$	5.6×10^{-2}	5.4×10^{-5}	
Citric acid (18 °C)	$H_3C_6H_5O_7$	7.1×10^{-4}	1.7×10^{-5}	6.3×10^{-6}

Calculate the concentrations of all the species produced in the ionization of 0.040 M H_2CO_3 as well as the pH of the solution.

ANALYSIS: As in any equilibrium problem, we begin with the chemical equations and the K_a expressions:

$$H_2CO_3 \rightleftharpoons H^+ + HCO_3^- \qquad K_{a_1} = \frac{[H^+][HCO_3^-]}{[H_2CO_3]} = 4.5 \times 10^{-7}$$

$$HCO_3^- \rightleftharpoons H^+ + CO_3^{2-} \qquad K_{a_2} = \frac{[H^+][CO_3^{2-}]}{[HCO_3^-]} = 4.7 \times 10^{-11}$$

We will want to calculate the concentrations of H^+, HCO_3^-, and CO_3^{2-}, and the concentration of H_2CO_3 that remains at equilibrium. As noted in the preceding discussion, the problem is simplified considerably by assuming that the second reaction occurs to a negligible extent compared to the first. This assumption (which we will justify later in the problem) allows us to calculate the H^+ and HCO_3^- concentrations as though the solute were a monoprotic acid. This type of problem is one we've worked on in Section 16.2.

To obtain $[CO_3^{2-}]$, we will have to use the second step in the ionization. Once again, the large difference between K_{a_1} and K_{a_2} permits some simplifications. They involve relationships we have already examined.

$$[H^+]_{equilib} \approx [H^+]_{formed\ in\ first\ step}$$

and

$$[HCO_3^-]_{equilib} \approx [HCO_3^-]_{formed\ in\ first\ step}$$

☐ Keep in mind that for a given solution, the values of H^+ used in the expressions for K_{a_1} and K_{a_2} are identical. At equilibrium there is only *one* equilibrium H^+ concentration.

SOLUTION: Treating H_2CO_3 as though it were a monoprotic acid yields a problem similar to many others we worked earlier in this chapter. We know some of the H_2CO_3 ionizes; let's call this amount x. If x moles per liter of H_2CO_3 ionizes, then x moles per liter of H^+ and HCO_3^- are formed, and the concentration of H_2CO_3 is reduced by x.

	H_2CO_3	$\rightleftharpoons$	H^+	$+$	HCO_3^-
Initial concentrations (M)	0.040		0		0
Changes in concentrations (M)	$-x$		$+x$		$+x$
Equilibrium concentrations (M)	$(0.040 - x)$		x		x
	≈ 0.040				

Substituting into the expression for K_{a_1} gives

$$\frac{x^2}{(0.040 - x)} \approx \frac{x^2}{0.040} = 4.5 \times 10^{-7}$$

Solving for x gives $x = 1.3 \times 10^{-4}$, so $[H^+] = [HCO_3^-] = 1.3 \times 10^{-4}$ M. From this we can now calculate the pH.

$$pH = -\log (1.3 \times 10^{-4}) = 3.89$$

Now let's calculate the concentration of CO_3^{2-}. We obtain this from the expression for K_{a_2}.

$$K_{a_2} = \frac{[H^+][CO_3^{2-}]}{[HCO_3^-]} = 4.7 \times 10^{-11}$$

In our analysis, we concluded that we can use the approximations

$$[H^+]_{equilib} \approx [H^+]_{first\ step}$$
$$[HCO_3^-]_{equilib} \approx [HCO_3^-]_{first\ step}$$

Substituting the values obtained above gives us

$$\frac{(1.3 \times 10^{-4})[CO_3^{2-}]}{1.3 \times 10^{-4}} = 4.7 \times 10^{-11}$$

$$[CO_3^{2-}] = 4.7 \times 10^{-11} = K_{a_2}$$

Let's summarize the results. At equilibrium, we have

$$[H_2CO_3] = 0.040 \ M$$

$$[H^+] = [HCO_3^-] = 1.3 \times 10^{-4} \ M \quad \text{(and pH} = 3.89)$$

$$[CO_3^{2-}] = 4.7 \times 10^{-11} \ M$$

ARE THE ANSWERS REASONABLE? First, we check our simplifying assumptions. The initial concentration was assumed to be much larger than the hydrogen ion concentration and it is $(0.040 - 0.00013 = 0.040)$. The second approximation was that the amount of CO_3^{2-} formed would be very small in relation to the HCO_3^- (and also H^+) concentration calculated in the first step. This assumption is true too $(1.3 \times 10^{-4} - 4.7 \times 10^{-11} = 1.3 \times 10^{-4})$. We can also check that the hydrogen ions added in the second step are inconsequential $(1.3 \times 10^{-4} + 4.7 \times 10^{-11} = 1.3 \times 10^{-4})$.

We've checked our assumptions and they are okay. The pH is what we expect from an acid. If more verification is needed you can always perform a quick check of the answers by substituting them into the appropriate mass action expressions:

$$\frac{(1.3 \times 10^{-4})(1.3 \times 10^{-4})}{0.040} = 4.2 \times 10^{-7}, \text{ which is very close to } K_{a_1}$$

$$\frac{(1.3 \times 10^{-4})(4.7 \times 10^{-11})}{(1.3 \times 10^{-4})} = 4.7 \times 10^{-11}, \text{ which equals } K_{a_2}$$

One last thing, the problem asked for all species produced in the ionization of H_2CO_3. Two other substances are in the reaction mixture, water and hydroxide ions. A rigorous solution would also include those species.

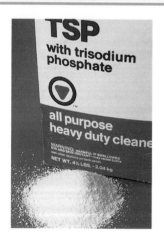

The salt Na_3PO_4 is sold under the name trisodium phosphate or TSP. Solutions of the salt in water are quite basic and are used as an aid in cleaning grime from painted surfaces. Some states restrict the sale of TSP because the phosphate ion it contains presents a pollution problem by promoting the growth of algae in lakes. *(Coco McCoy/Rainbow.)*

Practice Exercise 35: Write the three ionization steps for phosphoric acid, H_3PO_4, and write the K_a expressions for each step. (Hint: Recall that one proton is ionized in each step.)

Practice Exercise 36: Ascorbic acid (vitamin C) is a diprotic acid, $H_2C_6H_6O_6$. See Table 16.3. Calculate $[H^+]$, pH, and $[C_6H_6O_6^{2-}]$ in a 0.10 M solution of ascorbic acid.

One of the most interesting observations we can derive from the preceding example is that *in a solution that contains a polyprotic acid **as the only solute,** the concentration of the ion formed in the second step of the ionization equals K_{a_2}.*

Salts of polyprotic acids give basic solutions

You learned earlier that the pH of a salt solution is controlled by whether the salt's cation, anion, or both are able to react with water. For simplicity, the salts of polyprotic acids that we will discuss here will be limited to those containing *nonacidic* cations, such as sodium or potassium ion. In other words, we will study salts in which the anion alone is basic and thereby affects the pH of a solution.

A typical example of a salt of a polyprotic acid is sodium carbonate, Na_2CO_3. It is a salt of H_2CO_3, and the salt's carbonate ion is a Brønsted base that is responsible for *two* equilibria that furnish OH^- ion and thereby affect the pH of the solution. These equilibria and their corresponding expressions for K_b are as follows:

$$CO_3^{2-}(aq) + H_2O \rightleftharpoons HCO_3^-(aq) + OH^-(aq) \quad (16.13)$$

$$K_{b_1} = \frac{[HCO_3^-][OH^-]}{[CO_3^{2-}]}$$

$$HCO_3^-(aq) + H_2O \rightleftharpoons H_2CO_3(aq) + OH^-(aq) \qquad (16.14)$$

$$K_{b_2} = \frac{[H_2CO_3][OH^-]}{[HCO_3^-]}$$

The calculations required to determine the concentrations of the species involved in these equilibria are very much like those involving weak diprotic acids. The difference is that the chemical reactions here are those of bases instead of acids. In fact, *the simplifying assumptions in our calculations will be almost identical to those for weak polyprotic acids.*

First, let's compare the K_b values for the successive equilibria. To obtain these constants, we will use the relationship that $K_a \times K_b = K_w$ along with the values of K_{a_1} and K_{a_2} for H_2CO_3.

Notice that in the equilibrium in which CO_3^{2-} is the base (Equation 16.13), the conjugate acid is HCO_3^-. Therefore, to calculate K_b for CO_3^{2-} (which we called K_{b_1}), we must use the K_a for HCO_3^-, which corresponds to K_{a_2} for carbonic acid. Thus,

$$K_{b_1} = \frac{K_w}{K_{a_2}} = \frac{1.0 \times 10^{-14}}{4.7 \times 10^{-11}} = 2.1 \times 10^{-4}$$

Similarly, in the equilibrium in which HCO_3^- is the base (Equation 16.14), the conjugate acid is H_2CO_3. Therefore, to calculate K_b for HCO_3^- (which we called K_{b_2}), we must use the K_a for H_2CO_3, which is K_{a_1} for carbonic acid.

$$K_{b_2} = \frac{K_w}{K_{a_1}} = \frac{1.0 \times 10^{-14}}{4.5 \times 10^{-7}} = 2.2 \times 10^{-8}$$

Now we can compare the two K_b values. For CO_3^{2-}, $K_{b_1} = 2.1 \times 10^{-4}$, and for the (much) weaker base, HCO_3^-, K_{b_2} is 2.2×10^{-8}. Thus CO_3^{2-} has a K_b nearly 10,000 times that of HCO_3^-. This means that the reaction of CO_3^{2-} with water (Equation 16.13) generates far more OH^- than the reaction of HCO_3^- (Equation 16.14). The contribution of the latter to the total pool of OH^- is relatively so small that we can safely ignore it. The simplification here is very much the same as in our treatment of the ionization of weak polyprotic acids.

$$[OH^-]_{total} = [OH^-]_{formed\ in\ first\ step} + [OH^-]_{formed\ in\ second\ step}$$

$$[OH^-]_{formed\ in\ first\ step} \gg [OH^-]_{formed\ in\ second\ step}$$

$$[OH^-]_{total} \approx [OH^-]_{formed\ in\ first\ step}$$

Thus, if we wish to calculate the pH of a solution of a basic anion of a polyprotic acid, *we may work exclusively with K_{b_1} and ignore any further reactions.* Let's study an example of how this works.

□ In general, K_b values for anions of polyprotic acids are not tabulated. When needed, they are calculated from the appropriate K_a values for the acids.

□ Remember: K_{b_1} comes from K_{a_2}, and K_{b_2} comes from K_{a_1}.

EXAMPLE 16.18
Calculating the pH of a Solution of a Salt of a Weak Diprotic Acid

What is the pH of a 0.15 M solution of Na_2CO_3?

ANALYSIS: We can ignore the reaction of HCO_3^- with water, so the only relevant equilibrium is

$$CO_3^{2-} + H_2O \rightleftharpoons HCO_3^- + OH^- \qquad K_{b_1} = \frac{[HCO_3^-][OH^-]}{[CO_3^{2-}]} = 2.1 \times 10^{-4}$$

(The value of K_{b_1} was calculated in the discussion preceding this example.) Also, the initial concentration of CO_3^{2-} (0.15 M) is larger than $100 \times K_{b_1}$, so we can safely use 0.15 M as the equilibrium concentration of CO_3^{2-}.

SOLUTION: Some of the CO_3^{2-} will react; we'll let this be x mol L^{-1}. The concentration table, then, is as follows.

Some detergents that use sodium carbonate as their caustic ingredient. Detergents are best able to dissolve grease and grime if their solutions are basic. In these products, the basic ingredient is sodium carbonate. The salt Na_2CO_3 is relatively nontoxic and the carbonate ion it contains is a relatively strong base. The carbonate ion also serves as a water softener by precipitating Ca^{2+} ions as insoluble $CaCO_3$. *(Paul Silverman/Fundamental Photographs.)*

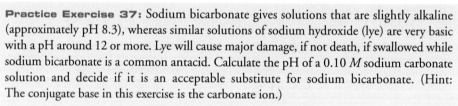

	$CO_3^{2-} + H_2O \rightleftharpoons HCO_3^- + OH^-$		
Initial concentrations (*M*)	0.15	0	0
Changes in concentrations caused by the ionization (*M*)	$-x$	$+x$	$+x$
Equilibrium concentrations (*M*)	$(0.15 - x) \approx 0.15$	x	x

Now we're ready to insert the values in the last row of the table into the equilibrium expression for the carbonate ion.

$$\frac{[HCO_3^-][OH^-]}{[CO_3^{2-}]} = \frac{(x)(x)}{0.15 - x} \approx \frac{(x)(x)}{0.15} = 2.1 \times 10^{-4}$$

$$x = [OH^-] = 5.6 \times 10^{-3} \, mol \, L^{-1}$$

and

$$pOH = -\log(5.6 \times 10^{-3}) = 2.25$$

Finally, we calculate the pH by subtracting pOH from 14.00.

$$pH = 14.00 - 2.25 = 11.75$$

Thus, the pH of 0.15 *M* Na_2CO_3 is calculated to be 11.75. Once again we see that an aqueous solution of a salt composed of a basic anion and a neutral cation is basic.

IS THE ANSWER REASONABLE? Our assumption is reasonable since 0.0056 is less than 5% of 0.015 (0.15− 0.0056 = 0.14). Also, the pH we obtained corresponds to a basic solution, which is what we expect when the anion of the salt reacts as a weak base. The answer seems reasonable.

Practice Exercise 37: Sodium bicarbonate gives solutions that are slightly alkaline (approximately pH 8.3), whereas similar solutions of sodium hydroxide (lye) are very basic with a pH around 12 or more. Lye will cause major damage, if not death, if swallowed while sodium bicarbonate is a common antacid. Calculate the pH of a 0.10 *M* sodium carbonate solution and decide if it is an acceptable substitute for sodium bicarbonate. (Hint: The conjugate base in this exercise is the carbonate ion.)

Practice Exercise 38: What is the pH of a 0.20 *M* solution of Na_2SO_3 at 25 °C? For the diprotic acid, H_2SO_3, $K_{a_1} = 1.2 \times 10^{-2}$ and $K_{a_2} = 6.6 \times 10^{-8}$.

Practice Exercise 39: Reasoning by analogy from what you learned about solutions of weak polyprotic acids, what is the molar concentration of H_2SO_3 in a 0.010 *M* solution of Na_2SO_3?

An acid–base titration. Phenolphthalein is often used as an indicator to detect the end point. *(Peter Lerman.)*

16.7	**ACID–BASE TITRATIONS HAVE SHARP CHANGES IN pH AT THE EQUIVALENCE POINT**

In Chapter 4 we studied the overall procedure for an acid–base titration, and we saw how titration data can be used in various stoichiometric calculations. In performing this procedure, the titration is halted at the **end point** when a change in color of an indicator occurs. Ideally, this end point should occur at the **equivalence point,** when stoichiometrically equivalent amounts of acid and base have combined. To obtain this ideal result, selecting an appropriate indicator requires foresight. We will understand this better by studying how the pH of the solution being titrated changes with the addition of titrant.

When the pH of a solution at different stages of a titration is plotted against the volume of titrant added, we obtain a **titration curve.** The values of pH in these plots can be measured using a pH meter during the titration, or it can be calculated by the procedures studied in this chapter.

We will use the calculation method, and also demonstrate that all titration curves can be described by four calculations. Two calculations describe single points on the curve, the starting point and the equivalence point. The other two calculations are simple limiting reactant calculations for mixtures (a) between the start and the equivalence point and (b) after the equivalence point.

Titration of a strong acid by a strong base uses four equations

TOOLS
Titration curves have four regions

The titration of HCl(*aq*) with a standardized NaOH solution illustrates the titration of a strong acid by a strong base. The molecular and net ionic equations are

$$HCl(aq) + NaOH(aq) \longrightarrow NaCl(aq) + H_2O$$

$$H^+(aq) + OH^-(aq) \longrightarrow H_2O$$

Let's consider what happens to the pH of a solution, initially 25.00 mL of 0.2000 *M* HCl, as small amounts of the titrant, 0.2000 *M* NaOH, are added. We will calculate the pH of the resulting solution at various stages of the titration, retaining only two significant figures, and plot the values against the volume of titrant.

◻ The *titrant* is the solution being slowly added from a buret to a solution in the receiving flask.

At the start, before any titrant has been added, the receiving flask contains only 0.2000 *M* HCl. Because this is a strong acid, we know that

$$[H^+] = [HCl] = 0.2000 \ M$$

So the initial pH is

$$pH = -\log(0.2000) = 0.70$$

After the start but before the equivalence point we need to determine the concentration of the excess reactant in a simple limiting reactant problem. Let's first calculate the amount of HCl initially present in 25.00 mL of 0.2000 *M* HCl.

$$25.00 \text{ mL HCl soln} \times \frac{0.2000 \text{ mol HCl}}{1000 \text{ mL HCl soln}} = 5.000 \times 10^{-3} \text{ mol HCl}$$

◻ Despite the high precision assumed for the molarity and the volume of the titrant, we will retain only two significant figures in the calculated pH. Precision higher than this is hard to obtain and seldom sought in actual lab work.

Now suppose we add 10.00 mL of 0.2000 *M* NaOH from the buret. The moles of NaOH added is

$$10.00 \text{ mL NaOH soln} \times \frac{0.2000 \text{ mol NaOH}}{1000 \text{ mL NaOH soln}} = 2.000 \times 10^{-3} \text{ mol NaOH}$$

We can see that we have more moles of HCl than NaOH (and the mole ratio is 1:1) so that the base neutralizes 2.000×10^{-3} mol of HCl, and the amount of HCl remaining is

$$(5.000 \times 10^{-3} - 2.000 \times 10^{-3}) \text{ mol HCl} = 3.000 \times 10^{-3} \text{ mol HCl remaining}$$

To obtain the concentration we divide by the total volume of the solution that is now (25.00 + 10.00) mL = 35.00 mL = 0.03500 L. The $[H^+]$ is

$$[H^+] = \frac{3.000 \times 10^{-3} \text{ mol}}{0.03500 \text{ L}} = 8.571 \times 10^{-2} \ M$$

◻ $[H^+] = \dfrac{M_A V_A - M_B V_B}{V_A + V_B}$

The corresponding pH is 1.07.

We can repeat this calculation for as many different volumes as we care to choose as long as the volume of NaOH is less than the equivalence point volume. A spreadsheet will allow us to quickly calculate the pH of large numbers of data points, but only a few are needed to see the nature of the curve.

At the equivalence point we can calculate the volume of NaOH added as

$$M_{HCl} \times V_{HCl} = M_{NaOH} \times V_{NaOH}$$

$$V_{NaOH}(\text{at eq pt}) = (0.2000 \ M_{HCl})(25.00 \text{ mL HCl})/(0.2000 \ M \text{ NaOH})$$

$$= 25.00 \text{ mL}$$

TABLE 16.4	Titration of 25.00 mL of 0.2000 M HCl with 0.2000 M NaOH						
Initial Volume of HCl (mL)	Initial Amount of HCl (mol)	Volume of NaOH added (mL)	Amount of NaOH (mol)	Amount of Excess Reagent (mol)	Total Volume of Solution (mL)	Molarity of Ion in Excess (mol L^{-1})	pH
25.00	5.000×10^{-3}	0.00	0.000	5.000×10^{-3} (H$^+$)	25.00	0.2000 (H$^+$)	0.70
25.00	5.000×10^{-3}	10.00	2.000×10^{-3}	3.000×10^{-3} (H$^+$)	35.00	8.571×10^{-2} (H$^+$)	1.07
25.00	5.000×10^{-3}	20.00	4.000×10^{-3}	1.000×10^{-3} (H$^+$)	45.00	2.222×10^{-2} (H$^+$)	1.65
25.00	5.000×10^{-3}	24.00	4.800×10^{-3}	2.000×10^{-4} (H$^+$)	49.00	4.082×10^{-3} (H$^+$)	2.39
25.00	5.000×10^{-3}	24.90	4.980×10^{-3}	2.000×10^{-5} (H$^+$)	49.90	4.000×10^{-4} (H$^+$)	3.40
25.00	5.000×10^{-3}	24.99	4.998×10^{-3}	2.000×10^{-6} (H$^+$)	49.99	4.000×10^{-5} (H$^+$)	4.40
25.00	5.000×10^{-3}	25.00	5.000×10^{-3}	0	50.00	0	7.00
25.00	5.000×10^{-3}	25.01	5.002×10^{-3}	2.000×10^{-6} (OH$^-$)	50.01	3.999×10^{-5} (OH$^-$)	9.60
25.00	5.000×10^{-3}	25.10	5.020×10^{-3}	2.000×10^{-5} (OH$^-$)	50.10	3.992×10^{-4} (OH$^-$)	10.60
25.00	5.000×10^{-3}	26.00	5.200×10^{-3}	2.000×10^{-4} (OH$^-$)	51.00	3.922×10^{-3} (OH$^-$)	11.59
25.00	5.000×10^{-3}	50.00	1.000×10^{-2}	5.000×10^{-3} (OH$^-$)	75.00	6.667×10^{-2} (OH$^-$)	12.82

◻ The pH of all strong acid–strong base titrations is 7.00 at the equivalence point.

◻ The equivalence point in a titration can be found using a pH meter by plotting pH versus volume of base added and noting the sharp rise in pH. If a pH meter is used, we don't have to use an indicator.

◻ $[OH^-] = \dfrac{M_B V_B - M_A V_A}{V_A + V_B}$

At this point we have exactly neutralized all of the acid with base and neither HCl nor NaOH are in excess. The solution contains only NaCl and we have already observed that NaCl solutions are neutral with a pH = 7.00. The pH at the equivalence point of all strong acid–strong base titrations is 7.00.

After the equivalence point we will have an excess of base. As we did before, we calculate the moles of acid and the moles of base. Now the moles of base will be larger and we subtract the moles of acid to find the excess moles of base. This is divided by the total volume to obtain the [OH$^-$] from which the pH is calculated.

Table 16.4 shows the results of calculating the pH of the solution in the receiving flask after the addition of further small volumes of the titrant. Figure 16.6 shows a plot of the pH of the solution in the receiving flask versus the volume of the 0.2000 M NaOH solution added—the *titration curve* for the titration of a strong acid with a strong base. Notice how the pH of the solution increases slowly until we are very close to the equivalence point, pH = 7.00. With the addition of a very small amount of base, the curve rises very sharply and then, almost as suddenly, levels off again to reflect just a gradual increase in pH.

Titration of a weak acid by a strong base uses four equations

The calculations for the titration of a weak acid by a strong base are a bit more complex than when both the acid and base are strong. This is because we have to consider the equilibria involving the weak acid and its conjugate base. As an example, let's do the calculations and

FIG. 16.6 **Titration curve for titrating a strong acid with a strong base.** Here we follow how the pH changes during the titration of 25.00 mL of 0.2000 M HCl with 0.2000 M NaOH.

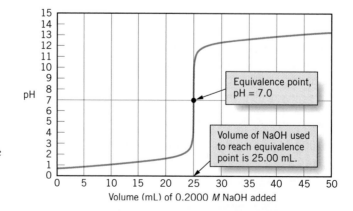

draw a titration curve for the titration of 25.00 mL of 0.2000 M $HC_2H_3O_2$ with 0.2000 M NaOH. The same four points are calculated but they use different equations.

The molecular and net ionic equations we will use are

$$HC_2H_3O_2(aq) + NaOH(aq) \longrightarrow NaC_2H_3O_2(aq) + H_2O$$

$$HC_2H_3O_2(aq) + OH^-(aq) \longrightarrow C_2H_3O_2^-(aq) + H_2O$$

Because the concentrations of both solutions are the same, and because the acid and base react in a one-to-one mole ratio, we know that we will need exactly 25.00 mL of the base to reach the equivalence point. With this as background, let's look at what is involved in calculating the pH at various points along the titration curve.

At the start the solution is simply a solution of the weak acid $HC_2H_3O_2$. We must use K_a to calculate the pH. We have seen that in many situations the simplifying assumptions hold and the calculations are summarized as

$$K_a = \frac{[H^+][C_2H_3O_2^-]}{[HC_2H_3O_2]} = \frac{(x)(x)}{(0.2000 - x)} \approx \frac{(x)(x)}{(0.2000)} = 1.8 \times 10^{-5}$$

$\square$ $[H^+] = \sqrt{K_a C_{HA}}$

$$x^2 = 3.6 \times 10^{-6} \quad \text{(rounded)}$$

$$x = [H^+] = 1.9 \times 10^{-3}$$

This result gives us a pH of 2.72. This is the pH before any NaOH is added.

Between the start and the equivalence point, as we add NaOH to the $HC_2H_3O_2$, the chemical reaction produces $C_2H_3O_2^-$, so the solution contains both $HC_2H_3O_2$ and $C_2H_3O_2^-$ (it is a buffer solution). Our equilibrium law can be rearranged to read

$$[H^+] = \frac{K_a[HC_2H_3O_2]}{[C_2H_3O_2^-]} = \frac{K_a(\text{mol } HC_2H_3O_2)}{(\text{mol } C_2H_3O_2^-)}$$

Now all we need to do is solve a limiting reactant calculation to determine the moles of acetic acid, $HC_2H_3O_2$, left after each addition of NaOH and at the same time calculate the moles of acetate ion, $C_2H_3O_2^-$, formed.

Let's see what happens when we add 10.00 mL of NaOH solution. The initial moles of acetic acid are

$$0.2000 \; M \; HC_2H_3O_2 \times 0.02500 \; L = 5.000 \times 10^{-3} \; \text{mol } HC_2H_3O_2$$

The moles of NaOH added are

$$0.2000 \; M \; NaOH \times 0.01000 \; L = 2.000 \times 10^{-3} \; \text{mol } NaOH$$

The moles of acetic acid left are

$$5.000 \times 10^{-3} \; \text{mol} - 2.000 \times 10^{-3} \; \text{mol} = 3.000 \times 10^{-3} \; \text{mol } HC_2H_3O_2$$

From the chemical equations above, the moles of NaOH added are stoichiometrically equal to the moles of acetate ion formed. We therefore have 2.000×10^{-3} mol $C_2H_3O_2^-$. Entering the values for the K_a and the moles of acetic acid and acetate ions we get

$$[H^+] = \frac{(1.8 \times 10^{-5})(3.000 \times 10^{-3} \; \text{mol } HC_2H_3O_2)}{(2.000 \times 10^{-3} \; \text{mol } C_2H_3O_2^-)} = 2.7 \times 10^{-5} \; M$$

$\square$ $[H^+] = K_a \dfrac{M_A V_A - M_B V_B}{M_B V_B}$

and the pH is 4.57.

At the equivalence point, all the $HC_2H_3O_2$ has reacted and the solution contains the salt $NaC_2H_3O_2$ (i.e., we have a mixture of the ions Na^+ and $C_2H_3O_2^-$).

We began with 5.000×10^{-3} mol of $HC_2H_3O_2$, so we now have 5.000×10^{-3} mol of $C_2H_3O_2^-$ (in 0.05000 L). The concentration of $C_2H_3O_2^-$ is

$$[C_2H_3O_2^-] = \frac{5.000 \times 10^{-3} \; \text{mol}}{0.05000 \; L} = 0.1000 \; M$$

Because $C_2H_3O_2^-$ is a base, we have to use K_b and write the chemical equation for the reaction of a base with water.

$$C_2H_3O_2^-(aq) + H_2O \rightleftharpoons HC_2H_3O_2(aq) + OH^-(aq)$$

$$K_b = \frac{[OH^-][HC_2H_3O_2]}{[C_2H_3O_2^-]} = \frac{K_w}{K_a} = 5.6 \times 10^{-10}$$

Substituting into the mass action expression gives

$$\frac{[OH^-][HC_2H_3O_2]}{[C_2H_3O_2^-]} = \frac{(x)(x)}{0.1000 - x} \approx \frac{(x)\,(x)}{0.1000} = 5.6 \times 10^{-10}$$

$$x^2 = 5.6 \times 10^{-11}$$

$$x = [OH^-] = 7.5 \times 10^{-6}$$

☐ $[OH^-] = \sqrt{K_b \dfrac{M_A V_A}{V_A + V_B}}$

The pOH calculates to be 5.12. Finally, the pH is (14.00 − 5.12) or 8.88. The pH at the equivalence point in this titration is 8.88, somewhat basic because the solution contains the Brønsted base, $C_2H_3O_2^-$. *In the titration of any weak acid with a strong base, the pH at the equivalence point will be greater than 7.*

☐ It is interesting that although we describe the overall reaction in the titration as *neutralization*, at the equivalence point the solution is slightly basic, not neutral.

After the equivalence point, the additional OH^- now shifts the following equilibrium to the left:

$$C_2H_3O_2^-(aq) + H_2O \rightleftharpoons HC_2H_3O_2(aq) + OH^-(aq)$$

The production of OH^- *by this route* is thus suppressed as we add more and more NaOH solution. The only source of OH^- that affects the pH is from the base added after the equivalence point. From here on, therefore, the pH calculations become identical to those for the last half of the titration curve for HCl and NaOH shown above. Each point is just a matter of calculating the additional number of moles of NaOH, calculating the new final volume, taking their ratio (to obtain the molar concentration), and then calculating pOH and pH.

☐ $[OH^-] = \dfrac{M_B V_B - M_A V_A}{V_A + V_B}$

Table 16.5 summarizes the titration data, and the titration curve is given in Figure 16.7. Once again, notice how the change in pH occurs slowly at first, then shoots up through the equivalence point, and finally looks just like the last half of the curve in Figure 16.6.

Practice Exercise 40: When a weak acid such as acetic acid, $HC_2H_3O_2$, is titrated with KOH what are ALL of the species in solution at (a) the equivalence point, (b) at the start of the titration, (c) after the equivalence point, and (d) before the equivalence point? For each part list the species in order from highest concentration to lowest. (Hint: H_2O should be the first item in all your lists and either $[H^+]$ or $[OH^-]$ should be the last.)

Practice Exercise 41: Suppose we titrate 20.0 mL of 0.100 M $HCHO_2$ with 0.100 M NaOH. Calculate the pH (a) before any base is added, (b) when half of the $HCHO_2$ has been neutralized, (c) after a total of 15.0 mL of base has been added, and (d) at the equivalence point.

Practice Exercise 42: Suppose 30.0 mL of 0.15 M NaOH is added to 50.0 mL of 0.20 M $HCHO_2$. What will be the pH of the resulting solution?

TABLE 16.5	Titration of 25.00 mL of 0.2000 M $HC_2H_3O_2$ with 0.2000 M NaOH	
Volume of Base Added (mL)	Molar Concentration of Species in Parentheses	pH
0.00	1.9×10^{-3} (H^+)	2.72
10.00	2.7×10^{-5} (H^+)	4.57
24.90	7.2×10^{-8} (H^+)	7.14
24.99	7.1×10^{-9} (H^+)	8.14
25.00	7.5×10^{-6} (OH^-)	8.88
25.01	4.0×10^{-5} (OH^-)	9.60
25.10	4.0×10^{-4} (OH^-)	10.60
26.00	3.9×10^{-3} (OH^-)	11.59
35.00	3.3×10^{-2} (OH^-)	12.52

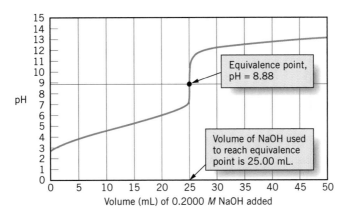

FIG. 16.7 Titration curve for titrating a weak acid with a strong base. In this titration, we follow the pH as 25.00 mL of 0.2000 *M* acetic acid is titrated with 0.2000 *M* NaOH.

Weak base–strong acid titrations also use four equations

The calculations involved here are nearly identical to those of the weak acid–strong base titration. We will review what is required but will not actually perform the calculations.

If we titrate 25.00 mL of 0.2000 *M* NH_3 with 0.2000 *M* HCl, the molecular and net ionic equations are

$$NH_3(aq) + HCl(aq) \longrightarrow NH_4Cl(aq)$$

$$NH_3(aq) + H^+(aq) \longrightarrow NH_4^+(aq)$$

Before the titration begins, the solution is simply a solution of the weak base, NH_3. Since the only solute is a base, we must use K_b to calculate the pH.

During the titration but before the equivalence point, as we add HCl to the NH_3, the neutralization reaction produces NH_4^+, so the solution contains both NH_3 and NH_4^+ (it is a buffer solution). We do a limiting reactant calculation to determine the moles of ammonia left and the moles of ammonium ions produced by the addition of HCl. We use the equilibrium law to perform the calculation as we did with the weak acid.

At the equivalence point, all the NH_3 has reacted and the solution contains the salt NH_4Cl. We calculate the concentration of ammonium ions and then use the techniques we developed to determine the pH of the conjugate acid of a weak base.

After the equivalence point, the H^+ introduced by further addition of HCl has nothing with which to react, so it causes the solution to become more and more acidic. The concentration of H^+ calculated from the excess of HCl is used to calculate the pH.

Figure 16.8 illustrates the titration curve for this system.

Titration curves for diprotic acids show two equivalence points

When a weak diprotic acid such as ascorbic acid (vitamin C) is titrated with a strong base, there are two protons to be neutralized and there are two equivalence points. Provided that

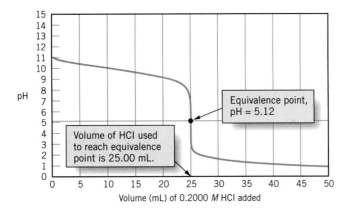

FIG. 16.8 Titration curve for the titration of a weak base with a strong acid. Here we follow the pH as 25.00 mL of 0.2000 *M* NH_3 is titrated with 0.2000 *M* HCl.

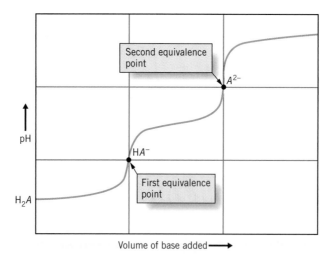

FIG. 16.9 **Titration of a diprotic acid, H₂A, by a strong base.** As each equivalence point is reached, there is a sharp rise in the pH.

the values of K_{a_1} and K_{a_2} differ by several powers of 10, the neutralization takes place stepwise and the resulting titration curve shows two sharp increases in pH. We won't perform the calculations here, because they're complex, but instead just look at the general shape of the titration curve, which is shown in Figure 16.9.

Acid–base indicators are weak acids

Most dyes that work as acid–base indicators are also weak acids. Therefore, let's represent an indicator by the formula H*In*. In its un-ionized state, H*In* has one color. Its conjugate base, *In*⁻, has a different color, the more strikingly different the better. In solution, the indicator is involved in a typical acid–base equilibrium:

$$H In(aq) \rightleftharpoons H^+(aq) + In^-(aq)$$

acid form   base form
(one color)   (another color)

The corresponding acid ionization constant, K_{In}, is given by

$$K_{In} = \frac{[H^+][In^-]}{[HIn]}$$

In a strongly acidic solution, when the H⁺ concentration is high, the equilibrium is shifted to the left and most of the indicator exists in its "acid form." Under these conditions, the color we observe is that of H*In*. If the solution is made basic, the H⁺ concentration drops and the equilibrium shifts to the right, toward *In*⁻, and the color we observe is that of the "base form" of the indicator.

The *observed* change in color for an indicator actually occurs gradually over a range of pH values. This is because of the human eye's limited ability to discern color changes. Sometimes a change of as much as 2 pH units is needed for some indicators—more for litmus—before the eye notices the color change. This is why tables of acid–base indicators, such as Table 15.5 on page 630, provide approximate pH ranges for the color changes.

How acid–base indicators work

In a typical acid–base titration, you've seen that as we pass the equivalence point, there is a sudden and large change in the pH. For example, in the titration of HCl with NaOH described earlier, the pH just one-half drop before the equivalence point (when 24.97 mL of the base has been added) is 3.92. Just one drop later (when 25.03 mL of base has been added) we have passed the equivalence point and the pH has risen to 10.08. This large swing in pH (from 3.92 to 10.08) causes a sudden shift in the position of equilibrium for the indicator, and we go from a condition where most of the indicator is in its acid form to a condition in which most is in the base form. This is observed visually as a change in color from that of the acid form to that of the base form.

SUMMARY

Acid and Base Ionization Constants. A weak acid H*A* ionizes according to the general equation

$$HA + H_2O \rightleftharpoons H_3O^+ + A^-$$

or more simply,

$$HA \rightleftharpoons H^+ + A^-$$

The equilibrium constant is called the **acid ionization constant, K_a** (sometimes called an *acid dissociation constant*).

$$K_a = \frac{[H^+][A^-]}{[HA]}$$

A weak base *B* ionizes by the general equation

$$B + H_2O \rightleftharpoons BH^+ + OH^-$$

The equilibrium constant is called the **base ionization constant, K_b** (sometimes called a *base dissociation constant*).

$$K_b = \frac{[OH^-][BH^+]}{[B]}$$

The smaller the values of K_a (or K_b), the weaker are the substances as Brønsted acids (or bases).

Another way to compare the relative strengths of acids or bases is to use the negative logarithms of K_a and K_b, called **pK_a** and **pK_b,** respectively.

$$pK_a = -\log K_a \qquad pK_b = -\log K_b$$

The *smaller* the pK_a or pK_b, the *stronger* is the acid or base. For a conjugate acid–base pair,

$$K_a \times K_b = K_w$$

and

$$pK_a + pK_b = 14.00 \qquad \text{(at 25 °C)}$$

Equilibrium Calculations—Determining K_a and K_b. The values of K_a and K_b can be obtained from initial concentrations of the acid or base and either the pH of the solution or the percentage ionization of the acid or base. The measured pH gives the equilibrium value for [H$^+$]. The **percentage ionization** is defined as

$$\text{Percentage ionization} = \frac{\text{amount ionized}}{\text{amount available}} \times 100\%$$

Equilibrium Calculations—Determining Equilibrium Concentrations when K_a or K_b Is Known. Problems fall into one of three categories: (1) the only solute is a weak acid (we must use the K_a expression), (2) the only solute is a weak base (we must use the K_b expression), and (3) the solution contains both a weak acid and its conjugate base (we can use either K_a or K_b).

When the initial concentration of the acid (or base) is larger than 400 times the value of K_a (or K_b), it is safe to use initial concentrations of acid or base as though they were equilibrium values in the mass action expression. When this approximation cannot be used, we can use the quadratic formula.

Ions as Acids or Bases. A solution of a salt is acidic if the cation is acidic but the anion is neutral. Metal ions with high charge densities generally are acidic, but those of Groups IA and IIA (except Be^{2+}) are not. Cations such as NH$_4^+$, which are the conjugate acids of weak *molecular* bases, are themselves proton donors and are acidic.

When the anion of a salt is the conjugate base of a *weak* acid, the anion is a weak base. Anions of strong acids, such as Cl$^-$ and NO$_3^-$, are such weak Brønsted bases that they cannot affect the pH of a solution.

If the salt is derived from a weak acid *and* a weak base, its net effect on pH has to be determined on a case by case basis by determining which of the two ions is the stronger.

Buffers. A solution that contains both a weak acid and a weak base (usually an acid–base conjugate pair) is called a **buffer,** because it is able to absorb [H$^+$] from a strong acid or [OH$^-$] from a strong base without suffering large changes in pH. For the general acid–base pair, H*A* and *A*$^-$, the following reactions neutralize H$^+$ and OH$^-$.

When H$^+$ is added to the buffer: $\qquad A^- + H^+ \longrightarrow HA$

When OH$^-$ is added to the buffer:

$$HA + OH^- \longrightarrow A^- + H_2O$$

The pH of a buffer is controlled by the ratio of weak acid to weak base, expressed either in terms of molarities or moles.

$$[H^+] = K_a \times \frac{[HA]}{[A^-]} = K_a \times \frac{\text{moles } HA}{\text{moles } A^-}$$

Because the [H$^+$] is determined by the mole ratio of H*A* to *A*$^-$, dilution does not change the pH of a buffer. The **Henderson–Hasselbalch equation,**

$$pH = pK_a + \log \frac{[A^-]}{[HA]}$$

can be used to calculate the pH directly from the pK_a of the acid and the concentrations of the conjugate acid, H*A*, and base, *A*$^-$.

In performing buffer calculations, the usually valid simplifications are

$$[HA]_{\text{equilib}} \approx [HA]_{\text{initial}}$$

$$[A^-]_{\text{equilib}} \approx [A^-]_{\text{initial}}$$

The value of [*A*$^-$]$_{\text{initial}}$ is found from the molarity of the *salt* of the weak acid in the buffer. Once [H$^+$] is found by this calculation, the pH is calculated.

Buffer calculations can also be performed using K_b for the weak base component. Similar equations apply, the principal difference being that it is the OH$^-$ concentration that is calculated. Thus, using K_b we have

$$[OH^-] = K_b \times \frac{[\text{conjugate base}]}{[\text{conjugate acid}]}$$

$$= K_b \times \frac{\text{moles conjugate base}}{\text{moles conjugate acid}}$$

A solution is buffered when the pK_a of the acid member of the buffer pair lies within ± 1 unit of the solution's pH.

Equilibria in Solutions of Polyprotic Acids.

A polyprotic acid has a K_a value for the ionization of each of its hydrogen ions. Successive values of K_a often differ by a factor of 10^4 to 10^5. This allows us to calculate the pH of a solution of a polyprotic acid by using just the value of K_{a_1}. If the polyprotic acid is the only solute, the anion formed in the second step of the ionization, A^{2-}, has a concentration equal to K_{a_2}.

The anions of weak polyprotic acids are bases that react with water in successive steps, the last of which has the molecular polyprotic acid as a product. For a diprotic acid, $K_{b_1} = K_w/K_{a_2}$ and $K_{b_2} = K_w/K_{a_1}$. Usually, $K_{b_1} \gg K_{b_2}$, so virtually all the OH^- produced in the solution comes from the first step. The pH of the solution can be calculated using just K_{b_1} and the reaction

$$A^{2-} + H_2O \rightleftharpoons HA^- + OH^-$$

Acid–Base Titrations and Indicators.

Neutralization titrations can be experimentally measured using a pH meter or they can be calculated using the principles developed in this chapter. Both methods yield the same result, a titration curve.

The titration curve contains important information about the chemical system including the equivalence point and equilibrium constant data.

Each calculated titration curve has four distinct calculations:

1. The starting pH of a solution that contains only an acid or base.
2. The pH values for titrant volumes between the start and the equivalence points.
3. The pH at the equivalence point.
4. The pH values for titrant volumes past the equivalence point.

A graph of the pH values versus the volume of titrant gives us a titration curve. Titration curves show a sharp change in pH at the equivalence point. Titration curves also have distinct differences in shape when strong acid–strong base titrations are compared to weak acid–weak base titrations.

Acid–base indicators are weak acids in which the conjugate acid and base have different colors. The sudden change in pH at the equivalence point causes a rapid shift from one color of the indicator to the other. If matched to the equivalence point, a pH indicator will change color abruptly when a titration reaches the equivalence point.

TOOLS FOR PROBLEM SOLVING

The concepts that you've learned in this chapter can be applied as tools in solving problems. Study each one carefully so that you know what each is used for. When faced with solving a problem, recall what each tool does and consider whether it will be helpful in finding a solution. This will aid you in selecting the tools you need. If necessary, refer to this table when working on the Review Exercises and Review Problems that follow.

General equations for the ionization of a weak acid *(page 643)* These are the two general equations for the ionization of weak acids in aqueous solution. We use these as a general outline for the reaction from which we can construct the correct K_a equation

$$HA + H_2O \rightleftharpoons H_3O^+ + A^- \quad \text{or} \quad HA \rightleftharpoons H^+ + A^-$$

General equation for the ionization of a weak base *(page 646)* This is the general equation for the ionization of a weak base in aqueous solution. We use this as a general outline for the reaction from which we can construct the correct K_b equation

$$B + H_2O \rightleftharpoons BH^+ + OH^-$$

Inverse relationships of acid and base constants *(page 648)* These two equations are used to convert between K_a and K_b or between pK_a and pK_b values

$$K_a \times K_b = K_w \quad \text{and} \quad pK_a + pK_b = pK_w = 14.00$$

Percentage ionization *(page 649)* Use this equation to calculate the percentage ionization from the initial concentration of acid (or base) and the change in the concentrations of the ions. If the percentage ionization is known, you can calculate the change in the concentration of the acid or base and then use that information to calculate the K_a (or K_b).

$$\text{Percentage ionization} = \frac{\text{moles per liter ionized}}{\text{moles per liter available}} \times 100\%$$

Identification of acidic cations and basic anions *(pages 657 and 658)* We use the concepts developed here to determine whether a salt solution is acidic, basic, or neutral. This is also the first step in calculating the pH of a salt solution.

Criterion for applying simplifications in acid–base equilibrium calculations *(page 663)* We use this to determine whether initial concentrations can be used as though they are equilibrium values in the mass action expression when working acid–base equilibrium problems. If the condition fails, then we have to use the quadratic equation or the method of successive approximations *(page 665)*.

$$[X]_{\text{initial}} > 400 \times K$$

Reactions when H⁺ or OH⁻ are added to a buffer *(page 666)* These reactions determine how the concentrations of conjugate acid and base change when a strong acid or strong base is added to a buffer. Adding H^+ decreases $[A^-]$ and increases $[HA]$; adding OH^- decreases $[HA]$ and increases $[A^-]$.

Ionization of polyprotic acids *(page 673)* Polyprotic acids have more than one ionizable proton in their formulas. Each proton will ionize sequentially and have a form similar to the monoprotic acid ionization tool above.

Four stages of a titration curve *(page 678)* A titration curve is a graph of the pH as a function of the volume of titrant added to a sample. To plot such a curve, there are four different stages of calculation. They are (1) the starting point, (2) the stage from the start to the equivalence point, (3) the equivalence point, and (4) after the equivalence point.

How acid-base indicators work *(page 684)* Acid-base indicators are weak acids that have one color for the conjugate acid and a different color for the conjugate base. Whether the indicator is in the conjugate acid or conjugate base form depends on the pH. The rapid, large change in pH at a titration equivalence point results in a distinct color change that signals a titration end point.

QUESTIONS, PROBLEMS, AND EXERCISES

Answers to problems whose numbers are printed in color are given in Appendix B. More challenging problems are marked with asterisks. ILW = Interactive Learningware solution is available at www.wiley.com/college/brady. OH = an Office Hours video is available for this problem.

REVIEW QUESTIONS

Acid and Base Ionization Constants: K_a, K_b, pK_a, and pK_b

16.1 Write the general equation for the ionization of a weak acid in water. Give the equilibrium law corresponding to K_a.

16.2 Write the chemical equation for the ionization of each of the following weak acids in water. (Some are polyprotic acids; for these write only the equation for the first step in the ionization.)

(a) HNO_2 (c) $HAsO_4^{2-}$

(b) H_3PO_4 (d) $(CH_3)_3NH^+$

16.3 For each of the acids in Question 16.2, write the appropriate K_a expression.

16.4 Write the general equation for the ionization of a weak base in water. Give the equilibrium law corresponding to K_b.

16.5 Write the chemical equation for the ionization of each of the following weak bases in water.

(a) $(CH_3)_3N$ (c) NO_2^-

(b) AsO_4^{3-} (d) $(CH_3)_2N_2H_2$

16.6 For each of the bases in Question 16.5, write the appropriate K_b expression.

16.7 The pK_a of HCN is 9.21 and that of HF is 3.17. Which is the stronger Brønsted base, CN^- or F^-?

16.8 Write the structural formulas for the conjugate acids of the following:

(a) $CH_3{-}CH_2{-}\overset{\overset{\displaystyle CH_3}{|}}{\underset{..}{N}}{-}H$ (b) a benzene ring with $\ddot{N}:$ (c) $H{-}\overset{..}{\underset{..}{O}}{-}\overset{}{\underset{..}{N}}{-}H$

16.9 Write the structural formulas for the conjugate bases of the following:

(a) a benzene ring with NH_3^+

(b) $\left[CH_3{-}\overset{\overset{\displaystyle CH_3}{|}}{\underset{\underset{\displaystyle CH_3}{|}}{N}}{-}H \right]^+$

(c) $\left[H{-}\overset{\overset{\displaystyle H}{|}}{\underset{..}{N}}{-}\overset{\overset{\displaystyle H}{|}}{\underset{\underset{\displaystyle H}{|}}{N}}{-}H \right]^+$

16.10 How is percentage ionization defined? Write the equation.

16.11 If a weak acid is 1.2% ionized in a 0.22 M solution, what is the molar concentration of H^+ in the solution?

16.12 What criterion do we use to determine whether or not the equilibrium concentration of an acid or base will be effectively the same as its initial concentration when we calculate the pH of the solution?

16.13 For which of the following are we permitted to make the assumption that the equilibrium concentration of the acid or base is the same as the initial concentration when we calculate the pH of the solution specified?

(a) 0.020 M $HC_2H_3O_2$ (c) 0.002 M N_2H_4

(b) 0.10 M CH_3NH_2 (d) 0.050 M $HCHO_2$

Acid–Base Properties of Salt Solutions

16.14 Aspirin is acetylsalicylic acid, a monoprotic acid whose K_a value is 3.27×10^{-4}. Does a solution of the sodium salt of aspirin in water test acidic, basic, or neutral? Explain.

16.15 The K_b value of the oxalate ion, $C_2O_4^{2-}$, is 1.9×10^{-10}. Is a solution of $K_2C_2O_4$ acidic, basic, or neutral? Explain.

16.16 Consider the following compounds and suppose that 0.5 M solutions are prepared of each: NaI, KF, $(NH_4)_2SO_4$, KCN, $KC_2H_3O_2$, $CsNO_3$, and KBr. Write the *formulas* of those that have solutions that are (a) acidic, (b) basic, and (c) neutral.

16.17 Will an aqueous solution of $AlCl_3$ turn litmus red or blue? Explain.

16.18 A solution of hydrazinium acetate is slightly acidic. Without looking at the tables of equilibrium constants, is K_a for acetic acid larger or smaller than K_b for hydrazine? Justify your answer.

16.19 When ammonium nitrate is added to a suspension of magnesium hydroxide in water, the $Mg(OH)_2$ dissolves. Write a net ionic equation to show how this occurs.

Buffers

16.20 Write ionic equations that illustrate how each pair of compounds can serve as a buffer pair.

(a) H_2CO_3 and $NaHCO_3$ (the "carbonate" buffer in blood)

(b) NaH_2PO_4 and Na_2HPO_4 (the "phosphate" buffer inside body cells)

(c) NH_4Cl and NH_3

16.21 Bicarbonate ion is able to act as a buffer all by itself. Write chemical equations that show how this ion reacts with (a) H^+ and (b) OH^-.

Ionization of Polyprotic Acids

16.22 When sulfur dioxide, an air pollutant from the burning of sulfur-containing coal or oil, dissolves in water, an acidic solution is formed that can be viewed as containing sulfurous acid, H_2SO_3.

$$H_2O + SO_2(g) \rightleftharpoons H_2SO_3(aq)$$

Write the expression for K_{a_1} and K_{a_2} for sulfurous acid.

16.23 Citric acid, found in citrus fruits, is a triprotic acid, $H_3C_6H_5O_7$. Write chemical equations for the three-step ionization of this acid in water and the corresponding K_a expressions.

16.24 What simplifying assumptions do we usually make in working problems involving the ionization of polyprotic acids? Why are they usually valid? Under what conditions do they fail?

Salts of Polyprotic Acids

16.25 Write the equations for the chemical equilibria that exist in solutions of (a) Na_2SO_3, (b) Na_3PO_4, and (c) $K_2C_4H_4O_6$.

16.26 What simplifying assumptions do we usually make in working problems involving equilibria of salts of polyprotic acids? Why are they usually valid? Under what conditions do they fail?

Titrations and Acid–Base Indicators

16.27 Define the terms *equivalence point* and *end point* as they apply to an acid–base titration.

16.28 When a formic acid solution is titrated with sodium hydroxide, will the solution be acidic, neutral, or basic at the equivalence point?

16.29 When a solution of hydrazine is titrated by hydrochloric acid, will the solution be acidic, neutral, or basic at the equivalence point?

16.30 Qualitatively, describe how an acid–base indicator works. Why do we want to use a minimum amount of indicator in a titration?

16.31 If you use methyl orange in the titration of $HC_2H_3O_2$ with NaOH, will the end point of the titration correspond to the equivalence point? Justify your answer.

REVIEW PROBLEMS

Acid and Base Ionization Constants: K_a, K_b, pK_a, and pK_b

16.32 The K_a for HF is 6.8×10^{-4}. What is the K_b for F^-?

16.33 The barbiturate ion, $C_4H_3N_2O_3^-$, has $K_b = 1.0 \times 10^{-10}$. What is K_a for barbituric acid?

16.34 Lactic acid, $HC_3H_5O_3$, is responsible for the sour taste of sour milk. At 25 °C, its $K_a = 1.4 \times 10^{-4}$. What is the K_b of its conjugate base, the lactate ion, $C_3H_5O_3^-$?

OH **16.35** Iodic acid, HIO_3, has a pK_a of 0.77. (a) What is the formula and the K_b of its conjugate base? (b) Is its conjugate base a stronger or a weaker base than the acetate ion?

Equilibrium Calculations

16.36 A 0.20 M solution of a weak acid, HA, has a pH of 3.22. What is the percentage ionization of the acid? What is the value of K_a for the acid?

16.37 If a weak base is 0.030% ionized in 0.030 M solution, what is the pH of the solution? What is the value of K_b for the base?

OH **16.38** Periodic acid, HIO_4, is an important oxidizing agent and a moderately strong acid. In a 0.10 M solution, $[H^+] = 3.8 \times 10^{-2}$ mol L^{-1}. Calculate the K_a and pK_a for periodic acid.

16.39 Chloroacetic acid, $HC_2H_2O_2Cl$, is a stronger monoprotic acid than acetic acid. In a 0.10 M solution, the pH is 1.96. Calculate the K_a and pK_a for chloroacetic acid.

ILW **16.40** Ethylamine, $CH_3CH_2NH_2$, has a strong, pungent odor similar to that of ammonia. Like ammonia, it is a Brønsted base. A 0.10 M solution has a pH of 11.86. Calculate the K_b and pK_b for ethylamine. What is the percentage ionization of ethylamine in the solution?

16.41 Hydroxylamine, $HONH_2$, like ammonia, is a Brønsted base. A 0.15 M solution has a pH of 10.12. What is the K_b and pK_b for hydroxylamine? What is the percentage ionization of the $HONH_2$?

ILW **16.42** What are the concentrations of all the solute species in 0.150 M lactic acid, $HC_3H_5O_2$? What is the pH of the solution? This acid has $K_a = 1.4 \times 10^{-4}$.

16.43 What are the concentrations of all the solute species in a 1.0 M solution of hydrogen peroxide, H_2O_2? What is the pH of the solution? For H_2O_2, $K_a = 1.8 \times 10^{-12}$.

16.44 Codeine, a cough suppressant extracted from crude opium, is a weak base with a pK_b of 5.79. What will be the pH of a 0.020 M solution of codeine? (Use *Cod* as a symbol for codeine.)

16.45 Pyridine, C_5H_5N, is a bad-smelling liquid that is a weak base in water. Its pK_b is 8.82. What is the pH of a 0.20 M aqueous solution of the compound?

16.46 A solution of acetic acid has a pH of 2.54. What is the concentration of acetic acid in this solution?

16.47 How many moles of NH_3 must be dissolved in water to give 500 mL of solution with a pH of 11.22?

Equilibrium Calculations when Simplifications Fail

16.48 What is the pH of a 0.0050 M solution of sodium cyanide?

16.49 What is the pH of a 0.020 M solution of chloroacetic acid, for which $K_a = 1.36 \times 10^{-3}$?

16.50 The compound *para*-aminobenzoic acid (PABA) is a powerful sun screening agent whose salts were once used widely in sun tanning and screening lotions. The parent acid, which we may symbolize as H-*Paba*, is a weak acid with a pK_a of 4.92 (at 25 °C). What is the $[H^+]$ and pH of a 0.030 M solution of the acid?

16.51 Barbituric acid, $HC_4H_3N_2O_3$ (which we will abbreviate H-*Bar*), was discovered by the Nobel prize–winning organic chemist Adolph von Baeyer and named after his friend, Barbara. It is the parent compound of widely used sleeping drugs, the barbiturates. Its pK_a is 4.01. What is the $[H^+]$ and pH of a 0.020 M solution of H-*Bar*?

Acid–Base Properties of Salt Solutions

16.52 Calculate the pH of 0.20 M NaCN. What is the concentration of HCN in the solution?

16.53 Calculate the pH of 0.40 M KNO$_2$. What is the concentration of HNO$_2$ in the solution?

ILW 16.54 Calculate the pH of 0.15 M CH$_3$NH$_3$Cl. For methylamine, CH$_3$NH$_2$, $K_b = 4.4 \times 10^{-4}$.

16.55 Calculate the pH of 0.10 M hydrazinium chloride, N$_2$H$_5$Cl.

16.56 A 0.18 M solution of the sodium salt of nicotinic acid (also known pharmaceutically as niacin) has a pH of 9.05. What is the value of K_a for nicotinic acid?

16.57 A weak base B forms the salt BHCl, composed of the ions BH$^+$ and Cl$^-$. A 0.15 M solution of the salt has a pH of 4.28. What is the value of K_b for the base B?

OH *16.58 Liquid chlorine bleach is really nothing more than a solution of sodium hypochlorite, NaOCl, in water. Usually, the concentration is approximately 5% NaOCl by weight. Use this information to calculate the approximate pH of a bleach solution, assuming no other solutes are in the solution except NaOCl. (Assume the bleach has a density of 1.0 g/mL.)

***16.59** The conjugate acid of a molecular base has the hypothetical formula, BH$^+$, which has a pK_a of 5.00. A solution of a salt of this cation, BHY, tests slightly basic. Will the conjugate acid of Y^-, HY, have a pK_a greater than 5.00 or less than 5.00? Explain.

Buffers

16.60 What is the pH of a solution that contains 0.15 M HC$_2$H$_3$O$_2$ and 0.25 M C$_2$H$_3$O$_2^-$? Use $K_a = 1.8 \times 10^{-5}$ for HC$_2$H$_3$O$_2$.

16.61 Rework the preceding problem using the K_b for the acetate ion. (Be sure to write the proper chemical equation and equilibrium law.)

OH 16.62 A buffer is prepared containing 0.25 M NH$_3$ and 0.45 M NH$_4^+$. Calculate the pH of the buffer using the K_b for NH$_3$.

16.63 Calculate the pH of the buffer in the preceding problem using the K_a for NH$_4^+$.

16.64 Suppose 25.0 mL of 0.10 M HCl is added to a 250 mL portion of a buffer composed of 0.25 M NH$_3$ and 0.20 M NH$_4$Cl. By how much will the concentrations of the NH$_3$ and NH$_4^+$ ions change after the addition of the strong acid?

16.65 A student added 100 mL of 0.10 M NaOH to 250 mL of a buffer that contained 0.15 M HC$_2$H$_3$O$_2$ and 0.25 M C$_2$H$_3$O$_2^-$. By how much did the concentrations of HC$_2$H$_3$O$_2$ and C$_2$H$_3$O$_2^-$ change after the addition of the strong base?

16.66 By how much will the pH change if 0.025 mol of HCl is added to 1.00 L of the buffer in Problem 16.60?

16.67 By how much will the pH change if 25.0 mL of 0.20 M NaOH is added to 500 mL of the buffer in Problem 16.60?

16.68 By how much will the pH change if 0.040 mol of HCl is added to 1.00 L of the buffer in Problem 16.62?

16.69 By how much will the pH change if 35 mL of 0.10 M KOH is added to 200 mL of the buffer in Problem 16.62?

16.70 How many grams of sodium acetate, NaC$_2$H$_3$O$_2$, would have to be added to 1.0 L of 0.15 M acetic acid (pK_a 4.74) to make the solution a buffer for pH 4.00?

16.71 How many grams of sodium formate, NaCHO$_2$, would have to be dissolved in 1.0 L of 0.12 M formic acid (pK_a 3.74) to make the solution a buffer for pH 3.50?

16.72 Suppose 30.00 mL of 0.100 M HCl is added to an acetate buffer prepared by dissolving 0.100 mol of acetic acid and 0.110 mol of sodium acetate in 100 mL of solution. What are the initial and final pH values? What would be the pH if the same amount of HCl solution were added to 100 mL of pure water?

16.73 How many milliliters of 0.15 M HCl would have to be added to the original 100 mL of the buffer described in Problem 16.72 to make the pH decrease by 0.05 pH unit? How many milliliters of the same HCl solution would, if added to 100 mL of pure water, make the pH decrease by 0.05 pH unit?

Solutions of Polyprotic Acids

ILW 16.74 Calculate the concentrations of all the solute species in a 0.15 M solution of ascorbic acid (vitamin C). What is the pH of the solution?

16.75 Tellurium, in the same family as sulfur, forms an acid analogous to sulfuric acid and called telluric acid. It exists, however, as H$_6$TeO$_6$ (which looks like the formula H$_2$TeO$_4$ + 2H$_2$O). It is a diprotic acid with $K_{a_1} = 2 \times 10^{-8}$ and $K_{a_2} = 1 \times 10^{-11}$. Calculate the concentrations of H$^+$, H$_5$TeO$_6^-$, and H$_4$TeO$_6^{2-}$ in a 0.25 M solution of H$_6$TeO$_6$. What is the pH of the solution?

OH 16.76 Calculate the concentrations of all of the solute species involved in the equilibria in a 2.0 M solution of H$_3$PO$_4$. Calculate the pH of the solution.

16.77 What is the pH of a 0.25 M solution of arsenic acid, H$_3$AsO$_4$? In this solution, what are the concentrations of H$_2$AsO$_4^-$ and HAsO$_4^{2-}$?

***16.78** Phosphorous acid, H$_3$PO$_3$, is actually a diprotic acid for which $K_{a_1} = 3.0 \times 10^{-2}$ and $K_{a_2} = 1.6 \times 10^{-7}$. What are the values of $[H^+]$, $[H_2PO_3^-]$, and $[HPO_3^{2-}]$ in a 1.0 M solution of H$_3$PO$_3$? What is the pH of the solution?

*16.79 What is the pH of a 0.20 M solution of oxalic acid, $H_2C_2O_4$?

Solutions of Salts of Polyprotic Acids

16.80 Calculate the pH of 0.24 M Na_2SO_3. What are the concentrations of HSO_3^- and H_2SO_3 in the solution?

16.81 Calculate the pH of 0.33 M K_2CO_3. What are the concentrations of HCO_3^- and H_2CO_3 in the solution?

16.82 Sodium citrate, $Na_3C_6H_5O_7$, is used as an anticoagulant in the collection of blood. What is the pH of a 0.10 M solution of this salt?

16.83 What is the pH of a 0.25 M solution of sodium oxalate, $Na_2C_2O_4$?

*16.84 What is the pH of a 0.50 M solution of Na_3PO_4? In this solution, what are the concentrations of HPO_4^{2-}, $H_2PO_4^-$, and H_3PO_4?

*16.85 The pH of a 0.10 M Na_2CO_3 solution is adjusted to 12.00 using a strong base. What is the concentration of CO_3^{2-} in this solution?

Acid–Base Titrations

16.86 When 50 mL of 0.050 M formic acid, $HCHO_2$, is titrated with 0.050 M sodium hydroxide, what is the pH at the equivalence point? (Be sure to take into account the change in volume during the titration.) Select a good indicator for this titration from Table 15.5.

OH 16.87 When 25 mL of 0.12 M aqueous ammonia is titrated with 0.12 M hydrobromic acid, what is the pH at the equivalence point? Select a good indicator for this titration from Table 15.5.

16.88 What is the pH of a solution prepared by mixing 25.0 mL of 0.180 M $HC_2H_3O_2$ with 40.0 mL of 0.250 M NaOH?

16.89 What is the pH of a solution prepared by mixing exactly 25.0 mL of 0.200 M $HC_2H_3O_2$ with 15.0 mL of 0.400 M KOH?

*16.90 For the titration of 75.00 mL of 0.1000 M acetic acid with 0.1000 M NaOH, calculate the pH (a) before the addition of any NaOH solution, (b) after 25.00 mL of the base has been added, (c) after half of the $HC_2H_3O_2$ has been neutralized, and (d) at the equivalence point.

*16.91 For the titration of 50.00 mL of 0.1000 M ammonia with 0.1000 M HCl, calculate the pH (a) before the addition of any HCl solution, (b) after 20.00 mL of the acid has been added, (c) after half of the NH_3 has been neutralized, and (d) at the equivalence point.

ADDITIONAL EXERCISES

16.92 Calculate the percentage ionization of acetic acid in solutions having concentrations of 1.0 M, 0.10 M, and 0.010 M. How does the percentage ionization of a weak acid change as the acid becomes more dilute?

16.93 What is the pH of a solution that is 0.100 M in HCl and also 0.125 M in $HC_2H_3O_2$? What is the concentration of acetate ion in this solution?

16.94 A solution is prepared by mixing 300 mL of 0.500 M NH_3 and 100 mL of 0.500 M HCl. Assuming that the volumes are additive, what is the pH of the resulting mixture?

16.95 A solution is prepared by dissolving 15.0 g of pure $HC_2H_3O_2$ and 25.0 g of $NaC_2H_3O_2$ in 750 mL of solution (the final volume). (a) What is the pH of the solution? (b) What would the pH of the solution be if 25.00 mL of 0.25 M NaOH were added? (c) What would the pH be if 25.0 mL of 0.40 M HCl were added to the original 750 mL of buffer solution?

*16.96 For an experiment involving what happens to the growth of a particular fungus in a slightly acidic medium, a biochemist needs 250 mL of an acetate buffer with a pH of 5.12. The buffer solution has to be able to hold the pH to within ±0.10 pH unit of 5.12 even if 0.0100 mol of NaOH or 0.0100 mol of HCl enters the solution.

(a) What is the minimum number of grams of acetic acid and of sodium acetate dihydrate that must be used to prepare the buffer?

(b) Describe the buffer by giving its molarity in acetic acid and its molarity in sodium acetate.

(c) What is the pH of an unbuffered solution made by adding 0.0100 mol of NaOH to 250 mL of pure water?

(d) What is the pH of an unbuffered solution made by adding 0.0100 mol of HCl to 250 mL of pure water?

16.97 Predict whether the pH of 0.120 M NH_4CN is greater than, less than, or equal to 7.00. Give your reasons.

*16.98 What is the pH of a 4.5×10^{-2} M solution of ammonium acetate, $NH_4C_2H_3O_2$?

*16.99 What is the approximate freezing point of a 0.50 M solution of dichloroacetic acid, $HC_2HO_2Cl_2$ ($K_a = 5.0 \times 10^{-2}$). Assume the density of the solution is 1.0 g/mL.

*16.100 How many milliliters of ammonia gas measured at 25 °C and 740 torr must be dissolved in 250 mL of 0.050 M HNO_3 to give a solution with a pH of 9.26?

*16.101 The hydrogen sulfate ion, HSO_4^-, is a moderately strong Brønsted acid with a K_a of 1.0×10^{-2}.
(a) Write the chemical equation for the ionization of the acid and give the appropriate K_a expression.
(b) What is the value of $[H^+]$ in 0.010 M HSO_4^- (furnished by the salt, $NaHSO_4$)? Do NOT make simplifying assumptions.
(c) What is the calculated $[H^+]$ in 0.010 M HSO_4^-, obtained by using the usual simplifying assumption?
(d) How much error is introduced by incorrectly using the simplifying assumption?

16.102 Some people who take megadoses of ascorbic acid will drink a solution containing as much as 6.0 g of ascorbic acid dissolved in a glass of water. Assuming the volume to be 250 mL, calculate the pH of the solution.

*16.103 For the titration of 25.00 mL of 0.1000 M HCl with 0.1000 M NaOH, calculate the pH of the reaction mixture after each of the following total volumes of base have been added to the original solution. (Remember to take into account the change in total volume.) Construct a graph showing the titration curve for this experiment.

(a) 0 mL   (d) 24.99 mL   (g) 25.10 mL
(b) 10.00 mL   (e) 25.00 mL   (h) 26.00 mL
(c) 24.90 mL   (f) 25.01 mL   (i) 50.00 mL

16.104 Below is a diagram illustrating a mixture HF and F^- in an aqueous solution. For this mixture, does pH equal pK_a for HF? Explain. Describe how the number of HF molecules and F^- ions will change after three OH^- ions are added. How will the number of HF and F^- change if two H^+ ions are added? Explain your answers by using chemical equations.

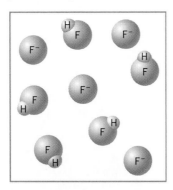

EXERCISES IN CRITICAL THINKING

16.105 Suppose that when doing a titration, a mistake causes an error of 10% in the concentration of hydronium ions. What is the error in terms of pH? Is the pH error the same for a $1.0 \times 10^{-3}\ M$ $[H^+]$ solution as compared to a $5.0 \times 10^{-6}\ M$ solution?

16.106 In the 1950s it was discovered that lakes in the northeastern United States had declining fish populations due to increased acidity. In order to address the problem of lake acidification, make a list of what you need to know in order to start addressing the problem.

16.107 Where are buffers found in everyday consumer products? Propose reasons why a manufacturer would use a buffer in a given product of your choice.

16.108 Why must the acid used for a buffer have a pK_a within one pH unit of the pH of the buffer? What happens if that condition is not met?

16.109 What conjugate acid–base pairs are used to buffer (a) over the counter drugs, (b) foods, (c) cosmetics, and (d) shampoos?

16.110 Your blood at 37 °C needs to be maintained within a narrow pH range of 7.35 to 7.45 to maintain optimal health. What possible conjugate acid–base pairs are present in blood that can buffer the blood and keep it within this range?

16.111 Develop a list of the uses of phosphoric acid in various consumer products.

16.112 Investigate the salts of phosphoric acid (i.e., those that contain the anions $H_2PO_4^-$, HPO_4^{2-}, and PO_4^{3-}) to find out how they are used in consumer products.

SOLUBILITY AND SIMULTANEOUS EQUILIBRIA

Small marine organisms called corals extract calcium ions and carbonate ions from sea water and precipitate calcium carbonate to form their shells. Over time, these small shells become the major structural feature of coral reefs, such as the one shown here. The equilibria involved in the solubility of metal salts constitute the major focus of this chapter. *(Scott Tuason/ Image Quest Marine)*

THIS CHAPTER IN CONTEXT   In the preceding chapters you learned how the principles of equ can be applied to aqueous solutions of acids and bases. In this chapter we extend these principles to a reactions that involve the formation and dissolving of precipitates (a topic we introduced in Chapter 4). Ma reactions are common in the world around us. For example, groundwater rich in carbon dioxide dissolves of calcium carbonate, producing vast underground caverns, and as the remaining calcium-containing solution g evaporates, stalactites and stalagmites form. Within living organisms, precipitation reactions form the hard carbonate shells of clams, oysters, and coral as well as the unwanted calcium oxalate and calcium phosphate we call kidney stones. Also, dilute acids in our mouths promote the dissolving of tooth enamel, which is cor of a mineral made up of calcium phosphate and calcium hydroxide.

In this chapter you will learn how we can calculate the solubilities of "insoluble" salts in water and in other solutions, and how the formation of substances called complex ions can affect solubilities. The concepts we develop here can tell us when precipitates will form and when they will dissolve, and we can use these in a practical lab setting in the separation of metal ions for chemical analysis.

17.1 AN INSOLUBLE SALT IS IN EQUILIBRIUM WITH THE SOLUTION AROUND IT

The equilibrium constant for an "insoluble" salt is called the solubility product constant, K_{sp}

None of the salts we described in Chapter 4 as being insoluble are *totally* insoluble. For example, the solubility rules tell us that AgCl is "insoluble," but if some solid AgCl is placed in water, a very small amount does dissolve. Once the solution has become saturated, the following equilibrium is established between the undissolved AgCl and its ions in the solution.

$$AgCl(s) \rightleftharpoons Ag^+(aq) + Cl^-(aq)$$

(In a saturated solution of AgCl)

This is a heterogeneous equilibrium because it involves a solid reactant (AgCl) in equilibrium with ions in aqueous solution. Using the procedure developed in Section 14.4 (page 579), we write the equilibrium law as follows, omitting the solid from the mass action expression.

$$[Ag^+][Cl^-] = K_{sp} \tag{17.1}$$

The equilibrium constant, K_{sp}, is called the **solubility product constant** (because the system is a *solubility* equilibrium and the constant equals a *product* of ion concentrations).

It's important that you understand the distinction between solubility and solubility product. The *solubility* of a salt is the amount of the salt that dissolves in a given amount of solvent to give a saturated solution. The *solubility product* is the product of the molar concentrations of the ions in the saturated solution, raised to appropriate powers (see below).

The solubilities of salts change with temperature, so a value of K_{sp} applies only at the temperature at which it was determined. Some typical K_{sp} values are in Table 17.1 and in Appendix C.

In solubility equilibria, the reaction quotient is called the ion product

In preceding chapters we described the value of the mass action expression as the reaction quotient, Q. For simple solubility equilibria like those discussed in this section, the mass action expression is a product of ion concentrations raised to appropriate powers, so Q is often called the **ion product** of the salt. Thus, for AgCl,

$$\text{Ion product} = [Ag^+][Cl^-] = Q$$

At any dilution of a salt throughout the range of possibilities for an *unsaturated* solution, there will be varying values for the ion concentrations and, therefore, for Q. However, Q acquires a constant value, K_{sp}, in a *saturated* solution. When a solution is less than saturated, the value of Q is less than K_{sp}. Thus, we can use the numerical value of Q for a given solution as a test for saturation by comparing it to the value of K_{sp}.

Many salts produce more than one of a given ion per formula unit when they dissociate, and this introduces exponents into the ion product expression. For example, when silver chromate, Ag_2CrO_4, precipitates (Figure 17.1), it enters into the following solubility equilibrium.

$$Ag_2CrO_4(s) \rightleftharpoons 2Ag^+(aq) + CrO_4^{2-}(aq)$$

The equilibrium law is obtained following the procedure we developed in Chapter 14, using coefficients as exponents in the mass action expression.

□ Recall that when salts dissolve, they dissociate essentially completely, so the equilibrium is between the solid and the ions that are in the solution.

TOOLS

Solubility product constant, K_{sp}

FIG. 17.1 **Silver chromate.** When sodium chromate is added to a solution of silver nitrate, deep red "insoluble" silver chromate, Ag_2CrO_4, precipitates. *(Michael Watson.)*

TABLE 17.1	Solubility Product Constants			
Type	Salt		Ions of Salt	K_{sp} (25 °C)
Halides	CaF_2	$\rightleftharpoons$	$Ca^{2+} + 2F^-$	3.9×10^{-11}
	$AgCl$	$\rightleftharpoons$	$Ag^+ + Cl^-$	1.8×10^{-10}
	$AgBr$	$\rightleftharpoons$	$Ag^+ + Br^-$	5.0×10^{-13}
	AgI	$\rightleftharpoons$	$Ag^+ + I^-$	8.3×10^{-17}
	PbF_2	$\rightleftharpoons$	$Pb^{2+} + 2F^-$	3.6×10^{-8}
	$PbCl_2$	$\rightleftharpoons$	$Pb^{2+} + 2Cl^-$	1.7×10^{-5}
	$PbBr_2$	$\rightleftharpoons$	$Pb^{2+} + 2Br^-$	2.1×10^{-6}
	PbI_2	$\rightleftharpoons$	$Pb^{2+} + 2I^-$	7.9×10^{-9}
Hydroxides	$Al(OH)_3$	$\rightleftharpoons$	$Al^{3+} + 3OH^-$	$3 \times 10^{-34\,(a)}$
	$Ca(OH)_2$	$\rightleftharpoons$	$Ca^{2+} + 2OH^-$	6.5×10^{-6}
	$Fe(OH)_2$	$\rightleftharpoons$	$Fe^{2+} + 2OH^-$	7.9×10^{-16}
	$Fe(OH)_3$	$\rightleftharpoons$	$Fe^{3+} + 3OH^-$	1.6×10^{-39}
	$Mg(OH)_2$	$\rightleftharpoons$	$Mg^{2+} + 2OH^-$	7.1×10^{-12}
	$Zn(OH)_2$	$\rightleftharpoons$	$Zn^{2+} + 2OH^-$	$3.0 \times 10^{-16\,(b)}$
Carbonates	Ag_2CO_3	$\rightleftharpoons$	$2Ag^+ + CO_3^{2-}$	8.1×10^{-12}
	$MgCO_3$	$\rightleftharpoons$	$Mg^{2+} + CO_3^{2-}$	3.5×10^{-8}
	$CaCO_3$	$\rightleftharpoons$	$Ca^{2+} + CO_3^{2-}$	$4.5 \times 10^{-9\,(c)}$
	$SrCO_3$	$\rightleftharpoons$	$Sr^{2+} + CO_3^{2-}$	9.3×10^{-10}
	$BaCO_3$	$\rightleftharpoons$	$Ba^{2+} + CO_3^{2-}$	5.0×10^{-9}
	$CoCO_3$	$\rightleftharpoons$	$Co^{2+} + CO_3^{2-}$	1.0×10^{-10}
	$NiCO_3$	$\rightleftharpoons$	$Ni^{2+} + CO_3^{2-}$	1.3×10^{-7}
	$ZnCO_3$	$\rightleftharpoons$	$Zn^{2+} + CO_3^{2-}$	1.0×10^{-10}
Chromates	Ag_2CrO_4	$\rightleftharpoons$	$2Ag^+ + CrO_4^{2-}$	1.2×10^{-12}
	$PbCrO_4$	$\rightleftharpoons$	$Pb^{2+} + CrO_4^{2-}$	$1.8 \times 10^{-14(d)}$
Sulfates	$CaSO_4$	$\rightleftharpoons$	$Ca^{2+} + SO_4^{2-}$	2.4×10^{-5}
	$SrSO_4$	$\rightleftharpoons$	$Sr^{2+} + SO_4^{2-}$	3.2×10^{-7}
	$BaSO_4$	$\rightleftharpoons$	$Ba^{2+} + SO_4^{2-}$	1.1×10^{-10}
	$PbSO_4$	$\rightleftharpoons$	$Pb^{2+} + SO_4^{2-}$	6.3×10^{-7}
Oxalates	CaC_2O_4	$\rightleftharpoons$	$Ca^{2+} + C_2O_4^{2-}$	2.3×10^{-9}
	MgC_2O_4	$\rightleftharpoons$	$Mg^{2+} + C_2O_4^{2-}$	8.6×10^{-5}
	BaC_2O_4	$\rightleftharpoons$	$Ba^{2+} + C_2O_4^{2-}$	1.2×10^{-7}
	FeC_2O_4	$\rightleftharpoons$	$Fe^{2+} + C_2O_4^{2-}$	2.1×10^{-7}
	PbC_2O_4	$\rightleftharpoons$	$Pb^{2+} + C_2O_4^{2-}$	2.7×10^{-11}

(a)Alpha form.   (b)Amorphous form.   (c)Calcite form.   (d)At 10 °C.

$$[Ag^+]^2[CrO_4^{2-}] = K_{sp}$$

Thus, the ion product contains the ion concentrations raised to powers equal to the number of ions released per formula unit. This means that to obtain the correct ion product expression you have to know the formulas of the ions that make up the salt. In other words, you have to realize that Ag_2CrO_4 is composed of Ag^+ and the polyatomic anion CrO_4^{2-}. If necessary, review the list of polyatomic ions in Table 2.8 on page 69.

Practice Exercise 1: Write the equation for the equilibrium involved in the solubility of barium phosphate, $Ba_3(PO_4)_2$, and write the equilibrium law corresponding to K_{sp}. (Hint: Remember that it's a heterogeneous equilibrium.)

Practice Exercise 2: What are the ion product expressions for the following salts? (a) barium oxalate, (b) silver sulfate

K_{sp} can be determined from molar solubilities

One way to determine the value of K_{sp} for a salt is to measure its solubility—how much of the salt is required to give a saturated solution in a specified amount of solution. It is useful to express this as the **molar solubility**, which equals *the number of moles of salt dissolved in one liter of its* **saturated** *solution.* The molar solubility can be used to calculate the K_{sp} under the assumption that all of the salt that dissolves is 100% dissociated into the ions implied in the salt's formula.[1]

TOOLS

Molar solubility

EXAMPLE 17.1

Calculating K_{sp} from Solubility Data

Silver bromide, AgBr, is the light-sensitive compound used in nearly all photographic film. The solubility of AgBr in water was measured to be 1.3×10^{-4} g L^{-1} at 25 °C. Calculate K_{sp} for AgBr at that temperature.

ANALYSIS: As usual, we begin with the chemical equation for the equilibrium, from which we construct the equilibrium law (here, the expression for K_{sp}).

$$AgBr(s) \rightleftharpoons Ag^+(aq) + Br^-(aq)$$
$$K_{sp} = [Ag^+][Br^-]$$

To calculate K_{sp}, we need the concentrations of the ions expressed in moles per liter. We can obtain these from the molar solubility—the number of moles of AgBr dissolved per liter. Therefore, the first step will be to change 1.3×10^{-4} g L^{-1} to moles per liter.

For problems dealing with solubility, the concentration table is an especially useful tool. In setting up the table, it is helpful if we imagine the formation of the saturated solution to occur stepwise. First, we will look at the composition of the solvent into which the salt will be placed. Does it contain any of the ions involved in the equilibrium? If it doesn't, the initial concentrations will be set equal to zero. However, if the solvent contains a solute that is a source of one of the ions in the equilibrium, we will use its concentration as the initial concentration of that ion.

When the salt dissolves, the concentrations of the ions increase, so the entries in the "change" row will be positive and will have values determined by the formula of the salt. We will obtain these from the molar solubility.

The entries in the last row, which are the equilibrium values, are obtained by adding the initial concentrations to the changes. Once we have the equilibrium ion concentrations, we substitute them into the ion product expression to calculate K_{sp}.

SOLUTION: First, we calculate the number of moles of AgBr dissolved per liter.

$$\text{Molar solubility} = \frac{1.3 \times 10^{-4} \text{ g AgBr}}{1.00 \text{ L soln}} \times \frac{1.00 \text{ mol AgBr}}{187.77 \text{ g AgBr}} = 6.9 \times 10^{-7} \text{ mol L}^{-1}$$

Now we can begin to set up the concentration table, which is shown on the next page. Notice first that there are no entries in the "reactant" column. This is because AgBr is a solid and doesn't appear in the mass action expression.

Initial Concentrations   In the first row, under the formulas of the ions, we enter the initial concentrations of Ag$^+$ and Br$^-$. *Remember, these are the concentrations of the ions present in the solvent before any of the AgBr dissolves.* In this case the solvent is pure water. Neither Ag$^+$ nor Br$^-$ are present in pure water, so we set the initial concentrations equal to zero.

---

[1] This assumption works reasonably well for slightly soluble salts made up of singly charged ions, like silver bromide. For simplicity, and to illustrate the nature of calculations involving solubility equilibria, we will work on the assumption that *all* salts behave as though they are 100% dissociated. This is not entirely true, especially for salts of multiply charged ions, so the accuracy of our calculations is limited. We discussed the reasons for the incomplete dissociation of salts in Section 12.9.

Changes in Concentrations In the "change" row, we enter data on how the concentrations of the $Ag^+(aq)$ and $Br^-(aq)$ change when the AgBr dissolves. Because dissolving the salt always increases these concentrations, these entries are always positive. They are also related to each other by the stoichiometry of the dissociation reaction. Thus, when AgBr dissolves, Ag^+ and Br^- ions are released in a 1:1 ratio. So, when 6.9×10^{-7} mol of AgBr dissolves (per liter), 6.9×10^{-7} mol of Ag^+ ion and 6.9×10^{-7} mol of Br^- ion go into solution. The concentrations of these species thus *change* (increase) by those amounts.

Equilibrium Concentrations As usual, we obtain the equilibrium values by adding the "initial concentrations" to the "changes."

	AgBr(s) $\rightleftharpoons$	$Ag^+(aq)$ +	$Br^-(aq)$
Initial concentrations (M)	No entries in this column	0	0
Changes in concentrations when AgBr dissolves (M)		$+6.9 \times 10^{-7}$	$+6.9 \times 10^{-7}$
Equilibrium concentrations (M)		6.9×10^{-7}	6.9×10^{-7}

☐ There are no entries in the column under AgBr(s) because this substance does not appear in the K_{sp} expression.

We now substitute the equilibrium ion concentrations into the K_{sp} expression.

$$K_{sp} = [Ag^+][Br^-]$$
$$= (6.9 \times 10^{-7})(6.9 \times 10^{-7})$$
$$= 4.8 \times 10^{-13}$$

☐ The K_{sp} we calculated from the solubility data here differs by only 4% from the value in Table 17.1.

The K_{sp} of AgBr is thus calculated to be 4.8×10^{-13} at 25 °C.

IS THE ANSWER REASONABLE? We've divided 1.3×10^{-4} by a number that's approximately 200, which would give a value of about 6.5×10^{-7}, so our molar solubility seems reasonable. (Also, we know AgBr has a very low solubility in water, so we expect the molar solubility to be very small.) The reasoning involved in the change row also makes sense; the number of moles of ions formed per liter must each equal the number of moles of AgBr that dissolve. Finally, if we round 6.9×10^{-7} to 7×10^{-7} and square it, we obtain $49 \times 10^{-14} = 4.9 \times 10^{-13}$. Our answer of 4.8×10^{-13} seems to be okay.

EXAMPLE 17.2
Calculating K_{sp} from Molar Solubility Data

The molar solubility of silver chromate, Ag_2CrO_4, in water is 6.7×10^{-5} mol L^{-1} at 25 °C. What is K_{sp} for Ag_2CrO_4?

ANALYSIS: We begin with the equilibrium equation and K_{sp} expression.

$$Ag_2CrO_4(s) \rightleftharpoons 2Ag^+(aq) + CrO_4^{2-}(aq) \qquad K_{sp} = [Ag^+]^2[CrO_4^{2-}]$$

Once again, we use the concentration table as our tool for analyzing the concentrations.

The solute is pure water, so neither Ag^+ nor CrO_4^{2-} are present before the salt dissolves; their initial concentrations are zero. For the "change" row, we have to be careful to take into account the formula of the salt. In a liter of water, when 6.7×10^{-5} mol of Ag_2CrO_4 dissolves, we obtain 6.7×10^{-5} mol of CrO_4^{2-} and $2 \times (6.7 \times 10^{-5}$ mol$)$ of Ag^+. With this information, we can fill in the "initial" and "change" rows.

SOLUTION: As usual, we add the values in the "initial" and "change" rows to obtain the equilibrium concentrations of the ions.

$Ag_2CrO_4(s) \rightleftharpoons$	$2Ag^+(aq)$	$+$	$CrO_4{}^{2-}(aq)$
Initial concentrations (M)	0		0
Changes in concentrations when Ag_2CrO_4 dissolves (M)	$+[2 \times (6.7 \times 10^{-5})]$ $= +1.3 \times 10^{-4}$		$+6.7 \times 10^{-5}$
Equilibrium concentrations (M)	1.3×10^{-4}		6.7×10^{-5}

Substituting the equilibrium concentrations into the mass action expression for K_{sp} gives

$$K_{sp} = (1.3 \times 10^{-4})^2 (6.7 \times 10^{-5})$$
$$= 1.1 \times 10^{-12}$$

So the K_{sp} of Ag_2CrO_4 at 25 °C is calculated to be 1.1×10^{-12}.

IS THE ANSWER REASONABLE? The critical step in solving the problem correctly is placing the correct quantities in the "initial" and "change" rows. The Ag_2CrO_4 is dissolved in water, so the initial concentrations of the ions must be zero; these entries are okay. For the "changes," it's important to remember that the quantities are related to each other by the coefficients in the chemical equation. That means the change for Ag^+ must be twice as large as the change for $CrO_4{}^{2-}$. Studying the table, we see that we've done this correctly. We can also see that we've added the "change" to the "initial" values correctly, and that we've performed the proper arithmetic in evaluating the mass action expression.

Practice Exercise 3: The solubility of thallium(I) iodide, TlI, in water at 20 °C is 5.9×10^{-3} g L^{-1}. Using this fact, calculate K_{sp} for TlI on the assumption that it is 100% dissociated in the solution. (Hint: What is the molar solubility of TlI?)

Practice Exercise 4: One liter of water is able to dissolve 2.15×10^{-3} mol of PbF_2 at 25 °C. Calculate the value of K_{sp} for PbF_2.

Now let's introduce a complication. Let's suppose that the aqueous system into which we're dissolving a slightly soluble salt is not pure water, but instead is a solution of a solute that provides one of the ions of the salt.

> **EXAMPLE 17.3**
> Calculating K_{sp} from Molar Solubility Data

The molar solubility of $PbCl_2$ in a 0.10 M NaCl solution is 1.7×10^{-3} mol L^{-1} at 25 °C. Calculate the K_{sp} for $PbCl_2$.

ANALYSIS: Again, we start by writing the equation for the equilibrium and the K_{sp} expression.

$$PbCl_2(s) \rightleftharpoons Pb^{2+}(aq) + 2Cl^-(aq) \qquad K_{sp} = [Pb^{2+}][Cl^-]^2$$

In this problem, the $PbCl_2$ is being dissolved not in pure water but in 0.10 M NaCl, which contains 0.10 M Cl$^-$. (It also contains 0.10 M Na$^+$, but that's not important here because Na$^+$ doesn't affect the equilibrium and so doesn't appear in the K_{sp} expression.) The initial concentration of Pb^{2+} is zero because none is in solution to begin with. The *initial* concentration of Cl$^-$, however, is 0.10 M.

For the change row, we note that when 1.7×10^{-3} mole of $PbCl_2$ dissolves per liter, the Pb^{2+} concentration increases by 1.7×10^{-3} M and the Cl$^-$ concentration increases by $2 \times (1.7 \times 10^{-3}$ $M)$. With these data we build the concentration table and evaluate the ion product to obtain K_{sp}.

SOLUTION: Here is the completed concentration table based on the analysis above.

	$PbCl_2(s) \rightleftharpoons$	$Pb^{2+}(aq)$	$+$	$2Cl^-(aq)$
Initial concentrations (M)		0		0.10 (because the solvent is 0.10 M NaCl)
Changes in concentrations when PbCl$_2$ dissolves (M)		$+1.7 \times 10^{-3}$		$+[2 \times (1.7 \times 10^{-3})]$ $= +3.4 \times 10^{-3}$
Equilibrium concentrations (M)		1.7×10^{-3}		$0.10 + 0.0034 = 0.10$ (rounded correctly)

Substituting the equilibrium concentrations into the K_{sp} expression gives

$$K_{sp} = (1.7 \times 10^{-3})(0.10)^2$$
$$= 1.7 \times 10^{-5}$$

The K_{sp} of PbCl$_2$ is calculated to be 1.7×10^{-5} at 25 °C.

IS THE ANSWER REASONABLE? The solvent here is 0.10 M NaCl, so we have Cl$^-$ in the mixture before any PbCl$_2$ dissolves. We check the "initial" row to be sure we've entered 0.10 M under Cl$^-$, and we have. Next, we check to be sure we've taken the stoichiometry of the equilibrium equation into account when placing values into the "change" row. We've done this correctly, too, because the change for Cl$^-$ is twice the change for Pb^{2+}. Finally, we can check to be sure we've performed the correct arithmetic on the equilibrium concentrations. We have, so our answer should be correct.

Practice Exercise 5: The molar solubility of Ag$_2$SO$_4$ in a solution containing 28.4 g Na$_2$SO$_4$ per liter is 4.3×10^{-3} M. What is K_{sp} for Ag$_2$SO$_4$? (Hint: What is the molarity of the Na$_2$SO$_4$ solution?)

Practice Exercise 6: At 25 °C, the molar solubility of CoCO$_3$ in a 0.10 M Na$_2$CO$_3$ solution is 1.0×10^{-9} mol L^{-1}. Calculate the value of K_{sp} for CoCO$_3$.

Practice Exercise 7: The molar solubility of PbF$_2$ in a 0.10 M Pb(NO$_3$)$_2$ solution at 25 °C is 3.1×10^{-4} mol L^{-1}. Calculate the value of K_{sp} for PbF$_2$.

Molar solubility can be calculated from K_{sp}

Besides calculating K_{sp} from solubility information, we can also compute solubilities from values of K_{sp}. The following examples illustrate the calculations.[2]

EXAMPLE 17.4
Calculating Molar Solubility from K_{sp}

What is the molar solubility of AgCl in pure water at 25 °C?

ANALYSIS: To solve this problem, we need the chemical equation, the equilibrium law, and the value of K_{sp} for AgCl (which we obtain from Table 17.1). The relevant equations are

$$AgCl(s) \rightleftharpoons Ag^+(aq) + Cl^-(aq) \qquad K_{sp} = [Ag^+][Cl^-] = 1.8 \times 10^{-10}$$

[2] As noted earlier, these calculations ignore the fact that the salt that dissolves is not truly 100% dissociated into the ions implied in the salt's formula. This is particularly a problem with the salts of multiply charged ions, so the solubilities of such salts, when calculated from their K_{sp} values, must be taken as rough estimates. In fact, many calculations involving K_{sp} give values that are merely estimates.

Now we can build a concentration table. First, we see that the solvent is pure water, so neither Ag^+ nor Cl^- ion is present in solution at the start; their *initial* concentrations are zero.

Next, we turn to the "change" row. If we knew what the changes were, we could calculate the equilibrium concentrations and figure out the molar solubility. But we don't know the changes, so we will have to find them algebraically. To do this, *we will define our unknown* x *as the molar solubility of the salt*—the number of moles of AgCl that dissolves in one liter. Because 1 mol of AgCl yields 1 mol Ag^+ and 1 mol Cl^-, the concentration of each of these ions increases by x (their changes are each $+x$).

SOLUTION: Our concentration table is as follows.

	$AgCl(s) \rightleftharpoons$	$Ag^+(aq)$	$+$	$Cl^-(aq)$
Initial concentrations (M)		0		0
Changes in concentrations when AgCl dissolves (M)		$+x$		$+x$
Equilibrium concentrations (M)		x		x

◻ By defining x as the molar solubility, the coefficients of x in the "change" row are the same as the coefficients of Ag^+ and Cl^- in the equation for the equilibrium.

We make the substitutions into the K_{sp} expression, using equilibrium quantities from the last row of the table:

$$(x)(x) = 1.8 \times 10^{-10}$$
$$x = 1.3 \times 10^{-5}$$

The calculated molar solubility of AgCl in water at 25 °C is 1.3×10^{-5} mol L^{-1}.

IS THE ANSWER REASONABLE? The solvent is water, so the initial concentrations are zero. If x is the molar solubility, then the changes in the concentrations of Ag^+ and Cl^- when the salt dissolves must also be equal to x. We can also check the algebra, which we've done correctly, so the answer seems to be okay.

EXAMPLE 17.5
Calculating Molar Solubility
from K_{sp}

Calculate the molar solubility of lead iodide in water from its K_{sp} at 25 °C.

ANALYSIS: First, we need the formula for lead iodide, which is PbI_2 (obtained from the rules of nomenclature in Chapter 2). To set up the problem, we begin with the equation for the equilibrium and the K_{sp} expression. We obtain K_{sp} from Table 17.1.

$$PbI_2(s) \rightleftharpoons Pb^{2+}(aq) + 2I^-(aq) \qquad K_{sp} = [Pb^{2+}][I^-]^2 = 7.9 \times 10^{-9}$$

The solvent is water, so the initial concentrations of the ions are zero. As before, we will define x as the molar solubility of the salt. By doing this, the coefficients of x in the "change" row will be identical to the coefficients of the ions in the chemical equation. This assures us that the changes in the concentrations are in the correct mole ratio.

SOLUTION: Here is the concentration table.

	$PbI_2(s) \rightleftharpoons$	$Pb^{2+}(aq)$	$+$	$2I^-(aq)$
Initial concentrations (M)		0		0
Changes in concentrations when PbI_2 dissolves (M)		$+x$		$+2x$
Equilibrium concentrations (M)		x		$2x$

A precipitate of yellow PbI_2 forms when the two colorless solutions, one with sodium iodide and the other of lead(II) nitrate, are mixed. (*Lawrence Migdale/Photo Researchers.*)

Substituting equilibrium quantities into the K_{sp} expression gives

$$K_{sp} = (x)(2x)^2 = 4x^3 = 7.9 \times 10^{-9}$$
$$x^3 = 2.0 \times 10^{-9}$$
$$x = 1.3 \times 10^{-3}$$

Thus, the molar solubility of PbI_2 is calculated to be 1.3×10^{-3} mol L^{-1}.

IS THE ANSWER REASONABLE?   We check the entries in the table. The solvent is water, so the initial concentrations are equal to zero. By setting x equal to the moles per liter of PbI_2 that dissolves (i.e., the molar solubility), the coefficients of x in the "change" row have to be the same as the coefficients of Pb^{2+} and Cl^- in the chemical equation. The entries in the "change" row are okay. In performing the algebra, notice that when we square $2x$, we get $4x^2$. Multiplying $4x^2$ by x gives $4x^3$. After that, the rest is straightforward.

FIG. 17.2   The common ion effect. The test tube shown here initially held a saturated solution of NaCl, where the equilibrium $NaCl(s) \rightleftharpoons$ $Na^+(aq) + Cl^-(aq)$ had been established. Addition of a few drops of concentrated HCl, containing a high concentration of the common ion Cl^-, forced the equilibrium to shift to the left. This caused some white crystals of solid NaCl to precipitate. *(Michael Watson.)*

Practice Exercise 8: Calculate the molar solubility of Ag_3PO_4 in water. Its $K_{sp} = 2.8 \times 10^{-18}$. (Hint: Review the algebra in the preceding example.)

Practice Exercise 9: What is the calculated molar solubility in water at 25 °C of (a) AgBr and (b) Ag_2CO_3?

A salt is less soluble if the solvent already contains an ion of the salt

Suppose that we stir some lead chloride (a compound having a low solubility) with water long enough to establish the following equilibrium.

$$PbCl_2(s) \rightleftharpoons Pb^{2+}(aq) + 2Cl^-(aq)$$

If we now add a concentrated solution of a soluble lead compound, such as $Pb(NO_3)_2$, the increased concentration of Pb^{2+} in the $PbCl_2$ solution will drive the position of equilibrium to the left, causing some $PbCl_2$ to precipitate. The phenomenon is simply an application of Le Châtelier's principle, the net result being that $PbCl_2$ is less soluble in a solution that contains Pb^{2+} from another source than it is in pure water. The same effect is produced if a concentrated solution of a soluble chloride salt such as NaCl is added to the saturated $PbCl_2$ solution. The added Cl^- will drive the equilibrium to the left, reducing the amount of dissolved $PbCl_2$.

The phenomenon described above is an example of the *common ion effect,* which we described in Chapter 16. In this case, Pb^{2+} is the common ion when we add $Pb(NO_3)_2$ and Cl^- is the common ion when we add NaCl. Figure 17.2 shows how even a relatively soluble salt, NaCl, can be forced out of its saturated solution simply by adding concentrated hydrochloric acid, which serves as a source of the common ion, Cl^-. The common ion effect can dramatically lower the solubility of a salt, as the next example demonstrates.

EXAMPLE 17.6
Calculations Involving the Common Ion Effect

What is the molar solubility of PbI_2 in a 0.10 M NaI solution?

ANALYSIS: We begin with the chemical equation for the equilibrium, the appropriate K_{sp} expression, and the value of K_{sp} obtained from Table 17.1.

$$PbI_2(s) \rightleftharpoons Pb^{2+}(aq) + 2I^-(aq) \qquad K_{sp} = [Pb^{2+}][I^-]^2 = 7.9 \times 10^{-9}$$

As usual, our tool to analyze what happens is the concentration table. As before, we imagine that we are adding the PbI_2 to a solvent into which it dissolves. This time, however, the solvent isn't water; it's a solution of NaI, which contains one of the ions of the salt PbI_2. Therefore, our initial concentrations will not both be zero. The solvent doesn't contain any lead compound, so the initial concentration of Pb^{2+} is equal to zero, but the solvent does contain 0.10 M NaI, which is completely dissociated and yields 0.10 M Na$^+$ and 0.10 M I$^-$. The initial concentration of I$^-$ is therefore 0.10 M. These are the values we place in the "initial" row.

Next, we let x be the molar solubility of PbI$_2$. When x mol of PbI$_2$ dissolves per liter, the concentration of Pb^{2+} changes by $+x$ and that of I$^-$ changes by twice as much, or $+2x$. Finally, the equilibrium concentrations are obtained by summing the initial concentrations and the changes.

SOLUTION: Here is the concentration table.

	PbI$_2$(s) $\rightleftharpoons$	Pb^{2+}(aq)	+	2I$^-$(aq)
Initial concentrations (M)		0		0.10
Changes in concentrations when PbI$_2$ dissolves (M)		$+x$		$+2x$
Equilibrium concentrations (M)		x		$0.10 + 2x$

Substituting equilibrium values into the K_{sp} expression gives

$$K_{sp} = (x)(0.10 + 2x)^2 = 7.9 \times 10^{-9}$$

Just a brief inspection reveals that solving this expression for x will be difficult if we cannot simplify the math. Fortunately, a simplification is possible, because the small value of K_{sp} for PbI$_2$ tells us that the salt has a very low solubility. This means very little of the salt will dissolve, so x (or even $2x$) will be quite small. Let's assume that $2x$ will be much smaller than 0.10. If this is so, then

$$0.10 + 2x \approx 0.10 \quad \text{(assuming } 2x \text{ is negligible compared to 0.10)}$$

Substituting 0.10 M for the I$^-$ concentration gives

$$K_{sp} = (x)(0.10)^2 = 7.9 \times 10^{-9}$$
$$x = \frac{7.9 \times 10^{-9}}{(0.10)^2}$$
$$= 7.9 \times 10^{-7} M$$

Thus, the molar solubility of PbI$_2$ in 0.10 M NaI solution is calculated to be $7.9 \times 10^{-7} M$.

IS THE ANSWER REASONABLE? Check the entries in the table. The initial concentrations come from the solvent, which contains no Pb^{2+} but does contain 0.10 M I$^-$. By letting x equal the molar solubility, the coefficients of x in the "change" row equal the coefficients in the equation for the equilibrium. *We should also check to see if our simplifying assumption is valid.* Notice that $2x$, which equals 1.6×10^{-6}, is indeed vastly smaller than 0.10, just as we anticipated. (If we add 1.6×10^{-6} to 0.10 and round correctly, we obtain 0.10.)

Practice Exercise 10: Calculate the molar solubility of AgI in 0.20 M CaI$_2$ solution. Compare the answer to the calculated molar solubility of AgI in pure water. (Hint: What is the I$^-$ concentration in 0.20 M CaI$_2$?)

Practice Exercise 11: Calculate the molar solubility of Fe(OH)$_3$ in a solution where the OH$^-$ concentration is initially 0.050 M. Assume the dissociation of Fe(OH)$_3$ is 100%.

A Mistake to Avoid

The most common mistake that students make with problems like Example 17.6 is to use the coefficient of an ion in the solubility equilibrium at the wrong moment in the calculation. The coefficient of I$^-$ in the PbI$_2$ equilibrium is 2. The mistake is to use this 2 to double the *initial* concentration of I$^-$. However, the *initial* concentration of I$^-$ was

□ READ THESE TWO
PARAGRAPHS!

provided not by PbI_2 but by NaI. When 0.10 mol of NaI dissociates, it gives 0.10 mol of I^-, not 2×0.10 mol. *The coefficients in the equation for the equilibrium are only used to obtain the quantities in the "change" row.*

To avoid mistakes, it is useful to always view the formation of the final solution as a two-step process. You begin with a solvent into which the "insoluble solid" will be placed. In some problems, the solvent may be pure water, in which case the initial concentrations of the ions will be zero. In other problems, like Example 17.6, the solvent will be a *solution* that contains a common ion. When this is so, first decide what the concentration of the common ion is and enter that value into the "initial concentration" row of the table. Next, imagine that the solid is added to the solvent and a little of it dissolves. *The amount that dissolves is what gives the values in the "change" row.* These entries must be in the same ratio as the coefficients in the equilibrium, which is accomplished if we let x be the molar solubility of the salt. Then the coefficients of x will be the same as the coefficients of the ions in the chemical equation for the equilibrium.

In Example 17.5 (page 699) we found that the molar solubility of PbI_2 in *pure* water is 1.3×10^{-3} M. In water that contains 0.10 M NaI (Example 17.6), the solubility of PbI_2 is 7.9×10^{-7} M, well over a thousand times smaller. As we said, the common ion effect can cause huge reductions in the solubilities of sparingly soluble compounds by shifting the equilibrium toward the formation of the solid.

We can use K_{sp} to determine if a precipitate will form in a solution

If we know the anticipated concentrations of the ions of a salt in a solution, we can use the value of K_{sp} for the salt to predict whether or not a precipitate should form. This is because the computed value for Q (the ion product) can tell us whether a solution is unsaturated, saturated, or supersaturated. *For a precipitate of a salt to form, the solution must be supersaturated.*

If the solution is unsaturated, its ion concentrations are less than required for saturation, Q is less than K_{sp}, and no precipitate should form. For a saturated solution, we have Q equal to K_{sp}, and no precipitate will form. (If a precipitate were to form, the solution would become unsaturated and the precipitate would redissolve.) If the solution is supersaturated, the ion concentrations exceed those required for saturation and Q is larger than K_{sp}. Only in this last instance should we expect a precipitate to form. This can be summarized as follows.

TOOLS

Ion product, Q, of a salt

Precipitate will form	$Q > K_{sp}$	(supersaturated)	
No precipitate will form	$\begin{cases} Q = K_{sp} \\ Q < K_{sp} \end{cases}$	(saturated) (unsaturated)	

Let's look at some sample calculations.

EXAMPLE 17.7
Predicting whether a Precipitate Will Form

Suppose we wish to prepare 0.500 L of a solution containing 0.0075 mol of NaCl and 0.075 mol of $Pb(NO_3)_2$. Knowing from the solubility rules that the chloride of Pb^{2+} is "insoluble," we are concerned that a precipitate of $PbCl_2$ might form. Will it?

ANALYSIS: Our tool for answering this question is the criteria described above, which tell us a precipitate will only form if the computed Q for the solution is larger than K_{sp}. Therefore, our first task is to compute the value of the ion product (Q) appropriate for $PbCl_2$ *using the concentrations of the ions in the solution to be prepared.* This means we need the correct form of the ion product, which we can obtain by writing the solubility equilibrium and the K_{sp} expression that applies to a saturated solution of $PbCl_2$.

$$PbCl_2(s) \rightleftharpoons Pb^{2+}(aq) + 2Cl^-(aq) \qquad K_{sp} = [Pb^{2+}][Cl^-]^2$$

From Table 17.1, $K_{sp} = 1.7 \times 10^{-5}$. Also, we have to convert moles to molarity, because these are the quantities that we have to substitute into the ion product expression.

SOLUTION: The planned solution would have the following molar concentrations.

$$[Pb^{2+}] = \frac{0.075 \text{ mol}}{0.500 \text{ L}} = 0.15 \, M \qquad [Cl^-] = \frac{0.0075 \text{ mol}}{0.500 \text{ L}} = 0.015 \, M$$

We use these values to compute the ion product for $PbCl_2$ in the solution.

$$Q = [Pb^{2+}][Cl^-]^2 = (0.15)(0.015)^2 = 3.4 \times 10^{-5}$$

This value of Q is larger than the K_{sp} of $PbCl_2$, 1.7×10^{-5}, which means that a precipitate of $PbCl_2$ is likely to form if we attempt to prepare this solution.

IS THE ANSWER REASONABLE? We can double-check that the molarities of the ions in the planned solution are correct. Then, we check the calculation of Q. All seems to be in order, so our answer is correct.

□ It is usually difficult to prevent the extra salt from precipitating out of a supersaturated solution. (Sodium acetate is a notable exception. Supersaturated solutions of this salt are easily made.)

Practice Exercise 12: Will a precipitate of $CaSO_4$ form in a solution if the Ca^{2+} concentration is 0.0025 M and the SO_4^{2-} concentration is 0.030 M? (Hint: What is the form of the ion product for $CaSO_4$?)

Practice Exercise 13: Will a precipitate form in a solution containing $3.4 \times 10^{-4} \, M$ CrO_4^{2-} and $4.8 \times 10^{-5} \, M \, Ag^+$?

EXAMPLE 17.8
Predicting whether a Precipitate
Will Form

What possible precipitate might form by mixing 50.0 mL of $1.0 \times 10^{-4} \, M$ NaCl with 50.0 mL of $1.0 \times 10^{-6} \, M$ AgNO$_3$? Will it form? (Assume the volumes are additive.)

ANALYSIS: In this problem we are being asked, in effect, whether a metathesis reaction will occur between NaCl and AgNO$_3$. We should be able to use the solubility rules in Chapter 4 as a tool to predict whether this *might* occur. If the solubility rules suggest a precipitate, we can then calculate the ion product for the compound using the concentrations of the ions in the final solution. If this ion product exceeds K_{sp} for the salt, then a precipitate is expected.

To calculate Q correctly requires that we use the concentrations of the ions *after the solutions have been mixed.* Therefore, before computing the ion product, we must first take into account the fact that mixing the solutions dilutes each of the solutes. Dilution problems were covered in Chapter 4, where you learned that the tool for working such calculations is Equation 4.6 (page 158).

□ To obtain the solution to this problem we must bring together tools from two different chapters.

SOLUTION: Let's begin by writing the equation for the potential metathesis reaction between NaCl and AgNO$_3$. Our tool is the solubility rules (page 147), which helps us determine whether each product is soluble or insoluble.

$$NaCl(aq) + AgNO_3(aq) \longrightarrow AgCl(s) + NaNO_3(aq)$$

The solubility rules indicate that we expect a precipitate of AgCl. But are the concentrations of Ag^+ and Cl^- actually high enough?

In the original solutions, the $1.0 \times 10^{-6} \, M$ AgNO$_3$ contains $1.0 \times 10^{-6} \, M \, Ag^+$ and the $1.0 \times 10^{-4} \, M$ NaCl contains $1.0 \times 10^{-4} \, M \, Cl^-$. What are the concentrations of these ions after dilution? To determine these we use the equation that applies to all dilution problems involving molarity (Equation 4.6, page 158).

$$V_{dil} \cdot M_{dil} = V_{conc} \cdot M_{conc} \qquad \text{(Equation 4.6)}$$

Solving for M_{dil} gives

$$M_{dil} = \frac{V_{conc} M_{conc}}{V_{dil}}$$

The initial volumes of the more concentrated solutions are 50.0 mL and when the two solutions are combined, the final total volume is 100 mL. Therefore,

$$[\text{Ag}^+]_{final} = \frac{(50.0 \text{ mL})(1.0 \times 10^{-6} M)}{100.0 \text{ mL}} = 5.0 \times 10^{-7} M$$

$$[\text{Cl}^-]_{final} = \frac{(50.0 \text{ mL})(1.0 \times 10^{-4} M)}{100.0 \text{ mL}} = 5.0 \times 10^{-5} M$$

Now we use these to calculate Q for AgCl, which we can obtain from the dissociation reaction of the salt.

$$\text{AgCl}(s) \rightleftharpoons \text{Ag}^+(aq) + \text{Cl}^-(aq)$$
$$Q = [\text{Ag}^+][\text{Cl}^-]$$

Substituting the concentrations computed above gives

$$Q = (5.0 \times 10^{-7})(5.0 \times 10^{-5}) = 2.5 \times 10^{-11}$$

In Table 17.1, the K_{sp} for AgCl is given as 1.8×10^{-10}. Notice that Q is *smaller* than K_{sp}, which means that the final solution is unsaturated in AgCl and a precipitate will *not* form.

IS THE ANSWER REASONABLE? There are several things we should check here. They include writing the equation for the metathesis, calculating the concentrations of the ions after dilution (we've doubled the volume, so the concentrations are halved), and setting up the correct ion product. All appear to be correct, so the answer should be okay.

Practice Exercise 14: What precipitate might be expected if we pour together 100.0 mL of $1.0 \times 10^{-3} M$ $\text{Pb(NO}_3)_2$ and 100.0 mL of $2.0 \times 10^{-3} M$ MgSO_4? Will some form? (Assume that the volumes are additive.) (Hint: What tools will you need to solve the problem?)

Practice Exercise 15: What precipitate might be expected if we pour together 50.0 mL of 0.10 M $\text{Pb(NO}_3)_2$ and 20.0 mL of 0.040 M NaCl? Will some form? (Assume that the volumes are additive.)

17.2 | SOLUBILITY EQUILIBRIA OF METAL OXIDES AND SULFIDES INVOLVE REACTION WITH WATER

Aqueous equilibria involving insoluble oxides and sulfides are more complex than those we've considered so far because of reactions of the anions with the solvent, water.

When a metal oxide dissolves in water, it does so by reacting with water instead of by a simple dissociation of ions that remain otherwise unchanged. Sodium oxide, for example, consists of Na^+ and O^{2-} ions, and it readily dissolves in water. The solution, however, does not contain the oxide ion, O^{2-}. Instead, the hydroxide ion forms. The equation for the reaction is

$$\text{Na}_2\text{O}(s) + \text{H}_2\text{O} \longrightarrow 2\text{NaOH}(aq)$$

This actually involves the reaction of oxide ions with water as the crystals of Na_2O break up.

$$\text{O}^{2-}(s) + \text{H}_2\text{O} \longrightarrow 2\text{OH}^-(aq)$$

The oxide ion is simply too powerful a base to exist in water at any concentration worthy of experimental note. We can understand why from the extraordinarily high (estimated) value of K_b for O^{2-}, 1×10^{22}. Thus there is no way to supply *oxide ions* to an aqueous solution in order to form an insoluble metal oxide directly. Oxide ions react with water, instead, to generate the hydroxide ion. When an insoluble metal *oxide* instead of an insoluble metal *hydroxide* does precipitate from a solution, it forms because the specific metal ion is able to react with OH^-, extract O^{2-}, and leave H^+ (or H_2O) in the solution. The silver ion, for example, precipitates as brown silver oxide, Ag_2O, when OH^- is added to aqueous silver salts (Figure 17.3).

$$2Ag^+(aq) + 2OH^-(aq) \longrightarrow Ag_2O(s) + H_2O$$

The reverse of this reaction, written as an equilibrium, corresponds to the solubility equilibrium for Ag_2O.

$$Ag_2O(s) + H_2O \rightleftharpoons 2Ag^+(aq) + 2OH^-(aq)$$

FIG. 17.3 Silver oxide. A brown, mudlike precipitate of silver oxide forms as sodium hydroxide solution is added to a solution of silver nitrate. *(Michael Watson.)*

Metal sulfides behave like oxides in their solubility equilibria

When we shift from oxygen to sulfur in Group VIA and consider metal sulfides, we find many similarities to oxides. One is that the sulfide ion, S^{2-}, like the oxide ion, is such a strong Brønsted base that it does not exist in any ordinary aqueous solution. The sulfide ion has not been detected in an aqueous solution even in the presence of 8 M NaOH where one might think that the reaction

$$OH^- + HS^- \longrightarrow H_2O + S^{2-}$$

could generate some detectable S^{2-}. An 8 M NaOH solution is at a concentration well outside the bounds of the "ordinary." Thus, Na_2S, like Na_2O, dissolves in water *by reacting with it*, not by releasing an otherwise unchanged divalent anion, S^{2-}.

$$Na_2S(s) + H_2O \longrightarrow 2Na^+(aq) + HS^-(aq) + OH^-(aq)$$

As with Na_2O, water reacts with the sulfide ion as the crystals break apart and the ions enter the solution.

$$S^{2-}(s) + H_2O \longrightarrow HS^-(aq) + OH^-(aq)$$

The sulfides of most metals have quite low solubilities in water. Simply bubbling hydrogen sulfide gas into an aqueous solution of any one of a number of metal ions—Cu^{2+}, Pb^{2+}, and Ni^{2+}, for example—causes their sulfides to precipitate. Many of these have distinctive colors (Figure 17.4) that can be used to help identify which metal ion is in solution.

To write the solubility equilibrium for an insoluble metal sulfide we have to take into account the reaction of the sulfide ion with water. For example, for CuS the equilibrium is best written as

$$CuS(s) + H_2O \rightleftharpoons Cu^{2+}(aq) + HS^-(aq) + OH^-(aq) \qquad (17.2)$$

This equation yields the ion product $[Cu^{2+}][HS^-][OH^-]$, and the solubility product constant for CuS is expressed by the equation.

$$K_{sp} = [Cu^{2+}][HS^-][OH^-]$$

▢ In the laboratory, the qualitative analysis of metal ions uses the precipitation of metal sulfides to separate some metal ions from others.

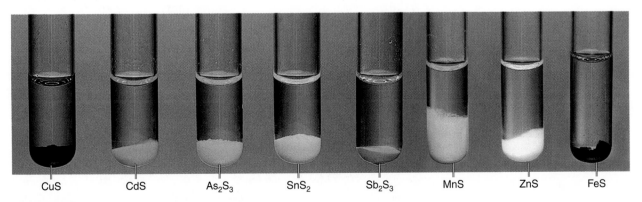

| CuS | CdS | As₂S₃ | SnS₂ | Sb₂S₃ | MnS | ZnS | FeS |

FIG. 17.4 The colors of some metal sulfides. *(OPC, Inc.)*

Values of K_{sp} of this form for a number of metal sulfides are given in the last column in Table 17.2. Notice particularly how much the K_{sp} values vary—from 2×10^{-53} to 3×10^{-11}, a spread of a factor of 10^{42}.

Acid-insoluble sulfides are so insoluble they don't dissolve in acid

Many metal sulfides are able to react with acid and thereby dissolve. An example is zinc sulfide.

$$ZnS(s) + 2H^+(aq) \longrightarrow Zn^{2+}(aq) + H_2S(aq)$$

However, some metal sulfides, referred to as the *acid-insoluble sulfides,* have K_{sp} values so low that they do not dissolve in acid. The cations in this group can be precipitated from the other cations simply by bubbling hydrogen sulfide into a sufficiently acidic solution that contains several metal ions.

When the solution is acidic, we have to treat the solubility equilibria differently. In acid, HS^- and OH^- would be neutralized, leaving their conjugate acids, H_2S and H_2O. Under these conditions, the equation for the solubility equilibrium becomes

$$CuS(s) + 2H^+(aq) \rightleftharpoons Cu^{2+}(aq) + H_2S(aq)$$

Acid solubility product, K_{spa}

This changes the mass action expression for the solubility product equilibrium, which we will now call the **acid solubility product, K_{spa}**. The *a* in the subscript indicates that the medium is acidic.

$$K_{spa} = \frac{[Cu^{2+}][H_2S]}{[H^+]^2}$$

Table 17.2 also gives K_{spa} values for the metal sulfides. Notice that all K_{spa} values are 10^{21} larger than the K_{sp} values. Metal sulfides are clearly vastly more soluble in dilute acid than in water. Yet several—the acid-insoluble sulfides—are so insoluble that even the most soluble of them, SnS, barely dissolves, even in moderately concentrated acid. So there are two families of sulfides, the *acid-insoluble sulfides* and the acid-soluble ones, otherwise

TABLE 17.2	Metal Ions Separable by Selective Precipitation of Sulfides[a]		
Metal Ion	Sulfide	K_{spa}	K_{sp}
Acid-Insoluble Sulfides			
Hg^{2+}	HgS (black form)	2×10^{-32}	2×10^{-53}
Ag^+	Ag_2S	6×10^{-30}	6×10^{-51}
Cu^{2+}	CuS	6×10^{-16}	6×10^{-37}
Cd^{2+}	CdS	3×10^{-7}	3×10^{-28}
Pb^{2+}	PbS	3×10^{-7}	3×10^{-28}
Sn^{2+}	SnS	1×10^{-5}	1×10^{-26}
Base-Insoluble Sulfides (Acid-Soluble Sulfides)			
Zn^{2+}	α-ZnS	3×10^{-4}	3×10^{-25}
	β-ZnS	3×10^{-2}	3×10^{-23}
Co^{2+}	CoS	5×10^{-1}	5×10^{-22}
Ni^{2+}	NiS	4×10^{1}	4×10^{-20}
Fe^{2+}	FeS	6×10^{2}	6×10^{-19}
Mn^{2+}	MnS (pink form)	3×10^{10}	3×10^{-11}
	MnS (green form)	3×10^{7}	3×10^{-14}

[a]Data are for 25 °C. See R.J. Meyers, *J. Chem. Ed.*, vol. 63, 1986, p. 689.

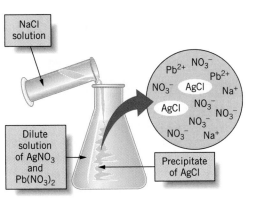

FIG. 17.5 Selective precipitation. When dilute sodium chloride is added to a - solution containing both Ag^+ ions and Pb^{2+} ions (both dissolved as their nitrate salts), the less soluble AgCl precipitates before the more soluble $PbCl_2$. Precipitation of the AgCl is nearly complete before any $PbCl_2$ begins to form. *(Andy Washnik.)*

known as the *base-insoluble sulfides.* As we discuss in the next section, the differing solubilities of their sulfides in acid provide a means of separating the two classes of metal ions from each other.

17.3 METAL IONS CAN BE SEPARATED BY SELECTIVE PRECIPITATION

Selective precipitation means causing one metal ion to precipitate while holding another in solution. Often this is possible because of large differences in the solubilities of salts that we would generally consider to be insoluble. For example, the K_{sp} values for AgCl and $PbCl_2$ are 1.8×10^{-10} and 1.7×10^{-5}, respectively, which gives them molar solubilities in water of 1.3×10^{-5} M for AgCl and 1.6×10^{-2} M for $PbCl_2$. In terms of molar solubilities, lead chloride is approximately 1200 times more soluble in water than AgCl. If we had a solution containing both 0.10 M Pb^{2+} and 0.10 M Ag^+ and began adding Cl^-, AgCl would precipitate first (Figure 17.5). In fact, we can calculate that before any $PbCl_2$ starts to precipitate, the concentration of Ag^+ will have been reduced to 1.4×10^{-8} M. Thus, nearly all the silver is removed from the solution without precipitating any of the lead, and the ions are effectively separated. All we need to do is find a way of adjusting the concentration of the Cl^- to achieve the separation.

Selective precipitation of metal sulfides is accomplished by controlling the pH

The large differences in K_{sp} values between the acid-insoluble and the base-insoluble metal sulfides make it possible to separate the corresponding cations from each other when they are in the same solution. The sulfides of the acid-insoluble cations are selectively precipitated by hydrogen sulfide from a solution kept at a pH that keeps the other cations in solution. A solution saturated in H_2S is used, for which the molarity of H_2S is 0.1 M.

Let's work an example to show how we can calculate the pH needed to allow the selective precipitation of two metal cations as their sulfides. We will use Cu^{2+} and Ni^{2+} ions to represent a cation from each class.

EXAMPLE 17.9
Selective Precipitation of the Sulfides of Acid-Insoluble Cations from Base-Insoluble Cations

Over what range of hydrogen ion concentrations (and pH) is it possible to separate Cu^{2+} from Ni^{2+} when both metal ions are present in a solution at a concentration of 0.010 M and the solution is made saturated in H_2S (where $[H_2S] = 0.1$ M)?

ANALYSIS: We must work with the chemical equilibria for the metal sulfides and their associated equilibrium expressions (the equations for their K_{spa}).

$$CuS(s) + 2H^+(aq) \rightleftharpoons Cu^{2+}(aq) + H_2S(aq) \qquad K_{spa} = \frac{[Cu^{2+}][H_2S]}{[H^+]^2} = 6 \times 10^{-16}$$

$$NiS(s) + 2H^+(aq) \rightleftharpoons Ni^{2+}(aq) + H_2S(aq) \qquad K_{spa} = \frac{[Ni^{2+}][H_2S]}{[H^+]^2} = 4 \times 10^1$$

The K_{spa} values (from Table 17.2) tell us that NiS is much more soluble in an acidic solution than CuS. Therefore, we want to make the H^+ concentration large enough to prevent NiS from precipitating, but small enough that CuS does precipitate.

The problem reduces to two questions. The first is, "What hydrogen ion concentration would be needed to keep the Cu^{2+} *in solution?*" (The answer to this question will give us the *upper limit* on $[H^+]$; we would really want a lower H^+ concentration so CuS *will* precipitate.) The second question is, "What is the hydrogen ion concentration just before NiS precipitates?" The answer to this will be the *lower limit* on $[H^+]$. At any lower H^+ concentration, NiS will precipitate, so we want an H^+ concentration equal to or larger than this value. Once we know these limits, we know that any hydrogen ion concentration in between them will permit CuS to precipitate but retain Ni^{2+} in solution.

SOLUTION: We will find the upper limit first. If CuS *does not precipitate*, the Cu^{2+} concentration will be the given value, 0.010 M, so we substitute this along with the H_2S concentration (0.1 M) into the expression for K_{spa}.

$$K_{spa} = \frac{[Cu^{2+}][H_2S]}{[H^+]^2} = \frac{(0.010)(0.1)}{[H^+]^2} = 6 \times 10^{-16}$$

Now we solve for $[H^+]$.

$$[H^+]^2 = \frac{(0.010)(0.1)}{6 \times 10^{-16}} = 2 \times 10^{12}$$

$$[H^+] = 1 \times 10^6\ M$$

If we could make $[H^+] = 1 \times 10^6\ M$, we could prevent CuS from forming. However, it isn't possible to have 10^6 or a *million* moles of H^+ per liter! What the calculated $[H^+]$ tells us, therefore, is that *no matter how acidic the solution is, we cannot prevent* CuS *from precipitating when we saturate the solution with* H_2S. (You can now see why CuS is classed as an "acid-insoluble sulfide.")

To obtain the lower limit, we calculate the $[H^+]$ required to give an equilibrium concentration of Ni^{2+} equal to 0.010 M. If we keep the value of $[H^+]$ *equal to or larger* than this value, then NiS will be prevented from precipitating. The calculation is exactly like the one above. First, we substitute values into the K_{spa} expression.

$$K_{spa} = \frac{[Ni^{2+}][H_2S]}{[H^+]^2} = \frac{(0.010)(0.1)}{[H^+]^2} = 4 \times 10^1$$

Once again, we solve for $[H^+]$.

$$[H^+]^2 = \frac{(0.010)(0.1)}{4 \times 10^1}$$

$$[H^+] = 5 \times 10^{-3}\ M$$

$$pH = 2.3$$

If we maintain the pH of the solution of 0.010 M Cu^{2+} and 0.010 M Ni^{2+} at 2.3 or lower (more acidic), as we make the solution saturated in H_2S, virtually all the Cu^{2+} will precipitate as CuS, but all the Ni^{2+} will stay in solution.

IS THE ANSWER REASONABLE? The K_{spa} values certainly tell us that CuS is quite insoluble in acid and that NiS is a lot more soluble, so from that standpoint the results seem reasonable. There's not much more we can do to check the answer, other than to review the entire set of calculations.

Practice Exercise 16: Suppose a solution contains 0.0050 M Co^{2+} and is saturated with H_2S (with $[H_2S]$ = 0.1 M). Would CoS precipitate if the solution has a pH of 3.5? (Hint: What relationship do we use to determine whether a precipitate is going to form in a solution?)

Practice Exercise 17: Consider a solution containing Hg^{2+} and Fe^{2+}, both at molarities of 0.010 M. It is to be saturated with H_2S. Calculate the highest pH that this solution could have that would keep Fe^{2+} in solution while causing Hg^{2+} to precipitate as HgS.

In actual lab work, separation of the acid-insoluble sulfides from the base-insoluble ones is performed with $[H^+] \approx 0.3$ M which corresponds to a pH of about 0.5. This ensures that the base-insoluble sulfides will not precipitate. The calculation above also demonstrated why NiS can be classified as a "base-insoluble sulfide." If the solution is *basic* when it is made saturated in H_2S, the pH will surely be larger than 2.3 and NiS will precipitate.

Selective precipitation can be applied to metal carbonates

The principles of selective precipitation by the control of pH apply to any system where the anion is that of a weak acid. The metal carbonates are examples, with many being quite insoluble in water (see Table 17.1). The dissociation of magnesium carbonate in water, for example, involves the following equilibrium and K_{sp} equations.

$$MgCO_3(s) \rightleftharpoons Mg^{2+}(aq) + CO_3^{2-}(aq) \qquad K_{sp} = 3.5 \times 10^{-8}$$

For strontium carbonate, the equations are

$$SrCO_3(s) \rightleftharpoons Sr^{2+}(aq) + CO_3^{2-}(aq) \qquad K_{sp} = 9.3 \times 10^{-10}$$

Would it be possible to separate the magnesium ion from the strontium ion by taking advantage of the difference in K_{sp} of their carbonates?

We can do so if we can control the carbonate ion concentration. Because the carbonate ion is a relatively strong Brønsted base, its control is available, indirectly, by adjusting the pH of the solution. This is because the hydrogen ion is one of the species in each of the following equilibria.[3]

$$H_2CO_3(aq) \rightleftharpoons H^+(aq) + HCO_3^-(aq) \qquad K_{a_1} = 4.5 \times 10^{-7}$$

$$HCO_3^-(aq) \rightleftharpoons H^+(aq) + CO_3^{2-}(aq) \qquad K_{a_2} = 4.7 \times 10^{-11}$$

You can see that if we increase the hydrogen ion concentration, both equilibria will shift to the left, in accordance with Le Châtelier's principle, and this will reduce the concentration of the carbonate ion. The value of $[CO_3^{2-}]$ thus decreases with decreasing pH. On the other hand, if we decrease the hydrogen ion concentration, making the solution more basic, we will cause the two equilibria to shift to the right. The concentration of the carbonate ion thus increases with increasing pH.

For the calculations ahead, it will be useful to combine the two hydrogen carbonate equilibria into one overall equation that relates the molar concentrations of carbonic acid, carbonate ion, and hydrogen ion. So we first add the two.

$$H_2CO_3(aq) \rightleftharpoons H^+(aq) + HCO_3^-(aq)$$
$$\underline{HCO_3^-(aq) \rightleftharpoons H^+(aq) + CO_3^{2-}(aq)}$$
$$H_2CO_3(aq) \rightleftharpoons 2H^+(aq) + CO_3^{2-}(aq) \qquad\qquad (17.3)$$

---

[3] The situation involving aqueous carbonic acid is complicated by the presence of dissolved CO_2, which we could represent in an equation as $CO_2(aq)$. In fact, this is how most of the dissolved CO_2 exists, namely, as $CO_2(aq)$, not as $H_2CO_3(aq)$. But we may use $H_2CO_3(aq)$ as a surrogate or stand-in for $CO_2(aq)$, because the latter changes smoothly to the former on demand. The following two successive equilibria involving carbonic acid exist in a solution of aqueous CO_2.

$$CO_2(aq) + H_2O \rightleftharpoons H_2CO_3(aq) \rightleftharpoons H^+(aq) + HCO_3^-(aq)$$

The value of K_{a_1} cited here for $H_2CO_3(aq)$ is really the product of the equilibrium constants of these two equilibria.

Recall from Chapter 14 that when we add two equilibria to get a third, the equilibrium constant of the latter is the product of the two equilibria that are combined. Thus, for Equation 17.3 the equilibrium constant, which we'll symbolize as K_a, is obtained as follows.

TOOLS

Combined K_a expression for a diprotic acid

$$K_a = K_{a_1} \times K_{a_2} = \frac{[H^+]^2[CO_3{}^{2-}]}{[H_2CO_3]} \qquad (17.4)$$

$$= (4.5 \times 10^{-7}) \times (4.7 \times 10^{-11})$$

$$= 2.1 \times 10^{-17}$$

☐ We can safely use Equation 17.4 *only* when two of the three concentrations are known.

With this K_a value we may now study how to find the pH range within which Mg^{2+} and Sr^{2+} can be separated by taking advantage of their difference in K_{sp} values. To perform such a separation we would saturate a solution with CO_2, which provides H_2CO_3 through the rapidly established equilibrium

$$CO_2(aq) + H_2O \rightleftharpoons H_2CO_3(aq)$$

Thus, a solution that contains 0.030 *M* CO_2 has an effective H_2CO_3 concentration of 0.030 *M*.

EXAMPLE 17.10

Separation of Metal Ions by the Selective Precipitation of Their Carbonates

A solution contains magnesium nitrate and strontium nitrate, each at a concentration of 0.10 *M*. Carbon dioxide is to be bubbled in to make the solution saturated in $CO_2(aq)$, approximately 0.030 *M*. What pH range would make it possible for the carbonate of one cation to precipitate but not that of the other?

ANALYSIS: There are really two parts to this. First, what is the range in values of $[CO_3{}^{2-}]$ that allow one carbonate to precipitate but not the other? Second, given this range, what are the values of the solution's pH that produce this range in $[CO_3{}^{2-}]$ values?

To answer the first question, we will use the K_{sp} values of the two carbonate salts and their molar concentrations to find the $CO_3{}^{2-}$ concentrations in their saturated solutions. To keep the more soluble carbonate from precipitating, the $CO_3{}^{2-}$ concentration must be at or below that required for saturation. For the less soluble of the two, we must have a $CO_3{}^{2-}$ concentration larger than in a saturated solution so that it will precipitate.

To answer the second question, we will use the combined K_a expression for H_2CO_3 to find the $[H^+]$ that gives the necessary $CO_3{}^{2-}$ concentrations obtained in answering the first question. Having these $[H^+]$, it is then a simple matter to convert them to pH values.

SOLUTION: The range in $[CO_3{}^{2-}]$ values is obtained by using the K_{sp} values of the two carbonates.

$$K_{sp} = [Mg^{2+}][CO_3{}^{2-}] = 3.5 \times 10^{-8}$$

$$K_{sp} = [Sr^{2+}][CO_3{}^{2-}] = 9.3 \times 10^{-10}$$

On the basis of the K_{sp} values, we see that $MgCO_3$ is the more soluble of the two. Let's find the $[CO_3{}^{2-}]$ values required to give saturated solutions of these two salts.

For Magnesium Carbonate:

$$[CO_3{}^{2-}] = \frac{K_{sp}}{[Mg^{2+}]} = \frac{3.5 \times 10^{-8}}{0.10} = 3.5 \times 10^{-7}\ M$$

For Strontium Carbonate:

$$[CO_3{}^{2-}] = \frac{K_{sp}}{[Sr^{2+}]} = \frac{9.3 \times 10^{-10}}{0.10} = 9.3 \times 10^{-9}\ M$$

For separation, we have to keep the $[CO_3{}^{2-}]$ less than or equal to 3.5×10^{-7} *M* and larger than 9.3×10^{-9} *M*.

$[CO_3^{2-}] > 9.3 \times 10^{-9} \, M$ (to precipitate $SrCO_3$)

$[CO_3^{2-}] \leq 3.5 \times 10^{-7} \, M$ (to prevent $MgCO_3$ from precipitating)

The second phase of our calculation now asks what values of $[H^+]$ correspond to the calculated limits on $[CO_3^{2-}]$. For this we will use the K_a expression given by Equation 17.4. First we solve for the square of $[H^+]$, using the molarity of the dissolved CO_2, 0.030 M, as the value of $[H_2CO_3]$. This gives us

$$[H^+]^2 = K_a \times \frac{[H_2CO_3]}{[CO_3^{2-}]} = 2.1 \times 10^{-17} \times \frac{0.030}{[CO_3^{2-}]}$$

We will use this equation for each of the two boundary values of $[CO_3^{2-}]$ to calculate the corresponding two values of $[H^+]^2$. Once we have them, the steps to values of $[H^+]$ and pH are easy.

For Magnesium Carbonate: To *prevent* the precipitation of $MgCO_3$, $[CO_3^{2-}]$ must be no higher than $3.5 \times 10^{-7} \, M$, so $[H^+]^2$ must not be less than

$$[H^+]^2 = 2.1 \times 10^{-17} \times \frac{0.030}{3.5 \times 10^{-7}} = 1.8 \times 10^{-12}$$

$$[H^+] = 1.3 \times 10^{-6} \, M$$

This corresponds to a pH of 5.89. At a higher (more basic) pH, magnesium carbonate precipitates. Thus, pH $\leq$ 5.89 prevents precipitation of $MgCO_3$.

For Strontium Carbonate: To have a saturated solution of $SrCO_3$ with $[Sr^{2+}] = 0.10 \, M$, the value of $[CO_3^{2-}]$ would be $9.3 \times 10^{-9} \, M$, as we calculated above. This corresponds to a value of $[H^+]^2$ found as follows.

$$[H^+]^2 = 2.1 \times 10^{-17} \times \frac{0.030}{9.3 \times 10^{-9}} = 6.8 \times 10^{-11}$$

$$[H^+] = 8.2 \times 10^{-6} \, M$$

$$pH = 5.09$$

To cause $SrCO_3$ to precipitate, the $[CO_3^{2-}]$ would have to be higher than $9.3 \times 10^{-9} \, M$, and that would require that $[H^+]$ be *less than* $8.2 \times 10^{-6} \, M$. If $[H^+]$ were less than $8.2 \times 10^{-6} \, M$, the pH would have to be higher than 5.09. Thus, to cause $SrCO_3$ to precipitate from the given solution, pH > 5.09.

In summary, when the pH of the given solution is kept above 5.09 and less than or equal to 5.89, Sr^{2+} will precipitate as $SrCO_3$ but Mg^{2+} will remain dissolved.

IS THE ANSWER REASONABLE?   The only way to be sure of the answer is to go back over the reasoning and the calculations. However, there is a sign that the answer is probably correct. Notice that the two K_{sp} values are not vastly different—they differ by just a factor of about 40. Therefore, it's not surprising that to achieve separation we would have to keep the pH within a rather narrow range (from 5.09 to 5.89).

> ☐ Because $CO_2(aq)$ can rapidly combine with water to give $H_2CO_3(aq)$, the value of $[H_2CO_3]$ is taken to be that of $[CO_2(aq)]$, namely, 0.030 M.

Practice Exercise 18: The K_{sp} for barium oxalate, BaC_2O_4, is 1.2×10^{-7} and for oxalic acid, $H_2C_2O_4$, $K_{a_1} = 5.6 \times 10^{-2}$ and $K_{a_2} = 5.4 \times 10^{-5}$. If a solution containing 0.10 M $H_2C_2O_4$ and 0.050 M $BaCl_2$ is prepared, what must the minimum H^+ concentration be in the solution to prevent the formation of a BaC_2O_4 precipitate? (Hint: Work with a combined K_a expression for $H_2C_2O_4$.)

Practice Exercise 19: A solution contains calcium nitrate and nickel nitrate, each at a concentration of 0.10 M. Carbon dioxide is to be bubbled in to make its concentration equal 0.030 M. What pH range would make it possible for the carbonate of one cation to precipitate but not that of the other?

FIG. 17.6 **The complex ion of Cu²⁺ and water.** A solution containing copper sulfate has a blue color because it contains the complex ion $Cu(H_2O)_4^{2+}$. *(Andy Washnik.)*

□ Recall that a *Lewis base* is an electron pair donor in the formation of a coordinate covalent bond.

FIG. 17.7 **The complex ion of Cu²⁺ and ammonia.** Ammonia molecules displace water molecules from $Cu(H_2O)_4^{2+}$ (left) to give the deep blue $Cu(NH_3)_4^{2+}$ ion (right). *(Andy Washnik.)*

17.4 COMPLEX IONS PARTICIPATE IN EQUILIBRIA IN AQUEOUS SOLUTIONS

Metal ions can combine with anions or neutral molecules to form complex ions

In our previous discussions of metal-containing compounds, we left you with the impression that the only kinds of bonds in which metals are ever involved are ionic bonds. For some metals, like the alkali metals of Group IA, this is close enough to the truth to warrant no modifications. But for many other metal ions, especially those of the transition metals and the post-transition metals, it is not. This is because the ions of many of these metals are able to behave as Lewis acids (i.e., as electron pair acceptors in the formation of coordinate covalent bonds). Thus, by participating in Lewis acid–base reactions they become *covalently* bonded to other atoms. Copper(II) ion is a typical example.

In aqueous solutions of copper(II) salts, like $CuSO_4$ or $Cu(NO_3)_2$, the copper is not present as simple Cu^{2+} ions. Instead, each Cu^{2+} ion becomes bonded to four water molecules to give a pale blue ion with the formula $Cu(H_2O)_4^{2+}$ (see Figure 17.6). We call this species a **complex ion** because it is composed of a number of simpler species (i.e., it is *complex*, not simple). The chemical equation for the formation of the $Cu(H_2O)_4^{2+}$ ion is

$$Cu^{2+} + 4H_2O \longrightarrow Cu(H_2O)_4^{2+}$$

which can be diagrammed using Lewis structures as follows.

$$Cu(H_2O)_4^{2+}$$

As you can see in this analysis, the Cu^{2+} ion accepts pairs of electrons from the water molecules, so Cu^{2+} is a Lewis acid and the water molecules are each Lewis bases.

The number of complex ions formed by metals, especially the transition metals, is enormous, and the study of the properties, reactions, structures, and bonding in complex ions like $Cu(H_2O)_4^{2+}$ has become an important specialty within chemistry. We will provide a more complete discussion of them in Chapter 21. For now, we will introduce you to some of the terminology that we use in describing these substances.

A Lewis base that attaches itself to a metal ion is called a **ligand** (from the Latin *ligare*, meaning "to bind"). Ligands can be neutral molecules with unshared pairs of electrons (like H_2O), or they can be anions (like Cl^- or OH^-). The atom in the ligand that actually provides the electron pair is called the **donor atom,** and the metal ion is the **acceptor.** The result of combining a metal ion with one or more ligands is a *complex ion*, or simply just a *complex*. The word "complex" avoids problems when the particle formed is electrically neutral, as sometimes happens. Compounds that contain complex ions are generally referred to as **coordination compounds** because the bonds in a complex ion can be viewed as coordinate covalent bonds. Sometimes the complex itself is called a *coordination complex*.

In an aqueous solution, the formation of a complex ion is really a reaction in which water molecules are replaced by other ligands. Thus, when NH_3 is added to a solution of copper ion, the water molecules in the $Cu(H_2O)_4^{2+}$ ion are replaced, one after another, by molecules of NH_3 until the deeply blue complex $Cu(NH_3)_4^{2+}$ is formed (Figure 17.7). Each successive reaction is an equilibrium, so the entire chemical system involves many species and is quite complicated. Fortunately, when the ligand concentration is *large* relative to that of the metal ion, the concentrations of the intermediate complexes are very small and we can work only with the *overall* reaction for the formation of the final complex. Our study of complex ion equilibria will be limited to these situations. The equilibrium equation for the formation of $Cu(NH_3)_4^{2+}$, therefore, can be written as though the complex forms in one step.

$$Cu(H_2O)_4^{2+}(aq) + 4NH_3(aq) \rightleftharpoons Cu(NH_3)_4^{2+}(aq) + 4H_2O$$

We will simplify this equation for the purposes of dealing quantitatively with the equilibria by omitting the water molecules. (It's safe to do this because the concentration of H_2O in aqueous solutions is taken to be effectively a constant and need not be included in mass action expressions.) In simplified form, we write the equilibrium above as follows:

$$Cu^{2+}(aq) + 4NH_3(aq) \rightleftharpoons Cu(NH_3)_4^{2+}(aq)$$

We have two goals here: to study such equilibria themselves and to learn how they can be used to influence the solubilities of metal ion salts.

☐ According to Le Châtelier's principle, when the concentration of ammonia is high, the position of equilibrium in this reaction is shifted far to the right, so effectively all complex ions with water molecules are changed to those with ammonia molecules.

Formation constants reflect the stabilities of complex ions

When the chemical equation for the equilibrium is written so that the complex ion is the product, the equilibrium constant for the reaction is called the **formation constant, K_{form}.** The equilibrium law for the formation of $Cu(NH_3)_4^{2+}$ in the presence of excess NH_3, for example, is

TOOLS
Formation constants of complexes

$$\frac{[Cu(NH_3)_4^{2+}]}{[Cu^{2+}][NH_3]^4} = K_{form}$$

Sometimes this equilibrium constant is called the **stability constant.** The larger its value, the greater is the concentration of the complex at equilibrium, and so the more stable is the complex.

Table 17.3 provides several more examples of complex ion equilibria and their associated equilibrium constants. (Additional examples are in Appendix C, Table C.6.) Notice that the most stable complex in the table, $Co(NH_3)_6^{3+}$, has, as you would expect, the largest value of K_{form}.

Instability constants are the inverse of formation constants

Some chemists prefer to describe the relative stabilities of complex ions differently. The *inverses* of formation constants are cited and are called **instability constants, K_{inst}.** This approach focuses attention on the *breakdown* of the complex, not its formation. Therefore,

TABLE 17.3	**Formation Constants and Instability Constants for Some Complex Ions**		
Ligand	Equilibrium	K_{form}	K_{inst}
NH_3	$Ag^+ + 2NH_3 \rightleftharpoons Ag(NH_3)_2^+$	1.6×10^7	6.3×10^{-8}
	$Co^{2+} + 6NH_3 \rightleftharpoons Co(NH_3)_6^{2+}$	5.0×10^4	2.0×10^{-5}
	$Co^{3+} + 6NH_3 \rightleftharpoons Co(NH_3)_6^{3+}$	4.6×10^{33}	2.2×10^{-34}
	$Cu^{2+} + 4NH_3 \rightleftharpoons Cu(NH_3)_4^{2+}$	1.1×10^{13}	9.1×10^{-14}
	$Hg^{2+} + 4NH_3 \rightleftharpoons Hg(NH_3)_4^{2+}$	1.8×10^{19}	5.6×10^{-20}
F^-	$Al^{3+} + 6F^- \rightleftharpoons AlF_6^{3-}$	1×10^{20}	1×10^{-20}
	$Sn^{4+} + 6F^- \rightleftharpoons SnF_6^{2-}$	1×10^{25}	1×10^{-25}
Cl^-	$Hg^{2+} + 4Cl^- \rightleftharpoons HgCl_4^{2-}$	5.0×10^{15}	2.0×10^{-16}
Br^-	$Hg^{2+} + 4Br^- \rightleftharpoons HgBr_4^{2-}$	1.0×10^{21}	1.0×10^{-21}
I^-	$Hg^{2+} + 4I^- \rightleftharpoons HgI_4^{2-}$	1.9×10^{30}	5.3×10^{-31}
CN^-	$Fe^{2+} + 6CN^- \rightleftharpoons Fe(CN)_6^{4-}$	1.0×10^{24}	1.0×10^{-24}
	$Fe^{3+} + 6CN^- \rightleftharpoons Fe(CN)_6^{3-}$	1.0×10^{31}	1.0×10^{-31}

the associated equilibrium equation is written as the reverse of the formation of the complex. The equilibrium for the copper–ammonia complex would be written as follows, for example:

$$Cu(NH_3)_4{}^{2+}(aq) \rightleftharpoons Cu^{2+}(aq) + 4NH_3(aq)$$

The equilibrium constant for this equilibrium is called the *instability constant*.

$$K_{inst} = \frac{[Cu^{2+}][NH_3]^4}{[Cu(NH_3)_4{}^{2+}]} = \frac{1}{K_{form}}$$

□ Among the complexes shown in Table 17.3, notice that Co^{3+} forms the most stable complex with NH_3 whereas Co^{2+} forms the least stable one.

Notice that K_{inst} is the reciprocal of K_{form}. The K_{inst} is called an *instability* constant because the larger its value, the more *unstable* the complex is. The data in the last column of Table 17.3 show this. The least stable complex in the table, $Co(NH_3)_6{}^{2+}$, has the largest value of K_{inst}.

| 17.5 | COMPLEX ION FORMATION INCREASES THE SOLUBILITY OF A SALT |

The silver halides are extremely insoluble salts, as we've learned. The K_{sp} of AgBr at 25 °C, for example, is only 5.0×10^{-13}. In a saturated aqueous solution, the concentration of each ion of AgBr is only 7.1×10^{-7} mol L^{-1}. Suppose that we start with a saturated solution in which undissolved AgBr is present and equilibrium exists. Now suppose that we begin to add aqueous ammonia to the system. Because NH_3 molecules bind strongly to silver ions, they begin to form $Ag(NH_3)_2{}^+$ with the trace amount of Ag^+ ions initially in solution. The reaction is

Complex ion equilibrium: $\quad Ag^+(aq) + 2NH_3(aq) \rightleftharpoons Ag(NH_3)_2{}^+(aq)$

Because the forward reaction removes *uncomplexed* Ag^+ ions from solution, it upsets the solubility equilibrium:

Solubility equilibrium: $\quad AgBr(s) \rightleftharpoons Ag^+(aq) + Br^-(aq)$

By withdrawing uncomplexed Ag^+ ions, the ammonia causes the solubility equilibrium to shift to the right to generate more Ag^+ ions from AgBr(s). The way the two equilibria are related can be viewed as follows.

$$AgBr(s) \rightleftharpoons Ag^+(aq) + Br^-(aq)$$
$$+$$

Addition of ammonia removes free silver ion from the solution, causing the solubility equilibrium to shift to the right.

$$2NH_3(aq)$$
$$\Updownarrow$$
$$Ag(NH_3)_2{}^+(aq)$$

Thus, adding ammonia causes more AgBr(s) to dissolve—an example of Le Châtelier's principle at work. Our example illustrates a general phenomenon:

> The solubility of a slightly soluble salt increases when one of its ions can be changed to a soluble complex ion.

To analyze what happens, let's put the two equilibria together.

Complex ion equilibrium: $\quad Ag^+(aq) + 2NH_3(aq) \rightleftharpoons Ag(NH_3)_2{}^+(aq)$

Solubility equilibrium: $\quad \underline{\quad\quad\quad AgBr(s) \rightleftharpoons Ag^+(aq) + Br^-(aq)}$

Sum of equilibria: $\quad AgBr(s) + 2NH_3(aq) \rightleftharpoons Ag(NH_3)_2{}^+(aq) + Br^-(aq)$

The equilibrium constant for the net overall reaction is written in the usual way. The term for [AgBr(s)] is omitted because it refers to a solid and so has a constant value.

$$K_c = \frac{[Ag(NH_3)_2{}^+][Br^-]}{[NH_3]^2}$$

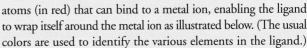

No More Soap Scum—Complex Ions and Solubility

A problem that has plagued homeowners with hard water—water that contains low concentrations of divalent cations, especially Ca^{2+}—is the formation of insoluble deposits of "soap scum" as well as "hard water spots" on surfaces such as shower tiles, shower curtains, and bathtubs. These deposits form when calcium ions interact with large anions in soap to form precipitates and also when hard water that contains bicarbonate ion evaporates, causing precipitation of calcium carbonate, $CaCO_3$.

$$Ca^{2+}(aq) + 2HCO_3^-(aq) \longrightarrow$$
$$CaCO_3(s) + CO_2(g) + H_2O$$

A variety of consumer products are sold that contain ingredients intended to prevent these precipitates from forming, and they accomplish this by forming complex ions with calcium ions, which has the effect of increasing the solubilities of the soap scum and calcium carbonate deposits. A principal ingredient in these products is an organic compound called *ethylenediaminetetraacetic* acid (mercifully abbreviated *EDTA*). The structure of the compound, which is also abbreviated as H_4EDTA to emphasize that it contains four acidic hydrogens which are part of carboxyl groups, is

A metal ion surrounded octahedrally by all six donor atoms if H_4EDTA loses all of the acidic hydrogens.

This molecule is an excellent complex-forming ligand; it contains a total of *six* donor atoms (in red) that can bind to a metal ion, enabling the ligand to wrap itself around the metal ion as illustrated below. (The usual colors are used to identify the various elements in the ligand.)

One consumer product, called Clean Shower (Figure 1), contains H_4EDTA along with substances called surfactants. When the EDTA binds with calcium ions, it releases just two H^+ ions

$$H_4EDTA(aq) + Ca^{2+}(aq) \longrightarrow$$
$$CaH_2EDTA(aq) + 2H^+(aq)$$

The H^+ combine with anions of the soap to form neutral organic compounds called fatty acids that are usually not water-soluble. The surfactants in the product, however, enable the fatty acids to dissolve, preventing formation of precipitates. The Clean Shower product is sprayed on the wet walls after you take a shower, forming the products described above. The next time you take a shower, the water washes away the soluble products, keeping soap scum from building up and keeping the shower walls clean.

$$HO-\overset{\displaystyle O}{\overset{\|}{C}}-CH_2$$
$$HO-\overset{\displaystyle O}{\overset{\|}{C}}-CH_2$$
$$N-CH_2-CH_2-N$$
$$CH_2-\overset{\displaystyle O}{\overset{\|}{C}}-OH$$
$$CH_2-\overset{\displaystyle O}{\overset{\|}{C}}-OH$$

H_4EDTA
Acidic hydrogens are shown in blue,
donor atoms are shown in red.

FIG. 1 The product Clean Shower contains EDTA, which prevents the formation of soap scum and hard water spots in showers and on bathtubs. (*Andy Washnik.*)

Because we have added two equations to obtain a third equation, K_c for this expression is the product of K_{form} and K_{sp}. The values for K_{form} for $Ag(NH_3)_2^+$ and K_{sp} for AgBr are known, so by multiplying the two, we find the overall value of K_c for the silver bromide–ammonia system.

$$K_c = (1.6 \times 10^7)(5.0 \times 10^{-13})$$
$$= 8.0 \times 10^{-6}$$

This approach thus gives us a way to calculate the solubility of a sparingly soluble salt when a substance able to form a complex with the metal ion is put into its solution. The next example shows how this works.

◻ Recall that when equilibria are added, their equilibrium constants are multiplied.

EXAMPLE 17.11

Calculating the Solubility of a Slightly Soluble Salt in the Presence of a Ligand

How many moles of AgBr can dissolve in 1.0 L of 1.0 M NH_3?

ANALYSIS: A few preliminaries have to be done before we can take advantage of a concentration table. We need the overall equation and its associated equation for the equilibrium constant, which serve as our tools for dealing with these kinds of problems. The overall equilibrium is

$$AgBr(s) + 2NH_3(aq) \rightleftharpoons Ag(NH_3)_2{}^+(aq) + Br^-(aq)$$

The equation for K_c is

$$K_c = \frac{[Ag(NH_3)_2{}^+][Br^-]}{[NH_3]^2} = 8.0 \times 10^{-6} \qquad \text{(as calculated earlier)}$$

Now let's prepare the concentration table. To do this, we imagine we are adding solid AgBr to the ammonia solution.

Before any reaction takes place, the concentration of NH_3 is 1.0 M and the concentration of $Ag(NH_3)_2{}^+$ is zero. The concentration of Br^- is also zero, because there is none of it in the ammonia solution.

If we define x as the molar solubility of the AgBr in the solution, then the concentrations of $Ag(NH_3)_2{}^+$ and Br^- both increase by x and the concentration of ammonia decreases by $2x$ (because of the coefficient of NH_3 in the equation).

The equilibrium values are obtained as usual by adding the initial and change rows. However, another comment is in order here. Letting the concentration of Br^- equal that of $Ag(NH_3)_2{}^+$ is valid because *and only because* K_{form} is such a large number. Essentially *all* Ag^+ ions that do dissolve from the insoluble AgBr are changed to the complex ion. There are relatively few uncomplexed Ag^+ ions in the solution, so the number of $Ag(NH_3)_2{}^+$ and Br^- ions in the solution are very nearly the same.

SOLUTION: Here is the concentration table, built using the reasoning above.

	AgBr(s) + 2NH$_3$(aq) $\rightleftharpoons$ Ag(NH$_3$)$_2{}^+$(aq) + Br$^-$(aq)		
Initial concentrations (M)	1.0	0	0
Changes in concentrations caused by NH$_3$ (M)	$-2x$	$+x$	$+x$
Equilibrium concentrations (M)	$(1.0 - 2x)$	x	x

We've done all the hard work. Now all we need to do is substitute the values in the last row of the concentration table into the equation for K_c:

$$K_c = \frac{(x)(x)}{(1.0 - 2x)^2} = 8.0 \times 10^{-6}$$

This can be solved by taking the square root of both sides, which gives

$$\frac{x}{(1.0 - 2x)} = \sqrt{8.0 \times 10^{-6}} = 2.8 \times 10^{-3}$$

Solving for x and rounding to the correct number of significant figures gives

$$x = 2.8 \times 10^{-3}$$

Because we've defined x as the molar solubility of AgBr in the ammonia solution, we can say that 2.8×10^{-3} mol of AgBr dissolves in 1.0 L of 1.0 M NH_3. (This is not very much, of course, but in contrast, only 7.1×10^{-7} mol of AgBr dissolves in 1.0 L of pure water. Thus AgBr is nearly 4000 times more soluble in the 1.0 M NH_3 than in pure water.)

IS THE ANSWER REASONABLE? Everything depends on the reasoning used in preparing the concentration table, particularly letting $-2x$ represent the change in the concentration of NH_3 as a result of the presence of AgBr and the formation of the complex. Additionally, we can see that the maximum solubility of AgBr if all the NH_3 were complexed is 0.5 M while the minimum solubility if the NH_3 had no effect is the solubility of AgBr in distilled water (7×10^{-7} M). Our result is between these two limits, so the answer is reasonable.

Practice Exercise 20: Calculate the solubility of silver chloride in 0.10 M NH_3 and compare it with its solubility in pure water. Refer to Table 17.1 for the K_{sp} for AgCl. [Hint: Assume all the Ag^+ from the AgCl becomes incorporated into $Ag(NH_3)_2^+$.]

Practice Exercise 21: How many moles of NH_3 have to be added to 1.0 L of water to dissolve 0.20 mol of AgCl? The complex ion $Ag(NH_3)_2^+$ forms.

SUMMARY

Solubility Equilibria for Salts. The mass action expression for a solubility equilibrium of a salt is called the **ion product.** It equals the product of the molar concentrations of its ions, each raised to a power equal to the subscript of the ion in the salt's formula. At a given temperature, the value of the ion product, Q, in a *saturated* solution of the salt equals a constant called the **solubility product constant,** or K_{sp}.

For solubility equilibria, the *common ion effect* is the ability of an ion of a soluble salt to suppress the solubility of a sparingly soluble compound that has the same (the "common") ion.

If soluble salts are mixed together in the same solution, a cation of one and an anion of another will precipitate if the ion product, Q, exceeds the solubility product constant of the salt formed from them.

Selective Precipitation. Metal sulfides are vastly more soluble in an acidic solution than in water. To express their solubility equilibria in acid, the **acid solubility constant** or K_{spa} is used.

Several metal sulfides have such low values of K_{spa} that they are insoluble even at low pH. These **acid-insoluble sulfides** can thus be selectively separated from the **base-insoluble sulfides** by making the solution both quite acidic as well as saturated in H_2S. By adjusting the pH, salts of other weak acids, like the carbonate salts, can also be selectively precipitated.

Complex Ions of Metals. **Coordination compounds** contain **complex ions** (also called **complexes** or **coordination complexes**), formed from a metal ion and a number of ligands. **Ligands** are Lewis bases and may be electrically neutral or negatively charged. Water and ammonia are common neutral ligands. The equilibrium constant for the formation of a complex in the presence of an excess of ligand is called the **formation constant, K_{form}**, of the complex. The larger the value of K_{form}, the more stable is the complex. Salts whose cations form stable complexes, like Ag^+ salts whose cation forms a stable complex with ammonia, $Ag(NH_3)_2^+$, are made more soluble when the ligand is present.

TOOLS FOR PROBLEM SOLVING

In this chapter you learned to apply the following concepts as tools in solving problems dealing with aspects of the solubility of salts. Study each tool carefully so that you know what each is used for. When faced with solving a problem, recall what each tool does and consider whether it will be helpful in finding a solution. This will aid you in selecting the tools you need.

Solubility product constant, K_{sp} *(page 693)* We use K_{sp} to calculate the molar solubility of a salt either in pure water or in a solution that contains a common ion. Comparing K_{sp} with the ion product of a potential precipitating salt permits us to decide whether a precipitate will form.

Molar solubility *(page 695)* This is used for calculating the value of K_{sp} for a salt. When calculating the solubility of a salt from K_{sp}, we let x represent the molar solubility in the concentration table.

Ion product, Q, of a salt *(page 702)* Compare Q with K_{sp} to determine whether a precipitate will form:

$$Q > K_{sp} \qquad \text{a precipitate forms}$$
$$Q \leq K_{sp} \qquad \text{a precipitate does not form}$$

Acid solubility product constant, K_{spa} *(page 706)* Use K_{spa} data to calculate the solubility of a metal sulfide at a given pH. We can use K_{spa} data for two or more metal sulfides to calculate the pH at which one will selectively precipitate from a solution saturated in H_2S.

Combined K_a expression for a diprotic acid *(page 710)* Combining expressions for K_{a_1} and K_{a_2} for a diprotic acid, H_2A, yields the equation

$$\frac{[H^+]^2[A^{2-}]}{[H_2A]} = K_a = K_{a_1} \times K_{a_2}$$

This equation can be used if (and only if) we know two of the three quantities in the combined mass action expression. This is a useful tool when working problems involving selective precipitation of salts of diprotic acids where the concentration of the anion A^{2-} is controlled by adjusting the pH of the solution.

Formation constants (stability constants) of complexes *(page 713)* We can use K_{form} values to make judgments concerning the relative stabilities of complexes. Along with K_{sp} values, we can use formation constants of complexes to determine the solubility of a sparingly soluble salt in a solution containing a ligand that's able to form a complex with the cation of the salt.

QUESTIONS, PROBLEMS, AND EXERCISES

Answers to problems whose numbers are printed in color are given in Appendix B. More challenging problems are marked with asterisks. ILW = Interactive Learningware solution is available at www.wiley.com/college/brady. OH = an Office Hours video is available for this problem.

REVIEW QUESTIONS

Solubility Products

17.1 What is the difference between an *ion product* and an *ion product constant*?

17.2 Use the equilibrium below to demonstrate why the K_{sp} expression does not include the concentration of $Ba_3(PO_4)_2$ in the denominator.

$$Ba_3(PO_4)_2(s) \rightleftharpoons 3Ba^{2+}(aq) + 2PO_4^{3-}(aq)$$

17.3 What is the *common ion effect*? How does Le Châtelier's principle explain it? Use the solubility equilibrium for AgCl to illustrate the common ion effect.

17.4 If sodium acetate is added to a solution of acetic acid, the pH increases. Explain how this is an example of the common ion effect.

17.5 With respect to K_{sp}, what conditions must be met if a precipitate is going to form in a solution?

17.6 What limits the accuracy and reliability of solubility calculations based on K_{sp} values?

Selective Precipitations

17.7 Potassium oxide is readily soluble in water, but the resulting solution contains essentially no oxide ion. Explain, using an equation, what happens to the oxide ion.

17.8 What chemical reaction takes place when solid sodium sulfide is dissolved in water? Write the chemical equation.

17.9 Consider cobalt(II) sulfide.
(a) Write its solubility equilibrium and K_{sp} equation for a saturated solution in water. (Remember, there is no free sulfide ion in the solution.)
(b) Write its solubility equilibrium and K_{spa} equation for a saturated solution in aqueous acid.

17.10 Use Le Châtelier's principle to explain how adjusting the pH enables the control of the concentration of $C_2O_4^{2-}$ in a solution of oxalic acid, $H_2C_2O_4$.

17.11 Suppose you wished to control the PO_4^{3-} concentration in a solution of phosphoric acid by controlling the pH of the solution. If you assume you know the H_3PO_4 concentration, what combined equation would be useful for that purpose?

Simultaneous and Complex Ion Equilibria

17.12 A solution of $MgBr_2$ can be changed to a solution of $MgCl_2$ by adding AgCl(s) and stirring the mixture well. In terms of the equilibria involved, explain how this happens.

17.13 On the basis of Le Châtelier's principle, explain how the addition of solid NH_4Cl to a beaker containing solid $Mg(OH)_2$ in contact with water is able to cause the $Mg(OH)_2$ to dissolve. Write equations for *all* the chemical equilibria that exist in the solution after the addition of the NH_4Cl.

17.14 Using Le Châtelier's principle, explain how the addition of aqueous ammonia dissolves silver chloride. If HNO_3 is added after the AgCl has dissolved in the NH_3 solution, it causes AgCl to re-precipitate. Explain why.

17.15 For $PbCl_3^-$, $K_{form} = 2.5 \times 10^1$. If a solution containing this complex ion is diluted with water, $PbCl_2$ precipitates. Write the equations for the equilibria involved and use them together with Le Châtelier's principle to explain how this happens.

REVIEW PROBLEMS

Solubility Products

17.16 Write the K_{sp} expressions for each of the following compounds.
(a) CaF_2 (c) $PbSO_4$ (e) PbI_2
(b) Ag_2CO_3 (d) $Fe(OH)_3$ (f) $Cu(OH)_2$

17.17 Write the K_{sp} expressions for each of the following compounds.
(a) AgI
(b) Ag_3PO_4
(c) $PbCrO_4$
(d) $Al(OH)_3$
(e) $ZnCO_3$
(f) $Zn(OH)_2$

Determining K$_{sp}$

17.18 In water, the solubility of lead(II) chloride is 0.016 M. Use that information to calculate the value of K_{sp} for $PbCl_2$.

OH 17.19 A student evaporated 100.0 mL of a saturated BaF_2 solution and found the solid BaF_2 she recovered weighed 0.132 g. From those data, calculate K_{sp} for BaF_2.

17.20 Barium sulfate is so insoluble that it can be swallowed without significant danger, even though Ba^{2+} is toxic. At 25 °C, 1.00 L of water dissolves only 0.00245 g of $BaSO_4$. Calculate K_{sp} for $BaSO_4$.

17.21 A student found that a maximum of 0.800 g silver acetate is able to dissolve in 100.0 mL of water. What is the molar solubility and the K_{sp} for the salt?

17.22 It was found that the molar solubility of $BaSO_3$ in 0.10 M $BaCl_2$ is 8.0×10^{-6} M. What is the value of K_{sp} for $BaSO_3$?

17.23 A student prepared a saturated solution of $CaCrO_4$ and found that when 156 mL of the solution was evaporated, 0.649 g of $CaCrO_4$ was left behind. What is the value of K_{sp} for the salt?

17.24 At 25 °C, the molar solubility of silver phosphate is 1.8×10^{-5} mol L^{-1}. Calculate K_{sp} for the salt.

17.25 The molar solubility of barium phosphate in water at 25 °C is 1.4×10^{-8} mol L^{-1}. What is the value of K_{sp} for the salt?

Using K$_{sp}$ to Calculate Solubilities

17.26 What is the molar solubility of $PbBr_2$ in water?

17.27 What is the molar solubility of Ag_2CrO_4 in water?

17.28 Calculate the molar solubility of Ag_2CO_3 in water. (Ignore the reaction of the CO_3^{2-} ion with water.)

17.29 Calculate the molar solubility of PbF_2 in water.

17.30 At 25 °C, the value of K_{sp} for LiF is 1.7×10^{-3}, and that for BaF_2 is 1.7×10^{-6}. Which salt, LiF or BaF_2, has the larger molar solubility in water? Calculate the solubility of each in units of mol L^{-1}.

17.31 At 25 °C, the value of K_{sp} for AgCN is 2.2×10^{-16} and that for $Zn(CN)_2$ is 3×10^{-16}. In terms of grams per 100 mL of solution, which salt is the more soluble in water?

17.32 A salt whose formula is MX has a K_{sp} equal to 3.2×10^{-10}. Another sparingly soluble salt, MX_3, must have what value of K_{sp} if the molar solubilities of the two salts are to be identical?

17.33 A salt having a formula of the type M_2X_3 has $K_{sp} = 2.2 \times 10^{-20}$. Another salt, M_2X, has to have what K_{sp} value if M_2X has twice the molar solubility of M_2X_3?

17.34 Calcium sulfate is found in plaster. At 25 °C the value of K_{sp} for $CaSO_4$ is 2.4×10^{-5}. What is the calculated molar solubility of $CaSO_4$ in water?

17.35 Chalk is $CaCO_3$, and at 25 °C its $K_{sp} = 4.5 \times 10^{-9}$. What is the molar solubility of $CaCO_3$? How many grams of $CaCO_3$ dissolve in 100 mL of aqueous solution? (Ignore the reaction of CO_3^{2-} with water.)

Common Ion Effect

ILW 17.36 Copper(I) chloride has $K_{sp} = 1.9 \times 10^{-7}$. Calculate the molar solubility of copper(I) chloride in (a) pure water, (b) 0.0200 M HCl solution, (c) 0.200 M HCl solution, and (d) 0.150 M $CaCl_2$ solution.

17.37 Gold(III) chloride has $K_{sp} = 3.2 \times 10^{-25}$. Calculate the molar solubility of gold(III) chloride in (a) pure water, (b) 0.010 M HCl solution, (c) 0.010 M $MgCl_2$ solution, and (d) 0.010 M $Au(NO_3)_3$ solution.

17.38 Calculate the molar solubility of $Mg(OH)_2$ in a solution that is basic with a pH of 12.50.

17.39 Calculate the molar solubility of $Al(OH)_3$ in a solution that is slightly basic with a pH of 9.50.

17.40 What is the highest concentration of Pb^{2+} that can exist in a solution of 0.10 M HCl?

17.41 Will lead(II) bromide be less soluble in 0.10 M $Pb(C_2H_3O_2)_2$ or in 0.10 M NaBr?

17.42 Calculate the molar solubility of Ag_2CrO_4 at 25 °C in (a) 0.200 M $AgNO_3$ and (b) 0.200 M Na_2CrO_4. For Ag_2CrO_4 at 25 °C, $K_{sp} = 1.2 \times 10^{-12}$.

17.43 What is the molar solubility of $Mg(OH)_2$ in (a) 0.20 M NaOH and (b) 0.20 M $MgSO_4$? For $Mg(OH)_2$, $K_{sp} = 7.1 \times 10^{-12}$.

17.44 How much will the percent ionization of the acetic acid change in 0.500 L of 0.10 M $HC_2H_3O_2$ if 0.050 mol of solid $NaC_2H_3O_2$ is added? (Assume no change in the volume of the solution.) How much will the pH change?

17.45 How much will the percent ionization of the acetic acid change in 0.500 L of 0.10 M $HC_2H_3O_2$ if 0.025 mol of gaseous HCl is dissolved in the solution? (Assume no change in volume.) How will the pH of the solution change?

*17.46 In an experiment 2.20 g of NaOH(s) is added to 250 mL of 0.10 M $FeCl_2$ solution. What mass of $Fe(OH)_2$ will be formed? What will the molar concentration of Fe^{2+} be in the final solution?

*17.47 Suppose that 1.75 g of NaOH(s) is added to 250 mL of 0.10 M $NiCl_2$ solution. What mass, in grams, of $Ni(OH)_2$ will be formed? What will be the pH of the final solution? For $Ni(OH)_2$, $K_{sp} = 6 \times 10^{-16}$.

17.48 What is the molar solubility of $Fe(OH)_2$ in a buffer that has a pH of 9.50?

17.49 What is the molar solubility of $Ca(OH)_2$ in (a) 0.10 M $CaCl_2$ and (b) 0.10 M NaOH?

Precipitation

17.50 Does a precipitate of $PbCl_2$ form when 0.0150 mol of $Pb(NO_3)_2$ and 0.0120 mol of NaCl are dissolved in 1.00 L of solution?

17.51 Silver acetate, $AgC_2H_3O_2$, has $K_{sp} = 2.3 \times 10^{-3}$. Does a precipitate form when 0.015 mol of $AgNO_3$ and 0.25 mol of $Ca(C_2H_3O_2)_2$ are dissolved in a total volume of 1.00 L of solution?

ILW 17.52 Does a precipitate of $PbBr_2$ form if 50.0 mL of 0.0100 M $Pb(NO_3)_2$ is mixed with (a) 50.0 mL of 0.0100 M KBr and (b) 50.0 mL of 0.100 M NaBr?

17.53 Would a precipitate of silver acetate form if 22.0 mL of 0.100 M $AgNO_3$ were added to 45.0 mL of 0.0260 M $NaC_2H_3O_2$? For $AgC_2H_3O_2$, $K_{sp} = 2.3 \times 10^{-3}$.

17.54 Both AgCl and AgI are very sparingly soluble salts, but the solubility of AgI is much less than that of AgCl, as can be seen by their K_{sp} values. Suppose that a solution contains both Cl^- and I^- with $[Cl^-] = 0.050$ M and $[I^-] = 0.050$ M. If solid $AgNO_3$ is added to 1.00 L of this mixture (so that no appreciable change in volume occurs), what is the value of $[I^-]$ when AgCl first begins to precipitate?

17.55 Suppose that Na_2SO_4 is added gradually to 100.0 mL of a solution that contains both Ca^{2+} ion (0.15 M) and Sr^{2+} ion (0.15 M). (a) What will the Sr^{2+} concentration be (in mol L^{-1}) when $CaSO_4$ just begins to precipitate? (b) What percentage of the strontium ion has precipitated when $CaSO_4$ just begins to precipitate?

17.56 Suppose 50.0 mL each of 0.0100 M solutions of NaBr and $Pb(NO_3)_2$ are poured together. Does a precipitate form? If so, calculate the molar concentrations of the ions at equilibrium.

17.57 If a solution of 0.10 M Mn^{2+} and 0.10 M Cd^{2+} is gradually made basic, what will the concentration of Cd^{2+} be when $Mn(OH)_2$ just begins to precipitate? Assume no change in the volume of the solution.

Selective Precipitation

ILW 17.58 What value of $[H^+]$ and what pH permits the selective pre-
OH cipitation of the sulfide of just one of the two metal ions in a solution that has a concentration of 0.010 M Pb^{2+} and 0.010 M Co^{2+}?

17.59 What pH would yield the maximum separation Mn^{2+} from Sn^{2+} in a solution that is 0.010 M in Mn^{2+}, 0.010 M in Sn^{2+}, and saturated in H_2S? (Assume the green form of MnS in Table 17.2.)

17.60 What range of pH would permit the selective precipitation of Cu^{2+} as $Cu(OH)_2$ from a solution that contains 0.10 M Cu^{2+} and 0.10 M Mn^{2+}? For $Mn(OH)_2$, $K_{sp} = 1.6 \times 10^{-13}$ and for $Cu(OH)_2$, $K_{sp} = 4.8 \times 10^{-20}$.

17.61 Kidney stones often contain insoluble calcium oxalate, CaC_2O_4, which has $K_{sp} = 2.3 \times 10^{-9}$. Calcium oxalate is considerably less soluble than magnesium oxalate, MgC_2O_4, which has $K_{sp} = 8.6 \times 10^{-5}$. Suppose a solution contained both Ca^{2+} and Mg^{2+} at a concentration of 0.10 M. What pH would be required to achieve maximum separation of these ions by precipitation of CaC_2O_4 if the solution also contains oxalic acid, $H_2C_2O_4$ at a concentration of 0.10 M? For $H_2C_2O_4$, $K_{a_1} = 5.6 \times 10^{-2}$ and $K_{a_2} = 5.4 \times 10^{-5}$.

Complex Ion Equilibria

17.62 Write the chemical equilibria and equilibrium laws that correspond to K_{form} for the following complexes:
(a) $CuCl_4^{2-}$
(b) AgI_2^-
(c) $Cr(NH_3)_6^{3+}$

17.63 Write the chemical equilibria and equilibrium laws that correspond to K_{form} for the following complexes:
(a) $Ag(S_2O_3)_2^{3-}$
(b) $Zn(NH_3)_4^{2+}$
(c) SnS_3^{2-}

OH 17.64 Write equilibria that correspond to K_{form} for each of the following complex ions and write the equations for K_{form}.
(a) $Co(NH_3)_6^{3+}$ (b) HgI_4^{2-} (c) $Fe(CN)_6^{4-}$

17.65 Write the equilibria that are associated with the equations for K_{form} for each of the following complex ions. Write also the equations for the K_{form} of each.
(a) $Hg(NH_3)_4^{2+}$ (b) SnF_6^{2-} (c) $Fe(CN)_6^{3-}$

17.66 For $PbCl_3^-$, $K_{form} = 2.5 \times 10^1$. Use this information plus the K_{sp} for $PbCl_2$ to calculate K_c for the reaction

$$PbCl_2(s) + Cl^-(aq) \rightleftharpoons PbCl_3^-(aq)$$

17.67 The overall formation constant for $Ag(CN)_2^-$ equals 5.3×10^{18}, and the K_{sp} for AgCN equals 1.2×10^{-16}. Calculate K_c for the reaction

$$AgCN(s) + CN^-(aq) \rightleftharpoons Ag(CN)_2^-(aq)$$

17.68 How many grams of solid NaCN have to be added to 1.2 L of water to dissolve 0.11 mol of $Fe(OH)_3$ in the form of $Fe(CN)_6^{3-}$? Use data as needed from Tables 17.1 and 17.3. (For simplicity, ignore the reaction of CN^- ion with water.)

17.69 In photography, unexposed silver bromide is removed from film by soaking the film in a solution of sodium thiosulfate, $Na_2S_2O_3$. Silver ion forms a soluble complex with thiosulfate ion, $S_2O_3^{2-}$, that has the formula $Ag(S_2O_3)_2^{3-}$, and formation of the complex causes the AgBr in the film to dissolve. The $Ag(S_2O_3)_2^{3-}$ complex has $K_{form} = 2.0 \times 10^{13}$. How many grams of AgBr ($K_{sp} = 5.0 \times 10^{-13}$) will dissolve in 125 mL of 1.20 M $Na_2S_2O_3$ solution?

17.70 Silver iodide is very insoluble and can be difficult to remove from glass apparatus, but it forms a relatively stable complex ion, AgI_2^- ($K_{form} = 1 \times 10^{11}$), that makes AgI fairly soluble in a solution containing I^-. When a solution containing the AgI_2^- ion is diluted with water, AgI precipitates. Explain why this happens in terms of the equilibria that are involved. How many grams of AgI will dissolve in 100 mL of 1.0 M KI solution?

17.71 Silver forms a sparingly soluble cyanide salt, AgCN, for which $K_{sp} = 1.2 \times 10^{-16}$. It also forms a soluble cyanide complex, $Ag(CN)_2^-$, for which $K_{form} = 5.3 \times 10^{18}$. How many grams of solid KCN must be added to 100 mL of water to dissolve 0.020 mol AgCN? For simplicity, ignore the reaction of CN^- with water. Be sure to include all the cyanide that's added to the solution.

17.72 The formation constant for $Ag(CN)_2^-$ equals 5.3×10^{18}. Use the data in Table 17.1 to determine the molar solubility of AgI in 0.010 M KCN solution.

17.73 Suppose that some dipositive cation, M^{2+}, is able to form a complex ion with a ligand, L, by the following equation.

$$M^{2+} + 2L \rightleftharpoons M(L)_2^{2+}$$

The cation also forms a sparingly soluble salt, MCl_2. In which of the following circumstances would a given quantity of ligand be more able to bring larger quantities of the salt into solution? Explain and justify the calculation involved.

(a) $K_{form} = 1 \times 10^2$ and $K_{sp} = 1 \times 10^{-15}$

(b) $K_{form} = 1 \times 10^{10}$ and $K_{sp} = 1 \times 10^{-20}$

17.74 The molar solubility of $Zn(OH)_2$ in 1.0 M NH_3 is 5.7×10^{-3} mol L^{-1}. Determine the value of the instability constant of the complex ion, $Zn(NH_3)_4^{2+}$. Ignore the reaction, $NH_3 + H_2O \rightleftharpoons NH_4^+ + OH^-$.

OH **17.75** Calculate the molar solubility of $Cu(OH)_2$ in 2.0 M NH_3. (For simplicity, ignore the reaction of NH_3 as a base.)

ADDITIONAL EXERCISES

*__17.76__ How many milliliters of 0.10 M HCl would have to be added to 100 mL of a saturated solution of $PbCl_2$ in contact with 50.0 g of solid $PbCl_2$ to reduce the Pb^{2+} concentration to 0.0050 M? (Don't forget to take into account the combined volumes of the two solutions.)

17.77 Magnesium hydroxide, $Mg(OH)_2$, found in milk of magnesia, has a solubility of 7.05×10^{-3} g L^{-1} at 25 °C. Calculate K_{sp} for $Mg(OH)_2$.

17.78 Does iron(II) sulfide dissolve in 8 M HCl? Perform the calculations that prove your answer.

17.79 As noted earlier, milk of magnesia is an aqueous suspension of $Mg(OH)_2$. If we assume that besides the $Mg(OH)_2$ the only other component is water, use K_{sp} to estimate the pH of milk of magnesia.

*__17.80__ Suppose that 25.0 mL of 0.10 M HCl is added to 1.000 L of saturated $Mg(OH)_2$ in contact with more than enough $Mg(OH)_2(s)$ to react with all the HCl. After reaction has ceased, what will the molar concentration of Mg^{2+} be? What will the pH of the solution be?

OH *__17.81__ Solid $Mn(OH)_2$ is added to a solution of 0.100 M $FeCl_2$. After reaction, what will be the molar concentrations of Mn^{2+} and Fe^{2+} in the solution? What will be the pH of the solution? For $Mn(OH)_2$, $K_{sp} = 1.6 \times 10^{-13}$.

*__17.82__ Suppose that 50.0 mL of 0.12 M $AgNO_3$ is added to 50.0 mL of 0.048 M NaCl solution. (a) What mass of AgCl would form? (b) Calculate the final concentrations of all of the ions in the solution that is in contact with the precipitate. (c) What percentage of the Ag^+ ions have precipitated?

*__17.83__ A sample of hard water was found to have 278 ppm Ca^{2+} ion. Into 1.00 L of this water, 1.00 g of Na_2CO_3 was dissolved. What is the new concentration of Ca^{2+} in parts per million? (Assume that the addition of Na_2CO_3 does not change the volume, and assume that the density of the aqueous solutions involved are all 1.00 g mL^{-1}.)

*__17.84__ What value of $[H^+]$ and what pH would allow the selective separation of the carbonate of just one of the two metal ions in a solution that has a concentration of 0.010 M La^{3+} and 0.010 M Pb^{2+}? For $La_2(CO_3)_3$, $K_{sp} = 4.0 \times 10^{-34}$; for $PbCO_3$, $K_{sp} = 7.4 \times 10^{-14}$. A saturated solution of CO_2 in water has a concentration of H_2CO_3 equal to 3.3×10^{-2} M.

*__17.85__ When solid NH_4Cl is added to a suspension of $Mg(OH)_2(s)$, some of the $Mg(OH)_2$ dissolves.

(a) Write equations for *all* the chemical equilibria that exist in the solution after the addition of the NH_4Cl.

(b) How many moles of NH_4Cl must be added to 1.0 L of a suspension of $Mg(OH)_2$ to dissolve 0.10 mol of $Mg(OH)_2$?

(c) What is the pH of the solution after the 0.10 mol of $Mg(OH)_2$ has dissolved in the solution containing the NH_4Cl?

*__17.86__ After solid $CaCO_3$ was added to a slightly basic solution, the pH was measured to be 8.50. What was the molar solubility of $CaCO_3$ in the solution?

17.87 In modern construction, walls and ceilings are constructed of "drywall," which consists of plaster sandwiched between sheets of heavy paper. Plaster is composed of calcium sulfate, $CaSO_4 \cdot 2H_2O$. Suppose you had a leak in a water pipe that was dripping water on a drywall ceiling 1/2 in. thick at a rate of 2.00 L per day. Use the K_{sp} of calcium sulfate to estimate how many days it would take to dissolve a hole 1.0 cm in diameter. Assume the density of the plaster is 0.97 g cm^{-3}.

17.88 What is the molar solubility of $Fe(OH)_3$ in water? (Hint: Don't forget the self-ionization of water.)

*__17.89__ In Example 17.11 (page 716) we say, "There are relatively few uncomplexed Ag^+ ions in the solution." Calculate the molar concentration of Ag^+ ion actually left after the complex forms as described in Example 17.11.

*__17.90__ What are the concentrations of Pb^{2+}, Br^-, and I^- in an aqueous solution that's in contact with both PbI_2 and $PbBr_2$?

*__17.91__ Will a precipitate form in a solution made by dissolving 1.0 mol of $AgNO_3$ and 1.0 mol $HC_2H_3O_2$ in 1.0 L of solution? For $AgC_2H_3O_2$, $K_{sp} = 2.3 \times 10^{-3}$ and for $HC_2H_3O_2$, $K_a = 1.8 \times 10^{-5}$.

*__17.92__ How many grams of solid sodium acetate must be added to 0.200 L of a solution containing 0.200 M $AgNO_3$ and 0.10 M nitric acid to cause silver acetate to begin to precipitate? For $HC_2H_3O_2$, $K_a = 1.8 \times 10^{-5}$ and for $AgC_2H_3O_2$, $K_{sp} = 2.3 \times 10^{-3}$.

*__17.93__ How many grams of solid potassium fluoride must be added to 200 mL of a solution that contains 0.20 M $AgNO_3$ and 0.10 M acetic acid to cause silver acetate to begin to precipitate? For HF, $K_a = 6.8 \times 10^{-4}$; for $HC_2H_3O_2$, $K_a = 1.8 \times 10^{-5}$; for $AgC_2H_3O_2$, $K_{sp} = 2.3 \times 10^{-3}$.

*__17.94__ What is the molar solubility of $Mg(OH)_2$ in 0.10 M NH_3 solution? Remember that NH_3 is a weak base.

*__17.95__ If 100 mL of 2.0 M NH_3 is added to 400 mL of a solution containing 0.10 M Mn^{2+} and 0.10 M Sn^{2+}, what minimum number of grams of HCl would have to be added to the mixture to prevent $Mn(OH)_2$ from precipitating? For $Mn(OH)_2$, $K_{sp} = 1.6 \times 10^{-13}$. Assume that virtually all the tin is precipitated as $Sn(OH)_2$ by the reaction

$$Sn^{2+}(aq) + 2NH_3(aq) + 2H_2O \longrightarrow$$
$$Sn(OH)_2(s) + 2NH_4^+(aq)$$

*__17.96__ What is the molar concentration of Cu^{2+} ion in a solution prepared by mixing 0.50 mol of NH_3 and 0.050 mol of $CuSO_4$ in 1.00 L of solution? For NH_3, $K_b = 1.8 \times 10^{-5}$; for $Cu(OH)_2$, $K_{sp} = 4.8 \times 10^{-20}$; and for $Cu(NH_3)_4^{2+}$, $K_{form} = 1.1 \times 10^{13}$.

*__17.97__ On the basis of the K_{sp} of $Al(OH)_3$, what would be the pH of a mixture consisting of solid $Al(OH)_3$ mixed with pure water? (Assume 100% dissociation of the aluminum hydroxide.)

17.98 You are given a sample containing NaCl(aq) and NaBr(aq), both with concentrations of 0.020 M. Some of the figures below represent a series of snapshots of what molecular level views of the sample would show as a 0.200 M Pb(NO$_3$)$_2$(aq) solution is slowly added. In these figures, Br$^-$ is red-brown and Cl$^-$ is green. Also, spectator ions are not shown, nor are ions whose concentrations are much less than the other ions. The K_{sp} constants for PbCl$_2$ and PbBr$_2$ are 1.7×10^{-5} and 2.1×10^{-6}, respectively.

(1) Arrange the figures in a time sequence to show what happens as the lead nitrate solution is added, excluding any that do not "make sense."

(2) Explain why you excluded any figures that did not belong in the observed time sequence.

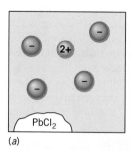

(a)

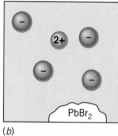

(b)

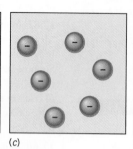

(c)

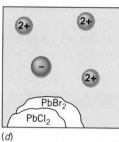

(d)

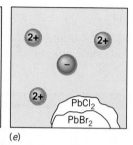

(e)

EXERCISES IN CRITICAL THINKING

17.99 Consider mercury(II) sulfide, HgS, which has a solubility product of 2×10^{-53}. Suppose some solid HgS was added to 1.0 L of water. How many ions of Hg^{2+} and S^{2-} are present in the water when equilibrium is reached? If your answer is accurate, is there a true equilibrium between HgS(s) and the ions in the solution? Explain your answer.

17.100 If aqueous ammonia is added gradually to a solution of copper sulfate, a pale blue precipitate forms that then dissolves to give a deep blue solution. Describe the chemical reactions that take place during these changes.

17.101 From a practical standpoint, can you effectively separate Pb^{2+} and Sr^{2+} ions by selective precipitation of their sulfates? Support your conclusions using calculations.

17.102 A salt with the formula of MX_2 is slightly soluble in water. Estimate the minimum reliable mass you can determine on your laboratory balance. Use that estimate to determine the smallest value of the solubility product of MX_2 that could be determined by evaporating a liter of a solution that is saturated in MX_2.

17.103 In older textbooks the solubility equilibrium for lead(II) sulfide was written as PbS(s) $\rightleftharpoons$ Pb^{2+}(aq) + S^{2-}(aq) with $K_{sp} = 3.0 \times 10^{-28}$. Calculate the solubility of lead sulfide using K_{sp} (assuming no reaction of S^{2-} with water) and with K_{spa}. Is there a difference between the two answers? Discuss the results of your calculations.

17.104 Suppose two silver wires, one coated with silver chloride and the other coated with silver bromide, are placed in a beaker containing pure water. Over time, what if anything will happen to the compositions of the coatings on the two wires? Justify your answer.

Once again you have an opportunity to test your understanding of concepts, your knowledge of scientific terms, and your skills at solving chemistry problems. Read through the following questions carefully, and answer each as fully as possible. Review topics when necessary. When you are able to answer these questions correctly, you are ready to go on to the next group of chapters.

1. List the factors that affect the speed of a chemical reaction.

2. At 25° C and $[OH^-] = 1.00\ M$, the reaction

$$I^-(aq) + OCl^-(aq) \longrightarrow OI^-(aq) + Cl^-(aq)$$

has the following rate law

$$\text{Rate} = (0.60\ L\ mol^{-1}\ s^{-1})[I^-][OCl^-]$$

Calculate the rate of the reaction when $[OH^-] = 1.00\ M$ and
   (a) $[I^-] = 0.0100\ M$ and $[OCl^-] = 0.0200\ M$
   (b) $[I^-] = 0.100\ M$ and $[OCl^-] = 0.0400\ M$

3. A reaction has the stoichiometry: $3A + B \longrightarrow C + D$. The following data were obtained for the initial rate of formation of C at various concentrations of A and B.

Initial Concentrations		Initial Rate of Formation
[A]	[B]	of C (mol $L^{-1}\ s^{-1}$)
0.010	0.010	2.0×10^{-4}
0.020	0.020	8.0×10^{-4}
0.020	0.010	8.0×10^{-4}

   (a) What is the rate law for the reaction?
   (b) What is the value of the rate constant?
   (c) What is the rate at which C is formed if $[A] = 0.017\ M$ and $[B] = 0.033\ M$?

4. If the concentration of a particular reactant is doubled and the rate of the reaction is cut in half, what must be the order of the reaction with respect to that reactant?

5. Organic compounds that contain large proportions of nitrogen and oxygen tend to be unstable and are easily decomposed. Hexanitroethane, $C_2(NO_2)_6$, decomposes according to the equation

$$C_2(NO_2)_6 \longrightarrow 2NO_2 + 4NO + 2CO_2$$

The reaction in CCl_4 as a solvent is first order with respect to $C_2(NO_2)_6$. At 70 °C, $k = 2.41 \times 10^{-6}\ s^{-1}$ and at 100 °C $k = 2.22 \times 10^{-4}\ s^{-1}$.
   (a) What is the half-life of $C_2(NO_2)_6$ at 70 °C? What is the half-life at 100 °C?
   (b) If 0.100 mol of $C_2(NO_2)_6$ is dissolved in CCl_4 at 70 °C to give 1.00 L of solution, what will be the $C_2(NO_2)_6$ concentration after 500 minutes?
   (c) What is the value of the activation energy of this reaction, expressed in kilojoules?
   (d) What is the reaction's rate constant at 120 °C?

6. Radioactive strontium-90, ^{90}Sr, has a half-life of 28 years.
   (a) What fraction of a sample of ^{90}Sr will remain after three half-lives?
   (b) What fraction of a sample of ^{90}Sr will remain after 168 years?
   (c) If the amount of ^{90}Sr remaining in a sample is only one-sixteenth of the amount originally present, how many

years has the sample been undergoing radioactive decay?
   (d) If the amount of ^{90}Sr remaining in a sample is only one-sixth of the amount originally present, how many years has the sample been undergoing radioactive decay?

7. The reaction $2A + 2B \longrightarrow M + N$ has this rate law: Rate $= k[A]^2$. At 25 °C, $k = 1.0 \times 10^{-4}\ L\ mol^{-1}\ s^{-1}$. If the initial concentrations of A and B are 0.250 M and 0.150 M, respectively
   (a) What is the half-life of the reaction?
   (b) What will be the concentrations of A and B after 30 minutes?

8. Define *reaction mechanism*, *rate-determining step*, and *elementary process*.

9. The decomposition of ozone, O_3, is believed to occur by the two-step mechanism

$$O_3 \longrightarrow O_2 + O \quad \text{(slow)}$$
$$\underline{O + O_3 \longrightarrow 2O_2 \quad \text{(fast)}}$$
$$2O_3 \longrightarrow 3O_2 \quad \text{(net reaction)}$$

If this is the mechanism, what is the reaction's rate law?

10. Draw a diagram showing how the potential energy varies during an exothermic reaction. Identify the activation energy for both the forward and reverse reactions. Also, identify the heat of reaction.

11. How does a heterogeneous catalyst increase the rate of a chemical reaction?

12. One possible mechanism for the decomposition of ethane, C_2H_6, into ethylene, C_2H_4, and hydrogen,

$$C_2H_6 \longrightarrow C_2H_4 + H_2$$

includes the following steps.

   (1) $\quad C_2H_6 \longrightarrow 2CH_3\cdot$
   (2) $\quad CH_3\cdot + C_2H_6 \longrightarrow CH_4 + C_2H_5\cdot$
   (3) $\quad C_2H_5\cdot \longrightarrow C_2H_4 + H\cdot$
   (4) $\quad H\cdot + C_2H_6 \longrightarrow C_2H_5\cdot + H_2$
   (5) $\quad H\cdot + C_2H_5\cdot \longrightarrow C_2H_6$

   (a) Which steps initiate the reaction?
   (b) Which are propagation steps?
   (c) Which is a termination step?

13. Write the appropriate mass action expression, using molar concentrations, for these reactions.
   (a) $NO_2(g) + N_2O(g) \rightleftharpoons 3NO(g)$
   (b) $CaSO_3(s) \rightleftharpoons CaO(s) + SO_2(g)$
   (c) $NiCO_3(s) \rightleftharpoons Ni^{2+}(aq) + CO_3^{2-}(aq)$

14. At a certain temperature, the reaction $2HF(g) \rightleftharpoons$ $2HF(g) + F_2(g)$ has $K_c = 1 \times 10^{-13}$. Does this reaction

proceed far toward completion when equilibrium is reached? If 0.010 mol HF was placed in a 1.00 L container and the system was permitted to come to equilibrium, what would be the concentrations of H_2 and F_2 in the container?

15. At 100°C, the reaction $2NO_2(g) \rightleftharpoons N_2O_4(g)$ has $K_p = 6.5 \times 10^{-2}$. What is the value of K_c at that temperature?

16. At 1000°C, the reaction $NO_2(g) + SO_2(g) \rightleftharpoons NO(g) + SO_3(g)$ has $K_c = 3.60$. If 0.100 mol NO_2 and 0.100 mol SO_2 are placed in a 5.00 L container and allowed to react, what will all the concentrations be when equilibrium is reached? What will the new equilibrium concentrations be if 0.010 mol NO and 0.010 mol SO_3 are added to the original equilibrium mixture?

17. For the reaction in the preceding question, $\Delta H° = -41.8$ kJ. How will the equilibrium concentration of NO be affected if
(a) More NO_2 is added to the container?
(b) Some SO_3 is removed from the container?
(c) The temperature of the reaction mixture is raised?
(d) Some SO_2 is removed from the mixture?
(e) The pressure of the gas mixture is lowered by expanding the volume to 10.0 L?

18. At 60°C, $K_w = 9.5 \times 10^{-14}$. What is the pH of pure water at that temperature? Why can we say that the water is neither acidic nor basic?

19. At 25 °C, the water in a natural pool of water in one of the western states was found to contain hydroxide ions at a concentration of 4.7×10^{-7} g OH^- per liter. Calculate the pH of the water and state if it is acidic, basic, or neutral.

20. Which is the stronger acid, H_3AsO_3 or H_3AsO_4? How can one tell without a table of weak and strong acids?

21. Which is the stronger acid, H_2S or H_2Te?

22. What are the conjugate acids of (a) HSO_3^- and (b) N_2H_4?

23. What are the conjugate bases of (a) HSO_3^-, (b) N_2H_4, and (c) $C_5H_5NH^+$?

24. Identify the conjugate acid–base pairs in the reaction

$$CH_3NH_2 + NH_4^+ \rightleftharpoons CH_3NH_3^+ + NH_3$$

25. What is the definition of an *amphoteric substance*? What is a *Lewis acid*? What is a *Lewis base*?

26. Use Lewis structures to diagram the reaction between the Lewis base OH^- and the Lewis acid SO_3.

27. X, Y, and Z are all nonmetallic elements in the same period of the periodic table where they occur, left to right, in the order given. Which would be a stronger binary acid than the binary acid of Y, the binary acid of X or the binary acid of Z? Explain.

28. The first antiseptic to be used in surgical operating rooms was phenol, C_6H_5OH, a weak acid and a potent bactericide. A 0.550 M solution of phenol in water was found to have a pH of 5.07.
(a) Write the chemical equation for the equilibrium involving C_6H_5OH in the solution.
(b) Write the equilibrium law corresponding to K_a for C_6H_5OH.
(c) Calculate the values of K_a and pK_a for phenol.
(d) Calculate the values of K_b and pK_b for the phenoxide ion, $C_6H_5O^-$.

29. The pK_a of saccharin, $HC_7H_3SO_3$, a sweetening agent, is 11.68.
(a) What is the pK_b of the saccharinate ion, $C_7H_3SO_3^-$?

(b) Does a solution of sodium saccharinate in water have a pH of 7, or is the solution acidic or basic? If the pH is not 7, calculate the pH of a 0.010 M solution of sodium saccharinate in water.

30. At 25 °C the value of K_b for codeine, a pain-killing drug, is 1.6×10^{-6}. Calculate the pH of a 0.0115 M solution of codeine in water.

31. Methylamine, CH_3NH_2, is a weak base. Write the chemical equation for the equilibrium that occurs in an aqueous solution of this solute. Write the equilibrium law corresponding to K_b for CH_3NH_2.

32. The pK_b of methylamine, CH_3NH_2, is 3.43. Calculate the pK_a of its conjugate acid, $CH_3NH_3^+$.

33. Ascorbic acid, $H_2C_6H_6O_6$, is a diprotic acid usually known as vitamin C. For this acid, pK_{a_1} is 4.10 and pK_{a_2} is 11.79. When 125 mL of a solution of ascorbic acid was evaporated to dryness, the residue of pure ascorbic acid had a mass of 3.12 g.
(a) Calculate the molar concentration of ascorbic acid in the solution before it was evaporated.
(b) Calculate the pH of the solution and the molar concentration of the ascorbate ion, $C_6H_6O_6^{2-}$, before the solution was evaporated.

34. What ratio of molar concentrations of sodium acetate to acetic acid can buffer a solution at a pH of 4.50?

35. Write a chemical equation for the reaction that would occur in a buffer composed of sodium acetate and acetic acid if
(a) Some HCl were added.
(b) Some NaOH were added.

36. If 0.020 mol of NaOH were added to 0.500 L of a sodium acetate–acetic acid buffer that contains 0.10 M $NaC_2H_3O_2$ and 0.15 M $HC_2H_3O_2$, by how many pH units will the pH of the buffer change?

37. A biology experiment requires the use of a nutrient fluid buffered at a pH of 4.85, and 625 mL of the solution is needed. It has to be buffered to be able to hold the pH to within ±0.10 pH unit of 5.00 even if 5.00×10^{-3} mol of OH^- or 5.00×10^{-3} mol of H^+ ion enter the buffer.
(a) Using tabulated data, pick the best acid and its sodium salt that could be used to prepare the solution.
(b) Calculate the minimum number of grams of the pure acid and its salt that are needed to prepare the buffer solution.
(c) What are the molar concentrations of the acid and of its salt in the solution?

38. How would each of the following aqueous solutions test, acidic, basic, or neutral? (Assume that each is at least 0.2 M.) (a) potassium nitrate, (b) chromium(III) chloride, (c) ammonium iodide, (d) potassium dihydrogen phosphate.

39. When 50.00 mL of an acid with a concentration of 0.115 M (for which $pK_a = 4.87$) is titrated with 0.100 M NaOH, what is the pH at the equivalence point? What would be a good indicator for the titration?

40. Calculate the pH of a 0.050 M solution of sodium ascorbate, $Na_2C_6H_6O_6$. For ascorbic acid, $H_2C_6H_6O_6$, $K_{a_1} = 7.9 \times 10^{-5}$ and $K_{a_2} = 1.6 \times 10^{-12}$.

41. When 25.0 mL of 0.100 M NaOH was added to 50.0 mL of a 0.100 M solution of a weak acid, HX, the pH of the mixture reached a value of 3.56. What is the value of K_a for the weak acid?

42. How many grams of solid NaOH would have to be added to 0.100 L of a 0.100 M solution of NH_4Cl to give a mixture with a pH of 9.26?

43. The molar solubility of silver chromate, Ag_2CrO_4, in water is 6.7×10^{-5} M. What is K_{sp} for Ag_2CrO_4?

44. What is the pH of a saturated solution of magnesium hydroxide?

45. What is the solubility of iron(II) hydroxide in grams per liter if the solution is buffered to a pH of 10.00?

46. Suppose 30.0 mL of 0.100 M $Pb(NO_3)_2$ is added to 20.0 mL of 0.500 M KI.

    (a) How many grams of PbI_2 will be formed?

    (b) What will the molar concentrations of all the ions be in the mixture after equilibrium has been reached?

47. How many moles of NH_3 must be added to 1.00 L of solution to dissolve 1.00 g of $CuCO_3$? For $CuCO_3$, $K_{sp} = 2.3 \times 10^{-10}$. Ignore hydrolysis of CO_3^{2-}, but consider the formation of the complex ion, $Cu(NH_3)_4^{2+}$.

48. Over what pH range must a solution be buffered to achieve a selective separation of the carbonates of barium, $BaCO_3$ ($K_{sp} = 5.0 \times 10^{-9}$), and lead, $PbCO_3$ ($K_{sp} = 7.4 \times 10^{-14}$)? The solution is initially 0.010 M in Ba^{2+} and 0.010 M in Pb^{2+}.

49. A solution containing 0.10 M Pb^{2+} and 0.10 M Ni^{2+} is to be saturated with H_2S. What range of pH values could the solution have so that when the procedure is completed one of the ions remains in solution while the other is precipitated as its sulfide?

50. A solution that contains 0.10 M Fe^{2+} and 0.10 M Sn^{2+} is maintained at a pH of 3.00 while H_2S is gradually added to it. What will be the concentration of Sn^{2+} in the solution when FeS just begins to precipitate?

51. A metal sulfide MS has a value of K_{sp} of 4.0×10^{-29}. (a) What is the value of K_{spa} for this compound? (b) Calculate the molar solubility of MS in 0.30 M HCl.

THERMODYNAMICS 1

A perfume serves its purpose because its aroma drifts spontaneously through the air as molecules of the perfume mix with those of the atmosphere. Such spontaneous events are predicted by thermodynamics. In this chapter you will learn about the factors that determine whether or not a process is spontaneous. *(Vincent Besnault/Sygma/Corbis)*

CHAPTER OUTLINE

18.1 Internal energy can be transferred as heat or work, but it cannot be created or destroyed

18.2 A spontaneous change is a change that continues without outside intervention

18.3 Spontaneous processes tend to proceed from states of lower probability to states of higher probability

18.4 All spontaneous processes increase the total entropy of the universe

18.5 The third law of thermodynamics makes experimental measurement of absolute entropies possible

18.6 The standard free energy change, $\Delta G°$, is ΔG at standard conditions

18.7 ΔG is the maximum amount of work that can be done by a process

18.8 ΔG is zero when a system is at equilibrium

18.9 Equilibrium constants can be estimated from standard free energy changes

18.10 Bond energies can be estimated from reaction enthalpy changes

THIS CHAPTER IN CONTEXT　　The chemistry we observe in our world is controlled both by w happen and what *cannot*. For example, hydrocarbon fuels such as octane (C_8H_{18}) *can* burn, forming CO_2 a and releasing heat. When combustion reactions are started, they proceed *spontaneously* (i.e., on their own, further assistance), and we use them to provide energy to move vehicles, generate electricity, and heat hon offices. On the other hand, if we mix CO_2 and H_2O, there is nothing we can do to entice them to react sponta to form hydrocarbons. These reactions *cannot* take place on their own. If they could, our problems with fossil fuel supplies and greenhouse gas production could easily be solved.

Observations like those described above raise the fundamental question, "What determines whether or not a chemical reaction is possible when substances are combined?" The answer to this question is found in the study of thermodynamics, which expands on topics introduced in Chapter 6—energy changes in chemical reactions. As you will see, not only will we be able to use thermodynamics to determine the possibility of reaction, but we will find another explanation of chemical equilibrium and another way of finding equilibrium constants.

18.1   INTERNAL ENERGY CAN BE TRANSFERRED AS HEAT OR WORK, BUT IT CANNOT BE CREATED OR DESTROYED

Chemical thermodynamics is the study of the role of energy in chemical change and in determining the behavior of materials. It is based on a few laws that summarize centuries of experimental observation. Each law is a statement about relationships between energy, heat, work, and temperature. Because the laws manifest themselves in so many different ways, and underlie so many different phenomena, there are many alternative but equivalent ways to state them. For ease of reference, the laws are identified by number and are called the first law, the second law, and the third law.

The **first law of thermodynamics,** which was discussed in Chapter 6, states that internal energy may be transferred as heat or work but it cannot be created or destroyed. This law, you recall, serves as the foundation for Hess's law, which we used in our computations involving enthalpy changes in Chapter 6. Let's review the first law in more detail.

Recall that the **internal energy** of a system, which is given the symbol E, is the system's total energy—the sum of all the kinetic and potential energies of its particles. For a chemical reaction, a change in the internal energy, ΔE, is defined as

$$\Delta E = E_{\text{products}} - E_{\text{reactants}}$$

Thus, ΔE is positive if energy flows into a system and negative if energy flows out.

The first law of thermodynamics considers two ways by which energy can be exchanged between a system and its surroundings. One is by the absorption or release of heat, which is given the symbol q. The other involves **work, w.** If *work is done on a system,* as in the compression of a gas, the system gains and stores energy. Conversely, if *the system does work on the surroundings,* as when a gas expands and pushes a piston, the system loses some energy by changing part of its potential energy to kinetic energy which is transferred to the surroundings. The first law of thermodynamics expresses the net change in energy mathematically by the equation

$$\Delta E = q + w$$

In Chapter 6 you learned that a positive sign on an energy change indicates energy gained by the system, whereas a negative sign indicates energy lost by the system. Thus, when...

q is (+)	Heat is absorbed by the system.
q is (−)	Heat is released by the system.
w is (+)	Work is done on the system.
w is (−)	Work is done by the system.

In Chapter 6 you also learned that ΔE is a state function, which means that its value does not depend on how a change from one state to another is carried out. On the other hand, q and w are not state functions.

When a chemical system expands, it does pressure-volume work on the surroundings

There are two kinds of work that chemical systems can do (or have done on them) that are of concern to us. One is electrical work, which is examined in the next chapter and

□ *Thermo* implies heat, *dynamics* implies movement.

Expanding gases can do work. In a steam engine, such as the one powering this locomotive, heat is absorbed by water to turn it into high temperature, high pressure steam (q is positive). The steam then expands, pushing pistons and causing the locomotive to move. In the expansion, the steam does work and w is negative. *(Richard A. Cooke III/Stone/Getty Images.)*

□ ΔE = (heat input) + (work input)

FIG. 18.1 **Work being done on a gas.** When a gas is *compressed* by an external pressure, w is positive because work is done on the gas. Because V decreases when the gas is compressed, the negative sign on ΔV assures that w will be positive for the compression of a gas. *(Lawrence Manning/ Corbis Images.)*

will be discussed there. The other is work associated with the expansion or contraction of a system under the influence of an external pressure. An example is the work you perform on a gas when you compress it to fill a tire (Figure 18.1). Such "pressure–volume" or P–V work was discussed in Chapter 6 where it was shown that this kind of work is given by the equation

$$w = -P\Delta V$$

where P is the *external pressure* on the system.

If P–V work is the only kind of work involved in a chemical change, the equation for ΔE takes the form

$$\Delta E = q + (-P\Delta V) = q - P\Delta V$$

In Chapter 6 we also showed that when a reaction takes place in a container whose volume cannot change, the entire energy change must appear as heat. Therefore, ΔE is called the heat at constant volume (q_v)

$$\Delta E = q_v$$

Practice Exercise 1: Molecules of an ideal gas have no intermolecular attractions and therefore undergo no change in potential energy on expansion of the gas. If the expansion is also at constant temperature, there is no change in the kinetic energy, so the isothermal (constant temperature) expansion of an ideal gas has $\Delta E = 0$. Suppose such a gas expands at constant temperature from a volume of 1.0 L to 12.0 L against a constant opposing pressure of 14.0 atm. In units of L atm, what are q and w for this change? (Hints: Is the system doing work, or is work done on the system? What must be the sum of q and w in this case?)

Practice Exercise 2: If a gas is compressed under adiabatic conditions (allowing no transfer of heat to or from the surroundings) by application of an external pressure, the temperature of the gas increases. Why?

Gases become hot when compressed. Diesel engines are used to power large trucks and other heavy equipment such as this diesel locomotive. In the cylinders of a diesel engine, air is compressed rapidly to very small volumes, raising the temperature to the point where fuel ignites spontaneously when injected into it. *(John Griffin/The Image Works.)*

Enthalpy is a convenient state function for studying heats of reaction under constant pressure

Rarely do we carry out reactions in containers of fixed volume. Usually, reactions take place in containers open to the atmosphere where they are exposed to a constant pressure. To study heats of reactions under constant pressure conditions, enthalpy was invented. Recall that the **enthalpy, H,** is defined by the equation

$$H = E + PV$$

In Section 6.5 we showed that at constant pressure, the **enthalpy change, ΔH,** is equal to q_p

$$\Delta H = q_p$$

where q_p is the **heat of reaction at constant pressure.** Thus, the value of ΔH for a system equals the heat at constant pressure.

The pressure-volume work is the difference between ΔE and ΔH for a chemical reaction

In Chapter 6 we noted that ΔE and ΔH are not equal. They differ by the pressure–volume work, $-P\Delta V$.

$$\Delta E - \Delta H = -P\Delta V$$

☐ The ΔV values for reactions involving only solids and liquids are very tiny, so ΔE and ΔH for the reactions are nearly the same size.

The only time ΔE and ΔH differ by a significant amount is when gases are formed or consumed in a reaction, and even then they do not differ by much. To calculate

ΔE from ΔH (or ΔH from ΔE), we must have a way of calculating the pressure–volume work.

If we assume the gases in the reaction behave as ideal gases, then we can use the ideal gas law. Solved for V this is

$$V = \frac{nRT}{P}$$

A volume change can therefore be expressed as

$$\Delta V = \Delta\left(\frac{nRT}{P}\right)$$

For a change at constant pressure and temperature we can rewrite this as

$$\Delta V = \Delta n\left(\frac{RT}{P}\right)$$

Thus, when the reaction occurs, the volume change is caused by a change in the number of moles of *gas*. Of course, in chemical reactions not all reactants and products need be gases, so to be sure we compute Δn correctly, let's express the change in the number of moles of gas as Δn_{gas}. It's defined as

$$\Delta n_{gas} = (n_{gas})_{products} - (n_{gas})_{reactants}$$

The $P\Delta V$ product is, therefore,

$$P\Delta V = P \cdot \Delta n_{gas}\left(\frac{RT}{P}\right) = \Delta n_{gas}RT$$

Substituting into the equation for ΔH gives

$$\Delta H = \Delta E + \Delta n_{gas}RT \qquad (18.1)$$

TOOLS
Converting between ΔE and ΔH

The following example illustrates how small the difference is between ΔE and ΔH.

EXAMPLE 18.1
Conversion between ΔE and ΔH

The decomposition of calcium carbonate in limestone is used industrially to make carbon dioxide.

$$CaCO_3(s) \longrightarrow CaO(s) + CO_2(g)$$

The reaction is endothermic and has $\Delta H° = +571$ kJ. What is the value of $\Delta E°$ for this reaction?

ANALYSIS: The problem asks us to convert between ΔE and ΔH, so the tool we need to use is Equation 18.1. The superscript ° on ΔH and ΔE tells us the temperature is 25 °C (standard temperature for measuring heats of reaction). It is also important to remember that in calculating Δn_{gas}, we count just the numbers of moles of gas. Also, because we wish to calculate the term nRT in units of kilojoules, we will use $R = 8.314$ J mol^{-1} K^{-1}.

SOLUTION: The equation we need is

$$\Delta H = \Delta E + \Delta n_{gas}RT$$

Solving for ΔE and applying the superscript ° gives

$$\Delta E° = \Delta H° - \Delta n_{gas}RT$$

To calculate Δn_{gas} we take the coefficients in the equation to represent numbers of moles. Therefore, there is one mole of gas among the products and no moles of gas among the reactants, so

$$\Delta n_{gas} = 1 - 0 = 1$$

The temperature is 298 K, and $R = 8.314$ J mol^{-1} K^{-1}. Substituting,

$$\Delta E° = +571 \text{ kJ} - (1 \text{ mol})(8.314 \text{ J mol}^{-1} \text{ K}^{-1})(298 \text{ K})$$
$$= +571 \text{ kJ} - 2.48 \text{ kJ}$$
$$= +569 \text{ kJ}$$

Notice that $\Delta H°$ and $\Delta E°$ differ by only 2 kJ, which is approximately 0.4%.

IS THE ANSWER REASONABLE? A gas is formed in the reaction, so the system must expand and push against the opposing pressure of the atmosphere when the reaction occurs at constant pressure. Energy must be supplied to accomplish this. At constant volume this expansion would not be necessary; the pressure would simply increase. Therefore, decomposing the $CaCO_3$ should require more energy at constant pressure ($\Delta H°$) than at constant volume ($\Delta E°$) by an amount equal to the work done pushing back the atmosphere, and we see that $\Delta H°$ is larger than $\Delta E°$, so the answer is reasonable.

Practice Exercise 3: Calculate the difference, in kilojoules, between ΔE and ΔH for the following exothermic reaction at 45 °C. Which is more exothermic, ΔE or ΔH? (Hint: Note the temperature.)

$$2N_2O(g) + 3O_2(g) \longrightarrow 4NO_2(g)$$

Practice Exercise 4: The reaction

$$CaO(s) + 2HCl(g) \longrightarrow CaCl_2(s) + H_2O(g)$$

has $\Delta H° = -217.1$ kJ. Calculate $\Delta E°$ for this reaction. What is the percentage difference between $\Delta E°$ and $\Delta H°$?

18.2 | A SPONTANEOUS CHANGE IS A CHANGE THAT CONTINUES WITHOUT OUTSIDE INTERVENTION

Now that we've reviewed the way thermodynamics treats energy changes, we turn our attention to one of our main goals in studying this subject—finding relationships among the factors that control whether events are spontaneous. By **spontaneous change** we mean one that occurs by itself, without continuous outside assistance. Examples are water flowing over a waterfall and the melting of ice cubes in a cold drink on a warm day. These are events that proceed on their own.

Some spontaneous changes occur very rapidly. An example is the detonation of a stick of dynamite, or the exposure of photographic film. Other spontaneous events, such as the rusting of iron or the erosion of stone, occur slowly and many years may pass before a change is noticed. Still others occur at such an extremely slow rate under ordinary conditions that they appear not to be spontaneous at all. Gasoline–oxygen mixtures appear perfectly stable indefinitely at room temperature because under those conditions they react very slowly. However, if heated, their rate of reaction increases tremendously and they react explosively.

Each day we also witness events that are obviously *not* spontaneous. We may pass by a pile of bricks in the morning and later in the day find that they have become a brick wall. We know from experience that the wall didn't get there by itself. A pile of bricks becoming a brick wall is *not* spontaneous; it requires the intervention of a bricklayer. Similarly, the decomposition of water into hydrogen and oxygen is not spontaneous. We see water all the time and we know that it's stable. Nevertheless, we can cause water to decompose by passing an electric current through it in a process called *electrolysis* (Figure 18.2.)

$$2H_2O(l) \xrightarrow{\text{electrolysis}} 2H_2(g) + O_2(g)$$

This decomposition will continue, however, only as long as the electric current is maintained. As soon as the supply of electricity is cut off, the decomposition ceases. This example demonstrates the difference between spontaneous and nonspontaneous changes. Once

FIG. 18.2 The electrolysis of water produces H_2 and O_2 gases. It is a nonspontaneous change that only continues as long as electricity is supplied. *(Charles D. Winters/Photo Researchers.)*

a spontaneous event begins, it has a tendency to continue until it is finished. A nonspontaneous event, on the other hand, can continue only as long as it receives some sort of outside assistance.

Nonspontaneous changes have another common characteristic. They are able to occur only when accompanied by some spontaneous change. For example, a bricklayer consumes food, and a series of spontaneous biochemical reactions then occur that supply the necessary muscle power to build a wall. Similarly, the nonspontaneous electrolysis of water requires some sort of spontaneous mechanical or chemical change to generate the needed electricity. In short, *all nonspontaneous events occur at the expense of spontaneous ones.* Everything that happens can be traced, either directly or indirectly, to spontaneous changes.

☐ The driving of nonspontaneous reactions to completion by linking them to spontaneous ones is an important principle in biochemistry.

Reaction rate affects the apparent spontaneity of reactions

The reaction of gasoline vapor with oxygen mentioned above illustrates an important observation about spontaneous changes. Even though the reaction between these substances has a strong tendency to occur, and is therefore spontaneous, the *rate of the reaction* at room temperature is so slow that the mixture appears to be stable. In other words, the reaction *appears* to be nonspontaneous because its rate is so slow. There are many reactions in nature that are spontaneous but occur at such a slow rate that they aren't observed. Biochemical reactions often fall into this category. Without the presence of a catalyst (an enzyme), these reactions are so slow that effectively they do not occur. Living systems control their chemical reactions by selectively making enzymes available when spontaneous reactions or their products are needed.

The direction of spontaneous change is often but not always in the direction of lower energy

What determines the direction of spontaneous change? Let's begin by examining some everyday events such as those depicted in Figure 18.3. When iron rusts, heat is released, so the reaction lowers the internal energy of the system. Similarly, the chemical substances in the gasoline–oxygen mixture lose chemical energy by evolving heat as the gasoline burns to produce CO_2 and H_2O.

We might be tempted to conclude (as some nineteenth century chemists did) that spontaneous events occur in the direction of lowest energy, so that energy lowering is a

FIG. 18.3 **Three common spontaneous events.** Iron rusts, fuel burns, and an ice cube melts at room temperature. *(left: George B. Diebold/Corbis Images; center: Lowell J. Georgia/Photo Resarchers; right: Susumu Sato/Corbis Images).*

☐ Most, but not all, chemical reactions that are exothermic occur spontaneously.

"driving force" behind spontaneous change. For example, we may argue that when we drop a book, it falls to the floor because that lowers its potential energy. Since a change that lowers the potential energy of a system can be said to be exothermic, we can state this factor another way—*exothermic changes have a tendency to proceed spontaneously.*

Yet if this is so, how do we explain the third photograph in Figure 18.3? The melting of ice at room temperature is clearly a spontaneous process. But ice absorbs heat from the surroundings as it melts. This absorbed heat gives the water from the melted ice cube a higher internal energy than the original ice had. This is an example of a spontaneous but endothermic process. There are many other examples of spontaneous endothermic processes: the evaporation of water from a lake, the expansion of carbon dioxide gas into a vacuum, or the operation of a chemical "cold pack."

In Chapter 12 we discussed the solution process, and we said that one of the principal driving forces in the formation of a solution is the fact that the mixed state is much more probable than the unmixed state. It turns out that arguments like this can be used to explain the direction of any spontaneous process.

18.3 | SPONTANEOUS PROCESSES TEND TO PROCEED FROM STATES OF LOWER PROBABILITY TO STATES OF HIGHER PROBABILITY

In Chapter 6 you learned that when a hot object is placed in contact with a colder one, heat will flow spontaneously from the hot object to the colder one. But why? Energy can be conserved no matter which direction the heat flows.

To analyze what happens in the spontaneous flow of heat, let's imagine a situation in which we have two objects in contact with one another, one with a high temperature and the other with a low temperature. Because of the relationship between average kinetic energy and temperature, we expect the high temperature object to have many rapidly moving molecules, whereas the low temperature object will have more slow speed molecules. With these objects in contact, how likely is it that no energy will be transferred between them?

Where the objects touch, many of the molecular collisions will involve fast-moving "hot" molecules and slow-moving "cold" ones. In such a collision, it is very unlikely that the fast molecule will gain kinetic energy at the expense of the slow one. Instead, the fast molecule will lose kinetic energy and slow down, while the slow molecule will gain kinetic

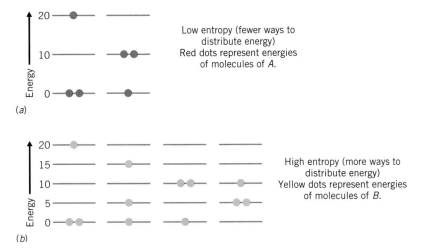

FIG. 18.4 A positive value for ΔS means an increase in the number of ways energy can be distributed among a system's molecules. Consider the reaction $A \longrightarrow B$, where A can take on energies that are multiples of 10 energy units, and B can take on energies that are multiples of 5 units. Suppose that the total energy of the reacting mixture is 20 units. (*a*) There are 2 ways to distribute 20 units of energy among 3 molecules of A. (*b*) There are 4 ways to distribute 20 units of energy among 3 molecules of B. The entropy of B is higher than the entropy of A because there are more ways to distribute the same amount of energy in B than in A.

energy and speed up. Over time, the result of many such collisions is that the hot object cools and the cool object warms. While this happens, the combined kinetic energy of the two objects becomes distributed over all the molecules in the system.

What we learn here is that heat flows because of the probable outcome of intermolecular collisions. Viewed on a larger scale, the uniform distribution of kinetic energy between the objects, caused by the flow of heat, is much more probable than a situation in which no heat flow occurs, which illustrates the role of probability in determining the direction of a spontaneous change. *Spontaneous processes tend to proceed from states of low probability to states of higher probability.* The higher probability states are those that allow more options for distributing energy among the molecules, so we can also say that *spontaneous processes tend to disperse energy.*

Entropy is a measure of the number of equivalent ways to distribute energy in the system

Because statistical probability is so important in determining the outcome of chemical and physical events, thermodynamics defines a quantity, called **entropy** (symbol S), that describes the number of equivalent ways that energy can be distributed in a system. The greater the number of energetically equivalent versions there are of the system, the larger is its statistical probability, and therefore the larger the value of the entropy (Figure 18.4).

☐ The greater the statistical probability of a particular state, the greater is the entropy.

(*a*) Two ways to count out $2 with paper money

(*b*) Five ways to count out $2 with 50¢ and 25¢ coins

Entropy. If energy were money, entropy would describe the number of different ways of counting it out. For example, there are only two ways of counting out $2 using American paper money. But there are five ways of counting out $2 using 50-cent and 25-cent coins. We could say that the "entropy" of a system that dealt in coins was higher than that of a system that dealt only in paper money.

In chemistry, we usually deal with systems that contain very large numbers of particles and it is usually impractical to count the number of ways that the particles can be arranged to produce a system with a particular energy. Fortunately, we will not need to do so. The entropy of the system can be related to experimental heat and temperature measurements.

Like enthalpy, entropy is a state function. It depends only on the state of the system, so an **entropy change, ΔS,** is independent of the path from start to finish. As with other thermodynamic quantities, ΔS is defined as "final minus initial" or "products minus reactants." Thus

$$\Delta S = S_{final} - S_{initial}$$

or, for a chemical system,

$$\Delta S = S_{products} - S_{reactants}$$

As you can see, when S_{final} is larger than $S_{initial}$ (or when $S_{products}$ is larger than $S_{reactants}$), the value of ΔS is positive. A positive value for ΔS means an increase in the number of energy-equivalent ways the system can be produced, and we have seen that this kind of change tends to be spontaneous. This leads to a general statement about entropy:

> Any event that is accompanied by an increase in the entropy of the system will have a *tendency* to occur spontaneously.

An increase in freedom of molecular motions corresponds to an increase in entropy

It is often possible to predict whether ΔS is positive or negative for a particular change. This is because several factors influence the magnitude of the entropy in predictable ways.

TOOLS

Factors affecting entropy: volume changes

Volume

For gases, the entropy increases with increasing volume, as illustrated in Figure 18.5. Below we see a gas confined to one side of a container, separated from a vacuum by a removable partition. Let's suppose the partition could be pulled away in an instant, as shown in Figure 18.5*b*. Now we find a situation in which all the molecules of the gas are at one end of a larger container. There are many more possible ways that the total kinetic energy can be distributed among the molecules in the larger volume. That makes the configuration in Figure 18.5*b* extremely unlikely. The gas expands spontaneously to achieve a more probable (higher entropy) particle distribution.

TOOLS

Factors affecting entropy: temperature changes

Temperature

The entropy is also affected by the temperature; the higher the temperature, the larger is the entropy. For example, when a substance is a solid at absolute zero, its particles are essentially motionless. There is relatively little kinetic energy, and so there are few ways to distribute kinetic energy among the particles; thus, the entropy of the solid is relatively low (Figure 18.6*a*).

FIG. 18.5 The expansion of a gas into a vacuum. (*a*) A gas in a container separated from a vacuum by a partition. (*b*) The gas at the moment the partition is removed. (*c*) The gas expands to achieve a more probable (higher entropy) particle distribution.

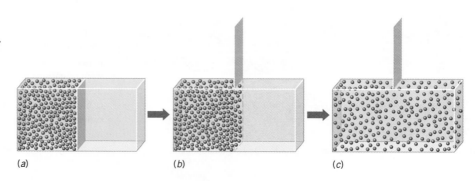

(*a*)   (*b*)   (*c*)

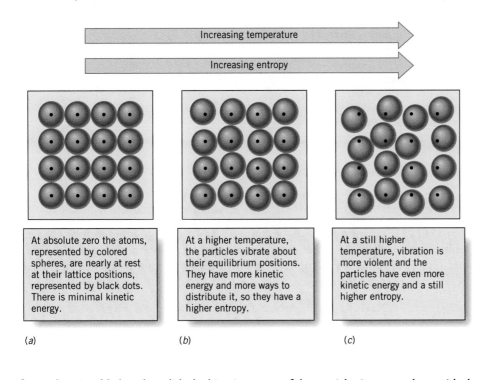

FIG. 18.6 Variation of entropy with temperature. (*a*) At absolute zero the atoms, represented by colored circles, rest at their equilibrium lattice positions, represented by black dots. Entropy is relatively low. (*b*) At a higher temperature, the particles vibrate about their equilibrium positions and there are more different ways to distribute kinetic energy among the molecules. Entropy is higher than in (*a*). (*c*) At a still higher temperature, vibration is more violent and at any instant the particles are found in even more arrangements. Entropy is higher than in (*b*).

If some heat is added to the solid, the kinetic energy of the particles increases along with the temperature. This causes the particles to move and vibrate within the crystal, so at a particular moment (pictured in Figure 18.6*b*) the particles are not found exactly at their lattice sites. There is more kinetic energy than at the lower temperature, and there are more ways to distribute it among the molecules, so the entropy is larger. If the temperature is raised further, the particles are given even more kinetic energy with an even larger number of possible ways to distribute it, causing the solid to have a still higher entropy (Figure 18.6*c*).

Physical state

One of the major factors that affects the entropy of a system is its physical state, which is demonstrated in Figure 18.7. Suppose that the diagrams represent ice, water, and steam at the same temperature. There is greater freedom of molecular movement in water than in ice at the same temperature, and so there are more ways to distribute kinetic energy among the molecules of liquid water than there are in ice. The water molecules in steam are free to move through the entire container. They are able to distribute their kinetic energies in a very large number of ways. In general, therefore, there are many more possible ways to distribute kinetic energy among gas molecules than there are in liquids and solids. In fact, a gas has such a large entropy compared with a liquid or solid that changes which produce gases from liquids or solids are almost always accompanied by increases in entropy.

TOOLS

Factors affecting entropy: physical state

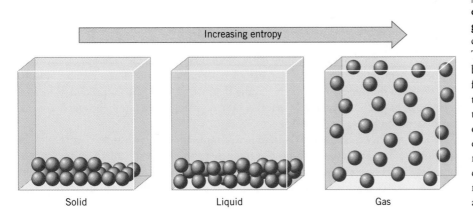

Solid | Liquid | Gas

FIG. 18.7 Comparison of the entropies of the solid, liquid, and gaseous states of a substance. The crystalline solid has a very low entropy. The liquid has a higher entropy because its molecules can move more freely and there are more ways to distribute kinetic energy among them. All the particles are still found at one end of the container. The gas has the highest entropy because the particles are randomly distributed throughout the entire container, so there are many, many ways to distribute kinetic energy among the molecules.

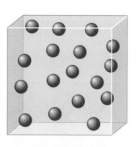

FIG. 18.8 Entropy is affected by number of particles. Adding additional particles to a system increases the number of ways that energy can be distributed in the system, so with all other things being equal, a reaction that produces more particles will have a positive value of ΔS.

Lower entropy　　Higher entropy

☐ As you will learn soon, absolute values for S can be obtained. This is entirely different from E and H, where we can only determine differences (i.e., ΔE and ΔH).

The sign of ΔS for a chemical reaction can sometimes be predicted by examining the chemical equation

When a chemical reaction produces or consumes gases, the sign of its entropy change is usually easy to predict. This is because the entropy of a gas is so much larger than that of either a liquid or solid. For example, the thermal decomposition of sodium bicarbonate produces two gases, CO_2 and H_2O.

$$2NaHCO_3(s) \xrightarrow{\text{heat}} Na_2CO_3(s) + CO_2(g) + H_2O(g)$$

Because the amount of gaseous products is larger than the amount of gaseous reactants, we can predict that the entropy change for the reaction is positive. On the other hand, the reaction

$$CaO(s) + SO_2(g) \longrightarrow CaSO_3(s)$$

(which can be used to remove sulfur dioxide from a gas mixture) has a negative entropy change.

TOOLS

Factors affecting entropy: number of particles

As the number of particles increases, the number of ways of distributing energy also increases

For chemical reactions, another major factor that affects the sign of ΔS is a change in the total number of molecules as the reaction proceeds. When more molecules are produced during a reaction, more ways of distributing the energy among the molecules are possible. *When all other things are equal, reactions that increase the number of particles in the system tend to have a positive entropy change*, as shown in Figure 18.8.

EXAMPLE 18.2
Predicting the Sign of ΔS

Predict the algebraic sign of ΔS for the reactions:

(a) $2NO_2(g) \longrightarrow N_2O_4(g)$
(b) $C_3H_8(g) + 5O_2(g) \longrightarrow 3CO_2(g) + 4H_2O(g)$

ANALYSIS: The tools we use in analyzing questions such as these are the factors that affect the entropy of a system. Thus, we look for changes in the number of moles of gas and changes in the number of particles on going from reactants to products.

SOLUTION: In reaction (a) we are forming fewer, more complex molecules (N_2O_4) from simpler ones (NO_2). Since we are forming fewer molecules, there are fewer ways to distribute energy among them, which means that the entropy must be decreasing. Therefore, ΔS must be negative. We reach the same conclusion by noting that one mole of gaseous product is formed from two moles of gaseous reactant. When there is a decrease in the number of moles of gas, the reaction tends to have a negative ΔS.

For reaction (b), we can count the number of molecules on both sides. On the left of the equation we have six molecules; on the right there are seven. There are more ways to distribute kinetic energy among seven molecules than among six, so for reaction (b), we expect ΔS to be positive. We reach the same conclusion by counting the number of moles of gas on both sides of the equation. On the left there are 6 moles of gas; on the right there are 7 moles of gas. Because the number of moles of gas is increasing, we expect ΔS to be positive.

ARE THE ANSWERS REASONABLE? The only check we can perform here is to carefully review our reasoning. It appears sound, so the answers appear to be correct.

Practice Exercise 5: Would you expect ΔS to be positive or negative for the following?

$$Ag^+(aq) + Cl^-(aq) \longrightarrow AgCl(s)$$

(Hint: How is the freedom of movement of the ions affected?)

Practice Exercise 6: Predict the sign of the entropy change for (a) the condensation of steam to liquid water and (b) the sublimation of a solid.

Practice Exercise 7: Predict the sign of ΔS for the following reactions:

(a) $2SO_2(g) + O_2(g) \longrightarrow 2SO_3(g)$
(b) $CO(g) + 2H_2(g) \longrightarrow CH_3OH(g)$

Practice Exercise 8: What is the expected sign of ΔS for the following reactions? Justify your answers.

(a) $2H_2(g) + O_2(g) \longrightarrow 2H_2O(l)$ (c) $Ca(OH)_2(s) \xrightarrow{H_2O} Ca^{2+}(aq) + 2OH^-(aq)$
(b) $N_2(g) + 3H_2(g) \longrightarrow 2NH_3(g)$

18.4 | ALL SPONTANEOUS PROCESSES INCREASE THE TOTAL ENTROPY OF THE UNIVERSE

You have learned that enthalpy and entropy are two factors that affect the spontaneity of a physical or chemical event. Sometimes they work together to favor a change, as in the combustion of gasoline where heat is given off (an exothermic change) and large volumes of gases are formed (an entropy increase).

In many situations, the enthalpy and entropy changes oppose each other, as in the melting of ice. Melting absorbs heat and is endothermic, which tends to make the process nonspontaneous. But the greater freedom of motion of the molecules that accompanies melting has the opposite effect and tends to make the change spontaneous.

When the enthalpy and entropy changes conflict, temperature becomes a critical factor that can influence the direction in which the change is spontaneous. For example, consider a mixture of solid ice and liquid water. If we attempt to raise the temperature of the mixture to 25 °C, all the solid will melt. At 25 °C the change *solid* $\longrightarrow$ *liquid* is spontaneous. On the other hand, if we attempt to cool the mixture to -25 °C, freezing occurs, so at -25 °C the opposite change (*liquid* $\longrightarrow$ *solid*) is spontaneous. *Thus, there are actually three factors that can influence spontaneity: the enthalpy change, the entropy change, and the temperature.* The balance between these factors comes into focus through the second law of thermodynamics.

The second law of thermodynamics states that all real processes increase the total entropy of the universe

One of the most far-reaching observations in science is incorporated into the **second law of thermodynamics,** which states, in effect, that *whenever a spontaneous event takes place in our universe, the total entropy of the universe increases* ($\Delta S_{total} > 0$). Notice that the increase in entropy that's referred to here is for the *total* entropy of the *universe* (system *plus* surroundings), not just the system alone. This means that a system's entropy can decrease, just as long as there is a larger increase in the entropy of the surroundings so that the *overall* entropy change is positive. Because everything that happens relies on spontaneous changes of some sort, the entropy of the universe is constantly rising.

Now let's examine more closely the total entropy change for the universe. As we've suggested, this quantity equals the sum of the entropy change for the system plus the entropy change for the surroundings.

$$\Delta S_{total} = \Delta S_{system} + \Delta S_{surroundings}$$

It can be shown that the entropy change for the surroundings is equal to the heat transferred *to* the surroundings *from* the system, $q_{surroundings}$, divided by the Kelvin temperature, T, at which it is transferred.

$$\Delta S_{surroundings} = \frac{q_{surroundings}}{T}$$

The law of conservation of energy requires that the heat transferred to the surroundings equals the negative of the heat added to the system, so we can write

$$q_{surroundings} = -q_{system}$$

In our study of the first law of thermodynamics we saw that for changes at constant temperature and pressure, $q_{system} = \Delta H$ for the system. By substitutions, therefore, we arrive at the relationship

$$\Delta S_{surroundings} = \frac{-\Delta H_{system}}{T}$$

and the entropy change for the entire universe becomes

$$\Delta S_{total} = \Delta S_{system} - \frac{\Delta H_{system}}{T}$$

By rearranging the right side of this equation, we obtain

$$\Delta S_{total} = \frac{T\Delta S_{system} - \Delta H_{system}}{T}$$

Now let's multiply both sides of the equation by T to give

$$T\Delta S_{total} = T\Delta S_{system} - \Delta H_{system}$$

or

$$T\Delta S_{total} = -(\Delta H_{system} - T\Delta S_{system})$$

Because ΔS_{total} must be positive for a spontaneous change, the quantity in parentheses, $(\Delta H_{system} - T\Delta S_{system})$, must be negative. Therefore, we can state that for a change to be spontaneous,

$$\Delta H_{system} - T\Delta S_{system} < 0 \qquad (18.2)$$

Equation 18.2 gives us a way of examining the balance between ΔH, ΔS, and temperature in determining the spontaneity of an event, and it becomes convenient at this point to introduce another thermodynamic state function. It is called the **Gibbs free energy, G,** named to honor one of America's greatest scientists, Josiah Willard Gibbs (1839–1903). (It's called **free energy** because it is related, as we will see later, to the maximum energy in a change that is "free" or "available" to do useful work.) The Gibbs free energy is defined as

☐ The origin of *free* in *free energy* is discussed in Section 18.7.

$$G = H - TS \qquad (18.3)$$

so for changes at constant T and P, the **Gibbs free energy change, ΔG,** becomes

TOOLS
Gibbs free energy

$$\Delta G = \Delta H - T\Delta S \qquad (18.4)$$

Because G is defined entirely in terms of state functions, it is also a state function. This means that

$$\Delta G = G_{final} - G_{initial} \qquad (18.5)$$

By comparing Equations 18.3 and 18.5, we arrive at the special importance of the free energy change:

> At constant temperature and pressure, a change can only be spontaneous if it is accompanied by a decrease in the free energy of the system.

In other words, for a change to be spontaneous, G_{final} must be less than G_{initial} and ΔG must be negative. With this in mind, we can now examine how ΔH, ΔS, and T are related in determining spontaneity.

When ΔH is negative and ΔS is positive, the process will be spontaneous

The combustion of octane (a component of gasoline),

$$2C_8H_{18}(l) + 25O_2(g) \longrightarrow 16CO_2(g) + 18H_2O(g)$$

is a very exothermic reaction. There is also a large increase in entropy because the number of particles in the system increases and large volumes of gases are formed. For this change, ΔH is negative and ΔS is positive, both of which favor spontaneity. Let's analyze how this affects the sign of ΔG.

$$\Delta H \text{ is negative } (-)$$
$$\Delta S \text{ is positive } (+)$$
$$\Delta G = \Delta H - T\Delta S$$
$$= (-) - [T(+)]$$

Notice that regardless of the Kelvin temperature, which must be a positive number, ΔG will be negative. This means that regardless of the temperature, such a change must be spontaneous. In fact, once started, fires will continue to consume all available fuel or oxygen at nearly any temperature because combustion reactions are always spontaneous (see Figure 18.9*a*).

When ΔH is positive and ΔS is negative, the process is not spontaneous

When a change is endothermic and is accompanied by a lowering of the entropy, both factors work against spontaneity.

TOOLS

ΔG as a predictor of spontaneity

☐ Reactions that occur with a free energy decrease are sometimes said to be **exergonic.** Those that occur with a free energy increase are sometimes said to be **endergonic.**

(a)

(b)

(c)

FIG. 18.9 **Process spontaneity can be predicted if ΔH, ΔS, and T are known.** (*a*) When ΔH is negative and ΔS is positive, as in any combustion reaction, the reaction is spontaneous at any temperature. (*b*) When ΔH is positive and ΔS is negative, the process is not spontaneous. Left to themselves, ash, carbon dioxide, and water will not spontaneously combine to form wood. (*c*) When ΔH and ΔS have the same sign, temperature determines whether the process is spontaneous or not. Water spontaneously becomes ice below 0 °C, and ice spontaneously melts into liquid water above 0 °C. (*left: Corbis images; center: Andrea Pistolesi/The Image Bank/Getty Images; right: John Berry/The Image Works*)

$$\Delta H \text{ is positive } (+)$$

$$\Delta S \text{ is negative } (-)$$

$$\Delta G = \Delta H - T\Delta S$$

$$= (+) - [T(-)]$$

Now, no matter what the temperature is, ΔG will be positive and the change must be nonspontaneous. An example would be carbon dioxide and water coming back together to form wood and oxygen again in a fire (Figure 18.9b).[1] If you saw such a thing happen on a film, experience would tell you that the film was being played backward.

When ΔH and ΔS have the same sign, temperature determines spontaneity

When ΔH and ΔS have the same algebraic sign, the temperature becomes the determining factor in controlling spontaneity. If ΔH and ΔS are both positive, then

$$\Delta G = (+) - [T(+)]$$

Thus, ΔG is the difference between two positive quantities, ΔH and $T\Delta S$. This difference will only be negative if the term $T\Delta S$ is larger in magnitude than ΔH, and this will only be true when the temperature is high. In other words, *when ΔH and ΔS are both positive, the change will be spontaneous at high temperature but not at low temperature.* A change noted above is the melting of ice.

$$H_2O(s) \longrightarrow H_2O(l)$$

This is a change that is endothermic and also accompanied by an increase in entropy. We know that at high temperatures (above 0 °C) melting is spontaneous, but at low temperatures (below 0 °C) it is not.

For similar reasons, when ΔH and ΔS are both negative, ΔG will be negative (and the change spontaneous) only when the temperature is low.

$$\Delta G = (-) - [T(-)]$$

Only when the negative value of ΔH is larger in magnitude than the negative value of $T\Delta S$ will ΔG be negative. Such a change is only spontaneous at low temperatures. An example is the freezing of water (see Figure 18.9c).

$$H_2O(l) \longrightarrow H_2O(s)$$

This is an exothermic change that is accompanied by a decrease in entropy; it is only spontaneous at low temperatures (i.e., below 0 °C).

Figure 18.10 summarizes the effects of the signs of ΔH and ΔS on ΔG, and hence on the spontaneity of physical and chemical events.

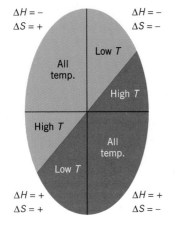

$\Delta H = -$
$\Delta S = +$

$\Delta H = -$
$\Delta S = -$

Low T

All temp.

High T

High T

All temp.

Low T

$\Delta H = +$
$\Delta S = +$

$\Delta H = +$
$\Delta S = -$

■ Spontaneous
■ Nonspontaneous

FIG. 18.10 Summary of the effects of the signs of ΔH and ΔS on spontaneity as a function of temperature. When ΔH and ΔS have the same sign, spontaneity is determined by the temperature.

18.5 | THE THIRD LAW OF THERMODYNAMICS MAKES EXPERIMENTAL MEASUREMENT OF ABSOLUTE ENTROPIES POSSIBLE

Earlier we described how the entropy of a substance depends on temperature, and we noted that at absolute zero the order within a crystal is a maximum and the entropy is a minimum. The **third law of thermodynamics** goes one step further by stating: *At absolute zero the entropy of a perfectly ordered pure crystalline substance is zero.*

$$S = 0 \quad \text{at} \quad T = 0 \text{ K}$$

[1] Plants can manufacture wood from carbon dioxide and water that they take in, but the reaction by itself is *not* spontaneous. Plant cells manufacture wood by coupling the nonspontaneous reaction to a complex series of reactions with negative values of ΔG, so that the entire chain of reactions *taken together* is spontaneous overall. The same trick is used to drive nonspontaneous processes forward in human cells. The high negative free energy change from the breakdown of sugar and other nutrients is coupled with the nonspontaneous synthesis of complex proteins from simple starting materials, driving cell growth and making life possible.

TABLE 18.1	Standard Entropies of Some Typical Substances at 298.15 K		
Substance	$S°$ (J mol^{-1} K^{-1})	Substance	$S°$ (J mol^{-1} K^{-1})
Ag(s)	42.55	$H_2O(g)$	188.7
AgCl(s)	96.2	$H_2O(l)$	69.96
Al(s)	28.3	HCl(g)	186.7
$Al_2O_3(s)$	51.00	$HNO_3(l)$	155.6
C(s, graphite)	5.69	$H_2SO_4(l)$	157
CO(g)	197.9	$HC_2H_3O_2(l)$	160
$CO_2(g)$	213.6	Hg(l)	76.1
$CH_4(g)$	186.2	Hg(g)	175
$CH_3Cl(g)$	234.2	K(s)	64.18
$CH_3OH(l)$	126.8	KCl(s)	82.59
$CO(NH_2)_2(s)$	104.6	$K_2SO_4(s)$	176
$CO(NH_2)_2(aq)$	173.8	$N_2(g)$	191.5
$C_2H_2(g)$	200.8	$NH_3(g)$	192.5
$C_2H_4(g)$	219.8	$NH_4Cl(s)$	94.6
$C_2H_6(g)$	229.5	NO(g)	210.6
$C_2H_5OH(l)$	161	$NO_2(g)$	240.5
$C_8H_{18}(l)$	466.9	$N_2O(g)$	220.0
Ca(s)	41.4	$N_2O_4(g)$	304
$CaCO_3(s)$	92.9	Na(s)	51.0
$CaCl_2(s)$	114	$Na_2CO_3(s)$	136
CaO(s)	40	$NaHCO_3(s)$	102
$Ca(OH)_2(s)$	76.1	NaCl(s)	72.38
$CaSO_4(s)$	107	NaOH(s)	64.18
$CaSO_4 \cdot \frac{1}{2}H_2O(s)$	131	$Na_2SO_4(s)$	149.49
$CaSO_4 \cdot 2H_2O(s)$	194.0	$O_2(g)$	205.0
$Cl_2(g)$	223.0	PbO(s)	67.8
Fe(s)	27	S(s)	31.9
$Fe_2O_3(s)$	90.0	$SO_2(g)$	248.5
$H_2(g)$	130.6	$SO_3(g)$	256.2

Because we know the point at which entropy has a value of zero, it is possible by *experimental measurement* and calculation to determine the total amount of entropy that a substance has at temperatures above 0 K. If the entropy of one mole of a substance is determined at a temperature of 298 K (25 °C) and a pressure of 1 atm, we call it the **standard entropy, $S°$.** Table 18.1 lists the standard entropies for a number of substances.[2] (Notice that entropy has the dimensions of energy/temperature (i.e., joules per kelvin); this is explained in Facets of Chemistry 18.1).

☐ 25 °C and 1 atm are the same standard conditions we used in our discussion of $\Delta H°$ in Chapter 6.

Once we have the entropies of a variety of substances, we can calculate the **standard entropy change, $\Delta S°$,** for chemical reactions in much the same way as we calculated $\Delta H°$ in Chapter 6.

$$\Delta S° = \text{(sum of } S° \text{ of the products)} - \text{(sum of } S° \text{ of the reactants)} \quad (18.6)$$

T૭OLS

Standard entropies

If the reaction we are working with happens to correspond to the formation of 1 mol of a compound from its elements, then the $\Delta S°$ that we calculate can be referred to as the **standard entropy of formation, $\Delta S_f°$.** Values of $\Delta S_f°$ are not tabulated, however; if we need them for some purpose, we must calculate them from tabulated values of $S°$.

☐ This is simply a Hess's law type of calculation. Note, however, that elements have nonzero $S°$ values, which must be included in the bookkeeping.

[2] In our earlier discussions of standard states (Chapter 6) we defined the *standard pressure* as 1 atm. This was the original pressure unit used by thermodynamicists. In the SI, however, the recognized unit of pressure is the pascal (Pa), not the atmosphere. After considerable discussion, the SI adopted the *bar* as the standard pressure for thermodynamic quantities: 1 bar = 10^5 Pa. One bar differs from one atmosphere by only 1.3%, and for thermodynamic quantities that we deal with in this text, their values at 1 atm and at 1 bar differ by an insignificant amount. Since most available thermodynamic data are still specified at 1 atm rather than 1 bar, we shall continue to use 1 atm for the standard pressure.

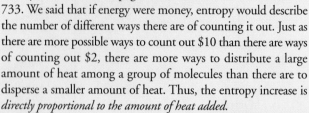

FACETS OF CHEMISTRY 18.1

Why the Units of Entropy Are Energy/Temperature

Entropy is a state function, just like enthalpy, so the value of ΔS doesn't depend on the "path" that is followed during a change. In other words, we can proceed from one state to another in any way we like and ΔS will be the same. If we choose a *reversible path* in which just a slight alteration in the system can change the direction of the process, we can measure ΔS directly. For example, at 25 °C an ice cube will melt and there is nothing we can do at that temperature to stop it. This change is *nonreversible* in the sense described above, so we couldn't use this path to measure ΔS. At 0 °C, however, it is simple to stop the melting process and reverse its direction. At 0 °C the melting of ice is a reversible process.

If we set up a change so that it is reversible, we can calculate the entropy change as $\Delta S = q/T$, where q is the heat added to the substance and T is the temperature at which the heat is added. The more energy we add to the system as heat, the more possible ways there are to distribute it among the molecules. To understand this, let's use the analogy between energy and money that we used on page 733. We said that if energy were money, entropy would describe the number of different ways there are of counting it out. Just as there are more possible ways to count out $10 than there are ways of counting out $2, there are more ways to distribute a large amount of heat among a group of molecules than there are to disperse a smaller amount of heat. Thus, the entropy increase is *directly proportional to the amount of heat added.*

Temperature also affects the size of the entropy increase. To see why, study Figure 18.6. At lower temperatures, the entropy of a material is low, so the change in entropy produced when a given amount of heat is added to the material will be greater than it would have been at higher temperatures. The low temperature material can distribute the energy in more ways than the higher temperature material can. For a given quantity of heat the entropy change is *inversely proportional to the temperature.* Thus, $\Delta S = q/T$, and entropy has units of energy divided by temperature (e.g., J K^{-1}).

EXAMPLE 18.3
Calculating $\Delta S°$ from Standard Entropies

Urea (a compound found in urine) is manufactured commercially from CO_2 and NH_3. One of its uses is as a fertilizer where it reacts slowly with water in the soil to produce ammonia and carbon dioxide. The ammonia provides a source of nitrogen for growing plants.

$$CO(NH_2)_2(aq) + H_2O(l) \longrightarrow CO_2(g) + 2NH_3(g)$$
$$\text{urea}$$

What is the standard entropy change when one mole of urea reacts with water?

ANALYSIS: This problem is a straightforward application of Equation 18.6 as a tool to compute the standard entropy change for the reaction. We'll need the standard entropies $S°$ of each reactant and product. The data we need can be found in Table 18.1 and are collected in the table below.

Substance	$S°$ (J/mol K)
$CO(NH_2)_2(aq)$	173.8
$H_2O(l)$	69.96
$CO_2(g)$	213.6
$NH_3(g)$	192.5

SOLUTION: Applying Equation 18.6, we have

$$\Delta S° = [S°_{CO_2(g)} + 2S°_{NH_3(g)}] - [S°_{CO(NH_2)_2(aq)} + S°_{H_2O(l)}]$$

$$= \left[1 \text{ mol} \times \left(\frac{213.6 \text{ J}}{\text{mol K}} \right) + 2 \text{ mol} \times \left(\frac{192.5 \text{ J}}{\text{mol K}} \right) \right]$$

$$- \left[1 \text{ mol} \times \left(\frac{173.8 \text{ J}}{\text{mol K}} \right) + 1 \text{ mol} \times \left(\frac{69.96 \text{ J}}{\text{mol K}} \right) \right]$$

$$= (598.6 \text{ J/K}) - (243.8 \text{ J/K})$$

$$= 354.8 \text{ J/K}$$

☐ Notice that the unit *mol* cancels in each term, so the units of $\Delta S°$ are joules per kelvin.

Thus, the standard entropy change for this reaction is $+354.8$ J/K (which we can also write as $+354.8$ J K^{-1}).

IS THE ANSWER REASONABLE? In the reaction, gases are formed from liquid reactants. Since gases have much larger entropies than liquids, we expect $\Delta S°$ to be positive, which agrees with our answer.

Practice Exercise 9: Calculate $\Delta S_f°$ for $NH_3(g)$. (Hint: Write the equation for the reaction.)

Practice Exercise 10: Calculate the standard entropy change, $\Delta S°$, in J K^{-1} for the following:

(a) $CaO(s) + 2HCl(g) \longrightarrow CaCl_2(s) + H_2O(l)$
(b) $C_2H_4(g) + H_2(g) \longrightarrow C_2H_6(g)$

18.6 | THE STANDARD FREE ENERGY CHANGE, ΔG°, IS ΔG AT STANDARD CONDITIONS

When ΔG is determined at 25 °C (298 K) and 1 atm, we call it the **standard free energy change, ΔG°**.[3] There are several ways of obtaining $\Delta G°$ for a reaction. One of them is to compute $\Delta G°$ from $\Delta H°$ and $\Delta S°$.

$$\Delta G° = \Delta H° - (298.15 \text{ K})\Delta S°$$

Experimental measurement of $\Delta G°$ is also possible, but we will discuss how this is done later.

TOOLS

Calculating $\Delta G°$ from $\Delta H°$ and $\Delta S°$

EXAMPLE 18.4
Calculating $\Delta G°$ from $\Delta H°$ and $\Delta S°$

Calculate $\Delta G°$ for the reaction of urea with water from values of $\Delta H°$ and $\Delta S°$.

$$CO(NH_2)_2(aq) + H_2O(l) \longrightarrow CO_2(g) + 2NH_3(g)$$

ANALYSIS: We can calculate $\Delta G°$ with the equation

$$\Delta G° = \Delta H° - T\Delta S°$$

To calculate $\Delta H°$, we can use Hess's law as a tool with the data in Table 6.2. To obtain $\Delta S°$, we normally would need to do a similar calculation using Equation 18.6 as a tool with data from Table 18.1. However, we already performed this calculation in Example 18.3.

SOLUTION: First we calculate $\Delta H°$ from data in Table 6.2.

$$\Delta H° = [\Delta H_{f\ CO_2(g)}° + 2\Delta H_{f\ NH_3(g)}°] - [\Delta H_{f\ CO(NH_2)_2(aq)}° + \Delta H_{f\ H_2O(l)}°]$$

$$= \left[1 \text{ mol} \times \left(\frac{-393.5 \text{ kJ}}{\text{mol}} \right) + 2 \text{ mol} \times \left(\frac{-46.19 \text{ kJ}}{\text{mol}} \right) \right]$$

$$- \left[1 \text{ mol} \times \left(\frac{-319.2 \text{ kJ}}{\text{mol}} \right) + 1 \text{ mol} \times \left(\frac{-285.9 \text{ kJ}}{\text{mol}} \right) \right]$$

$$= (-485.9 \text{ kJ}) - (-605.1 \text{ kJ})$$

$$= +119.2 \text{ kJ}$$

In Example 18.3 we found $\Delta S°$ to be +354.8 J K^{-1}. To calculate $\Delta G°$ we also need the Kelvin temperature, which we must express to at least four significant figures to match the number of significant figures in $\Delta S°$. Since standard temperature is *exactly* 25 °C, $T = (25.00 + 273.15)$ K $= 298.15$ K. Also, we must be careful to express $\Delta H°$ and $T\Delta S°$ in the same energy units, so

---

[3] Sometimes, the temperature is specified as a subscript in writing the symbol for the standard free energy change. For example, $\Delta G°$ can also be written $\Delta G_{298}°$. As you will see later, there are times when it is desirable to indicate the temperature explicitly.

□ 354.8 J K^{-1} = 0.3548 kJ K^{-1} we'll change the units of the entropy change to give $\Delta S° = +0.3548$ kJ K^{-1}. Substituting into the equation for $\Delta G°$,

$$\Delta G° = +119.2\text{ kJ} - (298.15\ \cancel{K})(0.3548\text{ kJ}\ \cancel{K^{-1}})$$
$$= +119.2\text{ kJ} - 105.8\text{ kJ}$$
$$= +13.4\text{ kJ}$$

Therefore, for this reaction, $\Delta G° = +13.4$ kJ.

IS THE ANSWER REASONABLE? We can estimate that the second term will be approximately 100, so the answer should be small, which it is. The answer is therefore reasonable.

Practice Exercise 11: Calculate $\Delta G_f°$ for N_2O_4 from $\Delta H_f°$ and $\Delta S_f°$ for N_2O_4. (Hint: Write the chemical equation.)

Practice Exercise 12: Use the data in Table 6.2 and Table 18.1 to calculate $\Delta G_f°$ for the formation of iron(III) oxide (the iron oxide in rust). The equation for the reaction is

$$4Fe(s) + 3O_2(g) \longrightarrow 2Fe_2O_3(s)$$

In Section 6.8 you learned that it is useful to have tabulated standard heats of formation, $\Delta H_f°$, because they can be used with Hess's law to calculate $\Delta H°$ for many different reactions. Standard free energies of formation, $\Delta G_f°$, can be used in similar calculations to obtain $\Delta G°$.

TOOLS
Using $\Delta G_f°$ values

$$\Delta G° = (\text{sum of }\Delta G_f°\text{ of products}) - (\text{sum of }\Delta G_f°\text{ of reactants}) \qquad (18.7)$$

The $\Delta G_f°$ values for some typical substances are found in Table 18.2. Example 18.5 shows how we can use them to calculate $\Delta G°$ for a reaction.

EXAMPLE 18.5
Calculating $\Delta G°$ from $\Delta G_f°$

Ethanol, C_2H_5OH (also called ethyl alcohol), is made from grain by fermentation and is used as an additive to gasoline to produce a fuel mix called E85 (85% ethanol, 15% gasoline). What is $\Delta G°$ for the combustion of liquid ethanol to give $CO_2(g)$ and $H_2O(g)$?

ANALYSIS: Our tool is Equation 18.7. To use it we will need the balanced chemical equation for the reaction and $\Delta G_f°$ for each reactant and product. The free energy data are available in Table 18.2.

SOLUTION: First, we construct the balanced equation for the reaction.

$$C_2H_5OH(l) + 3O_2(g) \longrightarrow 2CO_2(g) + 3H_2O(g)$$

Applying Equation 18.7, we have

$$\Delta G° = [2\Delta G_{f\,CO_2(g)}° + 3\Delta G_{f\,H_2O(g)}°] - [\Delta G_{f\,C_2H_5OH(l)}° + 3\Delta G_{f\,O_2(g)}°]$$

As with $\Delta H_f°$, the $\Delta G_f°$ for any element in its standard state is zero. Therefore, using the data from Table 18.2,

(© AP/Wide World Photos.)

$$\Delta G° = \left[2\ \cancel{mol} \times \left(\frac{-394.4\text{ kJ}}{\cancel{mol}}\right) + 3\ \cancel{mol} \times \left(\frac{-228.6\text{ kJ}}{\cancel{mol}}\right)\right]$$
$$- \left[1\ \cancel{mol} \times \left(\frac{-174.8\text{ kJ}}{\cancel{mol}}\right) + 3\ \cancel{mol} \times \left(\frac{0\text{ kJ}}{\cancel{mol}}\right)\right]$$
$$= (-1474.6\text{ kJ}) - (-174.8\text{ kJ})$$
$$= -1299.8\text{ kJ}$$

The standard free energy change for the reaction equals -1299.8 kJ.

IS THE ANSWER REASONABLE? As before, there's no easy way to estimate the answer. To check your answer, be sure you've got the correct algebraic sign for each term.

Practice Exercise 13: Calculate $\Delta G°$ for the reaction of iron(III) oxide with carbon monoxide to give elemental iron and carbon dioxide. (Hint: Be careful writing the chemical equation.)

Practice Exercise 14: Calculate $\Delta G°_{reaction}$ in kilojoules for the following reactions using the data in Table 18.2.

(a) $2NO(g) + O_2(g) \longrightarrow 2NO_2(g)$

(b) $Ca(OH)_2(s) + 2HCl(g) \longrightarrow CaCl_2(s) + 2H_2O(g)$

18.7	*ΔG* IS THE MAXIMUM AMOUNT OF WORK THAT CAN BE DONE BY A PROCESS

One of the chief uses of spontaneous chemical reactions is the production of useful work. For example, fuels are burned in gasoline or diesel engines to power automobiles and heavy machinery, and chemical reactions in batteries start our autos and run all sorts of modern electronic gadgets, including cellular phones, beepers, and laptop computers.

TABLE 18.2	**Standard Free Energies of Formation of Typical Substances at 298.15 K**		
Substance	$\Delta G_f°$ (kJ mol^{-1})	Substance	$\Delta G_f°$ (kJ mol^{-1})
$Ag(s)$	0	$H_2O(g)$	-228.6
$AgCl(s)$	-109.7	$H_2O(l)$	-237.2
$Al(s)$	0	$HCl(g)$	-95.27
$Al_2O_3(s)$	-1576.4	$HNO_3(l)$	-79.91
$C(s, \text{graphite})$	0	$H_2SO_4(l)$	-689.9
$CO(g)$	-137.3	$HC_2H_3O_2(l)$	-392.5
$CO_2(g)$	-394.4	$Hg(l)$	0
$CH_4(g)$	-50.79	$Hg(g)$	$+31.8$
$CH_3Cl(g)$	-58.6	$K(s)$	0
$CH_3OH(l)$	-166.2	$KCl(s)$	-408.3
$CO(NH_2)_2(s)$	-197.2	$K_2SO_4(s)$	-1316.4
$CO(NH_2)_2(aq)$	-203.8	$N_2(g)$	0
$C_2H_2(g)$	$+209$	$NH_3(g)$	-16.7
$C_2H_4(g)$	$+68.12$	$NH_4Cl(s)$	-203.9
$C_2H_6(g)$	-32.9	$NO(g)$	$+86.69$
$C_2H_5OH(l)$	-174.8	$NO_2(g)$	$+51.84$
$C_8H_{18}(l)$	$+17.3$	$N_2O(g)$	$+103.6$
$Ca(s)$	0	$N_2O_4(g)$	$+98.28$
$CaCO_3(s)$	-1128.8	$Na(s)$	0
$CaCl_2(s)$	-750.2	$Na_2CO_3(s)$	-1048
$CaO(s)$	-604.2	$NaHCO_3(s)$	-851.9
$Ca(OH)_2(s)$	-896.76	$NaCl(s)$	-384.0
$CaSO_4(s)$	-1320.3	$NaOH(s)$	-382
$CaSO_4 \cdot \frac{1}{2}H_2O(s)$	-1435.2	$Na_2SO_4(s)$	-1266.8
$CaSO_4 \cdot 2H_2O(s)$	-1795.7	$O_2(g)$	0
$Cl_2(g)$	0	$PbO(s)$	-189.3
$Fe(s)$	0	$S(s)$	0
$Fe_2O_3(s)$	-741.0	$SO_2(g)$	-300.4
$H_2(g)$	0	$SO_3(g)$	-370.4

☐ Gas and diesel engines are not very efficient, so most of the energy produced in the combustion of fuel appears as heat, not work. That's why these engines require cooling systems.

When chemical reactions occur, however, their energy is not always harnessed to do work. For instance, if gasoline is burned in an open dish, the energy evolved is lost entirely as heat and no useful work is accomplished. Engineers, therefore, seek ways to capture as much energy as possible in the form of work. One of their primary goals is to maximize the efficiency with which chemical energy is converted to work and to minimize the amount of energy transferred unproductively to the environment as heat.

Scientists have discovered that the maximum conversion of chemical energy to work occurs if a reaction is carried out under conditions that are said to be thermodynamically reversible. A process is defined as **thermodynamically reversible** if its driving force is opposed by another force that is just the slightest bit weaker, so that the slightest increase in the opposing force will cause the direction of the change to be reversed. An example of a nearly reversible process is illustrated in Figure 18.11, where we have a compressed gas in a cylinder pushing against a piston that's held in place by liquid water above it. If a water molecule evaporates, the external pressure drops slightly and the gas can expand just a bit, performing a small amount of work. Gradually, as one water molecule after another evaporates, the gas inside the cylinder slowly expands and performs work on the surroundings. At any time, however, the process can be reversed by the condensation of a water molecule.[4]

Although we could obtain the maximum work by carrying out a change reversibly, a thermodynamically reversible process requires so many steps that it proceeds at an extremely slow speed. If the work cannot be done at a reasonable rate, it is of little value to us. Our goal, then, is to approach thermodynamic reversibility for maximum efficiency, but to carry out the change at a pace that will deliver work at acceptable rates.

The relationship of useful work to thermodynamic reversibility was illustrated earlier (Section 6.5) in our discussion of the discharge of an automobile battery. Recall that when the battery is shorted with a heavy wrench, no work is done and all the energy appears as heat. In this case there is nothing opposing the discharge, and it occurs in the most thermodynamically irreversible manner possible. However, when the current is passed through a small electric motor, the motor itself offers resistance to the passage of the electricity and the discharge takes place slowly. In this instance, the discharge occurs in a more nearly thermodynamically reversible manner because of the opposition provided by the motor, and a relatively large amount of the available energy appears in the form of the work accomplished by the motor.

The preceding discussion leads naturally to the question: Is there a limit to the amount of the available energy in a reaction that can be harnessed as useful work? The answer to this question is to be found in the Gibbs free energy.

FIG. 18.11 **A reversible expansion of a gas.** As water molecules evaporate one at a time, the external pressure gradually decreases and the gas slowly expands, performing a small amount of work in each step. The process would be reversed if a molecule of water were to condense into the liquid. The ability of the expansion to be reversed by the slightest increase in the opposing pressure is what makes this a reversible process.

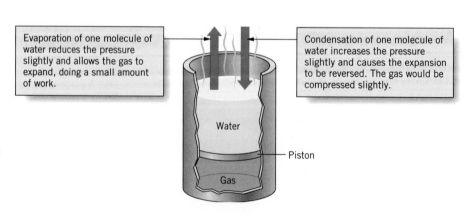

Evaporation of one molecule of water reduces the pressure slightly and allows the gas to expand, doing a small amount of work.

Condensation of one molecule of water increases the pressure slightly and causes the expansion to be reversed. The gas would be compressed slightly.

Water

Piston

Gas

[4] Although we sometimes say that a chemical reaction is "reversible" because it can run in both the forward and reverse directions, we cannot say the reaction is *thermodynamically reversible* unless the concentrations are only infinitesimally different from their equilibrium values as the reaction occurs.

> The maximum amount of energy produced by a reaction that can be *theoretically* harnessed as work is equal to ΔG.

This is the energy that need not be lost to the surroundings as heat and is therefore *free* to be used for work. Thus, by determining the value of ΔG, we can find out whether or not a given reaction will be an effective source of useful energy. Also, by comparing the actual amount of work derived from a given system with the ΔG values for the reactions involved, we can measure the efficiency of the system.

EXAMPLE 18.6
Calculating Maximum Work

Calculate the maximum work available, expressed in kilojoules, from the oxidation of 1 mol of octane, $C_8H_{18}(l)$, by oxygen to give $CO_2(g)$ and $H_2O(l)$ at 25 °C and 1 atm.

ANALYSIS: The maximum work is equal to ΔG for the reaction. Standard thermodynamic conditions are specified, so we need to calculate $\Delta G°$. The tool for this is Equation 18.7.

SOLUTION: First we need a balanced equation for the reaction. For the combustion of one mole of C_8H_{18} we have

$$C_8H_{18}(l) + 12\tfrac{1}{2}O_2(g) \longrightarrow 8CO_2(g) + 9H_2O(l)$$

Then we apply Equation 18.7.

$$\Delta G° = [8\Delta G°_{f\ CO_2(g)} + 9\Delta G°_{f\ H_2O(l)}] - [\Delta G°_{f\ C_8H_{18}(l)} + 12.5\Delta G°_{f\ O_2(g)}]$$

Referring to Table 18.2 and dropping the canceled mol units,

$$\Delta G° = [8 \times (-394.4)\ kJ + 9 \times (-237.2)\ kJ] - [1 \times (+17.3)\ kJ + 12.5 \times (0)\ kJ]$$
$$= (-5290\ kJ) - (+17.3\ kJ)$$
$$= -5307\ kJ$$

Thus, at 25 °C and 1 atm, we can expect no more than 5307 kJ of work from the oxidation of 1 mol of C_8H_{18}.

IS THE ANSWER REASONABLE? Be sure to check the algebraic signs of each of the terms in the calculation.

Practice Exercise 15: Calculate the maximum work that could be obtained from the combustion of 100 g of ethanol, $C_2H_5OH(l)$. How does it compare with the maximum work from the combustion of 100 g of $C_8H_{18}(l)$? Which is the better fuel? (Hint: The work available *per mole* has already been calculated in the worked examples.)

Practice Exercise 16: Calculate the maximum work that could be obtained at 25 °C and 1 atm from the oxidation of 1.00 mol of aluminum by $O_2(g)$ to give $Al_2O_3(s)$. (The oxidation of aluminum to aluminum oxide in booster rockets provides part of the energy that lifts the space shuttle off its launching pad.)

Blastoff of the space shuttle.
The large negative heat of formation of Al_2O_3 provides power to the solid booster rockets that lift the space shuttle from its launch pad. *(Courtesy Lockheed Missile and Space Co., Inc.)*

18.8 | ΔG IS ZERO WHEN A SYSTEM IS AT EQUILIBRIUM

We have seen that when the value of ΔG for a given change is negative, the change occurs spontaneously. We have also seen that a change is nonspontaneous when ΔG is positive. However, when ΔG is neither positive nor negative, the change is neither spontaneous nor nonspontaneous—the system is in a state of equilibrium. This occurs when ΔG is equal to zero.

> When a system is in a state of dynamic equilibrium,
>
> $$G_{\text{products}} = G_{\text{reactants}} \quad \text{and} \quad \Delta G = 0$$

Let's again consider the freezing of water.

$$H_2O(l) \rightleftharpoons H_2O(s)$$

Below 0 °C, ΔG for this change is negative and the freezing is spontaneous. On the other hand, above 0 °C we find that ΔG is positive and freezing is nonspontaneous. When the temperature is exactly 0 °C, $\Delta G = 0$ and an ice–water mixture exists in a condition of equilibrium. As long as heat isn't added or removed from the system, neither freezing nor melting is spontaneous and the ice and liquid water can exist together indefinitely.

No work can be done by a system at equilibrium

We have identified ΔG as a quantity that specifies the amount of work that is available from a system. Since ΔG is zero at equilibrium, the amount of work available is zero also. Therefore, when a system is at equilibrium, no work can be extracted from it. As an example, consider again the common lead storage battery that we use to start our car.

When the battery is fully charged, there are virtually no products of the discharge reaction present. The chemical reactants, however, are present in large amounts. Therefore, the total free energy of the reactants far exceeds the total free energy of products and, since $\Delta G = G_{\text{products}} - G_{\text{reactants}}$, the ΔG of the system has a large negative value. This means that a lot of energy is available to do work. As the battery discharges, the reactants are converted to products and G_{products} gets larger while $G_{\text{reactants}}$ gets smaller; thus ΔG becomes less negative, and less energy is available to do work. Finally, the battery reaches equilibrium. The total free energies of the reactants and the products have become equal, so $G_{\text{products}} - G_{\text{reactants}} = 0$ and $\Delta G = 0$. No further work can be extracted and we say the battery is dead.

Melting points and boiling points can be estimated from ΔH and ΔS

For a phase change such as $H_2O(l) \longrightarrow H_2O(s)$, equilibrium can only exist at one particular temperature at atmospheric pressure. For water, that temperature is 0 °C. Above 0 °C, only liquid water can exist, and below 0 °C all the liquid will freeze to give ice. This yields an interesting relationship between ΔH and ΔS for a phase change. Since $\Delta G = 0$,

$$\Delta G = 0 = \Delta H - T\Delta S$$

Therefore,

$$\Delta H = T\Delta S$$

and

$$\Delta S = \frac{\Delta H}{T} \tag{18.8}$$

Thus, if we know ΔH for the phase change and the temperature at which the two phases coexist, we can calculate ΔS for the phase change. Another interesting relationship that we can obtain is

$$T = \frac{\Delta H}{\Delta S} \qquad (18.9)$$

Thus, if we know ΔH and ΔS, we can calculate the temperature at which equilibrium will occur.

EXAMPLE 18.7
Estimating the Equilibrium
Temperature for a Phase Change

For the phase change $Br_2(l) \longrightarrow Br_2(g)$, $\Delta H° = +31.0$ kJ mol^{-1} and $\Delta S° = 92.9$ J mol^{-1} K^{-1}. Assuming that ΔH and ΔS are nearly temperature independent, calculate the approximate Celsius temperature at which $Br_2(l)$ will be in equilibrium with $Br_2(g)$ at 1 atm (i.e., the normal boiling point of liquid Br_2).

ANALYSIS: The temperature at which equilibrium exists is given by Equation 18.9,

$$T = \frac{\Delta H}{\Delta S}$$

If we assume that ΔH and ΔS do not depend much on temperature, then we can use $\Delta H°$ and $\Delta S°$ in this equation to approximate the boiling point. That is,

$$T \approx \frac{\Delta H°}{\Delta S°}$$

SOLUTION: Substituting the data given in the problem,

$$T \approx \frac{3.10 \times 10^4 \ \cancel{J} \ \text{mol}^{-1}}{92.9 \ \cancel{J} \ \text{mol}^{-1} \ K^{-1}}$$

$$= 334 \ K$$

The Celsius temperature is $334 - 273 = 61$ °C. Notice that we were careful to express $\Delta H°$ in joules, not kilojoules, so the units would cancel correctly. It is also interesting that the boiling point we calculated is quite close to the measured normal boiling point of 58.8 °C.

IS THE ANSWER REASONABLE? The $\Delta H°$ value equals 31,000 and the $\Delta S°$ value equals approximately 100, which means the temperature should be about 310 K. Our value, 334 K is not far from that, so the answer is reasonable.

☐ ΔH and ΔS do not change much with changes in temperature. This is because temperature changes affect the enthalpies and entropies of both the reactants and products by about the same amount, so the differences between reactants and products stays fairly constant.

Practice Exercise 17: The heat of vaporization of ammonia is 21.7 kJ mol^{-1} and the boiling point of ammonia is -33.3 °C. Estimate the entropy change for the vaporization of liquid ammonia. (Hint: What algebraic sign do we expect for the entropy change?)

Practice Exercise 18: The heat of vaporization of mercury is 60.7 kJ/mol. For $Hg(l)$, $S° = 76.1$ J mol^{-1} K^{-1} and for $Hg(g)$, $S° = 175$ J mol^{-1} K^{-1}. Estimate the normal boiling point of liquid mercury.

Free energy diagrams for chemical reactions show a minimum in free energy at equilibrium

One way to gain a better understanding of how the free energy changes during a reaction is by studying **free energy diagrams**. As an example, let's study a reaction you've seen before—the decomposition of N_2O_4 into NO_2.

$$N_2O_4(g) \longrightarrow 2NO_2(g)$$

In our discussion of chemical equilibrium in Chapter 14 (page 570), we noted that equilibrium in this system can be approached from *either* direction, with the same equilibrium concentrations being achieved provided we begin with the same overall system composition.

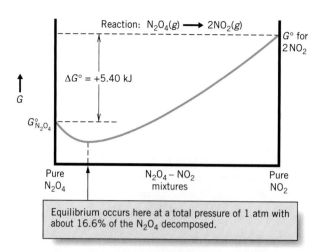

Reaction: $N_2O_4(g) \longrightarrow 2NO_2(g)$

$G°$ for $2NO_2$

$\Delta G° = +5.40$ kJ

G

$G°_{N_2O_4}$

Pure N_2O_4 — NO_2 Pure
N_2O_4 mixtures NO_2

Equilibrium occurs here at a total pressure of 1 atm with about 16.6% of the N_2O_4 decomposed.

FIG. 18.12 **Free energy diagram for the decomposition of $N_2O_4(g)$.** The minimum on the curve indicates the composition of the reaction mixture at equilibrium. Because $\Delta G°$ is positive, the position of equilibrium lies close to the reactants. The amount of product that will form by the time the system reaches equilibium will be small.

☐ When a system moves "downhill" on its free energy curve, $G_{final} < G_{initial}$ and ΔG is negative. Changes with negative ΔG are spontaneous.

Figure 18.12 shows the free energy diagram for the reaction, which depicts how the free energy changes as we proceed from the reactant to the product. On the left of the diagram we have the free energy of one mole of pure $N_2O_4(g)$, and on the right the free energy of two moles of pure $NO_2(g)$. Points along the horizontal axis represent mixtures of both substances. Notice that in going from reactant (N_2O_4) to product ($2NO_2$), the free energy has a minimum. It drops below that of either pure N_2O_4 or pure NO_2.

Any system will spontaneously seek the lowest point on its free energy curve. If we begin with pure $N_2O_4(g)$, the reaction will proceed from left to right and some $NO_2(g)$ will be formed, because proceeding in the direction of NO_2 leads to a lowering of the free energy. If we begin with pure $NO_2(g)$, a change also will occur. Going downhill on the free energy curve now takes place as the reverse reaction occurs [i.e., $2NO_2(g) \longrightarrow N_2O_4(g)$]. Once the bottom of the "valley" is reached, the system has come to equilibrium. As you learned in Chapter 14, if the system isn't disturbed, the composition of the equilibrium mixture will remain constant. Now we see that the reason is because any change (moving either to the left or right) would require an uphill climb. Free energy increases are not spontaneous, so this doesn't happen.

An important thing to notice in Figure 18.12 is that some reaction takes place spontaneously in the forward direction even though $\Delta G°$ is positive. However, the reaction doesn't proceed far before equilibrium is reached. For comparison, Figure 18.13 shows the shape of the free energy curve for a reaction with a negative $\Delta G°$. We see here that at equilibrium there has been a much greater conversion of reactants to products. Thus, $\Delta G°$ *tells us where the position of equilibrium lies between pure reactants and pure products.*

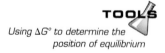

TOOLS

Using $\Delta G°$ to determine the position of equilibrium

$\Delta G°$ and the position of equilibrium

- When $\Delta G°$ is positive, the position of equilibrium lies close to the reactants and little reaction occurs by the time equilibrium is reached. The reaction will appear to be nonspontaneous.
- When $\Delta G°$ is negative, the position of equilibrium lies close to the products and a large amount of products will have formed by the time equilibrium is reached. The reaction will appear to be spontaneous.
- When $\Delta G° = 0$, the position of equilibrium will lie about midway between reactants and products. Substantial amounts of both reactants and products will be present when equilibrium is reached. The reaction will appear to be spontaneous whether we begin with pure reactants or pure products.

$\Delta G°$ can be used to predict the outcome of a chemical reaction

In general, the value of $\Delta G°$ for most reactions is much larger numerically than the $\Delta G°$ for the $N_2O_4 \longrightarrow NO_2$ reaction. In addition, the extent to which a reaction proceeds is very sensitive to the size of $\Delta G°$. If the $\Delta G°$ value for a reaction is reasonably large—about 20 kJ or more—almost no observable reaction will occur when $\Delta G°$ is positive. On the

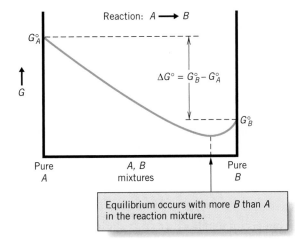

FIG. 18.13 Free energy curve for a reaction having a negative $\Delta G°$. Because $G_B°$ is lower than $G_A°$, $\Delta G°$ is negative for the reaction $A \longrightarrow B$. This causes the position of equilibrium to lie far to the right, near the products. When the system reaches equilibrium, there will be a large amount of products present and little reactants.

other hand, the reaction will go almost to completion if $\Delta G°$ is both large and negative.[5] From a practical standpoint, then, *the size and sign of $\Delta G°$ serve as indicators of whether an observable spontaneous reaction will occur.*

EXAMPLE 18.8
Using ΔG° as a Predictor of the Outcome of a Reaction

Would we expect to be able to observe the following reaction at 25 °C?

$$NH_4Cl(s) \longrightarrow NH_3(g) + HCl(g)$$

ANALYSIS: To answer this question, our tool is the magnitude and algebraic sign of $\Delta G°$. If $\Delta G°$ is reasonably large and positive, the reaction won't be observed. If it is reasonably large and negative, we can expect to see the reaction go nearly to completion.

SOLUTION: First let's calculate $\Delta G°$ for the reaction using the data in Table 18.2. The procedure is the same as that discussed earlier.

$$\Delta G° = [\Delta G_f°_{NH_3(g)} + \Delta G_f°_{HCl(g)}] - [\Delta G_f°_{NH_4Cl(s)}]$$
$$= [(-16.7 \text{ kJ}) + (-95.27 \text{ kJ})] - [-203.9 \text{ kJ}]$$
$$= +91.9 \text{ kJ}$$

Because $\Delta G°$ is large and positive, only extremely small amounts of products can form at this temperature.

IS THE ANSWER REASONABLE? Be sure to check the algebraic signs of each of the terms in the calculation.

Practice Exercise 19: Use the data in Table 18.2 to determine whether the reaction

$$SO_2(g) + O_2(g) \longrightarrow SO_3(g) + \tfrac{1}{2}O_2(g)$$

should "occur spontaneously" at 25 °C. (Hint: Be careful with algebraic signs.)

Practice Exercise 20: Use the data in Table 18.2 to determine whether we should expect to see the formation of $CaCO_3(s)$ in the following reaction at 25 °C.

$$CaCl_2(s) + H_2O(g) + CO_2(g) \longrightarrow CaCO_3(s) + 2HCl(g)$$

[5] As we discussed earlier, to actually see a change take place, the speed of a spontaneous reaction must be reasonably fast. For example, the decomposition of the nitrogen oxides into N_2 and O_2 is thermodynamically spontaneous ($\Delta G°$ is negative), but their rates of decomposition are so slow that these substances appear to be stable and some are obnoxious air pollutants.

The position of equilibrium changes with temperature because ΔG changes with temperature

So far, we have confined our discussion of the relationship of free energy and equilibrium to a special case, 25 °C. But what about other temperatures? Equilibria certainly can exist at temperatures other than 25 °C, and in Chapter 14 you learned how to apply Le Châtelier's principle to predicting the way temperature affects the position of equilibrium. Now let's see how thermodynamics deals with this.

You've learned that at 25 °C the position of equilibrium is determined by the difference between the free energy of pure products and the free energy of pure reactants. This difference is given by ΔG°_{298}, where we have now used the subscript "298" to indicate the temperature, 298 K. We define ΔG°_{298} as

□ 298 K = 25 °C

$$\Delta G^\circ_{298} = (G^\circ_{products})_{298} - (G^\circ_{reactants})_{298}$$

At temperatures other than 25 °C, it is still the difference between the free energies of the products and reactants that determines the position of equilibrium. We might write this as ΔG°_T. Thus, at a temperature other than 25 °C (298 K), we have

$$\Delta G^\circ_T = (G^\circ_{products})_T - (G^\circ_{reactants})_T$$

where $(G^\circ_{products})_T$ and $(G^\circ_{reactants})_T$ are the total free energies of the pure products and reactants, respectively, at that other temperature.

Next, we must find a way to compute ΔG°_T. Earlier we saw that ΔG° can be obtained from the equation

$$\Delta G^\circ = \Delta H^\circ - (298\ \text{K})\Delta S^\circ$$

At a different temperature, T, the equation becomes

$$\Delta G^\circ_T = \Delta H^\circ_T - T\Delta S^\circ_T$$

Now we seem to be getting closer to our goal. If we can compute or estimate the values of ΔH°_T and ΔS°_T for a reaction, we have solved our problem.

The size of ΔG°_T obviously depends very strongly on the temperature—the equation above has temperature as one of its variables. However, as noted in the margin comment on page 749, the magnitudes of the ΔH and ΔS for a reaction are relatively insensitive to the temperature. Therefore, we can use ΔH°_{298} and ΔS°_{298} as reasonable approximations of ΔH°_T and ΔS°_T. This allows us to rewrite the equation for ΔG°_T as

TOOLS
Calculating ΔG° at temperatures other than 25 °C

$$\Delta G^\circ_T \approx \Delta H^\circ_{298} - T\Delta S^\circ_{298} \qquad (18.10)$$

The following examples illustrate how this equation is useful.

EXAMPLE 18.9
ΔG° at Temperatures Other than 25 °C

Earlier we saw that at 25 °C the value of ΔG° for the reaction

$$N_2O_4(g) \longrightarrow 2NO_2(g)$$

has a value of $+5.40$ kJ. What is the approximate value of ΔG°_T for this reaction at 100 °C?

ANALYSIS: Equation 18.10 is the tool needed to solve the problem. To use it, we need values of ΔH° and ΔS°. The ΔH° for the reaction can be calculated from the data in Table 6.2 on page 236. Here we find the following standard heats of formation.

$$N_2O_4(g) \qquad \Delta H^\circ_f = +9.67\ \text{kJ/mol}$$
$$NO_2(g) \qquad \Delta H^\circ_f = +33.8\ \text{kJ/mol}$$

We combine these by a Hess's law calculation to compute ΔH° for the reaction. Next, we compute ΔS° for the reaction using absolute entropy data from Table 18.1.

$$N_2O_4(g) \qquad S^\circ = 304\ \text{J/mol K}$$
$$NO_2(g) \qquad S^\circ = 240.5\ \text{J/mol K}$$

Our tool for this calculation is Equation 18.6 on page 741, which is also a Hess's law kind of calculation.

SOLUTION: First, we compute $\Delta H°$ using Hess's law (Equation 6.14, page 238).

$$\Delta H° = [2\Delta H°_{f\ NO_2(g)}] - [\Delta H°_{f\ N_2O_4(g)}]$$

$$= \left[2\ \text{mol} \times \left(\frac{33.8\ \text{kJ}}{\text{mol}}\right)\right] - \left[1\ \text{mol} \times \left(\frac{9.67\ \text{kJ}}{\text{mol}}\right)\right]$$

$$= +57.9\ \text{kJ}$$

Next, we use Equation 18.6 to calculate $\Delta S°$.

$$\Delta S° = \left[2\ \text{mol} \times \left(\frac{240.5\ \text{J}}{\text{mol K}}\right)\right] - \left[1\ \text{mol} \times \left(\frac{304\ \text{J}}{\text{mol K}}\right)\right]$$

$$= +177\ \text{J K}^{-1}\ \text{or}\ 0.177\ \text{kJ K}^{-1}$$

The temperature is 100 °C, which is 373 K, so we can call the free energy change $\Delta G°_{373}$. Substituting into Equation 18.10 using $T = 373$ K, we have

$$\Delta G°_{373} \approx (+57.9\ \text{kJ}) - (373\ \text{K})(0.177\ \text{kJ K}^{-1})$$

$$\approx -8.1\ \text{kJ}$$

Notice that at this higher temperature, the sign of $\Delta G°_T$ has become negative.

IS THE ANSWER REASONABLE? As usual, we can double-check the algebraic signs to be sure we've performed the calculations correctly. For this problem, however, there's another check we can do.

Let's compare free energy diagrams for this reaction at 25 °C and 100 °C. At 25 °C, $\Delta G°$ is positive and the position of equilibrium lies toward the reactant (Figure 18.12). Because $\Delta G°$ is negative at 100 °C, the free energy diagram will resemble that in Figure 18.13, with the position of equilibrium closer to the product (see the figure in the margin). Raising the temperature has shifted the position of equilibrium of this *endothermic* reaction toward the products, which is just what we would have anticipated by applying Le Châtelier's principle. The answer is therefore reasonable.

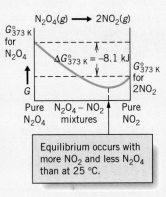

Equilibrium occurs with more NO_2 and less N_2O_4 than at 25 °C.

Practice Exercise 21: In Examples 18.3 and 18.4 we computed $\Delta S°$ and $\Delta H°$ for the reaction

$$CO(NH_2)_2(aq) + H_2O(l) \longrightarrow CO_2(g) + 2NH_3(g)$$

What is $\Delta G°_T$ for the reaction at 75 °C? (Hint: Be careful with the units.)

Practice Exercise 22: Use the data in Table 18.2 to determine $\Delta G°_{298}$ for the reaction

$$2NaHCO_3(s) \longrightarrow Na_2CO_3(s) + CO_2(g) + H_2O(g)$$

Then calculate the approximate value for $\Delta G°$ for the reaction at 200 °C using the data in Tables 6.2 and 18.1. How does the position of equilibrium for the reaction change as the temperature is increased?

18.9 | EQUILIBRIUM CONSTANTS CAN BE ESTIMATED FROM STANDARD FREE ENERGY CHANGES

In the preceding discussion, you learned in a qualitative way that the position of equilibrium in a reaction is determined by the sign and magnitude of $\Delta G°$. You also learned that the direction in which a reaction proceeds depends on where the system composition stands relative to the minimum on the free energy curve. Thus, the reaction will proceed spontaneously in the forward direction only if it will lead to a lowering of the free energy (i.e., if ΔG is negative).

Quantitatively, the relationship between ΔG and $\Delta G°$ is expressed by the following equation, which we will not attempt to justify.

Relating the reaction quotient to ΔG

□ Recall that in Chapter 14 we defined Q as the *reaction quotient*, the numerical value of the mass action expression.

$$\Delta G = \Delta G° + RT \ln Q \qquad (18.11)$$

Here R is the gas constant in appropriate energy units (e.g., 8.314 J mol⁻¹ K⁻¹), T is the Kelvin temperature, and ln Q is the natural logarithm of the reaction quotient. For gaseous reactions, Q is calculated using partial pressures expressed in atm[6]; for reactions in solution, Q is calculated from molar concentrations. Equation 18.11 allows us to predict the direction of the spontaneous change in a reaction mixture if we know $\Delta G°$ and the composition of the mixture, as illustrated in Example 18.10.

EXAMPLE 18.10
Determining the Direction of a Spontaneous Reaction

□ In Chapter 14, you learned that you can also predict the direction of a reaction by comparing Q with K (page 592)

The reaction $2NO_2(g) \rightleftharpoons N_2O_4(g)$ has $\Delta G°_{298} = -5.40$ kJ per mole of N_2O_4. In a reaction mixture, the partial pressure of NO_2 is 0.25 atm and the partial pressure of N_2O_4 is 0.60 atm. In which direction must this reaction proceed to reach equilibrium?

ANALYSIS: Since we know that reactions proceed spontaneously *toward* equilibrium, we are really being asked to determine whether the reaction will proceed spontaneously in the forward or reverse direction. We can use Equation 18.11 to calculate ΔG for the forward reaction. If ΔG is negative, then the forward reaction is spontaneous. However, if the calculated ΔG is positive, the forward reaction is nonspontaneous and it is really the reverse reaction that is spontaneous.

SOLUTION: First, we need the correct form for the mass action expression so we can calculate Q correctly. Expressed in terms of partial pressures, the mass action expression is

$$\frac{P_{N_2O_4}}{P_{NO_2}^2}$$

Therefore, the equation we will use is

$$\Delta G = \Delta G° + RT \ln \left(\frac{P_{N_2O_4}}{P_{NO_2}^2} \right)$$

Next, let's assemble the data:

$$\Delta G°_{298} = -5.40 \text{ kJ mol}^{-1} \qquad\qquad T = 298 \text{ K}$$
$$= -5.40 \times 10^3 \text{ J mol}^{-1} \qquad P_{N_2O_4} = 0.60 \text{ atm}$$
$$R = 8.314 \text{ J mol}^{-1} \text{K}^{-1} \qquad P_{NO_2} = 0.25 \text{ atm}$$

Notice we have changed the energy units of $\Delta G°$ to joules so they will be compatible with those calculated using R. The next step is to substitute into the equation for ΔG. In doing this, we leave off the units for the partial pressures because reaction quotients are always unitless quantities.[7] Here is the calculation.[8]

---

[6] Strictly speaking, we should express pressures in atmospheres or bars depending on which was used to obtain the $\Delta G°$ data. For simplicity, we will use the more familiar pressure unit atm in all our calculations. Because the atmosphere and bar differ by only about 1 percent, any errors that might be introduced will be very small.

[7] For reasons beyond the scope of this text, quantities in mass action expressions used to compute reaction quotients and equilibrium constants are actually ratios. For partial pressures, it's the pressure in atmospheres divided by 1 atm; for concentrations, it's the molarity divided by 1 M. This causes the units to cancel to give a unitless value for Q or K.

[8] As we noted in the footnote on page 535, when taking the logarithm of a quantity, the number of digits *after the decimal point* should equal the number of significant figures in the quantity. Since 0.60 atm and 0.25 atm both have two significant figures, the logarithm of the quantity in square brackets (2.26) is rounded to give two digits after the decimal point.

$$\Delta G = -5.40 \times 10^3 \text{ J mol}^{-1} + (8.314 \text{ J mol}^{-1} \text{ K}^{-1})(298 \text{ K}) \ln \left[\frac{0.60}{(0.25)^2} \right]$$

$$= -5.40 \times 10^3 \text{ J mol}^{-1} + (8.314 \text{ J mol}^{-1} \text{ K}^{-1})(298 \text{ K}) \ln (9.6)$$

$$= -5.40 \times 10^3 \text{ J mol}^{-1} + (8.314 \text{ J mol}^{-1} \text{ K}^{-1})(298 \text{ K})(2.26)$$

$$= -5.40 \times 10^3 \text{ J mol}^{-1} + 5.60 \times 10^3 \text{ J mol}^{-1}$$

$$= +2.0 \times 10^2 \text{ J mol}^{-1}$$

Since ΔG is positive, the forward reaction is nonspontaneous. The reverse reaction is the one that will occur, and to reach equilibrium, some N_2O_4 will have to decompose.

IS THE ANSWER REASONABLE? There is no simple check. However, we can check to be sure the energy units in both terms on the right are the same. Notice that here we have changed the units for $\Delta G°$ to joules to match those of R. Also notice that the temperature is expressed in kelvins, to match the temperature units in R.

Practice Exercise 23: Calculate ΔG for the reaction described in the preceding example if the partial pressure of NO_2 is 0.260 atm and the partial pressure of N_2O_4 is 0.598 atm. Where does the system stand relative to equilibrium? (Hint: What is ΔG for a system at equilibrium?)

Practice Exercise 24: In which direction will the reaction described in the preceding Example proceed to reach equilibrium if the partial pressure of NO_2 is 0.60 atm and the partial pressure of N_2O_4 is 0.25 atm?

The thermodynamic equilibrium constant K can be computed from $\Delta G°$

Earlier you learned that when a system reaches equilibrium the free energy of the products equals the free energy of the reactants and ΔG equals zero. We also know that at equilibrium the reaction quotient equals the equilibrium constant.

$$\text{At equilibrium} \quad \begin{cases} \Delta G = 0 \\ Q = K \end{cases}$$

If we substitute these into Equation 18.11, we obtain

$$0 = \Delta G° + RT \ln K$$

which can be rearranged to give

$$\Delta G° = -RT \ln K \qquad (18.12)$$

TOOLS

Determining thermodynamic equilibrium constants

The equilibrium constant K calculated from this equation is called the **thermodynamic equilibrium constant** and corresponds to K_P for reactions involving gases (with partial pressures expressed in bars) and to K_c for reactions in solution (with concentrations expressed in mol L^{-1}).[9]

Equation 18.12 is useful because it permits us to determine equilibrium constants from either measured or calculated values of $\Delta G°$. As you know, $\Delta G°$ can be determined by a Hess's law type of calculation from tabulated values of $\Delta G_f°$. It also allows us to obtain values of $\Delta G°$ from measured equilibrium constants.

[9] The thermodynamic equilibrium constant requires that gases *always* be included as partial pressures in mass action expressions. The pressure units must be standard pressure units (atmospheres or bars, depending on which convention was used for collecting the $\Delta G°$ data). For a heterogeneous equilibrium involving gases and substances in solution, the mass action expression will mix partial pressures (for the gases) with molarities (for the dissolved substances).

EXAMPLE 18.11
Thermodynamic Equilibrium Constants

The brownish haze often associated with air pollution is caused by nitrogen dioxide, NO_2, a red-brown gas. Nitric oxide, NO, is formed in auto engines and some of it escapes into the air where it is oxidized to NO_2 by oxygen.

$$2NO(g) + O_2(g) \rightleftharpoons 2NO_2(g)$$

The value of K_P for the reaction is 1.7×10^{12} at 25.00 °C. What is $\Delta G°$ for the reaction, expressed in joules per mole? In kilojoules per mole?

ANALYSIS: The tool relating thermodynamic data and equilibrium constants is Equation 18.12.

$$\Delta G° = -RT \ln K_P$$

We'll need the data below to calculate $\Delta G°$. Note that the temperature is given to the nearest hundredth of a degree so we'll use $T = t_C + 273.15$ to compute the Kelvin temperature.

$$R = 8.314 \text{ J mol}^{-1} \text{ K}^{-1}$$
$$T = 298.15 \text{ K}$$
$$K_P = 1.7 \times 10^{12}$$

☐ The units in this calculation give $\Delta G°$ on a per mole (mol^{-1}) basis. This reminds us that we are viewing the coefficients of the reactants and products as representing moles, rather than some other sized quantity.

SOLUTION: Substituting these values into the equation, we have

$$\Delta G° = -(8.314 \text{ J mol}^{-1} \text{ K}^{-1} \times 298.15 \text{ K}) \ln (1.7 \times 10^{12})$$
$$= -(8.314 \text{ J mol}^{-1} \text{ K}^{-1} \times 298.15 \text{ K}) \times (28.16)$$
$$= -6.980 \times 10^4 \text{ J mol}^{-1} \text{ (to four significant figures)}$$

Expressed in kilojoules, $\Delta G° = -69.80 \text{ kJ mol}^{-1}$.

IS THE ANSWER REASONABLE? The value of K_P tells us that the position of equilibrium lies far to the right, which means $\Delta G°$ must be large and negative. Therefore, the answer, $-69.80 \text{ kJ mol}^{-1}$, seems reasonable.

EXAMPLE 18.12
Thermodynamic Equilibrium Constants

Sulfur dioxide, which is sometimes present in polluted air, reacts with oxygen when it passes over the catalyst in automobile catalytic converters. The product is the very acidic oxide SO_3.

$$2SO_2(g) + O_2(g) \rightleftharpoons 2SO_3(g)$$

☐ To make the units cancel correctly, we have added the unit mol^{-1} to the value of $\Delta G°$. This just emphasizes that the amounts of reactants and products are specified in mole sized quantities.

For this reaction, $\Delta G° = -1.40 \times 10^2 \text{ kJ mol}^{-1}$ at 25 °C. What is the value of K_P?

ANALYSIS: Once again we use the equation

$$\Delta G° = -RT \ln K_P$$

Our data are

$$R = 8.314 \text{ J mol}^{-1} \text{ K}^{-1}$$
$$T = 298 \text{ K}$$
$$\Delta G° = -1.40 \times 10^2 \text{ kJ mol}^{-1}$$
$$= -1.40 \times 10^5 \text{ J mol}^{-1}$$

SOLUTION: To calculate K_P, let's first solve for $\ln K_P$.

$$\ln K_P = \frac{-\Delta G°}{RT}$$

Substituting values gives

$$\ln K_P = \frac{-(-1.40 \times 10^5 \; \cancel{J} \; \cancel{mol^{-1}})}{(8.314 \; \cancel{J} \; \cancel{mol^{-1}} \; \cancel{K^{-1}})(298 \; \cancel{K})}$$

$$= +56.5$$

To calculate K_P, we take the antilogarithm,

$$K_P = e^{56.5}$$

$$= 3 \times 10^{24}$$

Notice that we have expressed the answer to only one significant figure. As discussed earlier, when taking a logarithm, the number of digits written after the decimal place equals the number of significant figures in the number. Conversely, the number of significant figures in the antilogarithm equals the number of digits after the decimal in the logarithm.

IS THE ANSWER REASONABLE? The value of $\Delta G°$ is large and negative, so the position of equilibrium should favor the products. The large value of K_P is therefore reasonable.

Practice Exercise 25: The reaction $N_2(g) + 3H_2(g) \rightleftharpoons 2NH_3(g)$ has $K_P = 6.9 \times 10^5$ at 25.0 °C. Calculate $\Delta G°$ for this reaction in units of kilojoules. (Hint: Be careful with units and significant figures.)

Practice Exercise 26: The reaction $H_2(g) + I_2(g) \rightleftharpoons 2HI(g)$ has $\Delta G° = +3.3$ kJ mol^{-1} at 25.0 °C. What is the value of K_P at that temperature?

18.10 | BOND ENERGIES CAN BE ESTIMATED FROM REACTION ENTHALPY CHANGES

You have seen how thermodynamic data allow us to predict the spontaneity of chemical reactions as well as the nature of chemical systems at equilibrium. In addition to these useful and important benefits of the study of thermodynamics, there is a bonus. By studying heats of reaction, and heats of formation in particular, we can obtain fundamental information about the chemical bonds in the substances that react, because the origin of the energy changes in chemical reactions is changes in bond energies.

Recall that the **bond energy** is the amount of energy needed to break a chemical bond to give electrically neutral fragments. It is a useful quantity to know in the study of chemical properties, because during chemical reactions, bonds within the reactants are broken and new ones are formed as the products appear. The first step—bond breaking—is one of the factors that controls the reactivity of substances. Elemental nitrogen, for example, has a very low degree of reactivity, which is generally attributed to the very strong triple bond in N_2. Reactions that involve the breaking of this bond in a single step simply do not occur. When N_2 does react, it is by a stepwise involvement of its three bonds, one at a time.

□ The heats of formation of the nitrogen oxides are endothermic because of the large bond energy of the N_2 molecule.

Bond energies can be measured or calculated using Hess's law

The bond energies of simple diatomic molecules such as H_2, O_2, and Cl_2 are usually measured *spectroscopically*. A flame or an electric spark is used to excite (energize) the molecules, causing them to emit light. An analysis of the spectrum of emitted light allows scientists to compute the amount of energy needed to break the bond.

For more complex molecules, thermochemical data can be used to calculate bond energies in a Hess's law kind of calculation. We will use the standard heat of formation of methane to illustrate how this is accomplished. However, before we can attempt such a calculation, we must first define a thermochemical quantity that we will call the **atomization energy,** symbolized ΔH_{atom}. This is the amount of energy needed to rupture all the

□ The kind of bond breaking described here divides the electrons of the bond equally between the two atoms. It could be symbolized as

$$A{:}B \longrightarrow A{\cdot} + {\cdot}B$$

Two paths for the formation of methane from its elements in their standard states. As described in the text, steps 1, 2, and 3 of the upper path involve the formation of gaseous atoms of the elements and the formation of bonds in CH_4. The lower path corresponds to the direct combination of the elements in their standard states to give CH_4. Because ΔH is a state function, the sum of the enthalpy changes along the upper path must equal the enthalpy change for the lower path (ΔH_f°).

chemical bonds in one mole of gaseous molecules to give gaseous atoms as products. For example, the atomization of methane is

$$CH_4(g) \longrightarrow C(g) + 4H(g)$$

and the enthalpy change for the process is ΔH_{atom}. For this particular molecule, ΔH_{atom} corresponds to the total amount of energy needed to break all the C—H bonds in one mole of CH_4; therefore, division of ΔH_{atom} by 4 would give the average C—H bond energy in methane, expressed in kJ mol^{-1}.

Figure 18.14 shows how we can use the standard heat of formation, ΔH_f°, to calculate the atomization energy. Across the bottom we have the chemical equation for the formation of CH_4 from its elements. The enthalpy change for this reaction, of course, is ΔH_f°. In this figure we also can see an alternative three-step path that leads to $CH_4(g)$. One step is the breaking of H—H bonds in the H_2 molecules to give gaseous hydrogen atoms, another is the vaporization of carbon to give gaseous carbon atoms, and the third is the combination of the gaseous atoms to form CH_4 molecules. These changes are labeled 1, 2, and 3 in the figure.

Since ΔH is a state function, the net enthalpy change from one state to another is the same regardless of the path that we follow. This means that the sum of the enthalpy changes along the upper path must be the same as the enthalpy change along the lower path, ΔH_f°. Perhaps this can be more easily seen in Hess's law terms if we write the changes along the upper path in the form of thermochemical equations.

Steps 1 and 2 have enthalpy changes that are called *standard heats of formation of gaseous atoms*. Values for these quantities have been measured for many of the elements, and some are given in Table 18.3. Step 3 is the opposite of atomization, and its enthalpy change will therefore be the negative of ΔH_{atom} (recall that if we reverse a reaction, we change the sign of its ΔH).

☐ A more complete table of standard heats of formation of gaseous atoms is located in Appendix C.2.

(Step 1)	$2H_2(g) \longrightarrow 4H(g)$	$\Delta H_1^\circ = 4\Delta H_{f\ H(g)}^\circ$
(Step 2)	$C(s) \longrightarrow C(g)$	$\Delta H_2^\circ = \Delta H_{f\ C(g)}^\circ$
(Step 3)	$4H(g) + C(g) \longrightarrow CH_4(g)$	$\Delta H_3^\circ = -\Delta H_{atom}$
	$2H_2(g) + C(s) \longrightarrow CH_4(g)$	$\Delta H^\circ = \Delta H_{f\ CH_4(g)}^\circ$

Notice that by adding the first three equations, $C(g)$ and $4H(g)$ cancel and we get the equation for the formation of CH_4 from its elements in their standard states. This means that adding the ΔH° values of the first three equations should give ΔH_f° for CH_4.

$$\Delta H_1^\circ + \Delta H_2^\circ + \Delta H_3^\circ = \Delta H_{f\ CH_4(g)}^\circ$$

Let's substitute for ΔH_1°, ΔH_2°, and ΔH_3°, and then solve for ΔH_{atom}. First, we substitute for the ΔH° quantities.

$$4\Delta H_{f\ H(g)}^\circ + \Delta H_{f\ C(g)}^\circ + (-\Delta H_{atom}) = \Delta H_{f\ CH_4(g)}^\circ$$

Next, we solve for $(-\Delta H_{atom})$.

$$-\Delta H_{atom} = \Delta H_{f\ CH_4(g)}^\circ - 4\Delta H_{f\ H(g)}^\circ - \Delta H_{f\ C(g)}^\circ$$

Changing signs and rearranging the right side of the equation just a bit gives

$$\Delta H_{atom} = 4\Delta H_{f\ H(g)}^\circ + \Delta H_{f\ C(g)}^\circ - \Delta H_{f\ CH_4(g)}^\circ$$

Now all we need are values for the ΔH_f° terms on the right side. From Table 18.3 we obtain $\Delta H_{f\ H(g)}^\circ$ and $\Delta H_{f\ C(g)}^\circ$, and the value of $\Delta H_{f\ CH_4(g)}^\circ$ is obtained from Table 6.2. We will round these to the nearest 0.1 kJ/mol.

TABLE 18.3	Standard Heats of Formation of Some Gaseous Atoms from the Elements in Their Standard States
Atom	ΔH_f° per mole of atoms (kJ mol^{-1})^a
H	217.89
Li	161.5
Be	324.3
B	560
C	716.67
N	472.68
O	249.17
F	79.14
Si	450
P	332.2
S	276.98
Cl	121.47
Br	112.38
I	107.48

^{a}All values are positive because forming the gaseous atoms from the elements involves bond breaking and is endothermic.

$$\Delta H_{f\ H(g)}^\circ = +217.9 \text{ kJ/mol}$$

$$\Delta H_{f\ C(g)}^\circ = +716.7 \text{ kJ/mol}$$

$$\Delta H_{f\ CH_4(g)}^\circ = -74.8 \text{ kJ/mol}$$

Substituting these values gives

$$\Delta H_{atom} = 1663.1 \text{ kJ/mol}$$

and division by 4 gives an estimate of the average C—H bond energy in this molecule.

$$\text{Bond energy} = \frac{1663.1 \text{ kJ/mol}}{4}$$

$$= 415.8 \text{ kJ/mol of C—H bonds}$$

This value is quite close to the one in Table 18.4 on page 760, which is an average of the C—H bond energies in many different compounds. The other bond energies in Table 18.4 are also based on thermochemical data and were obtained by similar calculations.

Bond energies can be used to estimate heats of formation

An amazing thing about many covalent bond energies is that they are very nearly the same in many different compounds. This suggests, for example, that a C—H bond is very nearly the same in CH_4 as it is in a large number of other compounds that contain this kind of bond.

Because the bond energy doesn't vary much from compound to compound, we can use tabulated bond energies to estimate the heats of formation of substances. For example, let's calculate the standard heat of formation of methyl alcohol vapor, $CH_3OH(g)$. The structural formula for methanol is

$$\begin{array}{ccc} & H & \\ & | & \\ H— & C—O— & H \\ & | & \\ & H & \end{array}$$

To perform this calculation, we set up two paths from the elements to the compound, as shown in Figure 18.15. The lower path has an enthalpy change corresponding to $\Delta H_{f\ CH_3OH(g)}^\circ$, while the upper path takes us to the gaseous elements and then through the energy released when the bonds in the molecule are formed. This latter energy can be computed from the bond energies in Table 18.4. As before, the sum of the energy changes along

FIG. 18.15 Two paths for the formation of methyl alcohol vapor from its elements in their standard states. The numbered paths are referred to in the discussion.

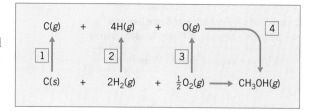

the upper path must be the same as the energy change along the lower path, and this permits us to compute $\Delta H^\circ_{f\ CH_3OH(g)}$.

Steps 1, 2, and 3 involve the formation of the gaseous atoms from the elements, and their enthalpy changes are obtained from Table 18.3.

$$\Delta H^\circ_1 = \Delta H^\circ_{f\ C(g)} = 1\ \text{mol} \times 716.7\ \text{kJ/mol} = 716.7\ \text{kJ}$$

$$\Delta H^\circ_2 = 4\Delta H^\circ_{f\ H(g)} = 4\ \text{mol} \times (217.9\ \text{kJ/mol}) = 871.6\ \text{kJ}$$

$$\Delta H^\circ_3 = \Delta H^\circ_{f\ O(g)} = 1\ \text{mol} \times (249.2\ \text{kJ/mol}) = 249.2\ \text{kJ}$$

The sum of these values, $+1837.5$ kJ, is the total energy input (the net ΔH°) for the first three steps.

The formation of the CH_3OH molecule from the gaseous atoms is exothermic because energy is always released when atoms become joined by covalent bonds. In this molecule we can count three $C-H$ bonds, one $C-O$ bond, and one $O-H$ bond. Their formation releases energy equal to their bond energies, which we obtain from Table 18.4.

Bond	Energy (kJ)
3(C—H)	3 × (412 kJ/mol) = 1236
C—O	360
O—H	463

Adding these together gives a total of 2059 kJ. Therefore, ΔH°_4 is -2059 kJ (because it is exothermic). Now we can compute the total enthalpy change for the upper path.

TABLE 18.4	Some Average Bond Energies
Bond	**Bond Energy (kJ mol^{-1})**
C—C	348
C=C	612
C≡C	960
C—H	412
C—N	305
C=N	613
C≡N	890
C—O	360
C=O	743
C—F	484
C—Cl	338
C—Br	276
C—I	238
H—H	436
H—F	565
H—Cl	431
H—Br	366
H—I	299
H—N	388
H—O	463
H—S	338
H—Si	376

$$\Delta H° = (+1837.5 \text{ kJ}) + (-2059 \text{ kJ})$$

$$= -222 \text{ kJ}$$

The value just calculated should be equal to $\Delta H_f°$ for $CH_3OH(g)$. For comparison, it has been found experimentally that $\Delta H_f°$ for this molecule (in the vapor state) is -201 kJ/mol. At first glance, the agreement doesn't seem very good, but on a relative basis the calculated value (-222 kJ) differs from the experimental one by only about 10%.

SUMMARY

First Law of Thermodynamics. The change in the **internal energy** of a system, ΔE, equals the sum of the heat absorbed by the system, q, and the work done on the system, w. ΔE is a state function, but q and w are not. For pressure–volume work, $w = -P\Delta V$, where P is the external pressure and $\Delta V = V_{final} - V_{initial}$. The heat at constant volume, q_v, is equal to ΔE, whereas the heat at constant pressure, q_p, is equal to ΔH. The value of ΔH differs from ΔE by the work expended in pushing back the atmosphere when the change occurs at constant atmospheric pressure. In general, the difference between ΔE and ΔH is quite small. For a chemical reaction, $\Delta H = \Delta E + \Delta n_{gas}RT$, where Δn_{gas} is the change in the number of moles of *gas* on going from reactants to products.

Spontaneity. A spontaneous change occurs without outside assistance, whereas a nonspontaneous change requires continuous help and can occur only if it is accompanied by and linked to some other spontaneous event.

Spontaneity is associated with statistical probability—spontaneous processes tend to proceed from lower probability states to those of higher probability. The thermodynamic quantity associated with the probability of a state is **entropy, S.** Entropy is a measure of the number of energetically equivalent ways a state can be realized. In general, gases have much higher entropies than liquids, which have somewhat higher entropies than solids. Entropy increases with volume for a gas and with the temperature. During a chemical reaction, the entropy tends to increase if the number of molecules increases.

Second Law of Thermodynamics. This law states that the entropy of the universe (system plus surroundings) increases whenever a spontaneous change occurs.

Gibbs Free Energy. The Gibbs free energy change, ΔG, allows us to determine the combined effects of enthalpy and entropy changes on the spontaneity of a chemical or physical change. A change is spontaneous only if the free energy of the system decreases (ΔG is negative). When ΔH and ΔS have the same algebraic sign, the temperature becomes the critical factor in determining spontaneity.

Third Law of Thermodynamics. The entropy of a pure crystalline substance is equal to zero at absolute zero (0 K). **Standard entropies, $S°$,** are calculated for 25 °C and 1 atm (Table 18.1) and can be used to calculate $\Delta S°$ for chemical reactions.

Standard Free Energy Changes. When ΔG is measured at 25 °C and 1 atm, it is the **standard free energy change, $\Delta G°$. Standard free energies of formation, $\Delta G_f°$,** can be used to obtain $\Delta G°$ for chemical reactions by a Hess's law type of calculation.

For any system, the value of ΔG is equal to the maximum amount of energy that can be obtained in the form of useful work, which can be obtained only if the change takes place by a **reversible process.** All real changes are irreversible and we always obtain less work than is theoretically available; the rest is lost as heat.

Free Energy and Equilibrium. When a system reaches equilibrium, $\Delta G = 0$ and no useful work can be obtained from it. For a phase change (e.g., solid $\rightleftharpoons$ liquid), ΔS and ΔH are related by the equation $\Delta S = \Delta H/T$, where T is the temperature at which the two phases are in equilibrium.

In chemical reactions, equilibrium occurs at a minimum on the free energy curve part way between pure reactants and pure products. The composition of the equilibrium mixture is determined by where the minimum lies along the reactant $\longrightarrow$ product axis; when it lies close to the products, the proportion of product to reactants is large and the reaction goes far toward completion.

When a reaction has a value of $\Delta G°$ that is both large and negative, it will appear to occur spontaneously because a lot of products will be formed by the time equilibrium is reached. If $\Delta G°$ is large and positive, it may be difficult to observe any reaction at all because only tiny amounts of products will be formed.

Thermodynamic Equilibrium Constants. The spontaneity of a reaction is determined by ΔG (how the free energy changes with a change in concentration). This is related to the standard free energy change, $\Delta G°$, by the equation $\Delta G = \Delta G° + RT \ln Q$, where Q is the reaction quotient for the system. At equilibrium, $\Delta G° = -RT \ln K$, where $K = K_p$ for gaseous reactions and $K = K_c$ for reactions in solution.

Bond Energies and Heats of Reaction. The bond energy equals the amount of energy needed to break a bond to give neutral fragments. The sum of all the bond energies in a molecule is the **atomization energy, ΔH_{atom},** and, on a mole basis, it corresponds to the energy needed to break one mole of molecules into individual atoms. The heat of formation of a gaseous compound equals the sum of the energies needed to form atoms of the elements that are found in the substance plus the negative of the atomization energy.

TOOLS FOR PROBLEM SOLVING

In this chapter you learned to apply the following concepts as tools in solving problems related to thermodynamics. Study each one carefully so that you know what each is used for. When faced with solving a problem, recall what each tool does and consider whether it will be helpful in finding a solution. This will aid you in selecting the tools you need.

Converting between ΔE and ΔH *(page 729)* Use the following equation when you need to find the difference between ΔE and ΔH, or when converting from one to the other.

$$\Delta H = \Delta E + \Delta n_{gas}RT$$

Use the coefficients of gaseous reactants and products to calculate Δn_{gas}.

Factors that affect the entropy *(pages 734 through 736)* You can sometimes anticipate the sign of the entropy change for a system because certain factors favor an increase in entropy.

- Volume: Entropy increases with increasing volume.
- Temperature: Entropy increases with increasing temperature.
- Physical state: $S_{gas} \gg S_{liquid} > S_{solid}$. When gases are formed in a reaction, ΔS is almost always positive.
- Number of particles: Entropy increases when the number of particles increases.

Gibbs free energy *(page 738)* The Gibbs free energy is defined in terms of ΔH and ΔS by the equation

$$\Delta G = \Delta H - T\Delta S$$

ΔG as a predictor of spontaneity *(page 739)* You can use the sign of ΔG to tell whether a particular change is spontaneous.

Standard entropies *(page 741)* Calculate the standard entropy change for a reaction using the following equation and standard entropy values from Table 18.1. The calculation is similar to the Hess's law calculation of $\Delta H°$ you learned in Chapter 6.

$$\Delta S° = (\text{sum of } S° \text{ of products}) - (\text{sum of } S° \text{of reactants})$$

Calculating $\Delta G°$ from $\Delta H°$ and $\Delta S°$ *(page 743)* By calculating $\Delta H°$ from data in Table 6.2 and $\Delta S°$ from data in Table 18.1 you can calculate $\Delta G°$ for a reaction. The equation is

$$\Delta G° = \Delta H° - (298.15 \text{ K})\Delta S°$$

Using standard free energies of formation to calculate $\Delta G°$ *(page 744)* When you want $\Delta G°$ for a reaction, use $\Delta G_f°$ data from Table 18.2 and the equation

$$\Delta G° = (\text{sum of } \Delta G_f° \text{ of products}) - (\text{sum of } \Delta G_f° \text{ of reactants})$$

Using $\Delta G°$ to judge qualitatively the position of equilibrium *(page 750)* The sign and magnitude of $\Delta G°$ can serve as a qualitative indicator of the position of equilibrium and lets us anticipate whether an observable amount of product will be formed in a reaction.

- $\Delta G°$ is large and positive: Position of equilibrium is close to reactants.
- $\Delta G°$ is large and negative: Position of equilibrium is close to products.
- $\Delta G° = 0$: Position of equilibrium lies about midway between reactants and products.

Calculating $\Delta G°$ at temperatures other than 25 °C *(page 752)* When you need $\Delta G°$ at some temperature other than 25 °C, assume $\Delta H°$ and $\Delta S°$ are nearly independent of temperature and use the equation

$$\Delta G_T° \approx \Delta H_{298}° - T\Delta S_{298}°$$

Such a calculation would be needed to estimate an equilibrium constant at a temperature other than 25 °C.

Testing where a reaction stands relative to equilibrium *(page 754)* We can tell whether a particular reaction mixture composition will lead to a spontaneous reaction in the forward direction or the reverse direction, or whether the reaction is at equilibrium, by calculating ΔG by the equation

$$\Delta G = \Delta G° + RT \ln Q$$

- ΔG is negative: The reaction is spontaneous in the forward direction.
- ΔG is positive: The reaction is spontaneous in the reverse direction.
- ΔG is zero: The reaction is at equilibrium.

Thermodynamic equilibrium constants *(page 755)* The following important equation lets us calculate equilibrium constants from thermodynamic data, or calculate $\Delta G°$ from measured equilibrium constants.

$$\Delta G° = -RT \ln K$$

Remember to use $R = 8.314 \text{ J mol}^{-1} \text{ K}^{-1}$, T in kelvins, and that $K = K_p$ for gaseous reactions and K_c for reactions in solution.

QUESTIONS, PROBLEMS, AND EXERCISES

Answers to problems whose numbers are printed in color are given in Appendix B. More challenging problems are marked with asterisks. ILW = Interactive Learningware solution is available at www.wiley.com/college/brady. OH = an Office Hours video is available for this problem.

REVIEW QUESTIONS

First Law of Thermodynamics

18.1 What is the origin of the name *thermodynamics*?

18.2 How is a change in the internal energy defined in terms of the initial and final internal energies?

18.3 What is the algebraic sign of ΔE for an endothermic change? Why?

18.4 State the first law of thermodynamics in words. What equation defines the change in the internal energy in terms of heat and work? Define the meaning of the symbols, including the significance of their algebraic signs.

18.5 Which quantities in the statement of the first law are state functions and which are not?

18.6 Which thermodynamic quantity corresponds to the heat at constant volume? Which corresponds to the heat at constant pressure?

18.7 What are the units of $P\Delta V$ if pressure is expressed in pascals and volume is expressed in cubic meters?

18.8 If there is a decrease in the number of moles of gas during an exothermic chemical reaction, which is numerically larger, ΔE or ΔH? Why?

18.9 Which of the following changes is accompanied by the most negative value of ΔE? (a) A spring is compressed and heated. (b) A compressed spring expands and is cooled. (c) A spring is compressed and cooled. (d) A compressed spring expands and is heated.

Spontaneous Change

18.10 What is a *spontaneous change*? What role does kinetics play in determining the apparent spontaneity of a chemical reaction?

18.11 List five changes that you have encountered recently that occurred spontaneously. List five changes that are nonspontaneous that you have caused to occur.

18.12 Which of the items that you listed in Question 18.11 are exothermic (leading to a lowering of the potential energy) and which are endothermic (accompanied by an increase in potential energy)?

18.13 At constant pressure, what role does the enthalpy change play in determining the spontaneity of an event?

18.14 How do the probabilities of the initial and final states in a process affect the spontaneity of the process?

Entropy

18.15 An instant cold pack purchased in a pharmacy contains a packet of solid ammonium nitrate surrounded by a pouch of water. When the packet of NH_4NO_3 is broken, the solid dissolves in water and a cooling of the mixture occurs because the solution process for NH_4NO_3 in water is endothermic. Explain, in terms of what happens to the molecules and ions, why this mixing occurs spontaneously.

18.16 What is *entropy*?

18.17 How is the entropy of a substance affected by (a) an increase in temperature, (b) a decrease in volume, (c) changing from a liquid to a solid, and (d) dissociating into individual atoms?

18.18 Will the entropy change for each of the following be positive or negative?
(a) Moisture condenses on the outside of a cold glass.
(b) Raindrops form in a cloud.
(c) Gasoline vaporizes in the carburetor of an automobile engine.
(d) Air is pumped into a tire.
(e) Frost forms on the windshield of your car.
(f) Sugar dissolves in coffee.

18.19 On the basis of our definition of entropy, suggest why entropy is a state function.

18.20 State the second law of thermodynamics.

18.21 How can a process have a negative entropy change for the system, and yet still be spontaneous?

Third Law of Thermodynamics and Standard Entropies

18.22 What is the third law of thermodynamics?

18.23 Would you expect the entropy of an alloy (a solution of two metals) to be zero at 0 K? Explain your answer.

18.24 Why does entropy increase with increasing temperature?

18.25 Does glass have $S = 0$ at 0 K? Explain.

Gibbs Free Energy

18.26 What is the equation expressing the change in the Gibbs free energy for a reaction occurring at constant temperature and pressure?

18.27 In terms of the algebraic signs of ΔH and ΔS, under what circumstances will a change be spontaneous:
(a) At all temperatures?

(b) At low temperatures but not at high temperatures?

(c) At high temperatures but not at low temperatures?

18.28 Under what circumstances will a change be nonspontaneous regardless of the temperature?

Free Energy and Work

18.29 How is free energy related to useful work?

18.30 What is a thermodynamically reversible process? How is the amount of work obtained from a change related to thermodynamic reversibility?

18.31 How is the *rate* at which energy is withdrawn from a system related to the amount of that energy which can appear as useful work?

18.32 When glucose is oxidized by the body to generate energy, part of the energy is used to make molecules of ATP (adenosine triphosphate). However, of the total energy released in the oxidation of glucose, only 38% actually goes to making ATP. What happens to the rest of the energy?

18.33 Why are real, observable changes not considered to be thermodynamically reversible processes?

Free Energy and Equilibrium

18.34 In what way is free energy related to equilibrium?

18.35 Considering the fact that the formation of a bond between two atoms is exothermic and is accompanied by an entropy decrease, explain why all chemical compounds decompose into individual atoms if heated to a high enough temperature.

18.36 When a warm object is placed in contact with a cold one, they both gradually come to the same temperature. On a molecular level, explain how this is related to entropy and spontaneity.

18.37 Sketch the shape of the free energy curve for a chemical reaction that has a positive $\Delta G°$. Indicate the composition of the reaction mixture corresponding to equilibrium.

18.38 Many reactions that have large, negative values of $\Delta G°$ are not actually observed to happen at 25 °C and 1 atm. Why?

Thermodynamics and Equilibrium

18.39 Suppose a reaction has a negative $\Delta H°$ and a negative $\Delta S°$. Will more or less product be present at equilibrium as the temperature is raised?

18.40 Write the equation that relates the free energy change to the value of the reaction quotient for a reaction.

18.41 How is the equilibrium constant related to the standard free energy change for a reaction? (Write the equation.)

18.42 What is the value of $\Delta G°$ for a reaction for which $K = 1$?

Bond Energies and Heats of Reaction

18.43 Define the term *atomization energy*.

18.44 Why are the heats of formation of gaseous atoms from their elements endothermic quantities?

18.45 The gaseous C_2 molecule has a bond energy of 602 kJ mol^{-1}. Why isn't the standard heat of formation of C(g) equal to half this value?

REVIEW PROBLEMS

First Law of Thermodynamics

18.46 A certain system absorbs 0.300 kJ of heat and has 0.700 kJ of work performed on it. What is the value of ΔE for the change? Is the overall change exothermic or endothermic?

18.47 The value of ΔE for a certain change is -1455 J. During the change, the system absorbs 812 J of heat. Did the system do work, or was work done on the system? How much work, expressed in joules, was involved?

18.48 Suppose that you were pumping an automobile tire with a hand pump that pushed 24.0 in.^{3} of air into the tire on each stroke, and that during one such stroke the opposing pressure in the tire was 30.0 lb/in.^{2} above the normal atmospheric pressure of 14.7 lb/in.^{2}. Calculate the number of joules of work accomplished during each stroke. (1 L atm = 101.325 J.)

OH 18.49 Consider the reaction between aqueous solutions of baking soda, $NaHCO_3$, and vinegar, $HC_2H_3O_2$.

$$NaHCO_3(aq) + HC_2H_3O_2(aq) \longrightarrow$$
$$NaC_2H_3O_2(aq) + H_2O(l) + CO_2(g)$$

If this reaction occurs at atmospheric pressure ($P = 1$ atm), how much work, expressed in *L atm*, is done by the system in pushing back the atmosphere when 1.00 mol $NaHCO_3$ reacts at a temperature of 25 °C? (*Hint:* Review the gas laws.)

18.50 Calculate $\Delta H°$ and $\Delta E°$ for the following reactions at 25 °C. (If necessary, refer to the data in Table C.1 in Appendix C.)
(a) $3PbO(s) + 2NH_3(g) \longrightarrow$
$$3Pb(s) + N_2(g) + 3H_2O(g)$$
(b) $NaOH(s) + HCl(g) \longrightarrow NaCl(s) + H_2O(l)$
(c) $Al_2O_3(s) + 2Fe(s) \longrightarrow Fe_2O_3(s) + 2Al(s)$
(d) $2CH_4(g) \longrightarrow C_2H_6(g) + H_2(g)$

18.51 Calculate $\Delta H°$ and $\Delta E°$ for the following reactions at 25 °C. (If necessary, refer to the data in Table C.1 in Appendix C.)
(a) $2C_2H_2(g) + 5O_2(g) \longrightarrow 4CO_2(g) + 2H_2O(g)$
(b) $C_2H_2(g) + 5N_2O(g) \longrightarrow$
$$2CO_2(g) + H_2O(g) + 5N_2(g)$$
(c) $NH_4Cl(s) \longrightarrow NH_3(g) + HCl(g)$
(d) $(CH_3)_2CO(l) + 4O_2(g) \longrightarrow 3CO_2(g) + 3H_2O(g)$

18.52 The reaction

$$2N_2O(g) \longrightarrow 2N_2(g) + O_2(g)$$

has $\Delta H° = -163.14$ kJ. What is the value of ΔE for the decomposition of 180 g of N_2O at 25 °C? If we assume that ΔH doesn't change appreciably with temperature, what is ΔE for this same reaction at 200 °C?

18.53 A 10.0 L vessel at 20 °C contains butane, $C_4H_{10}(g)$, at a pressure of 2.00 atm. What is the maximum amount of work that can be obtained by the combustion of this butane if the gas is first brought to a pressure of 1 atm and the temperature is brought to

25 °C? Assume the products are also returned to that same temperature and pressure.

Factors That Affect Spontaneity

OH 18.54 Use the data from Table 6.2 to calculate $\Delta H°$ for the following reactions. On the basis of their values of $\Delta H°$, which are favored to occur spontaneously?
(a) $CaO(s) + CO_2(g) \longrightarrow CaCO_3(s)$
(b) $C_2H_2(g) + 2H_2(g) \longrightarrow C_2H_6(g)$
(c) $3CaO(s) + 2Fe(s) \longrightarrow 3Ca(s) + Fe_2O_3(s)$

18.55 Use the data from Table 6.2 to calculate $\Delta H°$ for the following reactions. On the basis of their values of $\Delta H°$, which are favored to occur spontaneously?
(a) $NH_4Cl(s) \longrightarrow NH_3(g) + HCl(g)$
(b) $2C_2H_2(g) + 5O_2(g) \longrightarrow 4CO_2(g) + 2H_2O(g)$
(c) $C_2H_2(g) + 5N_2O(g) \longrightarrow$
$$2CO_2(g) + H_2O(g) + 5N_2(g)$$

18.56 What factors must you consider to determine the sign of ΔS for the reaction $2N_2O(g) \longrightarrow 2N_2(g) + O_2(g)$ if it occurs at constant temperature?

18.57 What factors must you consider to determine the sign of ΔS for the reaction $2HI(g) \longrightarrow H_2(g) + I_2(s)$?

18.58 Predict the algebraic sign of the entropy change for the following reactions.
(a) $PCl_3(g) + Cl_2(g) \longrightarrow PCl_5(g)$
(b) $SO_2(g) + CaO(s) \longrightarrow CaSO_3(s)$
(c) $CO_2(g) + H_2O(l) \longrightarrow H_2CO_3(aq)$
(d) $Ni(s) + 2HCl(aq) \longrightarrow H_2(g) + NiCl_2(aq)$

OH 18.59 Predict the algebraic sign of the entropy change for the following reactions.
(a) $I_2(s) \longrightarrow I_2(g)$
(b) $Br_2(g) + 3Cl_2(g) \longrightarrow 2BrCl_3(g)$
(c) $NH_3(g) + HCl(g) \longrightarrow NH_4Cl(s)$
(d) $CaO(s) + H_2O(l) \longrightarrow Ca(OH)_2(s)$

Third Law of Thermodynamics

18.60 Calculate $\Delta S°$ for the following reactions in J K^{-1} from the data in Table 18.1. On the basis of their values of $\Delta S°$, which of these reactions are favored to occur spontaneously?
(a) $N_2(g) + 3H_2(g) \longrightarrow 2NH_3(g)$
(b) $CO(g) + 2H_2(g) \longrightarrow CH_3OH(l)$
(c) $2C_2H_6(g) + 7O_2(g) \longrightarrow 4CO_2(g) + 6H_2O(g)$
(d) $Ca(OH)_2(s) + H_2SO_4(l) \longrightarrow CaSO_4(s) + 2H_2O(l)$
(e) $S(s) + 2N_2O(g) \longrightarrow SO_2(g) + 2N_2(g)$

18.61 Calculate $\Delta S°$ for the following reactions in J K^{-1}, using the data in Table 18.1.
(a) $Ag(s) + \frac{1}{2}Cl_2(g) \longrightarrow AgCl(s)$
(b) $H_2(g) + \frac{1}{2}O_2(g) \longrightarrow H_2O(g)$
(c) $H_2(g) + \frac{1}{2}O_2(g) \longrightarrow H_2O(l)$
(d) $CaCO_3(s) + H_2SO_4(l) \longrightarrow$
$$CaSO_4(s) + H_2O(g) + CO_2(g)$$
(e) $NH_3(g) + HCl(g) \longrightarrow NH_4Cl(s)$

OH 18.62 Calculate $\Delta S_f°$ for the following compounds in J mol^{-1} K^{-1}.
(a) $C_2H_4(g)$ (c) $HC_2H_3O_2(l)$
(b) $CaSO_4 \cdot 2H_2O(s)$

18.63 Calculate $\Delta S_f°$ for the following compounds in J mol^{-1} K^{-1}.
(a) $Al_2O_3(s)$ (c) $NH_4Cl(s)$
(b) $CaSO_4 \cdot \frac{1}{2}H_2O(s)$

18.64 Nitrogen dioxide, NO_2, an air pollutant, dissolves in rainwater to form a dilute solution of nitric acid. The equation for the reaction is
$$3NO_2(g) + H_2O(l) \longrightarrow 2HNO_3(l) + NO(g)$$
Calculate $\Delta S°$ for the reaction in J K^{-1}.

18.65 Good wine will turn to vinegar if it is left exposed to air because the alcohol is oxidized to acetic acid. The equation for the reaction is
$$C_2H_5OH(l) + O_2(g) \longrightarrow HC_2H_3O_2(l) + H_2O(l)$$
Calculate $\Delta S°$ for the reaction in J K^{-1}.

Gibbs Free Energy

ILW 18.66 Phosgene, $COCl_2$, was used as a war gas during World War I. It reacts with the moisture in the lungs to produce HCl, which causes the lungs to fill with fluid, and CO, which asphyxiates the victim. Both lead ultimately to death. For $COCl_2(g)$, $S° = 284$ J/mol K and $\Delta H_f° = -223$ kJ/mol. Use this information and the data in Table 18.1 to calculate $\Delta G_f°$ for $COCl_2(g)$ in kJ mol^{-1}.

OH 18.67 Aluminum oxidizes rather easily, but forms a thin protective coating of Al_2O_3 that prevents further oxidation of the aluminum beneath. Use the data for $\Delta H_f°$ (Table 6.2) and $S°$ (Table 18.1) to calculate $\Delta G_f°$ for $Al_2O_3(s)$ in kJ mol^{-1}.

18.68 Compute $\Delta G°$ in kJ for the following reactions, using the data in Table 18.2.
(a) $SO_3(g) + H_2O(l) \longrightarrow H_2SO_4(l)$
(b) $2NH_4Cl(s) + CaO(s) \longrightarrow$
$$CaCl_2(s) + H_2O(l) + 2NH_3(g)$$
(c) $CaSO_4(s) + 2HCl(g) \longrightarrow CaCl_2(s) + H_2SO_4(l)$

18.69 Compute $\Delta G°$ in kJ for the following reactions, using the data in Table 18.2.
(a) $2HCl(g) + CaO(s) \longrightarrow CaCl_2(s) + H_2O(g)$
(b) $2AgCl(s) + Ca(s) \longrightarrow CaCl_2(s) + 2Ag(s)$
(c) $3NO_2(g) + H_2O(l) \longrightarrow 2HNO_3(l) + NO(g)$

18.70 Given the following,
$$4NO(g) \longrightarrow 2N_2O(g) + O_2(g) \qquad \Delta G° = -139.56 \text{ kJ}$$
$$2NO(g) + O_2(g) \longrightarrow 2NO_2(g) \qquad \Delta G° = -69.70 \text{ kJ}$$
calculate $\Delta G°$ for the reaction
$$2N_2O(g) + 3O_2(g) \longrightarrow 4NO_2(g)$$

18.71 Given these reactions and their $\Delta G°$ values,
$$COCl_2(g) + 4NH_3(g) \longrightarrow CO(NH_2)_2(s) + 2NH_4Cl(s)$$
$$\Delta G° = -332.0 \text{ kJ}$$
$$COCl_2(g) + H_2O(l) \longrightarrow CO_2(g) + 2HCl(g)$$
$$\Delta G° = -141.8 \text{ kJ}$$
$$NH_3(g) + HCl(g) \longrightarrow NH_4Cl(s) \qquad \Delta G° = -91.96 \text{ kJ}$$

calculate the value of $\Delta G°$ for the reaction

$$CO(NH_2)_2(s) + H_2O(l) \longrightarrow CO_2(g) + 2NH_3(g)$$

Free Energy and Work

OH 18.72 Gasohol is a mixture of gasoline and ethanol (grain alcohol), C_2H_5OH. Calculate the maximum work that could be obtained at 25 °C and 1 atm by burning 1 mol of C_2H_5OH.

$$C_2H_5OH(l) + 3O_2(g) \longrightarrow 2CO_2(g) + 3H_2O(g)$$

18.73 What is the maximum amount of useful work that could possibly be obtained at 25 °C and 1 atm from the combustion of 48.0 g of natural gas, $CH_4(g)$, to give $CO_2(g)$ and $H_2O(g)$?

Free Energy and Equilibrium

18.74 Chloroform, formerly used as an anesthetic and now believed to be a carcinogen (cancer-causing agent), has a heat of vaporization $\Delta H_{vaporization} = 31.4$ kJ mol^{-1}. The change $CHCl_3(l) \longrightarrow CHCl_3(g)$ has $\Delta S° = 94.2$ J mol^{-1} K^{-1}. At what temperature do we expect $CHCl_3$ to boil (i.e., at what temperature will liquid and vapor be in equilibrium at 1 atm pressure)?

OH 18.75 For the melting of aluminum, $Al(s) \longrightarrow Al(l)$, $\Delta H° = 10.0$ kJ mol^{-1} and $\Delta S° = 9.50$ J/mol K. Calculate the melting point of Al. (The actual melting point is 660 °C.)

18.76 Isooctane, an important constituent of gasoline, has a boiling point of 99.3 °C and a heat of vaporization of 37.7 kJ mol^{-1}. What is ΔS (in J mol^{-1} K^{-1}) for the vaporization of 1 mol of isooctane?

18.77 Acetone (nail polish remover) has a boiling point of 56.2 °C. The change $(CH_3)_2CO(l) \longrightarrow (CH_3)_2CO(g)$ has $\Delta H° = 31.9$ kJ mol^{-1}. What is $\Delta S°$ for the change?

Free Energy and Spontaneity of Chemical Reactions

ILW 18.78 Determine whether the following reaction (equation unbalanced) will be spontaneous at 25 °C. (Do we expect appreciable amounts of products to form?)

$$C_2H_4(g) + HNO_3(l) \longrightarrow$$
$$HC_2H_3O_2(l) + H_2O(l) + NO(g) + NO_2(g)$$

18.79 Which of the following reactions (equations unbalanced) would be expected to be spontaneous at 25 °C and 1 atm?
(a) $PbO(s) + NH_3(g) \longrightarrow Pb(s) + N_2(g) + H_2O(g)$
(b) $NaOH(s) + HCl(g) \longrightarrow NaCl(s) + H_2O(l)$
(c) $Al_2O_3(s) + Fe(s) \longrightarrow Fe_2O_3(s) + Al(s)$
(d) $2CH_4(g) \longrightarrow C_2H_6(g) + H_2(g)$

Thermodynamic Equilibrium Constants

OH 18.80 Calculate the value of the thermodynamic equilibrium constant for the following reactions at 25 °C. (Equations are unbalanced. Refer to the data in Appendix C.)
(a) $PCl_3(g) + O_2(g) \rightleftharpoons POCl_3(g)$
(b) $SO_3(g) \rightleftharpoons SO_2(g) + O_2(g)$

18.81 Calculate the value of the thermodynamic equilibrium constant for the following reactions at 25 °C. (Equations are unbalanced. Refer to the data in Appendix C.)

(a) $N_2H_4(g) + O_2(g) \rightleftharpoons NO(g) + H_2O(g)$
(b) $N_2H_4(g) + H_2O_2(g) \rightleftharpoons NO_2(g) + H_2O(g)$

ILW 18.82 The reaction

$$NO_2(g) + NO(g) \rightleftharpoons N_2O(g) + O_2(g)$$

has $\Delta G_{1273}^0 = -9.67$ kJ. A 1.00 L reaction vessel at 1000 °C contains 0.0200 mol NO_2, 0.040 mol NO, 0.015 mol N_2O, and 0.0350 mol O_2. Is the reaction at equilibrium? If not, in which direction will the reaction proceed to reach equilibrium?

18.83 The reaction $CO(g) + H_2O(g) \rightleftharpoons HCHO_2(g)$ has $\Delta G_{673}° = +79.8$ kJ mol^{-1}. If a mixture at 400 °C contains 0.040 mol CO, 0.022 mol H_2O, and 3.8×10^{-3} mol $HCHO_2$ in a 2.50 L container, is the reaction at equilibrium? If not, in which direction will the reaction proceed spontaneously?

18.84 A reaction that can convert coal to methane (the chief component of natural gas) is

$$C(s) + 2H_2(g) \rightleftharpoons CH_4(g)$$

for which $\Delta G° = -50.79$ kJ mol^{-1}. What is the value of K_P for this reaction at 25 °C? Does this value of K_P suggest that studying this reaction as a means of methane production is worthwhile pursuing?

***18.85** One of the important reactions in living cells from which the organism draws energy is the reaction of adenosine triphosphate (ATP) with water to give adenosine diphosphate (ADP) and free phosphate ion.

$$ATP + H_2O \rightleftharpoons ADP + PO_4^{3-}$$

The value of $\Delta G_{310}°$ for the reaction at 37 °C (normal human body temperature) is -33 kJ mol^{-1}. Calculate the value of the equilibrium constant for the reaction at that temperature.

18.86 What is the value of the equilibrium constant for a reaction for which $\Delta G° = 0$? What will happen to the composition of the system if we begin the reaction with the pure products?

18.87 Methanol, a potential replacement for gasoline as an automotive fuel, can be made from H_2 and CO by the reaction

$$CO(g) + 2H_2(g) \rightleftharpoons CH_3OH(g)$$

At 500 K, this reaction has $K_P = 6.25 \times 10^{-3}$. Calculate $\Delta G_{500}°$ for this reaction in units of kilojoules.

Bond Energies and Heats of Reaction

18.88 Use the data in Table 18.4 to compute the approximate atomization energy of NH_3.

18.89 Approximately how much energy would be released during the formation of the bonds in one mole of acetone molecules? Acetone, the solvent usually found in nail polish remover, has the structural formula

```
      H  :O:  H
      |   ||   |
  H — C — C — C — H
      |        |
      H        H
```

OH 18.90 The standard heat of formation of ethanol vapor, $C_2H_5OH(g)$, is -235.3 kJ mol^{-1}. Use the data in Table 18.3 and the average bond energies for C—C, C—H, and O—H bonds to estimate the C—O bond energy in this molecule. The structure of the molecule is

$$\begin{array}{c} \text{H} \quad \text{H} \\ | \quad \quad | \\ \text{H} - \text{C} - \text{C} - \ddot{\text{O}} - \text{H} \\ | \quad \quad | \\ \text{H} \quad \text{H} \end{array}$$

18.91 The standard heat of formation of ethylene, $C_2H_4(g)$, is $+52.284$ kJ mol^{-1}. Calculate the $C{=}C$ bond energy in this molecule.

ILW 18.92 Carbon disulfide, CS_2, has the Lewis structure $:\ddot{S}{=}C{=}\ddot{S}:$, and for $CS_2(g)$, $\Delta H_f^\circ = +115.3$ kJ mol^{-1}. Use the data in Table 18.3 to calculate the average $C{=}S$ bond energy in this molecule.

18.93 Gaseous hydrogen sulfide, H_2S, has $\Delta H_f^\circ = -20.15$ kJ mol^{-1}. Use data in Table 18.3 to calculate the average $S{-}H$ bond energy in this molecule.

18.94 For $SF_6(g)$, $\Delta H_f^\circ = -1096$ kJ mol^{-1}. Use the data in Table 18.3 to calculate the average $S{-}F$ bond energy in SF_6.

18.95 Use the results of the preceding problem and the data in Table C.2 to calculate the standard heat of formation of $SF_4(g)$. The measured value of ΔH_f° for $SF_4(g)$ is -718.4 kJ mol^{-1}. What is the percentage difference between your calculated value of ΔH_f° and the experimentally determined value?

18.96 Use the data in Tables 18.3 and 18.4 to estimate the standard heat of formation of acetylene, $H{-}C{\equiv}C{-}H$, in the gaseous state.

18.97 What would be the approximate heat of formation of CCl_4 vapor at 25 °C and 1 atm?

18.98 Which substance should have the more exothermic heat of formation, CF_4 or CCl_4?

*18.99 Would you expect the value of ΔH_f° for benzene, C_6H_6, computed from tabulated bond energies, to be very close to the experimentally measured value of ΔH_f°? Justify your answer.

ADDITIONAL EXERCISES

18.100 If pressure is expressed in atmospheres and volume is expressed in liters, $P\Delta V$ has units of L atm (liters $\times$ atmospheres). In Chapter 10 you learned that 1 atm = 101,325 Pa, and in Chapter 1 you learned that 1 L = 1 dm^3. Use this information to determine the number of joules corresponding to 1 L atm.

18.101 Calculate the work, in joules, done by a gas as it expands at constant temperature from a volume of 3.00 L and a pressure of 5.00 atm to a volume of 8.00 L. The external pressure against which the gas expands is 1.00 atm. (1 atm = 101,325 Pa.)

*18.102 When an ideal gas expands at a constant temperature, $\Delta E = 0$ for the change. Why?

*18.103 When a real gas expands at a constant temperature, $\Delta E > 0$ for the change. Why?

18.104 An ideal gas in a cylinder fitted with a piston expands at constant temperature from a pressure of 5 atm and a volume of 12 L to a final volume of 30 L against a constant opposing pressure of 2.0 atm. How much heat does the gas absorb, expressed in units of L atm (liter $\times$ atm)? (Hint: See Problem 18.102)

*18.105 A cylinder fitted with a piston contains 5.00 L of a gas at a pressure of 4.00 atm. The entire apparatus is contained in a water bath to maintain a constant temperature of 25 °C.

The piston is released and the gas expands until the pressure inside the cylinder equals the atmospheric pressure outside, which is 1 atm. Assume ideal gas behavior and calculate the amount of work done by the gas as it expands at constant temperature.

*18.106 The experiment described in the preceding problem is repeated, but this time a weight, which exerts a pressure of 2 atm, is placed on the piston. When the gas expands, its pressure drops to 2 atm. Then the weight is removed and the gas is allowed to expand again to a final pressure of 1 atm. Throughout both expansions the temperature of the apparatus was held at a constant 25 °C. Calculate the amount of work performed by the gas in each step. How does the combined total amount of work in this two-step expansion compare with the amount of work done by the gas in the one-step expansion described in the preceding problem? How can even more work be obtained by the expansion of the gas?

18.107 When potassium iodide dissolves in water, the mixture becomes cool. For this change, which is of a larger magnitude, $T\Delta S$ or ΔH?

18.108 The enthalpy of combustion, $\Delta H_{combustion}^\circ$, of oxalic acid, $H_2C_2O_4(s)$, is -246.05 kJ mol^{-1}. Consider the following data:

Substance	ΔH_f° (kJ mol^{-1})	S° (J mol^{-1} K^{-1})
$C(s)$	0	5.69
$CO_2(g)$	-393.5	213.6
$H_2(g)$	0	130.6
$H_2O(l)$	-285.8	69.96
$O_2(g)$	0	205.0
$H_2C_2O_4(s)$	?	120.1

(a) Write the balanced thermochemical equation that describes the combustion of one mole of oxalic acid.

(b) Write the balanced thermochemical equation that describes the formation of one mole of oxalic acid.

(c) Use the information in the table above and the equations in parts (a) and (b) to calculate ΔH_f° for oxalic acid.

(d) Calculate ΔS_f° for oxalic acid and ΔS° for the combustion of one mole of oxalic acid.

(e) Calculate ΔG_f° for oxalic acid and ΔG° for the combustion of one mole of oxalic acid.

OH 18.109 Many biochemical reactions have positive values for ΔG° and seemingly should not be expected to be spontaneous. They occur, however, because they are chemically coupled with other reactions that have negative values of ΔG°. An example is the set of reactions that forms the beginning part of the sequence of reactions involved in the metabolism of glucose, a sugar. Given these reactions and their corresponding ΔG° values,

Glucose + phosphate $\longrightarrow$ glucose 6-phosphate + H_2O
$$\Delta G^\circ = +13.13 \text{ kJ}$$

ATP + H_2O $\longrightarrow$ ADP + phosphate
$$\Delta G^\circ = -32.22 \text{ kJ}$$

calculate ΔG° for the coupled reaction

Glucose + ATP $\longrightarrow$ glucose 6-phosphate + ADP

*18.110 The reaction

$$2C_4H_{10}(g) + 13O_2(g) \longrightarrow 8CO_2(g) + 10H_2O(g)$$

has $\Delta G° = -5407$ kJ. Determine the value of $\Delta G_f°$ for $C_4H_{10}(g)$. Calculate the value of K_c for the reaction at 25 °C.

*18.111 At 1500 °C, $K_c = 5.67$ for the reaction

$$CH_4(g) + H_2O(g) \rightleftharpoons CO(g) + 3H_2(g)$$

Calculate the value of $\Delta G_{1773}°$ for the reaction at that temperature.

18.112 Given the following reactions and their values of $\Delta G°$, calculate the value of $\Delta G_f°$ for $N_2O_5(g)$.

$$2H_2(g) + O_2(g) \longrightarrow 2H_2O(l) \qquad \Delta G° = -474.4 \text{ kJ}$$

$$N_2O_5(g) + H_2O(l) \longrightarrow 2HNO_3(l)$$
$$\Delta G° = -37.6 \text{ kJ}$$

$$\tfrac{1}{2}N_2(g) + \tfrac{3}{2}O_2(g) + \tfrac{1}{2}H_2(g) \longrightarrow HNO_3(l)$$
$$\Delta G° = -79.91 \text{ kJ}$$

18.113 Ethyl alcohol, C_2H_5OH, has been suggested as an alternative to gasoline as a fuel. In Example 18.5 we calculated $\Delta G°$ for combustion of 1 mol of C_2H_5OH; in Example 18.6 we calculated $\Delta G°$ for combustion of 1 mol of octane. Let's assume that gasoline has the same properties as octane (one of its constituents). The density of C_2H_5OH is 0.7893 g/mL; the density of octane, C_8H_{18}, is 0.7025 g/mL. Calculate the maximum work that could be obtained by burning 1 gallon (3.78 liters) each of C_2H_5OH and C_8H_{18}. On a *volume* basis, which is the better fuel?

*18.114 At room temperature (25 °C), the gas ClNO is impure because it decomposes slightly according to the equation

$$2ClNO(g) \rightleftharpoons Cl_2(g) + 2NO(g)$$

The extent of decomposition is about 5%. What is the approximate value of ΔG_{298} for the reaction at that temperature?

*18.115 The reaction

$$N_2O(g) + O_2(g) \rightleftharpoons NO_2(g) + NO(g)$$

has $\Delta H° = -42.9$ kJ and $\Delta S° = -26.1$ J/K. Suppose 0.100 mol of N_2O and 0.100 mol of O_2 are placed in a 2.00 L container at 500 °C and the equilibrium is established. What percentage of the N_2O has reacted? (Note: Assume that ΔH and ΔS are relatively insensitive to temperature, so $\Delta H_{298}°$ and $\Delta S_{298}°$ are about the same as $\Delta H_{773}°$ and $\Delta S_{773}°$, respectively.)

18.116 Use the data in Table 18.3 to calculate the bond energy in the nitrogen molecule and the oxygen molecule.

18.117 The heat of vaporization of carbon tetrachloride, CCl_4, is 29.9 kJ mol^{-1}. Using this information and data in Tables 18.3 and 18.4, estimate the standard heat of formation of liquid CCl_4.

*18.118 At 25 °C, 0.0560 mol O_2 and 0.020 mol N_2O were placed in a 1.00 L container where the following equilibrium was then established.

$$2N_2O(g) + 3O_2(g) \rightleftharpoons 4NO_2(g)$$

At equilibrium, the NO_2 concentration was 0.020 M. Calculate the value of $\Delta G°$ for the reaction.

18.119 For the substance $SO_2F_2(g)$, $\Delta H_f° = -858$ kJ mol^{-1}. The structure of the SO_2F_2 molecule is

Use the value of the S—F bond energy calculated in Problem 18.94 and the data in Table C.2 to determine the average S=O bond energy in SO_2F_2 in units of kJ mol^{-1}.

EXERCISES IN CRITICAL THINKING

18.120 On earth, we do not normally find collections of individual subatomic particles, such as protons, neutrons, and electrons. Rather, they are assembled into atoms of various kinds. On the other hand, in the interior of stars individual atoms don't exist. There, an atom would break apart into separate subatomic particles. Explain this in terms of the principles of thermodynamics.

18.121 The average C—H bond energy calculated using the procedure in Section 18.10 is not quite equal to the energy needed to cause the reaction $CH_4(g) \longrightarrow CH_3(g) + H(g)$. Suggest reasons why this is so.

18.122 Discuss the statement: A world near absolute zero would be controlled almost entirely by potential energy.

18.123 If a catalyst were able to affect the position of equilibrium in a reaction, it would be possible to construct a perpetual motion machine (a machine from which energy could be extracted without having to put energy into it). Imagine how such a machine could be made. Why would it violate the first law of thermodynamics?

18.124 At the beginning of this chapter we noted that the reaction of CO_2 with H_2O to form a hydrocarbon fuel is nonspontaneous. According to thermodynamics, where would the position of equilibrium lie for such a reaction. Why?

9 ELECTROCHEMISTRY

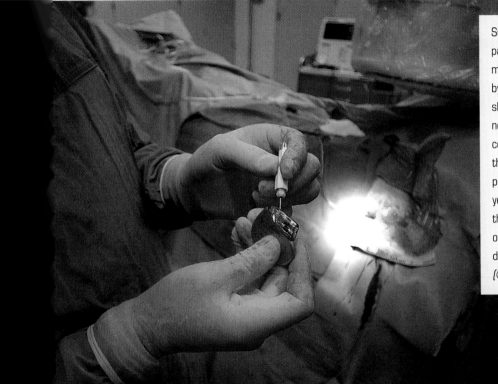

Surgeons implant a heart pacemaker to help this patient maintain a reasonable heart rate by providing a gentle electrical shock to the heart muscle as needed. The most critical component of the pacemaker is the battery that must remain in place and active for up to seven years at a time. Batteries and their design are important parts of the electrochemistry discussed in this chapter.
(© AP/Wide World Photos)

CHAPTER OUTLINE

19.1 Galvanic cells use redox reactions to generate electricity

19.2 Cell potentials can be related to reduction potentials

19.3 Standard reduction potentials can predict spontaneous reactions

19.4 Cell potentials are related to free energy changes

19.5 Concentrations in a galvanic cell affect the cell potential

19.6 Electrolysis uses electrical energy to cause chemical reactions

19.7 Stoichiometry of electrochemical reactions involves electric current and time

19.8 Practical applications of electrochemistry

CHAPTER IN CONTEXT   Oxidation and reduction (redox) reactions occur in many chemical ...s. Examples include our own respiratory system and the complementary photosynthetic system in plants. In ...n there's the toasting of bread, the rusting of iron, the action of bleach on stains, and the production and ...stion of petroleum that heats us, generates electricity, and moves our cars. In this chapter we will study how ...ssible to separate the processes of oxidation (electron loss) and reduction (electron gain) and cause them to ...n different physical locations. When we are able to do this, we can use spontaneous redox reactions to produce ...ity. And by reversing the process, we can use electricity to make nonspontaneous redox reactions happen to ...e important products by a process called electrolysis.

...cause electricity plays a role in these systems, the processes involved are described as **electrochemical** ...es. The study of such changes is called **electrochemistry.** As you will learn, electrical measurements and the principles of thermodynamics combine to give fundamental information about chemical reactions, such as free energy changes and equilibrium constants. In addition, you will learn some of the practical applications of electrochemistry.

The last section of this chapter describes modern batteries. Development of new, highly efficient, light weight and relatively inexpensive batteries and fuel cells is an area of intensive research. These devices will be important contributors to efforts to conserve fossil fuels.

19.1 | GALVANIC CELLS USE REDOX REACTIONS TO GENERATE ELECTRICITY

Batteries have become common sources of portable power for a wide range of consumer products, from cell phones to iPods to laptops and hybrid cars. The energy from a battery comes from a spontaneous redox reaction in which the electron transfer is forced to take place through a wire. The apparatus that provides electricity in this way is called a **galvanic cell,** after Luigi Galvani (1737–1798), an Italian anatomist who discovered that electricity can cause the contraction of muscles. [It is also called a **voltaic cell,** after another Italian scientist, Alessandro Volta (1745–1827), whose inventions led ultimately to the development of modern batteries.]

Galvanic cells form a useful electrical circuit

If a shiny piece of metallic copper is placed into a solution of silver nitrate, a spontaneous reaction occurs. Gradually, a grayish white deposit forms on the copper and the solution itself becomes pale blue as hydrated Cu^{2+} ions enter the solution (see Figure 19.1). The equation is

$$2Ag^+(aq) + Cu(s) \longrightarrow Cu^{2+}(aq) + 2Ag(s)$$

Although the reaction is exothermic, no usable energy can be harnessed from it because all the energy is dispersed as heat.

To produce useful *electrical* energy, the two half-reactions involved in the net reaction must be made to occur in separate containers or compartments called **half-cells.** When this is done, electrons must flow through an external circuit to power devices

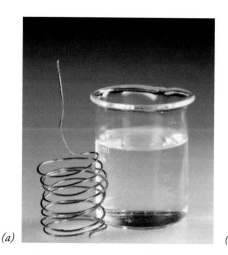

(a) (b) (c)

FIG. 19.1 **Reaction of copper with a solution of silver nitrate.** (*a*) A coil of copper wire stands next to a beaker containing a silver nitrate solution. (*b*) When the copper wire is placed in the solution, copper dissolves, giving the solution its blue color, and metallic silver deposits as glittering crystals on the wire. (*c*) After a while, much of the copper has dissolved and nearly all of the silver has deposited as the free metal. (*Michael Watson.*)

such as a laser pointer, a laptop computer, or your iPod. An apparatus to accomplish this—a **galvanic cell**—is made up of two half-cells, as illustrated in Figure 19.2. On the left, a silver electrode dips into a solution of $AgNO_3$, and, on the right, a copper electrode dips into a solution of $Cu(NO_3)_2$. The two electrodes are connected by an external electrical circuit and the two solutions are connected by a *salt bridge*, the function of which will be described shortly. When the circuit is completed by closing the switch, the reduction of Ag^+ to Ag occurs spontaneously in the half-cell on the left and oxidation of Cu to Cu^{2+} occurs spontaneously in the half-cell on the right. The reaction that takes place in each half-cell is a *half-reaction* of the type you learned to balance by the ion–electron method in Chapter 5. In the silver half-cell, the following half-reaction occurs.

$$Ag^+(aq) + e^- \longrightarrow Ag(s) \qquad \text{(reduction)}$$

In the copper half-cell, the half-reaction is

$$Cu(s) \longrightarrow Cu^{2+}(aq) + 2e^- \qquad \text{(oxidation)}$$

When these reactions take place, electrons, left behind by oxidation of the copper, travel through the external circuit to the other electrode where they are transferred to the silver ions, as Ag^+ is reduced to the familiar shiny silver metal.

□ When electrons appear as a reactant, the process is reduction; when they appear as a product, it is oxidation.

The cell reaction is the net overall reaction in the cell

The overall reaction that takes place in the galvanic cell is called the **cell reaction.** To obtain it, we combine the individual electrode half-reactions, making sure that the number of electrons gained in one half-reaction equals the number lost in the other. Thus, to obtain the cell reaction we multiply the half-reaction for the reduction of silver by 2 and then add the two half-reactions to obtain the net reaction. (Notice that $2e^-$ appear on each side, and so they cancel.) This is exactly the same as the process we used to balance redox reactions by the ion–electron method described in Section 5.2.

$$
\begin{aligned}
2Ag^+(aq) + 2e^- &\longrightarrow 2Ag(s) &&\text{(reduction)} \\
Cu(s) &\longrightarrow Cu^{2+}(aq) + 2e^- &&\text{(oxidation)} \\
\hline
2Ag^+(aq) + Cu(s) + \cancel{2e^-} &\longrightarrow 2Ag(s) + Cu^{2+}(aq) + \cancel{2e^-} &&\text{(cell reaction)}
\end{aligned}
$$

□ The two electrons canceled in this reaction are also the number of electrons transferred. These will be important later when we discuss the Nernst equation.

□ A galvanic cell is composed of two half-cells connected by an external circuit and a salt bridge.

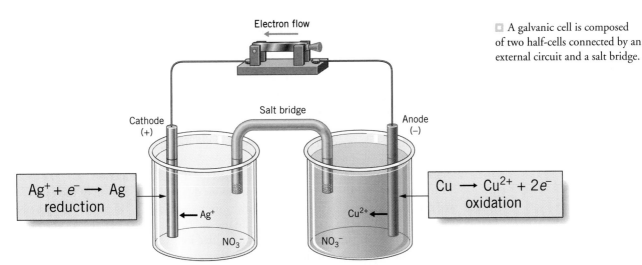

FIG. 19.2 **A galvanic cell.** The cell consists of two half-cells. Oxidation takes place in one half-cell and reduction in the other as indicated by the half-reactions.

Electrodes are named according to the chemical processes that occur at them

The electrodes in electrochemical systems are identified by the names *cathode* and *anode*. The names are *always* assigned according to the nature of the chemical changes that occur at the electrodes. In any electrochemical system:

TOOLS
Electrode reactions

> The **cathode** is the electrode at which reduction (electron gain) occurs.
> The **anode** is the electrode at which oxidation (electron loss) occurs.

Thus, in the galvanic cell we've been discussing, the silver electrode is the cathode and the copper electrode is the anode.

Conduction of charge occurs in two ways

In the external circuit of a galvanic cell, electrical charge is transported from one electrode to the other by the movement of *electrons* through the wires. This is called **metallic conduction,** and is how metals in general conduct electricity. In this external circuit, electrons always travel from the anode, where they are left behind by the oxidation process, to the cathode, where they are picked up by the substance being reduced.

In electrochemical cells another kind of electrical conduction also takes place. In a solution that contains ions (or in a molten ionic compound), *electrical charge is carried through the liquid by the movement of ions, not electrons.* The transport of electrical charge by ions is called **electrolytic conduction.**

When the reactions take place in the copper–silver galvanic cell, positive copper ions *enter* the liquid that surrounds the anode while positive silver ions *leave* the liquid that surrounds the cathode (Figure 19.3). For the galvanic cell to work, the solutions in both half-cells must remain electrically neutral. This requires that ions be permitted to enter or leave the solutions. For example, when copper is oxidized, the solution surrounding the anode becomes filled with Cu^{2+} ions, so negative ions are needed to balance their charge. Similarly, when Ag^+ ions are reduced, NO_3^- ions are left behind in the solution and positive ions are needed to maintain neutrality. The **salt bridge** shown in Figure 19.2 allows the movement of ions required to keep the solutions electrically neutral. The salt bridge is also essential to complete the electrical circuit.

☐ Often the salt bridge is prepared by saturating a hot agar-agar solution with KNO_3 or KCl. After pouring into a U-shaped tube the agar-agar solidifies on cooling. The salt ions can move but the agar-agar does not flow out of the salt bridge.

A salt bridge is a tube filled with a solution of a salt composed of ions not involved in the cell reaction. Often KNO_3 or KCl is used. The tube is fitted with porous plugs at each end that prevent the solution from pouring out but at the same time enable the solution in the salt bridge to exchange ions with the solutions in the half-cells.

During operation of the cell, negative ions can diffuse from the salt bridge into the copper half-cell, or, to a much smaller extent, Cu^{2+} ions can leave the solution and enter the salt bridge. Both processes help keep the copper half-cell electrically neutral. At the silver half-cell, positive ions from the salt bridge can enter or negative NO_3^- ions can, once again to a much smaller extent, leave the half-cell by entering the salt bridge, to keep it electrically neutral.

Without the salt bridge, electrical neutrality could not be maintained and no electrical current could be produced by the cell. Therefore, *electrolytic contact*—contact by means of a solution containing ions—must be maintained for the cell to function.

If we look closely at the overall movement of ions during the operation of the galvanic cell, we find that negative ions (*anions*) move away from the cathode, where they are present in excess, and *toward the anode*, where they are needed to balance the charge of the positive ions being formed. Similarly, we find that positive ions (*cations*) move away from the anode, where they are in excess, and *toward the cathode*, where they can balance the charge of the anions left in excess. In fact, the reason positive ions are called cations and negative ions are called anions is because of the nature of the electrodes toward which they move.

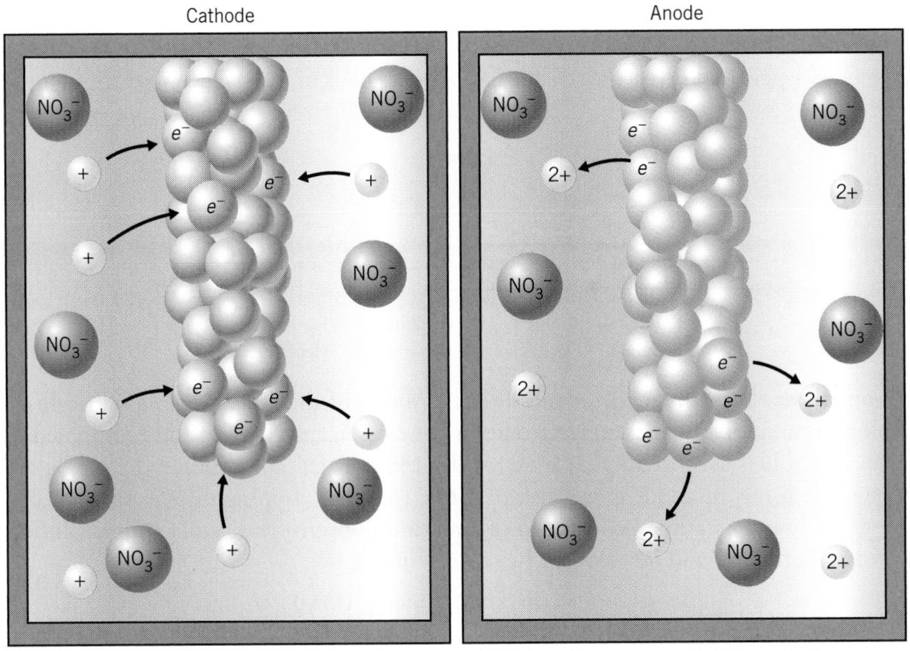

Cathode   Anode

Reduction of silver ions at the cathode extracts electrons from the electrode, so the electrode becomes positively charged.

Oxidation of copper atoms at the anode leaves electrons behind on the electrode, which becomes negatively charged.

FIG. 19.3 Expanded view of Figure 19.2 to show changes that take place at the anode and cathode in the copper–silver galvanic cell. (Not drawn to scale.) At the anode, Cu^{2+} ions enter the solution when copper atoms are oxidized, leaving electrons behind on the electrode. Unless Cu^{2+} ions move away from the electrode or NO_3^- ions move toward it, the solution around the electrode will become positively charged. At the cathode, Ag^+ ions leave the solution and become silver atoms by acquiring electrons from the electrode surface. Unless more silver ions move toward the cathode or negative ions move away, the solution around the electrode will become negatively charged.

In summary,

Cations move in the general direction of the cathode.
Anions move in the general direction of the anode.

Charges on the electrodes come from electron loss and gain

At the anode of the galvanic cell described in Figures 19.2 and 19.3, copper atoms spontaneously leave the electrode and enter the solution as Cu^{2+} ions. The electrons that are left behind give the anode a slight negative charge. (We say the anode has a *negative polarity*.) At the cathode, electrons spontaneously join Ag^+ ions to produce neutral atoms, but the effect is the same as if Ag^+ ions become part of the electrode, so the cathode acquires a slight positive charge. (The cathode has a *positive polarity*.) During the operation of the cell, the amount of positive and negative charge on the electrodes is kept small by the flow of electrons (an electric current) through the external circuit from the anode to the cathode when the circuit is complete. In fact, unless electrons can flow out of the anode and into the cathode, the chemical reactions that occur at their surfaces will cease.

☐ The small difference in charge between the electrodes is formed by the spontaneity of the overall reaction, that is, by the favorable free energy change. Nature's tendency toward electrical neutrality prevents a large buildup of charge on the electrodes and promotes the spontaneous flow of electricity through the external circuit.

Cell notation gives a shorthand description of a galvanic cell

As a matter of convenience, chemists have devised a shorthand way of describing the makeup of a galvanic cell. For example, the copper–silver cell that we have been using in our discussion is represented as follows.

$$Cu(s)\,|\,Cu^{2+}(aq)\,||\,Ag^+(aq)\,|\,Ag(s)$$

By convention, in **standard cell notation,** the anode half-cell is specified on the left, with the electrode material of the anode given first. In this case, the anode is copper metal. The single vertical bar represents a *phase boundary*—between the copper electrode and the solution that surrounds it. The double vertical bars represent the two phase boundaries, one at each

☐ Also, notice that for each half-cell, the reactant in the redox half-reaction is given first. In the anode compartment, Cu is the reactant and is oxidized to Cu^{2+}, whereas in the cathode compartment, Ag^+ is the reactant and is reduced to Ag.

end of the salt bridge, which connects the solutions in the two half-cells. On the right, the cathode half-cell is described, with the material of the cathode given last. Thus, the electrodes themselves (copper and silver) are specified at opposite ends of the cell description.

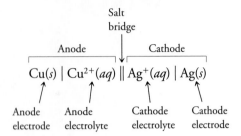

Sometimes, both the oxidized and reduced forms of the reactants in a half-cell are soluble and cannot be used as an electrode. In these cases, an inert electrode composed of platinum or gold is used to provide a site for electron transfer. For example, a galvanic cell can be made using an anode composed of a zinc electrode dipping into a solution containing Zn^{2+}, and a cathode composed of a platinum electrode dipping into a solution containing both Fe^{2+} and Fe^{3+} ions. The cell reaction is

$$2Fe^{3+}(aq) + Zn(s) \longrightarrow 2Fe^{2+}(aq) + Zn^{2+}(aq)$$

The cell notation for this galvanic cell is written as follows.

$$Zn(s)|Zn^{2+}(aq)||Fe^{3+}(aq), Fe^{2+}(aq)|Pt(s)$$

where we have separated the formulas for the two iron ions by a comma. In this cell, the reduction of the Fe^{3+} to Fe^{2+} takes place at the surface of the inert platinum electrode.

EXAMPLE 19.1
Describing Galvanic Cells

The following spontaneous reaction occurs when metallic zinc is dipped into a solution of copper sulfate.

$$Zn(s) + Cu^{2+}(aq) \longrightarrow Zn^{2+}(aq) + Cu(s)$$

Describe a galvanic cell that could take advantage of this reaction. What are the half-cell reactions? What is the standard cell notation? Make a sketch of the cell and label the cathode and anode, the charges on each electrode, the direction of ion flow, and the direction of electron flow.

ANALYSIS: Answering all these questions relies on identifying the anode and cathode in the equation for the cell reaction; this is often the key to solving problems of this type. By definition, the anode is the electrode at which oxidation happens, and the cathode is where reduction occurs. The first step, therefore, is to determine which reactant is oxidized and which is reduced. One way to do this is to divide the cell reaction into half-reactions and balance them by adding electrons. Then, if electrons appear as a product, the half-reaction is oxidation; if the electrons appear as a reactant, the half-reaction is reduction.

SOLUTION: The balanced half-reactions are as follows.

$$Zn(s) \longrightarrow Zn^{2+}(aq) + 2e^-$$
$$Cu^{2+}(aq) + 2e^- \longrightarrow Cu(s)$$

Zinc loses electrons and is oxidized, so it is the anode. The anode half-cell is therefore a zinc electrode dipping into a solution that contains Zn^{2+} [e.g., from dissolved $Zn(NO_3)_2$ or $ZnSO_4$]. Symbolically, the anode half-cell is written with the electrode material at the left of the vertical bar and the oxidation product at the right.

$$Zn(s)|Zn^{2+}(aq)$$

Copper ions gain electrons and are reduced to metallic copper, so the cathode half-cell consists of a copper electrode dipping into a solution containing Cu^{2+} [e.g., from dissolved

$Cu(NO_3)_2$ or $CuSO_4$]. The copper half-cell can be represented as follows, with the electrode material to the right of the vertical bar and the substance reduced on the left.

$$Cu^{2+}(aq)|Cu(s)$$

The standard cell notation places the zinc anode half-cell on the left and the copper cathode half-cell on the right separated by double bars that represent the salt bridge.

$$Zn(s)|Zn^{2+}(aq)||Cu^{2+}(aq)|Cu(s)$$
$$\text{anode} \qquad\qquad \text{cathode}$$

A sketch of the cell is shown in the margin. The anode always carries a negative charge in a galvanic cell, so the zinc electrode is negative and the copper electrode is positive. Electrons in the external circuit travel from the negative electrode to the positive electrode (i.e., from the Zn anode to the Cu cathode). Anions move toward the anode and cations move toward the cathode as shown.

ARE THE ANSWERS REASONABLE? All of the answers depend on determining which substance is oxidized and which is reduced, so we check that first. Oxidation is electron loss, and Zn must lose electrons to become Zn^{2+}, so zinc is oxidized and must be the anode. If zinc is the anode, then copper must be the cathode. We can then reason that the oxidation of zinc produces electrons that flow from the anode to the cathode.

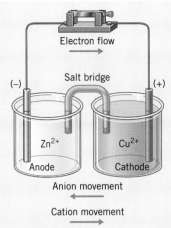

The zinc–copper cell. In the cell notation described in this example, we indicate the anode on the left and the cathode on the right. In this drawing of the apparatus, the anode half-cell is also shown on the left, but it could just as easily be shown on the right, as in Figure 19.2. Be sure you understand that where we place the apparatus on the lab bench doesn't affect which half-cell is the anode and which is the cathode.

Practice Exercise 1: Sketch and label a galvanic cell that makes use of the following spontaneous redox reaction.

$$Mg(s) + Fe^{2+}(aq) \longrightarrow Mg^{2+}(aq) + Fe(s)$$

Write the half-reactions for the anode and cathode. Give the standard cell notation. (Hint: Determine which reactant is being oxidized and which is being reduced.)

Practice Exercise 2: Write the anode and cathode half-reactions for the following galvanic cell. Write the equation for the overall cell reaction.

$$Al(s)|Al^{3+}(aq)||Ni^{2+}(aq)|Ni(s)$$

19.2 | CELL POTENTIALS CAN BE RELATED TO REDUCTION POTENTIALS

A galvanic cell has an ability to push electrons through the external circuit. The magnitude of this ability is expressed as a **potential.** Potential is expressed in an electrical unit called the **volt (V),** which is a measure of the amount of energy, in joules, that can be delivered per **coulomb, C,** (the SI unit of charge) as the charges move through the circuit. Thus, a charge flowing under a potential of 1 volt can deliver 1 joule of energy per coulomb.

$$1\ V = 1\ J/C \qquad\qquad (19.1)$$

□ The potential generated by a galvanic cell has also been called the *electromotive force (emf)*. Modern electrochemistry uses the preferred abbreviations E_{cell} or $E°_{cell}$ to note cell potentials and standard cell potentials, respectively.

The cell potential is the maximum potential produced by a galvanic cell

The voltage or potential of a galvanic cell varies with the amount of charge flowing through the circuit. The *maximum* potential that a given cell can generate is called its **cell potential, E_{cell},** and it depends on the composition of the electrodes, the concentrations of the ions in the half-cells, and the temperature. The standard state for electrochemistry is defined as a system where the temperature is 25 °C, all concentrations are 1.00 M, and any gases are at 1.00 atm pressure. When the system is at standard state, the potential of a galvanic cell is the **standard cell potential,** symbolized by $E°_{cell}$.

□ If charge flows from a cell, some of the cell's voltage is lost overcoming its own internal resistance, and the measured voltage is less than the original E_{cell}.

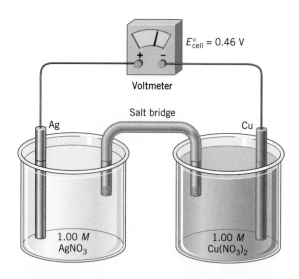

FIG. 19.4 A cell designed to generate the standard cell potential. The concentrations of the Cu^{2+} and Ag^+ ions in the half-cells are 1.00 M. It is very important to always connect the negative terminal of the voltmeter to the anode for correct readings.

Cell potentials are rarely larger than a few volts. For example, the standard cell potential for the galvanic cell constructed from silver and copper electrodes shown in Figure 19.4 is only 0.46 V, and one cell in an automobile battery produces only about 2 V. Batteries that generate higher voltages, such as an automobile battery, contain a number of cells arranged in series so that their potentials are additive.

Reduction potentials are a measure of the tendency of reduction half-reactions to occur

It is useful to think of each half-cell as having a certain natural tendency to acquire electrons and proceed as a *reduction*. The magnitude of this tendency is expressed by the half-reaction's **reduction potential.** When measured under standard conditions, namely, 25 °C, concentrations of 1.00 M for all solutes, and a pressure of 1 atm, the reduction potential is called the **standard reduction potential.** To represent a standard reduction potential, we will add a subscript to the symbol $E°$ that identifies the substance undergoing reduction. Thus, the standard reduction potential for the half-reaction

□ Standard reduction potentials are also called *standard electrode potentials.*

$$Cu^{2+}(aq) + 2e^- \longrightarrow Cu(s)$$

is specified as $E°_{Cu^{2+}}$.

When two half-cells are connected to make a galvanic cell, the one with the larger standard reduction potential (the one with the greater tendency to undergo reduction) acquires electrons from the half-cell with the lower standard reduction potential, which is therefore forced to undergo oxidation. The standard cell potential, which is always taken to be a positive number, represents the *difference* between the standard reduction potential of one half-cell and the standard reduction potential of the other. In general, therefore,

TOOLS

Standard reduction potentials are used to calculate $E°_{cell}$

$$E°_{cell} = \left(\begin{array}{c}\text{standard reduction potential}\\\text{of the substance reduced}\end{array}\right) - \left(\begin{array}{c}\text{standard reduction potential}\\\text{of the substance oxidized}\end{array}\right) \quad (19.2)$$

As an example, let's look at the copper–silver cell. From the cell reaction,

$$2Ag^+(aq) + Cu(s) \longrightarrow 2Ag(s) + Cu^{2+}(aq)$$

we can see that silver ions are reduced and copper is oxidized. If we compare the two possible reduction half-reactions,

$$Ag^+(aq) + e^- \longrightarrow Ag(s)$$

$$Cu^{2+}(aq) + 2e^- \longrightarrow Cu(s)$$

the one for Ag^+ must have a greater tendency to proceed than the one for Cu^{2+}, because it is the silver ion that is actually reduced. This means that the standard reduction potential of Ag^+ must be algebraically larger than the standard reduction potential of Cu^{2+}. In other words, if we knew the values of $E^\circ_{Ag^+}$ and $E^\circ_{Cu^{2+}}$, we could calculate E°_{cell} with Equation 19.2 by subtracting the smaller standard reduction potential (copper) from the larger one (silver).

$$E^\circ_{cell} = E^\circ_{Ag^+} - E^\circ_{Cu^{2+}}$$

Assigning standard reduction potentials requires a reference electrode

Unfortunately there is no way to measure the standard reduction potential of an isolated half-cell. All we can measure is the difference in potential produced when two half-cells are connected. Therefore, to assign numerical values for standard reduction potentials, a reference electrode has been arbitrarily chosen and its standard reduction potential has been defined as *exactly* 0 V. This reference electrode is called the **standard hydrogen electrode** (see Figure 19.5). Gaseous hydrogen at a pressure of 1.00 atm is bubbled over a platinum electrode coated with very finely divided platinum, which provides a large catalytic surface area on which the electrode reaction can occur. This electrode is surrounded by a solution whose temperature is 25 °C and in which the hydrogen ion concentration is 1.00 M. The half-cell reaction at the platinum surface, written as a reduction, is

$$2H^+(aq, 1.00\ M) + 2e^- \rightleftharpoons H_2(g, 1.00\ atm) \qquad E^\circ_{H^+} = 0\ V \text{ (exactly)}$$

The double arrows indicate only that the reaction is reversible, not that there is true equilibrium. Whether the half-reaction occurs as reduction or oxidation depends on the standard reduction potential of the half-cell with which it is paired.

Figure 19.6 illustrates the hydrogen electrode connected to a copper half-cell to form a galvanic cell. When we use a voltmeter to measure the potential of the cell, we find that the copper electrode carries a positive charge and the hydrogen electrode a negative charge. Therefore, copper must be the cathode, and Cu^{2+} is reduced to Cu when the cell operates. Similarly, hydrogen must be the anode, and H_2 is oxidized to H^+. The half-reactions and cell reaction, therefore, are

$$Cu^{2+}(aq) + 2e^- \longrightarrow Cu(s) \qquad \text{(cathode)}$$

$$\underline{\qquad H_2(g) \longrightarrow 2H^+(aq) + 2e^- \qquad} \text{(anode)}$$

$$Cu^{2+}(aq) + H_2(g) \longrightarrow Cu(s) + 2H^+(aq) \qquad \text{(cell reaction)}[1]$$

Using Equation 19.2, we can express E°_{cell} in terms of $E^\circ_{Cu^{2+}}$ and $E^\circ_{H^+}$.

$$E^\circ_{cell} = E^\circ_{Cu^{2+}} - E^\circ_{H^+}$$

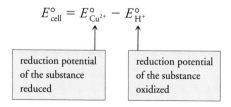

| reduction potential of the substance reduced | reduction potential of the substance oxidized |

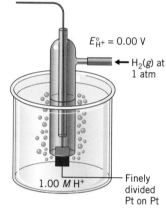

$E^\circ_{H^+} = 0.00$ V

← $H_2(g)$ at 1 atm

1.00 M H^+

Finely divided Pt on Pt

FIG. 19.5 **The hydrogen electrode.** The half-reaction is $2H^+(aq) + 2e^- \rightleftharpoons H_2(g)$.

[1] The cell notation for this cell is written as

$$Pt(s), H_2(g)|H^+(aq)||Cu^{2+}(aq)|Cu(s)$$

The notation for the hydrogen electrode (the anode in this case) is shown at the left of the double vertical bars. Although there is a phase boundary between H_2 and Pt, they are shown together to emphasize their simultaneous contact with the solution.

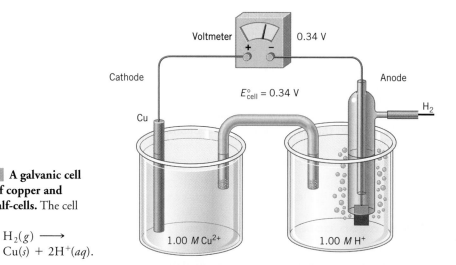

FIG. 19.6 **A galvanic cell composed of copper and hydrogen half-cells.** The cell reaction is
$$Cu^{2+}(aq) + H_2(g) \longrightarrow$$
$$Cu(s) + 2H^+(aq).$$

☐ In a galvanic cell, the measured cell potential is *always* taken to be a positive value. This is important to remember.

The measured standard cell potential is 0.34 V and $E^{\circ}_{H^+}$ equals 0.00 V.[2] Therefore,

$$0.34 \text{ V} = E^{\circ}_{Cu^{2+}} - 0.00 \text{ V}$$

Relative to the hydrogen electrode, then, the standard reduction potential of Cu^{2+} is +0.34 V. (We have written the value with a plus sign because some standard reduction potentials are negative, as we will see.)

Now let's look at a galvanic cell set up between a zinc electrode and a hydrogen electrode (see Figure 19.7). This time we find that the hydrogen electrode is positive and the zinc electrode is negative, which tells us that the hydrogen electrode is the cathode and the zinc electrode is the anode. This means that hydrogen ion is being reduced and zinc is being oxidized. The half-reactions and cell reaction are therefore

$$2H^+(aq) + 2e^- \longrightarrow H_2(g) \qquad \text{(cathode)}$$
$$\underline{Zn(s) \longrightarrow Zn^{2+}(aq) + 2e^- \qquad \text{(anode)}}$$
$$2H^+(aq) + Zn(s) \longrightarrow H_2(g) + Zn^{2+}(aq) \qquad \text{(cell reaction)[3]}$$

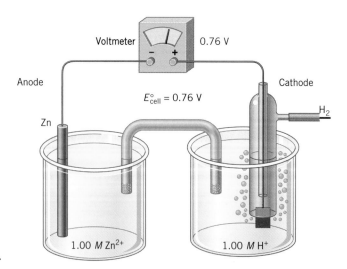

FIG. 19.7 **A galvanic cell composed of zinc and hydrogen half-cells.** The cell reaction is
$$Zn(s) + 2H^+(aq) \longrightarrow$$
$$Zn^{2+}(aq) + H_2(g).$$

[2] The standard reduction potential for the reduction of hydrogen ions is exactly zero. We will be writing its value in mathematical problems with the number of decimal places required to maintain the precision of the opposing electrode potential. In this case we used two decimal places (0.00) to match the two decimal places of the 0.34 V standard cell potential.

[3] This cell is represented as

$$Zn(s)|Zn^{2+}(aq)||H^+(aq)|H_2(g), Pt(s)$$

This time the hydrogen electrode is the cathode and appears at the right of the double vertical bars.

From Equation 19.2, the standard cell potential is given by

$$E^\circ_{cell} = E^\circ_{H^+} - E^\circ_{Zn^{2+}}$$

Substituting into this the measured standard cell potential of 0.76 V and $E^\circ_{H^+} = 0.00$ V, we have

$$0.76 \text{ V} = 0.00 \text{ V} - E^\circ_{Zn^{2+}}$$

which gives

$$E^\circ_{Zn^{2+}} = -0.76 \text{ V}$$

Notice that the standard reduction potential of zinc is negative. A negative standard reduction potential simply means that the substance is not as easily reduced as H^+. In this case, it tells us that Zn is oxidized when it is paired with the hydrogen electrode.

The standard reduction potentials of many half-reactions can be compared to that for the standard hydrogen electrode in the manner described above. Table 19.1 lists values obtained for some typical half-reactions. They are arranged in decreasing order—the

TABLE 19.1 Standard Reduction Potentials at 25 °C	
Half-Reaction	E° (volts)
$F_2(g) + 2e^- \rightleftharpoons 2F^-(aq)$	+2.87
$S_2O_8^{2-}(aq) + 2e^- \rightleftharpoons 2SO_4^{2-}(aq)$	+2.01
$PbO_2(s) + HSO_4^-(aq) + 3H^+(aq) + 2e^- \rightleftharpoons PbSO_4(s) + 2H_2O$	+1.69
$2HOCl(aq) + 2H^+(aq) + 2e^- \rightleftharpoons Cl_2(g) + 2H_2O$	+1.63
$MnO_4^-(aq) + 8H^+(aq) + 5e^- \rightleftharpoons Mn^{2+}(aq) + 4H_2O$	+1.51
$PbO_2(s) + 4H^+(aq) + 2e^- \rightleftharpoons Pb^{2+}(aq) + 2H_2O$	+1.46
$BrO_3^-(aq) + 6H^+(aq) + 6e^- \rightleftharpoons Br^-(aq) + 3H_2O$	+1.44
$Au^{3+}(aq) + 3e^- \rightleftharpoons Au(s)$	+1.42
$Cl_2(g) + 2e^- \rightleftharpoons 2Cl^-(aq)$	+1.36
$O_2(g) + 4H^+(aq) + 4e^- \rightleftharpoons 2H_2O$	+1.23
$Br_2(aq) + 2e^- \rightleftharpoons 2Br^-(aq)$	+1.07
$NO_3^-(aq) + 4H^+(aq) + 3e^- \rightleftharpoons NO(g) + 2H_2O$	+0.96
$Ag^+(aq) + e^- \rightleftharpoons Ag(s)$	+0.80
$Fe^{3+}(aq) + e^- \rightleftharpoons Fe^{2+}(aq)$	+0.77
$I_2(s) + 2e^- \rightleftharpoons 2I^-(aq)$	+0.54
$NiO_2(s) + 2H_2O + 2e^- \rightleftharpoons Ni(OH)_2(s) + 2OH^-(aq)$	+0.49
$Cu^{2+}(aq) + 2e^- \rightleftharpoons Cu(s)$	+0.34
$SO_4^{2-}(aq) + 4H^+(aq) + 2e^- \rightleftharpoons H_2SO_3(aq) + H_2O$	+0.17
$AgBr(s) + e^- \rightleftharpoons Ag(s) + Br^-(aq)$	+0.07
$2H^+(aq) + 2e^- \rightleftharpoons H_2(g)$	0
$Sn^{2+}(aq) + 2e^- \rightleftharpoons Sn(s)$	-0.14
$Ni^{2+}(aq) + 2e^- \rightleftharpoons Ni(s)$	-0.25
$Co^{2+}(aq) + 2e^- \rightleftharpoons Co(s)$	-0.28
$PbSO_4(s) + H^+(aq) + 2e^- \rightleftharpoons Pb(s) + HSO_4^-(aq)$	-0.36
$Cd^{2+}(aq) + 2e^- \rightleftharpoons Cd(s)$	-0.40
$Fe^{2+}(aq) + 2e^- \rightleftharpoons Fe(s)$	-0.44
$Cr^{3+}(aq) + 3e^- \rightleftharpoons Cr(s)$	-0.74
$Zn^{2+}(aq) + 2e^- \rightleftharpoons Zn(s)$	-0.76
$2H_2O + 2e^- \rightleftharpoons H_2(g) + 2OH^-(aq)$	-0.83
$Al^{3+}(aq) + 3e^- \rightleftharpoons Al(s)$	-1.66
$Mg^{2+}(aq) + 2e^- \rightleftharpoons Mg(s)$	-2.37
$Na^+(aq) + e^- \rightleftharpoons Na(s)$	-2.71
$Ca^{2+}(aq) + 2e^- \rightleftharpoons Ca(s)$	-2.76
$K^+(aq) + e^- \rightleftharpoons K(s)$	-2.92
$Li^+(aq) + e^- \rightleftharpoons Li(s)$	-3.05

☐ Substances located to the left of the double arrows are *oxidizing agents*, because they become reduced when the reactions proceed in the forward direction. The best oxidizing agents are those most easily reduced, and they are located at the top of the table (e.g., F_2).

☐ Substances located to the right of the double arrows are *reducing agents*; they become oxidized when the reactions proceed from right to left. The best reducing agents are those found at the bottom of the table (e.g., Li).

half-reactions at the top have the greatest tendency to occur as reduction, while those at the bottom have the least tendency to occur as reduction.

EXAMPLE 19.2
Calculating Standard Cell Potentials

We mentioned earlier that the standard cell potential of the silver–copper galvanic cell has a value of $+0.46$ V. The cell reaction is

$$2Ag^+(aq) + Cu(s) \longrightarrow 2Ag(s) + Cu^{2+}(aq)$$

and we have seen that the standard reduction potential of Cu^{2+}, $E^\circ_{Cu^{2+}}$, is $+0.34$ V. What is the value of $E^\circ_{Ag^+}$, the standard reduction potential of Ag^+?

ANALYSIS: Since we know the standard potential of the cell and one of the two standard reduction potentials, Equation 19.2 will be our tool to calculate the unknown standard reduction potential. This requires that we identify the substance oxidized and the substance reduced. We can do this by dividing the cell reaction into half-reactions, or we can observe how the oxidation numbers of the reactants change. Recall that if the oxidation number increases algebraically, the substance undergoes oxidation, whereas if the oxidation number decreases, the substance is reduced.

SOLUTION: Silver changes from Ag^+ to Ag; its oxidation number decreases from $+1$ to 0, so Ag^+ is reduced. Similar reasoning tells us that copper is oxidized from Cu to Cu^{2+}. Therefore, according to Equation 19.2,

$$E^\circ_{cell} = E^\circ_{Ag^+} - E^\circ_{Cu^{2+}}$$

| Standard reduction potential of substance reduced | | Standard reduction potential of substance oxidized |

Substituting values for E°_{cell} and $E^\circ_{Cu^{2+}}$,

$$0.46 \text{ V} = E^\circ_{Ag^+} - 0.34 \text{ V}$$

Then we solve for $E^\circ_{Ag^+}$.

$$E^\circ_{Ag^+} = 0.46 \text{ V} + 0.34 \text{ V}$$
$$= 0.80 \text{ V}$$

The standard reduction potential of silver ion is therefore $+0.80$ V.

IS THE ANSWER REASONABLE? We know the standard cell potential is the difference between the two standard reduction potentials. The difference between $+0.80$ V and $+0.34$ V (subtracting the smaller from the larger) is 0.46 V. Our calculated standard reduction potential for Ag^+ appears to be correct. You can also take a peek at Table 19.1 now for a final check.

Practice Exercise 3: Copper metal and zinc metal will both reduce Ag^+ ions under standard state conditions. Which metal, when used as an electrode in a galvanic cell, will have the larger E°_{cell} under these conditions? (Hint: Write the two possible chemical reactions.)

Practice Exercise 4: The galvanic cell described in Practice Exercise 1 has a standard cell potential of 1.93 V. The standard reduction potential of Mg^{2+} corresponding to the half-reaction $Mg^{2+}(aq) + 2e^- \rightleftharpoons Mg(s)$ is -2.37 V. Calculate the standard reduction potential of iron(II). Check your answer by referring to Table 19.1.

Corrosion of Iron and Cathodic Protection

A problem that has plagued humanity ever since the discovery of methods for obtaining iron and other metals from their ores has been corrosion—the reaction of a metal with substances in the environment. The rusting of iron in particular is a serious problem because iron and steel have so many uses.

The rusting of iron is a complex chemical reaction that involves both oxygen and moisture (see Figure 1). Iron won't rust in pure water that's oxygen free, and it won't rust in pure oxygen in the absence of moisture. The corrosion process is apparently electrochemical in nature, as shown in the accompanying diagram. At one place on the surface, iron becomes oxidized in the presence of water and enters solution as Fe^{2+}.

$$Fe(s) \longrightarrow Fe^{2+}(aq) + 2e^-$$

At this location the iron is acting as an anode.

The electrons that are released when the iron is oxidized travel through the metal to some other place where the iron is exposed to oxygen. This is where reduction takes place (it's a cathodic region on the metal surface), and oxygen is reduced to give hydroxide ion.

$$\tfrac{1}{2}O_2(aq) + H_2O + 2e^- \longrightarrow 2OH^-(aq)$$

The iron(II) ions that are formed at the anodic regions gradually diffuse through the water and eventually contact the hydroxide ions. This causes a precipitate of $Fe(OH)_2$ to form, which is very easily oxidized by O_2 to give $Fe(OH)_3$. This hydroxide readily loses water. In fact, complete dehydration gives the oxide,

$$2Fe(OH)_3 \longrightarrow Fe_2O_3 + 3H_2O$$

When partial dehydration of the $Fe(OH)_3$ occurs, *rust* is formed. It has a composition that lies between that of the hydroxide and that of the oxide, Fe_2O_3, and is usually referred to as a *hydrated oxide*. Its formula is generally represented as $Fe_2O_3 \cdot xH_2O$.

This mechanism for the rusting of iron explains one of the more interesting aspects of this damaging process. Perhaps you've noticed that when rusting occurs on the body of a car, the rust appears at and around a break (or a scratch) in the surface of the paint, but the damage extends under the painted surface for some distance. Apparently, the Fe^{2+} ions that are formed at the anode sites are able to diffuse rather long distances to the hole in the paint, where they finally react with air to form the rust.

Cathodic Protection

One way to prevent the rusting of iron is to coat it with another metal. This is done with "tin" cans, which are actually steel cans that have been coated with a thin layer of tin. However, if the layer of tin is scratched and the iron beneath is exposed, the corrosion is accelerated because iron has a lower reduction potential than tin; the iron becomes the anode in an electrochemical cell and is easily oxidized.

Another way to prevent corrosion is called *cathodic protection*. It involves placing the iron in contact with a metal that is *more easily* oxidized. This causes iron to be a cathode and the other metal to be the anode. If corrosion occurs, iron is protected from oxidation because it is cathodic and the other metal reacts instead.

Zinc is most often used to provide cathodic protection to other metals. For example, zinc sacrificial anodes can be attached to the rudder of a boat (see Figure 2). When the rudder is submerged, the zinc will gradually corrode but the metal of the rudder will not. Periodically, the anodes are replaced to provide continued protection.

Steel objects that must withstand the weather are often coated with a layer of zinc, a process called galvanizing. You've seen this on chain-link fences and metal garbage pails. Even if the steel is exposed through a scratch, it is prevented from being oxidized because it is in contact with a metal that is more easily oxidized.

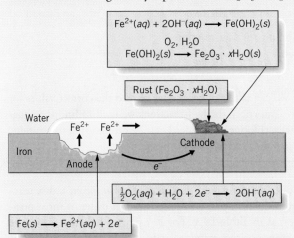

FIG. 1 **Corrosion of iron.** Iron dissolves in anodic regions to give Fe^{2+}. Electrons travel through the metal to cathodic sites where oxygen is reduced, forming OH^-. The combination of the Fe^{2+} and OH^-, followed by air oxidation, gives rust.

FIG. 2 **Cathodic protection.** Before launching, a shiny new zinc anode disk is attached to the bronze rudder of this boat to provide cathodic protection. Over time, the zinc will corrode instead of the less reactive bronze. (The rudder is painted with a special blue paint to inhibit the growth of barnacles.) *(Courtesy James Brady.)*

At this point you may have wondered why the term *cell potential* is used in some places, and *standard cell potential* is used in others. Based on our definitions, the term standard cell potential is used in places where the system is at standard state (i.e., 1.00 *M* concentrations, 1.00 atm pressures, and 25.0 °C). Cell potential is used for *any* set of concentrations, pressures, and temperatures, including the standard conditions. For convenience, our calculations in the next two sections will use standard cell potentials.

19.3 | STANDARD REDUCTION POTENTIALS CAN PREDICT SPONTANEOUS REACTIONS

Redox reactions can be predicted by comparing reduction potentials

It's easy to predict the spontaneous reaction between the substances in two half-reactions, at standard state, because we know that *the half-reaction with the more positive reduction potential always takes place as written (namely, as a reduction), while the other half-reaction is forced to run in reverse (as an oxidation).*

EXAMPLE 19.3
Predicting a Spontaneous Reaction

What spontaneous reaction occurs if Cl_2 and Br_2 are added to a solution that contains both Cl^- and Br^-? Assume that the cell is at standard state.

ANALYSIS: We know that in the spontaneous redox reaction, the more easily reduced substance will be the one that undergoes reduction. By assuming we are at standard state we can use the standard reduction potentials for Cl_2 and Br_2 to compare their $E°$ values and determine which is the more easily reduced, and then we will use that information to write the correct "cell reaction." This is the spontaneous reaction, *whether or not it occurs in a galvanic cell.*

SOLUTION: There are two possible reduction half-reactions.

$$Cl_2(g) + 2e^- \longrightarrow 2Cl^-(aq)$$
$$Br_2(aq) + 2e^- \longrightarrow 2Br^-(aq)$$

Referring to Table 19.1, we find that Cl_2 has a more positive standard reduction potential ($+1.36$ V) than does Br_2 ($+1.07$ V). This means Cl_2 will be reduced and the half-reaction for Br_2 will be reversed, changing to an oxidation. Therefore, the spontaneous reaction has the following half-reactions.

$$Cl_2(g) + 2e^- \longrightarrow 2Cl^-(aq) \quad \text{(a reduction)}$$
$$2Br^-(aq) \longrightarrow Br_2(aq) + 2e^- \quad \text{(an oxidation)}$$

The net reaction is obtained by combining the half-reactions.

$$Cl_2(g) + 2Br^-(aq) \longrightarrow Br_2(aq) + 2Cl^-(aq)$$

☐ Strictly speaking, the $E°$ values only tell us what to expect under standard conditions. However, only when $E°_{cell}$ is small can changes in the concentrations change the direction of the spontaneous reaction.

IS THE ANSWER REASONABLE? We can check to be sure we've read the correct values for $E°_{Cl_2}$ and $E°_{Br_2}$ from Table 19.1, and we can check the half-reactions we used to find the equation for the net reaction. (Experimentally, chlorine does indeed oxidize bromide ion to bromine, a fact used to recover bromine from seawater and natural brine solutions.)

When our cell is at standard state, reactants and products of *spontaneous* redox reactions are easy to spot when standard reduction potentials are listed in order of most positive to least positive (most negative), as in Table 19.1. For *any* pair of half-reactions, the one higher up in the table has the more positive standard reduction potential and occurs as a reduction. The other half-reaction is reversed and occurs as an oxidation. *Therefore, for a spontaneous reaction, the **reactants** are found on the left side of the higher half-reaction and on the right side of the lower half-reaction. (This is usually, but not always, true of systems that are not at standard state.)*

EXAMPLE 19.4
Predicting the Outcome of Redox Reactions

Predict the reaction that will occur, at 25 °C, when Ni and Fe are added to a solution that is 1.00 M in both Ni^{2+} and Fe^{2+}.

ANALYSIS: This system is at standard state and we can use the standard reduction potentials to predict the reaction. The first question we would ask is, "What *possible* reactions could occur?" We have a situation involving possible changes of ions to atoms or of atoms to ions. In other words, the system involves a possible redox reaction, and you've seen we can predict these using data in Table 19.1. One way to do this is to note the relative positions of the half-reactions when arranged as they are in Table 19.1.

$$Ni^{2+}(aq) + 2e^- \rightleftharpoons Ni(s) \qquad E^{\circ}_{Ni^{2+}} = -0.25$$

$$Fe^{2+}(aq) + 2e^- \rightleftharpoons Fe(s) \qquad E^{\circ}_{Fe^{2+}} = -0.44$$

In the table, the half-reaction higher up has the more positive (in this case, less negative) standard reduction potential, and will occur as a reduction. As a result, the reactants in the spontaneous reaction are related by the diagonal line that slants from upper left to lower right, as illustrated above. In other words, Ni^{2+} will react with Fe. The products are the substances on the opposite sides of the half-reaction, Ni and Fe^{2+}.

SOLUTION: We've done nearly all the work in our analysis of the problem. All that's left is to write the equation. The reactants are Ni^{2+} and Fe; the products are Ni and Fe^{2+}.

$$Ni^{2+}(aq) + Fe(s) \longrightarrow Ni(s) + Fe^{2+}(aq)$$

The equation is balanced in terms of both atoms and charges, so this is the reaction that will occur in the system specified in the problem.

IS THE ANSWER REASONABLE? Notice that we've predicted the reaction very easily using just the *positions* of the half-reactions relative to each other in the table; we really didn't have to use the values of their standard reduction potentials. We could check ourselves by proceeding as in Example 19.3. In the table, we see that Ni^{2+} has a more positive (less negative) standard reduction potential than Fe^{2+}, so Ni^{2+} is reduced and its half-cell reaction is written just as in Table 19.1. The half-cell reaction for Fe^{2+} in Table 19.1, however, must be reversed; it is Fe that will be oxidized.

$Ni^{2+}(aq) + 2e^- \longrightarrow Ni(s)$	(reduction)
$Fe(s) \longrightarrow Fe^{2+}(aq) + 2e^-$	(oxidation)
$Ni^{2+}(aq) + Fe(s) \longrightarrow Ni(s) + Fe^{2+}(aq)$	(net reaction)

Practice Exercise 5: Based only on the half-reactions in Table 19.1, determine what reaction will occur in each of the following mixtures, at standard state. (a) I_2, I^- and Fe^{2+}, Fe^{3+}, (b) Mg, Mg^{2+} and Cr, Cr^{3+}, (c) Co, Co^{2+} and H_2SO_3, SO_4^{2-}. (Hint: Use Table 19.1 to write the possible half-reactions and, if necessary, determine E°_{cell}.)

Practice Exercise 6: Use the positions of the half-reactions in Table 19.1 to predict the spontaneous reaction when Br^-, SO_4^{2-}, H_2SO_3, and Br_2 are mixed in an acidic solution at standard state.

Practice Exercise 7: From the positions of the respective half-reactions in Table 19.1, predict whether the following reaction will occur if all the ions are 1.0 M at 25 °C. If it is not, write the equation for the spontaneous reaction.

$$Ni^{2+}(aq) + 2Fe^{2+}(aq) \longrightarrow Ni(s) + 2Fe^{3+}(aq)$$

Standard reduction potentials predict the cell reaction and standard cell potential of a galvanic cell

We've just seen that we can use standard reduction potentials to predict spontaneous redox reactions. If we intend to use these reactions in a galvanic cell, we can also predict what the standard cell potential will be, as illustrated in the next example.

EXAMPLE 19.5
Predicting the Cell Reaction and Standard Cell Potential of a Galvanic Cell

A typical cell of a lead storage battery of the type used to start automobiles is constructed using electrodes made of lead and lead(IV) oxide (PbO_2) and with sulfuric acid as the electrolyte. The half-reactions and their standard reduction potentials in this system are

$$PbO_2(s) + 3H^+(aq) + HSO_4^-(aq) + 2e^- \rightleftharpoons PbSO_4(s) + 2H_2O$$
$$E^\circ_{PbO_2} = 1.69 \text{ V}$$

$$PbSO_4(s) + H^+(aq) + 2e^- \rightleftharpoons Pb(s) + HSO_4^-(aq)$$
$$E^\circ_{PbSO_4} = -0.36 \text{ V}$$

What is the cell reaction and what is the standard potential of the cell?

ANALYSIS: Our method for predicting spontaneous reactions specifies that the system should be at standard state. Although a battery is not at standard state, we will assume standard state to make the calculations easier. In the spontaneous cell reaction, the half-reaction with the larger (more positive) standard reduction potential will take place as reduction while the other half-reaction will be reversed and occur as oxidation. The standard cell potential is simply the difference between the two standard reduction potentials, calculated using Equation 19.2.

SOLUTION: PbO_2 has a larger, more positive standard reduction potential than $PbSO_4$, so the first half-reaction will occur in the direction written. The second must be reversed to occur as an oxidation. In the cell, therefore, the half-reactions are

$$PbO_2(s) + 3H^+(aq) + HSO_4^-(aq) + 2e^- \longrightarrow PbSO_4(s) + 2H_2O$$
$$Pb(s) + HSO_4^-(aq) \longrightarrow PbSO_4(s) + H^+(aq) + 2e^-$$

Adding the two half-reactions and canceling electrons gives the cell reaction,

$$PbO_2(s) + Pb(s) + 2H^+(aq) + 2HSO_4^-(aq) \longrightarrow 2PbSO_4(s) + 2H_2O$$

The cell standard potential is obtained by using Equation 19.2.

$$E^\circ_{cell} = (E^\circ \text{ of substance reduced}) - (E^\circ \text{ of substance oxidized})$$

Since the first half-reaction occurs as a reduction and the second as an oxidation,

$$E^\circ_{cell} = E^\circ_{PbO_2} - E^\circ_{PbSO_4}$$
$$= (1.69 \text{ V}) - (-0.36 \text{ V})$$
$$= 2.05 \text{ V}$$

□ Remember that half-reactions are combined following the same procedure used in the ion–electron method of balancing redox reactions (Section 5.2).

ARE THE ANSWERS REASONABLE? The half-reactions involved in the problem are located in Table 19.1, and their relative positions tell us that PbO_2 will be reduced and that lead will be oxidized. Therefore, we've combined the half-reactions correctly and we can feel confident that we've also applied Equation 19.2 correctly. In addition, the standard cell potential of 2.05 volts tells us that small differences from standard state will still allow us to come to the same conclusion.

At standard state, what would be the cell reaction and the standard cell potential of a galvanic cell employing the following half-reactions?

EXAMPLE 19.6
Predicting the Cell Reaction and
Standard Cell Potential of a
Galvanic Cell

$$Al^{3+}(aq) + 3e^- \rightleftharpoons Al(s) \qquad E°_{Al^{3+}} = -1.66 \text{ V}$$
$$Cu^{2+}(aq) + 2e^- \rightleftharpoons Cu(s) \qquad E°_{Cu^{2+}} = +0.34 \text{ V}$$

Which half-cell would be the anode?

ANALYSIS: This problem is very similar to the preceding one, so we expect to proceed in essentially the same way.

SOLUTION: Our method for predicting spontaneous reactions indicates that the half-reaction with the more positive standard reduction potential will occur as a reduction; the other will occur as an oxidation. In this cell, then, Cu^{2+} is reduced and Al is oxidized. To obtain the cell reaction, we add the two half-reactions, remembering that the electrons must cancel. This means we must multiply the copper half-reaction by three and the aluminum half-reaction by two.

$$3[Cu^{2+}(aq) + 2e^- \longrightarrow Cu(s)] \qquad \text{(reduction)}$$
$$\underline{2[Al(s) \longrightarrow Al^{3+}(aq) + 3e^-]} \qquad \text{(oxidation)}$$
$$3Cu^{2+}(aq) + 2Al(s) \longrightarrow 3Cu(s) + 2Al^{3+}(aq) \qquad \text{(cell reaction)}$$

The anode in the cell is aluminum because that is where oxidation takes place (by definition). To obtain the standard cell potential, we substitute into Equation 19.2.

$$E°_{cell} = E°_{Cu^{2+}} - E°_{Al^{3+}}$$
$$= (0.34 \text{ V}) - (-1.66 \text{ V})$$
$$= 2.00 \text{ V}$$

An important point to notice here is that *although we multiply the half-reactions by factors to make the electrons cancel, **we do not multiply the standard reduction potentials by these factors**.*[4] To obtain the standard cell potential, we simply subtract one standard reduction potential from the other.

ARE THE ANSWERS REASONABLE? If we locate the half-reactions in Table 19.1, their relative positions tell us we've written the correct equation for the spontaneous reaction. It also means we've identified correctly the substances reduced and oxidized, so we've correctly applied Equation 19.2.

Practice Exercise 8: What are the overall cell reaction and the standard cell potential of a galvanic cell employing the following half-reactions?

$$NiO_2(s) + 2H_2O + 2e^- \rightleftharpoons Ni(OH)_2(s) + 2OH^-(aq) \qquad E°_{NiO_2} = 0.49 \text{ V}$$
$$Fe(OH)_2(s) + 2e^- \rightleftharpoons Fe(s) + 2OH^-(aq) \qquad E°_{Fe(OH)_2} = -0.88 \text{ V}$$

(Hint: Recall that standard cell potentials are based on a spontaneous reaction.)

□ These are the reactions in an Edison cell, a type of rechargeable storage battery.

Practice Exercise 9: The four substances in the following two half-reactions are placed in the same beaker, at standard state. Write the balanced equation for the spontaneous reaction and determine the standard cell potential if the two reactions are used in a galvanic cell.

$$Cu^{2+}(aq) + 2e^- \rightleftharpoons Cu(s) \qquad E°_{Cu^{2+}} = +0.34 \text{ V}$$
$$Cr^{3+}(aq) + 3e^- \rightleftharpoons Cr(s) \qquad E°_{Cr^{3+}} = -0.74 \text{ V}$$

---

[4] Reduction potentials are intensive quantities; they have the units volts, which are joules *per coulomb*. The same number of joules are available for each coulomb of charge regardless of the total number of electrons shown in the equation. Therefore, reduction potentials are never multiplied by factors before they are subtracted to give the cell potential.

Practice Exercise 10: What are the overall cell reaction and the standard cell potential of a galvanic cell employing the following half-reactions at standard state?

$$Cr^{3+}(aq) + 3e^- \rightleftharpoons Cr(s) \qquad\qquad E^\circ_{Cr^{3+}} = -0.74 \text{ V}$$
$$MnO_4^-(aq) + 8H^+(aq) + 5e^- \rightleftharpoons Mn^{2+}(aq) + 4H_2O \qquad E^\circ_{MnO_4^-} = +1.51 \text{ V}$$

The calculated cell potential can tell us whether a reaction is spontaneous

Because we can predict the spontaneous redox reaction that will take place among a mixture of reactants, it also should be possible to predict whether or not a particular reaction, *as written*, can occur spontaneously. We can do this by calculating the standard cell potential that corresponds to the reaction in question and seeing if the standard potential is *positive*.

TOOLS

E°_{cell} and spontaneous reactions

> In a galvanic cell, the calculated standard cell potential for the spontaneous reaction is always positive. If the calculated standard cell potential is negative, the reaction is spontaneous in the reverse direction.

☐ These generalizations apply under standard conditions: 1 *M* concentrations of all ions, 1 atm pressure for gases, and 25 °C.

For example, to obtain the standard cell potential for a spontaneous reaction in our previous examples, we subtracted the standard reduction potentials in a way that gave a positive answer. Therefore, if we compute the standard cell potential for a particular reaction *based on the way the equation is written* and the standard potential comes out positive, we know the reaction is spontaneous. If the calculated standard cell potential comes out negative, however, the reaction is nonspontaneous. In fact, it is really spontaneous in the opposite direction.

EXAMPLE 19.7

Determining whether a Reaction Is Spontaneous by Using the Calculated Standard Cell Potential

Determine whether the following reactions, at standard state, are spontaneous as written. If a reaction is not spontaneous, write the equation for the reaction that is.

(1) $Cu(s) + 2H^+(aq) \longrightarrow Cu^{2+}(aq) + H_2(g)$

(2) $3Cu(s) + 2NO_3^-(aq) + 8H^+(aq) \longrightarrow 3Cu^{2+}(aq) + 2NO(g) + 4H_2O$

ANALYSIS: Our goal for each reaction will be to calculate the standard cell potential based on the reaction as written. Our tool for spontaneous reactions states that if E°_{cell} is positive, then the reaction is spontaneous. However, if E°_{cell} is negative, then the reaction is not spontaneous as written and reversing the equation will give the spontaneous reaction.

To calculate E°_{cell}, we need to divide the equation into its half-reactions, find the necessary standard reduction potentials in Table 19.1, and then use Equation 19.2 to calculate E°_{cell}. The signs of E°_{cell} will then tell us whether the reactions are spontaneous under standard conditions.

SOLUTION: (1) The half-reactions involved in this reaction are

$$Cu(s) \longrightarrow Cu^{2+}(aq) + 2e^- \qquad\qquad \text{(oxidation)}$$
$$2H^+(aq) + 2e^- \longrightarrow H_2(g) \qquad\qquad \text{(reduction)}$$

The H⁺ is reduced and Cu is oxidized, so Equation 19.2 will take the form

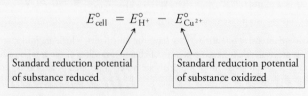

$$E^\circ_{cell} = E^\circ_{H^+} - E^\circ_{Cu^{2+}}$$

Standard reduction potential of substance reduced

Standard reduction potential of substance oxidized

Substituting values from Table 19.1 gives

$$E^\circ_{cell} = (0.00\ V) - (0.34\ V)$$
$$= -0.34\ V$$

The calculated standard cell potential is negative, so reaction (1) is not spontaneous in the forward direction. The spontaneous reaction is actually the reverse of (1).

$$Cu^{2+}(aq) + H_2(g) \longrightarrow Cu(s) + 2H^+(aq)$$
Reaction (1) reversed

(2) The half-reactions involved in this equation are

$$Cu(s) \longrightarrow Cu^{2+}(aq) + 2e^-$$
$$NO_3^-(aq) + 4H^+(aq) + 3e^- \longrightarrow NO(g) + 2H_2O$$

The Cu is oxidized while the NO_3^- is reduced. According to Equation 19.2,

$$E^\circ_{cell} = E^\circ_{NO_3^-} - E^\circ_{Cu^{2+}}$$

Substituting values from Table 19.1 gives

$$E^\circ_{cell} = (0.96\ V) - (0.34\ V)$$
$$= +0.62\ V$$

Because the calculated standard cell potential is positive, reaction 2 is spontaneous in the forward direction, as written.

□ Copper dissolves in HNO_3 because it contains the oxidizing agent NO_3^-.

ARE THE ANSWERS REASONABLE? By noting the relative positions of the half-reactions in Table 19.1, you can confirm that we've answered the questions correctly.

Practice Exercise 11: Determine if each of the following reactions, under standard state conditions, is spontaneous.

(a) $Br_2(aq) + 2I^-(aq) \longrightarrow 2Br^-(aq) + I_2(s)$

(b) $MnO_4^-(aq) + 5Ag(aq) + 8H^+(aq) \longrightarrow Mn^{2+}(aq) + 5Ag^+(s) + 4H_2O$

(Hint: Determine the sign of the calculated standard cell potential.)

Practice Exercise 12: Under standard state conditions, which of the following reactions occur spontaneously?

(a) $Br_2(aq) + Cl_2(g) + 2H_2O \longrightarrow 2Br^-(aq) + 2HOCl(aq) + 2H^+(aq)$

(b) $3Zn(s) + 2Cr^{3+}(aq) \longrightarrow 3Zn^{2+}(aq) + 2Cr(s)$

In the previous examples and exercises we have been rigorous in specifying that standard reduction potentials are used when the system is at standard state. If the cell is not at standard state, the cell potential will not be the same as the standard cell potential, but in the majority of cases, the algebraic sign of the calculated cell potential will be the same and we can reach the same conclusions.

19.4 | CELL POTENTIALS ARE RELATED TO FREE ENERGY CHANGES

The fact that cell potentials allow us to predict the spontaneity of redox reactions is no coincidence. There is a relationship between the cell potential and the free energy change for a reaction. In Chapter 18 we saw that ΔG for a reaction is a measure of the maximum useful work that can be obtained from a chemical reaction. Specifically, the relationship is

$$-\Delta G = \text{maximum work} \tag{19.3}$$

In an electrical system, work is supplied by the flow of electric charge created by the potential of the cell. It can be calculated from the equation

$$\text{Maximum work} = n\mathscr{F}E_{cell} \qquad (19.4)$$

Faraday constant

□ More precisely, one **Faraday** ($\mathscr{F}$) = 96,485 C.

where n is the number of moles of electrons transferred, $\mathscr{F}$ is a constant called the **Faraday constant** which is equal to the number of coulombs of charge equivalent to 1 mol of electrons (9.65×10^4 coulombs per mole of electrons), and E_{cell} is the potential of the cell in volts. To see that Equation 19.4 gives work (which has the units of energy) we can analyze the units. In Equation 19.1 you saw that 1 volt = 1 joule/coulomb. Therefore,

$$\text{Maximum work} = \overline{\text{mole } e^-} \times \left(\frac{\cancel{\text{coulombs}}}{\overline{\text{mole } e^-}}\right) \times \left(\frac{\text{joule}}{\cancel{\text{coulombs}}}\right) = \text{joule}$$

$$\Updownarrow \qquad\qquad \Updownarrow \qquad\qquad\quad \Updownarrow$$
$$n \qquad\qquad \mathscr{F} \qquad\qquad E_{cell}$$

Combining Equations 19.3 and 19.4 gives us

$$\Delta G = -n\mathscr{F}E_{cell} \qquad (19.5)$$

At standard state we are dealing with the *standard* cell potential, so we can calculate the *standard* free energy change.

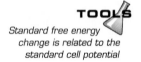

Standard free energy change is related to the standard cell potential

$$\Delta G° = -n\mathscr{F}E°_{cell} \qquad (19.6)$$

Referring back to Chapter 18, if ΔG has a negative value, a reaction will be spontaneous and this corresponds to a positive value of E_{cell}. Up to now we have been careful to predict spontaneity for standard state systems where $E°_{cell}$ is equal to E_{cell}. In Example 19.11 below we will see how to calculate E_{cell} and precisely predict if a reaction is spontaneous.

EXAMPLE 19.8
Calculating the Standard Free Energy Change

Calculate $\Delta G°$ for the following reaction, given that its standard cell potential is 0.320 V at 25 °C.

$$\text{NiO}_2(s) + 2\text{Cl}^-(aq) + 4\text{H}^+(aq) \longrightarrow \text{Cl}_2(g) + \text{Ni}^{2+}(aq) + 2\text{H}_2\text{O}$$

ANALYSIS: Our tool for solving this problem is Equation 19.6. Taking the coefficients in the equation to stand for *moles*, two moles of Cl^- are oxidized to Cl_2 and two moles of electrons are transferred to the NiO_2 ($n = 2$ mol e^-). We will also use the faraday constant, $1\mathscr{F} = 96,500$ C/mol e^- (recall that the SI abbreviation for coulomb is C).

$$1\mathscr{F} = \frac{96,500 \text{ C}}{1 \text{ mol } e^-}$$

SOLUTION: Using Equation 19.6, we have

$$\Delta G° = -(2 \text{ mol } e^-) \times \left(\frac{9.65 \times 10^4 \text{ C}}{1 \text{ mol } e^-}\right) \times \left(\frac{0.320 \text{ J}}{\text{C}}\right)$$

$$= -6.18 \times 10^4 \text{ J}$$

$$= -61.8 \text{ kJ}$$

IS THE ANSWER REASONABLE? Let's do some approximate arithmetic. The faraday constant equals approximately 100,000, or 10^5. The product $2 \times 0.32 = 0.64$, so $\Delta G°$ should be about 0.64×10^5 or 6.4×10^4 J. The answer seems to be okay.

Practice Exercise 13: A certain reaction has an $E°_{cell}$ of 0.107 volts and has a $\Delta G°$ of −30.9 kJ. How many electrons are transferred in the reaction? (Hint: See Equation 19.6.)

Practice Exercise 14: Calculate $\Delta G°$ for the reactions that take place in the galvanic cells described in Practice Exercises 11 and 12.

Equilibrium constants can be calculated from $E°_{cell}$

One useful application of electrochemistry is the determination of equilibrium constants. In Chapter 18 you saw that $\Delta G°$ is related to the equilibrium constant by the expression

$$\Delta G° = -RT \ln K_c$$

where we have used K_c for the equilibrium constant because electrochemical reactions occur in solution. We've seen in this chapter that $\Delta G°$ is also related to $E°_{cell}$

$$\Delta G° = -n\mathscr{F}E°_{cell}$$

Therefore, $E°_{cell}$ and the equilibrium constant are also related. Equating the right sides of the two equations, we have

$$-n\mathscr{F}E°_{cell} = -RT \ln K_c$$

Solving for $E°_{cell}$ gives[5]

$$E°_{cell} = \frac{RT}{n\mathscr{F}} \ln K_c \qquad (19.7)$$

TOOLS

Equilibrium constants are related to standard cell potentials

For the units to work out correctly, the value of R must be 8.314 J mol^{-1} K^{-1}, T must be the temperature in kelvins, $\mathscr{F}$ equals 9.65×10^4 C per mole of e^-, and n equals the number of moles of electrons transferred in the reaction.

EXAMPLE 19.9
Calculating Equilibrium Constants
from $E°_{cell}$

Calculate K_c for the reaction in Example 19.8.

ANALYSIS: Equation 19.7 is our tool for solving this problem. We need to collect the terms to insert in this equation to solve it. We need to find $E°_{cell}$, n, R, T, and $\mathscr{F}$. Remember that T is in kelvins and R must have the appropriate units of J mol^{-1} K^{-1}.

SOLUTION: The reaction in Example 19.8 has $E°_{cell} = 0.320$ V and $n = 2$. The temperature is 25 °C or 298 K. Let's solve Equation 19.7 for $\ln K_c$ and then substitute values.

$$\ln K_c = \frac{E°_{cell} \, n\mathscr{F}}{RT}$$

Substituting values and using the relationship that $1 \text{ V} = 1 \text{ J C}^{-1}$,

$$\ln K_c = \frac{0.320 \cancel{\text{ J C}^{-1}} \times 2 \times 9.65 \times 10^4 \cancel{\text{ C}} \cancel{\text{ mol}^{-1}}}{8.314 \cancel{\text{ J}} \cancel{\text{ mol}^{-1}} \cancel{\text{ K}^{-1}} \times 298 \cancel{\text{ K}}}$$

$$= 24.9$$

Taking the antilogarithm,

$$K_c = e^{24.9} = 7 \times 10^{10}$$

---

[5] For historical reasons, Equation 19.7 is sometimes expressed in terms of common logs (base 10 logarithms). Natural and common logarithms are related by the equation

$$\ln x = 2.303 \log x$$

For reactions at 25 °C (298 K), all of the constants (R, T, and $\mathscr{F}$) can be combined with the factor 2.303 to give 0.0592 joules/coulomb. Because joules/coulomb equals volts, Equation 19.7 reduces to

$$E°_{cell} = \frac{0.0592 \text{ V}}{n} \log K_c$$

where n is the number of moles of electrons transferred in the cell reaction as it is written.

IS THE ANSWER REASONABLE? As a rough check, we can look at the magnitude of E°_{cell} and apply some simple reasoning. When E°_{cell} is positive, ΔG° is negative, and in Chapter 18 you learned that when ΔG° is negative, the reaction proceeds far toward completion when equilibrium is reached. Therefore, we expect that K_c will be large, and that agrees with our answer.

A more complete check would require evaluating the fraction used to compute $\ln K_c$. First, we should check to be sure we've substituted correctly into the equation for $\ln K_c$. Next, we could do some approximate arithmetic to check the value of $\ln K_c$. Rounding all numbers to one significant figure we get

$$\ln K_c = \frac{0.3 \text{ J C}^{-1} \times 2 \times 10 \times 10^4 \text{ C mol}^{-1}}{10 \text{ J mol}^{-1}\text{K}^{-1} \times 300 \text{ K}} = \frac{6 \times 10^4}{3000} = 2 \times 10^1 = 20$$

This is close to the 24.9 we calculated above and we are confident the calculation was done correctly.

Practice Exercise 15: The calculated standard cell potential for the reaction

$$Cu^{2+}(aq) + 2Ag(s) \rightleftharpoons Cu(s) + 2Ag^+(aq)$$

is $E^\circ_{cell} = -0.46$ V. Calculate K_c for the reaction as written. Is the reaction spontaneous? If not, what is K_c for the spontaneous reaction? (Hint: The tool described by Equation 19.7 is important here.)

Practice Exercise 16: Use the following half-reactions and the data in Table 19.1 to write the equation for the spontaneous reaction. Write the equilibrium law for the reaction and use the standard cell potential to determine the value of the equilibrium constant. How is this related to the K_{sp} for AgBr?

$$Ag^+(aq) + e^- \longrightarrow Ag(s)$$
$$AgBr(s) + e^- \longrightarrow Ag(s) + Br^-(aq)$$

19.5 | CONCENTRATIONS IN A GALVANIC CELL AFFECT THE CELL POTENTIAL

At 25 °C when all of the ion concentrations in a cell are 1.00 M and when the partial pressures of any gases involved in the cell reaction are 1.00 atm, the cell potential is equal to the standard potential. When the concentrations or pressures change, however, so does the potential. For example, in an operating cell or battery, the potential gradually drops as the reactants are used up and as the cell reaction approaches its natural equilibrium status. When it reaches equilibrium, the potential has dropped to zero—the battery is dead.

The Nernst equation defines the relationship of cell potential to ion concentrations

The effect of concentration on the cell potential can be obtained from thermodynamics. In Chapter 18, you learned that the free energy change is related to the reaction quotient Q by the equation

$$\Delta G = \Delta G^\circ + RT \ln Q$$

Substituting for ΔG and ΔG° from Equations 19.5 and 19.6 gives

$$-n\mathscr{F}E_{cell} = -n\mathscr{F}E^\circ_{cell} + RT \ln Q$$

Dividing both sides by $-n\mathscr{F}$ gives

TOOLS
Nernst equation

$$E_{cell} = E^\circ_{cell} - \frac{RT}{n\mathscr{F}} \ln Q \qquad (19.8)$$

This equation is commonly known as the **Nernst equation,**[6] named after Walther Nernst, a German chemist and physicist. Notice, if $Q = 1$ then $\ln Q = 0$ and $E_{cell} = E°_{cell}$.

In writing the Nernst equation for a galvanic cell, we will construct the mass action expression (from which we calculate Q) using molar concentrations for ions and partial pressures in atmospheres for gases.[7] Thus, for the following cell using a hydrogen electrode (with the partial pressure of H_2 not necessarily equal to 1 atm) and having the reaction

$$Cu^{2+}(aq) + H_2(g) \longrightarrow Cu(s) + 2H^+(aq)$$

the Nernst equation would be written

$$E_{cell} = E°_{cell} - \frac{RT}{n\mathscr{F}} \ln \frac{[H^+]^2}{[Cu^{2+}]P_{H_2}}$$

□ This is a heterogeneous reaction, so we have not included the concentration of the solid, $Cu(s)$, in the mass action expression.

EXAMPLE 19.10
Calculating the Effect of Concentration on E_{cell}

Suppose a galvanic cell employs the following half-reactions.

$$Ni^{2+}(aq) + 2e^- \rightleftharpoons Ni(s) \qquad E°_{Ni^{2+}} = -0.25V$$
$$Cr^{3+}(aq) + 3e^- \rightleftharpoons Cr(s) \qquad E°_{Cr^{3+}} = -0.74\ V$$

Calculate the cell potential when $[Ni^{2+}] = 1.0 \times 10^{-4}\ M$ and $[Cr^{3+}] = 2.0 \times 10^{-3}\ M$.

ANALYSIS: Because the concentrations are not 1.00 M, we must use the Nernst equation (Equation 19.8) as our tool, but first we need the cell reaction. We need it to determine the number of electrons transferred, n, and we need it to determine the correct form of the mass action expression from which we calculate the numerical value of Q. We must also note that the reacting system is heterogeneous; both solid metals and a liquid solution of their dissolved ions are involved. We have to remember that a mass action expression does not contain concentration terms for solids, such as Ni and Cr.

SOLUTION: Nickel has the more positive (less negative) standard reduction potential, so its half-reaction will occur as a reduction. This means that chromium will be oxidized. Making electron gain equal to electron loss, the cell reaction is found as follows.

$$3[Ni^{2+}(aq) + 2e^- \longrightarrow Ni(s)] \qquad \text{(reduction)}$$
$$\underline{2[Cr(s) \longrightarrow Cr^{3+}(aq) + 3e^-]} \qquad \text{(oxidation)}$$
$$3Ni^{2+}(aq) + 2Cr(s) \longrightarrow 3Ni(s) + 2Cr^{3+}(aq) \qquad \text{(cell reaction)}$$

The total number of electrons transferred is six, which means $n = 6$. Now we can write the Nernst equation for the system.

$$E_{cell} = E°_{cell} - \frac{RT}{n\mathscr{F}} \ln \frac{[Cr^{3+}]^2}{[Ni^{2+}]^3}$$

Notice that we've constructed the mass action expression, from which we will calculate the reaction quotient, using the concentrations of the ions raised to powers equal to their coefficients in the net cell reaction, and that we have not included concentration terms for the two solids. This is the procedure we followed for heterogeneous equilibria in Chapter 14.

---

[6] Using common logarithms instead of natural logarithms and calculating the constants for 25 °C gives another form of the Nernst equation that is sometimes used:

$$E_{cell} = E°_{cell} - \frac{0.0592\ V}{n} \log Q$$

[7] Because of interionic attractions, ions do not always behave as though their concentrations are equal to their molarities. Strictly speaking, therefore, we should use effective concentrations (called activities) in the mass action expression. Effective concentrations are difficult to calculate, so for simplicity we will use molarities and accept the fact that our calculations are not entirely accurate.

Next we need E°_{cell}. Since Ni^{2+} is reduced,

$$E^\circ_{cell} = E^\circ_{Ni^{2+}} - E^\circ_{Cr^{3+}}$$
$$= (-0.25 \text{ V}) - (-0.74 \text{ V})$$
$$= 0.49 \text{ V}$$

Now we can substitute this value for E°_{cell} along with $R = 8.314$ J mol^{-1} K^{-1}, $T = 298$ K, $n = 6$, $\mathscr{F} = 9.65 \times 10^4$ C mol^{-1}, $[Ni^{2+}] = 1.0 \times 10^{-4}$ M, and $[Cr^{3+}] = 2.0 \times 10^{-3}$ M into the Nernst equation. This gives

$$E_{cell} = 0.49 \text{ V} - \frac{8.314 \text{ J mol}^{-1} \text{ K}^{-1} \times 298 \text{ K}}{6 \times 9.65 \times 10^4 \text{ C mol}^{-1}} \ln \frac{(2.0 \times 10^{-3})^2}{(1.0 \times 10^{-4})^3}$$
$$= 0.49 \text{ V} - (0.00428 \text{ V}) \ln (4.0 \times 10^6)$$
$$= 0.49 \text{ V} - (0.00428 \text{ V})(15.20)$$
$$= 0.49 \text{ V} - 0.0651 \text{ V}$$
$$= 0.42 \text{ V}$$

The potential of the cell is expected to be 0.42 V.

IS THE ANSWER REASONABLE? There's no simple way to check the answer. However, there are certain important points to consider. First, check that you've combined the half-reactions correctly to calculate E°_{cell} and given the balanced cell reaction, because we need the coefficients of the equation to obtain the correct superscripts in the Nernst equation. Then, be sure you've used the Kelvin temperature, $R = 8.314$ J mol^{-1} K^{-1}, and made the other substitutions correctly.

EXAMPLE 19.11

The Spontaneous Reaction May Be Concentration Dependent

The reaction of tin metal with acid can be written as

$$Sn(s) + 2H^+(aq) \longrightarrow Sn^{2+}(aq) + H_2(g)$$

Calculate the cell potential (a) when the system is at standard state, (b) when the pH is 2.00, and (c) when the pH is 5.00. Assume that $[Sn^{2+}] = 1.00$ M and the partial pressure of H_2 is also 1.00 atm.

ANALYSIS: In this reaction the tin metal is the substance that is oxidized and hydrogen ions are reduced. Part (a) is at standard state, and we have used our tool for combining standard reduction potentials to solve problems like that in Examples 19.6 and 19.7. For parts (b) and (c) we must use the Nernst equation as our tool. We determine the number of electrons transferred by noting that tin loses two electrons and each hydrogen gains an electron. Therefore two electrons are transferred from tin to the hydrogen ions. We can also set up Q for the Nernst equation by substituting 1.00 for both $[Sn^{2+}]$ and P_{H_2}:

$$Q = \frac{[Sn^{2+}]P_{H_2}}{[H^+]^2} = \frac{1.00}{[H^+]^2}$$

We can also calculate the hydrogen ion concentrations for the pH 2.00 and pH 5.00 solutions as 1.0×10^{-2} M and 1.0×10^{-5} M respectively.

SOLUTION: For part (a) we find the difference between standard reduction potentials as

$$E^\circ_{cell} = 0.00 \text{ V} - (-0.14) \text{ V} = +0.14 \text{ V}$$

For parts (b) and (c) we substitute into the Nernst equation

$$E_{cell} = E^{\circ}_{cell} - \frac{RT}{n\mathscr{F}} \ln \frac{1.00}{[H^+]^2}$$

(b) $E_{cell} = 0.14\,\text{V} - \dfrac{8.314\,\text{J}\,\cancel{\text{mol}^{-1}}\,\cancel{\text{K}^{-1}} \times 298\,\cancel{\text{K}}}{2 \times 9.65 \times 10^4\,\text{C}\,\cancel{\text{mol}^{-1}}} \ln \dfrac{1.00}{(1.0 \times 10^{-2})^2}$

$E_{cell} = 0.14\,\text{V} - 0.12\,\text{V} = +0.02\,\text{V}$

(c) $E_{cell} = 0.14\,\text{V} - \dfrac{8.314\,\text{J}\,\cancel{\text{mol}^{-1}}\,\cancel{\text{K}^{-1}} \times 298\,\cancel{\text{K}}}{2 \times 9.65 \times 10^4\,\text{C}\,\cancel{\text{mol}^{-1}}} \ln \dfrac{1.00}{(1.0 \times 10^{-5})^2}$

$E_{cell} = 0.14\,\text{V} - 0.30\,\text{V} = -0.16\,\text{V}$

At standard state the reaction is spontaneous. At pH 2.00 it is spontaneous but the potential is a small positive value. At pH 5.00 the reaction is not spontaneous.

ARE THE ANSWERS REASONABLE? The first question to answer is, "Does this make sense?" and indeed it does. Looking at the natural logarithm part of the equation we see that as the $[H^+]$ decreases, the ln term increases and makes a more negative adjustment to the E°_{cell}. Since a decrease in $[H^+]$ is an increase in pH, we expect E_{cell} will decrease as pH increases. We cannot easily estimate natural logarithms so a check of calculations may be easiest if the values are entered into your calculator in the reverse order from the first calculation.

Practice Exercise 17: A galvanic cell is constructed with a copper electrode dipping into a 0.015 M solution of Cu^{2+} ions and an electrode made of magnesium immersed in a 2.2×10^{-6} M solution of magnesium ions. Write the balanced chemical reaction. What is the cell potential at 25 °C? (Hint: Set up the Nernst equation for the reaction.)

Practice Exercise 18: In a certain zinc–copper cell,

$$Zn(s) + Cu^{2+}(aq) \longrightarrow Zn^{2+}(aq) + Cu(s)$$

the ion concentrations are $[Cu^{2+}] = 0.0100$ M and $[Zn^{2+}] = 1.0$ M. What is the cell potential at 25 °C?

Experimental cell potentials can be used to determine ion concentrations

One of the principal uses of the relationship between concentration and cell potential is for the measurement of concentrations of redox reactants and products in a galvanic cell. Experimental determination of cell potentials combined with modern developments in electronics has provided a means of monitoring and analyzing the concentrations of all sorts of substances in solution, even some that are not themselves ionic and that are not involved directly in electrochemical changes. In fact, the operation of a pH meter relies on the logarithmic relationship between hydrogen ion concentration and the potential of a special kind of electrode (Figure 19.8 on page 795)

EXAMPLE 19.12
Using the Nernst Equation to Determine Concentrations

To measure the concentration of Cu^{2+} in a large number of samples of water in which the copper ion concentration is expected to be quite small, an electrochemical cell was assembled that consists of a silver electrode, dipping into a 1.00 M solution of $AgNO_3$, connected by a salt bridge to a second half-cell containing a copper electrode. The copper half-cell was then filled with one water sample after another, with the cell potential being measured for each sample. In the analysis of one sample, the cell potential at 25 °C was measured to be 0.62 V. The copper electrode was observed to carry a negative charge, so it served as the anode. What was the concentration of copper ion in the sample?

ANALYSIS: In this problem, we've been given the cell potential, E_{cell}, and we can calculate $E°_{cell}$ from the standard reduction potentials in Table 19.1. The unknown quantity is one of the concentration terms in the Nernst equation that we use as our tool for solving this problem.

SOLUTION: The first step is to write the proper equation for the cell reaction, because we need it to compute $E°_{cell}$ and to construct the mass action expression for use in the Nernst equation. Because copper is the anode, it is being oxidized. This also means that Ag^+ is being reduced. Therefore, the equation for the cell reaction is

$$Cu(s) + 2Ag^+(aq) \longrightarrow Cu^{2+}(aq) + 2Ag(s)$$

Two electrons are transferred, so $n = 2$ and the Nernst equation is

$$E_{cell} = E°_{cell} - \frac{RT}{2\mathscr{F}} \ln \frac{[Cu^{2+}]}{[Ag^+]^2}$$

The value of $E°_{cell}$ can be obtained from the tabulated standard reduction potentials in Table 19.1. Following our usual procedure and recognizing that silver ion is reduced,

$$E°_{cell} = E°_{Ag^+} - E°_{Cu^{2+}}$$
$$= (0.80 \text{ V}) - (0.34 \text{ V})$$
$$= 0.46 \text{ V}$$

Now we can substitute values into the Nernst equation and solve for the concentration ratio in the mass action expression.

$$0.62 \text{ V} = 0.46 \text{ V} - \frac{8.314 \text{ J mol}^{-1} \text{ K}^{-1} \times 298 \text{ K}}{2 \times 9.65 \times 10^4 \text{ C mol}^{-1}} \ln \frac{[Cu^{2+}]}{[Ag^+]^2}$$

Solving for $\ln ([Cu^{2+}]/[Ag^+]^2)$ gives

$$\ln \frac{[Cu^{2+}]}{[Ag^+]^2} = -12$$

Taking the antilog gives us the value of the mass action expression.

$$\frac{[Cu^{2+}]}{[Ag^+]^2} = 6 \times 10^{-6}$$

Since we know that the concentration of Ag^+ is 1.00 M, we can now solve for the Cu^{2+} concentration.

$$\frac{[Cu^{2+}]}{(1.00)^2} = 6 \times 10^{-6}$$
$$[Cu^{2+}] = 6 \times 10^{-6} M$$

IS THE ANSWER REASONABLE? All we can do easily is check to be sure we've written the correct chemical equation, on which all the rest of the solution to the problem rests. Be careful about algebraic signs and that you select the proper value for R and the temperature in kelvins. Also, notice that we first solved for the logarithm of the ratio of concentration terms. Then, after taking the (natural) antilogarithm, we substitute the known value for $[Ag^+]$ and solve for $[Cu^{2+}]$.

As a final point, notice that the Cu^{2+} concentration is indeed very small, and that it can be obtained very easily by simply measuring the potential generated by the electrochemical cell. Determining the concentrations in many samples is also very simple—just change the water sample and measure the potential again.

☐ The ease of such operations and the fact that they lend themselves well to automation and computer analysis make electrochemical analyses especially attractive to scientists.

Practice Exercise 19: A galvanic cell is constructed with a copper electrode dipping into a 0.015 M solution of Cu^{2+} ions and a magnesium electrode immersed in a solution of Mg^{2+} ions. The cell potential is measured as 2.79 volts at 25 °C. What is the concentration of magnesium ions?

$$Mg(s) + Cu^{2+}(aq) \longrightarrow Mg^{2+}(aq) + Cu(s)$$

(Hint: Use the Nernst equation to solve for $[Mg^{2+}]$.)

Practice Exercise 20: In the analysis of two other water samples by the procedure described in Example 19.12, cell potentials (E_{cell}) of 0.57 V and 0.82 V were obtained. Calculate the Cu^{2+} ion concentration in each of these samples.

Practice Exercise 21: A galvanic cell was constructed by connecting a nickel electrode that was dipping into 1.20 M $NiSO_4$ solution to a chromium electrode that was dipping into a solution containing Cr^{3+} at an unknown concentration. The potential of the cell was measured to be 0.552 V, with the chromium serving as the anode. The standard cell potential for the system was determined to be 0.487 V. What was the concentration of Cr^{3+} in the solution of unknown concentration?

Concentration cells consist of two almost identical half-cells

The dependence of cell potential on concentration allows us to construct a galvanic cell from two half-cells composed of the same substances but having different concentrations of the solute species. An example would be a pair of copper electrodes dipping into solutions that have different concentrations of Cu^{2+}, say 0.10 M Cu^{2+} in one and 1.0 M in the other (Figure 19.9). When this cell operates, reactions take place that tend to bring the two Cu^{2+} concentrations toward the same value. Thus, in the half-cell containing 0.10 M Cu^{2+}, copper is oxidized, which adds Cu^{2+} to the more dilute solution. In the other cell, Cu^{2+} is reduced, removing Cu^{2+} from the more concentrated solution. This makes the more dilute half-cell the anode and the more concentrated half-cell the cathode.

$$Cu(s)|Cu^{2+}(0.10\ M)||Cu^{2+}(1.0\ M)|Cu(s)$$
$$\underset{\text{anode}}{\phantom{Cu(s)|Cu^{2+}(0.10\ M)}}\qquad\underset{\text{cathode}}{\phantom{Cu^{2+}(1.0\ M)|Cu(s)}}$$

The half-reactions in the spontaneous cell reaction are

$$Cu(s) \longrightarrow Cu^{2+}(0.10\ M) + 2e^-$$
$$Cu^{2+}(1.0\ M) + 2e^- \longrightarrow Cu(s)$$
$$\rule{6cm}{0.4pt}$$
$$Cu^{2+}(1.0\ M) \longrightarrow Cu^{2+}(0.10\ M)$$

The Nernst equation for this cell is

$$E_{cell} = E^{\circ}_{cell} - \frac{RT}{n\mathscr{F}} \ln \frac{[Cu^{2+}]_{dilute}}{[Cu^{2+}]_{conc}}$$

Because we're dealing with the same substances in the cell, $E^{\circ}_{cell} = 0$ V (exactly). When the cell operates, $n = 2$, and we'll take $T = 298$ K. Substituting values,

$$E_{cell} = 0\ V - \frac{8.314\ J\ \cancel{mol^{-1}}\ \cancel{K^{-1}} \times 298\ \cancel{K}}{2 \times 9.65 \times 10^4\ C\ \cancel{mol^{-1}}} \ln \left(\frac{0.10}{1.0} \right)$$
$$= 0.030\ V$$

In this concentration cell, one solution is ten times more concentrated than the other, yet the potential generated is only 0.03 V. In general, the potential generated by concentration differences are quite small. Yet they are significant in biological systems, where electrical potentials are generated across biological membranes by differences in ion concentrations (e.g., K^+). Membrane potentials are important in processes such as the transmission of nerve impulses.

These small differences in potential also illustrate that if Q, in a system that is not at standard state, is between 0.10 and 10 we can conclude that $E_{cell} \approx E^{\circ}_{cell}$ and we can generalize the results in Sections 19.2 and 19.3 when predicting spontaneous reactions.

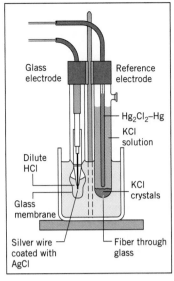

FIG. 19.8 Electrodes used with a pH meter. The electrode on the left is called a *glass electrode*. It contains a silver wire, coated with AgCl, dipping into a dilute solution of HCl. This half-cell has a potential that depends on the difference between the $[H^+]$ inside and outside a thin glass membrane at the bottom of the electrode. On the right is a reference electrode that forms the other half-cell. The galvanic cell formed by the two electrodes produces a potential that is proportional to the pH of the solution into which they are dipped.

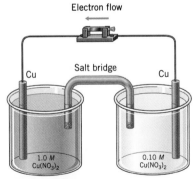

FIG. 19.9 A concentration cell. When the circuit is completed, reactions occur that tend to make the concentrations of Cu^{2+} the same in the two half-cells. Oxidation occurs in the more dilute half-cell, and reduction occurs in the more concentrated one.

19.6 ELECTROLYSIS USES ELECTRICAL ENERGY TO CAUSE CHEMICAL REACTIONS

In our preceding discussions, we've examined how spontaneous redox reactions can be used to generate electrical energy. We now turn our attention to the opposite process, the use of electrical energy to force nonspontaneous redox reactions to occur.

When electricity is passed through a molten (melted) ionic compound or through a solution of an electrolyte, a chemical reaction occurs that we call **electrolysis.** A typical electrolysis apparatus, called an **electrolysis cell** or **electrolytic cell,** is shown in Figure 19.10. This particular cell contains molten sodium chloride. (A substance undergoing electrolysis must be molten or in solution so its ions can move freely and conduction can occur.) *Inert electrodes*—electrodes that won't react with the molten NaCl—are dipped into the cell and then connected to a source of direct current (DC) electricity.

The DC source serves as an "electron pump," pulling electrons away from one electrode and pushing them through the external wiring onto the other electrode. The electrode from which electrons are removed becomes positively charged, while the other electrode becomes negatively charged. When electricity starts to flow, chemical changes begin to happen. At the positive electrode, oxidation occurs as electrons are pulled away from negatively charged chloride ions. Because of the nature of the chemical change, therefore, *the positive electrode becomes the anode.* The DC source pumps the electrons through the external electrical circuit to the negative electrode. Here reduction takes place as the electrons are forced onto positively charged sodium ions, so *the negative electrode is the cathode.*

The chemical changes that occur at the electrodes can be described by chemical equations.

$$Na^+(l) + e^- \longrightarrow Na(l) \qquad \text{(cathode)}$$
$$2Cl^-(l) \longrightarrow Cl_2(g) + 2e^- \qquad \text{(anode)}$$

As in a galvanic cell, the overall reaction that takes place in the electrolysis cell is called the *cell reaction.* To obtain it, we add the individual electrode half-reactions together, making sure that the number of electrons gained in one half-reaction equals the number lost in the other.

$$2Na^+(l) + 2e^- \longrightarrow 2Na(l) \qquad \text{(cathode)}$$
$$\underline{2Cl^-(l) \longrightarrow Cl_2(g) + 2e^- \qquad \text{(anode)}}$$
$$2Na^+(l) + 2Cl^-(l) + \cancel{2e^-} \longrightarrow 2Na(l) + Cl_2(g) + \cancel{2e^-} \qquad \text{(cell reaction)}$$

As you know, table salt is quite stable. It doesn't normally decompose because the reverse reaction, the reaction of sodium and chlorine to form sodium chloride, is highly spontaneous. Therefore, we often write the word *electrolysis* above the arrow in the equation to show that electricity is the driving force for this otherwise nonspontaneous reaction.

$$2Na^+(l) + 2Cl^-(l) \xrightarrow{\text{electrolysis}} 2Na(l) + Cl_2(g)$$

☐ To perform electrolysis, we must use direct current in which electrons move in only one direction, not in the oscillating, back and forth pattern of alternating current.

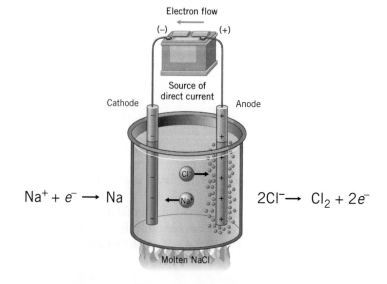

FIG. 19.10 **Electrolysis of molten sodium chloride.** In this electrolysis cell, the passage of an electric current decomposes molten sodium chloride into metallic sodium and gaseous chlorine. Unless the products are kept apart, they react on contact to re-form NaCl.

Electrolytic and galvanic cells have similarities and differences

In a galvanic cell, the spontaneous cell reaction deposits electrons on the anode and removes them from the cathode. As a result, the anode carries a slight negative charge and the cathode a slight positive charge. In most galvanic cells the reactants must be separated in separate compartments. In an *electrolysis cell*, the situation is reversed. Often the two electrodes are immersed in the same liquid. Also, the oxidation at the anode must be forced to occur, which requires that the anode be positive so it can remove electrons from the reactant at that electrode. On the other hand, the cathode must be made negative so it can force the reactant at the electrode to accept electrons.

Electrolytic Cell	Galvanic Cell
Cathode is negative (reduction).	Cathode is positive (reduction).
Anode is positive (oxidation).	Anode is negative (oxidation).
Anode and cathode are often in same compartment.	Anode and cathode are usually in separate compartments.

Even though the charges on the cathode and anode differ between electrolytic cells and galvanic cells, the ions in solution always move in the same direction. In both types of cells, positive ions (cations) move toward the cathode. They are attracted there by the negative charge on the cathode in an electrolysis cell; they diffuse toward the cathode in a galvanic cell to balance the charge of negative ions left behind when ions are reduced. Similarly, negative ions (anions) move toward the anode. They are attracted to the positive anode in an electrolysis cell, and they diffuse toward the anode in a galvanic cell to balance the charge of the positive ions entering the solution.

☐ By agreement among scientists, the names anode and cathode are assigned according to the nature of the reaction taking place at the electrode. If the reaction is oxidation, the electrode is called the anode; if it's reduction, the electrode is called the cathode.

Oxidation and reduction must occur for conduction to continue in an electrolytic cell

The electrical conductivity of a molten salt or a solution of an electrolyte is possible only because of the reactions that take place at the surface of the electrodes. For example, when charged electrodes are dipped into molten NaCl they become surrounded by a layer of ions of the opposite charge. Let's look closely at what happens at one of the electrodes, say the anode (Figure 19.11). Here the positive charge of the

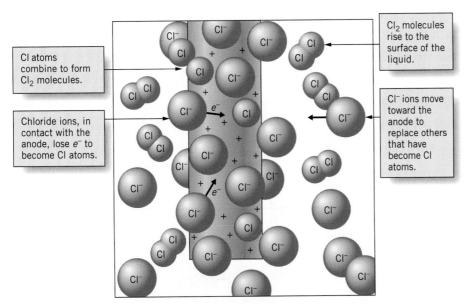

Cl atoms combine to form Cl_2 molecules.

Chloride ions, in contact with the anode, lose e^- to become Cl atoms.

Cl_2 molecules rise to the surface of the liquid.

Cl^- ions move toward the anode to replace others that have become Cl atoms.

FIG. 19.11 **A microscopic view of changes at the anode in the electrolysis of molten NaCl.** The positive charge of the electrode attracts a coating of Cl^- ions. At the surface of the electrode, electrons are pulled from the ions, yielding neutral Cl atoms, which combine to form Cl_2 molecules that move away from the electrode and eventually rise to the surface as a gas.

electrode attracts negative Cl^- ions, which form a coating on the electrode's surface. The charge on the anode pulls electrons from the ions, causing them to be oxidized and changing them into neutral Cl atoms that join to become Cl_2 molecules. Because the molecules are neutral, they are not held by the electrode and so move away from the electrode's surface. Their places are quickly taken by negative ions from the surrounding liquid, which tends to leave the surrounding liquid positively charged. Other negative ions from farther away move toward the anode to keep the liquid there electrically neutral. In this way, negative ions gradually migrate toward the anode. By a similar process, positive ions diffuse through the liquid toward the negatively charged cathode where they become reduced.

□ Cations (positive ions) move toward the cathode and anions (negative ions) migrate toward the anode. This happens in both electrolytic and galvanic cells.

Electrolysis reactions in aqueous solutions can involve oxidation and/or reduction of water

When electrolysis is carried out in an aqueous solution, the electrode reactions are more difficult to predict because at the electrodes there are competing reactions. We have to consider not only the possible oxidation and reduction of the solute, but also the oxidation and reduction of water. For example, consider what happens when electrolysis is performed on a solution of potassium sulfate (Figure 19.12). The products are hydrogen and oxygen. At the cathode, water is reduced, not K^+.

$$2H_2O(l) + 2e^- \longrightarrow H_2(g) + 2OH^-(aq) \qquad \text{(cathode)}$$

At the anode, water is oxidized, not the sulfate ion.

$$2H_2O(l) \longrightarrow O_2(g) + 4H^+(aq) + 4e^- \qquad \text{(anode)}$$

Color changes of an acid–base indicator dissolved in the solution confirm that the solution becomes basic around the cathode, where OH^- is formed, and acidic around the anode, where H^+ is formed (see Figure 19.13). In addition, the gases H_2 and O_2 can be separately collected.

We can understand why these redox reactions happen if we examine the standard reduction potential data from Table 19.1. For example, at the cathode we have the following competing reactions.

$$K^+(aq) + e^- \longrightarrow K(s) \qquad\qquad E^\circ_{K^+} = -2.92 \text{ V}$$

$$2H_2O(l) + 2e^- \longrightarrow H_2(g) + 2OH^-(aq) \qquad E^\circ_{H_2O} = -0.83 \text{ V}$$

Water has a much less negative (and therefore more positive) standard reduction potential than K^+, which means H_2O is much easier to reduce than K^+. As a result, when the

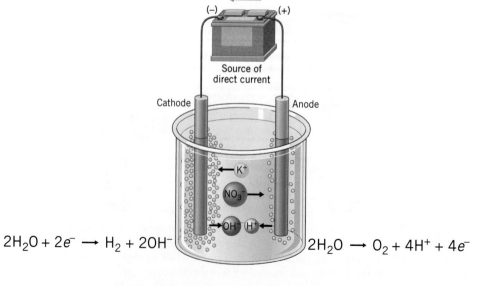

FIG. 19.12 **Electrolysis of an aqueous solution of potassium sulfate.** The products of the electrolysis are the gases hydrogen and oxygen as shown in the half-reactions for each half-cell.

$$2H_2O + 2e^- \longrightarrow H_2 + 2OH^-$$

$$2H_2O \longrightarrow O_2 + 4H^+ + 4e^-$$

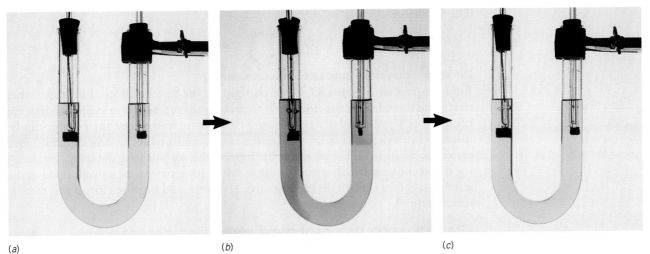

(a) (b) (c)

FIG. 19.13 **Electrolysis of an aqueous solution of potassium sulfate in the presence of acid–base indicators.** (*a*) The initial yellow color indicates that the solution is neutral (neither acidic nor basic). (*b*) As the electrolysis proceeds, H^+ is produced at the anode (along with O_2) and causes the solution there to become pink. At the cathode, H_2 is evolved and OH^- ions are formed, which turns the solution around that electrode a bluish violet. (*c*) After the electrolysis is stopped and the solution is stirred, the color becomes yellow again as the H^+ and OH^- ions formed by the electrolysis neutralize each other. (*Michael Watson*)

electrolysis is performed the more easily reduced substance is reduced and we observe H_2 being formed at the cathode.

At the anode we have the following possible oxidation half-reactions.

$$2SO_4^{2-}(aq) \longrightarrow S_2O_8^{2-}(aq) + 2e^-$$

$$2H_2O(l) \longrightarrow 4H^+(aq) + O_2(g) + 4e^-$$

In Table 19.1, we find them written in the opposite direction:

$$S_2O_8^{2-}(aq) + 2e^- \longrightarrow 2SO_4^{2-}(aq) \qquad E^\circ_{S_2O_8^{2-}} = +2.01 \text{ V}$$

$$O_2(g) + 4H^+(aq) + 4e^- \longrightarrow 2H_2O(l) \qquad E^\circ_{O_2} = +1.23 \text{ V}$$

The E° values tell us that $S_2O_8^{2-}$ is much more easily reduced than O_2. But if $S_2O_8^{2-}$ is the *more easily reduced*, then the product, SO_4^{2-}, must be *the less easily oxidized*. Stated another way, *the half-reaction with the smaller standard reduction potential is more easily reversed as an oxidation.* As a result, when electrolysis is performed, water is oxidized instead of SO_4^{2-} and we observe O_2 being formed at the anode.

The overall cell reaction for the electrolysis of the K_2SO_4 solution can be obtained as before. Because the number of electrons lost has to equal the number gained, the cathode reaction must occur twice each time the anode reaction occurs once.

$$2 \times [2H_2O(l) + 2e^- \longrightarrow H_2(g) + 2OH^-(aq)] \qquad \text{(cathode)}$$

$$2H_2O(l) \longrightarrow O_2(g) + 4H^+(aq) + 4e^- \qquad \text{(anode)}$$

After adding, we combine the coefficients for water and cancel the electrons from both sides to obtain the cell reaction.

$$6H_2O(l) \longrightarrow 2H_2(g) + O_2(g) + 4H^+(aq) + 4OH^-(aq)$$

Notice that hydrogen ions and hydroxide ions are produced in equal numbers. In Figure 19.13, we see that when the solution is stirred, they combine to form water.

$$6H_2O(l) \longrightarrow 2H_2(g) + O_2(g) + 4H^+(aq) + 4OH^-(aq)$$

$$H_2O$$

The net change, then, is

$$2H_2O \xrightarrow{\text{electrolysis}} 2H_2(g) + O_2(g)$$

What function does potassium sulfate serve?

Although neither K^+ nor SO_4^{2-} are changed by the reaction, K_2SO_4 or some other electrolyte is needed for the electrolysis to proceed. Its function is to maintain electrical neutrality at the electrodes. At the anode, H^+ ions are formed and their charge can be balanced by mixing with SO_4^{2-} ions of the solute. Similarly, at the cathode the K^+ ions are able to mix with OH^- ions as they are formed, thereby balancing the charge and keeping the solution electrically neutral. In this way, at any moment, each small region of the solution is able to contain the same number of positive and negative charges and thereby remain neutral.

Often we can use standard reduction potentials to predict electrolysis products

TOOLS
Predicting electrolysis products

Suppose we wished to know what products are expected in the electrolysis of an aqueous solution of copper(II) bromide, $CuBr_2$. Let's examine the possible electrode half-reactions and their respective standard reduction potentials.

At the cathode, possible reactions are the reduction of copper ion and the reduction of water. From Table 19.1,

$$Cu^{2+}(aq) + 2e^- \longrightarrow Cu(s) \qquad\qquad E^\circ_{Cu^{2+}} = +0.34\ V$$

$$2H_2O(l) + 2e^- \longrightarrow H_2(g) + 2OH^-(aq) \qquad E^\circ_{H_2O} = -0.83\ V$$

The much more positive standard reduction potential for Cu^{2+} tells us to anticipate that Cu^{2+} will be reduced at the cathode.

At the anode, possible reactions are the oxidation of Br^- and the oxidation of water. The half-reactions are

$$2Br^-(aq) \longrightarrow Br_2(aq) + 2e^-$$

$$2H_2O(l) \longrightarrow O_2(g) + 4H^+(aq) + 4e^-$$

In Table 19.1 they are written as reductions with the following E° values.

$$Br_2(aq) + 2e^- \longrightarrow 2Br^-(aq) \qquad E^\circ_{Br_2} = +1.07\ V$$

$$O_2(g) + 4H^+(aq) + 4e^- \longrightarrow 2H_2O(l) \qquad E^\circ_{O_2} = +1.23\ V$$

The data tell us that O_2 is more easily reduced than Br_2, which means that Br^- is more easily oxidized than H_2O. Therefore, we expect that Br^- will be oxidized at the anode.

In fact, our predictions are confirmed when we perform the electrolysis. The cathode, anode, and net cell reactions are

$$Cu^{2+}(aq) + 2e^- \longrightarrow Cu(s) \qquad\qquad \text{(cathode)}$$
$$\underline{\phantom{Cu^{2+}(aq) + }2Br^-(aq) \longrightarrow Br_2(aq) + 2e^- \qquad\qquad \text{(anode)}}$$
$$Cu^{2+}(aq) + 2Br^-(aq) \xrightarrow{\text{electrolysis}} Cu(s) + Br_2(aq) \qquad \text{(net reaction)}$$

EXAMPLE 19.13
Predicting the Products in an Electrolysis Reaction

Electrolysis is planned for an aqueous solution that contains a mixture of $0.50\ M\ ZnSO_4$ and $0.50\ M\ NiSO_4$. On the basis of standard reduction potentials, what products are expected to be observed at the electrodes? What is the expected net cell reaction?

ANALYSIS: We need to consider the competing reactions at the cathode and the anode. At the cathode, the half-reaction with the most positive (or least negative) standard reduction potential will be the one expected to occur. At the anode, the half-reaction with the *least* *positive* standard reduction potential is the one most easily reversed, and should occur as an oxidation.

SOLUTION: At the cathode, the competing reduction reactions involve the two cations and water. The reactions and their standard reduction potentials are

$$Ni^{2+}(aq) + 2e^- \rightleftharpoons Ni(s) \qquad E° = -0.25\,V$$
$$Zn^{2+}(aq) + 2e^- \rightleftharpoons Zn(s) \qquad E° = -0.76\,V$$
$$2H_2O + 2e^- \rightleftharpoons H_2(g) + 2OH^-(aq) \qquad E° = -0.83\,V$$

The least negative standard reduction potential is that of Ni^{2+}, so we expect that ion to be reduced at the cathode and solid nickel to be formed.

At the anode, the competing oxidation reactions are for water and SO_4^{2-} ion. In Table 19.1, substances oxidized are found on the right side of the half-reactions. The two half-reactions having these as products are

$$S_2O_8^{2-}(aq) + 2e^- \rightleftharpoons 2SO_4^{2-}(aq) \qquad E° = +2.01\,V$$
$$O_2(g) + 4H^+(aq) + 4e^- \rightleftharpoons 2H_2O \qquad E° = +1.23\,V$$

The half-reaction with the least positive $E°$ (the second one here) is most easily reversed as an oxidation, so we expect the oxidation half-reaction to be

$$2H_2O \rightleftharpoons O_2(g) + 4H^+(aq) + 4e^-$$

At the anode, we expect O_2 to be formed.

The predicted net cell reaction is obtained by combining the two expected electrode half-reactions, making the electron loss equal to the electron gain.

$$2H_2O \longrightarrow O_2(g) + 4H^+(aq) + 4e^- \qquad \text{(anode)}$$
$$\underline{2 \times [Ni^{2+}(aq) + 2e^- \longrightarrow Ni(s)]} \qquad \text{(cathode)}$$
$$2H_2O + 2Ni^{2+}(aq) \longrightarrow O_2(g) + 4H^+(aq) + 2Ni(s) \qquad \text{(net cell reaction)}$$

ARE THE ANSWERS REASONABLE? We can check the locations of the half-reactions in Table 19.1 to confirm our conclusions. For the reduction step, the higher up in the table a half-reaction is, the greater its tendency to occur as reduction. Among the competing half-reactions at the cathode, the one for Ni^{2+} is highest, so we expect that Ni^{2+} is the easiest to reduce and $Ni(s)$ should be formed at the cathode.

For the oxidation step, the lower down in the table a half-reaction is, the easier it is to reverse and cause to occur as oxidation. On this basis, the oxidation of water is easier than the oxidation of SO_4^{2-}, so we expect H_2O to be oxidized and O_2 to be formed at the anode.

Of course, we could also test our prediction by carrying out the electrolysis experimentally.

Practice Exercise 22: In the electrolysis of an aqueous solution containing Fe^{2+} and I^-, what product do we expect at the anode? (Hint: Write the three oxidation half-reactions possible at the anode.)

Practice Exercise 23: In the electrolysis of an aqueous solution containing both Cd^{2+} and Sn^{2+}, what product do we expect at the cathode? Under what conditions can the other ion be reduced?

Using standard reduction potentials to predict electrolysis doesn't always work

Although we can use standard reduction potentials to predict electrolysis reactions most of the time, there are occasions when standard reduction potentials do not successfully predict electrolysis products. Sometimes concentrations, far from standard conditions, will change the sign of the cell potential. The formation of complex ions can also interfere and produce unexpected results. And sometimes the electrodes themselves are the culprits. For example, in the electrolysis of aqueous NaCl using inert platinum electrodes, we find experimentally that Cl_2 is formed at the anode. Is this what we would have expected? Let's examine the standard reduction potentials of O_2 and Cl_2 to find out.

$$Cl_2(g) + 2e^- \rightleftharpoons 2Cl^-(aq) \qquad E° = +1.36\text{ V}$$
$$O_2(g) + 4H^+(aq) + 4e^- \rightleftharpoons 2H_2O \qquad E° = +1.23\text{ V}$$

Because of its less positive standard reduction potential, we would expect the oxygen half-reaction to be the easier to reverse (with water being oxidized to O_2). Thus, standard reduction potentials predict that O_2 should be formed, but experiment shows that Cl_2 is produced. The nature of the electrode surface and how it interacts with oxygen is part of the answer. Further explanation for why this happens is beyond the scope of this text, but the unexpected result does teach us that we must be cautious in predicting products in electrolysis reactions solely on the basis of standard reduction potentials.

Michael Faraday (1791–1867), a British scientist and both a chemist and a physicist, made key discoveries leading to electric motors, generators, and transformers. *(Courtesy Edgar Fahs Smith Collection, University of Pennsylvania.)*

19.7 STOICHIOMETRY OF ELECTROCHEMICAL REACTIONS INVOLVES ELECTRIC CURRENT AND TIME

In about 1833, Michael Faraday discovered that the amount of chemical change that occurs during electrolysis is directly proportional to the amount of electrical charge that is passed through an electrolysis cell. For example, the reduction of copper ion at a cathode is given by the equation

$$Cu^{2+}(aq) + 2e^- \longrightarrow Cu(s)$$

The equation tells us that to deposit one mole of metallic copper requires two moles of electrons. Thus, the half-reaction for an oxidation or reduction relates the amount of chemical substance consumed or produced to the amount of electrons that the electric current must supply. To use this information, however, we must be able to relate it to electrical measurements that can be made in the laboratory.

The SI unit of electric current is the **ampere (A)** and the SI unit of charge is the **coulomb (C).** A coulomb is the amount of charge that passes by a given point in a wire when an electric current of one ampere flows for one second. This means that coulombs are the product of amperes of current multiplied by seconds. Thus

$$1\text{ coulomb} = 1\text{ ampere} \times 1\text{ second}$$

$$\boxed{1\text{ C} = 1\text{ A s}}$$

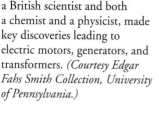

TOOLS

Coulombs are related to current in amperes and time in seconds.

For example, if a current of 4 A flows through a wire for 10 s, 40 C pass by a given point in the wire.

$$(4\text{ A}) \times (10\text{ s}) = 40\text{ A s}$$
$$= 40\text{ C}$$

As we noted earlier, it has been determined that 1 mol of electrons carries a charge of 9.65×10^4 C, which in honor of Michael Faraday is often called the Faraday constant, $\mathscr{F}$.

$$1\text{ mol }e^- \Leftrightarrow 9.65 \times 10^4\text{ C} \qquad \left(\begin{array}{c}\text{to three}\\ \text{significant figures}\end{array}\right)$$

$$1\ \mathscr{F} = 9.65 \times 10^4\text{ C/mol }e^-$$

Now we have a way to relate laboratory measurements to the amount of chemical change that occurs during an electrolysis. Measuring the current in amperes and the time in seconds allows us to calculate the charge sent through the system in coulombs. From this we can get the amount of electrons (in moles), which we can then use to calculate the amount of chemical change produced. The following examples demonstrate the principles involved for electrolysis, but similar calculations also apply to reactions in galvanic cells.

EXAMPLE 19.14
Calculations Related to
Electrolysis

How many grams of copper are deposited on the cathode of an electrolytic cell if an electric current of 2.00 A is run through a solution of $CuSO_4$ for a period of 20.0 min?

ANALYSIS: The balanced half-reaction serves as our tool for relating chemical change to amounts of electricity. The ion being reduced is Cu^{2+}, so the half-reaction is

$$Cu^{2+} + 2e^- \longrightarrow Cu$$

Therefore,

$$1 \text{ mol Cu} \Leftrightarrow 2 \text{ mol } e^-$$

The product of current (in amperes) and time (in seconds) is the tool that will give us charge (in coulombs). We can relate this to the number of moles of electrons by the Faraday constant, another of our tools. Then, from the number of moles of electrons we calculate moles of copper, from which we calculate the mass of copper by using the atomic mass. Here's a diagram of the path to the solution.

$$\boxed{\frac{1 \text{ mol } e^-}{9.65 \times 10^4 \text{ C}}} \quad \boxed{\frac{1 \text{ mol Cu}}{2 \text{ mol } e^-}}$$

$$\text{mol } e^- \qquad \boxed{\frac{63.55 \text{ g Cu}}{1 \text{ mol Cu}}}$$

$$\boxed{A \times s = C} \quad \text{coulombs} \qquad \text{mol Cu}$$

$$\text{current and time} \text{-------------------------->} \text{g Cu}$$

SOLUTION: First we convert minutes to seconds; $20.0 \text{ min} = 1.20 \times 10^3 \text{ s}$. Then we multiply the current by the time to obtain the number of coulombs ($1 \text{ A s} = 1 \text{ C}$).

$$(1.20 \times 10^3 \text{ s}) \times (2.00 \text{ A}) = 2.40 \times 10^3 \text{ A s}$$
$$= 2.40 \times 10^3 \text{ C}$$

Because $1 \text{ mol } e^- \Leftrightarrow 9.65 \times 10^4 \text{ C}$,

$$2.40 \times 10^3 \text{ C} \times \frac{1 \text{ mol } e^-}{9.65 \times 10^4 \text{ C}} = 0.02487 \text{ mol } e^-$$

Next, we use the relationship between mol e^- and mol Cu from the balanced half-reaction along with the atomic mass of copper.

$$0.02487 \text{ mol } e^- \times \left(\frac{1 \text{ mol Cu}}{2 \text{ mol } e^-}\right) \times \left(\frac{63.55 \text{ g Cu}}{1 \text{ mol Cu}}\right) = 0.7903 \text{ g Cu}$$

□ In stepwise calculations we always carry one or more extra significant figures until the final result to minimize rounding errors.

With proper rounding, the electrolysis will deposit 0.790 g of copper on the cathode.

We could have combined all the steps in a single calculation by stringing together the various conversion factors and using the factor-label method to cancel units.

$$2.00 \text{ A} \times 20.0 \text{ min} \times \frac{60 \text{ s}}{1 \text{ min}} \times \frac{1 \text{ mol } e^-}{9.65 \times 10^4 \text{ A s}} \times \frac{1 \text{ mol Cu}}{2 \text{ mol } e^-} \times \frac{63.55 \text{ g Cu}}{1 \text{ mol Cu}} = 0.790 \text{ g Cu}$$

IS THE ANSWER REASONABLE? As before, we round all numbers to one significant figure to estimate the answer.

$$\text{g Cu} = 2.00 \text{ A} \times 20.0 \text{ min} \times \frac{60 \text{ s}}{1 \text{ min}} \times \frac{1 \text{ mol } e^-}{10 \times 10^4 \text{ A s}} \times \frac{1 \text{ mol Cu}}{2 \text{ mol } e^-} \times \frac{60 \text{ g Cu}}{1 \text{ mol Cu}}$$

$$= \frac{40 \times 3600}{200000} = \frac{40 \times 0.36}{20} = 0.72 \text{ g Cu}$$

This is very close to our answer and we are even more confident that the calculation was correct when we check the cancellation of units.

EXAMPLE 19.15
Calculations Related
to Electrolysis

Electrolysis provides a useful way to deposit a thin metallic coating on an electrically conducting surface. This technique is called electroplating. How much time would it take in minutes to deposit 0.500 g of metallic nickel on a metal object using a current of 3.00 A? The nickel is reduced from the +2 oxidation state.

ANALYSIS: We need an equation for the reduction. Because the nickel is reduced to the free metal from the +2 state, we can write

$$Ni^{2+} + 2e^- \longrightarrow Ni(s)$$

This gives the relationship

$$1 \text{ mol Ni} \Leftrightarrow 2 \text{ mol } e^-$$

We wish to deposit 0.500 g of Ni, which we can convert to moles. Then we can calculate the number of moles of electrons required, which in turn is used with the tool for the Faraday constant to determine the number of coulombs required. Another of our tools tells us that this is the product of amperes and seconds, so we can calculate the time needed to deposit the metal. The calculation can be diagrammed as follows.

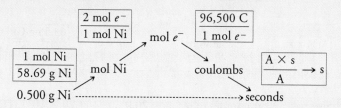

SOLUTION: First, we calculate the number of moles of electrons required (keeping at least one extra significant figure).

$$0.500 \text{ g Ni} \times \left(\frac{1 \text{ mol Ni}}{58.69 \text{ g Ni}} \right) \times \left(\frac{2 \text{ mol } e^-}{1 \text{ mol Ni}} \right) = 0.01704 \text{ mol } e^-$$

Then we calculate the number of coulombs needed.

$$0.01704 \text{ mol } e^- \times \left(\frac{9.65 \times 10^4 \text{ C}}{1 \text{ mol } e^-} \right) = 1.644 \times 10^3 \text{ C} = 1.644 \times 10^3 \text{ A s}$$

☐ Once we've calculated the number of coulombs required, we can calculate the time required if we know the current, or the current needed to perform the electrolysis in a given time.

This tells us that the product of current multiplied by time equals 1.644×10^3 A s. The current is 3.00 A. Dividing 1.644×10^3 A s by 3.00 A gives the time required in seconds, which we then convert to minutes.

$$\left(\frac{1.644 \times 10^3 \text{ A s}}{3.00 \text{ A}} \right) \times \left(\frac{1 \text{ min}}{60 \text{ s}} \right) = 9.133 \text{ min}$$

Properly rounded, this becomes 9.13 min. We could also have combined the calculations in a single string of conversion factors.

$$0.500 \text{ g Ni} \times \frac{1 \text{ mol Ni}}{58.69 \text{ g Ni}} \times \frac{2 \text{ mol } e^-}{1 \text{ mol Ni}} \times \frac{9.65 \times 10^4 \text{ A s}}{1 \text{ mol } e^-} \times \frac{1}{3.00 \text{ A}} \times \frac{1 \text{ min}}{60 \text{ s}} = 9.13 \text{ min}$$

IS THE ANSWER REASONABLE? As in the preceding example, let's round all numbers to one digit:

$$0.500 \text{ g Ni} \times \frac{1 \text{ mol Ni}}{60 \text{ g Ni}} \times \frac{2 \text{ mol } e^-}{1 \text{ mol Ni}} \times \frac{10 \times 10^4 \text{ A s}}{1 \text{ mol } e^-} \times \frac{1}{3.00 \text{ A}} \times \frac{1 \text{ min}}{60 \text{ s}} = \frac{100000 \text{ min}}{3600 \times 3} = \frac{100000 \text{ min}}{10000} = 10 \text{ min}$$

This result, along with the proper cancellation of units, indicates our calculations and setup were correct.

Practice Exercise 24: How many moles of hydroxide ion will be produced at the cathode during the electrolysis of water with a current of 4.00 A for a period of 200 s? The cathode reaction is

$$2e^- + 2H_2O \longrightarrow H_2 + 2OH^-$$

(Hint: The stepwise diagram in Example 19.15 will be helpful.)

Practice Exercise 25: How many minutes will it take for a current of 10.0 A to deposit 3.00 g of gold from a solution of $AuCl_3$?

Practice Exercise 26: What current must be supplied to deposit 3.00 g of gold from a solution of $AuCl_3$ in 20.0 min?

Practice Exercise 27: Suppose the solutions in the galvanic cell depicted in Figure 19.2 (page 771) have a volume of 125 mL and suppose the cell is operated for a period of 1.25 hr with a constant current of 0.100 A flowing through the external circuit. By how much will the concentration of the copper ion increase during that time?

19.8 | PRACTICAL APPLICATIONS OF ELECTROCHEMISTRY

Electrochemistry has many applications both in science and in our everyday lives. In this limited space, we can only touch on some of the more common and important examples.

Batteries are practical examples of galvanic cells

One of the most familiar uses of galvanic cells, popularly called *batteries*, is the generation of portable electrical energy.[8] These devices are classified as being either **primary cells** (cells not designed to be recharged; they are discarded after their energy is depleted) or **secondary cells** (cells designed for repeated use; they are able to be recharged).

The lead storage battery is used in most automobiles

The common **lead storage battery** used to start an automobile is composed of a number of secondary cells, each having a potential of about 2 V, that are connected in series so that their voltages are additive. Most automobile batteries contain six such cells and give about 12 V, but 6, 24, and 32 V batteries are also available.

A typical lead storage battery is illustrated in Figure 19.14. The anode of each cell is composed of a set of lead plates, the cathode consists of another set of plates that hold a coating of PbO_2, and the electrolyte is sulfuric acid. When the battery is discharging the electrode reactions are

$$PbO_2(s) + 3H^+(aq) + HSO_4^-(aq) + 2e^- \longrightarrow PbSO_4(s) + 2H_2O \qquad \text{(cathode)}$$

$$Pb(s) + HSO_4^-(aq) \longrightarrow PbSO_4(s) + H^+(aq) + 2e^- \text{ (anode)}$$

The net reaction taking place in each cell is

$$PbO_2(s) + Pb(s) + \underbrace{2H^+(aq) + 2HSO_4^-(aq)}_{2H_2SO_4} \longrightarrow 2PbSO_4(s) + 2H_2O$$

As the cell discharges, the sulfuric acid concentration decreases, which causes the density of the electrolyte to drop. The state of charge of the battery can be monitored with a **hydrometer,** which consists of a rubber bulb that is used to draw the battery fluid into

The oldest known electric battery in existence, discovered in 1938 in Baghdad, Iraq, consists of a copper tube surrounding an iron rod. If filled with an acidic liquid such as vinegar, the cell could produce a small electric current. (*Smith College Museum of Ancient Inventions.*)

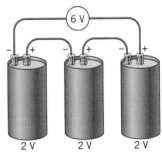

If three 2 volt cells are connected in series, their voltages are additive to provide a total of 6 volts. In today's autos, 12 volt batteries containing six cells are the norm.

---

[8] Strictly speaking, a cell is a single electrochemical unit consisting of a cathode and an anode. A battery is a collection of cells connected in series.

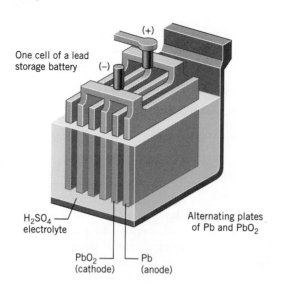

FIG. 19.14 **Lead storage battery.** A 12 volt lead storage battery, such as those used in most automobiles, consists of six cells like the one shown here. Notice that the anode and cathode each consist of several plates connected together. This allows the cell to produce the large currents necessary to start a car.

FIG. 19.15 **A battery hydrometer.** Battery acid is drawn into the glass tube. The depth to which the float sinks is inversely proportional to the concentration of the acid and, therefore, to the state of charge of the battery. *(OPC, Inc.)*

a glass tube containing a float (see Figure 19.15). The depth to which the float sinks is inversely proportional to the density of the liquid—the deeper the float sinks, the lower is the density of the acid and the weaker is the charge on the battery. The narrow neck of the float is usually marked to indicate the state of charge of the battery.

The principal advantage of the lead storage battery is that the cell reactions that occur spontaneously during discharge can be reversed by the application of a voltage from an external source. In other words, the battery can be recharged by electrolysis. The reaction for battery recharge is

$$2PbSO_4(s) + 2H_2O \xrightarrow{\text{electrolysis}} PbO_2(s) + Pb(s) + 2H^+(aq) + 2HSO_4^-(aq)$$

Improper recharging of lead–acid batteries can produce potentially explosive H_2 gas. Most modern lead storage batteries use a lead–calcium alloy as the anode. That reduces the need to have the individual cells vented, and the battery can be sealed, thereby preventing spillage of the corrosive electrolyte.

The zinc–manganese dioxide cell is our familiar dry cell

The ordinary, relatively inexpensive 1.5 V dry cell is the **zinc–manganese dioxide cell,** or **Leclanché cell** (named after its inventor George Leclanché). It is a primary cell used to power flashlights, remote TV, VCR, and DVD controllers, toys, and the like, but it is not really dry (see Figure 19.16). Its outer shell is made of zinc, which serves as the anode. The cathode—the positive terminal of the battery—consists of a carbon (graphite) rod surrounded by a moist paste of graphite powder, manganese dioxide, and ammonium chloride.

The anode reaction is simply the oxidation of zinc.

$$Zn(s) \longrightarrow Zn^{2+}(aq) + 2e^- \qquad \text{(anode)}$$

The cathode reaction is complex, and a mixture of products is formed. One of the major reactions is

$$2MnO_2(s) + 2NH_4^+(aq) + 2e^- \longrightarrow Mn_2O_3(s) + 2NH_3(aq) + H_2O \quad \text{(cathode)}$$

The ammonia that forms at the cathode reacts with some of the Zn^{2+} produced from the anode to form a complex ion, $Zn(NH_3)_4^{2+}$. Because of the complexity of the cathode half-cell reaction, no simple overall cell reaction can be written.

A more popular version of the Leclanché battery uses a basic, or *alkaline* electrolyte and is called an **alkaline battery** or **alkaline dry cell.** It too uses Zn and MnO_2 as reactants, but under basic conditions (Figure 19.17). The half-cell reactions are

☐ The alkaline battery is also a primary cell.

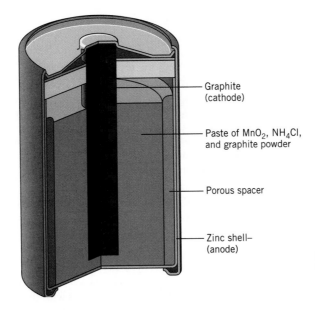

FIG. 19.16 A cutaway view of a zinc–carbon dry cell (Leclanché cell).

Graphite (cathode)

Paste of MnO_2, NH_4Cl, and graphite powder

Porous spacer

Zinc shell (anode)

$$Zn(s) + 2OH^-(aq) \longrightarrow ZnO(s) + H_2O + 2e^- \qquad \text{(anode)}$$

$$2MnO_2(s) + H_2O + 2e^- \longrightarrow Mn_2O_3(s) + 2OH^-(aq) \qquad \text{(cathode)}$$

$$Zn(s) + 2MnO_2(s) \longrightarrow ZnO(s) + Mn_2O_3(s) \qquad \text{(net cell reaction)}$$

and the voltage is about 1.54 V. It has a longer shelf-life and is able to deliver higher currents for longer periods than the less expensive zinc–carbon cell.

The nickel–cadmium storage cell is rechargeable

The **nickel–cadmium storage cell,** or **nicad battery,** is a secondary cell that produces a potential of about 1.4 V, which is slightly lower than that of the zinc–carbon cell. The electrode reactions in the cell during discharge are

$$Cd(s) + 2OH^-(aq) \longrightarrow Cd(OH)_2(s) + 2e^- \qquad \text{(anode)}$$

$$NiO_2(s) + 2H_2O + 2e^- \longrightarrow Ni(OH)_2(s) + 2OH^-(aq) \qquad \text{(cathode)}$$

$$Cd(s) + NiO_2(s) + 2H_2O \longrightarrow Ni(OH)_2(s) + Cd(OH)_2(s) \qquad \text{(net cell reaction)}$$

The nickel–cadmium battery can be recharged, in which case the anode and cathode reactions above are reversed to remake the reactants. The battery also can be sealed to prevent leakage, which is particularly important in electronic devices.

Nickel–cadmium batteries work especially well in applications such as portable power tools, CD players, and even electric cars. They have a high **energy density** (available energy per unit volume), they are able to release the energy quickly, and they can be rapidly recharged.

Nickel–metal hydride batteries store more energy than nicad batteries

These secondary cells, which are often referred to as Ni–MH batteries, have been used extensively in recent years to power devices such as cell phones, camcorders, and even electric vehicles. They are similar in many ways to the alkaline nickel–cadmium cells discussed above, except for the anode reactant, which is hydrogen. This is possible because certain metal alloys [e.g., $LaNi_5$ (an alloy of lanthanum and nickel) and Mg_2Ni (an alloy of magnesium and nickel)] have the ability to absorb and hold substantial amounts of hydrogen, and that the hydrogen can be made to participate in reversible electrochemical reactions. The term *metal hydride* is used to describe the hydrogen-holding alloy.

The cathode in the Ni–MH cell is NiO(OH), a compound of nickel in the +3 oxidation state, and the electrolyte is a solution of KOH. Using the symbol MH to stand for the metal hydride, the reactions in the cell during discharge are

$$MH(s) + OH^-(aq) \longrightarrow M(s) + H_2O + e^- \qquad \text{(anode)}$$

$$NiO(OH)(s) + H_2O + e^- \longrightarrow Ni(OH)_2(s) + OH^-(aq) \qquad \text{(cathode)}$$

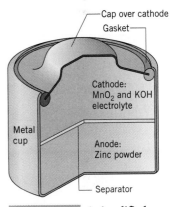

Cap over cathode

Gasket

Cathode: MnO_2 and KOH electrolyte

Metal cup

Anode: Zinc powder

Separator

FIG. 19.17 A simplified diagram of an alkaline zinc–carbon dry cell.

☐ If a battery can supply large amounts of energy and is contained in a small package, it will have a desirably high energy density.

☐ There are compounds of hydrogen with metals such as sodium that actually contain the *hydride ion,* H^-. The metal "hydrides" described here are not of that type.

The overall cell reaction is

$$MH(s) + NiO(OH)(s) \longrightarrow Ni(OH)_2(s) + M(s) \qquad E^°_{cell} = 1.35 \text{ V}$$

When the cell is recharged, the reactions are reversed.

The principal advantage of the Ni–MH cell over the Ni–Cd cell is that it can store about 50% more energy in the same volume. This means, for example, that comparing cells of the same size and weight, a nickel–metal hydride cell can power a laptop computer or a cell phone about 50% longer than a nickel–cadmium cell.

Lithium batteries combine high energy with low weight

Lithium has the most negative standard reduction potential of any metal (Table 19.1), so it has a lot of appeal as an anode material. Furthermore, lithium is a very lightweight metal, so a cell employing lithium as a reactant would also be lightweight. The major problem with using lithium in a galvanic cell is that the metal reacts vigorously with water to produce hydrogen gas and lithium hydroxide.

$$2Li(s) + 2H_2O \longrightarrow 2LiOH(aq) + H_2(g)$$

Therefore, to employ lithium in a galvanic cell scientists had to find a way to avoid aqueous electrolytes. This became possible in the 1970s with the introduction of organic solvents and solvent mixtures that were able dissolve certain lithium salts and thereby serve as electrolytes.

Today's lithium batteries fall into two categories, primary batteries that can be used once and then discarded when fully discharged, and rechargeable cells.

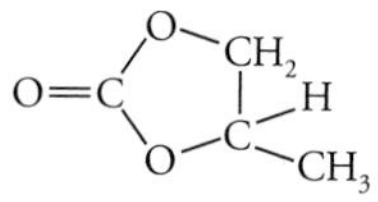

One of the most common nonrechargeable cells is the **lithium–manganese dioxide battery,** which accounts for about 80% of all primary lithium cells. This cell uses a solid lithium anode and a cathode made of heat-treated MnO_2. The electrolyte is a mixture of propylene carbonate and dimethoxyethane (see structures in the margin) containing a dissolved lithium salt such as $LiClO_4$. The cell reactions are as follows (superscripts are the oxidation numbers of the manganese):

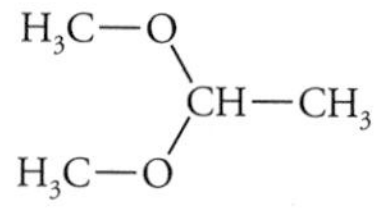

$$Li \longrightarrow Li^+ + e^- \qquad \text{(anode)}$$

$$\underline{Mn^{IV}O_2 + Li^+ + e^- \longrightarrow Mn^{III}O_2(Li^+)} \qquad \text{(cathode)}$$

$$Li + Mn^{IV}O_2 \longrightarrow Mn^{III}O_2(Li^+) \qquad \text{(net cell reaction)}$$

This cell produces a voltage of about 3.4 V, which is more than twice that of an alkaline dry cell, and because of the light weight of the lithium, it produces more than twice as much energy for a given weight. These cells are used in applications that require a higher current drain or energy pulses (e.g., photoflash).

Lithium ion cells are rechargeable

Rechargeable lithium batteries found in many cell phones, digital cameras, and laptop computers do not contain metallic lithium. They are called **lithium ion cells** and use lithium ions instead. In fact, the cell's operation doesn't actually involve true oxidation and reduction. Instead, it uses the transport of Li^+ ions through the electrolyte from one electrode to the other accompanied by the transport of electrons through the external circuit to maintain charge balance. Here's how it works.

It was discovered that Li^+ ions are able to slip between layers of atoms in certain crystals such as graphite[9] and $LiCoO_2$ (a process called **intercalation**). When the cell is constructed, it is in its "uncharged" state, with no Li^+ ions between the layers of carbon atoms in the graphite. When the cell is charged (Figure 19.18a), Li^+ ions leave $LiCoO_2$ and travel through the electrolyte to the graphite (represented below by the formula C_6).

Initial charging:

$$LiCoO_2 + C_6 \longrightarrow Li_{1-x}CoO_2 + Li_xC_6$$

When the cell spontaneously discharges to provide electrical power (Figure 19.18b), Li^+ ions move back through the electrolyte to the cobalt oxide while electrons move through

propylene carbonate

dimethoxyethane

☐ Pronounced in-*ter*-ca-*la*-tion. Rhymes with *percolation*.

---

[9] Graphite is one of the forms of elemental carbon and consists of layers of joined benzene-like rings.

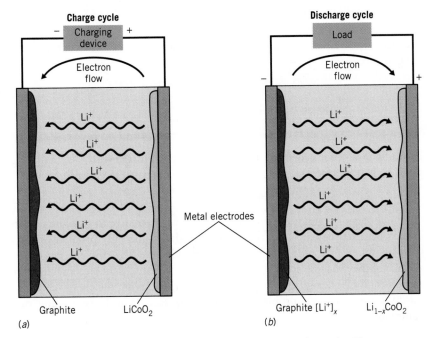

Charge cycle

Discharge cycle

FIG. 19.18 **Lithium ion cell.** (*a*) During the charging cycle, an external voltage forces electrons through the external circuit and causes lithium ions to travel from the $LiCoO_2$ electrode to the graphite electrode. (*b*) During discharge, the lithium ions spontaneously migrate back to the $LiCoO_2$ electrode, and electrons flow through the external circuit to balance the charge.

the external circuit from the graphite electrode to the cobalt oxide electrode. If we represent the amount of Li^+ transferring by y, the discharge "reaction" is

Discharge:

$$Li_{1-x}CoO_2 + Li_xC_6 \longrightarrow Li_{1-x+y}CoO_2 + Li_{x-y}C_6$$

Thus, the charging and discharging cycles simply sweep Li^+ ions back and forth between the two electrodes, with the electrons flowing through the external circuit to keep the charge in balance.

Fuel cells operate with a continuous supply of reactants

The galvanic cells we've discussed until now can only produce power for a limited time because the electrode reactants are eventually depleted. Fuel cells are different; they are electrochemical cells in which the electrode reactants are supplied continuously and are able to operate without theoretical limit as long as the supply of reactants is maintained. This makes fuel cells an attractive source of power where long-term generation of electrical energy is required.

Figure 19.19 illustrates an early design of a hydrogen–oxygen **fuel cell**. The electrolyte, a hot (~200 °C) concentrated solution of potassium hydroxide in the center

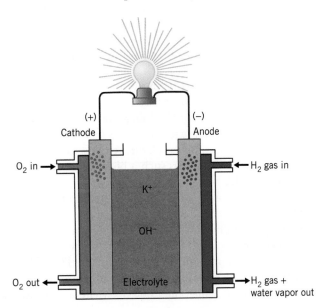

FIG. 19.19 **A hydrogen–oxygen fuel cell.**

compartment, is in contact with two porous electrodes that contain a catalyst (usually platinum) to facilitate the electrode reactions. Gaseous hydrogen and oxygen under pressure are circulated so as to come in contact with the electrodes. At the cathode, oxygen is reduced.

$$O_2(g) + 2H_2O + 4e^- \longrightarrow 4OH^-(aq) \qquad \text{(cathode)}$$

At the anode, hydrogen is oxidized to water.

$$H_2(g) + 2OH^-(aq) \longrightarrow 2H_2O + 2e^- \qquad \text{(anode)}$$

Part of the water formed at the anode leaves as steam mixed with the circulating hydrogen gas. The net cell reaction, after making electron loss equal to electron gain, is

$$2H_2(g) + O_2(g) \longrightarrow 2H_2O \qquad \text{(net cell reaction)}$$

Hydrogen–oxygen fuel cells are an attractive alternative to gasoline powered engines in part because they are essentially pollution-free—the only product of the reaction is harmless water. Fuel cells are also quite thermodynamically efficient, converting as much as 75% of the available energy to useful work, compared to approximately 25 to 30% for gasoline and diesel engines. Among the major obstacles are the energy costs of generating the hydrogen fuel and problems in providing storage and distribution of the highly flammable H_2.

Electrolysis has many industrial applications

Besides being a useful tool in the chemistry laboratory, electrolysis has many important industrial applications. Here we will briefly examine the chemistry of electroplating and the production of some of our most common chemicals.

Electroplating deposits metal on a surface

Electroplating, which was mentioned in Examples 19.14 and 19.15, is a procedure in which electrolysis is used to apply a thin (generally 0.03 to 0.05 mm thick) ornamental or protective coating of one metal over another. It is a common technique for improving the appearance and durability of metal objects. For instance, a thin, shiny coating of metallic chromium is applied over steel objects to make them attractive and to prevent rusting.

The exact composition of the electroplating bath varies, depending on the metal to be deposited, and it can affect the appearance and durability of the finished surface. For example, silver deposited from a solution of silver nitrate ($AgNO_3$) does not stick to other metal surfaces very well. However, if it is deposited from a solution of silver cyanide containing $Ag(CN)_2^-$, the coating adheres well and is bright and shiny. Other metals that are electroplated from a cyanide bath are gold and cadmium. Nickel, which can also be applied as a protective coating, is plated from a nickel sulfate solution, and chromium is plated from a chromic acid (H_2CrO_4) solution.

Aluminum is produced from aluminum oxide

Aluminum is a useful but highly reactive metal. It is so difficult to reduce that ordinary metallurgical methods for obtaining it do not work. Early efforts to produce aluminum by electrolysis failed because its anhydrous halide salts (those with no water of hydration) are difficult to prepare and are volatile, tending to evaporate rather than melt. On the other hand, its oxide, Al_2O_3, has such a high melting point (over 2000 °C) that no practical method of melting it could be found.

In 1886, Charles M. Hall discovered that Al_2O_3 dissolves in the molten form of a mineral called cryolite, Na_3AlF_6, to give a conducting mixture with a relatively low melting point from which aluminum could be produced electrolytically. The process was also discovered by Paul Héroult in France at nearly the same time, and today this method for producing aluminum is usually called the **Hall–Héroult process** (see Figure 19.20). Purified aluminum oxide, which is obtained from an ore called *bauxite*, is dissolved in molten cryolite in which the oxide dissociates to give Al^{3+} and O^{2-} ions. At the cathode,

This motorcycle sparkles with chrome plating that was deposited by electrolysis. The shiny hard coating of chromium is both decorative and a barrier to corrosion. *(Syracuse Newspapers/ The Image Works.)*

☐ Aluminum is used today as a structural metal, in alloys, and in such products as aluminum foil, electrical wire, window frames, and kitchen pots and pans.

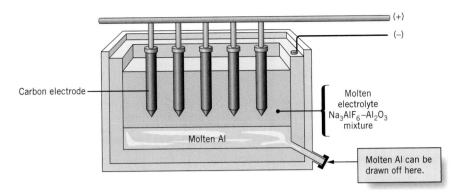

FIG. 19.20 **Production of aluminum by electrolysis.** In the apparatus used to produce aluminum electrolytically by the Hall–Héroult process, Al_2O_3 is dissolved in molten cryolite, Na_3AlF_6. Al^{3+} is reduced to metallic Al and O^{2-} is oxidized to O_2, which reacts with the carbon anodes to give CO_2. Periodically, molten aluminum is drawn off at the bottom of the cell and additional Al_2O_3 is added to the cryolite. The carbon anodes also must be replaced from time to time as they are consumed by their reaction with O_2.

aluminum ions are reduced to produce the free metal, which forms as a layer of molten aluminum below the less dense solvent. At the carbon anodes, oxide ion is oxidized to give free O_2.

$$Al^{3+} + 3e^- \longrightarrow Al(l) \qquad \text{(cathode)}$$
$$2O^{2-} \longrightarrow O_2(g) + 4e^- \qquad \text{(anode)}$$
$$\overline{4Al^{3+} + 6O^{2-} \longrightarrow 4Al(l) + 3O_2(g)} \qquad \text{(cell reaction)}$$

The oxygen formed at the anode attacks the carbon electrodes (producing CO_2), so the electrodes must be replaced frequently.

The production of aluminum consumes enormous amounts of electrical energy and is therefore very costly, not only in terms of dollars but also in terms of energy resources. For this reason, recycling of aluminum has a high priority as we seek to minimize our use of energy.

Sodium is made by electrolysis of sodium chloride

Sodium is prepared by the electrolysis of molten sodium chloride (see Section 19.6). The metallic sodium and the chlorine gas that form must be kept apart or they will react violently and re-form NaCl. A specialized apparatus called a **Downs cell** accomplishes this separation.

Both sodium and chlorine are commercially important. Chlorine is used largely to manufacture plastics such as polyvinyl chloride (PVC), many solvents, and industrial chemicals. A small percentage of the annual chlorine production is used to chlorinate drinking water.

Sodium has been used in the manufacture of tetraethyl lead, an octane booster for gasoline that has been phased out in the United States but which is still used in many other countries. Sodium is also used in the production of energy efficient sodium vapor lamps, which give street lights and other commercial lighting a bright yellow-orange color.

Refining of copper makes it suitable for electrical wire

When copper is first obtained from its ore, it is about 99% pure. The impurities—mostly silver, gold, platinum, iron, and zinc—decrease the electrical conductivity of the copper enough that even 99% pure copper must be further refined before it can be used in electrical wire.

The impure copper is used as the anode in an electrolysis cell that contains a solution of copper sulfate and sulfuric acid as the electrolyte (see Figure 19.21). The cathode is a thin sheet of very pure copper. When the cell is operated at the correct voltage, only copper and impurities more easily oxidized than copper (iron and zinc) dissolve at the anode. The less active metals simply fall off the electrode and settle to the bottom of the container. At the cathode, copper ions are reduced, but the zinc ions and iron ions remain

◻ The spectacular reaction of chlorine and sodium is captured in Figure 2.24 on page 62.

◻ PVC is used to make a large variety of products, from raincoats to wire insulation to pipes and conduits for water and sanitary systems. In the United States, the annual demand for PVC plastics is about 15 billion pounds.

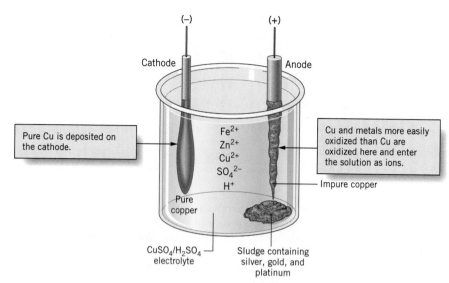

FIG. 19.21 Purification of copper by electrolysis. Impure copper anodes dissolve and pure copper is deposited on the cathodes. Metals less easily oxidized than copper settle to the bottom of the apparatus as "anode mud," while metals less easily reduced than copper remain in solution.

☐ Copper refining provides one-fourth of the silver and one-eighth of the gold produced annually in the United States.

Copper refining. Copper cathodes, 99.96% pure, are pulled from the electrolytic refining tanks at Kennecott's Utah copper refinery. It takes about 28 days for the impure copper anodes to dissolve and deposit the pure metal on the cathodes. *(Courtesy ASARCO, Inc.)*

☐ Sodium hydroxide is commonly known as *lye* or *caustic soda.*

in solution because they are more difficult to reduce than copper. Gradually, the impure copper anode dissolves and the copper cathode, about 99.96% pure, grows larger. The accumulating sludge—called anode mud—is removed periodically, and the value of the silver, gold, and platinum recovered from it virtually pays for the entire refining operation.

Electrolysis of brine produces several important chemicals

One of the most important commercial electrolysis reactions is the electrolysis of concentrated aqueous sodium chloride solutions called **brine.** At the cathode, water is much more easily reduced than sodium ion, so H_2 forms.

$$2H_2O(l) + 2e^- \longrightarrow H_2(g) + 2OH^-(aq) \qquad \text{(cathode)}$$

As we noted earlier, even though water is more easily oxidized than chloride ion, complicating factors at the electrodes actually allow chloride ion to be oxidized instead. At the anode, therefore, we observe the formation of Cl_2.

$$2Cl^-(aq) \longrightarrow Cl_2(g) + 2e^- \qquad \text{(anode)}$$

The net cell reaction is therefore

$$2Cl^-(aq) + 2H_2O(l) \longrightarrow H_2(g) + Cl_2(g) + 2OH^-(aq)$$

If we include the sodium ion, already in the solution as a spectator ion and not involved in the electrolysis directly, we can see why this is such an important reaction.

$$\underbrace{2Na^+(aq) + 2Cl^-(aq)}_{2NaCl(aq)} + 2H_2O \xrightarrow{\text{electrolysis}} H_2(g) + Cl_2(g) + \underbrace{2Na^+(aq) + 2OH^-(aq)}_{2NaOH(aq)}$$

Thus, the electrolysis converts inexpensive salt to valuable chemicals: H_2, Cl_2, and NaOH. The hydrogen is used to make other chemicals, including hydrogenated vegetable oils. The chlorine is used for the purposes mentioned earlier. Among the uses of sodium hydroxide, one of industry's most important bases, are the manufacture of soap and paper, the neutralization of acids in industrial reactions, and the purification of aluminum ores.

In the industrial electrolysis of brine, it is necessary to capture the H_2 and Cl_2 separately to prevent them from mixing and reacting (explosively). Second, the NaOH from the reaction is contaminated with unreacted NaCl. Third, if Cl_2 is left in the presence of NaOH, the solution becomes contaminated by hypochlorite ion (OCl^-), which forms by the reaction of Cl_2 with OH^-.

$$Cl_2(g) + 2OH^-(aq) \longrightarrow Cl^-(aq) + OCl^-(aq) + H_2O$$

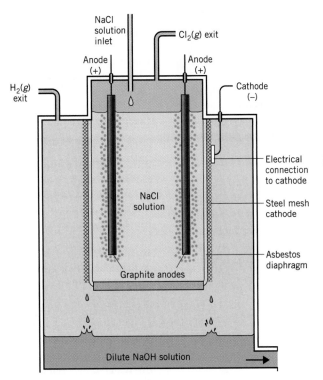

FIG. 19.22 **A diaphragm cell used in the commercial production of NaOH by the electrolysis of aqueous NaCl.** This is a cross section of a cylindrical cell in which the NaCl solution is surrounded by an asbestos diaphragm supported by a steel mesh cathode. (From J. E. Brady and G. E. Humiston, *General Chemistry: Principles and Structure*, 4th ed. Copyright © 1986, John Wiley & Sons, New York. Used by permission.)

In one manufacturing operation, however, the Cl_2 is not removed as it forms, and its reaction with hydroxide ion is used to manufacture aqueous sodium hypochlorite. For this purpose, the solution is stirred vigorously during the electrolysis so that very little Cl_2 escapes. As a result, a stirred solution of NaCl gradually changes during electrolysis to a solution of NaOCl, a dilute (5%) solution of which is sold as liquid laundry bleach (e.g., Clorox).

Most of the pure NaOH manufactured today is made in an apparatus called a **diaphragm cell.** The design varies somewhat, but Figure 19.22 illustrates its basic features. The cell consists of an iron wire mesh cathode that encloses a porous asbestos shell—the diaphragm. The NaCl solution is added to the top of the cell and seeps slowly through the diaphragm. When it contacts the iron cathode, hydrogen is evolved and is pumped out of the surrounding space. The solution, now containing dilute NaOH, drips off the cell into the reservoir below. Meanwhile, within the cell, chlorine is generated at the anodes dipping into the NaCl solution. Because there is no OH^- in this solution, the Cl_2 can't react to form OCl^- ion and simply bubbles out of the solution and is captured.

SUMMARY

Galvanic Cells. A **galvanic cell** is composed of two **half-cells,** each containing an **electrode** in contact with an electrolyte reactant. A spontaneous redox reaction is thus divided into separate oxidation and reduction half-reactions, with the electron transfer occurring through an external electrical circuit. Reduction occurs at the **cathode;** oxidation occurs at the **anode.** In a galvanic cell, the cathode is positively charged and the anode is negatively charged. The half-cells must be connected electrolytically by a **salt bridge** to complete the electrical circuit, which permits electrical neutrality to be maintained by allowing cations to move toward the cathode and anions toward the anode.

The **potential** (expressed in volts) produced by a cell is equal to the **standard cell potential** when all ion concentrations are 1.00 M and the partial pressures of any gases involved equal 1.00 atm and the temperature is 25.0 °C. The **standard cell potential** is the difference between the **standard reduction potentials** of the half-cells. In the spontaneous reaction, the half-cell with the higher standard reduction potential undergoes reduction and forces the other to undergo oxidation. The standard reduction potentials of isolated half-cells can't be measured, but values are assigned by choosing the **hydrogen electrode** as a reference electrode; its standard reduction potential is assigned a value of exactly 0 V. Species more easily reduced than H^+ have positive standard reduction potentials; those less easily reduced have negative standard reduction potentials. Standard reduction potentials can be used to predict the cell reaction. They can also be used to predict spontaneous redox reactions not occurring in galvanic cells and to predict whether or not a given reaction is spontaneous. Often, they can be used to determine the products of electrolysis reactions. Standard reduction potentials are used to calculate $E°_{cell}$. Since reduction potentials under nonstandard conditions are often numerically close to standard reduction potentials, we can usually use standard reduction potentials to make predictions about reactions with nonstandard conditions. The predictions above about spontaneous reactions, cell reactions, electrolysis products, and reactions outside of galvanic cells are usually valid under nonstandard conditions also.

Thermodynamics and Cell Potentials.

The values of $\Delta G°$ and K_c for a reaction can be calculated from $E°_{cell}$. They all involve the **faraday, $\mathscr{F}$,** a constant equal to the number of **coulombs (C)** of charge per mole of electrons (1 $\mathscr{F}$ = 96,500 C/mol e^-). The Nernst equation relates the cell potential to the standard cell potential and the reaction quotient. It allows the cell potential to be calculated for ion concentrations other than 1.00 M. The important equations are summarized as

$$\Delta G° = -n\mathscr{F}E°_{cell} = -RT \ln K_c$$

$$E_{cell} = E°_{cell} - \frac{RT}{n\mathscr{F}} \ln Q$$

Electrolysis.

In an **electrolytic cell,** a flow of electricity causes an otherwise nonspontaneous reaction to occur. A negatively charged **cathode** causes reduction of one reactant and a positively charged **anode** causes oxidation of another. Ion movement instead of electron transport occurs in the electrolyte. The electrode reactions are determined by which species is most easily reduced and which is most easily oxidized, but in aqueous solutions complex surface effects at the electrodes can alter the natural order.

In the electrolysis of water, an electrolyte must be present to maintain electrical neutrality at the electrodes.

Quantitative Aspects of Electrochemical Reactions.

The product of current (**amperes**) and time (seconds) gives coulombs. This relationship and the half-reactions that occur at the anode or cathode permit us to relate the amount of chemical change to measurements of current and time.

Practical Galvanic Cells.

The **lead storage battery** and the **nickel–cadmium (nicad) battery** are **secondary cells** and are rechargeable. The state of charge of the lead storage battery can be tested with a **hydrometer,** which measures the density of the sulfuric acid electrolyte. The **zinc–manganese dioxide cell** (the **Leclanché cell** or common dry cell) and the common **alkaline battery** (which uses essentially the same reactions as the less expensive dry cell) are **primary cells** and are not rechargeable. The rechargeable **nickel–metal hydride** (Ni–MH) battery uses hydrogen contained in a metal alloy as its anode reactant and has a higher **energy density** than the **nicad battery.** Primary **lithium–manganese dioxide cells** and rechargeable **lithium ion cells** produce a large cell potential and have a very high energy density. Lithium ion cells store and release energy by transferring lithium ions between electrodes where the Li$^+$ ions are **intercalated** between layers of atoms in the electrode materials. **Fuel cells,** which have high thermodynamic efficiencies, are able to provide continuous power because they consume fuel that can be fed continuously.

Applications of Electrolysis.

Electroplating, the production of aluminum, the refining of copper, and the electrolysis of molten and aqueous sodium chloride are examples of practical applications of electrolysis.

TOOLS FOR PROBLEM SOLVING

The table below lists the concepts that you've learned in this chapter which can be applied as tools in solving problems. Study each one carefully so that you know what each is used for. When faced with solving a problem, recall what each tool does and consider whether it will be helpful in finding a solution. This will aid you in selecting the tools you need. If necessary, refer to this table when working on the Review Questions and Review Problems that follow.

Electrode reactions *(page 772)* Chemists have agreed to call the electrode at which oxidation occurs the anode. The cathode is the electrode where reduction occurs.

Standard reduction potentials relate to $E°_{cell}$ In a galvanic cell, the difference between two standard reduction potentials equals the standard cell potential *(page 776)*.

$$E°_{cell} = \left(\begin{array}{c} \text{standard reduction potential} \\ \text{of the substance reduced} \end{array} \right) - \left(\begin{array}{c} \text{standard reduction potential} \\ \text{of the substance oxidized} \end{array} \right)$$

Standard cell potentials are always positive and the reaction that gives us a positive standard cell potential will be a spontaneous reaction at standard state *(page 786)*. Comparing standard reduction potentials also lets us predict the electrode reactions in electrolysis *(page 800)*.

Standard cell potentials are related to thermodynamic quantities The relationship between the standard cell potential, $E°_{cell}$, and the standard free energy, $\Delta G°$, is $\Delta G° = -n\mathscr{F}E°_{cell}$ *(page 788)*

The relationship between the standard cell potential, $E°_{cell}$, and the equilibrium constant, K_c, is $E°_{cell} = \frac{RT}{n\mathscr{F}} \ln K_c$ *(page 789)*.

Standard cell potentials are also needed in the Nernst equation (below) to relate concentrations of species in galvanic cells to the cell potential.

Nernst equation *(page 790)* The Nernst equation lets us relate the cell potential, E_{cell}, the standard cell potential, E_{cell}°, and concentration data.

$$E_{cell} = E_{cell}^\circ - \frac{RT}{n\mathscr{F}} \ln Q$$

We can also calculate the concentration of a species in solution from E_{cell}° and a measured value for E_{cell}.

Faraday constant *(page 788)* Besides being a constant in the equations above, the Faraday constant allows us to relate coulombs (obtained from the product of current and time) to moles of chemical change in electrochemical reactions.

$$1 \mathscr{F} = 9.65 \times 10^4 \text{ C/mol } e^-$$

Coulombs *(page 802)* Coulombs, C, can be experimentally determined as the current, in amperes, A, multiplied by time, in seconds. Combined with the faraday, the moles of electrons can be determined.

$$1 \text{ coulomb (C)} = 1 \text{ ampere (A)} \times 1 \text{ second (s)}$$

QUESTIONS, PROBLEMS, AND EXERCISES

Answers to problems whose numbers are printed in color are given in Appendix B. More challenging problems are marked with asterisks. ILW = Interactive Learningware solution is available at www.wiley.com/college/brady. (OH) = an Office Hours video is available for this problem.

REVIEW QUESTIONS

Galvanic Cells

19.1 What is a *galvanic cell*? What is a *half-cell*?

19.2 What is the function of a *salt bridge*?

19.3 In the copper–silver cell, why must the Cu^{2+} and Ag^+ solutions be kept in separate containers?

19.4 Which redox processes take place at the anode and cathode in a galvanic cell? What is the sign of the electrical charges on the anode and cathode in a galvanic cell?

19.5 In a galvanic cell, do electrons travel from anode to cathode, or from cathode to anode? Explain.

19.6 Explain how the movement of the ions relative to the electrodes is the same in both galvanic and electrolytic cells.

19.7 Aluminum will displace tin from solution according to the equation $2Al(s) + 3Sn^{2+}(aq) \rightarrow 2Al^{3+}(aq) + 3Sn(s)$. What would be the individual half-cell reactions if this were the cell reaction in a galvanic cell? Which metal would be the anode and which the cathode?

Cell Potentials and Reduction Potentials

19.8 What is the difference between a *cell potential* and a *standard cell potential*?

19.9 How are standard reduction potentials combined to give the standard cell potential for a spontaneous reaction?

19.10 Describe the hydrogen electrode. What is the value of its standard reduction potential?

19.11 What do the positive and negative signs of reduction potentials tell us?

19.12 If $E_{Cu^{2+}}^\circ$ had been chosen as the standard reference electrode and had been assigned a potential of 0.00 V, what would the reduction potential of the hydrogen electrode be relative to it?

19.13 If you set up a galvanic cell using metals not found in Table 19.1, what experimental information will tell you which is the anode and which is the cathode in the cell?

Using Standard Reduction Potentials

19.14 Compare Table 5.2 with Table 19.1. What can you say about the basis for the activity series for metals?

19.15 Make a sketch of a galvanic cell for which the cell notation is

$$Fe(s) \mid Fe^{3+}(aq) \| Ag^+(aq) \mid Ag(s)$$

(a) Label the anode and the cathode.

(b) Indicate the charge on each electrode.

(c) Indicate the direction of electron flow in the external circuit.

(d) Write the equation for the net cell reaction.

19.16 Make a sketch of a galvanic cell in which inert platinum electrodes are used in the half-cells for the system

$$Pt(s) \mid Fe^{2+}(aq), Fe^{3+}(aq) \| Br_2(aq), Br^-(aq) \mid Pt(s)$$

Label the diagram and indicate the composition of the electrolytes in the two cell compartments. Show the signs of the electrodes and label the anode and cathode. Write the equation for the net cell reaction.

Cell Potentials and Thermodynamics

19.17 Write the equation that relates the standard cell potential to the standard free energy change for a reaction.

19.18 What is the equation that relates the equilibrium constant to the cell potential?

19.19 Show how the equation that relates the equilibrium constant to the cell potential (Equation 19.7) can be derived from the Nernst equation (Equation 19.8).

The Effect of Concentration on Cell Potential

19.20 The cell reaction during the discharge of a lead storage battery is

$$Pb(s) + PbO_2(s) + 2H^+(aq) + 2HSO_4^-(aq) \longrightarrow$$
$$2PbSO_4(s) + 2H_2O$$

The standard cell potential is 2.05 V. What is the correct form of the Nernst equation for the reaction at 25 °C?

19.21 What is a *concentration cell*? Why is the E_{cell}° for such a cell equal to zero?

Electrolysis

19.22 What electrical charges do the anode and the cathode carry in an electrolytic cell? What does the term *inert electrode* mean?

19.23 Why must electrolysis reactions occur at the electrodes in order for electrolytic conduction to continue?

19.24 Why must NaCl be melted before it is electrolyzed to give Na and Cl_2? Write the anode, cathode, and overall cell reactions for the electrolysis of molten NaCl.

19.25 Write half-reactions for the oxidation and the reduction of water.

19.26 What happens to the pH of the solution near the cathode and anode during the electrolysis of K_2SO_4? What function does K_2SO_4 serve in the electrolysis of a K_2SO_4 solution?

Stoichiometric Relationships in Electrolysis

19.27 What is a *faraday*? What relationships relate faradays to current and time measurements?

19.28 Using the same current, which will require the greater length of time, depositing 0.10 mol Cu from a Cu^{2+} solution, or depositing 0.10 mol of Cr from a Cr^{3+} solution? Explain your reasoning.

19.29 An electric current is passed through two electrolysis cells connected in series (so the same amount of current passes through each of them). One cell contains Cu^{2+} and the other contains Ag^+. In which cell will the larger number of moles of metal be deposited? Explain your answer.

19.30 An electric current is passed through two electrolysis cells connected in series (so the same amount of current passes through each of them). One cell contains Cu^{2+} and the other contains Fe^{2+}. In which cell will the greater mass of metal be deposited? Explain your answer.

Practical Galvanic Cells

19.31 What are the anode and cathode reactions during the discharge of a lead storage battery? How can a battery produce a potential of 12 V if the cell reaction has a standard potential of only 2 V?

19.32 What are the anode and cathode reactions during the charging of a lead storage battery?

19.33 How is a hydrometer constructed? How does it measure density? Why can a hydrometer be used to check the state of charge of a lead storage battery?

19.34 What reactions occur at the electrodes in the ordinary dry cell?

19.35 What chemical reactions take place at the electrodes in an alkaline dry cell?

19.36 Give the half-cell reactions and the cell reaction that take place in a nicad battery during discharge. What are the reactions that take place during the charging of the cell?

19.37 How is hydrogen held as a reactant in a nickel–metal hydride battery? Write the chemical formula for a typical alloy used in this battery. What is the electrolyte?

19.38 What are the anode, cathode, and net cell reactions that take place in a nickel–metal hydride battery during discharge? What are the reactions when the battery is charged?

19.39 Give two reasons why lithium is such an attractive anode material for use in a battery. What are the problems associated with using lithium for this purpose?

19.40 What are the electrode materials in a typical primary lithium cell? Write the equations for the anode, cathode, and cell reactions.

19.41 What are the electrode materials in a typical lithium ion cell? Explain what happens when the cell is charged. Explain what happens when the cell is discharged.

19.42 Write the cathode, anode, and net cell reaction in a hydrogen–oxygen fuel cell.

19.43 What advantages do fuel cells offer over conventional means of obtaining electrical power by the combustion of fuels?

Applications of Electrolysis

19.44 What is *electroplating*? Sketch an apparatus to electroplate silver.

19.45 Describe the Hall–Héroult process for producing metallic aluminum. What half–reaction occurs at the anode? What half-reaction occurs at the cathode? What is the overall cell reaction?

19.46 In the Hall–Héroult process, why must the carbon anodes be replaced frequently?

19.47 How is metallic sodium produced? What are some uses of metallic sodium? Write equations for the anode and cathode reactions.

19.48 Describe the electrolytic refining of copper. What economic advantages offset the cost of electricity for this process? What chemical reactions occur at the anode and the cathode?

19.49 Describe the electrolysis of aqueous sodium chloride. How do the products of the electrolysis compare for stirred and unstirred reactions? Write chemical equations for the reactions that occur at the electrodes.

REVIEW PROBLEMS

Cell Notation

19.50 Write the half-reactions and the balanced cell reaction for the following galvanic cells.

(a) $Cd(s)|Cd^{2+}(aq)||Au^{3+}(aq)|Au(s)$

(b) $Fe(s)|Fe^{2+}(aq)||Br_2(aq), Br^-(aq)|Pt(s)$

(c) $Cr(s)|Cr^{3+}(aq)||Cu^{2+}(aq)|Cu(s)$

OH 19.51 Write the half-reactions and the balanced cell reaction for the following galvanic cells.

(a) $Zn(s)|Zn^{2+}(aq)||Cr^{3+}(aq)|Cr(s)$

(b) $Pb(s), PbSO_4(s)|HSO_4^-(aq), H^+(aq)||H^+(aq),$
$$HSO_4^-(aq)|PbO_2(s), PbSO_4(s)$$

(c) $Mg(s)|Mg^{2+}(aq)||Sn^{2+}(aq)|Sn(s)$

19.52 Write the cell notation for the following galvanic cells. For half-reactions in which all the reactants are in solution or are gases, assume the use of inert platinum electrodes.

(a) $NO_3^-(aq) + 4H^+(aq) + 3Fe^{2+}(aq) \longrightarrow$
$$3Fe^{3+}(aq) + NO(g) + 2H_2O$$

(b) $Cl_2(g) + 2Br^-(aq) \longrightarrow Br_2(aq) + 2Cl^-(aq)$

(c) $Au^{3+}(aq) + 3Ag(s) \longrightarrow Au(s) + 3Ag^+(aq)$

19.53 Write the cell notation for the following galvanic cells. For half-reactions in which all the reactants are in solution or are gases, assume the use of inert platinum electrodes.

(a) $Cd^{2+}(aq) + Fe(s) \longrightarrow Cd(s) + Fe^{2+}(aq)$

(b) $NiO_2(s) + 4H^+(aq) + 2Ag(s) \longrightarrow$
$$Ni^{2+}(aq) + 2H_2O + 2Ag^+(aq)$$

(c) $Mg(s) + Cd^{2+}(aq) \longrightarrow Mg^{2+}(aq) + Cd(s)$

Using Reduction Potentials

19.54 For each pair of substances, use Table 19.1 to choose the better reducing agent.

(a) $Sn(s)$ or $Ag(s)$ (c) $Co(s)$ or $Zn(s)$

(b) $Cl^-(aq)$ or $Br^-(aq)$ (d) $I^-(aq)$ or $Au(s)$

19.55 For each pair of substances, use Table 19.1 to choose the better oxidizing agent.

(a) $NO_3^-(aq)$ or $MnO_4^-(aq)$ (c) $PbO_2(s)$ or $Cl_2(g)$

(b) $Au^{3+}(aq)$ or $Co^{2+}(aq)$ (d) $NiO_2(s)$ or $HOCl(aq)$

OH 19.56 Use the data in Table 19.1 to calculate the standard cell potential for each of the following reactions:

(a) $NO_3^-(aq) + 4H^+(aq) + 3Fe^{2+}(aq) \longrightarrow$
$$3Fe^{3+}(aq) + NO(g) + 2H_2O$$

(b) $Br_2(aq) + 2Cl^-(aq) \longrightarrow Cl_2(g) + 2Br^-(aq)$

(c) $Au^{3+}(aq) + 3Ag(s) \longrightarrow Au(s) + 3Ag^+(aq)$

19.57 Use the data in Table 19.1 to calculate the standard cell potential for each of the following reactions:

(a) $Cd^{2+}(aq) + Fe(s) \longrightarrow Cd(s) + Fe^{2+}(aq)$

(b) $NiO_2(s) + 4H^+(aq) + 2Ag(s) \longrightarrow$
$$Ni^{2+}(aq) + 2H_2O + 2Ag^+(aq)$$

(c) $Mg(s) + Cd^{2+}(aq) \longrightarrow Mg^{2+}(aq) + Cd(s)$

19.58 From the positions of the half-reactions in Table 19.1, determine whether the following reactions are spontaneous under standard state conditions.

(a) $2Au^{3+} + 6I^- \longrightarrow 3I_2 + 2Au$

(b) $H_2SO_3 + H_2O + Br_2 \longrightarrow 4H^+ + SO_4^{2-} + 2Br^-$

(c) $3Ca + 2Cr^{3+} \longrightarrow 2Cr + 3Ca^{2+}$

19.59 Use the data in Table 19.1 to determine which of the following reactions should occur spontaneously under standard state conditions.

(a) $Br_2 + 2Cl^- \longrightarrow Cl_2 + 2Br^-$

(b) $3Fe^{2+} + 2NO + 4H_2O \longrightarrow 3Fe + 2NO_3^- + 8H^+$

(c) $Ni^{2+} + Fe \longrightarrow Fe^{2+} + Ni$

ILW 19.60 From the half-reactions below, determine the cell reaction and standard cell potential.

$BrO_3^- + 6H^+ + 6e^- \rightleftharpoons Br^- + 3H_2O$
$$E^\circ_{BrO_3^-} = 1.44 \text{ V}$$

$I_2 + 2e^- \rightleftharpoons 2I^-$ $E^\circ_{I_2} = 0.54 \text{ V}$

19.61 What is the standard cell potential and the net reaction in a galvanic cell that has the following half-reactions?

$MnO_2 + 4H^+ + 2e^- \rightleftharpoons Mn^{2+} + 2H_2O$
$$E^\circ_{MnO_2} = 1.23 \text{ V}$$

$PbCl_2 + 2e^- \rightleftharpoons Pb + 2Cl^-$ $E^\circ_{PbCl_2} = -0.27 \text{ V}$

OH 19.62 What will be the spontaneous reaction among H_2SO_3, $S_2O_3^{2-}$, $HOCl$, and Cl_2? The half-reactions involved are

$2H_2SO_3 + 2H^+ + 4e^- \rightleftharpoons S_2O_3^{2-} + 3H_2O$
$$E^\circ_{H_2SO_3} = 0.40 \text{ V}$$

$2HOCl + 2H^+ + 2e^- \rightleftharpoons Cl_2 + 2H_2O$ $E^\circ_{HOCl} = 1.63 \text{ V}$

19.63 What will be the spontaneous reaction among Br_2, I_2, Br^-, and I^-?

19.64 Will the following reaction occur spontaneously under standard state conditions?

$$SO_4^{2-} + 4H^+ + 2I^- \longrightarrow H_2SO_3 + I_2 + H_2O$$

Use E°_{cell} calculated from data in Table 19.1 to answer the question.

19.65 Determine whether the reaction

$S_2O_8^{2-} + Ni(OH)_2 + 2OH^- \longrightarrow$
$$2SO_4^{2-} + NiO_2 + 2H_2O$$

will occur spontaneously under standard state conditions. Use E°_{cell} calculated from the data below to answer the question.

$NiO_2 + 2H_2O + 2e^- \rightleftharpoons Ni(OH)_2 + 2OH^-$
$$E^\circ_{NiO_2} = 0.49 \text{ V}$$

$S_2O_8^{2-} + 2e^- \rightleftharpoons 2SO_4^{2-}$ $E^\circ_{S_2O_8^{2-}} = 2.01 \text{ V}$

Cell Potentials and Thermodynamics

ILW 19.66 Calculate ΔG° for the following reaction *as written*.

$$2Br^- + I_2 \longrightarrow 2I^- + Br_2$$

OH 19.67 Calculate ΔG° for the reaction
$2MnO_4^- + 6H^+ + 5HCHO_2 \longrightarrow$
$$2Mn^{2+} + 8H_2O + 5CO_2$$
for which $E^\circ_{cell} = 1.69 \text{ V}$.

19.68 Given the following half-reactions and their standard reduction potentials, calculate (a) E°_{cell}, (b) ΔG° for the cell reaction, and (c) the value of K_c for the cell reaction.

$2ClO_3^- + 12H^+ + 10e^- \rightleftharpoons Cl_2 + 6H_2O$
$$E^\circ_{ClO_3^-} = 1.47 \text{ V}$$

$S_2O_8^{2-} + 2e^- \rightleftharpoons 2SO_4^{2-}$ $E^\circ_{S_2O_8^{2-}} = 2.01 \text{ V}$

19.69 Calculate K_c for the system,

$$Ni^{2+} + Co \rightleftharpoons Ni + Co^{2+}$$

Use the data in Table 19.1. Assume $T = 298$ K.

19.70 The system $2AgI + Sn \rightleftharpoons Sn^{2+} + 2Ag + 2I^-$ has a calculated E°_{cell} of -0.015 V. What is the value of K_c for this system?

19.71 Determine the value of K_c at 25 °C for the reaction

$$2H_2O + 2Cl_2 \rightleftharpoons 4H^+ + 4Cl^- + O_2$$

The Effect of Concentration on Cell Potential

19.72 The cell reaction

$$NiO_2(s) + 4H^+(aq) + 2Ag(s) \longrightarrow$$
$$Ni^{2+}(aq) + 2H_2O + 2Ag^+(aq)$$

has $E°_{cell} = 2.48$ V. What will be the cell potential at a pH of 2.00 when the concentrations of Ni^{2+} and Ag^+ are each 0.030 M?

19.73 The $E°_{cell}$ is 0.135 V for the reaction

$$3I_2(s) + 5Cr_2O_7{}^{2-}(aq) + 34H^+ \longrightarrow$$
$$6IO_3{}^-(aq) + 10Cr^{3+}(aq) + 17H_2O$$

What is E_{cell} if $[Cr_2O_7{}^{2-}] = 0.010$ M, $[H^+] = 0.10$ M, $[IO_3{}^-] = 0.00010$ M, and $[Cr^{3+}] = 0.0010$ M?

OH *19.74** A cell was set up having the following reaction.

$$Mg(s) + Cd^{2+}(aq) \longrightarrow Mg^{2+}(aq) + Cd(s)$$
$$E°_{cell} = 1.97 \text{ V}$$

The magnesium electrode was dipping into a 1.00 M solution of $MgSO_4$ and the cadmium electrode was dipping into a solution of unknown Cd^{2+} concentration. The potential of the cell was measured to be 1.54 V. What was the unknown Cd^{2+} concentration?

***19.75** A silver wire coated with AgCl is sensitive to the presence of chloride ion because of the half-cell reaction

$$AgCl(s) + e^- \rightleftharpoons Ag(s) + Cl^- \qquad E°_{AgCl} = 0.2223 \text{ V}$$

A student, wishing to measure the chloride ion concentration in a number of water samples, constructed a galvanic cell using the AgCl electrode as one half-cell and a copper wire dipping into 1.00 M $CuSO_4$ solution as the other half-cell. In one analysis, the potential of the cell was measured to be 0.0895 V with the copper half-cell serving as the cathode. What was the chloride ion concentration in the water? (Take $E°_{Cu^{2+}} = +0.3419$ V.)

***19.76** At 25 °C, a galvanic cell was set up having the following half-reactions.

$$Fe^{2+}(aq) + 2e^- \rightleftharpoons Fe(s) \qquad E°_{Fe^{2+}} = -0.447 \text{ V}$$
$$Cu^{2+}(aq) + 2e^- \rightleftharpoons Cu(s) \qquad E°_{Cu^{2+}} = +0.3419 \text{ V}$$

The copper half-cell contained 100 mL of 1.00 M $CuSO_4$. The iron half-cell contained 50.0 mL of 0.100 M $FeSO_4$. To the iron half-cell was added 50.0 mL of 0.500 M NaOH solution. The mixture was stirred and the cell potential was measured to be 1.175 V. Calculate the value of K_{sp} for $Fe(OH)_2$.

***19.77** Suppose a galvanic cell was constructed at 25 °C using a Cu/Cu^{2+} half-cell (in which the molar concentration of Cu^{2+} was 1.00 M) and a hydrogen electrode having a partial pressure of H_2 equal to 1 atm. The hydrogen electrode dipped into a solution of unknown hydrogen ion concentration, and the two half-cells were connected by a salt bridge. The precise value of $E°_{Cu^{2+}}$ is +0.3419 V.

(a) Derive an equation for the pH of the solution with the unknown hydrogen ion concentration, expressed in terms of E_{cell} and $E°_{cell}$.

(b) If the pH of the solution were 5.15, what would be the observed potential of the cell?

(c) If the potential of the cell were 0.645 V, what would be the pH of the solution?

19.78 What is the potential of a concentration cell at 25.0 °C if it consists of silver electrodes dipping into two different solutions of $AgNO_3$, one with a concentration of 0.015 M and the other with a concentration of 0.50 M?

19.79 What would be the potential of the cell in the preceding problem if the temperature of the cell were 50 °C?

Quantitative Aspects of Electrochemical Reactions

19.80 How many moles of electrons are required to (a) reduce 0.20 mol Fe^{2+} to Fe, (b) oxidize 0.70 mol Cl^- to Cl_2, (c) reduce 1.50 mol Cr^{3+} to Cr, (d) oxidize 1.0×10^{-2} mol Mn^{2+} to $MnO_4{}^-$?

19.81 How many moles of electrons are required to (a) produce 5.00 g Mg from molten $MgCl_2$, (b) form 41.0 g Cu from a $CuSO_4$ solution?

ILW 19.82 How many grams of $Fe(OH)_2$ are produced at an iron anode when a basic solution undergoes electrolysis at a current of 8.00 A for 12.0 min?

19.83 How many grams of Cl_2 would be produced in the electrolysis of molten NaCl by a current of 4.25 A for 35.0 min?

ILW 19.84 How many hours would it take to produce 75.0 g of metallic chromium by the electrolytic reduction of Cr^{3+} with a current of 2.25 A?

19.85 How many hours would it take to generate 35.0 g of lead from $PbSO_4$ during the charging of a lead storage battery using a current of 1.50 A? The half-reaction is

$$Pb + HSO_4{}^- \longrightarrow PbSO_4 + H^+ + 2e^-$$

OH 19.86 How many amperes would be needed to produce 60.0 g of magnesium during the electrolysis of molten $MgCl_2$ in 2.00 hr?

19.87 A large electrolysis cell that produces metallic aluminum from Al_2O_3 by the Hall–Héroult process is capable of yielding 900 lb (409 kg) of aluminum in 24 hr. What current is required?

***19.88** The electrolysis of 250 mL of a brine solution (NaCl) was carried out for a period of 20.00 min with a current of 2.00 A in an apparatus that prevented Cl_2 from reacting with other products of the electrolysis. The resulting solution was titrated with 0.620 M HCl. How many milliliters of the HCl solution was required for the titration?

***19.89** An unstirred solution of 2.00 M NaCl was electrolyzed for a period of 25.0 min and then titrated with 0.250 M HCl. The titration required 15.5 mL of the acid. What was the average current in amperes during the electrolysis?

***19.90** A solution of NaCl in water was electrolyzed with a current of 2.50 A for 15.0 min. How many milliliters of Cl_2 gas would be formed if it was collected over water at 25 °C and a total pressure of 750 torr?

***19.91** How many milliliters of dry gaseous H_2, measured at 20 °C and 735 torr, would be produced at the cathode in the electrolysis of dilute H_2SO_4 with a current of 0.750 A for 15.00 min?

Predicting Electrolysis Reactions

19.92 If electrolysis is carried out on an aqueous solution of aluminum sulfate, what products are expected at the electrodes? Write the equation for the net cell reaction.

19.93 If electrolysis is carried out on an aqueous solution of cadmium iodide, what products are expected at the electrodes? Write the equation for the net cell reaction.

OH 19.94 What products would we expect at the electrodes if a solution containing both KBr and $CuSO_4$ were electrolyzed? Write the equation for the net cell reaction.

19.95 What products would we expect at the electrodes if a solution containing both $BaCl_2$ and CuI_2 were electrolyzed? Write the equation for the net cell reaction.

ADDITIONAL EXERCISES

*19.96 A watt is a unit of electrical power and is equal to one joule per second (1 watt = 1 J s^{-1}). How many hours can a calculator drawing 2.0×10^{-3} watt be operated by a mercury battery having a cell potential equal to 1.34 V if a mass of 1.00 g of HgO is available at the cathode? The cell reaction is

$$HgO(s) + Zn(s) \longrightarrow ZnO(s) + Hg(l)$$

*19.97 Suppose that a galvanic cell were set up having the net cell reaction

$$Zn(s) + 2Ag^+(aq) \longrightarrow Zn^{2+}(aq) + 2Ag(s)$$

The Ag^+ and Zn^{2+} concentrations in their respective half-cells initially are 1.00 M, and each half-cell contains 100 mL of electrolyte solution. If this cell delivers current at a constant rate of 0.10 A, what will the cell potential be after 15.00 hr?

*19.98 The value of K_{sp} for AgBr is 5.0×10^{-13}. What will be the potential of a cell constructed of a standard hydrogen electrode as one half-cell and a silver wire coated with AgBr dipping into 0.10 M HBr as the other half-cell? For the Ag/AgBr electrode,

$$AgBr(s) + e^- \rightleftharpoons Ag(s) + Br^-(aq) \qquad E^\circ_{AgBr} = +0.070 \text{ V}$$

*19.99 A student set up an electrolysis apparatus and passed a current of 1.22 A through a 3 M H_2SO_4 solution for 30.0 min. The H_2 formed at the cathode was collected and found to have a volume, over water at 27 °C, of 288 mL at a total pressure of 767 torr. Use the data to calculate the charge on the electron, expressed in coulombs.

*19.100 A hydrogen electrode is immersed in a 0.10 M solution of acetic acid at 25 °C. The electrode is connected to another consisting of an iron nail dipping into 0.10 M $FeCl_2$. What will be the measured potential of this cell? Assume $P_{H_2} = 1.00$ atm.

*19.101 What current would be required to deposit 1.00 m^2 of chrome plate having a thickness of 0.050 mm in 4.50 hr from a solution of H_2CrO_4? The density of chromium is 7.19 g cm^{-3}.

19.102 A solution containing vanadium (chemical symbol V) in an unknown oxidation state was electrolyzed with a current of 1.50 A for 30.0 min. It was found that 0.475 g of V was deposited on the cathode. What was the original oxidation state of the vanadium ion?

*19.103 What masses of H_2 and O_2 in grams would have to react each second in a fuel cell at 110 °C to provide 1.00 kilowatt (kW) of power if we assume a thermodynamic efficiency of 70%? (Hint: Use data in Chapters 6 and 18 to compute the value of

$\Delta G°$ for the reaction $H_2(g) + \frac{1}{2} O_2(g) \longrightarrow H_2O(g)$ at 110 °C. 1 watt = 1 J s^{-1}.)

*19.104 A Ag/AgCl electrode dipping into 1.00 M HCl has a standard reduction potential of +0.2223 V. The half-reaction is

$$AgCl(s) + e^- \rightleftharpoons Ag(s) + Cl^-(aq)$$

A second Ag/AgCl electrode is dipped into a solution containing Cl^- at an unknown concentration. The cell generates a potential of 0.0478 V, with the electrode in the solution of unknown concentration having a negative charge. What is the molar concentration of Cl^- in the unknown solution?

19.105 Consider the following galvanic cell

$$Ag(s)|Ag^+(0.00030 \ M)||Fe^{3+}(0.0011 \ M), Fe^{2+}(0.040 \ M)|Pt(s)$$

Calculate the cell potential. Determine the sign of the electrodes in the cell. Write the equation for the spontaneous cell reaction.

EXERCISES IN CRITICAL THINKING

19.106 In biochemical systems the normal standard state that requires $[H^+] = 1.00$ M is not realistic. (a) Which half-reactions in Table 19.1 will have different potentials if pH = 7.00 is defined as the standard state for hydronium ions? (b) What will the new standard reduction potentials be at pH = 7.00 for those reactions? These are called $E^{\circ\prime}_{cell}$ with the prime indicating the potential at pH = 7.00.

19.107 Calculate a new version of Table 19.1 using the lithium half-reaction to define zero. Does this change the results of any problems involving standard cell potentials?

19.108 In Problem 19.79 the potential at 50 °C was calculated. Does the change in molarity of the solutions, due to the change in density of water, have an effect on the potentials?

19.109 There are a variety of methods available for generating electricity. List as many methods as you can think of. Rank each of the methods based on your knowledge of (a) the efficiency of the method and (b) the environmental pollution caused by each method.

19.110 Using the cost of electricity in your area, how much will it cost to produce a case of 24 soda cans, each weighing 0.45 ounces? Assume that alternating current can be converted to direct current with 100% efficiency.

*19.111 Most flashlights use two or more batteries in series. Use the concepts of galvanic cells in this chapter to explain why a flashlight with two new batteries and one "dead" battery will give only a dim light if any light is obtained at all.

*19.112 If two electrolytic cells are placed in series, the same number of electrons must pass through both cells. One student argues you can get twice as much product if two cells are placed in series compared to a single cell and therefore the cost of production (i.e., the cost of electricity) will decrease greatly and profits will increase. Is the student correct? Explain your reasoning based on the principles of electrochemistry.

NUCLEAR REACTIONS AND THEIR ROLE IN CHEMISTRY

2

The nebula RCW49, shown in infrared light in this image from NASA's Spitzer Space Telescope, is a nursery for newborn stars. Nuclear fusion reactions involving hydrogen are responsible for the tremendous amounts of energy given off in stars. Reactions of this type are discussed in this chapter. *(Courtesy NASA/ JPL-Caltech/University of Wisconsin-madison)*

CHAPTER OUTLINE

20.1 Mass and energy are conserved in *all* of their forms

20.2 The energy required to break a nucleus into separate nucleons is called the nuclear binding energy

20.3 Radioactivity is an emission of particles and/or electromagnetic radiation by unstable atomic nuclei

20.4 Stable isotopes fall within a "band of stability" on a plot based on numbers of protons and neutrons

20.5 Transmutation is the change of one isotope into another

20.6 How is radiation measured?

20.7 Radionuclides have medical and analytical applications

20.8 Nuclear fission and nuclear fusion release large amounts of energy

THIS CHAPTER IN CONTEXT From the standpoint of chemistry, our interest in the atomic stems primarily from its role in determining the number and energies of an atom's electrons. This is becau the electron distribution in an atom that controls chemical properties. Although the nuclei of most isotop exceptionally stable, many of the elements of interest to us also have one or more isotopes with unstable nuc have unique properties which make them particularly useful in chemistry. These unstable nuclei tend to emit r consisting of particles and/or energy. In the pages ahead you will learn about the different kinds of nuclear ra how this radiation is detected and measured, and how the properties of unstable nuclei can be applied to practical problems.

One of the benefits that comes from studying nuclear transformations is an understanding of the enormous amounts of energy associated with certain nuclear changes. As you study this chapter you will come to appreciate the origin of the energy given off by stars, including our own sun. You will also learn how nuclear reactors work and how nuclear reactions have been applied to produce nuclear weapons.

20.1 MASS AND ENERGY ARE CONSERVED IN ALL OF THEIR FORMS

Changes involving unstable atomic nuclei generally involve large amounts of energy, amounts that are considerably greater than in chemical reactions. To understand how these energy changes arise, we begin our study by re-examining two physical laws that, until this chapter, have been assumed to be separate and independent, namely, the laws of conservation of energy and conservation of mass. They may be safely treated as distinct for chemical reactions but not for nuclear reactions. These two laws, however, are only different aspects of a deeper, more general law.

As atomic and nuclear physics developed in the early 1900s, physicists realized that the mass of a particle cannot be treated as a constant in all circumstances. The mass, m, of a particle depends on the particle's velocity, v, meaning the velocity relative to the observer. A particle's mass is related to this velocity, and to the velocity of light, c, by the following equation.

□ $c = 3.00 \times 10^8$ m s^{-1}, the speed of light.

$$m = \frac{m_0}{\sqrt{1 - (v/c)^2}} \qquad (20.1)$$

Notice what happens when v is zero and the particle has no velocity (relative to the observer). The ratio v/c is then zero, the whole denominator reduces to a value of 1, and Equation 20.1 becomes

$$m = m_0$$

This is why the symbol m_0 stands for the particle's *rest mass*.

Rest mass is what we measure in all lab operations, because any object, like a chemical sample, is either at rest (from our viewpoint) or is not moving extraordinarily rapidly. Only as the particle's velocity approaches the speed of light, c, does the v/c term in Equation 20.1 become important. As v approaches c, the ratio v/c approaches 1, and so $[1 - (v/c)^2]$ gets closer and closer to 0. The whole denominator, in other words, approaches a value of 0. If it actually reached 0, then m, which would be $(m_0 \div 0)$, would become infinity. In other words, the mass, m, of the particle moving at the velocity of light would be infinitely great, a physical impossibility. This is why the speed of light is seen as an absolute upper limit on the speed that any particle can approach.

□ Even at $v = 1000$ m s^{-1} (about 2250 mph), the denominator (not rounded) is 0.99999333, or within 7×10^{-4} % of 1.

At the velocities of everyday experience, the mass of anything calculated by Equation 20.1 equals the rest mass to four of five significant figures. The difference cannot be detected by weighing devices. Thus, in all of our normal work, mass appears to be conserved, and the law of conservation of mass functions this way in chemistry.

As a particle's velocity increases, energy is changed to mass

We know that matter cannot appear from nothing, so the extra mass an object acquires as it goes faster must come from the energy supplied to increase the object's velocity. Physicists therefore realized that mass and energy are interconvertible and that in the world of high energy physics, the laws of conservation of mass and conservation of energy are not separate and independent. What emerged was a single, deeper law now called the **law of conservation of mass–energy**.

> *Law of Conservation of Mass–Energy* The sum of all the energy and of all the mass (expressed as an equivalent in energy) in the universe is a constant.

The Einstein equation quantitatively relates rest mass and energy

Albert Einstein, perhaps the most famous physicist of the twentieth century, was able to show that when mass converts to energy, the change in energy, ΔE, is related to the change in rest mass, Δm_0, by the following equation, now called the **Einstein equation.**

Einstein equation

$$\Delta E = \Delta m_0 c^2 \tag{20.2}$$

Again, c is the velocity of light, 3.00×10^8 m s^{-1}.

☐ The Einstein equation is given as $E = mc^2$ in the popular press.

Because the velocity of light is very large, even if an energy change is enormous, the change in mass, Δm_0, is extremely small. For example, the combustion of methane releases considerable heat per mole.

$$CH_4(g) + 2O_2(g) \longrightarrow CO_2(g) + 2H_2O(l) \qquad \Delta H^\circ = -890 \text{ kJ}$$

The release of 890 kJ of heat energy corresponds to a loss of mass, which by the Einstein equation equals a loss of 9.89 ng. This is about $1 \times 10^{-7}\%$ of the mass of 1 mol of CH_4 and 2 mol of O_2. Such a tiny change in mass is not detectable by laboratory balances, so for all practical purposes, mass is conserved. Although the Einstein equation has no direct applications in chemistry, its importance certainly became clear when atomic fission (the breaking apart of heavy atoms to form lighter fragments) was first observed in 1939.

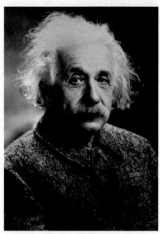

Albert Einstein (1879–1955);
Nobel prize, 1921 (physics).
(Photo Researchers.)

20.2 | THE ENERGY REQUIRED TO BREAK A NUCLEUS INTO SEPARATE NUCLEONS IS CALLED THE NUCLEAR BINDING ENERGY

As we will discuss further in Section 20.3, an atomic nucleus is held together by extremely powerful forces of attraction that are able to overcome the repulsions between protons. To break a nucleus into its individual nucleons therefore requires an enormous input of energy. This energy is called the **nuclear binding energy.**

Absorption of the binding energy would produce the individual nucleons—protons and neutrons—that had made up the nucleus. These nucleons would now carry extra mass corresponding to the mass-equivalent of the energy they had absorbed. If we add up their masses, the sum should be larger than the mass of the nucleus from which they had come. And this is exactly what is observed. *For a given atomic nucleus, the sum of the rest masses of all of its nucleons is always a little larger than the actual mass of the nucleus.* The mass difference is called the **mass defect,** and its energy equivalent is the nuclear binding energy.

Keep in mind that nuclear binding energy is not energy actually possessed by the nucleus but is, instead, the energy the nucleus would have to absorb to break apart. Thus, the *higher* the binding energy, the *more stable* is the nucleus.

The nuclear binding energy can be calculated

We can calculate nuclear binding energy using the Einstein equation. Helium-4, for example, has atomic number 2, so its nucleus consists of 4 nucleons (2 protons and 2 neutrons). The rest mass of one helium-4 nucleus is known to be 4.0015061792 u. However, the sum of the rest masses of its four separated nucleons is slightly more, 4.0318827650 u, which we can show as follows. The rest mass of an isolated proton is 1.0072764669 u and that of a neutron is 1.0086649156 u.

$$\text{For 2 protons: } 2 \times 1.0072764669 \text{ u} = 2.0145529338 \text{ u}$$

$$\text{For 2 neutrons: } 2 \times 1.0086649156 \text{ u} = \underline{2.0173298312 \text{ u}}$$

$$\text{Total rest mass of nucleons in } {}^4\text{He} = 4.0318827650 \text{ u}$$

The mass defect, the difference between the calculated and measured rest masses for the helium-4 nucleus, is 0.030375858 u, found by

$$\underset{\text{mass of the 4 nucleons}}{4.0318827650 \text{ u}} - \underset{\text{mass of nucleus}}{4.0015061792 \text{ u}} = \underset{\text{mass defect}}{0.0303765858 \text{ u}}$$

Using Einstein's equation, let's calculate to three significant figures the nuclear binding energy that is equivalent to the mass defect for the ^{4}He nucleus. We will round the mass defect to 0.0304 u. To obtain the energy in joules, we have to remember that $1 \text{ J} = 1 \text{ kg m}^2 \text{ s}^{-2}$, so the mass in atomic mass units (u) must be converted to kilograms. The table of constants inside the rear cover of the book gives $1 \text{ u} = 1.6605389 \times 10^{-24}$ g, which equals $1.6605389 \times 10^{-27}$ kg. Substituting into the Einstein equation gives

$$\Delta E = \Delta mc^2 = \underbrace{(0.0304 \text{ u}) \times \frac{1.66065389 \times 10^{-27} \text{ kg}}{1 \text{ u}}}_{\Delta m \text{ (in kg)}} \times \underbrace{(3.00 \times 10^8 \text{ m s}^{-1})^2}_{c^2}$$

$$= 4.54 \times 10^{-12} \text{ kg m}^2 \text{ s}^{-2}$$

$$= 4.54 \times 10^{-12} \text{ J}$$

There are four nucleons in the helium-4 nucleus, so the binding energy *per* nucleon is $(4.54 \times 10^{-12} \text{ J}/4 \text{ nucleons})$ or 1.14×10^{-12} J/nucleon.

The formation of just one nucleus of ^{4}He releases 4.54×10^{-12} J. If we could make Avogadro's number or 1 mol of ^{4}He nuclei (with a total mass of only 4 g) the net release of energy would be

$$(6.02 \times 10^{23} \text{ nuclei}) \times (4.54 \times 10^{-12} \text{ J/nucleus}) = 2.73 \times 10^{12} \text{ J}$$

This is a huge amount of energy from forming only 4 g of helium. It could keep a 100 watt lightbulb lit for nearly 900 years!

Binding energy per nucleon varies from one element to another

Figure 20.1 shows a plot of binding energies per nucleon versus mass numbers for most of the elements. The curve passes through a maximum at iron-56, which means that the nuclei of iron-56 atoms are the most stable of all. The plot in Figure 20.1, however, does not have a sharp maximum. Thus, a large number of elements with intermediate mass numbers in the broad center of the periodic table include the most stable isotopes in nature.

Nuclei of low mass number have small binding energies per nucleon. Joining two such nuclei to form a heavier nucleus, a process called **nuclear fusion,** leads to a more stable nucleus and a large increase in binding energy per nucleon. This extra energy is released when the two lighter nuclei fuse (join) and is the origin of the energy released in the cores of stars and the detonation of a hydrogen bomb. Nuclear fusion is discussed further in Section 20.8.

As we follow the plot of Figure 20.1 to the highest mass numbers, the nuclei decrease in stability as the binding energies decrease. Among the heaviest atoms, therefore, we might expect to find isotopes that could change to more stable forms by breaking up into lighter nuclei, by undergoing nuclear fission. **Nuclear fission,** also discussed in Section 20.8, is the spontaneous breaking apart of a nucleus to form isotopes of intermediate mass number.

□ Quite often you'll see the terms *atomic fusion* and *atomic fission* used for nuclear fusion and nuclear fission.

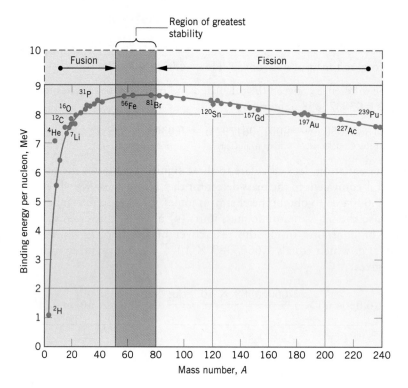

FIG. 20.1 **Binding energies per nucleon.** The energy unit here is the megaelectron volt or MeV: 1 MeV = 10^6 eV = 1.602×10^{-13} J. *(From D. Halliday and R. Resnick, Fundamentals of Physics, 2nd ed., Revised, 1986. John Wiley & Sons, Inc. Used by permission.)*

☐ Adjacent neutrons experience no electrostatic repulsion between each other, only the strong force (of attraction).

20.3 | RADIOACTIVITY IS AN EMISSION OF PARTICLES AND/OR ELECTROMAGNETIC RADIATION BY UNSTABLE ATOMIC NUCLEI

Except for hydrogen, all atomic nuclei have more than one proton, each of which carries a positive charge. Because like charges repel, we might wonder how any nucleus could be stable. Electrostatic forces of attraction and repulsion, such as the kinds present among the ions in a crystal of sodium chloride, are not the only forces at work in the nucleus, however. Protons do, indeed, repel each other electrostatically, but another force, a force of attraction called the *nuclear strong force,* also acts in the nucleus. The nuclear strong force, effective only at very short distances, overcomes the electrostatic force of repulsion between protons, and it binds both protons and neutrons into a nuclear package. Moreover, the neutrons, by helping to keep the protons farther apart, also lessen repulsions between protons.

One consequence of the difference between the nuclear strong force and the electrostatic force occurs among nuclei that have large numbers of protons but too few intermingled neutrons to dilute the electrostatic repulsions between protons. Such nuclei are often unstable; their nuclei carry more energy than do other arrangements of the same nucleons. To achieve a lower energy and thus more stability, unstable nuclei have a tendency to eject small nuclear fragments, and many simultaneously release high-energy electromagnetic radiation. The stream of particles (or photons) coming from the sample is called **nuclear radiation** or **atomic radiation** and the phenomenon is called **radioactivity.** Isotopes that exhibit this property are said to be **radioactive** and are called **radionuclides.** About 60 of the approximately 350 naturally occurring isotopes are radioactive.

In a sample of a given radionuclide, not all the atoms undergo change at once. The rate at which radiation is emitted (which translates into the intensity of the radiation) depends on the concentration of the isotope in the sample. Over time, as radioactive nuclei change into stable ones, the number of atoms of the radionuclide remaining in the sample decreases, causing the intensity of the radiation to drop, or *decay.* The radionuclide is said to undergo **radioactive decay.**

Naturally occurring atomic radiation consists principally of three kinds: alpha, beta, and gamma radiation, as discussed below.

Alpha radiation is a stream of helium nuclei

Alpha radiation consists of a stream of helium nuclei called **alpha particles** (α particles), symbolized as ^4_2He, where 4 is the mass number and 2 is the atomic number. The alpha particle bears a charge of $2+$, but the charge is omitted from the symbol.

Alpha particles are the most massive of those commonly emitted by radionuclides. When ejected (Figure 20.2), alpha particles move through the atom's electron orbitals, emerging from the atom at speeds of up to one-tenth the speed of light. Their size, however, prevents them from going far. After traveling at most only a few centimeters in air, alpha particles collide with air molecules, lose kinetic energy, pick up electrons, and become neutral helium atoms. Alpha particles cannot penetrate the skin, although enough exposure causes a severe skin burn. If carried in air or on food into the soft tissues of the lungs or the intestinal tract, emitters of alpha particles can cause serious harm, including cancer.

□ In Chapter 2 you learned that an isotope is identified by writing its mass number, A, as a superscript and its atomic number, Z, as a subscript in front of the chemical symbol, X, as in $^A_Z X$. We use this same notation in representing particles involved in nuclear reactions. For particles that are not atomic nuclei, Z stands for the charge on the particle.

Nuclear equations describe the decay of radioactive nuclei

To symbolize the decay of a nucleus, we construct a **nuclear equation**, which we can illustrate by the alpha decay of uranium-238 to thorium-234.

$$^{238}_{92}\text{U} \longrightarrow \, ^{234}_{90}\text{Th} + \, ^4_2\text{He}$$

Unlike chemical reactions, nuclear reactions produce new isotopes, so we need separate rules for balancing nuclear equations.

□ A nuclear transformation such as the alpha decay of ^{238}U does not depend on the chemical environment. The same nuclear equation applies whether the uranium is in the form of the free element or in a compound.

TOOLS

Nuclear equations

Rules for balancing a nuclear equation

1. The sum of the mass numbers on each side of the arrow must be the same.
2. The sum of the atomic numbers (nuclear charge) on each side of the arrow must be the same.

In the nuclear equation for the decay of uranium-238, the atomic numbers balance ($90 + 2 = 92$), and the mass numbers balance ($234 + 4 = 238$). Notice that electrical charges are not shown, even though they are there (initially). The alpha particle, for example, has a charge of $2+$. If it was emitted by a neutral uranium atom, then the thorium particle initially has a charge of $2-$. These charged particles, however, eventually pick up or lose electrons either from each other or from molecules in the matter through which they travel.

Beta radiation is a stream of electrons

Naturally occurring **beta radiation** consists of a stream of electrons, which in this context are called **beta particles**. In a nuclear equation, the beta particle has the symbol $^0_{-1}e$, because the electron's mass number is 0 and its charge is $1-$. Hydrogen-3 (tritium) is a beta emitter that decays by the following equation.

$$^3_1\text{H} \longrightarrow \, ^3_1\text{He} + \, ^0_{-1}e + \bar{\nu}$$

tritium   helium-3   beta particle   antineutrino
(electron)

□ Sometimes the beta particle is given the symbol $^0_{-1}\beta$, or simply $^-\beta$.

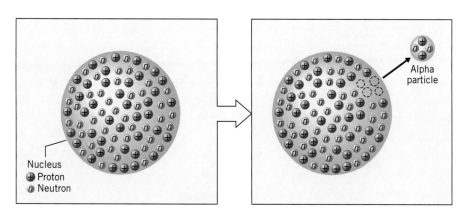

Nucleus
⊕ Proton
⊘ Neutron

Alpha particle

FIG. 20.2 Emission of an alpha particle from an atomic nucleus. Removal of ^4_2He from a nucleus decreases the atomic number by 2 and the mass number by 4.

Both the antineutrino (to be described further shortly) and the beta particle come from the atom's nucleus, not its electron shells. We do not think of them as having a prior existence in the nucleus, any more than a photon exists before its emission from an excited atom (see Figure 20.3). Both the beta particle and the antineutrino are created during the decay process in which a neutron is transformed into a proton.

$$\underset{\substack{\text{neutron} \\ \text{(in the} \\ \text{nucleus)}}}{{}^{1}_{0}n} \longrightarrow \underset{\substack{\text{beta particle} \\ \text{(emitted)}}}{{}^{0}_{-1}e} + \underset{\substack{\text{proton} \\ \text{(remains in} \\ \text{the nucleus)}}}{{}^{1}_{1}p} + \underset{\substack{\text{antineutrino} \\ \text{(emitted)}}}{\bar{\nu}}$$

Unlike alpha particles, which are all emitted with the same discrete energy from a given radionuclide, beta particles emerge from a given beta emitter with a continuous spectrum of energies. Their energies vary from zero to some characteristic fixed upper limit for each radionuclide. This fact once gave nuclear physicists considerable trouble, partly because it was an apparent violation of energy conservation. To solve this problem, Wolfgang Pauli proposed in 1927 that beta emission is accompanied by emission of yet another decay particle, this one electrically neutral and almost massless. Enrico Fermi suggested the name *neutrino* ("little neutral one"), but eventually it was named the *antineutrino*, symbolized by $\bar{\nu}$.

An electron is extremely small, so a beta particle is less likely to collide with the molecules of anything through which it travels. Depending on its initial kinetic energy, a beta particle can travel up to 300 cm (about 10 ft) in dry air, much farther than alpha particles. Only the highest energy beta particles can penetrate the skin, however.

Gamma radiation is very high energy electromagnetic radiation

☐ Gamma photons have the symbol ${}^{0}_{0}\gamma$ because they have no charge or mass.

Gamma radiation, which accompanies most nuclear decays, consists of high-energy photons given the symbol ${}^{0}_{0}\gamma$ or, often, simply γ in equations. Gamma radiation is extremely penetrating and is effectively blocked only by very dense materials, like lead.

The emission of gamma radiation involves transitions between energy levels *within* the nucleus. Nuclei have energy levels of their own, much as atoms have orbital energy levels. When a nucleus emits an alpha or beta particle, it sometimes is left in an excited energy state. By the emission of a gamma-ray photon, the nucleus relaxes into a more stable state.

The electron volt is an energy unit

The energy carried by a given radiation is usually described by an energy unit new to our study, the **electron volt,** abbreviated **eV;** 1 eV is the energy an electron receives when accelerated under the influence of 1 volt. It is related to the joule as follows.

☐ In the interconversion of mass and energy,

$1\text{eV} \Leftrightarrow 1.783 \times 10^{-36}\text{ kg}$

$1\text{MeV} \Leftrightarrow 1.78 \times 10^{-27}\text{ g}$

$1\text{ GeV} \Leftrightarrow 1.783 \times 10^{-24}\text{ g}$

$$1 \text{ eV} = 1.602 \times 10^{-19} \text{ J}$$

As you can see, the electron volt is an extremely small amount of energy, so multiples are commonly used, like the kilo-, mega-, and gigaelectron volt.

FIG. 20.3 **Emission of a beta particle from a tritium nucleus.** Emission of a beta particle changes a neutron into a proton. This results in a positively charged ion, which picks up an electron to become a neutral atom.

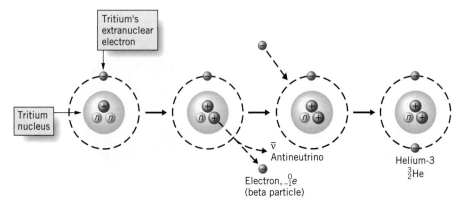

$$1 \text{ keV} = 10^3 \text{ eV}$$
$$1 \text{ MeV} = 10^6 \text{ eV}$$
$$1 \text{ GeV} = 10^9 \text{ eV}$$

An alpha particle emitted by radium-224 has an energy of 5 MeV. Hydrogen-3 (tritium) emits beta radiation at an energy of 0.05 to 1 MeV. The gamma radiation from cobalt-60, the radiation currently used to kill bacteria and other pests in certain foods, consists of photons with energies of 1.173 MeV and 1.332 MeV.

X rays are high energy electromagnetic radiation

X rays, like gamma rays, consist of high-energy electromagnetic radiation, but their energies are usually less than those of gamma radiation. Although X rays are emitted by some synthetic radionuclides, when needed for medical diagnostic work they are generated by focusing a high-energy electron beam onto a metal target.

□ X rays used in diagnosis typically have energies of 100 keV or less.

Some radioisotopes emit positrons or neutrons; others capture electrons

Many *synthetic isotopes* (isotopes not found in nature, but synthesized by methods discussed in Section 20.5) emit *positrons*, which are particles with the mass of an electron but a positive instead of a negative charge. A **positron** is a positive beta particle, a positive electron, and its symbol is ^0_1e. It forms in the nucleus by the conversion of a proton to a neutron (Figure 20.4). Positron emission, like beta emission, is accompanied by a chargeless and virtually massless particle, a *neutrino* (ν), the counterpart of the antineutrino $(\overline{\nu})$ in the realm of antimatter (defined below). Cobalt-54, for example, is a positron emitter and changes to a stable isotope of iron.

□ The symbol $^+\beta$ is sometimes used for the positron.

$$^{54}_{27}\text{Co} \longrightarrow {}^{54}_{26}\text{Fe} + {}^0_1e + \nu$$
$$\qquad\qquad\qquad\quad \text{positron} \quad \text{neutrino}$$

A positron, when emitted, eventually collides with an electron, and the two annihilate each other (Figure 20.5). Their masses change entirely into the energy of two gamma-ray photons called *annihilation radiation photons*, each with an energy of 511 keV.

$$^0_{-1}e + {}^0_1e \longrightarrow 2{}^0_0\gamma$$

Because a positron destroys a particle of ordinary matter (an electron), it is called a particle of antimatter. To be classified as **antimatter,** a particle must have a counterpart among one of ordinary matter, and the two must annihilate each other when they collide. For example, a neutron and an antineutron represent such a pair and annihilate each other when they come in contact.

Neutron emission, another kind of nuclear reaction, does not lead to an isotope of a different element. Krypton-87, for example, decays as follows to krypton-86.

$$^{87}_{36}\text{Kr} \longrightarrow {}^{86}_{36}\text{Kr} + {}^1_0n$$
$$\qquad\qquad\qquad\qquad \text{neutron}$$

Electron capture, yet another kind of nuclear reaction, is very rare among natural isotopes but common among synthetic radionuclides. For example, an electron can be captured from the orbital electron shell having $n = 1$ or $n = 2$ by a vanadium-50 nucleus, causing it to change to a stable ^{50}Ti nucleus. The transformation is accompanied by the emmision of X rays and a neutrino.

$$^{50}_{23}\text{V} + {}^0_{-1}e \xrightarrow{\text{Electron capture}} {}^{50}_{22}\text{Ti} + \text{X rays} + \nu$$

Proton
(in an atom's
nucleus)

ν
Neutrino

Positron
^0_1e

Neutron
(remains in
the nucleus)

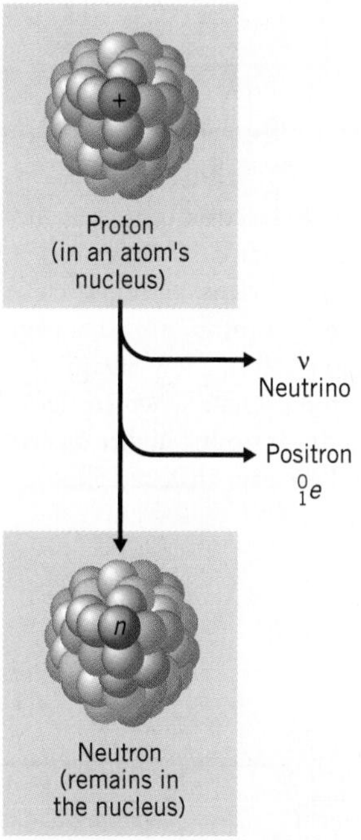

FIG. 20.4 The emission of a positron replaces a proton by a neutron.

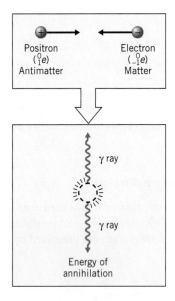

FIG. 20.5 **Gamma radiation is produced when a positron and an electron collide.** Annihilation of a positron and an electron leads to two gamma-ray photons.

The net effect in the nucleus of electron capture is the conversion of a proton into a neutron (Figure 20.6).

$$\underset{\substack{\text{proton} \\ \text{(in the} \\ \text{nucleus)}}}{^{1}_{1}p} + \underset{\substack{\text{electron} \\ \text{(captured} \\ \text{from the} \\ 1s \text{ orbital)}}}{^{0}_{-1}e} \longrightarrow \underset{\substack{\text{neutron} \\ \text{(in the} \\ \text{nucleus)}}}{^{1}_{0}n}$$

Electron capture does not change an atom's mass number, only its atomic number. It also leaves a hole in the first or second electron shell, and the atom emits photons of X rays as other orbital electrons drop down to fill the hole. Moreover, the nucleus that has just captured an orbital electron may be in an excited energy state and so can emit a gamma ray photon.

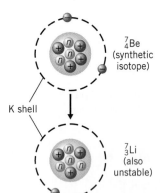

FIG. 20.6 **Electron capture.** Electron capture is the collapse of an orbital electron into the nucleus, and this changes a proton into a neutron. A gap is left in a low-energy electron orbital. When an electron drops from a higher orbital to fill the gap, an X-ray photon is emitted.

A radioactive disintegration series is a sequence of successive nuclear reactions

Sometimes a radionuclide does not decay directly to a stable isotope, but decays instead to another unstable radionuclide. The decay of one radionuclide after another will continue until a stable isotope forms. The sequence of such successive nuclear reactions is called a **radioactive disintegration series.** Four series occur naturally. Uranium-238 is at the head of one of them (Figure 20.7).

The rates of decay of radionuclides vary and are usually described by specifying their half lives, $t_{1/2}$, a topic we studied in Section 13.4. One *half-life* period in nuclear science is

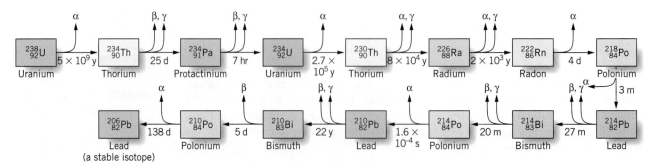

FIG. 20.7 **The uranium-238 radioactive disintegration series.** The time given beneath each arrow is the half-life period of the preceding isotope (y = year, m = month, d = day, hr = hour, and s = second).

TABLE 20.1	Typical Half-Life Periods		
Element	Isotope	Half-Life	Radiations or Mode of Decay
Naturally occurring radionuclides			
Potassium	$^{40}_{19}K$	1.3×10^9 yr	beta, gamma
Tellurium	$^{123}_{52}Te$	1.2×10^{13} yr	electron capture
Neodymium	$^{144}_{60}Nd$	5×10^{15} yr	alpha
Samarium	$^{149}_{62}Sm$	4×10^{14} yr	alpha
Rhenium	$^{187}_{75}Re$	7×10^{10} yr	beta
Radon	$^{222}_{86}Rn$	3.82 day	alpha
Radium	$^{226}_{88}Ra$	1590 yr	alpha, gamma
Thorium	$^{230}_{90}Th$	8×10^4 yr	alpha, gamma
Uranium	$^{238}_{92}U$	4.51×10^9 yr	alpha
Synthetic radionuclides			
Tritium	$^{3}_{1}T$	12.26 yr	beta
Oxygen	$^{15}_{8}O$	124 s	positron
Phosphorus	$^{32}_{15}P$	14.3 day	beta
Technetium[a]	$^{99m}_{43}Tc$	6.02 hr	gamma
Iodine	$^{131}_{53}I$	8.07 day	beta
Cesium	$^{137}_{55}Cs$	30 yr	beta, gamma
Strontium	$^{90}_{38}Sr$	28.1 yr	beta
Plutonium	$^{238}_{94}Pu$	87.8 yr	alpha
Americium	$^{243}_{95}Am$	7.37×10^3 yr	alpha

[a] The superscript 99m refers to a metastable isotope of technetium, which has a higher energy than technetium-99.

the time it takes for a given sample of a radionuclide to decay to one-half of its initial amount. Radioactive decay is a first-order process, so the period of time taken by one half-life is independent of the initial number of nuclei. The huge variations in the half-lives of several radionuclides are shown in Table 20.1.

Cesium-137, $^{137}_{55}Cs$, one of the radioactive wastes from a nuclear power plant or an atomic bomb explosion, emits beta and gamma radiation. Write the nuclear equation for the decay of cesium-137.

☐ Ions of cesium, which is in the same family as sodium, travel in the body to many of the same sites where sodium ions go.

ANALYSIS: We will start with an incomplete equation using the given information. Then we will use the requirements for a balanced nuclear equation as a tool to figure out any other data needed to complete the equation.

SOLUTION: The incomplete nuclear equation is

Mass number goes here.

Atomic symbol goes here.

$$^{137}_{55}Cs \longrightarrow \,^{0}_{-1}e \;+\; ^{0}_{0}\gamma \;+\; \underline{}\underline{}$$

Atomic number goes here.

The atomic symbol can be obtained from the table inside the front cover after we have determined the atomic number, Z. Z is found using the fact that the atomic number (55) on the left side of the equation must equal the sum of the atomic numbers on the right side.

$$55 = -1 + 0 + Z$$
$$Z = 56$$

The periodic table tells us that element 56 is Ba (barium). To determine which isotope of barium forms, we recall that the sums of the mass numbers on either side of the equation must also be equal. Letting A be the mass number of the barium isotope,

$$137 = 0 + 0 + A$$
$$A = 137$$

The balanced nuclear equation, therefore, is

$$^{137}_{55}\text{Cs} \longrightarrow {}^{0}_{-1}e + {}^{0}_{0}\gamma + {}^{137}_{56}\text{Ba}$$

IS THE ANSWER REASONABLE? Besides double-checking that element 56 is barium, the answer satisfies the requirements of a nuclear equation, namely, the sums of the mass numbers, 137, are the same on both sides as are the sums of the atomic numbers.

Practice Exercise 1: Marie Curie earned one of her two Nobel prizes for isolating the element radium, which soon became widely used to treat cancer. Radium-226, $^{226}_{88}\text{Ra}$, emits a gamma photon plus a particle to give radon-222. Write a balanced nuclear equation for its decay and identify the particle that's emitted. (Hint: Be sure to balance atomic number and mass.)

Practice Exercise 2: Write the balanced nuclear equation for the decay of strontium-90, a beta emitter. (Strontium-90 is one of the many radionuclides present in the wastes of operating nuclear power plants.)

20.4 | STABLE ISOTOPES FALL WITHIN A "BAND OF STABILITY" ON A PLOT BASED ON NUMBERS OF PROTONS AND NEUTRONS

When all known isotopes of each element, both stable and unstable, are arrayed on a plot according to numbers of protons and neutrons, an interesting zone can be defined (Figure 20.8). The two curved lines in the array of Figure 20.8 enclose this zone, called the **band of stability,** within which lie all stable nuclei. (No isotope above element 83, bismuth, is included in Figure 20.8 because none has a *stable* isotope.) Within the band of stability are also some unstable isotopes, because smooth lines cannot be drawn to exclude them.

Any isotope not represented anywhere on the array, inside or outside the band of stability, probably has a half-life too short to permit its detection. For example, an isotope with 50 neutrons and 60 protons would lie well below the band of stability and would likely be extremely unstable. Any attempt to make it would likely be a waste of time and money.

Notice that the band curves slightly upward as the number of protons increases. The curvature means that the *ratio* of neutrons to protons gradually increases from 1:1, a ratio indicated by the straight line in Figure 20.8. The reason is easy to understand. More protons require more neutrons to provide a compensating nuclear strong force and to dilute electrostatic proton–proton repulsions.

Isotopes occurring above and to the left of the band of stability tend to be beta emitters. Isotopes lying below and to the right of the band are positron emitters. The isotopes with atomic numbers above 83 tend to be alpha emitters. Are there any reasons for these tendencies?

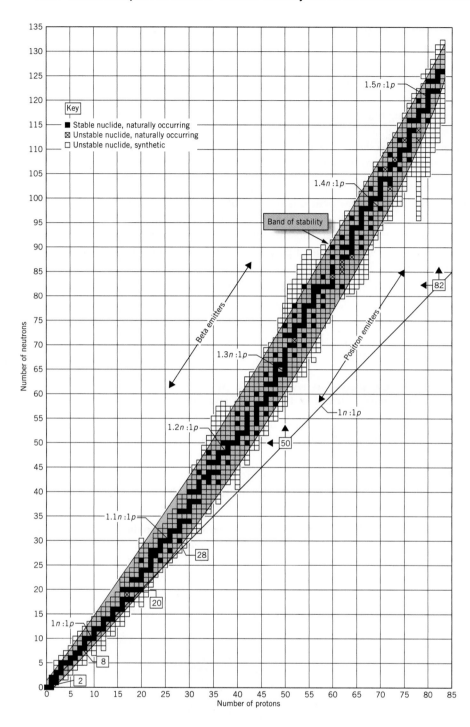

FIG. 20.8 The band of stability. Stable nuclei fall within a narrow band in a plot of number of neutrons versus number of protons. Nuclei far outside the band are too unstable to exist.

Alpha Emitters

The alpha emitters, as we said, occur mostly among the radionuclides above atomic number 83. Their nuclei have too many protons, and the most efficient way to lose protons is by the loss of an alpha particle.

Beta Emitters

Beta emitters are generally above the band of stability and so have neutron-to-proton ratios that evidently are too high. By beta decay a nucleus loses a neutron and gains a proton, thus decreasing the ratio.

$$\ _{0}^{1}n \longrightarrow \ _{1}^{1}p + \ _{-1}^{0}e + \bar{\nu}$$

☐ The proton can also be given the symbol $_{1}^{1}$H in nuclear equations.

For example, by beta decay fluorine-20 decreases its neutron-to-proton ratio from 11/9 to 10/10.

$$^{20}_{9}\text{F} \longrightarrow {}^{20}_{10}\text{Ne} + {}^{0}_{-1}e + \bar{\nu}$$

$$\frac{\text{neutron}}{\text{proton}} = \frac{11}{9} \qquad \frac{10}{10}$$

The surviving nucleus, that of neon-20, is closer to the center of the band of stability. Figure 20.9, an enlargement of the fluorine part of Figure 20.8, explains this change further. Figure 20.9 also shows how the beta decay of magnesium-27 to aluminum-27 also lowers the neutron-to-proton ratio.

Positron Emitters

In nuclei with too few neutrons to be stable, positron emission increases the neutron-to-proton ratio by changing a proton into a neutron. A fluorine-17 nucleus, for example, increases its neutron-to-proton ratio, improves its stability, and moves into the band of stability by emitting a positron and a neutrino and changing to oxygen-17 (see Figure 20.9).

$$^{17}_{9}\text{F} \longrightarrow {}^{17}_{8}\text{O} + {}^{0}_{1}e + \nu$$

$$\frac{\text{neutron}}{\text{proton}} = \frac{8}{9} \qquad \frac{9}{8}$$

Positron decay by magnesium-23 to sodium-23 produces a similarly favorable shift (also shown in Figure 20.9).

Nuclei with even numbers of protons and neutrons are likely to be stable

Study of the compositions of stable nuclei reveals an interesting relationship: Nature favors even numbers for protons and neutrons. This is summarized by the **odd–even rule**.

TOOLS
Odd–even rule

> *Odd–Even Rule* When the numbers of neutrons and protons in a nucleus are both even, the isotope is far more likely to be stable than when both numbers are odd.

◻ These five stable isotopes, $^{2}_{1}\text{H}$, $^{6}_{3}\text{Li}$, $^{10}_{5}\text{B}$, $^{14}_{7}\text{N}$, and $^{138}_{57}\text{La}$, all have odd numbers of both protons and neutrons.

Of the 264 stable isotopes, only five have odd numbers of both protons and neutrons, whereas 157 have even numbers of both. The rest have an odd number of one nucleon and an even number of the other. To see this, notice in Figure 20.8 how the horizontal lines

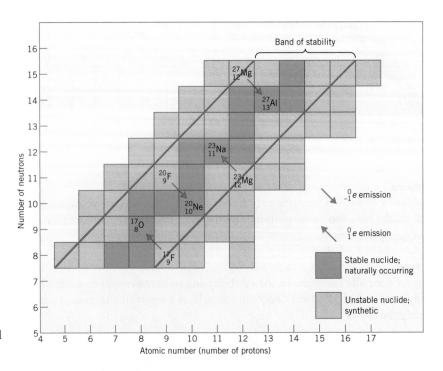

FIG. 20.9 **An enlarged section of the band of stability.** Beta decay from magnesium-27 and fluorine-20 reduces their neutron-to-proton ratio and moves them closer to the band of stability. Positron decay from magnesium-23 and fluorine-17 increases the ratio and moves those nuclides closer to the band of stability, too.

20.1

Positron Emission Tomography (PET)

Positron emitters are used in an important method for studying brain function called the PET scan, for *positron emission tomography*. The technique begins by chemically incorporating positron-emitting radionuclides into molecules, like glucose, that can be absorbed by the brain directly from the blood. It's like inserting radiation generators that act from within the brain rather than focusing X rays or gamma rays from the outside. Carbon-11, for example, is a positron emitter whose atoms can be used in place of carbon-12 atoms in glucose molecules, $C_6H_{12}O_6$. (One way to prepare such glucose is to let a leafy vegetable, Swiss chard, use $^{11}CO_2$ to make the glucose by photosynthesis.)

A PET scan using tiny amounts of carbon-11 glucose detects situations where glucose is not taken up normally, for example, in manic depression, schizophrenia, and Alzheimer's disease. After the carbon-11 glucose is ingested by the patient, radiation detectors outside the body pick up the annihilation radiation produced when electrons react with positrons emitted at specifically those brain sites that use glucose. By mapping the locations of the brain sites using the tagged glucose, a picture showing brain function can be formed. PET scan technology, for example, demonstrated that the uptake of glucose by the brains of smokers is less than that of nonsmokers, as shown in Figure 1.

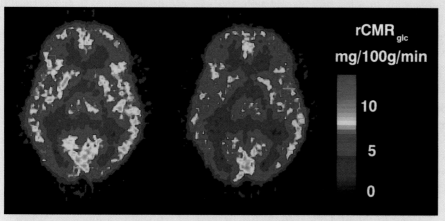

rCMR$_{glc}$
mg/100g/min

10

5

0

FIG. 1 **Positron emission tomography (PET) in the study of brain activity.** (*Left*) Normal brain. (*Right*) Brain affected by nicotine. The PET scan reveals widespread reduction in the rate of glucose metabolism when nicotine is present. (*Courtesy of E.D. London, National Institute of Drug Abuse.*)

The control, a PET scan of a normal brain.

The PET scan of the brain of a volunteer injected with nicotine.

The color code indicates the rates of glucose metabolism.

with the largest numbers of dark squares (stable isotopes) most commonly correspond to even numbers of neutrons. Similarly, the vertical lines with the most dark squares most often correspond to even numbers of protons.

The odd–even rule is related to the spins of nucleons. Both protons and neutrons behave as though they spin, like orbital electrons. When two protons or two neutrons have paired spins, meaning the spins are opposite, their combined energy is less than when the spins are unpaired. Only when there are even numbers of protons and neutrons can all the spins be paired and so give the nucleus a lower energy and greater stability. The least stable nuclei tend to be those with both an odd number of protons and an odd number of neutrons.

Isotopes with "magic numbers" are especially stable

Another rule of thumb for nuclear stability is based on *magic numbers* of nucleons. Isotopes with specific numbers of protons or neutrons, the **magic numbers,** are more stable than the rest. The magic numbers of nucleons are 2, 8, 20, 28, 50, 82, and 126, and where they fall is shown in Figure 20.8 (except for magic number 126).

When the numbers of both protons and neutrons are the same magic number, as they are in $^4_2$He, $^{16}_8$O, and $^{40}_{20}$Ca the isotope is very stable. $^{100}_{50}$Sn also has two identical magic numbers. Although this isotope of tin is unstable, having a half-life of only several seconds, it is much more stable than nearby radionuclides, whose half-lives are in milliseconds. Thus, although tin-100 lies well outside the band of stability, it is stable enough to be observed. One stable isotope of lead, $^{208}_{82}$Pb, involves two different magic numbers, 82 protons and 126 neutrons.

☐ Magic numbers do not cancel the need for a favorable neutron-to-proton ratio. An atom with 82 protons and 82 neutrons lies far outside the band of stability, and yet 82 is a magic number.

The existence of magic numbers supports the hypothesis that a nucleus has a shell structure with energy levels analogous to electron energy levels. Electron levels, as you already know, are associated with their own special numbers, those that equal the maximum number of electrons allowed in a principal energy level: 2, 8, 18, 32, 50, 72, and 98 (for principal levels with n equal to 1, 2, 3, 4, 5, 6, and 7, respectively). The total numbers of electrons in the atoms of the most chemically stable elements—the noble gases—also make up a special set: 2, 10, 18, 36, 54, and 86 electrons. Thus, special sets of numbers are not unique to nuclei.

20.5 TRANSMUTATION IS THE CHANGE OF ONE ISOTOPE INTO ANOTHER

The change of one isotope into another is called **transmutation,** and radioactive decay is only one cause. Transmutation can also be forced by the bombardment of nuclei with high-energy particles, such as alpha particles from natural emitters, neutrons from atomic reactors, or protons made by stripping electrons from hydrogen. To make them better bombarding missiles, protons and alpha particles can be accelerated in an electrical field (Figure 20.10). This gives them greater energy and enables them to sweep through the target atom's orbital electrons and become buried in its nucleus. Although beta particles can be accelerated, their disadvantage is that they are repelled by a target atom's own electrons.

Transmutation occurs when compound nuclei decay

☐ *Compound* here refers only to the idea of *combination*, not to a chemical.

Both the energy and the mass of a bombarding particle enter the target nucleus at the moment of capture. The energy of the new nucleus, called a **compound nucleus,** quickly becomes distributed among all of the nucleons, but the nucleus is nevertheless rendered somewhat unstable. To get rid of the excess energy, a compound nucleus generally ejects something (a neutron, proton, or electron) and often emits gamma radiation as well. This leaves a new nucleus of an isotope different than the original target, so a transmutation has occurred overall.

Ernest Rutherford observed the first example of artificial transmutation. When he let alpha particles pass through a chamber containing nitrogen atoms, an entirely new radiation was generated, one much more penetrating than alpha radiation. It proved to be a stream of protons (Figure 20.11). Rutherford was able to show that the protons came from the decay of the compound nuclei of fluorine-18, produced when nitrogen-14 nuclei captured bombarding alpha particles.

☐ The asterisk, *, symbolizes a high-energy nucleus, a *compound nucleus.*

$$^{4}_{2}\text{He} + {}^{14}_{7}\text{N} \longrightarrow {}^{18}_{9}\text{F}^{*} \longrightarrow {}^{17}_{8}\text{O} + {}^{1}_{1}p$$

| alpha particle | nitrogen nucleus | fluorine (compound nucleus) | oxygen (a rare but stable isotope) | proton (high energy) |

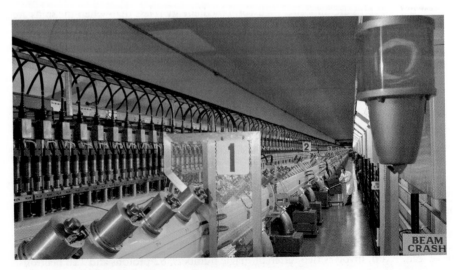

FIG. 20.10 Linear accelerator. In this linear accelerator at Brookhaven National Laboratory on Long Island, New York, protons can be accelerated to just under the speed of light and given up to 33 GeV of energy before they strike their target. (1 GeV = 10^9 eV.) *(Courtesy Brookhaven National Laboratory.)*

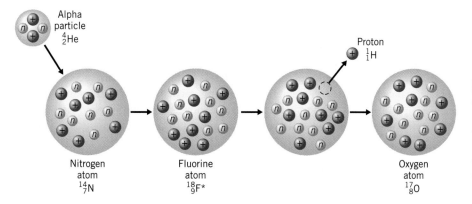

FIG. 20.11 **Transmutation of nitrogen into oxygen.** When the nucleus of nitrogen-14 captures an alpha particle it becomes a compound nucleus of fluorine-18. This then expels a proton and becomes the nucleus of oxygen-17.

In the synthesis of alpha particles from lithium-7, protons are used as bombarding particles. The resulting compound nucleus, that of beryllium-8, splits in two.

$$\underset{\text{proton}}{{}^{1}_{1}p} + \underset{\text{lithium}}{{}^{7}_{3}\text{Li}} \longrightarrow \underset{\text{beryllium}}{{}^{8}_{4}\text{Be*}} \longrightarrow \underset{\text{alpha particles}}{2\,{}^{4}_{2}\text{He}}$$

Compound nuclei can follow various decay modes

A given compound nucleus can be made in a variety of ways. Aluminum-27, for example, forms by any of the following routes.

$${}^{4}_{2}\text{He} + {}^{23}_{11}\text{Na} \longrightarrow {}^{27}_{13}\text{Al*}$$

$${}^{1}_{1}p + {}^{26}_{12}\text{Mg} \longrightarrow {}^{27}_{13}\text{Al*}$$

$$\underset{\text{deuteron}}{{}^{2}_{1}\text{H}} + {}^{25}_{12}\text{Mg} \longrightarrow {}^{27}_{13}\text{Al*}$$

Each path gives the compound nucleus ${}^{27}_{13}\text{Al*}$ a different amount of energy. Depending on this energy, different paths of decay are available, and all of the following routes have been observed. They illustrate how the synthesis of such a large number of synthetic isotopes, some stable and others unstable, has been possible.

□ A deuteron is the nucleus of a deuterium atom, just as a proton is the nucleus of a protium (hydrogen) atom.

$${}^{27}_{13}\text{Al*} \xrightarrow[\substack{\text{The mode of decay is} \\ \text{a function of the} \\ \text{nuclear energy of} \\ \text{aluminum-27.}}]{}$$

$$\longrightarrow \underset{\substack{\text{aluminum-27} \\ \text{(now stable)}}}{{}^{27}_{13}\text{Al}} + \underset{\substack{\text{gamma} \\ \text{radiation}}}{{}^{0}_{0}\gamma}$$

$$\longrightarrow \underset{\substack{\text{magnesium-26} \\ \text{(stable)}}}{{}^{26}_{12}\text{Mg}} + \underset{\substack{\text{proton} \\ \text{radiation}}}{{}^{1}_{1}p}$$

$$\longrightarrow \underset{\substack{\text{aluminum-26} \\ \text{(unstable;} \\ t_{1/2} = 7.4 \times 10^{5}\ \text{yr)}}}{{}^{26}_{13}\text{Al}} + \underset{\substack{\text{neutron} \\ \text{radiation}}}{{}^{1}_{0}n}$$

$$\longrightarrow \underset{\substack{\text{magnesium-25} \\ \text{(stable)}}}{{}^{25}_{12}\text{Mg}} + \underset{\substack{\text{neutron} \\ \text{radiation}}}{{}^{1}_{0}n} + \underset{\substack{\text{proton} \\ \text{radiation}}}{{}^{1}_{1}p}$$

$$\longrightarrow \underset{\substack{\text{sodium-23} \\ \text{(stable)}}}{{}^{23}_{11}\text{Na}} + \underset{\substack{\text{alpha} \\ \text{radiation}}}{{}^{4}_{2}\text{He}}$$

Transmutation is used to produce synthetic elements

Over a thousand isotopes have been made by transmutations. Most do not occur naturally; they appear in the band of stability (Figure 20.8) as open squares, nearly 900 in number. The naturally occurring radioactive isotopes above atomic number 83 all have very long half-lives. Others might have existed, but their half-lives probably were too short to permit them to last into our era. All of the elements beyond neptunium (atomic number 93 and higher, known as the **transuranium elements**) are synthetic. Elements from atomic numbers 93 to 103 complete the actinide series of the periodic table, which starts with element 90, thorium. Beyond this series, elements 104–116 and 118 have also been made.

To make the heaviest elements, bombarding particles larger than neutrons are used, such as alpha particles or the nuclei of heavier atoms. For example, element 110—darmstadtium, Ds—was made when a neutron was ejected from the compound nucleus formed by the fusion of nickel-62 and lead-208.

$$^{62}_{28}\text{Ni} + {}^{208}_{82}\text{Pb} \longrightarrow {}^{270}_{110}\text{Ds} \longrightarrow {}^{269}_{110}\text{Ds} + {}^{1}_{0}n$$

Similarly, some atoms of element 111 (roentgenium, Rg) formed when a neutron was lost from the compound nucleus made by bombarding bismuth-209 with nickel-64. Most of these heavy atoms are extremely unstable, with half-lives measured in fractions of milliseconds. An exception is element 114; two isotopes have been detected with half-lives reported to be in seconds.

☐ Element 110 was named after the place of its discovery, Darmstadt, Germany. Element 111 was named in honor of Wilhelm Roentgen, who discovered X rays in 1895.

20.6 HOW IS RADIATION MEASURED?

Atomic radiation is often described as **ionizing radiation** because it creates ions by knocking electrons from molecules in the matter through which the radiation travels. The generation of ions is behind some of the devices for detecting radiation.

The Geiger–Müller tube, one part of a **Geiger counter,** detects beta and gamma radiation having energy high enough to penetrate the tube's window. Inside the tube is a gas under low pressure in which ions form when radiation enters. The ions permit a pulse of electricity to flow, which activates a current amplifier, a pulse counter, and an audible click.

A **scintillation counter** (Figure 20.12) contains a sensor composed of a substance called a *phosphor* that emits a tiny flash of light when struck by a particle of ionizing radiation. These flashes can be magnified electronically and automatically counted.

The darkening of a photographic film exposed to radiation over a period of time is proportional to the total quantity of radiation received. **Film dosimeters** work on this principle (Figure 20.13), and people who work near radiation sources use them. Each person keeps a log of total exposure, and if a predetermined limit is exceeded, the worker must be reassigned to an unexposed workplace.

The rate of radioactive decay is measured in disintegrations per second

The **activity** of a radioactive material is the number of disintegrations per second. The SI unit of activity is the **becquerel (Bq),** and it equals one disintegration per second. A liter

☐ The becquerel is named after Henri Becquerel (1852–1908), the discoverer of radioactivity, who won a Nobel prize in 1903.

FIG. 20.12 Scintillation probe. Energy received from radiations striking the phosphor at the end of the probe is amplified by a photomultiplier unit and sent to the instrument where the intensity of the radiation is displayed on a meter. (*Research Products International Corp.*)

FIG. 20.13 **Badge dosimeter.** *(Cliff Moore/Photo Researchers, Inc.)*

Marie Curie (1867–1934); Nobel prizes 1903 (physics) and 1911 (chemistry). *(Courtesy College of Physicians of Philadelphia.)*

of air has an activity of about 0.04 Bq, due to carbon-14 in its carbon dioxide. A gram of natural uranium has an activity of about 2.6×10^4 Bq.

The **curie (Ci),** named after Marie Curie, the discoverer of radium, is an older unit, being equal to the activity of a 1.0 g sample of radium-226.

$$1 \text{ Ci} = 3.7 \times 10^{10} \text{ disintegrations s}^{-1} = 3.7 \times 10^{10} \text{ Bq} \qquad (20.3)$$

For a sufficiently large sample of a radioactive material, the activity is experimentally found to be proportional to the number of radioactive nuclei, N:

$$\text{Activity} = kN$$

The constant of proportionality, k, is called the **decay constant.** The decay constant is characteristic of the particular radioactive nuclide, and it gives the activity per nuclide in the sample. Since activity is the number of disintegrations per second, and therefore the change in the number of nuclei per second, we can write

$$\text{Activity} = -\frac{\Delta N}{\Delta t} = kN \qquad (20.4)$$

TOOLS
Law of radioactive decay

which is called the **law of radioactive decay.**[1] The law shows that radioactive decay is a first-order kinetic process, and the decay constant is really just a first-order rate constant in terms of number of nuclei, rather than concentrations.

Recall from Chapter 13 that the half-life of a first-order reaction is given by Equation 13.5:

$$t_{1/2} = \frac{\ln 2}{k}$$

TOOLS
Half-life of a radionuclide

If we know the half-life of a radioisotope, we can use this relationship to compute its decay constant and also the activity of a known mass of the radioisotope, as Example 20.2 demonstrates.

[1] Note that the minus sign is introduced to make the activity a positive number, since the change in the number of radioactive nuclei ΔN is negative.

EXAMPLE 20.2
Using the Law of Radioactive Decay

Deep space probes such as NASA's Cassini spacecraft need to keep their instruments warm enough to operate effectively. Since solar power is not available in the darkness of deep space, these craft generate heat from the radioactive decay of small pellets of plutonium dioxide. Each pellet is about the size of a pencil eraser and weighs about 2.7 g. If the pellets are pure PuO_2, with the plutonium being ^{238}Pu, what is the activity of one of the fuel pellets, in bequerels?

ANALYSIS: The tool for finding the activity is Equation 20.4. But to use the equation, we'll need the decay constant, k, and the number of plutonium-238 atoms, N, in the fuel pellet.

From Table 20.1, the half-life of ^{238}Pu is 87.8 years. We can rearrange Equation 13.5 to compute the decay constant k from the half-life:

$$k = \frac{\ln 2}{t_{1/2}}$$

We'll want the decay constant in terms of seconds because the becquerel is defined as disintegrations per second. We should therefore convert the half-life into seconds before substituting it into Equation 13.5.

We know that the pellet contains 2.7 g of PuO_2. To calculate N, we'll have to perform the following stoichiometric conversion:

$$2.7 \text{ g } PuO_2 \Leftrightarrow ? \text{ atoms Pu}$$

The tools here come from Chapter 3. We'll use the molar mass to find moles of PuO_2, the chemical formula to relate this to moles of Pu, and then Avogadro's number to find the number of atoms of Pu. Our strategy is to perform the following conversions:

$$2.7 \text{ g } PuO_2 \longrightarrow \text{mol } PuO_2 \longrightarrow \text{mol Pu} \longrightarrow \text{atoms Pu}$$

We'll need the formula mass of PuO_2 (270 g mol^{-1}) to perform the first conversion. For the second conversion, the formula of PuO_2 tells us that there is 1 mol Pu in 1 mol PuO_2. For the final conversion, recall that 1 mole of atoms is 6.02×10^{23} atoms.

SOLUTION: First, let's compute the decay constant from the half-life. We must convert the half-life into seconds:

$$87.8 \text{ years} \times \frac{365 \text{ days}}{1 \text{ year}} \times \frac{24 \text{ hours}}{1 \text{ day}} \times \frac{60 \text{ min}}{1 \text{ hour}} \times \frac{60 \text{ s}}{1 \text{ min}} = 2.77 \times 10^9 \text{ s}$$

Now we can solve Equation 13.5 for the decay constant:

$$k = \frac{\ln 2}{t_{1/2}}$$

$$= \frac{0.693}{2.77 \times 10^9 \text{ s}}$$

$$= 2.50 \times 10^{-10} \text{ s}^{-1}$$

Next, we need the number of ^{238}Pu atoms in the fuel pellet:

$$2.7 \text{ g } PuO_2 \times \frac{1 \text{ mol } PuO_2}{270 \text{ g } PuO_2} \times \frac{1 \text{ mol Pu}}{1 \text{ mol } PuO_2} \times \frac{6.02 \times 10^{23} \text{ atoms Pu}}{1 \text{ mol Pu}} = 6.0 \times 10^{21} \text{ atoms Pu}$$

From the law of radioactive decay, Equation 20.4, the activity of the fuel pellet is

$$\text{Activity} = kN = 2.50 \times 10^{-10} \text{ s}^{-1} \times 6.0 \times 10^{21} \text{ atoms Pu} = 1.5 \times 10^{12} \text{ atoms Pu/s}$$

Since the becquerel is defined as the number of disintegrations per second, and each plutonium atom corresponds to one disintegration, we can report the activity as 1.5×10^{12} Bq.

IS THE ANSWER REASONABLE? There is no easy way to check the size of the decay constant beyond checking the arithmetic. The number of Pu atoms in the pellet makes sense, because if we have 2.7 g PuO_2 and the formula mass is 270 g mol^{-1}, we have 1/100th of a mole of PuO_2 and so 1/100 a mole of Pu. We should have (1/100) of 6.02×10^{23} atoms, or 6.02×10^{21} atoms of Pu.

The fuel pellet has about 40 times the activity of a gram of radium-226, as indicated by Equation 20.3, so the activity of ^{238}Pu per gram is about 15 times the activity of ^{226}Ra per gram.

Practice Exercise 3: A 2.00 g sample of a mixture of plutonium with a nonradioactive metal has an activity of 6.22×10^{11} Bq. What is the percentage by mass of plutonium the sample? (Hint: How many atoms of Pu are in the sample?)

Practice Exercise 4: The EPA limit for radon-222 is 6 pCi (picocuries) per liter of air. How many atoms of ^{222}Rn per liter of air will produce that activity?

Other units are used to express amounts of radiation and its effects on tissue

Nuclear radiation can have varying effects depending on the energy of the radiation and its ability to be absorbed. The **gray (Gy)** is the SI unit of *absorbed dose,* and 1 gray corresponds to 1 joule of energy absorbed per kilogram of absorbing material. The **rad** is an older unit of absorbed dose, 1 rad being the absorption of 10^{-2} joule per kilogram of tissue. Thus, 1 Gy equals 100 rad. In terms of danger, if every individual in a large population received 450 rad (4.5 Gy), roughly half of the population would die in 60 days.

□ The *gray* is named after Harold Gray, a British radiologist. *Rad* stands for **rad**iation **a**bsorbed **d**ose.

The gray is not a good basis for comparing the biological effects of radiation in tissue, because these effects depend not just on the energy absorbed but also on the kind of radiation and the tissue itself. The **sievert (Sv),** the SI unit of *dose equivalent,* was invented to meet this problem. The **rem** is an older unit of dose equivalent, one still used in medicine. Its value is generally taken to equal 10^{-2} Sv. The U.S. government has set guidelines of 0.3 rem per week as the maximum exposure workers may receive. (For comparison, a chest X ray typically involves about 0.007 rem or 7 mrem.)

□ *Rem* stands for **r**oentgen **e**quivalent for **m**an, where the *roentgen* is a unit related to X ray and gamma radiation.

Radiation damages living tissue

A whole body dose of 25 rem (0.25 Sv) induces noticeable changes in human blood. A set of symptoms called *radiation sickness* develops at about 100 rem, becoming severe at 200 rem. Among the symptoms are nausea, vomiting, a drop in the white cell count, diarrhea, dehydration, prostration, hemorrhaging, and loss of hair. If each person in a large population absorbed 400 rem, half would die in 60 days. A 600 rem dose would kill everyone in the group in a week. Many workers received at least 400 rem in the moments following the steam explosion that tore apart one of the nuclear reactors at the Ukraine energy park near Chernobyl in 1986.

Radiation produces free radicals

Even small absorbed doses can be biologically harmful. The danger does not lie in the heat energy associated with the dose, which is usually very small. Rather, the harm is in the ability of ionizing radiation to create unstable ions or neutral species with odd (unpaired) electrons, species that can set off other reactions. Water, for example, can interact as follows with ionizing radiation.

$$H-\overset{..}{\underset{..}{O}}-H \xrightarrow{\text{radiation}} \left[H-\overset{.}{\underset{..}{O}}-H \right]^+ + {}_{-1}^{0}e$$

The new cation, $\left[H-\overset{.}{\underset{..}{O}}-H \right]^+$, is unstable and one breakup path is

$$\left[H-\overset{.}{\underset{..}{O}}-H \right]^+ \longrightarrow H^+ + \overset{.}{:\underset{..}{O}}-H$$

proton   hydroxyl radical

The proton might pick up a stray electron to become a hydrogen atom, H·.

□ Free radicals are discussed in more detail in Facets of Chemistry 13.1 on page 553.

Both the hydrogen atom and the hydroxyl radical are examples of **free radicals** (often simply called *radicals*), which are neutral or charged particles having one or more unpaired electrons. They are chemically very reactive. What they do once formed depends on the other chemical species nearby, but radicals can set off a series of totally undesirable chemical reactions inside a living cell. This is what makes the injury from absorbed radiation of far greater magnitude than the energy alone could inflict. A dose of 600 rem is a lethal dose in a human, but the same dose absorbed by pure water causes the ionization of only one water molecule in every 36 million.

Background radiation comes from a variety of sources

The presence of radionuclides in nature makes it impossible for us to be free from all exposure to ionizing radiation. Cosmic rays composed of high-energy photons shower on us from the sun and interstellar space. They interact with the air's nitrogen molecules to produce carbon-14, a beta emitter, which enters the food chain via photosynthesis, which converts CO_2 to sugars and starch. From soil and from building stone comes the radiation of radionuclides native to the earth's crust. The top 40 cm of soil holds an average of 1 gram of radium, an alpha emitter, per square kilometer. Naturally occurring potassium-40, a beta emitter, adds its radiation wherever potassium ions are found in the body. The presence of carbon-14 and potassium-40 together produce about 5×10^5 nuclear disintegrations per minute inside an adult human. Radon gas seeps into basements from underground formations. In fact, a little over half of the radiation we experience, on average, is from radon-222 and its decay products.

Diagnostic X rays, both medical and dental, also expose us to ionizing radiation. All these sources produce a combined **background radiation** that averages 360 mrem per person annually in the United States. The averages are roughly 82% from natural radiation and 18% from medical sources.

Radiation can be reduced by shielding and by distance

Gamma radiation and X rays are so powerful that they are effectively shielded only by very dense materials, like lead. Otherwise, one should stay as far from a source as possible, because the intensity of radiation diminishes with the *square* of the distance. This relationship is the **inverse square law,** which can be written mathematically as follows, where *d* is the distance from the source.

$$\text{Radiation intensity} \propto \frac{1}{d^2}$$

When the intensity, I_1, is known at distance d_1, then the intensity I_2 at distance d_2 can be calculated by the following equation.

TOOLS

Inverse square law

$$\frac{I_1}{I_2} = \frac{d_2^2}{d_1^2} \tag{20.5}$$

□ When the ratio is taken, the proportionality constant cancels, so we don't have to know what its value is.

This law applies only to a small source that radiates equally in all directions, with no intervening shields.

Practice Exercise 5: If the intensity of radiation from a radioactive source is 4.8 units at a distance of 5.0 m, how far from the source would you have to move to reduce the intensity to 0.30 units? (Hint: How does intensity vary with distance?)

Practice Exercise 6: If an operator 10 m from a small source is exposed to 1.4 units of radiation, what will be the intensity of the radiation if he moves to 1.2 m from the source?

20.7 | RADIONUCLIDES HAVE MEDICAL AND ANALYTICAL APPLICATIONS

Because chemical properties depend on the number and arrangement of orbital electrons and not on the specific makeup of nuclei, both radioactive and stable isotopes of an element behave the same chemically. This fact forms the basis for some uses of radionuclides. The chemical and physical properties enable scientists to get radionuclides into place in systems of interest. Then the radiation is exploited for medical or analytical purposes. Tracer analysis is an example.

Tracer analysis is used in medicine to study specific tissues in the body

In **tracer analysis,** the chemical form and properties of a radionuclide enable the system to distribute it to a particular location. The intensity of the radiation then tells something about how that site is working. In the form of the iodide ion, for example, iodine-131 is carried by the body to the thyroid gland, the only user of iodide ion in the body. The gland takes up the iodide ion to synthesize the hormone thyroxine. An underactive thyroid gland is unable to concentrate iodide ion normally and will emit less intense radiation under standard test conditions.

Tracer analyses are also used to pinpoint the locations of brain tumors, which are uniquely able to concentrate the pertechnetate ion, TcO_4^-, made from technetium-99*m*.[2] This strong gamma emitter, which resembles the chloride ion in some respects, is one of the most widely used radionuclides in medicine.

◻ Technetium-99*m* is also used in bone scans to detect and locate bone cancer. Active cancer sites concentrate the Tc, which can be detected using external scanning devices.

Neutron activation analysis is used to detect trace elements

A number of stable nuclei can be changed into emitters of gamma radiation by capturing neutrons, and this makes possible a procedure called **neutron activation analysis**. Neutron capture followed by gamma emission can be represented by the following equation (where A is a mass number and X is a hypothetical atomic symbol).

$$^{A}X \ + \ {}_{0}^{1}n \ \longrightarrow \ {}^{(A+1)}X* \ \longrightarrow \ {}^{(A+1)}X \ + \ {}_{0}^{0}\gamma$$

isotope   neutron   compound   more stable   gamma
of element   nucleus   form of a new radiation
X being   (unstable)   isotope of X
analyzed

A neutron-enriched compound nucleus emits gamma radiation at its own set of unique frequencies, and these sets of frequencies are now known for each isotope. (Not all isotopes, however, become gamma emitters by neutron capture.) The element can be identified by measuring the specific *frequencies* of gamma radiation emitted. The *concentration* of the element can be determined by measuring the *intensity* of the gamma radiation.

Neutron activation analysis is so sensitive that concentrations as low as $10^{-9}\%$ can be determined. A museum might have a lock of hair of some famous but long dead person suspected of having been slowly murdered by arsenic poisoning. If so, some arsenic would be in the hair, and neutron activation analysis could find it without destroying the specimen of hair.

Radiological dating determines the age of a sample using kinetics

The determination of the age of a geological deposit or an archaeological find by the use of the radionuclides that are naturally present is called **radiological dating.** It is based partly on the premise that the half-lives of radionuclides have been constant throughout the entire geological period. This premise is supported by the finding that half-lives are insensitive to all environmental forces such as heat, pressure, magnetism, or electrical stresses. Radiological dating of archaeological objects by carbon-14 analyses was described in Chapter 13 (page 539).

In geological dating, a pair of isotopes is sought that are related as a "parent" to a "daughter" in a radioactive disintegration series, like the uranium-238 series (Figure 20.7). Uranium-238 (as "parent") and lead-206 (as "daughter") have thus been used as a radiological dating pair of isotopes. The half-life of uranium-238 is very long, a necessary criterion for geological dating. Put simply, after the concentrations of uranium-238

---

[2] The *m* in technetium-99*m* means that the isotope is in a metastable form. Its nucleus is at a higher energy level than the nucleus in technetium-99, to which technetium-99*m* decays.

and lead-206 are determined in a rock specimen, the *ratio* of the concentrations together with the half-life of uranium-238 is used to calculate the age of the rock.

Probably the most widely used isotopes for dating rock are the potassium-40/argon-40 pair. Potassium-40 is a naturally occurring radionuclide with a half-life nearly as long as that of uranium-238. One of its modes of decay is electron capture, and argon-40 forms.

$$^{40}_{19}\text{K} + ^{0}_{-1}e \longrightarrow ^{40}_{18}\text{Ar}$$

The argon produced by the reaction remains trapped within the crystal lattices of the rock and is freed only when the rock sample is melted. How much has accumulated is measured with a mass spectrometer (page 47), and the observed ratio of argon-40 to potassium-40, together with the half-life of the parent, permits the age of the specimen to be estimated. Because the half-lives of uranium-238 and potassium-40 are so long, samples have to be at least 300,000 years old for either of the two parent–daughter isotope pairs to provide reliable results.

☐ For ^{238}U, $t_{1/2} = 4.51 \times 10^9$ yr.
For ^{40}K, $t_{1/2} = 1.3 \times 10^9$ yr.

Carbon-14 dating determines the age of organic objects

As discussed in detail in Chapter 13, measurements of the ^{14}C to ^{12}C ratio in an ancient organic sample, such as an object made of wood or bone, permits calculation of the sample's age.

There are two approaches to carbon-14 dating. The older method, introduced by its discoverer, Willard F. Libby (Nobel Prize in Chemistry, 1960), measures the *radioactivity* of a sample taken from the specimen. The radioactivity is proportional to the concentration of carbon-14.

☐ For carbon dating to be accurate, extraordinary precautions must be taken to ensure that specimens are not contaminated by more recent sources of carbon or carbon compounds.

The newer and current method of carbon-14 dating relies on a device resembling a mass spectrometer that is able to separate the atoms of carbon-14 from the other isotopes of carbon (as well as from nitrogen-14) *and count all of them*, not just the carbon-14 atoms that decay. This approach permits the use of smaller samples (0.5–5 mg versus 1–20 g for the Libby method); it works at much higher efficiencies; and it gives more precise dates. Objects of up to 70,000 years old can be dated, but the highest accuracy involves systems no older than 7000 years.

20.8 NUCLEAR FISSION AND NUCLEAR FUSION RELEASE LARGE AMOUNTS OF ENERGY

Nuclear fission is a process whereby a heavy atomic nucleus splits into two lighter fragments. **Nuclear fusion,** on the other hand, is a process whereby very light nuclei join to form a heavier nucleus. Both processes release large amounts of energy, as we will discuss shortly.

Nuclear fission is initiated by absorption of a neutron by an unstable nucleus

Because of their electrical neutrality, neutrons penetrate an atom's electron cloud relatively easily and so are able to enter the nucleus. Enrico Fermi discovered in the early 1930s that even slow-moving, *thermal neutrons* can be captured. (Thermal neutrons are those whose average kinetic energy puts them in thermal equilibrium with their surroundings at room temperature.) When he directed thermal neutrons at a uranium target, Fermi discovered that several different species of nuclei, all much lighter than uranium, were produced.

Without realizing it, what Fermi had observed was the nuclear fission of one particular isotope, uranium-235, present in small concentrations in naturally occurring uranium. The general reaction can be represented as follows.

$$^{235}_{92}\text{U} + ^{1}_{0}n \longrightarrow X + Y + b \, ^{1}_{0}n$$

X and Y can be a large variety of nuclei with intermediate atomic numbers. Over 30 have been identified. The coefficient b has an average value of 2.47, the average number of neutrons produced by fission events. A typical specific fission is

$$^{235}_{92}\text{U} + ^{1}_{0}n \longrightarrow ^{236}_{92}\text{U}^* \longrightarrow ^{94}_{36}\text{Kr} + ^{139}_{56}\text{Ba} + 3 \, ^{1}_{0}n$$

What actually undergoes fission is the compound nucleus of uranium-236. It has 144 neutrons and 92 protons, giving it a neutron-to-proton ratio of roughly 1.6. Initially, the emerging krypton and barium isotopes have the same ratio, and this is much too high for them. The neutron-to-proton ratio for stable isotopes with 36 to 56 protons is nearer 1.2 to 1.3 (Figure 20.8). Therefore, the initially formed, neutron-rich krypton and barium nuclides promptly eject neutrons, called *secondary neutrons,* that generally have much higher energies than thermal neutrons.

An isotope that can undergo fission after neutron capture is called a **fissile isotope.** The naturally occurring fissile isotope of uranium used in reactors is uranium-235, whose abundance among the uranium isotopes today is only 0.72%. Two other fissile isotopes, uranium-233 and plutonium-239, can be made in nuclear reactors.

Nuclear chain reactions require a critical mass of fissile material

The secondary neutrons released by fission become thermal neutrons as they are slowed by collisions with surrounding materials. They can now be captured by unchanged uranium-235 atoms. Because each fission event produces, on the average, more than two new neutrons, the potential exists for a **nuclear chain reaction** (Figure 20.14). A *chain reaction* is a self-sustaining process whereby products from one event cause one or more repetitions of the process.

If the sample of uranium-235 is small enough, the loss of neutrons to the surroundings is sufficiently rapid to prevent a chain reaction. However, at a certain *critical mass* of uranium-235, about 50 kilograms, this loss of neutrons is insufficient to prevent a sustained reaction. A virtually instantaneous fission of the sample ensues, in other words, an atomic bomb explosion. To trigger an atomic bomb, therefore, two or more subcritical masses of uranium-235 (or plutonium-239) are forced together to form a critical mass.

The energy yield from fission is very large

The binding energy per nucleon (Figure 20.1) in uranium-235 (about 7.6 MeV) is less than the binding energies of the new nuclides (about 8.5 MeV). The net change for a single

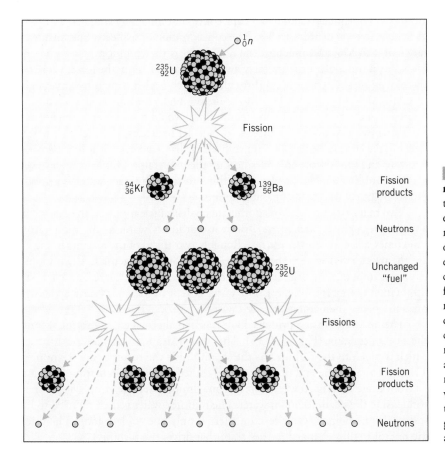

FIG. 20.14 **Nuclear chain reaction.** Whenever the concentration of a fissile isotope is high enough (at or above the critical mass), the neutrons released by one fission can be captured by enough unchanged nuclei to cause more than one additional fission event. In civilian nuclear reactors, the fissile isotope is too dilute for this to get out of control. In addition, control rods of nonfissile materials that are able to capture excess neutrons can be inserted or withdrawn from the reactor core to make sure that the heat generated can be removed as fast as it forms.

fission event can be calculated as follows (where we intend only *two* significant figures in each result).

Binding energy in krypton-94:

$$(8.5 \text{ MeV/nucleon}) \times 94 \text{ nucleons} = 800 \text{ MeV}$$

□ $1 \text{ MeV} = 1.602 \times 10^{-13} \text{ J}$

Binding energy in barium-139:

$$(8.5 \text{ MeV/nucleon}) \times 139 \text{ nucleons} = \underline{1200 \text{ MeV}}$$

$$\text{Total binding energy of products:} \quad 2000 \text{ MeV}$$

Binding energy in uranium-235:

$$(7.6 \text{ MeV/nucleon}) \times 235 \text{ nucleons} = 1800 \text{ MeV}$$

The difference in total binding energy is (2000 MeV − 1800 MeV), or 200 MeV (3.2×10^{-11} J), which has to be taken as just a rough calculation. This is the energy released by each fission event going by the equation given. The energy produced by the fission of 1 kg (4.25 mole) of uranium-235 is calculated to be roughly 8×10^{13} J, enough to keep a 100 watt lightbulb in energy for 3000 years.

□ The energy available from 1 kg of uranium-235 is equivalent to the energy of combustion of 3000 tons of soft coal or 13,200 barrels of oil.

Heat from fission reactions can be used to drive electrical generators

Virtually all civilian nuclear power plants throughout the world operate on the same general principles. The energy of fission is used, as heat, either directly or indirectly to increase the pressure of some gas that then drives an electrical generator.

The heart of a nuclear power plant is the *reactor*, where fission takes place in the *fuel core*. The nuclear fuel is generally uranium oxide, enriched to 2–4% in uranium-235 and formed into glasslike pellets. These are housed in long, sealed metal tubes called *cladding*. Bunches of tubes are assembled in spacers that permit a coolant to circulate around the tubes. A reactor has several such assemblies in its fuel core. The coolant carries away the heat of fission.

There is no danger of a nuclear power plant undergoing an atomic bomb explosion. An atomic bomb requires uranium-235 at a concentration of 85% or greater or plutonium-239 at a concentration of at least 93%. The concentration of fissile isotopes in a reactor is in the range of 2 to 4%, and much of the remainder is the common, nonfissile uranium-238. However, if the coolant fails to carry away the heat of fission, the reactor core can melt, and the molten mass might even go through the thick-walled containment vessel in which the reactor is kept. Or the high heat of the fission might split molecules of coolant water into hydrogen and oxygen, which, on recombining, would produce an immense explosion.

To convert secondary neutrons to thermal neutrons, the fuel core has a *moderator*, which is the coolant water itself in nearly all civilian reactors. Collisions between secondary neutrons and moderator molecules heat up the moderator. This heat energy eventually generates steam that enables an electric turbine to run. Ordinary water is a good moderator, but so are heavy water (D_2O) and graphite.

□ D_2O is deuterium oxide. Deuterium is an isotope of hydrogen, $_1^2H$.

Two main types of reactors dominate civilian nuclear power, the *boiling water reactor* and the *pressurized water reactor*. Both use ordinary water as the moderator and so are sometimes called *light water reactors*. Roughly two-thirds of the reactors in the United States are the pressurized-water type (Figure 20.15). Such a reactor has two loops, and water circulates in both. The primary loop moves water through the reactor core, where it picks up thermal energy from fission. The water is kept in the *liquid* state by being under high pressure (hence the name *pressurized* water reactor).

The hot water in the primary loop transfers thermal energy to the secondary loop at the steam generator (Figure 20.15). This makes steam at high temperature and pressure, which is piped to the turbine. As the steam drives the turbine, the steam pressure drops. The condenser at the end of the turbine, cooled by water circulating from a river or lake or from huge cooling towers, forces a maximum pressure drop within the turbine by condensing the steam to liquid water. The returned water is then recycled to high-pressure steam. (In the boiling water reactor, there is only one coolant loop. The water heated in the reactor itself is changed to the steam that drives the turbine.)

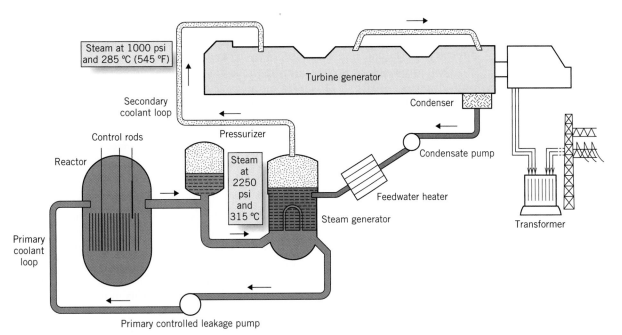

FIG. 20.15 **Pressurized water reactor, the type used in most of the nuclear power plants in the United States.** Water in the primary coolant loop is pumped around and through the fuel elements in the core, and it carries away the heat of the nuclear chain reactions. The hot water delivers its heat to the cooler water in the secondary coolant loop, where steam is generated to drive the turbines. *(Drawing from WASH-1261, U.S. Atomic Energy Commission, 1973.)*

Nuclear power plants produce several types of radioactive waste

Radioactive wastes from nuclear power plants occur as gases, liquids, and solids. The gases are mostly radionuclides of krypton and xenon but, with the exception of xenon-85 ($t_{1/2}$ = 10.4 years), the gases have short half-lives and decay quickly. During decay, they must be contained, and this is one function of the cladding. Other dangerous radionuclides produced by fission include iodine-131, strontium-90, and cesium-137.

Iodine-131 must be contained because the human thyroid gland concentrates iodide ion to make the hormone thyroxine. Once the isotope is in the gland, beta radiation from iodine-131 could cause harm, possibly thyroid cancer and possibly impaired thyroid function. An effective countermeasure to iodine-131 poisoning is to take doses of ordinary iodine (as sodium iodide). Statistically, this increases the likelihood that the thyroid will take up stable iodide ion rather than the unstable anion of iodine-131.

Cesium-137 and strontium-90 also pose problems to humans. Cesium is in Group IA together with sodium, so radiating cesium-137 cations travel to some of the same places in the body where sodium ions go. Strontium is in Group IIA with calcium, so strontium-90 cations can replace calcium ions in bone tissue, sending radiation into bone marrow and possibly causing leukemia. The half-lives of cesium-137 and strontium-90, however, are relatively short.

Some radionuclides in wastes are so long-lived that solid reactor wastes must be kept away from all human contact for dozens of centuries, longer than any nation has ever yet endured. Probably the most intensively studied procedure for making solid radioactive wastes secure is to convert them to glasslike or rocklike solids, and bury them deeply within a rock stratum or in a mountain believed to be geologically stable with respect to earthquakes or volcanoes. Finding a location for such a site has been the subject of much scientific and political debate.

▢ Cesium-137 has a half-life of 30 years; that of strontium-90 is 28.1 years. Both are beta emitters.

Nuclear fusion occurs when light nuclei join to form a heavier nucleus

In Section 20.2 we mentioned that joining, or *fusing,* two light nuclei that lie to the left of the peak in the nuclear binding energy curve in Figure 20.1 leads to a net increase in nuclear binding energy and a corresponding release of energy. The process is called *nuclear fusion,* and the amount of energy released is considerably greater than in fission. Harnessing this energy for peaceful purposes is still a long way off, however, because many immensely difficult scientific and engineering problems remain to be solved.

Deuterium, $_1^2\text{H}$, an isotope of hydrogen, is a key fuel in all approaches to fusion. It is naturally present as 0.015% of all hydrogen atoms, including those in water. Despite this low percentage, the earth has so much water that the supply of deuterium is virtually limitless.

The fusion reaction most likely to be used in a successful fusion reactor involves fusion of deuterium and another isotope of hydrogen, tritium, $_1^3\text{H}$.

$$_1^2\text{H} + _1^3\text{H} \longrightarrow _2^4\text{He} + _0^1n + 17.6\,\text{MeV}$$

deuterium   tritium   helium   neutron

This corresponds to an energy yield of 2.82×10^{-12} J for each atom of helium formed, or 1.70×10^9 kJ per mole of He formed. One problem with this reaction is that tritium is radioactive with a relatively short half-life, so it doesn't occur naturally. It can be made in several ways, however, from lithium or even deuterium via other nuclear reactions.

Comparing fission and fusion on a mass basis, fission of one kilogram of ^{235}U yields approximately 8×10^{13} J, whereas forming one kilogram of ^4He by the fusion reaction above yields 4.2×10^{14} J. Therefore, on a mass basis, fusion yields more than five times as much energy as fission. The potential energy yield from fusion is so great that the deuterium in just 0.005 cubic kilometers of ocean would supply the energy needs of the United States for one year.

Thermonuclear fusion uses high temperatures to overcome electrostatic repulsions between nuclei

The central scientific problem with fusion is to get the fusing nuclei close enough for a long enough time that the nuclear strong force (of attraction) can overcome the electrostatic force (of repulsion). As we learned in Section 20.3, the strong force acts over a much shorter range than the electrostatic force. Two nuclei on a collision course, therefore, repel each other virtually until they touch and get into the range of the strong force. The kinetic energies of two approaching nuclei must therefore be very substantial if they are to overcome this electrostatic barrier. Achieving such energies, moreover, must be accomplished by large numbers of nuclei all at once in batch after batch if there is to be any practical generation of electrical power by nuclear fusion. Relatively isolated fusion events achieved in huge accelerators will not do. The only practical way to give batch quantities of nuclei enough energy is to transfer *thermal* energy to them, and so the overall process is called *thermonuclear fusion.* Temperatures required to provide such thermal energy are very high—more than 100 million degrees Celsius!

The atoms whose nuclei we want to fuse must first be stripped of their electrons. Thus, a high energy cost is exacted from the start but, overall, the energy yield will more than pay for it. The product is an electrically neutral, gaseous mixture of nuclei and unattached electrons called a **plasma.** The plasma must then be made so dense that like-charged nuclei are within 2 fm (2×10^{-15} m) of each other, meaning a plasma density of roughly 200 g cm^{-3} as compared with 200 mg cm^{-3} under ordinary conditions. To achieve this, the plasma must be confined at a pressure of several billion atmospheres long enough for the separate nuclei to fuse. The temperature needed is several times the temperature at the center of our sun.

☐ The interior of the sun is at a temperature of approximately 15 million kelvins (15 MK).

Although practical peaceful uses for thermonuclear fusion are still in the distant future, military applications have been around for over 60 years. Thermonuclear fusion is the source of the energy released in the explosion of a hydrogen bomb. The energy needed to trigger the fusion is provided by the explosion of a fission bomb based on either uranium or plutonium.

Fusion reactions are the source of energy in stars

Nature has used thermonuclear fusion since the origin of the universe as the source of energy in stars, where high temperatures (over 15 megakelvins) and huge gravity provide the kinetic energy and high density needed to initiate fusion reactions. The chief process in solar-mass stars like our sun is called the proton–proton cycle:

The Proton–Proton Cycle

$$2\left[{}^{1}_{1}\text{H} + {}^{1}_{1}\text{H}\right] \longrightarrow 2\,{}^{2}_{1}\text{H} + 2\,{}^{0}_{1}e + 2\nu$$

$$2\left[{}^{1}_{1}\text{H} + {}^{2}_{1}\text{H}\right] \longrightarrow 2\,{}^{3}_{2}\text{He} + 2\gamma$$

$${}^{3}_{2}\text{He} + {}^{3}_{2}\text{He} \longrightarrow {}^{4}_{2}\text{He} + {}^{1}_{1}\text{H} + {}^{1}_{1}\text{H}$$

$$\text{Net:} \quad 4\,{}^{1}_{1}\text{H} \longrightarrow {}^{4}_{2}\text{He} + 2\,{}^{0}_{1}e + 2\nu + 2\gamma$$

The positrons produced combine with electrons in the plasma, annihilate each other, and generate additional energy and gamma radiation. Virtually all the neutrinos escape the sun and move into the solar system (and beyond), carrying with them a little less than 2% of the energy generated by the cycle. Not counting the energy of the neutrinos, each operation of one cycle generates 26.2 MeV or 4.20×10^{-12} J, which is equivalent to 2.53×10^{12} J per *mole* of alpha particles produced. This is the source of the solar energy radiated throughout our system, which can continue in this way for another 5 billion years.

☐ Even at a temperature of 15 megakelvins, the rate of energy production per cubic centimeter by fusion in the sun is quite small, only about 10^{-4} J s^{-1} cm^{-3}. (That's thousands of times less than the rate at which a human body generates heat!) But because the sun has such a large volume, the *total* rate of energy production is enormous.

SUMMARY

The Einstein Equation. Mass and energy are interconvertible. The **Einstein equation,** $\Delta E = \Delta mc^2$ (where c is the speed of light), lets us calculate one from the other. The total of the energy in the universe and all the mass calculated as an equivalent of energy is a constant, which is the **law of conservation of mass–energy.**

Nuclear Binding Energies. When a nucleus forms from its nucleons, some mass changes into energy. This amount of energy, the **nuclear binding energy,** would be required to break up the nucleus again. The higher the binding energy per nucleon, the more stable is the nucleus.

Radioactivity. The *electrostatic force* by which protons repel each other is overcome in the nucleus by the *nuclear strong force.* The ratio of neutrons to protons is a factor in nuclear stability. By radioactivity, the naturally occurring **radionuclides** adjust their neutron-to-proton ratios, lower their energies, and so become more stable by emitting **alpha** or **beta radiation,** sometimes gamma radiation as well.

The loss of an **alpha particle** leaves a nucleus with four fewer units of mass number and two fewer of atomic number. Loss of a **beta particle** leaves a nucleus with the same mass number and an atomic number one unit higher. **Gamma radiation** lets a nucleus lose some energy without a change in mass or atomic number. Depending on the specific isotope, synthetic radionuclides emit alpha, beta, and gamma radiation. Some emit **positrons** (positive electrons, a form of **antimatter**) that produce gamma radiation by annihilation collisions with electrons. Other synthetic radionuclides decay by **electron capture** and emit **X rays.** Some radionuclides emit neutrons.

Nuclear equations are balanced when the mass numbers and atomic numbers on either side of the arrow respectively balance. The energies of emission are usually described in **electron volts (eV)** or multiples thereof (1 eV $= 1.602 \times 10^{-19}$ J).

A few very long-lived radionuclides in nature, like ^{238}U, are at the heads of **radioactive disintegration series,** which represent the successive decays of "daughter" radionuclides until a stable isotope forms.

Nuclear Stability. Stable nuclides generally fall within a curving band, called the **band of stability,** when all known nuclides are plotted according to their numbers of neutrons and protons. Radionuclides that have too high neutron-to-proton ratios eject beta particles to adjust their ratios downward. Those with neutron-to-proton ratios too low generally emit positrons to change their ratios upward.

Isotopes whose nuclei consist of even numbers of both neutrons and protons are generally much more stable than those with odd numbers of both; this is the **odd–even rule.** Having all neutrons paired and all protons paired is energetically better (more stable) than having any nucleon unpaired. Isotopes with specific numbers of protons or neutrons, the **magic numbers** of 2, 8, 20, 28, 50, 82, and 126, are generally more stable than others.

Transmutation. When a bombardment particle—a proton, deuteron, alpha particle, or neutron—is captured, the resulting **compound nucleus** contains the energy of both the captured particle and its nucleons. The mode of decay of the compound nucleus is a function of its extra energy, not its extra mass. Many radionuclides have been made by these nuclear reactions, including all of the elements from atomic number 93 and higher.

Detecting and Measuring Radiations. Instruments to detect and measure **ionizing radiation—Geiger counters** or **scintillation counters,** for example—take advantage of the ability of radiation to generate ions in air or other matter. Such radiation can harm living tissue by producing **free radicals.**

The **curie (Ci)** and the **becquerel (Bq),** the SI unit, describe how active a source is; 1 Ci $= 3.7 \times 10^{10}$ Bq where 1 Bq $=$ 1 disintegration s^{-1}.

The SI unit of absorbed dose, the **gray (Gy),** is used to describe how much energy is absorbed by a unit mass of absorber; 1 Gy $= 1$ J kg^{-1}. An older unit, the **rad,** is equal to 0.01 Gy.

The **sievert,** an SI unit, and the **rem,** an older unit, are used to compare doses absorbed by different tissues and caused by different kinds of radiation. A 600 rem whole body dose is lethal.

The normal **background radiation** causes millirem exposures per year. Naturally occurring radon, cosmic rays, radionuclides in soil and stone building materials, medical X rays, and releases from nuclear tests or from nuclear power plants all contribute to this background.

Protection against radiation can be achieved by using dense shields (e.g., lead or thick concrete), by avoiding overuse of radionuclides or X rays in medicine, and by taking advantage of the **inverse square law.** This law tells us that the intensity of radiation decreases with the square of the distance from its source.

Applications. **Tracer analysis** uses small amounts of a radionuclide, which can be detected using devices like the scintillation counter, to follow the path of chemical and biological processes. In **neutron activation analysis,** neutron bombardment causes some elements to become γ emitters. The radiation can be detected and measured, giving the identity and concentration of the activated elements. **Radiological dating** uses the known half-lives of naturally occurring radionuclides to date geological and archeological objects.

Fission and Fusion. Uranium-235, which occurs naturally, and plutonium-239, which can be made from uranium-238, are **fissile isotopes** that serve as the fuel in present-day reactors. When either isotope captures a thermal neutron, the isotope splits in one of several ways to give two smaller isotopes plus energy and more neutrons. The neutrons can generate additional fission events, enabling a nuclear chain reaction. If a critical mass of a fissile isotope is allowed to form, the **nuclear chain reaction** proceeds out of control, and the material detonates as an atomic bomb explosion. *Pressurized water reactors* are the most commonly used fission reactors for power generation, and have two loops of circulating fluids. In the primary loop, water circulates around the reactor core and absorbs the heat of fission. In the secondary loop, water accepts the heat and changes to high-pressure steam, which drives the electrical generator. One major problem with nuclear energy is the storage of radioactive wastes.

Thermonuclear fusion joins two light nuclei to form a heavier nucleus with the release of more energy than nuclear fission. A typical reaction combines ^2_1H and ^3_1H to give ^4_2He and a neutron. High temperatures and pressures are necessary to initiate the fusion reaction. In stars, gravity is able to contain the high temperature **plasma** and allow fusion to occur. In a hydrogen bomb, the reaction is initiated by a fission bomb. Scientific and engineering hurdles must still be overcome before fusion can be a viable peaceful energy source.

TOOLS FOR PROBLEM SOLVING

In this chapter you learned to apply the following concepts as tools in solving problems related to nuclear changes and their applications. Study each tool carefully so that you know what each is used for. When faced with solving a problem, recall what each tool does and consider whether it will be helpful in finding a solution. This will aid you in selecting the tools you need.

The Einstein equation *(page 822)* This equation, $\Delta E = \Delta m_0 c^2$ (or often just $E = mc^2$), is used when you have to relate an amount of mass to its equivalent in energy. Be careful of units in using the equation. To obtain joules, mass must be in units of kilograms and c must have units of m/s (because $1\,J = 1\,kg\,m^2\,s^{-2}$).

Nuclear equations *(page 825)* When you have to write and balance a nuclear equation, remember to apply the following two criteria:

1. The sums of the mass numbers on each side of the arrow must be equal.
2. The sums of the atomic numbers on each side must be the same.

The odd–even rule *(page 832)* This rule allows you to judge and compare the likely stability of nuclei according to their numbers of protons and neutrons.

When the numbers of neutrons and protons in a nucleus are both even, the isotope is far more likely to be stable than when both numbers are odd.

Law of radioactive decay *(page 837)* Use this law to relate the *activity* (in units of disintegrations per second, or Bq) to the *decay constant, k* (a first-order rate constant), and the number of atoms of the radionuclide in the sample, *N*. The activity is a quantity that can be measured using a Geiger or scintillation counter.

$$\text{Activity} = -\frac{\Delta N}{\Delta t} = kN$$

Half-life of a radionuclide *(page 837)* When you know the half-life of an isotope (which is available in tables), you can calculate the decay constant, *k*. This is useful when you need to apply the law of radioactive decay (see above).

$$t_{1/2} = \frac{\ln 2}{k}$$

Inverse square law *(page 840)* This simple law lets you compute radiation intensity at various distances from a radioactive source. If the intensity, I_1, is known at distance d_1, then the intensity I_2 at distance d_2 can be calculated by

$$\frac{I_1}{I_2} = \frac{d_2^{\,2}}{d_1^{\,2}}$$

QUESTIONS, PROBLEMS, AND EXERCISES

Answers to problems whose numbers are printed in color are given in Appendix B. More challenging problems are marked with asterisks. ILW = Interactive Learningware solution is available at www.wiley.com/college/brady. OH = an Office Hours video is available for this problem.

REVIEW QUESTIONS

Conservation of Mass–Energy

20.1 In chemical calculations involving chemical reactions we can regard the law of conservation of mass as a law independent of the law of conservation of energy despite Einstein's union of the two. What fact(s) makes this possible?

20.2 How can we know that the speed of light is the absolute upper limit on the speed of any object?

20.3 State the following.
(a) law of conservation of mass–energy
(b) Einstein equation

20.4 Why isn't the sum of the masses of all nucleons in one nucleus equal to the mass of the actual nucleus?

Radioactivity

20.5 When a substance is described as *radioactive*, what does that mean? Why is the term *radioactive decay* used to describe the phenomenon?

20.6 Three kinds of radiation make up nearly all of the radiation observed from naturally occurring radionuclides. What are they?

20.7 Give the composition of each of the following.
(a) alpha particle   (c) positron
(b) beta particle   (d) deuteron

20.8 Why is the penetrating ability of alpha radiation less than that of beta or gamma radiation?

20.9 With respect to their formation, how do gamma rays and X rays differ?

20.10 How does electron capture generate X rays?

Nuclear Stability

20.11 What data are plotted and what criterion is used to identify the actual band in the band of stability?

20.12 Both barium-123 and barium-140 are radioactive, but which is more likely to have the *longer* half-life? Explain your answer.

20.13 Tin-112 is a stable nuclide but indium-112 is radioactive and has a very short half-life ($t_{1/2} = 14$ min). What does tin-112 have that indium-112 does not to account for this difference in stability?

20.14 Lanthanum-139 is a stable nuclide but lanthanum-140 is unstable ($t_{1/2} = 40$ hr). What rule of thumb concerning nuclear stability is involved?

20.15 As the atomic number increases, the neutron-to-proton ratio increases. What does this suggest is a factor in nuclear stability?

20.16 Radionuclides of high atomic number are far more likely to be alpha emitters than those of low atomic number. Offer an explanation for this phenomenon.

20.17 Although lead-164 has two magic numbers, 82 protons and 82 neutrons, this isotope is unknown. Lead-208, however, is known and stable. What problem accounts for the nonexistence of lead-164?

20.18 What decay particle is emitted from a nucleus of low to intermediate atomic number but a relatively high neutron-to-proton ratio? How does the emission of this particle benefit the nucleus?

20.19 What decay particle is emitted from a nucleus of low to intermediate atomic number but a relatively low neutron-to-proton ratio? How does the emission of this particle benefit the nucleus?

20.20 What does electron capture do to the neutron-to-proton ratio in a nucleus, increase it, decrease it, or leave it alone? Which kinds of radionuclides are more likely to undergo this change, those above or those below the band of stability?

Transmutations

20.21 Compound nuclei form and then decay almost at once. What accounts for the instability of a compound nucleus?

20.22 What explains the existence of several decay modes for the compound nucleus aluminum-27?

20.23 Rutherford theorized that a compound nucleus forms when helium nuclei hit nitrogen-14 nuclei. If this compound nucleus decayed by the loss of a neutron instead of a proton, what would be the other product?

Detecting and Measuring Radiations

20.24 What specific property of nuclear radiation is used by the Geiger counter?

20.25 Dangerous doses of radiation can actually involve very small quantities of energy. Explain.

20.26 What units, SI and common, are used to describe each of the following?
(a) the *activity* of a radioactive sample
(b) the *energy* of a particle or of a photon of radiation given off by a nucleus
(c) the amount of energy absorbed by a given mass from a dose of radiation
(d) dose equivalents for comparing biological effects

20.27 A sample giving 3.7×10^{10} disintegrations s^{-1} has what activity in Ci and in Bq?

20.28 Explain the necessity in health sciences for the *sievert*.

Applications of Radionuclides

20.29 Why should a radionuclide used in diagnostic work have a short half-life? If the half-life is too short, what problem arises?

20.30 An alpha emitter is not used in diagnostic work. Why?

20.31 In general terms, explain how neutron activation analysis is used and how it works.

20.32 What is one assumption in the use of the uranium/lead ratio for dating ancient geologic formations?

*__20.33__ If a sample used for carbon-14 dating is contaminated by air, there is a potentially serious problem with the method. What is it?

20.34 List some of the kinds of radiation that make up our background radiation.

Nuclear Fission and Fusion

20.35 Why is it easier for a nucleus to capture a neutron than a proton?

20.36 What do each of the following terms mean?
(a) thermal neutron
(b) nuclear fission
(c) fissile isotope
(d) nuclear fusion

20.37 Which fissile isotope occurs in nature?

20.38 What fact about the fission of uranium-235 makes it possible for a *chain reaction* to occur?

20.39 Explain in general terms why fission generates more neutrons than needed to initiate it.

20.40 Why would there be a *subcritical mass* of a fissile isotope? (Why isn't *any* mass of uranium-235 critical?)

20.41 What purpose is served by a *moderator* in a nuclear reactor?

20.42 Why is there no possibility of an atomic bomb explosion from a nuclear power plant?

20.43 Write the nuclear equation for the fusion reaction between deuterium and tritium. Why must tritium be synthesized for this reaction?

20.44 What obstacles make constructing a reactor for controlled nuclear fusion especially difficult?

REVIEW PROBLEMS

Conservation of Mass–Energy

20.45 Calculate the mass equivalent in grams of 1.00 kJ.

*20.46 Calculate the mass in kilograms of a 1.00 kg object when its velocity, relative to us, is (a) 3.00×10^7 m s^{-1}, (b) 2.90×10^8 m s^{-1}, and (c) 2.99×10^8 m s^{-1}. (Notice the progression of these numbers toward the velocity of light, 3.00×10^8 m s^{-1}.)

OH 20.47 Calculate the amount of mass in nanograms that is changed into energy when one mole of liquid water forms by the combustion of hydrogen, all measurements being made at 1 atm and 25 °C. What percentage is this of the total mass of the reactants?

20.48 Show that the mass equivalent to the energy released by the complete combustion of 1 mol of methane (890 kJ) is 9.89 ng.

Nuclear Binding Energies

ILW 20.49 Calculate the binding energy in joules per nucleon of the **OH** deuterium nucleus, whose mass is 2.0135 u.

20.50 Calculate the binding energy in joules per nucleon of the tritium nucleus, whose mass is 3.01550 u.

Radioactivity

20.51 Complete the following nuclear equations by writing the symbols of the missing particles
(a) $^{211}_{82}\text{Pb} \longrightarrow {}^{0}_{-1}e + \underline{\quad}$
(b) $^{177}_{73}\text{Ta} \xrightarrow{\text{electron capture}} \underline{\quad}$
(c) $^{220}_{86}\text{Rn} \longrightarrow {}^{4}_{2}\text{He} + \underline{\quad}$
(d) $^{19}_{10}\text{Ne} \longrightarrow {}^{0}_{1}e + \underline{\quad}$

20.52 Write the symbols of the missing particles to complete the following nuclear equations.
(a) $^{245}_{96}\text{Cm} \longrightarrow {}^{4}_{2}\text{He} + \underline{\quad}$
(b) $^{146}_{56}\text{Ba} \longrightarrow {}^{0}_{-1}e + \underline{\quad}$

(c) $^{58}_{29}\text{Cu} \longrightarrow {}^{0}_{1}e + \underline{\quad}$
(d) $^{68}_{32}\text{Ge} \xrightarrow{\text{electron capture}} \underline{\quad}$

20.53 Write a balanced nuclear equation for each of the following changes.
(a) alpha emission from plutonium-242
(b) beta emission from magnesium-28
(c) positron emission from silicon-26
(d) electron capture by argon-37

OH 20.54 Write the balanced nuclear equation for each of the following nuclear reactions.
(a) electron capture by iron-55
(b) beta emission by potassium-42
(c) positron emission by ruthenium-93
(d) alpha emission by californium-251

20.55 Write the symbols, including the atomic and mass numbers, for the radionuclides that would give each of the following products.
(a) fermium-257 by alpha emission
(b) bismuth-211 by beta emission
(c) neodymium-141 by positron emission
(d) tantalum-179 by electron capture

20.56 Each of the following nuclides forms by the decay mode described. Write the symbols of the parents, giving both atomic and mass numbers.
(a) rubidium-80 formed by electron capture
(b) antimony-121 formed by beta emission
(c) chromium-50 formed by positron emission
(d) californium-253 formed by alpha emission

20.57 Krypton-87 decays to krypton-86. What other particle forms?

20.58 Write the symbol of the nuclide that forms from cobalt-58 when it decays by electron capture.

Nuclear Stability

OH 20.59 If an atom of potassium-38 had the option of decaying by positron emission or beta emission, which route would it likely take, and why? Write the nuclear equation.

20.60 Suppose that an atom of argon-37 could decay by either beta emission or electron capture. Which route would it likely take, and why? Write the nuclear equation.

20.61 If we begin with 3.00 mg of iodine-131 ($t_{1/2} = 8.07$ days), how much remains after 6 half-life periods?

20.62 A sample of technetium-99m with a mass of 9.00 ng will have decayed to how much of this radionuclide after 4 half-life periods (about 1 day)?

Transmutations

20.63 When vanadium-51 captures a deuteron ($^{2}_{1}\text{H}$), what compound nucleus forms? (Write its symbol.) This particle expels a proton ($^{1}_{1}p$). Write the nuclear equation for the overall change from vanadium-51.

20.64 The alpha-particle bombardment of fluorine-19 generates sodium-22 and neutrons. Write the nuclear equation, including the intermediate compound nucleus.

OH 20.65 Gamma-ray bombardment of bromine-81 causes a transmutation in which a neutron is one product. Write the symbol of the other product.

20.66 Neutron bombardment of cadmium-115 results in neutron capture and the release of gamma radiation. Write the nuclear equation.

20.67 When manganese-55 is bombarded by protons, each ^{55}Mn nucleus releases a neutron. What else forms? Write the nuclear equation.

20.68 Which nuclide forms when sodium-23 is bombarded by alpha particles and the compound nucleus emits a gamma-ray photon?

20.69 The nuclei of which isotope of zinc-70 would be needed as bombardment particles to make nuclei of element 112 from lead-208 if the intermediate compound nucleus loses a neutron?

20.70 Write the symbol of the nuclide whose nuclei would be the target for bombardment by nickel-64 nuclei to produce nuclei of $^{272}_{111}$Rg after the intermediate compound nucleus loses a neutron.

Detecting and Measuring Radiations

20.71 Suppose that a radiologist who is 2.0 m from a small, unshielded source of radiation receives 2.8 units of radiation. To reduce the exposure to 0.28 units of radiation, to what distance from the source should the radiologist move?

20.72 By what percentage should a radiation specialist increase the distance from a small unshielded source to reduce the radiation intensity by 10.0%?

OH 20.73 If exposure from a distance of 1.60 m gave a worker a dose of 8.4 rem, how far should the worker move away from the source to reduce the dose to 0.50 rem for the same period?

20.74 During work with a radioactive source, a worker was told that he would receive 50 mrem at a distance of 4.0 m during 30 min of work. What would be the received dose if the worker moved closer, to 0.50 m, for the same period?

Law of Radioactive Decay

20.75 Smoke detectors contain a small amount of americium-241, which has a half-life of 1.70×10^5 days. If the detector contains 0.20 mg of ^{241}Am, what is the activity, in becquerels? In microcuries?

20.76 Strontium-90 is a dangerous radioisotope present in fallout produced by nuclear weapons. ^{90}Sr has a half-life of 1.00×10^4 days. What is the activity of 1.00 g of ^{90}Sr, in becquerels? In microcuries?

20.77 Iodine-131 is a radioisotope present in radioactive fallout that targets the thyroid gland. If 1.00 mg of ^{131}I has an activity of 4.6×10^{12} Bq, what is the decay constant for ^{131}I? What is the half-life, in seconds?

20.78 A 10.0 mg sample of thallium-201 has an activity of 7.9×10^{13} Bq. What is the decay constant for ^{201}Tl? What is the half-life of ^{201}Tl, in seconds?

Applications of Radionuclides

OH 20.79 What percentage of cesium chloride made from cesium-137 ($t_{1/2} = 30$ y; beta emitter) remains after 150 y? What *chemical* product forms?

20.80 A sample of waste has a radioactivity, caused solely by strontium-90 (beta emitter, $t_{1/2} = 28.1$ yr), of 0.245 Ci g^{-1}. How many years will it take for its activity to decrease to 1.00×10^{-6} Ci g^{-1}?

20.81 A worker in a laboratory unknowingly became exposed to a sample of radiolabeled sodium iodide made from iodine-131 (beta emitter, $t_{1/2} = 8.07$ days). The mistake was realized 28.0 days after the accidental exposure, at which time the activity of the sample was 25.6×10^{-5} Ci g^{-1}. The safety officer needed to know how active the sample was at the time of the exposure. Calculate that value in curies per gram.

20.82 Technetium-99*m* (gamma emitter, $t_{1/2} = 6.02$ hr) is widely used for diagnosis in medicine. A sample prepared in the early morning for use that day had an activity of 4.52×10^{-6} Ci. What will its activity be at the end of the day, that is, after 8.00 hr?

20.83 A 0.500 g sample of rock was found to have 2.45×10^{-6} mol of potassium-40 ($t_{1/2} = 1.3 \times 10^9$ yr) and 2.45×10^{-6} mol of argon-40. How old was the rock? (What assumption is made about the origin of the argon-40?)

20.84 If a rock sample was found to contain 1.16×10^{-7} mol of argon-40, how much potassium-40 would also have to be present for the rock to be 1.3×10^9 years old?

20.85 A tree killed by being buried under volcanic ash was found to have a ratio of carbon-14 atoms to carbon-12 atoms of 4.8×10^{-14}. How long ago did the eruption occur?

20.86 A wooden door lintel from an excavated site in Mexico would be expected to have what ratio of carbon-14 to carbon-12 atoms if the lintel is 9.0×10^3 y old?

Nuclear Energy

OH 20.87 Complete the following nuclear equation by supplying the symbol for the other product of the fission.

$$^{235}_{92}\text{U} + {}^{1}_{0}n \longrightarrow {}^{94}_{38}\text{Sr} + \underline{\quad\quad} + 2\,{}^{1}_{0}n$$

20.88 Both products of the fission in the previous problem are unstable. According to Figures 20.8 and 20.9, what is the most likely way for each of them to decay, by alpha emission, beta emission, or by positron emission? Explain. What are some of the possible fates of the extra neutrons produced by the fission shown in the previous problem?

ADDITIONAL EXERCISES

20.89 What is the nuclear equation for each of the following changes?
(a) beta emission from aluminum-30
(b) alpha emission from einsteinium-252
(c) electron capture by molybdenum-93
(d) positron emission by phosphorus-28

*20.90 Calculate to three significant figures the binding energy in joules per nucleon of the nucleus of an atom of iron-56. The observed mass of one *atom* is 55.9349 u. What information lets us know that no isotope has a *larger* binding energy per nucleon?

*20.91 Calculate to five significant figures the binding energy in joules per nucleon of uranium-235. The observed mass of one *atom* is 235.0439 u.

20.92 Give the nuclear equation for each of these changes.
(a) positron emission by carbon-10
(b) alpha emission by curium-243
(c) electron capture by vanadium-49
(d) beta emission by oxygen-20

*20.93 If a positron is to be emitted spontaneously, how much more *mass* (as a minimum) must an *atom* of the parent have than an *atom* of the daughter nuclide? Explain.

20.94 If a proton and an antiproton were to collide and produce two annihilation photons, what would the wavelength of the photons be, in meters? Which of the decimal multipliers in Table 1.4 (page 12) would be most appropriate for expressing this wavelength?

20.95 There is a gain in binding energy per nucleon when light nuclei fuse to form heavier nuclei. Yet, a tritium atom and a deuterium atom, in a mixture of these isotopes, does not spontaneously fuse to give helium (and energy). Explain why not.

20.96 ^{214}Bi decays to isotope *A* by alpha emission; *A* then decays to *B* by beta emission, which decays to *C* by another beta emission. Element *C* decays to *D* by still another beta emission, and *D* decays by alpha emission to a stable isotope, *E*. What is the proper symbol of element *E*? (Contributed by Prof. W. J. Wysochansky, Georgia Southern University.)

20.97 ^{15}O decays by positron emission with a half-life of 124 s. (a) Give the proper symbol of the product of the decay. (b) How much of a 750 mg sample of ^{15}O remains after 5.0 min of decay? (Contributed by Prof. W. J. Wysochansky, Georgia Southern University.)

20.98 Alpha decay of ^{238}U forms ^{234}Th. What kind of decay from ^{234}Th produces ^{234}Ac? (Contributed by Prof. Mark Benvenuto, University of Detroit—Mercy.)

20.99 A sample of rock was found to contain 2.07×10^{-5} mol of ^{40}K and 1.15×10^{-5} mol of ^{40}Ar. If we assume that all of the ^{40}Ar came from the decay of ^{40}K, what is the age of the rock in years ($t_{1/2} = 1.3 \times 10^9$ years for ^{40}K.)

20.100 The ^{14}C content of an ancient piece of wood was found to be one-eighth of that in living trees. How many years old is this piece of wood ($t_{1/2} = 5730$ years for ^{14}C)?

20.101 Dinitrogen trioxide, N_2O_3, is largely dissociated into NO and NO_2 in the gas phase where there exists the equilibrium, $N_2O_3 \rightleftharpoons NO + NO_2$. In an effort to determine the structure of N_2O_3, a mixture of NO and $^*NO_2$ was prepared containing isotopically labeled N in the NO_2. After a period of time the mixture was analyzed and found to contain substantial amounts of both $^*NO$ and $^*NO_2$. Explain how this is consistent with the structure for N_2O_3 being ONONO.

20.102 The reaction $(CH_3)_2Hg + HgI_2 \rightarrow 2CH_3HgI$ is believed to occur through a transition state with the structure

$$H_3C \diagdown \qquad \diagup I$$
$$Hg \qquad Hg$$
$$\diagup \qquad \diagdown$$
$$CH_3 \qquad I$$

If this is so, what should be observed if $(CH_3)_2Hg$ and $^*HgI_2$ are mixed, where the asterisk denotes a radioactive isotope of Hg? Explain your answer.

*__20.103__ A large, complex piece of apparatus has built into it a cooling system containing an unknown volume of cooling liquid. It is desired to measure the volume of the coolant without draining the lines. To the coolant was added 10.0 mL of methanol whose molecules included atoms of ^{14}C and that had a specific activity of 580 counts per minute per gram (cpm/g), determined using a Geiger counter. The coolant was permitted to circulate to assure complete mixing before a sample was withdrawn that was found to have a specific activity of 29 cpm/g. Calculate the volume of coolant in the system in milliliters. The density of methanol is 0.792 g/mL, and the density of the coolant is 0.884 g/mL.

*__20.104__ A complex ion of chromium(III) with oxalate ion was prepared from ^{51}Cr-labeled $K_2Cr_2O_7$, having a specific activity of 843 cpm/g (counts per minute per gram), and ^{14}C-labeled oxalic acid, $H_2C_2O_4$, having an specific activity of 345 cpm/g. Chromium-51 decays by electron capture with the emission of gamma radiation, whereas ^{14}C is a pure beta emitter. Because of the characteristics of the beta and gamma detectors, each of these isotopes may be counted independently. A sample of the complex ion was observed to give a gamma count of 165 cpm and a beta count of 83 cpm. From these data, determine the number of oxalate ions bound to each Cr(III) in the complex ion. (Hint: For the starting materials calculate the cpm per mole of Cr and oxalate, respectively.)

20.105 Iodine-131 is used to treat Graves disease, a disease of the thyroid gland. The amount of ^{131}I used depends on the size of the gland. If the dose is 86 microcuries per gram of thyroid gland, how many grams of ^{131}I should be administered to a patient with a thyroid gland weighing 20 g? Assume all the iodine administered accumulates in the thyroid gland.

20.106 The fuel for a thermonuclear bomb (hydrogen bomb) is lithium deuteride, a salt composed of the ions $^6_3Li^+$ and $^2_1H^-$. Considering the nuclear reaction

$$^6_3Li + \, ^1_1n \rightarrow \, ^4_2He + \, ^3_1H$$

explain how a ^{235}U fission bomb could serve as a trigger for a fusion bomb. Write appropriate nuclear equations.

20.107 In 2006, the confirmed synthesis of $^{294}_{118}$Uuo (an isotope of element 118) was reported to involve the bombardment of ^{245}Cf with ^{48}Ca. Write an equation for the nuclear reaction, being sure to include any other products of the reaction.

*__20.108__ Radon, a radioactive noble gas, is an environmental problem in some areas, where it can seep out of the ground and into homes. Exposure to radon-222, an alpha emitter with a half-life of 3.823 days, can increase the risk of lung cancer. At an exposure level of 4 pCi per liter (the level at which the EPA recommends action), the lifetime risk of death from lung cancer due to radon exposure is estimated to be 62 out of 1,000 for current smokers, compared with 73 out of 10,000 for nonsmokers. If the air in a home was analyzed and found to have an activity of 4.1 pCi L^{-1}, how many atoms of ^{222}Rn are there per liter of air?

*__20.109__ The isotope ^{145}Pr decays by emission of beta particles with an energy of 1.80 MeV each. Suppose a person swallowed, by accident, 1.0 mg of Pr having a specific activity (activity per gram) of 140 Bq g^{-1}. What would be the absorbed dose from ^{145}Pr in units of Gy and rad over a period of 10 minutes? Assume all the beta particles are absorbed by the person's body.

EXERCISES IN CRITICAL THINKING

20.110 A silver wire coated with nonradioactive silver chloride is placed into a solution of sodium chloride that is labeled with radioactive ^{36}Cl. After a while, the AgCl was analyzed and found to contain some ^{36}Cl. How do you interpret the results of this experiment?

20.111 Suppose you were given a piece of cotton cloth and told that it was believed to be 2000 years old. You performed a carbon dating test on a tiny piece of the cloth and your data indicated that it was only 800 years old. If the cloth really was 2000 years old, what factors might account for your results?

20.112 In 2006, the former Soviet spy Alexander Litvinenko was poisoned by the polonium isotope ^{210}Po. He died 23 days after ingesting the isotope, which is an alpha emitter. Find data on the Internet to answer the following: Assuming Litvinenko was fed 1 μg of ^{210}Po and that it became uniformly distributed through the cells in his body, how many atoms of ^{210}Po made their way into each cell in his body? (Assume his body contained the average number of cells found in an adult human.) Also calculate the number of cells affected by the radiation each second, being sure to take into account an estimate of the average number of cells affected by an alpha particle emitted by a ^{210}Po nucleus.

20.113 What would be the formula of the simplest hydrogen compound of element 116? Would a solution of that compound in water be acidic, basic, or neutral? Explain your reasoning.

20.114 Astatine is a halogen. Its most stable isotope, ^{210}At, has a half-life of only 8.3 hours, and only very minute amounts of the element are ever available for study (<0.001 μg). This amount is so small as to be virtually invisible. Describe experiments you might perfom that would tell you whether the silver salt of astatine, AgAt, is insoluble in water.

NONMETALS, METALLOIDS, METALS, AND METAL COMPLEXES

A chemical found in many brands of shampoo is EDTA, which is able to form stable complexes with ions found in hard water. These ions, which include Ca^{2+} and Mg^{2+}, can interfere with the action of soaps and some detergents and inhibit the formation of a nice lather, like the one shown here. Complexes of metal ions with EDTA and other substances are studied in detail in this chapter. *(Beauty Photo studio/Age Fotostock America, Inc.)*

CHAPTER OUTLINE

THIS CHAPTER IN CONTEXT   In previous chapters you learned many of the concepts that ch have used to develop their understanding of how the elements react with each other and the kinds of com they produce. For example, in our discussions of chemical kinetics, you learned how various factors affect th of reactions, and in our study of thermodynamics you learned how enthalpy and entropy changes affect the ity of observing chemical changes. Our focus, however, was primarily on the concepts themselves, with exam chemical behavior being used to reinforce and justify them. With these concepts available to us now, we wi our emphasis in the opposite direction and examine some of the physical and chemical properties of the elements and their compounds.

Our intent in this chapter is not to be encyclopedic. Instead, we will concentrate our attention on several aspects of the chemistries of the elements. We will study how the elements occur in nature and explore the methods used to obtain them in their free (uncombined) states. For metals, their extraction from compounds constitutes a vast commercial enterprise under the general heading of *metallurgy*.

In their free states, the nonmetallic elements exist in a broad range of structures, ranging from simple atoms to very complex molecular forms. We will study how the relative tendencies of the nonmetals to form strong σ and π bonds influences the kinds of structures observed.

The last part of the chapter is devoted to an in-depth look at complex ions of metals, a topic first introduced in Chapter 17. These substances, which have applications from food preservatives to catalyzing biochemical reactions, have a variety of structures and colors. We will study the kinds of substances that combine with metals to form complexes with various geometries, how complexes are named, and how the electronic structures and colors of complexes can be explained.

21.1 | NONMETALS AND METALLOIDS ARE FOUND AS FREE ELEMENTS AND IN COMPOUNDS

As you learned in Chapter 2, the nonmetals and metalloids are located at the right side of the periodic table (Figure 21.1). As suggested by their positions in the table, metalloids have properties that place them between those of metals and nonmetals. For instance, metalloids have a sheen that gives them the appearance of a metal, and they exhibit weak electrical conductivity (many are semiconductors). Chemically, however, they behave more like nonmetals. For example, metalloids combine with the more active metals in Groups IA and IIA to form compounds that are saltlike, containing anions such as Si^{4-}, As^{3-}, and Te^{2-} (more complex anions are also formed), and they also combine with nonmetals to form molecular compounds in which their oxidation numbers are positive.

A sample of crystalline elemental silicon exhibits a metallic sheen. *(Jeff J. Daly/ Fundamental Photographs.)*

Nonmetals occur in compounds and in the free state

Most chemical compounds contain one or more nonmetals. In compounds involving metals, nonmetals occur as either simple anions or in polyatomic anions. Many other compounds are composed of only nonmetals in combinations that range from simple (such as HCl) to very complex (such as DNA).

It is difficult to make general statements about the preparation of the elemental nonmetals. The noble gases, for example, are always found uncombined in nature. The atmosphere is the major source of the noble gases, even though their concentrations in air

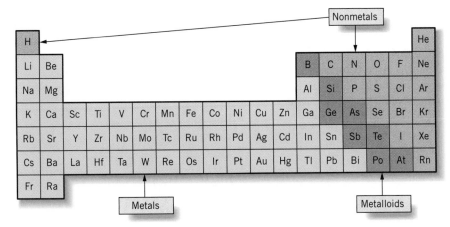

FIG. 21.1 Distribution of nonmetals and metalloids in the periodic table.

□ Noble gas atoms have completed *s* and *p* subshells in their outer shells and are very unreactive. They have very little tendency to form bonds to other atoms.

are very small. Physical methods are used to separate them from other gases with which they're mixed. Of the noble gases, only helium and radon are not obtained primarily from the atmosphere. Helium is found in gaseous deposits beneath the earth's crust where it has collected after being produced by the capture of electrons by alpha particles (helium nuclei, He^{2+}), which are formed during the radioactive decay of elements such as uranium. Radon itself is radioactive and is produced by the radioactive decay of radium.

$$^{226}Ra \longrightarrow {}^{222}Rn + {}^4He$$

Since radon spontaneously decomposes into other elements relatively quickly ($t_{1/2} = 3.8$ days), it occurs only in minute quantities in nature.

Other nonmetals, while present in many naturally occurring compounds, also are found extensively in the free state as well. For instance, our atmosphere is composed primarily of elemental nitrogen, N_2 (about 80%), and oxygen, O_2 (about 20%). Although nitrogen and oxygen are also found in a vast number of compounds, certainly their most economical source is simply the air itself. Sulfur and carbon are two other elements that occur naturally in both the combined and free states. There are, for instance, many naturally occurring sulfates (for example, $BaSO_4$ and $CaSO_4 \cdot 2H_2O$) and sulfides (FeS_2, CuS, HgS, PbS, and ZnS). In the free state, sulfur has been found in large underground deposits from which it is mined by forcing superheated water under pressure into the sulfur, causing the sulfur to melt. Once molten, the sulfur–water mixture is foamed to the surface using compressed air. Sulfur is also deposited on rock surfaces near volcanic vents and is called *brimstone.*

Turning to carbon, we find that most of its naturally occurring compounds are carbonates, for example, limestone ($CaCO_3$). In the free state most carbon is found in either of its two principal forms, diamond and graphite.

Elemental sulfur in nature.
Sulfur is one of the substances released from the earth during volcanic eruptions. Here we see molten sulfur pouring from a vent in the Kawah Ijen volcano in Indonesia. (© *API/Explorer/ Photo Researchers.)*

Nonmetals are obtained from compounds by either oxidation or reduction

Because nonmetals combine with each other as well as with metals, no simple generalizations can be made concerning their recovery from compounds. When combined with a metal, the nonmetal is found in a negative oxidation state, so an oxidation must be brought about to generate the free element. For example, the halogens Cl_2, Br_2, and I_2 can be conveniently prepared in the laboratory by reacting one of their salts with an oxidizing agent such as MnO_2 in an acidic solution:

$$2X^- + MnO_2 + 4H^+ \longrightarrow X_2 + Mn^{2+} + 2H_2O$$

where $X = $ Cl, Br, or I.

As you learned in Chapter 19, chlorine is a very important industrial chemical, and vast quantities (approximately 10 million tons annually) are produced by electrolysis of NaCl, both aqueous and molten. Chlorine is used in large amounts in water treatment, in the manufacture of pharmaceuticals, pesticides, and solvents, and in the production of vinyl chloride, which is used to manufacture vinyl plastics.

□ Remember, the larger the reduction potential, the greater is the tendency of the substance to acquire electrons and, therefore, to be an oxidizing agent.

The halogens themselves can also serve as oxidizing agents in replacement reactions. Since the tendency to acquire electrons (electronegativity) decreases as we proceed downward in a group, the ability of the halogen to serve as an oxidizing agent decreases too. This is seen in their reduction potentials (Table 21.1), which decrease from fluorine to iodine. As a result, a given halogen is a better oxidizing agent than the other halogens below it in Group VIIA and is able to displace them from their binary compounds with metals. Thus

TABLE 21.1 Reduction Potentials of the Halogens	
Reaction	$E°$(V)
$F_2(aq) + 2e^- \rightleftharpoons 2F^-(aq)$	2.87
$Cl_2(aq) + 2e^- \rightleftharpoons 2Cl^-(aq)$	1.36
$Br_2(aq) + 2e^- \rightleftharpoons 2Br^-(aq)$	1.07
$I_2(aq) + 2e^- \rightleftharpoons 2I^-(aq)$	0.54

F_2 will displace Cl^-, Br^-, and I^-, while Cl_2 will displace only Br^- and I^- but not F^-, and so on. This is illustrated by the following typical reactions.

For fluorine:

$$F_2 + \begin{Bmatrix} 2NaCl \\ 2NaBr \\ 2NaI \end{Bmatrix} \longrightarrow 2NaF + \begin{Bmatrix} Cl_2 \\ Br_2 \\ I_2 \end{Bmatrix}$$

For chlorine:

$$Cl_2 + \begin{Bmatrix} 2NaBr \\ 2NaI \end{Bmatrix} \longrightarrow 2NaCl + \begin{Bmatrix} Br_2 \\ I_2 \end{Bmatrix}$$

$$Cl_2 + 2NaF \longrightarrow \text{no reaction}$$

For bromine:

$$Br_2 + 2NaI \longrightarrow 2NaBr + I_2$$

$$Br_2 + \begin{Bmatrix} 2NaF \\ 2NaCl \end{Bmatrix} \longrightarrow \text{no reaction}$$

☐ Iodine cannot displace any of the other halogens from their compounds.

The relative oxidizing power of the halogens is used in the commercial preparation of Br_2. Bromine is isolated from seawater and brine solutions pumped from deep wells by passing Cl_2, followed by air, through the liquid. The Cl_2 oxidizes the Br^- to Br_2 and the air sweeps the volatile Br_2 from the solution.

Fluorine, because of its position as the most powerful chemical oxidizing agent, can only be obtained by electrolytic oxidation. This process must be carried out in the absence of water because water is more easily oxidized than the fluoride ion. In an aqueous solution, therefore, the oxidation

$$2H_2O(l) \longrightarrow O_2(g) + 4H^+(aq) + 4e^-$$

will occur in preference to

$$2F^-(aq) \longrightarrow F_2(g) + 2e^-$$

In practice, a molten mixture of KF and HF, which has a lower melting point than KF alone, is electrolyzed, producing H_2 at the cathode and F_2 at the anode.

☐ H^+ is more easily reduced than K^+, which is why H_2 appears at the cathode.

Nonmetals can also be extracted from their compounds by reduction if the nonmetal happens to exist in a positive oxidation state. For instance, elemental phosphorus is produced from a phosphate such as $Ca_3(PO_4)_2$, where it exists in the +5 oxidation state. To obtain the phosphorus, the $Ca_3(PO_4)_2$ is heated to approximately 1500 °C in an electric furnace with a mixture of carbon and SiO_2 (sand).[1]

$$Ca_3(PO_4)_2(s) + 3SiO_2(s) + 5C(s) \xrightarrow{\text{heat}} 3CaSiO_3(l) + 5CO(g) + 2P(g)$$

In this reaction, the SiO_2 is present to combine with the calcium to form calcium silicate, $CaSiO_3$, a compound with a relatively low melting point. Because the reduction of SiO_2 by carbon requires much higher temperatures (>1900 °C), only the phosphorus is reduced to the element at the lower temperatures used in the reaction.

☐ Most metal silicates contain polymeric anions with oxygen bridges between silicon atoms. Silicon dioxide itself has a complex structure consisting of SiO_4 tetrahedra in which each oxygen atom is shared by two silicon atoms.

Metalloids are found in nature in compounds

In most of their compounds, the metalloids are combined with nonmetals, either in a molecular structure such as SiO_2 (found in silica sand) or in an oxoanion such as those found in the silicates (found in many kinds of rocks). In such combinations, the

[1]Phosphorus was first produced in 1669 when alchemist Hennig Brandt heated a mixture of sand and dried urine. He condensed the vapors by passing them through water to give the new element. It was named phosphorus from the Greek *phosphoros* (light bringer) because the solid in a sealed bottle glowed in the dark. The glow is actually the result of slow oxidation of the phosphorus surface by residual oxygen in the container.

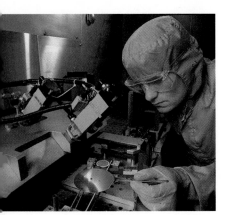

Uses of silicon as a semiconductor. A technician checks a silicon wafer during one stage in the manufacture of computer "chips." The silicon disk contains hundreds of individual chips, each consisting of thousands of electronic components. After all of the individual components have been added, the disk will be cut up to give separate chips that will be incorporated into parts for computer circuits. *(David Parker/Photo Researchers.)*

□ There are few aspects of modern life that are not impacted significantly by computer circuits embedded in silicon or germanium.

metalloid has a lower electronegativity than the nonmetal, so the metalloid exists in a positive oxidation state. To obtain the metalloid in its elemental state, therefore, a chemical reduction must be carried out. This is usually accomplished with either hydrogen or carbon as the reducing agent. For example, boron is obtained by passing a mixture of BCl_3 vapor and hydrogen gas over a hot wire, on which the following reaction takes place.

$$2BCl_3(g) + 3H_2(g) \longrightarrow 2B(s) + 6HCl(g)$$

On the other hand, elemental silicon is produced by heating SiO_2 with carbon in an electric furnace, where the reaction

$$SiO_2(s) + C(s) \longrightarrow Si(s) + CO_2(g)$$

occurs once the temperature exceeds approximately 3000 °C (below this temperature the reverse reaction is actually favored).

The remaining metalloids may be obtained from their oxides by heating them with either carbon or hydrogen; for example,

$$GeO_2(s) + C(s) \longrightarrow Ge(s) + CO_2(g)$$
$$GeO_2(s) + 2H_2(g) \longrightarrow Ge(s) + 2H_2O(g)$$

Similarly, we have

$$2As_2O_3(s) + 3C(s) \longrightarrow 4As(s) + 3CO_2(g)$$
$$As_2O_3(s) + 3H_2(g) \longrightarrow 2As(s) + 3H_2O(g)$$

and

$$2Sb_2O_3(s) + 3C(s) \longrightarrow 4Sb(s) + 3CO_2(g)$$
$$Sb_2O_3(s) + 3H_2(g) \longrightarrow 2Sb(s) + 3H_2O(g)$$

As you may recall, in very pure form, silicon and germanium have widespread applications in the electronics industry, where they are used in transistors and photoconduction devices. Sophisticated electronic circuits embedded in tiny wafers of silicon make possible a myriad of computer-controlled devices that we've come to take for granted, such as laptop computers; CD, DVD, and MP3 players; handheld computer games; computers that enable automobile engines to manage exhaust emission; cell phones; and digital cameras (and the list goes on).

21.2 NONMETALLIC ELEMENTS IN THEIR FREE STATES HAVE STRUCTURES OF VARYING COMPLEXITY

Only the noble gases exist in nature as single atoms. All the other nonmetallic elements are found in more complex forms in their free states—some as diatomic molecules and the rest in more complex molecular structures. In this section we will study what these structures are and use bonding theory to understand them. Let's begin by reviewing how atoms form covalent bonds.

You learned in Chapter 9 that atoms are able to share electrons in two basic ways. One is by the formation of σ bonds, which can involve the overlap of *s* orbitals or an end-to-end overlap of *p* orbitals or hybrid orbitals. The second kind of covalent bond is the π bond, which normally requires the sideways overlap of unhybridized *p* orbitals (Figure 21.2). (Pi bonds can also be formed by *d* orbitals, but we do not discuss them in this book.)

Not all atoms have the same tendency to form π bonds. The ability of an atom to form π bonds determines its ability to form multiple bonds, and this in turn greatly affects the kinds of molecular structures that the element produces. One of the most striking illustrations of this is the molecular structures of the elemental nonmetals and metalloids.

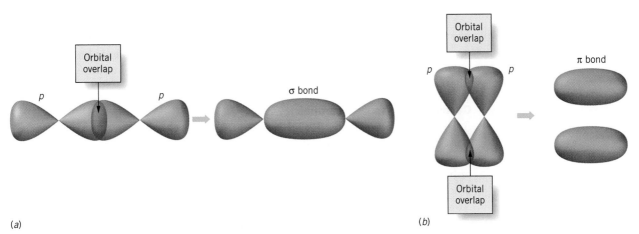

FIG. 21.2 **Formation of sigma and pi bonds.** (*a*) Sigma bonds formed by the head-to-head overlap of *p* orbitals. (*b*) Pi bonds formed by the side-by-side overlap of *p* orbitals.

Nonmetals in Period 2 form multiple bonds relatively easily

One of the controlling factors in determining the complexity of the molecular structures of the nonmetals and metalloids is their ability to form multiple bonds. Small atoms, such as those in Period 2, are able to approach each other closely. As a result, effective sideways overlap of their *p* orbitals can occur, and these atoms form strong π bonds. Therefore, carbon, nitrogen, and oxygen are able to form multiple bonds about as easily as they are able to form single bonds. On the other hand, when the atoms are large—which is the case for atoms from Periods 3, 4, and so on—π-type overlap between their *p* orbitals is relatively ineffective, so π bonds formed by large atoms are relatively weak compared to σ bonds. Therefore, rather than form a double bond consisting of one σ bond and one π bond, these elements prefer to use two separate σ bonds to bond their atoms together. This leads to a useful generalization: *Elements in Period 2 are able to form multiple bonds fairly readily, while elements below them in Periods 3, 4, 5, and 6 have a tendency to prefer single bonds.* Let's see how this affects the structures of the elemental nonmetallic elements.

Oxygen and nitrogen have six and five electrons, respectively, in their valence shells. This means that an oxygen atom needs two electrons to complete its valence shell, and a nitrogen atom needs three. Although a perfectly satisfactory Lewis structure for O_2 can't be drawn, experimental evidence suggests that the oxygen molecule does possess a double bond. The molecular orbital theory, which provides an excellent explanation of the bonding in O_2, also tells us that there is a double bond in the O_2 molecule. The nitrogen molecule, which we discussed earlier, contains a triple bond. Oxygen and nitrogen, because of their small size, are capable of multiple bonding because they are able to form strong π bonds. This allows them to form a sufficient number of bonds with just a single neighbor to complete their valence shells, so they are able to form diatomic molecules.

Oxygen, in addition to forming the stable species O_2 (dioxygen), also can exist in another very reactive molecular form called **ozone,** which has the formula O_3. The structure of ozone can be represented as a resonance hybrid

$$\ddot{O}{=}\overset{\displaystyle ..}{O}{-}\ddot{\underset{..}{O}}{:} \longleftrightarrow {:}\ddot{\underset{..}{O}}{-}\overset{\displaystyle ..}{O}{=}\ddot{O}{:}$$

□ ΔG_f° for O_3 is $+163$ kJ mol^{-1}, which indicates that the molecule has a strong tendency to decompose to give O_2.

This unstable molecule can be generated by the passage of an electric discharge through ordinary O_2, and the pungent odor of ozone can often be detected in the vicinity of high-voltage electrical equipment. It is also formed in limited amounts in the upper atmosphere by the action of ultraviolet radiation from the sun on O_2. The presence of ozone in the upper atmosphere shields the earth and its creatures from exposure to intense and harmful ultraviolet light from the sun.

The existence of an element in more than one form, either as the result of differences in molecular structure as with O_2 and O_3, or as the result of differences in the packing of molecules in the solid, is a phenomenon called **allotropy.** The different forms of the element are called **allotropes.** Thus, O_2 is one allotrope of oxygen and O_3 is another. Allotropy is not limited to oxygen, as you will soon see.

Carbon forms four allotropes

An atom of carbon, another Period 2 element, has four electrons in its valence shell, so it must share four electrons to complete its octet. There is no way for carbon to form a quadruple bond, so a simple C_2 species is not stable under ordinary conditions. Instead, carbon completes its octet in other ways, leading to four allotropic forms of the element. One of these is **diamond,** in which each carbon atom uses sp^3 hybrid orbitals to form covalent bonds to four other carbon atoms at the corners of a tetrahedron (Figure 21.3a).

In its other allotropes, carbon employs sp^2 hybrid orbitals to form ring structures with delocalized π systems covering their surfaces. The most stable form of carbon is **graphite,** which consists of layers of carbon atoms, each composed of many hexagonal "benzene-like" rings fused together in a structure reminiscent of chicken wire.

◻ Graphite is able to serve as a lubricant because the layers of carbon atoms in the structure are able to slide over each other relatively easily.

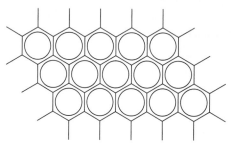

A fragment of a carbon layer in graphite

◻ Another figure showing the layer structure of graphite can be found on the rear cover of the book.

In graphite, these layers are stacked one on top of another, as shown in Figure 21.3b. Graphite is an electrical conductor because of the delocalized π electron system that extends across the layers. Electrons can be pumped in at one end of a layer and removed from the other.

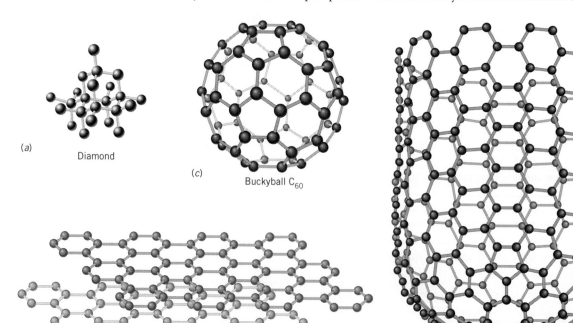

(a) Diamond

(c) Buckyball C_{60}

(b) Graphite

(d) Nanotube

FIG. 21.3 **Molecular forms of carbon.** (*a*) Diamond. (*b*) Graphite. (*c*) Buckminsterfullerene, or "buckyball," C_{60}. (*d*) A portion of a carbon nanotube showing one closed end.

In 1985, a new form of carbon was discovered that consists of tiny balls of carbon atoms, the simplest of which has the formula C_{60} (Figure 21.3c). They were named **fullerenes** and the C_{60} molecule itself was named **buckminsterfullerene** (nickname **buckyball**) in honor of R. Buckminster Fuller, the designer of a type of structure called a geodesic dome. The bonds between carbon atoms in the buckyball occur in a pattern of five- and six-membered rings arranged like the seams in a soccer ball as well as the structural elements of the geodesic dome.

Carbon nanotubes, discovered in 1991, are another form of carbon that is related to the fullerenes. They are formed, along with fullerenes, when an electric arc is passed between carbon electrodes. The nanotubes consist of tubular carbon molecules that we can visualize as rolled up sheets of graphite (with hexagonal rings of carbon atoms). The tubes are capped at each end with half of a spherical fullerene molecule, so a short tube would have a shape like a hot dog. A portion of a carbon nanotube is illustrated in Figure 21.3d. Carbon nanotubes have unusual properties that have made them the focus of much research in recent years.

◻ The front cover of the book illustrates the structure and formation of a carbon nanotube.

◻ Weight for weight, carbon nanotubes are about 100 times stronger than stainless steel and about 40 times stronger than the carbon fibers used to make tennis rackets and shafts for golf clubs.

Boron forms a complex structure containing B_{12} units

In Period 2 there is still one element whose structure we have not considered, namely, boron. This element, found in Group IIIA, is quite unlike any of the others, since there is no simple way for it to complete its valence shell. The boron atom has just three electrons in its valence shell. Crystalline boron contains clusters of 12 boron atoms located at the vertices of an icosahedron (a 20-sided geometric figure) as shown in Figure 21.4. In the solid, each of these is also joined to yet another boron atom outside the cluster (Figure 21.4b). The electrons available for bonding are therefore delocalized to a large extent over many boron atoms.

The linking together of B_{12} units produces a large three-dimensional covalent solid that is very difficult to break down. As a result, boron is very hard (it is the second hardest element) and has a very high melting point (about 2200 °C).

Nonmetallic elements below Period 2 have structures containing single bonds

In graphite, carbon exhibits multiple bonding, as do nitrogen and oxygen in their molecular forms. As we noted earlier, their ability to do this reflects their ability to form strong π bonds—a requirement for the formation of a double or triple bond. When we move to

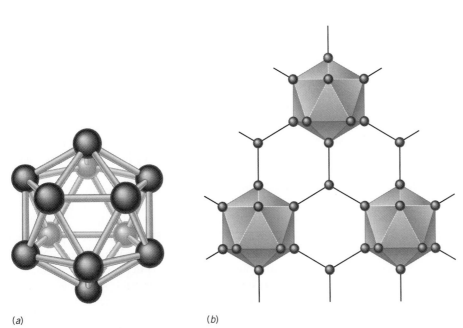

(a)   (b)

FIG. 21.4 **The structure of elemental boron.** (a) The arrangement of 12 boron atoms in a B_{12} cluster. (b) The element boron consists of an interconnecting network of B_{12} clusters that produces a very hard and high-melting solid.

the third and successive periods, a different state of affairs exists. Here, we have much larger atoms that are able to form relatively strong σ bonds but much weaker π bonds. Because their π bonds are so weak, these elements prefer single bonds (σ bonds), and the molecular structures of the free elements reflect this.

Elements of Group VIIA

Each of the elements in Group VIIA is diatomic in the free state. This is because π bonding is not necessary in any of their molecular structures. Chlorine, for example, requires just one electron to complete its octet, so it only needs to form one covalent bond with another atom. Therefore, it forms one σ bond to another chlorine atom and is able to exist as diatomic Cl_2. Bromine and iodine form diatomic Br_2 and I_2 molecules for the same reason. The structures of the remaining nonmetals and metalloids are considerably more complex, however.

Elements of Group VIA

Below oxygen in Group VIA is sulfur, which has the Lewis symbol

$$\cdot \ddot{S} \cdot$$

A sulfur atom requires two more electrons to obtain an octet, so it must form two covalent bonds. But sulfur doesn't form π bonds well to other sulfur atoms; instead, it prefers to form two stronger single bonds to *different* sulfur atoms. Each of these also prefers to bond to two different sulfur atoms, and this gives rise to a

$$-\ddot{S}-\ddot{S}-\ddot{S}-\ddot{S}-\ddot{S}-$$

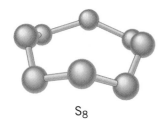

FIG. 21.5 **The structure of the puckered S_8 ring.**

sequence. Actually, in sulfur's most stable form, called **orthorhombic sulfur,** the sulfur atoms are arranged in an eight-membered ring to give a molecule with the formula S_8 (properly named cyclooctasulfur). The S_8 ring has a puckered crownlike shape, which is illustrated in Figure 21.5. Another allotrope is **monoclinic sulfur,** which also contains S_8 rings that are arranged in a slightly different crystal structure.

Selenium, below sulfur in Group VIA, also forms Se_8 rings in one of its allotropic forms. Both selenium and tellurium also can exist in a gray form in which there are long Se_x and Te_x chains (where the subscript x is a large number).

Elements of Group VA

Like nitrogen, the other elements in Group VA all have five valence electrons. Phosphorus is an example.

$$\cdot \dot{\underset{\cdot\cdot}{P}} \cdot$$

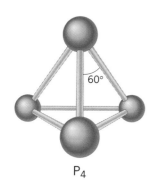

FIG. 21.6 **The molecular structure of white phosphorus, P_4.** The bond angles of 60° make the phosphorus–phosphorus bonds quite weak and causes the molecule to be very reactive.

To achieve a noble gas structure, the phosphorus atom must acquire three more electrons. Because there is little tendency for phosphorus to form multiple bonds, as nitrogen does when it forms N_2, the octet is completed by the formation of three single bonds to three *different* phosphorus atoms.

The simplest elemental form of phosphorus is a waxy solid called **white phosphorus** because of its appearance. It consists of P_4 molecules in which each phosphorus atom lies at a corner of a tetrahedron, as illustrated in Figure 21.6. Notice that in this structure each phosphorus is bound to three others. This allotrope of phosphorus is very reactive, partly because of the very small P—P—P bond angle of 60°. At this small angle, the p orbitals of the phosphorus atoms don't overlap very well, so the bonds are weak. As a result, breaking a P—P bond occurs easily. When a P_4 molecule reacts, this bond breaking is the first step, so P_4 molecules are readily attacked by other chemicals, especially oxygen. White phosphorus is so reactive toward oxygen that it ignites and burns spontaneously in air. For this reason, white phosphorus is used in military incendiary devices, and you've probably seen movies in which exploding phosphorus shells produce arching showers of smoking particles.

A second allotrope of phosphorus that is much less reactive is called **red phosphorus.** At the present time, its structure is unknown, although it has been suggested that it contains P_4 tetrahedra joined at the corners as shown in Figure 21.7. Red phosphorus is also used in explosives and fireworks, and it is mixed with fine sand and used on the

◻ The preferred angle between bonds formed by overlap of p orbitals is 90°. Each face of the P_4 tetrahedron is a triangle, however, with 60° angles between edges. This produces less than optimum overlap between the p orbitals in the bonds.

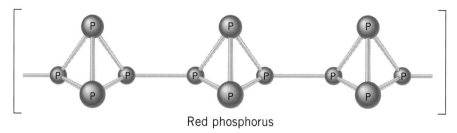

Red phosphorus

FIG. 21.7 **Proposed molecular structure of red phosphorus.** Red phosphorus is believed to be composed of long chains of P_4 tetrahedra connected at their corners.

striking surfaces of matchbooks. As a match is drawn across the surface, friction ignites the phosphorus, which then ignites the ingredients in the tip of the match.

A third allotrope of phosphorus is called **black phosphorus,** which is formed by heating white phosphorus at very high pressures. This variety has a layered structure in which each phosphorus atom in a layer is covalently bonded to three others in the same layer. As in graphite, these layers are stacked one atop another, with only weak forces between the layers. As you might expect, black phosphorus has many similarities to graphite.

The elements arsenic and antimony, which are just below phosphorus in Group VA, are also able to form somewhat unstable yellow allotropic forms containing As_4 and Sb_4 molecules, but their most stable forms have a metallic appearance with structures similar to black phosphorus.

Elements of Group IVA

Finally, we look at the heavier nonmetallic elements in Group IVA, silicon and germanium. To complete their octets, each must form four covalent bonds. Unlike carbon, however, they have very little tendency to form multiple bonds, so they don't form allotropes that have a graphite structure. Instead, each of them forms a solid with a structure similar to diamond.

21.3 METALS ARE PREPARED FROM COMPOUNDS BY REDUCTION

When metals form compounds, they almost always lose electrons (become oxidized) and exist in positive oxidation states. Therefore, isolating metals from compounds generally involves reduction. In this section we will look at some of the ways this can be accomplished. Before we do this, however, let's take a brief look at where in nature we find metal compounds.

Metals come from both the earth and the sea

Most metals are reactive enough that they do not occur as free elements in nature. Instead, they are found combined with other elements in compounds. Where we find such compounds depends a great deal on their solubilities in water. For example, you learned that salts of the alkali metals (metals of Group IA) are soluble in water. It is no surprise, therefore, to find Na^+ and K^+ ions in the sea. In fact, the oceans provide a huge storehouse of many minerals, as illustrated by the table in the margin. Sodium and magnesium (as Na^+ and Mg^{2+}) are the metal ions in largest concentration in seawater, partly because their natural abundance among the elements is large,[2] and also because their sulfates, halides, and carbonates are water soluble.

Oxygen is the earth's most abundant element, and because it is so reactive it is able to combine with nearly all metals. As you learned when studying the solubility rules in Chapter 4, most metal oxides are insoluble in water (exceptions are the oxides of the alkali metals and some of the oxides of the Group IIA metals). Because of these facts, many metals occur in nature as insoluble oxides found buried in the ground. An example is iron(III) oxide, which gives its rich rust-red color to iron ores and various clay minerals that contain Fe_2O_3 (Figure 21.8).

FIG. 21.8 **The color of iron oxide.** Red Fe_2O_3 gives the clay used by this sculptor its rich color. *(Dan Boler/Stone/Getty Images.)*

Concentrations of Ions in Seawater

Ion	Molarity
Chloride	0.550
Sodium	0.468
Magnesium	0.055
Sulfate	0.029
Calcium	0.011
Potassium	0.011
Bicarbonate	0.002

[2] On the earth, sodium is the fourth most abundant element on an atom basis (approximately 2.6% of the atoms on earth are Na); magnesium is the seventh most abundant (about 1.8%).

As you learned in Chapter 4, nearly all metal carbonates are also insoluble, and the ability of sea creatures, such as clams, oysters, and coral, to extract carbonate ions from seawater to construct their shells accounts for the large formations of carbonate minerals of calcium and magnesium present in many locations around the planet. Over eons of time, the calcium carbonate skeletons of these creatures have built up and then been moved by upheavals in the earth's crust. Such movements have often lifted them to heights far above sea level and at times subjected them to tremendous compressive forces that transformed them into limestone and marble.

◻ In most soils, phosphorus is the limiting nutrient, so phosphate fertilizers are essential to produce good crops.

Other anions yield insoluble compounds with metal ions as well, which accounts for deposits of metal sulfides, such as copper sulfides (CuS and Cu_2S), lead sulfide (PbS), and calcium phosphate, $Ca_3(PO_4)_2$. The latter mineral is the chief source of phosphate fertilizers, without which farmers could not hope to maintain the large crop harvests required to feed the world's growing population.

A few metals, most notably gold and platinum, do occur in the uncombined state in nature. These are metals with very low degrees of reactivity. Although they form many compounds, the metals are found free in nature because their compounds are not particularly stable and are easily decomposed by heat.

Reactive metals are often produced by electrolysis

◻ Recall that for metals, reactivity is a measure of how easily oxidized they are.

The method used to extract a metal from its compounds depends on how "reactive" the metal is. Metals that are easily oxidized, such as the alkali and alkaline earth metals, form compounds that are correspondingly difficult to reduce, and it is difficult and expensive to find chemical reducing agents that are up to the job. For this reason, electrolysis is usually the procedure used. For example, in Chapter 19 we described the elecrolytic production of two reactive metals, sodium and aluminum. Sodium is formed by electrolysis of its molten chloride, whereas aluminum is produced from its oxide by dissolving it in a salt such as Na_3AlF_6 which has a lower melting point.

In an interesting application of Le Châtelier's principle, potassium is usually made by passing sodium vapor over molten potassium chloride at high temperature. Although potassium ions are more difficult to reduce than sodium ions, the equilibrium

$$KCl(l) + Na(g) \rightleftharpoons NaCl(l) + K(g)$$

is shifted to the right because potassium has a higher vapor pressure than sodium. The less volatile sodium condenses as potassium vapor is swept away, thereby gradually shifting the position of equilibrium. The same procedure is used to make metallic rubidium and cesium.

Marble is a favorite stone of sculptors. The type of stone called marble is composed of calcium carbonate, which was deposited by sea creatures long ago and then transformed by heat and pressure caused by movements of the earth's crust. How fortunate for us, because it enabled the great sculptor Michelangelo to create this masterpiece known as *La Pietà*. (*Art Resource.*)

Many metals can be made using a chemical reducing agent

When a metal is of intermediate reactivity, it can be economically extracted from its compounds by reaction with a chemical reducing agent. For example, one of the most common agents used for the reduction of metal oxides is carbon. Tin and lead, for example, can be produced by heating their oxides with carbon, a process called **smelting.**

$$2SnO + C \xrightarrow{\text{heat}} 2Sn + CO_2$$

$$2PbO + C \xrightarrow{\text{heat}} 2Pb + CO_2$$

Carbon is used in large quantities in commercial metallurgy (Section 21.4) because of its abundance and low cost.

Hydrogen is another reducing agent that can be used to liberate metals of moderate chemical activity. For instance tin and lead oxides are also reduced when heated under a stream of H_2.

FACETS OF CHEMISTRY

Polishing Silver—The Easy Way

Using an active metal to reduce a compound of a less active metal has a number of practical applications. One that is handy around the home is using aluminum to remove the tarnish from silver. Generally, silver tarnishes by a gradual reaction with hydrogen sulfide, present in very small amounts in the air. The product of the reaction is silver sulfide, Ag_2S, which is black and forms a dull film over the bright metal. Polishing a silver object using a mild abrasive restores the shine, but it also gradually removes silver from the object as the silver sulfide is rubbed away.

An alternative method, and one that requires little effort, involves lining the bottom of a sink with aluminum foil, adding warm water and detergent (which acts as an electrolyte), and then submerging the tarnished silver object in the detergent–water mixture and placing it in contact with the aluminum (Figure 1). A galvanic cell is established in which the more active aluminum is the anode and the silver object is the cathode. In a short time, the silver sulfide is reduced, restoring the shine and depositing the freed silver metal on the object. As this happens, a small amount of the aluminum foil is oxidized and caused to dissolve. Besides requiring little physical effort, this silver polishing technique doesn't remove silver from the object being polished.

(a)   (b)   (c)

FIG. 1 **Using aluminum to remove tarnish from silver.** (*a*) A badly tarnished silver vase stands next to a container of detergent (Soilax) dissolved in water. The bottom of the container is lined with aluminum foil. (*b*) The vase, shown partly immersed in the detergent, rests on the aluminum foil. (*c*) After a short time, the vase is removed, rinsed with water, and wiped with a soft cloth. Where the vase was immersed in the liquid, much of the tarnish has been reduced to metallic silver. (*Andy Washnik.*)

$$SnO + H_2 \xrightarrow{\text{heat}} Sn + H_2O$$

$$PbO + H_2 \xrightarrow{\text{heat}} Pb + H_2O$$

The use of a more active metal to carry out the reduction is also possible. In Chapter 19 we saw that a galvanic cell could be established between two different metals, for example, Zn and Ag. In that cell the more active reducing agent, Zn, causes the Ag^+ to be reduced. Aluminum was first prepared in 1825 by the reaction of aluminum chloride with the more active metal, potassium.

$$AlCl_3 + 3K \longrightarrow 3KCl + Al$$

Some metal compounds are thermally unstable

Thermal decomposition of a compound involves the conversion of the substance into its elements by heat. Some metal compounds are extremely resistant to such decomposition. For example, magnesium oxide is used to make bricks to line the walls of high-temperature ovens because it has a very high melting point and virtually no tendency to undergo decomposition. On the other hand, mercury(II) oxide decomposes at a relatively low temperature. For example, Joseph Priestley (1733–1804), in his experiments leading to the discovery of oxygen, produced metallic mercury and oxygen from mercury(II) oxide by simply heating it with sunlight focused on the HgO by means of a magnifying glass.

In this case, HgO decomposes quite spontaneously at elevated temperatures (Figure 21.9). The equation for the decomposition is.

$$2HgO(s) \longrightarrow 2Hg(l) + O_2(g)$$

The practicality of using a thermal decomposition reaction of this type to produce a free metal depends on the extent to which the reaction proceeds to completion at a given temperature.

In Chapter 18 you learned that at 25 °C the position of equilibrium in a reaction is roughly governed by ΔG°_{298}. If ΔG°_{298} is negative, $K > 1$ and appreciable amounts of products will be expected at equilibrium. Taking ΔG°_T to be the equivalent of ΔG°_{298}, but at a higher temperature, we have the relationship

$$\Delta G^\circ_T = \Delta H^\circ_T - T\Delta S^\circ_T$$

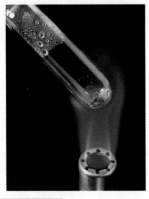

FIG. 21.9 Thermal decomposition of mercury(II) oxide. Heated to a temperature of only 400 °C, HgO turns black and releases oxygen. Drops of mercury metal begin to collect on the walls of the test tube as mercury vapor condenses on the cooler parts of the tube. *(Richard Megna/Fundamental Photographs.)*

For decomposition, ΔS°_T is positive (decomposition leads to formation of more particles). Most compounds have negative values of ΔH°_f, so we expect the ΔH°_T for the decomposition to be positive, too. That makes ΔG°_T equal to the difference between two positive quantities, ΔH°_T and $T\Delta S^\circ_T$. If ΔH°_T is not *too* positive, the temperature T needed to make ΔG°_T negative is not very large, and thermal decomposition should proceed to a significant degree at a reasonable temperature. *Stated another way, if ΔH°_f for a compound is not too negative, it should be susceptible to thermal decomposition at a reasonably low temperature.*

EXAMPLE 21.1

Calculating the Temperature Required for Thermal Decomposition

Above what temperature would the decomposition of Ag_2O be expected to proceed to an appreciable extent toward completion? At 25 °C, ΔH°_f for Ag_2O is -31.1 kJ mol^{-1}, and $\Delta S^\circ_f = -66.1$ J mol^{-1} K^{-1}.

ANALYSIS: The tool that we will use is Equation 18.10 (page 752), which allows us to estimate ΔG°_T assuming ΔH°_T and ΔS°_T are nearly independent of temperature:

$$\Delta G^\circ_T \approx \Delta H^\circ_{298} - T\Delta S^\circ_{298} \qquad \text{(Equation 18.10)}$$

The decomposition of Ag_2O, $Ag_2O(s) \longrightarrow 2Ag(s) + \frac{1}{2}O_2(g)$, is the reverse of its formation. Therefore, for this reaction at 25 °C we can write

$$\Delta H^\circ_{298} = -\Delta H^\circ_f = +31.1 \text{ kJ mol}^{-1}$$
$$\Delta S^\circ_{298} = -\Delta S^\circ_f = +66.1 \text{ J mol}^{-1} \text{ K}^{-1}$$

Let's calculate the temperature at which $\Delta G^\circ_T = 0$, because above that temperature ΔG°_T will be negative and the decomposition reaction will proceed to a significant extent.

SOLUTION: We will assume, as stated above, that ΔH°_T and ΔS°_T are approximately independent of temperature so that we can use ΔH°_{298} and ΔS°_{298} in the equation for ΔG°_T.

$$\Delta G^\circ_T \approx \Delta H^\circ_{298} - T\Delta S^\circ_{298}$$

When $\Delta G^\circ_T = 0$

$$0 = \Delta H^\circ_{298} - T\Delta S^\circ_{298}$$

Solving for T gives

$$T = \frac{\Delta H^\circ_{298}}{\Delta S^\circ_{298}}$$
$$= \frac{31,100 \text{ J mol}^{-1}}{66.1 \text{ J mol}^{-1} \text{ K}^{-1}}$$
$$= 470 \text{ K}$$

This corresponds to a Celsius temperature of 197 °C.

Because ΔH°_{298} and ΔS°_{298} are both positive, ΔG°_T will become negative at temperatures above 197 °C. This means that above 197 °C the reaction should become feasible, with much of the Ag_2O undergoing decomposition.

IS THE ANSWER REASONABLE?   There is no simple check on this answer, although we can check to be sure that the units cancel properly, and they do. Notice that we were careful to change the units of ΔH°_{298} from kilojoules to joules. If we had not done that, the units would not have canceled properly.

Practice Exercise 1: Above what temperature would Au_2O_3 decompose to give Au and O_2? At 25 °C, $\Delta H^\circ_f = +80.8$ kJ mol^{-1} for Au_2O_3. Also, for Au_2O_3, $S^\circ = 125$ J mol^{-1} K^{-1}; for Au, $S^\circ = 47.7$ J mol^{-1} K^{-1}; for O_2, $S^\circ = 205$ J mol^{-1} K^{-1}. (Hint: Can the absolute temperature be negative?)

Practice Exercise 2: Calculate the temperature required to observe a significant amount of thermal decomposition of MgO. At 25 °C, magnesium oxide has $\Delta H^\circ_f = -601.7$ kJ mol^{-1}; for Mg, $S^\circ = 32.5$ J mol^{-1} K^{-1}, and for O_2, $S^\circ = 205$ J mol^{-1} K^{-1}. For MgO, $S^\circ = 26.9$ J mol^{-1} K^{-1}.

21.4 | METALLURGY IS THE SCIENCE AND TECHNOLOGY OF METALS

Metals played an important role in the growth and development of civilization even before the beginning of recorded history. Archaeological evidence indicates that gold was used in making eating utensils and ornaments as early as 3500 BC. Silver was discovered at least as early as 2400 BC, and iron and steel have been used as construction materials since about 1000 BC. Since these earliest times, the methods for obtaining metals from their naturally occurring deposits have evolved, and today they constitute the subject we call metallurgy.

As the title of this section proclaims, **metallurgy** is defined as the science and technology of metals. In modern terms, it is primarily concerned with the procedures and chemical reactions that are used to separate metals from their ores and the preparation of metals for practical use. An **ore** is simply a mineral deposit that has a desirable component in a sufficiently high concentration to make its extraction economically profitable. The economics of the recovery operation, though, is what distinguishes an ore from just another rock. For example, magnesium is found in the mineral *olivine*, which has the formula Mg_2SiO_4. This compound contains over 30% magnesium, but there is no economical way to extract the metal from it. Instead, most magnesium is obtained from seawater, even though its concentration is a mere 0.13%. Although the concentration is much less in the water, a profitable method of obtaining the magnesium has been developed, so seawater is the principal source of magnesium.

Because of the wide variety of sources and the varying nature of the metal compounds in ores, no single method can be applied to the production of all metals. Nevertheless, the sequence of metallurgical processes can be divided into three principal steps.

1. *Concentration.* Ores that contain substantial amounts of impurities, such as rock, must often be treated to concentrate the metal-bearing component. Pretreatment of an ore is also carried out to convert some metal compounds into substances that can be more easily reduced.

2. *Reduction.* The particular procedure employed to reduce the metal compound to give the metal depends on how easily the compound is reduced.

3. *Refining.* Often, during reduction, substantial amounts of impurities become incorporated into the metal. Refining is the process whereby these impurities are removed and the composition of the metal adjusted (alloys formed) to meet the needs of specific applications.

Ores are often treated to enrich the metal-bearing component

When the source of a metal is an ore that is dug from the ground, considerable amounts of sand and dirt are usually mixed in with the ore. To reduce the volume of material that must be processed, the ore is normally concentrated before the metal is separated from it. How this is done depends on the physical and chemical properties of the ore itself, as well as those of the impurities.

□ Gangue is pronounced "gang."

In some cases, the unwanted rock and sand, called **gangue,** can be removed simply by washing the material with a stream of water. This flushes away the waste and leaves the enriched ore behind. Some iron ores are treated in this way. This procedure also forms the basis for the well-known technique called "panning for gold" that you've probably seen in movies. A sample of sand that might also contain gold is placed into a shallow pan partially filled with water. As the water is swirled around, it washes the less dense sand over the rim of the pan, but leaves any of the more dense bits of gold behind.

Flotation is a method commonly used to enrich the sulfide ores of copper and lead. The ore is crushed, mixed with water, and ground into a souplike slurry which is then transferred to flotation tanks (Figure 21.10) where it is mixed with detergents and oil. The oil adheres to the particles of sulfide ore, but not to the particles of sand and dirt. Air is blown through the mixture and the rising air bubbles become attached to the oil-coated ore particles, bringing them to the surface where they are held in a froth. The detergents in the mixture stabilize the bubbles long enough for the froth and its load of ore particles to be skimmed off. Meanwhile, the sand and dirt settle to the bottom of the tanks and are removed.

Many ores must undergo a second round of pretreatment before the metal can be obtained from them. For example, after enrichment, sulfide ores are usually heated in air. This procedure, called **roasting,** converts the sulfides to oxides which are more conveniently reduced than sulfides. Typical reactions that occur during roasting are

$$2Cu_2S + 3O_2 \longrightarrow 2Cu_2O + 2SO_2$$
$$2PbS + 3O_2 \longrightarrow 2PbO + 2SO_2$$

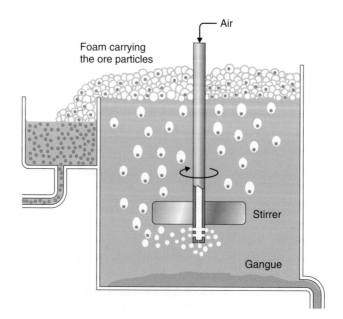

FIG. 21.10 **A flotation apparatus.**

A by-product of roasting is sulfur dioxide. In years past this was simply released to the atmosphere and was a major source of air pollution. Today we realize that the SO_2 cannot be allowed to escape into the air. One way to remove it from the exhaust gases is to allow it to react with calcium carbonate ($CaCO_3$).

$$CaCO_3(s) + SO_2(g) \longrightarrow CaSO_3(s) + CO_2(g)$$

This method creates another problem, however—the disposal of the solid calcium sulfite. Another way to dispose of the SO_2 is to oxidize it to SO_3. The SO_3 can be converted to sulfuric acid which is then sold.

Aluminum ore, called *bauxite*, must also be pretreated before it can be processed. Bauxite contains aluminum oxide, Al_2O_3, but a number of impurities are also present. To remove the impurities, use is made of aluminum oxide's amphoteric behavior. The ore is mixed with a concentrated sodium hydroxide solution, which dissolves the Al_2O_3.

◻ Aluminum oxide is also called alumina.

$$Al_2O_3(s) + 2OH^-(aq) \longrightarrow 2AlO_2^-(aq) + H_2O$$

The major impurities, however, are insoluble in base, so when the mixture is filtered, the impurities remain on the filter while the aluminum-containing solution passes through. The solution is then neutralized with acid, which precipitates aluminum hydroxide.

$$AlO_2^-(aq) + H^+(aq) + H_2O \longrightarrow Al(OH)_3(s)$$

When the precipitate is heated, water is driven off and the oxide is formed.

$$2Al(OH)_3(s) \xrightarrow{\text{heat}} Al_2O_3(s) + 3H_2O(g)$$

This purified Al_2O_3 then becomes the raw material for the Hall–Héroult process discussed in Section 19.8.

Most metals are obtained from their ores using chemical reducing agents

Except for very reactive metals such as sodium, magnesium, and aluminum, which are reduced using electrolysis (Section 19.8), most metals are formed from their compounds using chemical reduction. A plentiful, and therefore inexpensive, reducing agent that's often used is carbon, which is usually obtained from coal. When coal is heated strongly in the absence of air, volatile components are driven off and **coke** is formed. Coke is composed almost entirely of carbon. Carbon is an effective reducing agent for metal oxides because it combines with the oxygen to form carbon dioxide. For example, after it is roasted, lead oxide is mixed with coke and heated. As noted earlier, this method for reducing a metal oxide is known as *smelting*.

$$2PbO(s) + C(s) \xrightarrow{\text{heat}} 2Pb(l) + CO_2(g)$$

The high thermodynamic stability of CO_2 serves as one driving force for the reaction. The loss of CO_2 and the inability to reach an equilibrium is another.

Copper oxide ores can also be reduced with carbon.

$$2CuO + C \longrightarrow 2Cu + CO_2$$

This step is unnecessary for some copper sulfide ores if the conditions under which the ore is roasted are properly controlled. For example, heating an ore that contains Cu_2S in air can convert some of the Cu_2S to Cu_2O.

$$2Cu_2S + 3O_2 \longrightarrow 2Cu_2O + 2SO_2$$

At the appropriate time the supply of oxygen is cut off and the mixture of Cu_2S and Cu_2O reacts further to give metallic copper.

$$Cu_2S + 2Cu_2O \longrightarrow 6Cu + SO_2$$

Coke is made from coal. Coke is made in a battery of side-by-side coke ovens where coal is heated to drive off volatile materials. Here we see a fresh batch of white-hot coke being pushed from one of the ovens into a waiting railroad car. It will be delivered to a blast furnace nearby where it will be used to reduce iron ore to metallic iron. *(David M. Campione/Photo Researchers.)*

Reduction of iron ore is the first step in making steel

Without question, the most important use of carbon as a reducing agent is in the production of iron and steel. The chemical reactions take place in a huge tower called a **blast furnace**

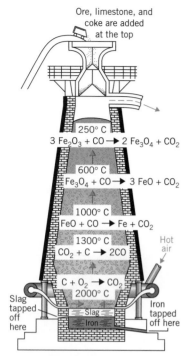

Ore, limestone, and coke are added at the top

250° C
$3 Fe_2O_3 + CO \longrightarrow 2 Fe_3O_4 + CO_2$

600° C
$Fe_3O_4 + CO \longrightarrow 3 FeO + CO_2$

1000° C
$FeO + CO \longrightarrow Fe + CO_2$

1300° C
$CO_2 + C \longrightarrow 2CO$

Hot air

$C + O_2 \longrightarrow CO_2$
2000° C

Slag tapped off here

Iron tapped off here

Slag
Iron

FIG. 21.11 **A typical blast furnace for the reduction of iron ore.** To make 1 ton of iron requires 1.75 tons of ore, 0.75 ton of coke, and 0.25 ton of limestone.

◻ The blast of hot air is what gives the blast furnace its name.

◻ The active reducing agent in the blast furnace is carbon monoxide.

◻ The acidic anhydride SiO_2 reacts with oxide ion in CaO to form the silicate ion, SiO_3^{2-}, in $CaSiO_3$. It's a Lewis acid–base reaction.

(see Figure 21.11). Some are as tall as a 15-story building and produce up to 2400 tons of iron a day. They are designed for continuous operation, so the raw materials can be added at the top and molten iron can be tapped off at the bottom. Once started, a typical blast furnace may run continuously for two years or longer before it is worn out and must be rebuilt.

The material put into the top of the blast furnace is called the **charge.** It consists of a mixture of iron ore, limestone, and coke. A typical iron ore consists of an iron oxide (Fe_2O_3, for example) plus impurities of sand and rock. The coke is added to reduce the iron oxide to the free metal. The limestone is added to react with the high-melting impurities to form a **slag,** which has a lower melting point. The slag can then be drained off as a liquid at the base of the furnace.

To understand what happens in the furnace, it is best to begin with the reactions that take place near the bottom. Here, heated air is blown into the furnace where carbon (from the coke) reacts with oxygen to form carbon dioxide.

$$C + O_2 \longrightarrow CO_2$$

The reaction is very exothermic, and the temperature in this part of the furnace rises to nearly 2000 °C. It is the hottest region of the furnace. The hot CO_2 rises and reacts with additional carbon to form carbon monoxide.

$$CO_2 + C \longrightarrow 2CO$$

This reaction is endothermic, which causes the temperature higher up in the furnace to drop to about 1300 °C. As the carbon monoxide rises through the charge, it reacts with the iron oxides and reduces them to the free metal. The reactions are

$$3Fe_2O_3(s) + CO(g) \longrightarrow 2Fe_3O_4(s) + CO_2(g)$$
$$Fe_3O_4(s) + CO(g) \longrightarrow 3FeO(s) + CO_2(g)$$
$$FeO(s) + CO(g) \longrightarrow Fe(l) + CO_2(g)$$

As the charge settles toward the bottom, molten iron trickles down and collects in a well at the base of the furnace.

The high temperature in the furnace also causes the limestone in the reaction mixture to decompose to give calcium oxide.

$$CaCO_3 \longrightarrow CaO + CO_2$$
limestone

The calcium oxide reacts with impurities such as silica (SiO_2) in the sand to form the slag.

$$CaO + SiO_2 \longrightarrow CaSiO_3$$
calcium silicate (slag)

The molten slag also trickles down through the charge. It collects as a liquid layer on top of the more dense molten iron. Periodically, the furnace is tapped and the iron and slag are drawn off. The iron, which still contains some impurities, is called **pig iron.**[3] It is usually treated further to produce steel. The slag itself is a valuable by-product. It is used to make insulating materials and is one of the chief ingredients in the manufacture of Portland cement.

Preparing metals for use is called refining

Before metals can be used, most must be purified, or **refined,** after they are reduced to the metallic state. Sometimes, reduction and purification can take place in a single step. For example, the ore for titanium (a metal used to make aircraft parts) is its oxide, TiO_2. Recovering the metal from the ore is difficult because the metal itself reacts at high temperature with both carbon and nitrogen. The solution is to heat the oxide with carbon

---

[3] The name pig iron comes from an early method of casting the molten iron into bars for shipment. The molten metal was run through a channel that fed into sand molds. The arrangement looked a little like a litter of pigs feeding from their mother.

in the presence of chlorine gas, which converts the titanium to $TiCl_4$, a volatile compound that is drawn off as a gas.

$$TiO_2(s) + C(s) + 2Cl_2(g) \longrightarrow TiCl_4(g) + CO_2(g)$$

The volatility of the $TiCl_4$ enables it to be removed from any impurities in the ore. After being separated from the CO_2, the $TiCl_4$ is allowed to react with magnesium to form essentially pure titanium metal.

$$TiCl_4 + 2Mg \longrightarrow Ti + 2MgCl_2$$

The purification of nickel also takes advantage of the volatility of one of its compounds. When nickel is heated mildly in the presence of carbon monoxide, it forms a compound called nickel carbonyl, $Ni(CO)_4$.

$$Ni(s) + 4CO(g) \xrightarrow{\text{warm}} Ni(CO)_4(g)$$
$$\text{nickel carbonyl}$$

Vapors of the $Ni(CO)_4$ compound are easily separated from impurities in the nickel, which don't form similarly volatile substances. Later the $Ni(CO)_4$ can be heated to high temperature, causing the substance to decompose and deposit highly purified nickel.[4]

For some metals, refining is accomplished by electrolysis. For example, metallic copper that comes from the smelting process is about 99% pure, but before being used in electrical wiring it is purified electrolytically as described in Chapter 19.

Refining of iron to make steel involves removing impurities and adding other metals

The conversion of pig iron to steel is the most important commercial refining process. The pig iron from a blast furnace consists of about 95% iron, 3 to 4% carbon, and smaller amounts of phosphorus, sulfur, manganese, and other elements. Steel contains much less carbon as well as certain other ingredients in very definite proportions. Converting pig iron to steel, therefore, involves removing the impurities and much of the carbon, and adding other metals in precisely controlled amounts.

Today, most steel is made by a method called the **basic oxygen process.** It uses a large pear-shaped reaction vessel that is mounted on pivots as shown in Figure 21.12. The vessel is lined with an insulating layer of refractory bricks composed of $MgCO_3$ or a mixture of $MgCO_3$ and $CaCO_3$. The charge consists of about 30% scrap iron and scrap steel and about 70% molten pig iron. A tube called an *oxygen lance* is dipped into the charge and pure oxygen is blown through the molten metal. The oxygen rapidly burns off the excess carbon and oxidizes impurities to their oxides. The heat generated also melts the scrap iron. The impurities form a slag with calcium oxide that comes from powdered limestone, which is also added. Finally, other metals are introduced in the proper proportions to give a product with the desired properties. After the steel is ready, the reaction vessel can be tipped to pour out its contents. This method of making steel is very fast. A batch of steel weighing 300 tons can be made in less than an hour.

21.5 | COMPLEX IONS ARE FORMED BY MANY METALS

In Section 17.4 (page 712), we introduced you to **complex ions** (or more simply, **complexes**) of metals. Recall that these are substances formed when molecules or anions become bonded covalently to metal ions to form more complex species. Two examples that were given were the pale blue $Cu(H_2O)_4{}^{2+}$ ion and the deep blue $Cu(NH_3)_4{}^{2+}$ ion. In Chapter 17 we discussed how the formation of complex ions can affect the solubilities of salts, but the importance of these substances reaches far beyond solubility equilibria. The number of complex ions formed by metals, especially the transition metals, is enormous, and the study of the properties, reactions, structures, and bonding in complexes like $Cu(NH_3)_4{}^{2+}$ has become an important specialty within chemistry. The study of metal

□ Nickel carbonyl is very toxic.

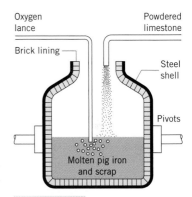

FIG. 21.12 The basic oxygen process for making steel. The reaction vessel is very large, being capable of holding up to 300 tons of steel.

A molten iron charge is added to a basic oxygen furnace. *(James Mejuto Photography.)*

---

[4] This method of purifying nickel is called the Mond process.

◻ In the space we have available here our goal will simply be to give you a taste of the subject.

complexes even extends into biochemistry. This is because, ultimately, nearly all the metals our bodies require become bound in complexes in order to perform their biochemical functions.

Before we proceed further, let's review some of the basic terminology we will use in our discussions. The molecules or ions that become attached to a metal ion [e.g., the NH_3 molecules in $Cu(NH_3)_4^{2+}$] are called **ligands.** Ligands are neutral molecules or anions that contain one or more atoms with at least one unshared electron pair that can be donated to the metal ion in the formation of a metal–ligand bond. The reaction of a ligand with a metal ion is therefore a Lewis acid–base reaction in which the ligand is the Lewis base (electron pair donor) and the metal ion is the Lewis acid (electron pair acceptor).

$$\underset{\substack{\text{silver ion}\\ \text{(Lewis acid)}}}{Ag^+} \quad + \quad \underset{\substack{\text{ammonia}\\ \text{molecule}\\ \text{(Lewis base)}}}{\overset{\displaystyle H}{\underset{\displaystyle H}{:\!N\!-\!H}}} \quad \longrightarrow \quad \underset{\substack{\text{complex ion}}}{\left[\overset{\displaystyle H}{\underset{\displaystyle H}{Ag\leftarrow N\!-\!H}}\right]^+}$$

Coordinate covalent bond between ammonia and the silver ion

◻ Recall that a coordinate covalent bond is one in which both of the shared electrons originate on the same atom. Once formed, of course, a coordinate covalent bond is just like any other covalent bond.

A ligand atom that donates an electron pair to the metal is said to be a **donor atom** and the metal is the **acceptor.** Thus, in the example above, the nitrogen of the ammonia molecule is the donor atom and the silver ion is the acceptor. Because of the way the metal–ligand bond is formed, it can be considered to be a coordinate covalent bond, and compounds that contain metal complexes are often called **coordination compounds.** The complexes themselves are sometimes referred to as **coordination complexes.**

Ligands are Lewis bases

As we've noted, ligands may be either anions or neutral molecules. In either case, *ligands are Lewis bases* and, therefore, contain at least one atom with one or more lone pairs (unshared pairs) of electrons.

Anions that serve as ligands include many simple monatomic ions such as the halide ions (F^-, Cl^-, Br^-, I^-) and the sulfide ion (S^{2-}). Common polyatomic anions that are ligands are nitrite ion (NO_2^-), cyanide ion (CN^-), hydroxide ion (OH^-), thiocyanate ion (SCN^-), and thiosulfate ion ($S_2O_3^{2-}$). (This is really only a small sampling, not a complete list.)

The most common neutral molecule that serves as a ligand is water, and most of the reactions of metal ions in aqueous solutions are actually reactions of their complex ions— ions in which the metal is attached to some number of water molecules. This number isn't always the same, however. Copper(II) ion, for example, forms the complex ion $Cu(H_2O)_4^{2+}$ (as we've noted earlier),[5] but cobalt(II) combines with water molecules to form $Co(H_2O)_6^{2+}$. Another common neutral ligand is ammonia, NH_3, which has one lone pair of electrons on the nitrogen atom. If ammonia is added to an aqueous solution containing the $Ni(H_2O)_6^{2+}$ ion, for example, the color changes dramatically from green to blue as ammonia molecules displace water molecules (see Figure 21.13).

$$\underset{\text{(green)}}{Ni(H_2O)_6^{2+}(aq)} + 5NH_3(aq) \longrightarrow \underset{\text{(blue)}}{Ni(NH_3)_5(H_2O)^{2+}(aq)} + 5H_2O$$

Each of the ligands that we have discussed so far is able to use just one atom to attach itself to a metal ion. Such ligands are called **monodentate ligands,** indicating that they have only "one tooth" with which to "bite" the metal ion.

FIG. 21.13 **Complex ions of nickel.** (*Left*) A solution of nickel chloride, which contains the green $Ni(H_2O)_6^{2+}$ ion. (*Right*) Adding ammonia to the nickel chloride solution leads to formation of the blue $Ni(NH_3)_5(H_2O)^{2+}$ ion. (*Andy Washnik.*)

[5] The formula $Cu(H_2O)_4^{2+}$ is actually an oversimplification. Copper(II) complexes in water usually have two additional water molecules loosely attached to the Cu^{2+} at a greater distance than the other four ligand atoms. Therefore, the copper(II) complex with water could also be written $Cu(H_2O)_6^{2+}$ to indicate the additional water molecules surrounding the Cu^{2+} ion.

There are also many ligands that have two or more donor atoms, and collectively they are referred to as **polydentate ligands.** The most common of these have two donor atoms, so they are called **bidentate ligands.** When they form complexes, *both* donor atoms become attached to the same metal ion. Oxalate ion and ethylenediamine (abbreviated *en* in writing the formula for a complex) are examples of bidentate ligands.

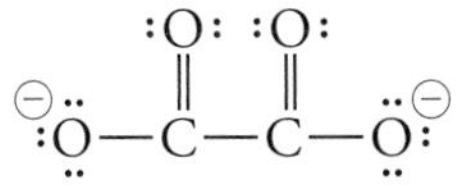

oxalate ion 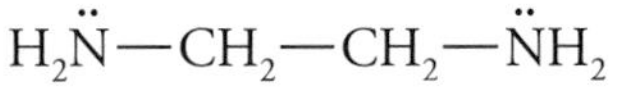   ethylenediamine, en

When these ligands become attached to a metal ion, ring structures are formed as shown below. Complexes that contain such ring structures are called **chelates.**[6]

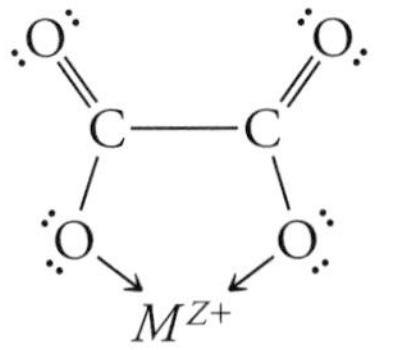

an oxalate complex 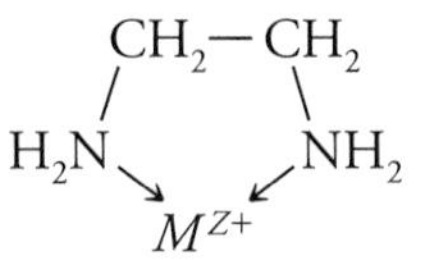   an ethylenediamine complex

Structures like these are important in "complex ion chemistry," as we shall see later in this chapter.

One of the most common polydentate ligands is a compound called ethylenediaminetetraacetic acid, mercifully abbreviated EDTA.

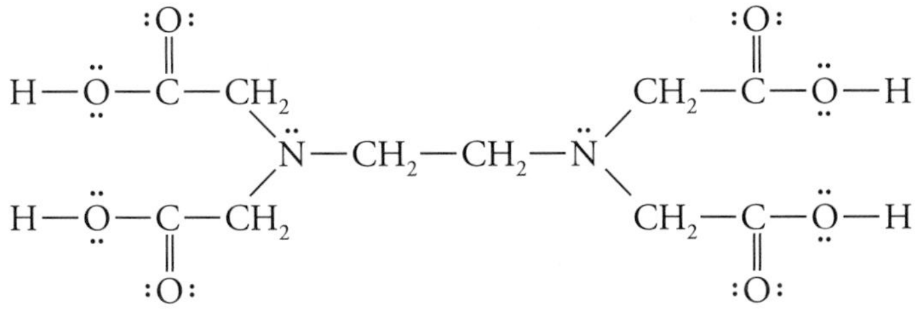

EDTA (often H_4EDTA)

The H atoms attached to the oxygen atoms are easily removed as protons, which gives an anion with a charge of $4-$. The structure of the anion, $EDTA^{4-}$, is shown below with the donor atoms in color.

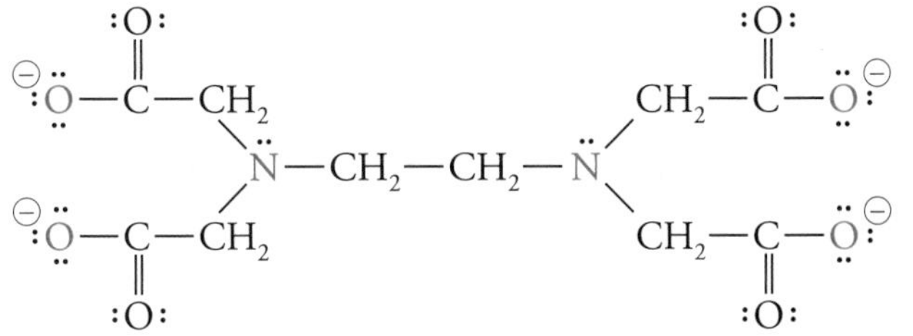

$EDTA^{4-}$

As you can see, the $EDTA^{4-}$ ion has six donor atoms, and this permits it to wrap itself around a metal ion and form very stable complexes.

EDTA is a particularly useful and important ligand. It is relatively nontoxic, which allows it to be used in small amounts in foods to retard spoilage. If you look at the labels on bottles of salad dressings, for example, you often will find that one of the ingredients is $CaNa_2EDTA$ (calcium disodium EDTA). The $EDTA^{4-}$ available from this salt forms

□ Sometimes the ligand EDTA is abbreviated using small letters (i.e., edta).

The structure of an EDTA complex. The nitrogen atoms are blue, oxygen is red, carbon is black, and hydrogen is white. The metal ion is in the center of the complex bonded to the two nitrogens and four oxygens.

□ The *calcium* salt of EDTA is used because the $EDTA^{4-}$ ion would otherwise extract Ca^{2+} ions from bones, and that would be harmful.

[6] The term *chelate* comes from the Greek *chele*, meaning claw. These bidentate ligands grasp the metal ions with two "claws" (donor atoms) somewhat like a crab holds its prey. (Who says scientists have no imagination?)

soluble complex ions with any traces of metal ions that might otherwise promote reactions of the salad oils with oxygen, and thereby lead to spoilage.

Many shampoos contain Na_4EDTA to soften water. The $EDTA^{4-}$ binds to Ca^{2+}, Mg^{2+}, and Fe^{3+} ions, which removes them from the water and prevents them from interfering with the action of detergents in the shampoo (see the photo at the beginning of this chapter). A similar application was described in Facets of Chemistry 17.1 on page 715.

EDTA is also sometimes added in small amounts to whole blood to prevent clotting. It ties up calcium ions, which the clotting process requires. EDTA has even been used as a treatment in cases of poisoning because it can help remove poisonous heavy metal ions, like Pb^{2+}, from the body when they have been accidentally ingested.

Formulas for complexes obey rules

When we write the formula for a complex, we follow rules.

1. The symbol for the metal ion is always given first, followed by the ligands.
2. When more than one kind of ligand is present, anionic ligands are written first (in alphabetical order), followed by neutral ligands (also in alphabetical order).
3. The charge on the complex is the algebraic sum of the charge on the metal ion and the charges on the ligands.

For example, the formula of the complex ion of Cu^{2+} and NH_3, which we mentioned earlier, was written $Cu(NH_3)_4{}^{2+}$ with the Cu first followed by the ligands. The charge on the complex is $2+$ because the copper ion has a charge of $2+$ and the ammonia molecules are neutral. Copper(II) ion also forms a complex ion with four cyanide ions, CN^-, $Cu(CN)_4{}^{2-}$. The metal ion contributes two $(+)$ charges and the four ligands contribute a total of four $(-)$ charges, one for each cyanide ion. The algebraic sum is therefore -2, so the complex ion has a charge of $2-$.

☐ Square brackets here do not mean molar concentration. It is usually clear from the context of a discussion whether we intend the brackets to mean molarity.

The formula for a complex ion is often placed within brackets, with the charge *outside*. The two complexes just mentioned would thus be written as $[Cu(H_2O)_4]^{2+}$ and $[Cu(CN)_4]^{2-}$. The brackets emphasize that the ligands are attached to the metal ion and are not free to roam about. One of the many complex ions formed by the chromium(III) ion contains five water molecules and one chloride ion as ligands. To indicate that all are attached to the Cr^{3+} ion, we use brackets and write the complex ion as $[CrCl(H_2O)_5]^{2+}$. When this complex is isolated as a chloride salt, the formula is written $[CrCl(H_2O)_5]Cl_2$, in which $[CrCl(H_2O)_5]^{2+}$ is the cation and so is written first. The formula $[CrCl(H_2O)_5]Cl_2$ clearly shows that five water molecules and a chloride ion are bonded to the chromium ion, and the other two chloride ions are present to provide electrical neutrality for the salt.

In Chapter 2 you learned about hydrates, and one was the beautiful blue hydrate of copper(II) sulfate, $CuSO_4 \cdot 5H_2O$ (see page 56). It was much too early then to make the distinction, but the formula should have been written as $[Cu(H_2O)_4]SO_4 \cdot H_2O$ to show that four of the five water molecules are held in the crystal as part of the complex ion $[Cu(H_2O)_4]^{2+}$. The fifth water molecule is held in the crystal by being hydrogen bonded to the sulfate ion.

☐ *Hexa-* means "six."

Many other hydrates of metal salts actually contain complex ions of the metals in which water is the ligand. Cobalt salts like cobalt(II) chloride, for example, crystallize from aqueous solutions as hexahydrates (meaning they contain six H_2O molecules per formula unit of the salt). The compound $CoCl_2 \cdot 6H_2O$ (Figure 21.14) actually is $[Co(H_2O)_6]Cl_2$, and it contains the pink complex $[Co(H_2O)_6]^{2+}$. This ion also gives solutions of cobalt(II) salts a pink color as can be seen in Figure 21.14. Although most hydrates of metal salts contain complex ions, the distinction is seldom made, and it's acceptable to write the formula for these hydrates in the usual fashion, e.g., $CuSO_4 \cdot 5H_2O$ instead of $[Cu(H_2O)_4]SO_4 \cdot H_2O$.

Write the formula for the complex ion formed by the metal ion Cr^{3+} and six NO_2^- ions as ligands. Decide whether the complex could be isolated as a chloride salt or a potassium salt, and write the formula for the appropriate salt.

ANALYSIS: The rules on page 874 are the tools we'll use to write the formula of the complex ion correctly. If the complex is a positive ion, it would require a negative ion to form a salt, so it could be isolated as a chloride salt; if the complex is a negative ion, then a potassium salt could form.

SOLUTION: Six NO_2^- ions contribute a total charge of $6-$; the metal contributes a charge of $3+$. The algebraic sum is $(6-) + (3+) = 3-$. The formula of the complex ion is therefore $[Cr(NO_2)_6]^{3-}$.

Because the complex is an anion, it requires a cation to form a neutral salt, so the complex could be isolated as a potassium salt, not as a chloride salt. For the salt to be electrically neutral, three K^+ ions are required for each complex ion, $[Cr(NO_2)_6]^{3-}$. The formula of the salt would therefore be $K_3[Cr(NO_2)_6]$. Notice that in writing the formula for the salt, we've specified the cation (K^+) first, followed by the anion.

IS THE ANSWER REASONABLE? Things to check: Have we written the formula with the metal ion first, followed by the ligands? (Yes.) Have we computed the charge on the complex correctly? (Yes.) Does the formula for the salt correspond to an electrically neutral substance? (Yes.) All seems to be okay.

Practice Exercise 3: Write the formula of the complex ion formed by Ag^+ and two thiosulfate ions, $S_2O_3^{2-}$. If we were able to isolate this complex ion as its ammonium salt, what would be the formula for the salt? (Hint: Remember, salts are electrically neutral.)

Practice Exercise 4: Aluminum chloride crystallizes from aqueous solutions as a hexahydrate. Write the formula for the salt and suggest a formula for the complex ion formed by aluminum ion and water.

The chelate effect leads to extra stability in complexes

An interesting aspect of the complexes formed by ligands such as ethylenediamine and oxalate ion is their stabilities compared to similar complexes formed by monodentate ligands. For example, the complex $[Ni(en)_3]^{2+}$ is considerably more stable than $[Ni(NH_3)_6]^{2+}$, even though both complexes have six nitrogen atoms bound to a Ni^{2+} ion. We can compare them quantitatively by examining their formation constants.

$$Ni^{2+}(aq) + 6NH_3(aq) \rightleftharpoons [Ni(NH_3)_6]^{2+}(aq) \qquad K_{form} = 2.0 \times 10^8$$
$$Ni^{2+}(aq) + 3en(aq) \rightleftharpoons [Ni(en)_3]^{2+}(aq) \qquad K_{form} = 1.4 \times 10^{17}$$

The ethylenediamine complex is more stable than the ammonia complex by a factor of 2×10^9 (2 billion)! This exceptional stability of complexes formed with polydentate ligands is called the **chelate effect,** so named because it occurs in compounds that have these *chelate ring* structures.

There are two related reasons for the chelate effect, which we can understand best if we examine the ease with which the complexes undergo dissociation once formed. One reason appears to be associated with the probability of the ligand being removed from the vicinity of the metal ion when a donor atom becomes detached. If one end of a bidentate ligand comes loose from the metal, the donor atom cannot wander very far because the other end of the ligand is still attached. There is a high probability that the loose end will become reattached to the metal ion before the other end can let go, so overall the ligand appears to be bound tightly. With a monodentate ligand, however, there is nothing to hold the ligand near the metal ion if it becomes detached. The ligand can easily wander off into

FIG. 21.14 Color of the cobalt(II) ion in hexahydrate salts. The ion $[Co(H_2O)_6]^{2+}$ is pink and gives its color both to crystals and to an aqueous solution of $CoCl_2 \cdot 6H_2O$. *(Michael Watson.)*

☐ Ammonia is a monodentate ligand, and each NH_3 can supply one donor atom to a metal. Ethylenediamine (en) is a bidentate ligand, and each has two nitrogen donor atoms. Therefore, six ammonia molecules and three ethylenediamine molecules supply the same number of donor atoms.

the surrounding solution and be lost. As a result, a mono-dentate ligand doesn't behave as if it is as firmly attached to the metal ion as a polydentate ligand.

The second reason is related to the entropy change for the dissociation. In Chapter 18 you learned that when there is an increase in the number of particles in a chemical reaction, the entropy change is positive. Dissociation of both complexes produces more particles, so the entropy change is positive for both of them. However, comparing the two reactions,

$$[Ni(NH_3)_6]^{2+}(aq) \rightleftharpoons Ni^{2+}(aq) + 6NH_3(aq) \qquad K_{inst} = 5.0 \times 10^{-9}$$
$$[Ni(en)_3]^{2+}(aq) \rightleftharpoons Ni^{2+}(aq) + 3en(aq) \qquad K_{inst} = 2.4 \times 10^{-18}$$

we see that dissociation of the ammonia complex gives a net increase of *six* in the number of particles, whereas dissociation of the ethylenediamine complex yields a net increase of *three*. This means the entropy change is more positive for the dissociation of the ammonia complex than for the ethylenediamine complex. The larger entropy change translates into a more favorable $\Delta G°$ for the decomposition, so at equilibrium the ammonia complex should be dissociated to a greater extent. This is, in fact, what is suggested by the values of their instability constants, K_{inst} (recall that $K_{inst} = 1/K_{form}$).

☐ Recall that $\Delta G°$ is related to the equilibrium constant. A more favorable $\Delta G°$ for dissociation should yield a larger equilibrium constant, and, indeed, we find the instability constant is larger for the ammonia complex.

21.6 | THE NOMENCLATURE OF METAL COMPLEXES FOLLOWS AN EXTENSION OF THE RULES DEVELOPED EARLIER

The naming of chemical compounds was introduced in Chapter 2 where we discussed the nomenclature system for simple inorganic compounds. This system, revised and kept up to date by the International Union of Pure and Applied Chemistry (IUPAC), has been extended to cover metal complexes. Below are some of the rules that have been developed to name coordination complexes. As you will see, some of the names arrived at by following the rules are difficult to pronounce at first, and may even sound a little odd. However, the primary purpose of this and any other system of nomenclature is to provide a method that gives each unique compound its own unique name and permits us to write the formula of the compound given the name.

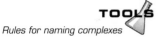

TOOLS

Rules for naming complexes

Rules of Nomenclature for Coordination Complexes

1. **Cationic species are named before anionic species.** This is the same rule that applies to other ionic compounds such as NaCl, where we name the cation first followed by the anion (i.e., sodium chloride).

2. **The names of anionic ligands always end in the suffix -o.**
   (a) Ligands whose names end in *-ide* have this suffix changed to *-o*.

Anion		Ligand
Chloride	Cl^-	chloro-
Bromide	Br^-	bromo-
Cyanide	CN^-	cyano-
Oxide	O^{2-}	oxo-

   (b) Ligands whose names end in *-ite* or *-ate* become *-ito* and *-ato*, respectively.

Anion		Ligand
Carbonate	CO_3^{2-}	carbonato-
Thiosulfate	$S_2O_3^{2-}$	thiosulfato-
Thiocyanate	SCN^-	thiocyanato- (when bonded through sulfur) isothiocyanato- (when bonded through nitrogen)
Oxalate	$C_2O_4^{2-}$	oxalato-
Nitrite	NO_2^-	nitrito- (when bonded through oxygen; written ONO in formula for complex)[a]

---
[a]An exception to this is when the nitrogen of the NO_2^- ion is bonded to the metal, in which case the ligand is named nitro-.

3. **A neutral ligand is given the same name as the neutral molecule.** By this rule, the molecule ethylenediamine, when serving as a ligand, is called ethylenediamine in the name of the complex. Two very important exceptions to this, however, are water and ammonia. These are named as follows when they serve as ligands.

$$H_2O \quad \text{aqua-} \qquad NH_3 \quad \text{ammine - (note the double } m)$$

4. **When there is more than one of a particular ligand, their number is specified by the prefixes di- = 2, tri- = 3, tetra- = 4, penta- = 5, hexa- = 6, and so forth. When confusion might result by using those prefixes, the following are used instead: bis- = 2, tris- = 3, tetrakis- = 4.** Following this rule, the presence of two chloride ligands in a complex would be indicated as *dichloro-* (notice, too, the ending on the ligand name). However, if two ethylenediamine ligands are present, use of the prefix *di-* might cause confusion. Someone reading the name might wonder whether diethylenediamine means two ethylenediamine molecules or one molecule of a substance called diethylenediamine. To avoid this problem we place the ligand name in parentheses preceded by *bis*; that is, *bis(ethylenediamine)*.

□ *Bis-* is employed here so that when the name is used in verbal communication it is clear that the meaning is two ethylenediamine molecules.

5. **As noted earlier, in the *formula* of a complex, the symbol for the metal is written first, followed by those of the ligands. Among the ligands, anionic ligands are written first (in alphabetical order), followed by neutral ligands (also in alphabetical order). In the *name* of the complex, the ligands are named first, in alphabetical order *without regard to charge,* followed by the name of the metal.** For example, suppose we had a complex composed of Co^{3+}, two Cl^- (chloro- ligands), one CN^- (cyano- ligand), and three NH_3 (ammine- ligands). The formula of the electrically neutral complex would be written $[CoCl_2(CN)(NH_3)_3]$. In the name of this complex, the ligands would be specified before the metal as *triamminedichlorocyano-* (*triammine-* for the three NH_3 ligands, *dichloro-* for the two Cl^- ligands, and *cyano-* for the CN^- ligand). Notice that in alphabetizing the names of the ligands, we ignore the prefixes *tri-* and *di-*. Thus *triammine-* is written before *dichloro-* because *ammine-* precedes *chloro-* alphabetically. For the same reason, *dichloro-* is written before *cyano-*. The complete name for the complex is given below under Rule 7.

□ In the formula, the metal ion appears first, followed by the ligands; in the name, the ligands are specified first, followed by the metal.

□ The ligands are alphabetized according to the first letter of the name of the ligand, not the first letter of the prefix.

6. **Negative (anionic) complex ions always end in the suffix *-ate.*** This suffix is appended to the English name of the metal atom in most cases. However, if the name of the metal ends in *-ium, -um,* or *-ese,* the ending is dropped and replaced by *-ate.*

Metal	Metal as Named in an Anionic Complex
Aluminum	aluminate
Chromium	chromate
Manganese	manganate
Nickel	nickelate
Cobalt	cobaltate
Zinc	zincate
Platinum	platinate
Vanadium	vanadate

For metals whose symbols are derived from their Latin names, the suffix *-ate* is appended to the Latin stem. (An exception, however, is mercury; in an anion it is named *mercurate.*)

Metal	Stem	Metal as Named in an Anionic Complex
Iron	ferr-	ferrate
Copper	cupr-	cuprate
Lead	plumb-	plumbate
Silver	argent-	argentate
Gold	aur-	aurate
Tin	stann-	stannate

For neutral or positively charged complexes, the metal is *always* specified with the English name for the element, *without any suffix.*

7. **The oxidation state of the metal in the complex is written in Roman numerals within parentheses following the name of the metal.** For example,

☐ As you learned earlier, the charge on the complex is the algebraic sum of the charges on the ligands and the charge on the metal ion.

$[CoCl_2(CN)(NH_3)_3]$ is triamminedichlorocyanocobalt(III)

$[Co(NH_3)_6]^{3+}$ is the hexaamminecobalt(III) ion

$[CuCl_4]^{2-}$ is the tetrachlorocuprate(II) ion

No Space

Notice that there are no spaces between the names of the ligands and the name of the metal, and that there is no space between the name of the metal and the parentheses that enclose the oxidation state expressed in Roman numerals.

The following are some additional examples. Study them carefully to see how the rules given above apply. Then try the practice exercises that follow.

☐ Notice, once again, that the alphabetical order of the ligands is determined by the first letter in the name of the ligand, not the first letter in the prefix.

$[Ni(CN)_4]^{2-}$	tetracyanonickelate(II) ion
$K_3[CoCl_6]$	potassium hexachlorocobaltate(III)
$[CoCl_2(NH_3)_4]^+$	tetraamminedichlorocobalt(III) ion
$Na_3[Co(NO_2)_6]$	sodium hexanitrocobaltate(III)
$[Ag(NH_3)_2]^+$	diamminesilver(I) ion
$[Ag(S_2O_3)_2]^{3-}$	dithiosulfatoargentate(I) ion
$[Mn(en)_3]Cl_2$	tris(ethylenediamine)manganese(II) chloride
$[PtCl_2(NH_3)_2]$	diamminedichloroplatinum(II)

Practice Exercise 5: Write the formula for each of the following: (a) hexachlorostannate(IV) ion and (b) ammonium diaquatetracyanoferrate(II). (Hint: Divide each name into its various parts.)

Practice Exercise 6: Name the following compounds: (a) $K_3[Fe(CN)_6]$ and (b) $[CrCl_2(en)_2]_2SO_4$.

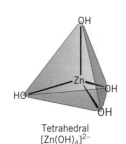

Tetrahedral
$[Zn(OH)_4]^{2-}$

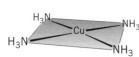

Square planar
$[Cu(NH_3)_4]^{2+}$

FIG. 21.15 **Tetrahedral and square planar geometries.** These are structures that occur for complexes in which the metal ion has a coordination number of 4. For the copper complex, we are viewing the square planar structure tilted back into the plane of the paper.

21.7 COORDINATION NUMBER AND STRUCTURE ARE OFTEN RELATED

One of the most interesting aspects of the study of complexes is the kinds of structures that they form. In many ways, this is related to the **coordination number** of the metal ion, which we define as *the number of donor atoms attached to the metal ion.* For example, in the complex $[Ni(CN)_4]^{2-}$ the nickel is surrounded by the four carbon atoms that belong to the cyanide ions, so the coordination number of Ni^{2+} in the complex is 4. Similarly, the coordination number of Cr^{3+} in the $[Cr(H_2O)_6]^{3+}$ ion is 6, and the coordination number of Ag^+ in $[Ag(NH_3)_2]^+$ is 2.

Sometimes the coordination number isn't immediately obvious from the formula of the complex. For example, you learned that there are many polydentate ligands which contain more than one donor atom that can bind simultaneously to a metal ion. Often, a metal is able to accommodate two or more polydentate ligands to give complexes with formulas such as $[Cr(H_2O)_2(en)_2]^{3+}$ and $[Cr(en)_3]^{3+}$. In each of these examples, the coordination number of the Cr^{3+} is 6. In the $[Cr(en)_3]^{3+}$ ion, there are three ethylenediamine ligands that each supply two donor atoms, for a total of 6, and in $[Cr(H_2O)_2(en)_2]^{3+}$, the two ethylenediamine ligands supply a total of 4 donor atoms and the two H_2O molecules supply another 2, so once again the total is 6.

☐ Ordinarily, the VSEPR model isn't used to predict the structures of transition metal complexes because it can't be relied on to give correct results when the metal has a partially filled *d* subshell.

Structures of complexes depend on coordination number

For metal complexes, there are certain geometries that are usually associated with particular coordination numbers.

Coordination Number 2. Examples are complexes such as $[Ag(NH_3)_2]^+$ and $[Ag(CN)_2]^-$. Usually, these complexes have a linear structure such as

$$[H_3N—Ag—NH_3]^+ \quad \text{and} \quad [NC—Ag—CN]^-$$

(Since the Ag^+ ion has a filled *d* subshell, it behaves as any of the representative elements as far as predicting geometry by VSEPR theory, so these structures are exactly what we would expect based on that theoretical model.)

Coordination Number 4. Two common geometries occur when four ligand atoms are bonded to a metal ion, namely, tetrahedral and square planar. These are illustrated in Figure 21.15. The tetrahedral geometry is usually found with metal ions that have completely filled *d* subshells, such as Zn^{2+}. The complexes $[Zn(NH_3)_4]^{2+}$ and $[Zn(OH)_4]^{2-}$ are examples.

Square planar geometries are observed for complexes of Cu^{2+}, Ni^{2+}, and especially Pt^{2+}. Examples are $[Cu(NH_3)_4]^{2+}$, $[Ni(CN)_4]^{2-}$, and $[PtCl_4]^{2-}$. The most well-studied square planar complexes are those of Pt^{2+}, because they are considerably more stable than the others.

Coordination Number 6. The most common coordination number for complex ions is 6. Examples are $[Al(H_2O)_6]^{3+}$, $[Co(C_2O_4)_3]^{3-}$, $[Ni(en)_3]^{2+}$, and $[Co(EDTA)]^-$. With few exceptions, all complexes with a coordination number of 6 are octahedral. This holds true for those formed from both monodentate and bidentate ligands, as illustrated in Figure 21.16. In describing the shapes of octahedral complexes, most chemists use one of the simplified drawings of the octahedron shown in Figure 21.17.

Practice Exercise 7: What is the coordination number of the metal ion in $[Cr(C_2O_4)_3]^{3-}$? (Hint: Identify the ligand and sketch its structure.)

Practice Exercise 8: What is the coordination number of the metal ion in (a) $[CoCl_2(C_2O_4)_2]^{3-}$, (b) $[Cr(C_2O_4)_2(en)]^-$, and (c) $[Co(H_2O)_2(en)_2]^{3+}$?

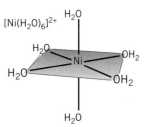

$[Ni(H_2O)_6]^{2+}$

Complex with monodentate ligands

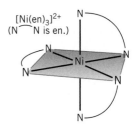

$[Ni(en)_3]^{2+}$
($N\frown N$ is en.)

Complex with bidentate ligands

FIG. 21.16 **Octahedral complexes.** Complexes with this geometry can be formed with either monodentate ligands such as water or with polydentate ligands such as ethylenediamine (en). To simplify the drawing of the ethylenediamine complex, the atoms joining the donor nitrogen atoms in the ligand, $—CH_2—CH_2—$, are represented as the curved line between the N atoms. Also notice that the nitrogen atoms of the bidentate ligand span adjacent positions within the octahedron. This is the case for all polydentate ligands that you will encounter in this book.

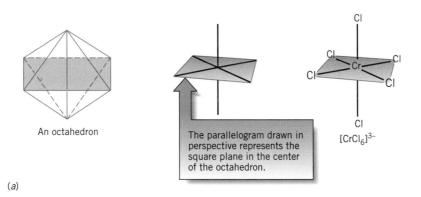

An octahedron

The parallelogram drawn in perspective represents the square plane in the center of the octahedron.

$[CrCl_6]^{3-}$

(a)

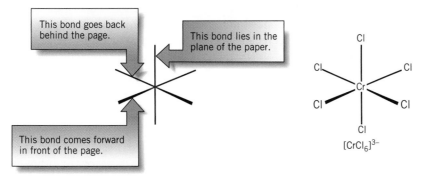

This bond goes back behind the page.

This bond lies in the plane of the paper.

This bond comes forward in front of the page.

$[CrCl_6]^{3-}$

(b)

FIG. 21.17 **Simplified representations of the octahedral complex, $[CrCl_6]^{3-}$.** (*a*) Drawings similar to those you learned to construct in Chapter 9. (*b*) An alternative method of representing the octahedron.

21.8 ISOMERS OF COORDINATION COMPLEXES ARE COMPOUNDS WITH THE SAME FORMULA BUT DIFFERENT STRUCTURES

When you write the chemical formula for a compound, you might be tempted to think that you should also be able to predict exactly what the structure of the molecule or ion is. As you may realize by now, this just isn't possible in many cases. Sometimes we can use simple rules to make reasonable structural guesses, as in the discussion of the drawing of Lewis structures in Chapter 8, but these rules apply only to simple molecules and ions. For more complex substances, there usually is no way of knowing for sure what the structure of the molecule or ion is without performing the necessary experiments to determine the structure.

One of the reasons that structures can't be predicted with certainty from chemical formulas alone is that there are usually many different ways that the atoms in the formula can be arranged. In fact, it is frequently possible to isolate two or more compounds that actually have the same chemical formula. For example, three different solids, each with its own characteristic color and other properties, can be isolated from a solution of chromium(III) chloride. All three have the same overall composition, and in the absence of other data, their formulas are written $CrCl_3 \cdot 6H_2O$. However, experiments have shown that these solids are actually the salts of three different complex ions. Their actual formulas (and colors) are

$[Cr(H_2O)_6]Cl_3$	purple
$[CrCl(H_2O)_5]Cl_2 \cdot H_2O$	blue-green
$[CrCl_2(H_2O)_4]Cl \cdot 2H_2O$	green

Chromium(III) chloride hexahydrate. The hydrated chromium(III) chloride purchased from chemical supply companies is actually $[CrCl_2(H_2O)_4]Cl \cdot 2H_2O$. Its green color in both the solid state and solution is due to the complex ion $[CrCl_2(H_2O)_4]^+$. *(Michael Watson.)*

Even though their overall compositions are the same, each of these substances is a distinct chemical compound with its own unique set of properties.

The existence of two or more compounds, each having the same chemical formula, is known as **isomerism.** In the example above, each salt is said to be an **isomer** of $CrCl_3 \cdot 6H_2O$. For coordination compounds, isomerism can occur in a variety of ways. In the example above, isomers exist because of the different possible ways that the water molecules and chloride ions can be held in the crystals. In one instance, all the water molecules serve as ligands, while in the other two, part of the water is present as water of hydration and some of the chloride is bonded to the metal ion. Another example, which is similar in some respects, is $Cr(NH_3)_5SO_4Br$. This "substance" can be isolated as two isomers.

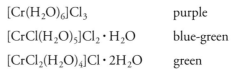

$$[CrSO_4(NH_3)_5]Br \quad \text{and} \quad [CrBr(NH_3)_5]SO_4$$

☐ Ag_2SO_4 is soluble but $BaSO_4$ is insoluble. $BaBr_2$ is soluble but AgBr is isoluble.

They can be distinguished chemically by their differing abilities to react with Ag^+ and Ba^{2+}. The first isomer reacts in aqueous solution with Ag^+ to give a precipitate of AgBr, but it doesn't react with Ba^{2+}. This tells us that Br^- exists as a free ion in the solution. It also suggests the SO_4^{2-} is bound to the chromium and is unavailable to react with Ba^{2+} to give insoluble $BaSO_4$.

The second isomer, $[CrBr(NH_3)_5]SO_4$, reacts in solution with Ba^{2+} to give a precipitate of $BaSO_4$, which means there is free SO_4^{2-} in the solution. There is no reaction with Ag^+, however, because Br^- is bonded to the chromium and is not available as free Br^- in the solution. Thus, we see that even though both isomers have the same overall composition, they behave chemically in quite different ways and are therefore distinctly different compounds.

Stereoisomerism relates to how atoms are arranged in space

One of the most interesting kinds of isomerism found among coordination compounds is called **stereoisomerism**, which is defined as *differences among isomers that arise as a result of the various possible orientations of their atoms in space.* In other words, when stereoisomerism exists, we have compounds in which the same atoms are attached to each other, but they differ in the way those atoms are arranged in space relative to one another.

One form of stereoisomerism is called **geometric isomerism;** it is best understood by considering an example. Consider the square planar complexes having the formula $PtCl_2(NH_3)_2$. There are two ways to arrange the ligands around the platinum, as illustrated below. In one isomer, called the **cis isomer,** the chloride ions are *next to each other* and the ammonia molecules are also next to each other. In the other isomer, called the **trans isomer,** identical ligands are *opposite each other*. In identifying (and naming) isomers, *cis* means "on the same side," and *trans* means "on opposite sides."

Cl   NH₃
\ /
Pt
/ \
Cl   NH₃

cis isomer
cis-diamminedichloroplatinum(II)

and

H₃N   Cl
\ /
Pt
/ \
Cl   NH₃

trans isomer
trans-diamminedichloroplatinum(II)

□ The isomer on the left, *cis*-$PtCl_2(NH_3)_2$, is the anticancer drug known as *cisplatin*. It is interesting that only the cis isomer of the compound is clinically active against tumors. The trans isomer is totally ineffective.

Geometric isomerism also occurs for octahedral complexes. For example, consider the ions $[CrCl_2(H_2O)_4]^+$ and $[CrCl_2(en)_2]^+$. Both can be isolated as cis and trans isomers.

H₂O
H₂O | Cl
\ | /
Cr
/ | \
H₂O | Cl
H₂O

cis

H₂O
H₂O | Cl
\ | /
Cr
/ | \
Cl | OH₂
H₂O

trans

$[CrCl_2(H_2O)_4]^+$

□ The structures of the octahedral complexes are being drawn following the method in Figure 21.17*b*.

Curved lines connecting nitrogen atoms represent —CH₂—CH₂—, which links the nitrogen atoms in ethylenediamine.

N
N | N
\ | /
Cr
/ | \
N | Cl
Cl

cis

Cl
N | N
\ | /
Cr
/ | \
N | N
Cl

trans

N‿N is en,
(ethylenediamine)
$NH_2CH_2CH_2NH_2$.

$[CrCl_2(en)_2]^+$

In the cis isomer, the chloride ligands are both on the same side of the metal ion; in the trans isomer, the chloride ligands are on opposite ends of a line that passes through the center of the metal ion.

FIG. 21.18 **One difference between left and right hands.** A left-hand glove won't fit the right hand. *(Michael Watson.)*

Chirality is a subtle type of isomerism

There is a second kind of stereoisomerism that is much more subtle than geometric isomerism. This occurs when molecules are exactly the same except for one small difference— they are *nonsuperimposable mirror images of each other*. They bear the same relationship to each other as do your left and right hands. (In fact this relationship between such isomers is sometimes referred to by the term *handedness*.)

Although similar in appearance, your two hands are not exactly alike. If you place one hand over the other, palms down, your thumbs point in opposite directions. **Superimposability** is the ability of two objects to fit "one within the other" with no mismatch of parts. Your left and right hands lack this ability, and we say they are *nonsuperimposable*. This is why your right hand doesn't fit into your left-hand glove (Figure 21.18); your right hand does not match *exactly* the space that corresponds to your left hand.

Your hands are also mirror images of each other. If you hold your left hand so it faces a mirror, and then look at its reflection as illustrated in Figure 21.19, you will see that it looks exactly like your right hand. If it were possible to reach "through the looking glass,"

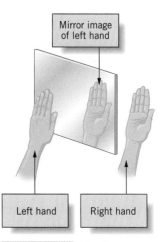

FIG. 21.19 **Hands are mirror images of each other.** The image of the left hand reflected in the mirror appears the same as the right hand.

FIG. 21.20 The two isomers of [Co(en)₃]³⁺. Isomer II is constructed as the mirror image of Isomer I. No matter how Isomer II is turned about, it is not superimposable on Isomer I.

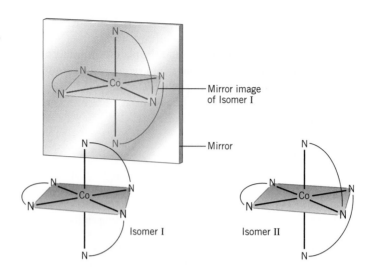

□ Chirality is the technical term for "handedness," meaning objects structurally related to each other as are our left and right hands.

Thumbtacks are not chiral. Thumbtacks and their mirror images are superimposable; they are not chiral and are identical. *(Andy Washnik.)*

your right-hand glove would fit the reflection of your left hand perfectly. Thus, your two hands are *nonsuperimposable mirror images* of each other.

If two objects are nonsuperimposable mirror images of each other, they are not identical and are said to be **chiral.** Your left and right hands have this property and are not exactly alike. A pair of thumbtacks, however, are mirror images of each other and *are* superimposable, so they are identical. Thumbtacks are not chiral.

Some complex ions exhibit chirality

The most common examples of chirality among coordination compounds occur with octahedral complexes that contain two or three bidentate ligands—for instance, $[CoCl_2(en)_2]^+$ and $[Co(en)_3]^{3+}$. For the complex $[Co(en)_3]^{3+}$, the two nonsuperimposable isomers, called **enantiomers,** are shown in Figure 21.20. For the complex $[CoCl_2(en)_2]^+$, only the *cis* isomer is chiral, as described in Figure 21.21.

As you can see, chiral isomers differ in only a very minor way from each other. This difference is so subtle that most of the properties of chiral isomers are identical. They have identical melting points and boiling points, and in nearly all of their reactions, their behavior is exactly alike. The only way that the difference between chiral molecules or ions manifests itself is in the way that they interact with physical or chemical "probes" that also

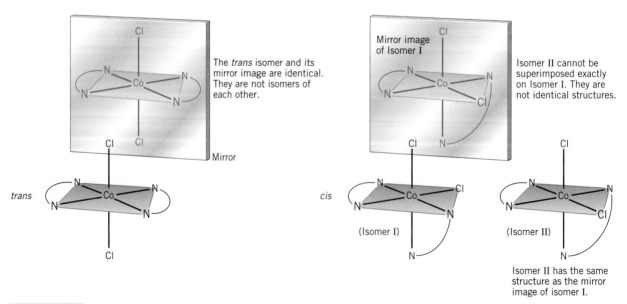

FIG. 21.21 Isomers of the $[CoCl_2(en)_2]^+$ ion. The mirror image of the trans isomer can be superimposed exactly on the original, so the trans isomer is not chiral. The cis isomer (Isomer I) is chiral, however, because its mirror image (Isomer II) cannot be superimposed on the original.

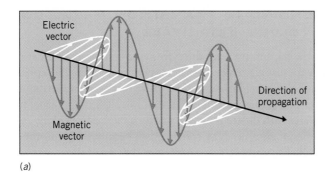

(a)

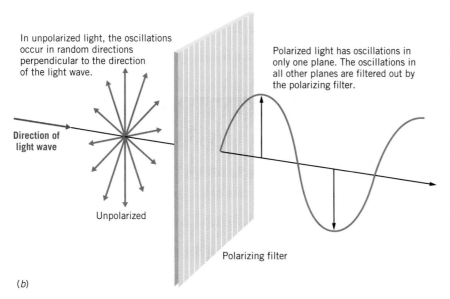

In unpolarized light, the oscillations occur in random directions perpendicular to the direction of the light wave.

Direction of light wave

Unpolarized

Polarized light has oscillations in only one plane. The oscillations in all other planes are filtered out by the polarizing filter.

Polarizing filter

(b)

FIG. 21.22 **Unpolarized and polarized light.** (*a*) Light possesses electric and magnetic components that oscillate perpendicular to the direction of propagation of the light wave. (*b*) In unpolarized light, the electromagnetic oscillations of the photons are oriented at random angles around the axis of propagation of the light wave. The polarizing filter has the effect of preventing oscillations from passing through unless they are in one particular plane. The result is called plane-polarized light.

have a handedness about them. For example, if two reactants are both chiral, then a given isomer of one of them will usually behave slightly differently toward each of the two isomers of the other reactant. This has very profound effects in biochemical reactions, in which nearly all of the molecules involved are chiral.

Chiral isomers can rotate plane-polarized light

One way that chiral isomers differ is in the way they affect polarized light. Light is *electromagnetic radiation* that possesses both electric and magnetic components that behave like vectors. These vectors oscillate in directions perpendicular to the direction in which the light wave is traveling (Figure 21.22*a*). In ordinary light, the oscillations of the electric and magnetic fields of the photons are oriented randomly around the direction of the light beam. In **plane-polarized light,** all the oscillations occur in the same plane (Figure 21.22*b*). Ordinary light can be polarized in several ways. One is to pass it through a special film of plastic, as in a pair of Polaroid sunglasses. This has the effect of filtering out all the vibrations except those that are in one plane (Figure 21.22*b*).

Chiral isomers like those described in Figures 21.20 and 21.21 are said to be **optically active** and have the ability to rotate plane-polarized light, as illustrated in Figure 21.23. Because of this phenomenon, chiral isomers are said to be **optical isomers.**

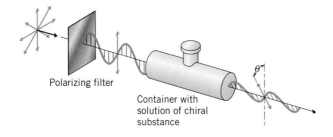

Polarizing filter

Container with solution of chiral substance

FIG. 21.23 **Rotation of polarized light by a chiral substance.** When plane-polarized light passes through a solution of a chiral substance, the plane of polarization is rotated either to the left or to the right. In this illustration, the plane of polarization of the light is rotated to the left by a measurable angle θ (as seen facing the light source).

21.9 | BONDING IN TRANSITION METAL COMPLEXES INVOLVES d ORBITALS

Complexes of the transition metals differ from the complexes of other metals in two special ways: (1) they are usually colored, whereas complexes of the representative metals are usually (but not always) colorless, and (2) their magnetic properties are often affected by the ligands attached to the metal ion. For example, it is not unusual for a given metal ion to form complexes with different ligands to give a rainbow of colors, as illustrated in Figure 21.24 for a series of complexes of cobalt. Also, because transition metal ions often have incompletely filled d subshells, we expect to find many of them with unpaired d electrons, and compounds that contain them should be paramagnetic. But for a given metal ion, the number of unpaired electrons is not always the same from one complex to another. For example, Fe^{2+} has four of its six $3d$ electrons unpaired in the $[Fe(H_2O)_6]^{2+}$ ion, but all of its electrons are paired in the $[Fe(CN)_6]^{4-}$ ion. As a result, the $[Fe(H_2O)_6]^{2+}$ ion is paramagnetic and the $[Fe(CN)_6]^{4-}$ ion is diamagnetic.

FIG. 21.24 **Colors of complex ions depend on the nature of the ligands.** Each of these brightly colored solutions contains a complex ion of Co^{3+}. The variety of colors arises because of the different ligands (molecules or anions) that are bonded to the cobalt ion in the complexes. *(Michael Watson.)*

Crystal field theory considers how d orbital energies are affected by the ligands

Any theory that attempts to explain the bonding in complex ions must also explain their colors and magnetic properties. One of the simplest theories that does this is the **crystal field theory.** The theory gets its name from its original use in explaining the behavior of transition metal ions in crystals. It was discovered later that the theory works well for transition metal complexes, too.

Crystal field theory ignores covalent bonding in complexes. It assumes that the primary stability comes from the electrostatic attractions between the positively charged metal ion and the negative charges of the ligand anions or dipoles. Crystal field theory's unique approach, though, is the way it examines how the negative charges on the ligands affect the energy of the complex by influencing the energies of the d orbitals of the metal ion, and this is what we will focus our attention on here. To understand the theory, therefore, it is essential that you know how the d orbitals are shaped and especially how they are oriented in space relative to each other. The d orbitals were described in Chapter 7, and they are illustrated again in Figure 21.25.

First, notice that four of the d orbitals have the same shape but point in different directions. These are the $d_{x^2-y^2}$, d_{xy}, d_{xz}, and d_{yz}. Each has four lobes of electron density. The fifth d orbital, labeled d_{z^2}, has two lobes that point in opposite directions along the z axis plus a small donut-shaped ring of electron density around the center that is concentrated in the xy plane.

Of prime importance to us are the *directions* in which the lobes of the d orbitals point. Notice that three of them—d_{xy}, d_{xz}, and d_{yz}—point *between* the x, y, and z axes. The other two—the d_{z^2} and $d_{x^2-y^2}$ orbitals—have their maximum electron densities *along* the x, y, and z axes.

◻ More complete theories consider the covalent nature of metal–ligand bonding, but crystal field theory nevertheless provides a useful model for explaining the colors and magnetic properties of complexes.

◻ The labels for the d orbitals come from the mathematics of quantum mechanics.

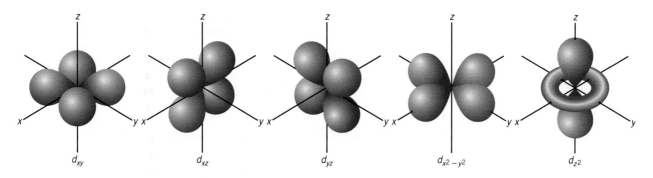

FIG. 21.25 The shapes and directional properties of the five *d* orbitals of a *d* subshell.

Now let's consider constructing an octahedral complex within this coordinate system. We can do this by bringing ligands in along each of the axes as shown in Figure 21.26. The question we want to answer is, "How do these ligands affect the energies of the *d* orbitals?"

In an isolated atom or ion, all the *d* orbitals of a given *d* subshell have the same energy. Therefore, an electron will have the same energy regardless of which *d* orbital it occupies. In an octahedral complex, however, this is no longer true. If the electron is in the $d_{x^2-y^2}$ or d_{z^2} orbital, it is forced to be nearer the negative charge of the ligands than if it is in a d_{xy}, d_{xz}, or d_{yz} orbital. Since the electron itself is negatively charged and is repelled by the charges of the ligands, the electron's potential energy will be higher in the $d_{x^2-y^2}$ and d_{z^2} orbitals than in a d_{xy}, d_{xz}, or d_{yz} orbital. Therefore, as the complex is formed, the *d* subshell actually splits into *two* new energy levels as shown in Figure 21.27. Here we see that regardless of which orbital the electron occupies, its energy increases because it is repelled by the negative charges of the approaching ligands. However, the electron is repelled *more* (and has a higher energy) if it is in an orbital that points directly at the ligands than if it occupies an orbital that points between them.

In an octahedral complex, the energy difference between the two sets of *d* orbital energy levels is called the **crystal field splitting.** It is usually given the symbol Δ (delta), and its magnitude depends on the following factors:

The nature of the ligand. *Some ligands produce a larger splitting of the energies of the d orbitals than others.* For a given metal ion, for example, cyanide always gives a large value of Δ and F⁻ always gives a small value. We will have more to say about this later.

The oxidation state of the metal. *For a given metal and ligand, the size of Δ increases with an increase in the oxidation number of the metal.* As electrons are removed from a metal and the charge on the ion becomes more positive, the ion becomes smaller. This

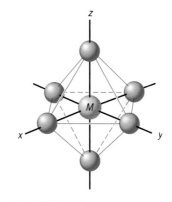

FIG. 21.26 **An octahedral complex ion with ligands that lie along the *x*, *y*, and *z* axes.**

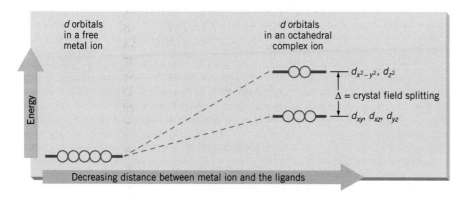

TOOLS
Crystal field splitting pattern for octahedral complexes

FIG. 21.27 **The changes in the energies of the *d* orbitals of a metal ion as an octahedral complex is formed.** As the ligands approach the metal ion, the *d* orbitals split into two new energy levels.

means that the ligands are attracted to the metal more strongly and they can approach the center of the complex more closely. As a result, they also approach the d orbitals along the x, y, and z axes more closely, and thereby cause a greater repulsion. This causes a greater splitting of the two d orbital energy levels and a larger value of Δ.

The row in which the metal occurs in the periodic table. *For a given ligand and oxidation state, the size of Δ increases going down a group.* In other words, for a given ligand, an ion of an element in the first row of transition elements has a smaller value of Δ than the ion of a heavier member of the same group. Thus, comparing complexes of Ni^{2+} and Pt^{2+} with the same ligand, we find that the platinum complex has the larger crystal field splitting. The explanation of this is that in the larger ion (e.g., Pt^{2+}), the d orbitals are larger and more diffuse and extend farther from the nucleus in the direction of the ligands. This produces a larger repulsion between the ligands and the orbitals that point at them.

The magnitude of Δ is very important in determining the properties of complexes, including the stabilities of oxidation states of the metal ions, the colors of complexes, and their magnetic properties. Let's look at some examples.

Crystal field theory can explain the relative stabilities of oxidation states

Comparing the cations formed by chromium, it is found that the Cr^{2+} ion is very easily oxidized to Cr^{3+}. This is easily explained by crystal field theory. In water, we expect the ions to exist as the complexes $[Cr(H_2O)_6]^{2+}$ and $[Cr(H_2O)_6]^{3+}$, respectively. Let's examine the energies and electron populations of the d orbital energy levels in each complex (Figure 21.28).

The element chromium has the electron configuration

$$Cr \quad [Ar]\, 3d^5 4s^1$$

Removing two electrons gives the Cr^{2+} ion, and removing three gives Cr^{3+}.

$$Cr^{2+} \quad [Ar]\, 3d^4$$

$$Cr^{3+} \quad [Ar]\, 3d^3$$

Next, we distribute the d electrons among the various d orbitals following Hund's rule, but for Cr^{2+} we have to make a choice. Should the electrons all be forced into the lower of the two energy levels, or should they be spread out? From the diagram we see that the fourth electron does not pair with one of the others in the lower energy d orbital level. Instead, three electrons populate the lower level and the fourth is in the upper level. We will discuss *why* this happens later, but for now, let's use the two energy diagrams to explain why Cr^{2+} is so easy to oxidize.

FIG. 21.28 **Energy level diagrams for the $[Cr(H_2O)_6]^{2+}$ and $[Cr(H_2O)_6]^{3+}$ ions.** The magnitude of Δ is larger for the chromium(III) complex because the Cr^{3+} ion is smaller than the Cr^{2+} ion and the ligands are drawn closer to the metal ion, thereby increasing repulsions felt by the $d_{x^2-y^2}$ and d_{z^2} orbitals.

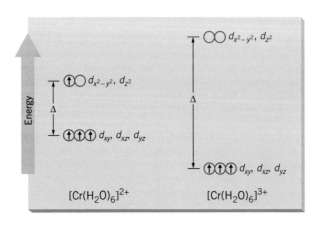

There are actually two factors that favor the oxidation of Cr(II) to Cr(III). First, the electron that is removed from Cr^{2+} to give Cr^{3+} comes from the *higher* energy level, so oxidizing the chromium(II) *removes* a high-energy electron. The second factor is the effect caused by increasing the oxidation state of the chromium. As we've pointed out, this increases the magnitude of Δ, and as you can see, the energy of the three electrons that remain is lowered. Thus, both the removal of a high-energy electron and the lowering of the energy of the electrons that are left behind help make the oxidation occur, and the $[Cr(H_2O)_6]^{2+}$ ion is very easily oxidized to $[Cr(H_2O)_6]^{3+}$.

Crystal field theory can explain the colors of complex ions

When light is absorbed by an atom, molecule, or ion, the energy of the photon raises an electron from one energy level to another. In many substances, such as sodium chloride, the energy difference between the highest energy populated level and the lowest energy unpopulated level is quite large, so the frequency of a photon that carries the necessary energy lies outside the visible region of the spectrum. The substance appears white because visible light is unaffected; it is reflected unchanged.

For complex ions of the transition metals, the energy difference between the *d* orbital energy levels is not very large, and photons with frequencies in the visible region of the spectrum are able to raise an electron from the lower energy set of *d* orbitals to the higher energy set. This is shown in Figure 21.29 for the $[Cr(H_2O)_6]^{3+}$ ion.

As you know, white light contains photons of all the frequencies and colors in the visible spectrum. If we shine white light through a solution of a complex, the light that passes through has all the colors *except* those that have been absorbed. It is not difficult to determine what will be seen if we know what colors are being absorbed. All we need is a color wheel like the one shown in Figure 21.30. Across from each other on the color wheel are *complementary colors*. Green-blue is the complementary color to red, and yellow is the complementary color to violet-blue. If a substance absorbs a particular color when bathed in white light, the perceived color of the reflected or transmitted light is the complementary color. In the case of the $[Cr(H_2O)_6]^{3+}$ ion, the light absorbed when the electron is raised from one set of *d* orbitals to the other has a frequency of 5.22×10^{14} Hz, which is the color of yellow light. This is why a solution of the ion appears violet.[7]

Because of the relationship between the energy and frequency of light, we see that the color of the light absorbed by a complex depends on the magnitude of Δ; the larger the size of Δ, the more energy the photon must have and the higher will be the frequency of the absorbed light. For a given metal in a given oxidation state, the size of Δ depends on the ligand. Some ligands give a large crystal field splitting, while others

> □ Remember, $E = h\nu$. The energy of the photon absorbed determines the frequency (and wavelength) of the absorbed light.

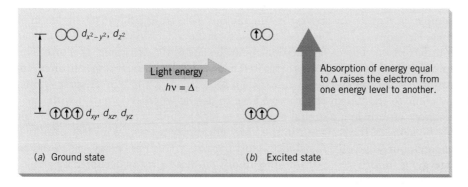

(a) Ground state

(b) Excited state

Light energy
$h\nu = \Delta$

Absorption of energy equal to Δ raises the electron from one energy level to another.

FIG. 21.29 Absorption of a photon by the $[Cr(H_2O)_6]^{3+}$ complex. (*a*) The electron distribution in the ground state of the $[Cr(H_2O)_6]^{3+}$ ion. (*b*) Light energy raises an electron from the lower energy set of *d* orbitals to the higher energy set.

[7] The perception of color is actually somewhat more complex than this because of the varying sensitivity of the human eye to various wavelengths. For example, the eye is much more sensitive to green than to red. If a compound reflects both of those colors with equal intensity, it will appear greenish simply because the eye sees green better than it sees red.

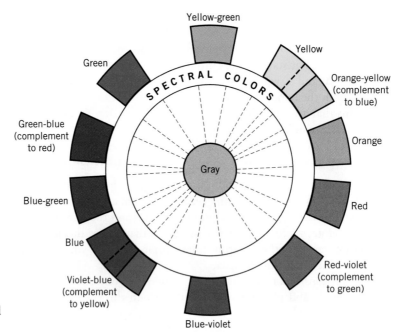

FIG. 21.30 **A color wheel.** Colors that are across from each other are called complementary colors. When a substance absorbs a particular color, light that is reflected or transmitted has the color of its complement. Thus something that absorbs red light appears green-blue, and vice versa.

☐ The order of the ligands can be determined by measuring the frequencies of the light absorbed by complexes.

TOOLS
Spectrochemical series

give a small splitting. For example, ammonia produces a larger splitting than water, so the complex $[Cr(NH_3)_6]^{3+}$ absorbs light of higher energy and higher frequency than $[Cr(H_2O)_6]^{3+}$. ($[Cr(NH_3)_6]^{3+}$ absorbs blue light and appears yellow.) Because changing the ligand changes Δ, the same metal ion is able to form a variety of complexes with a large range of colors.

A ligand that produces a large crystal field splitting with one metal ion also produces a large Δ in complexes with other metals. For example, cyanide ion is a very effective ligand and always gives a very large Δ, regardless of the metal to which it is bound. Ammonia is less effective than cyanide ion but more effective than water. Thus, ligands can be arranged in order of their effectiveness at producing a large crystal field splitting. This sequence is called the **spectrochemical series.** Such a series containing some common ligands arranged in order of their decreasing strength is

$$CN^- > NO_2^- > en > NH_3 > H_2O > C_2O_4^{2-} > OH^- > F^- > Cl^- > Br^- > I^-$$

For a given metal ion, cyanide ion produces the largest Δ and iodide produces the smallest.

Crystal field theory can explain the magnetic properties of complexes

Let's return to the question of the electron distribution among the d orbitals in Cr^{2+} complexes. As you saw above, this ion has four d electrons, and we noted that in placing these electrons in the d orbitals we had to make a decision about where to place the fourth electron. There's no question about the fate of the first three, of course. They just spread out across the three d orbitals in the lower level with their spins unpaired. In other words, we just follow Hund's rule, which we learned to apply in Chapter 7. But when we come to the fourth electron we have to decide whether to pair it with one of the electrons already in a d orbital of the lower set or to place it in one of the d orbitals of the higher set.[8] If we place it in the lower energy level, we give it extra stability (lower energy), but some of this stability is lost because it requires energy, called the **pairing energy,** P, to force the electron into an orbital that's already occupied by an electron. On the other hand, if we place it in the higher level, we are relieved of the burden of pairing the electron, but it also tends to give the electron a higher energy. Thus, for the

---

[8] We've never had to make this kind of decision before because the energy levels in atoms were always widely spaced. In complex ions, however, the spacing between the two d orbital energy levels is fairly small.

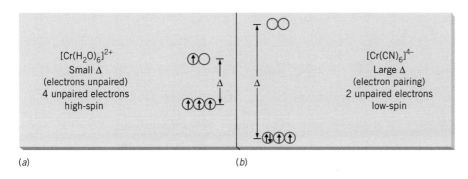

$[Cr(H_2O)_6]^{2+}$
Small Δ
(electrons unpaired)
4 unpaired electrons
high-spin

$[Cr(CN)_6]^{4-}$
Large Δ
(electron pairing)
2 unpaired electrons
low-spin

(a)   (b)

FIG. 21.31 The effect of Δ on the electron distribution in a complex with four *d* electrons. (*a*) When Δ is small, the electrons remain unpaired. (*b*) When Δ is large, the lower energy level accepts all four electrons and two electrons become paired.

fourth electron, "pairing" and "placing" work in opposite directions in the way they affect the energy of the complex.

The critical factor in determining whether the fourth electron enters the lower level and becomes paired, or whether it enters the higher level with the same spin as the other *d* electrons, is the magnitude of Δ. If Δ is larger than the pairing energy *P*, then greater stability is achieved if the fourth electron is paired with one in the lower level. If Δ is small compared to *P*, then greater stability is obtained by spreading the electrons out as much as possible. The complexes $[Cr(H_2O)_6]^{2+}$ and $[Cr(CN)_6]^{4-}$ illustrate this well.

Water is a ligand that does not produce a large Δ, so $P > \Delta$, and minimum pairing of electrons takes place. This explains the energy level diagram for the $[Cr(H_2O)_6]^{2+}$ complex in Figure 21.31*a*. When cyanide is the ligand, however, a very large Δ is obtained, and this leads to pairing of the fourth electron with one in the lower set of *d* orbitals. This is shown in Figure 21.31*b*. It is interesting to note that by measuring the degree of paramagnetism of the two complexes, it can be demonstrated experimentally that $[Cr(H_2O)_6]^{2+}$ has four unpaired electrons and the $[Cr(CN)_6]^{4-}$ ion has just two.

For octahedral chromium(II) complexes, there are two possibilities in terms of the number of unpaired electrons. They contain either four or two, depending on the magnitude of Δ. When there is the maximum number of unpaired electrons, the complex is described as being **high-spin;** when there is the minimum number of unpaired electrons it is described as being **low-spin.** High- and low-spin octahedral complexes are possible when the metal has a d^4, d^5, d^6, or d^7 electron configuration. Let's look at another example—one containing the Fe^{2+} ion, which has the electron configuration

$$Fe^{2+} \quad [Ar]\ 3d^6$$

At the beginning of this section we mentioned that the $[Fe(H_2O)_6]^{2+}$ ion is paramagnetic and has four unpaired electrons, while the $[Fe(CN)_6]^{4-}$ ion is diamagnetic, meaning it has no unpaired electrons. Now we can see why, by referring to Figure 21.32. Water produces a weak splitting and a minimum amount of pairing of electrons. When the six *d* electrons in the Fe^{2+} ion are distributed, one must be paired in the lower level after filling the upper level. The result is four unpaired *d* electrons, and a high-spin complex. Cyanide ion, however, produces a large splitting, so $\Delta > P$. This means that maximum pairing of electrons in the lower level takes place, and a low-spin complex is formed. Six electrons are just the right amount to completely fill all three of these *d* orbitals, and since all the electrons are paired, the complex is diamagnetic.

Crystal field theory also applies to other geometries

The crystal field theory can be extended to geometries other than octahedral. The effect that changing the structure of the complex has on the energies of the *d* orbitals is to change the splitting pattern.

Square planar complexes show additional splitting of the *d* orbital energies
We can form a square planar complex from an octahedral one by removing the ligands that lie along the *z* axis. As this happens, the ligands in the *xy* plane are able to approach the metal a little closer because they are no longer being repelled by ligands along the

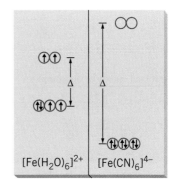

$[Fe(H_2O)_6]^{2+}$ $[Fe(CN)_6]^{4-}$

FIG. 21.32 The distribution of *d* electrons in $[Fe(H_2O)_6]^{2+}$ and $[Fe(CN)_6]^{4-}$. The magnitude of Δ for the cyanide complex is much larger than for the water complex. This produces a maximum pairing of electrons in the lower energy set of *d* orbitals in $[Fe(CN)_6]^{4-}$.

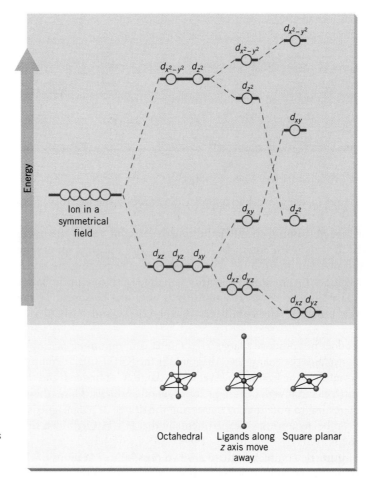

FIG. 21.33 Energies of *d* orbitals in complexes with various structures. The splitting pattern of the *d* orbitals changes as the geometry of the complex changes.

□ For Figure 21.33, as the energies of the *d* orbitals change, the d_{z^2} orbital drops in energy by the same amount as the $d_{x^2-y^2}$ rises. Similarly, the energies of the d_{xz} and d_{yz} orbitals drop only half as much as the energy of the d_{yz} rises. In this way, if all the *d* orbitals were filled, the changes in geometry would have no effect on the total energy of the complex.

$d_{x^2-y^2}$

d_{xy}

d_{z^2}

d_{xz}, d_{yz}

[Ni(CN)₄]²⁻

FIG. 21.34 Distribution of the electrons among the *d* orbitals of nickel in the diamagnetic [Ni(CN)₄]²⁻ ion.

z axis. The effect of these changes on the energies of the *d* orbitals is illustrated in Figure 21.33. The repulsions felt by the *d* orbitals that point in the *z* direction are reduced, so we find that the energies of the d_{z^2}, d_{xz}, and d_{yz} orbitals drop. At the same time, the energies of the orbitals in the *xy* plane feel greater repulsions, so the $d_{x^2-y^2}$ and d_{xy} orbitals rise in energy.

Nickel(II) ion (which has eight *d* electrons) forms a complex with cyanide ion that is square planar and diamagnetic. In this complex the strong field produced by the cyanide ions yields a large energy separation between the d_{xy} and $d_{x^2-y^2}$ orbitals, so that a low-spin complex results. The electron distribution in this complex is illustrated in Figure 21.34.

Tetrahedral complexes have a *d* orbital splitting pattern opposite that of octahedral complexes

The splitting pattern for the *d* orbitals in a tetrahedral complex is illustrated in Figure 21.35. Notice that the order of the energy levels is exactly opposite to that in an octahedral complex. In addition, the size of Δ is also much smaller for a tetrahedral complex than for an octahedral one. (Actually, $\Delta_{tet} \approx \frac{4}{9} \Delta_{oct}$ for the same metal ion with the same ligands.) This small Δ is always less than the pairing energy, so tetrahedral complexes are always high-spin complexes.

21.10 | METAL IONS SERVE CRITICAL FUNCTIONS IN BIOLOGICAL SYSTEMS

Most of the compounds in our bodies have structures based on carbon as the principal element, and their functions are usually related to the geometries assumed by carbon-containing compounds as well as the breaking and forming of carbon–carbon, carbon–oxygen, and carbon–nitrogen bonds. In Chapter 22 we will discuss some classes of biochemical molecules.

Our bodies also require certain metal ions in order to operate, and without them life cannot be sustained. For this reason, the study of metals in biological systems has become a very important branch of biochemistry, and a large number of research papers are published annually that deal with this topic. Table 21.2 lists some of the essential metals and the functions fulfilled by their ions.

A few metals, such as sodium and potassium, are found as simple monatomic ions in body fluids. Most metal ions, however, become bound by ligands and do their work as part of metal complexes. As examples, we will look briefly at two metals—iron and cobalt.

Iron is one of the essential elements required by our bodies. We obtain it in a variety of ways in our diets. Iron is involved in oxygen transport in our blood and in retaining oxygen in muscle tissue so that it's available when needed. The iron is present as Fe^{2+} held in a complex in which the basic ligand structure is

This ligand composition, with its square planar arrangement of nitrogen atoms that bind to a metal ion, is called a *porphyrin structure*. It is the ligand structure in a biologically active unit called heme. Heme is the oxygen-carrying component in the blood protein hemoglobin and in myoglobin, which is found in muscle tissue.

In the lungs, O_2 molecules are absorbed by the blood and become bound to Fe^{2+} ions in the heme units of hemoglobin (Figure 21.36). Blood circulation then carries the O_2 to tissues where it is needed, at which time it is released by the Fe^{2+}. One of the important functions of the porphyrin ligand in this process is to prevent the Fe^{2+} from being oxidized by the O_2. (In fact, if the iron is oxidized to Fe^{3+}, it no longer is able to carry O_2.) In muscle tissue, heme units in the protein myoglobin take O_2 from hemoglobin and hold it until it's needed. In this way, muscle tissue is able to store O_2 so that plenty of it is available when the muscle must work hard.

Heme units are also present in proteins called cytochromes where the iron is involved in electron transfer reactions that employ the +2 and +3 oxidation states of iron.

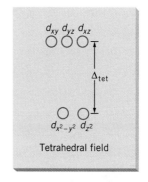

FIG. 21.35 Splitting pattern of the *d* orbitals for a tetrahedral complex. The crystal field splitting for the tetrahedral structure (Δ_{tet}) is smaller than that for the octahedral structure (Δ_{oct}). For complexes with the same ligands, $\Delta_{tet} \approx \frac{4}{9}\Delta_{oct}$.

☐ The porphyrin structure is present in chlorophyll, too, where the metal bound in the center is Mg^{2+}. Chlorophyll absorbs sunlight (solar energy), which is used by plants to convert carbon dioxide and water into glucose and oxygen.

☐ The iron in hemoglobin also binds CO_2 and helps transport it back to the lungs to be exhaled.

TABLE 21.2	Some Biologically Important Metals and their Corresponding Human Body Functions
Metal	Body Function
Na, Ca	Blood pressure and blood coagulation
Fe	Oxygen transport and storage
Ca	Teeth and bone formation
Ca	Urinary stone formation
Zn	Control of pH in blood
Ca, Mg	Muscle contraction
K	Maintenance of stomach acidity
Fe, Cu	Respiration
Cu	Bone health
Ca, Fe, Co	Cell division

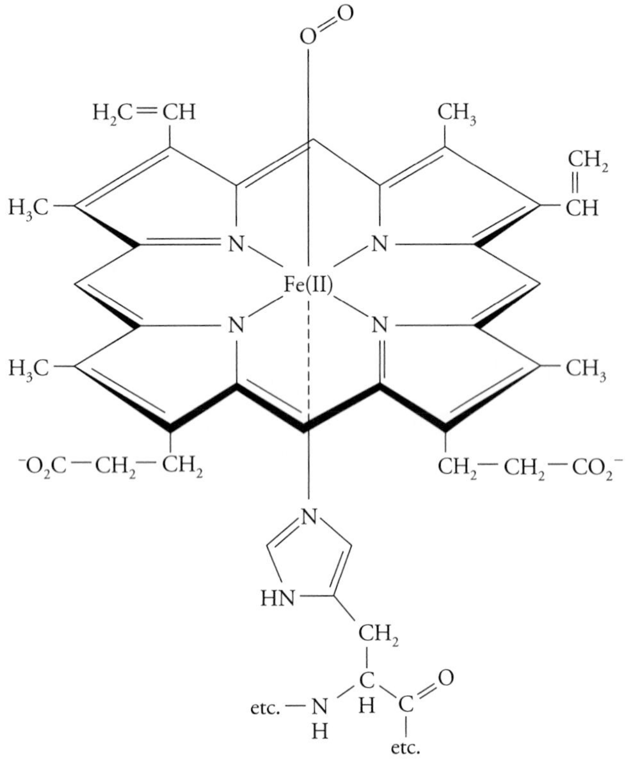

FIG. 21.36 Iron(II) bound to oxygen in heme. The porphyrin ring ligand in heme surrounds an Fe^{2+} ion that binds an O_2 molecule. In its oxygenated form, the Fe^{2+} is octahedrally coordinated in the structure.

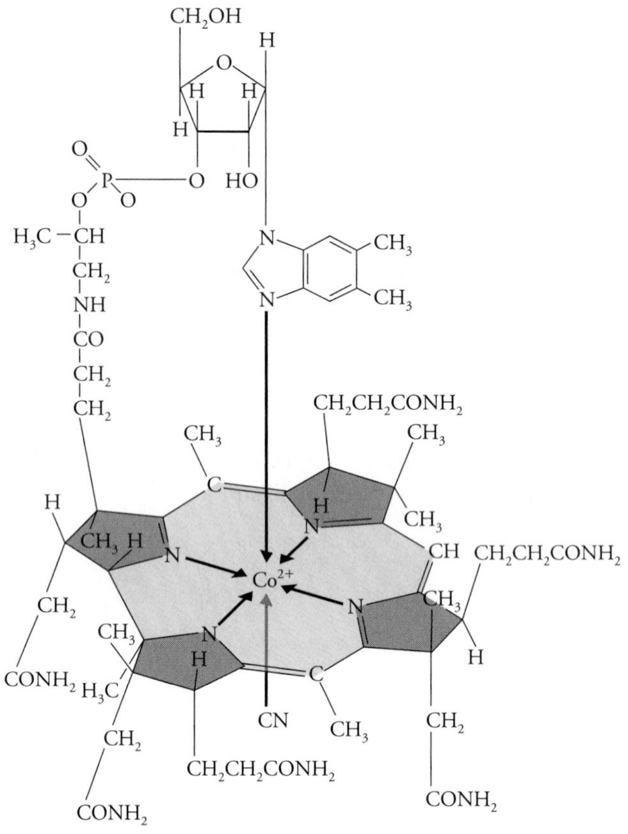

Vitamin B_{12}

FIG. 21.37 The structure of cyanocobalamin. Notice the cobalt ion in the center of the square planar arrangement of nitrogen atoms that are part of the ligand structure. Overall, the cobalt is surrounded octahedrally by donor atoms.

□ The ability of transition metals to exist in different oxidation states is one reason they are used in biological systems. They can easily take part in oxidation–reduction reactions. Copper(I) and copper(II) ions constitute another pair involved in catalyzing biochemical redox reactions.

A structure similar to heme is found in cyanocobalamin, the form of vitamin B_{12} found in vitamin pills (Figure 21.37). Here, a Co^{2+} ion is held in a square planar ligand structure (called a *corrin ring*) that is slightly different from that found in heme. Certain enzymes (biological catalysts) require cobalamins to function. Vitamin B_{12} is essential in our diets and a deficiency in the vitamin leads to a disease called pernicious anemia.

We have illustrated here just a few examples of the important roles that metal ions play in living systems. They are roles that cannot be fulfilled by other carbon-based compounds, some of which will be described in Chapter 22.

SUMMARY

Obtaining Nonmetallic Elements in Their Free States. Metalloids normally exist in positive oxidation states in compounds and are obtained by reduction. Common reducing agents are carbon and hydrogen. In nature, the noble gases are never found in compounds. Oxygen and nitrogen are obtained from air, and sulfur is found in natural deposits, often deep below the earth's surface. Carbon is found in coal and diamonds. Nonmetals are also found in naturally occurring compounds.

If the nonmetal is combined with a metal, oxidation is used to change it to the free element. The oxidizing strength of the halogens decreases from fluorine to iodine. In Group VIIA, a given halogen (e.g., F_2) is able to oxidize the halide ion below it (e.g., Cl^-), thereby displacing it from its compounds. Fluorine, being the most difficult element to oxidize, is obtained by electrolysis of molten mixtures of HF and KF. Elemental phosphorus is obtained from calcium phosphate by reaction with carbon and SiO_2.

Molecular Structures of the Nonmetals. Elements of Period 2, because of their small size, form strong π bonds. As a result, these elements easily participate in multiple bonding between like atoms, which accounts for diatomic molecules of O_2 and N_2, and the π-bonded structure of graphite. Elements of Periods 3, 4, and 5 are large and their p orbitals do not overlap well to form strong π bonds, so these elements prefer single σ bonds between like atoms, which leads to more complex molecular structures.

Different forms of the same element are called **allotropes.** Oxygen exists in two allotropic forms: dioxygen (O_2) and **ozone** (O_3). Carbon forms several allotropes including **diamond, graphite,** C_{60} molecules called **buckminsterfullerene** (one member of the **fullerene** family of structures), and **carbon nanotubes.** Elemental boron consists of B_{12} clusters linked through other boron atoms to give an extremely hard solid. Sulfur forms S_8 molecules that can be arranged in two different allotropic forms. Phosphorus occurs as **white phosphorus** (P_4), **red phosphorus,** and **black phosphorus.** Silicon only forms a diamondlike structure.

Preparation of Metals Most metals occur in compounds where they exist in positive oxidation states and are obtained from their compounds by reduction. Ions of sodium and potassium are found in seawater, along with magnesium. Insoluble carbonate deposits of Ca and Mg arise from the shells of marine animals. Many metals are found in the earth as oxides, sulfides, and phosphates. Active metals such as sodium, magnesium, and aluminum must generally be prepared by electrolysis. Metals of intermediate activity can be obtained using chemical reducing agents such as carbon and hydrogen. Reducing a metal oxide with carbon is called **smelting.** Compounds with small heats of formation tend to be thermally unstable and can be decomposed by heat.

Metallurgy. Usually, when an **ore** is dug from the ground, the metal-bearing component must be enriched by a pretreatment step that removes much of the unwanted **gangue. Flotation** is often used with lead and copper sulfide ores. Sulfide ores are usually **roasted** to convert them to oxides, which are more easily reduced. Aluminum's amphoteric character is exploited in purifying bauxite.

Carbon, in the form of **coke** made from coal, is a common chemical reducing agent because it is plentiful and inexpensive. Metallic iron forms in a **blast furnace** where a charge of iron ore, limestone, and coke reacts in a stream of heated air. Molten iron and **slag** flow to the bottom of the furnace and are periodically tapped. **Steel** is made from this impure iron mostly by the **basic oxygen process.**

Complex Ions of Metals. Coordination compounds contain **complex ions** (also called **complexes** or **coordination complexes**), formed from a metal ion and a number of ligands. **Ligands** are Lewis bases and may be **monodentate, bidentate,** or, in general, **polydentate,** depending on the number of **donor atoms** that they contain. Water is the most common monodentate ligand. Polydentate ligands bind to a metal through two or more donor atoms and yield ring structures called **chelates.** Common bidentate ligands are oxalate ion and ethylenediamine (en); a common polydentate ligand is ethylenediaminetetraacetic acid (EDTA), which has six donor atoms.

In the formula of a complex, the metal is written first, followed by the formulas of the ligands (anions first in alphabetical order followed by neutral ligands in alphabetical order). Brackets are often used to enclose the set of atoms that make up the complex, with the charge on the complex written outside the brackets. The charge on the complex is the algebraic sum of the charges on the metal ion and the charges on the ligands.

Complexes of polydentate ligands are more stable than similar complexes formed with monodentate ligands, partly because a polydentate ligand is less likely to be lost completely if one of its donor atoms becomes detached from the metal ion. The larger positive entropy change for dissociation of complexes with monodentate ligands also favors their dissociation compared with complexes of polydentate ligands. The phenomenon is called the **chelate effect.**

Nomenclature of Complexes. Complexes are named following a set of rules developed by the IUPAC. These are summarized on pages 876 to 878.

Coordination Number and Structure. The **coordination number** of a metal ion in a complex is the number of donor atoms attached to the metal ion. Polydentate ligands supply two or more donor atoms, which must be taken into account when determining the coordination number from the formula of the complex. Geometries associated with common coordination numbers are as follows: for coordination number 2, linear; for coordination number 4, tetrahedral and square planar (especially for Pt^{2+} complexes); and for coordination number 6, octahedral.

Isomers of Coordination Compounds. When two or more distinct compounds have the same chemical formula, they are **isomers** of each other. **Stereoisomers** have the same atoms attached to each other, but the atoms are arranged differently in space. In a **cis isomer,** attached groups of atoms are on the same side of some reference plane through the molecule. In a **trans isomer,** they are on opposite sides. Cis and trans isomerism is a form of **geometric isomerism. Chiral** isomers are exactly the same in every way but one—they are not **superimposable** on their mirror images. These kinds of isomers exist for complexes of the type $M(AA)_3$, where M is a metal ion and AA is a bidentate ligand, and also for complexes of the type cis-$M(AA)_2a_2$, where a is a monodentate ligand. Chiral isomers that are related as object to mirror images are said to be **enantiomers.** Because they are able to rotate **plane-polarized light,** they are called **optical isomers.**

Crystal Field Theory. In an octahedral complex, the ligands influence the energies of the d orbitals by splitting the d subshell into two energy sublevels. The lower energy one consists of the d_{xy}, d_{xz}, and d_{yz} orbitals; the higher energy level consists of the d_{z^2} and $d_{x^2-y^2}$ orbitals. The energy difference between the two new d sublevels is the **crystal field splitting,** Δ, and for a given ligand it increases with an increase in the oxidation state of the metal. For a given metal ion, Δ depends on the ligand, and it depends on the period number in which the metal is found.

In the **spectrochemical series,** ligands are arranged in order of their ability to cause a large Δ. Cyanide ion produces the largest crystal field splitting and iodide ion, the smallest. **Low-spin** complexes result when Δ is larger than the **pairing energy**—the energy needed to cause two electrons to become paired in the same orbital. **High-spin** complexes occur when Δ is smaller than the pairing energy. Light of energy equal to Δ is absorbed when an electron is raised from the lower energy set of d orbitals to the higher set, and the color of the complex is determined by the colors that remain in the transmitted light. Crystal field theory can also explain the relative stabilities of oxidation states, in many cases.

Different splitting patterns of the d orbitals occur for other geometries. The patterns for square planar and tetrahedral geometries are described in Figures 21.33 and 21.35, respectively. The value of Δ for a tetrahedral complex is only about 4/9 that of Δ for an octahedral complex.

Metals in Living Systems. Most metals required by living organisms perform their actions when bound as complex ions.

Heme contains Fe^{2+} held in a square planar porphyrin ligand and binds to O_2 in hemoglobin and myoglobin. Heme is also found in cytochromes where it participates in redox reactions involving Fe^{2+} and Fe^{3+}. Vitamin B_{12}, required by the body to prevent the vitamin deficiency disease called pernicious anemia, contains Co^{2+} in a corrin ring structure, which is similar to the porphyrin ring.

TOOLS FOR PROBLEM SOLVING

In this chapter you learned to apply the following concepts as tools in solving problems related to the properties of metal complexes. Study each tool carefully so that you know what each is used for. When faced with solving a problem, recall what each tool does and consider whether it will be helpful in finding a solution. This will aid you in selecting the tools you need.

Rules for writing formulas for complexes *(page 874)* The following rules apply whenever you have to write the formula for a complex ion:
1. The symbol for the metal ion is always given first, followed by the ligands.
2. When more than one kind of ligand is present, anionic ligands are written first (in alphabetical order), followed by neutral ligands (also in alphabetical order).
3. The charge on the complex is the algebraic sum of the charge on the metal ion and the charges on the ligands.

Rules for naming complexes *(pages 876 to 878)* Naming complexes follows rules that are an extension of the rules you learned earlier. You have to learn them and then apply them when you have to name a complex, or write a formula given the name.

Crystal field splitting pattern for an octahedral complex *(page 885)* Figure 21.27 forms the basis for applying the principles of crystal field theory to octahedral complexes. To use it, you need the electron configuration of the metal ion. First write the electron configuration for the metal under consideration. Then remove electrons from the atom starting with the outer s subshell first, followed if necessary by electrons from the underlying d subshell. For a complex under consideration, set up the splitting diagram and place electrons into the d orbitals following Hund's rule. For d^4, d^5, d^6, and d^7 configurations, you may have to decide whether a high- or low-spin configuration is preferred.

Spectrochemical series *(page 888)* Use the location of ligands in the spectrochemical series to compare their effects on the crystal field splitting. The series is

$$CN^- > NO_2^- > en > NH_3 > H_2O > C_2O_4^{2-} > OH^- > F^- > Cl^- > Br^- > I^-$$

QUESTIONS, PROBLEMS, AND EXERCISES

Answers to problems whose numbers are printed in color are given in Appendix B. More challenging problems are marked with asterisks. ILW = Interactive Learningware solution is available at www.wiley.com/college/brady. OH = an Office Hours video is available for this problem.

REVIEW QUESTIONS

Recovery of Nonmetals and Metalloids from Compounds

21.1 What is the major commercial source of N_2 and O_2?

21.2 Why is helium found in underground deposits? Why are only small quantities of radon observed in nature?

21.3 Chlorine, Cl_2, can be made in the lab by the reaction of HCl with $KMnO_4$, with $MnCl_2$ being among the products. Write a balanced net ionic equation for the reaction, keeping in mind that $KMnO_4$ is water soluble.

21.4 Complete the following chemical equations. If no reaction occurs, write N.R.

(a) $Cl_2 + KI \longrightarrow$

(b) $Br_2 + CaF_2 \longrightarrow$

(c) $I_2 + MgCl_2 \longrightarrow$

(d) $F_2 + SrCl_2 \longrightarrow$

21.5 How is Br_2 recovered from seawater?

21.6 Why can't fluorine be produced by the electrolysis of aqueous NaF? What products are formed at inert electrodes in the electrolysis of aqueous NaF?

21.7 Why is a molten mixture of KF and HF used in the production of F_2 by electrolysis rather than molten KF by itself?

21.8 Hydrogen fluoride is a gas that can be liquefied by cooling it to 19.6 °C (just slightly below room temperature). Why can't electrolysis be carried out on liquid HF to form F_2 and H_2?

21.9 Write the chemical equation for the production of elemental phosphorus from calcium phosphate and SiO_2. What is the reducing agent in the reaction? What is the function of the SiO_2? Why isn't SiO_2 reduced to Si in the reaction?

21.10 Under the proper conditions, iodide ion will react with H_2SO_4 to generate I_2 and H_2S. Write a balanced net ionic equation for the reaction.

21.11 Why are metalloids usually recovered from their compounds by chemical reduction of their compounds rather than by oxidation?

21.12 Write chemical equations for

(a) the chemical reduction of BCl_3 with hydrogen.

(b) the production of Si from SiO_2 using carbon as a reducing agent.

(c) the reduction of As_2O_3 with hydrogen.

Molecular Structures of the Nonmetals and Metalloids

21.13 Which of the nonmetals occur in nature in the form of isolated atoms?

21.14 Why are the Period 2 elements able to form much stronger π bonds than the nonmetals of Period 3? Why does a Period 3 nonmetal prefer to form all σ bonds instead of one σ bond and several π bonds?

21.15 Even though the nonmetals of Periods 3, 4, and 5 do not tend to form π bonds between like atoms, each of the halogens is able to form diatomic molecules (Cl_2, Br_2, I_2). Why?

21.16 What are *allotropes*? How do they differ from *isotopes*?

21.17 What are the two allotropes of oxygen?

21.18 Construct the molecular orbital diagram for O_2 and explain why it has two unpaired electrons. What is the net bond order in O_2?

21.19 Draw the Lewis structure for O_3. Is the molecule linear, based on the VSEPR theory? Assign formal charges to the atoms in the Lewis structure. Does this suggest the molecule is polar or nonpolar?

21.20 What beneficial function does ozone serve in the upper atmosphere?

21.21 Describe the structure of diamond. What kind of hybrid orbitals does carbon use to form bonds in diamond? What is the geometry around carbon in this structure?

21.22 Describe the structure of graphite. What kind of hybrid orbitals does carbon use in the formation of the molecular framework of graphite?

21.23 Why does graphite have lubricating properties?

21.24 Describe the C_{60} molecule. What is it called? What name is given to the series of similar substances?

21.25 How is the structure of a carbon nanotube related to the structure of graphite?

21.26 In elemental boron, there are clusters of boron atoms linked through other boron atoms. What is the formula for the boron clusters? What is the shape of a cluster?

21.27 What is the molecular structure of sulfur in its most stable allotropic form?

21.28 Make a sketch that describes the molecular structure of white phosphorus.

21.29 What are the P—P—P bond angles in the P_4 molecule? If phosphorus uses *p* orbitals to form the phosphorus–phosphorus bonds, what bond angle would give the best orbital overlap? On the basis of your answers to these two questions, explain why P_4 is so chemically reactive.

21.30 What structure has been proposed for red phosphorus? How do the reactivities of red and white phosphorus compare?

21.31 What is the molecular structure of black phosphorus? In what way does the structure of black phosphorus resemble that of graphite?

21.32 What is the molecular structure of silicon? Suggest a reason why silicon doesn't form an allotrope that's similar in structure to graphite.

Occurrence of Metals and Recovery of Metals from Compounds

21.33 Which are the three most abundant metals in seawater? Why don't we find large amounts of silver ion in seawater?

21.34 What is the origin of limestone?

21.35 Why are many metals found as oxides and sulfides in the earth?

21.36 Why is carbon used so often as an industrial reducing agent?

21.37 Write equations for the reduction of copper(II) oxide with hydrogen.

21.38 Why isn't thermal decomposition a practical method for obtaining metals such as sodium or magnesium?

21.39 In general, why do compounds tend to decompose at high temperatures but not at low temperatures?

21.40 In terms of thermodynamics, what must be true for us to be able to observe a substantial degree of decomposition of a compound?

21.41 The value of $\Delta G°$ for the decomposition of a metal oxide is negative if the heat of formation of the compound is positive. Why are we able to isolate such compounds at room temperature if they are unstable toward decomposition?

21.42 Many explosives have positive heats of formation. How does this explain why they tend to explode?

Metallurgy

21.43 Use your own words to define *metallurgy*.

21.44 What is an *ore*? What distinguishes an ore from some other potential source of a metal?

21.45 Many rocks are composed of minerals called aluminosilicates. One such mineral is called *orthoclase* and has the formula $KAlSi_3O_8$. Despite their high abundance, aluminosilicates are not considered aluminum ores. What is the probable reason for this?

21.46 What is *gangue*?

21.47 Why can gold be separated from impurities of rock and sand by *panning*?

21.48 Describe the *flotation process*.

21.49 Write chemical equations for the reactions that occur when Cu_2S and PbS are roasted in air. Write a chemical equation to show how SO_2 from the roasting can be kept from being released to the environment. Why might a sulfuric acid plant be located near a plant that roasts sulfide ores?

21.50 Write chemical equations that show how bauxite is purified.

21.51 Why is reduction, rather than oxidation, necessary to extract metals from their compounds?

21.52 Sodium, magnesium, and aluminum are produced by electrolysis instead of by reduction with chemical reducing agents. Why?

21.53 What is *coke*? How is it made?

21.54 Write chemical equations for the reduction of PbO and CuO with carbon.

21.55 Copper(I) sulfide can be converted to metallic copper without adding a reducing agent. Explain this using appropriate chemical equations.

21.56 Why is a blast furnace called a *blast* furnace?

21.57 What is the composition of the charge that's added to a blast furnace?

21.58 Describe the chemical reactions involved in the reduction of Fe_2O_3 that take place in a blast furnace. What is the active reducing agent in the blast furnace?

21.59 What is slag? Write a chemical equation for its formation in a blast furnace. What are some of its uses?

21.60 What does *refining* mean in metallurgy?

21.61 What is the difference between pig iron and steel?

21.62 Describe the basic oxygen process.

Complex Ions of Metals

21.63 The formation of the complex ion $[Cu(H_2O)_4]^{2+}$ is described as a Lewis acid–base reaction. Explain.
(a) What are the formulas of the Lewis acid and the Lewis base in the reaction?
(b) What is the formula of the ligand?
(c) What is the name of the species that provides the donor atom?
(d) What atom is the donor atom, and why is it so designated?
(e) What is the name of the species that is the acceptor?

21.64 To be a ligand, a substance should also be a Lewis base. Explain.

21.65 Why are substances that contain complex ions often called coordination compounds?

21.66 Give the names of two molecules mentioned in the text that are electrically neutral, monodentate ligands.

21.67 Give the formulas of four ions that have 1− charges and are monatomic, monodentate ligands.

21.68 Use Lewis structures to diagram the formation of $Cu(NH_3)_4^{2+}$ and $CuCl_4^{2-}$ ions from their respective components.

21.69 What must be true about the structure of a ligand classified as *bidentate*?

21.70 What is a *chelate*? Use Lewis structures to diagram the way that the oxalate ion, $C_2O_4^{2-}$, functions as a chelating agent.

21.71 How many donor atoms does EDTA^{4-} have?

21.72 Explain how a salt of EDTA^{4-} can retard the spoilage of salad dressing.

21.73 How does a salt of EDTA^{4-} in shampoo make the shampoo work better in hard water?

21.74 The cobalt(III) ion, Co^{3+}, forms a 1:1 complex with EDTA^{4-}. What is the net charge, if any, on this complex, and what would be a suitable formula for it (using the symbol EDTA)?

21.75 Which complex is more stable, $[Cr(NH_3)_6]^{3+}$ or $[Cr(en)_3]^{3+}$? Why?

Coordination Number and Structure

21.76 What is a *coordination number*? What structures are generally observed for complexes in which the central metal ion has a coordination number of 4? What is the most common structure observed for coordination number 6?

21.77 Sketch the structure of an octahedral complex that contains only identical monodentate ligands.

21.78 Sketch the structure of the octahedral $[Co(EDTA)]^-$ ion. Remember that donor atoms in a polydentate ligand span adjacent positions in the octahedron.

Isomers of Coordination Compounds

21.79 What are *isomers*?

21.80 Define *stereoisomerism, geometric isomerism, chiral isomers,* and *enantiomers*.

21.81 What are *cis* and *trans* isomers?

21.82 What condition must be fulfilled in order for a molecule or ion to be chiral?

21.83 What are *optical isomers*?

Bonding in Complexes

21.84 On appropriate coordinate axes, sketch and label the five *d* orbitals.

21.85 Which *d* orbitals point *between* the *x*, *y*, and *z* axes? Which point along the coordinate axes?

21.86 Explain why an electron in a $d_{x^2-y^2}$ or d_{z^2} orbital in an octahedral complex will experience greater repulsions because of the presence of the ligands than an electron in a d_{xy}, d_{xz}, or d_{yz} orbital.

21.87 Sketch the *d* orbital energy level diagram for a typical octahedral complex.

21.88 Explain why octahedral cobalt(II) complexes are easily oxidized to cobalt(III) complexes. Sketch the *d* orbital energy diagram and assume a large value of Δ when placing electrons in the *d* orbitals.

21.89 Explain how the same metal in the same oxidation state is able to form complexes of different colors.

21.90 If a complex appears red, what color light does it absorb? What color light is absorbed if the complex appears yellow?

21.91 What does the term *spectrochemical series* mean? How can the order of the ligands in the series be determined?

21.92 What do the terms *low-spin complex* and *high-spin complex* mean?

21.93 For which *d* orbital electron configurations are both high-spin and low-spin complexes possible?

21.94 Indicate by means of a sketch what happens to the *d* orbital electron configuration of the $[Fe(CN)_6]^{4-}$ ion when it absorbs a photon of visible light.

21.95 The complex $[Co(C_2O_4)_3]^{3-}$ is diamagnetic. Sketch the d orbital energy level diagram for the complex and indicate the electron populations of the orbitals.

21.96 Consider the complex $[MCl_4(H_2O)_2]^-$ illustrated below on the left. Suppose the structure of the complex is distorted to give the structure on the right, where the water molecules along the z axis have moved away from the metal somewhat and the four chloride ions along the x and y axes have moved closer. What effect will this distortion have on the energy level splitting pattern of the d orbitals? Use a sketch of the splitting pattern to illustrate your answer.

before distortion

after distortion

Metals in Living Systems

21.97 In what ways is the porphyrin structure important in biological systems?

21.98 If a metal ion is held in the center of a porphyrin ring structure, what is its coordination number? (Assume the porphyrin is the only ligand.)

21.99 What function does heme serve in hemoglobin? What does it do in myoglobin?

21.100 How are the ligand ring structures similar in vitamin B_{12} and in heme? What metal is coordinated in cobalamin?

21.101 What are some of the roles played by calcium ion in the body?

REVIEW PROBLEMS

Thermal Stability of Metal Compounds

OH 21.102 Estimate the temperature at which $\Delta G_T^\circ = 0$ for the decomposition of mercury(II) oxide according to the following equation.

$$2HgO(s) \longrightarrow 2Hg(g) + O_2(g)$$

For HgO, $\Delta H_f^\circ = -90.8$ kJ mol^{-1} and $S^\circ = 70.3$ J mol^{-1} K^{-1}; for Hg(g), $\Delta H_f^\circ = +61.3$ kJ mol^{-1} and $S^\circ = 175$ J mol^{-1} K^{-1}; for O$_2$, $S^\circ = 205$ J mol^{-1} K^{-1}.

OH 21.103 From the data below, estimate the temperature at which $K_P = 1$ for the reaction

$$CuO(s) \longrightarrow Cu(s) + \tfrac{1}{2}O_2(g)$$

For CuO, $\Delta H_f^\circ = -155$ kJ mol^{-1}. Absolute entropies: CuO(s), 42.6 J mol^{-1} K^{-1}; Cu(s), 33.2 J mol^{-1} K^{-1}; and O$_2$(g), 205 J mol^{-1} K^{-1}.

Complex Ions

21.104 The iron(III) ion forms a complex with six cyanide ions that is often called the ferricyanide ion. What is the net charge on the complex ion, and what is its formula? What is the IUPAC name for the complex?

21.105 The silver ion forms a complex ion with two ammonia molecules. What is the formula of the ion and what is its IUPAC name? Can the complex ion exist as a salt with the sodium ion or with the chloride ion? Write the formula of the possible salt. (Use brackets and parentheses correctly.)

21.106 Write the formula, including its correct charge, for a complex that contains Co^{3+}, two Cl$^-$, and two ethylenediamine ligands.

OH 21.107 Write the formula, including its correct charge, for a complex that contains Cr^{3+}, two NH$_3$ ligands, and four NO$_2^-$ ligands.

Naming Complexes

21.108 How would the following molecules or ions be named as ligands when writing the name of a complex ion?
(a) $C_2O_4^{2-}$
(b) S^{2-}
(c) Cl^-
(d) $(CH_3)_2NH$ (dimethylamine)

OH 21.109 How would the following molecules or ions be named as ligands when writing the name of a complex ion?
(a) NH_3
(b) N^{3-}
(c) SO_4^{2-}
(d) $C_2H_3O_2^-$

21.110 Give IUPAC names for each of the following.
(a) $[Ni(NH_3)_6]^{2+}$
(b) $[CrCl_3(NH_3)_3]^-$
(c) $[Co(NO_2)_6]^{3-}$
(d) $[Mn(CN)_4(NH_3)_2]^{2-}$
(e) $[Fe(C_2O_4)_3]^{3-}$

21.111 Give IUPAC names for each of the following.
(a) $[AgI_2]^-$
(b) $[SnS_3]^{2-}$
(c) $[Co(H_2O)_4(en)_2]_2(SO_4)_3$
(d) $[CrCl(NH_3)_5]SO_4$
(e) $K_3[Co(C_2O_4)_3]$

21.112 Write chemical formulas for each of the following.
(a) tetraaquadicyanoiron(III) ion
(b) tetraammineoxalatonickel(II)
(c) diaquatetracyanoferrate(III) ion
(d) potassium hexathiocyanatomanganate(III)
(e) tetrachlorocuprate(II) ion

21.113 Write chemical formulas for each of the following.
(a) tetrachloroaurate(III) ion
(b) bis(ethylenediamine)dinitroiron(III) ion
(c) tetraamminedicarbonatocobalt(III) nitrate
(d) ethylenediaminetetraacetatoferrate(II) ion
(e) diamminedichloroplatinum(II)

Coordination Number and Structure

21.114 In $[FeCl_2(H_2O)_2(en)]$, what is the coordination number of iron?

OH 21.115 What is the coordination number of nickel in $[Ni(NO_2)_2(C_2O_4)_2]^{4-}$?

21.116 NTA is the abbreviation for nitrilotriacetic acid, a substance that was used at one time in detergents. Its structure is

The four donor atoms of the ligand are shown in red. Sketch the structure of an octahedral complex containing the NTA ligand. Assume that two water molecules are also attached to the metal ion and that each oxygen donor atom in the NTA is bonded to a position in the octahedron that is adjacent to the nitrogen of the NTA.

21.117 The compound shown below is called diethylenetriamine and is abbreviated "dien."

$$H_2\ddot{N}—CH_2—CH_2—\ddot{N}H—CH_2—CH_2—\ddot{N}H_2$$

When it bonds to a metal, it is a ligand with three donor atoms.

(a) Which are most likely the donor atoms?

(b) What is the coordination number of cobalt in the complex $Co(dien)_2^{3+}$?

(c) Sketch the structure of the complex $[Co(dien)_2]^{3+}$.

(d) Which complex would be expected to be more stable in aqueous solution, $[Co(dien)_2]^{3+}$ or $[Co(NH_3)_6]^{3+}$?

(e) What would be the structure of triethylenetetraamine?

Isomers of Coordination Compounds

21.118 Below are two structures drawn for a complex. Are they actually different isomers, or are they identical? Explain your answer.

Structure I   Structure II

*21.119 Below is a structure for one of the isomers of the complex $[Co(H_2O)_3(dien)]^{3+}$. Are isomers of this complex chiral? Justify your answer.

N⌒N⌒N represents dien

21.120 Sketch and label the isomers of the square planar complex $[PtBrCl(NH_3)_2]$.

21.121 The complex $[CoCl_3(NH_3)_3]$ can exist in two isomeric forms. Sketch them.

21.122 Sketch the chiral isomers of $[Co(C_2O_4)_3]^{3-}$.

OH 21.123 Sketch the chiral isomers of $[CrCl_2(en)_2]^+$. Is there a nonchiral isomer of the complex?

Bonding in Complexes

21.124 In which complex do we expect to find the larger Δ?

(a) $[Cr(H_2O)_6]^{2+}$ or $[Cr(H_2O)_6]^{3+}$

(b) $[Cr(en)_3]^{3+}$ or $[CrCl_6]^{3-}$

21.125 Arrange the following complexes in order of increasing wavelength of the light absorbed by them: $[Cr(H_2O)_6]^{3+}$, $[CrCl_6]^{3-}$, $[Cr(en)_3]^{3+}$, $[Cr(CN)_6]^{3-}$, $[Cr(NO_2)_6]^{3-}$, $[CrF_6]^{3-}$, $[Cr(NH_3)_6]^{3+}$

OH 21.126 Which complex should be expected to absorb light of the highest frequency, $[Cr(H_2O)_6]^{3+}$, $[Cr(en)_3]^{3+}$, or $[Cr(CN)_6]^{3-}$?

21.127 Which complex should absorb light at the longer wavelength?

(a) $[Fe(H_2O)_6]^{2+}$ or $[Fe(CN)_6]^{4-}$

(b) $[Mn(CN)_6]^{3-}$ or $[Mn(CN)_6]^{4-}$

21.128 In each pair below, which complex is expected to absorb light of the shorter wavelength? Justify your answers.

(a) $[RuCl(NH_3)_5]^{2+}$ or $[FeCl(NH_3)_5]^{2+}$

(b) $[Ru(NH_3)_6]^{2+}$ or $[Ru(NH_3)_6]^{3+}$

21.129 A complex $[CoA_6]^{3+}$ is red. The complex $[CoB_6]^{3+}$ is green. Which ligand, A or B, produces the larger crystal field splitting, Δ? Explain your answer.

21.130 Referring to the two ligands, A and B, described in the preceding problem, which complex would be expected to be more easily oxidized, $[CoA_6]^{2+}$ or $[CoB_6]^{2+}$? Explain your answer.

21.131 Referring to the complexes in the preceding two problems, would the color of $[CoA_6]^{2+}$ more likely be red or blue?

21.132 Would the complex $[CoF_6]^{4-}$ more likely be low-spin or high-spin? Could it be diamagnetic?

21.133 Sketch the d orbital energy level diagrams for $[Fe(H_2O)_6]^{3+}$ and $[Fe(CN)_6]^{3-}$ and predict the number of unpaired electrons in each.

ADDITIONAL EXERCISES

*21.134 In the decomposition of HgO described in Problem 21.102, what are the equilibrium molar concentrations of $Hg(g)$ and $O_2(g)$ above solid HgO at the temperature at which $\Delta G_T^\circ = 0$?

OH 21.135 Estimate K_P at 100, 500, and 1000 °C for the reaction

$$MoO_3(s) \rightleftharpoons Mo(s) + \tfrac{3}{2}O_2(g)$$

given the following data:

	ΔH_f° (kJ mol^{-1})	S° (J mol^{-1} K^{-1})
$MoO_3(s)$	−754.3	78.2
$Mo(s)$	0.0	28.6
$O_2(g)$	0.0	205.0

21.136 Is the complex $[Co(EDTA)]^-$ chiral? Illustrate your answer with sketches.

21.137 The complex $[PtCl_2(NH_3)_2]$ can be obtained as two distinct isomeric forms. Make a model of a tetrahedron and show that if the complex were tetrahedral, two isomers would be impossible.

*21.138 A solution was prepared by dissolving 0.500 g of $CrCl_3 \cdot 6H_2O$ in 100 mL of water. A silver nitrate solution was added and gave a precipitate of AgCl that was filtered from the mixture, washed, dried, and weighed. The AgCl had a mass of 0.538 g.

(a) What is the formula of the complex ion of chromium in the compound?

(b) What is the correct formula for the compound?

(c) Sketch the structure of the complex ion in the compound.

(d) How many different isomers of the complex can be drawn?

*21.139 The compound $Cr_2(NH_3)_6Cl_6$ is a neutral salt in which the cation and anion are both octahedral complex ions. How many isomers (including possible structural and chiral isomers) are there that have this overall composition?

*21.140 The complex $[Co(CN)_6]^{4-}$ is not expected to be perfectly octahedral. Instead, the ligands in the xy plane are pulled closer to the Co^{2+} ion while those along the z axis move slightly farther away. Using information available in this chapter, explain why the distortion of the octahedral geometry leads to a net lowering of the energy of the complex.

EXERCISES IN CRITICAL THINKING

21.141 In Section 21.2 we assumed that $\Delta H_T^\circ \approx \Delta H_{298}^\circ$. Why is this just an approximation? What factors would cause ΔH_T° to differ from ΔH_{298}°?

21.142 Graphite is a reasonably good conductor in directions parallel to the planes of the carbon atoms, but is a poor conductor in a direction perpendicular to the planes. Why is this so? Would you expect carbon nanotubes to be good conductors of electricity along their length? Explain your answer.

21.143 Considering the fact that unshared electron pairs normally contribute to the polarity of a molecule, is the ozone molecule expected to be polar or nonpolar? How does your answer compare with the answer reached for Question 21.19?

21.144 It was mentioned on page 858 that d orbitals are capable of participating in the formation of π bonds. Make a sketch that illustrates how such a bond could be formed between two d orbitals and between a d and a p orbital.

21.145 The two chiral isomers of $[Co(C_2O_4)_3]^{3-}$ (shown below) can be viewed as propellers having either a right- or left-handed twist, respectively. They are identified by the labels Δ and Λ, as indicated. A 50–50 mixture of both isomers is said to be racemic and will not rotate plane-polarized light. Using various laboratory procedures the two isomers present in a racemic mixture can be separated from each other. For this complex, however, a solution of a single isomer is not stable and gradually reverts to a mixture of the two isomers by a process called racemization. Racemization involves the conversion of one isomer to the other until an equilibrium between the two isomers is achieved (i.e., $\Delta \rightleftharpoons \Lambda$). One mechanism proposed for the racemization of isomers of $[Co(C_2O_4)_3]^{3-}$ involves dissociation of an oxalate ion followed by rearrangement and then reattachment of $C_2O_4^{2-}$.

Δ isomer $C_2O_4^{2-}$ Λ isomer

What experiment could you perform to test whether this is really the mechanism responsible for the racemization of $[Co(C_2O_4)_3]^{3-}$?

ORGANIC COMPOUNDS, POLYMERS, AND BIOCHEMICALS

22

High-speed racing boats often are built with hulls made of a polymer called Kevlar. Because of the polymer's high strength, the hulls can be made thin, thereby reducing weight and increasing speed. How polymers form is one of the topics of this chapter. (Courtesy Extremeboat.com and Crash.net)

CHAPTER OUTLINE

22.1 Organic chemistry is the study of carbon compounds

22.2 Hydrocarbons consist of only C and H atoms

22.3 Ethers and alcohols are organic derivatives of water

22.4 Amines are organic derivatives of ammonia

22.5 Organic compounds with carbonyl groups include aldehydes, ketones, and carboxylic acids

22.6 Polymers are composed of many repeating molecular units

22.7 Most biochemicals are organic compounds

22.8 Nucleic acids carry our genetic information

THIS CHAPTER IN CONTEXT   A large proportion of the substances we encounter on a daily basis, including foods, fuels, and the many plastics and polymers used to make containers and fabrics, have molecular structures based on atoms of carbon linked to one another by covalent bonds. You've already seen a variety of organic compounds as examples used in discussions throughout this book. They include such substances as hydrocarbons, alcohols, ketones (such as acetone), and organic acids. The number of such compounds is enormous and their study constitutes the branch of chemistry called *organic chemistry,* so named because at one time it was believed that such substances could only be synthesized by living organisms.

At the molecular level of life, nature uses compounds of carbon. The amazing variety of living systems down to the uniqueness of each individual is possible largely because of the properties of this element. We'll take a look at some of carbon's properties in this chapter.

22.1 | ORGANIC CHEMISTRY IS THE STUDY OF CARBON COMPOUNDS

Organic chemistry is the study of the preparation, properties, identification, and reactions of those compounds of carbon not classified as inorganic. The latter include the oxides of carbon, the bicarbonates and carbonates of metal ions, the metal cyanides, and a handful of other compounds. There are several million known carbon compounds, and all but a very few are classified as organic.

Carbon has some unique properties that enable it to form so many compounds

What makes the existence of so many organic compounds possible is not just the multivalency of carbon—its atoms always have four bonds in organic compounds. Rather, carbon atoms are unique in their ability to form strong covalent bonds to each other *while at the same time bonding strongly to atoms of other nonmetals, such as H, N, and O.* For example, molecules in the plastic polyethylene have *carbon chains* that are thousands of carbon atoms long with hydrogen atoms attached to each carbon.

□ Sulfur atoms can also form long chains, but they are unable to hold the atoms of any other element strongly at the same time.

$$\text{H}-\underset{|}{\overset{|}{\text{C}}}-\underset{|}{\overset{|}{\text{C}}}-\underset{|}{\overset{|}{\text{C}}}-\underset{|}{\overset{|}{\text{C}}}-\underset{|}{\overset{|}{\text{C}}}-\underset{|}{\overset{|}{\text{C}}}-\underset{|}{\overset{|}{\text{C}}}-\underset{|}{\overset{|}{\text{C}}}-\underset{|}{\overset{|}{\text{C}}}-\underset{|}{\overset{|}{\text{C}}}-\underset{|}{\overset{|}{\text{C}}}-\underset{|}{\overset{|}{\text{C}}}-\underset{|}{\overset{|}{\text{C}}}-\text{etc.}$$

polyethylene (small segment of one molecule)

The longest known sequence of atoms of other members of the carbon family, each also bonded to hydrogens, is eight for silicon, five for germanium, two for tin, and one for lead.

Another reason for the huge number of organic compounds is *isomerism,* which was introduced in Chapter 21 (page 880) where we discussed isomers of complex ions. *Isomers,* recall, are compounds with identical molecular formulas but whose molecules have different structures. Examples are the isomers of butane, C_4H_{10}, and isomers of C_2H_6O (ethyl alcohol and dimethyl ether). See Figure 22.1.

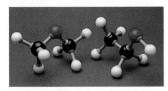

(a)

(b)

FIG. 22.1 Isomers. (*a*) The isomers of C_4H_{10}. Butane is on the left and 2-methylpropane (isobutane) is on the right. (*b*) The isomers of C_2H_6O. Dimethyl ether is on the left and ethanol is on the right. (*Robert Capece.*)

butane
BP −0.5 °C

isobutane
BP −11.7 °C

ethyl alcohol
BP 78.5 °C

dimethyl ether
BP −23 °C

Because the isomers have different structures, the effects of intermolecular attractions are different, which gives rise to differences in boiling points.

Organic compounds can also exhibit chirality, a property we discussed in Chapter 21 on page 881. When a carbon atom is bonded to four different atoms or groups, the carbon

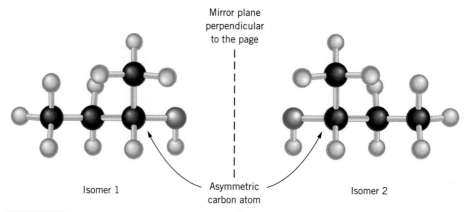

Mirror plane
perpendicular
to the page

Isomer 1

Asymmetric
carbon atom

Isomer 2

FIG. 22.2 **Chiral isomers of 2-butanol.** Isomer 2 is the mirror image of Isomer 1. No matter how you twist or turn Isomer 1, you cannot get it to fit exactly onto Isomer 2, which means the two isomers are nonsuperimposable mirror images of each other.

is a chiral center. It is called an **asymmetric carbon atom.** An example is 2-butanol, in which the asymmetric carbon, shown in red, is bonded to H, OH, CH_3, and CH_2CH_3.

$$\underset{\text{2-butanol}}{CH_3\overset{\overset{\displaystyle OH}{|}}{C}HCH_2CH_3}$$

The two nonsuperimposable mirror image isomers of this compound are shown in Figure 22.2.

As the number of carbons per molecule increases, the number of possible isomers for any given formula becomes astronomic.

Formula	Number of Isomers
C_8H_{18}	18
$C_{10}H_{22}$	75
$C_{20}H_{42}$	366,319
$C_{40}H_{82}$	6.25×10^{13} (estimated)

☐ Few of the possible isomers of the compounds with large numbers of carbon atoms have actually been made, but there is nothing except too much crowding within the molecules of some of them to prevent their existence.

Organic families are defined by their functional groups

The study of the huge number of organic compounds is manageable because they can be sorted into *organic families* defined by *functional groups*. A major goal of this chapter is to show how they enable us to organize and understand the properties of organic compounds.

Functional groups are small structural units within molecules at which most of the compound's chemical reactions occur (Table 22.1). For example, all *alcohols* have the *alcohol group*, and a molecule of the simplest member of the alcohol family, methyl alcohol, has only one carbon. Ethyl alcohol molecules have two carbons. All members of the family of *carboxylic acids* (organic acids) have the *carboxyl group*. The carboxylic acid with two carbons per molecule is the familiar weak acid, acetic acid.

alcohol group　　methyl alcohol　　carboxyl group　　acetic acid

One family in Table 22.1, the *alkane* family, has no functional group, just C—C and C—H single bonds. These bonds are virtually nonpolar, because C and H are so alike in electronegativity. Therefore, alkane molecules are the least able of all organic molecules to attract ions or polar molecules. Hence, they do not react, at least at room temperature, with

TABLE 22.1 **Some Important Families of Organic Compounds**

Family	Characteristic Structural Feature[a]	Example
Hydrocarbons	Only C and H present	
	Families of Hydrocarbons:	
	Alkanes: only single bonds	CH_3CH_3
	Alkenes: $C{=}C$	$CH_2{=}CH_2$
	Alkynes: $C{\equiv}C$	$HC{\equiv}CH$
	Aromatic: Benzene ring	⬡
Ethers	ROR′	CH_3OCH_3
Alcohols	ROH	CH_3CH_2OH
Aldehydes	$\overset{\displaystyle O}{\overset{\|}{R}}CH$	$CH_3\overset{\displaystyle O}{\overset{\|}{C}}H$
Ketones	$R\overset{\displaystyle O}{\overset{\|}{C}}R′$	$CH_3\overset{\displaystyle O}{\overset{\|}{C}}CH_3$
Carboxylic acids	$R\overset{\displaystyle O}{\overset{\|}{C}}OH$	$CH_3\overset{\displaystyle O}{\overset{\|}{C}}OH$
Esters	$R\overset{\displaystyle O}{\overset{\|}{C}}OR′$	$CH_3\overset{\displaystyle O}{\overset{\|}{C}}OCH_3$
Amines	RNH_2, RNHR′, RNR′R″	CH_3NH_2
		CH_3NHCH_3
		$CH_3\overset{\displaystyle CH_3}{\overset{\|}{N}}CH_3$
Amides	$R\overset{\displaystyle O}{\overset{\|}{C}}{-}\overset{\displaystyle R''(H)}{\overset{\|}{N}}R′(H)$	$CH_3\overset{\displaystyle O}{\overset{\|}{C}}NH_2$

[a] R, R′, and R″ represent hydrocarbon groups—*alkyl groups*—defined in the text.

TOOLS
Functional groups

polar or ionic reactants such as strong acids and bases nor with common oxidizing agents, like dichromate or permanganate ion.

Condensed structures save time and space

The structural formulas in Table 22.1 are "condensed" because this saves both space and time in writing structures *without sacrificing any structural information.* In condensed structures, C—H bonds are usually "understood." When three H atoms are attached to carbon, they are set alongside the C, as in CH_3, but sometimes H_3C. When a carbon is bonded to two other H atoms, the condensed symbol is usually CH_2, sometimes H_2C. Thus the condensed structure of ethanol is CH_3CH_2OH, and that of dimethyl ether is CH_3OCH_3 or H_3COCH_3.

Functional groups can react with polar reactants

When a polar group of atoms, like the OH group or even a halogen atom, is attached to carbon, the molecule has a polar site. It now can attract polar and ionic reactants and undergo chemical changes, but generally at or near just this functional group. This is why compounds of widely varying size but with the same functional group display very similar kinds of reactions.

For example, the reactions of *amines* (organic derivatives of ammonia, discussed in detail in Section 22.4) are similar from amine to amine. Therefore, we need only learn the handful of *kinds* of reactions exhibited by all amines and then adapt this knowledge to a specific example as needed. A special symbol makes this easy.

☐ Alkanes do react with fluorine, chlorine, bromine, and hot nitric acid. They also burn, a reaction with oxygen.

☐ We have used condensed structures in many of our earlier discussions.

In structural formulas R represents an alkane-like group

To focus on the general properties of a functional group, chemists use the symbol R in a structure to represent any and all purely alkane-like groups that do not react with a specific reactant. For example, one type of amine is represented by the formula, $R—NH_2$. R may be CH_3, CH_3CH_2, $CH_3CH_2CH_2$, and so forth. Because the amines are compounds with an ammonia-like group, they are all Brønsted bases and neutralize acids just as ammonia does. Therefore, we can summarize the reaction of hydrochloric acid with any amine of the $R—NH_2$ type, regardless of how large the hydrocarbon portion of the molecule is, by the following general equation.

$$R—NH_2 + HCl \longrightarrow R—NH_3^+ + Cl^-$$

□ The symbol R is from the German *radikal*.

Straight chain

Carbon forms open-chain and ring compounds

The continuous sequence of carbon atoms in polyethylene, shown above, is called a **straight chain.** This means *only* that no carbon atom is bonded to more than two other carbons, but it says nothing about the *conformation* of the molecule. If we made a molecular model of polyethylene and coiled it into a spiral, we would still say that its carbon skeleton has a straight chain. It has no branches.

Branched chains are also very common. Isooctane, for example, has a *main chain* of five carbon atoms (in black) carrying three CH_3 *branches* (shown in red).

Branched chain

□ Isooctane, one of the many alkanes in gasoline, is the standard for the octane ratings of various types of gasoline. Pure isooctane is assigned an octane rating of 100.

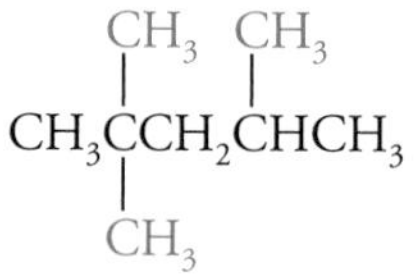

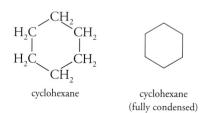

isooctane

Carbon rings are also common. Cyclohexane, for example, has a ring of six carbon atoms.

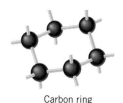

Carbon ring

$$\begin{array}{ccc} & CH_2 & \\ H_2C & & CH_2 \\ | & & | \\ H_2C & & CH_2 \\ & CH_2 & \end{array}$$

cyclohexane

cyclohexane
(fully condensed)

Just about everything is "understood" in the very convenient, fully condensed structure of cyclohexane. When polygons, like the hexagon, are used to represent rings, the following conventions are used.

TOOLS

Using polygons to represent rings

Using polygons to represent rings

1. C occurs at each corner unless O or N (or another multivalent atom) is explicitly written at a corner.
2. A line connecting two corners is a covalent bond between adjacent ring atoms.
3. Remaining bonds, as required by the covalence of the atom at a corner, are understood to hold H atoms.
4. Double bonds are always explicitly shown.

We can illustrate these rules with the following cyclic compounds.

cyclopropane    cyclobutane   cyclopentane   cyclohexane 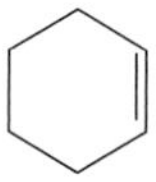   cyclohexene   bromocyclohexane

There is no theoretical upper limit to the size of a ring.

Many compounds have **heterocyclic** rings. Their molecules contain an atom other than carbon in a ring position, as in pyrrole, piperidine, and tetrahydropyran.

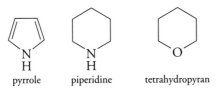

pyrrole   piperidine   tetrahydropyran

☐ The tetrahydropyran ring occurs in molecules of sugar.

The atom in the ring other than carbon is called the *heteroatom*, and any atoms of H or other element bonded to it are not "understood" but always shown.

General principles apply to structure and physical properties

One goal of organic chemistry is to enable the prediction of properties from molecular structure. Functional groups and molecular size determine, for example, whether a compound is soluble in water.

Functional groups affect water solubility

Piperidine and tetrahydropyran (shown below) are both freely soluble in water, whereas cyclohexane is insoluble. The cyclohexane molecule, having only nonpolar C—C and C—H single bonds, is unable to form hydrogen bonds or other polar attractions with water molecules (see page 481). Molecules of piperidine and tetrahydropyran, however, can form hydrogen bonds (shown as "dotted" bonds, ···) with water.

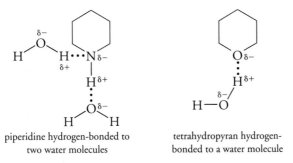

piperidine hydrogen-bonded to
two water molecules

tetrahydropyran hydrogen-
bonded to a water molecule

Thus organic compounds whose molecules have N and O atoms are more soluble in water than molecules of alkanes of about the same size.

Molecular size affects physical properties

Even with N or O atoms, a compound's solubility in water decreases as the hydrocarbon portion of its molecules becomes larger and larger. The cholesterol molecule, for example, has an OH group, but that group is overwhelmed by the huge hydrocarbon group. So cholesterol is practically insoluble in water.

☐ The insolubility of cholesterol in water accounts for its separation from the bloodstream as heart disease slowly develops.

cholesterol

Cholesterol, however, is correspondingly more soluble in organic solvents such as benzene, chloroform, and acetone.

22.2 HYDROCARBONS CONSIST OF ONLY C AND H ATOMS

□ Recall that in insufficient oxygen, some carbon monoxide and carbon also form when hydrocarbons burn.

□ The addition of H_2 to double or triple bonds is discussed further on page 912.

The alkanes make up just one family of a multifamily group of compounds called the **hydrocarbons** whose molecules consist only of C and H atoms. Besides the alkanes, the hydrocarbons include *alkenes, alkynes,* and *aromatic hydrocarbons* (Table 22.1). All are insoluble in water. All burn, giving carbon dioxide and water if sufficient oxygen is available.

Alkenes and alkynes are called **unsaturated compounds.** Because their molecules have double bonds or triple bonds, respectively, they are able to react with H_2 under appropriate conditions to yield alkanes. The alkanes are **saturated compounds,** compounds with only single bonds, and are unable to react with H_2. The aromatic hydrocarbons are also unsaturated because the carbon atoms of their rings, when represented by simple Lewis structures, also have double bonds. However, they do not react with hydrogen.

benzene
(Lewis structure)

benzene
(alternative structure)

Most hydrocarbons come from petroleum

Petroleum refinery. The towers of this petroleum refinery contain catalysts that break up large molecules in hot crude oil to sizes suitable for vehicle engines. *(Martin Bond/Photo Researchers.)*

The *fossil fuels*—coal, petroleum, and natural gas—supply us with virtually all of our hydrocarbons. One of the operations in petroleum refining is to boil crude oil (petroleum freed of natural gas) and selectively condense the vapors between preselected temperature ranges. The liquid collected at each range is called a *fraction*, and the operation is *fractional distillation*. Each fraction is a complex mixture made up almost entirely of hydrocarbons, mostly alkanes. *Gasoline*, for example, is the fraction boiling roughly between 40 and 200 °C. The *kerosene* and *jet fuel* fraction overlaps this range, going from 175 to 325 °C.

The alkanes in gasoline generally have 5 to 10 carbon atoms; those in kerosene, 12 to 18. *Paraffin wax* is part of the nonvolatile residue of petroleum refining, and it consists of alkanes with over 20 carbons per molecule. Low-boiling fractions of crude oil, those having molecules of 4 to 8 carbons, are used as nonpolar solvents.

Alkanes have only carbon–carbon single bonds

All open-chain **alkanes** (those without rings) have the general formula C_nH_{2n+2}, where *n* equals the number of carbon atoms. Table 22.2 gives the structures, names, and some properties of the first 10 unbranched open-chain alkanes. Their boiling points steadily increase with an increase in the number of atoms, illustrating how London forces become greater with molecular size. The alkanes are generally less dense than water.

TABLE 22.2	**Straight-Chain Alkanes**				
IUPAC Name	Molecular Formula	Structure	Boiling Point (°C)	Melting Point (°C)	Density (g mL^{-1}, 20 °C)
Methane	CH_4	CH_4	−161.5	−182.5	
Ethane	C_2H_6	CH_3CH_3	−88.6	−183.3	
Propane	C_3H_8	$CH_3CH_2CH_3$	−42.1	−189.7	
Butane	C_4H_{10}	$CH_3(CH_2)_2CH_3$	−0.5	−138.4	
Pentane	C_5H_{12}	$CH_3(CH_2)_3CH_3$	36.1	−129.7	0.626
Hexane	C_6H_{14}	$CH_3(CH_2)_4CH_3$	68.7	−95.3	0.659
Heptane	C_7H_{16}	$CH_3(CH_2)_5CH_3$	98.4	−90.6	0.684
Octane	C_8H_{18}	$CH_3(CH_2)_6CH_3$	125.7	−56.8	0.703
Nonane	C_9H_{20}	$CH_3(CH_2)_7CH_3$	150.8	−53.5	0.718
Decane	$C_{10}H_{22}$	$CH_3(CH_2)_8CH_3$	174.1	−29.7	0.730

An IUPAC system of nomenclature applies to organic compounds

The IUPAC rules for naming organic compounds follow a regular pattern. The last syllable in an IUPAC name designates the family of the compound. The names of all saturated hydrocarbons, for example, end in *-ane*. For each family there is a rule for picking out and naming the *parent chain* or *parent ring* within a specific molecule. The compound is then regarded as having *substituents* attached to its parent chain or ring. Let's see how these principles work with naming alkanes.

IUPAC Rules for Naming the Alkanes

IUPAC rules for naming compounds

1. The name ending for all alkanes (and cycloalkanes) is *-ane*.
2. The *parent chain* is the longest continuous chain of carbons in the structure. For example, the branched-chain alkane

$$\underset{\displaystyle CH_3CH_2CHCH_2CH_2CH_3}{\overset{\displaystyle CH_3}{\vert}}$$

is regarded as being "made" from (derived from) the following parent

$$CH_3CH_2CH_2CH_2CH_2CH_3$$

by replacing a hydrogen atom on the third carbon from the left with CH_3.

$$\underset{\displaystyle CH_3CH_2CHCH_2CH_2CH_3}{\overset{\displaystyle CH_3}{\underset{\displaystyle \diagdown /H}{\vert}}} \longrightarrow \underset{\displaystyle CH_3CH_2CHCH_2CH_2CH_3}{\overset{\displaystyle CH_3}{\vert}}$$

3. A prefix is attached to the name ending, *-ane,* to specify the number of carbon atoms *in the parent chain*. The prefixes through chain lengths of 10 carbons are as follows. The names in Table 22.2 illustrate how the prefixes are used.

meth-	1 C	hex-	6 C
eth-	2 C	hept-	7 C
prop-	3 C	oct-	8 C
but-	4 C	non-	9 C
pent-	5 C	dec-	10 C

The parent chain of our example has six carbons, so the parent is named hexane—*hex* for six carbons and *ane* for being in the alkane family. Therefore, the alkane whose name we are devising is viewed as a *derivative* of this parent, *hexane.*

4. The carbon atoms of the parent chain are numbered starting from whichever end of the chain gives the location of the first branch the lower of two possible numbers. Thus the correct direction for numbering our example is from left to right, not right to left, because this locates the branch (CH_3) at position 3, not position 4.

$$\underset{\substack{\text{(correct direction of numbering)}\\ 1\quad 2\quad 3\quad 4\quad 5\quad 6}}{\underset{\displaystyle CH_3CH_2CHCH_2CH_2CH_3}{\overset{\displaystyle CH_3}{\vert}}} \qquad \underset{\substack{\text{(incorrect direction of numbering)}\\ 6\quad 5\quad 4\quad 3\quad 2\quad 1}}{\underset{\displaystyle CH_3CH_2CHCH_2CH_2CH_3}{\overset{\displaystyle CH_3}{\vert}}}$$

5. Each branch attached to the parent chain is named, so we must now learn the names of some of the alkane-like branches.

Alkyl groups are alkane fragments that replace hydrogen in the parent alkane

Any branch that consists only of carbon and hydrogen and has only single bonds is called an **alkyl group,** and the names of all alkyl groups end in *-yl*. Think of an alkyl group as an alkane minus one of its hydrogen atoms. For example,

(Robert Capece.)

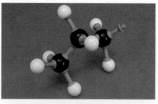

(Robert Capece.)

$$H-\overset{\overset{\displaystyle H}{|}}{\underset{\underset{\displaystyle H}{|}}{C}}-H \xrightarrow{\text{remove one H}} H-\overset{\overset{\displaystyle H}{|}}{\underset{\underset{\displaystyle H}{|}}{C}}- \quad \text{or} \quad CH_3-$$

methane   methyl

$$H-\overset{\overset{\displaystyle H}{|}}{\underset{\underset{\displaystyle H}{|}}{C}}-\overset{\overset{\displaystyle H}{|}}{\underset{\underset{\displaystyle H}{|}}{C}}-H \xrightarrow{\text{remove one H}} H-\overset{\overset{\displaystyle H}{|}}{\underset{\underset{\displaystyle H}{|}}{C}}-\overset{\overset{\displaystyle H}{|}}{\underset{\underset{\displaystyle H}{|}}{C}}- \quad \text{or} \quad CH_3CH_2-$$

ethane   ethyl

Two alkyl groups can be obtained from propane because the middle position in its chain of three is not equivalent to either of the end positions.

$$H-\overset{\overset{\displaystyle H}{|}}{\underset{\underset{\displaystyle H}{|}}{C}}-\overset{\overset{\displaystyle H}{|}}{\underset{\underset{\displaystyle H}{|}}{C}}-\overset{\overset{\displaystyle H}{|}}{\underset{\underset{\displaystyle H}{|}}{C}}-H \xrightarrow{\text{remove one H}} H-\overset{\overset{\displaystyle H}{|}}{\underset{\underset{\displaystyle H}{|}}{C}}-\overset{\overset{\displaystyle H}{|}}{\underset{\underset{\displaystyle H}{|}}{C}}-\overset{\overset{\displaystyle H}{|}}{\underset{\underset{\displaystyle H}{|}}{C}}- \quad \text{or} \quad CH_3CH_2CH_2-$$

propane   propyl

$$H-\overset{\overset{\displaystyle H}{|}}{\underset{\underset{\displaystyle H}{|}}{C}}-\overset{\overset{\displaystyle H}{|}}{\underset{\underset{\displaystyle H}{|}}{C}}-\overset{\overset{\displaystyle H}{|}}{\underset{\underset{\displaystyle H}{|}}{C}}-H \xrightarrow{\text{remove one H}} H-\overset{\overset{\displaystyle H}{|}}{\underset{\underset{\displaystyle H}{|}}{C}}-\overset{\overset{\displaystyle H}{|}}{\underset{\underset{\displaystyle H}{|}}{C}}-\overset{\overset{\displaystyle H}{|}}{\underset{\underset{\displaystyle H}{|}}{C}}-H \quad \text{or} \quad CH_3\overset{|}{C}HCH_3$$

propane   isopropyl

We will not need to know the IUPAC names for any alkyl groups with four or more carbon atoms.

6. The name of each alkyl group is attached to the name of the parent as a prefix, placing its chain location number in front and separating the number from the name by a hyphen. Thus, the original example is named 3-methylhexane.

$$\overset{\overset{\displaystyle CH_3}{|}}{CH_3CH_2CHCH_2CH_2CH_3}$$

3-methylhexane

7. When two or more groups are attached to the parent, each is named and located with a number. The names of alkyl substituents are assembled in their alphabetical order. Always use *hyphens* to separate numbers from words. Here is an application.

$$\underset{\overset{\displaystyle 7\ \ \ 6\ \ \ 5\ \ \ 4\ \ \ 3\ \ \ 2\ \ \ 1}{}}{CH_3CH_2CH_2\overset{\overset{\displaystyle CH_3CH_2}{|}}{C}HCH_2\overset{\overset{\displaystyle CH_3}{|}}{C}HCH_3}$$

4-ethyl-2-methylheptane

8. When two or more substituents are identical, multiplier prefixes are used: di- (for 2), tri- (for 3), tetra- (for 4), and so forth. The location number of every group must occur in the final name. Always separate a number from another number in a name by a *comma*. For example,

$$\overset{\overset{\displaystyle CH_3\ \ \ \ \ CH_3}{|\ \ \ \ \ \ \ \ \ |}}{CH_3CHCH_2CHCH_2CH_3}$$

Correct name: 2,4-dimethylhexane

Incorrect names: 2,4-methylhexane
3,5-dimethylhexane
2-methyl-4-methylhexane
2-4-dimethylhexane

9. When identical groups are on the *same* carbon, the number of this position is repeated in the name. For example,

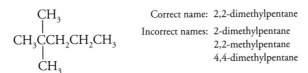

Correct name: 2,2-dimethylpentane

Incorrect names: 2-dimethylpentane
2,2-methylpentane
4,4-dimethylpentane

☐ *Common names* are still widely used for many compounds. For example, the common name of 2-methylpropane is *isobutane*.

These are not all of the IUPAC rules for alkanes, but they will handle all of our needs.

EXAMPLE 22.1
Using the IUPAC Rules to Name an Alkane

What is the IUPAC name for the following compound?

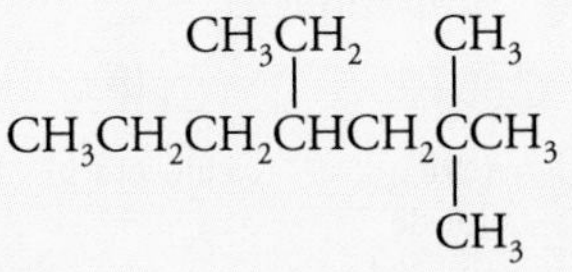

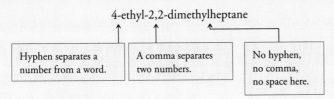

ANALYSIS: The compound is a hydrocarbon, and by studying the structure, we can see that there are only single bonds. Therefore, the substance is an alkane and we must use the IUPAC rules for naming alkanes.

SOLUTION: The ending to the name must be *-ane*. The longest chain is seven carbons long, so the name of the parent alkane is *heptane*. We have to number the chain from right to left in order to reach the first branch with the lower number.

At carbon 2 there are two one-carbon methyl groups. At carbon 4, there is a two-carbon ethyl group. Alphabetically, *ethyl* comes before *methyl*, so we must assemble these names as follows to make the final name. (Names of alkyl groups are alphabetized *before* any prefixes such as di- or tri- are affixed.)

4-ethyl-2,2-dimethylheptane

| Hyphen separates a number from a word. | A comma separates two numbers. | No hyphen, no comma, no space here. |

IS THE ANSWER REASONABLE? The most common mistake is to pick a shorter chain than the true "parent," a mistake we did not make. Another common mistake is to number the chain incorrectly. One overall check that some people use is to count the number of carbons implied by the name (in our example, 2 + 1 + 1 + 7 = 11) and compare it to the count obtained directly from the structure. If the counts don't match, you know you can't be right.

Practice Exercise 1: A student incorrectly named a compound 1,1,1-trimethylethane. What should the name be? (Hint: Write the structure of 1,1,1-trimethylethane.)

Practice Exercise 2: Write the IUPAC names of the following compounds. In searching for the parent chain, be sure to look for the longest continuous chain of carbons *even if the chain twists and goes around corners.*

(a) 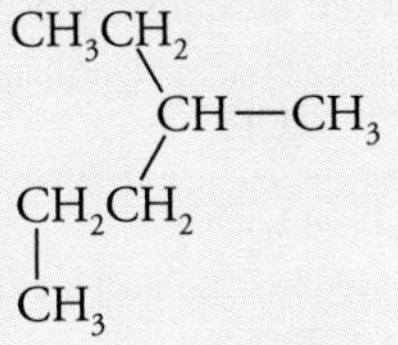 CH₃CH₂
           |
           CH—CH₃
           |
     CH₂CH₂
           |
           CH₃

(b) 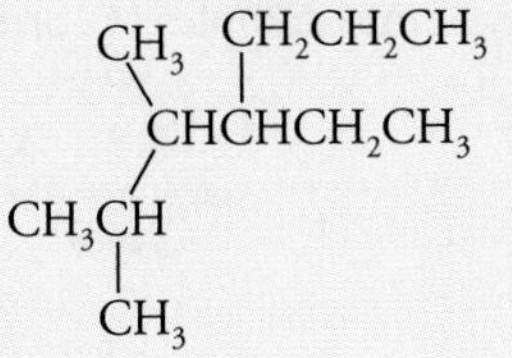 CH₃ CH₂CH₂CH₃
       | |
     CHCHCH₂CH₃
       |
     CH₃CH
           |
           CH₃

(c)

$$CH_3CH_2\overset{\overset{\displaystyle CH_3}{|}}{C}H\overset{\overset{\displaystyle CH_3}{|}}{C}HCH_2\overset{\overset{\displaystyle CH_3}{|}}{C}HCH_3$$
$$\overset{\displaystyle |}{\underset{\displaystyle CH_3CH_2}{}}$$

Alkanes undergo few chemical reactions

Alkanes, as we have indicated, are generally stable at room temperature toward such different reactants as concentrated sulfuric acid (or any other common acid), concentrated aqueous bases (like NaOH), and even the most reactive metals. Fluorine attacks virtually all organic compounds, including the alkanes, to give mixtures of products. Like all hydrocarbons, the alkanes burn in air to give carbon dioxide and water. *Hot* nitric acid, chlorine, and bromine also react with alkanes. The chlorination of methane, for example, can be made to yield the following compounds.

☐ These are the common names for the chlorinated derivatives of methane, not the IUPAC names.

CH_3Cl	CH_2Cl_2	$CHCl_3$	CCl_4
methyl chloride	methylene chloride	chloroform	carbon tetrachloride

When heated at high temperatures in the absence of air, alkanes "crack," meaning that they break up into smaller molecules. The cracking of methane, for example, yields finely powdered carbon and hydrogen.

$$CH_4 \xrightarrow{\text{high temperature}} C + 2H_2$$

The controlled cracking of ethane gives ethene, commonly called ethylene.

$$\underset{\text{ethane}}{CH_3CH_3} \xrightarrow{\text{high temperature}} \underset{\text{ethene}}{CH_2{=}CH_2} + H_2$$

☐ $HOCH_2CH_2OH$
ethylene glycol

Ethene ("ethylene"), from the cracking of ethane, is one of the most important raw materials in the organic chemicals industry. It is used to make polyethylene plastic as well as ethyl alcohol and ethylene glycol (an antifreeze).

Alkenes and alkynes have double and triple bonds

Hydrocarbons with one or more double bonds are members of the **alkene** family. Open-chain alkenes have the general formula, C_nH_{2n}. Hydrocarbons with triple bonds are in the **alkyne** family and have the general formula, C_nH_{2n-2} (when open-chain).

Alkenes and alkynes, like all hydrocarbons, are insoluble in water and are flammable. The most familiar alkenes are ethene and propene (commonly called ethylene and propylene, respectively), the raw materials for polyethylene and polypropylene, respectively. Ethyne ("acetylene"), an important alkyne, is the fuel for oxyacetylene torches.

☐ The IUPAC accepts both *ethene* and *ethylene* as the name of $CH_2{=}CH_2$. The common name of propene is *propylene*, and other simple alkenes have common names as well.

$CH_2{=}CH_2$	$CH_3CH{=}CH_2$	$HC{\equiv}CH$
ethene (ethylene)	propene (propylene)	ethyne (acetylene)

Alkenes have IUPAC names

The IUPAC rules for the names of alkenes are adaptations of those for alkanes, but with two important differences. First, the parent chain *must include the double bond* even if this means that the parent chain is shorter than another. Second, the parent alkene chain must be *numbered from whichever end gives the first carbon of the double bond the lower of two possible numbers.* This (lower) number, followed by a hyphen, precedes the name of the parent chain, unless there is no ambiguity about where the double bond occurs. The numbers for the locations of branches are not considered in numbering the chain. Otherwise, alkyl groups are named and located as before. Some examples of correctly named alkenes are as follows.

$CH_3CH_2CH{=}CH_2$
1-butene
(not 1,2-butene, not 3-butene)

$CH_3CH{=}CHCH_3$
2-butene

$CH_3CH_2\overset{\overset{\displaystyle CH_3}{|}}{C}HCH_2CH{=}\overset{\overset{\displaystyle CH_3}{|}}{C}CH_3$
2,5-dimethyl-2-heptene
(not 3,6-dimethyl-5-heptene)

cyclohexene

Notice that only one number is used to locate the double bond, the number of the first carbon of the double bond to be reached as the chain is numbered.

Some alkenes have two double bonds and are called *dienes*. Some have three double bonds and are called *trienes*, and so forth. Each double bond has to be located by a number.

$$CH_2\!\!=\!\!CHCH\!\!=\!\!CHCH_3 \qquad CH_2\!\!=\!\!CHCH_2CH\!\!=\!\!CH_2 \qquad CH_2\!\!=\!\!CHCH\!\!=\!\!CHCH\!\!=\!\!CH_2$$
1,3-pentadiene   1,4-pentadiene   1,3,5-hexatriene

Alkenes exhibit geometric isomerism

As explained in Section 9.6, there is no free rotation at a carbon–carbon double bond (see page 368). Many alkenes, therefore, exhibit **geometric isomerism.** Thus *cis*-2-butene and *trans*-2-butene (see below) are **geometric isomers** of each other. They not only have the same molecular formula, C_4H_8, but also the same skeletons and the same organization of atoms and bonds, namely, $CH_3CH\!\!=\!\!CHCH_3$. The two 2-butenes differ in the *directions* taken by the two CH_3 groups attached at the double bond.

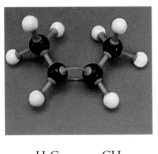

(Robert Capece.)

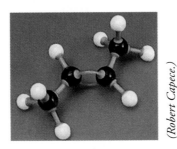

(Robert Capece.)

cis-2-butene
BP 3.72 °C

trans-2-butene
BP 0.88 °C

□ Because ring structures also lock out free rotation, geometric isomers of ring compounds are possible as well. These two isomers of 1, 2-dimethylcyclopropane are examples.

Cis means "on the same side"; *trans* means "on opposite sides." This difference in orientation gives the two geometric isomers of 2-butene measurable differences in physical properties, as their boiling points show. Because each has a double bond, however, the *chemical* properties of *cis*- and *trans*-2-butene are very similar.

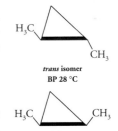

trans isomer
BP 28 °C

cis isomer
BP 37 °C

Alkenes undergo addition reactions

Electron-seeking species are naturally attracted to the electron density at the π bond of the double bond, so alkenes react readily with protons provided by strong proton donors. Alkenes thus undergo **addition reactions,** reactions in which the pieces of a reactant become separately attached to the carbons of a double bond. Ethene, for example, readily reacts with hydrogen chloride as follows.

$$CH_2\!\!=\!\!CH_2 + H\!-\!Cl(g) \longrightarrow Cl\!-\!CH_2\!-\!CH_3$$

We say that the hydrogen chloride molecule *adds across the double bond*, with the hydrogen of the HCl bonding to the carbon at one end and the chlorine bonding to the carbon at the other end. A pair of electrons of the π bond move out and take H^+ from HCl, which releases Cl^-. A positive (+) charge is left at one end of the original carbon–carbon double bond as a bond to H forms at the other end.

ethyl carbocation   chloroethane

□ Recall that curved arrows indicate how electron pairs rearrange; they usually are not used to signify the movement of atoms.

☐ A carbocation, having a carbon with only six valence electrons, not an octet, generally has only a fleeting existence.

The result of H^+ transfer is a very unstable cation called a *carbocation*, an ion with a positive charge on carbon. This charged site then quickly attracts the Cl^- ion to give the product, chloroethane.

Another example is 2-butene; like ethene, it too adds HCl.

$$CH_3CH\!=\!CHCH_3 + HCl \longrightarrow CH_3CHCH_2CH_3$$
2-butene

$$\underset{\text{2-chlorobutane}}{\overset{|}{Cl}}$$

Alkene double bonds also add hydrogen bromide, hydrogen iodide, and sulfuric acid ("hydrogen sulfate"). Alkynes undergo similar addition reactions.

A water molecule adds to a double bond if an acid catalyst, like sulfuric acid, is present. The catalyst participates in the first step by donating a proton to one end of the double bond to create a carbocation. This unstable species preferentially attracts what is the most abundant electron-rich species present, namely, the oxygen end of a water molecule.

☐ In the chemical equation, the notation

$$\xrightarrow{\;HSO_4^-\;}$$

means that one of the products of the reaction is HSO_4^-. Writing an equation this way lets us focus on the fate of the principal organic reactant(s).

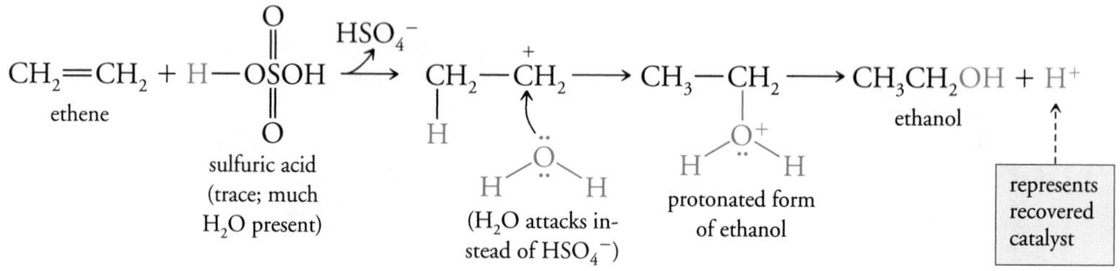

$$CH_2\!=\!CH_2 + H\!-\!O\underset{\overset{\|}{O}}{\overset{\overset{O}{\|}}{S}}OH \xrightarrow{\;HSO_4^-\;} \underset{\overset{|}{H}}{CH_2}\!-\!\overset{+}{CH_2} \longrightarrow CH_3\!-\!CH_2 \longrightarrow CH_3CH_2OH + H^+$$

ethene

sulfuric acid (trace; much H_2O present)

(H_2O attacks instead of HSO_4^-)

protonated form of ethanol

ethanol

represents recovered catalyst

Note that in the *overall* result, the pieces of the water molecule, H and OH, become attached at the different carbons of the double bond. 2-Butene (either cis or trans) gives a similar reaction.

Other inorganic compounds that add to an alkene double bond are chlorine, bromine, and hydrogen. Chlorine and bromine react rapidly at room temperature. Ethene, for example, reacts with bromine to give 1,2-dibromoethane.

$$CH_2\!=\!CH_2 + Br\!-\!Br \longrightarrow \underset{\underset{Br}{|}}{CH_2}\!-\!\underset{\underset{Br}{|}}{CH_2}$$

ethene

1,2-dibromoethane

Alkenes undergo hydrogenation by adding hydrogen

The product of the addition of hydrogen to an alkene is an alkane, and the reaction is called *hydrogenation*. It requires a catalyst—powdered platinum, for example—and sometimes a higher temperature and pressure than available under an ordinary room atmosphere. The hydrogenation of 2-butene (cis or trans) gives butane.

$$CH_3CH\!=\!CHCH_3 + H\!-\!H \xrightarrow[\text{catalyst}]{\text{heat, pressure}} \underset{\overset{|}{H}\;\;\overset{|}{H}}{CH_3CH\!-\!CHCH_3} \;\; \text{or} \;\; CH_3CH_2CH_2CH_3$$

2-butene (*cis* or *trans*)

butane

Double bonds react with ozone

☐ Ozone in smog attacks the double bonds in the chlorophyll of green plants, which is able to prevent photosynthesis and so kill the plants.

Ozone (O_3) reacts with anything that has carbon–carbon double or triple bonds, and the reaction breaks the molecules into fragments at each such site, giving a variety of products. Because many important compounds in living systems have alkene double bonds, ozone is a very dangerous material when it is formed in smog.

Aromatic hydrocarbons contain benzene rings

The most common **aromatic compounds** contain the *benzene ring*, a ring of six carbon atoms, each bonded to one H or one other atom or group (in addition to the two adjacent carbons). The benzene ring is represented as a hexagon either with alternating single and double bonds or with a circle. For example,

benzene   toluene   ethylbenzene
               (methylbenzene)

□ Hydrocarbons and their oxygen or nitrogen derivatives that are not aromatic are called *aliphatic compounds.*

The circle better represents the delocalized bonds of the benzene ring, which are described in Section 9.8.

In the molecular orbital view of benzene, discussed in Section 9.8, the delocalization of the ring's π electrons strongly stabilizes the ring. This explains why benzene does not easily undergo addition reactions; they would interfere with the delocalization of electron density. Instead, the benzene ring most commonly undergoes **substitution reactions** in which one of the ring H atoms is replaced by another atom or group. For example, benzene reacts with chlorine in the presence of iron(III) chloride to give chlorobenzene, instead of a 1,2-dichloro compound. To dramatize this point, we must use a resonance structure for benzene (see page 378).

chlorobenzene   (This would form if chlorine *added* to the double bond.)

You can infer that *substitution,* but not addition, leaves intact the closed-circuit, delocalized, and very stable π electron network of the benzene ring.

Provided that a suitable catalyst is present, benzene reacts by substitution with chlorine, bromine, and nitric acid as well as with sulfuric acid. (Recall that Cl_2 and Br_2 readily *add* to alkene double bonds.)

$$C_6H_6 + Br_2 \xrightarrow{\text{FeBr}_3 \text{ catalyst}} C_6H_5\!-\!Br \ + HBr$$
bromobenzene

$$C_6H_6 + HNO_3 \xrightarrow{\text{H}_2\text{SO}_4 \text{ catalyst}} C_6H_5\!-\!NO_2 + H_2O$$
nitrobenzene

$$C_6H_6 + H_2SO_4 \longrightarrow C_6H_5\!-\!SO_3H \ + H_2O$$
benzenesulfonic acid

22.3 ETHERS AND ALCOHOLS ARE ORGANIC DERIVATIVES OF WATER

Ethers have two alkyl groups attached to oxygen

Molecules of **ethers** contain two alkyl groups joined to one oxygen, the two R groups being alike or different. We give only the common names for the following examples.

CH_3OCH_3 $CH_3CH_2OCH_2CH_3$ $CH_3OCH_2CH_3$ R—O—R′
dimethyl ether   diethyl ether   methyl ethyl ether   ethers
BP −23 °C   BP 34.5 °C   BP 11 °C   (general structure)

□ Pentane (BP 36.1 °C), like diethyl ether in having no OH group but having nearly the identical number of atoms, has about the same boiling point as diethyl ether.

Diethyl ether is the "ether" once widely used as an anesthetic in surgery.

The contrasting boiling points of alcohols and ethers illustrate the influence of hydrogen bonding. Hydrogen bonds cannot exist between molecules of ethers and the simple ethers have very low boiling points, being substantially lower than those of alcohols of comparable molecular sizes. For example, 1-butanol, $CH_3CH_2CH_2CH_2OH$ (BP 117 °C) boils 83 degrees higher than its structural isomer, diethyl ether (BP 34.5 °C).

Alcohols can be represented by the formula ROH

An **alcohol** is any compound with an OH group and three other groups attached to a carbon atom by *single bonds*. Using the symbol R to represent any alkyl group, alcohols have ROH as their general structure.

The four structurally simplest alcohols are the following. (Their common names are in parentheses below their IUPAC names.)

$$CH_3OH \qquad CH_3CH_2OH \qquad CH_3CH_2CH_2OH \qquad \underset{\overset{|}{OH}}{CH_3CHCH_3}$$

methanol	ethanol	1-propanol	2-propanol
(methyl alcohol)	(ethyl alcohol)	(propyl alcohol)	(isopropyl alcohol)
BP 65 °C	BP 78.5 °C	BP 97 °C	BP 82 °C

Ethanol is the alcohol in beverages and is also added to gasoline to make "gasohol" and makes up 85% of the fuel E-85 (the rest is gasoline).

The name ending for an alcohol is *-ol*. It replaces the *-e* ending of the name of the hydrocarbon that corresponds to the parent. The parent chain of an alcohol must be the longest *that includes the carbon bonded to the OH group*. The chain is numbered to give the site of the OH group the lower number regardless of where alkyl substituents occur.

Reactions of alcohols include oxidation, dehydration, and substitution

Ethers are almost as chemically inert as alkanes. They burn (as do alkanes), and they are split apart when boiled in concentrated acids.

The alcohols, in contrast, have a rich chemistry. We'll look at their oxidation and dehydration reactions as well as some substitution reactions.

Oxidation products of alcohols depend on structure

When the carbon atom of the alcohol system, the *alcohol carbon atom,* also is bonded to at least one H, this H can be removed by an oxidizing agent. The H atom of the OH group also leaves, and the two Hs become part of a water molecule. We may think of the oxidizing agent as providing the O atom for H_2O. The number of H atoms left on the original alcohol carbon then determines the *family* of the product.

The oxidation of an alcohol of the RCH_2OH type, with two H atoms on the alcohol carbon, produces first an *aldehyde*, which is further oxidized to a *carboxylic acid*. (The nature of aldehydes and ketones are discussed further in Section 22.5.)

$$RCH_2OH \xrightarrow{\text{oxidation}} \underset{\text{aldehyde}}{\overset{\overset{\displaystyle O}{\|}}{RCH}} \xrightarrow{\overset{\text{further}}{\text{oxidation}}} \underset{\text{carboxylic acid}}{\overset{\overset{\displaystyle O}{\|}}{RCOH}}$$

The net ionic equation for the formation of the aldehyde when dichromate ion is used is

$$3RCH_2OH + Cr_2O_7^{2-} + 8H^+ \longrightarrow 3RCH{=}O + 2Cr^{3+} + 7H_2O$$

Aldehydes are much more easily oxidized than alcohols, so unless the aldehyde is removed from the solution as it forms, it will consume oxidizing agent that has not yet reacted and be changed to the corresponding carboxylic acid.

The oxidation of an alcohol of the R_2CHOH type produces a *ketone*. For example, the oxidation of 2-propanol gives propanone.

$$\underset{\text{2-propanol}}{3\overset{\overset{\displaystyle OH}{|}}{CH_3CHCH_3}} + Cr_2O_7^{2-} + 8H^+ \longrightarrow \underset{\substack{\text{propanone}\\\text{(acetone)}}}{3\overset{\overset{\displaystyle O}{\|}}{CH_3CCH_3}} + 2Cr^{3+} + 7H_2O$$

■ The aldehyde group, $CH{=}O$, is one of the most easily oxidized, and the carboxyl group, CO_2H, is one of the most oxidation resistant of the functional groups.

Ketones (discussed further in Section 22.5) strongly resist oxidation, so a ketone does not have to be removed from the oxidizing agent as it forms.

Alcohols of the type R_3COH have no removable H atom on the alcohol carbon, so they cannot be oxidized in a similar manner.

EXAMPLE 22.2
Alcohol Oxidation Products

What organic product can be made by the oxidation of 2-butanol with dichromate ion? If no oxidation can occur, state so.

ANALYSIS: We first have to look at the structure of 2-butanol.

$$\underset{\text{2-butanol}}{CH_3\overset{\overset{\displaystyle OH}{|}}{C}HCH_2CH_3}$$

2-Butanol can be oxidized because it has an H atom on the alcohol carbon (carbon 2). The oxidation results in the detachment of both this H atom and the one joined to the O atom, leaving a double bond to O.

SOLUTION: We carry out the changes that the analysis found. We simply erase the two H atoms that we identified and insert a double bond from C to O. The product is 2-butanone.

$$\underset{\text{2-butanone (a ketone)}}{CH_3\overset{\overset{\displaystyle O}{\|}}{C}CH_2CH_3}$$

The starting material had two alkyl groups, CH_3 and CH_2CH_3. It doesn't matter what the alkyl groups are, however, because the reaction takes the same course in all cases. All alcohols of the R_2CHOH type can be oxidized to ketones in this way.

IS THE ANSWER REASONABLE? The "skeleton" of heavy atoms, C and O, does not change in this kind of oxidation, and 2-butanone has the same skeleton as 2-butanol. The oxidation also produces a double bond from C to O, as we showed.

Practice Exercise 3: Oxidation of an alcohol gave the following product. What was the formula of the original alcohol? (Hint: How many hydrogens are removed from the alcohol carbon by oxidation?)

$$CH_3CH_2\overset{\overset{\displaystyle O}{\|}}{-C-}CH_2CH_3$$

Practice Exercise 4: What are the structures of the products that form by the oxidation of the following alcohols? (a) ethanol, (b) 3-pentanol

Dehydration reactions eliminate the components of water from alcohols

In the presence of a strong acid, like concentrated sulfuric acid, an alcohol molecule can undergo the loss of a water molecule, leaving behind a carbon–carbon double bond. This reaction, called **dehydration,** is one example of an **elimination reaction.** For example,

$$\underset{\text{ethanol}}{\overset{\displaystyle CH_2-CH_2}{\underset{\displaystyle H \qquad OH}{|\qquad\;\;|}}} \xrightarrow[\text{heat}]{\text{acid catalyst,}} \underset{\text{ethene}}{CH_2=CH_2} + H_2O$$

$$\underset{\text{1-propanol}}{\overset{\displaystyle CH_3CH-CH_2}{\underset{\displaystyle H \qquad OH}{|\qquad\;\;|}}} \xrightarrow[\text{heat}]{\text{acid catalyst,}} \underset{\text{propene}}{CH_3CH=CH_2} + H_2O$$

What makes the elimination of water possible is the proton-accepting ability of the O atom of the OH group. Alcohols resemble water in that they react like Brønsted bases toward concentrated strong acids to give an equilibrium mixture involving a protonated form. Ethanol, for example, reacts with (and dissolves in) concentrated sulfuric acid by the following reaction. (H_2SO_4 is written as $H—OSO_3H$.)[1]

□ Remember, the curved arrows in these diagrams show how electrons rearrange during the reaction. They don't indicate the movements of the atoms.

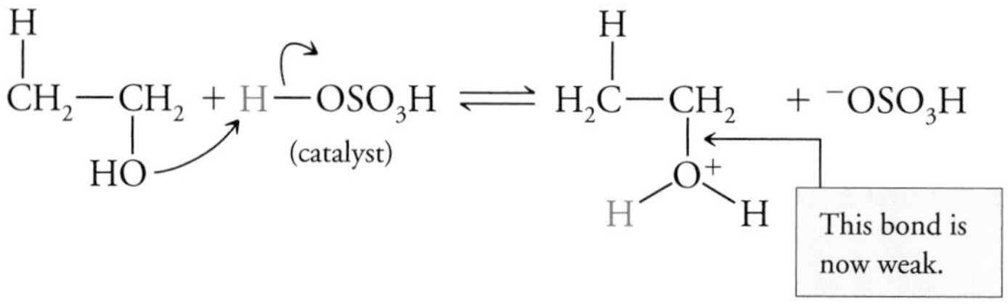

The organic cation is nothing more than the ethyl derivative of the hydronium ion, $CH_3CH_2OH_2{}^+$, and *all three bonds to oxygen in this cation are weak*, just like all three bonds to oxygen in H_3O^+.

A water molecule now leaves, taking with it the electron pair that held it to the CH_2 group. The remaining organic species is a carbocation.

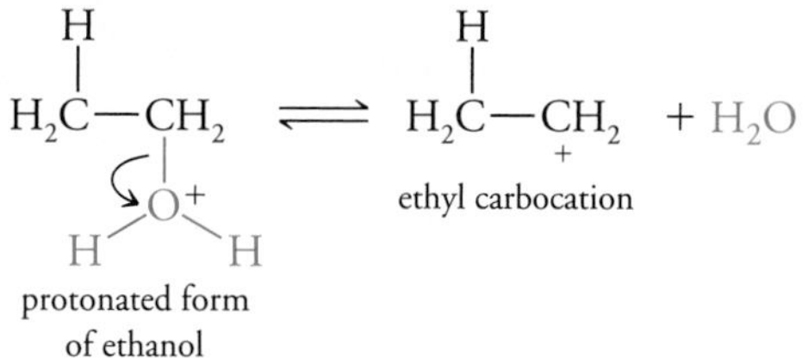

Carbocations, as we said, are unstable. The ethyl carbocation, $CH_3CH_2{}^+$, loses a proton to become more stable, donating it to some proton acceptor in the medium. The electron pair holding the departing proton stays behind to become the second bond of the new double bond in the product. All carbon atoms now have outer octets. We'll use the $HSO_4{}^-$ ion (written here as HSO_3O^-) as the proton acceptor.

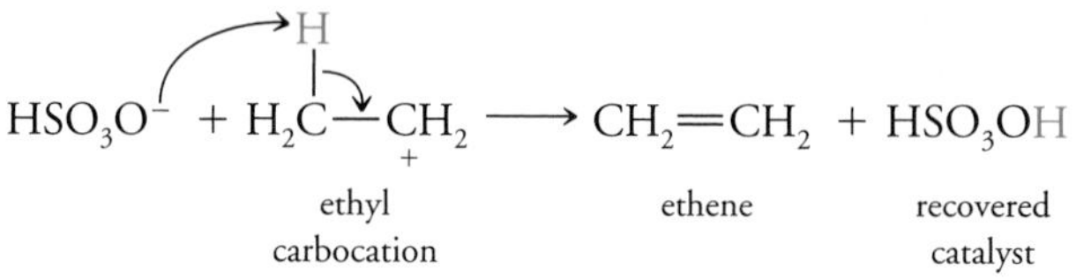

The last few steps in the dehydration of ethanol—the separation of H_2O, loss of the proton, formation of the double bond, and recovery of the catalyst—probably occur simultaneously. Notice two things about the catalyst, H_2SO_4. First, it works to convert a species with strong bonds, the alcohol, to one with weak bonds strategically located, the protonated alcohol. Second, the catalyst is recovered.

Alcohols participate in substitution reactions

Under acidic conditions, the OH group of an alcohol can be replaced by a halogen atom, using a concentrated hydrohalogen acid. For example,

$$CH_3CH_2OH + HI \text{ (conc.)} \xrightarrow{heat} CH_3CH_2I + H_2O$$
ethanol $\qquad\qquad\qquad\qquad$ iodoethane
$\qquad\qquad\qquad\qquad\qquad$ (ethyl iodide)

$$CH_3CH_2CH_2OH + HBr \text{ (conc.)} \xrightarrow{heat} CH_3CH_2CH_2Br + H_2O$$
1-propanol $\qquad\qquad\qquad\qquad$ 1-bromopropane
$\qquad\qquad\qquad\qquad\qquad\quad$ (propyl bromide)

---

[1] The first curved arrow illustrates how an atom attached to one molecule, like the O of the HO group, uses an unshared pair of electrons to pick up an atom of another molecule, like the H of the catalyst. The second curved arrow shows that *both* electrons of the bond from H to O in sulfuric acid remain in the hydrogen sulfate ion that forms. Thus H transfers as H^+.

These reactions, like the earlier reaction between chlorine and benzene, are **substitution reactions**. The first step in each is the transfer of H^+ to the OH of the alcohol to give the protonated form of the OH group.

$$R—OH + H^+ \longrightarrow R—OH_2{}^+$$

Once again, the acid catalyst works to weaken an important bond. Given the high concentration of halide ion, X^-, it is this species that successfully interacts with $R—OH_2{}^+$ to displace OH_2 (water) and yield $R—X$.

22.4 | AMINES ARE ORGANIC DERIVATIVES OF AMMONIA

Amines are organic derivatives of ammonia in which one, two, or three hydrocarbon groups have replaced hydrogens. Examples, together with their common (not IUPAC) names, are

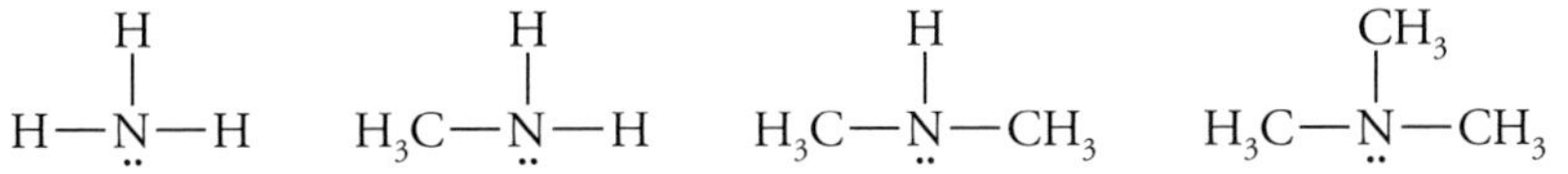

ammonia
BP −33.4 °C

methylamine
BP −8 °C

dimethylamine
BP 8 °C

trimethylamine
BP 3 °C

The N—H bond is not as polar as the O—H bond, so amines boil at lower temperatures than alcohols of comparable molecular size. Amines of low molecular mass are soluble in water. Hydrogen bonding between molecules of water and the amine facilitates this.

□ CH_3CH_2OH, BP 78.5 °C
$CH_3CH_2NH_2$, BP 17 °C
$CH_3CH_2CH_3$, BP −42 °C

The basicity of amines affects their reactions

As we said earlier, amines are Brønsted bases. Behaving like ammonia, amines that do dissolve in water establish an equilibrium in which a low concentration of hydroxide ion exists. For example,

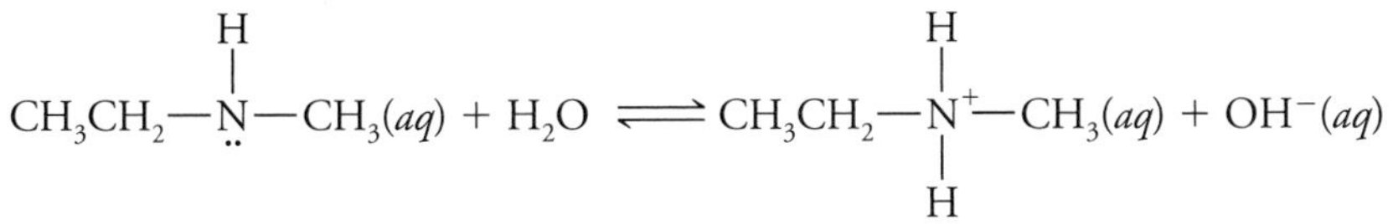

ethylmethylamine

ethylmethylammonium ion

As a result, aqueous solutions of amines test basic to litmus and have pH values above 7.

When an amine is mixed with an acid such as hydrochloric acid, the amine and acid react almost quantitatively (i.e., completely). The amine accepts a proton and changes almost 100% into its protonated form. For example,

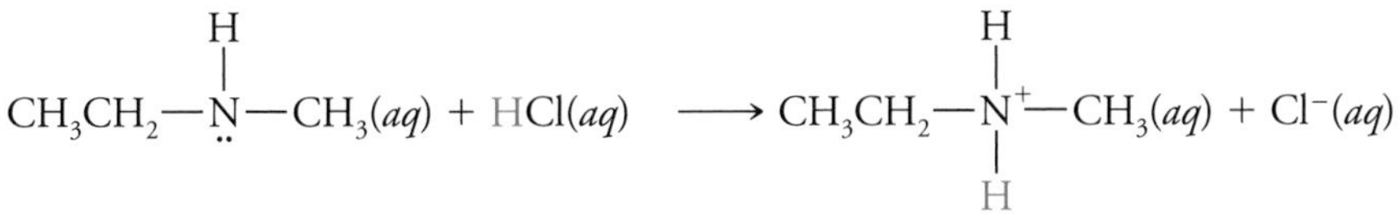

ethylmethylamine

ethylmethylammonium ion
(a protonated amine)

Even water-insoluble amines undergo this reaction, and the resulting salt is much more soluble in water than the original electrically neutral amine.

Many important medicinal chemicals, like quinine, are amines, but they are usually supplied to patients in protonated forms so that the drug can be administered as an aqueous solution, not as a solid. This strategy is particularly important for medicinals that must be given by intravenous drip.

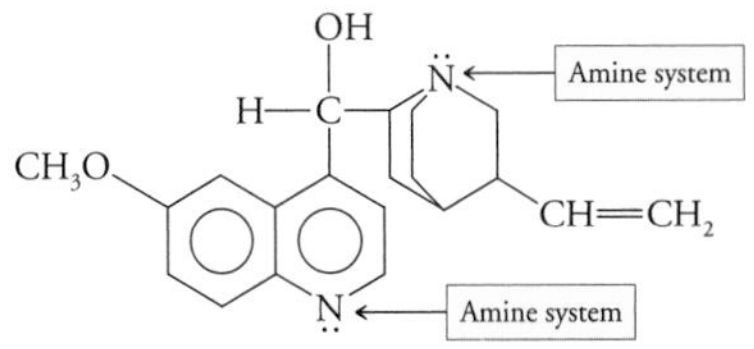

quinine
(an antimalarial drug)

Protonated amines are weak Brønsted acids

A protonated amine is a substituted ammonium ion. Like the ammonium ion itself, protonated amines are weak Brønsted acids. They can neutralize strong base. For example,

$$CH_3NH_3^+(aq) \; + \; OH^-(aq) \; \longrightarrow \; CH_3NH_2(aq) \; + \; H_2O$$

methylammonium ion   methylamine

This reverses the protonation of an amine and releases the uncharged amine molecule.

22.5 ORGANIC COMPOUNDS WITH CARBONYL GROUPS INCLUDE ALDEHYDES, KETONES, AND CARBOXYLIC ACIDS

Many organic compounds contain oxygen atoms doubly bonded to a carbon that is also bonded to two other atoms. This grouping of atoms, $>C=O$, is called a **carbonyl group,** and it occurs in several organic families. What is attached to the carbon atom in $C=O$ determines the specific family.

The carbonyl group is a polar group, and it helps to make compounds containing it much more soluble in water than hydrocarbons of roughly the same molecular size.

Aldehydes and ketones are carbonyl compounds

We've already encountered aldehydes and ketones in our discussion of the oxidation of alcohols. When the carbonyl group binds an H atom plus a hydrocarbon group (or a second H), the compound is an **aldehyde.** When $C=O$ is bonded to two hydrocarbon groups at C, the compound is a **ketone.**

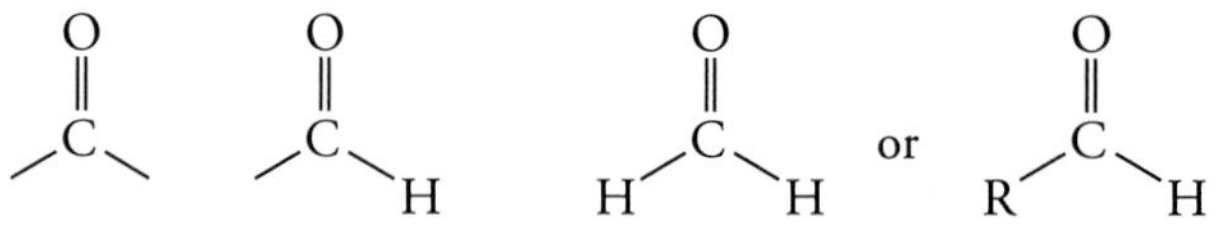

carbonyl group   aldehyde group   aldehydes

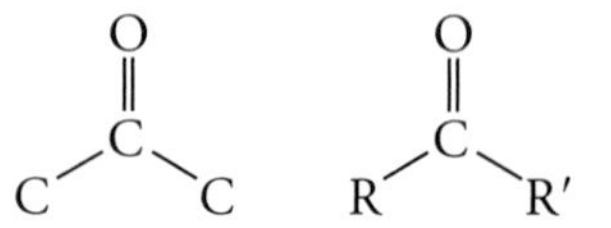

keto group   ketones

The *aldehyde group* is often condensed to CHO, the double bond of the carbonyl group being "understood." The *ketone group* is sometimes condensed to CO.

The carbonyl group occurs widely. As an aldehyde group, it's in the molecules of most sugars, like glucose. Another common sugar, fructose, has the keto group.

Names of aldehydes and ketones have characteristic endings

The IUPAC name ending for an aldehyde is *-al*. The parent chain is the longest chain *that includes the aldehyde group.* Thus, the three-carbon aldehyde is named *propanal*, because "propane" is the name of the three-carbon alkane and the *-e* in propane is replaced by *-al*. The numbering of the chain always starts by assigning the carbon of the aldehyde group position 1. This rule, therefore, makes it unnecessary to include the number locating the aldehyde group in the name, as illustrated by the name 2-methylpropanal.

HCH
methanal
BP −21 °C

CH₃CH
ethanal
BP 21 °C

CH₃CH₂CH
propanal
BP 49 °C

CH₃CH—CH
2-methylpropanal
(not 2-methyl-1-propanal)
BP 64 °C

Aldehydes cannot form hydrogen bonds between their own molecules, so they boil at lower temperatures than alcohols of comparable molecular masses.

The name ending for the IUPAC names of ketones is *-one*. The parent chain must include the carbonyl group and be numbered from whichever end reaches the carbonyl carbon first. The number of the ketone group's location must be part of the name whenever there would otherwise be uncertainty.

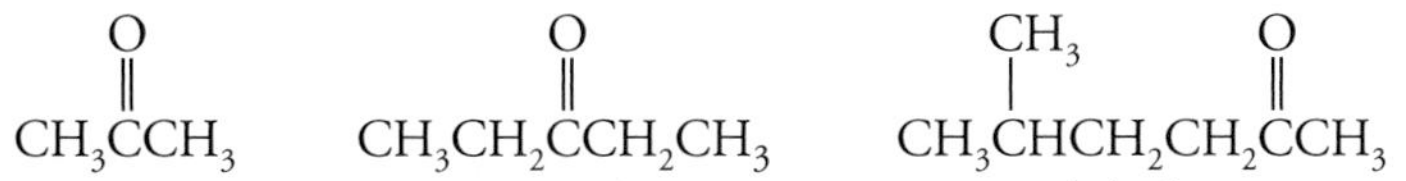

$$CH_3CCH_3 \qquad CH_3CH_2CCH_2CH_3 \qquad CH_3CHCH_2CH_2CCH_3$$

propanone
(acetone)
BP 56.5 °C

3-pentanone
BP 101.5 °C

5-methyl-2-hexanone
(not 2-methyl-5-hexanone)
BP 145 °C

☐ We need not write "2-propanone," because if the carbonyl carbon is anywhere else in a three-carbon chain, the compound is the *aldehyde*, propanal.

Aldehydes and ketones can be made to add hydrogen

Hydrogen is capable of adding across the double bond of the carbonyl group in both aldehydes and ketones. The reaction is just like the addition of hydrogen across the double bond of an alkene and takes place under roughly the same conditions, namely, with a metal catalyst, heat, and pressure. The reaction is called either *hydrogenation* or *reduction*. For example,

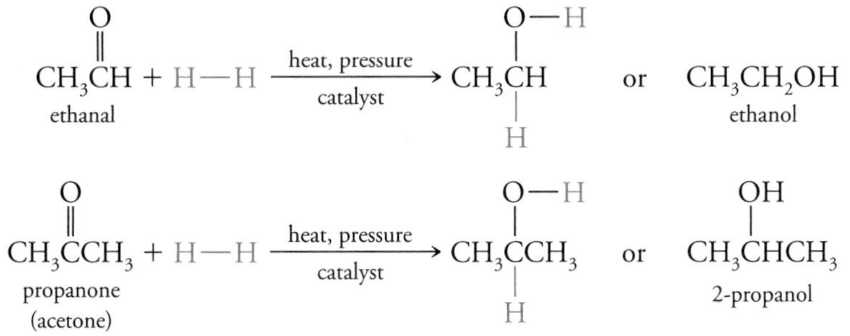

$$CH_3CH + H{-}H \xrightarrow[\text{catalyst}]{\text{heat, pressure}} CH_3CH \quad \text{or} \quad CH_3CH_2OH$$

ethanal

ethanol

$$CH_3CCH_3 + H{-}H \xrightarrow[\text{catalyst}]{\text{heat, pressure}} CH_3CCH_3 \quad \text{or} \quad CH_3CHCH_3$$

propanone
(acetone)

2-propanol

The H atoms take up positions at opposite ends of the carbonyl group's double bond, which then becomes a single bond holding an OH group.

Aldehydes are easily oxidized

Aldehydes and ketones are in separate families because of their remarkably different behavior toward oxidizing agents. As we noted on page 914, aldehydes are easily oxidized, but ketones strongly resist oxidation. Even in storage in a bottle, aldehydes are slowly oxidized by the oxygen of the air trapped in the bottle.

Compounds containing a carboxyl group are acids

A **carboxylic acid** carries an OH on the carbon of the carbonyl group.

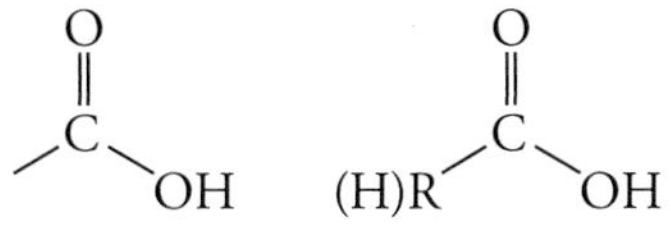

carboxyl
group

(H)R

carboxylic
acids

In condensed formulas the **carboxyl group** is often written as CO_2H or $COOH$.

The name ending of the IUPAC names of carboxylic acids is *-oic acid*. The parent chain must be the longest that includes the carboxyl carbon, which is numbered position 1. The name of the hydrocarbon with the same number of carbons as the parent is then changed by replacing the terminal *-e* with *-oic acid*. For example,

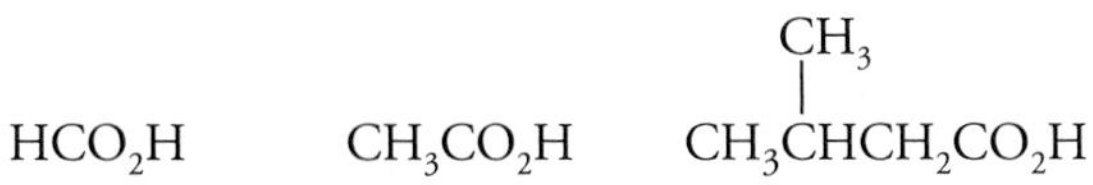

$$HCO_2H \qquad CH_3CO_2H \qquad CH_3CHCH_2CO_2H$$

methanoic acid
BP 101 °C

ethanoic acid
BP 118 °C

3-methylbutanoic acid
BP 176 °C

☐ Because carboxylic acids have both a lone oxygen and an OH group, their molecules strongly hydrogen bond to each other. Their high boiling points, relative to alcohols of comparable molecular size, reflect this.

The carboxyl group is a weakly acidic group, causing aqueous solutions of the compounds to be weakly acidic. In fact, we've used both formic acid and acetic acid in previous discussions of weak acids. All carboxylic acids, both water soluble and water insoluble, neutralize such bases as the hydroxide, bicarbonate, and carbonate ions. The general equation for the reaction with OH⁻ is

$$RCO_2H + OH^- \xrightarrow{H_2O} RCO_2^- + H_2O$$

The carboxyl group is present in all of the building blocks of proteins, the amino acids, which are discussed further on page 937.

Esters are derivatives of carboxylic acids

☐ A *derivative* of a carboxylic acid is a compound that can be made from the acid, or which can be changed to the acid by hydrolysis.

Carboxylic acids are used to synthesize two important kinds of derivatives, *esters* and *amides*. In **esters,** the OH of the carboxyl group is replaced by OR. (The H in parentheses means the group attached to the C of the carboxyl group can either be R or H.)

$$\text{(H)RCOR}' \quad \text{or} \quad \text{(H)RCO}_2\text{R}' \quad \text{for example,} \quad CH_3CO(CH_2)_7CH_3$$

esters

octyl ethanoate (fragrance of oranges)

☐ Esters are responsible for many pleasant fragrances in nature.

Ester	Aroma
$HCO_2CH_2CH_3$	Rum
$HCO_2CH_2CH(CH_3)_2$	Raspberry
$CH_3CO_2(CH_2)_4CH_3$	Banana
$CH_3CO_2(CH_2)_2CH(CH_3)_2$	Pear
$CH_3CO_2(CH_2)_7CH_3$	Orange
$CH_3(CH_2)_2CO_2CH_2CH_3$	Pineapple
$CH_3(CH_2)_2CO_2(CH_2)_4CH_3$	Apricot

The IUPAC name of an ester begins with the name of the alkyl group attached to the O atom. This is followed by a separate word, one taken from the name of the parent carboxylic acid but altered by changing *-ic acid* to *-ate*. For example,

$$HCO_2CH_3 \qquad CH_3CO_2CH_2CH_3 \qquad CH_3CHCH_2CO_2CHCH_3$$

methyl methanoate BP 31.5 °C

ethyl ethanoate BP 77 °C

isopropyl 3-methylbutanoate BP 142 °C

One way to prepare an ester is to heat a solution of the parent carboxylic acid and the alcohol in the presence of an acid catalyst. (We'll not go into the details of how this happens.) The following kind of equilibrium forms, but a substantial stoichiometric excess of the alcohol (usually the less expensive reactant) is commonly used to drive the position of the equilibrium toward the ester.

$$RCOH + HOR' \underset{heat}{\overset{H^+ catalyst}{\rightleftharpoons}} RCOR' + H_2O$$

carboxylic acid

alcohol

ester

For example,

$$CH_3CH_2CH_2COH + HOCH_2CH_3 \underset{heat}{\overset{H^+ catalyst}{\rightleftharpoons}} CH_3CH_2CH_2COCH_2CH_3 + H_2O$$

butanoic acid (BP 166 °C)

ethanol (BP 78.5 °C)

ethyl butanoate (BP 120 °C) (fragrance of pineapple)

Esters can be split by reaction with water or base

An ester is hydrolyzed to its parent acid and alcohol when the ester is heated together with a stoichiometric excess of water (plus an acid catalyst). The identical equilibrium as shown above forms, but in ester hydrolysis water is in excess, so the equilibrium shifts to the left to favor the carboxylic acid and alcohol, another illustration of Le Châtelier's principle.

Esters are also split apart by the action of aqueous base, only now the carboxylic acid emerges not as the free acid but as its anion. The reaction is called ester **saponification.** We may illustrate it by the action of aqueous sodium hydroxide on a simple ester, ethyl acetate.

$$CH_3COCH_2CH_3(aq) + NaOH(aq) \xrightarrow{heat} CH_3CO^-(aq) + Na^+(aq) + HOCH_2CH_3(aq)$$

ethyl ethanoate (ethyl acetate)

ethanoate ion (acetate ion)

ethanol

Ester groups abound among the molecules of the fats and oils in our diets. The hydrolysis of their ester groups occurs when we digest them, with an enzyme as the catalyst, not a strong acid. Because this digestion occurs in a region of the intestinal tract where the fluids are slightly basic, the anions of carboxylic acids form.

Amides are amine derivatives of carboxylic acids

Carboxylic acids can also be converted to *amides*, a functional group found in proteins. In **amides,** the OH of the carboxyl group is replaced by trivalent nitrogen, which may also be bonded to any combination of H atoms or hydrocarbon groups.

$$\underset{\text{simple amides}}{\overset{\displaystyle O \atop \displaystyle \|}{(H)RCNH_2}} \quad \text{or} \quad (H)RCONH_2, \quad \text{for example,} \quad \underset{\substack{\text{ethanamide} \\ \text{(acetamide)}}}{\overset{\displaystyle O \atop \displaystyle \|}{CH_3CNH_2}}$$

The *simple amides* are those in which the nitrogen bears no hydrocarbon groups, only 2 H atoms. In the place of either or both of these H atoms, however, there can be a hydrocarbon group, and the resulting substance is still in the amide family.

The IUPAC names of the simple amides are devised by first writing the name of the parent carboxylic acid. Then its ending, *-oic acid*, is replaced by *-amide*. For example:

$$\underset{\text{propanamide}}{CH_3CH_2CONH_2} \qquad \underset{\text{pentanamide}}{CH_3CH_2CH_2CH_2CONH_2} \qquad \underset{\text{4-methylpentanamide}}{\overset{\displaystyle CH_3 \atop \displaystyle |}{CH_3CHCH_2CH_2CONH_2}}$$

One of the ways to prepare simple amides parallels that of the synthesis of esters, that is, by heating a mixture of the carboxylic acid and an excess of ammonia.

In general: $\underset{\text{carboxylic acid}}{\overset{\displaystyle O \atop \displaystyle \|}{RCOH}} \;+\; \underset{\text{ammonia}}{H-NH_2} \;\xrightarrow{\text{heat}}\; \underset{\substack{\text{simple} \\ \text{amide}}}{\overset{\displaystyle O \atop \displaystyle \|}{RCNH_2}} + H_2O$

An example: $\underset{\text{ethanoic acid}}{\overset{\displaystyle O \atop \displaystyle \|}{CH_3COH}} \;+\; \underset{\text{ammonia}}{H-NH_2} \;\xrightarrow{\text{heat}}\; \underset{\text{ethanamide}}{\overset{\displaystyle O \atop \displaystyle \|}{CH_3CNH_2}} + H_2O$

Amides, like esters, can be hydrolyzed. When simple amides are heated with water, they change back to their parent carboxylic acids and ammonia. Both strong acids and strong bases promote the reaction. As the following equations show, the reaction is the reverse of the formation of an amide.

In general: $\underset{\text{simple amide}}{\overset{\displaystyle O \atop \displaystyle \|}{RCNH_2}} \;+\; H-OH \;\xrightarrow{\text{heat}}\; \underset{\text{carboxylic acid}}{\overset{\displaystyle O \atop \displaystyle \|}{RCOH}} \;+\; NH_3$

An example: $\underset{\text{ethanamide}}{\overset{\displaystyle O \atop \displaystyle \|}{CH_3CNH_2}} \;+\; H-OH \;\xrightarrow{\text{heat}}\; \underset{\text{ethanoic acid}}{\overset{\displaystyle O \atop \displaystyle \|}{CH_3COH}} \;+\; NH_3$

▢ Urea is an important nitrogen fertilizer because it reacts with soil moisture to release ammonia (and carbon dioxide).

$$\underset{\text{urea}}{\overset{\displaystyle O \atop \displaystyle \|}{NH_2CNH_2}}$$

Amides are not basic like amines

Despite the presence of the NH_2 group in simple amides, the amides are not Brønsted bases like amines or ammonia. This is can be understood by examining the following two resonance structures.

$$R-\overset{\overset{\displaystyle :\ddot{O}:}{\|}}{C}-\overset{\overset{\displaystyle }{|}}{\underset{\underset{\displaystyle H}{|}}{\ddot{N}}}-H \longleftrightarrow R-\overset{\overset{\displaystyle \overset{\ominus}{:}\ddot{O}:}{|}}{C}=\overset{\overset{\displaystyle \oplus}{}}{\underset{\underset{\displaystyle H}{|}}{N}}-H$$

Structure 1   Structure 2

Effectively, the lone pair on the nitrogen in Structure 1 becomes partially delocalized onto the oxygen, as shown in Structure 2. This makes the lone pair on the amide nitrogen less available for donation to an H^+ than the corresponding lone pair on the nitrogen of an amine. As a result, the amide nitrogen has little tendency to acquire a proton, so amides are neutral compounds in an acid–base sense.

Practice Exercise 5: Complete the following equation by drawing structural formulas for the products.

$$H_2N-CH_2CH_2CH_3 \ (aq) + CH_3CH_2-\overset{\overset{\displaystyle O}{\|}}{C}-OH \ (aq) \longrightarrow$$

(Hint: Identify the functional groups and their properties.)

Practice Exercise 6: Write the structural formula(s) for the principal organic product(s) in the following reactions:

(a) $CH_3CH_2-\overset{\overset{\displaystyle O}{\|}}{C}-OCH(CH_3)_2 \xrightarrow{OH^-(aq)}$

(b) $CH_3CH_2CH_2OH \xrightarrow[\text{conc.}]{H_2SO_4}$

<table>
<tr><td>22.6</td><td>

POLYMERS ARE COMPOSED OF MANY REPEATING MOLECULAR UNITS

</td></tr>
</table>

Nearly all of the compounds that we have studied so far have relatively low molecular masses. Both in nature and in the world of synthetics, however, many substances consist of **macromolecules** made up of hundreds or even thousands of atoms. Synthetics made of macromolecules are examples of how chemists have been able to take very ordinary substances in nature, like coal, oil, air, and water, and make new materials, never seen before, with useful applications. Recording tapes, skis, composites in recreational vehicles and their tires, backpacking gear, and all sorts of other recreational equipment derive strength from macromolecules. Materials that are made into thread and cloth consist of macromolecules, and when paints cure, some of their molecules change into other molecules of enormous sizes.

In nature, substances with macromolecules are almost everywhere you look. Trees and anything made of wood, for example, derive their strength from lignins and cellulose, both consisting of enormous molecules that overlap and intertwine. The proteins and the DNA found in our bodies are also huge molecules. Macromolecules of biological origin will be discussed in Section 22.7; in this section we will look at synthetic macromolecules and some of their uses.

Polymers have structural order

Some macromolecular substances have more structural order than others. A **polymer,** for example, is a macromolecular substance all of whose molecules have a small characteristic structural feature that repeats itself over and over. An example is polypropylene,

Lightweight synthetic fabrics have made it easier to pack strong tents into remote regions (here, the Wasatch Mountains of Utah). *(Richard Price/Taxi/ Getty Images.)*

a polymer with many uses, including dishwasher-safe food containers, indoor–outdoor carpeting, and artificial turf (Figure 22.3). The molecules of polypropylene have the following system.

FIG. 22.3 **Artificial turf on a football field is made of polypropylene fibers.** *(Robert Tringali Jr./Sports Chrome Inc.)*

$$\text{etc.}-CH_2-\underset{\underset{CH_3}{|}}{CH}-CH_2-\underset{\underset{CH_3}{|}}{CH}-CH_2-\underset{\underset{CH_3}{|}}{CH}-CH_2-\underset{\underset{CH_3}{|}}{CH}-CH_2-\underset{\underset{CH_3}{|}}{CH}-\text{etc.}$$

polypropylene

Notice that the polymer consists of a long carbon chain (the polymer's **backbone**) with CH_3 groups attached at periodic intervals.[2]

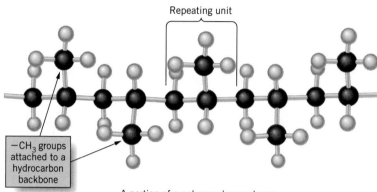

Repeating unit

—CH_3 groups attached to a hydrocarbon backbone

A portion of a polypropylene polymer

If you study this structure, you can see that one structural unit occurs repeatedly (actually thousands of times). In fact, the structure of a polymer is usually represented by the use of only its repeating unit, enclosed in parentheses, with a subscript n standing for several thousand units.

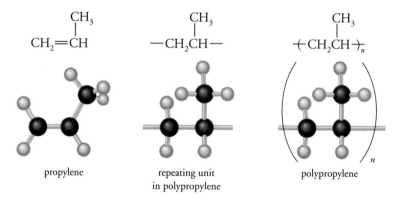

propylene

repeating unit in polypropylene

polypropylene

The value of n is not a constant for every molecule in a given polymer sample. A polymer, therefore, does not consist of molecules identical in *size*, just identical in *kind*; they have the same repeating unit. Notice that despite the *-ene* ending (which is used in naming alkenes), "polypropylene" has no double bonds. The polymer is named after its starting material, propylene.

The repeating unit of a polymer is contributed by a chemical raw material called a **monomer**. Thus propylene is the monomer for polypropylene. The reaction that makes a polymer out of a monomer is called **polymerization,** and the verb is "to polymerize." Most (but not all) useful polymers are formed from monomers that are considered to be organic compounds.

---

[2] The drawing of the molecule shows one way the CH_3 groups can be oriented relative to the backbone and each other. Other orientations are also possible, and they affect the physical properties of the polymer.

Some polymers form by addition of monomer units

There are basically two ways that monomers become joined to form polymers. One path involves the simple addition of one monomer unit to another, a process that continues over and over until a very long chain of monomer units is produced. Polymers formed by this process are called **addition polymers.** Polypropylene, discussed above, is an example. A simpler example is *polyethylene*, formed from ethylene ($CH_2=CH_2$) monomer units. Under the right conditions and with the aid of a substance called an **initiator**, a pair of electrons in the carbon–carbon double bond of ethylene becomes unpaired. The initiator binds to one carbon, leaving an unpaired electron on the other carbon. The result is a very reactive substance called a *free radical*, which can attack the double bond of another ethylene. In the attack, one of the electron pairs of the double bond becomes unpaired. One of the electrons becomes shared with the unpaired electron of the free radical, forming a bond that joins the two hydrocarbon units together. The other unpaired electron moves to the end of the chain, as illustrated below.

As the free radical approaches the ethylene molecule...

...electrons in one of the bonds unpair and move to opposite ends of the molecule.

A bond forms between the two hydrocarbon units and the unpaired electron moves to the end of the chain

This process is repeated over and over as a long hydrocarbon chain grows. Eventually the chain becomes terminated and the result is a polyethylene molecule. The molecule is so large that the initiator, which is still present at one end of the chain, is an insignificant part of the whole, so in writing the structure of the polymer, the initiator is generally ignored.

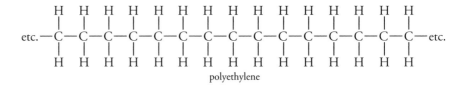

polyethylene

◻ Actually, after ethylene has polymerized, the repeating unit in polyethylene is simply CH_2.

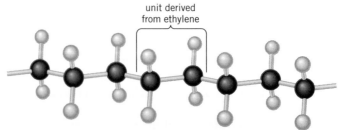

A portion of a polyethylene molecule. Although formed from a monomer with the formula C_2H_4, the actual repeating unit is CH_2.

The process by which the polymer forms has a significant influence on its ultimate structure. For example, the least expensive method for making polyethylene leads to **branching,** which means that polymer chains grow off the main backbone of the molecule as it grows longer (Figure 22.4). Other, more expensive procedures produce molecules without branching, and as we will discuss later, this has a significant effect on the properties of the polymer.

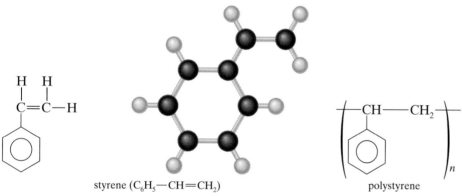

FIG. 22.4 **Branching of the polymer chain in polyethylene.** Segments of polyethylene grow off the main polymer backbone.

In addition to polyethylene and polypropylene, another very common addition polymer, called **polystyrene,** is formed by polymerizing styrene,

FIG. 22.5 **Styrofoam.** Made of polystyrene, Styrofoam is widely used as an insulation in construction. *(Michael Ventura/Bruce Coleman, Inc.)*

styrene (C_6H_5—CH=CH_2)   polystyrene

Notice that the monomer is similar to propylene, but with a benzene ring in place of the methyl group (—CH_3). Therefore, in the polymer we find C_6H_5— attached to every other atom in the hydrocarbon backbone. Polystyrene has almost as many uses as polyethylene. It's used to make clear plastic drinking glasses, molded car parts, and housings of things like computers and kitchen appliances. Sometimes a gas, like carbon dioxide, is blown through molten polystyrene as it is molded into articles. As the hot liquid congeals, tiny pockets of gas are trapped, and the product is a foamed plastic, like the familiar Styrofoam cups or insulation materials (Figure 22.5).

Hundreds of substances similar to ethylene, propylene, and styrene, as well as their halogen derivatives, have been tested as monomers, and Table 22.3 gives some examples.

☐ A "halogen derivative" is a compound in which one or more halogen atoms substitute for hydrogens in a parent molecule. Thus, CH_3Cl is a halogen derivative of CH_4.

EXAMPLE 22.3
Writing the Formula for an Addition Polymer

Use the information in Table 22.3 to write the structure of the polymer poly(vinyl chloride) showing three repeat units. Write the general formula for the polymer.

ANALYSIS: The polymer we're dealing with is an addition polymer, so we can anticipate that the entire CH_2=$CHCl$ molecule will repeat over and over. The polymer will be formed by opening the double bond, as we saw for ethylene.

SOLUTION: When the double bond opens, bonds to two other monomer units will form.

other monomer unit—$\overset{\overset{\displaystyle H}{|}}{\underset{\underset{\displaystyle H}{|}}{C}}$—$\overset{\overset{\displaystyle Cl}{|}}{\underset{\underset{\displaystyle H}{|}}{C}}$—other monomer unit

We need to attach three repeating units to have the answer to the problem.

repeating unit

The general formula for the polymer should indicate the repeating unit occurring *n* times.

IS THE ANSWER REASONABLE? There's not much to check here, other than to be sure that the repeating unit has the same molecular formula as the monomer, which it does.

Practice Exercise 7: Suppose 2-butene were polymerized. Make a sketch showing three repeating units of the monomer in the polymer. (Hint: What is the structure of 2-butene?)

Practice Exercise 8: Write a formula showing three repeating units of the monomer in the polymer Teflon.

TABLE 22.3	Some Addition Polymers Formed from Compounds Related to Ethylene, $CH_2=CH_2$	
Polymer	Monomer	Uses
Polyethylene	$CH_2=CH_2$	Grocery bags, bottles, children's toys, bulletproof vests
Polypropylene	$CH_2=CH$ with CH_3	Dishwasher-safe plastic kitchenware, indoor–outdoor carpeting, rope
Polystyrene	⬡—$CH=CH_2$	Plastic cups, toys, housings for kitchen appliances, Styrofoam insulation.
Poly(vinyl chloride) (PVC)	$CH_2=CHCl$	Insulation, credit cards, vinyl siding for houses, bottles, plastic pipe
Poly(tetrafluoroethylene) (Teflon)	$F_2C=CF_2$	Nonstick surfaces on cookware, valves
Poly(vinyl acetate) (PVA)	$CH_2=C$ with H, and $O-C=O$ bearing CH_3	Latex paint, coatings, glue, molded items
Poly(methyl methacrylate) (Lucite)	$CH_2=C$ with CH_3, and $C=O$, $O-CH_3$	Shatter-resistant windows, coatings, acrylic paints, molded items

Polymers can be formed by condensation reactions

The second way that monomer units can combine to form a polymer is by a process called **condensation,** in which a small molecule is eliminated when the two monomer units become joined. In a simplified way, we can diagram this as follows.

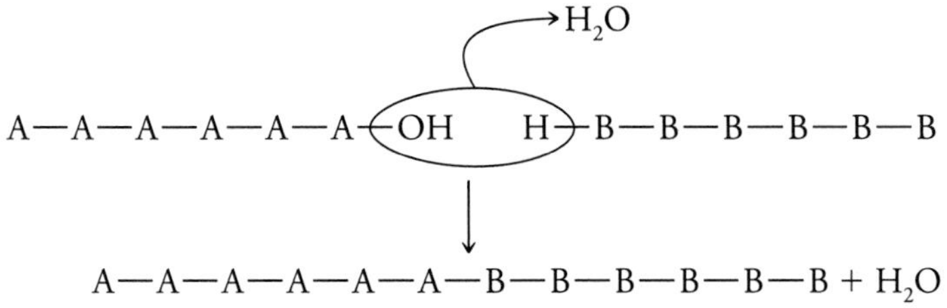

$$A-A-A-A-A-A(\!OH \qquad H\!)B-B-B-B-B-B \longrightarrow H_2O$$

$$A-A-A-A-A-A-B-B-B-B-B-B + H_2O$$

In this example, an OH group from one molecule combines with an H from another, forming a water molecule. At the same time, the two molecules A and B become joined by a covalent bond. If this can be made to happen at both ends of A and B, long chains are formed and a **condensation polymer** is the result.

The two most familiar condensation polymers are nylon and polyesters. Nylon is formed by combining two different compounds, so it's considered a **copolymer.** The first nylon to be manufactured is called **nylon 6,6** because it forms by combining two compounds each with six carbon atoms.

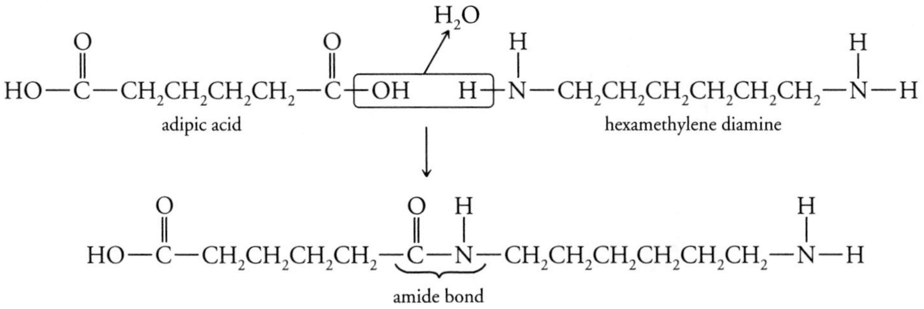

adipic acid   hexamethylene diamine

amide bond

Notice that adipic acid contains two carboxyl groups (it's called a dicarboxylic acid). The other compound is an amine (diamine, actually, because it has two amine groups). By the elimination of water, the two molecules become joined by a linkage called an *amide bond.* This same linkage is found in proteins, including silk (a fiber nylon was invented to replace) and proteins found in our bodies.

The molecule above with the amide bond still has a carboxyl group on one end and an amine group on the other, so further condensation can occur, ultimately leading to the formation of nylon 6,6.

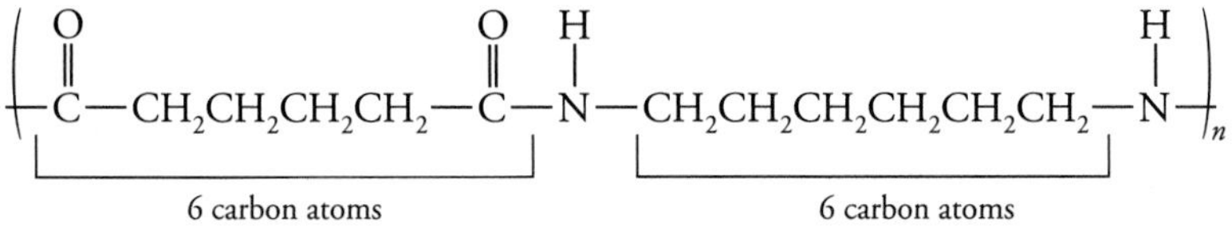

6 carbon atoms   6 carbon atoms

nylon 6,6

Nylon was invented in 1940 and became popular as a substitute for silk in women's stockings. It forms strong elastic fibers and is used to make fishing line as well as fibers found in all sorts of clothing and many other products.

An example of a polyester is shown below.

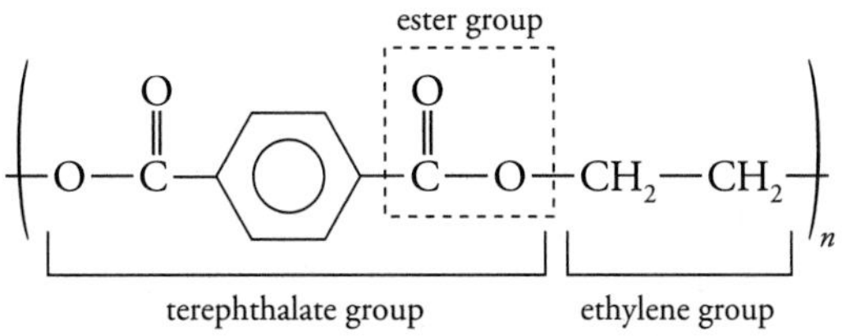

ester group

terephthalate group   ethylene group

poly(ethylene terephthalate), also known as PET

It is a copolymer made by condensation polymerization, the first step of which is

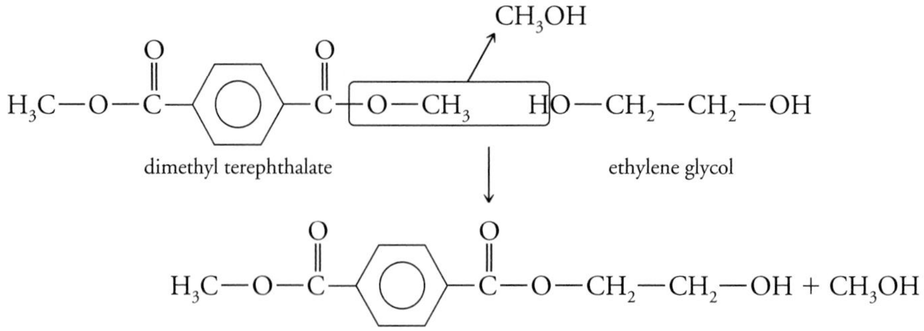

$$CH_3OH$$

H_3C—O—C(=O)—⟨benzene⟩—C(=O)[—O—CH_3   H]O—CH_2—CH_2—OH

dimethyl terephthalate   ethylene glycol

↓

H_3C—O—C(=O)—⟨benzene⟩—C(=O)—O—CH_2—CH_2—OH + CH_3OH

Notice that this time the small molecule that's displaced is CH_3OH, methyl alcohol. Continued polymerization ultimately leads to the PET polymer shown above. You probably have heard of this polymer because it also goes by the name *Dacron*.

A variety of starting materials can be used to form different polyesters with a range of properties. Their uses include fibers for fabrics, shatterproof plastic bottles for soft drinks, Mylar for making recording tapes and balloons that don't easily deflate, and shatterproof windows and eyeglasses. See Facets of Chemistry 22.1.

Cross-linking between polymer strands gives increased strength

When natural rubber latex was first discovered, it wasn't particularly useful. You couldn't make rubber tires out of it because when it got hot, the rubber became sticky and would melt; when it became cold, it became brittle and hard. In 1839, Charles Goodyear (of tire fame) discovered that adding sulfur to latex, and then heating it, drastically altered the properties of the rubber. He called his new product **vulcanized rubber.**

What happens when sulfur reacts with latex is that groups of sulfur atoms form bridges, called **cross-links,** between strands of the latex polymer (known technically as polyisoprene). This is shown in Figure 22.6. By linking the strands of polyisoprene together, they are no longer able to slip by each other when hot, so the rubber doesn't melt. The increased strength also prevents the polymer from becoming brittle and easily broken when cold. Cross-linking also gives the polymer a "memory," enabling it to snap back to its original shape when released after being stretched (a property you've experienced using rubber bands). The amount of sulfur used to vulcanize the latex also affects the properties of the finished product. If only a small amount of sulfur is used, the polymer is elastic. But as the amount of sulfur increases, so does the amount of cross-linking, and the product becomes harder and less resilient.

☐ Notice that the polyisoprene in Figure 22.6 has lots of bends and turns in it. When you stretch rubber, you tend to straighten out the polymer strands, but when you release it, the strands snap back to their original shapes.

Cross-linking provides strength to a variety of polymers you may be familiar with. Formica (used in kitchen countertops), epoxy resins (in epoxy glues), and polycarbonates (which have a polyester-like structure) made strong for use in shatterproof eyeglasses are examples. Even the material used to make soft contact lenses is a cross-linked polymer that's capable of absorbing lots of water.

Polymer crystallinity affects physical properties

Beyond chemical stability, physical properties are the features of polymers most sought after. Desirable properties of Teflon, for example, are its chemical inertness and its slipperiness toward just about anything. Nylon isn't eaten by moths—a chemical property, in fact—but its superior strength and its ability to be made into fibers and fabrics of great beauty are what make nylon valuable. Dacron (a polyester) resists mildewing and its fibers are not weakened by mildew like those of cotton. Dacron also has greater strength with lower mass than cotton, and Dacron fibers do not stretch as much, which are properties that account for Dacron's use for making sails.

In many ways, the physical properties of a polymer are related to how the individual polymer strands are able to pack in the solid. For example, earlier we noted that the least expensive way of making polyethylene yields a product that has branching. The branches

(a)

etc.—CH₂   CH₂ C=CH CH₂   CH₂ C=CH
      H₃C   H₃C

(The structural diagram shows two strands of polyisoprene molecules.)

(b)

crosslink to another polymer chain

sulfur crosslinks

crosslink to another polymer chain

FIG. 22.6 **Cross-linking of polymer chains in rubber by reaction with sulfur.** (*a*) Two strands of polyisoprene molecules. (*b*) Sulfur reacts by opening double bonds in the polymer molecules and forming bridges between adjacent strands.

prevent the molecules from lining up in an orderly fashion, so the molecules twist and intertwine to give an essentially amorphous solid (which means it lacks the kind of order found in crystalline solids). See Figure 22.7*a*. This amorphous product is called *low density polyethylene* (*LDPE*); the polymer molecules have a relatively low molecular mass and the solid has little structural strength. LDPE is the kind of polyethylene used to make the plastic bags grocery stores use to pack your purchases.

Following different methods, polyethylene can be made to form without branching and with molecular masses ranging from 200,000 to 500,000 u. This polymer is called *linear* polyethylene or *high density polyethylene* (*HDPE*). In HDPE, the polymer strands are able to line up alongside each other to produce a large degree of order (and therefore, crystallinity), as illustrated in Figure 22.7*b*. This enables the molecules to form fibers easily, and because the molecules are large and packed so well, the London forces between them are very strong. The result is a strong, tough fiber. DuPont's Tyvek, for example, is made from thin, crystalline HDPE polyethylene fibers randomly oriented and pressed together into a material resembling paper. It is lightweight, strong, and resists water, tears, punctures, and abrasion. Federal Express has been using it for years for envelopes, and builders use it to wrap new construction to prevent water and air intrusion, thereby lowering heating and cooling costs. Tyvek is also made into limited-use protective clothing for use in hazardous environments.

□ HDPE molecules contain approximately 30,000 CH₂ units linked end to end!

A new house under construction is wrapped with a Tyvek fabric to prevent water and air intrusion, thereby lowering heating and cooling costs. *(DuPont Tyvek Weatherization Systems.)*

□ UHMWPE molecules contain between 200,000 and 400,000 CH₂ units attached end to end!

Under the right conditions, linear polyethylene molecules can be made extremely long, yielding *ultrahigh molecular weight polyethylene* (*UHMWPE*) with molecules having molecular masses of three to six million. The fibers produced from this polymer are so strong that they are used to make bulletproof vests! Honeywell is producing an oriented polyethylene polymer they call Spectra, which forms flexible fibers that can be woven into a strong, cut-resistant fabric. It is used to make thin, lightweight liners for surgical gloves that resist cuts by scalpels, industrial work gloves, and even sails for sailboats (see Figure 22.8). Mixed with other plastics, it can be molded into strong rigid forms such as helmets for military or sporting applications.

Other good fiber-forming polymers also have long molecules with shapes that permit strong interactions between the individual polymer strands. Nylon, for example, possesses polar carbonyl groups, $>$C$=$O, and N—H bonds that form strong hydrogen bonds between the individual molecules.

(a) Two branched polymer chains become twisted with little order.

(b) Polymer chains are able to align, producing a tightly packed structure with a large degree of crystallinity.

FIG. 22.7 **Amorphous and crystalline polyethylene.**
(*a*) When branching occurs in LDPE, the polymer strands are not able to become aligned and an amorphous product results.
(*b*) Linear HDPE has a high degree of crystallinity, which makes for excellent strong fibers.

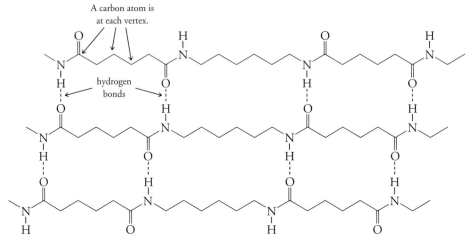

Three strands of nylon 6,6 bound to each other by hydrogen bonds.

Kevlar, another type of nylon, also forms strong hydrogen bonds between polymer molecules and is very crystalline. Its strong fibers are also used to make bulletproof vests. Because the fibers are so strong, they are also used to make thin yet strong hulls of racing boats. This lightweight construction improves speed and performance without sacrificing safety.

22.7 | MOST BIOCHEMICALS ARE ORGANIC COMPOUNDS

Biochemistry is the systematic study of the chemicals of living systems, their organization into cells, and their chemical interactions. Biochemicals have no life in themselves as isolated compounds, yet life has a molecular basis. Only when chemicals are organized into cells or tissues can interactions occur that enable tissue repair, cell reproduction, the generation of energy, the removal of wastes, and the management of a number of other

High-speed racing boats often are built with hulls made of Kevlar. Because of the polymer's high strength, the hulls can be made thin, thereby reducing weight and increasing speed. (*Tom Newby/Courtesy of Formula Powerboats.*)

FIG. 22.8 **Spectra fibers.**
Strong, lightweight sails made of Spectra fibers propelled Brad Van Liew to victory in the 2002–2003 "Around Alone" around-the-world yacht race. Van Liew sailed 31,094 miles in seven months to win the race. (*Photo courtesy Brad Van Liew and Tommy Hilfiger. Photo by Billy Black.*)

FACETS OF CHEMISTRY

22.1

Bioplastics and Biodegradable Polymers

Almost all the polymers we find incorporated in fabrics and consumer plastics are made from materials derived from petroleum. This leads to two major problems. First, there is only a finite amount of petroleum available on earth, so when we manufacture plastics, we are consuming a precious commodity that can't be renewed. Second, synthetic polymers and plastics are not readily attacked by microorganisms, so when placed in landfills or scattered into the environment, they do not degrade and pose a continuing pollution problem. But changes are in the wind.

DuPont, one of the world's leading chemical producers, is manufacturing a polyester polymer called *Sorona*, a versatile polymer with properties that make it excellent for apparel and upholstery fabrics (Figure 1). It is made by condensation polymerization of propanediol with terephthalic acid.

DuPont has been obtaining the propanediol from petroleum sources but has developed a genetically engineered microbe to produce it by fermentation of corn sugar. The terephthalic acid, however, is still made from petroleum.

Cargill Dow's *NatureWorks* is a completely bio-based polymer made by polymerization of lactic acid, which is also derived by fermentation of corn sugar. The reaction is

The NatureWorks polymer uses no petroleum products and is being used to make fibers for apparel where it is combined with cotton fibers. Other fabric blends for apparel include wool and silk. Clear cold drink cups are also being made with the polymer, which is biodegradable. It's expected that use of the polymer will spread to a variety of packaging materials, too (see Figure 2).

Metabolix, Inc., in Cambridge, Massachusetts, has found a way to avoid the chemical synthesis step in making polymers by using genetic engineering to develop microbes that convert plant matter directly into polymers that are similar to NatureWorks. Depending on the microbe used, a variety of polymers can be produced with the general formula

Different polymer properties are obtained depending on the value of x. At the present time, production of such polymers is at the pilot plant stage.

FIG. 1 **Sorona fibers in these fabrics have superior stretch recovery, soft touch, and good dye and print capabilities.** (*Anthony Farina/DuPont Media Relations.*)

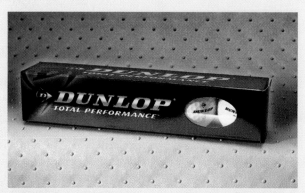

FIG. 2 **The plastic film used to package these golf balls is made from NatureWorks polylactide polymer.** (*Andy Washnik.*)

functions. The world of living things is composed mostly of organic compounds, including many natural polymers such as proteins, starch, cellulose, and the chemicals of genes.

There are three important requirements for life

A living system requires materials, energy, and information or "blueprints." Our focus in this section will be on the substances that supply them—*carbohydrates, lipids, proteins,* and *nucleic acids*—the basic materials whose molecules, together with water and a few kinds of ions, make up cells and tissues.

□ Starch, table sugar, and cotton are all *carbohydrates*.

Our brief survey of biochemistry will focus mainly on the *structures* of selected biochemical materials. This is where any study of biochemistry must begin, because the chemical, physical, and biological properties of biochemicals are determined by structure. Where appropriate, we'll describe some of their reactions, particularly with water.

A variety of compounds are required for cells to work. The membranes that enclose all of the cells of your body, for example, are made up mostly of lipid molecules, although molecules of proteins and carbohydrates are also incorporated. Most hormones are either in the lipid or the protein family. Essentially all cellular catalysts—enzymes—are proteins, but many enzyme molecules cannot function without the presence of relatively small molecules of vitamins or certain metal ions.

□ *Lipids* include the fats and oils in our diet, like butter, margarine, salad oils, and baking shortenings (e.g., lard). Meat and egg albumin are particularly rich in *proteins*.

Lipids and carbohydrates are also our major sources of the chemical energy we need to function. In times of fasting or starvation, however, the body is also able to draw on its proteins for energy.

The information needed to operate a living system is borne by molecules of nucleic acids. Their structures carry the *genetic code* that instructs cells how to make its proteins, including its enzymes. Hundreds of diseases, like cystic fibrosis and sickle-cell anemia, are caused by defects in the molecular structures of nucleic acids. Viruses, like the AIDS virus, work by taking over the genetic machinery of a cell.

Carbohydrates include sugars, starch, and cellulose

Carbohydrates are naturally occurring polyhydroxyaldehydes or polyhydroxyketones, or else they are compounds that react with water to give these. The carbohydrates include table sugar (sucrose) as well as starch and cellulose.

Most carbohydrates are polymers of simpler units called **monosaccharides.** The most common monosaccharide is glucose, a pentahydroxyaldehyde and probably the most widely occurring structural unit in the entire living world. Glucose is the chief carbohydrate in blood, and it provides the building unit for such important polysaccharides as cellulose and starch. Fructose, a pentahydroxyketone, is produced together with glucose when we digest table sugar. Honey is also rich in fructose.

$$CH_2CH—CH—CH—CH—CH\overset{\overset{\displaystyle O}{\|}}{} \qquad CH_2CH—CH—CHCCH_2\overset{\overset{\displaystyle O}{\|}}{}$$

glucose (open-chain form)
a polyhydroxyaldehyde

fructose (open-chain form)
a polyhydroxyketone

When dissolved in water, the molecules of most carbohydrates exist in a mobile equilibrium involving more than one structure. Glucose, for example, exists as two cyclic forms and one open-chain form in equilibrium in water (see Figure 22.9). The open-chain form, the only one with a free aldehyde group, is represented by less than 0.1% of the solute molecules. Yet, the solute in an aqueous glucose solution still gives the reactions of a polyhydroxyaldehyde. This is possible because the equilibrium between this form and the two cyclic forms shifts to supply more of any of its members when a specific reaction occurs to just one (in accordance with Le Châtelier's principle).

Disaccharides are composed to two monosaccharide units

Carbohydrates whose molecules are split into two monosaccharide molecules by reacting with water are called **disaccharides.** *Sucrose* (table sugar, cane sugar, or beet sugar) is an example, and its hydrolysis gives glucose and fructose.

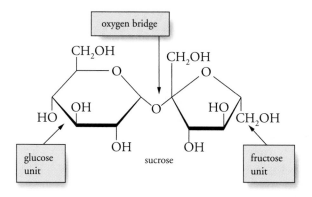

FIG. 22.9 **Structures of glucose.** Three forms of glucose are in equilibrium in an aqueous solution. The curved arrows in the open form show how bonds become reoriented as it closes into a cyclic form. Depending on how the CH=O group is turned at the moment of ring closure, the new OH group at C-1 takes up one of two possible orientations, α or β.

☐ The six-membered rings of the cyclic forms of monosaccharides are not actually *flat* rings. Glucose, for example, has the structure shown below.

To simplify, let's represent sucrose as Glu—O—Fru , where Glu is a glucose unit and Fru is a fructose unit, both joined by an oxygen bridge, —O— . The hydrolysis of sucrose, the chemical reaction by which we digest it, can thus be represented as follows.[3]

$$\text{Glu—O—Fru} + H_2O \xrightarrow[\text{(hydrolysis)}]{\text{digestion}} \text{glucose} + \text{fructose}$$
$$\underset{\text{sucrose}}{}$$

Lactose (milk sugar) hydrolyzes to glucose and galactose (Gal), an isomer of glucose, and this is the reaction by which we digest lactose.

$$\text{Gal—O—Glu} + H_2O \xrightarrow[\text{(hydrolysis)}]{\text{digestion}} \text{galactose} + \text{glucose}$$
$$\underset{\text{lactose}}{}$$

Polysaccharides are polymers of monosaccharides

Some of the most important naturally occurring polymers are the **polysaccharides,** carbohydrates whose molecules involve thousands of monosaccharide units linked to each other by oxygen bridges. They include starch, glycogen, and cellulose. The complete hydrolyses of all three yield only glucose, so their structural differences involve details of the oxygen bridges.

Plants store glucose units for energy needs in molecules of **starch,** found often in seeds and tubers (e.g., potatoes). Starch consists of two kinds of glucose polymers. The structurally simpler kind is *amylose,* which makes up roughly 20% of starch. We may represent its structure as follows, where O is the oxygen bridge linking glucose units.

$$\text{Glu}(\text{O—Glu})_n\text{OH}$$
$$\text{amylose (\textit{n} is very large)}$$

The average amylose molecule has over 1000 glucose units linked together by oxygen bridges. These are the sites that are attacked and broken when water reacts with amylose

---

[3] Considerable detail is lost with the simplified structure of sucrose (and other carbohydrates like it to come). We leave the details, however, to other books because we seek a broader view.

during digestion. Molecules of glucose are released and are eventually delivered into circulation in the bloodstream.

$$\text{Amylose} \; + \; n\text{H}_2\text{O} \; \xrightarrow[\text{(hydrolysis)}]{\text{digestion}} \; n \text{ glucose}$$

The bulk of starch is made up of *amylopectin,* whose molecules are even larger than those of amylose. The amylopectin molecule consists of several amylose molecules linked by oxygen bridges from the end of one amylose unit to a site somewhere along the "chain" of another amylose unit.

$$
\begin{array}{c}
\text{etc.} \\
| \\
\text{Glu}-\!\!\left(\text{O}-\text{Glu}\right)_{\!m}\!\!-\text{O} \\
| \\
\text{Glu}-\!\!\left(\text{O}-\text{Glu}\right)_{\!n}\!\!-\text{O} \\
| \\
\text{Glu}-\!\!\left(\text{O}-\text{Glu}\right)_{\!o}\!\!-\text{O} \\
| \\
\text{etc.}
\end{array}
$$

amylopectin (*m*, *n*, and *o* are large numbers)

Molecular masses ranging from 50,000 to several million are observed for amylopectin samples from the starches of different plant species. (A molecular mass of 1 million corresponds to about 6000 glucose units.)

Animals store glucose units for energy as **glycogen,** a polysaccharide with a molecular structure very similar to that of amylopectin. When we eat starchy foods and deliver glucose molecules into the bloodstream, any excess glucose not needed to maintain a healthy concentration in the blood is removed from circulation by particular tissues, like the liver and muscles. Liver and muscle cells convert glucose to glycogen. Later, during periods of high energy demand or fasting, glucose units are released from the glycogen reserves so that the concentration of glucose in the blood stays high enough for the needs of the brain and other tissues.

Cellulose is a carbohydrate that humans cannot digest

□ Cellulose is the chief material in a plant cell wall, and it makes up about 100% of cotton.

Cellulose is a polymer of glucose, much like amylose, but with the oxygen bridges oriented with different geometries. We lack the enzyme needed to hydrolyze its oxygen bridges, so we are unable to use cellulose materials like lettuce for food, only for fiber. Animals that eat grass and leaves, however, have bacteria living in their digestive tracts that convert cellulose into small molecules, which the host organism then appropriates for its own use.

Lipids comprise a family of water-insoluble compounds

Lipids are natural products that are water insoluble but tend to dissolve in nonpolar solvents such as diethyl ether or benzene. The lipid family is huge because the only structural requirement is that lipid molecules be relatively nonpolar with large segments that are entirely hydrocarbon-like. For example, the lipid family includes cholesterol as well as sex hormones, like estradiol and testosterone. You can see from their structures how largely hydrocarbon-like they are.

cholesterol

estradiol (a female sex hormone)

testosterone (a male sex hormone)

Triacylglycerols are esters of glycerol with long-chain carboxylic acids

The lipid family also includes the edible fats and oils in our diets—substances such as olive oil, corn oil, peanut oil, butterfat, lard, and tallow. These are **triacylglycerols,** that is, esters between glycerol, an alcohol with three OH groups, and any three of several long-chain carboxylic acids.

TABLE 22.4 Common Fatty Acids

Fatty Acid	Number of Carbon Atoms	Structure	Melting Point (°C)
Myristic acid	14	$CH_3(CH_2)_{12}CO_2H$	54
Palmitic acid	16	$CH_3(CH_2)_{14}CO_2H$	63
Stearic acid	18	$CH_3(CH_2)_{16}CO_2H$	70
Oleic acid	18	$CH_3(CH_2)_7CH{=}CH(CH_2)_7CO_2H$	4
Linoleic acid	18	$CH_3(CH_2)_4CH{=}CHCH_2CH{=}CH(CH_2)_7CO_2H$	−5
Linolenic acid	18	$CH_3CH_2CH{=}CHCH_2CH{=}CHCH_2CH{=}CH(CH_2)_7CO_2H$	−11

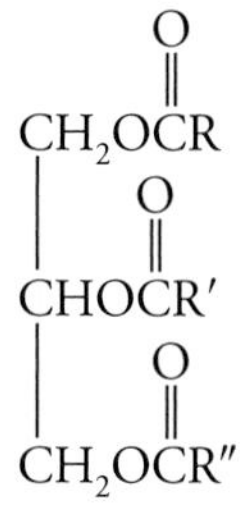
triacylglycerol (general structural features)

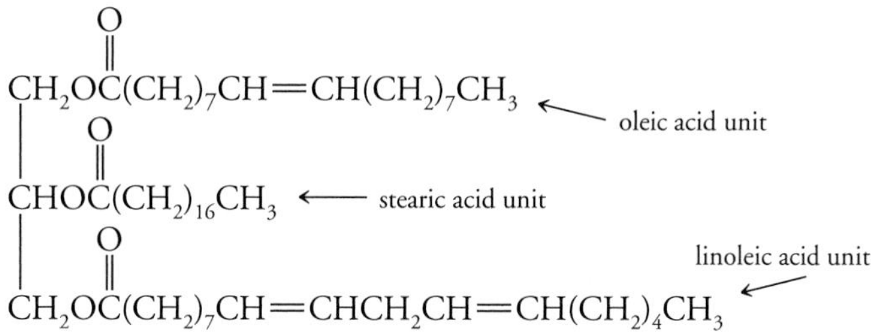

triacylglycerol—typical molecule present in a vegetable oil

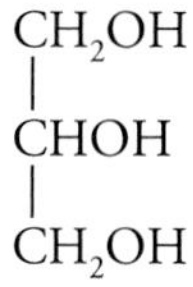
glycerol

The carboxylic acids used to make triacylglycerols are called **fatty acids** and generally have just one carboxyl group on an unbranched chain with an even number of carbon atoms (Table 22.4). Their long hydrocarbon chains make triacylglycerols mostly like hydrocarbons in physical properties, including insolubility in water. Many fatty acids have alkene groups.

Triacylglycerols obtained from vegetable sources, like olive oil, corn oil, and peanut oil, are called *vegetable oils* and are liquids at room temperature. Triacylglycerols from animal sources, like lard and tallow, are called *animal fats* and are solids at room temperature. The vegetable oils generally have more alkene double bonds per molecule than animal fats, and so are said to be *polyunsaturated.* The double bonds are usually cis, and so the molecules are kinked, making it more difficult for them to nestle close together, experience London forces, and so be in the solid state.

Cooking oils are advertised as *polyunsaturated* because of their several alkene groups per molecule.

Digestion of triacylglycerols involves hydrolysis

We digest the triacylglycerols by hydrolysis, meaning by their reaction with water. Our digestive juices in the upper intestinal tract have enzymes called *lipases* that catalyze these reactions. For example, the complete digestion of the triacylglycerol shown above occurs by the following reaction.

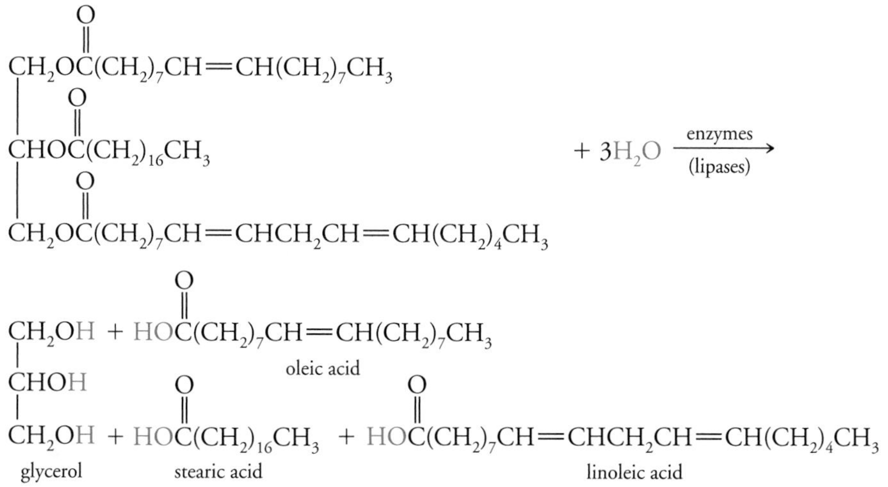

Actually, the *anions* of the acids form, because the medium in which lipid digestion occurs is basic.

When the hydrolysis of a triacylglycerol is carried out in the presence of sufficient base so as to release the fatty acids as their anions, the reaction is called *saponification.* The mixture of the salts of long-chain fatty acids is what makes up ordinary *soap.*

Hydrogenation of vegetable oils produces solid fats

Vegetable oils are generally less expensive to produce than butterfat, but because the oils are liquids, few people care to use them as bread spreads. Remember that animal fats, like butterfat, are solids at room temperature, and vegetable oils differ from animal fats only in the number of carbon–carbon double bonds per molecule. Simply adding hydrogen to the double bonds of a vegetable oil, therefore, changes the lipid from a liquid to a solid.

Partial hydrogenation of a vegetable oil can lead to rearrangement of the atoms around the double bonds from cis to trans. The resulting products are known as *trans fats.* Because ingestion of trans fats has been associated with coronary artery disease, food product labels are now required to show the amounts of those fats in the food.

Cell membranes in animals are composed of lipid bilayers

The lipids involved in the structures of cell membranes in animals are not triacylglycerols. Some are diacylglycerols with the third site on the glycerol unit taken up by an attachment to a phosphate unit. This, in turn, is joined to an amino alcohol unit by an ester-like network. The phosphate unit carries one negative charge, and the amino unit has a positive charge. These lipids are called *glycerophospholipids.* Lecithin is one example.

☐ The amino alcohol unit in lecithin is contributed by choline, a cation:

$$HOCH_2CH_2\overset{+}{N}(CH_3)_3$$

Ethanolamine (in its protonated form):

$$HOCH_2CH_2NH_3{}^+$$

is another amino alcohol that occurs in phospholipids.

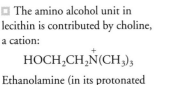

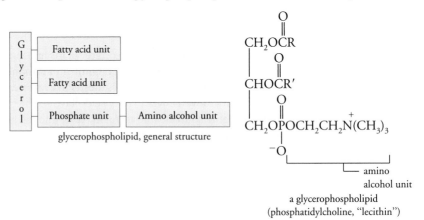

glycerophospholipid, general structure

a glycerophospholipid
(phosphatidylcholine, "lecithin")

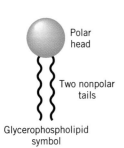

Glycerophospholipid symbol

The glycerophospholipids illustrate that it is possible for lipid molecules to carry polar, even ionic sites, and still not be very soluble in water. The combination of both nonpolar and polar or ionic units within the same molecule enable the glycerophospholipids and similar substances to be major building units for the membranes of animal cells.

The purely hydrocarbon-like portions of a glycerophospholipid molecule (the long R groups contributed by the fatty acid units) are **hydrophobic** ("water fearing"; they avoid water molecules). The portions bearing the electrical charges are **hydrophilic** ("water loving"; they are attracted to water molecules). In an aqueous medium, therefore, the molecules of a glycerophospholipid aggregate in a way that minimizes the exposure of the hydrophobic side chains to water and maximizes contact between the hydrophilic sites and water. These interactions are roughly what take place when glycerophospholipid molecules aggregate to form the *lipid bilayer* membrane of an animal cell (Figure 22.10). The hydrophobic side chains intermingle in the center of the layer where water molecules do not occur. The hydrophilic groups are exposed to the aqueous medium inside and outside of the cell. Not shown in Figure 22.10 are cholesterol and cholesterol ester molecules, which help to stiffen the membranes. Thus cholesterol is essential to the cell membranes of animals.

Cell membranes also include protein units, which provide several services. Some are molecular recognition sites for molecules such as hormones and neurotransmitters. Others provide channels for the movements of ions, like Na^+, K^+, Ca^{2+}, Cl^-, $HCO_3{}^-$, and others, into or out of the cell. Some are channels for the transfer of small organic molecules, like glucose.

☐ *Neurotransmitters* are small molecules that travel between the end of one nerve cell and the surface of the next to transmit the nerve impulse.

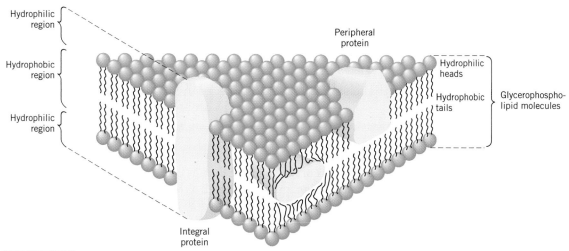

Hydrophilic region

Hydrophobic region

Hydrophilic region

Peripheral protein

Hydrophilic heads

Hydrophobic tails

Glycerophospho-lipid molecules

Integral protein

FIG. 22.10 **Animal cell membrane.** The lipid molecules of an animal cell membrane are organized as a bilayer.

Proteins are almost entirely polymers of amino acids

The proteins are a huge family of substances that make up about half of the human body's dry weight. They are found in all cells and in virtually all parts of cells. Proteins serve as enzymes, hormones, and neurotransmitters. They carry oxygen in the bloodstream as well as some of the waste products of metabolism. No other group of compounds has such a variety of functions in living systems.

The dominant structural units of **proteins** are macromolecules called **polypeptides**, which are made from a set of monomers called α-**amino acids.** Most protein molecules include, besides their polypeptide units, small organic molecules or metal ions, and the whole protein lacks its characteristic biological function without these species (Figure 22.11).

The monomer units for polypeptides are a group of about 20 α-amino acids all of which have structural features in common. Some examples of the set of 20 amino acids used to make proteins are given below. The symbol R stands for a structural group, an *amino acid side chain.* All are known by their common names. Each also has a three-letter symbol.

α-position

$$^{+}NH_3CHCO^{-}$$
|
R

α-amino acid, general structural features

R = H, glycine (Gly)

= CH_3, alanine (Ala)

= CH_2—⬡, phenylalanine (Phe)

= $CH_2CH_2CO_2H$, glutamic acid (Glu)

= $CH_2CH_2CH_2CH_2NH_2$, lysine (Lys)

= CH_2SH, cysteine (Cys)

The simplest amino acid is aminoacetic acid, or glycine, for which the "side chain" is H.

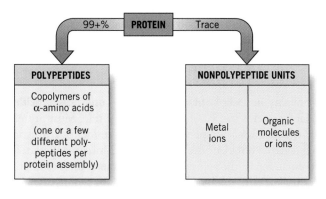

99+% **PROTEIN** Trace

POLYPEPTIDES

Copolymers of α-amino acids

(one or a few different poly-peptides per protein assembly)

NONPOLYPEPTIDE UNITS

Metal ions

Organic molecules or ions

FIG. 22.11 **Components of proteins.** Some proteins consist exclusively of polypeptide molecules, but most also have non-polypeptide units such as small organic molecules or metal ions, or both.

Glycine, like all of the amino acids in their pure states, exists as a *dipolar ion*. Such an ion results from an internal self-neutralization, by the transfer of a proton from the proton-donating carboxyl group to the proton-accepting amino group.

$$NH_2CH_2CO_2H \longrightarrow {}^+NH_3CH_2CO_2{}^-$$

aminoacetic acid   glycine, dipolar
(glycine)   ionic form

Polypeptides are polymers

☐ Polypeptides are elimination polymers, and they are similar to nylon in some ways. The peptide bond has the same structural features as the bond connecting monomer units in nylon (page 927).

Polypeptides are copolymers of the amino acids. The carboxyl group of one amino acid becomes joined to the amino group of another by means of the same kind of carbonyl–nitrogen bond found in amides, but here called the **peptide bond.** Let's see how two amino acids, glycine and alanine, can become linked by a (multistep) splitting out of water.

glycine (Gly)   alanine (Ala)   glycylalanine (Gly-Ala)

The product of the reaction, glycylalanine, is an example of a *dipeptide.* (Notice how the three-letter symbols for the amino acids make up what biochemists sometimes use as the *structural* formulas of such products.)

We could have taken glycine and alanine in different roles and written the equation for the formation of a different dipeptide, Ala-Gly.

alanine (Ala)   glycine (Gly)   alanylglycine (Ala-Gly)

☐ The artificial sweetener aspartame (NutraSweet) is the methyl ester of a dipeptide.

aspartame

We can think of the formation of these two dipeptides as being like the formation of two 2-letter words from the letters N and O. Taken in one order we get NO; in the other, ON. They have entirely different meanings, yet are made of the same pieces.

Notice that each dipeptide above has a $CO_2{}^-$ at one end of the chain and a $^+NH_3$ group at the other end. Each end of a dipeptide molecule, therefore, could become involved in the formation of yet another peptide bond involving any of the 20 amino acids. For example, if glycylalanine were to combine with phenylalanine (Phe), two different *tripeptides* could form with the sequences Gly-Ala-Phe or Phe-Gly-Ala. Each of these tripeptides has a $CO_2{}^-$ at one end and a $^+NH_3$ at the other end. Thus, you can see how very long sequences of amino acid units might be joined together.

As the length of a polypeptide chain grows, the number of possible combinations of amino acids becomes astronomical. For example, with just the three amino acids we've used (Gly, Ala, and Phe), six different polypeptide sequences are possible that differ only in the three side chains, H, CH_3, and $CH_2C_6H_5$, located at the α-carbon atoms.

Proteins usually contain more than one polypeptide chain

Many proteins consist of a single polypeptide. Most proteins, however, involve assemblies of two or more polypeptides. These are identical in some proteins, but in others the aggregating polypeptides are different. Moreover, a relatively small organic molecule may be included in the aggregation, and a metal ion is sometimes present, as well. Thus, the terms "protein" and "polypeptide" are not synonyms. Hemoglobin, for example, has all

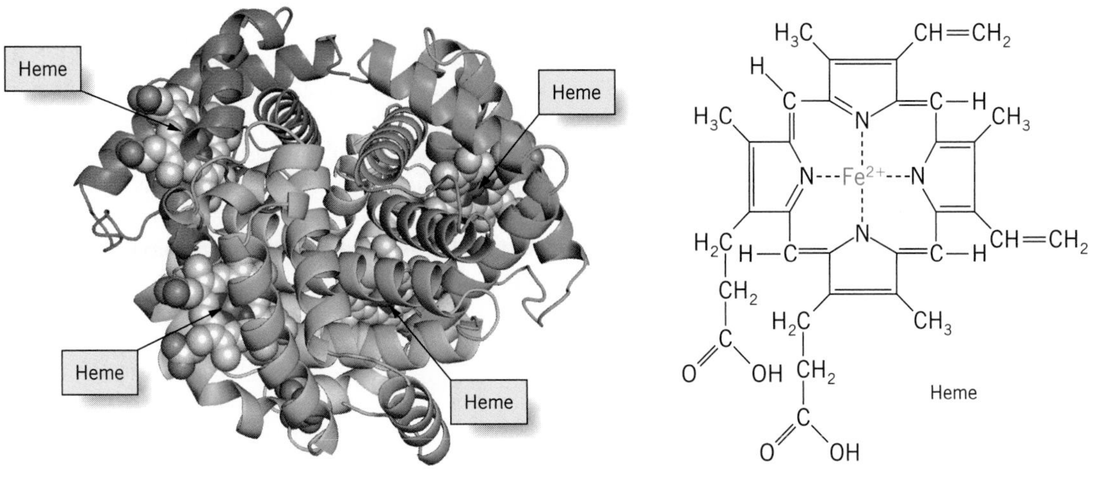

FIG. 22.12 **Hemoglobin.** Its four polypeptide chains, each shown as a different colored ribbon, twist and bend around the four embedded heme units. Each heme unit contains an Fe^{2+} ion in its center which is able to bind to O_2.

of the features just described (Figure 22.12). It is made of four polypeptides—two similar pairs—and four molecules of heme, the organic compound that causes the red color of blood. Heme, in turn, holds an iron(II) ion. The *entire* package is the protein, hemoglobin. If one piece is missing or altered in any way—for example, if iron occurs as Fe^{3+} instead of Fe^{2+}, the substance is not hemoglobin, and it does not transport oxygen in the blood.

Notice in Figure 22.12 how the strands of each polypeptide unit in hemoglobin are coiled and that the coils are kinked and twisted. Such shapes of polypeptides are determined by the amino acid sequence, because the side chains are of different sizes and some are hydrophilic and others are hydrophobic. Polypeptide molecules become twisted and coiled in whatever way minimizes the contact of hydrophobic groups with the surrounding water and maximizes the contacts of hydrophilic groups with water molecules.

The final shape of a protein, called its *native form,* is as critical to its ability to function as anything else about its molecular architecture. For example, just the exchange of one side-chain R group by another changes the shape of hemoglobin and causes a debilitating condition known as sickle-cell anemia.

Almost all enzymes are proteins
The catalysts in living cells are called **enzymes,** and virtually all are proteins. Some enzymes require metal ions, such as Mn^{2+}, Co^{2+}, Cu^{2+}, and Zn^{2+}, all of which are on the list of the *trace elements* that must be in a good diet. Some enzymes also require molecules of the B vitamins to be complete enzymes.

Some of our most dangerous poisons work by deactivating enzymes, often those needed for the transmission of nerve signals. For example, the botulinum toxin that causes botulism, a deadly form of food poisoning, deactivates an enzyme in the nervous system. Heavy metal ions, like Hg^{2+} or Pb^{2+}, are poisons because they deactivate enzymes.

□ Hemoglobin is the oxygen carrier in blood.

□ In one of the subunits of the hemoglobin in those with sickle-cell anemia an isopropyl group, $—CH(CH_3)_2$, is a side chain where a $—CH_2CH_2CO_2H$ side chain should be.

□ Heavy metal ions bond to the HS groups of cysteine side chains in polypeptides.

22.8 | NUCLEIC ACIDS CARRY OUR GENETIC INFORMATION

The enzymes of an organism are made under the chemical direction of a family of compounds called the *nucleic acids.* Both the similarities and the uniqueness of every species as well as every individual member of a species depend on structural features of these compounds.

DNA and RNA are types of nucleic acids

The **nucleic acids** occur as two broad types, namely, **RNA,** or ribonucleic acids, and **DNA,** or deoxyribonucleic acids. DNA is the actual chemical of a gene, the individual unit of heredity and the chemical basis through which we inherit all of our characteristics.

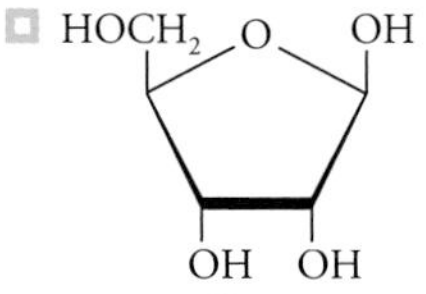

The main chains or "backbones" of DNA molecules consist of alternating units contributed by phosphoric acid and a monosaccharide (see Figure 22.13). In RNA the monosaccharide is ribose (hence the R in RNA). In DNA, the monosaccharide is deoxyribose (*deoxy* means "lacking an oxygen unit"). Thus, both DNA and RNA have the following systems, where *G* stands for *group,* each *G* unit representing a unique nucleic acid side chain or *base.*

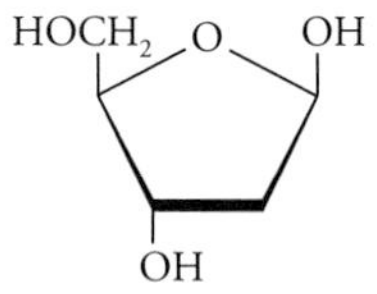

$$\overset{G^1}{\underset{|}{}} \qquad \overset{G^2}{\underset{|}{}} \qquad \overset{G^3}{\underset{|}{}}$$

phosphate—sugar—phosphate—sugar—phosphate—sugar—etc.

Backbone system in all nucleic acids–many thousands of repeating units long
(in DNA, the sugar is deoxyribose; in RNA, the sugar is ribose)

The side chains, *G,* are all heterocyclic amines whose molecular shapes have much to do with their function. Being amines, which are basic in water, they are referred to as the *bases* of the nucleic acids and are represented by single letters—A for adenine, T for thymine, U for uracil, G for guanine, and C for cytosine.

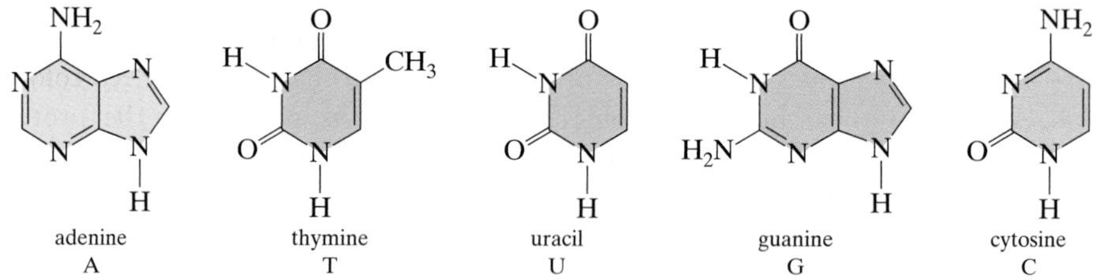

adenine
A

thymine
T

uracil
U

guanine
G

cytosine
C

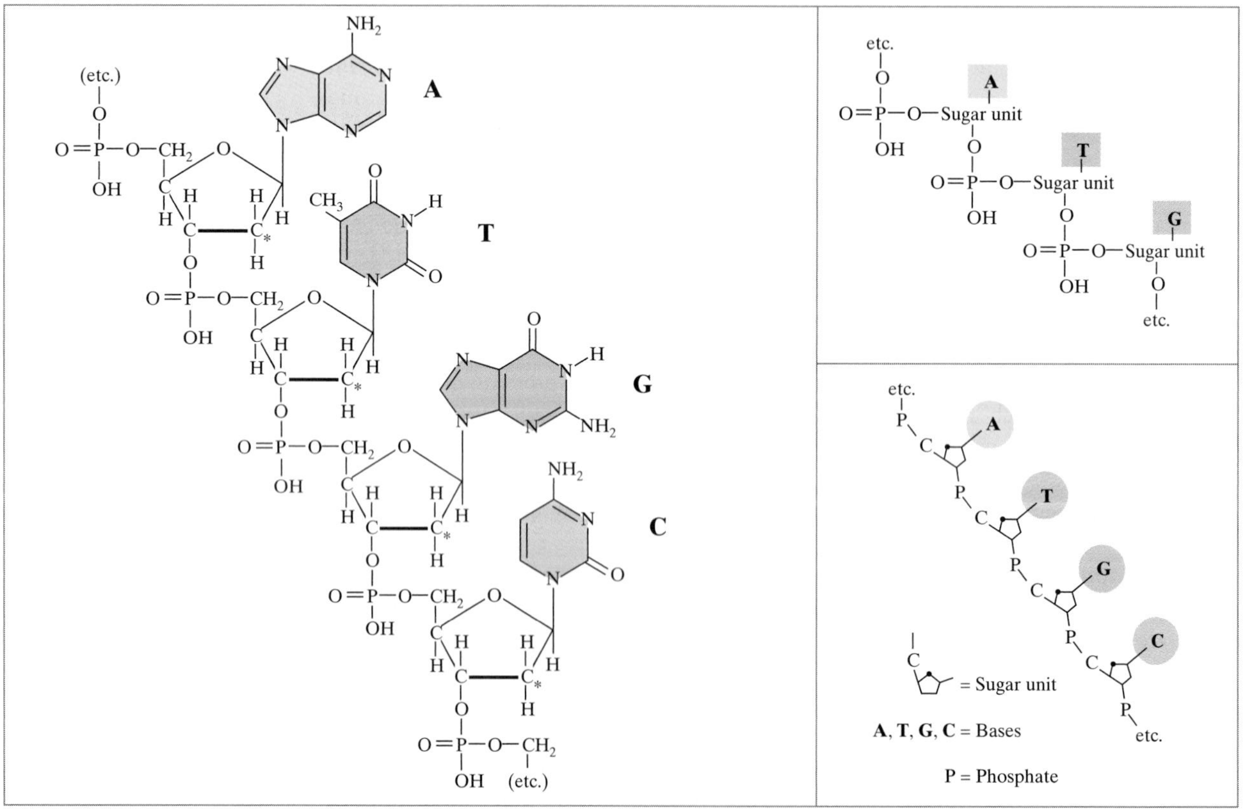

FIG. 22.13 **Nucleic acids.** A segment of a DNA chain featuring each of the four DNA bases. When the sites marked by asterisks each carry an OH group, the main "backbone" would be that of RNA. In RNA U replaces T. The insets show how simplified versions of a DNA strand can be drawn.

The bases A, T, G, and C occur in DNA, whereas A, U, G, and C are in RNA. These few bases are the "letters" of the genetic alphabet. The messages of all genes are composed with just four letters, A, T, G, and C.

DNA occurs as a double helix

In 1953, F. H. C. Crick of England and J. D. Watson, an American, deduced that DNA occurs in cells as two intertwined, oppositely running strands of molecules coiled like a spiral staircase and called the **DNA double helix** (Figure 22.14). Hydrogen bonds help to hold the two strands side by side, but other factors are also involved.

The bases have N—H and O=C groups, which enable hydrogen bonds ($\cdots$) to form between them.

$$\begin{matrix} \delta+ & & \delta- & & \\ N{-}H & \cdots & O & {=} & C \end{matrix}$$

However, the bases with the best "matching" molecular geometries for maximum hydrogen bonding occur only as particular *pairs* of bases. The functional groups of each pair are in exactly the right locations in their molecules to allow hydrogen bonds between pair members. Adenine (A) pairs with thymine (T) and cytosine (C) pairs with guanine (G) (see Figure 22.15). In DNA, A pairs only with T, never with G or C. Similarly, C pairs only with G, never with A or T. Thus opposite every G on one strand in a DNA double helix, a C occurs on the other. Opposite every A on one strand in DNA, a T is found on the other.

Adenine (A) can also pair with uracil (U), but U occurs in RNA. The A-to-U pairing is an important factor in the work of RNA.

The replication of DNA occurs through base pairing

Prior to cell division, the cell produces duplicate copies of its DNA so that each daughter cell will have a complete set. Such reproductive duplication is called DNA **replication.**

□ Crick and Watson shared the 1962 Nobel Prize in Physiology or Medicine with Maurice Wilkins, using X-ray data from Rosalind Franklin to deduce the helical structure of DNA.

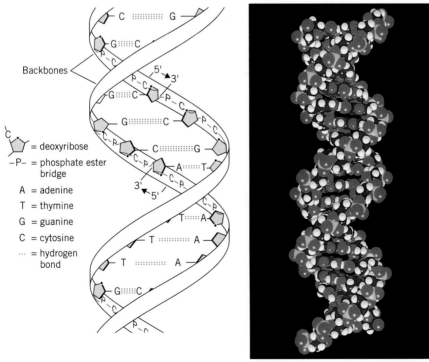

Backbones

= deoxyribose
–P– = phosphate ester bridge
A = adenine
T = thymine
G = guanine
C = cytosine
$\cdots$ = hydrogen bond

(a)

(b)

FIG. 22.14 The DNA double helix. (*a*) A schematic drawing in which the hydrogen bonds between the two strands are indicated by dotted lines (*b*) A model of a short section of a DNA double helix. (*Nelson Max/Peter Arnold, Inc.*)

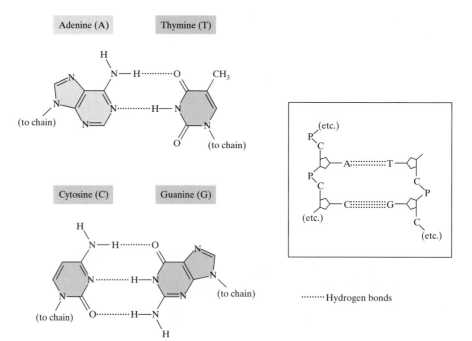

FIG. 22.15 **Base pairing in DNA.** The hydrogen bonds are indicated by dotted lines.

········ Hydrogen bonds

cytosine unit

a typical nucleotide, one using cytosine as its side chain

The accuracy of DNA replication results from the limitations of the base pairings: A only with T and C only with G (Figure 22.16). The unattached letters, A, T, G, and C, in Figure 22.16 here represent not just the bases but the whole monomer molecules of DNA. These are called *nucleotides* and are molecules made of a phosphate–sugar unit bonded to one particular base. The nucleotides are made by the cell and are present in the cellular "soup."

An enzyme catalyzes each step of replication. As replication occurs, the two strands of the parent DNA double helix separate, and the monomers for new strands assemble along the exposed single strands. Their order of assembling is determined entirely by the specificity of base pairing. For example, a base such as T on a parent strand can accept only a nucleotide with the base A. Two daughter double helices result that are identical to the parent, and each carries one strand from the parent. One new double helix goes to one daughter cell and the second goes to the other.

Genes are made up of segments along a DNA chain

A single human gene has between 1000 and 3000 bases, but they do not occur continuously on a DNA molecule. In multicelled organisms, a gene is neither a whole DNA molecule nor a continuous sequence in one. A single gene consists of the totality of particular *segments* of a DNA chain that, taken together, carry the necessary genetic

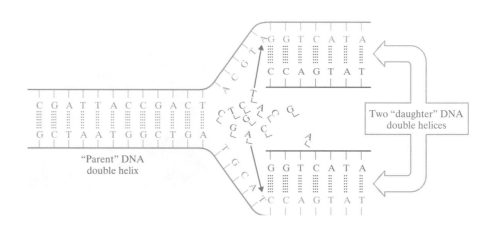

FIG. 22.16 **Base pairing and the replication of DNA.**

instruction for a particular polypeptide. The individual separated sections making up a gene are called **exons**—a unit that helps to *ex*press a message. The sections of a DNA strand between exons are called **introns**—units that *int*errupt the gene.

DNA directs the synthesis of polypeptides

Each polypeptide in a cell is made under the direction of its own gene. In broad outline, the steps between a gene and an enzyme occur as follows.

$$\text{DNA} \xrightarrow{\text{transcription}} \text{RNA} \xrightarrow{\text{translation}} \text{Polypeptide}$$

gene (The genetic message is read off in the cell nucleus and transferred to RNA.)

(The genetic message, now on RNA outside the nucleus, is used to direct the synthesis of a poly-peptide.)

☐ Something like 25,000 genes are needed to account for all of the kinds of proteins in a human body.

The step labeled **transcription** accomplishes just that—the genetic message, represented by a sequence of bases on DNA, is transcribed into a *complementary* sequence of bases on RNA, but U, not T, is on the RNA. **Translation** means the conversion of the base sequence on RNA into a side-chain sequence on a new polypeptide. It is like translating from one language (the DNA/RNA base sequences) to another language (the polypeptide side-chain sequence).

The cell tells which amino acid unit must come next in a growing polypeptide by means of a code that relates unique groups of nucleic acid bases to specific amino acids. The code, in other words, enables the cell to translate from the four-letter RNA alphabet (A, U, G, and C) to the 20-letter alphabet of amino acids (the amino acid side chains).

Four types of RNA are involved in polypeptide synthesis

Four types of RNA are involved in the connection between gene and polypeptide. One is called *ribosomal* RNA, or rRNA, and it is packaged together with enzymes in small granules called *ribosomes*. Ribosomes are manufacturing stations for polypeptides.

Another RNA is called *messenger* RNA, or mRNA, and it brings the blueprints for a specific polypeptide from the cell nucleus to the manufacturing station (a ribosome). mRNA is the carrier of the genetic message to the polypeptide assembly site.

The mRNA is made from another kind of RNA called *heterogeneous nuclear* RNA, or hnRNA. This is the RNA first made at the direction of a DNA unit, so it contains sections that were specified by both exons and introns (hence, *heterogeneous*).

The last type of RNA is called *transfer* RNA, or tRNA. It has responsibility for picking up the prefabricated parts, the amino acids, and getting them from the cell "soup" to the ribosome.

☐ Little agreement exists on the name *heterogeneous nuclear RNA* among biochemistry references. Some call it pre-RNA; others call it *primary transcript RNA*, or ptRNA.

When some chemical signal tells a cell to make a particular polypeptide, the cell nucleus makes the hnRNA that corresponds to the gene. As we indicated, the base sequence in hnRNA is an exact complement to a base sequence in the DNA being transcribed—both the exon sections of the DNA and the introns. Reactions and enzymes in the cell nucleus then remove those parts of the new hnRNA that were caused by introns. It is as if the message, now on hnRNA, is edited to remove nonsense sections. The result of this editing is messenger RNA.

The mRNA now moves outside the cell nucleus and becomes joined to a ribosome where the enzymes for polypeptide synthesis are found. The polypeptide manufacturing site now awaits the arrival of tRNA molecules bearing amino acid units. All is in readiness for polypeptide synthesis—for *translation*.

The genetic code consists of triplets of bases

To continue with our use of the language of coding, we can describe the genetic message as being written in code words made of three letters—three bases. For example, when the bases G, G, and U occur side by side on an mRNA chain, they together specify the amino acid glycine. Although three other triplets also mean glycine, one of the genetic codes for glycine is GGU. Similarly, GCU is a code "word" for alanine.

Each triplet of bases *as it occurs on mRNA* is called a **codon,** and each codon corresponds to a specific amino acid. Which amino acid goes with which codon constitutes the **genetic code.** One of the most remarkable features of the code is that it is essentially universal. The codon specifying alanine in humans, for example, also specifies alanine in the genetic machinery of bacteria, aardvarks, camels, rabbits, and stinkbugs. Our chemical kinship with the entire living world is profound (even humbling).

A triplet of bases complementary to a codon occurs on tRNA and is called an **anticodon.** A tRNA molecule, bearing the amino acid corresponding to its anticodon, can line up at a strand of mRNA only where the anticodon "fits" by hydrogen bonding to the matching codon. If the anticodon is ACC, then the A on the anticodon must find a U on the mRNA at the same time that its neighboring two C bases find neighboring G bases on the mRNA strand. Thus the anticodon and codon line up as shown in the margin, where the dotted lines indicate hydrogen bonds.

mRNA codons determine the sequence in which tRNA units can line up, and this sets the sequence in which amino acid units become joined in a polypeptide. Through this overall process, the sequence of bases in DNA are translated into a sequence of amino acids in the polypeptide.

Genetic defects are caused by "errors" in the base sequence in DNA

About 2000 diseases are attributed to various kinds of defects in the genetic machinery of cells. With so many steps from gene to polypeptide, we should expect many opportunities for things to go wrong. Suppose, for example, that just one base in a gene were wrong. Then one base on an mRNA strand would be the wrong base—"wrong" meaning with respect to getting the polypeptide we want. This would change every remaining codon. If the next three codons on mRNA, for example, were UCU—GGU—GCU—U—etc., and the first G were deleted, then the sequence would become

$$\text{UCU—GUG—CUU—etc.}$$

All remaining triplets change! You can imagine how this could lead to an entirely different polypeptide than what we want.

Or suppose that the GGU codon were replaced by, say, a GCU codon so that the UCU—GGU—GCU—etc. becomes

$$\text{UCU—GCU—GCU—etc.}$$

One amino acid in the resulting polypeptide would not be what we want. Something like this makes the difference, for example, between normal hemoglobin and sickle-cell hemoglobin and the difference between health and a tragic genetic disease.

Atomic radiation, like gamma rays, beta rays, or even X rays, as well as chemicals that mimic radiation can cause genetic defects, too. A stray high-energy photon hitting a gene might cause two opposite bases to fuse together chemically and so make the cell reproductively dead. When it came time for it to divide, the cell could not replicate its genes, could not divide, and that would be the end of it. If this happens to enough cells in a tissue, the organism might be fatally affected.

Viruses take over the genetic machinery in cells

Viruses are packages of chemicals usually consisting of nucleic acid and protein. Their nucleic acids are able to take over the genetic machinery of the cells of particular host tissues, manufacture more virus particles, and multiply enough to burst the host cell. Because cancer cells divide irregularly, and usually more rapidly than normal cells, some viruses are thought to be among the agents that can cause cancer. For example, strains of human papilloma virus (HPV) are known to cause cervical cancer.

□
```
 ⎰─A ⋮⋮⋮⋮⋮U─⎱
 ⎱─C ⋮⋮⋮⋮⋮⋮G─⎰
 ⎰─C ⋮⋮⋮⋮⋮⋮G─⎱
```
anticodon   codon on
on tRNA   mRNA

□ In 2001 scientists working on the *Human Genome Project*, a major scientific effort to "map" all of the genes of the body by locating where they are on the various chromosomes, announced the sequencing of the human genome. Knowledge of the locations and structures of genes is expected to help cure at least some genetic diseases.

□ The protein of a virus is a protective overcoat for its nucleic acid, and it provides an enzyme to catalyze a breakthrough by the virus into a host cell.

SUMMARY

Organic Compounds. Organic chemistry is the study of the covalent compounds of carbon, except for its oxides, carbonates, bicarbonates, and a few others. **Functional groups** attached to nonfunctional and hydrocarbon-like groups are the basis for the classification of organic compounds. Members of a family have the same kinds of chemical properties. Their physical properties are a function of the relative proportions of functional and nonfunctional groups. Opportunities for hydrogen bonding strongly influence the boiling points and water solubilities of compounds with OH or NH groups. Organic compounds exhibit isomerism because often there is more than one possible structure corresponding to a given molecular formula. Molecules containing an **asymmetric carbon atom** exhibit chirality.

Saturated Hydrocarbons. The **alkanes**—saturated compounds found chiefly in petroleum—are the least polar and the least reactive of the organic families. Their carbon skeletons can exist as **straight chains, branched chains,** or **rings.** When they are *open chain,* there is free rotation about single bonds. Rings can include heteroatoms, but **heterocyclic compounds** are not hydrocarbons.

By the IUPAC rules, the names of alkanes end in *-ane.* A prefix denotes the carbon content of the parent chain, the longest continuous chain, which is numbered from whichever end is nearest a branch. The **alkyl groups** are alkanes minus a hydrogen.

Alkanes in general do not react with strong acids or bases or strong redox reactants. At high temperatures, their molecules crack to give H_2 and unsaturated compounds.

Unsaturated Hydrocarbons. The lack of free rotation at a carbon–carbon double bond makes **geometric isomerism** possible. The pair of electrons of a π bond makes alkenes act as Brønsted bases, enabling alkenes to undergo **addition reactions** with hydrogen chloride and water (in the presence of an acid catalyst). Alkenes also add hydrogen (in the presence of a metal catalyst). Bromine and chlorine add to alkenes under mild, uncatalyzed conditions. Strong oxidizing agents, like ozone, readily attack alkenes and break their molecules apart.

Aromatic hydrocarbons, like benzene, do not give the addition reactions shown by alkenes. Instead, they undergo **substitution reactions** that leave the energy lowering, pi-electron network intact. In the presence of suitable catalysts, benzene reacts with chlorine, bromine, nitric acid, and sulfuric acid.

Alcohols and Ethers. The **alcohols,** ROH, and the **ethers,** ROR′, are alkyl derivatives of water. Ethers have almost as few chemical properties as alkanes. Alcohols undergo an **elimination reaction** that splits out H_2O and changes them to alkenes. Concentrated hydrohalogen acids, like HI, react with alcohols by a **substitution reaction,** which replaces the OH group by a halogen. Oxidizing agents convert alcohols of the type RCH_2OH first into aldehydes and then into carboxylic acids. Oxidizing agents convert alcohols of the type R_2CHOH into ketones. Alcohols form esters with carboxylic acids.

Amines. The simple **amines,** RNH_2, as well as the more substituted relatives, RNHR′ and RNR′R″, are organic derivatives of ammonia and thus are weak bases that can neutralize strong acids. The conjugate acids of amines are good proton donors and can neutralize strong bases.

Carbonyl Compounds. Aldehydes, RCH=O, among the most easily oxidized organic compounds, are oxidized to carboxylic acids. **Ketones,** RCOR′, strongly resist oxidation. Aldehydes and ketones add hydrogen to make alcohols.

The **carboxylic acids,** RCO_2H, are weak acids but neutralize strong bases. Their anions are Brønsted bases. Carboxylic acids can also be changed to esters by heating them with alcohols.

Esters, $RCO_2R′$, react with water to give back their parent acids and alcohols. When aqueous base is used for hydrolysis, the process is called *saponification* and the products are the salts of the parent carboxylic acids as well as alcohols.

The simple **amides,** $RCONH_2$, can be made from acids and ammonia, and they can be hydrolyzed back to their parent acids and trivalent nitrogen compounds. The amides are not basic.

Polymers. Polymers, which are **macromolecules,** are made up of a very large number of atoms in which a small characteristic feature repeats over and over many times. **Polypropylene,** an **addition polymer** that consists of a hydrocarbon **backbone** with a methyl group, CH_3, attached to every other carbon, is formed by **polymerization** of the **monomer** propylene. Polyethylene and polystyrene, which are also addition polymers, are formed from ethylene and styrene, respectively. **Condensation polymers** are formed by elimination of a small molecule such as H_2O or CH_3OH from two monomer units accompanied by the formation of a covalent bond between the monomers. **Nylons** and **polyesters** are **copolymers** because they are formed from two different monomers.

Cross-linking occurs when bridging groups of atoms link polymer chains together. Latex (polyisoprene) can be cross-linked by heating it with sulfur to give **vulcanized rubber.** Polymerization of ethylene can lead to **branching,** which produces an amorphous polymer called low density polyethylene (LDPE). High density polyethylene (HDPE) and ultrahigh molecular weight polyethylene (UHMWPE) are not branched and are more crystalline, which makes them stronger. Nylon's properties are affected by hydrogen bonding between polymer strands.

Carbohydrates. The glucose unit is present in starch, glycogen, cellulose, sucrose, lactose, and simply as a **monosaccharide** in honey. It's the chief "sugar" in blood. As a monosaccharide, glucose is a pentahydroxyaldehyde in one form but it also exists in two cyclic forms. The latter are joined by oxygen bridges in the **disaccharides** and **polysaccharides.** In lactose (milk sugar), a glucose and a galactose unit are joined. In sucrose (table sugar), glucose and fructose units are linked.

The major polysaccharides—**starch** (amylose and amylopectin), glycogen, and cellulose—are all polymers of glucose but with different patterns and geometries of branching. The digestion of the disaccharides and starch requires the hydrolyses of the oxygen bridges to give monosaccharides.

Lipids. Natural products in living systems that are relatively soluble in nonpolar solvents, but not in water, are all in a large group of compounds called **lipids.** They include sex hormones and cholesterol, the triacylglycerols of nutritional importance, and the glycerophospholipids and other phospholipids needed for cell membranes.

The **triacylglycerols** are triesters between glycerol and three of a number of long-chain, often unsaturated **fatty acids.** In the digestion of the triacylglycerols, hydrolysis of the ester groups occurs, and anions of fatty acids form (together with glycerol).

Molecules of glycerophospholipids have large segments that are hydrophobic and others that are hydrophilic. Glycerophospholipid molecules are the major components of cell membranes, where they are arranged in a lipid bilayer.

Amino Acids, Polypeptides, and Proteins. The **amino acids** in nature are mostly compounds with NH_3^+ and CO_2^- groups joined to the same carbon atom (called the alpha position of the amino acid). About 20 amino acids are important to the structures of polypeptides and proteins.

When two amino acids are linked by a **peptide bond** (an amide bond), the compound is a dipeptide. In **polypeptides,** several (sometimes thousands) of regularly spaced peptide bonds occur, involving as many amino acid units. The uniqueness of a polypeptide lies in its chain length and in the sequence of the side-chain groups.

Some **proteins** consist of only a polypeptide, but most proteins involve two or more (sometimes different) polypeptides and often a nonpolypeptide (an organic molecule) and a metal ion.

Nearly all **enzymes** are proteins. Major poisons work by deactivating enzymes.

Nucleic Acids. The formation of a polypeptide with the correct amino acid sequence needed for a given polypeptide is under the control of **nucleic acids.** These are polymers whose backbones are made of a repeating sequence of pentose sugar units. On each sugar unit is a **base,** a heterocyclic amine such as adenine (A), thymine (T), guanine (G), cytosine (C), or uracil (U). In **DNA,** the sugar is deoxyribose, and the bases are A, T, G, and C. In **RNA,** the sugar is ribose and the bases are A, U, G, and C.

DNA exists in cell nuclei as **double helices.** The two strands are associated side by side, with hydrogen bonds occurring between particular pairs of bases. In DNA, A is always paired to T; C is always paired to G. The base U replaces T in RNA, and A can also pair with U. The bases, A, U, G, and C, are the four letters of the genetic alphabet, and the specific combination that codes for one amino acid in polypeptide synthesis is three bases, side by side, on a strand. An individual gene in higher organisms consists of sections of a DNA chain, called **exons,** separated by other sections called **introns.** The **replication** of DNA is the synthesis by the cell of exact copies of the original two strands of a DNA double helix.

Polypeptide Synthesis. The DNA that carries the gene for a particular polypeptide is used to direct the synthesis of a molecule of hnRNA. The hnRNA is then modified by the removal of those segments corresponding to the introns of the DNA. This leaves messenger RNA, mRNA, the carrier of the message of the gene to the ribosomes. The ribosomes contain rRNA (ribosomal RNA). The overall change from gene to mRNA is called **transcription.** mRNA is like an assembly line at a factory (ribosomes) awaiting the arrival of parts—the amino acids. These are borne on transfer RNA molecules, tRNA.

A unit of three bases on mRNA constitutes a **codon** for one amino acid. A tRNA–amino acid unit has an **anticodon** that can pair to a codon on mRNA. In this way a tRNA–amino acid unit "recognizes" only one place on mRNA for delivering the amino acid to the polypeptide developing at the mRNA assembly line. The key that relates codons to specific amino acids is the **genetic code** and it is essentially the same code for all organisms in nature. The involvement of mRNA in directing the synthesis of a polypeptide is called **translation.**

Even small changes or deletions in the sequences of bases on DNA can have large consequences in the form of genetic diseases. Viruses are able to use their own nucleic acids to take over the genetic apparatus of the host tissue.

TOOLS FOR PROBLEM SOLVING

In this chapter you learned to apply the following concepts as tools in solving problems related to organic chemistry. Study each tool carefully so that you know what each is used for. When faced with solving a problem, recall what each tool does and consider whether it will be helpful in finding a solution. This will aid you in selecting the tools you need.

Functional group concept *(page 903)* If you can recognize a functional group in a molecule, you can place the structure into an organic family and so predict the kinds of reactions the compound can give. In particular, study Table 22.1.

Convention in using polygons to represent rings *(page 904)* A carbon atom is understood at each corner; other elements in the ring are explicitly written. Edges of the polygon represent covalent bonds; double bonds are explicitly shown. The remaining bonds, as required by the covalence of the atom at a corner, are understood to hold H atoms.

IUPAC rules of nomenclature *(pages 907, 910, 913, 914, and 917–921)* Each family of compounds has a characteristic name ending:

-ane	alkanes	-al	aldehydes
-ene	alkenes	-one	ketones
-yne	alkynes	-oic acid	carboxylic acids
-ol	alcohols	-oate	esters

Each member of a family has a defined "parent," which is the longest chain that includes the functional group. How the chain is numbered varies with the family, but generally the numbering starts from whichever end of the parent chain reaches the functional group with the lower number. The names of side chains, such as the alkyl groups, are included in the name ahead of the name of the parent, and their locations are designated by the numbers of the carbons at which they are attached to the parent.

QUESTIONS, PROBLEMS, AND EXERCISES

Answers to problems whose numbers are printed in color are given in Appendix B. More challenging problems are marked with asterisks.

REVIEW QUESTIONS

Structural Formulas

22.1 In general terms, what makes possible so many organic compounds?

22.2 What is the condensed structure of R if R—CH₃ represents the compound ethane?

22.3 Which of the following structures are possible, given the numbers of bonds that various atoms can form?
(a) $CH_2CH_2CH_3$
(b) $CH_3\!=\!CHCH_2CH_3$
(c) $CH_3CH\!=\!CHCH_2CH_3$

22.4 Write neat, condensed structures of the following.

(a)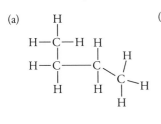

(b)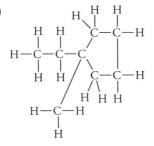

(c)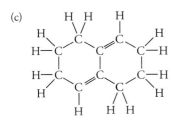

Families of Organic Compounds

22.5 In $CH_3CH_2NH_2$, the NH₂ group is called the *functional* group. In *general terms*, why is it called this?

22.6 In general terms, why do functional groups impart more chemical reactivity to families that have them? Why don't the alkanes display as many reactions as, say, the amines?

Isomers

22.7 What must be true about two substances if they are to be called *isomers* of each other?

22.8 What prevents free rotation about a double bond and so makes geometric isomers possible?

Properties and Structure

22.9 Explain why $CH_3CH_2CH_2OH$ is more soluble in water than $CH_3CH_2CH_2CH_3$.

22.10 Of the two compounds in Question 22.9, which has the higher boiling point? Explain.

22.11 Examine the structures of the following compounds.

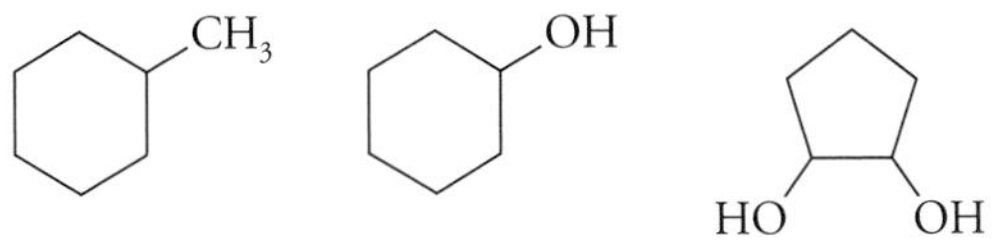

(a) Which has the highest boiling point? Explain.
(b) Which has the lowest boiling point? Explain.

22.12 Which of the following compounds is more soluble in water? Explain.

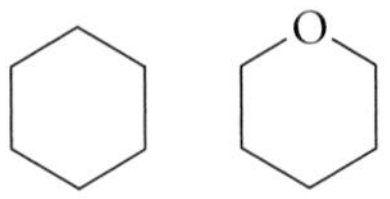

22.13 Which of the following compounds has the higher boiling point? Explain.

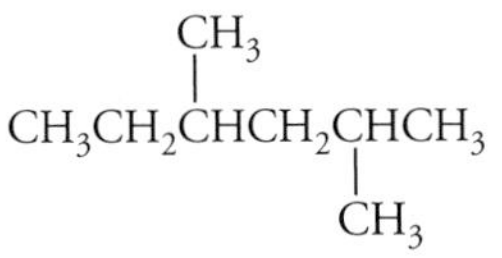

$$CH_3CH_2CHCH_2CHCH_3$$ with CH_3 groups   **A**

$$CH_3CH_2CH_2CH_2CH_3$$ **B**

22.14 Why do aldehydes and ketones have boiling points that are lower than those of their corresponding alcohols?

22.15 Acetic acid boils at 118 °C, higher even than 1-propanol, which boils at 97 °C. How can the higher boiling point of acetic acid be explained?

22.16 Methyl ethanoate has many more atoms than its parent acid, ethanoic acid. Yet methyl ethanoate (BP 59 °C) boils much lower than ethanoic acid (BP 118 °C). How can this be explained?

*22.17 Ethanamide is a solid at room temperature. 1-Aminobutane, which has about the same molecular mass, is a liquid. Explain.

22.18 Amines, RNH_2, do not have as high boiling points as alcohols with comparable numbers of atoms. Why?

Names

22.19 Write the condensed structures of the following compounds.
(a) 2,2-dimethyloctane
(b) 1,3-dimethylcyclopentane
(c) 1,1-diethylcyclohexane
(d) 6-ethyl-5-isopropyl-7-methyl-1-octene
(e) *cis*-2-pentene

22.20 Write condensed structures of the following compounds.
(a) 3-methylbutanal
(b) 4-methyl-2-octanone
(c) 2-chloropropanoic acid
(d) isopropyl ethanoate
(e) 2-methylbutanamide

22.21 Write condensed structures of the following compounds.
(a) 2,3-butanedione
(b) butanedicarboxylic acid
(c) 2-aminopropanal
(d) cyclohexyl 2-methylpropanoate
(e) sodium 2,3-dimethylbutanoate

22.22 "3-Butanol" is not a proper name, but a structure could still be written for it. What is this structure, and what IUPAC name should be used?

22.23 No number is needed to identify the location of the double bond in $CH_3CH=CH_2$, propene. Why?

Chemical Properties of Organic Compounds

22.24 What are the products of the complete combustion of any hydrocarbon, assuming an abundant supply of oxygen?

*22.25 Propene is known to react with concentrated sulfuric acid as follows.

$$CH_3CH=CH_2 + H_2SO_4 \longrightarrow CH_3\underset{\underset{OSO_3H}{|}}{C}HCH_3$$

The reaction occurs in two steps. Write the equation for the first.

*22.26 2-Methylpropene reacts with hydrogen chloride as follows.

$$CH_3\underset{\underset{CH_3}{|}}{C}=CH_2 + H-Cl \longrightarrow CH_3\underset{\underset{Cl}{|}}{\overset{\overset{CH_3}{|}}{C}}CH_3$$

The reaction occurs in two steps. Write the equation of each step.

22.27 The compound 2-butene exists as two isomers, but when both isomers are hydrogenated, the products are identical. Explain.

22.28 Briefly explain how the $C-O$ bond in isopropyl alcohol is weakened when a strong acid is present.

22.29 Which isomer of 1-butanol cannot be oxidized by dichromate ion? Write its structure and IUPAC name.

22.30 A monofunctional organic oxygen compound dissolves in aqueous base but not in aqueous acid. The compound is in which of the families of organic compounds that we studied? Explain.

22.31 A monofunctional organic nitrogen compound dissolves in aqueous hydrochloric acid but not in aqueous sodium hydroxide. What kind of organic compound is it?

22.32 Why are amides neutral while amines are basic?

*22.33 Hydrazine is a Brønsted base but urea does not exhibit basic properties. Offer an explanation.

$$NH_2NH_2 \qquad NH_2\overset{\overset{O}{||}}{C}NH_2$$
$$\text{hydrazine} \qquad \text{urea}$$

22.34 Write the equilibrium that is present when $CH_3CH_2CH_2NH_2$ is in an aqueous solution.

22.35 Predict which of the following species can neutralize the hydronium ion in dilute, aqueous HCl at room temperature.

(a) $CH_3\overset{\overset{O}{||}}{C}O^-$ (c) HO^- (e) $CH_3CH_2CH_2CH_3$

(b) CH_3NH_2 (d) $CH_3\overset{\overset{O}{||}}{C}NH_2$ (f) pyrrolidine ring with NH

22.36 Write the products that can be expected to form in the following situations. If no reaction occurs, write "N.R."
(a) $CH_3CH_2CH_2NH_2 + HBr(aq) \longrightarrow$
(b) $CH_3CH_2CH_2CH_3 + HI(aq) \longrightarrow$
(c) $CH_3CH_2CH_2NH_3^+ + H_3O^+ \longrightarrow$
(d) $CH_3CH_2CH_2NH_3^+ + OH^- \longrightarrow$

22.37 Write the equation for the equilibrium that is present in a solution of propanoic acid and methanol with a trace of strong acid.

Polymers

22.38 What is a *macromolecule*? Name two naturally occurring macromolecular substances.

22.39 What is a *polymer*? Are all macromolecules polymers?

22.40 What is a *monomer*? Draw structures for the monomers used to make (a) polypropylene, (b) poly(tetrafluoroethylene), and (c) poly(vinyl chloride).

22.41 What do we mean by the term *polymer backbone*?

22.42 What is the repeating unit in polypropylene? Write the formula for the polypropylene polymer. Give three uses for polypropylene.

22.43 How do propylene and the repeating unit in polypropylene differ?

22.44 What is the difference between an *addition polymer* and a *condensation polymer*?

22.45 Write the structure of polystyrene showing three of the repeating units. What are three uses for polystyrene plastic?

22.46 What is a *copolymer*?

22.47 Write the structural formula for (a) nylon 6,6 and (b) poly(ethylene terephthalate).

22.48 The structural formula for Kevlar is

Identify the amide bond in the polymer.

22.49 Polycarbonate polymers are polyesters. An example is

Identify the structural feature that makes it a polyester. Identify the structural feature that makes it a poly*carbonate*.

22.50 What is meant by the term *branching* as applied to polymers? How does branching affect the properties of low density polyethylene?

22.51 What is *cross-linking*? How does it affect the properties of a polymer?

22.52 What is *vulcanized rubber*?

22.53 How does polymer crystallinity affect the physical properties of the polymer?

22.54 Why doesn't low density polyethylene form strong crystalline polymer fibers?

22.55 Why does nylon form strong fibers?

22.56 Show how hydrogen bonding can bind Kevlar polymer chains together. (See Question 22.48.)

22.57 What are some applications of crystalline polymers such as HDPE, UHMWPE, and Kevlar?

Biochemistry

22.58 What is *biochemistry*?

22.59 What are the three fundamental needs for sustaining life and what are the general names for the substances that supply those needs?

Carbohydrates

22.60 How are *carbohydrates* defined?

22.61 What monosaccharide forms when the following polysaccharides are completely hydrolyzed? (a) starch, (b) glycogen, (c) cellulose

22.62 Glucose exists in three forms, only one of which is a polyhydroxyaldehyde. How then can an aqueous solution of any form of glucose undergo the reactions of an aldehyde?

22.63 Name the compounds that form when sucrose is digested.

22.64 The digestion of lactose gives what compounds? Name them.

22.65 The complete hydrolysis of the following compounds gives what product(s)? (Give the names only.)
(a) amylose   (b) amylopectin

22.66 Describe the relationships among amylose, amylopectin, and starch.

22.67 Why are humans unable to use cellulose as a source of glucose?

22.68 What function is served by glycogen in the body?

Lipids

22.69 How are *lipids* defined?

22.70 Why are lipids more soluble than carbohydrates in nonpolar solvents?

22.71 Cholesterol is not an ester, yet it is defined as a lipid. Why?

22.72 A product such as corn oil is advertised as "polyunsaturated," but all nutritionally important lipids have unsaturated $C{=}O$ groups. What does *polyunsaturated* refer to?

*22.73 Is it likely that the following compound could be obtained by the hydrolysis of a naturally occurring lipid? Explain.

$$CH_3(CH_2)_2CH{=}CHCH_2CH{=}CHCH_2CH{=}CH(CH_2)_7CO_2H$$

Amino Acids, Polypeptides, and Proteins

22.74 Describe the specific ways in which the monomers for all polypeptides are (a) alike and (b) different.

22.75 What is the *peptide bond*? How is it similar to the amide bond in nylon?

22.76 Describe the structural way in which two *isomeric* polypeptides would be different.

22.77 Describe the structural ways in which two different polypeptides can differ.

22.78 Why is a distinction made between the terms *polypeptide* and *protein*?

22.79 In general terms, what forces are at work that determine the final *shape* of a polypeptide strand?

22.80 What kind of substance makes up most enzymes?

22.81 The most lethal chemical poisons act on what kinds of substances? Give examples.

Nucleic Acids and Heredity

22.82 In general terms only, how does the body solve the problem of getting a particular amino acid sequence rather than a mixture of randomly organized sequences into a polypeptide?

22.83 In what specific structural way does DNA carry genetic messages?

22.84 What kind of force occurs between the two DNA strands in a double helix?

22.85 How are the two DNA strands in a double helix structurally related?

22.86 In what ways do DNA and RNA differ structurally?

22.87 Which base pairs with (a) A in DNA, (b) A in RNA, and (c) C in DNA or RNA?

22.88 A specific gene in the DNA of a higher organism is said to be *segmented* or *interrupted*. Explain.

22.89 On what kind of RNA are codons found?

22.90 On what kind of RNA are anticodons found?

22.91 What function does each of the following have in polypeptide synthesis?
(a) a ribosome   (b) mRNA   (c) tRNA

22.92 What kind of RNA forms directly when a cell uses DNA at the start of the synthesis of a particular enzyme? What kind of RNA is made from it?

22.93 The process of *transcription* begins with which nucleic acid and ends with which one?

22.94 The process of *translation* begins with which nucleic acid? What is the end result of translation?

22.95 What is a virus, and (in general terms only) how does it infect a tissue?

22.96 Use the internet to find what genetic engineering is able (in general terms) to accomplish.

REVIEW PROBLEMS

Structural Formulas

22.97 Write full (expanded) structures for each of the following molecular formulas. Remember how many bonds the various kinds of atoms must have. In some you will have to use double or triple bonds. (Hint: A trial-and-error approach will have to be used.)
(a) CH_5N (c) $CHCl_3$ (e) C_2H_2
(b) CH_2Br_2 (d) NH_3O (f) N_2H_4

22.98 Write full (expanded) structures for each of the following molecular formulas. Follow the guidelines of Problem 22.97.
(a) C_2H_6
(c) CH_2O
(e) C_3H_3N
(b) CH_2O_2
(d) HCN
(f) CH_4O

Families of Organic Compounds

22.99 Name the family to which each compound belongs.
(a) $CH_3CH=CH_2$
(b) CH_3CH_2OH
(c)

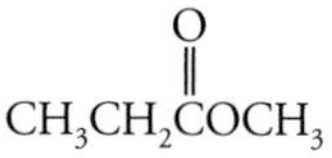

$$CH_3CH_2\overset{\overset{\displaystyle O}{\|}}{C}OCH_3$$

(d)

$$CH_3CH_2CH_2\overset{\overset{\displaystyle O}{\|}}{C}OH$$

(e) $CH_3CH_2CH_2NH_2$
(f) $HOCH_2CH_2CH_3$

22.100 To what organic family does each compound belong?
(a) $CH_3C\equiv CH$
(b)

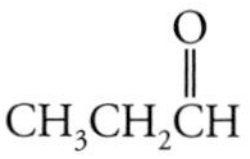

$$CH_3CH_2\overset{\overset{\displaystyle O}{\|}}{C}H$$

(c)

$$CH_3\overset{\overset{\displaystyle O}{\|}}{C}CH_2CH_2CH_3$$

(d) $CH_3-O-CH_2CH_3$
(e) $CH_3CH_2NH_2$

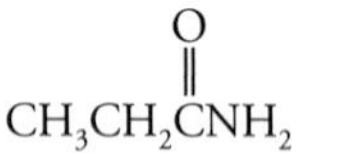

$$CH_3CH_2\overset{\overset{\displaystyle O}{\|}}{C}NH_2$$

22.101 Identify by letter the compounds in Problem 22.99 that are saturated compounds.

22.102 Which parts of Problem 22.100 give the structures of saturated compounds?

22.103 Classify the following compounds as amines or amides. If another functional group occurs, name it, too.
(a) $CH_3CH_2NH_2$
(c)

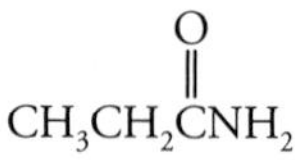

$$CH_3CH_2\overset{\overset{\displaystyle O}{\|}}{C}NH_2$$

(b) $CH_3CH_2NHCH_3$
(d)

$$CH_3\overset{\overset{\displaystyle O}{\|}}{C}CH_2NH_2$$

22.104 Name the functional groups present in each of the following structures.
(a)

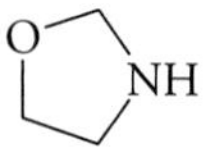

$$\overset{O}{\diagdown}\text{NH}$$

(c)

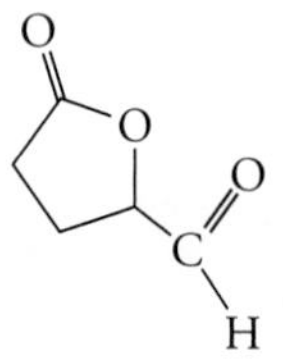

(b)

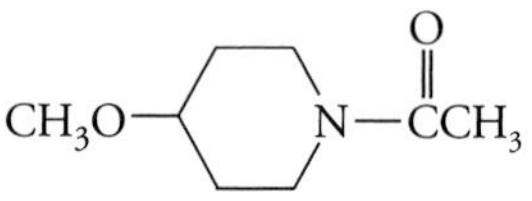

$$CH_3O-\text{(ring)}-N-\overset{\overset{\displaystyle O}{\|}}{C}CH_3$$

(d)

$$CH_3O\overset{\overset{\displaystyle O}{\|}}{C}CH_2CH_2\overset{\overset{\displaystyle O}{\|}}{C}OH$$

Isomers

22.105 Decide whether the members of each pair are identical, are isomers, or are unrelated.

(a) CH_3-CH_3 and

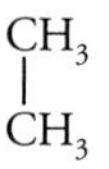

$$CH_3\underset{\underset{\displaystyle CH_3}{|}}{CH_3}$$

(b) CH_3 and CH_2 ...
CH_2 ...
CH_3 ...
CH_3 CH_3

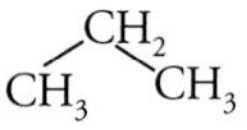

(c) CH_3CH_2OH and $CH_3CH_2CH_2OH$

(d) $CH_3CH=CH_2$ and

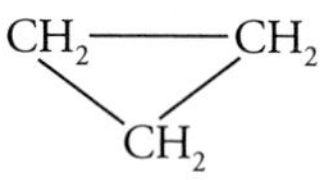

$$CH_2-CH_2$$
$$\diagdown CH_2 \diagup$$

(e)

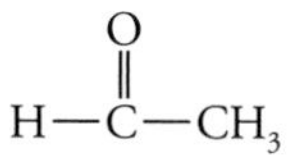

$$H-\overset{\overset{\displaystyle O}{\|}}{C}-CH_3 \quad \text{and} \quad CH_3-\overset{\overset{\displaystyle O}{\|}}{C}-H$$

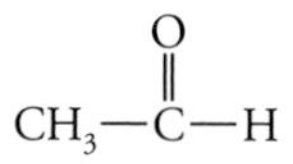

(f)

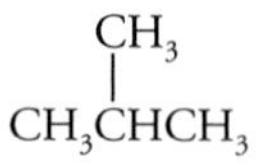

$$CH_3\underset{\underset{\displaystyle CH_3}{|}}{CH}CH_3 \quad \text{and} \quad CH_3\underset{\underset{\displaystyle CH_3}{|}}{CH}CH_3$$

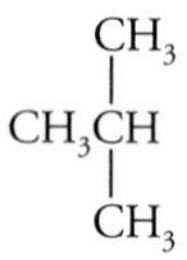

(g) $CH_3CH_2CH_2NH_2$ and $CH_3CH_2-NH-CH_3$

22.106 Examine each pair and decide if the two are identical, are isomers, or are unrelated.

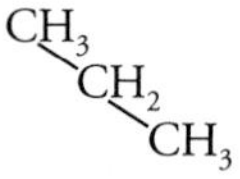

(a)

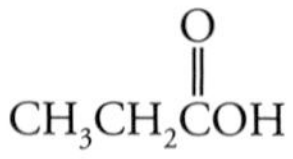

$$CH_3CH_2\overset{\overset{\displaystyle O}{\|}}{C}OH \quad \text{and} \quad HO\overset{\overset{\displaystyle O}{\|}}{C}CH_2CH_3$$

(b)

$$HCOCH_2CH_3 \quad \text{and} \quad CH_3CH_2\overset{\overset{\displaystyle O}{\|}}{C}OH$$

(c)

$$HCOCH_2CH_2OH \quad \text{and} \quad HOCH_2CH_2\overset{\overset{\displaystyle O}{\|}}{C}OH$$

(d)

$$CH_3\overset{\overset{\displaystyle O}{\|}}{C}CH_2CH_3 \quad \text{and} \quad CH_3CH_2\overset{\overset{\displaystyle O}{\|}}{C}CH_3$$

(e) $CH_3-CH-CH_3$
CH_2-CH_2 CH_3 CH_3
CH_2-C-CH
CH_3 CH_3

and

$$CH_3-\underset{}{CH}-CH_2-CH_2-CH_2-C-CH-CH_3$$
with CH_3 and CH_3 CH_3 substituents and CH_3 below.

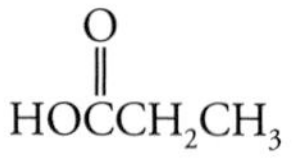

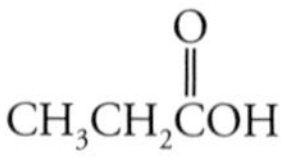

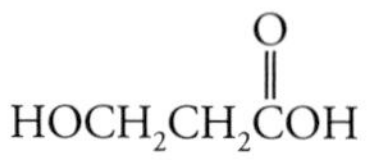

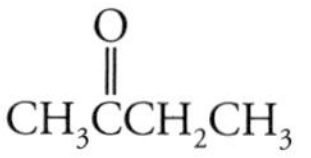

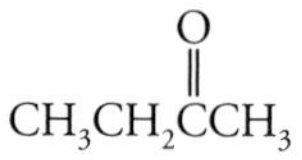

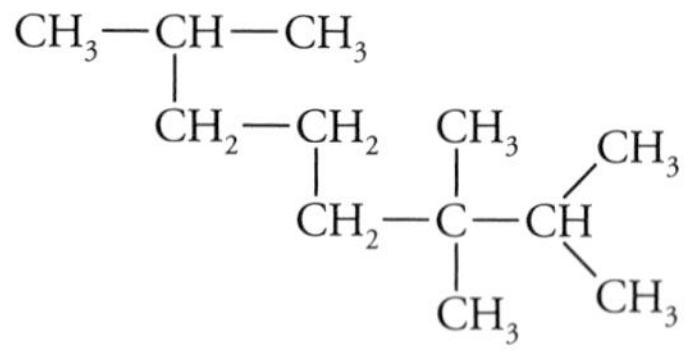

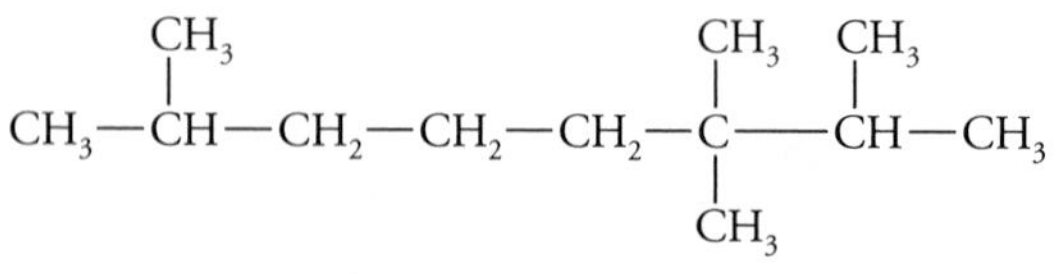

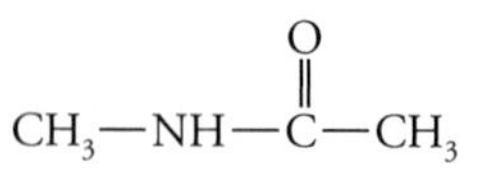

(f)

$$CH_3-NH-\overset{\overset{\displaystyle O}{\|}}{C}-CH_3 \quad \text{and} \quad CH_3CH_2\overset{\overset{\displaystyle O}{\|}}{C}NH_2$$

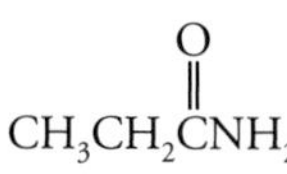

(g) $H-O-O-H$ and $H-O-H$

Names of Hydrocarbons

22.107 Write the IUPAC names of the following hydrocarbons.
(a) $CH_3CH_2CH_2CH_2CH_3$

(b) CH₃CH₂CH₂CHCH₃
              |
              CH₃

(c)
         CH₃
         |
CH₃CHCH₂CHCH₂CH₃
             |
             CH₃

22.108 Write the IUPAC names of the following compounds.

(a)
          CH₃
          |
CH₃CH₂CHCH₂CHCH₃
               |
               CH₃

(b) CH₃CH₂CH=CHCH₂CH₃

(c)
      CH₃
      |
CH₃CHCH=CHCH₃

Geometric Isomerism

22.109 Write the structures of the cis and trans isomers, *if any*, for the following.

(a) CH₂=CHBr

(b) CH₃CH=CHCH₂CH₃

(c)
     Br
     |
CH₃C=CHCl

22.110 Write the structures of the cis and trans isomers, if any, for the following compounds.

(a)
      CH₃
      |
CH₃C=CHCH₃

(b)
         CH₃
         |
CH₃CH=CCH₂CH₃

(c)
        Cl Cl
        | |
CH₃CH₂C=CCH₂CH₃

Chemical Reactions of Alkenes

22.111 Write the structures of the products that form when ethylene reacts with each of the following substances by an addition reaction. (Assume that needed catalysts or other conditions are provided.)

(a) H₂   (c) Br₂   (e) HBr(*g*)
(b) Cl₂   (d) HCl(*g*)   (f) H₂O (in acid)

22.112 The isopropyl cation is more stable than the propyl cation, so the former forms almost exclusively when propene undergoes addition reactions with proton-donating species. On the basis of this fact, predict the final products of the reaction of propene with each of the following reagents.

(a) hydrogen chloride   (b) hydrogen iodide
(c) water in the presence of an acid catalyst

22.113 Repeat Problem 22.111 using 2-butene.

22.114 Repeat Problem 22.112 using cyclohexene.

22.115 In general terms, why doesn't benzene undergo the same kinds of addition reactions as cyclohexene?

22.116 If benzene were to *add* one mole of Br₂, what would form? What forms, instead, when Br₂, benzene, and an FeBr₃ catalyst are heated together? (Write the structures.)

Structures and Properties of Other Functional Groups

22.117 Write condensed structures and the IUPAC names for all of the saturated alcohols with three or fewer carbon atoms per molecule.

22.118 Write the condensed structures and the IUPAC names for all of the possible alcohols with the general formula C₄H₁₀O.

22.119 Write the condensed structures of all of the possible ethers with the general formula C₄H₁₀O. Following the pattern for the common names of ethers given in the chapter, what are the likely common names of these ethers?

22.120 Write the structures of the isomeric alcohols of the formula C₄H₁₀O that could be oxidized to aldehydes. Write the structure of the isomer that could be oxidized to a ketone.

***22.121** Write the structures of the products of the acid-catalyzed dehydrations of the following compounds

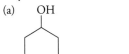

22.122 Write the structures of the substitution products that form when the alcohols of Problem 22.121 are heated with concentrated hydriodic acid.

22.123 Write the structures of the aldehydes or ketones that can be prepared by the oxidation of the compounds given in Problem 22.121.

***22.124** Write the structure of the product of the acid-catalyzed dehydration of 2-propanol. Write the mechanism of the reaction.

***22.125** When ethanol is heated in the presence of an acid catalyst, ethene and water form; an elimination reaction occurs. When 2-butanol is heated under similar conditions, *two* alkenes form (although not in equal quantities). Write the structures and IUPAC names of the two alkenes.

***22.126** If the formation of the two alkenes in Problem 22.125 were determined purely by statistics, then the mole ratio of the two alkenes should be in the ratio of what whole numbers? Why?

22.127 Which of the following two compounds could be easily oxidized? Write the structure of the product of the oxidation.

          O   O
          ‖   ‖
CH₃CH₂CH   CH₃CH₂CCHCH₃
                              |
                              CH₃

        A   **B**

22.128 Which of the following compounds has the chemical property given below? Write the structure of the product of the reaction.

$$CH_3CH_2CH_2OH \qquad CH_3CH_2\overset{O}{\overset{\|}{C}}OH \qquad CH_3CH_2\overset{O}{\overset{\|}{C}}H$$

A   **B**   **C**

(a) is easily oxidized
(b) neutralizes NaOH
(c) forms an ester with methyl alcohol
(d) can be oxidized to an aldehyde
(e) can be dehydrated to an alkene

22.129 Write the structures of the products that form in each of the following situations. If no reaction occurs, write "N.R."
(a) $CH_3CH_2CO_2^- + HCl(aq) \longrightarrow$

(b) $CH_3CH_2CO_2CH_3 + H_2O \xrightarrow{heat}$

(c) $CH_3CH_2CH_2CO_2H + NaOH(aq) \longrightarrow$

22.130 Write the structures of the products that form in each of the following situations. If no reaction occurs, write "N.R."

(a) $CH_3CH_2CO_2H + NH_3 \xrightarrow{heat}$

(b) $CH_3CH_2CH_2CONH_2 + H_2O \xrightarrow{heat}$

(c) $CH_3CH_2CO_2CH_3 + NaOH(aq) \xrightarrow{heat}$

*****22.131** What organic products with smaller molecules form when the following compound is heated with water?

$$CH_3CH_2\overset{O}{\overset{\|}{N}}CCH_3$$
$$\underset{CH_3CH_2}{|}$$

22.132 Which of the following species undergo the reaction specified? Write the structures of the products that form.

$$CH_3CH_2\overset{O}{\overset{\|}{C}}NH_2 \qquad CH_3CH_2CH_2NH_2 \qquad CH_3CH_2NH_3^+$$

(a) neutralizes dilute hydrochloric acid
(b) hydrolyzes (reacts with water)
(c) neutralizes dilute sodium hydroxide

Polymers

22.133 The structure of vinyl acetate is shown below. This compound forms an addition polymer in the same way as ethylene and propylene. Draw a segment of the poly(vinyl acetate) polymer that contains three of the repeating units.

$$\underset{H}{\overset{H}{\diagdown}}C=C\underset{O-\overset{O}{\overset{\|}{C}}-CH_3}{\overset{H}{\diagup}} \qquad \text{vinyl acetate}$$

22.134 If the following two compounds polymerized in the same way that Dacron forms, what would be the repeating unit of their polymer?

$$HO\overset{O}{\overset{\|}{C}}CH_2CH_2\overset{O}{\overset{\|}{C}}OH \qquad HOCH_2CH_2OH$$

22.135 Kodel, a polyester made from the following monomers, is used to make fibers for weaving crease-resistant fabrics.

$$HOCH_2 \text{—}⟨ \text{—} CH_2OH \qquad HO\overset{O}{\overset{\|}{C}}\text{—}◯\text{—}\overset{O}{\overset{\|}{C}}OH$$

monomers for Kodel

What is the structure of the repeating unit in Kodel?

22.136 If the following two compounds polymerized in the same way that nylon forms, what would be the repeating unit in the polymer?

$$HO\overset{O}{\overset{\|}{C}}\text{—}◯\text{—}\overset{O}{\overset{\|}{C}}OH \qquad NH_2CH_2CH_2CH_2CH_2NH_2$$

Lipids

22.137 Write the structure of a triacylglycerol that could be made from palmitic acid, oleic acid, and linoleic acid.

22.138 Write the structures of the products of the complete hydrolysis of the following triacylglycerol.

$$CH_2O\overset{O}{\overset{\|}{C}}(CH_2)_7CH=CHCH_2CH=CH(CH_2)_4CH_3$$
$$\underset{|}{\overset{O}{\overset{\|}{CHOC}}(CH_2)_{12}CH_3}$$
$$\underset{CH_2O\overset{O}{\overset{\|}{C}}(CH_2)_7CH=CH(CH_2)_7CH_3}{|}$$

22.139 Write the structure of the triacylglycerol that would result from the complete hydrogenation of the lipid whose structure is given in Problem 22.138.

22.140 If the compound in Problem 22.138 is saponified, what are the products? Give their names and structures.

22.141 What parts of glycerophospholipid molecules provide hydrophobic sites? Hydrophilic sites?

22.142 In general terms, describe the structure of the membrane of an animal cell. What kinds of molecules are present? How are they arranged? What forces keep the membrane intact? What functions are served by the protein components?

Amino Acids and Polypeptides

22.143 Write the structure of the dipeptide that could be hydrolyzed to give two molecules of glycine.

22.144 What is the structure of the tripeptide that could be hydrolyzed to give three molecules of alanine?

22.145 What are the structures of the two dipeptides that could be hydrolyzed to give glycine and phenylalanine?

22.146 Write the structures of the dipolar ionic forms of the amino acids that are produced by the complete digestion of the following compound.

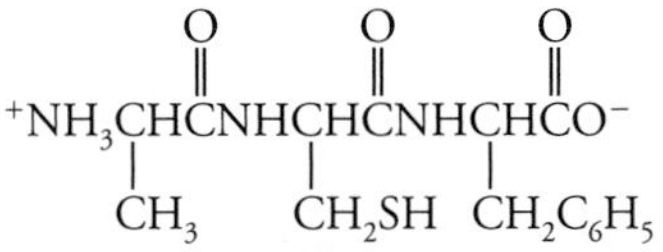

$$^+NH_3CHCNHCHCNHCHCO^-$$

with substituents CH_3, CH_2SH, $CH_2C_6H_5$ and three $C=O$ groups

ADDITIONAL EXERCISES

*22.147 The H_2SO_4-catalyzed addition of water to 2-methylpropene could give two isomeric alcohols.
(a) Write their condensed structures.
(b) Actually, only one forms. It is not possible to oxidize this alcohol to an aldehyde or to a ketone having four carbons. Which alcohol, therefore, is the product?
(c) Write the structures of the two possible carbocations that could form when sulfuric acid donates a proton to 2-methylpropene.
(d) One of the two carbocations of part (c) is more stable than the other. Which one is it, and how can you tell?

22.148 An unknown alcohol was either **A** or **B** below. When the unknown was oxidized with an *excess* of strong oxidizing agent, sodium dichromate in acid, the *organic* product isolated was able to neutralize sodium hydroxide.

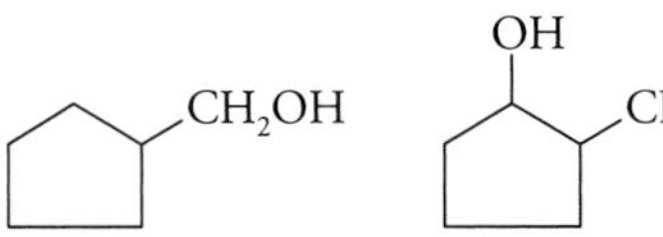

A (cyclopentyl-CH_2OH) **B** (cyclopentane with OH and CH_3)

(a) Which was the alcohol? Give the reasons for your choice.
(b) Write the balanced net ionic equation for the oxidation.

*22.149 Suggest a reason why trimethylamine, $(CH_3)_3N$, has a *lower* boiling point (BP 3 °C) than dimethylamine, $(CH_3)_2NH$ (BP 8 °C), despite having a larger number of atoms.

*22.150 Write the structures of the organic products that form in each situation. If no reaction occurs, write "N.R."

(a)
$$HOC\text{—}C_6H_4\text{—}COH + NaOH(aq) \xrightarrow{\text{excess}}$$

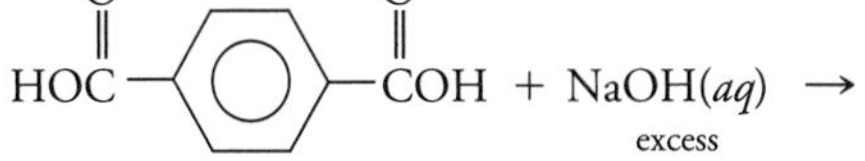

(b)
$$CH_3CCH_2CH_2CH_3 + H_2 \xrightarrow{\text{heat, pressure, catalyst}}$$

(c) $CH_3\overset{+}{N}H_2CH_2CH_2CH_3 + OH^-(aq) \longrightarrow$

(d)
$$CH_3CH_2OCH_2CH_2COCH_3 + H_2O \xrightarrow{\text{heat}}$$

(e)
$$\text{(cyclopentene)} + H_2O \xrightarrow[\text{catalyst}]{H_2SO_4}$$

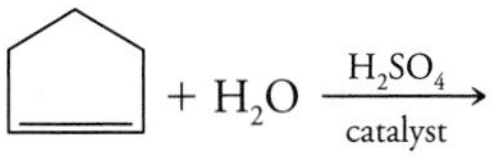

(f)
$$C_6H_5\text{—}CH=CH\text{—}C_6H_5 + HBr \longrightarrow$$

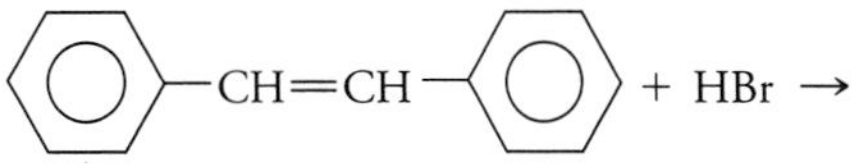

*22.151 How many tripeptides can be made from three different amino acids? If the three are glycine (Gly), alanine (Ala), and phenylalanine (Phe), what are the structures of the possible tripeptides? (Hint: Gly-Ala-Phe is one structure.)

*22.152 A 0.5574 mg sample of an organic acid, when burned in pure oxygen, gave 1.181 mg of CO_2 and 0.3653 mg H_2O. Calculate the empirical formula of the acid.

*22.153 When 0.2081 g of an organic acid was dissolved in 50.00 mL of 0.1016 M NaOH, it took 23.78 mL of 0.1182 M HCl to neutralize the NaOH that was not used up by the sample of the organic acid. Calculate the formula mass from the data given. Is the answer necessarily the *molecular mass* of the organic acid? Explain.

EXERCISES IN CRITICAL THINKING

22.154 The compound CH_2Cl_2 only exists as one isomer. Why does this support the statement that the atoms in the compound are arranged in a tetrahedral rather than a square planar structure?

22.155 The α-carbon atom in an amino acid is a chiral center (except for glycine). Of the two possible enantiomers of these optically active substances, only one is produced naturally. What does this suggest about the mechanism whereby amino acids are synthesized in living creatures?

22.156 Use resonance structures to explain why urea, $(NH_2)_2C=O$, is not basic like typical amines.

22.157 Below is the ring structure of a sugar molecule. How many chiral centers does this sugar molecule have? How many isomers are possible?

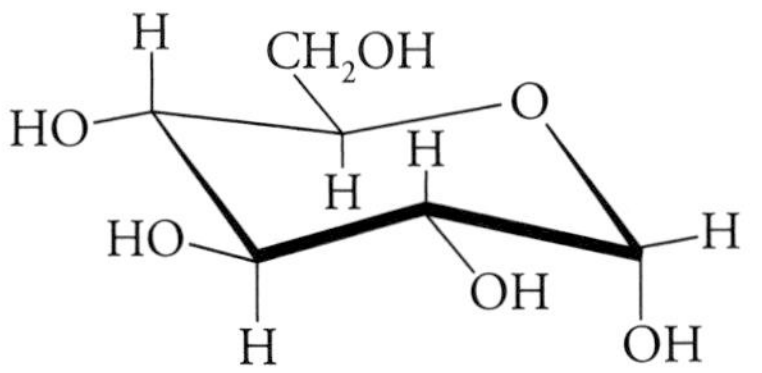

(sugar ring structure)

22.158 What would be the repeating unit of the polymer formed by condensation polymerization of the two monomers shown below?

$$CH_3O\text{—}C\text{—}CH_2\text{—}CH_2\text{—}CH_2\text{—}C\text{—}OCH_3$$
$$H_2N\text{—}CH_2\text{—}CH_2\text{—}NH_2$$

Again you have an opportunity to test your understanding of concepts, your knowledge of scientific terms, and your skills at solving chemistry problems. Read through the following questions carefully, and answer each as fully as possible. Review topics when necessary.

1. What is meant by the term *spontaneous change*?
2. Which of these are state functions: E, H, q, S, G, w, T?
3. How is entropy related to statistical probability?
4. What would be the algebraic signs of ΔS for the following reactions?
   (a) $Br_2(l) + Cl_2(g) \longrightarrow 2BrCl(g)$
   (b) $CaO(s) + CO_2(g) \longrightarrow CaCO_3(s)$
5. Which of the following states has the greatest entropy?
   (a) $2H_2O(l)$ (c) $2H_2(l) + O_2(g)$ (e) $4H(g) + 2O(g)$
   (b) $2H_2O(s)$ (d) $2H_2(g) + O_2(g)$
6. Calculate $\Delta S°$ (in J K^{-1}) for the following reactions.
   (a) $H_2O(l) + SO_3(g) \longrightarrow H_2SO_4(l)$
   (b) $2KCl(s) + H_2SO_4(l) \longrightarrow K_2SO_4(s) + 2HCl(g)$
   (c) $C_2H_4(g) + H_2O(g) \longrightarrow C_2H_5OH(l)$
7. Calculate $\Delta G°$ (in kJ) for the following reactions.
   (a) $CaSO_4 \cdot \frac{1}{2}H_2O(s) + \frac{3}{2}H_2O(l) \longrightarrow$
   $$CaSO_4 \cdot 2H_2O(s)$$
   (b) $CH_4(g) + Cl_2(g) \longrightarrow CH_3Cl(g) + HCl(g)$
   (c) $CaSO_4(s) + CO_2(s) \longrightarrow CaCO_3(s) + SO_3(g)$
8. Which of the reactions in the preceding question would appear to be spontaneous?
9. Calculate $\Delta S°$, $\Delta H°$, and $\Delta G°_T$ (at 400 °C) using energy units of joules or kilojoules for these reactions.
   (a) $CaSO_4 \cdot 2H_2O(s) \longrightarrow CaSO_4 \cdot \frac{1}{2}H_2O(s) + \frac{3}{2}H_2O(g)$
   (b) $NaOH(s) + NH_4Cl(s) \longrightarrow$
   $$NaCl(s) + NH_3(g) + H_2O(g)$$
   (c) $SO_3(g) \longrightarrow SO_2(g) + \frac{1}{2}O_2(g)$
10. For the reaction $3NO(g) \rightleftharpoons NO_2(g) + N_2O(g)$, calculate K_P at 25 °C using values of $\Delta G°_f$ from Table 18.2. Calculate the value of K_c at 25 °C for the reaction.
11. Consider the reaction

    $$CH_4(g) + Cl_2(g) \rightleftharpoons CH_3Cl(g) + HCl(g)$$

    (a) Calculate $\Delta G°_{473}$ for the reaction at 200 °C.
    (b) What is the value of K_P for the reaction at 200 °C?
    (c) What is the value of K_c for the reaction at 200 °C?
12. Glycine, one of the important amino acids, has the structure

    $$\begin{array}{ccc} & H & O \\ & | & \| \\ H-N-&C-&C-O-H \\ & | & | \\ & H & H \end{array}$$

    Calculate the atomization energy of the glycine molecule in units of kJ mol^{-1} from the data in Table 18.4.
13. Use bond energies in Table 18.4 to calculate the approximate energy that would be absorbed or given off in the formation of 25.0 g of C_2H_6 by the following reaction in the gas phase.

    $$\begin{array}{ccc} & & H \quad H \\ & & | \quad | \\ H-C\equiv C-H + 2H_2 \longrightarrow & H-C-C-H \\ & & | \quad | \\ & & H \quad H \end{array}$$

14. Sketch a diagram of an electrolysis cell in which a concentrated solution of NaCl is undergoing electrolysis.
    (a) Label the cathode and anode, including their charges.
    (b) Write half-reactions for the changes taking place at the electrodes.
    (c) Write a balanced equation for the net cell reaction.
15. Suppose that the electrolysis cell described in the previous question contains 250 mL of brine.
    (a) What will be the pH of the solution if the electrolysis is carried out for 20.0 minutes using a current of 1.00 A?
    (b) How many milliliters of H_2, measured at STP, would be evolved if the cell were operated at 5.00 A for 10.0 minutes?
16. What current would be required to deposit 0.100 g of nickel in 20.0 minutes from a solution of $NiSO_4$?
17. A large electrolysis cell can produce as much as 900 lb of aluminum in 1 day from Al_2O_3. What current is required to accomplish this? (Assume three significant figures.)
18. Sketch a diagram of a galvanic cell consisting of a copper electrode dipping into 1.00 M $CuSO_4$ solution and an iron electrode dipping into 1.00 M $FeSO_4$ solution.
    (a) Identify the cathode and the anode. Indicate the charge carried by each.
    (b) Write the equation for the net cell reaction.
    (c) Describe the cell by writing its standard cell notation.
    (d) What is the potential of the cell?
19. What is the purpose of a salt bridge in a galvanic cell?
20. Suppose the cell described in Question 18 contains 100 mL of each solution and is operated for a period of 50.0 hr at a constant current of 0.10 A. At the end of that time, what will be the concentrations of Cu^{2+} and Fe^{2+} in their respective solutions? What will the cell potential be at that point?
21. Use data from Table 19.1 to calculate the value of K_c at 25 °C for the reaction

    $$O_2(g) + 4Br^-(aq) + 4H^+(aq) \longrightarrow 2Br_2(aq) + 2H_2O$$

22. A galvanic cell was assembled as follows. In one compartment, a copper electrode was immersed in a 1.00 M solution of $CuSO_4$. In the other compartment, a manganese electrode was immersed in a 1.00 M solution of $MnSO_4$. The potential of the cell was measured to be 1.52 V, with the Mn electrode as the negative electrode. What is the value of $E°$ for the following half-reaction?

    $$Mn^{2+}(aq) + 2e^- \rightleftharpoons Mn(s)$$

23. Calculate $E°_{cell}$ for the reaction
    $$3Cu(s) + 2NO_3^-(aq) + 8H^+(aq) \longrightarrow$$
    $$2NO(g) + 4H_2O + 3Cu^{2+}(aq)$$

24. What is the value of K_c for the reaction described in the preceding question?

25. Consider a galvanic cell formed by using the half-reactions

$$NiO_2(s) + 2H_2O + 2e^- \rightleftharpoons Ni(OH)_2(s) + 2OH^-(aq)$$
$$E° = +0.49 \text{ V}$$

$$PbO_2(s) + H_2O + 2e^- \rightleftharpoons PbO(s) + 2OH^-(aq)$$
$$E° = +0.25 \text{ V}$$

(a) Write the equation for the spontaneous cell reaction.
(b) Calculate the value of $E°_{cell}$ for the system.
(c) Calculate $\Delta G°$ for the spontaneous cell reaction.

26. A galvanic cell was constructed in which one half-cell consists of a silver electrode coated with silver chloride dipping into a solution that contains chloride ion and the second half-cell consists of a nickel electrode dipping into a solution that contains Ni^{2+}. The half-cell reactions and their reduction potentials are

$$AgCl(s) + e^- \rightleftharpoons Ag(s) + Cl^-(aq) \quad E° = +0.222 \text{ V}$$
$$Ni^{2+}(aq) + 2e^- \rightleftharpoons Ni(s) \quad E° = -0.257 \text{ V}$$

(a) Write the equation for the spontaneous cell reaction.
(b) Calculate $E°_{cell}$ for the cell reaction.
(c) Write the Nernst equation for the cell.
(d) Calculate the cell potential if $[Cl^-] = 0.020 \ M$ and $[Ni^{2+}] = 0.10 \ M$.
(e) The galvanic cell was used to measure an unknown chloride ion concentration. The Ni^{2+} concentration was $0.200 \ M$ and the measured cell potential was 0.388 V. What was the chloride ion concentration?

27. Describe how a nickel–metal hydride cell works.

28. Describe how a lithium ion cell works. What does *intercalation* mean?

29. What factors involving the nucleus of helium might be responsible for the large abundance of helium in the universe?

30. What is the symbol for (a) an alpha particle, (b) a beta particle, (c) a positron?

31. What is the rest mass of a particle of gamma radiation?

32. Suppose that the total mass of the reactants in a chemical reaction was 100.00000 g. How many kilojoules of energy would have to evolve from this reaction if the total mass of the products could be no greater than 99.99900 g? If all this energy were used to heat water, how many liters of water could have its temperature raised from 10 °C to 100 °C?

33. Calculate the binding energy in joules per nucleon for the nucleus of the deuterium atom, ^2_1H. The mass of an atom of deuterium, including its electron, is 2.014102 u.

34. Which nuclear force acts over the longer distance, the electrostatic force or the nuclear strong force?

35. Why is an isotope of hydrogen a better candidate for nuclear fusion than an isotope of helium?

36. When an atom of uranium-238 absorbs a neutron, it can ultimately change to an atom of plutonium-239. Write a nuclear equation for the reaction. If the reaction occurs in two steps, what intermediate nucleus is formed?

37. If an atom of beryllium-7 decays by the capture of a K-electron, into which isotope does it change? Write the equation.

38. An atom of neodymium-144 decays by alpha emission. Write the nuclear equation.

39. Phosphorus-32 decays by beta emission. Write the nuclear equation.

40. The half-life of samarium-149, an alpha emitter, is 4×10^{14} years. The half-life of oxygen-15 is 124 seconds. Assuming that equimolar samples are compared, which is the more intensely radioactive?

41. The half-life of cesium-137 is 30 years. Of an initial 100 g sample, how much cesium-137 will remain after 300 years?

42. What are some "rules of thumb" that can be used to judge if a particular radionuclide might have a long enough half-life to warrant the effort to make it?

43. A particular compound nucleus can form from a variety of combinations of targets and bombarding particles, as in the example of aluminum on page 835. What determines how a compound nucleus breaks up?

44. Strontium-90, a beta emitter, has a half-life of 28.1 yr. If 36.2 mg of ^{90}Sr were incorporated in the bones of a growing child, how many beta particles would the child absorb from this source in 1.00 day?

45. Which kind of radiation poses a greater health risk, beta or alpha radiation? Why?

46. What reaction, if any, will occur when solutions of $KBr(aq)$ and $Cl_2(aq)$ are mixed?

47. Write the equation for the reduction of bismuth(III) oxide by hydrogen.

48. Why can't fluorine be produced by the electrolysis of aqueous NaF? Why can't liquid HF be electrolyzed to give F_2 and H_2?

49. Why doesn't phosphorus form a stable P_2 molecule similar to N_2?

50. Describe the structure of the ozone molecule. What effect does ozone in smog have on the chlorophyll in green plants?

51. What is the molecular structure of diamond? How are the structures of graphite, buckyballs, and carbon nanotubes related?

52. What must be true about the heat of formation of a metal compound if the compound is thermally unstable?

53. Why is carbon used as a reducing agent in industrial metallurgy? Write the equations that take place in a blast furnace during the reduction of Fe_2O_3 to metallic Fe?

54. The reaction

$$Ni(H_2O)_6{}^{2+} + 6NH_3 \longrightarrow Ni(NH_3)_6{}^{2+} + 6H_2O$$

can be described as the displacement of one Lewis base by another. Explain. What is the Lewis acid in the reaction?

55. Sketch the structures of the oxalate ion and ethylenediamine. Identify the donor atoms these ligands use when they form chelate complexes.

56. Sketch the chiral isomers of $[Cr(H_2O)_2(en)_2]^{3+}$. Is there a nonchiral isomer of the complex? What is the name of $[Cr(H_2O)_2(en)_2]Cl_3$?

57. Which complex would absorb light of a shorter wavelength, $[V(H_2O)_6]^{3+}$ or $[V(CN)_6]^{3-}$? Justify your answer.

58. Name the following organic compound.

$$\begin{array}{c} CH_3 \\ | \\ CH_3CHCH_2CH_2CH\!=\!CCH_2CH_3 \\ | \\ CH_2CH_2CH_3 \end{array}$$

59. Draw the structure of 2,2-dimethyl-4-ethylheptane.

60. Which of the following compounds (a) neutralizes NaOH, (b) neutralizes HCl, (c) yields an alcohol and an organic acid when hydrolyzed, (d) is easily oxidized to an acid, (e) would

be classified as aromatic, (f) would be oxidized to give a ketone?

(1)

$$CH_3O-\overset{\overset{\displaystyle O}{\|}}{C}CH_2CH_3$$

(2)

$$CH_3CH_2\overset{\overset{\displaystyle O}{\|}}{C}H$$

(3) 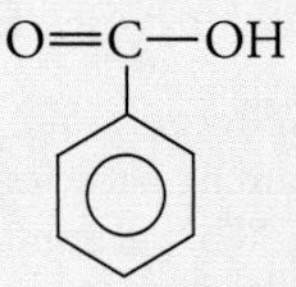 $O=\overset{|}{C}-OH$

(4)

$$\overset{\overset{\displaystyle OH}{|}}{CH_3CHCH_2CH_3}$$

(5) 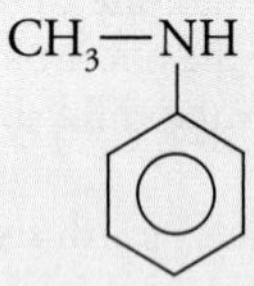 CH_3-NH

61. What would be the repeating structural unit if a condensation polymer were to form from the following monomers by the elimination of CH_3OH?

$$CH_3O-\overset{\overset{\displaystyle O}{\|}}{C}CH_2CH_2\overset{\overset{\displaystyle O}{\|}}{C}-OCH_3 \qquad H_2NCH_2CH_2CH_2NH_2$$

62. What effect does cross-linking have on the properties of a polymer?

63. What are the monomer units in (a) starch, (b) a polypeptide, and (c) DNA?

64. How do the water solubilities compare for monosaccharides and lipids?

65. How is the folding of a polypeptide chain affected by the hydrophobic and hydrophilic nature of its side chains?

66. Use data in Table 19.1 to calculate the value of K_{sp} for AgCl.

APPENDIX A

ELECTRON CONFIGURATIONS OF THE ELEMENTS

Atomic Number			Atomic Number			Atomic Number		
1	H	$1s^1$	40	Zr	$[Kr]\,5s^2\,4d^2$	79	Au	$[Xe]\,6s^1\,4f^{14}\,5d^{10}$
2	He	$1s^2$	41	Nb	$[Kr]\,5s^1\,4d^4$	80	Hg	$[Xe]\,6s^2\,4f^{14}\,5d^{10}$
3	Li	$[He]\,2s^1$	42	Mo	$[Kr]\,5s^1\,4d^5$	81	Tl	$[Xe]\,6s^2\,4f^{14}\,5d^{10}\,6p^1$
4	Be	$[He]\,2s^2$	43	Tc	$[Kr]\,5s^2\,4d^5$	82	Pb	$[Xe]\,6s^2\,4f^{14}\,5d^{10}\,6p^2$
5	B	$[He]\,2s^2\,2p^1$	44	Ru	$[Kr]\,5s^1\,4d^7$	83	Bi	$[Xe]\,6s^2\,4f^{14}\,5d^{10}\,6p^3$
6	C	$[He]\,2s^2\,2p^2$	45	Rh	$[Kr]\,5s^1\,4d^8$	84	Po	$[Xe]\,6s^2\,4f^{14}\,5d^{10}\,6p^4$
7	N	$[He]\,2s^2\,2p^3$	46	Pd	$[Kr]\,4d^{10}$	85	At	$[Xe]\,6s^2\,4f^{14}\,5d^{10}\,6p^5$
8	O	$[He]\,2s^2\,2p^4$	47	Ag	$[Kr]\,5s^1\,4d^{10}$	86	Rn	$[Xe]\,6s^2\,4f^{14}\,5d^{10}\,6p^6$
9	F	$[He]\,2s^2\,2p^5$	48	Cd	$[Kr]\,5s^2\,4d^{10}$	87	Fr	$[Rn]\,7s^1$
10	Ne	$[He]\,2s^2\,2p^6$	49	In	$[Kr]\,5s^2\,4d^{10}\,5p^1$	88	Ra	$[Rn]\,7s^2$
11	Na	$[Ne]\,3s^1$	50	Sn	$[Kr]\,5s^2\,4d^{10}\,5p^2$	89	Ac	$[Rn]\,7s^2\,6d^1$
12	Mg	$[Ne]\,3s^2$	51	Sb	$[Kr]\,5s^2\,4d^{10}\,5p^3$	90	Th	$[Rn]\,7s^2\,6d^2$
13	Al	$[Ne]\,3s^2\,3p^1$	52	Te	$[Kr]\,5s^2\,4d^{10}\,5p^4$	91	Pa	$[Rn]\,7s^2\,5f^2\,6d^1$
14	Si	$[Ne]\,3s^2\,3p^2$	53	I	$[Kr]\,5s^2\,4d^{10}\,5p^5$	92	U	$[Rn]\,7s^2\,5f^3\,6d^1$
15	P	$[Ne]\,3s^2\,3p^3$	54	Xe	$[Kr]\,5s^2\,4d^{10}\,5p^6$	93	Np	$[Rn]\,7s^2\,5f^4\,6d^1$
16	S	$[Ne]\,3s^2\,3p^4$	55	Cs	$[Xe]\,6s^1$	94	Pu	$[Rn]\,7s^2\,5f^6$
17	Cl	$[Ne]\,3s^2\,3p^5$	56	Ba	$[Xe]\,6s^2$	95	Am	$[Rn]\,7s^2\,5f^7$
18	Ar	$[Ne]\,3s^2\,3p^6$	57	La	$[Xe]\,6s^2\,5d^1$	96	Cm	$[Rn]\,7s^2\,5f^7\,6d^1$
19	K	$[Ar]\,4s^1$	58	Ce	$[Xe]\,6s^2\,4f^1\,5d^1$	97	Bk	$[Rn]\,7s^2\,5f^9$
20	Ca	$[Ar]\,4s^2$	59	Pr	$[Xe]\,6s^2\,4f^3$	98	Cf	$[Rn]\,7s^2\,5f^{10}$
21	Sc	$[Ar]\,4s^2\,3d^1$	60	Nd	$[Xe]\,6s^2\,4f^4$	99	Es	$[Rn]\,7s^2\,5f^{11}$
22	Ti	$[Ar]\,4s^2\,3d^2$	61	Pm	$[Xe]\,6s^2\,4f^5$	100	Fm	$[Rn]\,7s^2\,5f^{12}$
23	V	$[Ar]\,4s^2\,3d^3$	62	Sm	$[Xe]\,6s^2\,4f^6$	101	Md	$[Rn]\,7s^2\,5f^{13}$
24	Cr	$[Ar]\,4s^1\,3d^5$	63	Eu	$[Xe]\,6s^2\,4f^7$	102	No	$[Rn]\,7s^2\,5f^{14}$
25	Mn	$[Ar]\,4s^2\,3d^5$	64	Gd	$[Xe]\,6s^2\,4f^7\,5d^1$	103	Lr	$[Rn]\,7s^2\,5f^{14}\,6d^1$
26	Fe	$[Ar]\,4s^2\,3d^6$	65	Tb	$[Xe]\,6s^2\,4f^9$	104	Rf	$[Rn]\,7s^2\,5f^{14}\,6d^2$
27	Co	$[Ar]\,4s^2\,3d^7$	66	Dy	$[Xe]\,6s^2\,4f^{10}$	105	Db	$[Rn]\,7s^2\,5f^{14}\,6d^3$
28	Ni	$[Ar]\,4s^2\,3d^8$	67	Ho	$[Xe]\,6s^2\,4f^{11}$	106	Sg	$[Rn]\,7s^2\,5f^{14}\,6d^4$
29	Cu	$[Ar]\,4s^1\,3d^{10}$	68	Er	$[Xe]\,6s^2\,4f^{12}$	107	Bh	$[Rn]\,7s^2\,5f^{14}\,6d^5$
30	Zn	$[Ar]\,4s^2\,3d^{10}$	69	Tm	$[Xe]\,6s^2\,4f^{13}$	108	Hs	$[Rn]\,7s^2\,5f^{14}\,6d^6$
31	Ga	$[Ar]\,4s^2\,3d^{10}\,4p^1$	70	Yb	$[Xe]\,6s^2\,4f^{14}$	109	Mt	$[Rn]\,7s^2\,5f^{14}\,6d^7$
32	Ge	$[Ar]\,4s^2\,3d^{10}\,4p^2$	71	Lu	$[Xe]\,6s^2\,4f^{14}\,5d^1$	110	Ds	$[Rn]\,7s^2\,5f^{14}\,6d^8$
33	As	$[Ar]\,4s^2\,3d^{10}\,4p^3$	72	Hf	$[Xe]\,6s^2\,4f^{14}\,5d^2$	111	Rg	$[Rn]\,7s^2\,5f^{14}\,6d^9$
34	Se	$[Ar]\,4s^2\,3d^{10}\,4p^4$	73	Ta	$[Xe]\,6s^2\,4f^{14}\,5d^3$	112	Uub	$[Rn]\,7s^2\,5f^{14}\,6d^{10}$
35	Br	$[Ar]\,4s^2\,3d^{10}\,4p^5$	74	W	$[Xe]\,6s^2\,4f^{14}\,5d^4$	113	Uut	$[Rn]\,7s^2\,5f^{14}\,6d^{10}\,7p^1$
36	Kr	$[Ar]\,4s^2\,3d^{10}\,4p^6$	75	Re	$[Xe]\,6s^2\,4f^{14}\,5d^5$	114	Uuq	$[Rn]\,7s^2\,5f^{14}\,6d^{10}\,7p^2$
37	Rb	$[Kr]\,5s^1$	76	Os	$[Xe]\,6s^2\,4f^{14}\,5d^6$	115	Uup	$[Rn]\,7s^2\,5f^{14}\,6d^{10}\,7p^3$
38	Sr	$[Kr]\,5s^2$	77	Ir	$[Xe]\,6s^2\,4f^{14}\,5d^7$	116	Uuh	$[Rn]\,7s^2\,5f^{14}\,6d^{10}\,7p^4$
39	Y	$[Kr]\,5s^2\,4d^1$	78	Pt	$[Xe]\,6s^1\,4f^{14}\,5d^9$	118	Uuo	$[Rn]\,7s^2\,5f^{14}\,6d^{10}\,7p^6$

ANSWERS TO PRACTICE EXERCISES AND SELECTED REVIEW PROBLEMS

CHAPTER 1

Practice Exercises

1.1 meter^3 or m^3. **1.2** $kg\left(\dfrac{m}{s^2}\right)$ or kg m s^{-2}. **1.3** 187 °C.

1.4 10 °C, 293 K. **1.5** (a) 42.0 g, (b) 0.857 g/mL, (c) 149 cm.
1.6 (a) 30.0 mL, (b) 54.155 g, (c) 11.3 g, (d) 3.62 ft, (e) 0.48 m^2.
1.7 11.5 m^2. **1.8** (a) 108 in., (b) 1.25 × 10^5 cm, (c) 0.0107 ft,
(d) 8.59 km L^{-1}. **1.9** d = 16.5 g cm^{-3}. The object is not composed
of pure gold. **1.10** 647 lb. **1.11** 0.899 g/cm^3. **1.12** 0.0568 cm^3

Review Problems

1.26 (a) 0.01 m, (b) 1000 m, (c) 10^{12} pm, (d) 0.1 m,
(e) 0.001 kg, (f) 0.01 g. **1.28** (a)120 °F, (b) 50 °F, (c) −3.61 °C,
(d) 9.4 °C, (e) 333 K, (f) 243 K. **1.30** At 39.7 °C, this dog
has a fever; the temperature is out of normal canine range.
1.32 1.0 × 10^7 K − 2.5 × 10^7 K, 1.0 × 10^7 °C − 2.5 × 10^7 °C,
1.8 × 10^7 °F − 4.5 × 10^7 °F. **1.34** −269 °C. **1.36** (a) 4 significant
figures, (b) 5 significant figures, (c) 4 significant figures, (d) 2 significant figures, (e) 4 significant figures, (f) 2 significant figures.
1.38 (a) 0.72 m^2, (b) 84.24 kg, (c) 4.19 g/mL, (d) 19.42 g/mL,
(e) 857.7 cm^2. **1.40** (a) 11.5 km/h, (b) 8.2 × 10^6 µg/L,
(c) 7.53 × 10^{-5} kg, (d) 0.1375 L, (e) 25 mL, (f) 3.42 × 10^{-20} dm.
1.42 (a) 91 cm, (b) 2.3 kg, (c) 2800 mL, (d) 200 mL, (e) 88 km/hr,
(f) 80.4 km. **1.44** (a) 7,800 cm^2, (b) 577 km^2, (c) 6.54 × 10^6 cm^3.
1.46 4,000 pistachios. **1.48** 90 m/s. **1.50** 1520 mi/hr.
1.52 5.1 × 10^{13} mi. **1.54** 11,034 m. **1.56** 0.798 g/mL. **1.58**
31.6 mL. **1.60** 276 g. **1.62** 11 g/mL. **1.64** 0.0709 g/mL

CHAPTER 2

Practice Exercises

2.1 12.3 g Cd. **2.2** Compounds A and D are the same, as are
compounds B and C. **2.3** $^{240}_{94}$Pu 94 electrons. **2.4** $^{35}_{17}$Cl 17 protons,
17 electrons, and 18 neutrons. **2.5** We can discard the 17 since the
17 tells the number of protons which is information that the symbol
"Cl" also provides. In addition, the number of protons equals the
number of electrons in a neutral atom, so the symbol "Cl" also indicates the number of electrons. The 35 is necessary to state which isotope of chlorine is in question and therefore the number of neutrons
in the atom. **2.6** 26.9814 u. **2.7** 5.2955 times as heavy as carbon.
2.8 10.8 u. **2.9** (a) 1 Ni, 2 Cl, (b) 1 Fe, 1 S, 4 O, (c) 3 Ca, 2 P, 8 O,
(d) 1 Co, 2 N, 12 O, 12 H. **2.10** (a) 2 N nitrogen, 4 H hydrogen,
3 O oxygen, (b) 1 Fe iron, 1 N nitrogen, 4 H hydrogen, 2 S sulfur, 8
O oxygen, (c) 1 Mo molybdenum, 2 N nitrogen, 11 O oxygen,
10 H hydrogen, (d) 6 C carbon, 4 H hydrogen, 1 Cl chlorine,
1 N nitrogen, 2 O oxygen. **2.11** 1 Mg, 2 O, 4 H, and 2 Cl.
2.12 Mg(OH)$_2$(s) + 2HCl(aq) $\longrightarrow$ MgCl$_2$(aq) + 2H$_2$O.
2.13 6 N, 42 H, 2 P, 20 O, 3 Ba, and 12 C.
2.14 CH$_3$CH$_2$CH$_2$CH$_2$CH$_2$CH$_2$CH$_2$CH$_3$

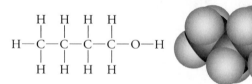

2.15 CH$_3$CH$_2$CH$_2$CH$_2$CH$_2$CH$_2$CH$_2$CH$_2$CH$_2$CH$_3$

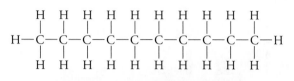

2.16 (a) CH$_3$CH$_2$CH$_2$OH

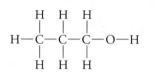

(b) CH$_3$CH$_2$CH$_2$CH$_2$OH

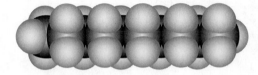

2.17 (a) 26 protons and 26 electrons, (b) 26 protons and 23
electrons, (c) 7 protons and 10 electrons, (d) 7 protons and 7
electrons. **2.18** (a) 8 protons and 8 electrons, (b) 8 protons and
10 electrons, (c) 13 protons and 10 electrons, (d) 13 protons
and 13 electrons.
2.19 (a) NaF, (b) Na$_2$O, (c) MgF$_2$, (d) Al$_4$C$_3$.
2.20 (a) Ca$_3$N$_2$, (b) AlBr$_3$, (c) Na$_3$P, d) CsCl. **2.21** (a) CrCl$_3$
and CrCl$_2$, Cr$_2$O$_3$ and CrO, (b) CuCl, CuCl$_2$, Cu$_2$O and CuO.
2.22 (a) Au$_2$S and Au$_2$S$_3$, Au$_3$N and AuN, (b) SnS and SnS$_2$,
Sn$_3$N$_2$ and Sn$_3$N$_4$.
2.23 (a) KC$_2$H$_3$O$_2$, (b) Sr(NO$_3$)$_2$, (c) Fe(C$_2$H$_3$O$_2$)$_3$.
2.24 (a) Na$_2$CO$_3$, (b) (NH$_4$)$_2$SO$_4$.
2.25 (a) phosphorous trichloride, (b) sulfur dioxide, (c) dichlorine
heptaoxide. **2.26** (a) AsCl$_5$, (b) SCl$_6$, (c) S$_2$Cl$_2$. **2.27** (a) K$_2$O,
(b) BaBr$_2$, (c) Na$_3$N, (d) Al$_2$S$_3$. **2.28** (a) aluminum chloride,
(b) barium sulfide, (c) sodium bromide, (d) calcium fluoride.
2.29 (a) postassium sulfide, (b) magnesium phosphide,
(c) nickel(II) chloride, (d) iron(III) oxide. **2.30** (a) Al$_2$S$_3$,
(b) SrF$_2$, (c) TiO$_2$, (d) Au$_2$O$_3$. **2.31** (a) lithium carbonate,
(b) iron(III) hydroxide. **2.32** (a) KClO$_3$, (b) Ni$_3$(PO$_4$)$_2$.
2.33 diiodine pentaoxide. **2.34** chromium(III) acetate

Review Problems

2.76 x = 29.3 g nitrogen. **2.78** 5.54 g ammonia.
2.80 2.286 g of O. **2.82** 1.008 u. **2.84** 2.01588 u.
2.86 (0.6917 × 62.9396 u) + (0.3083 × 64.9278 u) = 63.55 u.

2.88

	neutrons	protons	electrons
(a) Radium-226	138	88	88
(b) ^{206}Pb	124	82	82
(c) Carbon-14	8	6	6
(d) ^{23}Na	12	11	11

2.90 1 Cr, 6 C, 9 H, 6 O. **2.92** $MgSO_4$. **2.94** (a) 2 K, 2 C, 4 O, (b) 2 H, 1 S, 3 O, (c) 12 C, 26 H, (d) 4 H, 2 C, 2 O, (e) 9 H, 2 N, 1 P, 4 O. **2.96** (a) 1 Ni, 2 Cl, 8 O, (b) 1 Cu, 1 C, 3 O, (c) 2 K, 2 Cr, 7 O, (d) 2 C, 4 H, 2 O, (e) 2 N, 9 H, 1 P, 4 O. **2.98** (a) 6 N, 3 O, (b) 4 Na, 4 H, 4 C, 12 O, (c) 2 Cu, 2 S, 18 O, 20 H. **2.100** (a) 6, (b) 3, (c) 27. **2.102** (a) K^+, (b) Br^-, (c) Mg^{2+}, (d) S^{2-}, (e) Al^{3+}. **2.104** (a) NaBr, (b) KI, (c) BaO, (d) $MgBr_2$, (e) BaF_2. **2.106** (a) KNO_3, (b) $Ca(C_2H_3O_2)_2$, (c) NH_4Cl, (d) $Fe_2(CO_3)_3$, (e) $Mg_3(PO_4)_2$. **2.108** (a) PbO and PbO_2, (b) SnO and SnO_2, (c) MnO and Mn_2O_3, (d) FeO and Fe_2O_3, (e) Cu_2O and CuO. **2.110** (a) silicon dioxide, (b) xenon tetrafluoride, (c) tetraphosphorus decaoxide, (d) dichlorine heptaoxide. **2.112** (a) calcium sulfide, (b) aluminum bromide, (c) sodium phosphide, (d) barium arsenide, (e) rubidium sulfide. **2.114** (a) iron(II) sulfide, (b) copper(II) oxide, (c) tin(IV) oxide, (d) cobalt(II) chloride hexahydrate. **2.116** (a) sodium nitrite, (b) potassium permanganate, (c) magnesium sulfate heptahydrate, (d) potassium thiocyanate. **2.118** (a) ionic, chromium(II) chloride, (b) molecular, disulfur dichloride, (c) ionic, ammonium acetate, (d) molecular, sulfur trioxide, (e) ionic, potassium iodate, (f) molecular, tetraphosphorous hexaoxide, (g) ionic, calcium sulfite, (h) ionic, silver cyanide, (i) ionic, zinc(II) bromide, (j) molecular, hydrogen selenide. **2.120** (a) Na_2HPO_4, (b) Li_2Se, (c) $Cr(C_2H_3O_2)_3$, (d) S_2F_{10}, (e) $Ni(CN)_2$, (f) Fe_2O_3, (g) SbF_5. **2.122** (a) $(NH_4)_2S$, (b) $Cr_2(SO_4)_3\cdot6H_2O$, (c) SiF_4, (d) MoS_2, (e) $SnCl_4$, (f) H_2Se, (g) P_4S_7. **2.124** diselenium hexasulfide and diselenium tetrasulfide

CHAPTER 3

Practice Exercises

3.1 0.129 mol Al. **3.2** $\pm7.12 \times 10^{-5}$ mol Si. **3.3** Yes. **3.4** 3.5×10^{18} molecules of sucrose. **3.5** 0.0516 mol Al^{3+}. **3.6** 3.44 mol N atoms. **3.7** 59.5 g Fe. **3.8** 10.5 g Fe. **3.9** 27.9 g Fe. **3.10** 13.04% H, 52.17% C. It is likely that the compound contains another element. **3.11** 36.84% N, 63.16% O, There are no other elements present. **3.12** 30.45% N, 69.55% O.

3.13

N_2O:	63.65% N	36.34% O
NO:	46.68% N	53.32% O
NO_2:	30.45% N	69.55% O
N_2O_3:	36.86% N	63.14% O
N_2O_4:	30.45% N	69.55% O
N_2O_5:	25.94% N	74.06% O

The compound N_2O_3 corresponds to the data in Practice Exercise 3.11. **3.14** NO. **3.15** SO_2. **3.16** Al_2O_3. **3.17** N_2O_5. **3.18** Na_2SO_4. **3.19** C_9H_8O. **3.20** CS_2. **3.21** CH_2O. **3.22** $C_2H_4Cl_2$ and $C_6H_6Cl_6$. **3.23** N_2H_4. **3.24** $AlCl_3(aq) + Na_3PO_4(aq) \longrightarrow AlPO_4(s) + 3NaCl(aq)$. **3.25** $3CaCl_2(aq) + 2K_3PO_4(aq) \longrightarrow Ca_3(PO_4)_2(s) + 6KCl(aq)$. **3.26** 3.38 mol O_2. **3.27** 0.183 mol H_2SO_4. **3.28** 78.5 g Al_2O_3. **3.29** 1.18×10^2 g CO_2. **3.30** 55.0 g CO_2, 34 g HCl remaining. **3.31** 30.01 g NO. **3.32** 36.78 g $HOOCC_6H_4O_2C_2O_3$, 83.5%. **3.33** 30.9 g $HC_2H_3O_2$, 86.1%

Review Problems

3.25 1:2, 2 mol N to 4 mol O. **3.27** 2.59×10^{-3} mole Ta. **3.29** (a) 6 atom C:11 atom H, (b) 12 mole C:11 mole O, (c) 12 atom H:11 atom O, (d) 12 mole H:11 mole O. **3.31** 1.05 mol Bi. **3.33** 4.32 mol Cr.

3.35 (a) $\left(\dfrac{2 \text{ mol Al}}{3 \text{ mol S}}\right)$ or $\left(\dfrac{3 \text{ mol S}}{2 \text{ mol Al}}\right)$, (b) $\left(\dfrac{3 \text{ mol S}}{1 \text{ mol Al}_2(SO_4)_3}\right)$ or $\left(\dfrac{1 \text{ mol Al}_2(SO_4)_3}{3 \text{ mol S}}\right)$, (c) 0.600 mol Al, (d) 3.48 mol S. **3.37** 0.0725 mol N_2, 0.218 mole H_2. **3.39** 0.833 mol CF_4. **3.41** 9.33×10^{23} atoms C. **3.43** 3.76×10^{24} atoms. **3.45** 3.01×10^{23} atoms C–12. **3.47** (a) 75.4 g Fe, (b) 392 g O, (c) 35.1 g Ca. **3.49** 1.30×10^{-10} g K. **3.51** 0.302 mol Ni. **3.53** (a) $NaHCO_3$ 84.0066 g/mol, (b) $(NH_4)_2CO_3$ 96.0858 g/mol, (c) $CuSO_4\cdot5H_2O$ 249.685 g/mole, (d) $K_2Cr_2O_7$ 294.1846 g/mole, (e) $Al_2(SO_4)_3$ 342.151 g/mol. **3.55** (a) 388 g $Ca_3(PO_4)_2$, (b) 0.151 g $Fe(NO_3)_3$, (c) 34.9 g C_4H_{10}, (d) 1.39×10^{-4} g $(NH_4)_2CO_3$. **3.57** (a) 0.215 mol $CaCO_3$, (b) 9.16×10^{-11} mol NH_3, (c) 7.94×10^{-2} mol $Sr(NO_3)_2$, (d) 4.31×10^{-8} mol Na_2CrO_4. **3.59** 0.0750 mol Ca, 3.01 g Ca. **3.61** 1.30 mol N, 62.5 g $(NH_4)_2CO_3$. **3.63** 3.43 kg fertilizer. **3.65** Assume one mole total for each of the following.

(a) 19.2% Na	1.68% H	25.8% P	53.3% O
(b) 12.2% N	5.26% H	26.9% P	55.6% O
(c) 62.0% C	10.4% H	27.6% O	
(d) 23.3% Ca	18.6% S	55.7% O	2.34% H
(e) 23.3% Ca	18.6% S	55.7% O	2.34% H.

3.67 Heroin. **3.69** Freon 141b. **3.71** 22.9% P, 77.1% Cl. **3.73** These data are consistent with the experimental values cited in the problem. **3.75** 0.474 g O. **3.77** (a) SCl, (b) CH_2O (c) NH_3, (d) AsO_3, (e) HO. **3.79** $NaTcO_4$. **3.81** CCl_2. **3.83** $C_9H_8O_2$. **3.85** C_2H_6O. **3.87** $C_{19}H_{30}O_2$. **3.89** (a) $Na_2S_4O_6$, (b) $C_6H_4Cl_2$, (c) $C_6H_3Cl_3$. **3.91** $C_{19}H_{30}O_2$. **3.93** HgBr, Hg_2Br_2. **3.95** CHNO, $C_3H_3N_3O_3$. **3.97** 36 mol H. **3.99** $4Fe(s) + 3O_2(g) \longrightarrow 2Fe_2O_3(s)$. **3.101** (a) $Ca(OH)_2 + 2HCl \longrightarrow CaCl_2 + 2H_2O$, (b) $2AgNO_3 + CaCl_2 \longrightarrow Ca(NO_3)_2 + 2AgCl$, (c) $Pb(NO_3)_2 + Na_2SO_4 \longrightarrow PbSO_4 + 2NaNO_3$, (d) $2Fe_2O_3 + 3C \longrightarrow 4Fe + 3CO_2$, (e) $2C_4H_{10} + 13O_2 \longrightarrow 8CO_2 + 10H_2O$. **3.103** (a) $Mg(OH)_2 + 2HBr \longrightarrow MgBr_2 + 2H_2O$, (b) $2HCl + Ca(OH)_2 \longrightarrow CaCl_2 + 2H_2O$, (c) $Al_2O_3 + 3H_2SO_4 \longrightarrow Al_2(SO_4)_3 + 3H_2O$, (d) $2KHCO_3 + H_3PO_4 \longrightarrow K_2HPO_4 + 2H_2O + 2CO_2$, (e) $C_9H_{20} + 14O_2 \longrightarrow 9CO_2 + 10H_2O$. **3.105** $2FeCl_3 + SnCl_2 \longrightarrow 2FeCl_2 + SnCl_4$. **3.107** (a) 0.030 mol $Na_2S_2O_3$, (b) 0.24 mol HCl, (c) 0.15 mol H_2O, (d) 0.15 mol H_2O. **3.109** (a) 3.6 g Zn, (b) 22 g Au, (c) 55 g $Au(CN)_2^-$. **3.111** (a) $4P + 5O_2 \longrightarrow P_4O_{10}$, (b) 8.85 g O_2, (c) 14.2 g P_4O_{10}, (d) 3.26 g P. **3.113** 30.28 g HNO_3. **3.115** 0.47 kg O_2. **3.117** (a) Fe_2O_3, (b) 195 g Fe. **3.119** 26.7 g $FeCl_3$. **3.121** 0.913 mg HNO_3. **3.123** 66.98 g $BaSO_4$, 96.22%. **3.125** 88.72%. **3.127** 9.2 g C_7H_8

CHAPTER 4

Practice Exercises

4.1 (a) $FeCl_3(s) \longrightarrow Fe^{3+}(aq) + 3Cl^-(aq)$, (b) $K_3PO_4(s) \longrightarrow 3K^+(aq) + PO_4^{3-}(aq)$. **4.2** (a) $MgCl_2(s) \longrightarrow Mg^{2+}(aq) + 2Cl^-(aq)$, (b) $Al(NO_3)_3(s) \longrightarrow Al^{3+}(aq) + 3NO_3^-(aq)$, (c) $Na_2CO_3(s) \longrightarrow 2Na^+(aq) + CO_3^{2-}(aq)$. **4.3** molecular: $(NH_4)_2SO_4(aq) + Ba(NO_3)_2(aq) \longrightarrow BaSO_4(s) + 2NH_4NO_3(aq)$, ionic: $2NH_4^+(aq) + SO_4^{2-}(aq) + Ba^{2+}(aq) + 2NO_3^-(aq) \longrightarrow BaSO_4(s) + 2NH_4^+(aq) + 2NO_3^-(aq)$, net ionic: $Ba^{2+}(aq) + SO_4^{2-}(aq) \longrightarrow BaSO_4(s)$. **4.4** molecular: $CdCl_2(aq) + Na_2S(aq) \longrightarrow CdS(s) + 2NaCl(aq)$,

ionic: $Cd^{2+}(aq) + 2Cl^-(aq) + 2Na^+(aq) + S^{2-}(aq) \longrightarrow$
$$CdS(s) + 2Na^+(aq) + 2Cl^-(aq),$$
net ionic: $Cd^{2+}(aq) + S^{2-}(aq) \longrightarrow CdS(s)$.

4.5 $HCHO_2(aq) + H_2O \longrightarrow H_3O^+(aq) + CHO_2^-(aq)$.

4.6 $H_3C_6H_5O_7(s) + H_2O \longrightarrow H_3O^+(aq) + H_2C_6H_5O_7^-(aq)$,
$H_2C_6H_5O_7^-(aq) + H_2O \longrightarrow H_3O^+(aq) + HC_6H_5O_7^{2-}(aq)$,
$HC_6H_5O_7^{2-}(aq) + H_2O \longrightarrow H_3O^+(aq) + C_6H_5O_7^{3-}(aq)$.

4.7 $(C_2H_5)_3N(aq) + H_2O \longrightarrow (C_2H_5)_3NH^+(aq) + OH^-(aq)$.

4.8 $HONH_2(aq) + H_2O \longrightarrow HONH_3^+(aq) + OH^-(aq)$.

4.9 $CH_3NH_2(aq) + H_2O \rightleftharpoons CH_3NH_3^+(aq) + OH^-(aq)$.

4.10 $HNO_2(aq) + H_2O \rightleftharpoons H_3O^+(aq) + NO_2^-(aq)$.

4.11 Sodium arsenate. **4.12** Calcium formate. **4.13** HF: Hydrofluoric acid, sodium salt = sodium fluoride (NaF), HBr: Hydrobromic acid, sodium salt = sodium bromide (NaBr).

4.14 $NaHSO_3$, sodium hydrogen sulfite.

4.15 $H_3PO_4(aq) + NaOH(aq) \longrightarrow NaH_2PO_4(aq) + H_2O$
sodium dihydrogen phosphate,
$NaH_2PO_4(aq) + NaOH(aq) \longrightarrow Na_2HPO_4(aq) + H_2O$
sodium hydrogen phosphate,
$Na_2HPO_4(aq) + NaOH(aq) \longrightarrow Na_3PO_4(aq) + H_2O$
sodium phosphate.

4.16 molecular: $Zn(NO_3)_2(aq) + Ca(C_2H_3O_2)_2(aq) \longrightarrow$
$$Zn(C_2H_3O_2)_2(aq) + Ca(NO_3)_2(aq),$$
ionic: $Zn^{2+}(aq) + 2NO_3^-(aq) + Ca^{2+}(aq) + 2C_2H_3O_2^-(aq) \longrightarrow$
$$Zn^{2+}(aq) + 2C_2H_3O_2^-(aq) + Ca^{2+}(aq) + 2NO_3^-(aq),$$
net ionic: No reaction.

4.17 (a) molecular: $AgNO_3(aq) + NH_4Cl(aq) \longrightarrow$
$$AgCl(s) + NH_4NO_3(aq),$$
ionic: $Ag^+(aq) + NO_3^-(aq) + NH_4^+(aq) + Cl^-(aq) \longrightarrow$
$$AgCl(s) + NH_4^+(aq) + NO_3^-(aq),$$
net ionic: $Ag^+(aq) + Cl^-(aq) \longrightarrow AgCl(s)$,
(b) molecular: $Na_2S(aq) + Pb(C_2H_3O_2)_2(aq) \longrightarrow$
$$2NaC_2H_3O_2(aq) + PbS(s),$$
ionic: $2Na^+(aq) + S^{2-}(aq) + Pb^{2+}(aq) + 2C_2H_3O_2^-(aq) \longrightarrow$
$$2Na^+(aq) + 2C_2H_3O_2^-(aq) + PbS(s),$$
net ionic: $S^{2-}(aq) + Pb^{2+}(aq) \longrightarrow PbS(s)$.

4.18 molecular: $2HNO_3(aq) + Ca(OH)_2(aq) \longrightarrow$
$$Ca(NO_3)_2(aq) + 2H_2O,$$
ionic: $2H^+(aq) + 2NO_3^-(aq) + Ca^{2+}(aq) + 2OH^-(aq) \longrightarrow$
$$Ca^{2+}(aq) + 2NO_3^-(aq) + 2H_2O,$$
net ionic: $H^+(aq) + OH^-(aq) \longrightarrow H_2O$.

4.19 (a) molecular: $HCl(aq) + KOH(aq) \longrightarrow H_2O + KCl(aq)$,
ionic: $H^+(aq) + Cl^-(aq) + K^+(aq) + OH^-(aq) \longrightarrow$
$$H_2O + K^+(aq) + Cl^-(aq),$$
net ionic: $H^+(aq) + OH^-(aq) \longrightarrow H_2O$,
(b) molecular: $HCHO_2(aq) + LiOH(aq) \longrightarrow H_2O + LiCHO_2(aq)$,
ionic: $HCHO_2(aq) + Li^+(aq) + OH^-(aq) \longrightarrow$
$$H_2O + Li^+(aq) + CHO_2^-(aq),$$
net ionic: $HCHO_2(aq) + OH^-(aq) \longrightarrow H_2O + CHO_2^-(aq)$,
(c) molecular: $N_2H_4(aq) + HCl(aq) \longrightarrow N_2H_5Cl(aq)$,
ionic: $N_2H_4(aq) + H^+(aq) + Cl^-(aq) \longrightarrow N_2H_5^+(aq) + Cl^-(aq)$,
net ionic: $N_2H_4(aq) + H^+(aq) \longrightarrow N_2H_5^+(aq)$.

4.20 molecular: $CH_3NH_2(aq) + HCHO_2(aq) \longrightarrow$
$$CH_3NH_3CHO_2(aq),$$
ionic: $CH_3NH_2(aq) + HCHO_2(aq) \longrightarrow CH_3NH_3^+(aq) + CHO_2^-(aq)$,
net ionic: $CH_3NH_2(aq) + HCHO_2(aq) \longrightarrow$
$$CH_3NH_3^+(aq) + CHO_2^-(aq).$$

4.21 molecular: $2HCHO_2(aq) + Co(OH)_2(s) \longrightarrow$
$$Co(CHO_2)_2(aq) + 2H_2O,$$
ionic: $2HCHO_2(aq) + Co(OH)_2(s) \longrightarrow$
$$2CHO_2^-(aq) + Co^{2+}(aq) + 2H_2O,$$
net ionic: $2HCHO_2(aq) + Co(OH)_2(s) \longrightarrow$
$$2CHO_2^-(aq) + Co^{2+}(aq) + 2H_2O.$$

4.22 (a) Formic acid, a weak acid will form. Molecular:
$KCHO_2(aq) + HCl(aq) \longrightarrow KCl(aq) + HCHO_2(aq)$,

ionic: $K^+(aq) + CHO_2^-(aq) + H^+(aq) + Cl^-(aq) \longrightarrow$
$$K^+(aq) + Cl^-(aq) + HCHO_2(aq),$$
net ionic: $CHO_2^-(aq) + H^+(aq) \longrightarrow HCHO_2(aq)$,
(b) Carbonic acid will form and it will further dissociate to water and carbon dioxide:
$CuCO_3(s) + 2H^+(aq) \longrightarrow CO_2(g) + H_2O + Cu^{2+}(aq)$,
molecular: $CuCO_3(s) + 2HC_2H_3O_2(aq) \longrightarrow$
$$CO_2(g) + H_2O + Cu(C_2H_3O_2)_2(aq),$$
ionic: $CuCO_3(s) + 2HC_2H_3O_2(aq) \longrightarrow$
$$CO_2(g) + H_2O + Cu^{2+}(aq) + 2C_2H_3O_2^-(aq),$$
net ionic: $CuCO_3(s) + 2HC_2H_3O_2(aq) \longrightarrow$
$$CO_2(g) + H_2O + Cu^{2+}(aq) + 2C_2H_3O_2^-(aq),$$
c) NR, d) Insoluble nickel hydroxide will precipitate:
$Ni^{2+}(aq) + 2OH^-(aq) \longrightarrow Ni(OH)_2(s)$,
molecular: $NiCl_2(aq) + 2NaOH(aq) \longrightarrow Ni(OH)_2(s) + 2NaCl(aq)$,
ionic: $Ni^{2+}(aq) + 2Cl^-(aq) + 2Na^+(aq) + 2OH^-(aq) \longrightarrow$
$$Ni(OH)_2(s) + 2Na^+(aq) + 2Cl^-(aq),$$
net ionic: $Ni^{2+}(aq) + 2OH^-(aq) \longrightarrow Ni(OH)_2(s)$.

4.23 1.53 M HNO_3. **4.24** 0.1837 M NaCl.
4.25 0.0438 mol HCl. **4.26** 143 mL. **4.27** 2.11 g $Sr(NO_3)_2$.
4.28 0.531 g $AgNO_3$. **4.29** 250.0 mL. **4.30** 600 mL of water.
4.31 31.6 mL H_3PO_4. **4.32** 26.8 mL NaOH. **4.33** 0.40 M Fe^{3+}, 1.2 M Cl^-. **4.34** 0.750 M Na^+. **4.35** 0.0449 M $CaCl_2$.
4.36 60.0 mL KOH. **4.37** 0.605 g Na_2SO_4.
4.38 (a) 5.41×10^{-3} mol Ca^{2+}, (b) 5.41×10^{-3} moles Ca^{2+}, (c) 5.41×10^{-3} moles $CaCl_2$, (d) 0.600 g $CaCl_2$, (e) 30.0% $CaCl_2$.
4.39 0.178 M H_2SO_4. **4.40** 0.0220 M HCl, 0.0803%

Review Problems

4.49 (a) ionic:
$2NH_4^+(aq) + CO_3^{2-}(aq) + Mg^{2+}(aq) + 2Cl^-(aq) \longrightarrow$
$$2NH_4^+(aq) + 2Cl^-(aq) + MgCO_3(s),$$
net: $Mg^{2+}(aq) + CO_3^{2-}(aq) \longrightarrow MgCO_3(s)$,
(b) ionic: $Cu^{2+}(aq) + 2Cl^-(aq) + 2Na^+(aq) + 2OH^-(aq) \longrightarrow$
$$Cu(OH)_2(s) + 2Na^+(aq) + 2Cl^-(aq),$$
net: $Cu^{2+}(aq) + 2OH^-(aq) \longrightarrow Cu(OH)_2(s)$,
(c) ionic: $3Fe^{2+}(aq) + 3SO_4^{2-}(aq) + 6Na^+(aq) + 2PO_4^{3-}(aq) \longrightarrow$
$$Fe_3(PO_4)_2(s) + 6Na^+(aq) + 3SO_4^{2-}(aq),$$
net: $3Fe^{2+}(aq) + 2PO_4^{3-}(aq) \longrightarrow Fe_3(PO_4)_2(s)$,
(d) ionic: $2Ag^+(aq) + 2C_2H_3O_2^-(aq) + Ni^{2+}(aq) + 2Cl^-(aq) \longrightarrow$
$$2AgCl(s) + Ni^{2+}(aq) + 2C_2H_3O_2^-(aq),$$
net: $Ag^+(aq) + Cl^-(aq) \longrightarrow AgCl(s)$.

4.51 $HClO_4(l) + H_2O \longrightarrow H_3O^+(aq) + ClO_4^-(aq)$.

4.53 $N_2H_4(aq) + H_2O \rightleftharpoons N_2H_5^+(aq) + OH^-(aq)$.

4.55 $HNO_2(aq) + H_2O \rightleftharpoons H_3O^+(aq) + NO_2^-(aq)$.

4.57 $H_2CO_3(aq) + H_2O \rightleftharpoons H_3O^+(aq) + HCO_3^-(aq)$,
$HCO_3^-(aq) + H_2O \rightleftharpoons H_3O^+(aq) + CO_3^{2-}(aq)$

4.59 (a) ionic:
$3Fe^{2+}(aq) + 3SO_4^{2-}(aq) + 6K^+(aq) + 2PO_4^{3-}(aq) \longrightarrow$
$$Fe_3(PO_4)_2(s) + 6K^+(aq) + 3SO_4^{2-}(aq),$$
net: $3Fe^{2+}(aq) + 2PO_4^{3-}(aq) \longrightarrow Fe_3(PO_4)_2(s)$,
(b) ionic: $3Ag^+(aq) + 3C_2H_3O_2^-(aq) + Al^{3+}(aq) + 3Cl^-(aq) \longrightarrow$
$$3AgCl(s) + Al^{3+}(aq) + 3C_2H_3O_2^-(aq),$$
net: $Ag^+(aq) + Cl^-(aq) \longrightarrow AgCl(s)$.

4.61 molecular: $Na_2S(aq) + Cu(NO_3)_2(aq) \longrightarrow$
$$CuS(s) + 2NaNO_3(aq),$$
ionic: $2Na^+(aq) + S^{2-}(aq) + Cu^{2+}(aq) + 2NO_3^-(aq) \longrightarrow$
$$CuS(s) + 2Na^+(aq) + 2NO_3^-(aq),$$
net: $Cu^{2+}(aq) + S^{2-}(aq) \longrightarrow CuS(s)$.

4.63 (a), (b), and (d).

4.65 (a) molecular: $Ca(OH)_2(aq) + 2HNO_3(aq) \longrightarrow$
$$Ca(NO_3)_2(aq) + 2H_2O,$$
ionic: $Ca^{2+}(aq) + 2OH^-(aq) + 2H^+(aq) + 2NO_3^-(aq) \longrightarrow$
$$Ca^{2+}(aq) + 2NO_3^-(aq) + 2H_2O,$$
net: $H^+(aq) + OH^-(aq) \longrightarrow H_2O$,

(b) molecular: $Al_2O_3(s) + 6HCl(aq) \longrightarrow 2AlCl_3(aq) + 3H_2O$,
ionic: $Al_2O_3(s) + 6H^+(aq) + 6Cl^-(aq) \longrightarrow$
$$2Al^{3+}(aq) + 6Cl^-(aq) + 3H_2O,$$
net: $Al_2O_3(s) + 6H^+(aq) \longrightarrow 2Al^{3+}(aq) + 3H_2O$,
(c) molecular: $Zn(OH)_2(s) + H_2SO_4(aq) \longrightarrow ZnSO_4(aq) + 2H_2O$,
ionic: $Zn(OH)_2(s) + 2H^+(aq) + SO_4^{2-}(aq) \longrightarrow$
$$Zn^{2+}(aq) + SO_4^{2-}(aq) + 2H_2O,$$
net: $Zn(OH)_2(s) + 2H^+(aq) \longrightarrow Zn^{2+}(aq) + 2H_2O$.

4.67 The electrical conductivity would decrease gradually, until one solution had neutralized the other, forming a nonelectrolyte. Once the point of neutralization had been reached, the addition of excess sulfuric acid would cause the conductivity to increase, because sulfuric acid is a strong electrolyte itself.

4.69 (a) $2H^+(aq) + CO_3^{2-}(aq) \longrightarrow H_2O + CO_2(g)$,
(b) $NH_4^+(aq) + OH^-(aq) \longrightarrow NH_3(g) + H_2O$.

4.71 (a) formation of insoluble $Cr(OH)_3$, (b) formation of water, a weak electrolyte. **4.73** (a) molecular:
$3HNO_3(aq) + Cr(OH)_3(s) \longrightarrow Cr(NO_3)_3(aq) + 3H_2O$,
ionic: $3H^+(aq) + 3NO_3^-(aq) + Cr(OH)_3(s) \longrightarrow$
$$Cr^{3+}(aq) + 3NO_3^-(aq) + 3H_2O,$$
net: $3H^+(aq) + Cr(OH)_3(s) \longrightarrow Cr^{3+}(aq) + 3H_2O$,
(b) molecular: $HClO_4(aq) + NaOH(aq) \longrightarrow NaClO_4(aq) + H_2O$,
ionic: $H^+(aq) + ClO_4^-(aq) + Na^+(aq) + OH^-(aq) \longrightarrow$
$$Na^+(aq) + ClO_4^-(aq) + H_2O,$$
net: $H^+(aq) + OH^-(aq) \longrightarrow H_2O$,
(c) molecular: $Cu(OH)_2(s) + 2HC_2H_3O_2(aq) \longrightarrow$
$$Cu(C_2H_3O_2)_2(aq) + 2H_2O,$$
ionic: $Cu(OH)_2(s) + 2HC_2H_3O_2(aq) \longrightarrow$
$$Cu^{2+}(aq) + 2C_2H_3O_2^-(aq) + 2H_2O,$$
net: $Cu(OH)_2(s) + 2HC_2H_3O_2(aq) \longrightarrow$
$$Cu^{2+}(aq) + 2C_2H_3O_2^-(aq) + 2H_2O,$$
(d) molecular: $ZnO(s) + H_2SO_4(aq) \longrightarrow ZnSO_4(aq) + H_2O$,
ionic: $ZnO(s) + 2H^+(aq) + SO_4^{2-}(aq) \longrightarrow$
$$Zn^{2+}(aq) + SO_4^{2-}(aq) + H_2O,$$
net: $ZnO(s) + 2H^+(aq) \longrightarrow Zn^{2+}(aq) + H_2O$.

4.75 (a) molecular: $Na_2SO_3(aq) + Ba(NO_3)_2(aq) \longrightarrow$
$$BaSO_3(s) + 2NaNO_3(aq),$$
ionic: $2Na^+(aq) + SO_3^{2-}(aq) + Ba^{2+}(aq) + 2NO_3^-(aq) \longrightarrow$
$$BaSO_3(s) + 2Na^+(aq) + 2NO_3^-(aq),$$
net: $Ba^{2+}(aq) + SO_3^{2-}(aq) \longrightarrow BaSO_3(s)$,
(b) molecular: $2HCHO_2(aq) + K_2CO_3(aq) \longrightarrow$
$$CO_2(g) + H_2O + 2KCHO_2(aq),$$
ionic: $2HCHO_2(aq) + 2K^+(aq) + CO_3^{2-}(aq) \longrightarrow$
$$CO_2(g) + H_2O + 2K^+(aq) + 2CHO_2^-(aq),$$
net: $2HCHO_2(aq) + CO_3^{2-}(aq) \longrightarrow 2CHO_2^-(aq) + CO_2(g) + H_2O$,
(c) molecular: $2NH_4Br(aq) + Pb(C_2H_3O_2)_2(aq) \longrightarrow$
$$2NH_4C_2H_3O_2(aq) + PbBr_2(s),$$
ionic: $2NH_4^+(aq) + 2Br^-(aq) + Pb^{2+}(aq) + 2C_2H_3O_2^-(aq) \longrightarrow$
$$2NH_4^+(aq) + 2C_2H_3O_2^-(aq) + PbBr_2(s),$$
net: $Pb^{2+}(aq) + 2Br^-(aq) \longrightarrow PbBr_2(s)$,
(d) molecular: $2NH_4ClO_4(aq) + Cu(NO_3)_2(aq) \longrightarrow$
$$Cu(ClO_4)_2(aq) + 2NH_4NO_3(aq),$$
ionic: $2NH_4^+(aq) + 2ClO_4^-(aq) + Cu^{2+}(aq) + 2NO_3^-(aq) \longrightarrow$
$$Cu^{2+}(aq) + 2ClO_4^-(aq) + 2NO_3^-(aq) + 2NH_4^+(aq),$$
net: N.R.

4.77 There are numerous possible answers. One of many possible sets of answers would be,
(a) $NaHCO_3(aq) + HCl(aq) \longrightarrow NaCl(aq) + CO_2(g) + H_2O$,
(b) $FeCl_2(aq) + 2NaOH(aq) \longrightarrow Fe(OH)_2(s) + 2NaCl(aq)$,
(c) $Ba(NO_3)_2(aq) + K_2SO_3(aq) \longrightarrow BaSO_3(s) + 2KNO_3(aq)$,
(d) $2AgNO_3(aq) + Na_2S(aq) \longrightarrow Ag_2S(s) + 2NaNO_3(aq)$,
(e) $ZnO(s) + 2HCl(aq) \longrightarrow ZnCl_2(aq) + H_2O$.

4.79 (a) $1.00\ M$ NaOH, (b) $0.577\ M$ $CaCl_2$.
4.81 658 mL $NaC_2H_3O_2$. **4.83** (a) 1.46 g NaCl,
(b) 16.2 g $C_6H_{12}O_6$, (c) 6.13 g H_2SO_4. **4.85** $0.11\ M$ H_2SO_4.

4.87 300 mL. **4.89** 225 mL water. **4.91** (a) 0.0145 mol Ca^{2+}, 0.0290 mol Cl^-, (b) 0.020 mol Al^{3+}, 0.060 mol Cl^-.
4.93 (a) $0.25\ M$ Cr^{2+}, $0.50\ M$ NO_3^-, (b) $0.10\ M$ Cu^{2+}, $0.10\ M$ SO_4^{2-}, (c) $0.48\ M$ Na^+, $0.16\ M$ PO_4^{3-}, (d) $0.15\ M$ Al^{3+}, $0.22\ M$ SO_4^{2-}. **4.95** 1.0 g $Al_2(SO_4)_3$. **4.97** 12.0 mL $NiCl_2$ soln, 0.36 g $NiCO_3$. **4.99** $0.113\ M$ KOH, $KOH(aq) + HCl(aq) \longrightarrow$ $KCl(aq) + H_2O$. **4.101** 0.485 g $Al_2(SO_4)_3$.
4.103 2.00 mL $FeCl_3$ soln, 0.129 g AgCl. **4.105** 13.3 mL $AlCl_3$.
4.107 $0.167\ M$ Fe^{3+}, 3.67 g Fe_2O_3. **4.109** (a) 8.00×10^{-3} mol AgCl, (b) $0.160\ M$ NO_3^-, $0.220\ M$ Na^+, $0.060\ M$ Cl^-. **4.111** $0.114\ M$ HCl.
4.113 2.67×10^{-3} mol $HC_3H_5O_3$. **4.115** $MgSO_4 \cdot 7H_2O$.
4.117 48.40% Pb in the sample. **4.119** 58.6%

CHAPTER 5

Practice Exercises

5.1 Reduced. **5.2** Aluminum is oxidized and is the reducing agent, Chlorine is reduced and is the oxidizing agent. **5.3** $+3$.
5.4 (a) Ni $+2$; Cl -1, (b) Mg $+2$; Ti $+4$; O -2, (c) K $+1$; Cr $+6$; O -2, (d) H $+1$; P $+5$, O -2, (e) V $+3$; C 0; H $+1$; O -2.
5.5 $+8/3$. **5.6** $KClO_3$ is reduced and HNO_2 is oxidized.
5.7 Cl_2 is reduced and is the oxidizing agent. $NaClO_2$ is oxidized and is the reducing agent. **5.8** Water, since the oxidation number of oxygen drops from -1 to -2 in the formation of water.
5.9 $2Al(s) + 3Cu^{2+}(aq) \longrightarrow 2Al^{3+}(aq) + 3Cu(s)$.
5.10 $3Sn^{2+} + 16H^+ + 2TcO_4^- \longrightarrow 2Tc^{4+} + 8H_2O + 3Sn^{4+}$.
5.11 $4Cu + 2NO_3^- + 10H^+ \longrightarrow 4Cu^{2+} + N_2O + 5H_2O$.
5.12 $4OH^- + SO_2 \longrightarrow SO_4^{2-} + 2e^- + 2H_2O$.
5.13 $2MnO_4^- + 3C_2O_4^{2-} + 4OH^- \longrightarrow$
$$2MnO_2 + 6CO_3^{2-} + 2H_2O.$$
5.14 $Zn \longrightarrow Zn^{2+} + 2e^-$, $2H^+ + 2e^- \longrightarrow H_2$.
5.15 $HNO_3 + 9H^+ + 4Mg \longrightarrow NH_4^+ + 4Mg^{2+} + 3H_2O$.
5.16 (a) molecular: $Mg(s) + 2HCl(aq) \longrightarrow MgCl_2(aq) + H_2(g)$,
ionic: $Mg(s) + 2H^+(aq) + 2Cl^-(aq) \longrightarrow$
$$Mg^{2+}(aq) + 2Cl^-(aq) + H_2(g),$$
net ionic: $Mg(s) + 2H^+(aq) \longrightarrow Mg^{2+}(aq) + H_2(g)$,
(b) molecular: $2Al(s) + 6HCl(aq) \longrightarrow 2AlCl_3(aq) + 3H_2(g)$,
ionic: $2Al(s) + 6H^+(aq) + 6Cl^-(aq) \longrightarrow$
$$2Al^{3+}(aq) + 6Cl^-(aq) + 3H_2(g),$$
net ionic: $2Al(s) + 6H^+(aq) \longrightarrow 2Al^{3+}(aq) + 3H_2(g)$.
5.17 $Cu^{2+}(aq) + Mg(s) \longrightarrow Cu(s) + Mg^{2+}(aq)$.
5.18 (a) $2Al(s) + 3Cu^{2+}(aq) \longrightarrow 2Al^{3+}(aq) + 3Cu(s)$,
(b) $Ag(s) + Mg^{2+}(aq) \longrightarrow$ No reaction.
5.19 $2C_{20}H_{42}(s) + 21O_2(g) \longrightarrow 40C(s) + 42H_2O(g)$.
5.20 $2C_4H_{10}(g) + 13O_2(g) \longrightarrow 8CO_2(g) + 10H_2O(g)$.
5.21 $C_2H_5OH(l) + 3O_2(g) \longrightarrow 2CO_2(g) + 3H_2O(g)$.
5.22 $2Sr(s) + O_2(g) \longrightarrow 2SrO(s)$.
5.23 $4Fe(s) + 3O_2(g) \longrightarrow 2Fe_2O_3(s)$.
5.24 $0.06100\ M$ $H_2C_2O_4$. **5.25** 2.37 g $Na_2S_2O_3$.
5.26 (a) $5Sn^{2+} + 2MnO_4^- + 16H^+ \longrightarrow 5Sn^{4+} + 2Mn^{2+} + 8H_2O$,
(b) 0.120 g Sn, (c) 40.0% Sn, (d) 50.7% SnO_2

Review Problems

5.25 (a) S^{2-}: -2, (b) SO_2: S $+4$, O -2, (c) P_4: P 0, (d) PH_3: P -3, H $+1$. **5.27** (a) O: -2, Na: $+1$, Cl: $+1$, (b) O: -2, Na: $+1$, Cl: $+3$, (c) O: -2, Na: $+1$, Cl: $+5$, (d) O: -2, Na: $+1$, Cl: $+7$.
5.29 The sum of the oxidation numbers should be zero, (a) S: -2, Pb: $+2$, (b) Cl: -1, Ti: $+4$, (c) Cs $+1$, O $-1/2$, (d) F -1, O $+1$. **5.31** In the forward direction: Cl_2 is reduced and Cl_2 also oxidized. In the reverse direction: Cl^- is the reducing agent. HOCl must be the oxidizing agent. **5.33** (a) substance reduced (and oxidizing agent): HNO_3, substance oxidized (and reducing agent): H_3AsO_3, (b) substance reduced (and oxidizing agent): HOCl, substance oxidized (and reducing agent): NaI, (c) substance reduced (and oxidizing agent): $KMnO_4$, substance oxidized

(and reducing agent): $H_2C_2O_4$, (d) substance reduced (and oxidizing agent): H_2SO_4, substance oxidized (and reducing agent): Al.

5.35 (a) $OCl^- + 2S_2O_3^{2-} + 2H^+ \longrightarrow S_4O_6^{2-} + Cl^- + H_2O$,
(b) $2NO_3^- + Cu + 4H^+ \longrightarrow 2NO_2 + Cu^{2+} + 2H_2O$,
(c) $3AsO_3^{3-} + IO_3^- \longrightarrow I^- + 3AsO_4^{3-}$,
(d) $Zn + SO_4^{2-} + 4H^+ \longrightarrow Zn^{2+} + SO_2 + 2H_2O$,
(e) $NO_3^- + 4Zn + 10H^+ \longrightarrow 4Zn^{2+} + NH_4^+ + 3H_2O$,
(f) $2Cr^{3+} + 3BiO_3^- + 4H^+ \longrightarrow Cr_2O_7^{2-} + 3Bi^{3+} + 2H_2O$,
(g) $I_2 + 5OCl^- + H_2O \longrightarrow 2IO_3^- + 5Cl^- + 2H^+$,
(h) $2Mn^{2+} + 5BiO_3^- + 14H^+ \longrightarrow 2MnO_4^- + 5Bi^{3+} + 7H_2O$,
(i) $3H_3AsO_3 + Cr_2O_7^{2-} + 8H^+ \longrightarrow 3H_3AsO_4 + 2Cr^{3+} + 4H_2O$,
(j) $2I^- + HSO_4^- + 3H^+ \longrightarrow I_2 + SO_2 + 2H_2O$.
5.37 (a) $2CrO_4^{2-} + 3S^{2-} + 4H_2O \longrightarrow 2CrO_2^- + 3S + 8OH^-$,
(b) $3C_2O_4^{2-} + 2MnO_4^- + 4H_2O \longrightarrow 6CO_2 + 2MnO_2 + 8OH^-$,
(c) $4ClO_3^- + 3N_2H_4 \longrightarrow 4Cl^- + 6NO + 6H_2O$,
(d) $NiO_2 + 2Mn(OH)_2 \longrightarrow Ni(OH)_2 + Mn_2O_3 + H_2O$,
(e) $3SO_3^{2-} + 2MnO_4^- + H_2O \longrightarrow 3SO_4^{2-} + 2MnO_2 + 2OH^-$.
5.39 $4OCl^- + S_2O_3^{2-} + H_2O \longrightarrow 4Cl^- + 2SO_4^{2-} + 2H^+$.
5.41 $O_3 + Br^- \longrightarrow BrO_3^-$.
5.43 (a) $Mn(s) + 2HCl(aq) \longrightarrow MnCl_2(aq) + H_2(g)$,
$Mn(s) + 2H^+(aq) + 2Cl^-(aq) \longrightarrow Mn^{2+}(aq) + 2Cl^-(aq) + H_2(g)$,
$Mn(s) + 2H^+(aq) \longrightarrow Mn^{2+}(aq) + H_2(g)$,
(b) $Cd(s) + 2HCl(aq) \longrightarrow CdCl_2(aq) + H_2(g)$,
$Cd(s) + 2H^+(aq) + 2Cl^-(aq) \longrightarrow Cd^{2+}(aq) + 2Cl^-(aq) + H_2(g)$,
$Cd(s) + 2H^+(aq) \longrightarrow Cd^{2+}(aq) + H_2(g)$,
(c) $Sn(s) + 2HCl(aq) \longrightarrow SnCl_2(aq) + H_2(g)$,
$Sn(s) + 2H^+(aq) + 2Cl^-(aq) \longrightarrow Sn^{2+}(aq) + 2Cl^-(aq) + H_2(g)$,
$Sn(s) + 2H^+(aq) \longrightarrow Sn^{2+}(aq) + H_2(g)$.
5.45 (a) $3Ag(s) + 4HNO_3(aq) \longrightarrow$
$$3AgNO_3(aq) + 2H_2O + NO(g),$$
(b) $Ag(s) + 2HNO_3(aq) \longrightarrow AgNO_3(aq) + H_2O + NO_2(aq)$.
5.47 (a) N.R., (b) $2Cr(s) + 3Pb^{2+}(aq) \longrightarrow 2Cr^{3+}(aq) + 3Pb(s)$,
(c) $2Ag^+(aq) + Fe(s) \longrightarrow 2Ag(s) + Fe^{2+}(aq)$,
(d) $3Ag(s) + Au^{3+}(aq) \longrightarrow Au(s) + 3Ag^+(aq)$.
5.49 Pt, Ru, Tl, Pu.
5.51 $Cd(s) + 2TlCl(aq) \longrightarrow CdCl_2(aq) + 2Tl(s)$.
5.53 (a) $2C_6H_6(l) + 15O_2(g) \longrightarrow 12CO_2(g) + 6H_2O(g)$,
(b) $C_3H_8(g) + 5O_2(g) \longrightarrow 3CO_2(g) + 4H_2O(g)$,
(c) $C_{21}H_{44}(s) + 32O_2(g) \longrightarrow 21CO_2(g) + 22H_2O(g)$.
5.55 (a) $2C_6H_6(l) + 9O_2(g) \longrightarrow 12CO(g) + 6H_2O(g)$,
$2C_3H_8(g) + 7O_2(g) \longrightarrow 6CO(g) + 8H_2O(g)$,
$2C_{21}H_{44}(s) + 43O_2(g) \longrightarrow 42CO(g) + 44H_2O(g)$,
(b) $2C_6H_6(l) + 3O_2(g) \longrightarrow 12C(s) + 6H_2O(g)$,
$C_3H_8(g) + 2O_2(g) \longrightarrow 3C(s) + 4H_2O(g)$,
$C_{21}H_{44}(s) + 11O_2(g) \longrightarrow 21C(s) + 22H_2O(g)$.
5.57 $2CH_3OH(l) + 3O_2(g) \longrightarrow 2CO_2(g) + 4H_2O(g)$.
5.59 $2(CH_3)_2S(g) + 9O_2(g) \longrightarrow 4CO_2(g) + 6H_2O(g) + 2SO_2(g)$.
5.61 (a) $2Zn(s) + O_2(g) \longrightarrow 2ZnO(s)$,
(b) $4Al(s) + 3O_2(g) \longrightarrow 2Al_2O_3(s)$,
(c) $2Mg(s) + O_2(g) \longrightarrow 2MgO(s)$,
(d) $4Fe(s) + 3O_2(g) \longrightarrow 2Fe_2O_3(s)$.
5.63 (a) $IO_3^- + 3SO_3^{2-} \longrightarrow I^- + 3SO_4^{2-}$, (b) 9.55 g Na_2SO_3.
5.65 3.53 g Cu.
5.67 (a) $2MnO_4^- + 5Sn^{2+} + 16H^+ \longrightarrow 2Mn^{2+} + 5Sn^{4+} + 8H_2O$,
(b) 17.4 mL $KMnO_4$.
5.69 (a) $6.38 \times 10^{-3}\ M\ I_3^-$, (b) 1.01×10^{-3} g SO_2,
(c) 2.10×10^{-3}%, (d) 21 ppm.
5.71 (a) 9.463%, (b) 18.40%.
5.73 (a) 0.02994 g H_2O_2, (b) 2.994% H_2O_2.
5.75 (a) $2CrO_4^{2-} + 3SO_3^{2-} + H_2O \longrightarrow$
$$2CrO_2^- + 3SO_4^{2-} + 2OH^-,$$
(b) 0.875 g Cr in the original alloy., (c) 25.4% Cr.
5.77 (a) 5.405×10^{-3} mol $C_2O_4^{2-}$, (b) 0.5999 g $CaCl_2$,
(c) 24.35% $CaCl_2$

CHAPTER 6

Practice Exercises

6.1 55.1 J/°C. **6.2** 5.23 kJ, 1250 cal, 1.25 kcal. **6.3** 12.4 kJ °C^{-1}.
6.4 394 kJ/mol C. **6.5** -58 kJ mol^{-1}. **6.6** 3.7 kJ, 74 kJ/mol.
6.7 $\frac{1}{4} CH_4(g) + \frac{1}{2} O_2(g) \longrightarrow \frac{1}{4} CO_2(g) + \frac{1}{2} H_2O(l)$
$$\Delta H = 222.6\ kJ$$
6.8 $2.500\, H_2(g) + \dfrac{2.500}{2}\, O_2(g) \longrightarrow 2.500\, H_2O(l)\ \Delta H = -714.75\ kJ$

6.9

$2Cu(s)\ +\ O_2(g)$

The reaction is exothermic.

6.10 $NO(g) + \frac{1}{2} O_2(g)$

The reaction is endothermic.
6.11 $\Delta H = +857.7$ kJ. **6.12** $\Delta H = +99.2$ kJ.
6.13 $\Delta H° = -44.0$ kJ. **6.14** 385 kJ. **6.15** 2.62×10^6 kJ.
6.16 $\frac{1}{2} N_2(g) + 2H_2(g) + \frac{1}{2} Cl_2(g) \longrightarrow$
$$NH_4Cl(s)\ \Delta H_f° = -315.4\ kJ$$
6.17 $Na(s) + \frac{1}{2} H_2(g) + C(s) + \frac{3}{2} O_2(g) \longrightarrow$
$$NaHCO_3(s)\ \Delta H_f° = -947.7\ kJ/mol$$
6.18 $+800.34$ kJ.
6.19 $S(s) + \frac{3}{2} O_2(g) \longrightarrow SO_3(g) \quad \Delta H_f° = -395.2$ kJ/mol
$S(s) + O_2(g) \longrightarrow SO_2(g) \quad \Delta H_f° = -296.9$ kJ/mol
Reverse the first reaction and add the two reactions together to get
$SO_3(g) \longrightarrow SO_2(g) + \frac{1}{2} O_2(g) \quad \Delta H_f° = +98.3$ kJ
The answers for the enthalpy of reaction are the same using either
method. **6.20** (a) -113.1 kJ, (b) -177.8 kJ

Review Problems

6.41 -17 J. **6.43** $+100$ J. **6.45** -1320 J, -315 cal.
6.47 (a) 1.67×10^3 J, (b) 1.67×10^3 J, (c) 23.2 J °C^{-1},
(d) 4.64 J g^{-1} °C^{-1}. **6.49** 25.12 J/mol °C. **6.51** -30.4 kJ.
6.53 $HNO_3(aq) + KOH(aq) \longrightarrow KNO_3(aq) + H_2O(l)$,
$$3.8 \times 10^3\ J,\ 53\ kJ/mol.$$
6.55 (a) $C_3H_8(g) + 5O_2(g) \longrightarrow 3CO_2(g) + 4H_2O(l)$,
(b) 2.22×10^5 J, (c) -222 kJ/mol.
6.57 (a) $2CO(g) + O_2(g) \longrightarrow 2CO_2(g)$, $\Delta H° = -566$ kJ,
(b) -283 kJ/mol. **6.59** 162 kJ of heat are evolved.

6.61 $Ge(s) + O_2(g)$

$$\Delta H° = -280\ kJ$$
6.63 $2NO_2(g) \longrightarrow N_2O_4(g)$, $\Delta H° = -57.93$ kJ,
$2NO(g) + O_2(g) \longrightarrow 2NO_2(g)$, $\Delta H° = -113.14$ kJ,
$2NO(g) + O_2(g) \longrightarrow N_2O_4(g)$, $\Delta H° = -171.07$ kJ.
6.65 $\frac{1}{2} Na_2O(s) + HCl(g) \longrightarrow \frac{1}{2} H_2O(l) + NaCl(s)$,
$$\Delta H° = -253.66\ kJ,$$
$NaNO_2(s) \longrightarrow \frac{1}{2} Na_2O(s) + \frac{1}{2} NO_2(g) + \frac{1}{2} NO(g)$,
$$\Delta H° = +213.57\ kJ,$$
$\frac{1}{2} NO(g) + \frac{1}{2} NO_2(g) \longrightarrow \frac{1}{2} N_2O(g) + \frac{1}{2} O_2(g)$, $\Delta H° = -21.34$ kJ,

$\frac{1}{2}$ H$_2$O(l) + $\frac{1}{2}$ O$_2$(g) + $\frac{1}{2}$ N$_2$O(g) $\longrightarrow$ HNO$_2$(l),
$$\Delta H^\circ = -17.18 \text{ kJ},$$
HCl(g) + NaNO$_2$(s) $\longrightarrow$ HNO$_2$(l) + NaCl(s),
$$\Delta H^\circ = -78.61 \text{ kJ}.$$

6.67 $\frac{1}{2}$ CaO(s) + $\frac{1}{2}$ Cl$_2$(g) $\longrightarrow$ $\frac{1}{2}$ CaOCl$_2$(s)
$$\Delta H^\circ = \frac{1}{2} (-110.9 \text{ kJ}).$$
$\frac{1}{2}$H$_2$O(l) + $\frac{1}{2}$CaOCl$_2$(s) + NaBr(s) $\longrightarrow$
NaCl(s) + $\frac{1}{2}$Ca(OH)$_2$(s) + $\frac{1}{2}$Br$_2$ (l) $\quad \Delta H^\circ = \frac{1}{2} (-60.2 \text{ kJ}).$
$\frac{1}{2}$Ca(OH)$_2$(s) $\longrightarrow$ $\frac{1}{2}$CaO(s) + $\frac{1}{2}$H$_2$O(l) $\quad \Delta H^\circ = \frac{1}{2} (+65.1 \text{ kJ}).$
$\frac{1}{2}$Cl$_2$(g) + NaBr(s) $\longrightarrow$ NaCl(s) + $\frac{1}{2}$Br$_2$(l)
$$\Delta H^\circ = \frac{1}{2} (-160.1 \text{ kJ}) = -53 \text{ KJ}.$$

6.69 12NH$_3$(g) + 21O$_2$(g) $\longrightarrow$ 12NO$_2$(g) + 18H$_2$O(g)
$$\Delta H^\circ = 3(-1132 \text{ kJ}),$$
12NO$_2$(g) + 16NH$_3$(g) $\longrightarrow$ 14N$_2$(g) + 24H$_2$O(g)
$$\Delta H^\circ = 2(-2740 \text{ kJ}),$$
28NH$_3$(g) + 21O$_2$(g) $\longrightarrow$ 14N$_2$(g) + 42H$_2$O(g)
$$\Delta H^\circ = -8876 \text{ kJ},$$

Now divide this equation by 7 to get
4NH$_3$(g) + 3O$_2$(g) $\longrightarrow$ 2N$_2$(g) + 6H$_2$O(g)
$$\Delta H^\circ = 1/7(-8876 \text{ kJ}) = -1268 \text{ kJ}.$$

6.71 (a) 2C($graphite$) + 2H$_2$(g) + O$_2$(g) $\longrightarrow$ HC$_2$H$_3$O$_2$(l)
$$\Delta H_f^\circ = -487.0 \text{ kJ},$$
(b) 2C($graphite$) + $\frac{1}{2}$ O$_2$(g) + 3H$_2$(g) $\longrightarrow$ C$_2$H$_5$OH(l)
$$\Delta H_f^\circ = -277.63 \text{ kJ},$$
(c) Ca(s) + $\frac{1}{8}$ S$_8$(s) + 3O$_2$(g) + 2H$_2$(g) $\longrightarrow$ CaSO$_4$·2H$_2$O(s)
$$\Delta H_f^\circ = -2021.1 \text{ kJ}.$$

6.73 (a) -196.6 kJ, (b) -177.8 kJ.
6.75 C$_{12}$H$_{22}$O$_{11}$(s) + 12O$_2$(g) $\longrightarrow$ 12CO$_2$(g) + 11H$_2$O(l)
$\Delta H_f^\circ = -2021.1$ kJ mol^{-1} $\quad \Delta H^\circ_{combustion} = -5.65 \times 10^3$ kJ/mol.

CHAPTER 7

Practice Exercises

7.1 5.10×10^{14} Hz. **7.2** 3.00×10^{13} Hz. **7.3** 2.874 m.
7.4 2.63 μm. **7.5** 656.6 nm, red. **7.6** Shell 1 has 1 subshell, shell 2 has 2 subshells, shell 3 has 3 subshells, shell 4 has 4 subshells, shell 5 has 5 subshells, shell 6 has 6 subshells.
7.7 $n = 3$: s, p and d subshells, $n = 4$: s, p, d and f subshells.
7.8 (a) Mg: $1s^2 2s^2 2p^6 3s^2$,
(b) Ge: $1s^2 2s^2 2p^6 3s^2 3p^6 3d^{10} 4s^2 4p^2$,
(c) Cd: $1s^2 2s^2 2p^6 3s^2 3p^6 3d^{10} 4s^2 4p^6 4d^{10} 5s^2$,
(d) Gd: $1s^2 2s^2 2p^6 3s^2 3p^6 3d^{10} 4s^2 4p^6 4d^{10} 4f^7 5s^2 5p^6 5d^1 6s^2$.
7.9 The electron configuration of an element follows the periodic table. The electrons are filled in the order of the periodic table and the energy levels are determined by the row the element is in and the subshell is given by the column, the first two columns are the s-block, the last six columns are the p-block, the d-block has ten columns, and the f-block has 14 columns.
7.10 (a) O: $1s^2 2s^2 2p^4$, S: $1s^2 2s^2 2p^6 3s^2 3p^4$,
Se: $1s^2 2s^2 2p^6 3s^2 3p^6 3d^{10} 4s^2 4p^4$,
(b) P: $1s^2 2s^2 2p^6 3s^2 3p^3$, N: $1s^2 2s^2 2p^3$,
Sb: $1s^2 2s^2 2p^6 3s^2 3p^6 3d^{10} 4s^2 4p^6 4d^{10} 5s^2 5p^3$.
The elements have the same number of electrons in the valence shell, and the only differences between the valence shells are the energy levels.

7.11 (a) Na: (orbital diagram) $1s$ $2s$ $2p$ $3s$ $3p$ $4s$ $3d$
(b) S: (orbital diagram) $1s$ $2s$ $2p$ $3s$ $3p$ $4s$ $3d$
(c) Fe: (orbital diagram) $1s$ $2s$ $2p$ $3s$ $3p$ $4s$ $3d$

7.12 (a)
Mg: (orbital diagram) $1s$ $2s$ $2p$ $3s$ $3p$ $4s$ $3d$ $4p$
0 unpaired electrons
(b)
Ge: (orbital diagram) $1s$ $2s$ $2p$ $3s$ $3p$ $4s$ $3d$ $4p$
2 unpaired electrons
(c)
Cd: (orbital diagram) $1s$ $2s$ $2p$ $3s$ $3p$ $4s$ $3d$ $4p$
(orbital diagram) $5s$ $4d$
0 unpaired electrons
(d)
Gd: (orbital diagram) $1s$ $2s$ $2p$ $3s$ $3p$ $4s$ $3d$ $4p$
(orbital diagram) $5s$ $4d$ $5p$ $6s$ $5d$ $4f$
8 unpaired electrons

7.13 Yes, Ti, Cr, Fe, Ni and the elements in their groups have even numbers of electrons and are paramagnetic. Additionally, oxygen has eight electrons, but it is paramagnetic since it has two unpaired electrons in the $2p$ orbitals.

7.14 (a) P: [Ne]$3s^2 3p^3$
[Ne] (orbital diagram) $3s$ $3p$ (3 unpaired electrons),

(b) Sn: [Kr]$4d^{10} 5s^2 5p^2$
[Kr] (orbital diagram) $4d$ $5s$ $5p$ (2 unpaired electrons)

7.15 For representative elements the valence shell is defined as the occupied shell with the highest value of n. In a ground state atom, only s and p electrons fit that definition.
7.16 (a) Se: $4s^2 4p^4$, (b) Sn: $5s^2 5p^2$, (c) I: $5s^2 5p^5$.
7.17 (a) Sn, (b) Ga, (c) Cr, (d) S^{2-}.
7.18 (a) P, (b) Fe^{3+}, (c) Fe, (d) Cl$^-$.
7.19 (a) Be, (b) C. **7.20** (a) Na$^+$, (b) Mg^{2+}

Review Problems

7.73 6.98×10^{14} Hz. **7.75** 4.38×10^{13} Hz.
7.77 1.02×10^{15} Hz. **7.79** 2.97 m.
7.81 5.0×10^6 m, 5.0×10^3 km.
7.83 2.7×10^{-19} J, 1.6×10^5 J mol^{-1}.
7.85 (a) violet, (b) 7.307×10^{14} Hz, (c) 4.842×10^{-19} J.
7.87 1094 nm, We would not expect to see the light since it is not in the visible region.
7.89 1.737×10^{-6} m, infrared region. **7.91** (a) p, (b) f.
7.93 (a) $n = 3$, $\ell = 0$, (b) $n = 5$, $\ell = 2$.
7.95 0, 1, 2, 3, 4, 5. **7.97** (a) $m_\ell = 1, 0,$ or -1, (b) $m_\ell = 3, 2, 1, 0, -1, -2,$ or -3.
7.99 $\ell = 4$ $n = 5$.

7.101

n	ℓ	m_ℓ	m_s
2	1	-1	$+1/2$
2	1	-1	$-1/2$
2	1	0	$+1/2$
2	1	0	$-1/2$
2	1	$+1$	$+1/2$
2	1	$+1$	$-1/2$

7.103 21 electrons have $\ell = 1$, 20 electrons have $\ell = 2$.

7.105 (a) S $1s^22s^22p^63s^23p^4$, (b) K $1s^22s^22p^63s^23p^64s^1$,
(c) Ti $1s^22s^22p^63s^23p^63d^24s^2$,
(d) Sn $1s^22s^22p^63s^23p^63d^{10}4s^24p^64d^{10}5s^25p^2$.
7.107 (a) Mn paramagnetic, (b) As paramagnetic,
(c) S paramagnetic, (d) Sr not paramagnetic, (b) Ar not paramagnetic.
7.109 (a) Mg zero unpaired electrons, (b) P three unpaired
electrons, (c) V three unpaired electrons.
7.111 (a) Ni [Ar]$3d^84s^2$, (b) Cs [Xe]$6s^1$, (c) Ge [Ar]$3d^{10}4s^24p^2$,
(d) Br [Ar]$3d^{10}4s^24p^5$, (e) Bi [Xe]$4f^{14}5d^{10}6s^26p^3$.

7.113 (a) Mg:

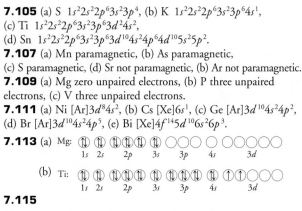

7.115

(a) 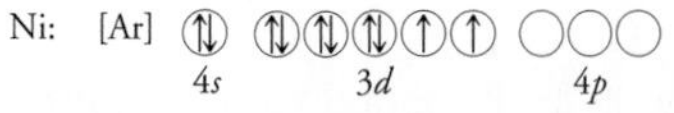 Ni: [Ar] ...
(b)  Cs: [Xe] ...
(c) 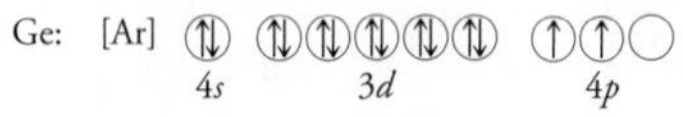 Ge: [Ar] ...
(d) 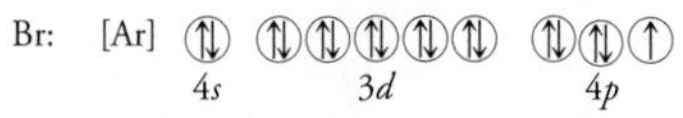 Br: [Ar] ...

7.117 (a) 5, (b) 4, (c) 4, (d) 6.

7.119 (a) $3s^1$, (b) $3s^23p^1$, (c) $4s^24p^2$, (d) $3s^23p^3$.

7.121 (a) 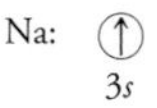 Na:
(b) 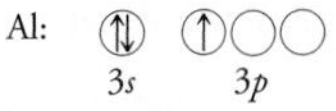 Al:
(c) 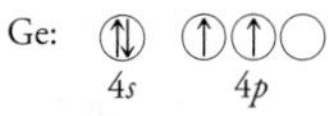 Ge:
(d) 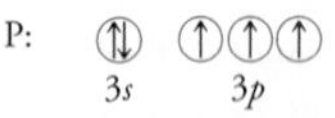 P:

7.123 (a) 1, (b) 6, (c) 7. **7.125** (a) Mg, (b) Bi. **7.127** Sb.
7.129 (a) Na, (b) Co^{2+}, (c) Cl$^-$. **7.131** (a) N, (b) S, (c) Cl.
7.133 (a) Br, (b) As. **7.135** Mg

CHAPTER 8

Practice Exercises

8.1 There is one electron missing, and it should go into
the $5s$ orbital, and the $5p$ orbital should be empty,
$1s^12s^22p^63s^23p^63d^{10}4s^24p^64d^{10}5s^2$.
8.2 (a) Cr^{2+}: [Ar]$3d^4$ The $4s$ electron and one $3d$ electron are lost,
(b) Cr^{3+}: [Ar]$3d^3$ The $4s$ electron and two $3d$ electrons are lost,
(c) Cr^{6+}: [Ar] The $4s$ electron and all of the $3d$ electrons are lost.
8.3 The electron configurations are identical.

8.4 :Ï· ·Ca· :Ï· ⟶ Ca^{2+} + 2[:Ï:]$^-$

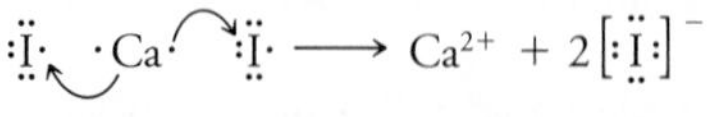

8.5 ·Ö: :Mg· ⟶ Mg^{2+} + [:Ö:]$^{2-}$

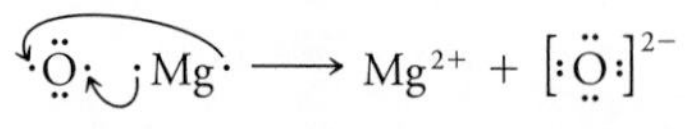

8.6 1.24 D. **8.7** 0.795 e^-, on Na: +0.795 e^-, on Cl: −0.795 e^-,
57.6% positive charge on the Na, 57.6% negative charge on the Cl.
8.8 The bond is polar and the Cl carries the negative charge.
8.9 (a) Br, (b) Cl, (c) Cl.
8.10

```
              O
    H   O   P   O   H
              O
```
32 valence electrons.

8.11

```
        O   S   O

            O
        O   N   O

            O
        O   Br   O   H

            H
            O
    H   O   As   O   H
            O
```

8.12 18 valence electrons, 32 valence electrons, 10 valence
electrons.

8.13 :F̈—Ö—F̈:

[H—N(H)—H]$^+$

[:Ö—N=Ö:]$^-$

Ö=S—Ö: :F̈—C̈l—F̈:   H—Ö—C̈l—Ö:
                                    :Ö:

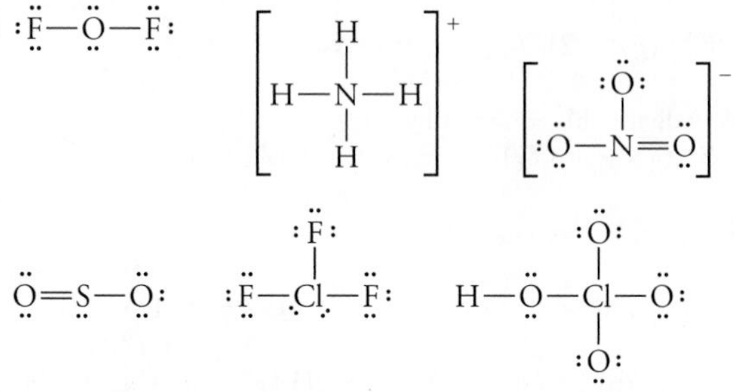

8.14 The negative sign should be on the oxygen, so two of the
oxygen atoms should have a single bond and three lone pairs and
the sulfur should have one double bond, two single bonds, and a
lone pair.

8.15 (a) 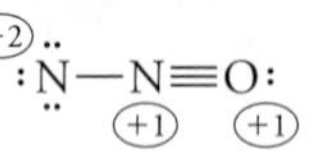 $^{(-2)}$:N̈—N≡O: $_{(+1)(+1)}$ (b) 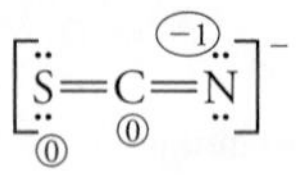 [S̈=C=N̈]$^-$ $_{0\ 0}^{(-1)}$

8.16 (a) 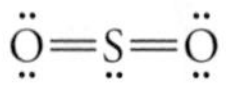 Ö=S=Ö

(b) 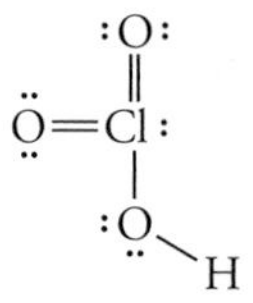 Ö=C̈l:
    with :O: above and :O—H below

(c) phosphorus structure with O, H, P=O

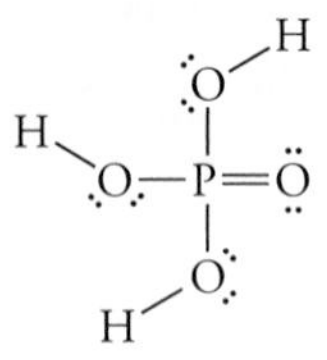

8.17

H—N(H)—H + H$^+$ ⟶ [H—N(H)—H]$^+$

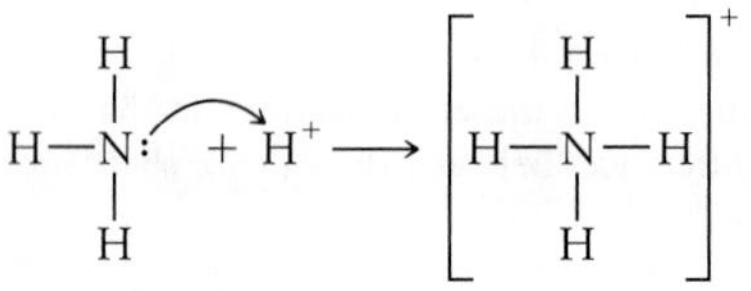

There is no difference between the coordinate covalent bond and
the other covalent bonds.

8.18 H—Ö:$^-$ + H$^+$ ⟶ H—Ö—H

coordinate covalent bond

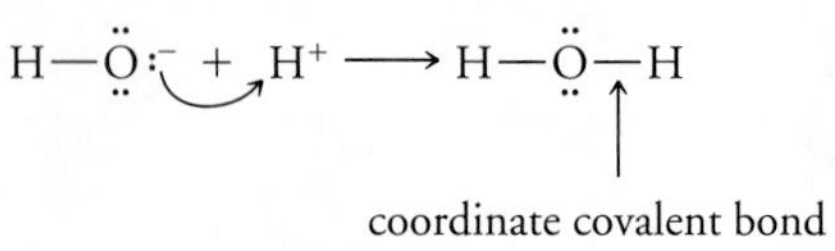

8.19

$$\left[\begin{array}{c} :\overset{..}{O}: \\ \overset{..}{O}=P-\overset{..}{O}: \\ :\overset{..}{O}: \end{array}\right]^{3-} \longleftrightarrow \left[\begin{array}{c} :\overset{..}{O}: \\ :\overset{..}{O}-P=\overset{..}{O} \\ :\overset{..}{O}: \end{array}\right]^{3-} \longleftrightarrow$$

$$\left[\begin{array}{c} :\overset{..}{O}: \\ :\overset{..}{O}-P-\overset{..}{O}: \\ :\overset{..}{O}: \end{array}\right]^{3-} \longleftrightarrow \left[\begin{array}{c} :O: \\ :\overset{..}{O}-P=O \\ :\overset{..}{O}: \end{array}\right]^{3-}$$

8.20

$$\left[\begin{array}{c} H \\ :\overset{..}{O}: \\ \overset{..}{O}=C-\overset{..}{O}: \end{array}\right]^{-} \longleftrightarrow \left[\begin{array}{c} H \\ :\overset{..}{O}: \\ :\overset{..}{O}-C=\overset{..}{O} \end{array}\right]^{-}$$

8.21

$$\left[\begin{array}{c} :\overset{..}{O}: \\ \overset{..}{O}\diagup^{Br}\diagdown\overset{..}{O}: \end{array}\right]^{-} \longleftrightarrow \left[\begin{array}{c} :\overset{..}{O}: \\ \overset{..}{O}\diagup^{Br}\diagdown\overset{..}{O} \end{array}\right]^{-} \longleftrightarrow \left[\begin{array}{c} :\overset{..}{O}: \\ \overset{..}{O}\diagup^{Br}\diagdown\overset{..}{O} \end{array}\right]^{-}$$

Review Problems

8.55 Magnesium loses two electrons, Bromine gains an electron: To keep the overall change of the formula unit neutral, two Br^- ions combine with one Mg^{2+} ion to form $MgBr_2$.

8.57 $[Xe]4f^{14}5d^{10}6s^2$, $[Xe]4f^{14}5d^{10}$.

8.59 $[Ar]3d^4$ 4 unpaired electrons.

8.61 (a) $\cdot\overset{..}{Si}\cdot$ (b) $:\overset{..}{Sb}\cdot$ (c) $\cdot Ba\cdot$ (d) $\cdot\overset{.}{Al}\cdot$ (e) $:\overset{.}{S}:$

8.63

(a) $:\overset{..}{Br}\overset{\curvearrowright}{\cdot}_j Ca \overset{\curvearrowleft}{\cdot}\overset{..}{Br}: \longrightarrow Ca^{2+} + 2\left[:\overset{..}{Br}:\right]^-$

(b) $\overset{..}{\cdot O}\cdot Al\cdot\overset{..}{O}\cdot Al\cdot\overset{..}{O}\cdot \longrightarrow 2Al^+ + 3\left[:\overset{..}{O}:\right]^{2-}$

(c) $K\cdot\overset{..}{S}\cdot K \longrightarrow 2K^+ + \left[:\overset{..}{S}:\right]^{2-}$

8.65 0.029 e^-, The nitrogen atom is positive. **8.67** 0.42 e^-.
8.69 1.4×10^3 g. **8.71** 344 nm, Ultraviolet region.
8.73

(a) $:\overset{..}{Br}\cdot + \cdot\overset{..}{Br}: \longrightarrow :\overset{..}{Br}-\overset{..}{Br}:$

(b) $2H\cdot + \cdot\overset{..}{O}\cdot \longrightarrow H-\overset{..}{O}:$
$\quad\quad\quad\quad\quad\quad\quad\quad\quad | $
$\quad\quad\quad\quad\quad\quad\quad\quad\quad H$

(c) $3H\cdot + \cdot\overset{..}{N}\cdot \longrightarrow H-N-H$
$\quad\quad\quad\quad\quad\quad\quad\quad\quad\quad | $
$\quad\quad\quad\quad\quad\quad\quad\quad\quad\quad H$

8.75 (a) H_2Se, (b) H_3As, (c) SiH_4. **8.77** (a) S, (b) Si, (c) Br, (d) C. **8.79** N—S.

8.81 (a)

	Cl	
Cl	Si	Cl
	Cl	

(b)

	F	
F	P	F

(c)

	H	
H	P	H

(d)

| Cl | S | Cl |

8.83 (a) 32, (b) 26, (c) 8, (d) 20.

8.85 (a)

$$\left[\begin{array}{c} :\overset{..}{Cl}: \\ :\overset{..}{Cl}-As-\overset{..}{Cl}: \\ :\overset{..}{Cl}: \end{array}\right]^{+}$$

(b) $\left[:\overset{..}{O}-\overset{..}{Cl}-\overset{..}{O}:\right]^-$

(c) $H-\overset{..}{O}-\overset{.}{N}=\overset{..}{O}$

(d) $:\overset{..}{F}-\overset{..}{Xe}-\overset{..}{F}:$

8.87 (a)

$$\begin{array}{c} :\overset{..}{Cl}: \\ :\overset{..}{Cl}-Si-\overset{..}{Cl}: \\ :\overset{..}{Cl}: \end{array}$$

(b)

$$\begin{array}{c} :\overset{..}{F}-P-\overset{..}{F}: \\ :\overset{..}{F}: \end{array}$$

(c) $H-P-H$
$\quad\quad\; |$
$\quad\quad\; H$

(d) $:\overset{..}{Cl}-\overset{..}{S}-\overset{..}{Cl}:$

8.89 (a) $\overset{..}{S}=C=\overset{..}{S}$ (b) $\left[:C\equiv N:\right]^-$

8.91 (a) $H-\overset{..}{As}-H$
$\quad\quad\quad\quad |$
$\quad\quad\quad\quad H$

(b) $H-\overset{..}{O}-\overset{..}{Cl}-\overset{..}{O}:$

(c)

$$\begin{array}{c} :O: \\ \| \\ H-\overset{..}{O}-Se-\overset{..}{O}-H \end{array}$$

(d)

$$\begin{array}{c} :\overset{..}{O}-H \\ :\overset{..}{O}-As-\overset{..}{O}: \\ | \\ H-\overset{..}{O}: \; H \end{array}$$

8.93 (a)

$$\begin{array}{c} H\diagdown \\ \quad\quad C=\overset{..}{O} \\ H\diagup \end{array}$$

(b)

$$\begin{array}{c} :O: \\ \| \\ :\overset{..}{Cl}-S-\overset{..}{Cl}: \end{array}$$

8.95 (a)

$$\overset{(0)}{H}-\overset{(0)}{\overset{..}{O}}-\overset{(1+)}{Cl}-\overset{(1-)}{\overset{..}{O}}:$$
$$\quad\quad\quad\quad\underset{(0)}{}$$

(b)

$$\begin{array}{c} :\overset{(1-)}{\overset{..}{O}}: \\ \| \\ \overset{(0)}{\overset{..}{O}}=\overset{(2+)}{S}-\overset{(1-)}{\overset{..}{O}}: \end{array}$$

(c) $\overset{(0)}{\overset{..}{O}}=\overset{(1+)}{S}-\overset{(1-)}{\overset{..}{O}}:$

8.97

$$\begin{array}{c} \overset{(1-)}{} \;:\overset{..}{O}: \\ \overset{(1-)}{:\overset{..}{O}}-\overset{(3+)}{Cl}-\overset{(0)}{\overset{..}{O}} \\ \quad\quad :\overset{..}{O}: \quad H \\ \quad\quad \overset{(1-)}{} \quad\quad \overset{(0)}{} \end{array}$$

$$\begin{array}{c} \overset{..}{O} \\ \overset{..}{O}-Cl=O \\ H\quad\quad \overset{..}{O}. \end{array}$$

8.99 The formal charges on all of the atoms of the left structure are zero, therefore, the potential energy of this molecule is lower and it is more stable.

8.101 The average bond order is 4/3

$$\left[\begin{array}{c} :\overset{..}{O}: \\ \overset{C}{} \\ \overset{..}{O}\quad\overset{..}{O}. \end{array}\right]^{2-} \longleftrightarrow \left[\begin{array}{c} :\overset{..}{O}: \\ \overset{C}{} \\ :\overset{..}{O}\quad\overset{..}{O}. \end{array}\right]^{2-} \longleftrightarrow \left[\begin{array}{c} :\overset{..}{O}: \\ \overset{C}{} \\ :\overset{..}{O}\quad\overset{..}{O} \end{array}\right]^{2-}$$

8.103 The N—O bond in NO_2^- should be shorter than that in NO_3^-.

8.105. :O≡C—Ö: ⟷ :Ö—C≡O:

These are not preferred structures, because in each Lewis diagram, one oxygen atom bears a formal charge of +1 whereas the other bears a formal charge of −1. The structure with the formal charges of zero has a lower potential energy and is more stable.

8.107

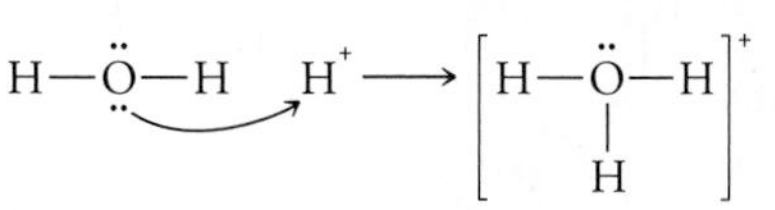

$$H—\overset{..}{\underset{..}{O}}—H \quad H^+ \longrightarrow \left[H—\overset{..}{\underset{|}{O}}—H \right]^+$$
$$\qquad\qquad\qquad\qquad\qquad\quad H$$

CHAPTER 9

Practice Exercises

9.1 Octahedral shape. **9.2** Trigonal bipyramidal. **9.3** Linear. **9.4** Linear. **9.5** Square planar. **9.6** SO_3^{2-} trigonal pyramidal, CO_3^{2-} planar triangular, XeO_4 tetrahedral, OF_2 bent. **9.7** Polar. **9.8** (a) SF_6 Not polar, (b) SO_2 Polar, (c) BrCl Polar, (d) AsH_3, Polar, (e) CF_2Cl_2 Polar. **9.9** The H—Cl bond is formed by the overlap of the half–filled $1s$ atomic orbital of a H atom with the half–filled $3p$ valence orbital of a Cl atom,

Cl atom in HCl (x = H electron):

$\qquad 3s \qquad\quad 3p$

The overlap that gives rise to the H—Cl bond is that of a $1s$ orbital of H with a $3p$ orbital of Cl.

9.10 The half–filled $1s$ atomic orbital of each H atom overlaps with a half–filled $3p$ atomic orbital of the P atom, to give three P–H bonds. This should give a bond angle of 90°,

P atom in PH_3 (x = H electron):

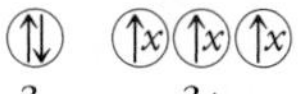

$\qquad 3s \qquad\quad 3p$

The orbital overlap that forms the P—H bond combines a $1s$ orbital of hydrogen with a $3p$ orbital of phosphorus:

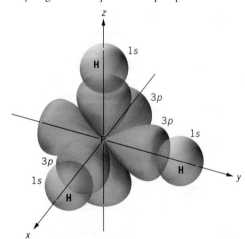

9.11 sp^2, The sp^2 hybrid orbitals on the B, x = Cl electron.

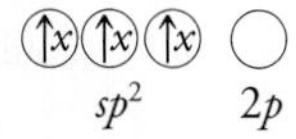

$\qquad sp^2 \qquad 2p$

9.12 sp, The sp hybrid orbitals on the Be; x = F electron.

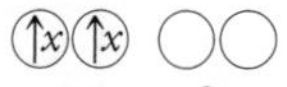

$\qquad sp \qquad 2p$

9.13 Since there are five bonding pairs of electrons on the central phosphorus atom, we choose sp^3d hybridization for the P atom. Each of phosphorus' five sp^3d hybrid orbitals overlaps with a $3p$ atomic orbital of a chlorine atom to form a total of five P—Cl single bonds. Four of the $3d$ atomic orbitals of P remain unhybridized.

9.14 sp^3

$\qquad sp^3$

9.15 Trigonal bipyramidal, sp^3d—p bonds. **9.16** sp^3d^2. **9.17** (a)sp^3, (b) sp^3d. **9.18** NH_3 is sp^3 hybridized. Three of the electron pairs are use for bonding with the three hydrogens. The fourth pair of electrons is a lone pair of electrons. This pair of electrons is used for the formation of the bond between the nitrogen of NH_3 and the hydrogen ion, H^+.

9.19 Octahedral. sp^3d^2,

P atom in PCl_6 (x = Cl electron):

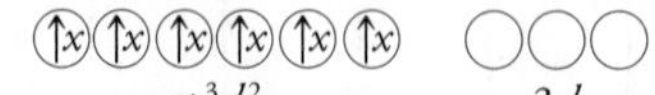

$\qquad sp^3d^2 \qquad\qquad 3d$

9.20 atom 1: sp^2, atom 2: sp^3, atom 3: sp^2, 10 σ bonds and 2 π bonds. **9.21** atom 1: sp, atom 2: sp^2, atom 3: sp^3, 9 σ bonds and 3 π bonds. **9.22** Bond order: 3 and this does agree with the Lewis structure.

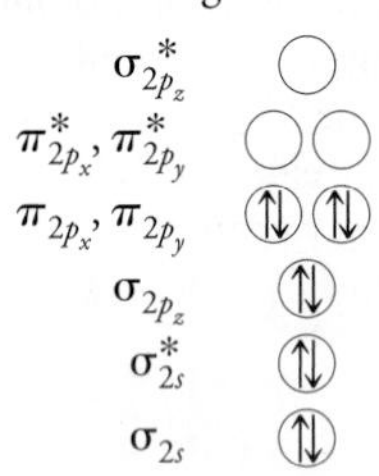

$\sigma_{2p_z}^*$

$\pi_{2p_x}^*, \pi_{2p_y}^*$

π_{2p_x}, π_{2p_y}

σ_{2p_z}

σ_{2s}^*

σ_{2s}

9.23

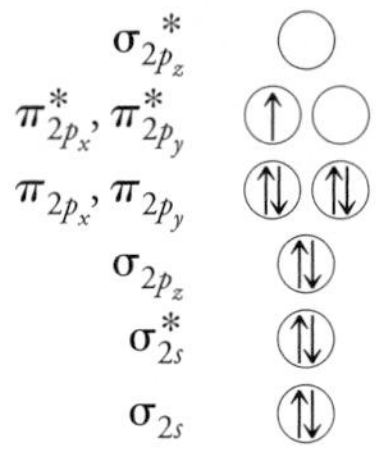

$\sigma_{2p_z}^*$

$\pi_{2p_x}^*, \pi_{2p_y}^*$

π_{2p_x}, π_{2p_y}

σ_{2p_z}

σ_{2s}^*

σ_{2s}

Bond order: 5/2:

Review Problems

9.50 (a) Bent, (b) Planar triangular, (c) T-shaped, (d) Linear, (e) Planar triangular. **9.52** (a) Nonlinear, (b) Trigonal bipyramidal, (c) Trigonal pyramidal, (d) Trigonal pyramidal, (e) Nonlinear. **9.54** (a) Tetrahedral, (b) Square planar, (c) Octahedral, (d) Tetrahedral, (e) Linear. **9.56** BrF_4^-. **9.58** 180°. **9.60** (a) 109.5°, (b) 109.5°, (c) 120°, (d) 180°, (e) 109.5°. **9.62** (a), (b), and (c). **9.64** All are polar. **9.66** In SF_6, although the individual bonds in this substance are polar bonds, the geometry of the bonds is symmetrical which serves to cause the individual dipole moments of the various bonds to cancel one another. In SF_5Br, one of the six bonds has a different polarity so the individual dipole moments of the various bonds do not cancel one another. **9.68** The $1s$ atomic orbitals of the hydrogen atoms overlap with the mutually perpendicular p atomic orbitals of the selenium atom.

Se atom in H_2Se (x = H electron):

$\qquad 4s \qquad\quad 4p$

9.70

Hybridized Be: (x = a Cl electron)

9.72 (a) sp^3

(b) sp^2

(c) sp^3

9.74 (a) sp^3,
The hybrid orbital diagram for As: (x = a Cl electron).

(b) sp^3d,
The hybrid orbital diagram for Cl: (x = a F electron).

9.76 Sb in SbF_6^-: (xx = an electron pair from the donor F^-).

sp^3d^2

9.78 (a) N in the C≡N system,

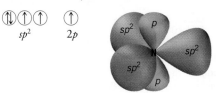

(b) pi bond,

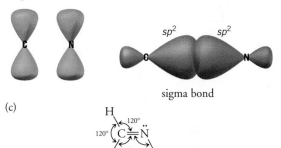

sigma bond

(c)

9.80 Each carbon atom is sp^2 hybridized, and each C—Cl bond is formed by the overlap of an sp^2 hybrid of carbon with a p atomic orbital of a chlorine atom. The C=C double bond consists first of a C—C σ bond formed by "head on" overlap of sp^2 hybrids from each C atom. Secondly, the C=C double bond consists of a side–to–side overlap of unhybridized p orbitals of each C atom, to give one π bond. The molecule is planar, and the expected bond angles are all 120°. **9.82** 1. sp^3, 2. sp, 3. sp^2, 4. sp^2. **9.84** (a) O_2^+, (b) O_2, (c) N_2. **9.86** (a) N_2^+, (b) NO, (c) O_2^-.

9.88

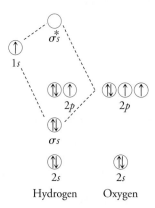

2 electrons in bonding MOs and 3 electrons in nonbonding MOs,
Bond order: 1

CHAPTER 10

Practice Exercises

10.1 14.1 psi, 28.7 in. Hg. **10.2** 88,800 Pascal, 666 torr.
10.3 1270 mm Hg, 270 mm Hg. **10.4** 663 mm Hg. **10.5** 2/3.
10.6 750 torr. **10.7** 688 torr. **10.8** 9.00 L O_2. **10.9** 64.3 L air.
10.10 495 mL O_2. **10.11** 15,000 g solid CO_2. **10.12** 1,130 g Ar.
10.13 26.0 g/mol. **10.14** 132 g mol^{-1}, Xenon. **10.15** Radon is almost eight times denser than air, the sensor should be in the basement. **10.16** 2.94 g L^{-1}. **10.17** P_2F_4. **10.18** 114 g mol^{-1}, 9 C and 6 H, 8 C and 18 H, 7 C and 30 H, 6 C and 42 H, 5 C and 54 H, 4 C and 66 H, 3 C and 78 H, 2 C and 90 H, 1 C and 102 H, 8 C and 18 H is the most likely combination.
10.19 2.80 L CO_2, 5.60 L SO_2, Total volume = 8.40 L.
10.20 1.00 g $CaCO_3$. **10.21** P_{Ar} = 6.01 atm, P_{N_2} = 8.59 atm, P_{O_2} = 7.53 atm, P_{total} = 22.13 atm. **10.22** 2713 g O_2.
10.23 743.18 torr, 0.0983 mol CH_4. **10.24** 732 torr 283 mL.
10.25 1.125 atm when just added, 0.750 atm when reaction is complete. **10.26** P_{H_2} = 0.996 atm, P_{NO} = 1.05 atm.
10.27 0.153, 15.3%. **10.28** 0.988. **10.29** HI

Review Problems

10.25 (a) 958 torr, (b) 0.974 atm, (c) 738 mm Hg, (d) 10.9 torr.
10.27 (a) 250 torr, (b) 350 torr.
10.29 4.5 cm Hg,

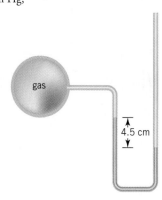

gas

4.5 cm

10.31 813 torr. **10.33** 125 torr. **10.35** 507 mL. **10.37** 4.28 L.
10.39 843 °C. **10.41** 796 torr. **10.43** 5.73 L.
10.45 −53.4 °C. **10.47** 6.24 × 10^4 mL torr mol^{-1} K^{-1}.
10.49 0.104 L. **10.51** 2340 torr. **10.53** 0.0398 g.
10.55 (a) 1.34 g L^{-1}, (b) 1.25 g L^{-1}, (c) 3.17 g L^{-1}, (d) 1.78 g L^{-1}.
10.57 1.28 g/L. **10.59** 88.2 g/mol. **10.61** 27.6 g/mol.
10.63 1.14 × 10^3 mL. **10.65** 10.7 L H_2. **10.67** 36.3 mL O_2.

10.69 217 mL. **10.71** 650 torr. **10.73** P_{N_2} = 228 torr, P_{O_2} = 152 torr, P_{He} = 304 torr, P_{CO_2} = 76 torr. **10.75** 736 torr, 260 mL. **10.77** 250 mL. **10.79** N_2, 1.25. **10.81** $^{235}UF_6$ 1.0043

CHAPTER 11

Practice Exercises

11.1 (a) $CH_3CH_2CH_2CH_2CH_3 < CH_3CH_2OH < Ca(OH)_2$, (b) $CH_3-O-CH_3 < CH_3CH_2NH_2 < HOCH_2CH_2CH_2CH_2OH$.
11.2 Propylamine, because of its ability to form hydrogen bonds.
11.3 Pushed in. **11.4** The total number of molecules remains the same. **11.5** (a) less than 10 °C. **11.6** 75 °C.
11.7 The equilibrium will shift to the right, producing more vapor.
11.8 Boiling,   Endothermic,
Melting,   Endothermic,
Condensing,   Exothermic,
Subliming,   Endothermic,
Freezing,   Exothermic,
No, each physical change is always exothermic, or always endothermic as shown. **11.9** 4 Ca^{2+} and 8 F^-. **11.10** 1 to 1.
11.11 Molecular crystal. **11.12** Covalent or network solid.
11.13 Molecular solid. **11.14** Vapor pressure curve, see Fig. 11.21.
11.15 Solid to gas. **11.16** Liquid.

Review Problems

11.78 Diethyl ether. **11.80** (a) London forces, dipole- dipole and hydrogen bonding, (b) London forces and dipole- dipole, (c) London forces, (d) London forces and dipole- dipole.
11.82 Chloroform would be expected to display larger dipole-dipole attractions because it has a larger dipole moment than bromoform. On the other hand, bromoform would be expected to show stronger London forces due to having larger electron clouds which are more polarizable than those of chlorine. Since bromoform in fact has a higher boiling point that chloroform, we must conclude that it experiences stronger intermolecular attractions than chloroform, which can only be due to London forces. Therefore, London forces are more important in determining the boiling points of these two compounds. **11.84** Ethanol.
11.86 ether < acetone < benzene < water < acetic acid.
11.88 305 kJ. **11.90** (a) 0 °C, (b) 47.9 g.
11.92 4 Zn^{2+}, 4 S^{2-}. **11.94** 3.51 Å., 351 pm. **11.96** 656 pm.
11.98 (a) 6.57°, (b) 27.3°. **11.100** 176 pm. **11.102** Molecular solid. **11.104** Metallic solid. **11.106** (a)molecular, (b) ionic, (c) ionic, (d) metallic, (e) covalent, (f) molecular, (g) ionic.
11.108

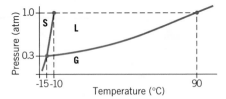

11.110 (a) solid, (b) gas, (c) liquid, (d) solid, liquid, and gas

CHAPTER 12

Practice Exercises

12.1 3.4 g L^{-1} atm^{-1}. Hydrogen sulfide is more soluble in water than nitrogen and oxygen. Hydrogen sulfide reacts with the water to form hydronium ions and $HS^-(aq)$ ions. **12.2** 0.899 mg of O_2, 1.48 mg of N_2. **12.3** 405.7 mL water. **12.4** 2.50 g NaBr, 248 g H_2O, 251 mL H_2O. **12.5** 2.0×10^1 g solution. **12.6** 1.239 m, Smaller. **12.7** 16.0 g CH_3OH. **12.8** (a) 28.3 g solution, (b) 70.7 g solution, (c) 1.41 g solution. **12.9** 25 m NaOH.

12.10 16.1 m. **12.11** 6.82 M. **12.12** 0.00469 M $Al(NO_3)_3$, 0.00470 m $Al(NO_3)_3$. **12.13** 9.02 torr. **12.14** 61.2 g stearic acid. **12.15** 55.4 torr. **12.16** 45.0 torr. **12.17** 100.16 °C.
12.18 209 g glucose. **12.19** 157 g/mol. **12.20** 125 g mol^{-1}.
12.21 3.75 mm Hg, 51.1 mm H_2O. **12.22** 0.051 g.
12.23 4.99×10^4 g mol^{-1}. **12.24** 5.38×10^2 g mol^{-1}.
12.25 −0.882 °C, −0.441 °C. **12.26** (a) 0.372 °C, (b) 0.0372 °C, (c) 0.00372 °C, The first freezing point depression could be measured using a laboratory thermometer that can measure 0.1 °C increments.

Review Problems

12.38
(a) $KCl(s) \longrightarrow K^+(g) + Cl^-(g)$, $\Delta H° = +690$ kJ mol^{-1}
(b) $K^+(g) + Cl^-(g) \longrightarrow K^+(aq) + Cl^-(aq)$, $\underline{\Delta H° = -686$ kJ $mol^{-1}}$
          $KCl(s) \longrightarrow K^+(aq) + Cl^-(aq)$, $\Delta H° = +4$ kJ mol^{-1}
12.40 0.038 g/L. **12.42** 0.020 g L^{-1}. **12.44** 3.35 m.
12.46 0.133 molal, 2.39×10^{-3}, 2.34%. **12.48** = 5.45%.
12.50 7.89%, 4.76 m. **12.52** 0.359 M $NaNO_3$, 3.00%, 6.49×10^{-3}. **12.54** 22.8 torr. **12.56** 52.7 torr. **12.58** 70 mol % toluene and 30 mol % benzene. **12.60** (a) 0.029, (b) 2.99×10^{-2} mol soute, (c) 278 g/mol. **12.62** 55.1 g. **12.64** 152 g/mol.
12.66 127 g/mol, $C_8H_4N_2$.

12.68 (a) $\dfrac{(g) \times (L\ atm\ mol^{-1}K^{-1}) \times (K)}{L \times atm} = \dfrac{g}{mol}$,
(b) 1.8×10^6 g/mol. **12.70** 15.3 torr. **12.72** 1.3×10^4 torr.
12.74 −1.1 °C. **12.76** 2. **12.78** 1.89

CHAPTER 13

Practice Exercises

13.1 Rate of production of I^- = 8.0×10^{-5} mol L^{-1} s^{-1}, Rate of production of SO_4^{2-} = 2.4×10^{-4} mol L^{-1} s^{-1}. **13.2** Rate of disappearance of O_2 = 0.45 mol L^{-1} s^{-1}. Rate of disappearance of H_2S = 0.30 mol L^{-1} s^{-1}. **13.3** -2.1×10^{-4} mol L^{-1} s^{-1}.
13.4 1×10^{-4} mol L^{-1} s^{-1} is correct.
13.5 (a) 9.8×10^{14} L^2 mol^{-2} s^{-1}, (b) L^2 mol^{-2} s^{-1}.
13.6 (a) 8.0×10^{-2} L mol^{-1} s^{-1}, (b) L mol^{-1} s^{-1}.
13.7 order of the reaction with respect to $[BrO_3^-]$ = 1, order of the reaction with respect to $[SO_3^{2-}]$ = 1, overall order of the reaction = 1 + 1 = 2. **13.8** Rate = $k[Cl_2]^2[NO]$.
13.9 k = 2.0×10^2 L^2 mol^{-2} s^{-1}. Each of the other data sets also gives the same value.
13.10 (a) The rate will increase nine–fold, (b) The rate will increase three–fold, (c) The rate will decrease by three fourths.
13.11 rate = $k[NO]^n$ $[H_2]^m$, (a) rate = $k[NO]^2$ $[H_2]^1$, (b) k = 2.1×10^5 mol^{-2} L^2 s^{-1}, (c) mol^{-2} L^2 s^{-1}.
13.12 (a) First order with respect to sucrose. (b) 6.17×10^{-4} s^{-1}.
13.13 (a) Rate = $k[A]^2[B]^2$, (b) k = 6.9×10^{-3} L^3 mol^{-3} s^{-1}, (c) L^3 mol^{-3} s^{-1}, (d) 4. **13.14** k = 2.56×10^{-2} yr^{-1}.
13.15 (a) 0.26 M, (b) 77 min. **13.16** 18.7 min, 37.4 min.
13.17 27.0 yr. **13.18** 1.72×10^4 yrs.
13.19 24,800 years BP, 424 years BP.
13.20 63 min. **13.21** 4.0×10^{-4} M.
13.22 1.03 L mol^{-1} s^{-1}, $t_{1/2}$ = 1.48×10^3 s.
13.23 The reaction is first–order. **13.24** 45 °C.
13.25 a) 1.4×10^2 kJ/mol, b) 0.30 L mol^{-1} s^{-1}.
13.26 (a), (b), and (e) may be elementary processes. Equations (c), (d), and (f) are not elementary processes because they have more than two molecules colliding at one time, and this is very unlikely.
13.27 Rate = $k[NO][O_3]$.

13.28 Rate = $\dfrac{k[NO_2Cl]^2}{[NO_2]}$

Review Problems

13.47

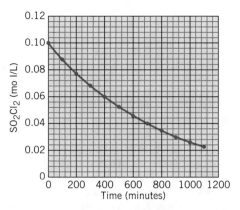

At 200 min: 1×10^{-4} M/s At 600 minutes: 7×10^{-5} M/s.

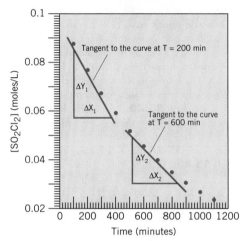

13.49 The rate of disappearance of hydrogen is three times the rate of disappearance of nitrogen. NH_3 appears twice as fast as N_2 disappears. **13.51** (a) rate for $O_2 = 11.4$ mol L^{-1} s^{-1}, (b) rate for $CO_2 = 7.20$ mol L^{-1} s^{-1}, (c) rate for $H_2O = 8.40$ mol L^{-1} s^{-1}.
13.53 rate $= 8.0 \times 10^{-11}$ mol L^{-1} s^{-1}.
13.55 rate $= 2.4 \times 10^{2}$ mol L^{-1} s^{-1}.
13.57 rate $= k \times [M][N]^2$, $k = 2.5 \times 10^3$ L^2 mol^{-2} s^{-1}.
13.59 rate $= k[OCl^-][I^-]$, $k = 6.1 \times 10^9$ L mol^{-1} s^{-1}.
13.61 rate $= k[ICl][H_2]$, $k = 1.5 \times 10^{-1}$ L mol^{-1} s^{-1}.
13.63

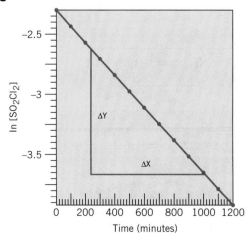

$k = 1.32 \times 10^{-3}$ min^{-1}.
13.65 (a) $x = 3.7 \times 10^{-3}$ M, (b) $x = 6.0 \times 10^{-4}$ M.

13.67 4.26×10^{-3} min^{-1}. **13.69** 1.3×10^4 min.
13.71 1/256. **13.73** Approximately 500 min, The reaction is first–order in SO_2Cl_2. **13.75** 1.3×10^9 years old.
13.77 2.7×10^4 years ago.
13.79 $E_a = 7.93 \times 10^4$ J/mol $= 79.3$ kJ/mol.
13.81 $E_a = 99$ kJ mol^{-1} and $A = 6.6 \times 10^9$ L mol^{-1} s^{-1}.
13.83 Use equation 13.10: (a) 1.9×10^{-5} s^{-1}, (b) 1.6×10^{-1} s^{-1}

CHAPTER 14

Practice Exercises

14.1 $2N_2O_3 + O_2 \rightleftharpoons 4NO_2$.

14.2 (a) $\dfrac{[H_2O]^2}{[H_2]^2[O_2]} = K_c$, (b) $\dfrac{[CO_2][H_2O]^2}{[CH_4][O_2]^2} = K_c$.

14.3 $K_c = 1.2 \times 10^{-13}$. **14.4** $K_c = 1.9 \times 10^5$.

14.5 $K_P = \dfrac{(P_{N_2O})^2}{(P_{N_2})^2(P_{O_2})}$. **14.6** $K_P = \dfrac{(P_{HI})^2}{(P_{H_2})(P_{I_2})}$.

14.7 $K_P = 1.8 \times 10^{36}$. **14.8** Smaller $K_c = 57$.

14.9 $K_c = \dfrac{1}{[NH_3(g)][HCl(g)]}$.

14.10 (a) $K_c = \dfrac{1}{[Cl_2(g)]}$,

(b) $K_c = [Na^+(aq)][OH^-(aq)][H_2(g)]$,

(c) $K_c = [Ag^+]^2[CrO_4^{2-}]$,

(d) $K_c = \dfrac{[Ca^{+2}(aq)][HCO_3^-(aq)]^2}{[CO_2(aq)]}$.

14.11 Reaction will proceed to the left. **14.12** Reaction (b).
14.13 There will be no change in the amount of H_3PO_4.
14.14 (a) Decreasing the concentration of Cl_2 at equilibrium, the value of K_P will be unchanged. (b) Increasing the amount of Cl_2 at equilibrium. The value of K_P will be unchanged, (c) Increasing the amount of Cl_2 at equilibrium. Decreasing the value of K_P. (d) Decreasing the concentration of Cl_2 at equilibrium, The value of K_P will be unchanged.
14.15 [CO] decreases by 0.060 mol/L and $[CO_2]$ increases by 0.060 mol/L. **14.16** $K_c = 4.06$.
14.17 (a) $[PCl_3] = 0.200$ M, $[Cl_2] = 0.100$ M, $[PCl_5] = 0.000$ M, (b) PCl_3 and Cl_2 have decreased by 0.080 M and PCl_5 has increased by 0.080 M. (c) $[PCl_3] = 0.120$ M. $[PCl_5] = 0.080$ M $[Cl_2] = 0.020$ M. (d) $K_c = 33$.
14.18 $[NO_2] = 1.04 \times 10^{-2}$ M.
14.19 $[C_2H_5OH] = 8.98 \times 10^{-3}$ M.
14.20 $[H_2] = [I_2] = 0.044$ M, $[HI] = 2(0.156) = 0.312$ M.
14.21 $[H_2] = 0.200 - 0.0934 = 0.107$ M, $[I_2] = 0.100 - 0.0934 = 0.0066$ M, $[HI] = 2(0.0934) = 0.1868$ M.
14.22 $[N_2] = 6.2 \times 10^{-4}$ M, $[H_2] = 1.9 \times 10^{-3}$ M.
14.23 [NO] $= 1.1 \times 10^{-17}$ M.

Review Problems

14.19 (a) $K_c = \dfrac{[POCl_3]^2}{[PCl_3]^2[O_2]}$, (b) $K_c = \dfrac{[SO_2]^2[O_2]}{[SO_3]^2}$,

(c) $K_c = \dfrac{[NO]^2[H_2O]^2}{[N_2H_4][O_2]^2}$, (d) $K_c = \dfrac{[NO_2]^2[H_2O]^8}{[N_2H_4][H_2O_2]^6}$,

(e) $K_c = \dfrac{[SO_2][HCl]^2}{[SOCl_2][H_2O]}$.

14.21 (a) $K_P = \dfrac{(P_{POCl_3})^2}{(P_{PCl_3})^2(P_{O_2})}$, (b) $K_P = \dfrac{(P_{SO_2})^2(P_{O_2})}{(P_{SO_3})^2}$,

(c) $K_P = \dfrac{(P_{NO})^2(P_{H_2O})^2}{(P_{N_2H_4})(P_{O_2})^2}$, (d) $K_P = \dfrac{(P_{NO_2})^2(P_{H_2O})^8}{(P_{N_2H_4})(P_{H_2O_2})^6}$,

(e) $K_P = \dfrac{(P_{SO_2})(P_{HCl})^2}{(P_{SOCl_2})(P_{H_2O})}$.

14.23 (a) $K_c = \dfrac{[Ag(NH_3)_2^+]}{[Ag^+][NH_3]^2}$, (b) $K_c = \dfrac{[Cd(SCN)_4^{2-}]}{[Cd^{2+}][SCN^-]^4}$.

14.25 $K = 1 \times 10^{85}$.

14.27 (a) $K_c = \dfrac{[HCl]^2}{[H_2][Cl_2]}$, (b) $K_c = \dfrac{[HCl]}{[H_2]^{1/2}[Cl_2]^{1/2}}$,

K_c for reaction (b) is the square root of K_c for reaction (a).
14.29 0.0375 M. **14.31** b. **14.33** $K_c = 11$.
14.35 $K_P = 2.7 \times 10^{-2}$. **14.37** $K_P = 5.4 \times 10^{-5}$.
14.39 (a) 55.5 M, (b) 55.5 M, (c) 55.5 M.

14.41 (a) $K_c = \dfrac{[CO]^2}{[O_2]}$, (b) $K_c = [H_2O][SO_2]$,

(c) $K_c = \dfrac{[CH_4][CO_2]}{[H_2O]^2}$, (d) $K_c = \dfrac{[H_2O][CO_2]}{[HF]^2}$,

(e) $K_c = [H_2O]^5$.
14.43 $[HI] = 1.47 \times 10^{-12}\ M$, $[Cl_2] = 7.37 \times 10^{-13}\ M$.
14.45 (a) The system shifts to the right to consume some of the added methane. (b) The system shifts to the left to consume some of the added hydrogen. (c) The system shifts to the right to make some more carbon disulfide. (d) The system shifts to the left to decrease the amount of gaseous moles. (e) The system shifts to the right to absorb some of the added heat.
14.47 (a) right, (b) left, (c) left, (d) right, (e) no effect, (f) left.
14.49 (a) No, (b) To the left. **14.51** $[CH_3OH] = 4.36 \times 10^{-3}\ M$.
14.53 $K_c = 0.398$. **14.55** $K_c = 0.0955$.
14.57 $K_c = 0.915$. **14.59** $[Br_2] = [Cl_2] = 0.011\ M$.
14.61 $[NO_2] = [SO_2] = 0.0497$ mol/L,
$[NO] = [SO_3] = 0.0703$ mol/L.
14.63 $[H_2] = [CO_2] = 7.7 \times 10^{-3}\ M$,
$[CO] = [H_2O] = 0.0123\ M$.
14.65 $[H_2] = [Cl_2] = 8.9 \times 10^{-19}\ M$.
14.67 $[CO] = 5.0 \times 10^{-4}\ M$. **14.69** $[PCl_5] = 3.0 \times 10^{-5}\ M$.
14.71 $[NO_2] = [SO_2] = 0.0281\ M$.
14.73 $[CO] = [H_2O] = 0.200\ M$.

CHAPTER 15

Practice Exercises

15.1 Conjugate acid base pairs (a), (c), and (f). (b) The conjugate base of HI is I^-. (d) The conjugate base of HNO_2 is NO_2^- and the conjugate base of NH_4^+ is NH_3. (e) The conjugate acid of CO_3^{2-} is HCO_3^- and the conjugate acid of CN^- is HCN.
15.2 (a) OH^-, (b) I^-, (c) NO_2^- (d) $H_2PO_4^-$, (e) HPO_4^{2-},
(f) PO_4^{3-}, (g) HS^- (h) NH_3. **15.3** (a) H_2O_2, (b) HSO_4^-,
(c) HCO_3^-, (d) HCN, (e) NH_3 (f) NH_4^+, (g) H_3PO_4
(h) $H_2PO_4^-$. **15.4** HCN and CN^-, HCl and Cl^-.
15.5 Brønsted acids: $H_2PO_4^-(aq)$ and $H_2CO_3(aq)$,
Brønsted bases: $HCO_3^-(aq)$ and $HPO_4^{2-}(aq)$.
15.6

conjugate pair

$$PO_4^{3-}(aq) + HC_2H_3O_2(aq) \rightleftharpoons HPO_4^{2-}(aq) + C_2H_3O_2^-(aq)$$
base · · · · · · acid · · · · · · · acid · · · · · · · · base

conjugate pair

15.7 (a) $H_2PO_4^-$ amphoteric since it can both accept and donate a proton, (b) HPO_4^{2-} amphoteric since it can both accept and

donate a proton, (c) H_2S amphoteric since it can both accept and donate a proton, (d) H_3PO_4 not amphoteric: it can only donate protons, (e) NH_4^+ not amphoteric: it can only donate protons, (f) H_2O amphoteric since it can both accept and donate a proton, (g) HI not amphoteric: it can only donate protons, (h) HNO_2 not amphoteric: it can only donate protons.
15.8 $HPO_4^{2-}(aq) + OH^-(aq) \longrightarrow PO_4^{3-}(aq) + H_2O$;
$HPO_4^{2-}(aq) + H_3O^+(aq) \longrightarrow H_2PO_4^- + H_2O$.
15.9 $HSO_4^-(aq) + HPO_4^{2-}(aq) \longrightarrow SO_4^{-2}(aq) + H_2PO_4^-(aq)$.
15.10 The substances on the right because they are the weaker acid and base. **15.11** (a) HF < HBr < HI, (b) PH_3 < H_2S < HCl,
(c) H_2O < H_2Se < H_2Te, (d) AsH_3 < H_2Se < HBr,
(e) PH_3 < H_2Se < HI. **15.12** (a) HBr, (b) H_2Te, (c) H_2S.
15.13 (a) $HClO_3$, (b) H_2SO_4. **15.14** (a) H_3AsO_4, (b) H_2TeO_4.
15.15 (a) HIO_4, (b) H_2TeO_4, (c) H_3AsO_4. **15.16** (a) H_2SO_4,
(b) H_3AsO_4. **15.17** (a) NH_3 Lewis base, H^+ Lewis acid, (b) CN^- Lewis base, H_2O Lewis acid, (c) Ag^+ Lewis acid, NH_3 Lewis base.
15.18 (a) Fluoride ions have a filled octet of electrons and are likely to behave as Lewis bases, i.e., electron pair donors. (b) $BeCl_2$ is a likely Lewis acid since it has an incomplete shell. The Be atom has only two valence electrons and it can easily accept a pair of electrons. (c) It could reasonably be considered a potential Lewis base since it contains three oxygens, each with lone pairs and partial negative charges. However, it is more effective as a Lewis acid, since the central sulfur bears a significant positive charge.
15.19 $8.3 \times 10^{-16}\ M$. **15.20** $1.3 \times 10^{-9}\ M$, Basic.
15.21 pOH = 9.75, $[H^+] = 5.62 \times 10^{-5}\ M$,
$[OH^-] = 1.78 \times 10^{-10}\ M$. **15.22** pH = 3.44, pOH = 10.56,
Basic. **15.23** 5.17. **15.24** CaO. **15.25** pH = 1.1,
pOH = 15.1. **15.26** (a) $[H^+] = 1.3 \times 10^{-3}\ M$,
$[OH^-] = 7.7 \times 10^{-12}\ M$, Acidic. (b) $[H^+] = 1.4 \times 10^{-4}\ M$,
$[OH^-] = 7.1 \times 10^{-11}\ M$, Acidic. (c) $[H^+] = 1.5 \times 10^{-11}\ M$,
$[OH^-] = 6.7 \times 10^{-4}\ M$, Basic. (d) $[H^+] = 7.8 \times 10^{-5}\ M$,
$[OH^-] = 1.3 \times 10^{-10}\ M$, Acidic. (e) $[H^+] = 2.5 \times 10^{-12}\ M$,
$[OH^-] = 4.0 \times 10^{-3}\ M$, Basic.
15.27 $[H^+] = 0.005\ M$, pH = 2.30, pOH = 11.70.
15.28 pOH = 1.068, pH = 12.932, $[H^+] = 1.17 \times 10^{-13}\ M$.
15.29 $[H^+] = 3.2 \times 10^{-6}\ M$.

Review Problems

15.41 (a) HF, (b) $N_2H_5^+$, (c) $C_5H_5NH^+$, (d) HO_2^-, (e) H_2CrO_4.
15.43

conjugate pair

(a) $HNO_3 + N_2H_4 \rightleftharpoons N_2H_5^+ + NO_3^-$
· · · · · acid · · · base · · · · · · acid · · · · base

conjugate pair

conjugate pair

(b) $N_2H_5^+ + NH_3 \rightleftharpoons NH_4^+ + N_2H_4$
· · · · · acid · · · base · · · · acid · · · · base

conjugate pair

conjugate pair

(c) $H_2PO_4^- + CO_3^{2-} \rightleftharpoons HCO_3^- + HPO_4^{2-}$
· · · · · acid · · · · base · · · · · acid · · · · · base

conjugate pair

conjugate pair

(d) $HIO_3 + HC_2O_4^- \rightleftharpoons H_2C_2O_4 + IO_3^-$
· · · · · acid · · · · base · · · · · acid · · · · · base

conjugate pair

15.45 (a) HBr, HBr bond is weaker, (b) HF, more electronegative F polarizes and weakens the bond, (c) HBr, larger Br forms a weaker bond with H. **15.47** (a) $HClO_2$, because it has more oxygen atoms, (b) H_2SeO_4, because it has more lone oxygen atoms. **15.49** (a) $HClO_3$, because Cl is more electronegative, (b) $HClO_3$, because the charge is more evenly distributed, (c) $HBrO_4$, because the negative charge is more evenly distributed.

15.51

Lewis bases: NH_2^- Lewis acid: H^+

15.53

15.55

15.57

Lewis bases: NH_2^- and OH^-; Lewis acid: H^+

15.59 $[D^+] = [OD^-] = 3.0 \times 10^{-8}$ M, pD = 7.52, pOD = 7.52.
15.61 (a) $[H^+] = 1.5 \times 10^{-12}$ M, pH = 11.83, pOH = 2.17,
(b) $[H^+] = 1.6 \times 10^{-10}$ M, pH = 9.81, pOH = 4.19,
(c) $[H^+] = 6.3 \times 10^{-7}$ M, pH = 6.20, pOH = 7.80,
(d) $[H^+] = 1.2 \times 10^{-3}$ M, pH = 2.91, pOH = 11.09.
15.63 4.72. **15.65** (a) $[H^+] = 7.2 \times 10^{-9}$ M,
$[OH^-] = 1.4 \times 10^{-6}$ M, (b) $[H^+] = 2.7 \times 10^{-3}$ M,
$[OH^-] = 3.6 \times 10^{-12}$ M, (c) $[H^+] = 5.6 \times 10^{-12}$ M,
$[OH^-] = 1.8 \times 10^{-3}$ M, (d) $[H^+] = 5.3 \times 10^{-14}$ M,
$[OH^-] = 1.9 \times 10^{-1}$ M, (e) $[H^+] = 2.0 \times 10^{-7}$ M,
$[OH^-] = 5.0 \times 10^{-8}$ M. **15.67** $[H^+] = 2.0 \times 10^{-6}$ M,
$[OH^-] = 5.0 \times 10^{-9}$ M. **15.69** pH = 3.19,
$[OH^-] = 1.55 \times 10^{-11}$ M. **15.71** 0.15 M OH^-,
pOH = 0.82, pH = 13.18, $[H^+] = 6.61 \times 10^{-14}$ M.
15.73 2.0×10^{-3} M $Ca(OH)_2$, 2.0×10^{-4} M $Ca(OH)_2$.
15.75 168 mL 0.0100 M KOH. **15.77** 5×10^{-12} M.

CHAPTER 16

Practice Exercises

16.1 (a) $HC_2H_3O_2 + H_2O \rightleftharpoons H_3O^+ + C_2H_3O_2^-$,
$$K_a = \frac{[H_3O^+][C_2H_3O_2^-]}{[HC_2H_3O_2]},$$

(b) $(CH_3)_3NH^+ + H_2O \rightleftharpoons H_3O^+ + (CH_3)_3N$,
$$K_a = \frac{[H_3O^+][(CH_3)_3N]}{[(CH_3)_3NH^+]},$$

(c) $H_3PO_4 + H_2O \rightleftharpoons H_3O^+ + H_2PO_4^-$,
$$K_a = \frac{[H_3O^+][H_2PO_4^-]}{[H_3PO_4]}.$$

16.2 (a) $HCHO_2 + H_2O \rightleftharpoons H_3O^+ + CHO_2^-$,
$$K_a = \frac{[H_3O^+][CHO_2^-]}{[HCHO_2]},$$

(b) $(CH_3)_2NH_2^+ + H_2O \rightleftharpoons H_3O^+ + (CH_3)_2NH$,
$$K_a = \frac{[H_3O^+][CH_3NH]}{[(CH_3)_2NH_2^+]},$$

(c) $H_2PO_4^- + H_2O \rightleftharpoons H_3O^+ + HPO_4^{2-}$,
$$K_a = \frac{[H_3O^+][HPO_4^{2-}]}{[H_2PO_4^-]}.$$

16.3 Barbituric acid. **16.4** HA is the strongest acid, For HA: $K_a = 6.9 \times 10^{-4}$, For HB: $K_a = 7.2 \times 10^{-5}$.
16.5 (a) $(CH_3)_3N + H_2O \rightleftharpoons (CH_3)_3NH^+ + OH^-$,
$$K_b = \frac{[(CH_3)_3NH^+][OH^-]}{[(CH_3)_3N]},$$

(b) $SO_3^{2-} + H_2O \rightleftharpoons HSO_3^- + OH^-$,
$$K_b = \frac{[HSO_3^-][OH^-]}{[SO_3^{2-}]},$$

(c) $NH_2OH + H_2O \rightleftharpoons NH_3OH^+ + OH^-$,
$$K_b = \frac{[NH_3OH^+][OH^-]}{[NH_2OH]}.$$

16.6 (a) $HSO_4^- + H_2O \rightleftharpoons H_2SO_4 + OH^-$,
$$K_b = \frac{[H_2SO_4][OH^-]}{[HSO_4^-]},$$

(b) $H_2PO_4^- + H_2O \rightleftharpoons H_3PO_4 + OH^-$,
$$K_b = \frac{[H_3PO_4][OH^-]}{[H_2PO_4^-]},$$

(c) $HPO_4^{2-} + H_2O \rightleftharpoons H_2PO_4^- + OH^-$,
$$K_b = \frac{[H_2PO_4^-][OH^-]}{[HPO_4^{2-}]},$$

(d) $HCO_3^- + H_2O \rightleftharpoons H_2CO_3 + OH^-$,
$$K_b = \frac{[H_2CO_3][OH^-]}{[HCO_3^-]},$$

(e) $HSO_3^- + H_2O \rightleftharpoons H_2SO_3 + OH^-$,
$$K_b = \frac{[H_2SO_3][OH^-]}{[HSO_3^-]}.$$

16.7 $K_b = 4.3 \times 10^{-4}$. **16.8** $K_b = 5.6 \times 10^{-11}$.
16.9 $K_a = 1.15 \times 10^{-3}$, p$K_a$ = 2.938.
16.10 $K_a = 1.7 \times 10^{-5}$, pK_a = 4.78.
16.11 $K_b = 1.6 \times 10^{-6}$, pK_b = 5.79.
16.12 $[H^+] = 5.4 \times 10^{-6}$ M, pH = 5.27.
16.13 $[H^+] = 8.4 \times 10^{-4}$ M, pH = 3.08.
16.14 pOH = 5.48. **16.15** pH = 8.59. **16.16** pH = 5.36.
16.17 (a) basic, (b) neutral, (c) acidic. **16.18** (a) neutral,
(b) basic, (c) acidic. **16.19** pH = 5.39. **16.20** pH = 8.07.
16.21 pH = 5.13. **16.22** basic. **16.23** neutral.

16.24 pH = 10.79. **16.25** Solving using the quadratic formula: pH = 2.38. Solving by simplification pH = 2.35. The difference is a difference of 0.03 pH units. **16.26** pH = 10.68. **16.27** Upon addition of a strong acid, the concentration of $HC_2H_3O_2$ will increase. When a strong base is added, it reacts with the acid to form more of the acetate ion, therefore the concentration of the acetic acid will decrease. **16.28** (a) $H^+ + NH_3 \longrightarrow NH_4^+$, (b) $OH^- + NH_4^+ \longrightarrow H_2O + NH_3$. **16.29** 4.84, the difference is due to rounding errors. **16.30** 4.61. **16.31** Acetic acid buffer, 26.2 g $NaC_2H_3O_2$, or hydrazoic acid buffer, 21.0 g NaN_3, or butanoic acid buffer, 29.6 g $NaC_4H_7O_2$, or propanoic acid buffer, 22.9 g $NaC_3H_5O_2$. **16.32** Yes, 0.692 mol $HCHO_2$ for 1 mol CHO_2^-, 4.7 g $NaCHO_2$. **16.33** 0.13 pH units. **16.34** pH = 9.76, pH = 9.67.

16.35 $H_3PO_4 \rightleftharpoons H^+ + H_2PO_4^-$ $K_a = \dfrac{[H^+][H_2PO_4^-]}{[H_3PO_4]}$,

$H_2PO_4^- \rightleftharpoons H^+ + HPO_4^{2-}$ $K_a = \dfrac{[H^+][HPO_4^{2-}]}{[H_2PO_4^-]}$,

$HPO_4^{2-} \rightleftharpoons H^+ + PO_4^{3-}$ $K_a = \dfrac{[H^+][PO_4^{3-}]}{[HPO_4^{2-}]}$.

16.36 $[H^+] = 2.6 \times 10^{-3}$ M, pH = 2.58, $[HC_6H_6O_6^-] = 2.7 \times 10^{-12}$.
16.37 pH = 11.66, It is not a substitute for $NaHCO_3$.
16.38 pH = 10.24. **16.39** $[H_2SO_3] = K_{b2}$ for SO_3^{2-}.
16.40 (a) H_2O, K^+, $HC_2H_3O_2$, H^+, $C_2H_3O_2^-$, and OH^-,
$[H_2O] > [K^+] > [C_2H_3O_2^-] > [OH^-] > [HC_2H_3O_2] > [H^+]$,
(b) H_2O, $HC_2H_3O_2$, H^+, $C_2H_3O_2^-$, and OH^-,
$[H_2O] > [HC_2H_3O_2] > [H^+] > [C_2H_3O_2^-] > [OH^-]$,
(c) H_2O, K^+, $HC_2H_3O_2$, H^+, $C_2H_3O_2^-$, and OH^-,
$[H_2O] > [K^+] > [OH^-] > [C_2H_3O_2^-] > [HC_2H_3O_2] > [H^+]$,
(d) H_2O, K^+, $HC_2H_3O_2$, H^+, $C_2H_3O_2^-$, and OH^-,
$[H_2O] > [HC_2H_3O_2] > [K^+] > [C_2H_3O_2^-] > [OH^-] > [H^+]$.
16.41 (a) 2.37, (b) 3.74, (c) 4.22, (d) 8.22. **16.42** pH = 3.66

Review Problems

16.32 1.5×10^{-11}. **16.34** 7.1×10^{-11}. **16.36** 0.30%, $K_a = 1.82 \times 10^{-6}$. **16.38** $K_a = 2.3 \times 10^{-2}$, $pK_a = 1.6$.
16.40 $K_b = 5.6 \times 10^{-4}$ $pK_b = 3.25$, 7.2%.
16.42 $[HC_3H_5O_2] = 0.145$, $[H^+] = 4.5 \times 10^{-3}$, $[C_3H_5O_2^-] = 4.5 \times 10^{-3}$, pH = 2.34. **16.44** 10.26.
16.46 $[HC_2H_3O_2] = 0.47$ M. **16.48** pH = 10.44.
16.50 $[H^+] = 6.0 \times 10^{-4}$ M, pH = 3.22.
16.52 pH = 11.26, $[HCN] = 1.8 \times 10^{-3}$ M.
16.54 pH = 5.72. **16.56** $K_a = 1.4 \times 10^{-5}$.
16.58 pH = 10.67. **16.60** pH = 4.97. **16.62** pH = 9.00.
16.64 $\Delta[NH_4^+] = -0.01$ M, $\Delta[NH_3] = -0.03$ M.
16.66 −0.12 pH units. **16.68** −0.11 pH units.
16.70 2.2 g $NaCHO_2$. **16.72** $pH_{initial} = 4.788$, $pH_{final} = 4.761$, pH = 1.63. **16.74** $[H_2C_6H_6O_6] \cong 0.15$ M, $[H_3O^+] = [HC_6H_6O_6^-] = 3.2 \times 10^{-3}$ M, $[C_6H_6O_6^{2-}] = 2.7 \times 10^{-12}$ M, $[OH^-] = 3.2 \times 10^{-12}$ M, pH = 2.5. **16.76** $[H^+] = [H_2PO_4^-] = 0.12$ M, $[H_3PO_4] = 2.0 - 0.12 = 1.9$ M, pH = 0.92, $[HPO_4^{2-}] = 6.3 \times 10^{-8}$, $[PO_4^{3-}] = 2.4 \times 10^{-19}$.
16.78 $[H^+] = [H_2PO_3^-] = 0.16$ M, $[HPO_3^{2-}] = 1.6 \times 10^{-7}$ M, pH = 0.80. **16.80** pH = 10.28, $[HSO_3^-] = 1.9 \times 10^{-4}$, $[H_2SO_3] = 8.3 \times 10^{-13}$. **16.82** pH = 9.10. **16.84** pH = 12.97, $[HPO_4^{2-}] = 9.4 \times 10^{-2}$ M, $[H_2PO_4^-] = 1.6 \times 10^{-7}$, $[H_3PO_4] = 2.4 \times 10^{-18}$. **16.86** pH = 8.07, Cresol red.
16.88 pH = 12.93. **16.90** (a) 2.8724, (b) 4.444, (c) 4.7447, (d) 8.7236

CHAPTER 17

Practice Exercises

17.1 $Ba_3(PO_4)_2(s) \rightleftharpoons 3Ba^{2+}(aq) + 2PO_4^{3-}(aq)$, $K_{sp} = [Ba^{2+}]^3[PO_4^{3-}]^2$.
17.2 (a) $K_{sp} = [Ba^{2+}][C_2O_4^{2-}]$, (b) $K_{sp} = [Ag^+]^2[SO_4^{2-}]$.
17.3 3.2×10^{-10}. **17.4** 3.98×10^{-8}. **17.5** 1.5×10^{-5}.
17.6 1.0×10^{-10}. **17.7** 3.9×10^{-8}. **17.8** 1.8×10^{-5} M Ag_3PO_4.
17.9 (a) 7.1×10^{-7} M AgBr, (b) 1.3×10^{-4} M Ag_2CO_3.
17.10 2.1×10^{-16} M of AgI will dissolve in a 0.20 M CaI_2 solution. In pure water, the solubility is 9.1×10^{-9} M.
17.11 1.3×10^{-35} M of $Fe(OH)_3$. **17.12** A precipitate will form. **17.13** No precipitate will form. **17.14** We expect $PbSO_4(s)$ since nitrates are soluble. A precipitate of $PbSO_4$ is not expected. **17.15** We expect a precipitate of $PbCl_2$ since nitrates are soluble. A precipitate of $PbCl_2$ is not expected.
17.16 No. **17.17** 2.9. **17.18** 0.35 M H^+.
17.19 5.40 to 6.13. **17.20** 4.9×10^{-3} M in 0.10 M NH_3; 1.3×10^{-5} M in pure water. **17.21** 4.1 mol NH_3

Review Problems

17.16 (a) $K_{sp} = [Ca^{2+}][F^-]^2$, (b) $K_{sp} = [Ag^+]^2[CO_3^{2-}]$, (c) $K_{sp} = [Pb^{2+}][SO_4^{2-}]$, (d) $K_{sp} = [Fe^{3+}][OH^-]^3$, (e) $K_{sp} = [Pb^{2+}][I^-]^2$, (f) $K_{sp} = [Cu^{2+}][OH^-]^2$.
17.18 1.6×10^{-5}. **17.20** 1.10×10^{-10}. **17.22** 8.0×10^{-7}.
17.24 2.8×10^{-18}. **17.26** 8.1×10^{-3} M. **17.28** 1.3×10^{-4} M.
17.30 4.1×10^{-2} M LiF, 7.5×10^{-3} M BaF_2, LiF is more soluble.
17.32 2.8×10^{-18}. **17.34** 4.9×10^{-3} M.
17.36 (a) 4.4×10^{-4} M, (b) 9.5×10^{-6} M, (c) 9.5×10^{-7} M, (d) 6.3×10^{-7} M. **17.38** 6.9×10^{-9} M. **17.40** 1.7×10^{-3} M.
17.42 (a) 3.0×10^{-11} mol/L, (b) 1.2×10^{-6} mol/L.
17.44 1.3 %, +1.8 pH units. **17.46** 2.2 g $Fe(OH)_2$, 2.0×10^{-12} M. **17.48** 7.9×10^{-7} M. **17.50** No precipitate will form. **17.52** (a) No precipitate will form, (b) A precipitate will form. **17.54** 2.3×10^{-8} M. **17.56** No precipitate forms.
17.58 $[H^+] = 0.045$ M, pH = 1.35. **17.60** pH = 4.8–8.1, $Mn(OH)_2$ will be soluble, but some $Cu(OH)_2$ will precipitate out of solution.
17.62 (a) $Cu^{2+}(aq) + 4Cl^-(aq) \rightleftharpoons CuCl_4^{2-}(aq)$

$$K_{form} = \frac{[CuCl_4^{2-}]}{[Cu^{2+}][Cl^-]^4},$$

(b) $Ag^+(aq) + 2I^-(aq) \rightleftharpoons AgI_2^-(aq)$ $K_{form} = \dfrac{[AgI_2^-]}{[Ag^+][I^-]^2}$,

(c) $Cr^{3+}(aq) + 6NH_3(aq) \rightleftharpoons Cr(NH_3)_6^{3+}(aq)$

$$K_{form} = \frac{[Cr(NH_3)_6^{3+}]}{[Cr^{3+}][NH_3]^6}.$$

17.64 (a) $Co^{3+}(aq) + 6NH_3(aq) \rightleftharpoons Co(NH_3)_6^{3+}(aq)$

$$K_{form} = \frac{[Co(NH_3)_6^{3+}]}{[Co^{3+}][NH_3]^6},$$

(b) $Hg^{2+}(aq) + 4I^-(aq) \rightleftharpoons HgI_4^{2-}(aq)$

$$K_{form} = \frac{[HgI_4^{2-}]}{[Hg^{2+}][I^-]^4},$$

(c) $Fe^{2+}(aq) + 6CN^-(aq) \rightleftharpoons Fe(CN)_6^{4-}(aq)$

$$K_{form} = \frac{[Fe(CN)_6^{4-}]}{[Fe^{2+}][CN^-]^6}.$$

17.66 4.3×10^{-4}. **17.68** 450 g NaCN are required.
17.70 1.9×10^{-4} g AgI. **17.72** 9.5×10^{-3} M.
17.74 $K_{inst} = 3.7 \times 10^{-10}$

CHAPTER 18

Practice Exercises

18.1 $+154$ L atm. **18.2** Energy is added to the system in the form of work. **18.3** -2.64 kJ, ΔE is more exothermic.
18.4 -214.6 kJ, 1.14 %. **18.5** negative.
18.6 (a) negative, (b) positive.
18.7 (a) negative, (b) negative.
18.8 (a) negative, (b) negative, (c) positive.
18.9 -99.1 J K^{-1}.
18.10 (a) -229 J/K, (b) -120.9 J/K.
18.11 $+98.3$ kJ/mol. **18.12** 1482 kJ.
18.13 -30.3 kJ/mol.
18.14 (a) -69.7 kJ/mol, (b) -120.1 kJ/mol.
18.15 2820 kJ work for $C_2H_5OH(l)$, 4650 kJ work for $C_8H_{18}(l)$, C_8H_{18} is a better fuel on a gram basis.
18.16 788 kJ. **18.17** $+90.5$ J mol^{-1} K^{-1}.
18.18 614 K (341 °C).
18.19 The reaction should be spontaneous.
18.20 We do not expect to see products formed from reactants.
18.21 -4.3 kJ. **18.22** $+32.8$ kJ, -29.1 kJ. The equilibrium shifts to products. **18.23** $\Delta G = 0$. The reaction is at equilibrium.
18.24 The reaction will proceed to the right. **18.25** -33 kJ.
18.16 0.26

Review Problems

18.46 $+1000$ J, Endothermic. **18.48** 121 J.
18.50 (a) $\Delta H° = +24.58$ kJ, $\Delta E° = 19.6$ kJ,
(b) $\Delta H° = -178$ kJ, $\Delta E° = -175$ kJ,
(c) $\Delta H° = 847.6$ kJ, $\Delta E° = \Delta H°$,
(d) $\Delta H° = 65.029$ kJ $\Delta E° = \Delta H°$.
18.52 $\Delta E = -677$ kJ, $\Delta E_{200\,°C} = -683$ kJ.
18.54 (a) -178 kJ spontaneous, (b) -311 kJ spontaneous,
(c) $+1084.3$ kJ not spontaneous. **18.56** number of moles of reactants and products, state of the reactants and products, and complexity of the molecules. **18.58** (a) negative, (b) negative, (c) negative, (d) positive. **18.60** (a) -198.3 J/K not spontaneous, (b) -332.3 J/K not spontaneous, (c) $+92.6$ J/K spontaneous, (d) $+14$ J/K spontaneous, (e) $+159$ J/K spontaneous.
18.62 (a) -52.8 J mol^{-1} K^{-1}, (b) -868.9 J mol^{-1} K^{-1}, (c) -318 J mol^{-1} K^{-1}.
18.64 -269.7 J/K.
18.66 -209 kJ/mol.
18.68 (a) -82.3 kJ, (b) -8.8 kJ, (c) $+70.7$ kJ.
18.70 $+0.16$ kJ. **18.72** 1299.8 kJ. **18.74** 333 K.
18.76 101 J mol^{-1} K^{-1}.
18.78 spontaneous.
18.80 (a) $K_P = 10^{263}$, (b) $K_P = 2.90 \times 10^{-25}$.
18.82 The system is not at equilibrium and must shift to the right to reach equilibrium.
18.84 $K_P = 8.000 \times 10^8$. This is a favorable reaction, since the equilibrium lies far to the side favoring products and is worth studying as a method for methane production.
18.86 If $\Delta G° = 0$, $K_c = 1$. If we start with pure products, the value of Q will be infinite (there are zero reactants) and, since $Q > K_c$, the reaction will proceed towards the reactants, i.e., the pure products will decompose to their elements.
18.88 1.16×10^3 kJ/mol. **18.90** 354 kJ/mol.
18.92 577.7 kJ/mol. **18.94** 308.0 kJ/mol.
18.96 85 kJ/mol.
18.98 The heat of formation of CF_4 should be more exothermic than that of CCl_4 because more energy is released on formation of a C—F bond than on formation of a C—Cl bond. Also, less energy is needed to form gaseous F atoms than to form gaseous Cl atoms.

CHAPTER 19

Practice Exercises

19.1 anode: $Mg(s) \longrightarrow Mg^{2+}(aq) + 2e^-$,
cathode: $Fe^{2+}(aq) + 2e^- \longrightarrow Fe(s)$,
cell notation: $Mg(s)\,|\,Mg^{2+}(aq)\,\|\,Fe^{2+}(aq)\,|\,Fe(s)$,

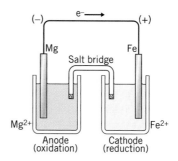

19.2 anode: $Al(s) \longrightarrow Al^{3+}(aq) + 3e^-$,
cathode: $Ni^{2+}(aq) + 2e^- \longrightarrow Ni(s)$,
overall: $3Ni^{2+}(aq) + 2Al(s) \longrightarrow 2Al^{3+}(aq) + 3Ni(s)$.
19.3 Zinc. **19.4** -0.44 V.
19.5 (a) $2I^-(aq) + 2Fe^{3+}(aq) \longrightarrow I_2(s) + 2Fe^{2+}(aq)$
(b) $3Mg(s) + 2Cr^{3+}(aq) \longrightarrow 2Cr(s) + 3Mg^{2+}(aq)$
(c) $Co(s) + 4H^+(aq) + 2SO_4^{2-}(aq) \longrightarrow$
$$H_2SO_3(aq) + H_2O + Co^{2+}(aq).$$
19.6 $Br_2(aq) + H_2SO_3(aq) + H_2O \longrightarrow$
$$2Br^-(aq) + SO_4^{2-}(aq) + 4H^+(aq).$$
19.7 Non spontaneous.
$$Ni(s) + 2Fe^{3+}(aq) \longrightarrow Ni^{2+}(aq) + 2Fe^{2+}(aq).$$
19.8 $NiO_2(s) + Fe(s) + 2H_2O \longrightarrow$
$$Ni(OH)_2(s) + Fe(OH)_2(s) \; E°_{cell} = 1.37 \text{ V.}$$
19.9 $2Cr(s) + 3Cu^{2+}(aq) \longrightarrow 2Cr^{3+}(aq) + 3Cu(s) \; E°_{cell} = 1.08$ V.
19.10 $3MnO_4^-(aq) + 24H^+(aq) + 5Cr(s) \longrightarrow$
$$5Cr^{3+}(aq) + 3Mn^{2+}(aq) + 12H_2O \; E°_{cell} = 2.25 \text{ V.}$$
19.11 (a) Spontaneous, (b) Spontaneous.
19.12 (a) Nonspontaneous, (b) Spontaneous. **19.13** 3 electrons.
19.14 $\Delta G° = -102$ kJ, -343 kJ, $+108$ kJ and -11.6 kJ, respectively. **19.15** $K_c = 2.7 \times 10^{-16}$, $K = 5.6 \times 10^{16}$.
19.16 $Ag^+(aq) + Br^-(aq) \longrightarrow AgBr(s)$,
$$K = \frac{1}{[Ag^+][Br^-]}, \; 2.2 \times 10^{12}.$$
19.17 $Cu^{2+}(aq) + Mg(s) \longrightarrow Mg^{2+}(aq) + Cu(s)$, 2.82 V.
19.18 1.04 V. **19.19** 2.9×10^{-5} M Mg^{2+}.
19.20 1.9×10^{-4} M, 6.6×10^{-13} M. **19.21** 6.6×10^{-4} M.
19.22 I_2. **19.23** Tin. **19.24** 8.29×10^{-3} mol OH$^-$.
19.25 7.33 min. **19.26** 3.67 A. **19.27** $+0.0187$ M.

Review Problems

19.50 (a) anode: $Cd(s) \longrightarrow Cd^{2+}(aq) + 2e^-$,
cathode: $Au^{3+}(aq) + 3e^- \longrightarrow Au(s)$,
cell: $3Cd(s) + 2Au^{3+}(aq) \longrightarrow 3Cd^{2+}(aq) + 2Au(s)$,
(b) anode: $Fe(s) \longrightarrow Fe^{2+}(aq) + 2e^-$,
cathode: $Br_2(aq) + 2e^- \longrightarrow 2Br^-(aq)$,
cell: $Fe(s) + Br_2(aq) \longrightarrow Fe^{2+}(aq) + 2Br^-(aq)$,
(c) anode: $Cr(s) \longrightarrow Cr^{3+}(aq) + 3e^-$,
cathode: $Cu^{2+}(aq) + 2e^- \longrightarrow Cu(s)$,
cell: $2Cr(s) + 3Cu^{2+}(aq) \longrightarrow 2Cr^{3+}(aq) + 3Cu(s)$.
19.52 (a) $Pt(s)\,|\,Fe^{2+}(aq),Fe^{3+}(aq)\,\|\,NO_3^-(aq),H^+(aq)\,|\,NO(g)\,|\,Pt(s)$,
(b) $Pt(s)\,|\,Cl^-(aq),Cl_2(g)\,\|\,Br_2(aq),Br^-(aq)\,|\,Pt(s)$,
(c) $Ag(s)\,|\,Ag^+(aq)\,\|\,Au^{3+}(aq)\,|\,Au(s)$.
19.54 (a) $Sn(s)$, (b) $Br^-(aq)$, (c) $Zn(s)$, (d) $I^-(aq)$.
19.56 (a) 0.19 V, (b) -0.29 V, (c) 0.62 V.
19.58 (a) Spontaneous. (b) Spontaneous. (c) Spontaneous.

19.60 $BrO_3^-(aq) + 6I^-(aq) + 6H^+(aq) \longrightarrow$
$\qquad 3I_2(s) + Br^-(aq) + 3H_2O$, net reaction.
$E^\circ_{cell} = 0.90V.$
19.62 $4HOCl(aq) + 2H^+(aq) + S_2O_3^{2-} \longrightarrow$
$\qquad 2Cl_2(g) + H_2O + 2H_2SO_3(aq)$

19.64 Not spontaneous. **19.66** 1.0×10^2 kJ.
19.68 (a) $E^\circ_{cell} = 0.54V$, (b) -5.2×10^2 kJ, (c) 2.1×10^{91}.
19.70 0.31. **19.72** 2.38 V. **19.74** $[Cd^{2+}] = 2.86 \times 10^{-15}$ M.
19.76 $K_{sp} = 1.96 \times 10^{-15}$. **19.78** 0.09 V.
19.80 (a) 0.40 mol e^-, (b) 0.70 mol e^-, (c) 4.50 mol e^-,
(d) 5.0×10^{-2} mol e^-. **19.82** 2.68 g Fe(OH).
19.84 51.5 hr. **19.86** 66.2 amp. **19.88** 40.1 mL.
19.90 298 mL Cl_2.
19.92 $2H_2O \rightleftharpoons 2H_2(g) + O_2(g)$, $E^\circ = -2.06$ V.
19.94 Br_2 and Cu, $Cu^{2+} + 2Br^- \rightleftharpoons Br_2 + Cu(s)$

CHAPTER 20

Practice Exercises

20.1 $^{226}_{88}Ra \longrightarrow ^{222}_{86}Rn + ^4_2He + ^0_0\gamma$.
20.2 $^{90}_{38}Sr \longrightarrow ^{90}_{39}Y + ^0_{-1}e$. **20.3** 50.0%.
20.4 1.10×10^5 atoms Rn-222. **20.5** 20 m. **20.6** 100 units

Review Problems

20.45 1.11×10^{-11} g. **20.47** -3.18 ng, $1.09 \times 10^{-5}\%$.
20.49 1.8×10^{-13} J/nucleon.
20.51 (a) $^{211}_{83}Bi$, (b) $^{177}_{72}Hf$, (c) $^{216}_{84}Po$, (d) $^{19}_9F$.
20.53 (a) $^{242}_{94}Pu \longrightarrow ^4_2He + ^{238}_{92}U$, (b) $^{28}_{12}Mg \longrightarrow ^0_{-1}e + ^{28}_{13}Al$,
(c) $^{26}_{14}Si \longrightarrow ^0_1e + ^{26}_{13}Al$, (d) $^{37}_{18}Ar + ^0_{-1}e \longrightarrow ^{37}_{17}Cl$.
20.55 (a) $^{261}_{102}No$, (b) $^{211}_{82}Pb$, (c) $^{141}_{61}Pm$, (d) $^{179}_{74}W$.
20.57 $^{87}_{36}Kr \longrightarrow ^{86}_{36}Kr + ^1_0n$. **20.59** The more likely process is
positron emission. $^{38}_{19}K \longrightarrow ^0_1e + ^{38}_{18}Ar$. **20.61** 0.0469 mg.
20.63 $^{53}_{24}Cr^*$; $^{51}_{23}V + ^2_1H \longrightarrow ^{53}_{24}Cr^* \longrightarrow ^1_1p + ^{52}_{23}V$.
20.65 $^{80}_{35}Br$. **20.67** $^{55}_{26}Fe$; $^{55}_{25}Mn + ^1_1p \longrightarrow ^1_0n + ^{55}_{26}Fe$.
20.69 $^{70}_{30}Zn + ^{208}_{82}Pb \longrightarrow ^{278}_{112}Uub \longrightarrow ^1_0n + ^{277}_{112}Uub$.
20.71 6.3 m. **20.73** 6.6 m.
20.75 2.4×10^7 Bq, 6.5×10^2 μCi.
20.77 $k = 1.0 \times 10^{-6}$ s^{-1}, $t_{1/2} = 6.9 \times 10^5$ s.
20.79 3.1% The chemical product is $BaCl_2$.
20.81 2.84×10^{-3} Ci/g.
20.83 1.3×10^9 years old.
20.85 2.7×10^4 years ago.
20.87 $^{235}_{92}U + ^1_0n \longrightarrow ^{94}_{38}Sr + ^{140}_{54}Xe + 2^1_0n$.

CHAPTER 21

Practice Exercises

21.1 At any temperature. **21.2** 5570 K.
21.3 $[Ag(S_2O_3)_2]^{3-}$, $(NH_4)_3[Ag(S_2O_3)_2]$.
21.4 $AlCl_3 \cdot 6H_2O$, $[Al(H_2O)_6]^{3+}$.
21.5 (a) $[SnCl_6]^{2-}$, (b) $(NH_4)_2[Fe(CN)_4(H_2O)_2]$.
21.6 (a) potassium hexacyanoferrate(III),
(b) dichlorobis(ethylenediamine)chromium(III) sulfate.
21.7 Six. **21.8** (a) Six, (b) Six, (c) Six.

Review Problems

21.102 734 K.
21.104 The net charge is -3, and the formula is $[Fe(CN)_6]^{3-}$,
hexacyanoferrate(III) ion. **21.106** $[CoCl_2(en)_2]^+$.
21.108 (a) oxalato, (b) sulfido or thio, (c) chloro,
(d) dimethylamine. **21.110** (a) hexaamminenickel(II) ion,
(b) triamminetrichlorochromate(II) ion,

(c) hexanitrocobaltate(III) ion,
(d) diamminetetracyanomanganate(II) ion,
(e) trioxalatoferrate(III) ion or trisoxalatoferrate(III) ion.
21.112 (a) $[Fe(CN)_2(H_2O)_4]^+$, (b) $[Ni(C_2O_4)(NH_3)_4]$,
(c) $[Fe(CN)_4(H_2O)_2]^-$, (d) $K_3[Mn(SCN)_6]$, (e) $[CuCl_4]^{2-}$.
21.114 Six.
21.116

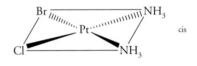

The curved lines represent $-CH_2-\overset{\overset{\displaystyle O}{\|}}{C}-$ groups.
21.118 Since both are the *cis* isomer, they are identical.
21.120

cis

trans

21.122

21.124 (a) $[Cr(H_2O)_6]^{3+}$, (b) $[Cr(en)_3]^{3+}$.
21.126 $[Cr(CN)_6]^{3-}$.
21.128 (a) $[RuCl(NH_3)_5]^{3+}$. The value of Δ increases down a
group., (b) $[Ru(NH_3)_6]^{3+}$. The value of Δ increases with oxidation
state of the metal.
21.130 This is the one with the strongest field ligand, since
Co^{2+} is a d^7 ion: CoA_6^{3+}.
21.132 This is a weak field complex of Co^{2+}, and it should be a
high–spin d^7 case. It cannot be diamagnetic.

CHAPTER 22

Practice Exercises

22.1 2,2-dimethylpropane.
22.2 (a) 3-methylhexane, (b) 4-ethyl-2,3-dimethylheptane,
(c) 5-ethyl-2,4,6-trimethyloctane.
22.3
$$\underset{\underset{\displaystyle CH_3CH_2-CH-CH_2CH_3}{}}{\overset{OH}{|}}$$
22.4 (a)
$$CH_3-\overset{\overset{\displaystyle O}{\|}}{CH} \quad \text{or} \quad CH_3-\overset{\overset{\displaystyle O}{\|}}{COH}$$
(b)
$$CH_3CH_2\overset{\overset{\displaystyle O}{\|}}{C}CH_2CH_3$$

22.5

$$CH_3CH_2-\overset{\overset{\displaystyle O}{\|}}{C}-NHCH_2CH_2CH_3$$

22.6 (a)

$$CH_3CH_2-\overset{\overset{\displaystyle O}{\|}}{C}-O^- + HOCH(CH_3)_2$$

(b) $CH_3CH=CH_2$

22.7

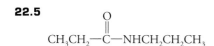

```
     H   CH3  H   CH3  H   CH3
     |    |   |    |   |    |
   —C———C———C———C———C———C—
     |    |   |    |   |    |
    CH3   H  CH3   H  CH3   H
        └─────┘
        Repeat
         unit
```

22.8

```
     F   F   F   F   F   F
     |   |   |   |   |   |
   —C———C———C———C———C———C—
     |   |   |   |   |   |
     F   F   F   F   F   F
       └───┘
       Repeat
        unit
```

Review Problems

22.97 (a)
```
        H   H
        |   |
    H—C—N—H
        |
        H
```
(b)
```
        H
        |
    Br—C—Br
        |
        H
```
(c)
```
        Cl
        |
    H—C—Cl
        |
        Cl
```
(d)
```
        H
        |
    H—N—O—H
```
(e) $H-C\equiv C-H$ (f)
```
      H   H
      |   |
    H—N—N—H
```

22.99 (a) alkene   (d) carboxylic acid
(b) alcohol   (e) amine
(c) ester   (f) alcohol.

22.101 b, e, and f.

22.103 (a) amine, (b) amine, (c) amide, (d) amine, ketone.

22.105 (a) identical, (b) identical, (c) unrelated, (d) isomers, (e) identical, (f) identical, (g) isomers.

22.107 (a) pentane, (b) 2-methylpentane, (c) 2,4-dimethylhexane.

22.109 (a) No isomers,
(b)
```
     H      H2C—CH3            H        H
      \    /                    \      /
       C=C              and      C=C
      /    \                    /      \
    H3C     H                 H3C      H2C—CH3
      trans                        cis
```
(c)
```
     Br      Cl               Br        H
      \     /                  \       /
       C=C            and       C=C
      /     \                  /       \
    H3C      H               H3C       Cl
       cis                       trans
```

22.111 (a) CH_3CH_3, (b) $ClCH_2CH_2Cl$, (c) $BrCH_2CH_2Br$, (d) CH_3CH_2Cl, (e) CH_3CH_2Br, (f) CH_3CH_2OH.

22.113 (a) $CH_3CH_2CH_2CH_3$,

(b)
```
      Cl  Cl
      |   |
  H3C—C———C—CH3
      |   |
      H   H
```
(c)
```
      Br  Br
      |   |
  H3C—C———C—CH3
      |   |
      H   H
```
(d)
```
      H   Cl
      |   |
  H3C—C———C—CH3
      |   |
      H   H
```
(e)
```
      H   Br
      |   |
  H3C—C———C—CH3
      |   |
      H   H
```
(f)
```
      H   OH
      |   |
  H3C—C———C—CH3
      |   |
      H   H
```

22.115 This sort of reaction would disrupt the π delocalization of the benzene ring. The subsequent loss of resonance energy would not be favorable.

22.117 CH_3OH:
IUPAC name = methanol;   common name = methyl alcohol.
CH_3CH_2OH:
IUPAC name = ethanol;   common name = ethyl alcohol.
$CH_3CH_2CH_2OH$:
IUPAC name = 1-propanol;   common name = propyl alcohol.

```
        CH3
        |
    H3C—CH—OH
```

IUPAC name = 2-propanol;   common name = isopropyl alcohol.

22.119 $CH_3CH_2CH_2-O-CH_3$ methyl propyl ether
$CH_3CH_2-O-CH_2CH_3$ diethyl ether
$(CH_3)_2CH-O-CH_3$ methyl 2-propyl ether

22.121 (a) ⬠   (b) Ph–CH=CH2

(c) Ph–CH=CH2

22.123 (a) cyclopentanone   (b)

(c)

22.125 The elimination of water can result in a $C=C$ double bond in two locations:
$CH_2=CHCH_2CH_3$ $CH_3CH=CHCH_3$
1-butene   2-butene

22.127 The aldehyde is more easily oxidized. The product is:

$$H_3C-CH_2-\overset{\overset{\displaystyle O}{\|}}{C}-OH$$

22.129 (a) $CH_3CH_2CO_2H$, (b) $CH_3CH_2CO_2H + CH_3OH$, (c) $Na^+ + CH_3CH_2CH_2CO_2^- + H_2O$

22.131 $CH_3CO_2H + CH_3CH_2NHCH_2CH_3$

22.133
```
        CH2      CH2      CH2      CH2
       /        /        /        /
     CH       CH       CH       CH
      |        |        |        |
      O        O        O        O
      |        |        |        |
     C=O      C=O      C=O      C=O
      |        |        |        |
     CH3      CH3      CH3      CH3
```

22.135

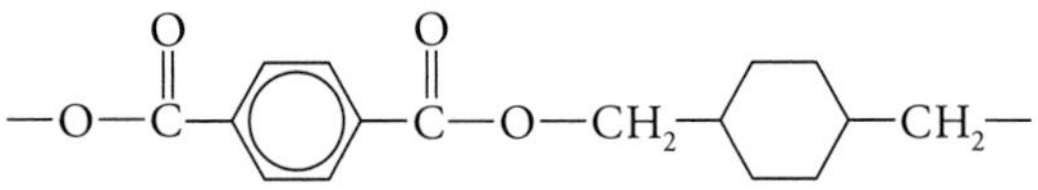

$$-O-\overset{O}{\overset{\|}{C}}-\bigcirc\!\!\!\!\!\!-\overset{O}{\overset{\|}{C}}-O-CH_2-\langle\,\rangle-CH_2-$$

22.137

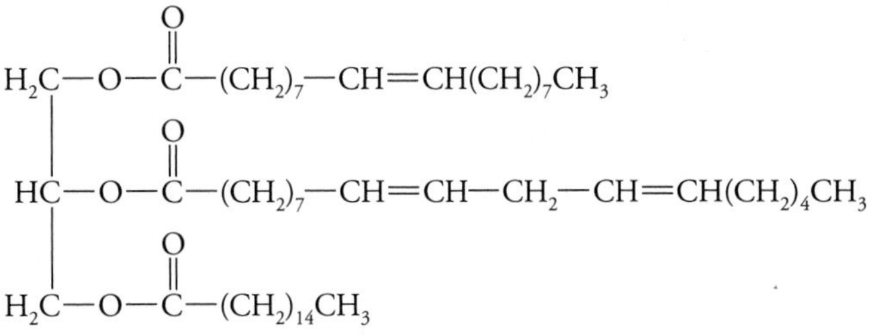

$$H_2C-O-\overset{O}{\overset{\|}{C}}-(CH_2)_7-CH=CH(CH_2)_7CH_3$$

$$HC-O-\overset{O}{\overset{\|}{C}}-(CH_2)_7-CH=CH-CH_2-CH=CH(CH_2)_4CH_3$$

$$H_2C-O-\overset{O}{\overset{\|}{C}}-(CH_2)_{14}CH_3$$

22.139

$$H_2C-O-\overset{O}{\overset{\|}{C}}-(CH_2)_{16}CH_3$$

$$HC-O-\overset{O}{\overset{\|}{C}}-(CH_2)_{12}CH_3$$

$$H_2C-O-\overset{O}{\overset{\|}{C}}-(CH_2)_{16}CH_3$$

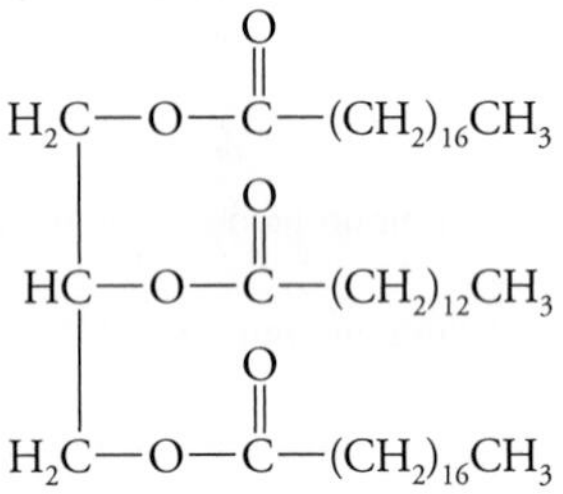

22.141 Hydrophobic sites are composed of fatty acid units.
Hydrophilic sites are composed of charged units.

22.143

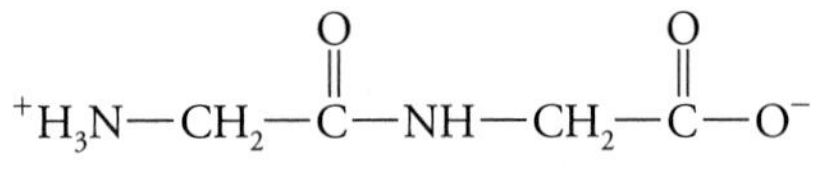

$$^+H_3N-CH_2-\overset{O}{\overset{\|}{C}}-NH-CH_2-\overset{O}{\overset{\|}{C}}-O^-$$

22.145

$$^+H_3N-CH_2-\overset{O}{\overset{\|}{C}}-NH-CH-\overset{O}{\overset{\|}{C}}-O^- \qquad ^+H_3N-CH-\overset{O}{\overset{\|}{C}}-NH-CH_2-\overset{O}{\overset{\|}{C}}-O^-$$

with CH_2-phenyl side chains

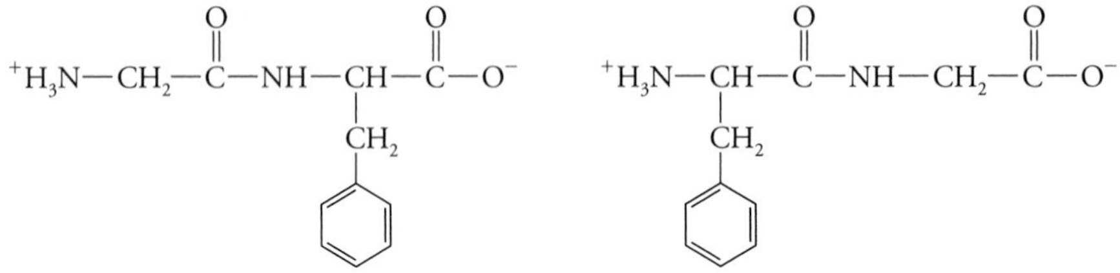

TABLES OF SELECTED DATA

TABLE C.1 Thermodynamic Data for Selected Elements, Compounds, and Ions (25 °C)

Substance	ΔH_f°(kJ mol^{-1})	S°(J mol^{-1} K^{-1})	ΔG_f°(kJ mol^{-1})	Substance	ΔH_f°(kJ mol^{-1})	S°(J mol^{-1} K^{-1})	ΔG_f°(kJ mol^{-1})
Aluminum				$CdCl_2(s)$	−392	115	−344
$Al(s)$	0	28.3	0	$CdO(s)$	−258.2	54.8	−228.4
$Al^{3+}(aq)$	−524.7		−481.2	$CdS(s)$	−162	64.9	−156
$AlCl_3(s)$	−704	110.7	−629	$CdSO_4(s)$	−933.5	123	−822.6
$Al_2O_3(s)$	−1669.8	51.0	−1576.4				
$Al_2(SO_4)_3(s)$	−3441	239	−3100	**Calcium**			
Arsenic				$Ca(s)$	0	41.4	0
$As(s)$	0	35.1	0	$Ca^{2+}(aq)$	−542.83	−53.1	−553.58
$AsH_3(g)$	+66.4	223	+68.9	$CaCO_3(s)$	−1207	92.9	−1128.8
$As_4O_6(s)$	−1314	214	−1153	$CaF_2(s)$	−741	80.3	−1166
$As_2O_5(s)$	−925	105	−782	$CaCl_2(s)$	−795.0	114	−750.2
$H_3AsO_3(aq)$	−742.2			$CaBr_2(s)$	−682.8	130	−663.6
$H_3AsO_4(aq)$	−902.5			$CaI_2(s)$	−535.9	143	
Barium				$CaO(s)$	−635.5	40	−604.2
$Ba(s)$	0	66.9	0	$Ca(OH)_2(s)$	−986.59	76.1	−896.76
$Ba^{2+}(aq)$	−537.6	9.6	−560.8	$Ca_3(PO_4)_2(s)$	−4119	241	−3852
$BaCO_3(s)$	−1219	112	−1139	$CaSO_3(s)$	−1156		
$BaCrO_4(s)$	−1428.0			$CaSO_4(s)$	−1433	107	−1320.3
$BaCl_2(s)$	−860.2	125	−810.8	$CaSO_4 \cdot \frac{1}{2}H_2O(s)$	−1575.2	131	−1435.2
$BaO(s)$	−553.5	70.4	−525.1	$CaSO_4 \cdot 2H_2O(s)$	−2021.1	194.0	−1795.7
$Ba(OH)_2(s)$	−998.22	−8	−875.3				
$Ba(NO_3)_2(s)$	−992	214	−795	**Carbon**			
$BaSO_4(s)$	−1465	132	−1353	$C(s, graphite)$	0	5.69	0
Beryllium				$C(s, diamond)$	+1.88	2.4	+2.9
$Be(s)$	0	9.50	0	$CCl_4(l)$	−134	214.4	−65.3
$BeCl_2(s)$	−468.6	89.9	−426.3	$CO(g)$	−110.5	197.9	−137.3
$BeO(s)$	−611	14	−582	$CO_2(g)$	−393.5	213.6	−394.4
Bismuth				$CO_2(aq)$	−413.8	117.6	−385.98
$Bi(s)$	0	56.9	0	$H_2CO_3(aq)$	−699.65	187.4	−623.08
$BiCl_3(s)$	−379	177	−315	$HCO_3^-(aq)$	−691.99	91.2	−586.77
$Bi_2O_3(s)$	−576	151	−497	$CO_3^{2-}(aq)$	−677.14	−56.9	−527.81
Boron				$CS_2(l)$	+89.5	151.3	+65.3
$B(s)$	0	5.87	0	$CS_2(g)$	+117	237.7	+67.2
$BCl_3(g)$	−404	290	−389	$HCN(g)$	+135.1	201.7	+124.7
$B_2H_6(g)$	+36	232	+87	$CN^-(aq)$	+150.6	94.1	+172.4
$B_2O_3(s)$	−1273	53.8	−1194	$CH_4(g)$	−74.848	186.2	−50.79
$B(OH)_3(s)$	−1094	88.8	−969	$C_2H_2(g)$	+226.75	200.8	+209
Bromine				$C_2H_4(g)$	+52.284	219.8	+68.12
$Br_2(l)$	0	152.2	0	$C_2H_6(g)$	−84.667	229.5	−32.9
$Br_2(g)$	+30.9	245.4	+3.11	$C_3H_8(g)$	−104	269.9	−23
$HBr(g)$	−36	198.5	+53.1	$C_4H_{10}(g)$	−126	310.2	−17.0
$Br^-(aq)$	−121.55	82.4	−103.96	$C_6H_6(l)$	+49.0	173.3	+124.3
Cadmium				$CH_3OH(l)$	−238.6	126.8	−166.2
				$C_2H_5OH(l)$	−277.63	161	−174.8
				$HCHO_2(g)$	−363	251	+335
				$HC_2H_3O_2(l)$	−487.0	160	−392.5
$Cd(s)$	0	51.8	0	$HCHO(g)$	−108.6	218.8	−102.5
$Cd^{2+}(aq)$	−75.90	−73.2	−77.61	$CH_3CHO(g)$	−167	250	−129

(Continued)

TABLE C.1 Thermodynamic Data for Selected Elements, Compounds, and Ions (25 °C) (Continued)

Substance	ΔH_f°(kJ mol^{-1})	S°(J mol^{-1} K^{-1})	ΔG_f°(kJ mol^{-1})	Substance	ΔH_f°(kJ mol^{-1})	S°(J mol^{-1} K^{-1})	ΔG_f°(kJ mol^{-1})
$(CH_3)_2CO(l)$	−248.1	200.4	−155.4	$H_2O_2(l)$	−187.6	109.6	−120.3
$C_6H_5CO_2H(s)$	−385.1	167.6	−245.3	$H_2Se(g)$	+76	219	+62.3
$CO(NH_2)_2(s)$	−333.19	104.6	−197.2	$H_2Te(g)$	+154	234	+138
$CO(NH_2)_2(aq)$	−391.2	173.8	−203.8	**Iodine**			
$CH_2(NH_2)CO_2H(s)$	−532.9	103.5	−373.4	$I_2(s)$	0	116.1	0
Chlorine				$I_2(g)$	+62.4	260.7	+19.3
$Cl_2(g)$	0	223.0	0	$HI(g)$	+26.6	206	+1.30
$Cl^-(aq)$	−167.2	56.5	−131.2	**Iron**			
$HCl(g)$	−92.30	186.7	−95.27	$Fe(s)$	0	27	0
$HCl(aq)$	−167.2	56.5	−131.2	$Fe^{2+}(aq)$	−89.1	−137.7	−78.9
$HClO(aq)$	−131.3	106.8	−80.21	$Fe^{3+}(aq)$	−48.5	−315.9	−4.7
Chromium				$Fe_2O_3(s)$	−822.2	90.0	−741.0
$Cr(s)$	0	23.8	0	$Fe_3O_4(s)$	−1118.4	146.4	−1015.4
$Cr^{3+}(aq)$	−232			$FeS(s)$	−100.0	60.3	−100.4
$CrCl_2(s)$	−326	115	−282	$FeS_2(s)$	−178.2	52.9	−166.9
$CrCl_3(s)$	−563.2	126	−493.7	**Lead**			
$Cr_2O_3(s)$	−1141	81.2	−1059	$Pb(s)$	0	64.8	0
$CrO_3(s)$	−585.8	72.0	−506.2	$Pb^{2+}(aq)$	−1.7	10.5	−24.4
$(NH_4)_2Cr_2O_7(s)$	−1807			$PbCl_2(s)$	−359.4	136	−314.1
$K_2Cr_2O_7(s)$	−2033.01			$PbO(s)$	−219.2	67.8	−189.3
Cobalt				$PbO_2(s)$	−277	68.6	−219
$Co(s)$	0	30.0	0	$Pb(OH)_2(s)$	−515.9	88	−420.9
$Co^{2+}(aq)$	−59.4	−110	−53.6	$PbS(s)$	−100	91.2	−98.7
$CoCl_2(s)$	−325.5	106	−282.4	$PbSO_4(s)$	−920.1	149	−811.3
$Co(NO_3)_2(s)$	−422.2	192	−230.5	**Lithium**			
$CoO(s)$	−237.9	53.0	−214.2	$Li(s)$	0	28.4	0
$CoS(s)$	−80.8	67.4	−82.8	$Li^+(aq)$	−278.6	10.3	
Copper				$LiF(s)$	−611.7	35.7	−583.3
$Cu(s)$	0	33.15	0	$LiCl(s)$	−408	59.29	−383.7
$Cu^{2+}(aq)$	+64.77	−99.6	+65.49	$LiBr(s)$	−350.3	66.9	−338.87
$CuCl(s)$	−137.2	86.2	−119.87	$Li_2O(s)$	−596.5	37.9	−560.5
$CuCl_2(s)$	−172	119	−131	$Li_3N(s)$	−199	37.7	−155.4
$Cu_2O(s)$	−168.6	93.1	−146.0	**Magnesium**			
$CuO(s)$	−155	42.6	−127	$Mg(s)$	0	32.5	0
$Cu_2S(s)$	−79.5	121	−86.2	$Mg^{2+}(aq)$	−466.9	−138.1	−454.8
$CuS(s)$	−53.1	66.5	−53.6	$MgCO_3(s)$	−1113	65.7	−1029
$CuSO_4(s)$	−771.4	109	−661.8	$MgF_2(s)$	−1124	79.9	−1056
$CuSO_4 \cdot 5H_2O(s)$	−2279.7	300.4	−1879.7	$MgCl_2(s)$	−641.8	89.5	−592.5
Fluorine				$MgCl_2 \cdot 2H_2O(s)$	−1280	180	−1118
$F_2(g)$	0	202.7	0	$Mg_3N_2(s)$	−463.2	87.9	−411
$F^-(aq)$	−332.6	−13.8	−278.8	$MgO(s)$	−601.7	26.9	−569.4
$HF(g)$	−271	173.5	−273	$Mg(OH)_2(s)$	−924.7	63.1	−833.9
Gold				**Manganese**			
$Au(s)$	0	47.7	0	$Mn(s)$	0	32.0	0
$Au_2O_3(s)$	+80.8	125	+163	$Mn^{2+}(aq)$	−223	−74.9	−228
$AuCl_3(s)$	−118	148	−48.5	$MnO_4^-(aq)$	−542.7	191	−449.4
Hydrogen				$KMnO_4(s)$	−813.4	171.71	−713.8
$H_2(g)$	0	130.6	0	$MnO(s)$	−385	60.2	−363
$H_2O(l)$	−285.9	69.96	−237.2	$Mn_2O_3(s)$	−959.8	110	−882.0
$H_2O(g)$	−241.8	188.7	−228.6	$MnO_2(s)$	−520.9	53.1	−466.1

(Continued)

TABLE C.1 Thermodynamic Data for Selected Elements, Compounds, and Ions (25 °C) *(Continued)*

Substance	ΔH_f°(kJ mol^{-1})	S°(J mol^{-1} K^{-1})	ΔG_f°(kJ mol^{-1})	Substance	ΔH_f°(kJ mol^{-1})	S°(J mol^{-1} K^{-1})	ΔG_f°(kJ mol^{-1})
$Mn_3O_4(s)$	−1387	149	−1280	$KBr(s)$	−393.8	95.9	−380.7
$MnSO_4(s)$	−1064	112	−956	$KI(s)$	−327.9	106.3	−324.9
Mercury				$KOH(s)$	−424.8	78.9	−379.1
$Hg(l)$	0	76.1	0	$K_2O(s)$	−361	98.3	−322
$Hg(g)$	+61.32	175	+31.8	$K_2SO_4(s)$	−1433.7	176	−1316.4
$Hg_2Cl_2(s)$	−265.2	192.5	−210.8	***Silicon***			
$HgCl_2(s)$	−224.3	146.0	−178.6	$Si(s)$	0	19	0
$HgO(s)$	−90.83	70.3	−58.54	$SiH_4(g)$	+33	205	+52.3
$HgS(s,red)$	−58.2	82.4	−50.6	$SiO_2(s,alpha)$	−910.0	41.8	−856
Nickel				***Silver***			
$Ni(s)$	0	30	0	$Ag(s)$	0	42.55	0
$NiCl_2(s)$	−305	97.5	−259	$Ag^+(aq)$	+105.58	72.68	+77.11
$NiO(s)$	−244	38	−216	$AgCl(s)$	−127.0	96.2	−109.7
$NiO_2(s)$			−199	$AgBr(s)$	−100.4	107.1	−96.9
$NiSO_4(s)$	−891.2	77.8	−773.6	$AgNO_3(s)$	−124	141	−32
$NiCO_3(s)$	−664.0	91.6	−615.0	$Ag_2O(s)$	−31.1	121.3	−11.2
$Ni(CO)_4(g)$	−220	399	−567.4	***Sodium***			
Nitrogen				$Na(s)$	0	51.0	0
$N_2(g)$	0	191.5	0	$Na^+(aq)$	−240.12	59.0	−261.91
$NH_3(g)$	−46.19	192.5	−16.7	$NaF(s)$	−571	51.5	−545
$NH_4^+(aq)$	−132.5	113	−79.37	$NaCl(s)$	−411.0	72.38	−384.0
$N_2H_4(g)$	+95.40	238.4	+159.3	$NaBr(s)$	−360	83.7	−349
$N_2H_4(l)$	+50.6	121.2	+149.4	$NaI(s)$	−288	91.2	−286
$NH_4Cl(s)$	−315.4	94.6	−203.9	$NaHCO_3(s)$	−947.7	102	−851.9
$NO(g)$	+90.37	210.6	+86.69	$Na_2CO_3(s)$	−1131	136	−1048
$NO_2(g)$	+33.8	240.5	+51.84	$Na_2O_2(s)$	−510.9	94.6	−447.7
$N_2O(g)$	+81.57	220.0	+103.6	$Na_2O(s)$	−510	72.8	−376
$N_2O_4(g)$	+9.67	304	+98.28	$NaOH(s)$	−426.8	64.18	−382
$N_2O_5(g)$	+11	356	+115	$Na_2SO_4(s)$	−1384.49	149.49	−1266.83
$HNO_3(l)$	−173.2	155.6	−79.91	***Sulfur***			
$NO_3^-(aq)$	−205.0	146.4	−108.74	$S(s, rhombic)$	0	31.9	0
Oxygen				$SO_2(g)$	−296.9	248.5	−300.4
$O_2(g)$	0	205.0	0	$SO_3(g)$	−395.2	256.2	−370.4
$O_3(g)$	+143	238.8	+163	$H_2S(g)$	−20.6	206	−33.6
$OH^-(aq)$	−230.0	−10.75	−157.24	$H_2SO_4(l)$	−811.32	157	−689.9
Phosphorus				$H_2SO_4(aq)$	−909.3	20.1	−744.5
$P(s,white)$	0	41.09	0	$SF_6(g)$	−1209	292	−1105
$P_4(g)$	+314.6	163.2	+278.3	***Tin***			
$PCl_3(g)$	−287.0	311.8	−267.8	$Sn(s,white)$	0	51.6	0
$PCl_5(g)$	−374.9	364.6	−305.0	$Sn^{2+}(aq)$	−8.8	−17	−27.2
$PH_3(g)$	+5.4	210.2	+12.9	$SnCl_4(l)$	−511.3	258.6	−440.2
$P_4O_6(s)$	−1640			$SnO(s)$	−285.8	56.5	−256.9
$POCl_3(g)$	−1109.7	646.5	−1019	$SnO_2(s)$	−580.7	52.3	−519.6
$POCl_3(l)$	−1186	26.36	−1035	***Zinc***			
$P_4O_{10}(s)$	−2984	228.9	−2698	$Zn(s)$	0	41.6	0
$H_3PO_4(s)$	−1279	110.5	−1119	$Zn^{2+}(aq)$	−153.9	−112.1	−147.06
Potassium				$ZnCl_2(s)$	−415.1	111	−369.4
$K(s)$	0	64.18	0	$ZnO(s)$	−348.3	43.6	−318.3
$K^+(aq)$	−252.4	102.5	−283.3	$ZnS(s)$	−205.6	57.7	−201.3
$KF(s)$	−567.3	66.6	−537.8	$ZnSO_4(s)$	−982.8	120	−874.5
$KCl(s)$	−435.89	82.59	−408.3				

TABLE C.2 Heats of Formation of Gaseous Atoms from Elements in Their Standard States

Element	$\Delta H_f^\circ (\text{kJ mol}^{-1})*$	Element	$\Delta H_f^\circ (\text{kJ mol}^{-1})*$
Group IA		*Group IVA*	
H	217.89	C	716.67
Li	161.5	Si	450
Na	107.8		
K	89.62	*Group VA*	
Rb	82.0	N	472.68
Cs	78.2	P	332.2
Group IIA		*Group VIA*	
Be	324.3	O	249.17
Mg	146.4	S	276.98
Ca	178.2		
Sr	163.6	*Group VIIA*	
Ba	177.8	F	79.14
Group IIIA		Cl	121.47
		Br	112.38
B	560	I	107.48
Al	329.7		

*All values in this table are positive because forming the gaseous atoms from the elements is endothermic: it involves bond breaking.

TABLE C.3 Average Bond Energies

Bond	Bond Energy (kJ mol^{-1})	Bond	Bond Energy (kJ mol^{-1})
C—C	348	C—Br	276
C=C	612	C—I	238
C≡C	960	H—H	436
C—H	412	H—F	565
C—N	305	H—Cl	431
C=N	613	H—Br	366
C≡N	890	H—I	299
C—O	360	H—N	388
C=O	743	H—O	463
C—F	484	H—S	338
C—Cl	338	H—Si	376

TABLE C.4 Vapor Pressure of Water as a Function of Temperature

Temp (°C)	Vapor Pressure (torr)	Temp (°C)	Vapor Pressure (torr)	Temp (°C)	Vapor Pressure (torr)	Temp (°C)	Vapor Pressure (torr)
0	4.58	11	9.84	22	19.8	33	37.7
1	4.93	12	10.5	23	21.1	34	39.9
2	5.29	13	11.2	24	22.4	35	41.2
3	5.68	14	12.0	25	23.8	36	44.6
4	6.10	15	12.8	26	25.2	37	47.1
5	6.54	16	13.6	27	26.7	38	49.7
6	7.01	17	14.5	28	28.3	39	52.4
7	7.51	18	15.5	29	30.0	40	55.3
8	8.04	19	16.5	30	31.8	41	58.3
9	8.61	20	17.5	31	33.7	42	61.5
10	9.21	21	18.7	32	35.7	43	64.8

(Continued)

TABLE C.4 Vapor Pressure of Water as a Function of Temperature (Continued)

Temp (°C)	Vapor Pressure (torr)	Temp (°C)	Vapor Pressure (torr)	Temp (°C)	Vapor Pressure (torr)	Temp (°C)	Vapor Pressure (torr)
44	68.3	59	142.6	74	277.2	89	506.1
45	71.9	60	149.4	75	289.1	90	525.8
46	75.6	61	156.4	76	301.4	91	546.0
47	79.6	62	163.8	77	314.1	92	567.0
48	83.7	63	171.4	78	327.3	93	588.6
49	88.0	64	179.3	79	341.0	94	610.9
50	92.5	65	187.5	80	355.1	95	633.9
51	97.2	66	196.1	81	369.7	96	657.6
52	102.1	67	205.0	82	384.9	97	682.1
53	107.2	68	214.2	83	400.6	98	707.3
54	112.5	69	223.7	84	416.8	99	733.2
55	118.0	70	233.7	85	433.6	100	760.0
56	123.8	71	243.9	86	450.9		
57	129.8	72	254.6	87	468.7		
58	136.1	73	265.7	88	487.1		

TABLE C.5 Solubility Product Constants

Salt	K_{sp}	Salt	K_{sp}
Fluorides		**Hydroxides**	
MgF_2	6.6×10^{-9}	$Mg(OH)_2$	7.1×10^{-12}
CaF_2	3.9×10^{-11}	$Ca(OH)_2$	6.5×10^{-6}
SrF_2	2.9×10^{-9}	$Mn(OH)_2$	1.6×10^{-13}
BaF_2	1.7×10^{-6}	$Fe(OH)_2$	7.9×10^{-16}
LiF	1.7×10^{-3}	$Fe(OH)_3$	1.6×10^{-39}
PbF_2	3.6×10^{-8}	$Co(OH)_2$	1×10^{-15}
		$Co(OH)_3$	3×10^{-45}
Chlorides		$Ni(OH)_2$	6×10^{-16}
$CuCl$	1.9×10^{-7}	$Cu(OH)_2$	4.8×10^{-20}
$AgCl$	1.8×10^{-10}	$V(OH)_3$	4×10^{-35}
Hg_2Cl_2	1.2×10^{-18}	$Cr(OH)_3$	2×10^{-30}
$TlCl$	1.8×10^{-4}	Ag_2O	1.9×10^{-8}
$PbCl_2$	1.7×10^{-5}	$Zn(OH)_2$	3.0×10^{-16}
$AuCl_3$	3.2×10^{-25}	$Cd(OH)_2$	5.0×10^{-15}
		$Al(OH)_3$	
Bromides		(alpha form)	3×10^{-34}
$CuBr$	5×10^{-9}		
$AgBr$	5.0×10^{-13}	**Cyanides**	
Hg_2Br_2	5.6×10^{-23}	$AgCN$	1.2×10^{-16}
$HgBr_2$	1.3×10^{-19}	$Zn(CN)_2$	3×10^{-16}
$PbBr_2$	2.1×10^{-6}		
		Sulfites	
		$CaSO_3$	3×10^{-7}
Iodides		Ag_2SO_3	1.5×10^{-14}
CuI	1×10^{-12}	$BaSO_3$	8×10^{-7}
AgI	8.3×10^{-17}		
Hg_2I_2	4.7×10^{-29}	**Sulfates**	
HgI_2	1.1×10^{-28}	$CaSO_4$	2.4×10^{-5}
PbI_2	7.9×10^{-9}	$SrSO_4$	3.2×10^{-7}

(Continued)

TABLE C.5 **Solubility Product Constants** (*Continued*)

Salt	K_{sp}	Salt	K_{sp}
$BaSO_4$	1.1×10^{-10}	Ag_2CO_3	8.1×10^{-12}
$RaSO_4$	4.3×10^{-11}	Hg_2CO_3	8.9×10^{-17}
Ag_2SO_4	1.5×10^{-5}	$ZnCO_3$	1.0×10^{-10}
Hg_2SO_4	7.4×10^{-7}	$CdCO_3$	1.8×10^{-14}
$PbSO_4$	6.3×10^{-7}	$PbCO_3$	7.4×10^{-14}
Chromates		***Phosphates***	
$BaCrO_4$	2.1×10^{-10}	$Ca_3(PO_4)_2$	2.0×10^{-29}
$CuCrO_4$	3.6×10^{-6}	$Mg_3(PO_4)_2$	6.3×10^{-26}
Ag_2CrO_4	1.2×10^{-12}	$SrHPO_4$	1.2×10^{-7}
Hg_2CrO_4	2.0×10^{-9}	$BaHPO_4$	4.0×10^{-8}
$CaCrO_4$	7.1×10^{-4}	$LaPO_4$	3.7×10^{-23}
$PbCrO_4$	1.8×10^{-14}	$Fe_3(PO_4)_2$	1×10^{-36}
		Ag_3PO_4	2.8×10^{-18}
Carbonates		$FePO_4$	4.0×10^{-27}
$MgCO_3$	3.5×10^{-8}	$Zn_3(PO_4)_2$	5×10^{-36}
$CaCO_3$	4.5×10^{-9}	$Pb_3(PO_4)_2$	3.0×10^{-44}
$SrCO_3$	9.3×10^{-10}	$Ba_3(PO_4)_2$	5.8×10^{-38}
$BaCO_3$	5.0×10^{-9}		
$MnCO_3$	5.0×10^{-10}	***Ferrocyanides***	
$FeCO_3$	2.1×10^{-11}	$Zn_2[Fe(CN)_6]$	2.1×10^{-16}
$CoCO_3$	1.0×10^{-10}	$Cd_2[Fe(CN)_6]$	4.2×10^{-18}
$NiCO_3$	1.3×10^{-7}	$Pb_2[Fe(CN)_6]$	9.5×10^{-19}
$CuCO_3$	2.5×10^{-10}		

TABLE C.6 **Formation Constants of Complexes (25 °C)**

Complex Ion Equilibrium	K_{form}	Complex Ion Equilibrium	K_{form}
Halide Complexes		$Hg^{2+} + 4NH_3 \rightleftharpoons [Hg(NH_3)_4]^{2+}$	1.8×10^{19}
$Al^{3+} + 6F^- \rightleftharpoons [AlF_6]^{3-}$	1×10^{20}	$Co^{2+} + 6NH_3 \rightleftharpoons [Co(NH_3)_6]^{2+}$	5.0×10^{4}
$Al^{3+} + 4F^- \rightleftharpoons [AlF_4]^-$	2.0×10^{8}	$Co^{3+} + 6NH_3 \rightleftharpoons [Co(NH_3)_6]^{3+}$	4.6×10^{33}
$Be^{2+} + 4F^- \rightleftharpoons [BeF_4]^{2-}$	1.3×10^{13}	$Cd^{2+} + 6NH_3 \rightleftharpoons [Cd(NH_3)_6]^{2+}$	2.6×10^{5}
$Sn^{4+} + 6F^- \rightleftharpoons [SnF_6]^{2-}$	1×10^{25}	$Ni^{2+} + 6NH_3 \rightleftharpoons [Ni(NH_3)_6]^{2+}$	2.0×10^{8}
$Cu^+ + 2Cl^- \rightleftharpoons [CuCl_2]^-$	3×10^{5}		
$Ag^+ + 2Cl^- \rightleftharpoons [AgCl_2]^-$	1.8×10^{5}	***Cyanide Complexes***	
$Pb^{2+} + 4Cl^- \rightleftharpoons [PbCl_4]^{2-}$	2.5×10^{15}	$Fe^{2+} + 6CN^- \rightleftharpoons [Fe(CN)_6]^{4-}$	1.0×10^{24}
$Zn^{2+} + 4Cl^- \rightleftharpoons [ZnCl_4]^{2-}$	1.6	$Fe^{3+} + 6CN^- \rightleftharpoons [Fe(CN)_6]^{3-}$	1.0×10^{31}
$Hg^{2+} + 4Cl^- \rightleftharpoons [HgCl_4]^{2-}$	5.0×10^{15}	$Ag^+ + 2CN^- \rightleftharpoons [Ag(CN)_2]^-$	5.3×10^{18}
$Cu^+ + 2Br^- \rightleftharpoons [CuBr_2]^-$	8×10^{5}	$Cu^+ + 2CN^- \rightleftharpoons [Cu(CN)_2]^-$	1.0×10^{16}
$Ag^+ + 2Br^- \rightleftharpoons [AgBr_2]^-$	1.7×10^{7}	$Cd^{2+} + 4CN^- \rightleftharpoons [Cd(CN)_4]^{2-}$	7.7×10^{16}
$Hg^{2+} + 4Br^- \rightleftharpoons [HgBr_4]^{2-}$	1×10^{21}	$Au^+ + 2CN^- \rightleftharpoons [Au(CN)_2]^-$	2×10^{38}
$Cu^+ + 2I^- \rightleftharpoons [CuI_2]^-$	8×10^{8}		
$Ag^+ + 2I^- \rightleftharpoons [AgI_2]^-$	1×10^{11}	***Complexes with Other Monodentate Ligands*** ***Methylamine (CH₃NH₂)***	
$Pb^{2+} + 4I^- \rightleftharpoons [PbI_4]^{2-}$	3×10^{4}	$Ag^+ + 2CH_3NH_2 \rightleftharpoons [Ag(CH_3NH_2)_2]^+$	7.8×10^{6}
$Hg^{2+} + 4I^- \rightleftharpoons [HgI_4]^{2-}$	1.9×10^{30}		
Ammonia Complexes		***Thiocyanate ion (SCN⁻)***	
$Ag^+ + 2NH_3 \rightleftharpoons [Ag(NH_3)_2]^+$	1.6×10^{7}	$Cd^{2+} + 4SCN^- \rightleftharpoons [Cd(SCN)_4]^{2-}$	1×10^{3}
$Zn^{2+} + 4NH_3 \rightleftharpoons [Zn(NH_3)_4]^{2+}$	7.8×10^{8}	$Cu^{2+} + 2SCN^- \rightleftharpoons [Cu(SCN)_2]$	5.6×10^{3}
$Cu^{2+} + 4NH_3 \rightleftharpoons [Cu(NH_3)_4]^{2+}$	1.1×10^{13}	$Fe^{3+} + 3SCN^- \rightleftharpoons [Fe(SCN)_3]$	2×10^{6}
		$Hg^{2+} + 4SCN^- \rightleftharpoons [Hg(SCN)_4]^{2-}$	5.0×10^{21}

(Continued)

TABLE C.6 Formation Constants of Complexes (25 °C) (Continued)

Complex Ion Equilibrium	K_{form}	Complex Ion Equilibrium	K_{form}
Hydroxide ion (OH$^-$)		$Ni^{2+} + 3$ bipy $\rightleftharpoons$ [Ni(bipy)$_3$]$^{2+}$	3.0×10^{20}
$Cu^{2+} + 4OH^- \rightleftharpoons$ [Cu(OH)$_4$]$^{2-}$	1.3×10^{16}	$Co^{2+} + 3$ bipy $\rightleftharpoons$ [Co(bipy)$_3$]$^{2+}$	8×10^{15}
$Zn^{2+} + 4OH^- \rightleftharpoons$ [Zn(OH)$_4$]$^{2-}$	2×10^{20}	$Mn^{2+} + 3$ phen $\rightleftharpoons$ [Mn(phen)$_3$]$^{2+}$	2×10^{10}
		$Fe^{2+} + 3$ phen $\rightleftharpoons$ [Fe(phen)$_3$]$^{2+}$	1×10^{21}
Complexes with Bidentate Ligands*		$Co^{2+} + 3$ phen $\rightleftharpoons$ [Co(phen)$_3$]$^{2+}$	6×10^{19}
$Mn^{2+} + 3$ en $\rightleftharpoons$ [Mn(en)$_3$]$^{2+}$	6.5×10^5	$Ni^{2+} + 3$ phen $\rightleftharpoons$ [Ni(phen)$_3$]$^{2+}$	2×10^{24}
$Fe^{2+} + 3$ en $\rightleftharpoons$ [Fe(en)$_3$]$^{2+}$	5.2×10^9	$Co^{2+} + 3C_2O_4{}^{2-} \rightleftharpoons$ [Co(C$_2$O$_4$)$_3$]$^{4-}$	4.5×10^6
$Co^{2+} + 3$ en $\rightleftharpoons$ [Co(en)$_3$]$^{2+}$	1.3×10^{14}	$Fe^{3+} + 3C_2O_4{}^{2-} \rightleftharpoons$ [Fe(C$_2$O$_4$)$_3$]$^{3-}$	3.3×10^{20}
$Co^{3+} + 3$ en $\rightleftharpoons$ [Co(en)$_3$]$^{3+}$	4.8×10^{48}		
$Ni^{2+} + 3$ en $\rightleftharpoons$ [Ni(en)$_3$]$^{2+}$	4.1×10^{17}	**Complexes of Other Polydentate Ligands***	
$Cu^{2+} + 2$ en $\rightleftharpoons$ [Cu(en)$_2$]$^{2+}$	3.5×10^{19}	$Zn^{2+} +$ EDTA$^{4-} \rightleftharpoons$ [Zn(EDTA)]$^{2-}$	3.8×10^{16}
$Mn^{2+} + 3$ bipy $\rightleftharpoons$ [Mn(bipy)$_3$]$^{2+}$	1×10^6	$Mg^{2+} + 2NTA^{3-} \rightleftharpoons$ [Mg(NTA)$_2$]$^{4-}$	1.6×10^{10}
$Fe^{2+} + 3$ bipy $\rightleftharpoons$ [Fe(bipy)$_3$]$^{2+}$	1.6×10^{17}	$Ca^{2+} + 2NTA^{3-} \rightleftharpoons$ [Ca(NTA)$_2$]$^{4-}$	3.2×10^{11}

*en = ethylenediamine

bipy = bipyridyl

bipyridyl

phen = 1,10-phenanthroline

1,10-phenanthroline

EDTA^{4-} = ethylenediaminetetraacetate ion

NTA^{3-} = nitrilotriacetate ion

TABLE C.7 Ionization Constants of Weak Acids and Bases (Alternative Formulas in Parentheses)

Monoprotic Acid	Name	K_a
HC$_2$O$_2$Cl$_3$ (Cl$_3$CCO$_2$H)	trichloroacetic acid	2.2×10^{-1}
HIO$_3$	iodic acid	1.69×10^{-1}
HC$_2$HO$_2$Cl$_2$ (Cl$_2$CHCO$_2$H)	dichloroacetic acid	5.0×10^{-2}
HC$_2$H$_2$O$_2$Cl (ClH$_2$CCO$_2$H)	chloroacetic acid	1.36×10^{-3}
HNO$_2$	nitrous acid	7.1×10^{-4}
HF	hydrofluoric acid	6.8×10^{-4}
HOCN	cyanic acid	3.5×10^{-4}
HCHO$_2$ (HCO$_2$H)	formic acid	1.8×10^{-4}
HC$_3$H$_5$O$_3$ [CH$_3$CH(OH)CO$_2$H]	lactic acid	1.38×10^{-4}
HC$_4$H$_3$N$_2$O$_3$	barbituric acid	9.8×10^{-5}
HC$_7$H$_5$O$_2$ (C$_6$H$_5$CO$_2$H)	benzoic acid	6.28×10^{-5}
HC$_4$H$_7$O$_2$ (CH$_3$CH$_2$CH$_2$CO$_2$H)	butanoic acid	1.52×10^{-5}
HN$_3$	hydrazoic acid	1.8×10^{-5}
HC$_2$H$_3$O$_2$ (CH$_3$CO$_2$H)	acetic acid	1.8×10^{-5}
HC$_3$H$_5$O$_2$ (CH$_3$CH$_2$CO$_2$H)	propanoic acid	1.34×10^{-5}
HC$_2$H$_4$NO$_2$	nicotinic acid (niacin)	1.4×10^{-5}
HOCl	hypochlorous acid	3.0×10^{-8}
HOBr	hypobromous acid	2.1×10^{-9}

(Continued)

TABLE C.7	Ionization Constants of Weak Acids and Bases (Alternative Formulas in Parentheses) *(Continued)*

Monoprotic Acid	Name	K_a
HCN	hydrocyanic acid	6.2×10^{-10}
HC_6H_5O	phenol	1.3×10^{-10}
HOI	hypoiodous acid	2.3×10^{-11}
H_2O_2	hydrogen peroxide	1.8×10^{-12}

Polyprotic Acid	Name	K_{a_1}	K_{a_2}	K_{a_3}
H_2SO_4	sulfuric acid	large	1.0×10^{-2}	
H_2CrO_4	chromic acid	5.0	1.5×10^{-6}	
$H_2C_2O_4$	oxalic acid	5.6×10^{-2}	5.4×10^{-5}	
H_3PO_3	phosphorous acid	3×10^{-2}	1.6×10^{-7}	
$H_2S(aq)$	hydrosulfuric acid	9.5×10^{-8}	1×10^{-19}	
H_2SO_3	sulfurous acid	1.2×10^{-2}	6.6×10^{-8}	
H_2SeO_4	selenic acid	large	1.2×10^{-2}	
H_2SeO_3	selenous acid	4.5×10^{-3}	1.1×10^{-8}	
H_6TeO_6	telluric acid	2×10^{-8}	1×10^{-11}	
H_2TeO_3	tellurous acid	3.3×10^{-3}	2.0×10^{-8}	
$H_2C_3H_2O_4$ ($HO_2CCH_2CO_2H$)	malonic acid	1.4×10^{-3}	2.0×10^{-6}	
$H_2C_8H_4O_4$	phthalic acid	1.1×10^{-3}	3.9×10^{-6}	
$H_2C_4H_4O_6$	tartaric acid	9.2×10^{-4}	4.3×10^{-5}	
$H_2C_6H_6O_6$	ascorbic acid	6.8×10^{-5}	2.7×10^{-12}	
H_2CO_3	carbonic acid	4.3×10^{-7}	4.7×10^{-11}	
H_3PO_4	phosphoric acid	7.1×10^{-3}	6.3×10^{-8}	4.5×10^{-13}
H_3AsO_4	arsenic acid	5.6×10^{-3}	1.7×10^{-7}	4.0×10^{-12}
$H_3C_6H_5O_7$	citric acid	7.1×10^{-4}	1.7×10^{-5}	6.3×10^{-6}

Weak Base	Name	K_b
$(CH_3)_2NH$	dimethylamine	9.6×10^{-4}
$C_4H_9NH_2$	butylamine	5.9×10^{-4}
CH_3NH_2	methylamine	4.4×10^{-4}
$CH_3CH_2NH_2$	ethylamine	4.3×10^{-4}
$(CH_3)_3N$	trimethylamine	7.4×10^{-5}
NH_3	ammonia	1.8×10^{-5}
$C_{21}H_{22}N_2O_2$	strychnine	1.0×10^{-6}
N_2H_4	hydrazine	9.6×10^{-7}
$C_{17}H_{19}NO_3$	morphine	7.5×10^{-7}
NH_2OH	hydroxylamine	6.6×10^{-9}
C_5H_5N	pyridine	1.5×10^{-9}
$C_6H_5NH_2$	aniline	4.1×10^{-10}
PH_3	phosphine	10^{-28}

TABLE C.8 Standard Reduction Potentials (25 °C)

$E°$ (Volts)	Half-Cell Reaction
+2.87	$F_2(g) + 2e^- \rightleftharpoons 2F^-(aq)$
+2.08	$O_3(g) + 2H^+(aq) + 2e^- \rightleftharpoons O_2(g) + H_2O$
+2.01	$S_2O_8^{2-}(aq) + 2e^- \rightleftharpoons 2SO_4^{2-}(aq)$
+1.82	$Co^{3+}(aq) + e^- \rightleftharpoons Co^{2+}(aq)$
+1.77	$H_2O_2(aq) + 2H^+(aq) + 2e^- \rightleftharpoons 2H_2O$
+1.695	$MnO_4^-(aq) + 4H^+(aq) + 3e^- \rightleftharpoons MnO_2(s) + 2H_2O$
+1.69	$PbO_2(s) + HSO_4^-(aq) + 3H^+(aq) + 2e^- \rightleftharpoons PbSO_4(s) + 2H_2O$
+1.63	$2HOCl(aq) + 2H^+(aq) + 2e^- \rightleftharpoons Cl_2(g) + 2H_2O$
+1.51	$Mn^{3+}(aq) + e^- \rightleftharpoons Mn^{2+}(aq)$
+1.51	$MnO_4^-(aq) + 8H^+(aq) + 5e^- \rightleftharpoons Mn^{2+}(aq) + 4H_2O$
+1.46	$PbO_2(s) + 4H^+(aq) + 2e^- \rightleftharpoons Pb^{2+}(aq) + 2H_2O$
+1.44	$BrO_3^-(aq) + 6H^+(aq) + 6e^- \rightleftharpoons Br^-(aq) + 3H_2O$
+1.42	$Au^{3+}(aq) + 3e^- \rightleftharpoons Au(s)$
+1.36	$Cl_2(g) + 2e^- \rightleftharpoons 2Cl^-(aq)$
+1.33	$Cr_2O_7^{2-}(aq) + 14H^+(aq) + 6e^- \rightleftharpoons 2Cr^{3+}(aq) + 7H_2O$
+1.24	$O_3(g) + H_2O + 2e^- \rightleftharpoons O_2(g) + 2OH^-(aq)$
+1.23	$MnO_2(s) + 4H^+(aq) + 2e^- \rightleftharpoons Mn^{2+}(aq) + 2H_2O$
+1.23	$O_2(g) + 4H^+(aq) + 4e^- \rightleftharpoons 2H_2O$
+1.20	$Pt^{2+}(aq) + 2e^- \rightleftharpoons Pt(s)$
+1.07	$Br_2(aq) + 2e^- \rightleftharpoons 2Br^-(aq)$
+0.96	$NO_3^-(aq) + 4H^+(aq) + 3e^- \rightleftharpoons NO(g) + 2H_2O$
+0.94	$NO_3^-(aq) + 3H^+(aq) + 2e^- \rightleftharpoons HNO_2(aq) + H_2O$
+0.91	$2Hg^{2+}(aq) + 2e^- \rightleftharpoons Hg_2^{2+}(aq)$
+0.87	$HO_2^-(aq) + H_2O + 2e^- \rightleftharpoons 3OH^-(aq)$
+0.80	$NO_3^-(aq) + 4H^+(aq) + 2e^- \rightleftharpoons 2NO_2(g) + 2H_2O$
+0.80	$Ag^+(aq) + e^- \rightleftharpoons Ag(s)$
+0.77	$Fe^{3+}(aq) + e^- \rightleftharpoons Fe^{2+}(aq)$
+0.69	$O_2(g) + 2H^+(aq) + 2e^- \rightleftharpoons H_2O_2(aq)$
+0.54	$I_2(s) + 2e^- \rightleftharpoons 2I^-(aq)$
+0.49	$NiO_2(s) + 2H_2O + 2e^- \rightleftharpoons Ni(OH)_2(s) + 2OH^-(aq)$
+0.45	$SO_2(aq) + 4H^+(aq) + 4e^- \rightleftharpoons S(s) + 2H_2O$
+0.401	$O_2(g) + 2H_2O + 4e^- \rightleftharpoons 4OH^-(aq)$
+0.34	$Cu^{2+}(aq) + 2e^- \rightleftharpoons Cu(s)$
+0.27	$Hg_2Cl_2(s) + 2e^- \rightleftharpoons 2Hg(l) + 2Cl^-(aq)$
+0.25	$PbO_2(s) + H_2O + 2e^- \rightleftharpoons PbO(s) + 2OH^-(aq)$
+0.2223	$AgCl(s) + e^- \rightleftharpoons Ag(s) + Cl^-(aq)$
+0.172	$SO_4^{2-}(aq) + 4H^+(aq) + 2e^- \rightleftharpoons H_2SO_3(aq) + H_2O$
+0.169	$S_4O_6^{2-}(aq) + 2e^- \rightleftharpoons 2S_2O_3^{2-}(aq)$
+0.16	$Cu^{2+}(aq) + e^- \rightleftharpoons Cu^+(aq)$
+0.15	$Sn^{4+}(aq) + 2e^- \rightleftharpoons Sn^{2+}(aq)$
+0.14	$S(s) + 2H^+(aq) + 2e^- \rightleftharpoons H_2S(g)$
+0.07	$AgBr(s) + e^- \rightleftharpoons Ag(s) + Br^-(aq)$
0 (exactly)	$2H^+(aq) + 2e^- \rightleftharpoons H_2(g)$
-0.13	$Pb^{2+}(aq) + 2e^- \rightleftharpoons Pb(s)$

(Continued)

TABLE C.8 **Standard Reduction Potentials (25 °C)** *(Continued)*

$E°$ (Volts)	Half-Cell Reaction
−0.14	$Sn^{2+}(aq) + 2e^- \rightleftharpoons Sn(s)$
−0.15	$AgI(s) + e^- \rightleftharpoons Ag(s) + I^-(aq)$
−0.25	$Ni^{2+}(aq) + 2e^- \rightleftharpoons Ni(s)$
−0.28	$Co^{2+}(aq) + 2e^- \rightleftharpoons Co(s)$
−0.34	$In^{3+}(aq) + 3e^- \rightleftharpoons In(s)$
−0.34	$Tl^+(aq) + e^- \rightleftharpoons Tl(s)$
−0.36	$PbSO_4(s) + H^+(aq) + 2e^- \rightleftharpoons Pb(s) + HSO_4^-(aq)$
−0.40	$Cd^{2+}(aq) + 2e^- \rightleftharpoons Cd(s)$
−0.44	$Fe^{2+}(aq) + 2e^- \rightleftharpoons Fe(s)$
−0.56	$Ga^{3+}(aq) + 3e^- \rightleftharpoons Ga(s)$
−0.58	$PbO(s) + H_2O + 2e^- \rightleftharpoons Pb(s) + 2OH^-(aq)$
−0.74	$Cr^{3+}(aq) + 3e^- \rightleftharpoons Cr(s)$
−0.76	$Zn^{2+}(aq) + 2e^- \rightleftharpoons Zn(s)$
−0.81	$Cd(OH)_2(s) + 2e^- \rightleftharpoons Cd(s) + 2OH^-(aq)$
−0.83	$2H_2O + 2e^- \rightleftharpoons H_2(g) + 2OH^-(aq)$
−0.88	$Fe(OH)_2(s) + 2e^- \rightleftharpoons Fe(s) + 2OH^-(aq)$
−0.91	$Cr^{2+}(aq) + e^- \rightleftharpoons Cr(s)$
−1.16	$N_2(g) + 4H_2O + 4e^- \rightleftharpoons N_2O_4(aq) + 4OH^-(aq)$
−1.18	$V^{2+}(aq) + 2e^- \rightleftharpoons V(s)$
−1.216	$ZnO_2^-(aq) + 2H_2O + 2e^- \rightleftharpoons Zn(s) + 4OH^-(aq)$
−1.63	$Ti^{2+}(aq) + 2e^- \rightleftharpoons Ti(s)$
−1.66	$Al^{3+}(aq) + 3e^- \rightleftharpoons Al(s)$
−1.79	$U^{3+}(aq) + 3e^- \rightleftharpoons U(s)$
−2.02	$Sc^{3+}(aq) + 3e^- \rightleftharpoons Sc(s)$
−2.36	$La^{3+}(aq) + 3e^- \rightleftharpoons La(s)$
−2.37	$Y^{3+}(aq) + 3e^- \rightleftharpoons Y(s)$
−2.37	$Mg^{2+}(aq) + 2e^- \rightleftharpoons Mg(s)$
−2.71	$Na^+(aq) + e^- \rightleftharpoons Na(s)$
−2.76	$Ca^{2+}(aq) + 2e^- \rightleftharpoons Ca(s)$
−2.89	$Sr^{2+}(aq) + 2e^- \rightleftharpoons Sr(s)$
−2.90	$Ba^{2+}(aq) + 2e^- \rightleftharpoons Ba(s)$
−2.92	$Cs^+(aq) + e^- \rightleftharpoons Cs(s)$
−2.92	$K^+(aq) + e^- \rightleftharpoons K(s)$
−2.93	$Rb^+(aq) + e^- \rightleftharpoons Rb(s)$
−3.05	$Li^+(aq) + e^- \rightleftharpoons Li(s)$

GLOSSARY

This glossary has the definitions of the key terms that were marked in boldface throughout the chapters plus a few additional terms. The numbers in parentheses that follow the definitions are the numbers of the sections in which the glossary entries received their principal discussions.

A

Absolute Zero: 0 K, -273.15 °C. Nature's lowest temperature. (1.5, 10.3)

Acceptor: A Lewis acid; the central metal ion in a complex ion. (17.4, 21.5)

Accuracy: Freedom from error. The closeness of a measurement to the true value. (1.6)

Acid: *Arrhenius theory:* A substance that produces hydronium ions (hydrogen ions) in water. (4.3)

    Brønsted theory: A proton donor. (15.1)

    Lewis theory: An electron-pair acceptor. (15.3)

Acid–Base Indicator: A dye with one color in acid and another color in base. (4.3, 4.8)

Acid–Base Neutralization: The reaction of an acid with a base. (4.3, 15.3)

Acid Ionization Constant (K_a):

$$K_a = \frac{[H^+][A^-]}{[HA]} \text{ for the equilibrium,}$$

$$HA \rightleftharpoons H^+ + A^-, \quad (16.1)$$

Acid Rain: Rain made acidic by dissolved sulfur and nitrogen oxides.

Acid Salt: A salt of a partially neutralized polyprotic acid, for example, $NaHSO_4$ or $NaHCO_3$. (4.4)

Acid Solubility Product: The special solubility product expression for metal sulfides in dilute acid and related to the equation for their dissolving. For a divalent metal sulfide, MS,

$$MS(s) + 2H^+(aq) \longrightarrow$$
$$M^{2+}(aq) + H_2S(aq)$$

$$K_{spa} = \frac{[M^{2+}][H_2S]}{[H^+]^2} \quad (17.2)$$

Acidic Anhydride: An oxide that reacts with water to make the solution acidic. (4.3)

Acidic Solution: An aqueous solution in which $[H^+] > [OH^-]$. (15.5)

Actinide Elements (Actinide Series): Elements 90–103. (2.3)

Activated Complex: The chemical species that exists with partly broken and partly formed bonds in the transition state. (13.5)

Activation Energy (E_a): The minimum kinetic energy that must be possessed by the reactants in order to give an effective collision (one that produces products). (13.5)

Activities: Effective concentrations which properly should be substituted into a mass action expression to satisfy the equilibrium law. The activity of a solid is defined as having a value of 1. (14.4)

Activity: For a radioactive material, the number of disintegrations per second. (20.6)

Activity Series: A list of metals in order of their reactivity as reducing agents. (5.4)

Actual Yield: See *Yield, Actual.*

Addition Compound: A molecule formed by the joining of two simpler molecules through formation of a covalent bond (usually a coordinate covalent bond). (8.6)

Addition Polymer: A polymer formed by the simple addition of one monomer unit to another, a process that continues over and over until a very long chain of monomer units is produced. (22.6)

Addition Reaction: The addition of a molecule to a double or triple bond. (22.2)

Adiabatic Change: A change within a system during which no energy enters or leaves the system. (6.3)

Alcohol: An organic compound whose molecules have the OH group attached to tetrahedral carbon. (2.6, 22.3)

Aldehyde: An organic compound whose molecules have the group $-CH=O$. (22.5)

Alkali Metals: The Group IA elements (except hydrogen)—lithium, sodium, potassium, rubidium, cesium, and francium. (2.3)

Alkaline Battery (Alkaline Dry Cell): A zinc–manganese dioxide galvanic cell of 1.54 V used commonly in flashlight batteries. (19.8)

Alkaline Earth Metals: The Group IIA elements—beryllium, magnesium, calcium, strontium, barium, and radium. (2.3)

Alkalis: (a) The alkali metals. (2.3) (b) Hydroxides of the alkali metals; strong bases. (4.3)

Alkane: A hydrocarbon whose molecules have only single bonds. (2.6, 22.2)

Alkene: A hydrocarbon whose molecules have one or more double bonds. (22.2)

Alkyl Group: An organic group of carbon and hydrogen atoms related to an alkane but with one less hydrogen atom (e.g., CH_3-, methyl; CH_3CH_2-, ethyl). (22.2)

Alkyne: A hydrocarbon whose molecules have one or more triple bonds. (22.2)

Allotrope: One of two or more forms of an element. (21.2)

Allotropy: The existence of an element in two or more molecular or crystalline forms called allotropes. (21.2)

Alpha Particle (^4_2He): The nucleus of a helium atom. (20.3)

Alpha Radiation: A high-velocity stream of alpha particles produced by radioactive decay. (20.3)

Alum: A double salt with the general formula $M^+M^{3+}(SO_4)_2 \cdot 12H_2O$, such as potassium alum: $KAl(SO_4)_2 \cdot 12H_2O$.

Amalgam: A solution of a metal in mercury.

Amide: An organic compound whose molecules have any one of the following groups: (22.5)

$$\overset{O}{\underset{\|}{-C}}NH_2 \quad \overset{O}{\underset{\|}{-C}}NHR \quad \overset{O}{\underset{\|}{-C}}NR_2$$

α-Amino Acid: One of about 20 monomers of polypeptides. (22.7)

Amine: An organic compound whose molecules contain the group NH_2, NHR, or NR_2. (22.4)

Amorphous Solid: A noncrystalline solid. A glass. (11.9)

Ampere (A): The SI unit for electric current; one coulomb per second. (19.7)

Amphiprotic Compound: A compound that can act either as a proton donor or as a proton acceptor; an amphoteric compound. (15.1)

Amphoteric Compound: A compound that can react as either an acid or a base. (15.1)

Amplitude: The height of a wave, which is a measure of the wave's intensity. (7.1)

amu: See *Atomic Mass Unit.*

Angstrom (Å): $1 \text{ Å} = 10^{-10} \text{ m} = 100 \text{ pm} = 0.1 \text{ nm}$. (7.8)

Anhydrous: Without water. (2.5)

Anion: A negatively charged ion. (2.8)

Anode: The positive electrode in a gas discharge tube. The electrode at which oxidation occurs during an electrochemical change. (19.1)

Antibonding Electrons: Electrons that occupy antibonding molecular orbitals. (9.7)

Antibonding Molecular Orbital: A molecular orbital that denies electron density to the space between nuclei and destabilizes a molecule when occupied by electrons. (9.7)

Anticodon: A triplet of bases on a tRNA molecule that pairs to a matching triplet—a codon—on an mRNA molecule during mRNA-directed polypeptide synthesis. (22.8)

Antimatter: Any particle annihilated by a particle of ordinary matter. (20.3)

Aqua Regia: One part concentrated nitric acid and three parts concentrated hydrochloric acid (by volume).

Aqueous Solution: A solution that has water as the solvent.

Aromatic Compound: An organic compound whose molecules have the benzene ring system. (22.2)

Arrhenius Acid: See *Acid*.

Arrhenius Base: See *Base*.

Arrhenius Equation: An equation that relates the rate constant of a reaction to the reaction's activation energy. (13.6)

Association: The joining together of molecules by hydrogen bonds. (12.9)

Asymmetric Carbon Atom: A carbon atom that is bonded to four different groups and which is a chiral center. (22.1)

Atmosphere, Standard (atm): 101,325 Pa. The pressure that supports a column of mercury 760 mm high at 0 °C; 760 torr. (6.5, 10.2)

Atmospheric Pressure: The pressure exerted by the mixture of gases in our atmosphere. (6.5, 10.2)

Atom: A neutral particle having one nucleus; the smallest representative sample of an element. (1.2)

Atomic Mass: The average mass (in u) of the atoms of the isotopes of a given element as they occur naturally. (2.2)

Atomic Mass Unit (u): $1.6605402 \times 10^{-24}$ g; 1/12th the mass of one atom of carbon-12. Sometimes given the symbol amu. (2.2)

Atomic Number: The number of protons in a nucleus. (2.2)

Atomic Radiation: Radiation consisting of particles or electromagnetic radiation given off by radioactive elements. (20.3)

Atomic Spectrum: The line spectrum produced when energized or excited atoms emit electromagnetic radiation. (7.2)

Atomic Weight: See *Atomic Mass*.

Atomization Energy (ΔH_{atom}): The energy needed to rupture all of the bonds in one mole of a substance in the gas state and produce its atoms, also in the gas state. (18.10)

Aufbau Principle: A set of rules enabling the construction of an electron structure of an atom from its atomic number. (7.5)

Average: See *Mean*.

Avogadro's Number (Avogadro's Constant): 6.022×10^{23}; the number of particles or formula units in one mole. (3.1)

Avogadro's Principle: Equal volumes of gases contain equal numbers of molecules when they are at identical temperatures and pressures. (10.4)

Axial Bonds: Covalent bonds oriented parallel to the vertical axis in a trigonal bipyramidal molecule. (9.1)

Azimuthal Quantum Number (ℓ): The quantum number ℓ. (See also *Secondary Quantum Number*.) (7.3)

B

Backbone (Polymer): The long chain of atoms in a polymer to which other groups are attached. (22.6)

Background Radiation: The atomic radiation from the natural radionuclides in the environment and from cosmic radiation. (20.6)

Balance: An apparatus for measuring mass. (1.5)

Balanced Equation: A chemical equation that has on opposites sides of the arrow the same number of each atom and the same net charge. (2.5, 3.4)

Band of Stability: The envelope that encloses just the stable nuclides in a plot of all nuclides constructed according to their numbers of neutrons versus their numbers of protons. (20.4)

Bar: The standard pressure for thermodynamic quantities; 1 bar = 10^5 pascals, 1 atm = 101,325 Pa. (6.5, 10.2)

Barometer: An apparatus for measuring atmospheric pressure. (10.2)

Base: *Arrhenius theory:* A substance that releases OH^- ions in water. (4.3)

Brønsted theory: A proton-acceptor. (15.1)

Lewis theory: An electron-pair acceptor. (15.3)

Base Ionization Constant, K_b:

$$K_b = \frac{[BH^+][OH^-]}{[B]} \text{ for the equilibrium,}$$

$$B + H_2O \rightleftharpoons BH^+ + OH^- \qquad (16.1)$$

Base Units: The units of the fundamental measurements of the SI. (1.5)

Basic Anhydride: An oxide that can neutralize acid or that reacts with water to give OH^-. (4.3)

Basic Oxygen Process: A method to convert pig iron into steel. (21.4)

Basic Solution: An aqueous solution in which $[H^+] < [OH^-]$. (15.5)

Battery: One or more galvanic cells arranged to serve as a practical source of electricity.

Becquerel (Bq): 1 disintegration s^{-1}. The SI unit for the activity of a radioactive source. (20.6)

Bent Molecule (V-Shaped Molecule): A molecule that is nonlinear. (9.2)

Beta Particle ($_{-1}^{0}e$): An electron emitted by radioactive decay. (20.3)

Beta Radiation: A stream of electrons produced by radioactive decay. (20.3)

Bidentate Ligand: A ligand that has two atoms that can become simultaneously attached to the same metal ion. (21.5)

Bimolecular Collision: A collision of two molecules. (13.7)

Binary Acid: An acid with the general formula H_nX, where X is a nonmetal. (4.4, 15.2)

Binary Compound: A compound composed of two different elements. (2.8)

Binding Energy, Nuclear: The energy equivalent of the difference in mass between an atomic nucleus and the sum of the masses of its nucleons. (20.2)

Biochemistry: The study of the organic substances in organisms. (22.7)

Biological Catalyst: Biological molecule such as an enzyme that catalyzes a chemical reaction. (13.8)

Black Phosphorus: An allotrope of phosphorus that has a layered structure. (21.2)

Blast Furnace: A structure in which iron ore is reduced to iron. (21.4)

Body-Centered Cubic (bcc) Unit Cell: A unit cell having identical atoms, molecules, or ions at the corners of a cube plus one more particle in the center of the cube. (11.9)

Boiling Point: The temperature at which the vapor pressure of the liquid equals the atmospheric pressure. (11.6)

Boiling Point Elevation: A colligative property of a solution by which the solution's boiling point is higher than that of the pure solvent. (12.7)

Bond Angle: The angle formed by two bonds that extend from the same atom. (9.1)

Bond Dipole: A dipole within a molecule associated with a specific bond. (9.3)

Bond Dissociation Energy: See *Bond Energy*.

Bond Distance: See *Bond Length*.

Bond Energy: The energy needed to break one mole of a particular bond to give electrically neutral fragments. (8.3, 18.10)

Bond Length: The distance between two nuclei that are held together by a chemical bond. (8.3)

Bond Order: The number of electron pairs shared between two atoms. The *net* number of pairs of bonding electrons. (8.6, 9.7)

Bond order = 1/2 × (no. of bonding e^- − no. of antibonding e^-)

Bonding Domain: A region between two atoms that contains one or more electron pairs in bonds and that influences molecular shape. (9.2)

Bonding Electrons: Electrons that occupy bonding molecular orbitals. (9.7)

Bonding Molecular Orbital: A molecular orbital that introduces a buildup of electron density between nuclei and stabilizes a molecule when occupied by electrons. (9.7)

Boundary: The interface between a system and its surroundings across which energy or matter might pass. (6.3)

Boyle's Law: See *Pressure–Volume Law.*

Bragg Equation: $n\lambda = 2d \sin \theta$. The equation used to convert X-ray diffraction data into a crystal structure. (11.10)

Branched-Chain Compound: An organic compound in whose molecules the carbon atoms do not all occur one after another in a continuous sequence. (22.1)

Branching (Polymer): The formation of side chains (branches) along the main backbone of a polymer. (22.6)

Branching Step: A step in a chain reaction that produces more chain-propagating species than it consumes. (Facets of Chemistry 13.1)

Brine: An aqueous solution of sodium chloride, often with other salts. (19.8)

Brønsted Acid: See *Acid.*

Brønsted Base: See *Base.*

Brownian Motion: The random, erratic motions of colloidally dispersed particles in a fluid. (2.6)

Buckminsterfullerene: The C_{60} molecule. Also called buckyball. (21.2)

Buckyball: See *Buckminsterfullerene.*

Buffer: (a) A pair of solutes that can keep the pH of a solution almost constant if either acid or base is added. (b) A solution containing such a pair of solutes. (16.5)

Buffer Capacity: A measure of how much strong acid or strong base is needed to change the pH of a buffer by some specified amount.

Buret: A long tube of glass usually marked in mL and 0.1 mL units and equipped with a stopcock for the controlled addition of a liquid to a receiving flask. (4.8)

By-product: The substances formed by side reactions. (3.6)

C

Calorie (cal): 4.184 J. The energy that will raise the temperature of 1.00 g of water from 14.5 to 15.5 °C. (In popular books on foods, the term *Calorie*, with a capital C, means 1000 cal or 1 kcal.) (6.1)

Calorimeter: An apparatus used in the determination of the heat of a reaction. (6.5)

Calorimetry: The science of measuring the quantities of heat that are involved in a chemical or physical change. (6.5)

Carbohydrates: Polyhydroxyaldehydes or polyhydroxyketones or substances that yield these by hydrolysis and that are obtained from plants or animals. (22.7)

Carbon Nanotube: Tubular carbon molecules that can be visualized as rolled up sheets of graphite (with hexagonal rings of carbon atoms) capped at each end by half of a spherical fullerene molecule. (21.2)

Carbon Ring: A series of carbon atoms arranged in a ring. (22.1)

Carbonyl Group: An organic functional group consisting of a carbon atom joined to an oxygen atom by a double bond; $C{=}O$. (22.5)

Carboxyl Group: $-CO_2H$. (8.3, 22.5)

Carboxylic Acid: An organic compound whose molecules have the carboxyl group $-CO_2H$. (8.3, 22.5)

Catalysis: Rate enhancement caused by a catalyst. (13.8)

Catalyst: A substance that in relatively small proportion accelerates the rate of a reaction without being permanently chemically changed. (13.8)

Catenation: The linking together of atoms of the same element to form chains.

Cathode: The negative electrode in a gas discharge tube. The electrode at which reduction occurs during an electrochemical change. (19.1)

Cathode Ray: A stream of electrons ejected from a hot metal and accelerated toward a positively charged site in a vacuum tube.

Cation: A positively charged ion. (2.8)

Cell Potential, E_{cell}: The potential (voltage) of a galvanic cell when no current is drawn from the cell. (19.2)

Cell Reaction: The overall chemical change that takes place in an electrolytic cell or a galvanic cell. (19.1)

Celsius Scale: A temperature scale on which water freezes at 0 °C and boils at 100 °C (at 1 atm) and that has 100 divisions called Celsius degrees between those two points. (1.5)

Centimeter (cm): 0.01 m. (1.5)

Chain Reaction: A self-sustaining change in which the products of one event cause one or more new events. (Facets of Chemistry 13.1, 20.8)

Change of State: Transformation of matter from one physical state to another. In thermochemistry, any change in a variable used to define the state of a particular system—a change in composition, pressure, volume, or temperature. (11.4)

Charge: The mixture of raw materials added to a blast furnace. (21.4)

Charles' Law: See *Temperature–Volume Law.*

Chelate: A complex ion containing rings formed by polydentate ligands. (21.5)

Chelate Effect: The extra stability found in complexes that contain chelate rings. (21.5)

Chemical Bond: The force of electrical attraction that holds atoms together in compounds. (2.6, 8 Introduction)

Chemical Change: A change that converts substances into other substances; a chemical reaction. (1.3)

Chemical Energy: The potential energy of chemicals that is transferred during chemical reactions. (6.1)

Chemical Equation: A before-and-after description that uses formulas and coefficients to represent a chemical reaction. (2.5)

Chemical Equilibrium: Dynamic equilibrium in a chemical system. (4.3, 14.1)

Chemical Formula: A formula written using chemical symbols and subscripts that describes the composition of a chemical compound or element. (2.5)

Chemical Kinetics: The study of rates of reaction. (13 Introduction)

Chemical Property: The ability of a substance, either by itself or with other substances, to undergo a change into new substances. (1.4)

Chemical Reaction: A change in which new substances (products) form from starting materials (reactants). (1.3)

Chemical Symbol: A formula for an element. (1.3)

Chemical Thermodynamics: See *Thermodynamics.*

Chemistry: The study of the compositions of substances and the ways by which their properties are related to their compositions. (1.1)

Chirality: The "handedness" of an object; the property of an object (like a molecule) that makes it unable to be superimposed onto a model of its own mirror image. (21.8, 22.1)

Cis Isomer: A stereoisomer whose uniqueness is in having two groups on the same side of some reference plane. (21.8, 22.2)

Clausius–Clapeyron Equation: The relationship between the vapor pressure, the temperature, and the molar heat of vaporization of a substance (where C is a constant). (Facets of Chemistry 11.1)

$$\ln P = \frac{\Delta H_{vap}}{RT} + C$$

Closed-End Manometer: See *Manometer.*

Closed System: A system that can absorb or release energy but not mass across the boundary between the system and its surroundings. (6.3)

Closest-Packed Structure: A crystal structure in which atoms or molecules are packed as efficiently as possible. (11.9)

Codon: An individual unit of hereditary instruction that consists of three, side by side, side chains on a molecule of mRNA. (22.8)

Coefficients: Numbers in front of formulas in chemical equations. (2.5)

Coinage Metals: Copper, silver, and gold.

Coke: Coal that has been strongly heated to drive off its volatile components and that is mostly carbon. (21.4)

Collapsing Atom Paradox: The paradox faced by classical physics that predicts a moving electron in an atom should emit energy and spiral into the nucleus. (7 Introduction)

Colligative Property: A property such as vapor pressure lowering, boiling point elevation, freezing point depression, and osmotic pressure whose physical value depends only on the ratio of the numbers of moles of solute and solvent particles and not on their chemical identities. (12.6)

Collision Theory: The rate of a reaction is proportional to the number of effective collisions that occur each second between the reactants. (13.5)

Combined Gas Law: See *Gas Law, Combined.*

Combustion: A rapid reaction with oxygen accompanied by a flame and the evolution of heat and light. (5.5)

Common Ion: The ion in a mixture of ionic substances that is common to the formulas of at least two. (16.5)

Common Ion Effect: The solubility of one salt is reduced by the presence of another having a common ion. (16.5, 17.1)

Competing Reaction: A reaction that reduces the yield of the main product by forming by-products (3.6)

Complex Ion (Complex): The combination of one or more anions or neutral molecules (ligands) with a metal ion. (17.4, 21.5)

Compound: A substance consisting of chemically combined atoms from two or more elements and present in a definite ratio. (1.3)

Compound Nucleus: An atomic nucleus carrying excess energy following its capture of some bombarding particle. (20.5)

Compressibility: Capable of undergoing a reduction in volume under increasing pressure. (10.1, 11.3)

Concentrated Solution: A solution that has a large ratio of the amounts of solute to solvent. (4.1)

Concentration: The ratio of the quantity of solute to the quantity of solution (or the quantity of solvent). (See *Molal Concentration, Molar Concentration, Mole Fraction, Percentage Concentration.*) (4.1)

Concentration Table: A part of the strategy for organizing data needed to make certain calculations, particularly any involving equilibria. (14.7, 16.2)

Conclusion: A statement that is based on what we think about a series of observations. (1.2)

Condensation: The change of a vapor to its liquid or solid state. (11.4)

Condensation Polymer: A polymer formed from monomers by splitting out a small molecule such as H_2O or CH_3OH. (22.6)

Condensation Polymerization: The process of forming a condensation polymer. (22.6)

Conformation: A particular relative orientation or geometric form of a flexible molecule. (9.5)

Conjugate Acid: The species in a conjugate acid–base pair that has the greater number of H^+ units. (15.1)

Conjugate Acid–Base Pair: Two substances (ions or molecules) whose formulas differ by only one H^+ unit. (15.1)

Conjugate Base: The species in a conjugate acid–base pair that has the fewer number of H^+ units. (15.1)

Conservation of Energy, Law of: See *Law of Conservation of Energy.*

Conservation of Mass–Energy, Law of: See *Law of Conservation of Mass–Energy.*

Continuous Spectrum: The electromagnetic spectrum corresponding to the mixture of frequencies present in white light. (7.2)

Contributing Structure: One of a set of two or more Lewis structures used in applying the theory of resonance to the structure of a compound. A resonance structure. (8.7)

Conversion Factor: A ratio constructed from the relationship between two units such as 2.54 cm/1 in., from 1 in. = 2.54 cm. (1.7)

Cooling Curve: A graph showing how the temperature of a substance changes as heat is removed from it at a constant rate as the substance undergoes changes in its physical state. (11.7)

Coordinate Covalent Bond: A covalent bond in which both electrons originated from one of the joined atoms, but otherwise like a covalent bond in all respects. (8.6)

Coordination Compound (Coordination Complex): A complex or its salt. (17.4, 21.5)

Coordination Number: The number of donor atoms that surround a metal ion. (21.7)

Copolymer: A polymer made from two or more different monomers. (22.6)

Core Electrons: The inner electrons of an atom that are not exposed to the electrons of other atoms when chemical bonds form. (7.6)

Corrosion: The slow oxidation of metals exposed to air or water. (5.5)

Coulomb (C): The SI unit of electrical charge; the charge on 6.25×10^{18} electrons; the amount of charge that passes a fixed point of a wire conductor when a current of 1 A flows for 1 s. (19.2, 19.7)

Covalent Bond: A chemical bond that results when atoms share electron pairs. (8.3)

Covalent Crystal (Network Solid): A crystal in which the lattice positions are occupied by atoms that are covalently bonded to the atoms at adjacent lattice sites. (11.11)

Critical Mass: The mass of a fissile isotope above which a self-sustaining chain reaction occurs. (20.8)

Critical Point: The point at the end of a vapor pressure versus temperature curve for a liquid and that corresponds to the critical pressure and the critical temperature. (11.12)

Critical Pressure (P_c): The vapor pressure of a substance at its critical temperature. (11.12)

Critical Temperature (T_c): The temperature above which a substance cannot exist as a liquid regardless of the pressure. (11.12)

Cross-Link: A bridge formed between polymer strands. (22.6)

Crystal Field Splitting (Δ): The difference in energy between sets of d orbitals in a complex ion. (21.9)

Crystal Field Theory: A theory that considers the effects of the polarities or the charges of the ligands in a complex ion on the energies of the d orbitals of the central metal ion. (21.9)

Crystal Lattice: The repeating symmetrical pattern of atoms, molecules, or ions that occurs in a crystal. (11.9)

Cubic Closest Packing (ccp): Efficient packing of spheres with an A-B-C-A-B-C. . . alternating stacking of layers of spheres. (11.9)

Cubic Meter (m^3): The SI derived unit of volume. (1.5)

Curie (Ci): A unit of activity for radioactive samples, equal to 3.7×10^{10} disintegrations per second. (20.6)

D

Dalton: One atomic mass unit, u.

Dalton's Atomic Theory: Matter consists of tiny, indestructible particles called atoms. All atoms of one element are identical. The atoms of different elements have different masses. Atoms combine in definite ratios by atoms when they form compounds. (2.1)

Dalton's Law of Partial Pressures: See *Partial Pressures, Law of.*

Data: The information (often in the form of physical quantities) obtained in an experiment or other experience or from references. (1.2)

Debye: Unit used to express dipole moments. 1 D = 3.34×10^{-30} C m (coulomb meter). (8.4)

Decay Constant: The first-order rate constant for radioactive decay. (20.6)

Decimal Multipliers: Factors—exponentials of 10 or decimals—that are used to define larger or smaller SI units. (1.5)

Decomposition: A chemical reaction that changes one substance into two or more simpler substances. (1.3)

Dehydration: Removal of water from a substance.

Dehydration Reaction: Formation of a carbon–carbon double bond by removal of the components of water from an alcohol. (22.3)

Deliquescent Compound: A compound able to absorb enough water from humid air to form a concentrated solution.

Delocalization Energy: The difference between the energy a substance would have if its molecules had no delocalized molecular orbitals and the energy it has because of such orbitals. (9.8)

Delocalized Molecular Orbital: A molecular orbital that spreads over more than two nuclei. (9.8)

ΔH_{fusion}: See *Molar Heat of Fusion*

$\Delta H_{sublimation}$: See *Molar Heat of Sublimation*

$\Delta H_{vaporization}$: See *Molar Heat of Vaporization*

Density: The ratio of an object's mass to its volume. (1.8)

Dependent Variable: The experimental variable of a pair of variables whose value is determined by the other, the independent variable.

Derived Unit: Any unit defined solely in terms of base units. (1.5)

Deuterium, $_1^2H$: The isotope of hydrogen with a mass number of 2. (20.8)

Diagonal Relationship: Physical or chemical properties that generally vary diagonally from one corner to the other in the periodic table (e.g., ionization energy, electron affinity, and electronegativity). (7.8)

Dialysis: The passage of small molecules and ions, but not species of a colloidal size, through a semipermeable membrane. (12.8)

Diamagnetism: The property experienced by a substance that contains no unpaired electrons whereby the substance is repelled weakly by a magnet. (7.4)

Diamond: A crystalline form of carbon in which each carbon atom is bonded tetrahedrally to four other carbon atoms. (21.2)

Diaphragm Cell: An electrolytic cell used to manufacture sodium hydroxide by the electrolysis of aqueous sodium chloride. (19.8)

Diatomic Substance (Diatomic Molecule): A molecular substance made from two atoms. (2.5)

Diffraction: Constructive and destructive interference by waves. (7.3)

Diffraction Pattern: The image formed on a screen or a photographic film caused by the diffraction of electromagnetic radiation such as visible light or X rays. (11.10)

Diffusion: The spontaneous intermingling of one substance with another. (10.7)

Dilute Solution: A solution in which the ratio of the quantities of solute to solvent is small. (4.1)

Dilution: The process whereby a concentrated solution is made more dilute. (4.6)

Dimensional Analysis: See *Factor-Label Method.*

Dimer: Two monomer units joined by chemical bonds or intramolecular forces. (12.9)

Dipole (Electric): Partial positive and partial negative charges separated by a distance. (8.4)

Dipole–Dipole Attraction: Attraction between molecules that are dipoles. (11.2)

Dipole Moment (μ): The product of the sizes of the partial charges in a dipole multiplied by the distance between them; a measure of the polarity of a molecule. (8.4)

Diprotic Acid: An acid that can furnish two H^+ per molecule. (4.3)

Disaccharide: A carbohydrate whose molecules can be hydrolyzed to two monosaccharides. (22.7)

Dispersion Forces: Another term for London forces. (11.2)

Disproportionation: A redox reaction in which a portion of a substance is oxidized at the expense of the rest, which is reduced.

Dissociation: The separation of preexisting ions when an ionic compound dissolves or melts. (4.2)

Distorted Tetrahedron: A description of a molecule in which the central atom is surrounded by five electron pairs, one of which is a lone pair of electrons. The central atom is bonded to four other atoms. The structure is also said to have a seesaw shape. (9.2)

Dissymmetric: Lacking or deficient in symmetry. In a dissymmetric molecule the effects of the individual bond dipoles do not cancel, causing the molecule as a whole to be polar. (9.3)

DNA: Deoxyribonucleic acid; a nucleic acid that hydrolyzes to deoxyribose, phosphate ion, adenine, thymine, guanine, and cytosine, and that is the carrier of genes. (22.8)

DNA Double Helix: Two oppositely running strands of DNA held in a helical configuration by interstrand hydrogen bonds. (22.8)

Donor Atom: The atom on a ligand that makes an electron pair available in the formation of a complex. (17.4, 21.5)

Double Bond: (a) A covalent bond formed by sharing two pairs of electrons. (8.3) (b) A covalent bond consisting of one sigma bond and one pi bond. (9.6)

Double Replacement Reaction (Metathesis Reaction): A reaction of two salts in which cations and anions exchange partners (e.g., $AgNO_3 + NaCl \longrightarrow AgCl + NaNO_3$). (4.5)

Downs Cell: An electrolytic cell for the industrial production of sodium. (19.8)

Ductility: A metal's ability to be drawn (or stretched) into wire. (2.4)

Dynamic Equilibrium: A condition in which two opposing processes are occurring at equal rates. (4.3, 14.1)

E

ΔE: See *Internal Energy Change.*

Effective Collision: A collision between molecules that is capable of leading to a net chemical change. (13.5)

Effective Nuclear Charge: The net positive charge an outer electron experiences as a result of the partial screening of the full nuclear charge by core electrons. (7.8)

Effusion: The movement of a gas through a very tiny opening into a region of lower pressure. (10.7)

Effusion, Law of (Graham's Law): The rates of effusion of gases are inversely proportional to the square roots of their densities when compared at identical pressures and temperatures.

$$\text{Effusion rate} \propto \frac{1}{\sqrt{d}} \quad \text{(constant } P \text{ and } T\text{)}$$

where d is the gas density. (10.7)

Einstein Equation: $\Delta E = \Delta m_0 c^2$ where ΔE is the energy obtained when a quantity of rest mass, Δm_0, is destroyed, or the energy lost when this quantity of mass is created. (20.1)

Electric Dipole: Two poles of electric charge separated by a distance. (8.4)

Electrochemical Change: A chemical change that is caused by or that produces electricity. (19 Introduction)

Electrochemistry: The study of electrochemical changes. (19 Introduction)

Electrolysis: The production of a chemical change by the passage of electricity through a solution that contains ions or through a molten ionic compound. (19.6)

Electrolysis Cell: An apparatus for electrolysis. (19.6)

Electrolyte: A compound that conducts electricity either in solution or in the molten state. (4.2)

Electrolytic Cell: See *Electrolysis Cell.*

Electrolytic Conduction: The transport of electrical charge by ions. (19.1)

Electromagnetic Spectrum: The distribution of frequencies of electromagnetic radiation among various types of such radiation—microwave, infrared, visible, ultraviolet, X, and gamma rays. (7.1)

Electromagnetic Wave (Electromagnetic Radiation): The successive series of oscillations in the strengths of electrical and magnetic fields associated with light, microwaves, gamma rays, ultraviolet rays, infrared rays, and the like. (7.1)

Electron (e^- or $_{-1}^0e$): (a) A subatomic particle with a charge of 1− and mass of 0.0005486 u (9.109383×10^{-28} g) that occurs outside an atomic nucleus.

The particle that moves when an electric current flows. (2.2) (b) A beta particle. (20.3)

Electron Affinity (EA): The energy change (usually expressed in kJ mol^{-1}) that occurs when an electron adds to an isolated gaseous atom or ion. (7.8)

Electron Capture: The capture by a nucleus of an orbital electron and that changes a proton into a neutron in the nucleus. (20.3)

Electron Cloud: Because of its wave properties, an electron's influence spreads out like a cloud around the nucleus. (7.7)

Electron Configuration: The distribution of electrons in an atom's orbitals. (7.5)

Electron Density: The concentration of the electron's charge within a given volume. (7.7)

Electron Domain: A region around an atom where one or more electron pairs are concentrated and which influences the shape of a molecule. (9.2)

Electron Domain Model: See *Valence Shell Electron Pair Repulsion Theory*.

Electron Pair Bond: A covalent bond. (8.3)

Electron Spin: The spinning of an electron about its axis that is believed to occur because the electron behaves as a tiny magnet. (7.4)

Electron Volt (eV): The energy an electron receives when it is accelerated under the influence of 1 V and equal to 1.6×10^{-19} J. (20.3)

Electronegativity: The relative ability of an atom to attract electron density toward itself when joined to another atom by a covalent bond. (8.4)

Electronic Structure: The distribution of electrons in an atom's orbitals. (7.5)

Electroplating: Depositing a thin metallic coating on an object by electrolysis. (19.8)

Element: A substance in which all of the atoms have the same atomic number. A substance that cannot be broken down by chemical reactions into anything that is both stable and simpler. (1.3, 2.2)

Elementary Process: One of the individual steps in the mechanism of a reaction. (13.7)

Elimination Reaction: The loss of a small molecule from a larger molecule as in the elimination of water from an alcohol. (22.3)

Emission Spectrum: See *Atomic Spectrum*.

Empirical Formula: A chemical formula that uses the smallest whole-number subscripts to give the proportions by atoms of the different elements present. (3.3)

Enantiomers: Stereoisomers whose molecular structures are related as an object to its mirror image but that cannot be superimposed. (21.8)

End Point: The moment in a titration when the indicator changes color and the titration is ended. (4.8, 16.7)

Endergonic: Descriptive of a change accompanied by an increase in free energy. (18.4)

Endothermic: Descriptive of a change in which a system's internal energy increases. (6.4)

Energy: Something that matter possesses by virtue of an ability to do work. (6.1)

Energy Density: For a galvanic cell, the ratio of the energy available to the volume of the cell. (19.8)

Energy Level: A particular energy an electron can have in an atom or a molecule. (7.2)

Enthalpy (H): The heat content of a system. (6.5, 18.1)

Enthalpy Change (ΔH): The difference in enthalpy between the initial state and the final state for some change. (6.5, 18.1)

Enthalpy Diagram: A graphical depiction of enthalpy changes following different paths from reactants to products. (6.7)

Enthalpy of Solution: See *Heat of Solution*.

Entropy (S): A thermodynamic quantity related to the number of equivalent ways the energy of a system can be distributed. The greater this number, the more probable is the state and the higher is the entropy. (18.3)

Entropy Change (ΔS): The difference in entropy between the initial state and the final state for some change. (18.3)

Enzyme: A catalyst in a living system and that consists of a protein. (13.8, 22.7)

Equation of State of an Ideal Gas: See *Gas Law, Ideal*.

Equatorial Bond: A covalent bond located in the plane perpendicular to the long axis of a trigonal bipyramidal molecule. (9.1)

Equilibrium: See *Dynamic Equilibrium*.

Equilibrium Constant, K: The value that the mass action expression has when the system is at equilibrium. (14.2)

Equilibrium Law: The mathematical equation for a particular equilibrium system that sets the mass action expression equal to the equilibrium constant. (14.2)

Equilibrium Vapor Pressure of a Liquid: The pressure exerted by a vapor in equilibrium with its liquid state. (11.5)

Equilibrium Vapor Pressure of a Solid: The pressure exerted by a vapor in equilibrium with its solid state. (11.5)

Equivalence: A relationship between two quantities expressed in different units. (1.8)

Equivalence Point: The moment in a titration when the number of equivalents of the

reactant added from a buret equals the number of equivalents of another reactant in the receiving flask. (16.7)

Error in a Measurement: The difference between a measurement and the "true" value we are trying to measure. (1.6)

Ester: An organic compound whose molecules have the ester group. (22.5)

$$\overset{\displaystyle O}{\underset{\text{ester group}}{-\overset{\|}{C}-O-C}}$$

Ether: An organic compound in whose molecules two hydrocarbon groups are joined to an oxygen. (22.3)

Ethyl Group: CH_3CH_2-. (22.2)

Evaporate: To change from a liquid to a vapor. (11.3)

Exact Number: A number obtained by a direct count or that results by a definition; and that is considered to have an infinite number of significant figures. (1.6)

Excess Reactant: The reactant left over once the limiting reactant is used up. (3.5)

Excited State: A term describing an atom or molecule where all of the electrons are not in their lowest possible energy levels. (7.2)

Exergonic: Descriptive of a change accompanied by a decrease in free energy. (18.4)

Exon: One of a set of sections of a DNA molecule (separated by introns) that, taken together, constitute a gene. (22.8)

Exothermic: Descriptive of a change in which energy leaves a system and enters the surroundings. (6.4)

Expansion Work: See *Pressure–Volume Work*.

Exponential Notation: See *Scientific Notation*.

Extensive Property: A property of an object that is described by a physical quantity whose magnitude is proportional to the size or amount of the object (e.g., mass or volume). (1.4)

F

Face-Centered Cubic (fcc) Unit Cell: A unit cell having identical atoms, molecules, or ions at the corners of a cube and also in the center of each face of the cube. (11.9)

Factor-Label Method: A problem-solving technique that uses the correct cancellation of the units of physical quantities as a guide for the correct setting up of the solution to the problem. (1.7)

Fahrenheit Scale: A temperature scale on which water freezes at 32 °F and boils at 212 °F (at 1 atm) and between which points there are 180 degree divisions called Fahrenheit degrees. (1.5)

Family of Elements: See *Group*.

Faraday (𝓕): One mole of electrons; 9.65×10^4 coulombs. (19.4)

Faraday Constant (𝓕): 9.65×10^4 coulombs/mol e^-. (19.4)

Fatty Acid: One of several long-chain carboxylic acids produced by the hydrolysis (digestion) of a lipid. (22.7)

Film Dosimeter: A device used by people working with radioactive isotopes that records doses of atomic radiation by the darkening of photographic film. (20.6)

First Law of Thermodynamics: A formal statement of the law of conservation of energy. $\Delta E = q + w$. (6.5, 18.1)

First-Order Reaction: A reaction with a rate law in which rate $= k[A]^1$, where A is a reactant. (13.3)

Fissile Isotope: An isotope capable of undergoing fission following neutron capture. (20.8)

Fission: The breaking apart of atomic nuclei into smaller nuclei accompanied by the release of energy, and the source of energy in nuclear reactors. (20.2, 20.8)

Flotation: A method for concentrating sulfide ores of copper and lead by bubbling air through a slurry of oil-coated ore particles. The sulfides, but not soil or other rock particles, stick to the rising air bubbles and collect in the foam at the surface. (21.4)

Force: Anything that can cause an object to change its motion or direction. (1.5)

Formal Charge: The apparent charge on an atom in a molecule or polyatomic ion as calculated by a set of rules. (8.6)

Formation Constant (K_{form}): The equilibrium constant for an equilibrium involving the formation of a complex ion. Also called the stability constant. (17.4)

Formula: See *Chemical Formula*.

Formula Mass: The sum of the atomic masses (in u) of all of the atoms represented in a chemical formula. Often used with units of g mol^{-1} to represent masses of ionic substances. See also *Molar Mass*. (3.1)

Formula Unit: A particle that has the composition given by the chemical formula. (2.7)

Forward Reaction: In a chemical equation, the reaction as read from left to right. (4.3)

Fossil Fuels: Coal, oil, and natural gas.

Free Element: An element that is not combined with another element in a compound. (2.5)

Free Energy: See *Gibbs Free Energy* or *Standard Free Energy Change*

Free Energy Diagram: A plot of the changes in free energy for a multicomponent system versus the composition. (18.8)

Free Radical: An atom, molecule, or ion that has one or more unpaired electrons. (13.7, 22.6)

Freezing Point Depression: A colligative property of a liquid solution by which the freezing point of the solution is lower than that of the pure solvent. (12.7)

Frequency (ν): The number of cycles per second of electromagnetic radiation. (7.1)

Frequency Factor: The proportionality constant, A, in the Arrhenius equation. (13.6)

Fuel Cell: An electrochemical cell in which electricity is generated from the redox reactions of common fuels. (19.8)

Fullerene: An allotrope of carbon made of an extended joining together of five- and six-membered rings of carbon atoms. (21.2)

Functional Group: The group of atoms of an organic molecule that enters into a characteristic set of reactions that are independent of the rest of the molecule. (22.1)

Fusion: (a) Melting. (11.7) (b) The formation of atomic nuclei by the joining together of the nuclei of lighter atoms. (20.2, 20.8)

G

G: See *Gibbs Free Energy*.

ΔG: See *Gibbs Free Energy Change*.

$\Delta G°$: See *Standard Free Energy Change*.

$\Delta G_f°$: See *Standard Free Energy of Formation*.

Galvanic Cell: An electrochemical cell in which a spontaneous redox reaction produces electricity. (19.1)

Gamma Radiation: Electromagnetic radiation with wavelengths in the range of 1 Å or less (the shortest wavelengths of the spectrum). (20.3)

Gangue: The unwanted rock and sand that is separated from an ore. (21.4)

Gas: One of the states of matter. A gas consists of rapidly moving widely spaced atomic or molecular sized particles. (1.4)

Gas Constant, Universal (R): $R = 0.0821$ liter atm mol^{-1} K^{-1} or $R = 8.314$ J mol^{-1} K^{-1} (10.5)

Gas Law, Combined: For a given mass of gas, the product of its pressure and volume divided by its Kelvin temperature is a constant. (10.3)

$$PV/T = \text{a constant}$$

Gas Law, Ideal: $PV = nRT$. (10.5)

Gay-Lussac's Law: See *Pressure–Temperature Law*.

Geiger Counter: A device that detects beta and gamma radiation (20.6)

Genetic Code: The correlation of codons with amino acids. (22.8)

Geometric Isomer: One of a set of isomers that differ only in geometry. (22.2)

Geometric Isomerism: The existence of isomers whose molecules have identical atomic organizations but different geometries; cis-trans isomers. (21.8, 22.2)

Gibbs Free Energy (G): A thermodynamic quantity that relates enthalpy (H), entropy (S), and temperature (T) by the equation: (18.4)

$$G = H - TS$$

Gibbs Free Energy Change (ΔG): The difference given by: (18.4)

$$\Delta G = \Delta H - T\Delta S$$

Glass: Any amorphous solid. (11.9)

Glycogen: A polysaccharide that animals use to store glucose units for energy. (22.7)

Graham's Law: See *Effusion, Law of*.

Gram (g): 0.001 kg. (1.5)

Graphite: The most stable allotrope of carbon, consisting of layers of joined six-membered rings of carbon atoms. (21.2)

Gray (Gy): The SI unit of radiation absorbed dose. (20.6)

$$1 \text{ Gy} = 1 \text{ J kg}^{-1}$$

Greenhouse Effect: The retention of solar energy made possible by the ability of the greenhouse gases (e.g., CO_2, CH_4, H_2O, and the chlorofluorocarbons) to absorb outgoing radiation and reradiate some of it back to earth.

Ground State: The lowest energy state of an atom or molecule. (7.2)

Group: A vertical column of elements in the periodic table. (2.3)

H

ΔH: See *Enthalpy Change*.

ΔH_{atom}: See *Atomization Energy*.

ΔH_c: See *Heat of Combustion*.

$\Delta H°$: See *Standard Heat of Reaction*.

$\Delta H_f°$: See *Standard Heat of Formation*.

ΔH_{fusion}: See *Molar Heat of Fusion*.

ΔH_{soln}: See *Heat of Solution*.

$\Delta H_{sublimation}$: See *Molar Heat of Sublimation*.

$\Delta H_{vaporization}$: See *Molar Heat of Vaporization*.

Half-Cell: That part of a galvanic cell in which either oxidation or reduction takes place. (19.1)

Half-Life ($t_{1/2}$): The time required for a reactant concentration or the mass of a radionuclide to be reduced by half. (13.4)

Half-Reaction: A hypothetical reaction that constitutes exclusively either the oxidation or the reduction half of a redox reaction and in whose equation the correct formulas for all species taking part in the change are given together with enough electrons to give the correct electrical balance. (5.2)

Hall–Héroult Process: A method for manufacturing aluminum by the electrolysis of aluminum oxide in molten cryolite. (19.8)

Halogen Family: Group VIIA in the periodic table—fluorine, chlorine, bromine, iodine, and astatine. (2.3)

Hard Water: Water with dissolved Mg^{2+}, Ca^{2+}, Fe^{2+}, or Fe^{3+} ions at a concentration high enough (above 25 mg L^{-1}) to interfere with the use of soap. (Facets of Chemistry 4.1)

Heat: Energy that flows from a hot object to a cold object as a result of their difference in temperature. (6.1)

Heat Capacity: The quantity of heat needed to raise the temperature of an object by 1 °C. (6.3)

Heat of Combustion: The heat evolved in the combustion of a substance. (6.5)

Heat of Formation, Standard: See *Standard Heat of Formation.*

Heat of Reaction: The heat exchanged between a system and its surroundings when a chemical change occurs in the system. (6.5)

Heat of Reaction at Constant Pressure (q_p): The heat of a reaction in an open system, ΔH. (6.5, 18.1)

Heat of Reaction at Constant Volume (q_v): The heat of a reaction in a sealed vessel, like a bomb calorimeter, ΔE. (6.5)

Heat of Reaction, Standard: See *Standard Heat of Reaction.*

Heat of Solution (ΔH_{soln}): The energy exchanged between the system and its surroundings when one mole of a solute dissolves in a solvent to make a dilute solution. (12.2)

Heating Curve: A graph showing how the temperature of a substance changes as heat is added to it at a constant rate as the substance undergoes changes in its physical state. (11.7)

Henderson–Hasselbalch Equation:

$$pH = pK_a + \log \frac{[A^-]_{initial}}{[HA]_{initial}} \quad \text{or}$$

$$pH = pK_a + \log \frac{[salt]}{[acid]}. \ (16.5)$$

Henry's Law: See *Pressure–Solubility Law.*

Hertz (Hz): 1 cycle s^{-1}; the SI unit of frequency. (7.1)

Hess's Law: For any reaction that can be written in steps, the standard heat of reaction is the same as the sum of the standard heats of reaction for the steps. (6.7)

Hess's Law Equation: For the change,

$$aA + bB + \dots \longrightarrow$$
$$nN + mM + \dots: \ (6.8)$$

$$\Delta H^\circ = \begin{pmatrix} \text{sum of } \Delta H_f^\circ \text{ of all} \\ \text{of the products} \end{pmatrix}$$
$$- \begin{pmatrix} \text{sum of } \Delta H_f^\circ \text{ of all} \\ \text{of the reactants} \end{pmatrix}$$

Heterocyclic Compound: A compound whose molecules have rings that include one or more multivalent atoms other than carbon. (22.1)

Heterogeneous Catalyst: A catalyst that is in a different phase than the reactants and onto whose surface the reactant molecules are adsorbed and where they react. (13.8)

Heterogeneous Equilibrium: An equilibrium involving more than one phase. (14.4)

Heterogeneous Mixture: A mixture that has two or more phases with different properties. (1.3)

Heterogeneous Reaction: A reaction in which not all of the chemical species are in the same phase. (13.1, 14.4)

Heteronuclear Molecule: A molecule in which not all atoms are of the same element. (9.7)

Hexagonal Closest Packing (hcp): Efficient packing of spheres with an A-B-A-B-. . . alternating stacking of layers of spheres. (11.9)

High-Spin Complex: A complex ion or coordination compound in which there is the maximum number of unpaired electrons. (21.9)

Homogeneous Catalyst: A catalyst that is in the same phase as the reactants. (13.8)

Homogeneous Equilibrium: An equilibrium system in which all components are in the same phase. (14.4)

Homogeneous Mixture: A mixture that has only one phase and that has uniform properties throughout; a solution. (1.3)

Homogeneous Reaction: A reaction in which all of the chemical species are in the same phase. (13.1, 14.4)

Homonuclear Diatomic Molecule: A diatomic molecule in which both atoms are of the same element. (9.7)

Hund's Rule: Electrons that occupy orbitals of equal energy are distributed with unpaired spins as much as possible among all such orbitals. (7.5)

Hybrid Atomic Orbitals: Orbitals formed by mixing two or more of the basic atomic orbitals of an atom and that make possible more effective overlaps with the orbitals of adjacent atoms than do ordinary atomic orbitals. (9.5)

Hydrate: A compound that contains molecules of water in a definite ratio to other components. (2.5)

Hydrated Ion: An ion surrounded by a cage of water molecules that are attracted by the charge on the ion. (4.2)

Hydration: The development in an aqueous solution of a cage of water molecules about ions or polar molecules of the solute. (12.1)

Hydration Energy: The enthalpy change associated with the hydration of gaseous ions or molecules as they dissolve in water. (12.2)

Hydride: (a) A binary compound of hydrogen. (2.6) (b) A compound containing the hydride ion (H^-).

Hydrocarbon: An organic compound whose molecules consist entirely of carbon and hydrogen atoms. (2.6, 22.2)

Hydrogen Bond: An extra strong dipole–dipole attraction between a hydrogen bound covalently to nitrogen, oxygen, or fluorine and another nitrogen, oxygen, or fluorine atom. (11.2)

Hydrogen Electrode: The standard of comparison for reduction potentials and for which $E_{H^+}^\circ$ has a value of 0.00 V at 25 °C, when $P_{H_2} = 1$ atm and $[H^+] = 1\ M$ in the reversible half-cell reaction: (19.2)

$$2H^+(aq) + 2e^- \rightleftharpoons H_2(g)$$

Hydrolysis: A reaction with water

Hydrometer: A device for measuring specific gravity. (19.8)

Hydronium Ion: H_3O^+. (4.3)

Hydrophilic Group: A polar molecular unit capable of having dipole–dipole attractions or hydrogen bonds with water molecules. (22.7)

Hydrophobic Group: A nonpolar molecular unit with no affinity for water. (22.7)

Hypertonic Solution: A solution that has a higher osmotic pressure than cellular fluids. (12.8)

Hypothesis: A tentative explanation of the results of experiments. (1.2)

Hypotonic Solution: A solution that has a lower osmotic pressure than cellular fluids. (12.8)

I

Ideal Gas: A hypothetical gas that obeys the gas laws exactly. (10.3)

Ideal Gas Law: $PV = nRT$. (10.5)

Ideal Solution: A hypothetical solution that would obey the vapor pressure–concentration law (Raoult's law) exactly. (12.2)

Immiscible: Mutually insoluble. Usually used to describe liquids that are insoluble in each other. (12.1)

Incompressible: Incapable of losing volume under increasing pressure. (11.3)

Independent Variable: The experimental variable of a pair of variables whose value is first selected and from which the value of the dependent variable then results.

Indicator: A chemical put in a solution being titrated and whose change in color signals the end point. (4.3, 15.5)

Induced Dipole: A dipole created when the electron cloud of an atom or a molecule is distorted by a neighboring dipole or by an ion. (11.2)

Inert Gas: Any of the noble gases—Group VIIIA of the periodic table. Any gas that has virtually no tendency to react. (2.3)

Initiation Step: The step in a chain reaction that produces reactive species that can start chain propagation steps. (Facets of Chemistry 13.1)

Inner Transition Elements: Members of the two long rows of elements below the main body of the periodic table—elements 58–71 and elements 90–103. (2.3)

Inorganic Compound: A compound made from any elements except those compounds of carbon classified as organic compounds. (2.9)

Instability Constant (K_{inst}): The reciprocal of the formation constant for an equilibrium in which a complex ion forms. (17.4)

Instantaneous Dipole: A momentary dipole in an atom, ion, or molecule caused by the erratic movement of electrons. (11.2)

Instantaneous Rate: The rate of reaction at any particular moment during a reaction. (13.2)

Integrated Rate Law: A rate law that relates concentration versus time. (13.4)

Intensive Property: A property whose physical magnitude is independent of the size of the sample, such as density or temperature. (1.4)

Intercalation: The insertion of small atoms or ions between layers in a crystal such as graphite. (19.8)

Interference Fringes: Pattern of light produced by waves that undergo diffraction. (7.3)

Intermolecular Forces (Intermolecular Attractions): Attractions *between* neighboring molecules. (11.2)

Internal Energy (E): The sum of all of the kinetic energies and potential energies of the particles within a system. (6.2, 18.1)

Internal Energy Change (ΔE): The difference in internal energy between the initial state and the final state for some change. (6.2, 6.5)

International System of Units (SI): The successor to the metric system of measurements that retains most of the units of the metric system and their decimal relation-ships but employs new reference standards. (1.5)

Intramolecular Forces: Forces of attraction within molecules; chemical bonds. (11.2)

Intron: One of a set of sections of a DNA molecule that separate the exon sections of a gene from each other. (22.8)

Inverse Square Law: The intensity of a radiation is inversely proportional to the square of the distance from its source. (20.6)

Ion: An electrically charged particle on the atomic or molecular scale of size. (2.7)

Ion–Dipole Attraction: The attraction between an ion and the charged end of a polar molecule. (11.2)

Ion–Electron Method: A method for balancing redox reactions that uses half-reactions. (5.2)

Ion–Induced Dipole Attraction: Attraction between an ion and a dipole induced in a neighboring molecule. (11.2)

Ion Pair: A more or less loosely associated pair of ions in a solution. (12.9)

Ion Product: The mass action expression for the solubility equilibrium involving the ions of a salt and equal to the product of the molar concentrations of the ions, each concentration raised to a power that equals the number of ions obtained from one formula unit of the salt. (17.1)

Ion Product Constant of Water (K_w): $K_w = [H^+][OH^-]$ (15.5)

Ionic Bond: The attractions between ions that hold them together in ionic compounds. (8.1)

Ionic Character: The extent to which a covalent bond has a dipole moment and is polarized. (8.4)

Ionic Compound: A compound consisting of positive and negative ions. (2.7)

Ionic Crystal: A crystal that has ions located at the lattice points. (11.11)

Ionic Equation: A chemical equation in which soluble strong electrolytes are written in dissociated or ionized form. (4.2)

Ionic Reaction: A chemical reaction in which ions are involved. (4.2)

Ionization Energy (IE): The energy needed to remove an electron from an isolated, gaseous atom, ion, or molecule (usually given in units of kJ mol^{-1}). (7.8)

Ionization Reaction: A reaction of chemical particles that produces ions. (4.3)

Ionizing Radiation: Any high-energy radiation—X rays, gamma rays, or radiations from radionuclides—that generates ions as it passes through matter. (20.6)

Isolated System: A system that cannot exchange matter or energy with its surroundings. (6.3)

Isomer: One of a set of compounds that have identical molecular formulas but different structures. (21.8)

Isomerism: The existence of sets of isomers. (21.8)

Isopropyl Group: $(CH_3)_2CH$ —. (22.2)

Isotonic Solution: A solution that has the same osmotic pressure as cellular fluids. (12.8)

Isotopes: Atoms of the same element with different atomic masses. Atoms of the same element with different numbers of neutrons in their nuclei. (2.2)

IUPAC Rules: The formal rules for naming substances as developed by the International Union of Pure and Applied Chemistry. (2.3, 2.9)

J

Joule (J): The SI unit of energy. (6.1)

$$1\ J = 1\ kg\ m^2\ s^{-2}$$

$$4.184\ J = 1\ cal\ (exactly)$$

K

K: See *Kelvin*.

K_a: See *Acid Ionization Constant*.

K_b: See *Base Ionization Constant*.

K_{form}: See *Formation Constant*.

K_{inst}: See *Instability Constant*.

K_{sp}: See *Solubility Product Constant*.

K_{spa}: See *Acid Solubility Product*.

K_w: See *Ion Product Constant of Water*.

K-Capture: See *Electron Capture*.

Kelvin (K): One degree on the Kelvin scale of temperature and identical in size to the Celsius degree. (1.5)

Kelvin Scale: The temperature scale on which water freezes at 273.15 K and boils at 373.15 K and that has 100 degree divisions called kelvins between these points. K = °C + 273.15. (1.5)

Ketone: An organic compound whose molecules have the carbonyl group (C=O) flanked by hydrocarbon groups. (22.5)

Kilocalorie (kcal): 1000 cal. (6.1)

Kilogram (kg): The base unit for mass in the SI and equal to the mass of a cylinder of platinum–iridium alloy kept by the International Bureau of Weights and Measures at Sevres, France. 1 kg = 1000 g. (1.5)

Kilojoule (kJ): 1000 J. (6.1)

Kinetic Energy (KE): Energy of motion. KE = $(1/2)mv^2$. (6.1)

Kinetic Molecular Theory: Molecules of a substance are in constant motion with a distribution of kinetic energies at a given temperature. The average kinetic energy of the molecules is proportional to the Kelvin temperature. (6.2)

Kinetic Molecular Theory of Gases: A set of postulates used to explain the gas laws. A gas consists of an extremely large number of very tiny, very hard particles in constant, random motion. They have negligible volume and, between collisions, experience no forces between themselves. (10.8)

L

Lanthanide Elements: Elements 58–71. (2.3)

Lattice: A symmetrical pattern of points arranged with constant repeat distances along lines oriented at constant angles. (11.9)

Lattice Energy: Energy released by the imaginary process in which isolated ions come together to form a crystal of an ionic compound. (8.1)

Law: A description of behavior (and not an *explanation* of behavior) based on the results of many experiments. (1.2)

Law of Combining Volumes: When gases react at the same temperature and pressure, their combining volumes are in ratios of simple whole numbers. (10.4)

Law of Conservation of Energy: The energy of the universe is constant; it can be neither created nor destroyed but only transferred and transformed. (6.1)

Law of Conservation of Mass: No detectable gain or loss in mass occurs in chemical reactions. Mass is conserved. (2.1)

Law of Conservation of Mass–Energy: The sum of all the mass in the universe and of all of the energy, expressed as an equivalent in mass (calculated by the Einstein equation), is a constant. (20.1)

Law of Definite Proportions: In a given chemical compound, the elements are always combined in the same proportion by mass. (2.1)

Law of Gas Effusion: See *Effusion, Law of.*

Law of Multiple Proportions: Whenever two elements form more than one compound, the different masses of one element that combine with the same mass of the other are in a ratio of small whole numbers. (2.1)

Law of Partial Pressures: See *Partial Pressures, Dalton's Law of.*

Law of Radioactive Decay:

$$\text{Activity} = -\frac{\Delta N}{\Delta t} = kN,$$

where ΔN is the change in the number of radioactive nuclei during the time span Δt, and k is the decay constant. (20.6)

Le Châtelier's Principle: When a system that is in dynamic equilibrium is subjected to a disturbance that upsets the equilibrium, the system undergoes a change that counteracts the disturbance and, if possible, restores the equilibrium. (11.8, 14.6)

Lead Storage Battery: A galvanic cell of about 2 V involving lead and lead(IV) oxide in sulfuric acid. (19.8)

Leclanché Cell: See *Zinc–Manganese Dioxide Cell.*

Lewis Acid: An electron-pair acceptor. (15.3)

Lewis Base: An electron-pair donor. (15.3)

Lewis Structure (Lewis Formula): A structural formula drawn with Lewis symbols and that uses dots and dashes to show the valence electrons and shared pairs of electrons. (8.3)

Lewis Symbol: The symbol of an element that includes dots to represent the valence electrons of an atom of the element. (8.2)

Ligand: A molecule or an anion that can bind to a metal ion to form a complex. (17.4, 21.5)

Like Dissolves Like Rule: Strongly polar and ionic solutes tend to dissolve in polar solvents and nonpolar solutes tend to dissolve in nonpolar solvents. (12.1)

Limiting Reactant: The reactant that determines how much product can form when nonstoichiometric amounts of reactants are used. (3.5)

Line Spectrum: An atomic spectrum. So named because the light emitted by an atom and focused through a narrow slit yields a series of lines when projected on a screen. (7.1)

Linear Molecule: A molecule all of whose atoms lie on a straight line. (9.1, 9.2)

Lipid: Any substance found in plants or animals that can be dissolved in nonpolar solvents. (22.7)

Liquid: One of the states of matter. A liquid consists of tightly packed atomic or molecular sized particles that can move past each other. (1.4)

Liter (L): 1 dm³. 1 L = 1000 mL = 1000 cm³. (1.5)

Lithium Ion Cell: A cell in which lithium ions are transferred between the electrodes through an electrolyte, while electrons travel through the external circuit. (19.8)

Lithium–Manganese Dioxide Battery: A battery that uses metallic lithium as the anode and manganese dioxide as the cathode. (19.8)

Localized Bond: A covalent bond in which the bonding pair of electrons is localized between two nuclei. (9.8)

London Forces (Dispersion Forces): Weak attractive forces caused by instantaneous dipole–induced dipole attractions. (11.2)

Lone Pair: A pair of electrons in the valence shell of an atom that is not shared with another atom. An unshared pair of electrons. (9.2)

Low-Spin Complex: A coordination compound or a complex ion with electrons paired as much as possible in the lower energy set of d orbitals. (21.9)

M

Macromolecule: A molecule whose molecular mass is very large. (22.6)

Magic Numbers: The numbers 2, 8, 20, 28, 50, 82, and 126, numbers whose significance in nuclear science is that a nuclide in which the number of protons or neutrons equals a magic number has nuclei that are relatively more stable than those of other nuclides nearby in the band of stability. (20.4)

Magnetic Quantum Number (m_ℓ): A quantum number that can have values from $-\ell$ to $+\ell$. (7.3)

Main Group Elements: Elements in any of the A groups in the periodic table. (2.3)

Main Reaction: The desired reaction between the reactants as opposed to competing reactions that give by-products. (3.6)

Malleability: A metal's ability to be hammered or rolled into thin sheets. (2.4)

Manometer: A device for measuring the pressure within a closed system. The two types—*closed end* and *open end*—differ according to whether the operating fluid (e.g., mercury) is exposed at one end to the atmosphere. (10.2)

Mass: A measure of the amount of matter that there is in a given sample. (1.3)

Mass Action Expression: A fraction in which the numerator is the product of the molar concentrations of the products, each raised to a power equal to its coefficient in the equilibrium equation, and the denominator is the product of the molar concentrations of the reactants, each also raised to the power that equals its coefficient in the equation. (For gaseous reactions, partial pressures can be used in place of molar concentrations.) (14.2)

Mass Defect: For a given isotope, it is the mass that changed into energy as the nucleons gathered to form the nucleus, this energy being released from the system. (20.2)

Mass Number: The numerical sum of the protons and neutrons in an atom of a given isotope. (2.2)

Matter: Anything that has mass and occupies space. (1.3)

Mean: The sum of N numerical values divided by N; the average. (1.6)

Measurement: A numerical observation. (1.5)

Mechanism of a Reaction: The series of individual steps (called elementary processes) in a chemical reaction that gives the net, overall change. (13.7)

Melting Point: The temperature at which a substance melts; the temperature at which a solid is in equilibrium with its liquid state. (11.4)

Meniscus: The interface between a liquid and a gas.

Metal: An element or an alloy that is a good conductor of electricity, that has a shiny surface, and that is malleable and ductile; an element that normally forms positive ions and has an oxide that is basic. (2.4, 4.3)

Metallic Conduction: Conduction of electrical charge by the movement of electrons. (19.1)

Metallic Crystal: A solid having positive ions at the lattice positions that are attracted to a "sea of electrons" that extends throughout the entire crystal. (11.11)

Metalloids: Elements with properties that lie between those of metals and nonmetals, and that are found in the periodic table around the diagonal line running from boron (B) to astatine (At). (2.4)

Metallurgy: The science and technology of metals, the procedures and reactions that separate metals from their ores, and the operations that create practical uses for metals. (21.4)

Metathesis Reaction: See *Double Replacement Reaction.*

Meter (m): The SI base unit for length. (1.5)

Methyl Group: CH_3—. (22.2)

Metric Units: A decimal system of units for physical quantities taken over by the SI. (1.5) See also *International System of Units.*

Millibar: 1 mb = 10^{-3} bar. (10.2)

Milliliter (mL): 0.001 L. 1000 mL = 1 L. (1.5)

Millimeter (mm): 0.001 m. 1000 mm = 1 m. (1.5)

Millimeter of Mercury (mm Hg): A unit of measurement that is proportional to pressure; equal to 1/760 atm. 760 mm Hg = 1 atm. 1 mm Hg = 1 torr. (10.2)

Miscible: Mutually soluble. (12.1)

Mixture: Any matter consisting of two or more substances physically combined in no particular proportion by mass. (1.3)

MO Theory: See *Molecular Orbital Theory.*

Model, Theoretical: A picture or a mental construction derived from a set of ideas and assumptions that are imagined to be true because they can be used to explain certain observations and measurements (e.g., the model of an ideal gas). (1.2)

Molal Boiling Point Elevation Constant (K_b): The number of degrees (°C) per unit of molal concentration that a boiling point of a solution is higher than that of the pure solvent. (12.7)

Molal Concentration (m): The number of moles of solute in 1000 g of solvent. (12.5)

Molal Freezing Point Depression Constant (K_f): The number of degrees (°C) per unit of molal concentration that a freezing point of a solution is lower than that of the pure solvent. (12.7)

Molality: The molal concentration. (12.5)

Molar Concentration (M): The number of moles of solute per liter of solution. The molarity of a solution. (4.6)

Molar Enthalpy of Solution: See *Heat of Solution.*

Molar Heat Capacity: The heat that can raise the temperature of 1 mol of a substance by 1 °C; the heat capacity per mole. (6.3)

Molar Heat of Fusion, ΔH_{fusion}: The heat absorbed when 1 mol of a solid melts to give 1 mol of the liquid at constant temperature and pressure. (11.7)

Molar Heat of Sublimation, $\Delta H_{sublimation}$: The heat absorbed when 1 mol of a solid sublimes to give 1 mol of its vapor at constant temperature and pressure. (11.7)

Molar Heat of Vaporization, $\Delta H_{vaporization}$: The heat absorbed when 1 mol of a liquid changes to 1 mol of its vapor at constant temperature and pressure. (11.7)

Molar Mass: The mass of one mole of a substance; the mass in grams equal to the sum of the atomic masses of the atoms in a substance, with units of g mol^{-1}. (3.1)

Molar Solubility: The number of moles of solute required to give 1 L of a saturated solution of the solute. (17.1)

Molar Volume, Standard: The volume of 1 mol of a gas at STP; 22.4 L mol^{-1}. (10.4)

Molarity: See *Molar Concentration.*

Mole (mol): The SI unit for amount of substance; the formula mass in grams of an element or compound; an amount of a chemical substance that contains 6.022×10^{23} formula units. (3.1)

Mole Fraction: The ratio of the number of moles of one component of a mixture to the total number of moles of all components. (10.6)

Mole Percent (mol%): The mole fraction of a component expressed as a percent; mole fraction × 100%. (10.6)

Molecular Compound: A compound consisting of electrically neutral molecules. (2.6)

Molecular Crystal: A crystal that has molecules or individual atoms at the lattice points. (11.11)

Molecular Equation: A chemical equation that gives the full formulas of all of the reactants and products and that is used to plan an actual experiment. (4.2)

Molecular Formula: A chemical formula that gives the actual composition of one molecule. (2.6, 3.3)

Molecular Kinetic Energy: The energy associated with the motions of and within molecules as they fly about, spinning and vibrating. (6.2)

Molecular Mass: The sum of the atomic masses (in u) of all of the atoms represented in a molecular chemical substance; also called the *molecular weight.* May be used with units of g mol^{-1}. See also *Molar Mass.* (3.1)

Molecular Orbital (MO): An orbital that extends over two or more atomic nuclei. (9.7)

Molecular Orbital Theory (MO Theory): A theory about covalent bonds that views a molecule as a collection of positive nuclei surrounded by electrons distributed among a set of bonding, antibonding, and nonbonding orbitals of different energies. (9.4, 9.7)

Molecular Weight: See *Molecular Mass.*

Molecule: A neutral particle composed of two or more atoms combined in a definite ratio of whole numbers. (1.2, 2.6)

Monatomic: A particle consisting of just one atom. (2.9)

Monoclinic Sulfur: An allotrope of sulfur. (21.2)

Monodentate Ligand: A ligand that can attach itself to a metal ion by only one atom. (21.5)

Monomer: A substance of relatively low formula mass that is used to make a polymer. (22.6)

Monoprotic Acid: An acid that can furnish one H^+ per molecule. (4.3)

Monosaccharide: A carbohydrate that cannot be hydrolyzed. (22.7)

N

Negative Charge: A type of electrical charge possessed by certain particles such as the electron. A negative charge is attracted by a positive charge and is repelled by another negative charge. (2.2)

Nernst Equation: An equation relating cell potential and concentration. (19.5)

$$E_{cell} = E^\circ_{cell} - \frac{RT}{n\mathscr{F}} \ln Q$$

Net Ionic Equation: An ionic equation from which spectator ions have been omitted. It is balanced when both atoms and electrical charge balance. (4.2)

Network Solid: See *Covalent Crystal.*

Neutralization, Acid–Base: See *Acid–Base Neutralization.*

Neutral Solution: A solution in which $[H^+] = [OH^-]$. (15.5)

Neutron (n, ^1_0n): A subatomic particle with a charge of zero, a mass of 1.0086649 u (1.674927×10^{-24} g) and that exists in all atomic nuclei except those of the hydrogen-1 isotope. (2.2)

Neutron Activation Analysis: A technique to analyze for trace impurities in a sample by studying the frequencies and intensities of the gamma radiations they emit after they have been rendered radioactive by neutron bombardment of the sample. (20.7)

Neutron Emission: A nuclear reaction in which a neutron is ejected. (20.3)

Nicad Battery: A nickel–cadmium cell. (19.8)

Nickel–Cadmium Storage Cell: A galvanic cell of about 1.4 V involving the reaction of cadmium with nickel(IV) oxide. (19.8)

Nitrogen Family: Group VA in the periodic table—nitrogen, phosphorus, arsenic, antimony, and bismuth. (2.3)

Noble Gases: Group VIIIA in the periodic table—helium, neon, argon, krypton, xenon, and radon. (2.3)

Nodal Plane: A plane that can be drawn to separate opposing lobes of p, d, and f orbitals. (7.7)

Node: A place where the amplitude or intensity of a wave is zero. (7.3)

Nomenclature: The names of substances and the rules for devising names. (2.9)

Nonbonding Domain: A region in the valence shell of an atom that holds an unshared pair of electrons and that influences the shape of a molecule. (9.2)

Nonbonding Molecular Orbital: A molecular orbital that has no net effect on the stability of a molecule when populated with electrons and that is localized on one atom in the molecule. (9.7)

Nonelectrolyte: A compound that in its molten state or in solution cannot conduct electricity. (4.2)

Nonlinear Molecule: A molecule in which the atoms do not lie in a straight line. (9.2)

Nonmetal: A nonductile, nonmalleable, nonconducting element that tends to form negative ions (if it forms them at all) far more readily than positive ions and whose oxide is likely to show acidic properties. (2.4)

Nonmetallic Element: An element without metallic properties; an element with poor electrical conductivity. (2.4)

Nonoxidizing acid: An acid in which the anion is a poorer oxidizing agent than the hydrogen ion (e.g., HCl, H_2SO_4, H_3PO_4). (5.3)

Nonpolar Covalent Bond: A covalent bond in which the electron pair(s) are shared equally by the two atoms. (8.4)

Nonpolar Molecule: A molecule that has no net dipole moment. (9.3)

Nonvolatile: Descriptive of a substance with a high boiling point, a low vapor pressure. and that does not evaporate. (12.6)

Normal Boiling Point: The temperature at which the vapor pressure of a liquid equals 1 atm. (11.6)

Nuclear Binding Energy: See *Binding Energy, Nuclear.*

Nuclear Chain Reaction: A self-sustaining nuclear reaction. (20.8)

Nuclear Equation: A description of a nuclear reaction that uses the special symbols of isotopes, that describes some kind of nuclear transformation or disintegration, and that is balanced when the sums of the atomic numbers on either side of the arrow are equal and the sums of the mass numbers are also equal. (20.3)

Nuclear Fission: See *Fission.*

Nuclear Fusion: See *Fusion.*

Nuclear Radiation: Alpha, beta, or gamma radiation emitted by radioactive nuclei. (20.3)

Nuclear Reaction: A change in the composition or energy of the nuclei of isotopes accompanied by one or more events such as the radiation of nuclear particles or electromagnetic energy, transmutation, fission, or fusion. (13.4, 20.3)

Nucleic Acids: Polymers in living cells that store and translate genetic information and whose molecules hydrolyze to give a sugar unit (ribose from ribonucleic acid, RNA, or deoxyribose from deoxyribonucleic acid, DNA), a phosphate, and a set of four of the five nitrogen-containing, heterocyclic bases (adenine, thymine, guanine, cytosine, and uracil). (22.8)

Nucleon: A proton or a neutron. (2.2)

Nucleus: The hard, dense core of an atom that holds the atom's protons and neutrons. (2.2)

Nylon 6,6: A polymer of a six-carbon dicarboxylic acid and a six-carbon diamine. (22.6)

O

Observation: A statement that accurately describes something we see, hear, taste, feel, or smell. (1.2)

Octahedral Molecule: A molecule in which a central atom is surrounded by six atoms located at the vertices of an imaginary octahedron. (9.1)

Octahedron: An eight-sided figure that can be envisioned as two square pyramids sharing the common square base. (9.1)

Octet (of Electrons): Eight electrons in the valence shell of an atom. (8.1)

Octet Rule: An atom tends to gain or lose electrons until its outer shell has eight electrons. (8.1, 8.3)

Odd–Even Rule: When the numbers of protons and neutrons in an atomic nucleus are both even, the isotope is more likely to be stable than when both numbers are odd. (20.4)

Open System: A system that can exchange both matter and energy with its surroundings. (6.3)

Open-End Manometer: See *Manometer.*

Optical Isomers: Stereoisomers other than geometric (cis–trans) isomers and that include substances that can rotate the plane of plane-polarized light. (21.8)

Orbital: An electron waveform with a particular energy and a unique set of values for the quantum numbers n, ℓ, and m_ℓ. (7.3)

Orbital Diagram: A diagram in which the electrons in an atom's orbitals are represented by arrows to indicate paired and unpaired spins. (7.5)

Order (of a Reaction): The sum of the exponents in the rate law is the *overall* order. Each exponent gives the order of the reaction with respect to a specific reactant. (13.3)

Ore: A substance in the earth's crust from which an element or compound can be extracted at a profit. (21.4)

Organic Acid: An acid that contains the carboxyl group, $-\overset{\overset{\displaystyle O}{\|}}{C}-OH$. (8.3, 22.6)

Organic Chemistry: The study of the compounds of carbon that are not classified as inorganic. (2.6, 22.1)

Organic Compound: Any compound of carbon other than a carbonate, bicarbonate, cyanide, cyanate, carbide, or gaseous oxide. (2.6)

Orthorhombic Sulfur: The most stable allotrope of sulfur, composed of S_8 rings. (21.2)

Osmosis: The passage of solvent molecules, but not those of solutes, through a semipermeable membrane; the limiting case of dialysis. (12.8)

Osmotic Membrane: A membrane that allows passage of solvent, but not solute particles. (12.8)

Osmotic Pressure: The back pressure that would have to be applied to prevent osmosis; one of the colligative properties. (12.8)

Outer Electrons: The electrons in the occupied shell with the largest principal quantum number. An atom's electrons in its valence shell. (7.6)

Outer Shell: The occupied shell in an atom having the highest principal quantum number (n). (7.6)

Overall Order of Reaction: The sum of the exponents on the concentration terms in a rate law. (13.3)

Overlap of Orbitals: A portion of two orbitals from different atoms that share the same space in a molecule. (9.4)

Oxidation: A change in which an oxidation number increases (becomes more positive). A loss of electrons. (5.1)

Oxidation Number: The charge that an atom in a molecule or ion would have if all of the electrons in its bonds belonged entirely to the more electronegative atoms; the oxidation state of an atom. (5.1)

Oxidation State: See *Oxidation Number.*

Oxidation–Reduction Reaction: A chemical reaction in which changes in oxidation numbers occur. (5.1)

Oxidizing Acid: An acid in which the anion is a stronger oxidizing agent than H^+ (e.g., $HClO_4$, HNO_3). (5.3)

Oxidizing Agent: The substance that causes oxidation and that is itself reduced. (5.1)

Oxoacid: An acid that contains oxygen besides hydrogen and another element (e.g., HNO_3, H_3PO_4, H_2SO_4). (4.4, 15.2)

Oxoanion: The anion of an oxoacid (e.g., ClO_4^-, SO_4^{2-}). (15.2)

Oxygen Family: Group VIA in the periodic table—oxygen, sulfur, selenium, tellurium, and polonium. (2.3)

Ozone: A very reactive allotrope of oxygen with the formula O_3. (21.2)

P

Pairing Energy: The energy required to force two electrons to become paired and occupy the same orbital. (21.9)

Paramagnetism: The weak magnetism of a substance whose atoms, molecules, or ions have one or more unpaired electrons. (7.4)

Partial Charge: Charges at opposite ends of a dipole that are fractions of full $1+$ or $1-$ charges. (8.4)

Partial Pressure: The pressure contributed by an individual gas to the total pressure of a gas mixture. (10.6)

Partial Pressure, Law of (Dalton's Law of Partial Pressures): The total pressure of a mixture of gases equals the sum of their partial pressures. (10.6)

Pascal (Pa): The SI unit of pressure equal to 1 newton m^{-2}; 1 atm = 101,325 Pa. (10.2)

Pauli Exclusion Principle: No two electrons in an atom can have the same values for all four of their quantum numbers. (7.4)

Peptide Bond: The amide linkage in molecules of polypeptides. (22.7)

Percentage by Mass (Percentage by Weight): (a) The number of grams of an element combined in 100 g of a compound. (3.3) (b) The number of grams of a substance in 100 g of a mixture or solution. (12.5)

Percentage Composition: A list of the percentages by weight of the elements in a compound. (3.3)

Percentage Concentration: A ratio of the amount of solute to the amount of solution expressed as a percent. (4.1)

Weight/weight: Grams of solute in 100 g of solution.

Weight/volume: Grams of solute in 100 mL of solution.

Volume/volume: Volumes of solute in 100 volumes of solution.

Percentage Ionization: An equation that quantifies the ionization of a substance in solution. (16.2)

Percentage ionization

$$= \frac{\text{amount of substance ionized}}{\text{initial amount of substance}} \times 100\%$$

Percentage Yield: The ratio (taken as a percent) of the mass of product obtained to the mass calculated from the reaction's stoichiometry. (3.6)

Period: A horizontal row of elements in the periodic table. (2.3)

Periodic Table: A table in which symbols for the elements are displayed in order of increasing atomic number and arranged so that elements with similar properties lie in the same column (group). (Inside front cover, 2.3)

pH: $-\log [H^+]$. (15.5)

Phase: A homogeneous region within a sample. (1.3)

Phase Diagram: A pressure–temperature graph on which are plotted the temperatures and the pressures at which equilibrium exists between the states of a substance. It defines regions of T and P in which the solid, liquid, and gaseous states of the substance can exist. (11.12)

Photon: A unit of energy in electromagnetic radiation equal to $h\nu$, where ν is the frequency of the radiation and h is Planck's constant. (7.1)

Photosynthesis: The use of solar energy by a plant to make high-energy molecules from carbon dioxide, water, and minerals. (6.4)

Physical Change: A change that is not accompanied by a change in chemical makeup. (1.3)

Physical Law: A relationship between two or more physical properties of a system, usually expressed as a mathematical equation, that describes how a change in one property affects the others.

Physical Property: A property that can be specified without reference to another substance and that can be measured without causing a chemical change. (1.4)

Physical State: The condition of aggregation of a substance's formula units, whether as a solid, a liquid, or a gas. (1.4)

Pi Bond (π Bond): A bond formed by the sideways overlap of a pair of p orbitals and that concentrates electron density into two separate regions that lie on opposite sides of a plane that contains an imaginary line joining the nuclei. (9.6)

Pig Iron: The impure iron made by a blast furnace. (21.4)

pK_a: $-\log K_a$. (16.1)

pK_b: $-\log K_b$. (16.1)

pK_w: $-\log K_w$. (15.5)

Planar Triangular Molecule: A molecule in which a central atom holds three other atoms located at the corners of an equilateral triangle and that includes the central atom at its center. (9.1)

Plane-Polarized Light: Light in which all the oscillations occur in one plane. (21.8)

Planck's Constant (h): The ratio of the energy of a photon to its frequency; $6.6260755 \times 10^{-34}$ J Hz^{-1}. (7.1)

pOH: $-\log [OH^-]$. (15.5)

Plasma: An electrically neutral, very hot gaseous mixture of nuclei and unattached electrons. (20.8)

Polar Covalent Bond (Polar Bond): A covalent bond in which more than half of the bond's negative charge is concentrated around one of the two atoms. (8.4)

Polar Molecule: A molecule in which individual bond polarities do not cancel and in which, therefore, the centers of density of negative and positive charges do not coincide. (8.4)

Polarizability: A term that describes the ease with which the electron cloud of a molecule or ion is distorted. (11.2)

Polyatomic Ion: An ion composed of two or more atoms. (2.8)

Polydentate Ligand: A ligand that has two or more atoms that can become simultaneously attached to a metal ion. (21.5)

Polymer: A substance consisting of macromolecules that have repeating structural units. (22.6)

Polymerization: A chemical reaction that converts a monomer into a polymer. (22.6)

Polypeptide: A polymer of α-amino acids that makes up all or most of a protein. (22.7)

Polyprotic Acid: An acid that can furnish more than one H^+ per molecule. (4.3)

Polysaccharide: A carbohydrate whose molecules can be hydrolyzed to hundreds of monosaccharide molecules. (22.7)

Polystyrene: An addition polymer of styrene with the following structure. (22.6)

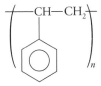

polystyrene

Position of Equilibrium: The relative amounts of the substances on both sides of the double arrows in the equation for an equilibrium. (4.3, 11.8)

Positive Charge: A type of electrical charge possessed by certain particles such as the proton. A positive charge is attracted by a negative charge and is repelled by another positive charge. (2.2)

Positron ($_0^1 p$): A positively charged particle with the mass of an electron. (20.3)

Post-transition Metal: A metal that occurs in the periodic table immediately to the right of a row of transition elements. (2.8)

Potential: See *Volt*.

Potential Energy (PE): Stored energy. (6.1)

Potential Energy Diagram: A diagram indicating the conversion of kinetic energy to potential energy and back again as atoms or molecules collide and then recoil in a chemical reaction. (13.5)

Precipitate: A solid that separates from a solution usually as the result of a chemical reaction. (4.1)

Precipitation Reaction: A reaction in which a precipitate forms. (4.1, 4.5)

Precision: How reproducible measurements are; the fineness of a measurement as indicated by the number of significant figures reported in the physical quantity. (1.6)

Pre-exponential Factor: A number or variable that precedes the exponential part of a number. (13.6)

Pressure: Force per unit area. (6.5, 10.2)

Pressure–Concentration Law: See *Vapor Pressure–Concentration Law.*

Pressure–Solubility Law (Henry's Law): The concentration of a gas dissolved in a liquid at any given temperature is directly proportional to the partial pressure of the gas above the solution. (12.4)

Pressure–Temperature Law (Gay-Lussac's Law): The pressure of a given mass of gas is directly proportional to its Kelvin temperature if the volume is kept constant. $P \propto T$. (10.3)

Pressure–Volume Law (Boyle's Law): The volume of a given mass of a gas is inversely proportional to its pressure if the temperature is kept constant. $V \propto 1/P$. (10.3)

Pressure–Volume Work (P–V Work): The energy transferred as work when a system expands or contracts against the pressure exerted by the surroundings. At constant pressure, $w = -P\Delta V$. (6.5)

Primary Cell: A galvanic cell (battery) not designed to be recharged; it is discarded after its energy is depleted. (19.8)

Primitive Cubic Unit Cell: A cubic unit cell that has atoms only at the corners of the cell. (11.9)

Principal Quantum Number (n): The quantum number that defines the principal energy levels and that can have values of $1, 2, 3, \ldots, \infty$. (7.3)

Products: The substances produced by a chemical reaction and whose formulas follow the arrows in chemical equations. (2.5)

Propagation Step: A step in a chain reaction for which one product must serve in a succeeding propagation step as a reactant and for which another (final) product accumulates with each repetition of the step. (Facets of Chemistry 13.1)

Property: A characteristic of matter. (1.4)

Propyl Group: $CH_3CH_2CH_2$—. (22.2)

Protein: A macromolecular substance found in cells that consists wholly or mostly of one or more polypeptides that often are combined with an organic molecule or a metal ion. (22.7)

Proton ($^{1}_{1}\text{p}$ or $^{1}_{1}\text{H}^+$): (a) A subatomic particle, with a charge of $1+$ and a mass of 1.0072765 u ($1.6726217 \times 10^{-24}$ g) and that is found in atomic nuclei. (2.2) (b) The name often used for the hydrogen ion and symbolized as H^+. (4.3)

Proton Acceptor: A Brønsted base. (15.1)

Proton Donor: A Brønsted acid. (15.1)

Pure Substance: An element or a compound. (1.3)

Q

Qualitative Analysis: The use of experimental procedures to determine what elements are present in a substance. (4.8)

Qualitative Observation: Observations that do not involve numerical information. (1.5)

Quanta: Packets of electromagnetic radiation now commonly called photons. (7.1)

Quantitative Analysis: The use of experimental procedures to determine the percentage composition of a compound or the percentage of a component of a mixture. (4.8)

Quantitative Observation: An observation involving a measurement and numerical information. (1.5)

Quantized: Descriptive of a discrete, definite amount as of *quantized energy*. (7.2)

Quantum: The energy of one photon. (7.1)

Quantum Mechanics: See *Wave Mechanics.*

Quantum Number: A number related to the energy, shape, or orientation of an orbital, or to the spin of an electron. (7.2)

Quantum Theory: The physics of objects that exhibit wave/particle duality.

R

R: See *Gas Constant, Universal.*

Rad (rd): A unit of radiation-absorbed dose and equal to 10^{-5} J g^{-1} or 10^{-2} Gy. (20.6)

Radioactive Decay: The change of a nucleus into another nucleus (or into a more stable form of the same nucleus) by the loss of a small particle or a gamma ray photon. (20.3)

Radioactive Disintegration Series: A sequence of nuclear reactions beginning with a very long-lived radionuclide and ending with a stable isotope of lower atomic number. (20.3)

Radioactivity: The emission of one or more kinds of radiation from an isotope with unstable nuclei. (20.3)

Radiological Dating: A technique for measuring the age of a geologic formation or an ancient artifact by determining the ratio of the concentrations of two isotopes, one radioactive and the other a stable decay product. (13.4, 20.7)

Radionuclide: A radioactive isotope. (20.3)

Raoult's Law: See *Vapor Pressure–Concentration Law.*

Rare Earth Metals: The lanthanides. (2.3)

Rate: A ratio in which a unit of time appears in the denominator, for example, 40 miles hr^{-1} or 3.0 mol L^{-1} s^{-1}. (13.2)

Rate Constant (k): The proportionality constant in the rate law; the rate of reaction when all reactant concentrations are $1\,M$. (13.3)

Rate Law: An equation that relates the rate of a reaction to the molar concentrations of the reactants raised to powers. (13.3)

Rate of Reaction: How quickly the reactants disappear and the products form and usually expressed in units of mol L^{-1} s^{-1}. (13.1)

Rate-Determining Step (Rate-Limiting Step): The slowest step in a reaction mechanism. (13.7)

Reactant, Limiting: See *Limiting Reactant.*

Reactants: The substances brought together to react and whose formulas appear before the arrow in a chemical equation. (2.5)

Reaction Coordinate: The horizontal axis of a potential energy diagram of a reaction. (13.5)

Reaction Quotient (Q): The numerical value of the mass action expression. See *Mass Action Expression.* (14.2)

Reactivity: A description of the tendency for a substance to undergo reaction. For a metal, it is the tendency to undergo oxidation. (8.5)

Red Phosphorus: A relatively unreactive allotrope of phosphorus. (21.2)

Redox Reaction: An oxidation–reduction reaction. (5.1)

Reducing Agent: A substance that causes reduction and is itself oxidized. (5.1)

Reduction: A change in which an oxidation number decrease (becomes less positive and more negative). A gain of electrons. (5.1)

Reduction Potential: A measure of the tendency of a given half-reaction to occur as a reduction. (19.2)

Refining: The industrial conversion of a compound (ore) containing a desired element into a pure form of the element. (21.4)

Refractory: A high-melting heat-resistant material used to line furnaces and rocket engines, and to shield the space shuttle from the high heat of re-entry. (21.4)

Rem: A dose in rads multiplied by a factor that takes into account the variations that different radiations have in their damage-causing abilities in tissue. (20.6)

Replication: In nucleic acid chemistry, the reproductive duplication of DNA double helices prior to cell division. (22.8)

Representative Element: An element in one of the A groups in the periodic table. (2.3)

Resonance: A concept in which the actual structure of a molecule or polyatomic ion is represented as a composite or average of two or more Lewis structures, which are called the resonance or contributing structures (and none of which has real existence). (8.7)

Resonance Energy: The difference in energy between a substance and its principal resonance (contributing) structure. (8.7)

Resonance Hybrid: The actual structure of a molecule or polyatomic ion taken as a composite or average of the resonance or contributing structures. (8.7)

Resonance Structure: A Lewis structure that contributes to the hybrid structure in resonance-stabilized systems; a contributing structure (8.7)

Reverse Reaction: In a chemical equation, the reaction as read from right to left. (4.3)

Reversible Process: A process that occurs by an infinite number of steps during which the driving force for the change is just barely greater than the force that resists the change. (18.7)

Reversible Reaction: A reaction capable of proceeding in either the forward or reverse direction. (13.5, 14.7, 18.7)

Ring, Carbon: A closed-chain sequence of carbon atoms. (22.1)

RNA: Ribonucleic acid; a nucleic acid that gives ribose, phosphate ion, adenine, uracil, guanine, and cytosine when hydrolyzed. It occurs in several varieties. (22.8)

Roasting: Heating a sulfide ore in air to convert it to an oxide. (21.4)

Rock Salt Structure: The face-centered cubic structure observed for sodium chloride, which is also possessed by crystals of many other compounds. (11.9)

Root Mean Square Speed (rms Speed): The square root of the average of the speeds-squared of the molecules in a substance. (10.8)

Rydberg Equation: An equation used to calculate the wavelengths of all the spectral lines of hydrogen. (7.2)

S

Salt: An ionic compound in which the anion is not OH^- or O^{2-} and the cation is not H^+. (4.2, 4.3)

Salt Bridge: A tube that contains an electrolyte that connects the two half-cells of a galvanic cell. (19.1)

Saponification: The reaction of an organic ester with a strong base to give an alcohol and the salt of the organic acid. (22.5)

Saturated Organic Compound: A compound whose molecules have only single bonds. (22.2)

Saturated Solution: A solution that holds as much solute as it can at a given temperature. A solution in which there is an equilibrium between the dissolved and the undissolved states of the solute. (4.1) (17.1)

Scanning Tunneling Microscope (STM): An instrument that enables the imaging of individual atoms on the surface of an electrically conducting specimen. (2.1)

Scientific Law: See *Law*.

Scientific Method: The observation, explanation, and testing of an explanation by additional experiments. (1.2)

Scientific Notation: The representation of a quantity as a decimal number between 1 and 10 multiplied by 10 raised to a power (e.g., 6.02×10^{23}). (1.5)

Scintillation Counter: A device for measuring nuclear radiation that contains a sensor composed of a substance called a *phosphor* that emits a tiny flash of light when struck by a particle of ionizing radiation. These flashes can be magnified electronically and automatically counted. (20.6)

Second Law of Thermodynamics: Whenever a spontaneous event takes place, it is accompanied by an increase in the entropy of the universe. (18.4)

Second-Order Reaction: A reaction with a rate law of the type: rate $= k[A]^2$ or rate $= k[A][B]$, where A and B are reactants. (13.3)

Secondary Cell: A galvanic cell (battery) designed for repeated use; it is able to be recharged. (19.8)

Secondary Quantum Number (ℓ): The quantum number whose values can be $0, 1, 2, \ldots, (n - 1)$, where n is the principal quantum number. (7.3)

Seesaw Shaped Molecule: A description given to a molecule in which the central atom has five electron pairs in its valence shell, one of which is a lone pair and the others are used in bonds to other atoms. See also *Distorted Tetrahedron*. (9.2)

Selective Precipitation: A technique that uses differences in the solubilities of specific salts to separate ions from each other. (17.3)

Semiconductor: A substance that conducts electricity weakly. (2.4)

Shell: All of the orbitals associated with a given value of n (the principal quantum number). (7.3)

SI (International System of Units): The modified metric system adopted in 1960 by the General Conference on Weights and Measures. (1.5)

Side Reaction: A reaction the occurs simultaneously with another reaction (the main reaction) in the same mixture to produce by-products. (3.6)

Sievert (Sv): The SI unit for dose equivalent. The dose equivalent H is calculated from D (the dose in grays), Q (a measure of the effectiveness of the radiation at causing harm), and N (a variable that accounts for other modifying factors). $H = DQN$. (20.6)

Sigma Bond (σ Bond): A bond formed by the head-to-head overlap of two atomic orbitals and in which electron density becomes concentrated along and around the imaginary line joining the two nuclei. (9.6)

Significant Figures (Significant Digits): The digits in a physical measurement that are known to be certain plus the first digit that contains uncertainty. (1.6)

Simple Cubic Unit Cell: See *Primitive Cubic Unit Cell*.

Simplest Formula: See *Empirical Formula*.

Single Bond: A covalent bond in which a single pair of electrons is shared. (8.3)

Single Replacement Reaction: A reaction in which one element replaces another in a compound; usually a redox reaction. (5.4)

Skeletal Structure: A diagram of the arrangement of atoms in a molecule, which is the first step in constructing the Lewis structure. (8.6)

Skeleton Equation: An unbalanced equation showing only the formulas of reactants and products. (5.2)

Slag: A relatively low melting mixture of impurities that forms in a blast furnace or other furnaces used to refine metals. (21.4)

Smelting: A process in which a metal oxide is heated with a reducing agent in order to obtain the free metal. (21.3)

Solid: One of the states of matter. A solid consists of tightly packed atomic or molecular sized particles held rigidly in place. (1.4)

Solubility: The ratio of the quantity of solute to the quantity of solvent in a saturated solution and that is usually expressed in units of (g solute)/(100 g solvent) at a specified temperature. (4.1)

Solubility Product Constant (K_{sp}): The equilibrium constant for the solubility of a salt and that, for a saturated solution, is equal to the product of the molar concentrations of the ions, each raised to a power equal to the number of its ions in one formula unit of the salt. (17.1) See also *Acid Solubility Product*.

Solubility Rules: A set of rules describing salts that are soluble and those that are insoluble. They enable the prediction of the formation of a precipitate in a metathesis reaction. (4.5)

Solute: Something dissolved in a solvent to make a solution. (4.1)

Solution: A homogeneous mixture in which all particles are of the size of atoms, small molecules, or small ions. (1.3, 4.1)

Solvation: The development of a cage-like network of a solution's solvent molecules about a molecule or ion of the solute. (12.1)

Solvation Energy: The enthalpy of the interaction of gaseous molecules or ions of solute with solvent molecules during the formation of a solution. (12.2)

Solvent: A medium, usually a liquid, into which something (a solute) is dissolved to make a solution. (4.1)

sp Hybrid Orbital: A hybrid orbital formed by mixing one s and one p atomic orbital. The angle between a pair of sp hybrid orbitals is 180°. (9.5)

sp^2 Hybrid Orbital: A hybrid orbital formed by mixing one s and two p atomic orbitals. sp^2 hybrids are planar triangular with the angle between two sp^2 hybrid orbitals being 120°. (9.5)

sp^3 Hybrid Orbital: A hybrid orbital formed by mixing one s and three p atomic orbitals. sp^3 hybrids point to the corners of a tetrahedron; the angle between two sp^3 hybrid orbitals is 109.5°. (9.5)

sp^3d Hybrid Orbital: A hybrid orbital formed by mixing one s, three p, and one d atomic orbital. sp^3d hybrids point to the corners of a trigonal bipyramid. (9.5)

sp^3d^2 Hybrid Orbital: A hybrid orbital formed by mixing one s, three p, and two d atomic orbitals. sp^3d^2 hybrids point to the corners of an octahedron. (9.5)

Specific Heat (Specific Heat Capacity): The quantity of heat that will raise the temperature of 1 g of a substance by 1 °C, usually in units of cal g^{-1} °C^{-1} or J g^{-1} °C^{-1}. (6.3)

Spectator Ion: An ion whose formula appears in an ionic equation identically on both sides of the arrow, that does not participate in the reaction, and that is excluded from the net ionic equation. (4.2)

Spectrochemical Series: A listing of ligands in order of their ability to produce a large crystal field splitting. (21.9)

Speed of Light (c): The speed at which light travels in a vacuum; 3.00×10^8 m s^{-1}. (7.1)

Spin Quantum Number (m_s): The quantum number associated with the spin of a subatomic particle and for the electron can have a value of $+\frac{1}{2}$ or $-\frac{1}{2}$. (7.4)

Spontaneous Change: A change that occurs by itself without outside assistance. (18.2)

Square Planar Molecule: A molecule with a central atom having four bonds that point to the corners of a square. (9.2)

Square Pyramid: A pyramid with four triangular sides and a square base. (9.2)

Stability Constant: See *Formation Constant.*

Stabilization Energy: See *Resonance Energy.*

Standard Atmosphere: See *Atmosphere, Standard*

Standard Cell Notation: A way of describing the anode and cathode half-cells in a galvanic cell. The anode half-cell is specified on the left, with the electrode material of the anode given first and a vertical bar representing the phase boundary between the electrode and the solution. Double bars represent the salt bridge between the half-cells. The cathode half-cell is specified on the right, with the material of the cathode given last. Once again, a single vertical bar represents the phase boundary between the solution and the electrode. (19.1)

Standard Cell Potential (E°_{cell}): The potential of a galvanic cell at 25 °C and when all ionic concentrations are exactly 1 M and the partial pressures of all gases are 1 atm. (19.2)

Standard Conditions of Temperature and Pressure (STP): Standard reference conditions for gases. 273 K (0 °C) and 1 atm (760 torr). (10.4)

Standard Enthalpy Change (ΔH°): See *Standard Heat of Reaction.*

Standard Enthalpy of Formation (ΔH°_f): See *Standard Heat of Formation.*)

Standard Entropy (S°): The entropy of 1 mol of a substance at 25 °C and 1 atm. (18.5)

Standard Entropy Change (ΔS°): The entropy change of a reaction when determined with reactants and products at 25 °C and 1 atm and on the scale of the mole quantities given by the coefficients of the balanced equation. (18.5)

Standard Entropy of Formation (ΔS°_f): The value of ΔS° for the formation of one mole of a substance from its elements in their standard states. (18.5)

Standard Free Energy Change (ΔG°): $\Delta G^\circ = \Delta H^\circ - T\Delta S^\circ$. (18.6)

Standard Free Energy of Formation (ΔG°_f): The value of ΔG° for the formation of *one* mole of a compound from its elements in their standard states. (18.6)

Standard Heat of Combustion (ΔH°_c): The enthalpy change for the combustion of one mole of a compound under standard conditions. (6.8)

Standard Heat of Formation (ΔH°_f): The amount of heat absorbed or evolved when one mole of the compound is formed from its elements in their standard states. (6.8)

Standard Heat of Reaction (ΔH°): The enthalpy change of a reaction when determined with reactants and products at 25 °C and 1 atm and on the scale of the mole quantities given by the coefficients of the balanced equation. (6.6)

Standard Hydrogen Electrode: See *Hydrogen Electrode.*

Standard Molar Volume: See *Molar Volume, Standard.*

Standard Reduction Potential E°_{cell}: The reduction potential of a half-reaction at 25 °C when all ion concentrations are 1 M and the partial pressures of all gases are 1 atm. Also called standard electrode potential. (19.2)

Standard Solution: Any solution whose concentration is accurately known. (4.8)

Standard State: The condition in which a substance is in its most stable form at 25 °C and 1 atm. (6.6, 6.8)

Standing Wave: A wave whose peaks and nodes do not change position. (7.3)

Starch: A polymer of glucose used by plants to store energy. (22.7)

State Function: A quantity whose value depends only on the initial and final states of the system and not on the path taken by the system to get from the initial to the final state. (P, V, T, H, S, and G are all state functions.) (6.2)

State of a System: The set of specific values of the physical properties of a system—its composition, physical form, concentration, temperature, pressure, and volume. (6.2)

State of Matter: A physical state of a substance: solid, liquid, or gas. See also *Standard State.* (1.4)

Stereoisomerism: The existence of isomers whose structures differ only in spatial orientations (e.g., geometric isomers and optical isomers). (21.8)

Stock System: A system of nomenclature that uses Roman numerals to specify oxidation states. (2.9)

Stoichiometric Equivalence: The ratio by moles between two elements in a formula or two substances in a chemical reaction. (3.2)

Stoichiometry: A description of the relative quantities by moles of the reactants and products in a reaction as given by the coefficients in the balanced equation. (3 Introduction)

Stopcock: A valve on a buret that is used to control the flow of titrant. (4.8)

Stored Energy: See *Potential Energy.*

STP: See *Standard Conditions of Temperature and Pressure.*

Straight-Chain Compound: An organic compound in whose molecules the carbon atoms are joined in one continuous open-chain sequence. (22.1)

Strong Acid: An acid that is essentially 100% ionized in water. A good proton donor. An acid with a large value of K_a. (4.3)

Strong Base: Any powerful proton acceptor. A base with a large value of K_b. A metal hydroxide that dissociates essentially 100% in water. (4.3)

Strong Electrolyte: Any substance that ionizes or dissociates in water to essentially 100%. (4.2, 4.3)

Structural Formula (Lewis Structure): A chemical formula that shows how the atoms of a molecule or polyatomic ion are arranged, to which other atoms they are bonded, and the kinds of bonds (single, double, or triple). (8.3)

Subatomic Particles: Electrons, protons, neutrons, and atomic nuclei. (2.2)

Sublimation: The conversion of a solid directly into a gas without passing through the liquid state. (11.3)

Subscript: In a chemical formula, a number after a chemical symbol, written below the line, and indicating the number of the preceding atoms in the formula (e.g., CH_4). Subscripts are also used to differentiate many variables such as the acid ionization constant (K_a) and the base ionization constant (K_b). (2.5)

Subshell: All of the orbitals of a given shell that have the same value of their secondary quantum number, ℓ. (7.3)

Substance: See *Pure Substance*.

Substitution Reaction: The replacement of an atom or group on a molecule by another atom or group. (22.2, 22.3)

Superconductor: A material in a state in which it offers no resistance to the flow of electricity.

Supercooled Liquid: A liquid at a temperature below its freezing point. An amorphous solid. (11.7)

Supercritical Fluid: A substance at a temperature above its critical temperature. (11.12)

Superheated Liquid: The condition of a substance in its liquid state above its boiling point. (11.7)

Superimposability: A test of structural chirality in which a model of one structure and a model of its mirror image are compared to see if the two could be made to blend perfectly, with every part of one coinciding simultaneously with the parts of the other. (21.8, 22.1)

Supersaturated Solution: A solution that contains more solute than it would hold if the solution were saturated. Supersaturated solutions are unstable and tend to produce precipitates. (4.1)

Surface Tension: A measure of the amount of energy needed to expand the surface area of a liquid. (11.3)

Surfactant: A substance that lowers the surface tension of a liquid and promotes wetting. (11.3)

Surroundings: That part of the universe other than the system being studied and separated from the system by a real or an imaginary boundary. (6.3)

Symmetric: An object is symmetric if it looks the same when rotated, reflected in a mirror, or reflected through a point. (9.3)

System: That part of the universe under study and separated from the surroundings by a real or an imaginary boundary. (6.3, 6.6)

T

$t_{1/2}$: See *Half-Life*.

T-Shaped Molecule: A molecule having five electron domains in its valence shell, two of which contain lone pairs. The other three are used in bonds to other atoms. The molecule has the shape of the letter T, with the central atom located at the intersection of the two crossing lines. (9.2)

Tarnishing: See *Corrosion*.

Temperature: A measure of the hotness or coldness of something. A property related to the average kinetic energy of the atoms and molecules in a sample. A property that determines the direction of heat flow—from high temperature to low temperature. (1.5, 6.1)

Temperature–Volume Law (Charles' Law): The volume of a given mass of a gas is directly proportional to its Kelvin temperature if the pressure is kept constant. $V \propto T$. (10.3)

Termination Step: A step in a chain reaction in which a reactive species needed for a chain propagation step disappears without helping to generate more of this species. (Facets of Chemistry 13.1)

Tetrahedral Molecule: A molecule with a central atom bonded to four other atoms located at the corners of an imaginary tetrahedron. (9.1)

Tetrahedron: A four-sided figure with four triangular faces and shaped like a pyramid. (9.1)

Theoretical Model: See *Model, Theoretical*.

Theoretical Yield: The yield of a product calculated from the reaction's stoichiometry. (3.6)

Theory: A tested explanation of the results of many experiments. (1.2)

Thermal Decomposition: The decomposition of a substance caused by heating it. (21.3)

Thermal Energy: The molecular kinetic energy possessed by molecules as a result of the temperature of the sample. Energy that is transferred as heat. (6.1)

Thermal Equilibrium: A condition reached when two or more substances in contact with each other come to the same temperature. (6.2)

Thermal Property: A physical property, like heat capacity or heat of fusion, that concerns a substance's ability to absorb heat without changing chemically.

Thermochemical Equation: A balanced chemical equation accompanied by the value of $\Delta H°$ that corresponds to the mole quantities specified by the coefficients. (6.6)

Thermochemistry: The study of the energy changes of chemical reactions. (6 Introduction)

Thermodynamic Equilibrium Constant (K): The equilibrium constant that is calculated from $\Delta G°$ (the standard free energy change) for a reaction at T K by the equation, $\Delta G° = RT \ln K$. (18.9)

Thermodynamics (Chemical Thermodynamics): The study of the role of energy in chemical change and in determining the behavior of materials. (6 Introduction, 18.1)

Third Law of Thermodynamics: For a pure crystalline substance at 0 K, $S = 0$. (18.5)

Titrant: The solution added from a buret during a titration. (4.8)

Titration: An analytical procedure in which a solution of unknown concentration is combined slowly and carefully with a standard solution until a color change of some indicator or some other signal shows that equivalent quantities have reacted. Either solution can be the titrant in a buret with the other solution being in a receiving flask. (4.8)

Titration Curve: For an acid–base titration, a graph of pH versus the volume of titrant added. (16.7)

Torr: A unit of pressure equal to 1/760 atm. 1 mm Hg. (10.2)

Tracer Analysis: The use of small amounts of a radioisotope to follow (trace) the course of a chemical or biological change. (20.7)

Transcription: The synthesis of mRNA at the direction of DNA. (22.8)

Trans Isomer: A stereoisomer whose uniqueness lies in having two groups that project on opposite sides of a reference plane. (21.8, 22.2)

Transition Elements: The elements located between Groups IIA and IIIA in the periodic table. (2.3)

Transition Metals: The transition elements. (2.3)

Transition State: The brief moment during an elementary process in a reaction mechanism when the species involved have acquired the minimum amount of potential energy needed for a successful reaction, an amount of energy that corresponds to the high point on a potential energy diagram of the reaction. (13.5)

Transition State Theory: A theory about the formation and breakup of activated complexes. (13.5)

Translation: The synthesis of a polypeptide at the direction of a molecule of mRNA. (22.8)

Transmutation: The conversion of one isotope into another. (20.5)

Transuranium Elements: Elements 93 and higher. (20.5)

Traveling Wave: A wave whose peaks and nodes move. (7.3)

Triacylglycerol: An ester of glycerol and three fatty acids. (22.7)

Trigonal Bipyramid: A six-sided figure made of two three-sided pyramids that share a common face. (9.1)

Trigonal Bipyramidal Molecule: A molecule with a central atom holding five other atoms that are located at the corners of a trigonal bipyramid. (9.1, 9.2)

Trigonal Pyramidal Molecule: A molecule that consists of an atom, situated at the top of a three-sided pyramid, that is bonded to three other atoms located at the corners of the base of the pyramid. (9.2)

Triple Bond: A covalent bond in which three pairs of electrons are shared. (8.3)

Triple Point: The temperature and pressure at which the liquid, solid, and vapor states of a substance can coexist in equilibrium. (11.12)

Triprotic Acid: An acid that can furnish three H^+ ions per molecule. (4.3)

U

u: See *Atomic Mass Unit.*

Ultraviolet Catastrophe: The term given to the fact that classical physics predicts large amounts of ultraviolet radiation should be emitted from heated materials. In fact, very little ultraviolet radiation is produced. (7 Introduction)

Uncertainty: The amount by which a measured quantity deviates from the true or actual value. (1.6)

Uncertainty Principle: There is a limit to our ability to measure a particle's speed and position simultaneously. (7.7)

Unit Cell: The smallest portion of a crystal that can be repeated over and over in all directions to give the crystal lattice. (11.9)

Unit of Measurement: A reference quantity, such as the meter or kilogram, in terms of which the sizes of measurements can be expressed. (1.5)

Universal Gas Constant (*R*): See *Gas Constant, Universal* .

Universe: The system and surroundings taken together. (6.3)

Unsaturated Compound: A compound whose molecules have one or more double or triple bonds. (22.2)

Unsaturated Solution: Any solution with a concentration less than that of a saturated solution of the same solute and solvent. (4.1)

V

V-Shaped Molecule: See *Bent Molecule.*

Vacuum: An enclosed space containing no matter whatsoever. A *partial vacuum* is an enclosed space containing a gas at a very low pressure.

Valence Bond Theory (VB Theory): A theory of covalent bonding that views a bond as being formed by the sharing of one pair of electrons between two overlapping atomic or hybrid orbitals. (9.4)

Valence Electrons: The electrons of an atom in its valence shell that participate in the formation of chemical bonds. (7.6)

Valence Shell: The electron shell with the highest principal quantum number, *n*, that is occupied by electrons. (7.6)

Valence Shell Electron Pair Repulsion Theory (VSEPR Theory): The bonding and nonbonding (lone pair) electron domains in the valence shell of an atom seek an arrangement that leads to minimum repulsions and thereby determine the geometry of a molecule. (9.2)

Van der Waals' Constants: Empirical constants that make the van der Waals' equation conform to the gas law behavior of a real gas. (10.9)

Van der Waals' Equation: An equation of state for a real gas that corrects *V* and *P* for the excluded volume and the effects of intermolecular attractions. (10.9)

Van der Waals' Forces: Attractive forces including dipole–dipole, ion–dipole, and induced dipole forces. (11.2)

Van't Hoff Factor (*i*): The ratio of the observed freezing point depression to the value calculated on the assumption that the solute dissolves as un-ionized molecules. (12.9)

Vapor Pressure: The pressure exerted by the vapor above a liquid (usually referring to the *equilibrium* vapor pressure when the vapor and liquid are in equilibrium with each other). (10.6, 11.5)

Vapor Pressure–Concentration Law (Raoult's Law): The vapor pressure of one component above a mixture of molecular compounds equals the product of its vapor pressure when pure and its mole fraction. (12.6)

Viscosity: A liquid's resistance to flow. (11.3)

Visible Spectrum: That region of the electromagnetic spectrum whose frequencies can be detected by the human eye. (7.1)

Volatile: Descriptive of a liquid that has a low boiling point, a high vapor pressure at room temperature, and therefore evaporates easily. (11.5)

Volt (V): The SI unit of electric potential or emf in joules per coulomb. (19.2)

$$1\ V = 1\ J\ C^{-1}$$

Voltaic Cell: See *Galvanic Cell.*

VSEPR Theory: See *Valence Shell Electron Pair Repulsion Theory.*

Vulcanized Rubber: Rubber that has been treated with a substance such as sulfur that forms cross-links and improves the properties of the rubber. (22.6)

W

Wave: An oscillation that moves outward from a disturbance. (7.1)

Wave Function (ψ): A mathematical function that describes the intensity of an electron wave at a specified location in an atom. The square of the wave function at a particular location specifies the probability of finding an electron there. (7.3)

Wave Mechanics (Quantum Mechanics): A theory of atomic structure based on the wave properties of matter. (7 Introduction)

Wave/Particle Duality: A particle such as the electron behaves like a particle in some experiments and like a wave in others. (7 Introduction)

Wavelength (λ): The distance between crests in the wavelike oscillations of electromagnetic radiations. (7.1)

Weak Acid: An acid with a low percentage ionization in solution; a poor proton donor; an acid with a low value of K_a. (4.3, 16.1)

Weak Base: A base with a low percentage ionization in solution; a poor proton acceptor; a base with a low value of K_b. (4.3, 16.1)

Weak Electrolyte: A substance that has a low percentage ionization or dissociation in solution. (4.3)

Weighing: The operation of measuring the mass of something using a balance. (1.5)

Weight: The force with which something is attracted to the earth by gravity. (1.3)

Weight Percent: See *Percentage by Mass.*

Wetting: The spreading of a liquid across a solid surface. (11.3)

White Phosphorus: A very reactive allotrope of phosphorus consisting of tetrahedral P_4 molecules. (21.2)

Work (*w*): The energy expended in moving an opposing force through some particular distance. Work has units of *force* × *distance*. (6.1, 6.5, 18.1)

X

X Ray: A stream of very high-energy photons emitted by substances when they are bombarded by high-energy beams of electrons or are emitted by radionuclides that have undergone K-electron capture. (20.3)

Y

Yield, Actual: The amount of a product obtained in a laboratory experiment. (3.6)

Yield, Percentage: The ratio, given as a percent, of the quantity of product actually obtained in a reaction to the theoretical yield. (3.6)

Yield, Theoretical: The amount of a product calculated by the stoichiometry of the reaction. (3.6)

Z

Zinc–Manganese Dioxide Dry Cell (Leclanché Cell): A galvanic cell of about 1.5 V involving zinc and manganese dioxide under mildly acidic conditions. (19.8)

Zero-Order Reaction: A reaction that occurs at a constant rate regardless of the concentration of the reactant. (13.3)

RELATIONSHIPS AMONG UNITS

(Values in boldface are exact.)

Length

1 in. = **2.54** cm
1 ft = **30.48** cm
1 yd = **91.44** cm
1 mi = **5280** ft
1 ft = **12** in.
1 yd = **36** in.

Volume

1 liq. oz = **29.57353** mL
1 qt = **946.352946** mL
1 gallon = **3.785411784** L
1 gallon = **4** qt = **8** pt
1 qt = **2** pt = **32** liq. oz

Mass

1 oz = **28.349523125** g
1 lb = **453.59237** g
1 lb = **16** oz

Pressure

1 atm = **760** torr
1 atm = **101,325** Pa
1 atm = 14.696 psi (lb/in.^{2})
1 atm = 29.921 in. Hg

Energy

1 cal = **4.184** J
1 ev = 1.6022 $\times$ 10^{-19} J
1 ev/molecule = 96.49 kJ/mol
1 ev/molecule = 23.06 kcal/mol
1 J = 1 kg m^2 s^{-2} = 10^7 erg

PHYSICAL CONSTANTS

Rest mass of electron	m_e = 5.485799094 $\times$ 10^{-4} u (9.1093821 $\times$ 10^{-28} g)	
Rest mass of proton	m_p = 1.0072764668 u (1.67262164 $\times$ 10^{-24} g)	
Rest mass of neutron	m_n = 1.0086649160 u (1.67492721 $\times$ 10^{-24} g)	
Electronic charge	e = 1.60217649 $\times$ 10^{-19} C	
Atomic mass unit	u = 1.66053878 $\times$ 10^{-24} g	
Gas constant	R = 0.0820575 L atm mol^{-1} K^{-1}	
	= 8.31447 J mol^{-1} K^{-1}	
	= 1.98721 cal mol^{-1} K^{-1}	
Molar volume, ideal gas	= 22.4140 L (at STP)	
Avogadro's number	= 6.0221418 $\times$ 10^{23} things/mol	
Speed of light in a vacuum	c = 2.99792458 $\times$ 10^8 m s^{-1} (Exactly)	
Planck's constant	h = 6.6260690 $\times$ 10^{-34} J s	
Faraday constant	F = 9.6485340 $\times$ 10^4 C mol^{-1}	

LABORATORY REAGENTS

(Values are for the average concentrated reagents available commercially.)

Reagent	Percent (w/w)	Mole Solute / Liter Solution	Gram Solute / 100 mL Solution
NH_3	29	15	26
$HC_2H_3O_2$	99.7	17	105
HCl	37	12	44
HNO_3	71	16	101
H_3PO_4	85	15	144
H_2SO_4	96	18	177